The Sporting News

BASEBALL GUIDE

1 9 9 2 E D I T I O N

Editor/Baseball Guide
CRAIG CARTER

The Sporting News

─── PUBLISHING CO. ───

Thomas G. Osenton, President and Chief Operating Officer; **Kathy Kinkeade**, Vice President/Production; **William N. Topaz**, Director/Information Development; **Gary Levy**, Editor; **Mike Nahrstedt**, Managing Editor; **Joe Hoppel**, Senior Editor; **Tom Dienhart and Dave Sloan**, Associate Editors; **Mark Shimabukuro**, Assistant Editor; **Bill Perry**, Director of Graphic Presentation; **Mike Bruner**, Art Director/Yearbooks and Books; **Gary Brinker**, Director of Information Systems.

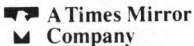 A Times Mirror
Company

World Series, A.L. Championship Series, N.L. Championship Series and All-Star Game highlights written by Joe Hoppel of THE SPORTING NEWS.

Major league statistics compiled by MLB-IBM Baseball Information System.

Minor league statistics compiled by Howe Sportsdata International Inc., Boston.

Additional assistance provided by Elias Sports Bureau, New York.

Copyright © 1992 by THE SPORTING NEWS Publishing Co. All rights reserved. Printed in the U.S.A.

Published in the United States by THE SPORTING NEWS Publishing Co., 1212 North Lindbergh Boulevard, St. Louis, Missouri 63132.

The Baseball Guide is protected by copyright. All information, in the form presented here, except playing statistics, was compiled by the publishers and proof is available.

No part of the Baseball Guide may be reproduced or transmitted in any form or by any means, electronic or mechanical, including photocopy, recording or any information storage and retrieval system now known or to be invented, without permission in writing from the publisher, except by a reviewer who wishes to quote brief passages in connection with a review written for inclusion in a magazine, newspaper or broadcast.

THE SPORTING NEWS is a registered trademark of THE SPORTING NEWS Publishing Co., a Times Mirror Company.

ISBN: 0-89204-418-7

10 9 8 7 6 5 4 3 2 1

CONTENTS

ON THE COVER: The San Francisco Giants struggled in 1991 despite a strong performance by first baseman Will Clark, who batted .301 with 29 homers and 116 RBIs. (Photo by Rich Pilling/The Sporting News)

1992
SEASON

MAJOR LEAGUE BASEBALL

COMMISSIONER'S OFFICE

Address
350 Park Avenue
New York, NY 10022
Telephone
212-371-7800
Teletype
910-380-9482
Commissioner
Francis T. Vincent Jr.

Deputy commissioner
Steven D. Greenberg
Director, broadcasting
David Alworth
Controller
Thomas Duffy
Director, special events
David Dziedzic
Director, security/facility management
Kevin Hallinan

Director, public relations
Richard Levin
Director, baseball operations
William Murray
General counsel
Thomas J. Ostertag
Director, broadcast administration
Leslie Sullivan
Exec. dir., licensing oper. and pres., MLBP
Rick White

AMERICAN LEAGUE

Address
350 Park Avenue
New York, NY 10022
Telephone
212-339-7600
President
Robert W. Brown, M.D.
Vice presidents
Gene Autry
Jean Yawkey
Special assistant to baseball
Dick Wagner
Supervisor of umpires
Martin J. Springstead
Coordinator of umpire operations
Philip Janssen
Special assistant to the president
Richard Butler
Director of public relations
Phyllis Merhige

Director, waivers and player records
Tim McCleary
Administrator of umpires/travel
Tess Basta
Administrative assistant
Carolyn Coen
Umpires
Lawrence Barnett
Joseph Brinkman
Alan Clark
Drew Coble
Terrance Cooney
Derryl Cousins
Donald Denkinger
James Evans
Dale Ford
Richard Garcia
Ted Hendry
John Hirschbeck
Mark Johnson

Jim Joyce
Kenneth Kaiser
Greg Kosc
Tim McClelland
Larry McCoy
James McKean
Durwood Merrill
Dan Morrison
Steve Palermo
David Phillips
Rick Reed
Michael Reilly
John (Rocky) Roe
Dale Scott
John Shulock
Tim Tschida
Vic Voltaggio
Tim Welke
Larry Young

NATIONAL LEAGUE

Address
350 Park Avenue
New York, NY 10022
Telephone
212-339-7700
President and treasurer
William D. White
Senior vice president and secretary
Phyllis B. Collins
Vice president, media and public affairs
Katy Feeney
Director of umpire supervision
Ed Vargo
Asst. secretary and mgr., player records
Nancy Crofts
Executive secretary
Valerie Dietrich

Administrative assistant, umpires
Cathy Davis
Umpires
Gregory Bonin
Gerald Crawford
Gary Darling
Robert Davidson
Gerald Davis
Dana DeMuth
Bruce Froemming
Eric Gregg
Thomas Hallion
Douglas Harvey
Mark Hirschbeck
William Hohn
Jerry Layne
Randall Marsh

John McSherry
Edward Montague
Frank Pulli
James Quick
Edward Rapuano
Charles Reliford
Laurence (Dutch) Rennert
Thomas Steven Rippley
Paul Runge
Terry Tata
Harry Wendelstedt
Joseph West
Charles Williams
Michael Winters

OTHER ORGANIZATIONS

NATIONAL BASEBALL HALL OF FAME AND MUSEUM

Address
P.O. Box 590
Cooperstown, NY 13326
Telephone
607-547-9988
607-547-5980 (FAX)
President
Edward W. Stack
Director
Howard C. Talbot Jr.

Associate director
William J. Guilfoile
Curator
William T. Spencer
Registrar
Peter P. Clark
Merchandising director
Jeffrey D. Stevens
Controller
Fran Althiser
Librarian
Thomas R. Heitz

ELIAS SPORTS BUREAU

Address
500 Fifth Ave.
New York, NY 10110
Telephone
212-869-1530
212-354-0980 (FAX)
General manager
Seymour Siwoff

HOWE SPORTSDATA INTERNATIONAL INC.
Address
Boston Fish Pier
West Building No. 2, Suite 306
Boston, MA 02210
Telephone
617-951-0070
617-951-1379 (stats request)
617-737-9960 (FAX)
President
Alan Goldfine
Executive vice president
Jay Virshbo

MAJOR LEAGUE BASEBALL PROPERTIES
Address
350 Park Avenue
New York, NY 10022
Telephone
212-339-7900
212-339-7628 (FAX)
President
Richard E. White
Vice president, design services
Anne Occi
Vice president, licensing operations
Frank Simio
Vice president, business development
Stu Upson
Manager, licensing information systems
Christopher Jones
Managing director of corporate sponsorship
Rick Dudley

PLAYER RELATIONS COMMITTEE
Address
350 Park Avenue
New York, NY 10022
Telephone
212-339-7400
212-371-2242 (FAX)
President and chief operating officer
Richard Ravitch
General counsel
Charles P. O'Connor
Associate counsels
Louis Melendez
John Westhoff
Contract administrator
Barbara Ernst
Director, public relations
Richard Levin

MAJOR LEAGUE BASEBALL PLAYERS ASSOCIATION
Address
805 Third Ave.
New York, NY 10022
Telephone
212-826-0808
212-752-3649 (FAX)
Executive director and general counsel
Donald M. Fehr
Special assistant
Mark Belanger
Associate general counsel
Eugene D. Orza
Assistant general counsels
Lauren Rich
Michael Weiner
Counsel
Arthur Schack
Director of marketing
Allyne Price

MAJOR LEAGUE UMPIRES ASSOCIATION
Address
1735 Market St., Suite 3420
Philadelphia, PA 19103
Telephone
215-979-3200
General counsel
Richard G. Phillips

MAJOR LEAGUE BASEBALL UMPIRE DEVELOPMENT
Address
P.O. Box A
St. Petersburg, FL 33731
Telephone
813-823-1286 and 813-823-3729
813-821-5819 (FAX)
Executive director
Edwin W. Lawrence
Director of field supervision
Mike Fitzpatrick

MAJOR LEAGUE SCOUTING BUREAU
Address
23712 Birtcher Dr., Suite A
El Toro, CA 92630
Telephone
714-458-7600
714-458-9454 (FAX)
Director
Donald F. Pries
Board of directors
Sandy Alderson
Dick Balderson
Lou Gorman
Jay Hankins
Roland Hemond
Joe McIlvaine
Bill Murray
Donald F. Pries
Art Stewart

NATIONAL ASSOCIATION OF PROFESSIONAL BASEBALL LEAGUES
Address
P.O. Box A
St. Petersburg, FL 33731
Telephone
813-822-6937
813-821-5819 (FAX)
Commissioner
Mike Moore
General counsel
George E. Yund
Director, information
Robert J. Sparks
Administrative assistant, information
Larry Wiederecht

ASS'N OF PROFESSIONAL BASEBALL PLAYERS OF AMERICA
Address
12062 Valley View, Suite 211
Garden Grove, CA 92645
Telephone
714-892-9900
714-897-0233 (FAX)
President
John J. McHale

MAJOR LEAGUE BASEBALL PLAYERS ALUMNI ASSOC.
Address
3637 4th St., North, Suite 101
St. Petersburg, FL 33704
Telephone
813-822-3399
813-822-6300 (FAX)
President
Brooks Robinson
Vice presidents
Hank Aguirre
Carl Erskine
Mike Hegan
Chuck Hinton
Al Kaline
Eddie Robinson
Mike Schmidt
Rusty Staub
Billy Williams
Secretary/treasurer
Fred Valentine
Chairman of the board
Bob Miller
Vice chairman
Jim Hannan
Board of directors
Bob Boone
Darrel Chaney
Jim (Mudcat) Grant
Rich Hand
Lou Klimchock
Tug McGraw
Jim Price
Dick Radatz
Ken Sanders
Fred Valentine
Carl Warwick

BASEBALL ASSISTANCE TEAM INC.
Address
350 Park Avenue
New York, NY 10022
Telephone
212-339-7800
Chairman
Ralph Branca
President
Joe Garagiola
Vice presidents
Joe Black
Rusty Staub
Earl Wilson
Executive director
Frank Slocum
Secretary/treasurer
Tom Ostertag

BASEBALL WRITERS' ASSOCIATION OF AMERICA
President
Pat Reusse,
Minneapolis Star Tribune
Vice president
Neil Hohlfeld, Houston Chronicle
Secretary/treasurer
Vern Plagenhoef, Booth Newspapers
Executive secretary
Jack Lang, Sportsticker
Board of directors
Paul Meyer,
Pittsburgh Post-Gazette
Claire Smith, New York Times
Kit Stier, Oakland Tribune
Mark Whicker,
Orange County Register

BALTIMORE ORIOLES
AMERICAN LEAGUE EAST DIVISION

1992 SCHEDULE

APRIL

S	M	T	W	T	F	S
5	6 CLE H	7	8 CLE H	9 N CLE H	10 N TOR H	11 TOR
12 TOR	13 BOS	14	15 BOS	16 N BOS	17 N DET H	18 DET H
19 DET H	20 N DET H	21 N KC	22 N KC	23 N KC	24 N NY	25 NY
26 NY	27 N MIN	28 N MIN	29 MIN	30		

MAY

S	M	T	W	T	F	S
					1 N SEA H	2 N SEA H
3 SEA H	4 N TEX H	5 N TEX H	6 N MIN H	7 N MIN H	8 N CHI H	9 N CHI H
10 CHI H	11	12 N TEX	13 N TEX	14	15 N CHI	16 N CHI
17 CHI	18 N OAK H	19 N OAK H	20 N OAK H	21	22 N CAL H	23 N CAL H
24 CAL H	25 N SEA	26 N SEA	27 SEA	28	29 N OAK	30 OAK
31 OAK						

JUNE

S	M	T	W	T	F	S
	1 N CAL	2 N CAL	3 CAL	4	5 N TOR H	6 N TOR H
7 TOR H	8 N BOS H	9 N BOS H	10 N BOS H	11 N DET	12 N DET	13 N DET
14 DET	15 N CLE	16 N CLE	17 CLE	18	19 N NY H	20 N NY H
21 N NY H	22 N NY H	23 N MIL	24 N MIL	25 MIL	26 N KC H	27 N KC H
28 KC H	29 N MIL H	30 N MIL H				

JULY

S	M	T	W	T	F	S
			1 MIL H	2	3 N MIN	4 MIN
5 MIN	6 N CHI H	7 N CHI H	8 N CHI H	9 N MIN H	10 N MIN H	11 N MIN H
12 MIN H	13	14 *	15	16 N TEX	17 N TEX	18 N TEX
19 N TEX	20 N CHI	21 N CHI	22 CHI	23 N TEX H	24 N TEX H	25 TEX H
26 TEX H	27	28 N NY	29 N NY	30 N NY	31 N BOS	

AUGUST

S	M	T	W	T	F	S
						1 BOS
2 BOS	3 N DET H	4 N DET H	5 N DET H	6	7 N CLE H	8 N CLE H
9 CLE H	10 TOR	11 N TOR	12 N TOR	13 N TOR	14 N KC	15 N KC
16 KC	17	18 N SEA H	19 N SEA H	20 N SEA H	21 N OAK H	22 N OAK H
23 OAK H	24 N CAL H	25 N CAL H	26 N CAL H	27	28 N SEA	29 N SEA
30 SEA	31 N OAK					

SEPTEMBER

S	M	T	W	T	F	S
		1 N OAK	2 N OAK	3	4 N CAL	5 N CAL
6 CAL	7 N NY H	8 N NY H	9 N NY H	10	11 N MIL H	12 N MIL H
13 MIL H	14 N KC H	15 N KC H	16 N KC H	17	18 N MIL	19 N MIL
20 MIL	21 N MIL	22 N TOR H	23 N TOR H	24 N TOR H	25 N BOS H	26 N BOS H
27 BOS H	28 N BOS H	29 N DET	30 N DET			

OCTOBER

S	M	T	W	T	F	S
				1 N CLE	2 N CLE	3 CLE
4 CLE	5	6	7	8	9	10

1992 SEASON

CLUB DIRECTORY

Chairman
Eli S. Jacobs
President
Lawrence Lucchino
Exec. vice president and general manager
Roland A. Hemond
Senior vice president/asst. to the chairman
Thomas A. Daffron
Vice president, administrative personnel
Calvin Hill
Vice president, business affairs
Robert R. Aylward
Vice president/sales
Louis I. Michaelson
Vice president and club counsel
Lon Babby
Vice president, planning and development
Janet Marie Smith
Vice president
Sven Erik Holmes
Vice president, marketing
Martin B. Conway
Asst. g.m./dir. of player personnel
R. Douglas Melvin
Assistant to the general manager
Frank Robinson
Director of scouting
Gary Nickels
Special assistants to the vice president
Gordon Goldsberry
Fred Uhlman Sr.
Chief financial officer
Aric Holsinger
Director of publications
Robert W. Brown
Traveling secretary
Philip E. Itzoe
Director of public relations
Richard L. Vaughn
Director of stadium services
Roy A. Sommerhof
Director of research and statistics
Eddie Epstein
Director of Orioles productions
Charles A. Steinberg, DDS
Director of sales operations
Vince Dunbar
Director, community relations
Julia A. Wagner
Director, computer services
James L. Kline
Special projects/baseball operations
Kenneth E. Nigro
Ticket office manager
Audrey Brown

Assistant director of public relations
Bob Miller
Assistant director of marketing
David Cope
Assistant director of sales operations
Matt Dryer
Assistant director of scouting
Fred Uhlman Jr.
Assistant directors of community relations
Stacey Beckwith
Jackie Patrick
Assistant ticket office managers
Joseph B. Codd
Denise C. Addicks
Publishing coordinator
Stephanie Kelly
Club physicians
Dr. Sheldon Goldgeier
Dr. Charles E. Silberstein
Trainers
Richie Bancells
Jamie Reed
Strength and conditioning
Allan Johnson
Scouts
Rick Arnold
Carlos Bernhardt
Jesus Carmona
John Cox
Ray Crone
Lane Decker
Manny Estrada
Paul Fryer
Jim Gilbert
Jesus Halabi
Rudy Hernandez
Jim Howard
Deacon Jones
Leo Labossiere
Mike Ledna
Ed Liberatore
Tim Luginbuhl
Miguel Machado
Curt Motton
Lamar North
Camilo Nunez
Fred Petersen
Harry Shelton
Ed Sprague
John Stockoe
Birdie Tebbetts
Mike Tullier
Logan White
Jerry Zimmerman

SCHEDULE KEY

H—Home game. *All-Star Game at San Diego/Jack Murphy Stadium.
N—Night game (any game starting after 5 p.m.).

SPRING TRAINING ROSTER

Manager—John Oates (26).

Coaches—Dick Bosman (31), Greg Biagini, Elrod Hendricks (44), Davey Lopes, Cal Ripken Sr. (7).

No.	PITCHERS	B/T	Ht./Wt.	Born	1991 clubs
34	Davis, Storm	R/R	6-4/225	12-26-61	Kansas City
	de la Rosa, Francisco	S/R	5-11/195	3-3-66	Rochester, Baltimore
46	Flanagan, Mike	L/L	6-0/199	12-16-51	Baltimore
49	Frohwirth, Todd	R/R	6-4/205	9-28-62	Rochester, Baltimore
	Hetzel, Eric	R/R	6-3/180	9-25-63	Pawtucket
	Lewis, Richie	R/R	5-10/175	1-25-66	Harrisburg, Indianapolis, Rochester
19	McDonald, Ben	R/R	6-7/214	11-24-67	Rochester, Baltimore
52	Mesa, Jose	R/R	6-3/222	5-22-66	Rochester, Baltimore
18	Milacki, Bob	R/R	6-4/232	7-28-64	Hagerstown, Baltimore
42	Mussina, Mike	R/R	6-2/182	12-8-68	Rochester, Baltimore
30	Olson, Gregg	R/R	6-4/206	10-11-66	Baltimore
	Oquist, Mike	R/R	6-2/170	5-30-68	Hagerstown
	Pennington, Brad	L/L	6-5/205	4-14-69	Frederick, Kane County
	Poole, Jim	L/L	6-2/203	4-28-66	Texas, Rochester, Baltimore
	Rhodes, Arthur	L/L	6-2/204	10-24-69	Hagerstown, Baltimore
40	Sutcliffe, Rick	L/R	6-7/215	6-21-56	Peoria, Iowa, Chicago NL
50	Telford, Anthony	R/R	6-0/189	3-6-66	Rochester, Baltimore
32	Williamson, Mark	R/R	6-0/177	7-21-59	Baltimore

No.	CATCHERS	B/T	Ht./Wt.	Born	1991 clubs
	Devares, Cesar	R/R	5-10/175	9-22-69	Frederick
23	Hoiles, Chris	R/R	6-0/206	3-20-65	Baltimore
41	Tackett, Jeff	R/R	6-2/206	12-1-65	Baltimore, Rochester

No.	INFIELDERS	B/T	Ht./Wt.	Born	1991 clubs
	Alexander, Manny	R/R	5-10/150	3-20-71	Hagerstown, Frederick
1	Bell, Juan	S/R	5-11/176	3-29-68	Baltimore
37	Davis, Glenn	R/R	6-3/211	3-28-61	Baltimore, Hagerstown
10	Gomez, Leo	R/R	6-0/202	3-2-67	Baltimore, Rochester
	Gutierrez, Ricky	R/R	6-1/175	5-23-70	Rochester, Hagerstown
15	Horn, Sam	L/L	6-5/247	11-2-63	Baltimore
36	Hulett, Tim	R/R	6-0/199	1-12-60	Baltimore
39	Milligan, Randy	R/R	6-1/234	11-27-61	Baltimore
3	Ripken, Bill	R/R	6-1/186	12-16-64	Baltimore, Hagerstown, Frederick
8	Ripken, Cal Jr.	R/R	6-4/224	8-24-60	Baltimore
21	Segui, David	S/L	6-1/200	7-19-66	Baltimore, Rochester
25	Worthington, Craig	R/R	6-0/200	4-17-65	Baltimore, Rochester

No.	OUTFIELDERS	B/T	Ht./Wt.	Born	1991 clubs
9	Anderson, Brady	L/L	6-1/185	1-18-64	Baltimore, Rochester
12	Devereaux, Mike	R/R	6-0/195	4-10-63	Baltimore
24	Evans, Dwight	R/R	6-3/180	11-3-51	Baltimore
14	Martinez, Chito	L/L	5-10/182	12-19-65	Baltimore, Rochester
11	Mercedes, Luis	R/R	6-0/193	2-20-68	Baltimore, Rochester
6	Orsulak, Joe	L/L	6-1/210	5-31-62	Baltimore
	Sherman, Darrell	L/L	5-9/160	12-4-67	Wichita

BALLPARK INFORMATION

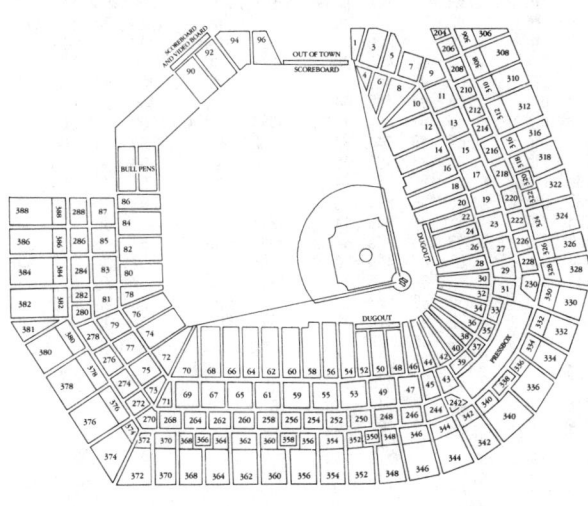

Ballpark (capacity, surface)
  Oriole Park at Camden Yards
  (48,000, grass)
Address
  333 W. Camden St.
  Baltimore, MD 21201
Business phone
  410-685-9800
Ticket information
  410-685-9800
Ticket prices
  $13 (lower boxes)
  $12 (terrace boxes)
  $10 (upper boxes)
  $8 (reserved seats)
  $4.75 (general admission, adult)
  $1 (g.a., 12 and under)
  $1 (g.a., senior citizens)
  $4 (bleachers)
Field dimensions (from home plate)
  To left field at foul line, 335 feet
  To center field, 400 feet
  To right field at foul line, 318
First game played
  Scheduled for April 6, 1992

MINOR LEAGUE AFFILIATES

Class	Team	League	Manager
AAA	Rochester	International	Jerry Narron
AA	Hagerstown	Eastern	Don Buford
A	Frederick	Carolina	Bob Miscik
A	Kane County	Midwest	Joel Youngblood
Rookie	Sarasota	Gulf Coast	Phil Wellman
Rookie	Bluefield	Appalachian	To be announced

☐ BROADCAST INFORMATION ☐

Radio: WBAL-AM (1090). Broadcasters: Joe Angel, Jon Miller, Chuck Thompson.
TV: WMAR-TV (Channel 2). Broadcasters: Scott Garceau, Keith Mills, Jack Dawson.
Cable TV: Home Team Sports. Broadcasters: Mel Procter, John Lowenstein.

SPRING TRAINING

Ballpark (city): Twin Lakes Park (Sarasota, Fla.) from February 20 through March 5; then home games will be played at Al Lang Stadium (St. Petersburg, Fla.).
Ticket information: 813-822-3384.

HISTORY

YEAR-BY-YEAR RECORDS

Year	Pos.	W	L	Pct.	*GB	Year	Pos.	W	L	Pct.	*GB
1901	8th	48	89	.350	35½	1949	7th	53	101	.344	44
1902	2nd	78	58	.574	5	1950	7th	58	96	.377	40
1903	6th	65	74	.468	26½	1951	8th	52	102	.338	46
1904	6th	65	87	.428	29	1952	7th	64	90	.416	31
1905	8th	54	99	.354	40½	1953	8th	54	100	.351	46½
1906	5th	76	73	.510	16	1954	7th	54	100	.351	57
1907	6th	69	83	.454	24	1955	7th	57	97	.370	39
1908	4th	83	69	.546	6½	1956	6th	69	85	.448	28
1909	7th	61	89	.407	36	1957	5th	76	76	.500	21
1910	8th	47	107	.305	57	1958	6th	74	79	.484	17½
1911	8th	45	107	.296	56½	1959	6th	74	80	.481	20
1912	7th	53	101	.344	53	1960	2nd	89	65	.578	8
1913	8th	57	96	.373	39	1961	3rd	95	67	.586	14
1914	5th	71	82	.464	28½	1962	7th	77	85	.475	19
1915	6th	63	91	.409	39½	1963	4th	86	76	.531	18½
1916	5th	79	75	.513	12	1964	3rd	97	65	.599	2
1917	7th	57	97	.370	43	1965	3rd	94	68	.580	8
1918	5th	58	64	.475	15	1966	1st	97	63	.606	+ 9
1919	5th	67	72	.482	20½	1967	T6th	76	85	.472	15½
1920	4th	76	77	.497	21½	1968	2nd	91	71	.562	12
1921	3rd	81	73	.526	17½	1969	1st†	109	53	.673	+19
1922	2nd	93	61	.604	1	1970	1st†	108	54	.667	+15
1923	7th	74	78	.487	24	1971	1st†	101	57	.639	+12
1924	4th	74	78	.487	17	1972	3rd	80	74	.519	5
1925	3rd	82	71	.536	15	1973	1st‡	97	65	.599	+ 8
1926	7th	62	92	.403	29	1974	1st‡	91	71	.562	+ 2
1927	7th	59	94	.336	50½	1975	2nd	90	69	.566	4½
1928	3rd	82	72	.532	19	1976	2nd	88	74	.543	10½
1929	4th	79	73	.520	26	1977	T2nd	97	64	.602	2½
1930	6th	64	90	.416	38	1978	4th	90	71	.559	9
1931	5th	63	91	.409	45	1979	1st†	102	57	.642	+ 8
1932	6th	63	91	.409	44	1980	2nd	100	62	.617	3
1933	8th	55	96	.364	43½	1981	2nd/4th	59	46	.562	§
1934	6th	67	85	.441	33	1982	2nd	94	68	.580	1
1935	7th	65	87	.428	28½	1983	1st†	98	64	.605	+ 6
1936	7th	57	95	.375	44½	1984	5th	85	77	.525	19
1937	8th	46	108	.299	56	1985	4th	83	78	.516	16
1938	7th	55	97	.362	44	1986	7th	73	89	.451	22½
1939	8th	43	111	.279	64½	1987	6th	67	95	.414	31
1940	6th	67	87	.435	23	1988	7th	54	107	.335	34½
1941	T6th	70	84	.455	31	1989	2nd	87	75	.537	2
1942	3rd	82	69	.543	19½	1990	5th	76	85	.472	11½
1943	6th	72	80	.474	25	1991	6th	67	95	.414	24
1944	1st	89	65	.578	+ 1						
1945	3rd	81	70	.536	6						
1946	7th	66	88	.429	38						
1947	8th	59	95	.383	38						
1948	6th	59	94	.386	37						

*Games behind winner. †Won Championship Series. ‡Lost Championship Series. §First half 31-23; second 28-23.

MANAGERS

Name	Record	Years
Hugh Duffy	48-89	1901
Jimmy McAleer	551-632	'02-09
Jack O'Connor	47-107	1910
Bobby Wallace	57-134	'11-12
George Stovall	91-158	'12-13
Branch Rickey	139-179	'13-15
Fielder Jones	158-196	'16-18
Jimmy Austin	29-38	'18, '23
Jimmy Burke	172-180	'18-20
Lee Fohl	226-183	'21-23
George Sisler	218-241	'24-26
Dan Howley	220-239	'27-29
Bill Killefer	224-329	'30-33
Al Sothoron	2-6	1933
Rogers Hornsby	255-381	'33-37
		1952
Jim Bottomley	21-56	1937
Gabby Street	55-97	1938
Fred Haney	125-227	'39-41
Luke Sewell	432-410	41-46
Zack Taylor	235-410	1946
		'48-51
Marty Marion	96-161	'52-53
Jimmie Dykes	54-100	1954
Paul Richards	517-539	'55-61
Lum Harris	17-10	1961
Billy Hitchcock	163-161	'62-63
Hank Bauer	407-318	'64-68
Earl Weaver	1481-1060	'68-82
		'85-86
Cal Ripken Sr.	67-101	'87-88
Frank Robinson	230-285	88-91
Johnny Oates	54-71	1991

DAY BY DAY

Date	Opp.	Res.	Score (inn.*)	Hits	Opp. hits	Winning pitcher	Losing pitcher	Save	Record	Pos.	GB
4-8	Chi.	L	1-9	4	10	McDowell	Ballard		0-1	T4th	1
4-10	Chi.	L	0-2	3	7	Hibbard	Mesa	Thigpen	0-2	7th	2
4-12	At Tex.	W	3-0	5	4	Johnson	Witt	Olson	1-2	5th	2
4-13	At Tex.	W	11-4	12	10	Ballard	Rogers		2-2	3rd	1
4-14	At Tex.	L	3-15	5	16	Ryan	Robinson		2-3	T4th	2
4-15	At Mil.	W	7-2	6	8	Mesa	Bosio	Williamson	3-3	3rd	2
4-17	At Mil.	L	3-7	12	10	Navarro	Johnson	Lee	3-4	6th	1½
4-18	At Mil.	L	3-4 (11)	6	7	Nunez	Bautista		3-5	6th	2
4-19	Tex.	W	5-0	10	5	Robinson	Rogers		4-5	T5th	2
4-20	Tex.	L	0-1	4	4	Ryan	Mesa	Russell	4-6	T5th	3
4-22	At Chi.	L	7-8	10	11	Fernandez	McDonald	Thigpen	4-7	6th	2½
4-23	At Chi.	L	4-10	9	12	McDowell	D. Johnson		4-8	7th	3½
4-24	At Chi.	W	5-1	10	7	Ballard	Hough		5-8	T5th	2½
4-26	Mil.	L	4-5	9	11	Holmes	Mesa	Nunez	5-9	7th	4
4-27	Mil.	L	2-5	7	12	August	Robinson		5-10	7th	4
4-28	Mil.	W	5-4	10	11	Milacki	Holmes	Olson	6-10	T6th	4
4-29	Sea.	L	1-10	8	15	DeLucia	Johnson		6-11	7th	4½
4-30	Sea.	L	3-6	6	10	Hanson	Ballard	Swan	6-12	7th	5
5-1	Sea.	W	2-1	3	7	Mesa	Johnson	Olson	7-12	6th	4
5-3	At Cal.	W	2-0	10	5	McDonald	McCaskill	Olson	8-12	6th	4
5-4	At Cal.	L	3-6	6	9	Langston	Robinson	Harvey	8-13	6th	5
5-5	At Cal.	L	4-6	8	8	J. Abbott	Ballard	Harvey	8-14	6th	6
5-6	At Cal.	W	7-0	10	7	Mesa	Lewis		9-14	6th	5½
5-7	At Oak.	L	3-11	8	12	Moore	McDonald		9-15	6th	5½
5-8	At Oak.	L	3-9	9	11	Young	Flanagan		9-16	6th	6½
5-10	At Sea.	L	1-3	6	7	DeLucia	Ballard	Jackson	9-17	7th	8
5-11	At Sea.	W	11-5	15	9	Mesa	Krueger		10-17	6th	8
5-12	At Sea.	L	4-5	6	6	Jackson	Olson		10-18	7th	8
5-14	Oak.	W	6-1	9	10	Robinson	Slusarski		11-18	7th	7½
5-15	Oak.	L	3-6	7	13	Welch	Ballard	Eckersley	11-19	7th	8½
5-16	Oak.	L	5-11	12	14	Klink	Mesa		11-20	7th	9
5-17	Cal.	W	5-1	11	6	McDonald	Lewis		12-20	T6th	8
5-18	Cal.	L	2-4	9	10	Finley	Williamson	Harvey	12-21	T6th	8
5-19	Cal.	L	2-10	7	15	McCaskill	Ballard		12-22	7th	8
5-20	At Det.	L	5-11	14	12	Gleaton	Milacki		12-23	7th	9
5-21	At Det.	W	5-4	9	9	Flanagan	Gibson	Olson	13-23	T6th	9
5-22	At Det.	L	5-9	9	9	Gullickson	McDonald		13-24	7th	10
5-24	N.Y.	L	1-7	3	10	Sanderson	Robinson		13-25	7th	10½
5-25	N.Y.	L	5-6	11	9	Farr	Flanagan	Guetterman	13-26	7th	10½
5-26	N.Y.	L	1-2 (11)	9	12	Habyan	Flanagan	Cadaret	13-27	7th	10½
5-27	Cle.	L	2-3	9	9	Candiotti	Milacki	Hillegas	13-28	7th	10½
5-28	Cle.	W	5-2	8	8	Smith	Nagy	Olson	14-28	7th	10½
5-29	Cle.	W	2-1	7	4	Robinson	Walker	Olson	15-28	7th	9½
5-30	At Bos.	W	9-3	10	6	Ballard	Young	Flanagan	16-28	7th	8½
5-31	At Bos.	L	2-7	6	13	Gardiner	Mesa		16-29	7th	9½
6-1	At Bos.	W	3-1	9	3	Hickey	Darwin	Olson	17-29	7th	8½
6-2	At Bos.	W	5-1	10	4	Smith	Clemens	Williamson	18-29	7th	7½
6-3	At Min.	L	2-3	8	8	Morris	Robinson	Aguilera	18-30	7th	8½
6-4	At Min.	L	3-4 (10)	11	13	Willis	Olson		18-31	7th	8½
6-5	At Min.	L	3-4	9	7	Tapani	Mesa	Aguilera	18-32	7th	9½
6-6	Tor.	W	6-4	6	9	Milacki	Timlin	Olson	19-32	7th	8½
6-7	Tor.	W	6-4	7	8	Smith	Guzman	Olson	20-32	7th	7½
6-8	Tor.	L	4-8	11	12	Key	Kilgus		20-33	7th	8½
6-9	Tor.	L	2-3	5	9	Stottlemyre	Ballard	Henke	20-34	7th	9½
6-11	K.C.	L	0-11	7	16	Gubicza	Mesa	Crawford	20-35	7th	9½
6-12	K.C.	L	8-9	11	8	M. Davis	Williamson	Montgomery	20-36	7th	10½
6-13	K.C.	L	4-6	9	12	M. Davis	Kilgus	Montgomery	20-37	7th	11½
6-14	At Tor.	L	1-9	8	12	Stottlemyre	Robinson		20-38	7th	12½
6-15	At Tor.	W	8-4	12	9	Ballard	Guzman	Williamson	21-38	7th	11½
6-16	At Tor.	W	13-8	13	12	Frohwirth	Ward		22-38	T6th	11
6-17	Min.	W	6-5	12	14	Williamson	Aguilera		23-38	6th	10
6-18	Min.	L	2-9	4	12	Erickson	Smith	Willis	23-39	6th	10
6-19	Min.	L	4-8	6	9	Morris	Olson		23-40	7th	10
6-20	At K.C.	L	2-3 (10)	8	9	Crawford	Frohwirth		23-41	7th	11½
6-22	At K.C.	W	1-0	3	3	Milacki	Gordon	Olson	24-41	6th	11½
6-23 (1)	At K.C.	W	11-8 (10)	17	14	Frohwirth	Montgomery	Olson	25-41	6th	11½
6-23 (2)	At K.C.	W	9-8 (12)	18	16	Olson	S. Davis	Kilgus	26-41	6th	11
6-25	At Cle.	W	5-3 (12)	11	14	Williamson	Jones	Olson	27-41	6th	10½
6-26	At Cle.	L	4-10	12	12	Swindell	Ballard	Shaw	27-42	6th	11½
6-27	At Cle.	W	7-2	15	10	Milacki	Mutis	Olson	28-42	6th	11½

BALTIMORE ORIOLES

1992 SEASON

BALTIMORE ORIOLES

Date	Opp.	Res.	Score (inn.*)	Hits	Opp. hits	Winning pitcher	Losing pitcher	Save	Record	Pos.	GB
6-28	Bos.	L	3-9	6	13	Harris	Mesa		28-43	6th	11½
6-29	Bos.	W	7-3	9	10	Smith	Darwin		29-43	6th	11½
6-30	Bos.	W	6-4	10	6	Williamson	Hesketh	Olson	30-43	6th	11½
7-1	Det.	W	10-2	10	5	McDonald	Gakeler		31-43	6th	11½
7-2	Det.	L	3-4	10	10	Gullickson	Ballard	Henneman	31-44	6th	12½
7-3	Det.	L	2-8	8	11	Tanana	Milacki		31-45	6th	13½
7-4	At N.Y.	L	2-3	6	8	Plunk	Smith	Guetterman	31-46	6th	13½
7-5	At N.Y.	W	7-4	15	8	Robinson	Leary	Olson	32-46	6th	13½
7-6	At N.Y.	L	5-13	10	13	Plunk	Frohwirth		32-47	6th	14½
7-7	At N.Y.	W	5-3	13	7	Ballard	Taylor	Olson	33-47	6th	14½
7-11	At Oak.	L	1-8	7	12	Stewart	Robinson		33-48	6th	15½
7-12	At Oak.	W	6-3	12	4	McDonald	Young	Olson	34-48	6th	15½
7-13	At Oak.	W	2-0	6	0	Milacki	Show	Olson	35-48	6th	15½
7-14	At Oak.	L	2-3 (11)	6	11	Burns	Olson		35-49	6th	15½
7-15	At Cal.	W	2-1	5	10	Ballard	Harvey	Frohwirth	36-49	6th	15½
7-16	At Cal.	L	1-2	6	3	Langston	Robinson		36-50	6th	15½
7-17	At K.C.	L	8-9 (15)	19	21	Aquino	Williamson		36-51	6th	16
7-18	At K.C.	L	1-5	7	7	Saberhagen	Milacki		36-52	6th	17
7-19	Sea.	W	4-1	7	7	Smith	DeLucia	Olson	37-52	6th	17
7-20	Sea.	L	1-5	9	9	Krueger	Ballard		37-53	6th	17
7-21	Sea.	L	4-6	10	9	Swan	Robinson	Swift	37-54	6th	17
7-23	Cal.	L	4-5	8	15	J. Abbott	McDonald	Harvey	37-55	6th	17
7-24	Cal.	W	5-2	9	6	Milacki	Finley	Olson	38-55	6th	17
7-25	Cal.	W	8-4	10	11	Frohwirth	McCaskill		39-55	6th	16
7-26	Oak.	L	9-12	8	14	Klink	Williamson	Chitren	39-56	6th	17
7-27	Oak.	L	1-9	2	13	Slusarski	Ballard		39-57	6th	17
7-28	Oak.	L	3-4	9	8	Honeycutt	McDonald	Eckersley	39-58	6th	17
7-29	At Sea.	L	4-11	8	11	Hanson	Milacki		39-59	6th	17
7-30	At Sea.	L	2-8	9	10	Krueger	Smith		39-60	6th	17
7-31	At Sea.	W	4-2 (11)	9	9	Flanagan	Swift	Olson	40-60	6th	16
8-2	At Chi.	W	3-0	5	8	McDonald	Fernandez	Olson	41-60	6th	16½
8-3	At Chi.	W	6-3	13	9	Milacki	McDowell	Olson	42-60	6th	15½
8-4	At Chi.	L	0-1	5	4	Hough	Mussina		42-61	6th	16½
8-5	Mil.	L	5-6	11	10	Henry	Williamson	Nunez	42-62	6th	17
8-6	Mil.	W	13-5	17	12	Johnson	Hunter		43-62	6th	17
8-7	Mil.	L	2-4	9	10	Navarro	McDonald		43-63	6th	18
8-8	Mil.	L	4-6	9	9	Wegman	Milacki	Nunez	43-64	6th	18
8-9	Chi.	L	4-7	7	13	Drahman	Mussina	Thigpen	43-65	6th	18
8-10	Chi.	L	4-6	7	9	Garcia	Flanagan	Thigpen	43-66	6th	18
8-11	Chi.	L	0-7	0	14	Alvarez	Johnson		43-67	6th	18
8-12	Chi.	W	5-4 (11)	10	6	Olson	Pall		44-67	6th	17
8-13 (1)	Tex.	W	4-3 (12)	6	13	Johnson	Rogers		45-67	6th	16
8-13 (2)	Tex.	W	8-7	12	13	Frohwirth	Guzman	Olson	46-67	6th	15½
8-14	Tex.	W	10-2	12	3	Mussina	Alexander		47-67	6th	14½
8-15	Tex.	W	9-2	14	3	Mesa	Boyd		48-67	6th	14½
8-16	At Mil.	L	5-8	11	13	August	Smith		48-68	6th	14½
8-17	At Mil.	L	6-7	12	11	Navarro	McDonald	Nunez	48-69	6th	15½
8-18	At Mil.	L	1-2	9	5	Wegman	Milacki	Henry	48-70	6th	16½
8-19	At Tex.	L	1-4	5	7	Ryan	Mussina	Mathews	48-71	6th	17
8-20	At Tex.	W	8-6	12	11	Johnson	Rosenthal	Flanagan	49-71	6th	17
8-21	At Tex.	W	4-3	10	7	Frohwirth	Brown	Olson	50-71	6th	16
8-23	Min.	W	5-4	9	10	Olson	Willis		51-71	6th	15½
8-24	Min.	L	2-5	5	8	Bedroaisn	Flanagan	Aguilera	51-72	6th	15½
8-25	Min.	W	7-3	9	7	Mussina	Erickson	Frohwirth	52-72	6th	15½
8-26	Tor.	L	2-5	10	11	Key	Johnson	Henke	52-73	6th	16½
8-27	Tor.	L	1-6	5	8	Guzman	Rhodes		52-74	6th	17½
8-28	Tor.	L	0-3	1	9	Candiotti	McDonald	Henke	52-75	6th	18½
8-30	At Min.	W	11-5	17	15	Milacki	Edens		53-75	6th	18
8-31	At Min.	L	2-5	7	11	Tapani	Mussina	Aguilera	53-76	6th	19
9-1	At Min.	L	3-14	7	16	Morris	Rhodes		53-77	6th	19
9-2	At Tor.	L	4-5 (12)	10	12	Timlin	Olson		53-78	6th	20
9-3	At Tor.	W	8-4	12	7	McDonald	Wells	Flanagan	54-78	6th	19
9-4	At Tor.	L	1-3	4	6	Stottlemyre	Milacki	Ward	54-79	6th	20
9-6	K.C.	W	6-2	9	6	Poole	Saberhagen		55-79	6th	20½
9-7	K.C.	L	4-7	7	12	Aquino	Mesa		55-80	6th	21½
9-8	K.C.	L	2-3	10	8	Johnston	Frohwirth	Montgomery	55-81	6th	22½
9-9	N.Y.	W	8-0	10	5	Milacki	Sanderson		56-81	6th	22
9-10	N.Y.	W	6-3	9	8	Frohwirth	Plunk		57-81	6th	21
9-11	N.Y.	W	4-2	7	8	Mussina	Taylor	Olson	58-81	6th	20
9-12	Cle.	L	5-6	12	10	Nagy	Mesa	Olin	58-82	6th	20½
9-13	Cle.	W	5-4	13	9	Olson	Shaw		59-82	6th	20½
9-14	Cle.	L	5-6 (11)	10	14	Bell	Flanagan	Olin	59-83	6th	21½
9-15	Cle.	W	4-3	4	5	Williamson	Blair	Olson	60-83	6th	20½
9-16	At Bos.	W	9-2	16	10	Mussina	Bolton		61-83	6th	19½

Date	Opp.	Res.	Score (inn.*)	Hits	Opp. hits	Winning pitcher	Losing pitcher	Save	Record	Pos.	GB
9-17	At Bos.	L	3-4	7	7	Morton	Mesa	Reardon	61-84	6th	19½
9-18	At Bos.	L	5-7	10	13	Gardiner	Johnson	Harris	61-85	6th	20½
9-20	At Cle.	W	2-1	6	7	Milacki	Otto	Olson	62-85	6th	19½
9-21	At Cle.	L	1-10	8	16	Swindell	Rhodes		62-86	6th	19½
9-22	At Cle.	L	1-2	3	7	Bell	Mussina		62-87	6th	20½
9-23	Bos.	W	4-3	5	9	Poole	Gardiner	Olson	63-87	6th	19½
9-26 (1)	Bos.	L	1-2	7	6	Clemens	Johnson		63-88	6th	21
9-26 (2)	Bos.	W	6-5	11	10	Frohwirth	Harris		64-88	6th	20½
9-27	At Det.	W	9-7	11	11	Williamson	Terrell	Olson	65-88	6th	20½
9-28	At Det.	L	4-5 (10)	9	9	Henneman	Olson		65-89	6th	20½
9-29	At Det.	W	7-4	12	10	Mesa	Aldred	Frohwirth	66-89	T5th	20½
9-30	At Det.	L	3-8	6	12	Leiter	Johnson		66-90	6th	20½
10-1	At N.Y.	L	2-3 (11)	10	8	Monteleone	Poole		66-91	6th	21½
10-2	At N.Y.	L	3-4	11	8	Cadaret	Flanagan	Farr	66-92	6th	22½
10-3	At N.Y.	L	6-9	11	11	Johnson	Ballard	Farr	66-93	6th	23
10-4	Det.	L	2-4 (14)	10	7	Haas	Poole	Cerutti	66-94	6th	24
10-5	Det.	W	7-3	9	8	Poole	Leiter	Williamson	67-94	6th	23
10-6	Det.	L	1-7	4	14	Tanana	Milacki		67-95	6th	24

Monthly records: April (6-12), May (10-17), June (14-14), July (10-17), August (13-16), September (13-14), Oct. (1-5).

HIGHLIGHTS

High point: The Orioles went 14-14 in June, the only month in which the club did not have a losing record.

Low point: From April 17 through May 10, Baltimore won just six of 20 games and fell into the American League East cellar.

Turning point: May 23, when Manager Frank Robinson was replaced by John Oates. The fortunes of the team did not change significantly, but the direction of the club did. Though no one conceded the season, Oates began building toward 1992 soon thereafter.

Most valuable player: Shortstop Cal Ripken. He had the best season of his career, batting .323 with 34 home runs and 114 runs batted in. He capped his season by winning his second A.L. Most Valuable Player award and first Gold Glove.

Most valuable pitcher: Righthander Todd Frohwirth. He came out of nowhere to establish himself as one of the league's premier middle relievers. He posted a 7-3 record with a 1.87 earned-run average in 51 games.

Most improved player: Rookie third baseman Leo Gomez. After disappointing during a call-up in '90, he led big-league rookies with 16 home runs in '91.

Most pleasant surprise: Right fielder Chito Martinez. Called up from Class AAA Rochester on July 5, Martinez hit 10 homers by September 1. He finished with 13 homers and 33 RBIs in 67 games.

Biggest disappointment: First baseman Glenn Davis. After coming to Baltimore from Houston in a big off-season trade, Davis injured his neck and subsequently lost strength in his shoulder. The injury forced him to miss 105 games.

Key injuries: Davis' neck injury hurt the team, as did the injuries suffered by righthanders Ben McDonald and Dave Johnson. McDonald was on the disabled list twice with elbow and shoulder problems. Johnson missed two months with a deep groin strain.

Notable: After 38 seasons and three world championships, Baltimore played its last game in Memorial Stadium on October 6. The Orioles lost to Detroit, 7-1. The club moves into Oriole Park at Camden Yards in 1992. . . . On July 13 at Oakland, Bob Milacki, Mike Flanagan, Mark Williamson and Gregg Olson combined to no-hit the A's, 2-0. . . . On August 11, Chicago's Wilson Alvarez threw the sixth and final no-hitter in Memorial Stadium. . . . Baltimore's bullpen threw a club record and big-league high 557⅔ innings.

—PETER SCHMUCK

RECORDS

1991 regular-season record: 67-95 (6th in A.L. East); 33-48 at home; 34-47 on road; 33-45 vs. East; 34-50 vs. West; 18-24 vs. LHP; 49-71 vs. RHP; 58-80 on grass; 9-15 on turf; 17-26 in daytime; 50-69 at night; 18-35 in one-run games; 6-12 in extra-inning games; 2-0-1 in doubleheaders.

Team record last five years: 351-457 (.434, ranks 13th in league in that span).

TEAM LEADERS

Batting average: Cal Ripken (.323).
At-bats: Cal Ripken (650).
Runs: Cal Ripken (99).
Hits: Cal Ripken (210).
Total bases: Cal Ripken (368).
Doubles: Cal Ripken (46).
Triples: Mike Devereaux (10).
Home runs: Cal Ripken (34).
Runs batted in: Cal Ripken (114).
Stolen bases: Mike Devereaux (16).
Slugging percentage: Cal Ripken (.566).
On-base percentage: Cal Ripken (.374).
Wins: Bob Milacki (10).
Earned-run average: Bob Milacki (4.01).
Complete games: Bob Milacki (3).
Shutouts: Jose Mesa, Bob Milacki (1).
Saves: Gregg Olson (31).
Innings pitched: Bob Milacki (184).
Strikeouts: Bob Milacki (108).

GAMES BY POSITION

Catcher: Chris Hoiles 89, Bob Melvin 72, Ernie Whitt 20, Jeff Tackett 6.
First base: Randy Milligan 106, David Segui 42, Glenn Davis 36, Leo Gomez 3, Chris Hoiles 2, Jeff McKnight 2, Chito Martinez 1.
Second base: Bill Ripken 103, Juan Bell 77, Tim Hulett 26, Shane Turner 1.
Third base: Leo Gomez 105, Tim Hulett 39, Craig Worthington 30.
Shortstop: Cal Ripken 162, Juan Bell 15, Tim Hulett 1.
Outfield: Mike Devereaux 149, Joe Orsulak 132, Brady Anderson 101, Dwight Evans 67, Chito Martinez 54, David Segui 33, Luis Mercedes 15, Randy Milligan 9, Jeff McKnight 7, Juan Bell 1.
Designated hitter: Sam Horn 102, Randy Milligan 25, Dwight Evans 21, Tim Hulett 15, Chris Hoiles 13, Glenn Davis 12, Leo Gomez 10, Juan Bell 4, Chito Martinez 4, Jeff McKnight 4, Bob Melvin 4, David Segui 4, Brady Anderson 3, Joe Orsulak 2, Ernie Whitt 2, Luis Mercedes 1, Shane Turner 1.

TOP 10 DRAFT CHOICES

1. **Mark Smith,** OF, University of Southern California.
2. **Shawn Curran,** C, Corona (Calif.) High School.
3. **Alex Ochoa,** OF, Miami Lakes High School, Hialeah, Fla.
4. **Vaughn Eshelman,** LHP, University of Houston.
5. **Jim Wawruck,** OF, University of Vermont.
6. **Daniel Fregoso,** RHP, Catalina High School, Tucson, Ariz.
7. **Jimmy Haynes,** RHP, Troup County High School, LaGrange, Ga.
8. **Terry Farrar,** LHP, Missouri Baptist College.
9. **Chris Lemp,** RHP, Sacramento (Calif.) Community College.
10. **Robert Waszgis,** C, McNeese State University.

BOSTON RED SOX
AMERICAN LEAGUE EAST DIVISION

1992 SCHEDULE

APRIL

S	M	T	W	T	F	S
5	6	7 NY	8	9 N NY	10	11 CLE
12 DH CLE	13 BAL H	14	15 BAL H	16 N BAL H	17 N TOR H	18 TOR H
19 TOR H	20 TOR H	21 N MIL	22 MIL	23 MIL	24 N TEX H	25 TEX H
26 TEX H	27	28 N CHI H	29 N CHI H	30		

MAY

S	M	T	W	T	F	S
					1 N KC	2 N KC H
3 KC H	4 MIN H	5 N MIN H	6 N CHI	7 CHI	8 N KC	9 KC
10 KC	11	12 N MIN	13 N MIN	14	15 N CAL H	16 CAL H
17 CAL H	18 SEA H	19 N SEA H	20 N SEA H	21	22 N OAK H	23 OAK H
24 OAK H	25	26 N CAL	27 CAL	28 N CAL	29 N SEA	30 N SEA
31 N SEA						

JUNE

S	M	T	W	T	F	S
	1 N OAK	2 N OAK	3 OAK	4	5 N CLE H	6 CLE H
7 CLE H	8 N BAL	9 N BAL	10 N BAL	11 N TOR	12 N TOR	13 TOR
14 TOR	15 N NY H	16 N NY H	17 N NY H	18 N NY H	19 N TEX	20 N TEX
21 N TEX	22 N DET H	23 N DET H	24 DET	25	26 N MIL H	27 MIL H
28 MIL H	29 N DET H	30 N DET H				

JULY

S	M	T	W	T	F	S
		1 N DET	2 N CHI	3 N CHI	4 N CHI	
5 CHI	6 N KC / CHI H	7 N KC / CHI H	8 N DET / CHI H	9	10 N CHI H	11 CHI H
12 CHI H	13	14 N *	15	16 N MIN	17 N MIN	18 MIN
19 MIN	20 N KC	21 N KC	22 N KC	23 N MIN H	24 N MIN H	25 MIN H
26 N MIN H	27 N TEX	28 N TEX	29 TEX	30		31 BAL H

AUGUST

S	M	T	W	T	F	S
						1 BAL H
2 BAL	3 N TOR H	4 N TOR H	5 N TOR H	6 NY H	7 N NY H	8 NY
9 NY	10 N CLE	11 N CLE	12 N CLE	13 N CLE	14 N MIL	15 N MIL
16 MIL	17	18 N CAL H	19 N CAL H	20 N CAL H	21 N SEA H	22 SEA H
23 SEA H	24 N OAK H	25 N OAK H	26 OAK H	27	28 N CAL	29 N CAL
30 CAL	31 N SEA					

SEPTEMBER

S	M	T	W	T	F	S
		1 N SEA	2 N SEA	3	4 N OAK	5 OAK
6 OAK	7 N TEX	8 N TEX	9 N TEX	10	11 N DET H	12 DET H
13 DET H	14	15 N MIL H	16 N MIL H	17 N MIL H	18 N DET	19 DET
20 DET	21 N CLE H	22 N CLE H	23 N CLE H	24 N CLE	25 N BAL	26 N BAL
27 BAL	28 N BAL	29 N TOR	30 N TOR			

OCTOBER

S	M	T	W	T	F	S
				1	2 N NY H	3 NY H
4 NY H	5	6	7	8	9	10

1992 SEASON

CLUB DIRECTORY

Owner/general partner
JRY Corporation
Majority owner and chairwoman of the brd.
Jean R. Yawkey
President
John L. Harrington
Vice president and treasurer
William B. Gutfarb
Owner/general partner
Haywood C. Sullivan
Senior vice president and general manager
James (Lou) Gorman
Executive vice president and counsel
John F. Donovan Jr.
Vice president and chief financial officer
Robert C. Furbush
Vice president, transportation
John J. Rogers
Director of scouting
Edward M. Kasko
Assistant general manager
Elaine W. Steward
Director of minor league operations
Edward P. Kenney
Administrative assistant to player develop.
Erwin L. Bryant
Special assistant to the general manager
John M. Pesky
Traveling secretary
Steven W. August
Medical director
Dr. Arthur M. Pappas
V.p., broadcasting and special projects
James P. Healey
Vice president, public relations
Richard L. Bresciani
Vice president, marketing
Lawrence C. Cancro
Vice president, stadium operations
Joseph F. McDermott
Dir. of comm. relations & personnel admin.
Linda G. Ezell
Director of facilities management
Thomas L. Queenan Jr.
Director of food services
Patricia T. Flanagan
Director of parking facilities
Michael L. Silva
Director of publicity
Josh S. Spofford

Director of statistics
James A. Samia
Director of ticket operations
Joseph P. Helyar
Superintendent of grounds and maintenance
Joseph F. Mooney
Treasurer
John J. Reilly
Controller
Stanley H. Tran
Staff accountant
Robin R. Yeingst
Manager of advertising
Karla K. O'Hara
Manager of corporate sales
Robert G. Capilli
Manager of publications
Debra A. Matson
Scouts
Rafael Batista
Milton Bolling
Ray Boone
Wayne Britton
Ray Crone
Luis Delgado
George Digby
Howard (Danny) Doyle
Bill Enos
Larry Flynn
Charles Koney
Jack Lee
Wilfred (Lefty) Lefebvre
Don Lenhardt
Howard McCullough
Frank Malzone
Sam Mele
Willie Paffen
Phillip Rossi
Alex Scott
Edward Scott
Matt Sczesny
Joe Stephenson
Larry Thomas
Fay Thompson
Charlie Wagner
Luke Wrenn
Jeff Zona

SCHEDULE KEY

H—Home game.   *All-Star Game at San Diego/Jack Murphy Stadium.
N—Night game (any game starting after 5 p.m.).   DH—Doubleheader.

SPRING TRAINING ROSTER

Manager—Butch Hobson.

Coaches—Gary Allenson, Al Bumbry (37), Rick Burleson, Rich Gale, Don Zimmer.

No.	PITCHERS	B/T	Ht./Wt.	Born	1991 clubs
50	Bolton, Tom	L/L	6-3/185	5-6-62	Boston
21	Clemens, Roger	R/R	6-4/220	8-4-62	Boston
44	Darwin, Danny	R/R	6-3/195	10-25-55	Boston
40	Dopson, John	R/R	6-4/235	7-14-63	Winter Haven, Boston
48	Fossas, Tony	L/L	6-0/187	9-23-57	Boston
47	Gardiner, Mike	S/R	6-0/200	10-19-65	Pawtucket, Boston
38	Gray, Jeff	R/R	6-1/190	4-10-63	Boston
27	Harris, Greg	S/R	6-0/175	11-2-55	Boston
55	Hesketh, Joe	L/L	6-2/170	2-15-59	Boston
	Hoy, Peter	L/R	6-7/220	6-29-66	New Britain, Pawtucket
59	Irvine, Daryl	R/R	6-3/195	11-15-64	Pawtucket, Boston
19	Kiecker, Dana	R/R	6-3/195	2-25-61	Pawtucket, Boston
51	Manzanillo, Josias	R/R	6-0/190	10-16-67	New Britain, Pawtucket, Boston
43	Morton, Kevin	R/L	6-2/185	8-3-68	Pawtucket, Boston
54	Plympton, Jeff	R/R	6-2/205	11-24-65	Pawtucket, Boston
	Quantrill, Paul	L/R	6-1/175	11-3-68	New Britain, Pawtucket
41	Reardon, Jeff	R/R	6-0/205	10-1-55	Boston
56	Taylor, Scott	L/L	6-1/185	8-2-67	New Britain, Pawtucket
16	Viola, Frank	L/L	6-4/210	4-19-60	New York NL
30	Young, Matt	L/L	6-3/210	8-9-58	Pawtucket, Boston

No.	CATCHERS	B/T	Ht./Wt.	Born	1991 clubs
20	Marzano, John	R/R	5-11/195	2-14-63	Boston
6	Pena, Tony	R/R	6-0/185	6-4-57	Boston
22	Wedge, Eric	R/R	6-3/215	1-27-68	Winter Haven, New Britain, Pawtucket, Boston

No.	INFIELDERS	B/T	Ht./Wt.	Born	1991 clubs
26	Boggs, Wade	L/R	6-2/197	6-15-58	Boston
25	Clark, Jack	R/R	6-3/210	11-10-55	Boston
45	Cooper, Scott	L/R	6-3/205	10-13-67	Pawtucket, Boston
11	Naehring, Tim	R/R	6-2/190	2-1-67	Boston
18	Quintana, Carlos	R/R	6-2/220	8-26-65	Boston
3	Reed, Jody	R/R	5-9/165	7-26-62	Boston
2	Rivera, Luis	R/R	5-9/175	1-3-64	Boston
	Valentin, John	R/R	6-0/170	2-18-67	New Britain, Pawtucket
42	Vaughn, Mo	L/R	6-1/230	12-15-67	Pawtucket, Boston

No.	OUTFIELDERS	B/T	Ht./Wt.	Born	1991 clubs
23	Brunansky, Tom	R/R	6-4/220	8-20-60	Boston
12	Burks, Ellis	R/R	6-2/205	9-11-64	Boston
39	Greenwell, Mike	L/R	6-0/205	7-18-63	Boston
17	Housie, Wayne	S/R	5-9/165	5-20-65	New Britain, Pawtucket, Boston
	McNeely, Jeff	R/R	6-2/190	10-18-69	Lynchburg
29	Plantier, Phil	L/R	5-11/195	1-27-69	Pawtucket, Boston
5	Winningham, Herm	L/R	5-11/190	12-1-61	Cincinnati
	Zupcic, Bob	R/R	6-4/225	8-18-66	Pawtucket, Boston

BALLPARK INFORMATION

Ballpark (capacity, surface)
Fenway Park (33,925, grass)

Address
4 Yawkey Way
Boston, MA 02215

Business phone
617-267-9440

Ticket information
617-267-8661

Ticket prices
$14 (upper box)
$10 (grandstand)
$7 (bleachers)
$7 (standing room)

Field dimensions (from home plate)
To left field at foul line, 315 feet
To center field, 420 feet
To right field at foul line, 302 feet

First game played
April 20, 1912 (Red Sox 7, New York
Highlanders 6)

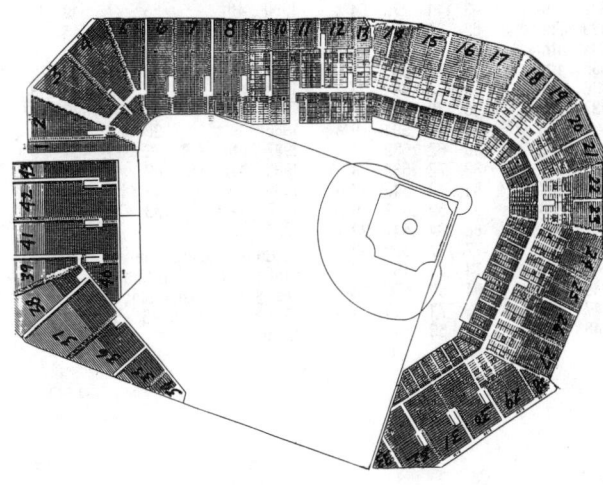

MINOR LEAGUE AFFILIATES

Class	Team	League	Manager
AAA	Pawtucket	International	Rico Petrocelli
AA	New Britain	Eastern	Jim Pankovits
A	Lynchburg	Carolina	Buddy Bailey
A	Winter Haven	Florida State	Felix Maldonado
A	Elmira	New York-Pennsylvania	Dave Holt
Rookie	Winter Haven Red Sox	Gulf Coast	Frank White

BROADCAST INFORMATION

Radio: WRKO-AM (680). Broadcasters: Bob Starr, Joe Castiglione.
TV: WSBK-TV (Channel 38). Broadcasters: Sean McDonough, Bob Montgomery.
Cable TV: New England Sports Network. Broadcasters: Ned Martin, Jerry Remy.

SPRING TRAINING

Ballpark (city): Chain O'Lakes Park (Winter Haven, Fla.).
Ticket information: 813-293-3900.

HISTORY

YEAR-BY-YEAR RECORDS

Year	Pos.	W	L	Pct.	*GB	Year	Pos.	W	L	Pct.	*GB
1901	2nd	79	57	.581	4	1949	2nd	96	58	.623	1
1902	3rd	77	60	.562	6½	1950	3rd	94	60	.610	4
1903	1st	91	47	.659	+14½	1951	3rd	87	67	.565	11
1904	1st	95	59	.617	+1½	1952	6th	76	78	.494	19
1905	4th	78	74	.513	16	1953	4th	84	69	.549	16
1906	8th	49	105	.318	45½	1954	4th	69	85	.448	42
1907	7th	59	90	.396	32½	1955	4th	84	70	.545	12
1908	5th	75	79	.487	15½	1956	4th	84	70	.545	13
1909	3rd	88	63	.583	9½	1957	3rd	82	72	.532	16
1910	4th	81	72	.529	22½	1958	3rd	79	75	.513	13
1911	5th	78	75	.510	24	1959	5th	75	79	.487	19
1912	1st	105	47	.691	+14	1960	7th	65	89	.422	32
1913	4th	79	71	.527	15½	1961	6th	76	86	.469	33
1914	2nd	91	62	.595	8½	1962	8th	76	84	.475	19
1915	1st	101	50	.669	+2½	1963	7th	76	85	.472	28
1916	1st	91	63	.591	+2	1964	8th	72	90	.444	27
1917	2nd	90	62	.592	9	1965	9th	62	100	.383	40
1918	1st	75	51	.595	+2½	1966	9th	72	90	.444	26
1919	6th	66	71	.482	20½	1967	1st	92	70	.568	+1
1920	5th	72	81	.471	25½	1968	4th	86	76	.531	17
1921	5th	75	79	.487	23½	1969	3rd	87	75	.537	22
1922	8th	61	93	.396	33	1970	3rd	87	75	.537	21
1923	8th	61	91	.401	37	1971	3rd	85	77	.525	18
1924	7th	67	87	.435	25	1972	2nd	85	70	.548	½
1925	8th	47	105	.309	49½	1973	2nd	89	73	.549	8
1926	8th	46	107	.301	44½	1974	3rd	84	78	.519	7
1927	8th	51	103	.331	59	1975	1st‡	95	65	.594	+4½
1928	8th	57	96	.373	43½	1976	3rd	83	79	.512	15½
1929	8th	58	96	.377	48	1977	T2nd	97	64	.602	2½
1930	8th	52	102	.338	50	1978	2nd§	99	64	.607	1
1931	6th	62	90	.408	45	1979	3rd	91	69	.569	11½
1932	8th	43	111	.279	64	1980	4th	83	77	.519	19
1933	7th	63	86	.423	34½	1981	5th/T2nd	59	49	.546	*
1934	4th	76	76	.500	24	1982	3rd	89	73	.549	6
1935	4th	78	75	.510	16	1983	6th	78	84	.481	20
1936	6th	74	80	.481	28½	1984	4th	86	76	.531	18
1937	5th	80	72	.526	21	1985	5th	81	81	.500	18½
1938	2nd	88	61	.591	9½	1986	1st‡	95	66	.590	+5½
1939	2nd	89	62	.589	17	1987	5th	78	84	.481	20
1940	T4th	82	72	.532	8	1988	1st•	89	73	.549	+1
1941	2nd	84	70	.545	17	1989	3rd	83	79	.512	6
1942	2nd	93	59	.612	9	1990	1st•	88	74	.543	+2
1943	7th	68	84	.447	29	1991	T2nd	84	78	.519	7
1944	4th	77	77	.500	12						
1945	7th	71	83	.461	17½						
1946	1st	104	50	.675	+12						
1947	3rd	83	71	.539	14						
1948	2nd†	96	59	.619	1						

*Games behind winner. †Lost pennant playoff. ‡Won Championship Series. §Lost division playoff. *First half 30-26; second 29-23. • Lost Championship Series.

MANAGERS

Name	Record	Years
Jimmy Collins	455-376	'01-06
Chick Stahl	14-26	1906
George Huff	2-6	1907
Bob Unglaub	9-20	1907
Deacon McGuire	98-123	'07-08
Fred Lake	110-80	'08-09
Patsy Donovan	159-147	'10-11
Jake Stahl	144-88	'12-13
Bill Carrigan	489-500	'13-16
		'27-29
Jack Barry	90-62	1917
Ed Barrow	213-203	'18-20
Hugh Duffy	136-172	'21-22
Frank Chance	61-91	1923
Lee Fohl	160-299	'24-26
Heinie Wagner	52-102	1930
Shano Collins	73-134	'31-32
Marty McManus	95-153	'32-33
Bucky Harris	76-76	1934
Joe Cronin	1071-916	'35-47
Joe McCarthy	223-145	'48-50
Steve O'Neill	150-99	'50-51
Lou Boudreau	229-232	'52-54
Pinky Higgins	560-556	'55-59
		'60-62
Billy Jurges	59-63	'59-60
Johnny Pesky	147-179	'63-64
		1980
Billy Herman	128-182	'64-66
Pete Runnels	8-8	1966
Dick Williams	260-217	'67-69
Eddie Popowski	5-4	1969
Eddie Kasko	346-295	'70-73
Darrell Johnson	220-188	'74-76
Don Zimmer	411-304	'76-80
Ralph Houk	312-282	'81-84
John McNamara	297-273	'85-88
Joe Morgan	301-262	'88-91

DAY BY DAY

Date	Opp.	Res.	Score (inn.*)	Hits	Opp. hits	Winning pitcher	Losing pitcher	Save	Record	Pos.	GB
4-8	At Tor.	W	6-2	5	7	Clemens	Stieb		1-0	T1st	...
4-9	At Tor.	L	3-4	9	8	Key	Harris	Henke	1-1	T3rd	½
4-10	At Tor.	L	3-5	7	4	Timlin	Gray	Henke	1-2	T5th	1½
4-11	Cle.	L	4-6	10	11	King	Darwin	Jones	1-3	6th	2
4-13	Cle.	W	4-0	9	3	Clemens	Swindell		2-3	T4th	1½
4-14	Cle.	L	0-6	5	13	Candiotti	Harris		2-4	T6th	2½
4-15	Cle.	L	0-1 (13)	6	5	Olin	Lamp	Jones	2-5	6th	3½
4-16	K.C.	W	5-2	8	6	Darwin	Appier	Reardon	3-5	6th	2½
4-17	K.C.	W	6-2	10	6	Bolton	S. Davis	Gray	4-5	5th	1½
4-18	K.C.	W	1-0	4	3	Clemens	Saberhagen	Reardon	5-5	4th	1
4-20	At Cle.	W	2-1	7	5	Harris	Candiotti	Reardon	6-5	3rd	1½
4-22	Tor.	W	6-4	10	8	Lamp	Wells	Reardon	7-5	T1st	...
4-23	Tor.	W	3-0	8	6	Clemens	Boucher	Reardon	8-5	1st	+1
4-24	Tor.	L	1-6	9	9	Stieb	Young		8-6	1st	...
4-26	At K.C.	L	3-5	6	7	Boddicker	Fossas	Montgomery	8-7	2nd	1½
4-27	At K.C.	W	6-4	12	8	Bolton	Appier	Reardon	9-7	2nd	½
4-28	At K.C.	W	2-1	10	7	Kiecker	Gordon	Reardon	10-7	2nd	½
4-30	At Min.	W	7-5	10	9	Gray	Bedrosian	Reardon	11-7	1st	+½
5-1	At Min.	L	0-1	2	4	Erickson	Gray		11-8	1st	+½
5-3	At Chi.	W	7-2	13	5	Clemens	McDowell		12-8	1st	...
5-4	At Chi.	W	4-0	5	5	Bolton	Perez		13-8	1st	+1
5-5	At Chi.	W	9-1	8	8	Young	Fernandez		14-8	1st	+1
5-7	Min.	L	3-9	7	13	Erickson	Harris		14-9	1st	+½
5-8	Min.	W	8-3	12	5	Clemens	Morris		15-9	1st	+½
5-9	Tex.	W	8-4	12	9	Lamp	Jeffcoat		16-9	1st	+½
5-10	Tex.	W	5-3	13	10	Young	Witt	Reardon	17-9	1st	+1½
5-11	Tex.	W	5-4	12	6	Kiecker	Brown	Reardon	18-9	1st	+2
5-12	Tex.	L	5-12	13	19	Rogers	Harris		18-10	1st	+1
5-13	Chi.	L	3-4 (10)	11	8	Thigpen	Gray		18-11	1st	...
5-14	Chi.	W	4-1	7	8	Bolton	Perez	Reardon	19-11	1st	...
5-15	Chi.	W	9-6	13	11	Hesketh	Pall	Reardon	20-11	1st	+1
5-17	At Tex.	L	4-6	12	11	Brown	Harris	Russell	20-12	1st	+1
5-18	At Tex.	L	5-13	9	17	Rogers	Clemens	Poole	20-13	1st	...
5-19	At Tex.	L	4-12	10	16	Alexander	Bolton		20-14	1st	...
5-20	Mil.	W	3-0	6	4	Young	Bosio	Reardon	21-14	1st	...
5-21	Mil.	W	10-6	14	13	Hesketh	Hunter		22-14	1st	...
5-22	Mil.	W	4-0	5	10	Darwin	Brown	Harris	23-14	1st	+1
5-23	At Det.	L	3-5	10	6	Henneman	Clemens	Gibson	23-15	1st	+½
5-24	At Det.	W	10-9	15	10	Bolton	Petry	Reardon	24-15	1st	+½
5-25	At Det.	L	2-3	7	5	Terrell	Young	Henneman	24-16	1st	+½
5-26	At Det.	L	4-9	13	11	Leiter	Kiecker	Gibson	24-17	1st	+½
5-27	At N.Y.	L	5-6	8	7	Guetterman	Reardon		24-18	1st	...
5-28	At N.Y.	W	6-2	12	4	Clemens	Leary		25-18	1st	+1
5-29	At N.Y.	L	0-7	5	8	Sanderson	Bolton		25-19	1st	...
5-30	Bal.	L	3-9	6	10	Ballard	Young	Flanagan	25-20	1st	...
5-31	Bal.	W	7-2	13	6	Gardiner	Mesa		26-20	1st	...
6-1	Bal.	L	1-3	3	9	Hickey	Darwin	Olson	26-21	1st	...
6-2	Bal.	L	1-5	4	10	Smith	Clemens	Williamson	26-22	1st	...
6-4	At Cal.	L	0-3	2	8	Finley	Bolton		26-23	2nd	½
6-5	At Cal.	L	2-7	8	7	McCaskill	Gardiner		26-24	2nd	1½
6-6	At Cal.	L	2-3	4	7	Langston	Darwin	Harvey	26-25	2nd	1½
6-7	At Oak.	W	3-1	6	4	Harris	Moore	Reardon	27-25	2nd	½
6-8	At Oak.	W	8-1	12	2	Clemens	Slusarski		28-25	2nd	½
6-9	At Oak.	L	0-8	5	13	Welch	Bolton		28-26	2nd	1½
6-10	At Sea.	W	6-2	7	9	Gardiner	Johnson		29-26	2nd	1
6-11	At Sea.	W	8-5	12	10	Darwin	Bankhead	Reardon	30-26	T1st	...
6-12	At Sea.	L	3-5	5	6	Krueger	Harris	Jackson	30-27	2nd	1
6-14	Cal.	W	9-4	11	8	Clemens	Robinson		31-27	2nd	1½
6-15	Cal.	W	13-3	16	6	Gardiner	Finley		32-27	2nd	½
6-16	Cal.	W	2-0	7	6	Bolton	McCaskill	Reardon	33-27	1st	+½
6-17	Cal.	L	2-4	7	7	Langston	Harris	Harvey	33-28	1st	...
6-18	Sea.	L	1-2	10	8	Krueger	Reardon		33-29	1st	...
6-19	Sea.	L	3-4	11	10	Swan	Clemens	Jackson	33-30	1st	...
6-20	Oak.	W	8-7	12	12	Gray	Chitren	Reardon	34-30	1st	...
6-21	Oak.	W	3-2	7	11	Bolton	Moore	Reardon	35-30	1st	...
6-22	Oak.	W	9-5	13	8	Harris	Slusarski		36-30	1st	...
6-23	Oak.	L	2-4	6	10	Welch	Darwin	Eckersley	36-31	2nd	1
6-25	N.Y.	L	4-6	10	10	Leary	Clemens	Farr	36-32	2nd	1½
6-26	N.Y.	L	1-5	8	12	Sanderson	Gardiner	Howe	36-33	2nd	2½
6-27	N.Y.	L	0-8	5	11	Taylor	Bolton		36-34	2nd	3½

— 17 —

Date	Opp.	Res.	Score (inn.*)	Hits	Opp. hits	Winning pitcher	Losing pitcher	Save	Record	Pos.	GB
6-28	At Bal.	W	9-3	13	6	Harris	Mesa		37-34	2nd	2 ½
6-29	At Bal.	L	3-7	10	9	Smith	Darwin		37-35	2nd	3 ½
6-30	At Bal.	L	4-6	6	10	Williamson	Hesketh	Olson	37-36	2nd	4 ½
7-1	At Mil.	W	6-0	10	5	Clemens	Navarro		38-36	2nd	4 ½
7-2	At Mil.	W	14-4	22	10	Lamp	Knudson		39-36	2nd	4 ½
7-3	At Mil.	W	5-3	7	8	Harris	August	Reardon	40-36	2nd	4 ½
7-4	Det.	L	1-6	9	11	Meacham	Darwin		40-37	2nd	4 ½
7-5	Det.	W	10-1	12	5	Morton	Terrell		41-37	2nd	4 ½
7-6	Det.	W	7-4	12	11	Clemens	Gibson	Reardon	42-37	2nd	4 ½
7-7	Det.	L	6-7	12	15	Gullickson	Bolton	Cerutti	42-38	2nd	5 ½
7-11	At Min.	L	3-7	13	8	Willis	Harris		42-39	2nd	6 ½
7-12	At Min.	L	4-5	6	11	Abbott	Clemens	Aguilera	42-40	2nd	7 ½
7-13	At Min.	L	1-3	5	10	Morris	Morton	Aguilera	42-41	2nd	8 ½
7-14	At Min.	W	5-3	11	8	Hesketh	West	Reardon	43-41	2nd	7 ½
7-15	At Chi.	L	1-7	5	13	Garcia	Gardiner	Patterson	43-42	3rd	8 ½
7-16	At Chi.	W	2-0	9	3	Harris	Hough	Reardon	44-42	3rd	7 ½
7-17	At Chi.	W	4-2 (10)	10	5	Fossas	Thigpen		45-42	3rd	7
7-18	Min.	L	3-11	5	12	Morris	Morton		45-43	3rd	8
7-19	Min.	L	2-3 (11)	10	14	Bedrosian	Harris	Aguilera	45-44	3rd	9
7-20	Min.	L	0-5	9	8	Erickson	Gardiner	Guthrie	45-45	3rd	9
7-21	Min.	L	1-14	5	18	Tapani	Bolton		45-46	4th	9
7-22	At Tex.	L	1-2	5	7	Guzman	Clemens	Russell	45-47	4th	9 ½
7-23	At Tex.	L	4-5	4	8	Ryan	Harris	Gossage	45-48	4th	9 ½
7-24	At Tex.	W	2-1	7	2	Hesketh	Boyd	Reardon	46-48	4th	9 ½
7-27 (1)	Chi.	L	8-10 (14)	10	14	Perez	Kiecker	Thigpen	46-49	4th	9 ½
7-27 (2)	Chi.	L	4-7	12	13	Garcia	Gardiner	Thigpen	46-50	4th	10
7-28	Chi.	L	2-5	7	9	Fernandez	Harris	Thigpen	46-51	4th	10
7-29	Tex.	L	2-7	8	13	Guzman	Hesketh	Rogers	46-52	4th	10
7-30	Tex.	W	11-6	12	12	Morton	Boyd		47-52	4th	9
7-31	Oak.	W	11-10 (14)	15	13	Harris	Chitren		48-52	3rd	9
8-1	Oak.	L	2-4	6	11	Klink	Lamp	Eckersley	48-53	4th	10
8-2	Tor.	W	5-3	6	5	Clemens	Candiotti		49-53	3rd	9
8-3	Tor.	W	4-1	8	7	Hesketh	Wells	Reardon	50-53	3rd	8
8-4	Tor.	L	1-2	7	7	Ward	Lamp	Henke	50-54	3rd	9
8-5	At K.C.	L	3-5	8	9	Montgomery	Fossas		50-55	3rd	9 ½
8-6	At K.C.	L	0-6	8	11	Boddicker	Gardiner		50-56	3rd	10 ½
8-7	At K.C.	L	0-2	4	7	Appier	Clemens		50-57	3rd	11 ½
8-9	At Tor.	W	12-7	21	15	Hesketh	Wells	Reardon	51-57	3rd	10
8-10	At Tor.	W	7-1	12	4	Harris	Stottlemyre		52-57	4th	9
8-11	At Tor.	W	9-6	16	10	Gardiner	Key	Reardon	53-57	3rd	8
8-12	At Tor.	W	11-8	18	13	Lamp	Ward	Reardon	54-57	3rd	7
8-13 (1)	At Cle.	L	6-8	13	12	Hillegas	Kiecker	Olin	54-58	3rd	7
8-13 (2)	At Cle.	W	7-5	10	10	Fossas	Nichols	Reardon	55-58	3rd	6 ½
8-14	At Cle.	W	2-1	9	9	Hesketh	Swindell	Reardon	56-58	3rd	5 ½
8-15	At Cle.	W	6-2	11	7	Gardiner	Otto		57-58	3rd	5 ½
8-16	K.C.	W	3-2	7	7	Fossas	S. Davis	Reardon	58-58	3rd	4 ½
8-17	K.C.	L	3-4	6	10	Aquino	Reardon	Montgomery	58-59	3rd	5 ½
8-18	K.C.	W	5-1	6	8	Morton	Appier		59-59	3rd	5 ½
8-21 (1)	Cle.	W	13-5	15	6	Hesketh	Swindell		60-59	3rd	5
8-21 (2)	Cle.	W	5-4	10	8	Harris	Olin		61-59	3rd	4 ½
8-22	Cle.	W	7-6 (10)	14	9	Harris	Olin		62-59	3rd	3 ½
8-23	At Cal.	L	1-4	6	8	J. Abbott	Young	Harvey	62-60	3rd	4 ½
8-24	At Cal.	L	0-1	4	3	McCaskill	Morton	Harvey	62-61	3rd	4 ½
8-25	At Cal.	L	5-9	9	12	Fetters	Hesketh	Eichhorn	62-62	3rd	5 ½
8-26	At Oak.	W	3-0	7	3	Clemens	Moore		63-62	3rd	5 ½
8-27	At Oak.	W	6-4	13	6	Gardiner	Welch	Reardon	64-62	3rd	5 ½
8-28	At Oak.	L	3-9	8	10	Stewart	Young		64-63	3rd	6 ½
8-30	At Sea.	W	3-2	9	8	Hesketh	Hanson	Reardon	65-63	3rd	6
8-31	At Sea.	W	4-1	10	4	Clemens	Krueger		66-63	3rd	6
9-1	At Sea.	W	13-2	18	8	Morton	Johnson		67-63	3rd	5
9-3	Cal.	L	0-2	4	7	Langston	Gardiner	Harvey	67-64	3rd	5 ½
9-4	Cal.	W	2-0	7	7	Hesketh	McCaskill	Reardon	68-64	3rd	5 ½
9-5	Sea.	W	4-3 (10)	8	10	Reardon	Murphy		69-64	3rd	5 ½
9-6	Sea.	W	6-5	13	8	Lamp	Jackson	Reardon	70-64	3rd	5 ½
9-7	Sea.	W	11-10	12	14	Bolton	Jones	Reardon	71-64	3rd	5 ½
9-8	Sea.	W	17-6	17	9	Gardiner	DeLucia		72-64	2nd	5 ½
9-9	At Cle.	W	4-3	9	8	Harris	Hillegas	Reardon	73-64	2nd	5
9-10	At Det.	W	4-0	7	2	Clemens	Tanana		74-64	2nd	4
9-11	At Det.	L	2-8	6	13	Terrell	Young		74-65	2nd	4
9-12	At N.Y.	W	7-2	11	8	Morton	Perez		75-65	2nd	3 ½
9-13	At N.Y.	W	5-4	9	10	Gardiner	Johnson	Reardon	76-65	2nd	3 ½
9-14	At N.Y.	L	1-3	5	9	Sanderson	Hesketh	Farr	76-66	2nd	4 ½
9-15	At N.Y.	W	5-4	9	8	Clemens	Guetterman	Reardon	77-66	2nd	3 ½
9-16	Bal.	L	2-9	10	16	Mussina	Bolton		77-67	2nd	3 ½

— 18 —

Date	Opp.	Res.	Score (inn.*)	Hits	Opp. hits	Winning pitcher	Losing pitcher	Save	Record	Pos.	GB
9-17	Bal.	W	4-3	7	7	Morton	Mesa	Reardon	78-67	2nd	2½
9-18	Bal.	W	7-5	13	10	Gardiner	Johnson	Harris	79-66	2nd	2½
9-20	N.Y.	W	2-0	7	3	Clemens	Sanderson		80-67	2nd	1½
9-21	N.Y.	W	12-1	14	4	Hesketh	Taylor		81-67	2nd	½
9-22	N.Y.	L	5-7 (10)	11	13	Farr	Young		81-68	2nd	1½
9-23	At Bal.	L	3-4	9	5	Poole	Gardiner	Olson	81-69	2nd	2½
9-26 (1)	At Bal.	W	2-1	6	7	Clemens	Johnson		82-69	2nd	3
9-26 (2)	At Bal.	L	5-6	10	11	Frohwirth	Harris		82-70	2nd	3½
9-27	At Mil.	L	5-7	8	8	Bosio	Morton	Machado	82-71	2nd	4½
9-28	At Mil.	L	1-4	4	8	Navarro	Gardiner	Henry	82-72	2nd	4½
9-29	At Mil.	L	4-5	7	8	Machado	Reardon	Henry	82-73	2nd	4½
9-30	At Mil.	W	9-8	11	13	Lamp	Ignasiak	Petry	83-73	2nd	4½
10-1	Det.	L	5-8	11	9	Tanana	Clemens		83-74	2nd	5½
10-2	Det.	W	5-3	13	7	Hesketh	Terrell	Fossas	84-74	2nd	5½
10-3	Det.	L	5-10	8	13	Gullickson	Morton		84-75	2nd	6
10-4	Mil.	L	2-3	9	7	Eldred	Gardiner	Henry	84-76	T2nd	7
10-5	Mil.	L	4-13	11	14	Ignasiak	Bolton		84-77	T2nd	7
10-6	Mil.	L	3-6	11	13	Machado	Clemens	Henry	84-78	T2nd	7

Monthly records: April (11-7), May (15-13), June (11-16), July (11-16), August (18-11), September (17-10), Oct. (1-5).

HIGHLIGHTS

High point: From August 9 through September 21, the Red Sox won 31 of 41 games to move from 10 games out of first place in the American League East to within half a game of the first-place Toronto Blue Jays.

Low point: After winning over 75 percent of its games during that torrid stretch, Boston lost 11 of its last 14 games to finish tied with Detroit for second place (seven games out).

Turning point: Boston could have moved into a first-place tie with Toronto with a win over New York on September 22. But Yankee outfielder Roberto Kelly hit a two-out, two-strike home run in the ninth inning off Jeff Reardon to tie the contest. Matt Young subsequently lost the game in the 10th inning, and Boston never recovered.

Most valuable player: Designated hitter Jack Clark. He overcame a horrible start to finish with a .249 average and a team-leading 28 homers and 87 RBIs. Fifteen of his 28 home runs either tied the game or gave Boston the lead.

Most valuable pitcher: Righthander Roger Clemens. The Rocket Man finished 18-10, leading the league in earned-run average (2.62), shutouts (four) and strikeouts (241). He capped his season by winning his third Cy Young Award.

Most improved player: Lefthander Joe Hesketh. After being 0-4 in 12 appearances in 1990 with the Red Sox, the free agent nobody wanted won a career-high 12 games with a 3.29 ERA.

Most pleasant surprise: Outfielder Phil Plantier. Called up twice last year, the lefthanded slugger hit .331 with 11 homers and 35 RBIs in just 53 games.

Biggest disappointments: Lefthander Matt Young and outfielder Ellis Burks. Young was 3-7 with a 5.18 ERA. He didn't win a game after May 30. Burks batted just .251 with 56 RBIs.

Key injuries: The loss of righthanders Danny Darwin (right shoulder) and Jeff Gray (slight stroke) in July hurt the pitching staff. Shortstop Tim Naehring played only 20 games before undergoing season-ending back surgery.

Notable: Two days after the season ended, Joe Morgan was fired as manager. Former Red Sox third baseman Butch Hobson, who managed Class AAA Pawtucket, was named Boston's new skipper. . . . Rookie first baseman Mo Vaughn hit three home runs in his first 27 at-bats. But in his final 192 at-bats he hit just one.

—JOE GIULIOTTI

RECORDS

1991 regular-season record: 84-78 (T2nd in A.L. East); 43-38 at home; 41-40 on road; 41-37 vs. East; 43-41 vs. West; 24-20 vs. LHP; 60-58 vs. RHP; 70-67 on grass; 14-11 on turf; 25-29 in daytime; 59-49 at night; 23-21 in one-run games; 4-5 in extra-inning games; 1-0-2 in doubleheaders. **Team record last five years:** 422-388 (.521, ranks 4th in league in that span).

TEAM LEADERS

Batting average: Wade Boggs (.332).
At-bats: Jody Reed (618).
Runs: Wade Boggs (93).
Hits: Wade Boggs (181).
Total bases: Wade Boggs (251).
Doubles: Wade Boggs, Jody Reed (42).
Triples: Mike Greenwell (6).
Home runs: Jack Clark (28).
Runs batted in: Jack Clark (87).
Stolen bases: Mike Greenwell (15).
Slugging percentage: Jack Clark (.466).
On-base percentage: Wade Boggs (.421).
Wins: Roger Clemens (18).
Earned-run average: Roger Clemens (2.62).
Complete games: Roger Clemens (13).
Shutouts: Roger Clemens (4).
Saves: Jeff Reardon (40).
Innings pitched: Roger Clemens (271⅓).
Strikeouts: Roger Clemens (241).

GAMES BY POSITION

Catcher: Tony Pena 140, John Marzano 48.
First base: Carlos Quintana 138, Mo Vaughn 49, Mike Marshall 5, Steve Lyons 2.
Second base: Jody Reed 152, Steve Lyons 16, Mike Brumley 7, Tim Naehring 1.
Third base: Wade Boggs 140, Mike Brumley 17, Scott Cooper 13, Steve Lyons 12, Tim Naehring 2.
Shortstop: Luis Rivera 129, Mike Brumley 31, Tim Naehring 17, Jody Reed 6, Steve Lyons 1.
Outfield: Mike Greenwell 143, Tom Brunansky 137, Ellis Burks 126, Steve Lyons 45, Phil Plantier 40, Bob Zupcic 16, Carlos Quintana 13, Kevin Romine 23, Mike Brumley 4, Wayne Housie 4.
Designated hitter: Jack Clark 135, Mo Vaughn 16, Kevin Romine 14, Mike Marshall 7, Phil Plantier 5, Mike Brumley 2, Ellis Burks 2, Wayne Housie 2, Steve Lyons 2, Tom Brunansky 1, Mike Greenwell 1, Carlos Quintana 1, Eric Wedge 1.

TOP 10 DRAFT CHOICES

1a. **Aaron Sele,** RHP, Washington St.
1b. **J.J. Johnson,** OF, Pine Plains (N.Y.) High School.
1c. **Scott Hatteberg,** C, Wash. St.
2a. **Terry Horn,** RHP, Yukon (Okla.) High School.
2b. **Chad Schoenvogel,** RHP, Blinn (Texas) Junior College.
3. **Joe Caruso,** RHP, Loyola Marymount.
4. **Joe Ciccarella,** 1B/LHP, Loyola Marymount University.
5. **Doug Carroll,** OF, Holliston (Mass.) High School.
6. **Donny Jones,** OF, Poway (Calif.) High School.
7. **Dan Collier,** OF, Enterprise State (Ala.) Junior College.
8. **Luis Ortiz,** 3B, Union (Tenn.) Univ.
9. **Dan McDonald,** 3B, Evans High School, Orlando, Fla.
10. **Luis Rodriguez,** SS, University of Charleston.

CALIFORNIA ANGELS
AMERICAN LEAGUE WEST DIVISION

1992 SCHEDULE

APRIL
S	M	T	W	T	F	S
5	6	7 N CHI H	8 N CHI H	9 N CHI H	10 N MIL H	11 N MIL H
12 MIL H	13 N TEX	14 N TEX	15 N TEX	16 N TEX	17 N KC	18 KC
19 KC	20 N OAK	21 N OAK	22 OAK	23	24 N SEA H	25 N SEA H
26 SEA H	27	28 N TOR	29 N TOR	30 CLE		

MAY
S	M	T	W	T	F	S
					1 N CLE	2 CLE
3 CLE	4 N DET	5 DET	6 N NY H	7 N NY H	8 N TOR H	9 N TOR H
10 N TOR H	11	12 N DET H	13 N DET H	14	15 N BOS	16 BOS
17 BOS	18 N NY	19 N NY	20 N NY	21	22 N BAL	23 N BAL
24 BAL	25	26 N BOS H	27 N BOS H	28 H BOS H	29 N CLE H	30 N CLE H
31 CLE H						

JUNE
S	M	T	W	T	F	S
	1 N BAL H	2 N BAL H	3 N BAL H	4	5 N MIL	6 N MIL
7 MIL	8 N CHI	9 N CHI	10 N CHI	11 CHI	12 N KC	13 N KC H
14	15 H TEX H	16 N TEX H	17 N TEX H	18	19 N OAK H	20 OAK H
21 OAK H	22 N MIN	23 N MIN	24 MIN	25 N SEA	26 N SEA	27 SEA
28 SEA	29 N MIN H	30 N MIN H				

JULY
S	M	T	W	T	F	S
			1 N MIN H	2	3 N TOR	4 TOR
5 TOR	6 N TOR	7 N CLE	8 N CLE	9 N DET	10 N DET	11 DET
12 DET	13	14 *	15	16 N NY	17 N NY H	18 N NY H
19 NY H	20 N TOR H	21 N TOR H	22 N DET H	23 N DET H	24 N DET H	25 DET H
26 DET	27 N SEA H	28 N SEA H	29 N SEA H	30 SEA H	31 N TEX	

AUGUST
S	M	T	W	T	F	S
						1 TEX
2 N TEX	3	4 N KC	5 N KC	6 N KC	7 N CHI H	8 H CHI H
9 CHI H	10 H MIL H	11 N MIL H	12 N MIL H	13 H OAK	14 N OAK	15 OAK
16 OAK	17	18 N BOS	19 N BOS	20 N BOS	21 N NY	22 NY
23 NY	24 N BAL	25 N BAL	26 N BAL	27	28 N BOS H	29 N BOS H
30 BOS H	31 N CLE H					

SEPTEMBER
S	M	T	W	T	F	S
		1 N CLE H	2 N CLE H	3	4 N BAL	5 N BAL
6	7 H OAK H	8 N OAK H	9 N OAK H	10	11 N MIL	12 MIL
13 MIN	14	15 N SEA	16 N SEA	17 MIN H	18 N MIN H	19 N MIN H
20 MIN H	21	22 N MIL	23 N MIL	24 N MIL	25 N CHI	26 CHI
27 CHI	28 N KC	29 N KC	30 N KC			

OCTOBER
S	M	T	W	T	F	S
				1	2 N KC H	3 N TEX H
4 TEX H	5	6	7	8	9	10

1992 SEASON

CLUB DIRECTORY

Chairman of the board
Gene Autry

Board of directors
Gene Autry
Jackie Autry
Richard M. Brown
Stanley B. Schneider
John P. Singleton
Peter V. Ueberroth

President and chief executive officer
Richard M. Brown

Executive vice president
Jackie Autry

V.p., treasurer and chief financial officer
Ron Shirley

V.p., public relations and broadcasting
Tom Seeberg

Senior v.p./director of player personnel
Whitey Herzog

Senior vice president, baseball operations
Daniel F. O'Brien

Assistant to the general manager
Preston Gomez

Director, minor league operations
Bill Bavasi

Director, scouting
Bob Fontaine Jr.

Coordinator of scouting operations
Tim Kelly

Executive assistant to president and CEO
Carmen Wesson-Goffney

Traveling secretary
Frank Sims

Assistant vice president, media relations
Tim Mead

Manager, baseball information
Larry Babcock

Director, community relations
Darrell Miller

Director, special projects
Corky Lippert

Manager, speakers bureau
Janet German

Director, creative services
John Sevano

Director, marketing
Bob Wagner

Manager, publications
Doug Ward

Director, sales and group promotions
Lynn Biggs

Manager, group sales and promotions
Marianne Zambrano

Controller
Catherine Sullivan

Asst. vice president, stadium operations
Kevin Uhlich

Equipment manager
Leonard Garcia

Director, ticket department
Carl Gordon

Assistant, ticket director
Gen Linhoff

Director, data operations
Ron Moore

Medical director
Dr. Robert K. Kerlan

Team physician, medicine
Dr. Jules Rasinski

Team physician, orthopedics
Dr. Lewis Yocum

Trainers
Ned Bergert
Rick Smith

Physical therapist
Roger Williams

Special assignment & scouting coordinators
Tom Davis
Rosey Gilhousen
Steve Gruwell
Bob Harrison
Rick Ingalls
Nick Kamzic
Hal Keller
Jon Neiderer
Paul Robinson
Rich Schlenker

Scouting supervisors
Ted Brzenk
Roger Ferguson
Red Gaskill
Kris Kline
Tom Kotchman
Tony Lacava
Steve McAllister
Jim McLaughlin
Tom Osowski
Vic Power
Dale Sutherland
Jack Uhey

Area scouts
Joe Caro
Joe Carpenter
Angelo Cerroni
Orv Franchuk
Bob Gardner
Dick Greene
Tom Gross
Fred Hatfield
Bill Lachemann Jr.
Don Long Sr.
David Martin
Dick Probola
Chris Royer

SCHEDULE KEY
H—Home game. *All-Star Game at San Diego/Jack Murphy Stadium.
N—Night game (any game starting after 5 p.m.).

SPRING TRAINING ROSTER

Manager—Buck Rodgers (7).

Coaches—Rod Carew (29), Deron Johnson (2), Bobby Knoop (1), Marcel Lachemann (53), Ken Macha (39), Jimmie Reese (50), Rick Turner (57), John Wathan (37).

No.	PITCHERS	B/T	Ht./Wt.	Born	1991 clubs
25	Abbott, Jim	L/L	6-3/210	9-19-67	California
43	Bailes, Scott	L/L	6-2/171	12-18-62	California
44	Butcher, Michael	R/R	6-1/200	5-10-65	Midland
32	Crim, Chuck	R/R	6-0/185	7-23-61	Milwaukee
45	Eichhorn, Mark	R/R	6-3/210	11-21-60	California
42	Erb, Michael	R/R	6-4/210	3-19-66	Edmonton
31	Finley, Chuck	L/L	6-6/214	11-26-62	California
51	Fortugno, Tim	L/L	6-0/185	4-11-62	El Paso, Denver
20	Grahe, Joe	R/R	6-0/200	8-14-67	Edmonton, California
34	Harvey, Bryan	R/R	6-2/212	6-2-63	California
23	Holdridge, David	R/R	6-3/185	2-5-69	Clearwater, Reading
27	Johnson, Dave	R/R	5-11/180	10-24-59	Hagerstown, Rochester, Baltimore
12	Langston, Mark	R/L	6-2/184	8-20-60	California
46	Lewis, Scott	R/R	6-3/178	12-5-65	California, Edmonton
40	Robinson, Don	R/R	6-4/240	6-8-57	San Francisco
41	Swingle, Paul	R/R	6-0/185	12-21-66	Palm Springs
35	Young, Cliff	L/L	6-4/210	8-2-64	Edmonton, California
38	Zappelli, Mark	R/R	6-0/160	7-21-66	Midland, Edmonton

No.	CATCHERS	B/T	Ht./Wt.	Born	1991 clubs
14	Orton, John	R/R	6-1/192	12-8-65	Edmonton, California
13	Parrish, Lance	R/R	6-3/224	6-15-56	California
24	Tingley, Ron	R/R	6-2/194	5-27-59	California, Edmonton

No.	INFIELDERS	B/T	Ht./Wt.	Born	1991 clubs
11	DiSarcina, Gary	R/R	6-1/178	11-19-67	Edmonton, California
4	Flora, Kevin	R/R	6-0/180	6-10-69	Midland, California
3	Gaetti, Gary	R/R	6-0/200	8-19-58	California
15	Phillips, J.R.	L/L	6-1/185	4-29-70	Palm Springs
6	Rose, Bobby	R/R	5-11/185	3-15-67	Edmonton, California
17	Schofield, Dick	R/R	5-10/179	11-21-62	California
10	Sojo, Luis	R/R	5-11/174	1-3-66	California
9	Stevens, Lee	L/L	6-4/219	7-10-67	Edmonton, California

No.	OUTFIELDERS	B/T	Ht./Wt.	Born	1991 clubs
16	Abner, Shawn	R/R	6-1/194	6-17-66	San Diego, California
8	Brooks, Hubie	R/R	6-0/205	9-24-56	New York NL
30	Curtis, Chad	R/R	5-10/175	11-6-68	Edmonton
18	Davis, Mark	R/R	6-0/170	11-25-64	Edmonton, California
48	Edmonds, James	L/L	6-1/190	6-27-70	Palm Springs
47	Felix, Junior	S/R	5-11/165	10-3-67	California, Palm Springs
9	Hayes, Von	L/R	6-5/188	8-31-58	Philadelphia, Scranton-W.B.
33	Morris, John	L/L	6-1/185	2-23-61	Philadelphia
22	Polonia, Luis	L/L	5-8/150	10-12-64	California
21	Salmon, Tim	R/R	6-3/200	8-24-68	Midland

BALLPARK INFORMATION

Ballpark (capacity, surface)
Anaheim Stadium (64,593, grass)
Address
2000 Gene Autry Way
Anaheim, CA 92806
Business phones
714-937-7200
213-625-1123
Ticket information
714-634-2000
Ticket prices
$11 (field and club box)
$9 (terrace box)
$8 (center field box)
$7 (view level, reserved)
$4 (view level, unreserved)
Field dimensions (from home plate)
To left field at foul line, 333 feet
To center field, 404 feet
To right field at foul line, 333 feet
First game played
April 19, 1966 (White Sox 3, Angels 1)

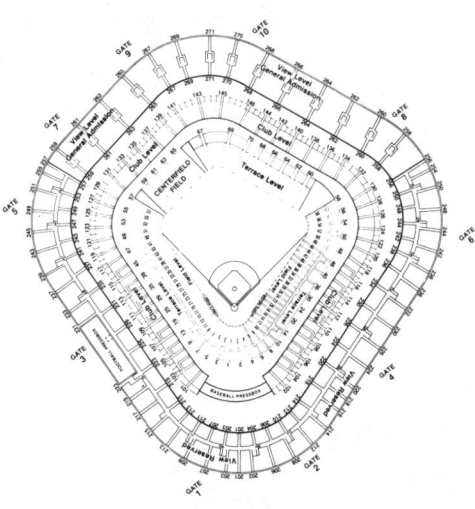

MINOR LEAGUE AFFILIATES

Class	Team	League	Manager
AAA	Edmonton	Pacific Coast	Max Oliveras
AA	Midland	Texas	Don Long
A	Palm Springs	California	Mario Mendoza
A	Quad City	Midwest	Mitch Seoane
A	Boise	Northwest	Tom Kotchman
Rookie	Mesa Angels	Arizona	Bill Lachemann

☐ BROADCAST INFORMATION ☐

Radio: KMPC-AM (710). Broadcasters: Al Conin, Bob Jamison. XPRS-AM (1090, Spanish language). Broadcasters: To be announced.
TV: KTLA-TV (Channel 5). Broadcasters: Ken Wilson, Ken Brett.
Cable TV: SportsChannel. Broadcasters: Ken Wilson, Ken Brett.

SPRING TRAINING

Ballpark (city): Gene Autry Park (Mesa, Ariz.) from March 6 through March 18; Angels Stadium (Palm Springs, Calif.) from March 20 through April 1.
Ticket information: 714-634-1300 (Ticketron); 619-323-4143 (Angels Stadium).

HISTORY

YEAR-BY-YEAR RECORDS

Year	Pos.	W	L	Pct.	*GB		Year	Pos.	W	L	Pct.	*GB
1961	8th	70	91	.435	38½		1978	T2nd	87	75	.537	5
1962	3rd	86	76	.531	10		1979	1st†	88	74	.543	+3
1963	9th	70	91	.435	34		1980	6th	65	95	.406	31
1964	5th	82	80	.506	17		1981	4th/7th	51	59	.464	‡
1965	7th	75	87	.463	27		1982	1st†	93	69	.574	+3
1966	6th	80	82	.494	18		1983	T5th	70	92	.432	29
1967	5th	84	77	.522	7½		1984	T2nd	81	81	.500	3
1968	8th	67	95	.414	36		1985	2nd	90	72	.556	1
1969	3rd	71	91	.438	26		1986	1st†	92	70	.568	+5
1970	3rd	86	76	.531	12		1987	T6th	75	87	.463	10
1971	4th	76	86	.469	25½		1988	4th	75	87	.463	29
1972	5th	75	80	.484	18		1989	3rd	91	71	.562	8
1973	4th	79	83	.488	15		1990	4th	80	82	.494	23
1974	6th	68	94	.420	22		1991	7th	81	81	.500	14
1975	6th	72	89	.447	25½							
1976	T4th	76	86	.469	14							
1977	5th	74	88	.457	28							

*Games behind winner. †Lost Championship Series. ‡First half 31-29; second 20-30.

MANAGERS

Name	Record	Years
Bill Rigney	625-707	'61-69
Lefty Phillips	222-225	'69-71
Del Rice	75-80	1972
Bobby Winkles	109-127	'73-74
Dick Williams	147-194	'74-76
Norm Sherry	76-71	'76-77
Dave Garcia	60-66	'77-78
Jim Fregosi	237-249	'78-81
Gene Mauch	379-332	'81-82
		'85-87
John McNamara	151-173	'83-84
Cookie Rojas	75-87	1988
Doug Rader	232-216	'89-91
Buck Rodgers	20-18	1991

DAY BY DAY

Date	Opp.	Res.	Score (inn.*)	Hits	Opp. hits	Winning pitcher	Losing pitcher	Save	Record	Pos.	GB
4-9	At Sea.	W	3-2	8	6	Finley	Hanson	Harvey	1-0	T1st	...
4-10	At Sea.	W	5-3	8	11	McCaskill	Johnson	Harvey	2-0	T1st	...
4-11	At Sea.	W	5-0	12	5	Langston	Holman		3-0	1st	+½
4-12	At Min.	L	0-6	7	10	Tapani	J. Abbott		3-1	T2nd	½
4-13	At Min.	W	15-9	21	13	Bailes	Guthrie		4-1	T2nd	½
4-14	At Min.	W	9-4	14	6	Finley	Morris		5-1	T2nd	...
4-15	Oak.	L	2-5	8	7	Welch	McCaskill	Eckersley	5-2	3rd	1
4-16	Oak.	L	5-8 (11)	14	12	Chitren	Bailes	Eckersley	5-3	3rd	2
4-17	Oak.	L	1-3	3	8	Moore	J. Abbott	Klink	5-4	3rd	3
4-18	Oak.	W	7-1	10	6	Lewis	Dressendorfer		6-4	3rd	2
4-19	Min.	W	2-0	7	2	Finley	Morris		7-4	3rd	1
4-20	Min.	W	2-1	4	3	McCaskill	Anderson	Harvey	8-4	T1st	...
4-21	Min.	L	3-4	8	8	Erickson	Eichhorn	Aguilera	8-5	T2nd	½
4-22	Sea.	L	3-4	6	8	Holman	J. Abbott	Jackson	8-6	T2nd	1½
4-23	Sea.	L	0-2	7	8	Bankhead	Lewis	Swan	8-7	4th	2½
4-24	Sea.	W	9-5	13	8	Finley	DeLucia	Harvey	9-7	T2nd	1½
4-26	At Oak.	L	1-4	5	6	Welch	McCaskill	Eckersley	9-8	4th	1½
4-27	At Oak.	L	3-4	8	7	Moore	Langston	Eckersley	9-9	T3rd	2½
4-28	At Oak.	L	3-7	7	11	Stewart	J. Abbott		9-10	T3rd	3½
4-30	Cle.	W	6-5 (11)	13	13	Harvey	Jones		10-10	T3rd	3
5-1	Cle.	L	1-5	5	9	Candiotti	Finley		10-11	T4th	4
5-3	Bal.	L	0-2	5	10	McDonald	McCaskill	Olson	10-12	4th	5
5-4	Bal.	W	6-3	9	6	Langston	Robinson	Harvey	11-12	4th	4
5-5	Bal.	W	6-4	8	8	J. Abbott	Ballard	Harvey	12-12	T3rd	3
5-6	Bal.	L	0-7	7	10	Mesa	Lewis		12-13	T5th	3½
5-7	N.Y.	W	7-4	8	4	Finley	Hawkins	Harvey	13-13	T5th	3½
5-8	N.Y.	L	5-10	12	11	Sanderson	McCaskill		13-14	T5th	4½
5-10	At Cle.	W	12-2	14	5	Langston	King		14-14	4th	3½
5-11	At Cle.	W	2-1	8	5	J. Abbott	Swindell	Harvey	15-14	4th	3½
5-12	At Cle.	L	1-4	3	11	Candiotti	Lewis		15-15	5th	3½
5-13	At Cle.	W	9-5	16	14	Finley	Olin	Robinson	16-15	T4th	2½
5-14	At N.Y.	L	1-7	5	11	Perez	McCaskill	Habyan	16-16	T5th	2½
5-15	At N.Y.	W	10-2	10	8	Langston	Cary		17-16	T4th	2½
5-16	At N.Y.	W	7-0	11	7	J. Abbott	Plunk		18-16	3rd	2½
5-17	At Bal.	L	1-5	6	11	McDonald	Lewis		18-17	T5th	3
5-18	At Bal.	W	4-2	10	9	Finley	Williamson	Harvey	19-17	T4th	3
5-19	At Bal.	W	10-2	15	7	McCaskill	Ballard		20-17	4th	2½
5-20	Chi.	W	6-3	8	9	Langston	Perez	Harvey	21-17	4th	2
5-21	Chi.	W	4-2	6	8	J. Abbott	Radinsky	Harvey	22-17	4th	1
5-22	Chi.	L	3-5	6	7	Hough	Lewis	Thigpen	22-18	4th	1½
5-24	Tor.	L	2-3	7	7	Timlin	Finley	Henke	22-19	4th	2½
5-25	Tor.	W	5-0	9	5	McCaskill	Stottlemyre		23-19	T3rd	2½
5-26	Tor.	W	6-2	10	5	Langston	Wells		24-19	3rd	2½
5-28	At Chi.	L	5-6	9	10	Pall	Harvey		24-20	3rd	3
5-29	At Chi.	W	8-4	15	11	Finley	Hibbard		25-20	3rd	2
5-30	At Chi.	W	7-6	11	12	McCaskill	McDowell	Harvey	26-20	3rd	2
5-31	At Tor.	L	1-5	5	9	Wells	Langston		26-21	3rd	2
6-1	At Tor.	W	11-8	13	16	Eichhorn	Fraser	Harvey	27-21	3rd	2
6-2	At Tor.	W	7-2	9	9	J. Abbott	Acker		28-21	3rd	1
6-4	Bos.	W	3-0	8	2	Finley	Bolton		29-21	2nd	1½
6-5	Bos.	W	7-2	7	8	McCaskill	Gardiner		30-21	2nd	1½
6-6	Bos.	W	3-2	7	4	Langston	Darwin	Harvey	31-21	2nd	1½
6-7	Det.	L	0-5	4	10	Tanana	Valenzuela		31-22	2nd	1½
6-8	Det.	L	3-4	8	6	Terrell	J. Abbott	Henneman	31-23	2nd	1½
6-9	Det.	W	7-3	14	9	Finley	Gakeler		32-23	2nd	1½
6-10	Mil.	L	2-7	10	10	Bosio	McCaskill		32-24	2nd	2½
6-11	Mil.	W	4-3	9	8	Langston	Brown	Harvey	33-24	2nd	1½
6-12	Mil.	L	0-8	4	13	Higuera	Valenzuela		33-25	3rd	2½
6-14	At Bos.	L	4-9	8	11	Clemens	Robinson		33-26	3rd	3
6-15	At Bos.	L	3-13	6	16	Gardiner	Finley		33-27	4th	3½
6-16	At Bos.	L	0-2	6	7	Bolton	McCaskill	Reardon	33-28	4th	4
6-17	At Bos.	W	4-2	7	7	Langston	Harris	Harvey	34-28	4th	3
6-18	At Mil.	L	6-10	11	14	Higuera	Grahe	Plesac	34-29	T4th	4
6-19	At Mil.	W	4-1	11	7	J. Abbott	Wegman	Harvey	35-29	T4th	4
6-20	At Det.	W	7-5	11	7	Grahe	Gibson	Harvey	36-29	T3rd	3½
6-21	At Det.	L	2-9	10	8	Gullickson	McCaskill		36-30	T4th	4½
6-22	At Det.	W	10-3	15	6	Langston	Ritz		37-30	T3rd	4½
6-23	At Det.	L	3-4 (10)	7	9	Gibson	Robinson		37-31	T3rd	4½
6-24	At K.C.	W	9-4	18	7	Finley	Wagner		38-31	3rd	4½
6-25	At K.C.	W	4-2	7	10	McCaskill	Boddicker	Harvey	39-31	T2nd	4½

CALIFORNIA ANGELS

1992 SEASON

CALIFORNIA ANGELS

Date	Opp.	Res.	Score (inn.*)	Hits	Opp. hits	Winning pitcher	Losing pitcher	Save	Record	Pos.	GB
6-26	At K.C.	W	10-5	16	7	Langston	Gubicza		40-31	2nd	3½
6-28	Tex.	W	10-8	11	17	Eichhorn	Rogers	Harvey	41-31	2nd	2
6-29	Tex.	L	4-7 (13)	15	16	Russell	Bailes		41-32	2nd	2
6-30	Tex.	L	1-2	2	7	Guzman	McCaskill		41-33	3rd	3
7-1	Tex.	W	6-2	10	6	Langston	Brown	Harvey	42-33	2nd	2
7-2	K.C.	W	10-3	15	10	J. Abbott	Gubicza	Robinson	43-33	2nd	1
7-3	K.C.	W	4-3	9	5	Finley	Aquino	Harvey	44-33	1st	...
7-4	K.C.	L	5-12	10	21	Appier	McCaskill		44-34	2nd	1
7-5	At Tex.	L	0-8	3	11	Guzman	Langston	Jeffcoat	44-35	3rd	1
7-6	At Tex.	L	3-4	7	8	Brown	J. Abbott	Russell	44-36	3rd	2
7-7	At Tex.	L	0-7	2	7	Ryan	Finley		44-37	3rd	2
7-11	N.Y.	L	0-2	1	11	Sanderson	McCaskill		44-38	4th	3
7-12	N.Y.	L	1-2 (10)	5	4	Howe	Harvey	Farr	44-39	5th	4
7-13	N.Y.	L	0-2	4	4	Johnson	J. Abbott	Farr	44-40	5th	5
7-14	N.Y.	W	10-2	15	9	Finley	Taylor		45-40	5th	4
7-15	Bal.	L	1-2	10	5	Ballard	Harvey	Frohwirth	45-41	5th	5
7-16	Bal.	W	2-1	3	6	Langston	Robinson		46-41	5th	4
7-18	Cle.	W	5-4	4	8	Harvey	Hillegas		47-41	2nd	4
7-19	Cle.	L	2-4 (11)	5	10	Orosco	Eichhorn	Olin	47-42	3rd	5
7-20	Cle.	L	1-4	6	7	Boucher	McCaskill	Olin	47-43	4th	6
7-21	Cle.	L	2-5	13	10	Nagy	Langston	Olin	47-44	5th	7
7-23	At Bal.	W	5-4	15	8	J. Abbott	McDonald	Harvey	48-44	5th	6
7-24	At Bal.	L	2-5	6	9	Milacki	Finley	Olson	48-45	5th	6
7-25	At Bal.	L	4-8	11	10	Frohwirth	McCaskill		48-46	6th	7
7-26	At N.Y.	W	5-1	10	7	Langston	Sanderson	Harvey	49-46	6th	7
7-27	At N.Y.	L	10-12	13	15	Cadaret	Fetters	Farr	49-47	6th	8
7-28	At N.Y.	W	8-4	12	8	J. Abbott	Kamieniecki		50-47	6th	7
7-29	At Cle.	W	10-2	17	8	Finley	Swindell		51-47	6th	7
7-30	At Cle.	W	4-2	8	7	McCaskill	Otto	Harvey	52-47	6th	7
7-31	At Det.	L	1-3	7	6	Terrell	Langston		52-48	6th	8
8-1	At Det.	L	3-5	10	11	Leiter	Fetters	Henneman	52-49	6th	8
8-2	Sea.	L	3-4	9	9	Jackson	J. Abbott	Schooler	52-50	6th	8
8-3	Sea.	L	3-9	6	12	Johnson	McCaskill	Swift	52-51	6th	9
8-4	Sea.	L	2-5 (12)	5	9	Jackson	Fetters	Schooler	52-52	7th	10
8-5	Min.	L	4-7	8	9	Tapani	Grahe	Aguilera	52-53	7th	11
8-6	Min.	L	4-7	7	9	Banks	Finley		52-54	7th	12
8-7	Min.	W	8-1	9	3	J. Abbott	Morris		53-54	7th	11
8-9	Oak.	L	4-5	8	8	Stewart	McCaskill	Eckersley	53-55	7th	12
8-10	Oak.	L	1-3	5	5	Darling	Langston	Eckersley	53-56	7th	12
8-11	Oak.	L	2-3	12	6	Moore	Grahe	Eckersley	53-57	7th	13
8-12	At Min.	L	3-4	7	9	Morris	Beasley	Aguilera	53-58	7th	14
8-13	At Min.	W	8-3	12	6	J. Abbott	Banks	Harvey	54-58	7th	13
8-14	At Min.	W	7-4	8	10	McCaskill	West	Harvey	55-58	7th	12
8-15	At Min.	W	9-1	11	6	Langston	Erickson		56-58	7th	11
8-16	At Sea.	L	3-5	8	7	Krueger	Grahe	Murphy	56-59	7th	12
8-17	At Sea.	W	4-1	8	9	Finley	DeLucia	Harvey	57-59	7th	12
8-18	At Sea.	W	4-3	9	11	J. Abbott	Holman	Harvey	58-59	7th	12
8-19	At Sea.	L	1-7	7	10	Johnson	McCaskill		58-60	7th	12
8-20	At Oak.	L	2-3	6	5	Darling	Langston	Eckersley	58-61	7th	13
8-21	At Oak.	L	0-2	4	11	Moore	Grahe	Eckersley	58-62	7th	14
8-22	At Oak.	L	1-2	4	5	Welch	Finley		58-63	7th	15
8-23	Bos.	W	4-1	8	6	J. Abbott	Young	Harvey	59-63	7th	14
8-24	Bos.	W	1-0	3	4	McCaskill	Morton	Harvey	60-63	7th	14
8-25	Bos.	W	9-5	12	9	Fetters	Hesketh	Eichhorn	61-63	7th	13
8-26	Det.	L	1-5	10	13	Leiter	Grahe	Gakeler	61-64	7th	14
8-27	Det.	W	4-2	9	6	Finley	Cerutti	Harvey	62-64	7th	13
8-28	Det.	W	1-0	5	4	J. Abbott	Gullickson	Harvey	63-64	7th	13
8-30	At Mil.	L	2-6	6	12	Wegman	McCaskill		63-65	7th	13
8-31	At Mil.	L	2-8	7	16	Lee	Grahe		63-66	7th	14
9-1	At Mil.	L	1-3	4	7	Navarro	Finley		63-67	7th	15
9-2	At Mil.	W	7-6	14	13	J. Abbott	August	Harvey	64-67	7th	15
9-3	At Bos.	W	2-0	7	4	Langston	Gardiner	Harvey	65-67	7th	14½
9-4	At Bos.	L	0-2	7	7	Hesketh	McCaskill	Reardon	65-68	7th	14½
9-6	Mil.	W	2-1	6	4	Grahe	Bosio		66-68	7th	14½
9-7	Mil.	W	1-0	3	5	Finley	Navarro	Harvey	67-68	7th	14½
9-8	Mil.	W	1-0	8	6	J. Abbott	Plesac	Harvey	68-68	6th	14½
9-9	Tex.	W	4-2	8	6	Langston	Boyd	Harvey	69-68	6th	14½
9-10	Tex.	L	1-6	6	10	Russell	K. Abbott		69-69	T6th	15½
9-11	Tex.	L	9-11 (12)	14	15	Manuel	Robinson		69-70	7th	15½
9-12	Chi.	W	7-4	12	7	Eichhorn	Perez	Harvey	70-70	7th	14½
9-13	Chi.	L	0-1	4	6	McDowell	J. Abbott		70-71	7th	15½
9-14	Chi.	W	3-2 (10)	12	7	Fetters	Radinsky		71-71	7th	14½
9-15	Chi.	L	2-9	8	14	Hough	K. Abbott		71-72	7th	14½
9-17	At Tex.	W	7-2	12	8	Lewis	Bohanon		72-72	7th	14

Date	Opp.	Res.	Score (inn.*)	Hits	Opp. hits	Winning pitcher	Losing pitcher	Save	Record	Pos.	GB
9-19 (1)	At Tex.	L	3-10	7	11	Ryan	Finley		72-73	7th	14
9-19 (2)	At Tex.	W	5-2	13	6	J. Abbott	Brown	Harvey	73-73	7th	13½
9-20	At Chi.	L	2-3 (11)	8	8	Perez	Eichhorn		73-74	7th	14½
9-21	At Chi.	W	4-3	9	5	K. Abbott	Drahman	Harvey	74-74	7th	14½
9-22	At Chi.	W	4-2	12	6	Grahe	Hibbard	Harvey	75-74	7th	14½
9-23	Tor.	W	10-9	14	12	Lewis	Candiotti	Harvey	76-74	T5th	14
9-24	Tor.	L	0-3 (10)	6	4	Wells	J. Abbott		76-75	T6th	15
9-25	Tor.	L	2-7	6	9	Key	Langston		76-76	T6th	15
9-26	At K.C.	L	2-3	8	6	Gubicza	Fetters	Montgomery	76-77	7th	15½
9-27	At K.C.	L	1-4	5	9	Saberhagen	McCaskill	Montgomery	76-78	7th	15½
9-28	At K.C.	W	4-3	10	6	Finley	Aquino	Harvey	77-78	7th	15½
9-29	At K.C.	L	4-8	7	9	Appier	J. Abbott		77-79	7th	15½
9-30	At Tor.	W	2-1	9	3	Langston	Key	Harvey	78-79	7th	15½
10-1	At Tor.	L	2-5	8	8	Guzman	Fetters	Ward	78-80	7th	16½
10-2	At Tor.	L	5-6	10	8	Timlin	Harvey		78-81	7th	17
10-4	K.C.	W	6-2	10	10	Young	Gordon		79-81	7th	15
10-5	K.C.	W	5-1	6	9	J. Abbott	Appier		80-81	7th	15
10-6	K.C.	W	3-1	4	5	Langston	M. Davis	Harvey	81-81	7th	14

Monthly records: April (10-10), May (16-11), June (15-12), July (11-15), August (11-18), September (15-13), Oct. (3-2).

HIGHLIGHTS

High point: On the morning of July 4, the Angels awoke in first place in the American League West by one percentage point, having won seven of nine games.

Low point: After their brief glimpse of first place, the Angels went 8-21 to fall into the A.L. West cellar August 6. California suffered two seven-game losing streaks during its 29-game skid.

Turning point: Despite a lineup with sluggers Dave Winfield, Dave Parker, Gary Gaetti, Lance Parrish and Wally Joyner, the Angels stopped hitting home runs in July. At one point the club went 419 consecutive plate appearances without a homer, a drought that coincided with the Angels' dive.

Most valuable player: First baseman Joyner. He led the club with a .301 average (the first time in his career he exceeded .300), reached the 20-homer mark (21) for the first time since 1987 and drove in a team-high 96 runs.

Most valuable pitcher: Righthander Bryan Harvey. He demolished Donnie Moore's club record for most saves in a season (31 in 1985) by saving 46 games. He struck out 101 batters while walking just 17 in 78⅔ innings and compiling a 1.60 earned-run average.

Most improved player: Lefthander Jim Abbott. One year earlier he was 10-14, and after a 0-4 start in 1991, Abbott heard public suggestions that he be sent to the minors. He silenced his critics by going 16-4 in his next 25 starts.

Most pleasant surprise: Righthander Mark Eichhorn. Not expected to make the team in spring training, he eventually became a reliable setup man for Harvey and finished with a 1.98 ERA.

Biggest disappointment: The Angels' inability to find a productive fifth starter. Four different pitchers who tried stumbled to a combined 1-16 record through the end of August.

Key injuries: Center fielder Junior Felix was able to play only 66 games because of a variety of ailments. A gaping hole in the rotation might have been plugged if veteran Bert Blyleven hadn't

been lost for the year in March because of a rotator cuff injury.

Notable: After posting a 61-63 mark, Doug Rader was fired as manager August 26 and replaced by Buck Rodgers, who closed the year with a 20-18 record.... Mark Langston (19-8), Abbott (18-11) and Chuck Finley (18-9) became the first trio of lefthanded teammates in major league history to win 18 or more games apiece in the same season.

—DAVID CUNNINGHAM

RECORDS

1991 regular-season record: 81-81 (7th in A.L. West); 40-41 at home; 41-40 on road; 44-40 vs. East; 37-41 vs. West; 25-18 vs. LHP; 56-63 vs. RHP; 64-71 on grass; 17-10 on turf; 22-18 in daytime; 59-63 at night; 23-21 in one-run games; 2-9 in extra-inning games; 0-0-1 in doubleheaders.

Team record last five years: 402-408 (.496, ranks 8th in league in that span).

TEAM LEADERS

Batting average: Wally Joyner (.301).
At-bats: Luis Polonia (604).
Runs: Luis Polonia (92).
Hits: Luis Polonia (179).
Total bases: Wally Joyner (269).
Doubles: Wally Joyner (34).
Triples: Luis Polonia (8).
Home runs: Dave Winfield (28).
Runs batted in: Wally Joyner (96).
Stolen bases: Luis Polonia (48).
Slugging percentage: Wally Joyner (.488).
On-base percentage: Wally Joyner (.360).
Wins: Mark Langston (19).
Earned-run average: Jim Abbott (2.89).
Complete games: Mark Langston (7).
Shutouts: Chuck Finley (2).
Saves: Bryan Harvey (46).
Innings pitched: Mark Langston (246⅓).
Strikeouts: Mark Langston (183).

GAMES BY POSITION

Catcher: Lance Parrish 111, Ron Tingley 45, John Orton 28.
First base: Wally Joyner 141, Lee Stevens 11, Chris Cron 5, Donnie Hill 3, Jack Howell 3, Lance Parrish 3, Bobby Rose 3, Barry Lyons 2, Mike Marshall 1.
Second base: Luis Sojo 107, Donnie Hill 39, Jack Howell 12, Bobby Rose 8, Gary DiSarcina 7, Ruben Amaro 4, Kevin Flora 3.
Third base: Gary Gaetti 152, Jack Howell 8, Bobby Rose 4, Gary DiSarcina 2, Luis Sojo 1.
Shortstop: Dick Schofield 133, Donnie Hill 29, Gary DiSarcina 10, Luis Sojo 2.
Outfield: Luis Polonia 143, Dave Winfield 115, Dave Gallagher 87, Junior Felix 65, Max Venable 65, Shawn Abner 38, Lee Stevens 9, Bobby Rose 7, Ruben Amaro 5, Jack Howell 5, Dave Marshall 4, Mark Davis 3, Luis Sojo 1.
Designated hitter: Dave Parker 119, Dave Winfield 34, Lance Parrish 5, Luis Polonia 4, Shawn Abner 3, Max Venable 3, Dave Gallagher 2, Ruben Amaro 1, Chris Cron 1, Jack Howell 1, Mike Marshall 1, John Orton 1, Luis Sojo 1.

TOP 10 DRAFT CHOICES

1a. Eduardo Perez, 1B, Florida State University.
1b. Jorge Fabregas, 3B/C, University of Miami.
2. Chris Pritchett, 1B, UCLA.
3. Mark Ratekin, RHP, Point Loma (Calif.) Nazarene College.
4. John Donati, 1B, De La Salle High School, Concord, Calif.
5. David Kennedy, RHP/OF, Montclair State College.
6. Brian Williard, RHP, Dixie Hollins High School, St. Petersburg, Fla.
7. Chris Turner, 3B/OF, Western Kentucky University.
8. Kurt Ehmann, SS, Arizona State University.
9. Mark Sweeney, OF, University of Maine.
10. Gary Hagy, SS, UCLA.

CHICAGO WHITE SOX
AMERICAN LEAGUE WEST DIVISION

1992 SCHEDULE

APRIL
S	M	T	W	T	F	S
5	6	7 N CAL	8 N CAL	9 N CAL	10 N OAK	11 N OAK
12 OAK	13 N SEA H	14	15 N SEA H	16 N SEA H	17 N MIN H	18 N MIN H
19 MIN H	20	21 N NY H	22 N NY H	23	24 N DET	25 N DET
26 DET	27	28 N BOS	29 N BOS	30 N TEX H		

MAY
S	M	T	W	T	F	S
					1 N TEX H	2 TEX H
3 TEX H	4 N MIL H	5 N MIL H	6 N BOS H	7 N BOS H	8 N BAL	9 N BAL
10 BAL	11	12 N MIL	13 N MIL	14	15 N BAL H	16 N BAL H
17 BAL H	18 N KC H	19 N KC H	20 N KC H	21	22 N TOR H	23 N TOR H
24 TOR H	25	26 N TEX	27 N TEX	28 N TEX	29 N TOR	30 TOR
31 TOR						

JUNE
S	M	T	W	T	F	S
	1 N KC	2 N KC	3 N KC	4	5 N OAK H	6 N OAK H
7 OAK H	8 N CAL H	9 N CAL H	10 N CAL H	11 N CAL H	12 N MIN	13 MIN
14 MIN	15 N SEA	16 N SEA	17 N SEA	18 N SEA	19 N DET H	20 N DET H
21 DET H	22 N CLE H	23 N CLE H	24 N CLE H	25	26 N NY	27 NY
28 N NY	29 N CLE	30 N CLE				

JULY
S	M	T	W	T	F	S
			1 N CLE	2 N BOS H	3 N BOS H	4 N BOS H
5 BOS H	6 N BAL	7 N BAL	8 N BAL	9 N BOS	10 N BOS	11 BOS
12 BOS	13	14 ★	15	16 N MIL H	17 N MIL H	18 N MIL H
19 MIL H	20 N BAL H	21 N BAL H	22 N BAL H	23 N MIL	24 N MIL	25 N MIL
26 MIL	27	28 N DET	29 N DET	30 N DET	31 N SEA H	

AUGUST
S	M	T	W	T	F	S
					1 N SEA H	2 N SEA H
2 SEA H	3	4 N MIN H	5 N MIN H	6 N MIN H	7 N CAL	8 N CAL
9 CAL	10 N OAK	11 N OAK	12 N OAK	13	14 N NY H	15 N NY H
16 NY H	17 N NY H	18 N TEX H	19 N TEX H	20 N TEX H	21 N KC H	22 N KC H
23 KC H	24 N TOR H	25 N TOR H	26 N TOR H	27	28 N TEX	29 TEX
30 N TEX	31 N TOR					

SEPTEMBER
S	M	T	W	T	F	S
		1 N TOR	2 N TOR	3 N KC	4 N KC	5 N KC
6 KC	7	8 N DET H	9 N DET H	10 N DET H	11 N CLE H	12 N CLE H
13 CLE H	14 N NY	15 N NY	16 N NY	17	18 N CLE	19 CLE
20 N CLE	21 N OAK H	22 N OAK H	23 N OAK H	24 N OAK H	25 N CAL H	26 N CAL H
27 CAL	28 N MIN	29 N MIN	30 N MIN			

OCTOBER
S	M	T	W	T	F	S
				1 N MIN	2 N SEA	3 N SEA
4 SEA	5	6	7	8	9	10

1992 SEASON

CLUB DIRECTORY

Chairman
Jerry Reinsdorf
Vice chairman
Eddie Einhorn
Executive vice president
Howard Pizer
Senior v.p., major league operations
Ron Schueler
Senior v.p., marketing and broadcasting
Rob Gallas
Senior vice president, baseball
Jack Gould
Vice president, finance
Tim Buzard
Vice president, stadium operations
Terry Savarise
V.p., scouting and major league operations
Larry Monroe
General counsel
Allan Muchin
Secretary
Gerald Penner
Director of baseball operations
Dan Evans
Special assistants to Ron Schueler
Ed Brinkman
Bart Johnson
Dave Yoakum
Director of scouting
Duane Shaffer
Director of minor league operations
Steve Noworyta
Director of minor league instruction
Buddy Bell
Traveling secretary
Glen Rosenbaum
Assistant to the director of scouting
Grace Guerrero Zwit
Asst. to the director of baseball operations
Jeff Chaney
Major league computer scouting analyst
Mike Maziarka
Trainers
Herm Schneider
Mark Anderson
Director of conditioning
Steve Odgers
Team physicians
Dr. James Boscardin
Dr. Hugo Cuadros
Dr. Robert Daley
Dr. Bernard Feldman
Dr. David Orth
Dr. Scott Price
Director of marketing and broadcasting
Mike Bucek
Director of advertising and promotions
Bob Grim

Director of p.r. and community affairs
Doug Abel
Director of ticket administration
Millie Johnson
Director of ticket sales
Bob Voight
Ticket manager
Bob Devoy
Controller
Bill Waters
Director of park operations
David Schaffer
Assistant director of public relations
Scott Reifert
Manager of publicity
Dana Noel
Manager of community relations
Dan Fabian
Scouting national cross-checker
George Bradley
Scouting supervisors
Mark Bernstein
Ed Pebley
Marti Wolever
Full-time scouts
Jose Bernhardt
Juan Ramon Bernhardt
Chuck Bizzell
Kevin Burrell
Joseph Butler
Scott Cerny
Alex Cosmidis
Warren Hughes
Miguel Ibarra
Douglas Laumann
Reginald Lewis
Guy Mader
David Owen
Gary Pellant
Victor Puig
Michael Rizzo
Alberto Rondon
Michael Sgobba
Ken Stauffer
John Tumminia
Part-time scouts
Steve Arnieri
Alonzo Ganther
Nino Giarratano
Joe Ingalls
Jack Jolly
George Kachigian
Bill Kahler
Dario Lodigiani
Jose Ortega
Al Otto
Robert Rikeman Jr.
Joe Thurman

SCHEDULE KEY

H—Home game.   *All-Star Game at San Diego/Jack Murphy Stadium.
N—Night game (any game starting after 5 p.m.).

SPRING TRAINING ROSTER

Manager—Gene Lamont (7).

Coaches—Terry Bevington (18), Jackie Brown (36), Walt Hriniak (6), Doug Mansolino (17), Joe Nossek (15), Mike Squires (38).

No.	PITCHERS	B/T	Ht./Wt.	Born	1991 clubs
40	Alvarez, Wilson	L/L	6-1/175	3-24-70	Birmingham, Chicago AL
41	Carter, Jeff	R/R	6-3/195	12-3-64	Vancouver, Chicago AL
50	Drahman, Brian	R/R	6-3/205	11-7-66	Chicago AL, Vancouver
45	Edwards, Wayne	L/L	6-5/185	3-7-64	Chicago AL, Vancouver
32	Fernandez, Alex	R/R	6-1/205	8-13-69	Chicago AL
43	Garcia, Ramon	R/R	6-2/200	12-9-69	Birmingham, Vancouver, Chicago AL
39	Hernandez, Roberto	R/R	6-4/220	11-11-64	Vancouver, Birmingham, Chicago AL
27	Hibbard, Greg	L/L	6-0/190	9-13-64	Chicago AL, Vancouver
49	Hough, Charlie	R/R	6-2/190	1-5-48	Chicago AL
56	Howard, Chris	R/L	6-0/185	11-18-65	Birmingham
28	McCaskill, Kirk	R/R	6-1/205	4-9-61	California
29	McDowell, Jack	R/R	6-5/180	1-16-66	Chicago AL
22	Pall, Donn	R/R	6-1/183	1-11-62	Chicago AL
34	Patterson, Ken	L/L	6-4/210	7-8-64	Chicago AL
42	Perschke, Greg	R/R	6-3/180	8-3-67	Vancouver
31	Radinsky, Scott	L/L	6-3/190	3-3-68	Chicago AL
47	Ruffin, Johnny	R/R	6-3/172	7-29-71	Sarasota
48	Scheid, Rich	L/L	6-3/185	2-3-65	Vancouver
37	Thigpen, Bobby	R/R	6-3/195	7-17-63	Chicago AL
51	Wapnick, Steve	R/R	6-2/200	9-25-65	Syracuse, Chicago AL

No.	CATCHERS	B/T	Ht./Wt.	Born	1991 clubs
72	Fisk, Carlton	R/R	6-2/223	12-26-47	Chicago AL
20	Karkovice, Ron	R/R	6-1/215	8-8-63	Chicago AL
5	Merullo, Matt	L/R	6-2/200	8-4-65	Chicago AL, Birmingham

No.	INFIELDERS	B/T	Ht./Wt.	Born	1991 clubs
28	Beltre, Esteban	R/R	5-10/155	12-26-67	Denver, Vancouver, Chicago AL
21	Cora, Joey	S/R	5-8/152	5-14-65	Chicago AL, South Bend
14	Grebeck, Craig	R/R	5-7/160	12-29-64	Chicago AL
13	Guillen, Ozzie	L/R	5-11/150	1-20-64	Chicago AL
53	Martin, Norberto	S/R	5-10/164	12-10-66	Vancouver
10	Sax, Steve	R/R	6-0/188	1-29-60	New York AL
35	Thomas, Frank	R/R	6-5/240	5-27-68	Chicago AL
23	Ventura, Robin	L/R	6-1/192	7-14-67	Chicago AL

No.	OUTFIELDERS	B/T	Ht./Wt.	Born	1991 clubs
12	Huff, Mike	R/R	6-1/180	8-11-63	Cleveland, Chicago AL
8	Jackson, Bo	R/R	6-1/235	11-30-62	Sarasota, Birmingham, Chicago AL
1	Johnson, Lance	L/L	5-11/160	7-6-63	Chicago AL
52	Lee, Derek	L/R	6-0/195	7-28-66	Birmingham, Vancouver
24	Newson, Warren	L/L	5-7/190	7-3-64	Vancouver, Chicago AL
44	Pasqua, Dan	L/L	6-0/203	10-17-61	Chicago AL
30	Raines, Tim	S/R	5-8/185	9-16-59	Chicago AL
25	Sosa, Sammy	R/R	6-0/175	11-12-68	Chicago AL, Vancouver

BALLPARK INFORMATION

Ballpark (capacity, surface)
Comiskey Park (44,177, grass)
Address
333 W. 35th St.
Chicago, IL 60616
Business phone
312-924-1000
Ticket information
312-924-1000
Ticket prices
$18 (club level)
$15 (lower deck box)
$12 (upper deck box)
$11 (lower deck reserved)
$8 (upper deck reserved)
$8 (bleacher reserved)
Field dimensions (from home plate)
To left field at foul line, 347 feet
To center field, 400 feet
To right field at foul line, 347 feet
First game played
April 18, 1991 (Tigers 16, White Sox 0)

MINOR LEAGUE AFFILIATES

Class	Team	League	Manager
AAA	Vancouver	Pacific Coast	Rick Renick
AA	Birmingham	Southern	Tony Franklin
A	Sarasota	Florida State	Rick Patterson
A	South Bend	Midwest	Terry Francona
A	Utica	New York-Pennsylvania	Mike Gellinger
Rookie	Gulf Coast White Sox	Gulf Coast	Mike Rojas

☐ BROADCAST INFORMATION ☐

Radio: WMAQ-AM (670). Broadcasters: John Rooney, Ed Farmer. WTAQ-AM (1300, Spanish language). Broadcasters: Chico Carrasquel, Teofilo Garcia, Frank Diaz.
TV: WGN-TV (Channel 9). Broadcasters: Tom Paciorek, Ken Harrelson.
Cable TV: SportsChannel. Broadcasters: Tom Paciorek, Ken Harrelson.

SPRING TRAINING

Ballpark (city): Ed Smith Stadium (Sarasota, Fla.).
Ticket information: 813-953-3388.

HISTORY

YEAR-BY-YEAR RECORDS

Year	Pos.	W	L	Pct.	*GB	Year	Pos.	W	L	Pct.	*GB
1901	1st	83	53	.610	+4	1949	6th	63	91	.409	34
1902	4th	74	60	.552	8	1950	6th	60	94	.390	38
1903	7th	60	77	.438	30½	1951	4th	81	73	.526	17
1904	3rd	89	65	.578	6	1952	3rd	81	73	.526	14
1905	2nd	92	60	.605	2	1953	3rd	89	65	.578	11½
1906	1st	93	58	.616	+3	1954	3rd	94	60	.610	17
1907	3rd	87	64	.576	5½	1955	3rd	91	63	.591	5
1908	3rd	88	64	.579	1½	1956	3rd	85	69	.552	12
1909	4th	78	74	.513	20	1957	2nd	90	64	.584	8
1910	6th	68	85	.444	35½	1958	2nd	82	72	.532	10
1911	4th	77	74	.510	24	1959	1st	94	60	.610	+5
1912	4th	78	76	.506	28	1960	3rd	87	67	.565	10
1913	5th	78	74	.513	17½	1961	4th	86	76	.531	23
1914	T6th	70	84	.455	30	1962	5th	85	77	.525	11
1915	3rd	93	61	.604	9½	1963	2nd	94	68	.580	10½
1916	2nd	89	65	.578	2	1964	2nd	98	64	.605	1
1917	1st	100	54	.649	+9	1965	2nd	95	67	.586	7
1918	6th	57	67	.460	17	1966	4th	83	79	.512	15
1919	1st	88	52	.629	+3½	1967	4th	89	73	.549	3
1920	2nd	96	58	.623	2	1968	T8th	67	95	.414	36
1921	7th	62	92	.403	36½	1969	5th	68	94	.420	29
1922	5th	77	77	.500	17	1970	6th	56	106	.346	42
1923	7th	69	85	.448	30	1971	3rd	79	83	.488	22½
1924	8th	66	87	.431	25½	1972	2nd	87	67	.565	5½
1925	5th	79	75	.513	18½	1973	5th	77	85	.475	17
1926	5th	81	72	.529	9½	1974	4th	80	80	.500	9
1927	5th	70	83	.458	29½	1975	5th	75	86	.466	22½
1928	5th	72	82	.468	29	1976	6th	64	97	.398	25½
1929	7th	59	93	.388	46	1977	3rd	90	72	.556	12
1930	7th	62	92	.403	40	1978	5th	71	90	.441	20½
1931	8th	56	97	.366	51	1979	5th	73	87	.456	14
1932	7th	49	102	.325	56½	1980	5th	70	90	.438	26
1933	6th	67	83	.447	31	1981	3rd/6th	54	52	.509	†
1934	8th	53	99	.349	47	1982	3rd	87	75	.537	6
1935	5th	74	78	.487	19½	1983	1st‡	99	63	.611	+20
1936	3rd	81	70	.536	20	1984	T5th	74	88	.457	10
1937	3rd	86	68	.558	16	1985	3rd	85	77	.525	6
1938	6th	65	83	.439	32	1986	5th	72	90	.444	20
1939	4th	85	69	.552	22½	1987	5th	77	85	.475	8
1940	T4th	82	72	.532	8	1988	5th	71	90	.441	32½
1941	3rd	77	77	.500	24	1989	7th	69	92	.429	29½
1942	6th	66	82	.446	34	1990	2nd	94	68	.580	9
1943	4th	82	72	.532	16	1991	2nd	87	75	.537	8
1944	7th	71	83	.461	18						
1945	6th	71	78	.477	15						
1946	5th	74	80	.481	30						
1947	6th	70	84	.455	27						
1948	8th	51	101	.336	44½						

*Game behind winner. †First half 31-22; second 23-30. ‡Lost Championship Series.

MANAGERS

Name	Record	Years
Clark Griffith	157-113	'01-02
Nixey Callahan	309-329	'03-04
		'12-14
Fielder Jones	426-293	'04-08
Billy Sullivan	78-74	1909
Hugh Duffy	145-159	'10-11
Pants Rowland	339-247	'15-18
Kid Gleason	392-364	'19-23
Johnny Evers	76-98	1924
Eddie Collins	160-147	'25-26
Ray Schalk	102-125	'27-28
Lena Blackburne	99-133	'28-29
Donie Bush	118-189	'30-31
Lew Fonseca	120-196	'32-34
Jimmie Dykes	899-940	'34-46
Ted Lyons	185-245	'46-48
Jack Onslow	71-133	'49-50
Red Corriden	52-72	1950
Paul Richards	406-362	'51-54
		1976
Marty Marion	179-138	'54-56
Al Lopez	840-650	'57-65
		'68-69
Eddie Stanky	206-197	'66-68
Don Gutteridge	109-172	'69-70
Chuck Tanner	401-414	'70-75
Bob Lemon	124-112	'77-78
Larry Doby	37-50	1978
Don Kessinger	46-60	1979
Tony La Russa	522-510	'79-86
Jim Fregosi	193-226	'86-88
Jeff Torborg	250-235	'89-91

DAY BY DAY

Date	Opp.	Res.	Score (inn.*)	Hits	Opp. hits	Winning pitcher	Losing pitcher	Save	Record	Pos.	GB
4-8	At Bal.	W	9-1	10	4	McDowell	Ballard		1-0	T1st	...
4-10	At Bal.	W	2-0	7	3	Hibbard	Mesa	Thigpen	2-0	T1st	...
4-12	At Det.	W	4-1	8	5	Fernandez	Searcy	Thigpen	3-0	1st	+½
4-13	At Det.	W	4-1	7	2	McDowell	Tanana		4-0	1st	+½
4-15	At N.Y.	W	6-5	13	5	Hibbard	Cadaret	Thigpen	5-0	1st	...
4-16	At N.Y.	W	4-3 (10)	8	5	Radinsky	Farr	Thigpen	6-0	1st	...
4-17	At N.Y.	L	1-10	4	12	Cary	Fernandez		6-1	2nd	1
4-18	Det.	L	0-16	7	19	Tanana	McDowell		6-2	2nd	1
4-20	Det.	L	1-2 (12)	9	11	Henneman	Radinsky	Gleaton	6-3	2nd	½
4-21	Det.	W	5-4	11	4	Drahman	Gibson		7-3	1st	+½
4-22	Bal.	W	8-7	11	10	Fernandez	McDonald	Thigpen	8-3	1st	+1½
4-23	Bal.	W	10-4	12	9	McDowell	D. Johnson		9-3	1st	+1½
4-24	Bal.	L	1-5	7	10	Ballard	Hough		9-4	1st	+1½
4-26	N.Y.	L	2-3 (11)	12	9	Cadaret	Drahman		9-5	1st	+½
4-27	N.Y.	W	14-9	20	13	Perez	Plunk		10-5	1st	+½
4-28	N.Y.	W	4-1	7	5	McDowell	Cary	Thigpen	11-5	1st	+½
4-30	At Mil.	L	2-8	10	13	Bosio	Fernandez	Crim	11-6	2nd	½
5-1	At Mil.	L	9-10 (19)	19	18	August	Edwards		11-7	2nd	1½
5-3	Bos.	L	2-7	5	13	Clemens	McDowell		11-8	2nd	2½
5-4	Bos.	L	0-4	5	5	Bolton	Perez		11-9	2nd	2½
5-5	Bos.	L	1-9	8	8	Young	Fernandez		11-10	2nd	2½
5-7	Mil.	W	2-1 (12)	9	9	Thigpen	Lee		12-10	2nd	2½
5-8	Mil.	W	2-1	7	7	McDowell	Navarro		13-10	2nd	2½
5-9	At Tor.	L	0-2	3	6	Wells	Perez	Ward	13-11	2nd	3
5-10	At Tor.	W	5-3 (12)	12	8	Radinsky	Fraser		14-11	2nd	2
5-11	At Tor.	L	2-5	7	6	Stieb	Hough	Ward	14-12	2nd	3
5-12	At Tor.	L	2-4	7	9	Key	Hibbard	Ward	14-13	3rd	3
5-13	At Bos.	W	4-3 (10)	8	11	Thigpen	Gray		15-13	3rd	2
5-14	At Bos.	L	1-4	8	7	Bolton	Perez	Reardon	15-14	4th	3
5-15	At Bos.	L	6-9	11	13	Hesketh	Pall	Reardon	15-15	6th	3
5-17	Tor.	W	5-3	11	9	Pall	Timlin	Thigpen	16-15	4th	3
5-18	Tor.	L	2-9	4	13	Key	Hibbard		16-16	6th	4
5-19	Tor.	W	5-4	9	9	Patterson	Timlin		17-16	5th	3½
5-20	At Cal.	L	3-6	9	8	Langston	Perez	Harvey	17-17	6th	4
5-21	At Cal.	L	2-4	8	6	J. Abbott	Radinsky	Harvey	17-18	6th	4
5-22	At Cal.	W	5-3	7	6	Hough	Lewis	Thigpen	18-18	5th	3½
5-23	At Oak.	W	11-1	17	5	Hibbard	Hawkins		19-18	5th	3
5-24	At Oak.	L	5-6	7	9	Eckersley	Thigpen		19-19	5th	3½
5-25	At Oak.	L	3-5 (10)	6	7	Klink	Edwards		19-20	5th	4½
5-26	At Oak.	L	2-6	10	7	Stewart	Fernandez	Klink	19-21	5th	6
5-28	Cal.	W	6-5	10	9	Pall	Harvey		20-21	5th	5½
5-29	Cal.	L	4-8	11	15	Finley	Hibbard		20-22	6th	5½
5-30	Cal.	L	6-7	12	11	McCaskill	McDowell	Harvey	20-23	6th	6½
5-31	Oak.	W	5-4	12	2	Thigpen	Chitren		21-23	6th	5½
6-1	Oak.	L	4-7	9	6	Klink	Fernandez	Eckersley	21-24	6th	6½
6-2	Oak.	W	4-3	10	4	Hough	Moore	Thigpen	22-24	6th	5½
6-3	Oak.	L	3-5	17	13	Slusarski	Hibbard	Eckersley	22-25	6th	6½
6-4	At Cle.	W	4-1	9	4	McDowell	Nichols		23-25	6th	6½
6-5	At Cle.	L	1-2	6	7	Hillegas	Garcia		23-26	6th	7½
6-6	At Cle.	W	2-1 (10)	10	8	Perez	Jones	Thigpen	24-26	6th	7½
6-7	At K.C.	W	2-0	5	6	Hough	Appier	Radinsky	25-26	6th	6½
6-8	At K.C.	W	14-7	18	12	Hibbard	Gordon		26-26	6th	5½
6-9	At K.C.	W	8-2	11	4	McDowell	Boddicker		27-26	6th	5½
6-10	At Tex.	W	3-2 (13)	6	6	Perez	Alexander	Thigpen	28-26	5th	5½
6-11	At Tex.	L	0-2	6	7	Ryan	Fernandez		28-27	6th	5½
6-12	At Tex.	L	2-4	7	2	Barfield	Hough	Russell	28-28	6th	6½
6-13	At Tex.	L	4-8	10	10	Alexander	Hibbard	Rogers	28-29	6th	7
6-14	K.C.	W	9-3	16	5	McDowell	Aquino	Radinsky	29-29	6th	6½
6-15	K.C.	L	3-5	7	9	Boddicker	Garcia	Montgomery	29-30	6th	7
6-16	K.C.	L	4-9	11	12	Gubicza	Fernandez		29-31	T6th	7½
6-18	Cle.	W	6-5	9	7	Hough	Candiotti	Thigpen	30-31	6th	7
6-19	Cle.	L	3-4	9	9	Nagy	Hibbard	Nichols	30-32	7th	8
6-20	Tex.	L	3-7	9	8	Jeffcoat	Thigpen		30-33	7th	8½
6-21	Tex.	W	6-5 (11)	9	9	Patterson	Schiraldi		31-33	7th	8½
6-22	Tex.	W	3-1	7	4	Fernandez	Barfield		32-33	T6th	8½
6-23	Tex.	W	6-5 (10)	7	8	Thigpen	Russell		33-33	6th	7½
6-24	Sea.	W	6-2	6	9	Hibbard	DeLucia	Radinsky	34-33	6th	7½
6-25	Sea.	W	4-0	9	3	McDowell	Burba		35-33	6th	7½
6-26	Sea.	L	4-5	4	10	Johnson	Garcia	Jackson	35-34	6th	7½
6-27	Sea.	W	5-2	10	8	Fernandez	Hanson	Thigpen	36-34	6th	6½

CHICAGO WHITE SOX

1992 SEASON

CHICAGO WHITE SOX

Date	Opp.	Res.	Score (inn.*)	Hits	Opp. hits	Winning pitcher	Losing pitcher	Save	Record	Pos.	GB
6-28	At Min.	W	4-2	8	8	Hough	Anderson	Thigpen	37-34	6th	5½
6-29	At Min.	W	8-4	16	7	Hibbard	Erickson		38-34	5th	4½
6-30	At Min.	L	0-3	6	9	Morris	McDowell		38-35	5th	5½
7-1	At Min.	W	5-4 (10)	6	10	Thigpen	Willis		39-35	5th	4½
7-2	At Sea.	W	5-4	10	10	Perez	Burba		40-35	4th	3½
7-3	At Sea.	W	3-2 (12)	13	4	Pall	Jones	Thigpen	41-35	4th	2½
7-4	At Sea.	L	2-3	7	6	DeLucia	Hibbard	Murphy	41-36	4th	3½
7-5	Min.	W	4-2	7	7	McDowell	Morris		42-36	T4th	2½
7-6	Min.	L	4-5	5	8	Willis	Radinsky	Aguilera	42-37	5th	3½
7-7	Min.	W	4-3	8	6	Patterson	Guthrie	Thigpen	43-37	4th	2½
7-11	At Mil.	L	1-5	6	9	Wegman	Hough		43-38	5th	3½
7-12	At Mil.	W	8-6	9	10	Perez	Plesac	Thigpen	44-38	4th	3½
7-13	At Mil.	L	2-8	7	12	August	Hibbard		44-39	3rd	4½
7-14	At Mil.	W	15-1	15	1	McDowell	Knudson		45-39	3rd	3½
7-15	Bos.	W	7-1	13	5	Garcia	Gardiner	Patterson	46-39	3rd	3½
7-16	Bos.	L	0-2	3	9	Harris	Hough	Reardon	46-40	4th	3½
7-17	Bos.	L	2-4 (10)	5	10	Fossas	Thigpen		46-41	T4th	4½
7-19	Mil.	W	14-3	16	9	McDowell	August		47-41	2nd	4½
7-20	Mil.	W	7-6 (10)	11	12	Thigpen	Plesac		48-41	2nd	4½
7-21	Mil.	L	1-2	6	3	Bosio	Hough		48-42	3rd	5½
7-22	Mil.	W	5-4	9	8	Hibbard	Wegman	Thigpen	49-42	3rd	5
7-23	Tor.	W	3-2	7	8	Thigpen	Candiotti		50-42	3rd	4
7-24	Tor.	L	1-2	7	10	Wells	McDowell	Henke	50-43	T2nd	4
7-25	Tor.	W	7-1	8	8	Hough	Stottlemyre		51-43	2nd	4
7-27 (1)	At Bos.	W	10-8 (14)	14	10	Perez	Kiecker	Thigpen	52-43	2nd	4
7-27 (2)	At Bos.	W	7-4	13	12	Garcia	Gardiner	Thigpen	53-43	2nd	4
7-28	At Bos.	W	5-2	9	7	Fernandez	Harris	Thigpen	54-43	2nd	3
7-29	At Tor.	W	12-4	11	6	McDowell	Wells		55-43	2nd	3
7-30	At Tor.	W	8-7	8	9	Radinsky	MacDonald	Thigpen	56-43	2nd	3
7-31	Tex.	W	10-8	14	11	Pall	Gossage		57-43	2nd	3
8-1	Tex.	W	13-2	11	10	Garcia	Witt		58-43	2nd	2
8-2	Bal.	L	0-3	8	5	McDonald	Fernandez	Olson	58-44	2nd	2
8-3	Bal.	L	3-6	9	13	Milacki	McDowell	Olson	58-45	2nd	3
8-4	Bal.	W	1-0	4	5	Hough	Mussina		59-45	2nd	3
8-6	N.Y.	W	14-5	15	9	Pall	Leary		60-45	2nd	3½
8-7	N.Y.	W	10-2	12	7	McDowell	Eiland		61-45	2nd	2½
8-8	N.Y.	W	4-1	7	5	Fernandez	Johnson	Radinsky	62-45	2nd	2
8-9	At Bal.	W	7-4	13	7	Drahman	Mussina	Thigpen	63-45	2nd	2
8-10	At Bal.	W	6-4	9	7	Garcia	Flanagan	Thigpen	64-45	2nd	1
8-11	At Bal.	W	7-0	14	0	Alvarez	Johnson		65-45	2nd	1
8-12	At Bal.	L	4-5 (11)	6	10	Olson	Pall		65-46	2nd	2
8-13 (1)	At Det.	L	9-11	16	10	Tanana	Fernandez		65-47	2nd	2½
8-13 (2)	At Det.	L	3-4	8	8	Gullickson	Hibbard	Henneman	65-48	2nd	2½
8-14	At Det.	W	9-8	12	8	Radinsky	Gibson	Thigpen	66-48	2nd	1½
8-15	At Det.	L	4-6	8	6	Leiter	Carter	Henneman	66-49	2nd	1½
8-16	At N.Y.	L	5-6	10	15	Monteleone	Radinsky		66-50	2nd	2½
8-17	At N.Y.	L	2-4	9	8	Taylor	McDowell	Farr	66-51	2nd	3½
8-18	At N.Y.	W	11-3	14	5	Hibbard	Johnson		67-51	2nd	3½
8-19	Det.	L	2-3	10	8	Tanana	Fernandez	Gibson	67-52	2nd	3½
8-20	Det.	L	0-5	6	11	Terrell	Hough		67-53	2nd	4½
8-21	Det.	L	9-12	12	10	Leiter	Alvarez		67-54	2nd	5½
8-23	At Cle.	L	3-4	12	10	Blair	Hibbard	Hillegas	67-55	2nd	6
8-24	At Cle.	L	1-2	5	4	Nagy	McDowell	Olin	67-56	2nd	7
8-25	At Cle.	L	0-3	3	11	Nichols	Fernandez		67-57	2nd	7
8-26	At K.C.	L	0-7	0	13	Saberhagen	Hough		67-58	2nd	8
8-27	At K.C.	L	2-3	6	9	M. Davis	Alvarez	Gordon	67-59	2nd	8
8-28	At K.C.	L	6-7	11	10	Montgomery	Thigpen		67-60	3rd	9
8-29	Cle.	W	7-2	13	7	McDowell	Blair		68-60	3rd	8½
8-30	Cle.	L	2-3	6	8	Nagy	Fernandez	Olin	68-61	4th	8½
8-31	Cle.	W	10-5	10	6	Pall	Otto	Radinsky	69-61	3rd	8½
9-1	Cle.	W	6-1	12	4	Alvarez	Swindell		70-61	3rd	8½
9-2	K.C.	W	5-1	8	3	Hernandez	Aquino		71-61	T2nd	8½
9-3	K.C.	L	0-8	5	12	Appier	McDowell		71-62	T2nd	9
9-4	K.C.	W	4-1	9	2	Fernandez	Boddicker	Thigpen	72-62	2nd	8
9-5	K.C.	W	11-2	13	7	Hough	Gubicza		73-62	2nd	7½
9-6	At Tex.	W	11-6	9	8	Pall	Rogers	Perez	74-62	2nd	7½
9-7	At Tex.	W	11-6	14	9	Hibbard	Witt		75-62	2nd	7½
9-8	At Tex.	L	6-7	8	6	Russell	Thigpen		75-63	2nd	8½
9-9	At Oak.	W	7-1	11	3	Fernandez	Darling		76-63	2nd	8½
9-10	At Oak.	W	3-1	7	6	Perez	Honeycutt	Thigpen	77-63	2nd	8½
9-11	At Oak.	L	5-6 (10)	10	9	Eckersley	Wapnick		77-64	2nd	8½
9-12	At Cal.	L	4-7	7	12	Eichhorn	Perez	Harvey	77-65	2nd	8½
9-13	At Cal.	W	1-0	6	4	McDowell	J. Abbott		78-65	2nd	8½
9-14	At Cal.	L	2-3 (10)	7	12	Fetters	Radinsky		78-66	2nd	8½

Date	Opp.	Res.	Score (inn.*)	Hits	Opp. hits	Winning pitcher	Losing pitcher	Save	Record	Pos.	GB
9-15	At Cal.	W	9-2	14	8	Hough	K. Abbott		79-66	2nd	7½
9-17	Oak.	W	1-0	2	3	Hibbard	Darling	Thigpen	80-66	2nd	7
9-18	Oak.	W	6-0	10	5	McDowell	Stewart		81-66	2nd	6
9-20	Cal.	W	3-2 (11)	8	8	Perez	Eichhorn		82-66	2nd	6
9-21	Cal.	L	3-4	5	9	K. Abbott	Drahman	Harvey	82-67	2nd	7
9-22	Cal.	L	2-4	6	12	Grahe	Hibbard	Harvey	82-68	2nd	8
9-24	At Min.	L	2-9	1	12	Erickson	McDowell		82-69	2nd	9
9-25	At Min.	W	6-1	7	8	Fernandez	Anderson		83-69	2nd	8
9-27	Sea.	L	8-10 (11)	14	14	Swan	Perez		83-70	2nd	8
9-28	Sea.	W	5-2	5	6	Hibbard	DeLucia	Radinsky	84-70	2nd	8
9-29	Sea.	L	1-2	6	2	Johnson	Hough	Swift	84-71	2nd	8
9-30	Min.	L	3-8	8	9	Edens	Fernandez		84-72	2nd	9
10-1	Min.	L	2-3	9	7	Guthrie	Perez	Aguilera	84-73	2nd	10
10-3 (1)	Min.	W	3-2 (10)	11	7	Radinsky	Aguilera		85-73	2nd	9
10-3 (2)	Min.	W	13-12 (12)	24	16	Drahman	Leach		86-73	2nd	8
10-4	At Sea.	L	4-6	7	11	Jones	Hough	Schooler	86-74	2nd	8
10-5	At Sea.	L	0-10	9	8	Krueger	Garcia	Harris	86-75	2nd	9
10-6	At Sea.	W	3-2	4	7	Alvarez	Hanson	Radinsky	87-75	2nd	8

Monthly records: April (11-6), May (10-17), June (17-12), July (19-8), August (12-18), September (15-11), Oct. (3-3).

HIGHLIGHTS

High point: Chicago extended its winning streak to seven games on August 11 behind rookie Wilson Alvarez's no-hitter at Baltimore in his club debut. The victory helped the White Sox close to within one game of the first-place Minnesota Twins in the American League West.

Low point: On the heels of Alvarez's gem, Chicago skidded to a 2-15 mark, getting no-hit by Kansas City's Bret Saberhagen on August 26 in the process. That horrid stretch dropped the White Sox nine games off the lead and eliminated them from contention.

Turning point: After stumbling to a 10-17 record in May, the White Sox posted a 17-12 mark in June and a 19-8 ledger in July, proving they were a contender for the second straight season.

Most valuable player: First baseman/designated hitter Frank Thomas. He became baseball's 38th player to reach base 300 times (317) in a season. He led the major leagues in on-base percentage (.453) and ranked fifth in the A.L. in home runs (32) and runs batted in (109) and ninth in hitting (.318).

Most valuable pitcher: Righthander Jack McDowell. He led the league in complete games (15) and his 17 wins were the most by a Chicago pitcher since Britt Burns won 18 in 1985.

Most improved player: Third baseman Robin Ventura. He won a Gold Glove and collected 18 home runs and 100 RBIs. His RBI total was the highest ever for a White Sox third baseman.

Most pleasant surprise: Infielder Craig Grebeck. He started games at shortstop and third and second base, while hitting .281 with six homers and 31 RBIs in just 224 at-bats.

Biggest disappointment: Outfielder Sammy Sosa. After registering double-figure totals in doubles, triples, homers and stolen bases in 1990, Sosa hit just .203 with 21 extra-base hits in '91.

Key injuries: For the second straight year, the White Sox did not suffer many key injuries. They did lose Thomas for four games in early September, though.

Notable: On April 18, the White Sox were humiliated by Detroit, 16-0, in the inaugural game in new Comiskey Park. . . . On April 3, Chicago signed Bo Jackson, who had been released by Kansas City in the wake of a serious hip injury. After a lengthy rehabilitation he played in 23 games and hit .225 with three homers and 14 RBIs. . . . The White Sox set an all-time attendance mark, drawing 2,934,154 fans.

—JOE GODDARD

RECORDS

1991 regular-season record: 87-75 (2nd in A.L. West); 46-35 at home; 41-40 on road; 45-39 vs. East; 42-36 vs. West; 21-27 vs. LHP; 66-48 vs. RHP; 74-64 on grass; 13-11 on turf; 23-20 in daytime; 64-55 at night; 32-27 in one-run games; 15-9 in extra-inning games; 1-1-0 in doubleheaders.

Team record last five years: 398-410 (.493, ranks 9th in league in that span).

TEAM LEADERS

Batting average: Frank Thomas (.318).
At-bats: Tim Raines (609).
Runs: Frank Thomas (104).
Hits: Frank Thomas (178).
Total bases: Frank Thomas (309).
Doubles: Frank Thomas (31).
Triples: Lance Johnson (13).
Home runs: Frank Thomas (32).
Runs batted in: Frank Thomas (109).
Stolen bases: Tim Raines (51).
Slugging percentage: Frank Thomas (.553).
On-base percentage: Frank Thomas (.453).
Wins: Jack McDowell (17).
Earned-run average: Jack McDowell (3.41).
Complete games: Jack McDowell (15).
Shutouts: Jack McDowell (3).
Saves: Bobby Thigpen (30).
Innings pitched: Jack McDowell (253⅔).
Strikeouts: Jack McDowell (191).

GAMES BY POSITION

Catcher: Carlton Fisk 106, Ron Karkovice 69, Matt Merullo 27, Don Wakamatsu 18.
First base: Dan Pasqua 83, Frank Thomas 56, Robin Ventura 31, Matt Merullo 16, Ron Kittle 15, Carlton Fisk 12.
Second base: Scott Fletcher 86, Joey Cora 80, Craig Grebeck 36, Mike Huff 2.
Third base: Robin Ventura 151, Craig Grebeck 49, Scott Fletcher 4.
Shortstop: Ozzie Guillen 149, Craig Grebeck 26, Esteban Beltre 8, Joey Cora 5.
Outfield: Lance Johnson 157, Tim Raines 133, Sammy Sosa 111, Dan Pasqua 59, Warren Newson 50, Mike Huff 48, Cory Snyder 29, Rodney McCray 8, Ron Karkovice 1.
Designated hitter: Frank Thomas 101, Bo Jackson 21, Tim Raines 19, Carlton Fisk 13, Dan Pasqua 8, Rodney McCray 6, Matt Merullo 6, Warren Newson 3, Joey Cora 2, Mike Huff 2, Sammy Sosa 2.

TOP 10 DRAFT CHOICES

1. **Scott Ruffcorn,** RHP, Baylor University.
2. **Larry Thomas,** LHP, University of Maine.
3. **Mike Robertson,** 1B, University of Southern California.
4. **Brian Boehringer,** RHP, University of Nevada-Las Vegas.
5. **Eric Richardson,** OF, Brenham (Texas) High School.
6. **Harold Henry,** OF, Northeast Louisiana University.
7. **Steve Olsen,** RHP, Eastern Kentucky University.
8. **Demond Thomas,** SS/OF, Elizabethtown (Ky.) High School.
9. **Troy Fryman,** 1B, Jefferson Davis State (Ala.) Junior College.
10. **Juan Thomas,** OF, Paul Blaser High School, Ashland, Ky.

CLEVELAND INDIANS
AMERICAN LEAGUE EAST DIVISION

1992 SCHEDULE

APRIL
S	M	T	W	T	F	S
5	6 BAL	7	8 N BAL	9 N BAL	10 N	11 BOS H
12 DH BOS H	13 DET H	14 N DET H	15 N DET H	16 N DET H	17 N NY	18 N NY
19 NY	20 NY	21 N TOR	22 N TOR	23 N TOR	24 N MIL H	25 MIL H
26 MIL H	27	28 N OAK H	29 N OAK H	30 CAL H		

MAY
S	M	T	W	T	F	S
					1 N CAL H	2 CAL H
3 CAL H	4 N KC H	5 N KC H	6 N KC H	7 N TEX	8 N MIN	9 N MIN
10 MIN	11	12 N KC	13 N KC	14	15 N MIN H	16 MIN H
17 MIN	18 N TEX H	19 N TEX H	20 N TEX H	21	22 N SEA	23 N SEA
24 N SEA	25 N OAK	26 N OAK	27 OAK	28	29 N CAL	30 N CAL
31 CAL						

JUNE
S	M	T	W	T	F	S
	1	2 N SEA H	3 N SEA H	4 N SEA H	5 N BOS	6 BOS
7 BOS	8 N DET	9 N DET	10 N DET	11	12 N NY	13 N NY H
14 NY	15 N BAL H	16 N BAL H	17 BAL H	18 N MIL	19 N MIL	20 N MIL
21 MIL	22 N CHI	23 N CHI	24 N CHI	25	26 N TOR H	27 N TOR H
28 TOR H	29 N CHI H	30 N CHI H				

JULY
S	M	T	W	T	F	S
			1 N CHI H	2 CHI H	3 N OAK H	4 N OAK H
5 OAK H	6 N OAK H	7 N CAL H	8 N CAL H	9 N TEX	10 N TEX	11 N TEX
12 N TEX	13	14 ★	15	16 N KC	17 N KC	18 N KC
19 KC	20 N MIN	21 N MIN	22	23 N MIN	24 N KC H	25 N KC H
26 KC H	27 N MIL H	28 N MIL H	29 MIL H	30	31 N DET H	

AUGUST
S	M	T	W	T	F	S
						1 DET H
2 DET H	3 N NY	4 N NY	5 N NY	6	7 N BAL	8 N BAL
9 BAL	10 N BOS H	11 N BOS H	12 N BOS H	13 N BOS H	14 N TOR H	15 N TOR H
16 TOR H	17	18 N MIN H	19 N MIN H	20 N MIN H	21 N TEX H	22 N TEX H
23 TEX H	24	25 N SEA	26 N SEA	27 N SEA	28 N OAK	29 N OAK
30 OAK	31 N CAL					

SEPTEMBER
S	M	T	W	T	F	S
		1 N CAL	2 N CAL	3	4 N SEA H	5 N SEA H
6 SEA H	7	8 N MIL	9 N MIL	10	11 N CHI	12 N CHI
13 CHI	14 N TOR	15 N TOR	16 N TOR	17	18 N CHI H	19 N CHI H
20 CHI H	21	22 N BOS	23 N BOS	24 N BOS	25 N DET	26 DET
27 DET	28 N NY H	29 N NY H	30 N NY H			

OCTOBER
S	M	T	W	T	F	S
				1 N BAL H	2 N BAL H	3 N BAL H
4 BAL H	5	6	7	8	9	10

1992 SEASON

CLUB DIRECTORY

Board of directors
 Richard E. Jacobs
 David H. Jacobs
 Martin J. Cleary
 Gary L. Bryenton
Chairman of the board and CEO
 Richard E. Jacobs
Vice chairman of the board
 David H. Jacobs
President and chief operating officer
 Rick Bay
Senior vice president, business
 Dennis Lehman
Vice president, baseball operations
 John Hart
Vice president, marketing
 Jeff Overton
Vice president, finance
 Gregg Olson
Vice president, public relations
 Bob DiBiasio
Vice president, stadium operations
 Carl Hoerig
Vice president
 Martin J. Cleary
Director, advertising
 Valerie Arcuri
Director, merchandising/licensing
 Jayne Churchmack
Director, ticket services
 Connie Minadeo
Director, scouting
 Mickey White
Director, player development
 Dan O'Dowd
Director, team travel
 Mike Seghi
Director, promotions/sales
 Jon Starrett
Director, community relations
 Glen Shumate
Controller
 Ken Stesanov
Assistant director, media relations
 Susie Gharrity
Assistant director, scouting
 Jay Green
Administrator, player personnel
 Wendy Hoppel
Manager, media relations
 John Maroon
Manager, promotions/sales
 Nadine Glinski

Manager, operations
 Kerry Wimsatt
Marketing representative
 Chris Previte
Account executive, ticket sales
 Devore Whitt
Director, telemarketing
 Scott Sterneckert
Speakers bureau
 Bob Feller
Indians equipment and clubhouse manager
 Cy Buynak
Medical director
 Dr. William T. Wilder
Orthopedic specialist
 Dr. Louis Keppler
Trainer
 Jim Warfield
Assistant trainer
 Paul Spicuzza
Team physicians
 Dr. John Brantigan
 Dr. Godofredo Domingo
 Dr. K.V. Gopal
 Dr. David Schultz
 Dr. Zenos Vangelos
National cross-checker scout
 Tony DeMacio
Scouting supervisors
 Buzzy Keller
 Shawn Pender
 Jay Robertson
Scouting regulars
 Luis Aponte
 Steve Avila
 Mark Baca
 Tom Chandler
 Ramon Conde
 Tom Couston
 Jeff Datz
 Joe Delucca
 Mark Germann
 Jerry LaPenta
 Bill Lawlor
 Alan Lewis
 Winston Llenas
 Rick Magnante
 Buddy Mercado
 Mark McKnight
 Jim Richardson
 Doug Takaragawa
 Mike Weidemaier

SCHEDULE KEY
H—Home game.   *All-Star Game at San Diego/Jack Murphy Stadium.
N—Night game (any game starting after 5 p.m.).   DH—Doubleheader.

SPRING TRAINING ROSTER

Manager—Mike Hargrove (21).

Coaches—Rick Adair (24), Ken Bolek (51), Dom Chiti (30), Ron Clark (6), Jose Morales (34), Dave Nelson (17), Jeff Newman (55).

No.	PITCHERS	B/T	Ht./Wt.	Born	1991 clubs
77	Armstrong, Jack	R/R	6-5/215	3-7-65	Cincinnati, Nashville
63	Bell, Eric	L/L	6-0/165	10-27-63	Canton-Akron, Colorado Springs, Cleveland
49	Boucher, Denis	R/L	6-1/195	3-7-68	Syracuse, Toronto, Cleveland, Colorado Springs
35	Christopher, Mike	R/R	6-5/205	11-3-63	Albuquerque, Los Angeles
36	Cook, Dennis	L/L	6-3/185	10-4-62	San Antonio, Albuquerque, Los Angeles
45	DiPoto, Jerry	R/R	6-2/203	5-24-68	Canton-Akron
46	Egloff, Bruce	R/R	6-2/215	4-10-65	Cleveland, Colorado Springs
38	Hillegas, Shawn	R/R	6-2/223	8-21-64	Cleveland
64	Kramer, Tom	S/R	6-0/185	1-9-68	Canton-Akron, Colorado Springs, Cleveland
26	Lilliquist, Derek	L/L	6-0/214	2-20-66	San Diego, Las Vegas
50	Mutis, Jeff	L/L	6-2/185	12-20-66	Canton-Akron, Cleveland
41	Nagy, Charles	L/R	6-3/200	5-5-67	Cleveland
54	Nichols, Rod	R/R	6-2/190	12-29-64	Cleveland
31	Olin, Steve	R/R	6-2/190	10-16-65	Cleveland, Colorado Springs
27	Otto, Dave	L/L	6-7/210	11-12-64	Colorado Springs, Cleveland
47	Scudder, Scott	R/R	6-2/185	2-14-68	Cincinnati
57	Shaw, Jeff	R/R	6-2/185	7-7-66	Colorado Springs, Cleveland
33	Thomas, Mike	L/L	6-1/175	9-2-69	Columbia, Sumter
53	Wickander, Kevin	L/L	6-2/202	1-4-65	Colorado Springs, Canton-Akron

No.	CATCHERS	B/T	Ht./Wt.	Born	1991 clubs
15	Alomar, Sandy	R/R	6-5/200	6-18-66	Cleveland, Colorado Springs
4	Skinner, Joel	R/R	6-4/204	2-21-61	Cleveland

No.	INFIELDERS	B/T	Ht./Wt.	Born	1991 clubs
9	Baerga, Carlos	S/R	5-11/165	11-4-68	Cleveland
14	Browne, Jerry	S/R	5-10/170	2-13-66	Cleveland
16	Fermin, Felix	R/R	5-11/170	10-9-63	Cleveland, Colorado Springs
44	Jefferson, Reggie	S/L	6-4/210	9-25-68	Nashville, Cincinnati, Cleveland, Canton-Akron, Colorado Springs
10	Lewis, Mark	R/R	6-1/190	11-30-69	Colorado Springs, Cleveland
42	Martinez, Carlos	R/R	6-5/175	8-11-65	Canton-Akron, Cleveland
20	Perezchica, Tony	R/R	5-11/165	4-20-66	Phoenix, San Francisco, Cleveland
22	Rohde, Dave	S/R	6-2/182	5-8-64	Houston, Tucson
25	Thome, Jim	L/R	6-3/200	8-27-70	Canton-Akron, Colorado Springs, Cleveland

No.	OUTFIELDERS	B/T	Ht./Wt.	Born	1991 clubs
29	Aldrete, Mike	L/L	5-11/185	1-29-61	San Diego, Colorado Springs, Cleveland
8	Belle, Albert	R/R	6-2/200	8-25-66	Cleveland, Colorado Springs
2	Cole, Alex	L/L	6-2/170	8-17-65	Cleveland, Colorado Springs
1	Hill, Glenallen	R/R	6-2/210	3-22-65	Toronto, Cleveland
28	Lofton, Kenny	L/L	6-0/180	5-31-67	Tucson, Houston
48	Pough, Clyde	R/R	6-0/173	12-25-69	Columbus (Ga.), Kinston, Colorado Springs
12	Tinsley, Lee	S/R	5-10/180	3-4-69	Huntsville, Canton-Akron
23	Whiten, Mark	S/R	6-3/215	11-25-66	Toronto, Cleveland

BALLPARK INFORMATION

Ballpark (capacity, surface)
Cleveland Stadium (74,483, grass)
Address
Cleveland Stadium
Cleveland, OH 44114
Business phone
216-861-1200
Ticket information
216-241-5555
Ticket prices
$11 (box seats)
$8.50 (reserved seats)
$5 (general admission, adult)
$4 (g.a., youth 14 and under)
$4 (g.a., senior citizen 60 and older)
$4 (bleachers)
Field dimensions (from home plate)
To left field at foul line, 320 feet
To center field, 404 feet
To right field at foul line, 320 feet
First game played
July 31, 1932 (Philadelphia Athletics 1, Indians 0)

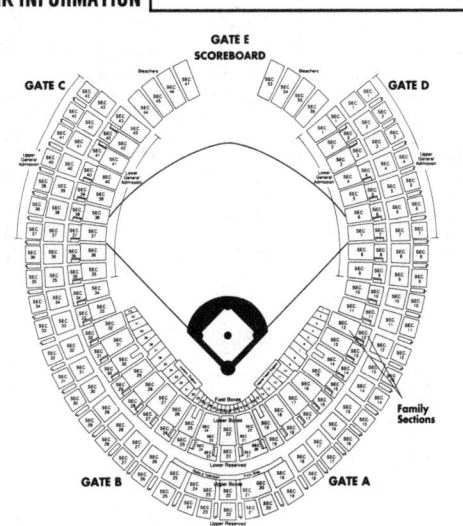

MINOR LEAGUE AFFILIATES

Class	Team	League	Manager
AAA	Colorado Springs	Pacific Coast	Charlie Manuel
AA	Canton/Akron	Eastern	Brian Graham
A	Kinston	Carolina	Dave Keller
A	Columbus, Ga.	South Atlantic	Mike Brown
A	Watertown	New York-Pennsylvania	Shawn Pender
Rookie	Burlington	Appalachian	Minnie Mendoza

☐ BROADCAST INFORMATION ☐

Radio: WKNR-AM (1220). Broadcasters: Tom Hamilton, Herb Score.
TV: WUAB-TV (Channel 43). Broadcasters: Mike Hegan, Jack Corrigan.
Cable TV: SportsChannel. Broadcasters: Rick Manning, John Sanders.

SPRING TRAINING

Ballpark (city): Hi Corbett Field (Tucson, Ariz.).
Ticket information: 602-791-4266.

HISTORY

YEAR-BY-YEAR RECORDS

Year	Pos.	W	L	Pct.	*GB	Year	Pos.	W	L	Pct.	*GB
1901	7th	54	82	.397	29	1948	1st†	97	58	.626 +	1
1902	5th	69	67	.507	14	1949	3rd	89	65	.578	8
1903	3rd	77	63	.550	15	1950	4th	92	62	.597	6
1904	4th	86	65	.570	7½	1951	2nd	93	61	.604	5
1905	5th	76	78	.494	19	1952	2nd	93	61	.604	2
1906	3rd	89	64	.582	5	1953	2nd	92	62	.597	8½
1907	4th	85	67	.559	8	1954	1st	111	43	.721 +	8
1908	2nd	90	64	.584	½	1955	2nd	93	61	.604	3
1909	6th	71	82	.464	27½	1956	2nd	88	66	.571	9
1910	5th	71	81	.467	32	1957	6th	76	77	.497	21½
1911	3rd	80	73	.523	22	1958	4th	77	76	.503	14½
1912	5th	75	78	.490	30½	1959	2nd	89	65	.578	5
1913	3rd	86	66	.566	9½	1960	4th	76	78	.494	21
1914	8th	51	102	.333	48½	1961	5th	78	83	.484	30½
1915	7th	57	95	.375	44½	1962	6th	80	82	.494	16
1916	6th	77	77	.500	14	1963	T5th	79	83	.488	25½
1917	3rd	88	66	.571	12	1964	T6th	79	83	.488	20
1918	2nd	73	54	.575	2½	1965	5th	87	75	.537	15
1919	2nd	84	55	.604	3½	1966	5th	81	81	.500	17
1920	1st	98	56	.636	+ 2	1967	8th	75	87	.463	17
1921	2nd	94	60	.610	4½	1968	3rd	86	75	.534	16½
1922	4th	78	76	.507	16	1969	6th	62	99	.385	46½
1923	3rd	82	71	.536	16½	1970	5th	76	86	.469	32
1924	6th	67	86	.438	24½	1971	6th	60	102	.370	43
1925	6th	70	84	.455	27½	1972	5th	72	84	.462	14
1926	2nd	88	66	.571	3	1973	6th	71	91	.438	26
1927	6th	66	87	.431	43½	1974	4th	77	85	.475	14
1928	7th	62	92	.403	39	1975	4th	79	80	.497	15½
1929	3rd	81	71	.533	24	1976	4th	81	78	.509	16
1930	4th	81	73	.536	21	1977	5th	71	90	.441	28½
1931	4th	78	76	.506	30	1978	6th	69	90	.434	29
1932	4th	87	65	.572	19	1979	6th	81	80	.503	22
1933	4th	75	76	.497	23½	1980	6th	79	81	.494	23
1934	3rd	85	69	.552	16	1981	6th/5th	52	51	.504	‡
1935	3rd	82	71	.536	12	1982	T6th	78	84	.481	17
1936	5th	80	74	.519	22½	1983	7th	70	92	.432	28
1937	4th	83	71	.539	19	1984	6th	75	87	.463	29
1938	3rd	86	66	.566	13	1985	7th	60	102	.370	39½
1939	3rd	87	67	.565	20½	1986	5th	84	78	.519	11½
1940	2nd	89	65	.578	1	1987	7th	61	101	.377	37
1941	T4th	75	79	.487	26	1988	6th	78	84	.481	11
1942	4th	75	79	.487	28	1989	6th	73	89	.451	16
1943	3rd	82	71	.536	15½	1990	4th	77	85	.475	11
1944	T5th	72	82	.468	17	1991	7th	57	105	.352	34
1945	5th	73	72	.503	11						
1946	6th	68	86	.442	36						
1947	4th	80	74	.519	17						

*Games behind winner. †Won pennant playoff. ‡First half 26-24; second 26-27.

MANAGERS

Name	Record	Years
Jimmy McAleer	54-82	1901
Bill Armour	232-195	'02-04
Nap Lajoie	377-309	'05-09
Deacon McGuire	91-117	'09-11
George Stovall	74-62	1911
Harry Davis	54-71	1912
Joe Birmingham	170-191	'12-15
Lee Fohl	327-310	'15-19
Tris Speaker	617-520	'19-26
Jack McCallister	66-87	1927
Rog. Peckinpaugh	490-481	'28-33
		1941
Walter Johnson	179-168	'33-35
Steve O'Neill	199-168	'35-37
Oscar Vitt	262-198	'38-40
Lou Boudreau	728-649	'42-50
Al Lopez	570-354	'51-56
Kerby Farrell	76-77	1957
Bobby Bragan	31-36	1958
Joe Gordon	184-19	'58-60
Jimmie Dykes	103-115	'60-61
Mel McGaha	80-82	1962
Birdie Tebbetts	269-298	'63-66
George Strickland	15-24	'66
Joe Adcock	75-87	1967
Alvin Dark	266-321	'68-71
Johnny Lipon	18-41	1971
Ken Aspromonte	220-260	'72-74
Frank Robinson	186-189	'75-77
Jeff Torborg	157-201	'77-79
Dave Garcia	247-244	'79-82
Mike Ferraro	40-60	1983
Pat Corrales	280-355	'83-87
Doc Edwards	173-207	'87-89
John Hart	8-11	1989
John McNamara	102-137	'90-91
Mike Hargrove	32-53	1991

DAY BY DAY

Date	Opp.	Res.	Score (inn.*)	Hits	Opp. hits	Winning pitcher	Losing pitcher	Save	Record	Pos.	GB
4-8	At K.C.	L	2-4	6	10	Saberhagen	Swindell	Montgomery	0-1	T4th	1
4-9	At K.C.	W	2-1	5	5	Candiotti	Boddicker	Jones	1-1	T3rd	½
4-10	At K.C.	L	0-1	7	7	Appier	Nagy	Montgomery	1-2	T5th	1½
4-11	At Bos.	W	6-4	11	10	King	Darwin	Jones	2-2	4th	1
4-13	At Bos.	L	0-4	3	9	Clemens	Swindell		2-3	T4th	1½
4-14	At Bos.	W	6-0	13	5	Candiotti	Harris		3-3	T2nd	1½
4-15	At Bos.	W	1-0 (13)	5	6	Olin	Lamp	Jones	4-3	2nd	1½
4-16	Tex.	L	1-3	3	8	Brown	King	Russell	4-4	T2nd	1½
4-18	Tex.	L	0-7	4	8	Witt	Swindell		4-5	5th	1½
4-20	Bos.	L	1-2	5	7	Harris	Candiotti	Reardon	4-6	T5th	3
4-22	K.C.	W	10-4	19	3	Nagy	Appier		5-6	5th	1½
4-23	K.C.	L	0-6	5	14	S. Davis	King		5-7	5th	2½
4-24	K.C.	L	2-4 (10)	14	7	Montgomery	Jones		5-8	T5th	2½
4-26	At Tex.	W	5-2	9	6	Olin	Ryan	Jones	6-8	T5th	3
4-27	At Tex.	L	1-4	6	12	Jeffcoat	Olin	Russell	6-9	T5th	3
4-28	At Tex.	W	4-2	9	6	King	Witt	Jones	7-9	5th	3
4-30	At Cal.	L	5-6 (11)	13	13	Harvey	Jones		7-10	5th	3½
5-1	At Cal.	W	5-1	9	5	Candiotti	Finley		8-10	5th	2½
5-3	At Oak.	L	3-4 (11)	10	7	Klink	Olin		8-11	5th	3½
5-4	At Oak.	W	20-6	20	10	King	Dressendorfer		9-11	5th	3½
5-5	At Oak.	W	15-6	19	12	Swindell	Welch		10-11	5th	3½
5-7	At Sea.	L	6-7	9	12	Jackson	Jones		10-12	5th	3½
5-8	At Sea.	L	2-6	8	9	Holman	Nagy	Swift	10-13	5th	4½
5-10	Cal.	L	2-12	5	14	Langston	King		10-14	5th	6
5-11	Cal.	L	1-2	5	8	J. Abbott	Swindell	Harvey	10-15	5th	7
5-12	Cal.	W	4-1	11	3	Candiotti	Lewis		11-15	5th	6
5-13	Cal.	L	5-9	14	16	Finley	Olin	Robinson	11-16	5th	6
5-14	Sea.	L	1-2	7	8	Holman	Nichols	Swift	11-17	6th	7
5-15	Sea.	L	4-6	8	10	DeLucia	King	Swift	11-18	6th	8
5-16	Sea.	L	1-3	8	8	Jackson	Swindell		11-19	6th	8½
5-17	Oak.	W	11-6	11	14	Candiotti	Moore		12-19	5th	7½
5-18	Oak.	L	0-3	4	7	Hawkins	Nagy	Eckersley	12-20	5th	7½
5-19	Oak.	L	4-9	7	13	Young	Nichols		12-21	5th	7½
5-20	N.Y.	W	3-1	8	6	King	Cary	Hillegas	13-21	5th	7½
5-21	N.Y.	W	5-2	11	8	Swindell	Eiland		14-21	5th	7½
5-22	N.Y.	L	1-8	8	11	Leary	Candiotti		14-22	5th	8½
5-23	At Mil.	L	3-7	9	14	August	Nagy	Holmes	14-23	T5th	8½
5-24	At Mil.	L	0-1	4	5	Navarro	Nichols		14-24	6th	9½
5-25	At Mil.	W	5-4	5	7	Jones	Machado		15-24	6th	8½
5-26	At Mil.	L	6-7 (10)	10	11	Crim	Jones		15-25	6th	8½
5-27	At Bal.	W	3-2	9	9	Candiotti	Milacki	Hillegas	16-25	6th	7½
5-28	At Bal.	L	2-5	8	8	Smith	Nagy	Olson	16-26	6th	8½
5-29	At Bal.	L	1-2	4	7	Robinson	Walker	Olson	16-27	6th	8½
5-31	Det.	W	11-9	16	14	S. Valdez	Ritz	Hillegas	17-27	6th	8
6-1	Det.	W	3-1	9	5	Swindell	Gullickson		18-27	6th	7
6-2	Det.	W	3-2	8	4	Candiotti	Tanana	Jones	19-27	6th	6
6-3	Det.	W	2-0	8	9	Nagy	Terrell	Hillegas	20-27	6th	6
6-4	Chi.	L	1-4	4	9	McDowell	Nichols		20-28	6th	6
6-5	Chi.	W	2-1	7	6	Hillegas	Garcia		21-28	6th	6
6-6	Chi.	L	1-2 (10)	8	10	Perez	Jones	Thigpen	21-29	6th	6
6-7	At Min.	L	0-2	2	5	Anderson	Candiotti	Aguilera	21-30	6th	6
6-8	At Min.	L	1-2	9	8	Erickson	Nagy	Aguilera	21-31	6th	7
6-9	At Min.	L	2-9	6	12	Morris	Nichols		21-32	6th	8
6-10	At Min.	L	5-8	13	14	Abbott	King	Aguilera	21-33	6th	8½
6-11	Tor.	W	2-1 (12)	9	7	Hillegas	Acker		22-33	6th	7½
6-12	Tor.	L	0-1	2	3	Timlin	Candiotti	Henke	22-34	6th	8½
6-13	Tor.	L	0-1	2	7	Key	Nagy		22-35	6th	9½
6-14	Min.	L	0-7	4	11	Morris	Shaw		22-36	6th	10½
6-15	Min.	L	7-11	9	15	Abbott	Mutis		22-37	6th	10½
6-16	Min.	L	2-4 (10)	7	9	Aguilera	Hillegas		22-38	T6th	11
6-18	At Chi.	L	5-6	7	9	Hough	Candiotti	Thigpen	22-39	7th	10½
6-19	At Chi.	W	4-3	9	9	Nagy	Hibbard	Nichols	23-39	6th	10
6-21	At Tor.	L	4-8	6	14	Wells	Swindell	Henke	23-40	6th	11
6-22	At Tor.	L	0-4	4	7	Guzman	Mutis	Ward	23-41	7th	12
6-23	At Tor.	L	1-3	8	10	MacDonald	Candiotti	Henke	23-42	7th	13
6-24	At Tor.	L	3-4	11	9	Ward	Nagy	Henke	23-43	7th	14
6-25	Bal.	L	3-5 (12)	14	11	Williamson	Jones	Olson	23-44	7th	14
6-26	Bal.	W	10-4	12	12	Swindell	Ballard	Shaw	24-44	7th	14
6-27	Bal.	L	2-7	10	15	Milacki	Mutis	Olson	24-45	7th	15
6-28	At Det.	L	1-7	5	9	Tanana	Boucher		24-46	7th	15

— 35 —

CLEVELAND INDIANS

1992 SEASON

CLEVELAND INDIANS

Date	Opp.	Res.	Score (inn.*)	Hits	Opp. hits	Winning pitcher	Losing pitcher	Save	Record	Pos.	GB
6-29	At Det.	L	4-9	10	15	Meacham	Nagy	Henneman	24-47	7th	16
6-30	At Det.	L	1-4	12	6	Terrell	Nichols	Leiter	24-48	7th	17
7-1	At N.Y.	L	2-6	9	11	Sanderson	Swindell	Guetterman	24-49	7th	18
7-2	At N.Y.	L	5-8	14	15	Taylor	York	Farr	24-50	7th	19
7-3	At N.Y.	L	2-3	5	5	Kamieniecki	Boucher	Farr	24-51	7th	20
7-4	Mil.	W	3-0	8	6	Nagy	Hunter		25-51	7th	19
7-5	Mil.	L	2-4	6	9	Wegman	Nichols	Plesac	25-52	7th	20
7-6	Mil.	W	2-0	5	4	Swindell	Navarro	Hillegas	26-52	7th	20
7-7	Mil.	L	6-10	18	16	Crim	Shaw	Plesac	26-53	7th	21
7-11	At Sea.	L	0-6	8	11	Holman	Nagy	Swift	26-54	7th	22
7-12	At Sea.	L	0-7	6	12	Johnson	Nichols		26-55	7th	23
7-13	At Sea.	W	6-3	12	4	Swindell	Jackson		27-55	7th	23
7-14	At Sea.	L	3-14	8	20	DeLucia	York		27-56	7th	23
7-15	At Oak.	L	1-6	4	12	Hawkins	Boucher		27-57	7th	24
7-16	At Oak.	L	6-7 (13)	12	13	Klink	Jones		27-58	7th	24
7-17	At Oak.	W	2-1	4	4	Nichols	Welch		28-58	7th	23½
7-18	At Cal.	L	4-5	8	4	Harvey	Hillegas		28-59	7th	24½
7-19	At Cal.	W	4-2 (11)	10	5	Orosco	Eichhorn	Olin	29-59	7th	24½
7-20	At Cal.	W	4-1	7	6	Boucher	McCaskill	Olin	30-59	7th	23½
7-21	At Cal.	W	5-2	10	13	Nagy	Langston	Olin	31-59	7th	22½
7-23	Oak.	L	7-10	16	14	Honeycutt	Shaw		31-60	7th	22½
7-24	Oak.	L	4-8	9	11	Show	Swindell		31-61	7th	23½
7-25	Oak.	W	8-7	9	6	York	Eckersley	Olin	32-61	7th	22½
7-26	Sea.	L	4-7	7	13	DeLucia	Boucher	Schooler	32-62	7th	23½
7-27	Sea.	W	6-1	13	6	Nagy	Holman		33-62	7th	22½
7-28	Sea.	L	5-6	7	15	Johnson	York		33-63	7th	22½
7-29	Cal.	L	2-10	8	17	Finley	Swindell		33-64	7th	22½
7-30	Cal.	L	2-4	7	8	McCaskill	Otto	Harvey	33-65	7th	22½
7-31	At Tor.	L	1-3	6	6	Key	King	Henke	33-66	7th	23½
8-1	At Tor.	L	5-7	8	10	Ward	Shaw	Henke	33-67	7th	24½
8-2	K.C.	L	4-6	13	13	Appier	Nichols	Montgomery	33-68	7th	24½
8-3	K.C.	W	3-1	10	7	Swindell	Gordon		34-68	7th	23½
8-4	K.C.	L	0-2	3	8	Saberhagen	Olin		34-69	7th	24½
8-5	At Tex.	W	9-0	19	2	King	Brown		35-69	7th	24
8-6	At Tex.	L	8-10	15	17	Rogers	York	Russell	35-70	7th	25
8-7	At Tex.	L	10-12	12	16	Jeffcoat	Hillegas	Russell	35-71	7th	26
8-9	At K.C.	L	2-4	4	10	Gubicza	Swindell	Montgomery	35-72	7th	25½
8-10	At K.C.	W	1-0	5	7	Otto	Saberhagen	Olin	36-72	7th	24½
8-11	At K.C.	L	2-3 (13)	9	8	Gordon	Olin		36-73	7th	24½
8-13 (1)	Bos.	W	8-6	12	13	Hillegas	Kiecker	Olin	37-73	7th	23½
8-13 (2)	Bos.	L	5-7	10	10	Fossas	Nichols	Reardon	37-74	7th	24
8-14	Bos.	L	1-2	9	9	Hesketh	Swindell	Reardon	37-75	7th	24
8-15	Bos.	L	2-6	7	11	Gardiner	Otto		37-76	7th	25
8-16 (1)	Tex.	L	3-5	8	12	Brown	King	Russell	37-77	7th	25
8-16 (2)	Tex.	W	13-9	12	11	Orosco	Jeffcoat		38-77	7th	24½
8-17	Tex.	L	0-2	7	7	Guzman	Blair	Russell	38-78	7th	25
8-18	Tex.	L	4-9	10	11	Bohanon	Nagy	Rosenthal	38-79	7th	26
8-21 (1)	At Bos.	L	5-13	6	15	Hesketh	Swindell		38-80	7th	26½
8-21 (2)	At Bos.	L	4-5	8	10	Harris	Olin		38-81	7th	27
8-22	At Bos.	L	6-7 (10)	9	14	Harris	Olin		38-82	7th	27
8-23	Chi.	W	4-3	10	12	Blair	Hibbard	Hillegas	39-82	7th	27
8-24	Chi.	W	2-1	4	5	Nagy	McDowell	Olin	40-82	7th	26
8-25	Chi.	W	3-0	11	3	Nichols	Fernandez		41-82	7th	26
8-26	Min.	L	3-5	7	10	Tapani	Otto	Aguilera	41-83	7th	27
8-27	Min.	W	2-1	11	6	Swindell	Morris	Olin	42-83	7th	27
8-28	Min.	L	2-4	7	13	West	King	Aguilera	42-84	7th	28
8-29	At Chi.	L	2-7	7	13	McDowell	Blair		42-85	7th	29
8-30	At Chi.	W	3-2	8	6	Nagy	Fernandez	Olin	43-85	7th	28
8-31	At Chi.	L	5-10	6	10	Pall	Otto	Radinsky	43-86	7th	29
9-1	At Chi.	L	1-6	4	12	Alvarez	Swindell		43-87	7th	29
9-2	At Min.	L	3-9	9	8	Erickson	King	Aguilera	43-88	7th	30
9-4	At Min.	W	8-4	12	10	Blair	West	Hillegas	44-88	7th	29½
9-5	Tor.	L	1-13	8	17	Key	Nagy		44-89	7th	30½
9-6	Tor.	L	4-7	9	9	Guzman	Otto	Ward	44-90	7th	31½
9-7	Tor.	L	1-4	5	9	Candiotti	Swindell		44-91	7th	32½
9-8	Tor.	L	5-11	10	14	Wells	King		44-92	7th	33½
9-9	Bos.	L	3-4	8	9	Harris	Hillegas	Reardon	44-93	7th	34
9-10	At Mil.	W	5-2	7	8	Jones	Wegman	Olin	45-93	7th	33
9-12	At Bal.	W	6-5	10	12	Nagy	Mesa	Olin	46-93	7th	32
9-13	At Bal.	L	4-5	9	13	Olson	Shaw		46-94	7th	33
9-14	At Bal.	W	6-5 (11)	14	10	Bell	Flanagan	Olin	47-94	7th	33
9-15	At Bal.	L	3-4	5	4	Williamson	Blair	Olson	47-95	7th	33
9-17	Det.	W	3-1	8	9	Jones	Terrell	Olin	48-95	7th	31½
9-18	Det.	W	3-2	6	8	Nagy	Gullickson		49-95	7th	31½

Date	Opp.	Res.	Score (inn.*)	Hits	Opp. hits	Winning pitcher	Losing pitcher	Save	Record	Pos.	GB
9-20	Bal.	L	1-2	7	6	Milacki	Otto	Olson	49-96	7th	31½
9-21	Bal.	W	10-1	16	8	Swindell	Rhodes		50-96	7th	30½
9-22	Bal.	W	2-1	7	3	Bell	Mussina		51-96	7th	30½
9-23	At Det.	L	1-2	6	8	Gullickson	King	Henneman	51-97	7th	30½
9-24	At Det.	L	2-7	9	10	Aldred	Nagy		51-98	7th	31½
9-25	At Det.	W	6-4	10	12	Jones	Leiter	Olin	52-98	7th	31½
9-26	At Det.	L	5-6	9	9	Cerutti	Otto	Henneman	52-99	7th	32
9-27	N.Y.	L	0-3	7	6	Perez	Swindell	Farr	52-100	7th	33
9-28	N.Y.	W	5-4	9	7	Bell	Cadaret	Olin	53-100	7th	32
9-29	N.Y.	W	5-2	10	10	King	Mills	Olin	54-100	7th	32
9-30	N.Y.	L	0-3	5	7	Sanderson	Nagy	Cadaret	54-101	7th	32
10-1 (1)	Mil.	L	0-11	7	18	Wegman	Nichols		54-102	7th	33
10-1 (2)	Mil.	W	6-2	12	13	Otto	Holmes		55-102	7th	32½
10-2	Mil.	L	4-11	11	15	Crim	Jones	Holmes	55-103	7th	33½
10-3	Mil.	L	3-9	10	14	Navarro	Swindell		55-104	7th	34
10-4	At N.Y.	W	3-2	7	9	Bell	Farr	Olin	56-104	7th	34
10-5	At N.Y.	W	7-5 (12)	11	19	Olin	Chapin	Jones	57-104	7th	33
10-6	At N.Y.	L	4-7	11	8	Eiland	Nagy	Habyan	57-105	7th	34

Monthly records: April (7-10), May (10-17), June (7-21), July (9-18), August (10-20), September (11-15), Oct. (3-4).

HIGHLIGHTS

High point: On June 5 the Indians were 21-28 after winning five of six games. But after that they lost 54 of their next 71, a winning percentage of .239.

Low point: With one out in the first inning of an August 3 game against Kansas City, Alex Cole caught George Brett's fly ball at the warning track in left field and ran off the field, thinking the inning was over. Brian McRae, meanwhile, tagged up and scored from second base.

Turning point: When Owners Richard and David Jacobs decided that to cut costs, either Tom Candiotti or Greg Swindell would not be retained past free agency. As a result, Candiotti was traded to Toronto on June 27, depleting Cleveland's already-thin starting pitching. Swindell was ultimately traded to Cincinnati in November.

Most valuable player: Outfielder Albert Belle. Despite missing 39 games, Belle proved he was a big-league slugger. He hit 28 home runs and collected 95 runs batted in.

Most valuable pitcher: Righthander Charles Nagy. In his first full big-league season, Nagy led Cleveland in wins (10) while posting a 4.13 earned-run average.

Most improved player: Infielder Carlos Baerga. Coming off his rookie season, Baerga was moved from third base to second and improved all of his offensive numbers, batting .288 with 11 homers and 69 RBIs.

Most pleasant surprise: Lefthander Dave Otto. He was only 2-8 with a 4.23 ERA, but he showed great promise after being recalled from Class AAA Colorado Springs on June 28.

Biggest disappointment: Righthander Doug Jones. After saving 112 games over the previous three seasons, Jones struggled and was sent to Class AAA on July 24. After he returned September 8, he became a starter and went 3-1 with a 3.77 ERA in that role.

Key injuries: A variety of ailments limited catcher Sandy Alomar to 51 games. Righthander John Farrell's season never got started due to recurring elbow problems.

Notable: Cleveland established a franchise record by losing 105 games. The previous mark was 102, attained in 1914, 1971 and 1985. ... John McNamara was fired as manager July 6 and replaced by Mike Hargrove, the skipper at Colorado Springs. ... Cleveland used a club-record 53 players.

—SHELDON OCKER

RECORDS

1991 regular-season record: 57-105 (7th in A.L. East); 30-52 at home; 27-53 on road; 29-49 vs. East; 28-56 vs. West; 14-30 vs. LHP; 43-75 vs. RHP; 53-85 on grass; 4-20 on turf; 19-29 in daytime; 38-76 at night; 21-30 in one-run games; 5-10 in extra-inning games; 0-1-3 in doubleheaders.

Team record last five years: 346-464 (.427, ranks 14th in league in that span).

TEAM LEADERS

Batting average: Carlos Baerga (.288).
At-bats: Carlos Baerga (593).
Runs: Carlos Baerga (80).
Hits: Carlos Baerga (171).
Total bases: Albert Belle (249).
Doubles: Albert Belle (31).
Triples: Mark Whiten (4).
Home runs: Albert Belle (28).
Runs batted in: Albert Belle (95).
Stolen bases: Alex Cole (27).
Slugging percentage: Carlos Baerga (.398).
On-base percentage: Carlos Baerga (.346).
Wins: Charles Nagy (10).
Earned-run average: Greg Swindell (3.48).
Complete games: Greg Swindell (7).
Shutouts: Eric King, Charles Nagy, Rod Nichols (1).
Saves: Steve Olin (17).
Innings pitched: Greg Swindell (238).
Strikeouts: Greg Swindell (169).

GAMES BY POSITION

Catcher: Joel Skinner 99, Sandy Alomar 46, Eddie Taubensee 25, Luis Lopez 12, Jeff Manto 5.

First base: Brook Jacoby 55, Mike Aldrete 47, Carlos Martinez 31, Reggie Jefferson 26, Chris James 15, Jeff Manto 14, Luis Lopez 10.

Second base: Carlos Baerga 75, Mark Lewis 50, Jerry Browne 47, Jose Escobar 4, Mike Huff 2, Tony Perezchica 2.

Third base: Carlos Baerga 89, Jeff Manto 32, James Thome 27, Jerry Browne 15, Brook Jacoby 15, Tony Perezchica 3, Jose Escobar 1, Luis Lopez 1.

Shortstop: Felix Fermin 129, Mark Lewis 36, Tony Perezchica 6, Jose Escobar 5, Carlos Baerga 2, Ever Magallanes 2.

Outfield: Alex Cole 107, Albert Belle 89, Mark Whiten 67, Mike Huff 48, Beau Allred 42, Chris James 39, Turner Ward 38, Glenallen Hill 33, Jose Gonzalez 32, Wayne Kirby 21, Jerry Browne 17, Mike Aldrete 16, Mitch Webster 10, Luis Lopez 1, Jeff Manto 1.

Designated hitter: Chris James 60, Carmelo Martinez 41, Albert Belle 32, Mike Aldrete 7, Jerry Browne 7, Alex Cole 6, Luis Lopez 6, Luis Medina 5, Sandy Alomar 4, Mark Whiten 3, Beau Allred 1, Glenallen Hill 1, Tony Perezchica 1.

TOP 10 DRAFT CHOICES

1. **Manny Ramirez**, 3B/OF, George Washington High School, New York.
2. **Herbert Perry**, 3B, University of Florida.
3. **Chad Ogea**, RHP, Louisiana State University.
4. **Paul Byrd**, RHP, Louisiana State University.
5. **Kevin Logsdon**, LHP, Linn-Benton (Ore.) Community College.
6. **Tom Vantiger**, OF, Iowa State University.
7. **Pep Harris**, RHP, Lancaster (S.C.) High School.
8. **Chris Coulter**, LHP, Pensacola (Fla.) Junior College.
9. **Paul Meade**, SS, Oral Roberts Univ.
10. **Scott Sharts**, 1B/RHP, Cal State Northridge.

DETROIT TIGERS
AMERICAN LEAGUE EAST DIVISION

1992 SEASON
DETROIT TIGERS

1992 SCHEDULE

APRIL

S	M	T	W	T	F	S
5	6 TOR H	7	8 TOR H	9 TOR H	10 N NY H	11 N NY H
12 NY H	13 CLE	14 N CLE	15 N CLE	16 CLE	17 N BAL	18 BAL
19 BAL	20 N BAL	21 N TEX	22 N TEX	23 N TEX	24 N CHI H	25 N CHI H
26 CHI H	27	28 N SEA H	29 H SEA H	30 N OAK H		

MAY

S	M	T	W	T	F	S
					1 N OAK H	2 N OAK H
3 OAK H	4 N CAL H	5 N CAL H	6 N OAK	7 N OAK	8 N SEA	9 N SEA
10 SEA	11	12 N CAL	13 N CAL	14	15 N KC	16 N KC
17 KC	18 N MIL H	19 N MIL H	20 N MIL H	21 N MIL H	22 N MIN H	23 MIN H
24 N MIN H	25	26 N KC H	27 H KC H	28 N KC H	29 N MIN	30 N MIN
31 MIN						

JUNE

S	M	T	W	T	F	S
	1 N NY	2 N NY	3	4 N NY	5 N NY	6 N NY
7 NY	8 N CLE H	9 N CLE H	10 H CLE H	11 N BAL H	12 N BAL H	13 N BAL H
14 BAL H	15	16 N TOR	17 N TOR	18 N TOR	19 N CHI	20 N CHI
21 CHI	22 N BOS H	23 H BOS H	24 N BOS H	25 N TEX H	26 N TEX H	27 TEX H
28 TEX H	29 N BOS	30 N BOS				

JULY

S	M	T	W	T	F	S
			1 N BOS	2	3 N SEA H	4 N SEA H
5 SEA H	6	7 N OAK H	8 N OAK H	9 N CAL H	10 N CAL H	11 N CAL H
12 CAL H	13	14 *	15	16 N OAK	17 N OAK	18 OAK
19 OAK	20 N SEA	21 N SEA	22 N SEA	23 N CAL	24 N CAL	25 CAL
26 CAL	27	28 N CHI H	29 H CHI H	30 N CHI H	31 N CLE	

AUGUST

S	M	T	W	T	F	S
						1 CLE
2 CLE	3 N BAL	4 N BAL	5 N BAL	6 N TOR H	7 N TOR H	8 N TOR H
9 TOR H	10 N NY H	11 N NY H	12 NY H	13	14 N TEX	15 N TEX
16 TEX	17 N KC	18 N KC	19 N KC	20	21 N MIL	22 N MIL
23 MIL	24 N MIN	25 N MIN	26 MIN	27	28 N KC H	29 KC H
30 KC H	31 N MIN H					

SEPTEMBER

S	M	T	W	T	F	S
		1 N MIN H	2 N MIN H	3	4 N MIL H	5 N MIL H
6 MIL H	7	8 N CHI	9 N CHI	10 N CHI	11 N BOS	12 BOS
13 BOS	14	15 N TEX H	16 N TEX H	17	18 N BOS H	19 N BOS H
20 BOS H	21 N NY	22 N NY	23 N NY	24 NY	25 N CLE	26 N CLE
27 CLE H	28	29 N BAL H	30 N BAL H			

OCTOBER

S	M	T	W	T	F	S
				1	2 N TOR	3 TOR
4 TOR	5	6	7	8	9	10

1992 SEASON

CLUB DIRECTORY

Owner
Thomas S. Monaghan
Board of directors
Thomas S. Monaghan
James A. Campbell
Douglas J. Dawson
Glenn E. (Bo) Schembechler
George Kell
John E. Fetzer
George W. Griffith
Chairman and chief executive officer
James A. Campbell
President and chief operating officer
Glenn E. (Bo) Schembechler
Sr. vice president, major league personnel
Jerry Walker
Senior vice president, finance
Alexander C. Callam
Senior v.p., planning and operations
William E. Haase
Senior v.p., player procurement and dev.
Joseph A. McDonald
Senior v.p., marketing, radio and TV
Jeff Odenwald
Vice president, assistant to the president
Alice Sloane
Vice president, stadium operations
Ralph E. Snyder
Vice president, controller
Michael Wilson
Vice president, media and public relations
Dan Ewald
Corporate secretary
Douglas J. Dawson
Director of radio and TV
Neal Fenkell
Director of media and public relations
Greg Shea
Director, ticket operations
Ken Marchetti
Director, minor league administration
Dave Miller
Scouting director
Jax Robertson
Director, field operations
Tom Petroff
Director, marketing services
Scott Nickle
Executive secretary/operations
Hazel McLane

Data processing manager
Richard Roy
Traveling secretary
Bill Brown
Executive consultant
Rick Ferrell
Manager, promotions
Mike Pyle
Community affairs coordinator
Vince Desmond
Group sales coordinator
Irwin Cohen
Assistant director of stadium operations
Frank Feneck
Assistant director of stadium operations
Ed Goward
Trainers
Russ Miller
Pio DiSalvo
Club physicians
Dr. Clarence S. Livingood
Dr. David Collon
Dr. Louis Saco
Scouts
Ruben Amaro
Arnie Beyeler
Wayne Blackburn
Mark Giegler
Jack Hays
Rich Henning
Joe Lewis
Dennis Lieberthal
Jeff Malinoff
Stan Meek
John Mirabelli
Mark Monahan
Ramon Pena
Dee Phillips
Joe Robinson
Donny Rowland
Bill Schudlich
Steve Souchock
Mike Wallace
Clyde Weir
Dick Wiencek
Rob Wilfong
Dick Wilson
Gary York

SCHEDULE KEY

H—Home game.   *All-Star Game at San Diego/Jack Murphy Stadium.
N—Night game (any game starting after 5 p.m.).

SPRING TRAINING ROSTER

Manager—Sparky Anderson (11).

Coaches—Billy Consolo (50), Larry Herndon (54), Billy Muffett (56), Gene Roof (52), Dick Tracewski (53), Dan Whitmer (59).

No.	PITCHERS	B/T	Ht./Wt.	Born	1991 clubs
30	Aldred, Scott	L/L	6-4/195	6-12-68	Toledo, Detroit
	Castillo, Tony	L/L	5-10/188	3-1-63	Richmond, Atlanta, New York NL
38	Cummings, Steve	S/R	6-2/205	7-15-64	Colorado Springs, Toledo
41	DeSilva, John	R/R	6-0/193	9-30-67	London, Toledo
44	Doherty, John	R/R	6-4/190	6-11-67	London
33	Gakeler, Dan	R/R	6-6/210	5-1-64	Toledo, Detroit
34	Gohr, Greg	R/R	6-3/210	10-29-67	London, Toledo
42	Groom, Buddy	L/L	6-2/200	7-10-65	London, Toledo
36	Gullickson, Bill	R/R	6-3/220	2-20-59	Detroit
16	Haas, David	R/R	6-1/200	10-19-65	Toledo, Detroit
39	Henneman, Mike	R/R	6-4/195	12-11-61	Detroit
46	Kiely, John	R/R	6-3/210	10-4-64	Toledo, Detroit
25	King, Eric	R/R	6-2/180	4-10-64	Cleveland, Colorado Springs
27	Knudsen, Kurt	R/R	6-2/185	2-20-67	London, Toledo
23	Leiter, Mark	R/R	6-3/210	4-13-63	Toledo, Detroit
43	Munoz, Mike	L/L	6-2/195	7-12-65	Toledo, Detroit
31	Ritz, Kevin	R/R	6-4/210	6-8-65	Toledo, Detroit
26	Tanana, Frank	L/L	6-3/195	7-3-53	Detroit
35	Terrell, Walt	R/R	6-2/205	5-11-58	Detroit

No.	CATCHERS	B/T	Ht./Wt.	Born	1991 clubs
12	Rowland, Rich	R/R	6-1/210	2-25-67	Toledo, Detroit
20	Tettleton, Mickey	S/R	6-2/212	9-16-60	Detroit

No.	INFIELDERS	B/T	Ht./Wt.	Born	1991 clubs
14	Bergman, Dave	L/L	6-2/190	6-6-53	Detroit
13	Brogna, Rico	L/L	6-2/190	4-18-70	London, Toledo
45	Fielder, Cecil	R/R	6-3/245	9-21-63	Detroit
24	Fryman, Travis	R/R	6-1/180	4-25-69	Detroit
7	Livingstone, Scott	L/R	6-0/190	7-15-65	Toledo, Detroit
4	Phillips, Tony	S/R	5-10/175	4-25-59	Detroit
8	Rosario, Victor	R/R	5-11/155	8-26-66	Richmond, Toledo
3	Trammell, Alan	R/R	6-0/175	2-21-58	Detroit
1	Whitaker, Lou	L/R	5-11/180	5-12-57	Detroit

No.	OUTFIELDERS	B/T	Ht./Wt.	Born	1991 clubs
9	Barnes, Skeeter	R/R	5-10/180	3-7-57	Toledo, Detroit
	Carreon, Mark	R/L	6-0/195	7-9-63	New York NL
22	Cuyler, Milt	S/R	5-10/175	10-7-68	Detroit
28	Deer, Rob	R/R	6-3/225	9-29-60	Detroit
32	Gladden, Dan	R/R	5-11/181	7-7-57	Minnesota
25	Hare, Shawn	L/R	6-2/190	3-26-67	London, Toledo, Detroit
21	Hurst, Jody	R/L	6-4/190	3-11-67	London
17	Ingram, Riccardo	R/R	6-0/198	9-10-66	London
40	Pegues, Steve	R/R	6-2/172	5-21-68	London, Toledo
18	Pemberton, Rudy	R/R	6-1/185	12-17-69	Lakeland

BALLPARK INFORMATION

Ballpark (capacity, surface)
Tiger Stadium (52,416, grass)

Address
Tiger Stadium
Detroit, MI 48216

Business phone
313-962-4000

Ticket information
313-962-4000

Ticket prices
$12.50 (box seats)
$10 (reserved seats)
$7 (grandstand reserved seats)
$4 (bleacher seats)

Field dimensions (from home plate)
To left field at foul line, 340 feet
To center field, 440 feet
To right field at foul line, 325 feet

First game played
April 20, 1912 (Cleveland Naps 6, Tigers 5)

MINOR LEAGUE AFFILIATES

Class	Team	League	Manager
AAA	Toledo	International	Joe Sparks
AA	London, Ont.	Eastern	Mark DeJohn
A	Fayetteville	South Atlantic	Gerry Groninger
A	Lakeland	Florida State	John Lipon
A	Niagara Falls	New York-Pennsylvania	Larry Parrish
Rookie	Bristol	Appalachian	Mark Wagner

☐ BROADCAST INFORMATION ☐

Radio: WJR-AM (760). Broadcasters: Rick Rizzs, Bob Rathbun.
TV: WDIV-TV (Channel 4). Broadcasters: Al Kaline, George Kell.
Cable TV: Pro Am Sports Systems. Broadcasters: Jim Northrup, Larry Osterman.

SPRING TRAINING

Ballpark (city): Marchant Stadium (Lakeland, Fla.).
Ticket information: 813-682-1401.

HISTORY

YEAR-BY-YEAR RECORDS

Year	Pos.	W	L	Pct.	*GB	Year	Pos.	W	L	Pct.	*GB
1901	3rd	74	61	.548	8½	1949	4th	87	67	.565	10
1902	7th	52	83	.385	30½	1950	2nd	95	59	.617	3
1903	5th	65	71	.478	25	1951	5th	73	81	.474	25
1904	7th	62	90	.408	32	1952	8th	50	104	.325	45
1905	3rd	79	74	.516	15½	1953	6th	60	94	.390	40½
1906	6th	71	78	.477	21	1954	5th	68	86	.442	43
1907	1st	92	58	.613 +	1½	1955	5th	79	75	.513	17
1908	1st	90	63	.588 +	½	1956	5th	82	72	.532	15
1909	1st	98	54	.645 +	3½	1957	4th	78	76	.506	20
1910	3rd	86	68	.558	18	1958	5th	77	77	.500	15
1911	2nd	89	65	.578	13½	1959	4th	76	78	.494	18
1912	6th	69	84	.451	36½	1960	6th	71	83	.461	26
1913	6th	66	87	.431	30	1961	2nd	101	61	.623	8
1914	4th	80	73	.523	19½	1962	4th	85	76	.528	10½
1915	2nd	100	54	.649	2½	1963	T5th	79	83	.488	25½
1916	3rd	87	67	.565	4	1964	4th	85	77	.525	14
1917	4th	78	75	.510	21½	1965	4th	89	73	.549	13
1918	7th	55	71	.437	20	1966	3rd	88	74	.543	10
1919	4th	80	60	.571	8	1967	T2nd	91	71	.562	1
1920	7th	61	93	.396	37	1968	1st	103	59	.636	+12
1921	6th	71	82	.464	27	1969	2nd	90	72	.556	19
1922	3rd	79	75	.513	15	1970	4th	79	83	.488	29
1923	2nd	83	71	.539	16	1971	2nd	91	71	.562	12
1924	3rd	86	68	.558	6	1972	1st†	86	70	.551 +	½
1925	4th	81	73	.526	16½	1973	3rd	85	77	.525	12
1926	6th	79	75	.513	12	1974	6th	72	90	.444	19
1927	4th	82	71	.536	27½	1975	6th	57	102	.358	37½
1928	6th	68	86	.442	33	1976	5th	74	87	.460	24
1929	6th	70	84	.455	36	1977	4th	74	88	.457	26
1930	5th	75	79	.487	27	1978	5th	86	76	.531	13½
1931	7th	61	93	.396	47	1979	5th	85	76	.528	18
1932	5th	76	75	.503	29½	1980	5th	84	78	.519	19
1933	5th	75	79	.487	25	1981	4th/T2d	60	49	.550	‡
1934	1st	101	53	.656 +	7	1982	4th	83	79	.512	12
1935	1st	93	58	.616 +	3	1983	2nd	92	70	.568	6
1936	2nd	83	71	.539	19½	1984	1st§	104	58	.642	+15
1937	2nd	89	65	.578	13	1985	3rd	84	77	.522	15
1938	4th	84	70	.545	16	1986	3rd	87	75	.537	8½
1939	5th	81	73	.526	26½	1987	1st†	98	64	.605 +	2
1940	1st	90	64	.584 +	1	1988	2nd	88	74	.543	1
1941	T4th	75	79	.487	26	1989	7th	59	103	.364	30
1942	5th	73	81	.474	30	1990	3rd	79	83	.488	9
1943	5th	78	76	.506	20	1991	T2nd	84	78	.519	7
1944	2nd	88	66	.571	1						
1945	1st	88	65	.575 +	1½						
1946	2nd	92	62	.597	12						
1947	2nd	85	69	.552	12						
1948	5th	78	76	.506	18½						

*Games behind winner. †Lost Championship Series. ‡First half 31-26; second 29-23. §Won Championship Series.

MANAGERS

Name	Record	Years
George Stallings	74-61	1901
Frank Dwyer	52-83	1902
Ed Barrow	97-117	'03-04
Bobby Lowe	30-44	1904
Bill Armour	150-152	'05-06
Hugh Jennings	1131-972	'07-20
Ty Cobb	479-444	'21-26
George Moriarty	150-157	'27-28
Bucky Harris	516-557	'29-33
		'55-56
Del Baker	392-336	1933
		'38-42
Mickey Cochrane	379-278	'34-38
Steve O'Neill	509-414	'43-48
Red Rolfe	278-256	'49-52
Fred Hutchinson	155-235	'52-54
Jack Tighe	99-104	'57-58
Bill Norman	58-64	'58-59
Jimmie Dykes	118-115	'59-60
Joe Gordon	26-31	1960
Bob Scheffing	210-173	'61-63
Chuck Dressen	221-189	'63-65
		1966
Bob Swift	56-43	'65, '66
Frank Skaff	40-39	1966
Mayo Smith	363-285	'67-70
Billy Martin	248-204	'71-73
Joe Schultz	14-14	1973
Ralph Houk	366-443	'74-78
Les Moss	27-26	'1979
Sparky Anderson	1058-938	'79-91

DAY BY DAY

Date	Opp.	Res.	Score (inn.*)	Hits	Opp. hits	Winning pitcher	Losing pitcher	Save	Record	Pos.	GB
4-8	N.Y.	W	6-4	8	10	Gibson	Cadaret	Henneman	1-0	T1st	...
4-10	N.Y.	L	0-4	1	8	Sanderson	Terrell		1-1	T3rd	1
4-11	N.Y.	W	11-5	10	10	Gibson	Habyan		2-1	2nd	½
4-12	Chi.	L	1-4	5	8	Fernandez	Searcy	Thigpen	2-2	T2nd	1½
4-13	Chi.	L	1-4	2	7	McDowell	Tanana		2-3	T4th	1½
4-15	Tor.	L	3-4	5	10	Stottlemyre	Terrell	Ward	2-4	5th	3
4-16	Tor.	W	6-2	8	6	Gullickson	Wells	Henneman	3-4	T4th	2
4-17	Tor.	W	5-4 (10)	9	7	Henneman	Ward		4-4	T2nd	1
4-18	At Chi.	W	16-0	19	7	Tanana	McDowell		5-4	T2nd	½
4-20	At Chi.	W	2-1 (12)	11	9	Henneman	Radinsky	Gleaton	6-4	2nd	1
4-21	At Chi.	L	4-5	4	11	Drahman	Gibson		6-5	T2nd	1
4-22	At N.Y.	W	10-5	12	9	Gleaton	Cadaret		7-5	T1st	...
4-23	At N.Y.	L	0-5	4	11	Eiland	Tanana		7-6	2nd	1
4-25	At Tor.	L	2-3	6	10	Key	Petry	Ward	7-7	3rd	1½
4-26	At Tor.	L	4-5	8	9	Stottlemyre	Terrell	Ward	7-8	4th	2½
4-27	At Tor.	W	4-2	5	6	Gullickson	Wells	Henneman	8-8	4th	1½
4-28	At Tor.	L	6-9	9	15	Timlin	Leiter	Ward	8-9	4th	2½
4-29	At K.C.	W	3-1	8	8	Searcy	Saberhagen	Gibson	9-9	T3rd	2
4-30	At K.C.	W	13-7	12	13	Leiter	Montgomery	Henneman	10-9	T3rd	1½
5-1	At K.C.	W	6-4	9	8	Gullickson	Boddicker	Henneman	11-9	T2nd	½
5-3	Tex.	W	7-6 (11)	9	10	Henneman	Arnsberg		12-9	4th	½
5-4	Tex.	L	5-6	6	10	Gossage	Gleaton		12-10	4th	1½
5-5	Tex.	W	8-7	12	16	Terrell	Brown		13-10	3rd	1½
5-7	K.C.	W	5-4	8	7	Gullickson	Appier	Gibson	14-10	2nd	½
5-8	K.C.	W	7-3	8	8	Tanana	S. Davis	Gibson	15-10	2nd	½
5-9	At Min.	W	3-0	5	7	Petry	Tapani	Gibson	16-10	2nd	½
5-10	At Min.	L	2-5	8	12	Guthrie	Terrell	Aguilera	16-11	2nd	1½
5-11	At Min.	L	4-5	8	12	Willis	Henneman	Aguilera	16-12	3rd	2½
5-12	At Min.	L	3-8	8	16	Erickson	Gullickson		16-13	3rd	2½
5-13	At Tex.	L	1-8	4	13	Barfield	Cerutti		16-14	3rd	2½
5-14	At Tex.	L	3-5	9	9	Chiamparino	Petry	Russell	16-15	3rd	3½
5-15	At Tex.	L	4-5 (12)	9	11	Gossage	Searcy		16-16	3rd	4½
5-17	Min.	L	1-8	7	13	Erickson	Gullickson	Bedrosian	16-17	3rd	4½
5-18	Min.	L	1-4	6	8	Guthrie	Tanana	Aguilera	16-18	T3rd	4½
5-19	Min.	W	8-3	8	8	Petry	Morris		17-18	T3rd	3½
5-20	Bal.	W	11-5	12	14	Gleaton	Milacki		18-18	3rd	3½
5-21	Bal.	L	4-5	9	9	Flanagan	Gibson	Olson	18-19	3rd	4½
5-22	Bal.	W	9-5	9	9	Gullickson	McDonald		19-19	3rd	4½
5-23	Bos.	W	5-3	6	10	Henneman	Clemens	Gibson	20-19	3rd	3½
5-24	Bos.	L	9-10	10	15	Bolton	Petry	Reardon	20-20	3rd	4½
5-25	Bos.	W	3-2	5	7	Terrell	Young	Henneman	21-20	3rd	3½
5-26	Bos.	W	9-4	11	13	Leiter	Kiecker	Gibson	22-20	3rd	2½
5-27	At Mil.	W	15-9 (14)	13	18	Henneman	Crim		23-20	3rd	1½
5-28	At Mil.	L	2-15	7	15	August	Tanana		23-21	3rd	2½
5-29	At Mil.	L	2-6	6	9	Navarro	Terrell		23-22	3rd	2½
5-31	At Cle.	L	9-11	14	16	S. Valdez	Ritz	Hillegas	23-23	3rd	3
6-1	At Cle.	L	1-3	5	9	Swindell	Gullickson		23-24	T3rd	3
6-2	At Cle.	L	2-3	4	8	Candiotti	Tanana	Jones	23-25	T3rd	3
6-3	At Cle.	L	0-2	9	8	Nagy	Terrell	Hillegas	23-26	4th	4
6-4	Sea.	L	6-8	9	10	Holman	Cerutti	Jackson	23-27	T4th	4
6-5	Sea.	W	7-1	11	4	Gleaton	DeLucia	Gibson	24-27	3rd	4
6-6	Sea.	W	5-4	8	10	Gullickson	Bankhead	Henneman	25-27	3rd	3
6-7	At Cal.	W	5-0	10	4	Tanana	Valenzuela		26-27	3rd	2
6-8	At Cal.	W	4-3	6	8	Terrell	J. Abbott	Henneman	27-27	3rd	2
6-9	At Cal.	L	3-7	9	14	Finley	Gakeler		27-28	3rd	3
6-10	At Oak.	L	6-12	8	15	Guzman	Henneman		27-29	T3rd	3½
6-11	At Oak.	W	5-1	11	4	Gullickson	Hawkins	Henneman	28-29	3rd	2½
6-12	At Oak.	L	1-3	3	5	Moore	Tanana	Eckersley	28-30	3rd	3½
6-13	At Sea.	L	5-6	4	9	Swift	Gibson	Jackson	28-31	3rd	4½
6-14	At Sea.	W	5-1	9	2	Gakeler	Holman		29-31	3rd	4½
6-15	At Sea.	L	2-15	5	10	Johnson	Ritz	Swift	29-32	3rd	4½
6-16	At Sea.	W	7-3	7	12	Gullickson	Rice		30-32	3rd	4
6-18	Oak.	W	2-0	3	4	Tanana	Welch	Henneman	31-32	3rd	2½
6-19	Oak.	L	4-5	8	13	Nelson	Terrell	Eckersley	31-33	3rd	2½
6-20	Cal.	L	5-7	7	11	Grahe	Gibson	Harvey	31-34	3rd	3½
6-21	Cal.	W	9-2	8	10	Gullickson	McCaskill		32-34	3rd	3½
6-22	Cal.	L	3-10	6	15	Langston	Ritz		32-35	3rd	4½
6-23	Cal.	W	4-3 (10)	9	7	Gibson	Robinson		33-35	3rd	4½
6-25	Mil.	L	3-11	10	12	Wegman	Terrell		33-36	3rd	5
6-26	Mil.	W	8-7 (13)	14	11	Cerutti	Machado		34-36	3rd	5

Date	Opp.	Res.	Score (inn.*)	Hits	Opp. hits	Winning pitcher	Losing pitcher	Save	Record	Pos.	GB
6-27	Mil.	L	3-9	4	11	Bosio	Gullickson		34-37	3rd	6
6-28	Cle.	W	7-1	9	5	Tanana	Boucher		35-37	3rd	5
6-29	Cle.	W	9-4	15	10	Meacham	Nagy	Henneman	36-37	3rd	5
6-30	Cle.	W	4-1	6	12	Terrell	Nichols	Leiter	37-37	3rd	5
7-1	At Bal.	L	2-10	5	10	McDonald	Gakeler		37-38	3rd	6
7-2	At Bal.	W	4-3	10	10	Gullickson	Ballard	Henneman	38-38	3rd	6
7-3	At Bal.	W	8-2	11	8	Tanana	Milacki		39-38	3rd	6
7-4	At Bos.	W	6-1	11	9	Meacham	Darwin		40-38	3rd	5
7-5	At Bos.	L	1-10	5	12	Morton	Terrell		40-39	3rd	6
7-6	At Bos.	L	4-7	11	12	Clemens	Gibson	Reardon	40-40	3rd	7
7-7	At Bos.	W	7-6	15	12	Gullickson	Bolton	Cerutti	41-40	3rd	7
7-11	K.C.	L	5-9	11	8	Appier	Gakeler		41-41	3rd	8
7-12	K.C.	W	6-3	7	12	Gibson	Magnante	Henneman	42-41	3rd	8
7-13	K.C.	W	8-5	10	10	Terrell	Saberhagen		43-41	3rd	8
7-14	K.C.	L	4-18	7	21	Gordon	Gullickson	Aquino	43-42	3rd	8
7-15	Tex.	W	8-7	12	14	Henneman	Jeffcoat		44-42	2nd	8
7-16	Tex.	W	6-5	8	6	Henneman	Brown		45-42	2nd	7
7-17	Tex.	W	6-4 (10)	6	9	Terrell	Rosenthal		46-42	2nd	6 ½
7-19	At K.C.	W	17-0	16	6	Gullickson	Gordon		47-42	2nd	7
7-20	At K.C.	L	4-8	12	11	Boddicker	Meacham	Aquino	47-43	2nd	7
7-21	At K.C.	L	4-8	7	10	Appier	Leiter		47-44	2nd	7
7-23	Min.	W	6-3	10	8	Tanana	Anderson	Henneman	48-44	2nd	6
7-24	Min.	W	6-3	11	8	Gullickson	West	Henneman	49-44	2nd	6
7-25	Min.	L	3-9	9	14	Erickson	Aldred	Bedrosian	49-45	2nd	6
7-26	At Tex.	W	3-2 (10)	9	14	Henneman	Russell		50-45	2nd	6
7-27	At Tex.	L	5-8	11	9	Alexander	Kiely	Rogers	50-46	2nd	6
7-28	At Tex.	L	6-10	9	13	Ryan	Tanana		50-47	2nd	6
7-29	At Min.	L	3-6	6	14	West	Gullickson	Aguilera	50-48	2nd	6
7-30	At Min.	L	7-9	12	17	Willis	Cerutti		50-49	2nd	6
7-31	Cal.	W	3-1	6	7	Terrell	Langston		51-49	2nd	6
8-1	Cal.	W	5-3	11	10	Leiter	Fetters	Henneman	52-49	2nd	6
8-2	N.Y.	W	7-3	9	9	Tanana	Kamieniecki		53-49	2nd	5
8-3	N.Y.	W	7-6	10	10	Gullickson	Johnson	Henneman	54-49	2nd	4
8-4	N.Y.	W	8-7 (10)	13	13	Henneman	Farr		55-49	2nd	4
8-5	N.Y.	L	5-7	8	10	Sanderson	Terrell	Guetterman	55-50	2nd	4 ½
8-6	At Tor.	L	1-2	5	7	Key	Cerutti	Henke	55-51	2nd	5 ½
8-7	At Tor.	L	2-5	4	8	Guzman	Tanana	Henke	55-52	2nd	6 ½
8-8	At Tor.	W	4-0 (14)	9	13	Gibson	Henke		56-52	2nd	5 ½
8-10 (1)	At N.Y.	W	5-1	8	6	Leiter	Sanderson		57-52	2nd	4
8-10 (2)	At N.Y.	W	4-0	6	4	Terrell	Taylor		58-52	2nd	3 ½
8-11 (1)	At N.Y.	L	6-12	9	13	Cadaret	Gakeler		58-53	2nd	3 ½
8-11 (2)	At N.Y.	L	8-10 (10)	8	14	Farr	Gibson		58-54	2nd	4
8-13 (1)	Chi.	W	11-9	10	16	Tanana	Fernandez		59-54	2nd	2 ½
8-13 (2)	Chi.	W	4-3	8	8	Gullickson	Hibbard	Henneman	60-54	2nd	2
8-14	Chi.	L	8-9	8	12	Radinsky	Gibson	Thigpen	60-55	2nd	2
8-15	Chi.	W	6-4	6	8	Leiter	Carter	Henneman	61-55	2nd	2
8-16	Tor.	W	5-2	7	6	Cerutti	Key	Gakeler	62-55	2nd	1
8-17	Tor.	L	5-7	5	8	MacDonald	Aldred	Henke	62-56	2nd	2
8-18	Tor.	L	2-4	3	7	Candiotti	Kaiser	Henke	62-57	2nd	3
8-19	At Chi.	W	3-2	8	10	Tanana	Fernandez	Gibson	63-57	2nd	2 ½
8-20	At Chi.	W	5-0	11	6	Terrell	Hough		64-57	2nd	2 ½
8-21	At Chi.	W	12-9	10	12	Leiter	Alvarez		65-57	2nd	1 ½
8-23	Sea.	W	8-6	9	15	Gullickson	Holman	Kaiser	66-57	2nd	1
8-24	Sea.	W	7-2	8	8	Tanana	Johnson		67-57	T1st	...
8-25	Sea.	W	4-3	11	9	Terrell	Schooler		68-57	1st	...
8-26	At Cal.	W	5-1	13	10	Leiter	Grahe	Gakeler	69-57	1st	...
8-27	At Cal.	L	2-4	6	9	Finley	Cerutti	Harvey	69-58	2nd	1
8-28	At Cal.	L	0-1	4	5	J. Abbott	Gullickson	Harvey	69-59	2nd	2
8-30	At Oak.	L	3-6 (10)	5	10	Eckersley	Gleaton		69-60	2nd	2 ½
8-31	At Oak.	L	8-9 (10)	11	12	Eckersley	Cerutti		69-61	2nd	3 ½
9-1	At Oak.	W	5-2	12	5	Leiter	Welch	Gleaton	70-61	2nd	2 ½
9-2	At Sea.	W	12-5	17	10	Gullickson	DeLucia	Gibson	71-61	2nd	2 ½
9-3	At Sea.	L	0-1	5	4	Holman	Aldred	Swift	71-62	2nd	2 ½
9-5	Oak.	L	1-4	7	8	Moore	Tanana	Eckersley	71-63	2nd	4
9-6	Oak.	W	11-2	14	5	Terrell	Welch		72-63	2nd	4
9-7	Oak.	L	1-3	8	9	Slusarski	Leiter	Eckersley	72-64	2nd	5
9-8	Oak.	L	4-7	8	11	Stewart	Gullickson	Eckersley	72-65	3rd	6
9-10	Bos.	L	0-4	2	7	Clemens	Tanana		72-66	3rd	6
9-11	Bos.	W	8-2	13	6	Terrell	Young		73-66	3rd	5
9-12	At Mil.	L	0-7	4	8	Bosio	Leiter		73-67	3rd	5 ½
9-13	At Mil.	W	3-2	11	6	Gullickson	Lee	Kaiser	74-67	3rd	5 ½
9-14	At Mil.	W	6-4	10	8	Aldred	Plesac		75-67	3rd	5 ½
9-15	At Mil.	L	3-5	10	8	Wegman	Tanana	Henry	75-68	3rd	5 ½
9-17	At Cle.	L	1-3	9	8	Jones	Terrell	Olin	75-69	3rd	5

Date	Opp.	Res.	Score (inn.*)	Hits	Opp. hits	Winning pitcher	Losing pitcher	Save	Record	Pos.	GB
9-18	At Cle.	L	2-3	8	6	Nagy	Gullickson		75-70	3rd	6
9-20	Mil.	L	5-8	6	10	Plesac	Leiter	Henry	75-71	3rd	6
9-21	Mil.	L	2-5	3	8	Wegman	Tanana	Henry	75-72	3rd	6
9-22	Mil.	L	5-9	7	14	Bosio	Terrell		75-73	3rd	7
9-23	Cle.	W	2-1	8	6	Gullickson	King	Henneman	76-73	3rd	6
9-24	Cle.	W	7-2	10	9	Aldred	Nagy		77-73	3rd	6
9-25	Cle.	L	4-6	12	10	Jones	Leiter	Olin	77-74	3rd	7
9-26	Cle.	W	6-5	9	9	Cerutti	Otto	Henneman	78-74	3rd	6½
9-27	Bal.	L	7-9	11	11	Williamson	Terrell	Olson	78-75	3rd	7½
9-28	Bal.	W	5-4 (10)	9	9	Henneman	Olson		79-75	3rd	6½
9-29	Bal.	L	4-7	10	12	Mesa	Aldred	Frohwirth	79-76	3rd	7½
9-30	Bal.	W	8-3	12	6	Leiter	Johnson		80-76	3rd	6½
10-1	At Bos.	W	8-5	9	11	Tanana	Clemens		81-76	3rd	6½
10-2	At Bos.	L	3-5	7	13	Hesketh	Terrell	Fossas	81-77	3rd	7½
10-3	At Bos.	W	10-5	13	8	Gullickson	Morton		82-77	3rd	7
10-4	At Bal.	W	4-2 (14)	7	10	Haas	Poole	Cerutti	83-77	T2nd	7
10-5	At Bal.	L	3-7	8	9	Poole	Leiter	Williamson	83-78	T2nd	7
10-6	At Bal.	W	7-1	14	4	Tanana	Milacki		84-78	T2nd	7

Monthly records: April (10-9), May (13-14), June (14-14), July (14-12), August (18-12), September (11-15), Oct. (4-2).

HIGHLIGHTS

High point: On August 26 the Tigers won their seventh straight game and stayed in a first-place tie with Toronto in the American League East for a third straight day.

Low point: That peak was immediately followed by a 9-18 dive from August 27 through September 27 that knocked the surprising Tigers out of the A.L. East race. Detroit finished tied for second place with Boston, seven games behind the Blue Jays with an 84-78 record.

Turning point: Third-string catcher Mark Salas' pinch-hit, three-run, 14th-inning home run off Tom Henke broke a scoreless tie and sparked a 4-0 win in Toronto on August 8. The Blue Jays had won the first two games of the three-game series and could have taken a 7½ game lead. Instead, the Tigers pulled within 5½ and caught the Jays for first place 16 days later.

Most valuable player: First baseman Cecil Fielder. He proved that his 51-homer 1990 season was no fluke by pacing the majors with 44 homers (tied with Oakland's Jose Canseco) and 133 runs batted in.

Most valuable pitcher: Righthander Bill Gullickson. A free-agent signee from Houston, the veteran won a career-high 20 games and anchored the staff by pitching 226⅓ innings.

Most improved player: Infielder Travis Fryman. The youngster collected 21 homers, 91 RBIs and 36 doubles. He also showed versatility by playing well at both shortstop and third base.

Most pleasant surprise: Center fielder Milt Cuyler. The rookie hit a decent .257 and stole 41 bases. He played excellent defense, too.

Biggest disappointment: Right fielder Rob Deer. He almost had a higher strikeout total than average (175-.179). In spite of his 25 homers and 64 RBIs he was benched for most of the final month.

Key injuries: Shortstop Alan Trammell missed 61 games with various injuries and played sporadically after suffering a sprained right ankle in a July 16 game. Closer Mike Henneman missed a month

with tendinitis in his pitching shoulder.

Notable: Radio voices Ernie Harwell and Paul Carey, with the team since 1960 and 1973, respectively, broadcast their final game. ... Tony Phillips became the first player in major league history to start at least 10 games at five positions in one season (second base, shortstop, third base, outfield and designated hitter).

—REID CREAGER

RECORDS

1991 regular-season record: 84-78 (T2nd in A.L. East); 49-32 at home; 35-46 on road; 39-39 vs. East; 45-39 vs. West; 23-21 vs. LHP; 61-57 vs. RHP; 74-63 on grass; 10-15 on turf; 25-26 in daytime; 59-52 at night; 24-18 in one-run games; 12-4 in extra-inning games; 2-1-0 in doubleheaders.

Team record last five years: 408-402 (.504, ranks 7th in league in that span).

TEAM LEADERS

Batting average: Tony Phillips (.284).
At-bats: Cecil Fielder (624).
Runs: Cecil Fielder (102).
Hits: Cecil Fielder (163).
Total bases: Cecil Fielder (320).
Doubles: Travis Fryman (36).
Triples: Milt Cuyler (7).
Home runs: Cecil Fielder (44).
Runs batted in: Cecil Fielder (133).
Stolen bases: Milt Cuyler (41).
Slugging percentage: Cecil Fielder (.513).
On-base percentage: Lou Whitaker (.391).
Wins: Bill Gullickson (20).
Earned-run average: Frank Tanana (3.77).
Complete games: Walt Terrell (8).
Shutouts: Frank Tanana, Walt Terrell (2).
Saves: Mike Henneman (21).
Innings pitched: Bill Gullickson (226⅓).
Strikeouts: Frank Tanana (107).

GAMES BY POSITION

Catcher: Mickey Tettleton 125, Andy Allanson 56, Mark Salas 11, Rich Rowland 2.

First base: Cecil Fielder 122, Dave Bergman 49, Skeeter Barnes 9, Mark Salas 5, Andy Allanson 2, Luis de los Santos 2, Mickey Tettleton 1.

Second base: Lou Whitaker 135, Tony Phillips 36, Skeeter Barnes 7, Johnny Paredes 7, Tony Bernazard 2.

Third base: Travis Fryman 86, Tony Phillips 46, Scott Livingstone 43, Skeeter Barnes 17, Luis de los Santos 2, Johnny Paredes 1.

Shortstop: Alan Trammell 92, Travis Fryman 71, Tony Phillips 13, Johnny Paredes 1.

Outfield: Milt Cuyler 151, Rob Deer 132, Lloyd Moseby 64, Tony Phillips 56, Pete Incaviglia 54, John Shelby 47, Skeeter Barnes 33, John Moses 12, Shawn Hare 6, Dave Bergman 4, Luis de los Santos 3, Mickey Tettleton 3.

Designated hitter: Cecil Fielder 42, Pete Incaviglia 41, Mickey Tettleton 24, Tony Phillips 18, Dave Bergman 13, Luis de los Santos 9, Mark Salas 8, Lloyd Moseby 7, Alan Trammell 6, John Shelby 4, Skeeter Barnes 3, Lou Whitaker 3, Tony Bernazard 2, Rob Deer 2, Shawn Hare 2, Johnny Paredes 2, Andy Allanson 1, Rich Rowland 1.

TOP 10 DRAFT CHOICES

1a. Justin Thompson, LHP, Klein Oak High School, Spring, Texas.

1b. Trever Miller, LHP, Trinity High School, Louisville.

2. Tarrik Brock, OF, Hawthorne (Calif.) High School.

3a. Brian Edmondson, RHP, Notre Vista High School, Riverside, Calif.

3b. Justin Mashore, OF, Clayton Valley High School, Concord, Calif.

4. Sean Bergman, RHP, S. Illinois Univ.

5. Paul Magrini, RHP, Wallington H.S.

6. Jason Pfaff, RHP, Univ. of Michigan.

7. Arthur Adams, RHP, Laney J.C.

8. Joe Perona, C, Northwestern Univ.

9. Clint Sodowsky, RHP, Connor St. J.C.

10. Thomas Gibson, OF, Mission J.C.

KANSAS CITY ROYALS
AMERICAN LEAGUE WEST DIVISION

1992 SCHEDULE

APRIL

S	M	T	W	T	F	S
5	6 N OAK	7	8 N OAK	9 OAK	10 N SEA	11 N SEA
12 SEA	13 OAK H	14 N OAK H	15 N OAK H	16 N OAK H	17 N CAL H	18 CAL H
19 CAL H	20	21 N BAL H	22 N BAL H	23 N BAL H	24 N TOR	25 TOR
26 N TOR	27	28 N MIL	29 N MIL	30		

MAY

S	M	T	W	T	F	S
					1 N BOS	2 BOS
3 BOS	4 N CLE	5 N CLE	6 N MIL H	7 N MIL H	8 N BOS H	9 BOS H
10 BOS H	11	12 N CLE H	13 N CLE H	14	15 N DET H	16 N DET H
17 DET H	18 N CHI	19 N CHI	20 N CHI	21 N TEX	22 N TEX	23 N TEX
24 TEX	25	26 N DET	27 N DET	28 N DET	29 N TEX H	30 N TEX H
31 TEX H						

JUNE

S	M	T	W	T	F	S
	1 N CHI H	2 N CHI H	3 N CHI H	4	5 N SEA H	6 N SEA H
7 SEA H	8 N MIN H	9 N MIN H	10 N MIN H	11	12 N CAL	13 N CAL
14 CAL	15 N MIN	16 N MIN	17 N MIN	18	19 N TOR H	20 N TOR H
21 TOR H	22	23 N NY H	24 N NY H	25 NY H	26 N BAL	27 N BAL
28 BAL	29 N NY	30 N NY				

JULY

S	M	T	W	T	F	S
			1 N NY	2 N MIL H	3 N MIL H	4 MIL H
5 MIL H	6 N BOS	7 N BOS	8 N BOS	9 N MIL	10 N MIL	11 N MIL
12 MIL	13	14 N ★	15	16 N CLE H	17 N CLE H	18 N CLE H
19 CLE H	20 N BOS H	21 N BOS H	22 N BOS H	23 N CLE	24 N CLE	25 N CLE
26 CLE	27	28 N TOR	29 N TOR	30 N TOR	31 N OAK H	

AUGUST

S	M	T	W	T	F	S
						1 OAK H
2 N OAK H	3	4 N CAL H	5 N CAL H	6 N CAL H	7 N OAK	8 OAK
9 OAK	10 N SEA	11 N SEA	12 SEA	13	14 N BAL H	15 N BAL H
16 BAL H	17 N DET H	18 N DET H	19 N DET H	20	21 N CHI	22 N CHI
23 CHI	24	25 N TEX	26 N TEX	27 N TEX	28 N DET	29 DET
30 DET	31 N TEX H					

SEPTEMBER

S	M	T	W	T	F	S
		1 N TEX H	2 N TEX H	3 N CHI H	4 N CHI H	5 N CHI H
6 CHI H	7 TOR H	8 N TOR H	9 N TOR H	10	11 N NY	12 NY
13 NY	14 N BAL	15 N BAL	16 N BAL	17	18 N NY H	19 N NY H
20 NY H	21 N SEA H	22 N SEA H	23 N SEA H	24 N SEA H	25 N MIN	26 N MIN
27 MIN	28 N CAL	29 N CAL	30 N CAL			

OCTOBER

S	M	T	W	T	F	S
				1 CAL	2 N MIN H	3 N MIN H
4 MIN H	5	6	7	8	9	10

1992 SEASON

CLUB DIRECTORY

Board of directors
  Joe Burke
  Charles Hughes
  Ewing Kauffman
  Mrs. Ewing Kauffman
Chairman of the board (owner)
  Ewing Kauffman
President
  Joe Burke
Exec. vice president and general manager
  Spencer (Herk) Robinson
Vice president, treasurer
  Charles Hughes
Vice president, finance
  Dale Rohr
Vice president, govt. and consumer affairs
  Merle Wood
Vice president, public relations
  Dean Vogelaar
Vice president, administration
  Dennis Cryder
Vice president, player personnel
  Joe Klein
Director of scouting
  Art Stewart
Assistant general manager
  Jay Hinrichs
Director of minor league operations
  Steve Schryver
Director of stadium operations
  Tom Folk
Director of season ticket sales
  Joe Grigoli
Director of group sales/Lancer coordinator
  Chris Muehlbach
Director of data processing
  Loretta Kratzberg
Director of benefits and compensation
  Tom Pfannenstiel
Director of accounting
  Ken Willeke
Ticket office manager
  Stacy Sherrow
Traveling secretary
  Dave Witty
Assistant director, player development
  Bob Hegman

Assistant directors of public relations
  Steve Fink
  Kevin Henderson
Assistant directors of marketing
  Mike Behymer
  Laura Collins
Assistant director of stadium operations
  John Johnson
Stadium engineers
  Duane Robinson
  Chris Frank
Production manager
  Larry Magariel
Executive secretary/baseball
  Peggy Mathews
Equipment manager
  Mike Burkhalter
Team physician
  Dr. Steve Joyce
Trainers
  Nick Swartz
  Steve Morrow
Scouts
  Allard Baird
  Carl Blando
  Bob Carter
  Floyd Chandler
  Balos Davis
  Boots Day
  Doug Deutsch
  Steve Flores
  Ken Gonzales
  Dave Herrera
  Ray Jackson
  Gary Johnson
  Al Kubski
  Tony Levato
  Ed Mathes
  Jeff McKay
  Chuck McMichael
  Brian Murphy
  Buck O'Neil
  Wil Rutenschroer
  Bob Schaefer
  Luis Silverio
  Jerry Stephens
  Terry Wetzel

SCHEDULE KEY

H—Home game.   *All-Star Game at San Diego/Jack Murphy Stadium.
N—Night game (any game starting after 5 p.m.).

SPRING TRAINING ROSTER

Manager—Hal McRae (11).

Coaches—Glenn Ezell (44), Adrian Garrett (41), Guy Hansen (43), Lynn Jones (35), Bruce Kison (42), Lee May (45).

No.	PITCHERS	B/T	Ht./Wt.	Born	1991 clubs
55	Appier, Kevin	R/R	6-2/200	12-6-67	Kansas City
27	Aquino, Luis	R/R	6-1/195	5-19-65	Kansas City
52	Boddicker, Mike	R/R	5-11/185	8-23-57	Kansas City
49	Clark, Dera	R/R	6-1/205	4-14-65	Omaha
50	Corbin, Archie	R/R	6-4/190	12-30-67	Memphis, Kansas City
48	Davis, Mark	L/L	6-4/210	10-19-60	Kansas City, Omaha
36	Gordon, Tom	R/R	5-9/180	11-18-67	Kansas City
23	Gubicza, Mark	R/R	6-5/225	8-14-62	Omaha, Kansas City
58	Johnston, Joel	R/R	6-4/220	3-8-67	Omaha, Kansas City
57	Magnante, Mike	L/L	6-1/180	6-17-65	Omaha, Kansas City
59	Maldonado, Carlos	R/R	6-1/215	10-18-66	Omaha, Kansas City
28	Meacham, Rusty	R/R	6-2/165	1-27-68	Toledo, Detroit
53	Moeller, Dennis	R/L	6-2/195	9-15-67	Memphis, Omaha
21	Montgomery, Jeff	R/R	5-11/180	1-7-62	Kansas City
58	Pichardo, Hipolito	R/R	6-1/160	8-22-69	Memphis
54	Pierce, Ed	L/L	6-1/185	10-6-68	Memphis
34	Wagner, Hector	R/R	6-3/200	11-26-68	Omaha, Kansas City

No.	CATCHERS	B/T	Ht./Wt.	Born	1991 clubs
15	Macfarlane, Mike	R/R	6-1/205	4-12-64	Kansas City
24	Mayne, Brett	L/R	6-1/190	4-19-68	Kansas City
2	Melvin, Bob	R/R	6-4/207	10-28-61	Baltimore
7	Spehr, Tim	R/R	6-2/205	7-2-66	Omaha, Kansas City

No.	INFIELDERS	B/T	Ht./Wt.	Born	1991 clubs
47	Berry, Sean	R/R	5-11/210	3-22-66	Omaha, Kansas City
5	Brett, George	L/R	6-0/205	5-15-53	Kansas City
39	Cole, Stu	R/R	6-1/175	2-7-66	Omaha, Kansas City
19	Conine, Jeff	R/R	6-1/220	6-27-66	Omaha
31	Howard, David	S/R	6-0/165	2-26-67	Kansas City, Omaha
9	Jefferies, Gregg	S/R	5-10/185	8-1-67	New York NL
12	Joyner, Wally	L/L	6-2/203	6-16-62	California
16	Miller, Keith	R/R	5-11/185	6-12-63	New York NL
33	Seitzer, Kevin	R/R	5-11/190	3-26-62	Kansas City
3	Shumpert, Terry	R/R	5-11/190	8-16-66	Kansas City

No.	OUTFIELDERS	B/T	Ht./Wt.	Born	1991 clubs
8	Eisenreich, Jim	L/L	5-11/200	4-18-59	Kansas City
30	Gibson, Kirk	L/L	6-3/225	5-28-57	Kansas City
29	Gwynn, Chris	L/L	6-0/210	10-13-64	Los Angeles
40	Koslofski, Kevin	L/R	5-8/165	9-24-66	Memphis, Omaha
56	McRae, Brian	S/R	6-0/185	8-27-67	Kansas City
22	McReynolds, Kevin	R/R	6-1/215	10-16-59	New York NL
31	Moore, Kerwin	R/R	6-1/190	10-29-70	Baseball City
51	Pulliam, Harvey	R/R	6-0/210	10-20-67	Omaha, Kansas City
25	Thurman, Gary	R/R	5-10/175	11-12-64	Kansas City

BALLPARK INFORMATION

Ballpark (capacity, surface)
 Royals Stadium (40,625, artificial)
Address
 P.O. Box 419969
 Kansas City, MO 64141
Business phone
 816-921-2200
Ticket information
 816-921-8000
Ticket prices
 $13 (club box)
 $12 (field box)
 $10 (plaza reserved)
 $9 (view upper box)
 $8 (view upper reserved)
 $4 (Royal nights)
 $5 (general admission)
Field dimensions (from home plate)
 To left field at foul line, 330 feet
 To center field, 410 feet
 To right field at foul line, 330 feet
First game played
 April 10, 1973 (Royals 12, Rangers 1)

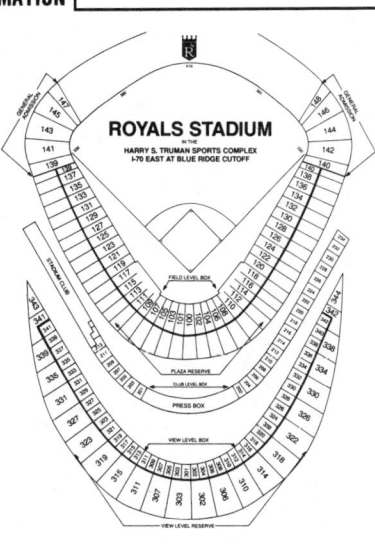

ROYALS STADIUM
HARRY S. TRUMAN SPORTS COMPLEX
I-70 EAST AT BLUE RIDGE CUTOFF

MINOR LEAGUE AFFILIATES

Class	Team	League	Manager
AAA	Omaha	American Association	Jeff Cox
AA	Memphis	Southern	Brian Poldberg
A	Baseball City	Florida State	Ron Johnson
A	Appleton	Midwest	Tom Poquette
A	Eugene	Northwest	Bobby Meacham
Rookie	Boardwalk Royals	Gulf Coast	Mike Jirschele

BROADCAST INFORMATION

Radio: WIBW-AM (580). Broadcasters: Denny Matthews, Fred White.
TV: WDAF-TV (Channel 4). Broadcasters: Denny Trease, Paul Splittorff.
Cable TV: None.

SPRING TRAINING

Ballpark (city): Baseball City Stadium (Baseball City, Fla.).
Ticket information: 813-424-2500.

HISTORY

YEAR-BY-YEAR RECORDS

Year	Pos.	W	L	Pct.	*GB	Year	Pos.	W	L	Pct.	*GB
1969	4th	69	93	.426	28	1983	2nd	79	83	.488	20
1970	T4th	65	97	.401	33	1984	1st†	84	78	.519	+ 3
1971	2nd	85	76	.528	16	1985	1st‡	91	71	.562	+ 1
1972	4th	76	78	.494	16½	1986	T3rd	76	86	.469	16
1973	2nd	88	74	.543	6	1987	2nd	83	79	.512	2
1974	5th	77	85	.475	13	1988	3rd	84	77	.522	19½
1975	2nd	91	71	.562	7	1989	2nd	92	70	.568	7
1976	1st†	90	72	.556	+ 2½	1990	6th	75	86	.466	27½
1977	1st†	102	60	.630	+ 8	1991	6th	82	80	.506	13
1978	1st†	92	70	.568	+ 5						
1979	2nd	85	77	.525	3						
1980	1st‡	97	65	.599	+14						
1981	5th/1st	50	53	.485	§*						
1982	2nd	90	72	.556	3						

*Games behind winner. †Lost Championship Series. ‡Won Championship Series. §First half 20-30; second 30-23. *Lost division playoff.

MANAGERS

Name	Record	Years
Joe Gordon	69-93	1969
Charlie Metro	19-33	1970
Bob Lemon	207-218	'70-72
Jack McKeon	215-205	'73-75
Whitey Herzog	410-304	'74-79
Jim Frey	127-105	'80-81
Dick Howser	404-365	'81-86
Mike Ferraro	36-38	1986
Billy Gardner	62-64	1987
John Wathan	288-270	'87-91
Hal McRae	66-58	1991

1991 REVIEW

DAY BY DAY

Date	Opp.	Res.	Score (inn.*)	Hits	Opp. hits	Winning pitcher	Losing pitcher	Save	Record	Pos.	GB
4-8	Cle.	W	4-2	10	6	Saberhagen	Swindell	Montgomery	1-0	T1st	...
4-9	Cle.	L	1-2	5	5	Candiotti	Boddicker	Jones	1-1	4th	½
4-10	Cle.	W	1-0	7	7	Appier	Nagy	Montgomery	2-1	3rd	½
4-12	N.Y.	W	9-5	15	9	S. Davis	Cary		3-1	T2nd	½
4-13	N.Y.	L	8-9	14	12	Leary	Saberhagen	Farr	3-2	4th	1½
4-14	N.Y.	W	5-3	13	6	Boddicker	Hawkins	Montgomery	4-2	4th	1
4-16	At Bos.	L	2-5	6	8	Darwin	Appier	Reardon	4-3	4th	2½
4-17	At Bos.	L	2-6	6	10	Bolton	S. Davis	Gray	4-4	4th	3½
4-18	At Bos.	L	0-1	3	4	Clemens	Saberhagen	Reardon	4-5	4th	3½
4-19	At N.Y.	L	1-3	3	7	Leary	Boddicker		4-6	T4th	3½
4-20	At N.Y.	W	5-2	10	6	Gordon	Sanderson	Montgomery	5-6	T4th	2½
4-22	At Cle.	L	4-10	3	19	Nagy	Appier		5-7	6th	3½
4-23	At Cle.	W	6-0	14	5	S. Davis	King		6-7	6th	3½
4-24	At Cle.	W	4-2 (10)	7	14	Montgomery	Jones		7-7	6th	2½
4-26	Bos.	W	5-3	7	6	Boddicker	Fossas	Montgomery	8-7	3rd	1½
4-27	Bos.	L	4-6	8	12	Bolton	Appier	Reardon	8-8	T4th	2½
4-28	Bos.	L	1-2	7	10	Kiecker	Gordon	Reardon	8-9	T3rd	3½
4-29	Det.	L	1-3	8	8	Searcy	Saberhagen	Gibson	8-10	T6th	4
4-30	Det.	L	7-13	13	12	Leiter	Montgomery	Henneman	8-11	7th	4½
5-1	Det.	L	4-6	8	9	Gullickson	Boddicker	Henneman	8-12	7th	5½
5-2	Tor.	L	1-3	2	9	Stottlemyre	Appier	Ward	8-13	7th	6
5-3	Tor.	L	1-5	9	11	Wells	S. Davis		8-14	7th	7
5-4	Tor.	W	6-5	11	10	Saberhagen	Boucher	Montgomery	9-14	7th	6
5-5	Tor.	L	0-3	3	8	Stieb	Gordon	Ward	9-15	7th	6
5-7	At Det.	L	4-5	7	8	Gullickson	Appier	Gibson	9-16	7th	7
5-8	At Det.	L	3-7	8	8	Tanana	S. Davis		9-17	7th	8
5-10	At Mil.	W	2-1	4	7	Saberhagen	Bosio		10-17	7th	7
5-11	At Mil.	W	4-2	11	5	Gordon	Wegman	Montgomery	11-17	7th	7
5-12	At Mil.	W	6-4	10	9	Boddicker	Brown	Montgomery	12-17	7th	6
5-13	At Tor.	L	2-4	6	7	Stottlemyre	S. Davis	Ward	12-18	7th	6
5-14	At Tor.	L	1-4	6	12	Wells	Gubicza	Timlin	12-19	7th	6
5-15	At Tor.	W	6-4	12	10	Saberhagen	Boucher		13-19	7th	6
5-17	Mil.	L	5-7 (10)	10	13	Crim	M. Davis	Machado	13-20	7th	7
5-18	Mil.	W	7-4	11	12	M. Davis	Lee	Montgomery	14-20	7th	7
5-19	Mil.	L	2-4	7	9	Navarro	Gubicza	Machado	14-21	7th	7½
5-20	Sea.	L	6-8	11	10	Swan	Montgomery	Jackson	14-22	7th	8
5-21	Sea.	W	4-3	8	5	Appier	Krueger		15-22	7th	7
5-22	Sea.	W	3-1	5	4	Gordon	Johnson		16-22	7th	6½
5-24	At Min.	L	2-3	5	9	Morris	S. Davis	Aguilera	16-23	7th	7½
5-25	At Min.	W	11-2	17	11	Gubicza	Guthrie		17-23	7th	7½
5-26	At Min.	W	5-1	11	8	Saberhagen	Tapani		18-23	7th	7½
5-27	At Sea.	W	6-3	8	4	Appier	Johnson		19-23	T6th	7½
5-28	At Sea.	W	6-5	11	8	Gordon	Hanson	M. Davis	20-23	T6th	7½
5-29	At Sea.	L	0-8	4	12	Holman	Boddicker		20-24	7th	6½
5-30	Min.	L	2-4	8	6	Guthrie	Gubicza	Aguilera	20-25	7th	7½
5-31	Min.	W	4-1	9	4	Saberhagen	Tapani		21-25	7th	6½
6-1	Min.	L	4-8	9	12	Anderson	Appier		21-26	7th	7½
6-2	Min.	L	1-4	5	11	Erickson	Gordon	Aguilera	21-27	7th	7½
6-4	Tex.	W	4-1	7	5	Boddicker	Guzman	Montgomery	22-27	7th	8
6-5	Tex.	W	3-2	5	6	Crawford	Brown	Montgomery	23-27	7th	8
6-6	Tex.	W	4-3 (18)	15	14	Boddicker	Rogers		24-27	7th	8
6-7	Chi.	L	0-2	6	5	Hough	Appier	Radinsky	24-28	7th	8
6-8	Chi.	L	7-14	12	18	Hibbard	Gordon		24-29	7th	8
6-9	Chi.	L	2-8	4	11	McDowell	Boddicker		24-30	7th	9
6-11	At Bal.	W	11-0	16	7	Gubicza	Mesa	Crawford	25-30	7th	8½
6-12	At Bal.	W	9-8	8	11	M. Davis	Williamson	Montgomery	26-30	7th	8½
6-13	At Bal.	W	6-4	12	9	M. Davis	Kilgus	Montgomery	27-30	7th	8
6-14	At Chi.	L	3-9	5	16	McDowell	Aquino	Radinsky	27-31	7th	8½
6-15	At Chi.	W	5-3	9	7	Boddicker	Garcia	Montgomery	28-31	7th	8
6-16	At Chi.	W	9-4	12	11	Gubicza	Fernandez		29-31	T6th	7½
6-17	At Tex.	L	9-10 (10)	12	19	Jeffcoat	Montgomery		29-32	7th	7½
6-18	At Tex.	W	12-5	15	10	Appier	Rogers	Aquino	30-32	7th	7½
6-19	At Tex.	W	15-2	20	5	Wagner	Guzman	S. Davis	31-32	6th	7½
6-20	Bal.	W	3-2 (10)	9	8	Crawford	Frohwirth		32-32	6th	7
6-22	Bal.	L	0-1	3	3	Milacki	Gordon	Olson	32-33	T6th	8½
6-23 (1)	Bal.	L	8-11 (10)	14	17	Frohwirth	Montgomery	Olson	32-34	7th	8½
6-23 (2)	Bal.	L	8-9 (12)	16	18	Olson	S. Davis	Kilgus	32-35	7th	9
6-24	Cal.	L	4-9	7	18	Finley	Wagner		32-36	7th	10
6-25	Cal.	L	2-4	10	7	McCaskill	Boddicker	Harvey	32-37	7th	11
6-26	Cal.	L	5-10	7	16	Langston	Gubicza		32-38	7th	11

Date	Opp.	Res.	Score (inn.*)	Hits	Opp. hits	Winning pitcher	Losing pitcher	Save	Record	Pos.	GB
6-28	At Oak.	W	11-0	14	5	Aquino	Welch		33-38	7th	9½
6-29	At Oak.	L	3-6	10	8	Stewart	S. Davis	Eckersley	33-39	7th	9½
6-30	At Oak.	L	2-3	5	5	Moore	Gordon	Eckersley	33-40	7th	10½
7-1	At Oak.	W	7-3	11	5	Boddicker	Hawkins	Montgomery	34-40	7th	9½
7-2	At Cal.	L	3-10	10	15	J. Abbott	Gubicza	Robinson	34-41	7th	9½
7-3	At Cal.	L	3-4	5	9	Finley	Aquino	Harvey	34-42	7th	9½
7-4	At Cal.	W	12-5	21	10	Appier	McCaskill		35-42	7th	9½
7-5	Oak.	L	3-9	7	8	Hawkins	Gordon	Chitren	35-43	7th	9½
7-6	Oak.	L	7-9	12	12	Welch	Boddicker	Eckersley	35-44	7th	10½
7-7	Oak.	W	7-5	10	9	Gubicza	Stewart		36-44	7th	9½
7-11	At Det.	W	9-5	8	11	Appier	Gakeler		37-44	7th	9½
7-12	At Det.	L	3-6	12	7	Gibson	Magnante	Henneman	37-45	7th	10½
7-13	At Det.	L	5-8	10	10	Terrell	Saberhagen		37-46	7th	11½
7-14	At Det.	W	18-4	21	7	Gordon	Gullickson	Aquino	38-46	7th	10½
7-15	Tor.	L	3-5 (12)	9	17	Timlin	Crawford	Henke	38-47	7th	11½
7-16	Tor.	W	2-1 (10)	7	5	Aquino	Candiotti		39-47	7th	10½
7-17	Bal.	W	9-8 (15)	21	19	Aquino	Williamson		40-47	7th	10
7-18	Bal.	W	5-1	7	7	Saberhagen	Milacki		41-47	7th	10
7-19	Det.	L	0-17	6	16	Gullickson	Gordon		41-48	7th	11
7-20	Det.	W	8-4	11	12	Boddicker	Meacham	Aquino	42-48	7th	11
7-21	Det.	W	8-4	10	7	Appier	Leiter		43-48	7th	11
7-23	Mil.	W	8-7	11	10	Gubicza	Navarro	Montgomery	44-48	7th	10
7-24	Mil.	W	7-4	15	6	S. Davis	Crim	Montgomery	45-48	7th	9
7-25	Mil.	W	2-0	6	4	Aquino	Hunter	Montgomery	46-48	7th	9
7-26	At Tor.	L	5-6 (11)	10	13	Ward	Gordon		46-49	7th	10
7-27	At Tor.	W	5-2 (10)	8	10	Gordon	Timlin	Montgomery	47-49	7th	10
7-28	At Tor.	W	10-4	16	12	Gubicza	Candiotti	S. Davis	48-49	7th	9
7-30	At Mil.	L	3-9	8	10	August	Saberhagen	Plesac	48-50	7th	10½
7-31	At Mil.	W	5-4	14	12	Aquino	Bosio	Montgomery	49-50	7th	10½
8-1	At Mil.	W	6-5 (11)	15	17	Gordon	Holmes	Montgomery	50-50	7th	9½
8-2	At Cle.	W	6-4	13	13	Appier	Nichols	Montgomery	51-50	7th	8½
8-3	At Cle.	L	1-3	7	10	Swindell	Gordon		51-51	7th	9½
8-4	At Cle.	W	2-0	8	3	Saberhagen	Olin		52-51	6th	9½
8-5	Bos.	W	5-3	9	8	Montgomery	Fossas		53-51	6th	9½
8-6	Bos.	W	6-0	11	8	Boddicker	Gardiner		54-51	6th	9½
8-7	Bos.	W	2-0	7	4	Appier	Clemens		55-51	6th	8½
8-9	Cle.	W	4-2	10	4	Gubicza	Swindell	Montgomery	56-51	T5th	8½
8-10	Cle.	L	0-1	7	5	Otto	Saberhagen	Olin	56-52	6th	8½
8-11	Cle.	W	3-2 (13)	8	9	Gordon	Olin		57-52	5th	8½
8-13 (1)	At N.Y.	W	5-0	11	3	Appier	Johnson		58-52	5th	8
8-13 (2)	At N.Y.	W	8-1	11	11	Boddicker	Eiland	Montgomery	59-52	4th	7½
8-14	At N.Y.	W	5-1 (11)	6	6	Gordon	Farr		60-52	5th	6½
8-15	At N.Y.	L	1-5	5	9	Sanderson	Gubicza		60-53	5th	6½
8-16	At Bos.	L	2-3	7	7	Fossas	S. Davis	Reardon	60-54	5th	7½
8-17	At Bos.	W	4-3	10	6	Aquino	Reardon	Montgomery	61-54	5th	7½
8-18	At Bos.	L	1-5	8	6	Morton	Appier		61-55	5th	8½
8-19	N.Y.	L	2-6	8	11	Cadaret	Boddicker		61-56	T5th	8½
8-20	N.Y.	L	3-7	6	10	Sanderson	Gubicza		61-57	T5th	9½
8-21	N.Y.	W	7-4	15	9	Saberhagen	Perez		62-57	5th	9½
8-22	Tex.	L	2-4	8	7	Rogers	Gordon		62-58	T5th	10½
8-23	Tex.	L	1-6	5	8	Bohanon	Appier		62-59	6th	10½
8-24	Tex.	W	8-1	13	9	Boddicker	Ryan		63-59	T4th	10½
8-25	Tex.	L	4-8 (11)	7	13	Mathews	S. Davis		63-60	5th	10½
8-26	Chi.	W	7-0	13	0	Saberhagen	Hough		64-60	5th	10½
8-27	Chi.	W	3-2	9	6	M. Davis	Alvarez	Gordon	65-60	5th	9½
8-28	Chi.	W	7-6	10	11	Montgomery	Thigpen		66-60	5th	9½
8-30	At Tex.	L	2-6	4	12	Ryan	Boddicker	Russell	66-61	5th	9½
8-31	At Tex.	W	3-2	5	9	Gubicza	Witt	Montgomery	67-61	5th	9½
9-1	At Tex.	L	4-6	6	10	Mathews	Saberhagen	Russell	67-62	5th	10½
9-2	At Chi.	L	1-5	3	8	Hernandez	Aquino		67-63	5th	11½
9-3	At Chi.	W	8-0	12	5	Appier	McDowell		68-63	5th	11
9-4	At Chi.	L	1-4	2	9	Fernandez	Boddicker	Thigpen	68-64	5th	11
9-5	At Chi.	L	2-11	7	13	Hough	Gubicza		68-65	5th	11½
9-6	At Bal.	L	2-6	6	9	Poole	Saberhagen		68-66	5th	12½
9-7	At Bal.	W	7-4	12	7	Aquino	Mesa		69-66	5th	12½
9-8	At Bal.	W	3-2	8	10	Johnston	Frohwirth	Montgomery	70-66	5th	12½
9-9	Min.	L	4-10	9	14	Edens	Boddicker	Wayne	70-67	5th	13½
9-10	Min.	L	2-7	8	12	Anderson	Gubicza	Aguilera	70-68	5th	14½
9-11	Min.	W	4-1	7	6	M. Davis	Tapani	Montgomery	71-68	5th	13½
9-13	Sea.	W	3-2 (12)	9	8	Montgomery	Jackson		72-68	5th	13
9-14	Sea.	L	3-4 (11)	8	9	Jackson	Crawford	Swift	72-69	5th	13
9-15	Sea.	L	7-14	12	17	DeLucia	Boddicker		72-70	T5th	13
9-16	At Min.	L	0-9	3	11	Tapani	Gubicza		72-71	6th	14
9-17	At Min.	W	4-1	9	6	Saberhagen	Morris	Montgomery	73-71	6th	13

Date	Opp.	Res.	Score (inn.*)	Hits	Opp. hits	Winning pitcher	Losing pitcher	Save	Record	Pos.	GB
9-18	At Min.	W	10-4	14	7	Aquino	Erickson		74-71	6th	12
9-19	At Sea.	L	5-10	9	13	Burba	Gordon	Swift	74-72	6th	12½
9-20	At Sea.	W	3-0	6	3	Boddicker	DeLucia	Montgomery	75-72	6th	12½
9-21	At Sea.	L	1-4	9	11	Fleming	Gubicza	Schooler	75-73	6th	13½
9-22	At Sea.	W	2-1	7	3	Saberhagen	Holman		76-73	T5th	13½
9-23	At Oak.	L	6-7	16	10	Klink	Gordon	Eckersley	76-74	5th	14
9-24	At Oak.	W	5-4	8	11	Appier	Slusarski	Montgomery	77-74	5th	14
9-25	At Oak.	L	4-8	8	14	Welch	M. Davis	Eckersley	77-75	5th	14
9-26	Cal.	W	3-2	6	8	Gubicza	Fetters	Montgomery	78-75	5th	13½
9-27	Cal.	W	4-1	9	5	Saberhagen	McCaskill	Montgomery	79-75	5th	12½
9-28	Cal.	L	3-4	6	10	Finley	Aquino	Harvey	79-76	5th	13½
9-29	Cal.	W	8-4	9	7	Appier	J. Abbott		80-76	5th	12½
9-30	Oak.	W	8-4	11	7	M. Davis	Welch		81-76	5th	12½
10-1	Oak.	L	0-4	6	8	Moore	Gubicza	Eckersley	81-77	5th	13½
10-2	Oak.	W	16-5	16	9	Crawford	Darling		82-77	5th	13
10-4	At Cal.	L	2-6	10	10	Young	Gordon		82-78	5th	12
10-5	At Cal.	L	1-5	9	6	J. Abbott	Appier		82-79	6th	13
10-6	At Cal.	L	1-3	5	4	Langston	M. Davis	Harvey	82-80	6th	13

Monthly records: April (8-11), May (13-14), June (12-15), July (16-10), August (18-11), September (14-15), Oct. (1-4).

HIGHLIGHTS

High point: From July 16 through August 14, the Royals won 22 of 27 games to pull within 6½ games of first place in the American League West.

Low point: After that impressive stretch, the Royals went 22-28 the rest of the season to fall out of the race. They finished 13 games behind division champion Minnesota.

Turning point: May 22, when Manager John Wathan was fired. The Royals were 15-22 and going nowhere at the time, but they showed signs of life under Wathan's replacement, Hal McRae, before finishing sixth with an 82-80 mark.

Most valuable player: Right fielder Danny Tartabull. He batted a career-high .316 with 31 home runs and 100 runs batted in. He led the league with a .593 slugging percentage.

Most valuable pitcher: Righthander Bret Saberhagen. He wasn't his normal brilliant self in an odd-numbered season, but no one in the rotation could better his 13-8 record and 3.07 earned-run average. At times he was dominating, such as when he tossed his first career no-hitter against the Chicago White Sox on August 26.

Most improved player: Infielder Bill Pecota. Given his first regular starting job when third baseman Kevin Seitzer was benched, Pecota batted .286 with 16 steals and played solid defense.

Most pleasant surprise: Catcher Mike Macfarlane. He was showing lots of pop in his bat before a July 15 knee injury sidelined him until September 14. In just 84 games he produced a .277 average, 13 homers and 41 RBIs.

Biggest disappointment: Left fielder Kirk Gibson. A free-agent acquisition, Gibson's fiery personality didn't spark the Royals. And he batted just .236.

Key injuries: Macfarlane's knee injury hurt, but designated hitter George Brett's April knee injury kept him out for a month and then nagged him the rest of the season. Tartabull and Saberhagen also suffered injuries.

Notable: Jeff Montgomery recorded 33 saves, more than any Royals pitcher since Dan Quisenberry (37) in 1985. ... Saberhagen's no-hitter was the Royals' first since Jim Colborn no-hit Texas in 1977. ... Kansas City posted a 40-41 mark at home, just the fifth losing record at home in club history and only the third since moving into Royals Stadium in 1973. ... The Royals used 45 players, one shy of the club record of 46 set in 1990.

—DICK KAEGEL

RECORDS

1991 regular-season record: 82-80 (6th in A.L. West); 40-41 at home; 42-39 on road; 46-38 vs. East; 36-42 vs. West; 20-29 vs. LHP; 62-51 vs. RHP; 31-31 on grass; 51-49 on turf; 22-24 in daytime; 60-56 at night; 24-17 in one-run games; 11-8 in extra-inning games; 1-1-0 in doubleheaders.

Team record last five years: 416-392 (.515, ranks 5th in league in that span).

TEAM LEADERS

Batting average: Danny Tartabull (.316).
At-bats: Brian McRae (629).
Runs: Brian McRae (86).
Hits: Brian McRae (164).
Total bases: Danny Tartabull (287).
Doubles: George Brett (40).
Triples: Brian McRae (9).
Home runs: Danny Tartabull (31).
Runs batted in: Danny Tartabull (100).
Stolen bases: Brian McRae (20).
Slugging percentage: Danny Tartabull (.593).
On-base percentage: Danny Tartabull (.397).
Wins: Kevin Appier, Bret Saberhagen (13).
Earned-run average: Bret Saberhagen (3.07).
Complete games: Bret Saberhagen (7).
Shutouts: Kevin Appier (3).
Saves: Jeff Montgomery (33).
Innings pitched: Kevin Appier (207⅔).
Strikeouts: Tom Gordon (167).

GAMES BY POSITION

Catcher: Brent Mayne 80, Mike Macfarlane 69, Tim Spehr 37, Jorge Pedre 9.
First base: Todd Benzinger 75, Carmelo Martinez 43, Warren Cromartie 29, Jim Eisenreich 15, George Brett 10, Russ Morman 8, Bill Pecota 8, Jorge Pedre 1.
Second base: Terry Shumpert 144, Bill Pecota 34, Dave Howard 26, Nelson Liriano 10, Stu Cole 5.
Third base: Bill Pecota 102, Kevin Seitzer 68, Sean Berry 30, Paul Zuvella 2, David Howard 1.
Shortstop: Kurt Stillwell 118, David Howard 63, Bill Pecota 9, Stu Cole 1.
Outfield: Brian McRae 150, Danny Tartabull 124, Jim Eisenreich 105, Kirk Gibson 94, Gary Thurman 72, Harvey Pulliam 15, Brad Moore 13, Warren Cromartie 6, Russ Morman 2, Dave Clark 1, Dave Howard 1, Bill Pecota 1, Terry Puhl 1.
Designated hitter: George Brett 118, Kirk Gibson 30, Danny Tartabull 6, Mike Macfarlane 4, Kevin Seitzer 3, Stu Cole 2, Bill Pecota 2, Terry Puhl 2, Todd Benzinger 1, Dave Clark 1, Warren Cromartie 1, Jim Eisenreich 1, David Howard 1, Carmelo Martinez 1, Brent Mayne 1, Russ Morman 1.

TOP 10 DRAFT CHOICES

1a. Joe Vitiello, OF/1B, University of Alabama.
1b. Jason Pruitt, RHP, Rockingham County High School, Wentworth, N.C.
2. Ryan Long, 3B, Doble High School, Pasadena, Texas.
3. None.
4. Dwayne Gerald, SS, St. Paul's (N.C.) High School.
5. Shane Halter, SS, University of Texas.
6. Mike Bovee, RHP, Mira Mesa High School, San Diego.
7. Paul Failla, SS, North Alleghany High School, Wexford, Pa.
8. Kevin Hodges, RHP, Klein Oak High School, Spring, Texas.
9. Steve Hinton, OF, Creighton University.
10. Mike Sweeney, C, Ontario (Calif.) High School.

MILWAUKEE BREWERS
AMERICAN LEAGUE EAST DIVISION

1992 SCHEDULE

APRIL

S	M	T	W	T	F	S
5	6 MIN H	7	8 N MIN H	9 N MIN H	10 N CAL	11 N CAL
12 CAL	13	14 N MIN	15 N MIN	16	17 N SEA H	18 N SEA H
19 SEA H	20	21 N BOS H	22 N BOS H	23 N BOS H	24 N CLE	25 N CLE
26 CLE	27	28 N KC H	29 N KC H	30 N TOR H		

MAY

S	M	T	W	T	F	S
					1 N TOR H	2 N TOR H
3 TOR H	4 N CHI	5 N CHI	6 N KC	7 N KC	8 N TEX	9 N TEX
10 TEX	11	12 N CHI H	13 N CHI H	14	15 N TEX H	16 N TEX H
17 TEX H	18 N DET	19 N DET	20 N DET	21 N DET	22 N NY	23 N NY
24 NY	25 N NY	26 N TOR	27 N TOR	28	29 N NY H	30 N NY H
31 NY H						

JUNE

S	M	T	W	T	F	S
	1 N DET H	2 N DET H	3 N DET H	4	5 N CAL H	6 N CAL H
7 CAL H	8 N OAK H	9 N OAK H	10 N OAK H	11	12 N SEA	13 N SEA
14 SEA	15 N OAK	16 N OAK	17 N OAK	18 N CLE H	19 N CLE H	20 N CLE H
21 CLE H	22	23 N BAL H	24 N BAL H	25 N BAL H	26 N BOS	27 BOS
28 BOS	29 N BAL	30 N BAL				

JULY

S	M	T	W	T	F	S
			1 N BAL	2 N KC	3 N KC	4 N KC
5 KC	6 N TEX	7 N TEX	8 N TEX	9 N KC H	10 N KC H	11 N KC H
12 KC H	13	14 ★	15	16 N CHI	17 N CHI	18 N CHI
19 CHI	20 N TEX H	21 N TEX H	22 N TEX H	23 N CHI H	24 N CHI H	25 N CHI H
26 CHI H	27 N CLE	28 N CLE	29 N CLE	30 N MIN	31 N MIN	

AUGUST

S	M	T	W	T	F	S
						1 N MIN
2 N MIN	3	4 N SEA H	5 N SEA H	6 N SEA H	7 N MIN H	8 N MIN H
9 MIN H	10 N CAL	11 N CAL	12 N CAL	13	14 N BOS H	15 N BOS H
16 BOS H	17	18 N TOR H	19 N TOR H	20 N TOR H	21 N DET H	22 N DET H
23 DET H	24 N NY	25 N NY	26 N NY	27 N TOR	28 N TOR	29 TOR
30 TOR H	31 N NY H					

SEPTEMBER

S	M	T	W	T	F	S
		1 N NY H	2 N NY H	3	4 N DET	5 N DET
6 DET	7 N CLE H	8 N CLE H	9 N CLE H	10	11 N BAL	12 N BAL
13 BAL	14 N BOS	15 N BOS	16 N BOS	17 N BAL H	18 N BAL H	19 N BAL H
20 BAL H	21 N CAL H	22 N CAL H	23 N CAL H	24 N OAK H	25 N OAK H	26 N OAK H
27 OAK H	28	29 N SEA	30 N SEA			

OCTOBER

S	M	T	W	T	F	S
				1 N SEA	2 N OAK	3 N OAK
4 OAK	5	6	7	8	9	10

1992 SEASON

CLUB DIRECTORY

President, chief executive officer
Allan H. (Bud) Selig
Senior vice president, baseball operations
Sal Bando
Senior vice president, special projects
Harry Dalton
Vice president, scouting and planning
Al Goldis
Vice president, government affairs
Dick Hackett
Vice president, broadcast operations
Bill Haig
Vice president, finance
Dick Hoffmann
Vice president, stadium operations
Gabe Paul Jr.
Asst. vice president, baseball operations
Bruce Manno
Senior consultant, baseball operations
Dee Fondy
Special assistants, baseball operations
Larry Haney
Chuck Tanner
General counsel
Wendy Selig
Assistant general counsel
Eugene (Pepi) Randolph
Director of baseball administration
Brian Small
Director of communications
Laurel Prieb
Director of community relations
Michael Downs
Director of corporate marketing
John Cordova
Director of electronic systems
Terry Ann Peterson
Director of grounds and maintenance
Gary Vandenberg
Director of media relations
Tom Skibosh
Director of player development
Fred Stanley
Director of player negotiations
Tom Gausden
Director of publications
Mario Ziino
Director of ticket operations
John Barnes
Director of ticket sales
Jeff Eisenberg
Traveling secretary
Jimmy Bank
Trainers
John Adam
Al Price
Strength and conditioning coach
Toby Oldham

Team physicians
Dr. Paul Jacobs
Dr. Dennis Sullivan
Director of national scouting
Lou Snipp
Director of international scouting
Dan Monzon
Midwest scout
Fred Beene
Eastern-northern region scout
Ken Califano
Latin America scout
Felix Delgado
Northeast scout
Ed Ford
Northwest scout
Dick Foster
Southwest scout
Jess Flores
Eastern-southern region scout
Rod Fridley
Special assignment scouts
Roland LeBlanc
Walter Youse
Scouts
Julio Blanco-Herrera
Al Bleser
Tom Calvano
Kevin Christman
Marc Cuseta
Preston Douglas
Ed Durkin
Miguel Flores
Steve Fuller
Mark Garcia
Dean Gruwell
Manola Hernandez
Pete Jones
Tommy Jones
Harvey Kuenn Jr.
Lou Laslo
Fred Long
Demie Mainieri
Gus Mureo
Frank Pena
Frank Piet
Mike Powers
Pedro Rivera
Ron Rizzi
Phil Rizzo
Jerry Salzano
Art Schuerman
Bob Sloan
Fermin Ubri
Thomas Walsh
Red Whitsett
Brian York
David Young

SCHEDULE KEY

H—Home game.   *All-Star Game at San Diego/Jack Murphy Stadium.
N—Night game (any game starting after 5 p.m.).

SPRING TRAINING ROSTER

Manager—Phil Garner (3).
Coaches—Bill Castro (35), Duffy Dyer (10), Mike Easler (22), Tim Foli (14), Don Rowe (45).

No.	PITCHERS	B/T	Ht./Wt.	Born	1991 clubs
42	Austin, Jim	R/R	6-2/200	12-7-63	Denver, Milwaukee
29	Bosio, Chris	R/R	6-3/225	4-3-63	Milwaukee
16	Brown, Kevin	L/L	6-1/185	3-5-66	Denver, Milwaukee
21	Eldred, Cal	R/R	6-4/215	11-24-67	Denver, Milwaukee
58	Elvira, Narciso	L/L	5-10/160	10-29-67	Denver
36	Fetters, Mike	R/R	6-4/212	12-19-64	Edmonton, California
59	George, Chris	R/R	6-2/200	9-24-66	Denver, Milwaukee
56	Green, Otis	L/L	6-2/192	3-11-64	Stockton, El Paso
28	Henry, Doug	R/R	6-4/185	12-10-63	Denver, Milwaukee
49	Higuera, Ted	S/L	5-10/178	11-9-58	Denver, Milwaukee
40	Holmes, Darren	R/R	6-0/199	4-25-66	Denver, Milwaukee
53	Ignasiak, Mike	S/R	5-11/175	3-12-66	Denver, Milwaukee
62	Kiefer, Mark	R/R	6-4/175	11-13-68	El Paso, Denver
34	Lee, Mark	L/L	6-3/200	7-20-64	Milwaukee
48	Machado, Julio	R/R	5-9/165	12-1-65	Milwaukee
43	Miranda, Angel	L/L	6-1/160	11-9-69	El Paso, Denver
31	Navarro, Jaime	R/R	6-4/210	3-27-67	Milwaukee
41	Nunez, Edwin	R/R	6-5/240	5-27-63	Beloit, Milwaukee
47	Orosco, Jesse	R/L	6-2/185	4-21-57	Cleveland
37	Plesac, Dan	L/L	6-5/215	2-4-62	Milwaukee
33	Robinson, Ron	R/R	6-4/235	3-24-62	Milwaukee
30	Ruffin, Bruce	R/L	6-2/209	10-4-63	Scranton-W.B., Philadelphia
46	Wegman, Bill	R/R	6-5/220	12-19-62	Beloit, Denver, Milwaukee

No.	CATCHERS	B/T	Ht./Wt.	Born	1991 clubs
27	Kmak, Joe	R/R	6-0/185	5-3-63	Denver
13	Nilsson, Dave	S/R	6-3/185	12-14-69	El Paso, Denver
5	Surhoff, B.J.	L/R	6-1/200	8-4-64	Milwaukee

No.	INFIELDERS	B/T	Ht./Wt.	Born	1991 clubs
57	Jaha, John	R/R	6-1/195	5-27-66	El Paso
52	Listach, Pat	R/R	5-9/170	9-12-67	El Paso, Denver
26	McIntosh, Tim	R/R	5-11/195	3-21-65	Denver, Milwaukee
4	Molitor, Paul	R/R	6-0/185	8-22-56	Milwaukee
11	Sheffield, Gary	R/R	5-11/190	11-18-68	Milwaukee
9	Spiers, Bill	L/R	6-2/190	6-5-66	Milwaukee
0	Stubbs, Franklin	L/L	6-2/209	10-21-60	Milwaukee
2	Suero, William	R/R	5-9/175	11-7-66	Syracuse, Denver
51	Tatum, Jim	R/R	6-2/200	10-9-67	El Paso

No.	OUTFIELDERS	B/T	Ht./Wt.	Born	1991 clubs
8	Bichette, Dante	R/R	6-3/225	11-18-63	Milwaukee
24	Hamilton, Darryl	L/R	6-1/180	12-3-64	Milwaukee
18	Olander, Jim	R/R	6-1/185	2-21-63	Denver, Milwaukee
23	Vaughn, Greg	R/R	6-0/193	7-3-65	Milwaukee
19	Yount, Robin	R/R	6-0/180	9-16-55	Milwaukee

BALLPARK INFORMATION

Ballpark (capacity, surface)
County Stadium (53,192, grass)
Address
County Stadium
Milwaukee, WI 53214
Business phone
414-933-4114
Ticket information
414-933-1818
Ticket prices
$14 (deluxe mezz. & mezzanine)
$13 (lower and upper box)
$10 (lower grandstand)
$7 (upper grandstand and g.a.)
$4 (bleachers)
Field dimensions (from home plate)
To left field at foul line, 315 feet
To center field, 402 feet
To right field at foul line, 315 feet
First game played
April 7, 1970 (Angels 12, Brewers 0)

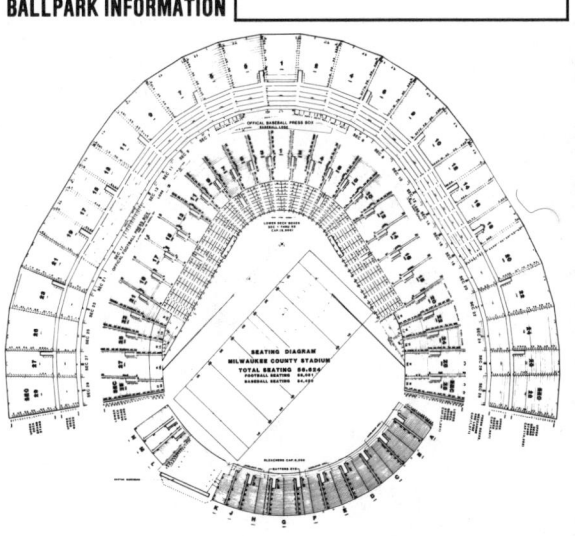

MINOR LEAGUE AFFILIATES

Class	Team	League	Manager
AAA	Denver	American Association	Tony Muser
AA	El Paso	Texas	Chris Bando
A	Stockton	California	Tim Ireland
A	Beloit	Midwest	Wayne Krenchicki
Rookie	Helena	Pioneer	Harry Dunlop
Rookie	Chandler Brewers	Arizona	Tommy Jones

BROADCAST INFORMATION

Radio: WTMJ-AM (620). Broadcasters: Bob Uecker, Pat Hughes.
TV: WCJV-TV (Channel 24). Broadcasters: To be announced.
Cable TV: None.

SPRING TRAINING

Ballpark (city): Compadre Stadium (Chandler, Ariz.).
Ticket information: 602-895-1200.

HISTORY

YEAR-BY-YEAR RECORDS

Year	Pos.	W	L	Pct.	*GB
1969	6th	64	98	.395	33
1970	T4th	65	97	.401	33
1971	6th	69	92	.429	32
1972	6th	65	91	.417	21
1973	5th	74	88	.457	23
1974	5th	76	86	.469	15
1975	5th	68	94	.420	28
1976	6th	66	95	.410	32
1977	6th	67	95	.414	33
1978	3rd	93	69	.574	6½
1979	2nd	95	66	.590	8
1980	3rd	86	76	.531	17
1981	3rd/1st	62	47	.569	†‡

Year	Pos.	W	L	Pct.	*GB
1982	1st§	95	67	.586	+1
1983	5th	87	75	.537	11
1984	7th	67	94	.416	36½
1985	6th	71	90	.441	28
1986	6th	77	84	.478	18
1987	3rd	91	71	.562	7
1988	T3rd	87	75	.537	2
1989	4th	81	81	.500	8
1990	6th	74	88	.457	14
1991	4th	83	79	.512	8

*Games behind winner. †First half 31-25; second 31-22. ‡Lost division playoff. §Won Championship Series.

MANAGERS

Name	Record	Years
Joe Schultz	64-98	1969
Dave Bristol	144-209	'70-72
Del Crandall	271-338	'72-75
Alex Grammas	133-190	'76-77
George Bamberger	377-351	'78-80
		'85-86
Buck Rodgers	124-102	'80-82
Harvey Kuenn	160-118	'82-83
Rene Lachemann	67-94	1984
Tom Trebelhorn	422-397	'86-91

1991 REVIEW

DAY BY DAY

Date	Opp.	Res.	Score (inn.*)	Hits	Opp. hits	Winning pitcher	Losing pitcher	Save	Record	Pos.	GB
4-8	At Tex.	W	5-4	10	8	Knudson	Ryan	Nunez	1-0	T1st	...
4-10	At Tex.	W	6-0	9	5	Bosio	Brown		2-0	1st	+½
4-11	At Tor.	L	3-7	9	13	Wells	Robinson		2-1	T2nd	½
4-12	At Tor.	L	4-5 (11)	7	12	Timlin	Plesac		2-2	T2nd	1½
4-13	At Tor.	W	7-3	10	7	Brown	Stieb	Crim	3-2	2nd	½
4-14	At Tor.	L	0-9	2	13	Key	August		3-3	T2nd	1½
4-15	Bal.	L	2-7	8	6	Mesa	Bosio	Williamson	3-4	4th	2½
4-17	Bal.	W	7-3	10	12	Navarro	Johnson	Lee	4-4	T2nd	1
4-18	Bal.	W	4-3 (11)	7	6	Nunez	Bautista		5-4	T2nd	½
4-19	Tor.	L	2-5	8	11	Stieb	August		5-5	T3rd	1½
4-20	Tor.	L	2-4	6	8	Key	Bosio	Ward	5-6	4th	2½
4-21	Tor.	W	11-8 (10)	11	11	Crim	Wills		6-6	4th	1½
4-23	Tex.	L	5-6 (11)	7	10	Gossage	Crim	Russell	6-7	4th	2
4-24	Tex.	L	2-8	5	12	Brown	Knudson		6-8	4th	2
4-25	Tex.	W	9-1	8	9	Bosio	Rogers		7-8	4th	2
4-26	At Bal.	W	5-4	11	9	Holmes	Mesa	Nunez	8-8	3rd	2
4-27	At Bal.	W	5-2	12	7	August	Robinson		9-8	3rd	1
4-28	At Bal.	L	4-5	11	10	Milacki	Holmes	Olson	9-9	3rd	2
4-30	Chi.	W	8-2	13	10	Bosio	Fernandez	Crim	10-9	T3rd	1½
5-1	Chi.	W	10-9 (19)	18	19	August	Edwards		11-9	T2nd	½
5-2	Min.	W	5-1	9	5	Brown	Tapani	Crim	12-9	2nd	...
5-3	Min.	W	6-5	9	10	Navarro	Aguilera	Nunez	13-9	2nd	...
5-4	Min.	L	4-7	7	15	Guthrie	Bosio	Bedrosian	13-10	T2nd	1
5-5	Min.	L	2-5 (10)	8	9	Aguilera	Nunez		13-11	4th	2
5-7	At Chi.	L	1-2 (12)	9	9	Thigpen	Lee		13-12	4th	2
5-8	At Chi.	L	1-2	7	7	McDowell	Navarro		13-13	4th	3
5-10	K.C.	L	1-2	7	4	Saberhagen	Bosio		13-14	4th	4½
5-11	K.C.	L	2-4	5	11	Gordon	Wegman	Montgomery	13-15	4th	5½
5-12	K.C.	L	4-6	9	10	Boddicker	Brown	Montgomery	13-16	4th	5½
5-14	At Min.	L	1-5	2	13	Morris	Navarro		13-17	4th	6
5-15	At Min.	W	4-2	9	7	Bosio	Tapani	Plesac	14-17	4th	6
5-16	At Min.	W	6-3	13	9	Wegman	Anderson	Holmes	15-17	4th	5½
5-17	At K.C.	W	7-5 (10)	13	10	Crim	M. Davis	Machado	16-17	T3rd	4½
5-18	At K.C.	L	4-7	12	11	M. Davis	Lee	Montgomery	16-18	T3rd	4½
5-19	At K.C.	W	4-2	9	7	Navarro	Gubicza	Machado	17-18	T3rd	3½
5-20	At Bos.	L	0-3	4	6	Young	Bosio	Reardon	17-19	4th	4½
5-21	At Bos.	L	6-10	13	14	Hesketh	Hunter		17-20	4th	5½
5-22	At Bos.	L	0-4	10	5	Darwin	Brown	Harris	17-21	4th	6½
5-23	Cle.	W	7-3	14	9	August	Nagy	Holmes	18-21	4th	5½
5-24	Cle.	W	1-0	5	4	Navarro	Nichols		19-21	4th	5½
5-25	Cle.	L	4-5	7	5	Jones	Machado		19-22	4th	5½
5-26	Cle.	W	7-6 (10)	11	10	Crim	Jones		20-22	4th	4½
5-27	Det.	L	9-15 (14)	18	13	Henneman	Crim		20-23	4th	4½
5-28	Det.	W	15-2	15	7	August	Tanana		21-23	4th	4½
5-29	Det.	W	6-2	9	6	Navarro	Terrell		22-23	4th	3½
5-31	At N.Y.	L	2-3	7	8	Howe	Crim		22-24	4th	4
6-1	At N.Y.	W	6-3	13	6	Wegman	Cary		23-24	T3rd	3
6-2	At N.Y.	L	4-7	10	13	Taylor	Higuera	Farr	23-25	T3rd	3
6-4	At Oak.	L	3-4	4	9	Welch	Navarro	Eckersley	23-26	3rd	3½
6-5	At Oak.	L	4-6	3	9	Stewart	Bosio	Chitren	23-27	4th	4½
6-6	At Oak.	L	8-9	8	12	Walton	Crim	Eckersley	23-28	T4th	4½
6-7	At Sea.	L	1-2	3	4	Krueger	Higuera	Jackson	23-29	5th	4½
6-8	At Sea.	L	2-6	5	9	DeLucia	Wegman	Burba	23-30	5th	5½
6-9	At Sea.	L	1-6	5	12	Holman	Navarro		23-31	5th	6½
6-10	At Cal.	W	7-2	10	10	Bosio	McCaskill		24-31	5th	6
6-11	At Cal.	L	3-4	8	9	Langston	Brown	Harvey	24-32	5th	6
6-12	At Cal.	W	8-0	13	4	Higuera	Valenzuela		25-32	5th	6
6-15 (1)	Oak.	W	6-4	6	6	Navarro	Stewart	Plesac	26-32	5th	6
6-15 (2)	Oak.	L	3-7	7	9	Hawkins	Brown	Chitren	26-33	T5th	6½
6-16	Oak.	W	11-7	13	14	Crim	Nelson		27-33	4th	6
6-17	Oak.	W	5-0	6	5	August	Moore		28-33	4th	5
6-18	Cal.	W	10-6	14	11	Higuera	Grahe	Plesac	29-33	4th	4
6-19	Cal.	L	1-4	7	11	J. Abbott	Wegman	Harvey	29-34	4th	4
6-20	Sea.	W	4-0	9	4	Navarro	Holman		30-34	4th	4
6-21	Sea.	L	1-5	4	9	Johnson	Bosio		30-35	4th	5
6-22	Sea.	L	0-5	4	7	Hanson	August		30-36	4th	6
6-23	Sea.	W	5-2	9	4	Higuera	Krueger	Plesac	31-36	4th	6
6-25	At Det.	W	11-3	12	10	Wegman	Terrell		32-36	4th	5½
6-26	At Det.	L	7-8 (13)	11	14	Cerutti	Machado		32-37	4th	6½
6-27	At Det.	W	9-3	11	4	Bosio	Gullickson		33-37	4th	6½

Date	Opp.	Res.	Score (inn.*)	Hits	Opp. hits	Winning pitcher	Losing pitcher	Save	Record	Pos.	GB
6-28	N.Y.	W	5-2	9	5	August	Kamieniecki	Plesac	34-37	4th	6½
6-29	N.Y.	L	8-9	10	13	Guetterman	Plesac	Farr	34-38	4th	7½
6-30	N.Y.	L	6-8	13	14	Cadaret	Lee	Farr	34-39	4th	7½
7-1	Bos.	L	0-6	5	10	Clemens	Navarro		34-40	5th	8½
7-2	Bos.	L	4-14	10	22	Lamp	Knudson		34-41	5th	9½
7-3	Bos.	L	3-5	8	7	Harris	August	Reardon	34-42	5th	10½
7-4	At Cle.	L	0-3	6	8	Nagy	Hunter		34-43	5th	10½
7-5	At Cle.	W	4-2	9	6	Wegman	Nichols	Plesac	35-43	5th	10½
7-6	At Cle.	L	0-2	4	5	Swindell	Navarro	Hillegas	35-44	5th	11½
7-7	At Cle.	W	10-6	16	18	Crim	Shaw	Plesac	36-44	5th	11½
7-11	Chi.	W	5-1	9	6	Wegman	Hough		37-44	5th	11½
7-12	Chi.	L	6-8	10	9	Perez	Plesac	Thigpen	37-45	5th	12½
7-13	Chi.	W	8-2	12	7	August	Hibbard		38-45	5th	12½
7-14	Chi.	L	1-15	1	15	McDowell	Knudson		38-46	5th	12½
7-15	Min.	L	7-11	12	14	Guthrie	Hunter	Bedrosian	38-47	5th	13½
7-16	Min.	W	4-3	10	10	Henry	Aguilera		39-47	5th	12½
7-17	Sea.	W	6-1	7	4	Wegman	Johnson		40-47	5th	12
7-18	Sea.	L	0-12	6	18	Hanson	Navarro		40-48	5th	13
7-19	At Chi.	L	3-14	9	16	McDowell	August		40-49	5th	14
7-20	At Chi.	L	6-7 (10)	12	11	Thigpen	Plesac		40-50	5th	14
7-21	At Chi.	W	2-1	3	6	Bosio	Hough		41-50	5th	13
7-22	At Chi.	L	4-5	8	9	Hibbard	Wegman	Thigpen	41-51	5th	13½
7-23	At K.C.	L	7-8	10	11	Gubicza	Navarro	Montgomery	41-52	5th	13½
7-24	At K.C.	L	4-7	6	15	S. Davis	Crim	Montgomery	41-53	5th	14½
7-25	At K.C.	L	0-2	4	6	Aquino	Hunter	Montgomery	41-54	5th	14½
7-26	At Min.	L	3-6	5	10	Tapani	Holmes	Aguilera	41-55	5th	15½
7-27	At Min.	L	4-7	11	11	Willis	Wegman		41-56	5th	15½
7-28	At Min.	W	11-2	22	10	Navarro	Morris		42-56	5th	14½
7-30	K.C.	W	9-3	10	8	August	Saberhagen	Plesac	43-56	5th	13
7-31	K.C.	L	4-5	12	14	Aquino	Bosio	Montgomery	43-57	5th	14
8-1	K.C.	L	5-6 (11)	17	15	Gordon	Holmes	Montgomery	43-58	5th	15
8-2	Tex.	L	1-15	6	18	Bohanon	Navarro		43-59	5th	15
8-3	Tex.	L	5-14	7	16	Guzman	Wegman		43-60	5th	15
8-4	Tex.	W	3-2	10	11	Crim	Russell		44-60	5th	15
8-5	At Bal.	L	6-5	10	11	Henry	Williamson	Nunez	45-60	5th	14½
8-6	At Bal.	L	5-13	12	17	Johnson	Hunter		45-61	5th	15½
8-7	At Bal.	W	4-2	10	9	Navarro	McDonald		46-61	5th	15½
8-8	At Bal.	W	6-4	9	9	Wegman	Milacki	Nunez	47-61	5th	14½
8-9	At Tex.	W	10-8	16	11	Bosio	Alexander	Nunez	48-61	5th	13½
8-10	At Tex.	W	5-2	9	8	Plesac	Boyd	Henry	49-61	5th	12½
8-11	At Tex.	L	4-5 (10)	12	10	Rogers	Machado		49-62	5th	12½
8-12	At Tex.	W	14-7	18	9	Navarro	Witt	Henry	50-62	5th	11½
8-13	Tor.	W	5-4	10	7	Crim	Henke		51-62	4th	10½
8-14	Tor.	W	5-3	9	7	Bosio	Wells	Henry	52-62	4th	9½
8-15	Tor.	L	1-4	4	7	Stottlemyre	Plesac	Henke	52-63	4th	10½
8-16	Bal.	W	8-5	13	11	August	Smith		53-63	4th	9½
8-17	Bal.	W	7-6	11	12	Navarro	McDonald	Nunez	54-63	4th	9½
8-18	Bal.	W	2-1	5	9	Wegman	Milacki	Henry	55-63	4th	9½
8-20	At Tor.	L	1-3	9	9	Stottlemyre	Bosio	Henke	55-64	5th	10½
8-21	At Tor.	W	3-0	9	2	Machado	Key	Nunez	56-64	4th	9½
8-22	At Tor.	W	8-7	13	10	Ignasiak	Ward	Henry	57-64	4th	8½
8-23	At Oak.	W	13-4	16	5	Navarro	Stewart		58-64	4th	8½
8-24	At Oak.	W	7-0	7	9	Wegman	Slusarski		59-64	4th	7½
8-25	At Oak.	W	8-2	16	6	Bosio	Darling		60-64	4th	7½
8-26	At Sea.	L	4-5 (14)	12	9	Schooler	Henry		60-65	4th	8½
8-27	At Sea.	L	4-6	9	12	DeLucia	August	Jackson	60-66	4th	9½
8-28	At Sea.	L	6-7	11	9	Holman	Navarro	Swift	60-67	4th	10½
8-30	Cal.	W	6-2	12	6	Wegman	McCaskill		61-67	4th	10
8-31	Cal.	W	8-2	16	7	Lee	Grahe		62-67	4th	10
9-1	Cal.	W	3-1	7	4	Navarro	Finley		63-67	4th	9
9-2	Cal.	L	6-7	13	14	J. Abbott	August	Harvey	63-68	4th	10
9-3	Oak.	W	5-3	7	8	Nunez	Eckersley		64-68	4th	9
9-4	Oak.	W	2-0	9	4	Wegman	Darling	Henry	65-68	4th	9
9-6	At Cal.	L	1-2	4	6	Grahe	Bosio		65-69	4th	10½
9-7	At Cal.	L	0-1	5	3	Finley	Navarro	Harvey	65-70	4th	11½
9-8	At Cal.	L	0-1	6	8	J. Abbott	Plesac	Harvey	65-71	4th	12½
9-10	Cle.	L	2-5	8	7	Jones	Wegman	Olin	65-72	4th	12½
9-12	Det.	W	7-0	8	4	Bosio	Leiter		66-72	4th	11½
9-13	Det.	L	2-3	6	11	Gullickson	Lee	Kaiser	66-73	4th	12½
9-14	Det.	L	4-6	8	10	Aldred	Plesac		66-74	4th	13½
9-15	Det.	W	5-3	8	10	Wegman	Tanana	Henry	67-74	4th	12½
9-16	At N.Y.	W	5-4	10	13	Lee	Taylor	Henry	68-74	4th	11½
9-17	At N.Y.	W	2-0	7	2	Bosio	Perez		69-74	4th	10½
9-18	At N.Y.	L	1-2 (10)	7	5	Farr	Navarro		69-75	4th	11½

Date		Opp.	Res.	Score (inn.*)	Hits	Opp. hits	Winning pitcher	Losing pitcher	Save	Record	Pos.	GB
9-20		At Det.	W	8-5	10	6	Plesac	Leiter	Henry	70-75	4th	10½
9-21		At Det.	W	5-2	8	3	Wegman	Tanana	Henry	71-75	4th	9½
9-22		At Det.	W	9-5	14	7	Bosio	Terrell		72-75	4th	9½
9-23		N.Y.	L	8-9	12	11	Monteleone	Lee	Farr	72-76	4th	9½
9-24		N.Y.	W	5-4	8	13	Eldred	Plunk	Henry	73-76	4th	9½
9-25		N.Y.	L	6-8 (11)	11	16	Mills	August		73-77	4th	10½
9-26		N.Y.	W	6-2	10	6	Wegman	Taylor		74-77	4th	10
9-27		Bos.	W	7-5	8	8	Bosio	Morton	Machado	75-77	4th	10
9-28		Bos.	W	4-1	8	4	Navarro	Gardiner	Henry	76-77	4th	9
9-29		Bos.	W	5-4	8	7	Machado	Reardon	Henry	77-77	4th	9
9-30		Bos.	L	8-9	13	11	Lamp	Ignasiak	Petry	77-78	4th	9
10-1	(1)	At Cle.	W	11-0	18	7	Wegman	Nichols		78-78	4th	9
10-1	(2)	At Cle.	L	2-6	13	12	Otto	Holmes		78-79	4th	9½
10-2		At Cle.	W	11-4	15	11	Crim	Jones	Holmes	79-79	4th	9½
10-3		At Cle.	W	9-3	14	10	Navarro	Swindell		80-79	4th	9
10-4		At Bos.	W	3-2	7	9	Eldred	Gardiner	Henry	81-79	4th	9
10-5		At Bos.	W	13-4	14	11	Ignasiak	Bolton		82-79	4th	8
10-6		At Bos.	W	6-3	13	11	Machado	Clemens	Henry	83-79	4th	8

Monthly records: April (10-9), May (12-15), June (12-15), July (9-18), August (19-10), September (15-11), Oct. (6-1).

HIGHLIGHTS

High point: From August 4 to the end of the season, Milwaukee's 40-19 record was the best in baseball. However, it wasn't enough for Tom Trebelhorn to keep his managerial job. His contract was not renewed after the season.

Low point: Following 15-1 and 14-5 defeats to Texas, the Brewers owned a 43-60 record on August 3 (15 games out of first place), their low-water mark of the season.

Turning point: The Brewers were three games below .500 and 6½ games out of first place before the bullpen blew sizable leads on June 29 and 30 to New York. That began a six-game losing streak that took Milwaukee out of the American League East race.

Most valuable player: Designated hitter Paul Molitor. He led the majors in hits (216) and runs (133) while tying for the A.L. lead in triples (13) and finishing fifth in the A.L. batting race (.325 average).

Most valuable pitcher: Righthander Bill Wegman. He returned from a rehabilitation assignment in early May and recorded a 15-7 record in 28 starts. Wegman's 2.84 earned-run average ranked third in the league, and after the All-Star break he posted an 11-4 mark with a 2.39 ERA.

Most improved player: Outfielder Greg Vaughn. When Candy Maldonado broke his foot in the second game of the season, Vaughn took over and proceeded to lead the Brewers with 27 homers and 98 runs batted in. He also improved his defensive play.

Most pleasant surprise: Righthander Doug Henry. Called up July 14, Henry converted 15 of 16 save opportunities and finished with a 2-1 record and 1.00 ERA in 36 innings.

Biggest disappointment: First baseman Franklin Stubbs. A free-agent acquisition from Houston, Stubbs hit just .213 with 11 homers and 38 RBIs.

Key injuries: Third baseman Gary Sheffield was limited to 50 games because of shoulder and wrist problems. Teddy Higuera tore his left rotator cuff in

spring training. Ron Robinson was lost for the season with an elbow injury after just one start.

Notable: Darryl Hamilton set career highs in virtually every offensive category, recording a 19-game hitting streak in the process. . . . The Brewers' designated hitters topped the league by batting .300 with 19 homers and 86 RBIs.

—BOB BERGHAUS

RECORDS

1991 regular-season record: 83-79 (4th in A.L. East); 43-37 at home; 40-42 on road; 45-33 vs. East; 38-46 vs. West; 20-26 vs. LHP; 63-53 vs. RHP; 75-62 on grass; 8-17 on turf; 26-19 in daytime; 57-60 at night; 19-30 in one-run games; 5-12 in extra-inning games; 0-0-2 in doubleheaders.

Team record last five years: 416-394 (.514, ranks 6th in league in that span).

TEAM LEADERS

Batting average: Willie Randolph (.327).
At-bats: Paul Molitor (665).
Runs: Paul Molitor (133).
Hits: Paul Molitor (216).
Total bases: Paul Molitor (325).
Doubles: Paul Molitor (32).
Triples: Paul Molitor (13).
Home runs: Greg Vaughn (27).
Runs batted in: Greg Vaughn (98).
Stolen bases: Paul Molitor (19).
Slugging percentage: Paul Molitor (.489).
On-base percentage: Willie Randolph (.424).
Wins: Jaime Navarro, Bill Wegman (15).
Earned-run average: Bill Wegman (2.84).
Complete games: Jaime Navarro (10).
Shutouts: Jaime Navarro, Bill Wegman (2).
Saves: Doug Henry (15).
Innings pitched: Jaime Navarro (234).
Strikeouts: Chris Bosio (117).

GAMES BY POSITION

Catcher: B.J. Surhoff 127, Rick Dempsey 56.

First base: Franklin Stubbs 92, Paul Molitor 46, Greg Brock 25, George Canale 19, Rick Dempsey 1, Tim McIntosh 1.

Second base: Willie Randolph 121, Jim Gantner 59, Dale Sveum 2, B.J. Surhoff 1.

Third base: Jim Gantner 90, Gary Sheffield 43, Dale Sveum 38, B.J. Surhoff 5, Dante Bichette 1.

Shortstop: Bill Spiers 128, Dale Sveum 51.

Outfield: Greg Vaughn 135, Dante Bichette 127, Darryl Hamilton 117, Robin Yount 117, Candy Maldonado 24, Jim Olander 9, Tim McIntosh 4, Franklin Stubbs 4, Matias Carrillo 3, B.J. Surhoff 2, Bill Spiers 1.

Designated hitter: Paul Molitor 112, Robin Yount 13, Greg Vaughn 10, B.J. Surhoff 6, Gary Sheffield 5, Franklin Stubbs 4, Jim Olander 3, Dale Sveum 3, Tim McIntosh 2, Willie Randolph 2, Bill Spiers 2.

TOP 10 DRAFT CHOICES

1a. Kenny Henderson, RHP, Ringgold (Ga.) High School.
1b. Tyrone Hill, LHP, Yucaipa (Calif.) High School.
2. Judd Wilstead, RHP, Dixie High School, St. George, Utah.
3. None.
4. Mike Harris, 1B, University of Kentucky.
5. Nomar Garciaparra, SS, St. John Bosco High School, Whittier, Calif.
6. Cecil Rodrigues, OF, Indian River (Fla.) Community College.
7. Derek Wachter, OF, Iona College.
8. Mike Matheny, C, University of Michigan.
9. Bill Dobrolsky, C, Shippensburg University.
10. Jim Wilke, RHP, Triton (Ill.) Junior College.

MINNESOTA TWINS
AMERICAN LEAGUE WEST DIVISION

1992 SCHEDULE

APRIL

S	M	T	W	T	F	S
5	6 MIL	7	8 MIL	9 MIL	10 N TEX H	11 N TEX H
12 TEX H	13	14 N MIL H	15 N MIL H	16	17 N CHI	18 CHI
19 CHI	20 N SEA	21 N SEA	22 N SEA	23 SEA	24 N OAK H	25 N OAK H
26 OAK H	27 N BAL H	28 N BAL H	29 BAL H	30		

MAY

S	M	T	W	T	F	S
					1 N NY	2 NY
3 NY	4 BOS	5 N BOS	6 N BAL	7 N BAL	8 N CLE H	9 N CLE H
10 CLE H	11	12 N BOS H	13 N BOS H	14	15 N CLE	16 CLE
17 CLE	18 TOR	19 N TOR	20 N TOR	21	22 N DET	23 DET
24 N DET	25	26 N NY H	27 N NY H	28	29 N DET H	30 N DET H
31 DET H						

JUNE

S	M	T	W	T	F	S
	1 N TOR H	2 N TOR H	3 N TOR H	4 TEX	5 N TEX	6 N TEX
7 N TEX	8 N KC	9 N KC	10 N KC	11	12 N CHI H	13 N CHI H
14 CHI H	15 N KC H	16 N KC H	17 N KC H	18 KC	19 N SEA H	20 N SEA H
21 SEA H	22 N CAL H	23 N CAL H	24 CAL H	25 OAK	26 N OAK	27 OAK
28 OAK	29 N CAL	30 N CAL				

JULY

S	M	T	W	T	F	S
			1 CAL	2	3 N BAL H	4 BAL H
5 BAL H	6 N NY	7 N NY	8 N NY	9 N BAL	10 N BAL	11 N BAL
12 BAL	13	14 *	15	16 N BOS H	17 N BOS H	18 N BOS H
19 BOS H	20 N CLE H	21 N CLE H	22	23 N CLE H	24 N BOS	25 BOS
26 N BOS	27 N OAK H	28 N OAK H	29 N OAK H	30 MIL H	31 N MIL H	

AUGUST

S	M	T	W	T	F	S
						1 MIL H
2 MIL H	3	4 N CHI	5 N CHI	6 N CHI	7 N MIL	8 N MIL
9 MIL	10 N TEX H	11 N TEX H	12 N TEX H	13 N TEX H	14 N SEA	15 SEA
16 SEA	17	18 N CLE	19 N CLE	20 CLE	21 N TOR H	22 N TOR H
23 TOR H	24 N DET H	25 N DET H	26 N DET H	27 N NY H	28 N NY H	29 N NY H
30 NY H	31 N DET					

SEPTEMBER

S	M	T	W	T	F	S
		1 N DET	2 DET	3	4 N TOR	5 TOR
6 TOR	7	8 N SEA H	9 N SEA H	10	11 N CAL H	12 CAL H
13 CAL H	14 N OAK	15 N OAK H	16 N OAK	17 CAL	18 N CAL	19 N CAL
20 CAL	21	22 N TEX	23 N TEX	24	25 N KC H	26 N KC H
27 KC H	28 N CHI H	29 N CHI H	30 N CHI H			

OCTOBER

S	M	T	W	T	F	S
				1	2 N CHI H	3 N KC
4 KC	5	6	7	8	9	10

1992 SEASON

CLUB DIRECTORY

Owner
Carl R. Pohlad

President
Jerry Bell

Chairman of executive committee
Howard Fox

Directors
Donald E. Benson
Paul R. Christen
James O. Pohlad
Robert C. Pohlad
William M. Pohlad
Robert E. Woolley

Executive v.p., baseball operations/g.m.
Andy MacPhail

Vice president, player personnel
Terry Ryan

Vice president, marketing
Dave Moore

Director of finance
Kevin Mather

Director of minor leagues
Jim Rantz

Director of scouting
Larry Corrigan

Assistant general manager
Bill Smith

Director of media relations
Rob Antony

Traveling secretary
Remzi Kiratli

Club physicians
Dr. Leonard J. Michienzi
Dr. John Steubs

Scouts
Floyd Baker
Vernon Borning
Ellsworth Brown
Don Cassidy
Murray Cook
Gene DeBoer
Dan Durst
Cal Ermer
Marty Esposito
Vern Followell
Earl Frishman
Angelo Giuliani
Scott Groot
Joel Lepel
Bill Lohr
Kevin Murphy
Mike Radcliff
Clair Rierson
Eddie Robinson
Edwin Rodriguez
Mike Ruth
Jeff Schugel
Herb Stein
Ricky Taylor
Jerry Terrell
Brad Weitzel
Steve Williams
John Wilson

International scouts
Enrique Brito
Howard Norsetter
Johnny Sierra

SCHEDULE KEY

H—Home game.   *All-Star Game at San Diego/Jack Murphy Stadium.
N—Night game (any game starting after 5 p.m.).

SPRING TRAINING ROSTER

Manager—Tom Kelly (10).

Coaches—Terry Crowley (46), Ron Gardenhire (35), Rick Stelmaszek (43), Dick Such (42), Wayne Terwilliger (45).

No.	PITCHERS	B/T	Ht./Wt.	Born	1991 clubs
37	Abbott, Paul	R/R	6-3/193	9-15-67	Portland, Minnesota
38	Aguilera, Rick	R/R	6-5/205	12-31-61	Minnesota
23	Banks, Willie	R/R	6-1/190	2-27-69	Portland, Minnesota
17	Casian, Larry	R/L	6-0/170	10-28-65	Minnesota, Portland
40	Cross, Jesse	R/R	5-10/195	1-15-68	Knoxville
59	Edens, Tom	L/R	6-2/185	6-9-61	Portland, Minnesota
19	Erickson, Scott	R/R	6-4/225	2-2-68	Minnesota
41	Garces, Richard	R/R	6-0/215	5-18-71	Portland, Orlando
53	Guthrie, Mark	S/L	6-4/196	9-22-65	Minnesota
50	Kipper, Bob	R/L	6-2/185	7-8-64	Pittsburgh
21	Mahomes, Pat	R/R	6-1/175	8-9-70	Orlando, Portland
22	Neagle, Denny	L/L	6-4/209	9-13-68	Portland, Minnesota
54	Newman, Alan	L/L	6-6/212	10-2-69	Visalia, Orlando
36	Tapani, Kevin	R/R	6-0/187	2-18-64	Minnesota
20	Trombley, Mike	R/R	6-2/200	4-14-67	Orlando
30	Tsamis, George	R/L	6-2/175	6-14-67	Orlando, Portland
55	Wassenaar, Rob	R/R	6-2/200	4-28-65	Orlando, Portland
48	Wayne, Gary	L/L	6-3/200	11-30-62	Portland, Minnesota
39	West, David	L/L	6-6/231	9-1-64	Orlando, Portland, Minnesota
51	Willis, Carl	L/R	6-4/212	12-28-60	Portland, Minnesota

No.	CATCHERS	B/T	Ht./Wt.	Born	1991 clubs
12	Harper, Brian	R/R	6-2/205	10-16-59	Minnesota
16	Parks, Derek	R/R	6-0/205	9-29-68	Orlando
15	Webster, Lenny	R/R	5-9/192	2-10-65	Portland, Minnesota

No.	INFIELDERS	B/T	Ht./Wt.	Born	1991 clubs
7	Gagne, Greg	R/R	5-11/172	11-12-61	Minnesota
2	Garcia, Cheo	S/R	5-11/165	4-27-68	Orlando
4	Gilbert, Shawn	R/R	5-9/170	3-12-65	Orlando
14	Hrbek, Kent	L/R	6-4/262	5-21-60	Minnesota
27	Jorgensen, Terry	R/R	6-4/213	9-2-66	Portland
11	Knoblauch, Chuck	R/R	5-9/175	7-7-68	Minnesota
9	Larkin, Gene	S/R	6-3/199	10-24-62	Minnesota
31	Leius, Scott	R/R	6-3/207	9-24-65	Minnesota
13	Pagliarulo, Mike	L/R	6-2/195	3-15-60	Minnesota
18	Sorrento, Paul	L/R	6-2/223	11-17-65	Portland, Minnesota

No.	OUTFIELDERS	B/T	Ht./Wt.	Born	1991 clubs
1	Brown, Jarvis	R/R	5-7/177	3-26-67	Portland, Minnesota
26	Bruett, J.T.	L/L	5-11/175	10-8-67	Portland
25	Bush, Randy	L/L	6-1/190	10-5-58	Minnesota
44	Davis, Chili	S/R	6-3/219	1-17-60	Minnesota
24	Mack, Shane	R/R	6-0/190	12-7-63	Minnesota
5	Munoz, Pedro	R/R	5-10/208	9-19-68	Portland, Minnesota
34	Puckett, Kirby	R/R	5-8/226	3-14-61	Minnesota

BALLPARK INFORMATION

Ballpark (capacity, surface)
Hubert H. Humphrey Metrodome (55,883, artificial)

Address
501 Chicago Ave. South
Minneapolis, MN 55415

Business phone
612-375-1366

Ticket information
612-375-7444

Ticket prices
$14 (club level)
$12 (lower deck reserved)
$10 (upper deck reserved)
$7 (g.a., lower left field)
$4 (g.a., upper deck outfield)

Field dimensions (from home plate)
To left field at foul line, 343 feet
To center field, 408 feet
To right field at foul line, 327 feet

First game played
April 6, 1982 (Mariners 11, Twins 7)

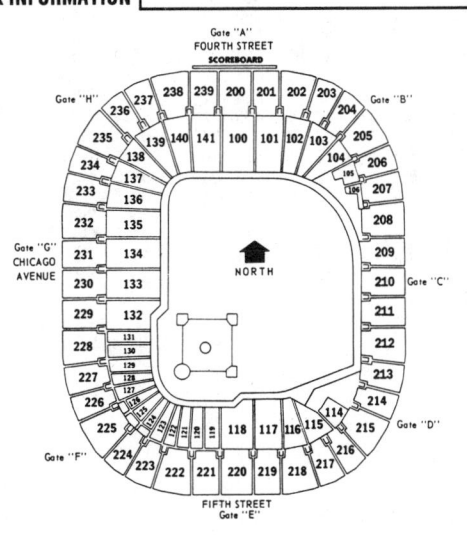

MINOR LEAGUE AFFILIATES

Class	Team	League	Manager
AAA	Portland	Pacific Coast	Scott Ullger
AA	Orlando	Southern	Phil Roof
A	Visalia	California	Steve Liddle
A	Kenosha	Midwest	Jim Dwyer
Rookie	Elizabethton	Appalachian	Jim Lemon
Rookie	Gulf Coast Twins	Gulf Coast	Dan Rohn

☐ BROADCAST INFORMATION ☐

Radio: WCCO-AM (830). Broadcasters: Herb Carneal, John Gordon.
TV: WCCO-TV (Channel 4). Broadcasters: Ted Robinson, Jim Kaat, Dick Bremer.
Cable TV: Midwest SportsChannel. Broadcasters: Ted Robinson, Jim Kaat, Dick Bremer.

SPRING TRAINING

Ballpark (city): Lee County Sports Complex (Fort Myers, Fla.).
Ticket information: 813-768-4200.

HISTORY

YEAR-BY-YEAR RECORDS

Year	Pos.	W	L	Pct.	*GB	Year	Pos.	W	L	Pct.	*GB
1901	6th	61	72	.459	20½	1949	8th	50	104	.325	47
1902	6th	61	75	.449	22	1950	5th	67	87	.435	31
1903	8th	43	94	.314	47½	1951	7th	62	92	.403	36
1904	8th	38	113	.251	55½	1952	5th	78	76	.506	17
1905	7th	64	87	.421	29½	1953	5th	76	76	.500	23½
1906	7th	55	95	.367	37½	1954	6th	66	88	.429	45
1907	8th	49	102	.325	43½	1955	8th	53	101	.344	43
1908	7th	67	85	.441	22½	1956	7th	59	95	.383	38
1909	8th	42	110	.276	56	1957	8th	55	99	.357	43
1910	7th	66	85	.437	36½	1958	8th	61	93	.396	31
1911	7th	64	90	.416	38½	1959	8th	63	91	.409	31
1912	2nd	91	61	.599	14	1960	5th	73	81	.474	24
1913	2nd	90	64	.584	6½	1961	7th	70	90	.438	38
1914	3rd	81	73	.526	19	1962	2nd	91	71	.562	5
1915	4th	85	68	.556	17	1963	3rd	91	70	.565	13
1916	7th	76	77	.497	14½	1964	T6th	79	83	.488	20
1917	5th	74	79	.484	25½	1965	1st	102	60	.630 +	7
1918	3rd	72	56	.563	4	1966	2nd	89	73	.549	9
1919	7th	56	84	.400	32	1967	T2nd	91	71	.562	1
1920	6th	68	84	.447	29	1968	7th	79	83	.488	24
1921	4th	80	73	.523	18	1969	1st†	97	65	.599 +	9
1922	6th	69	85	.448	25	1970	1st†	98	64	.605 +	9
1923	4th	75	78	.490	23½	1971	5th	74	86	.463	26½
1924	1st	92	62	.597 +	2	1972	3rd	77	77	.500	15½
1925	1st	96	55	.636 +	8½	1973	3rd	81	81	.500	13
1926	4th	81	69	.540	8	1974	3rd	82	80	.506	8
1927	3rd	85	69	.552	25	1975	4th	76	83	.478	20½
1928	4th	75	79	.487	26	1976	3rd	85	77	.525	5
1929	5th	71	81	.467	34	1977	4th	84	77	.522	17½
1930	2nd	94	60	.610	8	1978	4th	73	89	.451	19
1931	3rd	92	62	.597	16	1979	4th	82	80	.506	6
1932	3rd	93	61	.604	14	1980	3rd	77	84	.478	19½
1933	1st	99	53	.651 +	7	1981	7th/4th	41	68	.376	‡
1934	7th	66	86	.434	34	1982	7th	60	102	.370	33
1935	6th	67	86	.438	27	1983	T5th	70	92	.432	29
1936	4th	82	71	.536	20	1984	T2nd	81	81	.500	3
1937	6th	73	80	.477	28½	1985	T4th	77	85	.475	14
1938	5th	75	76	.497	23½	1986	6th	71	91	.438	21
1939	6th	65	87	.428	41½	1987	1st§	85	77	.525 +	2
1940	7th	64	90	.416	26	1988	2nd	91	71	.562	13
1941	T6th	70	84	.455	31	1989	5th	80	82	.494	19
1942	7th	62	89	.411	39½	1990	7th	74	88	.457	29
1943	2nd	84	69	.549	13½	1991	1st§	95	67	.586 +	8
1944	8th	64	90	.416	25						
1945	2nd	87	67	.565	1½						
1946	4th	76	78	.494	28						
1947	7th	64	90	.416	33						
1948	7th	56	97	.366	40						

*Games behind winner. †Lost Championship Series. ‡First half 17-39; second 24-29. §Won Championship Series.

MANAGERS

Name	Record	Years
Jimmy Manning	61-72	1901
Tom Loftus	104-169	'02-03
Patsy Donovan	38-113	1904
Jake Stahl	119-182	'05-06
Joe Cantillon	158-297	'07-09
Jimmy McAleer	130-175	'10-11
Clark Griffith	693-646	'12-20
George McBride	80-73	1921
Clyde Milan	69-85	1922
Donie Bush	75-78	1923
Bucky Harris	1336-1416	'24-28
		'35-42
		'50-54
Walter Johnson	350-264	'29-32
Joe Cronin	165-139	'33-34
Ossie Bluege	375-394	'43-47
Joe Kuhel	106-201	'48-49
Chuck Dressen	116-212	'55-57
Cookie Lavagetto	271-384	'57-61
Sam Mele	524-436	'61-67
Cal Ermer	145-129	'67-68
Billy Martin	97-65	1969
Bill Rigney	208-184	'70-72
Frank Quilici	280-287	'72-75
Gene Mauch	378-394	'76-80
Johnny Goryl	34-38	'80-81
Billy Gardner	268-353	'81-85
Ray Miller	109-130	'85-86
Tom Kelly	437-396	'86-91

DAY BY DAY

Date	Opp.	Res.	Score (inn.*)	Hits	Opp. hits	Winning pitcher	Losing pitcher	Save	Record	Pos.	GB
4-9	At Oak.	L	2-7	5	13	Stewart	Morris		0-1	T5th	1
4-10	At Oak.	W	4-1	6	4	Anderson	Welch	Aguilera	1-1	T4th	1
4-11	At Oak.	L	0-3	5	9	Slusarski	Erickson	Eckersley	1-2	5th	2
4-12	Cal.	W	6-0	10	7	Tapani	J. Abbott		2-2	5th	1½
4-13	Cal.	L	9-15	13	21	Bailes	Guthrie		2-3	5th	2½
4-14	Cal.	L	4-9	6	14	Finley	Morris		2-4	5th	3
4-15	At Sea.	L	4-8	7	12	Johnson	Anderson		2-5	5th	4
4-16	At Sea.	L	0-3	5	9	Holman	Erickson		2-6	T6th	5
4-17	At Sea.	L	3-4 (11)	10	10	Jackson	Aguilera		2-7	7th	6
4-19	At Cal.	L	0-2	2	7	Finley	Morris		2-8	7th	5½
4-20	At Cal.	L	1-2	3	4	McCaskill	Anderson	Harvey	2-9	7th	5½
4-21	At Cal.	W	4-3	8	8	Erickson	Eichhorn	Aguilera	3-9	7th	5
4-22	Oak.	W	3-2	10	8	Bedrosian	Klink	Aguilera	4-9	7th	5
4-23	Oak.	L	5-7	11	12	Dressendorfer	Guthrie	Eckersley	4-10	7th	6
4-24	Oak.	W	7-4	13	7	Morris	Stewart	Aguilera	5-10	7th	5
4-25	Sea.	W	4-3 (10)	13	8	Bedrosian	Jackson		6-10	7th	4½
4-26	Sea.	W	6-0	15	5	Erickson	Johnson		7-10	7th	3½
4-27	Sea.	W	7-2	10	6	Tapani	Holman		8-10	T6th	3½
4-28	Sea.	W	8-2	11	10	Morris	Bankhead		9-10	T3rd	3½
4-30	Bos.	L	5-7	9	10	Gray	Bedrosian	Reardon	9-11	6th	4
5-1	Bos.	W	1-0	4	2	Erickson	Gray		10-11	T4th	4
5-2	At Mil.	L	1-5	5	9	Brown	Tapani	Crim	10-12	T5th	4½
5-3	At Mil.	L	5-6	10	9	Navarro	Aguilera	Nunez	10-13	5th	5½
5-4	At Mil.	W	7-4	15	7	Guthrie	Bosio	Bedrosian	11-13	5th	4½
5-5	At Mil.	W	5-2 (10)	9	8	Aguilera	Nunez		12-13	T5th	3½
5-7	At Bos.	W	9-3	13	7	Erickson	Harris		13-13	T5th	3½
5-8	At Bos.	L	3-8	5	12	Clemens	Morris		13-14	T5th	4½
5-9	Det.	L	0-3	7	5	Petry	Tapani	Gibson	13-15	6th	5
5-10	Det.	W	5-2	12	8	Guthrie	Terrell	Aguilera	14-15	5th	4
5-11	Det.	W	5-4	12	8	Willis	Henneman	Aguilera	15-15	5th	4
5-12	Det.	W	8-3	16	8	Erickson	Gullickson		16-15	4th	3
5-14	Mil.	W	5-1	13	2	Morris	Navarro		17-15	3rd	1½
5-15	Mil.	L	2-4	7	9	Bosio	Tapani	Plesac	17-16	4th	2½
5-16	Mil.	L	3-6	9	13	Wegman	Anderson	Holmes	17-17	5th	3½
5-17	At Det.	W	8-1	13	7	Erickson	Gullickson	Bedrosian	18-17	5th	3
5-18	At Det.	W	4-1	8	6	Guthrie	Tanana	Aguilera	19-17	4th	3
5-19	At Det.	L	3-8	8	8	Petry	Morris		19-18	6th	3½
5-21	Tex.	L	5-6	6	10	Witt	Tapani	Russell	19-19	5th	3½
5-22	Tex.	L	2-5 (12)	10	12	Alexander	Willis	Russell	19-20	6th	4
5-23	Tex.	L	6-10 (11)	17	14	Russell	Bedrosian		19-21	6th	4½
5-24	K.C.	W	3-2	9	5	Morris	S. Davis	Aguilera	20-21	6th	4½
5-25	K.C.	L	2-11	11	17	Gubicza	Guthrie		20-22	6th	5½
5-26	K.C.	L	1-5	8	11	Saberhagen	Tapani		20-23	6th	6½
5-27	At Tex.	L	4-11	11	15	Brown	Anderson		20-24	6th	7½
5-28	At Tex.	W	3-0	9	7	Erickson	Guzman	Aguilera	21-24	6th	6½
5-29	At Tex.	W	9-1	10	4	Morris	Ryan		22-24	5th	5½
5-30	At K.C.	W	4-2	6	8	Guthrie	Gubicza	Aguilera	23-24	5th	5½
5-31	At K.C.	L	1-4	4	9	Saberhagen	Tapani		23-25	5th	5½
6-1	At K.C.	W	8-4	12	9	Anderson	Appier		24-25	5th	5½
6-2	At K.C.	W	4-1	11	5	Erickson	Gordon	Aguilera	25-25	5th	4½
6-3	Bal.	W	3-2	8	8	Morris	Robinson	Aguilera	26-25	5th	4½
6-4	Bal.	W	4-3 (10)	13	11	Willis	Olson		27-25	5th	4½
6-5	Bal.	W	4-3	7	9	Tapani	Mesa	Aguilera	28-25	5th	4½
6-7	Cle.	W	2-0	5	2	Anderson	Candiotti	Aguilera	29-25	4th	4
6-8	Cle.	W	2-1	8	9	Erickson	Nagy	Aguilera	30-25	4th	4
6-9	Cle.	W	9-2	12	6	Morris	Nichols		31-25	3rd	3
6-10	Cle.	W	8-5	14	13	Abbott	King	Aguilera	32-25	3rd	3
6-11	N.Y.	W	5-3	10	6	Tapani	Habyan	Aguilera	33-25	3rd	2
6-12	N.Y.	W	6-3	8	10	Anderson	Johnson	Bedrosian	34-25	2nd	2
6-13	N.Y.	W	10-3	13	12	Erickson	Witt		35-25	2nd	1½
6-14	At Cle.	W	7-0	11	4	Morris	Shaw		36-25	2nd	1½
6-15	At Cle.	W	11-7	15	9	Abbott	Mutis		37-25	2nd	½
6-16	At Cle.	W	4-2 (10)	9	7	Aguilera	Hillegas		38-25	1st	+½
6-17	At Bal.	L	5-6	14	12	Williamson	Aguilera		38-26	1st	+½
6-18	At Bal.	W	9-2	12	4	Erickson	Smith	Willis	39-26	1st	+1½
6-19	At Bal.	W	8-4	9	6	Morris	Olson		40-26	1st	+1½
6-21	At N.Y.	W	5-4	11	11	Guthrie	Sanderson	Aguilera	41-26	1st	+3
6-22	At N.Y.	W	4-3	6	9	Tapani	Taylor	Aguilera	42-26	1st	+4
6-23	At N.Y.	L	2-11	7	16	Kamieniecki	Anderson		42-27	1st	+3
6-24	At N.Y.	W	5-0	6	2	Erickson	Johnson		43-27	1st	+3½

MINNESOTA TWINS

1992 SEASON

MINNESOTA TWINS

Date	Opp.	Res.	Score (inn.*)	Hits	Opp. hits	Winning pitcher	Losing pitcher	Save	Record	Pos.	GB
6-25	Tor.	W	8-6	12	10	Morris	Stottlemyre	Aguilera	44-27	1st	+4½
6-26	Tor.	L	2-5	8	13	Wells	Guthrie	Henke	44-28	1st	+3½
6-27	Tor.	L	0-1	3	4	Guzman	Tapani	Henke	44-29	1st	+3
6-28	Chi.	L	2-4	8	8	Hough	Anderson	Thigpen	44-30	1st	+2
6-29	Chi.	L	4-8	7	16	Hibbard	Erickson		44-31	1st	+2
6-30	Chi.	W	3-0	9	6	Morris	McDowell		45-31	1st	+3
7-1	Chi.	L	4-5 (10)	10	6	Thigpen	Willis		45-32	1st	+2
7-2	At Tor.	L	3-4	4	16	Ward	Leach		45-33	1st	+1
7-3	At Tor.	L	0-4	6	12	Candiotti	Anderson		45-34	2nd	...
7-4	At Tor.	W	1-0	8	3	West	Key	Aguilera	46-34	1st	+1
7-5	At Chi.	L	2-4	7	7	McDowell	Morris	Thigpen	46-35	1st	+1
7-6	At Chi.	W	5-4	8	5	Willis	Radinsky	Aguilera	47-35	1st	+1
7-7	At Chi.	L	3-4	6	8	Patterson	Guthrie	Thigpen	47-36	2nd	...
7-11	Bos.	W	7-3	8	13	Willis	Harris		48-36	1st	+1
7-12	Bos.	W	5-4	11	6	Abbott	Clemens	Aguilera	49-36	1st	+2
7-13	Bos.	W	3-1	10	5	Morris	Morton	Aguilera	50-36	1st	+3
7-14	Bos.	L	3-5	8	11	Hesketh	West	Reardon	50-37	1st	+2
7-15	At Mil.	W	11-7	14	12	Guthrie	Hunter	Bedrosian	51-37	1st	+3
7-16	At Mil.	L	3-4	10	10	Henry	Aguilera		51-38	1st	+2½
7-18	At Bos.	W	11-3	12	5	Morris	Morton		52-38	1st	+4
7-19	At Bos.	W	3-2 (11)	14	10	Bedrosian	Harris	Aguilera	53-38	1st	+4½
7-20	At Bos.	W	5-0	8	9	Erickson	Gardiner	Guthrie	54-38	1st	+4½
7-21	At Bos.	W	14-1	18	5	Tapani	Bolton		55-38	1st	+5½
7-23	At Det.	L	3-6	8	10	Tanana	Anderson	Henneman	55-39	1st	+4
7-24	At Det.	L	3-6	8	11	Gullickson	West	Henneman	55-40	1st	+4
7-25	At Det.	W	9-3	14	9	Erickson	Aldred	Bedrosian	56-40	1st	+4
7-26	Mil.	W	6-3	10	5	Tapani	Holmes	Aguilera	57-40	1st	+4½
7-27	Mil.	W	7-4	11	11	Willis	Wegman		58-40	1st	+4
7-28	Mil.	L	2-11	10	22	Navarro	Morris		58-41	1st	+3
7-29	Det.	W	6-3	14	6	West	Gullickson	Aguilera	59-41	1st	+3
7-30	Det.	W	9-7	17	12	Willis	Cerutti		60-41	1st	+3
7-31	At N.Y.	W	12-3	20	8	Tapani	Sanderson		61-41	1st	+3
8-1	At N.Y.	L	3-8	9	9	Cadaret	Abbott		61-42	1st	+2
8-2	At Oak.	L	1-3	7	5	Welch	Morris		61-43	1st	+2
8-3	At Oak.	W	8-6	13	10	Bedrosian	Klink	Aguilera	62-43	1st	+3
8-4	At Oak.	W	6-2	11	6	Erickson	Stewart	Willis	63-43	1st	+3
8-5	At Cal.	W	7-4	9	8	Tapani	Grahe	Aguilera	64-43	1st	+3
8-6	At Cal.	W	7-4	9	7	Banks	Finley		65-43	1st	+3
8-7	At Cal.	L	1-8	3	9	J. Abbott	Morris		65-44	1st	+2½
8-9	At Sea.	W	5-2	9	7	West	Johnson	Aguilera	66-44	1st	+2
8-10	At Sea.	L	0-8	9	11	Hanson	Erickson		66-45	1st	+2
8-11	At Sea.	W	5-2	9	4	Tapani	Krueger		67-45	1st	+1
8-12	Cal.	W	4-3	9	7	Morris	Beasley	Aguilera	68-45	1st	+2
8-13	Cal.	L	3-8	6	12	J. Abbott	Banks	Harvey	68-46	1st	+2½
8-14	Cal.	L	4-7	10	8	McCaskill	West	Harvey	68-47	1st	+1½
8-15	Cal.	L	1-9	6	11	Langston	Erickson		68-48	1st	+1½
8-16	Oak.	W	5-4 (12)	14	9	Aguilera	Nelson		69-48	1st	+2½
8-17	Oak.	W	12-4	16	8	Morris	Welch		70-48	1st	+3½
8-18	Oak.	W	6-4	11	4	Willis	Honeycutt	Aguilera	71-48	1st	+3½
8-19	Oak.	L	7-8	13	11	Klink	Bedrosian	Eckersley	71-49	1st	+3½
8-20	Sea.	W	10-5	12	9	Erickson	Hanson	Guthrie	72-49	1st	+4½
8-21	Sea.	W	9-1	12	6	Tapani	Krueger		73-49	1st	+5½
8-22	Sea.	W	5-4 (10)	14	12	Aguilera	Schooler		74-49	1st	+6
8-23	At Bal.	L	4-5	10	9	Olson	Willis		74-50	1st	+6
8-24	At Bal.	W	5-2	8	5	Bedroaisn	Flanagan	Aguilera	75-50	1st	+7
8-25	At Bal.	L	3-7	7	9	Mussina	Erickson	Frohwirth	75-51	1st	+7
8-26	At Cle.	W	5-3	10	7	Tapani	Otto	Aguilera	76-51	1st	+8
8-27	At Cle.	L	1-2	6	11	Swindell	Morris	Olin	76-52	1st	+8
8-28	At Cle.	W	4-2	13	7	West	King	Aguilera	77-52	1st	+8
8-30	Bal.	L	5-11	15	17	Milacki	Edens		77-53	1st	+7
8-31	Bal.	W	5-2	11	7	Tapani	Mussina	Aguilera	78-53	1st	+7
9-1	Bal.	W	14-3	16	7	Morris	Rhodes		79-53	1st	+8
9-2	Cle.	W	9-3	8	9	Erickson	King	Aguilera	80-53	1st	+8½
9-4	Cle.	L	4-8	10	12	Blair	West	Hillegas	80-54	1st	+8
9-6	N.Y.	W	3-1	6	7	Tapani	Taylor	Aguilera	81-54	1st	+7½
9-7	N.Y.	W	3-2 (10)	13	5	Willis	Guetterman		82-54	1st	+7½
9-8	N.Y.	W	6-5	12	10	Erickson	Johnson	Bedrosian	83-54	1st	+8½
9-9	At K.C.	W	10-4	14	9	Edens	Boddicker	Wayne	84-54	1st	+8½
9-10	At K.C.	W	7-2	12	8	Anderson	Gubicza	Aguilera	85-54	1st	+8½
9-11	At K.C.	L	1-4	6	7	M. Davis	Tapani	Montgomery	85-55	1st	+8½
9-12	At Tex.	L	3-4	5	5	Ryan	Morris	Russell	85-56	1st	+8½
9-13	At Tex.	W	7-3 (10)	9	8	Leach	Rogers		86-56	1st	+8½
9-14	At Tex.	L	0-3	6	10	Boyd	Edens	Rogers	86-57	1st	+8½
9-15	At Tex.	L	2-4	6	8	Guzman	Anderson	Russell	86-58	1st	+7½

Date	Opp.	Res.	Score (inn.*)	Hits	Opp. hits	Winning pitcher	Losing pitcher	Save	Record	Pos.	GB
9-16	K.C.	W	9-0	11	3	Tapani	Gubicza		87-58	1st	+8
9-17	K.C.	L	1-4	6	9	Saberhagen	Morris	Montgomery	87-59	1st	+7
9-18	K.C.	L	4-10	7	14	Aquino	Erickson		87-60	1st	+6
9-20	Tex.	W	6-4	13	10	Wayne	Rosenthal	Aguilera	88-60	1st	+6
9-21	Tex.	W	8-4	12	8	Tapani	Guzman		89-60	1st	+7
9-22	Tex.	W	9-4	12	8	Morris	Fajardo		90-60	1st	+8
9-24	Chi.	W	9-2	12	1	Erickson	McDowell		91-60	1st	+9
9-25	Chi.	L	1-6	8	7	Fernandez	Anderson		91-61	1st	+8
9-27	At Tor.	L	2-7	3	9	Guzman	Tapani		91-62	1st	+8
9-28	At Tor.	W	5-0	10	6	Morris	Candiotti		92-62	1st	+8
9-29	At Tor.	L	1-2	6	5	Stottlemyre	Erickson	Ward	92-63	1st	+8
9-30	At Chi.	W	8-3	9	8	Edens	Fernandez		93-63	1st	+9
10-1	At Chi.	W	3-2	7	9	Guthrie	Perez	Aguilera	94-63	1st	+10
10-3 (1)	At Chi.	L	2-3 (10)	7	11	Radinsky	Aguilera		94-64	1st	+9
10-3 (2)	At Chi.	L	12-13 (12)	16	24	Drahman	Leach		94-65	1st	+8
10-4	Tor.	L	1-4	6	11	Stottlemyre	Neagle	Ward	94-66	1st	+8
10-5	Tor.	W	3-1	11	5	Erickson	Guzman	Aguilera	95-66	1st	+8
10-6	Tor.	L	2-3 (10)	6	6	Weathers	Anderson	Ward	95-67	1st	+8

Monthly records: April (9-11), May (14-14), June (22-6), July (16-10), August (17-12), September (15-10), Oct. (2-4).

HIGHLIGHTS

High point: The Twins won a club-record 15 straight games from June 1 through June 16. Minnesota jumped from fifth place (5½ games out of first place) to first (half-game lead) in the process. The Twins never were more than percentage points out of first place thereafter en route to winning their second world title in five seasons.

Low point: Forced to make two West Coast trips in the season's first two weeks, the Twins started 2-9.

Turning point: Entering their game in Texas on May 28, the Twins' 20-24 record relegated them to sixth place in the American League West, 7½ games out of first. But righthander Scott Erickson promised to end the Rangers' 14-game winning streak, and did. The 3-0 victory began a 22-2 run that gave the Twins control of the division.

Most valuable player: Designated hitter Chili Davis. By the end of June, the free-agent acquisition had 19 homers and 51 runs batted in. Though he cooled in the second half, Davis finished with 29 homers and 93 RBIs.

Most valuable pitcher: Righthander Jack Morris. He pitched 246⅔ innings and won 18 games. Morris also was the MVP of the World Series, throwing 10 shutout innings in an inspirational 1-0 victory in Game 7.

Most improved player: Third baseman Scott Leius. He moved to third base late in spring training and was the final player to make the roster. He proceeded to hit .286 while platooning with Mike Pagliarulo.

Most pleasant surprise: Second baseman Chuck Knoblauch. He jumped from Class AA and hit .281 en route to winning A.L. Rookie of the Year honors.

Biggest disappointment: Lefthander David West. He won only four games and finished the year in the bullpen. West still has not solved his control problems.

Key injuries: West was on the disabled list from the start of the season through July 2. Junior Ortiz sprained an ankle and missed the first two weeks of June. Erickson went on the D.L. July 2 with a strained elbow, an injury that would plague him for most of July and August. Dan Gladden missed four weeks with a strained abdominal muscle.

Notable: Tom Kelly was named the A.L. Manager of the Year. . . . Greg Gagne's 76-game errorless streak was the second-longest in A.L. history among shortstops.

— JEFF LENIHAN

RECORDS

1991 regular-season record: 95-67 (1st in A.L. West); 51-30 at home; 44-37 on road; 55-29 vs. East; 40-38 vs. West; 26-16 vs. LHP; 69-51 vs. RHP; 35-27 on grass; 60-40 on turf; 26-20 in day-time; 69-47 at night; 22-18 in one-run games; 9-7 in extra-inning games; 0-1-0 in doubleheaders.

1991 postseason record: Defeated Blue Jays, 4 games to 1, in A.L. playoffs; defeated Braves, 4 games to 3, in World Series.

Team record last five years: 425-385 (.525, ranks 3rd in league in that span).

TEAM LEADERS

Batting average: Kirby Puckett (.319).
At-bats: Kirby Puckett (611).
Runs: Kirby Puckett (92).
Hits: Kirby Puckett (195).
Total bases: Kirby Puckett (281).
Doubles: Chili Davis (34).
Triples: Dan Gladden (9).
Home runs: Chili Davis (29).
Runs batted in: Chili Davis (93).
Stolen bases: Chuck Knoblauch (25).
Slugging percentage: Chili Davis (.507).
On-base percentage: Chili Davis (.385).
Wins: Scott Erickson (20).
Earned-run average: Kevin Tapani (2.99).
Complete games: Jack Morris (10).
Shutouts: Scott Erickson (3).
Saves: Rick Aguilera (42).
Innings pitched: Jack Morris (246⅔).
Strikeouts: Jack Morris (163).

GAMES BY POSITION

Catcher: Brian Harper 119, Junior Ortiz 60, Lenny Webster 17.
First base: Kent Hrbek 128, Gene Larkin 39, Paul Sorrento 13, Randy Bush 12, Brian Harper 1, Al Newman 1.
Second base: Chuck Knoblauch 148, Al Newman 35, Gene Larkin 1, Mike Pagliarulo 1.
Third base: Mike Pagliarulo 118, Scott Leius 79, Al Newman 35, Gene Larkin 1.
Shortstop: Greg Gagne 137, Al Newman 55, Scott Leius 19, Chuck Knoblauch 2.
Outfield: Kirby Puckett 152, Shane Mack 140, Dan Gladden 126, Gene Larkin 47, Pedro Munoz 44, Randy Bush 38, Jarvis Brown 32, Carmen Castillo 4, Chili Davis 2, Scott Leius 2, Brian Harper 1, Al Newman 1.
Designated hitter: Chili Davis 150, Randy Bush 10, Jarvis Brown 4, Gene Larkin 4, Al Newman 3, Carmen Castillo 2, Brian Harper 2, Pedro Munoz 2, Paul Sorrento 2, Greg Gagne 1, Shane Mack 1.

TOP 10 DRAFT CHOICES

1a. David McCarty, 1B, Stanford University.
1b. Scott Stahoviak, 3B, Creighton University.
2. Mike Durant, C, Ohio State University.
3. Keith Legree, SS, Statesboro (Ga.) High School.
4. Brett Roberts, RHP, Morehead State University.
5. Shawn Miller, RHP, Beyer High School, Modesto, Calif.
6. Pedro Grifol, C, Florida State University.
7. Latroy Hawkins, RHP, West Side High School, Gary, Ind.
8. Brad Radke, RHP, Jesuit High School, Tampa.
9. Neil Stevens, RHP/C, Beekmantown Central High School, Plattsburg, N.Y.
10. Anthony Banks, OF, Hoover High School, San Diego.

NEW YORK YANKEES
AMERICAN LEAGUE EAST DIVISION

1992 SCHEDULE

APRIL
S	M	T	W	T	F	S
5	6	7 BOS H	8	9 N BOS H	10 N DET	11 DET
12 DET	13 N TOR	14 N TOR	15 N TOR	16 TOR	17 N CLE H	18 CLE H
19 CLE H	20 N CLE H	21 N CHI	22 N CHI	23	24 N BAL H	25 BAL H
26 BAL H	27 N TEX H	28 N TEX H	29 N TEX H	30		

MAY
S	M	T	W	T	F	S
					1 N MIN H	2 MIN H
3 MIN H	4 N SEA	5 N SEA	6 N CAL	7 N CAL	8 N OAK	9 OAK
10 OAK	11	12 N SEA H	13 N SEA H	14	15 N OAK H	16 OAK H
17 OAK H	18 N CAL H	19 N CAL H	20 N CAL H	21	22 N MIL H	23 MIL H
24 MIL H	25 MIL	26 N MIN	27 MIN	28	29 N MIL	30 N MIL
31 MIL						

JUNE
S	M	T	W	T	F	S
	1 N TEX	2 N TEX	3 N TEX	4 N DET H	5 N DET H	6 N DET H
7 DET H	8 N TOR H	9 N TOR H	10 N TOR H	11	12 N CLE	13 CLE
14 CLE	15 N BOS	16 N BOS	17 N BOS	18 N BOS	19 N BAL	20 N BAL
21 BAL	22 BAL	23 N KC	24 N KC	25 KC	26 N CHI H	27 CHI H
28 CHI H	29 N KC H	30 N KC H				

JULY
S	M	T	W	T	F	S
			1 N KC H	2	3 N TEX	4 N TEX
5 TEX	6 N MIN H	7 N MIN H	8 N MIN H	9 N SEA H	10 N SEA H	11 SEA H
12 SEA H	13	14*	15	16 N CAL	17 N CAL	18 N CAL
19 CAL	20 OAK	21 N OAK	22 OAK	23	24 N SEA	25 N SEA
26 SEA	27	28 N BAL H	29 N BAL H	30 N BAL H	31 TOR	

AUGUST
S	M	T	W	T	F	S
						1 TOR
2 TOR	3 N CLE H	4 N CLE H	5 N CLE H	6 BOS H	7 N BOS H	8 N BOS H
9 BOS H	10 N DET	11 N DET	12 N DET	13	14 N CHI	15 N CHI
16 CHI	17 N OAK H	18 N OAK H	19 N OAK H	20 N CAL H	21 N CAL H	22 N CAL H
23 CAL H	24 N MIL H	25 N MIL H	26 N MIL H	27 N MIN	28 N MIN	29 N MIN
30 MIN	31 N MIL					

SEPTEMBER
S	M	T	W	T	F	S
		1 N MIL	2 N MIL	3	4 N TEX H	5 TEX H
6 TEX H	7 N BAL	8 N BAL	9 N BAL	10	11 N KC	12 KC
13 KC	14 N CHI H	15 N CHI H	16 N CHI H	17	18 N KC H	19 N KC H
20 KC	21	22 N DET H	23 N DET H	24 DET H	25 N TOR H	26 TOR H
27 TOR H	28 N CLE	29 N CLE	30 N CLE			

OCTOBER
S	M	T	W	T	F	S
				1 CLE	2 N BOS	3 BOS
4 BOS	5	6	7	8	9	10

1992 SEASON

CLUB DIRECTORY

Principal owner
George M. Steinbrenner
Managing general partner
Robert E. Nederlander
Limited partners
Harold M. Bowman
Daniel M. Crown
James S. Crown
Lester Crown
Michael Friedman
Marvin Goldklang
Barry Halper
Harvey Leighton
Daniel McCarthy
Harry Nederlander
James Nederlander
William Rose Sr.
Edward Rosenthal
Jack Satter
Joan Z. Steinbrenner
Charlotte Witkind
Richard Witkind
Executive v.p. and chief operating officer
Leonard L. Kleinman
Vice president
Joseph Molloy
Senior vice president
Arthur Richman
Vice president and general manager
Gene Michael
Vice president, chief of operations
John C. Lawn
Vice president, marketing
John C. Fugazy
Vice president, community relations
Richard Kraft
Vice president
Ed Weaver
V.p., general counsel and secretary
David Sussman
Vice president, ticket operations
Frank Swaine
V.p., player development and scouting
Brian Sabean
Assistant general manager
Bill Bergesch
Director of minor league operations
Mitch Lukevics
Director of scouting
Bill Livesey
Traveling secretary
David Szen
Director of stadium operations
Timothy D. Hassett
Executive director of ticket operations
Jeff Kline
Director of media relations and publicity
Jeff Idelson

Asst. dir. of media relations and publicity
Brian Walker
Team physician
Dr. Stuart Hershon
Trainers
Gene Monahan
Steve Donohue
Scouting cross-checkers
Bill Livesey
Jack Gillis
Stan Saleski
Don Lindeberg
Area supervisor scouts
Fernando Arango
Mark Batchko
Joe DiCarlo
Lee Elder
Bill Geivett
Joel Grampietro
Dick Groch
Tim Kelly
Carl Moesche
Greg Orr
Joe Robison
Rudy Santin
Bill Schmidt
Jeff Taylor
Paul Turco
Leon Wurth
Associate scouts
Jack Carroll
Kermit Daimont
Ray Griffin
Bruce King
Special assignment scouts
Walt Dixon
Jack Llewellyn
Jim Naples
Coordinator of Canadian scouting
Dick Groch
Director of Latin American scouting
Herb Raybourn
Canadian/Latin American scouts
Luis Arroyo
Philip Elhage
Karl Heron
Pedro Ithier
Juan Joa
Leo Lacle
Raul Ortega
Atanacio Mendez
Arquimedes Rojas
Bruce Ross
Bill Saunders
Marc Pickard
Mike LaBossiere
Dale Tilleman
Dennis Springenatic

SCHEDULE KEY

H—Home game.   *All-Star Game at San Diego/Jack Murphy Stadium.
N—Night game (any game starting after 5 p.m.).

SPRING TRAINING ROSTER

Manager—Buck Showalter (11).

Coaches—Clete Boyer (47), Tony Cloninger (40), Mark Connor (52), Frank Howard (46), Monk Meyer (48), Ed Napoleon (50).

No.	PITCHERS	B/T	Ht./Wt.	Born	1991 clubs
25	Cadaret, Greg	L/L	6-3/215	2-27-62	New York AL
26	Farr, Steve	R/R	5-11/206	12-12-56	New York AL
49	Gardella, Mike	L/L	5-10/195	1-18-67	Albany
35	Guetterman, Lee	L/L	6-8/235	11-22-58	New York AL
42	Habyan, John	R/R	6-2/191	1-29-64	New York AL
57	Howe, Steve	L/L	5-11/196	3-10-58	Columbus, New York AL
43	Johnson, Jeff	R/L	6-3/206	8-4-66	Columbus, New York AL
33	Kamieniecki, Scott	R/R	6-0/197	4-19-64	Columbus, New York AL
54	Leary, Tim	R/R	6-3/218	12-23-58	New York AL
70	Martel, Ed	R/R	6-1/190	3-2-69	Albany
45	Mills, Alan	R/R	6-1/190	10-18-66	Columbus, New York AL
22	Monteleone, Rich	R/R	6-2/236	3-22-63	Columbus, New York AL
61	Munoz, Roberto	R/R	6-7/210	3-3-68	Ft. Lauderdale, Columbus
	Perez, Melido	R/R	6-4/180	2-15-66	Chicago AL
34	Perez, Pascual	R/R	6-3/184	5-17-57	New York AL
21	Sanderson, Scott	R/R	6-5/192	7-22-56	New York AL
59	Smith, Willie	R/R	6-6/240	8-27-67	Albany
68	Springer, Russ	R/R	6-4/195	11-7-68	Ft. Lauderdale, Albany
67	Stanford, Larry	R/R	6-3/205	9-24-67	Albany
41	Taylor, Wade	R/R	6-1/193	10-19-65	Columbus, New York AL

No.	CATCHERS	B/T	Ht./Wt.	Born	1991 clubs
53	Ausmus, Brad	R/R	5-11/185	4-14-69	Prince William, Albany
12	Leyritz, Jim	R/R	6-0/190	12-27-63	Columbus (O.), New York AL
38	Nokes, Matt	L/R	6-1/198	10-31-63	New York AL
44	Ramos, John	R/R	6-0/190	8-6-65	Columbus (O.), New York AL

No.	INFIELDERS	B/T	Ht./Wt.	Born	1991 clubs
20	Espinoza, Alvaro	R/R	6-0/190	2-19-62	New York AL
	Gallego, Mike	R/R	5-8/160	10-31-60	Oakland
14	Kelly, Pat	R/R	6-0/180	10-14-67	Columbus (O.), New York AL
24	Maas, Kevin	L/L	6-3/209	1-20-65	New York AL
23	Mattingly, Don	L/L	6-0/192	4-20-61	New York AL
63	Silvestri, Dave	R/R	6-0/180	9-29-67	Albany
71	Snow, J.T.	S/L	6-2/202	2-26-68	Albany
18	Velarde, Randy	R/R	6-0/190	11-24-62	New York AL

No.	OUTFIELDERS	B/T	Ht./Wt.	Born	1991 clubs
29	Barfield, Jesse	R/R	6-1/201	10-29-59	New York AL
27	Hall, Mel	L/L	6-1/214	9-16-60	New York AL
60	Humphreys, Mike	R/R	6-0/185	4-10-67	Columbus (O.), New York AL
39	Kelly, Roberto	R/R	6-2/192	10-1-64	New York AL
31	Meulens, Hensley	R/R	6-3/212	6-23-67	New York AL
	Tartabull, Danny	R/R	6-1/210	10-30-62	Kansas City
51	Williams, Bernie	S/R	6-2/196	9-13-68	Columbus (O.), New York AL
62	Williams, Gerald	R/R	6-2/190	8-10-66	Albany, Columbus (O.)

BALLPARK INFORMATION

Ballpark (capacity, surface)
Yankee Stadium (57,545, grass)

Address
Yankee Stadium
E. 161 St. and River Ave.
Bronx, NY 10451

Business phone
212-293-4300

Ticket information
212-293-6000

Ticket prices
$14.50 (lower and loge box seats)
$13.50 (tier box seats)
$12.50 (lower reserves)
$9.50 (tier reserves)
$1 (senior citizens)
$5.50 (bleachers)

Field dimensions (from home plate)
To left field at foul line, 312 feet
To center field, 410 feet
To right field at foul line, 310 feet

First game played
April 18, 1923 (Yankees 4, Red Sox 1)

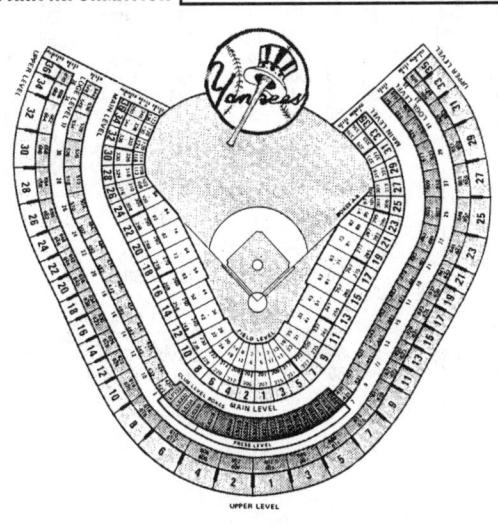

MINOR LEAGUE AFFILIATES

Class	Team	League	Manager
AAA	Columbus, O.	International	Rick Down
AA	Albany/Colonie	Eastern	Dan Radison
A	Prince William	Carolina	Mike Hart
A	Fort Lauderdale	Florida State	Brian Butterfield
A	Greensboro	South Atlantic	Trey Hillman
A	Oneonta	New York-Pennsylvania	To be announced
Rookie	Sarasota Yankees	Gulf Coast	Gary Denbo

BROADCAST INFORMATION

Radio: WABC-AM (770). Broadcasters: John Sterling, Michael Kay.
TV: WPIX (Channel 11). Broadcasters: Bobby Murcer, Phil Rizzuto, Tom Seaver.
Cable TV: Madison Square Garden Network. Broadcasters: Dewayne Staats, Tony Kubek, Al Trautwig.

SPRING TRAINING

Ballpark (city): Fort Lauderdale Stadium (Fort Lauderdale, Fla.).
Ticket information: 305-776-1921.

HISTORY

YEAR-BY-YEAR RECORDS

Year	Pos.	W	L	Pct.	*GB	Year	Pos.	W	L	Pct.	*GB
1901	5th	68	65	.511	13½	1949	1st	97	57	.630	+ 1
1902	8th	50	88	.362	34	1950	1st	98	56	.636	+ 3
1903	4th	72	62	.537	17	1951	1st	98	56	.636	+ 5
1904	2nd	92	59	.609	1½	1952	1st	95	59	.617	+ 2
1905	6th	71	78	.477	21½	1953	1st	99	52	.656	+ 8½
1906	2nd	90	61	.596	3	1954	2nd	103	51	.669	8
1907	5th	70	78	.473	21	1955	1st	96	58	.623	+ 3
1908	8th	51	103	.331	39½	1956	1st	97	57	.630	+ 9
1909	5th	74	77	.490	23½	1957	1st	98	56	.636	+ 8
1910	2nd	88	63	.583	14½	1958	1st	92	62	.597	+10
1911	6th	76	76	.500	25½	1959	3rd	79	75	.513	15
1912	8th	50	102	.329	55	1960	1st	97	57	.630	+ 8
1913	7th	57	94	.377	38	1961	1st	109	53	.673	+ 8
1914	T6th	70	84	.455	30	1962	1st	96	66	.593	+ 5
1915	5th	69	83	.454	32½	1963	1st	104	57	.646	+10½
1916	4th	80	74	.519	11	1964	1st	99	63	.611	+ 1
1917	6th	71	82	.464	28½	1965	6th	77	85	.475	25
1918	4th	60	63	.488	13½	1966	10th	70	89	.440	26½
1919	3rd	80	59	.576	7½	1967	9th	72	90	.444	20
1920	3rd	95	59	.617	3	1968	5th	83	79	.512	20
1921	1st	98	55	.641	+ 4½	1969	5th	80	81	.497	28½
1922	1st	94	60	.610	+ 1	1970	2nd	93	69	.574	15
1923	1st	98	54	.645	+16	1971	4th	82	80	.506	21
1924	2nd	89	63	.586	2	1972	4th	79	76	.510	6½
1925	7th	69	85	.448	30	1973	4th	80	82	.494	17
1926	1st	91	63	.591	+ 3	1974	2nd	89	73	.549	2
1927	1st	110	44	.714	+19	1975	3rd	83	77	.519	12
1928	1st	101	53	.656	+ 2½	1976	1st†	97	62	.610	+10½
1929	2nd	88	66	.571	18	1977	1st†	100	62	.617	+ 2½
1930	3rd	86	68	.558	16	1978	1st†‡	100	63	.613	+ 1
1931	2nd	94	59	.614	13½	1979	4th	89	71	.556	13½
1932	1st	107	47	.695	+13	1980	1st§	103	59	.636	+ 3
1933	2nd	91	59	.607	7	1981	1st/6th	59	48	.551	†‡*
1934	2nd	94	60	.610	7	1982	5th	79	83	.488	16
1935	2nd	89	60	.597	3	1983	3rd	91	71	.562	7
1936	1st	102	51	.667	+19½	1984	3rd	87	75	.537	17
1937	1st	102	52	.662	+13	1985	2nd	97	64	.602	2
1938	1st	99	53	.651	+ 9½	1986	2nd	90	72	.556	5½
1939	1st	106	45	.702	+17	1987	4th	89	73	.549	9
1940	3rd	88	66	.571	2	1988	5th	85	76	.528	3½
1941	1st	101	53	.656	+17	1989	5th	74	87	.460	14½
1942	1st	103	51	.669	+ 9	1990	7th	67	95	.414	21
1943	1st	98	56	.636	+13½	1991	5th	71	91	.438	20
1944	3rd	83	71	.539	6						
1945	4th	81	71	.533	6½						
1946	3rd	87	67	.565	17						
1947	1st	97	57	.630	+12						
1948	3rd	94	60	.610	2½						

*Games behind winner. †Won Championship Series. ‡Won division playoff. §Lost Championship Series. *First half 34-22; second 25-26.

MANAGERS

Name	Record	Years
John McGraw	94-96	'01-02
Wilbert Robinson	24-57	1902
Clark Griffith	419-370	'03-08
Kid Elberfeld	27-71	1908
George Stallings	152-136	'09-10
Hal Chase	86-80	'10-11
Harry Wolverton	50-102	1912
Frank Chance	117-168	'13-14
Rog. Peckinpaugh	10-10	1914
Bill Donovan	220-239	'15-17
Miller Huggins	1067-719	'18-29
Art Fletcher	6-5	1929
Bob Shawkey	86-68	1930
Joe McCarthy	1460-867	'31-46
Bill Dickey	57-48	1946
Johnny Neun	8-6	1946
Bucky Harris	191-117	'47-48
Casey Stengel	1149-696	'49-60
Ralph Houk	944-806	'61-63
		'66-73
Yogi Berra	192-148	1964
		'84-85
Johnny Keane	81-101	'65-66
Bill Virdon	142-124	'74-75
Billy Martin	501-345	'75-78
		'79, '83
		'85, '88
Bob Lemon	99-73	'78-79
		'81-82
Dick Howser	103-59	1980
Gene Michael	92-76	'81, '82
Clyde King	29-33	1982
Lou Piniella	224-193	'86-87
		1988
Dallas Green	56-65	1989
Bucky Dent	36-53	'89-90
Stump Merrill	120-155	'90-91

DAY BY DAY

Date	Opp.	Res.	Score (inn.*)	Hits	Opp. hits	Winning pitcher	Losing pitcher	Save	Record	Pos.	GB
4-8	At Det.	L	4-6	10	8	Gibson	Cadaret	Henneman	0-1	T4th	1
4-10	At Det.	W	4-0	8	1	Sanderson	Terrell		1-1	T3rd	1
4-11	At Det.	L	5-11	10	10	Gibson	Habyan		1-2	5th	1½
4-12	At K.C.	L	5-9	9	15	S. Davis	Cary		1-3	T6th	2½
4-13	At K.C.	W	9-8	12	14	Leary	Saberhagen	Farr	2-3	T4th	1½
4-14	At K.C.	L	3-5	6	13	Boddicker	Hawkins	Montgomery	2-4	T6th	2½
4-15	Chi.	L	5-6	5	13	Hibbard	Cadaret	Thigpen	2-5	T6th	3½
4-16	Chi.	L	3-4 (10)	5	8	Radinsky	Farr	Thigpen	2-6	7th	3½
4-17	Chi.	W	10-1	12	4	Cary	Fernandez		3-6	7th	2½
4-19	K.C.	W	3-1	7	3	Leary	Boddicker		4-6	7th	2½
4-20	K.C.	L	2-5	6	10	Gordon	Sanderson	Montgomery	4-7	7th	3½
4-22	Det.	L	5-10	9	12	Gleaton	Cadaret		4-8	7th	3
4-23	Det.	W	5-0	11	4	Eiland	Tanana		5-8	6th	3
4-26	At Chi.	W	3-2 (11)	9	12	Cadaret	Drahman		6-8	T5th	3
4-27	At Chi.	L	9-14	13	20	Perez	Plunk		6-9	T5th	3
4-28	At Chi.	L	1-4	5	7	McDowell	Cary	Thigpen	6-10	T6th	4
4-30	At Oak.	L	3-7	9	8	Welch	Eiland		6-11	6th	4½
5-1	At Oak.	L	4-7	7	10	Moore	Leary	Eckersley	6-12	7th	4½
5-3	At Sea.	W	5-0	6	3	Sanderson	Holman		7-12	7th	4½
5-4	At Sea.	L	2-3	11	7	Bankhead	Cary	Jackson	7-13	7th	5½
5-5	At Sea.	L	4-5 (16)	18	15	Krueger	Monteleone		7-14	7th	6½
5-6	At Sea.	L	2-4	7	9	Hanson	Leary	Swift	7-15	7th	7
5-7	At Cal.	L	4-7	4	8	Finley	Hawkins	Harvey	7-16	7th	7
5-8	At Cal.	W	10-5	11	12	Sanderson	McCaskill		8-16	7th	7
5-10	Oak.	W	5-3	7	6	Habyan	Klink	Farr	9-16	6th	7½
5-11	Oak.	L	2-10	2	10	Dressendorfer	Eiland		9-17	7th	8½
5-12	Oak.	W	10-6	15	12	Farr	Moore		10-17	6th	7½
5-13	Oak.	W	6-3	9	8	Sanderson	Young	Guetterman	11-17	6th	6½
5-14	Cal.	W	7-1	11	5	Perez	McCaskill	Habyan	12-17	5th	6½
5-15	Cal.	L	2-10	8	10	Langston	Cary		12-18	5th	7½
5-16	Cal.	L	0-7	7	11	J. Abbott	Plunk		12-19	5th	8
5-17	Sea.	L	0-1	4	3	Johnson	Leary	Swift	12-20	T6th	8
5-18	Sea.	L	1-4	6	11	Rice	Sanderson		12-21	T6th	8
5-19	Sea.	W	3-2	6	5	Howe	Holman	Guetterman	13-21	5th	7
5-20	At Cle.	L	1-3	6	8	King	Cary	Hillegas	13-22	6th	8
5-21	At Cle.	L	2-5	8	11	Swindell	Eiland		13-23	T6th	9
5-22	At Cle.	W	8-1	11	8	Leary	Candiotti		14-23	6th	9
5-24	At Bal.	W	7-1	10	3	Sanderson	Robinson		15-23	5th	8½
5-25	At Bal.	W	6-5	9	11	Farr	Flanagan	Guetterman	16-23	5th	7½
5-26	At Bal.	W	2-1 (11)	12	9	Habyan	Flanagan	Cadaret	17-23	5th	6½
5-27	Bos.	W	6-5	7	8	Guetterman	Reardon		18-23	5th	5½
5-28	Bos.	L	2-6	4	12	Clemens	Leary		18-24	5th	6½
5-29	Bos.	W	7-0	8	5	Sanderson	Bolton		19-24	5th	5½
5-31	Mil.	W	3-2	8	7	Howe	Crim		20-24	5th	5
6-1	Mil.	L	3-6	6	13	Wegman	Cary		20-25	5th	5
6-2	Mil.	W	7-4	13	10	Taylor	Higuera	Farr	21-25	5th	4
6-3	Tor.	L	3-5	8	12	Key	Leary	Henke	21-26	5th	5
6-4	Tor.	W	5-3	9	10	Sanderson	Stottlemyre	Farr	22-26	T4th	4
6-5	Tor.	L	1-4	4	9	Wells	Johnson	Henke	22-27	5th	5
6-7	Tex.	W	5-4	11	6	Habyan	Barfield		23-27	4th	3½
6-8	Tex.	W	10-7	14	16	Taylor	Petkovsek	Farr	24-27	4th	3½
6-9	Tex.	W	6-4	10	7	Habyan	Gossage	Farr	25-27	4th	3½
6-11	At Min.	L	3-5	6	10	Tapani	Habyan	Aguilera	25-28	4th	3½
6-12	At Min.	L	3-6	10	8	Anderson	Johnson	Bedrosian	25-29	4th	4½
6-13	At Min.	L	3-10	12	13	Erickson	Witt		25-30	4th	5½
6-14	At Tex.	L	4-8	12	9	Guzman	Taylor		25-31	4th	6½
6-15	At Tex.	L	3-4	12	8	Brown	Leary	Russell	25-32	T4th	6½
6-16	At Tex.	L	3-4 (15)	5	13	Bitker	Guetterman		25-33	5th	7
6-18	At Tor.	W	4-2	11	11	Kamieniecki	Timlin	Farr	26-33	5th	5½
6-19	At Tor.	W	3-0	10	6	Johnson	Key	Howe	27-33	5th	4½
6-20	At Tor.	L	1-6	8	9	Stottlemyre	Leary		27-34	5th	5½
6-21	Min.	L	4-5	11	11	Guthrie	Sanderson	Aguilera	27-35	5th	6½
6-22	Min.	L	3-4	9	6	Tapani	Taylor	Aguilera	27-36	5th	7½
6-23	Min.	W	11-2	16	7	Kamieniecki	Anderson		28-36	5th	7½
6-24	Min.	L	0-5	2	6	Erickson	Johnson		28-37	5th	8½
6-25	At Bos.	W	6-4	10	10	Leary	Clemens	Farr	29-37	5th	7½
6-26	At Bos.	W	5-1	12	8	Sanderson	Gardiner	Howe	30-37	5th	7½
6-27	At Bos.	W	8-0	11	5	Taylor	Bolton		31-37	5th	7½
6-28	At Mil.	L	2-5	5	9	August	Kamieniecki	Plesac	31-38	5th	7½
6-29	At Mil.	W	9-8	13	10	Guetterman	Plesac	Farr	32-38	5th	7½

NEW YORK YANKEES

1992 SEASON

NEW YORK YANKEES

Date	Opp.	Res.	Score (inn.*)	Hits	Opp. hits	Winning pitcher	Losing pitcher	Save	Record	Pos.	GB
6-30	At Mil.	W	8-6	14	13	Cadaret	Lee	Farr	33-38	5th	7 ½
7-1	Cle.	W	6-2	11	9	Sanderson	Swindell	Guetterman	34-38	4th	7 ½
7-2	Cle.	W	8-5	15	14	Taylor	York	Farr	35-38	4th	7 ½
7-3	Cle.	W	3-2	5	5	Kamieniecki	Boucher	Farr	36-38	4th	7 ½
7-4	Bal.	W	3-2	8	6	Plunk	Smith	Guetterman	37-38	4th	6 ½
7-5	Bal.	L	4-7	8	15	Robinson	Leary	Olson	37-39	4th	7 ½
7-6	Bal.	W	13-5	13	10	Plunk	Frohwirth		38-39	4th	7 ½
7-7	Bal.	L	3-5	7	13	Ballard	Taylor	Olson	38-40	4th	8 ½
7-11	At Cal.	W	2-0	11	1	Sanderson	McCaskill		39-40	4th	8 ½
7-12	At Cal.	W	2-1 (10)	4	5	Howe	Harvey	Farr	40-40	4th	8 ½
7-13	At Cal.	W	2-0	4	4	Johnson	J. Abbott	Farr	41-40	T3rd	8 ½
7-14	At Cal.	L	2-10	9	15	Finley	Taylor		41-41	4th	8 ½
7-15	At Sea.	L	1-5	7	11	Krueger	Cadaret		41-42	4th	9 ½
7-16	At Sea.	L	0-5	6	7	Holman	Sanderson		41-43	4th	9 ½
7-18	At Oak.	W	3-2	10	4	Kamieniecki	Show	Howe	42-43	4th	9 ½
7-19	At Oak.	W	3-0	6	4	Johnson	Moore	Farr	43-43	4th	9 ½
7-20	At Oak.	W	5-1	8	5	Taylor	Hawkins		44-43	3rd	8 ½
7-21	At Oak.	L	2-4	7	6	Stewart	Sanderson	Eckersley	44-44	3rd	8 ½
7-23	Sea.	L	1-6	6	11	Johnson	Kamieniecki		44-45	3rd	8 ½
7-24	Sea.	W	10-2	15	13	Johnson	Hanson		45-45	3rd	8 ½
7-25	Sea.	L	3-6	5	10	Krueger	Taylor	Murphy	45-46	3rd	8 ½
7-26	Cal.	L	1-5	7	10	Langston	Sanderson	Harvey	45-47	3rd	9 ½
7-27	Cal.	W	12-10	15	13	Cadaret	Fetters	Farr	46-47	3rd	8 ½
7-28	Cal.	L	4-8	8	12	J. Abbott	Kamieniecki		46-48	3rd	8 ½
7-29	Oak.	L	8-10	14	17	Campbell	Howe	Eckersley	46-49	3rd	8 ½
7-30	Oak.	L	5-6	4	10	Young	Taylor	Eckersley	46-50	3rd	8 ½
7-31	Min.	L	3-12	8	20	Tapani	Sanderson		46-51	4th	9 ½
8-1	Min.	W	8-3	9	9	Cadaret	Abbott		47-51	3rd	9 ½
8-2	At Det.	L	3-7	9	9	Tanana	Kamieniecki		47-52	4th	9 ½
8-3	At Det.	L	6-7	10	10	Gullickson	Johnson	Henneman	47-53	4th	9 ½
8-4	At Det.	L	7-8 (10)	13	13	Henneman	Farr		47-54	4th	10 ½
8-5	At Det.	W	7-5	10	8	Sanderson	Terrell	Guetterman	48-54	4th	10
8-6	At Chi.	L	5-14	9	15	Pall	Leary		48-55	4th	11
8-7	At Chi.	L	2-10	7	12	McDowell	Eiland		48-56	4th	12
8-8	At Chi.	L	1-4	5	7	Fernandez	Johnson	Radinsky	48-57	4th	12
8-10 (1)	Det.	L	1-5	6	8	Leiter	Sanderson		48-58	4th	11 ½
8-10 (2)	Det.	L	0-4	4	6	Terrell	Taylor		48-59	4th	12
8-11 (1)	Det.	W	12-6	13	9	Cadaret	Gakeler		49-59	4th	11
8-11 (2)	Det.	W	10-8 (10)	14	8	Farr	Gibson		50-59	4th	10 ½
8-13 (1)	K.C.	L	0-5	3	11	Appier	Johnson		50-60	4th	10
8-13 (2)	K.C.	L	1-8	11	11	Boddicker	Eiland	Montgomery	50-61	5th	10 ½
8-14	K.C.	L	1-5 (11)	6	6	Gordon	Farr		50-62	5th	10 ½
8-15	K.C.	W	5-1	9	5	Sanderson	Gubicza		51-62	5th	10 ½
8-16	Chi.	W	6-5	15	10	Monteleone	Radinsky		52-62	5th	9 ½
8-17	Chi.	W	4-2	8	9	Taylor	McDowell	Farr	53-62	5th	9 ½
8-18	Chi.	L	3-11	5	14	Hibbard	Johnson		53-63	5th	10 ½
8-19	At K.C.	W	6-2	11	8	Cadaret	Boddicker		54-63	5th	10
8-20	At K.C.	W	7-3	10	6	Sanderson	Gubicza		55-63	4th	10
8-21	At K.C.	L	4-7	9	15	Saberhagen	Perez		55-64	5th	10
8-23	At Tor.	L	5-6	15	9	Ward	Farr		55-65	5th	10 ½
8-24	At Tor.	W	6-5	11	7	Johnson	Wells		56-65	5th	9 ½
8-25	At Tor.	L	7-11	8	12	Acker	Guetterman		56-66	5th	10 ½
8-26	Tex.	L	2-10	5	12	Brown	Plunk		56-67	5th	11 ½
8-27	Tex.	L	2-7	7	12	Guzman	Perez	Rogers	56-68	5th	12 ½
8-28	Tex.	W	5-1	8	10	Taylor	Bohanon		57-68	5th	12 ½
8-29	Tor.	L	2-6	8	11	Wells	Johnson		57-69	5th	13 ½
8-30	Tor.	W	9-2	14	6	Sanderson	Stottlemyre		58-69	5th	12 ½
8-31	Tor.	L	0-5	3	12	Key	Cadaret	Ward	58-70	5th	13 ½
9-1	Tor.	W	4-2	7	5	Guetterman	MacDonald		59-70	5th	12 ½
9-2	At Tex.	L	2-7	10	11	Boyd	Leary		59-71	5th	13 ½
9-3	At Tex.	L	1-5	5	11	Guzman	Johnson		59-72	5th	13 ½
9-4	At Tex.	W	3-2	11	9	Cadaret	Bohanon	Farr	60-72	5th	13 ½
9-6	At Min.	L	1-3	7	6	Tapani	Taylor	Aguilera	60-73	5th	15
9-7	At Min.	L	2-3 (10)	5	13	Willis	Guetterman		60-74	5th	16
9-8	At Min.	L	5-6	10	12	Erickson	Johnson	Bedrosian	60-75	5th	17
9-9	At Bal.	L	0-8	5	10	Milacki	Sanderson		60-76	5th	17 ½
9-10	At Bal.	L	3-6	8	9	Frohwirth	Plunk		60-77	5th	17 ½
9-11	At Bal.	L	2-4	8	7	Mussina	Taylor	Olson	60-78	5th	17 ½
9-12	Bos.	L	2-7	8	11	Morton	Perez		60-79	5th	18
9-13	Bos.	L	4-5	10	9	Gardiner	Johnson	Reardon	60-80	5th	19
9-14	Bos.	W	3-1	9	5	Sanderson	Hesketh	Farr	61-80	5th	19
9-15	Bos.	L	4-5	8	9	Clemens	Guetterman	Reardon	61-81	5th	19
9-16	Mil.	L	4-5	13	10	Lee	Taylor	Henry	61-82	5th	19
9-17	Mil.	L	0-2	2	7	Bosio	Perez		61-83	5th	19

Date	Opp.	Res.	Score (inn.*)	Hits	Opp. hits	Winning pitcher	Losing pitcher	Save	Record	Pos.	GB
9-18	Mil.	W	2-1 (10)	5	7	Farr	Navarro		62-83	5th	19
9-20	At Bos.	L	0-2	3	7	Clemens	Sanderson		62-84	5th	19
9-21	At Bos.	L	1-12	4	14	Hesketh	Taylor		62-85	5th	19
9-22	At Bos.	W	7-5 (10)	13	11	Farr	Young		63-85	5th	19
9-23	At Mil.	W	9-8	11	12	Monteleone	Lee	Farr	64-85	5th	18
9-24	At Mil.	L	4-5	13	8	Eldred	Plunk	Henry	64-86	5th	19
9-25	At Mil.	W	8-6 (11)	16	11	Mills	August		65-86	5th	19
9-26	At Mil.	L	2-6	6	10	Wegman	Taylor		65-87	5th	19 ½
9-27	At Cle.	W	3-0	6	7	Perez	Swindell	Farr	66-87	5th	19 ½
9-28	At Cle.	L	4-5	7	9	Bell	Cadaret	Olin	66-88	5th	19 ½
9-29	At Cle.	L	2-5	10	10	King	Mills	Olin	66-89	T5th	20 ½
9-30	At Cle.	W	3-0	7	5	Sanderson	Nagy	Cadaret	67-89	5th	19 ½
10-1	Bal.	W	3-2 (11)	8	10	Monteleone	Poole		68-89	5th	19 ½
10-2	Bal.	W	4-3	8	11	Cadaret	Flanagan	Farr	69-89	5th	19 ½
10-3	Bal.	W	9-6	11	11	Johnson	Ballard	Farr	70-89	5th	19
10-4	Cle.	L	2-3	9	7	Bell	Farr	Olin	70-90	5th	20
10-5	Cle.	L	5-7 (12)	19	11	Olin	Chapin	Jones	70-91	5th	20
10-6	Cle.	W	7-4	8	11	Eiland	Nagy	Habyan	71-91	5th	20

Monthly records: April (6-11), May (14-13), June (13-14), July (13-13), August (12-19), September (9-19), Oct. (4-2).

HIGHLIGHTS

High point: Beginning with a three-game sweep at Boston on June 25-27 and ending with three straight wins at Oakland on July 18-20, the Yankees won 16 of 22 games to get over .500 (44-43) and within 8½ games of first place in the American League East.

Low point: Pitching in relief of Scott Sanderson on August 25, Tim Leary and Lee Guetterman squandered a 7-2, seventh-inning lead over Toronto, allowing the Blue Jays to claim an 11-7 victory. It marked the start of a 23-game stretch in which the Yankees lost 18 times and fell 22 games below .500.

Turning point: Don Mattingly's refusal to get a haircut August 15 proved to be a public relations disaster for General Manager Gene Michael, who had ordered Manager Stump Merrill to bench the first baseman if he did not comply with the club's grooming code. Mattingly revealed that he had asked Michael to seek a trade for him and used the incident to criticize the organization. What little control Merrill had of the clubhouse had vanished, and the Yankees skidded the rest of the way.

Most valuable player: Outfielder Mel Hall. He set personal standards in home runs (19) and runs batted in (80) while batting .285.

Most valuable pitcher: Sanderson. The righthander finished at 16-10 with a 3.81 earned-run average.

Most improved player: Catcher Matt Nokes. He made vast strides defensively and enjoyed his best season (.268 average, 24 homers, 77 RBIs) since his rookie year with Detroit in '87.

Most pleasant surprise: Righthander John Habyan. Two years removed from career-threatening shoulder surgery, the setup man went 4-2 with two saves and a 2.30 ERA in 66 games.

Biggest disappointment: Outfielder Hensley Meulens. The rookie lost his left-field job to Hall a month into the season and struggled throughout, batting .222 with six homers and 29 RBIs.

Key injuries: Jesse Barfield was leading the club in home runs (17) and RBIs (48) when he was lost for the season July 29 because of a fractured left foot. Roberto Kelly missed 33 games due to a sprained right wrist. Elbow problems ruined Mike Witt's season.

Notable: Merrill, fired the day after the season ended, was the first Yankees manager to last a full year since Lou Piniella in 1987. ... Sanderson, the team's lone All-Star representative, did not play in the All-Star Game, marking the first time ever a Yankee failed to participate.

—JACK O'CONNELL

RECORDS

1991 regular-season record: 71-91 (5th in A.L. East); 39-42 at home; 32-49 on road; 40-38 vs. East; 31-53 vs. West; 27-28 vs. LHP; 44-63 vs. RHP; 64-74 on grass; 7-17 on turf; 24-27 in daytime; 47-64 at night; 20-21 in one-run games; 8-7 in extra-inning games; 1-2-0 in doubleheaders.

Team record last five years: 386-422 (.478, ranks 11th in league in that span).

TEAM LEADERS

Batting average: Steve Sax (.304).
At-bats: Steve Sax (652).
Runs: Steve Sax (85).
Hits: Steve Sax (198).
Total bases: Steve Sax (270).
Doubles: Steve Sax (38).
Triples: Pat Kelly, Bernie Williams (4).
Home runs: Matt Nokes (24).
Runs batted in: Mel Hall (80).
Stolen bases: Roberto Kelly (32).
Slugging percentage: Mel Hall (.455).
On-base percentage: Steve Sax (.345).
Wins: Scott Sanderson (16).
Earned-run average: Scott Sanderson (3.81).
Complete games: Scott Sanderson (2).
Shutouts: Scott Sanderson (2).
Saves: Steve Farr (23).
Innings pitched: Scott Sanderson (208).
Strikeouts: Scott Sanderson (130).

GAMES BY POSITION

Catcher: Matt Nokes 130, Bob Geren 63, Jim Leyritz 5, John Ramos 5.
First base: Don Mattingly 127, Kevin Maas 36, Hensley Meulens 7, Jim Leyritz 3.
Second base: Steve Sax 149, Pat Kelly 19, Carlos Rodriguez 3.
Third base: Pat Kelly 80, Randy Velarde 50, Torey Lovullo 22, Jim Leyritz 18, Mike Blowers 14, Mike Humphreys 6, Steve Sax 5, Alvaro Espinoza 2.
Shortstop: Alvaro Espinoza 147, Randy Velarde 31, Carlos Rodriguez 11.
Outfield: Roberto Kelly 125, Mel Hall 120, Bernie Williams 85, Jesse Barfield 81, Hensley Meulens 73, Pat Sheridan 34, Mike Humphreys 9, Scott Lusader 4, Randy Velarde 2.
Designated hitter: Kevin Maas 109, Don Mattingly 22, Hensley Meulens 13, Mel Hall 10, Mike Humphreys 7, John Ramos 4, Steve Sax 4, Matt Nokes 3, Pat Sheridan 2, Jim Leyritz 1, Scott Lusader 1.

TOP 10 DRAFT CHOICES

1. **Brien Taylor,** LHP, East Carteret High School, Beaufort, N.C.
2. **None.**
3a. **Tim Flannelly,** 3B, University of Michigan.
3b. **Mark Hubbard,** RHP/OF, University of South Florida.
4. **Marc Gipner,** C, Dunedin (Fla.) High School.
5. **Lyle Mouton,** OF, Louisiana State University.
6. **Eric Knowles,** SS, St. Brenden High School, Miami.
7. **Tommy Carter,** LHP, Auburn University.
8. **Grant Sullivan,** LHP, University of Mississippi.
9. **Keith Garagozzo,** LHP, University of Delaware.
10. **Mike Muncy,** SS, Camarillo (Calif.) High School.

OAKLAND ATHLETICS
AMERICAN LEAGUE WEST DIVISION

1992 SCHEDULE

APRIL

S	M	T	W	T	F	S
5	6 N KC H	7	8 N KC H	9 KC H	10 N CHI H	11 CHI H
12 CHI H	13 KC	14 KC	15 N KC	16 N KC	17 TEX	18 TEX
19 TEX	20 N CAL H	21 N CAL H	22 CAL H	23	24 N MIN	25 MIN
26 MIN	27	28 N CLE	29 N CLE	30 N DET		

MAY

S	M	T	W	T	F	S
					1 N DET	2 N DET
3 DET	4 N TOR H	5 N TOR H	6 N DET H	7 DET H	8 N NY H	9 NY H
10 NY H	11	12 N TOR	13 N TOR	14	15 N NY	16 NY
17 NY H	18 N BAL	19 N BAL	20 N BAL	21	22 N BOS	23 BOS
24 BOS	25 N CLE H	26 N CLE H	27 CLE H	28	29 N BAL	30 BAL H
31 BAL H						

JUNE

S	M	T	W	T	F	S
	1 N BOS H	2 N BOS H	3 N BOS H	4	5 N CHI	6 N CHI
7 CHI	8 N MIL	9 N MIL	10 N MIL	11	12 N TEX H	13 TEX H
14 TEX	15 N MIL	16 N MIL	17 N MIL	18	19 N CAL	20 CAL
21 CAL	22 N SEA H	23 N SEA H	24 N SEA H	25 N MIN H	26 N MIN H	27 N MIN H
28 MIN H	29 N SEA	30 N SEA				

JULY

S	M	T	W	T	F	S
			1 N SEA	2	3 N CLE	4 CLE
5 N CLE	6 N CLE	7 DET	8 DET	9 N TOR	10 N TOR	11 TOR
12 TOR	13	14 ★	15	16 N DET H	17 N DET H	18 N DET H
19 DET H	20 N NY H	21 N NY H	22 N NY H	23 N TOR H	24 N TOR H	25 N TOR H
26 TOR H	27 N MIN	28 N MIN	29 N MIN	30	31 KC	

AUGUST

S	M	T	W	T	F	S
						1 KC
2 N KC	3 TEX	4 N TEX	5 N TEX	6 N TEX	7 N KC H	8 KC H
9 KC H	10 N CHI H	11 N CHI H	12 CHI H	13 N CAL H	14 N CAL H	15 CAL H
16 CAL H	17	18 N NY	19 N NY	20 N NY	21 N BAL	22 N BAL
23 BAL	24 N BOS	25 N BOS	26 BOS	27	28 N CLE H	29 CLE H
30 N CLE H	31 N BAL H					

SEPTEMBER

S	M	T	W	T	F	S
		1 N BAL H	2 N BAL H	3	4 N BOS H	5 BOS H
6 BOS H	7	8 N CAL	9 N CAL	10 N SEA H	11 N SEA H	12 SEA H
13 SEA H	14 N MIN H	15 N MIN H	16 MIN H	17	18 N SEA	19 SEA
20 N SEA	21 N CHI	22 N CHI	23 N CHI	24 N CHI	25 N MIL	26 MIL
27 MIL	28	29 N TEX H	30 N TEX H			

OCTOBER

S	M	T	W	T	F	S
				1	2 N TEX H	3 N MIL H
4 MIL H	5	6	7	8	9	10

1992 SEASON

CLUB DIRECTORY

Owner/managing general partner
Walter A. Haas Jr.
President/chief operating officer
Walter J. Haas
Vice president, baseball operations
Sandy Alderson
Vice president, business operations
Andy Dolich
Vice president, finance
Kathleen McCracken
Vice president, admin. and personnel
Raymond B. Krise Jr.
Asst. to the man. gen. partner, baseball
Bill Rigney
Director of player development
Keith Lieppman
Special assistant for baseball operations
Karl Kuehl
Director of scouting
Dick Bogard
Assistant director of scouting
Eric Kubota
Director of baseball administration
Walt Jocketty
Director of Latin American scouting
Juan Marichal
Director of team travel
Mickey Morabito
Director of baseball information
Jay Alves
Assistant director, baseball administration
Pamela Pitts
Administrative asst., baseball operations
Jennella Roark
Administrative assistant, baseball relations
Doreen Alves
Admin. asst., stats and desktop publishing
Mike Sellick
Director of broadcasting
Tom Cordova
Director of media relations
Kathy Jacobson
Dir. of community affairs/speakers bureau
Dave Perron
Director of stadium operations
Kevin Kahn

Director of broadcast operations
Bill King
Director of business administration
Alan Ledford
Director of sales
John Kamperschroer
Director of season tickets
Barbara Reilly
Director of group sales
Bettina Flores
Director of promotions
Sharon Kelly
Team physician
Dr. Allan Pont
Team orthopedist
Dr. Rick Bost
Trainers
Barry Weinberg
Larry Davis
Equipment manager
Frank Ciensczyk
Visiting clubhouse manager
Steve Vucinich
Scouts
Tony Arias
Billy Beane
Billy Bowman
Mark Conkin
Tim Corcoran
Ed Crosby
Grady Fuson
Bill Gayton
James Guinn
Michael Jones
John Kazanas
Billy Merkel
Bill Meyer
Marty Miller
Steve Nichols
Chris Pittaro
J.P. Ricciardi
Dave Roberts
Jeff Scott
Mike Stafford
Ron Vaughn
Craig Wallenbrock

SCHEDULE KEY

H—Home game.   ★All-Star Game at San Diego/Jack Murphy Stadium.
N—Night game (any game starting after 5 p.m.).

SPRING TRAINING ROSTER

Manager—Tony La Russa (10).

Coaches—Dave Duncan (18), Art Kusnyer (5), Rene Lachemann (15), Dave McKay (8), Doug Rader (11), Tommie Reynolds (47).

No.	PITCHERS	B/T	Ht./Wt.	Born	1991 clubs
53	Briscoe, John	R/R	6-3/185	9-22-67	Huntsville, Tacoma, Oakland
55	Campbell, Kevin	R/R	6-2/225	12-6-64	Tacoma, Oakland
49	Chitren, Steve	R/R	6-0/180	6-8-67	Oakland
17	Darling, Ron	R/R	6-3/195	8-19-60	New York NL, Montreal, Oakland
28	Dressendorfer, Kirk	R/R	5-11/190	4-8-69	Tacoma, Oakland
43	Eckersley, Dennis	R/R	6-2/195	10-3-54	Oakland
54	Erwin, Scott	R/L	6-2/210	8-21-67	Modesto, Huntsville
41	Guzman, Johnny	R/L	5-10/155	1-21-71	Huntsville, Tacoma, Oakland
32	Harris, Reggie	R/R	6-1/190	8-12-68	Tacoma, Oakland
40	Honeycutt, Rick	L/L	6-1/191	6-29-54	Madison, Modesto, Oakland
58	Klink, Joe	L/L	5-11/175	2-3-62	Modesto, Oakland
21	Moore, Mike	R/R	6-4/205	11-26-59	Oakland
19	Nelson, Gene	R/R	6-0/174	12-3-60	Oakland
48	Osteen, Gavin	R/L	6-0/195	11-27-69	Huntsville
30	Show, Eric	R/R	6-1/185	5-19-56	Modesto, Tacoma, Oakland
37	Slusarski, Joe	R/R	6-4/195	12-19-66	Tacoma, Oakland
34	Stewart, Dave	R/R	6-2/200	2-19-57	Oakland
59	Van Poppel, Todd	R/R	6-5/210	12-9-71	Huntsville, Oakland
50	Walton, Bruce	R/R	6-2/195	12-25-62	Tacoma, Oakland
35	Welch, Bob	R/R	6-3/198	11-3-56	Oakland

No.	CATCHERS	B/T	Ht./Wt.	Born	1991 clubs
39	Mercedes, Henry	R/R	5-11/185	7-23-69	Modesto
9	Quirk, Jamie	L/R	6-4/200	10-22-54	Oakland
36	Steinbach, Terry	R/R	6-1/195	3-2-62	Oakland

No.	INFIELDERS	B/T	Ht./Wt.	Born	1991 clubs
12	Blankenship, Lance	R/R	6-0/185	12-6-63	Tacoma, Oakland
46	Bordick, Mike	R/R	5-11/175	7-21-65	Tacoma, Oakland
45	Brosius, Scott	R/R	6-1/185	8-15-66	Tacoma, Oakland
31	Hemond, Scott	R/R	6-0/205	11-18-65	Tacoma, Oakland
23	Howitt, Dann	L/R	6-5/205	2-13-64	Tacoma, Oakland
4	Lansford, Carney	R/R	6-2/195	2-7-57	Tacoma, Oakland
25	McGwire, Mark	R/R	6-5/225	10-1-63	Oakland
20	Paquette, Craig	R/R	6-0/185	3-28-69	Huntsville
2	Ready, Randy	R/R	5-11/182	6-20-58	Philadelphia
22	Weiss, Walt	S/R	6-0/175	11-28-63	Oakland
57	Witmeyer, Ron	L/L	6-3/215	6-28-67	Tacoma, Oakland

No.	OUTFIELDERS	B/T	Ht./Wt.	Born	1991 clubs
3	Baines, Harold	L/L	6-2/195	3-15-59	Oakland
33	Canseco, Jose	R/R	6-4/240	7-2-64	Oakland
42	Henderson, Dave	R/R	6-2/220	7-21-58	Oakland
24	Henderson, Rickey	R/L	5-10/190	12-25-58	Oakland
13	Jennings, Doug	L/L	5-10/175	9-30-64	Tacoma, Oakland
6	Wilson, Willie	S/R	6-3/200	7-9-55	Oakland

BALLPARK INFORMATION

Ballpark (capacity, surface)
Oakland-Alameda County Coliseum
(47,313, grass)

Address
7000 Coliseum Way
Oakland, CA 94621-1918

Business phone
510-569-2121

Ticket information
510-639-7700

Ticket prices
$12 (field level)
$11 (plaza level)
$7 (upper reserved)
$4 (bleachers)

Field dimensions (from home plate)
To left field at foul line, 330 feet
To center field, 400 feet
To right field at foul line, 330 feet

First game played
April 17, 1968 (Orioles 4, Athletics 1)

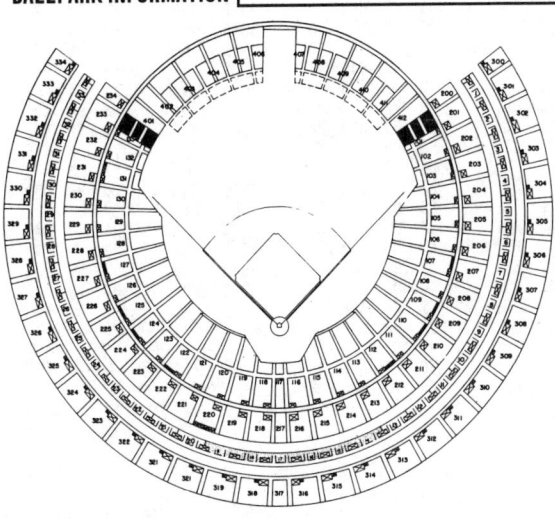

OAKLAND ATHLETICS

1992 SEASON

OAKLAND ATHLETICS

MINOR LEAGUE AFFILIATES

Class	Team	League	Manager
AAA	Tacoma	Pacific Coast	Bob Boone
AA	Huntsville	Southern	Casey Parsons
A	Modesto	California	Ted Kubiak
A	Reno	California	Gary Jones
A	Madison	Midwest	Dickie Scott
A	Southern Oregon	Northwest	To be announced
Rookie	Scottsdale Athletics	Arizona	Bruce Hines

BROADCAST INFORMATION

Radio: KSFO-AM (560). Broadcasters: Lon Simmons, Bill King, Ray Fosse. KNTA-AM (1430, Spanish language). Broadcasters: Amaury Pi-Gonzales, Erwin Higueros.
TV: KPIX-TV (Channel 5). Broadcasters: Monte Moore, Ray Fosse.
Cable TV: SportsChannel. Broadcasters: To be announced.

SPRING TRAINING

Ballpark (city): Phoenix Stadium (Phoenix, Ariz.).
Ticket information: 602-392-0074.

HISTORY

YEAR-BY-YEAR RECORDS

Year	Pos.	W	L	Pct.	*GB	Year	Pos.	W	L	Pct.	*GB
1901	4th	74	62	.544	9	1949	5th	81	73	.526	16
1902	1st	83	53	.610	+ 5	1950	8th	52	102	.338	46
1903	2nd	75	60	.556	14½	1951	6th	70	84	.455	28
1904	5th	81	70	.536	12½	1952	4th	79	75	.513	16
1905	1st	92	56	.622	+ 2	1953	7th	59	95	.383	41½
1906	4th	78	67	.538	12	1954	8th	51	103	.331	60
1907	2nd	88	57	.607	1½	1955	6th	63	91	.409	33
1908	6th	68	85	.444	22	1956	8th	52	102	.338	45
1909	2nd	95	58	.621	3½	1957	7th	59	94	.386	38½
1910	1st	102	48	.680	+14½	1958	7th	73	81	.474	19
1911	1st	101	50	.669	+13½	1959	7th	66	88	.429	28
1912	3rd	90	62	.592	15	1960	8th	58	96	.377	39
1913	1st	96	57	.627	+ 6½	1961	T9th	61	100	.379	47½
1914	1st	99	53	.651	+ 8½	1962	9th	72	90	.444	24
1915	8th	43	109	.283	58½	1963	8th	73	89	.451	31½
1916	8th	36	117	.235	54½	1964	10th	57	105	.352	42
1917	8th	52	98	.359	44½	1965	10th	59	103	.364	43
1918	8th	52	76	.406	24	1966	7th	74	86	.463	23
1919	8th	36	104	.257	52	1967	10th	62	99	.385	29½
1920	8th	48	106	.312	50	1968	6th	82	80	.506	21
1921	8th	53	100	.346	45	1969	2nd	88	74	.543	9
1922	7th	65	89	.422	29	1970	2nd	89	73	.549	9
1923	6th	69	83	.454	29	1971	1st†	101	60	.627	+16
1924	5th	71	81	.467	20	1972	1st‡	93	62	.600	+ 5½
1925	2nd	88	64	.579	8½	1973	1st‡	94	68	.580	+ 6
1926	3rd	83	67	.553	6	1974	1st‡	90	72	.556	+ 5
1927	2nd	91	63	.591	19	1975	1st†	98	64	.605	+ 7
1928	2nd	98	55	.641	2½	1976	2nd	87	74	.540	2½
1929	1st	104	46	.693	+18	1977	7th	63	98	.391	38½
1930	1st	102	52	.662	+ 8	1978	6th	69	93	.426	23
1931	1st	107	45	.704	+13½	1979	7th	54	108	.333	34
1932	2nd	94	60	.610	13	1980	2nd	83	79	.512	14
1933	3rd	79	72	.523	19½	1981	1st/2nd	64	45	.587	§†★
1934	5th	68	82	.453	31	1982	5th	68	94	.420	25
1935	8th	58	91	.389	34	1983	4th	74	88	.457	25
1936	8th	53	100	.346	49	1984	4th	77	85	.475	7
1937	7th	54	97	.358	46½	1985	T4th	77	85	.475	14
1938	8th	53	99	.349	46	1986	T3rd	76	86	.469	16
1939	7th	55	97	.362	51½	1987	3rd	81	81	.500	4
1940	8th	54	100	.351	36	1988	1st‡	104	58	.642	+13
1941	8th	64	90	.416	37	1989	1st‡	99	63	.611	+ 7
1942	8th	55	99	.357	48	1990	1st‡	103	59	.636	+ 9
1943	8th	49	105	.318	49	1991	4th	84	78	.519	11
1944	T5th	72	82	.468	17						
1945	8th	52	98	.347	34½						
1946	8th	49	105	.318	55						
1947	5th	78	76	.506	19						
1948	4th	84	70	.545	12½						

*Games behind winner. †Lost Championship Series. ‡Won Championship Series. §First half 37-23; second 27-22. ★Won division playoff.

MANAGERS

Name	Record	Years
Connie Mack	3582-3814	'01-50
Jimmie Dykes	198-254	'51-53
Eddie Joost	51-103	1954
Lou Boudreau	151-260	'55-57
Harry Craft	162-196	'57-59
Bob Elliott	58-96	1960
Joe Gordon	26-33	1961
Hank Bauer	187-226	'61-62
		1969
Eddie Lopat	90-124	'63-64
Mel McGaha	45-91	'64-65
Haywood Sullivan	54-82	1965
Alvin Dark	314-291	'66-67
		'74-75
Luke Appling	10-30	1967
Bob Kennedy	82-80	1968
John McNamara	97-78	'69-70
Dick Williams	288-190	'71-73
Chuck Tanner	87-74	1976
Jack McKeon	71-105	'77, '78
Bobby Winkles	61-86	'77-78
Jim Marshall	54-108	1979
Billy Martin	215-218	'80-82
Steve Boros	94-112	'83-84
Jackie Moore	163-190	'84-86
Tony La Russa	413-314	'86-91

DAY BY DAY

Date	Opp.	Res.	Score (inn.*)	Hits	Opp. hits	Winning pitcher	Losing pitcher	Save	Record	Pos.	GB
4-9	Min.	W	7-2	13	5	Stewart	Morris		1-0	T1st	...
4-10	Min.	L	1-4	4	6	Anderson	Welch	Aguilera	1-1	T4th	1
4-11	Min.	W	3-0	9	5	Slusarski	Erickson	Eckersley	2-1	T3rd	1
4-12	Sea.	W	6-1	13	7	Moore	Bankhead		3-1	T2nd	½
4-13	Sea.	W	4-2	7	5	Dressendorfer	DeLucia	Eckersley	4-1	T2nd	½
4-14	Sea.	W	7-6	8	8	Allison	Jackson		5-1	T2nd	...
4-15	At Cal.	W	5-2	7	8	Welch	McCaskill	Eckersley	6-1	2nd	...
4-16	At Cal.	W	8-5 (11)	12	14	Chitren	Bailes	Eckersley	7-1	2nd	...
4-17	At Cal.	W	3-1	8	3	Moore	J. Abbott	Klink	8-1	1st	+1
4-18	At Cal.	L	1-7	6	10	Lewis	Dressendorfer		8-2	1st	+1
4-19	At Sea.	L	7-11	10	13	DeLucia	Stewart	Murphy	8-3	1st	+½
4-20	At Sea.	L	2-3	5	9	Hanson	Eckersley		8-4	T1st	...
4-21	At Sea.	L	2-7	3	9	Johnson	Allison		8-5	T2nd	½
4-22	At Min.	L	2-3	8	10	Bedrosian	Klink	Aguilera	8-6	T2nd	1½
4-23	At Min.	W	7-5	12	11	Dressendorfer	Guthrie	Eckersley	9-6	2nd	1½
4-24	At Min.	L	4-7	7	13	Morris	Stewart	Aguilera	9-7	T2nd	1½
4-26	Cal.	W	4-1	6	5	Welch	McCaskill	Eckersley	10-7	2nd	½
4-27	Cal.	W	4-3	7	8	Moore	Langston	Eckersley	11-7	2nd	½
4-28	Cal.	W	7-3	11	7	Stewart	J. Abbott		12-7	2nd	½
4-30	N.Y.	W	7-3	8	9	Welch	Eiland		13-7	1st	+½
5-1	N.Y.	W	7-4	10	7	Moore	Leary	Eckersley	14-7	1st	+1½
5-3	Cle.	W	4-3 (11)	7	10	Klink	Olin		15-7	1st	+2½
5-4	Cle.	L	6-20	10	20	King	Dressendorfer		15-8	1st	+2½
5-5	Cle.	L	6-15	12	19	Swindell	Welch		15-9	1st	+2½
5-7	Bal.	W	11-3	12	8	Moore	McDonald		16-9	1st	+2½
5-8	Bal.	W	9-3	11	9	Young	Flanagan		17-9	1st	+2½
5-10	At N.Y.	L	3-5	6	7	Habyan	Klink	Farr	17-10	1st	+2
5-11	At N.Y.	W	10-2	10	2	Dressendorfer	Eiland		18-10	1st	+3
5-12	At N.Y.	L	6-10	12	15	Farr	Moore		18-11	1st	+2
5-13	At N.Y.	L	3-6	8	9	Sanderson	Young	Guetterman	18-12	1st	+1½
5-14	At Bal.	L	1-6	10	9	Robinson	Slusarski		18-13	1st	+½
5-15	At Bal.	W	6-3	13	7	Welch	Ballard	Eckersley	19-13	1st	+½
5-16	At Bal.	W	11-5	14	12	Klink	Mesa		20-13	1st	+½
5-17	At Cle.	L	6-11	14	11	Candiotti	Moore		20-14	2nd	½
5-18	At Cle.	W	3-0	7	4	Hawkins	Nagy	Eckersley	21-14	2nd	½
5-19	At Cle.	W	9-4	13	7	Young	Nichols		22-14	1st	+½
5-20	Tor.	L	0-1	3	4	Wells	Welch	Henke	22-15	2nd	½
5-21	Tor.	L	7-11	6	11	Acker	Dressendorfer	Timlin	22-16	2nd	½
5-22	Tor.	W	2-1	5	5	Moore	Stieb	Eckersley	23-16	1st	+½
5-23	Chi.	L	1-11	5	17	Hibbard	Hawkins		23-17	T2nd	½
5-24	Chi.	W	6-5	9	7	Eckersley	Thigpen		24-17	2nd	½
5-25	Chi.	W	5-3 (10)	7	6	Klink	Edwards		25-17	2nd	½
5-26	Chi.	W	6-2	7	10	Stewart	Fernandez	Klink	26-17	2nd	½
5-28	At Tor.	W	8-4	9	6	Moore	Acker	Eckersley	27-17	2nd	...
5-29	At Tor.	L	3-8	11	14	Key	Slusarski	Henke	27-18	2nd	...
5-30	At Tor.	W	8-6	10	12	Klink	Ward	Eckersley	28-18	1st	+1
5-31	At Chi.	L	4-5	2	12	Thigpen	Chitren		28-19	2nd	...
6-1	At Chi.	W	7-4	6	9	Klink	Fernandez	Eckersley	29-19	1st	+1
6-2	At Chi.	L	3-4	4	10	Hough	Moore	Thigpen	29-20	1st	+½
6-3	At Chi.	W	5-3	13	17	Slusarski	Hibbard	Eckersley	30-20	1st	+1
6-4	Mil.	W	4-3	9	4	Welch	Navarro	Eckersley	31-20	1st	+1½
6-5	Mil.	W	6-4	9	3	Stewart	Bosio	Chitren	32-20	1st	+1½
6-6	Mil.	W	9-8	12	8	Walton	Crim	Eckersley	33-20	1st	+1½
6-7	Bos.	L	1-3	4	6	Harris	Moore	Reardon	33-21	1st	+1½
6-8	Bos.	L	1-8	2	12	Clemens	Slusarski		33-22	1st	+1½
6-9	Bos.	W	8-0	13	5	Welch	Bolton		34-22	1st	+1½
6-10	Det.	W	12-6	15	8	Guzman	Henneman		35-22	1st	+2½
6-11	Det.	L	1-5	4	11	Gullickson	Hawkins	Henneman	35-23	1st	+1½
6-12	Det.	W	3-1	5	3	Moore	Tanana	Eckersley	36-23	1st	+2
6-15 (1)	At Mil.	L	4-6	6	6	Navarro	Stewart	Plesac	36-24	1st	...
6-15 (2)	At Mil.	W	7-3	9	7	Hawkins	Brown	Chitren	37-24	1st	+½
6-16	At Mil.	L	7-11	14	13	Crim	Nelson		37-25	2nd	½
6-17	At Mil.	L	0-5	5	6	August	Moore		37-26	2nd	½
6-18	At Det.	L	0-2	4	3	Tanana	Welch	Henneman	37-27	2nd	1½
6-19	At Det.	W	5-4	13	8	Nelson	Terrell	Eckersley	38-27	2nd	1½
6-20	At Bos.	L	7-8	12	12	Gray	Chitren	Reardon	38-28	2nd	2
6-21	At Bos.	L	2-3	11	7	Bolton	Moore	Reardon	38-29	2nd	3
6-22	At Bos.	L	5-9	8	13	Harris	Slusarski		38-30	2nd	4
6-23	At Bos.	W	4-2	10	6	Welch	Darwin	Eckersley	39-30	2nd	3
6-25	Tex.	L	1-6	7	11	Guzman	Stewart		39-31	T2nd	4½

— 71 —

Date	Opp.	Res.	Score (inn.*)	Hits	Opp. hits	Winning pitcher	Losing pitcher	Save	Record	Pos.	GB
6-26	Tex.	L	1-8	6	8	Brown	Nelson		39-32	3rd	4½
6-27	Tex.	L	6-9	12	11	Milacki	Mutis	Olson	39-33	4th	4½
6-28	K.C.	L	0-11	5	14	Aquino	Welch		39-34	T4th	4½
6-29	K.C.	W	6-3	8	10	Stewart	S. Davis	Eckersley	40-34	4th	3½
6-30	K.C.	W	3-2	5	5	Moore	Gordon	Eckersley	41-34	4th	3½
7-1	K.C.	L	3-7	5	11	Boddicker	Hawkins	Montgomery	41-35	4th	3½
7-2	At Tex.	L	6-9	4	19	Rogers	Honeycutt	Russell	41-36	5th	3½
7-3	At Tex.	W	5-0	10	3	Stewart	Barfield		42-36	5th	2½
7-4	At Tex.	L	4-5 (10)	5	9	Russell	Nelson		42-37	T4th	3½
7-5	At K.C.	W	9-3	8	7	Hawkins	Gordon	Chitren	43-37	T4th	2½
7-6	At K.C.	W	9-7	12	12	Welch	Boddicker	Eckersley	44-37	4th	2½
7-7	At K.C.	L	5-7	9	10	Gubicza	Stewart		44-38	5th	2½
7-11	Bal.	W	8-1	12	7	Stewart	Robinson		45-38	3rd	2½
7-12	Bal.	L	3-6	4	12	McDonald	Young	Olson	45-39	4th	3½
7-13	Bal.	L	0-2	0	6	Milacki	Show	Olson	45-40	4th	4½
7-14	Bal.	W	3-2 (11)	11	6	Burns	Olson		46-40	4th	3½
7-15	Cle.	W	6-1	12	4	Hawkins	Boucher		47-40	4th	3½
7-16	Cle.	W	7-6 (13)	13	12	Klink	Jones		48-40	2nd	2½
7-17	Cle.	L	1-2	4	4	Nichols	Welch		48-41	2nd	3
7-18	N.Y.	L	2-3	4	10	Kamieniecki	Show	Howe	48-42	3rd	4
7-19	N.Y.	L	0-3	4	6	Johnson	Moore	Farr	48-43	4th	5
7-20	N.Y.	L	1-5	5	8	Taylor	Hawkins		48-44	T4th	6
7-21	N.Y.	W	4-2	6	7	Stewart	Sanderson	Eckersley	49-44	4th	6
7-23	At Cle.	W	10-7	14	16	Honeycutt	Shaw		50-44	4th	5
7-24	At Cle.	W	8-4	11	9	Show	Swindell		51-44	4th	4
7-25	At Cle.	L	7-8	6	9	York	Eckersley	Olin	51-45	4th	5
7-26	At Bal.	W	12-9	14	8	Klink	Williamson	Chitren	52-45	3rd	5
7-27	At Bal.	W	9-1	13	2	Slusarski	Ballard		53-45	3rd	5
7-28	At Bal.	W	4-3	8	9	Honeycutt	McDonald	Eckersley	54-45	3rd	4
7-29	At N.Y.	W	10-8	17	14	Campbell	Howe	Eckersley	55-45	3rd	4
7-30	At N.Y.	W	6-5	10	4	Young	Taylor	Eckersley	56-45	3rd	4
7-31	At Bos.	L	10-11 (14)	13	15	Harris	Chitren		56-46	3rd	5
8-1	At Bos.	W	4-2	11	6	Klink	Lamp	Eckersley	57-46	3rd	4
8-2	Min.	W	3-1	5	7	Welch	Morris		58-46	3rd	3
8-3	Min.	L	6-8	10	13	Bedrosian	Klink	Aguilera	58-47	3rd	4
8-4	Min.	L	2-6	6	11	Erickson	Stewart	Willis	58-48	3rd	5
8-5	Sea.	W	3-0	12	2	Darling	Krueger	Eckersley	59-48	3rd	5
8-6	Sea.	W	3-0	7	7	Moore	DeLucia	Eckersley	60-48	3rd	5
8-7	Sea.	W	6-1	10	6	Welch	Holman		61-48	3rd	4
8-9	At Cal.	W	5-4	8	8	Stewart	McCaskill	Eckersley	62-48	3rd	4
8-10	At Cal.	W	3-1	5	5	Darling	Langston	Eckersley	63-48	3rd	4
8-11	At Cal.	W	3-2	6	12	Moore	Grahe	Eckersley	64-48	3rd	3
8-12	At Sea.	L	3-6	7	6	DeLucia	Welch		64-49	3rd	3
8-13	At Sea.	L	2-5	8	9	Holman	Stewart	Schooler	64-50	3rd	4
8-14	At Sea.	L	0-4	1	7	Johnson	Slusarski		64-51	3rd	4
8-15	At Sea.	L	6-8	14	11	Jones	Chitren	Schooler	64-52	3rd	4
8-16	At Min.	L	4-5 (12)	9	14	Aguilera	Nelson		64-53	3rd	5
8-17	At Min.	L	4-12	8	16	Morris	Welch		64-54	3rd	6
8-18	At Min.	L	4-6	4	11	Willis	Honeycutt	Aguilera	64-55	3rd	7
8-19	At Min.	W	8-7	11	13	Klink	Bedrosian	Eckersley	65-55	3rd	6
8-20	Cal.	W	3-2	5	6	Darling	Langston	Eckersley	66-55	3rd	6
8-21	Cal.	W	2-0	11	4	Moore	Grahe	Eckersley	67-55	3rd	6
8-22	Cal.	W	2-1	5	4	Welch	Finley		68-55	3rd	6
8-23	Mil.	L	4-13	5	16	Navarro	Stewart		68-56	3rd	6
8-24	Mil.	L	0-7	9	7	Wegman	Slusarski		68-57	3rd	7
8-25	Mil.	L	2-8	5	16	Bosio	Darling		68-58	3rd	7
8-26	Bos.	L	0-3	3	7	Clemens	Moore		68-59	3rd	8
8-27	Bos.	L	4-6	6	13	Gardiner	Welch	Reardon	68-60	3rd	8
8-28	Bos.	W	9-3	10	8	Stewart	Young		69-60	2nd	8
8-30	Det.	W	6-3 (10)	10	5	Eckersley	Gleaton		70-60	2nd	7
8-31	Det.	W	9-8 (10)	12	11	Eckersley	Cerutti		71-60	2nd	7
9-1	Det.	L	2-5	5	12	Leiter	Welch	Gleaton	71-61	2nd	8
9-3	At Mil.	L	3-5	8	7	Nunez	Eckersley		71-62	T2nd	9
9-4	At Mil.	L	0-2	4	9	Wegman	Darling	Henry	71-63	T3rd	9
9-5	At Det.	W	4-1	8	7	Moore	Tanana	Eckersley	72-63	3rd	8½
9-6	At Det.	L	2-11	5	14	Terrell	Welch		72-64	3rd	9½
9-7	At Det.	W	3-1	9	8	Slusarski	Leiter	Eckersley	73-64	3rd	9½
9-8	At Det.	W	7-4	11	8	Stewart	Gullickson	Eckersley	74-64	3rd	9½
9-9	Chi.	L	1-7	3	11	Fernandez	Darling		74-65	3rd	10½
9-10	Chi.	L	1-3	6	7	Perez	Honeycutt	Thigpen	74-66	3rd	11½
9-11	Chi.	W	6-5 (10)	9	10	Eckersley	Wapnick		75-66	3rd	10½
9-13	At Tor.	L	6-7	9	15	Guzman	Stewart	Henke	75-67	4th	11
9-14	At Tor.	L	0-6	5	8	Candiotti	Welch		75-68	4th	11
9-15	At Tor.	W	10-5	12	7	Moore	Stottlemyre	Eckersley	76-68	4th	10

Date	Opp.	Res.	Score (inn.*)	Hits	Opp. hits	Winning pitcher	Losing pitcher	Save	Record	Pos.	GB
9-17	At Chi.	L	0-1	3	2	Hibbard	Darling	Thigpen	76-69	4th	10½
9-18	At Chi.	L	0-6	5	10	McDowell	Stewart		76-70	4th	10½
9-20	Tor.	W	6-5 (11)	8	9	Eckersley	Ward		77-70	4th	10½
9-21	Tor.	W	4-0	6	5	Moore	Key		78-70	3rd	10½
9-22	Tor.	L	2-3	3	5	Guzman	Darling	Wells	78-71	3rd	11½
9-23	K.C.	W	7-6	10	16	Klink	Gordon	Eckersley	79-71	3rd	11
9-24	K.C.	L	4-5	11	8	Appier	Slusarski	Montgomery	79-72	4th	12
9-25	K.C.	W	8-4	14	8	Welch	M. Davis	Eckersley	80-72	4th	11
9-26	Tex.	W	10-0	14	4	Moore	Boyd		81-72	3rd	10½
9-27	Tex.	L	0-3	2	9	Guzman	Darling		81-73	4th	10½
9-28	Tex.	L	3-6 (10)	6	11	Mathews	Eckersley	Russell	81-74	4th	11½
9-29	Tex.	W	19-5	18	9	Slusarski	Brown		82-74	4th	10½
9-30	At K.C.	L	4-8	7	11	M. Davis	Welch		82-75	4th	11½
10-1	At K.C.	W	4-0	8	6	Moore	Gubicza	Eckersley	83-75	T3rd	11½
10-2	At K.C.	L	5-16	9	16	Crawford	Darling		83-76	T3rd	12
10-4	At Tex.	L	3-4	9	7	Rogers	Stewart		83-77	4th	11
10-5	At Tex.	W	12-5	15	9	Young	Fajardo		84-77	T3rd	11
10-6	At Tex.	L	2-4	4	5	Mathews	Nelson		84-78	4th	11

Monthly records: April (13-7), May (15-12), June (13-15), July (15-12), August (15-14), September (11-15), Oct. (2-3).

HIGHLIGHTS

High point: Despite suffering injuries in every key area, Oakland owned a 44-38 mark (just 2½ games off the lead in the American League West) at the All-Star break.

Low point: After winning six straight in early August, the A's lost seven in a row (four at Seattle and three at Minnesota) and fell seven games behind the Twins.

Turning point: Home and away series against the Twins in August showed that the A's weren't going to repeat as division champs. Oakland lost two of three at home. Then, in Minnesota, the A's were able to win just one game in the four-game series.

Most valuable player: Center fielder Dave Henderson. Sore legs forced him to slip at the end of the season, but he committed just one error in 140 games and hit a career-high 25 homers.

Most valuable pitcher: Righthander Dennis Eckersley. He saved 43 of Oakland's 84 wins to become the first pitcher ever to save 40-plus games in three straight seasons.

Most improved player: Second baseman Mike Gallego. He established career highs in several categories, and his 12 homers were one more than he had hit in 570 career games before last year.

Most pleasant surprise: Rookie shortstop Mike Bordick. When Walt Weiss was injured, Bordick came along and played steadily in 81 of the A's last 85 games.

Biggest disappointment: Left fielder Rickey Henderson and first baseman Mark McGwire. Henderson became baseball's all-time base thief when he swiped No. 939 on May 1. But other than that, the defending A.L. Most Valuable Player was pretty much a bust. McGwire finished with just 22 homers, 75 RBIs and a paltry .201 batting average.

Key injuries: The A's used the disabled list 16 times (one short of setting the club record). Injuries to Rick Honeycutt, Gene Nelson, Eric Show and Dave Stewart crippled the pitching staff. The loss of third baseman Carney Lansford and Weiss hampered the infield.

Notable: Bob Welch and Stewart, a combined 49-17 in 1990, were 23-24 in 1991. ... The third-base quartet of Lansford, Ernest Riles, Vance Law and Brook Jacoby combined to bat .208 (129-for-619) with five homers and 62 RBIs.... The A's were 0-65 when trailing entering the ninth inning.

—KIT STIER

RECORDS

1991 regular-season record: 84-78 (4th in A.L. West); 47-34 at home; 37-44 on road; 44-40 vs. East; 40-38 vs. West; 26-16 vs. LHP; 58-62 vs. RHP; 76-60 on grass; 8-18 on turf; 32-22 in daytime; 52-56 at night; 22-18 in one-run games; 9-4 in extra-inning games; 0-0-1 in doubleheaders.

Team record last five years: 471-339 (.581, ranks 1st in league in that span).

TEAM LEADERS

Batting average: Harold Baines (.295).
At-bats: Jose Canseco, Dave Henderson (572).
Runs: Jose Canseco (115).
Hits: Dave Henderson (158).
Total bases: Jose Canseco (318).
Doubles: Dave Henderson (33).
Triples: Mike Gallego, Ernest Riles, Willie Wilson (4).
Home runs: Jose Canseco (44).
Runs batted in: Jose Canseco (122).
Stolen bases: Rickey Henderson (58).
Slugging percentage: Jose Canseco (.556).
On-base percentage: Rickey Henderson (.400).
Wins: Mike Moore (17).
Earned-run average: Mike Moore (2.96).
Complete games: Bob Welch (7).
Shutouts: Mike Moore, Dave Stewart, Bob Welch (1).
Saves: Dennis Eckersley (43).
Innings pitched: Dave Stewart (226).
Strikeouts: Mike Moore (153).

GAMES BY POSITION

Catcher: Terry Steinbach 117, Jamie Quirk 54, Scott Hemond 8, Troy Afenir 4.

First base: Mark McGwire 152, Terry Steinbach 9, Jamie Quirk 8, Ron Witmeyer 8, Ernest Riles 5, Brook Jacoby 3, Dann Howitt 1, Vance Law 1.

Second base: Mike Gallego 135, Lance Blankenship 45, Scott Brosius 18, Scott Hemond 7, Ernest Riles 7, Mike Bordick 5, Fred Manrique 2, Dave Henderson 1.

Third base: Ernest Riles 69, Vance Law 67, Brook Jacoby 52, Lance Blankenship 14, Scott Brosius 7, Carney Lansford 4, Scott Hemond 2, Mike Bordick 1, Jamie Quirk 1.

Shortstop: Mike Bordick 84, Mike Gallego 55, Walt Weiss 40, Ernest Riles 20, Fred Manrique 7, Vance Law 3, Scott Hemond 1.

Outfield: Dave Henderson 140, Jose Canseco 131, Rickey Henderson 119, Willie Wilson 87, Lance Blankenship 28, Brad Komminsk 22, Dann Howitt 20, Scott Brosius 15, Harold Baines 12, Doug Jennings 6, Vance Law 3.

Designated hitter: Harold Baines 125, Jose Canseco 24, Rickey Henderson 10, Willie Wilson 9, Dave Henderson 7, Lance Blankenship 6, Scott Hemond 4, Terry Steinbach 2, Troy Afenir 1, Scott Brosius 1, Carney Lansford 1, Jamie Quirk 1.

TOP 10 DRAFT CHOICES

1a. Brent Gates, SS, Univ. of Minnesota.
1b. Mike Rossiter, RHP, Burroughs High School, Burbank, Calif.
2a. Mike Neill, OF, Villanova University.
2b. Russ Brock, RHP, University of Michigan.
3. Joel Wolfe, OF, UCLA.
4. Steve Wojciechowski, LHP, St. Xavier (Ill.) College.
5. Tim Smith, RHP, Ohio State.
6. Tim Doyle, LHP, Cal St. Sacramento.
7. Ricky Kimball, RHP, Florida State.
8. Scott Sheldon, SS, Univ. of Houston.
9. Damon Mashore, OF, Univ. of Arizona.
10. Zach Sawyer, RHP, Clinton (Mass.) High School.

SEATTLE MARINERS
AMERICAN LEAGUE WEST DIVISION

1992 SCHEDULE

APRIL

S	M	T	W	T	F	S
5	6 N	7 N	8 N	9 N	10 N	11 N
	TEX H	TEX H	TEX H	TEX H	KC H	KC H
12	13	14	15 N	16 N	17 N	18
KC H	CHI		CHI	CHI	MIL	MIL
19	20 N	21 N	22 N	23	24 N	25 N
MIL	MIN H	MIN H	MIN H	MIN H	CAL	CAL
26	27	28 N	29 N	30 N		
CAL		DET	DET	DET		

MAY

S	M	T	W	T	F	S
					1 N	2 N
					BAL	BAL
3	4 N	5 N	6 N	7 N	8 N	9 N
BAL	NY H	NY H	TOR H	TOR H	DET H	DET H
10	11	12 N	13 N	14	15 N	16
DET H		NY	NY	TOR	TOR	TOR
17	18 N	19 N	20 N	21	22 N	23 N
TOR	BOS	BOS	BOS		CLE H	CLE H
24 N	25 N	26 N	27	28	29 N	30 N
CLE H	BAL H	BAL H	BAL H		BOS H	BOS H
31 N						
BOS H						

JUNE

S	M	T	W	T	F	S
	1	2 N	3 N	4 N	5 N	6 N
		CLE	CLE	CLE	KC	KC
7	8 N	9 N	10 N	11	12 N	13 N
KC	TEX	TEX	TEX		MIL H	MIL H
14	15 N	16 N	17 N	18	19 N	20 N
MIL H	CHI H	CHI H	CHI H	CHI H	MIN	MIN
21	22 N	23 N	24 N	25 N	26 N	27 N
MIN H	OAK	OAK	OAK	CAL H	CAL H	CAL H
28	29 N	30 N				
CAL H	OAK H	OAK H				

JULY

S	M	T	W	T	F	S
			1 N	2	3 N	4 N
			OAK H		DET	DET
5	6 N	7 N	8 N	9 N	10 N	11
DET	DET	TOR	TOR	NY	NY	NY
12	13	14 *	15	16 N	17 N	18 N
NY				TOR H	TOR H	TOR H
19	20 N	21 N	22 N	23	24 N	25 N
TOR H	DET H	DET H	DET H	NY H	NY H	NY H
26	27 N	28 N	29 N	30 N	31 N	
NY	CAL	CAL	CAL	CAL	CHI	

AUGUST

S	M	T	W	T	F	S
						1 N
						CHI
2	3	4 N	5 N	6	7 N	8 N
CHI		MIL	MIL	MIL	TEX H	TEX H
9	10 N	11 N	12	13	14 N	15 N
TEX H	KC H	KC H	KC H		MIN H	MIN H
16	17	18 N	19 N	20	21 N	22
MIN H		BAL	BAL	BAL	BOS	BOS
23	24	25 N	26 N	27 N	28 N	29 N
BOS		CLE H	CLE H	CLE H	BAL H	BAL H
30	31 N					
BAL H	BOS H					

SEPTEMBER

S	M	T	W	T	F	S
		1 N	2 N	3	4 N	5 N
		BOS H	BOS H		CLE	CLE
6	7	8 N	9 N	10	11 N	12
CLE	MIN	MIN	MIN	OAK	OAK	OAK
13	14	15 N	16 N	17	18 N	19 N
OAK		CAL H	CAL H		OAK H	OAK H
20	21 N	22 N	23 N	24 N	25 N	26 N
OAK H	KC	KC	KC	KC	TEX	TEX
27	28	29 N	30 N			
TEX		MIL H	MIL H			

OCTOBER

S	M	T	W	T	F	S
				1 N	2 N	3 N
				MIL H	CHI H	CHI H
4	5	6	7	8	9	10
CHI H						

1992 SEASON

CLUB DIRECTORY

Chairman
Jeff Smulyan
President
Gary Kaseff
Vice president, baseball operations
Woody Woodward
Vice president, communications
Randy Adamack
Vice president, finance and administration
Brian Beggs
Vice president, marketing
Stuart Layne
V.p., scouting and player development
Roger Jongewaard
Director of baseball administration
Lee Pelekoudas
Asst. to vice president, baseball operations
George Zuraw
Farm director
Jim Beattie
Coordinator of minor league instruction
Jim Skaalen
Director of team travel
Craig Detwiler
Director of community relations
Joe Chard
Director of corporate sales
Greg Elliott
Director of promotions
Carl Weinstein
Director of public relations
Dave Aust
Director of stadium operations
Tony Pereira
Director of ticket sales
Chris McCartney
Director of ticket services
J.C. Crouch
Controller
Denise Podosek
Promotions manager
Kevin Martinez
Assistant director of public relations
Pete Vanderwarker
Exec. assistant to chairman and president
Janet O'Brien
Payroll manager
Shirley Shreve
Player development and scouting assistant
Larry Beinfest
Public relations assistant
Molly Magan
Trainer
Rick Griffin
Home clubhouse and equipment manager
Henry Genzale

Club physicians
Dr. Larry Pedegana
Dr. Mitchel Storey
Club dentist
Dr. Richard Leshgold
Head groundskeeper
Wilbur Loo
Public-address announcer
Tom Hutyler
Scouting national cross-checkers
Benny Looper
Bob Wadsworth
Special assignment scout
Bill Kearns
Scouting supervisors
Gordon Blakeley
Ron Hopkins
Ken Madeja
Regular scouts
Maximo Alvarez
Fernando Arguelles
Brian Ballantine
Al Bundy
John Burden
Kendall Carter
Ken Compton
Edward D'Alessio
Ramon de los Santos
Miguel Escobar
Ron Haffner
Matt Hall
Vic Harris
Gudadalupe Jabalera
Dan Jennings
Mark Jensen
Dave Karaff
Gary McGraw
Jerry Marik
Bill Miller
Omer Munoz
Glenn Murdock
Joe Nigro
Fran Oneto
Cliff Pastornicky
Myron Pines
Steve Pope
Phil Pote
John Ramey
Louis Scheuermann
Bill Sizemore
Chris Smith
Roberto Valdez
Ray Vince
Jack Webber
Archie White
Bill Young

SCHEDULE KEY

H—Home game.   *All-Star Game at San Diego/Jack Murphy Stadium.
N—Night game (any game starting after 5 p.m.).

SPRING TRAINING ROSTER

Manager—Bill Plummer (3).

Coaches—Gene Clines (16), Roger Hansen (25), Rusty Kuntz (22), Marty Martinez (14), Russ Nixon (5), Dan Warthen (49).

No.	PITCHERS	B/T	Ht./Wt.	Born	1991 clubs
55	DeLucia, Rich	R/R	6-0/180	10-7-64	Seattle
	Elliott, Don	R/R	6-5/200	9-20-68	Clearwater, Spartanburg
35	Fleming, Dave	L/L	6-3/200	11-7-69	Jacksonville, Seattle, Calgary
39	Hanson, Erik	R/R	6-6/210	5-18-65	Seattle, Calgary
47	Harris, Gene	R/R	5-11/190	12-5-64	Seattle, Calgary
36	Holman, Brian	R/R	6-4/185	1-25-65	Seattle
51	Johnson, Randy	R/L	6-10/225	9-10-63	Seattle
52	Jones, Calvin	R/R	6-3/185	9-26-63	Calgary, Seattle
27	Knackert, Brent	R/R	6-3/190	8-1-69	San Bernardino
40	Nelson, Jeff	R/R	6-8/225	11-17-66	Jacksonville, Calgary
33	Newlin, Jim	R/R	6-2/205	9-11-66	Jacksonville
	Remlinger, Mike	L/L	6-0/195	3-23-66	Phoenix, San Francisco
29	Schooler, Mike	R/R	6-3/220	8-10-62	Jacksonville, Seattle
37	Swan, Russ	L/L	6-4/215	1-3-64	Seattle
42	Woodson, Kerry	R/R	6-2/190	5-18-69	San Bernardino, Jacksonville
41	Zavaras, Clint	R/R	6-1/175	1-4-67	San Bernardino, Jacksonville

No.	CATCHERS	B/T	Ht./Wt.	Born	1991 clubs
9	Bradley, Scott	L/R	5-11/185	3-22-60	Seattle
31	Campanis, Jim	R/R	6-1/200	8-27-67	Jacksonville
43	Cochrane, Dave	S/R	6-2/180	1-31-63	Calgary, Seattle
45	Howard, Chris	R/R	6-2/200	2-27-66	Calgary, Seattle
20	Pirkl, Greg	R/R	6-5/225	8-7-70	San Bernardino, Peninsula
17	Sinatro, Matt	R/R	5-9/175	3-22-60	Calgary, Seattle
10	Valle, Dave	R/R	6-2/200	10-30-60	Seattle

No.	INFIELDERS	B/T	Ht./Wt.	Born	1991 clubs
8	Amaral, Rich	R/R	6-0/175	4-1-62	Calgary, Seattle
11	Martinez, Edgar	R/R	5-11/175	1-2-63	Seattle
23	Martinez, Tino	L/R	6-2/205	12-7-67	Calgary, Seattle
12	O'Brien, Pete	L/L	6-2/195	2-9-58	Seattle
4	Reynolds, Harold	S/R	5-11/165	11-26-60	Seattle
2	Schaefer, Jeff	R/R	5-10/170	5-31-60	Seattle
13	Vizquel, Omar	S/R	5-9/165	4-24-67	Seattle

No.	OUTFIELDERS	B/T	Ht./Wt.	Born	1991 clubs
1	Briley, Greg	L/R	5-8/165	5-24-65	Seattle
19	Buhner, Jay	R/R	6-3/205	8-13-64	Seattle
28	Cotto, Henry	R/R	6-2/180	1-5-61	Seattle
24	Griffey Jr., Ken	L/L	6-3/200	11-21-69	Seattle
26	Lennon, Pat	R/R	6-2/200	4-27-68	Calgary, Seattle
7	Mitchell, Kevin	R/R	5-11/210	1-13-62	San Francisco
	Powell, Alonzo	R/R	6-2/190	12-12-64	Calgary, Seattle

BALLPARK INFORMATION

Ballpark (capacity, surface)
The Kingdome (59,702, artificial)
Address
P.O. Box 4100
411 First Ave. S.
Seattle, WA 98104
Business phone
206-628-3555
Ticket information
206-628-3555
Ticket prices
$12.50 (box)
$11.50 (field)
$9.50 (club)
$6.50 (view)
$5.50 (general admission)
$5 (view, children 14 and under)
$4 (g.a., children 14 and under)
Field dimensions (from home plate)
To left field at foul line, 331 feet
To center field, 405 feet
To right field at foul line, 314 feet
First game played
April 6, 1977 (Angels 7, Mariners 0)

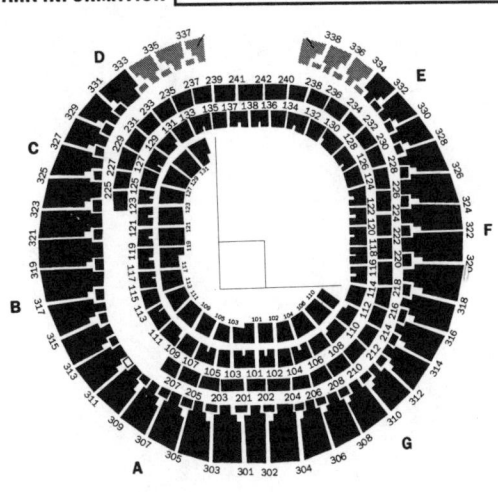

MINOR LEAGUE AFFILIATES

Class	Team	League	Manager
AAA	Calgary	Pacific Coast	Keith Bodie
AA	Jacksonville	Southern	Bob Hartsfield
A	San Bernardino	California	Ivan DeJesus
A	Peninsula	Carolina	Marc Hill
A	Bellingham	Northwest	Dave Myers
Rookie	Tempe Mariners	Arizona	Carlos Lezcano

BROADCAST INFORMATION

Radio: KIRO-AM (710). Broadcasters: Dave Niehaus; other(s) to be announced.
TV: To be announced. Broadcasters: To be announced.
Cable TV: None.

SPRING TRAINING

Ballpark (city): Tempe Stadium (Tempe, Ariz.).
Ticket information: 206-628-3555 (Mariners ticket office).

HISTORY

YEAR-BY-YEAR RECORDS

Year	Pos.	W	L	Pct.	*GB	Year	Pos.	W	L	Pct.	*GB
1977	6th	64	98	.395	38	1986	7th	67	95	.414	25
1978	7th	56	104	.350	35	1987	4th	78	84	.481	7
1979	6th	67	95	.414	21	1988	7th	68	93	.422	35½
1980	7th	59	103	.364	38	1989	6th	73	89	.451	26
1981	6th/5th	44	65	.404	†	1990	5th	77	85	.475	26
1982	4th	76	86	.469	17	1991	5th	83	79	.512	12
1983	7th	60	102	.370	39						
1984	T5th	74	88	.457	10						
1985	6th	74	88	.457	17						

*Games behind winner. †First half 21-36; second 23-29.

MANAGERS

Name	Record	Years
Darrell Johnson	226-362	'77-80
Maury Wills	26-56	'80-81
Rene Lachemann	140-180	'81-83
Del Crandall	93-141	'83-84
Chuck Cottier	98-120	'84-86
Dick Williams	159-192	'86-88
Jimmy Snyder	45-60	1988
Jim Lefebvre	233-253	'89-91

DAY BY DAY

Date	Opp.	Res.	Score (inn.*)	Hits	Opp. hits	Winning pitcher	Losing pitcher	Save	Record	Pos.	GB
4-9	Cal.	L	2-3	6	8	Finley	Hanson	Harvey	0-1	T5th	1
4-10	Cal.	L	3-5	11	8	McCaskill	Johnson	Harvey	0-2	T6th	2
4-11	Cal.	L	0-5	5	12	Langston	Holman		0-3	7th	3
4-12	At Oak.	L	1-6	7	13	Moore	Bankhead		0-4	7th	3½
4-13	At Oak.	L	2-4	5	7	Dressendorfer	DeLucia	Eckersley	0-5	7th	4½
4-14	At Oak.	L	6-7	8	8	Allison	Jackson		0-6	7th	5
4-15	Min.	W	8-4	12	7	Johnson	Anderson		1-6	7th	5
4-16	Min.	W	3-0	9	5	Holman	Erickson		2-6	T6th	5
4-17	Min.	W	4-3 (11)	10	10	Jackson	Aguilera		3-6	6th	5
4-19	Oak.	W	11-7	13	10	DeLucia	Stewart	Murphy	4-6	T4th	3½
4-20	Oak.	W	3-2	9	5	Hanson	Eckersley		5-6	T4th	2½
4-21	Oak.	W	7-2	9	3	Johnson	Allison		6-6	4th	2
4-22	At Cal.	W	4-3	8	6	Holman	J. Abbott	Jackson	7-6	4th	2
4-23	At Cal.	W	2-0	8	7	Bankhead	Lewis	Swan	8-6	3rd	2
4-24	At Cal.	L	5-9	8	13	Finley	DeLucia	Harvey	8-7	5th	2
4-25	At Min.	L	3-4 (10)	8	13	Bedrosian	Jackson		8-8	T4th	2½
4-26	At Min.	L	0-6	5	15	Erickson	Johnson		8-9	5th	2½
4-27	At Min.	L	2-7	6	10	Tapani	Holman		8-10	T6th	3½
4-28	At Min.	L	2-8	10	11	Morris	Bankhead		8-11	7th	4½
4-29	At Bal.	W	10-1	15	8	DeLucia	Johnson		9-11	6th	4
4-30	At Bal.	W	6-3	10	6	Hanson	Ballard	Swan	10-11	5th	3½
5-1	At Bal.	L	1-2	7	3	Mesa	Johnson	Olson	10-12	6th	4½
5-3	N.Y.	L	0-5	3	6	Sanderson	Holman		10-13	T5th	5½
5-4	N.Y.	W	3-2	7	11	Bankhead	Cary	Jackson	11-13	T5th	5½
5-5	N.Y.	W	5-4 (16)	15	18	Krueger	Monteleone		12-13	T5th	3½
5-6	N.Y.	W	4-2	9	7	Hanson	Leary	Swift	13-13	T3rd	3
5-7	Cle.	W	7-6	12	9	Jackson	Jones		14-13	4th	3
5-8	Cle.	W	6-2	9	8	Holman	Nagy	Swift	15-13	3rd	3
5-10	Bal.	W	3-1	7	6	DeLucia	Ballard	Jackson	16-13	T2nd	3
5-11	Bal.	L	5-11	9	15	Mesa	Krueger		16-14	T2nd	3
5-12	Bal.	W	5-4	6	6	Jackson	Olson		17-14	2nd	2
5-14	At Cle.	W	2-1	8	7	Holman	Nichols	Swift	18-14	2nd	½
5-15	At Cle.	W	6-4	10	8	DeLucia	King	Swift	19-14	2nd	½
5-16	At Cle.	W	3-1	8	8	Jackson	Swindell		20-14	2nd	½
5-17	At N.Y.	W	1-0	3	4	Johnson	Leary	Swift	21-14	1st	+½
5-18	At N.Y.	W	4-1	11	6	Rice	Sanderson		22-14	1st	+½
5-19	At N.Y.	L	2-3	5	6	Howe	Holman	Guetterman	22-15	2nd	½
5-20	At K.C.	W	8-6	10	11	Swan	Montgomery	Jackson	23-15	1st	+½
5-21	At K.C.	L	3-4	5	8	Appier	Krueger		23-16	1st	+½
5-22	At K.C.	L	1-3	4	5	Gordon	Johnson		23-17	2nd	½
5-24	Tex.	L	3-7	9	11	Rogers	holman	Barfield	23-18	3rd	1½
5-25	Tex.	L	6-8 (11)	12	16	Barfield	Swan		23-19	T3rd	2½
5-26	Tex.	L	4-6	7	14	Witt	Swift	Russell	23-20	4th	3½
5-27	K.C.	L	3-6	4	8	Appier	Johnson		23-21	4th	4½
5-28	K.C.	L	5-6	8	11	Gordon	Hanson	M. Davis	23-22	4th	4½
5-29	K.C.	W	8-0	12	4	Holman	Boddicker		24-22	4th	3½
5-30	At Tex.	W	11-4	11	9	DeLucia	Rogers		25-22	4th	3½
5-31	At Tex.	L	6-7	13	10	Alexander	Bankhead	Russell	25-23	4th	3½
6-1	At Tex.	W	12-8	13	11	Swan	Brown	Jackson	26-23	4th	3½
6-4	At Det.	W	8-6	10	9	Holman	Cerutti	Jackson	27-23	4th	3½
6-5	At Det.	L	1-7	4	11	Gleaton	DeLucia	Gibson	27-24	4th	4½
6-6	At Det.	L	4-5	10	8	Gullickson	Bankhead	Henneman	27-25	5th	5½
6-7	Mil.	W	2-1	4	3	Krueger	Higuera	Jackson	28-25	5th	4½
6-8	Mil.	W	6-2	9	5	DeLucia	Wegman	Burba	29-25	4th	3½
6-9	Mil.	W	6-1	12	5	Holman	Navarro		30-25	4th	3½
6-10	Bos.	L	2-6	9	7	Gardiner	Johnson		30-26	4th	4½
6-11	Bos.	L	5-8	10	12	Darwin	Bankhead	Reardon	30-27	4th	4½
6-12	Bos.	W	5-3	6	5	Krueger	Harris	Jackson	31-27	4th	4½
6-13	Det.	W	6-5	9	4	Swift	Gibson	Jackson	32-27	4th	4
6-14	Det.	L	1-5	2	9	Gakeler	Holman		32-28	5th	4½
6-15	Det.	W	15-2	10	5	Johnson	Ritz	Swift	33-28	5th	4½
6-16	Det.	L	3-7	12	7	Gullickson	Rice		33-29	5th	4½
6-18	At Bos.	W	2-1	8	10	Krueger	Reardon		34-29	T4th	4
6-19	At Bos.	W	4-3	10	11	Swan	Clemens	Jackson	35-29	T3rd	4
6-20	At Mil.	L	0-4	4	9	Navarro	Holman		35-30	5th	4½
6-21	At Mil.	W	5-1	9	4	Johnson	Bosio		36-30	T3rd	4½
6-22	At Mil.	W	5-0	7	4	Hanson	August		37-30	T3rd	4½
6-23	At Mil.	L	2-5	4	9	Higuera	Krueger	Plesac	37-31	T3rd	4½
6-24	At Chi.	L	2-6	9	6	Hibbard	DeLucia	Radinsky	37-32	4th	5½
6-25	At Chi.	L	0-4	3	9	McDowell	Burba		37-33	5th	6½

SEATTLE MARINERS

1992 SEASON

SEATTLE MARINERS

Date	Opp.	Res.	Score (inn.*)	Hits	Opp. hits	Winning pitcher	Losing pitcher	Save	Record	Pos.	GB
6-26	At Chi.	W	5-4	10	4	Johnson	Garcia	Jackson	38-33	5th	5½
6-27	At Chi.	L	2-5	8	10	Fernandez	Hanson	Thigpen	38-34	5th	5½
6-28	At Tor.	W	3-1	9	7	Krueger	Candiotti	Jackson	39-34	T4th	4½
6-29	At Tor.	L	0-4	7	6	Timlin	DeLucia	Ward	39-35	T5th	4½
6-30	At Tor.	L	1-6	4	8	Stottlemyre	Holman		39-36	6th	5½
7-1	At Tor.	L	3-4	7	4	Acker	Jackson		39-37	6th	5½
7-2	Chi.	L	4-5	10	10	Perez	Burba		39-38	6th	5½
7-3	Chi.	L	2-3 (12)	4	13	Pall	Jones	Thigpen	39-39	6th	5½
7-4	Chi.	W	3-2	6	7	DeLucia	Hibbard	Murphy	40-39	6th	5½
7-5	Tor.	L	1-2	7	6	MacDonald	Holman	Henke	40-40	6th	5½
7-6	Tor.	L	3-4 (10)	6	11	Timlin	Swan	Henke	40-41	6th	6½
7-7	Tor.	L	2-5	4	8	Guzman	Hanson		40-42	6th	6½
7-11	Cle.	W	6-0	11	8	Holman	Nagy	Swift	41-42	6th	6½
7-12	Cle.	W	7-0	12	6	Johnson	Nichols		42-42	6th	6½
7-13	Cle.	L	3-6	4	12	Swindell	Jackson		42-43	6th	7½
7-14	Cle.	W	14-3	20	8	DeLucia	York		43-43	6th	6½
7-15	N.Y.	W	5-1	11	7	Krueger	Cadaret		44-43	6th	6½
7-16	N.Y.	W	5-0	7	6	Holman	Sanderson		45-43	6th	5½
7-17	At Mil.	L	1-6	4	7	Wegman	Johnson		45-44	6th	6
7-18	At Mil.	W	12-0	18	6	Hanson	Navarro		46-44	6th	6
7-19	At Bal.	L	1-4	7	7	Smith	DeLucia	Olson	46-45	6th	7
7-20	At Bal.	W	5-1	9	9	Krueger	Ballard		47-45	6th	7
7-21	At Bal.	W	6-4	9	10	Swan	Robinson	Swift	48-45	6th	7
7-23	At N.Y.	W	6-1	11	6	Johnson	Kamieniecki		49-45	T5th	6
7-24	At N.Y.	L	2-10	13	15	Johnson	Hanson		49-46	T5th	6
7-25	At N.Y.	W	6-3	10	5	Krueger	Taylor	Murphy	50-46	5th	6
7-26	At Cle.	W	7-4	13	7	DeLucia	Boucher	Schooler	51-46	5th	6
7-27	At Cle.	L	1-6	6	13	Nagy	Holman		51-47	5th	7
7-28	At Cle.	W	6-5	15	7	Johnson	York		52-47	5th	6
7-29	Bal.	W	11-4	11	8	Hanson	Milacki		53-47	5th	6
7-30	Bal.	W	8-2	10	9	Krueger	Smith		54-47	5th	6
7-31	Bal.	L	2-4 (11)	9	9	Flanagan	Swift	Olson	54-48	5th	7
8-2	At Cal.	W	4-3	9	9	Jackson	J. Abbott	Schooler	55-48	5th	5½
8-3	At Cal.	W	9-3	12	6	Johnson	McCaskill	Swift	56-48	5th	5½
8-4	At Cal.	W	5-2 (12)	9	5	Jackson	Fetters	Schooler	57-48	4th	5½
8-5	At Oak.	L	0-3	2	12	Darling	Krueger	Eckersley	57-49	4th	6½
8-6	At Oak.	L	0-3	7	7	Moore	DeLucia	Eckersley	57-50	5th	7½
8-7	At Oak.	L	1-6	6	10	Welch	Holman		57-51	5th	7½
8-9	Min.	L	2-5	7	9	West	Johnson	Aguilera	57-52	T5th	8½
8-10	Min.	W	8-0	11	9	Hanson	Erickson		58-52	T4th	7½
8-11	Min.	L	2-5	4	9	Tapani	Krueger		58-53	6th	8½
8-12	Oak.	W	6-3	6	7	DeLucia	Welch		59-53	T4th	8½
8-13	Oak.	W	5-2	9	8	Holman	Stewart	Schooler	60-53	T4th	7½
8-14	Oak.	W	4-0	7	1	Johnson	Slusarski		61-53	T4th	6½
8-15	Oak.	W	8-6	11	14	Jones	Chitren	Schooler	62-53	4th	5½
8-16	Cal.	W	5-3	7	8	Krueger	Grahe	Murphy	63-53	4th	5½
8-17	Cal.	L	1-4	9	8	Finley	DeLucia	Harvey	63-54	4th	6½
8-18	Cal.	L	3-4	11	9	J. Abbott	Holman	Harvey	63-55	4th	7½
8-19	Cal.	W	7-1	10	7	Johnson	McCaskill		64-55	4th	6½
8-20	At Min.	L	5-10	9	12	Erickson	Hanson	Guthrie	64-56	4th	7½
8-21	At Min.	L	1-9	6	12	Tapani	Krueger		64-57	4th	8½
8-22	At Min.	L	4-5 (10)	12	14	Aguilera	Schooler		64-58	4th	9½
8-23	At Det.	L	6-8	15	9	Gullickson	Holman	Kaiser	64-59	T4th	9½
8-24	At Det.	L	2-7	8	8	Tanana	Johnson		64-60	T4th	10½
8-25	At Det.	L	3-4	9	11	Terrell	Schooler		64-61	6th	10½
8-26	Mil.	W	5-4 (14)	9	12	Schooler	Henry		65-61	6th	10½
8-27	Mil.	W	6-4	12	9	DeLucia	August	Jackson	66-61	6th	9½
8-28	Mil.	W	7-6	9	11	Holman	Navarro	Swift	67-61	T4th	9½
8-30	Bos.	L	2-3	8	9	Hesketh	Hanson	Reardon	67-62	T5th	9½
8-31	Bos.	L	1-4	4	10	Clemens	Krueger		67-63	6th	10½
9-1	Bos.	L	2-13	8	18	Morton	Johnson		67-64	6th	11½
9-2	Det.	L	5-12	10	17	Gullickson	DeLucia	Gibson	67-65	6th	12½
9-3	Det.	W	1-0	4	5	Holman	Aldred	Swift	68-65	6th	12
9-5	At Bos.	L	3-4 (10)	10	8	Reardon	Murphy		68-66	6th	12
9-6	At Bos.	L	5-6	8	13	Lamp	Jackson	Reardon	68-67	6th	13
9-7	At Bos.	L	10-11	14	12	Bolton	Jones	Reardon	68-68	6th	14
9-8	At Bos.	L	6-17	9	17	Gardiner	DeLucia		68-69	7th	15
9-10	At Tor.	W	5-4	6	9	Holman	Stottlemyre	Jones	69-69	T6th	15½
9-11	At Tor.	W	7-3	13	6	Hanson	Key		70-69	6th	14½
9-13	At K.C.	L	2-3 (12)	8	9	Montgomery	Jackson		70-70	6th	15
9-14	At K.C.	W	4-3 (11)	9	8	Jackson	Crawford	Swift	71-70	6th	14
9-15	At K.C.	W	14-7	17	12	DeLucia	Boddicker		72-70	T5th	13
9-16	Tor.	W	6-5 (11)	11	9	Swan	MacDonald		73-70	5th	13
9-17	Tor.	W	5-4 (11)	12	11	Schooler	Acker		74-70	5th	12

Date	Opp.	Res.	Score (inn.*)	Hits	Opp. hits	Winning pitcher	Losing pitcher	Save	Record	Pos.	GB
9-18	Tor.	L	3-5 (12)	9	8	Ward	Bankhead	Acker	74-71	T5th	12
9-19	K.C.	W	10-5	13	9	Burba	Gordon	Swift	75-71	5th	11½
9-20	K.C.	L	0-3	3	6	Boddicker	DeLucia	Montgomery	75-72	T5th	12½
9-21	K.C.	W	4-1	11	9	Fleming	Gubicza	Schooler	76-72	5th	12½
9-22	K.C.	L	1-2	3	7	Saberhagen	Holman		76-73	T5th	13½
9-23	Tex.	L	4-11 (11)	13	13	Russell	Schooler		76-74	T5th	14
9-24	Tex.	L	7-8	13	8	Russell	Jackson		76-75	T6th	15
9-25	Tex.	L	1-7	3	9	Ryan	DeLucia		76-76	T6th	15
9-27	At Chi.	W	10-8 (11)	14	14	Swan	Perez		77-76	6th	14
9-28	At Chi.	L	2-5	6	5	Hibbard	DeLucia	Radinsky	77-77	6th	15
9-29	At Chi.	W	2-1	2	6	Johnson	Hough	Swift	78-77	6th	14
9-30 (1)	At Tex.	W	3-2 (11)	8	8	Schooler	Rosenthal	Swift	79-77	6th	14
9-30 (2)	At Tex.	L	0-2	9	7	Bohanon	Krueger	Russell	79-78	6th	14½
10-1	At Tex.	W	8-1	11	3	Burba	Boyd	Jones	80-78	6th	14
10-2	At Tex.	W	4-3	7	4	Bankhead	Guzman	Swift	81-78	6th	13
10-4	Chi.	W	6-4	11	7	Jones	Hough	Schooler	82-78	T5th	12
10-5	Chi.	W	10-0	8	9	Krueger	Garcia	Harris	83-78	5th	12
10-6	Chi.	L	2-3	7	4	Alvarez	Hanson	Radinsky	83-79	5th	12

Monthly records: April (1Q-11), May (15-12), June (14-13), July (15-12), August (13-15), September (12-15), Oct. (4-1).

HIGHLIGHTS

High point: A four-run rally in the top of the ninth inning against the Chicago White Sox capped a comeback from a six-run deficit and set up a 10-8 victory September 27. The win pushed Seattle above .500 (77-76), and the Mariners went on to win six of their last nine games to post the first winning record (83-79) in franchise history.

Low point: On August 20, the Mariners went into the Metrodome trailing the Twins by 6½ games. They lost three straight and then went to Detroit for another three-game series. They were swept again and never got closer than 9½ games back.

Turning point: That winless six-game trip. Management had a big hand in the lousy trip by scheduling an August 19 game in Seattle as a night game. After beating California that night to go nine games over .500, the Mariners flew all night and arrived in Minnesota at 6 a.m. for a game that evening.

Most valuable player: Center fielder Ken Griffey Jr. His .327 average set a club record, and he also set team marks in doubles (42), slugging percentage (.527) and intentional walks (21).

Most valuable pitcher: Righthander Bill Swift. He was used in a career-high 71 games and led the team with 17 saves. His 1.99 earned-run average set a club record for relievers.

Most improved player: Right fielder Jay Buhner. He set career highs in virtually every hitting department. The slugger hit 27 homers and drove in 77 runs.

Most pleasant surprise: Lefthander Bill Krueger. He earned a starting assignment because of an injury to Erik Hanson in May and stayed in the rotation the rest of the season, posting a career-high 11 wins.

Biggest disappointment: Catcher Dave Valle and starting pitcher Hanson. Valle's batting average (.194) was one of the most discussed subjects of the season, and twice went on the disabled list. Hanson won only eight games and twice went on the disabled list.

Key injuries: Henry Cotto sustained a torn rotator cuff July 26, forcing him on

the disabled list shortly thereafter for the rest of the year. Starting pitchers Hanson, Randy Johnson, Scott Bankhead and Brian Holman all missed some starts because of injuries.

Notable: Seattle posted a league-high nine winning or losing streaks of at least five games. . . . Of their 83 wins, 39 were comeback victories, including 22 in the seventh inning or later.

—JIM STREET

RECORDS

1991 regular-season record: 83-79 (5th in A.L. West); 45-36 at home; 38-43 on road; 48-36 vs. East; 35-43 vs. West; 18-24 vs. LHP; 65-55 vs. RHP; 32-30 on grass; 51-49 on turf; 17-26 in daytime; 66-53 at night; 27-25 in one-run games; 9-10 in extra-inning games; 0-0-1 in doubleheaders.

Team record last five years: 379-430 (.468, ranks 12th in league in that span).

TEAM LEADERS

Batting average: Ken Griffey Jr. (.327).
At-bats: Harold Reynolds (631).
Runs: Edgar Martinez (98).
Hits: Ken Griffey Jr. (179).
Total bases: Ken Griffey Jr. (289).
Doubles: Ken Griffey Jr. (42).
Triples: Harold Reynolds (6).
Home runs: Jay Buhner (27).
Runs batted in: Ken Griffey Jr. (100).
Stolen bases: Harold Reynolds (28).
Slugging percentage: Ken Griffey Jr. (.527).
On-base percentage: Edgar Martinez (.405).
Wins: Brian Holman, Randy Johnson (13).
Earned-run average: Bill Krueger (3.60).
Complete games: Brian Holman (5).
Shutouts: Brian Holman (3).
Saves: Bill Swift (17).
Innings pitched: Randy Johnson (201⅓).
Strikeouts: Randy Johnson (228).

GAMES BY POSITION

Catcher: Dave Valle 129, Scott Bradley 65, Dave Cochrane 19, Chris Howard 9, Matt Sinatro 5.

First base: Pete O'Brien 132, Tino Martinez 29, Alvin Davis 14, Alonzo Powell 7, Dave Cochrane 4, Dave Valle 2, Rich Amaral 1, Scott Bradley 1.

Second base: Harold Reynolds 159, Jeff Schaefer 11, Rich Amaral 5, Greg Briley 1, Omar Vizquel 1.

Third base: Edgar Martinez 144, Jeff Schaefer 30, Dave Cochrane 13, Scott Bradley 4, Rich Amaral 2, Greg Briley 1.

Shortstop: Omar Vizquel 138, Jeff Schaefer 46, Rich Amaral 2.

Outfield: Ken Griffey Jr. 152, Jay Buhner 131, Greg Briley 125, Henry Cotto 56, Alonzo Powell 40, Tracy Jones 36, Dave Cochrane 26, Ken Griffey 26, Pete O'Brien 13, Patrick Lennon 1.

Designated hitter: Alvin Davis 126, Tracy Jones 37, Pete O'Brien 18, Alonzo Powell 7, Henry Cotto 6, Patrick Lennon 5, Tino Martinez 5, Rich Amaral 2, Scott Bradley 2, Greg Briley 2, Edgar Martinez 2, Dave Cochrane 1, Ken Griffey Jr. 1, Ken Griffey Sr. 1, Harold Reynolds 1, Jeff Schaefer 1.

TOP 10 DRAFT CHOICES

1. Shawn Estes, LHP, Douglas High School, Minden, Nev.
2. Tommy Adams, OF, Arizona State University.
3. Jim Mecir, RHP, Eckerd College.
4. Desi Reliford, SS, Sandalwood High School, Jacksonville, Fla.
5. Sean Rees, LHP, Arizona State University.
6. Craig Clayton, RHP/1B, Cal State Northridge.
7. Bruce Thompson, OF, Brandon (Fla.) High School.
8. Derek Lowe, RHP, Ford High School, Dearborn, Mich.
9. Trey Witte, RHP, Texas A&M University.
10. Jeff Borski, RHP, University of South Carolina-Aiken.

TEXAS RANGERS
AMERICAN LEAGUE WEST DIVISION

1992 SCHEDULE

APRIL

S	M	T	W	T	F	S
5	6 N	7 N	8 N	9 N	10 N	11 N
	SEA	SEA	SEA	SEA	MIN	MIN
12 N	13 N	14 N	15 N	16 N	17 N	18
MIN	CAL H	CAL H	CAL H	CAL H	OAK H	OAK H
19	20	21 N	22 N	23 N	24 N	25
OAK H		DET H	DET H	DET H	BOS	BOS
26	27 N	28 N	29 N	30 N		
BOS	NY	NY	CHI			

MAY

S	M	T	W	T	F	S
					1 N	2
					CHI	CHI
3	4 N	5	6 N	7 N	8 N	9 N
CHI	BAL	BAL	CLE H	CLE H	MIL H	MIL H
10	11	12 N	13 N	14	15 N	16
MIL H		BAL H	BAL H		MIL	MIL
17 N	18 N	19 N	20 N	21 N	22 N	23 N
MIL	CLE	CLE	CLE	KC H	KC H	KC H
24	25	26 N	27 N	28 N	29 N	30 N
KC H		CHI H	CHI H	CHI H	KC	KC
31						
KC						

JUNE

S	M	T	W	T	F	S
	1 N	2 N	3 N	4 N	5 N	6 N
	NY H	NY H	NY H	MIN H	MIN H	MIN H
7 N	8 N	9 N	10 N	11	12 N	13
MIN H	SEA H	SEA H	SEA H		OAK	OAK
14 N	15 N	16 N	17 N	18	19 N	20 N
OAK	CAL	CAL	CAL		BOS H	BOS H
21 N	22 N	23 N	24 N	25 N	26 N	27
BOS H	TOR H	TOR H	TOR H	DET	DET	DET
28	29 N	30 N				
DET	TOR	TOR				

JULY

S	M	T	W	T	F	S
			1	2	3 N	4 N
			TOR		NY H	NY H
5 N	6 N	7 N	8 N	9 N	10 N	11 N
NY H	MIL H	MIL H	MIL H	CLE H	CLE H	CLE H
12 N	13	14 ★	15	16 N	17 N	18 N
CLE H				BAL H	BAL H	BAL H
19 N	20 N	21 N	22 N	23 N	24 N	25
BAL H	MIL H	MIL H	MIL H	BAL	BAL	BAL
26 N	27 N	28 N	29 N	30 N	31 N	
BAL	BOS	BOS	BOS		CAL H	

AUGUST

S	M	T	W	T	F	S
						1 N
						CAL H
2 N	3 N	4 N	5 N	6 N	7 N	8 N
CAL H	OAK H	OAK H	OAK H	OAK H	SEA	SEA
9 N	10 N	11 N	12 N	13 N	14 N	15 N
SEA	MIN	MIN	MIN	MIN	DET H	DET H
16 N	17	18 N	19 N	20 N	21 N	22
DET H		CHI	CHI	CHI	CLE	CLE
23 N	24	25 N	26 N	27 N	28 N	29 N
CLE		KC H	KC H	KC H	CHI H	CHI H
30 N	31 N					
CHI H	KC					

SEPTEMBER

S	M	T	W	T	F	S
		1 N	2 N	3	4 N	5
		KC	KC		NY	NY
6	7 N	8 N	9 N	10	11 N	12 N
NY	BOS H	BOS H	BOS H		TOR H	TOR H
13	14	15 N	16 N	17	18 N	19
TOR H		DET	DET		TOR	TOR
20 N	21	22 N	23 N	24	25 N	26 N
TOR		MIN H	MIN H		SEA H	SEA H
27 N	28	29 N	30 N			
SEA H		OAK	OAK			

OCTOBER

S	M	T	W	T	F	S
				1 N	2 N	3 N
				OAK	CAL	CAL
4	5	6	7	8	9	10
CAL						

1992 SEASON

CLUB DIRECTORY

General partners
George W. Bush
Edward W. (Rusty) Rose
President
J. Thomas Schieffer
Vice president, general manager
Thomas A. Grieve
V.p., business operations/treasurer
John F. McMichael
Vice president, administration/secretary
Charles F. Wangner
Vice president, public relations
John C. Blake
Vice president, ballpark development
Jack W. Hill
General counsel
Gerald W. Haddock
Asst. g.m., player personnel and scouting
Sandy Johnson
Assistant general manager
Wayne Krivsky
Director, player development
Marty Scott
Dir., in-park entertainment/broadcasting
Chuck Morgan
Director, promotions
Dave Fendrick
Director, sales/customer service
Jay Miller
Director, stadium operations
Mat Stolley
Director, ticket operations
John Schriever
Director, group sales
Rich Billings
Traveling secretary
Dan Schimek
Controller
Steve McNeill
Director, community relations
Taunee Paur
Director, publications
Larry Kelly
Assistant director, ticket operations
Ben Marthaler
Assistant director, community relations
Ashley Brown

Assistant, special projects
Bobby Bragan
Major league scout/special assignments
Larry Hardy
Major league advance scout
Marc Sullivan
General manager, Charlotte Co. operations
Ted Guthrie
Medical director
Dr. Mike Mycoskie
Field superintendent
Jim Anglea
Assistant field superintendent
Brad Richards
Spring training director
John Welaj
Equipment and home clubhouse manager
Joe Macko
Visiting clubhouse manager
Zack Minasian
Scouts
Jim Benedict
Ray Blanco
Joe Branzell
Dick Coury
Mike Daughtry
Marc DelPlano
Jim Dreyer
Bill Earnhart
Kip Fagg
Jim Fairey
Doug Gassaway
Mike Grouse
Tim Hallgren
Bryan Lambe
Robert Lavallee
John Littlefield
Omar Minaya
Mike Piatnik
Pat Rigby
Don Shwery
Len Strelitz
Randy Taylor
Rudy Terrasas

SCHEDULE KEY

H—Home game.   *All-Star Game at San Diego/Jack Murphy Stadium.
N—Night game (any game starting after 5 p.m.).

SPRING TRAINING ROSTER

Manager—Bobby Valentine (2).

Coaches—Ray Burris (50), Orlando Gomez (13), Toby Harrah (11), Tom House (35), Dave Oliver (26), Tom Robson (31).

No.	PITCHERS	B/T	Ht./Wt.	Born	1991 clubs
48	Alexander, Gerald	R/R	5-11/200	3-26-68	Oklahoma City, Texas
27	Barfield, John	L/L	6-1/195	10-15-64	Texas
45	Bohanon, Brian	L/L	6-2/220	8-1-68	Charlotte, Tulsa, Oklahoma City, Texas
41	Brown, Kevin	R/R	6-4/195	3-14-65	Texas
43	Chiamparino, Scott	L/R	6-2/205	8-22-66	Texas
32	Fajardo, Hector	R/R	6-4/200	11-6-70	Augusta, Salem, Carolina, Pittsburgh, Buffalo, Texas
23	Guzman, Jose	R/R	6-3/195	4-9-63	Oklahoma City, Texas
44	Manuel, Barry	R/R	5-11/185	8-12-65	Tulsa, Texas
38	Mathews, Terry	L/R	6-2/225	10-5-64	Oklahoma City, Texas
42	Nen, Robb	R/R	6-4/200	11-28-69	Tulsa
59	Pavlik, Roger	R/R	6-2/220	10-4-67	Oklahoma City
37	Rogers, Kenny	L/L	6-1/205	11-10-64	Texas
40	Russell, Jeff	R/R	6-3/205	9-2-61	Texas
34	Ryan, Nolan	R/R	6-2/212	1-31-47	Texas
36	Witt, Bobby	R/R	6-2/205	5-11-64	Texas, Oklahoma City

No.	CATCHERS	B/T	Ht./Wt.	Born	1991 clubs
29	Haselman, Bill	R/R	6-3/205	5-25-66	Oklahoma City
12	Petralli, Geno	L/R	6-1/190	9-25-59	Texas, Oklahoma City
7	Rodriguez, Ivan	R/R	5-9/205	11-30-71	Tulsa, Texas

No.	INFIELDERS	B/T	Ht./Wt.	Born	1991 clubs
54	Colon, Cris	S/R	6-2/180	1-3-69	Charlotte, Tulsa
4	Fariss, Monty	R/R	6-4/205	10-13-67	Oklahoma City, Texas
14	Franco, Julio	R/R	6-1/190	8-23-61	Texas
51	Frye, Jeff	R/R	5-9/180	8-31-66	Tulsa
3	Hernandez, Jose	R/R	6-1/180	7-14-69	Tulsa, Oklahoma City, Texas
9	Huson, Jeff	L/R	6-3/180	8-15-64	Texas, Oklahoma City
39	Maurer, Rob	L/L	6-3/210	1-7-67	Oklahoma City, Texas
56	Oliva, Jose	R/R	6-1/160	3-3-71	Charlotte, Rangers (Gulf Coast)
25	Palmeiro, Rafael	L/L	6-0/188	9-24-64	Texas
16	Palmer, Dean	R/R	6-2/195	12-27-68	Oklahoma City, Texas
10	Thon, Dickie	R/R	5-11/176	6-20-58	Philadelphia

No.	OUTFIELDERS	B/T	Ht./Wt.	Born	1991 clubs
8	Daugherty, Jack	S/L	6-0/190	7-3-60	Texas, Oklahoma City
55	Downing, Brian	R/R	5-10/194	10-9-50	Texas
19	Gonzalez, Juan	R/R	6-3/210	10-16-69	Texas
33	Harris, Donald	R/R	6-1/185	11-12-67	Tulsa, Texas
53	Peltier, Dan	L/L	6-1/200	6-30-68	Oklahoma City
24	Pettis, Gary	S/R	6-1/160	4-3-58	Texas
47	Reimer, Kevin	L/R	6-2/230	6-28-64	Texas
21	Sierra, Ruben	S/R	6-1/200	10-6-65	Texas

BALLPARK INFORMATION

Ballpark (capacity, surface)
Arlington Stadium (43,521, grass)
Address
1250 Copeland Road, 11th floor
Arlington, TX 76010
Business phone
817-273-5222
Ticket information
817-273-5000
Ticket prices
$14 (infield box)
$13 (reserved box)
$9 (plaza)
$7 (grandstand reserved)
$4 (general admission, adults)
$2 (g.a., children 13 and under)
Field dimensions (from home plate)
To left field at foul line, 330 feet
To center field, 400 feet
To right field at foul line, 330 feet
First game played
April 21, 1972 (Rangers 7, Angels 6)

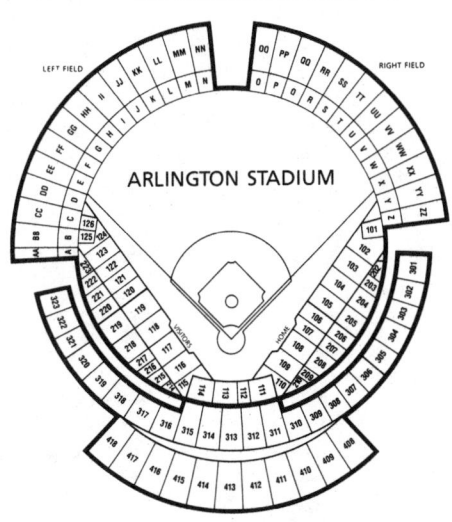

MINOR LEAGUE AFFILIATES

Class	Team	League	Manager
AAA	Oklahoma City	American Association	Tommy Thompson
AA	Tulsa	Texas	Bobby Jones
A	Charlotte	Florida State	Bump Wills
A	Gastonia	South Atlantic	Walt Williams
Rookie	Butte	Pioneer	Victor Ramirez
Rookie	Gulf Coast Rangers	Gulf Coast	Chino Cadahia

BROADCAST INFORMATION

Radio: WBAP-AM (820). Broadcasters: Mark Holtz, Eric Nadel.
TV: KTVT-TV (Channel 11). Broadcasters: Steve Busby, Jim Sundberg.
Cable TV: Home Sports Entertainment. Broadcasters: Greg Lucas, Norm Hitzges.

SPRING TRAINING

Ballpark (city): Charlotte County Stadium (Port Charlotte, Fla.).
Ticket information: 813-625-9500 or 813-624-2211.

HISTORY

YEAR-BY-YEAR RECORDS

Year	Pos.	W	L	Pct.	*GB	Year	Pos.	W	L	Pct.	*GB
1961	T9th	61	100	.379	47½	1978	T2nd	87	75	.537	5
1962	10th	60	101	.373	35½	1979	3rd	83	79	.512	5
1963	10th	56	106	.346	48½	1980	4th	76	85	.472	20½
1964	9th	62	100	.383	37	1981	2nd/3rd	57	48	.543	†
1965	8th	70	92	.432	32	1982	6th	64	98	.395	29
1966	8th	71	88	.447	25½	1983	3rd	77	85	.475	22
1967	T6th	76	85	.472	15½	1984	7th	69	92	.429	14½
1968	10th	65	96	.404	37½	1985	7th	62	99	.385	28½
1969	4th	86	76	.531	23	1986	2nd	87	75	.537	5
1970	6th	70	92	.432	38	1987	T6th	75	87	.463	10
1971	5th	63	96	.396	38½	1988	6th	70	91	.435	33½
1972	6th	54	100	.351	38½	1989	4th	83	79	.512	16
1973	6th	57	105	.352	37	1990	3rd	83	79	.512	20
1974	2nd	84	76	.525	5	1991	3rd	85	77	.525	10
1975	3rd	79	83	.488	19						
1976	T4th	76	86	.469	14						
1977	2nd	94	68	.580	8						

*Games behind winner. †First half 33-22; second 24-26.

MANAGERS

Name	Record	Years
Mickey Vernon	135-227	'61-63
Gil Hodges	321-444	'63-67
Jim Lemon	65-96	1968
Ted Williams	273-364	'69-72
Whitey Herzog	47-91	1973
Del Wilber	1-0	1973
Billy Martin	137-141	'73-75
Frank Lucchesi	142-149	'75-77
Eddie Stanky	1-0	1977
Connie Ryan	2-4	1977
Billy Hunter	146-108	'77-78
Pat Corrales	160-164	'78-80
Don Zimmer	95-106	'81-82
Darrell Johnson	26-40	1982
Doug Rader	155-200	'83-85
Bobby Valentine	536-564	'85-91

DAY BY DAY

Date	Opp.	Res.	Score (inn.*)	Hits	Opp. hits	Winning pitcher	Losing pitcher	Save	Record	Pos.	GB
4-8	Mil.	L	4-5	8	10	Knudson	Ryan	Nunez	0-1	7th	1
4-10	Mil.	L	0-6	5	9	Bosio	Brown		0-2	T6th	2
4-12	Bal.	L	0-3	4	5	Johnson	Witt	Olson	0-3	6th	3
4-13	Bal.	L	4-11	10	12	Ballard	Rogers		0-4	6th	4
4-14	Bal.	W	15-3	16	5	Ryan	Robinson		1-4	6th	3 ½
4-16	At Cle.	W	3-1	8	3	Brown	King	Russell	2-4	5th	4
4-18	At Cle.	W	7-0	8	4	Witt	Swindell		3-4	5th	3 ½
4-19	At Bal.	L	0-5	5	10	Robinson	Rogers		3-5	6th	3 ½
4-20	At Bal.	W	1-0	4	4	Ryan	Mesa		4-5	6th	2 ½
4-23	At Mil.	W	6-5 (11)	10	7	Gossage	Crim	Russell	5-5	5th	3
4-24	At Mil.	W	8-2	12	5	Brown	Knudson		6-5	4th	2
4-25	At Mil.	L	1-9	9	8	Bosio	Rogers		6-6	T5th	2 ½
4-26	Cle.	L	2-5	6	9	Olin	Ryan	Jones	6-7	6th	2 ½
4-27	Cle.	W	4-1	12	6	Jeffcoat	Olin	Russell	7-7	T3rd	3
4-28	Cle.	L	2-4	6	9	King	Witt	Jones	7-8	6th	3 ½
4-30	Tor.	W	8-5	12	11	Gossage	Acker	Russell	8-8	T3rd	3
5-1	Tor.	W	3-0	8	0	Ryan	Key		9-8	3rd	3
5-3	At Det.	L	6-7 (11)	10	9	Henneman	Arnsberg		9-9	3rd	3 ½
5-4	At Det.	W	6-5	10	6	Gossage	Gleaton		10-9	3rd	3
5-5	At Det.	L	7-8	16	12	Terrell	Brown		10-10	T3rd	3
5-7	At Tor.	W	3-2	11	8	Rogers	Key	Russell	11-10	3rd	3
5-8	At Tor.	L	2-4	6	4	Stottlmyre	Ryan	Ward	11-11	4th	4
5-9	At Bos.	L	4-8	9	12	Lamp	Jeffcoat		11-12	5th	4 ½
5-10	At Bos.	L	3-5	10	13	Young	Witt	Reardon	11-13	6th	4 ½
5-11	At Bos.	L	4-5	6	12	Kiecker	Brown	Reardon	11-14	6th	5 ½
5-12	At Bos.	W	12-5	19	13	Rogers	Harris		12-14	6th	4 ½
5-13	Det.	W	8-1	13	4	Barfield	Cerutti		13-14	6th	3 ½
5-14	Det.	W	5-3	9	9	Chiamparino	Petry	Russell	14-14	T5th	2 ½
5-15	Det.	W	5-4 (12)	11	9	Gossage	Searcy		15-14	3rd	2 ½
5-17	Bos.	W	6-4	11	12	Brown	Harris	Russell	16-14	3rd	2 ½
5-18	Bos.	W	13-5	17	9	Rogers	Clemens	Poole	17-14	3rd	2 ½
5-19	Bos.	W	12-4	16	10	Alexander	Bolton		18-14	3rd	2
5-21	At Min.	W	6-5	10	6	Witt	Tapani	Russell	19-14	3rd	1
5-22	At Min.	W	5-2 (12)	12	10	Alexander	Willis	Russell	20-14	2nd	½
5-23	At Min.	W	10-6 (11)	14	17	Russell	Bedrosian		21-14	1st	+ ½
5-24	At Sea.	W	7-3	11	9	Rogers	holman	Barfield	22-14	1st	+ ½
5-25	At Sea.	W	8-6 (11)	16	12	Barfield	Swan		23-14	1st	+ ½
5-26	At Sea.	W	6-4	14	7	Witt	Swift	Russell	24-14	1st	+ ½
5-27	Min.	W	11-4	15	11	Brown	Anderson		25-14	1st	+1
5-28	Min.	L	0-3	7	9	Erickson	Guzman	Aguilera	25-15	1st	...
5-29	Min.	L	1-9	4	10	Morris	Ryan		25-16	1st	...
5-30	Sea.	L	4-11	9	11	DeLucia	Rogers		25-17	2nd	1
5-31	Sea.	W	7-6	10	13	Alexander	Bankhead	Russell	26-17	1st	...
6-1	Sea.	L	8-12	11	13	Swan	Brown	Jackson	26-18	2nd	1
6-4	At K.C.	L	1-4	5	7	Boddicker	Guzman	Montgomery	26-19	3rd	2
6-5	At K.C.	L	2-3	6	5	Crawford	Brown	Montgomery	26-20	3rd	3
6-6	At K.C.	L	3-4 (18)	14	15	Boddicker	Rogers		26-21	3rd	4
6-7	At N.Y.	L	4-5	6	11	Habyan	Barfield		26-22	3rd	4
6-8	At N.Y.	L	7-10	16	14	Taylor	Petkovsek	Farr	26-23	5th	4
6-9	At N.Y.	L	4-6	7	10	Habyan	Gossage	Farr	26-24	5th	5
6-10	Chi.	L	2-3 (13)	6	6	Perez	Alexander	Thigpen	26-25	6th	6
6-11	Chi.	W	2-0	7	6	Ryan	Fernandez		27-25	5th	5
6-12	Chi.	W	4-2	7	2	Barfield	Hough	Russell	28-25	5th	5
6-13	Chi.	W	8-4	10	10	Alexander	Hibbard	Rogers	29-25	5th	4 ½
6-14	N.Y.	W	8-4	9	12	Guzman	Taylor		30-25	4th	4
6-15	N.Y.	W	4-3	8	12	Brown	Leary	Russell	31-25	3rd	3 ½
6-16	N.Y.	W	4-3 (15)	13	5	Bitker	Guetterman		32-25	3rd	3
6-17	K.C.	W	10-9 (10)	19	12	Jeffcoat	Montgomery		33-25	3rd	2
6-18	K.C.	L	5-12	10	15	Appier	Rogers	Aquino	33-26	3rd	3
6-19	K.C.	L	2-15	5	20	Wagner	Guzman	S. Davis	33-27	3rd	4
6-20	At Chi.	W	7-3	8	9	Jeffcoat	Thigpen		34-27	3rd	3 ½
6-21	At Chi.	L	5-6 (11)	9	9	Patterson	Schiraldi		34-28	3rd	4 ½
6-22	At Chi.	L	1-3	4	7	Fernandez	Barfield		34-29	5th	5 ½
6-23	At Chi.	L	5-6 (10)	8	7	Thigpen	Russell		34-30	5th	5 ½
6-25	At Oak.	W	6-1	11	7	Guzman	Stewart		35-30	4th	6
6-26	At Oak.	W	8-1	8	6	Brown	Nelson		36-30	4th	5
6-27	At Oak.	W	9-6	11	12	Milacki	Mutis	Olson	37-30	3rd	4
6-28	At Cal.	L	8-10	17	11	Eichhorn	Rogers	Harvey	37-31	3rd	4
6-29	At Cal.	W	7-4 (13)	16	15	Russell	Bailes		38-31	3rd	3
6-30	At Cal.	W	2-1	7	2	Guzman	McCaskill		39-31	2nd	3

TEXAS RANGERS

1992 SEASON

TEXAS RANGERS

Date	Opp.	Res.	Score (inn.*)	Hits	Opp. hits	Winning pitcher	Losing pitcher	Save	Record	Pos.	GB
7-1	At Cal.	L	2-6	6	10	Langston	Brown	Harvey	39-32	3rd	3
7-2	Oak.	W	9-6	19	4	Rogers	Honeycutt	Russell	40-32	3rd	2
7-3	Oak.	L	0-5	3	10	Stewart	Barfield		40-33	3rd	2
7-4	Oak.	W	5-4 (10)	9	5	Russell	Nelson		41-33	3rd	2
7-5	Cal.	W	8-0	11	3	Guzman	Langston	Jeffcoat	42-33	3rd	1
7-6	Cal.	W	4-3	8	7	Brown	J. Abbott	Russell	43-33	2nd	1
7-7	Cal.	W	7-0	7	2	Ryan	Finley		44-33	1st	...
7-11	At Tor.	L	0-2	5	9	Candiotti	Brown	Henke	44-34	2nd	1
7-12	At Tor.	L	2-6	5	12	Wells	Guzman	Ward	44-35	2nd	2
7-13	At Tor.	L	2-3	7	6	Timlin	Russell	Henke	44-36	2nd	3
7-14	At Tor.	W	8-6	11	7	Barfield	Key	Russell	45-36	2nd	2
7-15	At Det.	L	7-8	14	12	Henneman	Jeffcoat		45-37	2nd	3
7-16	At Det.	L	5-6	6	8	Henneman	Brown		45-38	3rd	3
7-17	At Det.	L	4-6 (10)	9	6	Terrell	Rosenthal		45-39	3rd	3½
7-18	Tor.	L	0-4	4	6	Wells	Ryan	Ward	45-40	T4th	4½
7-19	Tor.	L	2-7	8	14	Stottlemyre	Barfield	Timlin	45-41	5th	5½
7-20	Tor.	W	11-6	17	13	Jeffcoat	Key		46-41	3rd	5½
7-21	Tor.	W	6-5	9	10	Rogers	Timlin	Russell	47-41	2nd	5½
7-22	Bos.	W	2-1	7	5	Guzman	Clemens	Russell	48-41	2nd	5
7-23	Bos.	W	5-4	8	4	Ryan	Harris	Gossage	49-41	2nd	4
7-24	Bos.	L	1-2	2	7	Hesketh	Boyd	Reardon	49-42	2nd	4
7-26	Det.	L	2-3 (10)	14	9	Henneman	Russell		49-43	4th	5½
7-27	Det.	W	8-5	9	11	Alexander	Kiely	Rogers	50-43	4th	5½
7-28	Det.	W	10-6	13	9	Ryan	Tanana		51-43	4th	4½
7-29	At Bos.	W	7-2	13	8	Guzman	Hesketh	Rogers	52-43	4th	4½
7-30	At Bos.	L	6-11	12	12	Morton	Boyd		52-44	4th	5½
7-31	At Chi.	L	8-10	11	14	Pall	Gossage		52-45	4th	6½
8-1	At Chi.	L	2-13	10	11	Garcia	Witt		52-46	4th	6½
8-2	At Mil.	W	15-1	18	6	Bohanon	Navarro		53-46	4th	5½
8-3	At Mil.	W	14-5	16	7	Guzman	Wegman		54-46	4th	5½
8-4	At Mil.	L	2-3	11	10	Crim	Russell		54-47	5th	6½
8-5	Cle.	L	0-9	2	19	King	Brown		54-48	5th	7½
8-6	Cle.	W	10-8	17	15	Rogers	York	Russell	55-48	4th	7½
8-7	Cle.	W	12-10	16	12	Jeffcoat	Hillegas	Russell	56-48	4th	6½
8-9	Mil.	L	8-10	11	16	Bosio	Alexander	Nunez	56-49	4th	7½
8-10	Mil.	L	2-5	8	9	Plesac	Boyd	Henry	56-50	4th	7½
8-11	Mil.	W	5-4 (10)	10	12	Rogers	Machado		57-50	4th	7½
8-12	Mil.	L	7-14	9	18	Navarro	Witt	Henry	57-51	4th	8½
8-13 (1)	At Bal.	L	3-4 (12)	13	6	Johnson	Rogers		57-52		8½
8-13 (2)	At Bal.	L	7-8	13	12	Frohwirth	Guzman	Olson	57-53	6th	9
8-14	At Bal.	L	2-10	3	12	Mussina	Alexander		57-54	6th	9
8-15	At Bal.	L	2-9	3	14	Mesa	Boyd		57-55	6th	9
8-16 (1)	At Cle.	W	5-3	12	8	Brown	King	Russell	58-55	6th	9
8-16 (2).	At Cle.	L	9-13	11	12	Orosco	Jeffcoat		58-56	6th	9½
8-17	At Cle.	W	2-0	7	7	Guzman	Blair	Russell	59-56	6th	9½
8-18	At Cle.	W	9-4	11	10	Bohanon	Nagy	Rosenthal	60-56	6th	9½
8-19	Bal.	W	4-1	7	5	Ryan	Mussina	Mathews	61-56	T5th	8½
8-20	Bal.	L	6-8	11	12	Johnson	Rosenthal	Flanagan	61-57	T5th	9½
8-21	Bal.	L	3-4	7	10	Frohwirth	Brown	Olson	61-58	6th	10½
8-22	At K.C.	W	4-2	7	8	Rogers	Gordon		62-58	T5th	10½
8-23	At K.C.	W	6-1	8	5	Bohanon	Appier		63-58	4th	9½
8-24	At K.C.	L	1-8	9	13	Boddicker	Ryan		63-59	T4th	10½
8-25	At K.C.	W	8-4 (11)	13	7	Mathews	S. Davis		64-59	4th	9½
8-26	At N.Y.	W	10-2	12	5	Brown	Plunk		65-59	4th	9½
8-27	At N.Y.	W	7-2	12	7	Guzman	Perez	Rogers	66-59	4th	8½
8-28	At N.Y.	L	1-5	10	8	Taylor	Bohanon		66-60	T4th	9½
8-30	K.C.	W	6-2	12	4	Ryan	Boddicker	Russell	67-60	3rd	8½
8-31	K.C.	L	2-3	9	5	Gubicza	Witt	Montgomery	67-61	T4th	9½
9-1	K.C.	W	6-4	10	6	Mathews	Saberhagen	Russell	68-61	4th	9½
9-2	N.Y.	W	7-2	11	10	Boyd	Leary		69-61	4th	9½
9-3	N.Y.	W	5-1	11	5	Guzman	Johnson		70-61	T2nd	9
9-4	N.Y.	L	2-3	9	11	Cadaret	Bohanon	Farr	70-62	T3rd	9
9-6	Chi.	L	6-11	8	9	Pall	Rogers	Perez	70-63	4th	10
9-7	Chi.	L	6-11	8	14	Hibbard	Witt		70-64	4th	11
9-8	Chi.	W	7-6	6	8	Russell	Thigpen		71-64	4th	11
9-9	At Cal.	L	2-4	6	8	Langston	Boyd	Harvey	71-65	4th	12
9-10	At Cal.	W	6-1	10	6	Russell	K. Abbott		72-65	4th	12
9-11	At Cal.	W	11-9 (12)	15	14	Manuel	Robinson		73-65	4th	11
9-12	Min.	W	4-3	5	5	Ryan	Morris	Russell	74-65	3rd	10
9-13	Min.	L	3-7 (10)	8	9	Leach	Rogers		74-66	3rd	11
9-14	Min.	W	3-0	10	6	Boyd	Edens	Rogers	75-66	3rd	10
9-15	Min.	W	4-2	8	6	Guzman	Anderson	Russell	76-66	3rd	9
9-17	Cal.	L	2-7	8	12	Lewis	Bohanon		76-67	3rd	9½
9-19 (1)	Cal.	W	10-3	11	7	Ryan	Finley		77-67	3rd	8½

Date	Opp.	Res.	Score (inn.*)	Hits	Opp. hits	Winning pitcher	Losing pitcher	Save	Record	Pos.	GB
9-19 (2)	Cal.	L	2-5	6	13	J. Abbott	Brown	Harvey	77-68	3rd	9
9-20	At Min.	L	4-6	10	13	Wayne	Rosenthal	Aguilera	77-69	3rd	10
9-21	At Min.	L	4-8	8	12	Tapani	Guzman		77-70	4th	11
9-22	At Min.	L	4-9	8	12	Morris	Fajardo		77-71	4th	12
9-23	At Sea.	W	11-4 (11)	13	13	Russell	Schooler		78-71	4th	11½
9-24	At Sea.	W	8-7	8	13	Russell	Jackson		79-71	3rd	11½
9-25	At Sea.	W	7-1	9	3	Ryan	DeLucia		80-71	3rd	10½
9-26	At Oak.	L	0-10	4	14	Moore	Boyd		80-72	4th	11
9-27	At Oak.	W	3-0	9	2	Guzman	Darling		81-72	3rd	10
9-28	At Oak.	W	6-3 (10)	11	6	Mathews	Eckersley	Russell	82-72	3rd	10
9-29	At Oak.	L	5-19	9	18	Slusarski	Brown		82-73	3rd	10
9-30 (1)	Sea.	L	2-3 (11)	8	8	Schooler	Rosenthal	Swift	82-74	3rd	11
9-30 (2)	Sea.	W	2-0	7	9	Bohanon	Krueger	Russell	83-74	3rd	10½
10-1	Sea.	L	1-8	3	11	Burba	Boyd	Jones	83-75	T3rd	11½
10-2	Sea.	L	3-4	4	7	Bankhead	Guzman	Swift	83-76	T3rd	12
10-4	Oak.	W	4-3	7	9	Rogers	Stewart		84-76	3rd	10
10-5	Oak.	L	5-12	9	15	Young	Fajardo		84-77	T3rd	11
10-6	Oak.	W	4-2	5	4	Mathews	Nelson		85-77	3rd	10

Monthly records: April (8-8), May (18-9), June (13-14), July (13-14), August (15-16), September (16-13), Oct. (2-3).

HIGHLIGHTS

High point: From May 12-27, Texas set a club record with 14 consecutive victories to move from sixth place (5½ games back) into first place (one game ahead) in the American League West.

Low point: On May 27, the last day of the streak, starting pitcher Bobby Witt went on the disabled list. Fellow starter Scott Chiamparino preceded him the previous day. This started a pitching merry-go-round that featured the use of 13 different starters.

Turning point: Texas led the division at the All-Star break, but the Rangers lost eight of their first nine games in the second half, falling 5½ games out of first place. Texas was never closer than four games back the rest of the season, finishing in third place with an 85-77 record (10 games behind).

Most valuable player: Right fielder Ruben Sierra. He hit a career-high .307 with 25 home runs and 116 runs batted in.

Most valuable pitcher: Righthanded starter Jose Guzman. He had missed the previous two big-league seasons with a torn rotator cuff. But he rebounded to lead the staff with 13 victories. That effort earned him A.L. Comeback Player of the Year honors.

Most improved player: Second baseman Julio Franco. He won the A.L. batting title with a career-high .341 mark. He also set career highs in homers (15), stolen bases (36) and runs (108).

Most pleasant surprise: Rookie catcher Ivan Rodriguez. Only 19 years old when he was promoted from Class AA Tulsa on June 19, Rodriguez threw out 34 of 70 runners attempting to steal (48.6 percent), the best percentage in the A.L., and batted .264, the highest average for a teenage regular since Robin Yount hit .267 in 1975.

Biggest disappointment: Righthanded starter Oil Can Boyd. Texas traded three minor leaguers to Montreal on July 21 for Boyd. But the Can got kicked, going 2-7 with a 6.68 earned-run average in 12 starts.

Key injuries: The losses of Witt and Chi-amparino cut the heart out of the rotation, and left fielder Jack Daugherty missed most of the year with various injuries. In all, 18 players (including eight pitchers) spent 23 stints on the disabled list, the most in the majors.

Notable: Nolan Ryan threw his seventh career no-hitter May 1 against Toronto. . . . Texas finished over .500 for the third year in a row. It has never posted four consecutive winning seasons.

—PHIL ROGERS

RECORDS

1991 regular-season record: 85-77 (3rd in A.L. West); 46-35 at home; 39-42 on road; 42-42 vs. East; 43-35 vs. West; 24-19 vs. LHP; 61-58 vs. RHP; 71-66 on grass; 14-11 on turf; 17-13 in daytime; 68-64 at night; 21-23 in one-run games; 14-10 in extra-inning games; 0-1-3 in doubleheaders.

Team record last five years: 396-413 (.489, ranks 10th in league in that span).

TEAM LEADERS

Batting average: Julio Franco (.341).
At-bats: Ruben Sierra (661).
Runs: Rafael Palmeiro (115).
Hits: Rafael Palmeiro, Ruben Sierra (203).
Total bases: Rafael Palmeiro (336).
Doubles: Rafael Palmeiro (49).
Triples: Gary Pettis, Ruben Sierra (5).
Home runs: Juan Gonzalez (27).
Runs batted in: Ruben Sierra (116).
Stolen bases: Julio Franco (36).
Slugging percentage: Rafael Palmeiro (.532).
On-base percentage: Julio Franco (.408).
Wins: Jose Guzman (13).
Earned-run average: Nolan Ryan (2.91).
Complete games: Jose Guzman (5).
Shutouts: Nolan Ryan (2).
Saves: Jeff Russell (30).
Innings pitched: Kevin Brown (210⅔).
Strikeouts: Nolan Ryan (203).

GAMES BY POSITION

Catcher: Ivan Rodriguez 88, Geno Petralli 66, Mike Stanley 58, John Russell 5, Mark Parent 3, Chad Kreuter 1.
First base: Rafael Palmeiro 157, Mike Stanley 12, Jack Daugherty 11, Rob Maurer 4.
Second base: Julio Franco 146, Mario Diaz 20, Steve Buechele 13, Monty Fariss 4, Jeff Huson 2.
Third base: Steve Buechele 111, Dean Palmer 50, Denny Walling 14, Mario Diaz 8, Geno Petralli 7, Mike Stanley 6, Jose Hernandez 1, Jeff Huson 1.
Shortstop: Jeff Huson 116, Mario Diaz 65, Jose Hernandez 44, Gary Green 8, Steve Buechele 4.
Outfield: Ruben Sierra 161, Juan Gonzalez 136, Gary Pettis 126, Kevin Reimer 66, Jack Daugherty 37, Dean Palmer 29, Donald Harris 12, Monty Fariss 8, John Russell 8, Tony Scruggs 5, Denny Walling 5, Nick Capra 2, Mike Stanley 1.
Designated hitter: Brian Downing 109, Kevin Reimer 56, Mike Stanley 6, Dean Palmer 5, Geno Petralli 5, John Russell 5, Monty Fariss 4, Juan Gonzalez 4, Donald Harris 3, Gary Pettis 3, Rob Maurer 2, Rafael Palmeiro 2, Jack Daugherty 1, Mario Diaz 1.

TOP 10 DRAFT CHOICES

1. **Benji Gil**, SS/OF, Castle Park High School, Chula Vista, Calif.
2. **Terrell Lowery**, OF, Loyola Marymount University.
3. **Lawrence Hanlon**, SS, University of Texas-Arlington.
4. **Chris Curtis**, RHP, Blinn (Texas) Junior College.
5. **Mark O'Brien**, LHP, Deering High School, Portland, Maine.
6. **Steve Sadecki**, RHP, Vanderbilt University.
7. **Bert Gerhart**, RHP, New Hope High School, Columbus, Miss.
8. **Roger Luce**, C/RHP, University of Texas.
9. **Scott Eyre**, LHP, Junior College of Southern Idaho.
10. **Dave Geeve**, RHP, Bradley University.

TORONTO BLUE JAYS
AMERICAN LEAGUE EAST DIVISION

1992 SCHEDULE

APRIL
S	M	T	W	T	F	S
5	6 DET	7	8 DET	9 DET	10 BAL H	11 BAL H
12 BAL H	13 N NY H	14 N NY H	15 N NY H	16 N NY H	17 N BOS	18 BOS
19 BOS	20 BOS	21 N CLE H	22 N CLE H	23 N CLE H	24 N KC H	25 KC H
26 N KC H	27	28 N CAL H	29 N CAL H	30 N MIL		

MAY
S	M	T	W	T	F	S
					1 N MIL	2 MIL
3 MIL	4 OAK	5 N OAK	6 N SEA	7 SEA	8 N CAL	9 N CAL
10 N CAL	11 OAK H	12 N OAK H	13 N SEA H	14 N SEA H	15 N SEA H	16
17 SEA H	18 N MIN H	19 N MIN H	20 N MIN H	21	22 N CHI	23 N CHI
24 CHI	25	26 N MIL H	27 N MIL H	28	29 N CHI H	30 CHI H
31 CHI H						

JUNE
S	M	T	W	T	F	S
	1 N MIN	2 N MIN	3 N MIN	4	5 N BAL	6 BAL
7 BAL	8 N NY	9 N NY	10 N NY	11	12 N BOS H	13 BOS H
14 BOS H	15	16 N DET H	17 N DET H	18 DET H	19 N KC	20 KC
21 KC	22 N TEX	23 N TEX	24 N TEX	25	26 N CLE	27 CLE
28 CLE	29 N TEX H	30 N TEX H				

JULY
S	M	T	W	T	F	S
			1 TEX H	2	3 N CAL H	4 CAL H
5 CAL H	6 N CAL H	7 N SEA H	8 N SEA H	9 OAK H	10 N OAK H	11 OAK H
12 OAK H	13	14 ★	15	16 N SEA	17 N SEA	18 SEA
19 SEA	20 N CAL	21 N CAL	22 N CAL	23 OAK	24 N OAK	25 OAK
26 OAK	27	28 N KC H	29 N KC H	30 N KC H	31 N NY H	

AUGUST
S	M	T	W	T	F	S
						1 NY H
2 NY H	3 N BOS	4 N BOS	5 N BOS	6 DET	7 N DET	8 N DET
9 DET	10 N BAL H	11 N BAL H	12 N BAL H	13 CLE	14 N CLE	15 N CLE
16 CLE	17	18 N MIL	19 N MIL	20 MIL	21 N MIN	22 N MIN
23 MIN	24 N CHI	25 N CHI	26 N CHI	27 MIL H	28 N MIL H	29
30 MIL H	31 N CHI H					

SEPTEMBER
S	M	T	W	T	F	S
		1 N CHI H	2 N CHI H	3	4 N MIN H	5 MIN H
6 MIN H	7 N KC	8 N KC	9 N KC	10	11 N TEX	12 TEX
13 TEX	14 N CLE H	15 N CLE H	16 N CLE H	17 N TEX H	18 N TEX H	19
20 TEX H	21	22 N BAL	23 N BAL	24 N BAL	25 N NY	26 NY
27 NY	28	29 N BOS H	30 N BOS H			

OCTOBER
S	M	T	W	T	F	S
				1	2 N DET H	3 DET H
4 DET H	5	6	7	8	9	10

1992 SEASON

CLUB DIRECTORY

Chairman
P.N.T. Widdrington

President and chief executive officer
Paul Beeston

Executive vice president
Pat Gillick

Vice presidents, baseball
Bob Mattick
Al LaMacchia

Vice president, business
Bob Nicholson

Special asst. to the exec. v.p., baseball
Al Widmar

Assistant general manager
Gord Ash

Director, public relations
Howard Starkman

Director, stadium and ticket operations
George Holm

Director, marketing
Paul Markle

Director, finance
Susie Quigley

Director, scouting
Bob Engle

Director, international scouting
Wayne Morgan

Director, player development
Mel Queen

Director, Canadian scouting
Bob Prentice

Director, minor league business
Ken Carson

Administrator, player personnel
Bob Nelson

Administrator, scouting
Hank Zacharias

Assistant director, public relations
Mark Leno

Asst. dir., tickets and box office manager
Randy Low

Assistant director, operations
Len Frejlich

Manager, group sales
Maureen Haffey

Manager, team travel
John Brioux

Manager, promotions and advertising
Rick Amos

Manager, accounting
Cathy McNamara

Manager, employee compensations
Catharine Elwood

Manager, information systems
Hans Frauenlob

Manager, ticket vault
Paul Goodyear

Manager, ticket revenue
Mike Maunder

Managers, ticket mail services
Allan Koyanagi
Doug Barr

Manager, security
Fred Wootton

Manager, event personnel
Mario Coutinho

Systems administrator
Mark Graham

Supervisor, grounds
Brad Bujold

Supervisor, office services
Mick Bazinet

Trainers
Tommy Craig
Brent Andrews

Team physician
Dr. Ron Taylor

Coord., Latin American scouting & develop.
Epy Guerrero

Special assignment scouts
Moose Johnson
Gordon Lakey
Tim Wilken

Director, international scouting
Wayne Morgan

Advance scout
Jorge Rivera

Scouts
David Blume
Chris Bourjos
Chris Buckley
Ellis Clary
John Cole
Ellis Dungan
Joe Ford
Don Hara
Tim Hewes
Tom Hinkle
Jim Hughes
Duane Larson
Ted Lekas
Ben McLure
Bill Moore
Andy Pienovi
Earl Rapp
Alvin Rittman
Red Robbins
Joe Siers
Mark Snipp
Jerry Sobeck
Neil Summers
Ron Tostenson
Ramon Webster
Don Welke

SCHEDULE KEY

H—Home game.   *All-Star Game at San Diego/Jack Murphy Stadium.
N—Night game (any game starting after 5 p.m.).

SPRING TRAINING ROSTER

Manager—Cito Gaston (43).

Coaches—Bob Bailor (3), Galen Cisco (42), Rich Hacker (7), Larry Hisle (39), John Sullivan (8), Gene Tenace (18).

No.	PITCHERS	B/T	Ht./Wt.	Born	1991 clubs
46	Dayley, Ken	L/L	6-0/180	2-25-59	Dunedin, Syracuse, Toronto
66	Guzman, Juan	R/R	5-11/195	10-28-66	Syracuse, Toronto
50	Henke, Tom	R/R	6-5/225	12-21-57	Toronto
41	Hentgen, Pat	R/R	6-2/200	11-13-68	Syracuse, Toronto
26	Horsman, Vince	R/L	6-2/180	3-9-67	Knoxville, Toronto
22	Key, Jimmy	R/L	6-1/185	4-22-61	Toronto
28	Leiter, Al	L/L	6-3/215	10-23-65	Dunedin, Toronto
45	MacDonald, Bob	L/L	6-3/208	4-27-65	Syracuse, Toronto
47	Morris, Jack	R/R	6-3/200	5-16-55	Minnesota
37	Stieb, Dave	R/R	6-1/195	7-22-57	Toronto
30	Stottlemyre, Todd	L/R	6-3/195	5-20-65	Toronto
40	Timlin, Mike	R/R	6-4/205	3-10-66	Toronto
35	Trlicek, Ricky	R/R	6-3/200	4-26-69	Knoxville
31	Ward, Duane	R/R	6-4/215	5-28-64	Toronto
53	Weathers, Dave	R/R	6-3/205	9-25-69	Knoxville, Toronto
36	Wells, David	L/L	6-4/225	5-20-63	Toronto

No.	CATCHERS	B/T	Ht./Wt.	Born	1991 clubs
10	Borders, Pat	R/R	6-2/200	5-14-63	Toronto
27	Knorr, Randy	R/R	6-2/205	11-12-66	Knoxville, Syracuse, Toronto
21	Myers, Greg	L/R	6-2/205	4-14-66	Toronto
33	Sprague, Ed	R/R	6-2/215	7-25-67	Syracuse, Toronto

No.	INFIELDERS	B/T	Ht./Wt.	Born	1991 clubs
12	Alomar, Roberto	S/R	6-0/185	2-5-68	Toronto
17	Gruber, Kelly	R/R	6-0/185	2-26-62	Toronto
11	Kent, Jeff	R/R	6-1/185	3-7-68	Knoxville
4	Lee, Manuel	S/R	5-9/166	6-17-65	Toronto
19	Martinez, Domingo	R/R	6-2/215	6-4-67	Syracuse
5	Mulliniks, Rance	L/R	6-0/175	1-15-56	Toronto
9	Olerud, John	L/L	6-5/218	8-5-68	Toronto
16	Quinlan, Tom	R/R	6-3/210	3-27-68	Syracuse
15	Tabler, Pat	R/R	6-2/200	2-2-58	Toronto
1	Zosky, Eddie	R/R	6-0/175	2-10-68	Syracuse, Toronto

No.	OUTFIELDERS	B/T	Ht./Wt.	Born	1991 clubs
14	Bell, Derek	R/R	6-2/200	12-11-68	Syracuse, Toronto
29	Carter, Joe	R/R	6-3/225	3-7-60	Toronto
20	Ducey, Rob	L/R	6-2/180	5-24-65	Syracuse, Toronto
23	Maldonado, Candy	R/R	6-0/195	10-5-60	Milwaukee, Toronto
55	Perez, Robert	R/R	6-3/195	6-4-69	Dunedin, Syracuse
54	Thompson, Ryan	R/R	6-3/200	11-4-67	Knoxville
24	Ward, Turner	S/R	6-2/200	4-11-65	Syracuse, Toronto
25	White, Devon	S/R	6-2/182	12-29-62	Toronto
52	Wilson, Nigel	L/L	6-1/185	1-12-70	Dunedin
32	Winfield, Dave	R/R	6-6/246	10-3-51	California

BALLPARK INFORMATION

Ballpark (capacity, surface)
SkyDome (50,516, artificial)

Address
300 Bremner Blvd., Gate No. 9
Toronto, Ontario M5V 3B3

Business phone
416-341-1000

Ticket information
416-341-1111

Ticket prices
$17.50 (esplanade IF, club level OF)
$13.50 (skydeck IF, esplanade OF)
$10 (skydeck)
$4 (skydeck outfield)

Field dimensions (from home plate)
To left field at foul line, 330 feet
To center field, 400 feet
To right field at foul line, 330 feet

First game played
June 5, 1989 (Brewers 5, Blue Jays 3)

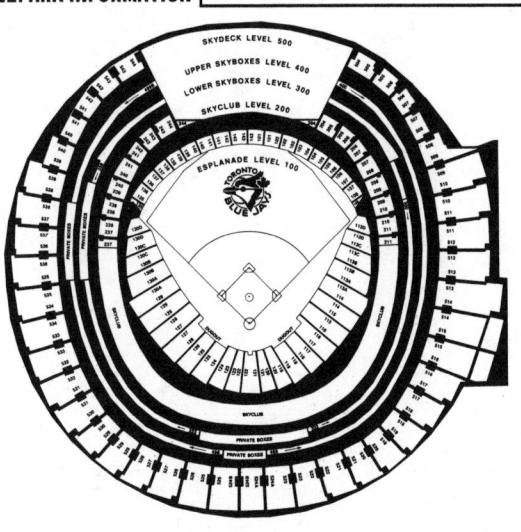

MINOR LEAGUE AFFILIATES

Class	Team	League	Manager
AAA	Syracuse	International	Nick Leyva
AA	Knoxville	Southern	Garth Iorg
A	Myrtle Beach	South Atlantic	Doug Ault
A	Dunedin	Florida State	Dennis Holmberg
A	St. Catharines	New York-Pennsylvania	J.J. Cannon
Rookie	Medicine Hat	Pioneer	Jim Nettles
Rookie	Gulf Coast Blue Jays	Gulf Coast	Omar Malave

BROADCAST INFORMATION

Radio: CJCL-AM (1430). Broadcasters: Tom Cheek, Jerry Howarth.
TV: CFTO-TV (Channel 9). Broadcasters: Don Chevrier, Tommy Hutton, Fergie Olver.
Cable TV: The Sports Network. Broadcasters: Jim Hughson, Buck Martinez.

SPRING TRAINING

Ballpark (city): Dunedin Stadium at Grant Field (Dunedin, Fla.).
Ticket information: 813-733-0429.

HISTORY

YEAR-BY-YEAR RECORDS

Year	Pos.	W	L	Pct.	*GB	Year	Pos.	W	L	Pct.	*GB
1977	7th	54	107	.335	45½	1986	4th	86	76	.531	9½
1978	7th	59	102	.366	40	1987	2nd	96	66	.593	2
1979	7th	53	109	.327	50½	1988	T3rd	87	75	.537	2
1980	7th	67	95	.414	36	1989	1st‡	89	73	.549 +	2
1981	7th/7th	37	69	.349	†	1990	2nd	86	76	.531	2
1982	T6th	78	84	.481	17	1991	1st‡	91	71	.562 +	7
1983	4th	89	73	.549	9		*Games behind winner. †First half				
1984	2nd	89	73	.549	15		16-42; second 21-27. ‡Lost Champion-				
1985	1st‡	99	62	.615 +	2		ship Series.				

MANAGERS

Name	Record	Years
Roy Hartsfield	166-318	'77-79
Bobby Mattick	104-164	'80-81
Bobby Cox	355-292	'82-85
Jimy Williams	281-241	'86-89
Cito Gaston	254-196	'89-91

DAY BY DAY

Date	Opp.	Res.	Score (inn.*)	Hits	Opp. hits	Winning pitcher	Losing pitcher	Save	Record	Pos.	GB
4-8	Bos.	L	2-6	7	5	Clemens	Stieb		0-1	T4th	1
4-9	Bos.	W	4-3	8	9	Key	Harris	Henke	1-1	T3rd	½
4-10	Bos.	W	5-3	4	7	Timlin	Gray	Henke	2-1	2nd	½
4-11	Mil.	W	7-3	13	9	Wells	Robinson		3-1	1st	+½
4-12	Mil.	W	5-4 (11)	12	7	Timlin	Plesac		4-1	1st	+1½
4-13	Mil.	L	3-7	7	10	Brown	Stieb	Crim	4-2	1st	+½
4-14	Mil.	W	9-0	13	2	Key	August		5-2	1st	+1
4-15	At Det.	W	4-3	10	5	Stottlemyre	Terrell	Ward	6-2	1st	+1½
4-16	At Det.	L	2-6	6	8	Gullickson	Wells	Henneman	6-3	1st	+1½
4-17	At Det.	L	4-5 (10)	7	9	Henneman	Ward		6-4	1st	+1
4-19	At Mil.	W	5-2	11	8	Stieb	August		7-4	1st	+1
4-20	At Mil.	W	4-2	8	6	Key	Bosio	Ward	8-4	1st	+1
4-21	At Mil.	L	8-11 (10)	11	11	Crim	Wills		8-5	1st	+1
4-22	At Bos.	L	4-6	8	10	Lamp	Wells	Reardon	8-6	3rd	...
4-23	At Bos.	L	0-3	6	8	Clemens	Boucher	Reardon	8-7	3rd	+1
4-24	At Bos.	W	6-1	9	9	Stieb	Young		9-7	2nd	...
4-25	Det.	W	3-2	10	6	Key	Petry	Ward	10-7	1st	+½
4-26	Det.	W	5-4	9	8	Stottlemyre	Terrell	Ward	11-7	1st	+1½
4-27	Det.	L	2-4	6	5	Gullickson	Wells	Henneman	11-8	1st	+½
4-28	Det.	W	9-6	15	9	Timlin	Leiter	Ward	12-8	1st	+½
4-30	At Tex.	L	5-8	11	12	Gossage	Acker	Russell	12-9	2nd	½
5-1	At Tex.	L	0-3	0	8	Ryan	Key		12-10	4th	½
5-2	At K.C.	W	3-1	9	2	Stottlemyre	Appier	Ward	13-10	3rd	...
5-3	At K.C.	W	5-1	11	9	Wells	S. Davis		14-10	2nd	...
5-4	At K.C.	L	5-6	10	11	Saberhagen	Boucher	Montgomery	14-11	3rd	1
5-5	At K.C.	W	3-0	8	3	Stieb	Gordon	Ward	15-11	2nd	1
5-7	Tex.	L	2-3	8	11	Rogers	Key	Russell	15-12	3rd	1
5-8	Tex.	W	4-2	4	6	Stottlmyre	Ryan	Ward	16-12	3rd	1
5-9	Chi.	W	2-0	6	3	Wells	Perez	Ward	17-12	3rd	1
5-10	Chi.	L	3-5 (12)	8	12	Radinsky	Fraser		17-13	3rd	2
5-11	Chi.	W	5-2	6	7	Stieb	Hough	Ward	18-13	2nd	2
5-12	Chi.	W	4-2	9	7	Key	Hibbard	Ward	19-13	2nd	1
5-13	K.C.	W	4-2	7	6	Stottlemyre	S. Davis	Ward	20-13	2nd	1
5-14	K.C.	W	4-1	12	6	Wells	Gubicza	Timlin	21-13	2nd	...
5-15	K.C.	L	4-6	10	12	Saberhagen	Boucher		21-14	2nd	1
5-17	At Chi.	L	3-5	9	11	Pall	Timlin	Thigpen	21-15	2nd	1
5-18	At Chi.	W	9-2	13	4	Key	Hibbard		22-15	2nd	...
5-19	At Chi.	L	4-5	9	9	Patterson	Timlin	Thigpen	22-16	2nd	...
5-20	At Oak.	W	1-0	4	3	Wells	Welch	Henke	23-16	2nd	...
5-21	At Oak.	W	11-7	11	6	Acker	Dressendorfer	Timlin	24-16	2nd	...
5-22	At Oak.	L	1-2	5	5	Moore	Stieb	Eckersley	24-17	2nd	1
5-24	At Cal.	W	3-2	7	7	Timlin	Finley	Henke	25-17	2nd	½
5-25	At Cal.	L	0-5	5	9	McCaskill	Stottlemyre		25-18	2nd	½
5-26	At Cal.	L	2-6	5	10	Langston	Wells		25-19	2nd	½
5-28	Oak.	L	4-8	6	9	Moore	Acker	Eckersley	25-20	2nd	1
5-29	Oak.	W	8-3	14	11	Key	Slusarski	Henke	26-20	2nd	...
5-30	Oak.	L	6-8	12	10	Klink	Ward	Eckersley	26-21	2nd	...
5-31	Cal.	W	5-1	9	5	Wells	Langston		27-21	2nd	...
6-1	Cal.	L	8-11	16	13	Eichhorn	Fraser	Harvey	27-22	2nd	...
6-2	Cal.	L	2-7	9	9	J. Abbott	Acker		27-23	2nd	...
6-3	At N.Y.	W	5-3	12	8	Key	Leary	Henke	28-23	1st	+½
6-4	At N.Y.	L	3-5	10	9	Sanderson	Stottlemyre	Farr	28-24	1st	+½
6-5	At N.Y.	W	4-1	9	4	Wells	Johnson	Henke	29-24	1st	+1½
6-6	At Bal.	L	4-6	9	6	Milacki	Timlin	Olson	29-25	1st	+1½
6-7	At Bal.	L	4-6	8	7	Smith	Guzman	Olson	29-26	1st	+½
6-8	At Bal.	W	8-4	12	11	Key	Kilgus		30-26	1st	+½
6-9	At Bal.	W	3-2	9	5	Stottlemyre	Ballard	Henke	31-26	1st	+1½
6-11	At Cle.	L	1-2 (12)	7	9	Hillegas	Acker		31-27	2nd	...
6-12	At Cle.	W	1-0	3	2	Timlin	Candiotti	Henke	32-27	1st	+1
6-13	At Cle.	W	1-0	7	2	Key	Nagy		33-27	1st	+1½
6-14	Bal.	W	9-1	12	8	Stottlemyre	Robinson		34-27	1st	+1½
6-15	Bal.	L	4-8	9	12	Ballard	Guzman	Williamson	34-28	1st	+½
6-16	Bal.	L	8-13	12	13	Frohwirth	Ward		34-29	2nd	½
6-18	N.Y.	L	2-4	11	11	Kamieniecki	Timlin	Farr	34-30	2nd	...
6-19	N.Y.	L	0-3	6	10	Johnson	Key	Howe	34-31	2nd	...
6-20	N.Y.	W	6-1	9	8	Stottlemyre	Leary		35-31	2nd	...
6-21	Cle.	W	8-4	14	6	Wells	Swindell	Henke	36-31	2nd	...
6-22	Cle.	W	4-0	7	4	Guzman	Mutis	Ward	37-31	2nd	...
6-23	Cle.	W	3-1	10	8	MacDonald	Candiotti	Henke	38-31	1st	+½
6-24	Cle.	W	4-3	9	11	Ward	Nagy	Henke	39-31	1st	+1½

TORONTO BLUE JAYS

1992 SEASON

TORONTO BLUE JAYS

Date	Opp.	Res.	Score (inn.*)	Hits	Opp. hits	Winning pitcher	Losing pitcher	Save	Record	Pos.	GB
6-25	At Min.	L	6-8	10	12	Morris	Stottlemyre	Aguilera	39-32	1st	+1½
6-26	At Min.	W	5-2	13	8	Wells	Guthrie	Henke	40-32	1st	+2½
6-27	At Min.	W	1-0	4	3	Guzman	Tapani	Henke	41-32	1st	+3½
6-28	Sea.	L	1-3	7	9	Krueger	Candiotti	Jackson	41-33	1st	+2½
6-29	Sea.	W	4-0	6	7	Timlin	DeLucia	Ward	42-33	1st	+3½
6-30	Sea.	W	6-1	8	4	Stottlemyre	Holman		43-33	1st	+4½
7-1	Sea.	W	4-3	4	7	Acker	Jackson		44-33	1st	+4½
7-2	Min.	W	4-3	16	4	Ward	Leach		45-33	1st	+4½
7-3	Min.	W	4-0	12	6	Candiotti	Anderson		46-33	1st	+4½
7-4	Min.	L	0-1	3	8	West	Key	Aguilera	46-34	1st	+4½
7-5	At Sea.	W	2-1	6	7	MacDonald	Holman	Henke	47-34	1st	+4½
7-6	At Sea.	W	4-3 (10)	11	6	Timlin	Swan	Henke	48-34	1st	+4½
7-7	At Sea.	W	5-2	8	4	Guzman	Hanson		49-34	1st	+5½
7-11	Tex.	W	2-0	9	5	Candiotti	Brown	Henke	50-34	1st	+6½
7-12	Tex.	W	6-2	12	5	Wells	Guzman	Ward	51-34	1st	+7½
7-13	Tex.	W	3-2	6	7	Timlin	Russell	Henke	52-34	1st	+8½
7-14	Tex.	L	6-8	7	11	Barfield	Key	Russell	52-35	1st	+7½
7-15	At K.C.	W	5-3 (12)	17	9	Timlin	Crawford	Henke	53-35	1st	+8
7-16	At K.C.	L	1-2 (10)	5	7	Aquino	Candiotti		53-36	1st	+7
7-18	At Tex.	W	4-0	6	4	Wells	Ryan	Ward	54-36	1st	+7
7-19	At Tex.	W	7-2	14	8	Stottlemyre	Barfield	Timlin	55-36	1st	+7
7-20	At Tex.	L	6-11	13	17	Jeffcoat	Key		55-37	1st	+7
7-21	At Tex.	L	5-6	10	9	Rogers	Timlin	Russell	55-38	1st	+7
7-23	At Chi.	L	2-3	8	7	Thigpen	Candiotti		55-39	1st	+6
7-24	At Chi.	W	2-1	10	7	Wells	McDowell	Henke	56-39	1st	+6
7-25	At Chi.	L	1-7	8	8	Hough	Stottlemyre		56-40	1st	+6
7-26	K.C.	W	6-5 (11)	13	10	Ward	Gordon		57-40	1st	+6
7-27	K.C.	L	2-5 (10)	10	8	Gordon	Timlin	Montgomery	57-41	1st	+6
7-28	K.C.	L	4-10	12	16	Gubicza	Candiotti	S. Davis	57-42	1st	+6
7-29	Chi.	L	4-12	6	11	McDowell	Wells		57-43	1st	+6
7-30	Chi.	L	7-8	9	8	Radinsky	MacDonald	Thigpen	57-44	1st	+6
7-31	Cle.	W	3-1	6	6	Key	King	Henke	58-44	1st	+6
8-1	Cle.	W	7-5	10	8	Ward	Shaw	Henke	59-44	1st	+6
8-2	At Bos.	L	3-5	5	6	Clemens	Candiotti		59-45	1st	+5
8-3	At Bos.	L	1-4	7	8	Hesketh	Wells	Reardon	59-46	1st	+4
8-4	At Bos.	W	2-1	7	7	Ward	Lamp	Henke	60-46	1st	+4
8-6	Det.	W	2-1	7	5	Key	Cerutti	Henke	61-46	1st	+5½
8-7	Det.	W	5-2	8	4	Guzman	Tanana	Henke	62-46	1st	+6½
8-8	Det.	L	0-4 (14)	13	9	Gibson	Henke		62-47	1st	+5½
8-9	Bos.	L	7-12	15	21	Hesketh	Wells	Reardon	62-48	1st	+5
8-10	Bos.	L	1-7	4	12	Harris	Stottlemyre		62-49	1st	+3½
8-11	Bos.	L	6-9	10	16	Gardiner	Key	Reardon	62-50	1st	+4
8-12	Bos.	L	8-11	13	18	Lamp	Ward	Reardon	62-51	1st	+3½
8-13	At Mil.	L	4-5	7	10	Crim	Henke		62-52	1st	+2
8-14	At Mil.	L	3-5	7	9	Bosio	Wells	Henry	62-53	1st	+2
8-15	At Mil.	W	4-1	7	4	Stottlemyre	Plesac	Henke	63-53	1st	+2
8-16	At Det.	L	2-5	6	7	Cerutti	Key	Gakeler	63-54	1st	+1
8-17	At Det.	W	7-5	8	5	MacDonald	Aldred	Henke	64-54	1st	+2
8-18	At Det.	W	4-2	7	3	Candiotti	Kaiser	Henke	65-54	1st	+3
8-20	Mil.	W	3-1	9	9	Stottlemyre	Bosio	Henke	66-54	1st	+2½
8-21	Mil.	L	0-3	2	9	Machado	Key	Nunez	66-55	1st	+1½
8-22	Mil.	L	7-8	10	13	Ignasiak	Ward	Henry	66-56	1st	+1
8-23	N.Y.	W	6-5	9	15	Ward	Farr		67-56	1st	+1
8-24	N.Y.	L	5-6	7	11	Johnson	Wells		67-57	T1st	...
8-25	N.Y.	W	11-7	12	8	Acker	Guetterman		68-57	T1st	...
8-26	At Bal.	W	5-2	11	10	Key	Johnson	Henke	69-57	T1st	...
8-27	At Bal.	W	6-1	8	5	Guzman	Rhodes		70-57	1st	+1
8-28	At Bal.	W	3-0	9	1	Candiotti	McDonald	Henke	71-57	1st	+2
8-29	At N.Y.	W	6-2	11	8	Wells	Johnson		72-57	1st	+2½
8-30	At N.Y.	L	2-9	6	14	Sanderson	Stottlemyre		72-58	1st	+2½
8-31	At N.Y.	W	5-0	12	3	Key	Cadaret	Ward	73-58	1st	+3½
9-1	At N.Y.	L	2-4	5	7	Guetterman	MacDonald		73-59	1st	+2½
9-2	Bal.	W	5-4 (12)	12	10	Timlin	Olson		74-59	1st	+2½
9-3	Bal.	L	4-8	7	12	McDonald	Wells	Flanagan	74-60	1st	+2½
9-4	Bal.	W	3-1	6	4	Stottlemyre	Milacki	Ward	75-60	1st	+3
9-5	At Cle.	W	13-1	17	8	Key	Nagy		76-60	1st	+4
9-6	At Cle.	W	7-4	9	9	Guzman	Otto	Ward	77-60	1st	+4
9-7	At Cle.	W	4-1	9	5	Candiotti	Swindell		78-60	1st	+5
9-8	At Cle.	W	11-5	14	10	Wells	King		79-60	1st	+5½
9-10	Sea.	L	4-5	9	6	Holman	Stottlemyre	Jones	79-61	1st	+4
9-11	Sea.	L	3-7	6	13	Hanson	Key		79-62	1st	+4
9-13	Oak.	W	7-6	15	9	Guzman	Stewart	Henke	80-62	1st	+3½
9-14	Oak.	W	6-0	8	5	Candiotti	Welch		81-62	1st	+4½
9-15	Oak.	L	5-10	7	12	Moore	Stottlemyre	Eckersley	81-63	1st	+3½

Date	Opp.	Res.	Score (inn.*)	Hits	Opp. hits	Winning pitcher	Losing pitcher	Save	Record	Pos.	GB
9-16	At Sea.	L	5-6 (11)	9	11	Swan	MacDonald		81-64	1st	+3½
9-17	At Sea.	L	4-5 (11)	11	12	Schooler	Acker		81-65	1st	+2½
9-18	At Sea.	W	5-3 (12)	8	9	Ward	Bankhead	Acker	82-65	1st	+2½
9-20	At Oak.	L	5-6 (11)	9	8	Eckersley	Ward		82-66	1st	+1½
9-21	At Oak.	L	0-4	5	6	Moore	Key		82-67	1st	+ ½
9-22	At Oak.	W	3-2	5	3	Guzman	Darling	Wells	83-67	1st	+1½
9-23	At Cal.	L	9-10	12	14	Lewis	Candiotti	Harvey	83-68	1st	+2½
9-24	At Cal.	W	3-0 (10)	4	6	Wells	J. Abbott		84-68	1st	+3
9-25	At Cal.	W	7-2	9	6	Key	Langston		85-68	1st	+3½
9-27	Min.	W	7-2	9	3	Guzman	Tapani		86-68	1st	+4½
9-28	Min.	L	0-5	6	10	Morris	Candiotti		86-69	1st	+4½
9-29	Min.	W	2-1	5	6	Stottlemyre	Erickson	Ward	87-69	1st	+4½
9-30	Cal.	L	1-2	3	9	Langston	Key	Harvey	87-70	1st	+4½
10-1	Cal.	W	5-2	8	8	Guzman	Fetters	Ward	88-70	1st	+5½
10-2	Cal.	W	6-5	8	10	Timlin	Harvey	Ward	89-70	1st	+5½
10-4	At Min.	W	4-1	11	6	Stottlemyre	Neagle	Ward	90-70	1st	+7
10-5	At Min.	L	1-3	5	11	Erickson	Guzman	Aguilera	90-71	1st	+7
10-6	At Min.	W	3-2 (10)	6	6	Weathers	Anderson	Ward	91-71	1st	+7

Monthly records: April (12-9), May (15-12), June (16-12), July (15-11), August (15-14), September (14-12), Oct. (4-1).

HIGHLIGHTS

High point: From June 20 through July 13, the Blue Jays won 18 of 21 games. In the process, they jumped from second place to first in the American League East, establishing an eight-game lead.

Low point: The Blue Jays started a seven-game losing streak by dropping a 14-inning marathon to Detroit on August 8. Included in that tailspin was a four-game sweep by Boston that let the Red Sox back in the race.

Turning point: After Toronto lost four of its first five games on its final West Coast trip in September, catcher Pat Borders hit a two-run home run that put the Blue Jays ahead for good in a 3-2 victory in Oakland. Borders hit another homer two nights later, this time a pinch-hit, three-run blast in the 10th inning for a 3-0 win over California.

Most valuable player: Second baseman Roberto Alomar. The switch-hitter posted career highs in doubles (41), runs batted in (69) and stolen bases (53), while also winning a Gold Glove.

Most valuable pitcher: Righthander Duane Ward. He switched from setup man to closer when Tom Henke was injured, logging a career-high 23 saves.

Most improved player: Center fielder Devon White. Not only did he win his third Gold Glove, but he also lifted his batting average from .217 (at California in 1990) to .282. He led the team in runs (110) and collected 67 extra-base hits and 33 stolen bases.

Most pleasant surprise: Rookie right-hander Juan Guzman. He set a club record for starters by posting 10 consecutive wins. He was the only Blue Jay starter to win a postseason game.

Biggest disappointment: Third baseman Kelly Gruber. For the fourth year in a row he experienced a hand injury. He missed 49 games, and his offensive numbers (.252 average, 20 homers, 65 RBIs) reflected it.

Key injuries: After nine starts, Dave Stieb was lost for the year due to shoulder and back problems. Ken Dayley (dizzy spells) missed almost the entire year. Henke missed five weeks with a pulled groin and made only two appearances after September 17 because of shoulder tendinitis.

Notable: Henke converted a major league-record 25 consecutive save opportunities before blowing his first save August 13 in Milwaukee. . . . The Blue Jays became the first major league team to top the four-million mark in attendance (4,001,526).

—NEIL MacCARL

RECORDS

1991 regular-season record: 91-71 (1st in A.L. East); 46-35 at home; 45-36 on road; 46-32 vs. East; 45-39 vs. West; 28-19 vs. LHP; 63-52 vs. RHP; 33-30 on grass; 58-41 on turf; 28-24 in daytime; 63-47 at night; 28-20 in one-run games; 8-10 in extra-inning games; 0-0 in doubleheaders.

1991 postseason record: Lost to Twins, 4 games to 1, in A.L. playoffs.

Team record last five years: 449-361 (.554, ranks 2nd in league in that span).

TEAM LEADERS

Batting average: Roberto Alomar (.295).
At-bats: Devon White (642).
Runs: Devon White (110).
Hits: Roberto Alomar (188).
Total bases: Joe Carter (321).
Doubles: Joe Carter (42).
Triples: Roberto Alomar (11).
Home runs: Joe Carter (33).
Runs batted in: Joe Carter (108).
Stolen bases: Roberto Alomar (53).
Slugging percentage: Joe Carter (.503).
On-base percentage: Roberto Alomar (.354).
Wins: Jimmy Key (16).
Earned-run average: Jimmy Key (3.05).
Complete games: Tom Candiotti (3).
Shutouts: Jimmy Key (2).
Saves: Tom Henke (32).
Innings pitched: Todd Stottlemyre (219).
Strikeouts: Duane Ward (132).

GAMES BY POSITION

Catcher: Greg Myers 104, Pat Borders 102, Randy Knorr 3, Ed Sprague 2.
First base: John Olerud 135, Ed Sprague 22, Pat Tabler 20, Cory Snyder 4, Rene Gonzales 2.
Second base: Roberto Alomar 160, Rene Gonzales 11.
Third base: Kelly Gruber 111, Ed Sprague 35, Rene Gonzales 26, Ray Giannelli 9, Rance Mulliniks 5, Cory Snyder 3.
Shortstop: Manny Lee 138, Rene Gonzales 36, Eddie Zosky 18.
Outfield: Devon White 156, Joe Carter 151, Candy Maldonado 52, Mark Whiten 42, Mookie Wilson 41, Rob Ducey 24, Cory Snyder 14, Derek Bell 13, Kenny Williams 9, Turner Ward 6, Pat Tabler 1.
Designated hitter: Rance Mulliniks 81, Pat Tabler 57, Mookie Wilson 34, Glenallen Hill 16, Joe Carter 11, Dave Parker 11, Candy Maldonado 9, Cory Snyder 3, Rob Ducey 2, Kelly Gruber 2, Ed Sprague 2, Kenny Williams 2, John Olerud 1.

TOP 10 DRAFT CHOICES

1a. Shawn Green, OF, Tustin (Calif.) High School.
1b. Jeff Ware, RHP, Old Dominion University.
1c. Dante Powell, SS, Millikan High School, Long Beach, Calif.
2a. Trevor Mallory, RHP, Lakewood High School, St. Petersburg, Fla.
2b. Dennis Gray, LHP, Long Beach State University.
3. Chris Stynes, SS, Boca Raton (Fla.) High School.
4. Roger Doman, RHP, Joplin (Mo.) High School.
5. Rickey Cradle, OF, Cerritos (Calif.) High School.
6. Jose Silva, RHP, Hilltop High School, Chula Vista, Calif.
7. Carlton Loewer, RHP, St. Edmund High School, Eunice, La.
8. Stoney Briggs, OF, Delaware Tech.
9. Pat Thacker, C, Millikan High School, Long Beach, Calif.
10. Kenny Robinson, RHP, Florida State.

ATLANTA BRAVES
NATIONAL LEAGUE WEST DIVISION

1992 SCHEDULE

APRIL

S	M	T	W	T	F	S
5	6	7 N HOU	8 N HOU	9 N SF H	10 N SF H	11 N SF H
12 SF H	13 N CIN	14 N CIN	15 CIN	16 N LA	17 N LA	18 LA
19 N LA	20 N SD	21 N SD	22 N SD	23	24 N HOU H	25 N HOU H
26 HOU H	27 CHI H	28 N CHI H	29 N CHI H	30		

MAY

S	M	T	W	T	F	S
					1 N NY H	2 NY H
3 NY H	4 N CHI	5 CHI	6 N PIT	7 N PIT	8 N STL	9 N STL
10 STL	11 N PIT	12 N PIT	13 N PIT	14 N MON H	15 N MON H	16 N MON H
17 MON H	18 STL	19 N STL	20 N STL	21	22 N MON	23 MON
24 MON	25 N PHI	26 PHI	27 N PHI	28	29 N NY	30 NY
31 NY						

JUNE

S	M	T	W	T	F	S
	1 N PHI	2 N PHI	3 N PHI	4	5 N SD	6 N SD
7 SD	8 N LA	9 N LA	10 LA	11	12 N SD	13 N SD
14 SD	15 N LA	16 N LA	17 N LA	18 N CIN	19 N CIN	20 N CIN
21 CIN H	22	23 N SF H	24 N SF H	25	26 N CIN	27 CIN
28 CIN H	29 N SF	30 SF				

JULY

S	M	T	W	T	F	S
			1 N SF	2	3 N CHI H	4 CHI H
5 CHI H	6 N NY H	7 N NY H	8 N NY H	9 N CHI	10 CHI	11 CHI
12 CHI	13	14 *	15	16 N HOU	17 N HOU	18 HOU
19 HOU	20	21 N STL	22 N STL	23	24 N PIT H	25 N PIT H
26 PIT H	27 N HOU H	28 N HOU H	29 N HOU H	30 N SF	31 SF	

AUGUST

S	M	T	W	T	F	S
						1 SF
2 SF	3	4 N CIN H	5 N CIN H	6 N CIN H	7 N LA H	8 LA H
9 LA H	10 N LA H	11 N SD H	12 N SD H	13 N SD H	14 N PIT	15 PIT
16 PIT	17 PIT	18 N MON	19 N MON	20 N MON	21 N STL H	22 STL H
23 STL H	24	25 N MON H	26 N MON H	27 MON H	28 N PHI	29 PHI
30 PHI	31 N NY					

SEPTEMBER

S	M	T	W	T	F	S
		1 N NY	2 N NY	3	4 N PHI H	5 N PHI H
6 PHI H	7	8 N LA	9 N LA	10 N CIN	11 N CIN	12 N HOU
13 HOU	14	15 N CIN	16 N CIN	17 CIN	18 N HOU H	19 N HOU H
20 HOU H	21 N LA	22 N LA	23 N SF	24 SF	25 N SD	26 N SD
27 SD	28	29 N SF H	30 N SF H			

OCTOBER

S	M	T	W	T	F	S
				1 N SF H	2 N SD H	3 N SD H
4 SD H	5	6	7	8	9	10

1992 SEASON

CLUB DIRECTORY

Chairman of the board
William C. Bartholomay
President
Stan Kasten
Sr. vice president and asst. to the president
Henry L. Aaron
Exec. vice president and general manager
John Schuerholz
Senior v.p., administration and finance
Charles S. Sanders
Director of player development and scouting
Chuck LaMar
Asst. v.p. and special asst. to the g.m.
Paul L. Snyder Jr.
Assistant general manager
Dean Taylor
Assistant scouting director
Scott Proefrock
Assistant director of player development
Rod Gilbreath
Minor league coordinator
Bobby Dews
V.p., director of marketing and broadcasting
Wayne Long
Dir. of team travel and equipment manager
Bill Acree
Director of public relations
Jim Schultz
Director of community relations
Danny Goodwin
Director of promotions
Miles McRea
Director of ticket sales
Jack Tyson
Director of ticket operations
Ed Newman
Assistant director of ticket operations
Sam Williams
Director of advertising
Peter Diffin
Director of merchandising
Robert A. Hope
Director of stadium operations and security
Terri Brennan
Assistant controller
Chip Moore
Public relations assistants
Glen Serra
Mike Ringering
Trainer
Dave Pursley
Assistant trainer
Jeff Porter
Club physician
Dr. David T. Watson

Associate physicians
Dr. John Cantwell
Dr. Robert Crow
Club orthopedist
Dr. Joe Chandler
Scouts
Mike Arbuckle
Butch Baccala
Ray Belanger
Sonny Bowers
Bart Braun
James Buchert
Stu Cann
Joe Caputo
Bill Clark
Roy Clark
Ray Corbett
Harold Cronin
Bob Dunning
Rob English
John Flannery
Ralph Garr
Steve Givens
Pedro Gonzalez
John Hagemann
Bob Isabelle
Jim Johnson
Dean Jongewaard
Steve Jongewaard
Brian Kohlscheen
Deric Ladnier
Bill Lajoie
Scott Littlefield
Gerardo Lopez
Robert Lucas
Robyn Lynch
Scott Nethery
Ernie Pederson
Rolando Petit
Julian Perez
Jack Pierce
Rance Pless
Carlos Rios
Fred Shaffer
Alex Smith
Charlie Smith
Paul Snyder
Ted Sparks
John Stewart
Tony Stiel
Bob Turzilli
Wes Westrum
Bill Wight
Dave Wilder
Don Williams
Bobby Wine

SCHEDULE KEY

H—Home game.   *All-Star Game at San Diego/Jack Murphy Stadium.
N—Night game (any game starting after 5 p.m.).

SPRING TRAINING ROSTER

Manager—Bobby Cox (6).

Coaches—Jim Beauchamp (37), Pat Corrales (39), Clarence Jones (28), Leo Mazzone (54), Jimy Williams (22), Ned Yost (52).

No.	PITCHERS	B/T	Ht./Wt.	Born	1991 clubs
33	Avery, Steve	L/L	6-4/190	4-14-70	Atlanta
48	Berenguer, Juan	R/R	5-11/220	11-30-54	Atlanta
36	Bielecki, Mike	R/R	6-3/195	7-31-59	Chicago NL, Atlanta
67	Burlingame, Dennis	R/R	6-4/200	6-17-69	Durham
40	Freeman, Marvin	R/R	6-7/222	4-10-63	Atlanta
47	Glavine, Tom	L/L	6-1/190	3-25-66	Atlanta
56	Gomez, Pat	L/L	5-11/185	3-17-68	Richmond, Greenville
32	Leibrandt, Charlie	R/L	6-3/200	10-4-56	Atlanta
50	Mercker, Kent	L/L	6-2/195	2-1-68	Atlanta
63	Murray, Matt	L/R	6-6/200	9-26-70	Durham
62	Nied, David	R/R	6-2/175	12-22-68	Greenville, Durham
26	Pena, Alejandro	R/R	6-1/203	6-25-59	New York NL, Atlanta
42	Reynoso, Armando	R/R	6-0/186	5-1-66	Atlanta, Richmond
51	Rivera, Ben	R/R	6-6/210	1-11-69	Greenville
25	Smith, Pete	R/R	6-2/200	2-27-66	Macon, Richmond, Atlanta
29	Smoltz, John	R/R	6-3/185	5-15-67	Atlanta
30	Stanton, Mike	L/L	6-1/190	6-2-67	Atlanta
43	Wohlers, Mark	R/R	6-4/207	1-23-70	Atlanta, Richmond

No.	CATCHERS	B/T	Ht./Wt.	Born	1991 clubs
11	Berryhill, Damon	S/R	6-0/205	12-3-63	Chicago NL, Atlanta
19	Cabrera, Francisco	R/R	6-4/193	10-10-66	Richmond, Atlanta
8	Heath, Mike	R/R	5-11/180	2-5-55	Atlanta
64	Lopez, Javier	R/R	6-3/185	11-5-70	Durham
10	Olson, Greg	R/R	6-0/200	9-6-60	Atlanta

No.	INFIELDERS	B/T	Ht./Wt.	Born	1991 clubs
2	Belliard, Rafael	R/R	5-6/160	10-24-61	Atlanta
4	Blauser, Jeff	R/R	6-0/170	11-8-65	Atlanta
12	Bream, Sid	L/L	6-4/220	8-3-60	Atlanta
65	Caraballo, Ramon	S/R	5-7/150	5-23-69	Durham
45	Castilla, Vinny	R/R	6-1/175	7-4-67	Richmond, Atlanta, Greenville
14	Hunter, Brian	R/L	6-0/195	3-4-68	Richmond, Atlanta
20	Lemke, Mark	S/R	5-9/167	8-13-65	Atlanta
18	Lyons, Steve	L/R	6-3/195	6-3-60	Boston
9	Pendleton, Terry	S/R	5-9/195	7-16-60	Atlanta
15	Treadway, Jeff	L/R	5-11/170	1-22-63	Atlanta

No.	OUTFIELDERS	B/T	Ht./Wt.	Born	1991 clubs
5	Gant, Ron	R/R	6-0/172	3-2-65	Atlanta
16	Gregg, Tommy	L/L	6-1/190	7-29-63	Atlanta
23	Justice, David	L/L	6-3/200	4-14-66	Atlanta
17	Mitchell, Keith	R/R	5-10/180	8-6-69	Atlanta, Greenville, Richmond
66	Nieves, Melvin	S/R	6-2/186	12-28-71	Durham
24	Sanders, Deion	L/L	6-1/195	8-9-67	Atlanta, Richmond
27	Smith, Lonnie	R/R	5-9/170	12-22-55	Atlanta

BALLPARK INFORMATION

Ballpark (capacity, surface)
Atlanta-Fulton County Stadium
(52,013, grass)

Address
P.O. Box 4064
Atlanta, GA 30302

Business phone
404-522-7630

Ticket information
404-522-7630

Ticket prices
$12 (club level)
$10 (field level)
$8 (upper level)
$8 (pavilion)
$4 (general admission)
$1 (g.a., children under 12)

Field dimensions (from home plate)
To left field at foul line, 330 feet
To center field, 402 feet
To right field at foul line, 330 feet

First game played
April 12, 1966 (Pirates 3, Braves 2)

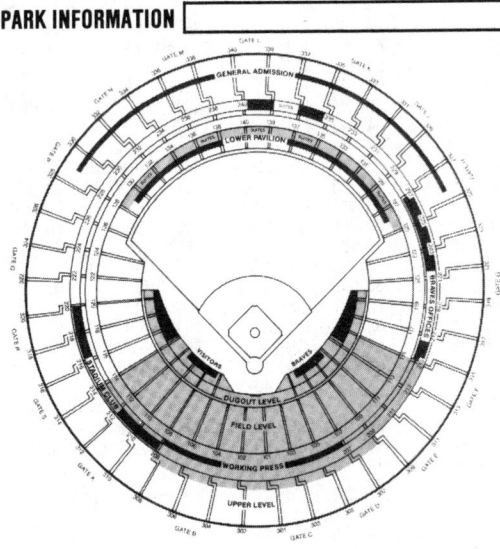

MINOR LEAGUE AFFILIATES

Class	Team	League	Manager
AAA	Richmond	International	Chris Chambliss
AA	Greenville	Southern	Grady Little
A	Durham	Carolina	Leon Roberts
A	Macon	South Atlantic	Brian Snitker
Rookie	Pulaski	Appalachian	Randy Ingle
Rookie	Idaho Falls	Pioneer	Dave Hilton
Rookie	Bradenton Braves	Gulf Coast	Jim Saul

BROADCAST INFORMATION

Radio: WGST-AM (640). Broadcasters: Skip Caray, Don Sutton, Pete Van Wieren; other to be announced. WPCH-FM (94.9). Broadcasters: Skip Caray, Don Sutton, Pete Van Wieren; other to be announced.
TV: TBS-TV (Channel 17). Broadcasters: Skip Caray, Don Sutton, Pete Van Wieren.
Cable TV: SportsSouth. Broadcasters: Chip Caray, Ernie Johnson.

SPRING TRAINING

Ballpark (city): Municipal Stadium (West Palm Beach, Fla.).
Ticket information: 407-683-6100.

HISTORY

YEAR-BY-YEAR RECORDS

Year	Pos.	W	L	Pct.	*GB	Year	Pos.	W	L	Pct.	*GB
1901	5th	69	69	.500	20½	1949	4th	75	79	.487	22
1902	3rd	73	64	.533	29	1950	4th	83	71	.539	8
1903	6th	58	80	.420	32	1951	4th	76	78	.494	20½
1904	7th	55	98	.359	51	1952	7th	64	89	.418	32
1905	7th	51	103	.331	54½	1953	2nd	92	62	.597	13
1906	8th	49	102	.325	66½	1954	3rd	89	65	.578	8
1907	7th	58	90	.392	47	1955	2nd	85	69	.552	13½
1908	6th	63	91	.409	36	1956	2nd	92	62	.597	1
1909	8th	45	108	.294	65½	1957	1st	95	59	.617	+8
1910	8th	53	100	.346	50½	1958	1st	92	62	.597	+8
1911	8th	44	107	.291	54	1959	T2nd	86	70	.551	2
1912	8th	52	101	.340	52	1960	2nd	88	66	.571	7
1913	5th	69	82	.457	31½	1961	4th	83	71	.539	10
1914	1st	94	59	.614	+10½	1962	5th	86	76	.531	15½
1915	2nd	83	69	.546	7	1963	6th	84	78	.519	15
1916	3rd	89	63	.586	4	1964	5th	88	74	.543	5
1917	6th	72	81	.471	25½	1965	5th	86	76	.531	11
1918	7th	53	71	.427	28½	1966	5th	85	77	.525	10
1919	6th	57	82	.410	38½	1967	7th	77	85	.475	24½
1920	7th	62	90	.408	30	1968	5th	81	81	.500	16
1921	4th	79	74	.516	15	1969	1st†	93	69	.574	+3
1922	8th	53	100	.346	39½	1970	5th	76	86	.469	26
1923	7th	54	100	.351	41½	1971	3rd	82	80	.506	8
1924	8th	53	100	.346	40	1972	4th	70	84	.455	25
1925	5th	70	83	.458	25	1973	5th	76	85	.472	22½
1926	7th	66	86	.434	22	1974	3rd	88	74	.543	14
1927	7th	60	94	.390	34	1975	5th	67	94	.416	40½
1928	7th	50	103	.327	44½	1976	6th	70	92	.432	32
1929	8th	56	98	.364	43	1977	6th	61	101	.377	37
1930	6th	70	84	.455	22	1978	6th	69	93	.426	26
1931	7th	64	90	.416	37	1979	6th	66	94	.413	23½
1932	5th	77	77	.500	13	1980	4th	81	80	.503	11
1933	4th	83	71	.539	9	1981	4th/5th	50	56	.472	‡
1934	4th	78	73	.517	16	1982	1st†	89	73	.549	+1
1935	8th	38	115	.248	61½	1983	2nd	88	74	.543	3
1936	6th	71	83	.461	21	1984	T2nd	80	82	.494	12
1937	5th	79	73	.520	16	1985	5th	66	96	.407	29
1938	5th	77	75	.507	12	1986	6th	72	89	.447	23½
1939	7th	63	88	.417	32½	1987	5th	69	92	.429	20½
1940	7th	65	87	.428	34½	1988	6th	54	106	.338	39½
1941	7th	62	92	.403	38	1989	6th	63	97	.394	28
1942	7th	59	89	.399	44	1990	6th	65	97	.401	26
1943	6th	68	85	.444	36½	1991	1st§	94	68	.580	+1
1944	6th	65	89	.422	40						
1945	6th	67	85	.441	30						
1946	4th	81	72	.529	15½						
1947	3rd	86	68	.558	8						
1948	1st	91	62	.595	+6½						

*Games behind winner. †Lost Championship Series. ‡First half 25-29; second 25-27. §Won Championship Series.

MANAGERS

Name	Record	Years
Frank Selee	69-69	1901
Al Buckenberger	186-242	'02-04
Fred Tenney	202-402	'05-07
		1911
Joe Kelley	63-91	1908
Frank Bowerman	23-55	1909
Harry Smith	22-53	1909
Fred Lake	53-100	1910
Johnny Kling	52-101	1912
George Stallings	579-597	'13-20
Fred Mitchell	186-274	'21-23
Dave Bancroft	249-363	'24-27
Jack Slattery	11-20	1928
Rogers Hornsby	39-83	1928
Emil Fuchs	56-98	1929
Bill McKechnie	560-666	'30-37
Casey Stengel	394-516	'38-43
Bob Coleman	107-140	'44-45
Del Bissonette	25-34	1945
Billy Southworth	424-358	'46-51
Tommy Holmes	61-69	'51-52
Charlie Grimm	341-285	'52-56
Fred Haney	341-231	'56-59
Chuck Dressen	159-124	'60-61
Birdie Tebbetts	98-89	'61-62
Bobby Bragan	310-287	'63-66
Billy Hitchcock	110-100	'66-67
Ken Silvestri	0-3	1967
Lum Harris	379-373	'68-72
Eddie Mathews	149-161	'72-74
Clyde King	96-101	'74-75
Connie Ryan	9-18	1975
Dave Bristol	131-192	'76-77
Ted Turner	0-1	1977
Bobby Cox	400-448	'78-81
		'90-91
Joe Torre	257-229	'82-84
Eddie Haas	50-71	1985
Bobby Wine	16-25	1985
Chuck Tanner	153-208	'86-88
Russ Nixon	130-216	'88-90

DAY BY DAY

Date	Opp.	Res.	Score (inn.*)	Hits	Opp. hits	Winning pitcher	Losing pitcher	Save	Record	Pos.	GB
4-10	L.A.	L	4-6	5	10	Belcher	Smoltz		0-1	4th	1½
4-11	L.A.	L	2-4	7	9	Martinez	Leibrandt		0-2	6th	2
4-13	At Cin.	W	7-5	9	12	Avery	Armstrong	Berenguer	1-2	6th	2
4-14	At Cin.	W	12-1	16	6	Glavine	Browning		2-2	T2nd	2
4-15	Hou.	L	1-3	5	6	Osuna	Mercker	Schilling	2-3	4th	3
4-16	Hou.	W	10-4	13	9	Sisk	Hernandez		3-3	T2nd	2
4-17	Hou.	L	3-4	6	7	Portugal	Avery	Schilling	3-4	5th	2
4-19	Cin.	L	3-8	5	8	Armstrong	Glavine		3-5	6th	2½
4-20	Cin.	L	0-3	4	11	Browning	Smoltz		3-6	6th	3
4-21	Cin.	W	3-2	5	6	Leibrandt	Rijo	Mercker	4-6	6th	2½
4-22	At L.A.	W	7-1	12	4	Avery	Ojeda		5-6	6th	2½
4-23	At L.A.	W	4-0	8	4	Glavine	Gross		6-6	3rd	2½
4-24	At L.A.	L	4-8	7	8	Morgan	Smoltz		6-7	6th	2½
4-26	At Hou.	W	7-2	9	9	Leibrandt	Deshaies		7-7	4th	2½
4-27	At Hou.	W	2-1 (13)	12	7	Sisk	Corsi	Parrett	8-7	3rd	1½
4-28	At Hou.	L	0-2	5	8	Jones	Glavine	Henry	8-8	4th	1½
4-29	At St.L.	L	3-4 (11)	8	9	L. Smith	Sisk		8-9	4th	1½
4-30	At St.L.	L	3-5	7	8	Carpenter	Leibrandt	L. Smith	8-10	4th	2½
5-1	At St.L.	W	5-4 (10)	8	9	Mercker	Perez		9-10	4th	1½
5-3	Chi.	W	5-2	8	4	Glavine	Boskie	Mercker	10-10	3rd	½
5-4	Chi.	W	4-2	8	11	Smoltz	Sutcliffe	Berenguer	11-10	3rd	½
5-5	Chi.	L	6-9	9	12	McElroy	Leibrandt	Smith	11-11	T3rd	1½
5-7	St.L.	W	9-2	12	8	Avery	B. Smith		12-11	2nd	1½
5-8	St.L.	W	17-1	17	6	Glavine	Hill		13-11	2nd	½
5-10	At Pit.	L	2-5	6	8	Smiley	Smoltz	Belinda	13-12	T1st	...
5-11	At Pit.	W	3-2	5	7	Leibrandt	Drabek	Mercker	14-12	T1st	...
5-12	At Pit.	W	6-1	9	4	Avery	Palacios	Berenguer	15-12	1st	+1
5-13	At Chi.	W	5-3	12	8	Glavine	Boskie		16-12	1st	+1
5-14	At Chi.	L	4-5	12	11	Assenmacher	Mercker	Smith	16-13	1st	...
5-15	At Chi.	L	1-6	7	8	Assenmacher	Berenguer		16-14	2nd	1
5-17	Pit.	W	9-3	12	7	Avery	Palacios		17-14	1st	...
5-19	Pit.	W	7-1	12	7	Glavine	Smith	Berenguer	18-14	2nd	½
5-20	S.D.	L	3-7	11	11	Whitson	Smoltz		18-15	2nd	½
5-21	S.D.	W	4-1	4	6	Mercker	Rosenberg		19-15	2nd	½
5-22	S.D.	L	2-7	6	13	Hurst	Avery		19-16	2nd	½
5-23	S.D.	L	10-11 (12)	12	15	Rosenberg	Parrett		19-17	T2nd	1½
5-24	S.F.	W	3-2	12	6	Glavine	Righetti		20-17	2nd	1½
5-25	S.F.	L	6-7	11	13	Downs	Smoltz	Brantley	20-18	2nd	2½
5-26	S.F.	L	6-10	12	15	Black	Leibrandt	Bass	20-19	2nd	2½
5-27	At S.D.	W	3-1	7	7	Avery	Hurst	Berenguer	21-19	2nd	2½
5-28	At S.D.	W	8-6	8	5	Stanton	Lefferts	Berenguer	22-19	2nd	2½
5-29	At S.D.	W	5-1	13	7	Glavine	Benes		23-19	2nd	1½
5-30	At S.F.	W	7-2	11	5	Smoltz	Downs		24-19	2nd	½
5-31	At S.F.	W	5-2	9	4	Leibrandt	Black	Stanton	25-19	2nd	½
6-1	At S.F.	L	2-8	4	8	Robinson	Avery	Oliveras	25-20	2nd	½
6-2	At S.F.	L	1-2	6	3	Wilson	Mercker	Righetti	25-21	2nd	1½
6-4	Phi.	W	9-5	12	12	Glavine	Mulholland		26-21	2nd	½
6-5	Phi.	L	11-12 (12)	12	16	Akerfelds	Parrett	DeJesus	26-22	2nd	1½
6-6	Phi.	W	9-4	13	6	Leibrandt	Combs		27-22	2nd	1½
6-7	Mon.	L	2-11	8	16	Boyd	Avery		27-23	2nd	2½
6-8	Mon.	W	7-6	11	11	Stanton	Burke	Mercker	28-23	2nd	1½
6-9	Mon.	W	8-6	16	11	Glavine	Gardner	Berenguer	29-23	2nd	1½
6-10	Mon.	L	1-7	7	12	Martinez	Smoltz	Ruskin	29-24	2nd	2½
6-11	At N.Y.	L	1-2	4	4	Viola	Leibrandt	Franco	29-25	2nd	3
6-12	At N.Y.	W	6-1	13	5	Avery	Darling		30-25	2nd	2
6-13	At N.Y.	W	3-2	6	4	Smith	Whitehurst	Berenguer	31-25	2nd	2
6-14	At Mon.	L	1-2	6	8	Gardner	Glavine	Ruskin	31-26	2nd	3
6-15	At Mon.	L	0-2	8	9	Martinez	Smoltz		31-27	2nd	3
6-16	At Mon.	L	6-7	12	10	Sampen	Stanton	Jones	31-28	3rd	4
6-17	At Phi.	L	3-4	7	11	Williams	Berenguer		31-29	3rd	5
6-18	At Phi.	L	4-8	8	10	DeJesus	Smith		31-30	3rd	6
6-19	At Phi.	W	9-2	14	6	Glavine	Mulholland		32-30	3rd	6
6-20	N.Y.	L	7-9	11	12	Gooden	Smoltz	Pena	32-31	3rd	7
6-21	N.Y.	W	4-2	6	5	Leibrandt	Viola	Berenguer	33-31	3rd	6
6-22	N.Y.	L	2-7	5	12	Darling	Avery		33-32	3rd	7
6-23	N.Y.	W	4-3	8	6	Mercker	Whitehurst	Berenguer	34-32	3rd	7
6-25	At Hou.	L	0-1	6	6	Harnisch	Glavine		34-33	4th	7
6-26	At Hou.	W	3-2	8	5	Stanton	Clancy	Berenguer	35-33	3rd	6
6-27	At Hou.	W	3-0	6	3	Leibrandt	Portugal		36-33	3rd	5½
6-28 (1)	L.A.	W	3-2 (10)	10	7	Mercker	Gott		37-33	3rd	4½

ATLANTA BRAVES
1992 SEASON
ATLANTA BRAVES

Date	Opp.	Res.	Score (inn.*)	Hits	Opp. hits	Winning pitcher	Losing pitcher	Save	Record	Pos.	GB
6-28 (2)	L.A.	L	2-8	5	14	Morgan	Mahler		37-34	3rd	5½
6-29	L.A.	L	1-2 (11)	7	5	Hartley	Berenguer	Gross	37-35	3rd	6½
6-30	L.A.	L	4-11	12	13	Hershiser	Smoltz	Gross	37-36	3rd	7½
7-2	Cin.	L	3-6	7	9	Armstrong	Leibrandt		37-37	3rd	8½
7-3	Cin.	W	8-6	17	11	Avery	Layana	Berenguer	38-37	3rd	8½
7-4	Cin.	L	4-10 (7)	6	14	Gross	Smith		38-38	3rd	8½
7-5	At L.A.	W	4-1	8	8	Glavine	Belcher		39-38	3rd	7½
7-6	At L.A.	L	6-7	8	9	Hershiser	Smoltz	Gross	39-39	3rd	8½
7-7	At L.A.	L	3-5	10	10	Martinez	Leibrandt	Morgan	39-40	3rd	9½
7-11	St.L.	W	4-1	8	2	Avery	DeLeon	Berenguer	40-40	3rd	8½
7-12	St.L.	W	6-2	10	7	Smoltz	B. Smith		41-40	3rd	7½
7-13	St.L.	W	10-5	10	9	Leibrandt	Hill		42-40	3rd	7
7-14	St.L.	W	2-1	6	6	Glavine	Tewksbury		43-40	3rd	5½
7-15	Chi.	L	4-6	8	8	Maddux	Smith	Assenmacher	43-41	3rd	5½
7-16	Chi.	W	8-5	12	5	Freeman	Scanlan	Berenguer	44-41	2nd	4½
7-17	Chi.	W	12-2	16	4	Smoltz	Lancaster		45-41	2nd	3½
7-19	At St.L.	W	8-3	12	8	Leibrandt	Hill	Berenguer	46-41	2nd	3
7-20	At St.L.	L	1-2	9	4	L. Smith	Stanton		46-42	2nd	4
7-21	At St.L.	W	5-1	7	3	Avery	Olivares		47-42	2nd	3
7-22	At Pit.	W	7-3	7	7	Smoltz	Smith		48-42	2nd	2½
7-23	At Pit.	L	3-12	4	16	Drabek	Leibrandt		48-43	2nd	3½
7-24	At Pit.	L	4-7	10	10	Smiley	Glavine	Belinda	48-44	2nd	4½
7-26	At Chi.	W	6-2	9	5	Avery	Castillo		49-44	2nd	5
7-27	At Chi.	L	5-7	10	6	Lancaster	Smoltz	McElroy	49-45	2nd	6
7-28	At Chi.	L	2-6	9	11	Bielecki	Leibrandt	Assenmacher	49-46	2nd	6
7-29 (1)	Pit.	W	7-5	8	8	Glavine	Drabek	Freeman	50-46	2nd	5½
7-29 (2)	Pit.	W	5-3	8	7	Mahler	Smiley	Mercker	51-46	2nd	4½
7-30	Pit.	W	10-3	13	9	Parrett	Landrum	Mercker	52-46	2nd	4½
7-31	Pit.	W	8-6	11	9	Smoltz	Palacios	Stanton	53-46	2nd	4½
8-2	S.D.	L	3-13	10	20	Hurst	Leibrandt		53-47	2nd	4½
8-3	S.D.	L	2-3	5	7	Benes	Glavine	Andersen	53-48	2nd	4½
8-4	S.D.	W	9-7	14	15	Avery	Rasmussen	Berenguer	54-48	2nd	3½
8-5	S.F.	W	5-2	8	6	Smoltz	Robinson		55-48	2nd	2½
8-6	S.F.	W	10-6	11	10	Clancy	McClellan		56-48	2nd	2½
8-7	S.F.	L	0-1	11	4	Black	Leibrandt	Righetti	56-49	2nd	3½
8-8	S.F.	L	1-8	8	13	Burkett	Glavine		56-50	2nd	4½
8-9	Hou.	W	7-2	11	9	Avery	Deshaies		57-50	2nd	3½
8-10	Hou.	W	4-0	8	4	Smoltz	Harnisch		58-50	2nd	2½
8-11	Hou.	W	3-1	8	4	Reynoso	Kile	Stanton	59-50	2nd	1½
8-12	At S.F.	W	2-1	4	6	Leibrandt	Black	Berenguer	60-50	2nd	1½
8-13	At S.F.	W	9-2	15	4	Glavine	Burkett		61-50	2nd	½
8-14	At S.F.	L	3-8	8	13	Wilson	Avery		61-51	2nd	1½
8-15	At S.D.	L	0-1	3	4	Harris	Smoltz		61-52	2nd	1½
8-16	At S.D.	W	3-2	7	6	Reynoso	Bones	Stanton	62-52	2nd	1½
8-17	At S.D.	W	2-1	6	3	Leibrandt	Hurst	Wohlers	63-52	2nd	1½
8-18	At S.D.	L	1-2	7	5	Benes	Glavine	Andersen	63-53	2nd	1½
8-20 (1)	At Cin.	L	2-8	5	12	Rijo	Avery		63-54	2nd	2½
8-20 (2)	At Cin.	W	5-1	8	5	Smoltz	Sanford		64-54	2nd	2½
8-21	At Cin.	W	10-9 (13)	15	14	Castillo	Myers		65-54	2nd	2½
8-22	At Cin.	W	4-1	8	6	Leibrandt	Scudder	Clancy	66-54	2nd	2
8-23	Phi.	W	4-2	13	6	Glavine	Mulholland	Wohlers	67-54	2nd	1
8-24	Phi.	L	5-6	7	10	Williams	Castillo		67-55	2nd	1
8-25	Phi.	L	5-6	10	9	Greene	Avery	Williams	67-56	2nd	1
8-26	Mon.	W	14-9	14	15	Wohlers	Sampen	Stanton	68-56	2nd	1
8-27	Mon.	W	3-2	9	4	Leibrandt	Nabholz	Clancy	69-56	T1st	...
8-28	N.Y.	W	3-1	7	4	Glavine	Viola		70-56	1st	+1
8-29	N.Y.	W	2-0	7	6	Smoltz	Young	Stanton	71-56	1st	+2
8-30	At Phi.	W	6-1	11	4	Avery	Greene		72-56	1st	+2
8-31	At Phi.	L	0-5	4	10	DeJesus	Reynoso		72-57	1st	+1
9-1	At Phi.	L	4-5 (10)	11	12	Williams	Wohlers		72-58	T1st	...
9-2	At Mon.	L	3-4	7	5	Sampen	Glavine		72-59	T1st	...
9-3	At Mon.	W	4-1	4	8	Smoltz	Barnes	Pena	73-59	T1st	...
9-4	At Mon.	L	4-8	5	14	Rojas	Clancy		73-60	2nd	1
9-6	At N.Y.	W	4-2	11	7	Pena	Whitehurst	Stanton	74-60	2nd	½
9-7	At N.Y.	W	6-1	9	6	Leibrandt	Viola		75-60	2nd	½
9-8	At N.Y.	W	7-5	11	7	Glavine	Franco	Pena	76-60	2nd	½
9-9	S.F.	W	8-3	7	9	Smoltz	Black	Clancy	77-60	2nd	½
9-10	S.F.	W	4-1	9	3	Avery	Burkett	Pena	78-60	1st	+½
9-11	S.D.	W	1-0	7	0	Mercker	Harris	Pena	79-60	1st	+½
9-12	S.D.	W	5-1	10	6	Leibrandt	Hurst		80-60	1st	+½
9-13	L.A.	L	2-5	4	11	Morgan	Glavine	McDowell	80-61	2nd	½
9-14	L.A.	W	3-2 (11)	10	9	Clancy	McDowell		81-61	1st	+½
9-15	L.A.	W	9-1	6	4	Avery	Martinez		82-61	1st	+1½
9-16	At S.F.	L	5-8	9	9	Oliveras	Clancy	Beck	82-62	1st	+½

Date	Opp.	Res.	Score (inn.*)	Hits	Opp. hits	Winning pitcher	Losing pitcher	Save	Record	Pos.	GB
9-17	At S.F.	L	2-3	4	5	Black	Stanton	Righetti	82-63	2nd	½
9-18	At S.D.	W	6-4	13	7	Glavine	Bones	Pena	83-63	2nd	½
9-19	At S.D.	W	4-2 (10)	7	6	Wohlers	Lefferts	Pena	84-63	2nd	½
9-20	At L.A.	W	3-0	5	6	Avery	Belcher		85-63	1st	+½
9-21	At L.A.	L	1-2	4	6	McDowell	Stanton		85-64	2nd	½
9-22	At L.A.	L	0-3	3	9	Martinez	Glavine	McDowell	85-65	2nd	1½
9-25 (1)	Cin.	W	2-1 (10)	9	6	Pena	Power		86-65	2nd	1½
9-25 (2)	Cin.	L	9-10 (10)	12	16	Hill	Stanton	Dibble	86-66	2nd	1½
9-26	Cin.	L	0-8	8	7	Rijo	Leibrandt		86-67	2nd	2
9-27	At Hou.	W	4-2	9	7	Wohlers	Mallicoat	Pena	87-67	2nd	2
9-28	At Hou.	W	5-4	7	7	Stanton	Hernandez	Pena	88-67	2nd	1
9-29	At Hou.	W	6-5 (13)	12	12	Clancy	Portugal		89-67	2nd	1
9-30	At Cin.	W	4-0	8	3	Smoltz	Armstrong		90-67	2nd	1
10-1	At Cin.	W	7-6	10	7	Stanton	Dibble	Pena	91-67	2nd	1
10-2	At Cin.	W	6-3	7	6	Glavine	Scudder	Pena	92-67	T1st	...
10-4	Hou.	W	5-2	8	4	Avery	Juden	Pena	93-67	1st	+1
10-5	Hou.	W	5-2	8	8	Smoltz	Portugal		94-67	1st	+2
10-6	Hou.	L	3-8	6	12	Harnisch	Leibrandt		94-68	1st	+1

Monthly records: April (8-10), May (17-9), June (12-17), July (16-10), August (19-11), September (18-10), Oct. (4-1).

HIGHLIGHTS

High point: From September 27 through October 2, the Braves won six straight road games to move into a first-place tie with the Los Angeles Dodgers in the National League West. Atlanta won its next two games at home to extend its winning steak to eight games and clinch the division title.

Low point: The Braves headed into the All-Star break having lost seven of nine games, dropping 9½ games behind the front-running Dodgers.

Turning point: Following that stretch, Atlanta started the second half of the season by winning nine of 11 games to close to within 2½ games of the lead.

Most valuable player: Third baseman Terry Pendleton. He hit .319 and won the N.L. batting title. Pendleton, who also won N.L. Most Valuable Player honors, hit a career-high 22 home runs and collected 86 runs batted in.

Most valuable pitcher: Lefthander Tom Glavine. The N.L. Cy Young Award winner became the first Braves lefty to win 20 games since Warren Spahn in 1963.

Most improved player: Outfielder Otis Nixon. Before he was suspended in September for violating baseball's drug policy, Nixon hit .297 and broke the club record for stolen bases (72).

Most pleasant surprise: First baseman/outfielder Brian Hunter. He was recalled from Class AAA Richmond on May 31 to replace the injured Sid Bream and proceeded to hit .251 with 12 homers and 50 RBIs in 97 games.

Biggest disappointment: Outfielder/infielder Tommy Gregg. The league's top pinch-hitter in 1990, he batted just .187 and drove in only four runs.

Key injuries: Mike Heath was lost for the season in July after elbow surgery, but the loss of David Justice (back) and Bream (knee) hurt more. Justice played in only 109 games, while Bream played in just 91. Juan Berenguer, who registered a career-high 17 saves, made his last appearance August 12 because of an injury to his forearm.

Notable: The Braves became the first N.L. team to go from last place to first

in consecutive seasons. Their World Series appearance was the first in Atlanta history. . . . Kent Mercker, Mark Wohlers and Alejandro Pena combined to no-hit San Diego on September 11. It represented the first combined no-hitter in N.L. annals, and it was the first Atlanta no-hitter since Phil Niekro stymied the Padres on August 5, 1973.

—BILL ZACK

RECORDS

1991 regular-season record: 94-68 (1st in N.L. West); 48-33 at home; 46-35 on road; 43-29 vs. East; 51-39 vs. West; 28-16 vs. LHP; 66-52 vs. RHP; 70-50 on grass; 24-18 on turf; 21-19 in daytime; 73-49 at night; 22-26 in one-run games; 8-6 in extra-inning games; 1-0-3 in doubleheaders.

1991 postseason record: Defeated Pirates, 4 games to 3, in N.L. playoffs; lost to Twins, 4 games to 3, in World Series.

Team record last five years: 345-460 (.429, ranks 12th in league in that span).

TEAM LEADERS

Batting average: Terry Pendleton (.319).
At-bats: Terry Pendleton (586).
Runs: Ron Gant (101).
Hits: Terry Pendleton (187).
Total bases: Terry Pendleton (303).
Doubles: Ron Gant (35).
Triples: Terry Pendleton (8).
Home runs: Ron Gant (32).
Runs batted in: Ron Gant (105).
Stolen bases: Otis Nixon (72).
Slugging percentage: Terry Pendleton (.517).
On-base percentage: Terry Pendleton (.363).
Wins: Tom Glavine (20).
Earned-run average: Tom Glavine (2.55).
Complete games: Tom Glavine (9).
Shutouts: Steve Avery, Tom Glavine, Charlie Leibrandt (1).
Saves: Juan Berenguer (17).
Innings pitched: Tom Glavine (246⅔).
Strikeouts: Tom Glavine (192).

GAMES BY POSITION

Catcher: Greg Olson 127, Mike Heath 45, Francisco Cabrera 17, Damon Berryhill 1, Jerry Willard 1.
First base: Sid Bream 85, Brian Hunter 85, Mike Bell 14, Francisco Cabrera 14, Tommy Gregg 13, Danny Heep 1.
Second base: Mark Lemke 110, Jeff Treadway 93, Jeff Blauser 32.
Third base: Terry Pendleton 148, Jeff Blauser 18, Mark Lemke 15.
Shortstop: Rafael Belliard 145, Jeff Blauser 85, Vinny Castilla 12, Rico Rossy 1.
Outfield: Ron Gant 148, Otis Nixon 115, Dave Justice 106, Lonnie Smith 99, Deion Sanders 44, Keith Mitchell 34, Tommy Gregg 14, Brian Hunter 6, Danny Heep 1.

TOP 10 DRAFT CHOICES

1. **Mike Kelly,** OF, Arizona State University.
2. **None** .
3. **Blase Sparma,** RHP, Ohio State University.
4. **Chris Seelbach,** RHP, Lufkin (Texas) High School.
5. **Vincent Moore,** OF, Elsik High School, Alief, Texas.
6. **Jose Rodriguez,** C, Cayey, Puerto Rico.
7. **Earl Nelson,** LHP, Clark High School, San Antonio.
8. **Jason Schmidt,** RHP, Kelso (Wash.) High School.
9. **Brad Ripplemeyer,** C/RHP, Kansas State University.
10. **Jerome Jones,** 3B, Carthage High School, Beckville, Texas.

CHICAGO CUBS
NATIONAL LEAGUE EAST DIVISION

1992 SCHEDULE

APRIL
S	M	T	W	T	F	S
5	6	7 PHI	8 N PHI	9 PHI	10 N STL H	11 STL H
12 STL H	13	14 N PIT	15 N PIT	16	17 N STL	18 STL
19 STL	20 PHI H	21 PHI H	22 PHI H	23 PHI H	24 PIT H	25 PIT H
26 PIT H	27 ATL	28 N ATL	29 ATL	30		

MAY
S	M	T	W	T	F	S
				1 N CIN	2 CIN	
3 CIN	4 N ATL H	5 ATL H	6 HOU H	7 N HOU H	8 CIN H	9 CIN H
10 CIN H	11 N HOU	12 N HOU	13 N HOU	14	15 N SF	16 SF
17 SF	18 N LA	19 N LA	20 N LA	21	22 N SD	23 N SD
24 SD	25	26 N SF H	27 SF H	28 N SF H	29 LA H	30 LA H
31 LA H						

JUNE
S	M	T	W	T	F	S
	1 N SD H	2 N SD H	3 N SD H	4	5 TN MON	6 MON
7 MON	8 N STL	9 N STL	10 N STL	11	12 MON H	13 MON H
14 MON H	15 N STL H	16 N STL H	17 STL H	18 N PHI	19 N PHI	20 N PHI
21 PHI	22 N NY	23 N NY	24 NY	25 NY	26 PHI H	27 PHI H
28 PHI H	29 NY H	30 N NY H				

JULY
S	M	T	W	T	F	S
			1 NY H	2	3 N ATL	4 ATL
5 ATL	6 N CIN H	7 N CIN H	8 N CIN H	9 N ATL H	10 H ATL H	11 ATL H
12 ATL H	13	14 ★	15	16 N PIT	17 N PIT	18 N PIT
19 N PIT	20 N CIN	21 N CIN	22 N CIN	23	24 N HOU	25 N HOU
26 HOU	27 N PIT H	28 PIT H	29 PIT H	30	31 N NY	

AUGUST
S	M	T	W	T	F	S
						1 N NY
2 NY	3 N MON	4 N MON	5 N MON	6 N NY	7 N NY H	8 NY H
9 N NY H	10	11	12 MON H	13 N HOU	14 N HOU	15 HOU
16 HOU H	17	18 N SF	19 SF	20 N SF	21 N LA	22 N LA
23 LA	24 N SD	25 N SD	26 SD	27	28 SF H	29 SF H
30 SF H	31 N LA H					

SEPTEMBER
S	M	T	W	T	F	S
		1 LA H	2 H LA H	3	4 SD H	5 SD H
6 SD H	7 PIT	8 N PIT	9 N PIT	10	11 N STL	12 N STL
13 N NY	14 N NY H	15 NY H	16 PHI H	17 H PHI H	18 N STL H	19 STL H
20 N STL	21 N NY	22 N NY	23 N PHI	24 N PHI	25 N MON	26 MON
27 MON	28 PIT H	29 N PIT H	30 PIT H			

OCTOBER
S	M	T	W	T	F	S
				1	2 N MON H	3 MON H
4 MON H	5	6	7	8	9	10

1992 SEASON

CLUB DIRECTORY

Board of directors
Stanton R. Cook
Thomas G. Ayers
Charles T. Brumback
Donald C. Grenesko
Andrew J. McKenna
Walter E. Massey
Exec. vice president, baseball operations
Larry Himes
Exec. vice president, business operations
Mark McGuire
Senior vice president, baseball operations
Jim Frey
Vice president, finance and info. systems
Keith Bode
Vice president, marketing and broadcasting
John McDonough
V.p., scouting and player development
Dick Balderson
Assistant general manager
Syd Thrift
Vice president, baseball administration
Ned Colletti
Director, human resources
Wendy Lewis
Director, media relations
Sharon Pannozzo
Director, minor league operations
Bill Harford Jr.
Director, stadium operations
Tom Cooper
Director, ticket operations
Frank Maloney
Corporate counsel
Geoff Anderson
Corporate secretary
Stanley Gradowski
Special player consultants
Hugh Alexander
Ed Lyons
Traveling secretary
Peter Durso
Assistant director, marketing
Connie Kowal
Assistant director, publications
Ernie Roth
Assistant director, stadium operations
Paul Rathje
Assistant director, scouting
Scott Nelson
Assistant director, ticket sales
Bill Galante
Assistant director, ticket services
Joe Kirchen
Equipment manager
Yosh Kowano
Team physician
Dr. John Marquardt

Head trainer
John Fierro
National scouting supervisor
Larry Maxie
Regional scouting supervisors
Frank DeMoss
Doug Mapson
Earl Winn
Latin American scouting coordinator
Luis Rosa
Area scouts
Billy Blitzer
Jeff Brookens
Bill Capps
Billy Champion
Bobby Gardner
John Gracio
Gene Handley
Elmore Hill
Joe Housey
Toney Howell
Spider Jorgensen
Gil Kubski
Dave Lottsfeldt
Gregg Patterson
Paul Provas
John Stockstill
Julio Valdez
Part-time scouts
Keith Bailey
Claudio Brito
Jose Cassino
Morley Freitas
Ralph Giansanti
Ben Gonzalez
Chad Granger
Jim Greenwald
John Hennessy
Carlos Hernandez
Diego Herrera
Vedie Himsl
Andres James
Pat Kane
Emilio Lisier
Bob Lofrano
Noe Maduro
Tony Malara
Jose Marcano
Abraham Martinez
William Moore
Lee Phillips
Hector Rivera
Milton Rosario
Joe Sayers
Chuck Sheldon
Jose Trujillo
Harry Von Suskil
Jim Willis

SCHEDULE KEY
H—Home game.   *All-Star Game at San Diego/Jack Murphy Stadium.
N—Night game (any game starting after 5 p.m.). TN—Twi-night doubleheader.

SPRING TRAINING ROSTER

Manager—Jim Lefebvre (5).

Coaches—Billy Connors (4), Chuck Cottier (15), Sammy Ellis (46), Jose Martinez (3), Tom Trebelhorn (41).

No.	PITCHERS	B/T	Ht./Wt.	Born	1991 clubs
45	Assenmacher, Paul	L/L	6-3/200	12-10-60	Chicago NL
47	Boskie, Shawn	R/R	6-3/205	3-28-67	Chicago NL, Iowa
52	Bullinger, Jim	R/R	6-2/185	8-21-65	Iowa, Charlotte
49	Castillo, Frank	R/R	6-1/180	4-1-69	Chicago NL, Iowa
33	Dickson, Lance	R/L	6-1/185	10-19-69	Iowa
22	Harkey, Mike	R/R	6-5/220	10-25-66	Chicago NL
44	Hartsock, Jeff	R/R	6-0/190	11-19-66	Albuquerque
32	Jackson, Danny	R/L	6-0/205	1-5-62	Chicago NL, Iowa
50	Lancaster, Les	R/R	6-2/200	4-21-62	Chicago NL
31	Maddux, Greg	R/R	6-0/175	4-14-66	Chicago NL
35	McElroy, Chuck	L/L	6-0/180	10-1-67	Chicago NL
36	Morgan, Mike	R/R	6-2/222	10-8-59	Los Angeles
30	Scanlan, Bob	R/R	6-7/215	8-9-66	Iowa, Chicago NL
51	Slocumb, Heathcliff	R/R	6-3/210	6-7-66	Iowa, Chicago NL
42	Smith, Dave	R/R	6-1/195	1-21-55	Chicago NL
43	Wendell, Turk	S/R	6-2/175	5-19-67	Greenville, Richmond

No.	CATCHERS	B/T	Ht./Wt.	Born	1991 clubs
7	Girardi, Joe	R/R	5-11/195	10-14-64	Chicago NL, Iowa
53	Pedre, George	R/R	5-11/210	10-12-66	Kansas City, Omaha, Memphis
19	Villanueva, Hector	R/R	6-1/220	10-2-64	Chicago NL, Iowa
2	Wilkins, Rick	L/R	6-2/210	6-4-67	Chicago NL, Iowa

No.	INFIELDERS	B/T	Ht./Wt.	Born	1991 clubs
21	Arias, Alex	R/R	6-3/185	11-20-67	Charlotte
37	Castellano, Pedro	R/R	6-1/175	3-11-70	Charlotte, Winston-Salem
12	Dunston, Shawon	R/R	6-1/175	3-21-63	Chicago NL
17	Grace, Mark	L/L	6-2/190	6-28-64	Chicago NL
9	Paulino, Elvin	L/R	6-1/190	11-6-67	Charlotte
10	Salazar, Luis	R/R	5-10/190	5-19-56	Chicago NL
6	Sanchez, Rey	R/R	5-9/165	10-5-67	Chicago NL, Iowa
23	Sandberg, Ryne	R/R	6-2/185	9-18-59	Chicago NL
25	Scott, Gary	R/R	6-0/175	8-22-68	Iowa, Chicago NL
1	Strange, Doug	S/R	6-2/170	4-13-64	Chicago NL, Iowa
16	Vizcaino, Jose	S/R	6-1/180	3-26-68	Chicago NL

No.	OUTFIELDERS	B/T	Ht./Wt.	Born	1991 clubs
11	Bell, George	R/R	6-1/202	10-21-59	Chicago NL
29	Dascenzo, Doug	S/L	5-8/160	6-30-64	Chicago NL
8	Dawson, Andre	R/R	6-3/197	7-10-54	Chicago NL
28	Landrum, Ced	L/R	5-8/170	9-3-63	Chicago NL, Iowa
27	May, Derrick	L/R	6-4/205	7-14-68	Chicago NL, Iowa
34	Roberson, Kevin	S/R	6-4/210	1-29-68	Charlotte
18	Smith, Dwight	L/R	5-11/175	11-8-63	Chicago NL
24	Walker, Chico	S/R	5-9/185	11-26-58	Chicago NL
20	Walton, Jerome	R/R	6-1/175	7-8-65	Chicago NL

BALLPARK INFORMATION

Ballpark (capacity, surface)
Wrigley Field (38,710, grass)

Address
1060 W. Addison St.
Chicago, IL 60613

Business phone
312-404-2827

Ticket information
312-404-2827

Ticket prices
$17 (field box)
$12 (terrace box)
$12 (upper deck box)
$9 (terrace reserved)
$7 (adult upper deck reserved)
$5 (under 14 upper deck reserved)
$7 (bleachers)
All tickets are $1 less for weekday afternoon games

Field dimensions (from home plate)
To left field at foul line, 355 feet
To center field, 400 feet
To right field at foul line, 353 feet

First game played
April 20, 1916 (Cubs 7, Reds 6)

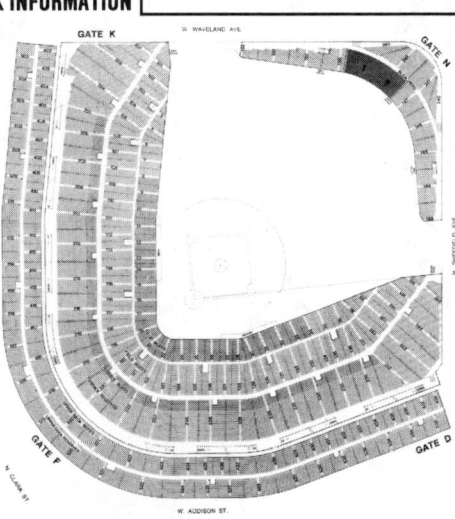

MINOR LEAGUE AFFILIATES

Class	Team	League	Manager
AAA	Iowa	American Association	Brad Mills
AA	Charlotte	Southern	Marv Foley
A	Winston-Salem	Carolina	Bill Hayes
A	Peoria	Midwest	Steve Roadcap
A	Geneva	New York-Pennsylvania	Greg Mahlberg
Rookie	Huntington	Appalachian	Phil Hannon

☐ BROADCAST INFORMATION ☐

Radio: WGN-AM (720). Broadcasters: Harry Caray, Thom Brennaman, Ron Santo.
TV: WGN-TV (Channel 9). Broadcasters: Harry Caray, Steve Stone, Thom Brennaman.
Cable TV: WGN subscription cable. Broadcasters: Harry Caray, Steve Stone.

SPRING TRAINING

Ballpark (city): HoHoKam Park (Mesa, Ariz.).
Ticket information: 602-964-4467.

HISTORY

YEAR-BY-YEAR RECORDS

Year	Pos.	W	L	Pct.	*GB	Year	Pos.	W	L	Pct.	*GB
1901	6th	53	86	.381	37	1948	8th	64	90	.416	27½
1902	5th	68	69	.496	34	1949	8th	61	93	.396	36
1903	3rd	82	56	.594	8	1950	7th	64	89	.418	26½
1904	2nd	93	60	.608	13	1951	8th	62	92	.403	34½
1905	3rd	92	61	.601	13	1952	5th	77	77	.500	19½
1906	1st	116	36	.763	+20	1953	7th	65	89	.422	40
1907	1st	107	45	.704	+17	1954	7th	64	90	.416	33
1908	1st	99	55	.643	+ 1	1955	6th	72	81	.471	26
1909	2nd	104	49	.680	6½	1956	8th	60	94	.390	33
1910	1st	104	50	.675	+13	1957	T7th	62	92	.403	33
1911	2nd	92	62	.597	7½	1958	T5th	72	82	.468	20
1912	3rd	91	59	.607	11½	1959	T5th	74	80	.481	13
1913	3rd	88	65	.575	13½	1960	7th	60	94	.390	35
1914	4th	78	76	.506	16½	1961	7th	64	90	.416	29
1915	4th	73	80	.477	17½	1962	9th	59	103	.364	42½
1916	5th	67	86	.438	26½	1963	7th	82	80	.506	17
1917	5th	74	80	.481	24	1964	8th	76	86	.469	17
1918	1st	84	45	.651	+10½	1965	8th	72	90	.444	25
1919	3rd	75	65	.536	21	1966	10th	59	103	.364	36
1920	T5th	75	79	.487	18	1967	3rd	87	74	.540	14
1921	7th	64	89	.418	30	1968	3rd	84	78	.519	13
1922	5th	80	74	.519	13	1969	2nd	92	70	.568	8
1923	4th	83	71	.539	12½	1970	2nd	84	78	.519	5
1924	5th	81	72	.529	12	1971	T3rd	83	79	.512	14
1925	8th	68	86	.442	27½	1972	2nd	85	70	.548	11
1926	4th	82	72	.532	7	1973	5th	77	84	.478	5
1927	4th	85	68	.556	8½	1974	6th	66	96	.407	22
1928	3rd	91	63	.591	4	1975	T5th	75	87	.463	17½
1929	1st	98	54	.645	+10½	1976	4th	75	87	.463	26
1930	2nd	90	64	.584	2	1977	4th	81	81	.500	20
1931	3rd	84	70	.545	17	1978	3rd	79	83	.488	11
1932	1st	90	64	.584	+ 4	1979	5th	80	82	.494	18
1933	3rd	86	68	.558	6	1980	6th	64	98	.395	27
1934	3rd	86	65	.570	8	1981	6th/5th	38	65	.369	†
1935	1st	100	54	.649	+ 4	1982	5th	73	89	.451	19
1936	T2nd	87	67	.565	5	1983	5th	71	91	.438	19
1937	2nd	93	61	.604	3	1984	1st‡	96	65	.596	+ 6½
1938	1st	89	63	.586	+ 2	1985	4th	77	84	.478	23½
1939	4th	84	70	.545	13	1986	5th	70	90	.438	37
1940	5th	75	79	.487	25½	1987	6th	76	85	.472	18½
1941	6th	70	84	.455	30	1988	4th	77	85	.475	24
1942	6th	68	86	.442	38	1989	1st‡	93	69	.574	+ 6
1943	5th	74	79	.484	30½	1990	T4th	77	85	.475	18
1944	4th	75	79	.487	30	1991	4th	77	83	.481	20
1945	1st	98	56	.636	+ 3						
1946	3rd	82	71	.536	14½						
1947	6th	69	85	.448	25						

*Games behind winner. †First half 15-37; second 23-28. ‡Lost Championship Series.

MANAGERS

Name	Record	Years
Tom Loftus	53-86	'01
Frank Selee	295-223	'02-05
Frank Chance	753-379	'05-12
Johnny Evers	130-121	'13, '21
Hank O'Day	78-76	1914
Roger Bresnahan	73-80	1915
Joe Tinker	67-86	1916
Fred Mitchell	308-269	'17-20
Bill Killefer	299-292	'21-25
Rabbit Maranville	23-30	1925
George Gibson	12-14	1925
Joe McCarthy	442-321	'26-30
Rogers Hornsby	141-114	'30-32
Charlie Grimm	946-784	'32-38
		'44-49
		1960
Gabby Hartnett	203-176	'38-40
Jimmy Wilson	213-258	'41-44
Roy Johnson	0-1	1944
Frank Frisch	141-196	'49-51
Phil Cavarretta	169-213	'51-53
Stan Hack	196-265	'54-56
Bob Scheffing	208-254	'57-59
Lou Boudreau	54-83	1960
Vedie Himsl*	10-21	1961
Harry Craft*	7-9	1961
Elvin Tappe*	46-69	'61-62
Lou Klein*	65-83	'61-62
		1965
Charlie Metro*	43-69	1962
Bob Kennedy	182-198	'63-65
Leo Durocher	535-526	'66-72
Whitey Lockman	157-162	'72-74
Jim Marshall	175-218	'74-76
Herman Franks	238-241	'77-79
Joe Amalfitano	66-116	1979
		'80-81
Preston Gomez	38-52	1980
Lee Elia	127-158	'82-83
Charlie Fox	17-22	1983
Jim Frey	196-182	'84-86
John Vukovich	1-1	1986
Gene Michael	114-124	'86-87
Frank Lucchesi	8-17	1987
Don Zimmer	265-259	'88-91
Jim Essian	59-63	1991

*College of Coaches.

DAY BY DAY

Date	Opp.	Res.	Score (inn.*)	Hits	Opp. hits	Winning pitcher	Losing pitcher	Save	Record	Pos.	GB
4-9	St.L.	L	1-4	5	8	B. Smith	Jackson	L. Smith	0-1	5th	1½
4-10	St.L.	W	2-0	8	7	Maddux	DeLeon	Smith	1-1	T3rd	½
4-11	St.L.	L	4-5	9	12	Hill	Harkey	L. Smith	1-2	T4th	1½
4-12	Pit.	L	1-3	4	8	Smiley	Boskie	Palacios	1-3	6th	2
4-13	Pit.	W	7-3	11	6	Bielecki	Drabek		2-3	T4th	1½
4-14	Pit.	W	6-4	7	9	Slocumb	Belinda	Smith	3-3	T2nd	1½
4-15	Phi.	W	5-4	8	4	Maddux	Grimsley	Smith	4-3	T2nd	1½
4-16	Phi.	W	4-3 (13)	8	8	Bielecki	Williams		5-3	2nd	½
4-17	Phi.	W	4-1	7	4	Boskie	Combs	Smith	6-3	1st	+½
4-18	At Pit.	W	3-2	7	4	Sutcliffe	Drabek	Assenmacher	7-3	1st	+1
4-19	At Pit.	L	4-5	3	8	Belinda	Smith		7-4	1st	+1
4-20	At Pit.	L	3-9	9	8	Smith	Maddux		7-5	T1st	...
4-21	At Pit.	L	12-13 (11)	13	13	Patterson	Bielecki		7-6	T3rd	1
4-22	At St.L.	L	2-3	4	5	Agosto	Smith		7-7	4th	1½
4-23	At St.L.	L	2-4	5	8	Tewksbury	Sutcliffe	L. Smith	7-8	4th	2½
4-24	At St.L.	W	1-0	6	3	Bielecki	DeLeon	Assenmacher	8-8	4th	2½
4-25	At Cin.	L	4-6	8	13	Power	McElroy	Myers	8-9	4th	3½
4-26	At Cin.	L	1-3	5	5	Rijo	Harkey	Dibble	8-10	4th	3½
4-27	At Cin.	W	8-3	11	11	Boskie	Charlton	Assenmacher	9-10	4th	3½
4-28	At Cin.	L	3-4	11	7	Hammond	Sutcliffe	Dibble	9-11	4th	4½
4-30	Hou.	W	10-3	12	7	Bielecki	Portugal		10-11	4th	3½
5-1	Hou.	W	11-8	12	10	Maddux	Deshaies		11-11	4th	3½
5-3	At Atl.	L	2-5	4	8	Glavine	Boskie	Mercker	11-12	4th	4½
5-4	At Atl.	L	2-4	11	8	Smoltz	Sutcliffe	Berenguer	11-13	T4th	4½
5-5	At Atl.	W	9-6	12	9	McElroy	Leibrandt	Smith	12-13	4th	3½
5-6	At Hou.	W	4-3	9	5	Maddux	Deshaies	Smith	13-13	4th	3½
5-7	At Hou.	W	4-3	8	8	Scanlan	Hernandez	Smith	14-13	4th	3½
5-8	At Hou.	L	2-4	8	7	Harnisch	Boskie	Schilling	14-14	4th	4½
5-10	Cin.	W	6-5	9	7	Sutcliffe	Browning	Smith	15-14	4th	4½
5-11	Cin.	L	2-12	8	12	Rijo	Bielecki		15-15	4th	4½
5-12	Cin.	L	3-5	8	10	Armstrong	Maddux	Dibble	15-16	5th	4½
5-13	Atl.	L	3-5	8	12	Glavine	Boskie		15-17	T5th	5
5-14	Atl.	W	5-4	11	12	Assenmacher	Mercker	Smith	16-17	4th	5
5-15	Atl.	W	6-1	8	7	Assenmacher	Berenguer		17-17	4th	5
5-17	At Phi.	L	0-1 (16)	10	10	Greene	Lancaster		17-18	T4th	4½
5-18	At Phi.	L	2-5	4	8	Boever	Assenmacher	Williams	17-19	T5th	5
5-19	At Phi.	W	2-1 (10)	9	6	Bielecki	McDowell	Smith	18-19	4th	5
5-21	At N.Y.	L	6-8	11	10	Gooden	Sutcliffe	Franco	18-20	T5th	6
5-22	At N.Y.	W	5-2	11	5	Maddux	Viola		19-20	T4th	5
5-23	At N.Y.	W	4-3	9	8	Lancaster	Franco	Assenmacher	20-20	T4th	4
5-24	Mon.	W	4-3	9	6	Scanlan	Gardner	Slocumb	21-20	4th	4
5-25	Mon.	W	6-1	10	6	Bielecki	Mahler	McElroy	22-20	4th	4
5-26	Mon.	W	8-6	11	11	Lancaster	Burke	Smith	23-20	4th	4
5-27	N.Y.	L	1-3	7	8	Viola	Maddux	Franco	23-21	4th	5
5-28	N.Y.	L	8-9	13	10	Pena	Assenmacher	Franco	23-22	4th	6
5-29	N.Y.	L	1-8	7	9	Cone	Scanlan		23-23	4th	7
5-31	At Mon.	W	7-2	14	8	Bielecki	Martinez	Lancaster	24-23	4th	7
6-1	At Mon.	W	2-1 (10)	7	5	McElroy	Jones	Smith	25-23	4th	7
6-2	At Mon.	W	4-3	7	3	Assenmacher	Ruskin	Smith	26-23	4th	7
6-4	S.D.	L	1-7	6	8	Benes	Scanlan		26-24	4th	7
6-5	S.D.	L	0-3	7	8	Rasmussen	Bielecki		26-25	4th	8
6-6	S.D.	W	6-2	12	5	Maddux	Melendez		27-25	4th	7
6-7	L.A.	L	2-3	6	9	Morgan	Boskie	Howell	27-26	4th	8
6-8	L.A.	W	4-3	9	6	McElroy	Gross	Smith	28-26	4th	7
6-9	L.A.	L	3-6	8	13	Hershiser	Jackson		28-27	4th	7
6-10	L.A.	L	5-13	14	16	Martinez	Bielecki	Hartley	28-28	4th	8
6-11	S.F.	L	6-8 (10)	11	13	Downs	Smith	Righetti	28-29	4th	8½
6-12	S.F.	W	6-1	8	7	Boskie	Robinson	Smith	29-29	4th	8½
6-13	S.F.	W	4-3	7	11	Bielecki	Wilson	Assenmacher	30-29	4th	7½
6-14	At S.D.	W	7-3	15	7	Jackson	Benes	Smith	31-29	4th	6½
6-15	At S.D.	L	2-6	8	11	Rasmussen	Bielecki		31-30	4th	6½
6-16	At S.D.	L	2-4	6	5	Melendez	Maddux	Andersen	31-31	4th	7½
6-17	At L.A.	L	4-6	10	7	Morgon	Boskie	Crews	31-32	4th	8½
6-18	At L.A.	L	5-6 (13)	8	13	Hartley	Bielecki		31-33	4th	9½
6-19	At L.A.	L	8-9	13	13	Howell	Assenmacher		31-34	T4th	4½
6-20	At S.F.	L	3-4	10	9	Oliveras	Lancaster	Righetti	31-35	5th	9½
6-21	At S.F.	L	2-4	12	6	Downs	Maddux	Righetti	31-36	5th	10½
6-22	At S.F.	L	3-6	11	8	Wilson	Boskie	Oliveras	31-37	5th	10½
6-23	At S.F.	L	1-2	7	5	Brantley	Smith		31-38	5th	10½
6-25	At Pit.	W	5-1	5	8	Lancaster	Smiley		32-38	5th	9½

Date	Opp.	Res.	Score (inn.*)	Hits	Opp. hits	Winning pitcher	Losing pitcher	Save	Record	Pos.	GB
6-26	At Pit.	L	6-7	10	11	Walk	Maddux	Landrum	32-39	5th	10½
6-27	At Pit.	L	3-4	9	7	Palacios	Assenmacher		32-40	5th	11½
6-28	St.L.	L	6-14	13	21	Olivares	Scanlan		32-41	5th	12½
6-29	St.L.	W	6-4	12	11	Lancaster	Tewksbury	Assenmacher	33-41	T4th	12½
6-30	St.L.	W	7-4	10	8	McElroy	DeLeon		34-41	4th	12½
7-1	Pit.	W	6-5 (13)	14	13	Scanlan	Belinda		35-41	4th	11½
7-2	Pit.	L	4-13	9	22	Drabek	Boskie		35-42	4th	12½
7-3	Pit.	L	7-11	9	11	Smith	Lancaster		35-43	4th	13½
7-4	Pit.	W	9-8 (11)	14	15	McElroy	Landrum		36-43	4th	12½
7-5	At St.L.	W	5-1	8	6	Castillo	DeLeon		37-43	4th	11½
7-6	At St.L.	W	12-2	13	4	Bielecki	B. Smith		38-43	4th	10½
7-7	At St.L.	L	7-8 (12)	11	16	Fraser	Renfroe		38-44	4th	11½
7-11	Hou.	L	4-6 (11)	9	8	Osuna	Smith	Capel	38-45	4th	12½
7-12	Hou.	W	5-2	10	4	Castillo	Portugal	Assenmacher	39-45	4th	12½
7-13	Hou.	W	4-3	9	10	Lancaster	Capel		40-45	4th	12½
7-14	Hou.	W	4-3	5	13	Bielecki	Kile	Assenmacher	41-45	4th	12½
7-15	At Atl.	W	6-4	8	8	Maddux	Smith	Assenmacher	42-45	4th	12½
7-16	At Atl.	L	5-8	5	12	Freeman	Scanlan	Berenguer	42-46	4th	13½
7-17	At Atl.	L	2-12	4	16	Smoltz	Lancaster		42-47	4th	13½
7-19	At Hou.	L	2-5	5	9	Harnisch	Scanlan	Osuna	42-48	4th	14½
7-20	At Hou.	W	6-0	10	8	Maddux	Kile		43-48	4th	13½
7-21	At Hou.	W	4-2	8	9	Castillo	Clancy		44-48	4th	13½
7-23	Cin.	W	8-5	9	9	Lancaster	Myers	Assenmacher	45-48	4th	13
7-24	Cin.	L	3-12	10	17	Browning	Bielecki		45-49	4th	14
7-25	Cin.	W	5-4 (13)	9	14	Slocumb	Layana		46-49	4th	13½
7-26	Atl.	L	2-6	5	9	Avery	Castillo		46-50	4th	14½
7-27	Atl.	W	7-5	6	10	Lancaster	Smoltz	McElroy	47-50	4th	14½
7-28	Atl.	W	6-2	11	9	Bielecki	Leibrandt	Assenmacher	48-50	4th	13½
7-30	At Cin.	L	5-6 (10)	10	13	Dibble	McElroy		48-51	4th	12½
7-31	At Cin.	L	1-5	8	9	Rijo	Castillo	Power	48-52	4th	12½
8-2	At N.Y.	W	4-2 (10)	11	8	Assenmacher	Pena		49-52	4th	11
8-3	At N.Y.	W	9-2	13	6	Scanlan	Viola		50-52	4th	10
8-4	At N.Y.	W	8-3	12	7	Maddux	Cone		51-52	4th	10
8-5	At N.Y.	W	7-2	11	9	Castillo	Schourek		52-52	4th	9½
8-6	At Phi.	L	2-6 (11)	10	11	Williams	Lancaster		52-53	4th	10½
8-7	At Phi.	L	4-5 (11)	10	14	Williams	Lancaster		52-54	4th	10½
8-8	At Phi.	L	1-11	6	12	Cox	Jackson		52-55	4th	10½
8-9	N.Y.	W	5-4	9	7	Maddux	Cone		53-55	4th	9½
8-10	N.Y.	W	6-2	9	3	Scanlan	Burke	Lancaster	54-55	4th	9½
8-11	N.Y.	W	3-2 (14)	9	11	Boskie	Schourek		55-55	4th	9½
8-12	N.Y.	W	3-2 (10)	9	6	Lancaster	Burke		56-55	4th	9½
8-13	Mon.	L	6-7	12	11	Sampen	Lancaster	Fassero	56-56	4th	10½
8-14	Mon.	L	0-2	2	6	Barnes	Maddux	Jones	56-57	4th	11½
8-15	Mon.	W	7-6	9	12	Assenmacher	Fassero	McElroy	57-57	T3rd	10½
8-16	Phi.	W	9-1	13	6	Sutcliffe	Ruffin		58-57	3rd	10½
8-17	Phi.	L	2-5	8	9	Mulholland	Bielecki	Williams	58-58	3rd	11½
8-18	Phi.	W	7-6 (10)	9	7	Assenmacher	Williams		59-58	3rd	11½
8-19	At Mon.	W	3-2 (11)	7	14	Assenmacher	Sampen		60-58	3rd	11
8-20	At Mon.	L	2-4	8	12	Haney	Scanlan	Rojas	60-59	3rd	11
8-21	At Mon.	W	3-1	7	5	Sutcliffe	Nabholz	Lancaster	61-59	3rd	10
8-23	S.D.	W	5-4	12	7	Lancaster	Lefferts		62-59	3rd	9½
8-24	S.D.	L	1-4	3	8	Benes	Maddux	Melendez	62-60	3rd	9½
8-25	S.D.	L	9-12	15	14	Maddux	Scanlan	Melendez	62-61	3rd	10½
8-26	L.A.	L	3-4	9	7	Gott	McElroy	Howell	62-62	3rd	10½
8-27	L.A.	W	2-1	7	3	Castillo	Martinez		63-62	3rd	10½
8-28	At S.F.	W	8-6	10	11	Bielecki	McClellan	Assenmacher	64-62	3rd	10½
8-29	At S.F.	W	5-4	11	8	Maddux	Oliveras		65-62	3rd	10½
8-30	At L.A.	L	0-2	4	6	Belcher	Jackson		65-63	3rd	11½
8-31	At L.A.	L	2-3	8	9	McDowell	Assenmacher	Howell	65-64	3rd	12½
9-1	At L.A.	L	3-12	8	15	Martinez	Castillo		65-65	3rd	12½
9-2	At S.D.	W	10-8	15	9	McElroy	Melendez		66-65	3rd	12½
9-3	At S.D.	L	1-4	7	8	Benes	Maddux		66-66	3rd	13½
9-4	At S.D.	L	1-5	6	7	Rasmussen	Jackson		66-67	3rd	14½
9-6	S.F.	W	3-2	9	5	Castillo	Hickerson	Smith	67-67	3rd	14
9-7	S.F.	W	2-1	5	4	Bielecki	McClellan	Assenmacher	68-67	3rd	13
9-8	S.F.	L	3-4	9	6	Wilson	Maddux	Righetti	68-68	3rd	13
9-9	Pit.	L	10-12	13	16	Belinda	Smith	Rodriguez	68-69	3rd	14
9-10	Pit.	W	6-2	13	8	Sutcliffe	Tomlin	Scanlan	69-69	3rd	13
9-11	N.Y.	L	1-4	6	9	T. Castillo	F. Castillo	Franco	69-70	3rd	14
9-12	N.Y.	L	3-6	5	10	Young	Bielecki	Whitehurst	69-71	3rd	14
9-13	Mon.	L	2-3	7	7	Martinez	Scanlan	Jones	69-72	T3rd	15
9-14	Mon.	W	7-5 (10)	10	8	Scanlan	Jones		70-72	3rd	15
9-15	Mon.	L	5-6 (10)	9	7	Rojas	Assenmacher	Fassero	70-73	3rd	15

Date	Opp.	Res.	Score (inn.*)	Hits	Opp. hits	Winning pitcher	Losing pitcher	Save	Record	Pos.	GB
9-16	At Pit.	L	4-5	6	9	Smith	Castillo	Mason	70-74	3rd	16
9-17	At Pit.	L	2-9	9	9	Drabek	Bielecki		70-75	T3rd	17
9-18	At N.Y.	W	4-1	9	5	Maddux	Viola		71-75	3rd	17
9-22 (1)	Mon.	L	2-6	6	9	Gardner	Sutcliffe		71-76	4th	18½
9-22 (2)	Mon.	L	3-5	7	13	Sampen	Castillo	Rojas	71-77	4th	19
9-23	Phi.	W	10-3	14	7	Maddux	Mulholland		72-77	T3rd	18½
9-24	Phi.	L	2-4	4	9	Ashby	Bielecki	Williams	72-78	T3rd	19½
9-25	Phi.	L	4-5	6	11	Greene	Boskie	Williams	72-79	5th	20
9-27	At St.L.	L	4-5	10	7	Tewksbury	Castillo	L. Smith	72-80	5th	20
9-28	At St.L.	L	2-3	7	6	Hill	Maddux	L. Smith	72-81	5th	20
9-29	At St.L.	W	5-3	8	7	Sutcliffe	B. Smith	Assenmacher	73-81	5th	20
9-30	At Phi.	L	5-6	9	9	Ritchie	Assenmacher		73-82	5th	21
10-1	At Phi.	L	5-6 (13)	9	13	Ruffin	Assenmacher		73-83	5th	22
10-2	At Phi.	W	1-0	3	3	Maddux	DeJesus		74-83	5th	21
10-5 (1)	St.L.	W	3-2	8	9	Scanlan	Fraser		75-83	4th	20½
10-5 (2)	St.L.	W	7-5	3	9	Perez	Agosto	Assenmacher	76-83	4th	20½
10-6	St.L.	W	7-3	10	6	Maddux	Olivares		77-83	4th	20

Monthly records: April (10-11), May (14-12), June (10-18), July (14-11), August (17-12), September (8-18), Oct. (4-1).

HIGHLIGHTS

High point: When Jim Essian replaced fired manager Don Zimmer on May 22, the Cubs posted a five-game winning streak. That surge gave Chicago a 23-20 mark on May 26, just four games out of first in the National League East.

Low point: When the Cubs lost 21 of their final 33 games to finish fourth (20 games out of first) with a 77-83 record. Essian was subsequently fired.

Turning point: The Cubs opened a 13-game road trip June 14 with a victory in San Diego. But by the time the journey ended June 27 in Pittsburgh, the Cubs had won just one more game.

Most valuable player: Second baseman Ryne Sandberg. He hit a team-high .291 with 26 homers and became the first big-league second baseman to drive in 100 runs or more in consecutive seasons since Boston's Bobby Doerr in 1949-50.

Most valuable pitcher: Righthander Greg Maddux. He led the league in innings pitched (263), and his 198 strikeouts were the most by a Cubs pitcher since Ferguson Jenkins' 263 in 1971. Maddux finished with a team-best 15-11 record and 3.35 ERA.

Most improved player: Third baseman/outfielder Chico Walker. After spending parts of 15 seasons in the minor leagues, Walker hit .257 with six homers and 34 runs batted in.

Most pleasant surprise: Lefthander Chuck McElroy. Obtained from Philadelphia in the Mitch Williams trade, McElroy was 6-2 with a 1.95 ERA in a club-rookie-record 71 appearances (all in relief).

Biggest disappointments: Free-agent pitchers Danny Jackson and Dave Smith. Jackson spent two stints on the disabled list and made only 14 starts, going 1-5 with a 6.75 ERA. Smith, who also spent time on the disabled list, finished with a team-high 17 saves. But he posted a 0-6 mark with a 6.00 ERA.

Key injuries: Jackson and Smith were joined on the DL by fellow pitchers Mike Harkey and Rick Sutcliffe. Harkey made just four starts before undergoing season-ending shoulder surgery May 2. Sutcliffe was disabled twice with shoulder weakness.

Notable: The Cubs have finished above .500 only twice (1984 and '89) since 1972. ... Chicago set club records for fewest errors (113) and highest fielding percentage (.982). ... Andre Dawson and Sandberg became the first Chicago teammates to each reach the 100-RBI mark in consecutive seasons since 1929-30, when Kiki Cuyler and Hack Wilson accomplished the feat. ... The Cubs' bullpen blew 27 of 67 save opportunities.

—DAVE van DYCK

RECORDS

1991 regular-season record: 77-83 (4th in N.L. East); 46-37 at home; 31-46 on road; 46-42 vs. East; 31-41 vs. West; 31-33 vs. LHP; 46-50 vs. RHP; 59-56 on grass; 18-27 on turf; 43-39 in day-time; 34-44 at night; 33-29 in one-run games; 12-11 in extra-inning games; 1-1-0 in doubleheaders.

Team record last five years: 400-407 (.496, ranks 8th in league in that span).

TEAM LEADERS

Batting average: Ryne Sandberg (.291).
At-bats: Mark Grace (619).
Runs: Ryne Sandberg (104).
Hits: Ryne Sandberg (170).
Total bases: Ryne Sandberg (284).
Doubles: Ryne Sandberg (32).
Triples: Shawon Dunston (7).
Home runs: Andre Dawson (31).
Runs batted in: Andre Dawson (104).
Stolen bases: Ced Landrum (27).
Slugging percentage: Andre Dawson (.488).
On-base percentage: Ryne Sandberg (.379).
Wins: Greg Maddux (15).
Earned-run average: Greg Maddux (3.35).
Complete games: Greg Maddux (7).
Shutouts: Greg Maddux (2).
Saves: Dave Smith (17).
Innings pitched: Greg Maddux (263).
Strikeouts: Greg Maddux (198).

GAMES BY POSITION

Catcher: Rick Wilkins 82, Hector Villanueva 55, Damon Berryhill 48, Joe Girardi 21, Erik Pappas 6.
First base: Mark Grace 160, Luis Salazar 7, Hector Villanueva 6.
Second base: Ryne Sandberg 157, Jose Vizcaino 9, Chico Walker 6, Rey Sanchez 2.
Third base: Luis Salazar 86, Jose Vizcaino 57, Chico Walker 57, Gary Scott 31, Doug Strange 3.
Shortstop: Shawon Dunston 142, Jose Vizcaino 33, Rey Sanchez 10.
Outfield: George Bell 146, Andre Dawson 137, Jerome Walton 101, Doug Dascenzo 86, Chico Walker 53, Ced Landrum 44, Dwight Smith 42, Derrick May 7, Luis Salazar 1.

TOP 10 DRAFT CHOICES

1. **Doug Glanville**, OF, University of Pennsylvania.
2. **None** .
3. **Bill Bliss**, LHP, Villanova University.
4. **Terry Adams**, RHP, Mary Montgomery High School, Semmes, Ala.
5. **Ozzie Timmons**, OF, University of Tampa.
6. **Hector Trinidad**, RHP, Pioneer High School, Whittier, Calif.
7. **Maceo Houston**, OF, Galileo High School, San Francisco.
8. **Steve Trachsel**, RHP, Long Beach State University.
9. **Jon Lieber**, RHP, University of South Alabama.
10. **Scott Weiss**, RHP, Stanford University.

CINCINNATI REDS
NATIONAL LEAGUE WEST DIVISION

1992 SCHEDULE

APRIL

S	M	T	W	T	F	S
5	6 SD H	7 N SD H	8 SD H	9 HOU	10 N HOU	11 N HOU
12 HOU	13 ATL H	14 N ATL H	15 ATL H	16	17 N SF	18 SF
19 SF	20 LA	21 N LA	22 N LA	23	24 N SD	25 N SD
26 SD	27	28 N PIT H	29 N PIT H	30		

MAY

S	M	T	W	T	F	S
					1 N CHI H	2 CHI H
3 CHI H	4 N PIT	5 N PIT	6 N NY	7 NY H	8 N CHI	9 CHI
10 CHI	11	12 N STL	13 N STL	14	15 N PHI H	16 N PHI H
17 PHI H	18 MON	19 N MON	20 N MON	21	22 N PHI	23 N PHI
24 PHI	25 NY	26 N NY	27 N NY	28	29 N MON H	30 N MON H
31 MON H						

JUNE

S	M	T	W	T	F	S
	1	2 N STL H	3 N STL H	4 LA	5 N LA	6 N LA
7 LA	8 N SF	9 N SF	10 SF	11	12 N LA H	13 LA H
14 N LA H	15 N SF	16 N SF	17 SF H	18 N ATL	19 N ATL	20 N ATL
21 ATL	22 N HOU H	23 N HOU H	24 N HOU H	25	26 N ATL H	27 ATL H
28 ATL H	29 N HOU	30 N HOU				

JULY

S	M	T	W	T	F	S
			1 HOU	2 N PIT	3 N PIT H	4 PIT
5 PIT	6 N CHI	7 CHI	8 CHI	9 N PIT H	10 N PIT H	11 N PIT H
12 PIT H	13	14 *	15	16 N STL H	17 N STL H	18 N STL H
19 STL H	20 N CHI H	21 N CHI H	22 N CHI H	23 N STL	24 N STL	25 N STL
26 STL	27 N SD	28 N SD	29 N SD	30	31 N HOU H	

AUGUST

S	M	T	W	T	F	S
						1 N HOU H
2 HOU H	3 HOU H	4 N ATL	5 N ATL	6 N ATL	7 N SF H	8 N SF H
9 SF H	10	11 N LA H	12 N LA H	13 N LA H	14 N SD	15 N SD
16 SD H	17 N PHI	18 N PHI	19 PHI	20	21 N MON	22 N MON
23 MON	24 N PHI H	25 N PHI H	26 N PHI H	27	28 N NY	29 NY
30 N NY	31 N MON H					

SEPTEMBER

S	M	T	W	T	F	S
		1 N MON H	2 N MON H	3 N NY	4 N NY	5 N NY
6 NY	7	8 N HOU	9 N HOU	10 N ATL	11 N SD	12 N SD
13 SD	14	15 N ATL H	16 N ATL H	17 N ATL H	18 N SD H	19 SD H
20 SD	21 N HOU H	22 HOU H	23 N LA	24 N LA	25 N SF	26 SF
27 SF	28	29 N LA H	30 N LA H			

OCTOBER

S	M	T	W	T	F	S
				1 LA H	2 N SF H	3 N SF H
4 SF H	5	6	7	8	9	10

1992 SEASON

CLUB DIRECTORY

General partner
Marge Schott
President and chief executive officer
Marge Schott
Vice president and general manager
Bob Quinn
Director, player development
Jim Bowden
Director, scouting
Julian Mock
Special player consultant
Sheldon Bender
Controller
Ernie Brubaker
Director, stadium operations
Tim O'Connell
Director, ticket department
John O'Brien
Director, season ticket sales
Pat McCaffrey
Director, group sales
Susan Toomey
Director, marketing
Chip Baker
Director, publicity
Jon Braude
Director, speakers bureau
Gordy Coleman
Traveling secretary
Joel Pieper
Assistant publicity director
Joe Kelley
Assistant ticket director
Ken Ayer
Chief administrative assistant
Joyce Pfarr

Administrative assistant, business
Ginny Kamp
Administrative assistant, scouting
Wilma Mann
Admin. assistant, player development
Lois Schneider
Trainers
Larry Starr
Dan Wright
Field superintendent
Tony Swain
Equipment manager
Bernie Stowe
Scouts
Johnny Almarez
Jeff Barton
Larry Barton Jr.
Ray Bellino
Gene Bennett
Jack Bowen
George Brill
Dave Calaway
Clay Daniel
Paul Faulk
Les Houser
Eddie Kolo
Tom Severtson
Bob Szymkowski
Marion (Bo) Trumbo
Tom Wilson
Jeff Zimmerman
Scouting consultants
Paul Campbell
Tony Robello

SCHEDULE KEY

H—Home game.   *All-Star Game at San Diego/Jack Murphy Stadium.
N—Night game (any game starting after 5 p.m.).

SPRING TRAINING ROSTER

Manager—Lou Piniella (41).
Coaches—John McLaren (8), Jackie Moore (4), Tony Perez (24), Sam Perlozzo (2), Larry Rothschild (3).

No.	PITCHERS	B/T	Ht./Wt.	Born	1991 clubs
62	Ayala, Bobby	R/R	6-2/190	7-8-69	Chattanooga
50	Bankhead, Scott	R/R	5-10/185	7-31-63	Seattle, San Bernardino, Bellingham, Calgary
31	Belcher, Tim	R/R	6-3/220	10-19-61	Los Angeles
32	Browning, Tom	L/L	6-1/195	4-28-60	Cincinnati
37	Charlton, Norm	S/L	6-3/205	1-6-63	Cincinnati
49	Dibble, Rob	L/R	6-4/230	1-24-64	Cincinnati
54	Foster, Steve	R/R	6-0/180	8-16-66	Chattanooga, Nashville, Cincinnati
61	Garcia, Victor	R/R	6-2/195	9-15-69	Chattanooga, Nashville
45	Hammond, Chris	L/L	6-1/190	1-21-66	Cincinnati
48	Henry, Dwayne	R/R	6-3/230	2-16-62	Houston
39	Hill, Milton	R/R	6-0/180	8-22-65	Nashville, Cincinnati
53	Hoffman, Trevor	R/R	6-0/200	10-13-67	Cedar Rapids, Chattanooga
43	Layana, Tim	R/R	6-2/190	3-2-64	Nashville, Cincinnati
33	Minutelli, Gino	L/L	6-0/190	5-23-64	Charleston (W.Va.), Nashville, Cincinnati
60	Powell, Ross	L/L	5-11/180	1-24-68	Nashville
55	Pugh, Tim	R/R	6-6/225	1-26-67	Chattanooga, Nashville
27	Rijo, Jose	R/R	6-2/210	5-13-65	Cincinnati
28	Ruskin, Scott	R/L	6-2/195	6-8-63	Montreal
36	Sanford, Mo	R/R	6-6/225	12-24-66	Chattanooga, Nashville, Cincinnati
63	Satre, Jason	R/R	6-1/180	8-24-70	Cedar Rapids, Chattanooga
29	Swindell, Greg	R/L	6-3/225	1-2-65	Cleveland

No.	CATCHERS	B/T	Ht./Wt.	Born	1991 clubs
25	Geren, Bob	R/R	6-3/225	9-22-61	New York AL
9	Oliver, Joe	R/R	6-3/210	7-24-65	Cincinnati
34	Reed, Jeff	L/R	6-2/190	11-12-62	Cincinnati
42	Sutko, Glenn	R/R	6-3/225	5-9-68	Chattanooga, Nashville, Cincinnati

No.	INFIELDERS	B/T	Ht./Wt.	Born	1991 clubs
12	Benavides, Freddie	R/R	6-2/185	4-7-66	Nashville, Cincinnati
58	Branson, Jeff	L/R	6-0/180	1-26-67	Chattanooga, Nashville
19	Doran, Bill	S/R	6-0/180	5-28-58	Cincinnati
51	Lane, Brian	R/R	6-3/215	6-15-69	DID NOT PLAY
11	Larkin, Barry	R/R	6-0/190	4-28-64	Cincinnati
23	Morris, Hal	L/L	6-4/215	4-9-65	Cincinnati
17	Sabo, Chris	R/R	6-0/185	1-19-62	Cincinnati

No.	OUTFIELDERS	B/T	Ht./Wt.	Born	1991 clubs
15	Braggs, Glenn	R/R	6-4/220	10-17-62	Cincinnati
46	Brumfield, Jacob	R/R	6-0/170	5-27-65	Omaha
22	Hatcher, Billy	R/R	5-10/190	10-4-60	Cincinnati
68	Hernandez, Cesar	R/R	6-0/160	9-28-66	Harrisburg
30	Martinez, Dave	L/L	5-10/175	9-26-64	Montreal
21	O'Neill, Paul	L/L	6-4/215	2-25-63	Cincinnati
10	Roberts, Bip	S/R	5-7/165	10-27-63	San Diego
16	Sanders, Reggie	R/R	6-1/180	12-1-67	Chattanooga, Cincinnati

BALLPARK INFORMATION

Ballpark (capacity, surface)
Riverfront Stadium (52,952, artificial)

Address
100 Riverfront Stadium
Cincinnati, OH 45202

Business phone
513-421-4510

Ticket information
513-421-7337

Ticket prices
$10 (blue level box seats)
$9 (green level box seats)
$9 (yellow level box seats)
$8 (red level box seats)
$7 (green level reserved seats)
$6 (red level reserved seats)
$3.50 ("top six" reserved seats)

Field dimensions (from home plate)
To left field at foul line, 330 feet
To center field, 404 feet
To right field at foul line, 330 feet

First game played
June 30, 1970 (Braves 8, Reds 2)

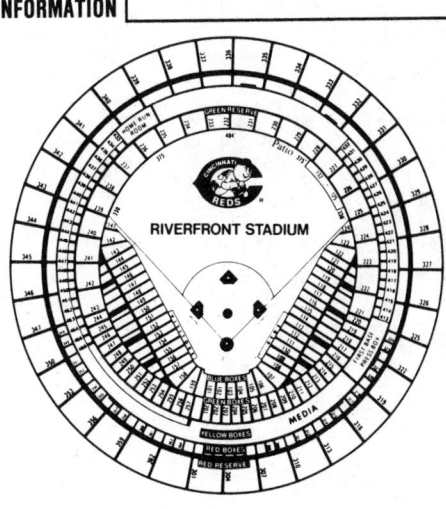

RIVERFRONT STADIUM

MINOR LEAGUE AFFILIATES

Class	Team	League	Manager
AAA	Nashville	American Association	Pete Mackanin
AA	Chattanooga	Southern	Dave Miley
A	Charleston, W.Va.	South Atlantic	P.J. Carey
A	Cedar Rapids	Midwest	Mark Berry
Rookie	Billings	Pioneer	Donnie Scott
Rookie	Plant City Reds	Gulf Coast	Sam Mejias

BROADCAST INFORMATION

Radio: WLW-AM (700). Broadcasters: Joe Nuxhall, Marty Brennaman.
TV: WLWT-TV (Channel 5). Broadcasters: Gordy Coleman, Steve LaMar, Marty Brennaman.
Cable TV: SportsChannel. Broadcasters: Steve LaMar, Gordy Coleman.

SPRING TRAINING

Ballpark (city): Plant City Stadium (Plant City, Fla.).
Ticket information: 813-752-7337.

HISTORY

YEAR-BY-YEAR RECORDS

Year	Pos.	W	L	Pct.	*GB	Year	Pos.	W	L	Pct.	*GB
1901	8th	52	87	.374	38	1949	7th	62	92	.403	35
1902	4th	70	70	.500	33½	1950	6th	66	87	.431	24½
1903	4th	74	65	.532	16½	1951	6th	68	86	.442	28½
1904	3rd	88	65	.575	18	1952	6th	69	85	.448	27½
1905	5th	79	74	.516	26	1953	6th	68	86	.442	37
1906	6th	64	87	.424	51½	1954	5th	74	80	.481	23
1907	6th	66	87	.431	41½	1955	5th	75	79	.487	23½
1908	5th	73	81	.474	26	1956	3rd	91	63	.591	2
1909	4th	77	76	.503	33½	1957	4th	80	74	.519	15
1910	5th	75	79	.487	29	1958	4th	76	78	.494	16
1911	6th	70	83	.458	29	1959	T5th	74	80	.481	13
1912	4th	75	78	.490	29	1960	6th	67	87	.435	28
1913	7th	64	89	.418	37½	1961	1st	93	61	.604 +	4
1914	8th	60	94	.390	34½	1962	3rd	98	64	.605	3½
1915	7th	71	83	.461	20	1963	5th	86	76	.531	13
1916	T7th	60	93	.392	33½	1964	T2nd	92	70	.549	1
1917	4th	78	76	.506	20	1965	4th	89	73	.549	8
1918	3rd	68	60	.531	15½	1966	7th	76	84	.475	18
1919	1st	96	44	.686 +	9	1967	4th	87	75	.537	14½
1920	3rd	82	71	.536	10½	1968	4th	83	79	.512	14
1921	6th	70	83	.458	24	1969	3rd	89	73	.549	4
1922	2nd	86	68	.558	7	1970	1st†	102	60	.630 +14½	
1923	2nd	91	63	.591	4½	1971	T4th	79	83	.488	11
1924	4th	83	70	.542	10	1972	1st†	95	59	.617 +10½	
1925	3rd	80	73	.523	15	1973	1st‡	99	63	.611 +	3½
1926	2nd	87	67	.565	2	1974	2nd	98	64	.605	4
1927	5th	75	78	.490	18½	1975	1st†	108	54	.667	+20
1928	5th	78	74	.513	16	1976	1st†	102	60	.630	+10
1929	7th	66	88	.429	33	1977	2nd	88	74	.543	10
1930	7tn	59	95	.383	33	1978	2nd	92	69	.571	2½
1931	8th	58	96	.377	43	1979	1st‡	90	71	.559 +	1½
1932	8th	60	94	.390	30	1980	3rd	89	73	.549	3½
1933	8th	58	94	.382	33	1981	2nd/2nd	66	42	.611	§
1934	8th	52	99	.344	42	1982	6th	61	101	.377	28
1935	6th	68	85	.444	31½	1983	6th	74	88	.457	17
1936	5th	74	80	.481	18	1984	5th	70	92	.432	22
1937	8th	56	98	.364	40	1985	2nd	89	72	.553	5½
1938	4th	82	68	.547	6	1986	2nd	86	76	.531	10
1939	1st	97	57	.630 +	4½	1987	2nd	84	78	.519	6
1940	1st	100	53	.654	+12	1988	2nd	87	74	.540	7
1941	3rd	88	66	.571	12	1989	5th	75	87	.463	17
1942	4th	76	76	.500	29	1990	1st†	91	71	.562 +	5
1943	2nd	87	67	.565	18	1991	5th	74	88	.457	20
1944	3rd	89	65	.578	16						
1945	7th	61	93	.396	37						
1946	6th	67	87	.435	30						
1947	5th	73	81	.474	21						
1948	7th	64	89	.418	27						

*Games behind winner. †Won Championship Series. ‡Lost Championship Series. §First half 35-21; second 31-21.

MANAGERS

Name	Record	Years
Biddy McPhee	79-124	'01-02
Frank Bancroft	9-7	1902
Joe Kelley	275-230	'02-05
Ned Hanlon	130-174	'06-07
John Ganzel	73-81	1908
Clark Griffith	222-238	'09-11
Hank O'Day	75-78	1912
Joe Tinker	64-89	1913
Buck Herzog	165-226	'14-16
Chris. Mathewson	164-176	'16-18
Heinie Groh	7-3	1918
Pat Moran	425-329	'19-23
Jack Hendricks	469-450	'24-29
Dan Howley	177-285	'30-32
Donie Bush	58-94	1933
Bob O'Farrell	30-60	1934
Chuck Dressen	214-282	'34-37
Bobby Wallace	5-20	1937
Bill McKechnie	747-632	'38-46
Johnny Neun	117-137	'47-48*
Bucky Walters	81-123	'48-49
Luke Sewell	176-234	'50-52
Rogers Hornsby	91-106	'52-53
Buster Mills	4-4	'1953
Birdie Tebbetts	372-357	'54-58
Jimmie Dykes	24-17	1958
Mayo Smith	35-45	1959
Fred Hutchinson	443-372	'59-64
Dick Sisler	121-94	'64-65
Don Heffner	37-46	1966
Dave Bristol	298-265	'66-69
Sparky Anderson	863-586	'70-78
John McNamara	279-244	'79-82
Russ Nixon	101-131	'82-83
Vern Rapp	51-70	1984
Pete Rose	426-388	'84-89
Tommy Helms	14-21	1989
Lou Piniella	165-159	'90-91

DAY BY DAY

Date	Opp.	Res.	Score (inn.*)	Hits	Opp. hits	Winning pitcher	Losing pitcher	Save	Record	Pos.	GB
4-8	Hou.	W	6-2	10	5	Browning	Scott	Dibble	1-0	1st	+½
4-10	Hou.	W	6-5	9	8	Power	Kile	Myers	2-0	T1st	...
4-11	Hou.	L	1-4	3	9	Harnisch	Charlton	Schilling	2-1	T2nd	½
4-13	Atl.	L	5-7	12	9	Avery	Armstrong	Berenguer	2-2	T2nd	1½
4-14	Atl.	L	1-12	6	16	Glavine	Browning		2-3	T4th	2½
4-15	At S.D.	L	2-3 (11)	6	9	Maddux	Power		2-4	5th	3½
4-16	At S.D.	W	1-0	5	4	Charlton	Benes	Myers	3-4	T4th	2½
4-17	At S.D.	W	5-1	9	7	Hammond	Harris	Scudder	4-4	T3rd	1½
4-19	At Atl.	W	8-3	8	5	Armstrong	Glavine		5-4	2nd	1
4-20	At Atl.	W	3-0	11	4	Browning	Smoltz		6-4	2nd	1
4-21	At Atl.	L	2-3	6	5	Leibrandt	Rijo	Mercker	6-5	2nd	1
4-22	At Hou.	L	1-2	4	9	Henry	Myers		6-6	2nd	2
4-23	At Hou.	W	3-1	10	5	Hammond	Corsi	Dibble	7-6	2nd	2
4-24	At Hou.	L	0-1 (13)	3	10	Henry	Scudder		7-7	2nd	2
4-25	Chi.	W	6-4	13	8	Power	McElroy	Myers	8-7	2nd	1½
4-26	Chi.	W	3-1	5	5	Rijo	Harkey	Dibble	9-7	2nd	1½
4-27	Chi.	L	3-8	11	11	Boskie	Charlton	Assenmacher	9-8	2nd	1½
4-28	Chi.	W	4-3	7	11	Hammond	Sutcliffe	Dibble	10-8	2nd	½
4-30	Pit.	W	4-3	8	4	Browning	Drabek	Dibble	11-8	1st	+1
5-1	Pit.	L	4-6	10	8	Belinda	Myers	Landrum	11-9	1st	...
5-3	St.L.	L	2-4	6	11	Carpenter	Scudder	L. Smith	11-10	1st	...
5-4	St.L.	W	3-1	6	5	Armstrong	Moyer	Dibble	12-10	1st	...
5-5	St.L.	W	4-2	8	6	Browning	L. Smith	Dibble	13-10	1st	...
5-6	At Pit.	L	1-3	3	9	Palacios	Rijo	Landrum	13-11	2nd	½
5-7	At Pit.	L	2-7	6	9	Tomlin	Hammond	Belinda	13-12	3rd	1½
5-8	At Pit.	L	2-7	4	7	Smith	Charlton		13-13	T3rd	1½
5-10	At Chi.	L	5-6	7	9	Sutcliffe	Browning	Smith	13-14	4th	1
5-11	At Chi.	W	12-2	12	8	Rijo	Bielecki		14-14	T3rd	1
5-12	At Chi.	W	5-3	10	8	Armstrong	Maddux	Dibble	15-14	T2nd	1
5-13	At St.L.	L	0-1	2	7	Hill	Myers	L. Smith	15-15	T3rd	2
5-14	At St.L.	W	3-1	7	6	Charlton	Moyer	Dibble	16-15	3rd	1
5-15	At St.L.	L	2-8	9	14	Tewksbury	Browning		16-16	3rd	2
5-17	S.D.	W	7-3	11	7	Myers	Hurst	Dibble	17-16	3rd	1
5-18	S.D.	L	2-5	7	12	Peterson	Armstrong		17-17	3rd	2
5-19	S.D.	L	2-3	9	8	Benes	Charlton	Lefferts	17-18	4th	3
5-21	S.F.	W	3-2	6	9	Browning	Black	Dibble	18-18	3rd	2½
5-22	S.F.	W	9-4	15	9	Rijo	Robinson		19-18	3rd	1½
5-23	S.F.	W	6-2	9	4	Armstrong	Wilson		20-18	3rd	1½
5-24	L.A.	L	3-11	9	13	Martinez	Hammond		20-19	3rd	2½
5-25	L.A.	L	1-8	8	11	Gross	Charlton		20-20	4th	3½
5-26	L.A.	W	3-0	6	4	Browning	Ojeda	Myers	21-20	3rd	2½
5-27	At S.F.	W	3-2	7	11	Rijo	Robinson	Dibble	22-20	3rd	2½
5-28	At S.F.	L	2-6	5	12	Wilson	Armstrong		22-21	3rd	3½
5-29	At S.F.	L	1-6	6	8	Oliveras	Hammond		22-22	3rd	3½
5-30	At L.A.	W	7-2	15	4	Scudder	Martinez		23-22	3rd	2½
5-31	At L.A.	L	4-7	10	8	Ojeda	Browning		23-23	3rd	3½
6-1	At L.A.	W	6-5 (10)	9	5	Myers	Howell	Dibble	24-23	3rd	2½
6-2	At L.A.	L	1-4	8	11	Belcher	Armstrong	Crews	24-24	4th	3½
6-4	N.Y.	L	2-4	4	7	Cone	Hammond	Franco	24-25	4th	3½
6-5	N.Y.	W	11-10	17	11	Browning	Gooden	Dibble	25-25	4th	3½
6-6	N.Y.	W	5-3	9	7	Power	Viola	Myers	26-25	4th	3½
6-7	Phi.	L	4-5	11	12	Greene	Armstrong	Williams	26-26	4th	4½
6-8	Phi.	L	1-4	5	10	DeJesus	Hammond	McDowell	26-27	4th	4½
6-9	Phi.	W	6-3	15	10	Browning	Mulholland	Dibble	27-27	4th	4½
6-10	Phi.	W	9-3	11	4	Rijo	Ashby		28-27	4th	4½
6-11	At Mon.	W	6-1	11	5	Charlton	Nabholz		29-27	3rd	4
6-12	At Mon.	L	9-10	16	14	Ruskin	Myers	Fassero	29-28	4th	4
6-13	At Mon.	W	3-2	9	5	Hammond	Barnes	Dibble	30-28	3rd	4
6-14	At Phi.	W	4-2	10	7	Browning	Mulholland	Dibble	31-28	3rd	4
6-15	At Phi.	W	3-1	4	5	Rijo	Ashby	Dibble	32-28	3rd	3
6-16	At Phi.	W	8-6	10	12	Myers	McDowell	Carman	33-28	2nd	3
6-17	At N.Y.	L	6-10	11	13	Darling	Scudder		33-29	2nd	4
6-18	At N.Y.	L	5-7	13	9	Pena	Myers		33-30	2nd	5
6-19	At N.Y.	W	7-6	12	12	Gross	Cone	Dibble	34-30	2nd	5
6-20	Mon.	L	0-1 (11)	3	7	Jones	Carman	Ruskin	34-31	2nd	6
6-21	Mon.	W	7-3	9	6	Scudder	Haney		35-31	2nd	5
6-22	Mon.	L	4-7	10	12	Boyd	Armstrong	Jones	35-32	2nd	6
6-23	Mon.	W	8-4	9	5	Myers	Sampen		36-32	2nd	5
6-25	S.D.	W	8-2	10	7	Hammond	Benes		37-32	2nd	5
6-26	S.D.	W	6-2	14	7	Scudder	Rasmussen	Myers	38-32	2nd	4

Date	Opp.	Res.	Score (inn.*)	Hits	Opp. hits	Winning pitcher	Losing pitcher	Save	Record	Pos.	GB
6-27	S.D.	W	3-0	5	5	Armstrong	Melendez	Dibble	39-32	2nd	3½
6-28	Hou.	W	8-5	14	9	Browning	Deshaies	Dibble	40-32	2nd	3
6-29	Hou.	L	2-6	9	8	Kile	Carman	Clancy	40-33	2nd	4
6-30	Hou.	W	5-4	11	8	Hammond	Harnisch	Dibble	41-33	2nd	4
7-2	At Atl.	W	6-3	9	7	Armstrong	Leibrandt		42-33	2nd	4
7-3	At Atl.	L	6-8	11	17	Avery	Layana	Berenguer	42-34	2nd	5
7-4	At Atl.	W	10-4 (7)	14	6	Gross	Smith		43-34	2nd	4
7-5	At Hou.	W	1-0	5	5	Hammond	Harnisch	Dibble	44-34	2nd	3
7-6	At Hou.	L	0-3	3	3	Jones	Armstrong		44-35	2nd	4
7-7	At Hou.	L	3-7	6	13	Portugal	Browning		44-36	2nd	5
7-11	Pit.	L	6-10	10	14	Palacios	Myers		44-37	2nd	5
7-12	Pit.	L	2-7	7	12	Drabek	Armstrong		44-38	2nd	5
7-13	Pit.	L	2-5	7	7	Smiley	Browning	Kipper	44-39	2nd	5½
7-14	Pit.	L	6-10	11	12	Walk	Gross	Patterson	44-40	2nd	5
7-15	St.L.	L	2-5	10	12	Olivares	Minutelli	L. Smith	44-41	2nd	5
7-16	St.L.	L	7-8	14	10	Fraser	Dibble	L. Smith	44-42	3rd	5
7-17	St.L.	L	5-6	9	10	B. Smith	Armstrong	L. Smith	44-43	3rd	5
7-19	At Pit.	L	2-7	6	13	Smiley	Browning		44-44	3rd	5½
7-20	At Pit.	W	3-2	5	8	Gross	Walk	Power	45-44	3rd	5½
7-21	At Pit.	L	0-6	3	8	Tomlin	Hammond		45-45	3rd	5½
7-23	At Chi.	L	5-8	9	9	Lancaster	Myers	Assenmacher	45-46	3rd	6½
7-24	At Chi.	W	12-3	17	10	Browning	Bielecki		46-46	3rd	6½
7-25	At Chi.	L	4-5 (13)	14	9	Slocumb	Layana		46-47	3rd	7½
7-26	At St.L.	L	1-5	8	10	Tewksbury	Hammond		46-48	3rd	8½
7-27	At St.L.	W	13-1	20	9	Gross	Olivares		47-48	3rd	8½
7-28	At St.L.	L	2-3	13	4	DeLeon	Myers	L. Smith	47-49	3rd	8½
7-30	Chi.	W	6-5 (10)	13	10	Dibble	McElroy		48-49	3rd	8
7-31	Chi.	W	5-1	9	8	Rijo	Castillo	Power	49-49	3rd	8
8-1	S.F.	L	1-8	7	17	McClellan	Gross		49-50	3rd	8½
8-2	S.F.	W	9-8	9	8	Myers	Black	Charlton	50-50	3rd	7½
8-3	S.F.	L	3-7	9	6	Burkett	Armstrong		50-51	3rd	7½
8-4	S.F.	W	6-5	8	8	Power	Brantley		51-51	3rd	6½
8-5	L.A.	W	10-6	13	9	Rijo	Martinez	Dibble	52-51	3rd	5½
8-6	L.A.	L	2-5	9	8	Hershiser	Gross	McDowell	52-52	3rd	6½
8-7	L.A.	L	0-2	3	7	Ojeda	Myers	McDowell	52-53	3rd	7½
8-8	L.A.	L	4-6	8	11	Morgan	Browning		52-54	3rd	8½
8-9	At S.D.	W	5-1	9	4	Sanford	Rasmussen		53-54	3rd	7½
8-10	At S.D.	L	0-1	6	6	Harris	Rijo		53-55	4th	7½
8-11	At S.D.	L	0-13	4	15	Bones	Gross		53-56	5th	7½
8-12	At L.A.	L	2-3	4	6	McDowell	Dibble		53-57	5th	8½
8-13	At L.A.	W	4-3 (10)	9	10	Dibble	McDowell		54-57	5th	7½
8-14	At L.A.	L	1-4	5	8	Belcher	Sanford	Howell	54-58	5th	8½
8-15	At S.F.	L	1-4	2	6	McClellan	Rijo	Righetti	54-59	5th	8½
8-16	At S.F.	W	5-0	8	5	Gross	Black		55-59	5th	8½
8-17	At S.F.	W	7-0	11	6	Scudder	Burkett		56-59	5th	8½
8-18	At S.F.	W	4-3 (11)	7	13	Dibble	Righetti		57-59	4th	7½
8-20 (1)	Atl.	W	8-2	12	5	Rijo	Avery		58-59	3rd	8
8-20 (2)	Atl.	L	1-5	5	8	Smoltz	Sanford		58-60	T3rd	8½
8-21	Atl.	L	9-10 (13)	14	15	Castillo	Myers		58-61	T3rd	9½
8-22	Atl.	L	1-4	6	8	Leibrandt	Scudder	Clancy	58-62	4th	10
8-23	At N.Y.	W	6-1	16	9	Browning	Viola		59-62	T3rd	9
8-24	At N.Y.	W	7-0	14	2	Rijo	Whitehurst		60-62	T3rd	8
8-25	At N.Y.	L	1-2	9	7	Cone	Myers	Franco	60-63	T3rd	8
8-26	Phi.	W	5-4	7	4	Gross	Hartley	Dibble	61-63	3rd	8
8-27	Phi.	W	4-2	9	7	Scudder	Ruffin	Dibble	62-63	3rd	7
8-28	Mon.	W	11-3	13	8	Browning	Martinez		63-63	3rd	7
8-29	Mon.	W	5-4	6	7	Rijo	Barnes	Dibble	64-63	3rd	7
8-30	N.Y.	L	2-3	9	6	Cone	Myers	Franco	64-64	3rd	8
8-31	N.Y.	L	7-8 (10)	13	10	Franco	Dibble		64-65	3rd	8
9-1	N.Y.	L	4-9	10	10	Whitehurst	Scudder	Simons	64-66	3rd	8
9-2	At Phi.	L	5-8	8	11	Mulholland	Browning	Williams	64-67	3rd	8
9-3	At Phi.	W	8-5	8	10	Rijo	Brantley	Dibble	65-67	3rd	8
9-4	At Phi.	W	5-1	12	4	Myers	Greene		66-67	3rd	8
9-6	At Mon.	L	1-4	4	11	Haney	Scudder	Rojas	66-68	4th	8½
9-7	At Mon.	L	5-7	8	10	Nabholz	Browning		66-69	4th	9½
9-8	At Mon.	L	2-4	7	11	Martinez	Armstrong	Jones	66-70	4th	10½
9-9	L.A.	L	4-10	10	12	Gross	Hill		66-71	4th	11½
9-10	L.A.	W	6-0	9	5	Rijo	Martinez	Power	67-71	4th	11
9-11	S.F.	L	2-4	8	8	Hickerson	Scudder	Righetti	67-72	4th	12
9-12	S.F.	W	7-3	9	5	Browning	McClellan	Dibble	68-72	4th	12
9-13	Hou.	W	13-2	17	7	Armstrong	Bowen		69-72	4th	11½
9-14	Hou.	L	3-7	7	12	Hernandez	Dibble	Schilling	69-73	4th	12
9-15	Hou.	W	10-0	11	6	Rijo	Gardner		70-73	4th	12
9-16	At L.A.	L	5-6 (12)	14	11	Wetteland	Power		70-74	4th	12

Date	Opp.	Res.	Score (inn.*)	Hits	Opp. hits	Winning pitcher	Losing pitcher	Save	Record	Pos.	GB
9-17	At L.A.	L	3-5	8	10	Ojeda	Browning	Wilson	70-75	4th	12½
9-18	At S.F.	L	2-7	5	9	Wilson	Armstrong		70-76	4th	13½
9-19	At S.F.	L	1-4	6	6	Oliveras	Myers	Righetti	70-77	4th	14½
9-20	At Hou.	L	2-3	4	7	Bowen	Rijo	Hernandez	70-78	4th	15
9-21	At Hou.	W	4-1	8	3	Scudder	Juden	Dibble	71-78	4th	14½
9-22	At Hou.	L	1-4	6	9	Hernandez	Browning	Portugal	71-79	4th	15½
9-25 (1)	At Atl.	L	1-2 (10)	6	9	Pena	Power		71-80	4th	16
9-25 (2)	At Atl.	W	10-9 (10)	16	12	Hill	Stanton	Dibble	72-80	4th	15½
9-26	At Atl.	W	8-0	7	8	Rijo	Leibrandt		73-80	4th	15
9-27	S.D.	L	3-8	7	11	Harris	Scudder	Andersen	73-81	4th	16
9-28	S.D.	L	2-4	8	13	Melendez	Browning	Maddux	73-82	4th	16
9-29	S.D.	W	8-1	14	7	Power	Bones		74-82	4th	16
9-30	Atl.	L	0-4	3	8	Smoltz	Armstrong		74-83	4th	17
10-1	Atl.	L	6-7	7	10	Stanton	Dibble	Pena	74-84	4th	18
10-2	Atl.	L	3-6	6	7	Glavine	Scudder	Pena	74-85	4th	18
10-4	At S.D.	L	2-3	7	6	Melendez	Browning	Hernandez	74-86	T4th	19
10-5	At S.D.	L	7-10	13	17	Maddux	Minutelli	Lefferts	74-87	5th	20
10-6	At S.D.	L	1-3	10	7	Benes	Rijo	Andersen	74-88	5th	20

Monthly records: April (11-8), May (12-15), June (18-10), July (8-16), August (15-16), September (10-18), Oct. (0-5).

HIGHLIGHTS

High point: The Reds won nine of 11 games from June 23 through July 5 to pull within three games of the first-place Los Angeles Dodgers in the National League West.

Low point: Cincinnati went 10-23 through September and October to finish with a 74-88 record, 20 games behind first-place Atlanta.

Turning point: Pitchers Jose Rijo, Norm Charlton and Scott Scudder all went on the disabled list during a 10-day stretch in late June. The Reds overcame the lack of pitching depth for a short time, but it finally caught up to them after the All-Star break.

Most valuable player: Third baseman Chris Sabo. Playing on bad knees for much of the season, Sabo hit .301 with 26 home runs and 88 runs batted in. He also played great defense.

Most valuable pitcher: Rijo. After missing five weeks with a fractured right ankle, the righthander made a late run at the Cy Young Award. He finished 15-6 with a 2.51 earned-run average and pitched a career-high 204⅓ innings.

Most improved player: Outfielder Paul O'Neill. He led the Reds with 28 homers, 91 RBIs, 36 doubles and 73 walks, all career highs. O'Neill also made the All-Star team for the first time.

Most pleasant surprise: Shortstop Barry Larkin. After never hitting more than 12 home runs in a season, Larkin belted 20 to tie Leo Cardenas' 1966 club season record for homers by a shortstop. He also tied a big-league record by hitting five homers in two games (two against San Diego on June 27 and three against Houston on June 28).

Biggest disappointment: Center fielder Eric Davis. He appeared in only 89 games, hitting .235 with 11 homers and 33 RBIs. Pitchers Jack Armstrong (7-13 record, 5.48 ERA) and Randy Myers (6-13 record, 3.55 ERA, six saves) and catcher Joe Oliver (.216 average) also had disappointing seasons.

Key injuries: The Reds placed 12 players on the disabled list a total of 15 times. Pitchers Norm Charlton, Scott Scudder and Davis each were disabled twice. Larkin missed 39 games with an elbow injury, a sore neck and a strained left Achilles tendon. Second baseman Bill Doran was plagued by a back injury.

Notable: Three Reds hit over .300 (Hal Morris, Larkin and Sabo), giving the team that many in one season (minimum 400 at-bats) for the first time since 1977. ... Sabo's 26 homers were the most by a Reds third baseman since 1970 (Tony Perez, 40).

—JERRY CRASNICK

RECORDS

1991 regular-season record: 74-88 (5th in N.L. West); 39-42 at home; 35-46 on road; 34-38 vs. East; 40-50 vs. West; 30-25 vs. LHP; 44-63 vs. RHP; 22-26 on grass; 52-62 on turf; 20-21 in daytime; 54-67 at night; 21-25 in one-run games; 5-8 in extra-inning games; 0-0-2 in doubleheaders.

Team record last five years: 411-398 (.508, ranks 5th in league in that span).

TEAM LEADERS

Batting average: Hal Morris (.318).
At-bats: Chris Sabo (582).
Runs: Chris Sabo (91).
Hits: Chris Sabo (175).
Total bases: Chris Sabo (294).
Doubles: Paul O'Neill (36).
Triples: Mariano Duncan, Barry Larkin (4).
Home runs: Paul O'Neill (28).
Runs batted in: Paul O'Neill (91).
Stolen bases: Barry Larkin (24).
Slugging percentage: Barry Larkin (.506).
On-base percentage: Barry Larkin (.378).
Wins: Jose Rijo (15).
Earned-run average: Jose Rijo (2.51).
Complete games: Jose Rijo (3).
Shutouts: Jose Rijo (1).
Saves: Rob Dibble (31).
Innings pitched: Tom Browning (230⅓).
Strikeouts: Jose Rijo (172).

GAMES BY POSITION

Catcher: Joe Oliver 90, Jeff Reed 89, Glenn Sutko 9, Donnie Scott 8.
First base: Hal Morris 128, Carmelo Martinez 25, Todd Benzinger 21, Bill Doran 4, Reggie Jefferson 2, Terry Lee 2.
Second base: Bill Doran 88, Mariano Duncan 62, Luis Quinones 33, Freddie Benavides 3.
Third base: Chris Sabo 151, Luis Quinones 19.
Shortstop: Barry Larkin 119, Mariano Duncan 32, Freddie Benavides 20, Luis Quinones 5.
Outfield: Paul O'Neill 150, Billy Hatcher 121, Eric Davis 81, Glenn Braggs 74, Herm Winningham 66, Chris Jones 26, Carmelo Martinez 16, Todd Benzinger 15, Reggie Sanders 9, Mariano Duncan 7, Bill Doran 6, Stan Jefferson 5, Hal Morris 1.

TOP 10 DRAFT CHOICES

1. **Calvin Reese,** SS, Lower Richland High School, Hopkins, S.C.
2. **Toby Rumfield,** C, Belton (Texas) High School.
3. **Joe DeBerry,** 1B, Clemson University.
4. **Kevin Bentley,** OF, Mansfield (Texas) High School.
5. **Mike Harrison,** C, University of California.
6. **Dave Tuttle,** RHP, Santa Clara University.
7. **Chris Reed,** RHP, Katella High School, Anaheim, Calif.
8. **John Courtright,** LHP, Duke University.
9. **Damon Montgomery,** OF, Fremont High School, Los Angeles.
10. **Armando Morales,** RHP, University of New Orleans.

HOUSTON ASTROS
NATIONAL LEAGUE WEST DIVISION

1992 SCHEDULE

APRIL
S	M	T	W	T	F	S
5	6	7 N ATL H	8 N ATL H	9 N CIN H	10 N CIN H	11 N CIN H
12 CIN H	13 N LA H	14 N LA H	15 LA H	16	17 N SD H	18 N SD H
19 SD H	20 N SF H	21 N SF H	22 N SF H	23	24 N ATL	25 N ATL
26 ATL	27	28 N NY	29 N NY	30 N NY		

MAY
S	M	T	W	T	F	S
					1 N PIT H	2 N PIT H
3 N PIT H	4 N NY H	5 N NY H	6 CHI	7 N CHI	8 N PIT	9 N PIT
10 PIT	11 N CHI H	12 N CHI H	13 N CHI H	14	15 N STL H	16 N STL H
17 STL H	18 N PHI	19 N PHI	20 N PHI	21	22 N STL	23 N STL
24 STL	25 N MON	26 N MON	27	28	29 N PHI H	30 N PHI H
31 PHI H						

JUNE
S	M	T	W	T	F	S
	1 N MON H	2 N MON H	3 N MON H	4 N SF	5 N SF	6 SF
7 SF	8 N SD	9 N SD	10 SD	11	12 N SF H	13 N SF H
14 SF	15 N SD H	16 N SD H	17 N SD H	18	19 N LA	20 LA
21 LA	22 N CIN	23 N CIN	24 N CIN	25 LA	26 N LA	27 N LA
28 LA	29 N CIN H	30 N CIN H				

JULY
S	M	T	W	T	F	S
			1 CIN H	2	3 N NY	4 N NY
5 NY	6 N PIT	7 N PIT	8 N PIT	9 N NY H	10 N NY H	11 N NY H
12 NY H	13 14 *	15	16 N ATL H	17 N ATL H	18 N ATL H
19 ATL H	20 N PIT H	21 N PIT H	22 N PIT H	23	24 N CHI	25 N CHI
26 CHI H	27 N ATL	28 ATL	29 ATL	30	31 N CIN	

AUGUST
S	M	T	W	T	F	S
						1 N CIN
2 CIN	3 CIN	4 N LA	5 N LA	6 N SD	7 N SD	8 SD
9 SD	10 N SF	11 SF	12 SF	13 N CHI	14 CHI	15 CHI
16 CHI	17	18 N STL	19 N STL	20 N STL	21 N PHI	22 N PHI
23 PHI	24	25 N STL H	26 N STL H	27 STL H	28 N MON H	29 N MON H
30 MON H	31 N PHI H					

SEPTEMBER
S	M	T	W	T	F	S
		1 N PHI H	2 N PHI H	3 N	4 N MON	5 N MON
6 MON	7 N CIN H	8 N CIN H	9 N SF	10 SF	11 N ATL H	12 N ATL H
13 ATL H	14 N SF H	15 N SF H	16 N SF H	17	18 N ATL	19 N ATL
20 ATL	21 N CIN	22 N CIN	23 N SD	24 SD	25 N LA	26 N LA
27 LA	28	29 N SD H	30 N SD H			

OCTOBER
S	M	T	W	T	F	S
				1 N SD H	2 N LA H	3 N LA H
4 LA H	5	6	7	8	9	10

1992 SEASON

CLUB DIRECTORY

Chairman of the board
Dr. John J. McMullen
Owners
Dr. John J. McMullen
Mrs. James (Catherine) Blake
H.L. Brown Jr.
Mrs. Thomas E. (Mimi) Dompier
James A. Elkins Jr.
Alfred C. Glassell Jr.
Mrs. Stephen (Mary) Mochary
Estate of Vivian L. Smith
Jack T. Trotter and Jacqueline
Peter and John McMullen
General manager
William J. Wood
Assistant general manager
Bob Watson
Director of minor league operations
Fred Nelson
Director of scouting
Dan O'Brien
Director of public relations
Rob Matwick
Traveling secretary
Barry Waters
Asst. director of minor leagues/scouting
Lew Temple
Assistant director of public relations
Chuck Pool
Assistant to general manager
Tim Hellmuth
Asst. dir. of scouting/dir. of intl. develop.
David Rawnsley
Staff publicist
Tyler Barnes
Vice president, marketing
Ted Haracz
Director of broadcasting
Jamie Hildreth
Director of sales
David Matlin
Director, group sales
Debra Fulmer
Club physicians
Dr. William Bryan
Dr. Michael Feltovich

HOUSTON SPORTS ASSOCIATION INC.
President and chief operating officer
Robert G. Harter
Executive vice president
Neal Gunn
V.p., Astrodome-Astrohall Stadium Corp.
John Elsner
Vice president, finance
Gary Brooks
Vice president, engineering
W. Gary Keller

Vice president, operations
Don Collins
Vice president, public affairs
Jim Weidler
General counsel
Frank Rynd
Treasurer
Adam C. Richards
Controller
Robert McBurnett
Scouts
Bob Blair
Jack Bloomfield
Stan Boroski
Ralph Bratton
Bill Buck
Gerry Craft
Clark Crist
Jug DeFord
Chuck Edmondson
Orlando Estevez
James Farrar
Ben Galante
Carl Greene
Sterling Housley
Dan Huston
Mark Johnson
Brian Keegan
Bill Kelso
Bob King
David Lakey
Bobby Macias
Mike Maggart
Walt Matthews
Walter Millies
Tom Mooney
Hal Newhouser
Joe Pittman
Jim Pransky
Ramee Richards
Deron Rombach
Ross Sapp
Rick Schroeder
Tad Slowik
Lynwood Stallings
Kevin Stein
Ronnie Stevens
Frankie Thon
Paul Weaver
Gene Wellman
Greg Whitworth
Advance scouts
Stan Benjamin
George Brophy
Charlie Fox
Howie Haak
Dick Hager

SCHEDULE KEY

H—Home game.   *All-Star Game at San Diego/Jack Murphy Stadium.
N—Night game (any game starting after 5 p.m.).

SPRING TRAINING ROSTER

Manager—Art Howe (18).

Coaches—Bob Cluck (55), Matt Galante (48), Rudy Jaramillo (42), Ed Ott (14), Tom Spencer (52).

No.	PITCHERS	B/T	Ht./Wt.	Born	1991 clubs
41	Blair, Willie	R/R	6-1/185	12-18-65	Colorado Springs, Cleveland
46	Bowen, Ryan	R/R	6-0/185	2-10-68	Tucson, Houston
35	Capel, Mike	R/R	6-1/175	10-13-61	Houston, Tucson
39	Gardner, Chris	R/R	6-0/175	3-30-69	Jackson, Houston
60	Griffiths, Brian	R/R	6-2/190	5-29-68	Osceola
27	Harnisch, Pete	R/R	6-0/207	9-23-66	Houston
50	Henry, Butch	L/L	6-1/195	10-7-68	Tucson
31	Hernandez, Xavier	L/R	6-2/185	8-16-65	Tucson, Houston
37	Jones, Jimmy	R/R	6-2/190	4-20-64	Houston
59	Jones, Todd	L/R	6-3/200	4-24-68	Osceola, Jackson
44	Juden, Jeff	R/R	6-7/245	1-19-71	Jackson, Tucson, Houston
57	Kile, Darryl	R/R	6-5/185	12-2-68	Houston
56	Mallicoat, Rob	L/L	6-3/180	11-16-64	Jackson, Tucson, Houston
29	Osuna, Al	L/L	6-3/200	8-10-65	Houston
51	Portugal, Mark	R/R	6-0/190	10-30-62	Houston
38	Reynolds, Shane	R/R	6-3/210	3-26-68	Jackson
19	Schilling, Curt	R/R	6-4/215	11-14-66	Tucson, Houston
47	Simon, Richie	R/R	6-2/200	11-29-65	Jackson
63	Turner, Matt	R/R	6-5/215	2-18-67	Richmond, Tucson
53	Williams, Brian	R/R	6-2/195	2-15-69	Osceola, Jackson, Tucson, Houston

No.	CATCHERS	B/T	Ht./Wt.	Born	1991 clubs
7	Biggio, Craig	R/R	5-11/180	12-14-65	Houston
10	Eusebio, Tony	R/R	6-2/180	4-27-67	Jackson, Tucson, Houston
9	Servais, Scott	R/R	6-2/195	6-4-67	Tucson, Houston
6	Taubensee, Ed	L/R	6-4/205	10-31-68	Cleveland, Colorado Springs
20	Tucker, Eddie	R/R	6-2/205	11-18-66	Shreveport

No.	INFIELDERS	B/T	Ht./Wt.	Born	1991 clubs
5	Bagwell, Jeff	R/R	6-0/195	5-27-68	Houston
11	Caminiti, Ken	S/R	6-0/200	4-21-63	Houston
1	Candaele, Casey	S/R	5-9/165	1-12-61	Houston
17	Cedeno, Andujar	R/R	6-1/168	8-21-69	Tucson, Houston
36	Cooper, Gary	R/R	6-1/200	8-13-64	Tucson, Houston
23	Guerrero, Juan	R/R	5-11/160	2-1-67	Shreveport
64	Miller, Orlando	R/R	6-1/180	1-13-69	Osceola, Jackson
23	Mota, Andy	R/R	5-10/180	3-4-66	Tucson, Houston
15	Yelding, Eric	R/R	5-11/165	2-22-65	Houston, Tucson

No.	OUTFIELDERS	B/T	Ht./Wt.	Born	1991 clubs
21	Anthony, Eric	L/L	6-2/195	11-8-67	Houston, Tucson
12	Finley, Steve	L/L	6-2/180	3-12-65	Houston
26	Gonzalez, Luis	L/R	6-2/180	9-3-67	Houston
4	Rhodes, Karl	L/L	5-11/170	8-21-68	Houston, Tucson
22	Simms, Mike	R/R	6-4/185	1-12-67	Tucson, Houston
2	Young, Gerald	S/R	6-2/185	10-22-64	Tucson, Houston

BALLPARK INFORMATION

Ballpark (capacity, surface)
The Astrodome (54,816, artificial)
Address
P.O. Box 288
Houston, TX 77001-0288
Business phone
713-799-9500
Ticket information
713-799-9555
Ticket prices
$12 (field box)
$10 (mezzanine)
$8 (loge)
$7 (upper box terrace)
$6 (upper box)
$5 (upper reserved)
Field dimensions (from home plate)
To left field at foul line, 330 feet
To center field, 400 feet
To right field at foul line, 330 feet
First game played
April 12, 1965 (Phillies 2, Astros 0)

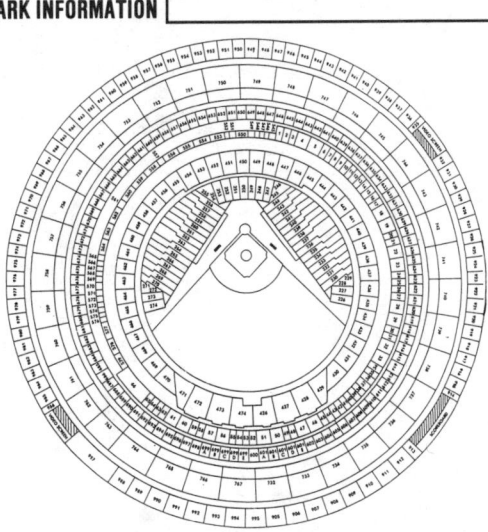

MINOR LEAGUE AFFILIATES

Class	Team	League	Manager
AAA	Tucson	Pacific Coast	Bob Skinner
AA	Jackson	Texas	Rick Sweet
A	Osceola	Florida State	Sal Butera
A	Burlington, Ia.	Midwest	Steve Curry
A	Asheville	South Atlantic	Tim Tolman
A	Auburn	New York-Pennsylvania	Steve Dillard
Rookie	Gulf Coast Astros	Gulf Coast	Julio Linares

☐ BROADCAST INFORMATION ☐

Radio: KPRC-AM (940). Broadcasters: Milo Hamilton, Larry Dierker, Bill Brown, Vince Cotroneo. KXYZ-AM (1320, Spanish language). Broadcasters: Rolando Becerra, Orlando Sanchez Diego.
TV: KTXH-TV (Channel 20). Broadcasters: Milo Hamilton, Larry Dierker, Bill Brown.
Cable TV: Home Sports Entertainment. Broadcasters: Milo Hamilton, Enos Cabell, Bill Worrell, Bill Brown.

SPRING TRAINING

Ballpark (city): Osceola County Stadium (Kissimmee, Fla.).
Ticket information: 407-933-2520.

HISTORY

YEAR-BY-YEAR RECORDS

Year	Pos.	W	L	Pct.	*GB	Year	Pos.	W	L	Pct.	*GB
1962	8th	64	96	.400	36½	1979	2nd	89	73	.549	1½
1963	9th	66	96	.407	33	1980	1st†‡	93	70	.571	+ 1
1964	9th	66	96	.407	27	1981	3rd/1st	61	49	.555	§*
1965	9th	65	97	.401	32	1982	5th	77	85	.475	12
1966	8th	72	90	.444	23	1983	3rd	85	77	.525	6
1967	9th	69	93	.426	32½	1984	T2nd	80	82	.494	12
1968	10th	72	90	.444	25	1985	T3rd	83	79	.512	12
1969	5th	81	81	.500	12	1986	1st‡	96	66	.593	+10
1970	4th	79	83	.488	23	1987	3rd	76	86	.469	14
1971	T4th	79	83	.488	11	1988	5th	82	80	.506	12½
1972	2nd	84	69	.549	10½	1989	3rd	86	76	.531	6
1973	4th	82	80	.506	17	1990	T4th	75	87	.463	16
1974	4th	81	81	.500	21	1991	6th	65	97	.401	29
1975	6th	64	97	.398	43½						
1976	3rd	80	82	.494	22						
1977	3rd	81	81	.500	17						
1978	5th	74	88	.457	21						

*Games behind winner. †Won division playoff. ‡Lost Championship Series. §Lost division playoff. ★First half 28-29; second 33-20.

MANAGERS

Name	Record	Years
Harry Craft	191-280	'62-64
Lum Harris	70-105	'64-65
Grady Hatton	164-221	'66-68
Harry Walker	355-353	'68-72
Leo Durocher	98-95	'72-73
Preston Gomez	128-161	'73-75
Bill Virdon	544-522	'75-82
Bob Lillis	276-261	'82-85
Hal Lanier	254-232	'86-88
Art Howe	226-260	'89-91

DAY BY DAY

Date	Opp.	Res.	Score (inn.*)	Hits	Opp. hits	Winning pitcher	Losing pitcher	Save	Record	Pos.	GB
4-8	At Cin.	L	2-6	5	10	Browning	Scott	Dibble	0-1	6th	1
4-10	At Cin.	L	5-6	8	9	Power	Kile	Myers	0-2	T5th	2
4-11	At Cin.	W	4-1	9	3	Harnisch	Charlton	Schilling	1-2	T4th	1½
4-12	S.F.	W	3-2	9	7	Portugal	Reuschel	Henry	2-2	4th	1
4-13	S.F.	L	2-16	6	19	Garrelts	Scott	Gunderson	2-3	T4th	2
4-14	S.F.	W	7-2	10	6	Jones	Burkett		3-3	T2nd	2
4-15	At Atl.	W	3-1	6	5	Osuna	Mercker	Schilling	4-3	2nd	2
4-16	At Atl.	L	4-10	9	13	Sisk	Hernandez		4-4	T2nd	2
4-17	At Atl.	W	4-3	7	6	Portugal	Avery	Schilling	5-4	2nd	1
4-19	At S.F.	L	2-5	8	9	Burkett	Jones	Brantley	5-5	T3rd	1½
4-20	At S.F.	L	0-4	5	9	Black	Deshaies		5-6	T3rd	2½
4-21	At S.F.	L	0-1	4	5	Righetti	Schilling		5-7	5th	2½
4-22	Cin.	W	2-1	9	4	Henry	Myers		6-7	T3rd	2½
4-23	Cin.	L	1-3	5	10	Hammond	Corsi	Dibble	6-8	T4th	3½
4-24	Cin.	W	1-0 (13)	10	3	Henry	Scudder		7-8	T3rd	3½
4-26	Atl.	L	2-7	9	9	Leibrandt	Deshaies		7-9	5th	3½
4-27	Atl.	L	1-2 (13)	7	12	Sisk	Corsi	Parrett	7-10	6th	3½
4-28	Atl.	W	2-0	8	5	Jones	Glavine	Henry	8-10	5th	2½
4-30	At Chi.	L	3-10	7	12	Bielecki	Portugal		8-11	5th	3
5-1	At Chi.	L	8-11	10	12	Maddux	Deshaies		8-12	5th	3
5-3	At Pit.	L	0-1	4	2	Smith	Harnisch		8-13	5th	3
5-4	At Pit.	W	8-3	13	8	Jones	Smiley	Clancy	9-13	5th	3
5-5	At Pit.	W	6-4	11	5	Portugal	Drabek	Schilling	10-13	5th	3
5-6	Chi.	L	3-4	5	9	Maddux	Deshaies	Smith	10-14	5th	3½
5-7	Chi.	L	3-4	8	8	Scanlan	Hernandez	Smith	10-15	5th	4½
5-8	Chi.	W	4-2	7	8	Harnisch	Boskie	Schilling	11-15	5th	3½
5-10	St.L.	L	5-7 (10)	12	11	Agosto	Schilling	L. Smith	11-16	5th	3
5-11	St.L.	W	6-1	10	3	Portugal	DeLeon		12-16	5th	3
5-12	St.L.	L	3-7	9	12	Carpenter	Osuna		12-17	5th	4
5-14	Pit.	L	3-6	9	12	Smith	Harnisch		12-18	5th	4½
5-15	Pit.	L	7-8	18	11	Kipper	Schilling	Landrum	12-19	5th	5½
5-16	Pit.	L	4-6	12	11	Drabek	Clancy	Belinda	12-20	5th	6
5-17	At St.L.	W	5-4	10	7	Deshaies	L. Smith	Osuna	13-20	5th	6
5-18	At St.L.	L	2-12	3	18	B. Smith	Hernandez		13-21	5th	6
5-19	At St.L.	L	2-9	4	13	Hill	Harnisch		13-22	5th	7
5-20	L.A.	W	4-1	8	4	Jones	Gross	Osuna	14-22	5th	6
5-21	L.A.	L	3-7	6	11	Ojeda	Corsi		14-23	5th	7
5-22	L.A.	W	3-2	9	3	Deshaies	Morgan	Osuna	15-23	5th	6
5-23	L.A.	L	0-2	6	7	Belcher	Hernandez	Howell	15-24	5th	7
5-24	S.D.	W	1-0	5	3	Schilling	Benes		16-24	5th	7
5-25	S.D.	L	2-4 (10)	7	8	Rodriguez	Osuna	Lefferts	16-25	5th	8
5-26	S.D.	W	13-3	14	8	Portugal	Whitson		17-25	5th	7
5-27	At L.A.	L	1-4	6	9	Morgan	Deshaies	Howell	17-26	5th	8
5-28	At L.A.	L	2-8	11	9	Belcher	Hernandez		17-27	5th	9
5-29	At L.A.	W	8-2	16	5	Harnisch	Hershiser	Osuna	18-27	5th	8
5-30	At S.D.	L	0-4	9	9	Rasmussen	Jones		18-28	5th	9
5-31	At S.D.	L	4-5	4	9	Melendez	Portugal	Lefferts	18-29	5th	9
6-1	At S.D.	L	2-7	7	8	Hurst	Deshaies		18-30	5th	9
6-2	At S.D.	L	1-3	2	5	Peterson	Hernandez	Lefferts	18-31	5th	10
6-4	Mon.	L	1-4	5	8	Gardner	Harnisch	Jones	18-32	6th	10
6-5	Mon.	L	2-8	8	14	Martinez	Jones		18-33	6th	11
6-6	Mon.	W	9-8	17	12	Schilling	Jones		19-33	6th	11
6-7	N.Y.	L	3-6	8	7	Simons	Schilling		19-34	6th	12
6-8	N.Y.	L	3-4 (11)	11	11	Pena	Capel	Franco	19-35	6th	12
6-9	N.Y.	W	1-0	3	3	Harnisch	Cone		20-35	6th	12
6-10	N.Y.	W	6-4	11	8	Schilling	Franco	Capel	21-35	6th	12
6-11	Phi.	W	1-0 (11)	8	6	Osuna	McDowell		22-35	6th	11½
6-12	Phi.	W	3-2	9	4	Osuna	Boever		23-35	5th	10½
6-13	Phi.	L	4-5	11	3	DeJesus	Kile	Williams	23-36	5th	11½
6-14	At N.Y.	W	4-1	11	4	Capel	Franco	Clancy	24-36	5th	11½
6-15	At N.Y.	L	0-6	3	9	Gooden	Jones		24-37	5th	11½
6-16	At N.Y.	W	5-4	11	9	Portugal	Viola	Osuna	25-37	5th	11½
6-17	At Mon.	L	2-3 (16)	12	6	Fassero	Schilling		25-38	5th	12½
6-18	At Mon.	L	2-3 (12)	8	4	Sampen	Corsi		25-39	5th	13½
6-19	At Mon.	L	1-3	5	5	Gardner	Harnisch	Fassero	25-40	6th	14½
6-20	At Phi.	L	3-7	5	14	Cox	Jones		25-41	6th	15½
6-21	At Phi.	L	0-3	4	5	Ruffin	Portugal	Williams	25-42	6th	15½
6-22	At Phi.	W	4-3 (10)	10	8	Osuna	McDowell	Capel	26-42	6th	15½
6-23	At Phi.	W	6-4	11	7	Kile	DeJesus	Clancy	27-42	6th	15½
6-25	Atl.	W	1-0	6	6	Harnisch	Glavine		28-42	6th	14½

HOUSTON ASTROS

1992 SEASON

HOUSTON ASTROS

Date	Opp.	Res.	Score (inn.*)	Hits	Opp. hits	Winning pitcher	Losing pitcher	Save	Record	Pos.	GB
6-26	Atl.	L	2-3	5	8	Stanton	Clancy	Berenguer	28-43	6th	14½
6-27	Atl.	L	0-3	3	6	Leibrandt	Portugal		28-44	6th	15
6-28	At Cin.	L	5-8	9	14	Browning	Deshaies	Dibble	28-45	6th	15½
6-29	At Cin.	W	6-2	8	9	Kile	Carman	Clancy	29-45	6th	15½
6-30	At Cin.	L	4-5	8	11	Hammond	Harnisch	Dibble	29-46	6th	16½
7-2	At S.F.	W	8-4	14	8	Portugal	Black		30-46	6th	16½
7-3	At S.F.	W	9-0	12	6	Deshaies	Burkett		31-46	6th	16½
7-4	At S.F.	W	14-6	13	14	Kile	Wilson		32-46	6th	15½
7-5	Cin.	L	0-1	5	5	Hammond	Harnisch	Dibble	32-47	6th	15½
7-6	Cin.	W	3-0	3	3	Jones	Armstrong		33-47	6th	15½
7-7	Cin.	W	7-3	13	6	Portugal	Browning		34-47	6th	15½
7-11	At Chi.	W	6-4 (11)	8	9	Osuna	Smith	Capel	35-47	T5th	14½
7-12	At Chi.	L	2-5	4	10	Castillo	Portugal	Assenmacher	35-48	T5th	14½
7-13	At Chi.	L	3-4	10	9	Lancaster	Capel		35-49	6th	15
7-14	At Chi.	L	3-4	13	5	Bielecki	Kile	Assenmacher	35-50	6th	14½
7-15	At Pit.	L	0-8	5	13	Tomlin	Jones		35-51	6th	14½
7-16	At Pit.	L	4-6	8	9	Smith	Kile	Belinda	35-52	6th	14½
7-17	At Pit.	W	10-2	15	9	Jones	Drabek	Osuna	36-52	6th	13½
7-19	Chi.	W	5-2	9	5	Harnisch	Scanlan	Osuna	37-52	6th	13
7-20	Chi.	L	0-6	8	10	Maddux	Kile		37-53	6th	14
7-21	Chi.	L	2-4	9	8	Castillo	Clancy		37-54	6th	14
7-22	At St.L.	L	1-9	7	7	DeLeon	Bowen		37-55	6th	14½
7-23	At St.L.	L	1-5	6	9	B. Smith	Deshaies		37-56	6th	15½
7-24	At St.L.	L	3-4	5	13	L. Smith	Osuna		37-57	6th	16½
7-26	Pit.	L	1-8	5	11	Heaton	Kile		37-58	6th	18
7-27	Pit.	L	5-11	10	16	Tomlin	Jones		37-59	6th	19
7-28	Pit.	W	9-7	12	9	Bowen	Smith	Clancy	38-59	6th	18
7-29	St.L.	W	6-2	10	9	Deshaies	B. Smith		39-59	6th	17
7-30	St.L.	W	7-5	10	7	Osuna	Carpenter		40-59	6th	17
7-31	St.L.	W	9-5	9	10	Kile	Tewksbury	Wilkins	41-59	6th	17
8-2	L.A.	W	9-8	9	12	Wilkins	Howell		42-59	6th	16
8-3	L.A.	W	2-1 (10)	8	7	Wilkins	Howell		43-59	6th	15
8-4	L.A.	W	2-1 (10)	6	5	Osuna	Gross		44-59	6th	14
8-5	S.D.	W	2-1 (12)	10	8	Henry	Andersen		45-59	6th	13
8-6	S.D.	W	6-1	10	5	Kile	Peterson	Osuna	46-59	6th	13
8-7	S.D.	L	4-7	8	10	Hurst	Wilkins	Andersen	46-60	6th	14
8-8	S.D.	L	3-5	9	9	Benes	Bowen	Lefferts	46-61	6th	15
8-9	At Atl.	L	2-7	9	11	Avery	Deshaies		46-62	6th	15
8-10	At Atl.	L	0-4	4	8	Smoltz	Harnisch		46-63	6th	15
8-11	At Atl.	L	1-3	4	8	Reynoso	Kile	Stanton	46-64	6th	15
8-12	At S.D.	L	5-6	6	13	Melendez	Capel	Lefferts	46-65	6th	16
8-13	At S.D.	W	12-9	12	6	Bowen	Maddux	Osuna	47-65	6th	15
8-14	At S.D.	L	1-4	5	9	Rasmussen	Deshaies	Andersen	47-66	6th	16
8-15	At L.A.	W	6-1	8	5	Harnisch	Martinez		48-66	6th	15
8-16	At L.A.	L	1-4 (13)	7	7	Gross	Corsi		48-67	6th	16
8-17	At L.A.	L	7-8 (10)	11	15	Howell	Henry		48-68	6th	17
8-18	At L.A.	W	8-4	12	9	Portugal	Morgan	Mallicoat	49-68	6th	16
8-20	S.F.	L	3-9	7	8	Downs	Jones	Brantley	49-69	6th	17½
8-21	S.F.	W	13-4	17	8	Harnisch	Black		50-69	6th	17½
8-22	S.F.	L	8-11	11	15	Brantley	Kile	Righetti	50-70	6th	18
8-23	Mon.	W	9-2	11	6	Bowen	Martinez		51-70	6th	17
8-24	Mon.	L	1-5	5	8	Rojas	Portugal		51-71	6th	17
8-25	Mon.	L	0-4	3	7	Gardner	Deshaies	Fassero	51-72	6th	17
8-26	N.Y.	L	4-6 (10)	9	11	Franco	Henry		51-73	6th	18
8-27	N.Y.	W	8-3	10	8	Kile	Whitehurst	Schilling	52-73	6th	17
8-28	At Phi.	L	10-11 (10)	15	11	Hartley	Osuna		52-74	6th	18
8-29	At Phi.	W	5-1	11	6	Portugal	Cox		53-74	6th	18
8-30	At Mon.	L	1-3	4	11	Gardner	Deshaies	Jones	53-75	6th	19
8-31	At Mon.	L	4-5 (10)	7	10	Fassero	Osuna		53-76	6th	19
9-1	At Mon.	L	1-6	4	9	Nabholz	Kile		53-77	6th	19
9-2	At N.Y.	W	3-0	12	6	Bowen	Viola	Osuna	54-77	6th	18
9-3	At N.Y.	L	1-6	8	10	Young	Portugal		54-78	6th	19
9-4	At N.Y.	W	8-3	10	10	Deshaies	Cone		55-78	6th	19
9-6	Phi.	W	3-1	6	4	Harnisch	DeJesus	Osuna	56-78	6th	18½
9-7	Phi.	W	6-0	9	5	Kile	Ruffin		57-78	6th	18½
9-8	Phi.	L	0-5	3	14	Mulholland	Bowen		57-79	6th	19½
9-9	S.D.	L	0-3	5	7	Benes	Portugal	Lefferts	57-80	6th	20½
9-10	S.D.	L	6-7	12	8	Rasmussen	Gardner	Lefferts	57-81	6th	21
9-11	L.A.	L	1-9	8	14	Hershiser	Harnisch		57-82	6th	22
9-12	L.A.	L	2-6 (10)	7	7	McDowell	Osuna		57-83	6th	23
9-13	At Cin.	L	2-13	7	17	Armstrong	Bowen		57-84	6th	23½
9-14	At Cin.	W	7-3	12	7	Hernandez	Dibble	Schilling	58-84	6th	23
9-15	At Cin.	L	0-10	6	11	Rijo	Gardner		58-85	6th	24
9-16	At S.D.	L	1-6	8	10	Harris	Williams	Andersen	58-86	6th	24

Date	Opp.	Res.	Score (inn.*)	Hits	Opp. hits	Winning pitcher	Losing pitcher	Save	Record	Pos.	GB
9-17	At S.D.	W	3-0	6	6	Harnisch	Hurst	Hernandez	59-86	6th	23½
9-18	At L.A.	L	4-5	9	8	Morgan	Mallicoat	Wilson	59-87	6th	24½
9-19	At L.A.	L	3-4	6	6	Gross	Portugal	McDowell	59-88	6th	25½
9-20	Cin.	W	3-2	7	4	Bowen	Rijo	Hernandez	60-88	6th	25
9-21	Cin.	L	1-4	3	8	Scudder	Juden	Dibble	60-89	6th	25½
9-22	Cin.	W	4-1	9	6	Hernandez	Browning	Portugal	61-89	6th	25½
9-23	S.F.	W	8-0	16	5	Harnisch	Wilson	Schilling	62-89	6th	25
9-24	S.F.	L	7-9	14	8	Beck	Portugal		62-90	6th	26
9-25	S.F.	L	1-2	6	4	Burkett	Kile	Brantley	62-91	6th	26
9-27	Atl.	L	2-4	7	9	Wohlers	Mallicoat	Pena	62-92	6th	27
9-28	Atl.	L	4-5	7	7	Stanton	Hernandez	Pena	62-93	6th	27
9-29	Atl.	L	5-6 (13)	12	12	Clancy	Portugal		62-94	6th	28
9-30	At S.F.	W	2-0	3	6	Gardner	Heredia	Hernandez	63-94	6th	28
10-1	At S.F.	L	4-6	11	7	Burkett	Kile	Brantley	63-95	6th	29
10-2	At S.F.	W	7-5	11	9	Bowen	McClellan	Osuna	64-95	6th	28
10-4	At Atl.	L	2-5	4	8	Avery	Juden	Pena	64-96	6th	29
10-5	At Atl.	L	2-5	8	8	Smoltz	Portugal		64-97	6th	30
10-6	At Atl.	W	8-3	12	6	Harnisch	Leibrandt		65-97	6th	29

Monthly records: April (8-11), May (10-18), June (11-17), July (12-13), August (12-17), September (10-18), Oct. (2-3).

HIGHLIGHTS

High point: After losing seven straight games, the Astros won a season-high nine consecutive games from July 28 through August 6. Included in that winning streak was a three-game sweep of one-run games from Los Angeles.

Low point: With a chance to play a spoiler's role in the National League West race, the Astros went 1-9 against Atlanta and Los Angeles in September and October. The Braves clinched the title against the Astros on October 5.

Turning point: The Astros won five of six games before the All-Star break and were within one game of getting out of last place. But in the next 15 games they were 3-12, virtually ensuring a last-place finish.

Most valuable player: First baseman Jeff Bagwell. He became the first Houston player to win the Rookie of the Year award, hitting .294 with a team-high 15 home runs and 82 runs batted in.

Most valuable pitcher: Righthander Pete Harnisch. Despite a lack of run support Harnisch finished 12-9 with a 2.70 earned-run average. He ranked among the league's top 10 in ERA, strikeouts (172) and shutouts (two).

Most improved player: Second baseman Casey Candaele. He got a chance to play every day and responded. Candaele hit .262 with 50 RBIs despite batting eighth most of the time.

Most pleasant surprise: Center fielder Steve Finley. He led the Astros in games played (159), at-bats (596), hits (170), triples (10) and stolen bases (34). Finley tied Bagwell for the lead in total bases (242) and played solid defensively.

Biggest disappointment: Lefthander Jim Deshaies. When Mike Scott was shelved early in the season with rotator cuff tendinitis, the Astros looked to Deshaies to anchor the rotation. But for the second straight season, Deshaies faltered, going 5-12 with a 4.98 ERA.

Key injuries: The Astros knew Scott's off-season rotator cuff surgery would make him a question mark in 1991. After two starts in April, his season was finished. Scott retired at the end of the year. Mark Portugal was 8-5 when he went on the disabled list with a groin injury July 19. He returned August 12 but went 2-7 the rest of the season.

Notable: Houston finished the season with a 37-44 home record, its first losing season at home since 1975. . . . The Astros' 65-97 record matched their highest loss total in club history and allowed the team to keep intact its streak as the only N.L. team never to have lost 100 games in a season.

— NEIL HOHLFELD

RECORDS

1991 regular-season record: 65-97 (6th in N.L. West); 37-44 at home; 28-53 on road; 28-44 vs. East; 37-53 vs. West; 23-39 vs. LHP; 42-58 vs. RHP; 18-30 on grass; 47-67 on turf; 15-23 in daytime; 50-74 at night; 19-28 in one-run games; 7-13 in extra-inning games; 0-0 in doubleheaders.

Team record last five years: 384-426 (.474), ranks 10th in league in that span).

TEAM LEADERS

Batting average: Craig Biggio (.295).
At-bats: Steve Finley (596).
Runs: Steve Finley (84).
Hits: Steve Finley (170).
Total bases: Jeff Bagwell, Steve Finley (242).
Doubles: Ken Caminiti (30).
Triples: Steve Finley (10).
Home runs: Jeff Bagwell (15).
Runs batted in: Jeff Bagwell (82).
Stolen bases: Steve Finley (34).
Slugging percentage: Jeff Bagwell (.437).
On-base percentage: Jeff Bagwell (.387).
Wins: Pete Harnisch (12).
Earned-run average: Pete Harnisch (2.70).
Complete games: Pete Harnisch (4).
Shutouts: Pete Harnisch (2).
Saves: Al Osuna (12).
Innings pitched: Pete Harnisch (216⅔).
Strikeouts: Pete Harnisch (172).

GAMES BY POSITION

Catcher: Craig Biggio 139, Carl Nichols 17, Scott Servais 14, Tony Eusebio 9.
First base: Jeff Bagwell 155, Ken Oberkfell 13, Jose Tolentino 10, Dave Rohde 1.
Second base: Casey Candaele 109, Andy Mota 27, Rafael Ramirez 27, Mark McLemore 19, Dave Rohde 4, Craig Biggio 3.
Third base: Ken Caminiti 152, Casey Candaele 11, Cary Cooper 4, Ken Oberkfell 4, Dave Rohde 3, Rafael Ramirez 2.
Shortstop: Eric Yelding 72, Andujar Cedeno 66, Rafael Ramirez 45, Dave Rohde 3.
Outfield: Steve Finley 153, Luis Gonzalez 133, Gerald Young 84, Mark Davidson 63, Karl Rhodes 44, Mike Simms 41, Eric Anthony 37, Casey Candaele 26, Javier Ortiz 24, Kenny Lofton 20, Eric Yelding 4, Craig Biggio 2, Jose Tolentino 1.

TOP 10 DRAFT CHOICES

1a. John Burke, RHP, Univ. of Florida.
1b. Shawn Livsey, SS, Simeon High School, Chicago.
1c. Jim Gonzalez, C, East Hartford (Conn.) High School.
1d. Mike Groppuso, 3B, Seton Hall University.
2a. Buck McNabb, OF, Fort Walton Beach (Fla.) High School.
2b. Jimmy Lewis, RHP, Florida State.
2c. Eddy Ramos, 3B, American High School, Hialeah, Fla.
3. Chris Durkin, OF, Youngstown State University.
4. Brian Holliday, RHP, San Diego State.
5. Dan Grapenthien, 1B/OF, Thornton Fractional South High School, Lansing, Ill.
6. Todd Hobson, OF, Indiana State.
7. James Mouton, OF, St. Mary's (Calif.) College.
8. Tom Anderson, RHP, Univ. of Iowa.
9. Angelo Lee, OF, Simeon High School, Chicago.
10. Joshua Spring, RHP, Lebanon (Ohio) High School.

— 115 —

LOS ANGELES DODGERS
NATIONAL LEAGUE WEST DIVISION

1992 SCHEDULE

APRIL

S	M	T	W	T	F	S
5	6 SF H	7 N SF H	8 N	9 N SD	10 N SD	11 N SD
12 SD	13 N HOU	14 N HOU	15 N HOU H	16 N ATL H	17 N ATL H	18 N ATL H
19 ATL H	20 N CIN	21 N CIN	22 N CIN H	23	24 N SF	25 SF
26 SF	27 N STL	28 N STL H	29 N PHI H	30 N PHI H		

MAY

S	M	T	W	T	F	S
					1 N MON H	2 N MON H
3 MON H	4	5 N PHI	6 N PHI	7	8 N NY	9 NY
10 NY	11 N MON	12 N MON	13 N MON	14	15 N NY H	16 N NY H
17 NY H	18 N CHI H	19 N CHI H	20 N CHI H	21	22 N PIT	23 N PIT
24 PIT H	25 STL	26 N STL	27 N STL	28	29 N CHI	30 CHI
31 CHI						

JUNE

S	M	T	W	T	F	S
	1 N PIT	2 N PIT	3 N PIT	4 N CIN H	5 N CIN H	6 N CIN H
7 CIN H	8 N ATL H	9 N ATL H	10 N ATL H	11	12 N CIN	13 CIN
14 CIN	15 N ATL	16 N ATL	17 N ATL	18	19 N HOU	20 HOU
21 HOU	22 N SD	23 N SD	24	25 N HOU H	26 N HOU H	27 N HOU H
28 HOU H	29 N SD H	30 N SD H				

JULY

S	M	T	W	T	F	S
			1 N SD H	2 H PHI	3 N PHI H	4 N PHI H
5 PHI H	6 N MON H	7 N MON H	8 N MON H	9 N STL	10 N STL H	11 STL H
12 STL H	13	14 ★	15	16 N PHI	17 PHI	18 N PHI
19 PHI	20 N NY	21 N NY	22 N NY	23	24 N MON	25 MON
26 MON	27 N SF	28 N SF	29 N SF	30 H SD	31 N SD H	

AUGUST

S	M	T	W	T	F	S
						1 N SD H
2 SD H	3	4 N HOU H	5 N HOU H	6	7 N ATL	8 ATL
9 ATL	10 N CIN	11 N CIN	12 N CIN	13 CIN	14 N SF H	15 N SF H
16 SF H	17 N NY H	18 N NY H	19 N NY H	20 N NY	21 N CHI H	22 N CHI H
23 CHI H	24 N PIT H	25 N PIT H	26 N PIT H	27	28 N STL	29 N STL
30 STL	31 N CHI					

SEPTEMBER

S	M	T	W	T	F	S
		1 N CHI	2 CHI	3	4 N PIT	5 N PIT
6 PIT	7 ATL	8 N ATL	9 N SD	10 N SD H	11 N SF H	12 N SF H
13 SF H	14 N SD	15 N SD	16 SD	17	18 N SF	19 SF
20 N SF	21 ATL H	22 N ATL H	23 N CIN H	24 N CIN H	25 N HOU H	26 N HOU H
27 HOU H	28	29 N CIN	30 N CIN			

OCTOBER

S	M	T	W	T	F	S
				1	2 N CIN	3 N HOU
4 HOU	5	6	7	8	9	10

1992 SEASON

CLUB DIRECTORY

Board of directors
Peter O'Malley
Harry M. Bardt
Roland Seidler
Mrs. Roland (Terry) Seidler

President
Peter O'Malley

Executive vice president, player personnel
Fred Claire

Vice president, communications
Tom Hawkins

Vice president, finance
Bob Graziano

Vice president, marketing
Barry Stockhamer

Vice president, stadium operations
Bob Smith

Vice president, ticket operations
Walter Nash

Vice president, treasurer
Roland Seidler

Vice president, Campo Las Palmas
Ralph Avila

Assistant to the president
Ike Ikuhara

Assistant secretary and general counsel
Santiago Fernandez

Director, accounting and finance
Bill Foltz

Director, advertising and special events
Paul Kalil

Director, broadcasting and publications
Brent Shyer

Director, community relations
Don Newcombe

Community relations
Roy Campanella

Dir., human resources and administration
Irene Tanji

Director, management information systems
Mike Mularky

Director, minor league operations
Charlie Blaney

Director, scouting
Terry Reynolds

Director, publicity
Jay Lucas

Assistant director, publicity
Chuck Harris

Traveling secretary
Bill DeLury

Director, stadium operations
Jim Italiane

Director, ticket operations
Debra Duncan

Director, ticket marketing
Allan Erselius

Club physicians
Dr. Frank W. Jobe
Dr. Michael F. Mellman
Dr. Herndon Harding

Scouts
Eleodoro Arias
Eddie Bane
Bill Barkley
Gil Bassetti
Rick Birmingham
Bob Bishop
Gib Bodet
Flores Bolivar
Mike Brito
Joe Campbell
Jim Chapman
Bob Darwin
Eddie Fajardo
Lin Garrett
Ossie Alvarez Gonzalez
Rafael Gonzalez
Michael Hankins
Dick Hanlon
Dennis Haren
Gail Henley
Hank Jones
Lon Joyce
John Keenan
Gary LaRocque
Juan Latigua
Don LeJohn
Carl Lowenstine
Manuel Lunar
Teodoro Mata
Dale McReynolds
Bob Miske
Tommy Mixon
Luis Angel Montalvo
Victor Nazario
Alberto Osorio
Deni Pacini
Camilo Pasqual
Pablo Peguero
Cornelio Pena
Jose Pena
Claude Pelletier
Bill Pleis
Silvano Quesada
Mark Sheehy
Jim Stoeckel
Dick Teed
Tom Thomas
Glen Van Proyen

Special assignment scouts
Mel Didier
Phil Regan
Jerry Stephenson
Gary Sutherland

SCHEDULE KEY

H—Home game.   *All-Star Game at San Diego/Jack Murphy Stadium.
N—Night game (any game starting after 5 p.m.).

SPRING TRAINING ROSTER

Manager—Tom Lasorda (2).

Coaches—Joe Amalfitano (8), Mark Cresse (58), Joe Ferguson (13), Ben Hines (37), Manny Mota (11), Ron Perranoski (16).

No.	PITCHERS	B/T	Ht./Wt.	Born	1991 clubs
56	Astacio, Pedro	R/R	6-2/174	11-28-69	Vero Beach, San Antonio
54	Candelaria, John	R/L	6-6/225	11-6-53	Los Angeles
49	Candiotti, Tom	R/R	6-2/200	8-31-57	Cleveland, Toronto
52	Crews, Tim	R/R	6-0/195	4-3-61	Los Angeles
35	Gott, Jim	R/R	6-4/220	8-3-59	Los Angeles
45	Gross, Kevin	R/R	6-5/215	6-8-61	Los Angeles
57	Gross, Kip	R/R	6-2/190	8-24-64	Nashville, Cincinnati
55	Hershiser, Orel	R/R	6-3/192	9-16-58	Bakersfield, San Antonio, Albuquerque, Los Angeles
50	Howell, Jay	R/R	6-3/220	11-26-55	Los Angeles
59	James, Mike	R/R	6-3/180	8-15-67	San Antonio, Albuquerque
45	Martinez, Pedro	R/R	5-11/150	7-25-71	Bakersfield, San Antonio, Albuquerque
48	Martinez, Ramon	L/R	6-4/173	4-22-68	Los Angeles
51	McAndrew, Jamie	R/R	6-2/190	9-2-67	Albuquerque
31	McDowell, Roger	R/R	6-1/182	12-21-60	Philadelphia, Los Angeles
17	Ojeda, Bob	L/L	6-1/195	12-17-57	Los Angeles
40	Seanez, Rudy	R/R	5-10/185	10-20-68	Colorado Springs, Cleveland, Canton-Akron
38	Wilson, Steve	L/L	6-4/195	12-13-64	Iowa, Chicago NL, Los Angeles
No.	CATCHERS	B/T	Ht./Wt.	Born	1991 clubs
61	Baar, Bryan	R/R	6-3/205	4-10-68	San Antonio
41	Hernandez, Carlos	R/R	5-11/185	5-24-67	Albuquerque, Los Angeles
60	Piazza, Mike	R/R	6-3/200	9-4-68	Bakersfield
14	Scioscia, Mike	L/R	6-2/220	11-27-58	Los Angeles
No.	INFIELDERS	B/T	Ht./Wt.	Born	1991 clubs
36	Benzinger, Todd	S/R	6-1/190	2-11-63	Cincinnati, Kansas City
3	Hamilton, Jeff	R/R	6-3/207	3-19-64	Albuquerque, Los Angeles
15	Hansen, Dave	L/R	6-0/180	11-24-68	Albuquerque, Los Angeles
29	Harris, Lenny	L/R	5-10/205	10-28-64	Los Angeles
23	Karros, Eric	R/R	6-4/205	11-4-67	Albuquerque, Los Angeles
30	Offerman, Jose	S/R	6-0/160	11-8-68	Albuquerque, Los Angeles
10	Samuel, Juan	R/R	5-11/170	12-9-60	Los Angeles
27	Sharperson, Mike	R/R	6-3/190	10-4-61	Los Angeles
21	Smith, Greg	S/R	5-11/170	4-5-67	Albuquerque, Los Angeles
52	Young, Eric	R/R	5-9/180	11-26-66	San Antonio, Albuquerque
No.	OUTFIELDERS	B/T	Ht./Wt.	Born	1991 clubs
63	Ashley, Billy	R/R	6-7/220	7-11-70	Vero Beach
22	Butler, Brett	L/L	5-10/160	6-15-67	Los Angeles
28	Daniels, Kal	L/R	5-11/205	8-20-63	Los Angeles
33	Davis, Eric	R/R	6-3/200	5-29-62	Cincinnati
47	Goodwin, Tom	L/R	6-1/165	7-27-68	Albuquerque, Los Angeles
5	Javier, Stan	S/R	6-0/185	1-9-64	Los Angeles
43	Mondesi, Raul	R/R	5-11/150	3-12-71	Bakersfield, San Antonio, Albuquerque
26	Rodriguez, Henry	L/L	6-1/180	11-8-67	Albuquerque
44	Strawberry, Darryl	L/L	6-6/200	3-12-62	Los Angeles

BALLPARK INFORMATION

Ballpark (capacity, surface)
Dodger Stadium (56,000, grass)
Address
1000 Elysian Park Ave.
Los Angeles, CA 90012
Business phone
213-224-1500
Ticket information
213-224-1400
Ticket prices
$11 (box seats)
$8 (reserved seats)
$6 (top deck and pavilion)
$3 (g.a., youth 12 and under)
Field dimensions (from home plate)
To left field at foul line, 330 feet
To center field, 395 feet
To right field at foul line, 330 feet
First game played
April 10, 1962 (Reds 6, Dodgers 3)

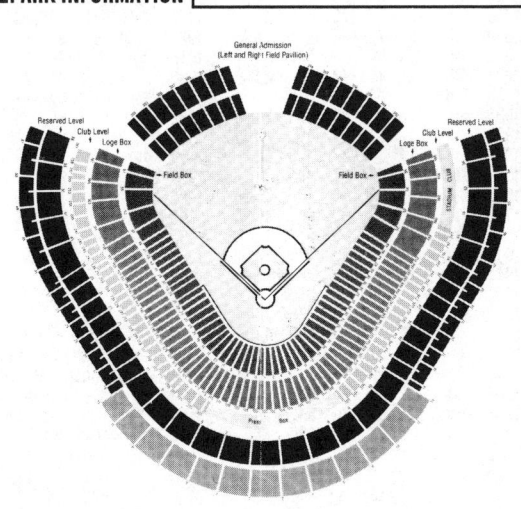

MINOR LEAGUE AFFILIATES

Class	Team	League	Manager
AAA	Albuquerque	Pacific Coast	Bill Russell
AA	San Antonio	Texas	Jerry Royster
A	Bakersfield	California	Tom Byers
A	Vero Beach	Florida State	Glenn Hoffman
A	Yakima	Northwest	Joe Vavra
Rookie	Great Falls	Pioneer	To be announced
Rookie	Port St. Lucie Dodgers	Gulf Coast	John Shoemaker

BROADCAST INFORMATION

Radio: KABC-AM (790). Broadcasters: Vin Scully, Don Drysdale, Ross Porter. KWKW-AM (1330, Spanish language). Broadcasters: Jaime Jarrin, Rene Cardenas.
TV: KTTV-TV (Channel 11). Broadcasters: Vin Scully, Don Drysdale, Ross Porter.
Cable TV: SportsChannel. Broadcasters: To be announced.

SPRING TRAINING

Ballpark (city): Holman Stadium (Vero Beach, Fla.).
Ticket information: 407-569-4900.

HISTORY

YEAR-BY-YEAR RECORDS

Year	Pos.	W	L	Pct.	*GB	Year	Pos.	W	L	Pct.	*GB
1901	3rd	79	57	.581	9½	1950	2nd	89	65	.578	2
1902	2nd	75	63	.543	27½	1951	2nd†	97	60	.618	1
1903	5th	70	66	.515	19	1952	1st	96	57	.627 + 4½	
1904	6th	56	97	.366	50	1953	1st	105	49	.682 +13	
1905	8th	48	104	.316	56½	1954	2nd	92	62	.597	5
1906	5th	66	86	.434	50	1955	1st	98	55	.641 +13½	
1907	5th	65	83	.439	40	1956	1st	93	61	.604 + 1	
1908	7th	53	101	.344	46	1957	3rd	84	70	.545	11
1909	6th	55	98	.359	55½	1958	7th	71	83	.461	21
1910	6th	64	90	.416	40	1959	1st‡	88	68	.564 + 2	
1911	7th	64	86	.427	33½	1960	4th	82	72	.532	13
1912	7th	58	95	.379	46	1961	2nd	89	65	.578	4
1913	6th	65	84	.436	34½	1962	2nd†	102	63	.618	1
1914	5th	75	79	.487	19½	1963	1st	99	63	.611 + 6	
1915	3rd	80	72	.526	10	1964	T6th	80	82	.494	13
1916	1st	94	60	.610 + 2½		1965	1st	97	65	.599 + 2	
1917	7th	70	81	.464	26½	1966	1st	95	67	.586 + 1½	
1918	5th	57	69	.452	25½	1967	8th	73	89	.451	28½
1919	5th	69	71	.493	27	1968	7th	76	86	.469	21
1920	1st	93	61	.604 + 7		1969	4th	85	77	.525	8
1921	5th	77	75	.507	16½	1970	2nd	87	74	.540	14½
1922	6th	76	78	.494	17	1971	2nd	89	73	.549	1
1923	6th	76	78	.494	19½	1972	3rd	85	70	.548	10½
1924	2nd	92	62	.597	1½	1973	2nd	95	66	.590	3½
1925	T6th	68	85	.444	27	1974	1st§	102	60	.630 + 4	
1926	6th	71	82	.464	17½	1975	2nd	88	74	.543	20
1927	6th	65	88	.425	28½	1976	2nd	92	70	.568	10
1928	6th	77	76	.503	17½	1977	1st§	98	64	.605 +10	
1929	6th	70	83	.458	28½	1978	1st§	95	67	.586 + 2½	
1930	4th	86	68	.558	6	1979	3rd	79	83	.488	11½
1931	4th	79	73	.520	21	1980	2nd★	92	71	.564	1
1932	3rd	81	73	.526	9	1981	1st/4th	63	47	.573	•§◆
1933	6th	65	88	.425	26½	1982	2nd	88	74	.543	1
1934	6th	71	81	.467	23½	1983	1st■	91	71	.652 + 3	
1935	5th	70	83	.458	29½	1984	4th	79	83	.488	13
1936	7th	67	87	.435	25	1985	1st■	95	67	.586 + 5½	
1937	6th	62	91	.405	33½	1986	5th	73	89	.451	23
1938	7th	69	80	.463	18½	1987	4th	73	89	.451	17
1939	3rd	84	69	.549	12½	1988	1st§	94	67	.584 + 7	
1940	2nd	88	65	.575	12	1989	4th	77	83	.481	14
1941	1st	100	54	.649 + 2½		1990	2nd	86	76	.531	5
1942	2nd	104	50	.675	2	1991	2nd	93	69	.574	1
1943	3rd	81	72	.529	23½						
1944	7th	63	91	.409	42						
1945	3rd	87	67	.565	11						
1946	2nd†	96	60	.615	2						
1947	1st	94	60	.610 + 5							
1948	3rd	84	70	.545	7½						
1949	1st	97	57	.630 + 1							

*Games behind winner. †Lost pennant playoff. ‡Won pennant playoff. §Won Championship Series. ★Lost division playoff. • Won division playoff. ◆First half 36-21; second 27-26. ■ Lost Championship Series.

MANAGERS

Name	Record	Years
Ned Hanlon	328-387	'01-05
Patsy Donovan	184-270	'06-08
Harry Lumley	55-98	1909
Bill Dahlen	251-355	'10-13
Wilbert Robinson	1375-1341	'14-31
Max Carey	146-161	'32-33
Casey Stengel	208-251	'34-36
Burleigh Grimes	131-171	'37-38
Leo Durocher	738-565	'39-46
		1948
Clyde Sukeforth	2-0	1947
Burt Shotton	326-215	1947
		'48-50
Chuck Dressen	298-166	'51-53
Walter Alston	2040-1613	'54-76
Tommy Lasorda	1278-1102	'76-91

DAY BY DAY

Date	Opp.	Res.	Score (inn.*)	Hits	Opp. hits	Winning pitcher	Losing pitcher	Save	Record	Pos.	GB
4-10	At Atl.	W	6-4	10	5	Belcher	Smoltz		1-0	T1st	½
4-11	At Atl.	W	4-2	9	7	Martinez	Leibrandt		2-0	1st	+½
4-12	S.D.	L	2-4	8	10	Harris	Ojeda	Gardner	2-1	T2nd	½
4-13	S.D.	L	3-6	9	14	Nolte	Gross	Maddux	2-2	T2nd	1½
4-14	S.D.	L	3-5	5	7	Whitson	Morgan	Lefferts	2-3	T4th	2½
4-15	At S.F.	W	2-1	5	6	Belcher	Black	Howell	3-3	3rd	2½
4-16	At S.F.	L	6-8	8	10	LaCoss	Martinez	Righetti	3-4	T4th	2½
4-17	At S.F.	W	6-2	11	5	Ojeda	Reuschel		4-4	T3rd	1½
4-18	At S.D.	L	5-10	13	14	Nolte	Gross		4-5	4th	2½
4-19	At S.D.	W	4-0	8	7	Morgan	Whitson		5-5	T3rd	1½
4-20	At S.D.	L	3-5	8	7	Andersen	Belcher	Lefferts	5-6	T3rd	2½
4-21	At S.D.	W	6-0	15	5	Martinez	Benes		6-6	T3rd	1½
4-22	Atl.	L	1-7	4	12	Avery	Ojeda		6-7	T3rd	2½
4-23	Atl.	L	0-4	4	8	Glavine	Gross		6-8	T4th	3½
4-24	Atl.	W	8-4	8	7	Morgan	Smoltz		7-8	3rd	2½
4-25	S.F.	W	7-1	8	5	Belcher	Black		8-8	3rd	2
4-26	S.F.	W	9-0	11	5	Martinez	LaCoss		9-8	3rd	2
4-27	S.F.	L	3-4	8	11	Downs	Ojeda	Brantley	9-9	4th	2
4-28	S.F.	W	7-3	9	10	Gross	Burkett		10-9	3rd	1
4-30	At Mon.	L	0-1	4	2	Martinez	Morgan		10-10	3rd	1½
5-1	At Mon.	L	3-9	9	11	Nabholz	Belcher		10-11	3rd	1½
5-3	At Phi.	W	7-1	13	4	Martinez	Cox		11-11	T3rd	1½
5-4	At Phi.	L	3-4	7	10	Mulholland	Howell	Williams	11-12	4th	½
5-5	At Phi.	W	3-2	12	9	Morgan	Boever	Howell	12-12	3rd	1½
5-7	At N.Y.	L	5-6	11	8	Viola	Belcher	Franco	12-13	4th	2½
5-8	At N.Y.	W	3-1	9	4	Martinez	Simons	Howell	13-13	3rd	1½
5-10	Phi.	W	3-1	9	7	Ojeda	Boever	Candelaria	14-13	T1st	...
5-11	Phi.	W	3-2	9	7	Morgan	Combs	Howell	15-13	T1st	...
5-12	Phi.	L	3-7	4	13	DeJesus	Belcher		15-14	T2nd	1
5-13	Mon.	W	8-3	8	8	Martinez	Boyd	Howell	16-14	2nd	1
5-14	Mon.	W	6-2	11	5	Gross	Gardner	Gott	17-14	2nd	...
5-15	Mon.	W	4-3	7	8	Crews	Jones	Howell	18-14	1st	+1
5-17	N.Y.	L	2-4	6	6	Viola	Morgan		18-15	2nd	...
5-18	N.Y.	W	4-3	5	11	Crews	Franco	Howell	19-15	1st	...
5-19	N.Y.	W	7-5	5	9	Martinez	Cone	Crews	20-15	1st	+½
5-20	At Hou.	L	1-4	4	8	Jones	Gross	Osuna	20-16	1st	+½
5-21	At Hou.	W	7-3	11	6	Ojeda	Corsi		21-16	1st	+½
5-22	At Hou.	L	2-3	3	9	Deshaies	Morgan	Osuna	21-17	1st	+½
5-23	At Hou.	W	2-0	7	6	Belcher	Hernandez	Howell	22-17	1st	+1½
5-24	At Cin.	W	11-3	13	9	Martinez	Hammond		23-17	1st	+1½
5-25	At Cin.	W	8-1	11	8	Gross	Charlton		24-17	1st	+2½
5-26	At Cin.	L	0-3	4	6	Browning	Ojeda	Myers	24-18	1st	+2½
5-27	Hou.	W	4-1	9	6	Morgan	Deshaies	Howell	25-18	1st	+2½
5-28	Hou.	W	8-2	9	11	Belcher	Hernandez		26-18	1st	+2½
5-29	Hou.	L	2-8	5	16	Harnisch	Hershiser	Osuna	26-19	1st	+1½
5-30	Cin.	L	2-7	4	15	Scudder	Martinez		26-20	1st	+½
5-31	Cin.	W	7-4	8	10	Ojeda	Browning		27-20	1st	+½
6-1	Cin.	L	5-6 (10)	5	9	Myers	Howell	Dibble	27-21	1st	+½
6-2	Cin.	W	4-1	11	8	Belcher	Armstrong	Crews	28-21	1st	+1½
6-4	At St.L.	L	2-3 (11)	10	7	L. Smith	Gott		28-22	1st	+½
6-5	At St.L.	W	2-0	6	4	Martinez	B. Smith		29-22	1st	+1½
6-6	At St.L.	W	1-0	6	4	Ojeda	Hill	Crews	30-22	1st	+1½
6-7	At Chi.	W	3-2	9	6	Morgan	Boskie	Howell	31-22	1st	+2½
6-8	At Chi.	L	3-4	6	9	McElroy	Gross	Smith	31-23	1st	+1½
6-9	At Chi.	W	6-3	13	8	Hershiser	Jackson		32-23	1st	+1½
6-10	At Chi.	W	13-5	16	14	Martinez	Bielecki	Hartley	33-23	1st	+2½
6-12	At Pit.	L	1-2	9	7	Drabek	Morgan	Landrum	33-24	1st	+2
6-13	At Pit.	W	3-2	7	6	Gott	Tomlin	Howell	34-24	1st	+2
6-14	St.L.	W	2-1	5	9	Howell	Terry		35-24	1st	+3
6-15	St.L.	L	4-5	10	9	B. Smith	Martinez	L. Smith	35-25	1st	+2
6-16	St.L.	W	7-2	16	4	Ojeda	Hill		36-25	1st	+3
6-17	Chi.	W	6-4	7	10	Morgon	Boskie	Crews	37-25	1st	+4
6-18	Chi.	W	6-5 (13)	13	8	Hartley	Bielecki		38-25	1st	+5
6-19	Chi.	W	9-8	13	13	Howell	Assenmacher		39-25	1st	+5
6-20	Pit.	W	3-2	9	5	Gross	Smiley		40-25	1st	+6
6-21	Pit.	L	1-5	9	10	Walk	Ojeda	Kipper	40-26	1st	+5
6-22	Pit.	W	4-1	8	3	Morgan	Drabek		41-26	1st	+6
6-23	Pit.	W	2-0	8	6	Belcher	Smith	Crews	42-26	1st	+6
6-25	S.F.	L	4-9	7	16	Remlinger	Hershiser		42-27	1st	+5
6-26	S.F.	L	2-3 (11)	11	4	Brangley	Crews		42-28	1st	+4

Date	Opp.	Res.	Score (inn.*)	Hits	Opp. hits	Winning pitcher	Losing pitcher	Save	Record	Pos.	GB
6-28 (1)	At Atl.	L	2-3 (10)	7	10	Mercker	Gott		42-29	1st	+3½
6-28 (2)	At Atl.	W	8-2	14	5	Morgan	Mahler		43-29	1st	+3
6-29	At Atl.	W	2-1 (11)	5	7	Hartley	Berenguer	Gross	44-29	1st	+4
6-30	At Atl.	W	11-4	13	12	Hershiser	Smoltz	Gross	45-29	1st	+4
7-2	At S.D.	W	4-1	4	6	Martinez	Rasmussen	Crews	46-29	1st	+4
7-3	At S.D.	W	6-3	10	10	Ojeda	Hurst		47-29	1st	+5
7-4	At S.D.	W	4-5 (12)	12	14	Melendez	Gott		47-30	1st	+4
7-5	Atl.	L	1-4	8	8	Glavine	Belcher		47-31	1st	+3
7-6	Atl.	W	7-6	9	8	Hershiser	Smoltz	Gross	48-31	1st	+4
7-7	Atl.	W	5-3	10	10	Martinez	Leibrandt	Morgan	49-31	1st	+5
7-11	At Mon.	L	2-3	7	7	Gardner	Ojeda	Ruskin	49-32	1st	+5
7-12	At Mon.	L	5-6	7	7	Ruskin	Gross		49-33	1st	+5
7-14 (1)	At Mon.	L	2-3	7	6	Boyd	Martinez	Jones	49-34	1st	+5
7-14 (2)	At Mon.	L	4-7	10	11	Barnes	Belcher	Jones	49-35	1st	+5
7-15	At Phi.	L	8-9	13	13	Searcy	Crews	Williams	49-36	1st	+5
7-16	At Phi.	L	1-3	7	9	Mulholland	Ojeda		49-37	1st	+4½
7-17	At Phi.	L	2-4	6	10	Greene	Candelaria	Williams	49-38	1st	+3½
7-18	At N.Y.	W	10-5	11	7	Gross	Cone		50-38	1st	+4
7-19	At N.Y.	L	2-6	5	10	Burke	Martinez		50-39	1st	+3
7-20	At N.Y.	W	11-7	16	12	Gott	Whitehurst		51-39	1st	+4
7-21	At N.Y.	L	4-9	8	11	Gooden	Ojeda		51-40	1st	+3
7-23	Phi.	W	6-5 (10)	9	10	Howell	McDowell		52-40	1st	+2½
7-24	Phi.	W	2-1	4	7	Candelaria	Searcy		53-40	1st	+3½
7-25	Phi.	W	5-0	14	5	Martinez	Ruffin		54-40	1st	+4½
7-26	Mon.	W	1-0 (10)	3	2	Howell	Gardner		55-40	1st	+5
7-27	Mon.	W	7-0	14	5	Ojeda	Haney		56-40	1st	+6
7-28	Mon.	L	0-2	0	4	Martinez	Morgan		56-41	1st	+6
7-29	N.Y.	L	1-5	3	10	Cone	Belcher		56-42	1st	+4½
7-30	N.Y.	W	3-1	6	6	Martinez	Schourek		57-42	1st	+4½
7-31	N.Y.	W	6-3	12	12	Gross	Burke		58-42	1st	+4½
8-2	At Hou.	L	8-9	12	9	Wilkins	Howell		58-43	1st	+4½
8-3	At Hou.	L	1-2 (10)	7	8	Wilkins	Howell		58-44	1st	+4½
8-4	At Hou.	L	1-2 (10)	5	6	Osuna	Gross		58-45	1st	+3½
8-5	At Cin.	L	6-10	9	13	Rijo	Martinez	Dibble	58-46	1st	+2½
8-6	At Cin.	W	5-2	8	9	Hershiser	Gross	McDowell	59-46	1st	+2½
8-7	At Cin.	W	2-0	7	3	Ojeda	Myers	McDowell	60-46	1st	+3½
8-8	At Cin.	W	6-4	11	8	Morgan	Browning		61-46	1st	+4½
8-9	At S.F.	L	0-1 (13)	9	6	Brantley	Gross		61-47	1st	+3½
8-10	At S.F.	L	3-4	8	12	Downs	Martinez	Righetti	61-48	1st	+2½
8-11	At S.F.	L	3-4	11	7	Downs	Gross	Downs	61-49	1st	+1½
8-12	Cin.	W	3-2	6	4	McDowell	Dibble		62-49	1st	+1½
8-13	Cin.	L	3-4 (10)	10	9	Dibble	McDowell		62-50	1st	+½
8-14	Cin.	W	4-1	8	5	Belcher	Sanford	Howell	63-50	1st	+1½
8-15	Hou.	L	1-6	5	8	Harnisch	Martinez		63-51	1st	+1½
8-16	Hou.	W	4-1 (13)	7	7	Gross	Corsi		64-51	1st	+1½
8-17	Hou.	W	8-7 (10)	15	11	Howell	Henry		65-51	1st	+1½
8-18	Hou.	L	4-8	9	12	Portugal	Morgan	Mallicoat	65-52	1st	+1½
8-19	S.D.	W	3-2 (10)	7	10	Gross	Andersen		66-52	1st	+2
8-20	S.D.	W	6-4	11	5	Martinez	Harris	Howell	67-52	1st	+2½
8-21	S.D.	W	9-5	9	11	Hershiser	Bones		68-52	1st	+2
8-23	At St.L.	L	1-2	9	4	Carpenter	Crews	L. Smith	68-53	1st	+1
8-24	At St.L.	L	3-7	7	10	Olivares	Morgan		68-54	1st	+1
8-25	At St.L.	L	2-5	12	11	Cormier	Belcher	L. Smith	68-55	1st	+1
8-26	At Chi.	W	4-3	7	9	Gott	McElroy	Howell	69-55	1st	+1
8-27	At Chi.	L	1-2	3	7	Castillo	Martinez		69-56	T1st	...
8-28	Pit.	L	4-6	8	11	Rodriguez	McDowell	Belinda	69-57	2nd	1
8-29	Pit.	L	1-4	7	7	Mason	Morgan	Landrum	69-58	2nd	2
8-30	Chi.	W	2-0	6	4	Belcher	Jackson		70-58	2nd	2
8-31	Chi.	W	3-2	9	8	McDowell	Assenmacher	Howell	71-58	2nd	1
9-1	Chi.	W	12-3	15	8	Martinez	Castillo		72-58	T1st	...
9-2	St.L.	L	4-7 (11)	8	15	Fraser	Howell		72-59	T1st	...
9-3	St.L.	L	5-4	7	6	Howell	Terry		73-59	T1st	...
9-4	St.L.	W	8-3	12	11	McDowell	McClure		74-59	1st	+1
9-6 (1)	At Pit.	W	4-3	8	6	McDowell	Belinda		75-59	1st	+1
9-6 (2)	At Pit.	L	1-3	3	10	Smith	Gross		75-60	1st	+½
9-7	At Pit.	W	5-1	9	8	Ojeda	Drabek	Gott	76-60	1st	+½
9-8	At Pit.	W	5-1	10	9	Morgan	Patterson		77-60	1st	+½
9-9	At Cin.	W	10-4	12	10	Gross	Hill		78-60	1st	+½
9-10	At Cin.	L	0-6	5	9	Rijo	Martinez	Power	78-61	2nd	½
9-11	At Hou.	W	9-1	14	8	Hershiser	Harnisch		79-61	2nd	½
9-12	At Hou.	W	6-2 (10)	7	7	McDowell	Osuna		80-61	2nd	½
9-13	At Atl.	W	5-2	11	4	Morgan	Glavine	McDowell	81-61	1st	+½
9-14	At Atl.	L	2-3 (11)	9	10	Clancy	McDowell		81-62	2nd	½
9-15	At Atl.	L	1-9	4	6	Avery	Martinez		81-63	2nd	1½

Date	Opp.	Res.	Score (inn.*)	Hits	Opp. hits	Winning pitcher	Losing pitcher	Save	Record	Pos.	GB
9-16	Cin.	W	6-5 (12)	11	14	Wetteland	Power		82-63	2nd	½
9-17	Cin.	W	5-3	10	8	Ojeda	Browning	Wilson	83-63	1st	+½
9-18	Hou.	W	5-4	8	9	Morgan	Mallicoat	Wilson	84-63	1st	+½
9-19	Hou.	W	4-3	6	6	Gross	Portugal	McDowell	85-63	1st	+½
9-20	Atl.	L	0-3	6	5	Avery	Belcher		85-64	2nd	½
9-21	Atl,	W	2-1	6	4	McDowell	Stanton		86-64	1st	+½
9-22	Atl.	W	3-0	9	3	Martinez	Glavine	McDowell	87-64	1st	+1½
9-24	At S.D.	W	5-2	7	6	Morgan	Bones	McDowell	88-64	1st	+2
9-25	At S.D.	L	2-8	8	8	Benes	Ojeda		88-65	1st	+2
9-27	S.F.	W	6-2	8	10	Belcher	Black		89-65	1st	+2
9-28	S.F.	L	1-4	4	7	Wilson	Martinez	Robinson	89-66	1st	+1
9-29	S.F.	W	3-2	13	8	Gott	Righetti		90-66	1st	+1
9-30	S.D.	W	7-2	10	4	Hershiser	Rasmussen		91-66	1st	+1
10-1	S.D.	W	3-1	8	6	Ojeda	Benes		92-66	1st	+1
10-2	S.D.	L	4-9	12	13	Harris	Gross		92-67	T1st	...
10-4	At S.F.	L	1-4	8	9	Black	Martinez	Brantley	92-68	2nd	1
10-5	At S.F.	L	0-4	2	4	Wilson	Morgan		92-69	2nd	2
10-6	At S.F.	W	2-0	8	7	Cook	Hickerson	Howell	93-69	2nd	1

Monthly records: April (10-10), May (17-10), June (18-9), July (13-13), August (13-16), September (20-8), Oct. (2-3).

HIGHLIGHTS

High point: Seven wins in nine games before the All-Star break enabled the Dodgers to take a five-game lead over Cincinnati and a 9½-game edge over Atlanta in the National League West.

Low point: Losing seven straight games immediately after the All-Star break. The Dodgers remained in first place despite suffering their longest losing streak of the season, but Atlanta closed their lead to 3½ games.

Turning point: Losing 20 of their first 26 road games after the All-Star break. A 24-15 road team the first half, the Dodgers finished 15-27 on the road in the second half as their five-game mid-season lead turned into a one-game deficit at the end of the season.

Most valuable player: Center fielder Brett Butler. The Dodgers' leading hitter (.296), Butler led the league in runs scored (112) and walks (108) and ranked second in hits (182) and on-base percentage (.401).

Most valuable pitcher: Righthander Mike Morgan. He had not posted a winning record in any of his 10 big-league seasons entering '91, but he went 14-10 with a 2.78 earned-run average.

Most improved player: Righthander Orel Hershiser. Brought along gingerly after undergoing career-threatening shoulder surgery in 1990, Hershiser finished 7-2 with a 3.46 ERA in 21 starts.

Most pleasant surprise: Second baseman Juan Samuel. Shunned following the 1990 season (.242 average, 126 strikeouts), Samuel batted .313 in the first half and made the All-Star team. He tailed off in the second half but still finished with a .271 average.

Biggest disappointment: A tossup between right fielder Darryl Strawberry's disappointing first half (.229 average, eight homers, 30 RBIs) and righthander Ramon Martinez's frustrating second half (5-10 record, 4.15 ERA).

Key injuries: Strawberry injured his right shoulder May 15 and missed 23 games. Shortstop Alfredo Griffin missed 53 games because of three injuries. Relief ace Jay Howell was disabled at mid-season and went from June 13 through August 14 without a save.

Notable: The Dodgers' home record (54-27) was the best in the majors. . . . The Dodgers were 1-1 in no-hitters pitched against them. On July 26, Montreal's Mark Gardner held the Dodgers hitless for nine innings but lost in 10 innings, 1-0. Two days later, Montreal's Dennis Martinez pitched a perfect game against Los Angeles. . . . Mike Scioscia caught in his 1,219th career game June 8 at Chicago to become the Dodgers' all-time leader in games caught.

—GORDON VERRELL

RECORDS

1991 regular-season record: 93-69 (2nd in N.L. West); 54-27 at home; 39-42 on road; 42-30 vs. East; 51-39 vs. West; 38-30 vs. LHP; 55-39 vs. RHP; 75-45 on grass; 18-24 on turf; 24-21 in daytime; 69-48 at night; 29-27 in one-run games; 9-11 in extra-inning games; 0-1-2 in doubleheaders.

Team record last five years: 423-384 (.524, ranks 4th in league in that span).

TEAM LEADERS

Batting average: Brett Butler (.296).
At-bats: Brett Butler (615).
Runs: Brett Butler (112).
Hits: Brett Butler (182).
Total bases: Darryl Strawberry (248).
Doubles: Eddie Murray (23).
Triples: Juan Samuel (6).
Home runs: Darryl Strawberry (28).
Runs batted in: Darryl Strawberry (99).
Stolen bases: Brett Butler (38).
Slugging percentage: Darryl Strawberry (.491).
On-base percentage: Brett Butler (.401).
Wins: Ramon Martinez (17).
Earned-run average: Tim Belcher (2.62).
Complete games: Ramon Martinez (6).
Shutouts: Ramon Martinez (4).
Saves: Jay Howell (16).
Innings pitched: Mike Morgan (236⅓).
Strikeouts: Tim Belcher (156).

GAMES BY POSITION

Catcher: Mike Scioscia 115, Gary Carter 68, Carlos Hernandez 13, Barry Lyons 6.

First base: Eddie Murray 149, Gary Carter 10, Eric Karros 10, Mike Sharperson 10, Stan Javier 2, Mitch Webster 1.

Second base: Juan Samuel 152, Lenny Harris 27, Mike Sharperson 5, Greg Smith 1.

Third base: Lenny Harris 113, Mike Sharperson 68, Jeff Hamilton 33, Dave Hansen 21, Carlos Hernandez 1, Eddie Murray 1.

Shortstop: Alfredo Griffin 109, Jose Offerman 50, Lenny Harris 20, Mike Sharperson 16, Jeff Hamilton 1, Dave Hansen 1.

Outfield: Brett Butler 161, Darryl Strawberry 136, Kal Daniels 132, Stan Javier 69, Chris Gwynn 41, Mitch Webster 36, Jose Gonzalez 27, Tom Goodwin 5, Roger McDowell 2, Lenny Harris 1.

TOP 10 DRAFT CHOICES

1. None.
2. None.
3a. **Todd Hollandsworth,** OF, Newport High School, Bellevue, Wash.
3b. **Todd LaRocca,** SS, The Lovett School, Atlanta.
4. **Mike Walkden,** LHP, Lake Stevens (Wash.) High School.
5. **Doug Bennett,** RHP, University of Arkansas.
6. **Mike Iglesias,** RHP, Hayward (Calif.) High School.
7. **Brandon Watts,** LHP, Ruston (La.) High School.
8. **Vince Jackson,** OF, Central High School, Davenport, Iowa.
9. **Dennis Winicki,** SS, Mona Shores High School, Muskegon, Mich.
10. **Lonnie Jackson,** OF, Washington High School, Oakland.

MONTREAL EXPOS
NATIONAL LEAGUE EAST DIVISION

1992 SCHEDULE

APRIL

S	M	T	W	T	F	S
5	6 N PIT	7	8 N PIT	9	10 NY	11 NY
12 NY	13 STL H	14 STL H	15 STL H	16	17 N NY	18 NY
19 NY H	20 PIT H	21 PIT H	22 PIT H	23 PIT H	24 N STL	25 N STL
26 STL	27 N SF	28 SF	29 N SD	30 SD		

MAY

S	M	T	W	T	F	S
					1 N LA	2 N LA
3 LA	4	5 N SD	6 N SD	7	8 N SF	9 SF H
10 SF H	11 N LA	12 H LA	13 N LA	14	15 N ATL	16 N ATL
17 ATL	18 CIN H	19 CIN H	20 N CIN H	21	22 N ATL	23 ATL H
24 ATL H	25 HOU H	26 N HOU H	27 HOU H	28	29 N CIN	30 N CIN
31 CIN						

JUNE

S	M	T	W	T	F	S
	1 N HOU	2 N HOU	3 N HOU	4	5 TN CHI H	6
7 CHI H	8 N NY	9 N NY	10 N NY	11	12 CHI	13 CHI
14 CHI	15 N NY	16 N NY	17 N NY	18 N PIT	19 N PIT	20 N PIT
21 PIT	22 N PHI H	23 N PHI H	24 PHI H	25	26 N PIT H	27 N PIT H
28 PIT H	29 N PHI	30 N PHI				

JULY

S	M	T	W	T	F	S
			1 N PHI	2 N SD	3 N SD	4 N SD
5 SD	6 N LA	7 N LA	8 LA	9	10 N SF	11 SF
12 SF	13	14 *	15	16 N SD	17 N SD H	18 N SD H
19 SD H	20 N SF H	21 N SF H	22 SF H	23	24 N LA	25 N LA H
26 LA	27 N STL	28 N STL	29 N STL	30 N PHI H	31 N PHI H	

AUGUST

S	M	T	W	T	F	S
						1 N PHI H
2 PHI H	3 N CHI H	4 N CHI H	5 N CHI H	6 N PHI	7 N PHI	8 N PHI
9 PHI	10 CHI	11 CHI	12 CHI	13	14 N STL H	15 N STL H
16 STL H	17	18 N ATL H	19 N ATL H	20 N ATL H	21 N CIN H	22 N CIN H
23 CIN H	24	25 N ATL	26 ATL	27 ATL	28 N HOU	29 HOU
30 HOU	31 N CIN					

SEPTEMBER

S	M	T	W	T	F	S
		1 N CIN	2 N CIN	3	4 N HOU H	5 N HOU H
6 HOU H	7	8 N STL H	9 N STL H	10	11 N NY	12 N NY H
13 N NY	14 N PHI	15 PHI	16 N PIT	17 N PIT	18 N NY	19 NY
20 NY	21 N PHI H	22 N PHI H	23 N PIT H	24 N PIT H	25 N CHI	26 N CHI H
27 CHI H	28 N STL	29 N STL	30 N STL			

OCTOBER

S	M	T	W	T	F	S
				1	2 CHI	3 CHI
4 CHI	5	6	7	8	9	10

1992 SEASON

CLUB DIRECTORY

President and general partner
Claude R. Brochu
Chairman of the board
Jacques Menard
Vice chairmen of the board
Jacques Berube
Claude Blanchet
Jocelyn Proteau
V.p., player personnel and general manager
Dan Duquette
Vice president, baseball operations
Bill Stoneman
Director, scouting
Kevin Malone
Director, minor league field operations
Kevin Kennedy
Director, minor league operations
Kent Qualls
Director, team travel
Erik Ostling
Director, Latin America operations
Fred Ferreira
Executive adviser, baseball operations
Eddie Haas
Special consultant, baseball operations
Jim Fanning
General mgr., West Palm Beach operations
Rob Rabenecker
Administrative assistant, scouting
Gregg Leonard
Administrator, baseball operations
Roberta Mazur
Vice president, marketing
Michel Lagace
Vice president, communications
Richard Morency
Vice president, business operations
Gerry Trudeau
Controller
Raymond St-Pierre
Director, marketing and communications
Carole Boivin
Director, ticket office
Luigi Carolo
Director, food concessions
Claude Delorme
Director, media services
Monique Giroux
Director, media relations
Richard Griffin
Director, advertising
Johanne Heroux

Director, stadium operations
Monique Lacas
Director, retailing
Susan LeBlanc
Director, ticket sales
Ronald Martineau
Director, corporate affairs
Pierre O. Touchette
Public relations representative
Ron Piche
Club physician
Dr. Robert Brodrick
Club orthopedist
Dr. Larry Coughlin
Scouts
Jesus Alou
Doug Carpenter
Emilio Carrasquel
Carl Cassell
Pepito Centeno
Ed Creech
Arturo DeFreitas
Richard DeHart
Brian Dermott
Phil Favia
Jim Fleming
Joe Frisina
Jim Holden
Bert Holt
Bob Johnson
Jeff Kahn
Randy Kierce
Dick Lemay
Dave Littlefield
Juan Loyola
Bill MacKenzie
Rene Marchand
Roy McMillan
Thomas Morales
Carlos Moreno
Mike Murphy
Bob Oldis
Rene Picota
Mark Servais
Keith Snider
Lynn Squires
Pat Sullivan
Ron Walters
Fred Wright
Stan Zielinski

SCHEDULE KEY

H—Home game.   *All-Star Game at San Diego/Jack Murphy Stadium.
N—Night game (any game starting after 5 p.m.). TN—Twi-night doubleheader.

SPRING TRAINING ROSTER

Manager—Tom Runnells (10).
Coaches—Felipe Alou (17), Tommy Harper (21), Joe Kerrigan (45), Jerry Manuel (6), Jay Ward (35).

No.	PITCHERS	B/T	Ht./Wt.	Born	1991 clubs
47	Barnes, Brian	L/L	5-9/170	3-25-67	Montreal, Indianapolis, West Palm Beach
46	Bottenfield, Kent	S/R	6-3/225	11-14-68	Indianapolis
49	Farmer, Howard	R/R	6-3/192	1-18-66	Indianapolis
39	Fassero, Jeff	L/L	6-1/195	1-5-63	Montreal, Indianapolis
41	Frey, Steve	R/L	5-9/170	7-29-63	Montreal, Indianapolis
28	Gardner, Mark	R/R	6-1/200	3-1-62	Montreal, Indianapolis
42	Haney, Chris	L/L	6-3/185	11-16-68	Harrisburg, Indianapolis, Montreal
44	Hill, Ken	R/R	6-2/175	12-14-65	St. Louis, Louisville
56	Hurst, Jonathan	R/R	6-3/175	10-20-66	Miami, Tulsa, Harrisburg
52	Karchner, Matt	R/R	6-4/225	6-28-67	Baseball City
32	Martinez, Dennis	R/R	6-1/180	5-14-55	Montreal
43	Nabholz, Chris	L/L	6-5/212	1-5-67	Montreal, Indianapolis
48	Piatt, Doug	L/R	6-1/190	9-26-65	Indianapolis, Montreal
50	Risley, Bill	R/R	6-2/215	5-29-67	Chattanooga, Nashville
51	Rojas, Mel	R/R	5-11/185	12-10-66	Indianapolis, Montreal
55	Sampen, Bill	R/R	6-2/195	1-18-63	Montreal, Indianapolis
40	Wainhouse, David	L/R	6-2/185	11-7-67	Harrisburg, Indianapolis, Montreal
57	Wetteland, John	R/R	6-2/195	8-21-66	Albuquerque, Los Angeles
60	Young, Pete	R/R	6-0/225	3-19-68	Harrisburg

No.	CATCHERS	B/T	Ht./Wt.	Born	1991 clubs
8	Carter, Gary	R/R	6-2/214	4-8-54	Los Angeles
15	Colbrunn, Greg	R/R	6-0/190	7-26-69	DID NOT PLAY
24	Fletcher, Darrin	L/R	6-1/199	10-3-66	Scranton-W.B., Philadelphia
54	Kremers, Jimmy	L/R	6-3/210	10-8-65	Indianapolis
53	Laker, Tim	R/R	6-2/185	11-27-69	Harrisburg, West Palm Beach
58	Natal, Robert	R/R	5-11/190	11-13-65	Indianapolis, Harrisburg
20	Reyes, Gilberto	R/R	6-2/212	12-10-63	Montreal

No.	INFIELDERS	B/T	Ht./Wt.	Born	1991 clubs
25	Barberie, Bret	S/R	5-11/180	8-16-67	Montreal, Indianapolis
26	Canale, George	L/R	6-1/190	8-11-65	Milwaukee, Denver
12	Cordero, Wilfredo	R/R	6-2/185	10-3-71	Indianapolis
4	DeShields, Delino	L/R	6-1/170	1-15-69	Montreal
16	Foley, Tom	L/R	6-1/175	9-9-59	Montreal
11	Owen, Spike	S/R	5-10/170	4-19-61	Montreal
29	Wallach, Tim	R/R	6-3/202	9-14-57	Montreal

No.	OUTFIELDERS	B/T	Ht./Wt.	Born	1991 clubs
18	Alou, Moises	R/R	6-3/190	7-3-66	DID NOT PLAY
22	Calderon, Ivan	R/R	6-1/221	3-19-62	Montreal
9	Grissom, Marquis	R/R	5-11/190	4-17-67	Montreal
5	Reed, Darren	R/R	6-1/205	10-16-65	DID NOT PLAY
59	Stairs, Matt	R/R	5-9/175	2-27-69	Harrisburg
23	VanderWal, John	L/L	6-2/190	4-29-66	Montreal, Indianapolis
33	Walker, Larry	L/R	6-3/215	12-1-66	Montreal

BALLPARK INFORMATION

Ballpark (capacity, surface)
Olympic Stadium (43,739, artificial)
Address
4549 Pierre-de-Coubertin Ave.
Montreal, QC H1V 3N7
Business phone
514-253-3434
Ticket information
514-253-3434
Ticket prices
$22 (VIP box seats)
$15.25 (box seats)
$9 (terrace)
$5.50 (general admission)
$4 (bleachers)
Field dimensions (from home plate)
To left field at foul line, 325 feet
To center field, 404 feet
To right field at foul line, 325 feet
First game played
April 15, 1977 (Phillies 7, Expos 2)

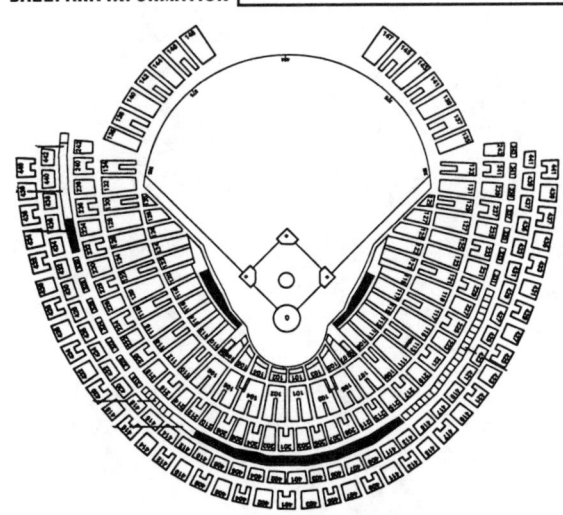

MINOR LEAGUE AFFILIATES

Class	Team	League	Manager
AAA	Indianapolis	American Association	Pat Kelly
AA	Harrisburg	Eastern	Mike Quade
A	West Palm Beach	Florida State	David Jauss
A	Rockford	Midwest	Rob Leary
A	Albany	South Atlantic	Lorenzo Bundy
A	Jamestown	New York-Pennsylvania	Q.V. Lowe
Rookie	Gulf Coast Expos	Gulf Coast	Nelson Norman

BROADCAST INFORMATION

Radio: CICQ-AM (600). Broadcasters: Dave VanHorne, Ken Singleton, Bobby Winkles, Elliott Price. CKAC-AM (73, French language). Broadcasters: Rodger Brulotte, Jacques Doucet, Claude Raymond.
TV: CFC-TV (Channel 12). Broadcasters: Ken Singleton, Dave VanHorne. CBFT (2, French language). Broadcasters: Claude Raymond, Raymond Lebrun.
Cable TV: The Sports Network. Broadcasters: Ken Singleton, Dave Van-Horne. RDS (French language). Broadcasters: Rodger Brulotte, Denis Cafavant.

SPRING TRAINING

Ballpark (city): Municipal Stadium (West Palm Beach, Fla.).
Ticket information: 407-684-6801.

HISTORY

YEAR-BY-YEAR RECORDS

Year	Pos.	W	L	Pct.	*GB	Year	Pos.	W	L	Pct.	*GB
1969	6th	52	110	.321	48	1982	3rd	86	76	.531	6
1970	6th	73	89	.451	16	1983	3rd	82	80	.506	8
1971	5th	71	90	.441	25 ½	1984	5th	78	83	.484	18
1972	5th	70	86	.449	26 ½	1985	3rd	84	77	.522	16 ½
1973	4th	79	83	.488	3 ½	1986	4th	78	83	.484	29 ½
1974	4th	79	82	.491	8 ½	1987	3rd	91	71	.562	4
1975	T5th	75	87	.463	17 ½	1988	3rd	81	81	.500	20
1976	6th	55	107	.340	46	1989	4th	81	81	.500	12
1977	5th	75	87	.463	26	1990	3rd	85	77	.525	10
1978	4th	76	86	.469	14	1991	6th	71	90	.441	26 ½
1979	2nd	95	65	.594	2						
1980	2nd	90	72	.556	1						
1981	3rd/1st	60	48	.556	†‡§						

*Games behind winner. †Won division playoff. ‡Lost Championship Series. §First half 30-25; second 30-23.

MANAGERS

Name	Record	Years
Gene Mauch	499-627	'69-75
Karl Kuehl	43-85	1976
Charlie Fox	12-22	1976
Dick Williams	350-322	'77-81
Jim Fanning	116-103	'81-82
		1984
Bill Virdon	146-147	'83-84
Buck Rodgers	520-499	'85-91
Tom Runnells	51-61	1991

DAY BY DAY

Date	Opp.	Res.	Score (inn.*)	Hits	Opp. hits	Winning pitcher	Losing pitcher	Save	Record	Pos.	GB
4-8	At Pit.	W	7-0	15	1	Martinez	Drabek		1-0	T1st	...
4-9	At Pit.	L	3-4	6	9	Kipper	Frey	Landrum	1-1	T3rd	1
4-10	At Pit.	L	3-6	7	10	Smith	Boyd	Belinda	1-2	T5th	1
4-11	At N.Y.	L	3-6	8	8	Whitehurst	Mahler	Franco	1-3	6th	2
4-12	At N.Y.	W	4-3 (11)	11	5	Burke	Franco	Frey	2-3	5th	1½
4-13	At N.Y.	L	3-5	7	7	Gooden	Martinez		2-4	6th	2
4-14	At N.Y.	L	1-7	5	9	Viola	Nabholz		2-5	6th	3
4-15	St.L.	L	4-5	5	9	Carpenter	Burke	L. Smith	2-6	6th	4
4-16	St.L.	W	4-1	9	6	Mahler	Hill	Burke	3-6	6th	3
4-17	St.L.	W	1-0	7	6	Sampen	Moyer	Jones	4-6	5th	2½
4-19	N.Y.	W	2-1	4	5	Martinez	Gooden	Burke	5-6	5th	2
4-20	N.Y.	L	1-3	9	6	Viola	Nabholz	Franco	5-7	5th	2
4-21	N.Y.	L	5-9	13	12	Cone	Boyd	Schourek	5-8	5th	3
4-23	Pit.	L	3-7	12	8	Smiley	Sampen		5-9	5th	4
4-24	Pit.	L	1-2	7	8	Drabek	Martinez	Landrum	5-10	5th	5
4-25	Pit.	L	0-8	4	14	Palacios	Nabholz		5-11	T5th	6
4-26	At St.L.	L	0-4	5	11	B. Smith	Boyd	Agosto	5-12	T3rd	6
4-27	At St.L.	L	1-2	6	10	Hill	Mahler	L. Smith	5-13	6th	7
4-28	At St.L.	W	9-6	17	12	Burke	Perez		6-13	6th	7
4-30	L.A.	W	1-0	2	4	Martinez	Morgan		7-13	6th	6
5-1	L.A.	W	9-3	11	9	Nabholz	Belcher		8-13	6th	6
5-3	S.D.	W	4-1	8	4	Boyd	Benes		9-13	6th	6
5-4	S.D.	L	5-6 (13)	13	8	Rodriguez	Fassero		9-14	6th	6
5-5	S.D.	L	3-6	7	9	Whitson	Barnes		9-15	6th	6
5-6	S.F.	W	10-4	14	12	Martinez	Robinson		10-15	6th	6
5-7	S.F.	W	3-2 (15)	10	5	Ruskin	Wilson		11-15	T5th	6
5-8	S.F.	W	5-4	10	8	Jones	Oliveras	Burke	12-15	T5th	6
5-10	At S.D.	W	6-4 (10)	13	9	Burke	Gardner		13-15	5th	6
5-11	At S.D.	W	5-1	6	7	Martinez	Peterson		14-15	5th	5
5-12	At S.D.	W	8-6	12	6	Sampen	Rodriguez	Jones	15-15	4th	4
5-13	At L.A.	L	3-8	8	8	Martinez	Boyd	Howell	15-16	4th	4½
5-14	At L.A.	L	2-6	5	11	Gross	Gardner	Gott	15-17	6th	5½
5-15	At L.A.	L	3-4	8	7	Crews	Jones	Howell	15-18	6th	6½
5-16	At S.F.	L	4-5	11	10	Robinson	Martinez	Oliveras	15-19	6th	7½
5-17	At S.F.	W	3-0	7	3	Jones	LaCoss	Ruskin	16-19	6th	6½
5-18	At S.F.	W	3-1	8	3	Boyd	Burkett	Burke	17-19	T5th	6
5-19	At S.F.	W	5-4 (13)	8	9	Sampen	LaCoss	Ruskin	18-19	T4th	5
5-21	Phi.	W	3-0	7	5	Martinez	Grimsley		19-19	4th	5
5-22	Phi.	L	1-8	9	10	Combs	Barnes		19-20	T4th	5
5-23	Phi.	L	0-2	0	8	Greene	Boyd		19-21	6th	5
5-24	At Chi.	L	3-4	6	9	Scanlan	Gardner	Slocumb	19-22	6th	6
5-25	At Chi.	L	1-6	6	10	Bielecki	Mahler	McElroy	19-23	6th	7
5-26	At Chi.	L	6-8	11	11	Lancaster	Burke	Smith	19-24	6th	8
5-27	At Phi.	W	8-1	8	5	Nabholz	Combs		20-24	T5th	8
5-28	At Phi.	L	0-12	3	12	Greene	Boyd		20-25	6th	9
5-29	At Phi.	L	1-2	7	5	Mulholland	Jones	Williams	20-26	6th	10
5-31	Chi.	L	2-7	8	14	Bielecki	Martinez	Lancaster	20-27	6th	11
6-1	Chi.	L	1-2 (10)	5	7	McElroy	Jones	Smith	20-28	6th	12
6-2	Chi.	L	3-4	3	7	Assenmacher	Ruskin	Smith	20-29	6th	13
6-4	At Hou.	W	4-1	8	5	Gardner	Harnisch	Jones	21-29	6th	12
6-5	At Hou.	W	8-2	14	8	Martinez	Jones		22-29	6th	12
6-6	At Hou.	L	8-9	12	17	Schilling	Jones		22-30	6th	12
6-7	At Atl.	W	11-2	16	8	Boyd	Avery		23-30	6th	12
6-8	At Atl.	L	6-7	11	11	Stanton	Burke	Mercker	23-31	6th	12
6-9	At Atl.	L	6-8	11	16	Glavine	Gardner	Berenguer	23-32	6th	12
6-10	At Atl.	W	7-1	12	7	Martinez	Smoltz	Ruskin	24-32	6th	12
6-11	Cin.	L	1-6	5	11	Charlton	Nabholz		24-33	6th	12½
6-12	Cin.	W	10-9	14	16	Ruskin	Myers	Fassero	25-33	T5th	12½
6-13	Cin.	L	2-3	5	9	Hammond	Barnes	Dibble	25-34	6th	12½
6-14	Atl.	W	2-1	8	6	Gardner	Glavine	Ruskin	26-34	T5th	11½
6-15	Atl.	W	2-0	9	8	Martinez	Smoltz		27-34	5th	10½
6-16	Atl.	W	7-6	10	12	Sampen	Stanton	Jones	28-34	5th	10½
6-17	Hou.	W	3-2 (16)	6	12	Fassero	Schilling		29-34	5th	10½
6-18	Hou.	W	3-2 (12)	4	8	Sampen	Corsi		30-34	5th	10½
6-19	Hou.	W	3-1	5	5	Gardner	Harnisch	Fassero	31-34	T4th	9½
6-20	At Cin.	W	1-0 (11)	7	3	Jones	Carman	Ruskin	32-34	4th	8½
6-21	At Cin.	L	3-7	6	9	Scudder	Haney		32-35	4th	8½
6-22	At Cin.	W	7-4	12	10	Boyd	Armstrong	Jones	33-35	4th	8½
6-23	At Cin.	L	4-8	5	9	Myers	Sampen		33-36	4th	8½
6-25	At N.Y.	L	5-8	9	9	Pena	Jones		33-37	4th	8½

Date	Opp.	Res.	Score (inn.*)	Hits	Opp. hits	Winning pitcher	Losing pitcher	Save	Record	Pos.	GB
6-26	At N.Y.	L	4-7	14	10	Viola	Gardner	Franco	33-38	4th	9½
6-27	At N.Y.	L	3-4	8	10	Cone	Boyd	Franco	33-39	4th	10½
6-28	Pit.	L	1-6	5	13	Smith	Haney		33-40	4th	11½
6-29	Pit.	L	1-2	8	6	Heaton	Ruskin	Landrum	33-41	T4th	12½
6-30	Pit.	L	1-2	7	7	Smiley	Martinez	Belinda	33-42	5th	13½
7-1	N.Y.	L	2-4	10	10	Viola	Gardner	Franco	33-43	5th	13½
7-2	N.Y.	L	1-2	8	4	Pena	Jones	Franco	33-44	5th	14½
7-3	N.Y.	L	0-4	2	10	Darling	Haney		33-45	5th	15½
7-4	N.Y.	L	1-5	4	7	Whitehurst	Burke		33-46	5th	15½
7-5	At Pit.	L	4-3	10	11	Martinez	Smiley		34-46	5th	14½
7-6	At Pit.	W	2-1	5	2	Gardner	Walk	Burke	35-46	5th	13½
7-7	At Pit.	L	1-6	6	10	Drabek	Boyd	Belinda	35-47	5th	14½
7-11	L.A.	W	3-2	7	7	Gardner	Ojeda	Ruskin	36-47	5th	14½
7-12	L.A.	W	6-5	7	7	Ruskin	Gross		37-47	5th	14½
7-14 (1)	L.A.	W	3-2	6	7	Boyd	Martinez	Jones	38-47	5th	14½
7-14 (2)	L.A.	W	7-4	11	10	Barnes	Belcher	Jones	39-47	5th	14½
7-15	S.D.	W	3-0	8	8	Haney	Benes	Fassero	40-47	5th	14½
7-16	S.D.	L	3-4	8	5	Hurst	Rojas	Andersen	40-48	5th	15½
7-17	S.D.	L	5-7	8	10	Melendez	Martinez	Andersen	40-49	5th	15½
7-19	S.F.	W	6-0	10	5	Boyd	Robinson		41-49	5th	15½
7-20	S.F.	L	3-5	12	9	Burkett	Darling	Brantley	41-50	5th	15½
7-21	S.F.	L	2-3	5	6	Wilson	Gardner	Brantley	41-51	5th	16½
7-23	At S.D.	L	1-2 (11)	8	9	Andersen	Schmidt		41-52	5th	17
7-24	At S.D.	W	8-2	13	6	Barnes	Rasmussen	Fassero	42-52	5th	17
7-25	At S.D.	L	5-6	12	10	Maddux	Jones		42-53	5th	17½
7-26	At L.A.	L	0-1 (10)	2	3	Howell	Gardner		42-54	5th	18½
7-27	At L.A.	L	0-7	5	14	Ojeda	Haney		42-55	5th	19½
7-28	At L.A.	W	2-0	4	0	Martinez	Morgan		43-55	5th	18½
7-29	At S.F.	L	5-6	8	10	Downs	Rojas	Righetti	43-56	5th	18
7-30	At S.F.	L	3-10	5	14	Wilson	Darling		43-57	5th	18
8-1	Phi.	L	1-4	3	8	Mulholland	Gardner		43-58	T5th	17½
8-2	Phi.	L	5-6 (11)	10	12	Williams	Rojas	Hartley	43-59	6th	17½
8-3	Phi.	L	1-7	7	7	Greene	Barnes		43-60	6th	17½
8-4	Phi.	L	2-3 (10)	6	6	Williams	Fassero		43-61	6th	18½
8-6	At St.L.	L	6-7 (10)	11	13	Terry	Jones		43-62	6th	19½
8-7	At St.L.	W	1-0	9	5	Gardner	Olivares	Jones	44-62	6th	18½
8-9	At Phi.	L	4-5	11	6	Williams	Wainhouse		44-63	6th	18
8-10	At Phi.	L	2-4	8	7	DeJesus	Ruskin	Williams	44-64	6th	19
8-11	At Phi.	L	4-5	5	7	Hartley	Fassero	Williams	44-65	6th	20
8-12	At Phi.	L	1-2	6	5	Mulholland	Martinez		44-66	6th	21
8-13	At Chi.	W	7-6	11	12	Sampen	Lancaster	Fassero	45-66	6th	21
8-14	At Chi.	W	2-0	6	2	Barnes	Maddux	Jones	46-66	6th	21
8-15	At Chi.	L	6-7	12	9	Assenmacher	Fassero	McElroy	46-67	6th	21
8-16	St.L.	L	2-4	5	7	Tewksbury	Nabholz	L. Smith	46-68	6th	22
8-17	St.L.	W	3-0	9	6	Martinez	DeLeon		47-68	6th	22
8-18	St.L.	L	1-4	7	10	Olivares	Gardner	L. Smith	47-69	6th	23
8-19	Chi.	L	2-3 (11)	14	7	Assenmacher	Sampen		47-70	6th	23½
8-20	Chi.	W	4-2	12	8	Haney	Scanlan	Rojas	48-70	6th	22½
8-21	Chi.	L	1-3	5	7	Sutcliffe	Nabholz	Lancaster	48-71	6th	22½
8-23	At Hou.	L	2-9	6	11	Bowen	Martinez		48-72	6th	23
8-24	At Hou.	W	5-1	8	5	Rojas	Portugal		49-72	6th	22
8-25	At Hou.	W	4-0	7	3	Gardner	Deshaies	Fassero	50-72	6th	22
8-26	At Atl.	L	9-14	15	14	Wohlers	Sampen	Stanton	50-73	6th	22
8-27	At Atl.	L	2-3	4	9	Leibrandt	Nabholz	Clancy	50-74	6th	23
8-28	At Cin.	L	3-11	8	13	Browning	Martinez		50-75	6th	24
8-29	At Cin.	L	4-5	7	6	Rijo	Barnes	Dibble	50-76	6th	25
8-30	Hou.	W	3-1	11	4	Gardner	Deshaies	Jones	51-76	6th	25
8-31	Hou.	W	5-4 (10)	10	7	Fassero	Osuna		52-76	6th	25
9-1	Hou.	W	6-1	9	4	Nabholz	Kile		53-76	6th	24
9-2	Atl.	W	4-3	5	7	Sampen	Glavine		54-76	6th	24
9-3	Atl.	L	1-4	8	4	Smoltz	Barnes	Pena	54-77	6th	25
9-4	Atl.	W	8-4	14	5	Rojas	Clancy		55-77	6th	25
9-6	Cin.	W	4-1	11	4	Haney	Scudder	Rojas	56-77	6th	24½
9-7	Cin.	W	7-5	10	8	Nabholz	Browning		57-77	6th	23½
9-8	Cin.	W	4-2	11	7	Martinez	Armstrong	Jones	58-77	6th	22½
9-9	At N.Y.	W	4-3	9	7	Barnes	Cone	Fassero	59-77	6th	22½
9-10	At N.Y.	L	0-9	1	11	Schourek	Gardner		59-78	6th	22½
9-11	At Phi.	W	6-5	8	12	Sampen	Ritchie	Jones	60-78	6th	22½
9-12	At Phi.	W	6-2	10	8	Nabholz	Ruffin		61-78	6th	21½
9-13	At Chi.	W	3-2	7	7	Martinez	Scanlan	Jones	62-78	6th	21½
9-14	At Chi.	L	5-7 (10)	8	10	Scanlan	Jones		62-79	6th	22½
9-15	At Chi.	W	6-5 (10)	7	9	Rojas	Assenmacher	Fassero	63-79	6th	21½
9-17 (1)	At N.Y.	W	5-4	11	11	Nabholz	Young	Rojas	64-79	6th	22½
9-17 (2)	At N.Y.	L	2-3	9	10	Whitehurst	Haney	Franco	64-80	6th	22½

Date	Opp.	Res.	Score (inn.*)	Hits	Opp. hits	Winning pitcher	Losing pitcher	Save	Record	Pos.	GB
9-18	At Phi.	L	0-1	2	7	Mulholland	Martinez		64-81	6th	23½
9-19	At Phi.	L	4-5 (10)	10	10	Williams	Ruskin		64-82	6th	24½
9-22 (1)	At Chi.	W	6-2	9	6	Gardner	Sutcliffe		65-82	6th	24½
9-22 (2)	At Chi.	W	5-3	13	7	Sampen	Castillo	Rojas	66-82	6th	24
9-23 (1)	At St.L.	L	1-10	3	9	B. Smith	Martinez		66-83	6th	24½
9-23 (2)	At St.L.	W	5-1	10	5	Nabholz	Clark		67-83	6th	24
9-24	At St.L.	L	3-4	9	6	Olivares	Haney	L. Smith	67-84	6th	25
9-25	At St.L.	W	7-2	10	10	Barnes	Cormier		68-84	6th	24½
9-27	At Pit.	W	12-8	15	9	Ruskin	Rodriguez		69-84	6th	23½
9-28	At Pit.	W	3-2	7	4	Nabholz	Drabek	Rojas	70-84	6th	22½
9-29	At Pit.	L	3-6	13	11	Walk	Sampen	Kipper	70-85	6th	23½
9-30	At St.L.	L	1-11	7	12	Clark	Haney	Agosto	70-86	6th	24½
10-1	At St.L.	L	1-3	8	8	Olivares	Barnes	L. Smith	70-87	6th	25½
10-2	At St.L.	L	4-6	9	6	Cormier	Gardner	L. Smith	70-88	6th	25½
10-4	At Pit.	W	3-1	13	8	Jones	Mason	Rojas	71-88	6th	24½
10-5	At Pit.	L	3-4	9	7	Walk	Fassero	Belinda	71-89	6th	25½
10-6	At Pit.	L	0-7	5	8	Smiley	Barnes		71-90	6th	26½

Monthly records: April (7-13), May (13-14), June (13-15), July (10-15), August (9-19), September (18-10), Oct. (1-4).

HIGHLIGHTS

High point: After Tom Runnells assumed managing duties from Buck Rodgers on June 3, the Expos won 12 of 17 games and moved from sixth place to fourth in the National League East (8½ games out of first).

Low point: Following that stretch, Montreal lost 11 straight games from June 23 through July 4. The Expos slipped to fifth place during the losing spell before sinking to their final resting place (the cellar) on August 2.

Turning point: On May 21, Montreal climbed to 19-19 (five games out of first) with a 3-0 win over Philadelphia. But the Expos proceeded to lose 10 of their next 11 games, falling 13 games off the pace.

Most valuable player: Left fielder Ivan Calderon. Despite missing 27 games with a left shoulder injury, he led the team in hitting (.300), home runs (19) and runs batted in (75).

Most valuable pitcher: Righthander Dennis Martinez. Besides pitching a perfect game at Los Angeles on July 28, Martinez led the major leagues in earned-run average (2.39) and shutouts (five) while tying for the N.L. lead in complete games (nine).

Most improved player: Right fielder Larry Walker. After opening the season as a platoon player, Walker became a regular because of his improved hitting (.241 in 1990 to .290 in '91). He also played excellent defense.

Most pleasant surprise: Infielder Bret Barberie. When Barberie was called up for a second time (on August 2) from Class AAA, he excelled. He finished with a .353 average in 57 games.

Biggest disappointment: First baseman Andres Galarraga. He continued a three-year slide after posting exceptional seasons in 1987 and '88. Galarraga was bothered by injury and hit just .219 with nine homers and 33 RBIs in 375 at-bats.

Key injuries: The Expos suffered 12 disabling injuries, costing them 794 playing days. Among the key losses were Darren Reed (broken forearm), Calderon (shoulder), Galarraga (hamstring) and Chris Nabholz (shoulder).

Notable: The Expos were forced to play their final 26 games on the road after a 55-ton cement beam fell from Olympic Stadium on September 13. No one was injured, but engineers needed time to determine if the facility was safe. Meanwhile, Montreal went 13-13 on the 28-day road trip. When the season ended, the Expos had played a major league-record 93 road games.

—IAN MacDONALD

RECORDS

1991 regular-season record: 71-90 (6th in N.L. East); 33-35 at home; 38-55 on road; 28-61 vs. East; 43-29 vs. West; 21-32 vs. LHP; 50-58 vs. RHP; 19-27 on grass; 52-63 on turf; 17-28 in daytime; 54-62 at night; 28-39 in one-run games; 9-10 in extra-inning games; 2-0-2 in doubleheaders.

Team record last five years: 409-400 (.506, ranks 7th in league in that span).

TEAM LEADERS

Batting average: Ivan Calderon (.300).
At-bats: Tim Wallach (577).
Runs: Delino DeShields (83).
Hits: Marquis Grissom (149).
Total bases: Ivan Calderon (226).
Doubles: Larry Walker (30).
Triples: Marquis Grissom (9).
Home runs: Ivan Calderon (19).
Runs batted in: Ivan Calderon (75).
Stolen bases: Marquis Grissom (76).
Slugging percentage: Ivan Calderon (.481).
On-base percentage: Ivan Calderon (.368).
Wins: Dennis Martinez (14).
Earned-run average: Dennis Martinez (2.39).
Complete games: Dennis Martinez (9).
Shutouts: Dennis Martinez (5).
Saves: Barry Jones (13).
Innings pitched: Dennis Martinez (222).
Strikeouts: Dennis Martinez (123).

GAMES BY POSITION

Catcher: Gilberto Reyes 80, Mike Fitzgerald 54, Ron Hassey 34, Nelson Santovenia 30.
First base: Andres Galarraga 105, Larry Walker 39, Tom Foley 31, Nelson Santovenia 7, Ivan Calderon 4, Eric Bullock 3, Mike Fitzgerald 3, Bret Barberie 1, Junior Noboa 1.
Second base: Delino DeShields 148, Bret Barberie 10, Junior Noboa 6, Tom Foley 2.
Third base: Tim Wallach 149, Bret Barberie 10, Tom Foley 6, Junior Noboa 2.
Shortstop: Spike Owen 133, Tom Foley 43, Bret Barberie 19, Junior Noboa 2.
Outfield: Marquis Grissom 138, Ivan Calderon 122, Dave Martinez 112, Larry Walker 102, Kenny Williams 24, John VanderWal 17, Eric Bullock 9, Junior Noboa 7, Mike Fitzgerald 3, Nikco Riesgo 2.

TOP 10 DRAFT CHOICES

1. **Cliff Floyd**, Thornwood High School, South Holland, Ill.
2a. **Scott Pisciotta**, RHP, Walton High School, Marietta, Ga.
2b. **Rodney Pedraza**, RHP, University of Texas.
3. **Jeff Hostetler**, RHP, Cleveland State (Tenn.) Junior College.
4. **Jim Austin**, 3B/OF, Arizona State University.
5. **Mike Daniel**, C, Oklahoma State University.
6. **Derrick White**, 1B, University of Oklahoma.
7. **Doug O'Neill**, OF, Cal Poly San Luis Obispo.
8. **Mark LaRosa**, RHP, Louisiana State University.
9. **Brett Jenkins**, 2B, University of Southern California.
10. **Brian Looney**, LHP, Boston College.

NEW YORK METS
NATIONAL LEAGUE EAST DIVISION

1992 SCHEDULE

APRIL

S	M	T	W	T	F	S
5	6 N	7 N	8 N	9	10	11
	STL	STL	STL	STL	MON H	MON H
12	13 N	14 N	15 N	16	17 N	18
MON H	PHI H	PHI H	PHI H		MON	MON
19	20	21 N	22 N	23	24 N	25 N
MON		STL H	STL H	STL H	PHI	PHI
26	27	28 N	29 N	30 N		
PHI		HOU H	HOU H	HOU H		

MAY

S	M	T	W	T	F	S
					1 N	2
					ATL	ATL
3	4 N	5	6 N	7	8 N	9
ATL	HOU	HOU	CIN	CIN	LA H	LA H
10	11 N	12 N	13 N	14	15 N	16 N
LA H	SD H	SD H	SD H		LA	LA
17	18 N	19 N	20 N	21	22 N	23
LA	SD	SD	SD	SD	SF	SF
24	25 N	26 N	27 N	28	29 N	30
SF	CIN H	CIN H	CIN H		ATL H	ATL H
31						
ATL H						

JUNE

S	M	T	W	T	F	S
	1 N	2 N	3		4 N	5 N	6 N
	SF H	SF H		PIT	PIT	PIT
7	8 N	9 N	10 N	11		12 N	13 N
PIT	MON	MON	MON		PIT H	PIT H
14	15 N	16 N	17 N	18 N	19 N	20 N
PIT H	MON H	MON H	MON H	STL H	STL H	STL H
21	22 N	23 N	24 N	25	26 N	27
STL H	CHI H	CHI H	CHI H	CHI H	STL	STL
28	29 N	30 N				
STL	CHI	CHI				

JULY

S	M	T	W	T	F	S
			1	2	3 N	4 N
			CHI		HOU H	HOU H
5	6 N	7 N	8 N	9 N	10 N	11 N
HOU H	ATL	ATL	ATL	HOU	HOU	HOU
12	13	14 ★	15		16 N	17 N	18 N
HOU				SF H	SF H	SF H
19	20 N	21 N	22	23		24 N	25 N
SF H	LA H	LA H	LA H		SD H	SD H
26	27 N	28 N	29 N	30		31 N
SD H	PHI	PHI	PHI		CHI H

AUGUST

S	M	T	W	T	F	S
						1 N
						CHI H
2	3	4 N	5 N	6 N	7	8
CHI H		PIT	PIT	CHI	CHI	CHI
9	10 N	11 N	12	13		14 N	15 N
CHI	PIT H	PIT H	PIT H		PHI H	PHI H
16	17	18 N	19 N	20 N	21 N	22 N
PHI H		LA	LA	LA		SD
23	24 N	25 N	26 N	27	28 N	29
SD	SF	SF	SF		CIN H	CIN H
30 N	31 N					
CIN H	ATL H					

SEPTEMBER

S	M	T	W	T	F	S
		1 N	2 N	3 N	4 N	5 N
		ATL H	ATL H	CIN	CIN	CIN
6	7 N	8 N	9 N	10		11 N	12 N
CIN	PHI	PHI	PHI		MON	MON
13 N	14 N	15	16 N	17 N	18 N	19
MON	CHI	CHI	STL H	STL H	MON H	MON H
20	21 N	22 N	23 N	24 N	25 N	26 N
MON H	CHI H	CHI H	STL	STL	PIT	PIT
27	28 N	29 N	30 N			
PIT	PHI H	PHI H	PHI H			

OCTOBER

S	M	T	W	T	F	S
				1	2 N	3
					PIT H	PIT H
4	5	6	7	8	9	10
PIT H						

1992 SEASON

CLUB DIRECTORY

Chairman of the board
Nelson Doubleday
President and chief executive officer
Fred Wilpon
Directors
Nelson Doubleday
Fred Wilpon
J. Frank Cashen
Saul Katz
Marvin Tepper
Special adviser to the board of directors
Richard Cummins
Chief operating officer and senior exec. v.p.
J. Frank Cashen
Executive v.p. and general manager
Alan E. Harazin
Asst. vice president, baseball operations
Gerald H. Hunsicker
Vice president, operations
Bob Mandt
Vice president, treasurer
Harold W. O'Shaughnessy
Vice president, marketing
James Ross
Vice president, broadcasting
Mike Ryan
Director of public relations
Jay Horwitz
Promotions director
James Plummer
Executive assistant to the general manager
Jean Coen
Director of ticket operations
Bill Iannicielo
Controller
Rick Iandoli
Traveling secretary
Bob O'Hara

Director of scouting
Roland Johnson
Stadium manager
John McCarthy
Director of amateur baseball relations
Tommy Holmes
Club physician
Dr. David Altchek
Team trainer
Steve Garland
Scouts
Paul Baretta
Larry Chase
Jim Eschen
Dick Gernert
Rob Guzik
R.J. Harrison
Marty Harvat
Ken Houp
Reginald Jackson
Darrell Johnson
Buddy Kerr
Andy Korenek
Craig Kornfield
Jim Marshall
Joe Mason
Bob Minor
Harry Minor
Carlos Pascual
Jim Reeves
Paul Ricciarini
Junior Roman
Bob Rossi
Daraka Shaheed
Eddy Toledo
Terry Tripp
Bob Wellman
Jim Woodward

SCHEDULE KEY

H—Home game.   *All-Star Game at San Diego/Jack Murphy Stadium.
N—Night game (any game starting after 5 p.m.).

SPRING TRAINING ROSTER

Manager—Jeff Torborg (10).

Coaches—Mike Cubbage (4), Barry Foote (26), Dave LaRoche (28), Tom McCraw (27), Mel Stottlemyre (5).

No.	PITCHERS	B/T	Ht./Wt.	Born	1991 clubs
46	Bross, Terry	R/R	6-9/230	3-30-66	Tidewater, Williamsport, New York NL
44	Burke, Tim	R/R	6-3/205	2-19-59	Montreal, New York NL
17	Cone, David	L/R	6-1/190	1-2-63	New York NL
50	Fernandez, Sid	L/L	6-1/230	10-12-62	St. Lucie, Williamsport, Tidewater, New York NL
31	Franco, John	L/L	5-10/185	9-17-60	New York NL
	Gibson, Paul	R/L	6-0/185	1-4-60	Detroit
16	Gooden, Dwight	R/R	6-3/210	11-16-64	New York NL
13	Hillman, Eric	L/L	6-10/225	4-27-66	Tidewater
40	Innis, Jeff	R/R	6-1/180	7-5-62	New York NL
38	Johnstone, John	R/R	6-3/195	11-25-68	Williamsport
	Marshall, Randy	L/L	6-3/170	10-12-66	London, Toledo
39	Rosenberg, Steve	L/L	6-0/185	10-31-64	Las Vegas, San Diego
18	Saberhagen, Bret	R/R	6-1/200	4-11-64	Kansas City
48	Schourek, Pete	L/L	6-5/195	5-10-69	New York NL, Tidewater
43	Simons, Doug	L/L	6-0/160	9-15-66	New York NL
34	Valera, Julio	R/R	6-2/215	10-13-68	Tidewater, New York NL
66	Vasquez, Julian	R/R	6-3/165	5-24-68	St. Lucie
63	Vitko, Joe	R/R	6-8/210	2-1-70	St. Lucie
47	Whitehurst, Wally	R/R	6-3/195	4-11-64	New York NL
19	Young, Anthony	R/R	6-2/200	1-19-66	Tidewater, New York NL

No.	CATCHERS	B/T	Ht./Wt.	Born	1991 clubs
64	Fordyce, Brook	R/R	6-1/185	5-7-70	St. Lucie
9	Hundley, Todd	S/R	5-11/185	5-27-69	Tidewater, New York NL
22	O'Brien, Charlie	R/R	6-2/190	5-1-61	New York NL
2	Sasser, Mackey	L/R	6-1/210	8-3-62	New York NL

No.	INFIELDERS	B/T	Ht./Wt.	Born	1991 clubs
11	Baez, Kevin	R/R	6-0/170	1-10-67	Tidewater
23	Donnels, Chris	L/R	6-0/185	4-21-66	Tidewater, New York NL
15	Elster, Kevin	R/R	6-2/200	8-3-64	New York NL
21	Hansen, Terrel	R/R	6-3/210	9-25-61	Tidewater
29	Magadan, Dave	L/R	6-3/200	9-30-62	New York NL
33	Murray, Eddie	S/R	6-2/222	2-24-56	Los Angeles
65	Navarro, Tito	S/R	5-10/155	9-12-70	Williamsport
3	Noboa, Junior	R/R	5-10/165	11-10-64	Montreal
32	Pecota, Bill	R/R	6-2/190	2-16-60	Kansas City
30	Randolph, Willie	R/R	5-11/171	7-6-54	Milwaukee

No.	OUTFIELDERS	B/T	Ht./Wt.	Born	1991 clubs
25	Bonilla, Bobby	S/R	6-3/240	2-23-63	Pittsburgh
6	Boston, Daryl	L/L	6-3/205	1-4-63	New York NL
1	Coleman, Vince	S/R	6-1/185	9-22-61	New York NL
8	Gallagher, Dave	R/R	6-0/184	9-20-60	California
62	Howell, Pat	S/R	5-11/155	8-31-68	Williamsport, St. Lucie
20	Johnson, Howard	S/R	5-10/195	11-29-60	New York NL

BALLPARK INFORMATION

Ballpark (capacity, surface)
Shea Stadium (55,601, grass)

Address
Roosevelt Ave. and 126th St.
Flushing, NY 11368

Business phone
718-507-6387

Ticket information
718-507-8499

Ticket prices
$15 (box)
$12 (upper level box)
$12 (loge and mezzanine reserved)
$6.50 (bk. rows, loge & mezz. res.)
$6.50 (upper level reserved)
$1 (senior citizens)

Field dimensions (from home plate)
To left field at foul line, 338 feet
To center field, 410 feet
To right field at foul line, 338 feet

First game played
April 17, 1964 (Pirates 4, Mets 3)

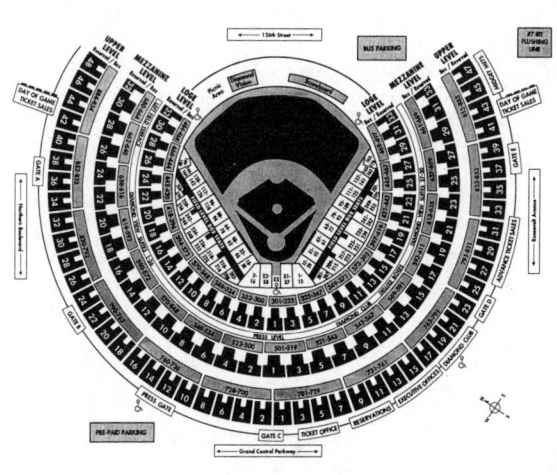

MINOR LEAGUE AFFILIATES

Class	Team	League	Manager
AAA	Tidewater	International	Clint Hurdle
AA	Binghamton	Eastern	Steve Swisher
A	St. Lucie	Florida State	John Tamargo
A	Columbia	South Atlantic	Tim Blackwell
A	Pittsfield	New York-Pennsylvania	Jim Thrift
Rookie	Kingsport	Appalachian	Andre David
Rookie	Sarasota Mets	Gulf Coast	Junior Roman

BROADCAST INFORMATION

Radio: WFAN-AM (660). Broadcasters: Gary Cohen, Bob Murphy.
TV: WWOR-TV (Channel 9). Broadcasters: Ralph Kiner, Tim McCarver.
Cable TV: SportsChannel. Broadcasters: Ralph Kiner, Fran Healy, Rusty Staub.

SPRING TRAINING

Ballpark (city): St. Lucie County Stadium (Port St. Lucie, Fla.).
Ticket information: 407-871-2115.

HISTORY

YEAR-BY-YEAR RECORDS

Year	Pos.	W	L	Pct.	*GB
1962	10th	40	120	.250	60½
1963	10th	51	111	.315	48
1964	10th	53	109	.327	40
1965	10th	50	112	.309	47
1966	9th	66	95	.410	28½
1967	10th	61	101	.377	40½
1968	9th	73	89	.451	24
1969	1st†	100	62	.617	+ 8
1970	3rd	83	79	512	6
1971	T3rd	83	79	.512	14
1972	3rd	83	73	.532	13½
1973	1st†	82	79	.509	+ 1½
1974	5th	71	91	.438	17
1975	T3rd	82	80	.506	10½
1976	3rd	86	76	.531	15
1977	6th	64	98	.395	37
1978	6th	66	96	.407	24
1979	6th	63	99	.389	35
1980	5th	67	95	.414	24
1981	5th/4th	41	62	.398	‡
1982	6th	65	97	.401	27
1983	6th	68	94	.420	22
1984	2nd	90	72	.556	6½
1985	2nd	98	64	.605	3
1986	1st†	108	54	.667	+21½
1987	2nd	92	70	.568	3
1988	1st§	100	60	.625	+15
1989	2nd	87	75	.537	6
1990	2nd	91	71	.562	4
1991	5th	77	84	.478	20½

*Games behind winner. †Won Championship Series. ‡First half 17-34; second 24-28. §Lost Championship Series.

MANAGERS

Name	Record	Years
Casey Stengel	175-404	'62-65
Wes Westrum	142-237	'65-67
Salty Parker	4-7	1967
Gil Hodges	339-309	'68-71
Yogi Berra	292-296	'72-75
Roy McMillan	26-27	1975
Joe Frazier	101-106	'76-77
Joe Torre	286-240	'77-81
George Bamberger	81-127	'82-83
Frank Howard	52-64	1983
Davey Johnson	595-417	'84-90
Bud Harrelson	145-129	'90-91
Mike Cubbage	3-4	1991

DAY BY DAY

NEW YORK METS

Date	Opp.	Res.	Score (inn.*)	Hits	Opp. hits	Winning pitcher	Losing pitcher	Save	Record	Pos.	GB
4-8	Phi.	W	2-1	6	6	Gooden	Mulholland	Franco	1-0	T 1st	...
4-9	Phi.	W	2-1 (10)	5	10	Simons	Boever		2-0	T 1st	½
4-10	Phi.	L	7-8 (10)	8	10	McDowell	Innis	Williams	2-1	T 1st	...
4-11	Mon.	W	6-3	8	8	Whitehurst	Mahler	Franco	3-1	1st	+½
4-12	Mon.	L	3-4 (11)	5	11	Burke	Franco	Frey	3-2	2nd	½
4-13	Mon.	W	5-3	7	7	Gooden	Martinez		4-2	1st	+½
4-14	Mon.	W	7-1	9	5	Viola	Nabholz		5-2	1st	+1½
4-15	At Pit.	W	9-3	16	9	Cone	Kipper		6-2	1st	+1½
4-16	At Pit.	L	2-4	6	9	Tomlin	Whitehurst	Belinda	6-3	1st	+½
4-17	At Pit.	L	0-4	1	5	Smiley	Darling		6-4	2nd	½
4-19	At Mon.	L	1-2	5	4	Martinez	Gooden	Burke	6-5	T2nd	1
4-20	At Mon.	W	3-1	6	9	Viola	Nabholz	Franco	7-5	T 1st	...
4-21	At Mon.	W	9-5	12	13	Cone	Boyd	Schourek	8-5	T 1st	...
4-23	At Phi.	W	2-1	3	6	Darling	Grimsley	Franco	9-5	T 1st	...
4-24	At Phi.	W	7-3	11	7	Schourek	Henry		10-5	T 1st	...
4-25	At Phi.	L	3-5	3	10	McDowell	Simons	Williams	10-6	2nd	1
4-26	Pit.	W	2-0	9	6	Viola	Smith	Franco	11-6	T 1st	...
4-27	Pit.	L	1-10	4	16	Tomlin	Cone		11-7	T2nd	1
4-28	Pit.	L	3-7	7	9	Smiley	Darling		11-8	T2nd	2
4-30	S.D.	W	6-3 (6½)	13	4	Gooden	Lilliquist	Pena	12-8	3rd	1
5-1	S.D.	L	7-8	12	9	Hurst	Viola	Lefferts	12-9	3rd	2
5-3	S.F.	W	3-0	6	5	Cone	Downs	Franco	13-9	3rd	2
5-4	S.F.	W	6-4 (12)	12	12	Schourek	LaCoss		14-9	2nd	1
5-5	S.F.	L	0-2	5	6	Black	Gooden		14-10	2nd	1
5-7	L.A.	W	6-5	8	11	Viola	Belcher		15-10	2nd	1½
5-8	L.A.	L	1-3	4	9	Martinez	Simons	Howell	15-11	2nd	2½
5-10	At S.F.	L	0-7	4	12	Black	Gooden		15-12	2nd	3½
5-11	At S.F.	W	6-2	12	7	Darling	Robinson	Pena	16-12	2nd	2½
5-12	At S.F.	L	4-2 (11)	12	10	Franco	Righetti		17-12	2nd	1½
5-13	At S.D.	L	2-5	7	9	Benes	Cone	Lefferts	17-13	2nd	2
5-14	At S.D.	W	6-1	10	4	Whitehurst	Nolte	Schourek	18-13	2nd	2
5-15	At S.D.	W	7-1	13	7	Gooden	Whitson		19-13	2nd	2
5-17	At L.A.	W	4-2	6	6	Viola	Morgan		20-13	2nd	1½
5-18	At L.A.	L	3-4	11	5	Crews	Franco	Howell	20-14	2nd	2
5-19	At L.A.	L	5-7	9	5	Martinez	Cone	Crews	20-15	2nd	2
5-21	Chi.	W	8-6	10	11	Gooden	Sutcliffe	Franco	21-15	2nd	2
5-22	Chi.	L	2-5	5	11	Maddux	Viola		21-16	2nd	2
5-23	Chi.	L	3-4	8	9	Lancaster	Franco	Assenmacher	21-17	3rd	2
5-24	St.L.	W	6-2	16	8	Cone	B. Smith		22-17	2nd	2
5-25	St.L.	L	2-7	7	9	Hill	Whitehurst		22-18	3rd	3
5-26	St.L.	L	4-14	8	23	Carpenter	Gooden		22-19	3rd	4
5-27	At Chi.	W	3-1	8	7	Viola	Maddux	Franco	23-19	3rd	4
5-28	At Chi.	W	9-8	10	13	Pena	Assenmacher	Franco	24-19	2nd	4
5-29	At Chi.	W	8-1	9	7	Cone	Scanlan		25-19	2nd	4
5-31	At St.L.	W	10-5	14	12	Whitehurst	Agosto		26-19	2nd	4
6-1	At St.L.	L	5-6 (10)	10	16	Agosto	Franco		26-20	2nd	5
6-2	At St.L.	L	1-3	6	7	Tewksbury	Darling	L. Smith	26-21	2nd	6
6-4	At Cin.	W	4-2	7	4	Cone	Hammond	Franco	27-21	2nd	5
6-5	At Cin.	L	10-11	11	17	Browning	Gooden	Dibble	27-22	2nd	6
6-6	At Cin.	L	3-5	7	9	Power	Viola	Myers	27-23	2nd	6
6-7	At Hou.	W	6-3	7	8	Simons	Schilling		28-23	2nd	6
6-8	At Hou.	W	4-3 (11)	11	11	Pena	Capel	Franco	29-23	2nd	5
6-9	At Hou.	L	0-1	3	3	Harnisch	Cone		29-24	2nd	5
6-10	At Hou.	L	4-6	8	11	Schilling	Franco	Capel	29-25	2nd	6
6-11	Atl.	W	2-1	4	4	Viola	Leibrandt	Franco	30-25	2nd	5½
6-12	Atl.	L	1-6	5	13	Avery	Darling		30-26	2nd	6½
6-13	Atl.	L	2-3	4	6	Smith	Whitehurst	Berenguer	30-27	3rd	6½
6-14	Hou.	L	1-4	4	11	Capel	Franco	Clancy	30-28	3rd	6½
6-15	Hou.	W	6-0	9	3	Gooden	Jones		31-28	3rd	5½
6-16	Hou.	L	4-5	9	11	Portugal	Viola	Osuna	31-29	3rd	6½
6-17	Cin.	W	10-6	13	11	Darling	Scudder		32-29	3rd	6½
6-18	Cin.	W	7-5	9	13	Pena	Myers		33-29	3rd	6½
6-19	Cin.	L	6-7	12	12	Gross	Cone	Dibble	33-30	3rd	6½
6-20	At Atl.	W	9-7	12	11	Gooden	Smoltz	Pena	34-30	3rd	5½
6-21	At Atl.	L	2-4	5	6	Leibrandt	Viola	Berenguer	34-31	3rd	6½
6-22	At Atl.	W	7-2	12	5	Darling	Avery		35-31	3rd	5½
6-23	At Atl.	L	3-4	6	8	Mercker	Whitehurst	Berenguer	35-32	3rd	5½
6-25	Mon.	W	8-5	9	9	Pena	Jones		36-32	3rd	4½
6-26	Mon.	W	7-4	10	14	Viola	Gardner	Franco	37-32	3rd	4½
6-27	Mon.	W	4-3	10	8	Cone	Boyd	Franco	38-32	3rd	4½

NEW YORK METS

1992 SEASON

Date	Opp.	Res.	Score (inn.*)	Hits	Opp. hits	Winning pitcher	Losing pitcher	Save	Record	Pos.	GB
6-28	Phi.	L	2-6	4	8	DeJesus	Darling		38-33	3rd	5 ½
6-29	Phi.	W	5-0	7	7	Whitehurst	Mulholland		39-33	3rd	5 ½
6-30	Phi.	L	9-10	10	17	Cox	Gooden	Williams	39-34	3rd	6 ½
7-1	At Mon.	W	4-2	10	10	Viola	Gardner	Franco	40-34	3rd	5 ½
7-2	At Mon.	W	2-1	4	8	Pena	Jones	Franco	41-34	3rd	5 ½
7-3	At Mon.	W	4-0	10	2	Darling	Haney		42-34	3rd	5 ½
7-4	At Mon.	W	5-1	7	4	Whitehurst	Burke		43-34	2nd	4 ½
7-5	At Phi.	W	3-1	6	4	Gooden	Cox	Franco	44-34	2nd	3 ½
7-6	At Phi.	W	2-1	8	6	Viola	Ruffin	Franco	45-34	2nd	2 ½
7-7	At Phi.	W	8-2	8	5	Cone	Greene		46-34	2nd	2 ½
7-11	S.D.	W	4-3	11	9	Franco	Andersen		47-34	2nd	2 ½
7-12	S.D.	W	6-3	9	3	Viola	Peterson	Pena	48-34	2nd	2 ½
7-13	S.D.	W	3-1	9	6	Cone	Rasmussen	Franco	49-34	2nd	2 ½
7-14	S.D.	L	1-2	1	5	Harris	Darling	Lefferts	49-35	2nd	3 ½
7-15	S.F.	L	3-4	6	6	Robinson	Whitehurst	Brantley	49-36	2nd	4 ½
7-16	S.F.	W	6-4	11	11	Gooden	Wilson	Franco	50-36	2nd	4 ½
7-17	S.F.	W	6-5	12	11	Pena	Righetti		51-36	2nd	3 ½
7-18	L.A.	L	5-10	7	11	Gross	Cone		51-37	2nd	4
7-19	L.A.	W	6-2	10	5	Burke	Martinez		52-37	2nd	4
7-20	L.A.	L	7-11	12	16	Gott	Whitehurst		52-38	2nd	4
7-21	L.A.	W	9-4	11	8	Gooden	Ojeda		53-38	2nd	4
7-23	At S.F.	L	2-4	6	5	Black	Viola	Righetti	53-39	2nd	4 ½
7-24	At S.F.	L	4-8	8	8	Burkett	Cone		53-40	2nd	5 ½
7-25	At S.F.	L	1-8	6	14	Wilson	Whitehurst		53-41	2nd	6
7-26	At S.D.	L	2-8	5	13	Hurst	Fernandez		53-42	2nd	7
7-27	At S.D.	W	4-0	8	4	Gooden	Peterson		54-42	2nd	7
7-28	At S.D.	L	0-2	5	5	Benes	Viola	Lefferts	54-43	2nd	7
7-29	At L.A.	W	5-1	10	3	Cone	Belcher		55-43	2nd	5 ½
7-30	At L.A.	L	1-3	6	6	Martinez	Schourek		55-44	2nd	5 ½
7-31	At L.A.	L	3-6	12	12	Gross	Burke		55-45	2nd	5 ½
8-2	Chi.	L	2-4 (10)	8	11	Assenmacher	Pena		55-46	2nd	5
8-3	Chi.	L	2-9	6	13	Scanlan	Viola		55-47	3rd	5
8-4	Chi.	L	3-8	7	12	Maddux	Cone		55-48	3rd	6
8-5	Chi.	L	2-7	9	11	Castillo	Schourek		55-49	3rd	6 ½
8-6	Pit.	L	1-3	4	8	Tomlin	Fernandez		55-50	3rd	7 ½
8-7	Pit.	W	7-1	11	4	Gooden	Smith		56-50	3rd	6 ½
8-8	Pit.	W	4-3	10	8	Viola	Drabek	Franco	57-50	3rd	5 ½
8-9	At Chi.	L	4-5	7	9	Maddux	Cone		57-51	3rd	5 ½
8-10	At Chi.	L	2-6	3	9	Scanlan	Burke	Lancaster	57-52	3rd	6 ½
8-11	At Chi.	L	2-3 (14)	11	9	Boskie	Schourek		57-53	3rd	7 ½
8-12	At Chi.	L	2-3 (10)	6	9	Lancaster	Burke		57-54	3rd	8 ½
8-13	At St.L.	L	4-7	9	12	Olivares	Viola	L. Smith	57-55	3rd	9 ½
8-14	At St.L.	L	4-5	9	12	Carpenter	Franco	L. Smith	57-56	3rd	10 ½
8-15	At St.L.	L	1-4	8	10	Cormier	Whitehurst	L. Smith	57-57	T3rd	10 ½
8-16	At Pit.	L	2-8	9	9	Tomlin	Fernandez		57-58	4th	11 ½
8-17	At Pit.	L	1-4	8	10	Smith	Gooden	Belinda	57-59	4th	12 ½
8-18	At Pit.	L	2-9	6	11	Drabek	Viola		57-60	4th	13 ½
8-21 (1)	St.L.	L	3-7	6	13	B. Smith	Cone		57-61	4th	13
8-21 (2)	St.L.	W	8-0	10	5	Fernandez	Cormier		58-61	4th	12 ½
8-22	St.L.	W	6-0	13	5	Gooden	Tewksbury	Burke	59-61	4th	11 ½
8-23	Cin.	L	1-6	9	16	Browning	Viola		59-62	4th	12 ½
8-24	Cin.	L	0-7	2	14	Rijo	Whitehurst		59-63	T4th	12 ½
8-25	Cin.	W	2-1	7	9	Cone	Myers	Franco	60-63	T4th	12 ½
8-26	At Hou.	W	6-4 (10)	11	9	Franco	Henry		61-63	4th	11 ½
8-27	At Hou.	L	3-8	8	10	Kile	Whitehurst	Schilling	61-64	4th	12 ½
8-28	At Atl.	L	1-3	4	7	Glavine	Viola		61-65	T4th	13 ½
8-29	At Atl.	L	0-2	6	7	Smoltz	Young	Stanton	61-66	T4th	14 ½
8-30	At Cin.	W	3-2	6	9	Cone	Myers	Franco	62-66	4th	14 ½
8-31	At Cin.	W	8-7 (10)	10	13	Franco	Dibble		63-66	4th	14 ½
9-1	At Cin.	W	9-4	10	10	Whitehurst	Scudder	Simons	64-66	4th	13 ½
9-2	Hou.	L	0-3	6	12	Bowen	Viola	Osuna	64-67	T4th	14 ½
9-3	Hou.	W	6-1	10	8	Young	Portugal		65-67	4th	14 ½
9-4	Hou.	L	3-8	10	10	Deshaies	Cone		65-68	4th	15 ½
9-6	Atl.	L	2-4	7	11	Pena	Whitehurst	Stanton	65-69	4th	16
9-7	Atl.	L	1-6	6	9	Leibrandt	Viola		65-70	4th	16
9-8	Atl.	L	5-7	7	11	Glavine	Franco	Pena	65-71	T4th	16
9-9	Mon.	L	3-4	7	9	Barnes	Cone	Fassero	65-72	T4th	17
9-10	Mon.	W	9-0	11	1	Schourek	Gardner		66-72	T4th	16
9-11	At Chi.	W	4-1	9	6	T. Castillo	F. Castillo	Franco	67-72	4th	16
9-12	At Chi.	W	6-3	10	5	Young	Bielecki	Whitehurst	68-72	4th	15
9-13	At St.L.	W	4-2 (10)	7	9	Burke	Fraser		69-72	T3rd	15
9-14	At St.L.	L	1-2	6	1	Olivares	Cone	L. Smith	69-73	4th	16
9-15	At St.L.	L	2-7	9	11	Cormier	Schourek		69-74	4th	16
9-17 (1)	Mon.	L	4-5	11	11	Nabholz	Young	Rojas	69-75	4th	17 ½

Date	Opp.	Res.	Score (inn.*)	Hits	Opp. hits	Winning pitcher	Losing pitcher	Save	Record	Pos.	GB
9-17 (2)	Mon.	W	3-2	10	9	Whitehurst	Haney	Franco	70-75	T3rd	17
9-18	Chi.	L	1-4	5	9	Maddux	Viola		70-76	4th	18
9-20	St.L.	W	1-0	6	1	Cone	Cormier		71-76	4th	17½
9-21	St.L.	W	5-3	8	6	Schourek	Tewksbury	Franco	72-76	3rd	17½
9-22	St.L.	L	1-2	2	7	Hill	Young	L. Smith	72-77	3rd	18½
9-24	Pit.	L	8-10	11	17	Patterson	Innis	Rodriguez	72-78	T3rd	19½
9-26 (1)	Pit.	L	3-4 (15)	11	12	Landrum	Whitehurst		72-79	4th	20½
9-26 (2)	Pit.	W	2-1	6	10	Burke	Mason	Franco	73-79	3rd	19½
9-27	Phi.	W	6-4	7	5	Schourek	DeJesus	Franco	74-79	3rd	18½
9-28	Phi.	L	2-6	7	10	Brantley	Young		74-80	3rd	18½
9-29	Phi.	W	4-3	7	10	Viola	Mulholland	Franco	75-80	3rd	18½
9-30	At Pit.	L	5-6	9	9	Landrum	Simons	Rodriguez	75-81	3rd	19½
10-1	At Pit.	L	1-2	8	5	Smiley	Cone	Belinda	75-82	4th	20½
10-2	At Pit.	W	9-6 (11)	16	12	Franco	Patterson		76-82	3rd	19½
10-4	At Phi.	L	4-5 (10)	11	11	Williams	Franco		76-83	4th	19½
10-5	At Phi.	L	0-1	8	5	Mulholland	Young		76-84	5th	20½
10-6	At Phi.	W	7-0	12	3	Cone	Ashby		77-84	5th	20½

Monthly records: April (12-8), May (14-11), June (13-15), July (16-11), August (8-21), September (12-15), Oct. (2-3).

HIGHLIGHTS

High point: Beginning July 1 with a 4-2 win at Montreal, the Mets embarked on a 10-game winning streak to pull within 2½ games of first place in the National League East.

Low point: Shortly after their 10-game winning streak the Mets fell apart, losing 23 of 27 games from July 23 through August 21. Included in that stretch was a 0-10 road trip to Chicago, St. Louis and Pittsburgh, the worst trip in club history.

Turning point: The Mets' midsummer collapse can be attributed to two events: First, Manager Bud Harrelson refused to act after center fielder Vince Coleman and coach Mike Cubbage engaged in a dispute July 26. Then, on August 5, Harrelson had pitching coach Mel Stottlemyre make a pitching change during a Mets loss. Harrelson admitted later that he didn't do it because he didn't want to get booed.

Most valuable player: Infielder Howard Johnson. HoJo registered 38 home runs, 117 runs batted in (a club record) and 76 extra-base hits, all N.L.-leading totals. He also stole 30 bases, allowing him to reach the 30-homer, 30-steal club for the third time.

Most valuable pitcher: Righthander David Cone. He paced a disappointing pitching staff, finishing 14-14 and leading the league in strikeouts (241) for the second straight year.

Most improved player: Shortstop Kevin Elster. He overcame off-season shoulder surgery and finished with a .241 average, the highest of his four-year major league career.

Most pleasant surprise: Utilityman Mackey Sasser. In the same year that Sasser's well-publicized throwing problem clouded his future as a catcher, he surprised the Mets by showing good athletic ability as a utility player.

Biggest disappointment: Outfielder Kevin McReynolds. The Mets gave McReynolds a three-year contract extension before the season started. He responded with his worst year in five seasons with the Mets, hitting .259 with 16 homers and 74 RBIs.

Key injuries: Injuries to Sid Fernandez (wrist and knee) and Dwight Gooden (shoulder) hurt the rotation. Coleman was leading the league in stolen bases when he strained his left hamstring June 14. He started only 15 games the rest of the season. Hubie Brooks (neck) didn't play after August 18.

Notable: New York finished in fifth place with a 77-84 record. It was the first time the Mets finished under .500 and lower than second place since 1983.

—JOHN HARPER

RECORDS

1991 regular-season record: 77-84 (5th in N.L. East); 40-42 at home; 37-42 on road; 44-45 vs. East; 33-39 vs. West; 32-32 vs. LHP; 45-52 vs. RHP; 54-61 on grass; 23-23 on turf; 24-29 in daytime; 53-55 at night; 20-29 in one-run games; 8-8 in extra-inning games; 0-0-3 in doubleheaders.

Team record last five years: 447-360 (.554, ranks 1st in league in that span).

TEAM LEADERS

Batting average: Greg Jefferies (.272).
At-bats: Howard Johnson (564).
Runs: Howard Johnson (108).
Hits: Howard Johnson (146).
Total bases: Howard Johnson (302).
Doubles: Howard Johnson (34).
Triples: Vince Coleman (5).
Home runs: Howard Johnson (38).
Runs batted in: Howard Johnson (117).
Stolen bases: Vince Coleman (37).
Slugging percentage: Howard Johnson (.535).
On-base percentage: Dave Magadan (.378).
Wins: David Cone (14).
Earned-run average: David Cone (3.29).
Complete games: David Cone (5).
Shutouts: David Cone (2).
Saves: John Franco (30).
Innings pitched: David Cone (232⅔).
Strikeouts: David Cone (241).

GAMES BY POSITION

Catcher: Rick Cerone 81, Charlie O'Brien 67, Mackey Sasser 43, Todd Hundley 20.

First base: Dave Magadan 122, Garry Templeton 25, Chris Donnels 15, Mackey Sasser 10, Kelvin Torve 1.

Second base: Gregg Jefferies 77, Keith Miller 60, Tom Herr 57, Jeff Gardner 3, Tim Teufel 1.

Third base: Howard Johnson 104, Gregg Jefferies 51, Chris Donnels 11, Tim Teufel 5, Keith Miller 2, Garry Templeton 2.

Shortstop: Kevin Elster 107, Garry Templeton 40, Howard Johnson 28, Jeff Gardner 8, Keith Miller 2.

Outfield: Kevin McReynolds 141, Daryl Boston 115, Hubie Brooks 100, Mark Carreon 77, Vince Coleman 70, Howard Johnson 30, Keith Miller 28, Mackey Sasser 21, Terry McDaniel 14, Chuck Carr 9, Garry Templeton 2.

TOP 10 DRAFT CHOICES

1a. Al Shirley. OF, George Washington High School, Danville, Va.

1b. Bobby Jones. RHP, Fresno State University.

2a. Bill Pulsipher. LHP, Fairfax (Va.) High School.

2b. Marc Kroon RHP, Shadow Mountain High School, Phoenix.

3. Jeff Kiraly, 1B, La Cueva High School, Albuquerque.

4. Erik Hiljus, RHP, Canyon High School, Santa Clarita, Calif.

5. Jared Osentowski, 3B, Kearney (Neb.) High School.

6. Eric Reichenbach, RHP, St. John's University.

7. Frank Jacobs, 1B, Notre Dame University.

8. Randy Curtis, OF, Riverside (Calif.) Community College.

9. Dave Swanson, RHP, Berlin High School, Kensington, Conn.

10. Dwight Robinson, 3B, Middle Tennessee State University.

PHILADELPHIA PHILLIES
NATIONAL LEAGUE EAST DIVISION

1992 SCHEDULE

APRIL
S	M	T	W	T	F	S
5	6	7 CHI H	8 N CHI H	9 N CHI H	10 N PIT H	11 N PIT H
12 PIT H	13 N NY H	14 N NY	15 N NY	16	17 PIT	18 PIT
19 PIT	20 N CHI	21 CHI	22 CHI	23 CHI	24 N NY	25 N NY H
26 NY H	27 N SD	28 N SD	29 N LA	30 N LA		

MAY
S	M	T	W	T	F	S
					1 N SF	2 SF
3 SF	4	5 N LA H	6 N LA H	7	8 N SD H	9 N SD H
10 SD H	11 N SF H	12 N SF H	13 N SF H	14	15 N CIN	16 N CIN
17 CIN	18 N HOU H	19 N HOU H	20 N HOU H	21	22 N CIN H	23 N CIN H
24 CIN H	25 N ATL H	26 N ATL H	27 N ATL H	28	29 N HOU	30 HOU
31 HOU						

JUNE
S	M	T	W	T	F	S
	1 N ATL	2 N ATL	3 ATL	4	5 N STL H	6 N STL H
7 N STL H	8 N PIT H	9 N PIT H	10 N PIT H	11	12 N STL	13 N STL
14 STL	15 N PIT	16 N PIT	17 N PIT	18 N CHI H	19 N CHI H	20 N CHI H
21 CHI	22 N MON	23 N MON	24 MON	25	26 CHI	27 CHI
28 CHI	29 N MON H	30 N MON H				

JULY
S	M	T	W	T	F	S
			1 N MON H	2 N LA	3 N LA	4 N LA
5 LA	6 N SF	7 N SF	8 N SF	9	10 N SD	11 N SD
12 N SD	13	14 ★	15	16	17 N LA H	18 N LA H
19 LA H	20 N SD H	21 N SD H	22 N SD H	23	24 N SF H	25 N SF H
26 SF H	27 N NY H	28 N NY H	29 N NY H	30 MON	31 N MON	

AUGUST
S	M	T	W	T	F	S
						1 N MON
2 MON	3 N STL	4 N STL	5 N STL	6 N MON H	7 N MON H	8 N MON H
9 MON H	10	11 N STL H	12 N STL H	13 N STL H	14 N NY	15 N NY
16 NY	17 N CIN H	18 N CIN H	19	20	21 N HOU H	22 N HOU H
23 HOU H	24 N CIN	25 N CIN	26 N CIN	27	28 N ATL	29 N ATL H
30 ATL H	31 N HOU					

SEPTEMBER
S	M	T	W	T	F	S
		1 N HOU	2 N HOU	3	4 N ATL	5 N ATL
6 ATL	7 N NY H	8 N NY H	9 N NY H	10	11 N PIT	12 N PIT
13 PIT	14 N MON H	15 N MON H	16	17 CHI	18 N PIT	19 N PIT
20 PIT	21 N MON	22 N MON	23 N CHI H	24 CHI H	25 N STL H	26 N STL H
27 STL H	28 N NY	29 NY	30 N NY			

OCTOBER
S	M	T	W	T	F	S
				1	2 N STL	3 STL
4 STL	5	6	7	8	9	10

1992 SEASON

CLUB DIRECTORY

President/CEO/general partner
Bill Giles
Partners
Claire S. Betz
Estate of John Drew Betz
Tri-Play Associates
Alexander K. Buck
J. Mahlon Buck Jr.
William C. Buck
Fitz Eugene Dixon Jr.
Mrs. Rochelle Levy
Executive v.p. and chief operating officer
David Montgomery
Executive secretary
Nancy Deren
Secretary and general counsel
William Y. Webb
Dir., planning/develop. and super boxes
Tom Hudson
Senior vice president, general manager
Lee Thomas
Player personnel administrator
Ed Wade
Director, player development
Del Unser
Director, scouting
Jay Hankins
Assistant to the president
Paul Owens
Business manager, minor leagues
Bill Gargano
Traveling secretary
Eddie Ferenz
Senior vice president, finance and planning
Jerry Clothier
Vice president, public relations
Larry Shenk
Broadcaster/director speakers' bureau
Chris Wheeler
Director, community relations
Regina Castellani
Assistant director, community relations
Karen Howard
Manager, media relations
Gene Dias
Manager, publicity
Leigh McDonald
Vice president, marketing
Dennis Mannion
Director, promotions
Frank Sullivan
Manager, advertising and broadcasting
Jo-Anne Levy-Lamoreaux
Assistant director, promotions
Chris Legault
Manager, corporate marketing
Dave Buck

Vice president, ticket sales and operations
Richard Deats
Director, sales
Rory McNeil
Director, ticket operations
Dan Goroff
Manager, group sales
Kathy Killian
Director, information systems
Brian Lamoreaux
Director, stadium operations
Mike DiMuzio
Club physician
Dr. Phillip Marone
Club trainers
Jeff Cooper
Mark Andersen
National cross-checker scouts
Tony Roig
Randy Waddill
Regional cross-checker scouts
Jim Baumer
Dick Lawlor
Bob Reasonover
Special assignment, major league scouts
Ray Shore
Jimmy Stewart
Advance scout, major leagues
Hank King
Special assignment scouts
Bing Devine
Larry Rojas
Regular scouts
Emil Belich
Oliver Bidwell
Jim Bierman
Carlos Cuervo
Tom Ferguson
Eli Grba
Bill Harper
Ken Hultzapple
Jerry Jordan
John Kennedy
Jerry Lafferty
George Lauzerique
Terry Logan
Fred Mazuca
Willie Montanez
Cotton Nye
Arthur Parrack
Jack Pastore
Bob Poole
Larry Reasonover
Larry Rojas
Gerald Sanders
Roy Tanner
Scott Trcka

SCHEDULE KEY

H—Home game.   *All-Star Game at San Diego/Jack Murphy Stadium.
N—Night game (any game starting after 5 p.m.).

SPRING TRAINING ROSTER

Manager—Jim Fregosi (11).

Coaches—Larry Bowa (2), Denis Menke (14), Johnny Podres (46), Mel Roberts (26), Mike Ryan (25), John Vukovich (18).

No.	PITCHERS	B/T	Ht./Wt.	Born	1991 clubs
47	Abbott, Kyle	L/L	6-4/200	2-18-68	Edmonton, California
40	Ashby, Andy	R/R	6-5/180	7-11-67	Scranton-W.B., Philadelphia
53	Ayrault, Bob	R/R	6-4/230	4-27-66	Scranton-W.B.
55	Borland, Toby	R/R	6-6/180	5-29-69	Reading
51	Brantley, Cliff	R/R	6-1/190	4-12-68	Reading, Scranton-W.B., Philadelphia
41	Chapin, Darrin	R/R	6-0/170	2-1-66	Columbus (O.), New York AL
21	Combs, Pat	L/L	6-4/207	10-29-66	Philadelphia, Scranton-W.B.
54	DeJesus, Jose	R/R	6-5/213	1-6-65	Philadelphia
49	Greene, Tommy	R/R	6-5/227	4-6-67	Philadelphia
48	Grimsley, Jason	R/R	6-3/182	8-7-67	Scranton-W.B., Philadelphia
42	Hartley, Mike	R/R	6-1/197	8-31-61	Los Angeles, Philadelphia
43	Howell, Ken	R/R	6-3/237	11-28-60	Scranton-W.B.
50	Jones, Barry	R/R	6-4/225	2-15-63	Montreal
45	Mulholland, Terry	R/L	6-3/206	3-9-63	Philadelphia
39	Ritchie, Wally	L/L	6-2/180	7-12-65	Scranton-W.B., Philadelphia
24	Searcy, Steve	L/L	6-1/195	6-5-64	Detroit, Philadelphia
28	Williams, Mitch	L/L	6-4/205	11-17-64	Philadelphia

No.	CATCHERS	B/T	Ht./Wt.	Born	1991 clubs
10	Daulton, Darren	L/R	6-2/200	1-3-62	Reading, Scranton-W.B., Philadelphia
57	Lindsey, Doug	R/R	6-2/200	9-22-67	Reading, Philadelphia
23	Pratt, Todd	R/R	6-3/195	2-9-67	Pawtucket

No.	INFIELDERS	B/T	Ht./Wt.	Born	1991 clubs
6	Backman, Wally	S/R	5-9/168	9-22-59	Philadelphia
5	Batiste, Kim	R/R	6-0/175	3-15-68	Scranton-W.B., Philadelphia
7	Duncan, Mariano	R/R	6-0/185	3-13-63	Cincinnati
8	Hayes, Charlie	R/R	6-0/210	5-29-65	Philadelphia
15	Hollins, Dave	S/R	6-1/207	5-25-66	Scranton-W.B., Philadelphia
17	Jordan, Ricky	R/R	6-3/209	5-26-65	Philadelphia
29	Kruk, John	L/L	5-10/200	2-9-61	Philadelphia
12	Morandini, Mickey	L/R	5-11/167	4-22-66	Scranton-W.B., Philadelphia
9	Sveum, Dale	S/R	6-3/185	11-23-63	Milwaukee

No.	OUTFIELDERS	B/T	Ht./Wt.	Born	1991 clubs
33	Amaro, Ruben	S/R	5-10/170	2-12-65	Edmonton, California
16	Castillo, Braulio	R/R	6-0/180	5-13-68	San Antonio, Scranton-W.B., Philadelphia
44	Chamberlain, Wes	R/R	6-2/210	4-13-66	Scranton-W.B., Philadelphia
57	Dostal, Bruce	L/L	6-0/195	3-10-65	Reading
4	Dykstra, Len	L/L	5-10/186	2-10-63	Philadelphia
19	Lindeman, Jim	R/R	6-1/200	1-10-62	Scranton-W.B., Philadelphia
27	Longmire, Anthony	L/R	6-1/195	6-12-68	Reading, Scranton-W.B.
3	Murphy, Dale	R/R	6-4/221	3-12-56	Philadelphia
58	Peguero, Julio	S/R	6-0/180	9-7-68	Scranton-W.B.
56	Williams, Cary	R/R	6-3/190	7-29-69	Reading

BALLPARK INFORMATION

Ballpark (capacity, surface)
Veterans Stadium (62,382, artificial)

Address
P.O. Box 7575
Philadelphia, PA 19101

Business phone
215-463-6000

Ticket information
215-463-1000

Ticket prices
$12 (field box)
$10 (sections 258-274)
$10 (terrace box)
$10 (loge box)
$7 (reserved, 600 level)
$4 (reserved, 700 level)

Field dimensions (from home plate)
To left field at foul line, 330 feet
To center field, 408 feet
To right field at foul line, 330 feet

First game played
April 10, 1971 (Phillies 4, Expos 1)

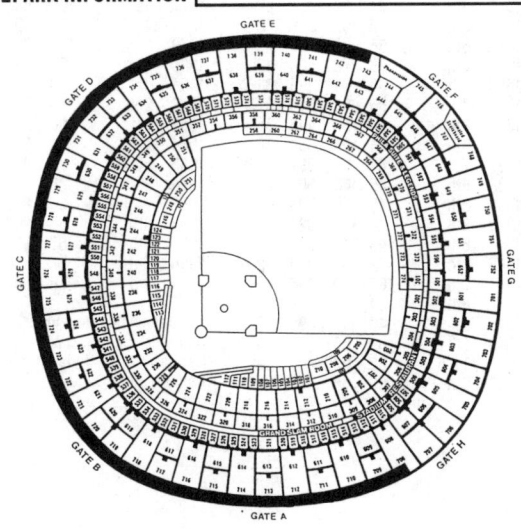

MINOR LEAGUE AFFILIATES

Class	Team	League	Manager
AAA	Scranton/Wilkes-Barre	International	Lee Elia
AA	Reading	Eastern	Don McCormack
A	Clearwater	Florida State	Bill Dancy
A	Spartanburg	South Atlantic	Roy Majtyka
A	Batavia	New York-Pennsylvania	Ramon Aviles
Rookie	Martinsville	Appalachian	Roly De Armas

☐ BROADCAST INFORMATION ☐

Radio: WOGL-AM (1210). Broadcasters: Harry Kalas, Richie Ashburn, Chris Wheeler, Andy Musser.
TV: WTXF-TV (Channel 29). Broadcasters: Andy Musser, Richie Ashburn, Harry Kalas.
Cable TV: PRISM, SportsChannel. Broadcasters: Garry Maddox, Chris Wheeler; other to be announced.

SPRING TRAINING

Ballpark (city): Jack Russell Stadium (Clearwater, Fla.).
Ticket information: 813-442-8496.

HISTORY

YEAR-BY-YEAR RECORDS

Year	Pos.	W	L	Pct.	*GB	Year	Pos.	W	L	Pct.	*GB
1901	2nd	83	57	.593	7½	1949	3rd	81	73	.526	16
1902	7th	56	81	.409	46	1950	1st	91	63	.591	+ 2
1903	7th	49	86	.363	39½	1951	5th	73	81	.474	23½
1904	8th	52	100	.342	53½	1952	4th	87	67	.565	9½
1905	4th	83	69	.546	21½	1953	T3rd	83	71	.539	22
1906	4th	71	82	.464	45½	1954	4th	75	79	.487	22
1907	3rd	83	64	.565	21½	1955	4th	77	77	.500	21½
1908	4th	83	71	.539	16	1956	5th	71	83	.461	22
1909	5th	74	79	.484	36½	1957	5th	77	77	.500	19
1910	4th	78	75	.510	25½	1958	8th	69	85	.448	23
1911	4th	79	73	.520	19½	1959	8th	64	90	.416	23
1912	5th	73	79	.480	30½	1960	8th	59	95	.383	36
1913	2nd	88	63	.583	12½	1961	8th	47	107	.305	46
1914	6th	74	80	.481	20½	1962	7th	81	80	.503	20
1915	1st	90	62	.592	+ 7	1963	4th	87	75	.537	12
1916	2nd	91	62	.595	2½	1964	T2nd	92	70	.568	1
1917	2nd	87	65	.572	10	1965	6th	85	76	.528	11½
1918	6th	55	68	.447	26	1966	4th	87	75	.537	8
1919	8th	47	90	.343	47½	1967	5th	82	80	.506	19½
1920	8th	62	91	.405	30½	1968	T7th	76	86	.469	21
1921	8th	51	103	.331	43½	1969	5th	63	99	.389	37
1922	7th	57	96	.373	35½	1970	5th	73	88	.453	15½
1923	8th	50	104	.325	45½	1971	6th	67	95	.414	30
1924	7th	55	96	.364	37	1972	6th	59	97	.378	37½
1925	T6th	68	85	.444	27	1973	6th	71	91	.438	11½
1926	8th	58	93	.384	29½	1974	3rd	80	82	.494	8
1927	8th	51	103	.331	43	1975	2nd	86	76	.531	6½
1928	8th	43	109	.283	51	1976	1st†	101	61	.623	+ 9
1929	5th	71	82	.464	27½	1977	1st†	101	61	.623	+ 5
1930	8th	52	102	.338	40	1978	1st†	90	72	.556	+ 1½
1931	6th	66	88	.429	35	1979	4th	84	78	.519	14
1932	4th	78	76	.506	12	1980	1st‡	91	71	.562	+ 1
1933	7th	60	92	.395	31	1981	1st/3rd	59	48	.551	§*
1934	7th	56	93	.376	37	1982	2nd	89	73	.549	3
1935	7th	64	89	.418	35½	1983	1st‡	90	72	.556	+ 6
1936	8th	54	100	.351	38	1984	4th	81	81	.500	15½
1937	7th	61	92	.399	34½	1985	5th	75	87	.463	26
1938	8th	45	105	.300	43	1986	2nd	86	75	.534	21½
1939	8th	45	106	.298	50½	1987	T4th	80	82	.494	15
1940	8th	50	103	.327	50	1988	6th	65	96	.404	35½
1941	8th	43	111	.279	57	1989	6th	67	95	.414	26
1942	8th	42	109	.278	62½	1990	T4th	77	85	.475	18
1943	7th	64	90	.416	41	1991	3rd	78	84	.481	20
1944	8th	61	92	.399	43½						
1945	8th	46	108	.299	52						
1946	5th	69	85	.448	28						
1947	T7th	62	92	.403	32						
1948	6th	66	88	.429	25½						

*Games behind winner. †Lost Championship Series. ‡Won Championship Series. §Lost division playoff. *First half 34-21; second 25-27.

MANAGERS

Name	Record	Years
Bill Shettsline	139-138	'01-02
Chief Zimmer	49-86	1903
Hugh Duffy	206-251	'04-06
Bill Murray	240-214	'07-09
Red Dooin	392-370	'10-14
Pat Moran	323-257	'15-18
Jack Coombs	18-44	1919
Gavvy Cravath	91-137	'19-20
Bill Donovan	31-71	1921
Kaiser Wilhelm	77-128	'21-22
Art Fletcher	231-378	'23-26
Stuffy McInnis	51-103	1927
Burt Shotton	370-439	'28-33
Jimmy Wilson	280-477	'34-38
Hans Lobert	42-111	'38, '42
Doc Prothro	138-320	'39-41
Bucky Harris	40-53	1943
Fred Fitzsimmons	102-179	'43-45
Ben Chapman	197-277	'45-48
Dusty Cooke	6-6	1948
Eddie Sawyer	390-424	'48-52
		'58-60
Steve O'Neill	182-140	'52-54
Terry Moore	35-42	1954
Mayo Smith	264-281	'55-58
Eddie Sawyer	94-132	'58-60
Andy Cohen	1-0	1960
Gene Mauch	645-684	'60-68
George Myatt	21-35	'68, '69
Bob Skinner	92-123	'68-69
Frank Lucchesi	166-233	'70-72
Paul Owens	161-158	1972
		'83-84
Danny Ozark	594-510	'73-79
Dallas Green	169-130	'79-81
Pat Corrales	132-115	'82-83
John Felske	190-194	'85-87
Lee Elia	111-142	'87-88
John Vukovich	5-4	1988
Nick Leyva	148-189	'89-91
Jim Fregosi	74-75	1991

DAY BY DAY

Date	Opp.	Res.	Score (inn.*)	Hits	Opp. hits	Winning pitcher	Losing pitcher	Save	Record	Pos.	GB
4-8	At N.Y.	L	1-2	6	6	Gooden	Mulholland	Franco	0-1	T5th	1
4-9	At N.Y.	L	1-2 (10)	10	5	Simons	Boever		0-2	6th	2
4-10	At N.Y.	W	8-7 (10)	10	8	McDowell	Innis	Williams	1-2	T5th	1
4-12	St.L.	W	11-4	14	12	Combs	Moyer		2-2	T3rd	1
4-13	St.L.	W	4-2	7	10	Mulholland	Tewksbury	Williams	3-2	T2nd	½
4-14	St.L.	L	7-11	8	12	B. Smith	LaPoint	L. Smith	3-3	T2nd	1½
4-15	At Chi.	L	4-5	4	8	Maddux	Grimsley	Smith	3-4	T4th	2½
4-16	At Chi.	L	3-4 (13)	8	8	Bielecki	Williams		3-5	5th	2½
4-17	At Chi.	L	1-4	4	7	Boskie	Combs	Smith	3-6	6th	3
4-19	At St.L.	L	1-3	5	6	Tewksbury	Mulholland	L. Smith	3-7	6th	3½
4-20 (1)	At St.L.	L	1-12	6	10	DeLeon	Grimsley	Olivares	3-8	6th	3½
4-20 (2)	At St.L.	W	6-5 (10)	12	7	McDowell	Carpenter	Williams	4-8	6th	3½
4-21	At St.L.	L	6-7 (10)	9	9	L. Smith	Williams		4-9	6th	4
4-23	N.Y.	L	1-2	6	3	Darling	Grimsley	Franco	4-10	6th	5
4-24	N.Y.	L	3-7	7	11	Schourek	Henry		4-11	6th	6
4-25	N.Y.	W	5-3	10	3	McDowell	Simons	Williams	5-11	T5th	6
4-26	S.D.	L	0-4	6	7	Hurst	DeJesus		5-12	T5th	6
4-27	S.D.	W	4-3 (12)	12	9	Akerfelds	Maddux		6-12	5th	6
4-28	S.D.	W	9-2	11	3	Grimsley	Nolte		7-12	5th	6
4-29	S.D.	W	7-2	12	6	Mulholland	Whitson		8-12	5th	5½
4-30	S.F.	W	11-9	14	11	Boever	Brantley	Williams	9-12	5th	4½
5-1	S.F.	W	4-1	7	4	Greene	LaCoss	McDowell	10-12	5th	4½
5-3	L.A.	L	1-7	4	13	Martinez	Cox		10-13	5th	5½
5-4	L.A.	W	4-3	10	7	Mulholland	Howell	Williams	11-13	T4th	4½
5-5	L.A.	L	2-3	9	12	Morgan	Boever	Howell	11-14	5th	4½
5-7	At S.D.	L	2-4	9	12	Hurst	DeJesus	Lefferts	11-15	T5th	6
5-8	At S.D.	W	5-2	9	5	Cox	Benes	McDowell	12-15	T5th	6
5-9	At S.D.	W	9-6	15	8	Mulholland	Lilliquist	Williams	13-15	5th	5½
5-10	At L.A.	L	1-3	7	9	Ojeda	Boever	Candelaria	13-16	6th	6½
5-11	At L.A.	L	2-3	7	9	Morgan	Combs	Howell	13-17	6th	6½
5-12	At L.A.	W	7-3	13	4	DeJesus	Belcher		14-17	6th	5½
5-13	At S.F.	W	3-2 (11)	6	6	Boever	Beck		15-17	T5th	5
5-14	At S.F.	W	9-0	14	8	Mulholland	Downs		16-17	T4th	5
5-15	At S.F.	L	2-4	5	9	Black	Grimsley	Brantley	16-18	5th	6
5-17	Chi.	W	1-0 (16)	10	10	Greene	Lancaster		17-18	T4th	5½
5-18	Chi.	W	5-2	8	4	Boever	Assenmacher	Williams	18-18	4th	5
5-19	Chi.	L	1-2 (10)	6	9	Bielecki	McDowell	Smith	18-19	T4th	5
5-21	At Mon.	L	0-3	5	7	Martinez	Grimsley		18-20	T5th	6
5-22	At Mon.	W	8-1	10	9	Combs	Barnes		19-20	T4th	5
5-23	At Mon.	W	2-0	8	0	Greene	Boyd		20-20	T4th	4
5-24	At Pit.	L	1-9	9	11	Smith	Mulholland		20-21	5th	5
5-25	At Pit.	L	2-4 (11)	4	9	Palacios	Boever		20-22	5th	6
5-26	At Pit.	L	2-5	5	9	Smiley	Grimsley	Landrum	20-23	5th	7
5-27	Mon.	L	1-8	5	8	Nabholz	Combs		20-24	T5th	8
5-28	Mon.	W	12-0	12	3	Greene	Boyd		21-24	5th	8
5-29	Mon.	W	2-1	5	7	Mulholland	Jones	Williams	22-24	5th	8
5-31	Pit.	L	1-5	5	7	Walk	Grimsley		22-25	5th	9
6-1	Pit.	L	3-5	9	9	Smiley	Combs	Landrum	22-26	5th	10
6-2	Pit.	L	3-5	12	11	Walk	Williams	Patterson	22-27	5th	11
6-4	At Atl.	L	5-9	12	12	Glavine	Mulholland		22-28	5th	11
6-5	At Atl.	W	12-11 (12)	16	12	Akerfelds	Parrett	DeJesus	23-28	5th	11
6-6	At Atl.	L	4-9	6	13	Leibrandt	Combs		23-29	5th	11
6-7	At Cin.	W	5-4	12	11	Greene	Armstrong	Williams	24-29	5th	11
6-8	At Cin.	W	4-1	10	5	DeJesus	Hammond	McDowell	25-29	5th	10
6-9	At Cin.	L	3-6	10	15	Browning	Mulholland	Dibble	25-30	5th	10
6-10	At Cin.	L	3-9	4	11	Rijo	Ashby		25-31	5th	11
6-11	At Hou.	L	0-1 (11)	6	8	Osuna	McDowell		25-32	5th	11½
6-12	At Hou.	L	2-3	4	9	Osuna	Boever		25-33	T5th	12½
6-13	At Hou.	W	5-4	3	11	DeJesus	Kile	Williams	26-33	5th	11½
6-14	Cin.	L	2-4	7	10	Browning	Mulholland	Dibble	26-34	T5th	11½
6-15	Cin.	L	1-3	5	4	Rijo	Ashby	Dibble	26-35	6th	11½
6-16	Cin.	L	6-8	12	10	Myers	McDowell	Carman	26-36	6th	12½
6-17	Atl.	W	4-3	11	7	Williams	Berenguer		27-36	6th	12½
6-18	Atl.	W	8-4	10	8	DeJesus	Smith		28-36	6th	12½
6-19	Atl.	L	2-9	6	14	Glavine	Mulholland		28-37	6th	12½
6-20	Hou.	W	7-3	14	5	Cox	Jones		29-37	6th	11½
6-21	Hou.	W	3-0	5	4	Ruffin	Portugal	Williams	30-37	6th	11½
6-22	Hou.	L	3-4 (10)	8	10	Osuna	McDowell	Capel	30-38	6th	11½
6-23	Hou.	L	4-6	7	11	Kile	DeJesus	Clancy	30-39	6th	11½
6-25	At St.L.	L	9-10	12	12	Terry	McDowell	L. Smith	30-40	6th	11½

Date	Opp.	Res.	Score (inn.*)	Hits	Opp. hits	Winning pitcher	Losing pitcher	Save	Record	Pos.	GB
6-26	At St.L.	L	1- 14	7	16	B. Smith	Combs		30-41	6th	12½
6-27	At St.L.	L	2- 4	3	5	Hill	Greene	L. Smith	30-42	6th	13½
6-28	At N.Y.	W	6- 2	8	4	DeJesus	Darling		31-42	6th	13½
6-29	At N.Y.	L	0- 5	7	7	Whitehurst	Mulholland		31-43	6th	14½
6-30	At N.Y.	W	10-9	17	10	Cox	Gooden	Williams	32-43	6th	14½
7-1	St.L.	L	0- 1	4	10	B. Smith	Ruffin	L. Smith	32-44	6th	14½
7-2	St.L.	L	1- 6	4	11	Hill	Greene	L. Smith	32-45	6th	15½
7-3	St.L.	L	3- 4	7	10	Olivares	DeJesus	L. Smith	32-46	6th	16½
7-4	St.L.	W	7- 1	9	6	Mulholland	Tewksbury		33-46	6th	15½
7-5	N.Y.	L	1- 3	4	6	Gooden	Cox	Franco	33-47	6th	15½
7-6	N.Y.	L	1- 2	6	8	Viola	Ruffin	Franco	33-48	6th	15½
7-7	N.Y.	L	2- 8	5	8	Cone	Greene		33-49	6th	16½
7-11	S.F.	W	3- 2	6	5	Mulholland	Wilson	Williams	34-49	6th	16½
7-12	S.F.	W	1- 0	3	3	Greene	Black	Williams	35-49	6th	16½
7-13	S.F.	L	5- 7	11	13	Oliveras	Ritchie	Righetti	35-50	6th	17½
7-14	S.F.	L	5- 17	6	22	Downs	Cox		35-51	6th	18½
7-15	L.A.	W	9- 8	13	13	Searcy	Crews	Williams	36-51	6th	18½
7-16	L.A.	W	3- 1	9	7	Mulholland	Ojeda		37-51	6th	18½
7-17	L.A.	W	4- 2	10	6	Greene	Candelaria	Williams	38-51	6th	17½
7-19	At S.D.	W	4- 1	7	4	DeJesus	Rasmussen	Williams	39-51	6th	17½
7-20	At S.D.	W	4- 0	10	2	Ruffin	Harris		40-51	6th	16½
7-21	At S.D.	L	2- 5	5	9	Hurst	Mulholland		40-52	6th	17½
7-23	At L.A.	L	5- 6 (10)	10	9	Howell	McDowell		40-53	6th	18
7-24	At L.A.	L	1- 2	7	4	Candelaria	Searcy		40-54	6th	19
7-25	At L.A.	L	0- 5	5	14	Martinez	Ruffin		40-55	6th	19½
7-26	At S.F.	L	2- 3	4	12	Downs	Mulholland	Righetti	40-56	6th	20½
7-27	At S.F.	L	0- 3	3	6	McClellan	Cox	Righetti	40-57	6th	21½
7-28	At S.F.	L	1- 2	6	7	Black	Greene	Brantley	40-58	6th	21½
7-30	S.D.	W	2- 1	6	8	DeJesus	Rasmussen	Williams	41-58	6th	19½
7-31	S.D.	W	9-3	11	9	Ruffin	Harris		42-58	6th	18½
8-1	At Mon.	W	4- 1	8	3	Mulholland	Gardner		43-58	T5th	17½
8-2	At Mon.	W	6- 5 (11)	12	10	Williams	Rojas	Hartley	44-58	5th	16½
8-3	At Mon.	W	7- 1	7	7	Greene	Barnes		45-58	5th	15½
8-4	At Mon.	W	3- 2 (10)	6	6	Williams	Fassero		46-58	5th	15½
8-6	Chi.	W	6- 2 (11)	11	10	Williams	Lancaster		47-58	5th	15½
8-7	Chi.	W	5- 4 (11)	14	10	Williams	Lancaster		48-58	5th	14½
8-8	Chi.	W	11- 1	12	6	Cox	Jackson		49-58	5th	13½
8-9	Mon.	W	5- 4	6	11	Williams	Wainhouse		50-58	5th	12½
8-10	Mon.	W	4- 2	7	8	DeJesus	Ruskin	Williams	51-58	5th	12½
8-11	Mon.	W	5- 4	7	5	Hartley	Fassero	Williams	52-58	5th	12½
8-12	Mon.	W	2- 1	5	6	Mulholland	Martinez		53-58	5th	12½
8-13	At Pit.	L	3- 4	8	12	Drabek	Cox	Belinda	53-59	5th	13½
8-14	At Pit.	L	3- 5	8	8	Smiley	Greene	Belinda	53-60	5th	14½
8-15	At Pit.	W	6- 4	12	9	DeJesus	Heaton	Williams	54-60	5th	13½
8-16	At Chi.	L	1- 9	6	13	Sutcliffe	Ruffin		54-61	5th	14½
8-17	At Chi.	W	5- 2	9	8	Mulholland	Bielecki	Williams	55-61	5th	14½
8-18	At Chi.	L	6- 7 (10)	7	9	Assenmacher	Williams		55-62	5th	15½
8-20	Pit.	W	6- 5	10	9	Searcy	Belinda		56-62	5th	14½
8-21	Pit.	W	6- 5	11	8	Williams	Kipper		57-62	5th	13½
8-22	Pit.	W	4- 3 (11)	7	9	Williams	Landrum		58-62	5th	12½
8-23	At Atl.	L	2- 4	6	13	Glavine	Mulholland	Wohlers	58-63	5th	13½
8-24	At Atl.	W	6- 5	10	7	Williams	Castillo		59-63	T4th	12½
8-25	At Atl.	W	6- 5	9	10	Greene	Avery	Williams	60-63	T4th	12½
8-26	At Cin.	L	4- 5	4	7	Gross	Hartley	Dibble	60-64	5th	12½
8-27	At Cin.	L	2- 4	7	9	Scudder	Ruffin	Dibble	60-65	5th	13½
8-28	Hou.	W	11- 10 (10)	11	15	Hartley	Osuna		61-65	T4th	13½
8-29	Hou.	L	1- 5	6	11	Portugal	Cox		61-66	T4th	14½
8-30	Atl.	L	1- 6	4	11	Avery	Greene		61-67	5th	15½
8-31	Atl.	W	5- 0	10	4	DeJesus	Reynoso		62-67	5th	15½
9-1	Atl.	W	5- 4 (10)	12	11	Williams	Wohlers		63-67	5th	14½
9-2	Cin.	W	8- 5	11	8	Mulholland	Browning	Williams	64-67	T4th	14½
9-3	Cin.	L	5- 8	10	8	Rijo	Brantley	Dibble	64-68	5th	15½
9-4	Cin.	L	1- 5	4	12	Myers	Greene		64-69	5th	16½
9-6	At Hou.	L	1- 3	4	6	Harnisch	DeJesus	Osuna	64-70	5th	17
9-7	At Hou.	L	0- 6	5	9	Kile	Ruffin		64-71	5th	17
9-8	At Hou.	W	5- 0	14	3	Mulholland	Bowen		65-71	T4th	16
9-9	At St.L.	L	2- 4	6	8	Olivares	Ashby	L. Smith	65-72	T4th	17
9-10	At St.L.	W	5- 2	12	6	Greene	Cormier	Williams	66-72	T4th	16
9-11	Mon.	L	5- 6	12	8	Sampen	Ritchie	Jones	66-73	5th	17
9-12	Mon.	L	2- 6	8	10	Nabholz	Ruffin		66-74	5th	17
9-13	Pit.	L	6- 8	13	12	Belinda	Williams	Rodriguez	66-75	5th	18
9-14	Pit.	L	3- 5	6	6	Smiley	Ashby	Palacios	66-76	5th	19
9-15	Pit.	W	8- 3	14	6	Greene	Tomlin	Williams	67-76	5th	18
9-16	St.L.	L	0- 3	7	8	Tewksbury	DeJesus	L. Smith	67-77	5th	19

Date	Opp.	Res.	Score (inn.*)	Hits	Opp. hits	Winning pitcher	Losing pitcher	Save	Record	Pos.	GB
9-17	St.L.	W	4-2	8	7	Brantley	Hill	Williams	68-77	5th	19
9-18	Mon.	W	1-0	7	2	Mulholland	Martinez		69-77	5th	19
9-19	Mon.	W	5-4 (10)	10	10	Williams	Ruskin		70-77	5th	19
9-20	At Pit.	W	8-3	15	5	Greene	Tomlin		71-77	5th	18
9-21	At Pit.	L	0-7	6	11	Smith	DeJesus		71-78	5th	19
9-22	At Pit.	L	1-2	7	3	Drabek	Brantley		71-79	5th	20
9-23	At Chi.	L	3-10	7	14	Maddux	Mulholland		71-80	5th	20½
9-24	At Chi.	W	4-2	9	4	Ashby	Bielecki	Williams	72-80	5th	20½
9-25	At Chi.	W	5-4	11	6	Greene	Boskie	Williams	73-80	4th	20
9-27	At N.Y.	L	4-6	5	7	Schourek	DeJesus	Franco	73-81	4th	20
9-28	At N.Y.	W	6-2	10	7	Brantley	Young		74-81	4th	19
9-29	At N.Y.	L	3-4	10	7	Viola	Mulholland	Franco	74-82	4th	20
9-30	Chi.	W	6-5	9	9	Ritchie	Assenmacher		75-82	4th	20
10-1	Chi.	W	6-5 (13)	13	9	Ruffin	Assenmacher		76-82	3rd	20
10-2	Chi.	L	0-1	3	3	Maddux	DeJesus		76-83	4th	20
10-4	N.Y.	W	5-4 (10)	11	11	Williams	Franco		77-83	3rd	19
10-5	N.Y.	W	1-0	5	8	Mulholland	Young		78-83	3rd	19
10-6	N.Y.	L	0-7	3	12	Cone	Ashby		78-84	3rd	20

Monthly records: April (9-12), May (13-13), June (10-18), July (10-15), August (20-9), September (13-15), Oct. (3-2).

HIGHLIGHTS

High point: The Phillies won 13 consecutive games from July 30 through August 12, the longest streak in the National League in 1991 and the club's best since 1977. Philadelphia gained nine games in the standings during that stretch.

Low point: The Phillies struggled at the start of the season, posting a 4-9 mark. Nick Leyva was dismissed as manager April 23 and replaced by Jim Fregosi.

Turning point: Any hope the Phillies had of contending was squashed from July 21 through 28, when the team lost seven consecutive games on a 2-7 West Coast trip. Philadelphia returned from the trip 18 games under .500 (40-58, 21½ games out of first).

Most valuable player: Outfielder/first baseman John Kruk. He enjoyed his best all-around season in the majors. Kruk became the first Phillie to lead the club in hitting (.294), homers (21) and runs batted in (92) since Greg Luzinski in 1977. Plus, he was the team's lone representative at the All-Star Game.

Most valuable pitcher: Lefthander Mitch Williams. The flame-throwing closer recorded 30 saves and 12 victories in 69 appearances.

Most improved player: Third baseman Dave Hollins. He began the year with the Phillies before being optioned to Class AAA on April 23, but he was recalled July 11. Upon his return, he took over the third-base job from Charlie Hayes and proceeded to hit .298 during his first real stint as a regular.

Most pleasant surprise: Righthander Tommy Greene. Not favored to make the team out of spring training, Greene emerged as a solid starter. He pitched a no-hitter May 23 at Montreal and finished with a 13-7 record and 3.38 earned-run average in 207⅔ innings.

Biggest disappointment: Outfielder Von Hayes. He was on the disabled list from June 15 through September 5 with a broken bone in his right arm. As a result, he batted a career-low .225 with no home runs and only 21 RBIs.

Key injuries: The Phillies played without leadoff hitter/center fielder Lenny Dykstra and catcher Darren Daulton for much of the season. Both players sustained injuries in a May 6 car accident. And both were re-injured upon their return.

Notable: The Phillies' third-place finish was their highest since finishing second in 1986.... Fregosi posted a 74-75 mark upon taking over the Phillies.... Kruk was hit by a pitch for the first time in his career after 2,681 plate appearances.

—BILL BROWN

RECORDS

1991 regular-season record: 78-84 (3rd in N.L. East); 47-36 at home; 31-48 on road; 43-47 vs. East; 35-37 vs. West; 30-32 vs. LHP; 48-52 vs. RHP; 17-25 on grass; 61-59 on turf; 20-26 in day-time; 58-58 at night; 36-27 in one-run games; 16-9 in extra-inning games; 0-0-1 in doubleheaders.

Team record last five years: 367-442 (.454, ranks 11th in league in that span).

TEAM LEADERS

Batting average: John Kruk (.294).
At-bats: Dale Murphy (544).
Runs: John Kruk (84).
Hits: John Kruk (158).
Total bases: John Kruk (260).
Doubles: Dale Murphy (33).
Triples: John Kruk (6).
Home runs: John Kruk (21).
Runs batted in: John Kruk (92).
Stolen bases: Len Dykstra (24).
Slugging percentage: John Kruk (.483).
On-base percentage: John Kruk (.367).
Wins: Terry Mulholland (16).
Earned-run average: Tommy Greene (3.38).
Complete games: Terry Mulholland (8).
Shutouts: Terry Mulholland (3).
Saves: Mitch Williams (30).
Innings pitched: Terry Mulholland (232).
Strikeouts: Tommy Greene (154).

GAMES BY POSITION

Catcher: Darren Daulton 88, Steve Lake 58, Darrin Fletcher 45, Doug Lindsey 1.
First base: John Kruk 102, Ricky Jordan 72, Dave Hollins 6, Jim Lindeman 1, Rick Schu 1.
Second base: Mickey Morandini 97, Randy Ready 66, Wally Backman 36.
Third base: Charlie Hayes 138, Dave Hollins 36, Wally Backman 20, Rod Booker 3, Rick Schu 3.
Shortstop: Dickie Thon 146, Rod Booker 20, Kim Batiste 7, Charlie Hayes 2.
Outfield: Dale Murphy 147, Wes Chamberlain 98, Von Hayes 72, Lenny Dykstra 63, John Morris 57, John Kruk 52, Jim Lindeman 30, Braulio Castillo 26, Sil Campusano 15.

TOP 10 DRAFT CHOICES

1. **Tyler Green,** RHP, Wichita State University.
2. **Kevin Stocker,** SS, University of Washington.
3. **Ronnie Allen,** RHP, Texas A&M University.
4. **Gene Schall,** OF, Villanova University.
5. **Steve Verdusco,** SS, Bellarmine Prep High School, Scotts Valley, Calif.
6. **Tommy Eason,** C, East Carolina University.
7. **Dave Tokheim,** OF, UCLA.
8. **Dave Hayden,** SS, University of Tennessee.
9. **Phil Geisler,** OF, University of Portland.
10. **Mike Grace,** RHP, Bradley University.

PITTSBURGH PIRATES
NATIONAL LEAGUE EAST DIVISION

1992 SCHEDULE

APRIL

S	M	T	W	T	F	S
5	6 N MON H	7	8 N MON H	9 N MON H	10 N PHI	11 N PHI
12 PHI	13	14 N CHI H	15 N CHI H	16	17 N PHI H	18 N PHI H
19 PHI H	20 MON	21 N MON	22 N MON	23 MON	24 CHI	25 CHI
26 CHI	27	28 N CIN	29 N CIN	30		

MAY

S	M	T	W	T	F	S
					1 N HOU	2 N HOU
3 N HOU	4 N CIN	5 N CIN H	6 N ATL H	7 N ATL H	8 N HOU H	9 N HOU H
10 HOU H	11	12 N ATL	13 N ATL	14 N ATL	15 N SD H	16 N SD H
17 SD H	18	19 N SF	20 N SF	21 SF	22 N LA	23 N LA
24 LA	25 N SD	26 N SD	27 N SD	28	29 N SF	30 N SF H
31 SF H						

JUNE

S	M	T	W	T	F	S
	1 N LA H	2 N LA H	3 N LA H	4 N NY	5 N NY H	6 N NY H
7 NY H	8 N PHI	9 N PHI	10 N PHI	11	12 N NY	13 N NY
14 NY	15 N PHI H	16 N PHI H	17 N PHI H	18 N MON H	19 N MON H	20 N MON H
21 MON H	22 N STL H	23 N STL H	24 N STL H	25	26 N MON	27 N MON
28 MON	29 N STL	30 N STL				

JULY

S	M	T	W	T	F	S
		1 N STL	2 N CIN H	3 N CIN H	4 N CIN H	5 N CIN H
5 CIN H	6 N HOU H	7 N HOU H	8 N HOU H	9 N CIN	10 N CIN	11 N CIN
12 CIN	13	14 ⋆	15	16 N CHI H	17 N CHI H	18 N CHI H
19 N CHI H	20 N HOU	21 N HOU	22 N HOU	23	24 N ATL	25 N ATL
26 ATL	27 N CHI	28 N CHI	29 CHI	30 N STL H	31 N STL H	

AUGUST

S	M	T	W	T	F	S
						1 STL H
2 STL H	3	4 N NY H	5 N NY H	6 N STL	7 N STL	8 N STL
9 STL	10 N NY	11 N NY	12 N NY	13	14 N ATL H	15 N ATL H
16 ATL H	17 N ATL H	18 N SD H	19 N SD H	20 N SD H	21 N SF	22 SF
23 SF	24 N LA	25 N LA	26 N LA	27 N SD	28	29 N SD
30 SD	31					

SEPTEMBER

S	M	T	W	T	F	S
		1 N SF H	2 N SF H	3 N SF H	4 N LA H	5 N LA H
6 LA H	7	8 N CHI H	9 N CHI H	10 N CHI H	11 N PHI	12 N PHI
13 LA H	14 N CHI	15 N CHI	16 N MON H	17 N MON H	18 N PHI H	19 N PHI H
20 PHI H	21 N STL	22 N STL	23 N MON	24 N MON	25 N NY H	26 N NY H
27 NY H	28 N CHI	29 N CHI	30 N CHI			

OCTOBER

S	M	T	W	T	F	S
				1	2 N NY	3 N NY
4 NY	5	6	7	8	9	10

1992 SEASON

CLUB DIRECTORY

Board of directors
Joe L. Brown
Frank V. Cahouet
Richard M. Cyert
Douglas D. Danforth
Eugene Litman
John Marous
Sophie Masloff
John H. McConnell
Thomas H. O'Brien
Paul H. O'Neill
David M. Roderick
Vincent A. Sarni
Harvey M. Walken
Chairman
Douglas D. Danforth
President and chief executive officer
Mark Sauer
Sr. v.p. and g.m./baseball oper. (interim)
Cam Bonifay
Sr. vice president for business operations
Doug Bureman
Vice president, finance and secretary
Kenneth C. Curcio
Vice president, public relations
Richard J. Cerrone
Vice president, marketing
Steven N. Greenberg
Assistant to the president
Ken Wilson
Assistant vice president, finance
Patti Mistick
Exec. dir. of broadcasting and adv. sales
Mark Driscoll
Traveling secretary
Greg Johnson
Manager of ticket operations
Gary Remlinger
Senior directors of sales and marketing
Bob Derda
Mark Norelli
Director of Bradenton baseball operations
Jeff Podobnik
Director of community relations
Patty Paytas
Director of community services and sales
Al Gordon
Director of corporate sales
Nellie Briles
Director of Diamond Club
Chris Cronin
Director of finance
Jim Plake

Director of in-game entertainment
Mike Gordon
Director of media relations
Jim Trdinich
Director of merchandising
Joe Billetdeaux
Director of minor league operations
Chet Montgomery
Director of promotions
Kathy Guy
Director of publications and special projects
Jim Lachimia
Director of stadium operations
Dennis DaPra
Director of telemarketing
Phillip Trozzi
Assistant director of public relations
Sally O'Leary
Assistant, baseball operations
John Sirignano
Club physician
Dr. Joseph Coroso
Team orthopedist
Dr. Jack Failla
Trainers
Kent Biggerstaff
Dave Tumbas
Equipment manager
Roger Wilson
Scouting coordinators
Bart Braun
Jerry Gardner
Don Mitchell
Scouting supervisors
Gene Baker
Joe L. Brown
Bill Bryk
Pablo Cruz
Larry D'Amato
Steve Demeter
Angel Figueroa
Steve Fleming
Jesse Flores
Dave Holliday
Leland Maddox
Rene Mons
Boyd Odom
Ed Roebuck
Paul Tinnell
Major league scout
Lenny Yochim
Minor league scout
Ken Parker

SCHEDULE KEY

H—Home game. ⋆All-Star Game at San Diego/Jack Murphy Stadium.
N—Night game (any game starting after 5 p.m.).

SPRING TRAINING ROSTER

Manager—Jim Leyland (10).
Coaches—Terry Collins, Rich Donnelly (45), Milt May (39), Ray Miller (31), Tommy Sandt (37).

No.	PITCHERS	B/T	Ht./Wt.	Born	1991 clubs
60	Ausanio, Joe	R/R	6-1/205	12-9-65	Carolina, Buffalo
	Batista, Miguel	R/R	6-0/160	2-19-71	Rockford
50	Belinda, Stan	R/R	6-3/200	8-6-66	Pittsburgh
	Cole, Victor	R/R	5-10/160	1-23-68	Omaha, Buffalo, Carolina
15	Drabek, Doug	R/R	6-1/185	7-25-62	Pittsburgh
26	Heaton, Neal	L/L	6-1/205	3-3-60	Pittsburgh
43	Landrum, Bill	R/R	6-2/205	8-17-58	Pittsburgh
48	Mason, Roger	R/R	6-6/220	9-18-58	Buffalo, Pittsburgh
64	Miller, Paul	R/R	6-5/215	4-27-65	Carolina, Buffalo, Pittsburgh
58	Palacios, Vicente	R/R	6-3/195	7-19-63	Pittsburgh, Buffalo
38	Patterson, Bob	R/L	6-2/192	5-16-59	Pittsburgh
34	Reed, Rick	R/R	6-0/205	8-16-64	Buffalo, Pittsburgh
30	Rodriguez, Rosario	R/L	6-0/195	7-8-69	Buffalo, Pittsburgh
35	Roesler, Mike	R/R	6-5/200	9-12-63	Carolina, Buffalo
57	Smiley, John	L/L	6-4/200	3-17-65	Pittsburgh
41	Smith, Zane	L/L	6-2/200	12-28-60	Pittsburgh
29	Tomlin, Randy	L/L	5-11/179	6-14-66	Pittsburgh
17	Walk, Bob	R/R	6-4/217	11-26-56	Pittsburgh, Carolina

No.	CATCHERS	B/T	Ht./Wt.	Born	1991 clubs
12	LaValliere, Mike	L/R	5-10/210	8-18-60	Pittsburgh
14	Prince, Tom	R/R	5-11/185	8-13-64	Pittsburgh, Buffalo
77	Romero, Mandy	S/R	5-11/196	10-19-67	Carolina
11	Slaught, Don	R/R	6-1/190	9-11-58	Pittsburgh

No.	INFIELDERS	B/T	Ht./Wt.	Born	1991 clubs
3	Bell, Jay	R/R	6-1/185	12-11-65	Pittsburgh
22	Buechele, Steve	R/R	6-2/200	9-26-61	Texas, Pittsburgh
51	Garcia, Carlos	R/R	6-1/185	10-15-67	Buffalo, Pittsburgh
7	King, Jeff	R/R	6-1/185	12-26-64	Pittsburgh, Buffalo
13	Lind, Jose	R/R	5-11/175	5-1-64	Pittsburgh
6	Merced, Orlando	S/R	5-11/175	11-2-66	Buffalo, Pittsburgh
2	Redus, Gary	R/R	6-1/195	11-1-56	Pittsburgh
27	Richardson, Jeff	R/R	6-2/180	8-26-65	Buffalo, Pittsburgh
	Shelton, Ben	R/L	6-3/210	9-21-69	Salem, Carolina
52	Wehner, John	R/R	6-3/204	6-29-67	Carolina, Buffalo, Pittsburgh

No.	OUTFIELDERS	B/T	Ht./Wt.	Born	1991 clubs
24	Bonds, Barry	L/L	6-1/190	7-24-64	Pittsburgh
47	Bullett, Scott	L/L	6-2/200	12-25-68	Augusta, Salem, Pittsburgh
	Martin, Albert	L/L	6-2/220	11-24-67	Greenville, Richmond
23	McClendon, Lloyd	R/R	5-11/210	1-11-59	Pittsburgh
	McDaniel, Terry	S/R	5-9/175	12-6-66	Tidewater, New York NL
	Ratliff, Daryl	R/R	6-1/180	10-15-69	Salem, Carolina
18	Van Slyke, Andy	L/R	6-2/195	12-21-60	Pittsburgh
42	Varsho, Gary	L/R	5-11/190	6-20-61	Pittsburgh

BALLPARK INFORMATION

Ballpark (capacity, surface)
Three Rivers Stadium (58,729, artificial)
Address
600 Stadium Circle
Pittsburgh, PA 15212
Business phone
412-323-5000
Ticket information
412-321-2827
Ticket prices
$14 (club boxes)
$10 (terrace boxes)
$8 (reserved seats)
$5 (general admission)
$2.50 (g.a., children 12 and under)
Field dimensions (from home plate)
To left field at foul line, 335 feet
To center field, 400 feet
To right field at foul line, 335 feet
First game played
July 16, 1970 (Reds 3, Pirates 2)

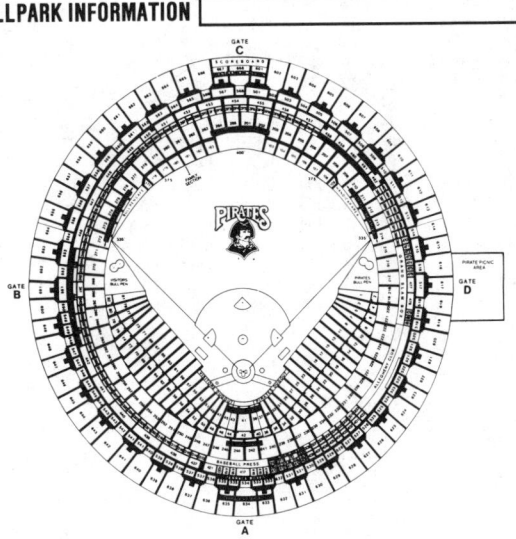

MINOR LEAGUE AFFILIATES

Class	Team	League	Manager
AAA	Buffalo	American Association	Marc Bombard
AA	Carolina	Southern	Don Werner
A	Salem	Carolina	John Wockenfuss
A	Augusta	South Atlantic	Scott Little
A	Welland, Ont.	New York-Pennsylvania	Trent Jewett
Rookie	Bradenton Pirates	Gulf Coast	Woody Huyke

BROADCAST INFORMATION

Radio: KDKA-AM (1020). Broadcasters: Lanny Frattare, Jim Rooker, Kent Derdivanis, Steve Blass.
TV: KDKA-TV (Channel 2). Broadcasters: Lanny Frattare, Jim Rooker, Kent Derdivanis, Steve Blass.
Cable TV: KBL Sports Network. Broadcasters: Lanny Frattare, Jim Rooker, Kent Derdivanis, Steve Blass.

SPRING TRAINING

Ballpark (city): McKechnie Field (Bradenton, Fla.).
Ticket information: 813-748-4610.

HISTORY

YEAR-BY-YEAR RECORDS

Year	Pos.	W	L	Pct.	*GB	Year	Pos.	W	L	Pct.	*GB
1901	1st	90	49	.647	+ 7½	1949	6th	71	83	.461	26
1902	1st	103	36	.741	+27½	1950	8th	57	96	.373	33½
1903	1st	91	49	.650	+ 6½	1951	7th	64	90	.416	32½
1904	4th	87	66	.569	19	1952	8th	42	112	.273	54½
1905	2nd	96	57	.627	9	1953	8th	50	104	.325	55
1906	3rd	93	60	.608	23½	1954	8th	53	101	.344	44
1907	2nd	91	63	.591	17	1955	8th	60	94	.390	38½
1908	T2nd	98	56	.636	1	1956	7th	66	88	.429	27
1909	1st	110	42	.724	+ 6½	1957	T7th	62	92	.403	33
1910	3rd	86	67	.562	17½	1958	2nd	84	70	.545	8
1911	3rd	85	69	.552	14½	1959	4th	78	76	.506	9
1912	2nd	93	58	.616	10	1960	1st	95	59	.617	+ 7
1913	4th	78	71	.523	21½	1961	6th	75	79	.487	18
1914	7th	69	85	.448	25½	1962	4th	93	68	.578	8
1915	5th	73	81	.474	18	1963	8th	74	88	.457	25
1916	6th	65	89	.422	29	1964	T6th	80	82	.494	13
1917	8th	51	103	.331	47	1965	3rd	90	72	.556	7
1918	4th	65	60	.520	17	1966	3rd	92	70	.568	3
1919	4th	71	68	.511	24½	1967	6th	81	81	.500	20½
1920	4th	79	75	.513	14	1968	6th	80	82	.494	17
1921	2nd	90	63	.588	4	1969	3rd	88	74	.543	12
1922	T3rd	85	69	.552	8	1970	1st†	89	73	.549	+ 5
1923	3rd	87	67	.565	8½	1971	1st‡	97	65	.599	+ 7
1924	3rd	90	63	.588	3	1972	1st†	96	59	.619	+11
1925	1st	95	58	.621	+ 8½	1973	3rd	80	82	.494	2½
1926	3rd	84	69	.549	4½	1974	1st†	88	74	.543	+ 1½
1927	1st	94	60	.610	+ 1½	1975	1st†	92	69	.571	+ 6½
1928	4th	85	67	.559	9	1976	2nd	92	70	.568	9
1929	2nd	88	65	.575	10½	1977	2nd	96	66	.593	5
1930	5th	80	74	.519	12	1978	2nd	88	73	.547	1½
1931	5th	75	79	.487	26	1979	1st‡	98	64	.605	+ 2
1932	2nd	86	68	.558	4	1980	3rd	83	79	.512	8
1933	2nd	87	67	.565	5	1981	4th/6th	46	56	.451	§
1934	5th	74	76	.493	19½	1982	4th	84	78	.519	8
1935	4th	86	67	.562	13½	1983	2nd	84	78	.519	6
1936	4th	84	70	.545	8	1984	6th	75	87	.463	21½
1937	3rd	86	68	.558	10	1985	6th	57	104	.354	43½
1938	2nd	86	64	.573	2	1986	6th	64	98	.395	44
1939	6th	68	85	.444	28½	1987	T4th	80	82	.494	15
1940	4th	78	76	.506	22½	1988	2nd	85	75	.531	15
1941	4th	81	73	.526	19	1989	5th	74	88	.457	19
1942	5th	66	81	.449	36½	1990	1st†	95	67	.586	+ 4
1943	4th	80	74	.519	25	1991	1st†	98	64	.605	+14
1944	2nd	90	63	.588	14½						
1945	4th	82	72	.532	16						
1946	7th	63	91	.409	34						
1947	T7th	62	92	.403	32						
1948	4th	83	71	.539	8½						

*Games behind winner. †Lost Championship Series. ‡Won Championship Series. §First half 25-23; second 21-33.

MANAGERS

Name	Record	Years
Fred Clarke	1343-909	'01-15
Jimmy Callahan	85-129	'16-17
Honus Wagner	1-4	1917
Hugo Bezdek	166-187	'17-19
George Gibson	401-330	'20-22
		'32-34
Bill McKechnie	409-293	'22-26
Donie Bush	246-178	'27-29
Jewel Ens	176-167	'29-31
Pie Traynor	457-406	'34-39
Frank Frisch	539-528	'40-46
Spud Davis	1-2	1946
Billy Herman	61-92	1947
Bill Burwell	1-0	1947
Billy Meyer	317-452	'48-52
Fred Haney	163-299	'53-55
Bobby Bragan	102-155	'56-57
Danny Murtaugh	1115-950	'57-64
		1967
		'70-71
		'73-76
Harry Walker	224-184	'65-67
Larry Shepard	164-155	'68-69
Alex Grammas	4-1	1969
Bill Virdon	163-128	'72-73
Chuck Tanner	711-685	'77-85
Jim Leyland	496-474	'86-91

DAY BY DAY

Date	Opp.	Res.	Score (inn.*)	Hits	Opp. hits	Winning pitcher	Losing pitcher	Save	Record	Pos.	GB
4-8	Mon.	L	0-7	1	15	Martinez	Drabek		0-1	T5th	1
4-9	Mon.	W	4-3	9	6	Kipper	Frey	Landrum	1-1	T3rd	1
4-10	Mon.	W	6-3	10	7	Smith	Boyd	Belinda	2-1	T1st	...
4-12	At Chi.	W	3-1	8	4	Smiley	Boskie	Palacios	3-1	1st	+½
4-13	At Chi.	L	3-7	6	11	Bielecki	Drabek		3-2	T2nd	½
4-14	At Chi.	L	4-6	9	7	Slocumb	Belinda	Smith	3-3	T2nd	1½
4-15	N.Y.	L	3-9	9	16	Cone	Kipper		3-4	T4th	2½
4-16	N.Y.	W	4-2	9	6	Tomlin	Whitehurst	Belinda	4-4	T3rd	1½
4-17	N.Y.	W	4-0	5	1	Smiley	Darling		5-4	3rd	1
4-18	Chi.	L	2-3	4	7	Sutcliffe	Drabek	Assenmacher	5-5	3rd	2
4-19	Chi.	W	5-4	8	3	Belinda	Smith		6-5	T2nd	1
4-20	Chi.	W	9-3	8	9	Smith	Maddux		7-5	T1st	...
4-21	Chi.	W	13-12 (11)	13	13	Patterson	Bielecki		8-5	T1st	...
4-23	At Mon.	W	7-3	8	12	Smiley	Sampen		9-5	T1st	...
4-24	At Mon.	W	2-1	8	7	Drabek	Martinez	Landrum	10-5	T1st	...
4-25	At Mon.	W	8-0	14	4	Palacios	Nabholz		11-5	1st	+1
4-26	At N.Y.	L	0-2	6	9	Viola	Smith	Franco	11-6	T1st	...
4-27	At N.Y.	W	10-1	16	4	Tomlin	Cone		12-6	1st	+1
4-28	At N.Y.	W	7-3	9	7	Smiley	Darling		13-6	1st	+2
4-30	At Cin.	L	3-4	4	8	Browning	Drabek	Dibble	13-7	1st	+½
5-1	At Cin.	W	6-4	8	10	Belinda	Myers	Landrum	14-7	1st	+1½
5-3	Hou.	W	1-0	2	4	Smith	Harnisch		15-7	1st	+1½
5-4	Hou.	L	3-8	8	13	Jones	Smiley	Clancy	15-8	1st	+1
5-5	Hou.	L	4-6	5	11	Portugal	Drabek	Schilling	15-9	1st	+1
5-6	Cin.	W	3-1	9	3	Palacios	Rijo	Landrum	16-9	1st	+1½
5-7	Cin.	W	7-2	9	6	Tomlin	Hammond	Belinda	17-9	1st	+1½
5-8	Cin.	W	7-2	7	4	Smith	Charlton		18-9	1st	+2½
5-10	Atl.	W	5-2	8	6	Smiley	Smoltz	Belinda	19-9	1st	+3½
5-11	Atl.	L	2-3	7	5	Leibrandt	Drabek	Mercker	19-10	1st	+2½
5-12	Atl.	L	1-6	4	9	Avery	Palacios	Berenguer	19-11	1st	+1½
5-14	At Hou.	W	6-3	12	9	Smith	Harnisch		20-11	1st	+2
5-15	At Hou.	W	8-7	11	18	Kipper	Schilling	Landrum	21-11	1st	+2
5-16	At Hou.	W	6-4	11	12	Drabek	Clancy	Belinda	22-11	1st	+2½
5-17	At Atl.	L	3-9	7	12	Avery	Palacios		22-12	1st	+1½
5-19	At Atl.	L	1-7	7	12	Glavine	Smith	Berenguer	22-13	1st	+2
5-21	St.L.	W	5-3	8	11	Smiley	Moyer	Landrum	23-13	1st	+2
5-22	St.L.	L	3-5	10	11	Carpenter	Drabek	L. Smith	23-14	1st	+2
5-23	St.L.	L	2-8	8	15	DeLeon	Tomlin	Terry	23-15	1st	+1½
5-24	Phi.	W	9-1	11	9	Smith	Mulholland		24-15	1st	+2
5-25	Phi.	W	4-2 (11)	9	4	Palacios	Boever		25-15	1st	+2½
5-26	Phi.	W	5-2	9	5	Smiley	Grimsley	Landrum	26-15	1st	+2½
5-27	At St.L.	W	8-0	15	1	Drabek	Tewksbury		27-15	1st	+3½
5-28	At St.L.	W	9-8	11	11	Belinda	DeLeon	Landrum	28-15	1st	+4
5-29	At St.L.	W	6-0	11	1	Z. Smith	B. Smith		29-15	1st	+4
5-31	At Phi.	W	5-1	7	5	Walk	Grimsley		30-15	1st	+4
6-1	At Phi.	W	5-3	9	9	Smiley	Combs	Landrum	31-15	1st	+5
6-2	At Phi.	W	5-3	11	12	Walk	Williams	Patterson	32-15	1st	+6
6-4	S.F.	L	3-5	6	12	Burkett	Smith	Righetti	32-16	1st	+5
6-5	S.F.	W	7-3	12	5	Walk	Downs		33-16	1st	+6
6-6	S.F.	L	3-6	5	11	Black	Smiley	Righetti	33-17	1st	+6
6-7	S.D.	W	1-0	7	13	Drabek	Hurst	Landrum	34-17	1st	+6
6-8	S.D.	L	0-11	4	18	Maddux	Tomlin		34-18	1st	+5
6-9	S.D.	L	3-5	6	10	Benes	Smith	Lefferts	34-19	1st	+5
6-10	S.D.	W	5-3	8	9	Palacios	Rasmussen	Landrum	35-19	1st	+6
6-12	L.A.	W	2-1	7	9	Drabek	Morgan	Landrum	36-19	1st	+6½
6-13	L.A.	L	2-3	6	7	Gott	Tomlin	Howell	36-20	1st	+6
6-14	At S.F.	L	2-3	4	8	Oliveras	Smith	Righetti	36-21	1st	+6
6-15	At S.F.	L	0-4	3	8	Remlinger	Smiley		36-22	1st	+5
6-16	At S.F.	W	4-3	6	8	Walk	Black	Landrum	37-22	1st	+6
6-17	At S.D.	W	3-2	8	10	Drabek	Hurst	Palacios	38-22	1st	+6
6-18	At S.D.	W	3-1	10	6	Landrum	Lefferts		39-22	1st	+6
6-19	At S.D.	L	5-6	10	10	Andersen	Heaton		39-23	1st	+5
6-20	At L.A.	L	2-3	5	9	Gross	Smiley		39-24	1st	+4½
6-21	At L.A.	W	5-1	10	9	Walk	Ojeda	Kipper	40-24	1st	+4½
6-22	At L.A.	L	1-4	3	8	Morgan	Drabek		40-25	1st	+4½
6-23	At L.A.	L	0-2	6	8	Belcher	Smith	Crews	40-26	1st	+4½
6-25	Chi.	L	1-5	8	5	Lancaster	Smiley		40-27	1st	+4
6-26	Chi.	W	7-6	11	10	Walk	Maddux	Landrum	41-27	1st	+4
6-27	Chi.	W	4-3	7	9	Palacios	Assenmacher		42-27	1st	+4
6-28	At Mon.	W	6-1	13	5	Smith	Haney		43-27	1st	+4

PITTSBURGH PIRATES

1992 SEASON

PITTSBURGH PIRATES

Date	Opp.	Res.	Score (inn.*)	Hits	Opp. hits	Winning pitcher	Losing pitcher	Save	Record	Pos.	GB
6-29	At Mon.	W	2-1	6	8	Heaton	Ruskin	Landrum	44-27	1st	+5
6-30	At Mon.	W	2-1	7	7	Smiley	Martinez	Belinda	45-27	1st	+6
7-1	At Chi.	L	5-6 (13)	13	14	Scanlan	Belinda		45-28	1st	+5
7-2	At Chi.	W	13-4	22	9	Drabek	Boskie		46-28	1st	+5
7-3	At Chi.	W	11-7	11	9	Smith	Lancaster		47-28	1st	+5
7-4	At Chi.	L	8-9 (11)	15	14	McElroy	Landrum		47-29	1st	+4½
7-5	Mon.	L	3-4	11	10	Martinez	Smiley		47-30	1st	+3½
7-6	Mon.	L	1-2	2	5	Gardner	Walk	Burke	47-31	1st	+2½
7-7	Mon.	W	6-1	10	6	Drabek	Boyd	Belinda	48-31	1st	+2½
7-11	At Cin.	W	10-6	14	10	Palacios	Myers		49-31	1st	+2½
7-12	At Cin.	W	7-2	12	7	Drabek	Armstrong		50-31	1st	+2½
7-13	At Cin.	W	5-2	7	7	Smiley	Browning	Kipper	51-31	1st	+2½
7-14	At Cin.	W	10-6	12	11	Walk	Gross	Patterson	52-31	1st	+3½
7-15	Hou.	W	8-0	13	5	Tomlin	Jones		53-31	1st	+4½
7-16	Hou.	W	6-4	9	8	Smith	Kile	Belinda	54-31	1st	+4½
7-17	Hou.	L	2-10	9	15	Jones	Drabek	Osuna	54-32	1st	+3½
7-19	Cin.	W	7-2	13	6	Smiley	Browning		55-32	1st	+4
7-20	Cin.	L	2-3	8	5	Gross	Walk	Power	55-33	1st	+4
7-21	Cin.	W	6-0	8	3	Tomlin	Hammond		56-33	1st	+4
7-22	Atl.	L	3-7	7	7	Smoltz	Smith		56-34	1st	+3½
7-23	Atl.	W	12-3	16	4	Drabek	Leibrandt		57-34	1st	+4½
7-24	Atl.	W	7-4	10	10	Smiley	Glavine	Belinda	58-34	1st	+5½
7-26	At Hou.	W	8-1	11	5	Heaton	Kile		59-34	1st	+7
7-27	At Hou.	W	11-5	16	10	Tomlin	Jones		60-34	1st	+7
7-28	At Hou.	L	7-9	9	12	Bowen	Smith	Clancy	60-35	1st	+7
7-29 (1)	At Atl.	L	5-7	8	8	Glavine	Drabek	Freeman	60-36	1st	+6½
7-29 (2)	At Atl.	L	3-5	7	8	Mahler	Smiley	Mercker	60-37	1st	+5½
7-30	At Atl.	L	3-10	9	13	Parrett	Landrum	Mercker	60-38	1st	+5½
7-31	At Atl.	L	6-8	9	11	Smoltz	Palacios	Stanton	60-39	1st	+5½
8-1	At St.L.	L	3-6	9	13	Olivares	Tomlin	L. Smith	60-40	1st	+5
8-2	At St.L.	L	3-4	6	5	McClure	Belinda		60-41	1st	+5
8-3	At St.L.	L	5-6 (10)	8	15	L. Smith	Patterson		60-42	1st	+4½
8-4	At St.L.	W	2-1	6	5	Smiley	Hill		61-42	1st	+5½
8-6	At N.Y.	W	3-1	8	4	Tomlin	Fernandez		62-42	1st	+5½
8-7	At N.Y.	L	1-7	4	11	Gooden	Smith		62-43	1st	+5½
8-8	At N.Y.	L	3-4	8	10	Viola	Drabek	Franco	62-44	1st	+5
8-9	St.L.	L	1-5	3	7	B. Smith	Smiley		62-45	1st	+4
8-10	St.L.	W	11-5	14	8	Heaton	Hill		63-45	1st	+5
8-11	St.L.	W	6-4	11	9	Mason	Tewksbury	Landrum	64-45	1st	+6
8-12	St.L.	W	4-3 (11)	6	12	Patterson	L. Smith		65-45	1st	+7
8-13	Phi.	W	4-3	12	8	Drabek	Cox	Belinda	66-45	1st	+7
8-14	Phi.	W	5-3	8	8	Smiley	Greene	Belinda	67-45	1st	+7
8-15	Phi.	L	4-6	9	12	DeJesus	Heaton	Williams	67-46	1st	+6
8-16	N.Y.	W	8-2	9	9	Tomlin	Fernandez		68-46	1st	+6
8-17	N.Y.	W	4-1	10	8	Smith	Gooden	Belinda	69-46	1st	+7
8-18	N.Y.	W	9-2	11	6	Drabek	Viola		70-46	1st	+7
8-20	At Phi.	L	5-6	9	10	Searcy	Belinda		70-47	1st	+6½
8-21	At Phi.	L	5-6	8	11	Williams	Kipper		70-48	1st	+6
8-22	At Phi.	L	3-4 (11)	9	7	Williams	Landrum		70-49	1st	+6
8-23	S.F.	W	8-0	14	7	Drabek	Burkett		71-49	1st	+6
8-24	S.F.	L	1-5	6	9	Wilson	Heaton		71-50	1st	+5
8-25	S.F.	W	8-3	10	12	Smiley	Oliveras	Belinda	72-50	1st	+5
8-26	S.D.	L	5-7 (10)	9	11	Lefferts	Landrum		72-51	1st	+4
8-27	S.D.	W	5-2	11	11	Smith	Bones	Mason	73-51	1st	+4
8-28	At L.A.	W	6-4	11	8	Rodriguez	McDowell	Belinda	74-51	1st	+5
8-29	At L.A.	W	4-1	7	7	Mason	Morgan	Landrum	75-51	1st	+6
8-30	At S.D.	W	4-1	9	4	Smiley	Rasmussen	Rodriguez	76-51	1st	+7
8-31	At S.D.	W	3-2 (12)	10	4	Landrum	Melendez	Kipper	77-51	1st	+8
9-1	At S.D.	L	4-7	7	10	Bones	Smith	Maddux	77-52	1st	+7
9-2	At S.F.	W	9-8	18	13	Belinda	Righetti	Rodriguez	78-52	1st	+7
9-3	At S.F.	W	5-3 (10)	8	8	Patterson	Oliveras		79-52	1st	+8
9-4	At S.F.	W	8-3	13	10	Smiley	Black	Mason	80-52	1st	+9
9-6 (1)	L.A.	L	3-4	6	8	McDowell	Belinda		80-53	1st	+9½
9-6 (2)	L.A.	W	3-1	10	3	Smith	Gross		81-53	1st	+10
9-7	L.A.	L	1-5	8	9	Ojeda	Drabek	Gott	81-54	1st	+10
9-8	L.A.	L	1-5	9	10	Morgan	Patterson		81-55	1st	+9½
9-9	At Chi.	W	12-10	16	13	Belinda	Smith	Rodriguez	82-55	1st	+9½
9-10	At Chi.	L	2-6	8	13	Sutcliffe	Tomlin	Scanlan	82-56	1st	+9½
9-11	At St.L.	W	3-1	10	6	Smith	Tewksbury		83-56	1st	+10½
9-12	At St.L.	L	0-1	7	5	Hill	Drabek	L. Smith	83-57	1st	+9½
9-13	At Phi.	W	8-6	12	13	Belinda	Williams	Rodriguez	84-57	1st	+10½
9-14	At Phi.	W	5-3	6	6	Smiley	Ashby	Palacios	85-57	1st	+10½
9-15	At Phi.	L	3-8	6	14	Greene	Tomlin	Williams	85-58	1st	+9½
9-16	Chi.	W	5-4	9	6	Smith	Castillo	Mason	86-58	1st	+9½

Date	Opp.	Res.	Score (inn.*)	Hits	Opp. hits	Winning pitcher	Losing pitcher	Save	Record	Pos.	GB
9-17	Chi.	W	9-2	9	9	Drabek	Bielecki		87-58	1st	+10½
9-18	St.L.	W	6-5	12	9	Mason	Fraser		88-58	1st	+11½
9-19	St.L.	W	5-1	6	6	Belinda	Olivares		89-58	1st	+12½
9-20	Phi.	L	3-8	5	15	Greene	Tomlin		89-59	1st	+12½
9-21	Phi.	W	7-0	11	6	Smith	DeJesus		90-59	1st	+13½
9-22	Phi.	W	2-1	3	7	Drabek	Brantley		91-59	1st	+13½
9-24	At N.Y.	W	10-8	17	11	Patterson	Innis	Rodriguez	92-59	1st	+13½
9-26 (1)	At N.Y.	W	4-3 (15)	12	11	Landrum	Whitehurst		93-59	1st	+13½
9-26 (2)	At N.Y.	L	1-2	10	6	Burke	Mason	Franco	93-60	1st	+14
9-27	Mon.	L	8-12	9	15	Ruskin	Rodriguez		93-61	1st	+13
9-28	Mon.	L	2-3	4	7	Nabholz	Drabek	Rojas	93-62	1st	+12
9-29	Mon.	W	6-3	11	13	Walk	Sampen	Kipper	94-62	1st	+13
9-30	N.Y.	W	6-5	9	9	Landrum	Simons	Rodriguez	95-62	1st	+13
10-1	N.Y.	W	2-1	5	8	Smiley	Cone	Belinda	96-62	1st	+13
10-2	N.Y.	L	6-9 (11)	12	16	Franco	Patterson		96-63	1st	+12
10-4	Mon.	L	1-3	8	13	Jones	Mason	Rojas	96-64	1st	+12
10-5	Mon.	W	4-3	7	9	Walk	Fassero	Belinda	97-64	1st	+13
10-6	Mon.	W	7-0	8	5	Smiley	Barnes		98-64	1st	+14

Monthly records: April (13-7), May (17-8), June (15-12), July (15-12), August (17-12), September (18-11), Oct. (3-2).

HIGHLIGHTS

High point: The Pirates, who had claimed a share of the lead in the National League East on April 20, pulled away from the competition with a season-best nine-game winning streak from May 24 through June 2.

Low point: Pittsburgh suffered a 2-11 stretch from July 28 through August 9 that included a season-high eight-game losing streak. Their lead at the start of the streak was seven games, but at the end it still was four.

Turning point: Barry Bonds' two-run homer in the 11th inning off Lee Smith gave the Pirates a 4-3 win over St. Louis on August 12. The win increased Pittsburgh's lead to seven games over the second-place Cardinals. Bonds' homer also allowed the Pirates to win three of four in the series and thereby regain the edge the Cardinals had taken by winning three of four the previous week in St. Louis.

Most valuable player: Left fielder Bonds. He hit .292 with 25 home runs and 116 RBIs. Bonds also stole 43 bases and played flawless defense.

Most valuable pitcher: Righthander Doug Drabek. With better run support and some breaks, Drabek (15-14) would have threatened the 20-win mark for the second consecutive season. But when the Pirates had to win big games, he was equal to the challenge.

Most improved player: Lefthander John Smiley. After posting a 9-10 mark with a 4.64 ERA in 1990, Smiley rebounded with a 20-8 mark and 3.08 ERA.

Most pleasant surprise: First baseman Orlando Merced. He filled the Pirates' needs for a leadoff hitter and a left-handed-hitting first baseman. He played good defense and managed a .373 on-base percentage.

Biggest disappointment: For the second straight year the Pirates' offense faded in the N.L. Championship Series. Pittsburgh was blanked three times in its seven-game series against Atlanta.

Key injuries: Third baseman Jeff King was limited to 33 games because of a lower-back strain. For the third con-secutive season righthander Bob Walk spent time on the disabled list. And catcher Don Slaught experienced his annual disabled stint.

Notable: The Pirates posted the major leagues' best road record at 46-32. . . . Bonds and Bobby Bonilla became the first teammates in franchise history to have consecutive 100-RBI seasons.

—JOHN MEHNO

RECORDS

1991 regular-season record: 98-64 (1st in N.L. East); 52-32 at home; 46-32 on road; 58-32 vs. East; 40-32 vs. West; 34-19 vs. LHP; 64-45 vs. RHP; 20-22 on grass; 78-42 on turf; 25-18 in day-time; 73-46 at night; 27-22 in one-run games; 6-6 in extra-inning games; 0-1-2 in doubleheaders.

1991 postseason record: Lost to Braves, 4 games to 3, in N.L. playoffs.

Team record last five years: 432-376 (.535, ranks 2nd in league in that span).

TEAM LEADERS

Batting average: Bobby Bonilla (.302).
At-bats: Jay Bell (608).
Runs: Bobby Bonilla (102).
Hits: Bobby Bonilla (174).
Total bases: Bobby Bonilla (284).
Doubles: Bobby Bonilla (44).
Triples: Jay Bell (8).
Home runs: Barry Bonds (25).
Runs batted in: Barry Bonds (116).
Stolen bases: Barry Bonds (43).
Slugging percentage: Barry Bonds (.514).
On-base percentage: Barry Bonds (.410).
Wins: John Smiley (20).
Earned-run average: Randy Tomlin (2.98).
Complete games: Zane Smith (6).
Shutouts: Zane Smith (3).
Saves: Bill Landrum (17).
Innings pitched: Doug Drabek (234⅔).
Strikeouts: Doug Drabek (142).

GAMES BY POSITION

Catcher: Mike LaValliere 105, Don Slaught 69, Tom Prince 19, Lloyd Mc-Clendon 2.
First base: Orlando Merced 105, Gary Redus 47, Lloyd McClendon 22, Carmelo Martinez 8, Bobby Bonilla 4, Gary Varsho 3, Tom Prince 1.
Second base: Jose Lind 149, Curtis Wilkerson 30, Carlos Garcia 1.
Third base: Bobby Bonilla 67, John Wehner 36, Jeff King 33, Steve Buechele 31, Curtis Wilkerson 14, Joe Redfield 9, Jeff Richardson 3, Carlos Garcia 2, Don Slaught 1.
Shortstop: Jay Bell 156, Curtis Wilkerson 15, Carlos Garcia 9, Jeff Richardson 2.
Outfield: Barry Bonds 150, Andy Van Slyke 135, Bobby Bonilla 104, Gary Varsho 54, Cecil Espy 35, Gary Redus 33, Lloyd McClendon 32, Mitch Webster 29, Jose Gonzalez 14, Orlando Merced 7, Scott Bullett 3.

TOP 10 DRAFT CHOICES

1. **John Farrell**, C/OF, Florida Junior College.
2a. **Dave Doorneweerd**, RHP, Ridgewood High School, Port Richey, Fla.
2b. **Dan Jones**, RHP, Northwestern University.
3. **Matt Ruebel**, LHP, University of Oklahoma.
4. **Benjamin Boka**, C, Barrington (Ill.) High School.
5. **Marty Neff**, OF, University of Oklahoma.
6. **Mickey Kerns**, OF, University of Alabama.
7. **Anthony Womack**, SS, Guilford (N.C.) College.
8. **Matt Pontbriant**, LHP, Brevard (Fla.) Community College.
9. **Deon Danner**, LHP, University of North Carolina-Charlotte.
10. **Chance Sanford**, SS/2B, San Jacinto (Texas) Junior College.

ST. LOUIS CARDINALS
NATIONAL LEAGUE EAST DIVISION

1992 SCHEDULE

APRIL

S	M	T	W	T	F	S
5	6 N	7 N	8 N	9	10	11
	NY H	NY H	NY H	NY H	CHI	CHI
12	13	14 N	15 N	16	17	18
CHI	MON	MON	MON		CHI H	CHI H
19	20	21 N	22 N	23	24 N	25 N
CHI H		NY	NY	NY	MON H	MON H
26	27 N	28 N	29	30		
MON H	LA	LA	SF	SF		

MAY

S	M	T	W	T	F	S
					1 N	2 N
					SD	SD
3	4	5 N	6 N	7	8 N	9 N
SD		SF H	SF H	SF H	ATL H	ATL H
10	11 N	12 N	13 N	14	15 N	16 N
ATL H	ATL H	CIN H	CIN H		HOU	HOU
17	18 N	19 N	20 N	21	22 N	23 N
HOU	ATL	ATL	ATL		HOU H	HOU H
24	25	26 N	27 N	28	29 N	30 N
HOU H	LA H	LA H	LA H		SD H	SD H
31						
SD H						

JUNE

S	M	T	W	T	F	S
	1	2 N	3	4	5 N	6 N
		CIN	CIN		PHI	PHI
7 N	8 N	9 N	10 N	11	12 N	13 N
PHI	CHI H	CHI H	CHI H		PHI H	PHI H
14	15 N	16 N	17	18 N	19 N	20 N
PHI H	CHI	CHI	CHI	NY	NY	NY
21	22 N	23 N	24 N	25	26 N	27
NY	PIT	PIT	PIT		NY H	NY H
28	29 N	30 N				
NY H	PIT H	PIT H				

JULY

S	M	T	W	T	F	S
			1	2 N	3 N	4 N
			PIT H	SF	SF	SF
5	6 N	7 N	8 N	9 N	10 N	11
SF	SD	SD	SD	LA	LA	LA
12	13	14 *	15	16 N	17 N	18 N
LA				CIN	CIN	CIN
19	20	21 N	22 N	23 N	24 N	25 N
CIN		ATL H	ATL H	CIN H	CIN H	CIN H
26	27 N	28 N	29 N	30 N	31 N	
CIN H	MON H	MON H	MON H	PIT	PIT	

AUGUST

S	M	T	W	T	F	S
						1
						PIT
2	3 N	4 N	5 N	6	7 N	8 N
PIT	PHI H	PHI H	PHI H	PIT	PIT H	PIT H
9	10	11 N	12 N	13 N	14 N	15 N
PIT H		PHI	PHI	PHI	MON	MON
16	17	18 N	19 N	20 N	21 N	22 N
MON		HOU H	HOU H	HOU H	ATL	ATL
23 N	24	25 N	26 N	27	28 N	29 N
ATL		HOU	HOU	HOU	LA H	LA H
30	31 N					
LA H	SD H					

SEPTEMBER

S	M	T	W	T	F	S
		1 N	2 N	3	4 N	5 N
		SD H	SD H		SF H	SF H
6	7	8 N	9 N	10	11 N	12 N
SF H	MON	MON	MON		CHI H	CHI H
13 N	14 N	15 N	16 N	17 N	18	
CHI H	PIT H	PIT H	NY		CHI	CHI
20	21 N	22 N	23 N	24 N	25 N	26 N
CHI	PIT	PIT	NY H	NY H	PHI	PHI
27	28 N	29 N	30 N			
PHI	MON H	MON H	MON H			

OCTOBER

S	M	T	W	T	F	S
				1	2 N	3
					PHI H	PHI H
4	5	6	7	8	9	10
PHI H						

1992 SEASON

CLUB DIRECTORY

Chairman of the board
August A. Busch III
Vice chairman
Fred L. Kuhlmann
President and chief executive officer
Stuart F. Meyer
Vice president, business operations
Mark Gorris
Controller
Brad Wood
Vice president, general manager
Dal Maxvill
Admin. asst. to the president and CEO
Elaine Milo
Admin. asst. to the v.p., general manager
Judy Carpenter Barada
Admin. asst., business operations
Renee Garrett
Vice president, marketing
Marty Hendin
Admin. asst. to the v.p., marketing
Mary Ellen Edmiston
Director of promotions
Nancy Trammell
Director of player development
Ted Simmons
Director of scouting
Fred McAlister
Assistant director of scouting
Marty Maier
Asst. to player development and scouting
Scott Smulczenski
Director of public relations
Jeff Wehling
Public relations manager
Brian Bartow
Dir. of broadcasting and market develop.
Dan Farrell
Promotions supervisor
Joe Strohm
Director of community relations
Joe Cunningham
Director of sales
Sue Ann McClaren
Director, target marketing
Ted Savage

Director, ticket systems
Josephine Arnold
Director, human resources
Marian Rhodes
Director, ticket services
Kevin Wade
Director, tickets and office administration
Colin Allsop
Manager, office services
Patti McCormick
Traveling secretary
C.J. Cherre
Club physician
Dr. Stan London
Scouting supervisors
Jorge Aranzamendi
Jim Bayens
Jim Belz
Vern Benson
Jim Johnston
Marty Keough
Tom McCormack
Joe Morlan
Mel Nelson
Joe Rigoli
Mike Roberts
Hal Smith
Charles (Tim) Thompson
Special assignment scout
Rube Walker
Regular scouts
James Brown
Roy Cromer
Roberto Diaz
John DiPuglia
Manuel Espinosa
Cecil Espy
Manuel Guerra
Juan Melo
Charles Menzhuber
Scott Nichols
Jay North
Ramon Ortiz
Joe Popek
Roger Smith
Kenneth Thomas

SCHEDULE KEY

H—Home game.   *All-Star Game at San Diego/Jack Murphy Stadium.
N—Night game (any game starting after 5 p.m.).

SPRING TRAINING ROSTER

Manager—Joe Torre (9).

Coaches—Don Baylor, Joe Coleman (40), Dave Collins (15), Bucky Dent (30), Gaylen Pitts (4), Red Schoendienst (2).

No.	PITCHERS	B/T	Ht./Wt.	Born	1991 clubs
49	Agosto, Juan	L/L	6-2/190	2-23-58	St. Louis
44	Carpenter, Cris	R/R	6-1/185	4-5-65	St. Louis
55	Clark, Mark	R/R	6-5/225	5-12-68	Arkansas, Louisville, St. Louis
	Compres, Fidel	R/R	6-0/165	5-10-65	Arkansas, Louisville
52	Cormier, Rheal	L/L	5-10/185	4-23-67	Louisville, St. Louis
48	DeLeon, Jose	R/R	6-3/226	12-20-60	St. Louis
35	DiPino, Frank	L/L	6-0/194	10-22-56	Louisville
66	Ericks, John	R/R	6-7/220	9-16-67	Arkansas
32	Magrane, Joe	R/L	6-6/230	7-2-64	DID NOT PLAY
22	McClure, Bob	R/L	5-11/188	4-29-53	California, St. Louis
73	Milchin, Mike	L/L	6-3/190	2-28-68	Arkansas, Louisville
26	Olivares, Omar	R/R	6-1/193	7-6-67	St. Louis, Louisville
36	Smith, Bryn	R/R	6-2/205	8-11-55	St. Louis
47	Smith, Lee	R/R	6-6/269	12-4-57	St. Louis
37	Terry, Scott	R/R	5-11/195	11-21-59	St. Louis
39	Tewksbury, Bob	R/R	6-4/208	11-30-60	St. Louis
38	Worrell, Todd	R/R	6-5/222	9-28-59	Louisville

No.	CATCHERS	B/T	Ht./Wt.	Born	1991 clubs
64	Fernandez, Jose	L/R	6-3/210	8-24-67	Arkansas
29	Gedman, Rich	L/R	6-0/211	9-26-59	St. Louis
19	Pagnozzi, Tom	R/R	6-1/190	7-30-62	St. Louis

No.	INFIELDERS	B/T	Ht./Wt.	Born	1991 clubs
18	Alicea, Luis	S/R	5-9/177	7-29-65	Louisville, St. Louis
33	Brewer, Rod	L/L	6-3/218	2-24-66	Louisville, St. Louis
67	Carmona, Greg	S/R	6-0/150	5-9-68	Arkansas, Louisville
41	Galarraga, Andres	R/R	6-3/235	6-18-61	Montreal
8	Jones, Tim	L/R	5-10/175	12-1-62	Louisville, St. Louis
11	Oquendo, Jose	S/R	5-10/171	7-4-63	St. Louis
7	Pena, Geronimo	S/R	6-1/195	3-29-67	St. Louis
21	Perry, Gerald	L/R	6-0/201	10-30-60	St. Louis
5	Royer, Stan	R/R	6-3/221	8-31-67	Louisville, St. Louis
1	Smith, Ozzie	S/R	5-10/168	12-26-54	St. Louis
12	Wilson, Craig	R/R	5-11/208	11-28-64	St. Louis
27	Zeile, Todd	R/R	6-1/190	9-9-65	St. Louis

No.	OUTFIELDERS	B/T	Ht./Wt.	Born	1991 clubs
23	Gilkey, Bernard	R/R	6-0/190	9-24-66	St. Louis, Louisville
28	Guerrero, Pedro	R/R	6-0/197	6-29-56	St. Louis, Louisville
10	Hudler, Rex	R/R	6-0/195	9-2-60	St. Louis
71	Jordan, Brian	R/R	6-1/205	3-29-67	Louisville
34	Jose, Felix	S/R	6-1/221	5-8-65	St. Louis
16	Lankford, Ray	L/L	5-11/198	6-5-67	St. Louis
51	Maclin, Lonnie	L/L	5-11/185	2-17-67	Louisville
25	Thompson, Milt	L/R	5-11/200	1-5-59	St. Louis

BALLPARK INFORMATION

Ballpark (capacity, surface)
Busch Stadium (56,627, artificial)
Address
250 Stadium Plaza
St. Louis, MO 63102
Business phone
314-421-3060
Ticket information
314-421-3060
Ticket prices
$12 (box)
$9.50 (reserved)
$5.50 (general admission)
$4 (bleachers)
Field dimensions (from home plate)
To left field at foul line, 330 feet
To center field, 402 feet
To right field at foul line, 330 feet
First game played
May 12, 1966 (Cardinals 4, Braves 3)

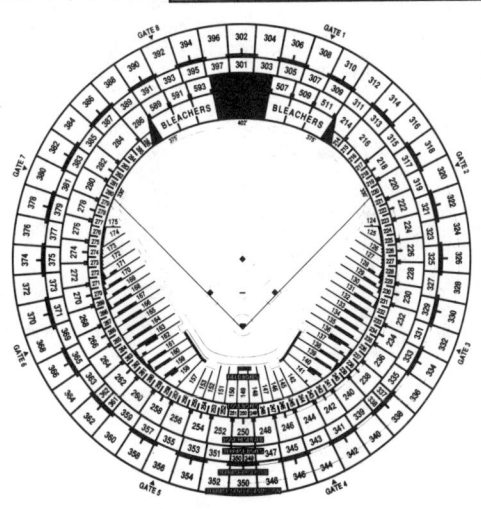

MINOR LEAGUE AFFILIATES

Class	Team	League	Manager
AAA	Louisville	American Association	Jack Krol
AA	Arkansas	Texas	Joe Pettini
A	St. Petersburg	Florida State	Dave Bialas
A	Springfield	Midwest	Rick Colbert
A	Savannah	South Atlantic	Mike Ramsey
A	Hamilton, Ont.	New York-Pennsylvania	Chris Maloney
Rookie	Johnson City	Appalachian	Steve Turco
Rookie	Peoria Cardinals	Arizona	Joe Cunningham III

BROADCAST INFORMATION

Radio: KMOX-AM (1120). Broadcasters: Jack Buck, Mike Shannon, Joe Buck.
TV: KPLR-TV (Channel 11). Broadcasters: George Grande, Al Hrabosky.
Cable TV: None.

SPRING TRAINING

Ballpark (city): Al Lang Stadium (St. Petersburg, Fla.).
Ticket information: 813-896-4641.

HISTORY

YEAR-BY-YEAR RECORDS

Year	Pos.	W	L	Pct.	*GB	Year	Pos.	W	L	Pct.	*GB
1901	4th	76	64	.543	14½	1948	2nd	85	69	.552	6½
1902	6th	56	78	.418	44½	1949	2nd	96	58	.623	1
1903	8th	43	94	.314	46½	1950	5th	78	75	.510	12½
1904	5th	75	79	.487	31½	1951	3rd	81	73	.526	15½
1905	6th	58	96	.377	47½	1952	3rd	88	66	.571	8½
1906	7th	52	98	.347	63	1953	T3rd	83	71	.539	22
1907	8th	52	101	.340	55½	1954	6th	72	82	.468	25
1908	8th	49	105	.318	50	1955	7th	68	86	.442	30½
1909	7th	54	98	.355	56	1956	4th	76	78	.494	17
1910	7th	63	90	.412	40½	1957	2nd	87	67	.565	8
1911	5th	75	74	.503	22	1958	T5th	72	82	.468	20
1912	6th	63	90	.412	41	1959	7th	71	83	.461	16
1913	8th	51	99	.340	49	1960	3rd	86	68	.558	9
1914	3rd	81	72	.529	13	1961	5th	80	74	.519	13
1915	6th	72	81	.471	18½	1962	6th	84	78	.519	17½
1916	T7th	60	93	.392	33½	1963	2nd	93	69	.574	6
1917	3rd	82	70	.539	15	1964	1st	93	69	.574 +	1
1918	8th	51	78	.395	33	1965	7th	80	81	.497	16½
1919	7th	54	83	.394	40½	1966	6th	83	79	.512	12
1920	T5th	75	79	.487	18	1967	1st	101	60	.627	+10½
1921	3rd	87	66	.569	7	1968	1st	97	65	.599	+ 9
1922	T3rd	85	69	.552	8	1969	4th	87	75	.537	13
1923	5th	79	74	.516	16	1970	4th	76	86	.469	13
1924	6th	65	89	.422	28½	1971	2nd	90	72	.556	7
1925	4th	77	76	.503	18	1972	4th	75	81	.481	21½
1926	1st	89	65	.578 +	2	1973	2nd	81	81	.500	1½
1927	2nd	92	61	.601	1½	1974	2nd	86	75	.534	1½
1928	1st	95	59	.617 +	2	1975	T3rd	82	80	.506	10½
1929	4th	78	74	.513	20	1976	5th	72	90	.444	29
1930	1st	92	62	.597 +	2	1977	3rd	83	79	.512	18
1931	1st	101	53	.656	+13	1978	5th	69	93	.426	21
1932	T6th	72	82	.468	18	1979	3rd	86	76	.531	12
1933	5th	82	71	.536	9½	1980	4th	74	88	.457	17
1934	1st	95	58	.621 +	2	1981	2nd/2nd	59	43	.578	‡
1935	2nd	96	58	.623	4	1982	1st§	92	70	.568	+ 3
1936	T2nd	87	67	.565	5	1983	4th	79	83	.488	11
1937	4th	81	73	.526	15	1984	3rd	84	78	.519	12½
1938	6th	71	80	.470	17½	1985	1st§	101	61	.623	+ 3
1939	2nd	92	61	.601	4½	1986	3rd	79	82	.491	28½
1940	3rd	84	69	.549	16	1987	1st§	95	67	.586	+ 3
1941	2nd	97	56	.634	2½	1988	5th	76	86	.469	25
1942	1st	106	48	.688 +	2	1989	3rd	86	76	.531	7
1943	1st	105	49	.682	+18	1990	6th	70	92	.432	25
1944	1st	105	49	.682	+14½	1991	2nd	84	78	.519	14
1945	2nd	95	59	.617	3						
1946	1st†	98	58	.628	+ 2						
1947	2nd	89	65	.578	5						

*Games behind winner. †Won pennant playoff. ‡First half 30-20; second 29-23. §Won Championship Series.

MANAGERS

Name	Record	Years
Patsy Donovan	175-236	'01-03
Kid Nichols	94-108	'04-05
Jimmy Burke	17-32	1905
Stanley Robison	22-35	1905
John McCloskey	153-304	'06-08
Roger Bresnahan	255-352	'09-12
Miller Huggins	346-415	'13-17
Jack Hendricks	51-78	1918
Branch Rickey	458-485	'19-25
Rogers Hornsby	153-116	'25-26
Bob O'Farrell	92-61	1927
Bill McKechnie	129-88	'28-29
Billy Southworth	620-346	1929
		'40-45
Gabby Street	312-242	'30-33
Frank Frisch	458-354	'33-38
Mike Gonzalez	9-13	'38, '40
Ray Blades	106-85	'39-40
Eddie Dyer	446-325	'46-50
Marty Marion	81-73	1951
Eddie Stanky	260-238	'52-55
Harry Walker	51-67	1955
Fred Hutchinson	232-220	'56-58
Stan Hack	3-7	1958
Solly Hemus	190-192	'59-61
Johnny Keane	317-249	'61-64
Red Schoendienst	1028-944	'65-76
		1980
Vern Rapp	89-90	'77-78
Ken Boyer	166-190	'78-80
Whitey Herzog	835-739	1980
		'81-90
Joe Torre	108-112	'90-91

Date	Opp.	Res.	Score (inn.*)	Hits	Opp. hits	Winning pitcher	Losing pitcher	Save	Record	Pos.	GB
4-9	At Chi.	W	4-1	8	5	B. Smith	Jackson	L. Smith	1-0	T1st	½
4-10	At Chi.	L	0-2	7	8	Maddux	DeLeon	Smith	1-1	T3rd	½
4-11	At Chi.	W	5-4	12	9	Hill	Harkey	L. Smith	2-1	T2nd	½
4-12	At Phi.	L	4-11	12	14	Combs	Moyer		2-2	T3rd	1
4-13	At Phi.	L	2-4	10	7	Mulholland	Tewksbury	Williams	2-3	T4th	1½
4-14	At Phi.	W	11-7	12	8	B. Smith	LaPoint	L. Smith	3-3	T2nd	1½
4-15	At Mon.	W	5-4	9	5	Carpenter	Burke	L. Smith	4-3	T2nd	1½
4-16	At Mon.	L	1-4	6	9	Mahler	Hill	Burke	4-4	T3rd	1½
4-17	At Mon.	L	0-1	6	7	Sampen	Moyer	Jones	4-5	4th	2
4-19	Phi.	W	3-1	6	5	Tewksbury	Mulholland	L. Smith	5-5	4th	1½
4-20 (1)	Phi.	W	12-1	10	6	DeLeon	Grimsley	Olivares	6-5	4th	½
4-20 (2)	Phi.	L	5-6 (10)	7	12	McDowell	Carpenter	Williams	6-6	4th	1
4-21	Phi.	W	7-6 (10)	9	9	L. Smith	Williams		7-6	T3rd	1
4-22	Chi.	W	3-2	5	4	Agosto	Smith		8-6	3rd	½
4-23	Chi.	W	4-2	8	5	Tewksbury	Sutcliffe	L. Smith	9-6	3rd	½
4-24	Chi.	L	0-1	3	6	Bielecki	DeLeon	Assenmacher	9-7	3rd	1½
4-26	Mon.	W	4-0	11	5	B. Smith	Boyd	Agosto	10-7	3rd	1
4-27	Mon.	W	2-1	10	6	Hill	Mahler	L. Smith	11-7	T2nd	1
4-28	Mon.	L	6-9	12	17	Burke	Perez		11-8	T2nd	2
4-29	Atl.	W	4-3 (11)	9	8	L. Smith	Sisk		12-8	2nd	1½
4-30	Atl.	W	5-3	8	7	Carpenter	Leibrandt	L. Smith	13-8	2nd	½
5-1	Atl.	L	4-5 (10)	9	8	Mercker	Perez		13-9	2nd	1½
5-3	At Cin.	W	4-2	11	6	Carpenter	Scudder	L. Smith	14-9	2nd	1½
5-4	At Cin.	L	1-3	5	6	Armstrong	Moyer	Dibble	14-10	3rd	1½
5-5	At Cin.	L	2-4	6	8	Browning	L. Smith	Dibble	14-11	3rd	1½
5-7	At Atl.	L	2-9	8	12	Avery	B. Smith		14-12	3rd	3
5-8	At Atl.	L	1-17	6	17	Glavine	Hill		14-13	3rd	4
5-10	At Hou.	W	7-5 (10)	11	12	Agosto	Schilling	L. Smith	15-13	3rd	4
5-11	At Hou.	L	1-6	3	10	Portugal	DeLeon		15-14	3rd	4
5-12	At Hou.	W	7-3	12	9	Carpenter	Osuna		16-14	3rd	3
5-13	Cin.	W	1-0	7	2	Hill	Myers	L. Smith	17-14	3rd	2½
5-14	Cin.	L	1-3	6	7	Charlton	Moyer	Dibble	17-15	3rd	3½
5-15	Cin.	W	8-2	14	9	Tewksbury	Browning		18-15	3rd	3½
5-17	Hou.	L	4-5	7	10	Deshaies	L. Smith	Osuna	18-16	3rd	4
5-18	Hou.	W	12-2	18	3	B. Smith	Hernandez		19-16	3rd	3½
5-19	Hou.	W	9-2	13	4	Hill	Harnisch		20-16	3rd	2½
5-21	At Pit.	L	3-5	11	8	Smiley	Moyer	Landrum	20-17	3rd	3½
5-22	At Pit.	W	5-3	11	10	Carpenter	Drabek	L. Smith	21-17	3rd	2½
5-23	At Pit.	W	8-2	15	8	DeLeon	Tomlin	Terry	22-17	2nd	1½
5-24	At N.Y.	L	2-6	8	16	Cone	B. Smith		22-18	3rd	2½
5-25	At N.Y.	W	7-2	9	7	Hill	Whitehurst		23-18	2nd	2½
5-26	At N.Y.	W	14-4	23	8	Carpenter	Gooden		24-18	2nd	2½
5-27	Pit.	L	0-8	1	15	Drabek	Tewksbury		24-19	2nd	3½
5-28	Pit.	L	8-9	11	11	Belinda	DeLeon	Landrum	24-20	3rd	4½
5-29	Pit.	L	0-6	1	11	Z. Smith	B. Smith		24-21	3rd	5½
5-31	N.Y.	L	5-10	12	14	Whitehurst	Agosto		24-22	3rd	6½
6-1	N.Y.	W	6-5 (10)	16	10	Agosto	Franco		25-22	3rd	6½
6-2	N.Y.	W	3-1	7	6	Tewksbury	Darling	L. Smith	26-22	3rd	6½
6-4	L.A.	W	3-2 (11)	7	10	L. Smith	Gott		27-22	3rd	5½
6-5	L.A.	L	0-2	4	6	Martinez	B. Smith		27-23	3rd	6½
6-6	L.A.	L	0-1	4	6	Ojeda	Hill	Crews	27-24	3rd	6½
6-7	S.F.	L	2-5	7	7	Robinson	Olivares	Righetti	27-25	3rd	7½
6-8	S.F.	W	3-2 (10)	11	5	Carpenter	Oliveras		28-25	3rd	6½
6-9	S.F.	L	2-3	4	7	Burkett	DeLeon	Brantley	28-26	3rd	6½
6-10	S.F.	W	3-2	8	6	Terry	Segura	L. Smith	29-26	3rd	6½
6-11	At S.D.	W	10-4	11	13	Hill	Melendez		30-26	3rd	6
6-12	At S.D.	L	2-7	4	9	Hurst	Carpenter		30-27	3rd	7
6-13	At S.D.	W	12-1	12	7	Tewksbury	Hammaker		31-27	2nd	6
6-14	At L.A.	L	1-2	9	5	Howell	Terry		31-28	2nd	6
6-15	At L.A.	W	5-4	9	10	B. Smith	Martinez	L. Smith	32-28	2nd	5
6-16	At L.A.	L	2-7	4	16	Ojeda	Hill		32-29	2nd	6
6-17	At S.F.	W	5-4	12	8	Agosto	Righetti	L. Smith	33-29	2nd	6
6-18	At S.F.	W	3-1	4	4	Tewksbury	Wilson	L. Smith	34-29	2nd	6
6-19	At S.F.	W	3-2	7	7	DeLeon	Burkett	L. Smith	35-29	2nd	5
6-21	S.D.	W	4-3	8	11	Agosto	Andersen		36-29	2nd	4½
6-22	S.D.	L	3-4	9	7	Melendez	Hill	Lefferts	36-30	2nd	4½
6-23	S.D.	L	2-3	7	7	Hurst	Agosto		36-31	2nd	4½
6-24	S.D.	L	1-4	5	9	Peterson	Tewksbury		36-32	2nd	5
6-25	Phi.	W	10-9	12	12	Terry	McDowell	L. Smith	37-32	2nd	4
6-26	Phi.	W	14-1	16	7	B. Smith	Combs		38-32	2nd	4

Date	Opp.	Res.	Score (inn.*)	Hits	Opp. hits	Winning pitcher	Losing pitcher	Save	Record	Pos.	GB
6-27	Phi.	W	4-2	5	3	Hill	Greene	L. Smith	39-32	2nd	4
6-28	At Chi.	W	14-6	21	13	Olivares	Scanlan		40-32	2nd	4
6-29	At Chi.	L	4-6	11	12	Lancaster	Tewksbury	Assenmacher	40-33	2nd	5
6-30	At Chi.	L	4-7	8	10	McElroy	DeLeon		40-34	2nd	6
7-1	At Phi.	W	1-0	10	4	B. Smith	Ruffin	L. Smith	41-34	2nd	5
7-2	At Phi.	W	6-1	11	4	Hill	Greene	L. Smith	42-34	2nd	5
7-3	At Phi.	W	4-3	10	7	Olivares	DeJesus	L. Smith	43-34	2nd	5
7-4	At Phi.	L	1-7	6	9	Mulholland	Tewksbury		43-35	3rd	5
7-5	Chi.	L	1-5	6	8	Castillo	DeLeon		43-36	3rd	5
7-6	Chi.	L	2-12	4	13	Bielecki	B. Smith		43-37	3rd	5
7-7	Chi.	W	8-7 (12)	16	11	Fraser	Renfroe		44-37	3rd	5
7-11	At Atl.	L	1-4	2	8	Avery	DeLeon	Berenguer	44-38	3rd	6
7-12	At Atl.	L	2-6	7	10	Smoltz	B. Smith		44-39	3rd	7
7-13	At Atl.	L	5-10	9	10	Leibrandt	Hill		44-40	3rd	8
7-14	At Atl.	L	1-2	6	6	Glavine	Tewksbury		44-41	3rd	9
7-15	At Cin.	W	5-2	12	10	Olivares	Minutelli	L. Smith	45-41	3rd	9
7-16	At Cin.	W	8-7	10	14	Fraser	Dibble	L. Smith	46-41	3rd	9
7-17	At Cin.	W	6-5	10	9	B. Smith	Armstrong	L. Smith	47-41	3rd	8
7-19	Atl.	L	3-8	8	12	Leibrandt	Hill	Berenguer	47-42	3rd	9
7-20	Atl.	W	2-1	4	9	L. Smith	Stanton		48-42	3rd	8
7-21	Atl.	L	1-5	3	7	Avery	Olivares		48-43	3rd	9
7-22	Hou.	W	9-1	7	7	DeLeon	Bowen		49-43	3rd	8
7-23	Hou.	W	5-1	9	6	B. Smith	Deshaies		50-43	3rd	8
7-24	Hou.	W	4-3	13	5	L. Smith	Osuna		51-43	3rd	8
7-26	Cin.	W	5-1	10	8	Tewksbury	Hammond		52-43	3rd	8
7-27	Cin.	L	1-13	9	20	Gross	Olivares		52-44	3rd	9
7-28	Cin.	W	3-2	4	13	DeLeon	Myers	L. Smith	53-44	3rd	8
7-29	At Hou.	L	2-6	9	10	Deshaies	B. Smith		53-45	3rd	7 ½
7-30	At Hou.	L	5-7	7	10	Osuna	Carpenter		53-46	3rd	7 ½
7-31	At Hou.	L	5-9	10	9	Kile	Tewksbury	Wilkins	53-47	3rd	7 ½
8-1	Pit.	W	6-3	13	9	Olivares	Tomlin	L. Smith	54-47	3rd	6 ½
8-2	Pit.	W	4-3	5	6	McClure	Belinda		55-47	3rd	5 ½
8-3	Pit.	W	6-5 (10)	15	8	L. Smith	Patterson		56-47	2nd	4 ½
8-4	Pit.	L	1-2	5	6	Smiley	Hill		56-48	2nd	5 ½
8-6	Mon.	W	7-6 (10)	13	11	Terry	Jones		57-48	2nd	5 ½
8-7	Mon.	L	0-1	5	9	Gardner	Olivares	Jones	57-49	2nd	5 ½
8-9	At Pit.	W	5-1	7	3	B. Smith	Smiley		58-49	2nd	4
8-10	At Pit.	L	5-11	8	14	Heaton	Hill		58-50	2nd	5
8-11	At Pit.	L	4-6	9	11	Mason	Tewksbury	Landrum	58-51	2nd	6
8-12	At Pit.	L	3-4 (11)	12	6	Patterson	L. Smith		58-52	2nd	7
8-13	N.Y.	W	7-4	12	9	Olivares	Viola	L. Smith	59-52	2nd	7
8-14	N.Y.	W	5-4	12	9	Carpenter	Franco	L. Smith	60-52	2nd	7
8-15	N.Y.	W	4-1	10	8	Cormier	Whitehurst	L. Smith	61-52	2nd	6
8-16	At Mon.	W	4-2	7	5	Tewksbury	Nabholz	L. Smith	62-52	2nd	6
8-17	At Mon.	L	0-3	6	9	Martinez	DeLeon		62-53	2nd	7
8-18	At Mon.	W	4-1	10	7	Olivares	Gardner	L. Smith	63-53	2nd	7
8-21(1)	At N.Y.	W	7-3	13	6	B. Smith	Cone		64-53	2nd	5 ½
8-21(2)	At N.Y.	L	0-8	5	10	Fernandez	Cormier		64-54	2nd	6
8-22	At N.Y.	L	0-6	5	13	Gooden	Tewksbury	Burke	64-55	2nd	6
8-23	L.A.	W	2-1	4	9	Carpenter	Crews	L. Smith	65-55	2nd	6
8-24	L.A.	W	7-3	10	7	Olivares	Morgan		66-55	2nd	5
8-25	L.A.	W	5-2	11	12	Cormier	Belcher	L. Smith	67-55	2nd	5
8-26	S.F.	W	7-6	9	13	Carpenter	Black	L. Smith	68-55	2nd	4
8-27	S.F.	W	5-4	8	10	Terry	Robinson	L. Smith	69-55	2nd	4
8-28	S.D.	L	1-2	6	3	Hurst	Terry	Lefferts	69-56	2nd	5
8-29	S.D.	L	0-1	2	4	Benes	Olivares		69-57	2nd	6
8-30	At S.F.	L	3-8	9	8	Black	Cormier	Brantley	69-58	2nd	7
8-31	At S.F.	L	1-6	5	11	Hickerson	B. Smith		69-59	2nd	8
9-1	At S.F.	W	14-1	18	7	Tewksbury	Burkett		70-59	2nd	7
9-2	At L.A.	W	7-4 (11)	15	8	Fraser	Howell		71-59	2nd	7
9-3	At L.A.	L	4-5	6	7	Howell	Terry		71-60	2nd	8
9-4	At L.A.	L	3-8	11	12	McDowell	McClure		71-61	2nd	9
9-5	At S.D.	L	1-3	3	7	Harris	Terry	Melendez	71-62	2nd	9 ½
9-6	At S.D.	L	2-6	9	11	Bones	Tewksbury		71-63	2nd	10
9-7	At S.D.	L	0-1 (10)	6	5	Maddux	Carpenter		71-64	2nd	10
9-9	Phi.	W	4-2	8	6	Olivares	Ashby	L. Smith	72-64	2nd	9 ½
9-10	Phi.	L	2-5	6	12	Greene	Cormier	Williams	72-65	2nd	9 ½
9-11	Pit.	L	1-3	6	10	Smith	Tewksbury		72-66	2nd	10 ½
9-12	Pit.	W	1-0	5	7	Hill	Drabek	L. Smith	73-66	2nd	9 ½
9-13	N.Y.	L	2-4 (10)	9	7	Burke	Fraser		73-67	2nd	10 ½
9-14	N.Y.	W	2-1	1	6	Olivares	Cone	L. Smith	74-67	2nd	10 ½
9-15	N.Y.	W	7-2	11	9	Cormier	Schourek		75-67	2nd	9 ½
9-16	At Phi.	W	3-0	8	7	Tewksbury	DeJesus	L. Smith	76-67	2nd	9 ½
9-17	At Phi.	L	2-4	7	8	Brantley	Hill	Williams	76-68	2nd	10 ½

Date	Opp.	Res.	Score (inn.*)	Hits	Opp. hits	Winning pitcher	Losing pitcher	Save	Record	Pos.	GB
9-18	At Pit.	L	5-6	9	12	Mason	Fraser		76-69	2nd	11½
9-19	At Pit.	L	1-5	6	6	Belinda	Olivares		76-70	2nd	12½
9-20	At N.Y.	L	0-1	1	6	Cone	Cormier		76-71	2nd	12½
9-21	At N.Y.	L	3-5	6	8	Schourek	Tewksbury	Franco	76-72	2nd	13½
9-22	At N.Y.	W	2-1	7	2	Hill	Young	L. Smith	77-72	2nd	13½
9-23 (1)	Mon.	W	10-1	9	3	B. Smith	Martinez		78-72	2nd	13
9-23 (2)	Mon.	L	1-5	5	10	Nabholz	Clark		78-73	2nd	13½
9-24	Mon.	W	4-3	6	9	Olivares	Haney	L. Smith	79-73	2nd	13½
9-25	Mon.	L	2-7	10	10	Barnes	Cormier		79-74	2nd	14
9-27	Chi.	W	5-4	7	10	Tewksbury	Castillo	L. Smith	80-74	2nd	13
9-28	Chi.	W	3-2	6	7	Hill	Maddux	L. Smith	81-74	2nd	12
9-29	Chi.	L	3-5	7	8	Sutcliffe	B. Smith	Assenmacher	81-75	2nd	13
9-30	Mon.	W	11-1	12	7	Clark	Haney	Agosto	82-75	2nd	13
10-1	Mon.	W	3-1	8	8	Olivares	Barnes	L. Smith	83-75	2nd	13
10-2	Mon.	W	6-4	6	9	Cormier	Gardner	L. Smith	84-75	2nd	12
10-5 (1)	At Chi.	L	2-3	9	8	Scanlan	Fraser		84-76	2nd	12
10-5 (2)	At Chi.	L	5-7	9	3	Perez	Agosto	Assenmacher	84-77	2nd	13
10-6	At Chi.	L	3-7	6	10	Maddux	Olivares		84-78	2nd	14

Monthly records: April (13-8), May (11-14), June (16-12), July (13-13), August (16-12), September (13-16), Oct. (2-3).

HIGHLIGHTS

High point: On August 9, the Cardinals beat Pittsburgh for the fourth time in their last five meetings to close to within four games of the division-leading Pirates.

Low point: From August 28 through September 7, St. Louis lost nine of 11 games against West Coast teams. That skid pushed the Cardinals 10 games out of first and eliminated them from contention in the National League East.

Turning point: When Ray Lankford scored from second base on a ball hit in the infield April 21. The rookie bowled over Philadelphia catcher Darren Daulton to score the winning run as the Cardinals rallied from a 5-0 deficit to win, 7-6, in 10 innings. That play typified the aggressive attitude the Cardinals would display most of the season.

Most valuable player: Righthander Lee Smith. The league's top fireman, Smith set an N.L. record by saving 47 games. The veteran fireballer won or saved 63 percent of the Cardinals' 84 victories.

Most improved player: Right fielder Felix Jose. He hit .300 from start to finish in 1991, finishing the year with a .305 average (fifth in the league). He also was named to the All-Star team.

Most pleasant surprise: Catcher Tom Pagnozzi. In his first full year as a regular catcher in the big leagues, Pagnozzi threw out 47 percent of would-be basestealers and batted a solid .264.

Biggest disappointment: Outfielder Bernard Gilkey. The Cardinals' opening-day left fielder, his season was marred by an injured right thumb and a trip to Class AAA Louisville. A .216 batting average in 81 games made his season a washout.

Key injuries: The broken leg suffered by first baseman Pedro Guerrero in a July 7 collision with Pagnozzi hurt the team's run-producing ability. Righthanders were scarce in the Cardinals' bullpen after injuries to Cris Carpenter and Scott Terry cost both pitchers virtually the entire last month of the season.

Notable: Smith recorded his 300th career save August 25. He finished the year third on the all-time saves list with 312. . . . Todd Zeile led the Cardinals with 11 home runs. His homer total was the lowest to lead St. Louis since 1920, when Austin McHenry hit a team-high 10. . . . Ozzie Smith committed just eight errors, setting an N.L. record (150 games minimum) for fewest errors by a shortstop in a season.
—RICK HUMMEL

RECORDS

1991 regular-season record: 84-78 (2nd in N.L. East); 52-32 at home; 32-46 on road; 49-41 vs. East; 35-37 vs. West; 35-37 vs. LHP; 49-41 vs. RHP; 15-27 on grass; 69-51 on turf; 24-22 in daytime; 60-56 at night; 37-22 in one-run games; 10-5 in extra-inning games; 0-1-3 in doubleheaders.
Team record last five years: 411-399 (.507, ranks 6th in league in that span).

TEAM LEADERS

Batting average: Felix Jose (.305).
At-bats: Felix Jose (568).
Runs: Ozzie Smith (96).
Hits: Felix Jose (173).
Total bases: Felix Jose (249).
Doubles: Felix Jose (40).
Triples: Ray Lankford (15).
Home runs: Todd Zeile (11).
Runs batted in: Todd Zeile (81).
Stolen bases: Ray Lankford (44).
Slugging percentage: Felix Jose (.438).
On-base percentage: Ozzie Smith (.380).
Wins: Bryn Smith (12).
Earned-run average: Jose DeLeon (2.71).
Complete games: Bryn Smith, Bob Tewksbury (3).
Shutouts: None.
Saves: Lee Smith (47).
Innings pitched: Bryn Smith (198⅔).
Strikeouts: Ken Hill (121).

GAMES BY POSITION

Catcher: Tom Pagnozzi 139, Rich Gedman 43, Ray Stephens 5.
First base: Pedro Guerrero 112, Gerald Perry 61, Rod Brewer 15, Rex Hudler 12, Craig Wilson 4, Jose Oquendo 3, Tom Pagnozzi 3.
Second base: Jose Oquendo 118, Geronimo Pena 83, Luis Alicea 11, Rex Hudler 5, Tim Jones 4, Craig Wilson 3.
Third base: Todd Zeile 154, Craig Wilson 12, Stan Royer 5, Luis Alicea 2.
Shortstop: Ozzie Smith 150, Jose Oquendo 22, Tim Jones 14, Luis Alicea 1.
Outfield: Felix Jose 153, Ray Lankford 149, Milt Thompson 91, Bernard Gilkey 74, Rex Hudler 58, Gerald Perry 5, Craig Wilson 5, Geronimo Pena 4, Rod Brewer 3.

TOP 10 DRAFT CHOICES

1a. Dmitri Young, 3B/OF, Rio Mesa High School, Oxnard, Calif.
1b. Allen Watson, LHP, New York Tech.
1c. Brian Barber, RHP, Dr. Phillips High School, Orlando, Fla.
1d. Tom McKinnon, RHP, Jordan High School, Long Beach, Calif.
1e. Dan Cholowsky, 3B, University of California.
2. Eddie Williams, C, Edison High School, Miami.
3. Basil Shabazz, OF, Pine Bluff (Ark.) High School.
4. Andy Bruce, 3B, Georgia Tech.
5. Darond Stovall, OF, Althoff High School, East St. Louis, Ill.
6. John Mabry, OF, West Chester University.
7. Doug Creek, LHP, Georgia Tech.
8. Antoine Henry, OF, Clairemont High School, San Diego.
9. Dennis Slininger, RHP, Largo (Fla.) High School.
10. Allen Battle, OF, University of South Alabama.

SAN DIEGO PADRES
NATIONAL LEAGUE WEST DIVISION

1992 SCHEDULE

APRIL

S	M	T	W	T	F	S
5	6 CIN	7 N CIN	8 N CIN	9 LA H	10 N LA H	11 N LA H
12 LA H	13	14 N SF	15 N SF	16 SF	17 N HOU	18 N HOU
19 HOU	20 N ATL H	21 N ATL H	22 N ATL H	23	24 N CIN H	25 N CIN H
26 CIN H	27 N PHI H	28 N PHI H	29 N MON H	30 MON H		

MAY

S	M	T	W	T	F	S
					1 N STL H	2 N STL H
3 STL H	4	5 N MON	6 N MON	7	8 N PHI	9 N PHI
10 PHI	11 N NY	12 N NY	13 N NY	14	15 N PIT	16 N PIT
17 PIT	18 N NY	19 N NY	20 N NY	21 N NY H	22 N CHI H	23 N CHI H
24 CHI H	25 N PIT H	26 N PIT H	27 N PIT H	28	29 N STL	30 N STL
31 STL						

JUNE

S	M	T	W	T	F	S
	1 N CHI	2 N CHI	3 CHI	4	5 N ATL H	6 N ATL H
7 ATL H	8 N HOU H	9 N HOU H	10 HOU H	11	12 N ATL	13 N ATL
14 ATL	15 N HOU	16 N HOU	17 HOU	18 N SF	19 N SF	20 SF
21 SF	22 N LA H	23 LA H	24	25 N SF H	26 N SF H	27 SF H
28 SF	29 N LA	30 N LA				

JULY

S	M	T	W	T	F	S
			1 LA	2 N MON H	3 N MON H	4 N MON H
5 MON H	6 N STL H	7 N STL H	8 N STL H	9	10 N PHI H	11 N PHI H
12 PHI H	13	14 *	15	16 N MON	17 N MON	18 N MON
19 MON	20 N PHI	21 N PHI	22 N PHI	23	24 N NY	25 N NY
26 N NY	27 N CIN H	28 N CIN H	29 N CIN H	30 H LA	31 N LA	

AUGUST

S	M	T	W	T	F	S
						1 N LA
2 LA	3 N SF	4 N SF H	5 N SF H	6 N HOU	7 N HOU H	8 N HOU H
9 HOU H	10	11 N ATL	12 N ATL	13 ATL	14 N CIN	15 N CIN
16 CIN	17	18 N PIT	19 N PIT	20 PIT	21	22 N NY H
23 NY H	24 N CHI H	25 N CHI H	26 N CHI H	27 PIT H	28	29 N PIT H
30 PIT H	31 N STL					

SEPTEMBER

S	M	T	W	T	F	S
		1 N STL	2 N STL	3	4 CHI	5 CHI
6 CHI	7 N SF	8 N SF	9 N LA	10 N LA	11 N CIN H	12 N CIN H
13 CIN H	14 N LA H	15 N LA H	16 N LA H	17	18 N CIN	19 CIN
20 CIN	21 N SF	22 N SF H	23 N HOU H	24 HOU H	25 N ATL H	26 N ATL H
27 ATL H	28	29 N HOU	30 N HOU			

OCTOBER

S	M	T	W	T	F	S
				1 N HOU	2 N ATL	3 N ATL
4 ATL	5	6	7	8	9	10

1992 SEASON

CLUB DIRECTORY

Chairman
Tom Werner
Vice chairmen
Art Engle
Russell Goldsmith
Art Rivkin
Partners
Malin Burnham
Bruce Corwin
John Earhart
Jack Goodall
Keith Matson
Michael Monk
Leon Parma
Robert Payne
Peter Peckham
Ernest Rady
Scott Wolfe
President
Dick Freeman
Executive v.p./baseball operations and g.m.
Joe McIlvaine
Vice president, business operations
Bill Adams
Vice president/finance
Bob Wells
Vice president/public relations
Andy Strasberg
Assistant vice president/assistant g.m.
John Barr
Major league scouts
Ken Bracey
Carmen Fusco
Director/administrative services
Lucy Freeman
Director/broadcasting
Jim Winters
Director/marketing
Don Johnson
Director/media relations
Jim Ferguson
Director/minor leagues
Ed Lynch
Director/promotions
Tom Ryba
Director/publications
Jim Geschke

Director/scouting
Reggie Waller
Director/stadium operations
Doug Duennes
Director/ticket sales
Dave Gilmore
Traveling secretary
John Mattei
Club physician
Scripps Clinic
National cross-checker scout
Brad Sloan
Scouting coordinators
Ray Coley
Andy Hancock
Joe Henderson
John Kosciak
Jim Miller
Damon Oppenheimer

Area scouts
Dave Bartosch
Dave Finley
Denny Galehouse
Ronquito Garcia
Brian Granger
Larry Harper
Kasey McKeon
Bobby Malkmus
Patrick Murtaugh
Hosken Powell
Greg Smith
Van Smith
Scipio Spinks
Craig Weissmann
Part-time scouts
Pedro Avila
Billy Castell
Julio Coronado
Ben Goodman
Cesar Jarquin
Darryl Milne
Charlie Ready
Blas Reyes
Earl Smith
Harry Stricklett
Jose Valentin

SCHEDULE KEY

H—Home game.   *All-Star Game at San Diego/Jack Murphy Stadium.
N—Night game (any game starting after 5 p.m.).

SPRING TRAINING ROSTER

Manager—Greg Riddoch (3).

Coaches—Bruce Kimm (34), Rob Picciolo (5), Merv Rettenmund (16), Mike Roarke (36), Jim Snyder (17).

No.	PITCHERS	B/T	Ht./Wt.	Born	1991 clubs
27	Andersen, Larry	R/R	6-3/205	5-6-53	San Diego
40	Benes, Andy	R/R	6-6/240	8-20-67	San Diego
56	Bones, Ricky	R/R	6-0/190	4-7-69	Las Vegas, San Diego
49	Brocail, Doug	L/R	6-5/220	5-16-67	Wichita
46	Harris, Greg	R/R	6-2/195	12-1-63	San Diego, Las Vegas
50	Hernandez, Jeremy	R/R	6-6/205	7-6-66	Las Vegas, San Diego
47	Hurst, Bruce	L/L	6-3/220	3-24-58	San Diego
11	Lefferts, Craig	L/L	6-1/210	9-29-57	San Diego
39	Lewis, Jim	R/R	6-2/215	7-20-64	Wichita, Las Vegas, San Diego
37	Linskey, Mike	L/L	6-5/220	6-18-66	Hagerstown, Rochester
51	Maddux, Mike	L/R	6-2/190	8-27-61	San Diego
48	Melendez, Jose	R/R	6-2/175	9-2-65	Las Vegas, San Diego
28	Myers, Randy	L/L	6-1/225	9-19-62	Cincinnati
32	Peterson, Adam	R/R	6-3/190	12-11-65	Las Vegas, San Diego
42	Rodriguez, Rich	R/L	6-0/200	3-1-63	San Diego
44	Seminara, Frank	R/R	6-2/205	5-16-67	Wichita
35	Valdez, Rafael	R/R	5-11/185	12-17-68	Las Vegas
31	Whitson, Ed	R/R	6-3/200	5-19-55	San Diego

No.	CATCHERS	B/T	Ht./Wt.	Born	1991 clubs
7	Bilardello, Dann	R/R	6-0/190	5-26-59	Las Vegas, San Diego
25	Lampkin, Tom	L/R	5-11/185	3-4-64	San Diego, Las Vegas
9	Santiago, Benito	R/R	6-1/185	3-9-65	San Diego

No.	INFIELDERS	B/T	Ht./Wt.	Born	1991 clubs
23	Faries, Paul	R/R	5-10/170	2-20-65	San Diego, High Desert, Las Vegas
1	Fernandez, Tony	S/R	6-2/175	6-30-62	San Diego
41	Gardner, Jeff	L/R	5-11/165	2-4-64	Tidewater, New York NL
53	Holbert, Ray	R/R	6-0/170	9-25-70	High Desert
14	Lopez, Luis	S/R	5-11/175	9-4-70	Wichita
29	McGriff, Fred	L/L	6-3/210	10-31-63	San Diego
10	Redington, Tom	R/R	6-1/200	2-13-69	Wichita
18	Shipley, Craig	R/R	6-1/185	1-7-63	Las Vegas, San Diego
28	Staton, Dave	R/R	6-5/215	4-12-68	Las Vegas
20	Teufel, Tim	R/R	6-0/175	7-7-58	New York NL, San Diego
8	Valentin, Jose	S/R	5-10/175	10-12-69	Wichita
15	Velasquez, Guillermo	L/R	6-3/220	4-23-68	Wichita

No.	OUTFIELDERS	B/T	Ht./Wt.	Born	1991 clubs
22	Azocar, Oscar	L/L	6-1/195	2-21-65	Las Vegas, San Diego
24	Clark, Jerald	R/R	6-4/205	8-10-63	San Diego
19	Gwynn, Tony	L/L	5-11/215	5-9-60	San Diego
33	Howard, Thomas	S/R	6-2/205	12-11-64	San Diego, Las Vegas
4	Jackson, Darrin	R/R	6-0/185	8-22-63	San Diego
57	Taylor, Will	R/R	6-2/170	8-19-68	Las Vegas
2	Vatcher, Jim	R/R	5-9/175	5-27-66	Las Vegas, San Diego

BALLPARK INFORMATION

Ballpark (capacity, surface)
San Diego/Jack Murphy Stadium (59,700, grass)
Address
P.O. Box 2000
San Diego, CA 92112-2000
Business phone
619-283-4494
Ticket information
619-283-4494
Ticket prices
$11 (field, plaza and press levels)
$9.50 (loge, view levels)
$7 (reserved grandstand)
$5 (general admission)
Field dimensions (from home plate)
To left field at foul line, 327 feet
To center field, 405 feet
To right field at foul line, 327 feet
First game played
April 8, 1969 (Padres 2, Astros 1)

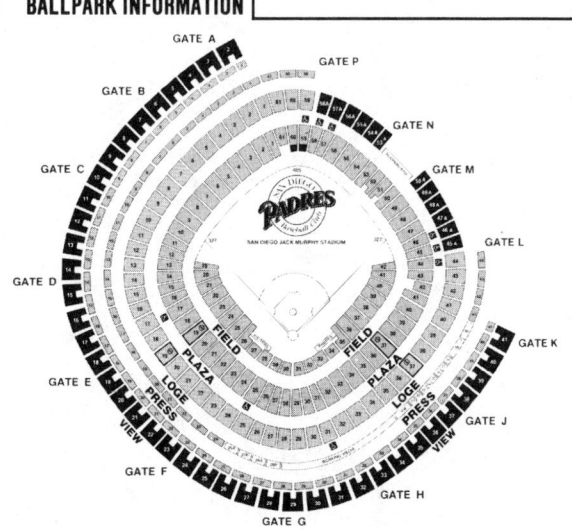

MINOR LEAGUE AFFILIATES

Class	Team	League	Manager
AAA	Las Vegas	Pacific Coast	Jim Riggleman
AA	Wichita	Texas	Bruce Bochy
A	High Desert	California	Bryan Little
A	Waterloo	Midwest	Keith Champion
A	Charleston, S.C.	South Atlantic	Dave Trembley
A	Spokane	Northwest	Ed Romero
Rookie	Scottsdale Padres	Arizona	Ken Berry

□ BROADCAST INFORMATION □

Radio: KFMB-AM (760). Broadcasters: Jerry Coleman, Rick Monday, Bob Chandler, Ted Leitner. XEXX-AM (1420, Spanish language). Broadcasters: Mario Thomas, Rogelio Escobar, Eduardo Ortega.
TV: KUSI-TV (Channel 51). Broadcasters: Jerry Coleman, Rick Monday.
Cable TV: San Diego Cable Sports Network. Broadcasters: Bob Chandler, Ted Leitner.

SPRING TRAINING

Ballpark (city): Desert Sun Stadium (Yuma, Ariz.).
Ticket information: 619-283-4494 (Padres' San Diego office).

HISTORY

YEAR-BY-YEAR RECORDS

Year	Pos.	W	L	Pct.	*GB		Year	Pos.	W	L	Pct.	*GB
1969	6th	52	110	.321	41		1982	4th	81	81	.500	8
1970	6th	63	99	.389	39		1983	4th	81	81	.500	10
1971	6th	61	100	.379	28½		1984	1st‡	92	70	.568	+12
1972	6th	58	95	.379	36½		1985	T3rd	83	79	.512	12
1973	6th	60	102	.370	39		1986	4th	74	88	.457	22
1974	6th	60	102	.370	42		1987	6th	65	97	.401	25
1975	4th	71	91	.438	37		1988	3rd	83	78	.516	11
1976	5th	73	89	.451	29		1989	2nd	89	73	.549	3
1977	5th	69	93	.426	29		1990	T4th	75	87	.463	16
1978	4th	84	78	.519	11		1991	3rd	84	78	.519	10
1979	5th	68	93	.422	22							
1980	6th	73	89	.451	19½							
1981	6th/6th	41	69	.373	†							

*Games behind winner. †First half 23-33; second 18-36. ‡Won Championship Series.

MANAGERS

Name	Record	Years
Preston Gomez	180-306	'69-72
Don Zimmer	114-186	'72-73
John McNamara	224-310	'74-77
Alvin Dark	49-65	1977
Roger Craig	152-171	'78-79
Jerry Coleman	73-89	1980
Frank Howard	41-69	1981
Dick Williams	337-311	'82-85
Steve Boros	74-88	1986
Larry Bowa	81-127	'87-88
Jack McKeon	193-164	'88-90
Greg Riddoch	122-122	'90-91

1991 REVIEW

DAY BY DAY

Date	Opp.	Res.	Score (inn.*)	Hits	Opp. hits	Winning pitcher	Losing pitcher	Save	Record	Pos.	GB
4-9	S.F.	W	7-4	13	4	Maddux	Wilson	Andersen	1-0	T1st	...
4-10	S.F.	W	4-3	5	5	Hurst	Black	Lefferts	2-0	T1st	...
4-11	S.F.	L	9-11 (10)	17	19	Righetti	Lefferts		2-1	T2nd	½
4-12	At L.A.	W	4-2	10	8	Harris	Ojeda	Gardner	3-1	1st	+½
4-13	At L.A.	W	6-3	14	9	Nolte	Gross	Maddux	4-1	1st	+1½
4-14	At L.A.	W	5-3	7	5	Whitson	Morgan	Lefferts	5-1	1st	+2
4-15	Cin.	W	3-2 (11)	9	6	Maddux	Power		6-1	1st	+2
4-16	Cin.	L	0-1	4	5	Charlton	Benes	Myers	6-2	1st	+2
4-17	Cin.	L	1-5	7	9	Hammond	Harris	Scudder	6-3	1st	+1
4-18	L.A.	W	10-5	14	13	Nolte	Gross		7-3	1st	+1½
4-19	L.A.	L	0-4	7	8	Morgan	Whitson		7-4	1st	+1
4-20	L.A.	W	5-3	7	8	Andersen	Belcher	Lefferts	8-4	1st	+1
4-21	L.A.	L	0-6	5	15	Martinez	Benes		8-5	1st	+1
4-22	At S.F.	W	7-5	12	10	Clements	Wilson	Lefferts	9-5	1st	+2
4-23	At S.F.	W	7-6	12	10	Nolte	Garrelts	Lefferts	10-5	1st	+2
4-24	At S.F.	L	1-6	6	9	Burkett	Whitson		10-6	1st	+2
4-26	At Phi.	W	4-0	7	6	Hurst	DeJesus		11-6	1st	+1½
4-27	At Phi.	L	3-4 (12)	9	12	Akerfelds	Maddux		11-7	1st	+1½
4-28	At Phi.	L	2-9	3	11	Grimsley	Nolte		11-8	1st	+½
4-29	At Phi.	L	2-7	6	12	Mulholland	Whitson		11-9	2nd	...
4-30	At N.Y.	L	3-6 (6½)	4	13	Gooden	Lilliquist	Pena	11-10	2nd	1
5-1	At N.Y.	W	8-7	9	12	Hurst	Viola	Lefferts	12-10	2nd	...
5-3	At Mon.	L	1-4	8	4	Boyd	Benes		12-11	2nd	...
5-4	At Mon.	W	6-5 (13)	8	13	Rodriguez	Fassero		13-11	2nd	...
5-5	At Mon.	W	6-3	9	7	Whitson	Barnes		14-11	2nd	...
5-7	Phi.	W	4-2	12	9	Hurst	DeJesus	Lefferts	15-11	1st	+1½
5-8	Phi.	L	2-5	5	9	Cox	Benes	McDowell	15-12	1st	+½
5-9	Phi.	L	6-9	8	15	Mulholland	Lilliquist	Williams	15-13	2nd	...
5-10	Mon.	L	4-6 (10)	9	13	Burke	Gardner		15-14	2nd	...
5-11	Mon.	L	1-5	7	6	Martinez	Peterson		15-15	3rd	1
5-12	Mon.	L	6-8	6	12	Sampen	Rodriguez	Jones	15-16	4th	2
5-13	N.Y.	W	5-2	9	7	Benes	Cone	Lefferts	16-16	T3rd	2
5-14	N.Y.	L	1-6	4	10	Whitehurst	Nolte	Schourek	16-17	4th	2
5-15	N.Y.	L	1-7	7	13	Gooden	Whitson		16-18	4th	3
5-17	At Cin.	L	3-7	7	11	Myers	Hurst	Dibble	16-19	4th	3
5-18	At Cin.	W	5-2	12	7	Peterson	Armstrong		17-19	4th	3
5-19	At Cin.	W	3-2	8	9	Benes	Charlton	Lefferts	18-19	3rd	3
5-20	At Atl.	W	7-3	11	11	Whitson	Smoltz		19-19	3rd	2
5-21	At Atl.	L	1-4	6	4	Mercker	Rosenberg		19-20	3rd	2½
5-22	At Atl.	W	7-2	13	6	Hurst	Avery		20-20	4th	2
5-23	At Atl.	W	11-10 (12)	15	12	Rosenberg	Parrett		21-20	4th	2
5-24	At Hou.	L	0-1	3	5	Schilling	Benes		21-21	4th	3
5-25	At Hou.	W	4-2 (10)	8	7	Rodriguez	Osuna	Lefferts	22-21	3rd	3
5-26	At Hou.	L	3-13	8	14	Portugal	Whitson		22-22	4th	3
5-27	Atl.	L	1-3	7	7	Avery	Hurst	Berenguer	22-23	4th	4
5-28	Atl.	L	6-8	5	8	Stanton	Lefferts	Berenguer	22-24	4th	5
5-29	Atl.	L	1-5	7	13	Glavine	Benes		22-25	4th	5
5-30	Hou.	W	4-0	9	9	Rasmussen	Jones		23-25	4th	4
5-31	Hou.	W	5-4	9	4	Melendez	Portugal	Lefferts	24-25	4th	4
6-1	Hou.	W	7-2	8	7	Hurst	Deshaies		25-25	4th	3
6-2	Hou.	W	3-1	5	2	Peterson	Hernandez	Lefferts	26-25	3rd	3
6-4	At Chi.	W	7-1	8	6	Benes	Scanlan		27-25	3rd	2
6-5	At Chi.	W	3-0	8	7	Rasmussen	Bielecki		28-25	3rd	2
6-6	At Chi.	L	2-6	5	12	Maddux	Melendez		28-26	3rd	3
6-7	At Pit.	L	0-1	13	7	Drabek	Hurst	Landrum	28-27	4th	4
6-8	At Pit.	W	11-0	18	4	Maddux	Tomlin		29-27	3rd	3
6-9	At Pit.	W	5-3	10	6	Benes	Smith	Lefferts	30-27	3rd	3
6-10	At Pit.	L	3-5	9	8	Palacios	Rasmussen	Landrum	30-28	3rd	4
6-11	St.L.	L	4-10	13	11	Hill	Melendez		30-29	4th	4½
6-12	St.L.	W	7-2	9	4	Hurst	Carpenter		31-29	3rd	3½
6-13	St.L.	L	1-12	7	12	Tewksbury	Hammaker		31-30	4th	4½
6-14	Chi.	L	3-7	7	15	Jackson	Benes	Smith	31-31	4th	5½
6-15	Chi.	W	6-2	11	8	Rasmussen	Bielecki		32-31	4th	4½
6-16	Chi.	W	4-2	5	6	Melendez	Maddux	Andersen	33-31	4th	4½
6-17	Pit.	L	2-3	10	8	Drabek	Hurst	Palacios	33-32	4th	5½
6-18	Pit.	L	1-3	6	10	Landrum	Lefferts		33-33	4th	6½
6-19	Pit.	W	6-5	10	10	Andersen	Heaton		34-33	4th	6½
6-21	At St.L.	L	3-4	11	8	Agosto	Andersen		34-34	4th	7
6-22	At St.L.	W	4-3	7	9	Melendez	Hill	Lefferts	35-34	4th	7
6-23	At St.L.	W	3-2	7	7	Hurst	Agosto		36-34	4th	7

— 155 —

Date	Opp.	Res.	Score (inn.*)	Hits	Opp. hits	Winning pitcher	Losing pitcher	Save	Record	Pos.	GB
6-24	At St.L.	W	4-1	9	5	Peterson	Tewksbury		37-34	3rd	6½
6-25	At Cin.	L	2-8	7	10	Hammond	Benes		37-35	3rd	6½
6-26	At Cin.	L	2-6	7	14	Scudder	Rasmussen	Myers	37-36	4th	6½
6-27	At Cin.	L	0-3	5	5	Armstrong	Melendez	Dibble	37-37	4th	7
6-28	S.F.	W	5-3	8	5	Hurst	Robinson	Andersen	38-37	4th	6½
6-29	S.F.	L	4-6	15	8	Wilson	Whitson	Righetti	38-38	4th	7½
6-30	S.F.	L	7-8 (10)	13	17	Brantley	Lefferts		38-39	4th	8½
7-2	L.A.	L	1-4	6	4	Martinez	Rasmussen	Crews	38-40	4th	9½
7-3	L.A.	L	3-6	10	10	Ojeda	Hurst		38-41	4th	10½
7-4	L.A.	W	5-4 (12)	14	12	Melendez	Gott		39-41	4th	9½
7-5	At S.F.	W	4-2	9	8	Whitson	Remlinger	Maddux	40-41	4th	8½
7-6	At S.F.	L	1-4	2	6	Robinson	Benes	Righetti	40-42	4th	9½
7-7	At S.F.	L	0-3	5	6	Burkett	Rasmussen		40-43	4th	10½
7-11	At N.Y.	L	3-4	9	11	Franco	Andersen		40-44	4th	10½
7-12	At N.Y.	L	3-6	3	9	Viola	Peterson	Pena	40-45	4th	10½
7-13	At N.Y.	L	1-3	6	9	Cone	Rasmussen	Franco	40-46	4th	11
7-14	At N.Y.	W	2-1	5	1	Harris	Darling	Lefferts	41-46	4th	9½
7-15	At Mon.	L	0-3	8	8	Haney	Benes	Fassero	41-47	4th	9½
7-16	At Mon.	W	4-3	5	8	Hurst	Rojas	Andersen	42-47	4th	8½
7-17	At Mon.	W	7-5	10	8	Melendez	Martinez	Andersen	43-47	4th	7½
7-19	Phi.	L	1-4	4	7	DeJesus	Rasmussen	Williams	43-48	4th	8
7-20	Phi.	L	0-4	2	10	Ruffin	Harris		43-49	4th	9
7-21	Phi.	W	5-2	9	5	Hurst	Mulholland		44-49	4th	8
7-23	Mon.	W	2-1 (11)	9	8	Andersen	Schmidt		45-49	4th	8
7-24	Mon.	L	2-8	6	13	Barnes	Rasmussen	Fassero	45-50	4th	9
7-25	Mon.	W	6-5	10	12	Maddux	Jones		46-50	4th	9
7-26	N.Y.	W	8-2	13	5	Hurst	Fernandez		47-50	4th	9
7-27	N.Y.	L	0-4	4	8	Gooden	Peterson		47-51	4th	10
7-28	N.Y.	W	2-0	5	5	Benes	Viola	Lefferts	48-51	4th	9
7-30	At Phi.	L	1-2	8	6	DeJesus	Rasmussen	Williams	48-52	5th	9½
7-31	At Phi.	L	3-9	9	11	Ruffin	Harris		48-53	5th	10½
8-2	At Atl.	W	13-3	20	10	Hurst	Leibrandt		49-53	5th	9½
8-3	At Atl.	W	3-2	7	5	Benes	Glavine	Andersen	50-53	5th	8½
8-4	At Atl.	L	7-9	15	14	Avery	Rasmussen	Berenguer	50-54	5th	8½
8-5	At Hou.	W	1-2 (12)	8	10	Henry	Andersen		50-55	5th	8½
8-6	At Hou.	L	1-6	5	10	Kile	Peterson	Osuna	50-56	5th	9½
8-7	At Hou.	W	7-4	10	8	Hurst	Wilkins	Andersen	51-56	5th	9½
8-8	At Hou.	W	5-3	9	9	Benes	Bowen	Lefferts	52-56	5th	9½
8-9	Cin.	L	1-5	4	9	Sanford	Rasmussen		52-57	5th	9½
8-10	Cin.	W	1-0	6	6	Harris	Rijo		53-57	5th	8½
8-11	Cin.	W	13-0	15	4	Bones	Gross		54-57	4th	7½
8-12	Hou.	W	6-5	13	6	Melendez	Capel	Lefferts	55-57	4th	7½
8-13	Hou.	L	9-12	6	12	Bowen	Maddux	Osuna	55-58	4th	7½
8-14	Hou.	W	4-1	9	5	Rasmussen	Deshaies	Andersen	56-58	4th	7½
8-15	Atl.	W	1-0	4	3	Harris	Smoltz		57-58	4th	6½
8-16	Atl.	L	2-3	6	7	Reynoso	Bones	Stanton	57-59	4th	7½
8-17	Atl.	L	1-2	3	6	Leibrandt	Hurst	Wohlers	57-60	4th	8½
8-18	Atl.	W	2-1	5	7	Benes	Glavine	Andersen	58-60	3rd	7½
8-19	At L.A.	L	2-3 (10)	10	7	Gross	Andersen		58-61	4th	8½
8-20	At L.A.	L	4-6	5	11	Martinez	Harris	Howell	58-62	5th	9½
8-21	At L.A.	L	5-9	11	9	Hershiser	Bones		58-63	5th	10½
8-23	At Chi.	L	4-5	7	12	Lancaster	Lefferts		58-64	5th	10½
8-24	At Chi.	W	4-1	8	3	Benes	Maddux	Melendez	59-64	5th	9½
8-25	At Chi.	W	12-9	14	15	Maddux	Scanlan	Melendez	60-64	5th	8½
8-26	At Pit.	W	7-5 (10)	11	9	Lefferts	Landrum		61-64	4th	8½
8-27	At Pit.	L	2-5	11	11	Smith	Bones	Mason	61-65	4th	8½
8-28	At St.L.	W	2-1	3	6	Hurst	Terry	Lefferts	62-65	4th	8½
8-29	At St.L.	W	1-0	4	2	Benes	Olivares		63-65	4th	8½
8-30	Pit.	L	1-4	4	9	Smiley	Rasmussen	Rodriguez	63-66	4th	9½
8-31	Pit.	L	2-3 (12)	4	10	Landrum	Melendez	Kipper	63-67	4th	9½
9-1	Pit.	W	7-4	10	7	Bones	Smith	Maddux	64-67	4th	8½
9-2	Chi.	L	8-10	9	15	McElroy	Melendez		64-68	4th	8½
9-3	Chi.	W	4-1	8	7	Benes	Maddux		65-68	4th	8½
9-4	Chi.	W	5-1	7	6	Rasmussen	Jackson		66-68	4th	8½
9-5	St.L.	W	3-1	7	3	Harris	Terry	Melendez	67-68	3rd	8
9-6	St.L.	W	6-2	11	9	Bones	Tewksbury		68-68	3rd	7½
9-7	St.L.	W	1-0 (10)	5	6	Maddux	Carpenter		69-68	3rd	7½
9-9	At Hou.	W	3-0	7	5	Benes	Portugal	Lefferts	70-68	3rd	8
9-10	At Hou.	W	7-6	8	12	Rasmussen	Gardner	Lefferts	71-68	3rd	7½
9-11	At Atl.	L	0-1	0	7	Mercker	Harris	Pena	71-69	3rd	8½
9-12	At Atl.	L	1-5	6	10	Leibrandt	Hurst		71-70	3rd	9½
9-13	At S.F.	W	13-2	15	4	Bones	Wilson		72-70	3rd	9
9-14	At S.F.	W	3-1	5	4	Benes	Heredia	Maddux	73-70	3rd	8½
9-15	At S.F.	L	2-7	8	11	Burkett	Rasmussen		73-71	3rd	9½

Date	Opp.	Res.	Score (inn.*)	Hits	Opp. hits	Winning pitcher	Losing pitcher	Save	Record	Pos.	GB
9-16	Hou.	W	6-1	10	8	Harris	Williams	Andersen	74-71	3rd	8½
9-17	Hou.	L	0-3	6	6	Harnisch	Hurst	Hernandez	74-72	3rd	9
9-18	Atl.	L	4-6	7	13	Glavine	Bones	Pena	74-73	3rd	10
9-19	Atl.	L	2-4 (10)	6	7	Wohlers	Lefferts	Pena	74-74	3rd	11
9-20	S.F.	W	10-5	11	11	Costello	Burkett	Hernandez	75-74	3rd	10½
9-21	S.F.	W	3-2	7	6	Harris	McClellan	Andersen	76-74	3rd	10
9-22	S.F.	W	6-3	7	8	Rodriguez	Oliveras	Lefferts	77-74	3rd	10
9-24	L.A.	L	2-5	6	7	Morgan	Bones	McDowell	77-75	3rd	11
9-25	L.A.	W	8-2	8	8	Benes	Ojeda		78-75	3rd	10
9-27	At Cin.	W	8-3	11	7	Harris	Scudder	Andersen	79-75	3rd	10
9-28	At Cin.	W	4-2	13	8	Melendez	Browning	Maddux	80-75	3rd	9
9-29	At Cin.	L	1-8	7	14	Power	Bones		80-76	3rd	10
9-30	At L.A.	L	2-7	4	10	Hershiser	Rasmussen		80-77	3rd	11
10-1	At L.A.	L	1-3	6	8	Ojeda	Benes		80-78	3rd	12
10-2	At L.A.	W	9-4	13	12	Harris	Gross		81-78	3rd	11
10-4	Cin.	W	3-2	6	7	Melendez	Browning	Hernandez	82-78	3rd	11
10-5	Cin.	W	10-7	17	13	Maddux	Minutelli	Lefferts	83-78	3rd	11
10-6	Cin.	W	3-1	7	10	Benes	Rijo	Andersen	84-78	3rd	10

Monthly records: April (11-10), May (13-15), June (14-14), July (10-14), August (15-14), September (17-10), Oct. (4-1).

HIGHLIGHTS

High point: On May 10, San Diego was in a first-place tie (15-14) in the National League West despite suffering three straight losses. But that was the last time the Padres would attain such lofty status. Additionally, the Padres won a season-high seven games from September 3 through 10, but by that stage of the season they were 7½ games out of first place.

Low point: From June 25 through July 15, the Padres lost 13 of 17 games and virtually fell out of contention.

Turning point: In early June, injuries to starting pitchers Greg Harris and Ed Whitson wrecked the rotation. By season's end, Andy Benes was the only member of the regular rotation who didn't miss a start because of injury.

Most valuable player: First baseman Fred McGriff. He didn't disappoint after arriving from Toronto in a blockbuster trade. He drove in a career-high 106 runs, and his 31 homers made him the first Padre since 1979 (Dave Winfield) to reach the 30-homer plateau.

Most valuable pitcher: Benes. From July 28 on, the righthander was 11-1 in 15 starts with a 1.77 earned-run average. He finished 15-11 with a 3.03 ERA.

Most improved player: Center fielder Darrin Jackson. Given 359 at-bats and 84 outfield starts, Jackson responded by belting 21 homers. Going into last season he had just 13 career homers.

Most pleasant surprise: Manager Greg Riddoch. Despite a season-long evaluation process by General Manager Joe McIlvaine and numerous rumors of his demise, Riddoch survived the 1991 season. He did so despite 11 players landing on the disabled list. He did so despite McIlvaine making just two in-season trades. Yet, San Diego's 84-78 record tied the 1978 team for the third-best mark in franchise history.

Biggest disappointment: Righthander Larry Andersen. Signed as a free agent, Andersen pitched in just 38 games due to a neck injury. Though he recorded a career-high 13 saves, he was not a dependable reliever.

Key injuries: Andersen, Whitson, Harris, Dennis Rasmussen and Bip Roberts were all disabled-list casualties. Additionally, Tony Gwynn and Bruce Hurst missed the latter portion of the year with injuries.

Notable: The Padres set team records for fewest errors (113) and best fielding percentage (.982). ... San Diego used a franchise-record 48 players.

—BARRY BLOOM

RECORDS

1991 regular-season record: 84-78 (3rd in N.L. West); 42-39 at home; 42-39 on road; 36-36 vs. East; 48-42 vs. West; 27-30 vs. LHP; 57-48 vs. RHP; 62-58 on grass; 22-20 on turf; 26-20 in daytime; 58-58 at night; 27-16 in one-run games; 8-8 in extra-inning games; 0-0 in doubleheaders.

Team record last five years: 396-413 (.489, ranks 9th in league in that span).

TEAM LEADERS

Batting average: Tony Gwynn (.317).
At-bats: Benito Santiago (580).
Runs: Fred McGriff (84).
Hits: Tony Gwynn (168).
Total bases: Fred McGriff (261).
Doubles: Tony Fernandez, Tony Gwynn (27).
Triples: Tony Gwynn (11).
Home runs: Fred McGriff (31).
Runs batted in: Fred McGriff (106).
Stolen bases: Bip Roberts (26).
Slugging percentage: Fred McGriff (.494).
On-base percentage: Fred McGriff (.396).
Wins: Andy Benes, Bruce Hurst (15).
Earned-run average: Andy Benes (3.03).
Complete games: Andy Benes, Bruce Hurst (4).
Shutouts: Greg Harris (2).
Saves: Craig Lefferts (23).
Innings pitched: Andy Benes (223).
Strikeouts: Andy Benes (167).

GAMES BY POSITION

Catcher: Benito Santiago 151, Dann Bilardello 13, Tom Lampkin 11.
First base: Fred McGriff 153, Jerald Clark 16, Tim Teufel 6, Brian Dorsett 2, Oscar Azocar 1.
Second base: Bip Roberts 68, Tim Teufel 65, Paul Faries 36, Craig Shipley 14, Jose Mota 3, Marty Barrett 2.
Third base: Scott Coolbaugh 54, Jack Howell 54, Tim Teufel 48, Jim Presley 16, Garry Templeton 15, Paul Faries 12, Marty Barrett 2.
Shortstop: Tony Fernandez 145, Craig Shipley 19, Paul Faries 8, Jose Mota 3, Garry Templeton 1.
Outfield: Tony Gwynn 134, Darrin Jackson 98, Jerald Clark 96, Thomas Howard 86, Bip Roberts 46, Shawn Abner 39, Oscar Azocar 13, Jim Vatcher 11, Mike Aldrete 5, Benito Santiago 1.

TOP 10 DRAFT CHOICES

1a. Joey Hamilton, RHP, Georgia Southern University.
1b. Greg Anthony, RHP/OF, Tavares (Fla.) High School.
2. Jon Barnes, RHP, Lancaster (S.C.) High School.
3. Antone Williamson, 3B, Torrance (Calif.) High School.
4. Sean Mulligan, C, University of Illinois.
5. Joey Long, LHP, Kent University.
6. Mike Grohs, RHP, Old Dominion University.
7. Homer Bush, SS, East St. Louis (Ill.) High School.
8. Manuel Cora, SS, Levittown, Puerto Rico.
9. Craig Hanson, RHP, Triton (Ill.) Junior College.
10. John Roberts, OF, Watson Chapel High School, Pine Bluff, Ark.

SAN FRANCISCO GIANTS
NATIONAL LEAGUE WEST DIVISION

1992 SCHEDULE

APRIL

S	M	T	W	T	F	S
5	6 LA	7 N LA	8 ATL	9 N ATL	10 N ATL	11 N ATL
12 ATL	13	14 N SD	15 SD H	16 SD H	17 N CIN	18 CIN H
19 CIN H	20 N HOU	21 N HOU	22 HOU	23	24 LA	25 LA H
26 LA H	27 N MON H	28 N MON H	29 STL	30 STL H		

MAY

S	M	T	W	T	F	S
					1 N PHI H	2 PHI H
3 PHI H	4	5 N STL	6 N STL	7 STL	8 N MON	9 MON
10 MON H	11 N PHI H	12 N PHI H	13 N PHI H	14	15 N CHI H	16 CHI H
17 CHI H	18	19 N PIT H	20 PIT H	21 PIT H	22 N NY H	23 NY H
24 NY H	25	26 N CHI	27 CHI	28 CHI	29 N PIT	30 N PIT
31 PIT						

JUNE

S	M	T	W	T	F	S
	1 N NY	2 N NY	3	4 N HOU H	5 N HOU H	6 HOU H
7 HOU H	8 N CIN H	9 N CIN H	10 CIN H	11	12 N HOU	13 N HOU
14 HOU H	15 N CIN	16 N CIN	17 CIN	18 N SD H	19 N SD H	20 SD H
21 SD H	22	23 N ATL	24 N ATL	25 N SD	26 N SD	27 N SD
28 SD	29 N ATL H	30 ATL H				

JULY

S	M	T	W	T	F	S
			1 ATL H	2 N STL H	3 N STL H	4 N STL H
5 STL H	6 N PHI H	7 N PHI H	8 N PHI H	9 MON H	10 N MON H	11 MON H
12 MON H	13	14 ★	15	16 N NY	17 N NY	18 N NY
19 NY H	20 N MON	21 N MON	22 N MON	23	24 N PHI	25 N PHI
26 PHI	27 N LA H	28 N LA H	29 LA H	30 N ATL H	31 N ATL H	

AUGUST

S	M	T	W	T	F	S
						1 ATL H
2 ATL H	3 N SD	4 N SD	5 N SD	6	7 N CIN	8 N CIN
9 CIN	10 N HOU H	11 HOU H	12 HOU H	13	14 N LA	15 N LA
16 LA	17 N LA	18 N CHI H	19 CHI H	20 CHI H	21 N PIT H	22 PIT H
23 PIT H	24 N NY H	25 N NY H	26 NY H	27	28 CHI	29 CHI
30 CHI	31					

SEPTEMBER

S	M	T	W	T	F	S
		1 N PIT	2 N PIT	3 N PIT	4 N STL	5 N STL
6 STL	7 N SD H	8 N SD H	9 N HOU H	10 HOU H	11 N LA	12 N LA
13 LA	14 N HOU	15 N HOU	16 HOU	17	18 N LA H	19 LA H
20 N LA H	21 N SD	22 SD	23 N ATL H	24 ATL H	25 N CIN H	26 CIN H
27 CIN H	28	29 N ATL	30 N ATL			

OCTOBER

S	M	T	W	T	F	S
				1 N ATL	2 N CIN	3 N CIN
4 CIN	5	6	7	8	9	10

1992 SEASON

CLUB DIRECTORY

Chairman
Bob Lurie

President and general manager
Al Rosen

Executive vice president, administration
Corey Busch

Vice president, baseball operations
Bob Kennedy

Senior vice president
Pat Gallagher

Vice president, assistant general manager
Ralph Nelson

Vice president, scouting operations
Bob Fontaine

Director of player development
Jack Hiatt

Director of minor leagues
Tony Siegle

Director of scouting
Dave Nahabedian

Director of travel
Dirk Smith

Special assistants to the president and g.m.
Willie Mays
Willie McCovey

Administrative assistant
Florence Myers

Vice president, public relations
Duffy Jennings

Director of media relations
Matt Fischer

Director of marketing
Mario Alioto

Director of sales
Pennie Lundberg

Vice president, stadium operations
Jorge Costa

Director of retail operations
Bob Tolifson

Vice president, ticket operations
Arthur Schulze

Director of ticket operations
Judy Jones

Controller
Jeannie Hurley

Promotions manager
Valerie McGuire

Director of community services
Dave Craig

Director of communications
Robin Carr Locke

Director of stadium operations
Gene Telucci

Staff counsel
Michael Shapiro Esq.

Assistant director of community services
Mike Sadek

Community representative
Vida Blue

Government affairs, broadcast coordinator
Bob Hartzell

Producer, broadcast services
Jeff Kuiper

Scouts
Harry Craft
Bob Cummings
Nino Escalera
George M. Genovese
Herman Hannah
Al Heist
Chuck Hensley Jr.
Elvio Jimenez
Mike Keenan
Richard Klaus
Tom Korenek
Alan Marr
Doug McMillan
Tony Michalak
Bob Miller
Rick Ragazzo
Gary Robinson
Mike Russell
Hank Sauer
John Shafer
Joe Strain
Todd Thomas
Gene Thompson
Mike Toomey
John Van Ornum
Elanis Westbrooks
Tom Zimmer

SCHEDULE KEY

H—Home game.　　*All-Star Game at San Diego/Jack Murphy Stadium.
N—Night game (any game starting after 5 p.m.).

SPRING TRAINING ROSTER

Manager—Roger Craig (38).

Coaches—Carlos Alfonso (16), Dusty Baker (12), Bob Brenly (14), Wendell Kim (20), Bob Lillis (5).

No.	PITCHERS	B/T	Ht./Wt.	Born	1991 clubs
30	Ard, Johnny	R/R	6-5/220	6-1-67	Phoenix, Shreveport
47	Beck, Rod	R/R	6-1/215	8-3-68	Phoenix, San Francisco
40	Black, Buddy	L/L	6-2/185	6-30-57	San Francisco
49	Brantley, Jeff	R/R	5-11/190	9-5-63	San Francisco
34	Burba, Dave	R/R	6-4/220	7-7-66	Calgary, Seattle
33	Burkett, John	R/R	6-2/210	11-28-64	San Francisco
37	Downs, Kelly	R/R	6-4/205	10-25-60	San Francisco
50	Garrelts, Scott	R/R	6-4/210	10-30-61	San Francisco
53	Gunderson, Eric	L/L	6-0/175	3-29-66	San Francisco, Phoenix
60	Hancock, Chris	L/L	6-3/175	9-12-69	San Jose
36	Heredia, Gil	R/R	6-1/190	10-26-65	Phoenix, San Francisco
41	Hickerson, Bryan	L/L	6-2/195	10-13-63	Shreveport, Phoenix, San Francisco
42	Jackson, Mike	R/R	6-0/200	12-22-64	Seattle
21	Masters, Dave	R/R	6-9/225	8-13-64	Indianapolis, Phoenix
54	Myers, Jim	R/R	6-1/185	4-28-69	Shreveport
45	Oliveras, Francisco	R/R	5-10/180	1-31-63	Phoenix, San Francisco
52	Quirico, Rafael	L/L	6-3/170	9-7-69	Greensboro
19	Righetti, Dave	L/L	6-4/212	11-28-58	San Francisco
58	Rogers, Kevin	S/L	6-1/190	8-20-68	Shreveport
26	Swift, Bill	R/R	6-0/180	10-27-61	Seattle
32	Wilson, Trevor	L/L	6-0/195	6-7-66	San Francisco

No.	CATCHERS	B/T	Ht./Wt.	Born	1991 clubs
35	Decker, Steve	R/R	6-3/205	10-25-65	San Francisco, Phoenix
8	Manwaring, Kirt	R/R	5-11/190	7-15-65	San Francisco, Phoenix, San Jose

No.	INFIELDERS	B/T	Ht./Wt.	Born	1991 clubs
18	Benjamin, Mike	R/R	6-2/175	11-22-65	San Francisco, Phoenix
22	Clark, Will	L/L	6-1/190	3-13-64	San Francisco
10	Clayton, Royce	R/R	6-0/175	1-2-70	Shreveport, San Francisco
15	Litton, Greg	R/R	6-0/190	7-13-64	San Francisco, Phoenix
57	Patterson, John	S/R	5-9/160	2-11-67	Shreveport
56	Santana, Andres	S/R	5-11/150	3-19-68	Phoenix
6	Thompson, Robby	R/R	5-11/170	5-10-62	San Francisco
23	Uribe, Jose	S/R	5-10/170	1-21-60	San Francisco, San Jose, Phoenix
9	Williams, Matt	R/R	6-2/210	11-28-65	San Francisco

No.	OUTFIELDERS	B/T	Ht./Wt.	Born	1991 clubs
17	Bass, Kevin	S/R	6-0/190	5-12-59	San Francisco, San Jose, Phoenix
25	Felder, Mike	S/R	5-8/160	11-18-62	San Francisco
7	Hosey, Steve	R/R	6-3/215	4-2-69	Shreveport
	James, Chris	R/R	6-1/190	10-4-62	Cleveland
1	Leonard, Mark	L/R	6-0/195	8-14-64	San Francisco, Phoenix
2	Lewis, Darren	R/R	6-0/175	8-28-67	Phoenix, San Francisco
51	McGee, Willie	S/R	6-1/195	11-2-58	San Francisco, Phoenix
39	Wood, Ted	L/L	6-2/178	1-4-67	Phoenix, San Francisco

BALLPARK INFORMATION

Ballpark (capacity, surface)
Candlestick Park (62,000, grass)
Address
Candlestick Park
San Francisco, CA 94124
Business phone
415-468-3700
Ticket information
415-467-8000
Ticket prices
$12.25 (lower box)
$11.25 (upper box)
$10.25 (lower reserved)
$8.25 (upper reserved)
$5.25 (pavilion)
$2.25 (general admission)
$1.25 (g.a., under 15 with adult)
Field dimensions (from home plate)
To left field at foul line, 335 feet
To center field, 400 feet
To right field at foul line, 330 feet
First game played
April 12, 1960 (Giants 3, Cardinals 1)

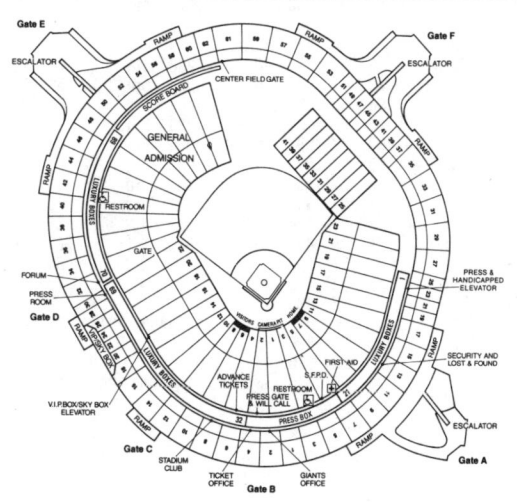

MINOR LEAGUE AFFILIATES

Class	Team	League	Manager
AAA	Phoenix	Pacific Coast	Bill Evers
AA	Shreveport	Texas	Bill Robinson
A	San Jose	California	Ron Wotus
A	Clinton	Midwest	Bill Stein
A	Everett	Northwest	Norm Sherry
Rookie	Scottsdale	Arizona	Alan Bannister

☐ BROADCAST INFORMATION ☐

Radio: KNBR-AM (680). Broadcasters: Hank Greenwald, Ron Fairly. KLOK-AM (1170, Spanish language). Broadcasters: Tito Fuentes, Eduardo Ortega.
TV: KTVU-TV (Channel 2). Broadcasters: Hank Greenwald, Duane Kuiper.
Cable TV: SportsChannel. Broadcasters: Duane Kuiper, Joe Morgan.

SPRING TRAINING

Ballpark (city): Scottsdale Stadium (Scottsdale, Ariz.).
Ticket information: 602-990-7972.

HISTORY

YEAR-BY-YEAR RECORDS

Year	Pos.	W	L	Pct.	*GB	Year	Pos.	W	L	Pct.	*GB
1901	7th	52	85	.380	37	1949	5th	73	81	.474	24
1902	8th	48	88	.353	53½	1950	3rd	86	68	.558	5
1903	2nd	84	55	.604	6½	1951	1st†	98	59	.624 +	1
1904	1st	106	47	.693	+13	1952	2nd	92	62	.597	4½
1905	1st	105	48	.686	+ 9	1953	5th	70	84	.455	35
1906	2nd	96	56	.632	20	1954	1st	97	57	.630 +	5
1907	4th	82	71	.536	25½	1955	3rd	80	74	.519	18½
1908	T2nd	98	56	.636	1	1956	6th	67	87	.435	26
1909	3rd	92	61	.601	18½	1957	6th	69	85	.448	26
1910	2nd	91	63	.591	13	1958	3rd	80	74	.519	12
1911	1st	99	54	.647	+ 7½	1959	3rd	83	71	.539	4
1912	1st	103	48	.682	+10	1960	5th	79	75	.513	16
1913	1st	101	51	.664	+12½	1961	3rd	85	69	.552	8
1914	2nd	84	70	.545	10½	1962	1st†	103	62	.624 +	1
1915	8th	69	83	.454	21	1963	3rd	88	74	.543	11
1916	4th	86	66	.566	7	1964	4th	90	72	.556	3
1917	1st	98	56	.636	+10	1965	2nd	95	67	.586	2
1918	2nd	71	53	.573	10½	1966	2nd	93	68	.578	1½
1919	2nd	87	53	.621	9	1967	2nd	91	71	.562	10½
1920	2nd	86	68	.558	7	1968	2nd	88	74	.543	9
1921	1st	94	59	.614	+ 4	1969	2nd	90	72	.556	3
1922	1st	93	61	.604	+ 7	1970	3rd	86	76	.531	16
1923	1st	95	58	.621	+ 4½	1971	1st‡	90	72	.556 +	1
1924	1st	93	60	.608	+ 1½	1972	5th	69	86	.445	26½
1925	2nd	86	66	.566	8½	1973	3rd	88	74	.543	11
1926	5th	74	77	.490	13½	1974	5th	72	90	.444	30
1927	3rd	92	62	.597	2	1975	3rd	80	81	.497	27½
1928	2nd	93	61	.604	2	1976	4th	74	88	.457	28
1929	3rd	84	67	.556	13½	1977	4th	75	87	.463	23
1930	3rd	87	67	.565	5	1978	3rd	89	73	.549	6
1931	2nd	87	65	.572	13	1979	4th	71	91	.438	19½
1932	T6th	72	82	.468	18	1980	5th	75	86	.466	17
1933	1st	91	61	.599	+ 5	1981	5th/3rd	56	55	.505	§
1934	2nd	93	60	.608	2	1982	3rd	87	75	.537	2
1935	3rd	91	62	.595	8½	1983	5th	79	83	.488	12
1936	1st	92	62	.597	+ 5	1984	6th	66	96	.407	26
1937	1st	95	57	.625	+ 3	1985	6th	62	100	.383	33
1938	3rd	83	67	.553	5	1986	3rd	83	79	.512	13
1939	5th	77	74	.510	18½	1987	1st‡	90	72	.556 +	6
1940	6th	72	80	.474	27½	1988	4th	83	79	.512	11½
1941	5th	74	79	.484	25½	1989	1st*	92	70	.568 +	3
1942	3rd	85	67	.559	20	1990	3rd	85	77	.525	6
1943	8th	55	98	.359	49½	1991	4th	75	87	.463	19
1944	5th	67	87	.435	38						
1945	5th	78	74	.513	19						
1946	8th	61	93	.396	36						
1947	4th	81	73	.526	13						
1948	5th	78	76	.506	13½						

*Games behind winner. †Won pennant playoff. ‡Lost Championship Series. §First half 27-32; second 29-23. *Won Championship Series.

MANAGERS

Name	Record	Years
George Davis	52-85	1901
Horace Fogel	18-23	1902
Heinie Smith	5-27	1902
John McGraw	2604-1801	'02-32
Bill Terry	823-661	'32-41
Mel Ott	464-530	'42-48
Leo Durocher	637-523	'48-55
Bill Rigney	406-430	'56-60
		1976
Tom Sheehan	46-50	1960
Alvin Dark	366-277	'61-64
Herman Franks	367-280	'65-68
Clyde King	109-95	'69-70
Charlie Fox	348-327	'70-74
Wes Westrum	118-129	'74-75
Joe Altobelli	225-239	'77-79
Dave Bristol	85-98	'79-80
Frank Robinson	264-277	'81-84
Danny Ozark	24-32	1984
Jim Davenport	56-88	1985
Roger Craig	514-476	'85-91

DAY BY DAY

Date	Opp.	Res.	Score (inn.*)	Hits	Opp. hits	Winning pitcher	Losing pitcher	Save	Record	Pos.	GB
4-9	At S.D.	L	4-7	4	13	Maddux	Wilson	Andersen	0-1	T5th	1
4-10	At S.D.	L	3-4	5	5	Hurst	Black	Lefferts	0-2	T5th	2
4-11	At S.D.	W	11-9 (10)	19	17	Righetti	Lefferts		1-2	T4th	1½
4-12	At Hou.	L	2-3	7	9	Portugal	Reuschel	Henry	1-3	5th	2
4-13	At Hou.	W	16-2	19	6	Garrelts	Scott	Gunderson	2-3	T4th	2
4-14	At Hou.	L	2-7	6	10	Jones	Burkett		2-4	6th	3
4-15	L.A.	L	1-2	6	5	Belcher	Black	Howell	2-5	6th	4
4-16	L.A.	W	8-6	10	8	LaCoss	Martinez	Righetti	3-5	6th	3
4-17	L.A.	L	2-6	5	11	Ojeda	Reuschel		3-6	6th	3
4-19	Hou.	W	5-2	9	8	Burkett	Jones	Brantley	4-6	5th	2½
4-20	Hou.	W	4-0	9	5	Black	Deshaies		5-6	T3rd	2½
4-21	Hou.	W	1-0	5	4	Righetti	Schilling		6-6	T3rd	1½
4-22	S.D.	L	5-7	10	12	Clements	Wilson	Lefferts	6-7	T3rd	2½
4-23	S.D.	L	6-7	10	12	Nolte	Garrelts	Lefferts	6-8	T4th	3½
4-24	S.D.	W	6-1	9	6	Burkett	Whitson		7-8	T3rd	2½
4-25	At L.A.	L	1-7	5	8	Belcher	Black		7-9	6th	3
4-26	At L.A.	L	0-9	5	11	Martinez	LaCoss		7-10	6th	4
4-27	At L.A.	W	4-3	11	8	Downs	Ojeda	Brantley	8-10	5th	3
4-28	At L.A.	L	3-7	10	9	Gross	Burkett		8-11	6th	3
4-30	At Phi.	L	9-11	11	14	Boever	Brantley	Williams	8-12	6th	3½
5-1	At Phi.	L	1-4	4	7	Greene	LaCoss	McDowell	8-13	6th	3½
5-3	At N.Y.	L	0-3	5	6	Cone	Downs	Franco	8-14	6th	3½
5-4	At N.Y.	L	4-6 (12)	12	12	Schourek	LaCoss		8-15	6th	3½
5-5	At N.Y.	W	2-0	6	5	Black	Gooden		9-15	6th	4½
5-6	At Mon.	L	4-10	12	14	Martinez	Robinson		9-16	6th	5
5-7	At Mon.	L	2-3 (15)	5	10	Ruskin	Wilson		9-17	6th	6
5-8	At Mon.	L	4-5	8	10	Jones	Oliveras	Burke	9-18	6th	6
5-10	N.Y.	W	7-0	12	4	Black	Gooden		10-18	6th	4½
5-11	N.Y.	L	2-6	7	12	Darling	Robinson	Pena	10-19	6th	5½
5-12	N.Y.	L	2-4 (11)	10	12	Franco	Righetti		10-20	6th	6½
5-13	Phi.	L	2-3 (11)	6	6	Boever	Beck		10-21	6th	7½
5-14	Phi.	L	0-9	8	14	Mulholland	Downs		10-22	6th	7½
5-15	Phi.	W	4-2	9	5	Black	Grimsley	Brantley	11-22	6th	7½
5-16	Mon.	W	5-4	10	11	Robinson	Martinez	Oliveras	12-22	6th	7
5-17	Mon.	L	0-3	3	7	Jones	LaCoss	Ruskin	12-23	6th	7
5-18	Mon.	L	1-3	3	8	Boyd	Burkett	Burke	12-24	6th	8
5-19	Mon.	L	4-5 (13)	9	8	Sampen	LaCoss	Ruskin	12-25	6th	9
5-21	At Cin.	L	2-3	9	6	Browning	Black	Dibble	12-26	6th	9½
5-22	At Cin.	L	4-9	9	15	Rijo	Robinson		12-27	6th	9½
5-23	At Cin.	L	2-6	4	9	Armstrong	Wilson		12-28	6th	10½
5-24	At Atl.	L	2-3	6	12	Glavine	Righetti		12-29	6th	11½
5-25	At Atl.	W	7-6	13	11	Downs	Smoltz	Brantley	13-29	6th	11½
5-26	At Atl.	W	10-6	15	12	Black	Leibrandt	Bass	14-29	6th	10½
5-27	Cin.	L	2-3	11	7	Rijo	Robinson	Dibble	14-30	6th	11½
5-28	Cin.	W	6-2	12	5	Wilson	Armstrong		15-30	6th	11½
5-29	Cin.	W	6-1	8	6	Oliveras	Hammond		16-30	6th	10½
5-30	Atl.	L	2-7	5	11	Smoltz	Downs		16-31	6th	10½
5-31	Atl.	L	2-5	9	9	Leibrandt	Black	Stanton	16-32	6th	11½
6-1	Atl.	W	8-2	8	4	Robinson	Avery	Oliveras	17-32	6th	10½
6-2	Atl.	W	2-1	3	6	Wilson	Mercker	Righetti	18-32	6th	10½
6-4	At Pit.	W	5-3	12	6	Burkett	Smith	Righetti	19-32	5th	9½
6-5	At Pit.	L	3-7	5	12	Walk	Downs		19-33	5th	10½
6-6	At Pit.	W	6-3	11	5	Black	Smiley	Righetti	20-33	5th	10½
6-7	At St.L.	W	5-2	7	7	Robinson	Olivares	Righetti	21-33	5th	10½
6-8	At St.L.	L	2-3 (10)	5	11	Carpenter	Oliveras		21-34	5th	10½
6-9	At St.L.	W	3-2	7	4	Burkett	DeLeon	Brantley	22-34	5th	10½
6-10	At St.L.	L	2-3	6	8	Terry	Segura	L. Smith	22-35	5th	11½
6-11	At Chi.	W	8-6 (10)	13	11	Downs	Smith	Righetti	23-35	5th	11
6-12	At Chi.	L	1-6	7	8	Boskie	Robinson	Smith	23-36	6th	11
6-13	At Chi.	L	3-4	11	7	Bielecki	Wilson	Assenmacher	23-37	6th	12
6-14	Pit.	W	3-2	8	4	Oliveras	Smith	Righetti	24-37	6th	12
6-15	Pit.	W	4-0	8	3	Remlinger	Smiley		25-37	5th	11
6-16	Pit.	L	3-4	8	6	Walk	Black	Landrum	25-38	6th	12
6-17	St.L.	L	4-5	8	12	Agosto	Righetti	L. Smith	25-39	6th	13
6-18	St.L.	L	1-3	4	4	Tewksbury	Wilson	L. Smith	25-40	6th	14
6-19	St.L.	L	2-3	7	7	DeLeon	Burkett	L. Smith	25-41	6th	15
6-20	Chi.	W	4-3	9	10	Oliveras	Lancaster	Righetti	26-41	5th	15
6-21	Chi.	W	4-2	6	12	Downs	Maddux	Righetti	27-41	5th	14
6-22	Chi.	W	6-3	8	11	Wilson	Boskie	Oliveras	28-41	5th	14
6-23	Chi.	W	2-1	5	7	Brantley	Smith		29-41	5th	14

SAN FRANCISCO GIANTS

1992 SEASON

SAN FRANCISCO GIANTS

Date	Opp.	Res.	Score (inn.*)	Hits	Opp. hits	Winning pitcher	Losing pitcher	Save	Record	Pos.	GB
6-25	At L.A.	W	9-4	16	7	Remlinger	Hershiser		30-41	5th	13
6-26	At L.A.	W	3-2 (11)	4	11	Brantley	Crews		31-41	5th	12
6-28	At S.D.	L	3-5	5	8	Hurst	Robinson	Andersen	31-42	5th	12½
6-29	At S.D.	W	6-4	8	15	Wilson	Whitson	Righetti	32-42	5th	12½
6-30	At S.D.	W	8-7 (10)	17	13	Brantley	Lefferts		33-42	5th	12½
7-2	Hou.	L	4-8	8	14	Portugal	Black		33-43	5th	13½
7-3	Hou.	L	0-9	6	12	Deshaies	Burkett		33-44	5th	14½
7-4	Hou.	L	6-14	14	13	Kile	Wilson		33-45	5th	14½
7-5	S.D.	L	2-4	8	9	Whitson	Remlinger	Maddux	33-46	5th	14½
7-6	S.D.	W	4-1	6	2	Robinson	Benes	Righetti	34-46	5th	14½
7-7	S.D.	W	3-0	6	5	Burkett	Rasmussen		35-46	5th	14½
7-11	At Phi.	L	2-3	5	6	Mulholland	Wilson	Williams	35-47	T5th	14½
7-12	At Phi.	L	0-1	3	3	Greene	Black	Williams	35-48	T5th	14½
7-13	At Phi.	W	7-5	13	11	Oliveras	Ritchie	Righetti	36-48	5th	14
7-14	At Phi.	W	17-5	22	6	Downs	Cox		37-48	5th	12½
7-15	At N.Y.	W	4-3	6	6	Robinson	Whitehurst	Brantley	38-48	5th	11½
7-16	At N.Y.	L	4-6	11	11	Gooden	Wilson	Franco	38-49	5th	11½
7-17	At N.Y.	L	5-6	11	12	Pena	Righetti		38-50	5th	11½
7-19	At Mon.	L	0-6	5	10	Boyd	Robinson		38-51	5th	12
7-20	At Mon.	W	5-3	9	12	Burkett	Darling	Brantley	39-51	5th	12
7-21	At Mon.	W	3-2	6	5	Wilson	Gardner	Brantley	40-51	5th	11
7-23	N.Y.	W	4-2	5	6	Black	Viola	Righetti	41-51	5th	11
7-24	N.Y.	W	8-4	8	8	Burkett	Cone		42-51	5th	11
7-25	N.Y.	W	8-1	14	6	Wilson	Whitehurst		43-51	5th	11
7-26	Phi.	W	3-2	12	4	Downs	Mulholland	Righetti	44-51	5th	11
7-27	Phi.	W	3-0	6	3	McClellan	Cox	Righetti	45-51	5th	11
7-28	Phi.	W	2-1	7	6	Black	Greene	Brantley	46-51	5th	10
7-29	Mon.	W	6-5	10	8	Downs	Rojas	Righetti	47-51	5th	9
7-30	Mon.	W	10-3	14	5	Wilson	Darling		48-51	4th	9
8-1	At Cin.	W	8-1	17	7	McClellan	Gross		49-51	4th	9
8-2	At Cin.	L	4-5	8	9	Myers	Black	Charlton	49-52	4th	9
8-3	At Cin.	W	7-3	6	9	Burkett	Armstrong		50-52	4th	8
8-4	At Cin.	L	5-6	8	8	Power	Brantley		50-53	4th	8
8-5	At Atl.	L	2-5	6	8	Smoltz	Robinson		50-54	4th	8
8-6	At Atl.	L	6-10	10	11	Clancy	McClellan		50-55	4th	9
8-7	At Atl.	W	1-0	4	11	Black	Leibrandt	Righetti	51-55	4th	9
8-8	At Atl.	W	8-1	13	8	Burkett	Glavine		52-55	4th	9
8-9	L.A.	W	1-0 (13)	6	9	Brantley	Gross		53-55	4th	8
8-10	L.A.	W	4-3	12	8	Downs	Martinez	Righetti	54-55	3rd	7
8-11	L.A.	W	4-3	7	11	Downs	Gross	Downs	55-55	3rd	6
8-12	Atl.	L	1-2	6	4	Leibrandt	Black	Berenguer	55-56	3rd	7
8-13	Atl.	L	2-9	4	15	Glavine	Burkett		55-57	3rd	7
8-14	Atl.	W	8-3	13	8	Wilson	Avery		56-57	3rd	7
8-15	Cin.	W	4-1	6	2	McClellan	Rijo	Righetti	57-57	3rd	6
8-16	Cin.	L	0-5	5	8	Gross	Black		57-58	3rd	7
8-17	Cin.	L	0-7	6	11	Scudder	Burkett		57-59	3rd	8
8-18	Cin.	L	3-4 (11)	13	7	Dibble	Righetti		57-60	5th	8
8-20	At Hou.	W	9-3	8	7	Downs	Jones	Brantley	58-60	T3rd	8½
8-21	At Hou.	L	4-13	8	17	Harnisch	Black		58-61	T3rd	9½
8-22	At Hou.	W	11-8	15	11	Brantley	Kile	Righetti	59-61	3rd	9
8-23	At Pit.	L	0-8	7	14	Drabek	Burkett		59-62	T3rd	9
8-24	At Pit.	W	5-1	9	6	Wilson	Heaton		60-62	T3rd	9
8-25	At Pit.	L	3-8	12	10	Smiley	Oliveras	Belinda	60-63	T3rd	8
8-26	At St.L.	L	6-7	13	9	Carpenter	Black	L. Smith	60-64	5th	9
8-27	At St.L.	L	4-5	10	8	Terry	Robinson	L. Smith	60-65	5th	9
8-28	Chi.	L	6-8	11	10	Bielecki	McClellan	Assenmacher	60-66	5th	10
8-29	Chi.	L	4-5	8	11	Maddux	Oliveras		60-67	5th	11
8-30	St.L.	W	8-3	8	9	Black	Cormier	Brantley	61-67	5th	11
8-31	St.L.	W	6-1	11	5	Hickerson	B. Smith		62-67	5th	10
9-1	St.L.	L	1-14	7	18	Tewksbury	Burkett		62-68	5th	10
9-2	Pit.	L	8-9	13	18	Belinda	Righetti	Rodriguez	62-69	5th	10
9-3	Pit.	L	3-5 (10)	8	8	Patterson	Oliveras		62-70	5th	11
9-4	Pit.	L	3-8	10	13	Smiley	Black	Mason	62-71	5th	12
9-6	At Chi.	L	2-3	5	9	Castillo	Hickerson	Smith	62-72	5th	12½
9-7	At Chi.	L	1-2	4	5	Bielecki	McClellan	Assenmacher	62-73	5th	13½
9-8	At Chi.	W	4-3	6	9	Wilson	Maddux	Righetti	63-73	5th	13½
9-9	At Atl.	L	3-8	9	7	Smoltz	Black	Clancy	63-74	5th	14½
9-10	At Atl.	L	1-4	3	9	Avery	Burkett	Pena	63-75	5th	15
9-11	At Cin.	W	4-2	8	8	Hickerson	Scudder	Righetti	64-75	5th	15
9-12	At Cin.	L	3-7	5	9	Browning	McClellan	Dibble	64-76	5th	16
9-13	S.D.	L	2-13	4	15	Bones	Wilson		64-77	5th	16½
9-14	S.D.	L	1-3	4	5	Benes	Heredia	Maddux	64-78	5th	17
9-15	S.D.	W	7-2	11	8	Burkett	Rasmussen		65-78	5th	17
9-16	Atl.	W	8-5	9	9	Oliveras	Clancy	Beck	66-78	5th	16

Date	Opp.	Res.	Score (inn.*)	Hits	Opp. hits	Winning pitcher	Losing pitcher	Save	Record	Pos.	GB
9-17	Atl.	W	3-2	5	4	Black	Stanton	Righetti	67-78	5th	15½
9-18	Cin.	W	7-2	9	5	Wilson	Armstrong		68-78	5th	15½
9-19	Cin.	W	4-1	6	6	Oliveras	Myers	Righetti	69-78	5th	15½
9-20	At S.D.	L	5-10	11	11	Costello	Burkett	Hernandez	69-79	5th	16
9-21	At S.D.	L	2-3	6	7	Harris	McClellan	Andersen	69-80	5th	16½
9-22	At S.D.	L	3-6	8	7	Rodriguez	Oliveras	Lefferts	69-81	5th	17½
9-23	At Hou.	L	0-8	5	16	Harnisch	Wilson	Schilling	69-82	5th	18
9-24	At Hou.	W	9-7	8	14	Beck	Portugal		70-82	5th	18
9-25	At Hou.	W	2-1	4	6	Burkett	Kile	Brantley	71-82	5th	17
9-27	At L.A.	L	2-6	10	8	Belcher	Black		71-83	5th	18
9-28	At L.A.	W	4-1	7	4	Wilson	Martinez	Robinson	72-83	5th	17
9-29	At L.A.	L	2-3	8	13	Gott	Righetti		72-84	5th	18
9-30	Hou.	L	0-2	6	3	Gardner	Heredia	Hernandez	72-85	5th	19
10-1	Hou.	W	6-4	7	11	Burkett	Kile	Brantley	73-85	5th	19
10-2	Hou.	L	5-7	9	11	Bowen	McClellan	Osuna	73-86	5th	19
10-4	L.A.	W	4-1	9	8	Black	Martinez	Brantley	74-86	T4th	19
10-5	L.A.	W	4-0	4	2	Wilson	Morgan		75-86	4th	19
10-6	L.A.	L	0-2	7	8	Cook	Hickerson	Howell	75-87	4th	19

Monthly records: April (8-12), May (8-20), June (17-10), July (15-9), August (14-16), September (10-18), Oct. (3-2).

HIGHLIGHTS

High point: On August 11, San Francisco completed a three-game sweep of first-place Los Angeles, giving the Giants 17 wins in their last 21 games and pulling them within six games of the National League West lead.

Low point: Following a three-game sweep in Cincinnati on May 23, San Francisco had a 12-28 record, the worst 40-game start in the club's 109-year history. The Giants were 10½ games out of first at that point.

Turning point: Center fielder Darren Lewis was called up from Class AAA on July 12, and the Giants went 14-4 in his first 18 games. He hit .301 in 36 games through August 22 as San Francisco improved from 35-48 to 59-61 in that stretch. But Lewis went 18-for-99 in his final 36 games, and the Giants also slumped out of contention.

Most valuable player: First baseman Will Clark. He was making a run for the Triple Crown until he fouled a ball off his right kneecap September 4. He was forced to "settle" for a .301 average, 29 homers and a career-high 116 runs batted in. He also won a Gold Glove.

Most valuable pitcher: Lefthander Trevor Wilson. He emerged as the Giants' most reliable pitcher, posting a 13-11 record with a 3.56 earned-run average.

Most improved player: Second baseman Robby Thompson. After hitting .245 with 15 homers in 1990, Thompson improved to .262 and 19, breaking the San Francisco season record for most homers by a second baseman.

Most pleasant surprise: Lefthander Bryan Hickerson. He threw seven shutout innings to win his first big-league start August 31. He also threw six shutout innings in an important start September 29 at Dodger Stadium.

Biggest disappointment: Lefthander Bud Black. Signed as a free agent, Black led the league with a career-high 16 losses. Some teammates said Black was bothered the second half of the season by a sore left arm, but he would not acknowledge it.

Key injuries: Outfielder Kevin Mitchell, who missed 49 games, was nagged by injuries for the second straight year. Righthander Scott Garrelts underwent reconstructive surgery on his right elbow July 18.

Notable: Catcher Steve Decker and shortstop Mike Benjamin became the first two rookies to crack San Francisco's opening-day lineup since Clark and Thompson in 1986. . . . The Giants' 11-game winning streak at the end of July was their longest since 1966.

—MARK NEWMAN

RECORDS

1991 regular-season record: 75-87 (4th in N.L. West); 43-38 at home; 32-49 on road; 32-40 vs. East; 43-47 vs. West; 23-25 vs. LHP; 52-62 vs. RHP; 58-62 on grass; 17-25 on turf; 34-27 in day-time; 41-60 at night; 23-32 in one-run games; 5-8 in extra-inning games; 0-0 in doubleheaders.

Team record last five years: 425-385 (.525, ranks 3rd in league in that span).

TEAM LEADERS

Batting average: Willie McGee (.312).
At-bats: Matt Williams (589).
Runs: Will Clark (84).
Hits: Will Clark (170).
Total bases: Will Clark (303).
Doubles: Will Clark (32).
Triples: Will Clark (7).
Home runs: Matt Williams (34).
Runs batted in: Will Clark (116).
Stolen bases: Mike Felder (21).
Slugging percentage: Will Clark (.536).
On-base percentage: Will Clark (.359).
Wins: Trevor Wilson (13).
Earned-run average: Trevor Wilson (3.56).
Complete games: Bud Black, John Burkett (3).
Shutouts: Bud Black (3).
Saves: Dave Righetti (24).
Innings pitched: Bud Black (214⅓).
Strikeouts: Trevor Wilson (139).

GAMES BY POSITION

Catcher: Steve Decker 78, Kirt Manwaring 67, Terry Kennedy 58, Greg Litton 1.
First base: Will Clark 144, Dave Anderson 16, Greg Litton 15, Mike Kingery 6, Terry Kennedy 2, Darnell Coles 1, Kevin Mitchell 1.
Second base: Robby Thompson 144, Tom Herr 15, Greg Litton 15, Dave Anderson 6, Tony Perezchica 6, Mike Felder 1.
Third base: Matt Williams 155, Dave Anderson 11, Greg Litton 11, Mike Felder 3, Tom Herr 3, Mike Benjamin 1.
Shortstop: Jose Uribe 87, Dave Anderson 63, Mike Benjamin 51, Tony Perezchica 13, Greg Litton 9, Royce Clayton 8, Matt Williams 4.
Outfield: Willie McGee 128, Mike Felder 107, Kevin Bass 101, Kevin Mitchell 100, Darren Lewis 68, Mike Kingery 38, Mark Leonard 34, Ted Wood 8, Greg Litton 6, Rick Parker 4, Darnell Coles 3, Tom Herr 1.

TOP 10 DRAFT CHOICES

1. **Steve Whitaker**, LHP, Long Beach State University.
2. None.
3. None.
4. **Chris Gambs**, RHP, Monte Vista High School, Danville, Calif.
5. **Billy Vanlandingham** RHP, University of Kentucky.
6. **Duane Thielen**, 3B, Mt. Hood (Ore.) Community College.
7. **Julian Frazier**, OF, Smackover (Ark.) High School.
8. **Dax Jones**, OF, Creighton University.
9. **Doug Vanderweele**, RHP, University of Nevada-Las Vegas.
10. **Jeff Martin**, RHP, Hazen High School, Renton, Wash.

CLUB DIRECTORY

Address
1700 Broadway, Suite 2100
Denver, CO 80290
Telephone
303-292-0200
303-830-8977 (FAX)
Chairman and chief executive officer
John Antonucci
President and chief operating officer
Steve Ehrhart
Exec. vice president, baseball operations
John McHale
Executive vice president/general counsel
Paul Jacobs
Senior vice president/general manager
Bob Gebhard
Special assistant to general manager
Larry Bearnarth
Senior vice president, business operations
Bernie Mullin
Senior vice president, public affairs
Dean Peeler
Vice president, finance
Michael Kent
Assistant general manager
Randy Smith
Director of scouting
Pat Daugherty
Assistant director of scouting
Paul Egins
Director of community relations
Roger Kinney

Director of ticket operations
Chuck Javernick
Director of corporate marketing
Dave Glazier
Director of merchandising
Mark Ehrhart
Special events coordinator
Alan Bossart
Executive administrator
Wendy Jobe
Assistant to chairman
Carolyn Shaffer
Assistant to president
Jennifer Moore
Asst. to senior v.p., business operations
Liz Stecklein
Administrators, baseball operations
Mary Cheney
Jeff Tamarkin
Administrative asst., baseball operations
Chris Rice
Administrative assistant, public affairs
Barb Maniscalco
Administrative assistant
Lisa Quarton
Secretary, scouting department
Penny Biever
Sales assistant
Jan Giovino
Scouting supervisors
Ty Coslow
Darwin Cox

Jimmy Lester
Lance Nichols
Ed Santa
Area scouting supervisor
Tom Wheeler
National cross-checker scout
Herb Hippauf
Regular scouts
Julian Gonzalez
Al Hargesheimer
Randy Johnson
Pat Jones
Danny Montgomery
Jorge Posada
Johnny Zizzo

CLUB DIRECTORY

Address
100 N.E. Third Ave., Third Floor
Fort Lauderdale, FL 33301
Telephone
305-779-7070
305-779-7130 (FAX)
President
Carl Barger
Exec. vice president and general manager
David Dombrowski
Vice president of business operations
Richard Andersen
Vice president of communications
Dean Jordan
Vice president/expansion coordinator
Don Smiley
Assistant general manager
Frank Wren
Senior adviser, player personnel
Whitey Lockman
Special assistant to the general manager
Cookie Rojas
Director of player development
John Boles
Director of minor league administration
Dan Lunetta
Director of season/group sales
Bill Galante
Ticket sales
William Beck
Staff assistants
Royal (Tripp) McKenney
Patrick McNamara

Archivist
Margo Malone
Dir., Latin Am. oper./consultant to the g.m.
Angel Vazquez
Dir. of scouting and special asst. to the g.m.
Gary Hughes
Scout/coordinator of team development
Jim Hendry
Major league scouts
Ken Kravec
Scott Reid
John Young
Scouts
J. Edward Bockman
Edmundo Borrome
Kelvin Bowles
Ty Brown
Julian Camilo
Joe Campise
John Castleberry
Murray Cook
Brad Del Barba
Scott Diez
Dick Egan
Orrin Freeman
Matthew King
Robert Laurie
Grady Mack
Steve Minor
Jim Moran
Levy Ochoa
Francis Oneto
James Pentland

Cucho Rodriguez
Jax Robertson
Bill Scherrer
Tim Schmidt
Bill Singer
George Tebbetts
Wally Walker
DeJon Watson
Jeff Wren
Greg Zunino

1991
REVIEW

YEAR IN REVIEW

By STEVE GIETSCHIER

The Minnesota Twins and Atlanta Braves brought the 1991 season to a memorable close in a tense, exhilarating, riveting seven-game World Series. The Twins won the championship October 27 with a 1-0 victory in Game 7 at the Metrodome, with the only run of the game coming home on a bases-loaded single by pinch-hitter Gene Larkin in the 10th inning. The game marked the third of the Series to go into extra innings, the fifth decided by one run and the fourth resolved on the game's final swing.

The season began with teams affixing U.S. and Canadian flag decals to batting helmets (intended to symbolize support for the military forces who fought in the recently concluded Persian Gulf War) and ended in a swirl of controversy surrounding the "tomahawk chop."

The "chop," a gesture expropriated by Braves fans from supporters of the Florida State Seminoles football team, was criticized by some Native American groups and others as demeaning. These protesters also condemned use of the word "Braves" and other team nicknames (Redskins, Indians, etc.) they deemed ethnically offensive. Commissioner Fay Vincent acknowledged the complaints and Braves President Stan Kasten said the team would address the issue after the World Series. Late in the year, Braves Owner Ted Turner said his team would retain its nickname but that he would ask fans to refrain from using the "chop" and its accompanying war chant.

The '91 season also marked a few special baseball anniversaries. Fifty years earlier, in 1941, Ted Williams batted .406 for the Boston Red Sox, the last player to hit .400 in a season. That same year, the Yankees' Joe DiMaggio hit safely in a record 56 consecutive games. And 40 years earlier, in 1951, Bobby Thomson won the National League pennant for the New York Giants in dramatic style by hitting a ninth-inning, game-winning homer against the Brooklyn Dodgers in the third game of a best-of-three playoff. In 1961, 30 years earlier, Roger Maris of the Yankees hit 61 home runs to surpass Babe Ruth's record total of 60 set in 1927.

Four division races

The Twins won a league-high 95 games to become the first American League team to rise from last place to first in consecutive years. Minnesota's patchwork roster included free agents (Jack Morris, Chili Davis, Mike Pagliarulo), discards from other clubs (Brian Harper, Shane Mack) and unproven youngsters (Scott Erickson, Chuck Knoblauch). This combination, abetted by such veteran Twins as Kirby Puckett and Kent Hrbek, brought the Twin Cities area its second world championship in five years.

The A.L. West remained a tough division despite the demise of three-time defending league champion Oakland, which finished 11 games behind the Twins. No division team finished below .500, and the last-place California Angels boasted four legitimate candidates for the league's Cy Young Award. The Twins, who vaulted into first place for the first time June 16 after winning their 15th consecutive game, withstood every challenge the remainder of the season. The Chicago White Sox came within a game of first place August 10 before folding dramatically and finishing in second place, eight games off the pace.

In the A.L. East, the Toronto Blue Jays won their third division title in seven seasons and second in three years. The Jays won 15 of 18 games prior to the All-Star break and had an eight-game lead July 15, enabling them to hold off an August challenge by Detroit and a September rally by Boston. The Tigers and defending division champion Red Sox ended up tied for second place, seven games behind Toronto.

Injuries sidelined many longtime Blue Jays regulars (pitchers Dave Stieb and Tom Henke and third baseman Kelly Gruber), but the team prevailed in large measure due to the contributions of three 1991 newcomers: outfielder Joe Carter and second baseman Roberto Alomar (acquired from San Diego the previous off-season) and outfielder Devon White (formerly of the California Angels).

Atlanta won its third N.L. West crown in 23 years (and its first since 1982) after rebounding from a 9½-game deficit at the All-Star break to hold off the Los Angeles Dodgers in a gripping, down-to-the-wire race. The Braves were consistent throughout the season—they never lost more than five games in a row—and were almost invincible at home in the second half (30-11). They won eight straight games from September 27 through October 5 to eliminate the Dodgers on the next-to-last day of the season.

The Braves used a combination of stifling pitching, timely hitting and solid defense en route to the title. Injuries to right fielder David Justice, first baseman Sid Bream and closer Juan Berenguer slowed the team somewhat, but newcomer Terry Pendleton hit .319 to win the batting title and Most Valuable Player Award while playing steady defense at third base. Center fielder Ron Gant became only the third player ever to hit at least 30 home runs and steal at least 30 bases in consecutive seasons. And four starting pitchers, including Cy Young Award winner Tom Glavine, combined for 67 of Atlanta's team-record 94 victories.

The Pittsburgh Pirates won the N.L. East crown to become the first N.L. team to repeat as division champion since Philadelphia and Los Angeles both did so in 1977-78. The Pirates moved into first place for good April 20 and clinched the title September 22 with a 2-1 win over the Phillies.

The Pirates overcame slow starts by outfielder Barry Bonds and pitcher Doug Drabek (the previous year's league MVP and Cy Young winner, respectively) and the lack of a dominant closer to pull away from the rest of the division. Only one regular—third baseman Jeff King—was sidelined by serious injury all season. When King's replacement, Pittsburgh native John Wehner, also was injured, the Pirates acquired veteran third baseman Steve Buechele in a trade with Texas.

Twins, Braves advance

Minnesota made quick work of Toronto in the A.L. Championship Series, ousting the Jays in five games to extend Toronto's skid of playoff losses to three (1985, 1989, 1991).

The teams split the first two games at the Metrodome in Minneapolis before the series shifted to Toronto's Skydome for Games 3, 4 and 5. The Twins won all three to become the first club to sweep three straight road games in A.L. playoff history.

The Twins took the series lead for good by winning Game 3 in 10 innings, 3-2. They erased a 2-0 deficit with single runs in the fifth and sixth innings before Mike Pagliarulo won it with a pinch homer in the 10th.

After a relatively easy victory in Game 4 (the score was 9-3), Minnesota captured its second A.L. pennant in five years with an 8-5 victory in Game 5. Toronto led, 5-2, after five innings before the Twins rallied with three runs in the sixth inning and three more in the eighth. In the meantime, three Minnesota relievers held the Blue Jays scoreless in Toronto's last five times at bat.

The N.L. Championship Series provided much more drama and excitement. It included one extra-inning game, four decided by one run and four shutouts, three of those by 1-0 scores.

The Pirates, who were seeking to return to the fall classic for the first time since 1979, seemed well on their way to doing so after winning two straight games at Atlanta-Fulton County Stadium to assume a three games-to-two series lead. But the Braves turned the tables on the Pirates with shutout victories in Games 6 and 7 at Three Rivers Stadium to win their first pennant since moving from Milwaukee to Atlanta in 1966.

The Braves, held scoreless for 26 straight innings at one point, used outstanding pitching to subdue Pittsburgh's big hitters. Glavine was the losing pitcher in two games, but the run the Pirates scored off him in the fifth inning of Game 5 would be their last of the series. Steve Avery, who had held the Bucs scoreless through 8⅓ innings

in Game 2, shut them out in Game 6. John Smoltz allowed only six hits in a complete-game, 4-0 victory in Game 7.

A memorable World Series

Many observers considered the 1991 World Series among the most competitive of all time.

Although Jack Morris was named MVP for wins in Games 1 and 7, the stars of the Series were primarily lesser-known players.

Scott Leius, a part-time third baseman during his 1991 rookie season, won Game 2 for Minnesota with an eighth-inning homer. Mark Lemke, an obscure middle infielder, drove in the winning run in Game 3 for the Braves and scored the winning run in Game 4 on a pinch-hit sacrifice fly by Jerry Willard, another relative unknown. In Game 7, Morris and John Smoltz locked horns for 9½ scoreless innings before pinch-hitter Gene Larkin, a reserve outfielder, singled home the Series-winning run for Minnesota.

Just as in 1987, the Twins won all four of their home games. Their success at the Metrodome in World Series play prompted some renewed talk that the facility provided an unfair advantage for the Twins, who are more familiar with the Metrodome's light-colored, Teflon-coated, fiberglass ceiling than are visiting National League teams. The ceiling makes it difficult to track down fly balls, a task made even more difficult by 55,000 fans waving Homer Hankies and screaming at the top of their lungs.

Each member of the Twins received a record winner's share of $119,579.66; each member of the Braves got a loser's share of $73,323.41.

Umpires get new contract

Major league club owners and the Major League Umpires Association reached agreement on a new labor contract on opening day after a two-day strike by umpires. However, the settlement came too late for the arbiters to work in seven of the eight season openers April 8, so replacement umpires were used that day.

Terms of the new four-year contract included a rise in minimum salary from $41,000 to $60,000 and in maximum salary from $105,000 after 20 years to $150,000 after 20 and $175,000 after 25 years; an increase in the postseason salary pool from $800,000 to $1.2 million, and enhancements in medical benefits, insurance coverage, expense money and pensions. Crew chiefs now earn an extra $6,000 (up from $4,000) a year.

In addition, the contract specified that umpires be selected for All-Star Game and postseason assignments strictly on merit. Vacations were increased from two weeks, chosen by seniority, to three weeks, scheduled by the leagues.

Henderson sets stolen-base record

Once the season began, much media attention focused on Oakland outfielder Rickey Henderson, who needed just three stolen bases to surpass Lou

Brock's career major league record of 938. Henderson stole one base in the Athletics' first game against Minnesota but suffered a strained muscle in his left calf before the season was a week old.

After spending 15 days on the disabled list, Henderson was stopped on his first four attempts to tie Brock's record. Finally, on April 28, he stole No. 938 in a 7-3 Oakland victory over California. Three days later, Henderson swiped third base against the New York Yankees to become the all-time leader. Immediately after being signaled safe, Henderson pulled the base from its mooring and, in a short speech to the fans at Oakland-Alameda County Coliseum, declared, "Today, I am the greatest of all time."

Ryan leads no-hit parade

Just hours after Henderson's achievement, 44-year-old Nolan Ryan of the Texas Rangers snatched a share of the next day's headlines by pitching the seventh no-hitter of his 25-year major league career. Ryan fanned 16 Toronto batters in a 3-0 victory at Arlington Stadium.

Ryan's May 1 masterpiece marked the start of another unusual season of no-hit games. After a 1990 season that included a modern-day-record nine no-hitters, eight more were thrown in 1991. Of those eight, two were joint efforts by several pitchers and one game went into extra innings. The no-hitters were thrown by Ryan; Philadelphia's Tommy Greene, who defeated Montreal, 2-0, on May 23; Bob Milacki, Mike Flanagan, Mark Williamson and Gregg Olson of the Baltimore Orioles, who combined to no-hit Oakland, 2-0, on July 13; Montreal's Mark Gardner, who pitched nine no-hit innings against Los Angeles on July 26 before yielding a run in the 10th and losing the game, 1-0; Montreal's Dennis Martinez, who hurled a 2-0, perfect-game victory over the Dodgers just two days after Gardner's performance (Martinez's was the 15th perfect game in major league history); Wilson Alvarez of the Chicago White Sox, who defeated Baltimore, 7-0, on August 11 (in only his second major league start); Kansas City's Bret Saberhagen, who beat the White Sox, 7-0, on August 26, and Kent Mercker, Mark Wohlers and Alejandro Pena of the Atlanta Braves, who combined for a 1-0 victory against San Diego on September 11. The Atlanta pitchers' performance was the sixth multiple-pitcher no-hitter in history and the first ever in the National League.

Other pitching achievements

Cy Young Award winner Tom Glavine (20-11) of Atlanta and Pittsburgh's John Smiley (20-8) were the National League's only 20-game winners. Glavine finished third in earned-run average (2.55), tied for first in complete games (nine), third in strikeouts (192) and second in innings pitched (246⅔). The Mets' David Cone led the league in strikeouts with 241, including 19 against Philadelphia on the last day of the season.

Roger Clemens (18-10) of the Red Sox won the Cy Young Award in the American League for the third time in his career. Clemens led the league in earned-run average (2.62), strikeouts (241) and innings pitched (271⅓). Clemens was the first A.L. starter to win the Cy Young Award without winning at least 20 games since Milwaukee's Pete Vuckovich in 1982.

Minnesota's Scott Erickson (20-8) and Detroit's Bill Gullickson (20-9) were the junior circuit's only 20-game winners.

Two pitchers attempted comebacks in 1991, one successfully, the other unsuccessfully.

The Dodgers' Orel Hershiser, the 1988 N.L. Cy Young winner, returned May 29 after a 13-month hiatus due to reconstructive surgery on his right (throwing) shoulder. Hershiser, who hadn't pitched in the majors since April 25, 1990, gave up nine hits and four runs in four innings in an 8-2 loss to Houston. He finished the season with a 7-2 record in 21 starts.

Righthander Jim Palmer, elected to the Hall of Fame only one year earlier, ended a brief comeback attempt with his old team, the Baltimore Orioles, after just one spring-training appearance. Palmer, who hadn't pitched competitively since 1984, was hit hard by the Red Sox and also aggravated a hamstring injury.

Outstanding hitting performances

Atlanta's Terry Pendleton won his first N.L. batting title by one point over runner-up Hal Morris of the Cincinnati Reds (.319 to .318). Morris went 3-for-4 on the last day of the season against the Padres while Pendleton sat out the Braves' final game against the Astros. Pittsburgh's Barry Bonds, the 1990 N.L. MVP, hit .292 with 25 home runs and 116 RBIs to finish behind Pendleton in the MVP balloting.

The Mets' Howard Johnson led the N.L. in home runs (38) and runs batted in (117), was second in runs scored (108) and slugging percentage (.535) and was third in total bases (302). He finished fifth in the MVP vote.

Detroit first baseman Cecil Fielder, who led the American League in RBIs (133) and tied for the league lead in home runs (44, with Oakland's Jose Canseco), was disappointed over his second straight runner-up finish in the A.L.'s MVP balloting. He lost out to Baltimore's Cal Ripken. The Orioles' shortstop hit .323 with 34 homers and 114 RBIs to earn his sixth Silver Slugger award, his first Gold Glove and a perfect 100 score in the Elias Sports Bureau's postseason player rankings. Ripken, who also received THE SPORTING NEWS' Major League Player of the Year Award, played in all 162 games to extend his consecutive-games streak to 1,573.

Bo Jackson returns from injury

Bo Jackson, one of baseball's most charismatic stars in recent years, made a dramatic return to the game in September after spending most of the year on the disabled list with a hip injury. Jackson, who sustained the injury in a National Football League playoff game January 13, made his comeback as a member of the Chicago White Sox after his old club, the Kansas City Royals, released him March 18.

The White Sox signed Jackson to a three-year contract April 3 after the two-sport star vowed to rehabilitate his injury through a vigorous conditioning program. Jackson recovered well enough to make his 1991 debut September 2, going 0-for-3 with a sacrifice fly in Chicago's 5-1 victory over the Royals at Comiskey Park.

Umpire Palermo wounded by gunshot

Steve Palermo, an A.L. umpire since 1977, was shot outside a Dallas restaurant in the early-morning hours of July 7 while trying to break up a robbery.

Palermo, who had worked third base in a Rangers-Angels game at Arlington Stadium the night before, was eating dinner when a bartender noticed four men robbing two waitresses in the restaurant parking lot. Palermo, 41, and several other people rushed to the scene.

Three of the suspects drove off in a car, only to return shortly thereafter and fire shots from a .32-caliber pistol. Palermo was shot once in the back, the bullet entering his right hip before exiting the left side of his body. The bullet traumatized Palermo's spinal cord and left him paralyzed from the waist down.

The umpire began his rehabilitation almost immediately. In October, wearing leg braces and using crutches, Palermo threw out the first ball in an emotional ceremony before Game 1 of the World Series. In November, he testified at the trial of his assailant, Kevin Bivins, who was convicted of aggravated robbery and sentenced to 75 years in prison.

In December, Palermo—whose goal is to return to baseball—took his first steps without crutches or braces.

Managerial changes

The old adage that managers are hired to be fired was never truer than in 1991. No fewer than 12 teams fired their field boss at some point during the 1991 calendar year, with the Chicago Cubs doing it twice.

Nick Leyva's April 23 firing in Philadelphia was the third-fastest in history. The Phillies' record at the time was 4-9. Leyva was replaced by Jim Fregosi, whose previous managerial experience consisted of stints with the White Sox and Angels.

Three managers were given pink slips on consecutive days in May: Don Zimmer by the Cubs on May 21, John Wathan by the Royals on May 22 and Frank Robinson by the Orioles on May 23. Their replacements were, respectively, Jim Essian, Hal McRae and Johnny Oates.

Four more managers lost their jobs later in the season. Those were Buck Rodgers, who was replaced by Tom Runnells in Montreal; John McNamara, replaced by Mike Hargrove in Cleveland; Doug Rader, replaced in California by Rodgers, and Bud Harrelson, who was replaced on an interim basis as New York Mets manager by Mike Cubbage.

The end of the regular season did not end the bloodletting. Four more managers got the ax on consecutive days: Stump Merrill of the Yankees on October 7, replaced by Buck Showalter; Joe Morgan of the Red Sox on October 8, replaced by Butch Hobson; Tom Trebelhorn of the Brewers on October 9, replaced by Phil Garner, and Jim Lefebvre of the Mariners on October 10, replaced by Bill Plummer.

The year ended with the Cubs replacing Essian with Lefebvre and the cross-town White Sox appointing Gene Lamont to succeed Jeff Torborg.

Torborg, who resigned as White Sox manager on October 10 to accept the same job with the Mets, was the only manager to depart voluntarily last year.

Two record-keeping revisions

Commissioner Vincent also played a part in revising two of baseball's record-keeping rules. In August, he announced that he would ask an eight-man committee for statistical accuracy to consider removing the parentheses noting that Roger Maris' 61 home runs during the 1961 season were compiled during a 162-game schedule.

"I think there should be one record," the commissioner said.

In September, the committee agreed with him, and in effect urged that Babe Ruth no longer be listed as a holder of the single-season home run record. Seymour Siwoff of the Elias Sports Bureau, publisher of one of the two recognized record books, said that Elias would comply with the committee's request. THE SPORTING NEWS said that it would continue to list records for both 154- and 162-game seasons in The Complete Baseball Record Book. THE SPORTING NEWS' policy applied not just to home runs, but to all other statistics as well.

The committee redefined no-hitters as games of nine innings or more that ended with no hits. Under such a designation, 50 games previously listed as no-hitters, including the one pitched by Montreal's Mark Gardner in 1991, no longer would be classified as no-hitters.

Disciplinary actions

Three players were involved in on-field incidents that resulted in disciplinary action.

Boston's Roger Clemens was able to pitch on opening day after appealing a five-game suspension and $10,000 fine imposed on him by A.L. President Bobby Brown after his ejection from Game 4 of the 1990 A.L. Championship Series. Clemens had first appealed the punishment to Brown, the original judge in the case, who sustained his initial judgment. Vincent then heard Clemens' appeal and upheld the penalties April 26.

Cincinnati pitcher Rob Dibble was suspended twice and fined once in three separate episodes. On April 11, he threw a pitch behind the back of Houston batter Eric Yelding, resulting in a three-game suspension. On April 28, he hit and injured a fan after hurling a ball into the center-field stands at Riverfront Stadium, a transgression that led to a four-game suspension. On July 23, Dibble threw a ball at the legs of Cubs batter Doug Dascenzo after Dascenzo had laid down a suicide-squeeze bunt. N.L. President Bill White imposed a fine after Dibble agreed to seek counseling. The amount of the fine was not disclosed.

Cleveland outfielder Albert Belle was suspended without pay for one week after throwing a ball at a fan seated in the stands.

Cincinnati Manager Lou Piniella also ran into some difficulties in 1991. After home-plate umpire Gary Darling reversed a home run call by first-base umpire Dutch Rennert in the Reds' 7-3 loss to the Giants on August 3, Piniella, in a postgame diatribe, accused Darling of bias against the Reds.

Piniella later retracted the charge after meeting with White, but Darling and the umpires association proceeded with a libel suit against the Cincinnati manager. The suit was settled out of court in December, but the terms were not revealed.

Two drug incidents

Two incidents occurred during 1991 that besmirched baseball's improving record in the area of drug and substance abuse.

Braves outfielder Otis Nixon was suspended for 60 days in September after testing positive twice for drugs in less than two months. The suspension, which could not be appealed, removed the Braves' leadoff man from their lineup at a critical time, with the club battling the Dodgers in the N.L. West race.

The players association later filed a grievance over the length of the suspension, but arbitrator George Nicolau ruled that the 60-day suspension was appropriate.

Yankees reliever Steve Howe, who had been suspended on five previous occasions for violations of baseball's drug policy, was arrested December 19 on cocaine charges in Kalispell, Mont. Howe, who had recently signed a contract that could have earned him $1.5 million in 1992, first underwent drug rehabilitation in 1982 while playing for the Dodgers.

Rose, Steinbrenner affairs

On January 7, Pete Rose, baseball's all-time hits leader, concluded serving two concurrent five-month sentences for filing false income tax returns.

Shortly after Rose's release from the Marion (Ill.) Federal Prison Camp, a special committee

charged with reviewing voting procedures for the Hall of Fame recommended that anyone on baseball's permanently ineligible list be kept off the Hall of Fame ballot. (Rose had been on that list since August 23, 1989.) The vote for the proposal was 7-3, with two committee members absent.

On February 4, the Hall of Fame's board of directors approved the committee's recommendations by a 12-0 vote. Four board members, including Commissioner Fay Vincent, were absent and did not vote. A.L. President Bobby Brown, who voted for the rule change, asserted that the decision was not directed specifically at Rose. Members of the Baseball Writers' Association of America voiced their opposition to the vote, calling it a rush to judgment and declaring that the fitness of anyone for election to the Hall should be left to voting members of the BBWAA to decide.

After leaving prison, Rose entered a halfway house in Cincinnati to begin working off the 1,000 hours of community service in his sentence. He left the halfway house in April, completed the community service in July and moved with his family to Florida. Near the end of the year, Rose hinted that he might seek reinstatement to baseball in 1992 and perhaps would like to work in broadcasting or for the Florida Marlins, one of the National League's two new expansion teams.

The possibility also arose that George Steinbrenner, principal owner of the New York Yankees, would apply for reinstatement following the conviction and sentencing of Howard Spira on extortion charges. Steinbrenner had admitted paying Spira, an admitted gambler, $40,000 in January 1990, and Vincent had ruled that the Steinbrenner-Spira association was not in the best interests of baseball. The commissioner intended to suspend Steinbrenner for two years, but the owner inexplicably asked for permanent removal instead.

In November, Spira was sentenced to 2½ years in prison. Shortly thereafter, Robert Nederlander, who succeeded Steinbrenner as the Yankees' managing general partner, resigned effective December 31. The following day, one of three lawsuits filed by Yankee officials against Major League Baseball was dropped. Steinbrenner did not comment on whether these moves presaged an appeal of his ban, but Vincent had said he would not consider reinstatement unless all three lawsuits were dropped.

Lenny Dykstra's problems

In March, Commissioner Vincent placed Philadelphia Phillies outfielder Lenny Dykstra on one-year probation for his involvement in high-stakes poker games. Earlier, Dykstra had been called as a prosecution witness in the federal trial of Herbert Kelso, accused of running illegal poker games. Kelso was acquitted, but Dykstra admitted losing $78,000 playing poker. Vincent required Dykstra to report to his office on a regular basis.

In May, Dykstra was arrested and charged with driving under the influence of alcohol after crashing his Mercedes-Benz automobile into a tree in suburban Philadelphia. Dykstra fractured his collarbone, cheekbone and three ribs in the one-car accident and was sidelined for two months. Phillies catcher Darren Daulton, the only passenger in the car, suffered a scratched left cornea and broken left eye socket.

Attendance records shattered

Major league baseball set a regular-season attendance record of 56,813,760 in 1991, the sixth time in seven years that a record had been established.

American League attendance rose nearly 6 percent to 32,117,588, led by Toronto's 4,001,527—the first time a team had reached the 4 million level. National League attendance rose less than 1 percent to 24,696,172.

Part of the A.L. increase was attributed to the debut of Chicago's new Comiskey Park at the beginning of the season, the last hurrah for Baltimore's Memorial Stadium and the uncertain fate of Tiger Stadium in Detroit.

The Montreal Expos had to vacate Olympic Stadium on September 13 when a 55-ton block of concrete dropped from its side. As a result, the Expos' last 13 home games became road games instead. The stadium has since been declared fit for use in 1992.

N.L. expands to Denver, Miami

The National League met its own timetable for expansion by announcing in June that franchises were being awarded to Denver and Miami. A four-man expansion committee headed by N.L. President Bill White recommended those two cities over four other finalists: Buffalo, Orlando, St. Petersburg, Fla., and Washington, D.C.

The two new teams, later named the Colorado Rockies and the Florida Marlins, will begin play in 1993. The Rockies, whose principal owner, John A. Antonucci, heads a wholesale beverage business, will play their home games in Mile High Stadium until Coors Field, a new park near downtown Denver, is ready, tentatively scheduled for 1995. The Marlins, owned by H. Wayne Huizenga of Blockbuster Entertainment Corp., will play in Joe Robbie Stadium, a facility originally built for football but since renovated for baseball as well.

Owners in both major leagues disagreed over how to divide the $95 million franchise fee assessed each new team. N.L. owners favored following the precedent that expansion fees generated in one league not be shared with the other. A.L. owners, for a variety of reasons, argued that the $190 million should be split into 26 equal parts.

Commissioner Vincent settled the dispute by awarding the American League $42 million (or $3 million per team), roughly 22 percent of the entire pot, and reserving the balance for the National

League ($12.3 million per team). Vincent also ruled that A.L. teams would have to participate in the three-round expansion draft to stock the new teams. Each existing team will be permitted to protect 15 players from its 40-man roster and cannot lose more than three players.

Salaries continue to rise

Following the season, the players association announced that the average player salary in 1991 was $851,492, an increase of 42.5 percent over 1990. Management's Player Relations Committee, which computes signing bonuses slightly differently, announced a similar figure of $845,383, up 43.4 percent over 1990.

The percentage increase was the second-highest ever, behind only the 1977 rise that followed the first year of free agency. The dollar increase more than doubled the previous record.

According to the players association, Oakland had the highest average salary at $1,394,119; Houston was the lowest at $395,444.

The highest individual salary belonged to Dodgers outfielder Darryl Strawberry, who received $3,800,000 in the first year of a five-year, $20.25 million contract signed in November 1990.

Before the season began, however, other players agreed to contracts that will vault some of them ahead of Strawberry in the future. Roger Clemens signed a four-year contract extension with Boston for $21.5 million, an average of $5.375 million a year. Other players who signed big contracts after January 1 included new-look free agents Gary Gaetti (California, 4 years, $11.4 million) and Jack Morris (Minnesota, 1 year, $3 million), as well as Tony Gwynn (San Diego, three-year extension, $12.25 million) and Dwight Gooden (New York Mets, three-year extension, $14.45 million).

Salary arbitration records

Commissioner Vincent attributed a good portion of the rising salaries to arbitration. Indeed, the 159 players who filed for arbitration in January 1991 earned an average salary increase of $540,000, a 104 percent hike over what they were paid in 1990.

Several records were set during the arbitration process. Glenn Davis, who sought $3.6 million from the Orioles (before reaching a salary accord with the club), and Bobby Bonilla, who asked for $3.475 million from the Pirates, both exceeded Robin Yount's 1990 demand of $3.4 million. Wally Joyner was awarded $2.1 million from the Angels, thereby surpassing the $1.975 million won by Don Mattingly in 1987. Joyner's record was short-lived as Pittsburgh's Doug Drabek was awarded $3.35 million. The Indians' Greg Swindell, who won his case, and the Pirates' Bonilla and Bobby Bonds, who both lost theirs, also exceeded Mattingly's previous high. Seventeen cases proceeded through the award stage, with the clubs winning 10 times.

Bonilla tops 1991-92 free agents

The 1991-92 class of free agents was composed of the 99 players who filed by the November 11 deadline. Early speculation that teams would not pursue these players with offers as lucrative as the previous year proved unfounded.

The Mets snared the biggest prize, outbidding several teams for former Pirates outfielder Bonilla, who signed a five-year, $29 million contract December 2.

Teams continued to bid fiercely for free agents despite dire predictions for baseball's economic future. Among the prominent players who agreed to terms were pitcher Mike Morgan (who signed a four-year, $12.5 million contract with the Chicago Cubs); first baseman Wally Joyner (Kansas City, one year, $4.2 million); pitcher Jack Morris (Toronto, two years, $10.85 million); pitcher Rick Sutcliffe (Baltimore, one year, $1.2 million), and outfielder Dave Winfield (Toronto, one year, $2.3 million).

When World Series hero Morris left his hometown Twins to sign with the Blue Jays in December, Minnesota Manager Tom Kelly said: "In the summer, baseball is a sport. In the winter, it's a business." Last summer, here's how the sport of baseball wound up:

FINAL STANDINGS

AMERICAN LEAGUE

EAST DIVISION

Team	Tor.	Det.	Bos.	Mil.	N.Y.	Bal.	Cle.	Min.	Chi.	Tex.	Oak.	Sea.	K.C.	Cal.	W	L	Pct.	GB
Toronto	...	8	4	7	7	8	12	8	5	6	6	7	7	6	91	71	.562	....
Detroit	5	...	8	4	8	8	6	4	8	6	4	8	8	7	84	78	.519	7
Boston	9	5	...	7	6	5	9	3	7	5	8	5	9	7	84	78	.519	7
Milwaukee	6	9	6	...	6	10	8	6	5	7	8	3	3	6	83	79	.512	8
New York	6	5	7	7	...	8	7	2	4	5	6	3	5	6	71	91	.438	20
Baltimore	5	5	8	3	5	...	7	4	4	9	3	4	4	4	67	95	.414	24
Cleveland	1	7	4	5	6	6	...	2	6	4	5	2	4	5	57	105	.352	34

WEST DIVISION

Team	Min.	Chi.	Tex.	Oak.	Sea.	K.C.	Cal.	Tor.	Det.	Bos.	Mil.	N.Y.	Bal.	Cle.	W	L	Pct.	GB
Minnesota	...	5	6	8	9	7	5	4	8	9	6	10	8	10	95	67	.586	....
Chicago	8	...	8	7	7	7	5	7	4	5	7	8	8	6	87	75	.537	8
Texas	7	5	...	9	8	6	8	6	6	7	5	7	3	8	85	77	.525	10
Oakland	5	6	4	...	6	7	12	6	8	4	4	6	9	7	84	78	.519	11
Seattle	4	6	5	7	...	6	7	5	4	3	9	9	8	10	83	79	.512	12
Kansas City	6	6	7	6	7	...	4	5	4	5	9	7	8	8	82	80	.506	13
California	8	8	5	1	6	9	...	6	5	8	6	6	6	7	81	81	.500	14

NATIONAL LEAGUE

EAST DIVISION

Team	Pit.	St.L.	Phi.	Chi.	N.Y.	Mon.	Atl.	L.A.	S.D.	S.F.	Cin.	Hou.	W	L	Pct.	GB
Pittsburgh	...	11	12	11	12	12	3	5	7	7	10	8	98	64	.605	....
St. Louis	7	...	12	8	11	11	3	6	3	8	8	7	84	78	.519	14
Philadelphia	6	6	...	10	7	14	7	5	9	6	3	5	78	84	.481	20
Chicago	7	10	8	...	11	10	6	2	4	6	4	9	77	83	.481	20
New York	6	7	11	6	...	14	3	5	7	6	7	5	77	84	.478	20½
Montreal	6	7	4	7	4	...	7	7	6	7	6	10	71	90	.441	26½

WEST DIVISION

Team	Atl.	L.A.	S.D.	S.F.	Cin.	Hou.	Pit.	St.L.	Phi.	Chi.	N.Y.	Mon.	W	L	Pct.	GB
Atlanta	...	7	11	9	11	13	9	9	5	6	9	5	94	68	.580	....
Los Angeles	11	...	10	8	12	10	7	6	7	10	7	5	93	69	.574	1
San Diego	7	8	...	11	10	12	5	9	3	8	5	6	84	78	.519	10
San Francisco	9	10	7	...	8	9	5	4	6	6	6	5	75	87	.463	19
Cincinnati	7	6	8	10	...	9	2	4	9	8	5	6	74	88	.457	20
Houston	5	8	6	9	9	...	4	5	7	3	7	2	65	97	.401	29

A.L. CHAMPIONSHIP SERIES

GAME 1

HIGHLIGHTS
MINNESOTA 5, TORONTO 4

Why the Twins won: They were on the attack from the outset before their boisterous, handkerchief-waving fans at the Metrodome. Minnesota came out hitting, running and scoring against a Toronto team that seemed unnerved by the frenzied atmosphere; in fact, after two innings, Minnesota had seven hits, three stolen bases and four runs.

Why the Blue Jays lost: Knuckleballer Tom Candiotti seemed to have a case of the butterflies while pitching in his first postseason game in the majors. The 34-year-old righthander, acquired from lowly Cleveland in late June, was raked for eight hits and five runs in 2⅔ innings and was no match for Twins veteran Jack Morris, who was appearing in his third League Championship Series. Morris didn't dazzle, but he took a 5-1 lead into the sixth before running into trouble.

The turning points:

1. Hoping to seize an early lead in an effort to keep the crowd out of the game, the Blue Jays wound up suffering the opposite fate. Toronto went down 1-2-3 in the first inning, but Minnesota's first two hitters rapped singles and eventually scored on Chili Davis' bloop single to left field. It was 2-0, Twins, after one inning and the joint was rocking.

2. When Morris ran out of gas in the sixth, an inning in which Toronto tallied three times, long-time minor leaguer Carl Willis came on in relief for Minnesota and pitched 2⅓ innings of scoreless ball. Twins bullpen stopper Rick Aguilera then finished the job.

Notable: The victory improved the Twins' postseason Metrodome record to 7-0. Minnesota had gone 2-0 at the indoor facility in its 1987 championship-series triumph over Detroit and posted a 4-0 record under the roof in its '87 World Series conquest of St. Louis. . . . The Metrodome's light-colored ceiling and tricky lighting created problems for both teams. The Twins benefited first when Shane Mack's third-inning drive shot over the head of Toronto right fielder Joe Carter for a run-scoring double. But in the sixth, Twins second baseman Chuck Knoblauch lost a high popup in the upper reaches of the dome and the Blue Jays went on to a big inning.

Quotable: Willis, 30, on Manager Tom Kelly's decision to use the little-known pitcher in a key situation: "When T.K. came to take me out, I told him I appreciated him having the confidence to bring me in."

BOX SCORE

TUESDAY, OCTOBER 8, AT MINNESOTA

Toronto	AB	R	H	RBI	PO	A
White, cf	4	1	1	0	5	0
Alomar, 2b	4	1	2	0	3	2
Carter, rf	4	2	2	0	2	1
Olerud, 1b	4	0	2	2	3	0
Gonzales, pr-1b	0	0	0	0	2	0
Gruber, 3b	4	0	2	2	1	1
Maldonado, lf	4	0	0	0	0	0
Mulliniks, dh	4	0	0	0	0	0
Borders, c	4	0	0	0	8	2
Lee, ss	3	0	0	0	0	1
Candiotti, p	0	0	0	0	0	0
Wells, p	0	0	0	0	0	0
Timlin, p	0	0	0	0	0	2
Totals	35	4	9	4	24	9

Minnesota	AB	R	H	RBI	PO	A
Gladden, lf	5	1	2	0	5	0
Knoblauch, 2b	3	1	2	1	0	5
Puckett, cf	4	0	0	0	3	1
Hrbek, 1b	4	0	1	0	7	1
Davis, dh	2	1	1	2	0	0
Harper, c	4	0	2	0	6	0
Ortiz, c	0	0	0	0	3	0
Mack, rf	3	1	2	1	0	0
Pagliarulo, 3b	2	0	0	0	1	0
Leius, ph-3b	1	0	0	0	1	0
Larkin, ph	1	0	0	0	0	0
Newman, 3b	0	0	0	0	0	0
Gagne, ss	4	1	1	1	0	2
Morris, p	0	0	0	0	0	1
Willis, p	0	0	0	0	0	0
Aguilera, p	0	0	0	0	0	0
Totals	33	5	11	5	27	10

Toronto	0 0 0	1 0 3	0 0 0—4
Minnesota	2 2 1	0 0 0	0 0 x—5

Toronto	IP	H	R	ER	BB	SO
Candiotti (L)	2⅔	8	5	5	1	2
Wells	3	2	0	0	2	2
Timlin	2⅓	1	0	0	1	2

Minnesota	IP	H	R	ER	BB	SO
Morris (W)	5⅓	8	4	4	0	4
Willis	2⅓	0	0	0	0	2
Aguilera (S)	1⅓	1	0	0	0	2

E—Gruber 2, Borders. DP—Toronto 1. LOB—Toronto 4, Minnesota 8. 2B—Carter, Harper, Mack. SB—Gruber, Knoblauch 2, Davis, Mack. CS—Knoblauch, Mack. U—Barnett, plate; Johnson, first; Roe, second; Welke, third; Reilly, left field; McKean, right field. T—3:17. A—54,766.

GAME 2

HIGHLIGHTS
TORONTO 5, MINNESOTA 2

Why the Blue Jays won: They took the Minnesota crowd out of the game early and got a cool performance from rookie pitcher Juan Guzman. With the decibel level at the Metrodome usually rising proportionally to the size of the Twins' lead, Toronto found the perfect answer to quieting the crowd: The Blue Jays led throughout. The Jays took a 1-0 edge in the first inning when Devon White singled, stole second, advanced to third on a sacrifice and scored on Joe Carter's single. In the third, Kelly Gruber delivered a two-run single that left Minnesota in a 3-0 hole and the throng in a funk. Entrusted with the lead, Guzman didn't let it get away—although he squandered some of it. Touched for single runs in the third and sixth innings, Guzman left after a solid 5⅔ innings—he allowed only four hits—and turned things over to the Toronto bullpen corps.

Why the Twins lost: They managed only five hits (all singles) against Guzman, Tom Henke and Duane Ward. Plus, Minnesota starter Kevin Tapani didn't settle down until the fourth inning—which proved too little too late.

The turning points:

1. For Toronto, one might actually have come the night before when the Blue Jays collected themselves amid the Metrodome frenzy and rallied from an early 5-0 deficit to close within 5-4. Manager Cito Gaston's team demonstrated it could perform in what is considered a house of horrors by other A.L. teams.

2. With two Twins on base in the first inning and one out and Minnesota threatening to make short work of Toronto's 1-0 lead, big guns Kent Hrbek and Chili Davis came up empty against Guzman. Hrbek popped out and Davis struck out. Yes, it was early in the game, but Guzman—who had a history of opening-inning woes—gained confidence by dodging the bullet and the Blue Jays overall got a much-needed boost by staying ahead and thereby silencing the crowd.

Notable: Twins rookie second baseman Chuck Knoblauch, seemingly immune to postseason pressure, had his second straight 2-for-3 performance at the plate.... Toronto's Gruber ran his runs-batted-in total to four in two games with his third-inning base hit. ... The defeat was Minnesota's first in eight postseason games played at the Metrodome.

Quotable: Guzman, on retiring Davis in the first inning with Dan Gladden and Kirby Puckett on base:

"That was my best pitch (of the day), when I struck him out."

BOX SCORE

WEDNESDAY, OCTOBER 9, AT MINNESOTA

Toronto	AB	R	H	RBI	PO	A
White, cf	4	3	2	0	2	0
Alomar, 2b	3	1	2	0	2	3
Carter, rf	3	0	1	2	2	0
Olerud, 1b	4	0	0	0	10	0
Gruber, 3b	4	0	2	2	2	2
Maldonado, lf	4	0	0	0	0	0
Mulliniks, dh	2	0	1	0	0	0
Tabler, ph-dh	1	0	0	0	0	0
Borders, c	4	0	1	0	8	0
Lee, ss	3	1	0	0	1	2
Guzman, p	0	0	0	0	0	0
Henke, p	0	0	0	0	0	1
Ward, p	0	0	0	0	0	0
Totals	32	5	9	4	27	8

Minnesota	AB	R	H	RBI	PO	A
Gladden, lf	3	0	0	0	6	0
Knoblauch, 2b	3	2	2	0	2	2
Puckett, cf	3	0	1	1	1	0
Hrbek, 1b	4	0	0	0	7	2
Davis, dh	3	0	0	0	0	0
Harper, c	4	0	1	1	5	1
Mack, rf	3	0	0	0	1	0
Larkin, ph	1	0	0	0	0	0
Pagliarulo, 3b	4	0	0	0	0	4
Gagne, ss	3	0	1	0	3	1
Tapani, p	0	0	0	0	2	0
Bedrosian, p	0	0	0	0	0	0
Guthrie, p	0	0	0	0	0	1
Totals	31	2	5	2	27	11

Toronto	1 0 2	0 0 0	2 0 0—5
Minnesota	0 0 1	0 0 1	0 0 0—2

Toronto	IP	H	R	ER	BB	SO
Guzman (W)	5⅔	4	2	2	4	2
Henke	1⅓	0	0	0	0	2
Ward (S)	2	1	0	0	0	4

Minnesota	IP	H	R	ER	BB	SO
Tapani (L)	6⅓	8	4	4	2	5
Bedrosian	⅓	1	0	1	0	0
Guthrie	2⅓	0	0	0	0	0

E—Mack. DP—Toronto 1, Minnesota 1. LOB—Toronto 5, Minnesota 6. 2B—White. SB—White, Alomar, Gladden. CS—Carter. SH—Alomar. SF—Carter. WP—Guzman. U—Johnson, plate; Roe, first; Welke, second; Reilly, third; McKean, left field; Barnett, right field. T—3:02. A—54,816.

GAME 3

HIGHLIGHTS

MINNESOTA 3, TORONTO 2

Why the Twins won: Relievers David West, Carl Willis, Mark Guthrie and Rick Aguilera held the Blue Jays scoreless over the last six innings of a 10-inning game while Minnesota scrounged for the tying run and then finally came up with the winner.

Why the Blue Jays lost: Actually, Toronto didn't score over the last nine innings after notching two first-inning runs against Twins starter Scott Erickson on Joe Carter's homer and Candy Maldonado's RBI double.

The turning points:

1. Minnesota's ability to break through against

Toronto's seemingly impenetrable bullpen. Entering the 10th inning of Game 3, Blue Jays relievers had not allowed a run in 11⅔ innings of the playoffs and had struck out 15 Twins batters. But pinch-hitter Mike Pagliarulo put an end to all that. Batting for fellow third baseman Scott Leius with one out in the 10th and the score tied 2-2, Pagliarulo sent a pitch from Toronto reliever Mike Timlin over the right-field wall.

2. Minnesota's ability to handle the din at somebody else's domed stadium. While Toronto's SkyDome doesn't hold the sound quite like the Metrodome does, the atmosphere at the Blue Jays' park—where the Jays, incredibly, crashed the 4,000,000 mark in attendance in 1991—is clearly

hostile. The Twins nevertheless rebounded from a 2-0 deficit with single runs in the fifth and sixth innings. In the fifth, Shane Mack tripled against Jays starter Jimmy Key—right fielder Carter twisted his ankle on the play—and raced home on Kent Hrbek's fielder's-choice grounder. In the sixth, Chuck Knoblauch laced a double and rode home on Kirby Puckett's single.

3. In three innings—the first, fourth and fifth—Toronto left runners stranded at both second and third base.

Notable: Knoblauch came through with his third consecutive two-hit game and boasted a series-leading .545 batting average. Knoblauch's counterpart at second base, Roberto Alomar, paced Toronto at this juncture with a .500 mark. . . . Carter, his ankle troubling him, left the game for a pinch-runner in the seventh inning and faced designated-hitter duty for the remainder of the A.L. playoffs.

Quotable: Kirby Puckett, on the Twins' resiliency: "To come in here and fall behind and then win in the 10th like we did says a lot about us." . . . Timlin, discussing the sinkerball that Pagliarulo deposited over the right-field barrier for the game-winning run: "The only movement it had was after he hit it."

BOX SCORE
FRIDAY, OCTOBER 11, AT TORONTO

Minnesota	AB	R	H	RBI	PO	A
Gladden, lf	5	0	0	0	4	0
Knoblauch, 2b	5	1	2	0	4	3
Puckett, cf	5	0	2	1	6	0
Davis, dh	4	0	1	0	0	0
Mack, rf	4	1	1	0	0	0
Hrbek, 1b	3	0	0	1	8	1
Gagne, ss	2	0	0	0	0	2
Sorrento, ph	1	0	0	0	0	0
Newman, ss	0	0	0	0	0	0
Ortiz, c	3	0	0	0	6	0
Larkin, ph	1	0	0	0	0	0

	AB	R	H	RBI	PO	A
Harper, c	0	0	0	0	1	0
Leius, 3b	3	0	0	0	0	4
Pagliarulo, ph-3b	1	1	1	1	0	0
Erickson, p	0	0	0	0	1	1
West, p	0	0	0	0	0	0
Willis, p	0	0	0	0	0	0
Guthrie, p	0	0	0	0	0	0
Aguilera, p	0	0	0	0	0	0
Totals	37	3	7	3	30	11

Toronto	AB	R	H	RBI	PO	A
White, cf	5	0	1	0	2	0
Alomar, 2b	3	0	1	0	3	3
Carter, rf	3	1	1	1	0	0
Ducey, pr-rf	1	0	0	0	0	0
Olerud, 1b	2	1	0	0	16	0
Gruber, 3b	5	0	1	0	0	2
Maldonado, lf	4	0	1	1	1	0
Mulliniks, dh	1	0	0	0	0	0
Tabler, ph	0	0	0	0	0	0
Wilson, pr-dh	1	0	0	0	0	0
Borders, c	3	0	0	0	7	0
Lee, ss	4	0	0	0	1	4
Key, p	0	0	0	0	0	3
Wells, p	0	0	0	0	0	1
Henke, p	0	0	0	0	0	1
Timlin, p	0	0	0	0	0	0
Totals	32	2	5	2	30	14

Minnesota	0 0 0	0 1 1	0 0 0	1—3
Toronto	2 0 0	0 0 0	0 0 0	0—2

Minnesota	IP	H	R	ER	BB	SO
Erickson	4	3	2	2	5	2
West	2⅔	1	0	0	3	3
Willis	2	1	0	0	0	1
Guthrie (W)	⅓	0	0	0	0	0
Aguilera (S)	1	0	0	0	0	0

Toronto	IP	H	R	ER	BB	SO
Key	6	5	2	2	1	1
Wells	1⅔	1	0	0	0	2
Henke	1⅓	0	0	0	1	3
Timlin (L)	1	1	1	1	0	1

E—Timlin. DP—Minnesota 1, Toronto 2. LOB—Minnesota 6, Toronto 10. 2B—Knoblauch, Puckett, Maldonado. 3B—Mack. HR—Carter, Pagliarulo. SH—Alomar, Borders. WP—West 2. U—Roe, plate; Welke, first; Reilly, second; McKean, third; Barnett, left field; Johnson, right field. T—3:36. A—51,454.

GAME 4

HIGHLIGHTS
MINNESOTA 9, TORONTO 3

Why the Twins won: Once Minnesota's major league-leading offense—the Twins batted .280 as a team in 1991—shifted into gear, it was lights out for Toronto. Shut out through the third inning by Blue Jays starter Todd Stottlemyre, the Twins proceeded to score in five of the last six innings.

Why the Blue Jays lost: Their pitching staff couldn't handle Dan Gladden and Kirby Puckett, two mainstays of Minnesota's 1987 World Series championship team, and Mike Pagliarulo, a free-agent signee of the Twins. Those Twins combined for eight hits in 13 at-bats and drove in seven runs.

The turning points:

1. The Blue Jays were up to their ol' Game 3 tricks in the third inning. Once again having runners stationed at second and third base, Toronto once again left them there. Looking to expand upon a 1-0 lead, the Jays got consecutive singles and a double steal from Devon White and Roberto Alomar in the third. With White perched on third and Alomar at second, Joe Carter struck out and John Olerud grounded out.

2. Down 4-1 entering the sixth inning but still in the ball game, Toronto needed to shut down the Twins' attack—but couldn't do it. Pagliarulo, a .188 batsman against lefthanded pitching during the regular season, rapped a run-scoring double to left-center off Jays lefthander David Wells, and Gladden knocked in Pagliarulo with a single to left. It was now 6-1, Twins, and veteran Minnesota starter Jack Morris had a comfortable working margin.

Notable: Pagliarulo, the hero of Game 3, drove in

Minnesota's go-ahead run in the Twins' four-run fourth inning. Manager Tom Kelly's team, facing a 1-0 deficit going into the fourth, got a game-tying home run from Puckett before Chili Davis doubled, advanced to third on a groundout and scored on Pagliarulo's single. Gladden later capped the inning with a two-run single. ... Toronto slugger Carter, relegated to DH duty because of the ankle injury he incurred in Game 3, went 0-for-5 and struck out three times. ... Toronto catcher Pat Borders went 3-for-4 and knocked in both of the runs scored against Morris, who gave way to reliever Steve Bedrosian in the ninth inning. Borders singled home Toronto's first run in the second inning and rapped an RBI double in the sixth.

Quotable: Gladden, commenting on the Minnesota offense's knack of supporting Morris: "We seem to pick it up a level behind him. You know he's out there busting his butt."

	AB	R	H	RBI	PO	A
Morris, p	0	0	0	0	2	1
Bedrosian, p	0	0	0	0	0	0
Totals	39	9	13	8	27	12
Toronto	AB	R	H	RBI	PO	A
White, cf	5	0	2	0	4	0
Alomar, 2b	5	0	2	1	2	1
Carter, dh	5	0	0	0	0	0
Olerud, 1b	5	0	1	0	4	1
Gruber, 3b	4	1	1	0	0	0
Maldonado, rf	4	1	1	0	2	0
Borders, c	4	0	3	2	9	1
Lee, ss	3	0	0	0	2	3
Mulliniks, ph	0	1	0	0	0	0
Wilson, lf	3	0	1	0	3	0
Stottlemyre, p	0	0	0	0	1	0
Wells, p	0	0	0	0	0	0
Acker, p	0	0	0	0	0	0
Timlin, p	0	0	0	0	0	0
MacDonald, p	0	0	0	0	0	0
Totals	38	3	11	3	27	6

Minnesota						
Minnesota	0 0 0	4 0 2	1 1 1—9			
Toronto	0 1 0	0 0 1	0 0 1—3			

Minnesota	IP	H	R	ER	BB	SO
Morris (W)	8	9	2	2	1	3
Bedrosian	1	2	1	0	1	2

Toronto	IP	H	R	ER	BB	SO
Stottlemyre (L)	3⅔	7	4	4	1	3
Wells	1⅔	2	2	2	0	3
Acker	⅔	1	0	0	0	1
Timlin	2	2	2	0	1	2
MacDonald	1	1	1	1	1	0

E—Gagne, Gruber, Lee. LOB—Minnesota 9, Toronto 10. 2B—Davis 2, Harper, Pagliarulo, Gruber, Borders. HR—Puckett. SB—Gladden, White, Alomar. CS—Gagne. SF—Puckett, Mack. HBP—By Stottlemyre (Gagne). WP—Morris 2. U—Welke, plate; Reilly, first; McKean, second; Barnett, third; Johnson, left field; Roe, right field. T—3:15. A—51,526.

BOX SCORE

SATURDAY, OCTOBER 12, AT TORONTO

Minnesota	AB	R	H	RBI	PO	A
Gladden, lf	5	1	3	3	2	0
Knoblauch, 2b	5	0	0	0	1	2
Puckett, cf	4	2	3	2	2	0
Hrbek, 1b	5	0	0	0	12	0
Davis, dh	4	1	2	0	0	0
Brown, pr-dh	0	1	0	0	0	0
Harper, c	5	1	1	0	5	0
Mack, rf	3	1	1	1	0	0
Pagliarulo, 3b	4	2	2	2	1	3
Leius, ph-3b	0	0	0	0	0	0
Gagne, ss	4	0	1	0	2	3

GAME 5

HIGHLIGHTS

MINNESOTA 8, TORONTO 5

Why the Twins won: Their offense, held in check for the most part over the first three games of the series, followed up its 13-hit salvo of Game 4 with a 14-hit attack in Game 5. Every member of the Twins' starting lineup collected at least one hit, with Kirby Puckett leading the way with a home run and two singles. Also, Minnesota's bullpen turned in another exemplary performance as David West, Carl Willis and Rick Aguilera combined for five scoreless innings.

Why the Blue Jays lost: Toronto starter Tom Candiotti, who was roughed up in Game 1, was hammered for nine hits and four runs (two earned) in five-plus innings in Game 5. Plus, the Jays' relief corps only fanned the fire.

The turning points:

1. Trailing, 5-2, Minnesota had runners at first and third base in the sixth inning when Dan Gladden hit a one-out ground ball to Jays third baseman Kelly Gruber. Attempting to cut off a run despite his team's healthy lead, Gruber fired home to catcher Pat Borders, who missed the tag on Minnesota's Shane Mack. Twins rookie second base-

man Chuck Knoblauch then doubled home two runs, tying the game at 5-5.

2. While Puckett drove in what proved to be the winning run with a two-out, eighth-inning single to right field, struggling Kent Hrbek applied the coup de grace. Following Puckett to the plate, Hrbek, 2-for-20 at that point in the series, stroked a two-run single to left off lefthander David Wells that gave Minnesota a three-run lead. Toronto went quietly in its final two at-bats.

Notable: The Twins' bullpen did not allow an earned run in 18⅓ innings against Toronto and yielded only seven hits. ... The defeat was the Blue Jays' fifth straight at home in League Championship Series play and seventh loss at home in 10 playoff games overall. ... Puckett, 1-for-7 in the first two games of the series, stung Toronto pitching for eight hits in his final 14 at-bats.

Quotable: Blue Jays reliever Duane Ward, explaining his eighth-inning strategy against Puckett (who was batting with Gladden on second after a single and a stolen base and Knoblauch on first following a base on balls): "I tried to pitch him inside because I felt if I pitched him outside, he might take it the other way. So, I pitch him inside and he took it the other way. He's just a great hitter."

BOX SCORE

SUNDAY, OCTOBER 13, AT TORONTO

Minnesota	AB	R	H	RBI	PO	A
Gladden, lf	5	2	1	0	3	0
Knoblauch, 2b	4	1	1	2	1	2
Puckett, cf	5	2	3	2	1	0
Hrbek, 1b	5	0	2	2	6	1
Davis, dh	4	1	1	0	0	0
Harper, c	5	0	1	0	6	0
Ortiz, c	0	0	0	0	1	0
Mack, rf	5	1	2	1	2	0
Pagliarulo, 3b	4	1	2	0	2	3
Gagne, ss	4	0	1	0	4	1
Tapani, p	0	0	0	0	1	0
West, p	0	0	0	0	0	0
Willis, p	0	0	0	0	0	0
Aguilera, p	0	0	0	0	0	0
Totals	41	8	14	7	27	7

Toronto	AB	R	H	RBI	PO	A
White, cf	4	1	1	0	3	0
Alomar, 2b	4	1	2	0	4	0
Carter, dh	4	0	1	1	0	0
Olerud, 1b	4	0	0	1	7	2
Gruber, 3b	4	0	0	0	0	1
Maldonado, rf	4	0	0	0	1	0
Borders, c	4	0	1	0	6	1
Lee, ss	3	2	2	0	4	6
Mulliniks, ph	1	0	0	0	0	0

	AB	R	H	RBI	PO	A
Gonzales, ss	0	0	0	0	0	0
Wilson, lf	4	1	1	0	1	0
Candiotti, p	0	0	0	0	0	2
Timlin, p	0	0	0	0	0	0
Ward, p	0	0	0	0	0	0
Wells, p	0	0	0	0	1	0
Totals	36	5	9	5	27	12

Minnesota	1 1 0	0 0 3	0 3 0—8			
Toronto	0 0 3	2 0 0	0 0 0—5			

Minnesota	IP	H	R	ER	BB	SO
Tapani	4	8	5	5	1	4
West (W)	3	0	0	0	1	1
Willis	1	1	0	0	0	0
Aguilera (S)	1	0	0	0	0	1

Toronto	IP	H	R	ER	BB	SO
Candiotti	*5	9	4	2	1	3
Timlin	⅓	1	1	1	0	0
Ward (L)	2 ⅓	3	3	3	1	2
Wells	1 ⅓	1	0	0	0	2

*Pitched to two batters in sixth.

E—Harper, Gagne, Borders. DP—Minnesota 1, Toronto 1. LOB—Minnesota 9, Toronto 6. 2B—Knoblauch, Carter. HR—Puckett. SB—Gladden, Mack, White, Wilson. CS—Gagne. SH—Pagliarulo. WP—Candiotti. PB—Borders 2. U—Reilly, plate; McKean, first; Barnett, second; Johnson, third; Roe, left field; Welke, right field. T—3:29. A—51,425.

STATISTICS

MINNESOTA TWINS' BATTING AND FIELDING AVERAGES

Player, position					BATTING										FIELDING		
	G	AB	R	H	TB	2B	3B	HR	RBI	BB	IBB	SO	Avg.	PO	A	E	Avg.
Puckett, cf	5	21	4	9	16	1	0	2	6	1	0	4	.429	13	1	0	1.000
Knoblauch, 2b	5	20	5	7	9	2	0	0	3	3	0	3	.350	8	14	0	1.000
Mack, rf	5	18	4	6	9	1	1	0	3	2	1	4	.333	3	0	1	.750
Pagliarulo, 3b-ph	5	15	4	5	9	1	0	1	3	0	0	2	.333	4	10	0	1.000
Davis, dh	5	17	3	5	7	2	0	0	2	5	1	8	.294	0	0	0	.000
Harper, c	5	18	1	5	7	2	0	0	1	0	0	2	.278	23	1	1	.960
Gladden, lf	5	23	4	6	6	0	0	0	0	1	0	3	.261	20	0	0	1.000
Gagne, ss	5	17	1	4	4	0	0	0	1	1	0	5	.235	9	9	2	.900
Hrbek, 1b	5	21	0	3	3	0	0	0	3	1	0	3	.143	40	8	0	1.000
Aguilera, p	3	0	0	0	0	0	0	0	0	0	0	0	.000	0	0	0	.000
Bedrosian, p	2	0	0	0	0	0	0	0	0	0	0	0	.000	0	0	0	.000
Brown, pr-dh	1	0	1	0	0	0	0	0	0	0	0	0	.000	0	0	0	.000
Erickson, p	1	0	0	0	0	0	0	0	0	0	0	0	.000	1	1	0	1.000
Guthrie, p	2	0	0	0	0	0	0	0	0	0	0	0	.000	0	1	0	1.000
Morris, p	2	0	0	0	0	0	0	0	0	0	0	0	.000	3	2	0	1.000
Newman, 3b-ss	2	0	0	0	0	0	0	0	0	0	0	0	.000	0	0	0	.000
Tapani, p	2	0	0	0	0	0	0	0	0	0	0	0	.000	3	0	0	1.000
West, p	2	0	0	0	0	0	0	0	0	0	0	0	.000	0	0	0	.000
Willis, p	3	0	0	0	0	0	0	0	0	0	0	0	.000	0	0	0	.000
Sorrento, ph	1	1	0	0	0	0	0	0	0	0	0	0	.000	0	0	0	.000
Larkin, ph	3	3	0	0	0	0	0	0	0	0	0	1	.000	0	0	0	.000
Ortiz, c	3	3	0	0	0	0	0	0	0	0	0	0	.000	10	0	0	1.000
Leius, ph-3b	3	4	0	0	0	0	0	0	0	1	0	1	.000	1	4	0	1.000
Totals	5	181	27	50	70	9	1	3	25	15	2	37	.276	138	51	4	.979

TORONTO BLUE JAYS' BATTING AND FIELDING AVERAGES

Player, position					BATTING										FIELDING		
	G	AB	R	H	TB	2B	3B	HR	RBI	BB	IBB	SO	Avg.	PO	A	E	Avg.
Alomar, 2b	5	19	3	9	9	0	0	0	4	2	0	3	.474	14	9	0	1.000
White, cf	5	22	5	8	9	1	0	0	0	2	0	3	.364	16	0	0	1.000
Gruber, 3b	5	21	1	6	7	1	0	0	4	0	0	4	.286	3	6	3	.750
Borders, c	5	19	0	5	6	1	0	0	2	0	0	0	.263	38	4	2	.955
Carter, rf-dh	5	19	3	5	10	2	0	1	4	1	1	5	.263	4	1	0	1.000
Wilson, pr-dh-lf	3	8	1	2	2	0	0	0	0	0	0	3	.250	0	0	0	.000
Olerud, 1b	5	19	1	3	3	0	0	0	3	3	0	1	.158	40	3	0	1.000
Lee, ss	5	16	3	2	2	0	0	0	0	1	0	5	.125	8	16	1	.960
Mulliniks, dh-ph	5	8	1	1	1	0	0	0	0	3	0	0	.125	0	0	0	.000
Maldonado, lf-rf	5	20	1	2	3	1	0	0	1	1	0	6	.100	4	0	0	1.000
Acker, p	1	0	0	0	0	0	0	0	0	0	0	0	.000	0	0	0	.000

Player, position	G	AB	R	H	TB	2B	3B	HR	RBI	BB	IBB	SO	Avg.	PO	A	E	Avg.
Candiotti, p	2	0	0	0	0	0	0	0	0	0	0	0	.000	0	2	0	1.000
Gonzales, pr-1b-ss	2	0	0	0	0	0	0	0	0	0	0	0	.000	2	0	0	1.000
Guzman, p	1	0	0	0	0	0	0	0	0	0	0	0	.000	0	0	0	.000
Henke, p	2	0	0	0	0	0	0	0	0	0	0	0	.000	0	2	0	1.000
Key, p	1	0	0	0	0	0	0	0	0	0	0	0	.000	0	3	0	1.000
MacDonald, p	1	0	0	0	0	0	0	0	0	0	0	0	.000	0	0	0	.000
Stottlemyre, p	1	0	0	0	0	0	0	0	0	0	0	0	.000	1	0	0	1.000
Timlin, p	4	0	0	0	0	0	0	0	0	0	0	0	.000	0	2	1	.667
Ward, p	2	0	0	0	0	0	0	0	0	0	0	0	.000	0	0	0	.000
Wells, p	4	0	0	0	0	0	0	0	0	0	0	0	.000	1	1	0	1.000
Ducey, pr-rf	1	1	0	0	0	0	0	0	0	0	0	0	.000	0	0	0	.000
Tabler, ph-dh	2	1	0	0	0	0	0	0	0	1	0	0	.000	0	0	0	.000
Totals	5	173	19	43	52	6	0	1	18	15	1	30	.249	135	49	7	.963

MINNESOTA TWINS' PITCHING RECORDS

Pitcher	G	GS	CG	IP	H	R	ER	HR	BB	IBB	SO	HB	WP	W	L	Pct.	ERA
West	2	0	0	5⅔	1	0	0	0	4	1	4	0	2	1	0	1.000	0.00
Willis	3	0	0	5⅓	2	0	0	0	0	0	3	0	0	0	0	.000	0.00
Aguilera	3	0	0	3⅓	1	0	0	0	0	0	3	0	0	0	0	.000	0.00
Guthrie	2	0	0	2⅔	0	0	0	0	0	0	0	0	0	1	0	1.000	0.00
Bedrosian	2	0	0	1⅓	3	2	0	0	2	0	2	0	0	0	0	.000	0.00
Morris	2	2	0	13⅓	17	6	6	0	1	0	7	0	2	2	0	1.000	4.05
Erickson	1	1	0	4	3	2	2	1	5	0	2	0	0	0	0	.000	4.50
Tapani	2	2	0	10⅓	16	9	9	0	3	0	9	0	0	0	1	.000	7.84
Totals	5	5	0	46	43	19	17	1	15	1	30	0	4	4	1	.800	3.33

No shutouts. Saves—Aguilera 3.

TORONTO BLUE JAYS' PITCHING RECORDS

Pitcher	G	GS	CG	IP	H	R	ER	HR	BB	IBB	SO	HB	WP	W	L	Pct.	ERA
Henke	2	0	0	2⅔	0	0	0	0	1	0	5	0	0	0	0	.000	0.00
Acker	1	0	0	⅔	1	0	0	0	0	1	0	0	0	0	0	.000	0.00
Wells	4	0	0	7⅔	6	2	2	0	2	1	9	0	0	0	0	.000	2.35
Key	1	1	0	6	5	2	2	0	1	0	1	0	0	0	0	.000	3.00
Guzman	1	1	0	5⅔	4	2	2	0	4	0	2	0	1	1	0	1.000	3.18
Timlin	4	0	0	5⅔	5	4	2	1	2	1	5	0	0	0	1	.000	3.18
Ward	2	0	0	4⅓	4	3	3	0	1	0	6	0	0	0	1	.000	6.23
Candiotti	2	2	0	7⅔	17	9	7	1	2	0	5	0	1	0	1	.000	8.22
MacDonald	1	0	0	1	1	1	1	0	1	0	0	0	0	0	0	.000	9.00
Stottlemyre	1	1	0	3⅔	7	4	4	1	1	0	3	1	0	0	1	.000	9.82
Totals	5	5	0	45	50	27	23	3	15	2	37	1	2	1	4	.200	4.60

No shutouts. Saves—Ward.

COMPOSITE SCORE BY INNINGS

Minnesota	3	3	2	4	1	7	1	4	1	1—27
Toronto	3	1	5	3	0	4	2	0	1	0—19

MISCELLANEOUS STATISTICS

Sacrifice hits—Alomar 2, Borders, Pagliarulo.
Sacrifice flies—Carter, Puckett, Mack.
Stolen bases—White 3, Gladden 3, Knoblauch 2, Mack 2, Alomar 2, Gruber, Davis, Wilson.
Caught stealing—Gagne 2, Knoblauch, Mack, Carter.
Double plays—Alomar and Olerud 2; Lee and Olerud; Pagliarulo, Knoblauch and Hrbek; Leius, Knoblauch and Hrbek; Key, Lee and Olerud; Knoblauch, Gagne and Hrbek; Candiotti, Lee and Olerud.
Left on bases—Minnesota 8, 6, 6, 9, 9—38; Toronto 4, 5, 10, 10, 6—35.
Hit by pitcher—By Stottlemyre (Gagne).
Passed balls—None.
Balks—None.
Time of games—First game, 3:17; second game, 3:02; third game, 3:36; fourth game, 3:15; fifth game, 3:29.
Attendance—First game, 54,766; second game, 54,816; third game, 51,454; fourth game, 51,526; fifth game, 51,425.
Umpires—Barnett, Johnson, Roe, Welke, Reilly and McKean.
Official scorers—Tom Mee, Minnesota official scorer; Joe Sawchuk, Toronto official scorer.

GAME 1

HIGHLIGHTS
PITTSBURGH 5, ATLANTA 1

Why the Pirates won: Andy Van Slyke, one-third of Pittsburgh's fence-busting trio that was silenced in the 1990 N.L. playoffs, boosted Pirate fans' hopes for a turnabout in the 1991 League Championship Series by hammering a bases-empty home run in the first inning and a run-scoring double in the third.

Why the Braves lost: Braves starter Tom Glavine, a 20-game winner but only 8-7 after the All-Star break, repeatedly encountered first-inning problems in the second half of the season and struggled again early in the championship-series opener. Besides allowing the homer to Van Slyke, Glavine issued two first-inning walks and, with an error thrown in, found himself in a two-out, bases-loaded jam. He escaped by inducing Don Slaught to ground out. After recording a 1-2-3 second inning, Glavine then was nicked for two third-inning runs on Jay Bell's single, Van Slyke's two-base hit and Bobby Bonilla's single.

The turning points:

1. Pittsburgh Manager Jim Leyland's decision to open the playoffs with righthander Doug Drabek. While fellow starters John Smiley and Zane Smith had compiled 20-8 and 16-10 records, respectively, compared with Drabek's 15-14 mark, the battle-tested Drabek was the choice to pitch the pressure-packed playoff opener. Drabek, the 1990 N.L. Cy Young Award winner and big-game pitcher (he fashioned a 1.65 ERA in the 1990 playoffs and hurled division-clinching victories in both '90 and '91), hurled shutout ball against the Braves for six innings, allowing only three singles.

2. The Braves' failure to break through in the fourth inning when trailing, 3-0. Mark Lemke reached base when his hard grounder went between the legs of first baseman Gary Redus, but he was thrown out attempting to go all the way to third on the play. Terry Pendleton followed with a walk and Dave Justice singled to center. However, Ron Gant and Sid Bream proceeded to fly out.

Notable: The ever-aggressive Drabek showed a bit too much enthusiasm in the sixth inning when he whacked a run-scoring double over center fielder Gant's head and tried to stretch his hit into a triple. Not only was Drabek thrown out, but he also suffered a hamstring injury and was forced to leave the game. Bob Walk finished up for the Pirates. . . . Van Slyke, 13-for-35 (.371) against lefthander Glavine after his big night, batted only .195 against lefthanders in the 1991 regular season.

Quotable: Leyland said Drabek's gung-ho approach "was one of the reasons he was my starting pitcher. I know a lot of people are going to say he should have stayed at second, and I wish he would have. But that's one of the reasons I love him so much. He only knows one way to play, and that's to bust his fanny."

BOX SCORE
WEDNESDAY, OCTOBER 9, AT PITTSBURGH

Atlanta	AB	R	H	RBI	PO	A
Smith, lf	4	0	0	0	2	1
Lemke, 2b	4	0	0	0	2	1
Pendleton, 3b	3	0	0	0	1	3
Justice, rf	3	1	2	1	1	0
Gant, cf	4	0	0	0	1	1
Bream, 1b	4	0	2	0	9	2
Olson, c	4	0	0	0	6	0
Belliard, ss	2	0	0	0	1	2
Willard, ph	1	0	0	0	0	0
Blauser, ss	0	0	0	0	0	1
Glavine, p	2	0	1	0	1	3
Gregg, ph	1	0	0	0	0	0
Wohlers, p	0	0	0	0	0	0
Stanton, p	0	0	0	0	0	0
Totals	32	1	5	1	24	14

Pittsburgh	AB	R	H	RBI	PO	A
Redus, 1b	4	0	1	0	10	0
Bell, ss	3	1	1	0	2	2
Van Slyke, cf	4	2	2	2	3	0
Bonilla, rf	3	1	2	1	1	1
Bonds, lf	2	0	0	0	2	0
Buechele, 3b	3	1	1	0	1	2
Slaught, c	3	0	0	0	6	1
Lind, 2b	3	0	0	1	0	6
Drabek, p	3	0	1	1	2	0
Walk, p	1	0	0	0	0	0
Totals	29	5	8	5	27	12

Atlanta	0	0	0	0	0	0	0	0	1	—1
Pittsburgh	1	0	2	0	0	1	0	1	x	—5

Atlanta	IP	H	R	ER	BB	SO
Glavine (L)	6	6	4	4	3	4
Wohlers	1	1	0	0	0	0
Stanton	1	1	1	1	2	1

Pittsburgh	IP	H	R	ER	BB	SO
Drabek (W)	6	3	0	0	2	5
Walk (S)	3	2	1	1	0	2

E—Belliard, Redus. DP—Atlanta 1. LOB—Atlanta 6, Pittsburgh 7. 2B—Drabek, Buechele, Van Slyke. HR—Van Slyke, Justice. SB—Redus. SH—Bell. SF—Lind. U—Harvey, plate; Pulli, first; DeMuth, second; Gregg, third; Davidson, left field; Froemming, right field. T—2:52. A—57,347.

GAME 2

HIGHLIGHTS
ATLANTA 1, PITTSBURGH 0

Why the Braves won: Second-year major leaguer

Steve Avery pitched with the poise and skill of a grizzled veteran, allowing six hits and no runs over 8⅓ innings. The 21-year-old lefthander, who was coming off an 18-8 season after going 3-11 as a rookie, struck out nine Pirates.

Why the Pirates lost: Not only were the Pirates unable to solve Avery, they even had a difficult time mounting a threat. And when Pittsburgh did stir up some trouble, Avery and relief pitcher Alejandro Pena were equal to the challenge.

The turning points:

1. The fact that Atlanta's Dave Justice, on base with a single, was running on the sixth-inning pitch that Greg Olson grounded to the left side of the infield. Instead of possibly being on the front end of a double play, Justice made it to second safely and was in position to score when Mark Lemke's ensuing bad-hop grounder down the third-base line skipped past third baseman Steve Buechele. Lemke's smash, ruled a double, produced the only run of the game.

2. The fact that Lemke made a run-squelching defensive play in the eighth inning. With two out, Pittsburgh's Gary Redus singled, stole second and appeared to be in position to score when Jay Bell hit a grounder that seemed bound for center field. However, second baseman Lemke made a diving stop on the play and prevented Redus from racing home with the tying run. Andy Van Slyke then grounded into a forceout.

Notable: Pena, who collected saves in all 11 of his opportunities after being acquired from the New York Mets in late August, came through once more for the Braves. With one out in the ninth and Bonilla at second base with a double, Pena uncorked a wild pitch before getting Buechele to ground back to the mound and pinch-hitter Curtis Wilkerson to strike out. ... The victory was the first postseason triumph for the Braves in their 26 seasons in Atlanta. The Braves were swept, three games to none, in both the 1969 and 1982 N.L. playoffs by the Mets and St. Louis Cardinals, respectively.

Quotable: Before giving way to Pena in the ninth, lefthander Avery was allowed to pitch to lefthanded-hitting Barry Bonds with no one out and Bonilla on second with a leadoff double. "He (Bonds) was trying to hit the ball out of the ballpark," said

Avery, referring to an at-bat in which Bonds popped out. Bonds' view: "In that situation, with no one out, my job is to get him over to third base. It won't happen again."

BOX SCORE

THURSDAY, OCTOBER 10, AT PITTSBURGH

Atlanta	AB	R	H	RBI	PO	A
L. Smith, lf	3	0	0	0	0	0
Mitchell, pr-lf	1	0	0	0	0	0
Pendleton, 3b	4	0	0	0	1	1
Gant, cf	3	0	2	0	0	0
Justice, rf	4	1	1	0	1	0
Hunter, 1b	4	0	1	0	7	1
Olson, c	4	0	2	0	11	0
Lemke, 2b	4	0	2	1	2	2
Belliard, ss	3	0	0	0	4	3
Avery, p	4	0	0	0	1	1
Pena, p	0	0	0	0	0	1
Totals	34	1	8	1	27	9

Pittsburgh	AB	R	H	RBI	PO	A
Redus, 1b	3	0	1	0	8	0
Bell, ss	4	0	1	0	1	2
Van Slyke, cf	4	0	0	0	3	0
Bonilla, rf	4	0	2	0	4	0
Bonds, lf	4	0	1	0	0	0
Buechele, 3b	3	0	0	0	0	3
Slaught, c	3	0	0	0	9	0
Wilkerson, ph	1	0	0	0	0	0
Lind, 2b	3	0	1	0	2	4
Z. Smith, p	2	0	0	0	0	1
Mason, p	0	0	0	0	0	0
McClendon, ph	1	0	0	0	0	0
Belinda, p	0	0	0	0	0	0
Totals	32	0	6	0	27	10

Atlanta	0 0 0	0 0 1	0 0 0—1
Pittsburgh	0 0 0	0 0 0	0 0 0—0

Atlanta	IP	H	R	ER	BB	SO
Avery (W)	8⅓	6	0	0	2	9
Pena (S)	⅔	0	0	0	0	1

Pittsburgh	IP	H	R	ER	BB	SO
Z. Smith (L)	7	8	1	1	2	5
Mason	1	0	0	0	0	1
Belinda	1	0	0	0	0	1

DP—Atlanta 1, Pittsburgh 1. LOB—Atlanta 9, Pittsburgh 7. 2B—Lemke, Bonilla. SB—Gant 3, Redus, Bonds 2. HBP—By Z. Smith (Gant). WP—Pena. U—Pulli, plate; DeMuth, first; Gregg, second; Davidson, third; Froemming, left field; Harvey, right field. T—2:46. A—57,533.

GAME 3

HIGHLIGHTS

ATLANTA 10, PITTSBURGH 3

Why the Braves won: They hauled out the heavy artillery and shelled both Pittsburgh starter John Smiley (five hits and four earned runs in two innings) and three of his four relievers (five hits and five earned runs in four innings). The big blow in the early going was struck by Braves catcher Greg Olson, who capped a four-run Atlanta outburst in the first inning with a two-run home run off Smiley. Olson had hit only six homers during the regular season.

Why the Pirates lost: Pittsburgh's pitching staff obviously didn't deliver—and neither did the Bucs'

offense, particularly the monster trio of Andy Van Slyke, Bobby Bonilla and Barry Bonds. Showing signs of regressing to their 1990 postseason form, Van Slyke, Bonilla and Bonds combined for two hits in 13 at-bats against Atlanta starter John Smoltz, a 24-year-old righthander, and three relievers.

The turning points:

1. The Braves' ability to get their chanting, tomahawk-chopping fans into the game early. Down 1-0 entering the bottom of the first, Atlanta got consecutive doubles from Ron Gant, Dave Justice and Brian Hunter. Then Olson did his thing.

2. The Braves' ability to strike back later in the game as well. After Pittsburgh had pared a 6-1

Atlanta lead to 6-3 in the top of the seventh, Gant drilled a bases-empty homer in the bottom half of the inning and then Sid Bream turned the game into a rout by blasting a three-run shot in the eighth.

Notable: The Braves' ability to beat up on the Pirates at Atlanta-Fulton County Stadium hardly came as news. In six regular-season meetings between the teams at Atlanta in 1991, the Braves went 6-0 and outscored the Pirates, 46-21. ... While the boisterous Atlanta crowd may have had some effect on the Pirates, it wasn't apparent at the outset of the game. In fact, Pittsburgh's Orlando Merced smacked Smoltz's first pitch of the day over the wall in right-center.

Quotable: "Everything was going my way (with) the first two hitters," said Smiley, reflecting on the fact he retired Lonnie Smith and Terry Pendleton in the first inning before running into a buzz saw. "And then it went downhill from there." Of course, two batters do not a game make. Or even an inning, for that matter. ... "We're going to have to get with it," Pirates Manager Jim Leyland said. "We've got to pitch better, hit better and manage better."

	AB	R	H	RBI	PO	A
Landrum, p	0	0	0	0	0	0
Varsho, ph	1	0	0	0	0	0
Patterson, p	0	0	0	0	0	0
Wilkerson, ph	1	0	0	0	0	0
Kipper, p	0	0	0	0	0	1
McClendon, ph-1b	0	0	0	0	0	0
Totals	37	3	10	3	24	7

Atlanta	AB	R	H	RBI	PO	A
Smith, lf	3	1	0	0	1	0
Mitchell, lf	1	0	0	0	1	0
Pendleton, 3b	5	0	2	1	1	0
Gant, cf	5	2	2	1	4	0
Justice, rf	3	1	1	1	4	0
Hunter, 1b	4	1	1	1	4	1
Pena, p	0	0	0	0	0	0
Olson, c	3	3	2	2	10	0
Lemke, 2b	2	1	0	0	0	0
Belliard, ss	3	0	1	1	0	0
Smoltz, p	3	0	0	1	0	1
Stanton, p	0	0	0	0	0	0
Wohlers, p	0	0	0	0	0	0
Bream, 1b	1	1	1	3	1	0
Totals	33	10	11	10	27	3

Pittsburgh	1	0	0		1	0	0		1	0	0— 3
Atlanta	4	1	1		0	0	0		1	3	x—10

Pittsburgh	IP	H	R	ER	BB	SO
Smiley (L)	2	5	5	4	0	2
Landrum	1	2	1	1	2	2
Patterson	2	1	0	0	0	3
Kipper	2	2	1	1	0	1
Rodriguez	1	1	3	3	2	1

Atlanta	IP	H	R	ER	BB	SO
Smoltz (W)	6⅓	8	3	3	2	7
Stanton	*⅔	1	0	0	0	0
Wohlers	⅓	1	0	0	1	1
Pena (S)	1⅔	0	0	0	0	0

*Stanton pitched to one batter in eighth.

E—Merced, Bell. LOB—Pittsburgh 11, Atlanta 5. 2B—Bell, Buechele, Pendleton, Gant, Justice, Hunter. HR—Gant, Olson, Bream, Merced, Bell. SB—Bonds, Olson, Smoltz. CS—Smith, Justice. SH—Belliard. HBP—By Smiley (Smith). WP—Stanton. U—DeMuth, plate; Gregg, first; Davidson, second; Froemming, third; Harvey, left field; Pulli, right field. T—3:22. A—50,905.

BOX SCORE

SATURDAY, OCTOBER 12, AT ATLANTA

Pittsburgh	AB	R	H	RBI	PO	A
Merced, 1b	5	1	1	1	3	0
Rodriguez, p	0	0	0	0	0	0
Bell, ss	5	1	3	1	3	1
Van Slyke, cf	3	0	1	0	1	0
Bonilla, rf	5	0	0	0	1	0
Bonds, lf	5	1	1	0	1	0
Buechele, 3b	4	0	2	0	2	2
LaValliere, c	2	0	0	0	7	2
Slaught, ph-c	1	0	1	0	1	0
Lind, 2b	4	0	1	1	5	0
Smiley, p	0	0	0	0	0	1
Espy, ph	1	0	0	0	0	0

GAME 4

HIGHLIGHTS

PITTSBURGH 3, ATLANTA 2

Why the Pirates won: Someone finally came through in the clutch. No, it wasn't Barry Bonds, who blasted 25 home runs and drove in 116 runs in the regular season. No, it wasn't Bobby Bonilla, who socked 18 homers and knocked in 100 runs. And, no, it wasn't Andy Van Slyke, who was coming off a 17-homer, 83-RBI year. Instead, Pittsburgh's man of the hour was Mike LaValliere, who in 1991 had three homers and 41 RBIs. With the score tied, 2-2, Van Slyke drew a leadoff base on balls in the top of the 10th inning. After Bonilla and Bonds were retired, Van Slyke stole second base and Steve Buechele walked. With righthanded-hitting Don Slaught due up next, Braves Manager Bobby Cox summoned rookie righthander Mark Wohlers to replace lefthanded reliever Kent Mercker. Pirates Manager Jim Leyland countered with left-handed hitter LaValliere. After falling behind in the

count at 0-2, LaValliere then spanked a tie-breaking single to center.

Why the Braves lost: Perhaps more than anything, their luck ran out. Or the law of averages simply came into play. When LaValliere stepped into the batter's box with the game on the line, the Pirates had managed only six hits in 40 at-bats with runners in scoring position.

The turning points:

1. Braves right fielder Dave Justice's costly throwing error in the fifth inning. With two out and Atlanta nursing a 2-1 lead, Gary Redus singled and raced to third base on Jay Bell's base hit. Justice, thinking he had a play on Redus, threw wildly to third and Redus sped home with the tying run.

2. Pittsburgh second baseman Jose Lind's heads-up play in the seventh inning. With one out in the deadlocked game, Atlanta's Lonnie Smith tried to stretch a single into a double when his hit bounded off the glove of center fielder Van Slyke. However, Smith was thrown out at second when

Lind quickly came up with the ball and fired it to shortstop Bell.

Notable: Buechele went 3-for-3 and stretched his consecutive-hit streak to five at-bats, which tied a League Championship Series record. ... Pittsburgh's Bell lashed three hits, boosting his total to eight over four games. ... The left side of the Bucs' infield—Bell and third baseman Buechele—was 14-for-30 overall (.467) after Game 4. ... Among regulars on both teams, the lowest average thus far in the National League playoffs belonged to Terry Pendleton, the 1991 N.L. batting champion. Pendleton was struggling at .118 (2-for-17).

Quotable: "I was surviving," LaValliere said of the two-on, two-out, two-strike situation he faced as a pinch-hitter in the 10th inning. "I was basically trying to guard the plate and not overswing."

	AB	R	H	RBI	PO	A
McClendon, ph	1	0	0	0	0	0
Belinda, p	0	0	0	0	0	1
Totals	37	3	11	2	30	12
Atlanta	AB	R	H	RBI	PO	A
Smith, lf	4	1	2	0	4	0
Pendleton, 3b	5	0	1	0	1	2
Gant, cf	5	0	0	1	1	1
Justice, rf	4	1	1	0	3	0
Hunter, 1b	3	0	1	0	9	0
Bream, ph-1b	1	0	0	0	1	1
Olson, c	3	0	1	1	9	1
Lemke, 2b	3	0	0	0	0	1
Belliard, ss	3	0	1	0	2	3
Leibrandt, p	1	0	0	0	0	1
Clancy, p	0	0	0	0	0	0
Gregg, ph	1	0	0	0	0	0
Stanton, p	0	0	0	0	0	2
Willard, ph	1	0	0	0	0	0
Mercker, p	0	0	0	0	0	0
Wohlers, p	0	0	0	0	0	0
Totals	34	2	7	2	30	12

Pittsburgh	0 1 0	0 1 0	0 0 0	1—3		
Atlanta	2 0 0	0 0 0	0 0 0	0—2		

Pittsburgh	IP	H	R	ER	BB	SO
Tomlin	6	6	2	2	2	1
Walk	2	1	0	0	0	0
Belinda (W)	2	0	0	0	1	1
Atlanta	IP	H	R	ER	BB	SO
Leibrandt	6⅔	8	2	1	3	6
Clancy	⅓	0	0	0	0	0
Stanton	2	2	0	0	0	2
Mercker (L)	⅔	0	1	1	2	0
Wohlers	⅓	1	0	0	0	0

E—Bonds, Justice. DP—Atlanta 1. LOB—Pittsburgh 10, Atlanta 7. 2B—Smith. SB—Van Slyke. CS—Bell, Bonilla. SH—Belliard, Leibrandt, Buechele. U—Gregg, plate; Davidson, first; Froemming, second; Harvey, third; Pulli, left field; DeMuth, right field. T—3:43. A—51,109.

BOX SCORE

SUNDAY, OCTOBER 13, AT ATLANTA

Pittsburgh	AB	R	H	RBI	PO	A
Redus, 1b	5	1	1	0	13	0
Bell, ss	5	0	3	0	1	5
Van Slyke, cf	3	1	0	0	4	0
Bonilla, rf	3	1	1	0	4	0
Bonds, lf	5	0	1	0	3	0
Buechele, 3b	3	0	3	0	2	3
Slaught, c	4	0	1	1	1	0
LaValliere, ph-c	1	0	1	1	1	0
Lind, 2b	4	0	0	0	0	3
Tomlin, p	2	0	0	0	1	0
Wilkerson, ph	1	0	0	0	0	0
Walk, p	0	0	0	0	0	0

GAME 5

HIGHLIGHTS

PITTSBURGH 1, ATLANTA 0

Why the Pirates won: They got clutch pitching from starter Zane Smith and reliever Roger Mason, plus just enough offense to manufacture a victory. Smith yielded seven hits and one walk over 7⅔ innings, while Mason worked out of jams in both the eighth and ninth innings. Mason relieved Smith after Terry Pendleton belted a two-out triple in the eighth and got power-hitting Ron Gant to pop out, thereby protecting the Pirates' 1-0 lead. In the ninth, Mason created a mess instead of inheriting one. However, with runners on the corners and two out, he induced Jeff Blauser to fly out. Offensively, the Bucs parlayed a walk to Steve Buechele and singles by Don Slaught and Jose Lind into the game's only run in the fifth inning.

Why the Braves lost: By game's end, they had been held scoreless in 18 consecutive innings.

The turning points:

1. Tom Glavine's botched suicide-bunt attempt in the second inning. With the bases full of Braves and one out, the Atlanta pitcher missed the signal but saw baserunner Brian Hunter breaking from third and tried belatedly to bunt on a 2-2 pitch.

Glavine missed the pitch for strike three and Hunter was retired on a rundown play.

2. Dave Justice's baserunning blunder in the fourth inning. Perched on second base after Pirates first baseman Gary Redus fielded his ground ball and made a bad throw to Smith (covering first base), Justice set sail for home when Mark Lemke singled to left. However, Justice stumbled as he approached third base and lost his rhythm before continuing to the plate. While he eluded Slaught's tag at home after Barry Bonds' throw from left field, Justice was called out for missing third base en route.

Notable: The Braves' offense was in a deep sleep, to be sure. However, the Pirates' offense was in the process of going into the ultimate snooze. Yes, the Bucs' fifth-inning run was enough to win Game 5, but the Pirates—unbeknown to anyone, of course—would not score again in this series.

Quotable: "Man, I know I touched it," said Justice, reflecting on the fourth-inning play in which he missed third base. "It was ugly. I'm not saying it was good, but I did touch it. I felt it with my spikes." ... Bonds, commenting on his 3-for-20 performance at the plate through Game 5: "Yes, but it's a hard .150 (average)." Not really. Bonds' hits were all singles and he had zero runs batted in. . . . Pittsburgh's Bobby Bonilla was walked intentionally twice to get to Bonds, and the Braves' strategy paid off. Bonds was retired each time.

BOX SCORE
MONDAY, OCTOBER 14, AT ATLANTA

Pittsburgh	AB	R	H	RBI	PO	A
Redus, 1b	4	0	0	0	9	0
Bell, ss	4	0	2	0	4	5
Van Slyke, cf	4	0	1	0	2	0
Bonilla, rf	2	0	1	0	2	0
Bonds, lf	4	0	0	0	1	1
Buechele, 3b	3	1	0	0	2	1
Slaught, c	3	0	1	0	7	2
Lind, 2b	4	0	1	1	0	2
Z. Smith, p	3	0	0	0	0	2
Mason, p	1	0	0	0	0	0
Totals	32	1	6	1	27	13

Atlanta	AB	R	H	RBI	PO	A
L. Smith, lf	4	0	2	0	1	0
Pena, p	0	0	0	0	1	1
Pendleton, 3b	4	0	1	0	1	1
Gant, cf	4	0	1	0	3	0
Justice, rf	4	0	0	0	3	0
Hunter, 1b	3	0	1	0	5	0
Gregg, ph	1	0	1	0	0	0
Olson, c	3	0	1	0	8	0
Lemke, 2b	4	0	2	0	4	3
Belliard, ss	2	0	0	0	1	3
Blauser, ph-ss	2	0	0	0	0	0
Glavine, p	2	0	0	0	0	0
Mitchell, ph-lf	1	0	0	0	0	0
Totals	34	0	9	0	27	8

Pittsburgh						
Pittsburgh	0 0 0	0 1 0	0 0 0—1			
Atlanta	0 0 0	0 0 0	0 0 0—0			

Pittsburgh	IP	H	R	ER	BB	SO
Z. Smith (W)	7 2/3	7	0	0	1	5
Mason (S)	1 1/3	2	0	0	0	1

Atlanta	IP	H	R	ER	BB	SO
Glavine (L)	8	6	1	1	3	7
Pena	1	0	0	0	0	1

E—Redus, Lind, Blauser. DP—Pittsburgh 2, Atlanta 1. LOB—Pittsburgh 8, Atlanta 8. 2B—Bell, Van Slyke, Bonilla. 3B—Pendleton. SB—Gant, L. Smith. CS—Hunter. SH—Slaught. U—Davidson, plate; Froemming, first; Harvey, second; Pulli, third; DeMuth, left field; Gregg, right field. T—2:51. A—51,109.

GAME 6

HIGHLIGHTS
ATLANTA 1, PITTSBURGH 0

Why the Braves won: Young lefthander Steve Avery gave another strong impersonation of Sandy Koufax.

Why the Pirates lost: The Pittsburgh offense gave another strong impersonation of the Hitless Wonders.

The turning points:

1. The Braves' collective at-bat, ninth inning. With Avery and Doug Drabek waging a sterling pitchers' duel, as a 0-0 score would suggest, Atlanta broke through when Ron Gant drew a one-out walk, stole second with two out and then scooted home on Greg Olson's double down the third-base line. The run snapped a Braves scoreless streak that had reached 26 innings.

2. The Pirates' collective at-bat, ninth inning. Alejandro Pena again came to Avery's rescue, this time at the beginning of the bottom half of the ninth inning. (Avery had given way to a pinch-hitter in the top half.) Things got a bit sticky as pinch-hitter Gary Varsho banged a leadoff single and advanced to second on Orlando Merced's sacrifice. Jay Bell then lined out, but Varsho moved up another base on a wild pitch. Pena, as was the case in his relief of Avery in Game 2, had wild-pitched the potential tying run within 90 feet of home plate. But, as also was the case in Game 2, Pena proceeded to close the door on the Pirates. He got Andy Van Slyke on a called third strike.

Notable: After two League Championship Series starts, Avery boasted dazzling statistics: 16 1/3 innings pitched, no runs and nine hits allowed, four walks given up and 17 strikeouts recorded. His won-lost record: 2-0. . . . The 1-0 outcome in Game 6 was the third such score in this series. . . . Gant's steal of second base in the ninth inning was his sixth theft of the playoffs, an N.L. Championship Series record.

Quotable: "I don't think he's 21," said Pirates third baseman Steve Buechele, alluding to Avery and his cool, veteran-like approach. "I think he's lying." . . . "If I would have gone out and looked nervous, I think it would have shown," Avery said. "I think it relaxes everyone out there if they think I'm relaxed." . . . Gant, praising the gutty performance of fellow Victoria, Tex., native Drabek, who had to leave Game 1 after six innings because of a hamstring injury: "He's got more courage than any pitcher I've seen. He's out there on one leg and he still had good stuff." . . . Olson, on Pena's game-ending pitch that seemed to freeze Van Slyke: "That's the first changeup he's thrown this series."

BOX SCORE
WEDNESDAY, OCTOBER 16, AT PITTSBURGH

Atlanta	AB	R	H	RBI	PO	A
Smith, lf	3	0	2	0	1	1
Mitchell, lf	0	0	0	0	0	0
Treadway, 2b	3	0	1	0	2	2
Lemke, 2b	0	0	0	0	1	0
Pendleton, 3b	4	0	0	0	0	3
Justice, rf	4	0	0	0	2	0
Gant, cf	3	1	1	0	2	0
Bream, 1b	4	0	0	0	8	1
Olson, c	4	0	1	1	10	0
Belliard, ss	3	0	1	0	1	2
Avery, p	3	0	0	0	0	1
Gregg, ph	1	0	0	0	0	0
Pena, p	0	0	0	0	0	0
Totals	32	1	7	1	27	10

Pittsburgh	AB	R	H	RBI	PO	A
Redus, 1b	3	0	0	0	11	0
Merced, ph	0	0	0	0	0	0

	AB	R	H	RBI	PO	A
Bell, ss	4	0	0	0	1	3
Van Slyke, cf	3	0	0	0	2	0
Bonilla, rf	2	0	0	0	0	0
Bonds, lf	3	0	0	0	2	0
Buechele, 3b	3	0	1	0	0	3
Slaught, c	3	0	1	0	6	2
Lind, 2b	3	0	1	0	4	4
Drabek, p	2	0	0	0	1	0
Varsho, ph	1	0	1	0	0	0
Totals	27	0	4	0	27	12

Atlanta		0 0 0	0 0 0	0 0 1—1		
Pittsburgh		0 0 0	0 0 0	0 0 0—0		

Atlanta	IP	H	R	ER	BB	SO
Avery (W)	8	3	0	0	2	8
Pena (S)	1	1	0	0	0	1

Pittsburgh	IP	H	R	ER	BB	SO
Drabek (L)	9	7	1	1	3	5

DP—Atlanta 2. LOB—Atlanta 8, Pittsburgh 3. 2B—Smith 2, Olson. SB—Gant 2. CS—Smith. SH—Treadway, Merced. WP—Pena. U—Froemming, plate; Harvey, first; Pulli, second; DeMuth, third; Gregg, left field; Davidson, right field. T—3:09. A—54,508.

GAME 7

HIGHLIGHTS

ATLANTA 4, PITTSBURGH 0

Why the Braves won: Righthander John Smoltz endured a shaky first inning and pitched brilliantly the rest of the way, finishing with a six-hitter and eight strikeouts. Plus, Smoltz's teammates gave him immediate support, scoring three first-inning runs on Ron Gant's sacrifice fly and rookie Brian Hunter's two-run homer.

Why the Pirates lost: Lefthander John Smiley, a 20-game winner in 1991, didn't last through the first inning. Also rocked in Game 3, Smiley finished with a 0-2 record and 23.63 ERA in the League Championship Series.

The turning points:

1. When Andy Van Slyke rocketed a first-inning Smoltz pitch toward the right-field wall, it appeared that he might have connected for a game-tying home run (Orlando Merced and Jay Bell had singled ahead of him). However, the ball didn't carry well enough and nestled into the glove of airborne Dave Justice.

2. Barry Bonds' inability to deliver in the eighth inning. With the Braves' lead having grown to 4-0 after Hunter's run-scoring double in the fifth inning, the Pirates had a chance to make a game of it in the eighth when they put runners on the corners. But the struggling Bonds hit an inning-ending fly ball to left, an out that seemed to symbolize the frustration and futility of Pittsburgh's sluggers in this series.

Notable: In the 1990 N.L. Championship Series against Cincinnati, Pittsburgh's vaunted offense was held to a .194 team batting average and Pirate big guns Bonds, Van Slyke and Bobby Bonilla combined for only 12 hits in 63 at-bats (.190) with five RBIs over six games; bound and determined to atone in 1991 postseason play, the Pirates went out and hit .224 as a team against the Braves as Bonds, Van Slyke and Bonilla batted .200 with a scant three RBIs. . . . The Bucs failed to score in the last 22 innings of the '91 playoffs and were shut out in the last 27 innings played in their home ballpark, Three Rivers Stadium. . . . Gant boosted his playoff-record stolen-base total to seven with a fifth-inning steal of second. . . . Bell set a record for most hits (12) in a seven-game championship series. However, he fell short of the overall mark of 13, established by San Francisco's Will Clark in the five-game League Championship Series of 1989. . . . Despite pleasant weather, Game 7 attracted only 46,932 fans—more than 11,000 short of capacity.

Quotable: "You don't know what it feels like to finish in last place three straight years (as Atlanta did in 1988, 1989 and 1990)," Smoltz said. "I can't say enough about our management and (Manager) Bobby Cox." . . . "Last year, I felt we were shot in the leg," Van Slyke said of the Bucs' disappointing playoff showing against the Reds. "This year, I feel like I've been shot right through the heart."

BOX SCORE

THURSDAY, OCTOBER 17, AT PITTSBURGH

Atlanta	AB	R	H	RBI	PO	A
Smith, lf	3	1	0	0	1	0
Mitchell, lf	1	0	0	0	1	0
Pendleton, 3b	5	1	1	0	0	1
Gant, cf	3	1	1	1	4	0
Justice, rf	3	0	0	0	3	0
Hunter, 1b	4	1	2	3	5	2
Olson, c	3	0	1	0	8	0
Lemke, 2b	3	0	0	0	3	1
Belliard, ss	3	0	1	0	0	2
Smoltz, p	2	0	0	0	2	0
Totals	30	4	6	4	27	6

Pittsburgh	AB	R	H	RBI	PO	A
Merced, 1b	4	0	1	0	10	0
Bell, ss	4	0	2	0	1	1
Van Slyke, cf	4	0	0	0	3	1
Bonilla, rf	4	0	1	0	0	0
Bonds, lf	4	0	1	0	5	0
Buechele, 3b	4	0	0	0	1	0
LaValliere, c	3	0	1	0	6	1
Lind, 2b	4	0	0	0	1	5
Smiley, p	0	0	0	0	0	0
Walk, p	1	0	0	0	0	0
Espy, ph	1	0	0	0	0	0
Mason, p	0	0	0	0	0	0
Wilkerson, ph	1	0	0	0	0	0
Belinda, p	0	0	0	0	0	1
Totals	34	0	6	0	27	9

Atlanta		3 0 0	0 1 0	0 0 0—4		
Pittsburgh		0 0 0	0 0 0	0 0 0—0		

Atlanta	IP	H	R	ER	BB	SO
Smoltz (W)	9	6	0	0	1	8

Pittsburgh	IP	H	R	ER	BB	SO
Smiley (L)	⅔	3	3	3	1	1
Walk	4⅓	2	1	1	3	3

	IP	H	R	ER	BB	SO
Mason	2	1	0	0	1	0
Belinda	2	0	0	0	2	2

E—Lemke. LOB—Atlanta 8, Pittsburgh 8. 2B—Hunter,

Bonds. HR—Hunter. SB—Gant. SH—Smoltz. SF—Gant. Balk—Walk. U—Harvey, plate; Pulli, first; DeMuth, second; Gregg, third; Davidson, left field; Froemming, right field. T—3:04. A—46,932.

STATISTICS

ATLANTA BRAVES' BATTING AND FIELDING AVERAGES

					BATTING									FIELDING		
Player, position	G	AB	R	H	TB	2B	3B	HR	RBI	BB	IBB	SO	Avg.	PO	A	E	Avg.
Olson, c	7	24	3	8	12	1	0	1	4	4	0	3	.333	62	1	0	1.000
Hunter, 1b	5	18	2	6	11	2	0	1	4	0	0	2	.333	30	4	0	1.000
Treadway, 2b	1	3	0	1	1	0	0	0	0	0	0	0	.333	2	2	0	1.000
Bream, 1b-ph	4	10	1	3	6	0	0	1	3	0	0	1	.300	19	4	0	1.000
Gant, cf	7	27	4	7	11	1	0	1	3	2	0	4	.259	15	2	0	1.000
L. Smith, lf	7	24	3	6	9	3	0	0	4	0	0	5	.250	10	2	0	1.000
Glavine, p	2	4	0	1	1	0	0	0	0	0	0	2	.250	1	3	0	1.000
Gregg, ph	4	4	0	1	1	0	0	0	0	0	0	2	.250	0	0	0	.000
Belliard, ss	7	19	0	4	4	0	0	0	1	3	2	3	.211	9	15	1	.960
Justice, rf	7	25	4	5	9	1	0	1	2	3	0	7	.200	17	0	1	.944
Lemke, 2b	7	20	1	4	5	1	0	0	1	4	1	0	.200	12	10	1	.957
Smoltz, p	2	5	0	1	1	0	0	0	0	1	0	4	.200	3	0	0	1.000
Pendleton, 3b	7	30	1	5	8	1	0	1	1	0	0	3	.167	5	11	0	1.000
Avery, p	2	7	0	1	1	0	0	0	0	0	0	4	.143	1	2	0	1.000
Clancy, p	1	0	0	0	0	0	0	0	0	0	0	0	.000	0	0	0	.000
Mercker, p	1	0	0	0	0	0	0	0	0	0	0	0	.000	0	0	0	.000
Pena, p	4	0	0	0	0	0	0	0	0	0	0	0	.000	1	2	0	1.000
Stanton, p	3	0	0	0	0	0	0	0	0	0	0	0	.000	0	2	0	1.000
Wohlers, p	3	0	0	0	0	0	0	0	0	0	0	0	.000	0	0	0	.000
Leibrandt, p	1	1	0	0	0	0	0	0	0	0	0	0	.000	0	1	0	1.000
Blauser, ss-ph	2	2	0	0	0	0	0	0	0	0	0	0	.000	0	1	1	.500
Willard, ph	2	2	0	0	0	0	0	0	0	0	0	1	.000	0	0	0	.000
Mitchell, pr-lf-ph	5	4	0	0	0	0	0	0	0	0	0	1	.000	2	0	0	1.000
Totals	7	229	19	53	80	10	1	5	19	22	3	42	.231	189	62	4	.984

PITTSBURGH PIRATES' BATTING AND FIELDING AVERAGES

					BATTING									FIELDING		
Player, position	G	AB	R	H	TB	2B	3B	HR	RBI	BB	IBB	SO	Avg.	PO	A	E	Avg.
Varsho, ph	2	2	0	1	1	0	0	0	0	0	0	1	.500	0	0	0	.000
Bell, ss	7	29	2	12	17	2	0	1	1	0	0	10	.414	13	19	1	.970
LaValliere, c-ph	3	6	0	2	2	0	0	0	1	2	0	0	.333	14	3	0	1.000
Bonilla, rf	7	23	2	7	9	2	0	0	1	6	2	2	.304	12	1	0	1.000
Buechele, 3b	7	23	2	7	9	2	0	0	4	4	0	6	.304	8	14	0	1.000
Slaught, c-ph	6	17	0	4	4	0	0	0	1	1	1	4	.235	30	5	0	1.000
Merced, 1b-ph	3	9	1	2	5	0	0	1	1	0	0	1	.222	13	0	1	.929
Drabek, p	2	5	0	1	2	1	0	0	1	0	0	2	.200	3	0	0	1.000
Lind, 2b	7	25	0	4	4	0	0	0	3	0	0	6	.160	12	24	1	.973
Van Slyke, cf	7	25	3	4	9	2	0	1	2	5	0	5	.160	18	1	0	1.000
Redus, 1b	5	19	1	3	3	0	0	0	0	1	0	4	.158	51	0	2	.962
Bonds, lf	7	27	1	4	5	1	0	0	0	2	0	4	.148	14	1	1	.938
Belinda, p	3	0	0	0	0	0	0	0	0	0	0	0	.000	0	2	0	1.000
Kipper, p	1	0	0	0	0	0	0	0	0	0	0	0	.000	0	1	0	1.000
Landrum, p	1	0	0	0	0	0	0	0	0	0	0	0	.000	0	0	0	.000
Patterson, p	1	0	0	0	0	0	0	0	0	0	0	0	.000	0	0	0	.000
Rodriguez, p	1	0	0	0	0	0	0	0	0	0	0	0	.000	0	1	0	1.000
Smiley, p	2	0	0	0	0	0	0	0	0	0	0	0	.000	0	0	0	.000
Mason, p	3	1	0	0	0	0	0	0	0	0	0	1	.000	0	0	0	.000
Espy, ph	2	2	0	0	0	0	0	0	0	0	0	2	.000	0	0	0	.000
McClendon, ph-1b	3	2	0	0	0	0	0	0	0	0	0	0	.000	1	0	0	1.000
Tomlin, p	1	2	0	0	0	0	0	0	0	0	0	0	.000	0	0	0	.000
Walk, p	3	2	0	0	0	0	0	0	0	0	0	2	.000	0	0	0	.000
Wilkerson, ph	4	4	0	0	0	0	0	0	0	0	0	3	.000	0	0	0	.000
Z. Smith, p	2	5	0	0	0	0	0	0	0	0	0	4	.000	0	3	0	1.000
Totals	7	228	12	51	70	10	0	3	11	22	3	57	.224	189	75	6	.978

ATLANTA BRAVES' PITCHING RECORDS

Pitcher	G	GS	CG	IP	H	R	ER	HR	BB	IBB	SO	HB	WP	W	L	Pct.	ERA
Avery	2	2	0	16⅓	9	0	0	0	4	0	17	0	0	2	0	1.000	0.00
Pena	4	0	0	4⅓	1	0	0	0	0	0	4	0	0	0	0	.000	0.00
Wohlers	3	0	0	1⅔	3	0	0	0	1	0	1	0	0	0	0	.000	0.00
Clancy	1	0	0	⅓	0	0	0	0	0	0	0	0	0	0	0	.000	0.00
Leibrandt	1	1	0	6⅔	8	2	1	0	3	0	6	0	0	0	0	.000	1.35
Smoltz	2	2	1	15⅓	14	3	3	2	3	0	15	0	2	1	0	1.000	1.76
Stanton	3	0	0	3⅔	4	1	1	0	3	1	3	0	1	0	0	.000	2.45

— 185 —

Pitcher	G	GS	CG	IP	H	R	ER	HR	BB	IBB	SO	HB	WP	W	L	Pct.	ERA
Glavine	2	2	0	14	12	5	5	1	6	2	11	0	0	0	2	.000	3.21
Mercker	1	0	0	⅔	0	1	1	0	2	0	0	0	0	0	1	.000	13.50
Totals	7	7	1	63	51	12	11	3	22	3	57	0	3	4	3	.571	1.57

Shutouts—Avery and Pena 2 (combined); Smoltz. Saves—Pena 3.

PITTSBURGH PIRATES' PITCHING RECORDS

Pitcher	G	GS	CG	IP	H	R	ER	HR	BB	IBB	SO	HB	WP	W	L	Pct.	ERA
Belinda	3	0	0	5	0	0	0	0	3	0	4	0	0	1	0	1.000	0.00
Mason	3	0	0	4⅓	3	0	0	0	1	0	2	0	0	0	0	.000	0.00
Patterson	1	0	0	2	1	0	0	0	0	0	3	0	0	0	0	.000	0.00
Drabek	2	2	0	15	10	1	1	0	5	1	10	0	0	1	1	.500	0.60
Z. Smith	2	2	0	14⅔	15	1	1	0	3	1	10	1	0	1	1	.500	0.61
Walk	3	0	0	9⅓	5	2	2	1	3	0	5	0	0	0	0	.000	1.93
Tomlin	1	1	0	6	6	2	2	0	2	0	1	0	0	0	0	.000	3.00
Kipper	1	0	0	2	2	1	1	1	0	0	1	0	0	0	0	.000	4.50
Landrum	1	0	0	1	2	1	1	0	2	1	2	0	0	0	0	.000	9.00
Smiley	2	2	0	2⅔	8	8	7	2	1	0	3	1	0	0	2	.000	23.63
Rodriguez	1	0	0	1	1	3	3	1	2	0	1	0	0	0	0	.000	27.00
Totals	7	7	1	63	53	19	18	5	22	3	42	2	0	3	4	.429	2.57

Shutout—Z. Smith and Mason (combined). Saves—Walk, Mason.

COMPOSITE SCORE BY INNINGS

Team												
Atlanta	9	1	1	0	1	1		1	3	2	0—19
Pittsburgh	2	1	2	1	2	1		1	1	0	1—12

MISCELLANEOUS STATISTICS

Sacrifice hits—Belliard 2, Bell, Leibrandt, Buechele, Slaught, Treadway, Merced, Smoltz.

Sacrifice flies—Lind, Gant.

Stolen bases—Gant 7 Bonds 3, Redus 2, Olson, Smoltz, Van Slyke, L. Smith.

Caught stealing—L. Smith 2, Justice, Bell, Bonilla, Hunter.

Double plays—L. Smith and Olson; Lemke, Belliard and Hunter; Lind, Bell and Redus; Olson, Belliard, Hunter; Bell and Redus; Slaught and Buechele; Belliard, Lemke and Hunter; Bream and Belliard; Pendleton, Treadway and Bream.

Left on bases—Atlanta 6, 9, 5, 7, 8, 8, 8—51; Pittsburgh 7, 7, 11, 10, 8, 3, 8—54.

Hit by pitcher—By Z. Smith (Gant), by Smiley (L. Smith).

Passed balls—None.

Balk—Walk.

Time of games—First game, 2:52; second game, 2:46; third game, 3:22; fourth game, 3:43; fifth game, 2:51; sixth game, 3:09; seventh game, 3:04.

Attendance—First game, 57,347; second game, 57,533; third game, 50,905; fourth game, 51,109; fifth game, 51,109; sixth game, 54,508; seventh game, 46,932.

Umpires—Harvey, Pulli, DeMuth, Gregg, Davidson and Froemming.

Official scorers—Tony Krizmanich, Pittsburgh official scorer; Nick Peters, San Francisco Chronicle; Paul Newberry, Atlanta official scorer.

WORLD SERIES

HIGHLIGHTS

MINNESOTA 5, ATLANTA 2

Why the Twins won: In the battle of worst-to-first teams (Minnesota and Atlanta became the first modern big-league teams to go from last place to first from one season to the next), the American League champions put forth the superior veteran pitcher, with 36-year-old Jack Morris outdueling the Braves' Charlie Leibrandt, 35. Morris, coming off an 18-12 season, had gone 2-0 in the 1991 A.L. Championship Series and, entering the '91 World Series, boasted a career postseason record of 5-1; Leibrandt, 15-13 in 1991, pitched well in his lone '91 playoff appearance—a no-decision outing—but had been luckless overall in postseason play (a career mark of 1-4 despite a 3.09 ERA). Morris pitched seven-plus innings against the Braves, yielding only five hits and two runs. Leibrandt made it only three batters into the fifth inning, giving up seven hits and four runs.

Why the Braves lost: Only Ron Gant could solve Minnesota pitching. He collected three of the Braves' six hits and drove in both Atlanta runs.

The turning points:

1. Greg Gagne's three-run home run off Leibrandt in the fifth inning. Kent Hrbek (double into the gap in right-center) and Scott Leius (bloop single to left) were on base for the Twins, who were guarding a 1-0 lead at that juncture.

2. Chuck Knoblauch's all-around play for Minnesota, with his eighth-inning defensive gem standing out. Trying to protect a 5-1 advantage, Morris walked two batters to open the eighth and was replaced by Mark Guthrie. The Braves' Terry Pendleton followed with a hard grounder to the right of second baseman Knoblauch, whose sprawling stop marked the start of a double play. Offensively, Knoblauch, a .350 batsman in the A.L. playoffs, contributed three hits and two stolen bases.

Notable: Atlanta designated hitter Lonnie Smith became the first player in history to appear in World Series competition with four different teams (Phillies, 1980; Cardinals, 1982; Royals, 1985, and Braves, 1991).... Hrbek hit a mammoth home run for the Twins in the sixth inning, an upper-deck shot to right-center field off Jim Clancy.... After two innings of scoreless relief by Guthrie and Rick Aguilera, the Minnesota bullpen had not yielded an earned run in 20⅓ innings of postseason play in 1991.

Quotable: Hrbek, discussing his approach to the sixth-inning at-bat in which he launched his 440-foot homer: "I try to go to the plate every time with an empty mind and a full bat." ... Pendleton, on Knoblauch's eighth-inning fielding play that robbed him of a hit: "I haven't hit well in this whole playoff scenario (five hits in 34 at-bats). When I do hit one, someone is stepping in there."

BOX SCORE

SATURDAY, OCTOBER 19, AT MINNESOTA

Atlanta (N.L.)	AB	R	H	RBI	PO	A
Smith, dh	3	1	0	0	0	0
Treadway, 2b	3	1	1	0	1	3
Pendleton, 3b	4	0	0	0	1	2
Justice, rf	2	0	1	0	1	1
Gant, cf	4	0	3	2	1	0
Bream, 1b	4	0	0	0	8	1
Hunter, lf	4	0	0	0	1	1
Olson, c	3	0	1	0	7	1
Belliard, ss	1	0	0	0	2	3
bBlauser, ss	2	0	0	0	2	0
Leibrandt, p	0	0	0	0	0	1
Clancy, p	0	0	0	0	0	0
Wohlers, p	0	0	0	0	0	0
Stanton, p	0	0	0	0	0	0
Totals	30	2	6	2	24	13

Minnesota (A.L.)	AB	R	H	RBI	PO	A
Gladden, lf	2	1	0	0	7	0
Knoblauch, 2b	3	0	3	1	1	2
Puckett, cf	4	0	0	0	2	0
Davis, dh	3	0	0	0	0	0
Harper, c	4	0	2	0	1	2
Mack, rf	4	0	0	0	0	0
Hrbek, 1b	4	2	2	1	12	0
Leius, 3b	2	1	1	0	0	1
aPagliarulo, 3b	1	0	0	0	1	0
Gagne, ss	3	1	1	3	3	5
Morris, p	0	0	0	0	0	0
Guthrie, p	0	0	0	0	0	0
Aguilera, p	0	0	0	0	0	0
Totals	30	5	9	5	27	13

Atlanta	0 0 0	0 0 1	0 1 0—2			
Minnesota	0 0 1	0 3 1	0 0 x—5			

Atlanta	IP	H	R	ER	BB	SO
Leibrandt (L)	*4	7	4	4	1	3
Clancy	2	1	1	1	2	0
Wohlers	1	1	0	0	1	1
Stanton	1	0	0	0	0	2

Minnesota	IP	H	R	ER	BB	SO
Morris (W)	†7	5	2	2	4	3
Guthrie	⅔	0	0	0	1	0
Aguilera (S)	1⅓	1	0	0	0	0

*Pitched to three batters in fifth.
†Pitched to two batters in eighth.

Bases on balls—Off Leibrandt 1 (Gladden), off Clancy 2 (Knoblauch, Davis), off Wohlers 1 (Gladden), off Morris 4 (Justice, Olson, Smith, Treadway), off Guthrie 1 (Justice). Strikeouts—By Leibrandt 3 (Puckett 2, Gagne), by Wohlers 1 (Davis), by Stanton 2 (Mack, Hrbek), by Morris 3 (Treadway 2, Bream). aGrounded out for Leius in sixth. bFlied out for Belliard in seventh. E—Treadway, Gladden. DP—Atlanta 2, Minnesota 2. LOB—Atlanta 7, Minnesota 5. 2B—Harper, Hrbek. HR—Gagne, Hrbek. SB—Gladden, Knoblauch 2. CS—Gladden. SH—Belliard. U—Denkinger (A.L.), plate; Wendelstedt (N.L.), first; Coble (A.L.), second; Tata (N.L.), third; Reed (A.L.), left field; Montague (N.L.), right field. T—3:00. A—55,108.

PLAY BY PLAY

FIRST INNING

Atlanta—Smith lined to left. Treadway struck out and was thrown out at first when the pitch briefly got away from the catcher. Pendleton grounded to short.

Minnesota—Gladden fouled to first. Knoblauch singled to center. Knoblauch stole second. Puckett struck out. Davis grounded to the pitcher.

SECOND INNING

Atlanta—Justice flied to left. Gant singled to right. Bream flied to left. Hunter grounded to the pitcher.

Minnesota—Harper doubled to right. Mack lined to shortstop, who threw to second baseman for a double play. Hrbek grounded to second.

THIRD INNING

Atlanta—Olson singled center. Belliard sacrificed to the pitcher. Smith grounded to third, Olson went to third. Treadway struck out and was thrown out at first when the pitch briefly got away from the catcher.

Minnesota—Leius grounded to first. Gagne struck out. Gladden walked. Gladden stole second. Knoblauch singled, scoring Gladden. Knoblauch was out after the run scored, right fielder to first baseman to shortstop.

FOURTH INNING

Atlanta—Pendleton grounded to the pitcher. Justice walked. Gant flied to center. Bream flied to left.

Minnesota—Puckett struck out. Davis lined to third. Harper singled to right. Mack flied to right.

FIFTH INNING

Atlanta—Hunter flied to left. Olson walked. Belliard grounded into a double play, short to first.

Minnesota—Hrbek doubled to right-center. Leius singled to left, Hrbek went to third. Gagne homered to left, scoring Hrbek

and Leius. Clancy now pitching. Gladden reached on an error by the second baseman. Knoblauch walked, Gladden went to second. Puckett flied to center, Gladden went to third. Knoblauch stole second. Davis was walked intentionally. Harper flied to left and Gladden was out at the plate when the left fielder threw to the third baseman, who relayed it to the catcher.

SIXTH INNING

Atlanta—Smith grounded to second. Treadway singled to center. Pendleton popped to second. Justice singled to center, Treadway went to second. Gant singled left, scoring Treadway as Justice went to third. Gant went to second on the left fielder's throwing error. Bream struck out.

Minnesota—Mack grounded to second. Hrbek homered to right. Pagliarulo, pinch-hitting for Leius, grounded to short. Gagne grounded to short.

SEVENTH INNING

Atlanta—Pagliarulo now at third. Hunter grounded to short. Olson fouled to third. Blauser, pinch-hitting for Belliard, flied to left.

Minnesota—Wohlers now pitching and Blauser at short. Gladden walked. Gladden caught stealing, catcher to shortstop. Knoblauch singled off pitcher's leg. Puckett forced Knoblauch, second to short. Davis struck out.

EIGHTH INNING

Atlanta—Smith and Treadway walked. Guthrie now pitching. Pendleton grounded into a double play, second to short to first, as Smith went to third. Justice walked. Aguilera now pitching. Gant singled to left, scoring Smith as Justice went to third. Bream flied to center.

Minnesota—Stanton now pitching. Harper grounded to third. Mack and Hrbek struck out.

NINTH INNING

Atlanta—Hunter lined to short. Olson grounded to short. Blauser flied to left.

GAME 2

HIGHLIGHTS

MINNESOTA 3, ATLANTA 2

Why the Twins won: Another unsung player came through in big-time style. In Game 1, it was shortstop Greg Gagne, who slugged a three-run home run. In Game 2, it was Scott Leius, who had only 199 at-bats in the regular season as the right-handed-hitting half of Minnesota's third-base platoon. Batting against Braves 20-game winner Tom Glavine with the score tied at 2-2, Leius led off the bottom of the eighth inning by stroking a homer into the left-field seats.

Why the Braves lost: Glavine, 0-2 in the 1991 National League Championship Series despite a 3.21 ERA, again pitched just well enough to lose. In eight innings against the Twins, he yielded only four hits—but two of them were homers that accounted for all of Minnesota's runs.

The turning points:

1. When the Twins' first hitter of the game, Dan Gladden, reached base on an error. Gladden sent a popup into short right field, with second baseman Mark Lemke and right fielder Dave Justice converging on the ball. As the Metrodome din drowned out either player's call for the ball, Lemke and Justice collided and the ball fell out of Lemke's glove. Justice was charged with a two-base error,

the Braves were a bit unnerved and the Twins had a threat going immediately. Chuck Knoblauch followed with a walk before Kirby Puckett hit a ground ball to third base. Terry Pendleton stepped on third and then rifled the ball to first for a double play. Just when it seemed that Glavine might escape the first-inning jam, Minnesota cleanup hitter Chili Davis strode to the plate and drilled a homer to left. Twins 2, Braves 0.

2. When the Braves' Ron Gant tried to scurry back to first base after a third-inning single. The two-out base hit sent Lonnie Smith, aboard via an error, to third base and seemed to give the Braves, down 2-1 at that point, a real chance at a productive inning. However, as Gant tried to retreat to first after rounding the bag, 250-pound first baseman Kent Hrbek took a throw from pitcher Kevin Tapani and seemed to lift the 172-pound Gant off the base while applying a tag. Umpire Drew Coble ruled that momentum had carried Gant off the bag and called the baserunner out. End of rally, end of inning.

Notable: The victory improved the Twins' postseason record at the Metrodome to 9-1. . . . Of the Twins' eight runs thus far in the '91 World Series, seven were driven in with home runs.

Quotable: Hrbek, discussing his body slam on Gant and speaking with a relatively straight face: "I just kept my glove on his foot and he came off the base. Did I help him? No, not at all." ... Gant's view: "I felt the whole force of him pulling me off the bag. He was definitely trying to pull me off the bag. When I was on the base, I was kind of falling back and he just grabbed me. I still don't understand the call. How can you pull a player off the base?" ... "It was a hell of a heads-up play by him (Hrbek)," Braves first-base coach Pat Corrales said.

BOX SCORE

SUNDAY, OCTOBER 20, AT MINNESOTA

Atlanta (N.L.)	AB	R	H	RBI	PO	A
Smith, dh	3	0	0	0	0	0
Pendleton, 3b	4	0	2	0	1	4
Gant, cf	4	0	1	0	2	0
Justice, rf	4	1	1	0	1	0
Bream, 1b	4	0	1	0	12	0
Hunter, lf	3	0	1	1	0	0
Olson, c	4	1	1	0	6	0
Lemke, 2b	3	0	0	0	2	5
aGregg	1	0	0	0	0	0
Belliard, ss	2	0	1	1	0	3
Glavine, p	0	0	0	0	0	1
Totals	32	2	8	2	24	13

Minnesota (A.L.)	AB	R	H	RBI	PO	A
Gladden, lf	4	0	0	0	5	1
Knoblauch, 2b	3	1	0	0	1	3
Puckctt, cf	4	0	0	0	2	0
Davis, dh	3	1	1	2	0	0
Harper, c	2	0	1	0	7	0
Mack, rf	3	0	0	0	3	0
Hrbek, 1b	2	0	0	0	8	2
Leius, 3b	3	1	1	1	0	2
Gagne, ss	3	0	1	0	1	2
Tapani, p	0	0	0	0	0	1
Aguilera, p	0	0	0	0	0	0
Totals	27	3	4	3	27	11

Atlanta	0 1 0	0 1 0	0 0 0—2
Minnesota	2 0 0	0 0 0	0 1 x—3

Atlanta	IP	H	R	ER	BB	SO
Glavine (L)	8	4	3	1	3	6

Minnesota	IP	H	R	ER	BB	SO
Tapani (W)	8	7	2	2	0	3
Aguilera (S)	1	1	0	0	0	3

Bases on balls—Off Glavine 3 (Knoblauch, Harper, Hrbek). Strikeouts—By Glavine 6 (Mack 2, Gladden, Puckett, Gagne, Hrbek), by Tapani 3 (Pendleton, Lemke, Hunter), by Aguilera 3 (Bream, Olson, Gregg). aStruck out for Lemke in ninth. E—Justice, Leius. DP—Atlanta 2. LOB—Atlanta 6, Minnesota 3. 2B—Bream, Olson. HR—Davis, Leius. SH—Smith. SF—Hunter, Belliard. Balk—Glavine. U—Wendelstedt (N.L.), plate; Coble (A.L.), first; Tata (N.L.), second; Reed (A.L.), third; Montague (N.L.), left field; Denkinger (A.L.), right field. T—2:37. A—55,145.

PLAY BY PLAY

FIRST INNING

Atlanta—Smith flied to left. Pendleton struck out. Gant grounded to third.

Minnesota—Gladden reached on a two-base error by the right fielder. Knoblauch walked. Puckett grounded into a double play, third to first, Knoblauch went to second. Davis homered to left, scoring Knoblauch. Harper walked. Mack grounded to second, forcing Harper.

SECOND INNING

Atlanta—Justice singled to right. Bream doubled to left, Justice went to third. Hunter hit a sacrifice fly to right, scoring Justice. Olson grounded to short. Lemke struck out.

Minnesota—Hrbek walked. Leius grounded into a double play, pitcher to second to first. Gagne grounded to short.

THIRD INNING

Atlanta—Belliard grounded to second. Smith reached on an error by the third baseman. Pendleton flied to center. Gant singled to left, Smith went to third. Gant was out after taking a big turn at first base, as the left fielder threw to the pitcher, who relayed the ball to the first baseman.

Minnesota—Gladden struck out. Knoblauch grounded to second. Puckett struck out.

FOURTH INNING

Atlanta—Justice flied to left. Bream popped to left. Hunter grounded to third.

Minnesota—Davis grounded to second. Harper grounded to third. Mack struck out.

FIFTH INNING

Atlanta—Olson doubled to left-center. Lemke grounded to second, Olson went to third. Belliard hit a sacrifice fly to right, scoring Olson. Smith flied to right.

Minnesota—Hrbek lined to right. Leius flied to center. Gagne struck out.

SIXTH INNING

Atlanta—Pendleton singled to left. Gant popped to center. Justice forced Pendleton, first to short. Bream grounded to second.

Minnesota—Gladden grounded to second. Knoblauch grounded to third. Puckett grounded to short.

SEVENTH INNING

Atlanta—Hunter struck out. Olson grounded to short. Lemke flied to left.

Minnesota—Davis grounded to third. Harper singled to left. Mack and Hrbek struck out.

EIGHTH INNING

Atlanta—Belliard hit a bunt single to third. Smith sacrificed Belliard, first baseman to second baseman covering the first base bag. Pendleton singled to right, Belliard went to third. Gant grounded to the catcher. Justice flied to left.

Minnesota—Leius homered to left. Gagne singled off the pitcher's foot. Gladden flied to center. Gagne went to second on a balk. Knoblauch grounded to second, Gagne went to third. Puckett grounded to short.

NINTH INNING

Atlanta—Aguilera now pitching. Bream struck out. Hunter singled to center. Olson struck out. Gregg, pinch-hitting for Lemke, struck out.

GAME 3

HIGHLIGHTS

ATLANTA 5, MINNESOTA 4

Why the Braves won: Second baseman Mark Lemke, whose error in the top of the 12th inning put At- lanta in a precarious position, delivered a two-out, game-winning single off Minnesota relief ace Rick Aguilera in the last of the 12th. With Atlanta's Dave Justice on second base after a single and a stolen base and Greg Olson on first via a walk,

Lemke rammed a single into left field. Justice, ever-mindful of his baserunning blunder in Game 5 of the N.L. playoffs, made sure he touched third base this time and then slid around catcher Brian Harper's tag after Harper had taken the throw from Dan Gladden.

Why the Twins lost: Minnesota starter Scott Erickson, who struggled in the second half of the season despite winning 20 games overall, was shaky once more, being tagged for five hits and four runs (three earned) in 4⅔ innings. Also, Twins slugger Kent Hrbek struck out in a key at-bat, going down against reliever Kent Mercker in the top of the 12th with one out and runners at the corners (Gladden had singled and advanced to third when Chuck Knoblauch reached base on Lemke's error). And the Minnesota bullpen finally gave up an earned run, doing so at a most inopportune time—in the game-deciding bottom of the 12th.

The turning points:

1. With Minnesota runners on first and second and two out in the 10th inning, reliever Mike Stanton kept the Braves in a 4-4 deadlock by striking out pinch-hitter Paul Sorrento.

2. Twins Manager Tom Kelly, unaccustomed to managing without the designated-hitter rule (the DH isn't used in World Series games played in National League ballparks), used all of his position players by the end of the 11th inning and had to employ reliever Aguilera as a pinch-hitter with the bases loaded and two out in the 12th. Aguilera was retired on a fly ball.

Notable: This was the first World Series game ever played in Atlanta. ... Braves lefthander Steve Avery, who was overwhelming in the N.L. playoffs, was merely outstanding in this game. He was nicked for four hits and three runs (two earned) in seven-plus innings.

Quotable: Lemke, reflecting on his game-winning hit, cracked: "As long as (Justice) touched third base, I was happy." ... Lemke said that while he felt no pressure to atone for his fielding misplay in the top of the 12th, "I thought it would be pretty damn good if I did." ... Hrbek received a not-so-warm welcome to Atlanta. With the Hrbek/Gant caper fresh in the minds of Braves fans, Minnesota's hulking first baseman heard the chant "Cheater, Cheater" as he walked to the plate in the first inning.

	AB	R	H	RBI	PO	A
dPagliarulo, 3b	1	0	0	0	0	0
jNewman, 3b	1	0	0	0	0	0
Gagne, ss	5	0	0	0	1	3
Ortiz, c	2	0	1	0	5	0
bHarper, c	3	1	1	0	1	0
Erickson, p	1	0	0	0	1	0
West, p	0	0	0	0	0	0
Leach, p	0	0	0	0	0	0
aLarkin	1	0	1	0	0	0
Bedrosian, p	0	0	0	0	0	1
cDavis	1	1	1	2	0	0
Brown, rf	0	0	0	0	0	0
eBush, rf	2	0	0	0	0	0
Totals	47	4	10	4	35	11

Atlanta (N.L.)	AB	R	H	RBI	PO	A
Smith, lf	4	1	1	1	1	0
Mitchell, lf	2	0	0	0	0	0
Pendleton, 3b	4	1	0	0	0	3
Gant, cf	6	0	0	0	4	0
Justice, rf	6	2	2	1	6	0
Bream, 1b	3	0	1	0	7	0
hHunter, 1b	2	0	0	0	0	0
Olson, c	3	1	1	1	14	0
Lemke, 2b	5	0	2	1	3	1
Bellaird, ss	3	0	1	1	1	2
iBlauser, ss	1	0	0	0	0	0
Avery, p	3	0	0	0	0	0
Pena, p	0	0	0	0	0	0
fTreadway	0	0	0	0	0	0
Stanton, p	0	0	0	0	0	0
kCabrera	1	0	0	0	0	0
Wohlers, p	0	0	0	0	0	0
Mercker, p	0	0	0	0	0	0
Clancy, p	0	0	0	0	0	0
Totals	43	5	8	5	36	6

Minnesota .... 1 0 0 0 0 0 1 2 0 0 0 0—4
Atlanta .... 0 1 0 1 2 0 0 0 0 0 0 1—5
Two out when winning run scored.

Minnesota	IP	H	R	ER	BB	SO
Erickson	4⅔	5	4	3	2	3
West	*0	0	0	0	2	0
Leach	⅓	0	0	0	0	1
Bedrosian	2	0	0	0	0	1
Willis	2	0	0	0	2	0
Guthrie	2	1	0	0	1	1
Aguilera (L)	⅔	2	1	1	1	1

Atlanta	IP	H	R	ER	BB	SO
Avery	†7	4	3	2	0	5
Pena	2	4	1	1	0	4
Stanton	2	1	0	0	1	3
Wohlers	⅓	1	0	0	0	0
Mercker	⅓	0	0	0	0	1
Clancy (W)	⅓	0	0	0	1	0

*Pitched to two batters in fifth.
†Pitched to one batter in eighth.

Bases on balls—Off Erickson 2 (Olson, Pendleton), off West 2 (Bream, Olson), off Willis 2 (Belliard, Pendleton), off Guthrie 1 (Lemke), off Aguilera 1 (Olson).

Strikeouts—By Erickson 3 (Smith, Justice, Avery), by Leach 1 (Lemke), by Bedrosian 1 (Avery), by Guthrie 1 (Mitchell), by Avery 5 (Puckett, Mack, Leius, Gladden, Erickson), by Pena 4 (Puckett, Mack, Pagliarulo, Bush), by Stanton 3 (Hrbek, Sorrento, Gagne), by Mercker 1 (Hrbek).

aSingled for Leach in sixth. bReached base on error for Ortiz in eighth. cHomered for Bedrosian in eighth. dStruck out for Leius in ninth. eStruck out for Brown in ninth. fSacrificed for Pena in ninth. gStruck out for Willis in 10th. hGrounded out for Bream in 10th. iPopped out for Belliard in 10th. jPopped out for Pagliarulo in 11th. kLined out for Stanton in 11th. lFlied out for Guthrie in 12th. E—Knoblauch, Pendleton, Lemke. LOB—Minnesota 10, Atlanta 12. 2B—Bream, Olson.

BOX SCORE

TUESDAY, OCTOBER 22, AT ATLANTA

Minnesota (A.L.)	AB	R	H	RBI	PO	A
Gladden, lf	6	1	3	0	2	0
Knoblauch, 2b	5	0	1	1	5	3
Hrbek, 1b	6	0	1	0	12	2
Puckett, cf	4	1	1	1	3	0
Mack, rf	4	0	0	0	3	0
Willis, p	0	0	0	0	0	0
gSorrento	1	0	0	0	0	0
Guthrie, p	0	0	0	0	0	1
lAguilera, p	1	0	0	0	0	0
Leius, 3b	3	0	0	0	2	1

3B—Gladden. HR—Justice, Smith, Puckett, Davis. SB—Knoblauch, Justice. SH—Treadway. SF—Knoblauch. U—Coble (A.L.), plate; Tata (N.L.), first; Reed (A.L.), second; Montague (N.L.), third; Denkinger (A.L.), left field; Wendelstedt (N.L.), right field. T—4:04. A—50,878.

PLAY BY PLAY

FIRST INNING

Minnesota—Gladden tripled to right. Knoblauch hit a sacrifice fly to right, scoring Gladden. Hrbek grounded to short. Puckett struck out.

Atlanta—Smith struck out. Pendleton lined to right. Gant grounded to short.

SECOND INNING

Minnesota—Mack and Leius struck out. Gagne fouled to the catcher.

Atlanta—Justice struck out. Bream lined to first. Olson walked. Lemke singled to right, Olson went to second. Belliard singled to left, scoring Olson, as Lemke went to third. Belliard went to second on the throw home. Avery grounded to second.

THIRD INNING

Minnesota—Ortiz popped to short. Erickson and Gladden struck out.

Atlanta—Smith fouled to right. Pendleton grounded to second. Gant flied to right.

FOURTH INNING

Minnesota—Knoblauch grounded to third. Hrbek flied to center. Puckett flied to right.

Atlanta—Justice homered to right. Bream doubled to right. Olson grounded to short. Lemke grounded to first baseman, who tossed to the pitcher covering first. Belliard grounded to second.

FIFTH INNING

Minnesota—Mack flied to right. Leius popped to second. Gagne grounded to short.

Atlanta—Avery struck out. Smith homered to left. Pendleton walked. Gant popped to second. Pendleton went to second on a wild pitch. Justice reached on an error by the second baseman, Pendleton went to third. West now pitching. Bream walked, Justice went to second. Olson walked, scoring Pendleton, as Justice went to third and Bream to second. Leach now pitching. Lemke struck out.

SIXTH INNING

Minnesota—Ortiz singled. Larkin, pinch-hitting for Leach, singled to left, Ortiz went to second. Gladden flied to left, Ortiz went to third. Knoblauch fouled to first. Hrbek flied to center.

Atlanta—Bedrosian now pitching. Belliard grounded to short. Avery struck out. Smith grounded to the pitcher.

SEVENTH INNING

Minnesota—Puckett homered to left. Mack grounded to third. Leius flied to right. Gagne popped to second.

Atlanta—Pendleton popped to third. Gant flied to left. Justice grounded to first.

EIGHTH INNING

Minnesota—Mitchell now in left. Harper, pinch-hitting for Ortiz, reached base on an error by the third baseman. Pena now pitching. Davis, pinch-hitting for Bedrosian, homered to left, scoring Harper. Gladden grounded to third. Knoblauch singled to right. Hrbek singled to center, Knoblauch went to third. Puckett and Mack struck out.

Atlanta—Willis now pitching, Harper catching and Brown in right. Bream popped center. Olson grounded to third. Lemke popped to third.

NINTH INNING

Minnesota—Pagliarulo, pinch-hitting for Leius, struck out. Gagne flied to right. Harper singled to center. Harper went to second on a wild pitch. Bush, pinch-hitting for Brown, struck out.

Atlanta—Pagliarulo now at third, Bush in right. Belliard walked. Treadway, pinch-hitting for Pena, sacrificed Belliard to second, first baseman to second baseman. Mitchell flied to center. Pendleton was walked intentionally. Gant lined to short.

10TH INNING

Minnesota—Stanton now pitching. Gladden singled to center. Knoblauch grounded to second, Gladden went to second. Hrbek struck out. Puckett was walked intentionally. Sorrento, pinch-hitting for Mack, struck out.

Atlanta—Guthrie now pitching. Justice flied to left. Hunter, pinch-hitting for Bream, grounded to the pitcher. Olson doubled to left-center. Lemke walked. Blauser, pinch-hitting for Belliard, popped to second.

11TH INNING

Minnesota—Hunter now at first and Blauser at short. Newman, pinch-hitting for Pagliarulo, popped to second. Gagne struck out. Harper flied to right.

Atlanta—Newman now at third. Cabrera, pinch-hitting for Stanton, lined to second. Mitchell struck out. Pendleton grounded to first.

12TH INNING

Minnesota—Wohlers now pitching. Bush flied to center. Gladden singled to right. Knoblauch reached on an error by the second baseman, Gladden went to third. Mercker now pitching. Hrbek struck out. Knoblauch stole second. Clancy now pitching. Puckett was walked intentionally. Aguilera, pinch-hitting for Guthrie, flied to center.

Atlanta—Aguilera now pitching. Gant flied to center. Justice singled to right. Hunter popped to second. Justice stole second. Olson walked. Lemke singled to left, scoring Justice.

GAME 4

HIGHLIGHTS

ATLANTA 3, MINNESOTA 2

Why the Braves won: Mark Lemke, not exactly a household name before this World Series, was fast becoming known in more than a few homes around America. The hero of Game 3 when he poked a decisive base hit to left field in the 12th inning, Lemke came to bat in the ninth inning of Game 4 with the score tied, 2-2, and drilled a one-out triple to left-center field. After Twins lefthanded reliever Mark Guthrie issued an intentional base on balls to Jeff Blauser, Braves Manager Bobby Cox sent up righthanded-hitting Francisco Cabrera to bat for bullpenner Mike Stanton. Twins Manager Tom Kelly then opted for righthander Steve Bedrosian, and Cox countered with lefthanded batter Jerry Willard. Once the managerial strategy had been played out, journeyman Willard, a 31-year-old catcher who had only three major league hits in 1991, drove a fly ball to right field. Shane Mack made the catch and followed with a strong throw to the plate, but Lemke slid past catcher Brian Harper and was called safe. While Harper begged to differ, the Braves proceeded to celebrate. The Series had been deadlocked.

Why the Twins lost: While third baseman Mike Pagliarulo went 3-for-3 (including a homer) and knocked in both of Minnesota's runs, the rest of the Twins contributed a measly four hits in 30 at-bats against Atlanta starter John Smoltz and relievers Mark Wohlers and Stanton. Also, Twins relievers Carl Willis and Guthrie couldn't fend off the Braves in the late going after Minnesota starter Jack Morris left with a 2-1 lead. Morris had allowed just one run and six hits over six innings.

The turning points:

1. While not crucial in a game-deciding sense, Harper's two fifth-inning defensive plays nonetheless kept Minnesota in the game at 1-1. After Atlanta's Lonnie Smith singled and stole second in the fifth, Terry Pendleton rapped a double to center field. Smith streaked for home on the play and, under a full head of steam, crashed into catcher Harper, who already had caught the relay throw and was braced for the impact. It was not a scene for the fainthearted. Harper somehow held onto the ball, though, and Smith was called out. Moments later, Pendleton tried to score from third on a wild pitch but was tagged out by Harper, who retrieved the ball and made a successful lunge at the Braves' baserunner.

2. A game-tying home run in the seventh inning by Atlanta's Smith.

Notable: Besides his ninth-inning triple, Lemke also singled and doubled for the Braves. . . . When the 24-year-old Smoltz was growing up in Michigan, his favorite player was Morris, a Detroit standout for a decade and Smoltz's mound opponent in this game.

Quotable: "I knew I couldn't go around him," said Smith, alluding to his crunching fifth-inning pileup with Harper. "And I knew I couldn't go under him because he was down. When I came to bat the next time, he (Harper) said it was the hardest he'd ever been hit. I told him, 'Don't feel bad because I'm not feeling that great either.' "

BOX SCORE

WEDNESDAY, OCTOBER 23, AT ATLANTA

Minnesota (A.L.)	AB	R	H	RBI	PO	A
Gladden, lf	4	0	0	0	6	0
Knoblauch, 2b	3	0	1	0	0	2
Puckett, cf	4	0	1	0	2	1
Hrbek, 1b	4	0	0	0	6	0
Harper, c	4	1	2	0	8	0
Mack, rf	4	0	0	0	3	0
Pagliarulo, 3b	3	1	3	2	0	2
eLeius, 3b	1	0	0	0	0	0
Bedrosian, p	0	0	0	0	0	0
Gagne, ss	3	0	0	0	0	2
Morris, p	2	0	0	0	1	1
aLarkin	1	0	0	0	0	0
Willis, p	0	0	0	0	0	0
Guthrie, p	0	0	0	0	0	0
Newman, 3b	0	0	0	0	0	0
Totals	33	2	7	2	26	8

Atlanta (N.L.)	AB	R	H	RBI	PO	A
Smith, lf	4	1	2	1	1	0
Pendleton, 3b	4	1	2	1	0	1
Gant, cf	3	0	1	0	3	0
Justice, rf	3	0	0	0	4	0
Bream, 1b	3	0	0	0	10	1
dHunter, 1b	1	0	0	0	0	0
Olson, c	3	0	0	0	6	3
Lemke, 2b	4	1	3	0	1	2
Bellaird, ss	2	0	0	0	1	4
bTreadway	1	0	0	0	0	0
Blauser, ss	0	0	0	0	0	0
Smoltz, p	2	0	0	0	1	0
cGregg	1	0	0	0	0	0
Wohlers, p	0	0	0	0	0	0
Stanton, p	0	0	0	0	0	0
fCabrera	0	0	0	0	0	0
gWillard	0	0	0	1	0	0
Totals	31	3	8	3	27	11

Minnesota ....0 1 0 0 0 0 1 0 0—2
Atlanta ....0 0 1 0 0 0 1 0 1—3

Two out when winning run scored.

Minnesota	IP	H	R	ER	BB	SO
Morris	6	6	1	1	3	4
Willis	1⅓	1	1	1	0	1
Guthrie (L)	1	1	1	1	1	1
Bedrosian	⅓	0	0	0	0	0

Atlanta	IP	H	R	ER	BB	SO
Smoltz	7	7	2	2	0	7
Wohlers	⅓	0	0	0	1	0
Stanton (W)	1⅔	0	0	0	0	1

Bases on balls—Off Morris 3 (Olson, Justice, Gant), off Guthrie 1 (Blauser), off Wohlers 1 (Knoblauch).

Strikeouts—By Morris 4 (Bream, Smoltz, Smith, Olson), by Willis 1 (Gregg), by Guthrie 1 (Justice), by Smoltz 7 (Gagne 3, Mack 2, Morris, Knoblauch).

aGrounded out for Morris in seventh. bFlied out for Belliard in seventh. cStruck out for Smoltz in seventh. dFlied out for Bream in eighth. eLined out for Pagliarulo in ninth. fAnnounced for Stanton in ninth. gHit sacrifice fly for Cabrera in ninth. LOB—Minnesota 5, Atlanta 7. 2B—Knoblauch, Harper, Pendleton, Lemke. 3B—Lemke. HR—Pendleton, Pagliarulo, Smith. SB—Gant, Smith, Knoblauch. CS—Mack. SF—Willard. WP—Morris. U—Tata (N.L.), plate; Reed (A.L.), first; Montague (N.L.), second; Denkinger (A.L.), third; Wendelstedt (N.L.), left field; Coble (A.L.), right field. T—2:57. A—50,878.

PLAY BY PLAY

FIRST INNING

Minnesota—Gladden grounded to short. Knoblauch doubled to right. Puckett flied to right. Hrbek grounded to the first baseman, who tossed to the pitcher covering.

Atlanta—Smith flied to center. Pendleton flied to left. Gant grounded to third.

SECOND INNING

Minnesota—Harper doubled to right. Mack struck out. Pagliarulo singled to left, scoring Harper. Pagliarulo went to second on the throw home. Gagne and Morris struck out.

Atlanta—Justice grounded to short. Bream struck out. Olson walked. Lemke singled to left-center, Olson went to second. Belliard fouled out to right.

THIRD INNING

Minnesota—Gladden and Knoblauch flied to center. Puckett singled to left. Hrbek popped to short.

Atlanta—Smoltz and Smith struck out. Pendleton homered to right. Gant singled to left. Gant stole second. Gant went to third on a wild pitch. Justice walked. Bream grounded to the pitcher, unassisted.

FOURTH INNING

Minnesota—Harper singled to left-center. Mack forced Harper, shortstop to second baseman. Pagliarulo singled to left, Mack went to third. On a failed squeeze, Mack was

— 192 —

caught stealing on a tag by the catcher. Gagne struck out and was thrown out at first when the pitch briefly got away from the catcher.

Atlanta—Olson struck out. Lemke doubled to right-center. Belliard flied to left. Smoltz grounded to second.

FIFTH INNING

Minnesota—Morris grounded to short. Gladden flied to center. Knoblauch struck out.

Atlanta—Smith singled to right. Smith stole second. Pendleton doubled to center, but Smith was out at the plate, center fielder to second baseman to catcher. Pendleton went to third on the play. Gant walked. Morris bounced a pitch which briefly got away from the catcher. Pendleton broke for home, but was tagged out by the catcher, as Gant went to second. Justice flied out to left.

SIXTH INNING

Minnesota—Puckett and Hrbek grounded to second. Harper grounded to short.

Atlanta—Bream flied to left. Olson grounded to the pitcher. Lemke flied to center.

SEVENTH INNING

Minnesota—Mack struck out. Pagliarulo homered to right.

Gagne struck out and was thrown out at first when the pitch briefly got away from the catcher. Larkin, pinch-hitting for Morris, grounded to first.

Atlanta—Willis now pitching. Treadway, pinch-hitting for Belliard, flied to left. Gregg, pinch-hitting for Smoltz, struck out. Smith homered to center. Pendleton flied to left.

EIGHTH INNING

Minnesota—Wohlers now pitching and Blauser at short. Gladden grounded to third. Knoblauch walked. Stanton now pitching. Puckett flied to right. Hrbek struck out and was thrown out at first when the pitch briefly got away from the catcher.

Atlanta—Gant grounded to third. Guthrie now pitching. Justice struck out. Hunter, pinch-hitting for Bream, flied to right.

NINTH INNING

Minnesota—Harper and Mack flied to right. Leius, pinch-hitting for Pagliarulo, flied to left.

Atlanta—Olson grounded to short. Lemke tripled to left. Blauser was walked intentionally. Cabrera was announced as a pinch-hitter for Stanton. Bedrosian now pitching and Newman at third. Willard, pinch-hitting for Cabrera, hit a sacrifice fly to right, scoring Leius.

GAME 5

HIGHLIGHTS
ATLANTA 14, MINNESOTA 5

Why the Braves won: They came out swinging—and connecting. Atlanta teed off on Kevin Tapani, Terry Leach, David West, Steve Bedrosian and Carl Willis for 17 hits, including two doubles, three triples and three home runs. Seven Atlanta players had two or more hits, while no Minnesota player had more than one.

Why the Twins lost: Tapani was ineffective, to be sure. But Minnesota's bullpen, impenetrable for most of postseason play in 1991, really unraveled in this game at Atlanta-Fulton County Stadium. The Twins' relievers gave up 11 hits and 10 earned runs in four innings.

The turning points:

1. When Atlanta hit the Twins with a four-run fourth—Dave Justice's two-run homer was the big blow—in a game that was scoreless to that point and had all the earmarks of another nail-biter.

2. When Atlanta hit the Twins with a six-run seventh after Minnesota had tried to make a game of it with a three-run sixth. Lonnie Smith triggered the Braves' outburst with his third homer in three games, and hot-as-a-firecracker Mark Lemke smashed a two-run triple to highlight the proceedings.

Notable: Lemke also tripled in a run in the fourth inning and boosted his World Series batting average to a cool .438. . . . Justice wound up with five runs batted in. After his homer, he accounted for three more RBIs with two ground balls and a single. . . . As was the case in their last World Series appearance, 1987, the Twins won the first two games of the fall classic at the Metrodome in Minneapolis, only to drop three straight at the opposition's ballpark (in '87, it was Busch Stadium in St. Louis).

Quotable: Seeing his batting mark in lights usually was a downer for Lemke, but not in this World Series. "By force of habit, I don't look at the scoreboard," Lemke said. "Most of the season, I don't want to look at my average." During the '91 regular season, Lemke batted .234; in 1990, he hit .226. . . . Masterful over the first five innings, Atlanta starter Tom Glavine lost it totally in the sixth, walking four batters in that frame and leaving in favor of Kent Mercker. "I just got out of rhythm," Glavine said. "I tried to relax too much (with a 5-0 lead). I think I was using reverse psychology. Normally, when I get in a funk like that, I know what I'm doing and I can make the adjustments. It was disheartening. We were in control, and I let them back in it." The Twins closed within 5-3, but an inning later they were down, 11-3.

BOX SCORE

THURSDAY, OCTOBER 24, AT ATLANTA

Minnesota (A.L.)	AB	R	H	RBI	PO	A
Gladden, lf	5	1	1	0	2	0
Knoblauch, 2b	3	1	1	0	2	1
Bedrosian, p	0	0	0	0	0	0
Ortiz, c	1	0	0	1	0	0
Puckett, cf	2	1	1	0	2	0
eBrown, cf	2	0	0	0	0	0
Davis, rf	3	2	1	0	1	0
Willis, p	0	0	0	0	1	0
Harper, c	2	0	0	1	6	0
fBush, rf	1	0	0	0	0	0
Leius, 3b	2	0	1	1	0	1
West, p	0	0	0	0	0	0
Newman, 2b	1	0	1	0	1	1
Hrbek, 1b	3	0	0	1	7	1
gSorrento, 1b	0	0	0	0	1	1
Gagne, ss	4	0	1	0	2	5
Tapani, p	1	0	0	0	0	1
aLarkin	1	0	0	0	0	0
Leach, p	0	0	0	0	0	0
cPagliarulo	2	0	0	0	0	0
Totals	33	5	7	5	24	11

Atlanta (N.L.)	AB	R	H	RBI	PO	A
Smith, lf	5	1	1	1	0	0
Mitchell, lf	0	0	0	0	0	0
Pendleton, 3b	4	3	2	0	0	3
Gant, cf	4	3	3	1	3	0
Justice, rf	5	2	2	5	2	0
Bream, 1b	2	0	0	0	13	1
dHunter, 1b	2	2	2	2	3	0
Olson, c	5	1	3	0	3	2
St. Claire, p	0	0	0	0	0	0
Lemke, 2b	4	2	2	3	2	7
Belliard, ss	4	0	2	2	1	3
Glavine, p	2	0	0	0	0	2
Mercker, p	0	0	0	0	0	0
bGregg	1	0	0	0	0	0
Clancy, p	1	0	0	0	0	0
Cabrera, c	0	0	0	0	0	0
Totals	39	14	17	14	27	18

Minnesota..........................0 0 0   0 0 3   0 1 1— 5
Atlanta.............................0 0 0   4 1 0   6 3 x—14

Minnesota	IP	H	R	ER	BB	SO
Tapani (L)	4	6	4	4	2	4
Leach	2	2	1	1	0	1
West	*0	2	4	4	2	0
Bedrosian	1	3	2	2	0	1
Willis	1	4	3	3	0	0

Atlanta	IP	H	R	ER	BB	SO
Glavine (W)	5⅓	4	3	3	4	2
Mercker	⅔	0	0	0	0	0
Clancy	2	2	1	1	1	2
St. Claire	1	1	1	1	0	0

*Pitched to four batters in seventh.

Bases on balls—Off Tapani 2 (Lemke, Bream), off West 2 (Pendleton, Gant), off Glavine 4 (Knoblauch, Davis, Harper, Leius), off Clancy 1 (Sorrento). Strikeouts—By Tapani 4 (Gant, Justice, Bream, Smith), by Leach 1 (Lemke), by Bedrosian 1 (Clancy), by Glavine 2 (Harper, Leius), by Clancy 2 (Gladden, Knoblauch). aGrounded into force out for Tapani in fifth. bFlied out for Mercker in sixth. cGrounded out for Leach in seventh. dSingled for Bream in seventh. eGrounded out for Puckett in eighth. fGrounded out for Harper in eighth. gWalked for Hrbek in eighth. E—Harper, Pendleton. DP—Minnesota 1. LOB—Minnesota 7, Atlanta 5. 2B—Gagne, Belliard, Pendleton. 3B—Lemke 2, Newman, Gant, Gladden. HR—Justice, Smith, Hunter. SB—Justice, Olson. CS—Leius. SH—Puckett. WP—Bedrosian. U—Reed (A.L.), plate; Montague (N.L.), first; Denkinger (A.L.), second; Wendelstedt (N.L.), third; Coble (A.L.), left field; Tata (N.L.), right field. T—2:59. A—50,878.

PLAY BY PLAY

FIRST INNING

Minnesota—Gladden grounded to second. Knoblauch flied to right. Puckett grounded to short.

Atlanta—Smith grounded to third. Pendleton grounded to the pitcher. Gant struck out.

SECOND INNING

Minnesota—Davis fouled to first. Harper grounded to second. Leius singled to right. Leius got caught stealing, pitcher to first baseman to shortstop.

Atlanta—Justice and Bream struck out. Olson singled to left-center. Olson stole second and continued to third after getting hit by an errant throw from the catcher. Lemke walked. Belliard forced Lemke, shortstop to second baseman.

THIRD INNING

Minnesota—Hrbek grounded to second. Gagne doubled to

right. Tapani grounded to second, Gagne went to third. Gladden grounded out, catcher to first baseman.

Atlanta—Glavine and Smith grounded to short. Pendleton flied to left.

FOURTH INNING

Minnesota—Knoblauch singled to center. Puckett sacrificed, pitcher to first baseman, Knoblauch went to second. Davis flied to center. Harper struck out.

Atlanta—Gant singled to left. Justice homered to left, scoring Gant. Bream walked. Olson singled, but Bream was declared out when the ball hit him on the foot. Lemke tripled to right, scoring Olson. Belliard doubled to left, scoring Lemke. Glavine grounded to second, Belliard went to third. Smith struck out.

FIFTH INNING

Minnesota—Leius struck out. Hrbek grounded to second. Gagne grounded to third and reached on an error by the third baseman. Larkin, pinch-hitting for Tapani, forced Gagne, third baseman to second baseman.

Atlanta—Leach now pitching. Pendleton singled off the pitcher's leg. Gant singled to left, Pendleton went to third. Justice forced Gant, first baseman to shortstop, scoring Pendleton. Bream flied to center. Olson popped to first.

SIXTH INNING

Minnesota—Gladden flied to center. Knoblauch walked. Puckett singled to right, Knoblauch went to third, and on the throw to third from right field, Puckett went to second. Davis walked. Harper walked, scoring Knoblauch, as Puckett went to third and Davis went to second. Leius walked, scoring Puckett, as Davis went to third and Harper to second. Mercker now pitching. Hrbek grounded to short, scoring Davis, as Harper went to third and Leius went to second. Gagne grounded to second.

Atlanta—Lemke struck out. Belliard grounded to short. Gregg, pinch-hitting for Mercker, flied to right.

SEVENTH INNING

Minnesota—Clancy now pitching. Pagliarulo, pinch-hitting for Leach, grounded to first. Gladden struck out. Knoblauch struck out and was thrown out at first when the pitch briefly got away from the catcher.

Atlanta—West now pitching and Pagliarulo at third. Smith homered to left. Pendleton and Gant walked. Justice singled to right, scoring Pendleton, as Gant went to third. Bedrosian now pitching, and Newman at second. Hunter, pinch-hitting for Bream, singled to left, scoring Gant, as Justice went to second. Olson flied to center. Lemke tripled to right, scoring Justice and Hunter. Belliard singled to center, scoring Lemke. Clancy struck out. Belliard went to second on a wild pitch. Smith flied to left.

EIGHTH INNING

Minnesota—Brown, pinch-hitting for Puckett, grounded to short. Davis singled to center. Bush, pinch-hitting for Harper, grounded to second, as Davis went to second. Newman tripled, scoring Davis. Sorrento, pinch-hitting for Hrbek, walked. Gagne forced Sorrento, third baseman to second baseman.

Atlanta—Willis now pitching, Ortiz catching, Brown in center, Bush in right and Sorrento at first. Pendleton doubled to right-center. Gant tripled to right-center, scoring Pendleton. Justice grounded to first baseman, who tossed to the pitcher covering, as Gant scored. Hunter homered to left. Olson singled to left. Lemke grounded into a double play, second to short to first.

NINTH INNING

Minnesota—St. Claire now pitching. Pagliarulo flied to right. Gladden tripled to right-center. Ortiz grounded to third, scoring Gladden. Brown flied to center.

HIGHLIGHTS

MINNESOTA 4, ATLANTA 3

Why the Twins won: Kirby Puckett, a .429 hitter with six RBIs in the A.L. playoffs but a .167 batsman with one RBI through five games of the World Series, was back in his familiar role: right in the middle of things. He belted a first-inning triple that thrust Minnesota into a 1-0 lead, delivered a fifth-inning sacrifice fly that sent the Twins ahead, 3-2, and then led off the bottom of the 11th inning with a home run to left-center field that gave Minnesota a 4-3 triumph.

Why the Braves lost: Charlie Leibrandt, who had a rough outing as a starter in Game 1 of the World Series, wore the goat horns in this one. Pitching in relief, he entered the game in the bottom of the 11th with the score tied at 3-3 and threw exactly four pitches, the last of which was deposited over the wall by Puckett.

The turning points:

1. Righthander Scott Erickson's ability to show at least some of his pre-All-Star-break form. A 12-3 pitcher in the first half of the season, Erickson experienced a so-so second half (8-5) and hadn't been any great shakes thus far in postseason play. This time, he shut out Atlanta through the first four innings and left after pitching to one batter in the seventh. His log: five hits and three runs allowed over six-plus innings.

2. Shane Mack's first-inning RBI for Minnesota. Coming to the plate in the throes of a 0-for-15 Series slump, he picked an ideal time to collect his first hit. With two out and Puckett on third base, Mack rapped a single to left, increasing the Twins' edge to 2-0. Minnesota was never headed after building that bulge, although the Braves did force two ties.

Notable: Puckett leaped high above the wall in left-center in the third inning, snaring Ron Gant's long smash and depriving the Braves' slugger of an extra-base hit. ... Atlanta's Terry Pendleton, making up for a poor N.L. playoffs performance, socked a game-tying, two-run homer in the fifth inning and went 4-for-5 overall. His average jumped to .400.

Quotable: With Puckett due to lead off the last of the 11th, some observers wondered why lefthander Leibrandt was brought in at that juncture. After all, Puckett had batted .406 against lefthanders in 1991. Plus, Leibrandt was in an unfamiliar relief role, having made starts in all 60 of his regular-season appearances with the Braves in 1990 and 1991. "I don't see how anybody could second-guess that move," Atlanta Manager Bobby Cox said. "I mean, why not? If someone else would have been in there and Puckett had homered, the first question everybody would have asked (was), 'Why didn't you use Leibrandt?' " More on Cox/Leibrandt: "He (Leibrandt) had been down there warming up for 25 minutes," Cox said. "It was just like he was making a start. What's the difference?"

BOX SCORE

SATURDAY, OCTOBER 26, AT MINNESOTA

Atlanta (N.L.)	AB	R	H	RBI	PO	A
Smith, dh	3	1	0	0	0	0
Pendleton, 3b	5	1	4	2	1	2
Gant, cf	5	0	0	1	2	0
Justice, rf	4	0	0	0	3	0
Bream, 1b	4	0	1	0	12	2
eMitchell, lf	0	0	0	0	0	0
Hunter, lf-1b	5	0	0	0	1	0
Olson, c	5	0	0	0	6	0
Lemke, 2b	4	1	2	0	2	3
Belliard, ss	2	0	1	0	1	4
aGregg	0	0	0	0	0	0
bBlauser, ss	2	0	1	0	1	3
Avery, p	0	0	0	0	1	0
Stanton, p	0	0	0	0	0	0
Pena, p	0	0	0	0	0	0
Leibrandt, p	0	0	0	0	0	0
Totals	39	3	9	3	30	14

Minnesota (A.L.)	AB	R	H	RBI	PO	A
Gladden, lf	4	1	0	0	1	0
Knoblauch, 2b	5	1	1	0	4	1
Puckett, cf	4	2	3	3	3	0
Davis, dh	4	0	0	0	0	0
Mack, rf	4	0	2	1	0	0
Leius, 3b	3	0	2	0	3	2
dPagliarulo, 3b	1	0	0	0	2	0
Hrbek, 1b	4	0	0	0	11	0
Ortiz, c	2	0	0	0	4	0
cHarper, c	2	0	0	0	0	1
Gagne, ss	4	0	1	0	5	6
Erickson, p	0	0	0	0	0	0
Guthrie, p	0	0	0	0	0	0
Willis, p	0	0	0	0	0	0
Aguilera, p	0	0	0	0	0	0
Totals	37	4	9	4	33	11

Atlanta ....0 0 0   0 2 0   1 0 0   0 0—3
Minnesota ....2 0 0   0 1 0   0 0 0   0 1—4
None out when winning run scored.

Atlanta	IP	H	R	ER	BB	SO
Avery	6	6	3	3	1	3
Stanton	2	2	0	0	0	1
Pena	2	0	0	0	0	2
Leibrandt (L)	†0	1	1	1	0	0

Minnesota	IP	H	R	ER	BB	SO
Erickson	*6	5	3	3	2	2
Guthrie	⅓	1	0	0	1	1
Willis	2⅔	1	0	0	0	1
Aguilera (W)	2	2	0	0	0	0

*Pitched to one batter in seventh.
†Pitched to one batter in 11th.

Bases on balls—Off Avery 1 (Gladden), off Erickson 2 (Justice, Bream), off Guthrie 1 (Smith). Strikeouts—By Avery 3 (Puckett, Ortiz, Davis), by Stanton 1 (Harper), by Pena 2 (Pagliarulo, Hrbek), by Erickson 2 (Belliard, Olson), by Guthrie 1 (Blauser), by Willis 1 (Justice).

aAnnounced for Belliard in seventh. bStruck out for Gregg in seventh. cStruck out for Ortiz in seventh. dStruck out for Leius in ninth. eRan for Bream in 11th. E—Harper. DP—Atlanta 2, Minnesota 2. LOB—Atlanta 7, Minnesota 5. 2B—Mack. 3B—Puckett. HR—Pendleton, Puckett.

SB—Gladden, Puckett. CS—Mitchell. SF—Puckett. HBP—By Erickson (Smith). WP—Guthrie. U—Montague (N.L.), plate; Denkinger (A.L.), first; Wendelstedt (N.L.), second; Coble (A.L.), third; Tata (N.L.), left field; Reed (A.L.), right field. T—3:36. A—55,155.

PLAY BY PLAY

FIRST INNING

Atlanta—Smith grounded to third. Pendleton singled to right. Gant grounded to first, Pendleton went to second. Justice walked. Bream flied to left.

Minnesota—Gladden grounded to short. Knoblauch singled to right. Puckett tripled to left, scoring Knoblauch. Davis flied to right. Mack singled to left, scoring Puckett. Leius singled to left, Mack went to third. Hrbek grounded to first.

SECOND INNING

Atlanta—Hunter lined to third. Olson grounded to short. Lemke singled to center. Belliard struck out.

Minnesota—Ortiz and Gagne grounded to third. Gladden grounded to short.

THIRD INNING

Atlanta—Smith was hit by a pitch. Pendleton forced Smith at second, first baseman to shortstop. Gant flied to center. Justice grounded to first.

Minnesota—Knoblauch grounded to short. Puckett struck out. Davis flied to right.

FOURTH INNING

Atlanta—Bream walked. Hunter lined to short. Olson struck out. Lemke grounded to short.

Minnesota—Mack doubled to right. Leius grounded to third. Hrbek reached on a two-base error by the left fielder, Mack went to third. Ortiz struck out. Gagne grounded to second.

FIFTH INNING

Atlanta—Belliard singled to third. Smith forced Belliard, third baseman to second baseman. Pendleton homered to center, scoring Smith. Gant grounded to short. Justice grounded to second.

Minnesota—Gladden walked and stole second. Knoblauch flied to right, Gladden went to third. Puckett hit a sacrifice fly to center, scoring Gladden. Davis struck out.

SIXTH INNING

Atlanta—Bream popped to third. Hunter popped to second. Olson flied to center.

Minnesota—Mack grounded to the first baseman, who tossed to the pitcher covering first. Leius singled to center. Hrbek grounded into a double play, first to short to first.

SEVENTH INNING

Atlanta—Lemke singled to center. Gregg was announced as a pinch-hitter for Belliard. Guthrie now pitching. Blauser, pinch-hitting for Gregg, struck out. Lemke went to second on a wild pitch. Smith walked. Pendleton singled to the infield, Lemke went to third and Smith to second. Willis now pitching. Gant forced Pendleton, shortstop to second baseman, as Lemke scored and Smith went to third. Justice struck out.

Minnesota—Stanton now pitching and Blauser at shortstop. Harper, pinch-hitting for Ortiz, struck out. Gagne singled to right-center. Gladden grounded into a double play, short to second to first.

EIGHTH INNING

Atlanta—Harper now catching. Bream flied to center. Hunter fouled to first. Olson grounded to short.

Minnesota—Knoblauch popped to short. Puckett singled to right. Davis flied to center. Puckett stole second. Mack flied to left.

NINTH INNING

Atlanta—Lemke popped to third. Blauser singled to center. Smith grounded into a double play, short to first.

Minnesota—Pena now pitching. Pagliarulo, pinch-hitting for Leius, struck out. Hrbek struck out. Harper grounded to short.

10TH INNING

Atlanta—Aguilera now pitching and Pagliarulo at third. Pendleton singled to center. Gant lined to the shortstop, who tagged Pendleton for a double play. Justice popped to third.

Minnesota—Gagne popped to second. Gladden grounded to second. Knoblauch grounded to short.

11TH INNING

Atlanta—Bream singled to right. Mitchell pinch-ran for Bream. Mitchell got caught stealing, catcher to second baseman. Hunter fouled to first. Olson popped to third.

Minnesota—Leibrandt now pitching. Puckett homered to left.

GAME 7

HIGHLIGHTS

MINNESOTA 1, ATLANTA 0

Why the Twins won: Veteran righthander Jack Morris, capping his first season with his "home" team, turned in the kind of clutch performance for which the St. Paul, Minn., native had become noted during a long career with the Detroit Tigers. Morris, who over a 10-year span (1979-1988) with Detroit never won fewer than 14 games and was an 18-game winner in 1991 for Minnesota (with whom he signed as a free agent), improved his career postseason record to a gaudy 7-1 by silencing the Braves on seven hits in a route-going, 10-inning masterpiece. He walked only two Atlanta batters and struck out eight.

Why the Braves lost: As good as Atlanta starter John Smoltz was (six hits and no runs allowed in 7⅓ innings), Morris was better.

The turning points:

1. The Atlanta eighth. Lonnie Smith led off the inning with a single and Terry Pendleton followed with a drive to deep left-center, a smash that bounded off the fence and seemed certain to snap the 0-0 deadlock. However, running with the pitch and not knowing where the ball was hit, Smith hesitated after rounding second base and could advance only to third on Pendleton's double. Atlanta still seemed in good shape to break the deadlock, but a groundout, an intentional walk and a double-play grounder kept the Braves scoreless.

2. The Minnesota 10th. After being thwarted in the eighth inning (Kent Hrbek's soft liner with the bases loaded and one out was turned into a double play) and again in the ninth (pinch-hitter Paul Sorrento struck out with runners at the corners), the Twins finally broke through. Dan Gladden opened the Minnesota 10th with a double and was sacrificed to third by Chuck Knoblauch. Two intentional walks followed, loading the bases with one out. Pinch-hitter Gene Larkin, facing reliever

Alejandro Pena, then ended one of the most fiercely contested Series in history by sending a drive into left-center, over a drawn-in outfield.

Notable: Morris won two games in both the American League Championship Series and the World Series in '91. . . . The Twins matched their 1987 feat of winning all four World Series games played at the Metrodome and boasted an 11-1 postseason record in their Minneapolis fun house.

Quotable: Smith, on his eighth-inning baserunning: "Evidently, what nobody realizes, I was going with the pitch on a delayed steal. I got about halfway and I heard the sound of the bat. I made the mistake of not looking in when I started running. I just assumed that the ball would be hit on the ground. (In fact, left fielder Gladden and center fielder Kirby Puckett were racing toward Pendleton's long smash.) Before I had a chance to look back, I saw the two (middle) infielders trying to glove something (as a decoy). Then I looked up and I happened to see Gladden running toward the outfield (fence), and I saw Kirby, and then I noticed the ball almost as it hit. And after I saw they weren't going to catch it, I started running as hard as I could. You know, if I saw the ball off the bat, there's a good chance I could have scored. But I didn't see it. I didn't take that look in. That's my mistake."

BOX SCORE

SUNDAY, OCTOBER 27, AT MINNESOTA

Atlanta (N.L.)	AB	R	H	RBI	PO	A
Smith, dh	4	0	2	0	0	0
Pendleton, 3b	5	0	1	0	0	5
Gant, cf	4	0	0	0	4	0
Justice, rf	3	0	1	0	4	0
Bream, 1b	4	0	0	0	7	2
Hunter, lf	4	0	1	0	1	0
Olson, c	4	0	0	0	5	0
Lemke, 2b	4	0	1	0	4	1
Belliard, ss	2	0	1	0	2	2
eBlauser, ss	1	0	0	0	0	0
Smoltz, p	0	0	0	0	1	1
Stanton, p	0	0	0	0	0	0
Pena, p	0	0	0	0	0	0
Totals	35	0	7	0	28	11
Minnesota (A.L.)	AB	R	H	RBI	PO	A
Gladden, lf	5	1	3	0	2	0
Knoblauch, 2b	4	0	1	0	2	2
Puckett, cf	2	0	0	0	2	0
Hrbek, 1b	3	0	0	0	10	2
Davis, dh	4	0	1	0	0	0
cBrown	0	0	0	0	0	0
fLarkin	1	0	1	1	0	0
Harper, c	4	0	2	0	10	2
Mack, rf	4	0	1	0	2	0
Pagliarulo, 3b	3	0	0	0	0	1
Gagne, ss	2	0	0	0	1	1
aBush	1	0	1	0	0	0
bNewman, ss	0	0	0	0	0	1
dSorrento	1	0	0	0	0	0
Leius, ss	0	0	0	0	0	1
Morris, p	0	0	0	0	1	0
Totals	34	1	10	1	30	10

Atlanta	0 0 0	0 0 0	0 0 0	0—0
Minnesota	0 0 0	0 0 0	0 0 1	1—1

One out when winning run scored.

Atlanta	IP	H	R	ER	BB	SO
Smoltz	7 1/3	6	0	0	1	4
Stanton	* 2/3	2	0	0	1	0
Pena (L)	1 1/3	2	1	1	3	1
Minnesota	IP	H	R	ER	BB	SO
Morris (W)	10	7	0	0	2	8

*Pitched to two batters in ninth.

Bases on balls—Off Smoltz 1 (Puckett), off Stanton 1 (Puckett), off Pena 3 (Pagliarulo, Puckett, Hrbek), off Morris 2 (Smith, Justice).
Strikeouts—By Smoltz 4 (Gladden, Davis, Puckett, Gagne), by Pena 1 (Sorrento), by Morris 8 (Gant 2, Hunter, Justice, Olson, Belliard, Lemke, Smith).
aSingled for Gagne in eighth. bRan for Bush in eighth. cRan for Davis in ninth. dStruck out for Newman in ninth. eFouled out for Belliard in 10th. fSingled for Brown in 10th. DP—Atlanta 3, Minnesota 1. LOB—Atlanta 8, Minnesota 12. 2B—Gladden 2, Hunter, Pendleton. SH—Belliard, Knoblauch. HBP—By Smoltz (Hrbek). PB—Harper. U—Denkinger (A.L.), plate; Wendelstedt (N.L.), first; Coble (A.L.), second; Tata (N.L.), third; Reed (A.L.), left field, Montague (N.L.), right field. T—3:23. A—55,118.

PLAY BY PLAY

FIRST INNING

Atlanta—Smith flied to right. Pendleton grounded to first. Gant struck out.

Minnesota—Gladden struck out. Knoblauch popped to right. Puckett grounded to the pitcher.

SECOND INNING

Atlanta—Justice, singled to center. Bream grounded to second, Justice went to second. Hunter struck out. Olson popped to second.

Minnesota—Hrbek lined to right. Davis struck out. Harper singled to center. Mack singled to center, Harper went to second. Pagliarulo grounded to the first baseman, who tossed to the pitcher covering first.

THIRD INNING

Atlanta—Lemke grounded to second. Belliard singled to right. Belliard went to second on a passed ball. Smith walked. Pendleton popped to left. Gant forced Smith at second, shortstop to second baseman.

Minnesota—Gagne grounded to third. Gladden doubled to left. Knoblauch flied to right. Puckett struck out.

FOURTH INNING

Atlanta—Justice struck out. Bream flied to left. Hunter doubled to left-center. Olson lined to right.

Minnesota—Hrbek was hit by a pitch. Davis flied to left. Harper flied to right. Mack popped to second.

FIFTH INNING

Atlanta—Lemke singled to right. Belliard sacrificed Lemke to second and was retired, catcher to first baseman. Smith singled to third base, Lemke went to third. Pendleton popped to short. Gant struck out.

Minnesota—Pagliarulo flied to center. Gagne struck out. Gladden singled to center. Knoblauch flied to center.

SIXTH INNING

Atlanta—Justice grounded to the first baseman, who tossed to the pitcher covering first. Bream grounded to first. Hunter flied to center.

Minnesota—Puckett walked. Hrbek flied to center. Davis grounded into a double play, first to short to first.

SEVENTH INNING

Atlanta—Olson struck out. Lemke flied to center. Belliard struck out.

Minnesota—Harper, Mack and Pagliarulo grounded to third.

EIGHTH INNING

Atlanta—Smith singled to right. Pendleton doubled to left-center, Smith went to third. Gant grounded to first. Justice was walked intentionally. Bream grounded into a double play, first to catcher to first.

Minnesota—Bush, pinch-hitting for Gagne, singled to center. Newman ran for Bush. Gladden flied to center. Knoblauch singled to right, Newman went to third. Stanton now pitching. Puckett was walked intentionally. Hrbek lined to the second baseman, who tagged second for a double play.

NINTH INNING

Atlanta—Newman now at shortstop. Hunter grounded to third. Olson grounded to short. Lemke struck out.

Minnesota—Davis singled to right-center. Brown pinch-ran

for Davis. Harper singled to second, Brown went to second. Pena now pitching. Mack grounded into a double play, second to short to first, and Brown went to third. Pagliarulo was walked intentionally. Sorrento, pinch-hitting for Newman, struck out.

10TH INNING

Atlanta—Leius now at shortstop. Blauser, pinch-hitting for Belliard, fouled to the catcher. Smith struck out. Pendleton grounded to short.

Minnesota—Gladden doubled to left-center. Knoblauch sacrificed Gladden to third and was retired, third to first. Puckett and Hrbek were walked intentionally. Larkin, pinch-hitting for Brown, singled to left-center, scoring Gladden.

STATISTICS

MINNESOTA TWINS' BATTING AND FIELDING AVERAGES

Player, position	G	AB	R	H	TB	2B	3B	HR	RBI	BB	IBB	SO	Avg.	PO	A	E	Avg.
Larkin, ph	4	4	0	2	2	0	0	0	1	0	0	0	.500	0	0	0	.000
Newman, ph-3b-2b-pr-ss	4	2	0	1	3	0	1	0	1	0	0	0	.500	0	2	0	1.000
Harper, c-ph	7	21	2	8	10	2	0	0	1	2	0	2	.381	33	5	2	.950
Leius, 3b-ph-ss	7	14	2	5	8	0	0	1	2	1	0	2	.357	5	8	1	.929
Knoblauch, 2b	7	26	3	8	9	1	0	0	2	4	0	2	.308	15	14	1	.967
Pagliarulo, ph-3b	6	11	1	3	6	0	0	1	2	1	1	2	.273	3	3	0	1.000
Puckett, cf	7	24	4	6	14	0	1	2	4	5	4	7	.250	16	1	0	1.000
Bush, ph-rf	3	4	0	1	1	0	0	0	0	0	0	1	.250	0	0	0	.000
Gladden, lf	7	30	5	7	13	2	2	0	3	0	0	4	.233	25	1	1	.963
Davis, dh-ph-rf	6	18	4	4	10	0	0	2	4	2	1	3	.222	1	0	0	1.000
Ortiz, c	3	5	0	1	1	0	0	0	1	0	0	1	.200	9	0	0	1.000
Gagne, ss	7	24	1	4	8	1	0	1	3	0	0	7	.167	13	24	0	1.000
Mack, rf	6	23	0	3	4	1	0	0	1	0	0	7	.130	11	0	0	1.000
Hrbek, 1b	7	26	2	3	7	1	0	1	2	2	1	6	.115	66	8	0	1.000
Bedrosian, p	3	0	0	0	0	0	0	0	0	0	0	0	.000	0	1	0	1.000
Leach, p	2	0	0	0	0	0	0	0	0	0	0	0	.000	0	0	0	.000
Guthrie, p	4	0	0	0	0	0	0	0	0	0	0	0	.000	0	1	0	1.000
West, p	2	0	0	0	0	0	0	0	0	0	0	0	.000	0	0	0	.000
Willis, p	4	0	0	0	0	0	0	0	0	0	0	0	.000	1	0	0	1.000
Aguilera, p-ph	4	1	0	0	0	0	0	0	0	0	0	0	.000	0	0	0	.000
Erickson, p	2	1	0	0	0	0	0	0	0	0	0	1	.000	1	0	0	1.000
Tapani, p	2	1	0	0	0	0	0	0	0	0	0	0	.000	0	2	0	1.000
Brown, rf-ph-cf-pr	3	2	0	0	0	0	0	0	0	0	0	0	.000	0	0	0	.000
Morris, p	3	2	0	0	0	0	0	0	0	0	0	1	.000	2	4	0	1.000
Sorrento, ph-1b	3	2	0	0	0	0	0	0	0	1	0	2	.000	1	1	0	1.000
Totals	7	241	24	56	96	8	4	8	24	21	7	48	.232	202	75	5	.982

Aguilera—Flied out for Guthrie in 12th inning of third game.
Brown—Grounded out for Puckett in eighth inning of fifth game; ran for Davis in ninth inning of seventh game.
Bush—Struck out for Brown in ninth inning of third game; grounded out for Harper in eighth inning of fifth game; singled for Gagne in eighth inning of seventh game.
Davis—Homered for Bedrosian in eighth inning of third game.
Harper—Reached base on error for Ortiz in eighth inning of third game; struck out for Ortiz in seventh inning of sixth game.
Larkin—Singled for Leach in sixth inning of third game; grounded out for Morris in seventh inning of fourth game; grounded into force out for Tapani in fifth inning of fifth game; singled for Brown in 10th inning of seventh game.
Leius—Lined out for Pagliarulo in ninth inning of fourth game.
Newman—Popped out for Pagliarulo in 11th inning of third game; ran for Bush in eighth inning of seventh game.
Pagliarulo—Grounded out for Leius in sixth inning of first game; struck out for Leius in ninth inning of third game; grounded out for Leach in seventh inning of fifth game; struck out for Leius in ninth inning of sixth game.
Sorrento—Struck out for Willis in 10th inning of third game; Walked for Hrbek in eighth inning of fifth game; struck out for Newman in ninth inning of seventh game.

ATLANTA BRAVES' BATTING AND FIELDING AVERAGES

Player, position	G	AB	R	H	TB	2B	3B	HR	RBI	BB	IBB	SO	Avg.	PO	A	E	Avg.
Lemke, 2b	6	24	4	10	17	1	3	0	4	2	0	4	.417	14	19	1	.971
Belliard, ss	7	16	0	6	7	1	0	0	4	1	0	2	.375	8	21	0	1.000
Pendleton, 3b	7	30	6	11	20	3	0	2	3	3	1	1	.367	3	20	2	.920
Gant, cf	7	30	3	8	10	0	1	0	4	2	0	3	.267	19	0	0	1.000
Justice, rf	7	27	5	7	13	0	0	2	6	5	1	5	.259	21	1	1	.957
Treadway, 2b-ph	3	4	1	1	1	0	0	0	0	1	0	2	.250	1	3	1	.800
Smith, dh-lf	7	26	5	6	15	0	0	3	3	3	0	4	.231	2	0	0	1.000
Olson, c	7	27	3	6	8	2	0	0	1	5	0	4	.222	47	6	0	1.000
Hunter, lf-ph-1b	7	21	2	4	8	1	0	1	3	0	0	2	.190	6	1	0	1.000
Blauser, ph-ss	5	6	0	1	1	0	0	0	0	1	1	1	.167	3	3	0	1.000

Player, position	BATTING													FIELDING			
	G	AB	R	H	TB	2B	3B	HR	RBI	BB	IBB	SO	Avg.	PO	A	E	Avg.
Bream, 1b	7	24	0	3	5	2	0	0	0	3	0	4	.125	69	7	0	1.000
Leibrandt, p	2	0	0	0	0	0	0	0	0	0	0	0	.000	0	1	0	1.000
Mercker, p	2	0	0	0	0	0	0	0	0	0	0	0	.000	0	0	0	.000
Pena, p	3	0	0	0	0	0	0	0	0	0	0	0	.000	0	0	0	.000
St. Claire, p	1	0	0	0	0	0	0	0	0	0	0	0	.000	0	0	0	.000
Stanton, p	5	0	0	0	0	0	0	0	0	0	0	0	.000	0	0	0	.000
Willard, ph	1	0	0	0	0	0	0	0	1	0	0	0	.000	0	0	0	.000
Wohlers, p	3	0	0	0	0	0	0	0	0	0	0	0	.000	0	0	0	.000
Cabrera, ph-c	3	1	0	0	0	0	0	0	0	0	0	1	.000	0	0	0	.000
Clancy, p	3	1	0	0	0	0	0	0	0	0	0	1	.000	0	0	0	.000
Glavine, p	2	2	0	0	0	0	0	0	0	0	0	0	.000	0	3	0	1.000
Mitchell, lf-pr	3	2	0	0	0	0	0	0	0	0	0	1	.000	0	0	0	.000
Smoltz, p	2	2	0	0	0	0	0	0	0	0	0	1	.000	2	1	0	1.000
Avery, p	2	3	0	0	0	0	0	0	0	0	0	2	.000	1	0	0	1.000
Gregg, ph	4	3	0	0	0	0	0	0	0	0	0	2	.000	0	0	0	.000
Totals	7	249	29	63	105	10	4	8	29	26	3	39	.253	196	86	5	.983

Blauser—Flied out for Belliard in seventh inning of first game; popped out for Belliard in 10th inning of third game; struck out for Gregg in seventh inning of sixth game; fouled out for Belliard in 10th inning of seventh game.

Cabrera—Lined out for Stanton in 11th inning of third game; announced for Stanton in ninth inning of fourth game.

Gregg—Struck out for Lemke in ninth inning of second game: struck out for Smoltz in seventh inning of fourth game; flied out for Mercker in sixth inning of fifth game; announced for Belliard in seventh inning of sixth game.

Hunter—Grounded out for Bream in 10th inning of third game; flied out for Bream in eighth inning of fourth game; singled for Bream in seventh inning of fifth game.

Mitchell—Ran for Bream in 11th inning of sixth game.

Treadway—Sacrificed for Pena in ninth inning of third game; flied out for Belliard in seventh inning of fourth game.

Willard—Hit sacrifice fly for Cabrera in ninth inning of fourth game.

MINNESOTA TWINS' PITCHING RECORDS

Pitcher	G	GS	CG	IP	H	R	ER	HR	BB	IBB	SO	HB	WP	W	L	Pct.	ERA
Morris	3	3	1	23	18	3	3	1	9	1	15	0	1	2	0	1.000	1.17
Aguilera	4	0	0	5	6	1	1	0	1	0	3	0	1	0	1	.500	1.80
Guthrie	4	0	0	4	3	1	1	0	4	1	3	0	1	0	1	.000	2.25
Leach	2	0	0	2⅓	2	1	1	0	0	0	2	0	0	0	0	.000	3.86
Tapani	2	2	0	12	13	6	6	1	2	0	7	0	0	1	1	.500	4.50
Erickson	2	2	0	10⅔	10	7	6	3	4	0	5	1	0	0	1	.000	5.06
Willis	4	0	0	7	6	4	4	2	2	1	2	0	0	0	0	.000	5.14
Bedrosian	3	0	0	3⅓	3	2	2	0	0	0	2	0	1	0	0	.000	5.40
West	2	0	0	*0	2	4	4	1	4	0	0	0	0	0	0	.000	....
Totals	7	7	1	67⅓	63	29	28	8	26	3	39	1	3	4	3	.571	3.74

*Pitched to two batters in fifth inning of third game and four batters in seventh inning of fifth game.
Shutout—Morris. Saves—Aguilera 2.

ATLANTA BRAVES' PITCHING RECORDS

Pitcher	G	GS	CG	IP	H	R	ER	HR	BB	IBB	SO	HB	WP	W	L	Pct.	ERA
Stanton	5	0	0	7⅓	5	0	0	0	2	2	7	0	0	1	0	1.000	0.00
Wohlers	3	0	0	1⅔	2	0	0	0	2	0	1	0	0	0	0	.000	0.00
Mercker	2	0	0	1	0	0	0	0	0	0	1	0	0	0	0	.000	0.00
Smoltz	2	2	0	14⅓	13	2	2	1	1	0	11	1	0	0	0	.000	1.26
Glavine	2	2	1	13⅓	8	6	4	2	7	0	8	0	0	1	1	.500	2.70
Pena	3	0	0	5⅓	6	2	2	1	3	3	7	0	0	0	1	.000	3.38
Avery	2	2	0	13	10	6	5	1	1	0	8	0	0	0	0	.000	3.46
Clancy	3	0	0	4⅓	3	2	2	1	4	2	2	0	0	1	0	1.000	4.15
St. Claire	1	0	0	1	1	1	1	0	0	0	0	0	0	0	0	.000	9.00
Leibrandt	2	1	0	4	8	5	5	2	1	0	3	0	0	0	2	.000	11.25
Totals	7	7	1	65⅓	56	24	21	8	21	7	48	1	0	3	4	.429	2.89

No shutouts or saves.

COMPOSITE SCORE BY INNINGS

Minnesota	5	1	1	0	4	4	2	4	1	1	1	0	—	24
Atlanta	0	2	1	5	6	1	8	4	1	0	0	1	—	29

MISCELLANEOUS STATISTICS

Sacrifice hits—Belliard 2, Smith, Treadway, Puckett, Knoblauch.
Sacrifice flies—Hunter, Belliard, Knoblauch, Willard, Puckett.
Stolen bases—Knoblauch 4, Gladden 2, Justice 2, Gant, Smith, Olson, Puckett.
Caught stealing—Gladden, Mack, Leius, Mitchell.
Double plays—Gagne and Hrbek 2; Bream, Belliard and Bream 2; Belliard and Treadway; Hunter, Pendleton and Olson; Knoblauch, Gagne and Hrbek; Pendleton and Bream; Glavine, Lemke and Bream; Newman, Gagne and Sorrento; Blauser, Lemke and Bream; Gagne (unassisted); Hrbek, Harper and Hrbek; Lemke (unassisted); Lemke, Belliard and Bream.
Left on bases--Minnesota 5, 3, 10, 5, 7, 5, 12—47; Atlanta 7, 6, 12, 7, 5, 7, 8—52.
Hit by pitcher—By Erickson (Smith), by Smoltz (Hrbek).
Passed ball—Harper.
Balk—Glavine.

Time of games—First game, 3:00, second game, 2:37; third game, 4:04; fourth game, 2:57; fifth game, 2:59; sixth game, 3:36; seventh game, 3:23.

Attendance—First game, 55,108; second game, 55,145; third game, 50,878; fourth game, 50,878; fifth game, 50,878; sixth game, 55,155; seventh game, 55,118.

Umpires—Denkinger (A.L.), Wendelstedt (N.L.), Coble (A.L.), Tata (N.L.), Reed (A.L.) and Montague (N.L.).

Official scorers—Red Foley, retired baseball writer; Tom Mee, Minnesota official scorer; Dave Nightingale, The Sporting News; Mark Fredrickson, Atlanta official scorer; Kit Stier, BBWAA.

ALL-STAR GAME

AT TORONTO'S SKYDOME, JULY 9, 1991

HIGHLIGHTS

AMERICAN LEAGUE 4, NATIONAL LEAGUE 2

Why the American League won: Cal Ripken did what he had been doing through the first three months of the season—hitting with power in key situations. Baltimore's Ripken, batting .348 with 18 home runs and 54 runs batted in at the midsummer break, rifled a three-run homer to center field in the third inning. The wallop, which came with Rickey Henderson and Wade Boggs aboard via singles, was struck against Montreal righthander Dennis Martinez.

Why the National League lost: The senior circuit displayed an anemic offense—again. Losing for the fourth consecutive time, the N.L. ran its four-year run total to six. And when the Chicago Cubs' Ryne Sandberg stroked a one-out double in the third inning, it marked the N.L.'s first extra-base hit since 1987.

The turning points:

1. When Martinez, pitching to longtime Orioles teammate Ripken, lost control of a third-inning slider and saw the pitch wind up right over the plate—and right over the center-field wall. It was Ripken's first homer in nine All-Star Games.

2. When the N.L., trailing 3-2, put its first two batters on base in the sixth inning against Jack McDowell of the Chicago White Sox but couldn't score. Will Clark started the inning with a base on balls and Bobby Bonilla singled. A.L. first baseman Cecil Fielder then made a nice stop on Felix Jose's grounder and threw to second base for a forceout. Pinch-hitter Paul O'Neill followed with a slow roller to the right side, which Fielder grabbed and fired home to catch a sliding Clark. Pinch-hitter Howard Johnson fouled out, ending the inning.

Notable: The Cubs' Andre Dawson, who in seven previous All-Star Games had failed to hit a home run or even collect an RBI, put an end to both futility streaks when he parked a Roger Clemens pitch over the center-field barrier in the fourth inning. Ripken, too, had yet to notch an All-Star RBI before getting three in one fell swoop.... The pitchers of record in this game played at Toronto's Sky-Dome were both from Canadian teams—winner Jimmy Key of the Blue Jays and loser Martinez of the Expos.... A.L. starting pitcher Jack Morris was struck on the right ankle by a shot off Bonilla's bat in the first inning. While X-rays were negative, the play reminded All-Star historians of Earl Averill's smash off Dizzy Dean's toe in the 1937 classic. Dean was never the same pitcher after incurring the injury.

Quotable: Ripken, responding to his prodigious performance in a home run-hitting contest the day before the game: "The worst thing a hitter in a good groove can do is start swinging for the fences. I was afraid it might carry over to the All-Star Game." Carry over it did—much to Ripken's delight, however.

BOX SCORE

National League	AB	R	H	RBI	PO	A
Gwynn, cf (Padres)	4	1	2	0	6	0
eButler, pr-cf (Dodgers) ...	1	0	0	0	0	0
Sandberg, 2b (Cubs)	3	0	1	0	2	1
Samuel, 2b (Dodgers)	1	0	1	0	2	1
Clark, 1b (Giants)	2	0	1	0	0	0
Murray, 1b (Dodgers)	1	0	0	0	3	0
Bonilla, dh (Pirates)	4	0	2	1	0	0
Dawson, rf (Cubs)	2	1	1	1	0	0
Jose, rf (Cardinals)	2	0	1	0	1	0
Calderon, lf (Expos)	2	0	1	0	1	0
aO'Neill, lf (Reds)	2	0	0	0	0	0
Sabo, 3b (Reds)	2	0	0	0	1	0
bJohnson, 3b (Mets)	2	0	0	0	0	0
Santiago, c (Padres)	3	0	0	0	4	0
Biggio, c (Astros)	1	0	0	0	2	0
O. Smith, ss (Cardinals)	1	0	0	0	0	1
Larkin, ss (Reds)	1	0	0	0	0	2
iBell (Cubs)	1	0	0	0	0	0
Glavine, p (Braves)	0	0	0	0	0	0
De. Martinez, p (Expos)	0	0	0	0	0	0
Viola, p (Mets)	0	0	0	0	0	0
Harnisch, p (Astros)	0	0	0	0	0	0
Smiley, p (Pirates)	0	0	0	0	0	0
Dibble, p (Reds)	0	0	0	0	0	0
Morgan, p (Dodgers)	0	0	0	0	0	1
Totals	**35**	**2**	**10**	**2**	**24**	**7**

American League	AB	R	H	RBI	PO	A
R. Henderson, lf (A's)	2	1	1	0	0	0
Carter, lf (Blue Jays)	1	1	1	0	1	0
Boggs, 3b (Red Sox)	2	1	1	0	1	2
fMolitor, 3b (Brewers)	0	0	0	0	0	0
C. Ripken, ss (Orioles)	3	1	2	3	2	1
gGuillen, ss (White Sox) ...	0	0	0	0	1	0
Fielder, 1b (Tigers)	3	0	0	0	6	2
hPalmeiro, 1b (Rangers) ...	0	0	0	0	2	0
Tartabull, dh (Royals)	2	0	0	0	0	0
cBaines, dh (A's)	1	0	0	1	0	0
D. Henderson, rf (A's)	2	0	0	0	2	0
dSierra, rf (Rangers)	2	0	0	0	0	0
Griffey Jr., cf (Mariners)	3	0	2	0	0	0
Puckett, cf (Twins)	1	0	0	0	0	0
S. Alomar, c (Indians)	2	0	0	0	2	0
Fisk, c (White Sox)	2	0	1	0	5	0
R. Alomar, 2b (Blue Jays) .	4	0	0	0	2	5
Morris, p (Twins)	0	0	0	0	0	1
Key, p (Blue Jays)	0	0	0	0	1	0
Clemens, p (Red Sox)	0	0	0	0	0	0
McDowell, p (White Sox) ..	0	0	0	0	0	0
Reardon, p (Red Sox)	0	0	0	0	0	0
Aguilera, p (Twins)	0	0	0	0	0	0
Eckersley, p (A's)	0	0	0	0	0	1
Totals	**30**	**4**	**8**	**4**	**27**	**12**

National League 1 0 0			1 0 0		0 0 0—2	
American League 0 0 3			0 0 0		1 0 x—4	

National League	IP	H	R	ER	BB	SO
Glavine (Braves)	2	1	0	0	1	3
De. Martinez (Expos) .	2	4	3	3	0	0
Viola (Mets)	1	0	0	0	1	0
Harnisch (Astros)	1	2	0	0	0	1

National League	IP	H	R	ER	BB	SO
Smiley (Pirates)	*0	1	1	1	0	0
Dibble (Reds)	1	0	0	0	1	1
Morgan (Dodgers)	1	0	0	0	0	1

*Pitched to two batters in seventh.

American League	IP	H	R	ER	BB	SO
Morris (Twins)	2	4	1	1	0	1
Key (Blue Jays)	1	1	0	0	0	1
Clemens (Red Sox)	1	1	1	1	0	0
McDowell (W. Sox).....	2	1	0	0	2	0
Reardon (Red Sox)	⅔	1	0	0	0	0
Aguilera (Twins)	1⅓	2	0	0	0	3
Eckersley (A's)..........	1	0	0	0	0	1

Winning pitcher—Key. Losing pitcher—De. Martinez. Save—Eckersley.

Molitor reached first base on catcher's interference.

aReached base on fielder's choice for Calderon in sixth. bFouled out for Sabo in sixth. cGrounded out for Tartabull in sixth. dStruck out for D. Henderson in sixth. eRan for Gwynn in seventh. fAwarded first base on catcher's interference for Boggs in seventh. gSacrificed for C. Ripken in seventh. hReceived intentional walk for Fielder in seventh. iStruck out for Larkin in 9th.—Biggio. E—Biggio. DP—A.L. 2. LOB—N.L. 8, A.L. 8. 2B—Sandberg. HR—C. Ripken, Dawson. SB—Calderon. SH—Guillen. SF—Baines. BB—Off Glavine 1 (Boggs), off Viola 1 (Carter), off Dibble 1 (Palmeiro), off McDowell 2 (O. Smith, Clark). SO—By Glavine 3 (Fielder, Tartabull, D. Henderson), by Harnisch 1 (Sierra), by Dibble 1 (Sierra), by Morgan 1 (Fisk), by Morris 1 (Santiago), by Key 1 (Bonilla), by Aguilera 3 (Murray, O'Neill, Johnson), by Eckersley 1 (Bell). U—Brinkman (A.L.), plate; McSherry (N.L.), first; Kaiser (A.L.), second; Quick (N.L.), third; Young (A.L.), left field; Bonin (N.L.), right field. Official scorers—Kit Stier (Oakland Tribune), Red Foley (BBWAA), Joe Sawchuk (Blue Jays official scorer). T—3:04. A—52,383.

Players listed on roster but not used: N.L.—Browning, Kruk, L. Smith. A.L.—Franco, Harvey, Langston, Sanderson.

PLAY BY PLAY

FIRST INNING

N.L.—Gwynn singled to left. Sandberg flied to right. Clark singled to right, Gwynn went to third. Bonilla hit a hard smash off the pitcher, Gwynn scored and Clark went to second. Dawson grounded into double play, third to second to first.

A.L.—R. Henderson fouled to first baseman. Boggs walked. C. Ripken singled to center, Boggs went to second. Fielder and Tartabull struck out.

SECOND INNING

N.L.—Calderon singled to right. Sabo grounded to pitcher, Calderon went to second. Santiago struck out as Calderon stole third. O. Smith lined to short.

A.L.—D. Henderson struck out. Griffey and S. Alomar flied to center.

THIRD INNING

N.L.—Key now pitching. Gwynn lined to first. Sandberg doubled to left-center. Clark grounded to first baseman, who tossed to pitcher covering, Sandberg went to third. Bonilla struck out.

A.L.—D. Martinez now pitching. R. Alomar flied to left. R. Henderson singled to center. Boggs singled to second base, R. Henderson went to second. C. Ripken homered to center, scoring R. Henderson and Boggs. Fielder grounded to second. Tartabull lined to third.

FOURTH INNING

N.L.—Clemens now pitching and Carter in left. Dawson homered to center. Calderon flied to center. Sabo flied to left. Santiago flied to center.

A.L.—Jose now in right. D. Henderson flied to center. Griffey singled to center. S. Alomar forced Griffey, shortstop to second baseman. R. Alomar lined to second.

FIFTH INNING

N.L.—McDowell now pitching and Fisk catching. O. Smith walked. Gwynn grounded into double play, third to second to first. Sandberg flied to right.

A.L.—Viola now pitching, Larkin at short and Samuel at second. Carter walked. Boggs flied to center, C. Ripken forced R. Henderson, shortstop to second baseman. Fielder flied to center.

SIXTH INNING

N.L.—Clark walked. Bonilla singled, Clark went to second. Jose forced Bonilla at second, first baseman to shortstop, Clark went to third. O'Neill, pinch-hitting for Calderon, reached base as first baseman threw to catcher to retire Clark at the plate, Jose went to second. Johnson, pinch-hitting for Sabo, fouled to third baseman.

A.L.—Harnisch now pitching, Murray at first, Johnson at third and O'Neill in left. Baines, pinch-hitting for Tartabull, grounded to second. Sierra, pinch-hitting for D. Henderson, struck out. Griffey singled to right. Fisk singled to center, Griffey went to third. R. Alomar flied to center.

SEVENTH INNING

N.L.—Reardon now pitching, Puckett in center and Sierra in right. Santiago grounded to second. Larkin grounded to short. Gwynn singled to left. Butler pinch-ran for Gwynn. Aguilera now pitching. Samuel singled to left, Butler went to second. Murray struck out.

A.L.—Smiley now pitching, Biggio catching and Butler in center. Carter singled to left. Molitor, pinch-hitting for Boggs, reached first on catcher's interference, Carter went to second. Dibble now pitching. Guillen, pinch-hitting for C. Ripken, sacrificed, pitcher to second baseman covering first, Carter went to third and Molitor went to second. Palmeiro, pinch-hitting for Fielder, was walked intentionally. Baines hit a sacrifice fly to right, Carter scored and Molitor went to third. Sierra struck out.

EIGHTH INNING

N.L.—Palmeiro now at first, Guillen at short and Molitor at third. Bonilla popped to short. Jose singled to right. O'Neill and Johnson struck out.

A.L.—Morgan now pitching. Puckett grounded to short. Fisk struck out. R. Alomar grounded to pitcher.

NINTH INNING

N.L.—Eckersley now pitching. Biggio grounded to second. Bell, pinch-hitting for Larkin, struck out. Butler grounded to pitcher.

BOX SCORES OF NO-HIT GAMES

NOLAN RYAN
MAY 1
Texas 3, Toronto 0 (N)

TORONTO	ab	r	h	bi	TEXAS	ab	r	h	bi
White, cf	4	0	0	0	Pettis, cf	4	1	1	0
Alomar, 2b	4	0	0	0	Daugherty, lf	4	0	1	0
Gruber, 3b	2	0	0	0	Palmeiro, 1b	4	1	2	0
Carter, lf	2	0	0	0	Sierra, rf	4	1	1	2
Olerud, 1b	3	0	0	0	Franco, 2b	4	0	0	0
Whiten, rf	3	0	0	0	Gonzalez, dh	3	0	1	0
Hill, dh	3	0	0	0	Stanley, c	3	0	1	0
Myers, c	3	0	0	0	Buechele, 3b	4	0	1	0
Lee, ss	3	0	0	0	Huson, ss	2	0	0	0
TOTALS	27	0	0	0	TOTALS	32	3	8	2

Toronto...0 0 0 0 0 0 0 0 0—0
Texas...0 0 3 0 0 0 0 0 x—3

E—Gruber (2), Myers (1), Lee (5), Palmeiro (1). LOB—Toronto 2, Texas 8. 2B—Stanley (1), Gonzalez (3). HR—Sierra (5). S—Huson. SB—Pettis (8). CS—Gonzalez (1).

TORONTO	IP	H	R	ER	BB	K
Key (L 4-1)	6	5	3	3	1	5
MacDonald	1	2	0	0	0	2
Fraser	1	1	0	0	0	0

TEXAS	IP	H	R	ER	BB	K
Ryan (W 3-2)	9	0	0	0	2	16

HBP: Gonzalez by Fraser. T—2:25. A—33,439. Umpires—HP, Tschida. 1B, Coble. 2B, Shulock. 3B, Johnson.

TOMMY GREENE
MAY 23
Philadelphia 2, Montreal 0 (N)

PHILADELPHIA	ab	r	h	bi	MONTREAL	ab	r	h	bi
Backman, 2b	4	0	1	0	DeShields, 2b	2	0	0	0
Booker, 3b	4	0	1	0	Grissom, cf	4	0	0	0
Kruk, lf	3	1	1	0	Calderon, lf	2	0	0	0
Jordan, 1b	4	0	2	1	Galarraga, 1b	4	0	0	0
V. Hayes, cf	4	1	1	0	Walker, rf	4	0	0	0
Fletcher, c	4	0	1	1	Wallach, 3b	2	0	0	0
Thon, ss	4	0	0	0	Hassey, c	2	0	0	0
Morris, rf	3	0	1	0	Owen, ss	3	0	0	0
Greene, p	4	0	0	0	Boyd, p	2	0	0	0
					Bullock, ph	0	0	0	0
					Ruskin, p	0	0	0	0
					Jones, p	0	0	0	0
TOTALS	34	2	8	2	TOTALS	25	0	0	0

Philadelphia....................................1 0 0 0 0 0 0 0 1—2
Montreal...0 0 0 0 0 0 0 0 0—0

E—None. LOB—Philadelphia 7, Montreal 6. 2B—Fletcher (4), V. Hayes (9), Kruk (6). 3B—Jordan (2). S—DeShields. SB—DeShields (18), Backman (1), Calderon (11). CS—DeShields (6).

PHILADELPHIA	IP	H	R	ER	BB	K
Greene (W 3-0)	9	0	0	0	7	10

MONTREAL	IP	H	R	ER	BB	K
Boyd (L 2-5)	8	6	1	1	1	6
Ruskin	0	2	1	1	0	0
Jones	1	0	0	0	1	0

Ruskin pitched to 2 batters in 9th.
WP—Boyd. T—2:25. A—8,833. Umpires—HP, Quick. 1B, Hallion. 2B, Darling. 3B, Rennert.

ORIOLES
JULY 13
Baltimore 2, Oakland 0 (D)

BALTIMORE	ab	r	h	bi	OAKLAND	ab	r	h	bi
Devereaux, cf	4	1	3	1	Wilson, lf	4	0	0	0
Orsulak, lf-rf	4	0	0	0	Blankenship, 2b	0	0	0	0

	ab	r	h	bi		ab	r	h	bi
C. Ripken, ss	4	0	0	0	D. Henderson, cf	3	0	0	0
Horn, dh	2	0	0	0	Canseco, rf	3	0	0	0
Segui, ph-dh	1	0	0	0	Baines, dh	3	0	0	0
Milligan, 1b	3	0	1	0	McGwire, 1b	3	0	0	0
Martinez, rf	3	1	1	0	Quirk, c	2	0	0	0
Anderson, pr-lf	0	0	0	0	Law, ph-3b	0	0	0	0
Gomez, 3b	4	0	0	0	Riles, 3b	2	0	0	0
Hoiles, c	4	0	1	1	Steinbach, ph-c	1	0	0	0
B. Ripken, 2b	3	0	0	0	Gallego, 2b-ss	3	0	0	0
					Bordick, ss	2	0	0	0
					R. Henderson, ph-lf	1	0	0	0
TOTALS	32	2	6	2	TOTALS	27	0	0	0

Baltimore...0 0 0 0 1 1 0 0 0—2
Oakland...0 0 0 0 0 0 0 0 0—0

E—Show (1). LOB—Baltimore 6, Oakland 4. 2B—Martinez (2). HR—Devereaux (11). CS—Devereaux (6).

BALTIMORE	IP	H	R	ER	BB	K
Milacki (W 5-3)	6	0	0	0	3	3
Flanagan (H,7)	1	0	0	0	1	0
Williamson (H,11)	1	0	0	0	0	0
Olson (S,19)	1	0	0	0	0	2

OAKLAND	IP	H	R	ER	BB	K
Show (L 0-1)	7	5	2	2	1	0
Chitren	⅓	1	0	0	0	0
Klink	⅔	0	0	0	0	1
Eckersley	1	0	0	0	2	2

T—2:38. A—40,047. Umpires—HP, Meriwether. 1B, Joyce. 2B, Cousins. 3B, McKean.

MARK GARDNER
JULY 26
Los Angeles 1, Montreal 0 (N)

MONTREAL	ab	r	h	bi	LOS ANGELES	ab	r	h	bi
DeShields, 2b	4	0	0	0	Butler, cf	4	0	0	0
Grissom, cf	4	0	1	0	Harris, 2b	4	1	1	0
Calderon, lf	3	0	0	0	Murray, 1b	3	0	1	0
Wallach, 3b	4	0	1	0	Strawberry, rf	4	0	1	1
Walker, rf	4	0	0	0	Daniels, lf	2	0	0	0
Galarraga, 1b	4	0	0	0	Scioscia, c	2	0	0	0
Reyes, c	3	0	0	0	Hansen, 3b	3	0	0	0
Owen, ss	2	0	0	0	Griffin, ss	3	0	0	0
Gardner, p	3	0	0	0	Hershiser, p	1	0	0	0
Fassero, p	0	0	0	0	Javier, ph	1	0	0	0
					Gross, p	0	0	0	0
					Gwynn, ph	1	0	0	0
					Howell, p	0	0	0	0
TOTALS	31	0	2	0	TOTALS	28	1	3	1

Montreal..0 0 0 0 0 0 0 0 0—0
Los Angeles.......................................0 0 0 0 0 0 0 0 1—1

None out when winning run scored.

E—None. DP—Montreal 1, Los Angeles 1. LOB—Montreal 3, Los Angeles 3. S—Scioscia. GDP—Galarraga. SB—Calderon (23).

MONTREAL	IP	H	R	ER	BB	K
Gardner (L 5-7)	9	2	1	1	2	4
Fassero	0	1	0	0	0	0

LOS ANGELES	IP	H	R	ER	BB	K
Hershiser	6	1	0	0	1	1
Gross	3	1	0	0	1	4
Howell (W 4-2)	1	0	0	0	0	0

Gardner pitched to 2 batters in 10th; Fassero pitched to 1 batter in 10th. T—2:29. A—38,957. Umpires—HP, DeMuth. 1B, Bonin. 2B, Poncino. 3B, Froemming.

NOTE: Mark Gardner held Los Angeles hitless for the first nine innings, but the Dodgers collected three singles in the 10th, including the game-winner off reliever Jeff Fassero, and beat Montreal, 1-0.

DENNIS MARTINEZ

JULY 28
Montreal 2, Los Angeles 0 (D)

MONTREAL	ab	r	h	bi	LOS ANGELES	ab	r	h	bi
DeShields, 2b	3	0	1	0	Butler, cf	3	0	0	0
Grissom, cf	4	0	0	0	Samuel, 2b	3	0	0	0
Da. Martinez, rf	4	1	0	0	Murray, 1b	3	0	0	0
Calderon, lf	3	0	0	0	Strawberry, rf	3	0	0	0
Wallach, 3b	4	0	0	0	Daniels, lf	3	0	0	0
Walker, 1b	4	1	1	1	Harris, 3b	3	0	0	0
Hassey, c	3	0	1	0	Scioscia, c	3	0	0	0
Owen, ss	3	0	0	0	Griffin, ss	2	0	0	0
De. Martinez, p	3	0	1	0	Javier, ph	1	0	0	0
					Morgan, p	2	0	0	0
					Gwynn, ph	1	0	0	0
TOTALS	31	2	4	1	TOTALS	27	0	0	0

Montreal ....0 0 0   0 0 0   2 0 0—2
Los Angeles ....0 0 0   0 0 0   0 0 0—0

E—Griffin 2 (20). LOB—Montreal 4. 3B—Walker (2). S—Calderon.
CS—Hassey (1).

MONTREAL	IP	H	R	ER	BB	K
De. Martinez (W 11-6)	9	0	0	0	0	5

LOS ANGELES	IP	H	R	ER	BB	K
Morgan (L 9-6)	9	4	2	0	1	5

WP—Morgan. T—2:14. A—45,560. Umpires—HP, Poncino. 1B, Froemming.
2B, DeMuth. 3B, Bonin.

WILSON ALVAREZ

AUGUST 11
Chicago 7, Baltimore 0 (D)

CHICAGO	ab	r	h	bi	BALTIMORE	ab	r	h	bi
Raines, lf	5	1	1	2	Devereaux, cf	4	0	0	0
Ventura, 3b	4	2	3	1	Bell, 2b	4	0	0	0
Thomas, dh	5	1	3	3	C. Ripken, ss	3	0	0	0
Pasqua, 1b	4	0	2	1	Evans, rf	2	0	0	0
Newson, rf	4	0	1	0	Milligan, lf	3	0	0	0
Huff, rf	1	0	0	0	Segui, lf	3	0	0	0
Johnson, cf	4	0	1	0	Hoiles, dh	3	0	0	0
Karkovice, c	3	1	1	0	Gomez, 3b	2	0	0	0
Cora, 2b	3	0	0	0	Melvin, c	3	0	0	0
Guillen, ss	3	2	2	0					
TOTALS	36	7	14	7	TOTALS	27	0	0	0

Chicago ....2 2 0   0 0 3   0 0 0—7
Baltimore ....0 0 0   0 0 0   0 0 0—0

E—Karkovice (2). DP—Chicago 1, Baltimore 3. LOB—Chicago 7, Baltimore 5. 2B—Raines (15), Thomas (25), Guillen (12). HR—Thomas (23).
S—Cora. GDP—Huff, Milligan, Newson 2. CS—Guillen (7).

CHICAGO	IP	H	R	ER	BB	K
Alvarez (W 1-0)	9	0	0	0	5	7

BALTIMORE	IP	H	R	ER	BB	K
Johnson (L 2-4)	1⅓	8	4	4	1	3
Frohwirth	4	3	3	3	2	3
Poole	2⅔	2	0	0	0	2
Olson	1	1	0	0	0	0

HBP: Pasqua by Frohwirth. T—2:45. A—40,455. Umpires—HP, Denkinger.
1B, McCoy. 2B, Merrill. 3B, McClelland.

BRET SABERHAGEN

AUGUST 26
Kansas City 7, Chicago 0 (N)

CHICAGO	ab	r	h	bi	KANSAS CITY	ab	r	h	bi
Raines, lf	4	0	0	0	McRae, cf	4	2	1	0
Cora, 2b	4	0	0	0	Gibson, lf	4	3	3	1
Thomas, 1b	4	0	0	0	Brett, dh	3	1	2	1
Ventura, 3b	3	0	0	0	Eisenreich, rf	3	0	1	1
Fisk, c	3	0	0	0	Benzinger, 1b	4	1	2	3
Pasqua, rf	2	0	0	0	Pecota, 3b	4	0	1	1
Johnson, cf	3	0	0	0	Mayne, c	4	0	1	0
Karkovice, c	2	0	0	0	Howard, ss	4	0	1	0
Merullo, c	0	0	0	0	Shumpert, 2b	4	0	1	0
Guillen, ss	3	0	0	0					
TOTALS	28	0	0	0	TOTALS	34	7	13	7

Chicago ....0 0 0   0 0 0   0 0 0—0
Kansas City ....2 0 3   2 0 0   0 0 x—7

E—Gibson (3), Patterson (3). LOB—Chicago 3, Kansas City 8.
2B—Benzinger (8), Pecota (17). 3B—Gibson (6). SF—Eisenreich, Brett.
SB—Benzinger (1).

CHICAGO	IP	H	R	ER	BB	K
Hough (L 7-8)	2⅔	8	5	5	1	0
Patterson	1	2	2	2	1	1
Pall	3⅓	2	0	0	0	1
Radinsky	1	1	0	0	0	0

KANSAS CITY	IP	H	R	ER	BB	K
Saberhagen (W 10-6)	9	0	0	0	2	5

HBP: McRae by Patterson. WP—Pall. PB—Karkovice. T—2:30. A—25,164.
Umpires—HP, Hendry. 1B, Hirschbeck. 2B, Phillips. 3B, Cedarstrom.

BRAVES

SEPTEMBER 11
Atlanta 1, San Diego 0 (D)

SAN DIEGO	ab	r	h	bi	ATLANTA	ab	r	h	bi
Fernandez, ss	4	0	0	0	Nixon, lf	4	0	0	0
Jackson, cf	4	0	0	0	Treadway, 2b	4	0	1	0
Gwynn, rf	3	0	0	0	Lemke, 2b	0	0	0	0
McGriff, 1b	3	0	0	0	Pendleton, 3b	4	1	2	1
Santiago, c	3	0	0	0	Justice, rf	4	0	0	0
Teufel, 3b-2b	3	0	0	0	Gant, cf	2	0	0	0
Clark, lf	2	0	0	0	Bream, 1b	3	0	1	0
Azocar, ph-lf	1	0	0	0	Mitchell, p	0	0	0	0
Shipley, 2b	1	0	0	0	Wohlers, p	0	0	0	0
Howell, ph-3b	1	0	0	0	L. Smith, ph	1	0	0	0
Harris, p	1	0	0	0	Rossy, pr	0	0	0	0
Roberts, ph	1	0	0	0	Pena, p	0	0	0	0
					Olson, c	4	0	2	0
					Belliard, ss	3	0	1	0
					Mercker, p	2	0	0	0
					Hunter, 1b	1	0	0	0
TOTALS	27	0	0	0	TOTALS	32	1	7	1

San Diego ....0 0 0   0 0 0   0 0 0—0
Atlanta ....0 0 0   0 1 0   0 0 x—1

E—Pendleton (20), Shipley (4). LOB—San Diego 3, Atlanta 9.
2B—Pendleton (27), Belliard (7). HR—Pendleton (20). S—Harris.

SAN DIEGO	IP	H	R	ER	BB	K
Harris (L 5-5)	8	7	1	1	2	7

ATLANTA	IP	H	R	ER	BB	K
Mercker (W 5-3)	6	0	0	0	2	6
Wohlers (H,1)	2	0	0	0	0	0
Pena (S,8)	1	0	0	0	0	0

T—2:11. A—20,477. Umpires—HP, Wendelstedt. 1B, Pulli. 2B, Williams. 3B,
Marsh.

LOW - HIT GAMES

AMERICAN LEAGUE

ONE - HIT GAMES

Date   Pitcher(s), Team, Opponent, Result—Player with hit

4-10   Scott Sanderson (8 innings) and Greg Cadaret (1 inning), New York at Detroit, W 4-0—Tony Phillips (double in
     ninth)

Date	Pitcher(s), Team, Opponent, Result—Player with hit
7-11	Scott Sanderson, New York at California, W 2-0—Luis Polonia (double in fourth)
7-14	Jack McDowell, Chicago at Milwaukee, W 15-1—Paul Molitor (home run in first)
8-14	Randy Johnson, Seattle vs. Oakland, W 4-0—Mike Gallego (single in ninth)
8-28	Tom Candiotti (8 innings) and Tom Henke (1 inning), Toronto at Baltimore, W 3-0—Joe Orsulak (single in first)
9-24	Scott Erickson (7 innings) and Mark Guthrie (2 innings), Minnesota vs. Chicago, W 9-2—Dan Pasqua (home run in seventh)

TWO-HIT GAMES

Date	Pitcher(s), Team, Opponent, Result—Player(s) with hits
4-13	Jack McDowell, Chicago at Detroit, W 4-1—Tony Phillips (home run in first), Dave Bergman (double in third)
4-14	Jimmy Key, Toronto vs. Milwaukee, W 9-0—Paul Molitor (single in third), Robin Yount (single in fourth)
4-19	Chuck Finley, California vs. Minnesota, W 2-0—Kirby Puckett (single in first), Greg Gagne (double in second)
5-1	Scott Erickson, Minnesota vs. Boston, W 1-0—Jody Reed (single in sixth), Tom Brunansky (double in seventh)
5-2	Todd Stottlemyre (7 innings), Mike Timlin (1 inning) and Duane Ward (1 inning), Toronto at Kansas City, W 3-1—Jim Eisenreich (single in second), Kurt Stillwell (single in seventh)
5-11	Kirk Dressendorfer (7 innings), Bruce Walton (1 inning) and Dana Allison (1 inning), Oakland at New York, W 10-2—Don Mattingly (single in first), Matt Nokes (home run in seventh)
5-14	Jack Morris, Minnesota vs. Milwaukee, W 5-1—Jim Gantner (doubles in fourth and seventh)
5-31	Ramon Garcia (7 innings), Scott Radinsky (1 inning) and Bobby Thigpen (1 inning), Chicago vs. Oakland, W 5-4—Mike Gallego (home run in second), Mark McGwire (single in seventh)
6-4	Chuck Finley, California vs. Boston, W 3-0—Ellis Burks (single in second), Mike Greenwell (single in seventh)
6-7	Allan Anderson (8 innings) and Rick Aguilera (1 inning), Minnesota vs. Cleveland, W 2-0—Mike Huff (single in fourth), Joel Skinner (double in eighth)
6-8	Roger Clemens (8 innings) and Dennis Lamp (1 inning), Boston at Oakland, W 8-1—Dave Henderson (home run in second), Ernest Riles (double in second)
6-12	Mike Timlin (6 innings), Bob MacDonald (1 inning), Jim Acker (⅔ inning) and Tom Henke (1⅓ innings), Toronto at Cleveland, W 1-0—Felix Fermin (single in sixth), Carlos Baerga (single in seventh)
6-12	Charlie Hough, Chicago at Texas, L 4-2—Ruben Sierra (triple in third), Steve Buechele (single in fourth)
6-13	Jimmy Key, Toronto at Cleveland, W 1-0—Joel Skinner and Felix Fermin (singles in third)
6-14	Dan Gakeler (7⅔ innings), Paul Gibson (⅔ inning) and Mike Henneman (⅔ inning), Detroit at Seattle, W 5-1—Greg Briley (single in third), Alvin Davis (single in eighth)
6-24	Scott Erickson, Minnesota at New York, W 5-0—Don Mattingly (single in first), Matt Nokes (double in second)
6-30	Jose Guzman, Texas at California, W 2-1—Dave Winfield (home run in fifth), Max Venable (single in fifth)
7-7	Nolan Ryan (8⅓ innings) and Kenny Rogers (⅔ inning), Texas vs. California, W 7-0—Dave Winfield (single in eighth), Gary Gaetti (double in eighth)
7-24	Joe Hesketh (6⅔ innings), Jeff Gray (1⅓ innings) and Jeff Reardon (1 inning), Boston at Texas, W 2-1—Rafael Palmeiro (single in first), Brian Downing (home run in fourth)
7-27	Joe Slusarski, Oakland at Baltimore, W 9-1—Chris Hoiles and Juan Bell (singles in third)
8-5	Eric King, Cleveland at Texas, W 9-0—Ruben Sierra (single in second), Jeff Huson (single in fifth)
8-5	Ron Darling (7 innings), Rick Honeycutt (⅔ inning) and Dennis Eckersley (1⅓ innings), Oakland vs. Seattle, W 3-0—Jay Buhner (single in second), Edgar Martinez (single in sixth)
8-21	Dan Plesac (4 innings), Julio Machado (4 innings) and Edwin Nunez (1 inning), Milwaukee at Toronto, W 3-0—Ed Sprague (single in second), Joe Carter (single in fourth)
9-4	Alex Fernandez (7 innings), Scott Radinsky (1 inning) and Bobby Thigpen (1 inning), Chicago vs. Kansas City, W 4-1—Danny Tartabull (single in first), Kurt Stillwell (home run in eighth)
9-10	Roger Clemens, Boston at Detroit, W 4-0—Alan Trammell (single in seventh), Milt Cuyler (single in ninth)
9-17	Ron Darling (7 innings), Rick Honeycutt (⅔ inning) and Gene Nelson (⅓ inning), Oakland at Chicago, L 1-0—Robin Ventura (single in first), Bo Jackson (home run in seventh)
9-17	Chris Bosio, Milwaukee at New York, W 2-0—Steve Sax (single in first), Torey Lovullo (single in ninth)
9-27	Jose Guzman, Texas at Oakland, W 3-0—Rickey Henderson (double in first), Mike Gallego (single in fifth)
9-29	Charlie Hough (8 innings) and Scott Radinsky (1 inning), Chicago vs. Seattle, L 2-1—Greg Briley (single in sixth), Pete O'Brien (single in seventh)

NATIONAL LEAGUE

ONE-HIT GAMES

Date	Pitcher(s), Team, Opponent, Result—Player with hit
4-8	Dennis Martinez (7 innings), Barry Jones (1 inning) and Scott Ruskin (1 inning), Montreal at Pittsburgh, W 7-0—Barry Bonds (single in seventh)
4-17	John Smiley, Pittsburgh vs. New York, W 4-0—Kevin McReynolds (double in second)
5-27	Doug Drabek, Pittsburgh at St. Louis, W 8-0—Bernard Gilkey (single in sixth)
5-29	Zane Smith, Pittsburgh at St. Louis, W 6-0—Jose Oquendo (triple in third)
7-14	Greg Harris (8⅓ innings) and Craig Lefferts (⅔ inning), San Diego at New York, W 2-1—Mackey Sasser (double in eighth)
9-10	Pete Schourek, New York vs. Montreal, W 9-0—Kenny Williams (single in fifth)
9-14	David Cone (7 innings) and Jeff Innis (1 inning), New York at St. Louis, L 2-1—Ray Lankford (single in fifth)
9-20	David Cone, New York vs. St. Louis, W 1-0—Felix Jose (double in eighth)

TWO-HIT GAMES

Date	Pitcher(s), Team, Opponent, Result—Player with hits
4-30	Mike Morgan, Los Angeles at Montreal, L 1-0—Tim Wallach (single in first), Delino DeShields (home run in ninth)
5-3	Pete Harnisch, Houston at Pittsburgh, L 1-0—Mike LaValliere (single in second), Orlando Merced (home run in third)
5-13	Ken Hill (8 innings) and Lee Smith (1 inning), St. Louis vs. Cincinnati, W 1-0—Jeff Reed (singles in third and eighth)
6-2	Adam Peterson (6 innings), Mike Maddux (1⅓ innings) and Craig Lefferts (1⅔ innings), San Diego vs. Houston, W 3-1—Steve Finley (home run in first and single in third)
7-3	Ron Darling (8 innings) and Alejandro Pena (1 inning), New York at Montreal, W 4-0—Dave Martinez (single in second), Spike Owen (single in eighth)

Date	Pitcher(s), Team, Opponent, Result—Player(s) with hits
7-6	Mark Gardner (8 innings), Jeff Fassero (⅔ inning) and Tim Burke (⅓ inning), Montreal at Pittsburgh, W 2-1—Barry Bonds (single in fifth), Jose Lind (double in fifth)
7-6	Don Robinson (8⅔ innings) and Dave Righetti (⅓ inning), San Francisco vs. San Diego, W 4-1—Benito Santiago (home run in fifth), Tony Gwynn (single in ninth)
7-11	Steve Avery (7⅓ innings) and Juan Berenguer (1⅔ innings), Atlanta vs. St. Louis, W 4-1—Rex Hudler (single in seventh), Ray Lankford (single in eighth)
7-20	Bruce Ruffin, Philadelphia at San Diego, W 4-0—Gerald Clark (double in fourth), Tim Teufel (single in seventh)
7-26	Orel Hershiser (6 innings), Kevin Gross (3 innings) and Jay Howell (1 inning), Los Angeles vs. Montreal, W 1-0—Tim Wallach (single in second), Marquis Grissom (single in ninth)
8-14	Brian Barnes (8⅓ innings) and Barry Jones (⅔ inning), Montreal at Chicago, W 2-0—Greg Maddux (single in third), Shawon Dunston (single in fourth)
8-15	Paul McClellan (7⅓ innings) and Dave Righetti (1⅔ innings), San Francisco vs. Cincinnati, W 4-1—Carmelo Martinez (home run in sixth), Billy Hatcher (single in ninth)
8-24	Jose Rijo, Cincinnati at New York, W 7-0—Gregg Jefferies (single in fifth), Kevin Elster (single in ninth)
8-29	Andy Benes, San Diego at St. Louis, W 1-0—Pedro Guerrero and Felix Jose (singles in fourth)
9-18	Terry Mulholland, Philadelphia at Montreal, W 1-0—Tim Wallach (single in second), Kenny Williams (single in third)
9-22	Ken Hill (8⅓ innings) and Lee Smith (⅔ innings), St. Louis at New York, W 2-1—Daryl Boston (double in sixth and home run in ninth)
10-5	Trevor Wilson, San Francisco vs. Los Angeles, W 4-0—Gary Carter (single in second), Mike Sharperson (double in ninth)

10-STRIKEOUT GAMES

AMERICAN LEAGUE

Team	No.	Pitchers
Seattle	9	Randy Johnson 7, Erik Hanson 2.
Texas	8	Nolan Ryan 6, Jose Guzman 1, Bobby Witt 1.
Boston	7	Roger Clemens 7.
Kansas City	6	Tom Gordon 3, Kevin Appier 2, Bret Saberhagen 1.
Chicago	5	Jack McDowell 3, Alex Fernandez 1, Melido Perez 1.
California	3	Jim Abbott 1, Chuck Finley 1, Mark Langston 1.
Cleveland	3	Greg Swindell 2, Doug Jones 1.
Milwaukee	3	Bill Wegman 1, Ted Higuera 1.
Toronto	3	Tom Candiotti 2, Juan Guzman 1.
Baltimore	2	Bob Milacki 1, Mike Mussina 1.
Detroit	2	Mark Leiter 2.
New York	2	Tim Leary 1, Scott Sanderson 1.
Minnesota	0	
Oakland	0	

NATIONAL LEAGUE

Team	No.	Pitchers
Atlanta	10	Tom Glavine 6, John Smoltz 2, Steve Avery 1, Charlie Leibrandt 1.
New York	7	David Cone 5, Dwight Gooden 1, Pete Schourek 1.
Philadelphia	5	Terry Mulholland 3, Jose DeJesus 1, Tommy Greene 1.
Houston	3	Pete Harnisch 3.
San Diego	3	Andy Benes 2, Bruce Hurst 1.
Chicago	2	Frank Castillo 1, Greg Maddux 1.
Cincinnati	2	Jose Rijo 2.
Montreal	2	Brian Barnes 1, Chris Nabholz 1.
Pittsburgh	2	Doug Drabek 1, John Smiley 1.
San Francisco	2	Bud Black 1, John Burkett 1.
Los Angeles	1	Tim Belcher 1.
St. Louis	0	

15-STRIKEOUT GAMES

Date	Pitcher, Team, Opponent	IP	H	R	ER	BB	SO	Result
5-1	Nolan Ryan, Texas vs. Toronto	9	0	0	0	2	16	W 3-0
10-6	David Cone, New York Mets at Philadelphia	9	3	0	0	1	19	W 7-0

1-0 GAMES

AMERICAN LEAGUE

Date	Winner	Loser	Inn.*	Site
4-10	†Kevin Appier, Kansas City	Charles Nagy, Cleveland	3	Kansas City
4-15	†Steve Olin, Cleveland	†Dennis Lamp, Boston	13	Boston
4-18	†Roger Clemens, Boston	†Bret Saberhagen, Kansas City	3	Boston
4-20	†Nolan Ryan, Texas	†Jose Mesa, Baltimore	5	Baltimore
5-1	Scott Erickson, Minnesota	Jeff Gray, Boston	8	Minnesota
5-17	†Randy Johnson, Seattle	†Tim Leary, New York	2	New York
5-20	†David Wells, Toronto	Bob Welch, Oakland	6	Oakland
5-24	Jaime Navarro, Milwaukee	Rod Nichols, Cleveland	3	Milwaukee
6-12	†Mike Timlin, Toronto	Tom Candiotti, Cleveland	1	Cleveland
6-13	Jimmy Key, Toronto	Charles Nagy, Cleveland	3	Cleveland
6-22	†Bob Milacki, Baltimore	†Tom Gordon, Kansas City	4	Kansas City
6-27	†Juan Guzman, Toronto	Kevin Tapani, Minnesota	4	Minnesota
7-4	†David West, Minnesota	†Jimmy Key, Toronto	2	Toronto
8-4	Charlie Hough, Chicago	†Mike Mussina, Baltimore	6	Baltimore
8-10	†Dave Otto, Cleveland	Bret Saberhagen, Kansas City	7	Kansas City
8-24	†Kirk McCaskill, California	†Kevin Morton, Boston	7	California
8-28	†Jim Abbott, California	Bill Gullickson, Detroit	6	California
9-3	†Brian Holman, Seattle	Scott Aldred, Detroit	3	Seattle
9-7	†Chuck Finley, California	Jaime Navarro, Milwaukee	1	California

Date	Winner	Loser	Inn.*	Site
9-8	†Jim Abbott, California	†Dan Plesac, Milwaukee	6	California
9-13	Jack McDowell, Chicago	Jim Abbott, California	6	California
9-17	†Greg Hibbard, Chicago	†Ron Darling, Oakland	7	Chicago

PLAYERS HITTING HOME RUNS IN 1-0 GAMES: 4-15—Brook Jacoby, Cleveland; 5-1—Dan Gladden, Minnesota; 8-4—Frank Thomas, Chicago; 8-24—Dave Winfield, California; 9-17—Bo Jackson, Chicago.

*Inning in which run was scored.   †Did not pitch complete game.

NATIONAL LEAGUE

Date	Winner	Loser	Inn.*	Site
4-16	†Norm Charlton, Cincinnati	†Andy Benes, San Diego	9	San Diego
4-17	†Bill Sampen, Montreal	†Jamie Moyer, St. Louis	1	Montreal
4-21	†Dave Righetti, San Francisco	†Curt Schilling, Houston	9	San Francisco
4-24	†Butch Henry, Houston	†Scott Scudder, Cincinnati	13	Houston
4-24	†Mike Bielecki, Chicago	†Jose DeLeon, St. Louis	2	St. Louis
4-30	Dennis Martinez, Montreal	Mike Morgan, Los Angeles	9	Montreal
5-3	Zane Smith, Pittsburgh	Pete Harnisch, Houston	3	Pittsburgh
5-13	†Ken Hill, St. Louis	†Randy Myers, Cincinnati	8	St. Louis
5-17	†Tommy Greene, Philadelphia	†Les Lancaster, Chicago	16	Philadelphia
5-24	†Curt Schilling, Houston	Andy Benes, San Diego	9	Houston
6-6	†Bob Ojeda, Los Angeles	†Ken Hill, St. Louis	1	St. Louis
6-7	†Doug Drabek, Pittsburgh	†Bruce Hurst, San Diego	2	Pittsburgh
6-9	Pete Harnisch, Houston	†David Cone, New York	4	Houston
6-11	†Al Osuna, Houston	†Roger McDowell, Philadelphia	11	Houston
6-20	†Barry Jones, Montreal	†Don Carman, Cincinnati	11	Cincinnati
6-25	Pete Harnisch, Houston	†Tom Glavine, Atlanta	3	Houston
7-1	†Bryn Smith, St. Louis	†Bruce Ruffin, Philadelphia	5	Philadelphia
7-5	‡Chris Hammond, Cincinnati	Pete Harnisch, Houston	3	Houston
7-12	†Tommy Greene, Philadelphia	†Bud Black, San Francisco	5	Philadelphia
7-26	†Jay Howell, Los Angeles	†Mark Gardner, Montreal	10	Los Angeles
8-7	†Mark Gardner, Montreal	†Omar Olivares, St. Louis	6	St. Louis
8-7	†Bud Black, San Francisco	†Charlie Leibrandt, Atlanta	1	Atlanta
8-9	†Jeff Brantley, San Francisco	†Kevin Gross, Los Angeles	13	San Francisco
8-10	Greg Harris, San Diego	†Jose Rijo, Cincinnati	3	San Diego
8-15	Greg Harris, San Diego	John Smoltz, Atlanta	8	San Diego
8-29	Andy Benes, San Diego	†Omar Olivares, St. Louis	4	St. Louis
9-7	†Greg Maddux, San Diego	†Cris Carpenter, St. Louis	10	San Diego
9-11	†Kent Mercker, Atlanta	Greg Harris, San Diego	5	Atlanta
9-12	†Ken Hill, St. Louis	†Doug Drabek, Pittsburgh	6	St. Louis
9-18	Terry Mulholland, Philadelphia	Dennis Martinez, Montreal	2	Philadelphia
9-20	David Cone, New York	Rheal Cormier, St. Louis	6	New York
10-2	Greg Maddux, Chicago	Jose DeJesus, Philadelphia	7	Philadelphia
10-5	Terry Mulholland, Philadelphia	†Anthony Young, New York	5	Philadelphia

PLAYERS HITTING HOME RUNS IN 1-0 GAMES: 4-21—Steve Decker, San Francisco; 4-24—Andre Dawson, Chicago; 4-30—Delino DeShields, Montreal; 5-3—Orlando Merced, Pittsburgh; 7-12—Darren Daulton, Philadelphia; 8-7—Darren Lewis, San Francisco; 9-7—Tim Teufel, San Diego; 9-11—Terry Pendleton, Atlanta.

*Inning in which run was scored.   †Did not pitch complete game.

FOUR OR MORE HITS IN ONE GAME

AMERICAN LEAGUE

Team	No.	Hitters
Milwaukee	20	Paul Molitor 7, B.J. Surhoff 4, Jim Gantner 2, Darryl Hamilton 2, Willie Randolph 2, Dante Bichette 1, Greg Vaughn 1, Robin Yount 1.
Boston	19	Wade Boggs 6, Mike Greenwell 4, Jody Reed 3, Jack Clark 1, Scott Cooper 1, Mike Marshall 1, Phil Plantier 1, Carlos Quintana 1, Luis Rivera 1.
Chicago	18	Tim Raines 4, Dan Pasqua 3, Robin Ventura 3, Scott Fletcher 2, Ozzie Guillen 2, Lance Johnson 2, Carlton Fisk 1, Frank Thomas 1.
California	15	Luis Polonia 4, Gary Gaetti 3, Dave Winfield 3, Junior Felix 1, Dave Gallagher 1, Wally Joyner 1, Luis Sojo 1, Max Venable 1.
Oakland	15	Harold Baines 4, Dave Henderson 3, Rickey Henderson 3, Jose Canseco 1, Mike Gallego 1, Ernest Riles 1, Terry Steinbach 1, Walt Weiss 1.
Kansas City	14	Todd Benzinger 3, George Brett 2, Jim Eisenreich 2, Kurt Stillwell 2, Warren Cromartie 1, Mike Macfarlane 1, Brian McRae 1, Kevin Seitzer 1, Gary Thurman 1.
Seattle	11	Ken Griffey Jr. 3, Edgar Martinez 2, Harold Reynolds 2, Scott Bradley 1, Alvin Davis 1, Dave Valle 1, Omar Vizquel 1.
Baltimore	10	Cal Ripken Jr. 3, Mike Devereaux 2, Randy Milligan 2, Dwight Evans 1, Bob Melvin 1, Joe Orsulak 1.
Detroit	10	Tony Phillips 2, Alan Trammell 2, Rob Deer 1, Travis Fryman 1, Lloyd Moseby 1, Johnny Paredes 1, Mickey Tettleton 1, Lou Whitaker 1.
New York	10	Steve Sax 4, Mel Hall 3, Roberto Kelly 1, Kevin Maas 1, Bernie Williams 1.
Texas	10	Rafael Palmeiro 4, Ruben Sierra 4, Kevin Reimer 1, Ivan Rodriguez 1.
Cleveland	9	Carlos Baerga 2, Sandy Alomar Jr. 1, Albert Belle 1, Alex Cole 1, Felix Fermin 1, Chris James 1, Carlos Martinez 1, Mark Whiten 1.
Minnesota	9	Kirby Puckett 3, Chuck Knoblauch 2, Chili Davis 1, Brian Harper 1, Shane Mack 1, Mike Pagliarulo 1.
Toronto	7	Devon White 2, Roberto Alomar 1, Joe Carter 1, Glenallen Hill 1, Manuel Lee 1, Greg Myers 1.

NATIONAL LEAGUE

Team	No.	Hitters
Montreal	14	Marquis Grissom 3, Dave Martinez 2, Larry Walker 2, Bret Barberie 1, Ivan Calderon 1, Delino DeShields 1, Andres Galarraga 1, Spike Owen 1, Tim Wallach 1, Kenny Williams 1.
Atlanta	13	Terry Pendleton 5, David Justice 2, Steve Avery 1, Jeff Blauser 1, Ron Gant 1, Brian Hunter 1, Greg Olson 1, Lonnie Smith 1.
Philadelphia	11	Wes Chamberlain 3, John Kruk 2, Dale Murphy 2, Charlie Hayes 1, Von Hayes 1, Ricky Jordan 1, Steve Lake 1.
San Diego	11	Bip Roberts 3, Benito Santiago 3, Tony Gwynn 2, Tony Fernandez 1, Darrin Jackson 1, Fred McGriff 1.
Chicago	9	Ryne Sandberg 4, Jose Vizcaino 2, Doug Dascenzo 1, Shawon Dunston 1, Mark Grace 1.
Cincinnati	9	Mariano Duncan 2, Paul O'Neill 2, Chris Sabo 2, Barry Larkin 1, Hal Morris 1, Luis Quinones 1.
New York	9	Kevin McReynolds 3, Dave Magadan 2, Vince Coleman 1, Tom Herr 1, Keith Miller 1, Mackey Sasser 1.
Pittsburgh	9	Jay Bell 3, Bobby Bonilla 2, John Wehner 2, Mike LaValliere 1, Andy Van Slyke 1.
St. Louis	9	Felix Jose 5, Ray Lankford 1, Tom Pagnozzi 1, Ozzie Smith 1, Todd Zeile 1.
San Francisco	8	Will Clark 2, Robby Thompson 2, Mike Felder 1, Willie McGee 1, Kevin Mitchell 1, Jose Uribe 1.
Los Angeles	7	Brett Butler 3, Gary Carter 1, Alfredo Griffin 1, Eddie Murray 1, Darryl Strawberry 1.
Houston	6	Craig Biggio 2, Steve Finley 2, Luis Gonzalez 1, Rafael Ramirez 1.

FIVE- AND SIX-HIT GAMES

Date	Player, Team, Opponent	AB	R	H	2B	3B	HR	RBI	Result
4-13	Dave Winfield, California at Minnesota	6	4	5	1	0	3	6	W 15-9
4-16	Dave Henderson, Oakland at California (11 inn.)	6	2	5	2	0	1	5	W 8-5
4-26	Brett Butler, Los Angeles vs. San Francisco	5	3	5	1	0	0	0	W 9-0
5-13	Luis Polonia, California at Cleveland	6	3	5	0	1	0	3	W 9-5
5-19	Dave Gallagher, California at Baltimore	5	2	5	0	0	0	3	W 10-2
5-23	Kirby Puckett, Minnesota vs. Texas (11 inn.)	7	2	6	0	1	0	0	L 10-6
6-1	Luis Polonia, California at Toronto	6	3	5	1	0	0	2	W 11-8
6-6	Kevin Reimer, Texas at Kansas City (18 inn.)	7	1	5	0	0	0	0	L 4-3
6-7	Marquis Grissom, Montreal at Atlanta	6	1	5	1	0	0	3	W 11-2
6-15	Bob Melvin, Baltimore at Toronto	5	2	5	1	0	1	2	W 8-4
6-17	Rafael Palmeiro, Texas vs. Kansas City (10 inn.)	5	2	5	2	0	0	1	W 10-9
6-23	Roberto Kelly, New York Yankees vs. Minnesota	5	2	5	0	0	1	3	W 11-2
6-24	Dave Winfield, California at Kansas City	5	3	5	1	1	1	3	W 9-4
6-25	Mike Felder, San Francisco at Los Angeles	6	4	5	0	0	0	0	W 9-4
6-26	Jay Bell, Pittsburgh vs. Chicago Cubs	5	1	5	1	0	0	1	W 7-6
6-26	Marquis Grissom, Montreal at New York Mets	5	1	5	0	0	0	1	L 7-4
7-4	Kevin Seitzer, Kansas City at California	5	2	5	0	0	0	0	W 12-5
7-14	Will Clark, San Francisco at Philadelphia	6	3	5	1	0	1	7	W 17-5
7-18	Omar Vizquel, Seattle at Milwaukee	5	2	5	0	0	0	1	W 12-0
7-18	Ken Griffey Jr., Seattle at Milwaukee	6	1	5	1	0	0	3	W 12-0
7-23	John Wehner, Pittsburgh vs. Atlanta	5	3	5	0	0	0	1	W 12-3
7-23	Carlos Baerga, Cleveland vs. Oakland	5	3	5	1	0	0	1	L 10-7
7-28	Paul Molitor, Milwaukee at Minnesota	6	2	5	0	0	0	0	W 11-2
7-28	Darryl Hamilton, Milwaukee at Minnesota	6	3	5	1	0	0	1	W 11-2
7-31	Wade Boggs, Boston vs. Oakland (14 inn.)	7	3	5	3	0	0	1	W 11-10
8-22	Jose Uribe, San Francisco at Houston	5	4	5	2	0	0	1	W 11-8
8-30	Joe Orsulak, Baltimore at Minnesota	5	3	5	1	0	0	0	W 11-5
9-13	Benito Santiago, San Diego at San Francisco	5	3	5	1	0	1	5	W 13-2
9-29	Rickey Henderson, Oakland vs. Texas	5	4	5	0	0	1	4	W 19-5
10-5	Bernie Williams, New York Yankees vs. Cleveland (12 inn.)	6	1	5	0	0	0	2	L 7-5

HITTING STREAKS OF 15 OR MORE GAMES

AMERICAN LEAGUE

G	Player, Team	Span of streak
22	Brian McRae, Kansas City	July 20-Aug. 13
21	Joe Orsulak, Baltimore	Aug. 2-Aug. 25
20	Chuck Knoblauch, Minnesota	Sept. 2-Sept. 25
19	Darryl Hamilton, Milwaukee	July 25-Aug. 14
18	Ruben Sierra, Texas	June 12-June 30
17	Mike Greenwell, Boston	June 7-June 26
	Kent Hrbek, Minnesota	Aug. 11-Aug. 30
16	Greg Vaughn, Milwaukee	April 24-May 12
	Wally Joyner, California	May 4-May 20
	Roberto Alomar, Toronto	May 24-June 9
	Don Mattingly, New York	June 18-July 3
	Kirby Puckett, Minnesota	July 6-July 26
	Carlos Martinez, Cleveland	July 16-Aug. 1
	Chili Davis, Minnesota	July 21-Aug. 7
15	Edgar Martinez, Seattle	April 15-April 30
	Ellis Burks, Boston	May 7-May 26
	Julio Franco, Texas	May 11-May 27
	Rafael Palmeiro, Texas	July 19-Aug. 4
	Dave Gallagher, California	July 21-Aug. 6
	Milt Cuyler, Detroit	Aug. 30-Sept. 15

NATIONAL LEAGUE

G	Player, Team	Span of streak
23	Brett Butler, Los Angeles	June 15-July 12
20	Otis Nixon, Atlanta	July 11-July 31
19	Willie McGee, San Francisco	May 26-June 15
	Mark Grace, Chicago	July 24-Aug. 13
	Barry Larkin, Cincinnati	Aug. 17-Sept. 6
18	Bobby Bonilla, Pittsburgh	Aug. 10-Aug. 28
15	Terry Pendleton, Atlanta	May 12-May 31
	Tony Gwynn, San Diego	May 25-June 9
	John Kruk, Philadelphia	Sept. 12-Sept. 28

MULTI-HOMER GAMES

AMERICAN LEAGUE

Team	No.	Hitters
Chicago	12	Robin Ventura 4, Carlton Fisk 3, Frank Thomas 2, Ron Karkovice 1, Dan Pasqua 1, Sammy Sosa 1.
Detroit	11	Cecil Fielder 5, Rob Deer 2, Mickey Tettleton 2, Dave Bergman 1, Lou Whitaker 1.
New York	10	Matt Nokes 5, Jesse Barfield 2, Mel Hall 1, Kevin Maas 1, Roberto Kelly 1.
Kansas City	8	Danny Tartabull 3, George Brett 1, Kirk Gibson 1, Mike Macfarlane 1, Brian McRae 1, Harvey Pulliam.
Oakland	8	Mark McGwire 3, Jose Canseco 2, Harold Baines 1, Dave Henderson 1, Rickey Henderson 1.
Baltimore	6	Randy Milligan 2, Cal Ripken 2, Mike Devereaux 1, Chito Martinez 1.
Milwaukee	6	Greg Vaughn 3, Dante Bichette 2, Bill Spiers 1.
Minnesota	6	Chili Davis 3, Randy Bush 1, Shane Mack 1, Mike Pagliarulo 1.
Texas	6	Rafael Palmeiro 2, Brian Downing 1, Juan Gonzalez 1, Dean Palmer 1, Ruben Sierra 1.
Toronto	6	Joe Carter 4, Roberto Alomar 1, John Olerud 1.
Boston	5	Carlos Quintana 2, Ellis Burks 1, Jack Clark 1, Phil Plantier 1.
Cleveland	5	Carlos Baerga 2, Albert Belle 1, Chris James 1, Mark Whiten 1.
Seattle	4	Jay Buhner 2, Edgar Martinez 1, Pete O'Brien 1.
California	3	Wally Joyner 1, Lance Parrish 1, Dave Winfield 1.

NATIONAL LEAGUE

Team	No.	Hitters
Cincinnati	10	Mariano Duncan 2, Barry Larkin 2, Paul O'Neill 2, Chris Sabo 2, Glenn Braggs 1, Eric Davis 1.
Chicago	8	Andre Dawson 2, George Bell 1, Mark Grace 1, Luis Salazar 1, Ryne Sandberg 1, Hector Villanueva 1, Chico Walker.
San Diego	7	Fred McGriff 3, Darrin Jackson 2, Jack Howell 1, Bip Roberts 1.
San Francisco	7	Will Clark 2, Kevin Mitchell 2, Matt Williams 2, Kevin Bass 1.
Atlanta	6	David Justice 2, Terry Pendleton 2, Francisco Cabrera 1, Lonnie Smith 1.
Philadelphia	6	Darren Daulton 2, Wes Chamberlain 1, Ricky Jordan 1, John Kruk 1, Dickie Thon 1.
Pittsburgh	6	Barry Bonds 2, Jay Bell 1, Bobby Bonilla 1, Lloyd McClendon 1, Gary Varsho 1.
Montreal	5	Ivan Calderon 2, Bret Barberie 1, Dave Martinez 1, Larry Walker 1.
St. Louis	4	Bernard Gilkey 1, Pedro Guerrero 1, Felix Jose 1, Ray Lankford 1.
New York	3	Howard Johnson 2, Hubie Brooks 1.
Los Angeles	2	Darryl Strawberry 2.
Houston	1	Luis Gonzalez 1.

THREE-HOMER GAMES

Date	Player, Team, Opponent	AB	R	H	2B	3B	HR	RBI	Result
4-13	Dave Winfield, California at Minnesota	6	4	5	1	0	3	6	W 15-9
5-7	Harold Baines, Oakland vs. Baltimore	4	4	4	1	0	3	7	W 11-3
6-28	Barry Larkin, Cincinnati vs. Houston	4	3	3	0	0	3	6	W 8-5
7-6	Danny Tartabull, Kansas City vs. Oakland	4	3	3	0	0	3	4	L 9-7
7-31	Jack Clark, Boston vs. Oakland (14 inn.)	7	4	4	0	0	3	6	W 11-10
8-3	Dave Henderson, Oakland vs. Minnesota	5	3	3	0	0	3	3	L 8-6

GRAND SLAMS

AMERICAN LEAGUE

Date	Batter	Pitcher	Inn.*	Site
4-8	Jack Clark, Boston	Dave Stieb, Toronto	3	Toronto
4-15	Sam Horn, Baltimore	Edwin Nunez, Milwaukee	8	Milwaukee
4-30	Rob Deer, Detroit	Luis Aquino, Kansas City	4	Kansas City
5-5	Kevin Romine, Boston	Alex Fernandez, Chicago	2	Chicago
5-10	Wally Joyner, California	Eric King, Cleveland	7	Cleveland
5-19	Milt Cuyler, Detroit	Jack Morris, Minnesota	1	Detroit
5-20	Pete Incaviglia, Detroit	Bob Milacki, Baltimore	1	Detroit
5-25	Kurt Stillwell, Kansas City	Larry Casian, Minnesota	9	Minnesota
5-31	Mike Gallego, Oakland	Ramon Garcia, Chicago	2	Chicago
6-1	Dave Winfield, California	Willie Fraser, Toronto	2	Toronto
6-6	Harold Baines, Oakland	Mark Lee, Milwaukee	7	Oakland
6-6	Dante Bichette, Milwaukee	Bruce Walton, Oakland	8	Oakland
6-7	Brian Downing, Texas	Mike Witt, New York	5	New York
6-12	Pedro Munoz, Minnesota	Jeff Johnson, New York	1	Minnesota
6-14	Shane Mack, Minnesota	Rod Nichols, Cleveland	5	Cleveland
6-16	Joe Orsulak, Baltimore	Duane Ward, Toronto	7	Toronto
6-16	Greg Vaughn, Milwaukee	Gene Nelson, Oakland	9	Milwaukee
6-18	Robin Ventura, Chicago	Tom Candiotti, Cleveland	6	Chicago
6-19	Kirk Gibson, Kansas City	Jeff Bitker, Texas	6	Texas
6-23	Chris Hoiles, Baltimore	Jeff Montgomery, Kansas City	9	Kansas City
6-24	Frank Thomas, Chicago	Mike Jackson, Seattle	8	Chicago
6-29	Harold Baines, Oakland	Storm Davis, Kansas City	7	Oakland

Date	Batter	Pitcher	Inn.*	Site
7-2	Max Venable, California	Mark Gubicza, Kansas City	2	California
7-4	Rickey Henderson, Oakland	Gerald Alexander, Texas	7	Texas
7-5	Jose Canseco, Oakland	Tom Gordon, Kansas City	4	Kansas City
7-11	Mike Macfarlane, Kansas City	Mark Leiter, Detroit	2	Detroit
7-14	Brian McRae, Kansas City	Dan Gakeler, Detroit	8	Detroit
7-15	Franklin Stubbs, Milwaukee	Scott Erickson, Minnesota	4	Milwaukee
7-23	Todd Benzinger, Kansas City	Julio Machado, Milwaukee	6	Kansas City
7-23	Ken Griffey Jr., Seattle	Lee Guetterman, New York	9	New York
7-23	Randy Milligan, Baltimore	Bryan Harvey, California	8	Baltimore
7-26	Dwight Evans, Baltimore	Gene Nelson, Oakland	7	Baltimore
7-26	Ernest Riles, Oakland	Dave Johnson, Baltimore	5	Baltimore
7-30	Ken Griffey Jr., Seattle	Roy Smith, Baltimore	2	Seattle
7-30	Carlos Quintana, Boston	Oil Can Boyd, Texas	3	Boston
7-31	Jack Clark, Boston	Dave Stewart, Oakland	3	Boston
7-31	Kent Hrbek, Minnesota	Scott Sanderson, New York	2	New York
7-31	Robin Ventura, Chicago	Rich Gossage, Texas	9	Chicago
8-11	Mickey Tettleton, Detroit	Lee Guetterman, New York	6	New York
8-14	Danny Tartabull, Kansas City	Steve Farr, New York	11	New York
8-18	Juan Gonzalez, Texas	Shawn Hillegas, Cleveland	6	Cleveland
9-1	Tom Brunansky, Boston	Scott Bankhead, Seattle	2	Seattle
9-2	Shane Mack, Minnesota	Steve Olin, Cleveland	8	Minnesota
9-5	Ozzie Guillen, Chicago	Storm Davis, Kansas City	4	Chicago
9-6	Dave Valle, Seattle	Matt Young, Boston	4	Boston
9-10	Reggie Jefferson, Cleveland	Bill Wegman, Milwaukee	6	Milwaukee
9-15	Jose Canseco, Oakland	Jim Acker, Toronto	9	Toronto
9-15	Craig Grebeck, Chicago	Kyle Abbott, California	3	California
9-19	Ken Griffey Jr., Seattle	Tom Gordon, Kansas City	6	Seattle
9-20	Bill Spiers, Milwaukee	Jeff Kaiser, Detroit	7	Detroit
9-23	Matt Nokes, New York	Mark Lee, Milwaukee	7	Milwaukee
9-29	Tim Spehr, Kansas City	Jim Abbott, California	2	Kansas City
10-3	Cecil Fielder, Detroit	Dan Petry, Boston	8	Boston
10-3	Carlton Fisk, Chicago	Steve Bedrosian, Minnesota	7	Chicago

*Inning in which grand slam was hit.

NATIONAL LEAGUE

Date	Batter	Pitcher	Inn.*	Site
4-19	Andre Dawson, Chicago	Stan Belinda, Pittsburgh	9	Pittsburgh
4-20	Mike LaValliere, Pittsburgh	Les Lancaster, Chicago	6	Pittsburgh
4-21	Andre Dawson, Chicago	Bob Patterson, Pittsburgh	11	Pittsburgh
4-24	Kal Daniels, Los Angeles	Doug Sisk, Atlanta	5	Los Angeles
4-28	Marquis Grissom, Montreal	Juan Agosto, St. Louis	8	St. Louis
5-8	Ricky Jordan, Philadelphia	Andy Benes, San Diego	6	San Diego
5-14	Hubie Brooks, New York	Eric Nolte, San Diego	3	San Diego
5-17	Sid Bream, Atlanta	Bob Patterson, Pittsburgh	7	Atlanta
6-10	Lenny Harris, Los Angeles	Chuck McElroy, Chicago	4	Chicago
6-18	Howard Johnson, New York	Tom Browning, Cincinnati	3	New York
6-25	Kevin McReynolds, New York	Scott Ruskin, Montreal	9	New York
6-25	Jeff Reed, Cincinnati	Andy Benes, San Diego	1	Cincinnati
7-4	Orlando Merced, Pittsburgh	Dave Smith, Chicago	8	Chicago
7-14	Will Clark, San Francisco	Amalio Carreno, Philadelphia	4	Philadelphia
7-15	Darren Daulton, Philadelphia	Tim Crews, Los Angeles	5	Philadelphia
7-19	Dave Hollins, Philadelphia	Dennis Rasmussen, San Diego	6	San Diego
7-23	Gary Redus, Pittsburgh	Rick Mahler, Atlanta	5	Pittsburgh
7-29	Ken Caminiti, Houston	Bryn Smith, St. Louis	4	Houston
8-2	Tim Teufel, San Diego	Charlie Leibrandt, Atlanta	3	Atlanta
8-6	Dale Murphy, Philadelphia	Les Lancaster, Chicago	11	Philadelphia
8-13	Fred McGriff, San Diego	Mark Portugal, Houston	3	San Diego
8-14	Fred McGriff, San Diego	Jim Deshaies, Houston	1	San Diego
8-20	Will Clark, San Francisco	Rob Mallicoat, Houston	7	Houston
8-21	Darryl Strawberry, New York	Ricky Bones, San Diego	5	New York
8-25	Darrin Jackson, San Diego	Bob Scanlan, Chicago	6	Chicago
8-26	Jeff Blauser, Atlanta	Chris Haney, Montreal	5	Atlanta
8-28	Charlie Hayes, Philadelphia	Ryan Bowen, Houston	1	Philadelphia
8-28	Chico Walker, Chicago	Paul McClellan, San Francisco	4	San Francisco
9-2	Ryne Sandberg, Chicago	Jim Lewis, San Diego	8	San Diego
9-15	Sid Bream, Atlanta	Ramon Martinez, Los Angeles	1	Atlanta
9-19	Curtis Wilkerson, Pittsburgh	Lee Smith, St. Louis	9	Pittsburgh
9-24	Daryl Boston, New York	Bob Walk, Pittsburgh	5	New York
9-25	John Kruk, Philadelphia	Shawn Boskie, Chicago	4	Chicago
9-30	Jay Bell, Pittsburgh	Doug Simons, New York	2	Pittsburgh
10-1	Joe Oliver, Cincinnati	Charlie Leibrandt, Atlanta	1	Cincinnati

*Inning in which grand slam was hit.

TRANSACTIONS

JANUARY 2
Cardinals signed C Alex Trevino, a free agent formerly with the Reds.

Yankees re-signed P Mike Witt, a free agent.

JANUARY 5
Astros signed P Mike Capel, a free agent.

JANUARY 7
Athletics signed 3B Vance Law, a free agent.

Yankees' Columbus affiliate signed OF Keith Hughes, a free agent.

Kinetsu Buffaloes of Japan Pacific League purchased OF Ozzie Canseco from Athletics.

Nippon Ham Fighters of Japan Pacific League signed IF Bill Bathe, a free agent.

JANUARY 8
Padres signed 2B Marty Barrett, a free agent.

Rangers organization re-signed P Craig McMurtry, a free agent.

White Sox signed 1B Rob Nelson, a free agent.

JANUARY 9
Cardinals' Louisville affiliate signed P Jamie Moyer, a free agent.

Padres re-signed P Dennis Rasmussen, a free agent.

Pirates signed IF Curtis Wilkerson, a free agent formerly with the Cubs.

JANUARY 10
Astros traded 1B Glenn Davis to Orioles for P Pete Harnisch, P Curt Schilling and OF Steve Finley.

Phillies signed 2B Wally Backman, a free agent formerly with the Pirates; Phillies' Scranton/Wilkes-Barre affiliate signed OF John Morris, a free agent.

JANUARY 11
Indians signed C-IF Luis Lopez, a free agent.

Orioles traded C Mickey Tettleton to Tigers for P Jeff M. Robinson.

JANUARY 13
Yankees released C Rick Cerone.

JANUARY 14
Rangers' Oklahoma City affiliate signed P Terry Wells, a free agent.

Tigers signed P John Cerutti, a free agent formerly with the Blue Jays.

Twins' Portland affiliate signed P Tom Edens, a free agent.

JANUARY 15
Orioles traded IF Rene Gonzales to Blue Jays for P Rob Blumberg; Orioles assigned Blumberg to Hagerstown.

Padres signed C Dann Bilardello and C Brian Dorsett, both free agents.

JANUARY 16
Indians' Colorado Springs affiliate signed P Dave Otto, a free agent.

Mariners' organization signed IF Steve Springer, a free agent.

JANUARY 17
Angels signed P Jeff D. Robinson, a free agent formerly with the Yankees.

JANUARY 20
Indians organization signed DH-1B Ron Kittle, a free agent formerly with the Orioles.

JANUARY 21
Mariners traded IF Todd Haney to Tigers for P Dave Richards.

Mets signed C Rick Cerone, a free agent.

Pirates' Buffalo affilate signed OF-3B Scott Little, a free agent.

Royals signed P Greg Mathews, a free agent.

Tigers' Toledo affiliate signed OF Skeeter Barnes.

JANUARY 22
Braves signed C Mike Heath, a free agent formerly with the Tigers.

JANUARY 23
Angels signed 3B Gary Gaetti, a free agent formerly with the Twins.

Red Sox organization signed P Tony Fossas, a free agent.

JANUARY 25
Braves re-signed P Doug Sisk, a free agent.

Pirates released OF-IF Mark Ryal.

Twins signed 3B Mike Pagliarulo, a free agent formerly with the Padres.

JANUARY 29
Braves signed P Juan Berenguer, a free agent formerly with the Twins, and OF Deion Sanders, a free agent.

Twins signed OF Chili Davis, a free agent formerly with the Angels.

JANUARY 31
Expos signed P Bill Long, a free agent.

FEBRUARY 1
Angels released IF Bobby Dean (Pete) Coachman.

Braves released OF Geronimo Berroa.

Rangers' Oklahoma City affiliate signed C John Russell, a free agent.

Red Sox signed OF John Moses, a free agent.

FEBRUARY 3
Giants signed P Gary Eave and P Jose Alvarez to minor-league contracts.

Padres' Las Vegas affiliate signed P Brian Holton, a free agent.

FEBRUARY 4
Rangers signed P Charley Kerfeld, a free agent to a minor-league contract and re-signed C Mike Stanley, a free agent.

FEBRUARY 5
Indians' Canton-Akron affiliate signed P Jeff Musselman, a free agent.

Pirates signed P Roger Mason, a free agent.

Twins signed P Jack Morris, a free agent formerly with the Tigers.

FEBRUARY 6
Astros signed P Don Carman, a free agent.

FEBRUARY 7
Yankees acquired OF Mike Humphreys from Padres to complete the trade in which the Yankees sent OF Oscar Azocar to Padres for a player to be named later (December 3, 1990).

FEBRUARY 8
Padres claimed OF Jim Vatcher on waivers from Braves and signed 3B Jim Presley, a free agent.

FEBRUARY 9
Padres' Las Vegas affiliate re-signed P Pat Clements, a free agent.

FEBRUARY 13
Braves signed OF Glenn Wilson, a free agent.

FEBRUARY 14
Padres released P Matthew Maysey.

FEBRUARY 15

Cardinals' Louisville affiliate signed C Rich Gedman, a free agent.

Expos signed C Ron Hassey to a minor-league contract.

White Sox acquired P Mario Brito from Expos to complete the trade in which the White Sox sent OF Ivan Calderon and P Barry Jones to Expos for OF Tim Raines, P Jeff Carter and a player to be named later (December 24, 1990).

FEBRUARY 17

Yankees released P Dave LaPoint.

FEBRUARY 23

White Sox granted 1B Carlos Martinez free agency.

FEBRUARY 27

Expos signed P Rick Mahler, a free agent, to a minor-league contract.

MARCH 1

Pirates organization re-signed P Doug Bair, a free agent.

MARCH 2

Indians signed 1B Carlos Martinez, a free agent.

MARCH 6

Astros' Tucson affiliate signed 2B Mark McLemore, a free agent.

MARCH 9

Braves' Richmond affiliate signed P Randy St. Claire, a free agent.

MARCH 11

Padres' Las Vegas affiliate signed IF Ed Romero, a free agent.

MARCH 13

Angels signed C Ed Hockenbury.

MARCH 14

Brewers traded OF Dave Parker to Angels for OF Dante Bichette.

Royals released P Jim Campbell.

MARCH 15

Tigers released P Clay Parker.

MARCH 17

Pirates re-signed P Jay Tibbs, a free agent.

MARCH 18

Cubs released P Jeff Pico.

Indians' Canton-Akron affiliate released P Jeff Musselman.

Royals released OF Bo Jackson and P Mel Stottlemyre Jr.

MARCH 19

Astros' Tuscon affiliate signed P Jim Corsi and P Jimmy Jones, both free agents.

Giants released OF Rick Leach.

Padres released P Candy Sierra.

Tigers traded IF Torey Lovullo to the New York Yankees for P Mark Leiter; Yankees assigned Lovullo to Columbus of the International League.

MARCH 20

Padres' Las Vegas affiliate released P Brian Holton.

MARCH 21

Mariners claimed OF Alan Cockrell on waivers from Indians and assigned him to Calgary of the Pacific Coast League.

MARCH 22

Cubs granted P Jose Nunez free agency.

Expos released P Drew Hall.

MARCH 24

Dodgers released IF Mickey Hatcher.

MARCH 25

Dodgers signed P John Candelaria, a free agent.

Indians released P Sergio Valdez.

Padres released P Mike Dunne.

Rangers released P Charley Kerfeld.

MARCH 26

Dodgers signed C Gary Carter, a free agent.

Orioles released IF Pete Stanicek.

Padres claimed P Jose Melendez on waivers from the Mariners.

Royals released P Greg Mathews.

MARCH 28

Braves released OF Oddibe McDowell.

Dodgers released P Fernando Valenzuela.

MARCH 29

Pirates traded OF Steve Carter to Cubs for OF Gary Varsho; released P Jay Tibbs.

Rangers released OF Pete Incaviglia.

Yankees reacquired P Ricky Rhodes from Blue Jays, who had selected him from Greensboro in 1990 major league draft; Yankees assigned him to Columbus of the International League.

MARCH 30

Astros granted P Brian Meyer free agency.

Expos released IF-OF Mike Aldrete.

Giants' Phoenix affiliate signed IF-OF Darnell Coles; released P Gary Eave and P Jose Alvarez.

Padres released P Calvin Schiraldi.

Tigers traded C Jim Baxter to Royals for C Andy Allanson.

MARCH 31

Blue Jays released C Carlos Diaz.

Cardinals released C Alex Trevino.

White Sox traded P Adam Peterson and P Steve Rosenberg to Padres for IF Joey Cora, IF Kevin Garner and OF Warren Newson; traded P Joe Borowski to Orioles for IF Pete Rose Jr.

APRIL 1

Angels released IF Fred Manrique and IF Rick Schu.

Braves released SS Andres Thomas.

Brewers released C Rick Wrona and P Mike Campbell.

Cubs released IF Domingo Ramos and OF Dave Clark.

Expos traded OF Otis Nixon and 3B Boi Rodriguez to Braves for C Jimmy Kremers and a player to be named later; Braves assigned Rodriguez to Richmond of the International League. Expos acquired P Keith Morrison to complete trade and assigned Morrison to Sumter of the South Atlantic League (June 3, 1991).

Indians released OF Stan Jefferson and DH-1B Ron Kittle.

Mets released OF Terry Puhl.

Red Sox traded P Rob Murphy to the Mariners for P Mike Gardiner; released P John Moses.

Yankees released IF Steve Balboni.

APRIL 2

Astros released P Don Carman.

Brewers released IF Edgar Diaz and OF Mike Felder; signed OF Candy Maldonado, C Rick Dempsey and 2B Willie Randolph, free agents.

Mets traded OF Darren Reed and OF Alex Diaz to the Montreal Expos for OF Terrel Hansen and P David Sommer; Mets assigned Hansen to Tidewater of the International League.

Orioles released P Kevin Hickey, P John Mitchell and P Dan Boone; signed P Mike Flanagan, a free agent.

Rangers released P Jose Guzman.

Twins released IF Nelson Liriano.

APRIL 3

Red Sox released P Cecilio Guante.

White Sox signed OF Bo Jackson, a free agent.

APRIL 4

Indians claimed C Eddie Taubensee on waivers from Athletics.

Mariners granted IF-OF Dave Cochrane free agency.

Pirates released P Doug Bair, P Joel Davis, P Joe Lazor, P Joe

Pacholec, C Tom Nieto, 1B Jeff Osborne and 1B Junior Vizcaino.

APRIL 5

Giants signed OF Mike Felder, a free agent.

Mets reacquired OF Pat Howell from Twins, who had selected him from Tidewater in the 1990 major league draft; Mets assigned Howell to Port St. Lucie of the Florida State League.

Padres signed IF-OF Mike Aldrete.

Phillies released P Guillermo Hernandez.

Reds reacquired Joe Turek from Athletics, who had selected him from Nashville in 1990 major league draft; Reds assigned Turek to Nashville of the American Association.

Royals signed IF-OF Warren Cromartie, a free agent.

Tigers released OF Chet Lemon; claimed IF Luis de los Santos on waivers from Royals.

Twins traded 1B Joey Meyer to Pirates for OF Greg Sims.

Yankees claimed OF Scott Lusader on waivers from Tigers.

APRIL 7

Cubs traded P Mitch Williams to Phillies for P Chuck McElroy and P Bob Scanlan.

Indians purchased the contract of P Kevin Burdick from Pirates.

Orioles signed C Ernie Whitt.

Phillies signed P Dave LaPoint, a free agent.

Rangers signed IF-OF Denny Walling, a free agent.

Reds signed P Don Carman, a free agent.

Tigers signed OF Pete Incaviglia, a free agent.

White Sox' Vancouver affiliate signed OF John Cangelosi, a free agent.

APRIL 8

Mariners' Calgary affiliate re-signed IF-OF Dave Cochrane, a free agent.

Orioles re-signed P Kevin Hickey, a free agent, and assigned him to Hagerstown of the Eastern League.

Rangers organization re-signed P Jose Guzman.

APRIL 10

Phillies' Scranton/Wilkes-Barre affiliate signed IF Rick Schu, a free agent.

APRIL 12

White Sox' Vancouver affiliate signed IF Danny Heep, a free agent.

APRIL 13

Rangers signed OF-DH Brian Downing, a free agent.

White Sox released IF-OF Steve Lyons.

APRIL 17

Astros' Tucson affiliate signed P Calvin Schiraldi.

Orioles signed OF Oddibe McDowell to a minor-league contract.

APRIL 18

Red Sox signed IF Steve Lyons, a free agent; released OF Randy Kutcher.

APRIL 23

Phillies released P Dave LaPoint.

APRIL 25

Royals signed OF Terry Puhl, a free agent.

APRIL 28

Rangers organization signed P Dan Boone.

APRIL 29

Royals' Omaha affiliate signed OF Dave Clark, a free agent.

MAY 1

Blue Jays signed P Guillermo Hernandez, a free agent, to a contract with Syracuse of the International League.

MAY 3

Pirates traded 1B-OF Carmelo Martinez to Royals for P Victor Cole; Pirates assigned Cole to Buffalo of the American Association.

MAY 6

Rangers' Tulsa affiliate signed P Mike Campbell, a free agent.

White Sox traded IF Danny Heep to the Atlanta Braves for IF Kevin Castleberry; White Sox assigned Castleberry to Birmingham of the Southern League.

MAY 7

Brewers purchased OF Chris Knabenshue from the Phillies' Scranton/Wilkes-Barre affiliate; Brewers assigned him to Denver of the American Association.

Phillies signed C Gary Tremblay, a free agent, and assigned him to Scranton/Wilkes-Barre of the International League.

Tigers released IF Tony Bernazard.

MAY 8

Phillies reclaimed OF Nikco Riesgo from Expos, who had drafted him from Scranton/Wilkes-Barre in the 1990 Major League draft.

MAY 9

Brewers organization signed P Dave LaPoint, a free agent.

Mets claimed P Mark Dewey on waivers from the Giants and assigned him to Tidewater of the International League.

Yankees released P Andy Hawkins.

MAY 10

Padres released OF Mike Aldrete.

Twins released OF Carmen Castillo.

MAY 11

Angels' Edmonton affiliate released P Ed Vosberg.

MAY 14

Padres' Las Vegas affiliate signed P Joe Price.

MAY 16

Indians traded OF Mitch Webster to Pirates for P Mike York; Indians assigned York to Colorado Springs.

MAY 17

Yankees traded 3B Mike Blowers to Seattle for a player to be named later and cash; Mariners assigned Blowers to Calgary. Yankees later acquired P Jim Blueberg from the Mariners to complete deal and assigned him to Albany of the Eastern League (June 22).

MAY 18

Athletics signed P Andy Hawkins, a free agent.

MAY 20

Angels signed P Fernando Valenzuela, a free agent, and assigned him to Palm Springs of the California League.

Padres released P Eric Nolte.

MAY 21

Indians traded P Steve Cummings to Tigers for a player to be named later; Indians acquired P Eric Stone to complete deal (July 8).

MAY 22

White Sox signed P Mike Dunne, a free agent, and assigned him to Vancouver of the Pacific Coast League.

MAY 23

Rangers signed P Eric Nolte and P Drew Hall, both free agents, and assigned them to Oklahoma City of the American Association.

White Sox traded OF John Cangelosi to Brewers for SS Esteban Beltre; White Sox assigned Beltre to Vancouver of the Pacific Coast League.

MAY 24

Expos signed OF Charles Lee, a free agent.

Mets signed OF Bert Bull, P Shawn Watson and IF Randy Farmer, free agents.

MAY 29

Royals released P Dan Schatzeder.

Twins' Orlando affiliate signed P Rusty Richards, a free agent.

MAY 31

Orioles claimed P Jim Poole on waivers from Rangers and assigned him to Rochester of the International League.

Padres traded SS Garry Templeton to Mets for IF Tim Teufel; released P Wes Gardner.

JUNE 2

Red Sox signed P-SS Frankie Rodriguez, a free agent.

JUNE 4

Expos claimed OF Kenny Williams on waivers from Blue Jays.

JUNE 6

Mets' Tidewater affiliate signed P Dan Schatzeder, a free agent.

JUNE 8

Padres released 3B Jim Presley.

JUNE 9

Royals released IF-OF Terry Puhl.

JUNE 10

Expos released P Rick Mahler.

JUNE 12

Dodgers granted C Barry Lyons free agency.

Royals' Omaha affiliate signed OF Jeffrey Leonard, a free agent.

JUNE 14

Braves signed P Rick Mahler, a free agent.

Reds traded 1B Reggie Jefferson to Indians for 1B Tim Costo; assigned Costo to Chattanooga of the Southern League.

Padres released 2B Marty Barrett.

JUNE 16

Angels released P Bob McClure.

Mets' Tidewater affiliate released P Dan Schatzeder.

JUNE 17

Braves released IF Danny Heep.

JUNE 19

Angels organization signed C Barry Lyons, a free agent, and assigned him to Edmonton of the Pacific Coast League.

Giants released P Rick Reuschel.

White Sox organization signed DH-1B Ron Kittle, a free agent, and assigned him to Vancouver of the Pacific Coast League.

JUNE 20

Astros traded P Calvin Schiraldi to Rangers for a player to be named later; claimed P David Richards on waivers from Mariners and assigned him to Jackson of the Texas League.

Rangers released P Mark Petkovsek.

JUNE 21

Rangers signed OF Billy Moore and assigned him to Oklahoma City of the American Association.

JUNE 22

Rangers released IF Denny Walling.

JUNE 23

Brewers organization released P Dave LaPoint.

JUNE 24

Cardinals signed P Bob McClure, a free agent.

JUNE 25

Astros released 2B Mark McLemore.

Orioles signed OF Ed Yacopino and assigned him to Hagerstown of the Eastern League.

Tigers traded P Dan Petry to the Braves for IF Victor Rosario; Tigers assigned Rosario to Toledo of the International League.

JUNE 26

Cardinals claimed P Willie Fraser on waivers from Blue Jays.

Royals' Omaha affiliate signed P Wes Gardner, a free agent.

White Sox traded P Grady Hall to Indians for P Robert Person and assigned Person to South Bend of the Midwest League.

Yankees traded P Steve Adkins to Cubs for P David Rosario and assigned Rosario to Columbus of the International League; Cubs assigned Adkins to Iowa of the American Association.

JUNE 27

Indians traded P Tom Candiotti and OF Turner Ward to Blue Jays for P Denis Boucher, OF Glenallen Hill, OF Mark Whiten and a player to be named later; Indians acquired cash instead of player to complete deal (October 15).

JUNE 28

Cubs' Iowa afilate signed P Dave LaPoint, a free agent.

JULY 3

Blue Jays claimed P Efrain Valdez on waivers from Indians and assigned him to Syracuse of the International League.

Brewers released 1B Greg Brock.

Pirates traded OF Mitch Webster to Dodgers for OF Jose Gonzalez.

Giants released P Mike LaCoss.

JULY 5

Angels released P Fernando Valenzuela.

Orioles released C Ernie Whitt; signed 2B Mark McLemore, a free agent and assigned him to Rochester of the International League.

JULY 8

Expos claimed P Chris Johnson on waivers from Brewers.

JULY 10

Angels organization signed P Fernando Valenzuela.

JULY 11

Orioles released P Kevin Hickey.

Reds traded 1B-OF Todd Benzinger to Royals for 1B-OF Carmelo Martinez.

JULY 12

Tigers granted P Steve Searcy free agency.

White Sox claimed OF Mike Huff on waivers from Indians.

JULY 14

White Sox traded OF Cory Snyder to Blue Jays for OF Shawn Jeter and a player to be named later; Blue Jays sent P Steve Wapnick to the White Sox to complete the deal (September 4).

JULY 15

Mets traded P Ron Darling and P Mike Thomas to Expos for P Tim Burke.

Phillies signed P Steve Searcy, a free agent.

JULY 16

Royals released P Andy McGaffigan.

JULY 18

Orioles signed OF Mark Smith and assigned him to Bluefield of the Appalachian League.

Reds released P Don Carman.

JULY 20

Red Sox released 1B-OF Mike Marshall.

JULY 21

Expos traded P Dennis Boyd to Rangers for P Jonathan Hurst, P Joey Eischen and a player to be named later; Expos assigned Hurst to Harrisburg of the Eastern League and Eischen to West Palm Beach of the Florida State League. Rangers sent P Travis Buckley to Expos to complete deal (September 1).

JULY 23

Expos sold the contract of P Scott Service to the Chunichi Dragons of the Japan Central League.

JULY 26

Indians traded IF Brook Jacoby to Athletics for OF Lee Tinsley and P Apolinar Garcia; Indians assigned Tinsley and Garcia to Canton-Akron of the Eastern League.

JULY 27

Angels signed 1B-OF Mike Marshall, a free agent, and assigned him to Edmonton of the Pacific Coast League.

Astros released IF Ken Oberkfell.

JULY 30
Padres traded OF Shawn Abner to Angels for 3B Jack Howell.

JULY 31
Astros traded P Jim Clancy to Braves for P Matt Turner and a player to be named later; Astros acquired P Earl Sanders to complete deal (November 15).

Expos traded P Ron Darling to Athletics for P Matt Grott and P Russell Cormier.

Phillies traded P Roger McDowell to Dodgers for P Mike Hartley and OF Braulio Castillo and assigned Hartley and Castillo to Scranton/Wilkes-Barre of the International League.

AUGUST 2
Expos released P Dave Schmidt.

AUGUST 5
Mets released 2B Tom Herr.

Tigers signed OF John Moses, a free agent.

AUGUST 6
Indians claimed IF Tony Perezchica on waivers from Giants.

AUGUST 7
Angels released IF-OF Mike Marshall.

Pirates' Carolina affiliate signed P Floyd Youmans.

AUGUST 8
Braves released P Rick Mahler.

Rangers signed P Dave Schmidt, a free agent, to a contract with Oklahoma City of the American Association.

Royals released P Wes Gardner.

AUGUST 9
Red Sox released OF Kevin Romine.

Brewers traded OF Candy Maldonado to Blue Jays for P Rob Wishnevski and a player to be named later; Brewers assigned Wishnevski to El Paso of the Texas League. Blue Jays sent IF William Suero to Brewers to complete the deal (August 14).

AUGUST 12
White Sox signed 1B Greg Brock, a free agent, and assigned him to Vancouver of the Pacific Coast League.

AUGUST 13
Tigers released OF John Shelby.

AUGUST 15
Giants signed 2B Tom Herr, a free agent.

Indians claimed OF Jose Gonzalez on waivers from Pirates.

White Sox released DH-1B Ron Kittle.

AUGUST 16
Braves traded P Dan Petry to Red Sox for a player to be named later; Braves acquired OF Mickey Pina to complete deal (November 13).

AUGUST 20
Athletics released P Andy Hawkins.

AUGUST 24
Orioles traded P Chris Myers to Expos for P Richie Lewis. Orioles sent Lewis to Rochester of the International League; Expos sent Myers to Indianapolis of the American Association.

AUGUST 25
Tigers released OF John Moses.

AUGUST 28
Mets traded P Alejandro Pena to Braves for P Tony Castillo and a minor league player to be named later; Braves sent P Joe Roa to the Mets to complete deal (August 29).

AUGUST 29
Angels released P Floyd Bannister.

AUGUST 30
Rangers traded 3B Steve Buechele to Pirates for P Kurt Miller and a player to be named later; Pirates sent P Hector Fajardo

to the Rangers to complete deal (September 6).

SEPTEMBER 5
Cubs released P Scott May and P Dave Pavlas.

SEPTEMBER 6
Dodgers traded P Jeff Hartsock to Cubs for P Steve Wilson.

SEPTEMBER 7
Angels released DH Dave Parker.

SEPTEMBER 10
Angels released P Fernando Valenzuela from his minor-league contract with Edmonton of the Pacific Coast League.

SEPTEMBER 14
Blue Jays signed DH Dave Parker, a free agent.

SEPTEMBER 15
Royals announced the retirement of DH Warren Cromartie.

SEPTEMBER 25
Astros claimed C-OF Eddie Tucker on waivers from the Giants.

SEPTEMBER 29
Cubs traded P Mike Bielecki and C Damon Berryhill to the Braves for P Turk Wendell and P Yorkis Perez.

OCTOBER 6
Giants released 2B Tom Herr and OF Mike Kingery.

OCTOBER 7
Indians released 1B Keith Hernandez and P Mike York.

Mets granted C Rick Cerone free agency.

Phillies granted P Darrel Akerfelds, OF Sil Campusano and P Amalio Carreno free agency.

White Sox granted C Don Wakamatsu and OF Rodney McCray free agency.

OCTOBER 8
Mets claimed IF Junior Noboa on waivers from the Montreal Expos.

Rangers granted C Mark Parent and P Mike Jeffcoat free agency.

OCTOBER 9
Brewers released C Rick Dempsey.

Phillies granted OF John Morris free agency.

OCTOBER 10
Mariners granted P Keith Comstock free agency.

OCTOBER 11
Athletics released IF Vance Law.

OCTOBER 14
Cardinals released P Jamie Moyer.

Rangers granted IF Gary Green and C Mike Stanley free agency.

OCTOBER 15
Brewers traded 1B George Canale to the Expos for OF Alex Diaz.

Indians granted C-IF Luis Lopez free agency.

Rangers granted IF Mario Diaz free agency.

Royals released OF Jeffrey Leonard.

White Sox granted P Tom Drees free agency.

Yankees released OF Pat Sheridan.

OCTOBER 16
Brewers granted P Don August free agency.

Orioles released P Paul Kilgus and IF Jeff McKnight.

Phillies granted P Chuck Malone free agency.

OCTOBER 17
Royals claimed P Alex Sanchez on waivers from Blue Jays.

Rangers granted P Brad Arnsberg free agency.

OCTOBER 18
Athletics granted P Todd Burns free agency.

Indians granted P Mario Gozzo free agency.

Orioles granted P Jeff Ballard free agency.

Phillies granted OF Ron Jones free agency.

OCTOBER 23

Royals claimed P Russell Meacham on waivers from the Tigers.

OCTOBER 24

Angels released IF Kent Anderson and C Barry Lyons.

OCTOBER 28

Blue Jays released OF Cory Snyder.

Rangers' Oklahoma City affiliate signed P Steve Fireovid.

Yankees released P Chuck Cary.

NOVEMBER 1

Mariners placed Ken Griffey Sr. on voluntarily retired list.

NOVEMBER 5

Cubs released C Erik Pappas.

NOVEMBER 7

Rangers organization signed OF John Cangelosi, a free agent.

NOVEMBER 12

Cardinals released C Carl Stephens Jr.

Orioles re-signed 1B Glenn Davis, a free agent.

Reds organization signed P Tim Drummond, P Tony Menendez, OF Geronimo Berroa, OF Jacob Brumfield, OF Dwight Taylor, OF Ruben Escalera, OF Nick Capra, OF Jeff Schulz, OF Jeff Stone, IF Darnell Coles, IF Gary Green, IF Mark Howie, IF Russ Morman, C Tom Nieto, C Joe Szekely and C Rick Wrona.

NOVEMBER 13

Angels released P Jeff Richardson and IF Chris Cron.

Orioles signed P Eric Hetzel, a free agent, and released P Jeff M. Robinson and P Brian DuBois.

NOVEMBER 15

Expos claimed C Gary Carter on waivers from Dodgers.

Indians traded P Greg Swindell to Reds for P Jack Armstrong, P Scott Scudder and P Joe Turek.

Reds organization signed C Troy Afenir, a free agent, and assigned him to Nashville of the American Association.

NOVEMBER 18

Astros released P Jim Corsi, OF Javier Ortiz and IF Jose Tolentino; placed P Mike Scott on voluntarily retired list.

Blue Jays granted IF Rene Gonzales free agency.

Expos released OF Kenny Williams.

NOVEMBER 19

Padres released P John Costello.

Pirates claimed OF Terry McDaniel on waivers from Mets.

NOVEMBER 20

Braves released P Randy St. Claire.

Indians claimed P Derek Lilliquist on waivers from Padres and released OF Jose Gonzalez.

Orioles released P Dave Johnson.

Padres claimed P Mike Linskey off waivers from Orioles.

Reds released IF Luis Quinones and 1B Terry Lee.

Yankees released P Eric Plunk.

NOVEMBER 22

Indians granted P John Farrell free agency.

NOVEMBER 25

Expos traded 1B Andres Galarraga to Cardinals for P Ken Hill.

NOVEMBER 26

Reds claimed P Dwayne Henry on waivers from Astros.

NOVEMBER 27

Indians released P Mike C. Walker and IF Jeff Manto.

Mets signed 1B Eddie Murray, a free agent formerly with Dodgers.

Reds traded OF Eric Davis and P Kip Gross to Dodgers for P Tim Belcher and P John Wetteland.

NOVEMBER 30

Braves released C Kelly Mann.

DECEMBER 2

Cubs claimed C George Pedre on waivers from Royals.

Mets signed OF Bobby Bonilla, a free agent formerly with Pirates.

Reds claimed C Bob Geren on waivers from Yankees and OF Cesar Hernandez on waivers from Expos.

DECEMBER 3

Cubs signed P Mike Morgan, a free agent formerly with Dodgers.

Dodgers re-signed P Orel Hershiser, a free agent, and signed P Tom Candiotti, a free agent formerly with Blue Jays.

DECEMBER 4

Rangers organization signed P Kevin Blankenship, P Bob Sebra, C Russ McGinnis and IF-OF Chuck Jackson; re-signed P Mike Campbell.

White Sox re-signed OF-1B Dan Pasqua, a free agent.

DECEMBER 5

Indians organization signed P Dave Walsh, a free agent.

Rangers organization signed P Tom Drees.

DECEMBER 6

Dodgers organization signed OF Mitch Webster, a free agent.

Indians traded P Jesse Orosco to Brewers for a player to be named later.

White Sox organization signed IF Chris Cron, IF Ever Magallanes and OF Brad Komminsk.

DECEMBER 7

Rangers re-signed C Geno Petralli and DH Brian Downing, both free agents.

DECEMBER 8

Giants organization signed P Don August.

Phillies traded OF-1B Von Hayes to Angels for P Kyle Abbott and OF Ruben Amaro Jr.

Reds traded P Randy Myers to the San Diego Padres for IF-OF Bip Roberts and a player to be named later; Reds acquired OF Craig Pueschner from Padres to complete deal (December 9).

Yakult Swallows of Japan Central League signed 3B Jack Howell, a free agent.

DECEMBER 9

Athletics re-signed 3B Carney Lansford, a free agent.

Braves released P Jeff Parrett.

Expos traded P Barry Jones to Phillies for C Darrin Fletcher and cash; released C Nelson Santovenia.

Giants released OF Rick Parker.

Mets traded P Blaine Beatty to Expos for OF Jeff Barry.

Phillies organization re-signed P Danny Cox, a free agent.

Pirates organization signed P Brian Fisher.

Royals signed 1B Wally Joyner, a free agent formerly with Angels.

DECEMBER 10

Brewers traded P Chuck Crim to Angels for P Mike Fetters and P Glenn Carter.

Dodgers traded P Dennis Cook and P Mike Christopher to Indians for P Rudy Seanez; signed C Don Wakamatsu, a free agent.

Indians traded P Willie Blair and C Eddie Taubensee to Astros for P Kenny Lofton and IF Dave Rohde.

Expos traded P Ben Vanryn to Dodgers for OF Mark Griffin; Expos organization signed P Dean Wilkins, P Tim Burcham, P Sergio Valdez, OF Shon Ashley and OF Jerome Nelson.

Mets traded OF Hubie Brooks to Angels for OF Dave Gallagher.

Orioles re-signed OF-DH Dwight Evans, a free agent.

Phillies signed IF Mariano Duncan, a free agent formerly with Reds.

Royals traded OF Bobby Moore to Braves for IF Rico Rossy.

Tigers re-signed 1B Dave Bergman, a free agent.

DECEMBER 11

Blue Jays organization signed IF Kent Anderson, 1B Julian Yan and OF Butch Davis.

Cubs released P Yorkis Perez.

Dodgers traded OF Chris Gwynn and 2B Domingo Mota to Royals for 1B-OF Todd Benzinger.

Giants traded OF Kevin Mitchell and P Mike Remlinger to Mariners for P Bill Swift, P Mike Jackson and P Dave Burba.

Mets traded OF Kevin McReynolds, IF Gregg Jefferies and 2B Keith Miller to Royals for P Bret Saberhagen and 2B Bill Pecota; traded IF Jeff Gardner to Padres for P Steve Rosenberg.

Orioles traded C Bob Melvin to Royals for P Storm Davis.

Phillies traded P Bruce Ruffin to Brewers for IF Dale Sveum.

Reds traded P John Wetteland and P Bill Risley to Expos for OF Dave Martinez, P Scott Ruskin and SS Willie Greene.

White Sox re-signed C Carlton Fisk, a free agent.

DECEMBER 12

Blue Jays' Syracuse affiliate signed P Eric Plunk.

Braves re-signed OF Otis Nixon, a free agent.

Pirates re-signed 3B Steve Buechele, a free agent.

DECEMBER 13

Indians organization signed OF Ron Jones, a free agent.

Mets traded OF Chuck Carr to Cardinals for P Clyde Keller; Mets organization signed OF Rodney McCray, a free agent.

Rangers signed SS Dickie Thon, a free agent formerly with Phillies.

Reds released OF Chris Jones.

DECEMBER 16

Angels signed OF John Morris, a free agent formerly with Phillies.

Brewers released OF Mickey Brantley.

Chiba Lotte of Japan signed OF Max Venable, a free agent.

Dodgers released P Jim Neidlinger.

Indians organization signed C Junior Ortiz, a free agent.

DECEMBER 17

Twins signed P Bob Kipper, a free agent formerly with Pirates.

DECEMBER 18

Blue Jays signed P Jack Morris, a free agent formerly with Twins.

Phillies re-signed P Mitch Williams, a free agent.

DECEMBER 19

Astros organization signed OF Chris Jones, a free agent.

Blue Jays signed OF Dave Winfield, a free agent formerly with Angels.

Orioles signed P Rick Sutcliffe, a free agent formerly with Cubs.

Red Sox re-signed P Joe Hesketh, a free agent.

Tigers organization signed P Mike C. Walker, a free agent.

Twins re-signed C Brian Harper, a free agent.

DECEMBER 20

Brewers re-signed 2B Jim Gantner, a free agent.

Mets signed 2B Willie Randolph, a free agent formerly with Brewers.

Nippon Ham Fighters of Japan Pacific League signed 1B-OF Mike Marshall, a free agent.

Rangers organization signed P Todd Burns, a free agent.

Tigers signed OF Dan Gladden, a free agent formerly with Twins.

DECEMBER 23

Cubs re-signed OF Chico Walker, a free agent.

DECEMBER 28

White Sox signed P Kirk McCaskill, a free agent formerly with Angels.

DECEMBER 31

Pirates re-signed P Bob Walk, a free agent.

AWARD WINNERS

THE SPORTING NEWS

AMERICAN LEAGUE

Player of the Year: Cal Ripken Jr., Baltimore, SS
Pitcher of the Year: Roger Clemens, Boston
Rookie Player of the Year: Chuck Knoblauch, Minnesota, 2B
Rookie Pitcher of the Year: Juan Guzman, Toronto, P
Fireman of the Year: Dennis Eckersley, Oakland
                    Bryan Harvey, California
Manager of the Year: Tom Kelly, Minnesota

NATIONAL LEAGUE

Player of the Year: Barry Bonds, Pittsburgh, OF
Pitcher of the Year: Tom Glavine, Atlanta
Rookie Player of the Year: Jeff Bagwell, Houston, 1B
Rookie Pitcher of the Year: Al Osuna, Houston
Fireman of the Year: Lee Smith, St. Louis
Manager of the Year: Bobby Cox, Atlanta

MAJOR LEAGUE

Player of the Year: Cal Ripken Jr., Baltimore
Executive of the Year: Andy MacPhail, Minnesota

MINOR LEAGUE

Player of the Year: Pedro Martinez, Albuquerque, Pacific Coast
Manager of the Year: Chris Chambliss, Greenville, Southern
Executive of the Year: Tom Maloney, Denver, Am. Association

BASEBALL WRITERS' ASSOCIATION OF AMERICA

AMERICAN LEAGUE

MOST VALUABLE PLAYER

Player, Team	1	2	3	4	5	6	7	8	9	10	Pts.
Cal Ripken, Baltimore	15	8	4	-	-	-	1	-	-	-	318
Cecil Fielder, Detroit	9	12	6	-	-	-	1	-	-	-	286
Frank Thomas, Chicago	1	4	5	5	4	4	1	2	-	2	181
Jose Canseco, Oakland	-	-	3	8	5	3	3	1	2	1	145
Joe Carter, Toronto	1	2	2	2	2	4	6	3	4	1	136
Roberto Alomar, Toronto	2	2	3	1	6	1	1	-	3	-	128
Kirby Puckett, Minnesota	-	-	2	3	2	2	2	3	1	-	78
Ruben Sierra, Texas	-	-	-	3	1	2	3	3	2	1	63
Ken Griffey Jr., Seattle	-	-	1	1	1	2	1	5	3	6	62
Roger Clemens, Boston	-	-	1	2	1	4	1	1	1	-	57
Paul Molitor, Milwaukee	-	-	-	2	2	1	2	1	3	3	51
Danny Tartabull, Kansas City	-	-	-	-	2	-	1	2	3	4	32
Jack Morris, Minnesota	-	-	-	-	-	3	3	-	-	2	29
Chili Davis, Minnesota	-	-	-	1	-	-	-	4	1	-	21
Julio Franco, Texas	-	-	-	-	1	-	1	1	1	2	17
Devon White, Toronto	-	-	-	-	-	1	-	1	2	3	15
Scott Erickson, Minnesota	-	-	1	-	-	-	1	-	-	-	12
Rick Aguilera, Minnesota	-	-	-	1	1	-	-	-	-	-	11
Rafael Palmeiro, Texas	-	-	-	-	-	-	-	1	1	1	6
Robin Ventura, Chicago	-	-	-	-	-	-	-	-	1	1	3
Dave Henderson, Oakland	-	-	-	-	-	-	-	-	-	1	1

Fourteen points awarded for a first-place vote, nine for second and on down to one for 10th.

CY YOUNG AWARD

Pitcher, Team	1	2	3	Pts.
Roger Clemens, Boston	21	4	2	119
Scott Erickson, Minnesota	3	12	5	56
Jim Abbott, California	-	5	11	26
Jack Morris, Minnesota	3	-	2	17
Bryan Harvey, California	-	3	1	10
Mark Langston, California	-	2	1	7
Kevin Tapani, Minnesota	1	-	1	6
Bill Gullickson, Detroit	-	-	5	5
Jack McDowell, Chicago	-	1	-	3
Duane Ward, Toronto	-	1	-	3

Five points awarded for a first-place vote, three for second and one for third.

MANAGER OF THE YEAR

Manager, Team	1	2	3	Pts.
Tom Kelly, Minnesota	27	1	-	138
Sparky Anderson, Detroit	1	14	3	50
Cito Gaston, Toronto	-	5	2	17
Jim Lefebvre, Seattle	-	4	4	16
Joe Morgan, Boston	-	3	7	16
Jeff Torborg, Chicago	-	-	6	6
Bobby Valentine, Texas	-	1	-	3
Hal McRae, Kansas City	-	-	3	3
Tony La Russa, Oakland	-	-	2	2
Stump Merrill, New York	-	-	1	1

Five points awarded for a first-place vote, three for second and one for third.

ROOKIE OF THE YEAR

Player, Team	1	2	3	Pts.
Chuck Knoblauch, Minnesota	26	2	-	136
Juan Guzman, Toronto	1	20	3	68
Milt Cuyler, Detroit	1	2	11	22
Ivan Rodriguez, Texas	-	2	4	10
Rich DeLucia, Seattle	-	2	1	7
Mike Timlin, Toronto	-	-	2	2
Mark Whiten, Tor.-Cle.	-	-	2	2

Player, Team	1	2	3	Pts.
Leo Gomez, Baltimore	-	-	1	1
Doug Henry, Milwaukee	-	-	1	1
Brent Mayne, Kansas City	-	-	1	1
Charles Nagy, Cleveland	-	-	1	1
Phil Plantier, Boston	-	-	1	1

Five points awarded for a first-place vote, three for second and one for third.

MOST VALUABLE PLAYER

Player, Team	1	2	3	4	5	6	7	8	9	10	Pts.
Terry Pendleton, Atlanta	12	10	2	-	-	-	-	-	-	-	274
Barry Bonds, Pittsburgh	10	10	1	3	-	-	-	-	-	-	259
Bobby Bonilla, Pittsburgh	1	3	14	3	2	1	-	-	-	-	191
Will Clark, San Francisco	-	-	3	1	7	3	4	4	-	2	118
Howard Johnson, New York	-	-	1	3	1	8	7	3	-	-	112
Ron Gant, Atlanta	-	-	1	5	3	3	5	3	1	3	110
Brett Butler, Los Angeles	1	1	1	4	1	3	3	2	2	1	103
Lee Smith, St. Louis	-	-	1	2	4	4	2	2	2	5	89
Darryl Strawberry, Los Angeles	-	-	-	3	3	2	-	6	4	1	76
Fred McGriff, San Diego	-	-	-	-	1	-	1	1	4	2	23
Tom Glavine, Atlanta	-	-	-	-	2	-	-	-	2	-	16
David Justice, Atlanta	-	-	-	-	-	-	1	1	2	-	11
Jay Bell, Pittsburgh	-	-	-	-	-	-	1	1	1	2	11
Andre Dawson, Chicago	-	-	-	-	-	-	-	1	1	-	5
John Smiley, Pittsburgh	-	-	-	-	-	-	-	-	2	1	5
Tony Gwynn, San Diego	-	-	-	-	-	-	-	-	2	-	4
John Kruk, Philadelphia	-	-	-	-	-	-	-	-	1	-	2
Ryne Sandberg, Chicago	-	-	-	-	-	-	-	-	-	2	2
Barry Larkin, Cincinnati	-	-	-	-	-	-	-	-	-	2	2
Dennis Martinez, Montreal	-	-	-	-	-	-	-	-	-	1	1
Chris Sabo, Cincinnati	-	-	-	-	-	-	-	-	-	1	1
Ozzie Smith, St. Louis	-	-	-	-	-	-	-	-	-	1	1

Fourteen points awarded for a first-place vote, nine for second and on down to one for 10th.

CY YOUNG AWARD

Pitcher, Team	1	2	3	Pts.
Tom Glavine, Atlanta	19	5	-	110
Lee Smith, St. Louis	4	12	4	60
John Smiley, Pittsburgh	-	4	14	26
Jose Rijo, Cincinnati	1	2	2	13
Dennis Martinez, Montreal	-	1	1	4
Steve Avery, Atlanta	-	-	1	1
Andy Benes, San Diego	-	-	1	1
Mitch Williams, Philadelphia	-	-	1	1

Five points awarded for a first-place vote, three for second and one for third.

ROOKIE OF THE YEAR

Player, Team	1	2	3	Pts.
Jeff Bagwell, Houston	23	1	-	118
Orlando Merced, Pittsburgh	1	13	9	53
Ray Lankford, St. Louis	-	7	7	28
Brian Hunter, Atlanta	-	1	4	7
Bret Barberie, Montreal	-	1	-	3
Wes Chamberlain, Philadelphia	-	-	3	3
Chuck McElroy, Chicago	-	1	-	3
Mike Stanton, Atlanta	-	-	1	1

Five points awarded for a first-place vote, three for second and one for third.

MANAGER OF THE YEAR

Manager, Team	1	2	3	Pts.
Bobby Cox, Atlanta	13	10	1	96
Jim Leyland, Pittsburgh	9	7	8	74
Joe Torre, St. Louis	2	7	10	41
Tommy Lasorda, Los Angeles	-	-	5	5

Five points awarded for a first-place vote, three for second and one for third.

MISCELLANEOUS

ATTENDANCE

AMERICAN LEAGUE

	Home	Road
Baltimore	2,552,753	2,129,408
Boston	2,562,435	2,311,280
California	2,416,236	2,336,299
Chicago	2,934,154	2,379,873
Cleveland	1,051,863	2,076,105
Detroit	1,641,661	2,396,528
Kansas City	2,161,537	2,189,767
Milwaukee	1,478,729	2,222,851
Minnesota	2,293,842	2,306,583
New York	1,863,733	2,381,481
Oakland	2,713,493	2,636,157
Seattle	2,147,905	2,205,667
Texas	2,297,720	2,302,254
Toronto	4,001,527	2,243,335
Totals	**32,117,588**	**32,117,588**

NATIONAL LEAGUE

	Home	Road
Atlanta	2,140,217	1,927,285
Chicago	2,314,250	2,039,465
Cincinnati	2,372,377	2,060,205
Houston	1,196,152	2,039,738
Los Angeles	3,348,170	2,483,818
Montreal	934,742	2,021,866
New York	2,284,484	2,139,475
Philadelphia	2,050,012	1,907,597
Pittsburgh	2,065,302	2,060,949
St. Louis	2,448,699	1,796,933
San Diego	1,804,289	2,025,196
San Francisco	1,737,478	2,193,645
Totals	**24,696,172**	**24,696,172**

DEBUTS

Player	Pos.	Team	Birth date	Birthplace	Debut
Abbott, Lawrence Kyle	P	California	2-18-68	Newbury Port, Mass.	9-10
Allison, Dana Eric	P	Oakland	8-14-66	Front Royal, Va.	4-12
Amaral, Richard Louis	SS	Seattle	4-1-62	Visalia, Calif.	5-27
Amaro, Ruben Jr.	PR	California	2-12-65	Philadelphia	6-8
Ashby, Andrew Jason	P	Philadelphia	7-11-67	Kansas City, Mo.	6-10
Austin, James Parker	P	Milwaukee	12-7-63	Farmville, Va.	7-4
Bagwell, Jeffrey Robert	1B	Houston	5-27-68	Boston	4-8
Banister, Jeffery Todd	PH	Pittsburgh	1-15-65	Weatherford, Okla.	7-23
Banks, Willie Anthony	P	Minnesota	2-27-69	Jersey City, N.J.	7-31
Barberie, Bret Edward	PH	Montreal	8-16-67	Long Beach, Calif.	6-16
Batiste, Kimothy Emil	SS	Philadelphia	3-15-68	New Orleans	9-8
Beasley, Christopher Charles	P	California	6-23-62	Jackson, Tenn.	7-20
Beck, Rodney Roy	P	San Francisco	8-3-68	Burbank, Calif.	5-6
Bell, Derek Nathaniel	OF	Toronto	12-11-68	Tampa, Fla.	6-28
Beltre, Esteban	SS	Chicago A.L.	12-26-67	Ingenio Quisfuella, D.R.	9-3
Benavides, Alfredo	SS	Cincinnati	4-7-66	Laredo, Tex.	5-23
Bones, Ricardo	P	San Diego	4-7-69	Salinas, Puerto Rico	8-11
Boucher, Denis	P	Toronto	3-7-68	Montreal	4-12
Bowen, Ryan Eugene	P	Houston	2-10-68	Hanford, Calif.	7-22
Brantley, Clifford	P	Philadelphia	4-12-68	Staten Island, N.Y.	9-3
Briscoe, John Eric	P	Oakland	9-22-67	La Grange, Ill.	4-18
Brosius, Scott David	OF	Oakland	8-15-66	Hillsboro, Ore.	8-7
Bross, Terrence Paul	P	New York N.L.	3-30-66	El Paso, Tex.	9-4
Brown, Jarvis Ardel	OF	Minnesota	3-26-67	Waukegan, Ill.	7-2
Bullett, Scott Douglas	PR	Pittsburgh	12-25-68	Martinsburg, W.Va.	9-3
Campbell, Kevin Wade	P	Oakland	12-6-64	Marianna, Ark.	7-19
Carreno, Amalio Rafael	P	Philadelphia	4-11-64	Chacachacare, Venezuela	7-7
Carrillo, Matias	OF	Milwaukee	2-24-63	Los Mochis, Sinaloa, Mex.	5-23
Carter, Jeffrey Allen	P	Chicago A.L.	12-3-64	Tampa, Fla.	7-31
Castilla, Vinicio	SS	Atlanta	7-4-61	Oaxaca, Mexico	9-1
Castillo, Braulio	OF	Philadelphia	5-13-68	Elias Pina, Dominican Republic	8-18
Castillo, Frank Anthony	P	Chicago N.L.	4-1-69	El Paso, Tex.	6-27
Chapin, Darrin John	P	New York A.L.	2-1-66	Warren, O.	9-21
Christopher, Michael Wayne	P	Los Angeles	11-3-63	Petersburg, Va.	9-10
Clark, Mark William	P	St. Louis	5-12-66	Bath, Ill.	9-13
Clayton, Royce Spencer	SS	San Francisco	1-2-70	Burbank, Calif.	9-20
Cole, Stewart Bryan	PH	Kansas City	2-7-66	Charlotte, N.C.	9-5
Cooper, Gary Clifton	PH	Houston	8-13-64	Lynwood, Calif.	9-15
Corbin, Archie Ray	P	Kansas City	12-30-67	Beaumont, Tex.	9-10
Cormier, Rheal Paul	P	St. Louis	4-23-67	Moneton, Canada	8-15
Cron, Christopher John	1B	California	3-31-64	Albuquerque, N.M.	9-25
Dalton, Michael Edward	P	Detroit	3-27-63	Palo Alto, Calif.	5-31
Davis, Mark Anthony	OF	California	11-25-64	Lemon Grove, Calif.	7-2
de la Rosa, Francisco	P	Baltimore	3-3-66	La Romana, Dominican Republic	9-7
Donnels, Chris Barton	3B	New York N.L.	4-21-66	Los Angeles	5-7
Drahman, Brian Stacy	P	Chicago A.L.	11-7-66	Kenton, Ky.	4-18
Drees, Thomas Kent	P	Chicago A.L.	6-17-63	Des Moines, Ia.	9-3
Dressendorfer, Kirk Richard	P	Oakland	4-8-69	Houston	4-13
Egloff, Bruce Edward	P	Cleveland	4-10-65	Denver	4-13

Player	Pos.	Team	Birth date	Birthplace	Debut
Eldred, Calvin John	P	Milwaukee	11-24-67	Cedar Rapids, Ia.	9-24
Escobar, Jose Elias	SS	Cleveland	10-30-60	Las Flores, Venezuela	4-13
Eusebio, Raul Antonio	C	Houston	4-27-67	Boca Chica, Dominican Republic	8-8
Fajardo, Hector	P	Pittsburgh	11- 6-70	Michoacan, Mexico	8-10
Fariss, Monty Ted	DH	Texas	10-13-67	Cordell, Okla.	9-6
Fassero, Jeffrey Joseph	P	Montreal	1- 5-63	Springfield, Ill.	5-4
Fleming, David Anthony	P	Seattle	11- 7-69	Queens, N.Y.	8-6
Flora, Kevin Scot	2B	California	6-10-69	Fontana, Calif.	9-27
Foster, Stephen Eugene	P	Cincinnati	8-16-66	Dallas	8-22
Gakeler, Daniel Michael	P	Detroit	5- 1-64	Mount Holly, N.J.	6-9
Garcia, Ramon Antonio	P	Chicago A.L.	12- 9-69	Guanare, Venezuela	5-31
Gardner, Christopher John	P	Houston	3-30-69	Long Beach, Calif.	9-10
Gardner, Jeffrey Scott	SS	New York N.L.	2- 4-64	Newport Beach, Calif.	9-10
George, Christopher Sean	P	Milwaukee	9-24-66	Pittsburgh	10-1
Giannelli, Raymond John	PH/3B	Toronto	2- 5-66	Brooklyn, N.Y.	5-4
Goodwin, Thomas Jones	OF	Los Angeles	7-27-68	Fresno, Calif.	9-1
Grater, Mark Anthony	P	St. Louis	1-19-64	Rochester, Pa.	6-12
Guzman, Dionini Ramon	P	Oakland	1-21-71	Hatillo Palma, D.R.	6-8
Guzman, Juan Andres	P	Toronto	10-28-66	Santo Domingo, Dominican Republic	6-7
Haas, Robert David	P	Detroit	10-19-65	Independence, Mo.	9-8
Haney, Christopher Deane	P	Montreal	11-16-68	Baltimore	6-21
Hare, Shawn Robert	PH/DH	Detroit	3-26-67	St. Louis	9-6
Harris, Donald	PR	Texas	11-12-67	Waco, Tex.	9-4
Henry, Richard Douglas	P	Milwaukee	12-10-63	Sacramento, Calif.	7-15
Hentgen, Patrick George	P	Toronto	11-13-68	Detroit	9-3
Heredia, Gilbert	P	San Francisco	10-26-65	Nogales, Ariz.	9-1
Hernandez, Jeremy Stuart	P	San Diego	7- 6-66	Burbank, Calif.	9-2
Hernandez, Jose Antonio	SS	Texas	7-14-69	Vega Alta, Puerto Rico	8-9
Hernandez, Roberto Manuel	P	Chicago A.L.	11-11-64	Santurce, Puerto Rico	9-2
Hickerson, Bryan David	P	San Francisco	10-13-63	Bemidji, Minn.	7-25
Hill, Milton Giles	P	Cincinnati	8-22-65	Atlanta	8-1
Horsman, Vincent Stanley	P	Toronto	3- 9-67	Halifax, Nova Scotia	9-5
Housie, Wayne Tyrone	PR/DH	Boston	5-20-65	Hampton, Va.	9-17
Howard, Christopher Hugh	C	Seattle	2-27-66	San Diego	9-15
Howard, David Wayne	2B	Kansas City	2-26-67	Sarasota, Fla.	4-14
Humphreys, Michael Butler	PH/OF	New York A.L.	4-10-67	Dallas	7-29
Hunter, Brian Ronald	1B	Atlanta	3- 4-68	El Toro, Calif.	5-31
Hunter, James MacGregor	P	Milwaukee	6-22-64	Jersey City, N.J.	5-17
Ignasiak, Michael James	P	Milwaukee	3-12-66	Mount Clemens, N.C.	8-22
Jefferson, Reginald Jirod	PH	Cincinnati	9-25-68	Tallahassee, Fla.	5-18
Johnson, William Jeffrey	P	New York A.L.	8- 4-66	Durham, N.C.	6-5
Johnston, Joel Raymond	P	Kansas City	3- 8-67	West Chester, Pa.	9-5
Jones, Calvin Douglas	P	Seattle	9-26-63	Compton, Calif.	6-14
Jones, Christopher Carlos	PR	Cincinnati	12-16-65	Utica, N.Y.	4-21
Jones, Joseph Stacy	P	Baltimore	5-26-67	Gadsden, Ala.	7-30
Juden, Jeffrey Daniel	P	Houston	1-19-71	Salem, Mass.	9-15
Kamieniecki, Scott Andrew	P	New York A.L.	4-19-64	Mount Clemens, Mich.	6-18
Karros, Eric Peter	PR/1B	Los Angeles	11- 4-67	Hackensack, N.J.	9-1
Kelly, Patrick Franklin	2B	New York A.L.	10-14-67	Philadelphia	5-20
Kiely, John Francis	P	Detroit	10- 4-64	Boston	7-26
Kile, Darryl Andrew	P	Houston	12- 2-68	Garden Grove, Calif.	4-8
Kirby, Wayne Leonard	OF	Cleveland	1-22-64	Williamsburg, Va.	9-12
Kiser, Garland Routhard	P	Cleveland	7- 8-68	Charlotte, N.C.	9-9
Knoblauch, Edward Charles	2B	Minnesota	7- 7-68	Houston	4-9
Knorr, Randy Duane	C	Toronto	11-12-68	San Gabriel, Calif.	9-5
Kramer, Thomas Joseph	P	Cleveland	1- 9-68	Cincinnati	9-12
Landrum, Cedric Bernard	PR/OF	Chicago N.L.	9- 3-63	Butler, Ala.	5-28
Lennon, Patrick Orlando	PH/DH	Seattle	4-27-68	Whiteville, N.C.	9-15
Lewis, James Steven	P	San Diego	7-20-64	Jackson, Mich.	8-9
Lewis, Mark David	SS	Cleveland	11-30-69	Hamilton, O.	4-26
Lindsey, Michael Douglas	C	Philadelphia	9-22-67	Austin, Tex.	10-6
Livingstone, Scott Louis	3B	Detroit	7-15-65	Dallas	7-19
Lofton, Kenneth	OF	Houston	5-31-67	East Chicago, Ind.	9-14
Magallanes, Everardo	SS	Cleveland	11- 6-65	Chihuahua, Mexico	5-17
Magnante, Michael Anthony	P	Kansas City	6-17-65	Glendale, Calif.	4-22
Manuel, Barry Paul	P	Texas	8-12-65	Mamou, La.	9-6
Manzanillo, Josias	P	Boston	10-16-67	San Pedro de Macoris, D.R.	10-5
Martinez, Reynaldo Igancio	OF	Baltimore	12-19-67	Belize, Central America	7-5
Mathews, Terry Alan	P	Texas	10- 5-64	Alexandria, La.	6-21
Maurer, Robert John	DH	Texas	1- 7-67	Evansville, Ind.	9-8
Mauser, Timothy Edward	P	Philadelphia	10- 4-66	Fort Worth, Tex.	7-7
McDaniel, Terrence Keith	OF	New York N.L.	12- 6-66	Kansas City, Mo.	8-30
Meacham, Russell Loren	P	Detroit	1-27-68	Stuart, Fla.	6-29
Mercedes, Luis Roberto	OF	Baltimore	2-20-68	San Pedro de Macoris, D.R.	9-8
Miller, Paul Robert	P	Pittsburgh	4-27-65	Burlington, Wis.	7-30
Mitchell, Keith Alexander	OF	Atlanta	8- 6-69	San Diego	7-23
Moore, Robert Vincent	PH/OF	Kansas City	10-27-65	Cincinnati	9-5

Player	Pos.	Team	Birth date	Birthplace	Debut
Morton, Kevin Joseph	P	Boston	8- 3-68	Norwalk, Conn.	7-5
Mota, Andres Alberto	2B	Houston	3- 4-66	Santo Domingo, D.R.	8-31
Mota, Jose Manuel	2B	San Diego	3-16-65	Santo Domingo, D.R.	5-24
Mussina, Michael Cole	P	Baltimore	12- 8-68	Williamsport, Pa.	8-4
Mutis, Jeffrey Thomas	P	Cleveland	12-20-66	Allentown, Pa.	6-15
Neagle, Dennis Edward	P	Minnesota	9-13-68	Prince Georges County, Md.	7-27
Newson, Warren Dale	PH	Chicago A.L.	7- 3-64	Newnan, Ga.	5-29
Olander, James Bentley	PH/OF	Milwaukee	2-21-63	Tucson, Ariz.	9-20
Pappas, Erik Daniel	C	Chicago N.L.	4-25-66	Chicago	4-19
Pedre, Jorge Enrique	C	Kansas City	10-12-66	Culver City, Calif.	9-7
Perez, Yorkis Miguel	P	Chicago N.L.	9-30-67	Bajos de Haina, D.R.	9-30
Petkovsek, Mark Joseph	P	Texas	11-18-65	Beaumont, Tex.	6-8
Piatt, Douglas William	P	Montreal	9-26-65	Beaver, Pa.	6-11
Plympton, Jeffrey Hunter	P	Boston	11-24-65	Framingham, Mass.	6-15
Pulliam, Harvey Jerome	OF	Kansas City	10-20-67	San Francisco	8-10
Ramos, John Joseph	C	New York A.L.	8- 6-65	Tampa, Fla.	9-18
Remlinger, Michael John	P	San Francisco	3-23-66	Middletown, N.Y.	6-15
Renfroe, Cohen Williams	P	Chicago N.L.	5- 9-62	Natchez, Miss.	7-3
Reynoso, Armando Martin	P	Atlanta	5- 1-66	San Luis Potosi, Mex.	8-11
Rhodes, Arthur Lee	P	Baltimore	10-24-69	Waco, Tex.	8-21
Rice, Patrick Edward	P	Seattle	11- 2-63	Rapid City, S.D.	5-18
Riesgo, Damon Nikco	OF	Montreal	1-11-67	Long Beach, Calif.	4-20
Rodriguez, Carlos	SS	New York A.L.	11- 1-67	Mexico City, Mex.	6-16
Rodriguez, Ivan	C	Texas	11-30-71	Vega Baja, Puerto Rico	6-20
Rosenthal, Wayne Scott	P	Texas	2-19-65	Brooklyn, N.Y.	6-26
Rossy, Elam Jose	PR	Atlanta	2-16-64	Santurce, Puerto Rico	9-11
Royer, Stanley Dean	PH	St. Louis	8-31-67	Olney, Ill.	9-11
Sanchez, Rey Francisco	SS	Chicago N.L.	10- 5-67	Rio Piedras, Puerto Rico	9-8
Sanders, Reginald Laverne	OF	Cincinnati	12- 1-67	Florence, S.C.	8-22
Sanford, Meredith Leroy	P	Cincinnati	12-24-66	Americus, Ga.	8-9
Scanlan, Robert Guy	P	Chicago N.L.	8- 9-66	Los Angeles	5-7
Schourek, Peter Alan	P	New York N.L.	5-10-69	Austin, Tex.	4-9
Scott, Gary Thomas	3B	Chicago N.L.	8-22-68	New Rochelle, N.Y.	4-9
Scott, Timothy Dale	P	San Diego	11-16-66	Hanford, Calif.	6-25
Scruggs, Anthony Raymond	PH/OF	Texas	3-19-66	Riverside, Calif.	4-8
Servais, Scott Daniel	PH	Houston	6- 4-67	LaCrosse, Wis.	7-12
Simons, Douglas Eugene	P	New York N.L.	9-15-66	Bakersfield, Calif.	4-9
Slocumb, Heath	P	Chicago N.L.	6- 7-66	Jamaica, N.Y.	4-11
Slusarski, Joseph Andrew	P	Oakland	12-19-66	Indianapolis	4-11
Spehr, Timothy Joseph	C	Kansas City	7- 2-66	Excelsior Springs, Mo.	7-18
Sprague, Edward Nelson	3B	Toronto	7-25-67	Castro Valley, Calif.	5-7
Tackett, Jeffery Wilson	C	Baltimore	12- 1-65	Fresno, Calif.	9-11
Taubensee, Edward Kenneth	C	Cleveland	10-31-68	Beeville, Tex.	9-6
Taylor, Wade Eric	P	New York A.L.	10-19-65	Mobile, Ala.	6-2
Thome, James Howard	3B	Cleveland	8-27-70	Peoria, Ill.	9-4
Timlin, Michael August	P	Toronto	3-10-66	Midland, Tex.	4-8
Tolentino, Jose Franco	PH	Houston	6- 3-61	Mexico City, Mex.	7-28
Vanderwal, John Henry	PH	Montreal	4-29-66	Grand Rapids, Mich.	9-6
Van Poppel, Todd Matthew	P	Oakland	12- 9-71	Hinsdale, Ill.	9-11
Vaughn, Maurice Samuel	1B	Boston	12-15-67	Norwalk, Conn.	6-27
Wainhouse, David Paul	P	Montreal	11- 7-67	Toronto	8-3
Wakamatsu, Wilbur Donald	C	Chicago A.L.	2-22-63	Hood River, Ore.	5-22
Walton, Bruce Kenneth	P	Oakland	12-25-62	Bakersfield, Calif.	5-11
Ward, Kevin Michael	OF	San Diego	9-28-61	Lansdale, Pa.	5-10
Weathers, John David	P	Toronto	9-25-69	Lawrenceburg, Tenn.	7-7
Wedge, Eric Michael	PH	Boston	1-27-68	Fort Wayne, Ind.	10-5
Wehner, John Paul	3B	Pittsburgh	6-29-67	Pittsburgh	7-17
Wilkins, Richard David	C	Chicago N.L.	7- 4-67	Jacksonville, Fla.	6-6
Williams, Bernabe	OF	New York A.L.	9-13-68	San Juan, Puerto Rico	7-7
Williams, Brian O'Neal	P	Houston	2-15-69	Lancaster, S.C.	9-16
Witmeyer, Ronald Herman	PH	Oakland	6-28-67	West Islip, N.Y.	8-25
Wohlers, Mark Edward	P	Atlanta	1-23-70	Holyoke, Mass.	8-17
Wood, Edward Robert	PH	San Francisco	1- 4-67	Mansfield, O.	9-4
Young, Anthony Wayne	P	New York N.L.	1-19-66	Houston	8-5
Zosky, Edward James	SS	Toronto	2-10-68	Whittier, Calif.	9-2
Zupcic, Robert	PR/OF	Boston	8-18-66	Pittsburgh	9-7

1991 FREE-AGENT FILINGS

AMERICAN LEAGUE

Baltimore: Glenn Davis, Dwight Evans.
Boston: Joe Hesketh, Dennis Lamp, Steve Lyons, Dan Petry.
California: Bert Blyleven, Donnie Hill, Wally Joyner, Kirk Mc-Caskill, Jeff Robinson, Dick Schofield, Max Venable, Dave Winfield.
Chicago: Carlton Fisk, Scott Fletcher, Dan Pasqua.
Detroit: Dave Bergman, John Cerutti, Jerry Don Gleaton, Pete Incaviglia, Lloyd Moseby, Mark Salas.
Kansas City: Steve Crawford, Jim Eisenreich, Kurt Stillwell, Danny Tartabull.
Milwaukee: Jim Gantner, Willie Randolph.
Minnesota: Steve Bedrosian, Dan Gladden, Brian Harper, Terry Leach, Jack Morris, Al Newman, Junior Ortiz, Mike Pagliarulo.
Oakland: Ron Darling, Mike Gallego, Brook Jacoby, Carney Lansford, Ernest Riles, Curt Young.
Seattle: Alvin Davis, Tracy Jones, Bill Krueger.
Texas: Oil Can Boyd, Brian Downing, Rich Gossage, Geno Petralli, John Russell.
Toronto: Jim Acker, Tom Candiotti, Dave Parker, Mookie Wilson.

NATIONAL LEAGUE

Atlanta: Jim Clancy, Otis Nixon, Alejandro Pena, Doug Sisk.
Chicago: Rick Sutcliffe.
Cincinnati: Mariano Duncan, Carmelo Martinez, Ted Power, Herm Winningham.
Houston: Jim Deshaies, Rafael Ramirez.
Los Angeles: Alfredo Griffin, Orel Hershiser, Jay Howell, Mike Morgan, Eddie Murray, Juan Samuel, Mitch Webster.
Montreal: Mike Fitzgerald, Ron Hassey.
New York: Daryl Boston, Garry Templeton, Frank Viola.
Philadelphia: Danny Cox, Steve Lake, Steve Ontiveros, Randy Ready, Rick Schu, Dickie Thon, Mitch Williams.
Pittsburgh: Bobby Bonilla, Steve Buechele, Bob Kipper, Mike LaValliere, Bob Walk, Curtis Wilkerson.
St. Louis: Pedro Guerrero.
San Diego: Atlee Hammaker, Jack Howell, Dennis Rasmussen, Tim Teufel.
San Francisco: Dave Anderson, Terry Kennedy, Don Robinson.

SALARY ARBITRATION RESULTS

WINNERS

Player, Team	Salary awarded	Team's offer
Mike Aldrete, Montreal	$510,000	$350,000
Roberto Alomar, Toronto	$1,250,000	$825,000
Doug Drabek, Pittsburgh	$3,350,000	$2,300,000
Paul Gibson, Detroit	$565,000	$350,000
Wally Joyner, California	$2,100,000	$1,650,000
Greg Swindell, Cleveland	$2,025,000	$1,400,000

LOSERS

Player, Team	Salary awarded	Player's request
Tim Belcher, Los Angeles	$900,000	$1,350,000
Barry Bonds, Pittsburgh	$2,300,000	$3,250,000
Bobby Bonilla, Pittsburgh	$2,400,000	$3,475,000
Jerry Browne, Cleveland	$800,000	$1,100,000
Jim Gantner, Milwaukee	$1,000,000	$2,000,000
Jack Howell, California	$652,500	$835,000
Jose Lind, Pittsburgh	$575,000	$950,000
Dan Petry, Detroit	$650,000	$1,350,000
Benito Santiago, San Diego	$1,650,000	$2,500,000
Cory Snyder, Chicago White Sox	$800,000	$1,020,000
Dickie Thon, Philadelphia	$1,250,000	$1,700,000

MAJOR LEAGUE DRAFT

(Listed in order of selection)

Player	Pos.	Drafted by	Drafted from (major league organization)
Mike Thomas	P	Cleveland	Indianapolis, American Association (Expos)
Juan Guerrero	3B	Houston	Phoenix, Pacific Coast League (Giants)
Darrell Sherman	OF	Baltimore	Las Vegas, Pacific Coast League (Padres)
Matt Karchner	P	Montreal	Omaha, American Association (Royals)
Dave Holdridge	P	California	Scranton/Wilkes-Barre, International League (Phillies)
Rafael Quirico	P	San Francisco	Columbus, International League (Yankees)
Don Elliott Jr.	P	Seattle	Scranton/Wilkes-Barre, International League (Phillies)
Todd Pratt	C	Philadelphia	Rochester, International League (Orioles)
Miguel Batista	P	Pittsburgh	Indianapolis, American Association (Expos)
Jesse Cross	P	Minnesota	Syracuse, International League (Blue Jays)
Tim Fortugno	P	California	Denver, American Association (Brewers)

NECROLOGY

DEATHS

Nate Andrews, 77, at Winston-Salem, N.C., on April 26. An eight-season major leaguer, this righthander won a total of 30 games for the Boston Braves in 1943 and 1944. He was a 20-game loser in '43.

Luke Appling, 81, at Cumming, Ga., on January 3. Appling, a Hall of Fame shortstop, batted .310 in 20 big-league seasons (all with the White Sox) and won two American League batting titles.

Tom Baker, 77, at Fort Worth, Tex., on January 3. Baker, a pitcher for the Brooklyn Dodgers and New York Giants, won three of 12 decisions from 1935 through 1938.

Heinz Becker, 76, at Dallas on November 11. A major leaguer for four seasons, he was a member of the 1945 National League champion Cubs. Becker was used primarily as a pinch-hitter for the Cubs' last pennant-winning team.

James (Cool Papa) Bell, 87, at St. Louis on March 7. Hall of Famer Bell, a gifted center fielder, was a longtime Negro leagues star. According to Satchel Paige, Bell was so fast that "he could turn out the light and be in bed before the room got dark."

Bill Bevens, 75, at Salem, Ore., on October 26. Bevens, pitching for the Yankees, hurled 8⅔ innings of no-hit ball against Brooklyn in Game 4 of the 1947 World Series, only to lose on Cookie Lavagetto's two-run pinch double in the ninth.

Marv Breuer, 76, at Rolla, Mo., on January 17. Righthander Breuer won a total of 17 games for the 1941 World Series champion Yankees and the 1942 A.L. pennant-winning Yanks.

Walter Brown, 75, at Westfield, N.Y., on February 3. Brown appeared in 19 big-league games, all in relief for the 1947 St. Louis Browns, and won his only decision.

George Brunet, 56, at Poza Rica, Mexico, on October 25. He pitched in professional baseball for 33 consecutive seasons, starting in 1953. Brunet had a 15-year career in the majors, posting a 69-93 record. He capped his career with a 13-year stint in the Mexican League, where he tossed 55 shutouts.

Smoky Burgess, 64, at Asheville, N.C., on September 15. Burgess, a catcher who hit .295 in 18 big-league seasons, ranks second in major league history with 145 career pinch hits.

Bill Byrd, 83, at Philadelphia on January 3. Byrd was a standout pitcher in the Negro leagues from 1932 through 1949.

Happy Chandler, 92, at Versailles, Ky., on June 15. Baseball's second commissioner (1945-1951), he presided over the integration of modern big-league baseball when Jackie Robinson joined the Brooklyn Dodgers in 1947.

Loyd Christopher, 71, at Richmond, Calif., on September 5. An outfielder, he played a total of 16 games in 1945 and 1947 for the Red Sox, Cubs and White Sox.

Red Conkwright, 94, at La Mesa, Calif., on July 30. He made five pitching appearances for the 1920 Tigers and won two of three decisions.

Bobby Coombs, 83, at Ogunquit, Me., on October 21. Coombs pitched in two major league seasons, 10 years apart (1933, 1943), and lost his only two decisions.

Jimmy Cooney, 96, at Warwick, R.I., on August 7. Playing for the Cubs in a May 30, 1927, game at Pittsburgh, shortstop Cooney completed the last unassisted triple play in National League history.

Walker Cooper, 76, at Scottsdale, Ariz., on April 11. He was the catching half of the brother combination (Mort was the pitcher) that paced the Cardinals to three pennants and two World Series crowns from 1942 through 1944.

Roy Cullenbine, 75, at Mount Clemens, Mich., on May 28. Outfielder Cullenbine batted .276 for six clubs in a 10-season

major league career that ended in 1947.

Leo Durocher, 86, at Palm Springs, Calif., on October 7. Durocher, shortstop for the Cardinals' 1934 Gas House Gang, managed 24 years in the majors and won three pennants and one World Series.

Bobby Estalella, 79, at Hialeah, Fla., on January 6. An outfielder/third baseman for nine big-league seasons, he was an effective wartime player, batting .298 and .299 for the Philadelphia Athletics in 1944 and 1945.

Hoot Evers, 69, at Houston on January 25. A major league outfielder for 12 years, Evers twice (1948, 1950) batted in more than 100 runs for the Tigers. He later served in front-office capacities with the Indians and Tigers.

John Fetzer, 89, at Honolulu on February 20. He headed a syndicate that bought the Tigers franchise in 1956 and owned it for more than a quarter of a century.

Jesse Flores, 77. Despite a seven-year major league record of 44-59, Flores fashioned a career earned-run average of 3.18 and threw 11 shutouts. In 1946, he went 9-7 with a 2.32 ERA for the Philadelphia A's.

Frank Gustine, 71, at Davenport, Ia., on April 1. Infielder Gustine played 10 of his 12 years in the majors for the Pirates, batting .290 for Pittsburgh in 1943 and .297 for the Bucs in 1947.

John Hallahan, 64, at Pittsburgh on September 11. Hallahan was the Pirates' equipment manager from 1957 until the time of his death and had served the N.L. club in various capacities since 1941.

Ed Hanyzewski, 71, at Fargo, N.D., on October 8. He pitched in a total of 58 big-league games, all for the Cubs, from 1942 through 1946. He posted a 12-13 record.

Jim Hardin, 47, in a plane crash at Key West, Fla., on March 8. A major league pitcher for six seasons, Hardin was an 18-game winner for the Orioles in 1968.

Lanny Harris, 51. Harris was a National League umpire from 1979 through 1985.

Johnny Johnson, 76, at Iron Mountain, Mich., on June 26. A reliever in 50 of his 51 games in the majors, he went 0-2 for the 1944 Yankees and 3-0 for the 1945 White Sox.

Smead Jolley, 89, at Alameda, Calif., on November 17. He hit .305 over four big-league seasons and drove in more than 100 runs in two of those years. A notoriously poor fielder, outfielder Jolley spent the bulk of his career in the minors, where he hit 336 homers, batted .404 one year and twice drove in more than 180 runs in a season.

Ken Jones, 87, at Hartford, Conn., on May 15. He pitched in one game for the 1924 Tigers and in eight games for the 1930 Boston Braves.

Sheldon Jones, 69, at Greenville, N.C., on February 22. Jones went 16-8 for the New York Giants in 1948 and won a total of 28 games for the club in the next two seasons. In 1951, he made two World Series appearances for the Giants.

Lyle Judy, 77, at Ormond Beach, Fla., on January 15. Judy stole 107 bases in the Western Association in 1935, earning a late-season promotion to the Cardinals, for whom he stole two bases in eight games.

Dick Kelley, 51, at Northridge, Calif., on December 12. A big-league pitcher for seven seasons, Kelly had his best year in 1966, when he went 7-5 for the Braves with a 3.22 ERA. He tossed two shutouts that season.

Ken Keltner, 75, at New Berlin, Wis., on December 12. A .276 batsman over 13 major league seasons, he hit .325 for Cleveland in 1939 and twice drove in more than 100 runs in a season. Playing third base for the Indians on July 17, 1941, he made two sparkling fielding plays that helped end Joe DiMaggio's 56-game hitting streak.

Clay Kirby, 43, at Arlington, Va., on October 11. A 20-game loser for the Padres in their first season, 1969, he went 75-104 in eight big-league seasons. In a 1970 game, he was taken out for a pinch-hitter after holding the Mets hitless through eight innings. (San Diego, behind 1-0 at the time, wound up losing, 3-0.)

Clem Koshorek, 66, at Royal Oak., Mich., on September 8. Infielder Koshorek played in 99 big-league games—98 of them for the 1952 Pirates, for whom he batted .261.

Frank Leja, 55, at Boston, on May 3. The Yankees' first "bonus baby" and a highly touted slugger, he wound up batting only 23 times in the majors (for the Yanks and Angels) and collecting one hit, a single.

Gene Lillard, 77, at Goleta, Calif., on April 12. A feared minor league slugger (345 homers, including 56 in one season), he saw brief big-league service—first as an infielder (1936), then as a pitcher (1939 and 1940).

Dale Long, 64, at Palm Coast, Fla., on January 27. Long, who played 10 seasons in the majors, set a big-league record with home runs in eight consecutive games for the Pirates in 1956.

Jim Magnuson, 44, at Green Bay, Wis., on May 30. A pitcher for the White Sox in 1970 and 1971 and for the Yankees In 1973, he compiled a 3-7 big-league record.

Hank Majeski, 74, at New York on August 9. Majeski, an infielder, batted .310 and drove in 120 runs for the Philadelphia Athletics in 1948. In 1954, he hit a pinch home run for Cleveland in the World Series.

Les Mallon, 85, at Granbury, Tex., on April 17. Infielder Mallon, who played for the Phillies in 1931 and 1932 and for the Braves in 1934 and 1935, had a .283 career average in the majors.

Alex McColl, 96, at Kingsville, O., on February 6. McColl compiled a 4-4 record while pitching for the Senators in 1933 and 1934 and appeared in the '33 World Series.

Ken Miller, 75, at St. Louis on April 3. Miller made four relief appearances for the 1944 New York Giants.

Johnny Moore, 89, at Bradenton, Fla., on April 4. A .307 hitter in 10 big-league seasons, he was the Cubs' center fielder at the time of Babe Ruth's alleged "called shot" homer to center in the 1932 World Series.

Chet Morgan, 81, at Pasadena, Tex., on September 20. Outfielder Morgan played a total of 88 games for the Tigers in 1935 and 1938.

Ed Moriarty, 78, at Holyoke, Mass., on September 29. Moriarty, a second baseman, played a total of 14 games for the Boston Braves/Bees in 1935 and 1936.

John W. Mullen, 66, at West Palm Beach, Fla., on April 3. Assistant general manager of the Braves, he also had served in the club's front office during the franchise's days in both Boston and Milwaukee.

Joe Munson, 91, at Drexel Hill, Pa., on February 24. Munson, an outfielder, played a total of 42 games for the Cubs in 1925 and 1926.

Marv Owen, 85, at Mountain View, Calif., on June 22. A .275 hitter over nine big-league seasons, he was the Detroit third baseman who was on the receiving end of Joe Medwick's hard slide in Game 7 of the 1934 World Series. St. Louis' Medwick subsequently was pelted with debris by Tiger fans and forced to leave the game.

Jimmy Pattison, 82, at Melbourne, Fla., on February 22. Pattison made six relief appearances for the 1929 Brooklyn Dodgers and lost his only decision.

Steve Peek, 77, at Syracuse, N.Y., on September 20. Peek won four of six decisions for the 1941 Yankees.

Pete Rambo, 84, at Camden, N.J., on June 19. He pitched in one game in the big leagues—for the Phillies, in 1926.

Les Rock, 79, at Davis, Calif., on September 9. He appeared in two games at first base for the 1936 White Sox.

Eric Rodin, 60, at Somerville, N.J., on January 4. Rodin, an outfielder, played five games for the New York Giants in their World Series championship year of 1954.

Pete Runnels, 63, at Pasadena, Tex., on May 20. Runnels was a two-time American League batting champion while playing for the Boston Red Sox, winning the 1960 crown with a .320 average and the 1962 title with a .326 mark.

Carl Sawatski, 64, at Little Rock, Ark., on November 24. An 11-year major leaguer, catcher Sawatski was a member of the 1957 World Series champion Milwaukee Braves. At the time of his death, he was president of the Texas League.

Pat Scantlebury, 65, at Glen Ridge, N.J., on May 24. A former Negro leagues pitcher and a longtime minor leaguer, he appeared in six games for the Reds in 1956.

Chris Short, 53, at Wilmington, Del., on August 1. In four seasons of a five-year stretch for the Phillies in the 1960s, the lefthanded pitcher posted victory totals of 17, 18, 19 and 20.

Ken Smith, 89, at Palatine Bridge, N.Y., on March 1. A longtime New York sportswriter, Smith worked 17 years for the Baseball Hall of Fame and was director of the shrine at the time of his retirement in 1979.

Bill Starr, 80, at La Jolla, Calif., on August 12. A catcher who saw brief action for the Washington Senators in 1935 and 1936, Starr later owned the San Diego Padres franchise in the Pacific Coast League.

Bryan Stephens, 71, at Santa Ana, Calif., on November 21. Pitcher Stephens went 5-10 for the 1947 Indians and 3-6 for the 1948 St. Louis Browns.

Cedric Tallis, 76, at Tampa, Fla., on May 7. Tallis, a baseball executive for 43 years, joined the Royals as general manager in 1968, a year before the expansion team began play, and was voted the 1971 Major League Executive of the Year while with the Royals.

Frank Umont, 72, at Fort Lauderdale, Fla., on June 20. Umont was an American League umpire from 1954 through 1973.

Johnny Vergez, 85, at Davis, Calif., on July 15. A big-league third baseman from 1931 through 1936, he played for the New York Giants, Phillies and Cardinals and batted .255 in 672 games.

Bucky Walters, 82, at Abington, Pa., on April 20. A three-time 20-game winner for the Reds, Walters won two games for Cincinnati in the 1940 World Series and posted 198 victories in 19 big-league seasons. He managed the Reds in 1948 and 1949.

Roy Weatherly, 75, at Woodville, Tex., on January 19. In 1936, rookie outfielder Weatherly hit .335 for the Indians in 349 at-bats. He played 10 seasons overall in the majors, batting .286.

Dick Weik, 63, at Harvey, Ill., on April 21. He posted a 6-22 record for the Washington Senators, Indians and Tigers in a five-season major league career that ended in 1954.

Sammy White, 63, at Princeville, Hawaii, on August 5. He caught 100 or more games in eight consecutive seasons for the Red Sox in the 1950s.

Alan Wiggins, 32, at Los Angeles on January 9. Wiggins, whose career was cut short because of drug problems, stole 70 bases for the 1984 N.L. champion Padres.

Harry Wilke, 90, at Hamilton, O., on June 21. Infielder Wilke played in three games for the 1927 Cubs.

Jim Zinn, 96, at Memphis, Tenn., on February 26. A noted minor league pitcher, he played 24 professional seasons—including five in the majors—in a career that began in 1915.

1991
A.L. STATISTICS

BATTING

TEAM

Team	Avg.	G	AB	R	H	TB	2B	3B	HR	RBI	SH	SF	BB	Int. BB	HP	SO	SB	CS	GI DP	LOB	ShO	Slg.	OBP
Minnesota	.280	162	5556	776	1557	2331	270	42	140	733	44	49	526	38	40	747	107	68	157	1137	8	.420	.344
Milwaukee	.271	162	5611	799	1523	2224	247	53	116	750	52	66	556	48	23	802	106	68	137	1122	11	.396	.336
Texas	.270	162	5703	829	1539	2420	288	31	177	774	55	41	596	51	59	1039	102	50	128	1187	9	.424	.341
Boston	.269	162	5530	731	1486	2219	305	25	126	691	50	51	593	49	32	820	59	50	143	1216	12	.401	.340
Kansas City	.264	162	5584	727	1475	2198	290	41	117	689	53	47	523	47	35	969	119	68	126	1117	9	.394	.328
Chicago	.262	162	5594	758	1464	2185	226	39	139	722	76	41	610	45	37	896	134	74	132	1183	12	.391	.336
Toronto	.257	162	5489	684	1412	2196	226	45	133	649	56	65	499	49	37	1043	148	53	108	1134	9	.400	.322
New York	.256	162	5541	674	1418	2146	249	19	147	630	37	50	473	38	39	861	109	36	125	1101	10	.387	.316
California	.255	162	5470	653	1396	2044	245	29	115	607	63	31	448	28	39	928	94	56	114	1073	15	.374	.314
Seattle	.255	162	5494	702	1400	2104	268	29	126	665	55	62	588	57	37	811	97	44	139	1150	10	.383	.328
Cleveland	.254	162	5470	576	1390	1915	236	26	79	546	62	46	449	24	43	888	84	58	146	1106	18	.350	.313
Baltimore	.254	162	5604	686	1421	2245	256	29	170	660	47	45	528	33	50	974	84	33	147	1162	6	.401	.319
Oakland	.248	162	5410	760	1342	2103	246	19	159	655	49	49	642	56	30	981	151	64	131	1105	14	.389	.331
Detroit	.247	162	5547	817	1372	2310	259	26	209	778	38	44	699	40	31	1185	109	47	90	1194	7	.416	.333
Totals	.260	1134	77603	10172	20195	30640	3680	453	1953	9610	733	687	7730	603	538	12944	1469	758	1823	15987	150	.395	.329

INDIVIDUAL

TOP 15 QUALIFIERS FOR BATTING CHAMPIONSHIP

Player, Team	Avg.	G	AB	R	H	TB	2B	3B	HR	RBI	SH	SF	BB	Int. BB	HP	SO	SB	CS	GI DP	Slg.	OBP
Franco, Julio, Texas	.341	146	589	108	201	279	27	3	15	78	0	2	65	8	3	78	36	9	13	.474	.408
Boggs, Wade, Boston*	.332	144	546	93	181	251	42	2	8	51	0	6	89	25	0	32	1	2	16	.460	.421
Randolph, Willie, Milwaukee	.327	124	431	60	141	161	14	2	0	54	3	6	75	3	1	38	4	2	10	.374	.424
Griffey, Ken Jr., Seattle*	.327	154	548	76	179	289	42	1	22	100	0	9	71	21	0	82	18	6	14	.527	.399
Molitor, Paul, Milwaukee	.325	158	665	133	216	325	32	13	17	75	1	1	77	16	6	62	19	8	11	.489	.399
Ripken, Cal Jr., Baltimore	.323	162	650	99	210	368	46	5	34	114	0	9	53	15	5	46	6	1	19	.566	.374
Palmeiro, Rafael, Texas*	.322	159	631	115	203	336	49	3	26	88	0	7	68	10	4	72	4	3	17	.532	.389
Puckett, Kirby, Minnesota	.319	152	611	92	195	281	29	6	15	89	2	8	31	4	6	72	11	5	27	.460	.352
Thomas, Frank, Chicago	.318	158	559	104	178	309	31	2	32	109	0	8	138	13	1	112	1	2	20	.553	.453
Tartabull, Danny, Kansas City	.316	132	484	78	153	287	35	3	31	100	0	5	65	13	3	121	6	3	17	.593	.397
Sierra, Ruben, Texas†	.307	161	661	110	203	332	44	5	25	116	0	9	56	6	7	91	16	4	17	.502	.357
Martinez, Edgar, Seattle	.307	150	544	98	167	246	35	1	14	52	2	4	84	9	8	72	0	3	19	.452	.405
Sax, Steve, New York	.304	158	652	85	198	270	38	2	10	56	6	3	41	2	1	38	31	11	15	.414	.345
Joyner, Wally, California*	.301	143	551	79	166	269	34	3	21	96	5	5	52	4	0	66	2	0	11	.488	.360
Greenwell, Mike, Boston*	.300	147	544	76	163	246	26	6	9	83	1	7	43	6	3	35	15	5	11	.419	.350

Minimum 502 plate appearances.   *Lefthanded batter.   †Switch-hitter.

DEPARTMENTAL LEADERS: G—Carter, Tor.; Fielder, Det.; C. Ripken, Bal., 162; AB—Molitor, Mil., 665; R—Molitor, Mil., 133; H—Molitor, Mil., 216; TB—C. Ripken, Bal., 368; 2B—Palmeiro, Tex., 49; 3B—Johnson, Chi.; Molitor, Mil., 13; HR—Canseco, Oak.; Fielder, Det., 44; RBI—Fielder, Det., 133; SH—Sojo, Cal., 19; SF—Davis, Sea.; Olerud, Tor., 10; HP—Carter, Tor., 10; BB—Thomas, Chi., 138; IBB—Boggs, Bos., 25; SO—Deer, Mil., 175; SB—R. Henderson, Oak., 58; CS—Polonia, Cal., 23; GIDP—Puckett, Min., 27; Slg. Pct.—Tartabull, K.C., .593; OB. Pct.—Thomas, Chi., .453.

ALL PLAYERS

*Lefthanded batter.   †Switch-hitter.

Player, Team	Avg.	G	AB	R	H	TB	2B	3B	HR	RBI	SH	SF	HP	BB	Int. BB	SO	SB	CS	GI DP	Slg.	OBP
Abner, Shawn, California	.228	41	101	12	23	37	6	1	2	9	0	0	0	4	0	18	1	2	3	.366	.257
Afenir, Troy, Oakland	.091	5	11	0	1	1	0	0	0	0	1	0	0	0	0	2	0	0	1	.091	.091
Aldrete, Mike, Cleveland*	.262	85	183	22	48	59	6	1	1	19	1	2	0	36	1	37	1	2	3	.322	.380
Allanson, Andy, Detroit	.232	60	151	10	35	48	10	0	1	16	2	2	0	7	0	31	0	1	3	.318	.266
Allred, Beau, Cleveland*	.232	48	125	17	29	41	3	0	3	12	0	2	0	25	2	35	2	1	5	.328	.359
Alomar, Roberto, Toronto†	.295	161	637	88	188	278	41	11	9	69	16	5	4	57	3	86	53	11	4	.436	.354
Alomar, Sandy, Cleveland	.217	51	184	10	40	49	9	0	0	7	2	1	4	8	1	24	0	4	5	.266	.264
Amaral, Rich, Seattle	.063	14	16	2	1	1	0	0	0	0	0	0	1	1	0	5	0	0	1	.063	.167
Amaro, Ruben, California†	.217	10	23	0	5	6	1	0	0	2	0	0	0	3	0	3	1	0	1	.261	.308
Anderson, Brady, Baltimore*	.230	113	256	40	59	83	12	3	2	27	4	3	5	38	0	44	12	5	1	.324	.338
Baerga, Carlos, Cleveland†	.288	158	593	80	171	236	28	2	11	69	11	3	6	48	5	74	3	2	12	.398	.346
Baines, Harold, Oakland*	.295	141	488	76	144	231	25	1	20	90	0	5	1	72	22	67	0	1	12	.473	.383
Barfield, Jesse, New York	.225	84	284	37	64	127	12	0	17	48	4	1	0	36	6	80	1	0	11	.447	.312
Barnes, Skeeter, Detroit	.289	75	159	28	46	78	13	2	5	17	2	0	0	9	0	24	10	7	1	.491	.325
Bell, Derek, Toronto	.143	18	28	5	4	4	0	0	0	1	0	0	0	6	0	5	3	2	0	.143	.314
Bell, Juan, Baltimore†	.172	100	209	26	36	52	9	2	1	15	4	1	0	8	2	51	3	1	0	.249	.201
Belle, Albert, Cleveland	.282	123	461	60	130	249	31	2	28	95	0	5	5	25	2	99	3	1	24	.540	.323
Beltre, Esteban, Chicago	.167	8	6	0	1	1	0	0	0	0	0	0	0	0	0	1	0	0	0	.167	.286
Benzinger, Todd, Kansas City†	.294	78	293	29	86	113	15	3	2	40	4	2	1	17	2	46	2	1	5	.386	.338
Bergman, Dave, Detroit*	.237	86	194	23	46	79	10	0	7	29	0	0	3	35	2	40	1	0	2	.407	.351
Bernazard, Tony, Detroit†	.167	6	12	0	2	2	0	0	0	0	0	1	0	0	0	4	0	0	0	.167	.167
Berry, Sean, Kansas City	.133	31	60	5	8	11	3	0	0	1	2	0	0	5	0	23	0	1	0	.183	.212
Bichette, Dante, Milwaukee	.238	134	445	53	106	175	18	3	15	59	1	6	1	22	4	107	14	8	9	.393	.272
Blankenship, Lance, Oakland	.249	90	185	33	46	63	8	0	3	21	2	3	3	23	0	42	12	3	2	.341	.336
Blowers, Mike, New York	.200	15	35	3	7	10	0	0	1	1	0	0	0	4	0	3	0	0	1	.286	.282
Boggs, Wade, Boston*	.332	144	546	93	181	251	42	2	8	51	6	6	1	89	25	32	1	2	16	.460	.421
Borders, Pat, Toronto	.244	105	291	22	71	103	17	0	5	36	6	3	3	11	0	45	0	2	8	.354	.271
Bordick, Mike, Oakland	.238	90	235	21	56	63	5	1	0	21	12	1	1	14	1	37	3	4	3	.268	.289
Bradley, Scott, Seattle*	.203	83	172	10	35	42	7	0	0	11	5	2	0	19	2	19	0	0	3	.244	.280
Brett, George, Kansas City*	.255	131	505	77	129	203	40	2	10	61	1	8	0	58	10	75	2	2	20	.402	.327
Briley, Greg, Seattle*	.260	139	381	39	99	128	17	3	2	26	1	3	1	27	0	51	23	11	7	.336	.307
Brock, Greg, Milwaukee*	.283	31	60	9	17	24	4	0	1	6	1	0	0	14	1	9	1	1	2	.400	.419
Brosius, Scott, Oakland	.235	36	68	9	16	27	5	0	2	4	1	0	1	3	0	11	3	1	0	.397	.268
Brown, Jarvis, Minnesota	.216	38	37	10	8	8	0	0	0	0	1	0	0	2	0	8	7	1	0	.216	.256
Browne, Jerry, Cleveland†	.228	107	290	28	66	78	14	2	1	29	12	0	1	27	0	29	2	4	5	.269	.292
Brumley, Mike, Boston†	.212	63	118	16	25	30	5	0	0	5	4	0	0	10	0	22	2	0	0	.254	.273
Brunansky, Tom, Boston	.229	142	459	54	105	179	24	1	16	70	10	8	3	49	2	72	1	2	8	.390	.303
Buechele, Steve, Texas	.267	121	416	58	111	186	17	2	18	66	2	4	5	39	4	69	0	1	11	.447	.335
Buhner, Jay, Seattle	.244	137	406	64	99	202	14	4	27	77	2	6	6	53	5	117	0	4	10	.498	.337
Burks, Ellis, Boston	.251	130	474	56	119	200	33	3	14	56	2	3	9	39	2	81	6	11	7	.422	.314
Bush, Randy, Minnesota*	.303	21	165	21	50	80	10	1	6	23	0	2	0	24	3	25	0	0	5	.485	.401
Canale, George, Milwaukee*	.176	21	34	6	6	17	2	0	1	10	0	0	0	8	0	6	0	0	5	.500	.318
Canseco, Jose, Oakland	.266	154	572	115	152	318	32	1	44	122	0	6	9	78	8	152	26	6	16	.556	.359

Player, Team	Avg.	G	AB	R	H	TB	2B	3B	HR	RBI	SH	SF	HP	BB	Int. BB	SO	SB	CS	GI DP	Slg.	OBP
Capra, Nick, Texas	.000	2	0	1	0	0	0	0	0	0	0	0	0	1	0	0	0	0	0	.000	1.000
Carter, Joe, Toronto	.273	162	638	89	174	321	42	3	33	108	0	9	0	49	12	112	20	9	6	.503	.330
Castillo, Carmen, Minnesota	.167	9	12	0	2	4	0	1	0	1	0	0	0	0	0	2	0	0	0	.333	.231
Clark, David, Kansas City*	.200	11	10	1	2	2	0	0	0	1	0	0	0	1	0	2	0	0	0	.200	.273
Clark, Jack, Boston	.249	140	481	75	120	224	18	0	28	87	0	5	3	96	3	133	0	2	17	.466	.374
Cochrane, Dave, Seattle†	.247	65	178	16	44	63	13	1	2	22	4	1	1	9	0	38	0	1	3	.354	.286
Cole, Alex, Cleveland*	.295	122	387	58	114	137	17	3	0	21	4	2	2	58	2	47	27	17	8	.354	.386
Cole, Stu, Kansas City	.143	9	7	1	1	1	0	0	0	0	0	0	0	0	0	2	0	0	0	.143	.333
Cooper, Scott, Boston*	.457	14	35	6	16	24	4	2	0	7	0	0	0	2	0	2	0	0	0	.686	.486
Cora, Joey, Chicago†	.241	100	228	37	55	63	6	1	0	18	8	3	5	20	0	21	11	6	1	.276	.313
Cotto, Henry, Seattle	.305	66	177	35	54	82	6	2	6	23	2	1	2	10	0	27	16	3	7	.463	.347
Cromartie, Warren, Kansas City*	.313	69	131	13	41	55	7	1	2	20	1	0	0	15	0	18	1	3	3	.420	.381
Cron, Chris, California	.133	6	15	0	2	2	0	0	0	0	0	0	0	2	0	5	0	0	0	.133	.235
Cuyler, Milt, Detroit†	.257	154	475	77	122	160	15	7	3	33	12	3	5	52	0	92	41	10	4	.337	.335
Daugherty, Jack, Texas†	.194	58	144	8	28	38	3	2	1	11	4	1	0	16	1	23	1	0	8	.264	.270
Davis, Alvin, Seattle*	.221	145	462	39	102	155	15	1	12	69	0	3	0	56	9	78	0	3	8	.335	.299
Davis, Chili, Minnesota†	.277	153	534	84	148	271	34	1	29	93	0	10	4	95	13	117	5	6	9	.507	.385
Davis, Glenn, Baltimore	.227	49	176	29	40	81	9	1	10	28	0	4	1	16	0	29	0	0	5	.460	.307
Davis, Mark, California	.000	3	2	0	0	0	0	0	0	0	0	0	0	0	0	0	0	0	0	.000	.000
de los Santos, Luis, Detroit	.167	16	30	1	5	7	2	0	0	0	1	0	0	2	0	4	0	0	2	.233	.219
Deer, Rob, Detroit	.179	134	448	64	80	173	14	2	25	64	0	3	3	89	1	175	1	3	3	.386	.314
Dempsey, Rick, Milwaukee	.231	61	147	15	34	51	5	0	4	21	1	2	2	23	1	20	1	2	7	.347	.329
Devereaux, Mike, Baltimore	.260	149	608	82	158	262	27	10	19	59	7	4	2	47	2	115	16	9	13	.431	.313
Diaz, Mario, Texas	.264	96	182	24	48	58	7	0	1	22	4	0	2	15	0	18	0	1	5	.319	.318
Disarcina, Gary, California	.211	18	57	5	12	14	2	0	0	3	2	1	0	4	0	4	1	0	0	.246	.274
Downing, Brian, Texas	.278	123	407	76	113	185	17	2	17	49	1	2	8	58	7	70	1	1	7	.455	.377
Ducey, Rob, Toronto*	.235	39	68	8	16	25	2	2	1	4	3	0	0	6	0	26	2	1	1	.368	.297
Eisenreich, Jim, Kansas City*	.301	135	375	47	113	147	22	3	2	47	3	6	1	20	1	35	5	3	10	.392	.333
Escobar, Jose, Cleveland	.200	10	15	1	3	3	0	0	0	0	1	0	0	0	0	4	0	0	0	.200	.250
Espinoza, Alvaro, New York	.256	148	480	51	123	165	23	1	5	33	9	2	2	16	0	57	4	1	10	.344	.282
Evans, Dwight, Baltimore	.270	101	270	35	73	102	9	1	6	38	1	2	1	54	3	54	0	7	7	.378	.393
Fariss, Monty, Texas	.258	19	31	5	8	12	1	0	1	6	0	0	0	11	0	11	0	3	0	.387	.395
Felix, Junior, California†	.283	66	230	32	65	85	10	2	2	26	6	0	3	7	0	55	7	5	5	.370	.321
Fermin, Felix, Cleveland	.262	129	424	30	111	128	13	2	0	31	13	3	6	26	2	27	5	4	17	.302	.307
Fielder, Cecil, Detroit	.261	162	624	102	163	320	25	0	44	133	0	6	7	78	12	151	0	0	17	.513	.347
Fisk, Carlton, Chicago	.241	134	460	42	111	190	25	0	18	74	1	3	3	32	4	86	1	4	19	.413	.299
Fletcher, Scott, Chicago	.206	90	248	14	51	66	10	1	0	28	6	2	3	17	0	26	1	2	3	.266	.262
Flora, Kevin, California	.125	3	8	1	1	1	0	0	0	0	0	0	0	1	0	5	1	0	0	.125	.222
Franco, Julio, Texas	.341	146	589	108	201	279	27	3	15	78	0	2	3	65	8	78	36	9	13	.474	.408
Fryman, Travis, Detroit	.259	149	557	65	144	249	36	3	21	91	0	6	6	40	3	149	12	5	13	.447	.309
Gaetti, Gary, California	.246	152	586	58	144	222	22	1	18	66	2	5	8	33	3	104	5	5	13	.379	.293
Gagne, Greg, Minnesota	.265	139	408	52	108	161	23	3	8	42	5	5	1	26	0	72	11	9	15	.395	.310
Gallagher, Dave, California	.293	90	270	32	79	99	17	0	1	30	10	3	0	24	3	43	2	4	6	.367	.355
Gallego, Mike, Oakland	.247	159	482	67	119	178	15	4	12	49	7	3	5	67	3	84	6	4	8	.369	.343
Gantner, Jim, Milwaukee*	.283	140	526	63	149	190	27	3	2	47	7	4	3	27	5	34	4	6	13	.361	.320
Geren, Bob, New York	.219	64	128	7	28	37	3	0	2	12	3	0	0	9	0	31	0	1	5	.289	.270

Player, Team	Avg.	G	AB	R	H	TB	2B	3B	HR	RBI	SH	SF	HP	BB	Int. BB	SO	SB	CS	GI DP	Slg.	OBP
Giannelli, Ray, Toronto*	.167	9	24	4	4	5	1	0	0	0	0	0	0	5	0	6	1	0	0	.208	.310
Gibson, Kirk, Kansas City*	.236	132	462	81	109	186	17	6	16	55	1	2	6	69	3	103	18	4	9	.403	.341
Gladden, Dan, Minnesota	.247	126	461	65	114	164	14	9	6	52	5	4	5	36	1	60	15	9	13	.356	.306
Gomez, Leo, Baltimore	.233	118	391	40	91	160	17	2	16	45	5	7	2	40	0	82	1	1	11	.409	.302
Gonzales, Rene, Toronto	.195	71	118	16	23	29	3	0	1	6	6	1	4	12	0	22	1	0	5	.246	.289
Gonzalez, Jesus, Cleveland	.159	33	69	10	11	18	2	1	1	4	0	0	1	11	0	27	8	4	2	.261	.284
Gonzalez, Juan, Texas	.264	142	545	78	144	261	34	1	27	102	0	3	5	42	7	118	4	3	10	.479	.321
Grebeck, Craig, Chicago	.281	107	224	37	63	103	16	3	0	31	4	1	1	38	0	40	1	0	0	.460	.386
Green, Gary, Texas	.150	8	20	0	3	4	1	0	0	1	2	0	0	1	0	6	0	0	0	.200	.190
Greenwell, Mike, Boston*	.300	147	544	76	163	228	26	6	9	83	1	7	3	43	6	35	15	5	11	.419	.350
Griffey Jr, Ken, Seattle*	.327	154	548	76	179	289	42	1	22	100	0	9	3	71	21	82	18	6	5	.527	.399
Griffey Sr, Ken, Seattle*	.282	30	85	10	24	34	7	0	1	9	4	1	1	13	0	13	0	6	2	.400	.380
Gruber, Kelly, Toronto	.252	113	429	58	108	190	18	2	20	65	0	5	6	31	5	70	12	7	7	.443	.308
Guillen, Ozzie, Chicago*	.273	154	524	52	143	178	20	3	3	49	13	7	0	11	0	38	21	15	7	.340	.284
Gullickson, Bill, Detroit	.000	35	0	0	0	0	0	0	0	0	0	0	0	0	0	0	0	0	0	.000	.000
Hall, Mel, New York*	.285	141	492	67	140	224	23	2	19	80	1	6	3	26	6	40	0	1	6	.455	.321
Hamilton, Darryl, Milwaukee*	.311	122	405	64	126	156	15	6	1	57	0	3	0	33	2	38	16	6	10	.385	.361
Hare, Shawn, Detroit*	.053	18	19	0	1	2	1	0	0	0	0	0	0	2	0	3	0	0	0	.105	.143
Harper, Brian, Minnesota	.311	123	441	54	137	197	28	1	10	69	2	6	6	14	3	22	1	2	14	.447	.336
Harris, Don, Texas	.375	18	8	4	3	6	0	0	1	2	0	0	0	1	0	3	1	0	0	.750	.444
Hemond, Scott, Oakland	.217	23	23	4	5	6	0	0	0	0	0	0	0	1	0	7	1	2	0	.217	.250
Henderson, Dave, Oakland	.276	150	572	86	158	266	33	0	25	85	0	2	4	58	3	113	6	6	9	.465	.346
Henderson, Rickey, Oakland	.268	134	470	105	126	199	17	1	18	57	1	3	7	98	0	73	58	18	7	.423	.400
Hernandez, Jose, Texas	.184	45	98	8	18	22	2	1	1	4	6	0	0	3	0	31	0	1	2	.224	.208
Hill, Donnie, California†	.239	77	209	36	50	63	8	2	1	20	3	3	0	30	1	21	1	0	7	.301	.335
Hill, Glenallen, Tor.-Cle.	.258	72	221	29	57	93	8	0	11	25	1	1	0	23	0	54	6	6	1	.421	.324
Hoiles, Chris, Baltimore	.243	107	341	36	83	131	15	0	11	31	0	3	1	29	1	61	0	2	11	.384	.304
Horn, Sam, Baltimore*	.233	121	317	45	74	159	16	0	23	61	0	1	3	41	4	99	0	0	10	.502	.326
Housie, Wayne, Boston†	.250	11	8	2	2	3	1	0	0	0	1	0	0	1	0	3	1	2	0	.375	.333
Howard, Chris, Seattle	.167	9	6	1	1	1	0	0	0	0	0	0	0	1	0	2	0	0	1	.333	.286
Howard, David, Kansas City†	.216	94	236	20	51	61	7	0	1	17	9	2	1	16	0	45	3	1	7	.258	.267
Howell, Jack, California*	.210	32	81	11	17	25	2	1	2	7	0	1	0	11	0	11	3	3	1	.309	.304
Howitt, Dann, Oakland*	.167	21	42	5	7	11	1	0	1	3	3	0	0	1	0	12	1	1	1	.262	.182
Hrbek, Kent, Minnesota*	.284	132	462	72	131	213	20	1	20	89	0	2	6	67	4	48	4	4	15	.461	.373
Huff, Mike, Cle.-Chi.	.251	102	243	42	61	84	10	1	3	25	3	2	1	37	2	48	14	4	7	.346	.361
Hulett, Tim, Baltimore	.204	79	206	29	42	72	9	0	7	18	6	0	0	13	0	49	0	0	3	.350	.255
Humphreys, Mike, New York	.200	25	40	9	8	8	0	0	0	3	1	1	0	9	0	7	1	0	6	.200	.347
Huson, Jeff, Texas*	.213	119	268	36	57	77	8	1	2	26	2	2	1	39	1	32	8	3	3	.287	.290
Incaviglia, Pete, Detroit	.214	97	337	38	72	119	12	1	11	38	0	1	0	36	3	92	1	2	13	.353	.274
Jackson, Bo, Chicago	.225	23	71	9	16	29	4	0	3	14	2	4	3	12	0	25	0	1	9	.408	.312
Jacoby, Brook, Cle.-Oak.	.224	122	419	28	94	139	21	0	4	44	0	2	4	27	2	54	2	3	6	.318	.273
James, Chris, Cleveland	.238	115	437	31	104	139	16	2	5	41	2	1	3	18	0	61	3	4	3	.318	.273
Jeffcoat, Mike, Texas*	1.000	70	1	0	1	2	1	0	0	0	0	0	0	0	0	0	0	0	0	2.000	1.000
Jennings, Doug, Oakland*	.198	26	101	10	20	29	3	0	2	12	0	1	0	3	0	22	0	0	1	.287	.219
Johnson, Lance, Chicago*	.274	159	588	72	161	201	14	13	0	49	6	3	1	26	2	58	26	11	14	.342	.304

Player, Team	Avg.	G	AB	R	H	TB	2B	3B	HR	RBI	SH	SF	HP	BB	Int. BB	SO	SB	CS	GI DP	Slg.	OBP
Jones, Tracy, Seattle	.251	79	175	30	44	63	8	3	3	24	1	2	1	18	2	22	2	0	8	.360	.321
Joyner, Wally, California*	.301	143	551	79	166	269	34	3	21	96	2	5	1	52	4	66	2	0	11	.488	.360
Karkovice, Ron, Chicago	.246	75	167	25	41	69	13	0	5	22	9	1	1	15	1	42	0	0	2	.413	.310
Kelly, Pat, New York	.242	96	298	35	72	101	12	4	3	23	2	1	5	15	0	52	12	5	5	.339	.288
Kelly, Roberto, New York	.267	126	486	68	130	216	22	2	20	69	2	5	5	45	2	77	32	9	14	.444	.333
Kirby, Wayne, Cleveland*	.209	21	43	4	9	11	2	0	0	5	1	1	0	2	0	6	1	2	2	.256	.239
Kittle, Ron, Chicago	.191	17	47	7	9	15	0	0	2	7	0	1	2	5	0	9	0	0	2	.319	.291
Knoblauch, Chuck, Minnesota	.281	151	565	78	159	198	24	6	1	50	6	5	4	59	0	40	25	5	8	.350	.351
Knorr, Randy, Toronto	.000	3	1	0	0	0	0	0	0	0	0	0	0	0	0	1	0	0	0	.000	.500
Komminsk, Brad, Oakland	.120	24	25	1	3	4	1	0	0	2	1	0	0	2	0	9	1	1	0	.160	.185
Kreuter, Chad, Texas†	.000	3	4	0	0	0	0	0	0	0	0	0	0	0	0	1	0	0	0	.000	.000
Lansford, Carney, Oakland	.063	5	16	0	1	1	0	0	0	1	0	0	0	2	0	2	0	0	0	.063	.063
Larkin, Gene, Minnesota*	.286	98	255	34	73	95	14	1	2	19	2	3	1	30	3	21	2	3	9	.373	.361
Law, Vance, Oakland	.209	74	134	11	28	37	7	1	0	9	5	2	1	18	0	27	2	0	4	.276	.303
Lee, Manuel, Toronto†	.234	138	445	41	104	128	18	3	0	29	10	4	2	24	1	107	7	2	11	.288	.274
Leius, Scott, Minnesota	.286	109	199	35	57	83	7	2	5	20	5	0	0	30	0	35	5	5	4	.417	.378
Lennon, Pat, Seattle	.125	9	8	1	1	2	1	0	0	0	0	0	0	3	0	1	0	0	0	.250	.364
Lewis, Mark, Cleveland	.264	84	314	29	83	100	15	1	0	30	2	5	1	15	0	45	2	2	12	.318	.293
Leyritz, Jim, New York	.182	32	77	8	14	17	3	0	0	4	1	0	0	13	0	15	0	1	0	.221	.300
Liriano, Nelson, Kansas City†	.409	10	22	5	9	9	0	0	0	1	1	0	0	0	0	2	0	1	0	.409	.409
Livingstone, Scott, Detroit*	.291	44	127	19	37	48	5	0	2	11	1	4	1	10	1	25	2	0	1	.378	.341
Lopez, Luis, Cleveland	.220	35	82	7	18	24	4	1	0	7	0	1	0	4	0	7	0	0	0	.293	.261
Lovullo, Torey, New York†	.176	22	51	2	9	11	2	0	0	2	3	0	1	5	1	7	0	0	0	.216	.250
Lusader, Scott, New York*	.143	11	7	1	1	1	0	0	0	0	0	0	0	0	0	3	0	0	0	.143	.250
Lyons, Barry, California	.200	2	5	0	1	1	0	0	0	0	1	0	0	1	0	0	0	0	0	.200	.200
Lyons, Steve, Boston*	.241	87	212	15	51	75	10	1	4	17	3	1	0	11	2	35	10	3	0	.354	.277
Maas, Kevin, New York*	.220	148	500	69	110	195	14	1	23	63	1	5	4	83	3	128	5	1	4	.390	.333
Macfarlane, Mike, Kansas City	.277	84	267	34	74	135	18	2	13	41	1	4	6	17	0	52	1	0	4	.506	.330
Mack, Shane, Minnesota	.310	143	442	79	137	234	27	8	18	74	2	5	6	34	1	79	13	9	11	.529	.363
Magallanes, Everardo, Cleveland*	.000	3	2	0	0	0	0	0	0	0	0	0	0	0	0	1	0	0	0	.000	.000
Maldonado, Candy, Mil.-Tor.	.250	86	288	37	72	123	15	0	12	48	0	3	6	36	4	76	4	0	8	.427	.342
Manrique, Fred, Oakland	.143	9	21	2	3	3	0	0	0	0	0	0	0	2	0	1	0	0	1	.143	.217
Manto, Jeff, Cleveland	.211	47	128	15	27	40	7	0	2	13	1	0	0	14	0	22	0	2	3	.313	.306
Marshall, Mike, Bos.-Cal.	.261	24	69	4	18	25	4	0	1	7	0	1	0	4	0	20	0	0	1	.362	.261
Martinez, Carmelo, Kansas City	.207	44	121	17	25	43	6	0	4	17	0	0	3	27	3	25	0	1	4	.355	.351
Martinez, Chito, Baltimore*	.269	67	216	32	58	111	12	0	13	33	0	1	2	11	0	51	1	1	2	.514	.303
Martinez, Carlos, Cleveland	.284	72	257	22	73	102	14	1	5	30	5	2	0	10	0	43	3	3	10	.397	.310
Martinez, Edgar, Seattle	.307	150	544	98	167	246	35	1	14	52	2	4	8	84	9	72	0	3	19	.452	.405
Martinez, Tino, Seattle*	.205	36	112	11	23	37	2	0	4	9	0	3	0	11	0	24	0	0	5	.330	.272
Marzano, John, Boston	.263	49	114	10	30	38	8	0	0	9	2	0	0	16	0	16	0	2	5	.333	.271
Mattingly, Don, New York*	.288	152	587	64	169	231	35	0	9	68	0	9	4	46	11	42	0	2	21	.394	.339
Maurer, Rob, Texas*	.063	13	16	0	1	2	1	0	0	2	0	0	0	2	0	6	0	0	0	.125	.211
Mayne, Brett, Kansas City*	.251	85	231	22	58	75	8	0	3	31	3	2	1	23	0	42	2	4	6	.325	.315
McCray, Rodney, Chicago	.286	17	7	2	2	2	0	0	0	0	0	0	0	0	0	2	2	1	0	.286	.286
McGwire, Mark, Oakland	.201	154	483	62	97	185	22	0	22	75	0	5	3	93	3	116	2	1	13	.383	.330
McIntosh, Tim, Milwaukee	.364	7	11	2	4	8	2	0	1	1	0	0	0	0	0	4	0	0	0	.727	.364

Player, Team	Avg.	G	AB	R	H	TB	2B	3B	HR	RBI	SH	SF	HP	BB	Int. BB	SO	SB	CS	GI DP	Slg.	OBP
McKnight, Jeff, Baltimore†	.171	16	41	2	7	8	1	0	0	2	0	0	0	2	0	7	1	0	0	.195	.209
McRae, Brian, Kansas City†	.261	152	629	86	164	234	28	9	8	64	3	5	2	24	1	99	20	11	12	.372	.288
Medina, Luis, Cleveland	.063	5	16	0	1	1	0	0	0	0	1	0	0	1	0	7	0	0	0	.063	.118
Melvin, Bob, Baltimore	.250	79	228	11	57	70	10	0	1	23	1	1	0	11	0	46	0	0	5	.307	.279
Mercedes, Luis, Baltimore	.204	19	54	10	11	13	2	0	0	3	1	0	0	4	0	9	0	0	1	.241	.259
Merullo, Matt, Chicago*	.229	80	140	8	32	48	1	0	5	21	1	2	4	9	0	18	0	0	7	.343	.268
Meulens, Hensley, New York	.222	96	288	37	64	92	8	1	6	29	0	2	2	18	1	97	3	5	3	.319	.276
Milligan, Randy, Baltimore	.263	141	483	57	127	196	17	2	16	70	0	2	6	84	4	108	0	5	23	.406	.373
Molitor, Paul, Milwaukee	.325	158	665	133	216	325	32	13	17	75	1	5	6	77	16	62	19	8	11	.489	.399
Moore, Bob, Kansas City	.357	18	14	3	5	6	1	0	0	0	1	0	0	1	0	2	3	0	0	.429	.400
Morman, Russ, Kansas City	.261	12	23	1	6	9	0	0	1	5	0	0	3	1	0	5	0	0	0	.396	.292
Moseby, Lloyd, Detroit*	.262	74	260	37	68	103	15	0	6	35	1	3	0	21	2	43	8	1	3	.396	.321
Moses, John, Detroit	.048	13	21	5	1	2	1	0	0	0	1	0	0	2	0	7	4	0	0	.095	.130
Mulliniks, Rance, Toronto*	.250	97	240	27	60	80	12	1	2	24	0	2	0	44	2	44	0	0	9	.333	.364
Munoz, Pedro, Minnesota	.283	51	138	15	39	69	7	1	7	26	1	2	1	9	0	31	3	1	2	.500	.327
Myers, Greg, Toronto*	.262	107	309	25	81	127	22	0	8	36	1	3	0	21	4	45	0	1	13	.411	.306
Naehring, Tim, Boston	.109	20	55	1	6	7	1	0	0	3	4	0	0	6	0	15	0	0	5	.127	.197
Newman, Al, Minnesota†	.191	118	246	25	47	52	5	0	0	19	5	3	1	23	0	21	4	2	5	.211	.260
Newson, Warren, Chicago*	.295	71	132	20	39	56	5	0	4	25	0	0	1	28	5	34	2	2	4	.424	.419
Nokes, Matt, New York*	.268	135	456	52	122	214	20	0	24	77	0	7	5	25	1	49	3	1	6	.469	.308
O'Brien, Pete, Seattle*	.248	152	560	58	139	225	29	3	17	88	0	9	1	44	7	61	0	1	14	.402	.300
Olander, Jim, Milwaukee	.000	12	9	0	0	0	0	0	0	0	0	0	0	2	0	5	0	0	0	.000	.182
Olerud, John, Toronto*	.256	139	454	64	116	199	30	1	17	68	3	3	6	68	9	84	0	2	12	.438	.353
Orsulak, Joe, Baltimore*	.278	143	486	57	135	174	22	1	5	43	2	2	4	28	1	45	6	3	9	.358	.321
Ortiz, Junior, Minnesota	.209	61	134	9	28	35	5	1	0	11	1	1	1	15	0	12	0	0	6	.261	.293
Orton, John, California	.203	29	69	7	14	18	4	0	0	3	4	0	3	10	0	17	0	1	2	.261	.313
Pagliarulo, Mike, Minnesota*	.279	121	365	38	102	140	20	0	6	36	2	3	3	21	3	55	1	2	9	.384	.322
Palmeiro, Rafael, Texas*	.322	159	631	115	203	336	49	3	26	88	0	7	6	68	10	72	4	3	17	.532	.389
Palmer, Dean, Texas	.187	81	268	38	50	108	9	2	15	37	1	1	3	32	0	98	0	2	4	.403	.281
Paredes, Johnny, Detroit	.333	16	18	4	6	6	0	0	0	0	4	0	0	3	0	1	1	1	0	.333	.333
Parent, Mark, Texas..	.000	3	1	0	0	0	0	0	0	0	0	0	0	0	0	1	0	0	0	.000	.000
Parker, Dave, Cal.-Tor.*	.239	132	502	47	120	183	26	2	11	59	0	3	3	33	3	98	3	3	9	.365	.288
Parrish, Lance, California	.216	119	402	38	87	156	12	0	19	51	0	5	5	35	1	117	0	1	7	.388	.285
Pasqua, Dan, Chicago*	.259	134	417	71	108	194	22	5	18	66	1	2	2	62	5	86	0	0	12	.465	.358
Pecota, Bill, Kansas City	.286	125	398	53	114	159	23	2	6	45	7	4	2	41	2	45	16	6	7	.399	.356
Pedre, Jorge, Kansas City	.263	10	19	2	5	8	1	0	0	3	1	0	0	3	0	5	0	0	0	.421	.364
Pena, Tony, Boston	.231	141	464	45	107	149	23	2	5	48	4	4	0	37	1	53	8	3	23	.321	.291
Perezchica, Tony, Cleveland	.364	17	22	4	8	10	2	0	0	2	0	0	0	3	0	5	0	0	0	.455	.440
Petralli, Geno, Texas*	.271	87	199	21	54	70	8	0	2	20	0	1	1	21	1	25	0	0	4	.352	.339
Pettis, Gary, Texas†	.216	137	282	37	61	78	7	5	0	19	6	1	3	54	0	91	29	13	4	.277	.341
Phillips, Tony, Detroit†	.284	146	564	87	160	247	28	4	17	72	3	6	3	79	5	95	10	5	8	.438	.371
Plantier, Phil, Boston*	.331	53	148	27	49	91	7	1	11	35	0	2	1	23	2	38	1	0	2	.615	.420
Polonia, Luis, California*	.296	150	604	92	179	229	28	8	2	50	2	2	1	52	4	74	48	23	11	.379	.352
Powell, Alonzo, Seattle	.216	57	111	16	24	41	6	1	3	12	3	0	1	11	0	24	2	2	3	.369	.288
Puckett, Kirby, Minnesota	.319	152	611	92	195	281	29	6	15	89	0	7	4	31	4	78	11	5	27	.460	.352
Puhl, Terry, Kansas City*	.222	15	18	0	4	4	0	0	0	3	0	0	0	3	1	2	0	0	1	.222	.333

Player, Team	Avg.	G	AB	R	H	TB	2B	3B	HR	RBI	SH	SF	HP	BB	Int. BB	SO	SB	CS	GI DP	Slg.	OBP
Pulliam, Harvey, Kansas City	.273	18	33	4	9	19	1	0	3	4	0	0	0	3	1	9	0	0	1	.576	.333
Quintana, Carlos, Boston	.295	149	478	69	141	197	21	4	11	71	6	3	2	61	1	66	1	3	17	.412	.375
Quirk, Jamie, Oakland*	.261	76	203	16	53	60	4	0	1	17	3	0	2	16	1	28	0	3	7	.296	.321
Raines, Tim, Chicago†	.268	155	609	102	163	210	20	6	5	50	9	3	5	83	9	68	51	15	7	.345	.359
Ramos, John, New York	.308	10	26	4	8	9	1	0	0	3	0	2	0	3	0	3	0	0	1	.346	.310
Randolph, Willie, Milwaukee	.327	124	431	60	141	161	14	3	0	54	3	3	0	75	3	38	4	2	14	.374	.424
Reed, Jody, Boston	.283	153	618	87	175	236	42	2	5	60	11	6	1	60	2	53	6	5	15	.382	.349
Reimer, Kevin, Texas*	.269	136	394	46	106	188	22	2	20	69	0	6	7	33	6	93	3	3	10	.477	.332
Reynolds, Harold, Seattle†	.254	161	631	95	160	215	34	6	3	57	14	6	5	72	2	63	28	8	11	.341	.332
Riles, Ernest, Oakland*	.214	108	281	30	60	91	8	4	0	32	4	4	1	31	3	42	3	2	11	.324	.290
Ripken, Bill, Baltimore	.216	104	287	24	62	75	11	1	0	14	11	2	0	15	0	31	4	1	14	.261	.253
Ripken, Cal, Baltimore	.323	162	650	99	210	368	46	5	34	114	0	9	5	53	15	46	6	1	19	.566	.374
Rivera, Luis, Boston	.258	129	414	64	107	159	22	3	8	40	12	4	3	35	0	86	4	4	10	.384	.318
Rodriguez, Carlos, New York†	.189	15	37	1	7	7	0	0	0	2	1	0	0	2	0	2	0	0	3	.189	.211
Rodriguez, Ivan, Texas	.264	88	280	24	74	99	16	0	3	27	7	0	1	5	0	42	0	1	10	.354	.276
Romine, Kevin, Boston	.164	44	55	7	9	14	2	0	1	7	2	0	0	3	0	10	1	0	1	.255	.207
Rowland, Rich, Detroit	.277	22	65	5	18	28	1	0	3	8	0	0	0	3	0	13	0	0	0	.431	.304
Russell, John, Texas	.250	4	4	0	1	1	0	0	0	1	0	0	0	1	0	2	0	0	0	.250	.333
Salas, Mark, Detroit*	.088	33	57	2	5	9	1	0	1	7	0	0	0	1	0	7	0	0	0	.158	.117
Sax, Steve, New York	.304	158	652	85	198	270	38	2	10	56	5	6	3	41	2	38	31	11	15	.414	.345
Schaefer, Jeff, Seattle	.250	84	164	19	41	53	7	0	1	11	6	0	1	5	0	25	3	1	7	.323	.272
Schofield, Dick, California	.225	134	427	44	96	111	9	3	0	31	7	0	3	50	2	69	8	4	3	.260	.310
Scruggs, Tony, Texas	.000	5	6	1	0	0	0	0	0	0	0	0	0	0	0	1	0	0	0	.000	.000
Segui, David, Baltimore†	.278	86	212	15	59	72	7	1	2	22	3	2	0	12	2	19	0	1	7	.340	.316
Seitzer, Kevin, Kansas City	.265	85	234	28	62	82	11	3	1	25	1	1	3	29	3	21	4	1	4	.350	.350
Sheffield, Gary, Milwaukee	.194	50	175	25	34	56	12	2	2	22	1	1	3	19	0	15	5	5	3	.320	.277
Shelby, John, Detroit†	.154	53	143	19	22	41	8	0	3	14	2	0	5	8	0	23	0	0	3	.287	.204
Sheridan, Pat, New York*	.204	62	113	13	23	38	3	0	4	7	5	1	0	13	0	30	1	6	6	.336	.286
Shumpert, Terry, Kansas City	.217	144	369	45	80	119	16	4	5	34	10	4	0	30	1	75	17	11	10	.322	.283
Sierra, Ruben, Texas†	.307	161	661	110	203	332	44	5	25	116	0	9	5	56	7	91	16	4	10	.502	.357
Sinatro, Matt, Seattle	.250	5	8	1	2	2	0	0	0	1	0	0	0	1	0	1	0	0	0	.250	.333
Skinner, Joel, Cleveland	.243	99	284	23	69	86	14	0	1	24	4	2	2	14	0	67	0	2	6	.303	.279
Snyder, Cory, Chi.-Tor.	.175	71	166	14	29	44	7	1	3	17	4	1	5	15	0	60	0	0	6	.265	.216
Sojo, Luis, California	.258	113	364	38	94	119	14	1	3	20	19	0	1	14	0	26	4	0	12	.327	.295
Sorrento, Paul, Minnesota*	.255	26	47	6	12	26	2	0	4	13	0	0	0	4	0	11	0	0	3	.553	.314
Sosa, Sammy, Chicago	.203	116	316	39	64	106	10	5	10	33	3	5	2	14	0	98	13	6	5	.335	.240
Spehr, Tim, Kansas City	.189	37	74	7	14	28	5	0	3	14	1	1	1	9	0	18	0	0	5	.378	.282
Spiers, Bill, Milwaukee*	.283	133	414	71	117	166	13	6	0	54	10	1	2	34	3	55	14	8	9	.401	.337
Sprague, Ed, Toronto	.275	61	160	17	44	63	7	1	4	20	1	1	3	19	0	43	0	3	2	.394	.361
Stanley, Mike, Texas	.249	95	181	25	45	69	13	1	3	25	5	5	2	34	0	44	0	2	15	.381	.372
Steinbach, Terry, Oakland	.274	129	456	50	125	176	31	1	6	67	6	9	7	22	4	70	2	1	15	.386	.312
Stevens, Lee, California*	.293	18	58	8	17	24	1	1	0	9	0	1	0	6	0	12	0	1	2	.414	.354
Stillwell, Kurt, Kansas City†	.265	122	385	44	102	139	17	7	6	51	5	4	2	33	5	56	3	4	8	.361	.322
Stubbs, Franklin, Milwaukee*	.213	103	362	48	77	130	16	2	11	38	0	9	0	35	3	71	13	4	4	.359	.282
Surhoff, B.J., Milwaukee*	.289	143	505	57	146	188	19	4	5	68	13	9	2	26	2	33	5	8	21	.372	.319

1991 A.L. STATISTICS

Player, Team	Avg.	G	AB	R	H	TB	2B	3B	HR	RBI	SH	SF	HP	BB	Int. BB	SO	SB	CS	GI DP	Slg.	OBP
Sveum, Dale, Milwaukee†	.241	90	266	33	64	97	19	1	4	43	5	4	1	32	0	78	2	4	8	.365	.320
Tabler, Pat, Toronto	.216	82	185	20	40	50	5	0	1	21	1	5	1	29	5	21	0	0	3	.270	.318
Tackett, Jeff, Baltimore	.125	6	8	1	1	1	0	0	0	0	2	0	0	2	0	2	0	0	0	.125	.300
Tanana, Frank, Detroit*	.000	33	1	0	0	0	0	0	0	0	0	0	0	0	0	1	0	0	0	.000	.000
Tartabull, Danny, Kansas City	.316	132	484	78	153	287	35	3	31	100	0	5	3	65	6	121	6	3	9	.593	.397
Taubensee, Ed, Cleveland*	.242	26	66	5	16	20	2	1	0	8	0	2	0	5	1	16	0	0	0	.303	.288
Tettleton, Mickey, Detroit†	.263	154	501	85	132	246	17	2	31	89	0	4	1	101	9	131	3	3	12	.491	.387
Thomas, Frank, Chicago	.318	158	559	104	178	309	31	2	32	109	0	2	1	138	13	112	1	2	20	.553	.453
Thome, Jim, Cleveland*	.255	27	98	7	25	36	4	2	1	9	3	0	1	5	0	16	1	1	4	.367	.298
Thurman, Gary, Kansas City	.277	80	184	24	51	66	9	0	2	13	4	2	1	11	0	42	15	5	1	.359	.320
Tingley, Ron, California	.200	45	115	11	23	33	7	0	1	13	5	1	1	8	0	34	1	1	4	.287	.258
Trammell, Alan, Detroit	.248	101	375	57	93	140	20	0	9	55	4	7	3	37	1	39	11	2	7	.373	.320
Turner, Shane, Baltimore*	.000	4	1	0	0	0	0	0	0	0	0	0	0	0	0	0	0	0	0	.000	.000
Valle, Dave, Seattle	.194	132	324	38	63	97	8	1	8	32	6	3	9	34	0	49	0	2	19	.299	.286
Vaughn, Greg, Milwaukee	.244	145	542	81	132	247	24	5	27	98	2	7	1	62	2	125	2	1	5	.456	.319
Vaughn, Mo, Boston*	.260	74	219	21	57	81	12	0	4	32	0	4	2	26	2	43	2	1	6	.370	.339
Velarde, Randy, New York	.245	80	184	19	45	61	11	1	1	15	5	0	3	18	0	43	3	1	6	.332	.322
Venable, Max, California*	.246	82	187	24	46	67	8	2	1	21	4	2	2	11	2	30	3	1	5	.358	.292
Ventura, Robin, Chicago*	.284	157	606	92	172	268	25	1	23	100	8	7	4	80	3	67	2	4	22	.442	.367
Vizquel, Omar, Seattle†	.230	142	426	42	98	125	16	4	1	41	8	3	0	45	0	37	7	2	8	.293	.302
Wakamatsu, Don, Chicago	.226	18	31	2	7	7	0	0	0	2	0	0	0	1	0	6	0	0	0	.226	.250
Walling, Denny, Texas*	.091	24	44	1	4	5	1	0	0	2	1	1	0	3	0	8	0	0	3	.114	.184
Ward, Turner, Cle.-Tor.†	.239	48	113	12	27	34	7	0	0	7	2	1	2	11	0	18	0	0	2	.301	.306
Webster, Lenny, Minnesota	.294	18	34	7	10	20	1	0	3	8	0	1	0	6	0	10	0	0	2	.588	.390
Webster, Mitch, Cleveland†	.125	13	32	2	4	4	0	0	0	0	1	0	0	3	0	9	2	0	0	.125	.200
Wedge, Eric, Boston	1.000	1	1	0	1	1	0	0	0	0	0	0	0	0	0	0	0	0	0	1.000	1.000
Weiss, Walt, Oakland†	.226	40	133	15	30	38	6	1	0	13	2	2	0	12	0	14	6	2	3	.286	.286
Whitaker, Lou, Detroit*	.279	138	470	94	131	230	26	2	23	78	2	8	2	90	6	45	4	3	3	.489	.391
White, Devon, Toronto†	.282	156	642	110	181	292	40	10	17	60	5	6	7	55	1	135	33	10	7	.455	.342
Whiten, Mark, Tor.-Cle.†	.243	116	407	46	99	158	18	7	9	45	5	5	3	30	2	85	4	3	13	.388	.297
Whitt, Ernie, Baltimore*	.242	35	62	5	15	17	2	0	0	3	0	0	0	8	0	12	0	0	3	.274	.329
Williams, Bernie, New York†	.238	85	320	43	76	112	19	4	3	34	2	3	1	48	0	57	10	5	4	.350	.336
Williams, Ken, Toronto	.207	13	29	5	6	11	2	0	1	3	0	0	0	5	0	5	1	0	1	.379	.314
Wilson, Mookie, Toronto†	.241	86	241	26	58	84	12	1	2	28	5	2	1	8	0	35	11	3	4	.349	.277
Wilson, Willie, Oakland†	.238	113	294	38	70	92	14	4	0	28	4	2	1	18	0	43	20	5	11	.313	.290
Winfield, Dave, California	.262	150	568	75	149	268	27	4	28	86	0	6	4	56	8	109	7	2	21	.472	.326
Witmeyer, Ron, Oakland*	.053	11	19	0	1	1	0	0	0	0	1	0	0	5	0	5	0	0	0	.053	.053
Worthington, Craig, Baltimore	.225	31	102	11	23	38	3	0	4	12	1	0	1	12	1	14	0	1	3	.373	.313
Yount, Robin, Milwaukee	.260	130	503	66	131	189	20	4	10	77	1	9	4	54	8	79	6	4	13	.376	.332
Zosky, Eddie, Toronto	.148	18	27	3	4	7	2	0	0	2	1	0	0	0	0	6	0	0	0	.259	.148
Zupcic, Bob, Boston	.160	18	25	3	4	7	0	0	0	3	0	0	0	1	0	6	0	0	0	.280	.192

AWARDED FIRST BASE ON CATCHER'S INTERFERENCE—Molitor, Milwaukee 3 (Mayne, Petralli, Steinbach); Clark, Boston 2 (Tettleton, Allanson); Knoblauch, Minnesota 2 (Petralli 2); Huff, Chicago (Parrish); Macfarlane, Kansas City (Myers); Plantier, Boston (Spehr); Shumpert, Kansas City (Steinbach); Thomas, Chicago (Sprague); Valle, Seattle (Steinbach).

PLAYERS WITH TWO OR MORE TEAMS

Player, Team	Avg.	G	AB	R	H	TB	2B	3B	HR	RBI	SH	SF	HP	BB	Int. BB	SO	SB	CS	GI DP	Slg.	OBP
Hill, Glenallen, Toronto	.253	35	99	14	25	43	5	2	3	11	0	2	0	7	0	24	2	2	2	.434	.296
Hill, Glenallen, Cleveland	.262	37	122	15	32	50	3	0	5	14	1	1	0	16	0	30	4	2	5	.410	.345
Huff, Mike, Cleveland	.240	51	146	28	35	49	6	1	2	10	3	1	4	25	0	30	11	2	2	.336	.364
Huff, Mike, Chicago	.268	51	97	14	26	35	4	1	1	15	3	1	2	12	2	18	3	1	2	.361	.357
Jacoby, Brook, Cleveland	.234	66	231	14	54	77	9	1	4	24	0	0	2	16	2	32	0	2	5	.333	.289
Jacoby, Brook, Oakland	.213	56	188	14	40	52	12	0	0	20	0	4	1	11	1	23	2	1	7	.277	.255
Maldonado, Candy, Milwaukee	.207	34	111	11	23	44	6	0	5	20	0	1	0	13	0	23	0	0	6	.396	.288
Maldonado, Candy, Toronto	.277	52	177	26	49	79	9	0	7	28	0	2	6	23	4	53	1	0	4	.446	.375
Marshall, Mike, Boston	.290	22	62	4	18	25	4	0	1	7	0	0	0	0	0	19	3	0	2	.403	.290
Marshall, Mike, California	.000	2	7	0	0	0	0	0	0	0	0	0	0	0	0	1	0	0	0	.000	.000
Parker, Dave, Toronto*	.232	119	466	45	108	167	22	2	11	56	0	3	0	29	3	91	3	2	9	.358	.279
Snyder, Cory, Chicago	.333	13	36	2	12	16	4	0	0	3	0	0	3	4	0	7	0	1	0	.444	.400
Snyder, Cory, Toronto	.188	50	117	10	22	35	4	0	3	11	3	1	0	6	1	41	0	0	5	.299	.228
Ward, Turner, Cleveland†	.143	21	49	4	7	9	0	1	0	6	1	0	0	3	0	19	0	0	1	.184	.189
Ward, Turner, Toronto†	.230	40	100	11	23	30	7	0	0	5	4	0	0	10	0	16	0	0	1	.300	.300
Ward, Turner, Toronto†	.308	8	13	1	4	4	0	0	0	2	0	0	1	1	0	2	0	0	1	.308	.357
Whiten, Mark, Toronto†	.221	46	149	12	33	49	4	3	2	19	0	3	1	11	1	35	4	1	5	.329	.274
Whiten, Mark, Cleveland†	.256	70	258	34	66	109	14	4	7	26	0	2	2	19	1	50	4	2	8	.422	.310

DESIGNATED HITTING

TEAM

Team	Avg.	AB	R	H	TB	3B	2B	HR	RBI	SH	SF	HP	BB	Int. BB	SO	SB	CS	GI DP	Slg.	OBP
Milwaukee	.300	664	113	199	312	13	30	19	86	2	4	4	76	11	84	13	3	11	.470	.373
Chicago	.296	601	102	178	301	3	33	28	103	1	6	1	129	11	130	11	6	22	.501	.418
Minnesota	.283	590	98	167	301	3	36	31	101	0	4	4	98	13	127	6	6	9	.512	.386
Oakland	.280	615	103	172	284	1	29	27	112	0	4	4	89	26	103	10	1	14	.462	.370
Texas	.263	649	106	171	291	3	30	28	83	3	7	3	80	10	136	4	3	8	.448	.351
Boston	.255	593	83	151	271	1	28	30	105	0	8	12	102	3	158	2	3	20	.457	.365
Toronto	.252	583	70	147	206	6	32	5	56	4	6	4	80	7	104	7	5	12	.353	.342
Cleveland	.252	647	57	163	231	2	31	11	63	4	5	2	29	3	106	12	5	25	.357	.286
Kansas City	.248	637	95	158	257	3	42	17	80	1	5	4	76	11	101	6	0	26	.403	.325
Detroit	.248	609	89	151	279	4	30	17	91	1	8	1	90	6	139	5	3	13	.458	.344
Baltimore	.240	601	84	144	272	0	26	34	105	1	5	2	85	5	160	3	3	18	.453	.338
California	.236	636	67	150	233	2	28	17	73	1	4	5	48	5	130	8	3	16	.366	.291
Seattle	.226	606	62	137	209	2	26	14	91	1	12	2	73	10	99	4	3	11	.345	.306
New York	.222	590	82	131	211	1	21	19	63	0	6	6	84	6	130	5	1	6	.358	.319

INDIVIDUAL

TOP 15 DESIGNATED HITTERS

Minimum 100 at-bats.

Player, Team	Avg.	G	AB	R	H	TB	2B	3B	HR	RBI	SH	SF	HP	BB	Int. BB	SO	SB	CS	GI DP	Slg.	OBP
Thomas, Frank, Chicago	.325	101	363	71	118	207	21	1	22	68	0	1	1	94	8	79	1	3	13	.570	.464
Molitor, Paul, Milwaukee	.321	112	476	88	153	226	23	10	10	45	0	0	4	50	11	50	11	1	6	.475	.391
Baines, Harold, Oakland*	.298	125	447	69	133	211	22	1	18	81	0	5	0	68	22	60	0	3	10	.472	.388
Belle, Albert, Cleveland	.287	32	129	18	37	66	12	1	5	24	0	2	1	4	0	19	0	1	12	.512	.304
Martinez, Carlos, Cleveland	.282	41	156	11	44	61	8	0	3	16	0	1	1	6	1	19	3	2	8	.391	.311
Davis, Chili, Minnesota†	.277	150	531	84	147	269	33	1	29	93	0	4	0	94	13	116	5	6	8	.507	.384
Downing, Brian, Texas	.272	109	393	75	107	178	16	2	17	45	1	2	8	58	7	69	1	0	4	.453	.375
Brett, George, Kansas City*	.261	118	463	73	121	195	40	2	10	60	0	8	0	56	10	66	2	0	20	.421	.336
Reimer, Kevin, Texas*	.258	56	178	23	46	83	10	1	9	27	1	1	3	13	2	45	0	0	4	.466	.312
Mulliniks, Rance, Toronto*	.258	81	217	25	56	76	12	0	2	20	0	1	0	43	0	40	0	0	8	.350	.379
Winfield, Dave, California	.256	34	125	14	32	52	5	0	5	16	0	1	1	16	1	31	3	3	6	.416	.338
Fielder, Cecil, Detroit	.254	42	169	21	43	88	9	0	12	33	0	2	0	19	1	40	0	0	6	.521	.326
Clark, Jack, Boston	.252	135	476	75	120	224	18	1	28	87	0	5	3	96	3	130	0	2	17	.471	.378
Tabler, Pat, Toronto	.250	57	116	13	29	34	5	0	1	12	2	4	1	18	5	14	0	0	13	.293	.345
Incaviglia, Pete, Detroit	.248	41	145	23	36	61	5	1	6	14	1	0	1	18	0	35	1	0	3	.421	.335

*Lefthanded batter. †Switch-hitter.

ALL DESIGNATED HITTERS

*Lefthanded batter. †Switch-hitter.

Player, Team	Avg.	G	AB	R	H	TB	2B	3B	HR	RBI	SH	SF	HP	BB	Int. BB	SO	SB	CS	GI DP	Slg.	OBP
Abner, Shawn, California	.000	3	0	1	0	0	0	0	0	0	0	0	0	0	0	0	0	0	0	.000	.000
Afenir, Troy, Oakland	.000	1	1	0	0	0	0	0	0	1	0	0	0	0	0	0	0	0	0	.000	.000
Aldrete, Mike, Cleveland*	.364	7	22	2	8	12	1	0	1	1	0	0	0	2	1	6	0	1	0	.545	.417
Allanson, Andy, Detroit	.000	1	1	0	0	0	0	0	0	0	0	0	0	0	0	0	0	0	0	.000	.000
Allred, Beau, Cleveland*	.000	1	0	0	0	0	0	0	0	0	0	0	0	1	0	0	0	0	0	.000	1.000
Alomar, Sandy, Cleveland	.167	4	18	1	3	3	0	0	0	0	0	0	0	0	0	4	0	0	0	.167	.167
Anderson, Brady, Baltimore*	.000	1	0	0	0	0	0	0	0	0	0	0	0	0	0	0	0	0	0	.000	.000
Baines, Harold, Oakland*	.298	125	447	69	133	211	22	1	18	81	0	5	1	68	22	60	0	1	10	.472	.388
Barnes, Skeeter, Detroit	.200	3	5	0	1	1	0	0	0	0	0	0	0	0	0	3	0	1	0	.200	.200
Bell, Jay, Baltimore†	.000	4	0	3	0	0	0	0	0	0	0	0	0	0	0	0	0	1	0	.200	.200
Belle, Albert, Cleveland	.287	32	129	18	37	66	12	1	5	24	0	2	0	4	0	22	2	1	12	.512	.304
Benzinger, Todd, Kansas City†	.400	1	5	0	2	2	0	0	0	1	0	0	0	0	0	4	0	0	0	.400	.400
Bergman, Dave, Detroit*	.226	13	31	4	7	12	2	0	1	5	0	0	0	7	2	2	0	0	0	.387	.368
Bernazard, Tony, Detroit†	.000	2	5	0	0	0	0	0	0	0	0	0	0	0	0	2	0	0	0	.000	.000
Blankenship, Lance, Oakland	.000	6	4	1	0	0	0	0	0	1	0	0	0	0	0	1	1	0	0	.000	.000
Bradley, Scott, Seattle*	.333	2	3	0	1	2	1	0	0	0	0	0	0	0	0	0	0	0	0	.667	.333
Brett, George, Kansas City*	.261	118	463	73	121	195	40	2	10	60	0	8	0	56	10	66	2	0	20	.421	.336
Briley, Greg, Seattle*	.000	1	2	0	0	0	0	0	0	0	0	0	0	0	0	0	0	0	0	.000	.000
Brosius, Scott, Oakland	.000	4	0	0	0	0	0	0	0	0	0	0	0	0	0	0	0	0	0	.000	.000
Brown, Jarvis, Minnesota	.000	7	2	3	0	0	0	0	0	0	0	0	0	0	0	2	1	0	0	.000	.000
Browne, Jerry, Cleveland†	.304	7	23	4	7	9	2	0	0	3	0	0	1	0	0	1	1	0	0	.391	.333
Brunansky, Tom, Boston	.000	1	1	0	0	0	0	0	0	0	0	0	0	1	0	0	0	0	0	.000	.500
Burks, Ellis, Boston	.500	2	4	0	2	3	1	0	0	4	0	0	0	1	0	1	0	0	0	.750	.600
Bush, Randy, Minnesota*	.346	10	26	5	9	15	1	1	1	4	0	0	0	2	0	6	1	0	0	.577	.375
Canseco, Jose, Oakland	.276	24	87	21	24	51	6	0	7	26	0	2	2	13	3	23	3	0	2	.586	.375
Carter, Joe, Toronto	.283	11	46	6	13	22	4	1	1	3	0	0	0	5	1	10	1	3	2	.478	.353
Castillo, Carmen, Minnesota	.500	2	4	0	2	4	2	0	0	0	0	0	0	0	0	0	0	0	0	1.000	.500
Clark, Dera, Kansas City*	.000	1	1	0	0	0	0	0	0	0	0	0	0	0	0	0	0	0	0	.000	.000
Clark, Jack, Boston	.252	135	476	75	120	224	18	1	28	87	0	5	3	96	3	130	0	2	17	.471	.378
Cochrane, Dave, Seattle†	.250	6	4	0	1	1	0	0	0	0	0	0	0	0	0	1	0	0	0	.250	.250
Cole, Alex, Cleveland*	.357	6	14	6	5	7	2	0	0	0	0	0	0	4	0	6	3	1	0	.500	.500
Cole, Stu, Kansas City	.000	2	0	0	0	0	0	0	0	0	0	0	0	0	0	0	0	0	0	.000	.000
Cora, Joey, Chicago†	.000	1	0	1	0	0	0	0	0	0	0	0	0	0	0	0	0	0	0	.000	.000
Cotto, Henry, Seattle	.143	6	7	2	1	1	0	0	0	0	1	0	0	1	0	0	3	1	0	.143	.250
Cromartie, Warren, Kansas City*	.000	1	1	0	0	0	0	0	0	0	0	0	0	0	0	0	0	0	0	.000	.000
Cron, Chris, California	.000	1	0	0	0	0	0	0	0	0	0	0	0	0	0	0	0	0	0	.000	.000
Daugherty, Jack, Texas†	.000	1	1	1	0	0	0	0	0	0	0	0	0	0	0	0	0	0	0	.000	.000
Davis, Alvin, Seattle*	.218	126	413	34	90	136	14	1	10	61	0	8	0	51	7	73	0	2	6	.329	.299
Davis, Chili, Minnesota†	.277	150	531	84	147	269	33	1	29	93	0	4	1	94	13	116	5	6	9	.507	.384
Davis, Glenn, Baltimore	.135	9	37	5	5	14	0	0	3	6	0	0	0	7	0	8	2	0	0	.378	.273
de los Santos, Luis, Detroit	.200	9	20	1	4	5	1	0	0	0	0	0	0	1	0	2	0	0	2	.250	.238

Player, Team	Avg.	G	AB	R	H	TB	2B	3B	HR	RBI	SH	SF	HP	BB	Int. BB	SO	SB	CS	GI DP	Slg.	OBP
Deer, Rob, Detroit	.000	2	3	0	0	0	0	0	0	0	0	0	0	1	0	0	0	0	0	.000	.250
Downing, Brian, Texas	.272	109	393	75	107	178	16	2	17	45	1	2	8	58	7	69	1	1	4	.453	.375
Ducey, Rob, Toronto*	.000	2	4	0	0	0	0	0	0	0	1	0	0	0	0	2	1	0	0	.000	.000
Eisenreich, Jim, Kansas City*	.250	2	4	0	1	1	0	0	0	0	0	0	0	0	0	0	0	0	0	.250	.250
Evans, Dwight, Baltimore	.282	21	39	5	11	16	2	0	1	6	0	2	0	12	0	8	0	0	3	.410	.451
Fariss, Monty, Texas	.250	4	4	0	1	2	1	0	0	0	0	0	0	0	0	3	0	0	0	.500	.250
Fielder, Cecil, Detroit	.254	42	169	21	43	88	9	0	12	33	0	2	0	19	1	40	0	0	6	.521	.326
Fisk, Carlton, Chicago	.182	13	44	2	8	13	2	0	1	7	0	0	0	4	0	7	0	0	5	.295	.240
Gallagher, Dave, California	1.000	2	2	0	2	3	1	0	0	0	0	0	0	0	0	0	0	0	0	1.500	1.000
Gibson, Kirk, Kansas City*	.196	30	107	16	21	44	1	1	7	14	1	0	0	15	1	24	3	1	3	.411	.295
Gomez, Leo, Baltimore	.208	10	24	1	5	6	1	0	0	0	0	0	1	3	0	6	0	0	2	.250	.296
Gonzalez, Juan, Texas	.263	4	19	1	5	8	0	0	1	3	0	0	0	1	0	6	0	0	1	.421	.333
Greenwell, Mike, Boston*	.000	1	4	0	0	0	0	0	0	0	0	0	0	0	0	1	0	0	0	.000	.000
Griffey Jr., Ken, Seattle	.000	1	4	0	0	0	0	0	0	0	0	0	0	0	0	0	0	0	0	.000	.000
Griffey Sr., Ken, Seattle*	1.000	1	1	1	1	1	0	0	0	0	0	0	0	0	0	0	0	0	0	1.000	1.000
Gruber, Kelly, Toronto	.286	2	7	1	2	3	1	0	0	0	0	0	0	2	0	1	1	0	0	.429	.444
Hall, Mel, New York*	.184	10	38	4	7	11	0	0	1	6	0	0	0	3	0	7	0	0	0	.289	.262
Hare, Shawn, Detroit*	.000	2	4	0	0	0	0	0	0	0	0	0	0	2	0	0	0	0	2	.000	.333
Harper, Brian, Minnesota	.600	2	5	2	3	4	1	0	0	1	0	1	0	0	0	0	0	0	0	.800	.667
Harris, Don, Texas	.000	3	0	0	0	0	0	0	0	0	0	0	0	0	0	0	0	0	0	.000	.000
Hemond, Scott, Oakland	.000	4	0	1	0	0	0	0	0	0	0	0	0	0	0	0	0	0	0	.000	.000
Henderson, Dave, Oakland	.211	7	19	4	4	4	0	0	0	0	0	0	0	1	0	5	0	0	0	.211	.250
Henderson, Rickey, Oakland	.143	10	35	5	5	11	0	0	2	3	0	0	1	7	3	7	2	1	1	.314	.286
Hill, Glenallen, Tor.-Cle.	.230	17	61	8	14	23	1	0	2	5	0	0	1	3	0	17	2	0	2	.377	.266
Hoiles, Chris, Baltimore	.250	13	36	9	9	16	1	0	2	6	0	1	0	6	0	5	0	0	1	.444	.357
Horn, Sam, Baltimore*	.232	102	302	42	70	148	15	0	21	58	0	1	3	40	4	93	0	0	8	.490	.327
Housie, Wayne, Boston†	.000	1	0	0	0	0	0	0	0	0	0	0	0	0	0	0	0	0	0	.000	.000
Howard, David, Kansas City†	.000	1	1	0	0	0	0	0	0	0	0	0	0	0	0	1	0	0	0	.000	.000
Howell, Jack, California*	.000	1	1	0	0	0	0	0	0	0	0	0	0	0	0	1	0	0	0	.000	.000
Huff, Mike, Chicago	.000	2	1	1	0	0	0	0	0	0	0	0	0	2	0	0	0	0	0	.000	.000
Hulett, Tim, Baltimore	.189	15	37	4	7	9	2	0	0	4	0	0	0	1	0	9	0	0	0	.243	.250
Humphreys, Mike, New York	.375	7	8	5	3	9	0	0	0	0	0	0	1	0	0	3	0	0	0	.375	.444
Incaviglia, Pete, Detroit	.248	41	145	23	36	61	5	1	6	14	0	0	3	18	0	35	0	3	3	.421	.335
Jackson, Bo, Chicago	.217	21	69	7	15	25	4	0	2	12	0	1	1	12	1	25	0	2	5	.362	.329
James, Craig, Cleveland	.227	60	233	13	53	66	5	0	2	16	1	0	3	10	1	35	3	2	3	.283	.267
Jones, Tracy, Seattle	.213	37	80	0	17	22	2	0	0	11	0	0	0	7	1	13	0	0	3	.275	.281
Lansford, Carney, Oakland	.000	1	2	0	0	0	0	0	0	0	0	0	0	0	0	2	0	0	0	.000	.000
Larkin, Gene, Minnesota†	.333	4	9	2	3	4	1	0	0	1	0	0	0	1	0	0	0	0	0	.444	.400
Lennon, Pat, Seattle	.167	5	6	0	1	2	1	0	0	1	0	0	0	2	0	1	0	0	0	.333	.375
Leyritz, Jim, New York	.333	1	3	1	1	2	1	0	0	0	0	0	0	0	0	1	0	0	0	.667	.333
Lopez, Luis, Cleveland	.167	6	18	0	3	4	1	0	0	2	0	0	0	0	0	1	0	0	1	.222	.167
Lyons, Steve, Boston*	.000	2	1	0	0	0	0	0	0	0	1	0	0	0	0	0	0	0	0	.000	.000
Maas, Kevin, New York*	.211	109	370	52	78	143	12	0	17	43	0	2	2	62	3	101	3	1	1	.386	.326
Macfarlane, Mike, Kansas City	.357	4	14	2	5	7	2	0	0	1	0	0	1	1	0	3	1	0	0	.500	.438
Mack, Shane, Minnesota	.000	1	2	0	0	0	0	0	0	0	0	0	0	0	0	1	0	0	0	.000	.000
Maldonado, Candy, Toronto	.192	9	26	3	5	12	1	0	2	6	0	0	0	5	0	5	0	0	2	.462	.323

Player, Team	Avg.	G	AB	R	H	TB	2B	3B	HR	RBI	SH	SF	HP	BB	Int. BB	SO	SB	CS	GI DP	Slg.	OBP
Marshall, Mike, Bos.-Cal.	.200	8	30	2	6	12	3	0	1	5	0	0	0	0	0	10	0	0	0	.400	.200
Martinez, Carmelo, Kansas City	.000	1	2	0	0	0	0	0	0	0	0	0	0	1	0	1	0	0	0	.000	.333
Martinez, Chito, Baltimore†	.467	4	15	7	7	20	1	0	4	9	0	0	1	0	0	2	0	0	0	1.333	.500
Martinez, Carlos, Cleveland	.282	41	156	11	44	61	8	0	3	16	0	1	0	6	1	19	3	1	8	.391	.311
Martinez, Edgar, Seattle	.375	2	8	0	3	5	2	0	0	1	0	0	0	1	0	1	0	0	1	.625	.444
Martinez, Tino, Seattle*	.417	5	12	1	5	6	1	0	0	1	0	0	0	0	0	2	0	0	0	.500	.444
Mattingly, Don, New York*	.244	22	86	9	21	27	3	0	1	7	0	2	0	11	2	7	0	0	3	.314	.323
Maurer, Rob, Texas*	.000	2	7	1	0	0	0	0	0	0	0	0	0	1	0	2	0	0	0	.000	.222
Mayne, Brett, Kansas City*	1.000	1	1	1	1	1	0	0	0	1	0	0	0	0	0	0	0	0	0	1.000	1.000
McCray, Rodney, Chicago	.000	6	0	1	0	0	0	0	0	0	0	0	0	0	0	0	1	0	0	.000	.000
McIntosh, Tim, Milwaukee	.444	2	9	1	4	8	1	0	1	7	0	0	0	0	0	3	0	0	1	.889	.444
McKnight, Jeff, Baltimore†	.222	4	9	2	2	3	1	0	0	2	1	0	0	0	0	1	1	0	1	.333	.222
Medina, Luis, Cleveland	.063	5	16	1	1	2	1	0	0	1	0	0	0	1	0	7	0	0	0	.063	.118
Melvin, Bob, Baltimore	.250	4	8	0	2	2	0	0	0	0	0	0	0	1	0	0	0	0	0	.250	.222
Mercedes, Luis, Baltimore	.000	1	1	0	0	0	0	0	0	0	0	0	0	0	0	0	0	0	0	.000	.000
Merullo, Matt, Chicago*	.143	6	14	2	2	5	0	0	1	3	0	1	0	2	0	0	0	0	0	.357	.222
Meulens, Hensley, New York	.214	13	42	7	9	11	2	0	0	4	0	0	0	2	0	14	2	0	1	.262	.244
Milligan, Randy, Baltimore	.289	25	83	12	24	36	3	0	3	11	0	2	1	13	1	28	2	2	4	.434	.392
Molitor, Paul, Milwaukee	.321	112	476	88	153	226	23	10	10	45	0	1	4	50	11	50	10	3	6	.475	.391
Morman, Russ, Kansas City	.000	7	0	0	0	0	0	0	0	0	0	0	0	0	0	0	0	0	0	.000	.000
Moseby, Lloyd, Detroit*	.368	7	19	5	7	10	3	0	0	1	0	0	0	1	0	1	1	0	0	.526	.400
Mulliniks, Rance, Toronto*	.258	81	217	25	56	76	12	1	2	20	0	1	0	43	2	40	0	0	8	.350	.379
Munoz, Pedro, Minnesota	.400	2	5	1	2	2	0	0	0	2	0	0	0	0	0	1	0	0	0	.400	.400
Newman, Al, Minnesota†	.000	3	1	1	0	0	0	0	0	0	1	0	0	1	0	0	0	0	0	.000	.000
Newson, Warren, Chicago*	1.000	3	3	2	3	4	1	0	0	3	0	0	0	1	0	0	0	0	0	1.333	1.000
Nokes, Matt, New York*	.182	3	11	0	2	2	0	0	0	0	0	0	0	0	0	2	0	0	1	.182	.250
O'Brien, Pete, Seattle*	.262	18	61	9	16	31	4	1	3	14	0	0	0	9	2	7	0	0	1	.508	.347
Olander, Jim, Milwaukee	.000	3	1	1	0	0	0	0	0	0	0	0	0	0	0	0	0	0	0	.000	.000
Olerud, John, Toronto*	.000	1	1	0	0	0	0	0	0	0	0	0	0	0	0	0	0	0	0	.000	.000
Orsulak, Joe, Baltimore*	.000	2	2	0	0	0	0	0	0	0	0	0	0	1	0	0	0	0	0	.000	.333
Palmeiro, Rafael, Texas*	.286	2	7	2	2	6	1	0	1	1	0	0	0	0	0	0	0	0	0	.857	.375
Palmer, Dean, Texas	.176	5	17	0	3	6	0	0	1	1	0	0	0	1	0	5	0	0	0	.353	.222
Paredes, Johnny, Detroit	.000	2	0	0	0	0	0	0	0	0	0	0	0	0	0	0	0	0	0	.000	.000
Parker, Dave, Cal.-Tor.*	.236	130	500	47	118	181	26	2	11	58	0	3	0	33	3	98	3	1	9	.362	.286
Parrish, Lance, California	.143	5	21	2	3	6	0	0	1	3	0	0	0	3	1	5	0	0	1	.286	.250
Pasqua, Dan, Chicago*	.200	8	20	2	4	5	1	0	0	3	0	0	0	3	1	5	0	0	0	.250	.304
Pecota, Bill, Kansas City	.000	2	11	0	0	0	0	0	0	0	0	0	0	1	0	2	1	0	0	.000	.000
Petralli, Geno, Texas*	.455	5	11	0	5	6	1	0	0	1	0	0	0	1	0	1	0	0	0	.545	.500
Pettis, Gary, Texas†	.000	3	2	0	0	0	0	0	0	0	0	0	0	2	0	1	1	0	0	.000	.500
Phillips, Tony, Detroit†	.274	18	62	13	17	32	3	0	3	15	0	0	0	16	1	14	1	0	1	.516	.413
Plantier, Phil, Boston*	.231	5	13	0	3	3	0	0	0	3	0	0	0	1	0	4	0	0	1	.231	.267
Polonia, Luis, California*	.313	4	16	3	5	5	0	0	0	0	0	0	0	0	0	0	2	1	0	.313	.313
Powell, Alonzo, Seattle	.333	7	3	1	1	2	1	0	0	1	0	0	0	0	0	3	0	1	0	.667	.500
Puhl, Terry, Kansas City*	.250	2	8	0	2	2	0	0	0	3	0	0	0	2	0	1	0	0	0	.250	.250
Quintana, Carlos, Boston	.000	1	2	0	0	0	0	0	0	0	0	0	0	0	0	0	0	0	0	.000	.000
Quirk, Jamie, Oakland*	.000	1	1	0	0	0	0	0	0	0	0	0	0	0	0	1	0	0	0	.000	.000

Player, Team	Avg.	G	AB	R	H	TB	2B	3B	HR	RBI	SH	SF	HP	BB	Int. BB	SO	SB	CS	GI DP	Slg.	OBP
Raines, Tim, Chicago†	.338	19	80	13	27	40	3	2	2	7	1	0	0	11	1	8	8	2	1	.500	.418
Ramos, John, New York	.222	4	9	2	2	2	0	0	0	1	0	1	0	0	0	1	0	0	0	.222	.273
Randolph, Willie, Milwaukee	.222	2	9	1	2	2	0	0	0	0	0	0	0	0	0	2	0	0	0	.222	.222
Reimer, Kevin, Texas*	.258	56	178	23	46	83	10	0	9	27	0	5	3	13	3	45	0	0	4	.466	.312
Reynolds, Harold, Seattle†	.000	1	4	0	0	0	0	0	0	0	0	0	0	0	0	0	0	0	0	.000	.000
Romine, Kevin, Boston	.000	14	1	1	0	0	0	0	0	0	0	0	0	0	0	0	0	0	0	.000	.000
Rowland, Rich, Detroit	.500	1	2	0	1	1	0	0	0	0	0	0	0	1	0	1	0	0	0	.500	.667
Russell, John, Texas	.000	5	3	1	0	0	0	0	0	0	0	0	0	0	0	5	0	0	1	.000	.250
Salas, Mark, Detroit*	.111	8	27	1	3	4	1	0	0	2	0	0	0	1	0	3	0	0	0	.148	.111
Sax, Steve, New York	.368	4	19	3	7	9	2	0	0	2	0	0	0	1	0	1	0	0	1	.474	.400
Segui, David, Baltimore†	.400	4	5	0	2	2	0	0	0	0	0	0	0	0	0	0	0	0	0	.400	.400
Seitzer, Kevin, Kansas City	.500	3	2	1	1	1	0	0	0	0	0	0	0	1	0	0	1	0	0	.500	.667
Sheffield, Gary, Milwaukee	.235	5	17	4	4	9	1	0	1	6	0	0	0	2	0	2	0	0	1	.529	.286
Shelby, John, Detroit†	.250	4	4	2	1	1	0	0	0	1	0	0	0	0	0	1	1	0	0	.250	.250
Sheridan, Pat, New York*	.250	2	4	1	1	4	0	0	1	0	0	0	0	1	0	2	0	0	0	1.000	.500
Snyder, Cory, Toronto	.250	3	4	1	1	1	0	0	0	0	0	0	0	1	0	0	0	0	0	.250	.400
Sojo, Luis, California	.000	1	0	1	0	0	0	0	0	0	0	0	0	0	0	0	0	0	0	.000	.000
Sorrento, Paul, Minnesota*	.125	2	8	1	1	4	1	0	1	1	0	0	0	0	0	2	0	0	0	.500	.125
Sosa, Sammy, Chicago	.000	2	3	0	0	0	0	0	0	0	0	0	0	1	0	2	1	0	0	.000	.250
Sprague, Ed, Toronto	.333	2	6	1	2	2	0	0	0	1	0	0	0	0	0	3	0	0	0	.333	.333
Stanley, Mike, Texas	.286	6	7	1	2	2	0	0	0	0	1	0	0	0	0	3	0	0	0	.286	.250
Steinbach, Terry, Oakland	.200	4	5	0	1	1	0	0	0	0	0	0	0	0	0	3	0	0	1	.200	.200
Stubbs, Franklin, Milwaukee*	.286	6	14	2	4	11	1	0	2	3	0	0	0	1	0	3	0	0	2	.786	.286
Surhoff, B.J., Milwaukee*	.333	4	21	1	7	12	2	0	1	2	2	0	0	1	0	1	0	0	0	.571	.364
Sveum, Dale, Milwaukee†	.300	3	10	0	3	3	0	0	0	1	0	0	0	0	0	1	0	0	0	.300	.345
Tabler, Pat, Toronto	.250	57	116	13	29	34	5	0	0	12	2	4	1	18	5	14	1	1	2	.293	.345
Tartabull, Danny, Kansas City	.160	6	25	1	4	4	0	0	0	0	0	0	1	2	2	7	0	0	2	.160	.222
Tettleton, Mickey, Detroit†	.277	24	83	11	23	48	4	0	7	17	0	0	1	17	2	28	1	1	13	.578	.402
Thomas, Frank, Chicago	.325	101	363	71	118	207	21	1	22	68	0	8	1	94	8	79	1	0	13	.570	.464
Trammell, Alan, Detroit	.250	6	20	3	5	6	1	0	0	1	0	0	0	3	0	3	2	0	0	.300	.348
Vaughn, Greg, Milwaukee	.200	10	30	7	6	14	2	0	2	8	0	0	1	11	0	7	1	0	2	.467	.405
Vaughn, Mo, Boston*	.302	16	63	4	19	28	6	0	1	9	0	1	0	4	0	12	0	1	2	.444	.353
Venable, Max, California*	.000	3	1	1	0	0	0	0	0	0	1	0	0	0	0	0	0	0	0	.000	.000
Wedge, Eric, Boston	1.000	3	1	1	1	1	0	0	0	1	0	0	0	0	0	1	0	0	1	1.000	1.000
Whitaker, Lou, Detroit*	.333	3	9	4	3	7	1	0	1	2	0	0	0	4	0	1	0	0	0	.778	.538
Whiten, Mark, Cleveland†	.077	3	13	1	1	1	0	0	0	0	2	0	0	0	0	4	1	0	0	.077	.071
Whitt, Ernie, Baltimore*	.000	2	2	0	0	0	0	0	0	0	0	0	0	0	0	0	0	0	0	.000	.000
Williams, Kenny, Toronto	.234	34	94	13	22	33	5	0	0	13	2	0	0	4	0	12	4	0	2	.351	.273
Wilson, Mookie, Toronto†	.500	9	10	5	5	6	1	0	0	2	0	0	0	0	0	2	4	1	0	.600	.500
Wilson, Willie, Oakland†	.256	34	125	14	32	52	5	2	5	16	1	1	0	16	1	31	3	1	6	.416	.338
Winfield, Dave, California	.256	34	125	14	32	52	5	2	5	16	1	1	0	16	1	31	3	1	6	.416	.338
Yount, Robin, Milwaukee	.212	13	52	4	11	15	2	2	0	10	1	1	0	6	0	8	2	0	0	.288	.288

DESIGNATED HITTERS WITH TWO OR MORE TEAMS

Player, Team	Avg.	G	AB	R	H	TB	2B	3B	HR	RBI	SH	SF	HP	BB	Int. BB	SO	SB	CS	GI DP	Slg.	OBP
Hill, Glenallen, Toronto	.232	16	56	8	13	22	1	1	2	5	0	0	0	3	0	16	2	0	2	.393	.271
Hill, Glenallen, Cleveland	.200	1	5	0	1	1	0	0	0	5	0	0	0	0	0	1	0	0	0	.200	.200
Marshall, Mike, Boston	.222	7	27	2	6	12	3	0	1	5	0	0	0	0	0	10	0	0	0	.444	.222
Marshall, Mike, California	.000	1	3	0	0	0	0	0	0	0	0	0	0	0	0	0	0	0	0	.000	.000
Parker, Dave, California*	.232	119	466	45	108	167	22	2	11	56	0	3	3	29	3	91	3	2	9	.358	.279
Parker, Dave, Toronto*	.294	11	34	2	10	14	4	0	0	2	0	0	0	4	0	7	0	1	0	.412	.368

The following designated hitters, each of whom appeared in at least one game, had no plate appearances: Amaral, Rich, Seattle (2); Brumley, Mike, Boston (2); Spiers, Bill, Milwaukee (2); Amaro, Ruben, California; Diaz, Mario, Texas; Gagne, Greg, Minnesota; Lusader, Scott, New York; Moore, Mike, Oakland; Orton, John, California; Perezchica, Tony, Cleveland; Schaefer, Jeff, Seattle; Turner, Shane, Baltimore.

PINCH-HITTING

TEAM

Team	Avg.	AB	R	H	TB	2B	3B	HR	RBI	SH	SF	HP	BB	Int. BB	SO	SB	CS	GI DP	Slg.	OBP
Minnesota	.304	158	18	48	72	4	1	6	30	2	1	1	22	4	30	1	1	4	.456	.390
New York	.265	113	16	30	47	5	0	4	18	0	2	2	22	5	31	2	1	1	.416	.384
Seattle	.260	181	18	47	58	9	1	0	23	1	0	1	17	4	37	1	2	6	.320	.333
Milwaukee	.258	62	10	16	19	3	0	0	6	0	0	3	14	2	12	1	0	1	.306	.403
Baltimore	.254	181	19	46	74	7	0	7	30	1	2	1	20	3	45	1	1	7	.409	.328
Kansas City	.254	193	16	49	73	5	2	5	23	1	0	1	19	2	43	0	0	5	.378	.321
Oakland	.250	148	13	37	54	6	1	3	19	1	1	0	12	1	29	4	0	1	.365	.309
Boston	.240	100	4	24	30	3	0	1	15	1	0	0	9	2	21	0	1	2	.300	.303
Toronto	.236	123	13	29	37	5	1	1	21	2	5	0	18	7	29	1	0	2	.301	.322
Cleveland	.233	120	10	28	33	2	0	1	9	1	1	3	15	1	29	0	0	1	.275	.329
California	.230	74	7	17	26	3	0	2	10	0	2	1	3	1	9	1	0	3	.351	.269
Chicago	.217	166	19	36	64	6	2	6	29	2	0	1	24	5	37	3	0	4	.386	.313
Texas	.214	206	13	44	65	12	0	3	33	0	4	1	19	3	59	1	0	6	.316	.281
Detroit	.178	129	16	23	41	3	0	5	27	0	3	2	14	4	35	3	0	3	.318	.264

INDIVIDUAL

TOP 15 PINCH-HITTERS

Minimum 20 at-bats. *Lefthanded batter. †Switch-hitter.

Player, Team	Avg.	G	AB	R	H	TB	2B	3B	HR	RBI	SH	SF	HP	BB	Int. BB	SO	SB	CS	GI DP	Slg.	OBP
Seitzer, Kevin, Kansas City	.550	23	20	1	11	15	2	1	0	3	0	0	0	2	0	0	0	0	0	.750	.591
Leius, Scott, Minnesota	.440	30	25	4	11	13	2	0	0	3	0	0	0	5	0	7	0	0	0	.520	.533
Tabler, Pat, Toronto	.429	33	21	6	9	11	2	0	0	6	1	2	0	8	4	1	0	1	0	.524	.548
Evans, Dwight, Baltimore	.400	32	25	3	10	15	2	0	1	6	0	0	0	7	0	5	0	0	2	.600	.531
Bush, Randy, Minnesota*	.382	47	34	4	13	21	1	2	1	8	0	2	0	8	2	4	0	1	2	.618	.500
Downing, Brian, Texas	.375	25	24	3	9	10	1	0	0	6	0	0	0	8	0	3	1	0	4	.417	.500
Newson, Warren, Chicago*	.364	28	22	3	8	10	2	0	0	5	0	0	1	6	1	6	0	0	1	.455	.481
Browne, Jerry, Cleveland†	.324	37	34	5	11	14	0	0	1	3	0	0	0	2	0	4	1	0	0	.412	.351
Jones, Tracy, Seattle	.300	30	20	4	6	8	1	0	0	1	0	1	0	1	0	4	0	0	1	.400	.320
Briley, Greg, Seattle*	.292	26	24	2	7	9	2	0	0	3	0	0	0	2	0	6	0	0	4	.375	.346
Horn, Sam, Baltimore*	.292	29	24	4	7	18	2	0	3	7	0	0	0	3	1	9	0	0	0	.750	.355
Reimer, Kevin, Texas*	.286	31	28	3	8	17	3	0	2	5	0	0	0	2	0	7	0	0	0	.607	.348
Wilson, Willie, Oakland†	.286	23	21	4	6	6	0	0	0	2	0	0	0	2	0	3	2	0	0	.333	.308
Segui, David, Baltimore†	.250	26	24	2	6	6	0	0	0	3	0	0	0	2	0	4	0	0	0	.250	.308
Newman, Al, Minnesota†	.238	24	21	1	5	5	0	0	0	1	1	0	0	1	0	5	0	1	0	.238	.261

ALL PINCH-HITTERS

*Lefthanded batter. †Switch-hitter.

Player, Team	Avg.	G	AB	R	H	TB	2B	3B	HR	RBI	SH	SF	HP	BB	Int. BB	SO	SB	CS	GI DP	Slg.	OBP
Abner, Shawn, California	.000	2	2	0	0	0	0	0	0	0	0	0	0	0	0	1	0	0	0	.000	.000
Afenir, Troy, Oakland	.000	1	1	1	0	0	0	0	0	0	0	0	0	0	0	1	0	0	0	.000	.000
Aldrete, Mike, Cleveland*	.143	19	14	1	2	3	1	0	0	3	0	0	0	4	0	1	0	0	0	.214	.333
Allanson, Andy, Detroit	.333	3	3	0	1	1	0	0	0	1	0	0	0	0	0	1	0	0	0	.333	.333
Allred, Beau, Cleveland*	.000	8	6	0	0	0	0	0	0	0	0	0	0	1	0	4	0	0	0	.000	.125
Alomar, Roberto, Toronto†	.000	1	1	0	0	0	0	0	0	0	0	0	0	0	0	0	0	0	0	.000	.000
Alomar, Sandy, Cleveland	.000	2	2	0	0	0	0	0	0	0	0	0	0	0	0	0	0	1	0	.000	.000
Amaral, Rich, Seattle	.000	2	2	0	0	0	0	0	0	0	0	0	0	0	0	1	0	0	0	.000	.000
Amaro, Ruben, California†	.000	2	2	0	0	0	0	0	0	0	0	0	0	0	0	0	1	0	1	.000	.000
Anderson, Brady, Baltimore*	.286	16	14	3	4	4	0	0	0	0	0	0	0	2	0	4	1	0	0	.286	.375
Baerga, Carlos, Cleveland†	.250	5	4	1	1	1	0	0	0	1	0	0	0	1	0	1	0	0	0	.250	.400
Baines, Harold, Oakland*	.455	11	11	1	5	8	0	0	1	3	0	0	0	0	0	1	0	0	0	.727	.455
Barfield, Jesse, New York	.500	8	4	2	2	6	1	0	1	2	0	0	0	4	2	2	0	0	0	1.500	.750
Barnes, Skeeter, Detroit	.000	15	11	3	0	0	0	0	0	0	0	0	0	2	0	1	3	0	1	.000	.154
Bell, Juan, Baltimore†	.000	5	5	0	0	0	0	0	0	0	0	0	0	1	0	1	0	0	0	.000	.167
Belle, Albert, Cleveland	.200	5	5	0	1	1	0	0	0	0	0	0	0	0	0	1	0	0	1	.200	.200
Benzinger, Todd, Kansas City†	.250	4	4	0	1	1	0	0	0	0	0	0	0	0	0	1	0	0	0	.250	.250
Bergman, Dave, Detroit*	.120	29	25	1	3	4	1	0	0	3	0	0	0	3	0	9	0	0	1	.160	.207
Bernazard, Tony, Detroit†	.000	3	3	0	0	0	0	0	0	0	0	0	0	0	0	2	0	0	0	.000	.000
Berry, Sean, Kansas City	.000	1	1	0	0	0	0	0	0	0	0	0	0	0	0	1	0	0	0	.000	.000
Bichette, Dante, Milwaukee	.400	14	10	3	4	5	1	0	0	1	0	0	0	3	0	1	1	0	0	.500	.538
Blankenship, Lance, Oakland	.000	11	8	0	0	0	0	0	0	0	0	0	0	3	0	1	1	0	0	.000	.273
Blowers, Mike, New York	.000	2	1	0	0	0	0	0	0	0	0	0	0	1	0	0	0	0	0	.000	.500
Boggs, Wade, Boston*	.667	4	3	0	2	2	0	0	0	2	0	0	0	1	0	0	0	0	0	.667	.750
Borders, Pat, Toronto	.278	21	18	2	5	10	2	0	1	6	0	0	0	2	0	3	0	0	0	.556	.300
Bordick, Mike, Oakland	.000	2	2	0	0	0	0	0	0	0	0	0	0	0	0	0	0	0	0	.000	.000
Bradley, Scott, Seattle*	.120	27	25	0	3	4	1	0	0	2	0	0	0	2	0	5	0	1	1	.160	.185
Brett, George, Kansas City*	.333	3	3	0	1	1	0	0	0	1	0	0	0	0	0	2	0	0	0	.333	.333
Briley, Greg, Seattle*	.292	26	24	2	7	9	2	0	0	1	0	0	0	1	0	6	0	1	0	.375	.320
Brock, Greg, Milwaukee*	.000	6	4	2	0	0	0	0	0	0	0	0	0	2	0	1	1	0	0	.000	.333
Brosius, Scott, Oakland	.500	4	4	0	2	2	0	0	0	0	0	0	0	0	0	0	0	0	0	.500	.500
Brown, Jarvis, Minnesota	.000	2	2	0	0	0	0	0	0	0	0	0	0	0	0	0	0	0	0	.000	.000
Browne, Jerry, Cleveland†	.324	37	34	5	11	14	0	0	1	3	0	1	0	2	0	4	0	0	0	.412	.351
Brumley, Mike, Boston†	.000	5	4	0	0	0	0	0	0	0	0	0	0	1	0	1	0	0	0	.000	.200
Brunansky, Tom, Boston	.400	7	5	0	2	3	1	0	0	3	0	0	0	2	0	0	0	0	1	.600	.571
Buechele, Steve, Texas	.400	5	5	1	2	2	0	0	0	2	0	0	0	0	0	2	0	0	0	.400	.400
Buhner, Jay, Seattle	.100	12	10	0	1	1	0	0	0	1	0	0	0	2	0	3	0	0	0	.100	.250
Burks, Ellis, Boston	.000	2	2	0	0	0	0	0	0	0	0	0	0	0	0	1	0	0	0	.000	.000
Bush, Randy, Minnesota*	.382	47	34	4	13	21	2	0	2	8	0	0	0	8	2	4	0	0	0	.618	.500
Canale, George, Milwaukee*	.000	1	1	0	0	0	0	0	0	0	0	0	0	0	0	1	0	0	0	.000	.000
Canseco, Jose, Oakland	.333	6	6	0	2	4	2	0	0	1	0	0	0	0	0	1	0	0	0	.667	.333

Player, Team	Avg.	G	AB	R	H	TB	2B	3B	HR	RBI	SH	SF	HP	BB	Int. BB	SO	SB	CS	GI DP	Slg.	OBP
Castillo, Carmen, Minnesota	.167	7	6	0	1	3	0	1	0	0	0	0	1	0	0	1	0	0	0	.500	.286
Clark, Dera, Kansas City*	.200	11	10	1	2	2	0	0	0	1	0	0	0	1	0	1	0	0	0	.200	.273
Clark, Jack, Boston	.000	6	6	0	0	0	0	0	0	0	0	0	0	0	0	3	0	0	0	.000	.000
Cochrane, Dave, Seattle†	.250	17	16	3	4	6	2	0	0	1	0	0	1	0	0	4	0	0	1	.375	.294
Cole, Alex, Cleveland*	.143	9	7	0	1	1	0	0	0	0	0	0	0	2	0	1	1	0	0	.143	.333
Cole, Stu, Kansas City	.000	2	2	0	0	0	0	0	0	0	0	0	0	0	0	1	0	0	0	.000	.000
Cooper, Scott, Boston*	.500	2	2	0	1	1	0	0	0	0	0	0	0	0	0	0	0	0	0	.500	.500
Cora, Joey, Chicago†	.143	9	7	1	1	1	0	0	0	0	0	0	0	2	0	1	0	0	0	.143	.333
Cotto, Henry, Seattle	.667	16	15	4	10	12	0	1	0	5	0	0	0	0	0	0	1	0	0	.800	.667
Cromartie, Warren, Kansas City*	.229	41	35	1	8	11	0	0	1	5	0	0	0	5	0	7	0	0	2	.314	.325
Cron, Chris, California	.000	1	1	0	0	0	0	0	0	0	0	0	0	0	0	0	0	0	0	.000	.000
Cuyler, Milt, Detroit†	.000	1	1	0	0	0	0	0	0	0	0	0	0	0	0	0	0	0	0	.000	.000
Daugherty, Jack, Texas†	.133	20	15	1	2	3	1	0	0	1	0	0	0	3	0	4	0	0	0	.200	.263
Davis, Alvin, Seattle*	.188	17	16	0	3	3	0	0	0	2	0	0	0	0	0	3	0	0	0	.188	.188
Davis, Chili, Minnesota†	.000	4	2	0	0	0	0	0	0	0	0	0	0	2	1	1	0	0	0	.000	.500
Davis, Glenn, Baltimore	.333	3	3	1	1	4	0	0	1	2	0	0	0	0	0	0	0	0	1	1.333	.333
de los Santos, Luis, Detroit	.200	5	5	0	1	1	0	0	0	0	0	0	0	0	0	0	0	0	0	.200	.200
Deer, Rob, Detroit	.000	3	1	0	0	0	0	0	0	0	0	0	0	2	1	1	0	0	0	.000	.667
Dempsey, Rick, Milwaukee	.500	5	4	0	2	2	0	0	0	2	0	0	0	1	0	0	0	0	0	.500	.600
Devereaux, Mike, Baltimore	.250	8	8	1	2	3	1	0	0	2	0	0	0	0	0	2	1	0	0	.375	.250
Diaz, Mario, Texas	.214	16	14	3	3	3	0	0	0	1	0	0	0	1	0	3	0	0	0	.214	.267
Downing, Brian, Texas	.375	25	24	3	9	10	1	0	0	2	0	0	0	1	1	6	0	0	4	.417	.400
Ducey, Rob, Toronto*	.214	14	14	3	3	3	0	0	0	0	0	0	0	0	0	5	0	0	0	.214	.214
Eisenreich, Jim, Kansas City*	.219	34	32	3	7	11	1	0	1	6	0	0	0	2	0	7	1	0	0	.344	.265
Espinoza, Alvaro, New York	.000	8	6	0	0	0	0	0	0	0	0	0	0	0	0	2	0	0	0	.000	.000
Evans, Dwight, Baltimore	.400	32	25	1	10	15	2	0	1	6	0	0	0	7	1	5	0	0	2	.600	.531
Fariss, Monty, Texas	.167	8	6	0	1	2	1	0	0	0	0	0	0	1	0	3	0	0	0	.333	.286
Felix, Junior, California†	.000	15	12	0	0	0	0	0	0	4	0	0	0	5	0	3	0	0	0	.000	.294
Fisk, Carlton, Chicago	.143	17	14	1	2	5	0	0	1	2	0	0	0	3	0	3	0	0	1	.357	.294
Fletcher, Scott, Chicago	.333	6	6	2	2	3	1	0	0	1	0	0	0	0	0	1	0	0	0	.500	.333
Franco, Julio, Texas	.500	2	2	1	1	1	0	0	0	1	0	0	0	0	0	0	0	0	1	.500	.500
Fryman, Travis, Detroit	1.000	1	1	0	1	1	0	0	0	0	0	0	0	0	0	0	0	0	0	1.000	1.000
Gaetti, Gary, California	1.000	1	1	0	1	1	0	0	0	0	0	0	0	0	0	0	0	0	0	1.000	1.000
Gagne, Greg, Minnesota	.500	2	2	0	1	1	0	0	0	1	0	0	0	0	0	0	0	0	0	.500	.500
Gallagher, Dave, California	.364	11	11	0	4	6	2	0	0	1	0	0	0	0	0	2	0	0	2	.545	.364
Gantner, Jim, Milwaukee*	.250	4	4	1	1	1	0	0	0	0	0	0	0	0	0	1	0	0	0	.250	.250
Geren, Bob, New York	.000	1	1	0	0	0	0	0	0	0	0	0	0	0	0	1	0	0	0	.000	.000
Giannelli, Ray, Toronto*	1.000	1	1	0	1	1	0	0	0	1	0	0	0	0	0	0	0	0	0	1.000	1.000
Gibson, Kirk, Kansas City*	.222	11	9	0	2	2	0	0	0	0	0	0	0	2	0	4	0	0	1	.222	.364
Gladden, Dan, Minnesota	.333	4	3	0	1	1	0	0	0	0	0	0	0	0	0	0	0	0	0	.333	.333
Gomez, Leo, Baltimore	.000	6	5	0	0	0	0	0	0	0	0	0	0	1	0	2	0	0	0	.000	.167
Gonzales, Rene, Toronto	.500	4	2	0	1	1	0	0	0	1	0	0	0	0	0	1	0	0	0	.500	.500
Gonzalez, Juan, Texas	.000	4	3	0	0	0	0	0	0	0	0	0	0	0	0	1	0	0	0	.000	.000
Gonzalez, Jesus, Cleveland	.000	4	3	0	0	0	0	0	0	0	0	0	0	1	0	3	0	0	0	.000	.250
Grebeck, Craig, Chicago	.214	19	14	3	3	9	1	1	1	3	0	0	0	2	0	3	0	0	0	.643	.333
Greenwell, Mike, Boston*	.250	4	4	0	1	1	0	0	0	3	0	0	0	0	0	0	0	0	0	.250	.250

Player, Team	Avg.	G	AB	R	H	TB	2B	3B	HR	RBI	SH	SF	HP	BB	Int. BB	SO	SB	CS	GI DP	Slg.	OBP
Griffey Jr., Ken, Seattle*	.250	6	4	0	1	1	0	0	0	0	0	0	0	2	1	1	0	0	0	.250	.500
Griffey Sr., Ken, Seattle*	.800	5	5	1	4	4	0	0	0	2	0	0	0	0	0	1	0	0	0	.800	.800
Gruber, Kelly, Toronto	.000	1	1	0	0	0	0	0	0	0	0	0	0	0	0	0	1	0	0	.000	.000
Guillen, Ozzie, Chicago*	.167	7	6	0	1	1	0	0	0	2	0	0	0	1	0	1	0	0	0	.167	.286
Hall, Mel, New York*	.286	17	14	1	4	5	1	0	0	4	0	1	0	1	0	3	1	0	0	.357	.313
Hamilton, Darryl, Milwaukee*	1.000	3	3	2	3	4	1	0	0	1	0	0	0	0	0	0	0	1	0	1.333	1.000
Hare, Shawn, Detroit*	.000	3	2	0	0	0	0	0	0	0	0	0	0	0	0	1	0	0	0	.000	.333
Harper, Brian, Minnesota	.000	2	2	0	0	0	0	0	0	0	0	0	0	0	0	1	0	0	0	.000	.000
Henderson, Dave, Oakland	.000	7	7	0	0	0	0	0	0	0	0	0	0	0	0	2	0	0	0	.000	.000
Henderson, Rickey, Oakland	.167	7	6	4	1	1	0	0	0	3	0	0	0	1	0	1	0	1	0	.167	.286
Hill, Donnie, California†	.188	19	16	0	3	4	1	0	0	0	1	0	0	2	0	3	0	0	0	.250	.278
Hill, Glenallen, Cleveland	.000	2	2	0	0	0	0	0	0	0	0	0	0	0	0	1	1	0	0	.000	.000
Hoiles, Chris, Baltimore	.167	6	6	0	1	1	0	0	0	0	0	0	0	0	0	0	0	0	0	.167	.167
Horn, Sam, Baltimore*	.292	29	24	4	7	18	2	0	3	7	0	0	0	2	1	9	0	0	4	.750	.346
Housie, Wayne, Boston†	1.000	2	1	1	1	1	0	0	0	0	0	0	0	0	0	0	0	0	0	1.000	1.000
Howard, David, Kansas City†	.000	1	1	0	0	0	0	0	0	0	0	1	0	0	0	0	0	0	0	.000	.000
Howell, Jack, California*	.250	6	4	0	1	1	0	0	0	0	0	0	0	2	0	0	1	0	0	.250	.250
Howitt, Dann, Oakland*	.167	6	6	0	1	4	0	0	1	1	0	0	0	0	0	3	0	0	0	.667	.167
Hrbek, Kent, Minnesota*	.750	4	4	2	3	6	0	0	1	2	0	0	0	0	0	0	0	0	0	1.500	.750
Huff, Mike, Cle.-Chi.	.000	16	12	1	0	0	0	0	0	0	0	0	0	3	0	4	0	0	0	.000	.200
Hulett, Tim, Baltimore	.200	11	10	1	2	3	1	0	0	2	0	0	0	1	0	4	0	0	1	.300	.273
Humphreys, Mike, New York	.000	5	2	2	0	0	0	0	0	0	0	0	0	3	0	0	0	0	0	.000	.600
Huson, Jeff, Texas*	.000	14	12	2	0	0	0	0	0	0	2	0	0	0	0	3	1	0	0	.000	.000
Incaviglia, Pete, Detroit	.500	4	2	1	1	2	1	0	0	2	0	0	3	0	0	0	0	0	0	1.000	.500
Jackson, Bo, Chicago	.500	2	2	0	1	4	0	0	1	1	0	0	0	0	0	1	0	0	2	2.000	.500
Jacoby, Brook, Cle.-Oak.	.000	10	6	0	0	0	0	0	0	0	0	0	0	2	0	2	0	0	0	.000	.333
James, Craig, Cleveland	.286	7	7	0	2	2	0	0	0	2	0	0	0	0	0	1	0	0	0	.286	.286
Jennings, Doug, Oakland*	.000	2	1	0	0	0	0	0	0	0	0	0	0	1	1	1	0	0	0	.000	.500
Johnson, Lance, Chicago*	.500	5	4	0	2	2	0	0	0	1	0	0	0	1	0	0	0	0	0	.500	.600
Jones, Tracy, Seattle	.300	30	20	4	6	8	2	0	0	3	0	0	1	6	0	4	0	0	1	.400	.481
Joyner, Wally, California*	.000	2	2	0	0	0	0	0	0	0	0	0	0	0	0	1	0	0	0	.000	.000
Karkovice, Ron, Chicago	.000	4	4	0	0	0	0	0	0	0	0	0	0	0	0	0	0	0	1	.000	.000
Kelly, Roberto, New York	.500	2	2	0	1	1	0	0	0	0	0	0	0	0	0	1	0	0	0	.500	.500
Kirby, Wayne, Cleveland*	.000	1	1	0	0	0	0	0	0	0	0	0	0	0	0	0	0	0	0	.000	.000
Kittle, Ron, Chicago	.000	2	2	0	0	0	0	0	0	0	0	0	0	1	0	2	0	0	0	.000	.000
Knoblauch, Chuck, Minnesota	.667	3	3	2	2	2	0	0	0	1	0	0	0	0	0	0	0	0	0	.667	.667
Knorr, Randy, Toronto	.000	1	0	0	0	0	0	0	0	0	0	0	0	1	0	0	0	0	0	.000	1.000
Komminsk, Brad, Oakland	.500	2	2	0	1	2	0	0	0	0	0	0	0	0	0	1	0	0	1	1.000	.500
Kreuter, Chad, Texas†	.000	1	1	0	0	0	0	0	0	0	0	0	0	0	0	0	0	0	0	.000	.000
Lansford, Carney, Oakland	.000	1	1	0	0	0	0	0	0	0	0	0	0	0	0	0	0	0	0	.000	.000
Larkin, Gene, Minnesota†	.158	24	19	2	3	3	0	0	0	2	0	0	0	5	0	2	0	0	0	.158	.333
Law, Vance, Oakland	.444	11	9	2	4	4	0	0	0	1	1	0	0	1	0	1	0	0	2	.444	.500
Leius, Scott, Minnesota	.440	30	25	4	11	13	2	0	0	2	1	0	0	5	0	7	0	0	0	.520	.533
Lennon, Pat, Seattle	.250	5	4	2	1	2	1	0	0	1	0	0	0	1	0	0	0	0	0	.500	.400
Lewis, Mark, Cleveland	1.000	2	2	1	2	3	1	0	0	0	0	0	0	0	0	0	0	0	1	1.500	1.000
Leyritz, Jim, New York	.222	10	9	1	2	2	0	0	0	0	0	0	0	1	0	2	0	0	0	.222	.300

Player, Team	Avg.	G	AB	R	H	TB	2B	3B	HR	RBI	SH	SF	HP	BB	Int. BB	SO	SB	CS	GI DP	Slg.	OBP
Livingstone, Scott, Detroit*	.500	2	2	0	1	2	1	0	0	0	0	0	0	0	0	1	0	0	0	1.000	.500
Lopez, Luis, Cleveland	.400	13	10	0	4	4	0	0	0	1	0	0	0	3	1	2	0	0	0	.400	.538
Lovullo, Torey, New York†	.000	1	0	0	0	0	0	0	0	1	0	0	0	1	1	0	0	0	0	.000	1.000
Lusader, Scott, New York*	.333	4	3	0	1	1	0	0	0	0	0	0	0	0	0	0	0	0	0	.333	.500
Lyons, Steve, Boston*	.048	24	21	0	1	1	0	0	0	0	0	0	0	0	0	4	0	0	0	.048	.048
Maas, Kevin, New York*	.222	9	9	1	2	2	0	0	0	0	0	0	0	0	0	4	0	0	0	.222	.222
Macfarlane, Mike, Kansas City	.308	13	13	0	4	5	1	0	0	3	0	0	0	0	0	3	0	0	1	.385	.308
Mack, Shane, Minnesota	.375	8	8	2	3	6	0	0	1	4	0	0	0	0	0	1	1	0	0	.750	.375
Magallanes, Everardo, Cleveland*	.000	1	1	0	0	0	0	0	0	0	0	0	0	0	0	1	0	0	0	.000	.000
Maldonado, Candy, Toronto	.000	5	3	0	0	0	0	0	0	0	0	0	1	1	0	0	0	0	0	.000	.400
Manto, Jeff, Cleveland	.000	1	0	0	0	0	0	0	0	0	0	0	1	0	0	0	0	0	0	.000	1.000
Marshall, Mike, Bos.-Cal.	.143	7	7	0	1	1	0	0	0	0	0	0	0	0	0	3	0	0	0	.143	.143
Martinez, Carlos, Cleveland	.000	2	2	0	0	0	0	0	0	2	0	0	0	0	0	0	0	0	0	.000	.000
Martinez, Carmelo, Kansas City	.667	5	3	3	2	8	0	0	2	2	0	0	0	2	0	0	0	0	0	2.667	.800
Martinez, Chito, Baltimore*	.125	9	8	1	1	4	0	0	1	1	0	0	0	0	0	2	0	0	0	.500	.125
Martinez, Edgar, Seattle	.333	4	3	0	1	1	0	0	0	1	0	0	0	1	0	1	0	0	0	.333	.500
Martinez, Tino, Seattle*	.400	5	5	0	2	2	0	0	0	2	0	1	0	0	0	0	0	0	1	.400	.400
Marzano, John, Boston	1.000	1	1	0	1	1	0	0	0	0	0	0	0	0	0	0	0	0	0	1.000	1.000
Mattingly, Don, New York*	.250	5	4	0	1	1	0	0	0	0	0	0	0	1	1	0	0	0	0	.250	.400
Maurer, Rob, Texas*	.000	8	6	2	0	0	0	0	0	0	0	0	0	2	0	4	0	0	0	.000	.250
Mayne, Brett, Kansas City*	.250	8	8	2	2	5	0	0	1	3	0	0	0	0	0	1	0	0	1	.625	.250
McGwire, Mark, Oakland	.250	4	4	1	1	4	0	0	1	0	0	0	0	0	0	1	0	0	0	1.000	.250
McIntosh, Tim, Milwaukee	.000	1	1	0	0	0	0	0	0	0	0	0	0	0	0	0	0	0	0	.000	.000
McKnight, Jeff, Baltimore†	.250	4	4	0	1	1	0	0	0	1	0	0	0	0	0	1	0	0	0	.250	.250
McRae, Brian, Kansas City†	.500	2	2	0	1	1	0	0	0	0	0	0	0	0	0	1	0	0	0	.500	.500
Melvin, Bob, Baltimore	.400	7	5	0	2	2	0	0	0	1	0	1	0	0	0	0	0	0	0	.400	.333
Mercedes, Luis, Baltimore	.500	2	2	2	1	1	0	0	0	0	0	0	0	0	0	0	0	0	0	.500	.500
Merullo, Matt, Chicago*	.171	47	41	2	7	13	0	0	2	8	0	0	0	1	0	10	0	0	1	.317	.178
Meulens, Hensley, New York	.364	12	11	2	4	8	0	0	1	4	0	0	0	1	0	4	0	0	0	.727	.417
Milligan, Randy, Baltimore	.167	7	6	0	1	1	0	0	0	2	1	0	0	1	0	3	0	0	0	.167	.286
Moore, Bob, Kansas City	.000	2	2	0	0	0	0	0	0	0	0	0	0	0	0	2	0	0	0	.000	.000
Morman, Russ, Kansas City	.000	5	4	0	0	0	0	0	0	4	0	0	0	0	0	2	0	0	0	.000	.000
Moseby, Lloyd, Detroit*	.273	11	11	2	3	3	0	0	0	1	0	0	0	0	0	4	0	0	0	.273	.273
Moses, John, Detroit†	.000	1	1	0	0	0	0	0	0	0	0	0	0	0	0	0	0	0	0	.000	.000
Mulliniks, Rance, Toronto*	.158	24	19	3	3	3	0	0	0	3	1	1	0	3	0	7	0	0	1	.158	.261
Munoz, Pedro, Minnesota	.167	6	6	0	1	1	0	0	0	5	0	0	0	0	0	1	0	0	0	.167	.167
Myers, Greg, Toronto*	.200	11	10	0	2	2	0	0	0	1	0	0	0	1	0	1	0	0	0	.200	.273
Naehring, Tim, Boston	.000	1	1	0	0	0	0	0	0	0	0	0	0	0	0	1	0	0	0	.000	.000
Newman, Al, Minnesota†	.238	24	21	1	5	5	0	0	0	2	0	1	0	1	0	5	0	0	0	.238	.261
Newson, Warren, Chicago*	.364	28	22	3	8	10	2	0	0	0	0	0	0	6	1	5	1	0	0	.455	.500
Nokes, Matt, New York*	.235	19	17	0	4	4	0	0	0	1	0	0	0	2	0	3	0	0	1	.235	.316
O'Brien, Pete, Seattle*	.667	3	3	0	2	2	0	0	0	2	0	0	0	0	0	1	0	0	0	.667	.667
Olander, Jim, Milwaukee	.000	1	0	0	0	0	0	0	0	0	0	1	0	0	0	0	0	0	0	.000	1.000
Olerud, John, Toronto*	.111	13	9	1	1	1	0	0	0	1	0	1	0	3	2	3	0	0	0	.111	.308
Orsulak, Joe, Baltimore*	.214	16	14	2	3	7	1	0	1	5	0	1	1	0	0	2	0	0	0	.500	.250
Ortiz, Junior, Minnesota	.000	1	1	0	0	0	0	0	0	0	0	1	0	0	0	0	0	0	0	.000	.000

Player, Team	Avg.	G	AB	R	H	TB	2B	3B	HR	RBI	SH	SF	HP	BB	Int. BB	SO	SB	CS	GI DP	Slg.	OBP
Pagliarulo, Mike, Minnesota *	.167	6	6	0	1	1	0	0	0	0	0	0	0	0	0	2	0	0	0	.167	.167
Palmeiro, Rafael, Texas *	.667	4	3	0	2	2	0	0	0	0	0	0	0	1	0	0	0	0	0	.667	.750
Palmer, Dean, Texas	.400	5	5	1	2	6	1	0	1	2	0	0	0	0	0	3	0	0	0	1.200	.400
Paredes, Johnny, Detroit	.000	2	2	0	0	0	0	0	0	0	0	0	0	0	0	1	0	0	0	.000	.000
Parker, Dave, Toronto*	.667	3	3	0	2	2	0	0	0	1	0	0	0	0	0	2	0	0	0	.667	.667
Parrish, Lance, California	.400	5	5	1	2	2	0	0	0	1	0	0	0	0	0	1	0	0	0	.400	.400
Pasqua, Dan, Chicago*	.231	16	13	2	3	4	1	0	0	2	0	0	0	3	1	6	0	0	0	.308	.375
Pecota, Bill, Kansas City	.333	6	6	0	2	2	0	0	0	1	0	0	0	0	0	1	0	0	0	.333	.333
Pena, Tony, Boston	.000	1	1	0	0	0	0	0	0	0	0	0	0	0	0	1	0	0	1	.000	.000
Perezchica, Tony, Cleveland	.400	5	5	2	2	2	0	0	0	0	0	0	0	0	0	2	0	0	0	.400	.400
Petralli, Geno, Texas*	.136	27	22	0	3	4	1	0	0	1	0	0	0	4	0	6	0	0	0	.182	.269
Pettis, Gary, Texas†	.000	10	10	2	0	0	0	0	0	0	0	0	0	0	0	4	0	0	1	.000	.000
Phillips, Tony, Detroit†	.333	8	6	0	2	5	0	0	1	2	0	0	0	2	0	1	0	0	0	.833	.500
Plantier, Phil, Boston*	.375	10	8	1	3	6	0	0	1	4	0	0	0	2	0	3	0	0	0	.750	.500
Polonia, Luis, California*	.200	5	5	0	1	1	0	0	0	1	0	0	0	0	0	1	1	0	0	.200	.200
Powell, Alonzo, Seattle	.154	14	13	1	2	3	1	0	0	0	0	0	0	1	0	5	0	0	0	.231	.214
Puhl, Terry, Kansas City*	.200	13	10	0	2	2	0	0	0	2	0	0	0	3	0	2	0	0	1	.200	.385
Pulliam, Harvey, Kansas City	.000	3	3	1	0	0	0	0	0	1	0	0	0	0	0	3	0	0	0	.000	.000
Quintana, Carlos, Boston	.294	18	17	2	5	6	1	0	0	4	0	0	0	1	0	3	0	0	1	.353	.333
Quirk, Jamie, Oakland*	.294	17	17	0	5	6	1	0	0	3	0	0	0	0	0	2	0	0	0	.353	.294
Raines, Tim, Chicago†	.000	5	5	1	0	0	0	0	0	1	0	0	0	0	0	0	0	0	0	.000	.000
Ramos, John, New York	.000	2	1	0	0	0	0	0	0	1	0	0	0	0	0	1	0	0	0	.000	.000
Randolph, Willie, Milwaukee	.500	8	8	0	4	5	1	0	0	3	0	0	0	0	0	0	0	0	1	.625	.500
Reimer, Kevin, Texas*	.286	31	28	3	8	17	3	0	2	5	0	0	0	3	0	7	0	0	0	.607	.355
Reynolds, Harold, Seattle†	.000	2	2	1	0	0	0	0	0	0	0	0	0	0	0	1	1	0	0	.000	.000
Riles, Ernest, Oakland*	.148	32	27	0	4	6	2	0	0	3	0	0	0	3	1	7	0	0	1	.222	.233
Rodriguez, Carlos, New York†	.000	2	2	0	0	0	0	0	0	0	0	0	0	0	0	0	0	0	0	.000	.000
Rodriguez, Ivan, Texas	.000	2	2	0	0	0	0	0	0	0	0	0	0	0	0	1	0	0	0	.000	.000
Romine, Kevin, Boston	.286	8	7	1	2	2	0	0	0	2	0	0	0	1	0	1	0	0	1	.286	.375
Rose, Bobby, California	.667	3	3	0	2	5	0	0	1	3	0	0	0	0	0	0	0	0	0	1.667	.667
Rowland, Rich, Detroit	.000	2	1	0	0	0	0	0	0	0	0	0	0	2	0	1	0	0	0	.000	.667
Russell, John, Texas	.111	9	9	0	1	1	0	0	0	0	0	0	0	0	0	4	0	0	0	.111	.111
Salas, Mark, Detroit*	.067	18	15	1	1	4	0	0	1	4	0	1	0	2	0	5	0	0	0	.267	.167
Schaefer, Jeff, Seattle	.000	3	3	0	0	0	0	0	0	0	0	0	0	0	0	1	0	0	0	.000	.000
Schofield, Dick, California	.000	3	3	0	0	0	0	0	0	0	0	0	0	0	0	0	0	0	0	.000	.000
Scruggs, Tony, Texas	.000	1	1	0	0	0	0	0	0	0	0	0	0	0	0	0	0	0	0	.000	.000
Segui, David, Baltimore†	.250	26	24	2	6	6	0	0	0	3	0	0	0	2	0	4	0	0	1	.250	.308
Seitzer, Kevin, Kansas City	.550	23	20	1	11	15	2	1	0	3	0	0	0	2	0	0	0	0	1	.750	.591
Sheffield, Gary, Milwaukee	.000	1	0	0	0	0	0	0	0	0	0	0	0	1	0	0	0	0	0	.000	1.000
Shelby, John, Detroit†	.000	7	6	2	0	0	0	0	0	0	0	0	0	0	0	2	0	0	1	.000	.000
Sheridan, Pat, New York*	.167	7	6	1	1	4	0	0	1	2	0	0	0	1	0	1	0	0	0	.667	.286
Sierra, Ruben, Texas†	.200	31	25	4	5	12	1	0	2	7	0	0	0	6	0	10	0	0	2	.480	.355
Snyder, Cory, Chi.-Tor.	1.000	1	1	0	1	1	0	0	0	1	0	0	0	0	0	0	0	0	0	1.000	1.000
Sojo, Luis, California	.133	16	15	1	2	3	1	0	0	2	0	0	0	1	0	5	0	0	0	.200	.188
Sorrento, Paul, Minnesota*	.250	4	4	1	1	3	0	1	0	1	0	0	0	0	0	3	0	0	1	.750	.308
Sosa, Sammy, Chicago	.286	10	7	1	2	5	0	0	1	1	0	0	0	2	0	1	1	0	0	.714	.444

Player, Team	Avg.	G	AB	R	H	TB	2B	3B	HR	RBI	SH	SF	HP	BB	Int. BB	SO	SB	CS	GI DP	Slg.	OBP
Spehr, Tim, Kansas City	.000	1	1	0	0	0	0	0	0	0	0	0	0	0	0	0	0	0	0	.000	.000
Spiers, Bill, Milwaukee*	.000	1	1	0	0	0	0	0	0	0	0	0	0	0	0	0	0	0	0	.000	.000
Sprague, Ed, Toronto	1.000	1	1	1	1	2	1	0	0	0	0	0	0	0	0	0	0	0	0	2.000	1.000
Stanley, Mike, Texas	.222	36	27	1	6	8	2	0	0	5	2	1	0	5	0	9	0	0	0	.296	.333
Steinbach, Terry, Oakland	.571	9	7	3	4	4	0	0	0	2	0	1	0	1	0	1	0	0	0	.571	.556
Stillwell, Kurt, Kansas City†	.111	20	18	2	2	5	0	0	1	1	0	1	0	1	0	3	1	0	0	.278	.158
Stubbs, Franklin, Milwaukee*	.200	5	5	0	1	1	0	0	0	0	0	0	0	0	0	3	0	0	0	.200	.200
Surhoff, B.J., Milwaukee*	.200	12	10	1	2	2	0	0	0	1	0	0	0	2	0	2	0	0	0	.200	.333
Sveum, Dale, Milwaukee†	.000	7	6	0	0	0	0	0	0	0	0	0	0	1	0	2	0	0	0	.000	.143
Tabler, Pat, Toronto	.429	33	21	6	9	11	2	0	0	6	0	0	0	8	4	1	0	0	0	.524	.548
Tartabull, Danny, Kansas City	.000	2	1	0	0	0	0	0	0	0	0	0	0	1	0	1	0	0	0	.000	.500
Taubensee, Ed, Cleveland*	.000	2	2	0	0	0	0	0	0	0	0	0	0	0	0	0	0	0	0	.000	.000
Tettleton, Mickey, Detroit†	.308	14	13	4	4	7	0	0	1	5	0	0	0	1	0	4	0	0	0	.538	.357
Thomas, Frank, Chicago	1.000	1	1	0	1	1	0	0	0	1	0	0	0	0	0	0	0	0	0	1.000	1.000
Thurman, Gary, Kansas City	.400	5	5	1	2	2	0	0	0	0	0	0	0	0	0	2	1	0	0	.400	.400
Trammell, Alan, Detroit	.250	6	4	0	1	2	1	0	0	1	0	0	0	1	0	0	0	0	0	.500	.400
Turner, Shane, Baltimore*	.000	1	1	0	0	0	0	0	0	0	0	0	0	1	0	1	0	0	0	.000	.400
Valle, Dave, Seattle	.000	5	3	0	0	0	0	0	0	0	0	0	0	0	0	3	0	0	0	.000	.000
Vaughn, Greg, Milwaukee	.333	3	3	0	1	1	0	0	0	0	0	0	0	0	0	1	0	0	0	.333	.333
Vaughn, Mo, Boston*	.333	10	9	0	3	4	1	0	0	2	0	0	0	1	0	2	0	0	0	.444	.400
Velarde, Randy, New York	.571	8	7	3	4	5	1	0	0	0	0	0	0	0	0	1	0	0	0	.714	.625
Venable, Max, California*	.188	19	16	1	3	6	0	0	1	1	0	0	0	1	0	3	0	0	0	.375	.278
Ventura, Robin, Chicago*	.000	3	3	0	0	0	0	0	0	0	0	0	0	0	0	0	0	0	0	.000	.000
Vizquel, Omar, Seattle†	.000	8	8	0	0	0	0	0	0	0	0	0	0	1	0	2	0	0	1	.000	.000
Wakamatsu, Don, Chicago	1.000	1	1	0	1	1	0	0	0	0	0	0	0	0	0	0	0	0	1	1.000	1.000
Walling, Denny, Texas*	.300	10	10	0	3	4	1	0	0	2	0	0	0	0	0	2	0	0	0	.400	.300
Ward, Turner, Cle.-Tor.†	.333	3	3	0	1	1	0	0	0	0	0	0	0	0	0	1	0	0	0	.333	.333
Webster, Lenny, Minnesota	.000	2	2	0	0	0	0	0	0	0	0	0	0	0	0	1	0	0	0	.000	.000
Webster, Mitch, Cleveland†	.333	3	3	0	1	1	0	0	0	0	0	0	0	1	0	2	0	0	1	.333	.333
Wedge, Eric, Boston	1.000	1	1	0	1	1	0	0	0	0	0	0	0	0	0	0	0	0	0	1.000	1.000
Weiss, Walt, Oakland†	1.000	1	1	0	1	1	0	0	0	0	0	0	0	0	0	0	0	0	0	1.000	1.000
Whitaker, Lou, Detroit*	.308	14	13	2	4	7	0	0	1	5	0	0	0	1	1	2	0	0	2	.538	.357
Whiten, Mark, Cleveland†	.000	5	5	0	0	0	0	0	0	0	0	0	0	0	0	2	0	0	0	.000	.000
Whitt, Ernie, Baltimore*	.250	20	16	1	4	4	0	0	0	1	0	0	0	4	0	4	1	0	2	.250	.400
Williams, Kenny, Toronto	.000	1	1	0	0	0	0	0	0	0	0	0	0	0	0	0	0	0	0	.000	.000
Wilson, Mookie, Toronto†	.111	10	9	1	1	1	0	0	0	0	0	0	0	0	0	3	1	0	0	.111	.200
Wilson, Willie, Oakland†	.286	23	21	4	6	7	1	0	0	1	1	0	0	0	0	3	2	0	0	.333	.348
Winfield, Dave, California	.000	4	4	0	0	0	0	0	0	0	0	0	0	0	0	3	0	0	0	.000	.000
Witmeyer, Ron, Oakland*	.000	1	1	0	0	0	0	0	0	0	0	0	0	0	0	1	0	0	0	.000	.000
Worthington, Craig, Baltimore	.000	1	1	0	0	0	0	0	0	0	0	0	0	0	0	0	0	0	0	.000	.000
Yount, Robin, Milwaukee	.000	1	1	0	0	0	0	0	0	0	0	0	0	0	0	1	0	0	0	.000	.000
Zosky, Eddie, Toronto	.000	1	1	0	0	0	0	0	0	0	0	0	0	0	0	0	0	0	0	.000	.000
Zupcic, Bob, Boston	.000	2	1	0	0	0	0	0	0	0	0	0	0	0	0	0	0	0	0	.000	.000

1991 A.L. STATISTICS

PINCH-HITTERS WITH TWO OR MORE TEAMS

Player, Team	Avg.	G	AB	R	H	TB	2B	3B	HR	RBI	SH	SF	HP	BB	Int. BB	SO	SB	CS	GI DP	Slg.	OBP
Huff, Mike, Cleveland	.000	9	8	0	0	0	0	0	0	0	0	0	0	1	0	4	0	0	0	.000	.111
Huff, Mike, Chicago	.000	7	4	1	0	0	0	0	0	0	0	0	0	2	1	0	0	0	0	.000	.333
Jacoby, Brook, Cleveland	.000	5	3	0	0	0	0	0	0	0	0	0	2	0	0	2	0	0	0	.000	.400
Jacoby, Brook, Oakland	.000	5	3	0	0	0	0	0	0	0	0	0	1	0	0	3	0	0	0	.000	.250
Marshall, Mike, Boston	.167	6	6	0	1	1	0	0	0	1	0	0	0	0	0	0	0	0	0	.167	.167
Marshall, Mike, California	.000	1	1	0	0	0	0	0	0	0	0	0	0	0	0	4	0	0	0	.000	.000
Snyder, Cory, Chicago	.200	11	10	1	2	3	1	0	0	0	0	0	0	1	0	1	0	0	0	.300	.273
Snyder, Cory, Toronto	.000	5	5	0	0	0	0	0	0	1	0	0	0	0	0	0	0	0	0	.000	.000
Ward, Turner, Cleveland†	.000	1	1	0	1	1	0	0	0	1	0	0	0	0	0	1	0	0	1	1.000	1.000
Ward, Turner, Toronto†	.000	2	2	0	0	0	0	0	0	0	0	0	0	0	0	0	0	0	0	.000	.000

PITCHING

TEAM

Team	W-L	ERA	G	CG	ShO	Sv.	IP	H	TBF	R	ER	HR	SH	SF	HB	BB	Int. BB	SO	WP	Bk.
Toronto	91-71	3.50	162	10	16	60	1462.2	1301	6136	622	569	121	53	45	43	523	41	971	55	8
California	81-81	3.69	162	18	16	50	1441.2	1351	6059	649	591	141	43	35	38	543	29	990	49	11
Minnesota	95-67	3.69	162	21	10	53	1449.1	1402	6101	652	595	139	46	49	27	488	39	876	57	5
Seattle	83-79	3.79	162	10	12	48	1464.1	1387	6261	674	616	136	51	35	31	628	39	1003	82	7
Chicago	87-75	3.79	162	28	13	40	1478.0	1302	6194	681	622	136	64	50	47	601	25	923	44	6
Kansas City	82-80	3.92	162	17	8	41	1466.0	1473	6310	722	639	105	55	41	43	529	44	1004	47	5
Boston	84-78	4.01	162	15	12	45	1439.2	1405	6126	712	642	147	42	46	31	530	59	999	42	5
Milwaukee	83-79	4.14	162	23	13	41	1463.2	1498	6302	744	674	147	60	47	45	527	31	859	53	4
Cleveland	57-105	4.23	162	22	11	33	1441.1	1551	6231	759	678	110	59	69	39	441	61	862	48	6
New York	71-91	4.42	162	3	8	37	1444.0	1510	6209	777	709	152	49	38	42	506	29	936	53	14
Texas	85-77	4.47	162	9	11	41	1479.0	1486	6487	814	734	151	52	56	45	662	37	1022	77	12
Detroit	84-78	4.51	162	18	8	38	1450.1	1570	6343	794	726	148	65	63	24	593	88	739	50	5
Oakland	84-78	4.57	162	14	10	49	1444.1	1425	6299	776	734	155	51	54	55	655	30	892	60	7
Baltimore	67-95	4.59	162	8	8	42	1457.2	1534	6247	796	743	147	43	45	28	504	40	868	49	8
Totals	1134-1134	4.09	1134	216	150	618	20382.0	20195	87305	10172	9272	1953	733	678	538	7730	603	12944	766	103

NOTE—Totals for earned runs for several clubs do not agree with the composite totals for all pitchers of each respective club due to instances in which provisions of Section 10.18(i) of the Scoring Rules were applied. The following differences are to be noted: Boston pitchers add to 643; Chicago pitchers add to 624; Cleveland pitchers add to 679; Detroit pitchers add to 731; Milwaukee pitchers add to 679; New York pitchers add to 711; Seattle pitchers add to 617; Texas pitchers add to 735.

INDIVIDUAL

TOP 15 QUALIFIERS FOR EARNED-RUN AVERAGE TITLE

Minimum 162 innings. *Lefthanded pitcher.

Pitcher, Team	W	L	ERA	G	GS	CG	ShO	GF	Sv.	IP	H	TBF	R	ER	HR	SH	SF	HB	BB	Int. BB	SO	WP	Bk.
Clemens, Roger, Boston	18	10	2.62	35	35	13	4	0	0	271.1	219	1077	93	79	15	6	8	5	65	12	241	6	0
Candiotti, Tom, Cle.-Tor.	13	13	2.65	34	34	6	0	0	0	238.0	202	981	82	70	12	4	11	7	73	1	167	11	0
Wegman, Bill, Milwaukee	15	7	2.84	28	28	7	1	0	0	193.1	176	785	76	61	16	6	4	7	40	0	89	6	0
Abbott, Jim, California*	18	11	2.89	34	34	5	0	1	0	243.0	222	1002	85	78	14	6	4	5	73	6	158	6	4
Ryan, Nolan, Texas	12	6	2.91	27	27	2	2	0	0	173.0	102	683	58	56	12	5	9	5	72	1	203	8	0
Moore, Mike, Oakland	17	8	2.96	33	33	4	1	0	0	210.0	176	887	80	69	11	5	6	2	105	1	153	14	3
Tapani, Kevin, Minnesota	16	9	2.99	34	34	7	2	0	0	244.0	225	974	84	81	23	9	2	6	40	0	135	3	3
Langston, Mark, California*	19	8	3.00	34	34	9	3	0	0	246.1	190	992	89	82	30	4	6	3	96	3	183	6	0
Key, Jimmy, Toronto*	16	12	3.05	33	33	6	2	0	0	209.1	207	877	84	71	12	5	5	9	44	5	125	1	1
Saberhagen, Bret, Kansas City	13	8	3.07	28	28	7	2	0	0	196.1	165	789	76	67	12	8	10	9	45	5	136	8	1
Guzman, Jose, Texas	13	7	3.08	25	25	5	1	0	0	169.2	152	730	67	58	10	2	3	4	84	1	125	4	1
Erickson, Scott, Minnesota	20	8	3.18	32	32	5	3	0	0	204.0	189	851	80	72	13	5	6	6	71	3	108	4	0
Bosio, Chris, Milwaukee	14	10	3.25	32	32	5	1	0	0	204.2	187	840	74	74	15	2	8	8	58	0	117	5	0
McDowell, Jack, Chicago	17	10	3.41	35	35	15	3	0	0	253.2	212	1028	97	96	19	8	4	4	82	2	191	10	1
Appier, Kevin, Kansas City	13	10	3.42	34	34	6	3	0	0	207.2	205	881	97	79	13	8	6	2	61	3	158	7	1

DEPARTMENTAL LEADERS: W—Erickson, Min., Gullickson, Det., 20; L—McCaskill, Cal., 19; G—Ward, Tor., 81; GS—Clemens, Bos., Gullickson, Det. McDowell, Chi., Morris, Min., Stewart, Oak., Welch, Oak., 35; CG—McDowell, Chi., 15; ShO—Clemens, Bos., 271.1; H—Terrell, Det., 257; TBF—Clemens, Bos., 1077; R—Stewart, Oak., 130; HR—DeLucia, Sea., 31; SH—Swindell, Cle., 13; SF—Hough, Chi., 16; HB—Boddicker, K.C., Brown, Tex., 13; TBB—Johnson, Sea., 152; IBB—Gullickson, Det., 13; SO—Clemens, Bos., 241; WP—Morris, Min., 15; Bk.—J. Abbott, Cal., Boucher, Tor.-Cle., 4.

1991 A.L. STATISTICS

ALL PITCHERS

*Lefthanded pitcher.

Pitcher, Team	W	L	ERA	G	GS	CG	ShO	GF	Sv.	IP	H	TBF	R	ER	HR	SH	SF	HB	BB	Int. BB	SO	WP	Bk.
Abbott, Jim, California*	18	11	2.89	34	34	5	0	0	0	243.0	222	1002	85	78	14	7	7	5	73	6	158	1	4
Abbott, Kyle, California*	1	2	4.58	5	5	0	0	0	0	19.2	22	90	11	10	2	7	0	1	13	1	12	1	1
Abbott, Paul, Minnesota	3	1	4.75	15	3	0	0	1	0	47.1	38	210	27	25	5	3	3	0	36	0	43	5	0
Acker, Jim, Toronto	3	5	5.20	54	0	0	0	11	1	88.1	77	374	53	51	16	7	5	2	36	6	44	7	0
Aguilera, Rick, Minnesota	4	5	2.35	63	0	0	0	60	42	69.0	44	275	20	18	3	6	3	1	30	2	61	3	0
Aldred, Scott, Detroit*	2	4	5.18	11	11	0	0	0	0	57.1	58	253	37	33	9	3	2	3	30	0	35	3	3
Alexander, Gerald, Texas	5	3	5.24	30	9	1	0	4	0	89.1	93	402	56	52	11	6	5	3	48	7	50	0	1
Allison, Dana, Oakland*	1	2	7.36	11	0	0	0	4	0	11.0	16	49	9	9	0	1	1	0	5	4	4	0	0
Alvarez, Wilson, Chicago*	3	2	3.51	10	9	2	1	0	0	56.1	47	237	26	22	9	3	1	1	29	0	32	2	0
Anderson, Allan, Minnesota*	5	11	4.96	29	22	2	0	4	0	134.1	148	584	82	74	24	4	6	5	42	4	51	3	1
Appier, Kevin, Kansas City	13	10	3.42	34	31	6	3	1	0	207.2	205	881	97	79	13	8	6	6	61	5	158	7	1
Aquino, Luis, Kansas City	8	4	3.44	38	18	0	0	9	3	157.0	152	661	67	60	10	6	7	4	47	5	80	1	1
Arnsberg, Brad, Texas	9	8	8.38	9	0	0	0	2	0	9.2	10	44	9	9	1	5	0	3	5	0	8	0	0
August, Don, Milwaukee	9	8	5.47	28	23	0	0	3	0	138.1	166	613	84	84	18	9	3	3	47	2	62	0	0
Austin, Jim, Milwaukee	0	0	8.31	5	0	0	0	1	0	8.2	8	46	8	8	1	0	1	1	11	0	3	1	2
Bailes, Scott, California*	0	2	4.18	42	0	0	0	14	0	51.2	41	219	26	24	5	5	3	4	22	5	41	2	0
Ballard, Jeff, Baltimore*	6	12	5.60	26	22	0	0	1	0	123.2	153	540	91	77	16	3	2	2	28	2	37	3	1
Bankhead, Scott, Seattle	3	6	4.90	17	9	0	0	2	0	60.2	73	271	35	33	8	1	2	2	21	1	28	0	0
Banks, Willie, Minnesota	1	1	5.71	5	3	0	0	2	0	17.1	21	85	15	11	1	0	0	0	12	0	16	3	0
Bannister, Floyd, California*	0	0	3.96	16	0	0	0	4	0	25.0	25	104	11	11	5	0	2	0	16	1	16	0	0
Barfield, John, Texas*	4	4	4.54	28	9	0	0	4	1	83.1	96	361	51	42	11	3	4	1	22	3	27	1	2
Bautista, Jose, Baltimore	0	1	16.88	5	0	0	0	3	0	5.1	13	34	10	10	1	0	0	0	3	0	3	0	2
Beasley, Chris, California	0	1	3.38	22	0	0	0	8	0	26.2	26	113	14	10	2	1	0	1	10	3	14	1	1
Bedrosian, Steve, Minnesota	5	3	4.42	56	0	0	0	22	6	77.1	70	332	42	38	11	2	4	3	35	6	44	2	0
Bell, Eric, Cleveland*	4	0	0.50	10	0	0	0	3	0	18.0	5	61	2	1	0	1	0	0	5	0	7	0	0
Bitker, Joe, Texas	0	0	6.75	9	0	0	0	4	0	14.2	17	70	11	11	4	0	2	0	8	3	16	2	0
Blair, Willie, Cleveland	2	3	6.75	11	5	0	0	0	0	36.0	58	168	27	27	7	1	1	1	10	0	13	1	0
Boddicker, Mike, Kansas City	12	12	4.08	30	29	1	0	0	0	180.2	188	775	89	82	13	3	0	13	59	0	79	3	2
Bohanon, Brian, Texas*	4	3	4.84	11	11	0	0	0	0	61.1	66	273	35	33	4	10	5	2	23	1	34	3	1
Bolton, Tom, Boston*	8	9	5.24	25	19	1	0	4	0	110.0	136	499	72	64	16	2	4	1	51	0	64	3	0
Bosio, Chris, Milwaukee	14	10	3.25	32	32	5	1	0	0	204.2	187	840	80	74	15	6	6	6	58	3	117	5	0
Boucher, Denis, Tor.-Cle.*	2	7	6.05	12	12	0	0	0	0	58.0	74	270	41	39	12	2	2	2	24	1	29	1	4
Boyd, Oil Can, Texas	0	2	6.68	12	12	0	0	0	0	62.0	81	277	47	46	12	3	1	0	17	0	33	0	0
Briscoe, John, Oakland	0	0	7.07	11	0	0	0	9	0	14.0	12	62	11	11	2	0	1	0	10	0	9	3	0
Brown, J. Kevin, Texas	9	12	4.40	33	33	0	0	0	0	210.2	233	934	116	103	17	6	4	13	90	5	96	12	3
Brown, Kevin D., Milwaukee*	2	2	5.51	15	10	0	0	0	0	63.2	66	285	39	39	6	5	5	0	34	2	30	6	0
Burba, Dave, Seattle	2	2	3.68	22	2	0	0	11	1	36.2	34	153	16	15	6	6	0	3	14	3	16	1	2
Burns, Todd, Oakland	1	0	3.38	9	0	0	0	5	0	13.1	10	57	5	5	2	0	2	1	8	0	3	1	1
Cadaret, Greg, New York*	6	8	3.62	68	0	0	0	17	3	121.2	110	517	52	49	8	6	3	2	59	6	105	3	0
Campbell, Kevin, Oakland	1	0	2.74	14	0	0	0	2	0	23.0	13	94	7	7	4	1	0	0	14	0	16	0	1
Candiotti, Tom, Cle.-Tor.	13	13	2.65	34	34	6	0	0	0	238.0	202	981	82	70	12	4	11	6	73	1	167	11	0

Pitcher, Team	W	L	ERA	G	GS	CG	ShO	GF	Sv.	IP	H	TBF	R	ER	HR	SH	SF	HB	BB	Int. BB	SO	WP	Bk.
Carter, Jeff, Chicago	0	1	5.25	5	2	0	0	1	0	12.0	8	49	8	7	1	6	0	0	5	2	2	2	0
Cary, Chuck, New York*	1	6	5.91	10	9	0	0	0	0	53.1	61	247	35	35	6	1	0	0	32	2	34	2	1
Casian, Larry, Minnesota*	2	1	7.36	15	0	0	0	4	0	18.1	28	87	16	15	4	0	3	1	7	2	6	1	0
Cerutti, John, Detroit*	3	6	4.57	38	8	1	0	10	2	88.2	94	389	49	45	9	7	3	0	37	9	29	4	1
Chapin, Darrin, New York	0	1	5.06	5	0	0	0	2	0	5.1	3	25	3	3	0	0	0	0	6	0	5	2	0
Chiamparino, Scott, Oakland	1	2	4.03	5	5	0	0	0	0	22.1	26	101	11	10	1	4	0	4	12	0	8	0	1
Chitren, Steve, Oakland	1	4	4.33	56	0	0	0	20	4	60.1	59	271	31	29	8	6	2	5	32	4	47	6	0
Clemens, Roger, Boston	18	10	2.62	35	35	13	4	0	0	271.1	219	1077	93	79	15	6	8	5	65	12	241	6	0
Comstock, Keith, Seattle*	0	0	54.00	1	0	0	0	0	0	0.1	2	4	2	2	0	0	0	0	1	0	0	0	1
Corbin, Archie, Kansas City	0	0	3.86	3	0	0	0	2	0	2.1	2	12	1	1	0	0	0	0	2	0	1	0	0
Crawford, Steve, Kansas City	3	2	5.98	33	0	0	0	17	1	46.2	60	216	31	31	3	3	3	1	18	5	38	5	3
Crim, Chuck, Milwaukee	8	5	4.63	66	0	0	0	29	3	91.1	115	408	52	47	9	3	0	2	25	9	39	3	3
Dalton, Mike, Detroit*	0	0	3.38	4	0	0	0	1	0	8.0	12	38	3	3	2	1	0	2	2	2	4	2	0
Darling, Ron, Oakland	3	7	4.08	12	12	0	0	0	0	75.0	64	319	34	34	7	5	4	2	38	2	60	0	0
Darwin, Danny, Boston	3	6	5.16	12	12	0	0	0	0	68.0	71	292	39	39	15	1	2	4	15	1	42	2	0
Davis, Mark, Kansas City*	6	3	4.45	29	5	0	0	8	1	62.2	55	276	36	31	6	2	5	1	39	9	47	1	0
Davis, Storm, Kansas City	3	9	4.96	51	9	0	1	22	2	114.1	140	515	69	63	11	6	4	1	46	9	53	3	0
Dayley, Ken, Toronto*	0	0	6.23	8	0	0	0	3	0	4.1	7	26	6	3	0	0	1	0	5	2	1	2	0
de la Rosa, Francisco, Baltimore	0	0	4.50	2	0	0	0	1	0	4.0	6	20	3	2	0	0	0	0	2	1	0	0	0
DeLucia, Rich, Seattle	12	13	5.09	32	31	0	0	0	0	182.0	176	779	107	103	31	5	14	4	78	4	98	10	0
Dempsey, Rick, Milwaukee	0	0	18.00	1	0	0	0	0	0	1.0	2	6	2	2	0	0	0	0	0	0	0	0	0
Dopson, John, Boston	3	3	3.23	28	0	0	0	8	0	30.2	21	125	12	11	2	2	1	0	13	1	18	0	0
Drahman, Brian, Chicago	3	2	12.27	4	0	0	0	1	0	7.1	10	37	10	10	4	1	1	0	6	0	2	2	0
Drees, Tom, Chicago*	0	0	5.45	7	7	0	0	0	0	34.2	33	159	28	21	5	5	0	1	21	0	17	3	0
Dressendorfer, Kirk, Oakland	3	3	2.96	67	0	0	0	59	43	76.0	60	299	26	25	11	2	2	5	9	3	87	1	0
Eckersley, Dennis, Oakland	5	4	4.09	8	8	0	0	0	0	33.0	34	143	15	15	2	1	0	1	10	0	19	1	0
Edens, Tom, Minnesota	2	2	3.86	13	6	0	0	3	0	23.1	22	106	14	10	2	0	2	1	17	3	12	2	0
Edwards, Wayne, Chicago*	0	0	4.76	6	0	0	0	3	0	5.2	8	28	3	3	0	2	0	2	4	1	8	2	0
Egloff, Bruce, Cleveland	3	3	1.98	70	0	0	0	23	1	81.2	63	311	21	18	8	0	3	2	13	2	49	2	3
Eichhorn, Mark, California	2	5	5.33	18	13	0	0	4	0	72.2	87	317	51	43	10	2	3	3	23	1	18	0	2
Eiland, Dave, New York	20	8	4.50	3	3	0	0	0	0	16.0	20	73	9	8	2	0	3	0	6	0	10	0	0
Eldred, Cal, Milwaukee	0	0	3.18	32	32	5	3	0	0	204.0	189	851	80	72	13	5	7	6	71	3	108	4	0
Erickson, Scott, Minnesota	0	0	0.00	1	0	0	0	1	0	0.2	0	2	0	0	0	0	0	0	0	0	0	0	0
Espinoza, Alvaro, New York	0	2	5.68	4	0	0	0	0	0	19.0	25	84	13	12	2	0	0	1	4	0	15	2	0
Fajardo, Hector, Texas	5	5	2.19	60	0	0	0	48	23	70.0	57	285	29	17	4	7	11	5	20	3	60	0	2
Farr, Steve, New York	9	13	4.51	34	32	0	0	0	0	191.2	186	827	100	96	16	6	2	8	88	2	145	4	4
Fernandez, Alex, Chicago	2	5	4.84	19	4	0	0	8	0	44.2	53	206	29	24	4	0	3	3	28	1	24	4	6
Fetters, Mike, California	18	9	3.80	34	34	4	2	0	0	227.1	205	955	102	96	23	5	0	8	101	6	171	6	3
Finley, Chuck, California*	2	7	2.38	64	0	0	0	24	3	98.1	84	391	27	26	6	3	0	3	25	6	55	2	2
Flanagan, Mike, Baltimore*	1	0	6.62	9	3	0	0	3	0	17.2	19	73	13	13	3	4	0	3	3	0	11	0	0
Fleming, Dave, Seattle*	3	2	3.47	64	0	0	0	18	1	57.0	49	244	27	22	8	5	2	3	28	9	29	2	2
Fossas, Tony, Boston*	0	2	6.15	13	1	0	0	6	0	26.1	33	123	20	18	4	3	0	1	11	3	12	0	0
Fraser, Willie, Toronto	7	3	1.87	51	0	0	0	10	3	96.1	64	372	24	20	2	2	3	1	29	7	77	7	0
Frohwirth, Todd, Baltimore	4	4	5.74	31	7	0	0	11	1	73.2	73	331	52	47	5	4	2	2	39	6	43	0	2
Gakeler, Dan, Detroit	4	4	5.40	16	15	0	0	0	2	78.1	79	332	50	47	13	3	2	2	31	2	40	2	2
Garcia, Ramon, Chicago																							

Pitcher, Team	W	L	ERA	G	GS	CG	ShO	GF	Sv.	IP	H	TBF	R	ER	HR	SH	SF	HB	BB	Int. BB	SO	WP	Bk.
Gardner, Mike, Boston	9	10	4.85	22	20	0	0	0	0	130.0	140	562	79	70	18	1	3	0	47	2	91	1	0
Gardner, Wes, Kansas City	0	0	1.59	3	0	0	0	2	0	5.2	5	26	4	1	0	1	0	0	2	0	3	0	0
George, Chris, Milwaukee	0	2	3.00	2	1	0	0	0	0	6.0	8	25	4	2	0	0	1	3	0	0	2	4	0
Gibson, Paul, Detroit*	5	7	4.59	68	0	0	0	28	8	96.0	112	432	51	49	10	2	2	3	48	8	52	4	0
Gleaton, Jerry Don, Detroit*	3	2	4.06	47	0	0	0	16	2	75.1	74	319	37	34	7	5	4	0	39	8	47	1	1
Gordon, Tom, Kansas City	9	14	3.87	45	14	1	0	11	1	158.0	129	684	76	68	16	5	3	4	87	6	167	5	0
Gossage, Goose, Texas	4	2	3.57	44	0	0	0	16	1	40.1	33	167	16	16	4	3	0	3	16	1	28	3	0
Gozzo, Mauro, Cleveland	0	0	19.29	2	0	0	0	0	0	4.2	11	28	10	9	0	0	1	0	7	0	3	0	0
Grahe, Joe, California	2	3	4.81	18	10	1	0	2	0	73.0	84	330	43	39	2	1	1	3	33	4	40	2	0
Gray, Jeff, Boston	2	3	2.34	50	0	0	0	20	1	61.2	39	231	17	16	7	3	1	1	10	1	41	2	0
Gubicza, Mark, Kansas City	9	12	5.68	26	26	0	0	0	0	133.0	168	601	90	84	10	1	5	6	42	4	89	5	0
Guetterman, Lee, New York*	3	4	3.68	64	0	0	0	37	6	88.0	91	376	42	36	6	3	8	3	25	13	35	4	0
Gullickson, Bill, Detroit	20	9	3.90	35	35	4	0	0	0	226.1	256	954	109	98	22	4	3	1	44	1	91	7	0
Guthrie, Mark, Minnesota*	7	5	4.32	41	12	0	0	13	2	98.0	116	432	52	47	11	8	3	4	41	0	72	4	0
Guzman, Jose, Texas	13	7	3.08	25	25	5	1	0	0	169.2	152	730	67	58	10	2	3	4	84	2	125	8	1
Guzman, Juan, Toronto	10	3	2.99	23	23	0	0	0	0	138.2	98	574	53	46	6	6	0	4	66	0	123	10	0
Guzman, Johnny, Oakland*	1	0	9.00	5	0	0	0	1	0	5.0	11	24	5	5	0	0	2	1	2	0	3	0	0
Haas, Dave, Detroit	1	0	6.75	11	0	0	0	0	0	10.2	8	50	8	8	2	0	1	1	12	3	6	1	2
Habyan, John, New York	4	2	2.30	66	0	0	0	16	2	90.0	73	349	28	23	7	2	2	5	20	3	70	1	1
Hanson, Erik, Seattle	8	8	3.81	27	27	2	1	0	0	174.2	182	744	82	74	16	2	8	0	56	0	143	1	1
Harris, Greg, Boston	11	12	3.85	53	21	2	0	15	2	173.0	157	731	79	74	13	4	8	5	69	2	127	6	1
Harris, Gene, Seattle	0	0	4.05	8	0	0	0	3	1	13.1	15	66	8	6	1	1	0	0	10	5	6	1	0
Harris, Reggie, Oakland	0	0	12.00	2	0	0	0	1	0	3.0	5	15	4	4	0	0	1	1	3	3	2	2	2
Harvey, Bryan, California	2	4	1.60	67	0	0	0	63	46	78.2	51	309	20	14	6	3	2	0	17	1	101	2	1
Hawkins, Andy, N.Y.-Oak.	4	6	5.52	19	17	1	0	2	0	89.2	91	399	56	55	10	2	3	5	42	0	45	1	1
Henke, Tom, Toronto	0	2	2.32	49	0	0	0	43	32	50.1	33	190	13	13	4	0	1	1	11	2	53	1	0
Henneman, Mike, Detroit	10	2	2.88	60	0	0	0	50	21	84.1	81	358	29	27	2	5	5	2	34	8	61	5	0
Henry, Doug, Milwaukee	2	1	1.00	32	0	0	0	25	15	36.0	16	137	4	4	1	2	2	1	14	0	28	0	0
Hentgen, Pat, Toronto	0	0	2.45	3	0	0	0	1	0	7.1	5	30	4	2	1	1	0	0	3	0	3	0	0
Hernandez, Roberto, Chicago	1	0	7.80	9	3	0	0	1	0	15.0	18	69	15	13	1	0	0	2	7	3	6	1	0
Hesketh, Joe, Boston*	12	4	3.29	39	17	0	0	5	0	153.1	142	631	59	56	19	7	3	0	53	1	104	8	0
Hibbard, Greg, Chicago*	11	11	4.31	32	29	5	0	0	0	194.0	196	806	107	93	23	8	2	2	57	3	71	1	0
Hickey, Kevin, Baltimore*	1	0	9.00	19	0	0	0	6	0	14.0	15	62	14	14	2	0	1	0	6	1	10	0	0
Higuera, Ted, Milwaukee*	3	2	4.46	7	6	1	0	1	0	36.1	37	153	18	18	8	4	7	1	10	0	33	0	0
Hillegas, Shawn, Cleveland	3	4	4.34	51	3	0	0	31	7	83.0	67	359	42	40	3	0	1	2	46	0	66	5	0
Holman, Brian, Seattle	13	14	3.69	30	30	5	3	0	0	195.1	199	839	86	80	16	6	7	10	77	6	108	8	0
Holmes, Darren, Milwaukee	1	4	4.72	40	0	0	0	9	3	76.1	90	344	43	40	6	8	6	6	27	7	59	6	0
Honeycutt, Rick, Oakland*	2	4	3.58	43	0	0	0	7	0	37.2	37	167	16	15	3	2	3	0	20	3	26	0	0
Horsman, Vince, Toronto*	0	0	0.00	4	0	0	0	1	0	4.0	2	16	0	0	0	0	0	1	3	0	2	0	0
Hough, Charlie, Chicago	9	10	4.02	31	29	4	1	0	0	199.1	167	858	98	89	21	8	16	11	94	2	107	5	1
Howe, Steve, New York*	3	1	1.68	37	0	0	0	10	3	48.1	39	189	12	9	2	1	1	3	7	2	34	2	0
Hunter, Jim, Milwaukee	2	1	7.26	8	6	0	0	0	0	31.0	45	152	26	25	3	2	1	4	17	0	14	3	0
Ignasiak, Mike, Milwaukee	0	0	5.68	4	1	0	0	0	0	12.2	7	51	8	8	2	0	0	0	6	1	10	0	0
Irvine, Daryl, Boston	0	0	6.00	9	0	0	0	5	0	18.0	25	90	13	12	2	1	0	2	9	1	8	1	0
Jackson, Mike, Seattle	7	7	3.25	72	0	0	0	35	14	88.2	64	363	35	32	5	4	4	6	34	11	74	3	0
Jeffcoat, Mike, Texas*	5	3	4.63	70	0	0	0	21	1	79.2	104	363	46	41	8	5	4	4	25	3	43	3	0

1991 A.L. STATISTICS

Pitcher, Team	W	L	ERA	G	GS	CG	ShO	GF	Sv.	IP	H	TBF	R	ER	HR	SH	SF	HB	BB	Int. BB	SO	WP	Bk.
Johnson, Dave, Baltimore	4	8	7.07	22	14	0	0	0	0	84.0	127	393	68	66	18	0	1	4	24	3	38	0	1
Johnson, Jeff, New York*	6	11	5.95	23	23	0	0	0	0	127.0	156	562	89	84	15	7	4	6	33	1	62	5	1
Johnson, Randy, Seattle*	13	10	3.98	33	33	2	2	0	0	201.1	151	889	96	89	15	9	8	12	152	0	228	12	2
Johnston, Joel, Kansas City	1	0	0.40	13	0	0	0	7	0	22.1	9	85	1	1	0	1	0	1	9	0	21	0	0
Jones, Cal, Seattle	2	0	2.53	27	0	0	0	6	0	46.1	33	194	14	13	0	6	2	1	29	5	42	6	0
Jones, Doug, Cleveland	4	8	5.54	36	0	0	0	29	7	63.1	87	293	42	39	7	2	2	0	17	5	48	1	0
Jones, Stacy, Baltimore	0	0	4.09	4	0	0	0	4	0	11.0	11	49	6	5	1	0	1	0	5	0	10	0	0
Kaiser, Jeff, Detroit*	0	0	9.00	10	0	0	0	6	0	5.0	6	26	5	5	1	0	0	0	5	2	4	0	0
Kamieniecki, Scott, New York	4	4	3.90	9	9	0	0	2	0	55.1	54	239	24	24	8	1	1	3	22	1	34	1	1
Key, Jimmy, Toronto*	16	12	3.05	33	33	2	2	0	0	209.1	207	877	84	71	12	0	5	3	44	3	125	1	2
Kiecker, Dana, Boston	2	2	7.36	18	5	0	0	3	0	40.1	56	194	34	33	6	2	5	2	23	4	21	3	0
Kiely, John, Detroit	0	0	14.85	7	0	0	0	3	0	6.2	13	42	11	11	0	2	1	0	9	2	1	1	0
Kilgus, Paul, Baltimore*	0	2	5.08	38	0	0	0	14	1	62.0	60	267	38	35	8	7	4	3	24	2	32	2	0
King, Eric, Cleveland	6	11	4.60	25	24	2	0	0	0	150.2	166	656	83	77	20	1	8	3	44	4	59	2	2
Kiser, Garland, Cleveland*	0	0	9.64	7	0	0	0	1	0	4.2	7	25	5	5	0	0	0	5	4	0	3	0	0
Klink, Joe, Oakland*	10	3	4.35	62	0	0	0	10	2	62.0	60	266	30	30	4	8	0	5	21	10	34	4	0
Knudson, Mark, Milwaukee	0	3	7.97	12	7	0	0	3	0	35.0	54	174	33	31	8	3	3	1	15	5	23	1	2
Kramer, Tom, Cleveland	0	0	17.36	4	0	0	0	1	0	4.2	10	30	9	9	1	0	3	0	6	0	4	0	0
Krueger, Bill, Seattle*	11	8	3.60	35	25	0	0	2	0	175.0	194	751	82	70	15	6	9	4	60	4	91	10	1
Lamp, Dennis, Boston	6	3	4.70	51	0	0	0	12	0	92.0	100	403	54	48	8	3	2	3	31	7	57	1	0
Langston, Mark, California*	19	8	3.00	34	34	7	0	0	0	246.1	190	992	89	82	30	4	6	2	96	3	183	6	1
Law, Vance, Oakland	0	0	0.00	1	0	0	0	1	0	0.2	0	4	0	0	0	0	0	0	0	0	0	0	0
Leach, Terry, Minnesota	1	2	3.61	50	0	0	0	22	0	67.1	82	292	28	27	3	3	1	0	14	5	32	0	0
Leary, Tim, New York*	4	10	6.49	28	18	0	0	4	0	120.2	150	551	89	87	20	7	1	4	57	1	83	10	1
Lee, Mark, Milwaukee*	2	0	3.86	62	0	0	0	9	1	67.2	72	291	33	29	10	4	2	1	31	7	43	0	0
Leiter, Al, Toronto*	0	0	27.00	3	0	0	0	1	0	1.2	3	13	5	5	0	1	0	0	5	0	1	0	0
Leiter, Mark, Detroit	9	7	4.21	38	15	1	0	7	1	134.2	125	578	66	63	16	5	6	6	50	4	103	2	0
Lewis, Scott, California	3	5	6.27	16	11	0	0	0	0	60.1	81	281	43	42	9	2	0	2	21	0	37	3	0
Lyons, Steve, Boston	0	0	0.00	1	0	0	0	0	0	1.0	2	5	0	0	0	0	0	0	0	0	2	0	0
Machado, Julio, Milwaukee	3	3	3.45	54	0	0	0	13	3	88.2	65	371	36	34	12	3	2	6	55	3	98	5	0
MacDonald, Bob, Toronto*	3	3	2.85	45	0	0	0	10	0	53.2	51	231	19	17	5	2	1	0	25	4	24	1	0
Magnante, Mike, Kansas City*	0	1	2.45	38	0	0	0	10	0	55.0	55	236	19	15	3	1	0	2	23	3	42	1	0
Maldonado, Carlos, Kansas City	0	0	8.22	5	0	0	0	2	0	7.2	11	43	9	7	0	8	1	1	9	1	5	4	0
Manuel, Barry, Texas	1	0	1.13	8	0	0	0	5	0	16.0	7	58	2	2	0	1	0	0	6	0	5	2	0
Manzanillo, Josias, Boston	0	0	18.00	1	0	0	0	1	0	1.0	7	8	2	2	1	0	0	1	3	0	1	0	1
Mathews, Terry, Texas	4	0	3.61	34	2	0	0	8	0	57.1	54	236	24	23	5	2	3	1	18	3	51	5	0
McCaskill, Kirk, California	10	19	4.26	30	30	1	0	0	0	177.2	193	762	93	84	19	6	0	3	66	0	71	6	2
McClure, Bob, California*	0	0	9.31	13	0	0	0	3	0	9.2	13	48	11	10	3	0	0	1	5	0	5	1	0
McDonald, Ben, Baltimore	6	8	4.84	21	21	1	1	0	0	126.1	126	532	71	68	16	2	3	1	43	2	85	3	0
McDowell, Jack, Chicago	17	10	3.41	35	35	15	3	0	0	253.2	212	1028	97	96	19	8	4	4	82	2	191	10	1
McGaffigan, Andy, Kansas City	0	1	4.50	4	0	0	0	2	0	8.0	14	39	5	4	1	0	1	1	2	0	3	0	0
Meacham, Russ, Detroit	2	1	5.20	10	4	0	0	0	0	27.2	35	126	17	16	4	1	3	0	11	2	14	0	0
Mesa, Jose, Baltimore	6	11	5.97	23	23	2	1	0	0	123.2	151	566	86	82	11	5	4	3	62	2	64	3	2
Milacki, Bob, Baltimore	10	9	4.01	31	26	3	0	1	0	184.0	175	758	86	82	17	7	5	5	53	0	108	11	2
Mills, Alan, New York	1	1	4.41	6	2	0	0	3	0	16.1	16	72	9	8	0	2	1	0	11	3	11	2	1
Monteleone, Rich, New York	3	1	3.64	26	0	0	0	10	0	47.0	42	201	27	19	5	2	2	0	19	3	34	1	1

1991 A.L. STATISTICS

Pitcher, Team	W	L	ERA	G	GS	CG	ShO	GF	Sv.	IP	H	TBF	R	ER	HR	SH	SF	HB	BB	Int. BB	SO	WP	Bk.
Montgomery, Jeff, Kansas City	4	8	2.90	67	0	0	0	55	33	90.0	83	376	32	29	6	6	2	4	28	1	77	6	0
Moore, Mike, Oakland	17	8	2.96	33	33	3	1	0	0	210.0	176	887	75	69	11	5	4	5	105	1	153	14	1
Morris, Jack, Minnesota	18	12	3.43	35	35	10	2	0	0	246.2	226	1032	107	94	18	5	8	5	92	5	163	15	1
Morton, Kevin, Boston*	6	5	4.59	16	15	1	0	0	0	86.1	93	379	49	44	9	3	7	5	40	2	45	1	0
Munoz, Mike, Detroit*	0	0	9.64	6	0	0	0	4	0	9.1	14	46	10	10	4	0	1	0	5	0	3	1	0
Murphy, Rob, Seattle*	0	1	3.00	57	0	0	0	26	4	48.0	47	211	17	16	7	3	0	1	19	4	34	4	0
Mussina, Mike, Baltimore	4	5	2.87	12	12	2	0	0	0	87.2	77	349	31	28	7	2	0	1	21	0	52	3	1
Mutis, Jeff, Cleveland*	0	3	11.68	3	3	0	0	0	0	12.1	23	68	16	16	1	5	1	0	7	0	6	1	0
Nagy, Charles, Cleveland	10	15	4.13	33	33	6	1	0	0	211.1	228	914	103	97	15	2	9	9	66	7	109	6	2
Navarro, Jaime, Milwaukee*	15	12	3.92	34	34	10	3	0	0	234.0	237	1002	117	102	18	5	8	6	73	3	114	10	0
Neagle, Dennis, Minnesota*	0	1	4.05	7	3	0	0	2	0	20.0	28	92	9	9	3	7	0	2	7	1	14	1	0
Nelson, Gene, Oakland	1	5	6.84	44	0	0	0	11	1	48.2	60	229	38	37	12	3	4	3	23	3	23	0	0
Nichols, Rod, Cleveland	2	11	3.54	31	16	3	0	4	0	137.1	145	578	63	54	6	6	6	6	30	3	76	3	0
Nolte, Eric, Texas*	0	0	3.38	3	0	0	0	1	0	2.2	3	14	1	1	0	0	0	0	3	0	1	0	0
Nunez, Edwin, Milwaukee	2	1	6.04	23	0	0	0	18	8	25.1	28	119	20	17	6	3	2	1	13	2	24	8	1
Olin, Steve, Cleveland	3	6	3.36	48	0	0	0	32	17	56.1	61	249	26	21	2	5	0	1	23	5	38	0	0
Olson, Gregg, Baltimore	4	6	3.18	72	0	0	0	62	31	73.2	74	319	28	26	1	1	1	1	29	8	72	8	0
Orosco, Jesse, Cleveland*	2	0	3.74	47	0	0	0	20	0	45.2	52	202	20	19	4	1	3	2	15	6	36	1	1
Otto, Dave, Cleveland*	2	8	4.23	18	14	1	0	0	0	100.0	108	425	52	47	7	8	1	3	27	6	47	3	0
Pall, Donn, Chicago	7	2	2.41	51	0	0	0	7	0	71.0	59	282	22	20	7	4	2	4	20	3	40	3	0
Patterson, Ken, Chicago*	3	0	2.83	43	0	0	0	13	1	63.2	48	265	22	20	5	0	2	2	35	3	32	2	0
Pecota, Bill, Kansas City	3	2	4.50	1	0	0	0	0	0	2.0	4	9	1	1	0	0	0	0	0	0	0	0	0
Perez, Melido, Chicago	8	7	3.12	49	8	0	0	16	1	135.2	111	553	49	47	15	3	0	5	52	0	128	11	2
Perez, Pascual, New York	2	4	3.18	14	14	0	0	0	0	73.2	68	299	26	26	4	0	1	0	24	0	41	3	0
Petkovsek, Mark, Texas	0	3	14.46	4	1	0	0	0	0	9.1	21	53	16	15	2	0	1	0	4	0	6	2	0
Petry, Dan, Det.-Bos.	2	7	4.79	30	6	0	0	8	1	77.0	87	338	52	41	12	1	3	3	31	5	30	2	0
Plesac, Dan, Milwaukee*	2	7	4.29	45	10	0	0	25	8	92.1	92	402	49	44	12	3	7	3	39	5	61	2	0
Plunk, Eric, New York	2	5	4.76	43	8	0	0	6	0	111.2	128	521	69	59	18	6	4	1	62	1	103	6	2
Plympton, Jeff, Boston	0	2	0.00	4	0	0	0	0	0	5.1	5	24	14	0	0	0	0	0	4	0	2	2	0
Poole, Jim, Tex.-Bal.*	3	2	2.36	29	0	0	0	5	0	42.0	29	166	11	11	3	3	4	0	12	2	38	2	0
Radinsky, Scott, Chicago*	5	5	2.02	67	0	0	0	19	8	71.1	53	289	18	16	4	4	2	2	23	3	49	0	0
Reardon, Jeff, Boston	1	4	3.03	57	0	0	0	51	40	59.1	54	248	21	20	9	0	3	4	16	3	44	0	0
Rhodes, Arthur, Baltimore*	0	3	8.00	8	2	0	0	0	0	36.0	47	174	35	32	4	1	2	1	23	1	23	0	0
Rice, Pat, Seattle	0	1	3.00	7	5	0	0	0	0	21.0	18	91	10	7	1	3	4	2	10	1	12	0	0
Ritz, Kevin, Detroit	0	3	11.74	11	1	0	0	3	0	15.1	17	86	22	20	9	0	2	2	22	1	9	3	1
Robinson, Jeff D., California	4	9	5.37	39	19	0	0	16	3	57.0	56	252	34	20	11	3	2	6	29	4	57	10	0
Robinson, Jeff M., Baltimore	4	9	5.18	21	19	0	0	0	0	104.1	119	472	62	60	12	0	6	1	51	2	65	8	1
Robinson, Ron, Milwaukee	1	1	6.23	1	1	0	0	0	0	4.1	6	21	3	3	0	0	0	0	3	0	0	0	0
Rogers, Kenny, Texas*	10	10	5.42	63	9	0	0	20	5	109.2	121	511	80	66	14	5	6	6	61	7	73	3	0
Rosenthal, Wayne, Texas	1	4	5.25	36	0	0	0	8	1	70.1	71	321	43	41	9	1	3	1	36	1	61	8	1
Russell, Jeff, Texas	6	4	3.29	68	0	0	0	56	30	79.1	71	336	36	29	11	3	5	1	26	8	52	6	0
Ryan, Nolan, Texas	12	6	2.91	27	27	2	2	0	0	173.0	102	683	58	56	12	2	9	5	72	0	203	8	1
Saberhagen, Bret, Kansas City	13	8	3.07	28	28	7	2	0	0	196.1	165	789	76	67	12	7	3	9	45	5	136	8	1
Sanderson, Scott, New York	16	10	3.81	34	34	2	0	0	0	208.0	200	837	95	88	22	2	5	3	29	0	130	4	1
Schatzeder, Dan, Kansas City*	0	0	9.45	8	0	0	0	2	1	6.2	11	37	9	7	0	3	0	0	7	1	4	0	0
Schiraldi, Calvin, Texas	0	1	11.57	3	0	0	0	1	0	4.2	5	25	6	6	3	1	0	0	5	1	1	0	0

1991 A.L. STATISTICS

Pitcher, Team	W	L	ERA	G	GS	CG	ShO	GF	Sv.	IP	H	TBF	R	ER	HR	SH	SF	HB	BB	Int. BB	SO	WP	Bk.
Schooler, Mike, Seattle	3	3	3.67	34	0	0	0	23	7	34.1	25	138	14	14	2	1	1	0	10	0	31	2	1
Seanez, Rudy, Cleveland	0	1	16.20	5	0	0	0	4	0	5.0	10	33	12	9	2	0	0	0	7	0	7	1	0
Searcy, Steve, Detroit*	0	2	8.41	16	5	0	0	6	0	40.2	52	201	40	38	8	2	3	4	30	0	32	4	0
Shaw, Jeff, Cleveland	0	5	3.36	29	1	0	0	9	1	72.1	72	311	34	27	6	1	4	0	27	5	31	6	0
Show, Eric, Oakland	1	2	5.92	23	5	0	0	6	0	51.2	62	231	34	34	5	1	4	4	17	1	20	2	1
Slusarski, Joe, Oakland	5	7	5.27	20	19	1	0	0	0	109.1	121	486	69	64	14	4	4	4	52	0	60	4	0
Smith, Roy, Baltimore	5	5	5.60	17	14	0	1	0	0	80.1	99	348	52	50	9	5	3	9	24	1	25	3	1
Stewart, Dave, Oakland	11	11	5.18	35	35	2	0	0	0	226.0	245	1014	135	130	24	4	15	5	105	0	144	13	0
Stieb, Dave, Toronto	4	3	3.17	9	9	1	0	0	0	59.2	52	244	22	21	4	5	1	2	23	0	29	0	0
Stottlemyre, Todd, Toronto	15	8	3.78	34	34	1	0	0	0	219.0	194	921	97	92	21	4	8	12	75	3	116	4	1
Swan, Russ, Seattle*	6	2	3.43	63	0	0	0	11	2	78.2	81	336	35	30	8	0	1	7	28	7	33	8	1
Swift, Bill, Seattle	1	2	1.99	71	0	0	0	30	17	90.1	74	359	22	20	3	6	0	1	26	3	48	2	1
Swindell, Greg, Cleveland*	9	16	3.48	33	33	7	2	0	0	238.0	241	971	112	92	21	2	8	3	31	1	169	3	1
Tanana, Frank, Detroit*	13	12	3.77	33	33	3	1	0	0	217.1	217	920	98	91	26	13	9	3	78	9	107	3	1
Tapani, Kevin, Minnesota	16	9	2.99	34	34	4	0	0	0	244.0	225	974	84	81	23	12	6	2	40	0	135	3	3
Taylor, Wade, New York	7	12	6.27	23	22	0	0	0	0	116.1	144	528	85	81	13	9	7	7	53	0	72	3	3
Telford, Anthony, Baltimore	0	0	4.05	9	1	0	0	4	0	26.2	27	109	12	12	3	2	0	5	6	2	24	0	3
Terrell, Walt, Detroit	12	14	4.24	35	33	8	2	1	0	218.2	257	954	115	103	16	10	9	9	79	10	80	8	0
Thigpen, Bobby, Chicago	7	5	3.49	67	0	0	0	58	30	69.2	63	309	32	27	10	7	2	4	38	8	47	6	0
Timlin, Mike, Toronto	11	6	3.16	63	3	0	0	17	3	108.1	94	463	43	38	6	6	1	3	50	11	85	2	0
Valdez, Efrain, Cleveland*	0	0	1.50	7	0	0	0	1	0	6.0	5	27	1	1	0	1	2	1	3	0	1	5	0
Valdez, Sergio, Cleveland	0	0	5.51	6	2	0	0	0	0	16.1	15	70	11	10	3	1	1	0	5	0	11	0	0
Valenzuela, Fernando, California*	0	2	12.15	2	2	0	0	0	0	6.2	14	36	10	9	1	1	1	2	2	0	5	1	0
Van Poppel, Todd, Oakland	0	1	9.64	1	1	0	0	0	0	4.2	7	21	5	5	1	0	0	0	2	0	6	1	0
Wagner, Hector, Kansas City	0	1	7.20	2	2	0	0	0	0	10.0	16	49	10	8	2	0	0	0	3	0	5	0	0
Walker, Mike, Cleveland	0	0	2.08	5	0	0	0	3	0	4.1	6	22	1	1	0	2	1	1	1	0	5	0	0
Walton, Bruce, Oakland	0	0	6.23	12	0	0	0	5	0	13.0	11	56	9	9	3	0	0	0	6	0	10	3	0
Wapnick, Steve, Chicago	0	0	1.80	6	0	0	0	4	0	5.0	2	22	1	1	0	0	0	1	4	0	1	0	0
Ward, Duane, Toronto	7	6	2.77	81	0	0	0	46	23	107.1	80	428	36	33	11	3	4	2	33	3	132	6	0
Wayne, Gary, Minnesota*	1	0	5.11	8	0	0	0	2	0	12.1	11	52	7	7	1	1	1	4	4	1	7	0	0
Weathers, Dave, Toronto	1	0	4.91	15	0	0	0	4	0	14.2	15	79	9	8	1	2	4	2	17	3	13	6	1
Wegman, Bill, Milwaukee	15	7	2.84	28	28	7	2	0	0	193.1	176	785	76	61	16	6	7	7	40	0	89	0	0
Welch, Bob, Oakland	12	13	4.58	35	35	7	0	0	0	220.0	220	950	124	112	25	6	6	11	91	1	101	6	2
Wells, David, Toronto*	15	10	3.72	40	28	2	0	3	1	198.1	188	811	88	82	24	6	6	5	49	0	106	3	3
West, David, Minnesota*	4	4	4.54	15	12	0	0	1	0	71.1	66	305	37	36	13	2	3	1	28	0	52	3	0
Weston, Mickey, Toronto	0	0	0.00	2	0	0	0	0	0	2.0	1	8	0	0	0	0	0	0	1	0	1	0	0
Williamson, Mark, Baltimore	5	5	4.48	65	0	0	0	21	4	80.1	87	357	42	40	9	5	5	1	35	7	53	7	2
Willis, Carl, Minnesota	8	3	2.63	40	0	0	0	9	2	89.0	76	355	31	26	4	3	4	0	19	5	53	4	0
Wills, Frank, Toronto	3	7	6.09	4	0	0	0	3	0	4.1	8	27	8	8	2	0	0	1	5	0	2	2	0
Witt, Bobby, Texas	3	7	6.62	17	16	1	1	0	0	88.2	84	413	66	60	8	3	4	1	74	3	82	8	1
Witt, Mike, New York	0	1	10.13	2	2	0	0	0	0	5.1	8	26	7	6	3	0	0	0	19	1	2	1	0
York, Mike, Cleveland*	1	4	6.75	14	4	0	0	3	0	34.2	45	163	29	26	2	3	4	2	34	0	19	2	3
Young, Curt, Oakland*	4	2	5.00	41	4	0	0	6	0	68.1	74	306	38	38	8	0	4	0	19	3	27	2	1
Young, Cliff, California*	1	0	4.26	11	1	0	0	6	0	12.2	12	49	6	6	3	0	0	0	3	1	6	5	0
Young, Matt, Boston*	3	7	5.18	19	16	0	0	1	0	88.2	92	404	55	51	4	1	2	2	53	2	69	5	0

PITCHERS WITH TWO OR MORE TEAMS

Pitcher, Team	W	L	ERA	G	GS	CG	ShO	Sv.	GF	IP	H	TBF	R	ER	HR	SH	SF	HB	BB	Int. BB	SO	WP	Bk.
Boucher, Denis, Toronto*	0	3	4.58	7	7	0	0	0	0	35.1	39	162	20	18	6	3	1	2	16	0	16	1	4
Boucher, Denis, Cleveland*	1	4	8.34	5	5	0	0	0	0	22.2	35	108	21	21	6	1	0	0	8	0	13	1	0
Candiotti, Tom, Cleveland	1	6	2.24	15	15	3	0	0	0	108.1	88	442	35	27	6	6	7	2	28	0	86	6	0
Candiotti, Tom, Toronto	6	7	2.98	19	19	3	0	0	0	129.2	114	539	47	43	6	3	4	4	45	1	81	5	0
Hawkins, Andy, New York	0	2	9.95	4	3	0	0	0	1	12.2	23	66	15	14	5	0	0	0	6	0	5	0	1
Hawkins, Andy, Oakland	2	4	4.79	15	14	1	0	0	1	77.0	68	333	41	41	9	5	3	1	36	3	40	0	0
Petry, Dan, Detroit	2	3	4.94	17	6	0	0	0	1	54.2	66	240	35	30	9	1	1	0	19	3	18	0	0
Petry, Dan, Boston	0	0	4.43	13	0	0	0	0	7	22.1	21	98	17	11	3	0	1	2	12	0	12	0	0
Poole, Jim, Texas*	0	0	4.50	5	0	0	0	1	1	6.0	10	31	4	3	0	0	0	1	3	0	4	0	0
Poole, Jim, Baltimore*	3	2	2.00	24	0	0	0	0	3	36.0	19	135	10	8	3	3	2	0	9	2	34	2	0

NOTE—The following pitchers combined to pitch shutout games: Baltimore (6)—Johnson, Kilgus, Williamson and Olson; Robinson and Kilgus; McDonald, Williamson, Flanagan and Olson; Milacki and Olson; Milacki, Flanagan, Williamson and Olson; McDonald, Flanagan, Williamson and Poole; Boston (9)—Clemens, Fossas and Reardon; Clemens, Gray and Reardon; Bolton, Gray, Fossas and Reardon; Young, Gray and Reardon; Darwin and Harris; Bolton and Reardon; Clemens and Gray; Harris, Gray and Reardon; Hesketh, Harris and Reardon; California (7)—J. Abbott, Eichhorn and Harvey 2; Langston and Robinson; McCaskill, Eichhorn and Harvey; McCaskill and Harvey; Langston, Eichhorn and Harvey; Finley, Eichhorn and Harvey; Chicago (3)—Hibbard and Thigpen; Hough and Radinsky; Hibbard, Perez and Thigpen; Cleveland (5)—Candiotti, Orosco, Olin and Jones; Nagy, Olin and Jones; Nagy and Hillegas; Swindell and Hillegas; Otto and Olin; Detroit (4)—Petry and Gibson; Tanana and Henneman; Gullickson and Cerutti; Gullickson, Henneman, Gleaton and Gibson; Kansas City (5)—Appier and Montgomery; Gubicza and Crawford; Aquino and Montgomery; Boddicker, Magnante and Davis; Boddicker, Magnante, Johnston and Montgomery; Milwaukee (5)—Bosio and Lee; Higuera, Machado and Plesac; Plesac, Machado and Nunez;

Wegman and Henry; Bosio, Machado, Lee and Henry; Minnesota (6)—Erickson and Aguilera; Anderson and Aguilera; Aguilera; Morris and Willis; West, Bedrosian and Aguilera; Erickson, Leach and Guthrie; Tapani and Abbott; New York (9)—Johnson and Farr 2; Sanderson and Cadaret; Eiland and Farr; Sanderson and Farr; Johnson, Habyan and Howe; Taylor, Cadaret and Guetterman; Perez and Farr; Sanderson, Habyan and Cadaret; Oakland (7)—Slusarski and Eckersley; Hawkins, Allison, Chitren, Klink and Eckersley; Darling, Honeycutt and Eckersley; Moore, Klink, Show, Honeycutt and Eckersley; Moore, Honeycutt and Eckersley; Moore and Eckersley; Moore, Klink and Eckersley; Seattle (8)—Holman and Swift 2; Bankhead and Swan; Johnson and Swift; Hanson and Murphy; Johnson, Schooler, Jackson and Murphy; Hanson and Schooler; Krueger and Harris; Texas (6)—Ryan and Russell; Guzman and Jeffcoat; Ryan and Rogers; Guzman and Russell; Boyd, Mathews and Rogers; Bohanon and Russell; Toronto (14)—Wells and Ward 2; Key, Timlin and Ward 2; Candiotti and Henke 2; Stieb, Timlin and Ward; Wells, Ward and Henke; Timlin, MacDonald, Acker and Henke; Guzman and Ward; Guzman, Ward and Henke; Candiotti, Ward and Henke; Candiotti, Ward and Timlin; Stottlemyre and Wells.

FIELDING

TEAM

Team	Pct.	G	PO	A	E	TC	DP	TP	PB
Baltimore	.985	162	4373	1807	91	6271	172	0	8
Minnesota	.985	162	4348	1779	95	6222	161	0	12
California	.984	162	4325	1858	102	6285	156	0	23
Detroit	.983	162	4351	1796	104	6251	171	0	12
Seattle	.983	162	4393	1783	110	6286	187	2	24
Oakland	.982	162	4333	1608	107	6048	150	0	8
Chicago	.982	162	4434	1740	116	6290	151	0	20
Boston	.981	162	4319	1768	116	6203	165	0	11
Milwaukee	.981	162	4391	1770	118	6279	176	0	16
Kansas City	.980	162	4398	1694	125	6217	141	0	11
Toronto	.980	162	4388	1686	127	6201	115	0	21
Texas	.979	162	4437	1712	134	6283	138	0	15
New York	.979	162	4332	1752	133	6217	181	0	13
Cleveland	.976	162	4324	1712	149	6185	150	0	19
Totals	.981	1134	61146	24465	1627	87238	2214	2	213

INDIVIDUAL

FIRST BASEMEN

*Throws lefthanded.

Leader, Team	Pct.	G	PO	A	E	TC	DP
O'BRIEN, Seattle	.997	132	1047	86	3	1136	124

Player, Team	Pct.	G	PO	A	E	TC	DP
Aldrete, Cleveland*	.994	47	313	22	2	337	31
Allanson, Detroit	1.000	2	7	0	0	7	2
Amaral, Seattle	1.000	1	6	1	0	7	1
Barnes, Detroit	1.000	9	24	1	0	25	2
Benzinger, K.C.	.996	75	651	38	3	692	57
Bergman, Detroit*	.997	49	364	29	1	394	42
Bradley, Seattle	.750	1	3	0	1	4	0
Brett, Kansas City	.989	10	87	5	1	93	6
Brock, Milwaukee	1.000	25	150	10	0	160	18
Bush, Minnesota*	.951	12	35	4	2	41	6
Canale, Milwaukee	.983	19	101	15	2	118	9
Cochrane, Seattle	1.000	4	21	1	0	22	2
Cromartie, K.C.*	.996	29	215	9	1	225	20
Cron, California	1.000	5	32	6	0	38	1
Daugherty, Texas*	1.000	11	68	3	0	71	4
Davis, Seattle	1.000	14	116	7	0	123	14
Davis, Baltimore	.976	36	288	38	8	334	35
de los Santos, Detroit	1.000	2	2	0	0	2	0
Dempsey, Milwaukee	.000	1	0	0	0	0	0
Eisenreich, K.C.*	.991	15	100	11	1	112	12
Fielder, Detroit	.993	122	1055	83	8	1146	110
Fisk, Chicago	.980	12	90	10	2	102	8
Gomez, Baltimore	1.000	3	16	0	0	16	0
Gonzales, Toronto	1.000	2	4	0	0	4	0
Harper, Minnesota	1.000	1	1	0	0	1	0
Hill, California	.947	3	15	3	1	19	2
Hoiles, Baltimore	1.000	2	10	1	0	11	1
Howell, California	1.000	3	18	2	0	20	2
Howitt, Oakland	1.000	1	8	0	0	8	0
Hrbek, Minnesota	.994	128	1138	95	8	1241	110
Jacoby, Cle.-Oak.	.989	58	404	35	5	444	30
James, Cleveland	1.000	15	95	8	0	103	7
Jefferson, Cleveland*	.993	26	252	24	2	278	28
Joyner, California*	.994	141	1335	98	8	1441	124
Kittle, Chicago	.982	15	101	6	2	109	8
Larkin, Minnesota	.997	39	281	19	1	301	22
Law, Oakland	1.000	1	2	0	0	2	0
Leyritz, New York	1.000	3	5	0	0	5	1
Lopez, Cleveland	.976	10	75	7	2	84	7
Lyons, California	1.000	2	10	1	0	11	0
Lyons, Boston	.000	2	0	0	0	0	0
Maas, New York*	.983	36	317	23	6	346	22
Manto, Cleveland	.975	14	75	3	2	80	5
Marshall, Bos.-Cal.	.984	6	60	1	1	62	6

Player, Team	Pct.	G	PO	A	E	TC	DP
Martinez, Kansas City	.991	43	307	35	3	345	30
Martinez, Baltimore*	1.000	1	4	0	0	4	0
Martinez, Cleveland	.968	31	229	12	8	249	30
T. Martinez, Seattle	.993	29	249	22	2	273	24
Mattingly, New York*	.996	127	1119	77	5	1201	135
Maurer, Texas*	1.000	4	7	3	0	10	2
McGwire, Oakland	.997	152	1191	101	4	1296	120
McIntosh, Milwaukee	1.000	1	1	0	0	1	0
McKnight, Baltimore	1.000	2	14	1	0	15	1
Merullo, Chicago	.989	16	80	6	1	87	10
Meulens, New York	.973	7	35	1	1	37	6
Milligan, Baltimore	.990	106	929	81	10	1020	92
Molitor, Milwaukee	.986	46	389	32	6	427	52
Morman, Kansas City	1.000	8	44	3	0	47	2
Newman, Minnesota	1.000	1	7	0	0	7	0
O'Brien, Seattle*	.997	132	1047	86	3	1136	124
Olerud, Toronto*	.996	135	1120	78	5	1203	77
Palmeiro, Texas*	.992	157	1305	96	12	1413	119
Parrish, California	1.000	3	12	0	0	12	0
Pasqua, Chicago*	.991	83	511	43	5	559	45
Pecota, Kansas City	1.000	8	39	0	0	39	3
Pedre, Kansas City	1.000	1	6	0	0	6	0
Powell, Seattle	1.000	7	18	2	0	20	4
Quintana, Boston	.993	138	1026	101	8	1135	101
Quirk, Oakland	1.000	8	44	6	0	50	4
Riles, Oakland	1.000	5	32	5	0	37	3
Rose, California	1.000	3	21	1	0	22	1
Salas, Detroit	1.000	5	6	1	0	7	0
Segui, Baltimore*	.996	42	206	22	1	229	22
Snyder, Chi.-Tor.	.993	22	133	8	1	142	10
Sorrento, Minnesota	1.000	13	70	7	0	77	7
Sprague, Toronto	1.000	22	143	11	0	154	12
Stanley, Texas	1.000	12	48	6	0	54	1
Steinbach, Oakland	.962	9	45	5	2	52	4
Stevens, California*	.989	11	85	6	1	92	5
Stubbs, Milwaukee*	.991	92	824	82	8	914	78
Tabler, Toronto	.985	20	182	14	3	199	11
Tettleton, Detroit	1.000	1	2	0	0	2	0
Thomas, Chicago	.996	56	459	27	2	488	43
Valle, Seattle	1.000	2	7	0	0	7	0
Vaughn, Boston	.985	49	378	26	6	410	43
Ventura, Chicago	1.000	31	91	4	0	95	8
Witmeyer, Oakland*	1.000	8	32	3	0	35	2

TRIPLE PLAYS: T. Martinez, Seattle; O'Brien, Seattle.

FIRST BASEMEN WITH TWO OR MORE TEAMS

Player, Team	Pct.	G	PO	A	E	TC	DP
Jacoby, Cleveland	.988	55	379	32	5	416	27
Jacoby, Oakland	1.000	3	25	3	0	28	3

FIELDING

1991 A.L. STATISTICS

FIELDING

Player, Team	Pct.	G	PO	A	E	TC	DP
Marshall, Boston	.979	5	46	0	1	47	4
Marshall, California	1.000	1	14	1	0	15	2
Snyder, Chicago	.991	18	107	6	1	114	10
Snyder, Toronto	1.000	4	26	2	0	28	0

SECOND BASEMEN

Leader, Team	Pct.	G	PO	A	E	TC	DP
WHITAKER, Detroit	.994	135	255	361	4	620	91

Player, Team	Pct.	G	PO	A	E	TC	DP
Alomar, Toronto	.981	160	333	447	15	795	79
Amaral, Seattle	1.000	5	4	11	0	15	4
Amaro, California	.917	4	6	5	1	12	1
Baerga, Cleveland	.971	75	163	238	12	413	59
Barnes, Detroit	1.000	7	5	10	0	15	0
Bell, Baltimore	.973	77	104	189	8	301	39
Bernazard, Detroit	.900	2	3	6	1	10	3
Blankenship, Oakland	.983	45	72	101	3	176	23
Bordick, Oakland	.929	5	9	4	1	14	2
Briley, Seattle	.000	1	0	0	0	0	0
Brosius, Oakland	1.000	18	4	5	0	9	1
Browne, Cleveland	.964	47	80	109	7	196	17
Brumley, Boston	1.000	7	12	21	0	33	8
Buechele, Texas	1.000	13	12	35	0	47	3
Cole, Kansas City	1.000	5	1	4	0	5	0
Cora, Chicago	.970	80	103	184	9	296	33
Diaz, Texas	1.000	20	22	26	0	48	6
Disarcina, California	1.000	7	12	11	0	23	2
Escobar, Cleveland	1.000	4	10	8	0	18	4
Fariss, Texas	1.000	4	4	9	0	13	3
Fletcher, Chicago	.992	86	177	191	3	371	49
Flora, California	.846	3	8	3	2	13	1
Franco, Texas	.979	146	294	372	14	680	80
Gallego, Oakland	.989	135	243	370	7	620	69
Gantner, Milwaukee	.977	59	109	190	7	306	31
Gonzales, Toronto	1.000	11	4	13	0	17	1
Grebeck, Chicago	.994	36	62	97	1	160	19
Hemond, Oakland	1.000	7	7	12	0	19	3
Henderson, Oakland	.000	1	0	0	0	0	0
Hill, California	.971	39	75	91	5	171	23
Howard, Kansas City	.990	26	36	60	1	97	10
Howell, California	.968	12	24	36	2	62	4
Huff, Cle.-Chi.	1.000	4	1	3	0	4	0
Hulett, Baltimore	.968	26	29	31	2	62	5
Huson, Texas	1.000	2	0	2	0	2	1
P. Kelly, New York	.976	19	35	47	2	84	15
Knoblauch, Minnesota	.975	148	249	460	18	727	94
Larkin, Minnesota	.000	1	0	0	0	0	0
Lewis, Cleveland	.966	50	87	140	8	235	29
Liriano, Kansas City	1.000	10	11	23	0	34	3
Lyons, Boston	.977	16	18	25	1	44	6
Manrique, Oakland	1.000	2	3	6	0	9	1
Naehring, Boston	1.000	1	1	2	0	3	0
Newman, Minnesota	.992	35	52	76	1	129	15
Pagliarulo, Minnesota	.000	1	0	0	0	0	0
Paredes, Detroit	.958	7	11	12	1	24	5
Pecota, Kansas City	1.000	34	46	34	0	80	8
Perezchica, Cleveland	1.000	2	1	6	0	7	0
Phillips, Detroit	.996	36	108	118	1	227	34
Randolph, Milwaukee	.969	121	237	378	20	635	96
Reed, Boston	.982	152	312	444	14	770	109
Reynolds, Seattle	.978	159	348	463	18	829	133
Riles, Oakland	1.000	7	10	12	0	22	4
B. Ripken, Baltimore	.986	103	201	284	7	492	75
Rodriguez, New York	1.000	3	0	1	0	1	0
Rose, California	1.000	8	12	26	0	38	6
Sax, New York	.990	149	274	443	7	724	107
Schaefer, Seattle	1.000	11	10	13	0	23	5
Shumpert, K.C.	.975	144	249	368	16	633	81
Sojo, California	.981	107	228	326	11	565	78
Surhoff, Milwaukee	.000	1	0	0	0	0	0
Sveum, Milwaukee	1.000	2	3	2	0	5	0
Turner, Baltimore	1.000	1	0	1	0	1	0
Vizquel, Seattle	.000	1	0	0	0	0	0
Whitaker, Detroit	.994	135	255	361	4	620	91

TRIPLE PLAY: Reynolds, Seattle.

SECOND BASEMEN WITH TWO OR MORE TEAMS

Player, Team	Pct.	G	PO	A	E	TC	DP
Huff, Cleveland	1.000	2	1	3	0	4	0
Huff, Chicago	.000	2	0	0	0	0	0

THIRD BASEMEN

Leader, Team	Pct.	G	PO	A	E	TC	DP
BUECHELE, Texas	.991	111	87	239	3	329	20

Player, Team	Pct.	G	PO	A	E	TC	DP
Amaral, Seattle	1.000	2	0	1	0	1	0
Baerga, Cleveland	.944	89	54	183	14	251	14
Barnes, Detroit	.939	17	9	22	2	33	2
Berry, Kansas City	.970	30	13	52	2	67	3
Bichette, Milwaukee	.000	1	0	0	0	0	0
Blankenship, Oakland	1.000	14	7	21	0	28	2
Blowers, New York	.870	14	4	16	3	23	1
Boggs, Boston	.968	140	89	276	12	377	34
Bordick, Oakland	.000	1	0	0	0	0	0
Bradley, Seattle	.667	4	0	2	1	3	0
Briley, Seattle	.000	1	0	0	0	0	0
Brosius, Oakland	1.000	7	3	10	0	13	1
Browne, Cleveland	.867	15	7	32	6	45	4
Brumley, Boston	.935	17	10	19	2	31	3
Buechele, Texas	.991	111	87	239	3	329	20
Cochrane, Seattle	.833	13	11	14	5	30	1
Cooper, Boston	.933	13	6	22	2	30	1
de los Santos, Detroit	.500	2	0	1	1	2	0
Diaz, Texas	1.000	8	3	7	0	10	1
Disarcina, California	1.000	2	2	6	0	8	1
Escobar, Cleveland	.000	1	0	0	0	0	0
Espinoza, New York	1.000	2	2	3	0	5	0
Fletcher, Chicago	1.000	4	1	1	0	2	0
Fryman, Detroit	.946	86	45	147	11	203	13
Gaetti, California	.965	152	111	353	17	481	39
Gantner, Milwaukee	.976	90	51	155	5	211	15
Giannelli, Toronto	.923	9	0	12	1	13	2
Gomez, Baltimore	.972	105	62	184	7	253	20
Gonzales, Toronto	.923	26	7	41	4	52	3
Grebeck, Chicago	.933	49	22	48	5	75	6
Gruber, Toronto	.962	111	97	231	13	341	16
Hemond, Oakland	1.000	2	3	0	0	3	0
Hernandez, Texas	1.000	1	1	1	0	2	1
Howard, Kansas City	.000	1	0	0	0	0	0
Howell, California	1.000	8	4	17	0	21	1
Hulett, Baltimore	.976	39	18	65	2	85	8
Humphreys, New York	.900	6	1	8	1	10	0
Huson, Texas	.000	1	0	0	0	0	0
Jacoby, Cle.-Oak.	.987	67	49	101	2	152	12
P. Kelly, New York	.926	80	43	157	16	216	14
Lansford, Oakland	1.000	4	0	3	0	3	0
Larkin, Minnesota	.000	1	0	0	0	0	0
Law, Oakland	.951	67	36	62	5	103	7
Leius, Minnesota	.953	79	41	100	7	148	8
Leyritz, New York	.909	18	9	21	3	33	2
Livingstone, Detroit	.980	43	32	67	2	101	6
Lopez, Cleveland	.000	1	0	0	0	0	0
Lovullo, New York	.940	22	14	33	3	50	7
Lyons, Boston	.929	12	9	17	2	28	0
Manto, Cleveland	.929	32	21	58	6	85	12
E. Martinez, Seattle	.962	144	84	299	15	398	25
Mulliniks, Toronto	1.000	5	2	3	0	5	0
Naehring, Boston	1.000	2	0	2	0	2	1
Newman, Minnesota	.963	35	8	18	1	27	1
Pagliarulo, Minnesota	.965	118	56	248	11	315	30
Palmer, Texas	.944	50	27	74	6	107	5
Paredes, Detroit	.000	1	0	0	0	0	0
Pecota, Kansas City	.983	102	69	158	4	231	14
Perezchica, Cleveland	1.000	3	0	1	0	1	0
Petralli, Texas	.750	7	1	5	2	8	2
Phillips, Detroit	.957	46	26	84	5	115	7
Quirk, Oakland	.000	1	0	0	0	0	0
Riles, Oakland	.939	69	54	101	10	165	14
Rose, California	1.000	4	2	4	0	6	0
Sax, New York	.824	5	3	11	3	17	0
Schaefer, Seattle	.960	30	4	20	1	25	3
Seitzer, Kansas City	.940	68	45	127	11	183	8

Player, Team	Pct.	G	PO	A	E	TC	DP
Sheffield, Milwaukee ...	.922	43	29	65	8	102	7
Snyder, Toronto	.875	3	0	7	1	8	0
Sojo, California	1.000	1	1	3	0	4	0
Sprague, Toronto	.870	35	19	61	12	92	2
Stanley, Texas	.833	6	1	4	1	6	1
Surhoff, Milwaukee	1.000	5	3	3	0	6	0
Sveum, Milwaukee	.957	38	26	62	4	92	9
Thome, Cleveland	.900	27	12	60	8	80	6
Velarde, New York	.935	50	31	85	8	124	8
Ventura, Chicago	.959	151	134	287	18	439	29
Walling, Texas	.950	14	6	13	1	20	0
Worthington, Bal.	.975	30	26	51	2	79	3
Zuvella, Kansas City ...	.000	2	0	0	0	0	0

TRIPLE PLAY: E. Martinez, Seattle.

THIRD BASEMEN WITH TWO OR MORE TEAMS

Player, Team	Pct.	G	PO	A	E	TC	DP
Jacoby, Cleveland	1.000	15	11	29	0	40	3
Jacoby, Oakland	.982	52	38	72	2	112	9

SHORTSTOPS

Leader, Team	Pct.	G	PO	A	E	TC	DP
C. RIPKEN, Baltimore .	.986	162	267	528	11	806	114

Player, Team	Pct.	G	PO	A	E	TC	DP
Amaral, Seattle	.750	2	3	3	2	8	1
Baerga, Cleveland	.000	2	0	0	1	1	0
Bell, Baltimore	.929	15	3	10	1	14	1
Beltre, Chicago	1.000	8	1	5	0	6	1
Bordick, Oakland	.972	84	137	209	10	356	44
Brumley, Boston	.950	31	19	76	5	100	9
Buechele, Texas	1.000	4	0	1	0	1	0
Cole, Kansas City	1.000	1	1	0	0	1	0
Cora, Chicago	.923	5	4	8	1	13	3
Diaz, Texas	.962	65	68	110	7	185	25
Disarcina, California ...	.915	10	15	28	4	47	2
Escobar, Cleveland	1.000	5	5	5	0	10	0
Espinoza, New York	.969	147	223	438	21	682	113
Fermin, Cleveland	.980	129	214	372	12	598	74
Fryman, Detroit	.963	71	108	207	12	327	48
Gagne, Minnesota	.984	137	181	377	9	567	69
Gallego, Oakland	.959	55	40	76	5	121	21
Gonzales, Toronto	.973	36	46	64	3	113	13
Grebeck, Chicago	.935	26	20	38	4	62	9
Green, Texas	.968	8	10	20	1	31	5
Guillen, Chicago	.970	149	249	439	21	709	88
Hemond, Cleveland	1.000	1	0	1	0	1	0
Hernandez, Texas	.975	44	48	110	4	162	17
Hill, California	.983	29	37	82	2	121	11
Howard, Kansas City	.962	63	93	188	11	292	30
Hulett, Baltimore	.000	1	0	0	0	0	0
Huson, Texas	.965	116	141	267	15	423	42
Knoblauch, Minnesota	.000	2	0	0	0	0	0
Law, Oakland	1.000	3	1	4	0	5	0
Lee, Toronto	.967	138	194	360	19	573	52
Leius, Minnesota	1.000	19	15	29	0	44	7
Lewis, Cleveland	.993	36	42	91	1	134	18
Lyons, Boston	1.000	1	1	1	0	2	0
Magallanes, Cleveland	1.000	2	0	1	0	1	0
Manrique, Oakland	.955	7	7	14	1	22	2
Naehring, Boston	.956	17	16	49	3	68	8
Newman, Minnesota	.987	55	63	90	2	155	23
Paredes, Detroit	.000	1	0	0	0	0	0
Pecota, Kansas City	1.000	9	8	14	0	22	3
Perezchica, Cleveland .	1.000	6	2	4	0	6	1
Phillips, Detroit	.981	13	21	32	1	54	10
Reed, Boston	1.000	6	2	5	0	7	1
Riles, Oakland	.977	20	17	25	1	43	5
C. Ripken, Baltimore	.986	162	267	528	11	806	114
Rivera, Boston	.959	129	180	386	24	590	87
Rodriguez, New York	.957	11	11	33	2	46	9
Schaefer, Seattle	.968	46	65	87	5	157	23
Schofield, California	.975	133	186	398	15	599	83
Sojo, California	1.000	2	2	6	0	8	0
Spiers, Milwaukee	.970	128	201	345	17	563	93
Stillwell, Kansas City ..	.959	118	163	263	18	444	66
Sveum, Milwaukee	.968	51	56	125	6	187	24
Trammell, Detroit	.979	92	131	296	9	436	60
Velarde, New York	.931	31	32	63	7	102	16
Vizquel, Seattle	.980	138	224	422	13	659	105
Weiss, Oakland	.970	40	64	99	5	168	21
Zosky, Toronto	1.000	18	12	26	0	38	5

OUTFIELDERS

*Throws lefthanded.

Leader, Team	Pct.	G	PO	A	E	TC	DP
WHITE, Toronto	.998	156	439	8	1	448	2

Player, Team	Pct.	G	PO	A	E	TC	DP
Abner, California	1.000	38	72	3	0	75	1
Aldrete, Cleveland*	1.000	16	21	1	0	22	0
Allred, Cleveland*	.972	42	105	1	3	109	0
Amaro, California	1.000	5	3	1	0	4	0
Anderson, Baltimore* .	.981	101	150	3	3	156	0
Baines, Oakland*	.923	12	11	1	1	13	0
Barfield, New York	1.000	81	178	10	0	188	3
Barnes, Detroit	1.000	33	54	5	0	59	0
Bell, Toronto	.889	13	16	0	2	18	0
Bell, Baltimore	.000	1	0	0	0	0	0
Belle, Cleveland	.952	89	170	8	9	187	1
Bergman, Detroit*	1.000	4	1	0	0	1	0
Bichette, Milwaukee	.976	127	270	14	7	291	7
Blankenship, Oakland .	1.000	28	44	0	0	44	0
Briley, Seattle	.980	125	187	5	4	196	1
Brosius, Oakland	1.000	13	24	1	0	25	1
Brown, Minnesota	.955	32	21	0	1	22	0
Browne, Cleveland	.963	17	26	0	1	27	0
Brumley, Boston	1.000	4	5	0	0	5	0
Brunansky, Boston	.989	137	265	5	3	273	2
Buhner, Seattle	.981	131	244	15	5	264	1
Burks, Detroit	.993	126	283	2	2	287	1
Bush, Minnesota*	1.000	38	50	1	0	51	1
Canseco, Oakland	.965	131	245	5	9	259	0
Capra, Texas	1.000	2	4	0	0	4	0
Carrillo, Milwaukee*	.000	3	0	0	0	0	0
Carter, Toronto	.974	151	283	13	8	304	2
Castillo, Minnesota	1.000	4	3	0	0	3	0
Clark, Kansas City	.000	1	0	0	0	0	0
Cochrane, Seattle	.969	26	31	0	1	32	0
Cole, Cleveland*	.970	107	256	6	8	270	1
Cotto, Seattle	.981	56	104	2	2	108	1
Cromartie, K.C.*	1.000	6	6	0	0	6	0
Cuyler, Detroit	.986	151	411	7	6	424	3
Daugherty, Texas*	.981	37	52	1	1	54	0
Davis, Minnesota	1.000	2	2	0	0	2	0
Davis, California	.500	3	1	0	1	2	0
de los Santos, Detroit ..	1.000	3	6	0	0	6	0
Deer, Detroit	.978	132	310	8	7	325	4
Devereaux, Baltimore ..	.993	149	399	10	3	412	1
Ducey, Toronto	.892	24	32	1	4	37	0
Eisenreich, K.C.*	.973	105	143	1	4	148	0
Evans, Baltimore	.984	67	116	6	2	124	2
Fariss, Texas	1.000	8	21	0	0	21	0
Felix, California	.977	65	126	1	3	130	0
Gallagher, California	1.000	87	180	8	0	188	1
Gibson, Kansas City* ..	.976	94	162	3	4	169	0
Gladden, Minnesota	.988	126	240	4	3	247	1
Gonzalez, Cleveland	.981	32	52	1	1	54	0
Gonzalez, Texas	.981	136	310	6	6	322	1
Greenwell, Boston	.989	143	263	9	3	275	3
Griffey Jr., Seattle*	.989	152	360	15	4	379	4
Griffey Sr., Seattle*	1.000	26	31	0	0	31	0
Hall, New York*	.987	120	221	8	3	232	2
Hamilton, Milwaukee ...	.996	117	234	3	1	238	0
Hare, Detroit*	1.000	6	9	1	0	10	0
Harper, Minnesota	.000	1	0	0	0	0	0
Harris, Texas	1.000	12	7	0	0	7	0
D. Henderson, Oakland	.997	140	362	10	1	373	0
R. Henderson, Oak.*	.970	119	249	10	8	267	0
Hill, Tor.-Cle.	.975	46	118	0	3	121	0

Player, Team	Pct.	G	PO	A	E	TC	DP
Housie, Boston	1.000	4	3	0	0	3	0
Howard, Kansas City	.000	1	0	0	0	0	0
Howell, California	1.000	5	7	0	0	7	0
Howitt, Oakland	1.000	20	28	0	0	28	0
Huff, Cle.-Chi.	.988	96	167	4	2	173	1
Humphreys, New York	1.000	9	9	0	0	9	0
Incaviglia, Detroit	.973	54	106	4	3	113	2
James, Cleveland	1.000	39	78	2	0	80	1
Jennings, Oakland*	1.000	6	8	0	0	8	0
Johnson, Chicago*	.995	158	425	11	2	438	3
T. Jones, Seattle	1.000	36	49	0	0	49	0
Karkovice, Chicago	.000	1	0	0	0	0	0
R. Kelly, New York	.986	125	268	8	4	280	1
Kirby, Cleveland	1.000	21	40	1	0	41	0
Komminsk, Oakland	1.000	22	18	1	0	19	0
Larkin, Minnesota	.968	47	59	1	2	62	1
Law, Oakland	.000	3	0	0	0	0	0
Leius, Minnesota	.000	2	0	0	0	0	0
Lennon, Seattle	1.000	1	2	0	0	2	0
Lopez, Cleveland	.000	1	0	0	0	0	0
Lusader, New York*	1.000	4	3	0	0	3	0
Lyons, Boston	1.000	45	90	0	0	90	0
Mack, Minnesota	.977	140	290	6	7	303	2
Maldonado, Mil.-Tor.	.986	76	139	2	2	143	0
Manto, Cleveland	.000	1	0	0	0	0	0
Marshall, California	1.000	4	3	0	0	3	0
Martinez, Baltimore*	.982	54	108	4	2	114	2
McCray, Chicago	1.000	8	10	0	0	10	0
McIntosh, Milwaukee	.000	4	0	0	0	0	0
McKnight, Baltimore	1.000	7	8	1	0	9	0
McRae, Kansas City	.993	150	405	2	3	410	0
Mercedes, Baltimore	1.000	15	20	0	0	20	0
Meulens, New York	.967	73	144	4	5	153	1
Milligan, Baltimore	.950	9	19	0	1	20	0
Moore, Kansas City	1.000	13	11	0	0	11	0
Morman, Kansas City	.000	2	3	0	0	3	0
Moseby, Detroit	.955	64	126	1	6	133	0
Moses, Detroit*	1.000	12	13	0	0	13	0
Munoz, Minnesota	.989	44	89	3	1	93	2
Newman, Minnesota	.000	1	0	0	0	0	0
Newson, Chicago*	.962	50	48	3	2	53	0
O'Brien, Seattle*	.905	13	18	1	2	21	1
Olander, Milwaukee	1.000	9	9	0	0	9	0
Orsulak, Baltimore*	.997	132	273	22	1	296	4
Palmer, Texas	.935	29	42	1	3	46	1
Pasqua, Chicago*	.988	59	76	3	1	80	2
Pecota, Kansas City	1.000	1	1	0	0	1	0
Pettis, Texas	.977	126	248	4	6	258	1
Phillips, Detroit	.992	56	114	3	1	118	0
Plantier, Boston	.976	40	80	1	2	83	0
Polonia, California*	.981	143	246	9	5	260	1
Powell, Seattle	.960	40	48	0	2	50	0
Puckett, Minnesota	.985	152	373	13	6	392	5
Puhl, Kansas City	.000	1	0	0	0	0	0
Pulliam, Kansas City	.917	15	21	1	2	24	0
Quintana, Boston	.941	13	15	1	1	17	0
Raines, Chicago	.990	133	273	12	3	288	0
Reimer, Texas	.948	66	110	0	6	116	0
Romine, Boston	.964	23	27	0	1	28	0
Rose, California	1.000	7	9	0	0	9	0
Jo. Russell, Texas	1.000	8	4	0	0	4	0
Scruggs, Texas	1.000	5	5	0	0	5	0
Segui, Baltimore*	.967	33	58	1	2	61	0
Shelby, Detroit	.982	47	108	4	2	114	0
Sheridan, New York	1.000	34	46	3	0	49	0
Sierra, Texas	.979	161	305	15	7	327	0
Snyder, Chi.-Tor.	.985	43	62	2	1	65	0
Sojo, California	1.000	1	2	0	0	2	0
Sosa, Chicago	.973	111	214	6	6	226	0
Spiers, Milwaukee	.000	1	0	0	0	0	0
Stanley, Texas	.000	1	0	0	0	0	0
Stevens, California*	1.000	9	15	0	0	15	0
Stubbs, Milwaukee*	.800	4	4	0	1	5	0
Surhoff, Milwaukee	1.000	2	2	0	0	2	0
Tabler, Toronto	1.000	1	1	0	0	1	0
Tartabull, Kansas City	.965	124	190	4	7	201	0

Player, Team	Pct.	G	PO	A	E	TC	DP
Tettleton, Detroit	1.000	3	2	0	0	2	0
Thurman, Kansas City	.970	72	129	2	4	135	0
Vaughn, Milwaukee	.994	135	315	5	2	322	1
Velarde, New York	1.000	2	1	0	0	1	0
Venable, California	.967	65	86	3	3	92	0
Walling, Texas	1.000	5	4	0	0	4	0
T. Ward, Cle.-Tor.	1.000	44	70	1	0	71	0
Webster, Cleveland*	1.000	10	24	0	0	24	0
White, Toronto	.998	156	439	8	1	448	2
Whiten, Tor.-Cle.	.975	109	256	13	7	276	2
Williams, New York	.979	85	230	3	5	238	0
Williams, Toronto	1.000	9	16	1	0	17	0
Wilson, Toronto	.973	41	71	2	2	75	0
Wilson, Oakland	.983	87	176	2	3	181	0
Winfield, California	.990	115	198	7	2	207	1
Yount, Milwaukee	.994	117	315	1	2	318	1
Zupcic, Boston	.875	16	14	0	2	16	0

OUTFIELDERS WITH TWO OR MORE TEAMS

Player, Team	Pct.	G	PO	A	E	TC	DP
Hill, Toronto	.967	13	29	0	1	30	0
Hill, Cleveland	.978	33	89	0	2	91	0
Huff, Cleveland	.990	48	96	3	1	100	1
Huff, Chicago	.986	48	71	1	1	73	0
Maldonado, Mil.	.976	24	41	0	1	42	0
Maldonado, Toronto	.990	52	98	2	1	101	0
Snyder, Chicago	.981	29	50	1	1	52	0
Snyder, Toronto	1.000	14	12	1	0	13	0
Ward, Cleveland	1.000	38	65	1	0	66	0
T. Ward, Toronto	1.000	6	5	0	0	5	0
Whiten, Toronto	1.000	42	90	2	0	92	0
Whiten, Cleveland	.962	67	166	11	7	184	2

CATCHERS

Leader, Team	Pct.	G	PO	A	E	TC	DP	PB
HOILES, Baltimore	.998	89	433	43	1	477	5	3

Player, Team	Pct.	G	PO	A	E	TC	DP	PB
Afenir, Oakland	1.000	4	18	1	0	19	1	0
Allanson, Detroit	.979	56	212	22	5	239	1	3
Alomar, Cleveland	.987	46	280	19	4	303	4	5
Borders, Toronto	.993	102	505	48	4	557	4	12
Bradley, Seattle	.993	65	285	16	2	303	4	3
Cochrane, Seattle	.981	19	42	10	1	53	0	6
Dempsey, Mil.	.993	56	246	23	2	271	4	5
Fisk, Chicago	.993	106	535	55	4	594	5	11
Geren, New York	.989	63	255	18	3	276	2	1
Harper, Minnesota	.988	119	642	33	8	683	7	9
Hemond, Oakland	.947	8	17	1	1	19	0	0
Hoiles, Baltimore	.998	89	433	43	1	477	5	3
Howard, Seattle	1.000	9	13	2	0	15	1	0
Karkovice, Chi.	.988	69	309	28	4	341	6	2
Knorr, Toronto	1.000	3	6	1	0	7	0	0
Kreuter, Texas	1.000	1	5	0	0	5	0	0
Leyritz, New York	1.000	5	24	0	0	24	0	0
Lopez, Cleveland	1.000	12	34	2	0	36	0	2
Macfarlane, K.C.	.993	69	391	28	3	422	4	4
Manto, Cleveland	1.000	5	13	2	0	15	0	2
Marzano, Boston	.985	48	174	20	3	197	0	6
Mayne, K.C.	.987	80	425	38	6	469	4	2
Melvin, Baltimore	.998	72	383	31	1	415	8	3
Merullo, Chicago	.989	27	79	8	1	88	1	3
Myers, Toronto	.979	104	484	37	11	532	5	9
Nokes, New York	.992	130	690	48	6	744	7	11
Ortiz, Minnesota	.995	60	203	17	1	221	2	3
Orton, California	.994	28	145	23	1	169	3	1
Parent, Texas	1.000	3	5	0	0	5	0	0
Parrish, California	.997	111	658	57	2	717	11	19
Pedre, K.C.	.971	9	29	4	1	34	0	0
Pena, Boston	.995	140	864	60	5	929	15	5
Petralli, Texas	.972	66	293	20	9	322	3	3
Quirk, Oakland	.982	54	293	32	6	331	2	2
Ramos, New York	1.000	5	23	1	0	24	0	1
Rodriguez, Texas.	.983	88	517	62	10	589	6	8
Rowland, Detroit.	1.000	2	2	1	0	3	0	0
Jo. Russell, Texas	1.000	5	20	0	0	20	0	1

Player, Team	Pct.	G	PO	A	E	TC	DP	PB
Salas, Detroit	1.000	11	22	1	0	23	0	0
Sinatro, Seattle	1.000	5	18	3	0	21	0	0
Skinner, Cle.	.991	99	504	38	5	547	4	6
Spehr, K.C.	.986	37	190	19	3	212	3	5
Sprague, Toronto	.714	2	5	0	2	7	0	0
Stanley, Texas	.980	58	239	10	5	254	0	3
Steinbach, Oak.	.980	117	594	48	13	655	7	6
Surhoff, Mil.	.995	127	660	68	4	732	11	11
Tackett, Baltimore	1.000	6	22	0	0	22	0	1
Taubensee, Cle.	.979	25	89	6	2	97	1	4
Tettleton, Detroit	.990	125	558	55	6	619	2	9
Tingley, California	.988	45	222	32	3	257	2	3
Valle, Seattle	.992	129	669	52	6	727	9	15
Wakamatsu, Chi.	1.000	18	47	2	0	49	2	4
Webster, Min.	.986	17	61	10	1	72	1	0
Whitt, Baltimore	1.000	20	72	8	0	80	0	1

TRIPLE PLAY: Valle, Seattle.

PITCHERS

*Throws lefthanded.

Leader, Team	Pct.	G	PO	A	E	TC	DP
McDOWELL, Chicago	1.000	35	19	32	0	51	1

Player, Team	Pct.	G	PO	A	E	TC	DP
J. Abbott, California*	.970	34	19	46	2	67	3
K. Abbott, California*	1.000	5	0	5	0	5	0
Abbott, Minnesota	1.000	15	3	4	0	7	0
Acker, Toronto	1.000	54	1	16	0	17	0
Aguilera, Minnesota	1.000	63	7	5	0	12	0
Aldred, Detroit*	1.000	11	3	8	0	11	0
Alexander, Texas	1.000	30	5	14	0	19	2
Allison, Oakland*	.000	11	0	0	0	0	0
Alvarez, Chicago*	1.000	10	1	7	0	8	1
Anderson, Minnesota*	1.000	29	8	19	0	27	1
Appier, Kansas City	.958	34	20	26	2	48	0
Aquino, Kansas City	.921	38	14	21	3	38	3
Arnsberg, Texas	.500	9	0	1	1	2	0
August, Milwaukee	1.000	28	11	21	0	32	1
Austin, Milwaukee	1.000	5	1	2	0	3	0
Bailes, California*	1.000	42	3	8	0	11	0
Ballard, Baltimore*	.950	26	4	15	1	20	3
Bankhead, Seattle	1.000	17	5	7	0	12	1
Banks, Minnesota	.000	5	0	0	0	0	0
Bannister, California*	1.000	16	0	1	0	1	0
Barfield, Texas*	.857	28	6	12	3	21	1
Bautista, Baltimore	1.000	5	0	1	0	1	0
Beasley, California	1.000	22	4	4	0	8	1
Bedrosian, Minnesota	1.000	56	6	5	0	11	0
Bell, Cleveland*	1.000	10	2	1	0	3	0
Bitker, Texas	1.000	9	0	1	0	1	0
Blair, Cleveland	1.000	11	2	5	0	7	1
Boddicker, K.C.	.960	30	12	36	2	50	1
Bohanon, Texas*	1.000	11	3	6	0	9	1
Bolton, Boston*	.889	25	1	15	2	18	3
Bosio, Milwaukee	.953	32	20	21	2	43	4
Boucher, Tor.-Cle.*	.882	12	2	13	2	17	2
Boyd, Texas	1.000	12	4	6	0	10	1
Briscoe, Oakland	1.000	11	0	1	0	1	0
Brown, Texas	.962	33	18	32	2	52	3
Brown, Milwaukee*	.944	15	6	11	1	18	0
Burba, Seattle	1.000	22	2	4	0	6	0
Burns, Oakland	1.000	9	3	2	0	5	0
Cadaret, New York*	.957	68	5	17	1	23	5
Campbell, Oakland	1.000	14	3	2	0	5	0
Candiotti, Cle.-Tor.	.979	34	19	28	1	48	1
Carter, Chicago	1.000	5	0	1	0	1	0
Cary, New York*	.778	10	0	7	2	9	4
Casian, Minnesota*	1.000	15	3	4	0	7	0
Cerutti, Detroit*	.875	38	1	20	3	24	0
Chapin, New York	1.000	3	0	1	0	1	0
Chiamparino, Texas	1.000	5	1	1	0	2	0
Chitren, Oakland	1.000	56	1	8	0	9	1
Clemens, Boston	.984	35	31	30	1	62	1
Comstock, Seattle*	.000	1	0	0	0	0	0
Corbin, Kansas City	.000	2	0	0	0	0	0
Crawford, Kansas City	1.000	33	4	5	0	9	0

Player, Team	Pct.	G	PO	A	E	TC	DP
Crim, Milwaukee	.957	66	8	14	1	23	0
Dalton, Detroit*	1.000	4	0	1	0	1	1
Darling, Oakland	1.000	12	8	9	0	17	1
Darwin, Boston	1.000	12	6	9	0	15	0
M. Davis, K.C.*	1.000	29	1	7	0	8	1
S. Davis, Kansas City	1.000	51	5	12	0	17	0
Dayley, Toronto*	1.000	8	1	1	0	2	0
de la Rosa, Baltimore	.000	2	0	0	0	0	0
Dempsey, Milwaukee	.000	2	0	0	0	0	0
DeLucia, Seattle	1.000	32	8	19	0	27	1
Dopson, Boston	1.000	1	0	1	0	1	0
Drahman, Chicago	.857	28	1	5	1	7	0
Drees, Chicago*	1.000	4	2	0	0	2	0
Dressendorfer, Oak.	1.000	7	2	3	0	5	0
Eckersley, Oakland	1.000	67	6	9	0	15	0
Edens, Minnesota	1.000	8	5	5	0	10	0
Edwards, Chicago*	1.000	13	1	2	0	3	0
Egloff, Cleveland	1.000	6	2	1	0	3	0
Eichhorn, California	1.000	70	4	18	0	22	2
Eiland, New York	1.000	18	6	2	0	8	0
Eldred, Milwaukee	1.000	3	2	1	0	3	0
Erickson, Minnesota	.980	32	19	31	1	51	3
Espinoza, New York	.000	1	0	0	0	0	0
Fajardo, Texas	1.000	4	1	1	0	2	0
Farr, New York	1.000	60	7	11	0	18	1
Fernandez, Chicago	.927	34	7	31	3	41	2
Fetters, California	.857	19	2	4	1	7	0
Finley, California*	.931	34	11	16	2	29	3
Flanagan, Baltimore*	1.000	64	6	23	0	29	2
Fleming, Seattle*	1.000	9	3	6	0	9	2
Fossas, Boston*	.900	64	6	12	2	20	2
Fraser, Toronto	1.000	13	2	3	0	5	0
Frohwirth, Baltimore*	.927	51	14	24	3	41	3
Gakeler, Detroit	1.000	31	5	12	0	17	0
Garcia, Chicago	.955	16	9	12	1	22	2
Gardiner, Boston	.962	22	12	13	1	26	2
Gardner, Kansas City	1.000	3	1	1	0	2	0
George, Milwaukee	.000	2	0	0	0	0	0
Gibson, Detroit*	1.000	68	6	13	0	19	0
Gleaton, Detroit*	1.000	47	4	11	0	15	1
Gordon, Kansas City	.935	45	12	17	2	31	1
Gossage, Texas	.800	44	2	2	1	5	0
Gozzo, Cleveland	.000	2	0	0	0	0	0
Grahe, California	.938	18	4	11	1	16	0
Gray, Boston	.944	50	7	10	1	18	0
Gubicza, Kansas City	.925	26	8	29	3	40	5
Guetterman, N.Y.*	.880	64	9	13	3	25	1
Gullickson, Detroit	1.000	35	14	21	0	35	0
Guthrie, Minnesota*	.938	41	5	10	1	16	0
Guzman, Texas	.978	25	12	32	1	45	2
Guzman, Toronto	.824	23	5	9	3	17	1
Guzman, Oakland*	1.000	5	0	1	0	1	1
Haas, Detroit	.000	11	0	0	0	0	0
Habyan, New York	1.000	66	6	12	0	18	0
Hanson, Seattle	.968	27	14	16	1	31	0
Harris, Boston	.956	53	11	32	2	45	0
Harris, Seattle	1.000	8	0	2	0	2	0
Harris, Oakland	.000	2	0	0	0	0	0
Harvey, California	.833	67	2	8	2	12	0
Hawkins, N.Y.-Oak.	1.000	19	6	18	0	24	2
Henke, Toronto	1.000	49	2	1	0	3	0
Henneman, Detroit	.889	60	6	10	2	18	1
Henry, Milwaukee	1.000	32	4	1	0	5	0
Hentgen, Toronto	1.000	3	0	2	0	2	1
Hernandez, Chicago	1.000	9	0	2	0	2	0
Hesketh, Boston*	.970	39	13	19	1	33	1
Hibbard, Chicago*	.949	32	9	28	2	39	2
Hickey, Baltimore*	1.000	19	1	1	0	2	0
Higuera, Milwaukee*	.857	7	1	5	1	7	0
Hillegas, Cleveland	1.000	51	7	8	0	15	1
Holman, Seattle	.962	30	17	33	2	52	2
Holmes, Milwaukee	.947	40	4	14	1	19	0
Honeycutt, Oakland*	1.000	43	4	4	0	8	1
Horsman, Toronto*	.000	4	0	0	0	0	0
Hough, Chicago	.977	31	12	31	1	44	1
Howe, New York*	.786	37	5	6	3	14	1
Hunter, Milwaukee	1.000	8	3	7	0	10	1

FIELDING

Player, Team	Pct.	G	PO	A	E	TC	DP
Ignasiak, Milwaukee ...	1.000	4	1	0	0	1	0
Irvine, Boston	.857	9	3	3	1	7	0
Jackson, Seattle	.909	72	2	8	1	11	1
Jeffcoat, Texas*	1.000	70	2	13	0	15	0
Johnson, Baltimore	1.000	22	7	7	0	14	1
Johnson, New York* ...	.903	23	4	24	3	31	3
Johnson, Seattle*	.821	33	0	23	5	28	3
Johnston, Kansas City	1.000	13	1	2	0	3	0
C. Jones, Seattle	1.000	27	1	8	0	9	1
Jones, Cleveland	1.000	36	7	10	0	17	1
Jones, Baltimore	1.000	4	2	1	0	3	0
Kaiser, Detroit*	1.000	10	0	1	0	1	0
Kamieniecki, N.Y.	1.000	9	5	9	0	14	0
Key, Toronto*	.967	33	22	37	2	61	3
Kiecker, Boston	.938	18	4	11	1	16	1
Kiely, Detroit	.000	7	0	0	0	0	0
Kilgus, Baltimore*	.931	38	14	13	2	29	2
King, Cleveland	.920	25	9	14	2	25	2
Kiser, Cleveland*	.000	7	0	0	0	0	0
Klink, Oakland*	1.000	62	4	8	0	12	1
Knudson, Milwaukee ..	1.000	12	4	3	0	7	0
Kramer, Cleveland	1.000	4	1	0	0	1	0
Krueger, Seattle*	1.000	35	5	30	0	35	2
Lamp, Boston	.933	51	2	12	1	15	2
Langston, California* .	.942	34	15	34	3	52	2
Law, Oakland	.000	1	0	0	0	0	0
Leach, Minnesota	1.000	50	8	13	0	21	2
Leary, New York	.955	28	9	12	1	22	3
Lee, Milwaukee*	1.000	62	0	13	0	13	2
Leiter, Toronto*	1.000	3	0	1	0	1	0
Leiter, Detroit	.952	38	3	17	1	21	1
Lewis, California	.923	16	4	8	1	13	0
Lyons, Boston	.000	1	0	0	0	0	0
Machado, Milwaukee ..	.917	54	4	7	1	12	1
MacDonald, Toronto* .	1.000	45	4	5	0	9	0
Magnante, K.C.*	.900	38	3	6	1	10	1
Maldonado, K.C.	.000	5	0	0	1	1	0
Manuel, Texas	1.000	8	0	6	0	6	0
Manzanillo, Boston......	.000	1	0	0	0	0	0
Mathews, Texas	1.000	34	8	5	0	13	0
McCaskill, California ..	.977	30	17	25	1	43	4
McClure, California* ...	1.000	13	0	2	0	2	0
McDonald, Baltimore ...	1.000	21	12	8	0	20	1
McDowell, Chicago......	1.000	35	19	32	0	51	1
McGaffigan, K.C.	.000	4	0	0	0	0	0
Meacham, Detroit	1.000	10	4	4	0	8	0
Mesa, Baltimore..........	1.000	23	17	17	0	34	0
Milacki, Baltimore	.959	31	23	24	2	49	4
Mills, New York	1.000	6	0	5	0	5	0
Monteleone, New York	.917	26	1	10	1	12	1
Montgomery, K.C.........	1.000	67	10	8	0	18	0
Moore, Oakland	.967	33	28	30	2	60	3
Morris, Minnesota	1.000	35	23	25	0	48	2
Morton, Boston*	1.000	16	4	16	0	20	2
Munoz, Detroit*	1.000	6	0	3	0	3	0
Murphy, Seattle*	.833	57	2	8	2	12	0
Mussina, Baltimore	1.000	12	4	11	0	15	1
Mutis, Cleveland*	1.000	3	1	1	0	2	0
Nagy, Cleveland	.949	33	17	20	2	39	4
Navarro, Milwaukee	.936	34	16	28	3	47	3
Neagle, Minnesota*	1.000	7	0	1	0	1	0
Nelson, Oakland	1.000	44	4	4	0	8	0
Nichols, Cleveland	.960	31	10	14	1	25	1
Nolte, Texas*	.000	3	0	0	0	0	0
Nunez, Milwaukee	.750	23	0	3	1	4	0
Olin, Cleveland	1.000	48	3	8	0	11	2
Olson, Baltimore	.850	72	6	11	3	20	0
Orosco, Cleveland*......	1.000	47	3	3	0	6	0
Otto, Cleveland*	.944	18	1	16	1	18	0
Pall, Chicago...............	.923	51	4	8	1	13	0
Patterson, Chicago*.....	.700	43	1	6	3	10	1
Pecota, Kansas City	.000	1	0	0	0	0	0
Perez, Chicago	.903	49	9	19	3	31	1
Perez, New York	.857	14	2	10	2	14	1
Petkovsek, Texas	1.000	4	1	0	0	1	0
Petry, Det.-Bos............	.963	30	8	18	1	27	3
Plesac, Milwaukee*	1.000	45	2	5	0	7	0
Plunk, New York	.846	43	4	7	2	13	0
Plympton, Boston	.000	4	0	0	0	0	0
Poole, Tex.-Bal.*	.889	29	2	6	1	9	0
Radinsky, Chicago*	1.000	67	6	11	0	17	0
Reardon, Boston	1.000	57	2	1	0	3	0
Rhodes, Baltimore*	1.000	8	0	1	0	1	0
Rice, Seattle.................	1.000	7	2	1	0	3	0
Ritz, Detroit.................	.833	11	1	4	1	6	0
Robinson, California....	1.000	39	3	7	0	10	0
Robinson, Baltimore	.882	21	5	10	2	17	0
Robinson, Milwaukee ..	1.000	1	0	2	0	2	0
Rogers, Texas*	.870	63	5	15	3	23	1
Rosenthal, Texas.........	.889	36	4	4	1	9	0
Je. Russell, Texas........	.960	68	6	18	1	25	1
Ryan, Texas.................	1.000	27	7	14	0	21	1
Saberhagen, K.C.	.959	28	17	30	2	49	2
Sanderson, New York..	.966	34	15	13	1	29	0
Schatzeder, K.C.*	.000	8	0	0	0	0	0
Schiraldi, Texas	1.000	3	1	1	0	2	0
Schooler, Seattle	1.000	34	2	2	0	4	0
Seanez, Cleveland	.000	5	0	0	0	0	0
Searcy, Detroit*	1.000	16	0	6	0	6	0
Shaw, Cleveland	.882	29	4	11	2	17	2
Show, Oakland	.778	23	3	4	2	9	0
Slusarski, Oakland	.944	20	7	10	1	18	0
Smith, Baltimore	1.000	17	9	8	0	17	0
Stewart, Oakland.........	.943	35	14	19	2	35	0
Stieb, Toronto	.944	9	5	12	1	18	2
Stottlemyre, Toronto ...	.962	34	30	21	2	53	2
Swan, Seattle*	.950	63	3	16	1	20	1
Swift, Seattle	.912	71	6	25	3	34	4
Swindell, Cleveland* ...	.974	33	7	30	1	38	2
Tanana, Detroit*	.980	33	12	36	1	49	3
Tapani, Minnesota	.981	34	26	26	1	53	2
Taylor, New York	1.000	23	2	21	0	23	3
Telford, Baltimore	1.000	9	2	2	0	4	0
Terrell, Detroit	1.000	35	18	26	0	44	5
Thigpen, Chicago	.947	67	3	15	1	19	0
Timlin, Toronto	.929	63	9	17	2	28	0
E. Valdez, Cleveland* .	1.000	7	0	1	0	1	0
S. Valdez, Cleveland	.000	6	0	0	0	0	0
Valenzuela, Cal.*	1.000	2	0	1	0	1	0
Van Poppel, Oakland ...	1.000	1	0	1	0	1	0
Wagner, Kansas City ..	.000	2	0	0	0	0	0
Walker, Cleveland	1.000	5	1	1	0	2	0
Walton, Oakland	1.000	12	1	0	0	1	0
Wapnick, Chicago	1.000	6	1	0	0	1	0
D. Ward, Toronto	.952	81	9	11	1	21	1
Wayne, Minnesota*	1.000	8	0	1	0	1	0
Weathers, Toronto	1.000	15	0	1	0	1	0
Wegman, Milwaukee ...	.939	28	28	34	4	66	1
Welch, Oakland	.957	35	15	29	2	46	1
Wells, Toronto*	.952	40	5	35	2	42	1
West, Minnesota*	.923	15	1	11	1	13	1
Weston, Baltimore*	.000	2	0	0	0	0	0
Williamson, Baltimore.	.889	65	7	9	2	18	0
Willis, Minnesota	.923	40	4	8	1	13	0
Wills, Toronto	1.000	4	0	2	0	2	0
Witt, Texas	.867	17	7	6	2	15	1
Witt, New York	1.000	2	1	1	0	2	0
York, Cleveland	1.000	14	2	3	0	5	0
Young, Oakland*	1.000	41	4	12	0	16	2
Young, California*	1.000	11	0	3	0	3	0
Young, Boston*	.933	19	4	10	1	15	1

PITCHERS WITH TWO OR MORE TEAMS

Player, Team	Pct.	G	PO	A	E	TC	DP
Boucher, Toronto*	.909	7	2	8	1	11	1
Boucher, Cleveland*	.833	5	0	5	1	6	1
Candiotti, Cleveland	1.000	15	9	10	0	19	0
Candiotti, Toronto	.966	19	10	18	1	29	0
Hawkins, New York	1.000	4	1	8	0	9	0
Hawkins, Oakland	1.000	15	5	10	0	15	2
Petry, Detroit	.952	17	6	14	1	21	3
Petry, Boston	1.000	13	2	4	0	6	0
Poole, Texas*	.000	5	0	0	0	0	0
Poole, Baltimore*	.889	24	2	6	1	9	0

MISCELLANEOUS

SHUTOUT GAMES

Read across for wins, down for losses.

Team	Tor.	Min.	K.C.	Bal.	Sea.	Det.	Tex.	N.Y.	Bos.	Mil.	Oak.	Cal.	Chi.	Cle.	W	L	Pct.
Toronto	..	2	1	1	1	0	2	1	0	1	2	1	1	3	16	9	.640
Minnesota	2	..	1	0	1	0	1	1	2	0	0	1	1	2	12	8	.600
Kansas City	0	0	..	1	1	0	0	1	2	1	1	0	2	3	12	9	.571
Baltimore	0	0	1	..	0	0	2	1	0	0	1	2	1	0	8	6	.571
Seattle	0	2	1	0	..	1	0	2	0	2	1	1	1	2	13	10	.565
Detroit	1	1	1	0	0	..	0	1	0	0	1	1	2	0	8	7	.533
Texas	1	1	0	1	1	0	..	0	0	0	1	2	1	2	10	9	.526
New York	1	0	0	0	1	2	0	..	2	0	1	2	0	2	11	10	.524
Boston	1	0	1	0	0	1	0	1	..	3	1	2	2	1	13	12	.520
Milwaukee	1	0	0	0	1	1	1	1	0	..	3	1	0	2	11	11	.500
Oakland	1	1	1	0	2	0	2	0	1	0	..	1	0	1	10	14	.417
California	1	1	0	0	1	1	0	1	3	2	0	..	0	0	10	15	.400
Chicago	0	0	1	3	1	0	0	0	0	0	2	1	..	0	8	12	.400
Cleveland	0	0	1	0	0	1	1	0	2	2	0	0	1	..	8	18	.308
Lost	9	8	9	6	10	7	9	10	12	11	14	15	12	18	150	150	.500

HOME RECORD

Read across for home wins, down for road losses.

Team	Min.	Det.	Oak.	Tor.	Tex.	Chi.	Sea.	Mil.	Bos.	K.C.	Cal.	N.Y.	Bal.	Cle.	W	L	Pct.
Minnesota	..	5	5	2	3	2	7	3	4	2	2	6	5	5	51	30	.630
Detroit	3	..	2	3	5	3	5	1	4	4	4	5	4	6	49	32	.605
Oakland	3	4	..	3	2	4	6	3	2	4	6	3	4	3	47	34	.580
Toronto	4	5	3	..	4	3	3	4	2	3	3	3	3	6	46	35	.568
Texas	4	5	4	4	..	4	2	1	5	3	4	5	2	3	46	35	.568
Chicago	4	1	4	4	5	..	4	5	1	4	2	5	3	4	46	35	.568
Seattle	4	3	7	2	0	3	..	6	1	3	2	5	4	5	45	36	.556
Milwaukee	3	4	5	3	2	4	3	..	3	1	4	3	5	3	43	37	.538
Boston	1	3	4	4	4	2	4	3	..	5	4	2	3	4	43	38	.531
Kansas City	2	2	3	2	4	3	3	4	4	..	3	3	3	2	40	41	.494
California	3	3	1	3	3	4	1	4	6	5	..	2	3	2	40	41	.494
New York	2	3	3	3	4	3	2	3	3	2	2	..	5	4	39	42	.481
Baltimore	3	2	1	2	5	1	2	2	4	1	3	3	..	4	33	48	.407
Cleveland	1	6	2	1	1	4	1	3	1	2	1	4	3	..	30	52	.366
Lost on road	37	46	44	36	42	40	43	42	40	39	40	49	47	53	598	536	.527

ROAD RECORD

Read across for road wins, down for home losses.

Team	Tor.	Min.	K.C.	Chi.	Cal.	Bos.	Mil.	Tex.	Sea.	Oak.	Det.	Bal.	N.Y.	Cle.	W	L	Pct.
Toronto	..	4	4	2	3	2	3	2	4	3	3	5	4	6	45	36	.556
Minnesota	2	..	5	3	3	5	3	3	2	3	3	3	4	5	44	37	.543
Kansas City	3	4	..	3	1	1	5	3	4	3	3	5	4	4	42	39	.519
Chicago	3	4	3	..	3	4	2	3	3	3	3	5	3	2	41	40	.506
California	3	5	4	4	..	2	2	2	5	0	2	3	4	5	41	40	.506
Boston	5	2	2	5	0	..	4	1	5	4	2	2	4	5	40	40	.506
Milwaukee	3	3	2	1	2	3	..	5	0	3	5	5	3	5	40	42	.488
Texas	2	3	3	1	4	2	4	..	6	5	1	1	2	5	39	42	.481
Seattle	3	0	3	3	5	2	3	5	..	0	1	4	4	5	38	44	.469
Oakland	3	2	3	2	6	2	1	2	0	..	4	5	3	4	37	44	.457
Detroit	2	1	4	5	3	4	3	1	3	2	..	4	3	0	35	46	.432
Baltimore	3	1	3	3	3	4	1	4	2	2	3	..	2	3	34	47	.420
New York	3	0	3	1	4	4	4	1	1	3	2	3	..	3	32	49	.395
Cleveland	0	1	2	2	4	3	2	3	1	3	1	3	2	..	27	53	.338
Lost at home	35	30	41	35	41	38	37	35	36	34	32	48	42	52	536	598	.473

PITCHING AGAINST EACH CLUB

BALTIMORE—67-95

Pitcher	Bos. W-L	Cal. W-L	Chi. W-L	Cle. W-L	Det. W-L	K.C. W-L	Mil. W-L	Min. W-L	N.Y. W-L	Oak. W-L	Sea. W-L	Tex. W-L	Tor. W-L	Totals W-L
Ballard	1-0	1-2	1-1	0-1	0-1	0-0	0-0	0-0	1-1	0-2	0-3	1-0	1-1	6-12
Bautista	0-0	0-0	0-0	0-0	0-0	0-0	0-1	0-0	0-0	0-0	0-0	0-0	0-0	0-1
Flanagan	0-0	0-0	0-1	0-1	1-0	0-0	0-0	0-1	0-3	0-1	1-0	0-0	0-0	2-7
Frohwirth	1-0	1-0	0-0	0-0	0-0	1-2	0-0	0-0	1-1	0-0	0-0	2-0	1-0	7-3
Hickey	1-0	0-0	0-0	0-0	0-0	0-0	0-0	0-0	0-0	0-0	0-0	0-0	0-0	1-0

Pitcher	Bos. W-L	Cal. W-L	Chi. W-L	Cle. W-L	Det. W-L	K.C. W-L	Mil. W-L	Min. W-L	N.Y. W-L	Oak. W-L	Sea. W-L	Tex. W-L	Tor. W-L	Totals W-L
Johnson	0-2	0-0	0-2	0-0	0-1	0-0	1-1	0-0	0-0	0-0	0-1	3-0	0-1	4-8
Kilgus	0-0	0-0	0-0	0-0	0-0	0-1	0-0	0-0	0-0	0-0	0-0	0-0	0-1	0-2
McDonald.....	0-0	2-1	1-1	0-0	1-1	0-0	0-2	0-0	0-0	1-2	0-0	0-0	1-1	6-8
Mesa...........	0-3	1-0	0-1	0-1	1-0	0-2	1-1	0-1	0-0	0-1	2-0	1-1	0-0	6-11
Milacki	0-0	1-0	1-0	2-1	0-3	1-1	1-2	1-0	1-0	1-0	0-1	0-0	1-1	10-9
Mussina	1-0	0-0	0-2	0-1	0-0	0-0	0-0	1-1	1-0	0-0	0-0	1-1	0-0	4-5
Olson	0-0	0-0	1-0	1-0	0-1	1-0	0-0	1-2	0-0	0-1	0-1	0-0	0-1	4-6
Poole	1-0	0-0	0-0	0-0	1-1	1-0	0-0	0-0	0-0	0-1	0-0	0-0	0-0	3-2
Rhodes	0-0	0-0	0-0	0-1	0-0	0-0	0-0	0-1	0-0	0-0	0-0	0-0	0-0	0-3
Robinson	0-0	0-2	0-0	1-0	0-0	0-0	0-1	0-1	1-1	1-1	0-1	1-1	0-1	4-9
Smith...........	2-0	0-0	0-0	1-0	0-0	0-0	0-1	0-1	0-1	0-0	1-1	0-0	1-0	5-4
Williamson...	1-0	0-1	0-0	2-0	1-0	0-2	0-1	1-0	0-0	0-1	0-0	0-0	0-0	5-5
Totals	**8-5**	**6-6**	**4-8**	**7-6**	**5-8**	**4-8**	**3-10**	**4-8**	**5-8**	**3-9**	**4-8**	**9-3**	**5-8**	**67-95**

No-decisions—de la Rosa, Jones, Telford.

BOSTON—84-78

Pitcher	Bal. W-L	Cal. W-L	Chi. W-L	Cle. W-L	Det. W-L	K.C. W-L	Mil. W-L	Min. W-L	N.Y. W-L	Oak. W-L	Sea. W-L	Tex. W-L	Tor. W-L	Totals W-L
Bolton..........	0-1	1-1	2-0	0-0	1-1	2-0	0-1	0-1	0-2	1-1	1-0	0-1	0-0	8-9
Clemens	1-1	1-0	1-0	1-0	2-2	1-1	1-1	1-1	3-1	2-0	1-1	0-2	3-0	18-10
Darwin	0-2	0-1	0-0	0-1	0-1	1-0	1-0	0-0	0-0	0-1	1-0	0-0	0-0	3-6
Fossas.........	0-0	0-0	1-0	1-0	0-0	1-2	0-0	0-0	0-0	0-0	0-0	0-0	0-0	3-2
Gardiner.......	2-1	1-2	0-2	1-0	0-0	0-1	0-2	0-1	1-1	1-0	2-0	0-0	1-0	9-10
Gray	0-0	0-0	0-1	0-0	0-0	0-0	0-0	1-1	0-0	1-0	0-0	0-0	0-1	2-3
Harris..........	1-1	0-1	1-1	4-1	0-0	0-0	1-0	0-3	0-0	3-0	0-1	0-3	1-1	11-12
Hesketh........	0-1	1-1	1-0	2-0	1-0	0-0	1-0	1-0	1-1	0-0	1-0	1-1	2-0	12-4
Kiecker........	0-0	0-0	0-1	0-1	0-1	1-0	0-0	0-0	0-0	0-0	1-0	0-0	0-0	2-3
Lamp...........	0-0	0-0	0-0	0-1	0-0	0-0	2-0	0-0	0-0	0-1	1-0	1-0	2-1	6-3
Morton	1-0	0-1	0-0	0-0	1-1	1-0	0-1	0-2	1-0	0-0	1-0	1-0	0-0	6-5
Reardon	0-0	0-0	0-0	0-0	0-0	0-1	0-1	0-0	0-1	0-0	1-1	0-0	0-0	1-4
Young..........	0-1	0-1	1-0	0-0	0-2	0-0	1-0	0-0	0-1	0-1	0-0	1-0	0-1	3-7
Totals	**5-8**	**4-8**	**7-5**	**9-4**	**5-8**	**7-5**	**7-6**	**3-9**	**6-7**	**8-4**	**9-3**	**5-7**	**9-4**	**84-78**

No-decisions—Dopson, Irvine, Lyons, Manzanillo, Petry, Plympton.

CALIFORNIA—81-81

Pitcher	Bal. W-L	Bos. W-L	Chi. W-L	Cle. W-L	Det. W-L	K.C. W-L	Mil. W-L	Min. W-L	N.Y. W-L	Oak. W-L	Sea. W-L	Tex. W-L	Tor. W-L	Totals W-L
J. Abbott	2-0	1-0	1-1	1-0	1-1	2-1	3-0	2-1	2-1	0-2	1-2	1-1	1-1	18-11
K. Abbott......	0-0	0-0	1-1	0-0	0-0	0-0	0-0	0-0	0-0	0-0	0-1	0-0	0-0	1-2
Bailes	0-0	0-0	0-0	0-0	0-0	0-0	0-0	1-0	0-0	0-1	0-0	0-1	0-0	1-2
Beasley	0-0	0-0	0-0	0-0	0-0	0-0	0-0	0-1	0-0	0-0	0-0	0-0	0-0	0-1
Eichhorn	0-0	0-0	1-1	0-1	0-0	0-0	0-0	0-1	0-0	1-0	0-0	1-0	1-0	3-3
Fetters.........	0-0	1-0	1-0	0-0	0-1	0-0	0-0	0-0	0-1	0-0	0-1	0-0	0-1	2-5
Finley..........	1-1	1-1	1-0	2-1	2-0	3-0	1-1	2-1	2-0	0-1	3-0	0-2	0-1	18-9
Grahe	0-0	0-0	1-0	0-0	1-1	0-0	1-2	0-1	0-0	0-2	0-1	0-0	0-0	3-7
Harvey	0-1	0-0	0-1	2-0	0-0	0-0	0-0	0-0	0-1	0-0	0-0	0-0	0-1	2-4
Langston......	2-0	3-0	1-0	1-1	1-1	2-0	1-0	1-0	2-0	0-3	1-0	2-1	2-2	19-8
Lewis...........	0-2	0-0	0-1	0-1	0-1	0-0	0-0	0-0	0-0	1-0	0-1	1-0	1-0	3-5
McCaskill.....	1-2	2-2	1-0	1-1	0-1	1-2	0-2	2-0	0-3	0-3	1-2	0-1	1-0	10-19
Robinson	0-0	0-1	0-0	0-0	0-1	0-0	0-0	0-0	0-0	0-0	0-1	0-0	0-0	0-3
Valenzuela ...	0-0	0-0	0-0	0-0	0-1	0-0	0-1	0-0	0-0	0-0	0-0	0-0	0-0	0-2
Young..........	0-0	0-0	0-0	0-0	0-0	1-0	0-0	0-0	0-0	0-0	0-0	0-0	0-0	1-0
Totals	**6-6**	**8-4**	**8-5**	**7-5**	**5-7**	**9-4**	**6-6**	**8-5**	**6-6**	**1-12**	**6-7**	**5-8**	**6-6**	**81-81**

No-decisions—Bannister, McClure.

CHICAGO—87-75

Pitcher	Bal. W-L	Bos. W-L	Cal. W-L	Cle. W-L	Det. W-L	K.C. W-L	Mil. W-L	Min. W-L	N.Y. W-L	Oak. W-L	Sea. W-L	Tex. W-L	Tor. W-L	Totals W-L
Alvarez........	1-0	0-0	0-0	1-0	0-1	0-1	0-0	0-0	0-0	0-0	1-0	0-0	0-0	3-2
Carter..........	0-0	0-0	0-0	0-0	0-1	0-0	0-0	0-0	0-0	0-0	0-0	0-0	0-0	0-1
Drahman	1-0	0-0	0-1	0-0	1-0	0-0	1-0	0-1	0-0	0-0	0-0	0-0	0-0	3-2
Edwards.......	0-0	0-0	0-0	0-0	0-0	0-0	0-1	0-0	0-0	0-1	0-0	0-0	0-0	0-2
Fernandez....	1-1	1-1	0-0	0-2	1-2	1-1	0-1	1-1	1-1	1-2	1-0	1-1	0-0	9-13
Garcia	1-0	2-0	0-0	0-1	0-0	0-1	0-0	0-0	0-0	0-0	0-2	1-0	0-0	4-4
Hernandez....	0-0	0-0	0-0	0-0	0-0	0-0	1-0	0-0	0-0	0-0	0-0	0-0	0-0	1-0
Hibbard	1-0	0-0	0-2	0-2	0-1	1-0	1-1	1-0	2-0	2-1	2-1	1-1	0-2	11-11
Hough..........	1-1	0-1	2-0	1-0	0-1	2-1	0-2	1-0	0-0	1-0	0-2	0-1	1-1	9-10
McDowell	2-1	0-1	1-1	2-1	1-1	2-1	3-0	1-2	2-1	1-0	1-0	0-0	1-1	17-10
Pall..............	0-1	0-1	1-0	1-0	0-0	0-0	0-0	0-0	1-0	0-0	1-0	2-0	1-0	7-2
Patterson	0-0	0-0	0-0	0-0	0-0	0-0	0-0	1-0	0-0	0-0	0-0	1-0	1-0	3-0
Perez	0-0	1-2	1-2	1-0	0-0	0-0	0-0	0-1	1-0	1-0	1-1	1-0	0-1	8-7

Pitcher	Bal.	Bos.	Cal.	Cle.	Det.	K.C.	Mil.	Min.	N.Y.	Oak.	Sea.	Tex.	Tor.	Totals
	W-L	W-L	W-L	W-L	W-L	W-L	W-L	W-L	W-L	W-L	W-L	W-L	W-L	W-L
Radinsky	0-0	0-0	0-2	0-0	1-1	0-0	0-0	1-1	1-1	0-0	0-0	0-0	2-0	5-5
Thigpen	0-0	1-1	0-0	0-0	0-0	0-1	2-0	1-0	0-0	1-1	0-0	1-2	1-0	7-5
Wapnick	0-0	0-0	0-0	0-0	0-0	0-0	0-0	0-0	0-0	0-1	0-0	0-0	0-0	0-1
Totals	8-4	5-7	5-8	6-6	4-8	7-6	7-5	8-5	8-4	7-6	7-6	8-5	7-5	87-75

No-decisions—Drees.

CLEVELAND—57-105

Pitcher	Bal.	Bos.	Cal.	Chi.	Det.	K.C.	Mil.	Min.	N.Y.	Oak.	Sea.	Tex.	Tor.	Totals
	W-L	W-L	W-L	W-L	W-L	W-L	W-L	W-L	W-L	W-L	W-L	W-L	W-L	W-L
Bell	2-0	0-0	0-0	0-0	0-0	0-0	0-0	0-0	2-0	0-0	0-0	0-0	0-0	4-0
Blair	0-1	0-0	0-0	1-1	0-0	0-0	0-0	1-0	0-0	0-0	0-0	0-1	0-0	2-3
Boucher	0-0	0-0	1-0	0-0	0-1	0-0	0-0	0-0	0-1	0-1	0-1	0-0	0-0	1-4
Candiotti	1-0	1-1	2-0	0-1	1-0	1-0	0-0	0-1	0-1	1-0	0-0	0-0	0-2	7-6
Hillegas	0-0	1-1	0-1	1-0	0-0	0-0	0-0	0-1	0-0	0-0	0-0	0-1	1-0	3-4
Jones	0-1	0-0	0-1	0-1	2-0	0-1	2-2	0-0	0-0	0-1	0-1	0-0	0-0	4-8
King	0-0	1-0	0-1	0-0	0-1	0-1	0-1	0-0	0-3	2-0	1-0	2-2	0-2	6-11
Mutis	0-1	0-0	0-0	0-0	0-0	0-0	0-0	0-1	0-0	0-0	0-0	0-0	0-1	0-3
Nagy	1-1	0-0	1-0	3-0	2-2	1-1	1-1	0-1	0-2	0-1	1-2	0-1	0-3	10-15
Nichols	0-0	0-1	0-0	1-1	0-1	0-1	0-3	0-1	0-0	1-1	0-2	0-0	0-0	2-11
Olin	0-0	1-2	0-1	0-0	0-0	0-1	0-0	0-0	1-0	0-1	0-0	1-1	0-0	3-6
Orosco	0-0	0-0	1-0	0-0	0-0	0-0	0-0	0-0	0-0	0-0	1-0	0-0	0-0	2-0
Otto	0-1	0-1	0-1	0-1	0-1	1-1	1-0	0-1	0-0	0-0	0-0	0-0	0-1	2-8
Shaw	0-1	0-0	0-0	0-0	0-0	0-0	0-0	0-1	0-1	0-1	0-0	0-0	0-1	0-5
Swindell	2-0	0-3	0-2	0-1	1-0	1-2	1-1	1-0	1-2	1-1	1-1	0-1	0-2	9-16
S. Valdez	0-0	0-0	0-0	0-0	1-0	0-0	0-0	0-0	0-0	0-0	0-0	0-0	0-0	1-0
Walker	0-1	0-0	0-0	0-0	0-0	0-0	0-0	0-0	0-0	0-0	0-0	0-0	0-0	0-1
York	0-0	0-0	0-0	0-0	0-0	0-0	0-0	0-0	0-1	1-0	0-2	0-1	0-0	1-4
Totals	6-7	4-9	5-7	6-6	7-6	4-8	5-8	2-10	6-7	5-7	2-10	4-8	1-12	57-105

No-decisions—Egloff, Gozzo, Kiser, Kramer, Seanez, E. Valdez.

DETROIT—84-78

Pitcher	Bal.	Bos.	Cal.	Chi.	Cle.	K.C.	Mil.	Min.	N.Y.	Oak.	Sea.	Tex.	Tor.	Totals
	W-L	W-L	W-L	W-L	W-L	W-L	W-L	W-L	W-L	W-L	W-L	W-L	W-L	W-L
Aldred	0-1	0-0	0-0	0-0	1-0	0-0	1-0	0-1	0-0	0-0	0-1	0-0	0-1	2-4
Cerutti	0-0	0-0	0-1	0-0	1-0	0-0	1-0	0-1	0-0	0-1	0-1	0-1	1-1	3-6
Gakeler	0-1	0-0	0-1	0-0	0-0	0-1	0-0	0-0	0-0	0-0	1-0	0-1	0-0	1-4
Gibson	0-1	0-1	1-1	0-2	0-0	1-0	0-0	0-0	2-1	0-0	0-1	0-0	1-0	5-7
Gleaton	1-0	0-0	0-0	0-0	0-0	0-0	0-0	0-0	1-0	0-1	1-0	0-1	0-0	3-2
Gullickson	2-0	2-0	1-1	1-0	1-2	3-1	1-1	1-3	1-0	1-1	4-0	0-0	2-0	20-9
Haas	1-0	0-0	0-0	0-0	0-0	0-0	0-0	0-0	0-0	0-0	0-0	0-0	0-0	1-0
Henneman	1-0	1-0	0-0	1-0	0-0	0-0	1-0	0-1	1-0	0-1	0-0	4-0	1-0	10-2
Kaiser	0-0	0-0	0-0	0-0	0-0	0-0	0-0	0-0	0-0	0-0	0-0	0-0	0-1	0-1
Kiely	0-0	0-0	0-0	0-0	0-0	0-0	0-0	0-0	0-0	0-0	0-1	0-0	0-0	0-1
Leiter	1-1	1-0	2-0	2-0	0-1	1-1	0-2	0-0	1-0	1-1	0-0	0-0	0-1	9-7
Meacham	0-0	1-0	0-0	0-0	1-0	0-1	0-0	0-0	0-0	0-0	0-0	0-0	0-0	2-1
Petry	0-0	0-1	0-0	0-0	0-0	0-0	0-0	2-0	0-0	0-0	0-0	0-1	0-1	2-3
Ritz	0-0	0-0	0-1	0-0	0-1	0-0	0-0	0-0	0-0	0-0	0-1	0-0	0-0	0-3
Searcy	0-0	0-0	0-0	0-1	0-0	1-0	0-0	0-0	0-0	0-0	0-0	0-1	0-0	1-2
Tanana	2-0	1-1	1-0	3-1	1-1	1-0	0-3	1-1	1-1	1-2	1-0	0-1	0-1	13-12
Terrell	0-1	2-2	2-0	1-0	1-2	1-0	0-3	0-1	1-2	1-1	1-0	2-0	0-2	12-14
Totals	8-5	8-5	7-5	8-4	6-7	8-4	4-9	4-8	8-5	4-8	8-4	6-6	5-8	84-78

No-decisions—Dalton, Munoz.

KANSAS CITY—82-80

Pitcher	Bal.	Bos.	Cal.	Chi.	Cle.	Det.	Mil.	Min.	N.Y.	Oak.	Sea.	Tex.	Tor.	Totals
	W-L	W-L	W-L	W-L	W-L	W-L	W-L	W-L	W-L	W-L	W-L	W-L	W-L	W-L
Appier	0-0	1-3	2-1	1-1	2-1	2-1	0-0	0-1	1-0	1-0	2-0	1-1	0-1	13-10
Aquino	2-0	0-0	0-2	0-2	0-0	0-0	2-0	1-0	1-0	1-0	0-0	0-0	1-0	8-4
Boddicker	0-0	2-0	0-1	1-2	0-1	1-1	1-0	0-1	2-2	1-1	1-2	3-1	0-0	12-12
Crawford	1-0	0-0	0-0	0-0	0-0	0-0	0-0	0-0	0-0	1-0	0-1	1-0	0-1	3-2
S. Davis	0-1	0-2	0-0	0-0	1-0	0-1	1-0	0-1	1-0	0-1	0-0	0-1	0-2	3-9
M. Davis	2-0	0-0	0-1	1-0	0-0	0-0	1-1	1-0	0-0	1-1	0-0	0-0	0-0	6-3
Gordon	0-1	0-1	0-1	0-1	1-1	1-1	2-0	0-1	2-0	0-3	2-1	0-1	1-2	9-14
Gubicza	1-0	0-0	1-2	1-1	1-0	0-0	1-1	1-3	0-2	1-1	0-1	1-0	1-1	9-12
Johnston	1-0	0-0	0-0	0-0	0-0	0-0	0-0	0-0	0-0	0-0	0-0	0-0	0-0	1-0
Magnante	0-0	0-0	0-0	0-0	0-0	0-0	0-0	0-1	0-0	0-0	0-0	0-0	0-0	0-1
Montgomery	0-1	1-0	0-0	1-0	1-0	0-0	0-0	0-0	0-0	0-0	1-1	0-0	0-0	4-4
Saberhagen	1-1	0-1	1-0	1-0	2-1	0-2	0-1	1-0	3-0	1-1	1-0	0-1	2-0	13-8
Wagner	0-0	0-0	0-1	0-0	0-0	0-0	0-0	0-0	0-0	0-0	1-0	0-0	0-0	1-1
Totals	8-4	5-7	4-9	6-7	8-4	4-8	9-3	6-7	7-5	6-7	7-6	7-6	5-7	82-80

No-decisions—Corbin, Gardner, Maldonado, McGaffigan, Pecota, Schatzeder.

MILWAUKEE—83-79

Pitcher	Bal. W-L	Bos. W-L	Cal. W-L	Chi. W-L	Cle. W-L	Det. W-L	K.C. W-L	Min. W-L	N.Y. W-L	Oak. W-L	Sea. W-L	Tex. W-L	Tor. W-L	Totals W-L
August	2-0	0-1	0-1	2-1	1-0	1-0	1-0	0-0	1-1	1-0	0-2	0-0	0-2	9-8
Bosio	0-1	1-1	1-1	2-0	0-0	3-0	0-2	1-1	1-0	1-1	0-1	3-0	1-2	14-10
Brown	0-0	0-1	0-1	0-0	0-0	0-0	0-1	1-0	0-0	0-1	0-0	0-0	1-0	2-4
Crim	0-0	0-0	0-0	0-0	3-0	0-1	1-1	0-0	0-1	1-1	0-0	1-1	2-0	8-5
Eldred	0-0	1-0	0-0	0-0	0-0	0-0	0-0	0-0	1-0	0-0	0-0	0-0	0-0	2-0
Henry	1-0	0-0	0-0	0-0	0-0	0-0	0-0	1-0	0-0	0-0	0-1	0-0	0-0	2-1
Higuera	0-0	0-0	2-0	0-0	0-0	0-0	0-0	0-0	0-1	0-0	1-1	0-0	0-0	3-2
Holmes	1-1	0-0	0-0	0-0	0-1	0-0	0-1	0-1	0-0	0-0	0-0	0-0	0-0	1-4
Hunter	0-1	0-1	0-0	0-0	0-1	0-0	0-0	0-1	0-0	0-0	0-0	0-0	0-0	0-5
Ignasiak	0-0	1-1	0-0	0-0	0-0	0-0	0-0	0-0	0-0	0-0	0-0	0-0	1-0	2-1
Knudson	0-0	0-1	0-0	0-1	0-0	0-0	0-0	0-0	0-0	0-0	0-0	1-1	0-0	1-3
Lee	0-0	0-0	1-0	0-1	0-0	0-1	0-1	0-0	1-2	0-0	0-0	0-0	0-0	2-5
Machado	0-0	2-0	0-0	0-0	0-1	0-1	0-0	0-0	0-0	0-0	0-0	0-1	1-0	3-3
Navarro	3-0	1-1	1-1	0-1	2-1	1-0	1-1	2-1	0-1	2-1	1-3	1-1	0-0	15-12
Nunez	1-0	0-0	0-0	0-0	0-0	0-0	0-0	0-1	0-0	1-0	0-0	0-0	0-0	2-1
Plesac	0-0	0-0	0-1	0-2	0-0	1-1	0-0	0-0	0-1	0-0	0-0	1-0	0-2	2-7
Robinson	0-0	0-0	0-0	0-0	0-0	0-0	0-0	0-0	0-0	0-0	0-0	0-0	0-1	0-1
Wegman	2-0	0-0	1-1	1-1	2-1	3-0	0-1	1-1	2-0	2-0	1-1	0-1	0-0	15-7
Totals	10-3	6-7	6-6	5-7	8-5	9-4	3-9	6-6	6-7	8-4	3-9	7-5	6-7	83-79

No-decisions—Austin, Dempsey, George.

MINNESOTA—95-67

Pitcher	Bal. W-L	Bos. W-L	Cal. W-L	Chi. W-L	Cle. W-L	Det. W-L	K.C. W-L	Mil. W-L	N.Y. W-L	Oak. W-L	Sea. W-L	Tex. W-L	Tor. W-L	Totals W-L
Abbott	0-0	1-0	0-0	0-0	2-0	0-0	0-0	0-0	0-1	0-0	0-0	0-0	0-0	3-1
Aguilera	0-1	0-0	0-0	0-1	1-0	0-0	0-0	1-2	0-0	1-0	1-1	0-0	0-0	4-5
Anderson	0-0	0-0	0-1	0-2	1-0	0-1	2-0	0-1	1-1	1-0	0-1	0-2	0-2	5-11
Banks	0-0	0-0	1-1	0-0	0-0	0-0	0-0	0-0	0-0	0-0	0-0	0-0	0-0	1-1
Bedrosian	1-0	1-1	0-0	0-0	0-0	0-0	0-0	0-0	2-1	1-0	0-1	0-1	0-0	5-3
Edens	0-1	0-0	0-0	1-0	0-0	0-0	1-0	0-0	0-0	0-0	0-1	0-0	0-0	2-2
Erickson	1-1	3-0	1-1	1-1	2-0	3-0	1-1	0-0	3-0	1-1	2-2	1-0	1-1	20-8
Guthrie	0-0	0-0	0-1	1-1	0-0	2-0	1-1	2-0	1-0	0-1	0-0	0-0	0-1	7-5
Leach	0-0	0-0	0-0	0-1	0-0	0-0	0-0	0-0	0-0	0-0	0-0	1-0	0-1	1-2
Morris	3-0	2-1	1-3	1-1	2-1	0-1	1-1	1-1	0-0	2-2	1-0	2-1	2-0	18-12
Neagle	0-0	0-0	0-0	0-0	0-0	0-0	0-0	0-0	0-0	0-0	0-0	0-0	0-1	0-1
Tapani	2-0	1-0	2-0	0-0	1-0	0-1	1-3	1-2	4-0	0-0	3-0	1-1	0-2	16-9
Wayne	0-0	0-0	0-0	0-0	0-0	0-0	0-0	0-0	0-0	0-0	0-0	1-0	0-0	1-0
West	0-0	0-1	0-1	0-0	1-1	1-1	0-0	0-0	0-0	0-0	1-0	0-0	1-0	4-4
Willis	1-1	1-0	0-0	1-1	0-0	2-0	0-0	1-0	1-0	1-0	0-0	0-1	0-0	8-3
Totals	8-4	9-3	5-8	5-8	10-2	8-4	7-6	6-6	10-2	8-5	9-4	6-7	4-8	95-67

No-decisions—Casian.

NEW YORK—71-91

Pitcher	Bal. W-L	Bos. W-L	Cal. W-L	Chi. W-L	Cle. W-L	Det. W-L	K.C. W-L	Mil. W-L	Min. W-L	Oak. W-L	Sea. W-L	Tex. W-L	Tor. W-L	Totals W-L
Cadaret	1-0	0-0	1-0	1-1	0-1	1-2	1-0	1-0	1-0	0-0	0-1	1-0	0-1	8-6
Cary	0-0	0-0	0-1	1-1	0-1	0-0	0-1	0-1	0-0	0-0	0-1	0-0	0-0	1-6
Chapin	0-0	0-0	0-0	0-0	0-1	0-0	0-0	0-0	0-0	0-0	0-0	0-0	0-0	0-1
Eiland	0-0	0-0	0-0	0-1	1-1	1-0	0-1	0-0	0-0	0-2	0-0	0-0	0-0	2-5
Farr	1-0	1-0	0-0	0-1	0-1	1-1	0-1	1-0	0-0	1-0	0-0	0-0	0-1	5-5
Guetterman	0-0	1-1	0-0	0-0	0-0	0-0	0-0	0-0	0-1	0-0	0-0	0-1	1-1	3-4
Habyan	1-0	1-0	0-0	0-0	0-0	0-0	0-1	0-0	0-0	0-1	1-0	0-0	2-0	4-2
Hawkins	0-0	0-0	0-1	0-0	0-0	0-0	0-0	0-0	0-0	0-0	0-0	0-0	0-0	0-2
Howe	0-0	0-0	1-0	0-0	0-0	0-0	0-0	1-0	0-0	0-1	1-0	0-0	0-0	3-1
Johnson	1-0	0-1	1-0	0-2	0-0	0-1	0-0	0-0	0-3	1-0	1-0	0-1	2-2	6-11
Kamieniecki	0-0	0-0	0-1	0-0	1-0	0-0	0-0	0-1	1-0	1-0	0-1	0-0	1-0	4-4
Leary	0-1	1-1	0-0	0-1	1-0	0-0	2-0	0-0	0-0	0-1	0-2	0-2	0-2	4-10
Mills	0-0	0-0	0-0	0-0	0-1	0-0	0-0	0-0	1-0	0-0	0-0	0-0	0-0	1-1
Monteleone	1-0	0-0	0-0	1-0	0-0	0-0	0-0	0-0	1-0	0-0	0-1	0-0	0-0	3-1
Perez	0-0	0-1	1-0	0-0	1-0	0-0	0-1	0-1	0-0	0-0	0-0	0-1	0-0	2-4
Plunk	2-1	0-0	0-1	0-1	0-1	0-0	0-0	0-1	0-0	0-0	0-0	0-1	0-0	2-5
Sanderson	1-1	3-1	2-1	0-0	2-0	2-1	2-1	0-0	0-2	1-1	1-2	0-0	2-0	16-10
Taylor	0-2	1-1	0-1	1-0	1-0	0-1	0-0	1-2	0-2	1-1	0-1	2-1	0-0	7-12
Witt	0-0	0-0	0-0	0-0	0-0	0-0	0-0	0-0	0-1	0-0	0-0	0-0	0-0	0-1
Totals	8-5	7-6	6-6	4-8	7-6	5-8	5-7	7-6	2-10	6-6	3-9	5-7	6-7	71-91

No-decisions—Espinoza.

OAKLAND—84-78

Pitcher	Bal. W-L	Bos. W-L	Cal. W-L	Chi. W-L	Cle. W-L	Det. W-L	K.C. W-L	Mil. W-L	Min. W-L	N.Y. W-L	Sea. W-L	Tex. W-L	Tor. W-L	Totals W-L
Allison	0-0	0-0	0-0	0-0	0-0	0-0	0-0	0-0	0-0	0-0	1-1	0-0	0-0	1-1
Burns	1-0	0-0	0-0	0-0	0-0	0-0	0-0	0-0	0-0	0-0	0-0	0-0	0-0	1-0

Pitcher	Bal. W-L	Bos. W-L	Cal. W-L	Chi. W-L	Cle. W-L	Det. W-L	K.C. W-L	Mil. W-L	Min. W-L	N.Y. W-L	Sea. W-L	Tex. W-L	Tor. W-L	Totals W-L
Campbell	0-0	0-0	0-0	0-0	0-0	0-0	0-0	0-0	0-0	1-0	0-0	0-0	0-0	1-0
Chitren	0-0	0-2	1-0	0-1	0-0	0-0	0-0	0-0	0-0	0-0	0-1	0-0	0-0	1-4
Darling	0-0	0-0	2-0	0-2	0-0	0-0	0-1	0-2	0-0	0-0	1-0	0-1	0-1	3-7
Dres'ndorfer	0-0	0-0	0-1	0-0	0-1	0-0	0-0	0-0	1-0	1-0	1-0	0-0	0-1	3-3
Eckersley	0-0	0-0	0-0	2-0	0-1	2-0	0-0	0-1	0-0	0-0	0-1	0-1	1-0	5-4
Guzman	0-0	0-0	0-0	0-0	0-0	1-0	0-0	0-0	0-0	0-0	0-0	0-0	0-0	1-0
Hawkins	0-0	0-0	0-0	0-1	0-0	0-1	1-1	1-0	0-0	0-1	0-0	0-0	0-0	4-4
Honeycutt	1-0	0-0	0-0	0-1	1-0	0-0	0-0	0-0	0-1	0-0	0-0	0-2	0-0	2-4
Klink	2-0	1-0	0-0	2-0	2-0	0-0	1-0	0-0	1-2	0-1	0-0	0-0	1-0	10-3
Moore	1-0	0-3	4-0	0-1	0-1	2-0	2-0	0-1	0-0	1-2	2-0	1-0	4-0	17-8
Nelson	0-0	0-0	0-0	0-0	0-0	1-0	0-0	0-1	0-1	0-0	0-0	0-3	0-0	1-5
Show	0-1	0-0	0-0	0-0	1-0	0-0	0-0	0-0	0-0	0-1	0-0	0-0	0-0	1-2
Slusarski	1-1	0-2	0-0	1-0	0-0	0-0	0-1	0-1	1-0	0-0	0-1	1-0	0-1	5-7
Stewart	1-0	1-0	2-0	1-1	0-0	1-0	1-1	1-2	1-2	1-0	0-2	1-2	0-1	11-11
Walton	0-0	0-0	0-0	0-0	0-0	0-0	0-0	0-0	1-0	0-0	0-0	0-0	0-0	1-0
Welch	1-0	2-1	3-0	0-0	0-2	0-3	2-2	1-0	1-2	1-0	1-1	0-0	0-2	12-13
Young	1-1	0-0	0-0	0-0	1-0	0-0	0-0	0-0	0-0	1-1	0-0	1-0	0-0	4-2
Totals	9-3	4-8	12-1	6-7	7-5	8-4	7-6	4-8	5-8	6-6	6-7	4-9	6-6	84-78

No-decisions—Briscoe, Harris, Law, Van Poppel.

SEATTLE—83-79

Pitcher	Bal. W-L	Bos. W-L	Cal. W-L	Chi. W-L	Cle. W-L	Det. W-L	K.C. W-L	Mil. W-L	Min. W-L	N.Y. W-L	Oak. W-L	Tex. W-L	Tor. W-L	Totals W-L
Bankhead	0-0	0-1	1-0	0-0	0-0	0-1	0-0	0-0	0-1	1-0	0-1	1-1	0-1	3-6
Burba	0-0	0-0	0-0	0-2	0-0	0-0	1-0	0-0	0-0	0-0	0-0	1-0	0-0	2-2
DeLucia	2-1	0-0	0-2	1-2	3-0	0-2	1-1	2-0	0-0	0-0	2-2	1-1	0-1	12-13
Fleming	0-0	0-0	0-0	0-0	0-0	0-0	1-0	0-0	0-0	0-0	0-0	0-0	0-0	1-0
Hanson	2-0	0-1	0-1	0-2	0-0	0-0	0-1	2-0	1-1	1-1	1-0	0-0	1-1	8-8
Holman	0-0	0-0	1-2	0-0	3-1	2-2	1-1	2-1	1-1	1-2	1-1	0-1	1-2	13-14
Jackson	1-0	0-1	2-0	0-0	2-1	0-0	0-1	0-0	1-0	0-1	0-1	0-1	0-1	7-7
Johnson	0-1	0-2	2-1	2-0	2-0	1-1	0-2	1-1	1-2	2-0	2-0	0-0	0-0	13-10
C. Jones	0-0	0-1	0-0	1-1	0-0	0-0	0-0	0-0	0-0	1-0	0-0	0-0	0-0	2-2
Krueger	2-1	2-1	1-0	1-0	0-0	0-0	0-1	1-1	0-2	3-0	0-1	0-1	1-0	11-8
Murphy	0-0	0-1	0-0	0-0	0-0	0-0	0-0	0-0	0-0	0-0	0-0	0-0	0-0	0-1
Rice	0-0	0-0	0-0	0-0	0-0	0-1	0-0	0-0	0-0	1-0	0-0	0-0	0-0	1-1
Schooler	0-0	0-0	0-0	0-0	0-0	0-1	0-0	1-0	0-1	0-0	0-0	1-1	0-0	3-3
Swan	1-0	1-0	0-0	1-0	0-0	0-0	1-0	0-0	0-0	0-0	1-1	1-1	0-0	6-2
Swift	0-1	0-0	0-0	0-0	0-0	1-0	0-0	0-0	0-0	0-0	0-0	0-1	0-0	1-2
Totals	8-4	3-9	7-6	6-7	10-2	4-8	6-7	9-3	4-9	9-3	7-6	5-8	5-7	83-79

No-decisions—Comstock, Harris.

TEXAS—85-77

Pitcher	Bal. W-L	Bos. W-L	Cal. W-L	Chi. W-L	Cle. W-L	Det. W-L	K.C. W-L	Mil. W-L	Min. W-L	N.Y. W-L	Oak. W-L	Sea. W-L	Tor. W-L	Totals W-L
Alexander	0-1	1-0	0-0	1-1	0-0	1-0	0-0	0-1	1-0	0-0	0-0	1-0	0-0	5-3
Arnsberg	0-0	0-0	0-0	0-0	0-0	0-1	0-0	0-0	0-0	0-0	0-0	0-0	0-0	0-1
Barfield	0-0	0-0	0-0	1-1	0-0	1-0	0-0	0-0	0-0	0-1	0-1	1-0	1-1	4-4
Bitker	0-0	0-0	0-0	0-0	0-0	0-0	0-0	0-0	0-0	1-0	0-0	0-0	0-0	1-0
Bohanon	0-0	0-0	0-1	0-0	1-0	0-0	1-0	1-0	0-0	0-2	0-0	1-0	0-0	4-3
Boyd	0-1	0-2	0-1	0-0	0-0	0-0	0-0	0-1	1-0	1-0	0-1	0-1	0-0	2-7
Brown	0-1	1-1	1-2	0-0	2-1	0-2	0-1	1-1	1-0	2-0	1-1	0-1	0-1	9-12
Chiamparino	0-0	0-0	0-0	0-0	0-0	1-0	0-0	0-0	0-0	0-0	0-0	0-0	0-0	1-0
Fajardo	0-0	0-0	0-0	0-0	0-0	0-0	0-0	0-0	0-1	0-0	0-0	0-0	0-0	0-2
Gossage	0-0	0-0	0-0	0-1	0-0	0-0	2-0	0-0	1-0	0-0	0-1	0-0	0-0	4-2
Guzman	0-1	2-0	3-0	0-0	1-0	0-0	0-2	1-0	1-2	3-0	2-0	0-1	0-1	13-7
Jeffcoat	0-0	0-1	0-0	1-0	2-1	0-1	1-0	0-0	0-0	0-0	0-0	0-0	1-0	5-3
Manuel	0-0	0-0	1-0	0-0	0-0	0-0	0-0	0-0	0-0	0-0	0-0	0-0	0-0	1-0
Mathews	0-0	0-0	0-0	0-0	0-0	0-0	2-0	0-0	0-0	2-0	0-0	0-0	0-0	4-0
Petkovsek	0-0	0-0	0-0	0-0	0-0	0-0	0-0	0-0	0-0	0-1	0-0	0-0	0-0	0-1
Rogers	0-3	2-0	0-1	0-1	1-0	0-0	1-2	1-1	0-1	0-0	2-0	1-1	2-0	10-10
Rosenthal	0-1	0-0	0-0	0-0	0-0	0-1	0-0	0-0	0-0	0-1	1-0	0-1	0-0	1-4
Je. Russell	0-0	0-0	0-1	1-1	0-0	0-1	0-0	0-1	1-0	0-0	1-0	2-0	0-1	6-4
Ryan	3-0	1-0	2-0	1-0	0-1	1-0	1-1	0-1	1-1	0-0	0-0	0-0	1-2	12-6
Schiraldi	0-0	0-0	0-0	0-1	0-0	0-0	0-0	0-0	0-0	0-0	0-0	0-0	0-0	0-1
Witt	0-1	0-1	0-0	0-2	1-1	0-0	0-1	0-1	1-0	0-0	0-0	1-0	0-0	3-7
Totals	3-9	7-5	8-5	5-8	8-4	6-6	6-7	5-7	7-6	7-5	9-4	8-5	6-6	85-77

No-decisions—Nolte, Poole.

TORONTO—91-71

Pitcher	Bal. W-L	Bos. W-L	Cal. W-L	Chi. W-L	Cle. W-L	Det. W-L	K.C. W-L	Mil. W-L	Min. W-L	N.Y. W-L	Oak. W-L	Sea. W-L	Tex. W-L	Totals W-L
Acker	0-0	0-0	0-1	0-0	0-1	0-0	0-0	0-0	0-0	1-0	1-1	1-1	0-1	3-5
Boucher	0-0	0-1	0-0	0-0	0-0	0-0	0-2	0-0	0-0	0-0	0-0	0-0	0-0	0-3

Pitcher	Bal. W-L	Bos. W-L	Cal. W-L	Chi. W-L	Cle. W-L	Det. W-L	K.C. W-L	Mil. W-L	Min. W-L	N.Y. W-L	Oak. W-L	Sea. W-L	Tex. W-L	Totals W-L
Candiotti	1-0	0-1	0-1	0-1	1-0	1-0	0-2	0-0	1-1	0-0	1-0	0-1	1-0	6-7
Fraser..........	0-0	0-0	0-1	0-1	0-0	0-0	0-0	0-0	0-0	0-0	0-0	0-0	0-0	0-2
Guzman	1-2	0-0	1-0	0-0	2-0	1-0	0-0	0-0	2-1	0-0	2-0	1-0	0-0	10-3
Henke	0-0	0-0	0-0	0-0	0-0	0-1	0-0	0-1	0-0	0-0	0-0	0-0	0-0	0-2
Key	2-0	1-1	1-1	2-0	3-0	2-1	0-0	2-1	0-1	2-1	1-1	0-1	0-4	16-12
MacDonald...	0-0	0-0	0-0	0-1	1-0	1-0	0-0	0-0	0-1	0-0	0-0	1-1	0-0	3-3
Stieb............	0-0	1-1	0-0	1-0	0-0	0-0	0-0	1-0	1-1	0-0	0-0	0-1	0-0	4-3
Stottlemyre ..	3-0	0-1	0-1	0-1	0-0	2-0	2-0	2-0	2-1	1-2	0-1	1-1	2-0	15-8
Timlin	1-1	1-0	2-0	0-2	1-0	1-0	1-1	1-0	0-0	0-1	0-0	2-0	1-1	11-6
D. Ward	0-1	1-1	0-0	0-0	2-0	0-0	1-0	0-1	1-0	0-2	1-0	0-0	0-0	7-6
Weathers	0-0	0-0	0-0	0-0	0-0	0-0	0-0	0-0	1-0	0-0	0-0	0-0	0-0	1-0
Wells	0-1	0-3	2-1	2-1	2-0	0-2	2-0	1-1	1-0	2-1	1-0	0-0	2-0	15-10
Wills	0-0	0-0	0-0	0-0	0-0	0-0	0-0	0-1	0-0	0-0	0-0	0-0	0-0	0-1
Totals........	8-5	4-9	6-6	5-7	12-1	8-5	7-5	7-6	8-4	7-6	6-6	7-5	6-6	91-71

No-decisions—Dayley, Hentgen, Horsman, Leiter, Weston.

HOME RUNS BY PARKS

	At Bal.	At Bos.	At Cal.	At Chi.	At Cle.	At Det.	At K.C.	At Mil.	At Min.	At N.Y.	At Oak.	At Sea.	At Tex.	At Tor.	Totals 1991	1990
Baltimore	80	12	8	5	5	8	4	8	4	8	6	6	7	9	170	132
Boston..................	6	69	2	6	0	5	2	7	4	6	3	9	1	6	126	106
California	7	0	59	4	2	6	2	2	12	6	2	6	2	5	115	147
Chicago................	6	5	6	74	0	8	2	6	5	7	5	4	2	9	139	106
Cleveland	3	8	6	7	22	3	2	4	2	5	7	2	7	1	79	110
Detroit..................	5	13	6	10	1	109	8	7	8	9	5	10	9	9	209	172
Kansas City	8	2	4	9	3	9	47	3	4	5	7	3	9	4	117	100
Milwaukee............	5	3	4	3	3	8	0	62	7	1	6	0	7	7	116	128
Minnesota............	4	5	5	11	6	7	7	5	62	11	6	3	7	1	140	100
New York..............	3	6	5	3	3	6	3	7	7	82	7	4	6	5	147	147
Oakland................	7	8	8	5	5	6	5	6	6	4	76	8	8	7	159	164
Seattle.................	10	2	7	5	3	5	2	3	2	5	2	69	5	6	126	107
Texas...................	4	9	8	8	7	10	2	8	8	12	8	11	79	3	177	110
Toronto	4	3	5	3	3	8	1	7	6	5	3	3	7	75	133	167
1991 total..........	152	145	133	153	63	198	87	135	137	166	143	138	156	147	1953	....
1990 total..........	156	105	144	94	138	167	88	119	115	142	121	109	123	175	....	1796

AT BALTIMORE (152):

Baltimore (80)—C. Ripken 16, Horn 12, Devereaux 10, Martinez 8, Milligan 8, Gomez 7, Hoiles 5, Evans 4, Davis 3, Orsulak 3, Anderson 1, Hulett 1, Segui 1, Worthington 1. **Boston (6)**—Clark 2, Boggs 1, Greenwell 1, Plantier 1, Vaughn 1. **California (7)**—Parker 2, Gaetti 1, Gallagher 1, Joyner 1, Polonia 1, Winfield 1. **Chicago (6)**—Sosa 2, Fisk 1, Guillen 1, Newson 1, Thomas 1. **Cleveland (3)**—Allred 1, Belle 1, Jacoby 1. **Detroit (5)**—Whitaker 2, Fielder 1, Livingstone 1, Tettleton 1. **Kansas City (8)**—Tartabull 4, Brett 1, Gibson 1, Pecota 1, Shumpert 1. **Milwaukee (5)**—Vaughn 2, Hamilton 1, Molitor 1, Stubbs 1. **Minnesota (4)**—Davis 2, Mack 2. **New York (3)**—Hall 1, Maas 1, Mattingly 1. **Oakland (7)**—Baines 2, Canseco 2, D. Henderson 1, R. Henderson 1, Riles 1. **Seattle (10)**—Buhner 2, Cotto 2, Valle 2, Davis 1, Griffey Jr. 1, E. Martinez 1, Reynolds 1. **Texas (4)**—Gonzalez 2, Buechele 1, Reimer 1. **Toronto (4)**—White 3, Carter 1.

AT BOSTON (145):

Baltimore (12)—Milligan 3, Devereaux 2, Gomez 2, Horn 2, Davis 1, Hoiles 1, C. Ripken 1. **Boston (69)**—Clark 18, Brunansky 10, Burks 8, Boggs 6, Plantier 6, Greenwell 5, Rivera 4, Reed 3, Lyons 2, Pena 2, Quintana 2, Vaughn 1. **California—None. **Chicago (5)**—Ventura 3, Merullo 1, Thomas 1. **Cleveland (8)**—Belle 3, Baerga 2, Hill 2, Jacoby 1. **Detroit (13)**—Deer 3, Fielder 3, Fryman 2, Incaviglia 2, Barnes 1, Bergman 1, Tettleton 1. **Kansas City (2)**—Cromartie 1, Stillwell 1. **Milwaukee (3)**—Bichette 2, Brock 1. **Minnesota (5)**—Bush 1, Davis 1, Leius 1, Mack 1, Puckett 1. **New York (6)**—R. Kelly 2, Geren 1, Hall 1, Nokes 1, Sax 1. **Oakland (8)**—Canseco 2, McGwire 2, Blankenship 1, D. Henderson 1, R. Henderson 1, Steinbach 1. **Seattle (2)**—Valle 2. **Texas (9)**—Gonzalez 4, Downing 1, Franco 1, Palmeiro 1, Palmer 1, Sierra 1. **Toronto (3)**—Carter 2, Gruber 1.

AT CALIFORNIA (133):

Baltimore (8)—Devereaux 2, Gomez 1, Horn 1, Hulett 1, Martinez 1, C. Ripken 1, Worthington 1. **Boston (2)**—Brunansky 2. **California (59)**—Winfield 13, Gaetti 12, Joyner 10, Parrish 9, Parker 6, Felix 2, Venable 2, Abner 1, Hill 1, Polonia 1, Sojo 1, Tingley 1. **Chicago (6)**—Fisk 1, Grebeck 1, Raines 1, Sosa 1, Thomas 1, Ventura 1. **Cleveland (6)**—Belle 5, Hill 1. **Detroit (6)**—Phillips 2, Whitaker 2, Fryman 1, Trammell 1. **Kansas City (4)**—Tartabull 2, McRae 1, Spehr 1. **Milwaukee (4)**—Molitor 2, Bichette 1, Gantner 1. **Minnesota (5)**—Davis 2, Larkin 1, Puckett 1. **New York (5)**—R. Kelly 2, Hall 1, Maas 1, Williams 1. **Oakland (8)**—Canseco 3, D. Henderson 3, Gallego 1, Riles 1. **Seattle (7)**—Buhner 4, Davis 1, Griffey Jr. 1, O'Brien 1. **Texas (8)**—Palmeiro 3, Sierra 2, Buechele 1, Downing 1, Palmer 1. **Toronto (5)**—Borders 1, Gruber 1, Maldonado 1, Olerud 1, Williams 1.

AT CHICAGO (153):

Baltimore (5)—Davis 2, Hulett 1, Orsulak 1, C. Ripken 1. **Boston (6)**—Boggs 1, Brunansky 1, Clark 1, Pena 1, Quintana 1, Romine 1. **California (4)**—Winfield 2, Joyner 1, Parrish 1. **Chicago (74)**—Thomas 24, Ventura 16, Pasqua 10, Fisk 9, Grebeck 3, Jackson 3, Sosa 3, Snyder 2, Guillen 1, Merullo 1, Newson 1, Raines 1. **Cleveland (7)**—Baerga 3, Aldrete 1, Belle 1, Gonzalez 1, Martinez 1. **Detroit (10)**—Deer 3, Fielder 3, Barnes 1, Moseby 1, Phillips 1, Tettleton 1. **Kansas City (9)**—Tartabull 2, Gibson 2, Shumpert 2, Macfarlane 1, Stillwell 1. **Milwaukee (3)**—Vaughn 2, Spiers 1. **Minnesota (11)**—Hrbek 2, Munoz 2, Bush 1, Gagne 1, Gladden 1, Harper 1, Leius 1, Puckett 1, Sorrento 1. **New York (3)**—Barfield 1, Hall 1, Nokes 1. **Oakland (5)**—Baines 1, Blankenship 1,

Canseco 1, Gallego 1, Quirk 1. **Seattle (5)** —Griffey Jr. 1, T. Martinez 1, E. Martinez 1, O'Brien 1, Schaefer 1. **Texas (8)** —Franco 2, Gonzalez 2, Sierra 2, Palmeiro 1, Palmer 1. **Toronto (3)** —Olerud 2, Sprague 1.

AT CLEVELAND (63):

Baltimore (5) —C. Ripken 2, Hoiles 1, Horn 1, Milligan 1. **Boston**—None. **California (2)** —Gaetti 1, Joyner 1. **Chicago**—None. **Cleveland (22)** —Belle 8, Martinez 3, Baerga 2, Jacoby 2, Whiten 2, Browne 1, Hill 1, Huff 1, James 1, Jefferson 1. **Detroit (1)** —Bergman 1. **Kansas City (3)** —Gibson 3. **Milwaukee (3)** —Bichette 1, Molitor 1, Vaughn 1. **Minnesota (6)** —Mack 2, Puckett 2, Harper 1, Hrbek 1. **New York (3)** —Maas 1, Meulens 1, Nokes 1. **Oakland (5)** —Canseco 2, D. Henderson 2, Steinbach 1. **Seattle (3)** —Cotto 1, E. Martinez 1, Powell 1. **Texas (7)** —Gonzalez 2, Downing 1, Franco 1, Palmeiro 1, Palmer 1, Reimer 1. **Toronto (3)** —Gruber 2, Carter 1.

AT DETROIT (198):

Baltimore (8) —C. Ripken 3, Horn 2, Davis 1, Hulett 1, Martinez 1. **Boston (5)** —Rivera 2, Burks 1, Quintana 1, Reed 1. **California (6)** —Gaetti 2, Parker 2, Parrish 2. **Chicago (8)** —Karkovice 2, Fisk 1, Guillen 1, Huff 1, Kittle 1, Raines 1, Ventura 1. **Cleveland (3)** —Belle 2, Martinez 1. **Detroit (109)** —Fielder 27, Tettleton 15, Whitaker 15, Deer 12, Phillips 9, Fryman 8, Incaviglia 6, Trammell 6, Moseby 4, Bergman 2, Shelby 2, Barnes 1, Cuyler 1, Livingstone 1. **Kansas City (9)** —Macfarlane 4, McRae 2, Benzinger 1, Brett 1, Tartabull 1. **Milwaukee (8)** —Molitor 2, Spiers 2, Vaughn 2, Canale 1, Stubbs 1. **Minnesota (7)** —Pagliarulo 2, Davis 1, Hrbek 1, Leius 1, Mack 1, Puckett 1. **New York (6)** —Maas 2, Blowers 1, Hall 1, R. Kelly 1, Mattingly 1. **Oakland (6)** —Baines 3, Canseco 2, McGwire 1. **Seattle (5)** —Valle 2, Cotto 1, T. Jones 1, O'Brien 1. **Texas (10)** —Franco 2, Palmeiro 2, Sierra 2, Stanley 2, Gonzalez 1, Huson 1. **Toronto (8)** —Gruber 3, Alomar 1, Maldonado 1, Myers 1, Olerud 1, White 1.

AT KANSAS CITY (87):

Baltimore (4) —Anderson 1, Hoiles 1, Hulett 1, Milligan 1. **Boston (2)** —Brunansky 1, Clark 1. **California (2)** —Winfield 2. **Chicago (2)** —Fisk 2. **Cleveland (2)** —Belle 1, Manto 1. **Detroit (8)** —Tettleton 3, Bergman 1, Deer 1, Fielder 1, Fryman 1, Whitaker 1. **Kansas City (47)** —Tartabull 13, Macfarlane 6, Gibson 4, Pecota 4, Brett 3, Martinez 3, McRae 3, Eisenreich 2, Mayne 2, Pulliam 2, Benzinger 1, Shumpert 1, Spehr 1, Stillwell 1, Thurman 1. **Milwaukee**—None. **Minnesota (7)** —Davis 3, Webster 2, Munoz 1, Puckett 1. **New York (3)** —R. Kelly 1, Maas 1, Nokes 1. **Oakland (5)** —Canseco 2, Baines 1, Gallego 1, McGwire 1. **Seattle (2)** —Davis 1, Griffey Jr. 1. **Texas (2)** —Gonzalez 2. **Toronto (1)** —Alomar 1.

AT MILWAUKEE (135):

Baltimore (8) —C. Ripken 3, Davis 1, Devereaux 1, Gomez 1, Horn 1, Martinez 1. **Boston (7)** —Plantier 2, Brunansky 1, Burks 1, Clark 1, Greenwell 1, Vaughn 1. **California (2)** —Joyner 1, Winfield 1. **Chicago (6)** —Merullo 1, Newson 1, Pasqua 1, Raines 1, Thomas 1, Ventura 1. **Cleveland (4)** —Belle 2, Baerga 1, Jefferson 1. **Detroit (7)** —Fielder 2, Tettleton 2, Allanson 1, Deer 1, Shelby 1. **Kansas City (3)** —Brett 1, Gibson 1, Mayne 1. **Milwaukee (62)** —Vaughn 16, Stubbs 8, Yount 8, Molitor 7, Bichette 6, Maldonado 3, Surhoff 3, Sveum 3, Dempsey 2, Sheffield 2, Canale 1, Gantner 1, McIntosh 1, Spiers 1. **Minnesota (5)** —Gagne 2, Harper 2, Mack 1. **New York (7)** —Maas 3, Barfield 1, Espinoza 1, R. Kelly 1, Nokes 1. **Oakland (6)** —Canseco 2, McGwire 2, R. Henderson 1, Howitt 1. **Seattle (3)** —Buhner 1, Cochrane 1, Davis 1. **Texas (8)** —Buechele 2, Reimer 2, Downing 1, Gonzalez 1, Palmeiro 1, Sierra 1. **Toronto (7)** —Carter 2, Olerud 2, Gruber 1, Maldonado 1, Mulliniks 1.

AT MINNESOTA (137):

Baltimore (4) —Gomez 1, Martinez 1, Milligan 1, Segui 1. **Boston (4)** —Greenwell 1, Pena 1, Quintana 1, Rivera 1. **California (12)** —Parrish 5, Winfield 4, Abner 1, Joyner 1, Sojo 1. **Chicago (5)** —Pasqua 2, Fisk 1, Snyder 1, Sosa 1. **Cleveland (2)** —Belle 1, Huff 1. **Detroit (8)** —Fryman 3, Fielder 2, Deer 1, Phillips 1, Tettleton 1. **Kansas City (4)** —Brett 2, McRae 1, Stillwell 1. **Milwaukee (7)** —Maldonado 2, Bichette 1, Molitor 1, Stubbs 1, Sveum 1, Yount 1. **Minnesota (62)** —Davis 14, Hrbek 11, Puckett 7, Harper 4, Mack 4, Munoz 4, Pagliarulo 4, Gagne 3, Gladden 3, Bush 2, Leius 2, Sorrento 2, Knoblauch 1, Webster 1. **New York (7)** —Barfield 2, Hall 1, R. Kelly 1, Maas 1, Nokes 1, Sheridan 1. **Oakland (6)** —Canseco 4, R. Henderson 1, Steinbach 1. **Seattle (2)** —Davis 1, Griffey Jr. 1. **Texas (8)** —Palmer 3, Buechele 1, Daugherty 1, Gonzalez 1, Palmeiro 1, Sierra 1. **Toronto (6)** —Alomar 1, Ducey 1, Gruber 1, Myers 1, Olerud 1, White 1.

AT NEW YORK (166):

Baltimore (8) —Horn 3, Devereaux 1, Gomez 1, Hoiles 1, Hulett 1, Milligan 1. **Boston (6)** —Greenwell 1, Lyons 1, Plantier 1, Quintana 1, Reed 1, Rivera 1. **California (6)** —Joyner 3, Parrish 1, Rose 1, Venable 1. **Chicago (7)** —Fletcher 1, Karkovice 1, Newson 1, Pasqua 1, Sosa 1, Thomas 1, Ventura 1. **Cleveland (5)** —Whiten 2, Baerga 1, Belle 1, Thome 1. **Detroit (9)** —Tettleton 3, Bergman 2, Deer 1, Fryman 1, Phillips 1, Whitaker 1. **Kansas City (5)** —Gibson 2, Tartabull 2, Pulliam 1. **Milwaukee (1)** —Canale 1. **Minnesota (11)** —Mack 4, Bush 2, Davis 2, Gladden 1, Hrbek 1, Puckett 1. **New York (82)** —Hall 13, Nokes 13, Barfield 11, R. Kelly 11, Maas 8, Mattingly 7, Sax 6, Meulens 4, P. Kelly 3, Espinoza 2, Sheridan 2, Geren 1, Williams 1. **Oakland (4)** —Canseco 1, D. Henderson 1, McGwire 1, Steinbach 1. **Seattle (5)** —Buhner 1, Davis 1, Griffey Jr. 1, E. Martinez 1, O'Brien 1. **Texas (12)** —Buechele 2, Gonzalez 2, Palmeiro 2, Petralli 2, Downing 1, Franco 1, Reimer 1, Sierra 1. **Toronto (5)** —Carter 2, Hill 1, White 1, Wilson 1.

AT OAKLAND (143):

Baltimore (6) —C. Ripken 2, Devereaux 1, Hoiles 1, Hulett 1, Martinez 1. **Boston (3)** —Clark 1, Plantier 1, Quintana 1. **California (2)** —Howell 1, Joyner 1. **Chicago (5)** —Fisk 2, Pasqua 2, Merullo 1. **Cleveland (7)** —James 2, Allred 1, Baerga 1, Belle 1, Hill 1, Skinner 1. **Detroit (5)** —Cuyler 1, Fryman 1, Incaviglia 1, Tettleton 1, Trammell 1. **Kansas City (7)** —Tartabull 4, Gibson 1, Pecota 1, Shumpert 1. **Milwaukee (6)** —Bichette 2, Vaughn 2, Molitor 1, Spiers 1. **Minnesota (6)** —Davis 1, Harper 2, Gagne 1, Mack 1. **New York (7)** —Nokes 3, Barfield 1, Espinoza 1, Sax 1, Sheridan 1. **Oakland (76)** —Canseco 16, D. Henderson 15, McGwire 15, Baines 11, R. Henderson 8, Gallego 6, Riles 3, Brosius 1, Steinbach 1. **Seattle (2)** —Buhner 1, E. Martinez 1. **Texas (8)** —Palmer 2, Sierra 2, Buechele 1, Gonzalez 1, Harris 1, Reimer 1. **Toronto (3)** —Borders 2, White 1.

AT SEATTLE (138):

Baltimore (6) —C. Ripken 2, Bell 1, Devereaux 1, Evans 1, Worthington 1. **Boston (9)** —Burks 3, Clark 2, Quintana 2, Brunansky 1, Vaughn 1. **California (6)** —Gaetti 2, Joyner 2, Parker 1, Sojo 1. **Chicago (4)** —Fisk 1, Merullo 1, Pasqua 1, Raines 1. **Cleveland (2)** —Allred 1, Whiten 1. **Detroit (10)** —Fielder 3, Barnes 2, Cuyler 1, Deer 1, Fryman 1, Phillips 1, Whitaker 1. **Kansas City (3)** —Macfarlane 1, Spehr 1, Tartabull 1. **Milwaukee**—None. **Minnesota (3)** —Mack 2, Hrbek 1. **New York (4)** —Maas 2, Meulens 1, Williams 1. **Oakland (8)** —D. Henderson 2, R. Henderson 2, Blankenship 1, Brosius 1, Gallego 1, Steinbach 1. **Seattle**

(69)—Griffey Jr. 16, Buhner 14, O'Brien 12, E. Martinez 8, Davis 6, T. Martinez 3, Briley 2, Cotto 2, Cochrane 1, Griffey Sr. 1, T. Jones 1, Powell 1, Reynolds 1, Vizquel 1. **Texas (11)**—Downing 4, Buechele 2, Franco 1, Gonzalez 1, Palmeiro 1, Reimer 1, Sierra 1. **Toronto (3)**—Olerud 2, Gruber 1.

AT TEXAS (156):

Baltimore (7)—C. Ripken 2, Davis 1, Gomez 1, Hoiles 1, Horn 1, Worthington 1. **Boston (1)**—Lyons 1. **California (2)**—Parrish 1, Winfield 1. **Chicago (2)**—Grebeck 1, Sosa 1. **Cleveland (7)**—Belle 2, Whiten 2, Baerga 1, James 1, Manto 1. **Detroit (9)**—Fryman 2, Incaviglia 2, Tettleton 2, Fielder 1, Moseby 1, Phillips 1. **Kansas City (9)**—Brett 2, Gibson 2, Stillwell 2, Martinez 1, Seitzer 1, Tartabull 1. **Milwaukee (7)**—Vaughn 2, Bichette 1, Molitor 1, Spiers 1, Surhoff 1, Yount 1. **Minnesota (7)**—Hrbek 3, Davis 1, Gagne 1, Gladden 1, Larkin 1. **New York (6)**—Maas 2, Sax 2, Nokes 1, Velarde 1. **Oakland (8)**—R. Henderson 3, Baines 2, Canseco 2, Gallego 1. **Seattle (5)**—Buhner 3, T. Jones 1, Valle 1. **Texas (79)**—Reimer 13, Palmeiro 12, Sierra 12, Downing 8, Buechele 7, Franco 7, Gonzalez 7, Palmer 6, Rodriguez 3, Diaz 1, Fariss 1, Huson 1, Stanley 1. **Toronto (7)**—Carter 2, Gruber 2, Myers 1, Olerud 1, White 1.

AT TORONTO (147):

Baltimore (9)—Gomez 2, Davis 1, Devereaux 1, Evans 1, Melvin 1, Milligan 1, Orsulak 1, C. Ripken 1. **Boston (6)**—Clark 2, Quintana 2, Burks 1, Pena 1. **California (5)**—Winfield 4, Howell 1. **Chicago (9)**—Thomas 3, Karkovice 2, Grebeck 1, Kittle 1, Pasqua 1, Sosa 1. **Detroit (9)**—Deer 2, Fielder 1, Fryman 1, Phillips 1, Salas 1, Tettleton 1, Trammell 1, Whitaker 1. **Kansas City (4)**—Howard 1, Macfarlane 1, McRae 1, Thurman 1. **Milwaukee (7)**—Dempsey 2, Spiers 2, Bichette 1, Molitor 1, Surhoff 1. **Minnesota (1)**—Sorrento 1. **New York (5)**—Barfield 1, Espinoza 1, R. Kelly 1, Maas 1, Nokes 1. **Oakland (7)**—Canseco 5, Gallego 1, R. Henderson 1. **Seattle (6)**—Buhner 1, E. Martinez 1, O'Brien 1, Powell 1, Reynolds 1, Valle 1. **Texas (3)**—Buechele 1, Gonzalez 1, Palmeiro 1. **Toronto (75)**—Carter 23, White 9, Gruber 8, Olerud 7, Alomar 6, Myers 5, Maldonado 4, Sprague 3, Borders 2, Hill 2, Whiten 2, Gonzales 1, Mulliniks 1, Tabler 1, Wilson 1.

1991
N.L. STATISTICS

BATTING

1991 N.L. STATISTICS

TEAM

Team	Avg.	G	AB	R	H	TB	2B	3B	HR	RBI	SH	SF	HP	BB	Int. BB	SO	SB	CS	GI DP	LOB	ShO	Slg.	OBP
Pittsburgh	.263	162	5449	768	1433	2170	259	50	126	725	99	66	35	620	62	901	124	46	111	1188	6	.398	.338
Cincinnati	.258	162	5501	689	1419	2215	250	27	164	654	72	41	32	488	54	1006	124	56	85	1110	9	.403	.320
Atlanta	.258	162	5456	749	1407	2145	255	30	141	704	86	45	32	563	55	906	165	76	104	1110	9	.393	.328
St. Louis	.255	162	5362	651	1366	1915	239	53	68	599	58	47	21	532	48	857	202	110	94	1072	14	.357	.322
Chicago	.253	160	5522	695	1395	2156	232	26	159	654	75	55	36	442	41	879	123	64	87	1074	8	.390	.309
Los Angeles	.253	162	5408	665	1366	1939	191	29	108	605	94	46	28	583	59	957	126	68	109	1151	8	.359	.326
San Francisco	.246	162	5463	649	1345	2079	215	29	141	605	90	33	40	471	59	973	95	57	91	1110	13	.381	.309
Montreal	.246	161	5412	579	1329	1934	236	42	95	536	64	47	28	484	51	1056	221	100	97	1074	10	.357	.308
Houston	.244	162	5504	605	1345	1908	240	43	79	570	63	43	35	502	45	1027	125	68	87	1131	16	.347	.309
San Diego	.244	162	5408	636	1321	1960	204	36	121	591	78	38	32	501	53	1069	101	64	122	1080	12	.362	.310
New York	.244	161	5359	640	1305	1954	250	24	117	605	60	52	27	578	53	789	153	70	97	1114	9	.365	.317
Philadelphia	.241	162	5521	629	1332	1979	248	33	111	590	52	49	21	490	48	1026	92	30	114	1108	12	.358	.303
Totals	.250	970	65365	7955	16363	24354	2819	441	1430	7438	891	562	367	6254	626	11446	1651	809	1198	13323	122	.373	.317

INDIVIDUAL

TOP 15 QUALIFIERS FOR BATTING CHAMPIONSHIP

Minimum 502 plate appearances. *Lefthanded batter. †Switch-hitter.

Player, Team	Avg.	G	AB	R	H	TB	2B	3B	HR	RBI	SH	SF	HP	BB	Int. BB	SO	SB	CS	GI DP	Slg.	OBP
Pendleton, Terry, Atlanta†	.319	153	586	94	187	303	34	8	22	86	7	7	1	43	8	70	10	2	16	.517	.363
Morris, Hal, Cincinnati*	.318	136	478	72	152	229	33	14	4	59	5	7	1	46	7	61	10	4	4	.479	.374
Gwynn, Tony, San Diego*	.317	134	530	69	168	229	27	11	4	62	5	5	0	34	8	19	8	8	11	.432	.355
McGee, Willie, San Francisco†	.312	131	497	67	155	203	30	3	4	43	8	2	2	34	3	74	17	8	11	.408	.357
Jose, Felix, St. Louis†	.305	154	568	69	173	249	40	6	8	77	0	5	2	50	3	113	20	12	12	.438	.360
Larkin, Barry, Cincinnati	.302	123	464	88	140	235	27	4	20	69	3	2	3	55	1	64	24	6	7	.506	.378
Bonilla, Bobby, Pittsburgh†	.302	157	577	102	174	284	44	6	18	100	0	11	3	90	12	67	2	4	14	.492	.391
Clark, Will, San Francisco*	.301	148	565	84	170	303	32	7	29	116	0	4	2	51	12	91	4	2	5	.536	.359
Sabo, Chris, Cincinnati	.301	153	582	91	175	294	35	3	26	88	5	3	6	44	3	79	19	6	13	.505	.354
Calderon, Ivan, Montreal	.300	134	470	69	141	226	22	3	19	75	4	10	6	53	4	64	31	16	7	.481	.368
Butler, Brett, Los Angeles*	.296	161	615	112	182	211	13	5	2	38	4	1	1	108	4	79	38	28	3	.343	.401
Biggio, Craig, Houston	.295	149	546	79	161	204	23	4	4	46	5	3	2	53	3	71	19	6	6	.374	.358
Bagwell, Jeff, Houston	.294	156	554	79	163	242	26	4	15	82	1	7	13	75	5	116	7	4	12	.437	.387
Kruk, John, Philadelphia*	.294	152	538	84	158	260	27	6	21	92	0	9	1	67	16	100	7	4	11	.483	.367
Bonds, Barry, Pittsburgh*	.292	153	510	95	149	262	28	5	25	116	0	13	0	107	25	73	43	13	8	.514	.410

DEPARTMENTAL LEADERS: G—Butler, L.A., 161; AB—Grace, Chi., 619; R—Butler, L.A., 112; H—Pendleton, Atl. 187; TB—Clark, S.F., Pendleton, Atl, 303; 1B—Butler, L.A., 162; 2B—Bonilla, Pit., 44; 3B—Lankford, St.L., 15; HR—Johnson, N.Y., 38; RBI—Johnson, N.Y., 117; SH—Bell, Pit., 30; SF—Johnson, N.Y., 15; HP—Bagwell, Hou., 13; BB—Butler, L.A., 108; IBB—McGriff, S.D., 26; SO—DeShields, Mon., 151; SB—Grissom, Mon., 76; CS—Butler, L.A., 28; GIDP—Santiago, S.D., 21; Slg. Pct.—Clark, S.F., .536; OB. Pct.—Bonds, Pit., .410.

ALL PLAYERS

*Lefthanded batter. †Switch-hitter.

Player, Team	Avg.	G	AB	R	H	TB	2B	3B	HR	RBI	SH	SF	HP	BB	Int. BB	SO	SB	CS	GI DP	Slg.	OBP
Abner, Shawn, San Diego	.165	53	115	15	19	28	4	1	1	5	1	1	1	7	4	25	0	0	3	.243	.218
Agosto, Juan, St. Louis*	.333	72	3	0	1	1	0	0	0	0	1	0	0	1	0	2	0	0	1	.333	.500
Akerfelds, Darrell, Philadelphia	.000	30	3	0	0	0	0	0	0	0	0	0	0	0	0	3	0	0	0	.000	.000
Aldrete, Mike, San Diego*	.000	12	15	0	0	0	0	0	0	0	0	0	0	3	0	4	0	1	0	.000	.167
Alicea, Luis, St. Louis†	.191	56	68	5	13	16	3	0	0	0	1	0	0	8	2	19	0	0	0	.235	.276
Andersen, Larry, San Diego	.000	38	2	0	0	0	0	0	0	0	0	0	0	0	0	1	0	0	0	.000	.000
Anderson, Dave, San Francisco	.248	100	226	24	56	71	5	2	2	13	2	2	0	12	2	35	2	4	8	.314	.286
Anthony, Eric, Houston*	.153	39	118	11	18	27	6	0	1	7	0	2	0	12	1	41	1	0	2	.229	.227
Armstrong, Jack, Cincinnati	.093	27	43	3	4	5	1	0	0	2	5	0	0	1	0	18	0	0	1	.116	.114
Ashby, Andy, Philadelphia	.083	8	12	0	1	1	0	0	0	0	1	0	0	0	0	9	0	0	0	.083	.083
Assenmacher, Paul, Chicago*	.250	75	4	1	1	1	0	0	0	0	5	0	0	1	1	1	0	0	0	.250	.400
Avery, Steve, Atlanta*	.215	37	79	4	17	20	1	1	0	2	2	0	0	4	0	31	1	0	1	.253	.253
Azocar, Oscar, San Diego*	.246	38	57	5	14	16	2	0	0	9	0	1	0	1	1	9	2	2	2	.281	.267
Backman, Wally, Philadelphia†	.243	94	185	20	45	57	12	0	0	15	1	3	0	30	5	30	3	4	12	.308	.344
Bagwell, Jeff, Houston	.294	156	554	79	163	242	26	4	15	82	2	7	13	75	5	116	7	4	12	.437	.387
Banister, Jeff, Pittsburgh	1.000	1	1	0	1	1	0	0	0	0	0	0	0	0	0	0	0	0	0	1.000	1.000
Barberie, Bret, Montreal†	.353	57	136	16	48	70	12	2	2	18	1	3	2	20	2	22	0	0	4	.515	.435
Barnes, Brian, Montreal*	.082	28	49	1	4	4	0	0	0	1	7	0	0	7	0	19	0	0	0	.082	.196
Barrett, Marty, San Diego	.188	12	16	1	3	7	1	0	0	3	0	0	0	0	0	3	0	0	0	.438	.235
Bass, Kevin, San Francisco†	.233	124	361	43	84	132	10	4	10	40	2	3	4	36	8	56	7	4	12	.366	.307
Batiste, Kim, Philadelphia	.222	10	27	2	6	6	0	0	0	1	0	0	0	0	1	8	0	0	0	.222	.250
Beck, Rod, San Francisco	.500	31	2	0	1	1	0	0	0	0	0	0	0	0	0	0	0	0	0	.500	.500
Belcher, Tim, Los Angeles	.119	33	67	3	8	10	2	0	0	3	7	0	0	2	0	26	0	0	1	.149	.119
Belinda, Stan, Pittsburgh	.000	60	7	0	0	0	0	0	0	0	2	0	0	0	0	5	0	0	0	.000	.000
Bell, George, Chicago	.285	149	558	63	159	261	27	0	25	86	0	9	4	32	6	62	2	6	10	.468	.323
Bell, Jay, Pittsburgh	.270	157	608	96	164	260	32	8	16	67	30	3	2	52	1	99	10	6	15	.428	.330
Bell, Mike, Atlanta*	.133	17	30	4	4	7	0	0	1	1	0	1	0	2	0	7	0	0	4	.233	.188
Belliard, Rafael, Atlanta	.249	149	353	36	88	101	9	2	0	27	7	1	1	22	2	63	3	4	4	.286	.296
Benavides, Freddie, Cincinnati	.286	24	63	11	18	19	1	0	0	3	1	0	2	1	1	15	1	0	1	.302	.303
Benes, Andy, San Diego	.032	33	62	4	2	5	3	0	0	1	6	0	0	6	2	29	0	0	1	.081	.143
Benjamin, Mike, San Francisco	.123	54	106	12	13	22	3	0	2	8	7	2	0	7	0	26	3	0	2	.208	.188
Benzinger, Todd, Cincinnati†	.187	51	123	7	23	33	3	2	1	11	1	1	2	10	2	20	2	0	2	.268	.244
Berenguer, Juan, Atlanta	.000	49	5	0	0	0	0	0	0	0	0	0	0	0	0	3	0	0	0	.000	.000
Berryhill, Damon, Chi.-Atl.†	.188	63	160	13	30	52	7	0	5	14	4	1	0	11	1	42	0	2	2	.325	.243
Bielecki, Mike, Chi.-Atl.	.065	41	46	1	3	3	0	0	0	7	5	0	0	3	0	21	1	0	1	.065	.122
Biggio, Craig, Houston	.295	149	546	79	161	204	23	4	4	46	4	3	2	53	3	71	19	6	2	.374	.358
Bilardello, Dann, San Diego	.269	15	26	4	7	11	1	0	1	5	5	1	0	3	0	4	0	0	0	.423	.345
Black, Bud, San Francisco*	.183	35	71	3	13	16	3	0	0	6	9	0	0	3	0	20	0	0	0	.225	.183
Blauser, Jeff, Atlanta	.259	129	352	49	91	144	14	3	11	54	4	3	2	54	4	59	5	6	4	.409	.358
Boever, Joe, Philadelphia	.333	68	3	0	1	1	0	0	0	0	0	0	0	0	0	3	0	0	0	.333	.333
Bonds, Barry, Pittsburgh*	.292	153	510	95	149	262	28	5	25	116	0	13	4	107	25	73	43	13	8	.514	.410
Bones, Ricky, San Diego	.077	11	13	0	1	1	0	0	0	1	4	0	0	2	0	5	0	0	0	.077	.200
Bonilla, Bobby, Pittsburgh†	.302	157	577	102	174	284	44	6	18	100	0	11	2	90	8	67	2	4	14	.492	.391

1991 N.L. STATISTICS

Player, Team	Avg.	G	AB	R	H	TB	2B	3B	HR	RBI	SH	SF	HP	BB	Int. BB	SO	SB	CS	GI DP	Slg.	OBP
Booker, Rod, Philadelphia*	.226	28	53	3	12	13	1	0	0	7	1	0	0	3	1	7	0	0	1	.245	.236
Boskie, Shawn, Chicago	.171	30	41	3	7	12	0	1	1	2	3	1	0	3	0	15	0	0	0	.293	.227
Boston, Daryl, New York*	.275	137	255	40	70	106	16	4	4	21	0	1	0	30	0	42	15	8	2	.416	.350
Bowen, Ryan, Houston	.182	17	22	2	4	5	1	0	0	0	3	0	0	3	0	11	0	0	0	.227	.280
Boyd, Oil Can, Montreal	.083	19	36	1	3	3	0	0	0	2	2	0	0	0	0	19	0	0	0	.083	.154
Braggs, Glenn, Cincinnati	.260	85	250	36	65	108	10	0	11	39	0	4	2	23	3	46	11	3	4	.432	.323
Brantley, Cliff, Philadelphia	.000	6	8	0	0	0	0	0	0	0	2	0	0	0	0	4	0	0	0	.000	.000
Brantley, Jeff, San Francisco	.000	67	6	0	0	0	0	0	0	0	1	0	0	0	0	1	0	0	0	.000	.000
Bream, Sid, Atlanta*	.253	91	265	32	67	112	12	0	11	45	4	4	0	25	5	31	0	3	8	.423	.313
Brewer, Rod, St. Louis*	.077	19	13	0	1	1	0	0	0	1	0	0	0	0	0	5	0	0	0	.077	.077
Brooks, Hubie, New York*	.238	103	357	48	85	146	11	1	16	50	0	3	3	44	8	62	3	1	7	.409	.324
Browning, Tom, Cincinnati*	.171	36	70	3	12	18	3	0	1	5	10	0	0	3	0	19	0	1	3	.257	.205
Buechele, Steve, Pittsburgh	.246	31	114	16	28	47	5	1	4	19	1	1	2	10	0	28	1	1	0	.412	.315
Bullett, Scott, Pittsburgh*	.000	11	4	2	0	0	0	0	0	0	0	0	0	0	0	3	1	0	0	.000	.200
Bullock, Eric, Montreal*	.222	73	72	6	16	23	4	0	1	6	1	0	0	9	0	13	6	1	3	.319	.305
Burke, Tim, Mon.-N.Y.	.000	72	6	0	0	0	0	0	0	0	0	0	0	0	0	4	0	0	0	.000	.000
Burkett, John, San Francisco	.091	36	55	0	5	6	1	0	0	1	9	0	0	3	0	26	0	0	0	.109	.138
Butler, Brett, Los Angeles*	.296	161	615	112	182	211	13	5	2	38	4	2	3	108	4	79	38	28	3	.343	.401
Cabrera, Francisco, Atlanta	.242	44	95	7	23	41	6	0	4	23	0	1	0	6	0	20	1	0	5	.432	.284
Calderon, Ivan, Montreal	.300	134	470	69	141	226	22	3	19	75	1	10	3	53	4	64	31	16	7	.481	.368
Caminiti, Ken, Houston†	.253	152	574	65	145	220	30	3	13	80	3	4	5	46	7	85	4	5	18	.383	.312
Campusano, Sil, Philadelphia	.114	15	35	2	4	7	0	0	1	2	1	0	0	1	0	10	0	0	0	.200	.139
Candaele, Casey, Houston†	.262	151	461	44	121	167	20	0	4	50	3	0	3	40	7	49	9	3	5	.362	.319
Carman, Don, Cincinnati*	.000	28	5	0	0	0	0	0	0	0	0	0	0	0	0	3	0	0	0	.000	.000
Carpenter, Cris, St. Louis	.333	59	3	0	1	1	0	0	0	1	1	0	0	0	0	0	0	0	1	.333	.333
Carr, Chuck, New York†	.182	28	11	1	2	2	0	0	0	1	0	0	0	0	0	1	2	1	0	.182	.182
Carreno, Amalio, Philadelphia	.000	3	1	0	0	0	0	0	0	0	0	0	0	0	0	1	0	0	0	.000	.000
Carreon, Mark, New York	.260	106	254	18	66	84	6	0	4	21	1	2	2	12	2	26	2	2	13	.331	.297
Carter, Gary, Los Angeles	.246	101	248	22	61	93	14	0	6	26	1	7	2	22	1	26	2	1	11	.375	.323
Castilla, Vince, Atlanta	.200	12	5	1	1	1	0	0	0	0	0	0	0	0	0	2	0	0	0	.200	.200
Castillo, Braulio, Philadelphia	.173	28	52	3	9	12	3	0	0	2	2	0	0	1	0	15	1	0	1	.231	.189
Castillo, Frank, Chicago	.143	18	35	0	5	5	0	0	0	0	6	0	0	2	0	13	0	0	0	.143	.189
Castillo, Tony, Atl.-N.Y.*	.000	17	4	0	0	0	0	0	0	0	2	0	0	0	0	0	0	0	0	.000	.000
Cedeno, Andujar, Houston	.243	67	251	27	61	105	13	2	9	36	2	2	1	9	1	74	4	3	3	.418	.270
Cerone, Rick, New York	.273	90	227	18	62	81	13	0	2	16	1	2	0	30	2	24	1	1	9	.357	.360
Chamberlain, Wes, Philadelphia	.240	101	383	51	92	153	16	3	13	50	4	1	2	31	1	73	9	4	8	.399	.300
Charlton, Norm, Cincinnati†	.043	41	23	1	1	2	1	0	0	2	1	0	0	0	0	10	0	0	0	.087	.043
Clancy, Jim, Hou.-Atl.	.000	54	6	0	0	0	0	0	0	0	4	0	0	0	0	2	0	0	0	.000	.000
Clark, Jerald, San Diego	.228	118	369	26	84	130	16	0	10	47	0	4	6	31	3	90	0	1	10	.352	.295
Clark, Mark, St. Louis	.000	7	7	0	0	0	0	0	0	0	0	0	0	0	0	2	0	0	0	.000	.000
Clark, Will, San Francisco*	.301	148	565	84	170	303	32	7	29	116	0	7	2	51	12	91	4	2	5	.536	.359
Clayton, Royce, San Francisco	.115	9	26	0	3	4	1	0	0	2	0	0	0	1	0	6	0	1	0	.154	.148
Clements, Pat, San Diego	.000	12	1	0	0	0	0	0	0	0	0	0	0	0	0	0	0	0	0	.000	.000
Coleman, Vince, New York†	.255	72	278	45	71	91	7	5	1	17	2	0	1	39	0	47	37	14	3	.327	.347
Coles, Darnell, San Francisco	.214	11	14	1	3	3	0	0	0	0	0	0	0	1	0	2	0	0	1	.214	.214
Combs, Pat, Philadelphia*	.133	14	15	5	2	2	0	0	0	0	2	0	0	2	0	7	0	0	0	.133	.278

1991 N.L. STATISTICS

Player, Team	Avg.	G	AB	R	H	TB	2B	3B	HR	RBI	SH	SF	HP	BB	Int. BB	SO	SB	CS	GI DP	Slg.	OBP
Cone, David, New York*	.125	34	72	3	9	9	0	0	0	5	6	1	2	3	0	14	0	0	3	.125	.179
Cook, Dennis, Los Angeles*	.000	20	1	0	0	0	0	0	0	0	1	0	0	0	0	1	0	0	0	.000	.000
Coolbaugh, Scott, San Diego	.217	60	180	12	39	55	8	1	2	15	4	1	1	19	2	45	0	3	8	.306	.294
Cooper, Gary, Houston	.250	9	16	1	4	5	1	0	0	2	0	0	0	3	0	6	0	0	0	.313	.368
Cormier, Rheal, St. Louis*	.238	11	21	2	5	5	0	0	0	1	2	0	0	0	0	5	0	0	0	.238	.238
Corsi, Jim, Houston	.000	47	1	0	0	0	0	0	0	0	0	0	0	0	0	1	0	0	0	.000	.000
Costello, John, San Diego	.000	27	1	0	0	0	0	0	0	0	0	0	0	0	0	1	0	0	0	.000	.000
Cox, Danny, Philadelphia	.103	23	29	4	3	3	0	0	0	0	1	0	0	2	0	16	0	0	0	.103	.161
Crews, Tim, Los Angeles	.000	60	1	0	0	0	0	0	0	0	0	0	0	1	0	1	0	0	0	.000	.500
Daniels, Kal, Los Angeles*	.249	137	461	54	115	183	15	1	17	73	0	6	1	63	4	116	6	1	9	.397	.337
Darling, Ron, N.Y.-Mon.	.125	20	40	0	5	9	0	1	1	3	4	0	0	0	0	16	0	0	3	.225	.125
Dascenzo, Doug, Chicago†	.255	118	239	40	61	75	11	0	0	18	6	1	2	24	2	26	14	7	4	.314	.327
Daulton, Darren, Philadelphia*	.196	89	285	36	56	104	12	0	12	42	6	5	2	41	4	66	5	1	2	.365	.297
Davidson, Mark, Houston	.190	85	142	10	27	39	6	0	2	15	2	0	2	12	2	28	0	0	0	.275	.263
Davis, Butch, Los Angeles	.000	1	1	0	0	0	0	0	0	0	0	0	0	0	0	0	0	0	0	.000	.000
Davis, Eric, Cincinnati	.235	89	285	39	67	110	10	0	11	33	0	2	5	48	5	92	14	2	4	.386	.353
Dawson, Andre, Chicago	.272	149	563	69	153	275	21	4	31	104	0	6	5	22	3	80	4	5	10	.488	.302
DeJesus, Jose, Philadelphia	.129	31	62	3	8	8	0	0	0	0	4	0	0	2	0	39	0	0	0	.129	.156
DeLeon, Jose, St. Louis	.043	28	46	0	2	2	0	0	0	0	5	0	0	0	0	17	0	0	0	.043	.043
Decker, Steve, San Francisco	.206	79	233	11	48	72	7	1	5	24	2	4	3	16	1	44	0	0	7	.309	.262
DeShields, Delino, Montreal*	.238	151	563	83	134	187	15	4	10	51	8	5	4	95	2	151	56	23	6	.332	.347
DeShaies, Jim, Houston*	.098	28	41	1	4	4	0	0	0	0	8	0	0	1	0	16	0	0	0	.098	.178
Dibble, Rob, Cincinnati*	.000	67	2	0	0	0	0	0	0	0	1	0	0	0	0	0	0	0	0	.000	.000
Donnels, Chris, New York*	.225	37	89	7	20	22	2	0	0	5	1	0	0	14	1	19	1	1	0	.247	.330
Doran, Bill, Cincinnati†	.280	111	361	51	101	135	12	2	6	35	0	3	3	46	1	39	5	4	4	.374	.359
Dorsett, Brian, San Diego	.083	11	12	1	1	1	0	0	0	1	0	0	0	0	0	3	0	0	0	.083	.083
Downs, Kelly, San Francisco	.087	45	23	3	2	2	0	0	0	0	2	1	1	1	0	5	0	0	0	.087	.125
Drabek, Doug, Pittsburgh	.179	36	84	6	15	16	1	0	0	2	4	0	3	1	0	28	0	0	0	.190	.188
Duncan, Mariano, Cincinnati.	.258	100	333	46	86	137	7	4	12	40	5	3	4	12	1	57	5	4	9	.411	.288
Dunston, Shawon, Chicago	.260	142	492	59	128	200	22	7	12	50	4	4	1	23	5	64	21	6	4	.407	.292
Dykstra, Len, Philadelphia*	.297	63	246	48	73	105	13	5	3	12	0	0	1	37	6	20	24	4	1	.427	.391
Elster, Kevin, New York.	.241	115	348	33	84	122	16	2	6	36	1	4	4	40	6	53	0	3	4	.351	.318
Espy, Cecil, Pittsburgh†	.244	43	82	7	20	27	4	0	1	11	3	2	0	5	0	17	4	0	0	.329	.281
Eusebio, Tony, Houston	.105	10	19	4	2	3	1	0	0	0	0	0	0	6	0	8	0	0	1	.158	.320
Fajardo, Hector, Pittsburgh	.000	2	2	0	0	0	0	0	0	0	0	0	0	0	0	1	0	0	0	.000	.000
Faries, Paul, San Diego	.177	57	130	13	23	28	3	1	0	7	4	0	0	14	0	21	3	1	5	.215	.262
Fassero, Jeff, Montreal*	.000	51	3	0	0	0	0	0	0	0	2	0	0	0	0	2	0	0	1	.000	.250
Felder, Mike, San Francisco†	.264	132	348	51	92	114	10	6	0	18	4	0	2	30	2	31	21	6	6	.328	.325
Fernandez, Sid, New York*	.154	8	13	1	2	3	1	0	0	0	1	0	0	0	0	7	0	0	0	.231	.154
Fernandez, Tony, San Diego†	.272	145	558	81	152	201	27	5	4	38	7	6	2	55	5	74	23	9	12	.360	.337
Finley, Steve, Houston*	.285	159	596	84	170	242	28	10	8	54	11	3	6	42	5	65	34	18	8	.406	.331
Fitzgerald, Mike, Montreal	.202	71	198	17	40	61	8	1	6	28	1	3	0	22	5	35	0	2	5	.308	.278
Fletcher, Darrin, Philadelphia*	.228	46	136	5	31	42	8	0	1	12	1	3	0	14	4	15	0	1	4	.309	.255
Foley, Tom, Montreal*	.208	86	168	12	35	48	11	1	0	15	1	3	1	14	4	30	2	0	4	.286	.269
Franco, John, New York*	.000	52	0	0	0	0	0	0	0	0	0	0	0	0	0	0	0	0	0	.000	.000
Fraser, Willie, St. Louis	.000	35	2	0	0	0	0	0	0	0	0	0	0	0	0	2	0	0	0	.000	.000

Player, Team	Avg.	G	AB	R	H	TB	2B	3B	HR	RBI	SH	SF	HP	BB	Int. BB	SO	SB	CS	GI DP	Slg.	OBP
Freeman, Marvin, Atlanta	.000	34	7	0	0	0	0	0	0	0	0	0	0	0	0	5	0	0	0	.000	.000
Frey, Steve, Montreal*	.000	31	2	0	0	0	0	0	0	0	0	0	0	0	0	2	0	0	0	.000	.000
Galarraga, Andres, Montreal	.219	107	375	34	82	126	13	2	9	33	0	5	2	23	0	86	5	6	6	.336	.268
Gant, Ron, Atlanta	.251	154	561	101	141	278	35	3	32	105	0	5	5	71	8	104	34	15	6	.496	.338
Garcia, Carlos, Pittsburgh	.250	12	24	2	6	10	0	0	0	1	0	0	0	1	0	8	0	0	1	.417	.280
Gardner, Chris, Houston	.000	5	5	0	0	0	0	0	0	0	0	0	0	1	0	0	0	0	0	.000	.167
Gardner, Jeff, New York*	.162	13	37	3	6	6	0	0	0	1	0	0	0	4	0	6	0	0	0	.162	.238
Gardner, Mark, Montreal	.091	27	55	1	5	5	0	0	0	0	4	0	0	1	0	18	0	0	0	.091	.107
Gardner, Wes, San Diego	.000	14	4	0	0	0	0	0	0	0	0	0	0	0	0	2	0	0	0	.000	.000
Garrelts, Scott, San Francisco	.000	11	2	0	0	0	0	0	0	0	0	0	0	0	0	1	0	0	2	.000	.000
Gedman, Rich, St. Louis*	.106	46	94	7	10	20	1	0	3	8	1	2	0	4	0	15	0	0	14	.213	.140
Gilkey, Bernard, St. Louis*	.216	81	268	28	58	84	7	2	5	20	1	2	1	39	1	33	14	8	0	.313	.316
Girardi, Joe, Chicago	.191	21	47	3	9	11	2	0	0	6	0	0	0	6	0	6	1	0	1	.234	.283
Glavine, Tom, Atlanta*	.230	36	74	1	17	18	1	0	0	6	15	1	1	6	0	19	0	0	0	.243	.288
Gonzalez, Jose, L.A.-Pit.	.042	58	48	5	2	2	0	0	0	3	2	0	0	2	0	15	1	0	0	.104	.078
Gonzalez, Luis, Houston*	.254	137	473	51	120	205	28	9	13	69	1	4	8	40	4	101	10	7	9	.433	.320
Gooden, Dwight, New York	.238	27	63	7	15	21	3	0	1	6	8	0	0	0	0	9	0	1	1	.333	.238
Goodwin, Tom, Los Angeles*	.143	16	7	3	1	1	0	0	0	0	0	0	0	0	0	0	1	0	0	.143	.143
Gott, Jim, Los Angeles	.500	55	2	0	1	1	0	0	0	0	1	0	1	0	0	1	0	0	0	.500	.500
Grace, Mark, Chicago*	.273	160	619	87	169	231	28	5	8	58	4	7	3	70	7	53	3	4	6	.373	.346
Greene, Tommy, Philadelphia	.268	38	71	4	19	27	2	1	2	7	3	0	0	4	0	15	0	0	1	.380	.307
Gregg, Tommy, Atlanta*	.187	72	107	13	20	33	8	1	1	4	0	2	0	12	2	24	2	2	1	.308	.275
Griffin, Alfredo, Los Angeles†	.243	109	350	27	85	95	6	2	0	27	7	5	1	22	5	49	5	4	5	.271	.286
Grimsley, Jason, Philadelphia	.059	12	17	2	1	1	0	0	0	0	1	0	1	2	0	6	0	0	0	.059	.158
Grissom, Marquis, Montreal	.267	148	558	73	149	208	23	9	6	39	4	5	0	34	0	89	76	17	8	.373	.333
Gross, Kevin, Los Angeles	.280	48	25	4	7	8	1	0	0	3	4	0	0	2	0	14	0	0	0	.320	.333
Gross, Kip, Cincinnati	.091	29	22	4	2	2	0	0	0	1	2	0	0	0	0	6	0	0	0	.091	.091
Guerrero, Pedro, St. Louis	.272	115	427	41	116	154	12	1	8	70	0	7	1	37	2	46	4	2	12	.361	.326
Gwynn, Chris, Los Angeles*	.252	94	139	18	35	57	5	1	5	22	0	3	1	10	1	23	1	0	5	.410	.301
Gwynn, Tony, San Diego*	.317	134	530	69	168	229	27	11	4	62	7	5	1	34	8	19	8	8	11	.432	.355
Hamilton, Jeff, Los Angeles	.223	41	94	4	21	28	4	0	1	14	0	2	0	4	0	21	0	0	2	.298	.255
Hammaker, Atlee, San Diego†	.000	20	1	0	0	0	0	0	0	0	1	0	0	0	0	1	0	0	0	.000	.000
Hammond, Chris, Cincinnati*	.353	20	34	4	12	15	3	0	0	1	7	0	0	2	0	10	0	0	1	.441	.389
Haney, Chris, Montreal*	.074	16	27	1	2	2	0	0	0	0	2	0	0	2	0	3	0	0	0	.074	.074
Hansen, Dave, Los Angeles*	.268	53	56	3	15	22	4	0	1	5	0	0	0	4	0	12	0	0	2	.393	.293
Harkey, Mike, Chicago	.400	9	5	2	2	2	0	0	0	0	4	0	1	0	0	0	0	0	0	.400	.500
Harnisch, Pete, Houston	.097	33	62	2	6	7	0	0	0	4	12	1	1	0	0	21	0	1	1	.113	.149
Harris, Greg, San Diego	.083	20	36	0	3	3	0	0	0	2	2	0	0	0	0	13	0	0	0	.083	.132
Harris, Lenny, Los Angeles*	.287	145	429	59	123	150	16	1	3	38	7	2	5	37	5	32	12	3	16	.350	.349
Hartley, Mike, L.A.-Phi.	.000	58	5	5	0	0	0	0	0	0	2	0	0	0	0	0	0	0	1	.000	.000
Hassey, Ron, Montreal*	.227	52	119	9	27	38	8	0	1	14	0	1	0	13	1	16	0	1	5	.319	.301
Hatcher, Billy, Cincinnati	.262	138	442	45	116	159	25	4	4	41	4	3	3	26	4	55	11	9	9	.360	.312
Hayes, Charlie, Philadelphia	.230	142	460	34	106	167	23	1	12	53	2	5	3	16	3	75	3	2	13	.363	.257
Hayes, Von, Philadelphia*	.225	77	284	43	64	81	15	1	0	21	2	1	1	31	5	42	9	9	6	.285	.303
Heath, Mike, Atlanta	.209	49	139	4	29	37	3	1	1	12	2	1	0	7	0	26	0	0	4	.266	.250
Heaton, Neal, Pittsburgh*	.286	44	14	0	4	5	1	0	0	1	4	0	0	1	0	2	0	0	0	.357	.333

1991 N.L. STATISTICS

Player, Team	Avg.	G	AB	R	H	TB	2B	3B	HR	RBI	SH	SF	HP	BB	Int. BB	SO	SB	CS	GI DP	Slg.	OBP
Heep, Danny, Atlanta*	.417	14	12	4	5	6	1	0	0	3	0	0	0	1	0	4	0	1	0	.500	.462
Henry, Dwayne, Houston	.000	52	7	0	0	0	0	0	0	0	2	0	0	1	0	1	0	0	0	.000	.000
Heredia, Gil, San Francisco	.429	7	7	1	3	3	0	0	0	0	0	0	0	0	0	1	1	0	0	.429	.500
Hernandez, Carlos, Los Angeles	.214	15	14	0	3	4	1	0	0	1	0	1	0	0	0	5	0	0	2	.286	.250
Hernandez, Jeremy, San Diego	.000	9	7	0	0	0	0	0	0	0	2	0	0	0	0	1	0	0	0	.000	.000
Hernandez, Xavier, Houston*	.000	32	10	0	0	0	0	0	0	0	4	1	0	2	0	7	0	0	2	.000	.167
Herr, Tom, N.Y.-S.F.†	.209	102	215	23	45	58	8	0	1	21	2	2	0	45	5	28	9	2	4	.270	.344
Hershiser, Orel, Los Angeles	.258	21	31	6	8	10	2	0	0	2	4	0	0	3	0	8	1	0	0	.323	.324
Hickerson, Bryan, San Francisco*	.000	17	12	0	0	0	0	0	0	0	1	0	0	0	0	6	0	0	0	.000	.000
Hill, Ken, St. Louis	.100	30	50	2	5	5	0	0	0	3	7	0	0	4	0	12	0	0	0	.100	.167
Hill, Milt, Cincinnati	.000	22	1	0	0	0	0	0	0	0	0	0	0	0	0	1	0	0	0	.000	.000
Hollins, Dave, Philadelphia†	.298	56	151	18	45	77	10	2	6	21	0	1	3	17	1	26	1	1	2	.510	.378
Howard, Thomas, San Diego†	.249	106	281	30	70	100	12	3	4	22	2	1	0	24	4	57	10	7	4	.356	.309
Howell, Jack, San Diego*	.206	58	160	24	33	56	3	1	6	16	1	0	0	18	1	33	0	0	1	.350	.287
Hudler, Rex, St. Louis	.227	101	207	21	47	64	10	0	1	15	2	2	1	10	0	29	12	8	1	.309	.260
Hundley, Todd, New York	.133	21	60	5	8	13	0	1	1	7	1	1	0	6	0	14	0	0	3	.217	.221
Hunter, Brian, Atlanta	.251	97	271	32	68	122	16	1	12	50	0	2	1	17	6	48	0	2	6	.450	.296
Hurst, Bruce, San Diego*	.134	31	67	3	9	10	1	0	0	6	12	0	0	4	0	23	0	0	1	.149	.183
Innis, Jeff, New York	.000	69	2	0	0	0	0	0	0	0	0	0	0	0	0	1	0	0	0	.000	.000
Jackson, Danny, Chicago	.087	17	23	1	2	2	0	0	0	1	2	0	0	0	0	13	0	0	0	.087	.087
Jackson, Darrin, San Diego	.262	122	359	51	94	171	12	1	21	49	3	3	2	27	2	66	5	3	5	.476	.315
Javier, Stan, Los Angeles†	.205	121	176	21	36	50	5	3	1	11	3	2	0	16	0	36	7	1	4	.284	.268
Jefferies, Gregg, New York†	.272	136	486	59	132	182	19	2	9	62	3	3	2	47	2	38	26	5	12	.374	.336
Jefferson, Reggie, Cincinnati†	.143	5	7	0	1	1	0	0	0	1	0	0	0	1	0	2	0	0	0	.250	.250
Jefferson, Stan, Cincinnati†	.053	13	19	2	1	1	0	0	0	1	0	0	1	0	0	3	2	0	0	.053	.100
Johnson, Howard, New York†	.259	156	564	108	146	302	34	4	38	117	0	5	1	78	12	120	30	16	4	.535	.342
Jones, Barry, Montreal	.000	77	0	0	0	0	0	0	0	0	1	0	0	0	0	0	0	0	0	.000	.000
Jones, Chris, Cincinnati	.292	52	89	14	26	37	1	2	2	6	0	1	2	2	0	31	2	1	2	.416	.304
Jones, Jimmy, Houston	.184	28	38	4	7	8	1	0	0	0	2	0	0	3	0	11	0	0	1	.211	.244
Jones, Ron, Philadelphia*	.154	26	26	0	4	6	2	0	0	3	0	0	1	2	0	9	0	0	0	.231	.214
Jones, Tim, St. Louis*	.167	16	24	1	4	6	2	0	0	2	0	1	0	2	1	6	0	1	0	.250	.222
Jordan, Ricky, Philadelphia	.272	101	301	38	82	136	21	3	9	49	0	5	2	14	2	49	0	2	11	.452	.304
Jose, Felix, St. Louis†	.305	154	568	69	173	249	40	6	8	77	3	5	2	50	8	113	20	12	12	.438	.360
Juden, Jeff, Houston	.000	4	5	0	0	0	0	0	0	0	0	0	0	0	0	3	0	0	0	.000	.000
Justice, David, Atlanta*	.275	109	396	67	109	199	25	1	21	87	0	5	3	65	9	81	8	8	4	.503	.377
Karros, Eric, Los Angeles	.071	14	14	0	1	2	1	0	0	1	0	0	0	1	0	6	0	0	0	.143	.133
Kennedy, Terry, San Francisco*	.234	69	171	12	40	58	7	0	3	13	0	1	1	11	4	31	0	0	4	.339	.283
Kile, Darryl, Houston	.000	37	38	2	0	0	0	0	0	1	4	0	0	3	0	23	0	0	1	.000	.073
King, Jeff, Pittsburgh	.239	33	109	16	26	41	2	1	4	18	0	1	1	14	3	15	3	1	3	.376	.328
Kingery, Mike, San Francisco*	.182	91	110	13	20	26	2	2	0	8	2	0	0	15	1	21	1	0	3	.236	.280
Kipper, Bob, Pittsburgh	.000	52	1	0	0	0	0	0	0	0	0	0	0	0	0	0	0	0	0	.000	.000
Kruk, John, Philadelphia*	.294	152	538	84	158	260	27	6	21	92	0	9	1	67	16	100	7	0	11	.483	.367
LaCoss, Mike, San Francisco	.222	18	9	2	2	2	0	0	0	1	4	0	0	1	0	6	0	0	0	.222	.300
Lake, Steve, Philadelphia	.228	58	158	12	36	45	4	1	1	11	1	0	0	2	1	26	0	0	5	.285	.238
Lampkin, Tom, San Diego*	.190	38	58	4	11	16	3	1	0	3	4	0	0	3	0	9	0	0	0	.276	.230
Lancaster, Les, Chicago	.179	64	28	2	5	7	2	0	0	2	6	0	0	0	0	13	0	0	0	.250	.179

Player, Team	Avg.	G	AB	R	H	TB	2B	3B	HR	RBI	SH	SF	HP	BB	Int. BB	SO	SB	CS	GI DP	Slg.	OBP
Landrum, Bill, Pittsburgh	.000	61	4	0	0	0	0	0	0	0	0	0	0	0	0	3	0	0	0	.000	.000
Landrum, Ced, Chicago*	.233	56	86	28	20	24	2	1	0	6	3	0	0	10	0	18	27	5	2	.279	.313
Lankford, Ray, St. Louis*	.251	151	566	83	142	222	23	15	9	69	4	3	1	41	1	114	44	20	4	.392	.301
LaPoint, Dave, Philadelphia*	.000	2	2	0	0	0	0	0	0	0	4	0	0	0	0	1	0	0	0	.000	.000
Larkin, Barry, Cincinnati	.302	123	464	88	140	235	27	4	20	69	3	2	3	55	4	64	24	6	7	.506	.378
LaValliere, Mike, Pittsburgh*	.289	108	336	25	97	121	11	2	3	41	1	5	2	33	4	27	2	1	10	.360	.351
Layana, Tim, Cincinnati	.000	23	1	0	0	0	0	0	0	0	0	0	0	0	0	1	0	0	0	.000	.000
Lee, Terry, Cincinnati	.000	3	6	0	0	0	0	0	0	0	0	0	0	0	0	2	0	0	0	.000	.000
Lefferts, Craig, San Diego*	.000	54	6	0	0	0	0	0	0	0	2	0	0	0	0	2	0	0	0	.000	.000
Leibrandt, Charlie, Atlanta	.043	36	70	1	3	7	0	0	0	0	12	0	0	3	0	18	1	0	1	.100	.082
Lemke, Mark, Atlanta†	.234	136	269	36	63	84	11	2	2	23	6	4	1	29	2	27	1	1	9	.312	.305
Leonard, Mark, San Francisco*	.240	64	129	14	31	46	7	1	2	14	1	2	1	12	1	25	0	0	3	.357	.306
Lewis, Darren, San Francisco	.248	72	222	41	55	69	5	3	1	15	7	0	1	36	0	30	13	7	3	.311	.358
Lewis, Jim, San Diego	.000	12	2	0	0	0	0	0	0	0	0	0	0	0	0	1	0	0	0	.000	.000
Lilliquist, Derek, San Diego*	.000	6	2	0	0	0	0	0	0	1	0	0	0	0	0	0	0	0	0	.000	.000
Lind, Jose, Pittsburgh	.265	150	502	53	133	170	16	6	3	54	5	6	2	30	10	56	7	4	20	.339	.306
Lindeman, Jim, Philadelphia	.337	65	95	13	32	37	5	0	0	12	2	1	0	13	0	14	1	1	0	.389	.413
Lindsey, Doug, Philadelphia	.000	3	3	0	0	0	0	0	0	0	0	0	0	0	0	3	0	0	0	.000	.000
Litton, Greg, San Francisco	.181	59	127	13	23	35	7	1	1	15	3	0	1	11	0	25	0	2	1	.276	.250
Lofton, Kenny, Houston*	.203	20	74	9	15	16	1	0	0	0	0	0	0	5	0	19	2	1	0	.216	.253
Lyons, Barry, Los Angeles	.000	9	9	0	0	0	0	0	0	0	0	0	0	0	0	2	0	0	0	.000	.000
Maddux, Greg, Chicago	.205	39	88	8	18	23	2	0	1	7	11	0	0	2	0	24	1	0	0	.261	.222
Maddux, Mike, San Diego*	.077	64	13	1	1	1	0	0	0	0	3	0	0	0	0	4	0	0	0	.077	.200
Magadan, Dave, New York*	.258	124	418	58	108	143	23	0	4	51	7	7	2	83	3	50	1	1	5	.342	.378
Mahler, Rick, Mon.-Atl.	.143	23	14	0	2	3	1	0	0	0	4	0	0	0	0	4	0	0	0	.214	.143
Mallicoat, Rob, Houston*	.000	24	1	0	0	0	0	0	0	0	0	0	0	0	0	0	0	0	0	.000	.000
Manwaring, Kirt, San Francisco	.225	67	178	16	40	49	9	0	0	19	9	2	3	9	0	22	1	0	2	.275	.271
Martinez, Carmelo, Pit.-Cin.	.234	64	154	13	36	59	5	0	6	19	0	3	3	16	1	39	0	0	3	.383	.301
Martinez, Dave, Montreal*	.295	124	396	47	117	166	18	5	7	42	5	3	2	20	3	54	16	7	1	.419	.332
Martinez, Dennis, Montreal	.153	32	72	8	11	15	4	0	0	4	10	0	0	1	0	24	0	0	1	.208	.164
Martinez, Ramon, Los Angeles*	.117	33	77	6	9	13	1	0	1	9	8	0	0	1	0	25	0	0	1	.169	.128
Mason, Roger, Pittsburgh	.000	24	0	0	0	0	0	0	0	0	1	0	0	1	0	0	0	0	0	.000	1.000
Mauser, Tim, Philadelphia	.000	3	3	0	0	0	0	0	0	0	0	0	0	0	0	2	0	0	0	.000	.000
May, Derrick, Chicago*	.227	15	22	4	5	10	2	0	1	3	0	0	0	2	0	3	0	1	1	.455	.280
McClellan, Paul, San Francisco	.143	13	21	0	3	3	0	0	0	0	2	0	0	0	0	23	0	0	2	.143	.182
McClendon, Lloyd, Pittsburgh	.288	85	163	24	47	75	7	1	7	24	0	1	2	18	0	23	2	1	2	.460	.366
McClure, Bob, St. Louis	1.000	32	1	1	1	1	0	0	0	0	0	0	0	0	0	0	0	0	0	1.000	1.000
McDaniel, Terry, New York†	.207	23	29	3	6	7	1	0	0	2	0	0	0	0	0	11	2	0	0	.241	.233
McDowell, Roger, Phi.-L.A.	.000	72	2	0	0	0	0	0	0	0	2	0	0	0	0	3	0	0	0	.000	.000
McElroy, Chuck, Chicago*	.300	71	10	1	3	4	1	0	0	2	3	0	0	0	0	3	0	1	0	.400	.300
McGee, Willie, San Francisco	.312	131	497	67	155	203	30	3	4	43	8	2	2	34	3	74	17	9	11	.408	.357
McGriff, Fred, San Diego*	.278	153	528	84	147	261	19	1	31	106	0	7	1	105	26	135	4	1	14	.494	.396
McLemore, Mark, Houston†	.148	21	61	6	9	10	1	0	0	2	1	0	2	6	0	13	0	1	0	.164	.221
McReynolds, Kevin, New York	.259	143	522	65	135	217	32	1	16	74	0	4	2	49	7	46	6	6	8	.416	.322
Melendez, Jose, San Diego	.100	31	20	1	2	3	1	0	0	0	4	0	0	1	0	14	0	0	0	.150	.143
Merced, Orlando, Pittsburgh†	.275	120	411	83	113	164	17	2	10	50	1	4	1	64	4	81	8	4	6	.399	.373

Player, Team	Avg.	G	AB	R	H	TB	2B	3B	HR	RBI	SH	SF	HP	BB	Int. BB	SO	SB	CS	GI DP	Slg.	OBP
Mercker, Kent, Atlanta*	.100	50	10	0	1	1	0	1	0	0	0	0	0	0	0	7	0	0	0	.100	.182
Miller, Keith, New York	.280	98	275	41	77	113	22	1	4	23	0	1	5	23	0	44	14	4	2	.411	.345
Miller, Paul, Pittsburgh	.000	1	3	0	0	0	0	0	0	0	0	0	0	0	0	0	0	0	0	.000	.000
Minutelli, Gino, Cincinnati*	.000	16	3	0	0	0	0	0	0	0	0	0	0	0	0	1	0	0	0	.000	.000
Mitchell, Kevin, San Francisco	.256	113	371	52	95	191	13	1	27	69	0	4	5	43	8	57	2	3	6	.515	.338
Mitchell, Keith, Atlanta	.318	48	66	11	21	27	1	1	2	5	0	0	0	8	0	12	3	1	1	.409	.392
Morandini, Mickey, Philadelphia*	.249	98	325	38	81	103	11	4	1	20	6	2	2	29	0	45	13	4	7	.317	.313
Morgan, Mike, Los Angeles	.092	34	76	2	7	7	0	0	0	3	8	0	0	0	0	11	0	0	1	.092	.101
Morris, Hal, Cincinnati*	.318	136	478	72	152	229	33	1	14	59	5	7	1	46	7	61	10	4	4	.479	.374
Morris, John, Philadelphia*	.220	85	127	15	28	35	2	1	1	6	0	2	1	12	4	25	2	0	1	.276	.293
Mota, Andy, Houston	.189	27	90	4	17	22	2	0	1	6	0	0	0	2	0	17	2	0	0	.244	.198
Mota, Jose, San Diego†	.222	17	36	4	8	8	0	0	0	2	2	0	1	2	0	7	1	0	0	.222	.282
Moyer, Jamie, St. Louis*	.000	8	8	0	0	0	0	0	0	0	5	0	0	0	0	4	0	0	0	.000	.000
Mulholland, Terry, Philadelphia	.088	35	80	3	7	7	0	0	0	0	2	0	0	1	0	32	1	0	2	.088	.111
Murphy, Dale, Philadelphia	.252	153	544	66	137	226	33	1	18	81	0	7	1	48	3	93	1	0	20	.415	.309
Murray, Eddie, Los Angeles†	.260	153	576	69	150	232	23	1	19	96	0	8	0	55	17	74	10	3	17	.403	.321
Myers, Randy, Cincinnati*	.172	58	29	5	5	5	0	0	0	1	6	0	0	3	0	16	0	0	0	.172	.200
Nabholz, Chris, Montreal*	.115	24	52	3	6	6	0	0	0	3	2	0	0	1	0	14	0	0	2	.115	.164
Nichols, Carl, Houston	.196	24	51	3	10	13	3	0	0	6	0	0	0	5	0	17	0	0	2	.255	.268
Nixon, Otis, Atlanta†	.297	124	401	81	119	131	10	1	0	26	7	3	0	47	3	40	72	21	5	.327	.371
Noboa, Junior, Montreal	.242	67	95	5	23	29	3	0	1	11	2	1	1	3	1	8	2	3	1	.305	.250
Nolte, Eric, San Diego*	.111	6	9	2	1	1	0	0	0	0	2	0	0	0	0	6	0	0	0	.111	.111
Oberkfell, Ken, Houston*	.229	53	70	7	16	20	4	0	0	14	0	2	0	14	4	8	0	0	0	.286	.357
O'Brien, Charlie, New York	.185	69	168	16	31	43	6	0	2	14	3	2	4	17	1	25	0	3	5	.256	.272
Offerman, Jose, Los Angeles†	.195	52	113	10	22	24	2	0	0	3	2	0	1	25	2	32	3	2	5	.212	.345
Ojeda, Bob, Los Angeles*	.161	31	56	3	9	12	0	1	0	3	6	1	0	10	0	32	0	0	5	.214	.200
Olivares, Omar, St. Louis	.226	28	53	4	12	15	3	0	0	6	4	0	0	2	0	16	0	0	2	.283	.255
Oliver, Joe, Cincinnati	.216	94	269	21	58	102	11	0	11	41	0	3	3	18	5	53	0	0	14	.379	.265
Oliveras, Francisco, San Francisco	.200	55	10	2	2	2	0	0	0	0	4	0	0	0	0	4	0	0	0	.200	.200
Olson, Greg, Atlanta	.241	133	411	46	99	142	25	0	6	44	2	4	3	44	3	48	1	1	13	.345	.316
O'Neill, Paul, Cincinnati*	.256	152	532	71	136	256	36	0	28	91	0	4	1	73	14	107	12	7	8	.481	.346
Oquendo, Jose, St. Louis†	.240	127	366	37	88	110	11	4	1	26	6	3	1	67	13	48	1	2	5	.301	.357
Ortiz, Javier, Houston	.277	47	83	7	23	32	4	1	1	5	0	0	0	14	0	14	1	0	3	.386	.381
Osuna, Al, Houston	.000	71	2	0	0	0	0	0	0	0	1	0	0	0	0	1	0	0	0	.000	.000
Owen, Spike, Montreal†	.255	139	424	39	108	155	22	8	3	26	4	4	1	42	11	61	2	6	11	.366	.321
Pagnozzi, Tom, St. Louis	.264	140	459	38	121	161	24	5	2	57	6	5	1	36	6	63	9	13	10	.351	.319
Palacios, Vicente, Pittsburgh	.071	36	14	1	1	1	0	0	0	0	5	0	0	0	0	7	0	0	0	.071	.071
Pappas, Erik, Chicago	.176	7	17	1	3	3	1	0	0	2	0	0	0	1	0	5	0	0	0	.176	.222
Parker, Rick, San Francisco	.071	13	14	0	1	1	0	0	0	0	0	0	0	1	0	5	0	0	0	.071	.133
Parrett, Jeff, Atlanta	.000	18	0	0	0	0	0	0	0	0	0	0	0	0	0	0	0	0	0	.000	1.000
Patterson, Bob, Pittsburgh	.250	54	4	1	1	1	0	0	0	0	0	0	0	0	0	2	0	0	0	.250	.250
Pena, Alejandro, N.Y.-Atl.	.000	59	6	0	0	0	0	0	0	0	0	0	0	0	0	1	0	0	0	.000	.000
Pena, Geronimo, St. Louis†	.243	104	185	38	45	74	8	3	5	17	0	1	3	18	1	45	15	5	1	.400	.322
Pendleton, Terry, Atlanta†	.319	153	586	94	187	303	34	8	22	86	0	7	0	43	8	70	10	2	16	.517	.363
Perezchica, Tony, San Francisco	.229	23	48	2	11	17	3	0	1	3	3	0	0	2	1	12	1	1	1	.354	.260
Perry, Gerald, St. Louis*	.240	109	242	29	58	92	8	4	6	36	0	3	0	22	1	34	15	8	2	.380	.300

Player, Team	Avg.	G	AB	R	H	TB	2B	3B	HR	RBI	SH	SF	HP	BB	Int. BB	SO	SB	CS	GI DP	Slg.	OBP
Peterson, Adam, San Diego	.000	13	13	0	0	0	0	0	0	0	1	0	0	2	0	9	0	0	0	.000	.133
Petry, Dan, Atlanta	.200	10	5	1	1	1	0	0	0	0	0	0	0	0	0	4	0	0	0	.200	.200
Platt, Doug, Montreal*	.000	5	1	0	0	0	0	0	0	0	0	0	0	0	0	0	0	0	0	.000	.000
Portugal, Mark, Houston	.196	33	46	4	9	10	1	0	0	3	6	0	1	4	0	4	0	0	0	.217	.269
Power, Ted, Cincinnati	.000	68	3	0	0	0	0	0	0	1	0	1	1	1	1	3	0	0	2	.000	.250
Presley, Jim, San Diego	.136	20	59	3	8	11	0	0	1	5	0	1	1	7	0	16	0	1	3	.186	.200
Prince, Tom, Pittsburgh	.265	26	34	4	9	15	3	0	1	2	1	1	0	3	1	3	0	1	2	.441	.405
Quinones, Luis, Cincinnati†	.222	97	212	15	47	69	4	3	4	20	1	2	1	21	3	31	1	2	3	.325	.297
Ramirez, Rafael, Houston	.236	101	233	17	55	68	10	0	1	20	3	0	0	13	1	40	3	3	2	.292	.274
Rasmussen, Dennis, San Diego*	.136	25	44	3	6	7	1	0	0	0	3	0	0	5	0	12	0	0	5	.159	.224
Ready, Randy, Philadelphia	.249	76	205	32	51	66	10	1	1	20	1	4	2	47	3	25	2	3	5	.322	.385
Redfield, Joe, Pittsburgh	.111	11	18	1	2	2	0	0	0	0	1	0	0	4	0	1	1	0	0	.111	.273
Redus, Gary, Pittsburgh	.246	98	252	45	62	99	12	2	7	24	1	4	3	28	2	39	17	3	6	.393	.324
Reed, Jeff, Cincinnati*	.267	91	270	20	72	100	15	2	3	31	4	5	1	23	3	38	0	0	6	.370	.321
Reed, Rick, Pittsburgh	.500	1	2	0	1	2	1	0	0	2	0	0	0	1	0	0	0	0	0	1.000	.500
Remlinger, Mike, San Francisco*	.000	8	7	1	0	0	0	0	0	0	4	0	0	1	0	0	0	0	0	.000	.125
Renfroe, Laddie, Chicago†	.000	4	1	0	0	0	0	0	0	0	0	0	0	0	0	0	0	0	0	.000	.000
Reuschel, Rick, San Francisco	.000	4	2	0	0	0	0	0	0	0	1	0	0	0	0	2	0	0	0	.000	.000
Reyes, Gilberto, Montreal	.217	83	207	11	45	54	9	0	0	13	1	1	0	19	2	51	2	4	3	.261	.285
Reynoso, Armando, Atlanta	.000	6	6	0	0	0	0	0	0	0	0	0	0	0	0	5	0	0	0	.000	.125
Rhodes, Karl, Houston*	.213	44	136	7	29	37	3	0	1	12	1	0	1	14	3	26	2	2	1	.272	.289
Richardson, Jeff, Pittsburgh	.250	6	4	0	1	1	0	0	0	0	0	0	0	0	0	3	0	0	0	.250	.250
Riesgo, Damon, Montreal	.143	4	7	1	1	1	0	0	0	0	1	0	0	3	0	1	0	0	0	.143	.400
Righetti, Dave, San Francisco*	.000	61	3	0	0	0	0	0	0	0	1	0	0	0	0	2	0	1	1	.000	.000
Rijo, Jose, Cincinnati	.209	31	67	7	14	14	0	0	0	5	9	0	0	2	0	13	0	0	0	.209	.232
Ritchie, Wally, Philadelphia*	.000	39	3	0	0	0	0	0	0	0	0	0	0	0	0	2	0	0	0	.000	.000
Roberts, Bip, San Diego†	.281	117	424	66	119	147	13	3	0	32	4	3	4	37	0	71	26	11	6	.347	.342
Robinson, Don, San Francisco	.150	35	40	1	6	7	1	0	0	4	3	0	0	0	0	13	0	0	0	.175	.171
Rodriguez, Rosario, Pittsburgh*	.000	18	1	0	0	0	0	0	0	0	0	0	0	0	0	0	0	0	0	.000	.000
Rodriguez, Rich, San Diego*	.000	65	5	0	0	0	0	0	0	0	2	0	0	0	0	2	0	0	0	.000	.000
Rohde, Dave, Houston†	.122	29	41	3	5	5	0	0	0	0	1	0	0	5	0	8	0	0	1	.122	.217
Rojas, Mel, Montreal	.000	37	4	0	0	0	0	0	0	0	3	0	0	0	0	3	0	0	0	.000	.000
Rosenberg, Steve, San Diego*	.000	10	1	0	0	0	0	0	0	0	0	0	0	0	0	1	0	0	0	.000	.000
Rossy, Rico, Atlanta	.286	5	21	1	6	7	1	0	0	0	1	0	0	1	0	1	0	0	0	.333	.318
Royer, Stan, St. Louis	.000	8	24	0	0	0	0	0	0	0	0	0	0	0	0	7	0	0	0	.000	.000
Ruffin, Bruce, Philadelphia†	.000	31	24	0	0	0	0	0	0	0	6	0	0	1	0	2	0	0	0	.000	.143
Ruskin, Scott, Montreal	.000	64	2	1	0	0	0	0	0	0	5	0	0	4	0	18	0	0	0	.000	.333
Sabo, Chris, Cincinnati	.301	153	582	91	175	294	35	3	26	88	5	3	6	44	3	79	19	6	13	.505	.354
St. Claire, Randy, Atlanta	.500	19	2	1	1	1	0	0	0	0	2	0	0	0	0	0	0	0	0	.500	.500
Salazar, Luis, Chicago	.258	103	333	34	86	144	14	1	14	38	2	2	3	15	4	45	2	3	8	.432	.292
Sampen, Bill, Montreal	.231	43	13	2	3	3	0	0	0	1	2	0	0	0	0	6	0	0	0	.231	.231
Samuel, Juan, Los Angeles	.271	153	594	74	161	231	22	6	12	58	10	3	3	49	4	133	23	8	8	.389	.328
Sanchez, Rey, Chicago	.261	23	23	6	6	6	0	0	0	2	0	0	0	4	0	3	0	0	0	.261	.370
Sandberg, Ryne, Chicago	.291	158	585	104	170	284	32	2	26	100	1	9	2	87	4	89	22	8	9	.485	.379
Sanders, Deion, Atlanta*	.191	54	110	16	21	38	2	0	4	13	0	0	0	12	0	23	11	3	1	.345	.270
Sanders, Reggie, Cincinnati	.200	9	40	6	8	11	1	0	1	3	0	0	0	0	0	9	1	1	1	.275	.200

1991 N.L. STATISTICS

Player, Team	Avg.	G	AB	R	H	TB	2B	3B	HR	RBI	SH	SF	HP	BB	Int. BB	SO	SB	CS	GI DP	Slg.	OBP
Sanford, Mo, Cincinnati	.000	5	8	0	0	0	0	0	0	0	2	0	0	0	0	5	0	0	0	.000	.000
Santiago, Benito, San Diego	.267	152	580	60	155	234	22	3	17	87	2	7	4	23	5	114	8	10	21	.403	.296
Santovenia, Nelson, Montreal	.250	41	96	7	24	35	5	0	2	14	0	4	0	9	2	18	0	0	4	.365	.255
Sasser, Mackey, New York*	.272	96	228	18	62	95	14	2	5	35	1	4	1	1	2	19	0	2	6	.417	.298
Scanlan, Bob, Chicago	.042	40	24	0	1	1	0	0	0	1	2	0	0	0	0	10	0	0	3	.042	.080
Schilling, Curt, Houston	.333	56	3	0	1	1	0	0	0	0	0	0	0	0	0	0	0	0	0	.333	.333
Schourek, Pete, New York*	.136	35	22	0	3	4	1	0	0	3	5	0	0	2	0	9	0	0	0	.182	.208
Schu, Rick, Philadelphia	.091	17	22	1	2	2	0	0	0	2	0	0	0	0	0	7	0	0	1	.091	.125
Schulz, Jeff, Pittsburgh*	.000	3	2	0	0	0	0	0	0	0	0	0	0	0	0	2	0	0	0	.000	.000
Scioscia, Mike, Los Angeles*	.264	119	345	39	91	135	16	2	8	40	5	4	3	47	3	32	4	3	5	.391	.353
Scott, Donnie, Cincinnati†	.158	10	19	0	3	3	0	0	0	0	1	0	0	0	0	2	0	0	0	.158	.158
Scott, Gary, Chicago	.165	31	79	8	13	19	3	0	1	5	2	0	3	13	4	14	0	1	2	.241	.305
Scott, Mike, Houston	.000	2	1	0	0	0	0	0	0	0	0	0	0	0	0	0	0	0	0	.000	.000
Scudder, Scott, Cincinnati	.103	27	29	2	3	3	0	0	0	0	5	0	0	0	0	11	0	0	0	.103	.103
Searcy, Steve, Philadelphia*	.000	18	4	0	0	0	0	0	0	0	1	0	0	0	0	3	0	0	0	.000	.000
Servais, Scott, Houston	.162	16	37	0	6	9	3	0	0	6	2	0	1	4	0	8	0	1	2	.243	.244
Sharperson, Mike, Los Angeles	.278	105	216	24	60	81	11	2	2	20	10	2	1	25	2	24	1	3	3	.375	.355
Shipley, Craig, San Diego	.275	37	91	6	25	31	3	0	1	6	1	0	0	2	0	14	1	0	2	.341	.298
Simms, Mike, Houston	.203	49	123	18	25	39	5	0	3	16	0	0	3	18	1	38	0	0	2	.317	.301
Simons, Doug, New York*	.000	42	3	0	0	0	0	0	0	0	2	0	0	0	0	0	0	0	0	.000	.000
Slaught, Don, Pittsburgh	.295	77	220	19	65	87	17	1	1	29	1	1	3	21	0	32	1	0	6	.395	.363
Slocumb, Heath, Chicago	.000	52	1	0	0	0	0	0	0	0	0	0	0	0	0	0	0	0	0	.000	.000
Smiley, John, Pittsburgh*	.100	33	70	3	7	7	0	0	0	3	6	0	0	3	0	24	1	0	1	.100	.137
Smith, Bryn, St. Louis	.246	31	65	6	16	17	1	0	0	8	7	0	0	3	3	11	0	0	0	.262	.254
Smith, Dave, Chicago	.000	35	1	0	0	0	0	0	0	0	0	0	0	0	0	0	0	0	0	.000	.000
Smith, Dwight, Chicago*	.228	90	167	16	38	58	7	2	3	21	1	1	1	11	2	32	2	3	2	.347	.279
Smith, Greg, Los Angeles†	.000	5	1	1	0	0	0	0	0	0	0	0	0	0	0	2	0	0	0	.000	.000
Smith, Lonnie, Atlanta	.275	122	353	58	97	139	19	1	7	44	2	2	9	50	3	64	9	5	4	.394	.377
Smith, Ozzie, St. Louis†	.285	150	550	96	157	202	30	3	3	50	6	1	0	83	2	36	35	9	8	.367	.380
Smith, Pete, Atlanta	.167	14	12	1	2	2	0	0	0	0	1	0	0	0	0	5	0	0	0	.167	.231
Smith, Zane, Pittsburgh*	.183	36	71	7	13	16	3	0	0	10	13	0	0	5	0	28	0	0	8	.225	.224
Smoltz, John, Atlanta	.108	38	65	3	7	10	3	0	0	3	8	0	0	1	0	28	0	0	0	.154	.171
Stanton, Mike, Atlanta*	.500	74	6	0	3	3	0	0	0	1	0	0	0	1	0	1	0	0	0	.667	.571
Stephens, Ray, St. Louis	.286	6	7	0	2	2	0	0	0	0	0	0	0	1	0	3	0	0	0	.286	.375
Stephenson, Phil, San Diego*	.286	11	7	0	2	2	0	0	0	0	0	0	0	2	0	3	1	0	0	.286	.444
Strange, Doug, Chicago†	.444	3	9	0	4	5	1	0	0	1	0	0	0	0	0	1	0	0	0	.556	.455
Strawberry, Darryl, Los Angeles*	.265	139	505	86	134	248	22	4	28	99	0	5	3	75	4	125	10	8	8	.491	.361
Sutcliffe, Rick, Chicago*	.094	20	32	2	3	4	1	0	0	2	5	0	0	1	0	6	0	0	1	.125	.121
Sutko, Glenn, Cincinnati	.100	10	10	0	1	1	0	0	0	0	0	0	0	0	0	9	0	0	0	.100	.250
Templeton, Garry, S.D.-N.Y.†	.221	112	276	25	61	84	10	0	3	26	4	3	0	10	3	38	3	2	10	.304	.246
Terry, Scott, St. Louis	.143	65	7	0	1	1	0	0	0	0	2	0	0	0	0	2	0	0	0	.143	.143
Teufel, Tim, N.Y.-S.D.	.217	117	341	41	74	126	16	0	12	44	4	2	1	51	4	77	9	3	8	.370	.319
Tewksbury, Bob, St. Louis	.155	30	58	5	9	10	1	0	0	2	7	0	0	4	0	16	0	0	3	.172	.210
Thompson, Milt, St. Louis*	.307	115	326	55	100	144	16	5	6	34	2	4	0	32	7	53	16	9	4	.442	.368
Thompson, Robby, San Francisco	.262	144	492	74	129	220	24	5	19	48	11	1	6	63	2	95	14	7	5	.447	.352
Thon, Dickie, Philadelphia	.252	146	539	44	136	189	18	4	9	44	2	1	0	25	6	84	11	5	9	.351	.283

1991 N.L. STATISTICS

Player, Team	Avg.	G	AB	R	H	TB	2B	3B	HR	RBI	SH	SF	HP	BB	Int. BB	SO	SB	CS	GI DP	Slg.	OBP
Tolentino, Jose, Houston*	.259	44	54	6	14	21	4	0	1	6	0	1	0	4	0	9	0	0	2	.389	.305
Tomlin, Randy, Pittsburgh*	.192	32	52	0	10	11	1	0	0	2	13	0	0	2	0	18	0	0	2	.212	.222
Torve, Kelvin, New York*	.000	10	8	0	0	0	0	0	0	0	2	0	0	0	0	1	0	0	1	.000	.000
Treadway, Jeff, Atlanta*	.320	106	306	41	98	128	17	2	3	32	2	3	2	23	1	19	2	2	8	.418	.368
Uribe, Jose, San Francisco†	.221	90	231	23	51	70	8	4	1	12	2	0	0	20	6	33	3	2	2	.303	.283
VanderWal, John, Montreal*	.213	21	61	4	13	22	4	1	1	8	1	1	4	7	0	18	0	0	4	.361	.222
Van Slyke, Andy, Pittsburgh*	.265	138	491	87	130	219	24	7	17	83	0	11	2	71	11	85	10	3	5	.446	.355
Varsho, Gary, Pittsburgh*	.273	99	187	23	51	78	11	2	4	23	1	0	2	19	2	34	9	0	2	.417	.344
Vatcher, Jim, San Diego	.200	17	20	3	4	4	0	0	0	2	1	0	0	4	0	6	0	0	0	.200	.333
Villanueva, Hector, Chicago	.276	71	192	23	53	104	10	0	13	32	0	1	4	21	3	30	0	3	3	.542	.346
Viola, Frank, New York*	.127	35	71	2	9	11	2	0	0	2	10	0	0	2	1	13	1	1	1	.155	.151
Vizcaino, Jose, Chicago†	.262	93	145	7	38	43	5	1	0	10	2	2	0	5	0	18	2	1	1	.297	.283
Walk, Bob, Pittsburgh	.205	25	39	2	8	12	1	0	1	5	2	0	0	1	0	11	0	0	3	.308	.225
Walker, Chico, Chicago†	.257	124	374	51	96	126	10	1	6	34	2	3	1	33	2	57	13	5	3	.337	.315
Walker, Larry, Montreal*	.290	137	487	59	141	223	30	2	16	64	1	4	5	42	5	102	14	9	7	.458	.349
Wallach, Tim, Montreal	.225	151	577	60	130	193	22	1	13	73	0	4	6	50	8	100	2	4	12	.334	.292
Walton, Jerome, Chicago	.219	123	270	42	59	89	13	2	5	17	3	3	3	19	0	55	7	4	7	.330	.275
Ward, Kevin, San Diego	.243	44	107	13	26	43	7	1	2	8	1	0	3	9	0	27	1	3	3	.402	.308
Webster, Mitch, Pit.-L.A.†	.222	94	171	21	38	62	8	5	2	19	1	1	1	18	0	52	7	4	3	.363	.296
Wehner, John, Pittsburgh	.340	37	106	15	36	43	7	0	0	7	1	0	0	7	0	17	3	0	0	.406	.381
Whitehurst, Wally, New York	.125	36	24	1	3	6	0	0	0	0	5	0	0	2	0	6	0	0	0	.125	.229
Whitson, Ed, San Diego	.188	13	16	2	3	7	1	1	0	1	2	0	0	1	0	6	0	1	0	.212	.160
Wilkerson, Curtis, Pittsburgh†	.188	85	191	20	36	53	9	1	2	18	2	4	0	15	0	40	2	0	2	.277	.243
Wilkins, Dean, Houston	.000	7	1	0	0	0	0	0	0	0	7	0	0	0	0	1	0	0	0	.000	.000
Wilkins, Rick, Chicago*	.222	86	203	21	45	72	9	0	6	22	2	0	6	19	2	56	3	3	3	.355	.307
Willard, Jerry, Atlanta*	.214	17	14	1	3	6	0	0	1	4	0	0	0	2	0	5	0	0	0	.429	.313
Williams, Brian, Houston	.000	2	3	0	0	0	0	0	0	0	2	0	0	0	0	0	0	0	0	.000	.000
Williams, Kenny, Montreal	.271	34	70	11	19	28	5	2	0	7	1	0	1	3	0	22	2	1	1	.400	.311
Williams, Mitch, Philadelphia*	.000	69	0	0	0	0	0	0	0	0	0	0	0	3	0	1	0	0	0	.000	.500
Williams, Matt, San Francisco	.268	157	589	72	158	294	24	5	34	98	0	7	6	33	6	128	5	5	11	.499	.310
Wilson, Craig, St. Louis	.171	60	82	5	14	16	2	0	0	13	3	0	0	6	0	10	2	0	2	.195	.222
Wilson, Steve, Chi.-L.A.*	.000	20	2	0	0	0	0	0	0	0	1	0	0	0	0	1	0	0	0	.000	.000
Winningham, Herm, Cincinnati*	.225	98	169	17	38	49	6	0	1	4	2	0	0	11	1	40	4	4	2	.290	.272
Wohlers, Mark, Atlanta	.000	17	1	0	0	0	0	0	0	0	0	0	0	0	0	1	0	0	0	.000	.000
Wood, Ted, San Francisco*	.120	10	25	0	3	3	0	0	0	1	0	0	0	2	0	11	0	0	0	.120	.185
Yelding, Eric, Houston	.243	78	276	19	67	83	11	1	1	20	3	1	0	13	0	46	11	9	4	.301	.276
Young, Anthony, New York	.143	10	14	0	2	3	1	0	0	0	1	0	0	0	0	4	0	0	0	.214	.143
Young, Gerald, Houston†	.218	108	142	26	31	39	3	1	1	11	2	2	0	24	3	17	16	5	3	.275	.327
Zeile, Todd, St. Louis	.280	155	565	76	158	233	36	3	11	81	0	6	5	62	3	94	17	11	15	.412	.353

AWARDED FIRST BASE ON CATCHER'S INTERFERENCE—Herr, New York (Wilkins); Kingery, San Francisco (Santiago).

PLAYERS WITH TWO OR MORE TEAMS

Player, Team	Avg.	G	AB	R	H	TB	2B	3B	HR	RBI	SH	SF	HP	BB	Int. BB	SO	SB	CS	GI DP	Slg.	OBP
Berryhill, Damon, Chicago†	.189	62	159	13	30	52	7	0	5	14	0	1	0	11	1	41	1	2	2	.327	.244
Berryhill, Damon, Atlanta†	.000	1	1	0	0	0	0	0	0	0	0	0	0	0	0	0	0	0	1	.000	.000
Bielecki, Mike, Chicago	.065	39	46	1	3	3	0	0	0	0	4	0	0	3	0	21	0	0	0	.065	.122
Bielecki, Mike, Atlanta	.000	2	0	1	0	0	0	0	0	0	0	0	0	0	0	0	0	0	0	.000	.000
Burke, Tim, Montreal	.000	37	1	0	0	0	0	0	0	0	0	0	0	0	0	0	0	0	0	.000	.000
Burke, Tim, New York*	.000	35	5	0	0	0	0	0	0	0	2	0	0	0	0	4	0	0	0	.000	.000
Castillo, Tony, Atlanta*	.000	7	0	0	0	0	0	0	0	0	0	0	0	0	0	0	0	0	0	.000	.000
Castillo, Tony, New York*	.000	10	4	0	0	0	0	0	0	0	2	0	0	0	0	1	0	0	0	.000	.000
Clancy, Jim, Houston	.000	30	3	0	0	0	0	0	0	0	1	0	0	0	0	1	0	0	0	.000	.000
Clancy, Jim, Atlanta	.000	24	3	0	0	0	0	0	0	0	5	0	0	0	0	1	0	0	0	.000	.000
Darling, Ron, New York	.118	17	34	0	4	7	3	0	0	1	7	0	0	2	0	14	0	0	0	.206	.118
Darling, Ron, Montreal	.167	3	6	0	1	2	1	0	0	2	2	0	0	0	0	2	0	0	0	.333	.167
Gonzalez, Jose, Los Angeles	.000	42	28	3	0	0	0	0	0	0	0	0	0	2	0	9	0	0	0	.000	.067
Gonzalez, Jose, Pittsburgh	.100	16	20	2	2	5	0	0	0	3	2	0	0	0	0	6	0	0	0	.250	.095
Hartley, Mike, Los Angeles	.000	40	4	0	0	0	0	0	0	0	0	1	0	0	0	1	0	1	0	.000	.000
Hartley, Mike, Philadelphia	.000	18	1	0	0	0	0	0	0	0	0	0	0	0	0	0	0	0	0	.000	.000
Herr, Tom, New York†	.194	70	155	17	30	40	7	1	0	14	2	2	0	32	4	21	7	2	1	.258	.328
Herr, Tom, San Francisco†	.250	32	60	6	15	18	1	1	0	7	3	2	0	13	1	7	2	2	3	.300	.384
Mahler, Rick, Montreal	.111	10	9	0	1	1	0	0	0	0	3	0	0	1	0	2	0	0	0	.111	.111
Mahler, Rick, Atlanta	.200	13	5	0	1	2	1	0	0	0	1	0	0	0	0	2	0	0	0	.400	.200
Martinez, Carmelo, Pittsburgh	.250	11	16	1	4	4	0	0	0	0	0	0	0	1	0	2	0	0	2	.250	.294
Martinez, Carmelo, Cincinnati	.232	53	138	12	32	55	5	0	6	19	0	3	0	15	0	37	0	0	0	.399	.301
McDowell, Roger, Philadelphia	.000	38	2	0	0	0	0	0	0	0	4	0	0	0	0	0	0	0	0	.000	.000
McDowell, Roger, Los Angeles	.000	34	0	0	0	0	0	0	0	0	2	0	0	0	0	0	0	0	0	.000	.000
Pena, Alejandro, New York	.000	44	0	0	0	0	0	0	0	0	0	1	0	0	0	0	0	0	0	.000	.000
Pena, Alejandro, Atlanta	.000	15	0	0	0	0	0	0	0	0	0	0	0	0	0	1	0	0	0	.000	.000
Templeton, Garry, San Diego†	.193	32	57	5	11	17	1	1	1	6	4	2	0	3	3	9	0	1	3	.298	.203
Templeton, Garry, New York†	.228	80	219	20	50	67	9	1	2	20	4	2	0	9	3	29	3	1	7	.306	.257
Teufel, Tim, New York	.118	20	34	4	4	7	0	0	1	2	0	0	1	2	1	8	1	1	0	.206	.167
Teufel, Tim, San Diego	.228	97	307	39	70	119	16	0	11	42	0	2	1	49	1	69	8	2	8	.388	.334
Webster, Mitch, Pittsburgh†	.175	36	97	9	17	31	3	4	1	9	1	0	0	9	0	31	0	0	3	.320	.245
Webster, Mitch, Los Angeles†	.284	58	74	12	21	31	5	1	0	10	1	0	0	9	0	21	1	0	0	.419	.361
Wilson, Steve, Chicago*	.000	9	1	0	0	0	0	0	0	0	0	0	0	0	0	0	0	0	0	.000	.000
Wilson, Steve, Los Angeles*	.000	11	1	0	0	0	0	0	0	0	0	0	0	0	0	0	0	0	0	.000	.000

PINCH-HITTING

TEAM

Team	Avg.	AB	R	H	TB	2B	3B	HR	RBI	SH	SF	HP	BB	Int. BB	SO	SB	CS	GI DP	Slg.	OBP
St. Louis	.254	209	22	53	72	9	2	2	38	2	5	1	27	4	43	7	4	3	.344	.332
Philadelphia	.241	245	21	59	78	13	2	2	33	3	4	1	30	2	53	2	0	5	.318	.321
Montreal	.239	213	16	51	76	8	1	5	25	3	3	1	22	2	47	4	1	7	.357	.310
Atlanta	.233	253	24	59	79	11	0	3	26	5	1	0	25	4	62	1	3	5	.312	.301
Chicago	.233	223	29	52	87	8	3	7	35	2	1	1	17	3	45	3	2	0	.390	.289
Pittsburgh	.226	217	25	49	79	8	2	6	29	3	1	2	30	2	50	3	0	5	.364	.324
Cincinnati	.222	234	19	52	78	4	2	6	22	0	2	0	19	3	50	3	0	3	.333	.278
San Francisco	.216	259	30	56	69	7	3	0	26	2	2	0	31	4	61	2	0	9	.266	.298
New York	.212	231	24	49	76	3	0	8	28	0	2	1	28	5	41	2	2	11	.329	.298
Houston	.182	274	22	50	71	12	0	3	35	1	4	0	44	5	51	3	0	11	.259	.292
Los Angeles	.180	305	28	55	81	10	2	4	42	8	1	3	26	5	56	2	1	11	.266	.251
San Diego	.176	238	16	42	66	8	2	2	28	2	0	2	19	0	68	0	1	5	.277	.243

INDIVIDUAL

TOP 15 PINCH-HITTERS

Minimum 20 at-bats. *Lefthanded batter. †Switch-hitter.

Player, Team	Avg.	G	AB	R	H	TB	2B	3B	HR	RBI	SH	SF	HP	BB	Int. BB	SO	SB	CS	GI DP	Slg.	OBP
Walker, Chico, Chicago†	.406	38	32	4	13	17	2	1	0	6	0	0	0	6	1	4	2	0	3	.531	.500
Winningham, Herm, Cincinnati*	.394	36	33	4	13	13	0	0	0	2	0	0	0	2	1	8	2	0	0	.394	.429
Lindeman, Jim, Philadelphia	.361	40	36	4	13	14	1	0	0	2	0	0	0	1	0	5	1	1	1	.389	.395
Thompson, Milt, St. Louis*	.357	34	28	6	10	15	2	0	1	6	0	0	1	0	0	5	3	0	0	.536	.455
Carreon, Mark, New York	.343	40	35	7	12	22	1	0	3	7	0	1	0	4	0	7	0	0	4	.629	.425
Lemke, Mark, Atlanta†	.333	28	27	2	9	10	1	0	0	5	1	0	0	0	0	4	0	0	1	.370	.333
Jordan, Ricky, Philadelphia	.321	31	28	1	9	12	3	0	0	6	0	1	0	2	1	7	1	0	1	.429	.355
Hansen, Dave, Los Angeles*	.313	35	32	1	10	15	2	0	1	4	0	0	0	1	0	5	0	1	1	.469	.333
Jones, Chris, Cincinnati	.308	27	26	6	8	13	2	0	1	3	0	0	0	1	0	7	1	0	0	.500	.333
Noboa, Junior, Montreal	.304	48	46	5	14	19	2	0	1	2	0	2	0	1	0	6	1	1	0	.413	.319
Wilson, Craig, St. Louis	.297	43	37	4	11	13	2	0	0	11	0	0	0	3	1	6	0	0	1	.351	.333
Redus, Gary, Pittsburgh	.290	36	31	8	9	13	1	0	1	3	0	0	0	5	0	8	2	0	0	.419	.389
Felder, Mike, San Francisco†	.278	42	36	7	10	11	1	0	0	3	1	0	0	2	1	1	1	0	0	.306	.366
McClendon, Lloyd, Pittsburgh	.273	40	33	5	9	16	2	1	1	8	0	0	2	5	0	6	0	0	1	.485	.400
Sharperson, Mike, Los Angeles	.273	28	22	3	6	7	0	0	0	3	2	0	0	4	0	4	0	1	0	.318	.385

ALL PINCH-HITTERS

*Lefthanded batter. †Switch-hitter.

Player, Team	Avg.	G	AB	R	H	TB	2B	3B	HR	RBI	SH	SF	HP	BB	Int. BB	SO	SB	CS	GI DP	Slg.	OBP
Abner, Shawn, San Diego	.154	13	13	0	2	2	0	0	0	0	0	0	0	1	0	5	0	0	0	.154	.154
Aldrete, Mike, San Diego*	.000	7	6	1	0	0	0	0	0	0	0	0	0	0	0	2	0	0	0	.000	.143

1991 N.L. STATISTICS

Player, Team	Avg.	G	AB	R	H	TB	2B	3B	HR	RBI	SH	SF	HP	BB	Int. BB	SO	SB	CS	GI DP	Slg.	OBP
Alicea, Luis, St. Louis†	.205	46	39	2	8	9	1	0	0	2	0	0	0	6	0	10	0	1	0	.231	.311
Anderson, Dave, San Francisco	.138	32	29	1	4	5	1	0	0	2	0	0	0	3	0	3	0	0	1	.172	.219
Anthony, Eric, Houston*	.000	3	2	0	0	0	0	0	0	0	0	0	0	1	0	1	0	0	0	.000	.333
Avery, Steve, Atlanta*	.000	1	0	0	0	0	0	0	0	0	2	0	0	0	0	0	0	0	0	.000	.000
Azocar, Oscar, San Diego*	.200	28	25	2	5	6	1	0	0	4	0	0	1	0	0	6	0	0	0	.240	.231
Backman, Wally, Philadelphia†	.184	49	38	2	7	11	4	0	0	8	0	0	0	8	0	10	1	0	0	.289	.319
Bagwell, Jeff, Houston	.500	4	4	1	2	6	1	0	1	2	0	0	0	0	0	1	0	0	0	1.500	.500
Banister, Jeff, Pittsburgh	1.000	1	1	0	1	1	0	0	0	0	0	0	0	0	0	0	0	0	0	1.000	1.000
Barberie, Bret, Montreal†	.063	22	16	0	1	2	1	0	0	1	0	0	1	2	0	7	0	0	1	.125	.211
Barrett, Marty, San Diego	.375	8	8	1	3	7	1	0	1	3	0	0	0	0	0	0	0	0	2	.875	.375
Bass, Kevin, San Francisco*	.125	28	24	4	3	6	0	0	1	3	0	0	0	3	0	2	1	0	2	.250	.222
Batiste, Kim, Philadelphia	.000	2	2	0	0	0	0	0	0	0	0	0	0	0	0	1	0	0	0	.000	.000
Bell, George, Chicago	.500	4	4	1	2	2	0	0	0	2	0	0	0	0	0	1	0	0	0	.500	.500
Bell, Jay, Pittsburgh	.000	2	2	0	0	0	0	0	0	0	0	0	0	0	0	0	0	0	0	.000	.000
Bell, Mike, Atlanta*	.000	4	4	1	0	0	0	0	0	0	0	0	0	0	0	1	0	0	0	.000	.000
Belliard, Rafael, Atlanta	.000	2	2	0	0	0	0	0	0	0	0	1	0	1	0	1	0	0	0	.000	.250
Benavides, Freddie, Cincinnati	.000	2	2	0	0	0	0	0	0	0	0	0	0	0	0	0	0	0	0	.000	.000
Benjamin, Mike, San Francisco	.111	20	18	0	2	2	0	0	0	1	0	1	0	1	0	2	0	0	0	.111	.150
Benzinger, Todd, Cincinnati†	.118	17	17	0	2	2	0	0	0	1	0	0	0	0	0	7	0	0	0	.118	.118
Berryhill, Damon, Atlanta†	.333	11	9	0	3	5	2	0	0	2	0	0	0	2	0	4	0	0	0	.556	.455
Biggio, Craig, Houston	.000	2	2	0	0	0	0	0	0	0	0	0	0	0	0	0	0	0	0	.000	.000
Bilardello, Dann, San Diego	.000	1	1	0	0	0	0	0	0	0	0	0	0	0	0	0	0	0	0	.000	.000
Black, Bud, San Francisco*	.231	29	26	2	6	6	0	0	0	3	2	0	0	2	0	5	0	0	0	.231	.286
Blauser, Jeff, Atlanta	.333	5	3	2	1	2	1	0	0	0	0	0	0	2	0	0	0	0	0	.667	.600
Bonds, Barry, Pittsburgh*	.000	2	2	0	0	0	0	0	0	0	0	0	0	1	1	0	0	0	0	.000	.333
Bonilla, Bobby, Pittsburgh†	.333	5	3	0	1	1	0	0	0	1	0	0	0	0	0	0	0	0	0	.333	.333
Booker, Rod, Philadelphia*	.000	1	1	0	0	0	0	0	0	0	0	0	0	0	0	0	0	0	0	.000	.000
Boskie, Shawn, Chicago	.000	1	1	0	0	0	0	0	0	0	0	0	0	0	0	0	0	0	0	.000	.000
Boston, Daryl, New York*	.222	30	27	2	6	7	1	0	0	4	0	0	0	2	1	4	0	0	2	.259	.276
Braggs, Glenn, Cincinnati	.267	16	15	2	4	10	0	0	2	3	0	0	0	1	0	7	0	0	0	.667	.313
Bream, Sid, Atlanta*	.556	11	9	2	5	12	1	0	2	7	0	0	0	1	0	0	0	0	1	1.333	.600
Brewer, Rod, St. Louis*	.000	5	4	0	0	0	0	0	0	0	0	0	0	1	0	1	0	0	0	.000	.200
Brooks, Hubie, New York*	.000	1	1	0	0	0	0	0	0	0	0	0	0	0	0	0	0	0	0	.000	.000
Bullett, Scott, Pittsburgh*	.000	1	1	0	0	0	0	0	0	0	0	0	0	0	0	4	0	0	0	.000	.000
Bullock, Eric, Montreal*	.208	57	48	3	10	12	2	0	0	3	0	0	0	6	0	9	0	0	0	.250	.304
Butler, Brett, Los Angeles*	.000	1	1	0	0	0	0	0	0	0	0	0	0	0	0	1	0	0	0	.000	.000
Cabrera, Francisco, Atlanta	.167	18	18	2	3	4	1	0	0	4	0	0	0	0	0	8	0	0	1	.222	.167
Calderon, Ivan, Montreal	.400	11	10	1	4	7	0	0	1	3	0	1	0	0	0	2	1	0	0	.700	.364
Caminiti, Ken, Houston†	.000	2	2	0	0	0	0	0	0	0	0	0	0	0	0	1	0	0	0	.000	.000
Campusano, Sil, Philadelphia	.333	3	3	1	1	1	0	0	0	1	0	0	0	0	0	0	0	0	0	.333	.333
Candaele, Casey, Houston†	.158	21	19	2	3	3	0	0	0	0	0	0	0	2	0	1	0	0	0	.158	.238
Carr, Chuck, New York†	.000	3	3	0	0	0	0	0	0	0	0	0	0	0	0	1	0	0	0	.000	.000
Carreon, Mark, New York	.343	40	35	7	12	22	1	0	3	7	0	0	1	4	1	7	0	0	4	.629	.425
Carter, Gary, Los Angeles	.074	31	27	1	2	3	1	0	0	3	0	0	0	4	1	5	0	0	3	.111	.194
Cedeno, Andujar, Houston	.000	1	1	0	0	0	0	0	0	0	0	0	0	0	0	0	0	0	0	.000	.000
Cerone, Rick, New York	.286	17	14	0	4	4	0	0	0	0	0	0	0	3	0	4	0	0	1	.286	.412

Player, Team	Avg.	G	AB	R	H	TB	2B	3B	HR	RBI	SH	SF	HP	BB	Int. BB	SO	SB	CS	GI DP	Slg.	OBP
Chamberlain, Wes, Philadelphia	.000	3	3	0	0	0	0	0	0	0	0	0	0	0	0	0	0	0	0	.000	.000
Clark, Jerald, San Diego	.200	10	10	1	2	3	1	0	0	1	0	0	0	0	0	2	0	0	1	.300	.200
Clark, Will, San Francisco*	.333	5	3	0	1	1	0	0	0	0	0	0	0	2	0	0	0	0	0	.333	.600
Coleman, Vince, New York†	.000	2	2	0	0	0	0	0	0	0	0	0	0	0	0	2	0	0	0	.000	.000
Coles, Darnell, San Francisco	.286	7	7	0	2	2	0	0	0	1	0	0	0	0	0	2	0	0	0	.286	.286
Coolbaugh, Scott, San Diego	.000	6	6	0	0	0	0	0	0	0	0	0	0	0	0	2	0	0	0	.000	.000
Cooper, Gary, Houston	.200	5	4	0	1	2	1	0	0	3	0	0	0	1	0	2	0	0	0	.400	.200
Daniels, Kal, Los Angeles*	.200	5	5	0	1	2	1	0	0	1	0	0	0	0	0	4	0	0	1	.143	.167
Dascenzo, Doug, Chicago†	.107	31	28	3	3	4	1	0	0	1	1	0	0	1	0	4	0	0	0	.143	.167
Daulton, Darren, Philadelphia*	.250	6	4	0	1	1	0	0	0	2	0	2	0	0	0	4	0	0	0	.250	.167
Davidson, Mark, Houston	.138	35	29	2	4	4	0	0	0	3	1	0	0	6	1	4	0	0	0	.138	.286
Davis, Butch, Los Angeles	.000	1	1	0	0	0	0	0	0	0	0	0	0	0	0	0	0	0	0	.000	.000
Davis, Eric, Cincinnati	.250	9	8	0	2	3	1	0	0	1	0	0	0	1	0	4	0	0	0	.375	.333
Dawson, Andre, Chicago	.167	12	12	0	2	8	0	0	2	5	0	0	0	0	0	4	0	0	0	.667	.167
DeShields, Delino, Montreal*	.000	6	5	0	0	0	0	0	0	0	0	0	0	1	0	4	0	0	0	.000	.167
Decker, Steve, San Francisco	.250	4	4	0	1	1	0	0	0	0	0	0	0	0	0	0	0	0	0	.250	.250
Donnels, Chris, New York*	.077	15	13	0	1	1	0	0	0	5	0	0	0	2	1	5	0	0	0	.077	.200
Doran, Bill, Cincinnati†	.267	20	15	2	4	7	0	0	1	1	0	0	0	4	0	2	1	0	0	.467	.421
Dorsett, Brian, San Diego	.100	10	10	0	1	1	0	0	0	0	0	0	0	0	0	4	0	0	0	.100	.100
Duncan, Mariano, Cincinnati	.500	8	8	0	2	2	0	0	0	0	0	0	0	0	0	0	0	0	0	.250	.250
Dunston, Shawon, Chicago	.500	2	2	0	1	1	0	0	0	0	0	0	0	0	0	2	0	0	0	.500	.500
Dykstra, Len, Philadelphia*	1.000	11	1	1	1	2	1	0	0	0	0	0	0	0	0	0	0	0	0	2.000	1.000
Elster, Kevin, New York	.222	8	9	1	2	2	0	0	0	2	0	0	0	1	0	2	0	0	0	.222	.273
Espy, Cecil, Pittsburgh†	.333	8	6	1	2	3	1	0	0	0	0	0	0	1	0	2	0	0	0	.500	.429
Eusebio, Tony, Houston	.000	1	1	0	0	0	0	0	0	0	0	0	0	0	0	1	0	0	0	.000	.000
Faries, Paul, San Diego	.222	2	2	0	0	0	0	0	0	0	0	0	0	0	0	0	1	0	0	.000	.000
Felder, Mike, San Francisco†	.278	42	36	7	10	11	1	0	0	3	0	0	0	5	1	1	0	1	0	.306	.366
Fernandez, Tony, San Diego†	.000	2	2	0	0	0	0	0	0	0	0	0	0	0	0	0	0	0	0	.000	.000
Finley, Steve, Houston*	.222	9	9	0	2	3	1	0	0	0	0	0	0	0	0	2	0	0	0	.333	.222
Fitzgerald, Mike, Montreal	.250	12	8	0	2	5	0	0	1	7	0	1	0	2	0	1	0	0	0	.625	.364
Fletcher, Darrin, Philadelphia*	.000	1	1	0	0	0	0	0	0	0	0	0	0	0	0	1	0	0	0	.000	.000
Foley, Tom, Montreal*	.214	15	14	0	3	4	1	0	0	3	0	0	0	1	0	5	0	0	0	.286	.267
Galarraga, Andres, Montreal	.000	4	2	0	0	0	0	0	0	0	0	0	0	1	0	2	0	0	0	.000	.333
Gant, Ron, Atlanta	.000	8	6	0	0	0	0	0	0	0	0	0	0	2	0	3	0	0	0	.000	.250
Garcia, Carlos, Pittsburgh	.000	1	1	0	0	0	0	0	0	0	0	0	0	0	0	0	0	0	0	.000	.000
Gardner, Jeff, New York*	.500	2	2	0	1	1	0	0	0	0	0	0	0	0	0	0	1	0	0	.500	.500
Gedman, Rich, St. Louis*	.000	7	6	0	0	0	0	0	0	2	0	0	0	0	0	2	0	0	0	.000	.000
Gilkey, Bernard, St. Louis	.143	8	7	1	1	2	1	0	0	0	0	0	0	1	0	0	1	0	0	.286	.250
Girardi, Joe, Chicago	1.000	1	1	1	1	1	0	0	0	0	0	0	0	0	0	0	0	0	1	1.000	1.000
Glavine, Tom, Atlanta*	.000	1	0	1	0	0	0	0	0	0	0	0	0	1	0	0	0	0	0	.000	1.000
Gonzalez, Jose, L.A.-Pit.	.000	17	15	1	0	0	0	0	0	0	1	0	0	1	0	6	0	0	0	.000	.063
Gonzalez, Luis, Houston*	.200	10	5	1	0	1	0	0	0	2	0	0	0	1	0	2	0	0	0	.200	.500
Goodwin, Tom, Los Angeles*	.000	1	1	0	0	0	0	0	0	0	0	0	0	0	0	1	1	0	0	.000	.000
Grace, Mark, Chicago*	.000	4	4	0	0	0	0	0	0	0	0	0	0	0	0	0	0	0	0	.000	.000
Greene, Tommy, Philadelphia	.000	2	4	0	0	0	0	0	0	0	0	0	0	0	0	8	0	1	0	.000	.000
Gregg, Tommy, Atlanta*	.231	46	39	4	9	13	4	0	0	2	0	0	0	6	1	8	1	1	0	.333	.333

Player, Team	Avg.	G	AB	R	H	TB	2B	3B	HR	RBI	SH	SF	HP	BB	Int. BB	SO	SB	CS	GI DP	Slg.	OBP
Grissom, Marquis, Montreal	.125	8	8	0	1	1	0	0	0	0	0	0	0	0	0	2	0	0	0	.125	.125
Gross, Kevin, Los Angeles	.500	2	2	1	1	1	0	0	0	0	0	0	0	0	0	0	0	0	0	.500	.500
Guerrero, Pedro, St. Louis	.667	3	3	0	2	2	0	0	0	1	0	0	0	0	0	0	0	0	0	.667	.667
Gwynn, Chris, Los Angeles*	.232	64	56	5	13	21	2	0	2	13	0	1	1	3	1	10	0	0	3	.375	.279
Gwynn, Tony, San Diego*	.000	1	1	0	0	0	0	0	0	0	0	0	0	0	0	0	0	0	0	.000	.000
Hamilton, Jeff, Los Angeles	.000	11	11	0	0	0	0	0	0	0	0	0	0	0	0	3	0	0	0	.000	.000
Hansen, Dave, Los Angeles*	.313	35	32	1	10	15	2	0	1	4	0	0	0	1	1	5	1	0	2	.469	.333
Harris, Lenny, Los Angeles*	.125	27	24	4	3	3	0	0	0	2	0	0	0	2	0	5	0	0	0	.125	.192
Hassey, Ron, Montreal*	.154	18	13	0	2	2	0	0	0	0	1	0	0	1	0	3	0	0	1	.154	.214
Hatcher, Billy, Cincinnati	.158	19	19	1	3	3	0	0	0	1	0	0	0	0	0	5	1	0	0	.158	.158
Hayes, Charlie, Philadelphia	.500	9	8	1	4	4	0	0	0	0	0	0	0	1	0	1	0	0	0	.500	.556
Hayes, Von, Philadelphia*	.250	5	4	1	1	2	1	0	0	1	0	0	0	1	0	1	1	0	0	.500	.400
Heath, Mike, Atlanta	.167	7	6	2	1	1	0	0	0	0	0	0	0	1	0	2	0	0	0	.167	.286
Heaton, Neal, Pittsburgh*	.000	1	0	0	0	0	0	0	0	0	0	0	0	1	0	0	0	0	0	.000	1.000
Heep, Danny, Atlanta*	.417	13	12	3	5	6	1	0	0	3	0	0	0	1	0	4	0	0	1	.500	.462
Hernandez, Carlos, Los Angeles	.000	3	2	0	0	0	0	0	0	0	0	0	0	1	0	1	0	0	0	.000	.333
Herr, Tom, N.Y.-S.F.†	.179	34	28	3	5	5	0	0	0	2	0	0	0	5	0	9	0	0	1	.179	.303
Hollins, Dave, Philadelphia†	.214	16	14	3	3	6	0	0	1	2	0	0	0	2	0	1	0	0	0	.429	.313
Howard, Thomas, San Diego†	.115	30	26	1	3	7	1	0	1	3	1	0	0	2	1	8	0	0	1	.269	.179
Howell, Jack, San Diego*	.273	13	11	1	3	3	0	0	0	3	0	0	0	2	0	2	0	0	0	.273	.385
Hudler, Rex, St. Louis	.148	33	27	1	4	6	2	0	0	1	1	0	0	3	0	7	2	1	0	.222	.226
Hundley, Todd, New York†	.333	3	3	1	1	4	0	0	1	3	0	0	0	0	0	0	0	0	0	1.333	.333
Hunter, Brian, Atlanta	.167	19	18	3	3	7	1	0	1	2	0	0	0	0	0	6	0	0	0	.389	.158
Jackson, Darrin, San Diego	.130	29	23	5	3	6	0	0	1	0	0	0	0	5	0	7	0	0	0	.261	.286
Javier, Stan, Los Angeles†	.096	59	52	3	5	7	2	0	0	3	0	0	0	4	0	14	1	0	1	.135	.161
Jefferies, Gregg, New York†	.222	12	9	3	2	5	0	0	1	0	3	0	0	3	0	2	0	0	0	.556	.417
Jefferson, Reggie, Cincinnati†	.000	3	2	0	0	0	0	0	0	1	0	0	0	1	0	0	0	0	0	.000	.333
Jefferson, Stan, Cincinnati†	.000	4	4	1	0	0	0	0	0	2	0	0	0	2	0	2	1	0	0	.000	.333
Johnson, Howard, New York†	.000	1	1	0	0	0	0	0	0	1	0	0	0	0	0	1	0	0	0	.000	.000
Jones, Chris, Cincinnati	.308	27	26	4	8	13	2	0	1	3	0	0	0	1	0	7	0	0	1	.500	.333
Jones, Ron, Philadelphia*	.154	28	26	0	4	6	2	0	0	0	0	0	0	2	0	9	0	0	1	.231	.214
Jordan, Ricky, Philadelphia	.321	31	28	1	9	12	3	0	0	3	0	1	0	2	0	7	0	1	1	.429	.355
Jose, Felix, St. Louis†	1.000	1	1	1	1	2	1	0	0	2	0	0	0	0	0	0	0	0	0	2.000	1.000
Justice, David, Atlanta*	.250	5	4	0	1	2	1	0	0	2	0	0	0	1	0	3	0	0	0	.500	.400
Karros, Eric, Los Angeles	.308	15	13	2	4	4	0	0	0	0	0	0	0	1	0	2	0	0	1	.308	.357
Kennedy, Terry, San Francisco*	.250	55	44	6	11	13	2	0	0	2	0	0	0	8	1	4	0	0	0	.295	.365
Kingery, Mike, San Francisco*	.222	10	9	2	2	5	0	0	1	2	1	0	0	1	0	8	0	0	0	.556	.300
Kruk, John, Philadelphia*	.222	10	9	0	2	2	0	0	0	1	0	0	0	1	0	1	0	0	0	.222	.250
LaValliere, Mike, Pittsburgh*	.208	27	24	2	5	8	3	0	0	1	0	0	0	2	0	5	0	0	1	.333	.269
Lampkin, Tom, San Diego*	.000	4	2	0	0	0	0	0	0	0	0	0	0	1	0	5	0	0	0	.000	.333
Landrum, Ced, Chicago*	.000	2	2	1	0	0	0	0	0	0	0	0	0	0	0	3	0	0	0	.000	.000
Lankford, Ray, St. Louis*	.200	6	5	1	1	1	0	0	0	1	0	0	0	1	0	3	0	0	0	.200	.333
Larkin, Barry, Cincinnati	.000	2	1	0	0	0	0	0	0	0	0	0	0	0	0	1	0	0	0	.000	.000
Lee, Terry, Cincinnati	.000	2	2	0	0	0	0	0	0	0	0	0	0	1	0	1	0	0	0	.000	.333
Lemke, Mark, Atlanta†	.333	28	27	2	9	10	1	0	0	5	1	0	0	0	0	4	0	0	1	.370	.333
Leonard, Mark, San Francisco*	.269	32	26	4	7	11	2	1	0	5	0	2	0	3	0	5	0	0	2	.423	.323

Player, Team	Avg.	G	AB	R	H	TB	2B	3B	HR	RBI	SH	SF	HP	BB	Int. BB	SO	SB	CS	GI DP	Slg.	OBP
Lewis, Darren, San Francisco	.250	5	4	0	1	1	0	0	0	1	0	0	0	1	0	1	0	0	0	.250	.400
Lind, Jose, Pittsburgh	.000	2	1	0	0	0	0	0	0	0	0	0	0	1	0	0	0	0	0	.000	.500
Lindeman, Jim, Philadelphia	.361	40	36	4	13	14	1	0	0	2	0	0	0	2	1	5	0	0	1	.389	.395
Litton, Greg, San Francisco	.231	13	13	1	3	4	1	0	0	2	0	0	0	0	0	1	0	0	0	.308	.231
Lofton, Kenny, Houston*	.000	1	1	0	0	0	0	0	0	0	0	0	0	0	0	1	0	0	0	.000	.000
Lyons, Barry, Los Angeles	.500	4	4	0	2	2	0	0	0	1	0	0	0	0	0	1	0	0	0	.500	.500
Maddux, Greg, Chicago	.500	2	2	1	1	1	0	0	0	1	0	0	0	0	0	1	0	0	0	.500	.500
Magadan, Dave, New York*	.750	6	4	1	3	3	0	0	0	1	0	0	0	2	0	0	0	0	0	.750	.833
Manwaring, Kirk, San Francisco	1.000	1	1	0	1	1	0	0	0	1	0	0	0	0	0	0	0	0	0	1.000	1.000
Martinez, Carmelo, Pit.-Cin.	.188	17	16	0	3	6	0	0	1	1	0	0	0	0	0	3	0	0	1	.375	.188
Martinez, Dennis, Montreal	.000	1	0	0	0	0	0	0	0	0	1	0	0	0	0	0	0	0	0	.000	.000
Martinez, Dave, Montreal*	.364	12	11	1	4	5	1	0	0	2	0	0	0	1	0	0	0	0	0	.455	.417
May, Derrick, Chicago*	.143	8	7	0	1	4	0	0	1	1	0	0	0	1	0	3	0	0	0	.571	.250
McClendon, Lloyd, Pittsburgh	.273	40	33	5	9	16	1	0	2	8	0	0	0	5	1	6	0	0	1	.485	.400
McDaniel, Terry, New York†	.200	7	5	1	1	1	0	0	0	1	0	0	0	1	0	2	0	0	0	.200	.333
McGee, Willie, San Francisco†	.500	4	4	2	2	2	0	0	0	0	0	0	0	0	0	1	1	0	0	.500	.500
McLemore, Mark, Houston†	.000	2	2	0	0	0	0	0	0	0	0	0	0	0	0	0	0	0	0	.000	.000
McReynolds, Kevin, New York	.500	4	4	1	2	5	0	0	1	2	0	0	0	0	0	2	0	0	0	1.250	.500
Merced, Orlando, Pittsburgh†	.353	20	17	4	6	9	0	0	1	3	0	0	0	3	0	7	0	0	0	.529	.450
Miller, Keith, New York	.182	13	11	0	2	2	0	0	0	1	0	0	0	2	0	1	1	0	0	.182	.308
Minutelli, Gino, Cincinnati*	.000	1	1	0	0	0	0	0	0	0	1	0	0	0	0	1	0	0	0	.000	.000
Mitchell, Keith, Atlanta	.200	13	10	0	2	2	0	0	0	1	0	0	0	3	0	2	0	0	1	.200	.385
Mitchell, Kevin, San Francisco	.000	14	13	2	0	0	0	0	0	0	0	0	0	1	1	5	1	0	0	.000	.071
Morris, Hal, Cincinnati*	.333	10	9	2	3	7	1	0	1	2	0	0	0	0	0	1	0	0	0	.778	.333
Morris, John, Philadelphia*	.214	31	28	2	6	6	0	0	0	2	0	0	1	2	0	6	1	0	0	.214	.290
Mota, Jose, San Diego†	.000	1	1	0	0	0	0	0	0	0	0	0	0	0	0	1	0	0	0	.000	.000
Murphy, Dale, Philadelphia	.333	10	9	0	3	4	1	0	0	3	0	0	0	1	0	1	0	0	0	.444	.400
Murray, Eddie, Los Angeles†	.667	5	3	1	2	5	0	0	1	5	0	0	0	2	1	0	0	0	0	1.667	.800
Nichols, Carl, Houston	.000	4	4	0	0	0	0	0	0	0	0	0	0	0	0	2	0	0	0	.000	.000
Nixon, Otis, Atlanta†	.375	10	8	1	3	5	0	1	0	1	0	0	0	1	0	1	1	0	0	.625	.444
Noboa, Junior, Montreal	.304	48	46	5	14	19	2	0	1	2	0	0	0	1	0	6	1	1	0	.413	.319
Oberkfell, Ken, Houston†	.188	39	32	1	6	8	2	0	0	2	1	0	0	3	0	6	0	1	0	.250	.316
Oliver, Joe, Cincinnati	.000	7	7	0	0	0	0	0	0	0	0	0	0	0	0	3	0	0	1	.000	.000
Olson, Greg, Atlanta	.286	7	7	1	2	2	0	0	0	0	0	0	0	0	0	1	0	0	0	.286	.286
Ortiz, Javier, Houston	.238	26	21	0	5	7	2	0	0	1	0	0	0	5	0	3	0	0	0	.333	.385
Owen, Spike, Montreal†	.333	9	6	0	2	2	0	0	0	0	0	0	0	2	0	1	0	0	0	.333	.500
O'Brien, Charlie, New York	.000	2	2	0	0	0	0	0	0	0	0	0	0	0	0	1	0	0	0	.000	.000
O'Neill, Paul, Cincinnati*	.250	5	4	1	1	1	0	0	0	0	0	0	0	1	0	1	0	0	0	.250	.400
Pagnozzi, Tom, St. Louis	.000	2	0	0	0	0	0	0	0	0	1	0	0	0	0	0	0	0	0	.000	.000
Pappas, Erik, Chicago	1.000	1	1	0	1	1	0	0	0	0	0	0	0	0	0	0	0	0	0	1.000	1.000
Parker, Rick, San Francisco	.000	9	8	0	0	0	0	0	0	0	0	0	0	1	0	3	0	0	0	.000	.111
Pena, Geronimo, St. Louis†	.273	13	11	0	3	5	2	0	0	0	0	0	0	0	0	2	0	0	0	.455	.273
Pendleton, Terry, Atlanta†	.250	5	4	1	1	1	0	0	0	1	0	0	0	1	0	1	0	0	1	.250	.400
Perezchica, Tony, San Francisco	.000	4	4	0	0	0	0	0	0	0	0	0	0	0	0	1	0	0	0	.000	.000
Perry, Gerald, St. Louis*	.268	48	41	4	11	16	0	1	1	13	0	1	0	6	1	8	2	1	1	.390	.354

Player, Team	Avg.	G	AB	R	H	TB	2B	3B	HR	RBI	SH	SF	HP	BB	Int. BB	SO	SB	CS	GI DP	Slg.	OBP
Presley, Jim, San Diego	.250	4	4	0	1	1	0	0	0	0	0	0	0	0	0	2	0	0	1	.250	.250
Prince, Tom, Pittsburgh	.000	6	5	2	0	0	0	0	0	0	0	0	0	1	0	1	0	0	1	.000	.167
Quinones, Luis, Cincinnati†	.167	43	36	3	6	9	2	0	0	4	0	1	0	6	0	5	0	0	1	.250	.279
Ramirez, Rafael, Houston	.231	45	39	3	9	11	2	0	0	7	0	1	0	5	0	7	0	0	2	.282	.311
Rasmussen, Dennis, San Diego*	.000	3	1	0	0	0	0	0	0	0	0	0	0	0	0	1	0	0	0	.000	.000
Ready, Randy, Philadelphia	.167	20	12	3	2	2	0	0	0	2	0	0	0	8	0	3	0	0	0	.167	.500
Redfield, Joe, Pittsburgh	.000	3	3	0	0	0	0	0	0	0	0	0	0	0	0	1	0	0	0	.000	.000
Redus, Gary, Pittsburgh	.290	36	31	8	9	13	1	0	1	3	0	0	0	5	0	8	2	0	0	.419	.389
Reed, Jeff, Cincinnati†	.250	4	4	1	1	2	1	0	0	1	0	0	0	0	0	1	0	0	0	.500	.250
Reyes, Gilberto, Montreal	.500	3	2	0	1	1	0	0	0	0	0	0	0	1	0	0	0	0	0	.500	.667
Rhodes, Karl, Houston*	.000	3	3	0	0	0	0	0	0	0	0	0	0	0	0	1	0	0	0	.000	.000
Richardson, Jeff, Pittsburgh	.000	3	3	0	0	0	0	0	0	0	0	0	0	0	0	1	0	0	0	.000	.000
Riesgo, Damon, Montreal	.000	1	1	0	0	0	0	0	0	0	0	0	0	0	0	0	0	0	1	.000	.000
Rijo, Jose, Cincinnati	.000	1	2	0	0	0	0	0	0	0	0	1	0	0	0	0	0	0	0	.000	.000
Roberts, Bip, San Diego†	.143	9	7	2	1	1	0	0	0	0	0	0	0	1	0	4	0	0	1	.143	.250
Robinson, Don, San Francisco	.000	2	7	0	0	0	0	0	0	0	0	0	0	0	0	0	0	0	0	.000	.000
Rohde, Dave, Houston†	.118	21	17	2	2	2	0	0	0	0	0	0	0	3	0	4	0	0	1	.118	.250
Rossy, Rico, Atlanta	.000	1	1	0	0	0	0	0	0	0	0	0	0	0	0	0	0	0	0	.000	.000
Royer, Stan, St. Louis	.333	4	3	0	1	1	0	0	0	0	0	0	0	1	0	2	0	0	0	.333	.500
Sabo, Chris, Cincinnati	.500	2	2	0	1	1	0	0	0	2	0	0	0	0	0	0	0	0	0	.500	.500
Salazar, Luis, Chicago	.154	13	13	1	2	3	1	0	0	1	0	0	0	0	0	2	0	0	0	.231	.154
Samuel, Juan, Los Angeles	.500	2	2	0	1	1	0	0	0	1	0	0	0	0	0	0	0	0	0	.500	.500
Sanchez, Rey, Chicago	.000	3	4	1	0	0	0	0	0	0	0	0	0	0	0	2	0	0	0	.000	.000
Sandberg, Ryne, Chicago	.333	3	3	0	1	1	0	0	0	0	0	0	0	0	0	0	0	0	0	.333	.333
Sanders, Deion, Atlanta*	.000	4	4	0	0	0	0	0	0	0	0	0	0	0	0	1	0	0	0	.000	.000
Santiago, Benito, San Diego	1.000	2	2	0	2	3	1	0	0	2	0	0	0	0	0	0	0	0	0	1.000	1.000
Santovenia, Nelson, Montreal	.429	10	7	3	3	6	0	0	1	1	0	0	0	2	1	2	0	0	0	.857	.556
Sasser, Mackey, New York*	.263	41	38	4	10	16	3	0	1	7	0	1	0	1	0	4	0	0	2	.421	.275
Schu, Rick, Philadelphia	.077	13	13	0	1	1	0	0	0	0	0	0	0	0	0	3	0	0	1	.077	.077
Schulz, Jeff, Pittsburgh*	.000	3	3	0	0	0	0	0	0	0	0	0	0	0	0	2	0	0	0	.000	.000
Scioscia, Mike, Los Angeles*	.375	9	8	1	3	3	0	0	0	2	0	0	1	2	0	1	0	0	0	.375	.444
Scott, Donnie, Cincinnati†	.000	2	2	0	0	0	0	0	0	0	0	0	0	0	0	1	0	0	0	.000	.000
Servais, Scott, Houston	.000	2	2	0	0	0	0	0	0	0	0	0	0	0	0	1	0	0	0	.000	.000
Sharperson, Mike, Los Angeles	.273	28	22	3	6	7	1	0	0	3	2	0	0	4	0	4	1	0	1	.318	.385
Shipley, Craig, San Diego	.000	4	4	0	0	0	0	0	0	0	0	1	0	0	0	2	0	0	0	.000	.000
Simms, Mike, Houston	.125	10	8	1	1	4	0	1	0	2	0	0	0	1	0	3	0	0	1	.500	.200
Slaught, Don, Pittsburgh	.154	16	13	1	2	5	0	0	1	3	0	0	0	2	0	7	0	0	0	.385	.267
Smith, Dwight, Chicago*	.244	50	45	5	11	16	2	1	0	6	0	0	0	2	1	10	1	0	0	.356	.277
Smith, Greg, Los Angeles†	.000	4	3	0	0	0	0	0	0	0	0	0	0	0	0	4	0	0	0	.000	.000
Smith, Lonnie, Atlanta	.182	24	22	2	4	4	0	0	0	0	0	0	1	1	0	1	0	0	0	.182	.217
Smith, Zane, Pittsburgh*	.000	1	1	0	0	0	0	0	0	0	0	0	0	0	0	0	0	0	0	.000	.000
Stephenson, Phil, San Diego*	.286	11	7	0	2	2	0	0	0	1	0	0	0	2	0	3	0	0	0	.286	.444
Strawberry, Darryl, Los Angeles*	.333	3	3	0	0	1	0	0	0	0	0	0	0	0	0	1	0	0	0	.333	.333
Sutcliffe, Rick, Chicago*	.000	1	0	0	0	0	0	0	0	0	1	0	0	0	0	0	0	0	0	.000	.000
Sutko, Glenn, Cincinnati	.000	1	1	0	0	0	0	0	0	0	0	0	0	2	1	1	0	0	0	1.000	1.000
Templeton, Garry, S.D.-N.Y.†	.111	38	36	3	4	9	2	0	1	5	0	0	0	2	1	5	0	0	2	.250	.158

1991 N.L. STATISTICS

Player, Team	Avg.	G	AB	R	H	TB	2B	3B	HR	RBI	SH	SF	HP	BB	Int. BB	SO	SB	CS	GI DP	Slg.	OBP
Teufel, Tim, N.Y.-S.D.	.083	16	12	2	1	2	1	0	0	0	0	0	0	3	0	5	1	0	0	.167	.267
Thompson, Milt, St. Louis*	.357	34	28	6	10	15	0	1	1	6	0	0	0	5	1	5	3	1	0	.536	.455
Thon, Dickie, Philadelphia*	.000	1	1	0	0	0	0	0	0	0	0	0	0	0	0	1	0	0	0	.000	.000
Tolentino, Jose, Houston*	.200	35	30	3	6	10	0	0	0	6	0	0	0	2	0	6	0	0	1	.333	.242
Torve, Kelvin, New York*	.000	10	8	0	0	0	0	0	0	5	0	0	0	0	0	1	0	0	0	.000	.000
Treadway, Jeff, Atlanta*	.286	16	14	2	4	4	0	0	0	0	0	0	0	0	0	2	0	0	2	.286	.333
Uribe, Jose, San Francisco†	.000	1	1	0	0	0	0	0	0	0	0	0	0	0	0	0	0	0	0	.000	.000
VanderWal, John, Montreal*	.250	4	4	0	1	1	0	0	0	1	0	0	0	1	0	1	0	0	1	.250	.250
Van Slyke, Andy, Pittsburgh*	.000	6	4	0	0	0	0	0	0	0	0	0	0	2	1	0	0	0	0	.000	.200
Varsho, Gary, Pittsburgh*	.220	43	41	4	9	14	2	0	1	6	0	0	0	1	0	10	3	0	1	.341	.256
Vatcher, Jim, San Diego	.250	9	8	1	2	2	0	0	0	1	0	0	0	1	0	3	0	0	0	.250	.333
Villanueva, Hector, Chicago	.231	15	13	1	3	5	1	0	0	1	0	0	0	2	0	2	0	0	0	.385	.333
Vizcaino, Jose, Chicago†	.167	7	6	0	1	1	0	0	0	0	0	0	0	0	0	1	0	0	0	.167	.167
Walker, Chico, Chicago†	.406	38	32	4	13	17	1	0	1	6	0	1	0	6	1	4	2	0	0	.531	.500
Walker, Larry, Montreal*	.500	3	2	1	1	4	0	0	1	1	0	0	0	0	0	1	0	0	2	2.000	.500
Walton, Jerome, Chicago	.200	27	25	3	5	6	1	0	0	0	0	0	1	2	0	7	0	1	0	.240	.222
Ward, Kevin, San Diego	.300	13	10	0	3	6	0	0	1	2	0	0	0	0	0	9	0	0	0	.600	.462
Webster, Mitch, Pit.-L.A.†	.188	42	32	5	6	10	2	1	0	6	0	0	0	6	0	0	0	0	0	.313	.316
Wehner, Jeff, Pittsburgh	.667	3	3	0	2	3	1	0	0	0	0	0	1	0	0	0	0	0	0	1.000	.667
Wilkerson, Curtis, Pittsburgh†	.212	37	33	2	7	12	2	0	1	5	0	0	0	3	0	4	0	0	0	.364	.270
Wilkins, Rick, Chicago*	.400	7	5	2	2	6	1	0	1	2	0	1	0	2	0	2	0	0	0	1.200	.571
Willard, Jerry, Atlanta*	.167	16	12	0	2	2	0	0	0	2	0	0	0	2	0	5	0	0	0	.167	.286
Williams, Kenny, Montreal	.222	9	9	1	2	5	0	0	1	2	0	0	0	0	0	3	0	0	0	.556	.222
Williams, Matt, San Francisco	.000	3	3	0	0	0	0	0	0	0	0	0	0	0	0	1	0	0	0	.000	.000
Wilson, Craig, St. Louis	.297	43	37	4	11	13	2	0	0	11	0	2	0	3	0	6	0	0	1	.351	.333
Winningham, Herm, Cincinnati*	.394	36	33	4	13	13	0	0	0	6	0	0	0	0	0	8	2	0	0	.394	.429
Wood, Ted, San Francisco*	.333	3	3	0	1	1	0	0	0	0	0	0	0	0	0	1	0	0	0	.333	.333
Yelding, Eric, Houston	.429	7	7	1	3	4	1	0	0	0	0	0	0	0	0	0	4	0	0	.571	.429
Young, Gerald, Houston†	.130	29	23	3	3	3	0	0	0	0	0	0	0	6	1	4	3	0	0	.130	.310
Zeile, Todd, St. Louis	.000	1	1	0	0	0	0	0	0	0	0	0	0	0	0	0	0	0	0	.000	1.000

PINCH-HITTERS WITH TWO OR MORE TEAMS

Player, Team	Avg.	G	AB	R	H	TB	2B	3B	HR	RBI	SH	SF	HP	BB	Int. BB	SO	SB	CS	GI DP	Slg.	OBP
Gonzalez, Jose, Los Angeles	.000	14	13	1	0	0	0	0	0	0	0	0	0	1	0	5	0	0	0	.000	.071
Gonzalez, Jose, Pittsburgh	.000	3	2	0	0	0	0	0	0	0	0	0	0	0	0	1	0	0	0	.000	.000
Herr, Tom, New York†	.071	17	14	0	1	1	0	0	0	0	1	0	0	2	0	7	0	0	0	.071	.188
Herr, Tom, San Francisco†	.286	17	14	3	4	4	0	0	0	1	0	0	0	3	0	2	0	0	1	.286	.412
Martinez, Carmelo, Pittsburgh	.500	3	2	0	1	2	0	0	0	0	0	0	0	0	0	0	0	0	0	.500	.500
Martinez, Carmelo, Cincinnati	.143	14	14	1	2	5	0	0	1	1	0	0	0	0	0	3	0	0	1	.357	.143
Templeton, Garry, San Diego†	.150	20	20	2	3	7	1	0	1	4	0	0	0	0	0	4	0	0	2	.350	.150
Templeton, Garry, New York†	.063	18	16	1	1	2	1	0	0	0	0	0	0	2	1	1	0	0	0	.125	.167
Teufel, Tim, New York	.000	10	7	1	0	0	0	0	0	0	0	0	0	2	0	1	0	0	0	.000	.222
Teufel, Tim, San Diego	.200	6	5	1	1	2	1	0	0	0	0	0	0	1	0	4	0	0	0	.400	.333
Webster, Mitch, Pittsburgh†	.000	8	5	0	0	0	0	0	0	0	0	0	0	2	0	1	0	0	0	.000	.286
Webster, Mitch, Los Angeles†	.222	34	27	5	6	10	2	1	0	6	1	0	0	4	0	8	0	0	0	.370	.323

PITCHING

TEAM

Team	W-L	ERA	G	CG	ShO	Sv	IP	H	TBF	R	ER	HR	SH	SF	HB	BB	Int. BB	SO	WP	Bk.
Los Angeles	93-69	3.06	162	15	14	40	1458.0	1312	6089	565	496	96	74	39	28	500	77	1028	48	12
Pittsburgh	98-64	3.44	162	18	11	51	1456.2	1411	6046	632	557	117	59	34	30	401	34	919	40	12
Atlanta	94-68	3.49	162	18	7	48	1452.2	1304	6051	644	563	118	74	39	28	481	39	969	66	13
New York	77-84	3.56	161	12	11	39	1437.1	1403	6030	646	568	108	83	46	25	410	41	1028	59	14
San Diego	84-78	3.57	162	14	11	47	1452.2	1385	6092	646	577	139	72	50	13	457	56	921	49	13
Montreal	71-90	3.64	161	12	14	39	1440.1	1304	6061	655	583	111	67	33	32	584	42	909	51	9
St. Louis	84-78	3.69	162	9	5	51	1435.1	1367	5996	648	588	114	75	52	47	454	52	822	33	7
Cincinnati	74-88	3.83	162	7	11	43	1440.0	1372	6133	691	613	127	73	52	28	560	41	997	60	9
Philadelphia	78-84	3.86	162	16	11	35	1463.0	1346	6332	680	628	111	78	61	43	670	58	988	81	6
Houston	65-97	4.00	162	7	13	36	1453.0	1347	6255	717	646	129	69	52	29	651	62	1033	46	17
San Francisco	75-87	4.03	162	10	10	45	1442.0	1397	6132	697	646	143	71	46	36	544	36	905	44	14
Chicago	77-83	4.03	160	12	4	40	1456.2	1415	6224	734	653	117	96	58	28	542	64	927	48	12
Totals	970-970	3.68	970	150	122	514	17387.2	16363	73441	7955	7118	1430	891	562	367	6254	626	11446	625	138

NOTE—Totals for earned runs for several clubs do not agree with the composite totals for all pitchers of each respective club due to instances in which provisions of Section 10.18(i) of the Scoring Rules were applied. The following differences are to be noted: Atlanta pitchers add to 564; Chicago pitchers add to 655; Los Angeles pitchers add to 497; New York pitchers add to 569; San Diego pitchers add to 578.

INDIVIDUAL

TOP 15 QUALIFIERS FOR EARNED-RUN AVERAGE TITLE

Minimum 162 innings.   *Lefthanded pitcher.

Pitcher, Team	W	L	ERA	G	GS	CG	ShO	GF	Sv	IP	H	TBF	R	ER	HR	SH	SF	HB	BB	Int. BB	SO	WP	Bk.
Martinez, Dennis, Montreal	14	11	2.39	31	31	9	5	0	0	222.0	187	905	70	59	9	7	3	4	62	3	123	3	0
Rijo, Jose, Cincinnati	15	6	2.51	30	30	3	1	0	0	204.1	165	825	69	57	8	7	8	4	55	3	172	6	2
Glavine, Tom, Atlanta*	20	11	2.55	34	34	9	1	0	0	246.2	201	989	83	70	17	7	6	2	69	6	192	10	4
Belcher, Tim, Los Angeles	10	9	2.62	33	33	2	1	0	0	209.1	189	880	76	61	11	11	3	2	75	3	156	7	2
Harnisch, Pete, Houston	12	9	2.70	33	33	4	2	0	0	216.2	169	900	71	65	14	9	7	5	83	3	172	5	0
DeLeon, Jose, St. Louis	5	9	2.71	28	28	1	0	0	0	162.2	144	679	57	49	15	6	5	6	61	1	118	1	2
Morgan, Mike, Los Angeles*	14	10	2.78	34	33	5	2	0	1	236.1	197	949	85	73	12	10	4	3	61	10	140	6	1
Tomlin, Randy, Pittsburgh*	8	7	2.98	31	27	4	2	0	1	175.0	170	736	75	58	9	5	2	6	54	4	104	4	3
Benes, Andy, San Diego	15	11	3.03	33	33	4	2	0	0	223.0	194	908	76	75	23	5	4	2	59	7	167	4	4
Drabek, Doug, Pittsburgh	15	14	3.07	35	35	5	2	0	0	234.2	245	977	92	80	16	12	6	6	62	6	142	5	4
Smiley, John, Pittsburgh*	20	8	3.08	33	32	2	1	0	0	207.2	194	836	78	71	11	11	4	3	44	0	129	4	1
Ojeda, Bob, Los Angeles*	12	9	3.18	31	31	2	1	0	0	189.1	181	802	78	67	15	15	9	3	70	9	120	4	2
Smith, Zane, Pittsburgh*	16	10	3.20	35	35	3	0	0	0	228.0	234	916	95	81	15	7	5	5	29	5	120	1	0
Tewksbury, Bob, St. Louis	11	12	3.25	30	30	3	0	0	0	191.0	206	798	86	69	13	12	10	5	38	2	75	0	0
Martinez, Ramon, Los Angeles	17	13	3.27	33	33	6	4	0	0	220.1	190	916	89	80	18	8	4	7	69	4	150	6	0

DEPARTMENTAL LEADERS: W—Glavine, Atl., Smiley, Pit., 20; L—Black, S.F., 16; G—Jones, Mon., 77; GS—Maddux, Chi., 37; CG—Glavine, Atl., De. Martinez, Mon., 9; ShO—De. Martinez, Mon., 5; GF—L. Smith, St.L., 61; Sv.—L. Smith, St.L., 47; IP—Maddux, Chi., 263.0; H—Viola, N.Y., 259; TBF—Maddux, Chi., 1070; R—Browning, Cin., 124; ER—Browning, Cin., 107; HR—Browning, Cin., 32; SH—Leibrandt, Atl., 19; SF—Greene, Phi., 11; HB—Burkett, S.F., 10; TBB—DeJesus, Phi., 128; IBB—McDowell, Phi.-L.A., 20; SO—Cone, N.Y., 241; WP—Smoltz, Atl., 20; Bk.—Black, S.F., 6.

1991 N.L. STATISTICS

ALL PITCHERS

*Lefthanded pitcher.

Pitcher, Team	W	L	ERA	G	GS	CG	ShO	GF	Sv.	IP	H	TBF	R	ER	HR	SH	SF	HB	BB	Int. BB	SO	WP	Bk.
Agosto, Juan, St. Louis*	5	3	4.81	72	0	0	0	22	2	86.0	92	377	52	46	4	11	3	8	39	4	34	6	0
Akerfelds, Darrell, Philadelphia	2	1	5.26	30	0	0	0	11	0	49.2	49	229	30	29	5	6	2	2	27	4	31	4	0
Andersen, Larry, San Diego	3	4	2.30	38	0	0	0	24	13	47.0	39	188	13	12	0	4	2	0	13	3	40	1	0
Armstrong, Jack, Cincinnati	7	13	5.48	27	24	1	0	1	0	139.2	158	611	90	85	25	6	9	2	54	3	93	2	1
Ashby, Andy, Philadelphia	1	5	6.00	8	8	0	0	0	0	42.0	41	186	28	28	5	6	3	2	19	0	26	1	0
Assenmacher, Paul, Chicago*	7	8	3.24	75	0	0	0	31	15	102.2	85	427	41	37	10	8	4	3	31	6	117	4	0
Avery, Steve, Atlanta*	18	8	3.38	35	35	3	1	0	0	210.1	189	868	89	79	21	8	5	3	65	2	137	4	1
Barnes, Brian, Montreal*	5	8	4.22	28	27	1	0	1	0	160.0	135	684	82	75	16	9	5	6	84	1	117	5	1
Beatty, Blaine, New York*	0	0	2.79	5	0	0	0	1	0	9.2	9	42	3	3	0	1	1	0	4	2	7	0	0
Beck, Rod, San Francisco	1	1	3.78	31	0	0	0	10	1	52.1	53	214	22	22	4	4	3	1	13	4	38	0	0
Belcher, Tim, Los Angeles	10	9	2.62	33	33	2	1	0	0	209.1	189	880	76	61	10	4	3	2	75	3	156	7	0
Belinda, Stan, Pittsburgh	7	5	3.45	60	0	0	0	37	16	78.1	50	318	30	30	10	4	3	4	35	3	71	3	0
Benes, Andy, San Diego	15	11	3.03	33	33	4	1	0	0	223.0	194	908	76	75	23	5	2	4	59	7	167	3	4
Berenguer, Juan, Atlanta	0	3	2.24	49	0	0	0	35	17	64.1	43	255	18	16	5	2	2	2	20	2	53	6	0
Bielecki, Mike, Chi. - Atl.	13	11	4.46	41	25	0	0	9	0	173.2	171	727	91	86	18	10	6	3	56	6	75	6	0
Black, Bud, San Francisco*	12	16	3.99	34	34	3	0	0	0	214.1	201	893	104	95	25	11	7	4	71	8	104	6	6
Boever, Joe, Philadelphia	0	3	3.84	68	0	0	0	27	0	98.1	90	431	45	42	9	3	6	0	54	11	89	6	1
Bones, Ricky, San Diego	4	6	4.83	11	11	1	0	0	0	54.0	57	234	33	29	3	5	4	0	18	0	31	4	0
Boskie, Shawn, Chicago	4	9	5.23	28	20	1	0	2	0	129.0	150	582	78	75	14	8	6	5	52	4	62	4	0
Bowen, Ryan, Houston	6	4	5.15	14	13	0	0	0	0	71.2	73	319	43	41	4	2	4	1	36	1	49	8	2
Boyd, Oil Can, Montreal	6	8	3.52	19	19	1	1	0	0	120.1	115	496	49	47	9	0	3	2	40	2	82	2	3
Brantley, Cliff, Philadelphia	2	2	3.41	6	5	0	0	3	0	31.2	26	140	12	12	0	2	3	5	19	0	25	6	0
Brantley, Jeff, San Francisco	5	2	2.45	67	0	0	0	39	15	95.1	78	411	27	26	8	4	0	1	52	10	81	0	0
Bross, Terry, New York	0	0	1.80	8	0	0	0	4	0	10.0	7	39	2	2	1	4	0	0	3	0	5	1	0
Brown, Keith, Cincinnati	0	0	2.25	11	0	0	0	3	0	12.0	15	56	4	3	0	1	0	0	6	1	4	0	0
Browning, Tom, Cincinnati*	14	14	4.18	36	36	1	0	0	0	230.1	241	983	124	107	32	8	9	4	56	4	115	3	1
Burke, Tim, Mon. - N.Y.	6	7	3.36	72	0	0	0	31	6	101.2	96	421	46	38	8	3	8	0	26	8	59	3	0
Burkett, John, San Francisco	12	11	4.18	36	34	3	1	0	0	206.2	223	890	103	96	19	8	3	10	60	2	131	5	1
Candelaria, John, Los Angeles*	1	1	3.74	59	0	0	0	10	2	33.2	31	138	16	14	3	1	1	2	11	2	38	1	0
Capel, Mike, Houston	3	3	3.03	25	0	0	0	13	0	32.2	33	143	14	11	3	3	1	1	15	1	23	0	0
Carman, Don, Cincinnati*	0	2	5.25	28	0	0	0	10	0	36.0	40	164	21	21	8	3	1	1	19	2	15	2	0
Carpenter, Cris, St. Louis	10	4	4.23	59	0	0	0	19	0	66.0	53	266	31	31	6	6	2	0	20	9	47	1	0
Carreno, Amalio, Philadelphia	0	0	16.20	3	0	0	0	6	0	3.1	5	20	6	6	1	0	3	2	2	0	2	1	0
Castillo, Frank, Chicago	6	7	4.35	18	18	4	0	0	0	112.1	107	467	56	54	15	6	3	3	33	2	73	5	1
Castillo, Tony, Atl. - N.Y.*	2	1	3.34	17	3	0	0	6	0	32.1	40	148	16	12	4	2	1	1	11	3	18	0	0
Charlton, Norm, Cincinnati*	3	5	2.91	39	11	1	0	9	0	108.1	92	438	37	35	6	7	0	6	34	4	77	11	0
Christopher, Mike, Los Angeles	0	0	0.00	3	0	0	0	2	0	4.0	2	15	0	0	0	2	0	0	3	0	2	0	0
Clancy, Jim, Hou. - Atl.	3	5	3.91	54	0	0	0	22	8	89.2	73	368	42	39	8	2	4	1	34	4	50	10	0
Clark, Mark, St. Louis	1	1	4.03	7	2	0	0	4	0	22.1	17	93	10	10	3	0	3	6	11	0	13	2	0
Clements, Pat, San Diego*	1	0	3.77	12	0	0	0	4	0	14.1	13	63	9	6	0	1	1	1	9	4	8	0	0
Combs, Pat, Philadelphia*	2	6	4.90	14	13	1	0	0	0	64.1	64	300	41	35	7	5	2	2	43	7	41	7	1
Cone, David, New York	14	14	3.29	34	34	5	2	0	0	232.2	204	966	95	85	13	13	7	5	73	2	241	17	1
Cook, Dennis, Los Angeles*	1	0	0.51	20	1	0	0	5	0	17.2	12	69	3	1	0	1	2	0	7	1	8	0	0

Pitcher, Team	W	L	ERA	G	GS	CG	ShO	GF	Sv.	IP	H	TBF	R	ER	HR	SH	SF	HB	BB	Int. BB	SO	WP	Bk.
Cormier, Rheal, St. Louis*	4	5	4.12	11	10	2	0	1	0	67.2	74	281	35	31	5	3	3	2	8	1	38	2	1
Corsi, Jim, Houston	0	5	3.71	47	0	0	0	15	0	77.2	76	322	37	32	6	3	2	0	23	5	53	1	1
Costello, John, San Diego	1	0	3.09	27	0	0	0	6	0	35.0	37	157	15	12	2	4	1	0	17	3	24	2	0
Cox, Danny, Philadelphia	4	6	4.57	23	17	0	0	2	0	102.1	98	433	57	52	14	6	7	0	39	3	46	7	1
Crews, Tim, Los Angeles	2	2	3.43	60	0	0	0	17	0	76.0	75	318	30	29	7	4	2	1	19	11	53	3	1
Darling, Ron, N.Y.-Mon.	5	8	4.37	20	20	0	0	0	0	119.1	121	508	66	58	15	7	4	0	33	1	69	13	4
Dascenzo, Doug, Chicago*	0	0	0.00	3	0	0	0	3	0	4.0	2	15	2	0	0	1	0	0	2	0	2	0	0
DeJesus, Jose, Philadelphia	10	9	3.42	31	28	3	1	0	0	181.2	147	801	74	69	7	11	3	4	128	4	118	10	1
DeLeon, Jose, St. Louis	5	9	2.71	28	28	0	0	1	0	162.2	144	679	57	49	15	5	4	6	61	1	118	0	1
Deshaies, Jim, Houston*	5	12	4.98	28	28	1	0	0	0	161.0	156	686	90	89	19	4	7	1	72	5	98	5	5
Dibble, Rob, Cincinnati	3	5	3.17	67	0	0	0	57	31	82.1	67	334	32	29	5	5	3	3	25	9	124	5	0
Downs, Kelly, San Francisco	10	4	4.19	45	11	0	0	4	0	111.2	99	479	59	52	9	4	4	3	53	6	62	4	1
Drabek, Doug, Pittsburgh	15	14	3.07	35	35	5	2	0	0	234.2	245	977	92	80	16	12	4	3	62	0	142	5	0
Fajardo, Hector, Pittsburgh	0	0	9.95	2	2	0	0	0	0	6.1	10	35	7	7	1	0	0	0	7	0	8	3	0
Fassero, Jeff, Montreal*	2	5	2.44	51	0	0	0	30	8	55.1	39	223	17	15	5	6	0	1	17	7	42	0	0
Fernandez, Sid, New York*	1	3	2.86	8	8	0	0	0	0	44.0	36	177	18	14	4	5	0	0	9	0	31	1	0
Foster, Steve, Cincinnati	0	1	1.93	11	0	0	0	5	0	14.0	7	53	3	3	1	2	0	1	4	4	11	1	0
Franco, John, New York*	5	9	2.93	52	0	0	0	48	30	55.1	61	247	27	18	2	0	3	3	18	3	45	6	2
Fraser, Willie, St. Louis	3	3	4.93	35	0	0	0	16	0	49.1	44	210	28	27	9	1	3	3	21	3	25	4	2
Freeman, Marvin, Atlanta	1	0	3.00	34	0	0	0	6	1	48.0	37	190	19	16	5	1	2	2	13	4	34	4	3
Frey, Steve, Montreal*	0	1	4.99	31	0	0	0	5	0	39.2	43	182	31	22	3	3	0	2	23	1	21	3	0
Gardner, Chris, Houston	1	2	4.01	5	4	0	0	0	0	24.2	19	103	12	11	3	2	2	0	14	1	12	0	1
Gardner, Mark, Montreal	9	11	3.85	27	27	2	1	0	0	168.1	139	692	78	72	17	7	7	4	75	1	107	2	0
Gardner, Wes, San Diego	0	1	7.08	14	3	0	0	2	0	20.1	27	99	16	16	5	0	0	4	12	0	9	1	0
Garrelts, Scott, San Francisco	1	1	6.41	8	3	0	0	2	0	19.2	25	90	14	14	1	0	1	0	9	0	8	0	0
Glavine, Tom, Atlanta*	20	11	2.55	34	34	9	1	0	0	246.2	201	989	83	70	17	7	6	6	69	6	192	10	2
Gott, Jim, Los Angeles	13	7	2.96	55	0	0	0	26	2	76.0	63	322	28	25	12	5	4	3	56	7	150	5	3
Grater, Mark, St. Louis	0	0	0.00	3	0	0	0	2	0	3.0	5	15	0	0	0	6	1	0	2	0	0	0	0
Greene, Tommy, Philadelphia	13	7	3.38	36	27	3	2	0	0	207.2	177	857	85	78	19	9	11	3	66	4	154	4	3
Grimsley, Jason, Philadelphia	1	7	4.87	12	10	0	0	2	0	61.0	54	272	34	33	4	3	2	3	41	0	42	14	1
Gross, Kevin, Los Angeles	10	11	3.58	46	10	0	0	16	3	115.2	123	509	55	46	10	6	4	2	50	6	95	3	0
Gross, Kip, Cincinnati	6	4	3.47	29	9	1	0	6	1	85.2	93	381	43	33	8	6	2	0	40	2	40	5	1
Gunderson, Eric, San Francisco*	0	0	5.40	2	1	0	0	1	0	3.1	8	18	4	2	0	2	0	0	1	0	2	1	0
Hammaker, Atlee, San Diego*	0	1	5.79	7	1	0	0	6	0	4.2	6	27	7	3	3	6	0	0	3	0	1	0	0
Hammond, Chris, Cincinnati*	7	7	4.06	20	18	0	0	2	0	99.2	92	425	51	45	4	6	1	2	48	3	50	3	0
Haney, Chris, Montreal*	3	7	4.04	16	16	0	0	0	0	84.2	94	387	49	38	6	6	1	0	43	1	51	9	1
Harkey, Mike, Chicago	0	2	5.30	4	4	0	0	0	0	18.2	21	84	11	11	3	0	0	0	6	1	15	1	0
Harnisch, Pete, Houston	12	9	2.70	33	33	4	2	0	0	216.2	169	900	71	65	14	9	7	5	83	3	172	5	2
Harris, Greg, San Diego	9	5	2.23	20	20	3	0	0	0	133.0	116	537	42	33	16	2	2	6	27	6	95	2	0
Hartley, Mike, L.A.-Phi.	4	1	4.21	58	0	0	0	16	2	83.1	74	368	39	39	11	3	1	8	47	8	63	10	0
Heaton, Neal, Pittsburgh*	3	3	4.33	42	1	0	0	5	0	68.2	72	293	37	33	6	7	6	4	21	2	34	5	1
Henry, Dwayne, Houston	3	2	3.19	52	0	0	0	25	2	67.2	51	282	25	24	4	6	2	2	39	7	51	5	0
Heredia, Gil, San Francisco	0	0	3.82	7	4	0	0	0	0	33.0	27	126	14	14	4	2	1	0	7	2	13	5	0
Hernandez, Jeremy, San Diego	0	0	0.00	9	0	0	0	8	3	14.1	8	56	1	0	0	0	1	0	5	0	9	2	0
Hernandez, Xavier, Houston	2	7	4.71	32	6	0	0	8	3	63.0	66	285	34	33	7	0	1	0	32	7	55	0	0

1991 N.L. STATISTICS

Pitcher, Team	W	L	ERA	G	GS	CG	ShO	GF	Sv.	IP	H	TBF	R	ER	HR	SH	SF	HB	BB	Int. BB	SO	WP	Bk.
Hershiser, Orel, Los Angeles	7	2	3.46	21	21	0	0	0	0	112.0	112	473	43	43	3	2	1	5	32	6	73	2	4
Hickerson, Bryan, San Francisco*	2	2	3.60	17	6	0	0	4	0	50.0	53	212	20	20	3	2	0	7	17	6	43	2	1
Hill, Ken, St. Louis	11	10	3.57	30	30	0	0	0	0	181.1	147	743	76	72	15	7	7	6	67	4	121	7	1
Hill, Milt, Cincinnati	2	1	3.78	22	0	0	0	8	0	33.1	36	137	14	14	1	5	3	6	8	3	20	0	0
Howell, Jay, Los Angeles	6	5	3.18	44	0	0	0	35	16	51.0	39	202	19	18	1	4	2	0	11	3	40	0	0
Huismann, Mark, Pittsburgh	0	0	7.20	5	0	0	0	0	0	5.0	7	25	4	4	0	0	0	0	2	1	5	0	0
Hurst, Bruce, San Diego*	15	8	3.29	31	31	4	0	0	0	221.2	201	909	89	81	17	8	4	3	59	6	141	5	1
Innis, Jeff, New York	0	2	2.66	69	0	0	0	29	0	84.2	89	336	30	25	2	6	5	0	23	6	47	5	0
Jackson, Danny, Chicago*	1	5	6.75	17	14	0	0	1	0	70.2	89	347	59	53	8	8	2	1	48	4	31	1	1
Jackson, Darrin, San Diego	0	0	9.00	1	0	0	0	1	0	2.0	3	10	3	2	0	0	0	0	2	0	0	0	0
Jones, Barry, Montreal	4	9	3.35	77	0	0	0	46	13	88.2	76	353	35	33	8	7	3	1	33	8	46	0	1
Jones, Jimmy, Houston	6	8	4.39	26	22	1	1	0	0	135.1	143	593	73	66	9	7	3	3	51	3	88	4	0
Juden, Jeff, Houston	0	1	6.00	4	3	0	0	0	0	18.0	19	81	14	12	3	2	2	1	7	0	11	0	0
Kile, Darryl, Houston	7	11	3.69	37	22	0	1	5	0	153.2	144	689	81	63	16	9	5	6	84	4	100	5	4
Kipper, Bob, Pittsburgh*	2	2	4.65	52	0	0	0	18	4	60.0	66	264	34	31	7	1	2	0	22	3	38	0	2
LaCoss, Mike, San Francisco	2	5	7.23	18	5	0	0	6	0	47.1	61	225	39	38	4	3	2	4	24	2	30	2	0
Lancaster, Les, Chicago	9	7	3.52	64	11	0	0	21	3	156.0	150	653	68	61	13	9	4	4	49	7	102	2	2
Landrum, Bill, Pittsburgh	4	4	3.18	61	0	0	0	43	17	76.1	76	322	32	27	4	1	1	1	19	5	45	3	2
LaPoint, Dave, Philadelphia*	0	1	16.20	2	2	0	0	0	0	5.0	10	32	10	9	0	1	0	1	6	0	3	0	0
Layana, Tim, Cincinnati	0	0	6.97	22	0	0	0	9	0	20.2	23	95	18	16	1	1	0	0	10	5	14	3	0
Lefferts, Craig, San Diego*	1	6	3.91	54	0	0	0	40	23	69.0	74	290	35	30	5	10	5	1	14	6	48	3	1
Leibrandt, Charlie, Atlanta*	15	13	3.49	36	36	0	1	0	0	229.2	212	949	105	89	18	19	6	4	56	3	128	5	3
Lewis, Jim, San Diego	0	0	4.15	12	0	0	0	2	0	13.0	14	64	7	6	2	2	0	0	11	2	10	1	0
Lilliquist, Derek, San Diego*	0	2	8.79	6	1	0	0	1	0	14.1	25	70	14	14	3	0	1	3	4	0	7	0	0
Litton, Greg, San Francisco	0	0	9.00	1	0	0	0	1	0	1.0	1	7	1	1	0	0	0	0	3	0	0	0	0
Long, Bill, Montreal	0	0	10.80	3	0	0	0	1	0	1.2	4	12	2	2	0	0	0	0	4	1	0	0	0
Maddux, Greg, Chicago	15	11	3.35	37	37	7	2	0	0	263.0	232	1070	113	98	18	16	3	6	66	9	198	6	3
Maddux, Mike, San Diego	7	2	2.46	64	1	0	0	27	5	98.2	78	388	30	27	4	5	2	1	27	3	57	5	0
Mahler, Rick, Mon.-Atl.	2	4	4.50	23	8	0	0	8	1	66.0	70	291	37	33	2	5	1	2	28	3	27	1	0
Mallicoat, Rob, Houston*	0	2	3.86	24	0	0	0	4	0	23.1	22	103	10	10	3	1	2	1	13	1	18	1	0
Martinez, Dennis, Montreal	14	11	2.39	31	31	9	5	0	0	222.0	187	905	70	59	9	7	3	4	62	3	123	3	2
Martinez, Ramon, Los Angeles	17	13	3.27	33	33	6	4	0	0	220.1	190	916	89	80	18	8	1	7	69	4	150	6	1
Mason, Roger, Pittsburgh	3	2	3.03	24	0	0	0	6	0	29.2	21	114	11	10	3	1	1	0	6	2	21	2	0
Mauser, Tim, Philadelphia	0	0	7.59	3	0	0	0	3	0	10.2	18	53	10	9	3	0	0	0	3	0	6	0	0
May, Scott, Chicago	0	0	18.00	2	0	0	0	1	0	2.0	6	12	4	4	0	0	0	0	3	0	1	1	0
McClellan, Paul, San Francisco	3	6	4.56	13	12	1	0	0	0	71.0	68	300	41	36	12	3	3	1	25	2	44	5	0
McClure, Bob, St. Louis*	1	1	3.13	32	0	0	0	9	0	23.0	24	98	8	8	1	11	3	1	8	0	15	0	2
McDowell, Roger, Phi.-LA	9	9	2.93	71	0	0	0	34	10	101.1	100	445	40	33	4	9	1	2	48	20	50	2	0
McElroy, Chuck, Chicago*	6	2	1.95	71	0	0	0	12	3	101.1	73	419	33	22	7	9	6	7	57	7	92	0	3
Melendez, Jose, San Diego	8	5	3.27	31	9	0	0	10	0	93.2	77	381	35	34	11	2	6	1	24	3	60	3	0
Mercker, Kent, Atlanta*	5	3	2.58	50	4	0	0	28	6	73.1	56	306	23	21	5	2	2	0	35	3	62	4	1
Miller, Paul, Pittsburgh	0	0	5.40	1	1	0	0	0	0	5.0	4	21	3	3	0	1	0	0	3	0	2	0	0
Minutelli, Gino, Cincinnati*	0	2	6.04	16	3	0	0	2	0	25.1	30	124	17	17	5	0	2	1	18	0	21	0	0
Morgan, Mike, Los Angeles	14	10	2.78	34	33	5	0	1	0	236.1	197	949	85	73	12	10	4	3	61	10	140	6	3
Moyer, Jamie, St. Louis*	0	5	5.74	8	7	0	0	1	0	31.1	38	142	21	20	5	4	2	1	16	0	20	2	0
Mulholland, Terry, Philadelphia*	16	13	3.61	34	34	8	3	0	0	232.0	231	956	100	93	15	11	6	3	49	2	142	3	0

Pitcher, Team	W	L	ERA	G	GS	CG	ShO	GF	Sv.	IP	H	TBF	R	ER	HR	SH	SF	HB	BB	Int. BB	SO	WP	Bk.
Myers, Randy, Cincinnati*	6	13	3.55	58	12	1	0	18	6	132.0	116	575	61	52	8	8	6	2	80	5	108	2	1
Nabholz, Chris, Montreal*	8	7	3.63	24	24	1	0	0	0	153.2	134	631	66	62	5	2	4	0	57	0	99	3	1
Nolte, Eric, San Diego*	3	2	11.05	6	6	0	0	0	0	22.0	37	111	27	27	6	0	3	0	10	0	15	1	1
Ojeda, Bob, Los Angeles*	12	9	3.18	31	31	2	1	0	0	189.1	181	802	78	67	15	15	9	3	70	9	120	4	2
Olivares, Omar, St. Louis	11	7	3.71	28	24	0	0	2	1	167.1	148	688	72	69	13	5	2	5	61	4	91	3	2
Oliveras, Francisco, San Francisco	6	6	3.86	55	1	0	0	17	3	79.1	69	316	36	34	12	1	0	1	22	4	48	2	0
Oquendo, Jose, St. Louis	0	0	27.00	1	0	0	0	0	0	1.0	2	7	3	3	0	0	0	0	2	0	1	0	0
Osuna, Al, Houston*	7	6	3.42	71	0	0	0	32	12	81.2	59	353	39	31	5	6	5	3	46	5	68	3	2
Palacios, Vicente, Pittsburgh	6	3	3.75	36	7	1	1	8	3	81.2	69	347	34	34	12	4	1	1	38	2	64	6	0
Parrett, Jeff, Atlanta	1	2	6.33	18	0	0	0	9	0	21.1	31	109	18	15	2	2	2	0	12	1	14	4	1
Patterson, Bob, Pittsburgh*	4	3	4.11	54	1	0	0	19	2	65.2	67	270	32	30	7	2	2	0	15	4	57	0	0
Pavlas, Dave, Chicago	0	0	18.00	1	0	0	0	1	0	1.0	3	5	2	2	0	1	0	0	0	0	0	1	0
Pena, Alejandro, N.Y.-Atl.	8	1	2.40	59	0	0	0	36	15	82.1	74	331	23	22	6	3	4	1	22	4	62	2	2
Perez, Mike, St. Louis	0	1	5.82	14	0	0	0	2	0	17.0	19	75	11	11	1	0	2	1	7	2	7	2	0
Perez, Yorkis, Chicago*	0	0	2.08	3	0	0	0	2	0	4.1	2	16	1	1	0	0	0	0	2	0	3	1	1
Peterson, Adam, San Diego	3	4	4.45	13	11	0	0	0	0	54.2	50	241	33	27	10	4	2	0	28	2	37	2	1
Petry, Dan, Atlanta	0	0	5.55	10	0	0	0	4	0	24.1	29	116	17	15	2	3	2	0	14	1	9	7	0
Platt, Doug, Montreal	0	0	2.60	21	0	0	0	3	0	34.2	29	145	11	10	3	2	6	0	17	5	29	2	1
Portugal, Mark, Houston	10	12	4.49	32	27	1	0	3	1	168.1	163	710	91	84	19	6	4	2	59	5	120	4	0
Power, Ted, Cincinnati	5	3	3.62	68	0	0	0	22	3	87.0	87	371	37	35	6	6	6	2	31	3	51	6	1
Rasmussen, Dennis, San Diego*	6	13	3.74	24	24	1	1	0	0	146.2	155	633	74	61	12	4	4	2	49	0	75	2	1
Reed, Rick, Pittsburgh	0	0	10.38	1	1	0	0	0	0	4.1	8	21	6	5	1	0	0	0	1	0	2	0	0
Remlinger, Mike, San Francisco*	2	1	4.37	8	6	0	0	1	0	35.0	36	155	17	17	5	1	0	1	20	0	19	2	0
Renfroe, Laddie, Chicago	0	2	13.50	4	0	0	0	0	0	4.2	11	27	7	7	1	0	0	0	2	1	1	0	0
Reuschel, Rick, San Francisco	2	2	4.22	4	4	0	0	0	0	10.2	17	54	5	5	0	1	0	0	7	1	4	1	0
Reynoso, Armando, Atlanta	2	1	6.17	6	5	0	0	1	0	23.1	26	103	18	16	4	3	2	1	10	1	10	2	0
Righetti, Dave, San Francisco*	2	7	3.39	61	0	0	0	49	24	71.2	64	304	29	27	8	2	2	0	28	6	51	1	0
Rijo, Jose, Cincinnati	15	6	2.51	30	30	3	1	0	0	204.1	165	825	69	57	8	8	8	3	55	4	172	2	4
Ritchie, Wally, Philadelphia*	1	2	2.50	39	0	0	0	13	0	50.1	44	213	17	14	4	4	5	2	17	5	26	1	0
Robinson, Don, San Francisco	5	9	4.38	34	16	0	0	7	0	121.1	123	525	64	59	12	2	1	1	50	7	78	2	0
Rodriguez, Rosario, Pittsburgh*	1	1	4.11	18	0	0	0	8	0	15.1	14	67	7	7	1	4	0	0	10	5	10	0	1
Rodriguez, Rich, San Diego*	3	1	3.26	64	1	0	0	19	0	80.0	66	335	31	29	8	7	2	0	44	8	40	4	2
Rojas, Mel, Montreal	3	3	3.75	37	0	0	0	13	6	48.0	42	200	21	20	4	0	0	1	13	1	37	3	1
Rosenberg, Steve, San Diego*	1	1	6.94	10	0	0	0	5	0	11.2	11	49	9	9	3	0	0	1	5	1	6	0	0
Ruffin, Bruce, Philadelphia*	4	7	3.78	31	15	0	0	2	0	119.0	125	508	52	50	9	6	4	3	38	3	85	4	0
Ruskin, Scott, Montreal*	4	4	4.24	64	0	0	0	24	6	63.2	57	275	31	30	4	5	4	0	30	2	46	5	0
Sampen, Bill, Montreal	9	5	4.00	43	8	0	0	8	2	92.1	96	409	49	41	13	5	4	6	46	7	52	3	1
Sanford, Mo, Cincinnati	1	2	3.86	6	5	0	0	0	0	28.0	19	118	14	12	1	0	0	3	15	2	31	4	0
Sauveur, Rich, New York*	0	0	10.80	5	0	0	0	1	0	3.1	7	19	4	4	1	0	0	0	2	0	4	1	0
Scanlan, Bob, Chicago	7	8	3.89	40	13	0	0	16	1	111.0	114	482	60	48	5	8	6	3	40	3	44	4	0
Schilling, Curt, Houston	3	5	3.81	56	0	0	0	34	8	75.2	79	336	35	32	2	5	5	7	39	7	71	4	0
Schmidt, Dave, Montreal	0	0	10.38	4	0	0	0	0	0	4.1	9	24	5	5	2	0	0	0	2	0	3	0	0
Schourek, Pete, New York*	5	4	4.27	35	8	0	0	7	0	86.1	82	385	41	41	7	5	4	2	43	4	67	3	1
Scott, Mike, Houston	0	2	12.86	2	2	0	0	0	0	7.0	11	35	10	10	1	0	0	0	4	1	3	1	0
Scott, Tim, San Diego	0	0	9.00	2	0	0	0	1	0	1.0	2	5	2	1	0	0	0	0	0	0	1	0	0
Scudder, Scott, Cincinnati	6	9	4.35	27	14	0	0	4	1	101.1	91	443	52	49	6	8	3	6	56	4	51	7	0

1991 N.L. STATISTICS

Pitcher, Team	W	L	ERA	G	GS	CG	ShO	GF	Sv.	IP	H	TBF	R	ER	HR	SH	SF	HB	BB	Int. BB	SO	WP	Bk.
Searcy, Steve, Philadelphia*	2	1	4.15	18	0	0	0	4	0	30.1	29	134	16	8	2	3	2	0	14	1	21	1	1
Segura, Jose, San Francisco	0	1	4.41	10	0	0	0	2	0	16.1	20	72	11	8	1	1	0	2	5	0	10	2	0
Sherrill, Tim, St. Louis*	0	0	8.16	10	0	0	0	3	0	14.1	20	67	13	13	2	1	2	2	3	1	4	1	0
Simons, Doug, New York*	2	3	5.19	42	1	0	0	11	1	60.2	55	258	40	35	5	9	4	2	19	5	38	3	0
Sisk, Doug, Atlanta	2	1	5.02	14	0	0	0	2	0	14.1	21	73	14	8	1	1	1	0	8	2	5	0	0
Slocumb, Heath, Chicago	2	3	3.45	52	0	0	0	21	1	62.2	53	274	29	24	3	6	6	3	30	6	34	9	0
Smiley, John, Pittsburgh*	20	8	3.08	33	32	2	2	0	0	207.2	194	836	78	71	17	11	4	6	44	0	129	3	1
Smith, Bryn, St. Louis	12	9	3.85	31	31	1	0	0	0	198.2	188	818	95	85	16	9	7	7	45	3	94	1	1
Smith, Dave, Chicago	0	6	6.00	35	0	0	0	28	17	33.0	39	151	22	22	6	2	0	1	19	5	16	3	1
Smith, Lee, St. Louis	6	3	2.34	67	0	0	0	61	47	73.0	70	300	22	19	5	5	7	0	13	5	67	1	1
Smith, Pete, Atlanta*	1	3	5.06	14	10	0	0	2	0	48.0	48	211	33	27	5	5	4	2	22	3	29	1	0
Smith, Zane, Pittsburgh*	16	10	3.20	35	35	6	3	0	0	228.0	234	916	95	81	15	7	5	3	29	3	120	1	2
Smoltz, John, Atlanta	14	13	3.80	36	36	5	0	0	0	229.2	206	947	101	97	16	9	9	7	77	1	148	20	0
St. Claire, Randy, Atlanta	0	0	4.08	19	0	0	0	5	0	28.2	31	123	17	13	4	3	1	1	9	6	30	4	2
Stanton, Mike, Atlanta*	5	5	2.88	74	0	0	0	20	7	78.0	62	314	27	25	6	6	5	5	21	6	54	0	0
Sutcliffe, Rick, Chicago	6	5	4.10	19	18	0	0	0	0	96.2	96	422	52	44	4	4	8	4	45	3	52	2	2
Terry, Scott, St. Louis	4	4	2.80	65	0	0	0	13	0	80.1	76	339	31	25	7	5	0	0	32	14	52	0	0
Tewksbury, Bob, St. Louis	11	12	3.25	30	30	3	0	0	0	191.0	206	798	86	69	13	12	10	5	38	2	75	0	3
Tomlin, Randy, Pittsburgh*	8	7	2.98	31	27	4	0	0	0	175.0	170	736	75	58	9	5	5	6	54	4	104	2	0
Valera, Julio, New York*	0	0	0.00	2	0	0	0	0	0	2.0	0	11	0	0	0	0	1	0	4	0	3	0	1
Viola, Frank, New York*	13	15	3.97	35	35	3	0	0	0	231.1	259	980	112	102	25	15	5	1	54	4	132	6	1
Wainhouse, Dave, Montreal	0	1	6.75	2	0	0	0	1	0	2.2	2	14	2	2	0	0	1	0	4	0	1	2	0
Walk, Bob, Pittsburgh	9	2	3.60	25	20	0	0	3	0	115.0	104	484	53	46	10	7	4	5	35	2	67	11	2
Wetteland, John, Los Angeles	1	0	0.00	6	0	0	0	6	0	9.0	5	36	2	0	0	0	0	4	9	3	9	0	0
Whitehurst, Wally, New York	7	12	4.19	36	20	0	0	6	1	133.1	142	556	67	62	12	6	3	4	25	3	87	3	4
Whitson, Ed, San Diego	4	6	5.03	13	12	0	0	0	0	78.2	93	337	47	44	13	6	2	0	17	3	40	1	1
Wilkins, Dean, Houston	2	0	11.25	7	0	0	0	3	0	8.0	16	51	14	10	0	0	0	0	10	0	4	0	0
Williams, Brian, Houston	0	1	3.75	2	2	0	0	0	0	12.0	11	49	5	5	2	2	1	0	4	0	4	4	1
Williams, Mitch, Philadelphia*	12	5	2.34	69	0	0	0	60	30	88.1	56	386	24	23	4	4	1	8	62	5	84	4	0
Wilson, Steve, Chi.-L.A.*	0	2	2.61	19	0	0	0	5	2	20.2	14	81	7	6	1	4	5	0	9	0	14	1	1
Wilson, Trevor, San Francisco*	13	11	3.56	44	29	2	1	6	0	202.0	173	841	87	80	13	14	5	5	77	4	139	5	3
Wohlers, Mark, Atlanta	3	1	3.20	17	0	0	0	4	2	19.2	17	89	7	7	1	2	1	1	13	3	13	0	0
Young, Anthony, New York	2	5	3.10	10	8	0	0	2	0	49.1	48	202	20	17	4	1	1	1	12	1	20	5	0

PITCHERS WITH TWO OR MORE TEAMS

Pitcher, Team	W	L	ERA	G	GS	CG	ShO	GF	Sv.	IP	H	TBF	R	ER	HR	SH	SF	HB	BB	Int. BB	SO	WP	Bk.
Bielecki, Mike, Chicago	13	11	4.50	39	25	0	0	8	0	172.0	169	718	91	86	18	10	6	2	54	6	72	6	0
Bielecki, Mike, Atlanta	0	0	0.00	2	0	0	0	0	0	1.2	0	9	0	0	0	0	0	0	2	0	3	0	0
Burke, Tim, Montreal	3	4	4.11	37	0	0	0	16	5	46.0	41	190	24	21	3	2	1	4	14	6	25	1	0
Burke, Tim, New York	3	3	2.75	35	0	0	0	15	1	55.2	55	231	22	17	5	1	2	0	12	2	34	2	0
Castillo, Tony, Atlanta*	1	0	7.27	7	0	0	0	5	0	8.2	13	44	9	7	3	1	0	0	5	1	8	0	0
Castillo, Tony, New York*	1	0	1.90	10	0	0	0	1	0	23.2	27	104	7	5	1	1	0	1	6	0	10	0	0
Clancy, Jim, Houston	0	3	2.78	30	0	0	0	13	5	55.0	37	215	19	17	5	1	2	2	20	3	33	5	0
Clancy, Jim, Atlanta	3	2	5.71	24	0	0	0	9	3	34.2	36	153	23	22	3	1	1	1	14	1	17	5	0

Pitcher, Team	W	L	ERA	G	GS	CG	ShO	GF	Sv.	IP	H	TBF	R	ER	HR	SH	SF	HB	BB	Int. BB	SO	WP	Bk.
Darling, Ron, New York	5	6	3.87	17	17	0	0	0	0	102.1	96	427	50	44	9	7	4	6	28	1	58	9	4
Darling, Ron, Montreal	0	2	7.41	3	3	0	0	0	0	17.0	25	81	16	14	6	0	1	1	5	0	11	4	1
Hartley, Mike, Los Angeles	2	0	4.42	40	0	0	0	11	1	57.0	53	258	29	28	7	1	1	3	37	7	44	8	1
Hartley, Mike, Philadelphia	2	1	3.76	18	0	0	0	5	0	26.1	21	110	11	11	4	1	0	0	10	0	19	2	1
Mahler, Rick, Montreal	1	3	3.62	10	6	0	0	1	0	37.1	37	158	17	15	2	4	1	2	15	1	17	0	1
Mahler, Rick, Atlanta	1	1	5.65	13	2	0	0	1	0	28.2	33	133	20	18	2	1	0	3	13	2	10	1	0
McDowell, Roger, Philadelphia	3	6	3.20	38	0	0	0	16	3	59.0	61	271	28	21	3	7	2	2	32	12	28	1	0
McDowell, Roger, Los Angeles	6	3	2.55	33	0	0	0	18	7	42.1	39	174	12	12	3	4	0	0	16	8	22	1	0
Pena, Alejandro, New York	6	1	2.71	44	0	0	0	24	4	63.0	63	261	20	19	5	2	4	0	19	4	49	1	2
Pena, Alejandro, Atlanta	2	0	1.40	15	0	0	0	12	11	19.1	11	70	3	3	1	0	0	0	3	0	13	0	0
Wilson, Steve, Los Angeles*	0	0	0.00	11	0	0	0	3	2	8.1	1	28	0	0	0	1	1	0	4	0	5	0	0
Wilson, Steve, Chicago*	0	0	4.38	8	0	0	0	2	0	12.1	13	53	7	6	1	0	0	0	5	1	9	0	0

NOTE—The following pitchers combined to pitch shutout games: Atlanta (4)—Smoltz, Stanton and Berenguer; Smoltz and Stanton; Mercker, Wohlers and Pena; Smoltz and Bielecki; Chicago (2)—Maddux and Smith; Bielecki and Assenmacher; Cincinnati (10)—Charlton and Myers; Browning and Dibble; Browning and Myers; Armstrong, Power and Dibble; Hammond, Myers and Dibble; Gross and Dibble; Scudder, Charlton and Power; Rijo and Power; Rijo and Hill; Rijo, Charlton and Foster; Houston (10)—Harnisch and Schilling 2; Kile, Osuna, Schilling and Henry; Jones, Osuna and Henry; Portugal and Osuna; Deshaies and Clancy; Bowen, Mallicoat and Osuna; Kile, Mallicoat and Hernandez; Harnisch, Schilling, Mallicoat and Hernandez; Gardner, Mallicoat and Hernandez; Los Angeles (7)—Belcher, Candelaria and Howell; Ojeda, Candelaria and Crews; Belcher and Crews; Hershiser, Gross and Howell; Ojeda, Gross and McDowell; Martinez, Wilson and McDowell; Cook, Crews, Wilson, Christopher and Howell; Montreal (8)—De. Martinez, Jones and Ruskin 2; Sampen and Jones; Mahler, Jones and Ruskin; Haney and Fassero; Gardner and Jones; Barnes and Jones; Gardner, Rojas and Fassero; New York (7)—Viola and Franco; Cone and Franco; Whitehurst, Innis and Pena; Darling and Pena; Gooden and Franco; Fernandez and Pena; Gooden, Schourek and Burke; Philadelphia (5)—Mulholland and Boever; Combs, McDowell, Boever and Greene; Ruffin and Williams; Greene, Ritchie and Williams; DeJesus and Boever; Pittsburgh (2)—Drabek, Patterson, Belinda and Landrum; Smiley, Tomlin and Landrum; St. Louis (5)—B. Smith and Agosto; Hill and L. Smith; B. Smith, Carpenter and L. Smith; Hill, McClure, Terry and L. Smith; Tewksbury, Fraser and L. Smith; San Diego (7)—Benes and Lefferts 2; Hurst, Andersen and Maddux; Rasmussen, Andersen and Rodriguez; Maddux, Costello and Rodriguez; Bones, Lewis and Rodriguez; Hurst and Maddux; San Francisco (4)—LaCoss and Righetti; McClellan, Oliveras and Righetti; Black and Righetti; Wilson, Oliveras, Righetti and Brantley.

FIELDING

TEAM

Team	Pct.	G	PO	A	E	TC	DP	TP	PB
St. Louis	.982	162	4306	1689	107	6102	133	1	8
San Francisco	.982	162	4326	1753	109	6188	151	0	9
Chicago	.982	160	4370	1830	113	6313	120	0	19
San Diego	.982	162	4358	1731	113	6202	130	0	9
Pittsburgh	.981	162	4370	1846	120	6336	134	0	9
Philadelphia	.981	162	4389	1623	119	6131	111	1	9
Los Angeles	.980	162	4374	1795	123	6292	126	0	8
Cincinnati	.979	162	4320	1615	125	6060	131	0	20
Montreal	.979	161	4321	1796	133	6250	128	1	22
Atlanta	.978	162	4358	1834	138	6330	122	0	14
New York	.977	161	4312	1766	143	6221	112	0	12
Houston	.974	162	4359	1617	161	6137	129	2	16
Totals	**.980**	**970**	**52163**	**20895**	**1504**	**74562**	**1527**	**5**	**155**

INDIVIDUAL

FIRST BASEMEN

*Throws lefthanded.

Leader, Team	Pct.	G	PO	A	E	TC	DP
CLARK, S.F.*	.997	144	1273	110	4	1387	115

Player, Team	Pct.	G	PO	A	E	TC	DP
Anderson, S.F.	1.000	16	85	9	0	94	3
Azocar, San Diego*	1.000	1	5	0	0	5	0
Bagwell, Houston	.991	155	1270	106	12	1388	97
Barberie, Montreal	1.000	1	1	0	0	1	0
Bell, Atlanta*	.975	14	72	5	2	79	7
Benzinger, Cincinnati..	.986	21	123	13	2	138	7
Bonilla, Pittsburgh	1.000	4	28	2	0	30	6
Bream, Atlanta*	.996	85	668	50	3	721	53
Brewer, St. Louis*	1.000	15	27	3	0	30	2
Bullock, Montreal*	.933	3	11	3	1	15	0
Cabrera, Atlanta	.973	14	65	7	2	74	3
Calderon, Montreal	1.000	4	28	2	0	30	4
Carter, Los Angeles	1.000	10	47	7	0	54	3
Clark, San Diego	.989	16	85	5	1	91	4
Clark, San Francisco*.	.997	144	1273	110	4	1387	115
Coles, San Francisco..	1.000	1	4	0	0	4	0
Donnels, New York	1.000	15	123	12	0	135	10
Doran, Cincinnati	1.000	4	19	0	0	19	3
Dorsett, San Diego	1.000	2	4	1	0	5	0
Fitzgerald, Montreal	1.000	3	15	3	0	18	1
Foley, Montreal	.994	31	148	9	1	158	8
Galarraga, Montreal	.991	105	887	80	9	976	68
Grace, Chicago*	.995	160	1520	167	8	1695	106
Gregg, Atlanta*	1.000	13	105	9	0	114	6
Guerrero, St. Louis	.985	112	953	66	16	1035	73
Heep, Atlanta*	1.000	1	1	0	0	1	0
Hollins, Philadelphia	.979	6	42	4	1	47	4
Hudler, St. Louis	1.000	12	30	0	0	30	5
Hunter, Atlanta*	.988	85	622	46	8	676	42
Javier, Los Angeles	.920	2	20	3	2	25	1
R. Jefferson, Cin.*	1.000	2	14	1	0	15	3
Jordan, Philadelphia	.987	72	626	37	9	672	37
Karros, Los Angeles	1.000	10	33	2	0	35	5
Kennedy, S.F.	1.000	2	3	0	0	3	0
Kingery, S.F.*	1.000	6	21	2	0	23	2
Kruk, Philadelphia*	.997	102	735	49	2	786	54
Lee, Cincinnati	1.000	2	8	4	0	12	0
Lindeman, Phi.	1.000	1	4	0	0	4	1
Litton, San Francisco.	.989	15	75	11	1	87	10
Magadan, New York	.996	122	1035	90	5	1130	73
Martinez, Pit.-Cin.	.977	33	239	12	6	257	15
McClendon, Pit.	.986	22	132	10	2	144	12
McGriff, San Diego*	.990	153	1370	87	14	1471	111
Merced, Pittsburgh	.988	105	911	60	12	983	64
Mitchell, S.F.	.000	1	0	0	0	0	0
Morris, Cincinnati*	.992	128	979	100	9	1088	87
Murray, Los Angeles	.995	149	1327	128	7	1462	96

Player, Team	Pct.	G	PO	A	E	TC	DP
Noboa, Montreal	1.000	1	1	0	0	1	0
Oberkfell, Houston	1.000	13	66	8	0	74	6
Oquendo, St. Louis	.000	3	0	0	0	0	0
Pagnozzi, St. Louis	1.000	3	9	0	0	9	1
Perry, St. Louis	.989	61	407	28	5	440	30
Prince, Pittsburgh	1.000	1	1	0	0	1	0
Redus, Pittsburgh	.990	47	377	25	4	406	35
Rohde, Houston	1.000	1	3	0	0	3	0
Salazar, Chicago	.969	7	30	1	1	32	2
Santovenia, Montreal..	1.000	7	31	4	0	35	4
Sasser, New York	.988	10	80	5	1	86	5
Schu, Philadelphia	1.000	1	13	1	0	14	0
Sharperson, L.A.	.983	10	46	12	1	59	5
Templeton, New York ..	.994	25	152	12	1	165	9
Teufel, San Diego	1.000	6	47	2	0	49	1
Tolentino, Houston*	.982	10	49	5	1	55	3
Torve, New York	1.000	1	0	2	0	2	0
Varsho, Pittsburgh	1.000	3	11	0	0	11	0
Villanueva, Chicago	1.000	6	17	1	0	18	2
Walker, Montreal	.988	39	313	30	4	347	28
Webster, L.A.*	1.000	1	2	0	0	2	1
Wilson, St. Louis	1.000	4	14	1	0	15	2

TRIPLE PLAYS: Bagwell, Houston; Foley, Montreal; Guerrero, St. Louis; Jordan, Philadelphia.

FIRST BASEMEN WITH TWO OR MORE TEAMS

Player, Team	Pct.	G	PO	A	E	TC	DP
Martinez, Pittsburgh	.945	8	51	1	3	55	2
Martinez, Cincinnati	.985	25	188	11	3	202	13

SECOND BASEMEN

Leader, Team	Pct.	G	PO	A	E	TC	DP
SANDBERG, Chicago	.995	157	267	515	4	786	66

Player, Team	Pct.	G	PO	A	E	TC	DP
Alicea, St. Louis	1.000	11	17	22	0	39	3
Anderson, S.F.	1.000	6	6	3	0	9	1
Backman, Phi.	.981	36	50	52	2	104	12
Barberie, Montreal	1.000	10	22	25	0	47	7
Barrett, San Diego	1.000	2	7	4	0	11	2
Benavides, Cincinnati .	1.000	3	7	4	0	11	1
Biggio, Houston	.929	3	5	8	1	14	1
Blauser, Atlanta	.983	32	48	66	2	116	15
Candaele, Houston	.982	109	197	301	9	507	52
DeShields, Montreal	.962	148	285	405	27	717	72
Doran, Cincinnati	.981	88	153	208	7	368	47
Duncan, Cincinnati	.974	62	116	144	7	267	29
Faries, San Diego	.988	36	67	92	2	161	18
Felder, San Francisco .	1.000	1	0	2	0	2	0
Foley, Montreal	1.000	2	6	8	0	14	3
Garcia, Pittsburgh	1.000	1	2	0	0	2	0

FIELDING

1991 N.L. STATISTICS

FIELDING

Player, Team	Pct.	G	PO	A	E	TC	DP
Gardner, New York	1.000	3	4	9	0	13	0
Harris, Los Angeles	.988	27	33	49	1	83	12
Herr, N.Y.-S.F.	1.000	72	114	148	0	262	33
Hudler, St. Louis	1.000	5	3	2	0	5	1
Jefferies, New York	.982	77	144	177	6	327	15
Jones, St. Louis	1.000	4	0	3	0	3	0
Lemke, Atlanta	.978	110	159	205	8	372	39
Lind, Pittsburgh	.989	149	349	438	9	796	79
Litton, San Francisco	1.000	15	29	24	0	53	7
McLemore, Houston	.975	19	25	54	2	81	8
Miller, New York	.972	60	129	148	8	285	28
Morandini, Phi.	.986	97	183	254	6	443	45
Mota, Houston	.970	27	30	66	3	99	11
Mota, San Diego	.962	13	24	27	2	53	5
Noboa, Montreal	.962	6	11	14	1	26	3
Oquendo, St. Louis	.988	118	244	346	7	597	60
Pena, St. Louis	.976	83	95	146	6	247	28
Perezchica, S.F.	1.000	6	6	7	0	13	3
Quinones, Cincinnati	.975	33	45	74	3	122	16
Ramirez, Houston	.978	27	35	52	2	89	9
Ready, Philadelphia	.989	66	127	145	3	275	22
Roberts, San Diego	.978	68	128	185	7	320	35
Rohde, Houston	1.000	4	7	12	0	19	1
Samuel, Los Angeles	.978	152	300	442	17	759	73
Sanchez, Chicago	1.000	2	1	8	0	9	0
Sandberg, Chicago	.995	157	267	515	4	786	66
Sharperson, L.A.	1.000	5	5	8	0	13	3
Shipley, San Diego	.982	14	18	36	1	55	8
Smith, Los Angeles	.000	1	0	0	0	0	0
Teufel, N.Y.-S.D.	.987	66	102	124	3	229	22
Thompson, S.F.	.985	144	320	402	11	733	98
Treadway, Atlanta	.960	93	155	206	15	376	33
Vizcaino, Chicago	.929	9	8	18	2	28	4
Walker, Chicago	1.000	6	11	16	0	27	1
Wilkerson, Pittsburgh	.992	30	50	80	1	131	15
Wilson, St. Louis	1.000	3	0	2	0	2	1

TRIPLE PLAYS: Candaele, Houston; DeShields, Montreal; Pena, St. Louis; Ready, Philadelphia.

SECOND BASEMEN WITH TWO OR MORE TEAMS

Player, Team	Pct.	G	PO	A	E	TC	DP
Herr, N.Y.	1.000	57	100	121	0	221	29
Herr, S.F.	1.000	15	14	27	0	41	4
Teufel, N.Y.	1.000	1	1	2	0	3	0
Teufel, San Diego	.987	65	101	122	3	226	22

THIRD BASEMEN

Leader, Team	Pct.	G	PO	A	E	TC	DP
WALLACH, Montreal	.968	149	107	310	14	431	27

Player, Team	Pct.	G	PO	A	E	TC	DP
Alicea, St. Louis	1.000	2	1	0	0	1	0
Anderson, S.F.	.842	11	8	8	3	19	0
Backman, Phi.	.939	20	4	27	2	33	1
Barberie, Montreal	1.000	10	11	17	0	28	1
Barrett, San Diego	1.000	2	0	2	0	2	0
Benjamin, S.F.	.000	1	0	0	0	0	0
Blauser, Atlanta	.911	18	13	28	4	45	1
Bonilla, Pittsburgh	.932	67	43	134	13	190	13
Booker, Philadelphia	1.000	3	1	4	0	5	0
Buechele, Pittsburgh	.956	31	22	64	4	90	5
Caminiti, Houston	.948	152	129	293	23	445	29
Candaele, Houston	.958	11	7	16	1	24	1
Coolbaugh, San Diego	.952	54	32	108	7	147	8
Cooper, Houston	.833	4	3	2	1	6	0
Donnels, New York	.938	11	8	22	2	32	3
Faries, San Diego	1.000	12	5	13	0	18	0
Felder, San Francisco	.857	3	1	5	1	7	1
Foley, Montreal	.857	6	1	5	1	7	0
Garcia, Pittsburgh	1.000	2	4	5	0	9	0
Hamilton, Los Angeles	.928	33	21	43	5	69	2
Hansen, Los Angeles	1.000	21	4	18	0	22	1
Harris, Los Angeles	.943	113	77	155	14	246	16
C. Hayes, Philadelphia	.958	138	85	237	14	336	25
Hernandez, L.A.	.000	1	0	0	0	0	0

Player, Team	Pct.	G	PO	A	E	TC	DP
Herr, San Francisco	1.000	3	2	3	0	5	0
Hollins, Philadelphia	.922	36	25	58	7	90	2
Howell, San Diego	.985	54	33	98	2	133	7
Jefferies, New York	.916	51	26	94	11	131	6
Johnson, New York	.927	104	55	173	18	246	11
King, Pittsburgh	.975	33	15	62	2	79	0
Lemke, Atlanta	.867	15	3	10	2	15	1
Litton, San Francisco	.958	11	5	18	1	24	1
Miller, New York	1.000	2	2	1	0	3	0
Murray, Los Angeles	.000	1	0	0	0	0	0
Noboa, Montreal	1.000	2	1	3	0	4	1
Oberkfell, Houston	.818	4	4	5	2	11	0
Pendleton, Atlanta	.950	148	108	349	24	481	31
Presley, San Diego	.923	16	13	23	3	39	0
Quinones, Cincinnati	.914	19	12	20	3	35	2
Ramirez, Houston	1.000	2	0	1	0	1	0
Redfield, Pittsburgh	.917	9	4	7	1	12	3
Richardson, Pit.	.000	3	0	0	0	0	0
Rohde, Houston	1.000	3	0	3	0	3	0
Royer, St. Louis	1.000	5	5	4	0	9	0
Sabo, Cincinnati	.966	151	86	255	12	353	24
Salazar, Chicago	.956	86	46	151	9	206	5
Schu, Philadelphia	.667	3	2	0	1	3	0
Scott, Chicago	.969	31	13	50	2	65	6
Sharperson, L.A.	.981	68	30	71	2	103	5
Slaught, Pittsburgh	.000	1	0	0	0	0	0
Strange, Chicago	.800	3	1	3	1	5	0
Templeton, S.D.-N.Y.	.967	17	4	25	1	30	3
Teufel, N.Y.-S.D.	.947	53	29	79	6	114	4
Vizcaino, Chicago	.947	57	10	26	2	38	1
Walker, Chicago	.929	57	22	69	7	98	7
Wallach, Montreal	.968	149	107	310	14	431	27
Wehner, Pittsburgh	.936	36	23	65	6	94	9
Wilkerson, Pittsburgh	.974	14	14	24	1	39	4
Williams, S.F.	.964	155	131	293	16	440	30
Wilson, St. Louis	.905	12	8	11	2	21	3
Zeile, St. Louis	.943	154	124	290	25	439	18

TRIPLE PLAYS: Barberie, Montreal; Caminiti, Houston; Zeile, St. Louis.

THIRD BASEMEN WITH TWO OR MORE TEAMS

Player, Team	Pct.	G	PO	A	E	TC	DP
Templeton, San Diego	.950	15	2	17	1	20	2
Templeton, New York	1.000	2	2	8	0	10	1
Teufel, New York	1.000	5	1	5	0	6	0
Teufel, San Diego	.944	48	28	74	6	108	4

SHORTSTOPS

Leader, Team	Pct.	G	PO	A	E	TC	DP
O. SMITH, St. Louis	.987	150	244	387	8	639	79

Player, Team	Pct.	G	PO	A	E	TC	DP
Alicea, St. Louis	1.000	1	1	1	0	2	1
Anderson, S.F.	.956	63	68	107	8	183	25
Barberie, Montreal	.931	19	19	48	5	72	7
Batiste, Philadelphia	.970	7	10	22	1	33	4
Bell, Pittsburgh	.968	156	239	491	24	754	78
Belliard, Atlanta	.967	145	168	361	18	547	53
Benavides, Cincinnati	.974	20	26	49	2	77	5
Benjamin, S.F.	.984	51	64	123	3	190	23
Blauser, Atlanta	.948	85	75	125	11	211	21
Booker, Philadelphia	1.000	20	16	29	0	45	2
Castilla, Atlanta	1.000	12	6	6	0	12	0
Cedeno, Houston	.930	66	88	151	18	257	36
Clayton, S.F.	.880	4	16	6	3	25	1
Duncan, Cincinnati	.983	32	46	68	2	116	12
Dunston, Chicago	.968	142	261	383	21	665	69
Elster, New York	.970	107	149	299	14	462	39
Faries, San Diego	1.000	8	8	12	0	20	2
Fernandez, San Diego	.972	145	247	440	20	707	78
Foley, Montreal	.967	43	45	71	4	120	12
Garcia, Pittsburgh	.947	9	5	13	1	19	3
Gardner, New York	.818	8	7	20	6	33	2
Griffin, Los Angeles	.961	109	186	349	22	557	45
Hamilton, Los Angeles	.000	1	0	0	0	0	0

Player, Team	Pct.	G	PO	A	E	TC	DP
Hansen, Los Angeles...	1.000	1	1	1	0	2	1
Harris, Los Angeles.....	.924	20	15	46	5	66	7
C. Hayes, Philadelphia	.857	2	3	3	1	7	0
Johnson, New York......	.924	28	45	88	11	144	15
Jones, St. Louis	1.000	14	5	13	0	18	3
Larkin, Cincinnati.......	.976	119	226	372	15	613	65
Litton, San Francisco..	1.000	9	7	12	0	19	3
Miller, New York	.667	2	1	3	2	6	1
Mota, San Diego	.750	3	1	2	1	4	0
Noboa, Montreal	1.000	2	0	2	0	2	0
Offerman, Los Angeles	.945	50	50	121	10	181	17
Oquendo, St. Louis	.961	22	27	22	2	51	5
Owen, Montreal	.986	133	189	376	8	573	64
Perezchica, S.F.	.947	13	14	22	2	38	3
Quinones, Cincinnati...	.958	5	11	12	1	24	5
Ramirez, Houston	.953	45	51	71	6	128	13
Richardson, Pit...........	1.000	2	0	1	0	1	0
Rohde, Houston	1.000	3	3	8	0	11	1
Rossy, Atlanta	.000	1	0	0	0	0	0
Sanchez, Chicago........	1.000	10	10	17	0	27	1
Sharperson, L.A.	.960	16	8	16	1	25	2
Shipley, San Diego......	.902	19	21	34	6	61	6
O. Smith, St. Louis	.987	150	244	387	8	639	79
Templeton, S.D.-N.Y...	.963	41	54	104	6	164	18
Thon, Philadelphia	.969	146	234	412	21	667	65
Uribe, San Francisco....	.966	87	98	218	11	327	35
Vizcaino, Chicago.........	.972	33	31	74	3	108	14
Wilkerson, Pittsburgh.	1.000	15	9	20	0	29	5
Williams, S.F..............	1.000	4	3	2	0	5	2
Yelding, Houston	.939	72	113	166	18	297	31

TRIPLE PLAY: Cedeno, Houston.

SHORTSTOPS WITH TWO OR MORE TEAMS

Player, Team	Pct.	G	PO	A	E	TC	DP
Templeton, San Diego .	1.000	1	1	0	0	1	0
Templeton, New York ..	.963	40	53	104	6	163	18

OUTFIELDERS

*Throws lefthanded.

Leader, Team	Pct.	G	PO	A	E	TC	DP
BUTLER, L.A.*............	1.000	161	372	8	0	380	3

Player, Team	Pct.	G	PO	A	E	TC	DP
Abner, San Diego	1.000	39	86	1	0	87	0
Aldrete, San Diego*.....	1.000	5	7	1	0	8	0
Anthony, Houston*......	.986	37	64	5	1	70	1
Azocar, San Diego*.....	.875	13	14	0	2	16	0
Bass, San Francisco ...	.977	101	159	9	4	172	2
Bell, Chicago..............	.962	146	249	6	10	265	0
Benzinger, Cincinnati..	1.000	15	23	0	0	23	0
Biggio, Houston	1.000	2	0	1	0	1	0
Bonds, Pittsburgh*......	.991	150	321	13	3	337	1
Bonilla, Pittsburgh	.989	104	176	8	2	186	0
Boston, New York*......	.981	115	156	2	3	161	1
Braggs, Cincinnati	.966	74	139	2	5	146	1
Brewer, St. Louis*.......	.750	3	3	0	1	4	0
Brooks, New York	.972	100	166	6	5	177	0
Bullett, Pittsburgh*......	1.000	3	2	0	0	2	0
Bullock, Montreal*	1.000	9	11	0	0	11	0
Butler, Los Angeles*....	1.000	161	372	8	0	380	3
Calderon, Montreal......	.974	122	256	3	7	266	1
Campusano, Phi.	1.000	15	27	1	0	28	0
Candaele, Houston	1.000	26	40	1	0	41	0
Carr, New York	1.000	9	9	0	0	9	0
Carreon, New York*.....	.971	77	96	4	3	103	1
Castillo, Philadelphia .	.977	26	40	2	1	43	1
Chamberlain, Phi.......	.985	98	199	4	3	206	0
Clark, San Diego	.994	96	160	5	1	166	2
Coleman, New York	.979	70	132	5	3	140	0
Coles, San Francisco...	.000	3	0	0	0	0	0
Daniels, Los Angeles...	.979	132	220	9	5	234	0
Dascenzo, Chicago*.....	.985	86	134	0	2	136	0
Davidson, Houston......	1.000	63	71	1	0	72	0
Davis, Cincinnati	.985	81	190	5	3	198	2
Dawson, Chicago........	.988	137	243	7	3	253	2

Player, Team	Pct.	G	PO	A	E	TC	DP
Doran, Cincinnati	1.000	6	11	0	0	11	0
Duncan, Cincinnati......	1.000	7	7	0	0	7	0
Dykstra, Phi.*.............	.977	63	167	3	4	174	2
Espy, Pittsburgh........	.966	35	54	3	2	59	2
Felder, San Francisco .	.985	107	192	3	3	198	2
Finley, Houston*.........	.985	153	323	13	5	341	2
Fitzgerald, Montreal	1.000	3	10	0	0	10	0
Gant, Atlanta	.983	148	338	7	6	351	1
Gilkey, St. Louis..........	.994	74	164	6	1	171	1
Gonzalez, L.A.-Pit......	1.000	41	38	1	0	39	0
Gonzalez, Houston......	.984	133	294	6	5	305	1
Goodwin, Los Angeles .	1.000	5	8	0	0	8	0
Gregg, Atlanta*...........	1.000	14	16	0	0	16	0
Grissom, Montreal	.984	138	350	15	6	371	2
Gwynn, Los Angeles*..	1.000	41	37	2	0	39	0
Gwynn, San Diego*	.990	134	291	8	3	302	2
Harris, Los Angeles.....	.000	1	0	0	0	0	0
Hatcher, Cincinnati......	.981	121	248	4	5	257	0
V. Hayes, Phi.	.990	72	202	3	2	207	2
Heep, Atlanta*............	.000	1	0	0	0	0	0
Herr, San Francisco	.000	1	0	0	0	0	0
Howard, San Diego	.995	86	182	4	1	187	1
Hudler, St. Louis	.981	58	97	4	2	103	0
Hunter, Atlanta*..........	1.000	6	2	0	0	2	0
Jackson, San Diego	.992	98	243	2	2	247	2
Javier, Los Angeles	.986	69	70	1	1	72	0
S. Jefferson, Cin........	1.000	5	4	0	0	4	0
Johnson, New York	.970	30	61	3	2	66	0
Jones, Cincinnati........	1.000	26	27	1	0	28	0
Jose, St. Louis	.990	153	268	15	3	286	2
Justice, Atlanta*.........	.968	106	204	9	7	220	0
Kingery, S.F.*.............	.975	38	39	0	1	40	0
Kruk, Philadelphia*.....	.992	52	113	4	1	118	1
Landrum, Chicago.......	.968	44	61	0	2	63	0
Lankford, St. Louis*.....	.984	149	367	7	6	380	2
Leonard, S.F...............	1.000	34	41	0	0	41	0
Lewis, San Francisco..	1.000	68	159	2	0	161	0
Lindeman, Phi.............	1.000	30	31	1	0	32	0
Litton, San Francisco...	1.000	6	2	0	0	2	0
Lofton, Houston*........	.977	20	41	1	1	43	0
Martinez, Cincinnati.....	1.000	16	35	1	0	36	0
Da. Martinez, Mon.*....	.982	112	213	10	4	227	0
May, Chicago..............	1.000	7	11	1	0	12	0
McClendon, Pit.	.966	32	26	2	1	29	1
McDaniel, New York	1.000	14	18	0	0	18	0
McDowell, L.A.............	.000	2	0	0	0	0	0
McGee, San Francisco	.978	128	259	6	6	271	3
McReynolds, N.Y.	.993	141	281	9	2	292	1
Merced, Pittsburgh......	1.000	7	5	0	0	5	0
Miller, New York	1.000	28	33	2	0	35	1
Mitchell, S.F..............	.970	100	188	6	6	200	1
Mitchell, Atlanta	.970	34	31	1	1	33	0
Morris, Cincinnati*.......	.000	1	0	0	0	0	0
Morris, Philadelphia*..	.974	57	73	1	2	76	0
Murphy, Philadelphia .	.983	147	287	6	5	298	0
Nixon, Atlanta	.987	115	218	6	3	227	1
Noboa, Montreal	1.000	7	7	0	0	7	0
O'Neill, Cincinnati*......	.994	150	301	13	2	316	2
Ortiz, Houston	1.000	24	27	2	0	29	1
Parker, San Francisco	1.000	4	5	0	0	5	0
Pena, St. Louis............	1.000	4	6	0	0	6	0
Perry, St. Louis............	1.000	5	6	1	0	7	0
Redus, Pittsburgh........	.931	33	26	1	2	29	0
Rhodes, Houston*	.958	44	87	4	4	95	1
Riesgo, Montreal	.500	2	0	1	1	2	0
Roberts, San Diego	.974	46	111	0	3	114	0
Salazar, Chicago..........	.000	1	0	0	0	0	0
Sanders, Atlanta*	.952	44	57	3	3	63	0
Sanders, Cincinnati.....	1.000	9	22	0	0	22	0
Santiago, San Diego	.000	1	0	0	0	0	0
Sasser, New York	.967	21	26	3	1	30	1
Simms, Houston	.889	41	44	4	6	54	0
Dw. Smith, Chicago.....	.962	42	73	3	3	79	1
L. Smith, Atlanta	.965	99	134	5	5	144	2
Strawberry, L.A.*........	.978	136	209	11	5	225	2
Templeton, New York ..	.000	2	0	0	0	0	0

Player, Team	Pct.	G	PO	A	E	TC	DP
Thompson, St. Louis ...	.991	91	207	8	2	217	1
Tolentino, Houston*....	1.000	1	4	0	0	4	0
VanderWal, Montreal*	1.000	17	29	0	0	29	0
Van Slyke, Pittsburgh .	.996	135	273	8	1	282	1
Varsho, Pittsburgh......	.989	54	84	2	1	87	1
Vatcher, San Diego......	.900	11	8	1	1	10	0
Walker, Chicago..........	.987	53	73	4	1	78	1
Walker, Montreal.........	.991	102	223	6	2	231	2
Walton, Chicago..........	.983	101	170	2	3	175	1
Ward, San Diego......	.982	33	54	0	1	55	0
Webster, Pit.-L.A.*	.978	65	85	2	2	89	0
Williams, Montreal......	.957	24	42	3	2	47	0
Wilson, St. Louis.........	1.000	5	8	0	0	8	0
Winningham, Cin.........	.953	66	99	2	5	106	0
Wood, San Francisco*	.909	8	10	0	1	11	0
Yelding, Houston	.333	4	1	0	2	3	0
Young, Houston	1.000	84	96	4	0	100	1

TRIPLE PLAY: Simms, Houston.

OUTFIELDERS WITH TWO OR MORE TEAMS

Player, Team	Pct.	G	PO	A	E	TC	DP
Gonzalez, Los Angeles	1.000	27	20	0	0	20	0
Gonzalez, Pittsburgh ..	1.000	14	18	1	0	19	0
Webster, Pittsburgh*..	.963	29	50	2	2	54	0
Webster, L.A.*	1.000	36	35	0	0	35	0

CATCHERS

Leader, Team	Pct.	G	PO	A	E	TC	DP	PB
LaVALLIERE, Pit.	.998	105	565	46	1	612	4	5

Player, Team	Pct.	G	PO	A	E	TC	DP	PB
Berryhill, Chi.-Atl.	.967	49	214	24	8	246	2	8
Biggio, Houston	.990	139	889	64	10	963	10	13
Bilardello, S.D.	1.000	13	59	6	0	65	1	0
Cabrera, Atlanta....	.987	17	72	6	1	79	0	3
Carter, L.A.	.988	68	355	45	5	405	2	4
Cerone, New York .	.987	81	424	36	6	466	0	6
Daulton, Phi......	.985	88	493	33	8	534	5	2
Decker, S.F.	.984	78	385	41	7	433	5	7
Eusebio, Houston .	.981	9	49	4	1	54	0	1
Fitzgerald, Mon.....	.994	54	306	24	2	332	3	2
Fletcher, Phi.	.992	45	242	22	2	266	1	1
Gedman, St. Louis	.976	43	192	13	5	210	4	3
Girardi, Chicago ...	.972	21	95	11	3	109	1	1
Hassey, Montreal .	.989	34	172	13	2	187	1	4
Heath, Atlanta	.991	45	192	33	2	227	1	6
Hernandez, L.A......	.966	13	24	4	1	29	0	1
Hundley, N.Y........	1.000	20	85	11	0	96	1	1
Kennedy, S.F........	.978	58	237	36	6	279	2	2
Lake, Philadelphia	.993	58	277	25	2	304	1	5
Lampkin, S.D.	1.000	11	49	5	0	54	0	1
LaValliere, Pit.......	.998	105	565	46	1	612	4	5
Lindsey, Phi..........	1.000	1	8	0	0	8	0	0
Litton, S.F.............	1.000	1	3	0	0	3	0	0
Lyons, L.A.............	1.000	6	12	1	0	13	1	0
Manwaring, S.F.....	.988	67	315	28	4	347	7	0
McClendon, Pit......	1.000	2	5	0	0	5	0	0
Nichols, Houston ..	.971	17	86	14	3	103	2	2
O'Brien, New York	.991	67	396	37	4	437	7	2
Oliver, Cincinnati..	.980	90	496	40	11	547	6	10
Olson, Atlanta	.995	127	721	48	4	773	7	5
Pagnozzi, St.L.......	.991	139	673	81	7	761	8	5
Pappas, Chicago ...	1.000	6	35	1	0	36	0	0
Prince, Pittsburgh	.984	19	52	9	1	62	0	1
Reed, Cincinnati ...	.991	89	527	29	5	561	7	7
Reyes, Montreal....	.975	80	375	61	11	447	4	10
Santiago, S.D.	.985	151	830	100	14	944	14	8
Santovenia, Mon...	.976	30	109	12	3	124	3	6
Sasser, New York .	.994	43	165	13	1	179	0	3
Scioscia, L.A........	.990	115	677	51	7	735	8	3
Scott, Cincinnati....	1.000	8	19	0	0	19	0	2
Servais, Houston ..	.988	14	77	4	1	82	0	1
Slaught, Pit..........	.987	69	338	31	5	374	4	3
Stephens, St.L.	1.000	6	16	2	0	18	0	0
Sutko, Cincinnati..	.875	9	16	5	3	24	0	1

Player, Team	Pct.	G	PO	A	E	TC	DP	PB
Villanueva, Chi.	.979	55	259	26	6	291	2	4
Wilkins, Chicago ..	.993	82	373	42	3	418	6	6
Willard, Atlanta	1.000	1	3	0	0	3	0	0

CATCHERS WITH TWO OR MORE TEAMS

Player, Team	Pct.	G	PO	A	E	TC	DP	PB
Berryhill, Chi.........	.967	48	211	24	8	243	0	8
Berryhill, Atl.	1.000	1	3	0	0	3	0	0

PITCHERS

*Throws lefthanded.

Leader, Team	Pct.	G	PO	A	E	TC	DP
GLAVINE, Atlanta*......	1.000	34	16	45	0	61	4

Player, Team	Pct.	G	PO	A	E	TC	DP
Agosto, St. Louis*	.000	72	5	17	2	24	2
Akerfelds, Phi.	.933	30	2	12	1	15	0
Andersen, San Diego...	.923	38	5	7	1	13	0
Armstrong, Cincinnati.	.941	27	16	16	2	34	0
Ashby, Philadelphia	1.000	8	7	4	0	11	1
Assenmacher, Chi.*	.933	75	4	10	1	15	0
Avery, Atlanta*	.976	35	9	31	1	41	2
Barnes, Montreal*.......	.950	28	7	31	2	40	1
Beatty, New York*.......	1.000	5	1	1	0	2	0
Beck, San Francisco ...	1.000	31	1	10	0	11	0
Belcher, Los Angeles...	.939	33	11	20	2	33	2
Belinda, Pittsburgh	1.000	60	5	5	0	10	1
Benes, San Diego........	1.000	33	8	29	0	37	3
Berenguer, Atlanta	1.000	49	7	5	0	12	0
Bielecki, Chi.-Atl.	1.000	41	22	24	0	46	3
Black, San Francisco*	1.000	34	14	38	0	52	4
Boever, Philadelphia ...	1.000	68	1	10	0	11	0
Bones, San Diego........	1.000	11	1	2	0	3	0
Boskie, Chicago	.946	28	14	21	2	37	0
Bowen, Houston	.778	14	4	3	2	9	0
Boyd, Montreal	1.000	19	7	11	0	18	0
Brantley, Philadelphia.	.875	6	2	5	1	8	0
Brantley, S.F...............	1.000	67	4	9	0	13	1
Bross, New York	.000	8	0	0	0	0	0
Brown, Cincinnati........	.800	11	2	2	1	5	0
Browning, Cincinnati*	.865	36	8	24	5	37	2
Burke, New York........	.923	72	3	21	2	26	1
Burkett, S.F.................	.974	36	13	25	1	39	2
Candelaria, L.A.*	1.000	59	0	2	0	2	0
Capel, Houston	1.000	25	3	4	0	7	1
Carman, Cincinnati* ...	1.000	28	1	8	0	9	1
Carpenter, St. Louis	1.000	59	4	8	0	12	0
Carreno, Philadelphia..	.000	3	0	0	0	0	0
Castillo, Chicago	1.000	18	6	16	0	22	0
Castillo, Atl.-N.Y.*	1.000	17	3	6	0	9	0
Charlton, Cincinnati*..	.960	39	4	20	1	25	1
Christopher, L.A.	1.000	3	0	1	0	1	0
Clancy, Hou.-Atl.	.923	54	3	9	1	13	0
Clark, St. Louis	1.000	7	2	1	0	3	0
Clements, San Diego* .	1.000	12	0	3	0	3	1
Combs, Philadelphia*..	1.000	14	2	9	0	11	0
Cone, New York	.917	34	18	26	4	48	2
Cook, Los Angeles*	1.000	20	0	4	0	4	0
Cormier, St. Louis*......	1.000	11	3	8	0	11	0
Corsi, Houston	.955	47	6	15	1	22	1
Costello, San Diego......	1.000	27	0	5	0	5	0
Cox, Philadelphia.........	1.000	23	10	11	0	21	1
Crews, Los Angeles	.944	60	7	10	1	18	0
Darling, N.Y.-Mon.	.824	20	10	18	6	34	1
Dascenzo, Chicago*....	.000	3	0	0	0	0	0
DeJesus, Philadelphia.	.957	31	4	18	1	23	0
DeLeon, St. Louis.	1.000	28	5	17	0	22	0
Deshaies, Houston*	.880	28	4	18	3	25	1
Dibble, Cincinnati........	.917	67	4	7	1	12	0
Downs, San Francisco	.966	45	9	19	1	29	1
Drabek, Pittsburgh.......	.932	35	27	41	5	73	1
Fajardo, Pittsburgh	.000	2	0	0	0	0	0
Fassero, Montreal*	.933	51	3	11	1	15	1
Fernandez, New York*	1.000	8	1	11	0	12	0
Foster, Cincinnati........	1.000	11	2	1	0	3	0

— 303 —

Player, Team	Pct.	G	PO	A	E	TC	DP
Franco, New York*	.929	52	3	10	1	14	1
Fraser, St. Louis	1.000	35	1	3	0	4	0
Freeman, Atlanta	1.000	34	3	4	0	7	0
Frey, Montreal*	1.000	31	1	4	0	5	0
Gardner, Houston	.900	5	3	6	1	10	1
Gardner, Montreal	.964	27	12	15	1	28	1
Gardner, San Diego	1.000	14	0	4	0	4	0
Garrelts, S.F.	1.000	8	4	1	0	5	1
Glavine, Atlanta*	1.000	34	16	45	0	61	4
Gooden, New York	.956	27	15	28	2	45	3
Gott, Los Angeles	1.000	55	10	9	0	19	1
Grater, St. Louis	.500	3	1	0	1	2	0
Greene, Philadelphia	.968	36	14	16	1	31	0
Grimsley, Philadelphia	.941	12	2	14	1	17	3
Gross, Los Angeles	.958	46	9	14	1	24	0
Gross, Cincinnati	.909	29	5	15	2	22	0
Gunderson, S.F.*	1.000	2	0	1	0	1	0
Hammaker, S.D.*	1.000	1	0	1	0	1	0
Hammond, Cincinnati*	.923	20	6	18	2	26	1
Haney, Montreal*	.923	16	6	18	2	26	1
Harkey, Chicago	1.000	4	1	3	0	4	0
Harnisch, Houston	.962	33	7	18	1	26	0
Harris, San Diego	.960	20	10	14	1	25	0
Hartley, L.A.-Phi.	.941	58	10	6	1	17	2
Heaton, Pittsburgh*	.900	42	1	8	1	10	0
Henry, Houston	1.000	52	4	5	0	9	1
Heredia, S.F.	1.000	7	2	2	0	4	0
Hernandez, San Diego .	1.000	9	0	3	0	3	1
Hernandez, Houston	1.000	32	6	9	0	15	0
Hershiser, L.A.	.968	21	12	18	1	31	1
Hickerson, S.F.*	1.000	17	0	1	0	1	0
Hill, St. Louis	.953	30	15	26	2	43	1
Hill, Cincinnati	1.000	22	2	2	0	4	0
Howell, Los Angeles	.917	44	5	6	1	12	1
Huismann, Pittsburgh.	1.000	5	1	1	0	2	0
Hurst, San Diego*	.952	31	7	33	2	42	2
Innis, New York	.975	69	13	26	1	40	1
Jackson, Chicago*	.917	17	4	7	1	12	0
Jackson, San Diego	.000	1	0	0	0	0	0
Jones, Montreal	.889	77	5	19	3	27	1
Jones, Houston	.944	26	8	26	2	36	2
Juden, Houston	.400	4	0	2	3	5	0
Kile, Houston	.889	37	7	17	3	27	1
Kipper, Pittsburgh*	.778	52	1	6	2	9	0
LaCoss, S.F.	.900	18	4	5	1	10	0
Lancaster, Chicago	1.000	64	13	14	0	27	1
Landrum, Pittsburgh	1.000	61	4	8	0	12	0
LaPoint, Philadelphia*	.667	2	0	2	1	3	0
Layana, Cincinnati	.875	22	3	4	1	8	1
Lefferts, San Diego*	1.000	54	3	12	0	15	1
Leibrandt, Atlanta*	.971	36	14	53	2	69	1
Lewis, San Diego	.833	12	0	5	1	6	0
Lilliquist, San Diego*	1.000	6	1	4	0	5	0
Litton, San Francisco..	.000	1	0	0	0	0	0
Long, Montreal	.000	3	0	0	0	0	0
Maddux, Chicago	.978	37	39	50	2	91	5
Maddux, San Diego	.964	64	9	18	1	28	1
Mahler, Mon.-Atl.	.952	23	7	13	1	21	0
Mallicoat, Houston*	.500	24	1	0	1	2	0
De. Martinez, Montreal	.945	31	21	48	4	73	5
Martinez, Los Angeles.	.956	33	22	21	2	45	0
Mason, Pittsburgh	1.000	24	1	5	0	6	1
Mauser, Philadelphia .	1.000	3	0	1	0	1	0
May, Chicago	.000	2	0	0	0	0	0
McClellan, S.F.	1.000	13	4	6	0	10	1
McClure, St. Louis*	1.000	32	1	3	0	4	0
McDowell, Phi.-L.A.	.917	71	8	25	3	36	3
McElroy, Chicago*	1.000	71	8	14	0	22	1
Melendez, San Diego	.882	31	4	11	2	17	0
Mercker, Atlanta*	.900	50	2	7	1	10	1
Miller, Pittsburgh	.000	1	0	0	0	0	0
Minutelli, Cincinnati* ..	1.000	16	1	5	0	6	0
Morgan, Los Angeles	.971	34	25	41	2	68	3
Moyer, St. Louis*	1.000	8	0	5	0	5	0
Mulholland, Phi.*	.889	34	12	28	5	45	2
Myers, Cincinnati*	.900	58	6	12	2	20	0

Player, Team	Pct.	G	PO	A	E	TC	DP
Nabholz, Montreal*	.974	24	9	28	1	38	2
Nolte, San Diego*	1.000	6	0	3	0	3	0
Ojeda, Los Angeles*	1.000	31	14	32	0	46	1
Olivares, St. Louis	.958	28	16	30	2	48	5
Oliveras, S.F.	.938	55	3	12	1	16	0
Oquendo, St. Louis	.000	1	0	0	0	0	0
Osuna, Houston*	.933	71	4	10	1	15	2
Palacios, Pittsburgh.	1.000	36	4	9	0	13	0
Parrett, Atlanta	.889	18	3	5	1	9	1
Patterson, Pit.*	1.000	54	4	9	0	13	1
Pavlas, Chicago	.000	1	0	0	0	0	0
Pena, N.Y.-Atl.	.938	59	6	9	1	16	1
Perez, St. Louis	1.000	14	0	2	0	2	0
Perez, Chicago*	1.000	3	0	1	0	1	0
Peterson, San Diego	1.000	13	4	5	0	9	1
Petry, Atlanta	1.000	10	4	4	0	8	0
Piatt, Montreal	1.000	21	2	4	0	6	1
Portugal, Houston	.917	32	16	17	3	36	1
Power, Cincinnati	1.000	68	8	10	0	18	1
Rasmussen, S.D.*	.975	24	5	34	1	40	0
Reed, Pittsburgh	.000	1	0	0	0	0	0
Remlinger, S.F.*	.875	8	1	6	1	8	0
Renfroe, Chicago	1.000	4	0	1	0	1	0
Reuschel, S.F.	1.000	4	0	1	0	1	0
Reynoso, Atlanta	1.000	6	3	12	0	15	0
Righetti, S.F.*	1.000	61	3	13	0	16	1
Rijo, Cincinnati	.929	30	17	22	3	42	2
Ritchie, Philadelphia* .	1.000	39	1	8	0	9	0
Robinson, S.F.	1.000	34	7	16	0	23	0
Rodriguez, Pit.*	1.000	18	2	2	0	4	0
Rodriguez, San Diego*	1.000	64	2	13	0	15	1
Rojas, Montreal	1.000	37	2	5	0	7	0
Rosenberg, S.D.*	1.000	10	0	1	0	1	0
Ruffin, Philadelphia*	.920	31	8	15	2	25	1
Ruskin, Montreal*	.917	64	1	10	1	12	1
Sampen, Montreal	.923	43	3	9	1	13	0
Sanford, Cincinnati	1.000	5	2	1	0	3	0
Sauveur, New York*	1.000	6	0	2	0	2	0
Scanlan, Chicago	.926	40	9	16	2	27	0
Schilling, Houston	.909	56	6	4	1	11	0
Schmidt, Montreal	1.000	4	0	1	0	1	0
Schourek, New York*	1.000	35	6	14	0	20	1
Scott, Houston	1.000	2	0	1	0	1	0
Scott, San Diego	.000	2	0	0	0	0	0
Scudder, Cincinnati	1.000	27	10	11	0	21	0
Searcy, Philadelphia* .	1.000	18	1	4	0	5	0
Segura, San Francisco	.667	11	1	1	1	3	0
Sherrill, St. Louis*	1.000	10	1	3	0	4	0
Simons, New York*	1.000	42	6	16	0	22	0
Sisk, Atlanta	1.000	14	3	2	0	5	1
Slocumb, Chicago	.938	52	5	10	1	16	0
Smiley, Pittsburgh*	.975	33	5	34	1	40	0
B. Smith, St. Louis	1.000	31	12	26	0	38	2
Da. Smith, Chicago	1.000	35	0	5	0	5	0
L. Smith, St. Louis	1.000	67	3	6	0	9	0
P. Smith, Atlanta	1.000	14	3	6	0	9	0
Smith, Pittsburgh*	.944	35	12	39	3	54	5
Smoltz, Atlanta	.980	36	15	34	1	50	5
St. Claire, Atlanta	1.000	19	2	5	0	7	0
Stanton, Atlanta*	1.000	74	6	16	0	22	0
Sutcliffe, Chicago	1.000	19	10	12	0	22	2
Terry, St. Louis	1.000	65	7	16	0	23	1
Tewksbury, St. Louis	.956	30	9	34	2	45	2
Tomlin, Pittsburgh*	.957	31	9	36	2	47	0
Valera, New York	.000	2	0	0	0	0	0
Viola, New York*	.909	35	6	34	4	44	1
Wainhouse, Montreal.	.000	2	0	0	0	0	0
Walk, Pittsburgh	.923	25	9	15	2	26	1
Wetteland, L.A.	.750	6	1	2	1	4	0
Whitehurst, New York.	.946	36	11	24	2	37	2
Whitson, San Diego	1.000	13	5	9	0	14	0
Wilkins, Houston	1.000	7	1	0	0	1	0
Williams, Houston	1.000	2	1	2	0	3	0
Williams, Phi.*	.727	69	0	8	3	11	0
Wilson, Chi.-L.A.*	.000	19	0	0	0	0	0
Wilson, S.F.*	.981	44	9	42	1	52	4

Player, Team	Pct.	G	PO	A	E	TC	DP
Wohlers, Atlanta	1.000	17	0	3	0	3	1
Young, New York	.889	10	4	4	1	9	0

PITCHERS WITH TWO OR MORE TEAMS

Player, Team	Pct.	G	PO	A	E	TC	DP
Bielecki, Chicago	1.000	39	22	24	0	46	3
Bielecki, Atlanta	.000	2	0	0	0	0	0
Burke, Montreal	.909	37	1	9	1	11	0
Burke, New York	.933	35	2	12	1	15	1
Castillo, Atlanta*	1.000	7	1	0	0	1	0
Castillo, New York*	1.000	10	2	6	0	8	0
Clancy, Houston	.800	30	0	4	1	5	0
Clancy, Atlanta	1.000	24	3	5	0	8	0
Darling, New York	.828	17	7	17	5	29	0
Darling, Montreal	.800	3	3	1	1	5	1
Hartley, Los Angeles	.933	40	10	4	1	15	2
Hartley, Philadelphia	1.000	18	0	2	0	2	0
Mahler, Montreal	1.000	10	3	9	0	12	0
Mahler, Atlanta	.889	13	4	4	1	9	0
McDowell, Phi.	.875	38	4	17	3	24	2
McDowell, L.A.	1.000	33	4	8	0	12	1
Pena, New York	.923	44	5	7	1	13	0
Pena, Atlanta	1.000	15	1	2	0	3	1
Wilson, Chicago*	.000	8	0	0	0	0	0
Wilson, Los Angeles*	.000	11	0	0	0	0	0

MISCELLANEOUS

SHUTOUT GAMES

Read across for wins, down for losses.

Team	Pit.	L.A.	Mon.	N.Y.	Cin.	Chi.	S.D.	Phi.	Hou.	Atl.	S.F.	St.L.	W	L	Pct.
Pittsburgh	..	0	2	1	1	0	1	1	2	0	1	2	11	6	.647
Los Angeles	1	..	2	0	1	1	2	1	1	1	2	2	14	8	.636
Montreal	1	2	..	0	1	1	1	1	1	1	2	3	14	10	.583
New York	1	0	2	..	0	0	1	2	1	0	1	3	11	9	.550
Cincinnati	0	2	0	1	..	0	2	0	2	2	2	0	11	9	.550
Chicago	0	0	0	0	0	..	0	1	1	0	0	2	4	4	.500
San Diego	1	0	0	1	2	1	..	1	2	1	0	2	11	12	.478
Philadelphia	0	0	3	1	0	1	1	..	2	1	2	2	11	12	.478
Houston	0	0	0	2	2	0	2	2	..	2	3	0	13	16	.448
Atlanta	0	2	0	1	0	1	0	2	0	..	0	0	7	9	.438
San Francisco	1	2	0	2	0	0	1	1	2	1	..	0	10	13	.435
St. Louis	1	0	1	0	1	0	0	2	0	0	0	..	5	14	.263
Lost	6	8	10	9	9	4	12	12	16	9	13	14	122	122	.500

HOME RECORD

Read across for home wins, down for road losses.

Team	L.A.	St.L.	Pit.	Atl.	Phi.	Chi.	S.F.	S.D.	N.Y.	Mon.	Cin.	Hou.	W	L	Pct.
Los Angeles	..	4	3	5	5	6	5	5	4	5	6	6	54	27	.667
St. Louis	4	..	4	3	7	5	4	1	7	8	4	5	52	32	.619
Pittsburgh	2	6	..	3	7	7	3	3	7	6	5	3	52	32	.619
Atlanta	3	6	6	..	3	4	5	4	4	4	3	6	48	33	.593
Philadelphia	4	4	4	4	..	7	4	5	3	8	1	3	47	36	.566
Chicago	2	6	5	4	6	..	4	2	4	5	3	5	46	37	.554
San Francisco	6	2	2	5	4	4	..	4	4	3	5	4	43	38	.531
San Diego	4	4	2	2	2	4	6	..	3	2	6	7	42	39	.519
New York	3	5	4	1	5	1	4	4	..	8	3	2	40	42	.488
Montreal	6	3	0	5	1	1	4	2	1	..	4	6	33	35	.485
Cincinnati	3	2	1	1	4	5	6	5	2	4	..	6	39	42	.481
Houston	5	4	1	2	4	2	4	4	3	2	6	..	37	44	.457
Lost on road	42	46	32	35	48	46	49	39	42	55	46	53	533	437	.549

ROAD RECORD

Read across for road wins, down for home losses.

Team	Pit.	Atl.	S.D.	L.A.	N.Y.	Cin.	St.L.	Mon.	Chi.	S.F.	Phi.	Hou.	W	L	Pct.
Pittsburgh	..	0	4	3	5	5	5	6	4	4	5	5	46	32	.590
Atlanta	3	..	7	4	5	8	3	1	2	4	2	7	46	35	.568
San Diego	3	5	..	4	2	4	5	4	4	5	1	5	42	39	.519
Los Angeles	4	6	5	..	3	6	2	0	4	3	2	4	39	42	.481
New York	2	2	3	2	..	4	2	6	5	2	6	3	37	42	.468
Cincinnati	1	6	3	3	3	..	2	2	3	4	5	3	35	46	.432
St. Louis	3	0	2	2	4	4	..	3	3	4	5	2	32	46	.410
Montreal	6	2	2	1	3	2	4	..	6	3	3	4	38	55	.409
Chicago	2	2	2	0	7	1	4	5	..	2	2	4	31	46	.403
San Francisco	3	4	3	4	2	3	2	2	2	..	2	5	32	49	.395
Philadelphia	2	3	4	1	4	2	2	6	3	2	..	2	31	48	.392
Houston	3	3	2	3	4	3	1	0	1	5	3	..	28	53	.346
Lost at home	32	33	39	27	42	42	32	35	37	38	36	44	437	533	.451

PITCHING AGAINST EACH CLUB

ATLANTA—94-68

Pitcher	Chi. W-L	Cin. W-L	Hou. W-L	L.A. W-L	Mon. W-L	N.Y. W-L	Phi. W-L	Pit. W-L	St.L. W-L	S.D. W-L	S.F. W-L	Totals W-L
Avery	1-0	2-1	2-1	3-0	0-1	1-1	1-1	2-0	3-0	2-1	1-2	18-8
Berenguer	0-1	0-0	0-0	0-1	0-0	0-0	0-1	0-0	0-0	0-0	0-0	0-3
Castillo	0-0	1-0	0-0	0-0	0-0	0-0	0-1	0-0	0-0	0-0	0-0	1-1
Clancy	0-0	0-0	1-0	1-0	0-1	0-0	0-0	0-0	0-0	0-0	1-1	3-2
Freeman	1-0	0-0	0-0	0-0	0-0	0-0	0-0	0-0	0-0	0-0	0-0	1-0
Glavine	2-0	2-1	0-2	2-2	1-2	2-0	3-0	2-1	2-0	2-2	2-1	20-11
Leibrandt	0-2	2-2	2-1	0-2	1-0	2-1	1-0	1-1	2-1	2-1	2-2	15-13

Pitcher	Chi. W-L	Cin. W-L	Hou. W-L	L.A. W-L	Mon. W-L	N.Y. W-L	Phi. W-L	Pit. W-L	St.L. W-L	S.D. W-L	S.F. W-L	Totals W-L
Mahler	0-0	0-0	0-0	0-1	0-0	0-0	0-0	1-0	0-0	0-0	0-0	1-1
Mercker	0-1	0-0	0-1	1-0	0-0	1-0	0-0	0-0	1-0	2-0	0-1	5-3
Parrett	0-0	0-0	0-0	0-0	0-0	0-0	0-1	1-0	0-0	0-1	0-0	1-2
Pena	0-0	1-0	0-0	0-0	0-0	1-0	0-0	0-0	0-0	0-0	0-0	2-0
Reynoso	0-0	0-0	1-0	0-0	0-0	0-0	0-1	0-0	0-0	1-0	0-0	2-1
Sisk	0-0	0-0	2-0	0-0	0-0	0-0	0-0	0-0	0-1	0-0	0-0	2-1
P. Smith	0-1	0-1	0-0	0-0	0-0	1-0	0-1	0-0	0-0	0-0	0-0	1-3
Smoltz	2-1	2-1	2-0	0-4	1-2	1-1	0-0	2-1	1-0	0-2	3-1	14-13
Stanton	0-0	1-1	2-0	0-1	1-1	0-0	0-0	0-0	0-1	1-0	0-1	5-5
Wohlers	0-0	0-0	1-0	0-0	1-0	0-0	0-1	0-0	0-0	1-0	0-0	3-1
Totals	6-6	11-7	13-5	7-11	5-7	9-3	5-7	9-3	9-3	11-7	9-9	94-68

No-decisions—Bielecki, Petry, St. Claire.

CHICAGO—77-83

Pitcher	Atl. W-L	Cin. W-L	Hou. W-L	L.A. W-L	Mon. W-L	N.Y. W-L	Phi. W-L	Pit. W-L	St.L. W-L	S.D. W-L	S.F. W-L	Totals W-L
Assenmacher	2-0	0-0	0-0	0-2	3-1	1-1	0-1	0-0	0-0	0-0	0-0	7-8
Bielecki	1-0	0-2	2-0	0-2	2-0	0-1	2-2	1-2	2-0	0-2	3-0	13-11
Boskie	0-2	1-0	0-1	0-2	0-0	1-0	1-1	0-2	0-0	0-0	1-1	4-9
Castillo	0-1	0-1	2-0	1-1	0-1	1-1	0-0	0-1	1-1	0-0	1-0	6-7
Harkey	0-0	0-1	0-0	0-0	0-0	0-0	0-0	0-0	0-1	0-0	0-0	0-2
Jackson	0-0	0-0	0-0	0-2	0-0	1-0	0-1	0-0	0-1	1-1	0-0	1-5
Lancaster	1-1	1-0	1-0	0-0	1-1	2-0	0-3	1-1	1-0	1-0	0-1	9-7
Maddux	1-0	0-1	3-0	0-0	0-1	4-1	3-0	0-2	2-1	1-3	1-2	15-11
McElroy	1-0	0-1	0-0	1-1	1-0	0-0	0-0	1-0	1-0	1-0	0-0	6-2
Perez	0-0	0-0	0-0	0-0	0-0	0-0	0-0	0-0	1-0	0-0	0-0	1-0
Renfroe	0-0	0-0	0-0	0-0	0-0	0-0	0-0	0-0	0-1	0-0	0-0	0-1
Scanlan	0-1	0-0	1-1	0-0	2-2	2-1	0-0	1-0	1-1	0-2	0-0	7-8
Slocumb	0-0	1-1	0-0	0-0	0-0	0-0	0-0	1-0	0-0	0-0	0-0	2-1
Da. Smith	0-0	0-0	0-1	0-0	0-0	0-0	0-0	0-2	0-1	0-0	0-2	0-6
Sutcliffe	0-1	1-1	0-0	0-0	1-1	0-1	1-0	2-0	1-1	0-0	0-0	6-5
Totals	6-6	4-8	9-3	2-10	10-7	11-6	8-10	7-11	10-8	4-8	6-6	77-83

No-decisions—Dascenzo, S. May, Pavlas, Wilson.

CINCINNATI—74-88

Pitcher	Atl. W-L	Chi. W-L	Hou. W-L	L.A. W-L	Mon. W-L	N.Y. W-L	Phi. W-L	Pit. W-L	St.L. W-L	S.D. W-L	S.F. W-L	Totals W-L
Armstrong	2-2	1-0	1-1	0-1	0-2	0-0	0-1	0-1	1-1	1-1	1-3	7-13
Browning	1-1	1-1	2-2	1-3	1-1	2-0	2-1	1-2	1-1	0-2	2-0	14-14
Carman	0-0	0-0	0-1	0-0	0-1	0-0	0-0	0-0	0-0	0-0	0-0	0-2
Charlton	0-0	0-1	0-1	0-1	1-0	0-0	0-0	0-1	1-0	1-1	0-0	3-5
Dibble	0-1	1-0	0-1	1-1	0-0	0-1	0-0	0-0	0-1	0-0	1-0	3-5
Gross	1-0	0-0	0-0	0-1	0-0	1-0	1-0	1-1	1-0	0-1	1-1	6-4
Hammond	0-0	1-0	3-0	0-1	1-0	0-1	0-1	0-2	0-1	2-0	0-1	7-7
Hill	1-0	0-0	0-0	0-1	0-0	0-0	0-0	0-0	0-0	0-0	0-0	1-1
Layana	0-1	0-1	0-0	0-0	0-0	0-0	0-0	0-0	0-0	0-0	0-0	0-2
Minutelli	0-0	0-0	0-0	0-0	0-0	0-0	0-0	0-0	0-1	0-1	0-0	0-2
Myers	0-1	0-1	0-1	1-1	1-1	0-3	2-0	0-2	0-2	1-0	1-1	6-13
Power	0-1	1-0	1-0	0-1	0-0	1-0	0-0	0-0	0-0	1-1	1-0	5-3
Rijo	2-1	3-0	1-1	2-0	1-0	1-0	3-0	0-1	0-0	0-2	2-1	15-6
Sanford	0-1	0-0	0-0	0-1	0-0	0-0	0-0	0-0	0-0	1-0	0-0	1-2
Scudder	0-2	0-0	1-1	1-0	1-1	0-2	1-0	0-0	0-1	1-1	1-1	6-9
Totals	7-11	8-4	9-9	6-12	6-6	5-7	9-3	2-10	4-8	8-10	10-8	74-88

No-decisions—Brown, Foster.

HOUSTON—65-97

Pitcher	Atl. W-L	Chi. W-L	Cin. W-L	L.A. W-L	Mon. W-L	N.Y. W-L	Phi. W-L	Pit. W-L	St.L. W-L	S.D. W-L	S.F. W-L	Totals W-L
Bowen	0-0	0-0	1-1	0-0	1-0	1-0	0-1	1-0	0-1	1-1	1-0	6-4
Capel	0-0	0-1	0-0	0-0	0-0	1-1	0-0	0-0	0-0	0-1	0-0	1-3
Clancy	0-1	0-1	0-0	0-0	0-0	0-0	0-0	0-1	0-0	0-0	0-0	0-3
Corsi	0-1	0-0	0-1	0-2	0-1	0-0	0-0	0-0	0-0	0-0	0-0	0-5
Deshaies	0-2	0-2	0-1	1-1	0-2	1-0	0-0	0-0	2-1	0-2	1-1	5-12
Gardner	0-0	0-0	0-1	0-0	0-0	0-0	0-0	0-0	0-0	0-1	1-0	1-2
Harnisch	2-1	2-0	1-2	2-1	0-2	1-0	1-0	0-2	0-1	1-0	2-0	12-9
Henry	0-0	0-0	2-0	0-1	0-0	0-1	0-0	0-0	0-0	1-0	0-0	3-2
Hernandez	0-2	0-1	2-0	0-2	0-0	0-0	0-0	0-0	0-1	0-1	0-0	2-7
Jones	1-0	0-0	1-0	1-0	0-1	0-1	0-1	2-2	0-0	0-1	1-2	6-8
Juden	0-1	0-0	0-1	0-0	0-0	0-0	0-0	0-0	0-0	0-0	0-0	0-2
Kile	0-1	0-2	1-1	0-0	0-1	1-0	2-1	0-2	1-0	1-0	1-3	7-11
Mallicoat	0-1	0-0	0-0	0-1	0-0	0-0	0-0	0-0	0-0	0-0	0-0	0-2

MISCELLANEOUS

Pitcher	Atl. W-L	Chi. W-L	Cin. W-L	L.A. W-L	Mon. W-L	N.Y. W-L	Phi. W-L	Pit. W-L	St.L. W-L	S.D. W-L	S.F. W-L	Totals W-L
Osuna	1-0	1-0	0-0	1-1	0-1	0-0	3-1	0-0	1-2	0-1	0-0	7-6
Portugal	1-3	0-2	1-0	1-1	0-1	1-1	1-1	1-0	1-0	1-2	2-1	10-12
Schilling	0-0	0-0	0-0	0-0	1-1	1-1	0-0	0-1	0-1	1-0	0-1	3-5
Scott	0-0	0-0	0-1	0-0	0-0	0-0	0-0	0-0	0-0	0-0	0-1	0-2
Wilkins	0-0	0-0	0-0	2-0	0-0	0-0	0-0	0-0	0-0	0-1	0-0	2-1
Williams	0-0	0-0	0-0	0-0	0-0	0-0	0-0	0-0	0-0	0-1	0-0	0-1
Totals	5-13	3-9	9-9	8-10	2-10	7-5	7-5	4-8	5-7	6-12	9-9	65-97

LOS ANGELES—93-69

Pitcher	Atl. W-L	Chi. W-L	Cin. W-L	Hou. W-L	Mon. W-L	N.Y. W-L	Phi. W-L	Pit. W-L	St.L. W-L	S.D. W-L	S.F. W-L	Totals W-L
Belcher	1-2	1-0	2-0	2-0	0-2	0-2	0-1	1-0	0-1	0-1	3-0	10-9
Candelaria	0-0	0-0	0-0	0-0	0-0	0-0	1-1	0-0	0-0	0-0	0-0	1-1
Cook	0-0	0-0	0-0	0-0	0-0	0-0	0-0	0-0	0-0	1-0	0-0	1-0
Crews	0-0	0-0	0-0	0-0	1-0	1-0	0-1	0-0	0-1	0-0	0-1	2-3
Gott	0-1	1-0	0-0	0-0	0-0	1-0	0-0	1-0	0-1	0-1	1-0	4-3
Gross	0-1	0-1	2-0	2-2	1-1	2-0	0-0	1-1	0-0	1-3	1-2	10-11
Hartley	1-0	1-0	0-0	0-0	0-0	0-0	0-0	0-0	0-0	0-0	0-0	2-0
Hershiser	2-0	1-0	1-0	1-1	0-0	0-0	0-0	0-0	0-0	2-0	0-1	7-2
Howell	0-0	1-0	0-1	1-2	1-0	0-0	1-1	0-0	2-1	0-0	0-0	6-5
Martinez	3-1	2-1	1-3	0-1	1-1	3-1	2-0	0-0	1-1	3-0	1-4	17-13
McDowell	1-1	1-0	1-1	1-0	0-0	0-0	0-0	1-1	1-0	0-0	0-0	6-3
Morgan	3-0	2-0	1-0	2-2	0-2	0-1	2-0	2-2	0-1	2-1	0-1	14-10
Ojeda	0-1	0-0	3-1	1-0	1-1	0-1	1-1	1-1	2-0	2-2	1-1	12-9
Wetteland	0-0	0-0	1-0	0-0	0-0	0-0	0-0	0-0	0-0	0-0	0-0	1-0
Totals	11-7	10-2	12-6	10-8	5-7	7-5	7-5	7-5	6-6	10-8	8-10	93-69

No-decisions—Christopher, Wilson.

MONTREAL—71-90

Pitcher	Atl. W-L	Chi. W-L	Cin. W-L	Hou. W-L	L.A. W-L	N.Y. W-L	Phi. W-L	Pit. W-L	St.L. W-L	S.D. W-L	S.F. W-L	Totals W-L
Barnes	0-1	1-0	0-2	0-0	1-0	1-0	0-2	0-1	1-1	1-1	0-0	5-8
Boyd	1-0	0-0	1-0	0-0	1-1	0-2	0-2	0-2	0-1	1-0	2-0	6-8
Burke	0-1	0-1	0-0	0-0	0-0	1-1	0-0	0-0	1-1	1-0	0-0	3-4
Darling	0-0	0-0	0-0	0-0	0-0	0-0	0-0	0-0	0-0	0-0	0-2	0-2
Fassero	0-0	0-1	0-0	2-0	0-0	0-0	0-2	0-1	0-0	0-1	0-0	2-5
Frey	0-0	0-0	0-0	0-0	0-0	0-0	0-0	0-1	0-0	0-0	0-0	0-1
Gardner	1-1	1-1	0-0	4-0	1-2	0-3	0-1	1-0	1-2	0-0	0-1	9-11
Haney	0-0	1-0	1-1	0-0	0-1	0-2	0-0	0-1	0-2	1-0	0-0	3-7
Jones	0-0	0-2	1-0	0-1	0-1	0-2	0-1	1-0	0-1	0-1	2-0	4-9
Mahler	0-0	0-1	0-0	0-0	0-0	0-1	0-0	0-0	1-1	0-0	0-0	1-3
De. Martinez	2-0	1-1	1-1	1-1	2-0	1-1	1-2	2-2	1-1	1-1	1-1	14-11
Nabholz	0-1	0-1	1-1	1-0	1-0	1-2	2-0	1-1	1-1	0-0	0-0	8-7
Rojas	1-0	1-0	0-0	1-0	0-0	0-0	0-1	0-0	0-0	0-1	0-1	3-3
Ruskin	0-0	0-1	1-0	0-0	1-0	0-0	0-2	1-1	0-0	0-0	1-0	4-4
Sampen	2-1	2-1	0-1	1-0	0-0	0-0	1-0	0-2	1-0	1-0	1-0	9-5
Schmidt	0-0	0-0	0-0	0-0	0-0	0-0	0-0	0-0	0-0	0-1	0-0	0-1
Wainhouse	0-0	0-0	0-0	0-0	0-0	0-0	0-1	0-0	0-0	0-0	0-0	0-1
Totals	7-5	7-10	6-6	10-2	7-5	4-14	4-14	6-12	7-11	6-6	7-5	71-90

No-decisions—Long, Piatt.

NEW YORK—77-84

Pitcher	Atl. W-L	Chi. W-L	Cin. W-L	Hou. W-L	L.A. W-L	Mon. W-L	Phi. W-L	Pit. W-L	St.L. W-L	S.D. W-L	S.F. W-L	Totals W-L
Burke	0-0	0-2	0-0	0-0	1-1	0-0	0-0	1-0	1-0	0-0	0-0	3-3
Castillo	0-0	1-0	0-0	0-0	0-0	0-0	0-0	0-0	0-0	0-0	0-0	1-0
Cone	0-0	1-2	3-1	0-2	1-2	2-1	2-0	1-2	2-2	1-1	1-1	14-14
Darling	1-1	0-0	1-0	0-0	0-0	1-0	1-1	0-2	0-1	0-1	1-0	5-6
Fernandez	0-0	0-0	0-0	0-0	0-0	0-0	0-0	0-2	1-0	0-1	0-0	1-3
Franco	0-1	0-1	1-0	1-2	0-1	0-1	0-1	1-0	0-2	1-0	1-0	5-9
Gooden	1-0	1-0	0-1	1-0	1-0	1-1	2-1	1-1	1-1	3-0	1-2	13-7
Innis	0-0	0-0	0-0	0-0	0-0	0-0	0-1	0-1	0-0	0-0	0-0	0-2
Pena	0-0	1-1	1-0	1-0	0-0	2-0	0-0	0-0	0-0	0-0	1-0	6-1
Schourek	0-0	0-2	0-0	0-0	0-1	1-0	2-0	0-0	1-1	0-0	1-0	5-4
Simons	0-0	0-0	0-0	1-0	0-1	0-0	1-1	0-1	1-0	0-0	0-0	2-3
Viola	1-3	1-3	0-2	0-2	2-0	4-0	2-0	2-1	0-1	1-2	0-1	13-15
Whitehurst	0-3	0-0	1-1	0-1	0-1	3-0	1-0	0-2	1-2	1-0	0-2	7-12
Young	0-1	1-0	0-0	1-0	0-0	0-1	0-2	0-0	0-1	0-0	0-0	2-5
Totals	3-9	6-11	7-5	5-7	5-7	14-4	11-7	6-12	7-11	7-5	6-6	77-84

No-decisions—Beatty, Bross, Sauveur, Valera.

PHILADELPHIA—78-84

Pitcher	Atl. W-L	Chi. W-L	Cin. W-L	Hou. W-L	L.A. W-L	Mon. W-L	N.Y. W-L	Pit. W-L	St.L. W-L	S.D. W-L	S.F. W-L	Totals W-L
Akerfelds	1-0	0-0	0-0	0-0	0-0	0-0	0-1	0-0	0-0	1-0	0-0	2-1
Ashby	0-0	1-0	0-2	0-0	0-0	0-0	0-1	0-1	0-1	0-0	0-0	1-5
Boever	0-0	1-0	0-0	0-1	0-2	0-0	0-1	0-1	0-0	0-0	2-0	3-5
Brantley	0-0	0-0	0-1	0-0	0-0	0-0	1-0	0-1	1-0	0-0	0-0	2-2
Combs	0-1	0-1	0-0	0-0	0-1	1-1	0-0	0-1	1-1	0-0	0-0	2-6
Cox	0-0	1-0	0-0	1-1	0-1	0-0	1-1	0-1	0-0	1-0	0-2	4-6
DeJesus	2-0	0-1	1-0	1-2	1-0	1-0	1-1	1-1	0-2	2-2	0-0	10-9
Greene	1-1	2-0	1-1	0-0	1-0	3-0	0-1	2-1	1-2	0-0	2-1	13-7
Grimsley	0-0	0-1	0-0	0-0	0-0	0-1	0-1	0-2	0-1	1-0	0-1	1-7
Hartley	0-0	0-0	0-1	1-0	0-0	1-0	0-0	0-0	0-0	0-0	0-0	2-1
LaPoint	0-0	0-0	0-0	0-0	0-0	0-0	0-0	0-0	0-1	0-0	0-0	0-1
McDowell	0-0	0-1	0-1	0-2	0-1	0-0	2-0	0-0	1-1	0-0	0-0	3-6
Mulholland	0-3	1-1	1-2	1-0	2-0	4-0	1-3	0-1	2-1	2-1	2-1	16-13
Ritchie	0-0	1-0	0-0	0-0	0-0	0-1	0-0	0-0	0-0	0-0	0-1	1-2
Ruffin	0-0	1-1	0-1	1-1	0-1	0-1	0-1	0-0	0-1	2-0	0-0	4-7
Searcy	0-0	0-0	0-0	0-0	1-1	0-0	0-0	1-0	0-0	0-0	0-0	2-1
Williams	3-0	2-2	0-0	0-0	0-0	4-0	1-0	2-2	0-1	0-0	0-0	12-5
Totals	7-5	10-8	3-9	5-7	5-7	14-4	7-11	6-12	6-12	9-3	6-6	78-84

No-decisions—Carreno, Mauser.

PITTSBURGH—98-64

Pitcher	Atl. W-L	Chi. W-L	Cin. W-L	Hou. W-L	L.A. W-L	Mon. W-L	N.Y. W-L	Phi. W-L	St.L. W-L	S.D. W-L	S.F. W-L	Totals W-L
Belinda	0-0	2-2	1-0	0-0	0-1	0-0	0-0	1-1	2-1	0-0	1-0	7-5
Drabek	1-2	2-2	1-1	1-2	1-2	2-2	1-1	2-0	1-2	2-0	1-0	15-14
Heaton	0-0	0-0	0-0	1-0	0-0	1-0	0-0	0-1	1-0	0-1	0-1	3-3
Kipper	0-0	0-0	0-0	1-0	0-0	1-0	0-1	0-1	0-0	0-0	0-0	2-2
Landrum	0-1	0-1	0-0	0-0	0-0	0-0	2-0	0-1	0-0	2-1	0-0	4-4
Mason	0-0	0-0	0-0	0-0	1-0	0-1	0-1	0-0	2-0	0-0	0-0	3-2
Palacios	0-3	1-0	2-0	0-0	0-0	1-0	0-0	1-0	0-0	1-0	0-0	6-3
Patterson	0-0	1-0	0-0	0-0	0-1	0-0	1-1	0-0	1-1	0-0	1-0	4-3
Rodriguez	0-0	0-0	0-0	0-0	1-0	0-1	0-0	0-0	0-0	0-0	0-0	1-1
Smiley	2-1	1-1	2-0	0-1	0-1	3-1	3-0	4-0	2-1	1-0	2-2	20-8
Smith	0-2	3-0	1-0	3-1	1-1	2-0	1-2	2-0	2-0	1-2	0-2	16-10
Tomlin	0-0	0-1	2-0	2-0	0-1	0-0	4-0	0-2	0-2	0-1	0-0	8-7
Walk	0-0	1-0	1-1	0-0	1-0	2-1	0-0	2-0	0-0	0-0	2-0	9-2
Totals	3-9	11-7	10-2	8-4	5-7	12-6	12-6	12-6	11-7	7-5	7-5	98-64

No-decisions—Fajardo, Huismann, Miller, Reed.

ST. LOUIS—84-78

Pitcher	Atl. W-L	Chi. W-L	Cin. W-L	Hou. W-L	L.A. W-L	Mon. W-L	N.Y. W-L	Phi. W-L	Pit. W-L	S.D. W-L	S.F. W-L	Totals W-L
Agosto	0-0	1-1	0-0	1-0	0-0	0-0	1-1	0-0	0-0	1-1	1-0	5-3
Carpenter	1-0	0-0	1-0	1-1	1-0	1-0	2-0	0-1	1-0	0-2	2-0	10-4
Clark	0-0	0-0	0-0	0-0	0-0	1-1	0-0	0-0	0-0	0-0	0-0	1-1
Cormier	0-0	0-0	0-0	0-0	1-0	1-1	2-2	0-1	0-0	0-0	0-1	4-5
DeLeon	0-1	0-4	1-0	1-1	0-0	0-1	0-0	1-0	1-1	0-0	1-1	5-9
Fraser	0-0	1-1	0-0	0-0	1-0	0-0	0-1	0-0	0-1	0-0	0-0	3-3
Hill	0-3	2-0	1-0	1-0	0-2	1-1	2-0	2-1	1-2	1-1	0-0	11-10
McClure	0-0	0-0	0-0	0-0	0-0	0-0	0-0	0-0	1-0	0-0	0-0	1-1
Moyer	0-0	0-0	0-2	0-0	0-0	0-1	0-0	0-1	0-1	0-0	0-0	0-5
Olivares	0-1	1-1	1-1	0-0	1-0	3-1	2-0	2-0	1-1	0-1	0-1	11-7
Perez	0-1	0-0	0-0	0-0	0-0	0-1	0-0	0-0	0-0	0-0	0-0	0-2
B. Smith	0-2	1-2	1-0	2-1	1-1	2-0	1-1	3-0	1-1	0-0	0-1	12-9
L. Smith	2-0	0-0	0-1	1-1	1-0	0-0	0-0	1-0	1-1	0-0	0-0	6-3
Terry	0-0	0-0	0-0	0-0	0-2	1-0	0-0	1-0	0-0	0-2	2-0	4-4
Tewksbury	0-1	2-1	2-0	0-1	0-0	1-0	1-2	2-2	0-3	1-2	2-0	11-12
Totals	3-9	8-10	8-4	7-5	6-6	11-7	11-7	12-6	7-11	3-9	8-4	84-78

No-decisions—Grater, Oquendo, Sherrill.

SAN DIEGO—84-78

Pitcher	Atl. W-L	Chi. W-L	Cin. W-L	Hou. W-L	L.A. W-L	Mon. W-L	N.Y. W-L	Phi. W-L	Pit. W-L	St.L. W-L	S.F. W-L	Totals W-L
Andersen	0-0	0-0	0-0	0-1	1-1	1-0	0-1	0-0	1-0	0-1	0-0	3-4
Benes	2-1	3-1	2-2	2-1	1-2	0-2	2-0	0-1	1-0	1-0	1-1	15-11
Bones	0-2	0-0	1-1	0-0	0-2	0-0	0-0	0-0	1-1	1-0	1-0	4-6
Clements	0-0	0-0	0-0	0-0	0-0	0-0	0-0	0-0	0-0	0-0	1-0	1-0
Costello	0-0	0-0	0-0	0-0	0-0	0-0	0-0	0-0	0-0	1-0	0-0	1-0
Gardner	0-0	0-0	0-0	0-0	0-0	0-1	0-0	0-0	0-0	0-0	0-0	0-1
Hammaker	0-0	0-0	0-0	0-0	0-0	0-0	0-0	0-0	0-0	0-1	0-0	0-1

Pitcher	Atl. W-L	Chi. W-L	Cin. W-L	Hou. W-L	L.A. W-L	Mon. W-L	N.Y. W-L	Phi. W-L	Pit. W-L	St.L. W-L	S.F. W-L	Totals W-L
Harris	1-1	0-0	2-1	1-0	2-1	0-0	1-0	0-2	0-0	1-0	1-0	9-5
Hurst	2-3	0-0	0-1	2-1	0-1	1-0	2-0	3-0	0-2	3-0	2-0	15-8
Lefferts	0-2	0-1	0-0	0-0	0-0	0-0	0-0	0-0	1-1	0-0	0-2	1-6
Lilliquist	0-0	0-0	0-0	0-0	0-0	0-0	0-1	0-1	0-0	0-0	0-0	0-2
Maddux	0-0	1-0	2-0	0-1	0-0	1-0	0-0	0-1	1-0	1-0	1-0	7-2
Melendez	0-0	1-2	2-1	2-0	1-0	1-0	0-0	0-0	0-1	1-1	0-0	8-5
Nolte	0-0	0-0	0-0	0-0	2-0	0-0	0-1	0-1	0-0	0-0	1-0	3-2
Peterson	0-0	0-0	1-0	1-1	0-0	0-1	0-2	0-0	0-0	1-0	0-0	3-4
Rasmussen	0-1	3-0	0-2	3-0	0-2	0-1	0-1	0-2	0-2	0-0	0-2	6-13
Rodriguez	0-0	0-0	0-0	1-0	0-0	1-1	0-0	0-0	0-0	0-0	1-0	3-1
Rosenberg	1-1	0-0	0-0	0-0	0-0	0-0	0-0	0-0	0-0	0-0	0-0	1-1
Whitson	1-0	0-0	0-0	0-1	1-1	1-0	0-1	0-1	0-0	0-0	1-2	4-6
Totals	7-11	8-4	10-8	12-6	8-10	6-6	5-7	3-9	5-7	9-3	11-7	84-78

No-decisions—Hernandez, Jackson, Lewis, Scott.

SAN FRANCISCO—75-87

Pitcher	Atl. W-L	Chi. W-L	Cin. W-L	Hou. W-L	L.A. W-L	Mon. W-L	N.Y. W-L	Phi. W-L	Pit. W-L	St.L. W-L	S.D. W-L	Totals W-L
Beck	0-0	0-0	0-0	1-0	0-0	0-0	0-0	0-1	0-0	0-0	0-0	1-1
Black	3-3	0-0	0-3	1-2	1-3	0-0	3-0	2-1	1-2	1-1	0-1	12-16
Brantley	0-0	1-0	0-1	1-0	2-0	0-0	0-0	0-1	0-0	0-0	1-0	5-2
Burkett	1-2	0-0	1-1	3-2	0-1	1-1	1-0	0-0	1-1	1-2	3-1	12-11
Downs	1-1	2-0	0-0	1-0	3-0	1-0	0-1	2-1	0-1	0-0	0-0	10-4
Garrelts	0-0	0-0	0-0	1-0	0-0	0-0	0-0	0-0	0-0	0-0	0-1	1-1
Heredia	0-0	0-0	0-0	0-1	0-0	0-0	0-0	0-0	0-0	0-0	0-1	0-2
Hickerson	0-0	0-1	1-0	0-0	0-0	0-0	0-0	0-0	1-0	0-0	0-1	2-2
LaCoss	0-0	0-0	0-0	0-0	1-1	0-2	0-1	0-1	0-0	0-0	0-0	1-5
McClellan	0-1	0-2	2-1	0-0	0-0	0-0	1-0	0-0	0-0	0-1	0-1	3-6
Oliveras	1-0	1-1	2-0	0-0	0-0	0-1	0-0	1-0	1-2	0-1	0-1	6-6
Remlinger	0-0	0-0	0-0	0-0	1-0	0-0	0-0	1-0	0-0	0-0	0-1	2-1
Reuschel	0-0	0-0	0-0	0-1	0-1	0-0	0-0	0-0	0-0	0-0	0-0	0-2
Righetti	0-1	0-0	0-1	1-0	0-1	0-0	0-2	0-0	0-1	0-1	1-0	2-7
Robinson	1-1	0-1	0-2	0-0	0-0	1-2	1-1	0-0	0-0	1-1	1-1	5-9
Segura	0-0	0-0	0-0	0-0	0-0	0-0	0-0	0-1	0-0	0-0	0-0	0-1
Wilson	2-0	2-1	2-1	0-2	2-0	2-1	1-1	0-1	1-0	0-1	1-3	13-11
Totals	9-9	6-6	8-10	9-9	10-8	5-7	6-6	6-6	5-7	4-8	7-11	75-87

No-decisions—Gunderson, Litton.

HOME RUNS BY PARKS

	At Atl.	At Chi.	At Cin.	At Hou.	At L.A.	At Mon.	At N.Y.	At Phi.	At Pit.	At St.L.	At S.D.	At S.F.	Totals 1991	1990
Atlanta	83	4	7	3	5	2	6	4	7	4	7	9	141	162
Chicago	8	93	8	4	3	1	9	4	10	6	7	6	159	136
Cincinnati	9	9	104	1	8	3	5	5	3	1	7	9	164	125
Houston	6	5	8	27	8	1	3	3	3	3	5	7	79	94
Los Angeles	6	4	2	11	57	2	8	3	2	2	9	2	108	129
Montreal	9	11	7	3	2	35	2	7	7	3	4	5	95	114
New York	5	4	9	2	3	5	57	6	9	8	5	4	117	172
Philadelphia	4	12	6	0	1	4	8	61	2	3	6	4	111	103
Pittsburgh	6	15	9	6	3	5	3	3	61	3	5	4	126	138
St. Louis	2	2	6	4	1	2	1	6	4	32	3	5	68	73
San Diego	10	7	3	4	5	5	2	6	3	3	65	7	121	123
San Francisco	8	2	12	6	7	4	5	7	2	5	14	69	141	152
1991 total	156	168	181	71	103	68	112	114	116	73	137	131	1430	....
1990 total	155	148	143	82	127	110	138	114	122	90	141	151	....	1521

AT ATLANTA (156):

Atlanta (83)—Gant 18, Pendleton 13, Justice 11, Blauser 7, Hunter 7, Olson 6, L. Smith 6, Bream 3, Cabrera 2, Lemke 2, Sanders 2, Bell 1, Gregg 1, Heath 1, Mitchell 1, Treadway 1, Willard 1. **Chicago (8)**—Bell 2, Sandberg 2, Dascenzo 1, Grace 1, Salazar 1, Wilkins 1. **Cincinnati (9)**—Oliver 3, Sabo 2, Doran 1, Duncan 1, Larkin 1, Sanders 1. **Houston (6)**—Bagwell 2, Biggio 1, Caminiti 1, Cedeno 1, Simms 1. **Los Angeles (6)**—Daniels 1, Gwynn 1, Javier 1, Murray 1, Samuel 1, Strawberry 1. **Montreal (9)**—Wallach 3, Calderon 2, Walker 2, DeShields 1, Da. Martinez 1. **New York (5)**—Brooks 2, Jefferies 2, Gooden 1. **Philadelphia (4)**—C. Hayes 2, Jordan 1, Kruk 1. **Pittsburgh (6)**—McClendon 2, Bonds 1, Bonilla 1, LaValliere 1, Redus 1. **St. Louis (2)**—Gilkey 1, Pena 1. **San Diego (10)**—Jackson 3, Gwynn 2, McGriff 2, Fernandez 1, Santiago 1, Teufel 1. **San Francisco (8)**—Bass 3, Benjamin 1, Clark 1, Lewis 1, Thompson 1, Williams 1.

AT CHICAGO (168):

Atlanta (4)—Pendleton 2, Gant 1, Hunter 1. **Chicago (93)**—Dawson 22, Sandberg 15, Villanueva 11, Bell 9, Salazar 8, Dunston 7, Grace 5, Walker 4, Berryhill 3, Walton 3, Dw. Smith 2, Wilkins 2, D. May 1, Scott 1. **Cincinnati (9)**—Davis 2, O'Neill 2, Sabo 2, Hatcher 1, Morris 1, Reed 1. **Houston (5)**—Gonzalez 3, Finley 1, Rhodes 1. **Los Angeles (4)**—Daniels 2, Harris 1, Samuel 1. **Mont-**

real (11)—DeShields 2, Da. Martinez 2, Calderon 1, Fitzgerald 1, Galarraga 1, Noboa 1, Santovenia 1, Vanderwal 1, Walker 1. **New York (4)**—Brooks 2, Johnson 2. **Philadelphia (12)**—Daulton 3, Kruk 3, Murphy 3, Chamberlain 2, C. Hayes 1. **Pittsburgh (15)**—Merced 3, Van Slyke 3, Bonilla 2, McClendon 2, Varsho 2, Bell 1, Bonds 1, Walk 1. **St. Louis (2)**—Gilkey 2. **San Diego (7)**—Fernandez 2, Jackson 2, McGriff 1, Santiago 1, Teufel 1. **San Francisco (2)**—Mitchell 1, Williams 1.

AT CINCINNATI (181):

Atlanta (7)—Cabrera 2, Pendleton 2, Bream 1, Hunter 1, Justice 1. **Chicago (8)**—Bell 3, Dunston 2, Boskie 1, Dawson 1, Salazar 1. **Cincinnati (104)**—O'Neill 20, Larkin 16, Sabo 15, Duncan 10, Morris 9, Braggs 8, Oliver 7, Davis 5, Doran 3, Hatcher 2, Martinez 2, Quinones 2, Benzinger 1, R. Jefferson 1, Reed 1, Scudder 1, Winningham 1. **Houston (8)**—Bagwell 2, Biggio 2, Gonzalez 2, Candaele 1, Ramirez 1. **Los Angeles (2)**—Harris 1, Strawberry 1. **Montreal (7)**—Wallach 3, Calderon 2, Da. Martinez 1, Walker 1. **New York (9)**—Johnson 3, Brooks 1, Coleman 1, Jefferies 1, McReynolds 1, Miller 1, O'Brien 1. **Philadelphia (6)**—Murphy 2, Daulton 1, C. Hayes 1, Kruk 1, Thon 1. **Pittsburgh (9)**—Bonds 3, Bonilla 3, Bell 1, Lind 1, Van Slyke 1. **St. Louis (6)**—Perry 2, Gedman 1, Oquendo 1, Pena 1, Zeile 1. **San Diego (3)**—McGriff 2, Shipley 1. **San Francisco (12)**—Mitchell 3, Williams 3, Bass 2, Clark 2, Thompson 1, Uribe 1.

AT HOUSTON (71):

Atlanta (3)—Blauser 1, Bream 1, Justice 1. **Chicago (4)**—Bell 3, Berryhill 1. **Cincinnati (1)**—Braggs 1. **Houston (27)**—Caminiti 9, Bagwell 6, Cedeno 4, Gonzalez 4, Candaele 1, Davidson 1, Simms 1, Tolentino 1. **Los Angeles (11)**—Strawberry 6, Murray 2, Scioscia 2, Daniels 1. **Montreal (3)**—DeShields 2, Grissom 1. **New York (2)**—Brooks 1, Johnson 1. **Philadelphia—None. Pittsburgh (6)**—Bell 4, Bonilla 1, Van Slyke 1. **St. Louis (4)**—Jose 1, Lankford 1, Perry 1, Thompson 1. **San Diego (4)**—McGriff 2, Coolbaugh 1, Teufel 1. **San Francisco (6)**—Mitchell 3, Clark 1, Thompson 1, Williams 1.

AT LOS ANGELES (103):

Atlanta (5)—Blauser 1, Gant 1, Justice 1, Sanders 1, Treadway 1. **Chicago (3)**—Dawson 1, Dunston 1, Sandberg 1. **Cincinnati (8)**—O'Neill 2, Braggs 1, Davis 1, Jones 1, Martinez 1, Quinones 1, Sabo 1. **Houston (8)**—Finley 3, Bagwell 1, Cedeno 1, Gonzalez 1, Ortiz 1, Simms 1. **Los Angeles (57)**—Strawberry 14, Daniels 12, Murray 11, Samuel 4, Carter 3, Gwynn 3, Scioscia 3, Butler 2, Hamilton 1, Harris 1, Martinez 1, Sharperson 1, Webster 1. **Montreal (2)**—DeShields 1, Galarraga 1. **New York (3)**—McReynolds 2, Johnson 1. **Philadelphia (1)**—Murphy 1. **Pittsburgh (3)**—Redus 2, Bonds 1. **St. Louis (1)**—Lankford 1. **San Diego (5)**—Howell 3, Santiago 2. **San Francisco (7)**—Clark 2, McGee 2, Williams 2, Mitchell 1.

AT MONTREAL (68):

Atlanta (2)—Bream 1, Gant 1. **Chicago (1)**—Grace 1. **Cincinnati (3)**—Sabo 2, Reed 1. **Houston (1)**—Young 1. **Los Angeles (2)**—Carter 1, Ojeda 1. **Montreal (35)**—Calderon 7, Walker 5, Wallach 5, DeShields 3, Galarraga 3, Grissom 3, Da. Martinez 3, Barberie 2, Bullock 1, Fitzgerald 1, Owen 1, Santovenia 1. **New York (5)**—Elster 2, Johnson 2, Jefferies 1. **Philadelphia (4)**—Thon 2, Chamberlain 1, Murphy 1. **Pittsburgh (5)**—Bonds 2, Bell 1, Bonilla 1, Van Slyke 1. **St. Louis (2)**—Guerrero 2. **San Diego (4)**—McGriff 2, Presley 1, Santiago 1. **San Francisco (4)**—Mitchell 2, Thompson 1, Williams 1.

AT NEW YORK (112):

Atlanta (6)—Hunter 2, Justice 2, Bream 1, Pendleton 1. **Chicago (9)**—Sandberg 2, Bell 1, Berryhill 1, Dawson 1, Dunston 1, Salazar 1, Villanueva 1, Walker 1. **Cincinnati (5)**—O'Neill 2, Duncan 1, Larkin 1. **Houston (3)**—Bagwell 1, Biggio 1, Mota 1. **Los Angeles (8)**—Strawberry 3, Murray 2, Carter 1, Gwynn 1, Hansen 1. **Montreal (2)**—Walker 1, Wallach 1. **New York (57)**—Johnson 21, McReynolds 7, Jefferies 5, Brooks 4, Carreon 3, Elster 3, Sasser 3, Boston 2, Magadan 2, Miller 2, Cerone 1, Hundley 1, O'Brien 1, Templeton 1, Teufel 1. **Philadelphia (8)**—Kruk 2, Campusano 1, Chamberlain 1, C. Hayes 1, Lake 1, Murphy 1, Thon 1. **Pittsburgh (3)**—Bonilla 1, Buechele 1, McClendon 1. **St. Louis (1)**—Jose 1. **San Diego (5)**—McGriff 2, Santiago 2, Jackson 1. **San Francisco (5)**—Mitchell 2, Williams 2, Clark 1.

AT PHILADELPHIA (114):

Atlanta (4)—Justice 2, Gant 1, Pendleton 1. **Chicago (4)**—Sandberg 2, Salazar 1, Dw. Smith 1. **Cincinnati (5)**—Larkin 2, Braggs 1, Morris 1, Sabo 1. **Houston (3)**—Anthony 1, Caminiti 1, Finley 1. **Los Angeles (3)**—Samuel 2, Murray 1. **Montreal (7)**—Calderon 3, Walker 2, Fitzgerald 1, Galarraga 1. **New York (6)**—Boston 2, McReynolds 2, Brooks 1, Miller 1. **Philadelphia (61)**—Chamberlain 9, Murphy 9, Daulton 8, Kruk 8, C. Hayes 6, Jordan 5, Thon 4, Dykstra 3, Hollins 3, Greene 2, Fletcher 1, Morandini 1, Morris 1, Ready 1. **Pittsburgh (6)**—Bonds 2, King 1, Merced 1, Van Slyke 1, Varsho 1. **St. Louis (6)**—Guerrero 2, Jose 1, Lankford 1, Perry 1, Zeile 1. **San Diego (2)**—Benes 1, Clark 1. **San Francisco (7)**—Williams 3, Clark 2, Anderson 1, Mitchell 1.

AT PITTSBURGH (116):

Atlanta (7)—Gant 2, Bream 1, Hunter 1, Justice 1, Pendleton 1, Treadway 1. **Chicago (10)**—Wilkins 3, Bell 2, Dawson 2, Salazar 1, Sandberg 1, Villanueva 1. **Cincinnati (3)**—Davis 2, Hatcher 1. **Houston (3)**—Bagwell 1, Davidson 1, Finley 1. **Los Angeles (2)**—Daniels 1, Scioscia 1. **Montreal (7)**—Galarraga 2, Calderon 1, DeShields 1, Fitzgerald 1, Hassey 1, Owen 1. **New York (9)**—Johnson 3, Brooks 1, Carreon 1, Cerone 1, Elster 1, McReynolds 1, Sasser 1. **Philadelphia (2)**—Kruk 1, Thon 1. **Pittsburgh (61)**—Bonds 12, Bonilla 9, Van Slyke 8, Bell 7, Merced 5, King 3, Redus 3, Buechele 2, Lind 2, McClendon 2, Wilkerson 2, Espy 1, Gonzalez 1, LaValliere 1, Varsho 1, Webster 1. **St. Louis (4)**—Zeile 2, Pena 1, O. Smith 1. **San Diego (6)**—Teufel 2, Ward 2, Gwynn 1, Jackson 1. **San Francisco (2)**—Clark 1, Williams 1.

AT ST. LOUIS (73):

Atlanta (4)—Gant 2, Bream 1, Sanders 1. **Chicago (6)**—Dawson 3, Bell 1, Sandberg 1, Walton 1. **Cincinnati (1)**—Sabo 1. **Houston (3)**—Finley 1, Gonzalez 1, Yelding 1. **Los Angeles (2)**—Samuel 1, Strawberry 1. **Montreal (3)**—Calderon 1, Grissom 1, Wallach 1. **New York (8)**—Brooks 3, Johnson 2, McReynolds 2, Magadan 1, Sasser 1. **Philadelphia (2)**—Kruk 2, C. Hayes 1. **Pittsburgh (3)**—Bell 1, Bonds 1, Merced 1. **St. Louis (32)**—Zeile 7, Guerrero 4, Lankford 4, Thompson 4, Jose 3, Gilkey 2, Pagnozzi 2, O. Smith 2, Gedman 1, Hudler 1, Pena 1, Perry 1. **San Diego (3)**—Clark 1, Santiago 1, Teufel 1. **San Francisco (5)**—Clark 2, Litton 1, Thompson 1, Williams 1.

AT SAN DIEGO (137):

Atlanta (7)—Gant 2, Pendleton 2, Bream 1, Justice 1, L. Smith 1. **Chicago (7)**—Bell 2, Grace 1, Maddux 1, Salazar 1, Sandberg 1, Walton 1. **Cincinnati (7)**—Browning 1, Doran 1, Martinez 1, Morris 1, O'Neill 1, Quinones 1, Sabo 1. **Houston (5)**—Bagwell 1,

Caminiti 1, Cedeno 1, Finley 1, Gonzalez 1. **Los Angeles (9)**—Samuel 3, Strawberry 2, Carter 1, Murray 1, Scioscia 1, Sharperson 1. **Montreal (4)**—Walker 2, Grissom 1, Owen 1. **New York (5)**—Brooks 1, Johnson 1, Magadan 1, McReynolds 1, Templeton 1. **Philadelphia (6)**—Jordan 3, Hollins 2, Kruk 1. **Pittsburgh (5)**—Bonds 2, LaValliere 1, Redus 1, Slaught 1. **St. Louis (3)**—Pena 1, Perry 1, Thompson 1. **San Diego (65)**—McGriff 18, Jackson 12, Clark 8, Santiago 6, Teufel 5, Howard 4, Howell 3, Roberts 3, Abner 1, Barrett 1, Coolbaugh 1, Fernandez 1, Gwynn 1, Templeton 1. **San Francisco (14)**—Mitchell 5, Thompson 3, Leonard 2, Benjamin 1, Decker 1, Kennedy 1, Williams 1.

AT SAN FRANCISCO (131):

Atlanta (9)—Gant 4, Blauser 2, Bream 1, Justice 1, Mitchell 1. **Chicago (6)**—Bell 2, Dawson 1, Dunston 1, Sandberg 1, Walker 1. **Cincinnati (9)**—Martinez 2, Morris 2, Davis 1, Jones 1, Oliver 1, O'Neill 1, Sabo 1. **Houston (7)**—Candaele 2, Cedeno 2, Bagwell 1, Caminiti 1, Gonzalez 1. **Los Angeles (2)**—Murray 1, Scioscia 1. **Montreal (5)**—Calderon 2, Walker 2, Galarraga 1. **New York (4)**—Johnson 2, Brooks 1, Herr 1. **Philadelphia (4)**—Kruk 2, Hollins 1, Murphy 1. **Pittsburgh (4)**—Bell 1, Buechele 1, Prince 1, Van Slyke 1. **St. Louis (5)**—Jose 2, Lankford 2, Gedman 1. **San Diego (7)**—Santiago 3, Jackson 2, McGriff 2. **San Francisco (69)**—Clark 17, Williams 17, Thompson 11, Mitchell 9, Bass 5, Decker 4, Kennedy 2, McGee 2, Anderson 1, Wilson 1.

HISTORY

ALL-TIME RESULTS

WORLD SERIES

Year	Winner	Loser
1903	Boston A.L. over Pittsburgh N.L., 5 games to 3.	
1904	No Series.	
1905	New York N.L. over Philadelphia A.L., 4-1.	
1906	Chicago A.L. over Chicago N.L., 4-2.	
1907	Chicago N.L. over Detroit A.L., 4-0 with 1 tie.	
1908	Chicago N.L. over Detroit A.L., 4-1.	
1909	Pittsburgh N.L. over Detroit A.L., 4-3.	
1910	Philadelphia A.L. over Chicago N.L., 4-1.	
1911	Philadelphia A.L. over New York N.L., 4-2.	
1912	Boston A.L. over New York N.L., 4-3 with 1 tie.	
1913	Philadelphia A.L. over New York N.L., 4-1.	
1914	Boston N.L. over Philadelphia A.L., 4-0.	
1915	Boston A.L. over Philadelphia N.L., 4-1.	
1916	Boston A.L. over Brooklyn N.L., 4-1.	
1917	Chicago A.L. over New York N.L., 4-2.	
1918	Boston A.L. over Chicago N.L., 4-2.	
1919	Cincinnati N.L. over Chicago A.L., 5-3.	
1920	Cleveland A.L. over Brooklyn N.L., 5-2.	
1921	New York N.L. over New York A.L., 5-3.	
1922	New York N.L. over New York A.L., 4-0 with 1 tie.	
1923	New York A.L. over New York N.L., 4-2.	
1924	Washington A.L. over New York N.L., 4-3.	
1925	Pittsburgh N.L. over Washington A.L., 4-3.	
1926	St. Louis N.L. over New York A.L., 4-3.	
1927	New York A.L. over Pittsburgh, N.L., 4-0.	
1928	New York A.L. over St. Louis N.L., 4-0.	
1929	Philadelphia A.L. over Chicago N.L., 4-1.	
1930	Philadelphia A.L. over St. Louis N.L., 4-2.	
1931	St. Louis N.L. over Philadelphia A.L., 4-3.	
1932	New York A.L. over Chicago N.L., 4-0.	
1933	New York N.L. over Washington A.L., 4-1.	
1934	St. Louis N.L. over Detroit A.L., 4-3.	
1935	Detroit A.L. over Chicago N.L., 4-2.	
1936	New York A.L. over New York N.L., 4-2.	
1937	New York A.L. over New York N.L., 4-1.	
1938	New York A.L. over Chicago N.L., 4-0.	
1939	New York A.L. over Cincinnati N.L., 4-0.	
1940	Cincinnati N.L. over Detroit A.L., 4-3.	
1941	New York A.L. over Brooklyn N.L., 4-1.	
1942	St. Louis N.L. over New York A.L., 4-1.	
1943	New York A.L. over St. Louis, N.L., 4-1.	
1944	St. Louis N.L. over St. Louis A.L., 4-2.	
1945	Detroit A.L. over Chicago N.L., 4-3.	
1946	St. Louis N.L. over Boston A.L., 4-3.	
1947	New York A.L. over Brooklyn, N.L., 4-3.	
1948	Cleveland A.L. over Boston N.L., 4-2.	
1949	New York A.L. over Brooklyn N.L., 4-1.	
1950	New York A.L. over Philadelphia N.L., 4-0.	
1951	New York A.L. over New York N.L., 4-2.	
1952	New York A.L. over Brooklyn N.L., 4-3.	
1953	New York A.L. over Brooklyn N.L., 4-2.	
1954	New York N.L. over Cleveland A.L., 4-0.	
1955	Brooklyn N.L. over New York A.L., 4-3.	
1956	New York A.L. over Brooklyn N.L., 4-3.	
1957	Milwaukee N.L. over New York A.L., 4-3.	
1958	New York A.L. over Milwaukee N.L., 4-3.	
1959	Los Angeles N.L. over Chicago A.L., 4-2.	
1960	Pittsburgh N.L. over New York A.L., 4-3.	
1961	New York A.L. over Cincinnati N.L., 4-1.	
1962	New York A.L. over San Francisco N.L., 4-3.	
1963	Los Angeles N.L. over New York A.L., 4-0.	
1964	St. Louis N.L. over New York A.L., 4-3.	
1965	Los Angeles N.L. over Minnesota A.L., 4-3.	
1966	Baltimore A.L. over Los Angeles N.L., 4-0.	
1967	St. Louis N.L. over Boston A.L., 4-3.	
1968	Detroit A.L. over St. Louis N.L., 4-3.	
1969	New York N.L. over Baltimore A.L., 4-1.	
1970	Baltimore A.L. over Cincinnati N.L., 4-1.	
1971	Pittsburgh N.L. over Baltimore A.L., 4-3.	
1972	Oakland A.L. over Cincinnati N.L., 4-3.	
1973	Oakland A.L. over New York N.L., 4-3.	
1974	Oakland A.L. over Los Angeles N.L., 4-1.	
1975	Cincinnati N.L. over Boston A.L., 4-3.	
1976	Cincinnati N.L. over New York A.L., 4-0.	
1977	New York A.L. over Los Angeles N.L., 4-2.	
1978	New York A.L. over Los Angeles N.L., 4-2.	
1979	Pittsburgh N.L. over Baltimore A.L., 4-3.	
1980	Philadelphia N.L. over Kansas City A.L., 4-2.	
1981	Los Angeles N.L. over New York A.L., 4-2.	
1982	St. Louis N.L. over Milwaukee A.L., 4-3.	
1983	Baltimore A.L. over Philadelphia N.L., 4-1.	
1984	Detroit A.L. over San Diego N.L., 4-1.	
1985	Kansas City A.L. over St. Louis N.L., 4-3.	
1986	New York N.L. over Boston A.L., 4-3.	
1987	Minnesota A.L. over St. Louis N.L., 4-3.	
1988	Los Angeles N.L. over Oakland A.L., 4-1.	
1989	Oakland A.L. over San Francisco N.L., 4-0.	
1990	Cincinnati N.L. over Oakland A.L., 4-0.	
1991	Minnesota A.L. over Atlanta N.L., 4-3.	

CHAMPIONSHIP SERIES

AMERICAN LEAGUE

Year	Winner	Loser
1969	Baltimore (East) over Minnesota (West), 3 games to 0.	
1970	Baltimore (East) over Minnesota (West), 3-0.	
1971	Baltimore (East) over Oakland (West), 3-0.	
1972	Oakland (West) over Detroit (East), 3-2.	
1973	Oakland (West) over Baltimore (East), 3-2.	
1974	Oakland (West) over Baltimore (East), 3-1.	
1975	Boston (East) over Oakland (West), 3-0.	
1976	New York (East) over Kansas City (West), 3-2.	
1977	New York (East) over Kansas City (West), 3-2.	
1978	New York (East) over Kansas City (West), 3-1.	
1979	Baltimore (East) over California (West), 3-1.	
1980	Kansas City (West) over New York (East), 3-0.	
1981	New York (East) over Oakland (West), 3-0.	
1982	Milwaukee (East) over California (West), 3-2.	
1983	Baltimore (East) over Chicago (West), 3-1.	
1984	Detroit (East) over Kansas City (West), 3-0.	
1985	Kansas City (West) over Toronto (East), 4-3.	
1986	Boston (East) over California (West), 4-3.	
1987	Minnesota (West) over Detroit (East), 4-1.	

NATIONAL LEAGUE

Year	Winner	Loser
1969	New York (East) over Atlanta (West), 3 games to 0.	
1970	Cincinnati (West) over Pittsburgh (East), 3-0.	
1971	Pittsburgh (East) over San Francisco (West), 3-1.	
1972	Cincinnati (West) over Pittsburgh (East), 3-2.	
1973	New York (East) over Cincinnati (West), 3-2.	
1974	Los Angeles (West) over Pittsburgh (East), 3-1.	
1975	Cincinnati (West) over Pittsburgh (East), 3-0.	
1976	Cincinnati (West) over Philadelphia (East), 3-0.	
1977	Los Angeles (West) over Philadelphia (East), 3-1.	
1978	Los Angeles (West) over Philadelphia (East), 3-1.	
1979	Pittsburgh (East) over Cincinnati (West), 3-0.	
1980	Philadelphia (East) over Houston (West), 3-2.	
1981	Los Angeles (West) over Montreal (East), 3-2.	
1982	St. Louis (East) over Atlanta (West), 3-0.	
1983	Philadelphia (East) over Los Angeles (West), 3-1.	
1984	San Diego (West) over Chicago (East), 3-2.	
1985	St. Louis (East) over Los Angeles (West), 4-2.	
1986	New York (East) over Houston (West), 4-2.	
1987	St. Louis (East) over San Francisco (West), 4-3.	

Year	Winner	Loser
1988—Oakland (West) over Boston (East), 4-0.		
1989—Oakland (West) over Toronto (East), 4-1.		
1990—Oakland (West) over Boston (East), 4-0.		
1991—Minnesota (West) over Toronto (East), 4-1.		

Year	Winner	Loser
1988—Los Angeles (West) over New York (East), 4-3.		
1989—San Francisco (West) over Chicago (East), 4-1.		
1990—Cincinnati (West) over Pittsburgh (East), 4-2.		
1991—Atlanta (West) over Pittsburgh (East), 4-3.		

ALL-STAR GAME

Date	Site	Score (Winner)	Winning pitcher (Losing pitcher)	Winning manager (Losing manager)	Att.
7-6-33	Comiskey Park Chicago	4-2 (A.L.)	Lefty Gomez, Yankees (Bill Hallahan, Cardinals)	Connie Mack, Athletics (John McGraw, Giants)	47,595
7-10-34	Polo Grounds New York	9-7 (A.L.)	Mel Harder, Indians (Van Mungo, Dodgers)	Joe Cronin, Senators (Bill Terry, Giants)	48,363
7-8-35	Municipal Stadium Cleveland	4-1 (A.L.)	Lefty Gomez, Yankees (Bill Walker, Cardinals)	Mickey Cochrane, Tigers (Frankie Frisch, Cardinals)	69,831
7-7-36	Braves Field Boston	4-3 (N.L.)	Dizzy Dean, Cardinals (Lefty Grove, Red Sox)	Charlie Grimm, Cubs (Joe McCarthy, Yankees)	25,556
7-7-37	Griffith Stadium Washington	8-3 (A.L.)	Lefty Gomez, Yankees (Dizzy Dean, Cardinals)	Joe McCarthy, Yankees (Bill Terry, Giants)	31,391
7-6-38	Crosley Field Cincinnati	4-1 (N.L.)	Johnny Vander Meer, Reds (Lefty Gomez, Yankees)	Bill Terry, Giants (Joe McCarthy, Yankees)	27,067
7-11-39	Yankee Stadium New York	3-1 (A.L.)	Tommy Bridges, Tigers (Bill Lee, Cubs)	Joe McCarthy, Yankees (Gabby Hartnett, Cubs)	62,892
7-9-40	Sportsman's Park St. Louis	4-0 (N.L.)	Paul Derringer, Reds (Red Ruffing, Yankees)	Bill McKechnie, Reds (Joe Cronin, Red Sox)	32,373
7-8-41	Briggs Stadium Detroit	7-5 (A.L.)	Ed Smith, White Sox (Claude Passeau, Cubs)	Del Baker, Tigers (Bill McKechnie, Reds)	54,674
7-6-42	Polo Grounds New York	3-1 (A.L.)	Spud Chandler, Yankees (Mort Cooper, Cardinals)	Joe McCarthy, Yankees (Leo Durocher, Dodgers)	34,178
7-13-43	Shibe Park Philadelphia	5-3 (A.L.)	Dutch Leonard, Senators (Mort Cooper, Cardinals)	Joe McCarthy, Yankees (Billy Southworth, Cardinals)	31,938
7-11-44	Forbes Field Pittsburgh	7-1 (N.L.)	Ken Raffensberger, Phillies (Tex Hughson, Red Sox)	Billy Southworth, Cardinals (Joe McCarthy, Yankees)	29,589
1945	No game played.				
7-9-46	Fenway Park Boston	12-0 (A.L.)	Bob Feller, Indians (Claude Passeau, Cubs)	Steve O'Neill, Tigers (Charlie Grimm, Cubs)	34,906
7-8-47	Wrigley Field Chicago	2-1 (A.L.)	Frank Shea, Yankees (Johnny Sain, Braves)	Joe Cronin, Red Sox (Eddie Dyer, Cardinals)	41,123
7-13-48	Sportsman's Park St. Louis	5-2 (A.L.)	Vic Raschi, Yankees (Johnny Schmitz, Cubs)	Bucky Harris, Yankees (Leo Durocher, Dodgers)	34,009
7-12-49	Ebbets Field Brooklyn	11-7 (A.L.)	Virgil Trucks, Tigers (Don Newcombe, Dodgers)	Lou Boudreau, Indians (Billy Southworth, Braves)	32,577
7-11-50	Comiskey Park Chicago	4-3* (N.L.)	Ewell Blackwell, Reds (Ted Gray, Tigers)	Burt Shotton, Dodgers (Casey Stengel, Yankees)	46,127
7-10-51	Briggs Stadium Detroit	8-3 (N.L.)	Sal Maglie, Giants (Ed Lopat, Yankees)	Eddie Sawyer, Phillies (Casey Stengel, Yankees)	52,075
7-8-52	Shibe Park Philadelphia	3-2† (N.L.)	Bob Rush, Cubs (Bob Lemon, Indians)	Leo Durocher, Giants (Casey Stengel, Yankees)	32,785
7-14-53	Crosley Field Cincinnati	5-1 (N.L.)	Warren Spahn, Braves (Allie Reynolds, Yankees)	Chuck Dressen, Dodgers (Casey Stengel, Yankees)	30,846
7-13-54	Municipal Stadium Cleveland	11-9 (A.L.)	Dean Stone, Senators (Gene Conley, Braves)	Casey Stengel, Yankees (Walter Alston, Dodgers)	68,751
7-12-55	Milwaukee Co. Stadium Milwaukee	6-5‡ (N.L.)	Gene Conley, Braves (Frank Sullivan, Red Sox)	Leo Durocher, Giants (Al Lopez, Indians)	45,643
7-10-56	Griffith Stadium Washington	7-3 (N.L.)	Bob Friend, Pirates (Billy Pierce, White Sox)	Walter Alston, Dodgers (Casey Stengel, Yankees)	28,843
7-9-57	Busch Stadium St. Louis	6-5 (A.L.)	Jim Bunning, Tigers (Curt Simmons, Phillies)	Casey Stengel, Yankees (Walter Alston, Dodgers)	30,693
7-8-58	Memorial Stadium Baltimore	4-3 (A.L.)	Early Wynn, White Sox (Bob Friend, Pirates)	Casey Stengel, Yankees (Fred Haney, Braves)	48,829
7-7-59	Forbes Field Pittsburgh	5-4 (N.L.)	Johnny Antonelli, Giants (Whitey Ford, Yankees)	Fred Haney, Braves (Casey Stengel, Yankees)	35,277
8-3-59	Memorial Coliseum Los Angeles	5-3 (A.L.)	Jerry Walker, Orioles (Don Drysdale, Dodgers)	Casey Stengel, Yankees (Fred Haney, Braves)	55,105
7-11-60	Municipal Stadium Kansas City	5-3 (N.L.)	Bob Friend, Pirates (Bill Monbouquette, Red Sox)	Walter Alston, Dodgers (Al Lopez, White Sox)	30,619
7-13-60	Yankee Stadium New York	6-0 (N.L.)	Vernon Law, Pirates (Whitey Ford, Yankees)	Walter Alston, Dodgers (Al Lopez, White Sox)	38,362
7-11-61	Candlestick Park San Francisco	5-4§ (N.L.)	Stu Miller, Giants (Hoyt Wilhelm, Orioles)	Danny Murtaugh, Pirates (Paul Richards, Orioles)	44,115
7-31-61	Fenway Park Boston	1-1 (tie)		Paul Richards, Orioles (A.L.) Danny Murtaugh, Pirates (N.L.)	31,851
7-10-62	District of Col. Stad. Washington	3-1 (N.L.)	Juan Marichal, Giants (Camilo Pascual, Twins)	Fred Hutchinson, Reds (Ralph Houk, Yankees)	45,480
7-30-62	Wrigley Field Chicago	9-4 (A.L.)	Ray Herbert, White Sox (Art Mahaffey, Phillies)	Ralph Houk, Yankees (Fred Hutchinson, Reds)	38,359

Date	Site	Score (Winner)	Winning pitcher (Losing pitcher)	Winning manager (Losing manager)	Att.
7-9-63	Municipal Stadium Cleveland	5-3 (N.L.)	Larry Jackson, Cubs (Jim Bunning, Tigers)	Alvin Dark, Giants (Ralph Houk, Yankees)	44,160
7-7-64	Shea Stadium New York	7-4 (N.L.)	Juan Marichal, Giants (Dick Radatz, Red Sox)	Walter Alston, Dodgers (Al Lopez, White Sox)	50,850
7-13-65	Metropolitan Stadium Bloomington, Minn.	6-5 (N.L.)	Sandy Koufax, Dodgers (Sam McDowell, Indians)	Gene Mauch, Phillies (Al Lopez, White Sox)	46,706
7-12-66	Busch Stadium St. Louis	2-1§ (N.L.)	Gaylord Perry, Giants (Pete Richert, Senators)	Walter Alston, Dodgers (Sam Mele, Twins)	49,936
7-11-67	Anaheim Stadium Anaheim, Calif.	2-1* (N.L.)	Don Drysdale, Dodgers (Jim Hunter, Athletics)	Walter Alston, Dodgers (Hank Bauer, Orioles)	46,309
7-9-68	Astrodome Houston	1-0 (N.L.)	Don Drysdale, Dodgers (Luis Tiant, Indians)	Red Schoendienst, Cardinals (Dick Williams, Red Sox)	48,321
7-23-69	R.F.K. Stadium Washington	9-3 (N.L.)	Steve Carlton, Cardinals (Mel Stottlemyre, Yankees)	Red Schoendienst, Cardinals (Mayo Smith, Tigers)	45,259
7-14-70	Riverfront Stadium Cincinnati	5-4‡ (N.L.)	Claude Osteen, Dodgers (Clyde Wright, Angels)	Gil Hodges, Mets (Earl Weaver, Orioles)	51,838
7-13-71	Tiger Stadium Detroit	6-4 (A.L.)	Vida Blue, Athletics (Dock Ellis, Pirates)	Earl Weaver, Orioles (Sparky Anderson, Reds)	53,559
7-25-72	Atlanta Stadium Atlanta	4-3§ (N.L.)	Tug McGraw, Mets (Dave McNally, Orioles)	Danny Murtaugh, Pirates (Earl Weaver, Orioles)	53,107
7-24-73	Royals Stadium Kansas City	7-1 (N.L.)	Rick Wise, Cardinals (Bert Blyleven, Twins)	Sparky Anderson, Reds (Dick Williams, Athletics)	40,849
7-23-74	Three Rivers Stadium Pittsburgh	7-2 (N.L.)	Ken Brett, Pirates (Luis Tiant, Red Sox)	Yogi Berra, Mets (Dick Williams, Athletics)	50,706
7-15-75	Milwaukee Co. Stadium Milwaukee	6-3 (N.L.)	Jon Matlack, Mets (Jim Hunter, Yankees)	Walter Alston, Dodgers (Alvin Dark, Athletics)	51,480
7-13-76	Veterans Stadium Philadelphia	7-1 (N.L)	Randy Jones, Padres (Mark Fidrych, Tigers)	Sparky Anderson, Reds (Darrell Johnson, Red Sox)	63,974
7-19-77	Yankee Stadium New York	7-5 (N.L.)	Don Sutton, Dodgers (Jim Palmer, Orioles)	Sparky Anderson, Reds (Billy Martin, Yankees)	56,683
7-11-78	San Diego Stadium San Diego	7-3 (N.L.)	Bruce Sutter, Cubs (Rich Gossage, Yankees)	Tommy Lasorda, Dodgers (Billy Martin, Yankees)	51,549
7-17-79	Kingdome Seattle	7-6 (N.L.)	Bruce Sutter, Cubs (Jim Kern, Rangers)	Tommy Lasorda, Dodgers (Bob Lemon, Yankees)	58,905
7-8-80	Dodger Stadium Los Angeles	4-2 (N.L.)	Jerry Reuss, Dodgers (Tommy John, Yankees)	Chuck Tanner, Pirates (Earl Weaver, Orioles)	56,088
8-9-81	Municipal Stadium Cleveland	5-4 (N.L.)	Vida Blue, Giants (Rollie Fingers, Brewers)	Dallas Green, Phillies (Jim Frey, Royals)	72,086
7-13-82	Olympic Stadium Montreal	4-1 (N.L.)	Steve Rogers, Expos (Dennis Eckersley, Red Sox)	Tommy Lasorda, Dodgers (Billy Martin, Athletics)	59,057
7-6-83	Comiskey Park Chicago	13-3 (A.L.)	Dave Stieb, Blue Jays (Mario Soto, Reds)	Harvey Kuenn, Brewers (Whitey Herzog, Cardinals)	43,801
7-10-84	Candlestick Park San Francisco	3-1 (N.L.)	Charlie Lea, Expos (Dave Stieb, Blue Jays)	Paul Owens, Phillies (Joe Altobelli, Orioles)	57,756
7-16-85	Metrodome Minneapolis	6-1 (N.L.)	LaMarr Hoyt, Padres (Jack Morris, Tigers)	Dick Williams, Padres (Sparky Anderson, Tigers)	54,960
7-15-86	Astrodome Houston	3-2 (A.L.)	Roger Clemens, Red Sox (Dwight Gooden, Mets)	Dick Howser, Royals (Whitey Herzog, Cardinals)	45,774
7-14-87	Oak.-Alameda Co. Col. Oakland	2-0• (N.L.)	Lee Smith, Cubs (Jay Howell, Athletics)	Dave Johnson, Mets (John McNamara, Red Sox)	49,671
7-12-88	Riverfront Stadium Cincinnati	2-1 (A.L.)	Frank Viola, Twins (Dwight Gooden, Mets)	Tom Kelly, Twins (Whitey Herzog, Cardinals)	55,837
7-11-89	Anaheim Stadium Anaheim, Calif.	5-3 (A.L.)	Nolan Ryan, Rangers (John Smoltz, Braves)	Tony La Russa, Athletics (Tommy Lasorda, Dodgers)	64,036
7-10-90	Wrigley Field Chicago	2-0 (A.L.)	Bret Saberhagen, Royals (Jeff Brantley, Giants)	Tony La Russa, Athletics (Roger Craig, Giants)	39,071
7-9-91	SkyDome Toronto	4-2 (A.L.)	Jimmy Key, Blue Jays (Dennis Martinez, Expos)	Tony La Russa, Athletics (Lou Piniella, Reds)	52,383

*14 innings.   †5 innings (rain).   ‡12 innings.   §10 innings.   *15 innings.   •13 innings.

AWARD WINNERS

THE SPORTING NEWS

MOST VALUABLE PLAYER

AMERICAN LEAGUE

Year	Player, Team, Pos.	Points
1929—	Al Simmons, Philadelphia, OF	40
1930—	Joe Cronin, Washington, SS	52
1931—	Lou Gehrig, New York, 1B	40
1932—	Jimmie Foxx, Philadelphia, 1B	46
1933—	Jimmie Foxx, Philadelphia, 1B	49
1934—	Lou Gehrig, New York, 1B	51
1935—	Hank Greenberg, Detroit, 1B	64
1936—	Lou Gehrig, New York, 1B	55
1937—	Charley Gehringer, Detroit, 2B	78
1938—	Jimmie Foxx, Boston, 1B	304
1939—	Joe DiMaggio, New York, OF	280
1940—	Hank Greenberg, Detroit, OF	292
1941—	Joe DiMaggio, New York, OF	291
1942—	Joe Gordon, New York, 2B	270
1943—	Spud Chandler, New York, P	246
1944—	Bobby Doerr, Boston, 2B	
1945—	Eddie Mayo, Detroit, 2B	

NATIONAL LEAGUE

Year	Player, Team, Pos.	Points
1929—	No selection	
1930—	Bill Terry, New York, 1B	47
1931—	Chuck Klein, Philadelphia, OF	40
1932—	Chuck Klein, Philadelphia, OF	46
1933—	Carl Hubbell, New York, P	64
1934—	Dizzy Dean, St. Louis, P	57
1935—	Arky Vaughan, Pittsburgh, SS	42
1936—	Carl Hubbell, New York, P	61
1937—	Joe Medwick, St. Louis, OF	70
1938—	Ernie Lombardi, Cincinnati, C	229
1939—	Bucky Walters, Cincinnati, P	303
1940—	Frank McCormick, Cincinnati, 1B	274
1941—	Dolf Camilli, Brooklyn, 1B	300
1942—	Mort Cooper, St. Loius, P	263
1943—	Stan Musial, St. Louis, OF	267
1944—	Marty Marion, St. Louis, SS	
1945—	Tommy Holmes, Boston, OF	

PLAYER AND PITCHER OF THE YEAR

AMERICAN LEAGUE

Year	Player, Team, Pos.
1948—	Lou Boudreau, Cleveland, SS
	Bob Lemon, Cleveland, P
1949—	Ted Williams, Boston, OF
	Ellis Kinder, Boston, P
1950—	Phil Rizzuto, New York, SS
	Bob Lemon, Cleveland, P
1951—	Ferris Fain, Philadelphia, 1B
	Bob Feller, Cleveland, P
1952—	Luke Easter, Cleveland, 1B
	Bobby Shantz, Philadelphia, P
1953—	Al Rosen, Cleveland, 3B
	Bob Porterfield, Washington, P
1954—	Bobby Avila, Cleveland, 2B
	Bob Lemon, Cleveland, P
1955—	Al Kaline, Detroit, OF
	Whitey Ford, New York, P
1956—	Mickey Mantle, New York, OF
	Billy Pierce, Chicago, P
1957—	Ted Williams, Boston, OF
	Billy Pierce, Chicago, P
1958—	Jackie Jensen, Boston, OF
	Bob Turley, New York, P
1959—	Nellie Fox, Chicago, 2B
	Early Wynn, Chicago, P
1960—	Roger Maris, New York, OF
	Chuck Estrada, Baltimore, P
1961—	Roger Maris, New York, OF
	Whitey Ford, New York, P
1962—	Mickey Mantle, New York, OF
	Dick Donovan, Cleveland, P
1963—	Al Kaline, Detroit, OF
	Whitey Ford, New York, P
1964—	Brooks Robinson, Baltimore, 3B
	Dean Chance, Los Angeles, P
1965—	Tony Oliva, Minnesota, OF
	Jim Grant, Minnesota, P
1966—	Frank Robinson, Baltimore, OF
	Jim Kaat, Minnesota, P
1967—	Carl Yastrzemski, Boston, OF
	Jim Lonborg, Boston, P
1968—	Ken Harrelson, Boston, OF
	Denny McLain, Detroit, P
1969—	Harmon Killebrew, Minnesota, 1B-3B
	Denny McLain, Detroit, P

NATIONAL LEAGUE

Year	Player, Team, Pos.
1948—	Stan Musial, St. Louis, OF-1B
	Johnny Sain, Boston, P
1949—	Enos Slaughter, St. Louis, OF
	Howard Pollet, St. Louis, P
1950—	Ralph Kiner, Pittsburgh, OF
	Jim Konstanty, Philadelphia, P
1951—	Stan Musial, St. Louis, OF
	Preacher Roe, Brooklyn, P
1952—	Hank Sauer, Chicago, OF
	Robin Roberts, Philadelphia, P
1953—	Roy Campanella, Brooklyn, C
	Warren Spahn, Milwaukee, P
1954—	Willie Mays, New York, OF
	Johnny Antonelli, New York, P
1955—	Duke Snider, Brooklyn, OF
	Robin Roberts, Philadelphia, P
1956—	Hank Aaron, Milwaukee, OF
	Don Newcombe, Brooklyn, P
1957—	Stan Musial, St. Louis, 1B
	Warren Spahn, Milwaukee, P
1958—	Ernie Banks, Chicago, SS
	Warren Spahn, Milwaukee, P
1959—	Ernie Banks, Chicago, SS
	Sam Jones, San Francisco, P
1960—	Dick Groat, Pittsburgh, SS
	Vern Law, Pittsburgh, P
1961—	Frank Robinson, Cincinnati, OF
	Warren Spahn, Milwaukee, P
1962—	Maury Wills, Los Angeles, SS
	Don Drysdale, Los Angeles, P
1963—	Hank Aaron, Milwaukee, OF
	Sandy Koufax, Los Angeles, P
1964—	Ken Boyer, St. Louis, 3B
	Sandy Koufax, Los Angeles, P
1965—	Willie Mays, San Francisco, OF
	Sandy Koufax, Los Angeles, P
1966—	Roberto Clemente, Pittsburgh, OF
	Sandy Koufax, Los Angeles, P
1967—	Orlando Cepeda, St. Louis, 1B
	Mike McCormick, San Francisco, P
1968—	Pete Rose, Cincinnati, OF
	Bob Gibson, St. Louis, P
1969—	Willie McCovey, San Francisco, 1B
	Tom Seaver, New York, P

Year	Player, Team, Pos.	Year	Player, Team, Pos.
1970	Harmon Killebrew, Minnesota, 3B	1970	Johnny Bench, Cincinnati, C
	Sam McDowell, Cleveland, P		Bob Gibson, St. Louis, P
1971	Tony Oliva, Minnesota, OF	1971	Joe Torre, St. Louis, 3B
	Vida Blue, Oakland, P		Ferguson Jenkins, Chicago, P
1972	Dick Allen, Chicago, 1B	1972	Billy Williams, Chicago, OF
	Wilbur Wood, Chicago, P		Steve Carlton, Philadelphia, P
1973	Reggie Jackson, Oakland, OF	1973	Bobby Bonds, San Francisco, OF
	Jim Palmer, Baltimore, P		Ron Bryant, San Francisco, P
1974	Jeff Burroughs, Texas, OF	1974	Lou Brock, St. Louis, OF
	Jim Hunter, Oakland, P		Mike Marshall, Los Angeles, P
1975	Fred Lynn, Boston, OF	1975	Joe Morgan, Cincinnati, 2B
	Jim Palmer, Baltimore, P		Tom Seaver, New York, P
1976	Thurman Munson, New York, C	1976	George Foster, Cincinnati, OF
	Jim Palmer, Baltimore, P		Randy Jones, San Diego, P
1977	Rod Carew, Minnesota, 1B	1977	George Foster, Cincinnati, OF
	Nolan Ryan, California, P		Steve Carlton, Philadelphia, P
1978	Jim Rice, Boston, OF	1978	Dave Parker, Pittsburgh, OF
	Ron Guidry, New York, P		Vida Blue, San Francisco, P
1979	Don Baylor, California, OF	1979	Keith Hernandez, St. Louis, 1B
	Mike Flanagan, Baltimore, P		Joe Niekro, Houston, P
1980	George Brett, Kansas City, 3B	1980	Mike Schmidt, Philadelphia, 3B
	Steve Stone, Baltimore, P		Steve Carlton, Philadelphia, P
1981	Tony Armas, Oakland, OF	1981	Andre Dawson, Montreal, OF
	Jack Morris, Detroit, P		Fernando Valenzuela, Los Angeles, P
1982	Robin Yount, Milwaukee, SS	1982	Dale Murphy, Atlanta, OF
	Dave Stieb, Toronto, P		Steve Carlton, Philadelphia, P
1983	Cal Ripken Jr., Baltimore, SS	1983	Dale Murphy, Atlanta, OF
	LaMarr Hoyt, Chicago, P		John Denny, Philadelphia, P
1984	Don Mattingly, New York, 1B	1984	Ryne Sandberg, Chicago, 2B
	Willie Hernandez, Detroit, P		Rick Sutcliffe, Chicago, P
1985	Don Mattingly, New York, 1B	1985	Willie McGee, St. Louis, OF
	Bret Saberhagen, Kansas City, P		Dwight Gooden, New York, P
1986	Don Mattingly, New York, 1B	1986	Mike Schmidt, Philadelphia, 3B
	Roger Clemens, Boston, P		Mike Scott, Houston, P
1987	George Bell, Toronto, OF	1987	Andre Dawson, Chicago, OF
	Jimmy Key, Toronto, P		Rick Sutcliffe, Chicago, P
1988	Jose Canseco, Oakland, OF	1988	Andy Van Slyke, Pittsburgh, OF
	Frank Viola, Minnesota, P		Orel Hershiser, Los Angeles, P
1989	Ruben Sierra, Texas, OF	1989	Kevin Mitchell, San Francisco, OF
	Bret Saberhagen, Kansas City, P		Mark Davis, San Diego, P
1990	Cecil Fielder, Detroit, 1B	1990	Barry Bonds, Pittsburgh, OF
	Bob Welch, Oakland, P		Doug Drabek, Pittsburgh, P
1991	Cal Ripken Jr., Baltimore, SS	1991	Barry Bonds, Pittsburgh, OF
	Roger Clemens, Boston, P		Tom Glavine, Atlanta, P

ROOKIE OF THE YEAR

1946 — Combined selection — Del Ennis, Philadelphia NL, OF
1947 — Combined selection — Jackie Robinson, Brooklyn NL, 1B
1948 — Combined selection — Richie Ashburn, Philadelphia NL, OF

AMERICAN LEAGUE

NATIONAL LEAGUE

Year	Player, Team, Pos.	Year	Player, Team, Pos.
1949	Roy Sievers, St. Louis, OF	1949	Don Newcombe, Brooklyn, P
1950	Combined selection — Whitey Ford, New York, A.L., P		
1951	Minnie Minoso, Chicago, OF	1951	Willie Mays, New York, OF
1952	Clint Courtney, St. Louis, C	1952	Joe Black, Brooklyn, P
1953	Harvey Kuenn, Detroit, SS	1953	Jim Gilliam, Brooklyn, 2B
1954	Bob Grim, New York, P	1954	Wally Moon, St. Louis, OF
1955	Herb Score, Cleveland, P	1955	Bill Virdon, St. Louis, OF
1956	Luis Aparicio, Chicago, SS	1956	Frank Robinson, Cincinnati, OF
1957	Tony Kubek, New York, IF-OF	1957	Ed Bouchee, Philadelphia, 1B
	(No pitcher named)		Jack Sanford, Philadelphia, P
1958	Albie Pearson, Washington, OF	1958	Orlando Cepeda, San Francisco, 1B
	Ryne Duren, New York, P		Carlton Willey, Milwaukee, P
1959	Bob Allison, Washington, OF	1959	Willie McCovey, San Francisco, 1B
1960	Ron Hansen, Baltimore, SS	1960	Frank Howard, Los Angeles, OF
1961	Dick Howser, Kansas City, SS	1961	Billy Williams, Chicago, OF
	Don Schwall, Boston, P		Ken Hunt, Cincinnati, P
1962	Tom Tresh, New York, OF-SS	1962	Ken Hubbs, Chicago, 2B
1963	Pete Ward, Chicago, 3B	1963	Pete Rose, Cincinnati, 2B
	Gary Peters, Chicago, P		Ray Culp, Philadelphia, P
1964	Tony Oliva, Minnesota, OF	1964	Dick Allen, Philadelphia, 3B
	Wally Bunker, Baltimore, P		Billy McCool, Cincinnati, P
1965	Curt Blefary, Baltimore, OF	1965	Joe Morgan, Houston, 2B
	Marcelino Lopez, California, P		Frank Linzy, San Francisco, P

Year	Player, Team, Pos.
1966	Tommie Agee, Chicago, OF
	Jim Nash, Kansas City, P
1967	Rod Carew, Minnesota, 2B
	Tom Phoebus, Baltimore, P
1968	Del Unser, Washington, OF
	Stan Bahnsen, New York, P
1969	Carlos May, Chicago, OF
	Mike Nagy, Boston, P
1970	Roy Foster, Cleveland, OF
	Bert Blyleven, Minnesota, P
1971	Chris Chambliss, Cleveland, 1B
	Bill Parsons, Milwaukee, P
1972	Carlton Fisk, Boston, C
	Dick Tidrow, Cleveland, P
1973	Al Bumbry, Baltimore, OF
	Steve Busby, Kansas City, P
1974	Mike Hargrove, Texas, 1B
	Frank Tanana, California, P
1975	Fred Lynn, Boston, OF
	Dennis Eckersley, Cleveland, P
1976	Butch Wynegar, Minnesota, C
	Mark Fidrych, Detroit, P
1977	Mitchell Page, Oakland, OF
	Dave Rozema, Detroit, P
1978	Paul Molitor, Milwaukee, 2B
	Rich Gale, Kansas City, P
1979	Pat Putnam, Texas 1B
	Mark Clear, California, P
1980	Joe Charboneau, Cleveland, OF
	Britt Burns, Chicago, P
1981	Rich Gedman, Boston, C
	Dave Righetti, New York, P
1982	Cal Ripken Jr., Baltimore, SS-3B
	Ed Vande Berg, Seattle, P
1983	Ron Kittle, Chicago, OF
	Mike Boddicker, Baltimore, P
1984	Alvin Davis, Seattle, 1B
	Mark Langston, Seattle, P
1985	Ozzie Gullen, Chicago, SS
	Teddy Higuera, Milwaukee, P
1986	Jose Canseco, Oakland, OF
	Mark Eichhorn, Toronto, P
1987	Mark McGwire, Oakland, 1B
	Mike Henneman, Detroit, P
1988	Walt Weiss, Oakland, SS
	Bryan Harvey, California, P
1989	Craig Worthington, Baltimore, 3B
	Tom Gordon, Kansas City, P
1990	Sandy Alomar Jr., Cleveland, C
	Kevin Appier, Kansas City, P
1991	Chuck Knoblauch, Minnesota, 2B
	Juan Guzman, Toronto, P

Year	Player, Team, Pos.
1966	Tommy Helms, Cincinnati, 3B
	Don Sutton, Los Angeles, P
1967	Lee May, Cincinnati, 1B
	Dick Hughes, St. Louis, P
1968	Johnny Bench, Cincinnati, C
	Jerry Koosman, New York, P
1969	Coco Laboy, Montreal, 3B
	Tom Griffin, Houston, P
1970	Bernie Carbo, Cincinnati, OF
	Carl Morton, Montreal, P
1971	Earl Williams, Atlanta, C
	Reggie Cleveland, St. Louis, P
1972	Dave Rader, San Francisco, C
	Jon Matlack, New York, P
1973	Gary Matthews, San Francisco, OF
	Steve Rogers, Montreal, P
1974	Greg Gross, Houston, OF
	John D'Acquisto, San Francisco, P
1975	Gary Carter, Montreal, OF-C
	John Montefusco, San Francisco, P
1976	Larry Herndon, San Francisco, OF
	Butch Metzger, San Diego, P
1977	Andre Dawson, Montreal, OF
	Bob Owchinko, San Diego, P
1978	Bob Horner, Atlanta, 3B
	Don Robinson, Pittsburgh, P
1979	Jeff Leonard, Houston, OF
	Rick Sutcliffe, Los Angeles, P
1980	Lonnie Smith, Philadelphia, OF
	Bill Gullickson, Montreal, P
1981	Tim Raines, Montreal, OF
	Fernando Valenzuela, Los Angeles, P
1982	Johnny Ray, Pittsburgh, 2B
	Steve Bedrosian, Atlanta, P
1983	Darryl Strawberry, New York, OF
	Craig McMurtry, Atlanta, P
1984	Juan Samuel, Philadelphia, 2B
	Dwight Gooden, New York, P
1985	Vince Coleman, St. Louis, OF
	Tom Browning, Cincinnati, P
1986	Robby Thompson, San Francisco, 2B
	Todd Worrell, St. Louis, P
1987	Benito Santiago, San Diego, C
	Mike Dunne, Pittsburgh, P
1988	Mark Grace, Chicago, 1B
	Tim Belcher, Los Angeles, P
1989	Jerome Walton, Chicago, OF
	Andy Benes, San Diego, P
1990	David Justice, Atlanta, OF
	Mike Harkey, Chicago, P
1991	Jeff Bagwell, Houston, 1B
	Al Osuna, Houston, P

FIREMAN OF THE YEAR

AMERICAN LEAGUE

Year	Player, Team
1960	Mike Fornieles, Boston
1961	Luis Arroyo, New York
1962	Dick Radatz, Boston
1963	Stu Miller, Baltimore
1964	Dick Radatz, Boston
1965	Eddie Fisher, Chicago
1966	Jack Aker, Kansas City
1967	Minnie Rojas, California
1968	Wilbur Wood, Chicago
1969	Ron Perranoski, Minnesota
1970	Ron Perranoski, Minnesota
1971	Ken Sanders, Milwaukee
1972	Sparky Lyle, New York
1973	John Hiller, Detroit
1974	Terry Forster, Chicago
1975	Rich Gossage, Chicago
1976	Bill Campbell, Minnesota
1977	Bill Campbell, Boston
1978	Rich Gossage, New York

NATIONAL LEAGUE

Year	Player, Team
1960	Lindy McDaniel, St. Louis
1961	Stu Miller, San Francisco
1962	Roy Face, Pittsburgh
1963	Lindy McDaniel, Chicago
1964	Al McBean, Pittsburgh
1965	Ted Abernathy, Chicago
1966	Phil Regan, Los Angeles
1967	Ted Abernathy, Cincinnati
1968	Phil Regan, L.A.-Chicago
1969	Wayne Granger, Cincinnati
1970	Wayne Granger, Cincinnati
1971	Dave Giusti, Pittsburgh
1972	Clay Carroll, Cincinnati
1973	Mike Marshall, Montreal
1974	Mike Marshall, Los Angeles
1975	Al Hrabosky, St. Louis
1976	Rawly Eastwick, Cincinnati
1977	Rollie Fingers, San Diego
1978	Rollie Fingers, San Diego

Year	Player, Team		Year	Player, Team
1979—	Mike Marshall, Minnesota		1979—	Bruce Sutter, Chicago
	Jim Kern, Texas			
1980—	Dan Quisenberry, Kansas City		1980—	Rollie Fingers, San Diego
				Tom Hume, Cincinnati
1981—	Rollie Fingers, Milwaukee		1981—	Bruce Sutter, St. Louis
1982—	Dan Quisenberry, Kansas City		1982—	Bruce Sutter, St. Louis
1983—	Dan Quisenberry, Kansas City		1983—	Al Holland, Philadelphia
				Lee Smith, Chicago
1984—	Dan Quisenberry, Kansas City		1984—	Bruce Sutter, St. Louis
1985—	Dan Quisenberry, Kansas City		1985—	Jeff Reardon, Montreal
1986—	Dave Righetti, New York		1986—	Todd Worrell, St. Louis
1987—	Dave Righetti, New York		1987—	Steve Bedrosian, Philadelphia
	Jeff Reardon, Minnesota			
1988—	Dennis Eckersley, Oakland		1988—	John Franco, Cincinnati
1989—	Jeff Russell, Texas		1989—	Mark Davis, San Diego
1990—	Bobby Thigpen, Chicago		1990—	John Franco, New York
1991—	Dennis Eckersley, Oakland		1991—	Lee Smith, St. Louis
	Bryan Harvey, California			

MAJOR LEAGUE PLAYER OF THE YEAR

Year	Player, Team	Year	Player, Team	Year	Player, Team
1936—	Carl Hubbell, New York NL	1955—	Duke Snider, Brooklyn NL	1973—	Reggie Jackson, Oakland AL
1937—	Johnny Allen, Cleveland AL	1956—	Mickey Mantle, New York AL	1974—	Lou Brock, St. Louis NL
1938—	Johnny Vander Meer, Cin. NL	1957—	Ted Williams, Boston AL	1975—	Joe Morgan, Cincinnati NL
1939—	Joe DiMaggio, New York AL	1958—	Bob Turley, New York AL	1976—	Joe Morgan, Cincinnati NL
1940—	Bob Feller, Cleveland AL	1959—	Early Wynn, Chicago AL	1977—	Rod Carew, Minnesota AL
1941—	Ted Williams, Boston AL	1960—	Bill Mazeroski, Pittsburgh NL	1978—	Ron Guidry, New York AL
1942—	Ted Williams, Boston AL	1961—	Roger Maris, New York AL	1979—	Willie Stargell, Pittsburgh NL
1943—	Spud Chandler, New York AL	1962—	Maury Wills, Los Angeles NL	1980—	George Brett, Kansas City AL
1944—	Marty Marion, St. Louis NL		Don Drysdale, Los Angeles NL	1981—	Fernando Valenzuela, L.A. NL
1945—	Hal Newhouser, Detroit AL	1963—	Sandy Koufax, Los Angeles NL	1982—	Robin Yount, Milwaukee AL
1946—	Stan Musial, St. Louis NL	1964—	Ken Boyer, St. Louis NL	1983—	Cal Ripken Jr., Baltimore AL
1947—	Ted Williams, Boston AL	1965—	Sandy Koufax, Los Angeles NL	1984—	Ryne Sandberg, Chicago NL
1948—	Lou Boudreau, Cleveland AL	1966—	Frank Robinson, Baltimore AL	1985—	Don Mattingly, New York AL
1949—	Ted Williams, Boston AL	1967—	Carl Yastrzemski, Boston AL	1986—	Roger Clemens, Boston AL
1950—	Phil Rizzuto, New York AL	1968—	Denny McLain, Detroit AL	1987—	George Bell, Toronto AL
1951—	Stan Musial, St. Louis NL	1969—	Willie McCovey, San Fran. NL	1988—	Orel Hershiser, Los Angeles NL
1952—	Robin Roberts, Philadelphia NL	1970—	Johnny Bench, Cincinnati NL	1989—	Kevin Mitchell, San Fran. NL
1953—	Al Rosen, Cleveland AL	1971—	Joe Torre, St. Louis NL	1990—	Barry Bonds, Pittsburgh NL
1954—	Willie Mays, New York NL	1972—	Billy Williams, Chicago NL	1991—	Cal Ripken Jr., Baltimore AL

MAJOR LEAGUE MANAGER OF THE YEAR

Year	Manager, Team	Year	Manager, Team	Year	Manager, Team
1936—	Joe McCarthy, New York AL	1957—	Fred Hutchinson, St. Louis NL	1978—	George Bamberger, Mil. AL
1937—	Bill McKechnie, Boston NL	1958—	Casey Stengel, New York AL	1979—	Earl Weaver, Baltimore AL
1938—	Joe McCarthy, New York AL	1959—	Walter Alston, Los Angeles NL	1980—	Bill Virdon, Houston NL
1939—	Leo Durocher, Brooklyn NL	1960—	Danny Murtaugh, Pit. NL	1981—	Billy Martin, Oakland AL
1940—	Bill McKechnie, Cincinnati NL	1961—	Ralph Houk, New York AL	1982—	Whitey Herzog, St. Louis NL
1941—	Billy Southworth, St. Louis NL	1962—	Bill Rigney, Los Angeles AL	1983—	Tony La Russa, Chicago AL
1942—	Billy Southworth, St. Louis NL	1963—	Walter Alston, Los Angeles NL	1984—	Jim Frey, Chicago NL
1943—	Joe McCarthy, New York AL	1964—	Johnny Keane, St. Louis NL	1985—	Bobby Cox, Toronto AL
1944—	Luke Sewell, St. Louis AL	1965—	Sam Mele, Minnesota AL	1986—	John McNamara, Boston AL
1945—	Ossie Bluege, Washington AL	1966—	Hank Bauer, Baltimore AL		Hal Lanier, Houston NL
1946—	Eddie Dyer, St. Louis NL	1967—	Dick Williams, Boston AL	1987—	Sparky Anderson, Detroit AL
1947—	Bucky Harris, New York AL	1968—	Mayo Smith, Detroit AL		Buck Rodgers, Montreal NL
1948—	Bill Meyer, Pittsburgh NL	1969—	Gil Hodges, New York NL	1988—	Tony La Russa, Oakland AL
1949—	Casey Stengel, New York AL	1970—	Danny Murtaugh, Pit. NL		Tom Lasorda, L.A. NL (tie)
1950—	Red Rolfe, Detroit AL	1971—	Charlie Fox, San Francisco NL		Jim Leyland, Pit. NL (tie)
1951—	Leo Durocher, New York NL	1972—	Chuck Tanner, Chicago AL	1989—	Frank Robinson, Baltimore AL
1952—	Eddie Stanky, St. Louis NL	1973—	Gene Mauch, Montreal NL		Don Zimmer, Chicago NL
1953—	Casey Stengel, New York AL	1974—	Bill Virdon, New York AL	1990—	Jeff Torborg, Chicago AL
1954—	Leo Durocher, New York AL	1975—	Darrell Johnson, Boston AL		Jim Leyland, Pittsburgh NL
1955—	Walter Alston, Brooklyn NL	1976—	Danny Ozark, Philadelphia NL	1991—	Tom Kelly, Minnesota AL
1956—	Birdie Tebbetts, Cincinnati NL	1977—	Earl Weaver, Baltimore AL		Bobby Cox, Atlanta NL

MAJOR LEAGUE EXECUTIVE OF THE YEAR

Year	Executive, Team	Year	Executive, Team	Year	Executive, Team
1936—	Branch Rickey, St. Louis NL	1943—	Clark Griffith, Washington AL	1950—	George Weiss, New York AL
1937—	Ed Barrow, New York AL	1944—	Billy DeWitt, St. Louis AL	1951—	George Weiss, New York AL
1938—	Warren Giles, Cincinnati NL	1945—	Phil Wrigley, Chicago NL	1952—	George Weiss, New York AL
1939—	Larry MacPhail, Brooklyn NL	1946—	Tom Yawkey, Boston AL	1953—	Lou Perini, Milwaukee NL
1940—	Walter Briggs Sr., Detroit AL	1947—	Branch Rickey, Brooklyn NL	1954—	Horace Stoneham, New York NL
1941—	Ed Barrow, New York AL	1948—	Bill Veeck, Cleveland AL	1955—	Walter O'Malley, Brooklyn NL
1942—	Branch Rickey, St. Louis NL	1949—	Bob Carpenter, Philadelphia NL	1956—	Gabe Paul, Cincinnati NL

Year	Executive, Team	Year	Executive, Team	Year	Executive, Team
1957—	Frank Lane, St. Louis NL	1969—	John Murphy, New York NL	1981—	John McHale, Montreal NL
1958—	Joe Brown, Pittsburgh NL	1970—	Harry Dalton, Baltimore AL	1982—	Harry Dalton, Milwaukee AL
1959—	Buzzie Bavasi, L.A. NL	1971—	Cedric Tallis, Kansas City AL	1983—	Hank Peters, Baltimore AL
1960—	George Weiss, New York AL	1972—	Roland Hemond, Chicago AL	1984—	Dallas Green, Chicago NL
1961—	Dan Topping, New York AL	1973—	Bob Howsam, Cincinnati NL	1985—	John Schuerholz, K.C. AL
1962—	Fred Haney, Los Angeles AL	1974—	Gabe Paul, New York AL	1986—	Frank Cashen, New York NL
1963—	Bing Devine, St. Louis NL	1975—	Dick O'Connell, Boston AL	1987—	Al Rosen, San Francisco NL
1964—	Bing Devine, St. Louis NL	1976—	Joe Burke, Kansas City AL	1988—	Fred Claire, Los Angeles NL
1965—	Cal Griffith, Minnesota AL	1977—	Bill Veeck, Chicago AL	1989—	Roland Hemond, Baltimore AL
1966—	Lee MacPhall, Comm. Office	1978—	Spec Richardson, San Fran. NL	1990—	Bob Quinn, Cincinnati NL
1967—	Dick O'Connell, Boston AL	1979—	Hank Peters, Baltimore AL	1991—	Andy MacPhail, Minnesota AL
1968—	Jim Campbell, Detroit AL	1980—	Tal Smith, Houston NL		

GOLD GLOVE TEAMS

1957
MAJORS
P—Bobby Shantz, N.Y. AL
C—Sherm Lollar, Chicago AL
1B—Gil Hodges, Brooklyn NL
2B—Nellie Fox, Chicago AL
3B—Frank Malzone, Boston AL
SS—Roy McMillan, Cin. NL
OF—Minnie Minoso, Chicago AL
OF—Willie Mays, N.Y. NL
OF—Al Kaline, Detroit AL

1958
AMERICAN LEAGUE
P—Bobby Shantz, New York
C—Sherm Lollar, Chicago
1B—Vic Power, Cleveland
2B—Frank Bolling, Detroit
3B—Frank Malzone, Boston
SS—Luis Aparicio, Chicago
OF—Norm Siebern, New York
OF—Jimmy Piersall, Boston
OF—Al Kaline, Detroit

NATIONAL LEAGUE
P—Harvey Haddix, Cincinnati
C—Del Crandall, Milwaukee
1B—Gil Hodges, Los Angeles
2B—Bill Mazeroski, Pitt.
3B—Ken Boyer, St. Louis
SS—Roy McMillan, Cin.
OF—Frank Robinson, Cin.
OF—Willie Mays, San Fran.
OF—Hank Aaron, Milwaukee

1959
AMERICAN LEAGUE
P—Bobby Shantz, New York
C—Sherm Lollar, Chicago
1B—Vic Power, Cleveland
2B—Nellie Fox, Chicago
3B—Frank Malzone, Boston
SS—Luis Aparicio, Chicago
OF—Minnie Minoso, Cleveland
OF—Al Kaline, Detroit
OF—Jackie Jensen, Boston

NATIONAL LEAGUE
P—Harvey Haddix, Pittsburgh
C—Del Crandall, Milwaukee
1B—Gil Hodges, Los Angeles
2B—Charley Neal, Los Angeles
3B—Ken Boyer, St. Louis
SS—Roy McMillan, Cincinnati
OF—Jackie Brandt, San Fran.
OF—Willie Mays, San Francisco
OF—Hank Aaron, Milwaukee

1960
AMERICAN LEAGUE
P—Bobby Shantz, New York
C—Earl Battey, Washington
1B—Vic Power, Cleveland
2B—Nellie Fox, Chicago
3B—Brooks Robinson, Baltimore
SS—Luis Aparicio, Chicago
OF—Minnie Minoso, Chicago
OF—Jim Landis, Chicago
OF—Roger Maris, New York

NATIONAL LEAGUE
P—Harvey Haddix, Pittsburgh
C—Del Crandall, Milwaukee
1B—Bill White, St. Louis
2B—Bill Mazeroski, Pittsburgh
3B—Ken Boyer, St. Louis
SS—Ernie Banks, Chicago
OF—Wally Moon, Los Angeles
OF—Willie Mays, San Francisco
OF—Hank Aaron, Milwaukee

1961
AMERICAN LEAGUE
P—Frank Lary, Detroit
C—Earl Battey, Chicago
1B—Vic Power, Cleveland
2B—Bobby Richardson, N.Y.
3B—Brooks Robinson, Baltimore
SS—Luis Aparicio, Chicago
OF—Al Kaline, Detroit
OF—Jimmy Piersall, Cleveland
OF—Jim Landis, Chicago

NATIONAL LEAGUE
P—Bobby Shantz, Pittsburgh
C—John Roseboro, Los Angeles
1B—Bill White, St. Louis
2B—Bill Mazeroski, Pittsburgh
3B—Ken Boyer, St. Louis
SS—Maury Wills, Los Angeles
OF—Willie Mays, San Francisco
OF—Roberto Clemente, Pittsburgh
OF—Vada Pinson, Cincinnati

1962
AMERICAN LEAGUE
P—Jim Kaat, Minnesota
C—Earl Battey, Minnesota
1B—Vic Power, Minnesota
2B—Bobby Richardson, N.Y.
3B—Brooks Robinson, Baltimore
SS—Luis Aparicio, Chicago
OF—Jim Landis, Chicago
OF—Mickey Mantle, New York
OF—Al Kaline, Detroit

NATIONAL LEAGUE
P—Bobby Shantz, St. Louis
C—Del Crandall, Milwaukee
1B—Bill White, St. Louis
2B—Ken Hubbs, Chicago
3B—Jim Davenport, S.F.
SS—Maury Wills, Los Angeles
OF—Willie Mays, San Francisco
OF—Roberto Clemente, Pittsburgh
OF—Bill Virdon, Pittsburgh

1963
AMERICAN LEAGUE
P—Jim Kaat, Minnesota
C—Elston Howard, New York
1B—Vic Power, Minnesota
2B—Bobby Richardson, N.Y.
3B—Brooks Robinson, Baltimore
SS—Zoilo Versalles, Minnesota
OF—Al Kaline, Detroit
OF—Carl Yastrzemski, Boston
OF—Jim Landis, Chicago

NATIONAL LEAGUE
P—Bobby Shantz, St. Louis
C—Johnny Edwards, Cincinnati
1B—Bill White, St. Louis
2B—Bill Mazeroski, Pittsburgh
3B—Ken Boyer, St. Louis
SS—Bobby Wine, Philadelphia
OF—Willie Mays, San Francisco
OF—Roberto Clemente, Pittsburgh
OF—Curt Flood, St. Louis

1964
AMERICAN LEAGUE
P—Jim Kaat, Minnesota
C—Elston Howard, New York
1B—Vic Power, Los Angeles
2B—Bobby Richardson, N.Y.
3B—Brooks Robinson, Baltimore
SS—Luis Aparicio, Baltimore
OF—Al Kaline, Detroit
OF—Jim Landis, Chicago
OF—Vic Davalillo, Cleveland

NATIONAL LEAGUE
P—Bobby Shantz, Philadelphia
C—Johnny Edwards, Cincinnati
1B—Bill White, St. Louis
2B—Bill Mazeroski, Pittsburgh
3B—Ron Santo, Chicago
SS—Ruben Amaro, Philadelphia
OF—Willie Mays, San Francisco
OF—Roberto Clemente, Pittsburgh
OF—Curt Flood, St. Louis

1965
AMERICAN LEAGUE
P—Jim Kaat, Minnesota
C—Bill Freehan, Detroit
1B—Joe Pepitone, New York
2B—Bobby Richardson, N.Y.
3B—Brooks Robinson, Baltimore
SS—Zoilo Versalles, Minnesota
OF—Al Kaline, Detroit
OF—Tom Tresh, New York
OF—Carl Yastrzemski, Boston

NATIONAL LEAGUE
P—Bob Gibson, St. Louis
C—Joe Torre, Atlanta
1B—Bill White, St. Louis
2B—Bill Mazeroski, Pittsburgh
3B—Ron Santo, Chicago
SS—Leo Cardenas, Cincinnati
OF—Willie Mays, San Francisco
OF—Roberto Clemente, Pittsburgh
OF—Curt Flood, St. Louis

1966
AMERICAN LEAGUE
P—Jim Kaat, Minnesota
C—Bill Freehan, Detroit
1B—Joe Pepitone, New York
2B—Bobby Knoop, California
3B—Brooks Robinson, Balt.
SS—Luis Aparicio, Baltimore
OF—Al Kaline, Detroit
OF—Tommie Agee, Chicago
OF—Tony Oliva, Minnesota

NATIONAL LEAGUE
P—Bob Gibson, St. Louis
C—John Roseboro, Los Angeles
1B—Bill White, Philadelphia
2B—Bill Mazeroski, Pittsburgh
3B—Ron Santo, Chicago
SS—Gene Alley, Pittsburgh
OF—Willie Mays, San Francisco
OF—Curt Flood, St. Louis
OF—Roberto Clemente, Pittsburgh

1967
AMERICAN LEAGUE
P—Jim Kaat, Minnesota
C—Bill Freehan, Detroit
1B—George Scott, Boston
2B—Bobby Knoop, California
3B—Brooks Robinson, Balt.
SS—Jim Fregosi, California
OF—Carl Yastrzemski, Boston
OF—Paul Blair, Baltimore
OF—Al Kaline, Detroit

NATIONAL LEAGUE
P—Bob Gibson, St. Louis
C—Randy Hundley, Chicago
1B—Wes Parker, Los Angeles
2B—Bill Mazeroski, Pittsburgh
3B—Ron Santo, Chicago
SS—Gene Alley, Pittsburgh
OF—Roberto Clemente, Pittsburgh
OF—Curt Flood, St. Louis
OF—Willie Mays, San Francisco

1968
AMERICAN LEAGUE
P—Jim Kaat, Minnesota
C—Bill Freehan, Detroit
1B—George Scott, Boston
2B—Bobby Knoop, California
3B—Brooks Robinson, Balt.
SS—Luis Aparicio, Chicago
OF—Mickey Stanley, Detroit
OF—Carl Yastrzemski, Boston
OF—Reggie Smith, Boston

NATIONAL LEAGUE
P—Bob Gibson, St. Louis
C—Johnny Bench, Cincinnati
1B—Wes Parker, Los Angeles
2B—Glenn Beckert, Chicago
3B—Ron Santo, Chicago
SS—Dal Maxvill, St. Louis
OF—Willie Mays, San Francisco
OF—Roberto Clemente, Pittsburgh
OF—Curt Flood, St. Louis

1969
AMERICAN LEAGUE
P—Jim Kaat, Minnesota
C—Bill Freehan, Detroit
1B—Joe Pepitone, New York
2B—Dave Johnson, Baltimore
3B—Brooks Robinson, Balt.
SS—Mark Belanger, Baltimore
OF—Paul Blair, Baltimore
OF—Mickey Stanley, Detroit
OF—Carl Yastrzemski, Boston

NATIONAL LEAGUE
P—Bob Gibson, St. Louis
C—Johnny Bench, Cincinnati
1B—Wes Parker, Los Angeles
2B—Felix Millan, Atlanta
3B—Clete Boyer, Atlanta
SS—Don Kessinger, Chicago
OF—Roberto Clemente, Pittsburgh
OF—Curt Flood, St. Louis
OF—Pete Rose, Cincinnati

1970
AMERICAN LEAGUE
P—Jim Kaat, Minnesota
C—Ray Fosse, Cleveland
1B—Jim Spencer, California
2B—Dave Johnson, Baltimore
3B—Brooks Robinson, Balt.
SS—Luis Aparicio, Chicago
OF—Mickey Stanley, Detroit
OF—Paul Blair, Baltimore
OF—Ken Berry, Chicago

NATIONAL LEAGUE
P—Bob Gibson, St. Louis
C—Johnny Bench, Cincinnati
1B—Wes Parker, Los Angeles
2B—Tommy Helms, Cincinnati
3B—Doug Rader, Houston
SS—Don Kessinger, Chicago
OF—Roberto Clemente, Pittsburgh
OF—Tommie Agee, New York
OF—Pete Rose, Cincinnati

1971
AMERICAN LEAGUE
P—Jim Kaat, Minnesota
C—Ray Fosse, Cleveland
1B—George Scott, Boston
2B—Dave Johnson, Baltimore
3B—Brooks Robinson, Balt.
SS—Mark Belanger, Baltimore
OF—Paul Blair, Baltimore
OF—Amos Otis, Kansas City
OF—Carl Yastrzemski, Boston

NATIONAL LEAGUE
P—Bob Gibson, St. Louis
C—Johnny Bench, Cincinnati
1B—Wes Parker, Los Angeles
2B—Tommy Helms, Cincinnati
3B—Doug Rader, Houston
SS—Bud Harrelson, New York
OF—Roberto Clemente, Pittsburgh
OF—Bobby Bonds, San Francisco
OF—Willie Davis, Los Angeles

1972
AMERICAN LEAGUE
P—Jim Kaat, Minnesota
C—Carlton Fisk, Boston
1B—George Scott, Milwaukee
2B—Doug Griffin, Boston
3B—Brooks Robinson, Baltimore
SS—Ed Brinkman, Detroit
OF—Paul Blair, Baltimore
OF—Bobby Murcer, New York
OF—Ken Berry, California

NATIONAL LEAGUE
P—Bob Gibson, St. Louis
C—Johnny Bench, Cincinnati
1B—Wes Parker, Los Angeles
2B—Felix Millan, Atlanta
3B—Doug Rader, Houston
SS—Larry Bowa, Philadelphia
OF—Roberto Clemente, Pittsburgh
OF—Cesar Cedeno, Houston
OF—Willie Davis, Los Angeles

1973
AMERICAN LEAGUE
P—Jim Kaat, Chicago
C—Thurman Munson, New York
1B—George Scott, Milwaukee
2B—Bobby Grich, Baltimore
3B—Brooks Robinson, Baltimore
SS—Mark Belanger, Baltimore
OF—Paul Blair, Baltimore
OF—Amos Otis, Kansas City
OF—Mickey Stanley, Detroit

NATIONAL LEAGUE
P—Bob Gibson, St. Louis
C—Johnny Bench, Cincinnati
1B—Mike Jorgensen, Montreal
2B—Joe Morgan, Cincinnati
3B—Doug Rader, Houston
SS—Roger Metzger, Houston
OF—Bobby Bonds, San Francisco
OF—Cesar Cedeno, Houston
OF—Willie Davis, Los Angeles

1974
AMERICAN LEAGUE
P—Jim Kaat, Chicago
C—Thurman Munson, New York
1B—George Scott, Milwaukee
2B—Bobby Grich, Baltimore
3B—Brooks Robinson, Baltimore
SS—Mark Belanger, Baltimore
OF—Paul Blair, Baltimore
OF—Amos Otis, Kansas City
OF—Joe Rudi, Oakland

NATIONAL LEAGUE
P—Andy Messersmith, Los Angeles
C—Johnny Bench, Cincinnati
1B—Steve Garvey, Los Angeles
2B—Joe Morgan, Cincinnati
3B—Doug Rader, Houston
SS—Dave Concepcion, Cincinnati
OF—Cesar Cedeno, Houston
OF—Cesar Geronimo, Cincinnati
OF—Bobby Bonds, San Francisco

1975
AMERICAN LEAGUE
P—Jim Kaat, Chicago
C—Thurman Munson, New York
1B—George Scott, Milwaukee
2B—Bobby Grich, Baltimore
3B—Brooks Robinson, Baltimore
SS—Mark Belanger, Baltimore
OF—Paul Blair, Baltimore
OF—Joe Rudi, Oakland
OF—Fred Lynn, Boston

NATIONAL LEAGUE
P—Andy Messersmith, Los Angeles
C—Johnny Bench, Cincinnati
1B—Steve Garvey, Los Angeles
2B—Joe Morgan, Cincinnati
3B—Ken Reitz, St. Louis
SS—Dave Concepcion, Cincinnati
OF—Cesar Cedeno, Houston
OF—Cesar Geronimo, Cincinnati
OF—Garry Maddox, Philadelphia

1976
AMERICAN LEAGUE
P—Jim Palmer, Baltimore
C—Jim Sundberg, Texas
1B—George Scott, Milwaukee
2B—Bobby Grich, Baltimore
3B—Aurelio Rodriguez, Detroit
SS—Mark Belanger, Baltimore
OF—Joe Rudi, Oakland
OF—Dwight Evans, Boston
OF—Rick Manning, Cleveland

NATIONAL LEAGUE
P—Jim Kaat, Philadelphia
C—Johnny Bench, Cincinnati
1B—Steve Garvey, Los Angeles
2B—Joe Morgan, Cincinnati
3B—Mike Schmidt, Philadelphia
SS—Dave Concepcion, Cincinnati
OF—Cesar Cedeno, Houston
OF—Cesar Geronimo, Cincinnati
OF—Garry Maddox, Philadelphia

1977
AMERICAN LEAGUE
P—Jim Palmer, Baltimore
C—Jim Sundberg, Texas
1B—Jim Spencer, Chicago
2B—Frank White, Kansas City
3B—Graig Nettles, New York
SS—Mark Belanger, Baltimore
OF—Juan Beniquez, Texas
OF—Carl Yastrzemski, Boston
OF—Al Cowens, Kansas City

NATIONAL LEAGUE
P—Jim Kaat, Philadelphia
C—Johnny Bench, Cincinnati
1B—Steve Garvey, Los Angeles
2B—Joe Morgan, Cincinnati
3B—Mike Schmidt, Philadelphia
SS—Dave Concepcion, Cincinnati
OF—Cesar Geronimo, Cincinnati
OF—Garry Maddox, Philadelphia
OF—Dave Parker, Pittsburgh

1978
AMERICAN LEAGUE
P—Jim Palmer, Baltimore
C—Jim Sundberg, Texas
1B—Chris Chambliss, New York
2B—Frank White, Kansas City
3B—Graig Nettles, New York
SS—Mark Belanger, Baltimore
OF—Fred Lynn, Boston
OF—Dwight Evans, Boston
OF—Rick Miller, California

NATIONAL LEAGUE
P—Phil Niekro, Atlanta
C—Bob Boone, Philadelphia
1B—Keith Hernandez, St. Louis
2B—Dave Lopes, Los Angeles
3B—Mike Schmidt, Philadelphia
SS—Larry Bowa, Philadelphia
OF—Garry Maddox, Philadelphia
OF—Dave Parker, Pittsburgh
OF—Ellis Valentine, Montreal

1979
AMERICAN LEAGUE
P—Jim Palmer, Baltimore
C—Jim Sundberg, Texas
1B—Cecil Cooper, Milwaukee
2B—Frank White, Kansas City
3B—Buddy Bell, Texas
SS—Rick Burleson, Boston
OF—Dwight Evans, Boston
OF—Sixto Lezcano, Milwaukee
OF—Fred Lynn, Boston

NATIONAL LEAGUE
P—Phil Niekro, Atlanta
C—Bob Boone, Philadelphia
1B—Keith Hernandez, St. Louis
2B—Manny Trillo, Philadelphia
3B—Mike Schmidt, Philadelphia
SS—Dave Concepcion, Cincinnati
OF—Garry Maddox, Philadelphia
OF—Dave Parker, Pittsburgh
OF—Dave Winfield, San Diego

1980
AMERICAN LEAGUE
P—Mike Norris, Oakland
C—Jim Sundberg, Texas
1B—Cecil Cooper, Milwaukee
2B—Frank White, Kansas City
3B—Buddy Bell, Texas
SS—Alan Trammell, Detroit
OF—Fred Lynn, Boston
OF—Dwayne Murphy, Oakland
OF—Willie Wilson, Kansas City

NATIONAL LEAGUE
P—Phil Niekro, Atlanta
C—Gary Carter, Montreal
1B—Keith Hernandez, St. Louis
2B—Doug Flynn, New York
3B—Mike Schmidt, Philadelphia
SS—Ozzie Smith, San Diego
OF—Andre Dawson, Montreal
OF—Garry Maddox, Philadelphia
OF—Dave Winfield, San Diego

1981
AMERICAN LEAGUE
P—Mike Norris, Oakland
C—Jim Sundberg, Texas
1B—Mike Squires, Chicago
2B—Frank White, Kansas City
3B—Buddy Bell, Texas
SS—Alan Trammell, Detroit
OF—Dwayne Murphy, Oakland
OF—Dwight Evans, Boston
OF—Rickey Henderson, Oakland

NATIONAL LEAGUE
P—Steve Carlton, Philadelphia
C—Gary Carter, Montreal
1B—Keith Hernandez, St. Louis
2B—Manny Trillo, Philadelphia
3B—Mike Schmidt, Philadelphia
SS—Ozzie Smith, San Diego
OF—Andre Dawson, Montreal
OF—Garry Maddox, Philadelphia
OF—Dusty Baker, Los Angeles

1982
AMERICAN LEAGUE
P—Ron Guidry, New York
C—Bob Boone, California
1B—Eddie Murray, Baltimore
2B—Frank White, Kansas City
3B—Buddy Bell, Texas
SS—Robin Yount, Milwaukee
OF—Dwight Evans, Boston
OF—Dave Winfield, New York
OF—Dwayne Murphy, Oakland

NATIONAL LEAGUE
P—Phil Niekro, Atlanta
C—Gary Carter, Montreal
1B—Keith Hernandez, St. Louis
2B—Manny Trillo, Philadelphia
3B—Mike Schmidt, Philadelphia
SS—Ozzie Smith, St. Louis
OF—Andre Dawson, Montreal
OF—Dale Murphy, Atlanta
OF—Garry Maddox, Philadelphia

1983
AMERICAN LEAGUE
P—Ron Guidry, New York
C—Lance Parrish, Detroit
1B—Eddie Murray, Baltimore
2B—Lou Whitaker, Detroit
3B—Buddy Bell, Texas
SS—Alan Trammell, Detroit
OF—Dwight Evans, Boston
OF—Dave Winfield, New York
OF—Dwayne Murphy, Oakland

NATIONAL LEAGUE
P—Phil Niekro, Atlanta
C—Tony Pena, Pittsburgh
1B—Keith Hernandez, St.L.-N.Y.
2B—Ryne Sandberg, Chicago
3B—Mike Schmidt, Philadelphia
SS—Ozzie Smith, St. Louis
OF—Andre Dawson, Montreal
OF—Dale Murphy, Atlanta
OF—Willie McGee, St. Louis

1984
AMERICAN LEAGUE
P—Ron Guidry, New York
C—Lance Parrish, Detroit
1B—Eddie Murray, Baltimore
2B—Lou Whitaker, Detroit
3B—Buddy Bell, Texas
SS—Alan Trammell, Detroit
OF—Dwight Evans, Boston
OF—Dave Winfield, New York
OF—Dwayne Murphy, Oakland

NATIONAL LEAGUE
P—Joaquin Andujar, St. Louis
C—Tony Pena, Pittsburgh
1B—Keith Hernandez, New York
2B—Ryne Sandberg, Chicago
3B—Mike Schmidt, Philadelphia
SS—Ozzie Smith, St. Louis
OF—Dale Murphy, Atlanta
OF—Bob Dernier, Chicago
OF—Andre Dawson, Montreal

1985
AMERICAN LEAGUE
P—Ron Guidry, New York
C—Lance Parrish, Detroit
1B—Don Mattingly, New York
2B—Lou Whitaker, Detroit
3B—George Brett, Kansas City
SS—Alfredo Griffin, Oakland
OF—Gary Pettis, California
OF—Dave Winfield, New York
OF—Dwight Evans, Boston (tie)
    Dwayne Murphy, Oakland (tie)

NATIONAL LEAGUE
P—Rick Reuschel, Pittsburgh
C—Tony Pena, Pittsburgh
1B—Keith Hernandez, New York
2B—Ryne Sandberg, Chicago
3B—Tim Wallach, Montreal
SS—Ozzie Smith, St. Louis
OF—Willie McGee, St. Louis
OF—Dale Murphy, Atlanta
OF—Andre Dawson, Montreal

1986
AMERICAN LEAGUE
P—Ron Guidry, New York
C—Bob Boone, California
1B—Don Mattingly, New York
2B—Frank White, Kansas City
3B—Gary Gaetti, Minnesota
SS—Tony Fernandez, Toronto
OF—Gary Pettis, California
OF—Jesse Barfield, Toronto
OF—Kirby Puckett, Minnesota

NATIONAL LEAGUE
P—Fernando Valenzuela, L.A.
C—Jody Davis, Chicago
1B—Keith Hernandez, New York
2B—Ryne Sandberg, Chicago
3B—Mike Schmidt, Philadelphia
SS—Ozzie Smith, St. Louis
OF—Tony Gwynn, San Diego
OF—Dale Murphy, Atlanta
OF—Willie McGee, St. Louis

1987
AMERICAN LEAGUE
P—Mark Langston, Seattle
C—Bob Boone, California
1B—Don Mattingly, New York
2B—Frank White, Kansas City
3B—Gary Gaetti, Minnesota
SS—Tony Fernandez, Toronto
OF—Jesse Barfield, Toronto
OF—Kirby Puckett, Minnesota
OF—Dave Winfield, New York

NATIONAL LEAGUE
P—Rick Reuschel, Pitt.-S.F.
C—Mike LaValliere, Pittsburgh
1B—Keith Hernandez, New York
2B—Ryne Sandberg, Chicago
3B—Terry Pendleton, St. Louis
SS—Ozzie Smith, St. Louis
OF—Eric Davis, Cincinnati
OF—Tony Gwynn, San Diego
OF—Andre Dawson, Chicago

1988
AMERICAN LEAGUE
P—Mark Langston, Seattle
C—Bob Boone, California
1B—Don Mattingly, New York
2B—Harold Reynolds, Seattle
3B—Gary Gaetti, Minnesota
SS—Tony Fernandez, Toronto
OF—Kirby Puckett, Minnesota
OF—Devon White, California
OF—Gary Pettis, Detroit

NATIONAL LEAGUE
P—Orel Hershiser, Los Angeles
C—Benito Santiago, San Diego
1B—Keith Hernandez, New York
2B—Ryne Sandberg, Chicago
3B—Tim Wallach, Montreal
SS—Ozzie Smith, St. Louis
OF—Andy Van Slyke, Pittsburgh
OF—Eric Davis, Cincinnati
OF—Andre Dawson, Chicago

1989
AMERICAN LEAGUE
P—Bret Saberhagen, Kansas City
C—Bob Boone, Kansas City
1B—Don Mattingly, New York
2B—Harold Reynolds, Seattle
3B—Gary Gaetti, Minnesota
SS—Tony Fernandez, Toronto
OF—Kirby Puckett, Minnesota
OF—Devon White, California
OF—Gary Pettis, Detroit

NATIONAL LEAGUE
P—Ron Darling, New York
C—Benito Santiago, San Diego
1B—Andres Galarraga, Montreal
2B—Ryne Sandberg, Chicago
3B—Terry Pendleton, St. Louis
SS—Ozzie Smith, St. Louis
OF—Andy Van Slyke, Pittsburgh
OF—Tony Gwynn, San Diego
OF—Eric Davis, Cincinnati

1990
AMERICAN LEAGUE
P—Mike Boddicker, Boston
C—Sandy Alomar Jr., Cleveland
1B—Mark McGwire, Oakland
2B—Harold Reynolds, Seattle
3B—Kelly Gruber, Toronto
SS—Ozzie Guillen, Chicago
OF—Ken Griffey Jr., Seattle
OF—Ellis Burks, Boston
OF—Gary Pettis, Texas

NATIONAL LEAGUE
P—Greg Maddux, Chicago
C—Benito Santiago, San Diego
1B—Andres Galarraga, Montreal
2B—Ryne Sandberg, Chicago
3B—Tim Wallach, Montreal
SS—Ozzie Smith, St. Louis
OF—Barry Bonds, Pittsburgh
OF—Andy Van Slyke, Pittsburgh
OF—Tony Gwynn, San Diego

1991
AMERICAN LEAGUE
P—Mark Langston, California
C—Tony Pena, Boston
1B—Don Mattingly, New York
2B—Roberto Alomar, Toronto
3B—Robin Ventura, Chicago
SS—Cal Ripken, Baltimore
OF—Ken Griffey Jr., Seattle
OF—Kirby Puckett, Minnesota
OF—Devon White, Toronto

NATIONAL LEAGUE
P—Greg Maddux, Chicago
C—Tom Pagnozzi, St. Louis
1B—Will Clark, San Francisco
2B—Ryne Sandberg, Chicago
3B—Matt Williams, San Francisco
SS—Ozzie Smith, St. Louis
OF—Barry Bonds, Pittsburgh
OF—Andy Van Slyke, Pittsburgh
OF—Tony Gwynn, San Diego

AWARD WINNERS

HISTORY

1980
AMERICAN LEAGUE
1B—Cecil Cooper, Milwaukee
2B—Willie Randolph, New York
3B—George Brett, Kansas City
SS—Robin Yount, Milwaukee
OF—Ben Oglivie, Milwaukee
OF—Al Oliver, Texas
OF—Willie Wilson, Kansas City
C—Lance Parrish, Detroit
DH—Reggie Jackson, New York

NATIONAL LEAGUE
1B—Keith Hernandez, St. Louis
2B—Manny Trillo, Philadelphia
3B—Mike Schmidt, Philadelphia
SS—Garry Templeton, St. Louis
OF—Dusty Baker, Los Angeles
OF—Andre Dawson, Montreal
OF—George Hendrick, St. Louis
C—Ted Simmons, St. Louis
P—Bob Forsch, St. Louis

1981
AMERICAN LEAGUE
1B—Cecil Cooper, Milwaukee
2B—Bobby Grich, California
3B—Carney Lansford, Boston
SS—Rick Burleson, California
OF—Rickey Henderson, Oakland
OF—Dwight Evans, Boston
OF—Dave Winfield, New York
C—Carlton Fisk, Chicago
DH—Al Oliver, Texas

NATIONAL LEAGUE
1B—Pete Rose, Philadelphia
2B—Manny Trillo, Philadelphia
3B—Mike Schmidt, Philadelphia
SS—Dave Concepcion, Cincinnati
OF—Andre Dawson, Montreal
OF—George Foster, Cincinnati
OF—Dusty Baker, Los Angeles
C—Gary Carter, Montreal
P—Fernando Valenzuela, L.A.

1982
AMERICAN LEAGUE
1B—Cecil Cooper, Milwaukee
2B—Damaso Garcia, Toronto
3B—Doug DeCinces, California
SS—Robin Yount, Milwaukee
OF—Dave Winfield, New York
OF—Willie Wilson, Kansas City
OF—Reggie Jackson, California
C—Lance Parrish, Detroit
DH—Hal McRae, Kansas City

NATIONAL LEAGUE
1B—Al Oliver, Montreal
2B—Joe Morgan, San Francisco
3B—Mike Schmidt, Philadelphia
SS—Dave Concepcion, Cincinnati
OF—Dale Murphy, Atlanta
OF—Pedro Guerrero, Los Angeles
OF—Leon Durham, Chicago
C—Gary Carter, Montreal
P—Don Robinson, Pittsburgh

1983
AMERICAN LEAGUE
1B—Eddie Murray, Baltimore
2B—Lou Whitaker, Detroit
3B—Wade Boggs, Boston
SS—Cal Ripken Jr., Baltimore
OF—Jim Rice, Boston
OF—Dave Winfield, New York
OF—Lloyd Moseby, Toronto
C—Lance Parrish, Detroit
DH—Don Baylor, New York

NATIONAL LEAGUE
1B—George Hendrick, St. Louis
2B—Johnny Ray, Pittsburgh
3B—Mike Schmidt, Philadelphia
SS—Dickie Thon, Houston
OF—Andre Dawson, Montreal
OF—Dale Murphy, Atlanta
OF—Jose Cruz, Houston
C—Terry Kennedy, San Diego
P—Fernando Valenzuela, L.A.

1984
AMERICAN LEAGUE
1B—Eddie Murray, Baltimore
2B—Lou Whitaker, Detroit
3B—Buddy Bell, Texas
SS—Cal Ripken Jr., Baltimore
OF—Tony Armas, Boston
OF—Jim Rice, Boston
OF—Dave Winfield, New York
C—Lance Parrish, Detroit
DH—Andre Thornton, Cleveland

NATIONAL LEAGUE
1B—Keith Hernandez, New York
2B—Ryne Sandberg, Chicago
3B—Mike Schmidt, Philadelphia
SS—Garry Templeton, San Diego
OF—Dale Murphy, Atlanta
OF—Jose Cruz, Houston
OF—Tony Gwynn, San Diego
C—Gary Carter, Montreal
P—Rick Rhoden, Pittsburgh

1985
AMERICAN LEAGUE
1B—Don Mattingly, New York
2B—Lou Whitaker, Detroit
3B—George Brett, Kansas City
SS—Cal Ripken Jr., Baltimore
OF—Rickey Henderson, New York
OF—Dave Winfield, New York
OF—George Bell, Toronto
C—Carlton Fisk, Chicago
DH—Don Baylor, New York

NATIONAL LEAGUE
1B—Jack Clark, St. Louis
2B—Ryne Sandberg, Chicago
3B—Tim Wallach, Montreal
SS—Hubie Brooks, Montreal
OF—Willie McGee, St. Louis
OF—Dale Murphy, Atlanta
OF—Dave Parker, Cincinnati
C—Gary Carter, New York
P—Rick Rhoden, Pittsburgh

1986
AMERICAN LEAGUE
1B—Don Mattingly, New York
2B—Frank White, Kansas City
3B—Wade Boggs, Boston
SS—Cal Ripken Jr., Baltimore
OF—George Bell, Toronto
OF—Kirby Puckett, Minnesota
OF—Jesse Barfield, Toronto
C—Lance Parrish, Detroit
DH—Don Baylor, Boston

NATIONAL LEAGUE
1B—Glenn Davis, Houston
2B—Steve Sax, Los Angeles
3B—Mike Schmidt, Philadelphia
SS—Hubie Brooks, Montreal
OF—Tony Gwynn, San Diego
OF—Tim Raines, Montreal
OF—Dave Parker, Cincinnati
C—Gary Carter, New York
P—Rick Rhoden, Pittsburgh

1987
AMERICAN LEAGUE
1B—Don Mattingly, New York
2B—Lou Whitaker, Detroit
3B—Wade Boggs, Boston
SS—Alan Trammell, Detroit
OF—George Bell, Toronto
OF—Dwight Evans, Boston
OF—Kirby Puckett, Minnesota
C—Matt Nokes, Detroit
DH—Paul Molitor, Milwaukee

NATIONAL LEAGUE
1B—Jack Clark, St. Louis
2B—Juan Samuel, Philadelphia
3B—Tim Wallach, Montreal
SS—Ozzie Smith, St. Louis
OF—Andre Dawson, Chicago
OF—Eric Davis, Cincinnati
OF—Tony Gwynn, San Diego
C—Benito Santiago, San Diego
P—Bob Forsch, St. Louis

1988
AMERICAN LEAGUE
1B—George Brett, Kansas City
2B—Julio Franco, Cleveland
3B—Wade Boggs, Boston
SS—Alan Trammell, Detroit
OF—Kirby Puckett, Minnesota
OF—Jose Canseco, Oakland
OF—Mike Greenwell, Boston
C—Carlton Fisk, Chicago
DH—Paul Molitor, Milwaukee

NATIONAL LEAGUE
1B—Andres Galarraga, Montreal
2B—Ryne Sandberg, Chicago
3B—Bobby Bonilla, Pittsburgh
SS—Barry Larkin, Cincinnati
OF—Darryl Strawberry, New York
OF—Andy Van Slyke, Pittsburgh
OF—Kirk Gibson, Los Angeles
C—Benito Santiago, San Diego
P—Tim Leary, Los Angeles

AWARD WINNERS

1989

AMERICAN LEAGUE

1B—Fred McGriff, Toronto
2B—Julio Franco, Texas
3B—Wade Boggs, Boston
SS—Cal Ripken Jr., Baltimore
OF—Kirby Puckett, Minnesota
OF—Ruben Sierra, Texas
OF—Robin Yount, Milwaukee
C—Mickey Tettleton, Baltimore
DH—H. Baines, Chicago-Texas

NATIONAL LEAGUE

1B—Will Clark, San Francisco
2B—Ryne Sandberg, Chicago
3B—Howard Johnson, New York
SS—Barry Larkin, Cincinnati
OF—Kevin Mitchell, San Francisco
OF—Tony Gwynn, San Diego
OF—Eric Davis, Cincinnati
C—Craig Biggio, Houston
P—Don Robinson, San Francisco

1990

AMERICAN LEAGUE

1B—Cecil Fielder, Detroit
2B—Julio Franco, Texas
3B—Kelly Gruber, Toronto
SS—Alan Trammell, Detroit
OF—Rickey Henderson, Oakland
OF—Jose Canseco, Oakland
OF—Ellis Burks, Boston
C—Lance Parrish, California
DH—Dave Parker, Milwaukee

NATIONAL LEAGUE

1B—Eddie Murray, Los Angeles
2B—Ryne Sandberg, Chicago
3B—Matt Williams, San Francisco
SS—Barry Larkin, Cincinnati
OF—Barry Bonds, Pittsburgh
OF—Bobby Bonilla, Pittsburgh
OF—Darryl Strawberry, New York
C—Benito Santiago, San Diego
P—Don Robinson, San Francisco

1991

AMERICAN LEAGUE

1B—Cecil Fielder, Detroit
2B—Julio Franco, Texas
3B—Wade Boggs, Boston
SS—Cal Ripken Jr., Baltimore
OF—Jose Canseco, Oakland
OF—Joe Carter, Toronto
OF—Ken Griffey Jr., Seattle
C—Mickey Tettleton, Detroit
DH—Frank Thomas, Chicago

NATIONAL LEAGUE

1B—Will Clark, San Francisco
2B—Ryne Sandberg, Chicago
3B—Howard Johnson, New York
SS—Barry Larkin, Cincinnati
OF—Barry Bonds, Pittsburgh
OF—Bobby Bonilla, Pittsburgh
OF—Ron Gant, Atlanta
C—Benito Santiago, San Diego
P—Tom Glavine, Atlanta

MAJOR LEAGUE ALL-STAR TEAMS

1925

1B—Jim Bottomley, St. Louis NL
2B—Rogers Hornsby, St. Louis NL
SS—Glenn Wright, Pittsburgh NL
3B—Pie Traynor, Pittsburgh NL
OF—Kiki Cuyler, Pittsburgh NL
OF—Max Carey, Pittsburgh NL
OF—Goose Goslin, Washington AL
C—Mickey Cochrane, Phil. AL
P—Walter Johnson, Washington AL
P—Ed Rommel, Philadelphia AL
P—Dazzy Vance, Brooklyn NL

1926

1B—George Burns, Cleveland AL
2B—Rogers Hornsby, St. Louis NL
SS—Joe Sewell, Cleveland AL
3B—Pie Traynor, Pittsburgh NL
OF—Goose Goslin, Washington AL
OF—John Mostil, Chicago AL
OF—Babe Ruth, New York AL
C—Bob O'Farrell, St. Louis NL
P—Herb Pennock, New York AL
P—George Uhle, Cleveland AL
P—Grover Alexander, St. Louis NL

1927

1B—Lou Gehrig, New York AL
2B—Rogers Hornsby, New York NL
SS—Travis Jackson, New York NL
3B—Pie Traynor, Pittsburgh NL
OF—Babe Ruth, New York AL
OF—Al Simmons, Philadelphia AL
OF—Paul Waner, Pittsburgh NL
C—Gabby Hartnett, Chicago NL
P—Charley Root, Chicago NL
P—Ted Lyons, Chicago AL

1928

1B—Lou Gehrig, New York AL
2B—Rogers Hornsby, Boston NL
SS—Travis Jackson, New York NL
3B—Fred Lindstrom, New York NL
OF—Babe Ruth, New York AL
OF—Heinie Manush, St. Louis AL
OF—Paul Waner, Pittsburgh NL
C—Mickey Cochrane, Phil. AL
P—Lefty Grove, Philadelphia AL
P—Waite Hoyt, New York AL

1929

1B—Jimmie Foxx, Philadelphia AL
2B—Rogers Hornsby, Chicago NL
SS—Travis Jackson, New York NL
3B—Pie Traynor, Pittsburgh NL
OF—Al Simmons, Philadelphia AL
OF—Hack Wilson, Chicago NL
OF—Babe Ruth, New York AL
C—Mickey Cochrane, Phil. AL
P—Lefty Grove, Philadelphia AL
P—Burleigh Grimes, Pittsburgh NL

1930

1B—Bill Terry, New York NL
2B—Frank Frisch, St. Louis NL
SS—Joe Cronin, Washington AL
3B—Fred Lindstrom, New York NL
OF—Al Simmons, Philadelphia AL
OF—Hack Wilson, Chicago NL
OF—Babe Ruth, New York AL
C—Mickey Cochrane, Phil. AL
P—Lefty Grove, Philadelphia AL
P—Wes Ferrell, Cleveland AL

1931

1B—Lou Gehrig, New York AL
2B—Frank Frisch, St. Louis NL
SS—Joe Cronin, Washington AL
3B—Pie Traynor, Pittsburgh NL
OF—Al Simmons, Philadelphia AL
OF—Earl Averill, Cleveland AL
OF—Babe Ruth, New York AL
C—Mickey Cochrane, Phil. AL
P—Lefty Grove, Philadelphia AL
P—George Earnshaw, Phil. AL

1932

1B—Jimmie Foxx, Philadelphia AL
2B—Tony Lazzeri, New York AL
SS—Joe Cronin, Washington AL
3B—Pie Traynor, Pittsburgh NL
OF—Lefty O'Doul, Brooklyn NL
OF—Earl Averill, Cleveland AL
OF—Chuck Klein, Philadelphia NL
C—Bill Dickey, New York AL
P—Lefty Grove, Philadelphia AL
P—Lon Warneke, Chicago NL

1933

1B—Jimmie Foxx, Philadelphia AL
2B—Charley Gehringer, Detroit AL
SS—Joe Cronin, Washington AL
3B—Pie Traynor, Pittsburgh NL
OF—Al Simmons, Chicago AL
OF—Wally Berger, Boston NL
OF—Chuck Klein, Philadelphia NL
C—Bill Dickey, New York AL
P—Alvin Crowder, Washington AL
P—Carl Hubbell, New York NL

1934

1B—Lou Gehrig, New York AL
2B—Charley Gehringer, Detroit AL
SS—Joe Cronin, Washington AL
3B—Mike Higgins, Philadelphia AL
OF—Al Simmons, Chicago AL
OF—Earl Averill, Cleveland AL
OF—Mel Ott, New York NL
C—Mickey Cochrane, Detroit AL
P—Lefty Gomez, New York AL
P—Schoolboy Rowe, Detroit AL
P—Dizzy Dean, St. Louis NL

1935

1B—Hank Greenberg, Detroit AL
2B—Charley Gehringer, Detroit AL
SS—Arky Vaughan, Pittsburgh NL
3B—Pepper Martin, St. Louis NL
OF—Joe Medwick, St. Louis NL
OF—Doc Cramer, Philadelphia AL
OF—Mel Ott, New York NL
C—Mickey Cochrane, Detroit AL
P—Carl Hubbell, New York NL
P—Dizzy Dean, St. Louis NL

1936

1B—Lou Gehrig, New York AL
2B—Charley Gehringer, Detroit AL
SS—Luke Appling, Chicago AL
3B—Mike Higgins, Philadelphia AL
OF—Joe Medwick, St. Louis NL
OF—Earl Averill, Cleveland AL
OF—Mel Ott, New York NL
C—Bill Dickey, New York AL
P—Carl Hubbell, New York NL
P—Dizzy Dean, St. Louis NL

1937

1B—Lou Gehrig, New York AL
2B—Charley Gehringer, Detroit AL
SS—Dick Bartell, New York NL
3B—Red Rolfe, New York AL
OF—Joe Medwick, St. Louis NL
OF—Joe DiMaggio, New York AL
OF—Paul Waner, Pittsburgh NL
C—Gabby Hartnett, Chicago NL
P—Carl Hubbell, New York NL
P—Red Ruffing, New York AL

1938

1B—Jimmie Foxx, Boston AL
2B—Charley Gehringer, Detroit AL
SS—Joe Cronin, Boston AL
3B—Red Rolfe, New York AL
OF—Joe Medwick, St. Louis NL
OF—Joe DiMaggio, New York AL
OF—Mel Ott, New York NL
C—Bill Dickey, New York AL
P—Red Ruffing, New York AL
P—Lefty Gomez, New York AL
P—Johnny Vander Meer, Cin. NL

1939

1B—Jimmie Foxx, Boston AL
2B—Joe Gordon, New York AL
SS—Joe Cronin, Boston AL
3B—Red Rolfe, New York AL
OF—Joe Medwick, St. Louis NL
OF—Joe DiMaggio, New York AL
OF—Ted Williams, Boston AL
C—Bill Dickey, New York AL
P—Red Ruffing, New York AL
P—Bob Feller, Cleveland AL
P—Bucky Walters, Cincinnati NL

1940

1B—Frank McCormick, Cin. NL
2B—Joe Gordon, New York AL
SS—Luke Appling, Chicago AL
3B—Stan Hack, Chicago NL
OF—Hank Greenberg, Detroit AL
OF—Joe DiMaggio, New York AL
OF—Ted Williams, Boston AL
C—Harry Danning, New York NL
P—Bob Feller, Cleveland AL
P—Bucky Walters, Cincinnati NL
P—Paul Derringer, Cincinnati NL

1941

1B—Dolf Camilli, Brooklyn NL
2B—Joe Gordon, New York AL
SS—Cecil Travis, Washington AL
3B—Stan Hack, Chicago NL
OF—Ted Williams, Boston AL
OF—Joe DiMaggio, New York AL
OF—Pete Reiser, Brooklyn NL
C—Bill Dickey, New York AL
P—Bob Feller, Cleveland AL
P—Whitlow Wyatt, Brooklyn NL
P—Bill Lee, Chicago NL

1942

1B—Johnny Mize, New York NL
2B—Joe Gordon, New York AL
SS—Johnny Pesky, Boston AL
3B—Stan Hack, Chicago NL
OF—Ted Williams, Boston AL
OF—Joe DiMaggio, New York AL
OF—Enos Slaughter, St. Louis NL
C—Mickey Owen, Brooklyn NL
P—Mort Cooper, St. Louis NL
P—Tiny Bonham, New York AL
P—Tex Hughson, Boston AL

1943

1B—Rudy York, Detroit AL
2B—Billy Herman, Brooklyn NL
SS—Luke Appling, Chicago AL
3B—Billy Johnson, New York AL
OF—Dick Wakefield, Detroit AL
OF—Stan Musial, St. Louis NL
OF—Bill Nicholson, Chicago NL
C—Walker Cooper, St. Louis NL
P—Spud Chandler, New York AL
P—Mort Cooper, St. Louis NL
P—Rip Sewell, Pittsburgh NL

1944

1B—Ray Sanders, St. Louis NL
2B—Bobby Doerr, Boston AL
SS—Marty Marion, St. Louis NL
3B—Bob Elliott, Pittsburgh NL
OF—Stan Musial, St. Louis NL
OF—Dick Wakefield, Detroit AL
OF—Dixie Walker, Brooklyn, NL
C—Walker Cooper, St. Louis NL
P—Hal Newhouser, Detroit AL
P—Mort Cooper, St. Louis NL
P—Dizzy Trout, Detroit AL

1945

1B—Phil Cavarretta, Chicago NL
2B—George Stirnweiss, New York AL
SS—Marty Marion, St. Louis NL
3B—Whitey Kurowski, St. Louis NL
OF—Tommy Holmes, Boston NL
OF—Andy Pafko, Chicago NL
OF—Goody Rosen, Brooklyn NL
C—Paul Richards, Detroit AL
P—Hal Newhouser, Detroit AL
P—Boo Ferriss, Boston AL
P—Hank Borowy, Chicago NL

1946

1B—Stan Musial, St. Louis NL
2B—Bobby Doerr, Boston AL
SS—Johnny Pesky, Boston AL
3B—George Kell, Detroit AL
OF—Ted Williams, Boston AL
OF—Dom DiMaggio, Boston AL
OF—Enos Slaughter, St. Louis NL
C—Aaron Robinson, New York AL
P—Hal Newhouser, Detroit AL
P—Bob Feller, Cleveland AL
P—Boo Ferriss, Boston AL

1947

1B—Johnny Mize, New York NL
2B—Joe Gordon, Cleveland AL
SS—Lou Boudreau, Cleveland AL
3B—George Kell, Detroit AL
OF—Ted Williams, Boston AL
OF—Joe DiMaggio, New York AL
OF—Ralph Kiner, Pittsburgh NL
C—Walker Cooper, New York NL
P—Ewell Blackwell, Cincinnati NL
P—Bob Feller, Cleveland AL
P—Ralph Branca, Brooklyn NL

1948

1B—Johnny Mize, New York NL
2B—Joe Gordon, Cleveland AL
SS—Lou Boudreau, Cleveland AL
3B—Bob Elliott, Boston NL
OF—Ted Williams, Boston AL
OF—Joe DiMaggio, New York AL
OF—Stan Musial, St. Louis NL
C—Birdie Tebbetts, Boston AL
P—Johnny Sain, Boston NL
P—Bob Lemon, Cleveland AL
P—Harry Brecheen, St. Louis NL

1949

1B—Tommy Henrich, New York AL
2B—Jackie Robinson, Brooklyn NL
SS—Phil Rizzuto, New York AL
3B—George Kell, Detroit AL
OF—Ted Williams, Boston AL
OF—Stan Musial, St. Louis NL
OF—Ralph Kiner, Pittsburgh NL
C—Roy Campanella, Brooklyn NL
P—Mel Parnell, Boston AL
P—Ellis Kinder, Boston AL
P—Joe Page, New York AL

1950

1B—Walt Dropo, Boston AL
2B—Jackie Robinson, Brooklyn NL
SS—Phil Rizzuto, New York AL
3B—George Kell, Detroit AL
OF—Stan Musial, St. Louis NL
OF—Ralph Kiner, Pittsburgh NL
OF—Larry Doby, Cleveland AL
C—Yogi Berra, New York AL
P—Vic Raschi, New York AL
P—Bob Lemon, Cleveland AL
P—Jim Konstanty, Philadelphia NL

1951

1B—Ferris Fain, Philadelphia AL
2B—Jackie Robinson, Brooklyn NL
SS—Phil Rizzuto, New York AL
3B—George Kell, Detroit AL
OF—Stan Musial, St. Louis NL
OF—Ted Williams, Boston AL
OF—Ralph Kiner, Pittsburgh AL
C—Roy Campanella, Brooklyn NL
P—Sal Maglie, New York NL
P—Preacher Roe, Brooklyn NL
P—Allie Reynolds, New York AL

1952

1B—Ferris Fain, Philadelphia AL
2B—Jackie Robinson, Brooklyn NL
SS—Phil Rizzuto, New York AL
3B—George Kell, Boston AL
OF—Stan Musial, St. Louis NL
OF—Hank Sauer, Chicago NL
OF—Mickey Mantle, New York AL
C—Yogi Berra, New York AL
P—Robin Roberts, Philadelphia NL
P—Bobby Shantz, Philadelphia AL
P—Allie Reynolds, New York AL

1953

1B—Mickey Vernon, Washington AL
2B—Red Schoendienst, St. Louis NL
SS—Pee Wee Reese, Brooklyn NL
3B—Al Rosen, Cleveland AL
OF—Stan Musial, St. Louis NL
OF—Duke Snider, Brooklyn NL
OF—Carl Furillo, Brooklyn NL
C—Roy Campanella, Brooklyn NL
P—Robin Roberts, Philadelphia NL
P—Warren Spahn, Milwaukee NL
P—Bob Porterfield, Washington AL

1954

1B—Ted Kluszewski, Cincinnati NL
2B—Bobby Avila, Cleveland AL
SS—Alvin Dark, New York AL
3B—Al Rosen, Cleveland AL
OF—Willie Mays, New York NL
OF—Stan Musial, St. Louis NL
OF—Duke Snider, Brooklyn NL
C—Yogi Berra, New York AL
P—Bob Lemon, Cleveland AL
P—Johnny Antonelli, New York NL
P—Robin Roberts, Philadelphia NL

1955

1B—Ted Kluszewski, Cincinnati NL
2B—Nellie Fox, Chicago AL
SS—Ernie Banks, Chicago NL
3B—Ed Mathews, Milwaukee NL
OF—Duke Snider, Brooklyn NL
OF—Ted Williams, Boston AL
OF—Al Kaline, Detroit AL
C—Roy Campanella, Brooklyn NL
P—Robin Roberts, Philadelphia NL
P—Don Newcombe, Brooklyn NL
P—Whitey Ford, New York AL

1956

1B—Ted Kluszewski, Cincinnati NL
2B—Nellie Fox, Chicago AL
SS—Harvey Kuenn, Detroit AL
3B—Ken Boyer, St. Louis NL
OF—Mickey Mantle, New York AL
OF—Hank Aaron, Milwaukee NL
OF—Ted Williams, Boston AL
C—Yogi Berra, New York AL
P—Don Newcombe, Brooklyn NL
P—Whitey Ford, New York AL
P—Billy Pierce, Chicago AL

1957

1B—Stan Musial, St. Louis NL
2B—Red Schoendienst, N.Y.-Mil. NL
SS—Gil McDougald, New York AL
3B—Ed Mathews, Milwaukee NL
OF—Mickey Mantle, New York AL
OF—Ted Williams, Boston AL
OF—Willie Mays, New York NL
C—Yogi Berra, New York AL
P—Warren Spahn, Milwaukee NL
P—Billy Pierce, Chicago NL
P—Jim Bunning, Detroit AL

1958

1B—Stan Musial, St. Louis NL
2B—Nellie Fox, Chicago AL
SS—Ernie Banks, Chicago NL
3B—Frank Thomas, Pittsburgh NL
OF—Ted Williams, Boston AL
OF—Willie Mays, San Francisco NL
OF—Hank Aaron, Milwaukee NL
C—Del Crandall, Milwaukee NL
P—Bob Turley, New York AL
P—Warren Spahn, Milwaukee NL
P—Bob Friend, Pittsburgh NL

1959

1B—Orlando Cepeda, S.F. NL
2B—Nellie Fox, Chicago AL
SS—Ernie Banks, Chicago NL
3B—Ed Mathews, Milwaukee NL
OF—Minnie Minoso, Cleveland AL
OF—Willie Mays, San Francisco NL
OF—Hank Aaron, Milwaukee NL
C—Sherm Lollar, Chicago AL
P—Early Wynn, Chicago AL
P—Sam Jones, San Francisco NL
P—Johnny Antonelli, S.F. NL

1960

1B—Bill Skowron, New York AL
2B—Bill Mazeroski, Pittsburgh NL
SS—Ernie Banks, Chicago NL
3B—Ed Mathews, Milwaukee NL
OF—Minnie Minoso, Chicago AL
OF—Willie Mays, San Francisco NL
OF—Roger Maris, New York AL
C—Del Crandall, Milwaukee NL
P—Vernon Law, Pittsburgh NL
P—Warren Spahn, Milwaukee NL
P—Ernie Broglio, St. Louis NL

1961

AMERICAN LEAGUE

1B—Norm Cash, Detroit
2B—Bobby Richardson, New York
SS—Tony Kubek, New York
3B—Brooks Robinson, Baltimore
OF—Mickey Mantle, New York
OF—Roger Maris, New York
OF—Rocky Colavito, Detroit
C—Elston Howard, New York
P—Whitey Ford, New York
P—Frank Lary, Detroit

NATIONAL LEAGUE

1B—Orlando Cepeda, San Francisco
2B—Frank Bolling, Milwaukee
SS—Maury Wills, Los Angeles
3B—Ken Boyer, St. Louis
OF—Willie Mays, San Francisco
OF—Frank Robinson, Cincinnati
OF—Roberto Clemente, Pittsburgh
C—Smoky Burgess, Pittsburgh
P—Joey Jay, Cincinnati
P—Warren Spahn, Milwaukee

1962

AMERICAN LEAGUE

1B—Norm Siebern, Kansas City
2B—Bobby Richardson, New York
SS—Tom Tresh, New York
3B—Brooks Robinson, Baltimore
OF—Leon Wagner, Los Angeles
OF—Mickey Mantle, New York
OF—Al Kaline, Detroit
C—Earl Battey, Minnesota
P—Ralph Terry, New York
P—Dick Donovan, Cleveland

NATIONAL LEAGUE

1B—Orlando Cepeda, San Francisco
2B—Bill Mazeroski, Pittsburgh
SS—Maury Wills, Los Angeles
3B—Ken Boyer, St. Louis
OF—Tommy Davis, Los Angeles
OF—Willie Mays, San Francisco
OF—Frank Robinson, Cincinnati
C—Del Crandall, Milwaukee
P—Don Drysdale, Los Angeles
P—Bob Purkey, Cincinnati

1963

AMERICAN LEAGUE

1B—Joe Pepitone, New York
2B—Bobby Richardson, New York
SS—Luis Aparicio, Baltimore
3B—Frank Malzone, Boston
OF—Carl Yastrzemski, Boston
OF—Albie Pearson, Los Angeles
OF—Al Kaline, Detroit
C—Elston Howard, New York
P—Whitey Ford, New York
P—Gary Peters, Chicago

NATIONAL LEAGUE

1B—Bill White, St. Louis
2B—Jim Gilliam, Los Angeles
SS—Dick Groat, St. Louis
3B—Ken Boyer, St. Louis
OF—Tommy Davis, Los Angeles
OF—Willie Mays, San Francisco
OF—Hank Aaron, Milwaukee
C—John Edwards, Cincinnati
P—Sandy Koufax, Los Angeles
P—Juan Marichal, San Francisco

1964

AMERICAN LEAGUE

1B—Dick Stuart, Boston
2B—Bobby Richardson, New York
SS—Jim Fregosi, Los Angeles
3B—Brooks Robinson, Baltimore
OF—Harmon Killebrew, Minnesota
OF—Mickey Mantle, New York
OF—Tony Oliva, Minnesota
C—Elston Howard, New York
P—Dean Chance, Los Angeles
P—Gary Peters, Chicago

NATIONAL LEAGUE

1B—Bill White, St. Louis
2B—Ron Hunt, New York
SS—Dick Groat, St. Louis
3B—Ken Boyer, St. Louis
OF—Billy Williams, Chicago
OF—Willie Mays, San Francisco
OF—Roberto Clemente, Pittsburgh
C—Joe Torre, Milwaukee
P—Sandy Koufax, Los Angeles
P—Jim Bunning, Philadelphia

1965

AMERICAN LEAGUE

1B—Fred Whitfield, Cleveland
2B—Bobby Richardson, New York
SS—Zoilo Versalles, Minnesota
3B—Brooks Robinson, Baltimore
OF—Carl Yastrzemski, Boston
OF—Jimmie Hall, Minnesota
OF—Tony Oliva, Minnesota
C—Earl Battey, Minnesota
P—Jim Grant, Minnesota
P—Mel Stottlemyre, New York

NATIONAL LEAGUE

1B—Willie McCovey, San Francisco
2B—Pete Rose, Cincinnati
SS—Maury Wills, Los Angeles
3B—Deron Johnson, Cincinnati
OF—Willie Stargell, Pittsburgh
OF—Willie Mays, San Francisco
OF—Hank Aaron, Milwaukee
C—Joe Torre, Milwaukee
P—Sandy Koufax, Los Angeles
P—Juan Marichal, San Francisco

1966

AMERICAN LEAGUE

1B—Boog Powell, Baltimore
2B—Bobby Richardson, New York
SS—Luis Aparicio, Baltimore
3B—Brooks Robinson, Baltimore
OF—Frank Robinson, Baltimore
OF—Al Kaline, Detroit
OF—Tony Oliva, Minnesota
C—Paul Casanova, Washington
P—Jim Kaat, Minnesota
P—Earl Wilson, Detroit

NATIONAL LEAGUE

1B—Felipe Alou, Atlanta
2B—Pete Rose, Cincinnati
SS—Gene Alley, Pittsburgh
3B—Ron Santo, Chicago
OF—Willie Stargell, Pittsburgh
OF—Willie Mays, San Francisco
OF—Roberto Clemente, Pittsburgh
C—Joe Torre, Atlanta
P—Sandy Koufax, Los Angeles
P—Juan Marichal, San Francisco

1967
AMERICAN LEAGUE
1B—Harmon Killebrew, Minnesota
2B—Rod Carew, Minnesota
SS—Jim Fregosi, California
3B—Brooks Robinson, Baltimore
OF—Carl Yastrzemski, Boston
OF—Al Kaline, Detroit
OF—Frank Robinson, Baltimore
C—Bill Freehan, Detroit
P—Jim Lonborg, Boston
P—Earl Wilson, Detroit

NATIONAL LEAGUE
1B—Orlando Cepeda, St. Louis
2B—Bill Mazeroski, Pittsburgh
SS—Gene Alley, Pittsburgh
3B—Ron Santo, Chicago
OF—Hank Aaron, Atlanta
OF—Jim Wynn, Houston
OF—Roberto Clemente, Pittsburgh
C—Tim McCarver, St. Louis
P—Mike McCormick, San Francisco
P—Ferguson Jenkins, Chicago

1968
AMERICAN LEAGUE
1B—Boog Powell, Baltimore
2B—Rod Carew, Minnesota
SS—Luis Aparicio, Chicago
3B—Brooks Robinson, Baltimore
OF—Ken Harrelson, Boston
OF—Willie Horton, Detroit
OF—Frank Howard, Washington
C—Bill Freehan, Detroit
P—Dave McNally, Baltimore
P—Denny McLain, Detroit

NATIONAL LEAGUE
1B—Willie McCovey, San Francisco
2B—Tommy Helms, Cincinnati
SS—Don Kessinger, Chicago
3B—Ron Santo, Chicago
OF—Billy Williams, Chicago
OF—Curt Flood, St. Louis
OF—Pete Rose, Cincinnati
C—Johnny Bench, Cincinnati
P—Bob Gibson, St. Louis
P—Juan Marichal, San Francisco

1969
AMERICAN LEAGUE
1B—Boog Powell, Baltimore
2B—Rod Carew, Minnesota
SS—Rico Petrocelli, Boston
3B—Harmon Killebrew, Minnesota
OF—Frank Howard, Washington
OF—Paul Blair, Baltimore
OF—Reggie Jackson, Oakland
C—Bill Freehan, Detroit
RHP—Denny McLain, Detroit
LHP—Mike Cuellar, Baltimore

NATIONAL LEAGUE
1B—Willie McCovey, San Francisco
2B—Glenn Beckert, Chicago
SS—Don Kessinger, Chicago
3B—Ron Santo, Chicago
OF—Cleon Jones, New York
OF—Matty Alou, Pittsburgh
OF—Hank Aaron, Atlanta
C—Johnny Bench, Cincinnati
RHP—Tom Seaver, New York
LHP—Steve Carlton, St. Louis

1970
AMERICAN LEAGUE
1B—Boog Powell, Baltimore
2B—Dave Johnson, Baltimore
SS—Luis Aparicio, Chicago
3B—Harmon Killebrew, Minnesota
OF—Frank Howard, Washington
OF—Reggie Smith, Boston
OF—Tony Oliva, Minnesota
C—Ray Fosse, Cleveland
RHP—Jim Perry, Minnesota
LHP—Sam McDowell, Cleveland

NATIONAL LEAGUE
1B—Willie McCovey, San Francisco
2B—Glenn Beckert, Chicago
SS—Don Kessinger, Chicago
3B—Tony Perez, Cincinnati
OF—Billy Williams, Chicago
OF—Bobby Tolan, Cincinnati
OF—Hank Aaron, Atlanta
C—Johnny Bench, Cincinnati
RHP—Bob Gibson, St. Louis
LHP—Jim Merritt, Cincinnati

1971
AMERICAN LEAGUE
1B—Norm Cash, Detroit
2B—Cookie Rojas, Kansas City
SS—Leo Cardenas, Minnesota
3B—Brooks Robinson, Baltimore
OF—Merv Rettenmund, Baltimore
OF—Bobby Murcer, New York
OF—Tony Oliva, Minnesota
C—Bill Freehan, Detroit
RHP—Jim Palmer, Baltimore
LHP—Vida Blue, Oakland

NATIONAL LEAGUE
1B—Lee May, Cincinnati
2B—Glenn Beckett, Chicago
SS—Bud Harrelson, New York
3B—Joe Torre, St. Louis
OF—Willie Stargell, Pittsburgh
OF—Willie Davis, Los Angeles
OF—Hank Aaron, Atlanta
C—Manny Sanguillen, Pittsburgh
RHP—Ferguson Jenkins, Chicago
LHP—Steve Carlton, St. Louis

1972
AMERICAN LEAGUE
1B—Dick Allen, Chicago
2B—Rod Carew, Minnesota
SS—Luis Aparicio, Boston
3B—Brooks Robinson, Baltimore
OF—Joe Rudi, Oakland
OF—Bobby Murcer, New York
OF—Richie Scheinblum, Kansas City
C—Carlton Fisk, Boston
RHP—Gaylord Perry, Cleveland
LHP—Wilbur Wood, Chicago

NATIONAL LEAGUE
1B—Willie Stargell, Pittsburgh
2B—Joe Morgan, Cincinnati
SS—Chris Speier, San Francisco
3B—Ron Santo, Chicago
OF—Billy Williams, Chicago
OF—Cesar Cedeno, Houston
OF—Roberto Clemente, Pittsburgh
C—Johnny Bench, Cincinnati
RHP—Ferguson Jenkins, Chicago
LHP—Steve Carlton, Philadelphia

1973
AMERICAN LEAGUE
1B—John Mayberry, Kansas City
2B—Rod Carew, Minnesota
SS—Bert Campaneris, Oakland
3B—Sal Bando, Oakland
OF—Reggie Jackson, Oakland
OF—Amos Otis, Kansas City
OF—Bobby Murcer, New York
C—Thurman Munson, New York
RHP—Jim Palmer, Baltimore
LHP—Ken Holtzman, Oakland

NATIONAL LEAGUE
1B—Tony Perez, Cincinnati
2B—Dave Johnson, Atlanta
SS—Bill Russell, Los Angeles
3B—Darrell Evans, Atlanta
OF—Bobby Bonds, San Francisco
OF—Cesar Cedeno, Houston
OF—Pete Rose, Cincinnati
C—Johnny Bench, Cincinnati
RHP—Tom Seaver, New York
LHP—Ron Bryant, San Francisco

1974
AMERICAN LEAGUE
1B—Dick Allen, Chicago
2B—Rod Carew, Minnesota
SS—Bert Campaneris, Oakland
3B—Sal Bando, Oakland
OF—Joe Rudi, Oakland
OF—Paul Blair, Baltimore
OF—Jeff Burroughs, Texas
C—Thurman Munson, New York
DH—Tommy Davis, Baltimore
RHP—Jim Hunter, Oakland
LHP—Mike Cuellar, Baltimore

NATIONAL LEAGUE
1B—Steve Garvey, Los Angeles
2B—Joe Morgan, Cincinnati
SS—Dave Concepcion, Cincinnati
3B—Mike Schmidt, Philadelphia
OF—Lou Brock, St. Louis
OF—Jim Wynn, Los Angeles
OF—Richie Zisk, Pittsburgh
C—Johnny Bench, Cincinnati
RHP—Andy Messersmith, Los Angeles
LHP—Don Gullett, Cincinnati

1975
AMERICAN LEAGUE
1B—John Mayberry, Kansas City
2B—Rod Carew, Minnesota
SS—Toby Harrah, Texas
3B—Graig Nettles, New York
OF—Jim Rice, Boston
OF—Fred Lynn, Boston
OF—Reggie Jackson, Oakland
C—Thurman Munson, New York
DH—Willie Horton, Detroit
RHP—Jim Palmer, Baltimore
LHP—Jim Kaat, Chicago

NATIONAL LEAGUE
1B—Steve Garvey, Los Angeles
2B—Joe Morgan, Cincinnati
SS—Larry Bowa, Philadelphia
3B—Bill Madlock, Chicago
OF—Greg Luzinski, Philadelphia
OF—Al Oliver, Pittsburgh
OF—Dave Parker, Pittsburgh
C—Johnny Bench, Cincinnati
RHP—Tom Seaver, New York
LHP—Randy Jones, San Diego

1976

AMERICAN LEAGUE
1B—Chris Chambliss, New York
2B—Bobby Grich, Baltimore
3B—George Brett, Kansas City
SS—Mark Belanger, Baltimore
OF—Joe Rudi, Oakland
OF—Mickey Rivers, New York
OF—Reggie Jackson, Baltimore
C—Thurman Munson, New York
DH—Hal McRae, Kansas City
RHP—Jim Palmer, Baltimore
LHP—Frank Tanana, California

NATIONAL LEAGUE
1B—Willie Montanez, San Fran.-Atl.
2B—Joe Morgan, Cincinnati
3B—Mike Schmidt, Philadelphia
SS—Dave Concepcion, Cincinnati
OF—George Foster, Cincinnati
OF—Cesar Cedeno, Houston
OF—Ken Griffey, Cincinnati
C—Bob Boone, Philadelphia
RHP—Don Sutton, Los Angeles
LHP—Randy Jones, San Diego

1977

AMERICAN LEAGUE
1B—Rod Carew, Minnesota
2B—Willie Randolph, New York
3B—Graig Nettles, New York
SS—Rick Burleson, Boston
OF—Jim Rice, Boston
OF—Larry Hisle, Minnesota
OF—Bobby Bonds, California
C—Carlton Fisk, Boston
DH—Hal McRae, Kansas City
RHP—Nolan Ryan, California
LHP—Frank Tanana, California

NATIONAL LEAGUE
1B—Steve Garvey, Los Angeles
2B—Joe Morgan, Cincinnati
3B—Mike Schmidt, Philadelphia
SS—Garry Templeton, St. Louis
OF—George Foster, Cincinnati
OF—Dave Parker, Pittsburgh
OF—Greg Luzinski, Philadelphia
C—Ted Simmons, St. Louis
RHP—Rick Reuschel, Chicago
LHP—Steve Carlton, Philadelphia

1978

AMERICAN LEAGUE
1B—Rod Carew, Minnesota
2B—Frank White, Kansas City
3B—Graig Nettles, New York
SS—Robin Yount, Milwaukee
OF—Jim Rice, Boston
OF—Larry Hisle, Milwaukee
OF—Fred Lynn, Boston
C—Jim Sundberg, Texas
DH—Rusty Staub, Detroit
RHP—Jim Palmer, Baltimore
LHP—Ron Guidry, New York

NATIONAL LEAGUE
1B—Steve Garvey, Los Angeles
2B—Dave Lopes, Los Angeles
3B—Pete Rose, Cincinnati
SS—Larry Bowa, Philadelphia
OF—George Foster, Cincinnati
OF—Dave Parker, Pittsburgh
OF—Jack Clark, San Francisco
C—Ted Simmons, St. Louis
RHP—Gaylord Perry, San Diego
LHP—Vida Blue, San Francisco

1979

AMERICAN LEAGUE
1B—Cecil Cooper, Milwaukee
2B—Bobby Grich, California
3B—George Brett, Kansas City
SS—Roy Smalley, Minnesota
OF—Jim Rice, Boston
OF—Fred Lynn, Boston
OF—Ken Singleton, Baltimore
C—Darrell Porter, Kansas City
DH—Don Baylor, California
RHP—Jim Kern, Texas
LHP—Mike Flanagan, Baltimore

NATIONAL LEAGUE
1B—Keith Hernandez, St. Louis
2B—Dave Lopes, Los Angeles
3B—Mike Schmidt, Philadelphia
SS—Garry Templeton, St. Louis
OF—Dave Kingman, Chicago
OF—Omar Moreno, Pittsburgh
OF—Dave Winfield, San Diego
C—Ted Simmons, St. Louis
RHP—Joe Niekro, Houston
LHP—Steve Carlton, Philadelphia

1980

AMERICAN LEAGUE
1B—Cecil Cooper, Milwaukee
2B—Willie Randolph, New York
3B—George Brett, Kansas City
SS—Robin Yount, Milwaukee
OF—Ben Oglivie, Milwaukee
OF—Al Bumbry, Baltimore
OF—Reggie Jackson, New York
DH—Reggie Jackson, New York
C—Rick Cerone, New York
RHP—Steve Stone, Baltimore
LHP—Tommy John, New York

NATIONAL LEAGUE
1B—Keith Hernandez, St. Louis
2B—Manny Trillo, Philadelphia
3B—Mike Schmidt, Philadelphia
SS—Garry Templeton, St. Louis
OF—Dusty Baker, Los Angeles
OF—Cesar Cedeno, Houston
OF—George Hendrick, St. Louis
C—Gary Carter, Montreal
RHP—Jim Bibby, Pittsburgh
LHP—Steve Carlton, Philadelphia

1981

AMERICAN LEAGUE
1B—Cecil Cooper, Milwaukee
2B—Bobby Grich, California
3B—Buddy Bell, Texas
SS—Rick Burleson, California
OF—Rickey Henderson, Oakland
OF—Dwayne Murphy, Oakland
OF—Tony Armas, Oakland
C—Jim Sundberg, Texas
DH—Richie Zisk, Seattle
RHP—Jack Morris, Detroit
LHP—Ron Guidry, New York

NATIONAL LEAGUE
1B—Pete Rose, Philadelphia
2B—Manny Trillo, Philadelphia
3B—Mike Schmidt, Philadelphia
SS—Dave Concepcion, Cincinnati
OF—George Foster, Cincinnati
OF—Andre Dawson, Montreal
OF—Pedro Guerrero, Los Angeles
C—Gary Carter, Montreal
RHP—Tom Seaver, Cincinnati
LHP—Fernando Valenzuela, Los Ang.

1982

AMERICAN LEAGUE
1B—Cecil Cooper, Milwaukee
2B—Damaso Garcia, Toronto
3B—Doug DeCinces, California
SS—Robin Yount, Milwaukee
OF—Dave Winfield, New York
OF—Gorman Thomas, Milwaukee
OF—Dwight Evans, Boston
C—Lance Parrish, Detroit
DH—Hal McRae, Kansas City
RHP—Dave Stieb, Toronto
LHP—Geoff Zahn, California

NATIONAL LEAGUE
1B—Al Oliver, Montreal
2B—Manny Trillo, Philadelphia
3B—Mike Schmidt, Philadelphia
SS—Ozzie Smith, St. Louis
OF—Lonnie Smith, St. Louis
OF—Dale Murphy, Atlanta
OF—Pedro Guerrero, Los Angeles
C—Gary Carter, Montreal
RHP—Steve Rogers, Montreal
LHP—Steve Carlton, Philadelphia

1983

AMERICAN LEAGUE
1B—Eddie Murray, Baltimore
2B—Lou Whitaker, Detroit
3B—Wade Boggs, Boston
SS—Cal Ripken, Baltimore
OF—Jim Rice, Boston
OF—Dave Winfield, New York
OF—Lloyd Moseby, Toronto
C—Carlton Fisk, Chicago
DH—Greg Luzinski, Chicago
RHP—LaMarr Hoyt, Chicago
LHP—Ron Guidry, New York

NATIONAL LEAGUE
1B—George Hendrick, St. Louis
2B—Glenn Hubbard, Atlanta
3B—Mike Schmidt, Philadelphia
SS—Dickie Thon, Houston
OF—Dale Murphy, Atlanta
OF—Andre Dawson, Montreal
OF—Tim Raines, Montreal
C—Tony Pena, Pittsburgh
RHP—John Denny, Philadelphia
LHP—Larry McWilliams, Pittsburgh

1984

AMERICAN LEAGUE
1B—Don Mattingly, New York
2B—Lou Whitaker, Detroit
3B—Buddy Bell, Texas
SS—Cal Ripken, Baltimore
OF—Tony Armas, Boston
OF—Dwight Evans, Boston
OF—Dave Winfield, New York
C—Lance Parrish, Detroit
DH—Dave Kingman, Oakland
RHP—Mike Boddicker, Baltimore
LHP—Willie Hernandez, Detroit

NATIONAL LEAGUE
1B—Keith Hernandez, New York
2B—Ryne Sandberg, Chicago
3B—Mike Schmidt, Philadelphia
SS—Ozzie Smith, St. Louis
OF—Dale Murphy, Atlanta
OF—Jose Cruz, Houston
OF—Tony Gwynn, San Diego
C—Gary Carter, Montreal
RHP—Rick Sutcliffe, Chicago
LHP—Mark Thurmond, San Diego

1985
AMERICAN LEAGUE
1B—Don Mattingly, New York
2B—Damaso Garcia, Toronto
3B—Wade Boggs, Boston
SS—Cal Ripken, Baltimore
OF—Rickey Henderson, New York
OF—Harold Baines, Chicago
OF—Phil Bradley, Seattle
C—Carlton Fisk, Chicago
DH—Don Baylor, New York
RHP—Bret Saberhagen, Kansas City
LHP—Ron Guidry, New York

NATIONAL LEAGUE
1B—Keith Hernandez, New York
2B—Tom Herr, St. Louis
3B—Tim Wallach, Montreal
SS—Ozzie Smith, St. Louis
OF—Dave Parker, Cincinnati
OF—Willie McGee, St. Louis
OF—Dale Murphy, Atlanta
C—Gary Carter, New York
RHP—Dwight Gooden, New York
LHP—John Tudor, St. Louis

1986
AMERICAN LEAGUE
1B—Don Mattingly, New York
2B—Tony Bernazard, Cleveland
3B—Wade Boggs, Boston
SS—Tony Fernandez, Toronto
OF—Jim Rice, Boston
OF—George Bell, Toronto
OF—Kirby Puckett, Minnesota
C—Rich Gedman, Boston
DH—Don Baylor, Boston
RHP—Roger Clemens, Boston
LHP—Teddy Higuera, Milwaukee

NATIONAL LEAGUE
1B—Keith Hernandez, New York
2B—Steve Sax, Los Angeles
3B—Mike Schmidt, Philadelphia
SS—Ozzie Smith, St. Louis
OF—Tim Raines, Montreal
OF—Tony Gwynn, San Diego
OF—Dave Parker, Cincinnati
C—Gary Carter, New York
RHP—Mike Scott, Houston
LHP—Fernando Valenzuela, Los Ang.

1987
AMERICAN LEAGUE
1B—Don Mattingly, New York
2B—Willie Randolph, New York
3B—Wade Boggs, Boston
SS—Alan Trammell, Detroit
OF—George Bell, Toronto
OF—Kirby Puckett, Minnesota
OF—Dwight Evans, Boston
C—Matt Nokes, Detroit
DH—Paul Molitor, Milwaukee
RHP—Roger Clemens, Boston
LHP—Jimmy Key, Toronto

NATIONAL LEAGUE
1B—Jack Clark, St. Louis
2B—Juan Samuel, Philadelphia
3B—Tim Wallach, Montreal
SS—Ozzie Smith, St. Louis
OF—Andre Dawson, Chicago
OF—Tony Gwynn, San Diego
OF—Eric Davis, Cincinnati
C—Benito Santiago, San Diego
RHP—Rick Sutcliffe, Chicago
LHP—Zane Smith, Atlanta

1988
AMERICAN LEAGUE
1B—George Brett, Kansas City
2B—Johnny Ray, California
3B—Wade Boggs, Boston
SS—Alan Trammell, Detroit
OF—Kirby Puckett, Minnesota
OF—Mike Greenwell, Boston
OF—Jose Canseco, Oakland
C—Ernie Whitt, Toronto
DH—Harold Baines, Chicago
RHP—Dave Stewart, Oakland
LHP—Frank Viola, Minnesota

NATIONAL LEAGUE
1B—Will Clark, San Francisco
2B—Ryne Sandberg, Chicago
3B—Bobby Bonilla, Pittsburgh
SS—Barry Larkin, Cincinnati
OF—Darryl Strawberry, New York
OF—Andy Van Slyke, Pittsburgh
OF—Kevin McReynolds, New York
C—Mike LaValliere, Pittsburgh
RHP—Orel Hershiser, Los Angeles
LHP—Danny Jackson, Cincinnati

1989
AMERICAN LEAGUE
1B—Fred McGriff, Toronto
2B—Julio Franco, Texas
3B—Carney Lansford, Oakland
SS—Cal Ripken, Baltimore
OF—Ruben Sierra, Texas
OF—Kirby Puckett, Minnesota
OF—Robin Yount, Milwaukee
C—Mickey Tettleton, Baltimore
DH—Harold Baines, Chicago-Texas
RHP—Bret Saberhagen, Kansas City
LHP—Chuck Finley, California

NATIONAL LEAGUE
1B—Will Clark, San Francisco
2B—Ryne Sandberg, Chicago
3B—Howard Johnson, New York
SS—Shawon Dunston, Chicago
OF—Tony Gwynn, San Diego
OF—Kevin Mitchell, San Francisco
OF—Eric Davis, Cincinnati
C—Benito Santiago, San Diego
RHP—Mike Scott, Houston
LHP—Mark Davis, San Diego

1990
AMERICAN LEAGUE
1B—Cecil Fielder, Detroit
2B—Julio Franco, Texas
3B—Kelly Gruber, Toronto
SS—Alan Trammell, Detroit
OF—Rickey Henderson, Oakland
OF—Jose Canseco, Oakland
OF—Ellis Burks, Boston
C—Carlton Fisk, Chicago
DH—Dave Parker, Milwaukee
RHP—Bob Welch, Oakland
LHP—Chuck Finley, California

NATIONAL LEAGUE
1B—Eddie Murray, Los Angeles
2B—Ryne Sandberg, Chicago
3B—Matt Williams, San Francisco
SS—Barry Larkin, Cincinnati
OF—Barry Bonds, Pittsburgh
OF—Bobby Bonilla, Pittsburgh
OF—Darryl Strawberry, New York
C—Mike Scioscia, Los Angeles
RHP—Doug Drabek, Pittsburgh
LHP—Frank Viola, New York

1991
AMERICAN LEAGUE
1B—Cecil Fielder, Detroit
2B—Julio Franco, Texas
3B—Wade Boggs, Boston
SS—Cal Ripken, Baltimore
OF—Jose Canseco, Oakland
OF—Joe Carter, Toronto
OF—Ken Griffey Jr., Seattle
C—Mickey Tettleton, Detroit
RHP—Roger Clemens, Boston
LHP—Jim Abbott, California

NATIONAL LEAGUE
1B—Will Clark, San Francisco
2B—Ryne Sandberg, Chicago
3B—Terry Pendleton, Atlanta
SS—Barry Larkin, Cincinnati
OF—Barry Bonds, Pittsburgh
OF—Bobby Bonilla, Pittsburgh
OF—Ron Gant, Atlanta
C—Benito Santiago, San Diego
RHP—Jose Rijo, Cincinnati
LHP—Tom Glavine, Atlanta

MINOR LEAGUE PLAYER OF THE YEAR

Year	Player, Team, League
1936	John Vander Meer, Durham, Piedmont
1937	Charlie Keller, Newark, International
1938	Fred Hutchinson, Seattle, Pacific Coast
1939	Lou Novikoff, Tulsa-Los Angeles
1940	Phil Rizzuto, Kansas City, American Association
1941	John Lindell, Newark, International
1942	Dick Barrett, Seattle, Pacific Coast
1943	Chet Covington, Scranton, Eastern

Year	Player, Team, League
1944	Rip Collins, Albany, Eastern
1945	Gil Coan, Chattanooga, Southern
1946	Sibby Sisti, Indianapolis, American Association
1947	Hank Sauer, Syracuse, International
1948	Gene Woodling, San Francisco, Pacific Coast
1949	Orie Arntzen, Albany, Eastern
1950	Frank Saucier, San Antonio, Texas
1951	Gene Conley, Hartford, Eastern

Year	Player, Team, League
1952—	Bill Skowron, Kansas City, American Association
1953—	Gene Conley, Toledo, American Association
1954—	Herb Score, Indianapolis, American Association
1955—	John Murff, Dallas, Texas
1956—	Steve Bilko, Los Angeles, Pacific Coast
1957—	Norm Siebern, Denver, American Association
1958—	Jim O'Toole, Nashville, Southern
1959—	Frank Howard, Victoria-Spok.
1960—	Willie Davis, Spokane, Pacific Coast
1961—	Howie Koplitz, Birmingham, Southern
1962—	Bob Bailey, Columbus, International
1963—	Don Buford, Indianapolis, International
1964—	Mel Stottlemyre, Richmond, International
1965—	Joe Foy, Toronto, International
1966—	Mike Epstein, Rochester, International
1967—	Johnny Bench, Buffalo, International
1968—	Merv Rettenmund, Rochester, International
1969—	Danny Walton, Oklahoma City, American Association
1970—	Don Baylor, Rochester, International
1971—	Bobby Grich, Rochester, International
1972—	Tom Paciorek, Albuquerque, Pacific Coast

Year	Player, Team, League
1973—	Steve Ontiveros, Phoenix, Pacific Coast
1974—	Jim Rice, Pawtucket, International
1975—	Hector Cruz, Tulsa, American Association
1976—	Pat Putnam, Asheville, W. Car.
1977—	Ken Landreaux, S.L.C., Pacific Coast-El Paso, Tex.
1978—	Champ Summers, Indianapolis, American Association
1979—	Mark Bomback, Vancouver, Pacific Coast
1980—	Tim Raines, Denver, American Association
1981—	Mike Marshall, Albuquerque, Pacific Coast
1982—	Ron Kittle, Edmonton, Pacific Coast
1983—	Kevin McReynolds, Las Vegas, Pacific Coast
1984—	Alan Knicely, Wichita, American Association
1985—	Jose Canseco, Hunt., Southern-Tac., Pacific Coast
1986—	Tim Pyznarski, Las Vegas, Pacific Coast
1987—	Randy Milligan, Tidewater, International
1988—	Sandy Alomar Jr., Las Vegas, Pacific Coast
	Gary Sheffield, Denver, American Association (tie)
1989—	Sandy Alomar Jr., Las Vegas, Pacific Coast
1990—	Jose Offerman, Albuquerque, Pacific Coast
1991—	Pedro Martinez, Albuquerque, Pacific Coast

MINOR LEAGUE MANAGER OF THE YEAR

Year	Manager, Team, League
1936—	Al Sothoron, Milwaukee, American Association
1937—	Jake Flowers, Salisbury, Eastern Sh.
1938—	Paul Richards, Atlanta, Southern
1939—	Bill Meyer, Kansas City, American Association
1940—	Larry Gilbert, Nashville, Southern
1941—	Burt Shotton, Columbus, American Association
1942—	Eddie Dyer, Columbus, American Association
1943—	Nick Cullop, Columbus, American Association
1944—	Al Thomas, Baltimore, International
1945—	Lefty O'Doul, San Francisco, Pacific Coast
1946—	Clay Hopper, Montreal, International
1947—	Nick Cullop, Milwaukee, American Association
1948—	Casey Stengel, Oakland, Pacific Coast
1949—	Fred Haney, Hollywood, Pacific Coast
1950—	Rollie Hemsley, Columbus, American Association
1951—	Charlie Grimm, Milwaukee, American Association
1952—	Luke Appling, Memphis, Southern
1953—	Bobby Bragan, Hollywood, Pacific Coast
1954—	Kerby Farrell, Indianapolis, American Association
1955—	Bill Rigney, Minneapolis, American Association
1956—	Kerby Farrell, Indianapolis, American Association
1957—	Ben Geraghty, Wichita, American Association
1958—	Cal Ermer, Birmingham, Southern
1959—	Pete Reiser, Victoria, Texas
1960—	Mel McGaha, Toronto, International
1961—	Kerby Farrell, Buffalo, International
1962—	Ben Geraghty, Jacksonville, International
1963—	Rollie Hemsley, Indianapolis, International

Year	Manager, Team, League
1964—	Harry Walker, Jacksonville, International
1965—	Grady Hatton, Oklahoma City, Pacific Coast
1966—	Bob Lemon, Seattle, Pacific Coast
1967—	Bob Skinner, San Diego, Pacific Coast
1968—	Jack Tighe, Toledo, International
1969—	Clyde McCullough, Tidewater, International
1970—	Tom Lasorda, Spokane, Pacific Coast
1971—	Del Rice, Salt Lake City, Pacific Coast
1972—	Hank Bauer, Tidewater, International
1973—	Joe Morgan, Charleston, International
1974—	Joe Altobelli, Rochester, International
1975—	Joe Frazier, Tidewater, International
1976—	Vern Rapp, Denver, American Association
1977—	Tommy Thompson, Arkan., Texas
1978—	Les Moss, Evansville, American Association
1979—	Vern Benson, Syracuse, International
1980—	Hal Lanier, Springfield, American Association
1981—	Del Crandall, Albuquerque, Pacific Coast
1982—	George Scherger, Indianapolis, American Association
1983—	Bill Dancy, Reading, Eastern
1984—	Bob Rodgers, Indianapolis, American Association
1985—	Jim Fregosi, Louisville, American Association
1986—	Joe Sparks, Indianapolis, American Association
1987—	Terry Collins, Albuquerque, Pacific Coast
1988—	Joe Sparks, Indianapolis, American Association
1989—	Bob Bailor, Syracuse, International
1990—	Sal Rende, Omaha, American Association
1991—	Chris Chambliss, Greenville, Southern

MINOR LEAGUE EXECUTIVE OF THE YEAR (HIGHER CLASSIFICATIONS)

(Restricted to Class AAA starting in 1963)

Year	Executive, Team, League
1936—	Earl Mann, Atlanta, Southern
1937—	Robert LaMotte, Savannah, Sally
1938—	Louis McKenna, St. Paul, American Association
1939—	Bruce Dudley, Louisville, American Association
1940—	Roy Hamey, Kansas City, American Association
1941—	Emil Sick, Seattle, Pacific Coast
1942—	Bill Veeck, Milwaukee, American Association
1943—	Clarence Rowland, Los Angeles, Pacific Coast
1944—	William Mulligan, Seattle, Pacific Coast
1945—	Bruce Dudley, Louisville, American Association
1946—	Earl Mann, Atlanta, Southern
1947—	William Purnhage, Waterloo, I.I.I.
1948—	Edward Glennon, Birmingham, Southern
1949—	Ted Sullivan, Indianapolis, American Association
1950—	Clearnce (Brick) Laws, Oakland, Pacific Coast
1951—	Robert Howsam, Denver, West
1952—	Jack Cooke, Toronto, International
1953—	Richard Burnett, Dallas, Texas

Year	Executive, Team, League
1954—	Edward Stumpf, Indianapolis, American Association
1955—	Dewey Soriano, Seattle, Pacific Coast
1956—	Robert Howsam, Denver American Association
1957—	John Stiglmeier, Buffalo, International
1958—	Edward Glennon, Birmingham, Southern
1959—	Edward Leishman, Salt Lake City, Pacific Coast
1960—	Ray Winder, Little Rock, Southern
1961—	Elten Schiller, Omaha, American Association
1962—	George Sisler Jr., Rochester, International
1963—	Lewis Matlin, Hawaii, Pacific Coast
1964—	Edward Leishman, San Diego, Pacific Coast
1965—	Harold Cooper, Columbus, International
1966—	John Quinn Jr., Hawaii, Pacific Coast
1967—	Hillman Lyons, Richmond, International
1968—	Gabe Paul Jr., Tulsa, Pacific Coast
1969—	Bill Gardner, Louisville, International
1970—	Dick King, Wichita, American Association
1971—	Carl Steinfeldt Jr., Rochester, International

Year	Executive, Team, League	Year	Executive, Team, League
1972—	Don Labbruzzo, Evansville, American Association	1982—	A. Ray Smith, Louisville, American Association
1973—	Merle Miller, Tucson, Pacific Coast	1983—	A. Ray Smith, Louisville, American Association
1974—	John Carbray, Sacramento, Pacific Coast	1984—	Mike Tamburro, Pawtucket, International
1975—	Stan Naccarato, Tacoma, Pacific Coast	1985—	Patty Cox Hampton, Oklahoma City, Amer. Assoc.
1976—	Art Teece, Salt Lake City, Pacific Coast	1986—	Bob Goughan, Rochester, International
1977—	George Sisler Jr., Columbus, International	1987—	Stu Kehoe, Vancouver, Pacific Coast
1978—	Willie Sanchez, Albuquerque, Pacific Coast	1988—	Bob Rich, Buffalo, American Association
1979—	George Sisler Jr., Columbus, International	1989—	Larry Schmittou, Nashville, American Association
1980—	Jim Burris, Denver, American Association	1990—	Greg Corns, Phoenix, Pacific Coast
1981—	Pat McKernan, Albuquerque, Pacific Coast	1991—	Tom Maloney, Denver, American Association

MINOR LEAGUE EXECUTIVE OF THE YEAR (LOWER CLASSIFICATIONS, 1950-1990)

(Separate awards for Class AA and Class A started in 1963; for Short Class A in 1988)

Year	Executive, Team, League	Year	Executive, Team, League
1950—	H. Cooper, Hutch'son, West. A.	1975—	Jim Paul, El Paso, Texas
1951—	O. W. (Bill) Hayes, Triple, B.S.		Cordy Jensen, Eugene, Northwest
1952—	Hillman Lyons, Danville, MOV	1976—	Woodrow Reid, Chattanooga, Southern
1953—	Carl Roth, Peoria, I.I.I.		Don Buchheister, Cedar Rapids, Midwest
1954—	James Meagham, Cedar Rapids, I.I.I.	1977—	Jim Paul, El Paso, Texas
1955—	John Petrakis, Dubuque, MOV		Harry Pells, Quad Cities, Midwest
1956—	Marvin Milkes, Fresno, California	1978—	Larry Schmittou, Nashville, Southern
1957—	Richard Wagner, Lincoln, West.		Dave Hersh, Appleton, Midwest
1958—	Gerald Waring, Macon, Sally	1979—	Bill Rigney Jr., Midland, Texas
1959—	Clay Dennis, Des Moines, I.I.I.		Tom Romenesko, Greensboro, W.C.
1960—	Hubert Kittle, Yakima, Northwest	1980—	Frances Crockett, Charlotte, Southern
1961—	David Steele, Fresno, California		Tom Romenesko, Greensboro, W.C.
1962—	John Quinn Jr., San Jose, California	1981—	Allie Prescott, Memphis, Southern
1963—	Hugh Finnerty, Tulsa, Texas		Dan Overstreet, Hagerstown, Caro.
	Ben Jewell, M. Valley, Pioneer	1982—	Art Clarkson, Birmingham, Southern
1964—	Glynn West, Birmingham, Southern		Bob Carruesco, Stockton, California
	Jas. Bayens, Rock Hill, W. Car.	1983—	Edward Kenney, New Britain, Eastern
1965—	Dick Butler, Dallas-Ft. Worth, Texas		Terry Reynolds, Vero Beach, Florida State
	Ken. Blackman, Quad Cities, Midwest	1984—	Bruce Baldwin, Greenville, Southern
1966—	Tom Fleming, Evansville, Southern		Dave Tarrolly, Beloit, Midwest
	Cappy Harada, Lodi, California	1985—	Ben Bernard, Albany-Colonie, Eastern
1967—	Robert Quinn, Reading, Eastern		Pete Vonachen, Peoria, Midwest
	Pat Williams, Spar'burg, W.C.	1986—	Bill Davidson, Midland, Texas
1968—	Phil Howser, Charlotte, Southern		Rob Dlugozima, Durham, Carolina
	Merle Miller, Burlington, Midwest	1987—	Joe Preseren, Tulsa, Texas
1969—	Charlie Blaney, Albuquerque, Texas		Skip Weisman, Greensboro, South Atlantic
	Bill Gorman, Visalia, California	1988—	Bill Valentine, Arkansas, Texas
1970—	Carl Sawatski, Arkansas, Texas		Dennis Bastien, Charleston (W.Va.), South Atlantic
	Bob Williams, Bakersfield, California		Bob Beban, Eugene, Northwest
1971—	Miles Wolff, Savannah, Dixie A.	1989—	Chuck Domino, Reading, Eastern
	Ed Holtz, Appleton, Midwest		John Baxter, South Bend, Midwest
1972—	John Begzos, S. Antonio, Texas		Bill Pereira, Boise, Northwest
	Bob Piccinini, Modesto, California	1990—	Joe Preseren, Tulsa, Texas
1973—	Dick Kravitz, Jacksonville, Southern		Dan Chapman, Stockton, California
	Fritz Colschen, Clinton, Midwest		Dave Baggott, Salt Lake City, Pioneer
1974—	Jim Paul, El Paso, Texas		
	Bing Russell, Portland, Northwest		

BASEBALL WRITERS' ASSOCIATION OF AMERICA

MOST VALUABLE PLAYER

AMERICAN LEAGUE

Year	Player, Team, Pos.	Points
1931—	Lefty Grove, Philadelphia, P	78
1932—	Jimmie Foxx, Philadelphia, 1B	75
1933—	Jimmie Foxx, Philadelphia, 1B	74
1934—	Mickey Cochrane, Detroit, C	67
1935—	Hank Greenberg, Detroit, 1B	*80
1936—	Lou Gehrig, New York, 1B	73
1937—	Charley Gehringer, Detroit, 2B	78
1938—	Jimmie Foxx, Boston, 1B	305
1939—	Joe DiMaggio, New York, OF	280
1940—	Hank Greenberg, Detroit, OF	292
1941—	Joe DiMaggio, New York, OF	291
1942—	Joe Gordon, New York, 2B	270
1943—	Spud Chandler, New York, P	246
1944—	Hal Newhouser, Detroit, P	236
1945—	Hal Newhouser, Detroit, P	236
1946—	Ted Williams, Boston, OF	224

NATIONAL LEAGUE

Year	Player, Team, Pos.	Points
1931—	Frank Frisch, St. Louis, 2B	65
1932—	Chuck Klein, Philadelphia, OF	78
1933—	Carl Hubbell, New York, P	77
1934—	Dizzy Dean, St. Louis, P	78
1935—	Gabby Hartnett, Chicago, C	75
1936—	Carl Hubbell, New York, P	60
1937—	Joe Medwick, St. Louis, OF	70
1938—	Ernie Lombardi, Cincinnati, C	229
1939—	Bucky Walters, Cincinnati, P	303
1940—	Frank McCormick, Cincinnati, 1B	274
1941—	Dolf Camilli, Brooklyn, 1B	300
1942—	Mort Cooper, St. Louis, P	263
1943—	Stan Musial, St. Louis, OF	267
1944—	Marty Marion, St. Louis, SS	190
1945—	Phil Cavarretta, Chicago, 1B	279
1946—	Stan Musial, St. Louis, 1B	319

Year	Player, Team, Pos.	Points
1947—	Joe DiMaggio, New York, OF	202
1948—	Lou Boudreau, Cleveland, SS	324
1949—	Ted Williams, Boston, OF	272
1950—	Phil Rizzuto, New York SS	284
1951—	Yogi Berra, New York, C	184
1952—	Bobby Shantz, Philadelphia, P	280
1953—	Al Rosen, Cleveland, 3B	*336
1954—	Yogi Berra, New York, C	230
1955—	Yogi Berra, New York, C	218
1956—	Mickey Mantle, New York, OF	*336
1957—	Mickey Mantle, New York, OF	233
1958—	Jackie Jensen, Boston, OF	233
1959—	Nellie Fox, Chicago, 2B	295
1960—	Roger Maris, New York, OF	225
1961—	Roger Maris, New York, OF	202
1962—	Mickey Mantle, New York, OF	234
1963—	Elston Howard, New York, C	248
1964—	Brooks Robinson, Baltimore, 3B	269
1965—	Zoilo Versalles, Minnesota, SS	275
1966—	Frank Robinson, Baltimore, OF	*280
1967—	Carl Yastrzemski, Boston, OF	275
1968—	Denny McLain, Detroit, P	*280
1969—	Harmon Killebrew, Minnesota, 1B-3B	294
1970—	Boog Powell, Baltimore, 1B	234
1971—	Vida Blue, Oakland, P	268
1972—	Dick Allen, Chicago, 1B	321
1973—	Reggie Jackson, Oakland, OF	*336
1974—	Jeff Burroughs, Texas, OF	248
1975—	Fred Lynn, Boston, OF	326
1976—	Thurman Munson, New York, C	304
1977—	Rod Carew, Minnesota, 1B	273
1978—	Jim Rice, Boston, OF	352
1979—	Don Baylor, California, OF	347
1980—	George Brett, Kansas City, 3B	335
1981—	Rollie Fingers, Milwaukee, P	319
1982—	Robin Yount, Milwaukee, SS	385
1983—	Cal Ripken, Baltimore, SS	322
1984—	Willie Hernandez, Detroit, P	306
1985—	Don Mattingly, New York, 1B	367
1986—	Roger Clemens, Boston, P	339
1987—	George Bell, Toronto, OF	332
1988—	Jose Canseco, Oakland, OF	*392
1989—	Robin Yount, Milwaukee, OF	256
1990—	Rickey Henderson, Oakland, OF	317
1991—	Cal Ripken, Baltimore, SS	318

*Unanimous selection.

Year	Player, Team, Pos.	Points
1947—	Bob Elliott, Boston, 3B	205
1948—	Stan Musial, St. Louis, OF	303
1949—	Jackie Robinson, Brooklyn, 2B	264
1950—	Jim Konstanty, Philadelphia, P	286
1951—	Roy Campanella, Brooklyn, C	243
1952—	Hank Sauer, Chicago, OF	226
1953—	Roy Campanella, Brooklyn, C	297
1954—	Willie Mays, New York, OF	283
1955—	Roy Campanella, Brooklyn, C	226
1956—	Don Newcombe, Brooklyn, P	223
1957—	Hank Aaron, Milwaukee, OF	239
1958—	Ernie Banks, Chicago, SS	283
1959—	Ernie Banks, Chicago, SS	232½
1960—	Dick Groat, Pittsburgh, SS	276
1961—	Frank Robinson, Cincinnati, OF	219
1962—	Maury Wills, Los Angeles, SS	209
1963—	Sandy Koufax, Los Angeles, P	237
1964—	Ken Boyer, St. Louis, 3B	243
1965—	Willie Mays, San Francisco, OF	224
1966—	Roberto Clemente, Pittsburgh, OF	218
1967—	Orlando Cepeda, St. Louis, 1B	*280
1968—	Bob Gibson, St. Louis, P	242
1969—	Willie McCovey, San Francisco, 1B	265
1970—	Johnny Bench, Cincinnati, C	326
1971—	Joe Torre, St. Louis, 3B	318
1972—	Johnny Bench, Cincinnati, C	263
1973—	Pete Rose, Cincinnati, OF	274
1974—	Steve Garvey, Los Angeles, 1B	270
1975—	Joe Morgan, Cincinnati, 2B	321½
1976—	Joe Morgan, Cincinnati, 2B	311
1977—	George Foster, Cincinnati, OF	291
1978—	Dave Parker, Pittsburgh, OF	320
1979—	Willie Stargell, Pittsburgh, 1B	216
	Keith Hernandez, St. Louis, 1B	216
1980—	Mike Schmidt, Philadelphia, 3B	*336
1981—	Mike Schmidt, Philadelphia, 3B	321
1982—	Dale Murphy, Atlanta, OF	283
1983—	Dale Murphy, Atlanta, OF	318
1984—	Ryne Sandberg, Chicago, 2B	326
1985—	Willie McGee, St. Louis, OF	280
1986—	Mike Schmidt, Philadelphia, 3B	287
1987—	Andre Dawson, Chicago, OF	269
1988—	Kirk Gibson, Los Angeles, OF	272
1989—	Kevin Mitchell, San Francisco, OF	314
1990—	Barry Bonds, Pittsburgh, OF	331
1991—	Terry Pendleton, Atlanta, 3B	274

CY YOUNG MEMORIAL AWARD

Year	Pitcher, Team	Votes
1956—	Don Newcombe, Brooklyn	10
1957—	Warren Spahn, Milwaukee	15
1958—	Bob Turley, New York AL	5
1959—	Early Wynn, Chicago AL	13
1960—	Vernon Law, Pittsburgh	8
1961—	Whitey Ford, New York AL	9
1962—	Don Drysdale, Los Angeles NL	14
1963—	Sandy Koufax, Los Angeles NL	*20
1964—	Dean Chance, Los Angeles AL	17
1965—	Sandy Koufax, Los Angeles NL	*20
1966—	Sandy Koufax, Los Angeles NL	*20
1967—	A. L.—Jim Lonborg, Boston	18
	N. L.—Mike McCormick, San Francisco	18
1968—	A. L.—Denny McLain, Detroit	*20
	N. L.—Bob Gibson, St. Louis	*20
1969—	A. L.—Denny McLain, Detroit	10
	Mike Cuellar, Baltimore	10
	N. L.—Tom Seaver, New York	23
1970—	A. L.—Jim Perry, Minnesota	55
	N. L.—Bob Gibson, St. Louis	118
1971—	A. L.—Vida Blue, Oakland	98
	N. L.—Fergie Jenkins, Chicago	97
1972—	A. L.—Gaylord Perry, Cleveland	64
	N. L.—Steve Carlton, Philadelphia	*120
1973—	A. L.—Jim Palmer, Baltimore	88
	N. L.—Tom Seaver, New York	71

Year	Pitcher, Team	Votes
1974—	A. L.—Jim Hunter, Oakland	90
	N. L.—Mike Marshall, Los Angeles	96
1975—	A. L.—Jim Palmer, Baltimore	98
	N. L.—Tom Seaver, New York	98
1976—	A. L.—Jim Palmer, Baltimore	108
	N. L.—Randy Jones, San Diego	96
1977—	A. L.—Sparky Lyle, New York	56½
	N. L.—Steve Carlton, Philadelphia	*104
1978—	A. L.—Ron Guidry, New York	*140
	N. L.—Gaylord Perry, San Diego	116
1979—	A. L.—Mike Flanagan, Baltimore	136
	N. L.—Bruce Sutter, Chicago	72
1980—	A. L.—Steve Stone, Baltimore	100
	N. L.—Steve Carlton, Philadelphia	118
1981—	A. L.—Rollie Fingers, Milwaukee	126
	N. L.—Fernando Valenzuela, Los Angeles	70
1982—	A. L.—Pete Vuckovich, Milwaukee	87
	N. L.—Steve Carlton, Philadelphia	112
1983—	A. L.—LaMarr Hoyt, Chicago	116
	N. L.—John Denny, Philadelphia	103
1984—	A. L.—Willie Hernandez, Detroit	88
	N. L.—Rick Sutcliffe, Chicago	*120
1985—	A. L.—Bret Saberhagen, Kansas City	127
	N. L.—Dwight Gooden, New York	*120
1986—	A. L.—Roger Clemens, Boston	*140
	N. L.—Mike Scott, Houston	98

Year	Pitcher, Team	Votes
1987— A. L.—Roger Clemens, Boston	124
N. L.—Steve Bedrosian, Philadelphia	57
1988— A. L.—Frank Viola, Minnesota	138
N. L.—Orel Hershiser, Los Angeles	*120
1989— A. L.—Bret Saberhagen, Kansas City	138
N. L.—Mark Davis, San Diego	107

Year	Pitcher, Team	Votes
1990— A. L.—Bob Welch, Oakland	107
N. L.—Doug Drabek, Pittsburgh	118
1991— A. L.—Roger Clemens, Boston	119
N. L.—Tom Glavine, Atlanta	110

*Unanimous selection.

ROOKIE OF THE YEAR

1947—Combined selection—Jackie Robinson, Brooklyn NL, 1B.
1948—Combined selection—Alvin Dark, Boston NL, SS.

AMERICAN LEAGUE

Year	Player, Team, Pos.	Votes
1949— Roy Sievers, St. Louis, OF	10
1950— Walt Dropo, Boston, 1B	15
1951— Gil McDougald, New York, 3B	13
1952— Harry Byrd, Philadelphia, P	9
1953— Harvey Kuenn, Detroit, SS	23
1954— Bob Grim, New York, P	15
1955— Herb Score, Cleveland, P	18
1956— Luis Aparicio, Chicago, SS	22
1957— Tony Kubek, New York, IF-OF	23
1958— Albie Pearson, Washington, OF	14
1959— Bob Allison, Washington, OF	18
1960— Ron Hansen, Baltimore, SS	22
1961— Don Schwall, Boston, P	7
1962— Tom Tresh, New York, OF-SS	13
1963— Gary Peters, Chicago, P	10
1964— Tony Oliva, Minnesota, OF	19
1965— Curt Blefary, Baltimore, OF	12
1966— Tommie Agee, Chicago, OF	16
1967— Rod Carew, Minnesota, 2B	19
1968— Stan Bahnsen, New York, P	17
1969— Lou Piniella, Kansas City, OF	9
1970— Thurman Munson, New York, C	23
1971— Chris Chambliss, Cleveland, 1B	11
1972— Carlton Fisk, Boston, C	*24
1973— Al Bumbry, Baltimore, OF	13½
1974— Mike Hargrove, Texas, 1B	16½
1975— Fred Lynn, Boston, OF	23
1976— Mark Fidrych, Detroit, P	22
1977— Eddie Murray, Baltimore, DH-1B	12½
1978— Lou Whitaker, Detroit, 2B	21
1979— John Castino, Minnesota, 3B	7
Alfredo Griffin, Toronto, SS	7
1980— Joe Charboneau, Cleveland, OF	103
1981— Dave Righetti, New York, P	127
1982— Cal Ripken, Baltimore, SS-3B	132
1983— Ron Kittle, Chicago, OF	104
1984— Alvin Davis, Seattle, 1B	134
1985— Ozzie Guillen, Chicago, SS	101
1986— Jose Canseco, Oakland, OF	110
1987— Mark McGwire, Oakland, 1B	*140
1988— Walt Weiss, Oakland, SS	103
1989— Gregg Olson, Baltimore, P	136
1990— Sandy Alomar Jr., Cleveland, C	*140
1991— Chuck Knoblauch, Minnesota, 2B	136

*Unanimous selection. †Three writers did not vote.

NATIONAL LEAGUE

Year	Player, Team, Pos.	Votes
1949— Don Newcombe, Brooklyn, P	21
1950— Sam Jethroe, Boston, OF	11
1951— Willie Mays, New York, OF	18
1952— Joe Black, Brooklyn, P	19
1953— Jim Gilliam, Brooklyn, 2B	11
1954— Wally Moon, St. Louis, OF	17
1955— Bill Virdon, St. Louis, OF	15
1956— Frank Robinson, Cincinnati, OF	*24
1957— Jack Sanford, Philadelphia, P	16
1958— Orlando Cepeda, San Francisco, 1B	*†21
1959— Willie McCovey, San Francisco, 1B	*24
1960— Frank Howard, Los Angeles, OF	12
1961— Billy Williams, Chicago, OF	10
1962— Ken Hubbs, Chicago, 2B	19
1963— Pete Rose, Cincinnati, 2B	17
1964— Dick Allen, Philadelphia, 3B	18
1965— Jim Lefebvre, Los Angeles, 2B	13
1966— Tommy Helms, Cincinnati, 3B	12
1967— Tom Seaver, New York, P	11
1968— Johnny Bench, Cincinnati, C	10½
1969— Ted Sizemore, Los Angeles, 2B	14
1970— Carl Morton, Montreal, P	11
1971— Earl Williams, Atlanta, C	18
1972— Jon Matlack, New York, P	19
1973— Gary Matthews, San Francisco, OF	11
1974— Bake McBride, St. Louis, OF	16
1975— John Montefusco, San Francisco, P	12
1976— Butch Metzger, San Diego, P	11
Pat Zachry, Cincinnati, P	11
1977— Andre Dawson, Montreal, OF	10
1978— Bob Horner, Atlanta, 3B	12½
1979— Rick Sutcliffe, Los Angeles, P	20
1980— Steve Howe, Los Angeles, P	80
1981— Fernando Valenzuela, Los Angeles, P	107
1982— Steve Sax, Los Angeles, 2B	63
1983— Darryl Strawberry, New York, OF	109
1984— Dwight Gooden, New York, P	118
1985— Vince Coleman, St. Louis, OF	*120
1986— Todd Worrell, St. Louis, P	118
1987— Benito Santiago, San Diego, C	*120
1988— Chris Sabo, Cincinnati, 3B	79
1989— Jerome Walton, Chicago, OF	116
1990— Dave Justice, Atlanta, OF	118
1991— Jeff Bagwell, Houston, 1B	118

MANAGER OF THE YEAR

AMERICAN LEAGUE

Year	Manager, Team	Points
1983— Tony La Russa, Chicago	17
1984— Sparky Anderson, Detroit	96
1985— Bobby Cox, Toronto	104
1986— John McNamara, Boston	95
1987— Sparky Anderson, Detroit	90
1988— Tony La Russa, Oakland	103
1989— Frank Robinson, Baltimore	125
1990— Jeff Torborg, Chicago	128
1991— Tom Kelly, Minnesota	138

NATIONAL LEAGUE

Year	Manager, Team	Points
1983— Tommy Lasorda, Los Angeles	10
1984— Jim Frey, Chicago	101
1985— Whitey Herzog, St. Louis	86
1986— Hal Lanier, Houston	108
1987— Buck Rodgers, Montreal	92
1988— Tommy Lasorda, Los Angeles	101
1989— Don Zimmer, Chicago	118
1990— Jim Leyland, Pittsburgh	99
1991— Bobby Cox, Atlanta	96

EARLY MOST VALUABLE PLAYER AWARDS

CHALMERS AWARD

AMERICAN LEAGUE

Year	Player, Team, Pos.	Points
1911	Ty Cobb, Detroit, OF	64
1912	Tris Speaker, Boston, OF	59
1913	Walter Johnson, Washington, P	54
1914	Eddie Collins, Philadelphia, 2B	63

NATIONAL LEAGUE

Year	Player, Team, Pos.	Points
1911	Frank Schulte, Chicago, OF	29
1912	Larry Doyle, New York, 2B	48
1913	Jake Daubert, Brooklyn, 1B	50
1914	Johnny Evers, Boston, 2B	50

LEAGUE AWARDS

AMERICAN LEAGUE

Year	Player, Team, Pos.	Points
1922	George Sisler, St. Louis, 1B	59
1923	Babe Ruth, New York, OF	64
1924	Walter Johnson, Washington, P	55
1925	Roger Peckinpaugh, Washington, SS	45
1926	George Burns, Cleveland, 1B	63
1927	Lou Gehrig, New York, 1B	56
1928	Mickey Cochrane, Philadelphia, C	53
1929	No selection	

NATIONAL LEAGUE

Year	Player, Team, Pos.	Points
1922	No selection	
1923	No selection	
1924	Dazzy Vance, Brooklyn, P	74
1925	Rogers Hornsby, St. Louis, 2B	73
1926	Bob O'Farrell, St. Louis, C	79
1927	Paul Waner, Pittsburgh, OF	72
1928	Jim Bottomley, St. Louis, 1B	76
1929	Rogers Hornsby, Chicago, 2B	60

HALL OF FAME

ROSTER OF MEMBERS

Name	Des.*	Elec. year	Votes rec.†	Votes cast‡	% of vote	Teams as player
Aaron, Hank	P	1982	406	415	97.8	Milwaukee NL, Atlanta NL, Milwaukee AL
Alexander, Grover C.	P	1938	212	262	80.9	Philadelphia NL, Chicago NL, St. Louis NL
Alston, Walter	M	1983	CV	—	—	St. Louis NL
Anson, Cap	P	1939	C1	—	—	Chicago NL
Aparicio, Luis	P	1984	341	403	84.6	Chicago AL, Baltimore AL, Boston AL
Appling, Luke	P	1964	189	225	84	Chicago AL
Averill, Earl	P	1975	CV	—	—	Cleveland AL, Detroit AL, Boston AL
Baker, Home Run	P	1955	CV	—	—	Philadelphia AL, New York AL
Bancroft, Dave	P	1971	CV	—	—	Philadelphia NL, New York NL, Boston NL, Brooklyn NL
Banks, Ernie	P	1977	321	383	83.8	Chicago NL
Barlick, Al	U	1989	CV	—	—	
Barrow, Ed	E	1953	CV	—	—	
Beckley, Jake	P	1971	CV	—	—	Pittsburgh NL, Pittsburgh PL, New York NL, Cincinnati NL, St. Louis NL
Bell, Cool Papa	P	1974	SCNL	—	—	Negro Leagues
Bench, Johnny	P	1989	431	447	96.4	Cincinnati NL
Bender, Chief	P	1953	CV	—	—	Philadelphia AL, Philadelphia NL, Chicago AL
Berra, Yogi	P	1972	339	396	85.6	New York AL, New York NL
Bottomley, Jim	P	1974	CV	—	—	St. Louis NL, Cincinnati NL, St. Louis AL
Boudreau, Lou	P	1970	232	300	77.3	Cleveland AL, Boston AL
Bresnahan, Roger	P	1945	C2	—	—	Washington NL, Chicago NL, Baltimore AL, New York NL, St. Louis NL
Brock, Lou	P	1985	315	395	79.7	Chicago NL, St. Louis NL
Brouthers, Dan	P	1945	C2	—	—	Troy NL, Buffalo NL, Detroit NL, Boston NL, Boston PL, Boston AA, Brooklyn NL, Baltimore NL, Louisville NL, Philadelphia NL, New York NL
Brown, Three Finger	P	1949	C2	—	—	St. Louis NL, Chicago NL, Cincinnati NL
Bulkeley, Morgan	E	1937	CC	—	—	
Burkett, Jesse	P	1946	C2	—	—	New York NL, Cleveland NL, St. Louis NL, St. Louis AL, Boston AL
Campanella, Roy	P	1969	270	340	79.4	Brooklyn NL
Carew, Rod	P	1991	401	447	89.7	Minnesota AL, California AL
Carey, Max	P	1961	CV	—	—	Pittsburgh NL, Brooklyn NL
Cartwright, Alexander	O	1938	CC	—	—	
Chadwick, Henry	O	1938	CC	—	—	
Chance, Frank	P	1946	C2	—	—	Chicago NL, New York AL
Chandler, Happy	E	1982	CV	—	—	
Charleston, Oscar	P	1976	SCNL	—	—	Negro Leagues
Chesbro, Jack	P	1946	C2	—	—	Pittsburgh NL, New York AL, Boston AL
Clarke, Fred	P	1945	C2	—	—	Louisville NL, Pittsburgh NL
Clarkson, John	P	1963	CV	—	—	Worcester NL, Chicago NL, Boston NL, Cleveland NL
Clemente, Roberto	P	1973	393	424	92.7	Pittsburgh NL
Cobb, Ty	P	1936	222	226	98.2	Detroit AL, Philadelphia AL
Cochrane, Mickey	P	1947	128	161	79.5	Philadelphia AL, Detroit AL
Collins, Eddie	P	1939	213	274	77.7	Philadelphia AL, Chicago AL
Collins, Jimmy	P	1945	C2	—	—	Boston NL, Louisville NL, Boston AL, Philadelphia AL
Combs, Earle	P	1970	CV	—	—	New York AL
Comiskey, Charley	F/P	1939	C1	—	—	St. Louis AA, Chicago PL, Cincinnati NL
Conlan, Jocko	U	1974	CV	—	—	Chicago AL
Connolly, Tommy	U	1953	CV	—	—	
Connor, Roger	P	1976	CV	—	—	Troy NL, New York NL, New York PL, Philadelphia NL, St. Louis NL
Coveleski, Stan	P	1969	CV	—	—	Philadelphia AL, Cleveland AL, Washington AL, New York AL
Crawford, Sam	P	1957	CV	—	—	Cincinnati NL, Detroit AL
Cronin, Joe	P	1956	152	193	78.8	Pittsburgh NL, Washington AL, Boston AL
Cummings, Candy	P	1939	C1	—	—	Hartford NL, Cincinnati NL
Cuyler, Kiki	P	1968	CV	—	—	Pittsburgh NL, Chicago NL, Cincinnati NL, Brooklyn NL
Dandridge, Ray	P	1987	CV	—	—	Negro Leagues
Dean, Dizzy	P	1953	209	264	79.2	St. Louis NL, Chicago NL, St. Louis AL
Delahanty, Ed	P	1945	C2	—	—	Philadelphia NL, Cleveland PL, Washington AL
Dickey, Bill	P	1954	202	252	80.2	New York AL
Dihigo, Martin	P	1977	SCNL	—	—	Negro Leagues
DiMaggio, Joe	P	1955	223	251	88.8	New York AL
Doerr, Bobby	P	1986	CV	—	—	Boston AL
Drysdale, Don	P	1984	316	403	78.4	Brooklyn NL, Los Angeles NL
Duffy, Hugh	P	1945	C2	—	—	Chicago NL, Chicago PL, Boston AA, Boston NL, Milwaukee AL, Philadelphia NL
Evans, Billy	U	1973	CV	—	—	
Evers, Johnny	P	1946	C2	—	—	Chicago NL, Boston NL, Philadelphia NL, Chicago AL
Ewing, Buck	P	1939	C1	—	—	Troy NL, New York NL, New York PL, Cleveland NL, Cincinnati NL

Name	Des.*	Elec. year	Votes rec.†	Votes cast‡	% of vote	Teams as player
Faber, Red	P	1964	CV	—	—	Chicago AL
Feller, Bob	P	1962	150	160	93.8	Cleveland AL
Ferrell, Rick	P	1984	CV	—	—	St. Louis AL, Boston AL, Washington AL
Fingers, Rollie	P	1992	349	430	81.2	Oakland AL, San Diego NL, Milwaukee AL
Flick, Elmer	P	1963	CV	—	—	Philadelphia NL, Philadelphia AL, Cleveland AL
Ford, Whitey	P	1974	284	365	77.8	New York AL
Foster, Rube	P	1981	CV	—	—	Negro Leagues
Foxx, Jimmie	P	1951	179	226	79.2	Philadelphia AL, Boston AL, Chicago NL, Philadelphia NL
Frick, Ford	E	1970	CV	—	—	
Frisch, Frank	P	1947	136	161	84.5	New York NL, St. Louis NL
Galvin, Pud	P	1965	CV	—	—	Buffalo NL, Pittsburgh AA, Pittsburgh NL, Pittsburgh PL, St. Louis NL
Gehrig, Lou	P	1939	SE	—	—	New York AL
Gehringer, Charley	P	1949	159	187	85.0	Detroit AL
Gibson, Bob	P	1981	337	401	84.0	St. Louis NL
Gibson, Josh	P	1972	SCNL	—	—	Negro Leagues
Giles, Warren	E	1979	CV	—	—	
Gomez, Lefty	P	1972	CV	—	—	New York AL, Washington AL
Goslin, Goose	P	1968	CV	—	—	Washington AL, St. Louis AL, Detroit AL
Greenberg, Hank	P	1956	164	193	85.0	Detroit AL, Pittsburgh NL
Griffith, Clark	M	1946	C2	—	—	St. Louis AA, Boston AA, Chicago NL, Chicago AL, New York AL, Cincinnati NL, Washington AL
Grimes, Burleigh	P	1964	CV	—	—	Pittsburgh NL, Brooklyn NL, New York NL, Boston NL, St. Louis NL, Chicago NL, New York AL
Grove, Lefty	P	1947	123	161	76.4	Philadelphia AL, Boston AL
Hafey, Chick	P	1971	CV	—	—	St. Louis NL, Cincinnati NL
Haines, Jesse	P	1970	CV	—	—	Cincinnati NL, St. Louis NL
Hamilton, Billy	P	1961	CV	—	—	Kansas City AA, Philadelphia NL, Boston NL
Harridge, Will	E	1972	CV	—	—	
Harris, Bucky	M	1975	CV	—	—	Washington AL, Detroit AL
Hartnett, Gabby	P	1955	195	251	77.7	Chicago NL, New York NL
Heilmann, Harry	P	1952	203	234	86.8	Detroit AL, Cincinnati NL
Herman, Billy	P	1975	CV	—	—	Chicago NL, Brooklyn NL, Boston NL, Pittsburgh NL
Hooper, Harry	P	1971	CV	—	—	Boston AL, Chicago AL
Hornsby, Rogers	P	1942	182	233	78.1	St. Louis NL, New York NL, Boston NL, Chicago NL, St. Louis AL
Hoyt, Waite	P	1969	CV	—	—	New York NL, Boston AL, New York AL, Detroit AL, Philadelphia AL, Brooklyn NL, Pittsburgh NL
Hubbard, Cal	U	1976	CV	—	—	
Hubbell, Carl	P	1947	140	161	87.0	New York NL
Huggins, Miller	M	1964	CV	—	—	Cincinnati NL, St. Louis NL
Hunter, Catfish	P	1987	315	413	76.3	Kansas City AL, Oakland AL, New York AL
Irvin, Monte	P	1973	SCNL	—	—	New York NL, Chicago NL, Negro Leagues
Jackson, Travis	P	1982	CV	—	—	New York NL
Jenkins, Ferguson	P	1991	334	447	74.7	Philadelphia NL, Chicago NL, Texas AL, Boston AL
Jennings, Hugh	P	1945	C2	—	—	Louisville AA, Louisville NL, Baltimore NL, Brooklyn NL, Philadelphia NL, Detroit AL
Johnson, Ban	E	1937	CC	—	—	
Johnson, Judy	P	1975	SCNL	—	—	Negro Leagues
Johnson, Walter	P	1936	189	226	83.6	Washington AL
Joss, Addie	P	1978	CV	—	—	Cleveland AL
Kaline, Al	P	1980	340	385	88.3	Detroit AL
Keefe, Tim	P	1964	CV	—	—	Troy NL, New York AA, New York NL, New York PL, Philadelphia NL
Keeler, Willie	P	1939	207	274	75.5	New York NL, Brooklyn NL, Baltimore NL, New York AL
Kell, George	P	1983	CV	—	—	Philadelphia AL, Detroit AL, Boston AL, Chicago AL, Baltimore AL
Kelley, Joe	P	1971	CV	—	—	Boston NL, Pittsburgh NL, Baltimore NL, Brooklyn NL, Baltimore AL, Cincinnati NL
Kelly, George	P	1973	CV	—	—	New York NL, Pittsburgh NL, Cincinnati NL, Chicago NL, Brooklyn NL
Kelly, Mike	P	1945	C2	—	—	Cincinnati NL, Chicago NL, Boston NL, Boston PL, Cincinnati AA, Boston AA, New York NL
Killebrew, Harmon	P	1984	335	403	83.1	Washington AL, Minnesota AL, Kansas City AL
Kiner, Ralph	P	1975	273	362	75.4	Pittsburgh NL, Chicago NL, Cleveland AL
Klein, Chuck	P	1980	CV	—	—	Philadelphia NL, Chicago NL, Pittsburgh NL
Klem, Bill	U	1953	CV	—	—	
Koufax, Sandy	P	1972	344	396	86.9	Brooklyn NL, Los Angeles NL
Lajoie, Nap	P	1937	168	201	83.6	Philadelphia NL, Philadelphia AL, Cleveland AL
Landis, Kenesaw M.	E	1944	C2	—	—	
Lazzeri, Tony	P	1991	CV	—	—	New York AL, Chicago NL, Brooklyn NL, New York NL
Lemon, Bob	P	1976	305	388	78.6	Cleveland AL
Lindstrom, Fred	P	1976	CV	—	—	New York NL, Pittsburgh NL, Chicago NL, Brooklyn NL
Lloyd, John Henry	P	1977	SCNL	—	—	Negro Leagues
Lombardi, Ernie	P	1986	CV	—	—	Brooklyn NL, Cincinnati NL, Boston NL, New York NL
Lopez, Al	M	1977	CV	—	—	Brooklyn NL, Boston NL, Pittsburgh NL, Cleveland AL
Lyons, Ted	P	1955	217	251	86.5	Chicago AL

Name	Des.*	Elec. year	Votes rec.†	Votes cast‡	% of vote	Teams as player
Mack, Connie	M	1937	CC	—	—	Washington NL, Buffalo PL, Pittsburgh NL
MacPhail, Larry	E	1978	CV	—	—	
Mantle, Mickey	P	1974	322	365	88.2	New York AL
Manush, Heinie	P	1964	CV	—	—	Detroit AL, St. Louis AL, Washington AL, Boston AL, Brooklyn NL, Pittsburgh NL
Maranville, Rabbit	P	1954	209	252	82.9	Boston NL, Pittsburgh NL, Chicago NL, Brooklyn NL, St. Louis NL
Marichal, Juan	P	1983	313	374	83.7	San Francisco NL, Boston AL, Los Angeles NL
Marquard, Rube	P	1971	CV	—	—	New York NL, Brooklyn NL, Cincinnati NL, Boston NL
Mathews, Eddie	P	1978	301	379	79.4	Boston NL, Milwaukee NL, Atlanta NL, Houston NL, Detroit AL
Mathewson, Christy	P	1936	205	226	90.7	New York NL, Cincinnati NL
Mays, Willie	P	1979	409	432	94.7	New York (Giants)NL, San Francisco NL, New York (Mets)NL
McCarthy, Joe	M	1957	CV	—	—	
McCarthy, Tommy	P	1946	C2	—	—	Boston UA, Boston NL, Philadelphia NL, St. Louis AA, Brooklyn NL
McCovey, Willie	P	1986	346	425	81.4	San Francisco NL, San Diego NL, Oakland AL
McGinnity, Joe	P	1946	C2	—	—	Baltimore NL, Brooklyn NL, Baltimore AL, New York NL
McGraw, John	M	1937	CC	—	—	Baltimore AA, Baltimore NL, St. Louis NL, Baltimore AL, New York NL
McKechnie, Bill	M	1962	CV	—	—	Pittsburgh NL, Boston NL, New York AL, New York NL, Cincinnati NL
Medwick, Joe	P	1968	240	283	84.8	St. Louis NL, Brooklyn NL, New York NL, Boston NL
Mize, Johnny	P	1981	CV	—	—	St. Louis NL, New York NL, New York AL
Morgan, Joe	P	1990	363	444	81.8	Houston NL, Cincinnati NL, San Francisco NL, Philadelphia NL, Oakland AL
Musial, Stan	P	1969	317	340	93.2	St. Louis NL
Nichols, Kid	P	1949	C2	—	—	Boston NL, St. Louis NL, Philadelphia NL
O'Rourke, Jim	P	1945	C2	—	—	Boston NL, Providence NL, Buffalo NL, New York NL, Washington NL, New York PL
Ott, Mel	P	1951	197	226	87.2	New York NL
Paige, Satchel	P	1971	SCNL	—	—	Cleveland AL, St. Louis AL, Kansas City AL, Negro Leagues
Palmer, Jim	P	1990	411	444	92.6	Baltimore AL
Pennock, Herb	P	1948	94	121	77.7	Philadelphia AL, Boston AL, New York AL
Perry, Gaylord	P	1991	342	447	76.5	San Francisco NL, Cleveland AL, Texas AL, San Diego NL, New York AL, Atlanta NL, Seattle AL, Kansas City AL
Plank, Eddie	P	1946	C2	—	—	Philadelphia AL, St. Louis AL
Radbourn, Hoss	P	1939	C1	—	—	Buffalo NL, Providence NL, Boston NL, Boston PL, Cincinnati NL
Reese, Pee Wee	P	1984	CV	—	—	Brooklyn NL, Los Angeles NL
Rice, Sam	P	1963	CV	—	—	Washington AL, Cleveland AL
Rickey, Branch	E	1967	CV	—	—	St. Louis AL, New York AL
Rixey, Eppa	P	1963	CV	—	—	Philadelphia NL, Cincinnati NL
Roberts, Robin	P	1976	337	388	86.9	Philadelphia NL, Baltimore AL, Houston NL, Chicago NL
Robinson, Brooks	P	1983	344	374	92.0	Baltimore AL
Robinson, Frank	P	1982	370	415	89.2	Cincinnati NL, Baltimore AL, Los Angeles NL, California AL, Cleveland AL
Robinson, Jackie	P	1962	124	160	77.5	Brooklyn NL
Robinson, Wilbert	M	1945	C2	—	—	Philadelphia AA, Baltimore AA, Baltimore NL, St. Louis NL, Baltimore AL
Roush, Edd	P	1962	CV	—	—	Chicago AL, New York NL, Cincinnati NL
Ruffing, Red	P	1967	266	306	86.9	Boston AL, New York AL, Chicago AL
Rusie, Amos	P	1977	CV	—	—	Indianapolis NL, New York NL, Cincinnati NL
Ruth, Babe	P	1936	215	226	95.1	Boston AL, New York AL, Boston NL
Schalk, Ray	P	1955	CV	—	—	Chicago AL, New York NL
Schoendienst, Red	P	1989	CV	—	—	St. Louis NL, New York (Giants)NL, Milwaukee NL
Seaver, Tom	P	1992	425	430	98.8	New York NL, Cincinnati NL, Chicago AL, Boston AL
Sewell, Joe	P	1977	CV	—	—	Cleveland AL, New York AL
Simmons, Al	P	1953	199	264	75.4	Philadelphia AL, Chicago AL, Detroit AL, Washington AL, Boston NL, Cincinnati NL, Boston AL
Sisler, George	P	1939	235	274	85.8	St. Louis AL, Washington AL, Boston NL
Slaughter, Enos	P	1985	CV	—	—	St. Louis NL, New York AL, Kansas City AL, Milwaukee NL
Snider, Duke	P	1980	333	385	86.5	Brooklyn NL, Los Angeles NL, New York NL, San Francisco NL
Spahn, Warren	P	1973	316	380	83.2	Boston NL, Milwaukee NL, New York NL, San Francisco NL
Spalding, Al	P	1939	C1	—	—	Chicago NL
Speaker, Tris	P	1937	165	201	82.1	Boston AL, Cleveland AL, Washington AL, Philadelphia AL
Stargell, Willie	P	1988	352	427	82.4	Pittsburgh NL
Stengel, Casey	M	1966	CV	—	—	Brooklyn NL, Pittsburgh NL, Philadelphia NL, New York NL, Boston NL
Terry, Bill	P	1954	195	252	77.4	New York NL
Thompson, Sam	P	1974	CV	—	—	Detroit NL, Philadelphia NL, Detroit AL
Tinker, Joe	P	1946	C2	—	—	Chicago NL, Cincinnati NL
Traynor, Pie	P	1948	93	121	76.9	Pittsburgh NL
Vance, Dazzy	P	1955	205	251	81.7	Pittsburgh NL, New York AL, Brooklyn NL, St. Louis NL, Cincinnati NL
Vaughan, Arky	P	1985	CV	—	—	Pittsburgh NL, Brooklyn NL
Veeck, Bill	E	1991	CV	—	—	
Waddell, Rube	P	1946	C2	—	—	Louisville NL, Pittsburgh NL, Chicago NL, Philadelphia AL, St. Louis AL

Name	Des.*	Elec. year	Votes rec.†	Votes cast‡	% of vote	Teams as player
Wagner, Honus	P	1936	215	226	95.1	Louisville NL, Pittsburgh NL
Wallace, Bobby	P	1953	CV	—	—	Cleveland NL, St. Louis NL, St. Louis AL
Walsh, Ed	P	1946	C2	—	—	Chicago AL, Boston NL
Waner, Lloyd	P	1967	CV	—	—	Pittsburgh NL, Boston NL, Cincinnati NL, Philadelphia NL, Brooklyn NL
Waner, Paul	P	1952	195	234	83.3	Pittsburgh NL, Brooklyn NL, Boston NL, New York AL
Ward, John Montgomery	P	1964	CV	—	—	Providence NL, New York NL, Brooklyn PL, Brooklyn NL
Weiss, George	E	1971	CV	—	—	
Welch, Mickey	P	1973	CV	—	—	Troy NL, New York NL
Wheat, Zack	P	1959	CV	—	—	Brooklyn NL, Philadelphia AL
Wilhelm, Hoyt	P	1985	331	395	83.8	New York NL, St. Louis NL, Cleveland AL, Baltimore AL, Chicago AL, California AL, Atlanta NL, Chicago NL, Los Angeles NL
Williams, Billy	P	1987	354	413	85.7	Chicago NL, Oakland AL
Williams, Ted	P	1966	282	302	93.4	Boston AL
Wilson, Hack	P	1979	CV	—	—	New York NL, Chicago NL, Brooklyn NL, Philadelphia NL
Wright, George	M	1937	CC	—	—	Boston NL, Providence NL
Wright, Harry	M	1953	CV	—	—	Boston NL
Wynn, Early	P	1972	301	396	76.0	Washington AL, Cleveland AL, Chicago AL
Yastrzemski, Carl	P	1989	423	447	94.6	Boston AL
Yawkey, Tom	E	1980	CV	—	—	
Young, Cy	P	1937	153	201	76.1	Cleveland NL, St. Louis NL, Boston AL, Cleveland AL, Boston NL
Youngs, Ross	P	1972	CV	—	—	New York NL

*Designation for which he was honored. Abbreviations: E—executive; F—founder; M—manager; O—organizer; P—player; U—umpire.

†Where an abbreviation is listed rather than a vote total, the enshrinee was selected by one of the following groups: Centennial Commission (CC), committee of old-time players and writers (C1), committee on old-timers (C2), Committee on Veterans (CV), special election by Baseball Writers' Association of America (SE) or Special Committee on Negro Leagues (SCNL).

‡Votes cast by eligible members of the Baseball Writers' Association of America.

League abbreviations: AA—American Association; AL—American League; NL—National League; PL—Players League; UA—Union Association.

MINOR LEAGUES

FARM SYSTEMS

AMERICAN LEAGUE

BALTIMORE (6): AAA—Rochester. AA—Hagerstown. A—Frederick, Kane County. Rookie—Sarasota, Bluefield.

BOSTON (6): AAA—Pawtucket. AA—New Britain. A—Lynchburg, Winter Haven, Elmira. Rookie—Winter Haven Red Sox.

CALIFORNIA (6): AAA—Edmonton. AA—Midland. A—Palm Springs, Quad City, Boise. Rookie—Mesa Angels.

CHICAGO (6): AAA—Vancouver. AA—Birmingham. A—Sarasota, South Bend, Utica. Rookie—Gulf Coast White Sox.

CLEVELAND (6): AAA—Colorado Springs. AA—Canton/Akron. A—Kinston, Columbus (Ga.), Watertown. Rookie—Burlington.

DETROIT (6): AAA—Toledo. AA—London (Ont.). A—Fayetteville, Lakeland, Niagara Falls. Rookie—Bristol.

KANSAS CITY (6): AAA—Omaha. AA—Memphis. A—Baseball City, Appleton, Eugene. Rookie—Boardwalk Royals.

MILWAUKEE (6): AAA—Denver. AA—El Paso. A—Stockton, Beloit. Rookie—Helena, Chandler Brewers.

MINNESOTA (6): AAA—Portland. AA—Orlando. A—Visalia, Kenosha. Rookie—Elizabethton, Gulf Coast Twins.

NEW YORK (7): AAA—Columbus, O. AA—Albany/Colonie. A—Prince William, Fort Lauderdale, Greensboro, Oneonta. Rookie—Sarasota Yankees.

OAKLAND (7): AAA—Tacoma. AA—Huntsville. A—Modesto, Reno, Madison, Southern Oregon. Rookie—Scottsdale Athletics.

SEATTLE (6): AAA—Calgary. AA—Jacksonville. A—San Bernardino, Peninsula, Bellingham. Rookie—Tempe Mariners.

TEXAS (6): AAA—Oklahoma City. AA—Tulsa. A—Charlotte, Gastonia. Rookie—Butte, Gulf Coast Rangers.

TORONTO (7): AAA—Syracuse. AA—Knoxville. A—Dunedin, Myrtle Beach, St. Catharines. Rookie—Medicine Hat, Gulf Coast Blue Jays.

NATIONAL LEAGUE

ATLANTA (7): AAA—Richmond. AA—Greenville. A—Durham, Macon. Rookie—Pulaski, Idaho Falls, Bradenton Braves.

CHICAGO (6): AAA—Iowa. AA—Charlotte. A—Winston-Salem, Peoria, Geneva. Rookie—Huntington.

CINCINNATI (6): AAA—Nashville. AA—Chattanooga. A—Charleston (W.Va.), Cedar Rapids. Rookie—Billings, Plant City Reds.

HOUSTON (7): AAA—Tucson. AA—Jackson. A—Osceola, Asheville, Burlington (Ia.), Auburn. Rookie—Gulf Coast Astros.

LOS ANGELES (7): AAA—Albuquerque. AA—San Antonio. A—Bakersfield, Vero Beach, Yakima. Rookie—Great Falls, Port St. Lucie Dodgers.

MONTREAL (7): AAA—Indianapolis. AA—Harrisburg. A—West Palm Beach, Rockford, Albany, Jamestown. Rookie—Gulf Coast Expos.

NEW YORK (7): AAA—Tidewater. AA—Binghamton. A—St. Lucie, Columbia, Pittsfield. Rookie—Kingsport, Sarasota Mets.

PHILADELPHIA (6): AAA—Scranton/Wilkes-Barre. AA—Reading. A—Clearwater, Spartanburg, Batavia. Rookie—Martinsville.

PITTSBURGH (6): AAA—Buffalo. AA—Carolina. A—Salem, Augusta, Welland (Ont.). Rookie—Bradenton Pirates.

ST. LOUIS (8): AAA—Louisville. AA—Arkansas. A—St. Petersburg, Springfield, Savannah, Hamilton (Ont.). Rookie—Johnson City, Peoria Cardinals.

SAN DIEGO (7): AAA—Las Vegas. AA—Wichita. A—High Desert, Waterloo, Charleston (S.C.), Spokane. Rookie—Scottsdale Padres.

SAN FRANCISCO (6): AAA—Phoenix. AA—Shreveport. A—San Jose, Clinton, Everett. Rookie—Scottsdale.

AMERICAN ASSOCIATION

FINAL STANDINGS

EASTERN DIVISION

Team	W	L	T	Pct.	GB
Buffalo (Pirates)	81	62	0	.566	....
Indianapolis (Expos)	75	68	0	.524	6
Nashville (Reds)	65	78	0	.455	16
Louisville (Cardinals)	51	92	0	.357	30

WESTERN DIVISION

Team	W	L	T	Pct.	GB
Denver (Brewers)	79	65	0	.549	....
Iowa (Cubs)	78	66	0	.542	1
Omaha (Royals)	73	71	0	.507	6
Oklahoma City (Rangers)	52	92	0	.361	27

COMPOSITE

Team	Buf.	Den.	Iowa	Ind.	Oma.	Nash.	O.C.	Lou.	W	L	T	Pct.	GB
Buffalo (Pirates)	....	4	9	16	7	11	8	11	81	62	0	.566	....
Denver (Brewers)	8	....	12	4	15	7	16	8	79	65	0	.549	2½
Iowa (Cubs)	3	12	....	5	14	8	16	9	78	66	0	.542	3½
Indianapolis (Expos)	4	8	7	....	3	12	9	12	75	68	0	.524	6
Omaha (Royals)	5	9	14	9	....	5	16	8	73	71	0	.507	8½
Nashville (Reds)	7	5	4	6	7	....	7	12	65	78	0	.455	16
Oklahoma City (Rangers)	4	12	8	3	8	5	....	5	52	92	0	.361	29½
Louisville (Cardinals)	7	4	3	6	4	7	7	....	51	92	0	.357	30

Major league affiliations in parentheses.

Iowa club represented Des Moines, Ia.

Playoffs—Denver defeated Buffalo, three games to two, to win league championship. Denver defeated Columbus (International League), four games to one, to win Triple-A Alliance Championship.

Regular-season attendance—Buffalo, 1,188,972; Denver, 550,135; Indianapolis, 348,089; Iowa, 308,814; Louisville, 565,716; Nashville, 454,575; Oklahoma City, 347,427; Omaha, 329,797. Total, 4,093,525. Playoffs (5 games), 54,242. Alliance Playoffs (5 games), 38,865. Class AAA All-Star Game at Louisville, 20,725.

Managers—Buffalo, Terry Collins; Denver, Tony Muser; Indianapolis, Jerry Manuel (through June 2), Pat Kelly (June 3 through end of season); Iowa, Jim Essian (through May 20), Mick Kelleher (May 21 through end of season); Louisville, Mark DeJohn; Nashville, Pete Mackanin; Oklahoma City, Tommy Thompson; Omaha, Sal Rende. Managerial records of teams with more than one manager: Indianapolis, Manuel 29-22, Kelly 46-46; Iowa, Essian 22-15, Kelleher 56-51.

All-Star team—1B—Rob Maurer, Oklahoma City; 2B—Todd Haney, Indianapolis; 3B—Dean Palmer, Oklahoma City; SS—Rey Sanchez, Iowa; OF—Mickey Brantley, Denver; Jim Olander, Denver; John VanderWal, Indianapolis; C—Tim Spehr, Omaha; DH—Terry Lee, Nashville; RHP—Rick Reed, Buffalo; LHP—Bob Buchanan, Omaha; Most Valuable Player—Jim Olander, Denver; Most Valuable Pitcher—Rick Reed, Buffalo; Rookie of the Year—Rob Maurer, Oklahoma City; Manager of the Year—Tony Muser, Denver.

BATTING

TEAM

Team	Avg.	G	AB	R	OR	H	TB	2B	3B	HR	RBI	SH	SF	HP	BB	Int. BB	SO	SB	CS	LOB
Denver	.271	144	4826	735	638	1309	1934	202	63	99	678	49	40	37	573	22	768	127	73	1053
Iowa	.267	144	4803	674	678	1281	1884	249	48	86	625	87	38	55	513	43	795	93	78	1004
Indianapolis	.261	143	4754	631	616	1242	1875	252	42	99	587	59	45	36	500	29	921	77	43	1037
Buffalo	.260	143	4637	643	546	1204	1748	232	66	60	582	84	45	56	517	39	783	153	61	1010
Omaha	.259	144	4729	627	611	1225	1793	212	55	82	569	38	49	29	456	15	761	129	97	937
Oklahoma City	.258	144	4743	660	779	1223	1910	247	37	122	619	43	41	29	692	22	1060	74	64	1124
Nashville	.248	143	4695	525	614	1163	1672	177	40	84	496	66	23	29	434	31	851	84	60	968
Louisville	.241	143	4665	514	697	1123	1647	203	33	85	483	56	29	38	518	17	940	82	65	1009

INDIVIDUAL

(Leading qualifiers for batting championship—389 or more plate appearances)

*Bats lefthanded.   †Switch-hitter.

Player, Team	Avg.	G	AB	R	H	TB	2B	3B	HR	RBI	SH	SF	HP	BB	Int. BB	SO	SB	CS
Olander, Jim, Denver	.325	134	498	89	162	241	32	10	9	78	3	2	4	64	5	83	14	2
Haney, Todd, Indianapolis	.312	132	510	68	159	203	32	3	2	39	7	4	9	47	3	49	12	11
Espy, Cecil, Buffalo†	.312	102	398	69	124	177	27	10	2	43	4	4	0	36	1	65	22	10
Lee, Terry, Nashville	.304	126	437	70	133	207	21	4	15	67	0	4	5	62	1	80	12	6
Brantley, Mickey, Denver	.301	122	478	78	144	219	20	5	15	78	4	7	2	38	2	45	10	9
Clark, Dave, Omaha*	.301	104	359	45	108	177	24	3	13	64	0	2	0	30	4	53	6	4
Maurer, Rob, Oklahoma City*	.301	132	459	76	138	245	41	3	20	77	0	6	3	96	8	135	2	3
Schulz, Jeff, Buffalo*	.300	122	437	55	131	165	20	4	2	54	2	8	1	42	8	41	7	2
VanderWal, John, Indianapolis*	.293	133	478	84	140	237	36	8	15	71	1	4	2	79	4	118	8	1
Strange, Doug, Iowa†	.293	131	509	76	149	218	35	5	8	56	7	1	1	49	10	75	10	5

Departmental leaders: G—Royer, 138; AB—Royer, 523; R—Olander, 89; H—Olander, 162; TB—Maurer, 245; 2B—Maurer, 41; 3B—Carter, Tubbs, 11; HR—Palmer, 22; RBI—McIntosh, 91; SH—R. Moore, 13; SF—Leonard, Schulz, Shines, 8; HP—Carter, Redfield, 15; BB—Maurer, 96; IBB—Strange, 10; SO—Fariss, 143; SB—Brumfield, 36; CS—Brumfield, 16.

(All players—listed alphabetically)

Player, Team	Avg.	G	AB	R	H	TB	2B	3B	HR	RBI	SH	SF	HP	BB	Int. BB	SO	SB	CS
Adkins, Steve, Iowa*	.000	13	6	0	0	0	0	0	0	0	1	0	0	0	0	6	0	0
Alicea, Luis, Louisville†	.393	31	112	26	44	68	6	3	4	16	2	2	2	14	1	8	5	4
Alvarez, Jose, Nashville	.000	16	1	0	0	0	0	0	0	0	0	0	0	0	0	0	0	0
Armstrong, Jack, Nashville	.125	6	8	0	1	1	0	0	0	1	3	0	0	1	0	1	0	0
Ausanio, Joe, Buffalo	.000	22	1	0	0	0	0	0	0	0	0	0	0	0	0	0	0	0
Balboni, Steve, Oklahoma City	.269	83	301	44	81	158	15	1	20	63	0	4	1	33	2	74	0	2
Baldwin, Jeff, Iowa*	.210	25	62	5	13	18	2	0	1	8	1	0	0	5	0	16	0	1
Banister, Jeff, Buffalo	.244	79	234	23	57	72	7	1	2	21	0	1	1	28	2	57	1	2
Barberie, Bret, Indianapolis†	.312	71	218	45	68	116	14	4	10	48	1	2	3	59	2	47	10	5
Barnes, Brian, Indianapolis*	.250	2	4	1	1	1	0	0	0	0	0	0	0	0	0	1	0	0

— 343 —

Player, Team	Avg.	G	AB	R	H	TB	2B	3B	HR	RBI	SH	SF	HP	BB	Int. BB	SO	SB	CS
Bates, Billy, Nashville*	.242	49	165	22	40	58	3	3	3	15	4	2	0	2	0	17	1	2
Baxter, Jim, Omaha	.000	3	4	0	0	0	0	0	0	0	0	0	0	0	0	1	0	0
Bearse, Kevin, Indianapolis*	.500	12	2	0	1	1	0	0	0	0	1	0	0	0	0	1	0	0
Beeler, Pete, Nashville	.308	4	13	2	4	5	1	0	0	0	0	0	0	2	0	1	0	0
Belcher, Kevin, Oklahoma City	.210	52	205	23	43	59	6	2	2	15	2	0	2	26	0	49	7	6
Beltre, Esteban, Denver	.179	27	78	11	14	21	1	3	0	9	0	0	0	9	0	16	3	2
Benavides, Freddie, Nashville	.242	94	331	24	80	88	8	0	0	21	3	0	0	16	3	55	7	7
Bennett, Chris, Indianapolis	.000	6	1	0	0	0	0	0	0	0	0	0	0	0	0	0	0	0
Berger, Mike, Oklahoma City	.315	67	213	27	67	97	15	3	3	31	0	3	0	36	3	50	2	2
Berry, Sean, Omaha	.264	103	368	62	97	169	21	9	11	54	0	5	3	48	2	70	8	6
Berryhill, Damon, Iowa†	.330	26	97	20	32	62	4	1	8	24	0	2	0	12	0	25	0	3
Bierley, Brad, Iowa*	.228	110	382	48	87	152	21	4	12	60	2	4	1	39	4	75	5	3
Blair, Paul, Iowa†	.111	13	9	2	1	1	0	0	0	0	0	0	0	2	0	2	0	0
Blankenship, Kevin, Buffalo	.048	28	21	3	1	1	0	0	0	1	3	0	0	1	0	6	0	0
Boskie, Shawn, Iowa	.000	7	13	0	0	0	0	0	0	0	1	0	0	0	0	2	0	0
Bottenfield, Kent, Indianapolis†	.034	29	29	3	1	2	1	0	0	0	5	0	0	1	0	13	0	0
Branson, Jeff, Nashville*	.241	43	145	10	35	41	4	1	0	11	1	0	0	8	2	31	5	4
Brantley, Mickey, Denver	.301	122	478	78	144	219	20	5	15	78	4	7	2	38	2	45	10	9
Brewer, Rod, Louisville*	.225	104	382	39	86	133	21	1	8	52	0	1	6	35	1	57	4	1
Bridges, Tony, Omaha	.318	7	22	1	7	8	1	0	0	2	0	0	0	1	0	6	0	0
Brown, Keith, Nashville†	.000	47	3	0	0	0	0	0	0	0	0	0	0	0	0	2	0	0
Brown, Kevin, Denver*	.000	14	2	0	0	0	0	0	0	0	0	0	0	0	0	0	0	0
Brumfield, Jacob, Omaha	.267	111	397	62	106	143	14	7	3	43	2	3	1	33	0	64	36	16
Bullinger, Jim, Iowa	.250	8	4	1	1	3	0	1	0	0	0	0	0	1	0	1	0	0
Burgos, Paco, Oklahoma City†	.192	9	26	3	5	5	0	0	0	1	2	0	0	2	0	3	0	0
Burrell, Kevin, Omaha*	.227	67	211	22	48	72	10	1	4	17	1	1	2	17	0	43	1	2
Canale, George, Denver*	.234	88	274	36	64	108	10	2	10	47	0	3	2	51	0	49	6	2
Canan, Dick, Iowa	.266	32	64	14	17	23	6	0	0	6	1	0	0	10	0	19	2	1
Cangelosi, John, Denver†	.294	83	303	69	89	112	8	3	3	25	1	0	2	59	2	29	26	13
Capra, Nick, Oklahoma City	.272	127	485	74	132	189	34	4	5	39	8	1	4	87	1	57	27	14
Carmona, Greg, Louisville†	.175	56	143	16	25	35	2	1	2	10	2	1	0	13	0	25	7	1
Carrillo, Matias, Denver*	.276	120	421	56	116	168	18	5	8	56	5	3	0	32	2	85	10	13
Carter, Steve, Iowa*	.287	136	519	79	149	226	31	11	8	67	6	2	15	36	3	78	11	11
Casillas, Adam, Nashville*	.275	128	422	44	116	154	17	3	5	52	4	3	2	47	3	28	3	2
Castaneda, Nick, Louisville*	.271	49	140	24	38	60	11	1	3	18	0	1	1	28	3	38	0	0
Castillo, Carmen, Denver	.302	92	334	41	101	170	19	4	14	72	1	3	4	17	1	79	2	1
Castillo, Frank, Iowa	.000	4	3	0	0	0	0	0	0	0	0	0	0	0	0	2	0	0
Castillo, Juan, Denver	.174	13	46	3	8	11	1	1	0	7	1	0	0	6	1	9	2	1
Christian, Rick, Louisville	.118	16	17	2	2	3	1	0	0	1	0	0	0	2	0	8	0	1
Clark, Dave, Omaha*	.301	104	359	45	108	177	24	3	13	64	0	2	0	30	4	53	6	4
Clark, Mark, Louisville	.091	7	11	0	1	1	0	0	0	0	0	0	0	0	0	3	0	0
Clarke, Stan, Louisville*	.120	20	25	2	3	5	0	1	0	1	3	0	0	3	0	13	0	0
Clary, Marty, 33 Lou. -7 Buf.	.154	40	13	0	2	3	1	0	0	1	1	0	0	1	0	2	0	0
Cole, Stu, Omaha	.261	120	441	64	115	151	13	7	3	39	5	2	1	42	0	61	11	10
Cole, Victor, 6 Oma. - 19 Buf.†	.000	25	1	0	0	0	0	0	0	0	0	0	0	0	0	0	0	0
Conine, Jeff, Omaha	.257	51	171	23	44	64	9	1	3	15	0	1	0	26	2	39	0	6
Cordero, Wil, Indianapolis	.261	98	360	48	94	151	16	4	11	52	0	2	3	26	2	89	9	2
Cormier, Rheal, Louisville†	.118	21	17	1	2	2	0	0	0	0	0	5	0	0	1	0	7	0	0
Crosby, Todd, Louisville†	.211	96	227	26	48	57	5	2	0	15	3	2	0	55	0	56	1	3
Daugherty, Jack, Oklahoma City†	.143	22	77	4	11	13	2	0	0	4	0	0	0	8	2	14	1	0
Davidson, Bob, Louisville	.000	52	4	0	0	0	0	0	0	0	0	0	0	1	0	2	0	0
Davis, Mike, Indianapolis*	.236	58	178	27	42	66	11	2	3	20	0	2	1	19	1	29	0	4
DeFrancesco, Tony, Nashville	.156	55	141	9	22	29	1	0	2	12	8	0	0	27	0	45	0	1
Diaz, Alex, Indianapolis†	.243	108	370	48	90	115	14	4	1	21	3	2	1	27	2	46	17	3
Diaz, Carlos, Denver	.000	1	1	0	0	0	0	0	0	0	0	0	0	0	0	0	0	0
Dickson, Lance, Iowa	.133	18	15	0	2	2	0	0	0	1	0	0	0	0	0	8	0	0
Dixon, Eddie, Indianapolis	.100	54	20	1	2	2	0	0	0	0	3	0	0	1	0	10	0	0
Dorsett, Brian, Buffalo	.272	29	103	17	28	40	6	0	2	18	0	4	1	8	1	19	0	0
Dulin, Tim, Buffalo	.071	14	28	4	2	5	0	0	1	1	2	0	0	2	1	10	0	0
Dunbar, Tommy, 11 Oma. - 19 Buf.*	.174	30	69	6	12	16	1	0	1	4	0	1	0	4	0	9	0	0
Edge, Greg, Buffalo†	.235	12	17	2	4	4	0	0	0	2	0	0	1	0	0	3	1	1
Espy, Cecil, Buffalo†	.312	102	398	69	124	177	27	10	2	43	4	4	0	36	1	65	22	10
Fariss, Monty, Oklahoma City	.271	137	494	84	134	222	31	9	13	73	3	2	0	91	4	143	5	7
Farmer, Howard, Indianapolis	.182	20	22	1	4	6	2	0	0	2	3	0	0	0	0	6	0	0
Fassero, Jeff, Indianapolis*	1.000	18	1	0	1	1	0	0	0	0	0	0	0	0	0	0	0	0
Fernandez, Joey, Louisville*	.237	104	316	40	75	126	14	2	11	31	3	2	2	57	2	63	3	4
Figueroa, Bien, Louisville	.204	97	269	18	55	68	9	2	0	14	5	0	2	20	2	27	1	5
Filer, Tom, Iowa	.375	18	16	3	6	7	1	0	0	2	0	0	0	1	0	5	0	0
Fireovid, Steve, Buffalo†	.208	35	24	1	5	5	0	0	0	3	3	0	0	0	0	5	0	0
Fitzgerald, Mike, Indianapolis	.222	10	27	5	6	10	1	0	1	4	0	2	0	6	0	3	0	1
Foster, Steve, Nashville	.000	41	1	1	0	0	0	0	0	0	0	0	0	0	0	0	0	0
Frey, Steve, Indianapolis	.000	30	1	0	0	0	0	0	0	0	0	0	0	1	0	1	0	0
Fulton, Ed, Louisville*	.197	45	132	10	26	34	8	0	0	15	0	0	0	15	1	35	0	0
Gainey, Ty, Buffalo*	.357	9	14	3	5	6	1	0	0	1	0	0	0	4	1	2	2	0
Garber, Jeff, Nashville	.277	34	94	12	26	38	3	3	1	13	2	1	0	6	0	21	0	2
Garcia, Carlos, Buffalo	.266	127	463	62	123	177	21	6	7	60	6	3	7	33	5	78	30	7
Garcia, Leo, Nashville*	.244	125	450	49	110	159	12	5	9	37	6	2	0	32	4	57	17	9
Garcia, Victor, Nashville	.000	15	1	0	0	0	0	0	0	0	0	0	0	0	0	0	0	0
Gardner, Mark, Indianapolis	.143	6	7	0	1	1	0	0	0	1	1	0	0	0	0	4	0	0
Garner, Darrin, Oklahoma City	.273	5	11	3	3	5	0	1	0	1	0	0	0	2	0	0	0	1
George, Chris, Denver	.000	44	0	0	0	0	0	0	0	0	0	0	0	0	0	0	0	0
Gilkey, Bernard, Louisville	.146	11	41	5	6	8	2	0	0	2	0	0	0	6	0	10	1	3
Girardi, Joe, Iowa	.222	12	36	3	8	9	1	0	0	4	1	0	0	4	0	8	2	0
Goff, Jerry, Indianapolis*	.251	57	191	32	48	89	10	2	9	37	0	0	3	22	2	51	2	0
Gonzalez, Angel, Nashville	.243	103	309	31	75	111	10	7	4	42	5	1	3	19	2	36	3	2
Gonzalez, Denny, Nashville	.289	74	242	41	70	116	17	1	9	38	1	1	3	49	1	40	3	5
Green, Gary, Oklahoma City	.218	100	308	36	67	81	4	2	2	30	9	5	3	35	0	57	1	3
Gross, Kip, Nashville	.167	14	6	1	1	1	0	0	0	0	0	0	0	0	0	1	0	0
Guerrero, Pedro, Louisville	.455	3	11	2	5	8	0	0	1	2	0	0	0	0	0	2	0	0
Guerrero, Sandy, Denver*	.282	73	216	29	61	92	11	4	4	32	2	2	1	27	2	28	2	3
Guinn, Brian, Iowa†	.236	109	343	46	81	108	11	2	4	32	11	1	4	49	0	70	10	10
Hamelin, Bob, Omaha*	.189	37	127	13	24	41	3	1	4	19	1	4	0	16	0	32	0	0
Hamilton, Carl, Buffalo*	.300	18	10	1	3	4	1	0	0	1	1	0	0	0	0	2	0	0
Haney, Chris, Indianapolis*	.500	2	2	0	1	1	0	0	0	0	0	0	0	0	0	0	0	0
Haney, Todd, Indianapolis	.312	132	510	68	159	203	32	3	2	39	7	4	9	47	3	49	12	11

Player, Team	Avg.	G	AB	R	H	TB	2B	3B	HR	RBI	SH	SF	HP	BB	Int. BB	SO	SB	CS
Haselman, Bill, Oklahoma City	.256	126	442	57	113	166	22	2	9	60	1	4	1	61	1	89	10	7
Hecht, Steve, Indianapolis*	.243	89	210	34	51	75	8	2	4	26	6	1	0	12	0	51	9	3
Hernandez, Jose, Oklahoma City	.304	14	46	6	14	20	1	1	1	3	3	1	0	4	0	10	0	0
Hill, Milton, Nashville	.000	37	4	0	0	0	0	0	0	0	1	0	0	0	0	0	0	0
Hines, Tim, Buffalo*	.333	17	33	4	11	15	2	1	0	7	0	0	3	1	0	5	0	0
Hinkle, Mike, Louisville	.222	11	9	2	2	2	0	0	0	2	1	0	0	0	0	3	0	0
Hinzo, Tommy, Omaha†	.250	9	20	4	5	6	1	0	0	4	1	0	2	1	0	3	0	1
Houston, Mel, Indianapolis	.114	15	35	5	4	8	1	0	1	1	0	0	1	4	0	10	0	1
Howard, Dave, Omaha†	.122	14	41	2	5	5	0	0	0	2	2	0	1	7	0	11	1	1
Huismann, Mark, 13 Buf.-32 Oma.	.000	45	1	0	0	0	0	0	0	0	0	0	0	0	0	1	0	0
Huson, Jeff, Oklahoma City*	.500	2	6	0	3	4	1	0	0	2	0	0	0	0	0	1	0	0
Imes, Rodney, Nashville	.000	25	12	0	0	0	0	0	0	0	1	1	0	0	0	11	0	0
Jackson, Danny, Iowa	.000	1	1	0	0	0	0	0	0	0	0	0	0	0	0	1	0	0
Jefferson, Reggie, Nashville†	.320	28	103	15	33	47	3	1	3	20	0	0	4	10	1	22	3	1
Jefferson, Stanley, Nashville†	.244	27	78	10	19	35	4	3	2	5	0	1	4	4	0	19	2	0
Jones, Chris, Nashville	.243	73	267	29	65	105	5	4	9	33	0	1	2	19	1	65	10	5
Jones, Tim, Louisville*	.255	86	306	34	78	104	9	1	5	29	4	3	0	36	1	59	19	5
Jordan, Brian, Louisville	.264	61	212	35	56	87	11	4	4	24	1	0	8	17	1	41	10	3
Jose, Manny, Nashville†	.224	37	67	5	15	16	1	0	0	2	3	1	0	8	2	19	5	1
King, Jeff, Buffalo	.222	9	18	3	4	7	1	1	0	2	0	0	0	6	0	3	1	0
Kmak, Joe, Denver	.237	100	295	34	70	94	17	2	1	33	7	1	5	28	0	45	7	3
Knabenshue, Chris, Denver*	.207	12	29	5	6	10	1	0	1	3	0	0	0	5	0	9	1	0
Koslofski, Kevin, Omaha*	.298	25	94	13	28	41	3	2	2	19	2	1	1	15	0	19	4	3
Kraemer, Joe, Iowa*	.000	20	13	2	0	0	0	0	0	1	2	0	0	1	0	7	0	0
Kremers, Jimmy, Indianapolis*	.241	98	290	34	70	117	14	0	11	42	5	4	0	40	6	99	1	1
Kreuter, Chad, Oklahoma City†	.271	24	70	14	19	28	6	0	1	12	0	1	0	18	0	16	2	0
Landrum, Cedric, Iowa*	.336	38	131	14	44	59	8	2	1	11	2	0	0	5	0	21	13	3
Laureano, Frank, Omaha	.158	6	19	2	3	6	0	0	1	5	0	1	0	2	0	5	0	0
Layana, Tim, Nashville	.000	26	4	1	0	0	0	0	0	1	0	0	0	1	0	1	0	0
Lee, Terry, Nashville	.304	126	437	70	133	207	21	4	15	67	0	4	5	62	1	80	12	6
Leonard, Jeffrey, Omaha	.244	68	258	28	63	104	9	1	10	50	0	8	2	12	0	46	1	4
Lewis, Richie, Indianapolis	.000	5	7	0	0	0	0	0	0	0	0	0	0	0	0	2	0	0
Liddell, Dave, Denver	.270	32	89	15	24	33	4	1	1	13	1	0	1	12	0	15	0	0
Liriano, Nelson, Omaha†	.274	86	292	50	80	120	16	9	2	36	3	3	2	31	3	39	6	8
Listach, Pat, Denver	.252	89	286	51	72	93	10	4	1	31	3	4	0	45	1	66	23	8
Little, Scott, Buffalo	.242	62	165	22	40	51	5	3	0	18	1	0	2	28	0	28	3	3
Lockhart, Keith, Nashville*	.260	116	411	53	107	162	25	3	8	36	2	1	2	24	2	64	3	7
Long, Bill, Indianapolis	.000	10	2	0	0	0	0	0	0	0	1	0	0	0	0	1	0	0
Lopez, Rob, Nashville*	.000	4	2	0	0	0	0	0	0	0	0	0	0	0	0	0	0	1
Loynd, Mike, Louisville	.000	9	9	0	0	0	0	0	0	1	0	0	0	0	0	7	0	0
Luecken, Rick, Iowa	.000	5	1	0	0	0	0	0	0	0	0	0	0	0	0	0	0	0
Mack, Quinn, Indianapolis*	.272	120	416	35	113	164	20	8	5	49	1	3	3	12	0	42	4	5
Maclin, Lonnie, Louisville*	.287	84	327	35	94	122	12	2	4	37	2	1	0	16	0	50	19	12
Magallanes, Willie, Louisville	.224	41	116	10	26	35	4	1	1	6	0	3	0	10	0	39	0	0
Magrann, Tom, Buffalo	.273	8	11	0	3	3	0	0	0	0	0	0	0	6	0	1	0	0
Marchok, Chris, Indianapolis*	.000	11	3	0	0	0	0	0	0	0	1	0	0	0	0	2	0	0
Martinez, Julian, Louisville	.226	135	402	52	91	148	21	3	10	40	3	3	4	63	1	84	8	11
Mason, Roger, Buffalo	.182	34	11	0	2	2	0	0	0	2	0	0	0	0	0	6	0	0
Masters, Dave, Indianapolis	.333	27	9	1	3	3	0	0	0	1	0	0	0	1	0	2	0	0
Maurer, Rob, Oklahoma City*	.301	132	459	76	138	245	41	3	20	77	0	6	3	96	8	135	2	3
May, Derrick, Iowa*	.297	82	310	47	92	127	18	4	3	49	1	3	4	19	4	38	7	8
May, Scott, Iowa	.000	57	5	1	0	0	0	0	0	0	1	0	0	1	0	1	0	0
Maysey, Matt, Indianapolis	.000	12	10	0	0	0	0	0	0	0	2	0	0	0	0	4	0	0
McGinnis, Russ, Iowa	.281	111	374	70	105	172	18	2	15	70	1	4	6	63	6	68	3	2
McIntosh, Tim, Denver	.292	122	462	69	135	226	19	9	18	91	0	7	11	37	3	60	2	5
McPhail, Marlin, Indianapolis	.273	100	319	40	87	135	23	2	7	38	4	6	3	30	3	53	1	2
Meeks, Tim, Buffalo	.000	36	17	0	0	0	0	0	0	0	6	0	0	1	0	4	0	0
Mendez, Jesus, Louisville*	.268	98	213	15	57	72	8	2	1	18	6	3	0	8	1	18	1	4
Merced, Orlando, Buffalo†	.167	3	12	1	2	2	0	0	0	0	0	0	0	1	0	4	1	0
Meyer, Joey, Buffalo	.250	75	292	27	73	108	13	2	6	35	0	3	0	15	0	58	0	1
Milchin, Mike, Louisville*	.500	20	18	7	9	17	2	0	2	6	1	0	0	3	0	2	0	0
Millay, Gar, Oklahoma City	.233	93	257	38	60	92	12	1	6	27	4	3	5	58	0	48	1	1
Miller, Keith, Buffalo†	.261	133	441	63	115	183	27	7	9	68	8	2	3	70	5	71	9	5
Miller, Paul, Buffalo	.048	10	21	1	1	1	0	0	0	0	2	0	0	0	0	8	0	0
Minor, Blas, Buffalo	.000	17	3	0	0	0	0	0	0	0	1	0	0	0	0	2	0	0
Minutelli, Gino, Nashville*	.059	16	17	0	1	2	1	0	0	0	3	0	0	0	0	5	0	0
Mitchell, Charlie, Nashville	.476	37	21	8	10	14	2	1	0	1	2	0	0	0	0	3	0	0
Montoyo, Charlie, Denver	.239	120	394	68	94	145	13	1	12	45	6	4	5	69	0	50	15	3
Moore, Billy, Oklahoma City	.220	37	123	16	27	53	11	0	5	16	0	2	2	20	0	30	0	2
Moore, Bobby, Omaha	.243	130	494	65	120	139	13	3	0	34	13	2	3	37	0	41	35	14
Moreno, Armando, Buffalo	.226	96	221	39	50	80	11	2	5	30	6	4	4	30	1	40	2	1
Morman, Russ, Omaha	.263	88	316	46	83	125	15	3	7	50	1	6	2	43	1	53	10	6
Moses, John, Buffalo†	.273	3	11	2	3	3	0	0	0	0	0	0	0	0	0	0	0	0
Mount, Chuck, Iowa	.000	10	2	0	0	0	0	0	0	0	2	0	0	0	0	0	0	0
Moyer, Jamie, Louisville*	.263	20	19	3	5	5	0	0	0	0	2	0	0	3	0	6	0	0
Munoz, Omer, Indianapolis	.283	27	92	7	26	28	2	0	0	12	6	0	3	3	1	13	0	0
Myers, Chris, Indianapolis*	.000	2	4	0	0	0	0	0	0	0	0	0	0	0	0	1	0	0
Natal, Rob, Indianapolis	.317	16	41	2	13	17	4	0	0	6	0	1	0	6	1	9	1	0
Nichols, Scott, Louisville	.222	28	54	9	12	24	1	1	3	8	2	0	3	12	0	14	1	0
Nieto, Tom, Louisville	.263	19	57	5	15	21	3	0	1	4	0	0	0	5	0	10	0	1
Nilsson, Dave, Denver*	.232	28	95	10	22	33	8	0	1	14	0	0	0	17	0	16	1	1
Nipper, Al, Louisville	.000	5	7	0	0	0	0	0	0	0	0	0	0	0	0	2	0	0
Noce, Doug, Indianapolis	.083	9	12	0	1	1	0	0	0	0	0	0	0	0	0	5	0	0
Nunez, Jose, Iowa	.000	28	15	0	0	0	0	0	0	0	1	0	0	1	0	6	0	0
Nunez, Mauricio, Louisville	.261	6	23	1	6	7	1	0	0	3	0	0	0	0	0	7	0	0
Olander, Jim, Denver	.325	134	498	89	162	241	32	10	9	78	3	2	4	64	5	83	14	2
Olivares, Omar, Louisville	.000	6	5	0	0	0	0	0	0	0	1	0	1	0	0	4	0	0
Osteen, Dave, Louisville	.200	29	5	1	1	2	1	0	0	0	2	0	0	1	0	1	0	0
Palacios, Vicente, Buffalo	1.000	3	1	0	1	1	0	0	0	0	0	0	0	0	0	0	0	0
Palmer, Dean, Oklahoma City	.299	60	234	45	70	151	11	2	22	59	1	2	2	20	2	61	4	6
Pappas, Erik, Iowa	.275	88	284	41	78	120	19	1	7	48	4	3	4	45	3	47	5	3
Parent, Mark, Oklahoma City	.250	5	8	2	2	2	0	0	0	0	0	0	0	0	0	1	0	0
Pavlas, Dave, Iowa	.250	61	4	0	1	1	0	0	0	1	1	0	0	0	0	2	0	0
Pearson, Kevin, Nashville	.240	91	229	23	55	70	13	1	0	19	2	1	2	21	2	38	3	1
Pedre, Jorge, Omaha	.216	31	116	12	25	32	4	0	1	4	0	0	4	10	0	18	2	1

Player, Team	Avg.	G	AB	R	H	TB	2B	3B	HR	RBI	SH	SF	HP	BB	Int. BB	SO	SB	CS
Peltier, Dan, Oklahoma City*	.229	94	345	38	79	112	16	4	3	32	2	2	0	43	2	71	6	5
Petralli, Geno, Oklahoma City*	.267	4	15	1	4	5	1	0	0	2	0	0	0	2	0	1	0	0
Picota, Len, Louisville	.091	29	11	2	1	2	1	0	0	1	2	0	0	1	0	8	0	0
Piskor, Kirk, Omaha	.500	3	8	3	4	8	1	0	1	4	0	0	0	0	0	0	0	0
Polidor, Gus, Denver	.272	30	103	8	28	32	2	1	0	5	6	0	0	4	0	8	0	3
Pose, Scott, Nashville*	.192	15	52	7	10	10	0	0	0	3	2	0	2	2	0	9	3	1
Postier, Paul, Oklahoma City	.242	70	219	22	53	60	4	0	1	20	3	1	0	13	0	43	1	2
Powell, Ross, Nashville*	.160	24	25	1	4	5	1	0	0	1	2	0	0	0	0	9	0	0
Presley, Jim, Indianapolis	.271	51	207	30	56	88	10	2	6	29	2	1	2	16	0	64	1	0
Prince, Tom, Buffalo	.208	80	221	29	46	78	8	3	6	32	2	3	7	37	1	31	3	4
Prybylinski, Don, Louisville	.254	24	67	6	17	21	4	0	0	4	2	1	1	7	0	13	0	0
Pugh, Tim, Nashville	.042	23	24	0	1	1	0	0	0	0	3	0	0	1	0	11	0	0
Pulliam, Harvey, Omaha	.257	104	346	35	89	129	18	2	6	39	1	3	1	31	0	62	2	4
Redfield, Joe, Buffalo	.275	105	356	60	98	152	21	6	7	50	10	1	15	54	2	50	21	4
Reed, Rick, Buffalo	.156	25	32	2	5	5	0	0	0	4	5	2	1	2	0	9	0	0
Renfroe, Laddie, Iowa†	.000	63	1	0	0	0	0	0	0	0	0	0	0	0	0	0	0	0
Renteria, Rich, Indianapolis	.236	20	72	6	17	25	5	0	1	5	0	1	0	6	0	9	0	0
Richardson, Dave, Louisville*	.333	13	3	0	1	1	0	0	0	0	0	0	0	0	0	1	0	0
Richardson, Jeff, Buffalo	.258	62	186	21	48	71	16	2	1	24	9	3	2	18	8	29	5	3
Ridenour, Dana, Indianapolis	.333	57	3	1	1	1	0	0	0	0	2	0	0	1	0	1	0	0
Risley, Bill, Nashville	.125	8	8	0	1	1	0	0	0	1	0	0	0	0	0	3	0	0
Rodriguez, Rosario, Buffalo	.000	48	0	0	0	0	0	0	0	0	1	0	0	0	0	0	0	0
Rojas, Mel, Indianapolis	.067	14	15	1	1	2	1	0	0	2	2	0	0	0	0	8	0	0
Roomes, Rolando, Denver	.164	20	61	9	10	16	0	3	0	2	0	1	0	11	2	21	0	0
Rosario, Dave, Iowa*	.000	33	2	0	0	0	0	0	0	0	0	0	0	0	0	2	0	0
Ross, Mike, Louisville	.211	67	251	21	53	76	9	1	4	20	1	2	0	13	1	45	1	1
Royer, Stan, Louisville	.254	138	523	48	133	217	30	6	14	74	0	6	3	43	1	126	1	2
Sampen, Bill, Indianapolis	.182	7	11	1	2	2	0	0	0	1	0	0	0	0	0	4	0	0
Sanchez, Rey, Iowa	.290	126	417	60	121	153	16	5	2	46	11	2	7	37	2	27	13	7
Sanford, Mo, Nashville	.200	5	5	0	1	2	1	0	0	1	1	0	0	0	0	2	0	0
Santovenia, Nelson, Indianapolis	.262	61	195	23	51	78	7	1	6	26	0	2	0	21	1	25	0	1
Scanlan, Bob, Iowa	.000	4	1	0	0	0	0	0	0	0	1	0	0	0	0	0	0	0
Schmidt, Dave, 13 Ind.- 11 O.C.	1.000	24	1	0	1	1	0	0	0	0	1	0	0	0	0	0	0	0
Schulz, Jeff, Buffalo*	.300	122	437	55	131	165	20	4	2	54	2	8	1	42	8	41	7	2
Scott, Donnie, Nashville†	.178	84	225	19	40	57	8	0	3	18	3	3	0	25	4	41	0	2
Scott, Gary, Iowa	.208	63	231	21	48	71	10	2	3	34	3	2	6	20	2	45	0	6
Scruggs, Tony, Oklahoma City	.203	53	182	19	37	50	4	0	3	21	3	3	4	20	0	41	4	4
Service, Scott, Indianapolis	.056	18	18	1	1	1	0	0	0	0	2	0	0	0	0	10	0	0
Sherrill, Tim, Louisville*	.000	42	2	0	0	0	0	0	0	0	0	0	0	0	0	1	0	0
Shines, Razor, Indianapolis†	.251	136	471	61	118	167	28	0	7	60	0	8	2	65	1	82	2	2
Simonds, Dan, Iowa	.125	20	32	6	4	4	0	0	0	3	3	1	1	7	0	6	1	2
Smajstrla, Craig, Iowa†	.278	117	385	55	107	143	17	5	3	38	7	2	3	47	3	53	7	3
Small, Jeff, Iowa	.295	36	122	11	36	46	8	1	0	11	3	1	0	5	0	19	2	3
Smith, D.L., Denver	.213	94	291	34	62	78	7	3	1	22	7	2	0	28	0	46	0	5
Sodders, Mike, Iowa	.000	16	1	0	0	0	0	0	0	0	1	0	0	0	0	1	0	0
Sparks, Greg, Buffalo*	.180	55	128	13	23	39	7	0	3	16	2	2	0	12	0	31	1	0
Spehr, Tim, Omaha	.274	72	215	27	59	95	14	2	6	26	3	4	3	25	1	48	3	2
Stephens, Ray, Louisville	.279	60	165	16	46	74	7	0	7	28	2	0	4	24	1	39	0	3
Stockstill, David, Indianapolis*	.240	18	50	9	12	26	3	1	3	11	0	0	5	0	7	0	1
Strange, Doug, Iowa†	.293	131	509	76	149	218	35	5	8	56	7	7	1	49	10	75	10	5
Strauss, Julio, Iowa	.000	6	1	0	0	0	0	0	0	0	0	0	0	0	0	0	0	0
Suero, William, Denver	.386	20	70	20	27	34	3	2	0	15	2	1	0	10	0	8	3	0
Sullivan, Glenn, Iowa*	.247	99	247	35	61	92	17	1	4	30	6	1	2	42	4	30	1	5
Sutcliffe, Rick, Iowa*	.000	3	4	0	0	0	0	0	0	0	0	0	0	0	0	2	0	0
Sutko, Glenn, Nashville	.209	45	134	9	28	41	2	1	3	15	0	0	0	22	3	67	1	0
Thomas, Andres, Omaha	.288	19	66	6	19	30	5	0	2	7	0	1	0	3	0	7	0	0
Thomas, Orlando, Louisville	.273	4	11	1	3	3	0	0	0	1	0	0	0	0	0	7	0	0
Tracy, Jim, Buffalo	.000	11	10	1	0	0	0	0	0	0	0	0	0	4	0	0	0
Trafton, Todd, Nashville	.285	75	263	37	75	120	16	1	9	41	2	3	3	28	0	46	1	0
Tubbs, Greg, Buffalo	.273	121	373	71	102	151	18	11	3	34	5	2	5	48	1	62	34	11
Turek, Joe, Nashville	.167	14	12	0	2	2	0	0	0	1	3	0	0	0	0	2	0	0
VanderWal, John, Indianapolis*	.293	133	478	84	140	237	36	8	15	71	1	4	2	79	4	118	8	1
Vasquez, Luis, Nashville	.091	8	11	0	1	1	0	0	0	0	0	0	0	0	0	4	0	0
Vierra, Joey, Nashville*	.067	62	15	2	1	1	0	0	0	0	1	0	0	0	0	5	0	0
Villanueva, Hector, Iowa	.360	6	25	2	9	18	3	0	2	9	0	1	0	1	1	6	0	0
Walker, Bernie, Nashville*	.226	16	31	2	7	10	1	1	0	1	0	0	3	0	13	2	1
Walling, Denny, Oklahoma City*	.500	3	10	0	5	6	1	0	0	3	0	1	0	1	0	2	0	0
Wehner, John, Buffalo	.304	31	112	18	34	50	9	2	1	15	0	2	0	14	1	12	6	4
Wilkins, Rick, Iowa*	.271	38	107	12	29	49	3	1	5	14	2	2	1	11	1	17	1	2
Williams, Kenny, Indianapolis	.234	18	47	7	11	22	3	1	2	7	0	1	2	5	0	16	1	0
Wilson, Steve, Iowa*	.000	25	9	0	0	0	0	0	0	0	1	0	0	0	0	2	0	0
Winston, Darrin, Indianapolis	.000	27	0	0	0	0	0	0	0	0	1	0	0	0	0	0	0	0
York, Mike, Buffalo	.400	9	10	2	4	5	1	0	0	1	1	0	0	2	0	0	0	0
Young, Kevin, Buffalo	.222	4	9	1	2	3	1	0	0	1	0	0	1	0	0	1	0	0
Zambrano, Eddie, Buffalo	.340	48	144	19	49	76	8	5	3	35	2	4	2	17	1	25	1	1
Zuvella, Paul, Omaha	.269	64	219	28	59	78	14	1	1	20	1	2	3	23	1	15	3	2

The following pitchers, listed alphabetically by club, with games in parentheses, had no plate appearances, primarily through use of designated hitters:

BUFFALO—Fajardo, Hector (8); Neely, Jeff (42); Roesler, Mike (33); Wakefield, Tim (1).

DENVER—Alba, Gibson (7); August, Don (1); Austin, Jim (20); Davins, Jim (25); Eldred, Cal (29); Elvira, Narciso (19); Fisher, Brian (44); Fortugno, Tim (26); Henry, Doug (32); Hernandez, Manny (5); Higuera, Ted (2); Holmes, Darren (1); Hunter, Jim (14); Ignasiak, Mike (24); Kaiser, Jeff (8); Kiefer, Mark (17); Knudson, Mark (13); LaPoint, Dave (7); Mathews, Greg (13); McGaffigan, Andy (10); Miranda, Angel (11); Puig, Ed (11); Sadler, Alan (2); Wegman, Bill (1).

INDIANAPOLIS—Davis, Bret (7); Grewal, Ranbir (2); Nabholz, Chris (4); Piatt, Doug (44); Ryan, Bob (2); Stewart, Tito (3); Wainhouse, David (14).

IOWA—LaPoint, Dave (26); Slocumb, Heathcliff (12).

LOUISVILLE—Baker, Ernie (2); Compres, Fidel (10); Corona, John (12); DiPino, Frank (2); Grater, Mark (58); Hill, Ken (1); Perez, Mike (37); Walter, Gene (4); Worrell, Todd (3).

NASHVILLE—Hall, Drew (8).

OKLAHOMA CITY—Alexander, Gerald (2); Arnsberg, Brad (9); Bautista, Jose (11); Bitker, Joe (23); Bohanon, Brian (7); Boone, Dan (24); Bronkey, Jeff (7); Campbell, Mike (1); Gossage, Goose (2); Guzman, Jose (3); Hall, Drew (15); Hayward, Ray (19); Laskey, Bill (31); Mathews, Terry (18); Menendez, Tony (21); Mielke, Gary (10); Murphy, Dan (2); Nolte, Eric (25); Pavlik, Roger (8); Peters, Steve (24); Petkovsek, Mark

(25); Poole, Jim (10); Rosenthal, Wayne (32); Schiraldi, Calvin (18); Smith, Dan (28); Thompson, Rich (16); Wells, Terry (12); Witt, Bobby (2).

OMAHA—Buchanan, Bob (32); Carman, Don (14); Centala, Scott (18); Clark, Dera (25); Davis, Mark (6); Encarnacion, Luis (50); Everson, Greg (16); Gardner, Wes (9); Gubicza, Mark (3); Johnston, Joel (47); LeMasters, Jim (21); Magnante, Mike (10); Maldonado, Carlos (41); McGaffigan, Andy (23); Moeller, Dennis (14); Smith, Daryl (23); Wagner, Hector (17).

GRAND SLAMS—Balboni, Barberie, Carmona, Carrillo, Carter, C. Castillo, C. Garcia, Green, Haselman, R. Jefferson, Lee, Martinez, D. May, K. Miller, B. Moore, Olander, Strange, VanderWal, Zambrano, 1 each.

AWARDED FIRST BASE ON CATCHER'S INTERFERENCE—Banister (Goff); Casillas (Knorr); C. Jones (Lyden); McIntosh (Kremers).

PITCHING

TEAM

Team	ERA	G	CG	ShO	Sv.	IP	H	R	ER	HR	HB	BB	Int. BB	SO	WP	Bk.
Buffalo	3.53	143	17	16	36	1240.0	1222	546	486	82	35	446	28	750	53	13
Indianapolis	3.65	143	10	9	36	1246.1	1136	616	505	87	50	549	43	956	82	16
Nashville	3.77	143	11	14	35	1245.2	1132	614	522	90	41	561	27	886	65	19
Omaha	3.80	144	5	5	44	1247.1	1206	611	527	95	38	566	14	871	74	6
Denver	4.13	144	13	6	36	1254.1	1239	638	576	104	66	533	28	888	50	20
Iowa	4.20	144	13	7	38	1276.0	1238	678	596	99	38	562	25	896	91	10
Louisville	4.50	143	9	12	28	1240.0	1390	697	620	93	39	502	55	714	70	12
Oklahoma City	4.98	144	10	6	22	1236.1	1387	779	684	85	36	559	28	875	76	17

INDIVIDUAL

(Leading qualifiers for earned-run average leadership—115 or more innings)

*Throws lefthanded.

Pitcher, Team	W	L	Pct.	ERA	G	GS	CG	GF	ShO	Sv.	IP	H	R	ER	HR	HB	BB	Int. BB	SO	WP
Reed, Buffalo	14	4	.778	2.15	25	25	5	0	2	0	167.2	151	45	40	3	2	26	2	102	2
Fireovid, Buffalo	9	8	.529	2.90	34	18	1	6	0	3	130.1	127	51	42	5	6	43	6	72	8
Dixon, Indianapolis	6	7	.462	2.91	53	8	0	16	0	5	117.2	120	50	38	5	2	30	8	63	1
Service, Indianapolis	6	7	.462	2.97	18	17	3	1	1	0	121.1	83	42	40	7	6	39	0	91	5
Mason, Buffalo	9	5	.643	3.08	34	15	2	6	1	0	122.2	115	47	42	11	6	44	1	80	2
Buchanan, Omaha*	11	7	.611	3.26	32	22	2	0	0	0	157.1	147	67	57	12	4	66	0	79	9
Eldred, Denver	13	9	.591	3.75	29	29	3	0	1	0	185.0	161	82	77	13	12	84	2	168	8
Moyer, Louisville*	5	10	.333	3.80	20	20	1	0	0	0	125.2	125	64	53	16	3	43	4	69	8
Pugh, Nashville	7	11	.389	3.81	23	23	3	0	1	0	148.2	130	68	63	9	10	56	2	89	9
Meeks, Buffalo	4	8	.333	3.89	36	18	2	4	1	1	143.1	146	72	62	11	3	31	1	66	1

Departmental leaders: G—Renfroe, 63; W—Reed, 14; L—Dan. Smith, 17; Pct.—Reed, .778; GS—Eldred, 29; CG—Bottenfield, Reed, 5; GF—Grater, 41; ShO—Cormier, 3; Sv.—Renfroe, 18; IP—Eldred, 185.0; H—Dan. Smith, 195; R—Dan. Smith, 114; ER—Dan. Smith, 93; HR—Moyer, 16; HB—Eldred, 12; BB—Nunez, 87; IBB—Neely, 10; SO—Eldred, 168; WP—D. Clark.

(All pitchers—listed alphabetically)

Pitcher, Team	W	L	Pct.	ERA	G	GS	CG	GF	ShO	Sv.	IP	H	R	ER	HR	HB	BB	Int. BB	SO	WP
Adkins, Iowa*	4	4	.500	5.14	13	12	0	0	0	0	63.0	57	41	36	6	2	32	0	48	8
Alba, Denver*	0	0	.000	7.20	7	0	0	3	0	0	5.0	7	4	4	0	0	2	0	6	2
Alexander, Oklahoma City	1	1	.500	4.22	2	2	0	0	0	0	10.2	10	5	5	0	0	4	0	10	0
Alvarez, Nashville	2	2	.500	2.03	16	1	0	6	0	1	31.0	19	8	7	2	1	16	1	28	1
Armstrong, Nashville	2	0	1.000	2.65	6	6	2	0	0	0	37.1	31	14	11	4	1	5	0	28	0
Arnsberg, Oklahoma City	1	0	1.000	1.69	9	0	0	6	0	1	10.2	3	2	2	1	0	3	0	10	0
August, Denver	1	0	1.000	0.00	1	1	0	0	0	0	5.0	3	0	0	0	0	0	0	1	0
Ausanio, Buffalo	2	2	.500	3.86	22	0	0	14	0	3	30.1	33	17	13	5	0	19	3	26	2
Austin, Denver	6	3	.667	2.45	20	3	0	10	0	3	44.0	35	12	12	4	2	24	3	37	1
Baker, Louisville	0	0	.000	2.25	2	0	0	1	0	0	4.0	4	1	1	0	0	1	0	3	0
Barnes, Indianapolis*	2	0	1.000	1.64	2	2	0	0	0	0	11.0	6	2	2	0	1	6	0	10	0
Bautista, Oklahoma City	0	3	.000	5.29	11	3	0	4	0	0	32.1	38	19	19	4	1	6	0	22	0
Bearse, Indianapolis*	0	2	.000	3.15	12	3	0	3	0	0	34.1	33	16	12	3	2	10	0	17	1
Bennett, Indianapolis	1	0	1.000	7.94	6	0	0	1	0	0	11.1	12	10	10	3	1	1	0	5	0
Bierley, Iowa	0	0	.000	0.00	1	0	0	1	0	0	0.2	0	0	0	0	0	0	0	0	0
Bitker, Oklahoma City	0	5	.000	4.00	23	0	0	20	0	7	27.0	30	16	12	1	0	9	2	33	2
Blankenship, Buffalo	8	9	.471	4.30	27	21	2	1	1	0	125.2	127	63	60	3	2	61	0	77	10
Bohanon, Oklahoma City*	0	4	.000	2.91	7	7	0	0	0	0	46.1	49	19	15	2	1	15	1	37	2
Boone, Oklahoma City*	5	7	.417	4.28	24	16	3	3	0	0	115.2	131	61	55	15	1	36	1	67	6
Boskie, Iowa	2	2	.500	3.57	7	6	2	0	0	0	45.1	43	19	18	1	2	11	0	29	1
Bottenfield, Indianapolis	8	15	.348	4.06	29	27	5	0	2	0	166.1	155	97	75	15	4	61	7	108	5
Bronkey, Oklahoma City*	1	0	1.000	10.80	7	0	0	1	0	0	10.0	16	13	12	2	1	4	0	7	2
Brown, Nashville	2	5	.286	3.48	47	1	0	32	0	16	62.0	64	26	24	3	2	32	4	53	5
Brown, Denver*	4	3	.571	4.67	12	11	1	1	0	0	61.2	71	36	32	4	2	34	0	31	2
Buchanan, Omaha*	11	7	.611	3.26	32	22	2	2	0	0	157.1	147	67	57	12	4	66	0	79	9
Bullinger, Iowa	3	4	.429	5.40	8	8	0	0	0	0	46.2	47	32	28	6	0	23	0	30	7
Campbell, Oklahoma City	0	0	.000	13.50	1	1	0	0	0	0	3.1	5	5	5	2	0	1	0	3	0
Canan, Iowa	0	0	.000	0.00	1	0	0	0	0	0	0.2	0	0	0	0	0	1	0	1	0
Cangelosi, Denver	0	0	.000	2.45	2	0	0	2	0	0	3.2	3	1	1	0	0	2	0	1	0
Capra, Oklahoma City	0	0	.000	0.00	1	0	0	1	0	0	3.0	3	2	0	0	0	1	0	2	0
Carman, Omaha*	3	3	.500	3.96	14	2	0	1	0	0	25.0	29	12	11	0	0	13	1	14	2
Casillas, Nashville*	0	0	.000	0.00	2	0	0	1	0	0	3.0	1	0	0	0	1	2	0	2	0
Castillo, Iowa	3	1	.750	2.52	4	4	1	0	1	0	25.0	20	7	7	0	0	7	0	20	3
Centala, Omaha	6	9	.400	3.58	18	18	0	0	0	0	100.2	109	56	40	11	4	37	2	64	5
Clark, Omaha	6	9	.400	4.51	25	23	0	1	0	0	129.2	126	76	65	10	4	74	0	108	17
Clark, Louisville	3	2	.600	2.98	7	6	1	0	1	0	45.1	43	17	15	4	0	15	0	29	2
Clarke, Louisville*	5	7	.417	4.60	20	20	2	0	1	0	121.1	130	71	62	11	4	52	2	74	4
Clary, Buffalo	5	8	.385	4.31	40	12	1	7	1	1	100.1	108	53	48	8	2	36	1	42	7
Cole, Buffalo	2	3	.400	3.89	25	1	0	10	0	0	37.0	32	17	16	3	1	29	1	36	3
Compres, Louisville	0	2	.000	3.07	10	0	0	4	0	0	14.2	22	5	5	0	0	8	2	7	1
Cormier, Louisville*	7	9	.438	4.23	21	21	3	0	3	0	127.2	140	64	60	5	6	31	2	74	6
Corona, Louisville*	1	0	1.000	5.40	12	0	0	3	0	0	16.2	18	12	10	2	0	11	1	19	2
Crosby, Louisville	0	0	.000	8.10	4	0	0	4	0	0	3.1	4	3	3	1	0	1	0	0	0
Davidson, Louisville	3	5	.375	4.29	51	0	0	10	0	0	107.0	134	58	51	7	2	34	8	61	5
Davins, Denver	1	2	.333	8.06	25	0	0	19	0	5	22.1	21	20	20	5	3	10	0	20	0

— 347 —

Pitcher, Team	W	L	Pct.	ERA	G	GS	CG	GF	ShO	Sv.	IP	H	R	ER	HR	HB	BB	Int. BB	SO	WP
Davis, Indianapolis	1	0	1.000	4.97	7	0	0	3	0	0	12.2	16	11	7	0	0	3	1	8	0
Davis, Omaha*	4	1	.800	2.02	6	6	0	0	0	0	35.2	27	11	8	1	1	9	0	36	1
Dickson, Iowa*	4	4	.500	3.11	18	18	1	0	1	0	101.1	85	39	35	5	0	57	1	101	5
DiPino, Louisville*	0	0	.000	36.00	2	0	0	1	0	0	1.0	2	4	4	0	0	3	0	0	0
Dixon, Indianapolis	6	7	.462	2.91	53	8	0	16	0	5	117.2	120	50	38	5	2	30	8	63	1
Eldred, Denver	13	9	.591	3.75	29	29	3	0	1	0	185.0	161	82	77	13	12	84	2	168	8
Elvira, Denver*	0	4	.000	5.96	18	13	1	0	0	0	80.0	100	62	53	8	4	40	1	52	3
Encarnacion, Omaha	3	3	.500	3.76	50	0	0	18	0	4	93.1	77	42	39	8	2	41	2	65	3
Everson, Omaha	0	0	.000	4.88	16	0	0	6	0	1	31.1	33	19	17	3	1	19	0	19	0
Fajardo, Buffalo	1	0	1.000	0.96	8	0	0	4	0	1	9.1	6	1	1	0	0	3	0	12	0
Farmer, Indianapolis	6	4	.600	3.86	20	19	0	0	0	0	105.0	93	55	45	5	6	37	0	67	6
Fassero, Indianapolis*	3	0	1.000	1.47	18	0	0	11	0	4	18.1	11	3	3	1	1	7	3	12	1
Filer, Iowa	8	3	.727	4.37	18	18	2	0	1	0	113.1	126	62	55	12	1	29	0	47	7
Fireovid, Buffalo	9	8	.529	2.90	34	18	1	6	0	3	130.1	127	51	42	5	6	43	6	72	8
Fisher, Denver	10	6	.625	4.78	44	2	1	15	0	2	98.0	98	54	52	10	9	39	5	66	1
Fortugno, Denver*	0	1	.000	3.57	26	0	0	10	0	2	35.1	30	15	14	1	3	20	2	39	4
Foster, Nashville	2	3	.400	2.14	41	0	0	25	0	12	54.2	46	17	13	4	1	29	5	52	0
Frey, Indianapolis*	3	1	.750	1.51	30	0	0	15	0	3	35.2	25	6	6	1	1	15	2	45	1
Garcia, Nashville	2	0	1.000	2.63	15	0	0	9	0	0	24.0	15	7	7	2	1	14	0	12	2
Gardner, Indianapolis	2	0	1.000	3.48	6	6	0	0	0	0	31.0	26	13	12	3	3	16	0	38	2
Gardner, Omaha	3	1	.750	4.91	9	1	0	3	0	1	18.1	27	11	10	0	0	5	0	12	3
George, Denver	4	5	.444	2.33	43	1	0	16	0	4	85.0	74	31	22	6	0	26	5	65	4
Gossage, Oklahoma City	0	0	.000	18.00	2	0	0	1	0	0	2.0	2	4	4	1	1	0	0	3	1
Grater, Louisville	3	5	.375	2.02	58	0	0	41	0	12	80.1	68	20	18	1	3	33	7	53	4
Grewal, Indianapolis	0	0	.000	0.00	2	0	0	0	0	0	3.0	2	0	0	0	0	3	0	1	0
Gross, Nashville	5	3	.625	2.08	14	6	1	3	1	0	47.2	39	13	11	3	4	16	0	28	3
Gubicza, Omaha	2	1	.667	3.31	3	3	0	0	0	0	16.1	20	7	6	0	0	4	0	12	4
Guzman, Oklahoma City	1	1	.500	3.92	3	3	0	0	0	0	20.2	18	9	9	1	0	4	0	18	2
Hall, 8 Nash. - 15 O.C.*	1	3	.250	6.75	23	1	0	9	0	0	32.0	34	28	24	3	0	27	1	17	5
Hamilton, Buffalo*	4	3	.571	4.92	18	10	1	2	0	1	67.2	77	39	37	6	5	24	1	29	6
Haney, Indianapolis*	1	1	.500	4.35	2	2	0	0	0	0	10.1	14	10	5	2	1	6	0	8	2
Hayward, Oklahoma City*	3	3	.500	4.88	19	3	0	5	0	1	48.0	59	32	26	3	1	21	1	27	5
Henry, Denver	3	2	.600	2.18	32	0	0	27	0	14	57.2	47	16	14	4	3	20	3	47	4
Hernandez, Denver	1	1	.500	0.54	5	0	0	3	0	1	16.2	14	3	1	0	0	4	1	8	2
Higuera, Denver*	1	0	1.000	2.08	2	2	0	0	0	0	8.2	6	3	2	1	0	6	0	6	0
Hill, Louisville	0	0	.000	0.00	1	0	0	1	0	0	1.0	0	0	0	0	0	0	0	2	0
Hill, Nashville	3	3	.500	2.94	37	0	0	16	0	3	67.1	59	26	22	3	0	15	1	62	3
Hinkle, Louisville	1	2	.333	4.65	6	6	0	0	0	0	31.0	42	17	16	4	1	10	1	15	2
Holmes, Denver	0	0	.000	9.00	1	0	0	1	0	0	1.0	1	1	1	0	0	2	0	2	0
Huismann, 13 Buf. -32 Oma.	6	5	.545	3.16	45	1	0	37	0	17	68.1	70	28	24	7	1	18	3	51	2
Hunter, Denver	7	4	.636	3.30	14	14	0	0	0	0	87.1	94	38	32	6	5	27	0	43	2
Ignasiak, Denver	9	5	.643	4.25	24	22	1	1	0	1	137.2	119	68	65	14	6	57	2	103	4
Imes, Nashville	3	7	.300	6.30	25	16	0	5	0	0	85.2	103	75	60	7	1	49	0	49	1
Jackson, Iowa*	0	0	.000	1.80	1	1	0	0	0	0	5.0	2	1	1	0	0	2	0	4	0
Johnston, Omaha	4	7	.364	5.21	47	1	0	27	0	8	74.1	60	43	43	12	1	42	2	63	6
Kaiser, Denver*	0	1	.000	3.86	8	1	0	1	0	0	18.2	16	9	8	0	1	13	1	12	1
Kiefer, Denver	9	5	.643	4.62	17	17	3	0	2	0	101.1	104	55	52	7	9	41	0	68	6
Knudson, Denver	4	4	.500	5.40	13	10	2	2	0	1	51.2	73	34	31	5	2	13	1	28	1
Kraemer, Iowa*	8	7	.533	4.60	20	19	1	0	1	0	119.1	127	66	61	12	3	48	1	77	6
LaPoint, 7 Den. -26 Iowa*	3	2	.600	6.47	33	8	0	11	0	1	65.1	85	56	47	6	5	25	1	42	1
Laskey, Oklahoma City	3	5	.375	4.40	31	0	0	13	0	2	47.0	50	29	23	2	0	30	4	33	1
Layana, Nashville	3	1	.750	3.23	26	2	0	4	0	1	47.1	41	17	17	3	2	28	0	43	6
LeMasters, Omaha	2	7	.222	5.42	21	12	0	2	0	0	74.2	88	48	45	5	4	37	1	45	3
Lewis, Indianapolis	1	0	1.000	3.58	5	4	0	0	0	0	27.2	35	12	11	1	0	20	1	22	2
Little, Buffalo	0	0	.000	36.00	1	0	0	1	0	0	1.0	4	4	4	1	0	0	0	0	0
Long, Indianapolis	1	4	.200	5.13	10	4	0	1	0	1	33.1	32	20	19	6	0	14	0	17	1
Lopez, Nashville	1	1	.500	4.50	3	3	0	0	0	0	16.0	11	9	8	1	0	4	0	11	1
Loynd, Louisville	3	6	.333	5.09	9	8	0	0	0	0	46.0	43	30	26	7	3	15	0	36	3
Luecken, Iowa	0	0	.000	9.82	5	0	0	1	0	0	7.1	12	8	8	1	0	8	1	3	2
Mack, Indianapolis*	0	0	.000	27.00	2	0	0	2	0	0	2.0	4	6	6	2	1	3	0	0	0
Magnante, Omaha*	6	1	.857	3.02	10	10	2	0	0	0	65.2	53	23	22	2	1	23	0	50	2
Maldonado, Omaha	1	1	.500	4.28	41	0	0	31	0	9	61.0	67	31	29	6	2	42	1	46	6
Marchok, Indianapolis*	2	2	.500	4.13	11	3	0	2	0	0	28.1	24	13	13	1	1	13	1	10	1
Mason, Buffalo	9	5	.643	3.08	34	15	2	6	1	0	122.2	115	47	42	11	6	44	1	80	2
Masters, Indianapolis	4	6	.400	6.04	27	9	1	5	0	1	70.0	82	56	47	7	1	63	2	64	16
Mathews, Denver	6	3	.667	3.86	13	9	1	1	1	0	60.2	62	32	26	7	2	27	1	25	0
Mathews, Oklahoma City	5	6	.455	3.49	18	13	1	2	0	1	95.1	98	39	37	2	2	34	3	63	4
May, Iowa	4	4	.500	2.97	57	2	0	26	0	10	94.0	75	38	31	7	2	54	3	93	6
Maysey, Indianapolis	3	6	.333	5.14	12	12	0	0	0	0	63.0	60	45	36	7	2	33	2	45	6
McGaffigan, 23 Oma. - 10 Den.	2	2	.500	3.58	33	4	0	13	0	7	65.1	72	33	26	5	2	26	1	45	6
Meeks, Buffalo	4	8	.333	3.89	36	18	2	4	1	1	143.1	146	72	62	11	3	31	1	66	1
Menendez, Oklahoma City	5	5	.500	5.20	21	19	0	1	0	0	116.0	107	70	67	6	6	62	2	82	8
Mielke, Oklahoma City	2	1	.667	9.74	10	0	0	7	0	0	20.1	34	23	22	3	2	6	0	14	2
Milchin, Louisville*	5	9	.357	5.07	18	18	2	0	1	0	94.0	132	64	53	4	4	40	5	47	5
Miller, Buffalo	5	2	.714	1.48	10	10	2	0	0	0	67.0	41	17	11	2	5	29	0	30	1
Minor, Buffalo	2	2	.500	5.75	17	3	0	3	0	0	36.0	46	27	23	7	0	15	0	25	1
Minutelli, Nashville*	4	7	.364	1.90	13	13	1	0	1	0	80.1	57	25	17	3	1	35	2	64	6
Miranda, Denver*	0	1	.000	6.17	11	0	0	8	0	2	11.2	10	9	8	0	0	17	1	14	1
Mitchell, Nashville	6	9	.400	4.17	35	12	0	12	0	0	108.0	110	59	50	12	3	33	6	61	6
Moeller, Omaha*	7	3	.700	3.22	14	14	0	0	0	0	78.1	70	36	28	4	3	40	0	51	3
Morman, Omaha	0	0	.000	0.00	1	0	0	1	0	0	1.0	0	0	0	0	0	0	0	0	0
Mount, Iowa	1	2	.333	5.40	10	3	0	0	0	0	23.1	29	15	14	4	0	18	0	15	0
Moyer, Louisville*	5	10	.333	3.80	20	20	1	0	0	0	125.2	125	64	53	16	3	43	4	69	8
Murphy, Oklahoma City	0	1	.000	81.00	2	1	0	0	0	0	1.0	7	13	9	1	1	5	0	1	0
Myers, Indianapolis*	0	1	.000	3.29	2	2	0	0	0	0	13.2	15	5	5	0	0	5	0	9	0
Nabholz, Indianapolis*	2	2	.500	1.86	4	4	0	0	0	0	19.1	13	5	4	2	0	5	0	16	0
Neely, Buffalo	2	5	.286	4.63	42	0	0	25	0	7	58.1	67	32	30	5	2	27	10	45	3
Nipper, Louisville	0	3	.000	5.72	5	5	0	0	0	0	28.1	36	18	18	3	2	9	1	10	1
Nolte, Oklahoma City*	1	3	.250	5.91	25	9	0	6	0	1	56.1	74	39	37	4	2	31	0	40	3
Nunez, Iowa	12	9	.571	4.58	28	25	4	0	0	0	165.0	157	95	84	8	7	87	0	118	13
Olivares, Louisville	1	2	.333	3.47	6	6	0	0	0	0	36.1	39	15	14	1	1	16	1	27	2
Osteen, Louisville	1	5	.167	6.41	29	5	0	3	0	0	59.0	74	49	42	4	3	31	4	25	2
Palacios, Buffalo	0	0	.000	1.42	3	0	0	2	0	2	6.1	7	1	1	0	0	2	0	8	2
Pavlas, Iowa	5	6	.455	3.98	61	0	0	29	0	7	97.1	92	49	43	5	5	43	9	54	13

Pitcher, Team	W	L	Pct.	ERA	G	GS	CG	GF	ShO	Sv.	IP	H	R	ER	HR	HB	BB	Int. BB	SO	WP
Pavlik, Oklahoma City	0	5	.000	5.19	8	7	0	0	0	0	26.0	19	21	15	1	1	26	1	43	5
Pearson, Nashville	0	0	.000	6.75	3	0	0	3	0	0	4.0	2	3	3	0	0	6	0	2	0
Perez, Louisville	3	5	.375	6.13	37	0	0	23	0	4	47.0	54	38	32	5	2	25	6	39	5
Peters, Oklahoma City*	3	3	.500	5.57	24	0	0	6	0	0	32.1	43	21	20	3	0	19	1	27	3
Petkovsek, Oklahoma City	9	8	.529	4.93	25	24	3	0	1	0	149.2	162	89	82	9	7	38	2	67	10
Piatt, Indianapolis	6	4	.600	3.45	44	0	0	32	0	13	47.0	40	24	18	2	3	27	1	61	5
Picota, Louisville	3	6	.333	5.83	28	11	0	3	0	0	88.0	112	62	57	5	3	51	5	42	6
Poole, Oklahoma City*	0	0	.000	0.00	10	0	0	7	0	3	12.1	4	0	0	0	0	1	0	14	0
Postier, Oklahoma City	1	0	1.000	5.40	4	0	0	3	0	0	6.2	8	4	4	1	0	5	0	3	0
Powell, Oklahoma City*	8	8	.500	4.37	24	24	1	0	0	0	129.2	125	74	63	10	2	63	1	82	3
Pugh, Nashville	7	11	.389	3.81	23	23	3	0	1	0	148.2	130	68	63	9	10	56	2	89	9
Puig, Denver*	0	2	.000	5.14	11	0	0	9	0	0	14.0	13	8	8	3	0	3	0	5	0
Reed, Buffalo	14	4	.778	2.15	25	25	5	0	2	0	167.2	151	45	40	3	2	26	2	102	2
Renfroe, Iowa	8	5	.615	4.21	63	1	0	40	0	18	98.1	101	52	46	10	3	32	5	52	2
Richardson, Louisville*	1	0	1.000	7.15	13	0	0	4	0	1	22.2	29	18	18	1	0	16	2	8	3
Ridenour, Indianapolis	5	3	.625	3.12	57	0	0	21	0	6	80.2	69	31	28	2	6	50	8	92	16
Risley, Nashville*	3	5	.375	4.91	8	8	1	0	0	0	44.0	45	27	24	7	1	26	2	32	3
Rodriguez, Buffalo*	4	3	.571	3.00	48	0	0	21	0	8	51.0	38	22	17	1	2	31	2	43	3
Roesler, Buffalo	5	4	.556	3.56	33	0	0	21	0	8	48.0	46	19	19	3	1	21	1	34	3
Rojas, Indianapolis	4	2	.667	4.10	14	10	0	2	0	1	52.2	50	29	24	4	1	14	1	55	3
Rosario, Iowa*	3	1	.750	2.18	33	0	0	5	0	1	33.0	21	10	8	1	0	11	0	31	2
Rosenthal, Oklahoma City	3	2	.600	4.03	32	0	0	16	0	5	51.1	52	24	23	2	3	22	2	59	3
Ryan, Indianapolis*	1	0	1.000	1.80	2	0	0	0	0	0	5.0	5	2	1	0	1	0	0	3	1
Sadler, Denver	0	2	.000	11.81	2	1	0	0	0	0	5.1	7	7	7	1	0	5	0	1	3
Sampen, Indianapolis	4	0	1.000	2.04	7	7	1	0	0	0	39.2	33	13	9	1	1	19	0	41	2
Sanford, Nashville	3	0	1.000	1.60	5	5	2	0	2	0	33.2	19	7	6	0	1	22	0	38	3
Scanlan, Iowa	2	0	1.000	2.95	4	3	0	1	0	0	18.1	14	8	6	0	0	10	1	15	3
Schiraldi, Oklahoma City	1	2	.333	5.64	18	0	0	6	0	0	30.1	32	19	19	2	1	23	2	24	3
Schmidt, 13 Ind. - 11 O.C.	0	3	.000	2.92	24	4	0	7	0	1	37.0	39	17	12	3	0	17	6	19	0
Service, Indianapolis	6	7	.462	2.97	18	17	3	1	1	0	121.1	83	42	40	7	6	39	0	91	5
Sherrill, Louisville*	5	5	.500	3.13	42	0	0	29	0	10	60.1	56	21	21	5	0	26	3	38	2
Shines, Louisville	0	0	.000	0.00	3	0	0	3	0	0	2.1	0	0	0	0	0	0	0	2	0
Simonds, Iowa	0	0	.000	0.00	1	0	0	1	0	0	0.1	0	0	0	0	0	1	0	0	0
Slocumb, Iowa	1	0	1.000	4.05	12	0	0	6	0	1	13.1	10	8	6	0	1	6	0	9	1
Smith, Oklahoma City*	4	17	.190	5.52	28	27	3	1	0	0	151.2	195	114	93	10	4	75	1	85	5
Smith, Omaha	4	5	.444	3.39	23	14	0	4	0	0	93.0	82	38	35	10	4	33	1	94	4
Sodders, Iowa*	2	4	.333	6.69	16	5	0	3	0	0	37.2	48	31	28	5	1	18	1	33	2
Stewart, Indianapolis*	0	0	.000	8.10	3	0	0	2	0	1	3.1	5	3	3	1	0	3	0	1	0
Strauss, Iowa	1	0	1.000	0.87	6	0	0	1	0	0	10.1	9	2	1	0	0	2	0	8	0
Sutcliffe, Iowa	1	2	.333	9.69	3	2	0	1	0	0	13.0	23	14	14	2	0	6	0	8	2
Thompson, Oklahoma City	0	2	.000	6.51	16	0	0	9	0	0	27.2	47	26	20	1	0	11	0	16	1
Tracy, Buffalo	2	2	.500	5.17	11	8	0	1	0	0	47.0	61	27	27	8	0	10	0	20	1
Turek, Nashville	3	6	.333	4.99	14	14	0	0	0	0	79.1	88	45	44	5	2	29	0	49	3
Vasquez, Nashville	1	2	.333	5.12	8	7	0	0	0	0	38.2	40	28	22	4	2	29	0	15	3
Vierra, Nashville*	5	4	.556	4.33	62	2	0	15	0	2	95.2	81	60	46	8	6	43	2	84	5
Wagner, Omaha	5	6	.455	3.44	17	14	1	0	0	0	86.1	88	45	33	4	5	38	0	36	0
Wainhouse, Indianapolis	2	0	1.000	4.08	14	0	0	8	0	1	28.2	28	14	13	1	3	15	1	13	3
Wakefield, Buffalo	0	1	.000	11.57	1	1	0	0	0	0	4.2	8	6	6	3	0	1	0	4	0
Walter, Louisville*	0	0	.000	0.00	4	0	0	2	0	0	6.0	2	0	0	0	0	2	0	4	0
Wegman, Denver	0	0	.000	2.57	1	1	0	0	0	0	7.0	6	2	2	0	0	1	0	1	0
Wells, Oklahoma City*	1	3	.250	7.15	12	6	0	2	0	0	34.0	40	34	27	2	1	33	0	29	5
Wilson, Iowa*	3	8	.273	3.87	25	16	1	4	0	0	114.0	102	55	49	11	7	45	2	83	8
Winston, Indianapolis	1	0	1.000	1.45	27	0	0	4	0	0	31.0	26	10	5	3	1	21	5	23	2
Witt, Oklahoma City	1	1	.500	1.13	2	2	0	0	0	0	8.0	3	1	1	0	0	8	0	12	0
Worrell, Louisville	0	0	.000	18.00	3	0	0	0	0	0	3.0	4	6	6	1	0	3	0	4	1
York, Buffalo	5	1	.833	2.91	7	7	1	0	0	0	43.1	36	17	14	0	0	23	0	22	2

BALKS—Nunez, 6; Dan. Smith, 5; Masters, 4; M. Hill, LaPoint, G. Mathews, Mitchell, Moeller, Moyer, Turek, Vasquez, 3 each; Alba, Kev. Brown, Clarke, Clary, Davidson, Dixon, Eldred, Farmer, Fireovid, Fisher, Henry, Meeks, Nolte, Peters, Schmidt, Dar. Smith, Tracy, Vierra, 2 each; Ausanio, Bennett, Blankenship, Osteen, Cormier, Hayward, Imes, Elvira, Picota, Ignasiak, Olivares, Sutcliffe, Reed, Service, Gross, Dickson, Pavlik, Layana, LeMasters, T. Mathews, Menendez, Miller, Minutelli, Petkovsek, Higuera, Kaiser, Rojas, Piatt, Boskie, Pugh, Puig, Frey, Rodriguez, Guzman, Rosenthal, Hinkle, Bottenfield, Thompson, 1 each.

COMBINATION SHUTOUTS—Reed-Roesler 2, Blankenship-Meeks-Rodriguez-Roesler, Clary-Roesler, Mason-Huismann-Rodriguez, Mason-Rodriguez, Mason-Roesler, Miller-Cole, Reed-Meeks-Fajardo-Tracy, Reed-Rodriguez-Neely, Buffalo; Eldred-Henry, Hunter-Davins, Denver; Barnes-Bottenfield-Long, Bottenfield-Dixon, Dixon-Marchok-Ridenour, Nabholz-Dixon-Frey-Piatt, Powell-Hill, Schmidt-Frey-Davis-Ridenour, Indianapolis; Dickson-Pavlas, Sodders-May, Wilson-May, Iowa; Cormier-Perez, Davidson-Perez, Loynd-Grater, Moyer-Grater-Sherrill, Moyer-Sherrill, Osteen-Sherrill, Louisville; Layana-Foster-Brown, Lopez-Gross, Minutelli-Brown-Foster, Mitchell-Foster-Vierra, Powell-Hill, Powell-Hill-Brown, Powell-Mitchell, Risley-Brown, Turek-Vierra-Brown, Nashville; Alexander-Bronkey-Bitker, Boone-Schmidt, Mathews-Hayward, Mathews-Thompson, Petkovsek-Arnsberg, Oklahoma City; Buchanan-Encarnacion, Clark-McGaffigan, Magnante-McGaffigan, Smith-Maldonado, Wagner-Maldonado, Omaha.

NO-HIT GAME—Pavlik-Peters, Oklahoma City, lost to Indianapolis, 1-0, April 17.

FIELDING

TEAM

Team	Pct.	G	PO	A	E	DP	PB	Team	Pct.	G	PO	A	E	DP	PB
Iowa	.977	144	3828	1621	127	138	17	Omaha	.973	144	3742	1480	144	145	11
Denver	.976	144	3763	1488	130	127	15	Nashville	.972	143	3737	1536	151	110	21
Louisville	.974	143	3720	1565	139	153	12	Oklahoma City	.970	144	3709	1446	161	116	24
Buffalo	.974	143	3720	1485	138	126	11	Indianapolis	.969	143	3739	1557	169	143	25

Triple play—Nashville.

INDIVIDUAL

*Throws lefthanded.

FIRST BASEMEN

Player, Team	Pct.	G	PO	A	E	DP
Balboni, Oklahoma City	.971	9	62	6	2	6
Banister, Buffalo	.889	3	7	1	1	2
Barberie, Indianapolis	1.000	1	1	1	0	0
Berger, Oklahoma City	1.000	14	108	10	0	5
Bierley, Iowa	1.000	2	12	3	0	2
Brewer, Louisville*	.996	66	501	40	2	52
Burrell, Omaha	1.000	4	36	0	0	3
Canale, Denver	.992	67	480	29	4	32

CLASS AAA — AMERICAN ASSOCIATION

Player, Team	Pct.	G	PO	A	E	DP
Cangelosi, Denver*	1.000	1	1	0	0	0
Carrillo, Denver*	.976	5	38	2	1	2
Casillas, Nashville*	1.000	4	20	3	0	1
Castaneda, Louisville	1.000	15	118	5	0	15
Da. Clark, Omaha	.995	19	172	9	1	14
S. Cole, Omaha	1.000	4	30	4	0	3
Conine, Omaha	.988	43	380	40	5	38
DeFrancesco, Nashville	.929	2	13	0	1	2
Dorsett, Buffalo	.951	19	124	11	7	19
Dunbar, Buffalo*	1.000	1	3	0	0	0
Fernandez, Louisville	.999	76	624	50	1	64
Goff, Indianapolis	.947	6	34	2	2	5
Guerrero, Denver	1.000	3	10	1	0	1
Guerrero, Louisville	.933	3	14	0	1	0
Guinn, Iowa	1.000	7	28	2	0	1
Hamelin, Omaha*	1.000	6	55	4	0	6
Haselman, Oklahoma City	1.000	4	23	1	0	2
R. Jefferson, Nashville*	.991	19	196	13	2	20
Kremers, Indianapolis	.989	19	159	16	2	11
LEE, Nashville	.991	110	936	74	9	95
Leonard, Omaha	1.000	2	13	0	0	1
Liddell, Denver	.941	3	15	1	1	2
Little, Buffalo	.947	7	32	4	2	4
Maurer, Oklahoma City*	.985	120	941	84	16	83
McGinnis, Iowa	.990	70	557	41	6	55
McIntosh, Denver	.989	78	572	54	7	64
McPhail, Indianapolis	1.000	6	33	0	0	3
Mendez, Louisville*	1.000	14	60	7	0	5
Merced, Buffalo	1.000	3	29	2	0	4
Meyer, Buffalo	.994	70	611	46	4	44
K. Miller, Buffalo	1.000	21	94	7	0	10
Morman, Omaha	.990	70	547	40	6	63
Nilsson, Denver	1.000	6	29	2	0	4
Pappas, Iowa	1.000	9	80	4	0	7
Pearson, Nashville	1.000	5	41	2	0	4
Pedre, Omaha	1.000	4	25	2	0	0
Postier, Oklahoma City	1.000	1	8	1	0	1
Redfield, Buffalo	.970	7	31	1	1	2
Santovenia, Indianapolis	.979	6	41	5	1	6
Schulz, Buffalo	1.000	6	37	5	0	4
Shines, Indianapolis	.989	121	998	74	12	102
Smith, Denver	1.000	1	2	0	0	0
Sparks, Buffalo*	.993	45	278	24	2	23
Strange, Iowa	.992	16	115	11	1	17
Sullivan, Iowa*	.996	72	496	32	2	41
Trafton, Nashville	.985	7	62	3	1	2
Young, Buffalo	1.000	2	3	2	0	0

Triple play—Lee.

SECOND BASEMEN

Player, Team	Pct.	G	PO	A	E	DP
Alicea, Louisville	.970	30	68	95	5	32
Barberie, Indianapolis	.955	17	38	47	4	16
Bates, Nashville	.970	28	52	77	4	16
Benavides, Nashville	1.000	10	13	19	0	7
Berry, Omaha	1.000	2	3	7	0	0
Branson, Nashville	1.000	11	17	18	0	9
Bridges, Omaha	1.000	1	2	2	0	3
Capra, Oklahoma City	.778	4	6	8	4	2
S. Cole, Omaha	.978	21	30	58	2	12
Crosby, Louisville	.987	56	100	133	3	31
Diaz, Indianapolis	1.000	1	5	1	0	1
Dulin, Buffalo	1.000	11	13	21	0	3
Edge, Buffalo	1.000	7	3	11	0	3
Fariss, Oklahoma City	.961	132	276	366	26	63
Figueroa, Louisville	.988	42	69	91	2	22
Garber, Omaha	.971	9	14	19	1	3
A. Gonzalez, Nashville	.982	64	94	130	4	23
Guerrero, Denver	.967	13	28	30	2	5
Guinn, Iowa	.942	13	25	24	3	5
HANEY, Indianapolis	.974	129	230	381	16	74
Hecht, Indianapolis	.889	2	4	4	1	1
Hinzo, Omaha	.938	5	7	8	1	1
Howard, Omaha	.969	6	9	22	1	5
Jones, Louisville	.906	16	28	30	6	9
Laureano, Omaha	.929	6	8	18	2	2
Liriano, Omaha	.980	77	141	199	7	42
Listach, Denver	.983	69	153	194	6	50
Lockhart, Nashville	.970	47	96	133	7	32
K. Miller, Buffalo	.980	46	88	110	4	20
Montoyo, Denver	.991	48	80	130	2	19
Moreno, Buffalo	.987	55	88	137	3	26
Pearson, Nashville	.974	11	18	20	1	6
Postier, Oklahoma City	1.000	12	18	23	0	5
Redfield, Buffalo	1.000	4	6	4	0	1
Renteria, Indianapolis	1.000	2	3	1	0	1
Richardson, Buffalo	.984	51	100	144	4	31
Ross, Louisville	.978	17	36	55	2	14
Smajstrla, Iowa	.982	88	162	226	7	53
Small, Iowa	.952	26	46	53	5	15
Strange, Iowa	.976	39	87	115	5	28
Suero, Denver	.976	19	63	57	3	15
Zuvella, Omaha	.990	23	36	65	1	19

Triple play—Pearson.

THIRD BASEMEN

Player, Team	Pct.	G	PO	A	E	DP
Barberie, Indianapolis	.932	45	32	77	8	11
Berry, Omaha	.930	96	70	195	20	18
Bierley, Iowa	1.000	1	0	1	0	0
Canale, Denver	.929	16	9	17	2	0
Canan, Iowa	1.000	3	1	3	0	0
Capra, Oklahoma City	.913	8	5	16	2	1
J. Castillo, Denver	.889	12	9	15	3	0
S. Cole, Omaha	1.000	14	7	28	0	2
Diaz, Indianapolis	1.000	7	1	7	0	1
Garber, Omaha	.865	15	11	21	5	1
Goff, Indianapolis	.800	15	10	22	8	4
A. Gonzalez, Nashville	.833	5	0	5	1	0
D. Gonzalez, Nashville	.927	65	51	115	13	12
Guerrero, Denver	.927	51	36	78	9	9
Guinn, Iowa	.900	10	3	15	2	3
Haselman, Oklahoma City	1.000	1	2	1	0	0
Hinzo, Omaha	1.000	1	1	3	0	0
Jones, Louisville	1.000	7	3	12	0	1
King, Buffalo	.909	6	2	8	1	1
Little, Buffalo	.750	2	1	2	1	0
Lockhart, Nashville	.961	59	42	107	6	11
Martinez, Louisville	.833	8	4	1	1	0
McGinnis, Iowa	1.000	1	0	2	0	0
McPhail, Indianapolis	.886	58	45	103	19	15
K. Miller, Buffalo	.938	5	5	10	1	0
Montoyo, Denver	1.000	13	8	33	0	5
Moreno, Buffalo	.964	16	8	19	1	0
Palmer, Oklahoma City	.932	58	45	105	11	5
Pearson, Nashville	.947	29	15	56	4	5
Polidor, Denver	1.000	12	7	17	0	0
Postier, Oklahoma City	.913	30	21	42	6	3
Presley, Oklahoma City	.958	51	31	82	5	6
REDFIELD, Buffalo	.947	96	75	157	13	14
Renteria, Indianapolis	.982	18	10	44	1	2
Ross, Louisville	1.000	4	1	6	0	1
Royer, Louisville	.932	135	100	299	29	32
Scott, Nashville	.875	2	1	6	1	1
Scott, Iowa	.963	55	36	94	5	4
Shines, Indianapolis	.931	13	13	14	2	3
Smajstrla, Iowa	1.000	1	0	1	0	0
Small, Iowa	1.000	6	2	8	0	1
Smith, Denver	.964	62	43	90	5	9
Spehr, Omaha	.800	5	2	6	2	0
Strange, Iowa	.930	81	55	144	15	15
Thomas, Omaha	.857	3	4	2	1	1
Wehner, Buffalo	.925	31	30	69	8	3
Young, Buffalo	.778	3	3	4	2	2
Zuvella, Omaha	.978	14	12	32	1	1

Triple play—Lockhart.

SHORTSTOPS

Player, Team	Pct.	G	PO	A	E	DP
Barberie, Indianapolis	.980	14	12	37	1	6
Bates, Nashville	.914	8	12	20	3	3
Beltre, Denver	.899	26	52	64	13	14
Benavides, Nashville	.972	84	135	250	11	54
Berry, Omaha	1.000	3	2	4	0	0
Branson, Nashville	.937	33	44	75	8	13
Bridges, Omaha	.933	5	3	11	1	0
Burgos, Oklahoma City	.829	8	17	12	6	0
Capra, Oklahoma City	.857	3	5	1	1	0
Carmona, Louisville	.922	46	67	134	17	23
J. Castillo, Denver	1.000	1	0	1	0	0
S. Cole, Omaha	.947	76	111	174	16	51
Cordero, Indianapolis	.943	97	157	287	27	69
Diaz, Indianapolis	.927	12	20	31	4	3
Edge, Buffalo	.895	4	8	9	2	1
Figueroa, Louisville	.966	54	80	145	8	32
Garber, Omaha	.860	10	18	25	7	5
Garcia, Louisville	.946	126	212	332	31	69
Garner, Oklahoma City	1.000	3	6	5	0	2
A. Gonzalez, Nashville	.911	25	42	60	10	18
Green, Oklahoma City	.956	100	171	245	19	55
Guinn, Iowa	.953	22	25	36	3	9
T. Haney, Indianapolis	1.000	2	2	4	0	0
Hernandez, Oklahoma City	.962	14	32	43	3	11
Howard, Omaha	.955	8	21	21	2	10
Huson, Oklahoma City	1.000	2	5	3	0	0
Jones, Louisville	.976	65	80	165	6	38
Knabenshue, Denver	1.000	1	0	2	0	0
Liriano, Omaha	.931	7	8	19	2	3
Listach, Denver	.959	19	27	43	3	7
Martinez, Louisville	1.000	5	1	10	0	4
Montoyo, Denver	.937	57	98	153	17	26
Moreno, Buffalo	1.000	6	8	12	0	1
Munoz, Indianapolis	.939	27	37	70	7	9
Pearson, Nashville	1.000	5	4	9	0	2
Polidor, Denver	.956	18	43	43	4	11
Postier, Oklahoma City	.975	28	26	51	2	11
Richardson, Buffalo	.982	13	21	35	1	7
SANCHEZ, Iowa	.971	124	204	375	17	81
Scott, Iowa	.917	8	11	22	3	1

Player, Team	Pct.	G	PO	A	E	DP
Small, Iowa	.931	10	8	19	2	0
Smith, Denver	.985	34	41	91	2	16
Strange, Iowa	1.000	2	3	3	0	0
Thomas, Omaha	.984	15	22	38	1	12
Zuvella, Omaha	.941	28	51	76	8	20

OUTFIELDERS

Player, Team	Pct.	G	PO	A	E	DP
Baldwin, Iowa*	1.000	15	11	0	0	0
Belcher, Oklahoma City	.972	51	101	4	3	2
Berger, Oklahoma City	.970	30	63	2	2	1
Bierley, Iowa	.99505	98	198	3	1	0
Brantley, Denver	.965	90	153	12	6	5
Brewer, Louisville*	.989	47	87	2	1	1
Brumfield, Omaha	.992	111	227	10	2	2
Canan, Iowa	.864	14	18	1	3	1
Cangelosi, Denver*	.977	66	117	9	3	1
Capra, Oklahoma City	.981	98	202	8	4	3
Carrillo, Denver*	.984	110	241	5	4	1
Carter, Iowa	.983	133	324	19	6	3
Casillas, Nashville*	.959	106	182	6	8	1
Castaneda, Louisville	.960	11	22	2	1	2
C. Castillo, Denver	.963	16	26	0	1	0
Christian, Louisville	1.000	15	10	0	0	0
Da. Clark, Omaha	.969	52	92	2	3	1
S. Cole, Omaha	1.000	7	17	2	0	0
Conine, Omaha	.867	8	12	1	2	1
Daughtry, Oklahoma City*	.967	13	27	2	1	1
M. Davis, Oklahoma City*	.964	23	27	0	1	0
DeFrancesco, Nashville	.667	1	2	0	1	0
Diaz, Indianapolis	.979	87	181	6	4	1
Dunbar, 7 Oma.-5 Buf.*	.913	12	20	1	2	0
Espy, Buffalo	.970	100	215	10	7	2
Fariss, Oklahoma City	.875	8	12	2	2	0
Fitzgerald, Indianapolis	1.000	3	6	0	0	0
Gainey, Buffalo	1.000	6	5	0	0	0
L. Garcia, Nashville*	.982	117	256	12	5	2
Gilkey, Louisville	1.000	11	33	1	0	0
D. Gonzalez, Nashville	1.000	1	1	0	0	0
Guinn, Iowa	.972	53	103	2	3	0
Haselman, Oklahoma City	.900	6	8	1	1	0
Hecht, Indianapolis	.968	64	91	1	3	0
Houston, Indianapolis	.889	11	16	0	2	0
S. Jefferson, Nashville	1.000	16	45	4	0	0
Jones, Nashville	.950	66	110	5	6	0
Jones, Louisville	1.000	8	9	0	0	0
Jordan, Louisville	.987	61	144	3	2	2
Jose, Nashville	.921	22	33	2	3	0
Knabenshue, Denver	1.000	9	13	3	0	2
Koslofski, Omaha	.985	25	61	3	1	1
Landrum, Iowa	.940	37	43	4	3	1
Lee, Nashville	1.000	12	18	1	0	0
Leonard, Omaha	.889	10	15	1	2	0
Listach, Denver	1.000	2	2	0	0	0
Little, Buffalo	.987	45	68	6	1	1
Lockhart, Nashville	1.000	13	15	1	0	0
Mack, Indianapolis*	.973	103	174	8	5	1
Maclin, Louisville*	.981	78	157	1	3	0
Magallanes, Louisville	.957	26	42	2	2	0
Martinez, Louisville	.961	123	224	21	10	3
D. May, Iowa	.964	81	130	2	5	0
McIntosh, Denver	1.000	19	21	0	0	0
McPhail, Indianapolis	.952	25	39	1	2	1
Mendez, Louisville*	.955	68	102	4	5	1
Millay, Oklahoma City	.956	71	122	9	6	2
K. Miller, Buffalo	.985	68	130	4	2	2
Moore, Omaha	.994	130	296	15	2	6
Moore, Oklahoma City*	1.000	33	59	0	0	0
Moreno, Buffalo	1.000	4	3	0	0	0
Morman, Omaha	.947	9	17	1	1	0
Moses, Buffalo*	1.000	3	5	0	0	0
Nichols, Louisville	1.000	3	0	1	0	0
Nunez, Louisville	1.000	6	13	0	0	0
Olander, Denver	.990	132	307	3	3	3
Palmer, Oklahoma City	1.000	1	4	0	0	0
Pappas, Iowa	1.000	18	21	0	0	0
Pearson, Nashville	1.000	24	26	1	0	0
Peltier, Oklahoma City*	.966	89	161	7	6	2
Pose, Nashville	.958	14	23	0	1	0
Pulliam, Omaha	.983	102	162	12	3	0
Roomes, Denver	.944	15	32	2	2	1
Ross, Louisville	.988	44	75	6	1	2
Schulz, Buffalo	.989	84	168	6	2	2
Scott, Nashville	1.000	1	1	0	0	0
Scruggs, Oklahoma City	1.000	52	128	1	0	1
Sparks, Buffalo*	1.000	1	1	0	0	0
Stockstill, Indianapolis	.947	14	18	0	1	0
Strange, Iowa	1.000	1	3	0	0	0
Sullivan, Iowa*	1.000	18	27	4	0	0
Trafton, Nashville	1.000	65	124	5	0	1
Tubbs, Buffalo	.988	109	237	3	3	1
VANDERWAL, Indianapolis*	.99512	125	197	7	1	1
Walker, Nashville	1.000	7	12	0	0	0
Williams, Indianapolis	1.000	16	30	3	0	0
Zambrano, Buffalo	1.000	48	86	2	0	1

CATCHERS

Player, Team	Pct.	G	PO	A	E	DP	PB
Banister, Buffalo	.972	60	296	22	9	1	4
Baxter, Omaha	1.000	3	5	1	0	0	0
Beeler, Nashville	1.000	3	15	0	0	0	0
Berger, Oklahoma City	.980	16	94	6	2	3	9
Berryhill, Iowa	.981	16	90	14	2	2	3
Burrell, Omaha	.983	56	321	29	6	5	2
DeFrancesco, Nashville	.979	41	251	24	6	3	4
Dorsett, Buffalo	1.000	14	62	9	0	0	0
Fitzgerald, Indianapolis	1.000	7	25	2	0	1	3
Fulton, Louisville	.991	42	192	17	2	5	4
Girardi, Iowa	.957	11	62	5	3	1	2
Goff, Indianapolis	.984	27	160	20	3	3	4
Haselman, Oklahoma City	.987	109	673	68	10	5	12
Hines, Buffalo	.949	7	34	3	2	1	1
KMAK, Denver	.992	98	579	77	5	10	9
Kremers, Indianapolis	.975	73	441	66	13	7	15
Kreuter, Oklahoma City	.960	23	146	23	7	5	3
Liddell, Denver	.981	25	129	25	3	5	2
Magrann, Buffalo	1.000	4	22	2	0	0	1
McGinnis, Iowa	.990	30	177	21	2	4	3
McIntosh, Denver	.991	18	105	10	1	1	1
Natal, Indianapolis	.971	14	62	5	2	0	1
Nichols, Louisville	.980	19	87	10	2	2	0
Nieto, Louisville	.965	19	77	5	3	1	1
Nilsson, Denver	.985	22	117	14	2	0	4
Noce, Indianapolis	1.000	2	2	0	0	0	2
Pappas, Iowa	.984	59	319	54	6	5	4
Parent, Oklahoma City	1.000	4	4	0	0	0	2
Pedre, Omaha	.979	29	170	18	4	1	3
Petralli, Oklahoma City	1.000	2	13	1	0	0	0
Piskor, Omaha	1.000	3	15	0	0	0	0
Prince, Buffalo	.989	78	379	61	5	8	6
Prybylinski, Louisville	.960	24	111	8	5	0	3
Royer, Louisville	1.000	1	1	0	0	0	1
Santovenia, Indianapolis	.988	42	292	28	4	3	1
Scott, Nashville	.976	70	409	42	11	5	11
Simonds, Iowa	1.000	14	55	7	0	2	1
Spehr, Omaha	.987	66	400	47	6	6	6
Stephens, Louisville	.980	58	261	28	6	4	6
Sutko, Nashville	.985	42	228	39	4	4	6
Thomas, Louisville	.962	4	24	1	1	1	0
Villanueva, Iowa	1.000	2	15	0	0	0	0
Wilkins, Iowa	.987	32	204	24	3	3	4

PITCHERS

Player, Team	Pct.	G	PO	A	E	DP
Adkins, Iowa*	.923	13	2	10	1	0
Alexander, Oklahoma City	1.000	2	0	2	0	0
Alvarez, Nashville	1.000	16	3	8	0	0
Armstrong, Nashville	.818	6	3	6	2	1
Arnsberg, Oklahoma City	1.000	9	2	3	0	0
August, Denver	1.000	1	0	1	0	0
Ausanio, Buffalo	.667	22	0	2	1	0
Austin, Denver	1.000	20	4	4	0	0
Baker, Louisville	1.000	2	0	1	0	0
Barnes, Indianapolis*	1.000	2	1	2	0	0
Bautista, Oklahoma City	1.000	11	1	3	0	0
Bearse, Indianapolis*	1.000	12	2	9	0	2
Bennett, Indianapolis	1.000	6	1	5	0	1
Bitker, Oklahoma City	1.000	23	1	5	0	1
Blankenship, Buffalo	.839	27	4	22	5	1
Bohanon, Oklahoma City*	.900	7	1	8	1	0
Boone, Oklahoma City*	1.000	24	13	32	0	1
Boskie, Iowa	.875	7	1	6	1	0
Bottenfield, Indianapolis	.977	29	8	34	1	4
Bronkey, Oklahoma City	1.000	7	1	1	0	0
Brown, Nashville	1.000	47	4	9	0	1
Brown, Denver*	.900	12	5	13	2	0
Buchanan, Omaha*	1.000	32	5	37	0	2
Bullinger, Iowa	1.000	8	4	7	0	2
Cangelosi, Denver*	1.000	2	0	1	0	0
Capra, Oklahoma City	1.000	1	1	0	0	0
Carman, Omaha*	1.000	14	0	4	0	0
Casillas, Nashville*	1.000	2	1	0	0	0
Castillo, Omaha	1.000	4	3	3	0	0
Centala, Omaha	.842	18	5	11	3	0
De. Clark, Omaha	1.000	25	10	17	0	2
Clark, Louisville	1.000	7	2	7	0	0
Clarke, Louisville*	.926	20	3	22	2	2
Clary, 33 Lou.-7 Buf.	.958	40	11	12	1	1
V. Cole, 6 Oma.-19 Buf.	1.000	25	2	4	0	0
Compres, Louisville	1.000	10	1	3	0	0
Cormier, Louisville*	.949	21	7	30	2	6
Corona, Louisville*	1.000	12	0	3	0	0
Crosby, Louisville	1.000	4	0	1	0	0
Davidson, Louisville	.957	51	10	12	1	0
Davins, Denver	1.000	25	1	4	0	0
Davis, Omaha*	.800	6	1	3	1	0
Dickson, Iowa*	.967	18	3	26	1	1
Dixon, Indianapolis	.974	53	13	25	1	2
Eldred, Denver	.960	29	6	18	1	0
Elvira, Denver*	.897	18	4	22	3	2

Player, Team	Pct.	G	PO	A	E	DP
Encarnacion, Omaha	1.000	50	9	9	0	0
Everson, Omaha	1.000	16	6	11	0	3
Fajardo, Buffalo	1.000	8	0	1	0	0
Farmer, Indianapolis	.933	20	12	16	2	2
Fassero, Indianapolis*	1.000	18	4	1	0	0
Filer, Iowa	1.000	18	13	23	0	3
Fireovid, Buffalo	.923	34	15	21	3	2
Fisher, Denver	.933	44	2	12	1	1
Fortugno, Denver*	1.000	26	1	3	0	1
Foster, Nashville	.867	41	4	9	2	0
Frey, Indianapolis*	1.000	30	0	5	0	0
V. Garcia, Nashville	1.000	15	1	2	0	1
Gardner, Indianapolis	.500	6	0	1	1	0
Gardner, Omaha	1.000	9	0	1	0	0
George, Denver	.667	43	5	5	5	0
Grater, Louisville	.960	58	8	16	1	1
Grewal, Indianapolis	1.000	2	0	2	0	0
Gross, Nashville	.955	14	7	14	1	1
Gubicza, Omaha	1.000	3	2	4	0	1
Guzman, Oklahoma City	1.000	3	0	2	0	0
Hall, 8 Nash. - 15 O.C.*	1.000	23	1	5	0	1
Hamilton, Buffalo	.923	18	5	7	1	1
C. Haney, Indianapolis*	1.000	2	3	0	0	0
Hayward, Oklahoma City*	.923	19	2	10	1	1
Henry, Denver	1.000	32	5	4	0	0
Hernandez, Denver	1.000	5	1	5	0	0
Higuera, Denver*	1.000	2	0	1	0	1
Hill, Nashville	1.000	37	2	7	0	0
Hinkle, Louisville	.938	6	6	9	1	1
Huismann, 13 Buf.-32 Oma.	.929	45	4	9	1	0
Hunter, Denver	.952	14	4	16	1	5
Ignasiak, Denver	.971	24	16	17	1	3
Imes, Nashville	1.000	25	6	11	0	1
Johnston, Omaha	.917	47	5	6	1	1
Kaiser, Denver*	1.000	8	2	6	0	1
Kiefer, Denver	.964	17	11	16	1	1
Knudson, Denver	1.000	13	2	5	0	0
Kraemer, Iowa*	1.000	20	4	24	0	3
LaPoint, 7 Den.-26 Iowa*	.950	33	3	16	1	0
Laskey, Oklahoma City	.889	31	3	5	1	2
Layana, Nashville	.909	26	5	15	2	1
LeMasters, Omaha	.952	21	6	14	1	1
Lewis, Indianapolis	1.000	5	2	8	0	1
Long, Indianapolis	1.000	10	1	4	0	0
Lopez, Nashville	.750	3	1	2	1	0
Loynd, Louisville	.750	9	1	5	2	0
Luecken, Iowa	1.000	5	0	3	0	0
Magnante, Omaha*	.929	10	5	8	1	3
Maldonado, Omaha	.882	41	4	11	2	2
Marchok, Indianapolis*	1.000	11	1	4	0	1
Mason, Buffalo	1.000	34	8	14	0	1
Masters, Indianapolis	.800	27	5	7	3	1
Mathews, Denver*	.800	13	1	7	2	0
Mathews, Oklahoma City	.920	18	6	17	2	1
S. May, Iowa	.947	57	6	12	1	1
Maysey, Iowa	.917	12	4	7	1	0
McGaffigan, 23 Oma.- 10 Den.	.889	33	5	11	2	2
Meeks, Indianapolis	.929	36	10	16	2	3
Menendez, Oklahoma City	.955	21	10	11	1	2
Mielke, Oklahoma City	1.000	10	0	1	0	0
Milchin, Louisville	1.000	18	9	11	0	1
P. Miller, Buffalo	.923	10	3	9	1	1
Minor, Buffalo	1.000	17	1	11	0	0
Minutelli, Nashville*	.882	13	2	13	2	0
Mitchell, Nashville	.980	35	17	31	1	1
Moeller, Omaha*	.882	14	2	13	2	0
Mount, Iowa	1.000	10	1	5	0	0
Moyer, Louisville*	1.000	20	16	19	0	0
Myers, Indianapolis*	1.000	2	1	1	0	0
Nabholz, Indianapolis*	.909	4	3	7	1	1
Neely, Buffalo	.952	42	5	15	1	2
Nipper, Louisville	1.000	5	2	6	0	1
Nolte, Oklahoma City*	.833	25	3	7	2	0
Nunez, Iowa	.824	28	8	20	6	1
Olivares, Louisville	.900	6	1	8	1	0
Osteen, Louisville	.938	29	3	12	1	1
Palacios, Buffalo	1.000	3	0	1	0	0
Pavlas, Iowa	1.000	61	7	24	0	0
Pavlik, Oklahoma City	.750	8	0	3	1	0
Perez, Louisville	1.000	37	2	8	0	0
Peters, Oklahoma City*	1.000	24	1	5	0	0
PETKOVSEK, Oklahoma City	1.000	25	15	40	0	1
Piatt, Indianapolis	1.000	44	3	3	0	0
Picota, Louisville	.969	28	12	19	1	2
Poole, Oklahoma City*	1.000	10	0	1	0	0
Postier, Oklahoma City	1.000	4	2	2	0	0
Powell, Nashville*	.889	24	3	13	2	1
Pugh, Nashville	.929	23	10	16	2	3
Puig, Denver*	1.000	11	1	2	0	0
Reed, Buffalo	.971	25	8	25	1	2
Renfroe, Iowa	.968	63	7	23	1	1
Richardson, Louisville*	1.000	13	1	2	0	0
Ridenour, Indianapolis	1.000	57	5	7	0	2
Risley, Nashville	.889	8	2	6	1	0
Rodriguez, Buffalo*	.857	48	5	7	2	2
Roesler, Buffalo	1.000	33	1	6	0	0
Rojas, Indianapolis	1.000	14	0	6	0	0
Rosario, Iowa*	1.000	33	2	8	0	0
Rosenthal, Oklahoma City	.917	32	5	6	1	1
Ryan, Indianapolis*	1.000	2	1	0	0	0
Sadler, Denver	1.000	2	0	1	0	0
Sampen, Indianapolis	.800	7	2	2	1	1
Sanford, Nashville	.778	5	3	4	2	0
Scanlan, Iowa	.750	4	1	2	1	0
Schiraldi, Oklahoma City	.917	18	3	8	1	0
Schmidt, 13 Ind. - 11 O.C.	1.000	24	5	4	0	1
Service, Indianapolis	.933	18	12	16	2	4
Sherrill, Louisville*	1.000	42	3	6	0	0
Slocumb, Iowa	.875	12	1	6	1	0
Smith, Oklahoma City*	.971	28	7	26	1	2
Smith, Omaha	.750	23	1	8	3	0
Sodders, Iowa*	1.000	16	1	7	0	0
Stewart, Indianapolis*	1.000	3	0	1	0	0
Strauss, Iowa	1.000	6	1	2	0	0
Sutcliffe, Iowa	1.000	3	1	0	0	0
Thompson, Oklahoma City	1.000	16	0	9	0	1
Tracy, Buffalo	.909	11	6	4	1	0
Turek, Iowa	1.000	14	2	8	0	1
Vasquez, Nashville	.938	8	4	11	1	0
Vierra, Nashville*	.947	62	2	16	1	0
Wagner, Omaha	1.000	17	5	16	0	1
Wainhouse, Indianapolis	1.000	14	3	4	0	0
Wakefield, Indianapolis	1.000	1	0	1	0	0
Walter, Louisville*	1.000	4	0	2	0	0
Wegman, Denver	1.000	1	1	4	0	1
Wells, Oklahoma City*	.600	12	1	2	2	0
Wilson, Iowa*	.941	25	5	11	1	0
Winston, Indianapolis*	.900	27	4	5	1	1
Witt, Oklahoma City	1.000	2	2	0	0	0
York, Buffalo	1.000	2	2	6	0	1

The following players did not have any fielding statistics at the positions indicated or appeared only as a designated hitter, pinch-hitter or pinch-runner: Alba, p; Beeler, 3b; Bierley, p; Blair, 2b, ss; Branson, of; Burgos, 3b; Campbell, p; Canan, p; B. Davis, p; C. Diaz, ph; DiPino, p; Fernandez, of; A. Gonzalez, c; Gossage, p; Hecht, 3b; K. Hill, p; Hinzo, of; Holmes, p; Jackson, p; Little, p; Mack, p; Miranda, p; Morman, p; Murphy, p; Nilsson, 3b; Pearson, p; Redfield, ss; Shines, p; Simonds, p; Walling, dh; Wilkins, of; Worrell, p.

LEAGUE CHAMPIONS

Year	Team	Pct.
1902 — Indianapolis		.683
1903 — St. Paul		.657
1904 — St. Paul		.646
1905 — Columbus		.658
1906 — Columbus		.615
1907 — Columbus		.584
1908 — Indianapolis		.601
1909 — Louisville		.554
1910 — Minneapolis		.637
1911 — Minneapolis		.600
1912 — Minneapolis		.636
1913 — Milwaukee		.599
1914 — Milwaukee		.590
1915 — Minneapolis		.597
1916 — Louisville		.605
1917 — Indianapolis		.588
1918 — Kansas City		.589
1919 — St. Paul		.610
1920 — St. Paul		.701
1921 — Louisville		.583
1922 — St. Paul		.641
1923 — Kansas City		.675
1924 — St. Paul		.578
1925 — Louisville		.635
1926 — Louisville		.629
1927 — Toledo		.601
1928 — Indianapolis		.593
1929 — Kansas City		.665
1930 — Louisville		.608
1931 — St. Paul		.623
1932 — Minneapolis		.595
1933 — Columbus*		.604
Minneapolis		.562
1934 — Minneapolis		.570
Columbus*		.556
1935 — Minneapolis		.591
1936 — Milwaukee†		.584
1937 — Columbus†		.584
1938 — St. Paul		.596
Kansas City (2nd)‡		.556
1939 — Kansas City		.695
Louisville (4th)‡		.490
1940 — Kansas City		.625
Louisville (4th)‡		.500
1941 — Columbus†		.621
1942 — Kansas City		.549
Columbus (3rd)‡		.532
1943 — Milwaukee		.596
Columbus (3rd)‡		.532
1944 — Milwaukee		.667
Louisville (3rd)‡		.574
1945 — Milwaukee		.604
Louisville (3rd)‡		.545
1946 — Louisville†		.601
1947 — Kansas City		.608
Milwaukee (3rd)†		.513
1948 — Indianapolis		.649
St. Paul (3rd)‡		.558
1949 — St. Paul		.608
Indianapolis (2nd)‡		.604

Year	Team	Pct.
1950—	Minneapolis	.584
	Columbus (3rd)‡	.549
1951—	Milwaukee†	.623
1952—	Milwaukee	.656
	Kansas City (2nd)‡	.578
1953—	Toledo	.584
	Kansas City (2nd)‡	.571
1954—	Indianapolis	.625
	Loiusville (2nd)‡	.556
1955—	Minneapolis†	.597
1956—	Indianapolis†	.597
1957—	Wichita	.604
	Denver (2nd)†	.584
1958—	Charleston	.589
	Minneapolis (3rd)‡	.536
1959—	Louisville§	.599
	Omaha§	.516
	Minneapolis (2nd)‡	.586
1960—	Denver	.571
	Louisville (2nd)‡	.556
1961—	Indianapolis	.573
	Louisville (2nd)‡	.533
1962—	Indianapolis	.605
	Louisville (4th)‡	.486

Year	Team	Pct.
1963-1968—Did not operate.		
1969—	Omaha	.607
1970—	Omaha*	.529
	Denver	.504
1971—	Indianapolis	.604
	Denver*	.521
1972—	Wichita	.621
	Evansville*	.593
1973—	Iowa	.610
	Tulsa*	.504
1974—	Indianapolis	.578
	Tulsa*	.567
1975—	Evansville*	.566
	Denver	.596
1976—	Denver*	.632
	Omaha	.574
1977—	Omaha	.563
	Denver*	.522
1978—	Indianapolis	.578
	Omaha*	.489
1979—	Evansville*	.574
	Oklahoma City	.533
1980—	Denver	.676
	Springfield*	.551

Year	Team	Pct.
1981—	Omaha	.581
	Denver*	.559
1982—	Indianapolis*	.551
	Omaha	.518
1983—	Louisville	.578
	Denver‡	.545
1984—	Denver	.513
	Louisville‡	.510
1985—	Oklahoma City	.556
	Louisville*	.521
1986—	Indianapolis*	.563
	Denver	.535
1987—	Denver	.564
	Indianapolis‡	.536
1988—	Indianapolis*	.627
	Omaha	.570
1989—	Indianapolis*	.596
	Omaha	.507
1990—	Omaha*	.589
	Nashville	.585
1991—	Buffalo	.566
	Denver*	.549

*Won playoff (East vs. West). †Won championship and four-team playoff. ‡Won four-team playoff. §Respective Eastern and Western division winners.

CLASS AAA

AMERICAN ASSOCIATION

AMERICAN ASSOCIATION

INTERNATIONAL LEAGUE

FINAL STANDINGS

EASTERN DIVISION

Team	W	L	T	Pct.	GB
Pawtucket (Red Sox)	79	64	0	.552	....
Rochester (Orioles)	76	68	0	.528	3½
Syracuse (Blue Jays)	73	71	0	.507	6½
Scranton-Wilkes Barre (Phillies)	65	78	0	.455	14

WESTERN DIVISION

Team	W	L	T	Pct.	GB
Columbus (Yankees)	85	59	0	.590	....
Tidewater (Mets)	77	65	0	.542	7
Toledo (Tigers)	74	70	0	.514	11
Richmond (Braves)	65	79	0	.451	20

COMPOSITE

Team	Col.	Paw.	Tid.	Roc.	Tol.	Syr.	SWB	Rich.	W	L	T	Pct.	GB
Columbus (Yankees)	....	6	7	8	11	8	9	11	85	59	0	.590	....
Pawtucket (Red Sox)	8	....	9	11	7	10	13	7	79	64	0	.552	5½
Tidewater (Mets)	9	5	....	6	8	9	7	11	77	65	0	.542	7
Rochester (Orioles)	6	11	8	....	5	13	10	8	76	68	0	.528	9
Toledo (Tigers)	5	7	8	9	....	7	10	8	74	70	0	.514	11
Syracuse (Blue Jays)	6	12	5	11	7	....	13	9	73	71	0	.507	12
Scranton-Wilkes Barre (Phillies)	5	10	7	12	4	9	....	8	65	78	0	.455	19½
Richmond (Braves)	5	7	5	6	8	5	6	....	65	79	0	.451	20

Tidewater club represented Norfolk and Portsmouth, Va.

Major league affiliations in parentheses.

Playoffs—Columbus defeated Pawtucket, three games to none, to win league championship. Denver (American Association) defeated Columbus, four games to one, to win Triple-A Alliance Championship.

Regular-season attendance—Columbus, 570,605; Pawtucket, 349,338; Richmond, 434,994; Rochester, 345,167; Scranton-Wilkes Barre, 535,725; Syracuse, 307,993; Tidewater, 196,998; Toledo, 217,662. Total—2,958,482. Playoffs (3 games)—13,672. Alliance Playoffs (5 games)—38,865. Class AAA All-Star Game at Louisville—20,725.

Managers—Columbus, Rick Down; Pawtucket, Butch Hobson; Richmond, Phil Niekro; Rochester, Greg Biagini; Scranton-Wilkes Barre, Bill Dancy; Syracuse, Bob Bailor; Tidewater, Steve Swisher; Toledo, Joe Sparks.

All-Star team—1B—Domingo Martinez, Syracuse; 2B—Jeff Gardner, Tidewater; 3B—Scott Cooper, Pawtucket; SS—Eddie Zosky, Syracuse; OF—Derek Bell, Syracuse; Phil Plantier, Pawtucket; Luis Mercedes, Rochester; C—Todd Hundley, Tidewater; DH—Mitch Lyden, Toledo; SP—Mike Mussina, Rochester; RP—Daryl Irvine, Pawtucket; Most Valuable Player—Derek Bell, Syracuse; Most Valuable Pitcher—Mike Mussina, Rochester; Rookie of the Year—Luis Mercedes, Rochester; Manager of the Year—Butch Hobson, Pawtucket.

BATTING

TEAM

Team	Avg.	G	AB	R	OR	H	TB	2B	3B	HR	RBI	SH	SF	HP	BB	Int. BB	SO	SB	CS	LOB
Syracuse	.275	144	4974	703	709	1367	2002	225	43	108	644	54	42	50	545	35	946	102	72	1113
Columbus	.274	144	4722	749	624	1295	1937	239	59	95	685	36	61	47	621	25	761	178	99	984
Rochester	.273	144	4767	710	658	1302	1886	209	39	99	647	45	37	41	617	21	845	123	78	1073
Scranton W.B.	.269	144	4799	666	700	1290	1943	238	59	99	618	38	49	37	442	17	797	101	63	981
Toledo	.266	144	4764	668	646	1265	1821	236	37	82	604	58	42	44	479	27	777	138	72	948
Richmond	.258	144	4862	604	628	1252	1780	222	33	80	555	75	40	47	477	30	882	72	60	1046
Pawtucket	.257	143	4711	699	677	1213	1981	251	29	153	665	71	51	42	648	38	811	62	42	1085
Tidewater	.256	142	4687	613	600	1201	1690	219	33	68	543	61	51	58	562	37	861	73	49	1054

INDIVIDUAL

(Leading qualifiers for batting championship—389 or more plate appearances)

*Bats lefthanded. †Switch-hitter.

Player, Team	Avg.	G	AB	R	H	TB	2B	3B	HR	RBI	SH	SF	HP	BB	Int. BB	SO	SB	CS
Bell, Derek, Syracuse	.346	119	457	89	158	243	22	12	13	93	0	5	9	57	7	69	27	13
Mercedes, Luis, Rochester	.334	102	374	68	125	155	14	5	2	36	6	4	5	65	0	63	23	13
Schu, Rick, Scranton W.B.	.321	106	355	69	114	196	30	5	14	57	0	4	4	50	2	38	7	1
Martinez, Domingo, Syracuse	.313	126	467	61	146	217	16	2	17	83	5	6	6	41	0	107	6	4
Ramos, John, Columbus	.308	104	377	52	116	170	18	3	10	63	1	9	3	56	3	54	1	5
Rosario, Victor, 60 Rich.-56 Tol.	.300	116	423	59	127	174	20	12	1	48	4	3	1	21	4	87	12	6
Batiste, Kim, Scranton W.B.	.292	122	462	54	135	175	25	6	1	41	10	4	4	11	0	72	18	13
Gardner, Jeff, Tidewater*	.292	136	504	73	147	181	23	4	1	56	7	5	3	84	4	48	6	5
Legg, Greg, Scranton W.B.	.290	111	352	58	102	134	15	4	3	41	6	5	3	44	2	33	3	0
Shields, Tommy, Rochester	.289	116	412	69	119	161	18	3	6	52	5	3	11	32	1	73	16	8

Departmental leaders: G—Rossy, 139; AB—Paredes, 514; R—D. Bell, 89; H—D. Bell, 158; TB—D. Bell, 243; 2B—Schu, 30; 3B—D. Bell, Rosario, 12; HR—Lancellotti, 21; RBI—D. Bell, 93; SH—Paredes, 16; SF—Ramos, 9; HP—Hansen, 20; BB—Gardner, 84; IBB—Cooper, 11; SO—Quinlan, 163; SB—Walewander, 54; CS—Walewander, 19.

(All players—listed alphabetically)

Player, Team	Avg.	G	AB	R	H	TB	2B	3B	HR	RBI	SH	SF	HP	BB	Int. BB	SO	SB	CS
Agostinelli, Sal, Scranton W.B.	.167	14	18	0	3	3	0	0	0	0	0	0	0	1	0	4	0	0
Aguayo, Luis, Pawtucket	.284	65	204	31	58	101	14	1	9	37	5	0	3	22	1	35	0	0
Akerfelds, Darrel, Scranton W.B.	.143	11	7	1	1	1	0	0	0	3	0	0	0	1	0	3	0	0
Alexander, Gary, Scranton W.B.	.239	79	209	31	50	110	9	0	17	48	1	3	1	17	1	50	1	1
Allaire, Karl, Toledo*	.262	129	385	57	101	139	21	4	3	34	13	2	1	64	2	68	4	3
Alva, John, Richmond	.287	44	129	16	37	49	3	0	3	17	2	0	0	6	0	26	2	0
Anderson, Brady, Rochester*	.385	7	26	5	10	13	3	0	0	2	0	0	0	7	0	4	4	1
Ashby, Andy, Scranton W.B.	.211	26	19	2	4	6	2	0	0	1	1	0	0	0	0	4	0	0
Ayrault, Bob, Scranton W.B.	.000	68	4	0	0	0	0	0	0	0	0	0	0	0	0	2	0	0
Baez, Kevin, Tidewater	.171	65	210	18	36	44	8	0	0	13	5	4	4	12	1	32	0	1
Barnes, Skeeter, Toledo	.330	62	233	48	77	118	14	1	9	40	2	2	4	23	1	26	27	7
Barrett, Tom, Pawtucket†	.269	102	331	43	89	106	15	1	0	27	5	8	1	54	3	39	8	10

Player, Team	Avg.	G	AB	R	H	TB	2B	3B	HR	RBI	SH	SF	HP	BB	Int. BB	SO	SB	CS
Batiste, Kim, Scranton W.B.	.292	122	462	54	135	175	25	6	1	41	10	4	4	11	0	72	18	13
Beatty, Blaine, Tidewater*	.250	29	20	4	5	5	0	0	0	2	0	1	0	2	0	1	0	0
Bell, Derek, Syracuse	.346	119	457	89	158	243	22	12	13	93	0	5	9	57	7	69	27	13
Bell, Mike, Richmond*	.249	91	341	37	85	116	12	2	5	29	2	2	2	26	2	68	2	3
Benton, Butch, Toledo	.133	9	30	1	4	4	0	0	0	0	0	0	1	0	0	9	0	0
Beyeler, Arnie, Toledo	.174	29	69	14	12	14	2	0	0	2	4	0	3	4	0	8	0	2
Bogar, Tim, Tidewater	.257	65	218	23	56	70	11	0	1	23	4	2	1	20	2	35	1	0
Brantley, Cliff, Scranton W.B.	.000	8	2	0	0	0	0	0	0	0	0	0	0	0	0	0	0	0
Brogna, Rico, Toledo*	.220	41	132	13	29	43	6	1	2	13	1	0	1	4	2	26	2	0
Bross, Terry, Tidewater	1.000	27	1	0	1	2	1	0	0	1	0	0	0	0	0	0	0	0
Brumley, Mike, Pawtucket†	.269	32	108	25	29	47	2	2	4	16	1	0	1	24	1	21	8	4
Burgos, John, Scranton W.B.*	.200	24	5	0	1	1	0	0	0	0	0	0	0	0	0	0	0	1
Cabrera, Francisco, Richmond	.261	32	119	22	31	61	7	1	7	24	0	1	3	10	0	21	0	1
Campusano, Sil, Scranton W.B.	.262	94	305	44	80	118	12	1	8	47	0	3	2	23	0	63	9	6
Carr, Chuck, Tidewater†	.195	64	246	34	48	59	6	1	1	11	1	0	1	18	0	37	27	8
Carreno, Amalio, Scranton W.B.	.000	33	3	0	0	0	0	0	0	0	0	0	0	0	0	1	0	0
Casarotti, Rich, Richmond†	.200	29	85	10	17	21	2	1	0	8	1	1	0	3	1	18	2	1
Castilla, Vinny, Richmond	.225	67	240	25	54	90	7	4	7	36	0	5	3	14	2	32	1	1
Castillo, Braulio, Scranton W.B.	.350	16	60	14	21	32	9	1	0	15	0	1	0	6	0	7	2	1
Castillo, Tony, Richmond*	.143	24	14	0	2	2	0	0	0	0	2	0	0	1	0	5	0	0
Chamberlain, Wes, Scranton W.B.	.257	39	144	12	37	54	7	2	2	20	0	4	0	8	1	13	7	4
Chance, Tony, Rochester	.251	111	355	61	89	151	14	3	14	55	2	0	2	41	0	98	4	4
Cinnella, Doug, Tidewater	.250	12	4	1	1	1	0	0	0	0	0	0	0	0	0	3	0	0
Clark, Phil, Toledo	.254	110	362	47	92	126	14	4	4	45	3	2	5	21	0	49	6	6
Combs, Pat, Scranton W.B.*	.333	6	6	2	2	2	0	0	0	0	2	0	0	0	0	0	0	0
Contreras, Joaquin, Rochester†	.000	3	6	0	0	0	0	0	0	0	0	0	0	0	2	0	3	0	1
Cooper, Scott, Pawtucket*	.277	137	483	55	134	204	21	2	15	72	4	6	7	50	11	58	3	5
Cox, Danny, Scranton W.B.	.000	1	1	0	0	0	0	0	0	0	1	0	0	0	0	0	0	0
Crabbe, Bruce, Richmond	.264	65	178	21	47	57	10	0	0	20	2	1	1	35	0	27	1	5
Cruz, Ivan, Toledo*	.138	8	29	2	4	7	0	0	1	4	0	0	1	2	0	12	0	0
Dalton, Mike, Toledo	.000	39	0	0	0	0	0	0	0	0	1	0	0	0	0	0	0	0
Daulton, Darren, Scranton W.B.*	.222	2	9	1	2	5	0	0	1	1	0	0	0	0	0	0	0	0
Davis, John, Richmond	.000	5	1	0	0	0	0	0	0	0	0	0	0	0	0	0	0	0
DeCillis, Dean, Toledo	.308	39	143	20	44	57	7	0	2	18	3	1	1	17	3	11	3	2
DeKneef, Michael, Pawtucket	.188	6	16	3	3	3	0	0	0	0	0	0	0	2	0	0	0	0
Delgado, Carlos, Syracuse*	.000	1	3	0	0	0	0	0	0	0	0	0	0	0	0	2	0	0
de los Santos, Luis, Toledo	.284	41	141	12	40	54	8	0	2	22	0	2	1	16	0	19	0	0
Dewey, Mark, Tidewater	.000	48	1	0	0	0	0	0	0	0	1	0	0	0	0	0	0	0
Dickerson, Bobby, Rochester	.333	2	6	0	2	3	1	0	0	0	0	0	0	0	0	1	0	0
Distefano, Benny, Rochester*	.267	124	427	52	114	195	23	2	18	83	2	3	4	41	7	52	5	2
Donnels, Chris, Tidewater*	.303	84	287	45	87	134	19	2	8	56	0	3	1	62	3	56	1	4
Dozier, D.J., Tidewater	.269	43	171	19	46	66	7	5	1	22	2	2	4	13	0	41	8	6
Ducey, Rob, Syracuse*	.293	72	266	53	78	118	10	3	8	40	4	2	0	51	4	58	5	7
Dunbar, Tommy, Rochester*	.300	20	60	13	18	30	3	0	3	8	0	0	0	12	1	8	0	1
Eberle, Mike, Rochester	.178	42	90	8	16	18	2	0	0	5	1	0	1	9	0	24	0	1
Fernandez, Sid, Tidewater*	.500	3	2	0	1	1	0	0	0	0	0	0	0	0	0	0	0	0
Fields, Bruce, 37 Rich.-42 Syr.*	.250	79	260	28	65	81	10	0	2	21	1	1	2	26	3	36	1	1
Flaherty, John, Pawtucket	.186	45	156	18	29	45	7	0	3	13	4	0	0	15	0	14	0	1
Fletcher, Darrin, Scranton W.B.*	.284	90	306	39	87	126	13	1	8	50	1	6	3	23	4	29	1	3
Ford, Curt, Toledo*	.268	102	366	52	98	139	24	4	3	38	7	5	1	42	0	38	8	10
Garces, Jesus, Scranton W.B.	.125	3	8	0	1	1	0	0	0	0	1	0	0	1	0	6	0	0
Gardner, Jeff, Tidewater*	.292	136	504	73	147	181	23	4	1	56	7	5	3	84	4	48	6	5
Gomez, Leo, Rochester	.257	28	101	13	26	50	6	0	6	19	0	2	2	16	0	18	0	0
Gomez, Pat, Richmond*	.111	16	9	1	1	1	0	0	0	0	0	0	1	0	0	2	0	0
Gonzalez, Javier, Tidewater	.333	1	3	0	1	1	0	0	0	0	0	0	0	0	0	0	0	0
Gregg, Tommy, Richmond*	.462	3	13	3	6	9	0	0	1	4	0	0	0	1	0	2	1	1
Grimsley, Jason, Scranton W.B.	1.000	10	2	0	2	2	0	0	0	0	0	0	0	0	0	0	0	0
Grotewold, Jeff, Scranton W.B.*	.257	87	276	33	71	109	13	5	5	38	2	0	1	25	1	61	0	2
Gutierrez, Ricky, Rochester	.306	49	157	23	48	59	5	3	0	15	3	1	0	24	1	27	4	1
Hansen, Terrel, Tidewater	.272	107	368	54	100	160	20	2	12	62	0	3	20	40	2	82	0	0
Hare, Shawn, Toledo*	.310	80	252	44	78	127	18	2	9	42	1	5	2	30	1	53	1	2
Hayes, Von, Scranton W.B.*	.250	2	8	2	2	3	1	0	0	0	0	0	0	0	0	3	0	0
Hillman, Eric, Tidewater*	.059	27	17	0	1	1	0	0	0	0	0	4	0	0	0	4	0	0
Hollins, Dave, Scranton W.B.†	.266	72	229	37	61	108	11	6	8	35	0	2	4	43	3	43	4	1
Housie, Wayne, Pawtucket†	.329	21	79	14	26	41	9	0	2	8	0	0	1	6	0	20	2	2
Howell, Ken, Scranton W.B.	.000	6	4	0	0	0	0	0	0	0	0	0	0	0	0	0	0	0
Hughes, Keith, Columbus*	.271	130	424	64	115	173	18	8	8	66	0	8	3	60	2	74	6	5
Humphreys, Mike, Columbus	.283	117	413	71	117	195	23	5	9	53	1	6	3	63	2	62	34	9
Hundley, Todd, Tidewater†	.273	125	454	62	124	198	24	4	14	66	4	8	2	51	2	95	1	2
Hunter, Brian, Richmond	.260	48	181	28	47	84	7	0	10	30	2	3	1	11	1	24	3	2
Jeltz, Steve, 64 Roch.-7 Syr.†	.188	71	224	26	42	57	6	3	1	26	1	0	3	41	1	34	5	5
Jeter, Shawn, Syracuse*	.264	70	242	36	64	90	15	1	3	26	6	0	0	15	5	55	5	5
Jimenez, Al, Syracuse	.208	114	331	36	69	92	9	1	4	32	4	1	3	41	4	60	0	2
Jones, Ron, Scranton W.B.*	.253	48	150	17	38	57	7	0	4	26	0	1	1	19	5	20	3	1
Kelly, Pat, Columbus	.336	31	116	27	39	61	9	2	3	19	1	0	1	16		8	2	
Kilgus, Paul, Rochester*	.000	9	3	0	0	0	0	0	0	0	0	1	0	0	0	0	0	0
Kingwood, Tyrone, Rochester	.312	37	138	20	43	58	8	2	1	18	1	3	1	9	0	22	12	3
Kline, Doug, Tidewater	.000	2	1	0	0	0	0	0	0	0	0	0	0	0	0	0	0	0
Knabenshue, Chris, Scranton W.B.*	.200	17	35	3	7	9	2	0	0	8	1	0	0	10	1	12	1	0
Knoblauch, Jay, Columbus	.309	31	94	16	29	44	4	3	1	19	0	2	2	7	0	18	2	2
Knorr, Randy, Syracuse	.260	91	342	29	89	124	20	0	5	44	0	4	3	23	3	58	1	0
Kramer, Randy, Richmond	.000	11	8	0	0	0	0	0	0	0	0	0	1	0	0	0	0	0
Kutcher, Randy, Toledo	.232	70	237	26	55	77	11	1	3	28	2	3	1	31	2	37	0	4
Lancellotti, Rick, Pawtucket*	.209	102	330	43	69	149	15	1	21	64	4	6	2	44	2	75	1	0
Legg, Greg, Scranton W.B.	.290	111	352	58	102	134	15	4	3	41	6	5	3	44	2	33	3	0
Leiper, Tim, Tidewater*	.252	93	282	33	71	90	11	1	2	30	4	4	1	35	5	32	0	3
Leyritz, Jim, Columbus	.267	79	270	50	72	131	24	1	11	48	1	3	8	38	1	50	1	2
Lindeman, Jim, Scranton W.B.	.275	11	40	7	11	20	1	1	2	7	0	0	0	5	0	6	0	0
Livingstone, Scott, Toledo*	.302	92	331	48	100	128	13	3	3	62	3	6	2	40	3	52	2	1
Lofton, Rod, Rochester	.000	3	3	0	0	0	0	0	0	0	1	0	0	0	0	0	0	0
Loggins, Mike, Richmond†	.165	25	91	7	15	15	0	0	0	6	0	0	1	8	1	11	3	0
Longmire, Tony, Scranton W.B.*	.261	36	111	11	29	36	3	2	0	9	1	0	0	8	1	20	4	4
Lovullo, Torey, Columbus†	.271	106	395	74	107	171	24	5	10	75	2	6	0	59	4	54	4	4
Lusader, Scott, Columbus*	.282	76	284	48	80	126	13	6	7	32	1	1	1	27	4	55	7	0
Lyden, Mitch, Toledo	.224	101	340	34	76	145	11	2	18	55	0	7	0	15	4	108	0	0

Player, Team	Avg.	G	AB	R	H	TB	2B	3B	HR	RBI	SH	SF	HP	BB	Int. BB	SO	SB	CS
Maas, Jason, Columbus*	.352	30	71	16	25	36	6	1	1	6	0	0	2	12	0	15	6	2
Magrann, Tom, Pawtucket	.146	13	41	5	6	10	1	0	1	2	2	1	0	4	0	3	0	0
Maksudian, Mike, Syracuse*	.330	31	97	13	32	47	6	3	1	13	1	0	0	10	0	17	0	0
Malone, Chuck, Scranton W.B.	.000	5	1	0	0	0	0	0	0	0	0	0	0	0	0	0	0	0
Mangham, Eric, Toledo	.241	124	378	60	91	117	12	1	4	35	1	1	3	53	1	59	29	10
Mann, Kelly, Richmond	.184	64	196	24	36	52	7	0	3	14	3	0	6	23	1	41	1	2
Marak, Paul, Richmond	.077	29	13	0	1	1	0	0	0	0	4	0	0	2	0	7	0	0
Martin, Al, Richmond*	.278	44	151	20	42	70	11	1	5	18	0	0	1	7	0	33	11	2
Martinez, Chito, Rochester*	.322	60	211	42	68	138	8	1	20	50	0	2	0	26	3	69	2	2
Martinez, Domingo, Syracuse	.313	126	467	61	146	217	16	2	17	83	5	6	6	41	0	107	6	4
Mauser, Tim, Scranton W.B.	.200	27	15	2	3	5	2	0	0	1	0	0	0	3	0	6	0	0
May, Lee, Tidewater†	.257	29	113	16	29	45	6	5	0	8	2	1	2	9	1	42	5	3
McCarthy, Tom, Richmond	.000	21	3	0	0	0	0	0	0	0	0	0	0	0	0	2	0	0
McDaniel, Terry, Tidewater†	.248	118	399	63	99	161	23	6	9	42	2	0	5	50	4	117	18	4
McDougal, Julius, Syracuse*	.253	59	182	26	46	64	9	3	1	11	2	2	1	18	0	42	1	1
McDowell, Oddibe, Rochester*	.231	78	264	31	61	90	13	2	4	22	7	5	1	35	1	45	12	9
McKnight, Jeff, Rochester†	.383	22	81	19	31	45	7	2	1	18	0	1	0	14	0	10	1	2
McLemore, Mark, Rochester†	.281	57	228	32	64	86	11	4	1	28	2	2	0	27	0	29	12	5
Meadows, Louie, Scranton W.B.*	.210	73	186	23	39	66	9	3	4	16	1	1	3	27	2	40	2	1
Meadows, Scott, Rochester	.329	74	249	45	82	115	16	1	5	42	5	0	5	41	1	38	3	2
Mercado, Orlando, Tidewater	.270	55	159	13	43	67	12	0	4	26	3	6	0	11	3	28	0	1
Mercedes, Luis, Rochester	.334	102	374	68	125	155	14	5	2	36	6	4	5	65	0	63	23	13
Milstien, Dave, Pawtucket	.203	19	59	2	12	12	0	0	0	4	0	0	3	3	0	8	0	0
Mitchell, Keith, Richmond	.326	25	95	16	31	45	6	1	2	17	2	3	1	9	0	13	0	2
Montalvo, Rob, Syracuse	.000	1	3	0	0	0	0	0	0	0	0	0	0	0	0	0	0	0
Moore, Brad, Tidewater	.167	50	6	0	1	1	0	0	0	0	0	0	1	0	0	0	0	0
Morandini, Mickey, Scranton W.B.*	.261	12	46	7	12	19	4	0	1	9	0	1	0	5	0	6	2	0
Nelson, Jerome, Richmond†	.288	63	215	34	62	81	7	6	0	18	0	1	1	36	1	46	10	5
Ontiveros, Steve, Scranton W.B.	.500	7	2	0	1	1	0	0	0	0	0	0	0	1	0	0	0	0
Pankovits, Jim, Pawtucket	.265	65	215	29	57	86	14	0	5	30	3	4	2	15	1	39	1	2
Paredes, Johnny, Toledo	.284	135	514	82	146	186	25	6	1	53	16	2	11	47	3	51	36	16
Parrett, Jeff, Richmond	.100	19	10	0	1	1	0	0	0	0	0	0	0	0	0	2	0	0
Pederson, Stu, Syracuse*	.263	108	373	49	98	146	20	2	8	54	9	6	5	66	6	68	3	5
Pedrique, Al, Tidewater	.269	79	182	24	49	55	6	0	0	12	7	1	3	23	2	19	2	0
Peguero, Julio, Scranton W.B.†	.273	133	506	71	138	182	20	9	2	39	5	2	1	40	3	69	21	15
Pegues, Steve, Toledo	.225	68	222	21	50	81	13	3	4	23	1	0	3	3	0	31	8	5
Perez, Robert, Syracuse	.200	4	20	2	4	5	1	0	0	1	0	0	0	0	0	2	0	0
Perez, Yorkis, Richmond*	.250	36	8	0	2	2	0	0	0	0	1	0	0	0	0	1	0	0
Perry, Pat, Scranton W.B.*	.000	36	0	0	0	0	0	0	0	0	1	0	0	0	0	0	0	0
Peterek, Jeff, Richmond	.000	6	1	0	0	0	0	0	0	0	0	0	0	0	0	0	0	0
Pevey, Marty, Syracuse*	.280	55	193	24	54	75	8	2	3	23	1	0	0	20	5	41	1	2
Pina, Mickey, Pawtucket	.208	105	298	39	62	99	11	1	8	33	2	3	1	28	0	94	2	1
Plantier, Phil, Pawtucket*	.305	84	298	69	91	166	19	4	16	61	0	0	5	65	2	64	6	1
Plummer, Dale, Tidewater	.222	46	9	2	2	2	0	0	0	0	1	0	0	0	0	6	0	0
Polley, Dale, Richmond	.000	50	6	0	0	0	0	0	0	0	0	0	0	0	0	0	0	0
Pratt, Todd, Pawtucket	.292	68	219	27	64	113	16	0	11	41	5	0	3	23	2	42	0	3
Quinlan, Tom, Syracuse	.240	132	466	56	112	178	24	6	10	49	3	2	5	72	3	163	9	4
Ramos, John, Columbus	.308	104	377	52	116	170	18	3	10	63	1	9	3	56	3	54	1	5
Rayford, Floyd, Scranton W.B.	.357	5	14	5	5	7	2	0	0	5	0	1	0	1	0	3	0	0
Reynoso, Armando, Richmond	.167	22	24	2	4	8	1	0	1	3	1	1	0	1	0	5	0	0
Richards, Rusty, Richmond*	.000	7	1	0	0	0	0	0	0	0	0	0	0	0	0	1	0	0
Rodriguez, Boi, Richmond*	.281	105	392	50	110	161	25	1	8	49	2	5	2	34	5	100	1	3
Rodriguez, Carlos, Columbus†	.255	73	212	32	54	69	9	3	0	21	5	5	1	42	0	13	1	4
Rosario, Victor, 60 Rich.-56 Tol.	.300	116	423	59	127	174	20	12	1	48	4	3	1	21	4	87	12	6
Roseboro, Jaime, Tidewater	.294	89	279	34	82	100	12	0	2	29	2	4	5	28	2	36	0	4
Ross, Mark, Richmond	.000	39	1	0	0	0	0	0	0	0	0	0	2	0	0	0	0	0
Rossy, Rico, Richmond	.257	139	482	58	124	157	25	1	2	48	13	3	5	67	1	44	4	8
Rowland, Rich, Toledo	.272	109	383	56	104	169	26	0	13	68	0	1	3	60	3	77	4	2
Ruffin, Bruce, Scranton W.B.†	.077	13	13	1	1	1	0	0	0	0	1	0	0	0	0	6	0	0
St. Claire, Randy, Richmond	.000	29	8	0	0	0	0	0	0	0	0	0	0	0	0	7	0	0
Sanders, Deion, Richmond*	.262	29	130	20	34	61	6	3	5	16	0	1	0	10	0	28	12	4
Sauveur, Rich, Tidewater*	.000	43	6	0	0	0	0	0	0	0	0	0	0	0	0	3	0	0
Sax, Dave, Columbus	.285	99	270	45	77	124	19	2	8	54	1	3	0	51	2	39	1	0
Scarsone, Steve, Scranton W.B.	.274	111	405	52	111	161	20	6	6	38	2	7	7	19	1	81	10	5
Schatzeder, Dan, Tidewater*	.250	9	4	0	1	1	0	0	0	0	0	0	0	0	0	0	0	0
Schourek, Pete, Tidewater*	.000	4	4	0	0	0	0	0	0	0	0	0	1	0	0	1	0	0
Schu, Rick, Scranton W.B.	.321	106	355	69	114	196	30	5	14	57	0	4	4	50	2	38	7	1
Schunk, Jerry, Syracuse	.248	92	327	34	81	105	9	0	5	29	10	0	4	8	0	26	0	3
Scott, Shawn, Syracuse†	.231	12	39	4	9	11	0	1	0	3	0	1	0	5	0	10	0	2
Segui, David, Rochester†	.271	28	96	9	26	31	2	0	1	10	0	1	1	15	1	6	1	1
Shamburg, Ken, Rochester	.150	13	40	4	6	7	1	0	0	3	0	0	0	5	1	10	0	0
Sheridan, Pat, Columbus*	.271	21	70	15	19	32	3	2	2	12	0	0	0	10	0	26	2	0
Shields, Tommy, Rochester	.289	116	412	69	119	161	18	3	6	52	5	3	11	32	1	73	16	8
Skeels, Andy, Columbus*	.140	14	43	0	6	9	1	1	0	5	0	0	0	2	0	10	0	1
Smith, Pete, Richmond	.286	10	7	1	2	2	0	0	0	1	0	1	0	0	1	0	0	0
Snider, Van, Columbus*	.267	66	247	28	66	112	17	1	9	44	1	0	4	21	2	54	4	3
Snyder, Cory, Syracuse	.269	17	67	11	18	39	3	0	6	17	0	2	1	4	0	16	0	0
Soff, Ray, Tidewater	.074	28	27	1	2	2	0	0	0	1	0	0	0	1	0	4	0	0
Sparks, Don, Columbus	.257	52	152	11	39	49	6	2	0	25	3	2	4	12	0	27	0	0
Sprague, Ed, Syracuse	.364	23	88	24	32	55	8	0	5	25	0	2	2	10	0	21	2	0
Stankiewicz, Andy, Columbus	.272	125	372	47	101	124	12	4	1	41	8	5	8	29	0	46	29	16
Stone, Jeff, Pawtucket*	.281	104	352	63	99	155	14	9	8	44	2	1	5	31	0	65	18	1
Suero, William, Syracuse	.198	98	393	49	78	101	18	1	1	28	4	3	7	38	0	51	17	13
Szekely, Joe, Richmond*	.260	83	227	24	59	80	10	1	3	30	3	2	2	20	2	45	1	2
Tackett, Jeff, Rochester	.236	126	433	64	102	142	18	2	6	50	4	3	2	54	0	59	3	3
Tomberlin, Andy, Richmond*	.234	93	329	47	77	100	13	2	2	24	9	1	8	41	3	85	10	6
Torve, Kelvin, Richmond*	.274	103	336	57	92	143	20	2	9	49	1	6	1	62	2	58	4	4
Tremblay, Gary, Scranton W.B.	.245	53	147	18	36	52	7	0	3	16	1	2	0	15	0	25	1	0
Turner, Matt, Richmond	.000	23	2	0	0	0	0	0	0	0	1	0	0	0	0	0	0	0
Turner, Shane, Rochester*	.282	110	404	49	114	134	13	2	1	57	1	2	3	47	1	75	6	7
Twardoski, Mike, Pawtucket*	.253	110	367	52	93	129	20	2	4	26	14	1	3	62	4	64	0	2
Valentin, John, Pawtucket	.264	100	329	52	87	144	22	4	9	49	6	4	0	60	2	42	0	1
Valera, Julio, Tidewater	.125	26	24	0	3	3	0	0	0	1	3	0	1	0	0	5	0	0
Vaughn, Mo, Pawtucket*	.274	69	234	35	64	116	10	0	14	50	0	4	3	60	7	44	2	1
Veres, Randy, Richmond	.000	9	3	0	0	0	0	0	0	0	0	0	1	0	0	2	0	0

Player, Team	Avg.	G	AB	R	H	TB	2B	3B	HR	RBI	SH	SF	HP	BB	Int. BB	SO	SB	CS
Voigt, Jack, Rochester	.270	83	267	46	72	110	12	4	6	35	5	2	1	40	2	53	9	2
Wade, Scott, Scranton W.B.	.262	112	309	48	81	136	14	7	9	43	1	2	3	32	0	70	5	5
Walewander, Jim, Columbus†	.225	126	408	81	92	118	11	3	3	38	7	3	5	69	1	66	54	19
Waller, Casey, Scranton W.B.†	.071	4	14	1	1	1	0	0	0	0	0	0	0	0	0	2	0	0
Ward, Turner, Syracuse†	.330	59	218	40	72	110	11	3	7	32	1	0	0	47	1	22	9	6
Watkins, Darren, Richmond	.273	3	11	1	3	3	0	0	0	0	0	0	0	1	0	5	0	0
Wedge, Eric, Pawtucket	.233	53	163	24	38	69	14	1	5	18	2	5	1	25	0	26	0	2
Wendell, Turk, Richmond*	1.000	3	2	2	2	3	1	0	0	0	0	0	0	0	0	0	0	0
Wetherby, Jeffrey, Rochester*	.143	25	70	2	10	15	2	0	1	5	0	0	1	10	0	17	1	2
Willard, Jerry, Richmond*	.300	91	277	42	83	131	24	0	8	39	2	1	5	45	4	46	1	3
Williams, Bernie, Columbus	.294	78	306	52	90	140	14	6	8	37	4	3	2	38	2	43	9	8
Williams, Gerald, Columbus	.258	61	198	20	51	71	8	3	2	27	0	5	1	16	1	39	9	11
Williams, Kenny, Syracuse	.333	15	54	14	18	40	1	0	7	19	1	1	1	6	0	12	6	2
Wilson, Gary, Scranton W.B.	.091	40	11	1	1	1	0	0	0	1	2	0	0	0	0	4	0	0
Wilson, Glenn, Richmond	.270	29	100	13	27	37	4	0	2	15	0	1	0	13	0	21	1	1
Woodson, Tracy, Richmond	.277	120	441	43	122	166	20	3	6	56	3	8	2	28	1	43	1	4
Woodward, Rob, Rochester	.000	47	3	0	0	0	0	0	0	0	0	0	0	0	0	1	0	0
Worthington, Craig, Rochester	.298	19	57	10	17	27	4	0	2	9	0	1	0	6	0	10	0	1
Young, Anthony, Tidewater	.211	27	19	1	4	5	1	0	0	1	3	0	1	0	0	10	0	1
Zosky, Eddie, Syracuse	.264	149	511	69	135	179	18	4	6	39	7	5	5	35	1	82	9	4
Zupcic, Bob, Pawtucket	.240	129	429	70	103	186	27	1	18	70	12	8	1	55	2	58	11	6

The following pitchers, listed alphabetically by club, with games in parentheses, had no plate appearances, primarily through use of designated hitters:

COLUMBUS—Adkins, Steve (14); Bond, Daven (32); Cary, Chuck (8); Chapin, Darrin (55); Clayton, Royal (32); Cook, Andy (13); Draper, Mike (4); Eiland, Dave (9); Garcia, Victor (5); Howe, Steve (12); Hutton, Mark (1); Johnson, Jeff (10); Kamieniecki, Scott (11); Mills, Alan (38); Mmahat, Kevin (12); Monteleone, Rich (32); Munoz, Roberto (1); Newell, Tom (2); Pena, Hipolito (6); Rosario, Dave (29); Rub, Jerry (44); Seiler, Keith (2); Sellers, Jeff (6); Stanford, Don (15); Taylor, Wade (9); Witt, Mike (1).

PAWTUCKET—Conroy, Brian (17); Finnvold, Gar (3); Fischer, Tom (2); Gale, Rich (1); Gardiner, Mike (8); Hetzel, Eric (19); Hoy, Peter (15); Irvine, Daryl (27); Kiecker, Dana (8); Livernois, Derek (5); Manzanillo, Josias (20); Morton, Kevin (16); O'Neill, Dan (55); Owen, Dave (2); Plympton, Jeff (41); Quantrill, Paul (25); Ryan, Ken (9); Shikles, Larry (41); Taylor, Scott (7); Walter, Gene (22); Walters, Dave (48); Young, Matt (2).

RICHMOND—Alba, Gibson (3); Grant, Mark (1); Holman, Shawn (4); Sisk, Doug (9); Wohlers, Mark (23).

ROCHESTER—Ballard, Jeff (7); Bautista, Jose (6); Codiroli, Chris (7); de la Rosa, Francisco (38); Frohwirth, Todd (20); Hernandez, Julio (2); Johnson, Dave (2); Jones, Stacy (33); Lewis, Richie (2); Linskey, Mike (10); Martinez, David (37); McDonald, Ben (2); McKeon, Joel (3); Mesa, Jose (8); Miller, Dave (1); Mussina, Mike (19); Myers, Chris (23); Peraza, Oswaldo (8); Poole, Jim (27); Price, Joe (7); Robinson, Jeff (8); Sanchez, Israel (24); Smith, Roy (11); Telford, Anthony (27).

SCRANTON WILKES-BARRE—Baller, Jay (61); Bearse, Kevin (6); Elli, Rocky (18); Ritchie, Wally (7); Searage, Ray (3); Sims, Mark (45).

SYRACUSE—Bair, Doug (8); Blohm, Pete (37); Boucher, Denis (8); Dayley, Ken (10); Fraser, Willie (7); Gordon, Don (26); Guzman, Juan (12); Hentgen, Pat (31); Hernandez, Guillermo (8); Linton, Doug (30); MacDonald, Rob (7); Manzanillo, Ravelo (12); Sanchez, Alex (14); Shea, John (35); Valdez, Efrain (21); Wapnick, Steve (53); Weston, Mickey (27); Williams, Woody (31); Wills, Frank (22).

TIDEWATER—Hernandez, Manny (1); Trautwein, Dave (12).

TOLEDO—Aldred, Scott (22); Bair, Doug (5); Cummings, Steve (30); DeSilva, John (11); Gakeler, Dan (23); Gohr, Greg (26); Groom, Buddy (24); Haas, David (28); Kaiser, Jeff (16); Kiely, John (42); Knudson, Kurt (12); Leiter, Mark (5); Marshall, Randy (1); Meacham, Rusty (26); Munoz, Mike (38); Nosek, Randy (1); Rightnowar, Ron (23); Ritz, Kevin (20); Vesling, Don (12).

GRAND SLAMS—Campusano, Lancellotti, Pederson, 2 each; Aguayo, M. Bell, Brumley, Chance, Distefano, Hare, Hundley, C. Martinez, McDowell, McLemore, Pankovits, Quinlan, Rowland, Schunk, Shields, Vaughn, Wedge, Woodson, Zupcic, 1 each.

AWARDED FIRST BASE ON CATCHER'S INTERFERENCE—M. Bell 3 (Flaherty, Liddell, Sprague); L. Gomez (DeFrancesco); Hansen (Scott); Kutcher (Santovenia); Pina (Fletcher).

PITCHING

TEAM

Team	ERA	G	CG	ShO	Sv.	IP	H	R	ER	HR	HB	BB	Int. BB	SO	WP	Bk.
Columbus	3.76	144	18	9	46	1264.0	1149	624	528	73	38	588	20	850	71	20
Tidewater	3.79	142	14	13	34	1253.1	1227	600	528	82	42	521	45	734	54	18
Richmond	3.93	144	9	10	34	1277.0	1273	628	558	82	46	513	27	850	67	15
Toledo	3.95	144	12	11	36	1259.1	1218	646	553	88	42	565	29	899	66	11
Rochester	4.13	144	17	9	34	1247.1	1311	663	573	98	36	463	8	902	62	10
Pawtucket	4.23	143	11	5	49	1253.1	1246	677	589	131	39	509	26	827	65	15
Syracuse	4.35	144	11	2	37	1286.0	1336	709	622	114	41	548	19	807	88	15
Scranton W.B.	4.41	143	11	10	29	1233.0	1245	700	604	98	48	609	36	853	87	15

INDIVIDUAL

(Leading qualifiers for earned-run average leadership—115 or more innings)

*Throws lefthanded.

Pitcher, Team	W	L	Pct.	ERA	G	GS	CG	GF	ShO	Sv.	IP	H	R	ER	HR	HB	BB	Int. BB	SO	WP
Reynoso, Richmond	10	6	.625	2.61	22	19	3	1	3	0	131.0	117	44	38	9	10	39	1	97	9
Mussina, Rochester*	10	4	.714	2.87	19	19	3	0	1	0	122.1	108	42	39	9	2	31	0	107	6
Castillo, Richmond*	5	6	.455	2.90	23	17	0	0	0	0	118.0	89	47	38	4	1	32	0	78	2
Meacham, Toledo	9	7	.563	3.09	26	17	3	4	1	2	125.1	117	53	43	8	1	40	3	70	5
Ritz, Toledo	8	7	.533	3.28	20	19	3	1	0	0	126.1	116	50	46	9	3	60	2	105	6
Ashby, Scranton W.-B.	11	11	.500	3.46	26	26	6	0	3	0	161.1	144	78	62	12	9	60	2	113	7
Soff, Tidewater	8	7	.533	3.52	28	18	3	2	3	0	138.0	118	56	54	7	4	48	3	84	6
Hetzel, Pawtucket	9	5	.643	3.57	19	19	0	0	0	0	116.0	110	60	46	14	4	58	3	83	9
Mauser, Scranton W.-B.	6	11	.353	3.72	26	18	1	3	0	1	128.1	119	66	53	11	2	55	2	75	4
A. Young, Tidewater	7	9	.438	3.73	25	25	3	0	1	0	164.0	172	74	68	13	1	67	2	93	6

Departmental leaders: G—Ayrault, 68; W—Several pitchers tied with 12; L—Marak, 13; Pct.—Dewey, Perez, .800; GS—Beatty, Haas, Hentgen, 28; CG—Ashby, Quantrill, 6; GF—Baller, 51; ShO—Ashby, Reynoso, Soff, 3; Sv.—Wapnick, 20; IP—Valera, 176.1; H—Marak, 220; R—Marak, 123; ER—Marak, 112; HR—Linton, 21; HB—Hillman, Linton, Reynoso, 10; BB—Hentgen, 90; IBB—Moore, 8; SO—Hentgen, 155; WP—Gohr, 14.

(All pitchers—listed alphabetically)

Pitcher, Team	W	L	Pct.	ERA	G	GS	CG	GF	ShO	Sv.	IP	H	R	ER	HR	HB	BB	Int. BB	SO	WP
Adkins, Columbus*	4	5	.444	5.60	14	13	3	1	0	0	80.1	75	59	50	7	0	57	1	52	5
Agostinelli, Scranton W.-B.	0	0	.000	0.00	1	0	0	0	1	0	1.0	0	0	0	0	0	1	0	0	0

Pitcher, Team	W	L	Pct.	ERA	G	GS	CG	GF	ShO	Sv.	IP	H	R	ER	HR	HB	BB	Int. BB	SO	WP
Akerfelds, Scranton W.-B.	3	3	.500	6.32	11	11	0	0	0	0	52.2	52	37	37	9	0	39	0	36	5
Alba, Richmond*	0	0	.000	2.25	3	0	0	2	0	0	4.0	1	1	1	0	0	3	0	3	0
Aldred, Toledo*	8	8	.500	3.92	22	20	2	2	0	1	135.1	127	65	59	7	4	72	1	95	5
Ashby, Scranton W.-B.	11	11	.500	3.46	26	26	6	0	3	0	161.1	144	78	62	12	9	60	2	113	7
Ayrault, Scranton W.-B.	8	5	.615	4.83	68	0	0	21	0	3	98.2	91	58	53	12	5	47	4	103	5
Bair, 5 Tol.-8 Syr.	0	1	.000	2.50	13	0	0	8	0	0	18.0	21	10	5	0	0	6	1	21	0
Ballard, Rochester	3	3	.500	4.41	7	7	3	0	0	0	51.0	63	27	25	2	0	10	0	19	1
Baller, Scranton W.-B.	4	4	.500	4.98	61	1	0	51	0	17	72.1	84	43	40	10	3	33	6	79	11
Bautista, Rochester	1	0	1.000	0.59	6	0	0	5	0	1	15.1	8	1	1	1	0	3	2	7	0
Bearse, Scranton W.-B.*	1	1	.500	5.79	6	5	0	1	0	0	23.1	30	18	15	3	0	12	0	14	1
Beatty, Tidewater*	12	9	.571	4.11	28	28	3	0	1	0	175.1	192	86	80	18	5	43	6	74	0
Blohm, Syracuse	2	5	.286	4.71	37	7	0	16	0	2	99.1	96	53	52	15	2	43	3	45	8
Bogar, Tidewater	0	0	.000	27.00	1	0	0	0	0	0	0.1	0	1	1	0	1	0	0	1	0
Bond, Columbus	4	8	.333	5.70	32	9	0	5	0	1	85.1	103	61	54	5	4	41	2	52	8
Boucher, Syracuse*	2	1	.667	3.18	8	8	1	0	0	0	56.2	57	24	20	5	3	19	1	28	2
Brantley, Scranton W.-B.	2	4	.333	3.80	8	8	0	0	0	0	47.1	44	26	20	2	2	25	0	28	0
Bross, Tidewater	2	0	1.000	4.36	27	0	0	10	0	2	33.0	31	21	16	0	1	32	2	23	3
Burgos, Scranton W.-B.*	1	3	.250	2.95	24	6	1	1	1	0	64.0	54	25	21	3	1	29	1	32	3
Carreno, Scranton W.-B.	4	8	.333	5.33	33	8	1	12	0	1	81.0	88	51	48	7	6	26	2	52	4
Cary, Columbus*	5	3	.625	5.72	8	8	0	0	0	0	45.2	44	31	29	9	1	26	0	27	6
Castillo, Richmond*	5	6	.455	2.90	23	17	0	0	0	0	118.0	89	47	38	4	1	32	0	78	2
Chance, Rochester	0	0	.000	0.00	1	0	0	1	0	0	1.0	0	0	0	0	0	2	0	0	0
Chapin, Columbus	10	3	.769	1.95	55	0	0	28	0	12	78.1	54	23	17	5	1	40	3	69	5
Cinnella, Tidewater	2	2	.500	2.51	12	2	0	4	0	0	28.2	26	17	8	1	2	15	0	15	2
Clayton, Columbus	11	7	.611	3.84	32	19	1	2	0	0	150.0	152	76	64	15	2	53	1	100	2
Codiroli, Columbus	0	0	.000	13.50	7	0	0	1	0	0	8.0	20	13	12	1	0	6	0	5	2
Combs, Scranton W.-B.*	2	2	.500	6.67	6	6	1	0	0	0	27.0	39	23	20	0	0	16	0	14	1
Conroy, Pawtucket	6	4	.600	4.58	17	16	1	1	0	0	98.1	95	60	50	13	2	51	1	66	3
Cook, Columbus	5	5	.500	3.52	13	13	2	0	0	0	79.1	63	34	31	0	4	38	1	40	1
Cox, Scranton W.-B.	1	0	1.000	3.00	1	1	0	0	0	0	6.0	5	2	2	0	0	2	0	3	0
Cummings, Toledo	5	5	.500	4.68	30	7	0	15	0	5	75.0	72	42	39	4	6	29	3	41	2
Dalton, Toledo*	3	3	.500	4.13	39	0	0	18	0	4	65.1	72	33	30	7	2	24	4	28	7
Davis, Richmond	0	1	.000	9.00	5	0	0	4	0	0	8.0	11	9	8	1	0	6	3	6	1
Dayley, Syracuse*	0	1	.000	9.64	10	0	0	2	0	1	14.0	26	16	15	2	0	11	0	13	2
de la Rosa, Rochester	4	1	.800	2.67	38	4	0	16	0	3	84.1	71	28	25	6	0	33	1	61	2
DeSilva, Toledo	5	4	.556	4.60	11	11	1	0	0	0	58.2	62	33	30	10	1	21	0	56	1
Dewey, Tidewater	12	3	.800	3.34	48	0	0	32	0	9	64.2	61	30	24	2	0	36	6	38	5
Draper, Columbus	1	3	.250	3.77	4	4	2	0	0	0	28.2	36	21	12	1	0	5	0	13	0
Eiland, Columbus	6	1	.857	2.40	9	9	2	0	0	0	60.0	54	22	16	5	2	7	0	18	1
Elli, Scranton W.-B.*	1	0	1.000	4.26	18	0	0	4	0	0	19.0	23	13	9	0	0	20	2	13	3
Fernandez, Tidewater*	1	0	1.000	1.15	3	3	0	0	0	0	15.2	9	2	2	0	0	6	0	22	0
Finnvold, Pawtucket	1	2	.333	6.60	3	3	0	0	0	0	15.0	19	13	11	4	0	7	0	12	0
Fischer, Pawtucket	0	2	.000	9.58	2	2	0	0	0	0	10.1	14	11	11	3	1	2	0	8	2
Fraser, Syracuse	0	1	.000	3.68	7	0	0	2	0	1	14.2	12	7	6	1	0	6	1	12	1
Frohwirth, Rochester	1	3	.250	3.65	20	0	0	16	0	8	24.2	17	12	10	1	2	5	0	15	1
Gakeler, Toledo	2	3	.400	3.50	23	2	0	12	0	4	43.2	44	22	17	0	1	13	1	32	3
Gale, Pawtucket	0	0	.000	1.59	1	0	0	1	0	0	5.2	4	1	1	0	0	1	0	1	1
Garcia, Columbus*	0	1	.000	3.86	5	5	0	0	0	0	28.0	20	16	12	2	1	20	0	11	3
Gardiner, Pawtucket	7	1	.875	2.34	8	8	2	0	1	0	57.2	39	16	15	2	1	11	0	42	0
Gohr, Toledo	10	8	.556	4.61	26	26	2	0	1	0	148.1	125	86	76	11	3	66	0	96	14
Gomez, Richmond*	2	9	.182	4.39	16	14	0	0	0	0	82.0	99	55	40	3	2	41	0	41	3
Gordon, Syracuse	2	2	.500	1.69	26	0	0	9	0	1	48.0	48	11	9	2	1	9	0	29	4
Grant, Richmond	0	0	.000	0.00	1	0	0	0	0	0	3.0	2	0	0	1	1	0	0	3	0
Grimsley, Scranton W.-B.	2	3	.400	4.35	9	9	0	0	0	0	51.2	48	28	25	3	2	37	2	43	7
Groom, Toledo*	2	5	.286	4.32	24	6	0	4	0	1	75.0	75	39	36	7	4	25	2	49	1
Guzman, Syracuse	4	5	.444	4.03	12	11	0	0	0	0	67.0	46	39	30	4	2	42	0	67	7
Haas, Toledo	8	10	.444	5.26	28	28	1	0	0	0	157.1	187	103	92	11	8	77	3	133	8
Hentgen, Syracuse	8	9	.471	4.47	31	28	1	2	0	0	171.0	146	91	85	17	2	90	1	155	11
Hernandez, Syracuse*	1	1	.500	4.22	8	0	0	2	0	0	10.2	10	5	5	2	1	4	0	9	0
Hernandez, Rochester	0	0	.000	10.50	2	1	0	0	0	0	6.0	10	7	7	1	0	3	0	3	0
Hernandez, Tidewater	1	2	.333	8.03	3	3	0	0	0	0	12.1	17	11	11	0	0	8	0	4	0
Hetzel, Pawtucket	9	5	.643	3.57	19	19	0	0	0	0	116.0	110	60	46	14	4	58	3	83	9
Hillman, Tidewater*	5	12	.294	4.01	27	27	2	0	0	0	161.2	184	89	72	8	10	58	0	91	13
Holman, Richmond	0	1	.000	7.36	4	0	0	4	0	0	7.1	7	7	6	1	0	5	2	5	0
Howe, Columbus*	2	1	.667	0.00	12	0	0	9	0	5	18.0	11	1	0	0	1	8	2	13	1
Howell, Scranton W.-B.	2	0	1.000	5.11	6	6	0	0	0	0	24.2	30	15	14	3	2	16	0	20	4
Hoy, Pawtucket	1	2	.333	2.38	15	0	0	13	0	5	22.2	18	8	6	2	0	10	1	12	2
Hutton, Columbus	1	0	1.000	1.50	1	1	0	0	0	0	6.0	3	2	1	0	0	5	0	5	0
Irvine, Pawtucket	1	1	.500	3.00	27	0	0	25	0	17	33.0	27	11	11	2	0	13	1	19	10
Johnson, Rochester	0	1	.000	4.15	2	2	1	0	0	0	13.0	18	7	6	1	0	5	0	8	1
Johnson, Columbus*	4	0	1.000	2.61	10	10	0	0	0	0	62.0	58	27	18	1	1	25	0	40	1
Jones, Rochester	4	4	.500	3.38	33	1	0	21	0	8	50.2	53	22	19	4	0	20	2	47	2
Kaiser, Toledo*	3	0	1.000	2.08	16	3	0	6	0	1	34.2	35	9	8	3	1	11	0	28	5
Kamieniecki, Columbus	6	3	.667	2.36	11	11	3	0	1	0	76.1	61	25	20	2	3	20	0	58	2
Kiecker, Pawtucket	2	3	.400	3.79	8	7	0	0	0	0	38.0	42	24	16	4	3	19	2	23	2
Kiely, Toledo	4	2	.667	2.13	42	0	0	27	0	6	72.0	55	25	17	3	3	35	3	60	2
Kilgus, Rochester	2	2	.500	5.76	8	0	0	2	0	0	45.1	58	32	29	3	0	10	0	29	1
Kline, Tidewater	2	0	1.000	0.00	2	0	0	1	0	0	5.0	0	0	0	0	0	2	0	5	0
Knudsen, Toledo	1	2	.333	1.47	12	0	0	3	0	0	18.1	13	11	3	1	0	10	1	28	2
Kramer, Richmond	3	3	.500	2.80	11	10	1	0	0	0	64.1	60	22	20	2	2	24	0	26	7
Legg, Scranton W.-B.	0	0	.000	9.00	1	0	0	1	0	0	1.0	3	1	1	0	0	0	0	0	0
Leiper, Tidewater	0	0	.000	27.00	1	0	0	1	0	0	1.0	4	3	3	1	0	0	0	0	0
Lewis, Rochester	1	0	1.000	2.81	2	2	0	0	0	0	16.0	13	5	5	1	0	7	0	18	1
Linskey, Rochester*	1	5	.167	7.24	10	9	0	0	0	0	41.0	67	34	33	5	3	17	0	25	1
Linton, Syracuse	10	12	.455	5.01	30	26	3	1	1	0	161.2	181	108	90	21	10	56	2	93	5
Livernois, Pawtucket	1	2	.333	10.53	5	5	0	0	0	0	19.2	27	25	23	4	0	17	0	14	1
Lusader, Columbus	0	0	.000	0.00	1	0	0	0	0	0	2.0	3	1	0	0	0	1	0	1	0
MacDonald, Syracuse*	1	0	1.000	4.50	7	0	0	5	0	1	6.0	3	3	3	1	0	5	0	8	3
Malone, Scranton W.-B.	0	3	.000	17.31	5	5	0	0	0	0	13.0	16	27	25	3	3	32	0	9	1
Manzanillo, Pawtucket	5	5	.500	5.61	20	16	0	0	0	0	102.2	109	69	64	12	4	53	0	65	9
Manzanillo, Syracuse*	3	0	1.000	3.42	12	0	0	4	0	1	23.2	26	10	9	3	0	14	0	20	4
Marak, Richmond	10	13	.435	5.85	29	26	2	1	1	0	172.1	220	123	112	18	7	80	1	57	6
Marshall, Toledo*	1	0	1.000	9.00	1	1	0	0	0	0	5.0	5	6	5	1	0	2	0	2	0
Martinez, Rochester	0	5	.000	5.28	37	4	0	9	0	1	87.0	98	58	51	8	3	43	1	73	10

Pitcher, Team	W	L	Pct.	ERA	G	GS	CG	GF	ShO	Sv.	IP	H	R	ER	HR	HB	BB	Int. BB	SO	WP
Mauser, Scranton W.-B.	6	11	.353	3.72	26	18	1	3	0	1	128.1	119	66	53	11	2	55	3	75	4
McCarthy, Richmond	4	6	.400	4.24	21	13	1	2	0	0	85.0	80	43	40	3	3	34	3	51	3
McDonald, Rochester	0	1	.000	7.71	2	2	0	0	0	0	7.0	10	7	6	1	0	5	0	7	1
McKeon, Rochester*	0	0	.000	9.00	3	0	0	3	0	0	2.0	2	2	2	0	0	2	0	1	1
Meacham, Toledo	9	7	.563	3.09	26	17	3	4	1	2	125.1	117	53	43	8	1	40	3	70	5
Mesa, Rochester	3	3	.500	3.86	8	8	1	0	1	0	51.1	37	25	22	4	2	30	0	48	3
Miller, Rochester	0	0	.000	0.00	1	0	0	1	0	0	0	0	0	0	0	0	0	0	0	0
Mills, Columbus	7	5	.583	4.43	38	15	0	18	0	8	113.2	109	65	56	3	6	75	1	77	12
Milstien, Pawtucket	0	0	.000	9.00	1	0	0	1	0	0	1.0	3	1	1	0	0	1	0	0	0
Mmahat, Columbus*	3	3	.500	3.58	12	11	2	0	2	0	65.1	54	26	26	2	2	34	0	59	2
Monteleone, Columbus	1	3	.250	2.12	32	0	0	25	0	17	46.2	36	15	11	1	0	7	0	52	3
Moore, Tidewater	8	5	.615	3.33	50	1	0	35	0	13	78.1	73	36	29	4	5	45	8	53	5
Morton, Pawtucket*	7	3	.700	3.49	16	15	1	0	1	0	98.0	91	41	38	8	2	30	1	80	3
Munoz, Toledo*	2	3	.400	3.83	38	1	0	19	0	8	54.0	44	30	23	4	0	35	4	38	3
Munoz, Columbus	0	1	.000	24.00	1	1	0	0	0	0	3.0	8	8	8	0	0	3	0	2	0
Mussina, Rochester	10	4	.714	2.87	19	19	3	0	1	0	122.1	108	42	39	9	2	31	0	107	6
Myers, Rochester	8	7	.533	4.49	23	21	0	0	0	0	118.1	141	63	59	9	4	44	0	57	6
Newell, Columbus	0	0	.000	23.63	2	0	0	1	0	0	2.2	5	8	7	0	1	6	0	2	2
Nosek, Toledo	0	0	.000	0.00	1	1	0	0	0	0	0.2	0	4	0	0	1	4	0	1	0
O'Neill, Pawtucket*	5	7	.417	5.30	55	0	0	16	0	1	69.2	76	46	41	10	1	44	4	54	3
Ontiveros, Scranton W.-B.	2	1	.667	2.90	7	7	0	0	0	0	31.0	29	11	10	2	0	10	0	21	2
Owen, Pawtucket*	0	1	.000	17.36	2	2	0	0	0	0	4.2	9	9	9	0	0	6	0	3	0
Parrett, Richmond	2	7	.222	4.52	19	14	0	2	0	0	79.2	72	45	40	2	1	46	1	88	5
Pederson, Syracuse*	0	0	.000	3.00	1	0	0	1	0	0	3.0	2	1	1	0	0	0	0	1	0
Pena, Columbus*	1	0	1.000	8.38	6	0	0	1	0	0	9.2	11	9	9	1	0	9	0	7	2
Peraza, Rochester	3	4	.429	5.20	8	8	0	0	0	0	45.0	45	29	26	4	1	21	0	40	5
Perez, Richmond*	12	3	.800	3.79	36	10	0	5	0	1	107.0	99	47	45	7	2	53	1	102	7
Perry, Scranton W.-B.*	2	4	.333	3.98	36	1	0	12	0	4	54.1	60	26	24	3	3	21	0	36	12
Peterek, Richmond	0	1	.000	4.38	6	0	0	4	0	0	12.1	10	6	6	3	0	4	1	9	1
Plummer, Tidewater	4	3	.571	3.99	46	4	0	14	0	3	97.0	95	49	43	8	6	32	6	33	3
Plympton, Pawtucket	2	6	.250	3.12	41	1	0	26	0	7	69.1	65	31	24	11	6	29	2	58	1
Polley, Richmond*	2	3	.400	3.26	50	1	0	27	0	4	66.1	70	24	24	2	4	30	5	38	0
Poole, Rochester	3	2	.600	2.79	27	0	0	19	0	9	29.0	29	11	9	1	0	9	0	25	3
Price, Rochester*	0	1	.000	16.20	7	0	0	2	0	0	5.0	13	9	9	4	0	4	0	3	1
Quantrill, Pawtucket	10	7	.588	4.45	25	23	6	0	2	0	155.2	169	81	77	14	4	30	1	75	2
Reynoso, Richmond	10	6	.625	2.61	22	19	3	1	0	0	131.0	117	44	38	9	10	39	1	97	9
Richards, Richmond	1	2	.333	7.47	6	2	0	1	0	0	15.2	25	15	13	0	1	7	1	8	0
Rightnowar, Toledo	1	1	.500	3.94	23	0	0	14	0	3	29.2	30	15	13	2	1	15	2	5	0
Ritchie, Scranton W.-B.*	1	0	1.000	2.42	7	2	0	3	0	2	26.0	17	8	7	2	0	7	1	25	0
Ritz, Toledo	8	7	.533	3.28	20	19	3	1	0	0	126.1	116	50	46	9	3	60	2	105	4
Robinson, Rochester	1	2	.333	6.43	8	1	0	3	0	1	21.0	23	18	15	3	1	15	0	13	2
Rosario, Columbus*	4	0	1.000	2.11	29	0	0	14	0	2	47.0	30	11	11	2	1	22	0	34	0
Ross, Richmond	3	6	.333	3.50	39	1	0	22	0	9	82.1	84	35	32	2	1	13	7	50	1
Rub, Columbus*	3	2	.600	3.44	44	0	0	16	0	1	52.1	42	22	20	2	1	30	3	51	9
Ruffin, Scranton W.-B.*	4	5	.444	4.66	13	13	1	0	0	0	75.1	82	43	39	4	0	41	1	50	3
Ryan, Pawtucket	1	0	1.000	4.91	9	0	0	4	0	0	18.1	15	11	10	2	1	11	1	14	2
St. Claire, Richmond	0	0	.000	1.19	29	0	0	14	0	2	68.0	39	10	9	2	4	11	2	60	8
Sanchez, Syracuse	1	4	.200	10.29	14	5	0	8	0	1	28.0	33	33	32	2	1	35	0	12	14
Sanchez, Syracuse*	6	2	.750	3.42	24	12	4	6	1	2	94.2	94	43	36	3	4	33	0	74	1
Sauveur, Tidewater*	2	2	.500	2.38	42	0	0	21	0	6	45.1	31	14	12	0	0	23	5	49	3
Schatzeder, Tidewater*	0	0	.000	7.36	9	1	0	2	0	0	14.2	22	13	12	1	0	13	3	10	0
Schourek, Tidewater*	1	1	.500	2.52	4	4	0	0	0	0	25.0	18	7	7	3	0	10	0	17	0
Searage, Scranton W.-B.*	1	0	1.000	5.79	3	0	0	2	0	0	4.2	5	4	3	1	0	2	0	3	1
Seiler, Columbus	0	0	.000	3.86	2	0	0	1	0	0	2.1	3	1	1	0	0	3	0	1	0
Sellers, Columbus	0	1	.000	4.84	6	4	0	2	0	0	22.1	17	14	12	1	2	17	0	11	3
Shea, Syracuse*	12	10	.545	4.55	35	24	3	5	0	2	172.0	198	104	87	15	8	78	2	76	4
Shields, Rochester	0	0	.000	0.00	2	1	0	1	0	0	2.0	1	0	0	0	2	0	0	1	0
Shikles, Pawtucket	8	4	.667	3.95	41	10	0	11	0	3	127.2	130	64	56	12	4	34	3	74	5
Sims, Scranton W.-B.*	4	3	.571	3.05	45	0	0	15	0	2	65.0	61	32	22	3	1	33	6	38	6
Sisk, Richmond	0	0	.000	1.59	9	0	0	4	0	2	11.1	14	3	2	0	0	4	0	2	1
Smith, Rochester	6	2	.750	3.50	11	11	2	0	0	0	74.2	65	31	29	3	3	17	0	40	2
Smith, Richmond	3	3	.500	7.24	10	10	1	0	0	0	51.0	66	44	41	10	0	24	0	41	2
Soff, Tidewater	8	7	.533	3.52	28	18	3	2	3	0	138.0	118	56	54	7	4	48	3	84	6
Stanford, Columbus	3	3	.500	4.01	15	1	0	2	0	0	33.2	30	15	15	2	1	15	3	14	2
Stankiewicz, Columbus	0	0	.000	0.00	1	1	0	0	0	0	0.1	0	0	0	0	1	0	0	0	0
Taylor, Pawtucket*	3	3	.500	3.46	7	7	1	0	0	0	39.0	32	19	15	3	1	17	0	35	1
Taylor, Columbus	4	1	.800	3.54	9	9	3	0	1	0	61.0	59	27	24	4	3	22	1	36	0
Telford, Rochester	12	9	.571	3.95	27	25	3	0	0	0	157.1	166	82	69	17	4	48	2	115	7
Trautwein, Tidewater	0	0	.000	6.35	12	0	0	8	0	1	17.0	22	12	12	4	1	13	0	5	0
Turner, Richmond	1	3	.250	4.75	23	0	0	17	0	5	36.0	33	21	19	5	2	20	0	33	4
Turner, Rochester	0	0	.000	0.00	1	0	0	1	0	0	1.0	0	0	0	0	0	0	0	0	0
Valdez, Syracuse*	3	2	.600	5.36	21	1	0	4	0	0	43.2	50	27	26	7	0	25	0	30	3
Valera, Tidewater	10	10	.500	3.83	26	26	3	0	1	0	176.1	152	79	75	12	6	70	4	117	8
Veres, Richmond	0	2	.000	5.04	9	3	0	4	0	0	25.0	32	14	14	4	1	10	0	12	2
Vesling, Toledo*	0	1	1.000	5.48	12	2	0	1	0	0	23.0	28	17	14	0	2	19	0	20	2
Walter, Pawtucket*	4	3	.571	4.81	22	6	0	7	0	3	58.0	61	37	31	4	2	29	2	34	3
Walters, Pawtucket	5	3	.625	3.07	48	1	0	27	0	12	85.0	83	35	29	7	3	30	4	48	6
Wapnick, Syracuse	6	3	.667	2.76	53	0	0	42	0	20	71.2	68	23	22	4	2	25	4	58	4
Wendell, Richmond	0	2	.000	3.43	3	3	1	0	0	0	21.0	20	9	8	3	1	6	0	18	2
Weston, Syracuse	12	6	.667	3.74	27	25	3	1	0	0	166.0	193	85	69	7	3	36	1	60	10
Williams, Syracuse	3	4	.429	4.12	31	0	0	16	0	6	54.2	52	27	25	2	3	27	3	37	4
Wills, Syracuse	3	5	.375	4.84	22	9	0	8	0	1	61.1	71	35	33	4	3	21	0	38	2
Wilson, Scranton W.-B.	3	7	.300	4.92	40	10	0	5	0	0	104.1	121	65	57	5	8	45	6	46	12
Witt, Columbus	0	0	.000	9.00	1	1	0	0	0	0	4.0	7	4	4	0	1	3	0	5	1
Wohlers, Richmond	1	0	1.000	1.03	23	0	0	21	0	11	26.1	23	4	3	1	1	12	1	22	1
Woodward, Rochester	7	7	.500	4.23	47	0	0	21	0	1	72.1	80	50	34	6	6	39	0	60	2
Young, Tidewater	7	9	.438	3.73	25	25	3	0	1	0	164.0	172	74	68	13	1	67	2	93	6
Young, Pawtucket*	1	0	1.000	4.50	2	2	0	0	0	0	8.0	8	4	4	0	0	6	0	7	0

BALKS—Reynoso, 6; Wills, 4; Baller, Gohr, J. Johnson, Kamieniecki, Sauveur, Shea, Valera, 3 each; Adkins, Bond, Brantley, Bross, Cary, Castillo, Cook, de la Rosa, Grimsley, Guzman, Hentgen, Hetzel, Hillman, Kaiser, Morton, Perez, Perry, Quantrill, Shikles, Soff, Telford, 2 each; Akerfelds, Ayrault, Bair, Bearse, Beatty, Carreno, Chapin, Cinnella, Clayton, Conroy, Cummings, Dewey, Garcia, Gomez, Gordon, Groom, Haas, Howell, Jones, Linskey, Livernois, J. Manzanillo, R. Manzanillo, Marak, Mesa, Mills, Moore, Mussina, O'Neill, Peraza, Peterek, Plympton, Ritz, I. Sanchez, Schatzeder, Sims, P. Smith, Stanford, S. Taylor, W. Taylor, Vesling, Walters, Wapnick, Williams, Wohlers, A. Young, 1 each.

COMBINATION SHUTOUTS—Bond-Chapin-Monteleone, Cook-Monteleone, Johnson-Howe, Mmahat-Clayton-Chapin, Rosario-Rub-Stanford, Columbus; Morton-Irvine, Pawtucket; Castillo-McCarthy-Wohlers, Castillo-St. Claire, McCarthy-Parrett, Parrett-Reynoso-Wohlers, Perez-Wohlers, Reynoso-Ross, Richmond; de la Rosa-Jones, Mesa-Poole-Jones, Mussina-de la Rosa, Sanchez-Jones, Shields-Turner-Kilgus, Smith-Woodward-Price-Frohwirth, Rochester; Brantley-Baller, Brantley-Sims, Grimsley-Wilson-Sims-Baller, Mauser-Baller, Mauser-Sims, Mauser-Sims-Baller, Scranton-Wilkes Barre; Shea-Wills, Syracuse; Beatty-Dewey, Beatty-Schatzeder-Dewey-Young-Moore, Fernandez-Bross, Schourek-Dewey, Soff-Plummer, Valera-Moore, Valera-Sauveur-Dewey, Tidewater; Aldred-Rightnowar, Cummings-Munoz, DeSilva-Groom, Haas-Aldred, Kaiser-Kiely, Kaiser-Kiely-Cummings, Meacham-Munoz-Rightnowar, Meacham-Ritz, Ritz-Rightnowar, Toledo.

NO-HIT GAME—Mmahat, Columbus, defeated Louisville, 6-0, July 5.

FIELDING

TEAM

Team	Pct.	G	PO	A	E	DP	PB	Team	Pct.	G	PO	A	E	DP	PB
Richmond	.977	144	3831	1576	129	161	11	Scranton W.B.	.972	143	3699	1496	148	145	8
Tidewater	.974	142	3760	1699	143	170	11	Columbus	.972	144	3792	1569	154	121	24
Rochester	.974	144	3742	1391	137	126	14	Syracuse	.971	144	3858	1579	161	154	13
Pawtucket	.973	143	3760	1466	144	138	11	Toledo	.970	144	3778	1610	166	167	16

Triple plays—Columbus, Syracuse.

INDIVIDUAL

*Throws lefthanded.

FIRST BASEMEN

Player, Team	Pct.	G	PO	A	E	DP
Alexander, Scranton-W.B.	.992	51	327	26	3	36
Allaire, Toledo	.990	14	90	8	1	16
Barnes, Toledo	1.000	18	137	13	0	13
Bell, Richmond*	.995	66	616	41	3	74
Bogar, Tidewater	1.000	1	1	0	0	1
Brogna, Toledo*	.986	41	311	37	5	35
Cabrera, Richmond	.989	11	87	6	1	7
Crabbe, Richmond	1.000	2	12	1	0	1
Cruz, Toledo*	1.000	8	70	7	0	12
de los Santos, Toledo	.989	33	247	17	3	30
Distefano, Rochester*	.992	84	621	37	5	59
Dunbar, Rochester*	1.000	3	14	0	0	1
Fletcher, Scranton-W.B.	1.000	6	35	2	0	3
Gomez, Rochester	1.000	1	10	0	0	0
Grotewold, Scranton-W.B.	.988	41	305	28	4	33
Hansen, Tidewater	.989	12	84	4	1	14
Hare, Toledo*	.979	25	168	16	4	13
Hollins, Scranton-W.B.	1.000	5	17	1	0	2
Hughes, Columbus*	.983	37	326	20	6	28
Hundley, Tidewater	1.000	1	2	0	0	0
Jimenez, Tidewater*	.990	99	844	76	9	90
Kutcher, Toledo	.970	8	62	2	2	9
Lancellotti, Pawtucket*	1.000	7	66	1	0	6
Leiper, Tidewater	1.000	1	3	0	0	0
Lindeman, Scranton-W.B.	.917	3	21	1	2	2
Livingstone, Toledo	.941	3	15	1	1	4
Lovullo, Columbus	.991	28	206	22	2	14
Lyden, Toledo	1.000	20	157	7	0	16
Maksudian, Syracuse	.986	9	67	4	1	12
MARTINEZ, Syracuse	.993	125	1110	103	9	106
R. Martinez, Rochester*	.992	16	109	10	1	7
McLemore, Rochester	1.000	1	2	0	0	0
Meadows, Rochester	1.000	1	9	0	0	0
Mercado, Tidewater	.750	2	3	0	1	0
Mercedes, Rochester	1.000	1	2	0	0	0
Pedrique, Tidewater	1.000	5	19	3	0	1
Pevey, Syracuse	1.000	6	43	2	0	6
Pratt, Pawtucket	1.000	2	10	1	0	2
Quinlan, Syracuse	.921	4	35	0	3	1
Rodriguez, Richmond	.982	20	156	6	3	22
Sax, Columbus	.985	35	237	26	4	18
Schu, Scranton-W.B.	.993	65	509	29	4	56
Schunk, Syracuse	.974	9	66	9	2	5
Segui, Rochester*	1.000	20	149	13	0	12
Shamburg, Rochester	.963	12	73	4	3	13
Shields, Rochester	1.000	1	2	0	0	0
Snider, Columbus	.984	36	290	11	5	26
Sparks, Columbus	.987	29	216	17	3	20
Szekely, Richmond	.978	8	36	8	1	1
Tackett, Rochester	1.000	2	15	0	0	0
Torve, Tidewater	.993	45	391	23	3	51
Twardoski, Pawtucket*	.996	88	715	58	3	74
Vaughn, Pawtucket	.993	53	432	24	3	40
Voigt, Rochester	.991	16	95	11	1	8
Walewander, Columbus	1.000	4	16	0	0	1
Wetherby, Rochester*	1.000	8	59	9	0	6
Willard, Richmond	.991	24	203	13	2	15
Woodson, Richmond	.996	26	219	16	1	18

SECOND BASEMEN

Player, Team	Pct.	G	PO	A	E	DP
Aguayo, Pawtucket	.990	20	45	57	1	14
Allaire, Toledo	1.000	5	7	7	0	2
Alva, Richmond	.991	23	38	75	1	12

Player, Team	Pct.	G	PO	A	E	DP
Barrett, Pawtucket	.957	83	148	209	16	47
Beyeler, Toledo	.931	8	9	18	2	2
Bogar, Tidewater	.991	22	53	55	1	21
Brumley, Pawtucket	1.000	5	7	11	0	3
Casarotti, Richmond	.975	15	33	46	2	10
Crabbe, Richmond	.971	5	15	18	1	7
DeCillis, Toledo	.941	3	8	8	1	3
DeKneef, Pawtucket	1.000	4	13	14	0	6
Dickerson, Rochester	1.000	2	3	4	0	1
Donnels, Tidewater	.987	17	27	50	1	8
Garces, Scranton-W.B.	.667	2	1	1	1	0
Gardner, Tidewater	.995	96	231	312	3	75
Jeltz, 19 Roch.-2 Syr.	.990	21	41	54	1	12
Kelly, Columbus	.974	30	53	97	4	20
Kutcher, Toledo	1.000	2	2	3	0	0
Legg, Scranton-W.B.	1.000	38	60	105	0	19
Leiper, Tidewater	1.000	1	1	0	0	0
Leyritz, Columbus	1.000	1	0	2	0	0
Lofton, Rochester	1.000	2	2	2	0	0
Lovullo, Columbus	.968	15	24	37	2	5
McDougal, Syracuse	.955	21	42	63	5	12
McKnight, Rochester	.971	7	12	21	1	1
McLemore, Rochester	.983	57	132	166	5	38
Meadows, Rochester	.912	9	13	18	3	4
Milstien, Pawtucket	.960	12	19	29	2	5
Morandini, Scranton-W.B.	.983	12	19	38	1	6
Pankovits, Pawtucket	.956	31	57	73	6	22
Paredes, Tidewater	.975	132	292	421	18	101
Pedrique, Tidewater	.988	21	34	45	1	11
Pevey, Syracuse	1.000	1	1	1	0	0
Rossy, Richmond	.983	112	234	344	10	89
Scarsone, Scranton-W.B.	.963	100	209	318	20	82
Schu, Scranton-W.B.	1.000	1	4	5	0	1
Schunk, Syracuse	.987	27	59	89	2	18
Stankiewicz, Columbus	.988	81	164	236	5	42
Suero, Rochester	.963	97	178	318	19	62
Turner, Rochester	.958	60	101	126	10	26
Walewander, Columbus	.993	28	58	91	1	20

Triple play—Schunk.

THIRD BASEMEN

Player, Team	Pct.	G	PO	A	E	DP
Aguayo, Pawtucket	1.000	8	5	11	0	2
Alexander, Scranton-W.B.	1.000	4	1	6	0	0
Allaire, Toledo	.955	27	15	48	3	5
Barnes, Toledo	.925	25	22	52	6	5
Beyeler, Toledo	1.000	4	0	1	0	0
Bogar, Tidewater	.976	15	10	31	1	2
Chance, Rochester	.714	3	0	5	2	0
Cooper, Pawtucket	.929	134	106	232	26	22
Crabbe, Richmond	1.000	17	11	20	0	1
DeCillis, Toledo	.800	16	10	26	9	6
de los Santos, Toledo	.750	2	2	1	1	1
Donnels, Tidewater	.939	70	61	139	13	15
GARDNER, Tidewater	1.000	2	0	4	0	0
Gomez, Rochester	.938	24	14	46	4	3
Gutierrez, Rochester	1.000	1	0	2	0	0
Hollins, Scranton-W.B.	.939	66	50	104	10	13
Humphreys, Columbus	.937	21	18	41	4	5
Kutcher, Toledo	.952	9	4	16	1	1
Legg, Scranton-W.B.	.959	45	22	72	4	12
Leiper, Tidewater	.908	41	28	81	11	12
Leyritz, Columbus	.894	21	12	30	5	3
Livingstone, Toledo	.925	73	50	136	15	17
Lovullo, Columbus	.926	60	46	105	12	7
McDougal, Syracuse	.750	3	3	0	1	0
Meadows, Rochester	1.000	4	1	7	0	1
Milstien, Pawtucket	1.000	1	1	3	0	0

Player, Team	Pct.	G	PO	A	E	DP
Pankovits, Pawtucket	.824	8	7	7	3	0
Pedrique, Tidewater	.901	30	15	49	7	6
QUINLAN, Syracuse	.942	129	103	222	20	26
Rodriguez, Richmond	.927	45	17	85	8	9
Rossy, Richmond	1.000	6	5	8	0	0
Schu, Scranton-W.B.	.933	41	21	35	4	2
Schunk, Syracuse	.909	11	5	25	3	4
Shields, Rochester	.947	68	51	110	9	9
Snider, Columbus	.857	3	2	4	1	0
Sparks, Columbus	.806	13	7	18	6	0
Sprague, Syracuse	1.000	3	6	8	0	0
Stankiewicz, Columbus	.941	8	10	6	1	1
Tackett, Rochester	.800	4	3	5	2	0
Torve, Tidewater	1.000	2	2	0	0	0
Turner, Rochester	.937	40	33	41	5	2
Voigt, Rochester	1.000	7	2	16	0	1
Walewander, Columbus	.951	39	29	68	5	3
Waller, Scranton-W.B.	1.000	3	1	4	0	1
Woodson, Richmond	.920	85	58	150	18	22
Worthington, Rochester	.958	13	10	13	1	1

Triple play—Quinlan.

SHORTSTOPS

Player, Team	Pct.	G	PO	A	E	DP
Aguayo, Pawtucket	.934	14	20	37	4	7
Allaire, Toledo	.957	83	125	229	16	56
Baez, Tidewater	.959	65	128	227	15	47
Batiste, Scranton-W.B.	.934	121	181	344	37	78
Beyeler, Toledo	.923	18	15	45	5	6
Bogar, Tidewater	.941	31	46	97	9	24
Brumley, Pawtucket	.939	27	41	66	7	14
Casarotti, Richmond	1.000	1	0	1	0	0
Castilla, Richmond	.962	66	93	208	12	39
Cooper, Pawtucket	1.000	4	9	9	0	3
Crabbe, Richmond	1.000	1	2	5	0	2
DeKneef, Pawtucket	.750	1	0	3	1	0
Gardner, Tidewater	.969	44	55	130	6	26
Gutierrez, Rochester	.959	49	61	127	8	24
Jeltz, 42 Roch.-1 Syr.	.961	43	72	100	7	24
Legg, Scranton-W.B.	.963	19	21	57	3	10
McDougal, Syracuse	.972	9	13	22	1	2
McKnight, Rochester	.938	14	21	39	4	5
Milstien, Pawtucket	.885	5	9	14	3	5
Montalvo, Syracuse	.857	1	2	4	1	0
Pedrique, Tidewater	.984	22	29	34	1	8
Rodriguez, Columbus	.971	73	138	236	11	45
Rosario, 57 Rich.-56 Tol.	.944	113	188	305	29	76
Rossy, Richmond	.936	24	47	56	7	19
Scarsone, Scranton-W.B.	.974	9	13	25	1	7
Schunk, Syracuse	.944	18	31	53	5	9
Shields, Rochester	.930	46	72	100	13	24
Stankiewicz, Columbus	.934	31	46	82	9	17
Turner, Rochester	1.000	2	3	0	0	0
Valentin, Pawtucket	.951	99	184	300	25	65
Walewander, Columbus	.939	48	76	139	14	19
ZOSKY, Syracuse	.961	119	221	371	24	88

Triple play—Stankiewicz.

OUTFIELDERS

Player, Team	Pct.	G	PO	A	E	DP
Allaire, Toledo	1.000	2	1	0	0	0
Alva, Richmond	1.000	7	10	0	0	0
Anderson, Rochester*	1.000	7	19	1	0	0
Barnes, Toledo	.982	27	50	4	1	2
Bell, Syracuse	.948	117	278	15	16	7
Bell, Richmond*	.970	18	29	3	1	1
Brumley, Pawtucket	1.000	2	1	0	0	0
Cabrera, Richmond	1.000	3	5	0	0	0
Campusano, Scranton-W.B.	.960	87	161	8	7	3
Carr, Tidewater	.961	62	141	8	6	1
Castillo, Scranton-W.B.	1.000	16	29	1	0	0
Chamberlain, Scranton-W.B.	.956	34	63	2	3	0
Chance, Rochester	.962	93	171	7	7	1
Clark, Toledo	.936	78	128	3	9	2
Contreras, Rochester*	1.000	2	3	0	0	0
Crabbe, Richmond	1.000	30	48	3	0	0
Distefano, Rochester*	1.000	16	26	3	0	2
Dozier, Tidewater	.951	43	75	2	4	0
Ducey, Tidewater	1.000	63	120	1	0	0
Fields, 25 Rich.-7 Syr.	.940	32	63	0	4	0
FORD, Toledo	.995	97	187	7	1	2
Gregg, Richmond*	1.000	2	5	0	0	0
Hansen, Tidewater	.972	78	133	7	4	0
Hare, Toledo*	.985	37	63	3	1	0
Hayes, Scranton-W.B.	1.000	2	3	0	0	0
Housie, Pawtucket	1.000	21	49	1	0	0
Hughes, Columbus*	.979	75	141	2	3	1
Humphreys, Columbus	.978	101	170	10	4	3
Hunter, Richmond*	.969	48	121	4	4	2
Jeltz, 2 Roch.-4 Syr.	1.000	6	16	1	0	0
Jeter, Syracuse	.975	70	145	12	4	4
Jimenez, Tidewater*	1.000	4	7	0	0	0

Player, Team	Pct.	G	PO	A	E	DP
Jones, Scranton-W.B.	.936	25	44	0	3	0
Kingwood, Rochester	.930	33	78	2	6	0
Knabenshue, Scranton-W.B.	1.000	12	18	2	0	0
Knoblauh, Columbus	.985	29	65	2	1	1
Kutcher, Toledo	.971	44	63	4	2	3
Lancellotti, Pawtucket*	1.000	50	99	3	0	1
Leiper, Tidewater	.988	37	77	2	1	1
Lindeman, Scranton-W.B.	1.000	5	9	1	0	0
Loggins, Richmond*	.984	25	59	2	1	0
Longmire, Scranton-W.B.	.932	33	54	1	4	1
Lovullo, Columbus	1.000	2	1	0	0	0
Lusader, Columbus*	.975	70	109	8	3	2
Maas, Columbus	1.000	7	7	0	0	0
Mangham, Toledo	.980	117	242	8	5	2
Martin, Richmond*	.975	42	73	4	2	1
R. Martinez, Rochester*	.965	38	81	2	3	1
May, Tidewater	.982	28	51	4	1	1
McDaniel, Richmond	.960	115	207	8	9	0
McDowell, Rochester*	.989	73	168	4	2	2
McKnight, Rochester	1.000	1	1	0	0	0
Meadows, Rochester	.986	32	68	2	1	1
Meadows, Scranton-W.B.*	.968	53	87	4	3	0
Mercedes, Rochester	.958	95	173	10	8	0
Mitchell, Richmond	.982	25	56	0	1	0
Nelson, Richmond	.984	61	119	4	2	2
Paredes, Toledo	1.000	2	1	1	0	0
Pederson, Syracuse*	.936	64	114	3	8	2
Pedrique, Tidewater	1.000	1	2	0	0	0
Peguero, Scranton-W.B.	.988	127	317	12	4	2
Pegues, Toledo	.958	64	84	7	4	1
Perez, Syracuse	.833	4	5	0	1	0
Pevey, Syracuse	1.000	8	12	0	0	0
Pina, Pawtucket	.989	104	172	10	2	1
Plantier, Pawtucket	1.000	79	173	6	0	1
Rodriguez, Richmond	.970	26	29	3	1	1
Roseboro, Tidewater	.979	32	134	7	3	1
Sanders, Richmond*	.987	29	73	1	1	1
Schunk, Syracuse	.956	22	42	1	2	0
Scott, Syracuse	1.000	11	22	2	0	0
Segui, Rochester*	1.000	8	16	2	0	0
Sheridan, Columbus	1.000	16	34	0	0	0
Shields, Rochester	1.000	2	6	0	0	0
Snider, Columbus	.949	25	36	1	2	0
Snyder, Columbus	1.000	17	25	0	0	0
Stone, Pawtucket	.979	86	179	10	4	0
Tomberlin, Richmond*	.995	91	192	1	1	1
Torve, Tidewater	.960	18	23	1	1	0
Turner, Rochester	.933	9	13	1	1	0
Twardoski, Pawtucket*	1.000	7	15	0	0	0
Voigt, Rochester	.981	53	101	5	2	2
Wade, Scranton-W.B.	.972	84	131	8	4	1
Walewander, Columbus	1.000	1	2	0	0	0
Ward, Syracuse	1.000	50	136	5	0	2
Watkins, Richmond	.750	3	3	0	1	0
Wetherby, Rochester*	1.000	1	1	0	0	0
B. Williams, Columbus	.994	77	164	2	1	0
Ge. Williams, Columbus	.977	58	124	5	3	0
K. Williams, Syracuse	1.000	14	31	1	0	0
Wilson, Richmond	.930	25	40	0	3	0
Woodson, Richmond	.000	1	0	0	1	0
Zupcic, Pawtucket	.993	128	255	13	2	3

CATCHERS

Player, Team	Pct.	G	PO	A	E	DP	PB
Agostinelli, Scranton-W.B.	.963	9	24	2	1	0	0
Benton, Toledo	.955	9	52	11	3	0	1
Bogar, Tidewater	1.000	1	1	0	0	0	0
Cabrera, Richmond	.984	8	53	7	1	0	0
Clark, Toledo	.951	11	68	9	4	4	4
Daulton, Scranton-W.B.	1.000	2	14	1	0	0	0
Delgado, Syracuse	1.000	1	5	0	0	0	0
Eberle, Rochester	.989	41	169	16	2	3	0
Flaherty, Pawtucket	.970	44	270	18	9	1	2
Fletcher, Scranton-W.B.	.990	77	456	42	5	7	4
Gonzalez, Tidewater	1.000	1	11	3	0	1	0
Grotewold, Scranton-W.B.	.987	25	139	10	2	1	1
Hundley, Tidewater	.986	110	583	63	9	12	8
Knorr, Syracuse	.987	86	477	49	7	7	3
Leyritz, Columbus	1.000	34	197	16	0	1	5
Lyden, Toledo	.987	35	211	15	3	2	3
Magrann, Pawtucket	1.000	13	75	12	0	4	3
Maksudian, Syracuse	.986	13	64	6	1	2	0
Mann, Richmond	.989	61	327	36	4	6	8
Mercado, Tidewater	.995	36	177	27	1	2	3
Pevey, Syracuse	.980	32	180	14	4	2	1
Pratt, Pawtucket	.984	38	226	20	4	4	3
Ramos, Columbus	.989	84	487	41	6	5	9
Rayford, Scranton-W.B.	1.000	1	0	0	0	0	0
ROWLAND, Toledo	.994	96	614	78	4	10	8
Sax, Columbus	.974	31	137	10	4	2	8
Skeels, Columbus	.952	11	55	5	3	1	2
Sprague, Syracuse	.950	16	105	9	6	1	9
Szekely, Richmond	.997	50	291	31	1	6	9
Tackett, Rochester	.993	122	761	85	6	12	14

— 361 —

Player, Team	Pct.	G	PO	A	E	DP	PB
Tremblay, Scranton-W.B.	.989	49	258	16	3	0	3
Turner, Rochester	1.000	1	1	0	0	0	0
Wedge, Pawtucket	.981	53	282	36	6	3	3
Willard, Richmond	.983	36	208	24	4	2	3

PITCHERS

Player, Team	Pct.	G	PO	A	E	DP
Adkins, Columbus*	.667	14	2	8	5	2
Akerfelds, Scranton-W.B.	.833	11	2	3	1	0
Aldred, Toledo*	.861	22	5	26	5	1
Ashby, Scranton-W.B.	.906	26	13	16	3	2
Ayrault, Scranton-W.B.	.938	68	4	11	1	1
Bair, 5 Tol.-8 Syr.	1.000	13	1	4	0	0
Ballard, Rochester*	1.000	7	3	3	0	0
Baller, Scranton-W.B.	.917	61	2	9	1	0
Bautista, Rochester	.667	6	3	1	2	0
Bearse, Scranton-W.B.*	1.000	6	1	3	0	0
Beatty, Tidewater*	.978	28	12	32	1	2
Blohm, Syracuse	.889	37	7	9	2	0
Bond, Columbus	.810	32	8	9	4	1
Boucher, Syracuse*	.950	8	7	12	1	2
Brantley, Scranton-W.B.	1.000	8	2	10	0	2
Bross, Tidewater	1.000	27	0	2	0	0
Burgos, Scranton-W.B.*	.933	24	1	13	1	1
Carreno, Scranton-W.B.	.950	33	4	15	1	1
Cary, Columbus*	1.000	8	0	6	0	0
CASTILLO, Richmond*	1.000	23	4	29	0	1
Chapin, Columbus	1.000	55	4	9	0	0
Cinnella, Tidewater	.857	12	1	5	1	0
Clayton, Columbus	1.000	32	11	21	0	0
Combs, Scranton-W.B.*	1.000	6	1	2	0	1
Conroy, Pawtucket	1.000	17	8	11	0	1
Cook, Columbus	1.000	13	7	17	0	3
Cox, Scranton-W.B.	1.000	1	1	0	0	0
Cummings, Toledo	.917	30	4	7	1	0
Dalton, Toledo*	1.000	39	7	18	0	2
Davis, Richmond	1.000	5	1	0	0	0
Dayley, Syracuse*	1.000	10	0	1	0	0
de la Rosa, Rochester	.923	38	4	8	1	0
DeSilva, Toledo	1.000	11	6	5	0	1
Dewey, Tidewater	1.000	48	6	10	0	1
Draper, Columbus	.750	4	1	2	1	0
Eiland, Columbus	.960	9	10	14	1	2
Elli, Scranton-W.B.*	1.000	18	3	7	0	1
Finnvold, Pawtucket	.000	3	0	0	1	0
Fraser, Syracuse	1.000	7	1	3	0	0
Frohwirth, Rochester	1.000	20	1	4	0	0
Gakeler, Toledo	1.000	23	4	6	0	0
Gale, Pawtucket	1.000	1	0	1	0	0
Garcia, Columbus*	.857	5	1	5	1	0
Gardiner, Pawtucket	.941	8	9	7	1	1
Gohr, Toledo	.972	26	14	21	1	3
Gomez, Richmond*	1.000	16	4	14	0	2
Gordon, Syracuse	.875	26	8	6	2	0
Grant, Richmond	1.000	1	0	1	0	0
Grimsley, Scranton-W.B.	1.000	9	5	7	0	0
Groom, Toledo*	.824	24	3	11	3	0
Guzman, Syracuse	.917	12	5	6	1	0
Haas, Toledo	.882	28	13	17	4	1
Hentgen, Syracuse	.962	31	7	18	1	2
Hernandez, Syracuse*	1.000	8	0	3	0	1
Hernandez, Rochester	1.000	2	1	1	0	1
Hernandez, Tidewater	1.000	3	3	3	0	1
Hetzel, Pawtucket	.769	19	5	5	3	0
Hillman, Tidewater*	.875	27	5	30	5	1
Holman, Richmond	1.000	4	1	1	0	0
Howe, Columbus*	.875	12	2	5	1	2
Howell, Scranton-W.B.	.833	6	2	3	1	0
Hoy, Pawtucket	1.000	15	0	6	0	1
Irvine, Pawtucket	.857	27	1	5	1	0
Johnson, Rochester	1.000	2	0	2	0	0
Johnson, Columbus*	1.000	10	2	18	0	1
Jones, Rochester	.889	33	3	5	1	1
Kaiser, Toledo*	.923	16	5	7	1	1
Kamieniecki, Columbus	.895	11	5	12	2	1
Kiecker, Pawtucket	.909	8	1	9	1	1
Kiely, Toledo	1.000	42	4	12	0	0
Kilgus, Rochester*	1.000	9	8	8	0	0
Kramer, Richmond	.947	11	8	10	1	1
Leiter, Toledo*	1.000	5	1	2	0	0
Lewis, Rochester	1.000	2	0	2	0	0
Linskey, Rochester*	.750	10	2	1	1	0
Linton, Syracuse	.931	30	8	19	2	1

Player, Team	Pct.	G	PO	A	E	DP
Livernois, Pawtucket	.875	5	2	5	1	0
Lusader, Columbus*	1.000	1	0	1	0	0
Malone, Scranton-W.B.	.500	5	0	1	1	0
Manzanillo, Pawtucket	1.000	20	4	13	0	2
Manzanillo, Syracuse*	1.000	12	2	2	0	0
Marak, Richmond	.902	29	16	21	4	3
D. Martinez, Rochester	1.000	37	4	11	0	1
Mauser, Scranton-W.B.	.950	26	11	8	1	0
McCarthy, Richmond	1.000	21	4	15	0	1
McDonald, Rochester	1.000	2	0	1	0	0
Meacham, Toledo	1.000	26	12	19	0	3
Mesa, Rochester	.909	8	5	5	1	0
Mills, Columbus	.800	38	8	12	5	0
Mmahat, Columbus*	1.000	12	3	11	0	0
Monteleone, Columbus	.900	32	2	7	1	0
Moore, Tidewater	.913	50	5	16	2	2
Morton, Pawtucket*	.909	16	1	9	1	0
Munoz, Toledo*	.733	38	3	8	4	1
Munoz, Columbus	1.000	1	0	1	0	0
Mussina, Rochester	1.000	19	6	14	0	0
Myers, Rochester*	.941	23	3	13	1	0
O'Neill, Pawtucket	1.000	55	4	11	0	1
Ontiveros, Scranton-W.B.	1.000	7	4	6	0	0
Owen, Pawtucket*	1.000	2	0	1	0	0
Parrett, Richmond	.889	19	4	4	1	1
Peraza, Rochester	1.000	8	1	5	0	0
Perez, Richmond*	.933	36	5	9	1	2
Perry, Scranton-W.B.*	.944	36	4	13	1	0
Peterek, Richmond	1.000	6	2	1	0	0
Plummer, Tidewater	.938	46	11	19	2	1
Plympton, Pawtucket	.857	41	3	9	2	0
Polley, Richmond*	.947	50	3	15	1	0
Poole, Rochester*	.909	27	4	6	1	1
Price, Rochester*	1.000	7	0	1	0	0
Quantrill, Pawtucket	.974	25	11	26	1	1
Reynoso, Richmond	.938	22	6	24	2	2
Richards, Richmond	1.000	6	1	3	0	1
Rightnowar, Toledo	1.000	23	1	4	0	0
Ritchie, Scranton-W.B.*	1.000	7	1	5	0	0
Ritz, Toledo	.952	20	7	13	1	2
Robinson, Rochester	.800	8	1	3	1	0
Rosario, Columbus*	1.000	29	4	7	0	0
Ross, Richmond	1.000	39	0	18	0	0
Rub, Columbus*	.800	44	5	3	2	0
Ruffin, Scranton-W.B.*	.769	13	2	8	3	1
Ryan, Pawtucket	1.000	9	0	2	0	0
St. Claire, Richmond	1.000	29	5	11	0	0
Sanchez, Syracuse	.917	14	4	7	1	0
Sanchez, Syracuse*	1.000	24	9	17	0	2
Sauveur, Tidewater*	.857	42	1	5	1	1
Schatzeder, Tidewater*	.833	9	1	4	1	1
Schourek, Tidewater*	1.000	4	0	4	0	0
Searage, Scranton-W.B.*	1.000	3	0	1	0	0
Sellers, Columbus	.800	6	3	1	1	0
Shea, Syracuse*	.935	35	5	24	2	1
Shikles, Pawtucket	.906	41	8	21	3	1
Sims, Scranton-W.B.*	1.000	45	4	21	0	0
Sisk, Richmond	1.000	9	0	3	0	1
Smith, Rochester	.900	11	3	6	1	0
Smith, Richmond	.917	10	4	7	1	0
Soff, Tidewater	.969	28	6	25	1	1
Stanford, Columbus	1.000	15	6	1	0	1
Taylor, Pawtucket*	.917	7	4	7	1	2
Taylor, Columbus	1.000	9	5	12	0	0
Telford, Rochester	.943	27	15	35	3	3
Trautwein, Tidewater	1.000	12	2	2	0	0
Turner, Richmond	.750	23	0	3	1	0
Valdez, Syracuse*	.857	21	0	6	1	0
Valera, Tidewater	.941	26	7	25	2	2
Veres, Richmond	1.000	9	0	2	0	1
Vesling, Toledo*	1.000	12	4	4	0	0
Walter, Pawtucket*	1.000	21	3	15	0	1
Walters, Pawtucket	.947	49	5	13	1	1
Wapnick, Syracuse	1.000	53	1	8	0	0
Wendell, Richmond	.875	3	1	6	1	0
Weston, Syracuse	.975	27	21	18	1	2
Gr. Williams, Syracuse	1.000	31	4	7	0	0
Wills, Syracuse	1.000	22	7	11	0	0
Wilson, Scranton-W.B.	1.000	40	7	23	0	3
Witt, Columbus	1.000	1	0	1	0	0
Wohlers, Richmond	.500	23	0	1	1	0
Woodward, Rochester	.895	47	2	15	2	0
Young, Tidewater	.884	25	11	27	5	2
Young, Pawtucket*	1.000	2	1	2	0	0

The following players did not have any fielding statistics at the positions indicated or appeared only as a designated hitter, pinch-hitter or pinch-runner: Agostinelli, p; Alba, p; Bogar, of, p; Chance, p; Codiroli, p; Fernandez, p; Fischer, p; Garces, 3b; Hutton, p; Kline, p; Knudsen, p; Legg, p; Leiper, p; Leyritz, p; Maas, 2b; MacDonald, p; Marshall, p; McKeon, p; Miller, p; Milstein, p; Newell, p; Nosek, p; Pederson, p; Pena, p; Plantier, 3b; Seiler, p; Schu, of; Shields, 2b, c, p; Stankiewicz, p; S. Turner, 1b, p; Wade, 1b.

LEAGUE CHAMPIONS

Year	Team	Pct.
1884—	Trenton	.520
1885—	Syracuse	.584
1886—	Utica	.646
1887—	Toronto	.644
1888—	Syracuse	.723
1889—	Detroit	.649
1890—	Detroit	.617
1891—	Buffalo (reg. season)	.727
	Buffalo (supplem'l)	.680
1892—	Providence	.615
	Binghamton*	.667
1893—	Erie	.606
1894—	Providence	.696
1895—	Springfield	.687
1896—	Providence	.602
1897—	Syracuse	.632
1898—	Montreal	.586
1899—	Rochester	.624
1900—	Providence	.616
1901—	Rochester	.642
1902—	Toronto	.669
1903—	Jersey City	.642
1904—	Buffalo	.657
1905—	Providence	.638
1906—	Buffalo	.607
1907—	Toronto	.619
1908—	Baltimore	.593
1909—	Rochester	.596
1910—	Rochester	.601
1911—	Rochester	.645
1912—	Toronto	.595
1913—	Newark	.625
1914—	Providence	.617
1915—	Buffalo	.632
1916—	Buffalo	.586
1917—	Toronto	.604
1918—	Toronto	.693
1919—	Baltimore	.671
1920—	Baltimore	.719
1921—	Baltimore	.717
1922—	Baltimore	.689
1923—	Baltimore	.677
1924—	Baltimore	.709
1925—	Baltimore	.633
1926—	Toronto	.657
1927—	Buffalo	.667
1928—	Rochester	.549
1929—	Rochester	.613
1930—	Rochester	.629
1931—	Rochester	.601
1932—	Newark	.649

Year	Team	Pct.
1933—	Newark	.622
	Buffalo (4th)+	.494
1934—	Newark	.608
	Toronto (3rd)+	.559
1935—	Montreal	.597
	Syracuse (2nd)+	.565
1936—	Buffalo‡	.610
1937—	Newark‡	.717
1938—	Newark‡	.684
1939—	Jersey City	.582
	Rochester (2nd)+	.556
1940—	Rochester	.611
	Newark (2nd)+	.594
1941—	Newark	.649
	Montreal (2nd)+	.584
1942—	Newark	.601
	Syracuse (3rd)+	.513
1943—	Toronto	.625
	Syracuse (3rd)+	.536
1944—	Baltimore‡	.553
1945—	Montreal	.621
	Newark (2nd)+	.582
1946—	Montreal‡	.649
1947—	Jersey City	.610
	Syracuse (3rd)+	.575
1948—	Montreal‡	.614
1949—	Buffalo	.584
	Montreal (3rd)+	.545
1950—	Rochester	.609
	Baltimore (3rd)+	.556
1951—	Montreal‡	.617
1952—	Montreal	.629
	Rochester (3rd)+	.619
1953—	Rochester	.630
	Montreal (2nd)+	.586
1954—	Toronto	.630
	Syracuse (4th)§	.510
1955—	Montreal	.617
	Rochester (4th)+	.497
1956—	Toronto	.566
	Rochester (2nd)+	.553
1957—	Toronto	.575
	Buffalo (2nd)+	.571
1958—	Montreal‡	.588
1959—	Buffalo	.582
	Havana (3rd)+	.523
1960—	Toronto‡	.649
1961—	Columbus	.597
	Buffalo (3rd)+	.559
1962—	Jacksonville	.610
	Atlanta (3rd)+	.539

Year	Team	Pct.
1963—	Syracuse x	.533
	Indianapolis‡	.562
1964—	Jacksonville	.589
	Rochester (4th)+	.532
1965—	Columbus	.582
	Toronto (3rd)+	.556
1966—	Rochester	.565
	Toronto (2nd-tied)+	.558
1967—	Richmond	.574
	Toledo (3rd)+	.525
1968—	Toledo	.565
	Jacksonville (4th)+	.514
1969—	Tidewater	.563
	Syracuse (3rd)+	.536
1970—	Syracuse‡	.600
1971—	Rochester‡	.614
1972—	Louisville	.563
	Tidewater (3rd)+	.545
1973—	Charleston	.586
	Pawtucket y+	.534
1974—	Memphis	.613
	Rochester x‡	.611
1975—	Tidewater‡	.610
1976—	Rochester	.638
	Syracuse (2nd)+	.590
1977—	Pawtucket	.571
	Charleston (2nd)‡	.557
1978—	Charleston	.607
	Richmond (4th)+	.511
1979—	Columbus‡	.612
1980—	Columbus‡	.593
1981—	Columbus‡	.633
1982—	Richmond	.590
	Tidewater (3rd)+	.540
1983—	Columbus	.593
	Tidewater (4th)+	.511
1984—	Columbus	.590
	Pawtucket (4th)+	.536
1985—	Syracuse	.564
	Tidewater (4th)+	.540
1986—	Richmond‡	.571
1987—	Tidewater	.579
	Columbus+	.550
1988—	Rochester z	.546
	Tidewater	.546
1989—	Syracuse	.572
	Richmond z	.555
1990—	Rochester z	.614
	Columbus	.596
1991—	Columbus z	.590
	Pawtucket	.552

*Won split-season playoff. +Won four-team playoff. ‡Won championship and four-team playoff. §Defeated Havana in game to decide fourth place, then won four-team playoff. xLeague was divided into Northern, Southern divisions. yLeague divided into American, National divisions. zLeague divided into Eastern, Western divisions; won playoffs. (NOTE—Known as Eastern League in 1884, New York State League in 1885, International League in 1886-87, International Association in 1888, International League in 1889-90, Eastern Association in 1891 and Eastern League from 1892 until 1912.)

MEXICAN LEAGUE

FINAL STANDINGS

NORTHERN ZONE

Team	M.S.	N.L.	M.I.	Jal.	U.L.	Sal.	Mva.	S.L.	M.R.	Leo.	Cam.	Yuc.	M.T.	Cor.	Tab.	Ags.	W	L	T	Pct.	GB
Monterrey Sultans	..	8	8	8	10	12	13	10	0	0	1	3	2	1	3	3	82	38	0	.683	......
Nuevo Laredo	5	..	8	7	9	7	9	7	2	2	3	2	2	0	1	3	67	54	0	.554	15 ½
Monterrey Industrials	5	6	..	10	4	9	10	8	0	0	1	1	1	3	2	1	61	56	1	.521	19 ½
Jalisco	6	7	4	..	10	4	6	10	1	2	0	1	1	2	1	2	57	62	2	.479	24 ½
Union Laguna	4	4	10	3	..	8	8	9	1	2	1	3	0	1	1	2	57	63	1	.475	25
Saltillo	2	7	4	10	8	..	7	7	0	3	1	0	2	2	0	2	55	68	0	.447	28 ½
Monclova	1	7	4	5	6	7	..	8	0	1	0	0	2	2	3	3	49	71	1	.408	33
San Luis	4	6	6	5	5	7	5	..	3	0	1	0	2	0	2	1	47	74	0	.388	35 ½

SOUTHERN ZONE

Team	M.S.	N.L.	M.I.	Jal.	U.L.	Sal.	Mva.	S.L.	M.R.	Leo.	Cam.	Yuc.	M.T.	Cor.	Tab.	Ags.	W	L	T	Pct.	GB
Mexico City Reds	3	1	3	2	2	3	3	0	..	5	7	7	10	9	8	11	74	44	2	.627	......
Leon	3	1	3	1	1	0	2	3	7	..	11	8	6	9	7	11	73	45	2	.619	1
Campeche	2	0	2	3	2	2	3	2	6	3	..	9	7	11	9	9	70	50	1	.583	5
Yucatan	0	1	2	2	0	3	3	3	7	6	7	..	7	9	10	10	70	52	1	.574	6
Mexico City Tigers	1	1	0	2	3	1	1	1	6	7	7	7	..	6	9	10	62	56	1	.525	12
Cordoba	2	3	0	1	1	1	1	3	4	3	2	4	8	..	10	5	48	68	1	.414	25
Tabasco	0	2	1	2	1	3	0	1	5	6	5	3	4	5	..	8	46	72	1	.390	28
Aguascalientes	0	0	1	1	1	1	0	2	2	5	3	4	2	8	6	..	36	81	4	.308	37 ½

Playoffs—Monterrey Sultans defeated Jalisco, four games to one; Monterrey Industrials defeated Nuevo Laredo, four games to none; Mexico City Reds defeated Yucatan, four games to none; Leon defeated Campeche, four games to one. Monterrey Sultans defeated Monterrey Industrials, four games to two, in Northern Zone finals; Mexico City Reds defeated Leon, four games to three, in Southern Zone finals. Monterrey Sultans defeated Mexico City Reds, four games to three, in final series to capture league championship.

(Compiled by Ana Luisa Talarico, League Statistician, Mexico, D.F.)

BATTING

TEAM

Team	Avg.	G	AB	R	OR	H	TB	2B	3B	HR	RBI	SH	SF	HP	BB	Int. BB	SO	SB	CS	LOB
Mexico City Reds	.337	120	4123	891	670	1388	2247	216	26	197	823	19	32	29	430	33	605	75	22	851
Leon	.316	120	3963	760	634	1252	1982	240	38	138	697	33	31	37	442	53	522	76	44	836
Aguascalientes	.305	121	4141	760	986	1261	2012	225	35	152	675	53	35	24	422	28	535	32	17	857
Saltillo	.304	123	4069	681	704	1237	1780	222	45	77	635	52	30	44	494	42	695	91	67	943
San Luis	.302	121	3910	630	868	1179	1814	190	26	131	570	54	24	42	456	39	649	48	39	896
Union Laguna	.301	121	3982	721	757	1199	1875	202	36	134	644	49	34	41	486	47	708	45	22	911
Nuevo Laredo	.300	121	3934	707	641	1180	1813	155	17	148	648	42	40	41	451	42	503	127	49	823
Mexico City Tigers	.299	119	3944	761	688	1180	1842	184	26	142	683	53	30	46	511	32	571	42	28	868
Monterrey Sultans	.299	120	4035	744	525	1205	1889	212	23	142	676	49	48	47	506	64	651	81	42	902
Jalisco	.297	121	3974	722	750	1182	1781	202	35	109	646	46	40	43	512	44	560	106	38	871
Monclova	.294	121	3948	646	791	1160	1640	151	40	83	563	48	37	28	466	44	727	66	58	878
Cordoba	.293	117	3879	638	679	1136	1767	176	22	137	564	30	32	46	384	24	675	74	59	781
Monterrey Ind'tr'ls	.293	118	3764	572	508	1104	1538	155	18	81	511	67	30	33	394	44	556	43	33	854
Campeche	.291	121	3939	705	615	1146	1835	184	11	161	631	38	31	32	471	50	569	56	31	823
Yucatan	.291	123	4046	635	645	1176	1681	145	27	102	558	56	30	30	480	49	556	184	85	881
Tabasco	.280	119	3729	520	632	1043	1452	155	22	70	463	44	28	28	373	25	624	75	63	800

INDIVIDUAL

(Leading qualifiers for batting championship—356 or more plate appearances)

*Bats lefthanded.

Player, Team	Avg.	G	AB	R	H	TB	2B	3B	HR	RBI	SH	SF	HP	BB	Int. BB	SO	SB	CS
Renteria, Ricardo, Jalisco	.442	104	382	90	169	283	30	6	24	106	0	4	6	50	13	30	17	4
Rivera, German, Monterrey Sultans	.385	114	413	82	159	265	27	2	25	99	0	6	5	52	10	36	10	5
Stockstill, David, Union Laguna	.384	104	378	80	145	243	30	1	22	95	2	6	2	68	11	47	1	3
Steels, James, Mexico City Reds	.374	120	468	131	175	311	29	1	35	121	3	6	5	60	11	59	30	3
Diaz, Luis Fernando, Nuevo Laredo	.371	110	367	77	136	235	24	3	23	89	4	2	1	54	7	53	5	4
Shepherd, Ron, Leon	.370	99	354	97	131	263	26	2	34	98	1	1	2	55	7	70	5	1
Tillman, Rusty, Tabasco	.364	114	396	81	144	238	26	1	22	83	0	5	3	51	8	68	24	5
Garbey, Barbaro, Mexico City Tigers	.363	118	454	100	165	281	29	0	29	115	2	3	7	38	4	49	2	1
Martinez, Grimaldo, Monclova	.361	99	371	70	134	170	13	7	3	40	9	2	3	34	1	66	15	5
Garcia, Cornelio, Yucatan	.361	105	347	55	111	154	14	3	10	50	5	5	1	75	1	64	52	11

Departmental leaders: G—Five players tied with 121; AB—R. Vizcarra, 481; R—Steels, 131; H—Steels, 175; 2B—R. Vizcarra, 49; 3B—Esquer, 13; HR—Johnson, 37; RBI—See, 129; SH—R. Almodobar, Ju. Rodriguez, 14; SF—Blocker, 8; HP—Ge. Sanchez, 17; BB—Johnson, 110; IBB—Johnson, 25; SO—J. Reyes, 102; SB—Taylor, 72; CS—Taylor, 24.

(All players—listed alphabetically)

Player, Team	Avg.	G	AB	R	H	TB	2B	3B	HR	RBI	SH	SF	HP	BB	Int. BB	SO	SB	CS
Abrego, Jesus, Jalisco	.291	97	326	75	95	144	30	2	5	43	3	4	6	50	4	36	2	4
Abril, Ramon, Jalisco	.268	77	184	22	49	59	4	3	0	19	9	1	0	18	0	11	4	5
Acosta, Carlos, Tabasco	.500	1	2	0	1	0	0	0	0	0	0	0	0	0	0	0	0	0
Agamez, Miguel, Mexico City Tigers	.273	90	22	3	6	0	0	0	0	0	0	0	0	0	0	0	0	0
Aganza, Ruben, Monclova	.276	92	297	37	82	125	10	3	9	42	4	0	0	25	2	66	1	2
Agramon, Antonio, Saltillo	.320	105	347	55	111	154	27	2	4	60	5	5	7	4	28	3	63	5	3

Player, Team	Avg.	G	AB	R	H	TB	2B	3B	HR	RBI	SH	SF	HP	BB	Int. BB	SO	SB	CS
Aguilar, Enrique, San Luis	.336	118	444	71	149	231	23	1	19	82	3	5	4	42	6	47	2	1
Aguilera, Antonio, Monterrey Sultans	.306	116	471	107	144	247	17	4	26	61	3	2	8	75	13	88	25	14
Aikens, Willie, Monterrey Industrials	.299	111	361	52	108	179	14	0	19	80	0	3	4	80	16	59	2	2
Almeida, Shammar, Saltillo	.296	30	54	11	16	25	3	0	2	10	0	0	0	5	0	14	2	0
Almodobar, Francisco, Cordoba*	.149	33	47	8	7	0	0	0	0	3	3	0	0	8	0	13	0	0
Almodobar, Ricardo, Jalisco*	.243	90	189	26	45	54	5	2	0	14	14	0	4	18	0	23	9	1
Alvarez, Chris, Mexico City Tigers	.352	93	330	79	116	162	17	1	9	59	1	3	4	69	4	24	2	5
Alvarez, Hector, Mexico City Tigers	.324	92	299	54	97	153	15	1	13	52	5	1	4	29	1	38	3	1
Alvarez, Heriberto, Yucatan	.200	35	70	4	14	17	0	0	1	5	1	1	2	9	3	13	2	0
Alvarez, Juan Carlos, Jalisco	.200	30	57	8	12	16	1	0	1	6	2	0	1	6	0	10	0	0
Amador, Arturo, Nuevo Laredo	.152	22	46	5	7	0	2	0	0	2	1	1	0	2	1	7	0	0
Arce, Francisco Javier, San Luis	.309	109	360	43	111	168	17	2	12	41	3	1	4	28	1	47	0	1
Arias, Everardo, Mexico City Tigers	.264	56	163	23	43	64	5	2	4	21	6	2	2	13	0	37	0	2
Arnold, Larry, Monclova	.237	13	36	4	8	0	0	0	0	5	0	1	0	4	0	7	2	2
Arredondo, Luis, Jalisco	.319	102	335	71	107	141	10	6	4	44	4	2	5	34	2	60	28	7
Arzate, Martin, Leon	.318	109	340	59	108	145	20	1	5	45	3	3	0	33	2	29	0	2
Avila Torres, Ruben, Nuevo Laredo	.310	120	423	75	131	213	18	2	20	76	6	7	8	45	4	84	5	2
Avina, Reyes, Leon	.183	46	60	17	11	14	3	0	0	5	0	0	0	11	0	10	1	0
Baca, Manuel, Aguascalientes	.332	102	388	75	129	214	31	3	16	82	2	3	3	36	1	53	4	2
Banuelos, Fidel, Union Laguna	.233	81	160	29	37	53	6	2	2	12	1	2	3	19	3	43	9	2
Barajas, Mario, Aguascalientes	.241	75	145	25	35	51	8	1	2	14	3	1	1	11	1	21	1	1
Barandica, Juan Carlos, Cordoba	.238	62	168	27	40	49	5	2	0	10	3	1	0	13	0	26	1	5
Barrera, Jesus Antonio, Tabasco	.282	117	386	59	109	133	14	2	2	32	6	1	2	32	0	25	5	3
Barrera, Nelson, Mexico City Reds	.299	110	394	79	118	242	14	1	36	102	0	3	0	50	9	64	1	3
Becerra, Juan, Nuevo Laredo*	.167	39	90	8	15	24	3	0	2	11	1	0	1	9	0	22	0	0
Bellazetin, Jose Juan, M.C. Tigers	.283	71	180	33	51	64	7	0	2	18	1	1	2	37	3	12	1	4
Bellino, Frank, San Luis	.360	102	359	76	129	221	23	6	19	73	1	2	2	52	6	45	3	4
Beltran, Gerardo, Cordoba	.270	83	252	42	68	99	11	1	6	39	0	1	6	31	3	44	5	5
Beristain, Gregorio, Monterrey Sultans	.256	57	90	17	23	29	2	2	0	9	0	0	0	8	0	15	2	1
Birriel, Jose, Jalisco*	.292	26	72	15	21	41	8	0	4	21	0	2	1	14	2	11	0	0
Blocker, Terry, Leon	.358	112	430	85	154	251	29	7	18	106	3	8	0	47	13	60	10	4
Bocardo, Manuel, Monclova	.272	70	146	25	40	57	8	0	3	18	3	1	4	35	1	35	0	2
Brown, Todd, Yucatan	.372	24	86	19	32	52	6	1	4	20	0	2	1	12	1	12	3	4
Brummer, Jeff, Mexico City Tigers	.229	8	35	4	8	13	2	0	1	5	0	0	1	0	0	6	2	2
Burke, Norberto, Yucatan	.233	89	232	24	54	73	7	0	4	32	1	1	2	47	0	35	0	3
Bustamante, Miguel Angel, M.C. Tigers	.214	89	168	40	36	47	7	2	0	18	4	0	2	44	0	44	6	1
Camacho, Adulfo, Mexico City Tigers	.259	61	197	61	51	80	11	0	6	27	4	1	1	58	0	39	7	3
Camarero M., Rolando, Union Laguna	.269	58	182	35	49	67	7	1	3	15	4	1	3	16	0	29	0	0
Camargo, Alonso, Aguascalientes	.239	48	138	23	33	51	9	0	3	19	0	0	1	15	0	28	0	0
Cangas, Rosendo, Tabasco	.000	1	1	0	0	0	0	0	0	0	0	0	0	0	0	0	0	0
Cantu, Gerardo, Cordoba	.262	72	183	15	48	66	6	0	4	23	1	1	2	19	2	35	2	3
Carlson, Bill, San Luis*	.281	59	203	40	57	102	13	1	10	29	1	1	0	27	2	42	2	1
Carter, Denny, Monclova	.286	26	98	16	28	54	3	1	7	26	0	0	1	10	0	24	0	1
Castaneda, Aurelio, Jalisco	.000	1	1	0	0	0	0	0	0	0	0	0	0	0	0	0	0	0
Castaneda, Rafael, Mexico City Tigers	.290	94	259	37	75	98	10	2	3	36	6	3	2	39	3	45	2	4
Castelan, Miguel Angel, Monclova	.262	86	262	42	68	98	9	3	5	36	1	5	0	40	6	40	11	6
Castillo, Juan, Aguascalientes	.364	52	195	63	71	116	13	4	8	30	0	3	2	32	0	29	11	2
Castillo, Raul, Tabasco	.233	73	210	17	49	69	8	0	4	27	0	2	0	16	0	48	2	1
Castro, Eddie, Cordoba*	.317	104	319	65	101	170	9	3	18	66	2	5	6	84	14	83	2	3
Cavia, Jesus, San Luis	.257	21	35	6	9	0	1	0	2	5	1	0	0	1	0	8	0	0
Cazarin, Manuel, Leon	.321	115	439	75	141	229	26	7	16	72	3	3	3	25	3	52	4	2
Cepeda, Alejandro, Monclova	.320	10	25	4	8	0	1	0	0	2	0	0	0	2	0	3	0	1
Cervera, Francisco J., Cordoba	.302	105	328	56	99	169	19	3	15	51	5	2	9	21	0	75	10	2
Chan, Armando, Monclova	.182	14	22	2	4	0	1	0	0	3	0	0	0	1	0	7	0	1
Chavez, Heriberto, Tabasco	.264	65	140	18	37	53	5	1	3	13	5	0	3	8	0	31	2	0
Chavez, Orlando, Mont. Industrials	.364	7	11	2	4	0	0	0	0	3	0	0	0	1	0	4	0	0
Clayton, Leonardo, San Luis*	.181	41	83	6	15	18	3	0	0	9	2	2	1	13	5	12	0	1
Cole, Mike, Monterrey Industrials*	.371	70	240	61	89	110	6	3	3	37	9	2	4	41	4	20	24	9
Contreras, Cuitlahuac, Union Laguna	.239	92	242	43	58	92	16	3	4	38	1	1	2	35	5	67	1	0
Contreras, Silvano, Cordoba	.257	31	70	4	18	25	4	0	1	6	0	1	1	4	0	21	1	1
Cooper, Gary, Tabasco	.320	72	269	44	86	117	16	0	5	35	0	3	1	27	0	42	0	3
Cosey, Tim, Monclova	.241	25	83	15	20	40	3	1	5	17	0	3	2	16	2	24	0	0
Cruz, Fernando, Cordoba	.256	81	246	26	63	78	9	0	2	30	0	3	2	21	3	42	1	8
Cruz Borbon, Luis Alfonso, U. Laguna	.331	112	423	74	140	252	26	7	24	98	2	2	5	34	6	69	5	5
Cruz Galindo, Marco Antonio, N.L.	.288	32	60	9	17	18	1	0	0	6	2	1	1	4	0	10	0	0
Cueto, Raul, Tabasco	.211	14	19	2	4	0	0	0	0	0	0	0	1	0	0	7	0	0
Cuevas, Jaime, Monclova	.162	35	37	10	6	7	1	0	0	0	0	0	0	5	0	4	0	2
Daut, Manuel, Monclova	.258	89	236	32	61	79	9	0	3	30	4	2	4	15	0	51	2	1
DeAngelis, Steve, San Luis	.329	43	139	22	45	69	6	0	6	24	0	0	3	14	3	34	0	1
de los Santos, Carlos E., Cordoba	.000	3	6	0	0	0	0	0	0	0	0	0	0	0	0	1	0	0
de los Santos, Luis, Jalisco	.356	26	101	19	36	59	5	0	6	24	0	1	2	11	1	18	1	0
Diaz, Luis Fernando, Nuevo Laredo	.369	110	367	77	136	235	24	3	23	89	4	2	1	54	7	53	5	4
Diaz, Remigio, Monterrey Sultans	.262	34	122	29	32	40	6	1	0	10	2	2	1	9	1	18	2	1
Dixon, Dee, Tabasco*	.280	20	82	14	23	36	6	2	1	9	1	0	7	1	9	9	2	—
Dominguez, David, San Luis	.288	120	419	66	121	231	20	3	28	79	0	2	6	70	9	97	1	1
Dominguez, Fausto, Union Laguna	.239	73	207	23	45	52	4	0	1	14	7	1	0	4	1	45	3	0
Durham, Leon, San Luis	.158	7	23	2	5	0	1	0	0	8	0	2	0	1	0	6	0	0
Elizondo, Fernando, Aguascalientes	.306	36	144	26	44	76	11	0	7	27	5	0	0	9	0	17	0	3
Espinoza, Antonio, San Luis	.247	71	166	28	41	59	9	0	3	18	10	0	3	24	0	42	2	3
Espinoza, Javier, Mexico City Reds	.290	56	100	22	29	35	2	2	0	13	1	0	1	15	0	17	1	1
Esquer, Ramon, Leon	.337	111	418	88	141	219	25	13	9	55	8	1	6	55	3	46	23	10
Estrada, Asdrubal, Tabasco	.273	19	66	12	18	18	0	0	0	9	0	0	0	9	2	6	0	0
Estrada, Francisco, Leon	.279	75	229	23	64	77	8	1	1	36	2	1	5	24	2	12	0	2
Estrada, Hector, Mexico City Reds	.356	92	331	49	118	171	21	1	10	57	0	2	1	16	1	32	2	0
Estrada, Roberto, Mont. Industrials*	.315	102	302	46	95	123	9	5	3	29	5	0	2	23	1	29	3	5
Estrada, Ruben, Nuevo Laredo	.225	66	102	16	23	34	5	0	2	9	1	2	2	7	0	24	3	3
Fentanes, Oscar, Cordoba	.000	3	4	0	0	0	0	0	0	0	0	0	0	0	0	1	0	0
Fernandez, Daniel, Mexico City Reds	.359	111	434	101	156	199	22	3	5	55	4	5	2	59	2	40	13	2
Firova, Dan, Nuevo Laredo	.263	78	248	33	65	87	13	0	3	25	6	0	5	19	1	34	0	1
Forrester, Tom, Monclova	.292	101	359	62	105	187	15	5	19	82	0	3	1	55	14	78	1	2
Francois, Manuel, Cordoba	.347	74	271	56	94	148	18	3	10	42	2	2	1	31	1	40	12	4
Gainey, Ty, Mexico City Reds	.427	29	103	35	44	79	6	1	9	36	0	0	2	5	3	24	5	0
Garbey, Barbaro, Mexico City Tigers	.363	118	454	100	165	281	29	0	29	115	2	3	7	38	4	49	2	1
Garcia, Butch, Saltillo*	.247	26	100	17	25	39	5	0	3	14	0	2	2	8	1	16	0	2
Garcia, Carlos Miguel, San Luis	.238	64	96	24	24	31	5	1	0	9	1	0	0	12	0	23	5	2

Player, Team	Avg.	G	AB	R	H	TB	2B	3B	HR	RBI	SH	SF	HP	BB	Int. BB	SO	SB	CS
Garcia, Cornelio, Yucatan	.361	92	310	78	112	162	14	3	10	50	5	5	1	75	1	64	52	11
Garcia, Heberto, San Luis	.227	92	178	27	41	49	2	3	0	18	6	1	0	16	0	23	3	5
Garcia, Juan Manuel, Aguascalientes	.295	88	207	25	61	87	9	4	3	32	3	1	0	26	1	18	0	1
Garcia Valdez, Martin, Mont. Indus.	.270	91	227	29	61	77	10	0	2	28	9	3	3	26	2	48	4	2
Garibay, Roberto, Leon	.500	7	10	2	5	0	1	0	0	1	1	1	0	1	0	2	0	0
Garza Garza, Gerardo, Mont. Indus.	.311	111	348	48	108	133	22	0	1	43	12	3	3	21	2	34	2	2
Garzon, Eliseo, Mexico City Reds	.269	65	197	49	53	107	11	2	13	45	0	1	1	39	0	59	0	1
Garzon, Felix, Cordoba	.286	5	14	1	4	0	1	0	0	0	0	0	0	4	0	3	0	0
Gassos, Genaro, Tabasco	.186	62	113	6	21	26	2	0	1	10	0	2	0	12	1	14	1	4
Gastelum, Carlos, San Luis	.279	66	201	16	55	65	7	0	1	18	10	1	0	16	1	43	0	1
Gomez, Alejandro, Aguascalientes	.233	102	313	42	73	96	11	3	2	25	10	3	1	17	0	40	3	0
Gonzalez, Carlos, Campeche*	.188	42	64	7	12	15	3	0	0	6	4	0	0	9	0	13	0	0
Gonzalez, Jesus, Campeche	.302	121	469	60	142	173	16	0	5	43	4	2	1	36	1	29	4	2
Gonzalez, Mario A., Yucatan	.260	32	50	9	13	21	1	2	1	5	1	0	0	7	0	6	0	2
Gonzalez, Pedro, Yucatan	.250	6	16	1	4	0	1	0	2	5	0	0	0	3	0	2	0	1
Guajardo, Octavio, Mont. Industrials	1.000	1	1	0	1	0	0	0	0	0	0	0	0	0	0	0	0	0
Guerrero, Francisco, Union Laguna	.330	70	276	63	91	88	17	1	6	35	2	3	2	43	2	45	5	1
Guerrero, Jaime, Monterrey Sultans	.252	99	330	40	85	118	15	6	2	38	9	4	8	23	0	67	15	6
Guerrero, Leobardo, Leon	.314	42	105	6	33	35	2	0	0	14	1	2	0	4	1	20	3	1
Guerrero Solis, Fran. Javier, Mon. Ind.	.119	38	42	3	5	0	1	0	0	1	2	0	1	4	0	12	0	0
Gutierrez, Andres, San Luis	.261	20	23	3	7	0	2	0	0	3	0	0	0	8	0	3	2	2
Gutierrez, Arnoldo Ivan, Tabasco	.224	57	125	11	28	36	5	0	1	10	2	1	0	4	0	39	0	2
Gutierrez, Felipe, Campeche	.287	116	457	82	131	182	20	2	9	63	7	3	8	18	1	38	3	3
Gutierrez, Jose Luis, Jalisco	.246	66	187	30	46	78	8	3	6	30	4	1	4	29	0	38	1	0
Guzman, Marco Antonio, Campeche	.314	106	373	67	117	200	15	1	22	71	3	7	0	43	3	31	1	0
Guzman Lopez, Andres, Campeche	.100	5	10	0	1	0	1	0	0	2	0	0	0	1	0	2	0	0
Hernandez, Eduardo, Saltillo	.222	29	45	5	9	0	2	0	0	3	0	0	0	4	0	9	0	1
Hernandez, Juan, Jalisco	.300	14	20	2	6	0	2	0	0	4	0	0	0	3	0	5	1	0
Hernandez, Leo, Yucatan	.300	54	207	32	62	124	14	0	16	56	0	5	0	15	2	27	0	0
Hernandez, Miguel, Monterrey Sultans	.246	98	277	38	69	81	9	0	1	25	5	2	2	39	0	33	0	1
Hernandez, Rodolfo, Jalisco	.232	74	203	28	47	71	6	0	6	35	1	2	1	33	5	25	0	0
Herrera, Isidro, Campeche	.299	106	310	65	93	122	16	2	3	40	4	2	1	66	6	35	8	4
Herrera, Ricardo, Jalisco	.304	118	451	96	136	190	21	6	7	51	7	3	2	67	2	46	30	12
Herrera, Roberto, Leon	.000	1	1	1	0	0	0	0	0	0	0	0	0	0	0	0	0	0
Hinzo, Tommy, Yucatan	.330	112	451	91	149	215	18	9	10	48	2	2	10	43	6	51	61	14
Hithe, Victor, Leon	.316	56	187	36	59	83	15	0	3	31	2	1	1	35	1	34	8	7
Holman, Shawn, Nuevo Laredo	.000	1	2	0	0	0	0	0	0	0	0	0	0	0	0	0	0	0
Hurtado, Hector Hugo, Leon	.177	47	96	9	17	23	3	0	1	4	2	0	3	1	0	39	0	2
Ibarra, Jose A., Campeche*	.196	78	139	15	26	37	8	0	1	13	0	4	0	29	4	51	3	0
Infante, Kennedy, Mexico City Tigers	.294	22	85	10	25	40	3	0	4	11	1	1	1	10	0	10	0	0
Iturbe, Pedro, Cordoba	.239	71	176	35	42	59	4	5	1	17	4	0	2	20	0	41	2	2
Jarrell, Joe, Campeche	.234	32	128	18	30	50	8	0	4	20	0	0	1	4	0	23	0	1
Jimenez, Eduardo, Aguascalientes	.350	118	408	103	143	267	30	2	30	91	1	7	1	82	9	70	4	2
Jimenez, Jose Antonio, Mont. Indus.	.229	46	48	11	11	13	0	1	0	2	1	0	2	6	1	13	1	2
Jimenez, Leopoldo, Tabasco	.287	105	345	55	99	153	18	3	10	50	5	2	2	44	3	70	3	3
Johnson, Roy, Campeche	.345	119	408	115	139	274	22	1	37	98	0	5	2	110	25	38	2	1
Jurak, Ed, Mexico City Reds	.356	115	427	98	152	224	24	6	12	88	0	3	4	59	0	69	7	1
Knabenshue, Chris, Saltillo	.323	42	133	35	43	67	9	3	3	30	1	0	0	47	4	34	4	1
Landrum, Tito, Jalisco	.249	59	213	46	53	92	7	1	10	33	0	4	6	34	1	41	9	1
Lavagnino, Jose Ernesto, M.C. Tigers	.000	4	2	0	0	0	0	0	0	0	0	0	0	0	0	3	0	2
Leal, Jose Guadalupe, Mont. Sultans	.243	102	309	40	75	122	13	2	10	49	3	5	1	20	5	53	3	1
Ledezma, Victor Manuel, Leon	.333	12	15	2	5	0	0	1	0	3	0	0	0	5	0	0	0	1
Leyva, German, Monclova	.357	121	473	77	169	210	24	4	3	61	5	7	3	53	11	41	10	11
Lizarraga, Alejandro, Tabasco	.281	13	32	3	9	0	2	0	1	4	1	1	1	1	0	2	0	0
Lopez, Antonio, Cordoba	.203	18	59	8	12	21	0	0	3	8	0	0	1	3	2	5	0	0
Lopez, Gonzalo, Monclova	.305	100	315	68	96	132	13	7	3	41	7	2	1	36	0	54	8	8
Lopez, Pablo, Leon	.300	11	20	2	6	0	0	0	3	0	0	1	0	3	0	3	0	0
Lopez, Salvador, Aguascalientes	.322	97	345	75	111	192	18	6	17	50	6	1	1	29	2	32	4	2
Loredo, Jorge Luis, Campeche	.263	110	299	42	79	97	12	0	2	32	12	1	4	30	0	56	3	6
Luna, Jose Luis, Aguascalientes	.229	55	140	10	32	38	4	1	0	9	0	0	1	9	0	11	0	0
Machiria, Pablo, Mexico City Tigers	.348	114	448	90	156	271	22	6	27	95	2	2	7	32	2	48	2	0
Magana, Gabriel, Yucatan	.200	11	5	4	1	0	0	0	0	0	0	0	0	1	0	2	0	0
Marquez, Victor, Cordoba	.000	7	8	0	0	0	0	0	0	0	0	0	0	1	0	2	0	0
Marte, Alexi, Tabasco	.200	5	5	0	1	0	0	0	0	1	0	0	0	0	0	2	0	0
Martinez, Grimaldo, Monclova	.358	99	371	70	134	170	13	7	3	40	9	2	3	34	1	66	15	5
Martinez, Jesus Asencion, M.I.	.250	10	8	3	2	0	0	0	0	1	0	0	1	0	0	3	0	0
Martinez, Raul, Jalisco	.292	104	352	57	104	175	16	2	17	57	2	2	4	36	6	45	2	0
Melendez, Francisco, Cordoba*	.347	48	176	30	61	102	6	1	11	40	0	2	1	21	3	26	0	0
Mena, Evaristo, Monclova	.000	3	2	0	0	0	0	0	0	0	0	0	0	0	0	0	0	0
Mendez, Ramon, Aguascalientes	.000	7	0	0	0	0	0	0	0	0	0	0	0	0	0	0	0	0
Mercado, Felipe, Leon	1.000	7	1	1	1	0	0	0	0	0	0	0	0	0	0	0	0	0
Mere, Pedro, Nuevo Laredo	.271	107	365	55	99	160	12	2	15	57	2	2	4	38	6	59	6	2
Meza, Alfredo, Monterrey Sultans	.214	10	14	1	3	0	0	0	1	1	1	1	0	2	0	5	0	0
Michel, Domingo, Saltillo	.310	36	126	32	39	57	6	3	2	27	2	1	1	28	0	35	4	2
Micheu, Budy, Tabasco	.077	4	13	1	1	0	0	0	0	0	1	0	0	1	0	4	0	0
Minshaw, George, Mont. Indus.	.182	4	11	1	2	0	0	0	0	3	0	1	0	1	0	3	0	0
Miranda, Julio Cesar, Aguascalientes	1.000	1	1	0	1	0	0	0	0	0	0	0	0	0	0	0	0	0
Monell, John, San Luis	.356	60	236	37	84	128	19	2	7	39	2	0	1	15	0	16	9	4
Mora Ibarra, Andres, Nuevo Laredo	.293	117	413	65	121	216	11	0	28	96	1	5	3	54	2	60	0	1
Morales, Florentino, San Luis	.304	119	424	83	129	182	22	5	7	38	6	4	13	69	1	68	8	4
Morales, Manuel, Aguascalientes	.111	17	27	0	3	0	1	0	0	1	2	0	0	2	0	2	0	0
Moreno, Leonardo, Mexico City Tigers	.286	28	56	6	16	21	2	0	1	14	2	0	0	4	0	2	0	1
Moreno, Lorenzo, Mexico City Reds	.215	34	79	10	17	21	1	0	1	6	0	1	0	6	0	19	0	0
Moreno, Roberto, Monclova	.260	95	296	38	77	106	11	3	4	37	5	2	1	15	0	71	1	0
Morones, Martin, Cordoba	.305	112	433	71	132	215	23	3	18	60	5	2	3	35	1	68	10	12
Morris, Angel, Aguascalientes	.282	71	262	52	74	155	10	1	23	68	0	2	1	36	4	53	0	0
Motley, Darryl, Monterrey Sultans	.339	117	449	123	152	269	31	4	26	103	2	5	8	61	7	86	8	3
Munoz, Noe, Mexico City Reds	.200	10	15	0	3	0	0	0	0	1	0	0	0	1	0	3	0	0
Navarro, Luis Alberto, Saltillo	.000	5	4	0	0	0	0	0	0	0	0	0	0	0	0	0	0	0
Navarro, Ruben, Mont. Industrials*	.278	82	223	28	62	81	8	1	3	27	2	1	1	25	3	35	1	2
Nelson, Jerome, Saltillo	.347	50	174	39	61	88	10	1	5	22	0	2	0	41	1	17	12	5
Nelson, John, Saltillo	.143	2	7	2	1	0	0	0	0	0	0	0	0	0	0	1	0	0
Nichols, Howard, Leon*	.306	88	301	73	92	160	19	2	15	57	1	7	8	44	5	38	2	0
Noriega, Luis Antonio, Jalisco	.279	64	190	23	52	75	11	0	4	30	0	2	2	26	0	30	1	1
Noris, Rogelio, Mexico City Reds	.301	54	146	22	44	54	6	2	0	19	3	0	0	10	0	30	1	0

Player, Team	Avg.	G	AB	R	H	TB	2B	3B	HR	RBI	SH	SF	HP	BB	Int. BB	SO	SB	CS
Ortiz, Alejandro, Nuevo Laredo	.311	119	405	87	126	220	13	0	27	98	1	4	2	84	11	55	9	2
Osuna, Hector, Saltillo	.260	57	131	19	34	43	5	2	0	13	2	0	2	10	0	23	2	1
Oviedo, Rolando, Mexico City Tigers	.333	7	3	0	1	0	0	0	0	0	1	0	0	0	0	1	0	0
Pacho, Juan Jose, Yucatan	.284	119	391	72	111	130	13	3	0	30	11	1	1	45	0	38	7	8
Padget, Chris, San Luis	.326	13	51	12	16	23	2	1	1	13	0	0	0	7	3	7	0	0
Pardo, Victor Manuel, Cordoba	.182	44	88	15	16	18	2	0	0	4	2	0	0	13	0	14	0	0
Pena, Luis Alberto, Mont. Industrials*	.271	102	336	43	91	147	17	0	13	52	0	1	1	41	6	77	1	3
Peralta, Alfredo, Union Laguna	.232	18	56	5	13	17	4	0	0	9	0	1	0	4	0	15	1	0
Peralta, Amado, Saltillo	.339	102	327	57	111	181	22	6	12	75	0	4	4	56	8	68	6	2
Perez, Alfredo, Mexico City Tigers	.000	1	0	0	0	0	0	0	0	0	0	0	0	0	0	0	0	0
Perez, Francisco, Mexico City Tigers	.277	90	260	60	72	131	14	6	11	54	4	0	3	20	3	68	8	1
Perkins, Harold, Mont. Industrials*	.205	23	88	13	18	27	4	1	1	6	1	0	1	8	1	22	1	3
Perry, Jeff, Union Laguna	.000	1	0	0	0	0	0	0	0	0	1	0	0	0	0	0	0	0
Picos, Tereso, Jalisco	.000	4	3	3	1	0	0	1	0	0	0	0	0	1	0	0	0	0
Placencia, Obed, Nuevo Laredo	.291	61	172	20	51	72	6	3	3	19	4	3	2	18	2	19	0	1
Ponce, Hector, Yucatan	.289	109	391	38	113	138	11	4	2	39	4	3	1	17	0	30	15	5
Quintero, Guadalupe, Union Laguna*	.211	45	76	8	15	18	3	0	0	7	2	0	1	12	1	12	0	0
Quintero, Guillermo, Mont. Sultans	.294	8	18	5	5	0	1	0	0	1	0	1	0	2	0	6	0	0
Quintero, Victor, Saltillo	.301	58	133	19	41	54	8	1	1	22	1	0	0	16	1	12	1	1
Quiroz, Jose Julian, Mont. Industrials	.265	81	211	40	56	76	6	1	4	17	4	1	1	19	3	45	0	2
Ramirez, Enrique, Nuevo Laredo	.298	121	430	61	128	149	10	1	3	50	6	4	0	32	2	21	18	1
Ramirez, Gustavo, Monclova	.205	19	44	2	9	0	0	1	0	4	1	0	0	2	0	4	0	0
Ramos, Enrique, Monterrey Sultans	.000	3	3	1	0	0	0	0	0	0	0	0	0	0	0	1	0	0
Reid, Jessie, Union Laguna	.327	95	324	84	106	224	22	3	30	86	0	2	1	85	11	70	6	0
Renteria, Ricardo, Jalisco	.442	104	382	90	169	283	30	6	24	106	0	4	6	50	13	30	17	4
Reyes, Enrique, Aguascalientes	.308	76	201	21	62	79	9	1	2	27	6	3	4	22	0	25	0	0
Reyes, Luis, Monterrey Sultans	.305	114	423	70	129	241	32	1	26	101	3	2	3	46	11	102	2	1
Reyna, Luis, Cordoba	.311	108	392	72	122	223	23	0	26	77	0	4	1	43	5	64	20	5
Reynolds, Ron, Tabasco	.238	56	185	17	44	65	6	0	5	24	1	0	2	25	3	43	0	3
Rivera, Alberto, Jalisco	.211	38	42	8	9	0	2	0	0	6	1	0	0	5	0	13	0	0
Rivera, Eleazar, San Luis	.257	76	209	25	54	86	14	0	6	23	3	0	0	11	2	56	1	2
Rivera, German, Monterrey Sultans	.385	114	413	82	159	265	27	2	25	99	0	6	5	52	10	36	10	5
Rodriguez, Adelaido, Mont. Sultans	.263	27	54	5	13	15	2	0	0	5	0	0	0	12	1	13	0	1
Rodriguez, Cecilio, Mont. Industrials	.284	108	352	41	99	115	14	1	0	39	11	4	2	52	1	30	4	5
Rodriguez, Genaro, Aguascalientes	.335	63	221	55	74	130	11	3	13	56	0	3	2	11	2	26	2	0
Rodriguez, Guillermo, M.C. Tigers	.262	100	359	57	94	161	14	1	17	56	3	1	6	36	8	54	3	0
Rodriguez, Gustavo, Mont. Indus.*	.289	27	76	11	22	25	0	0	1	6	0	1	5	1	1	12	1	2
Rodriguez, Jose Luis, Saltillo	.309	106	311	47	96	131	21	4	2	45	5	1	6	23	2	56	5	3
Rodriguez, Juan Francisco, M.S.	.325	103	400	79	130	161	20	1	3	61	14	6	5	50	3	20	6	3
Rojas, Homar, Mexico City Tigers	.324	59	216	53	70	127	14	2	13	52	0	5	0	39	4	26	0	0
Romero, Oscar, Cordoba	.318	109	387	74	123	179	16	2	12	45	2	4	4	36	1	49	5	4
Romero Tirado, Marco A., N. Laredo	.329	83	313	75	103	168	20	0	15	64	1	4	0	29	2	33	3	4
Rubio, Marco Antonio, Leon	.333	53	132	28	44	59	4	1	3	20	4	0	2	16	1	15	1	1
Ruiz, Demetrio, Campeche	.339	24	59	10	20	27	7	0	0	10	1	0	0	6	0	1	0	1
Ruiz, Juan De Dios, Union Laguna	.308	40	146	27	45	68	9	1	4	19	2	1	2	7	0	26	2	4
Saenz, Ricardo, Saltillo*	.322	112	400	69	128	219	29	1	20	77	4	4	9	37	3	97	3	3
Saiz Aguilar, Herminio, Union Laguna	.321	115	374	60	120	166	15	5	7	53	7	1	7	47	1	64	3	2
Salazar, Leonardo, Mexico City Tigers	.216	21	37	3	8	0	0	0	0	2	1	1	0	3	0	12	0	0
Salcido, Mario, Saltillo	.217	8	23	3	5	0	0	0	1	2	0	0	0	8	0	8	0	0
Salgado, Eduardo, Nuevo Laredo	.059	7	17	3	1	0	0	0	0	0	1	0	0	1	0	5	0	1
Salinas, Luis Guillermo, Monclova	.235	28	84	6	20	25	2	0	1	11	0	1	6	4	0	18	0	0
Samaniego, Manuel, Yucatan	.223	88	274	22	61	70	1	1	2	21	7	1	0	22	1	31	3	8
Sanchez, Alejandro, Campeche	.293	115	430	81	126	259	27	2	34	115	2	6	13	26	3	87	16	2
Sanchez, Andres, Tabasco	.265	107	324	37	86	110	14	2	2	29	13	2	1	41	1	44	6	8
Sanchez, Armando, Mexico City Reds	.227	19	44	2	10	12	2	0	0	4	0	1	0	5	0	4	0	0
Sanchez, Gerardo, Nuevo Laredo	.307	121	450	98	138	221	15	1	22	78	5	6	17	59	3	41	11	3
Sanchez, Gilberto, Yucatan	.111	9	9	0	1	0	1	0	0	0	1	0	0	1	0	3	0	0
Sanchez, Martin, Mont. Indus.	.000	2	2	0	0	0	0	0	0	0	1	0	0	0	0	1	0	0
Sanchez, Orlando, Monterrey Sultans	.349	79	289	48	101	161	15	0	15	56	0	2	2	41	8	35	3	3
Sanchez, Zoilo, Tabasco	.353	6	17	0	6	0	1	0	0	2	0	0	0	4	1	1	0	0
Sandoval, Jose Luis, Mexico City Reds	.340	117	421	90	143	249	23	4	25	80	0	4	3	31	1	66	2	5
Santana, Miguel, Tabasco	.292	73	281	42	82	101	9	5	0	14	5	1	2	29	3	39	16	15
See, Larry, Mexico City Reds	.338	114	450	102	152	287	23	5	34	129	0	4	3	37	4	59	13	2
Serratos, Miguel, Campeche*	.261	24	59	4	12	17	2	0	1	6	0	1	0	2	0	13	0	0
Shaw, Teo, Union Laguna	.000	1	1	0	0	0	0	0	0	0	0	0	0	0	0	0	0	0
Shepherd, Ron, Leon	.370	99	354	97	131	263	26	2	34	98	1	1	2	55	7	70	5	1
Smith, Gregory, Saltillo	.205	20	78	6	17	21	4	0	0	9	1	0	1	5	1	10	0	1
Sommers, Jesus, Jalisco	.280	114	411	57	115	165	17	3	9	81	1	7	3	57	6	65	2	1
Soto, Carlos, San Luis	.320	72	174	21	56	91	5	0	10	29	0	1	3	18	2	25	0	2
Spagnola, Glenn, Nuevo Laredo	.000	1	1	0	0	0	0	0	0	0	0	0	0	1	0	0	0	0
Steels, James, Mexico City Reds	.374	120	468	131	175	311	29	1	35	121	3	6	5	60	11	59	30	3
Stockstill, David, Union Laguna	.384	104	378	80	145	243	30	1	22	95	2	6	2	68	11	47	1	3
Taylor, Dwight, Nuevo Laredo	.327	118	471	96	153	202	20	7	5	46	6	3	6	43	5	63	72	24
Tellez, Alonso, Monterrey Industrials	.358	118	469	83	168	265	31	3	20	77	2	3	3	23	5	39	4	4
Threadgill, George, Tabasco	.313	11	32	4	10	11	1	0	0	6	0	1	1	6	0	7	1	1
Tillman, Rusty, Tabasco	.364	114	396	81	144	238	26	1	22	83	0	5	3	51	8	68	24	5
Tiquet, Lazaro, Tabasco	.285	110	358	54	102	126	11	2	3	42	4	0	5	35	0	52	4	6
Tirado, Federico, Mexico City Tigers	.226	73	177	17	40	53	7	0	2	28	3	6	2	23	0	29	0	1
Tirado, Victor, Yucatan	.286	56	147	28	42	64	7	0	5	26	3	3	5	6	0	22	2	2
Torres, Eduardo, Saltillo	.302	115	401	74	120	204	19	7	17	80	1	1	3	66	9	51	21	19
Torres, Guillermo, Saltillo	.236	51	108	15	25	39	6	1	2	11	3	1	0	9	0	26	1	1
Torres, Raymundo, Campeche*	.229	105	354	66	81	179	8	0	30	66	0	2	8	60	2	101	11	4
Trevino, Alejandro, Monterrey Sultans	.267	36	116	20	31	46	6	0	3	21	3	4	2	19	0	14	3	2
Ulin, Sergio T., Campeche	.185	17	29	2	5	0	0	0	0	0	0	0	0	2	0	4	0	0
Uribe Moreno, Jorge, Campeche	.254	46	189	35	48	77	4	2	7	22	2	0	2	16	3	46	10	6
Uzcanga, Ali, Aguascalientes	.288	87	288	43	83	108	13	3	2	29	7	0	2	16	0	37	1	1
Valdez, Baltazar, Yucatan	.332	91	298	40	99	157	13	0	15	65	2	2	4	31	6	41	3	5
Valdez, Jesus, Jalisco	.288	113	400	65	115	175	28	1	10	67	3	6	5	37	3	69	2	3
Valdez, Luis Alberto, Aguascalientes	.340	107	365	55	124	163	20	2	5	49	7	1	1	21	0	27	0	3
Valdez C., Francisco Javier, M.I.	.333	44	57	11	19	24	2	0	1	4	2	1	0	5	1	7	0	0
Valencia, Carlos, Monterrey Sultans*	.288	93	317	52	92	135	14	1	9	49	4	4	7	25	0	42	3	1
Valenzuela, Armando, Saltillo	.337	102	419	68	141	166	15	5	0	38	7	4	9	21	0	47	21	13
Valenzuela, Eduardo, Saltillo	.324	72	187	26	60	76	10	0	2	23	2	0	1	8	0	15	0	2
Valenzuela, Horacio, Leon	.264	113	382	60	101	161	14	2	14	69	1	3	4	42	10	65	1	0
Valenzuela, Jose Luis, Aguascalientes	.220	34	59	14	13	16	3	0	0	3	0	1	0	10	0	14	1	0

Player, Team	Avg.	G	AB	R	H	TB	2B	3B	HR	RBI	SH	SF	HP	BB	Int. BB	SO	SB	CS
Valenzuela, Leonardo, Monclova	.334	121	413	87	138	200	19	2	13	67	6	3	1	71	6	60	10	6
Valle, Guadalupe, San Luis	.245	21	49	5	12	16	1	0	1	7	0	1	0	7	0	10	0	1
Valle, Jose Luis, Leon	.333	37	69	11	23	24	1	0	0	12	2	1	0	4	1	8	1	0
Valverde, Raul, Union Laguna	.309	100	376	60	117	163	15	8	5	43	6	2	1	29	0	43	1	1
Vargas, Antonio, Tabasco	.261	109	348	44	91	150	20	3	11	65	1	7	1	15	3	83	3	6
Vargas, Hediberto, Aguascalientes	.347	70	239	46	83	154	12	1	19	56	0	3	2	35	5	33	0	1
Vargas, Ignacio, Aguascalientes	1.000	9	1	2	1	0	0	0	0	0	0	0	0	0	0	0	1	0
Vargas, Trinidad, Yucatan	.254	89	213	34	54	70	6	2	2	19	7	1	0	15	0	52	5	3
Verdugo, Vincente, Mexico City Reds	.327	114	450	88	147	194	23	0	8	57	8	1	7	30	1	37	0	4
Vergara, Salvador, Leon	.000	10	4	1	0	0	0	0	0	1	0	0	0	2	0	1	0	1
Villaescusa, Fernando, Yucatan	.304	71	224	32	68	79	5	0	2	39	9	1	0	23	5	10	8	8
Villagomez, David, Campeche	.295	70	193	24	57	73	7	0	3	19	3	2	0	17	0	28	0	1
Villegas, Fernando, Saltillo	.250	8	4	3	1	0	0	0	0	0	0	0	0	0	0	2	0	0
Villela, Carlos, Monterrey Industrials	.286	111	434	73	124	173	16	6	7	65	8	5	1	31	2	57	2	0
Vizcarra, Marco A., Union Laguna	.233	84	240	39	56	70	7	2	1	22	8	2	4	28	0	26	3	0
Vizcarra, Roberto, Leon	.322	119	481	108	155	278	49	1	24	87	0	2	4	50	5	35	18	10
Vizcarra, Sergio Hugo, San Luis*	.000	4	10	1	0	0	0	0	0	0	0	0	1	0	0	1	0	0
Williams, Reggie, Monclova	.264	26	87	15	23	32	1	1	2	12	0	1	0	17	1	18	0	3
Young, Elwing, Monterrey Industrials ...	.316	12	38	5	12	16	1	0	1	4	1	0	0	6	1	9	0	0
Yuriar, Jesus, Monclova	.248	83	255	33	63	84	8	2	3	29	3	4	1	26	0	54	5	5
Zamudio, Rafael, Campeche	.333	13	15	1	5	0	2	0	1	0	0	0	1	0	0	3	0	0
Zazueta, Mauricio, Mexico City Reds	.341	55	164	35	56	94	11	0	9	24	1	1	0	12	1	40	1	1
Zulueta, Felix, Yucatan	.257	69	183	25	47	72	7	0	6	31	1	0	1	19	1	47	2	2
Zuniga, Armando, Saltillo	.260	78	197	26	51	66	5	2	2	17	2	2	1	16	1	48	1	5

The following pitchers, listed alphabetically by name, with games in parentheses, had no plate appearances, primarily through use of designated hitters:

AGUASCALIENTES—Acosta, Martin (33); Aguilar, Miguel (29); Beltran, Eleazar (1); Calderon, Jose (12); Cardenas, Benito (23); Cedeno, Vinicio (10); Cruz, Jesus (4); Espinoza, Salvador (8); Granillo, Carlos (2); Jaime Granillo, Ismael (43); Leon, Maximino (1); Lopez, Jonas (23); Medina, Gilberto (2); Neri, Braulio (44); Ojeda, Jorge (5); Padilla, Raymundo (22); Quinonez, Enrique (26); Steward, Hector (6); Toliver, Fred (12); Urrea, Leonel (28); Velazquez, Luis A. (1); Villa, Jose (8).

CAMPECHE—Browning, Mike (46); Childress, Rocky (6); Diaz, Alejandro (16); Dominguez, Herminio (13); Guzman, Gelacio (14); Hernandez, Roberto (8); Huerta, Luis Enrique (24); Lopez, Jose Ramon (27); Manzano, Fernando (27); Raygoza, Martin (26); Tejeda, Juan (23); Tinoco, Ruben (26); Toledo, Mario (21); Vazquez, Adrian (6); Velazquez, Ildefonso (24); Villegas, Ramon (38); Zamorano, Gabriel (12); Zavaleta, Marcelino (4).

CORDOBA—Cruz, Javier (28); Flores, Jose Alberto (10); Jones, Al (36); Lopez, Emigdio (26); Martinez, Victor (40); Moreno, Juan de Dios (27); Perez, Joaquin (32); Pruneda, Armando (14); Quiroz, Emanuel (5); Ramos, Emilio (2); Ruelas, Hugo (5); Salas, Ernesto (11); Sanchez, Felipe (9); Soto, Ernesto (1); Valenzuela, Saul (33); Villarreal, Antonio (16); Weber, Wes (1).

JALISCO—Carranza, Javier (30); Cervera, Vicente (8); Chadwick, Ray (4); Espizona, Rogelio (6); Ibarra, Carlos (25); Kerfeld, Charley (25); Leon, Danilo (5); Lugo, Urbano (25); Malave, Benito (25); Mojica, Hector (15); Morales, Isidro (27); Noles, Dickie (9); Romo, Manuel (16); Schwabe, Mike (18); Sosa, Victor (19); Soto, Alvaro (17); Veliz, Alberto Arturo (15).

LEON—Alvarado, Joaquin (12); Bowden, Mark (5); Cerros, Alberto (1); DeLeon, Luis (23); Diaz, Octavio (18); Duarte, Adolfo (1); Hernandez, Julio (31); Jusaino, Martin (4); Olivas, Anselmo (17); Orozco, Jaime (14); Pelcastregui, Leo (2); Purata, Julio (23); Sinohui, David (26); Soto, Fernando (27); Torres, Sotero (3); Velazquez, Israel (27); Villanueva, Luis (41).

MEXICO CITY REDS—Alvarez, Juan Carlos (14); Angulo, Julian (8); Barojas, Salome (41); Cano, Jose (4); Felix, Antonio (25); Jimenez, Saul (25); Leyva, Filiberto (22); Luevano, Juan (17); Macias, Abraham (23); Martinez, Ramon (27); Mendez, Luis Fernando (20); Mendoza, Marco Antonio (21); Moreno, Leobardo (18); Osuna, Ricardo (24); Tejeda, Felix (15).

MEXICO CITY TIGERS—Easley, Logan (24); Garcia, Juan (22); Grajales, Norberto (35); Herrera, Calixto (23); Medina, Eugenio (3); Mora, Eleazar (22); Moreno, Angel (24); Noriega, Eduardo (27); Perea, Juan Alberto (15); Puig, Eddie (15); Reyes, Jesus Manuel (23); Rios, Jesus (23); Robles, Felix (17); Rodriguez, Raul (11); Ruiz, Cecilio (24).

MONCLOVA—Arias, Daniel (29); Campos, Jorge (4); Cano, Ezequiel (24); Chavez, Guadalupe (28); Cosio, Mario Alberto (23); Espinoza, Carlos A. (19); Gracia, Anselmo (15); Murillo, Felipe (21); Normand, Guy (22); Solano, Julio (52); Valdez, Rodolfo (19); Vazquez, Florentino (10); Velazquez, Ernesto A. (35).

MONTERREY INDUSTRIALS—Clay, Danny (4); Escamilla, Sergio (24); Flores, Jose Angel (4); Garcia Garcia, Jorge Luis (23); Jimenez, Isaac (22); Jones, Odell (18); Medvin, Scott (15); Ochoa, Porfirio (53); Ontiveros, Juan (36); Serafin, Luis Antonio (4); Thompson, Richie (8); Valdez, Armando (24); Villegas, Jose Angel (24).

MONTERREY SULTANS—Acosta, Aaron (19); Alicea, Miguel (32); Garza, Alejandro (20); Gonzalez, Arturo (11); Heredia, Hector (24); Jimenez, German (20); Madrid, Alejandro (8); Osuna, Roberto (24); Sandoval, Guillermo (15); Serna, Ramon (16); Uribe, Juan Carlos (40); Valenzuela, Ramon Loreto (30); Veliz Arballo, Francisco (27).

NUEVO LAREDO—Alvarez, Juan Jesus (26); Barraza, Ernesto (29); Castillo, Luis Trinidad (6); Couch, Enrique (18); Cruz, Miguel (14); Moreno, Jesus (21); Navidad, Miguel Angel (17); Peterek, Jeff (21); Quiroz, Aaron (24); Scherrer, Bill (4); Solis, Jesus (46); Valdez, Jose Luis (34); Valenzuela, Mario (5).

SALTILLO—Alvarez, Martin (51); Barron, Avelino (37); Castellanos, Humberto (26); Castro, Rodrigo (37); Cesena, Jose Isabel (42); Garcia, Miguel (4); Garza, Adrian (9); Lara, Eddie (7); Lizarraga, Hugo (23); Mendez, Martin (8); Miranda, Pedro (1); Morrow, Ben (33); Munoz, Miguel (30); Pulido, Alfonso (27); Sanchez, Hector (39); Silva, Ramon (4); Smith, Mike (13).

SAN LUIS—Cabrales, Gabriel (26); Cazares, Juan (24); Chavarin, Jose Angel (19); Contreras, Benjamin (3); Garcia, Horacio (31); Guzman, Benjamin (43); Lopez, Raul (21); Meza, Evaristo (7); Moore, Robert (5); Ordaz, Reynaldo (8); Ortega, Alfredo (1); Pena, Ramon Arturo (57); Pulido, Antonio (35); Ramirez, Emilio (22); Rodriguez, Ignacio (27); Rodriguez, Mario (28); Sandoval, Carlos (16); Soto, Ramon Eugenio (16); Valdez, Pedro (6).

TABASCO—Camarena, Martin (22); Enriquez, Martin (49); Gonzalez, Maximino (5); Hernandez, Martin (15); Herrera, Enrique (32); Ledon, Juan Carlos (3); Navarro, Adolfo (21); Ortiz, Gregorio (13); Retes, Lorenzo (21); Romero, Juan (29); Saldana, Edgardo (23); Serafin, Hector (23); Sibate, Pedro (5); Sosa, Mario (23); Zamudio, Aurelio (8).

UNION LAGUNA—Acosta, Martin (20); Castaneda, Maximiliano (20); Cervantes, Lauro (27); Diaz Garcia, Cesar (32); Esquivias, Ruben (1); Gonzalez, Fernando (28); Medina, Carlos (1); Palafox, Juan Manuel (28); Pimentel, Roberto (7); Quintero, Victor Hugo (10); Renteria, Hilario (24); Rincon, Ricardo (24); Rios, Jose Luis (22); Talamantes, Porfirio (14); Tirado, Sebastian (16).

YUCATAN—Antunez, Martin (50); Chavez, Humberto (10); Colorado, Salvador (22); Cruz, Andres (5); Delgadillo, Gustavo (17); Dozier, Thomas (21); Esquer, Mercedes (22); Hernandez, Encarnacion (25); Lara, Gerardo (8); Montano, Francisco (22); Puerto, Carlos (21); Sombra, Francisco (31).

GRAND SLAMS—Jurak, R. Torres, 3 each; Mora, Morris, Renteria, Al. Sanchez, 2 each; Agramon, Aikens, Arce, N. Barrera, Birriel, Brown, Camacho, L.F. Diaz, D. Dominguez, H. Estrada, L. Hernandez, E. Jimenez, Johnson, G. Lopez, S. Lopez, Motley, Ortiz, Am. Peralta, F. Perez, Saiz, Ge. Sanchez, O. Sanchez, Soto, Tillman, V. Tirado, J. Valdez, H. Vargas, Villaescusa, Villagomez, Villela, 1 each.

AWARDED FIRST BASE ON CATCHER'S INTERFERENCE—M.A. Cruz (R. Martinez); F. Gutierrez (F. Cruz); S. Lopez (F. Dominguez); Mora (R. Martinez).

PITCHING

TEAM

Team	ERA	G	CG	ShO	Sv.	IP	H	R	ER	HR	HB	BB	Int. BB	SO	WP	Bk.
Monterrey Sultans	3.92	120	19	11	36	1035.2	1078	525	451	99	34	390	26	581	48	7
Monterrey Industrials	4.06	118	25	9	21	963.1	1054	508	435	84	40	372	44	634	50	5
Campeche	4.79	121	23	5	36	977.2	1133	615	520	139	35	313	28	490	34	5
Yucatan	4.83	123	26	12	29	1045.0	1191	645	561	146	25	353	31	586	43	5
Tabasco	4.93	119	19	8	23	957.2	1129	632	525	104	34	392	28	506	54	3
Leon	5.05	120	28	7	27	982.0	1149	634	551	106	35	470	30	645	61	3
Nuevo Laredo	5.10	121	18	7	26	1004.1	1084	641	569	118	45	526	31	685	76	4
Cordoba	5.38	117	26	4	14	968.0	1166	679	579	113	33	459	63	627	68	10
Mexico City Tigers	5.48	119	28	3	15	985.1	1191	688	600	154	38	437	38	641	44	2
Mexico City Reds	5.50	120	29	1	30	975.2	1099	670	596	122	33	539	22	554	76	6
Saltillo	5.55	123	10	3	28	1016.0	1248	704	626	120	38	457	46	648	56	4
Jalisco	5.65	121	18	5	19	1006.1	1280	750	632	115	41	458	30	659	65	2
Monclova	5.96	121	7	2	30	996.1	1229	791	660	120	35	532	59	649	65	2
Union Laguna	6.01	121	23	3	22	987.0	1287	757	659	129	41	421	59	632	70	4
San Luis	6.91	121	12	4	21	981.0	1285	868	753	136	43	560	59	571	60	4
Aguascalientes	8.07	121	10	2	11	1004.0	1425	986	900	199	47	599	66	598	69	5

INDIVIDUAL

(Leading qualifiers for earned-run average leadership— 106 or more innings)

*Throws lefthanded.

Pitcher, Team	W	L	Pct.	ERA	G	GS	CG	GF	ShO	Sv.	IP	H	R	ER	HR	HB	BB	Int. BB	SO	WP
Jones, Monterrey Industrials	9	4	.692	2.67	18	18	5	0	2	0	107.2	93	38	32	11	5	33	3	94	4
Garza, Monterrey Sultans	13	6	.684	2.72	20	19	4	1	1	0	129.0	110	45	39	6	4	58	2	86	4
Esquer, Yucatan	15	3	.833	3.12	22	22	7	0	4	0	153.0	148	57	53	21	3	33	1	136	5
Jimenez, Monterrey Sultans	7	3	.700	3.20	20	20	5	0	2	0	132.0	152	65	47	6	2	33	2	77	6
Lugo, Jalisco	12	7	.632	3.29	25	24	8	1	3	1	150.2	150	69	55	9	4	49	0	110	9
Acosta, Monterrey Sultans	12	3	.800	3.32	19	19	5	0	2	2	124.2	129	58	46	8	2	46	3	66	10
Moreno, Mexico City Tigers	12	4	.750	3.61	24	24	9	0	1	0	154.2	181	75	62	11	4	47	3	115	2
Lopez, Cordoba	11	7	.611	3.62	26	25	7	1	2	0	169.0	184	79	68	11	5	52	12	103	2
Garcia Garcia, Mont. Industrials..	7	7	.500	3.63	23	17	4	6	2	1	116.2	128	56	47	11	2	39	6	55	7
Osuna, Monterrey Sultans	8	4	.667	3.65	24	17	1	7	0	2	130.2	142	60	53	13	2	49	3	71	1

Departmental leaders: G—Garibay, 60; W—Palafox, 17; L—Carranza, Saldana, Veliz Arballo, 12; Pct.—Barojas, .909; GS—Cervantes, Morrow, Palafox, 26; CG—F. Gonzalez, A. Moreno, Raygoza, Je, Rios V., 9; GF—Garibay, 60; ShO—Esquer, 4; Sv.—Browning, 34; IP—Raygoza, 182.2; H—Palafox, 231; R—Carranza, 118; ER—Quinonez, 106; HR—Quinonez, 29; HB—A. Valdez, 12; BB—Felix, 114; IBB—Cervantes, 16; SO—Morrow, 144; WP—Carranza, 17.

(All pitchers—listed alphabetically)

Pitcher, Team	W	L	Pct.	ERA	G	GS	CG	GF	ShO	Sv.	IP	H	R	ER	HR	HB	BB	Int. BB	SO	WP
Acosta, Monterrey Sultans	12	3	.800	3.32	19	19	5	0	2	2	124.2	129	58	46	8	2	46	3	66	10
Acosta C., Union Laguna	1	1	.500	8.92	20	0	0	20	0	0	35.1	48	37	35	3	5	28	3	20	7
Acosta V., Aguascalientes	3	7	.300	8.68	33	11	0	22	0	0	84.1	124	99	88	16	1	66	11	42	4
Aguilar, Aguascalientes	9	9	.357	6.73	29	20	1	9	1	0	119.0	144	99	89	17	7	48	7	75	6
Alicea, Monterrey Sultans	5	5	.500	2.98	32	0	0	32	0	14	42.1	38	15	14	5	0	13	4	32	0
Alvarado, Leon	1	4	.200	10.20	12	0	0	12	0	3	15.0	20	17	17	4	1	10	0	11	1
Alvarez, Mexico City Reds	7	4	.636	4.90	14	13	6	1	0	0	82.2	87	51	45	11	4	33	2	31	2
Alvarez, Nuevo Laredo	7	5	.583	4.75	26	22	4	4	1	0	136.2	142	79	69	13	5	70	5	93	6
Alvarez, Saltillo	5	4	.556	5.05	51	4	0	47	0	0	66.2	70	42	38	6	2	35	4	45	8
Angulo, Mexico City Reds	0	0	.000	2.16	8	0	0	8	0	1	8.1	6	2	2	0	0	5	0	6	2
Antunez, Yucatan	7	2	.778	3.31	50	2	0	48	0	10	73.1	72	30	27	7	1	27	4	47	3
Arias, Monclova	4	7	.364	5.24	29	8	0	21	0	1	88.0	92	59	51	5	4	57	8	48	6
Arzate, Leon	0	0	.000	15.43	3	0	0	3	0	0	1.2	4	4	4	1	0	2	0	4	0
Barojas, Mexico City Reds	10	1	.909	2.43	41	0	0	41	0	25	77.1	60	25	21	4	2	35	4	49	2
Barraza, Nuevo Laredo	7	5	.583	4.94	29	20	1	9	1	0	123.0	125	82	67	7	7	95	3	74	7
Barron, Saltillo	4	7	.364	5.61	37	13	0	24	0	3	94.0	123	66	59	9	8	59	4	56	5
Bellino, San Luis	0	0	.000	21.60	1	0	0	1	0	0	1.2	6	6	4	0	0	2	0	1	1
Beltran, Aguascalientes	0	0	.000	0.00	1	1	0	0	0	0	1.0	1	0	0	0	0	1	0	0	0
Birriel, Monterrey Sultans	0	0	.000	0.00	1	1	0	0	0	0	2.1	1	0	0	0	0	3	0	1	1
Bowden, Leon	0	1	.000	9.95	5	0	0	5	0	0	6.1	9	7	7	0	0	1	0	3	1
Browning, Campeche	3	4	.429	1.48	46	0	0	46	0	34	72.2	51	13	12	1	3	10	2	39	1
Cabrales, San Luis	4	10	.286	6.87	26	22	2	4	0	1	115.1	153	97	88	15	7	57	9	57	4
Calderon, Aguascalientes	1	4	.200	7.18	12	4	0	8	0	0	31.1	34	29	25	9	0	29	5	19	2
Camarena, Tabasco	7	8	.467	5.11	22	21	3	1	2	0	123.1	133	84	70	21	6	35	0	58	3
Campos, Monclova	0	0	.000	31.50	4	0	0	4	0	0	2.0	7	7	7	0	1	5	2	0	0
Cano, Monclova	6	9	.400	6.24	24	23	2	1	0	0	132.2	171	111	92	19	9	42	4	95	7
Cano, Mexico City Reds	3	0	1.000	6.18	4	4	1	0	0	0	27.2	35	20	19	3	1	12	1	16	2
Cardenas, Aguascalientes*	0	2	.000	5.92	23	3	0	20	0	0	62.2	76	44	41	7	5	29	1	23	5
Carranza, Jalisco*	7	12	.368	6.19	30	25	3	5	1	0	148.1	183	118	102	21	5	82	4	123	17
Castaneda, Jalisco	4	11	.267	6.06	27	21	2	6	0	0	117.0	165	94	79	9	9	56	1	63	7
Castaneda, Union Laguna	1	2	.333	7.97	20	0	0	20	0	0	35.0	59	34	31	4	1	15	4	20	1
Castaneda, Mexico City Tigers	0	0	.000	0.00	1	0	0	1	0	0	2.0	4	1	0	1	0	0	0	1	0
Castellanos, Saltillo	7	11	.389	5.05	26	25	2	1	0	0	146.0	172	96	82	19	3	46	5	111	0
Castillo, Nuevo Laredo	0	2	.000	6.30	6	1	0	5	0	1	10.0	15	8	7	1	2	7	1	4	4
Castro, Saltillo	3	4	.429	3.99	37	9	1	28	0	0	88.0	95	53	39	8	7	35	6	45	10
Cazares, San Luis	8	5	.615	5.46	24	13	2	11	1	0	86.1	95	62	53	6	4	54	1	38	6
Cedeno, Aguascalientes	0	6	.143	8.86	10	9	1	1	0	0	41.2	60	47	41	10	0	36	1	21	3
Cerros, Leon	0	0	.....		1	0	0	1	0	0	0.0	1	1	0	0	0	1	0	0	1
Cervantes, Union Laguna	12	10	.545	4.53	27	26	6	1	0	0	151.0	164	98	76	23	3	59	16	97	10
Cervera, Jalisco	0	0	.000	6.08	8	0	0	8	0	0	13.1	18	11	9	2	0	11	0	5	0
Cesena, Saltillo	8	4	.667	6.04	42	2	0	40	0	10	53.2	59	38	36	4	5	45	8	53	6
Chadwick, Jalisco	0	2	.000	6.75	4	3	0	1	0	0	14.2	14	12	11	1	0	13	0	14	0
Chavarin, San Luis*	1	0	1.000	7.03	19	0	0	19	0	0	32.0	39	31	25	4	0	15	1	16	6
Chavez, Monclova*	5	4	.556	7.41	28	8	0	20	0	0	75.1	101	69	62	12	5	37	6	62	3
Chevez, Yucatan	0	0	.000	6.00	10	0	0	10	0	0	11.0	16	9	6	1	0	7	0	5	1
Childress, Campeche	2	3	.400	6.23	6	6	0	0	0	0	26.0	36	20	18	6	0	5	1	11	2

Pitcher, Team	W	L	Pct.	ERA	G	GS	CG	GF	ShO	Sv.	IP	H	R	ER	HR	HB	BB	Int. BB	SO	WP
Clay, Monterrey Industrials	1	3	.250	5.96	4	4	1	0	0	0	22.2	25	16	15	3	1	13	0	12	1
Colorado, Yucatan	9	8	.529	5.18	22	22	6	0	2	0	144.1	171	96	83	23	3	18	2	49	0
Contreras, San Luis	0	0	.000	10.80	3	0	0	3	0	0	1.2	3	3	2	0	0	0	0	2	0
Cosio, Monclova	2	7	.222	7.55	23	13	1	10	0	0	87.2	131	87	73	12	2	49	10	36	7
Couch, Nuevo Laredo	1	6	.143	6.34	18	8	3	10	0	1	55.1	67	44	39	12	1	33	1	28	4
Cruz, Yucatan	1	1	.500	4.50	5	5	1	0	1	0	30.0	30	17	15	4	1	11	0	14	4
Cruz, Cordoba	3	6	.333	7.27	28	10	1	18	0	0	91.2	122	80	74	14	0	54	3	54	13
Cruz, Aguascalientes	0	0	.000	9.45	4	0	0	4	0	0	7.1	12	8	7	2	0	1	0	5	4
Cruz, Nuevo Laredo	1	1	.500	5.82	14	1	0	13	0	1	23.0	30	17	14	4	1	19	0	11	1
DeLeon, Leon*	2	1	.667	6.29	23	0	0	23	0	6	24.1	29	19	17	1	0	7	2	20	1
Delgadillo, Yucatan*	2	0	1.000	8.44	17	2	1	15	0	0	43.0	58	41	40	7	1	14	2	7	1
Diaz, Campeche	1	2	.333	4.37	16	1	0	15	0	0	22.2	30	19	11	4	2	4	0	12	0
Diaz, Leon*	3	0	1.000	5.50	18	2	1	16	0	0	37.2	42	24	23	5	1	18	0	24	1
Diaz Garcia, Union Laguna	1	4	.200	6.61	32	2	0	30	0	7	49.0	57	40	35	11	0	25	5	36	3
Dominguez, Campeche	7	4	.636	3.92	13	13	3	0	2	0	82.2	90	42	36	6	1	22	1	33	2
Dozier, Yucatan	11	8	.579	4.23	21	21	8	0	2	0	151.0	138	79	71	21	2	47	1	98	7
Duarte, Leon	0	0	.000	0.00	0	0	0	0	0	0	0.0	0	0	0	0	0	0	0	0	0
Easley, Mexico City Tigers	4	4	.500	7.05	24	3	1	21	0	7	44.2	54	37	35	8	0	12	3	30	2
Enriquez, Tabasco	5	6	.455	3.50	49	0	0	49	0	14	60.2	58	27	25	3	5	33	9	39	10
Escamilla, Mont. Industrials	2	5	.286	4.24	24	5	1	19	0	0	68.0	64	36	32	10	2	27	2	44	4
Espinoza, Monclova	2	3	.400	6.99	19	4	0	15	0	0	46.0	68	44	38	9	1	24	3	25	2
Espinoza, Jalisco	0	0	.000	19.29	6	1	0	6	0	0	5.2	12	12	10	1	0	4	0	2	0
Espinoza, Aguascalientes	0	1	.000	15.43	8	1	0	7	0	0	7.0	15	13	12	2	0	10	1	1	0
Esquer, Yucatan	15	3	.833	3.12	22	22	7	0	4	0	153.0	148	57	53	21	3	33	1	136	5
Esquivias, Union Laguna	0	0	.000	94.50	1	0	0	1	0	0	0.1	5	5	5	0	0	0	0	0	0
Felix, Mexico City Reds	11	7	.611	6.16	25	23	6	2	1	1	125.2	125	93	86	13	3	114	2	93	14
Flores, Mont. Industrials	0	0	.000	4.11	4	0	0	4	0	0	3.0	5	1	1	0	0	2	0	0	1
Flores R., Cordoba*	0	0	.000	23.63	10	0	0	10	0	0	11.1	21	19	16	8	1	8	2	5	3
Forrester, Monclova	0	2	.000	18.00	3	0	0	3	0	1	1.0	1	4	2	0	1	4	0	0	0
Garcia, San Luis	0	3	.000	9.41	31	1	0	30	0	0	58.2	93	71	61	15	6	58	4	43	11
Garcia, Jalisco	0	1	.000	11.81	10	0	0	10	0	0	5.1	14	9	7	1	0	3	0	3	1
Garcia, Mexico City Tigers	9	5	.643	4.99	22	19	4	3	0	0	122.2	128	77	68	24	8	61	6	66	4
Garcia, Saltillo	2	2	.000	9.00	4	3	0	1	0	0	15.0	22	18	15	4	0	12	0	11	3
Garcia Garcia, Mont. Industrials	7	7	.500	3.63	23	17	4	6	2	1	116.2	128	56	47	11	2	39	6	55	7
Garibay, Yucatan	8	5	.615	3.07	60	0	0	60	0	16	84.0	86	42	29	4	3	51	10	44	6
Garza, Saltillo	0	0	.000	3.52	9	0	0	9	0	0	7.2	6	3	3	0	0	8	0	6	1
Garza, Monterrey Sultans	13	6	.684	2.72	20	19	4	1	1	0	129.0	110	45	39	6	4	58	2	86	4
Gonzalez, Monterrey Sultans	4	3	.571	3.32	11	11	0	0	0	0	62.1	73	32	23	7	2	19	2	31	4
Gonzalez, Union Laguna*	9	11	.450	4.99	28	25	9	3	0	0	168.2	203	111	94	18	3	49	7	138	8
Gonzalez, Yucatan	0	0	.000	22.50	2	0	0	2	0	0	2.0	6	5	5	1	0	1	0	1	1
Gonzalez, Tabasco	0	0	.000	13.50	5	0	0	5	0	0	8.0	19	12	12	1	0	3	0	3	0
Gracia, Monclova	0	0	.000	5.28	15	0	0	15	0	0	29.0	38	19	17	2	1	15	1	18	4
Grajales, Mexico City Tigers	4	4	.500	7.14	35	2	0	33	0	2	63.1	97	67	50	12	1	32	2	38	5
Granillo, Aguascalientes	0	0	.000	10.13	2	2	0	0	0	0	5.1	11	7	6	1	0	5	0	3	0
Guajardo, Monterrey Industrials	0	0	.000	4.66	12	1	0	11	0	0	16.2	20	10	9	1	2	14	0	9	1
Guzman, San Luis	6	5	.545	7.52	43	2	0	41	0	1	73.1	110	78	61	13	7	49	7	33	3
Guzman Z., Campeche	1	0	1.000	11.74	14	0	0	14	0	0	7.2	15	11	10	2	0	6	0	4	1
Heredia, Monterrey Sultans	8	3	.727	2.34	24	9	4	15	2	10	88.1	83	26	23	4	1	16	1	49	3
Hernandez, Yucatan	7	11	.389	5.43	25	21	3	4	0	0	127.2	171	89	76	18	2	42	4	56	4
Hernandez, Leon	3	4	.429	4.68	31	9	2	22	2	4	83.1	99	51	44	3	1	56	1	55	7
Hernandez, Tabasco*	2	6	.250	8.13	15	11	0	4	0	0	58.2	87	55	51	11	0	15	3	44	7
Hernandez, Campeche	0	0	.000	8.76	8	1	0	7	0	0	12.1	15	16	12	2	2	6	0	2	2
Herrera, Mexico City Tigers	2	5	.286	6.75	23	2	0	21	0	1	46.0	64	37	35	9	0	31	4	40	6
Herrera, Tabasco	2	2	.500	3.97	32	0	0	32	0	2	47.1	58	31	23	7	4	24	1	34	9
Herrera, Leon	7	3	.700	4.53	57	0	0	57	0	10	97.1	112	61	50	12	5	49	10	60	11
Holman, Nuevo Laredo	3	2	.600	1.73	9	3	0	6	0	0	26.0	14	7	5	0	1	14	2	16	1
Huerta, Campeche	10	11	.476	3.96	24	23	4	1	0	0	145.1	154	84	64	16	4	45	5	78	3
Ibarra, Jalisco*	1	1	.500	9.71	25	6	0	19	0	0	59.1	104	68	64	18	2	21	3	29	6
Iturbe, Cordoba	0	0	.000	3.86	2	0	0	2	0	0	2.1	0	1	1	0	0	4	0	3	1
Jaime Granillo, Aguascalientes*	5	5	.500	8.51	43	5	0	38	0	0	75.2	126	80	70	4	4	31	7	31	1
Jimenez, Monterrey Sultans*	7	3	.700	3.20	20	20	5	0	2	0	132.0	152	65	47	6	2	33	2	77	6
Jimenez, Monterrey Industrials	7	9	.438	4.31	22	22	3	0	2	0	121.0	131	69	58	10	4	68	3	78	6
Jimenez, Mexico City Reds	6	0	1.000	4.24	25	0	0	25	0	0	46.2	47	28	20	3	3	32	0	27	2
Jones, Cordoba*	6	7	.462	2.86	36	8	4	28	0	7	94.0	78	39	30	5	3	39	6	97	4
Jones, Monterrey Industrials	9	4	.692	2.67	18	18	5	0	2	0	107.2	93	38	32	11	5	33	4	94	4
Jurak, Mexico City Reds	0	0	.000	3.86	2	0	0	2	0	0	2.1	1	1	1	0	0	3	0	0	0
Jusaino, Leon	1	0	1.000	2.57	4	0	0	4	0	0	7.0	5	2	2	1	0	3	1	7	0
Kerfeld, Jalisco	5	2	.714	0.97	25	0	0	25	0	10	46.1	28	9	5	0	1	13	1	62	4
Lara, Saltillo	0	0	.000	17.05	7	1	0	6	0	0	6.1	8	12	12	0	1	12	0	4	0
Lara, Yucatan	0	0	.000	9.53	8	0	0	8	0	0	11.1	17	16	12	3	0	13	0	6	0
Ledon, Tabasco	0	0	.000	11.57	3	0	0	3	0	0	4.2	11	7	6	2	0	3	0	2	0
Leon, Jalisco	0	2	.000	13.86	5	5	0	0	0	0	12.1	18	19	19	1	1	19	0	8	2
Leon, Aguascalientes	0	0	.000	0.00	1	1	0	0	0	0	2.0	4	1	0	0	2	1	2	0	0
Leyva, Mexico City Reds	0	1	.000	16.10	12	0	0	12	0	1	17.1	29	32	31	8	2	20	1	6	5
Lizarraga, Saltillo*	1	6	.143	9.77	23	12	0	11	0	0	72.0	109	80	76	13	1	55	3	45	3
Lopez, Cordoba	11	7	.611	3.57	26	25	7	1	2	0	169.0	184	79	68	11	5	52	12	103	3
Lopez, Campeche	2	2	.500	6.23	27	0	0	27	0	1	43.0	38	32	28	8	0	15	0	21	1
Lopez, San Luis*	7	8	.467	6.16	21	21	3	0	0	0	107.2	139	72	70	13	0	43	2	72	3
Lopez J., Aguascalientes	2	6	.250	9.40	23	8	2	15	0	0	59.1	89	67	62	9	3	29	3	35	2
Luevano, Mexico City Reds	5	1	.833	5.77	17	3	0	14	0	0	43.2	71	30	28	4	2	18	2	19	3
Lugo, Jalisco	12	7	.632	3.29	25	24	8	1	3	1	150.2	150	69	55	9	4	49	0	110	9
Macias, Mexico City Reds	0	0	.000	6.28	23	0	0	23	0	0	43.0	46	31	30	11	4	33	4	23	8
Madrid, Monterrey Sultans	3	2	.600	6.60	8	7	1	0	0	0	45.0	61	36	33	6	2	12	0	13	0
Malave, Jalisco	3	2	.600	3.15	25	1	0	24	0	7	40.0	46	29	17	1	3	29	3	46	3
Manzano, Campeche	0	0	.000	2.45	2	0	0	2	0	0	3.2	2	1	1	0	0	2	0	2	0
Martinez, Mexico City Reds	7	8	.467	6.31	27	20	4	7	0	1	108.1	127	90	76	12	2	73	0	61	12
Martinez, Cordoba	2	2	.500	3.46	40	0	0	40	0	2	26.0	30	11	10	3	2	10	3	12	5
Medina, Union Laguna	0	0	.000	0.00	1	0	0	1	0	0	0.1	2	2	2	0	0	0	0	0	0
Medina, Mexico City Tigers	0	2	.000	16.20	3	0	0	3	0	0	5.0	12	9	9	0	0	7	2	2	3
Medina, Aguascalientes	0	1	.000	23.63	2	1	0	1	0	0	2.2	6	7	7	2	0	3	0	1	0
Medvin, Monterrey Industrials	4	3	.571	4.73	15	4	1	11	1	1	45.2	52	28	24	3	3	20	4	46	1
Mena, Monclova	1	1	.500	8.90	29	1	0	28	0	0	59.2	82	65	59	8	7	53	3	32	14
Mendez, Mexico City Reds	8	8	.500	5.59	20	20	6	0	0	0	125.2	159	84	78	21	2	30	2	74	2
Mendez, Saltillo	2	0	1.000	6.17	8	1	0	8	0	0	11.2	15	9	8	2	1	5	0	10	4
Mendoza, Mexico City Reds	3	3	.500	4.68	21	1	0	20	0	1	32.2	28	20	17	2	2	31	0	37	3

Pitcher, Team	W	L	Pct.	ERA	G	GS	CG	GF	ShO	Sv.	IP	H	R	ER	HR	HB	BB	Int. BB	SO	WP
Meza, San Luis	1	0	1.000	1.08	7	1	0	6	0	0	16.2	14	4	2	1	0	12	1	9	1
Miranda, Aguascalientes	6	8	.429	5.70	55	1	1	54	0	8	79.1	94	57	50	10	5	52	12	81	5
Miranda, Saltillo	0	0	.000	.....	1	0	0	1	0	0	0.0	1	2	2	0	0	1	0	0	0
Mojica, Jalisco	1	1	.500	6.43	15	0	0	15	0	0	28.0	34	21	20	2	1	18	0	18	3
Montano, Yucatan	6	8	.429	5.24	22	21	0	1	0	0	122.0	143	85	71	15	5	64	4	82	5
Moore, San Luis	1	2	.333	8.83	5	4	2	1	0	0	17.1	22	18	17	3	1	10	2	8	1
Mora, Mexico City Tigers	3	2	.600	6.64	22	7	0	15	0	1	42.0	51	32	31	3	3	23	3	34	1
Morales, Jalisco*	3	1	.750	5.26	27	9	0	18	0	0	77.0	86	50	45	13	0	38	1	39	4
Moreno, Mexico City Tigers	12	4	.750	3.61	24	24	9	0	1	0	154.2	181	75	62	11	4	47	3	115	2
Moreno, Nuevo Laredo	8	5	.615	4.93	21	21	7	0	1	0	131.1	144	75	72	15	5	35	1	86	3
Moreno, Cordoba	4	2	.667	4.40	27	4	3	23	0	0	74.2	86	46	37	9	6	34	3	22	2
Moreno, Mexico City Reds	3	0	1.000	3.80	18	2	0	16	0	0	47.1	52	24	20	4	1	21	1	38	7
Morrow, Saltillo*	9	8	.529	5.19	33	26	4	7	1	1	157.1	184	100	87	11	2	62	3	144	5
Munoz, Saltillo	3	10	.231	6.91	30	17	3	13	0	3	109.1	160	95	84	16	1	34	6	52	0
Murillo, Monclova	3	6	.333	7.04	21	14	0	7	0	0	69.2	94	69	55	12	2	34	2	26	1
Navarro, Tabasco*	4	8	.333	5.45	21	20	2	1	0	0	109.0	125	71	66	12	3	53	1	67	8
Navidad, Nuevo Laredo	0	0	.000	6.21	17	0	0	17	0	0	37.2	41	29	26	4	2	25	3	20	0
Neri, Aguascalientes	0	1	.000	9.50	44	4	0	40	0	0	54.0	81	61	57	15	8	42	0	29	9
Noles, Jalisco	3	5	.375	8.16	9	7	2	2	0	0	32.0	50	35	29	2	4	7	0	12	0
Noriega, Mexico City Tigers	3	4	.429	6.35	27	4	0	23	0	2	62.1	74	53	44	12	7	48	3	34	8
Normand, Monclova	8	8	.500	4.32	22	22	2	0	0	0	118.2	127	72	57	11	1	73	3	91	5
Ochoa, Monterrey Industrials	7	4	.636	2.57	53	1	0	52	0	16	91.2	89	37	26	9	1	20	5	61	4
Ojeda, Aguascalientes	1	2	.333	5.84	5	4	0	1	0	0	24.2	24	18	16	4	2	17	1	8	3
Olivas, Leon	1	0	1.000	5.73	17	0	0	17	0	0	21.2	31	17	14	2	0	16	2	12	4
Ontiveros, Mont. Industrials*	4	3	.571	3.49	36	0	0	36	0	2	59.0	58	30	23	6	1	17	3	33	1
Ordaz, San Luis	2	0	1.000	12.19	8	0	0	8	0	0	10.1	16	16	14	1	1	15	3	3	1
Orozco, Leon	6	3	.667	4.43	14	14	4	0	1	0	89.1	118	53	44	15	0	17	1	36	1
Ortega, San Luis	0	0	.000	0.00	0	0	0	0	0	0	0.0	0	0	0	0	0	0	0	0	0
Ortiz, Tabasco*	1	1	.500	11.85	13	1	0	12	0	0	13.2	22	19	18	2	1	17	0	5	6
Osuna, Mexico City Reds	9	9	.500	5.87	24	24	6	0	0	0	130.1	149	94	85	19	5	53	3	51	8
Osuna, Monterrey Sultans	8	4	.667	3.65	24	17	1	7	0	2	130.2	142	60	53	13	2	49	3	71	1
Padilla, Aguascalientes*	0	1	.000	8.58	22	0	0	22	0	0	35.2	56	39	34	16	3	17	1	13	0
Palafox, Union Laguna	17	4	.810	5.63	28	26	8	2	1	0	164.2	231	117	103	15	11	46	4	84	8
Pelcastregui, Monterrey Sultans	0	0	.000	0.00	2	0	0	2	0	0	1.1	2	0	0	0	0	1	0	0	0
Pena, San Luis	5	6	.455	4.97	57	0	0	57	0	19	82.0	100	52	42	11	2	18	7	62	3
Perea, Mexico City Tigers	2	1	.667	6.52	15	0	0	15	0	0	29.0	33	22	21	7	3	15	2	9	5
Perez, Cordoba*	3	4	.429	6.09	32	2	0	30	0	2	68.0	85	55	46	14	2	43	4	28	2
Perry, Union Laguna	8	9	.471	3.82	54	5	3	49	0	14	122.2	128	59	52	8	4	56	7	105	11
Peterek, Nuevo Laredo	9	6	.600	5.37	21	19	3	2	1	0	119.0	144	77	71	18	1	42	0	100	8
Pimentel, Union Laguna	1	1	.500	3.12	7	0	0	7	0	0	16.1	21	7	5	1	1	4	0	12	0
Pruneda, Cordoba*	1	6	.143	7.29	14	11	0	3	0	0	47.2	61	47	37	7	1	38	1	21	5
Puerto, Yucatan	1	1	.500	6.60	21	0	0	21	0	1	43.2	62	33	32	10	2	8	1	11	1
Pulg, Mexico City Tigers	4	3	.571	5.30	15	3	1	12	0	1	37.1	47	27	22	2	1	15	1	27	1
Pulido, Saltillo	9	9	.500	5.05	27	24	3	3	0	0	132.0	164	79	74	18	1	31	3	59	2
Pulido, San Luis*	3	8	.273	5.20	35	0	0	35	0	8	45.0	52	35	29	6	2	20	8	31	1
Purata, Leon	12	5	.706	5.70	23	23	2	0	0	0	120.0	145	88	76	8	2	69	1	75	7
Quinonez, Aguascalientes	5	11	.313	8.30	26	23	2	3	0	0	115.0	175	112	106	29	7	55	1	62	5
Quintero V., Union Laguna	0	3	.000	5.83	10	5	0	5	0	0	29.1	29	20	19	6	2	16	2	13	2
Quiroz, Nuevo Laredo	13	7	.650	5.59	24	24	0	0	0	0	132.0	154	89	82	25	8	58	1	94	15
Quiroz, Cordoba	0	1	.000	16.71	5	1	0	4	0	0	7.0	16	14	13	2	1	4	0	4	4
Quiroz, Mont. Industrials	1	2	.333	2.92	19	0	0	19	0	1	12.1	8	5	4	1	0	10	3	10	0
Ramirez, San Luis	0	3	.000	6.59	22	3	1	19	0	0	27.1	34	22	20	9	0	17	2	25	3
Ramos, Cordoba	0	1	.000	12.15	2	1	0	1	0	0	6.2	9	9	9	1	1	8	0	3	3
Raygoza, Campeche	16	7	.696	3.70	26	25	9	1	0	0	182.2	190	93	75	24	5	58	2	108	13
Renteria, Union Laguna	5	10	.333	7.20	24	23	3	1	1	0	104.1	167	91	84	14	3	25	7	61	4
Retes, Tabasco	0	8	.000	5.35	21	9	0	12	0	2	65.1	73	42	39	9	5	29	0	41	2
Reyes, Mexico City Tigers*	1	3	.250	8.18	16	5	1	11	0	1	44.0	81	44	40	13	0	19	2	11	0
Rincon, Union Laguna	2	8	.200	6.75	32	9	0	23	0	1	74.1	99	60	54	12	2	48	3	66	7
Rios V., Mex. City Tigers	10	8	.556	4.36	23	23	9	0	2	0	152.2	154	82	74	22	1	52	6	128	1
Rios V., Union Laguna	0	1	.000	6.30	22	0	0	22	0	0	50.0	66	42	35	4	3	23	4	13	4
Robles, Mexico City Tigers	1	2	.333	4.76	17	1	0	16	0	0	39.1	38	23	21	7	2	28	0	17	2
I. Rodriguez, San Luis*	2	8	.200	7.47	27	18	0	9	0	0	93.1	109	91	78	8	5	67	4	53	6
M. Rodriguez, San Luis*	3	7	.300	5.81	28	13	1	15	0	0	96.1	122	69	63	13	7	38	8	54	3
Rodriguez, Mex. City Tigers	1	3	.250	6.38	11	9	2	2	0	0	46.0	71	42	34	13	2	15	0	23	1
Romero, Tabasco	3	2	.600	5.46	29	1	0	28	0	0	64.1	73	52	39	8	2	39	4	32	5
Romo, Jalisco	0	2	.000	5.81	16	0	0	16	0	0	26.1	31	20	17	3	1	13	4	13	2
Ruelas, Cordoba	1	1	.500	9.00	5	0	0	5	0	0	10.0	13	11	10	0	1	9	0	4	0
Ruiz, Mexico City Tigers	7	9	.438	5.63	24	22	2	2	0	0	131.0	166	92	82	21	6	48	3	73	2
Salas, Cordoba	2	1	1.000	7.36	11	0	0	11	0	0	18.1	27	16	15	2	2	9	1	13	1
Saldana, Tabasco	7	12	.368	4.29	23	22	8	1	0	0	136.1	157	74	65	11	2	47	2	64	8
Sanchez, Cordoba	2	0	1.000	3.60	9	0	0	9	0	0	16.2	25	8	8	3	1	11	3	8	0
Sanchez, Saltillo	4	3	.571	5.27	39	2	0	37	0	1	71.2	88	43	42	6	1	17	2	29	2
Sanchez, Mont. Industrials*	5	4	.556	6.31	43	3	0	40	0	3	73.1	93	59	51	8	1	44	8	54	15
Sandoval, San Luis	0	0	.000	1.69	6	0	0	6	0	0	5.1	3	1	1	0	0	6	1	1	0
Sandoval, Monterrey Sultans	4	2	.667	4.97	15	8	2	7	0	2	67.0	76	39	37	10	2	21	3	43	4
Scherrer, Nuevo Laredo	1	0	1.000	3.86	4	0	0	4	0	1	4.2	3	2	2	0	0	5	0	3	1
Schwabe, Jalisco	9	5	.643	4.20	18	13	2	5	0	0	94.1	115	54	44	4	2	16	1	59	9
Serafin, Tabasco*	1	7	.125	5.76	23	8	0	15	0	2	59.1	81	52	38	10	2	24	1	36	2
Serafin, Mont. Industrials	0	0	.000	27.00	4	0	0	4	0	0	3.0	13	10	9	2	0	3	0	5	0
Serna, Monterrey Sultans	2	2	.500	6.64	16	6	0	10	0	1	39.1	42	33	29	5	1	20	0	26	2
Shaw, Union Laguna	5	5	.500	4.93	11	10	1	1	0	0	49.1	57	41	27	6	3	26	4	23	4
Sibate, Tabasco	0	0	.000	4.50	5	0	0	5	0	0	8.0	9	4	4	0	2	4	1	2	0
Silva, Saltillo	0	0	.000	3.18	4	0	0	4	0	1	5.2	10	2	2	0	0	1	0	4	0
Sinohui, Leon	11	4	.733	5.66	26	24	4	2	0	0	146.1	178	107	92	19	8	69	2	92	13
Smith, Saltillo	4	3	.571	5.25	13	10	0	3	0	1	58.1	73	38	34	8	0	41	0	50	10
Solano, Monclova	7	9	.467	2.90	52	0	0	52	0	25	88.2	83	38	29	2	1	30	6	86	7
Solis, Nuevo Laredo	9	4	.692	4.92	46	1	0	45	0	10	75.1	64	45	41	9	8	53	9	61	5
Sombra, Yucatan*	2	4	.333	7.16	31	6	0	25	0	3	43.2	66	45	35	7	1	20	3	26	3
Sosa, Tabasco	9	8	.529	4.45	23	22	3	1	2	0	119.1	140	69	61	10	6	52	0	59	1
Sosa, Jalisco	2	0	1.000	7.99	19	0	0	19	0	0	23.2	30	23	22	4	0	19	6	11	0
Soto, Jalisco	4	3	.571	5.70	17	8	1	9	0	0	60.1	87	45	38	7	2	20	2	35	1
Soto, Cordoba	0	0	.000	3.86	1	0	0	1	0	0	1.0	1	1	1	1	0	1	0	0	0
Soto, Leon	11	11	.500	4.48	27	23	7	4	0	0	154.2	181	88	77	15	7	67	6	103	3
Soto, San Luis	1	1	.500	10.65	16	0	0	16	0	0	23.2	36	28	28	8	1	15	1	17	2
Spagnola, Nuevo Laredo	6	5	.545	2.90	32	0	0	32	0	11	62.0	52	28	20	1	1	25	2	70	7

MEXICAN LEAGUE

CLASS AAA

MEXICAN LEAGUE

Pitcher, Team	W	L	Pct.	ERA	G	GS	CG	GF	ShO	Sv.	IP	H	R	ER	HR	HB	BB	Int. BB	SO	WP
Steward, Aguascalientes	0	0	.000	10.80	6	0	0	6	0	0	6.2	11	8	8	0	0	10	3	5	2
Talamantes, Union Laguna	0	1	.000	8.03	14	0	0	14	0	0	12.1	18	13	11	1	0	9	1	14	2
Tejeda, Mexico City Reds	2	2	.500	5.57	15	10	0	5	0	0	53.2	70	39	33	7	0	22	0	22	1
Tejeda, Campeche	0	5	.000	8.74	23	8	0	15	0	0	45.2	76	48	44	12	1	21	3	20	2
Thompson, Mont. Industrials	2	5	.286	3.42	8	7	2	1	1	1	47.1	53	21	18	2	3	7	2	23	1
Tinoco, Campeche	8	2	.800	5.06	26	12	0	14	0	0	85.1	107	56	48	7	3	25	3	35	3
Tirado, Union Laguna	1	1	.500	8.37	16	5	0	11	0	0	33.1	48	33	31	4	1	19	3	22	0
Toledo, Campeche	2	0	1.000	6.28	21	0	0	21	0	0	14.1	19	11	10	0	2	10	1	11	0
Toliver, Aguascalientes	4	5	.444	5.97	12	11	2	1	0	0	69.1	90	49	46	11	2	42	4	47	4
Torres, Leon	0	0	.000	19.29	3	1	0	2	0	0	2.1	8	6	5	0	0	2	0	0	1
Uribe, Monterrey Sultans	6	2	.750	3.76	40	1	0	39	0	6	52.2	53	28	22	6	7	23	3	23	3
Urrea, Aguascalientes*	1	5	.167	8.47	28	1	0	27	0	1	62.2	105	69	59	13	3	19	2	39	1
Valdez, Mont. Industrials	12	9	.571	3.99	26	25	7	1	1	0	149.0	162	74	66	11	12	48	4	101	7
Valdez, Nuevo Laredo	1	5	.167	7.11	34	0	0	34	0	1	62.0	83	54	49	8	2	38	2	25	10
Valdez, San Luis	0	2	.000	5.93	6	2	0	4	0	0	13.2	12	11	9	1	0	10	0	9	3
Valdez, Monclova*	7	8	.467	6.08	19	17	1	2	0	0	96.1	112	77	66	13	1	50	4	66	3
Valenzuela, Nuevo Laredo	1	1	.500	7.11	5	1	0	4	0	0	6.1	6	5	5	1	1	7	1	3	4
Valenzuela, Mont. Sultans	7	1	.875	3.80	34	0	0	34	0	1	83.0	77	39	36	9	5	32	3	38	3
Valenzuela, Cordoba	0	7	.000	6.75	33	5	0	28	0	1	46.2	63	44	35	6	2	31	9	28	7
Vargas, Aguascalientes	2	1	.667	8.49	29	2	0	27	0	0	53.0	70	51	50	12	2	30	3	34	2
Vasquez, Campeche	1	1	.500	5.88	6	6	0	0	0	0	26.0	30	17	17	4	2	10	2	20	1
Vazquez, Monclova	0	2	.000	0.00	10	8	0	2	0	0	29.1	39	25	19	4	1	22	2	19	3
Velazquez, Monclova	4	3	.571	4.23	35	0	0	35	0	0	70.2	78	50	34	9	1	37	7	37	4
Velazquez, Campeche	13	6	.684	5.01	24	24	7	0	1	0	161.2	195	103	90	28	9	45	2	62	1
Velazquez, Leon	12	6	.667	4.27	27	24	8	3	2	1	147.2	151	81	70	15	7	66	2	113	5
Velazquez, Aguascalientes	0	0	.000	16.20	1	1	0	0	0	0	1.2	3	3	3	0	0	3	0	1	3
Velez, Jalisco	0	1	.000	13.06	15	2	0	13	0	0	20.2	37	33	31	5	1	28	0	10	5
Veliz Arballo, Mont. Sultans*	4	12	.250	7.98	27	18	3	9	1	0	93.2	129	99	83	12	5	53	4	63	5
Villa, Aguascalientes	1	0	1.000	6.19	8	0	0	8	0	1	16.0	19	11	11	2	1	13	1	12	2
Villanueva, Leon	2	1	.667	1.14	41	0	0	41	0	2	23.2	20	5	4	0	3	7	1	22	0
Villarreal, Cordoba*	3	5	.375	6.14	16	12	1	4	0	0	70.1	100	55	48	11	2	44	5	30	7
Villegas, Mont. Industrials	4	2	.667	6.35	24	10	1	14	0	0	66.2	100	51	47	5	1	26	4	37	3
Villegas, Campeche*	6	11	.353	6.79	38	6	0	32	0	1	85.0	115	61	53	22	4	28	11	43	1
Weber, Cordoba	0	1	.000	7.71	1	1	0	0	0	0	2.1	4	4	2	2	0	2	0	1	0
Zamorano, Campeche	0	1	.000	7.80	12	0	0	12	0	0	15.0	21	14	12	6	0	7	1	6	1
Zamudio, Tabasco	2	3	.400	6.43	8	8	0	0	0	0	35.0	40	32	25	5	0	22	0	13	2
Zavaleta, Campeche	0	1	.000	3.00	4	0	0	4	0	0	6.0	5	3	2	1	0	3	0	3	0
Zulueta, Yucatan	0	0	.000	.....	1	0	0	1	0	0	0.0	3	4	4	0	0	2	0	0	1

BALKS—R. Martinez, 4; F. Gonzalez, Rincon, R.L. Valenzuela, 3 each; J.J. Alvarez, Camarena, J. Cruz, Esquer, Neri, Pruneda, 2 each; Acosta C., M. Alvarez, Antunez, Castro, Cazares, Clay, A. Cruz, Juan Garcia, Garcia Garcia, Al. Garza, E. Hernandez, J. Hernandez, E. Herrera, Huerta, Jaime Granillo, I. Jimenez, Kerfeld, Lara, Lizarraga, E. Lopez, J.R. Lopez, Macias, Mena, L.F. Mendez, Mora, Ju. Moreno, Murillo, Navidad, Ontiveros, Ortiz, Ro. Osuna, Pena, Perez, Peterek, J.J. Quiroz, Raygoza, Reyes, Serafin, R.E. Soto, Toledo, Torres, Uribe, Urrea, Veliz Arballo, Villanueva, Zamorano, 1 each.

COMBINATION SHUTOUTS—Jaime Granillo-Aguilar, Aguascalientes; Childress-Toledo-Browning, Tinoco-R. Villegas, Campeche; E. Lopez-F. Gonzalez, Cordoba; Schwabe-V. Sosa, Jalisco; Orozco-Alvarado, Is. Velazquez-DeLeon-R. Herrera, Leon; Normand-Solano, F. Vazquez-Solano, Monclova; O. Jones-Ochoa, Monterrey Industrials; Acosta-Alicea, Al. Garza-Alicea, Al. Garza-Heredia, Al. Garza-Uribe-Alicea, Navarro-Uribe-Alicea, Monterrey Sultans; Barraza-Solis, Peterek-Spagnola, A. Quiroz-Scherrer-Solis, Nuevo Laredo; Barron-Jones, Castro-Barron, Castro-Castellanos, Saltillo; Cabrales-B. Guzman-Pena, R. Lopez-Cazares-Pena, San Luis; Jimenez-Enriquez, M. Sosa-Enriquez, Zamudio-Max. Gonzalez, Tabasco; Rincon-Perry, Union Laguna; Dozier-Garibay, Esquer-Garibay, Montano-Antunez, Yucatan.

NO-HIT GAME—Felix, Mexico City Reds, defeated Monterrey Sultans, 7-0, June 5.

FIELDING

TEAM

Team	Pct.	G	PO	A	E	DP	PB	Team	Pct.	G	PO	A	E	DP	PB
Yucatan	.976	123	3135	1287	107	97	11	Union Laguna	.971	121	2961	1287	128	110	15
Monterrey Sultans	.975	120	3107	1265	112	130	12	Mexico City Tigers	.970	119	2956	1135	125	125	14
Leon	.973	120	2946	1332	117	119	16	Monterrey Industrials	.967	118	2890	1242	141	121	14
Saltillo	.972	123	3048	1346	127	126	17	Jalisco	.967	121	3019	1374	152	118	8
Aguascalientes	.972	121	3012	1332	126	143	12	San Luis	.966	121	2943	1325	148	153	24
Mexico City Reds	.971	120	2927	1221	123	120	12	Cordoba	.965	117	2904	1148	146	112	23
Nuevo Laredo	.971	121	3013	1260	127	129	24	Campeche	.965	121	2933	1295	153	130	11
Tabasco	.971	119	2873	1179	121	104	24	Monclova	.962	121	2989	1166	165	113	17

Triple plays—Mexico City Reds, Monclova, Monterrey Industrials, Nuevo Laredo, Saltillo.

INDIVIDUAL

FIRST BASEMEN

Player, Team	Pct.	G	PO	A	E	DP	Player, Team	Pct.	G	PO	A	E	DP
Cruz Borbon, Union Laguna	1.000	11	96	4	0	5	Sanchez, Monterrey Sultans	.990	77	666	41	7	77
Contreras, Cordoba	1.000	11	66	4	0	5	Hernandez, Jalisco	.990	11	88	9	1	7
Rivera, Monterrey Sultans	1.000	12	103	1	0	10	Rodriguez, Mex. C. Tigers	.989	95	783	55	9	76
Rubio, Leon	1.000	10	33	1	0	2	Valverde, Union Laguna	.989	22	173	7	2	13
Garcia, Yucatan	1.000	12	108	6	0	7	Hernandez, Yucatan	.989	10	85	5	1	4
Morris, Aguascalientes	.998	52	438	42	1	56	Castro, Tabasco	.989	89	750	35	9	77
Valdez, Yucatan	.997	74	630	47	2	65	Clayton, San Luis	.988	23	157	12	2	21
Cooper, Tabasco	.997	66	561	43	2	45	Vargas, Tabasco	.988	20	156	3	2	15
Zulueta, Yucatan	.996	36	267	14	1	19	Quiroz, Monterrey Industrials	.987	65	435	37	6	47
Peralta, Saltillo	.995	23	188	10	1	16	Ibarra, Campeche	.987	54	370	20	5	43
Valenzuela, Leon	.995	106	889	41	5	98	Villagomez, Campeche	.987	22	147	8	2	19
Tillman, Tabasco	.994	19	165	8	1	18	Garbey, Mexico City Tigers	.987	17	141	10	2	23
Birriel, Jalisco	.994	21	158	14	1	21	Soto, San Luis	.987	11	71	4	1	14
Avila Torres, Union Laguna	.994	72	630	54	4	67	de los Santos, Jalisco	.987	23	196	29	3	21
Romero Tirado, Nuevo Laredo	.993	80	661	56	5	73	Diaz, Nuevo Laredo	.987	36	281	16	4	28
Arce, San Luis	.993	89	765	73	6	83	Rodriguez, Aguascalientes	.986	29	192	16	3	31
Valdez, Jalisco	.992	39	314	40	3	26	Reyna, Cordoba	.986	26	192	12	3	20
Sommers, Jalisco	.991	44	409	46	4	35	Camargo, Aguascalientes	.985	34	248	12	4	27
Almeida, Saltillo	.991	14	96	11	1	17	Michel, Saltillo	.985	36	307	16	5	34
							Melendez, Cordoba	.984	47	399	31	7	43
							Aganza, Monclova	.984	70	495	43	9	48

Player, Team	Pct.	G	PO	A	E	DP
Carlson, San Luis	.983	41	326	21	6	36
Forrester, Monclova	.983	43	381	19	7	38
Lopez, Cordoba	.982	10	106	6	2	10
Jurak, Mexico City Reds	.982	114	991	69	19	106
Sanchez, Campeche	.982	17	157	4	3	20
Pena, Monterrey Industrials	.977	95	785	29	19	85
Arnold, Monclova	.964	10	74	7	3	8

(Fewer Than Ten Games)

Player, Team	Pct.	G	PO	A	E	DP
Peralta, Union Laguna	1.000	2	13	1	0	1
Padget, San Luis	1.000	8	63	4	0	4
Durham, San Luis	1.000	2	10	2	0	0
Salinas, Monclova	1.000	3	24	0	0	4
Navarro, Mont. Industrials	1.000	6	19	2	0	0
Valdez C., Monterrey Industrials	1.000	2	4	0	0	1
Jimenez, Mont. Industrials	1.000	6	15	0	0	1
Beltran, Cordoba	1.000	2	16	1	0	0
Cantu, Cordoba	1.000	1	4	0	0	0
Trevino, Monterrey Sultans	1.000	4	24	1	0	1
Vargas, Aguascalientes	1.000	4	22	4	0	3
Garcia, Aguascalientes	1.000	3	26	0	0	2
Mora Ibarra, Nuevo Laredo	1.000	8	73	4	0	8
Estrada, Nuevo Laredo	1.000	3	8	0	0	1
Alvarez, Mexico City Tigers	1.000	8	34	0	0	2
Steels, Mexico City Reds	1.000	6	31	1	0	4
Barrera, Mexico City Reds	1.000	2	3	0	0	1
Nichols, Leon	1.000	9	80	6	0	11
Cazarin, Leon	1.000	1	5	0	0	0
Arzate, Leon	1.000	3	11	0	0	2
Vergara, Leon	1.000	7	21	2	0	1
Burke, Yucatan	1.000	3	11	1	0	2
Villaescusa, Yucatan	1.000	7	36	2	0	2
Osuna, Saltillo	1.000	5	31	1	0	1
Zuniga, Saltillo	1.000	2	18	0	0	1
Guzman, Campeche	1.000	6	33	2	0	5
Jimenez, Tabasco	1.000	1	1	0	0	0
Gassos, Tabasco	1.000	2	10	2	0	1
Reynolds, Tabasco	1.000	6	32	2	0	3
Estrada, Tabasco	1.000	4	36	3	0	7
Castillo, Tabasco	1.000	3	21	0	0	2
Garcia, Saltillo	.988	9	75	7	1	9
Garzon, Cordoba	.979	5	42	4	1	6
See, Mexico City Reds	.972	6	34	1	1	4
Agamez, Mexico City Tigers	.958	3	22	1	1	3
Bellino, San Luis	.955	7	37	5	2	0
Jarrell, Campeche	.952	8	58	2	3	7
Lopez, Leon	.920	8	45	1	4	0
Aikens, Monterrey Industrials	.917	2	8	3	1	0
Espinoza, Mexico City Tigers	.900	2	8	1	1	0
Amador, Nuevo Laredo	.875	2	7	0	1	2
Chan, Monclova	.857	5	6	0	1	1
Gutierrez, Union Laguna	.750	2	5	1	2	3

Triple plays—Aganza, Jurak, Quiroz, Romero Tirado.

SECOND BASEMEN

Player, Team	Pct.	G	PO	A	E	DP
Ruiz, Union Laguna	1.000	10	20	23	0	7
Zuniga, Saltillo	1.000	16	16	21	0	4
Castaneda, Mex. City Tigers	.994	38	84	95	1	29
Barandica, Cordoba	.988	40	69	92	2	18
Diaz, Monterrey Sultans	.988	17	32	47	1	7
Uzcanga, Aguascalientes	.982	18	26	30	1	6
Contreras, Union Laguna	.982	64	113	164	5	24
Gonzalez, Campeche	.981	121	273	363	12	100
Zazueta, Mexico City Reds	.981	29	44	57	2	11
Sanchez, Mexico City Reds	.980	12	25	25	1	7
Villela, Monterrey Industrials	.979	109	285	286	12	85
Lopez, Monclova	.979	23	40	54	2	10
Valdez, Aguascalientes	.979	98	231	280	11	29
Pardo, Cordoba	.979	30	29	63	2	13
Rodriguez, Mont. Sultans	.978	102	222	259	11	79
Wong, Saltillo	.977	117	234	312	13	85
Barrera, Tabasco	.974	116	281	284	15	63
Esquer, Leon	.972	111	274	346	18	89
Mere, Nuevo Laredo	.970	107	246	306	17	85
Verdugo, Mexico City Reds	.969	93	174	230	13	65
Vargas, Yucatan	.969	14	36	26	2	7
Hinzo, Yucatan	.969	112	238	317	18	67
Vizcarra, Union Laguna	.967	45	87	120	7	30
Herrera, Jalisco	.966	31	73	71	5	13
Camacho, Mexico City Tigers	.965	59	127	124	9	35
Martinez, Monclova	.964	96	216	266	18	63
Morales, San Luis	.962	119	278	324	24	74
Abril, Jalisco	.961	70	145	176	13	45
Noriega, Jalisco	.955	33	75	93	8	14
Arias, Mexico City Tigers	.955	19	45	60	5	13
Francois, Cordoba	.951	73	151	177	17	50
Estrada, Nuevo Laredo	.949	16	32	24	3	3
Barajas, Aguascalientes	.942	40	54	59	7	15
Camarero M., Union Laguna	.924	26	31	42	6	7

(Fewer Than Ten Games)

Player, Team	Pct.	G	PO	A	E	DP
Peralta, Union Laguna	1.000	1	1	1	0	1
Gutierrez, San Luis	1.000	6	6	8	0	2
Rodriguez, Monclova	1.000	2	4	1	0	0
Rodriguez, Mont. Industrials	1.000	4	17	7	0	1
Garcia Valdez, Mont. Industrials	1.000	1	1	0	0	0
Guerrero Solis, Mont. Industrials	1.000	9	9	22	0	2
Chavez, Monterrey Industrials	1.000	2	0	3	0	0
Almodobar, Mont. Sultans	1.000	3	1	1	0	0
Beristain, Monterrey Sultans	1.000	7	9	10	0	0
Quintero, Monterrey Sultans	1.000	2	3	3	0	0
Hernandez, Jalisco	1.000	1	1	0	0	0
Castillo, Aguascalientes	1.000	3	5	10	0	1
Sanchez, Nuevo Laredo	1.000	4	4	1	0	0
Salgado, Nuevo Laredo	1.000	2	5	3	0	1
Garbey, Mexico City Tigers	1.000	2	3	1	0	1
Perez, Mexico City Tigers	1.000	1	2	0	0	0
Infante, Mexico City Tigers	1.000	1	0	1	0	0
Valle, Leon	1.000	2	4	3	0	0
Avina, Leon	1.000	7	11	6	0	2
Villaescusa, Yucatan	1.000	2	2	7	0	1
Magana, Yucatan	1.000	5	2	4	0	1
Hernandez, Saltillo	1.000	1	1	0	0	0
Gonzalez, Campeche	1.000	3	3	5	0	1
Loredo, Campeche	1.000	1	1	3	0	0
Chavez, Tabasco	1.000	5	7	9	0	2
Sanchez, Tabasco	.964	9	10	17	1	2
Vizcarra, Leon	.953	8	19	22	2	4
Rivera, Jalisco	.952	8	9	11	1	2
Leyva, Monclova	.914	7	17	15	3	3
Barrera, Mexico City Reds	.800	1	3	1	1	0
Sandoval, Mexico City Reds	.750	4	0	3	1	0
Jurak, Mexico City Reds	.750	1	2	1	1	1
Mercado, Jalisco	.714	4	3	2	2	1

Triple plays—Martinez, Mere, Verdugo, Villela, Wong.

THIRD BASEMEN

Player, Team	Pct.	G	PO	A	E	DP
Rivera, Jalisco	1.000	13	5	11	0	1
Estrada, Nuevo Laredo	1.000	12	6	4	0	3
Castaneda, Mex. City Tigers	.967	48	28	60	3	4
Renteria, Jalisco	.962	103	68	210	11	20
Aguilar, San Luis	.959	118	79	228	13	19
Cazarin, Leon	.958	95	62	215	12	20
Sanchez, Tabasco	.957	13	7	15	1	0
Rodriguez, Mont. Industrials	.953	62	50	114	8	15
Vargas, Tabasco	.952	10	5	15	1	2
Jimenez, Tabasco	.949	94	67	173	13	16
Uzcanga, Aguascalientes	.949	52	34	95	7	13
Saiz Aguilar, Union Laguna	.946	114	81	202	16	16
Beristain, Monterrey Sultans	.943	26	9	24	2	5
Garcia Valdez, Mont. Industrials	.940	28	19	44	4	7
Elizondo, Aguascalientes	.940	32	29	80	7	11
Noriega, Jalisco	.939	12	6	25	2	1
Ortiz, Nuevo Laredo	.938	116	88	199	19	20
Rivera, Monterrey Sultans	.938	109	84	218	20	22
Hernandez, Yucatan	.938	18	19	26	3	2
Barrera, Mexico City Reds	.934	107	96	174	19	16
Rubio, Leon	.934	32	18	53	5	2
Leyva, Monclova	.934	115	127	212	24	22
Vargas, Yucatan	.933	56	38	102	10	5
Quintero, Saltillo	.933	14	4	10	1	1
Zuniga, Saltillo	.932	32	15	54	5	2
Romero, Cordoba	.925	109	77	182	21	18
Serratos, Monterrey Industrials	.925	23	15	34	4	1
Burke, Yucatan	.923	67	43	124	14	10
Infante, Mexico City Tigers	.922	18	12	47	5	1
Peralta, Saltillo	.918	84	76	137	19	15
Garbey, Mexico City Tigers	.909	67	46	113	16	13
Loredo, Campeche	.907	105	84	209	30	27
Ulin, Campeche	.895	17	6	11	2	1
Castillo, Aguascalientes	.880	40	35	75	15	0
Verdugo, Mexico City Reds	.879	11	8	28	5	3
Serratos, Campeche	.878	16	8	28	5	3
Contreras, Union Laguna	.824	14	7	7	3	2
Jarrell, Campeche	.786	16	6	27	9	3

(Fewer Than Ten Games)

Player, Team	Pct.	G	PO	A	E	DP
Cruz Borbon, Union Laguna	1.000	3	1	4	0	0
Aganza, Monclova	1.000	2	1	2	0	0
Valdez C., Monterrey Industrials	1.000	6	2	7	0	1
Pardo, Cordoba	1.000	1	0	1	0	1
Fentanes, Cordoba	1.000	1	0	1	0	1
Trevino, Monterrey Sultans	1.000	2	1	1	0	0
See, Mexico City Reds	1.000	3	1	4	0	0
Jurak, Mexico City Reds	1.000	2	3	0	0	0
Zazueta, Mexico City Reds	1.000	1	0	1	0	0
Guerrero, Leon	1.000	1	0	4	0	0
Villaescusa, Yucatan	1.000	1	0	3	0	0
Sanchez, Yucatan	1.000	4	2	2	0	0

Player, Team	Pct.	G	PO	A	E	DP
Quintero, Saltillo	1.000	2	3	4	0	2
Valenzuela, Saltillo	1.000	1	1	0	0	0
Estrada, Tabasco	.944	6	4	13	1	0
Chavez, Monterrey Industrials	.900	5	3	6	1	1
Hernandez, Saltillo	.867	9	2	11	2	1
Cepeda, Monclova	.857	7	8	10	3	2
Valencia, Cordoba	.857	3	2	4	1	1
Barajas, Aguascalientes	.833	4	1	4	1	0
Romero Tirado, Nuevo Laredo	.833	3	3	7	2	0
Gonzalez, Campeche	.833	9	5	5	2	2
Ruiz, Union Laguna	.818	4	1	8	2	0
Arce, San Luis	.800	3	2	2	1	0
Rodriguez, Mex. City Tigers	.800	4	0	4	1	0
Almodobar, Mont. Sultans	.750	5	0	3	1	1
Picos, Jalisco	.600	5	3	0	2	0
Carlson, Campeche	.571	1	0	4	3	0
Vizcarra, Leon	.400	1	1	1	3	1

Triple plays—Barrera, Leyva, Ortiz, Peralta, Rodriguez.

SHORTSTOPS

Player, Team	Pct.	G	PO	A	E	DP
Gomez, Aguascalientes	.979	98	151	320	10	81
Guerrero, Union Laguna	.979	69	132	233	8	54
Valdez, Aguascalientes	.977	16	12	30	1	4
Zuniga, Saltillo	.973	24	35	72	3	12
Bustamante, Mexico City Tigers	.972	62	87	118	6	27
Uzcanga, Aguascalientes	.971	13	14	20	1	5
Ramirez, Nuevo Laredo	.970	121	221	362	18	79
Pacho, Yucatan	.968	119	194	351	18	69
Valle, Cordoba	.966	24	17	39	2	7
Diaz, Monterrey Sultans	.963	18	27	51	3	9
Valenzuela, Saltillo	.958	101	189	360	24	86
Vizcarra, Leon	.957	111	184	349	24	82
Sandoval, Mexico City Reds	.957	109	208	323	24	81
Garcia, San Luis	.954	82	114	216	16	51
Guerrero, Monterrey Sultans	.951	97	207	281	25	71
Chavez, Tabasco	.951	52	76	97	9	27
Sanchez, Tabasco	.948	91	123	244	20	38
Gonzalez, Campeche	.946	21	16	54	4	12
Cervera, Cordoba	.942	104	190	267	28	56
Gutierrez, Campeche	.942	115	181	338	32	80
Lopez, Monclova	.941	43	61	82	9	18
Barandica, Cordoba	.937	21	22	37	4	5
Herrera, Jalisco	.936	95	148	246	27	47
Rodriguez, Mont. Industrials	.934	46	68	145	15	31
Moreno, Monclova	.933	94	159	232	28	51
Ruiz, Union Laguna	.932	25	47	63	8	14
Garcia Valdez, Mont. Industrials	.931	59	79	136	16	23
Valle, San Luis	.929	20	25	40	5	5
Morales, Aguascalientes	.929	13	16	23	3	4
Hernandez, Saltillo	.929	11	5	21	2	2
Vizcarra, Union Laguna	.927	31	50	89	11	9
Magana, Yucatan	.925	11	12	25	3	3
Almodobar, Jalisco	.922	84	103	191	25	34
Young, Monterrey Industrials	.920	11	13	33	4	11
Arias, Mexico City Tigers	.918	35	58	76	12	20
Garcia, San Luis	.894	48	51	75	15	18
Guerrero Solis, Mont. Industrials	.872	23	15	26	6	3

(Fewer Than Ten Games)

Player, Team	Pct.	G	PO	A	E	DP
Aguilar, San Luis	1.000	1	2	1	0	0
Leyva, Monclova	1.000	1	0	1	0	0
Almodobar, Cordoba	1.000	1	0	1	0	0
Estrada, Nuevo Laredo	1.000	5	2	1	0	0
Beristain, Monterrey Sultans	.958	8	9	14	1	3
Camacho, Mexico City Tigers	.950	7	6	13	1	4
Loredo, Campeche	.950	6	8	11	1	2
de los Santos, Cordoba	.917	3	1	10	1	1
Quintero, Monterrey Sultans	.900	3	3	6	1	0
Zazueta, Mexico City Reds	.857	2	2	4	1	1
Vizcarra, San Luis	.769	3	2	8	3	0
Saiz Aguilar, Union Laguna	.750	1	1	2	1	1

OUTFIELDERS

Player, Team	Pct.	G	PO	A	E	DP
Stockstill, Union Laguna	1.000	88	139	13	0	1
Salinas, Monclova	1.000	11	11	0	0	0
Tellez, Monterrey Industrials	1.000	118	227	9	0	2
Trevino, Monterrey Sultans	1.000	15	24	0	0	1
Rodriguez, Monterrey Sultans	1.000	23	25	2	0	1
Bellazetin, Mexico City Tigers	1.000	21	26	0	0	0
Moreno, Mexico City Reds	1.000	14	8	0	0	0
Avina, San Luis	1.000	10	2	0	0	0
Alvarez, Yucatan	1.000	14	9	0	0	0
Gonzalez, Yucatan	1.000	13	10	1	0	0
Ponce, Yucatan	1.000	107	232	11	0	0
Machiria, Mexico City Tigers	.995	113	176	7	1	3
Shepherd, Leon	.993	92	136	7	1	0
Motley, Monterrey Sultans	.990	117	200	8	2	1
Sanchez, Nuevo Laredo	.990	119	203	5	2	1
Fernandez, Mexico City Reds	.989	111	257	5	3	0
Leal, Monterrey Sultans	.988	99	152	9	2	2
Valenzuela, Monclova	.987	120	220	5	3	1
Knabenshue, Saltillo	.987	41	72	3	1	1
Morones, Cordoba	.987	48	73	1	1	0
Navarro, Mont. Industrials	.986	54	69	2	1	2
See, Mexico City Reds	.986	96	130	9	2	1
Iturbe, Cordoba	.984	60	121	3	2	1
Noris, Mexico City Reds	.984	40	57	4	1	0
Tillman, Saltillo	.984	58	115	7	2	0
Dominguez, San Luis	.984	120	174	6	3	0
Blocker, Leon	.982	111	212	5	4	0
Herrera, Campeche	.982	99	156	4	3	0
Cole, Monterrey Industrials	.980	69	88	11	2	4
Villagomez, Campeche	.980	28	46	2	1	1
Steels, Mexico City Reds	.979	111	174	14	4	1
Garcia, Yucatan	.978	80	130	6	3	0
Aguilera, Monterrey Sultans	.978	116	261	7	6	1
Lopez, Aguascalientes	.977	90	205	8	5	1
Agramon, Saltillo	.977	92	154	13	4	1
Torres, Campeche	.976	109	198	6	5	1
Baca, Aguascalientes	.976	101	186	14	5	3
Alvarez, Mexico City Tigers	.976	54	79	1	2	0
Cruz Borbon, Union Laguna	.975	101	187	11	5	0
Placencia, Nuevo Laredo	.975	49	79	0	2	0
Castelan, Monclova	.973	61	107	0	3	0
Espinoza, Mexico City Tigers	.972	28	33	2	1	0
Sanchez, Campeche	.972	98	190	15	6	7
Taylor, Nuevo Laredo	.971	118	228	9	7	0
Alvarez, Mexico City Tigers	.970	81	159	4	5	0
Beltran, Cordoba	.970	77	121	7	4	1
Jimenez, Aguascalientes	.970	108	179	12	6	1
Torres, Saltillo	.969	112	210	10	7	0
Wright, Yucatan	.968	118	258	17	9	0
Nelson, Saltillo	.968	50	88	3	3	0
Moreno, Mexico City Tigers	.968	17	27	3	1	2
Estrada, Mont. Industrials	.966	83	105	7	4	0
Rodriguez, Aguascalientes	.966	18	27	1	1	0
Bellino, San Luis	.965	84	133	6	5	0
Arredondo, Jalisco	.965	99	187	7	7	0
Arzate, Leon	.965	93	106	4	4	0
Saenz, Saltillo	.963	104	202	7	8	2
Reyna, Cordoba	.962	60	98	4	4	0
Vargas, Tabasco	.962	38	48	2	2	0
Reid, Union Laguna	.961	75	117	5	5	1
Johnson, Campeche	.961	39	69	4	3	0
Valverde, Union Laguna	.960	46	46	2	2	0
Uribe Moreno, Campeche	.959	44	117	1	5	0
Carter, Monclova	.959	26	46	1	2	0
Hithe, Leon	.959	54	86	8	4	1
Jimenez, Mont. Industrials	.958	16	22	1	1	0
Tiquet, Monclova	.958	107	192	13	9	1
Cosey, Monclova	.957	25	42	3	2	0
Gutierrez, Tabasco	.957	47	84	4	4	0
Santana, Tabasco	.955	73	185	8	9	2
Garcia, Aguascalientes	.955	43	57	7	3	0
Diaz, Nuevo Laredo	.953	75	95	6	5	2
Espinoza, San Luis	.952	63	118	2	6	2
Gutierrez, Jalisco	.952	60	96	4	5	2
Perkins, Monterrey Industrials	.950	12	19	0	1	0
Monell, San Luis	.950	56	128	4	7	0
Yuriar, Monclova	.949	76	140	9	8	1
Landrum, Jalisco	.946	59	133	7	8	3
Perez, Mexico City Tigers	.945	74	134	3	8	2
Zulueta, Yucatan	.944	13	17	0	1	0
Abrego, Jalisco	.944	87	138	13	9	2
Banuelos, Union Laguna	.944	57	64	3	4	1
Dixon, Tabasco	.940	22	45	2	3	0
Almodobar, Cordoba	.938	16	14	1	1	0
Valencia, Monterrey Sultans	.938	79	95	10	7	4
Brown, Monclova	.936	24	41	3	3	0
Valdez, Jalisco	.933	70	93	4	7	0
Cuevas, Monclova	.929	19	12	1	1	0
Valenzuela, Aguascalientes	.929	30	25	1	2	0
Lopez, Monclova	.919	25	31	3	3	0
Rodriguez, Saltillo	.919	32	30	4	3	1
Quiroz, Monterrey Industrials	.917	11	10	1	1	0
DeAngelis, San Luis	.915	24	41	2	4	0
Williams, Monclova	.905	24	36	2	4	0
Threadgill, Tabasco	.882	10	14	1	2	0
Noriega, Jalisco	.846	12	9	2	2	1
Jimenez, Tabasco	.818	13	9	0	2	0

(Fewer Than Ten Games)

Player, Team	Pct.	G	PO	A	E	DP
Contreras, Union Laguna	1.000	1	1	0	0	0
Clayton, San Luis	1.000	1	3	0	0	0
Padget, San Luis	1.000	7	12	1	0	0
Gutierrez, San Luis	1.000	9	6	0	0	0
Mena, Monclova	1.000	2	2	0	0	0
Bocardo, Monclova	1.000	2	2	0	0	0
Minshaw, Monterrey Industrials	1.000	4	7	0	0	0
Ramos, Monterrey Sultans	1.000	1	2	0	0	0

Player, Team	Pct.	G	PO	A	E	DP
Almodobar, Jalisco	1.000	2	2	0	0	0
Hernandez, Jalisco	1.000	8	4	0	0	0
Estrada, Nuevo Laredo	1.000	2	1	0	0	0
Amador, Nuevo Laredo	1.000	8	4	1	0	1
Sandoval, Mexico City Reds	1.000	7	5	0	0	0
Gainey, Mexico City Reds	1.000	6	7	0	0	0
Nichols, San Luis	1.000	3	6	0	0	0
Garibay, Leon	1.000	7	4	0	0	0
Guerrero, Leon	1.000	6	5	1	0	1
Ledezma, Leon	1.000	7	2	1	0	0
Garcia, Saltillo	1.000	1	2	0	0	0
Hernandez, Saltillo	1.000	1	1	0	0	0
Salcido, Saltillo	1.000	8	6	2	0	0
Nelson, Tabasco	1.000	3	9	0	0	0
Marte, Tabasco	1.000	2	2	0	0	0
Chavez, Tabasco	1.000	4	4	1	0	0
Brummer, Mexico City Tigers	.941	8	15	1	1	1
Lizarraga, Tabasco	.900	8	8	1	1	0
Zamudio, Campeche	.875	7	7	0	1	0
Estrada, Tabasco	.846	6	11	0	2	0
Salgado, Nuevo Laredo	.833	3	3	2	1	0
Navarro, Saltillo	.667	5	2	0	1	0
Villegas, Saltillo	.600	3	2	1	2	0
Chan, Monclova	.500	3	1	0	1	0
Martinez, Mont. Industrials	.500	4	1	0	1	0

CATCHERS

Player, Team	Pct.	G	PO	A	E	DP	PB
Ramirez, Monclova	1.000	16	43	2	0	0	2
Alvarez, Jalisco	1.000	31	107	13	0	2	2
Salazar, Mex. C. Tigers	1.000	22	91	5	0	0	8
Cazarin, Leon	.993	21	125	13	1	0	2
Tirado, M. C. Tigers	.992	72	319	36	3	8	5
Reynolds, Tabasco	.991	46	208	17	2	0	3
Trevino, Mont. Sultans	.989	19	78	8	1	1	1
Reyes, Aguascalientes	.988	74	318	25	4	4	4
Luna, Aguascalientes	.988	49	220	29	3	2	4
Ruiz, Campeche	.988	21	71	11	1	1	1
Garzon, Mex. C. Reds	.988	35	151	10	2	1	3
Hernandez, Mont. Sul.	.988	97	481	80	7	10	7
Castillo, Tabasco	.987	64	272	37	4	4	12
Estrada, Leon	.986	74	395	42	6	2	6
See, Mexico City Reds	.986	16	62	10	1	0	0
Tirado, Yucatan	.986	50	199	14	3	0	4
Cavia, San Luis	.986	15	64	6	1	1	2
Martinez, Jalisco	.986	101	549	79	9	10	5
Estrada, M. C. Reds	.985	77	369	35	6	1	9
Cantu, Cordoba	.984	62	228	17	4	3	6
Gastelum, San Luis	.984	65	315	47	6	4	13
Valdez C., Mont. Ind.	.982	22	51	5	1	0	0
Samaniego, Yucatan	.982	89	451	42	9	3	7
Osuna, Saltillo	.981	49	198	11	4	1	3
Garza Garza, Mont. Ind.	.981	110	636	71	14	14	14
Valenzuela, Saltillo	.981	66	313	39	7	4	6
Firova, Nuevo Laredo	.980	78	449	53	10	8	17
Guzman, Campeche	.980	96	429	50	10	4	6
Rojas, Mex. City Tigers	.980	46	268	19	6	4	1
Rivera, San Luis	.978	59	236	36	6	3	9
Cruz, Cordoba	.977	78	401	33	10	7	14
Dominguez, U. Laguna	.975	74	388	35	11	3	12
Becerra, Nuevo Laredo	.973	39	162	20	5	3	6
Quintero, U. Laguna	.972	38	124	15	4	0	4
Daut, Monclova	.970	85	431	52	15	5	9
Torres, Saltillo	.969	45	163	24	6	2	8
Cruz Galindo, N. Lar.	.967	28	134	13	5	3	2
Avila Torres, U. Lag.	.966	56	223	35	9	5	3
Bocardo, Monclova	.965	54	203	16	8	1	6
Cueto, Tabasco	.963	12	24	2	1	1	1
Hurtado, Leon	.953	45	166	18	9	0	8
Morris, Aguascalientes	.941	24	104	8	7	4	4

(Fewer Than Ten Games)

Player, Team	Pct.	G	PO	A	E	DP	PB
Melendez, Cordoba	1.000	1	0	0	0	0	1
Lopez, Cordoba	1.000	1	2	0	0	0	1
Meza, Monterrey Ind.	1.000	9	27	9	0	0	0
Estrada, Nuevo Lar.	1.000	1	1	1	0	0	0
Oviedo, Mex. C. Tigers	1.000	1	2	0	0	0	0
Gonzalez, Yucatan	1.000	2	1	1	0	0	0
Vargas, Tabasco	1.000	5	14	1	0	0	3
Micheu, Tabasco	1.000	4	26	1	0	1	4
Gassos, Tabasco	1.000	6	17	1	0	0	1
Abrego, Jalisco	.964	5	23	4	1	0	1
Guzman Lopez, Camp.	.889	5	13	3	2	0	3
Marquez, Cordoba	.882	6	13	2	2	0	1
Munoz, Mex. City Reds	.867	5	12	1	2	0	0

Triple play—Valenzuela.

PITCHERS

Player, Team	Pct.	G	PO	A	E	DP
Palafox, Union Laguna	1.000	28	8	28	0	3
Shaw, Union Laguna	1.000	11	3	5	0	1
Diaz Garcia, Union Laguna	1.000	32	2	6	0	0
Tirado, Union Laguna	1.000	16	0	2	0	0
Talamantes, Union Laguna	1.000	14	0	1	0	0
Acosta C., Union Laguna	1.000	20	0	6	0	2
Quintero V., Union Laguna	1.000	10	3	3	0	0
Rodriguez, San Luis	1.000	27	2	12	0	1
Lopez, San Luis	1.000	21	8	15	0	0
Chavarin, San Luis	1.000	19	1	1	0	0
Rodriguez, San Luis	1.000	28	7	15	0	4
Garcia, San Luis	1.000	31	1	11	0	0
Soto, San Luis	1.000	16	2	4	0	1
Valdez, Monclova	1.000	19	6	9	0	2
Velazquez, Monclova	1.000	35	4	11	0	2
Mena, Monclova	1.000	29	0	4	0	0
Espinoza, Monclova	1.000	19	1	7	0	0
Gracia, Monclova	1.000	15	1	2	0	0
Vazquez, Monclova	1.000	10	2	8	0	3
Ochoa, Monterrey Industrials	1.000	53	3	19	0	1
Escamilla, Monterrey Industrials	1.000	24	3	6	0	0
Villegas, Mont. Industrials	1.000	24	4	13	0	0
Medvin, Monterrey Industrials	1.000	15	1	10	0	2
Quiroz, Mont. Industrials.	1.000	19	2	6	0	0
Flores R., Cordoba	1.000	10	3	0	0	0
Jones, Cordoba	1.000	36	3	17	0	1
Martinez, Cordoba	1.000	40	0	7	0	1
Cruz, Cordoba	1.000	28	6	8	0	0
Lopez, Cordoba	1.000	26	13	38	0	5
Osuna, Monterrey Sultans	1.000	24	10	20	0	3
Garza, Monterrey Sultans	1.000	20	3	16	0	2
Alicea, Monterrey Sultans	1.000	32	1	8	0	2
Lugo, Jalisco	1.000	25	5	24	0	1
Schwabe, Jalisco	1.000	18	7	19	0	1
Kerfeld, Jalisco	1.000	23	2	5	0	0
Morales, Jalisco	1.000	27	0	11	0	3
Romo, Jalisco	1.000	16	2	5	0	0
Sosa, Jalisco	1.000	19	0	3	0	0
Garcia, Jalisco	1.000	10	1	1	0	0
Velez, Jalisco	1.000	15	0	4	0	0
Padilla, Aguascalientes	1.000	22	1	3	0	0
Cardenas, Aguascalientes	1.000	23	6	9	0	2
Vargas, Aguascalientes	1.000	29	3	2	0	0
Toliver, Aguascalientes	1.000	12	10	7	0	2
Peterek, Nuevo Laredo	1.000	21	7	16	0	2
Cruz, Nuevo Laredo	1.000	14	1	3	0	1
Navidad, Nuevo Laredo	1.000	17	1	6	0	1
Valdez, Nuevo Laredo	1.000	34	2	15	0	0
Puig, Mexico City Tigers	1.000	15	0	7	0	0
Garcia, Mexico City Tigers	1.000	22	9	20	0	1
Perea, Mexico City Tigers	1.000	15	2	2	0	0
Herrera, Mexico City Tigers	1.000	23	3	8	0	1
Mora, Mexico City Tigers	1.000	22	2	5	0	0
Easley, Mexico City Tigers	1.000	24	3	13	0	2
Robles, Mexico City Tigers	1.000	17	5	4	0	0
Felix, Mexico City Reds	1.000	25	6	12	0	3
Barojas, Mexico City Reds	1.000	41	8	20	0	2
Leyva, Mexico City Reds	1.000	12	1	1	0	0
Jimenez, Mexico City Reds	1.000	25	3	5	0	1
Mendoza, Mexico City Reds	1.000	21	0	1	0	0
DeLeon, Leon	1.000	23	1	4	0	1
Diaz, Leon	1.000	18	0	5	0	0
Purata, Leon	1.000	23	3	22	0	1
Soto, Leon	1.000	27	7	9	0	0
Alvarado, Leon	1.000	12	0	3	0	0
Olivas, Leon	1.000	17	0	4	0	0
Delgadillo, Yucatan	1.000	17	1	3	0	0
Sombra, Yucatan	1.000	31	2	5	0	0
Colorado, Yucatan	1.000	22	7	15	0	0
Antunez, Yucatan	1.000	50	1	10	0	2
Dozier, Yucatan	1.000	21	3	17	0	2
Chevez, Yucatan	1.000	10	2	0	0	0
Sanchez, Saltillo	1.000	39	2	11	0	0
Barron, Saltillo	1.000	87	4	16	0	1
Cesena, Saltillo	1.000	42	3	10	0	1
Alvarez, Saltillo	1.000	51	0	15	0	1
Smith, Saltillo	1.000	13	6	12	0	1
Dominguez, Campeche	1.000	13	3	20	0	1
Browning, Campeche	1.000	46	6	19	0	1
Villegas, Campeche	1.000	36	1	19	0	0
Velazquez, Campeche	1.000	24	9	12	0	1
Tinoco, Campeche	1.000	26	1	21	0	4
Guzman Z., Campeche	1.000	14	0	1	0	1
Diaz, Campeche	1.000	16	0	5	0	0
Lopez, Campeche	1.000	27	1	2	0	0
Tejeda, Campeche	1.000	23	1	3	0	0
Hernandez, Tabasco	1.000	15	2	11	0	0
Retes, Tabasco	1.000	21	2	10	0	0
Herrera, Tabasco	1.000	32	1	7	0	0
Enriquez, Tabasco	1.000	49	3	8	0	0
Moreno, Mexico City Tigers	.978	24	7	37	1	2
Valdez, Monterrey Industrials	.975	26	8	31	1	0
Esquer, Yucatan	.971	22	5	28	1	0
Velazquez, Leon	.968	27	4	26	1	2
Jimenez, Monterrey Sultans	.964	20	6	21	1	4
Mendez, Mexico City Reds	.963	30	4	22	1	1
Solis, Nuevo Laredo	.962	46	5	20	1	1
Sosa, Tabasco	.962	23	2	23	1	1

Player, Team	Pct.	G	PO	A	E	DP
Herrera, Leon	.958	57	3	20	1	3
Osuna, Mexico City Reds	.957	24	11	33	2	2
Hernandez, Leon	.957	31	3	19	1	1
Raygoza, Campeche	.956	26	20	45	3	4
Normand, Monclova	.955	22	5	16	1	1
Jones, Monterrey Industrials	.955	18	7	14	1	1
Hernandez, Yucatan	.955	25	5	16	1	2
Garibay, Yucatan	.952	60	9	11	1	0
Castro, Saltillo	.952	37	3	17	1	0
Arias, Monclova	.950	29	5	14	1	2
Uribe, Monterrey Sultans	.950	40	3	16	1	0
Alvarez, Mexico City Reds	.950	14	4	15	1	1
Munoz, Saltillo	.950	30	8	30	2	3
Heredia, Monterrey Sultans	.947	24	1	17	1	1
Cazares, San Luis	.944	24	5	29	2	1
Valenzuela, Mont. Sultans	.944	34	6	11	1	1
Ibarra, Jalisco	.944	25	5	12	1	1
Acosta V., Aguascalientes	.944	33	6	11	1	4
Pulido, Saltillo	.944	27	9	25	2	3
Cervantes, Union Laguna	.943	27	10	23	2	3
Renteria, Union Laguna	.941	24	3	13	1	2
Jamie Granillo, Agua.	.941	43	5	11	1	1
Pena, San Luis	.938	57	1	14	1	1
Cosio, Monclova	.938	23	3	12	1	0
Sandoval, Monterrey Sultans	.938	15	4	11	1	0
Montano, Yucatan	.935	22	12	17	2	0
Rios V., Union Laguna	.933	22	5	9	1	0
Moreno, Mexico City Reds	.933	18	3	11	1	0
Saldana, Tabasco	.933	23	12	30	3	4
Rincon, Union Laguna	.929	32	4	9	1	1
Cano, Monclova	.929	24	8	18	2	4
Ontiveros, Monterrey Industrials	.929	36	1	12	1	2
Perez, Cordoba	.929	32	6	7	1	1
Grajales, Mexico City Tigers	.929	35	4	9	1	2
Carranza, Jalisco	.926	30	4	21	2	2
Valenzuela, Cordoba	.923	33	5	7	1	0
Spagnola, Nuevo Laredo	.923	32	3	9	1	2
Acosta, Monterrey Sultans	.920	19	6	17	2	2
Quinonez, Aguascalientes	.920	26	10	13	2	3
Huerta, Campeche	.920	24	4	19	2	1
Murillo, Monclova	.917	21	5	6	1	0
Chavez, Monclova	.917	28	4	7	1	1
Urrea, Aguascalientes	.917	28	5	6	1	0
Aguilar, Aguascalientes	.917	29	1	10	1	0
Ruiz, Mexico City Tigers	.917	24	4	18	2	2
Martinez, Mexico City Reds	.917	21	1	21	2	0
Macias, Mexico City Reds	.909	23	2	8	1	0
Miranda, Aguascalientes	.905	55	4	15	2	1
Castellanos, Saltillo	.905	26	7	12	2	2
Perry, Union Laguna	.903	54	7	21	3	0
Moreno, Nuevo Laredo	.902	21	6	31	4	2
Gonzalez, Union Laguna	.900	28	5	31	4	0
Solano, Monclova	.900	52	3	15	2	0
Moreno, Cordoba	.900	27	1	8	1	0
Malave, Aguascalientes	.900	25	1	8	1	0
Mojica, Jalisco	.900	15	4	5	1	0
Rios V., Mexico City Tigers	.900	23	7	11	2	0
Romero, Tabasco	.900	29	2	7	1	0
Castaneda, Union Laguna	.889	20	4	4	1	0
Sanchez, Mont. Industrials	.889	43	4	12	2	0
Castaneda, Jalisco	.889	27	5	19	3	2
Puerto, Yucatan	.889	21	4	4	1	0
Morrow, Saltillo	.885	33	4	19	3	1
Villarreal, Cordoba	.882	16	2	13	2	2
Gonzalez, Monterrey Sultans	.882	11	3	12	2	2
Jimenez, Monterrey Industrials	.875	22	5	44	7	2
Soto, Jalisco	.875	17	3	11	2	0
Barraza, Nuevo Laredo	.875	29	6	22	4	4
Reyes, Mexico City Tigers	.875	16	0	7	1	0
Lizarraga, Saltillo	.875	23	1	6	1	1
Ortiz, Tabasco	.875	13	0	7	1	1
Quiroz, Nuevo Laredo	.870	24	5	15	3	3
Lopez J., Aguascalientes	.867	23	4	9	2	1
Navarro, Tabasco	.867	21	2	11	2	0

Player, Team	Pct.	G	PO	A	E	DP
Neri, Aguascalientes	.862	44	8	17	4	1
Serna, Monterrey Sultans	.857	16	1	5	1	0
Noriega, Mexico City Tigers	.857	27	0	6	1	0
Orozco, Leon	.857	14	8	10	3	0
Alvarez, Nuevo Laredo	.852	26	4	19	4	2
Sinohui, Leon	.846	26	3	19	4	0
Cabrales, San Luis	.839	26	9	17	5	4
Pruneda, Cordoba	.833	14	1	4	1	0
Serafin, Tabasco	.833	23	3	7	2	2
Camarena, Tabasco	.824	22	4	10	3	0
Guzman, San Luis	.813	43	3	10	3	1
Veliz Arballo, Monterrey Sultans	.810	27	5	12	4	0
Cedeno, Aguascalientes	.800	10	2	2	1	0
Calderon, Aguascalientes	.800	12	1	3	1	0
Rodriguez, Mexico City Tigers	.800	11	3	5	2	1
Toledo, Campeche	.800	21	0	4	1	0
Luevano, Mexico City Reds	.778	17	1	6	2	1
Garcia Garcia, Mont. Industrials	.750	23	3	9	4	0
Guajardo, Monterrey Industrials	.750	12	0	3	1	0
Tejeda, Mexico City Reds	.750	15	0	6	2	2
Pulido, San Luis	.727	35	1	7	3	0
Couch, Nuevo Laredo	.727	18	1	7	3	0
Salas, Cordoba	.667	11	0	2	1	0
Villanueva, Leon	.667	41	0	2	1	0
Zamorano, Campeche	.667	12	0	2	1	0
Ramirez, San Luis	.500	22	1	0	1	0

(Fewer Than Ten Games)

Player, Team	Pct.	G	PO	A	E	DP
Pimentel, Union Laguna	1.000	7	2	2	0	0
Meza, San Luis	1.000	7	0	4	0	1
Moore, San Luis	1.000	5	1	1	0	0
Valdez, San Luis	1.000	6	0	3	0	0
Campos, Monclova	1.000	4	0	1	0	0
Thompson, Mont. Industrials	1.000	8	2	16	0	0
Flores, Monterrey Industrials	1.000	4	0	2	0	0
Ruelas, Cordoba	1.000	5	0	2	0	0
Ramos, Cordoba	1.000	2	1	2	0	0
Sanchez, Cordoba	1.000	9	2	4	0	1
Iturbe, Cordoba	1.000	2	1	0	0	0
Quiroz, Cordoba	1.000	5	0	1	0	0
Weber, Cordoba	1.000	1	1	0	0	0
Espinoza, Jalisco	1.000	6	0	1	0	0
Cervera, Jalisco	1.000	8	0	5	0	0
Leon, Jalisco	1.000	5	1	3	0	0
Chadwick, Jalisco	1.000	4	0	2	0	0
Ojeda, Aguascalientes	1.000	5	1	2	0	0
Steward, Aguascalientes	1.000	6	0	2	0	0
Villa, Aguascalientes	1.000	8	..	5	0	0
Valenzuela, Nuevo Laredo	1.000	5	..	1	0	0
Castillo, Nuevo Laredo	1.000	6	..	1	0	0
Angulo, Mexico City Reds	1.000	4	..	1	0	0
Jusaino, Leon	1.000	4	..	1	0	0
Lara, Yucatan	1.000	5	..	1	0	0
Cruz, Yucatan	1.000	5	..	2	0	0
Mendez, Saltillo	1.000	8	..	1	0	0
Garcia, Saltillo	1.000	4	..	5	0	1
Zavaleta, Campeche	1.000	4	..	2	0	0
Hernandez, Campeche	1.000	8	..	2	0	0
Vazquez, Campeche	1.000	6	..	2	0	0
Childress, Campeche	1.000	6	..	6	0	0
Manzano, Campeche	1.000	2	..	1	0	0
Zamudio, Tabasco	.923	8	..	7	1	1
Noles, Jalisco	.917	9	..	9	1	1
Cano, Mexico City Reds	.917	4	..	6	1	0
Madrid, Monterrey Sultans	.857	8	..	4	1	0
Clay, Monterrey Industrials	.833	4	..	3	1	0
Holman, Nuevo Laredo	.833	9	..	3	1	0
Ledon, Tabasco	.750	3	..	3	1	0
Ordaz, San Luis	.667	8	..	1	1	1
Granillo, Aguascalientes	.000	2	..	0	1	0
Torres, Leon	.000	3	..	0	1	0

LEAGUE CHAMPIONS

Year	Team	Pct.
1955—	Mexico City Tigers*	.539
1956—	Mexico City Reds	.692
1957—	Yucatan	.567
	Mex. C. Reds (2nd)†	.550
1958—	Nuevo Laredo	.625
1959—	Poza Rica	.575
	Mex. C. Reds (3rd)†	.507
1960—	Mexico City Reds	.538
1961—	Veracruz	.575
1962—	Monterrey	.592
1963—	Puebla	.606
1964—	Mexico City Reds	.586
1965—	Mexico City Tigers	.590
1966—	Mexico City Tigers†	.614
	Mexico City Reds	.571
1967—	Jalisco	.607
1968—	Mexico City Reds	.586

Year	Team	Pct.
1969—	Reynosa	.591
1970—	Aguila§	.580
	Mexico City Reds	.607
1971—	Jalisco§	.558
	Saltillo	.593
1972—	Saltillo	.636
	Cordoba§	.541
1973—	Saltillo	.656
	Mexico City Reds x	.590
1974—	Jalisco	.627
	Mexico City Reds x	.551
1975—	Tampico x	.541
	Cordoba	.649
1976—	Mexico City Reds	.543
	Union Laguna	.547
1977—	Mexico City Reds	.623
	Nuevo Laredo x	.507

Year	Team	Pct.
1978—	Aguascalientes x	.589
	Union Laguna	.523
1979—	Saltillo	.704
	Puebla x	.628
1980—	No champion y	
1981—	Mexico City Reds	.615
	Reynosa	.492
1982—	Ciudad Juarez x	.570
	Mexico City Tigers	.508
1983—	Campeche z	.614
	Ciudad Juarez	.535
1984—	Yucatan x	.560
	Ciudad Juarez	.509
1985—	Mexico City Reds z	.606
	Nuevo Laredo	.5275
1986—	Puebla z	.682
	Monclova	.598

Year	Team	Pct.	Year	Team	Pct.	Year	Team	Pct.
1987—	Mexico City Reds z	.605	1989—	Nuevo Laredo z	.621	1991—	Monterrey z	.683
	Monterrey	.536		Yucatan	.539		Mexico City Reds	.627
1988—	Mexico City Reds z	.646	1990—	Nuevo Laredo	.618			
	Nuevo Laredo	.602		Leon z	.565			

*Defeated Nuevo Laredo, two games to none, in playoff for pennant. †Won four-team playoff. ‡Won split-season playoff. §League divided into Northern, Southern divisions; won two-team playoff. xLeague divided into Northern, Southern zones; sub-divided into Eastern, Western divisions, won eight-team playoff. yA players strike on July 1 forced the cancellation of the regular season and playoff schedule. zLeague divided into Northern, Southern zones; four clubs from each zone qualified for postseason play. Won final series for league championship.

PACIFIC COAST LEAGUE

FINAL STANDINGS

FIRST HALF

NORTHERN DIVISION

Team	W	L	T	Pct.	GB
Portland (Twins)	36	32	0	.529	....
Edmonton (Angels)	33	33	0	.500	2
Tacoma (Athletics)	33	37	0	.471	4
Calgary (Mariners)	27	40	0	.403	8 ½
Vancouver (White Sox)	27	42	0	.391	9 ½

SOUTHERN DIVISION

Team	W	L	T	Pct.	GB
Tucson (Astros)	45	25	0	.643	....
Phoenix (Giants)	39	30	0	.565	5 ½
Albuquerque (Dodgers)	38	30	0	.559	6
Las Vegas (Padres)	36	34	0	.514	9
Colorado Springs (Indians)	30	41	0	.423	15 ½

SECOND HALF

NORTHERN DIVISION

Team	W	L	T	Pct.	GB
Calgary (Mariners)	45	24	0	.652	....
Edmonton (Angels)	37	33	0	.529	8 ½
Portland (Twins)	34	36	0	.486	11 ½
Tacoma (Athletics)	30	36	0	.455	13 ½
Vancouver (White Sox)	22	44	0	.333	21 ½

SOUTHERN DIVISION

Team	W	L	T	Pct.	GB
Colorado Springs (Indians)	42	26	0	.618	....
Albuquerque (Dodgers)	42	28	0	.600	1
Tucson (Astros)	34	36	0	.486	9
Phoenix (Giants)	29	40	0	.420	13 ½
Las Vegas (Padres)	29	41	0	.414	14

COMPOSITE

Team	Alb.	Tuc.	Cal.	C.S.	Edm.	Port.	Phoe.	L.V.	Tac.	Van.	W	L	T	Pct.	GB
Albuquerque (Dodgers)	....	8	3	14	5	7	14	19	5	5	80	58	0	.580	....
Tucson (Astros)	16	....	7	14	6	3	15	9	3	6	79	61	0	.564	2
Calgary (Mariners)	5	1	....	5	14	13	1	6	14	13	72	64	0	.529	7
Colorado Springs (Indians)	12	11	3	....	4	6	13	14	5	4	72	67	0	.518	8 ½
Edmonton (Angels)	3	2	10	3	....	4	6	4	12	18	70	66	0	.515	9
Portland (Twins)	1	5	11	2	12	....	3	4	12	20	70	68	0	.507	10
Phoenix (Giants)	10	11	6	11	2	5	....	13	6	4	68	70	0	.493	12
Las Vegas (Padres)	6	16	2	11	4	4	12	....	4	6	65	75	0	.464	16
Tacoma (Athletics)	3	5	12	3	12	12	2	4	....	10	63	73	0	.463	16
Vancouver (White Sox)	2	2	10	4	7	6	4	2	12	....	49	86	0	.363	29 ½

Major league affiliations in parentheses.

Playoffs—Calgary defeated Portland, three games to none; Tucson defeated Colorado Springs, three games to one; Tucson defeated Calgary, three games to two, to win league championship.

Regular-season attendance—Albuquerque, 340,685; Calgary, 325,965; Colorado Springs, 174,731; Edmonton, 252,813; Las Vegas, 330,699; Phoenix, 247,791; Portland, 181,116; Tacoma, 293,418; Tucson, 317,347; Vancouver, 288,978. Total, 2,753,543. Playoffs (12 games)—44,815. Class AAA All-Star Game at Louisville—20,725.

Managers—Albuquerque, Kevin Kennedy; Calgary, Keith Bodie; Colorado Springs, Charlie Manuel; Edmonton, Max Oliveras; Las Vegas, Jim Riggleman; Phoenix, Duane Espy; Portland, Russ Nixon; Tacoma, Jeff Newman; Tucson, Bob Skinner; Vancouver, Marv Foley (through June 14), Moe Drabowsky (June 15 to 16), Doug Mansolino (June 17 to 21), Rick Renick (June 22 to end of season). Managerial records of teams with more than one manager: Vancouver, Foley 24-39, Drabowsky 0-3, Mansolino 3-1, Renick 22-43.

All-Star team—1B—Tino Martinez, Calgary; 2B—Andres Santana, Phoenix; 3B—Gary Cooper, Tucson; SS—Andujar Cedeno, Tucson; OF—Ken Lofton, Tucson; Ruben Amaro, Edmonton; Geronimo Berroa, Colorado Springs; C—Carlos Hernandez, Albuquerque; DH—Luis Medina, Colorado Springs; LHP—Kyle Abbott, Edmonton; RHP—Tom Edens, Portland; RP—Dean Wilkins, Tucson; Most Valuable Player—Tino Martinez, Calgary; Manager of the Year—Bob Skinner, Tucson.

BATTING

TEAM

Team	Avg.	G	AB	R	OR	H	TB	2B	3B	HR	RBI	SH	SF	HP	BB	Int. BB	SO	SB	CS	LOB
Colorado Springs	.298	139	4704	780	690	1400	2122	269	48	119	720	25	54	30	492	28	759	68	51	1021
Albuquerque	.294	138	4678	730	668	1375	1948	237	63	70	660	59	44	24	427	41	654	153	85	926
Tucson	.292	140	4809	762	716	1406	1995	258	59	71	698	61	46	44	511	38	905	122	85	1035
Calgary	.292	136	4659	808	770	1359	2123	291	37	133	751	29	47	20	544	26	796	98	56	974
Phoenix	.289	138	4673	747	755	1351	1974	226	50	99	681	30	55	34	519	30	833	151	71	1017
Edmonton	.286	136	4498	735	699	1286	1941	262	42	103	662	53	47	59	503	22	740	185	73	947
Las Vegas	.285	140	4809	838	830	1370	2022	239	46	107	675	56	42	27	541	42	804	133	69	1028
Portland	.277	138	4581	660	597	1267	1831	225	33	91	596	46	40	44	478	24	644	89	44	1001
Tacoma	.266	136	4561	641	718	1211	1770	221	49	80	596	49	53	49	531	21	762	85	35	1061
Vancouver	.261	135	4493	562	720	1173	1618	197	34	60	499	46	38	35	457	19	764	101	71	975

INDIVIDUAL

(Leading qualifiers for batting championship—378 or more plate appearances)

*Bats lefthanded.   †Switch-hitter.

Player, Team	Avg.	G	AB	R	H	TB	2B	3B	HR	RBI	SH	SF	HP	BB	Int. BB	SO	SB	CS
Amaral, Rich, Calgary	.346	86	347	79	120	159	26	2	3	36	3	3	3	53	0	37	30	7
Lennon, Pat, Calgary	.329	112	416	75	137	221	29	5	15	74	1	1	4	46	4	68	12	5
Munoz, Jose, Albuquerque†	.326	101	389	49	127	153	18	4	0	65	6	5	2	20	0	36	15	10
Amaro, Ruben, Edmonton†	.326	121	472	95	154	217	42	6	3	42	9	2	6	63	2	48	36	18
Martinez, Tino, Calgary*	.326	122	442	94	144	242	34	5	18	86	0	8	3	82	7	44	3	3
Medina, Luis, Colorado Springs	.324	117	450	81	146	267	28	6	27	98	0	8	2	47	2	100	0	1
Berroa, Geronimo, Colorado Springs	.322	125	478	81	154	253	31	7	18	91	1	3	2	35	2	88	2	1
Santana, Andres, Phoenix†	.316	113	456	84	144	164	7	5	1	35	2	1	4	36	0	46	45	19
Karros, Eric, Albuquerque	.316	132	488	88	154	269	33	8	22	101	0	5	6	58	8	80	3	2
Curtis, Chad, Edmonton	.316	115	431	81	136	205	28	7	9	61	4	4	3	51	1	56	46	11

Departmental leaders: G—T. Wood, 137; AB—Lofton, 545; R—Amaro, 95; H—Lofton, 168; TB—Karros, 269; 2B—Amaro, 42; 3B—Lofton, 17; HR—B. Brito, Medina, 27; RBI—T. Wood, 109; SH—Reboulet, 17; SF—Cron, 11; HP—Jennings, 11; BB—T. Wood, 86; IBB—Karros, Tolentino, 8; SO—M. Davis, 114; SB—Taylor, 62; CS—Goodwin, Lofton, 23.

(All players—listed alphabetically)

Player, Team	Avg.	G	AB	R	H	TB	2B	3B	HR	RBI	SH	SF	HP	BB	Int. BB	SO	SB	CS
Afenir, Troy, Tacoma	.244	80	262	35	64	112	12	3	10	38	3	6	3	22	1	59	0	0
Aldrete, Mike, Colorado Springs*	.289	23	76	4	22	27	5	0	0	8	0	0	0	8	1	17	0	0
Aldrete, Rich, Phoenix*	.302	82	215	29	65	75	10	0	0	18	0	3	0	19	3	33	0	5
Allen, Harold, Tucson*	.500	5	2	0	1	1	0	0	0	1	0	0	0	1	0	1	0	0
Allred, Beau, Colorado Springs*	.250	53	148	39	37	73	12	3	6	21	0	2	3	34	1	55	1	1
Alomar, Sandy, Colorado Springs	.400	12	35	5	14	19	2	0	1	10	0	1	0	5	2	0	0	0
Amaral, Rich, Calgary	.346	86	347	79	120	159	26	2	3	36	3	3	3	53	0	37	30	7
Amaro, Ruben, Edmonton†	.326	121	472	95	154	217	42	6	3	42	9	2	6	63	2	48	36	18
Anderson, Kent, Edmonton	.210	84	271	30	57	76	9	2	2	26	3	1	0	26	0	32	6	3
Anthony, Eric, Tucson*	.336	79	318	57	107	160	22	2	9	63	0	3	3	25	6	58	11	5
Ard, Johnny, Phoenix	.286	10	7	0	2	2	0	0	0	0	0	0	0	1	0	4	0	0
Azocar, Oscar, Las Vegas*	.296	107	361	51	107	157	23	3	7	50	1	5	1	21	3	26	4	4
Bailey, Mark, Phoenix†	.301	63	186	33	56	92	16	1	6	36	0	2	1	30	5	39	1	5
Baker, Doug, Tucson†	.183	73	164	17	30	38	1	2	1	15	3	1	1	14	0	23	0	0
Barns, Jeff, Edmonton	.176	7	17	1	3	4	1	0	0	0	0	0	1	3	1	4	0	0
Barrett, Marty, Las Vegas	.319	16	47	5	15	21	4	1	0	4	0	1	0	11	3	3	0	0
Bass, Kevin, Phoenix†	.317	10	41	8	13	24	3	1	2	7	0	1	0	2	0	4	1	0
Bean, Billy, Albuquerque*	.297	103	259	35	77	117	22	6	2	35	2	2	3	23	3	32	7	7
Beck, Rod, Phoenix	.200	23	10	1	2	2	0	0	0	1	0	0	0	0	0	1	0	0
Belle, Albert, Colorado Springs	.328	16	61	9	20	33	3	2	2	16	0	2	1	2	0	8	1	1
Beltre, Esteban, Vancouver	.271	88	347	48	94	111	11	3	0	30	7	1	0	23	0	61	8	8
Benjamin, Mike, Phoenix	.204	64	226	34	46	81	13	2	6	31	1	4	2	20	3	67	3	2
Bernhardt, Cesar, Vancouver	.260	87	323	40	84	107	10	5	1	30	2	2	1	18	1	26	12	6
Berroa, Geronimo, Colorado Springs	.322	125	478	81	154	253	31	7	18	91	1	3	2	35	2	88	2	1
Bilardello, Dann, Las Vegas	.314	44	140	17	44	71	13	1	4	29	0	2	0	9	3	19	2	0
Blankenship, Lance, Tacoma	.294	30	109	19	32	42	7	0	1	11	0	3	2	22	0	27	9	1
Blowers, Mike, Calgary	.289	90	329	56	95	146	20	2	9	59	1	6	3	40	1	74	3	1
Bones, Ricky, Las Vegas	.179	25	28	2	5	6	1	0	0	1	3	0	0	2	0	6	0	0
Bordick, Mike, Tacoma	.272	26	81	15	22	34	4	1	2	14	1	0	1	17	0	10	0	1
Bournigal, Rafael, Albuquerque	.293	66	215	34	63	78	5	5	0	29	8	4	0	14	1	13	4	1
Bowen, Ryan, Tucson	.176	20	17	3	3	4	1	0	0	1	2	0	0	3	0	6	0	0
Bowie, Jim, Calgary*	.340	14	50	9	17	23	3	0	1	7	0	0	0	2	0	8	0	0
Brito, Bernardo, Portland	.259	115	428	65	111	213	17	2	27	83	0	7	7	28	1	110	1	0
Brito, Jorge, Tacoma	.233	22	73	6	17	22	2	0	1	3	0	0	4	0	20	0	0
Brock, Greg, Vancouver*	.143	2	7	0	1	1	0	0	0	0	0	0	0	1	0	1	0	0
Brooks, Jerry, Albuquerque	.294	125	429	64	126	199	20	7	13	82	1	4	6	29	5	49	4	3
Brosius, Scott, Tacoma	.286	65	245	28	70	116	16	3	8	31	1	2	2	18	0	29	4	2
Brown, Jarvis, Portland	.289	108	436	62	126	156	5	8	3	37	3	1	6	36	1	66	27	12
Brown, Kurt, Vancouver	.248	84	274	22	68	96	12	2	4	27	1	2	2	18	1	47	2	0
Brown, Marty, Colorado Springs	.301	121	396	65	119	192	24	2	15	69	5	9	2	49	2	77	3	7
Bruett, J.T., Portland*	.284	99	345	51	98	110	6	3	0	35	9	0	3	40	1	41	21	9
Brundage, Dave, Calgary*	.310	105	365	75	113	151	23	3	3	32	1	1	1	70	3	66	7	6
Buckley, Troy, Portland	.400	3	5	2	2	2	0	0	0	0	0	0	0	0	0	1	0	0
Burdick, Kevin, Colorado Springs	.235	36	132	24	31	43	6	0	2	17	0	2	1	12	2	9	3	1
Cangelosi, John, Vancouver†	.245	30	102	15	25	26	1	0	0	10	1	1	2	11	0	8	9	2
Capel, Mike, Tucson	.000	30	4	0	0	0	0	0	0	1	0	1	0	0	0	1	0	0
Carter, Jeff, Phoenix†	.272	92	246	47	67	82	5	2	2	24	2	1	0	34	1	51	11	7
Cedeno, Andujar, Tucson	.303	93	347	49	105	157	19	6	7	55	3	7	5	19	2	68	5	3
Childress, Rocky, Tucson	.000	7	1	0	0	0	0	0	0	0	0	0	0	0	0	0	0	0
Christopher, Mike, Albuquerque	.000	63	2	0	0	0	0	0	0	0	0	0	0	0	0	0	0	0
Clark, Terry, Tucson	.207	29	29	2	6	6	0	0	0	4	0	0	0	0	0	8	0	0
Coachman, Pete, Tacoma	.271	97	306	64	83	107	16	1	2	36	5	5	6	49	0	42	16	2
Cochrane, Dave, Calgary†	.321	47	190	25	61	81	11	0	3	37	0	3	1	8	1	36	2	0
Cockrell, Alan, Calgary	.290	117	435	77	126	189	26	2	11	81	1	3	4	45	1	74	7	5
Colbert, Craig, Phoenix	.246	42	142	9	35	51	6	2	2	13	0	1	0	11	2	38	0	1
Cole, Alex, Colorado Springs*	.188	8	32	6	6	8	0	1	0	3	0	0	1	4	0	3	1	3
Coles, Darnell, Phoenix	.290	83	328	43	95	140	23	2	6	65	1	3	6	27	2	43	0	0
Colombino, Carlo, Tucson	.273	81	198	38	54	71	12	1	1	25	5	1	1	13	1	32	0	2
Cook, Dennis, Albuquerque*	.250	14	8	0	2	2	0	0	0	2	0	0	0	0	0	4	0	0
Coolbaugh, Scott, Las Vegas	.287	60	209	29	60	94	9	2	7	29	0	2	0	34	2	53	2	2
Cooper, Gary, Tucson	.305	120	406	86	124	203	25	6	14	75	2	5	3	66	5	107	7	8
Correia, Ron, Tacoma	.250	17	56	9	14	17	0	0	1	7	3	0	1	4	0	6	0	0
Corsi, Jim, Tucson	.000	2	1	0	0	0	0	0	0	0	0	0	0	0	0	0	0	0
Costello, John, Las Vegas	.333	17	3	0	1	1	0	0	0	0	0	0	0	0	0	1	0	0
Cron, Chris, Edmonton	.293	123	461	74	135	224	21	1	22	91	2	11	10	47	3	103	6	5
Curtis, Chad, Edmonton	.316	115	431	81	136	205	28	7	9	61	4	4	3	51	1	56	46	11
Davis, Butch, Albuquerque	.313	91	284	55	89	149	19	10	7	44	0	2	2	18	6	51	12	5
Davis, Doug, Edmonton	.274	33	113	12	31	44	4	0	3	18	3	1	1	11	1	23	1	3
Davis, Kevin, Edmonton	.237	34	118	14	28	45	7	2	2	20	6	2	0	3	0	20	2	3
Davis, Mark, Edmonton	.278	116	424	86	118	189	20	6	13	58	8	2	8	71	1	114	32	13
Dean, Kevin, Tucson	.333	17	48	14	16	24	4	2	0	5	0	0	1	11	0	17	1	1
DeButch, Mike, Vancouver	.000	2	1	0	0	0	0	0	0	0	0	0	0	0	0	0	0	0
Decker, Steve, Phoenix	.252	31	111	20	28	53	5	1	6	14	0	0	1	13	0	29	0	0
Diaz, Carlos, Colorado Springs	.237	36	93	7	22	26	4	0	0	7	1	0	2	0	0	17	0	0
Diaz, Edgar, Las Vegas	.232	24	56	6	13	15	0	1	0	4	1	1	0	5	1	4	1	0
Disarcina, Gary, Edmonton	.310	119	390	61	121	162	21	4	4	58	4	3	9	29	1	32	16	5
Dorsett, Brian, Las Vegas	.307	62	215	36	66	120	13	1	13	38	0	1	1	17	0	43	0	0
Ebel, Dino, Albuquerque	.000	2	0	1	0	0	0	0	0	0	0	0	0	0	0	0	0	0
Engle, Dave, Tucson	.000	1	1	0	0	0	0	0	0	0	0	0	0	0	0	0	0	0
Escobar, Jose, Colorado Springs	.204	33	93	12	19	26	5	1	0	11	0	1	0	4	0	16	0	0
Eusebio, Tony, Tucson	.400	5	20	5	8	9	1	0	0	2	0	0	0	0	0	3	1	1
Faries, Paul, Las Vegas	.307	20	75	16	23	30	2	1	1	12	2	1	0	12	0	5	7	3
Fermin, Felix, Colorado Springs	.250	2	8	1	2	2	0	0	0	1	0	0	0	0	0	0	0	0
Fernandez, Danny, Phoenix	.000	4	3	0	0	0	0	0	0	0	0	0	0	0	0	1	0	0
Finken, Steve, Albuquerque	.282	11	39	8	11	15	2	1	0	5	0	0	1	6	0	9	0	0
Fox, Eric, Tacoma†	.270	127	522	85	141	193	24	8	4	52	9	4	2	57	4	82	17	11
Freeland, Dean, Tucson	.500	22	4	1	2	2	0	0	0	0	0	0	0	0	0	1	0	0
Garrison, Webster, Tacoma	.215	75	237	28	51	72	11	2	2	28	7	2	2	26	0	34	4	0
Gilmore, Terry, Las Vegas	.125	26	8	0	1	1	0	0	0	0	0	0	2	0	0	4	0	0

Player, Team	Avg.	G	AB	R	H	TB	2B	3B	HR	RBI	SH	SF	HP	BB	Int. BB	SO	SB	CS
Gonzales, Lawrence, Edmonton	.000	2	3	0	0	0	0	0	0	0	0	0	0	1	0	1	0	0
Goodwin, Tom, Albuquerque*	.273	132	509	84	139	169	19	4	1	45	10	3	2	59	0	83	48	23
Grunhard, Dan, Edmonton*	.267	100	326	62	87	137	19	2	9	45	1	5	1	49	4	63	12	5
Gunderson, Eric, Phoenix	.240	40	25	4	6	8	0	1	0	2	0	1	0	0	0	8	1	0
Hale, Chip, Portland*	.241	110	352	45	85	110	16	3	1	37	5	5	0	47	4	22	3	3
Hall, Joe, Vancouver	.248	118	427	41	106	136	16	1	4	39	3	4	4	23	2	45	11	11
Hamilton, Jeff, Albuquerque	.000	2	7	0	0	0	0	0	0	0	0	0	0	0	0	2	0	0
Hammaker, Atlee, Las Vegas†	.500	3	2	1	1	2	1	0	0	0	0	0	0	0	0	0	0	0
Hansen, Dave, Albuquerque*	.303	68	254	42	77	105	11	1	5	40	0	7	0	49	3	33	4	3
Harris, Greg, Las Vegas	.333	4	3	0	1	1	0	0	0	1	1	0	0	0	0	1	0	0
Hartgraves, Dean, Tucson	.000	16	7	0	0	0	0	0	0	0	0	1	0	0	0	3	0	0
Hartsock, Jeff, Albuquerque	.120	29	25	2	3	4	1	0	0	3	2	0	0	1	0	11	0	0
Hatcher, Mickey, Albuquerque	.160	17	25	2	4	4	0	0	0	0	0	0	0	2	1	4	0	0
Hawks, Larry, Las Vegas	.500	1	4	0	2	2	0	0	0	2	0	0	0	0	0	1	0	0
Heep, Danny, Vancouver*	.243	20	70	2	17	23	6	0	0	10	0	1	0	4	0	9	1	1
Heffernan, Bert, Albuquerque*	.242	67	161	17	39	51	10	1	0	13	3	2	0	22	1	19	1	3
Hemond, Scott, Tacoma	.272	92	327	50	89	127	19	5	3	31	5	1	7	39	1	69	11	8
Henley, Dan, Vancouver	.195	70	190	30	37	47	5	1	1	13	7	3	1	14	1	35	3	1
Hennis, Randy, Tucson	.077	11	13	1	1	1	0	0	0	0	1	0	0	1	0	8	0	0
Henry, Butch, Tucson*	.192	28	26	3	5	5	0	0	0	4	4	0	0	4	0	6	0	0
Heredia, Gil, Phoenix	.278	33	18	0	5	5	0	0	0	1	2	0	0	0	0	3	0	0
Hernandez, Carlos, Albuquerque	.345	95	345	60	119	171	24	2	8	44	0	2	1	24	5	36	5	5
Hernandez, Jeremy, Las Vegas	.000	56	1	0	0	0	0	0	0	0	0	0	0	1	0	1	0	0
Hernandez, Xavier, Tucson*	.000	16	2	0	0	0	0	0	0	0	1	0	0	0	0	1	0	0
Hershiser, Orel, Albuquerque	.000	1	0	0	0	0	0	0	0	0	0	0	0	0	0	0	0	0
Hickerson, Bryan, Phoenix*	.667	12	3	1	2	2	0	0	0	0	1	0	0	0	0	0	0	0
Higgins, Kevin, Las Vegas*	.288	130	403	53	116	145	12	4	3	45	10	3	2	47	5	38	2	2
Hill, Orsino, Vancouver*	.288	106	347	39	100	128	14	1	4	45	2	6	2	42	4	76	4	6
Hillemann, Charlie, Las Vegas	.283	15	46	5	13	23	1	0	3	5	0	0	2	0	9	0	0	
Holton, Brian, Albuquerque	.133	29	15	1	2	3	1	0	0	0	4	0	0	1	0	3	0	0
Hood, Dennis, Albuquerque	.178	103	314	52	56	102	9	2	11	44	7	0	2	34	0	97	18	6
Howard, Chris, Calgary	.246	82	293	32	72	110	12	1	8	36	3	1	2	16	1	56	1	2
Howard, Thomas, Las Vegas†	.309	25	94	22	29	40	3	1	2	16	1	2	0	10	3	16	11	5
Howitt, Dann, Tacoma*	.267	122	449	58	120	202	28	6	14	73	1	5	2	49	2	92	6	2
Hubbard, Trent, Tucson†	.000	2	4	0	0	0	0	0	0	0	0	0	0	0	0	0	0	0
Ilsley, Blaise, Tucson*	.400	49	15	3	6	10	1	0	1	2	0	0	0	2	0	1	0	0
Jackson, Chuck, Calgary	.285	121	488	80	139	222	28	5	15	85	3	5	2	37	0	53	2	7
James, Mike, Albuquerque	.250	13	4	1	1	2	1	0	0	0	0	0	0	0	0	1	0	0
Jefferson, Reggie, Colorado Springs†	.309	39	136	29	42	62	11	0	3	21	0	2	1	16	1	28	0	0
Jefferson, Stan, Colorado Springs†	.284	28	74	11	21	31	2	1	2	9	1	1	0	5	0	9	3	2
Jelic, Chris, Las Vegas	.275	49	91	23	25	41	5	1	3	23	2	0	0	26	0	17	1	1
Jennings, Doug, Tacoma*	.268	95	332	43	89	119	17	2	3	44	1	9	11	47	1	65	5	1
Jeter, Shawn, Vancouver*	.299	43	144	24	43	53	5	1	1	13	1	1	2	11	2	28	4	2
Johnson, Brian, Colorado Springs	.340	21	53	13	18	28	4	0	2	3	0	0	1	8	1	14	0	0
Johnson, Erik, Phoenix	.324	16	34	6	11	14	1	1	0	4	0	1	0	3	1	5	0	0
Jones, Barry, 28 C.S. -64 Port.*	.264	92	296	42	78	118	17	4	5	40	1	1	2	17	2	42	9	7
Jones, Chris, Albuquerque	.000	29	1	0	0	0	0	0	0	0	0	0	0	0	0	1	0	0
Jorgensen, Terry, Portland	.298	126	456	74	136	198	29	0	11	59	2	2	4	54	1	41	1	0
Juden, Jeff, Tucson	.333	10	3	1	1	1	0	0	0	0	2	0	0	0	0	1	0	0
Karros, Eric, Albuquerque	.316	132	488	88	154	269	33	8	22	101	0	5	6	58	8	80	3	2
Kelley, Dean, Las Vegas*	.253	84	221	33	56	78	13	3	1	24	2	0	0	17	0	47	6	1
King, Bryan, Calgary	.571	2	7	2	4	6	2	0	0	1	0	0	0	3	0	2	0	0
Kingery, Mike, Phoenix*	.341	13	44	8	15	21	3	0	1	13	0	2	0	6	0	6	0	1
Kirby, Wayne, Colorado Springs*	.294	118	385	66	113	138	14	4	1	39	5	3	2	34	2	36	29	14
Kittle, Ron, Vancouver	.310	17	71	9	22	40	4	1	4	21	0	0	0	6	0	13	1	1
Komminsk, Brad, Tacoma	.293	74	270	38	79	117	15	4	5	43	1	1	3	29	0	49	11	1
Kutzler, Jerry, Vancouver*	.000	30	1	0	0	0	0	0	0	0	0	0	0	0	0	1	0	0
Lambert, Reese, Las Vegas*	.000	11	4	0	0	0	0	0	0	0	0	0	0	0	0	2	0	0
Lampkin, Tom, Las Vegas*	.317	45	164	25	52	71	11	1	2	29	0	1	2	10	1	19	2	1
Lansford, Carney, Tacoma	.304	8	23	1	7	10	1	1	0	1	0	0	2	0	1	0	0	0
Law, Vance, Tacoma	.200	18	65	7	13	14	1	0	0	6	0	0	0	12	0	12	0	0
Lawton, Marcus, Edmonton†	.279	12	43	9	12	16	0	2	0	1	3	0	1	9	1	8	5	3
Lee, Derek, Vancouver*	.296	87	318	54	94	150	28	5	6	44	3	1	2	35	2	62	4	3
Lennon, Pat, Calgary	.329	112	416	75	137	221	29	5	15	74	1	1	4	46	4	68	12	5
Leonard, Mark, Phoenix*	.253	41	146	27	37	68	7	0	8	25	0	2	0	21	1	29	1	0
Letterio, Shane, Calgary	.174	17	46	6	8	10	2	0	0	2	0	0	1	8	0	9	0	2
Lewis, Darren, Phoenix	.340	81	315	63	107	145	12	10	0	52	4	5	2	41	1	36	32	10
Lewis, Jim, Las Vegas	.000	48	5	0	0	0	0	0	0	0	0	0	0	0	0	3	0	0
Lewis, Mark, Colorado Springs	.279	46	179	29	50	72	10	3	2	31	0	6	0	18	0	23	3	1
Liebert, Allen, Vancouver*	.235	21	51	3	12	18	3	0	1	7	1	1	0	8	1	5	0	0
Lilliquist, Derek, Las Vegas*	.207	37	29	3	6	9	3	0	0	6	2	0	2	2	0	7	0	0
Litton, Greg, Phoenix	.407	8	27	9	11	24	1	0	4	9	0	0	0	8	0	5	0	0
Lofton, Kenny, Tucson*	.308	130	545	93	168	227	19	17	2	50	8	2	0	52	5	95	40	23
Lopez, Luis, Colorado Springs	.347	41	176	29	61	83	11	4	1	31	0	0	3	9	0	10	0	0
Lynch, David, Albuquerque	.000	33	1	0	0	0	0	0	0	0	0	0	0	0	0	0	0	0
Lyons, Barry, Edmonton	.309	47	165	15	51	70	13	0	2	23	0	1	3	10	1	11	0	0
Magallanes, Ever, Colorado Springs*	.285	94	305	37	87	105	13	1	1	33	1	1	2	23	1	36	1	2
Mallicoat, Rob, Tucson*	.000	19	2	0	0	0	0	0	0	0	2	0	0	0	0	0	0	0
Manrique, Fred, Tacoma	.268	12	41	6	11	14	0	0	1	4	0	1	1	3	0	9	0	0
Manto, Jeff, Colorado Springs	.320	43	153	36	49	83	16	0	6	36	0	3	3	33	2	24	1	0
Manwaring, Kirt, Phoenix	.222	24	81	8	18	30	0	0	4	14	0	1	0	8	0	15	0	0
Martin, Norberto, Vancouver†	.278	93	338	39	94	103	9	0	0	20	10	2	3	21	0	38	11	8
Martinez, Luis, Albuquerque	.282	67	170	20	48	61	11	1	0	13	4	1	0	12	0	14	1	1
Martinez, Pedro, Albuquerque	.333	6	9	0	3	4	1	0	0	3	2	0	0	0	0	1	0	0
Martinez, Tino, Calgary*	.326	122	442	94	144	242	34	5	18	86	0	8	3	82	7	44	3	3
Massarelli, John, Tucson	.268	46	127	19	34	43	7	1	0	16	1	1	0	15	1	18	10	2
Masters, Dave, Phoenix	.200	8	5	1	1	2	1	0	0	0	0	1	0	0	0	1	0	0
McAndrew, Jamie, Albuquerque	.294	29	34	7	10	10	0	0	0	4	1	0	1	0	0	9	0	0
McCament, Randy, Las Vegas	.500	30	2	0	1	1	0	0	0	0	0	0	0	0	0	1	0	0
McClellan, Paul, Phoenix	.200	5	5	0	1	1	0	0	0	0	0	0	0	0	0	2	0	0
McCray, Rod, Vancouver	.230	83	222	37	51	70	9	5	0	13	2	2	8	26	0	48	14	10
McGee, Willie, Phoenix†	.500	4	10	4	5	6	1	0	0	0	0	1	0	1	0	2	0	0
McGriff, Terry, Tucson	.288	51	146	18	42	59	15	1	0	24	0	2	3	16	0	20	0	1
McGuire, Bill, Colorado Springs	.286	11	28	0	8	9	1	0	0	4	1	0	0	7	0	2	0	0
McLemore, Mark, Tucson†	.357	4	14	2	5	6	1	0	0	0	0	0	0	2	0	1	0	0

Player, Team	Avg.	G	AB	R	H	TB	2B	3B	HR	RBI	SH	SF	HP	BB	Int. BB	SO	SB	CS
McMurtry, Craig, Phoenix	.053	27	19	0	1	1	0	0	0	1	4	0	0	0	0	9	0	0
McNamara, Jim, Phoenix*	.170	17	53	3	9	10	1	0	0	2	1	0	0	6	0	12	0	0
McWilliam, Tim, Las Vegas	.200	2	5	1	1	1	0	0	0	0	0	0	0	0	0	0	0	0
Medina, Luis, Colorado Springs	.324	117	450	81	146	267	28	6	27	98	0	8	2	47	2	100	0	1
Melendez, Jose, Las Vegas	.286	9	7	0	2	2	0	0	0	1	1	0	0	1	0	5	0	0
Mikulik, Joe, Tucson	.500	2	4	2	2	2	0	0	0	0	0	0	0	0	0	0	1	0
Mondesi, Raul, Albuquerque	.333	2	9	3	3	5	0	1	0	0	0	0	0	0	0	1	1	0
Morgan, Kenny, Portland*	.148	13	27	1	4	5	1	0	0	1	0	0	0	2	0	4	1	0
Moses, John, Colorado Springs†	.295	74	298	58	88	121	18	3	3	31	4	3	1	36	1	32	11	7
Mota, Andy, Tucson	.299	123	462	65	138	171	19	4	2	46	4	2	7	22	3	76	14	9
Mota, Jose, Las Vegas†	.289	107	377	56	109	126	10	2	1	37	6	3	2	54	2	48	15	10
Munoz, Jose, Albuquerque†	.326	101	389	49	127	153	18	4	0	65	6	5	2	20	0	36	15	10
Munoz, Pedro, Portland	.316	56	212	33	67	105	19	2	5	28	0	1	1	19	3	42	9	5
Naveda, Ed, Portland	.269	87	245	42	66	101	10	2	7	32	0	2	2	38	1	33	6	1
Neel, Troy, Tacoma*	.237	18	59	7	14	19	3	1	0	7	0	0	1	7	0	14	0	0
Neidlinger, Jim, Albuquerque†	.143	23	14	2	2	3	1	0	0	1	5	0	0	1	0	4	0	0
Nelson, Rob, 86 Van.-25 Tuc.*	.249	111	361	40	90	159	17	2	16	62	1	1	1	49	2	112	1	2
Newson, Warren, Vancouver*	.369	33	111	19	41	61	12	1	2	19	0	2	0	30	1	26	5	4
Nichols, Carl, Tucson	.215	36	121	13	26	41	4	1	3	17	2	0	1	17	0	27	0	0
Nixon, Donnell, Colorado Springs	.304	11	23	4	7	8	1	0	0	1	1	1	1	1	0	3	3	2
Noce, Paul, Phoenix	.143	16	21	3	3	3	0	0	0	2	0	1	1	1	0	4	1	0
Novoa, Rafael, Phoenix*	.250	18	24	7	6	12	3	0	1	4	1	0	0	2	0	3	1	0
Offerman, Jose, Albuquerque†	.298	79	289	58	86	102	8	4	0	29	4	0	0	47	3	58	32	15
Opperman, Dan, Albuquerque	.500	11	10	3	5	5	0	0	0	1	0	0	1	0	1	0	0	0
Ortiz, Javier, Tucson	.323	34	127	20	41	63	13	0	3	22	0	2	0	10	0	22	0	3
Orton, John, Edmonton	.224	76	245	39	55	86	14	1	5	32	4	2	5	31	1	66	5	0
Parker, Rick, Phoenix	.300	85	297	41	89	135	10	9	6	41	0	6	2	26	1	35	16	3
Patterson, Dave, Phoenix	.314	54	169	23	53	71	8	2	2	22	0	0	0	25	0	19	5	2
Perezchica, Tony, Phoenix	.293	51	191	41	56	98	10	4	8	34	1	3	6	18	0	43	1	0
Peters, Reed, Edmonton	.266	78	207	32	55	73	13	1	1	19	4	1	2	26	0	18	10	2
Peterson, Adam, Las Vegas	.000	8	5	0	0	0	0	0	0	0	1	0	0	0	0	4	0	0
Phelps, Ken, Phoenix*	.318	7	22	1	7	8	1	0	0	3	0	0	1	2	1	1	0	0
Polidor, Gus, Tacoma	.297	53	182	22	54	70	8	4	0	14	9	2	2	12	1	15	0	0
Pough, Clyde, Colorado Springs	.000	2	2	0	0	0	0	0	0	0	0	0	0	0	0	0	0	0
Powell, Alonzo, Calgary	.375	53	192	45	72	125	18	7	7	43	0	5	0	31	2	33	2	6
Price, Joe, Las Vegas	.000	26	1	0	0	0	0	0	0	0	0	0	0	0	0	0	0	0
Pye, Eddie, Albuquerque	.433	12	30	4	13	17	1	0	1	8	1	0	0	4	0	4	1	2
Rambo, Dan, Phoenix	.500	3	2	0	1	1	0	0	0	0	0	0	0	0	0	1	0	0
Rasmussen, Dennis, Las Vegas*	.000	5	5	0	0	0	0	0	0	0	0	0	0	0	0	3	0	0
Reboulet, Jeff, Portland	.248	134	391	50	97	139	27	3	3	46	17	2	1	57	2	52	5	2
Reed, Steve, Phoenix	.000	41	1	0	0	0	0	0	0	0	0	0	0	0	0	1	0	0
Remlinger, Mike, Phoenix*	.111	19	18	1	2	2	0	0	0	0	1	0	0	3	0	8	0	0
Rhodes, Karl, Tucson*	.260	84	308	45	80	102	17	1	1	46	5	4	0	38	1	47	5	8
Rice, Lance, Albuquerque†	.333	1	3	0	1	2	1	0	0	0	0	0	0	0	0	0	0	0
Ritchie, Gregg, Phoenix*	.287	67	157	23	45	53	8	0	0	16	0	2	0	19	2	29	13	4
Rodriguez, Henry, Albuquerque*	.271	121	446	61	121	183	22	5	10	67	1	5	1	25	3	62	4	5
Rodriguez, Victor, Portland	.304	83	270	36	82	117	17	0	6	32	4	4	2	20	0	22	0	0
Rohde, Dave, Tucson†	.372	73	253	36	94	115	10	4	1	40	2	5	5	52	3	34	15	6
Romero, Ed, Las Vegas	.284	28	74	16	21	28	4	0	1	14	4	4	1	13	3	9	1	0
Roomes, Rolando, Portland	.235	50	136	21	32	54	4	3	4	25	2	3	3	13	1	45	6	2
Rose, Bobby, Edmonton	.298	62	242	35	72	114	14	5	6	55	1	8	5	21	1	41	3	0
Rosenberg, Steve, Las Vegas*	.143	36	7	1	1	1	0	0	0	1	0	0	0	0	0	4	0	0
Roth, Greg, Vancouver*	.190	7	21	2	4	8	1	0	1	2	0	0	0	0	0	7	0	0
Sager, A.J., Las Vegas	.346	19	26	3	9	10	1	0	0	2	4	0	1	1	0	5	0	0
Sammons, Lee, Tacoma	.200	2	5	1	1	1	0	0	0	0	0	0	0	1	0	1	0	0
Santana, Andres, Phoenix†	.316	113	456	84	144	164	7	5	1	35	2	1	4	36	0	46	45	19
Schilling, Curt, Tucson	.667	13	3	0	2	2	0	0	0	1	0	0	0	0	0	1	0	0
Schiraldi, Calvin, Tucson	.250	15	8	2	2	2	0	0	0	0	0	0	0	0	0	3	0	0
Scott, Tim, Las Vegas	.313	42	16	5	5	11	3	0	1	2	0	0	0	0	0	6	0	0
Sebra, Bob, Tucson	.250	30	4	0	1	1	0	0	0	0	0	0	0	0	0	0	0	0
Segura, Jose, Phoenix	.000	32	2	0	0	0	0	0	0	0	0	0	0	0	0	2	0	0
Servais, Scott, Tucson	.324	60	219	34	71	89	12	0	2	27	3	1	6	13	2	19	0	4
Sheaffer, Danny, Portland	.303	93	330	46	100	121	14	2	1	43	3	3	5	26	1	35	2	2
Shinall, Zak, Albuquerque	.000	29	2	0	0	0	0	0	0	0	0	0	0	0	0	1	0	0
Shipley, Craig, Las Vegas†	.300	65	230	27	69	103	9	5	5	34	0	4	0	10	1	32	2	2
Simmons, Nelson, Tacoma†	.272	118	427	48	116	162	18	2	8	67	0	7	0	48	6	56	0	1
Simms, Mike, Tucson	.246	85	297	53	73	142	20	2	15	59	1	7	4	36	0	94	2	2
Sinatro, Matt, Calgary	.260	40	131	13	34	51	8	0	3	19	3	2	1	16	0	20	1	1
Siwa, Joe, Portland	.000	1	3	0	0	0	0	0	0	0	0	0	0	1	0	1	0	0
Smith, Greg, Albuquerque†	.217	48	161	25	35	42	3	2	0	17	1	1	0	10	1	30	11	0
Smith, Jack, Calgary	.272	63	202	26	55	98	14	1	9	41	3	0	0	25	1	43	2	4
Smith, Keith, Colorado Springs	.317	71	205	28	65	87	10	0	4	31	3	2	1	32	1	25	1	3
Smithberg, Roger, Las Vegas	.188	17	16	1	3	4	1	0	0	0	3	0	0	1	0	5	0	0
Sorrento, Paul, Portland*	.308	113	409	59	126	199	30	2	13	79	0	6	8	62	5	65	1	0
Sosa, Sammy, Vancouver	.267	32	116	19	31	51	7	2	3	19	0	3	1	10	0	32	9	3
Springer, Steve, Calgary	.257	109	412	62	106	186	25	2	17	70	3	2	0	28	5	76	8	2
Stark, Matt, Vancouver	.284	118	394	47	112	165	21	1	10	68	0	2	3	79	2	37	0	3
Staton, Dave, Las Vegas	.267	107	375	61	100	187	19	1	22	74	0	3	3	44	4	89	1	0
Stephenson, Phil, Las Vegas*	.222	7	18	1	4	6	0	1	0	5	0	1	0	1	0	1	0	0
Stevens, Lee, Edmonton*	.314	123	481	75	151	243	29	3	19	96	0	4	2	37	4	79	3	2
Tatarian, Dean, Vancouver	.316	10	19	3	6	6	0	0	0	3	0	0	0	2	0	6	1	1
Tatis, Bernie, Colorado Springs†	.250	7	20	4	5	11	0	0	2	2	0	0	0	3	0	5	1	1
Taubensee, Eddie, Colorado Springs*	.310	91	281	53	89	157	23	3	13	39	0	0	3	31	5	61	0	0
Taylor, Will, Las Vegas	.259	125	468	82	121	154	11	5	4	33	4	3	0	56	1	101	62	22
Tejada, Wil, Tacoma	.186	22	59	7	11	16	1	2	0	6	1	0	1	6	0	11	0	0
Thome, Jim, Colorado Springs*	.285	41	151	20	43	62	7	3	2	28	0	3	0	12	0	29	0	0
Thurmond, Mark, Phoenix*	.000	26	2	0	0	0	0	0	0	0	0	0	0	0	0	0	0	0
Tingley, Ron, Edmonton	.291	17	55	11	16	30	5	0	3	15	1	0	1	8	0	14	1	0
Tolentino, Jose, Tucson*	.290	90	303	44	88	140	24	5	6	51	0	1	2	44	8	44	2	3
Traxler, Brian, Albuquerque*	.357	18	28	3	10	18	3	1	1	8	0	0	3	0	5	0	0	0
Tunnell, Lee, Tucson	.167	20	12	2	2	2	0	0	0	0	0	0	0	1	0	4	0	0
Turner, Matt, Tucson	.000	13	2	0	0	0	0	0	0	0	0	0	0	0	0	2	0	0
Uribe, Jose, Phoenix†	.341	11	41	7	14	17	1	1	0	4	0	0	0	0	0	2	0	0
Valdez, Rafael, Las Vegas	1.000	5	1	0	1	1	0	0	0	0	0	0	0	0	0	0	0	0

Player, Team	Avg.	G	AB	R	H	TB	2B	3B	HR	RBI	SH	SF	HP	BB	Int. BB	SO	SB	CS
Vatcher, Jim, Las Vegas	.266	117	395	67	105	196	28	6	17	67	3	2	3	53	3	76	4	12
Veres, Dave, Albuquerque....................	.333	57	6	1	2	2	0	0	0	1	0	0	0	0	0	3	0	0
Veres, Randy, Phoenix	.500	19	2	1	1	1	0	0	0	0	1	0	0	0	0	1	0	0
Waggoner, Aubrey, Vancouver*	.205	50	156	23	32	47	4	4	1	10	1	1	2	19	0	39	5	3
Wakamatsu, Don, Vancouver	.198	55	172	20	34	54	8	0	4	19	4	2	1	12	0	39	0	0
Walters, Dan, Las Vegas	.317	96	293	39	93	127	22	0	4	44	0	0	0	22	5	35	0	0
Ward, Kevin, Las Vegas	.322	83	276	51	89	136	17	6	6	43	1	5	7	58	2	53	10	4
Ward, Turner, Colorado Springs†	.196	14	51	5	10	16	1	1	1	3	1	0	0	6	0	9	2	1
Wasinger, Mark, Edmonton	.118	13	34	3	4	6	2	0	0	2	0	0	1	7	0	7	1	0
Webster, Lenny, Albuquerque	.252	87	325	43	82	121	18	0	7	34	0	3	1	24	2	32	1	4
Wells, Terry, Albuquerque*	.000	29	0	0	0	0	0	0	0	0	1	0	0	0	0	0	0	0
Wetteland, John, Albuquerque	.500	42	2	0	1	1	0	0	0	1	0	0	0	0	0	1	0	0
Wilkins, Dean, Tucson	.000	65	3	0	0	0	0	0	0	0	0	0	3	0	0	2	0	0
Williams, Brian, Tucson	.286	9	7	0	2	2	0	0	0	1	0	0	0	0	0	2	0	0
Williams, Jimmy, Phoenix*	.130	30	23	5	3	4	1	0	0	5	0	0	1	0	0	13	0	0
Wilson, Jim, Phoenix	.300	116	433	62	130	223	30	0	21	78	0	5	4	45	3	89	5	5
Witmeyer, Ron, Tacoma* ◄	.262	122	431	64	113	184	18	4	15	80	2	5	2	57	5	59	2	5
Wood, Brian, Las Vegas*	.000	47	3	0	0	0	0	0	0	0	0	0	0	0	0	3	0	0
Wood, Ted, Phoenix*	.311	137	512	90	159	242	38	6	11	109	0	10	4	86	4	96	12	7
Yelding, Eric, Tucson	.395	11	43	6	17	20	3	0	0	3	0	0	2	4	0	4	4	2
Young, Eric, Albuquerque	.400	1	5	0	2	2	0	0	0	0	0	0	0	0	0	0	0	0
Young, Gerald, Tucson†	.304	24	79	14	24	32	2	3	0	17	1	1	0	14	1	8	3	1
Zambrano, Roberto, Colorado Springs...	.297	35	91	12	27	42	2	2	3	14	1	1	1	10	1	13	0	0

The following pitchers, listed alphabetically by club, with games in parentheses, had no plate appearances, primarily through use of designated hitters:

ALBUQUERQUE—Marquez, Isidro (1); Walsh, Dave (14).

CALGARY—Balabon, Rick (17); Bankhead, Scott (5); Barton, Shawn (17); Burba, Dave (23); Comstock, Keith (15); Cook, Mike (10); Eave, Gary (21); Fleming, Dave (3); Givens, Brian (3); Hanson, Erik (1); Harris, Gene (25); Helton, Keith (30); Jones, Calvin (20); Kramer, Randy (16); Lovelace, Vance (13); Meyer, Brian (18); Mitchell, John (2); Nelson, Jeff (28); Powell, Dennis (27); Rice, Pat (21); Richards, Dave (10); Rojas, Ricky (16); Salkeld, Roger (4); Vande Berg, Ed (47); Vosberg, Ed (16).

COLORADO SPRINGS—Bell, Eric (4); Birkbeck, Mike (3); Bittiger, Jeff (27); Blair, Willie (26); Boucher, Denis (3); Bruske, Jim (7); Chamberlain, Craig (1); Cummings, Steve (5); Curtis, Mike (20); Egloff, Bruce (15); Gozzo, Mauro (25); Hall, Drew (5); Hall, Grady (3); Horton, Ricky (22); Jones, Doug (17); King, Eric (3); Kramer, Tom (10); Olin, Steve (22); Otto, Dave (17); Roscoe, Greg (3); Seanez, Rudy (16); Shaw, Jeff (12); Valdez, Efrain (14); Valdez, Sergio (26); Ward, Colby (29); Wickander, Kevin (11); York, Mike (5).

EDMONTON—Abbott, Kyle (27); Beasley, Chris (23); Berrios, Hector (17); Bockus, Randy (4); Buckels, Gary (51); Burcham, Tim (31); Corbett, Sherm (41); Erb, Mike (31); Fetters, Mike (11); Grahe, Joe (14); Leiper, Dave (13); Lewis, Scott (17); Montalvo, Rafael (25); Pawlowski, John (10); Sontag, Alan (3); Toliver, Fred (18); Valenzuela, Fernando (7); Vosberg, Ed (12); Young, Cliff (34); Zappelli, Mark (17).

LAS VEGAS—Clements, Pat (11).

PHOENIX—Dewey, Mark (10); Hickey, Kevin (5); Oliveras, Francisco (19); Prentice, Tony (1); Rodriguez, Rick (3); Tate, Stuart (8).

PORTLAND—Abbott, Paul (8); Anderson, Allan (5); Banks, Willie (25); Casian, Larry (34); Delkus, Pete (2); Drummond, Tim (56); Edens, Tom (25); Garces, Richard (10); Mahomes, Pat (9); Neagle, Denny (19); Pulido, Carlos (2); Savage, Jack (38); Scott, Charles (19); Tsamis, George (29); Wassenaar, Rob (40); Wayne, Gary (15); West, David (4); Willis, Carl (3).

TACOMA—Allison, Dana (18); Briscoe, John (22); Burns, Todd (13); Campbell, Kevin (35); Dressendorfer, Kirk (8); Eskew, Dan (7); Garcia, Apolinar (7); Guzman, Johnny (17); Harris, Reggie (17); McCoy, Tim (4); Mielke, Gary (10); Musselman, Jeff (25); Parker, Clay (25); Pico, Jeff (45); Schock, Will (16); Show, Eric (9); Slusarski, Joe (7); Strebeck, Ricky (5); Waggoner, Jimmy (1); Walton, Bruce (38); Weber, Weston (15); Wernig, Pat (39).

VANCOUVER—Brito, Mario (19); Carter, Jeff (41); Drahman, Brian (22); Drees, Tom (22); Dunne, Mike (17); Edwards, Wayne (14); Garcia, Ramon (4); Hall, Grady (19); Hasler, Curt (11); Hernandez, Roberto (17); Hibbard, Greg (1); Kennedy, Bo (17); Perschke, Greg (27); Scheid, Rich (48); Stephens, Ron (53).

GRAND SLAMS—Cooper, 3; Afenir, Bilardello, B. Brito, J. Brown, Cochrane, Cockrell, Coolbaugh, Disarcina, Grunhard, Hood, C. Howard, Jackson, Lee, M. Lewis, A. Mota, Perezchica, Powell, Pye, Shipley, Simmons, Springer, Stark, Vatcher, Witmeyer, 1 each.

AWARDED FIRST BASE ON CATCHER'S INTERFERENCE—K. Brown 2 (J. Brito, Orton); Lee (Hemond); Grunhard (Walters); Hale (Servais).

PITCHING

TEAM

Team	ERA	G	CG	ShO	Sv.	IP	H	R	ER	HR	HB	BB	Int. BB	SO	WP	Bk.
Portland	3.81	138	13	13	66	1178.2	1180	597	499	70	36	507	23	756	51	8
Albuquerque	4.26	138	5	3	43	1201.1	1256	668	569	100	25	524	18	879	92	25
Tucson	4.34	140	8	11	37	1236.0	1399	716	596	58	36	526	35	873	71	23
Colorado Springs	4.49	139	13	5	33	1169.2	1262	690	584	96	43	478	33	744	77	24
Edmonton	4.72	136	16	9	34	1157.2	1311	699	607	106	37	440	28	747	68	10
Tacoma	4.73	136	7	10	32	1177.0	1274	718	619	96	35	560	13	757	56	23
Phoenix	4.75	138	17	6	29	1185.2	1388	755	626	102	25	490	30	678	52	14
Vancouver	4.88	135	13	7	26	1158.1	1262	720	628	94	43	529	29	659	43	12
Calgary	5.08	136	8	2	29	1178.0	1399	770	665	115	52	507	17	674	85	21
Las Vegas........................	5.15	140	7	4	24	1228.1	1467	830	703	96	41	442	65	894	61	13

INDIVIDUAL

(Leading qualifiers for earned-run average leadership—112 or more innings)

*Throws lefthanded.

Pitcher, Team	W	L	Pct.	ERA	G	GS	CG	GF	ShO	Sv.	IP	H	R	ER	HR	HB	BB	Int. BB	SO	WP
Heredia, Phoenix	9	11	.450	2.82	33	15	5	7	1	1	140.1	155	60	44	3	2	28	5	75	4
Edens, Portland	10	7	.588	3.01	25	24	3	0	1	0	161.1	145	67	54	6	7	62	3	100	4
Tsamis, Portland*	10	8	.556	3.27	29	27	2	0	1	0	167.2	183	75	61	11	5	66	0	71	7
Drees, Vancouver*	8	8	.500	3.52	22	22	3	0	3	0	143.0	130	70	56	15	3	62	0	89	2
Parker, Tacoma	7	6	.538	3.67	25	24	3	2	1	0	132.1	123	65	54	6	2	44	0	78	5
Hartsock, Albuquerque	12	6	.667	3.80	29	26	0	0	0	0	154.0	153	80	65	12	3	78	0	123	10
Bittiger, Colorado Springs ...	9	12	.429	3.90	27	27	2	0	0	0	147.2	158	89	64	12	6	83	0	93	13
K. Abbott, Edmonton*	14	10	.583	3.99	27	27	4	0	2	0	180.1	173	84	80	22	1	46	1	120	7
S. Valdez, Colorado Springs ...	4	12	.250	4.11	26	15	4	6	0	0	131.1	139	67	60	12	7	27	6	71	9
Powell, Calgary*	9	8	.529	4.15	27	26	5	1	1	0	173.2	200	90	80	20	6	59	0	96	12

Departmental leaders: G—Wilkins, 65; W—K. Abbott, Clark, 14; L—Bittiger, Perschke, S. Valdez, 12; Pct.—Campbell, .818; GS—J. Williams, 28;

CG—Heredia, Kutzler, Powell, 5; GF—Wilkins, 47; ShO—Drees, 3; Sv.—Wilkins, 21; IP—K. Abbott, 180.1; H—Clark, Powell, 200; R—J. Williams, 120; ER—J. Williams, 106; HR—K. Abbott, 22; HB—Kutzler, 9; BB—J. Williams, 93; IBB—J. Hernandez, 10; SO—Hartsock, 123; WP—Banks, Ward, 14.

(All pitchers—listed alphabetically)

Pitcher, Team	W	L	Pct.	ERA	G	GS	CG	GF	ShO	Sv.	IP	H	R	ER	HR	HB	BB	Int. BB	SO	WP
Abbott, Edmonton*	14	10	.583	3.99	27	27	4	0	2	0	180.1	173	84	80	22	1	46	1	120	7
Abbott, Portland	2	3	.400	3.89	8	8	1	0	1	0	44.0	36	19	19	2	3	28	1	40	1
Aldrete, Phoenix*	0	0	.000	0.00	1	0	0	1	0	0	1.1	4	5	0	0	0	2	0	0	0
Allen, Tucson*	0	2	.000	19.50	5	4	0	0	0	0	12.0	25	27	26	0	1	22	0	6	3
Allison, Tacoma*	3	1	.750	4.37	18	0	0	4	0	0	22.2	25	12	11	2	1	11	2	13	0
Anderson, Portland*	4	1	.800	3.06	5	5	2	0	0	0	32.1	33	15	11	2	2	7	0	16	1
Ard, Phoenix	3	5	.375	5.78	10	10	1	0	0	0	62.1	76	42	40	6	2	33	0	30	1
Baker, Tucson	0	0	.000	3.00	3	0	0	3	0	0	3.0	7	7	1	0	0	3	0	1	3
Balabon, Calgary	6	6	.500	6.41	17	15	0	0	0	0	87.0	109	71	62	14	4	43	1	42	10
Bankhead, Calgary	0	0	.000	1.04	5	0	0	2	0	1	8.2	7	1	1	0	0	1	0	10	0
Banks, Portland	9	8	.529	4.55	24	24	1	1	1	0	146.1	156	81	74	6	6	76	1	63	14
Barton, Calgary*	2	0	1.000	2.61	17	0	0	6	0	1	31.0	25	11	9	3	0	8	0	22	1
Beasley, Edmonton	3	5	.375	5.26	23	10	1	3	1	1	89.0	99	55	52	10	5	26	3	51	3
Beck, Phoenix	4	3	.571	2.02	23	5	3	14	0	6	71.1	56	18	16	3	2	13	2	35	2
Bell, Colorado Springs*	2	1	.667	2.13	4	4	1	0	1	0	25.1	23	6	6	1	0	11	1	16	1
Berrios, Edmonton*	3	1	.750	3.86	17	0	0	5	0	1	16.1	15	7	7	1	0	8	1	12	1
Birkbeck, Colorado Springs	0	0	.000	0.00	3	1	0	2	0	0	7.0	4	1	0	0	0	3	0	3	0
Bittiger, Colorado Springs	9	12	.429	3.90	27	27	2	0	0	0	147.2	158	89	64	12	6	83	0	93	13
Blair, Colorado Springs	9	6	.600	4.99	26	15	0	10	0	4	113.2	130	74	63	10	2	30	2	57	3
Bockus, Edmonton	0	0	.000	16.62	4	0	0	3	0	0	4.1	13	10	8	2	0	3	1	3	0
Bones, Las Vegas	8	6	.571	4.22	23	23	1	0	0	0	136.1	155	90	64	10	4	43	3	95	6
Boucher, Colorado Springs*	1	0	1.000	5.02	3	3	0	0	0	0	14.1	14	8	8	1	0	2	0	9	0
Bowen, Tucson	5	5	.500	4.38	18	18	2	0	2	0	98.2	114	56	48	3	3	56	2	78	9
Briscoe, Tacoma	3	5	.375	3.66	22	9	0	6	0	1	76.1	73	35	31	7	5	44	1	66	3
Brito, Vancouver	0	10	.000	7.12	19	13	1	2	0	0	78.1	106	69	62	8	3	25	1	41	0
Brundage, Calgary*	0	0	.000	2.25	4	0	0	4	0	0	4.0	5	1	1	0	0	4	0	4	2
Bruske, Colorado Springs	4	0	1.000	2.45	7	1	0	3	0	2	25.2	19	9	7	3	0	8	0	13	1
Buckels, Edmonton	5	3	.625	4.18	51	0	0	21	0	7	56.0	66	27	26	4	0	20	5	34	5
Burba, Calgary	6	4	.600	3.53	23	9	0	9	0	4	71.1	82	35	28	4	4	27	0	42	3
Burcham, Edmonton	7	7	.500	4.98	31	20	1	6	0	5	137.1	161	83	76	15	4	57	0	70	8
Burns, Tacoma	0	2	.000	5.33	13	0	0	4	0	2	25.1	30	16	15	5	0	7	2	24	2
Campbell, Tacoma	9	2	.818	1.80	35	0	0	12	0	2	75.0	53	18	15	1	3	35	1	56	5
Capel, Tucson	4	2	.667	2.40	30	0	0	9	0	3	56.1	49	16	15	1	5	17	2	44	4
Carter, Vancouver	3	7	.300	3.05	41	4	0	26	0	4	79.2	78	33	27	3	1	35	5	40	3
Casian, Portland*	3	2	.600	3.46	34	6	0	10	0	1	52.0	51	25	20	3	1	16	1	24	0
Chamberlain, Colorado Springs	0	1	.000	12.60	1	1	0	0	0	0	5.0	7	9	7	1	1	2	0	0	0
Childress, Tucson	0	1	.000	6.92	7	1	0	4	0	0	13.0	21	13	10	3	0	2	0	6	0
Christopher, Albuquerque	7	2	.778	2.44	63	0	0	34	0	16	77.1	73	25	21	2	3	30	5	67	7
Clark, Portland	14	7	.667	4.66	26	26	2	0	0	0	164.0	200	104	85	5	6	37	0	97	9
Clements, Las Vegas*	0	0	.000	6.75	11	0	0	4	0	0	12.0	15	9	9	3	0	5	1	4	1
Coachman, Tacoma	0	0	.000	9.00	1	0	0	0	0	0	2.0	4	2	2	0	0	3	0	2	0
Comstock, Calgary*	3	1	.750	3.28	15	0	0	4	0	2	35.2	25	16	13	4	0	16	0	38	2
Cook, Albuquerque*	7	3	.700	3.63	14	14	1	0	0	0	91.2	73	46	37	9	2	32	0	84	5
Cook, Tucson	2	4	.333	9.68	10	6	0	1	0	0	30.2	45	35	33	5	1	24	0	18	1
Corbett, Edmonton*	4	3	.571	3.92	41	2	0	17	0	6	62.0	58	30	27	4	2	33	5	34	5
Corsi, Tucson	0	0	.000	0.00	2	0	0	2	0	0	3.0	2	0	0	0	0	0	0	4	0
Costello, Las Vegas	1	2	.333	2.15	17	0	0	5	0	3	29.1	31	16	7	1	2	7	1	24	1
Cron, Edmonton	0	0	.000	0.00	1	0	0	1	0	0	2.0	2	0	0	0	0	0	0	0	0
Cummings, Colorado Springs	0	4	.000	6.08	5	5	0	0	0	0	26.2	36	24	18	3	0	6	0	15	1
Curtis, Colorado Springs*	2	4	.333	3.83	20	2	0	8	0	1	44.2	43	26	19	4	1	23	3	32	4
Delkus, Portland	0	0	.000	11.25	2	0	0	0	0	0	4.0	7	5	5	2	0	2	0	0	0
Dewey, Phoenix	1	2	.333	3.97	10	0	0	10	0	4	11.1	16	7	5	0	1	7	5	4	0
Drahman, Vancouver	2	3	.400	4.44	22	0	0	21	0	12	24.1	21	12	12	2	0	13	1	17	1
Drees, Vancouver*	8	8	.500	3.52	22	22	3	0	3	0	143.0	130	70	56	15	3	62	0	89	2
Dressendorfer, Tacoma	1	3	.250	10.88	8	7	0	0	0	0	24.0	31	29	29	4	1	20	0	19	2
Drummond, Portland	5	8	.385	4.65	56	1	0	37	0	7	79.1	87	52	41	6	1	32	4	45	6
Dunne, Vancouver	2	2	.500	5.40	17	5	1	7	0	2	55.0	66	37	33	5	2	19	0	21	1
Eave, Calgary	3	6	.333	5.52	21	17	0	1	0	0	93.0	120	71	57	6	8	50	2	39	8
Edens, Portland	10	7	.588	3.01	25	24	3	0	1	0	161.1	145	67	54	6	7	62	3	100	4
Edwards, Vancouver*	3	9	.250	6.26	14	12	0	1	0	0	64.2	73	50	45	5	4	37	0	35	4
Egloff, Colorado Springs	1	2	.333	3.38	15	0	0	7	0	2	29.1	31	14	11	2	1	13	2	17	1
Erb, Edmonton	1	0	1.000	3.76	31	1	0	19	0	5	40.2	40	18	17	3	2	23	0	26	3
Eskew, Tacoma	0	3	.000	9.91	7	5	0	0	0	0	26.1	46	29	29	2	0	19	0	23	1
Fetters, Edmonton	2	7	.222	4.87	11	11	1	0	0	0	61.0	65	39	33	5	3	26	0	43	2
Fleming, Calgary*	2	0	1.000	1.13	3	2	1	0	0	0	16.0	11	2	2	1	0	3	0	16	0
Fox, Tacoma*	0	0	.000	36.00	1	0	0	0	0	0	1.0	3	4	4	1	0	3	0	0	0
Freeland, Tucson	1	3	.250	6.42	17	0	0	10	0	0	40.2	63	36	29	3	0	25	6	30	5
Garces, Portland	0	1	.000	4.85	10	0	0	8	0	3	13.0	10	7	7	1	1	8	1	13	0
Garcia, Tacoma	0	4	.000	10.92	7	5	0	0	0	0	29.2	49	45	36	5	1	20	1	12	4
Garcia, Vancouver	2	2	.500	4.05	4	4	0	0	0	0	26.2	24	13	12	3	0	7	0	17	0
Garrison, Tacoma	0	0	.000	18.00	1	0	0	0	0	0	2.0	5	4	4	1	0	1	0	0	0
Gilmore, Las Vegas	2	7	.222	6.90	26	10	0	5	0	0	73.0	128	66	56	7	2	17	5	52	4
Givens, Calgary*	1	0	1.000	4.91	3	3	0	0	0	0	14.2	16	8	8	1	1	6	0	8	4
Gozzo, Colorado Springs	10	6	.625	5.25	25	20	3	4	0	1	130.1	143	86	76	9	6	68	3	81	7
Grahe, Edmonton	9	3	.750	4.01	14	14	3	0	1	0	94.1	121	55	42	3	3	30	0	55	6
Gunderson, Phoenix*	7	6	.538	6.14	40	14	0	8	0	3	107.0	153	85	73	10	3	44	4	53	3
Guzman, Tacoma*	2	5	.286	6.78	17	13	0	2	0	0	79.2	113	74	60	8	2	51	0	40	4
A. Hall, Colorado Springs*	1	0	1.000	1.86	5	0	0	3	0	0	9.2	6	5	2	0	0	6	2	8	0
G. Hall, 19 Van.-3 C.S.*	1	5	.167	5.57	22	10	0	7	0	1	72.2	97	54	45	7	6	45	1	36	7
Hammaker, Las Vegas*	0	0	.000	6.46	3	3	0	0	0	0	15.1	21	11	11	1	0	3	0	9	2
Hanson, Calgary	0	0	.000	1.50	1	1	0	0	0	0	6.0	1	1	1	0	0	2	0	5	0
Harris, Calgary	4	0	1.000	3.34	25	0	0	18	0	4	35.0	37	16	13	2	1	11	1	23	2
Harris, Las Vegas	1	2	.333	7.40	4	4	0	0	0	0	20.2	24	20	17	1	0	8	2	16	0
Harris, Tacoma	5	4	.556	4.99	16	15	0	0	0	0	83.0	83	55	46	11	3	58	0	72	5
Hartgraves, Tucson*	1	0	1.000	3.09	16	3	1	4	1	0	43.2	47	17	15	2	0	20	1	18	2
Hartsock, Albuquerque	12	6	.667	3.80	29	26	0	0	0	0	154.0	153	80	65	12	3	78	0	123	10
Hasler, Vancouver	0	2	.000	7.81	11	0	0	6	0	0	27.2	44	28	24	5	3	16	3	17	1
Heffernan, Albuquerque	0	0	.000	0.00	2	0	0	0	0	0	2.0	4	0	0	0	0	1	0	0	0
Helton, Calgary*	4	7	.364	6.46	30	13	1	4	0	0	110.0	148	86	79	12	6	51	1	55	6

Pitcher, Team	W	L	Pct.	ERA	G	GS	CG	GF	ShO	Sv.	IP	H	R	ER	HR	HB	BB	Int. BB	SO	WP
Henley, Vancouver	0	0	.000	9.00	1	0	0	1	0	0	2.0	3	2	2	1	0	2	0	1	1
Hennis, Tucson	4	0	1.000	3.36	11	10	0	0	0	0	61.2	69	28	23	5	1	31	1	41	0
Henry, Tucson*	10	11	.476	4.80	27	27	2	0	0	0	153.2	192	92	82	10	1	42	2	97	5
Heredia, Phoenix	9	11	.450	2.82	33	15	5	7	1	1	140.1	155	60	44	3	2	28	5	75	4
Hernandez, Las Vegas	4	8	.333	4.74	56	0	0	45	0	13	68.1	76	36	36	1	4	25	10	67	2
Hernandez, Vancouver	4	1	.800	3.22	7	7	0	0	0	0	44.2	41	17	16	2	0	23	0	40	1
Hernandez, Tucson	2	1	.667	2.75	16	3	0	8	0	4	36.0	35	16	11	1	2	9	0	34	4
Hershiser, Albuquerque	0	0	.000	0.00	1	1	0	0	0	0	5.0	5	0	0	0	0	0	0	5	1
Hibbard, Vancouver*	0	0	.000	3.38	1	1	0	0	0	0	5.1	4	3	2	0	0	3	0	3	0
Hickerson, Phoenix*	1	1	.500	3.80	12	0	0	7	0	2	21.1	29	10	9	1	0	5	1	21	1
Hickey, Phoenix*	0	0	.000	20.65	5	0	0	1	0	0	5.2	18	13	13	3	0	1	0	5	1
Hill, Vancouver	0	0	.000	9.00	1	0	0	1	0	0	1.0	1	1	1	0	0	1	0	1	0
Holton, Albuquerque	7	7	.500	3.87	29	16	0	4	0	0	107.0	121	58	46	7	3	19	1	77	3
Horton, Colorado Springs*	3	2	.600	6.67	22	0	0	6	0	1	27.0	37	21	20	4	0	7	1	18	0
Ilsley, Tucson*	8	6	.571	4.27	46	4	0	17	0	4	86.1	105	51	41	7	3	27	1	52	2
James, Albuquerque	1	3	.250	6.60	13	8	0	3	0	0	45.0	51	36	33	7	2	30	0	39	5
Jones, Calgary	1	1	.500	3.91	20	0	0	15	0	7	23.0	19	12	10	1	2	19	1	25	6
Jones, Albuquerque	4	1	.800	4.97	29	1	0	8	0	0	54.1	68	34	30	6	0	23	1	23	5
Jones, Colorado Springs	2	2	.500	3.28	17	2	1	14	1	7	35.2	30	14	13	3	1	5	0	29	0
Juden, Tucson	3	2	.600	3.18	10	10	0	0	0	0	56.2	56	28	20	2	0	25	0	51	7
Kennedy, Vancouver	3	4	.429	7.85	17	5	0	5	0	0	36.2	56	39	32	3	2	29	1	25	0
King, Colorado Springs	1	0	1.000	9.53	3	3	0	0	0	0	11.1	18	12	12	1	0	5	0	3	1
Kramer, Calgary	4	4	.500	5.86	16	11	0	0	0	0	66.0	87	57	43	3	5	25	0	24	7
Kramer, Colorado Springs	1	0	1.000	0.79	10	1	0	6	0	4	11.1	5	1	1	1	0	5	0	18	1
Kutzler, Vancouver	5	10	.333	5.06	29	24	5	2	1	0	158.1	199	98	89	9	9	62	4	64	5
Lambert, Las Vegas*	1	0	1.000	3.86	11	2	0	2	0	0	28.0	24	12	12	3	1	12	2	21	4
Leiper, Edmonton*	1	0	1.000	7.64	13	0	0	6	0	1	17.2	30	15	15	4	0	5	1	8	1
Lewis, Las Vegas	6	3	.667	3.38	48	0	0	15	0	3	85.1	93	41	32	4	3	34	4	76	2
Lewis, Edmonton	3	9	.250	4.50	17	17	4	0	0	0	110.0	132	71	55	7	8	26	2	87	5
Lilliquist, Las Vegas*	4	6	.400	5.38	33	14	0	8	0	2	105.1	142	79	63	10	2	33	7	89	4
Lovelace, Calgary*	0	2	.000	7.58	13	0	0	4	0	0	19.0	21	18	16	1	1	22	0	6	1
Lynch, Albuquerque*	1	3	.250	6.63	33	0	0	8	0	0	36.2	51	28	27	2	0	26	1	29	2
Mahomes, Portland	3	5	.375	3.44	9	9	2	0	0	0	55.0	50	26	21	2	0	36	1	41	2
Mallicoat, Tucson*	4	4	.500	5.48	19	6	0	4	0	1	47.2	43	32	29	3	2	38	4	32	2
Marquez, Albuquerque	0	0	.000	0.00	1	0	0	1	0	0	1.0	1	0	0	0	0	1	0	1	0
Martinez, Albuquerque	3	3	.500	3.66	6	6	0	0	0	0	39.1	28	17	16	3	0	16	0	35	3
Masters, Phoenix	1	2	.333	6.46	8	4	0	2	0	0	30.2	34	24	22	3	0	17	0	28	1
McAndrew, Albuquerque	12	10	.545	5.04	28	26	0	2	0	0	155.1	167	105	87	11	3	76	1	91	7
McCament, Las Vegas	2	1	.667	6.85	30	0	0	6	0	0	47.1	61	42	36	6	6	19	2	15	7
McClellan, Phoenix	2	2	.500	2.82	5	5	2	0	0	0	38.1	27	12	12	2	0	21	2	18	2
McCoy, Tacoma*	0	1	.000	7.36	4	0	0	3	0	0	7.1	8	6	6	1	1	9	0	5	1
McMurtry, Phoenix	10	6	.625	4.38	27	15	1	4	1	0	113.0	117	70	55	8	2	44	1	67	4
Melendez, Las Vegas	7	0	1.000	3.99	9	8	1	1	0	0	58.2	54	27	26	8	3	11	0	45	0
Meyer, Calgary	2	3	.400	4.01	18	0	0	6	0	1	33.2	39	18	15	4	4	10	2	10	4
Mielke, Tacoma	1	0	1.000	5.93	10	0	0	3	0	0	13.2	14	9	9	1	1	9	0	6	0
Mitchell, Calgary	0	2	.000	7.88	2	2	0	0	0	0	8.0	17	10	7	2	0	2	0	1	1
Montalvo, Edmonton	1	0	1.000	6.84	25	0	0	10	0	2	26.1	39	26	20	1	3	12	2	15	0
Musselman, Tacoma*	5	9	.357	5.79	25	24	2	1	1	0	138.1	176	100	89	6	1	69	1	81	7
Naveda, Portland	0	0	.000	0.00	2	0	0	2	0	0	2.1	1	0	0	0	0	4	0	0	0
Neagle, Portland*	9	4	.692	3.27	19	17	1	1	1	0	104.2	101	41	38	6	2	32	1	94	4
Neidlinger, Albuquerque	7	7	.500	4.75	23	23	3	0	1	0	130.2	165	81	69	19	0	39	0	80	12
Nelson, Calgary	3	4	.429	3.90	28	0	0	21	0	7	32.1	39	19	14	1	0	15	3	26	2
Novoa, Phoenix*	6	6	.500	5.96	17	17	0	0	0	0	93.2	135	83	62	16	5	37	3	46	3
Olin, Colorado Springs	3	2	.600	4.47	22	0	0	16	0	6	44.1	45	25	22	1	6	10	5	36	2
Oliveras, Phoenix	2	0	1.000	2.45	3	3	1	0	1	0	18.1	18	5	5	1	1	7	0	12	1
Opperman, Albuquerque	5	4	.556	5.95	11	10	1	0	0	0	59.0	74	43	39	4	2	34	2	32	5
Otto, Colorado Springs*	5	6	.455	4.75	17	15	1	1	0	0	94.2	110	56	50	7	1	43	2	62	7
Parker, Tacoma	7	6	.538	3.67	25	20	3	2	1	0	132.1	123	65	54	6	2	44	0	78	5
Pawlowski, Edmonton	0	0	.000	3.97	10	0	0	5	0	1	11.1	16	6	5	2	0	3	1	10	1
Perschke, Vancouver	7	12	.368	4.65	27	27	3	0	0	0	176.0	170	104	91	18	7	62	0	98	8
Peters, Edmonton	0	0	.000	54.00	1	0	0	0	0	0	0.1	0	2	2	0	0	2	0	0	0
Peterson, Las Vegas	2	2	.500	4.50	8	8	0	0	0	0	42.0	41	25	21	3	2	20	2	37	3
Pico, Tacoma	4	8	.333	3.00	45	0	0	25	0	4	75.0	82	28	25	4	1	29	4	50	2
Powell, Calgary*	9	8	.529	4.15	27	26	5	1	1	0	173.2	200	90	80	20	6	59	0	96	12
Prentice, Phoenix	0	0	.000	3.00	1	0	0	1	0	0	3.0	3	1	1	0	1	0	2	2	0
Price, Las Vegas*	2	1	.667	2.19	26	0	0	5	0	1	24.2	16	9	6	1	0	15	2	24	2
Pulido, Portland*	0	0	.000	16.20	2	0	0	2	0	0	1.2	4	3	3	1	0	1	0	2	0
Rambo, Phoenix	0	1	.000	4.61	3	2	0	0	0	0	13.2	18	8	7	1	0	6	0	10	0
Rasmussen, Las Vegas*	1	3	.250	5.47	5	5	1	0	0	0	26.1	23	18	16	2	2	15	0	12	1
Reed, Phoenix	2	3	.400	4.31	41	0	0	24	0	6	56.1	62	33	27	5	2	12	0	46	1
Remlinger, Phoenix*	5	5	.500	6.38	19	19	1	0	1	0	108.2	134	86	77	15	1	59	0	68	6
Rice, Calgary	13	4	.765	5.03	21	21	1	1	0	0	121.2	138	70	68	18	2	37	0	59	5
Richards, Calgary*	0	2	.000	7.63	10	0	0	2	0	0	15.1	27	14	13	3	0	13	3	13	3
Ritchie, Phoenix*	0	0	.000	5.40	1	0	0	1	0	0	1.2	2	1	1	0	0	2	0	2	2
Rodriguez, Phoenix	0	0	.000	4.91	3	0	0	1	0	0	3.2	2	4	2	0	0	4	0	4	1
Rojas, Calgary	0	0	.000	9.10	16	5	0	7	0	0	29.2	54	31	30	4	1	14	0	19	0
Roomes, Portland	0	0	.000	9.00	1	0	0	1	0	0	1.0	3	1	1	0	0	0	0	0	0
Roscoe, Colorado Springs	2	1	.667	5.74	3	2	0	0	0	0	15.2	20	11	10	1	1	9	0	6	3
Rosenberg, Las Vegas*	2	4	.333	7.54	36	8	0	9	0	0	68.0	95	62	57	6	2	26	5	61	2
Sager, Las Vegas	7	5	.583	4.71	18	18	3	0	2	0	109.0	127	63	57	5	1	20	3	61	4
Salkeld, Calgary	2	1	.667	5.12	4	4	0	0	0	0	19.1	18	16	11	2	4	13	0	21	1
Savage, Portland	2	4	.333	6.56	38	1	0	12	0	1	60.1	77	52	44	3	1	38	1	45	4
Scheid, Vancouver*	6	7	.462	6.08	47	0	0	20	0	3	66.2	65	46	45	7	2	33	4	57	6
Schilling, Tucson	0	1	.000	3.42	13	0	0	5	0	3	23.2	16	9	9	0	0	12	1	21	0
Schiraldi, Tucson	3	3	.500	4.47	15	8	0	0	0	0	54.1	62	28	27	2	1	21	1	49	4
Schock, Tacoma	6	7	.462	5.74	16	15	0	1	0	0	89.1	102	60	57	12	5	30	0	41	4
Scott, Portland	3	6	.333	3.83	18	11	1	3	0	0	80.0	75	51	34	9	3	30	1	59	2
Scott, Las Vegas	8	8	.500	5.19	41	11	0	9	0	0	111.0	133	78	64	8	1	39	8	74	1
Seanez, Colorado Springs	0	0	.000	7.27	16	0	0	11	0	0	17.1	17	14	14	2	1	22	0	19	5
Sebra, Tucson	4	2	.667	3.75	30	2	0	13	0	4	60.0	64	33	25	3	2	32	5	52	2
Segura, Phoenix	5	5	.500	3.43	32	0	0	27	0	4	39.1	46	15	15	4	1	17	2	21	3
Shaw, Colorado Springs	6	3	.667	4.64	12	12	1	0	0	0	75.2	77	47	39	9	4	25	0	55	1
Sheaffer, Portland	0	0	.000	18.00	1	0	0	1	0	0	2.0	6	4	4	0	1	1	0	0	1
Shinall, Albuquerque	2	0	1.000	3.07	29	0	0	11	0	1	41.0	48	15	14	3	2	10	0	22	3

Pitcher, Team	W	L	Pct.	ERA	G	GS	CG	GF	ShO	Sv.	IP	H	R	ER	HR	HB	BB	Int. BB	SO	WP
Show, Tacoma	3	2	.600	2.68	8	8	1	0	1	0	40.1	36	15	12	4	0	9	0	27	1
Slusarski, Tacoma	4	2	.667	2.72	7	7	0	0	0	0	46.1	42	20	14	4	0	10	0	25	0
Smithberg, Las Vegas	3	7	.300	6.61	17	15	1	0	0	0	79.0	112	65	58	8	3	33	1	34	8
Sontag, Edmonton	1	1	.500	10.57	3	1	0	1	0	0	7.2	13	10	9	2	0	5	0	6	0
Stephens, Vancouver	3	4	.429	3.42	53	1	0	27	0	4	105.1	103	50	40	3	2	58	9	59	3
Strebeck, Tacoma	0	0	.000	6.43	5	0	0	1	0	0	7.0	7	5	5	0	0	10	0	3	0
Tate, Phoenix	0	0	.000	4.50	8	0	0	3	0	0	18.0	20	10	9	2	0	11	0	6	1
Tejada, Tacoma	0	0	.000	9.00	2	0	0	2	0	0	3.0	3	3	3	1	0	5	0	1	0
Thurmond, Phoenix*	0	3	.000	3.42	26	0	0	7	0	2	23.2	29	17	9	0	0	12	3	15	0
Tolentino, Tucson*	0	0	.000	0.00	1	0	0	1	0	0	1.0	1	1	0	0	0	1	0	0	0
Toliver, Edmonton	7	4	.636	4.15	18	18	2	0	1	0	95.1	89	48	44	6	0	49	1	68	11
Tsamis, Portland*	10	8	.556	3.27	29	27	2	0	1	0	167.2	183	75	61	11	5	66	0	71	7
Tunnell, Tucson	5	3	.625	3.84	20	11	1	0	0	0	72.2	78	38	31	3	1	27	2	41	1
Turner, Tucson	1	1	.500	4.15	13	0	0	5	0	1	26.0	27	12	12	0	1	14	2	25	1
E. Valdez, Colorado Springs*	3	1	.750	3.82	14	1	0	5	0	1	30.2	26	15	13	1	0	13	3	25	1
Valdez, Las Vegas	0	2	.000	5.94	5	5	0	0	0	0	16.2	22	13	11	2	0	16	2	9	0
S. Valdez, Colorado Springs	4	12	.250	4.11	26	15	4	6	0	0	131.1	139	67	60	12	7	27	6	71	9
Valenzuela, Edmonton*	3	3	.500	7.12	7	7	0	0	0	0	36.2	48	34	29	9	1	17	1	36	0
Vande Berg, Calgary*	5	3	.625	4.26	47	1	0	16	0	6	69.2	71	35	33	3	1	24	3	37	2
Vatcher, Las Vegas	1	0	1.000	0.00	1	0	0	1	0	0	3.0	1	0	0	0	1	2	1	1	0
Veres, Albuquerque	7	6	.538	4.47	57	3	0	16	0	5	100.2	89	52	50	8	3	52	5	81	9
Veres, Phoenix	3	0	1.000	3.56	19	1	0	2	0	1	43.0	42	26	17	1	2	14	2	41	3
Vosberg, 12 Edm.-16 Cal.*	0	3	.000	6.87	28	0	0	11	0	2	38.0	57	36	29	4	1	17	0	29	3
Walsh, Albuquerque*	0	0	.000	1.13	14	0	0	1	0	0	8.0	8	4	1	1	0	6	0	2	2
Walton, Tacoma	1	1	.500	1.35	38	0	0	38	0	20	46.2	39	11	7	0	0	5	1	49	2
Ward, Colorado Springs	2	1	.667	4.50	28	2	0	17	0	2	48.0	56	28	24	5	2	28	1	33	14
Wassenaar, Portland	4	4	.500	3.26	40	0	0	14	0	5	77.1	75	31	28	3	1	25	5	62	1
Wayne, Portland*	4	5	.444	2.79	51	0	0	32	0	8	67.2	63	27	21	4	1	31	4	66	4
Weber, Tacoma	2	0	1.000	1.99	15	0	0	11	0	1	31.2	28	14	7	0	2	7	0	15	1
Wells, Albuquerque*	1	0	1.000	4.78	29	0	0	9	0	0	32.0	29	22	17	1	1	25	1	29	7
Wernig, Tacoma*	7	8	.467	4.91	39	8	1	12	1	2	99.0	99	59	54	10	6	51	0	48	7
West, Portland*	1	1	.500	6.32	4	4	0	0	0	0	15.2	12	11	11	3	0	12	0	15	0
Wetteland, Albuquerque	4	3	.571	2.79	41	4	0	34	0	20	61.1	48	22	19	5	1	26	1	55	6
Wickander, Colorado Springs*	1	0	1.000	2.31	12	0	0	7	0	2	11.2	9	3	3	0	0	5	2	10	1
Wilkins, Tucson	8	7	.533	4.20	65	0	0	47	0	21	83.2	84	47	39	2	5	43	5	65	5
Williams, Tucson	0	1	.000	4.93	7	7	0	0	0	0	38.1	39	25	21	3	2	22	0	29	3
Williams, Phoenix*	7	9	.438	5.96	30	28	3	1	0	0	160.0	192	120	106	17	1	93	0	69	12
Willis, Portland	1	1	.500	1.64	3	1	0	1	0	0	11.0	5	4	2	0	1	0	0	0	0
Wood, Las Vegas	3	8	.273	5.74	47	6	0	18	0	2	69.0	73	48	44	6	2	39	4	68	7
York, Colorado Springs	0	1	.000	5.88	5	0	0	0	0	0	26.0	40	19	17	2	1	16	0	13	1
Young, Edmonton*	4	8	.333	4.90	34	8	0	15	0	5	71.2	88	53	39	2	4	25	1	39	8
Zappelli, Edmonton	2	1	.667	4.44	17	0	0	5	0	0	24.1	24	16	12	1	1	19	3	16	0

BALKS—Guzman, 6; D. Cook, McAndrew, J. Williams, 5 each; Gozzo, Helton, Henry, Holton, D. Veres, B. Williams, 4 each; Bones, Dunne, Egloff, Fetters, Hennis, Ch. Jones, S. Lewis, Lilliquist, Otto, Perschke, Show, 3 each; Balabon, Burba, Clark, Comstock, Cummings, Eskew, Freeland, X. Hernandez, Ca. Jones, Olin, Oliveras, Parker, Rojas, Sebra, Slusarski, Stephens, Toliver, Turner, E. Valdez, S. Valdez, Wayne, Wernig, 2 each; Allison, Banks, Bittiger, Blair, Bruske, Christopher, Clements, Corbett, Delkus, Drahman, Drees, Drummond, Eave, Garces, A. Garcia, Givens, G. Hall, Hammaker, Ge. Harris, Gr. Harris, Hartsock, Horton, James, Kennedy, King, R. Kramer, Mahomes, Masters, McClellan, McCoy, McMurtry, Nelson, Novoa, Pawlowski, Peterson, Powell, Rasmussen, Remlinger, Rosenberg, Sager, Schiraldi, Schock, Shaw, Tejada, Thurmond, Tsamis, Tunnell, Vande Berg, R. Veres, Weber, Wetteland, 1 each.

COMBINATION SHUTOUTS—Holton-Wetteland-Christopher, Martinez-Holton-Shinall, Albuquerque; Cook-Vande Berg, Calgary; Bittiger-Olin, Blair-Ward, King-Valdez, Colorado Springs; Beasley-Buckels-Leiper, Burcham-Young, Grahe-Pawlowski, Tolliver-Corbett-Beasley-Berrios-Buckels, Edmonton; Peterson-Clements-Costello, Rosenberg-Lewis-Wood-Hernandez, Las Vegas; McMurtry-Reed, Oliveras-Tate, Phoenix; Edens-Drummond, Edens-Savage-Drummond, Edens-Wayne, Neagle-Drummond-Wayne, Neagle-Tsamis-Garces, Neagle-Wassenaar, Tsamis-Neagle, Tsamis-Wassenaar-Casian-Drummond, Portland; Dressendorfer-Campbell-Walton, Guzman-Allison-Briscoe, Harris-Briscoe, Harris-Briscoe-Wernig-Pico-Walton, Schock-Wernig-Walton, Show-Campbell-Allison, Tacoma; Bowen-Hernandez 2, Clark-Capel, Ilsley-Turner-Hartgraves-Wilkins, Juden-Sebra, Mallicoat-Schilling-Wilkins, Tunnell-Ilsley-Wilkins-Corsi, Tunnell-Wilkins, Tucson; Carter-Stephens-Scheid-Drahman, Drees-Carter, Perschke-Carter-Hall, Vancouver.

NO-HIT GAMES—Wernig, Tacoma, defeated Vancouver, 1-0, June 10; Neidlinger, Albuquerque, defeated Las Vegas, 3-0, August 6.

FIELDING

TEAM

Team	Pct.	G	PO	A	E	DP	PB	Team	Pct.	G	PO	A	E	DP	PB
Tacoma	.977	136	3531	1527	121	146	19	Colorado Springs	.968	139	3509	1525	169	141	18
Albuquerque	.976	138	3604	1548	129	144	15	Vancouver	.968	135	3475	1414	164	84	21
Portland	.974	138	3536	1557	138	144	18	Tucson	.967	140	3708	1572	179	163	23
Edmonton	.971	136	3473	1606	151	158	10	Las Vegas	.966	140	3685	1518	182	124	19
Calgary	.968	136	3534	1617	171	162	30	Phoenix	.964	138	3557	1570	189	132	18

INDIVIDUAL

*Throws lefthanded.

FIRST BASEMEN

Player, Team	Pct.	G	PO	A	E	DP	Player, Team	Pct.	G	PO	A	E	DP
Afenir, Tacoma	1.000	2	19	1	0	2	Colbert, Phoenix	1.000	3	21	0	0	5
Aldrete, Colorado Springs*	.985	9	58	7	1	4	Coles, Phoenix	.926	4	23	2	2	4
Aldrete, Phoenix*	.985	58	486	37	8	43	Cooper, Tucson	.990	17	95	5	1	5
Amaro, Edmonton	1.000	1	8	0	0	0	Cron, Edmonton	.990	80	738	51	8	72
Anthony, Tucson*	1.000	3	23	0	0	2	Dorsett, Las Vegas	.971	18	124	10	4	10
Azocar, Las Vegas*	.993	16	127	6	1	10	Garrison, Tacoma	1.000	1	2	0	0	0
Bailey, Phoenix	1.000	1	1	0	0	0	Grunhard, Edmonton*	1.000	1	1	0	0	1
Baker, Tucson	1.000	1	1	0	0	0	Heep, Vancouver*	1.000	5	8	1	0	0
Bilardello, Las Vegas	.955	8	36	6	2	4	J. Hall, Vancouver	1.000	4	20	5	0	0
Blowers, Calgary	1.000	1	9	0	0	1	Higgins, Las Vegas	.985	51	303	24	5	36
Bowie, Calgary*	1.000	13	105	6	0	14	Howitt, Tacoma	.996	24	243	22	1	24
Brock, Vancouver	1.000	1	5	1	0	0	R. Jefferson, Colorado Springs*.	.991	36	289	25	3	26
Brown, Vancouver	1.000	1	1	0	0	0	Jelic, Las Vegas	1.000	5	18	3	0	1
Brown, Colorado Springs	1.000	3	17	0	0	0	Karros, Albuquerque	.991	127	1095	109	11	119
Cockrell, Calgary	1.000	4	29	4	0	5	Kittle, Vancouver	.979	11	87	7	2	10
							Lampkin, Las Vegas	1.000	5	32	2	0	5
							Lee, Vancouver	1.000	2	1	0	0	0

CLASS AAA — PACIFIC COAST LEAGUE

Player, Team	Pct.	G	PO	A	E	DP
Lopez, Colorado Springs	.995	19	186	20	1	13
Lyons, Edmonton	.970	12	94	4	3	6
Manto, Colorado Springs	.986	15	128	10	2	12
MARTINEZ, Calgary	.992	118	1078	106	9	122
Medina, Colorado Springs*	.998	50	439	29	1	52
Moses, Colorado Springs*	.976	12	113	10	3	13
Naveda, Portland	1.000	2	10	2	0	2
Nelson, 67 Van.-22 Tuc.*	.987	89	701	64	9	53
Noce, Phoenix	1.000	2	4	0	0	0
Patterson, Phoenix	.988	11	79	2	1	8
Phelps, Phoenix*	1.000	4	22	4	0	1
A. Powell, Calgary	1.000	1	4	0	0	1
Rodriguez, Albuquerque*	.975	12	71	8	2	8
Rodriguez, Portland	.993	15	130	10	1	13
Rohde, Tucson	.971	4	31	2	1	3
Rose, Edmonton	1.000	1	11	0	0	1
Roth, Vancouver	1.000	1	5	0	0	0
Sheaffer, Portland	.983	20	157	17	3	18
Simms, Tucson	.978	30	243	22	6	26
Sorrento, Portland	.986	106	925	56	14	95
Springer, Calgary	1.000	3	26	3	0	3
Stark, Vancouver	.988	60	461	28	6	35
Staton, Las Vegas	.980	64	526	52	12	36
Stevens, Edmonton*	.991	52	426	30	4	64
Tolentino, Tucson*	.984	79	690	55	12	88
Traxler, Albuquerque*	1.000	6	39	3	0	2
Wakamatsu, Vancouver	1.000	1	1	0	0	0
Walters, Las Vegas	.982	8	50	6	1	5
Wilson, Phoenix	.990	72	650	40	7	58
Witmeyer, Tacoma*	.992	113	955	58	8	106

SECOND BASEMEN

Player, Team	Pct.	G	PO	A	E	DP
Amaral, Calgary	.966	26	41	74	4	18
Amaro, Edmonton	.947	4	9	9	1	2
Anderson, Edmonton	.974	64	127	171	8	47
Baker, Tucson	.962	9	11	14	1	3
Barrett, Las Vegas	1.000	16	28	39	0	7
Bernhardt, Vancouver	.978	77	161	188	8	34
Blankenship, Tacoma	.956	11	15	28	2	5
Bournigal, Albuquerque	.981	12	23	29	1	9
Brosius, Tacoma	1.000	1	0	2	0	0
Brown, Colorado Springs	.939	28	51	72	8	14
Burdick, Colorado Springs	.978	32	60	75	3	22
Carter, Phoenix	.992	30	48	76	1	17
Coachman, Tacoma	.982	76	162	221	7	58
Cochrane, Calgary	.837	10	22	19	8	3
Colombino, Tucson	1.000	1	2	3	0	1
Correia, Tacoma	.909	5	13	7	2	1
Curtis, Edmonton	.945	25	55	83	8	20
K. Davis, Edmonton	.976	24	52	70	3	22
DeButch, Vancouver	1.000	1	0	2	0	0
Diaz, Las Vegas	.909	6	11	9	2	2
Disarcina, Edmonton	1.000	1	2	6	0	1
Escobar, Colorado Springs	.951	8	16	23	2	6
Garrison, Tacoma	.986	20	33	39	1	11
HALE, Portland	.982	108	236	306	10	85
Hemond, Tacoma	.990	36	88	105	2	34
Henley, Vancouver	1.000	7	13	15	0	2
Higgins, Las Vegas	.944	16	18	33	3	7
Hubbard, Tucson	1.000	1	1	2	0	0
Jackson, Calgary	.972	58	136	177	9	54
Johnson, Phoenix	.920	6	16	7	2	2
Kelley, Las Vegas	.973	54	83	137	6	25
Kirby, Colorado Springs	1.000	5	2	7	0	0
Letterio, Calgary	.963	17	29	49	3	10
Lewis, Colorado Springs	.941	3	4	12	1	1
Litton, Phoenix	1.000	1	1	2	0	0
Magallanes, Colorado Springs	.983	60	110	171	5	42
Manrique, Tacoma	1.000	1	2	2	0	0
Martin, Vancouver	.977	55	115	143	6	16
McLemore, Tucson	1.000	4	8	6	0	3
Mota, Tucson	.967	116	214	307	18	71
Mota, Las Vegas	.985	76	126	208	5	38
Munoz, Albuquerque	.971	70	151	217	11	46
Naveda, Portland	1.000	6	7	16	0	3
Noce, Phoenix	1.000	4	5	10	0	2
Perezchica, Phoenix	.956	16	41	45	4	14
Pye, Las Vegas	.947	11	18	18	2	5
Rodriguez, Portland	.988	40	68	94	2	24
Rohde, Tucson	.967	22	47	71	4	20
Rose, Edmonton	.960	26	54	66	5	20
Roth, Vancouver	1.000	4	8	7	0	0
Santana, Phoenix	.956	90	193	265	21	54
Shipley, Las Vegas	1.000	2	3	2	0	1
Smith, Albuquerque	.971	43	76	126	6	34
Smith, Calgary	.909	3	6	4	1	1
Smith, Colorado Springs	.988	21	30	49	1	15
Springer, Calgary	.942	32	76	85	10	27
Tatarian, Vancouver	1.000	2	2	3	0	0
Tatis, Colorado Springs	1.000	1	2	1	0	1
Vatcher, Las Vegas	.667	1	2	0	1	0
Wasinger, Edmonton	1.000	1	2	2	0	1
Young, Albuquerque	1.000	1	1	2	0	1

THIRD BASEMEN

Player, Team	Pct.	G	PO	A	E	DP
Anderson, Edmonton	.800	1	3	1	1	0
Baker, Tucson	.962	34	21	55	3	4
Barns, Edmonton	1.000	1	0	1	0	0
Beltre, Vancouver	.889	16	9	31	5	1
Bilardello, Las Vegas	.889	8	3	13	2	0
Blankenship, Tacoma	1.000	3	2	11	0	2
Blowers, Calgary	.915	75	45	160	19	13
Bournigal, Albuquerque	.944	9	3	14	1	3
Brosius, Tacoma	.939	65	46	155	13	16
Brown, Colorado Springs	.903	60	32	126	17	9
Burdick, Colorado Springs	.727	6	2	6	3	0
Carter, Phoenix	.857	3	1	5	1	1
Cochrane, Calgary	1.000	3	0	3	0	0
Colbert, Phoenix	.864	6	5	14	3	1
Coles, Phoenix	.920	55	46	115	14	12
Colombino, Tucson	.921	48	52	77	11	7
Coolbaugh, Las Vegas	.886	59	36	112	19	8
Cooper, Tucson	.962	60	33	118	6	11
Correia, Tacoma	.978	12	10	34	1	2
Cron, Edmonton	.869	41	19	74	14	8
Curtis, Edmonton	.918	58	36	133	15	14
K. Davis, Edmonton	.846	7	5	17	4	2
Diaz, Las Vegas	.667	3	2	4	3	3
Dorsett, Las Vegas	1.000	1	3	3	0	0
Ebel, Albuquerque	1.000	2	0	1	0	0
Finken, Albuquerque	.895	10	4	13	2	2
Garrison, Tacoma	.944	8	3	14	1	5
J. HALL, Vancouver	.938	99	69	202	18	6
Hansen, Albuquerque	.965	68	42	124	6	11
Hatcher, Albuquerque	1.000	1	0	1	0	0
Hemond, Tacoma	.893	24	14	53	8	4
Henley, Vancouver	.878	24	23	42	9	4
Higgins, Las Vegas	.931	41	33	62	7	5
Jackson, Calgary	.978	31	25	63	2	8
Jelic, Las Vegas	.000	1	0	0	1	0
Jorgensen, Portland	.925	125	91	277	30	32
Lansford, Tacoma	1.000	6	1	4	0	1
Law, Tacoma	.951	18	5	34	2	3
Lennon, Calgary	1.000	1	1	0	0	0
Lewis, Colorado Springs	.667	1	1	1	1	0
Litton, Phoenix	.857	4	1	5	1	0
Lopez, Colorado Springs	.935	14	10	33	3	3
Magallanes, Colorado Springs	1.000	6	4	14	0	0
Manrique, Tacoma	.967	10	6	23	1	2
Manto, Colorado Springs	.846	17	6	27	6	2
L. Martinez, Albuquerque	.909	22	13	37	5	5
Mota, Las Vegas	.750	4	2	4	2	0
Munoz, Albuquerque	.895	33	26	51	9	3
Naveda, Portland	.786	5	1	10	3	0
Noce, Phoenix	1.000	1	0	1	0	0
Parker, Phoenix	.882	13	11	19	4	2
Patterson, Phoenix	.930	41	26	81	8	6
Perezchica, Phoenix	.917	24	14	52	6	9
Rodriguez, Portland	.933	13	8	20	2	4
Rohde, Tucson	.939	24	20	42	4	5
Rose, Edmonton	.952	33	16	64	4	3
Roth, Vancouver	.833	3	2	3	1	0
Sheaffer, Portland	.000	2	0	0	1	0
Smith, Calgary	1.000	2	1	3	0	0
Smith, Colorado Springs	1.000	1	0	2	0	0
Springer, Calgary	.921	29	17	65	7	7
Staton, Las Vegas	.883	41	27	64	12	7
Tatarian, Vancouver	.857	5	2	4	1	0
Thome, Colorado Springs	.949	40	28	84	6	5
Wasinger, Edmonton	1.000	2	0	2	0	0

SHORTSTOPS

Player, Team	Pct.	G	PO	A	E	DP
Amaral, Calgary	.966	63	107	210	11	46
Anderson, Edmonton	.977	20	30	54	2	9
Baker, Tucson	.959	24	22	48	3	11
Beltre, Vancouver	.941	73	120	212	21	27
Benjamin, Phoenix	.976	64	109	252	9	38
Blankenship, Tacoma	.940	14	28	51	5	13
Blowers, Calgary	1.000	1	2	3	0	1
Bordick, Tacoma	.974	26	35	79	3	13
Bournigal, Albuquerque	.969	45	74	145	7	31
Brosius, Tacoma	.933	4	3	11	1	4
Brown, Colorado Springs	1.000	1	1	3	0	0
Burdick, Colorado Springs	1.000	2	3	1	0	0
Carter, Phoenix	.890	17	17	56	9	8
Cedeno, Tucson	.927	90	131	262	31	68
Cochrane, Calgary	.895	3	6	11	2	4
Colbert, Phoenix	1.000	2	1	1	0	0
K. Davis, Edmonton	1.000	2	3	8	0	2
Diaz, Las Vegas	.921	11	14	21	3	3
DISARCINA, Edmonton	.968	117	189	419	20	99
Escobar, Colorado Springs	.944	25	24	61	5	16
Faries, Las Vegas	.980	20	33	65	2	13
Fermin, Colorado Springs	1.000	2	2	5	0	0
Garrison, Tacoma	.955	48	63	149	10	32
Hansen, Albuquerque	1.000	1	1	1	0	1

Player, Team	Pct.	G	PO	A	E	DP
Hemond, Tacoma	1.000	2	2	2	0	0
Henley, Vancouver	.947	26	32	75	6	11
Jackson, Calgary	1.000	9	15	28	0	7
Johnson, Phoenix	.848	7	9	19	5	4
Jorgensen, Portland	1.000	2	0	1	0	0
King, Calgary	1.000	2	4	4	0	0
Lewis, Colorado Springs	.958	41	60	122	8	29
Litton, Phoenix	.870	4	4	16	3	4
Magallanes, Colorado Springs	.957	29	46	89	6	21
Manrique, Tacoma	1.000	1	1	1	0	1
Manto, Colorado Springs	.941	5	5	11	1	1
Martin, Vancouver	.953	39	81	122	10	23
L. Martinez, Albuquerque	.948	20	17	38	3	8
Mota, Las Vegas	.947	35	44	98	8	18
Naveda, Portland	.897	9	6	20	3	1
Noce, Phoenix	1.000	2	3	6	0	0
Offerman, Albuquerque	.956	76	126	241	17	54
Parker, Phoenix	.918	13	21	35	5	9
Perezchica, Phoenix	.898	11	16	28	5	6
Polidor, Tacoma	.953	53	64	140	10	27
Reboulet, Portland	.951	134	202	415	32	85
Rodriguez, Portland	1.000	5	2	6	0	2
Rohde, Tucson	.986	30	45	93	2	21
Romero, Las Vegas	.933	28	35	62	7	11
Santana, Phoenix	.838	15	20	37	11	8
Shipley, Las Vegas	.977	62	80	175	6	37
Smith, Albuquerque	.885	8	4	19	3	1
Smith, Calgary	.947	57	93	194	16	44
Smith, Colorado Springs	.958	47	69	135	9	35
Springer, Calgary	1.000	9	12	33	0	10
Tatarian, Vancouver	.875	2	2	5	1	1
Uribe, Phoenix	.980	11	16	34	1	4
Yelding, Tucson	.958	11	22	24	2	4

OUTFIELDERS

Player, Team	Pct.	G	PO	A	E	DP
Aldrete, Colorado Springs*	1.000	10	19	1	0	1
Aldrete, Phoenix*	.750	2	3	0	1	0
Allred, Colorado Springs*	.980	52	92	4	2	0
Amaro, Edmonton	.976	94	150	14	4	2
Anthony, Tucson*	.972	70	131	9	4	0
Azocar, Las Vegas*	.978	77	133	3	3	0
Baker, Tucson	1.000	1	1	0	0	0
Bass, Phoenix	1.000	10	20	0	0	0
Bean, Albuquerque*	.992	74	112	5	1	1
Belle, Colorado Springs	.952	11	19	1	1	0
Berroa, Colorado Springs	.971	83	151	14	5	2
Blankenship, Tacoma	.857	3	6	0	1	0
Brito, Portland	1.000	1	1	0	0	0
Brooks, Albuquerque	.989	97	175	7	2	3
Brown, Portland	.984	108	243	11	4	3
Brown, Colorado Springs	.840	20	19	2	4	0
Bruett, Portland*	.991	97	211	10	2	0
BRUNDAGE, Calgary*	.995	94	193	8	1	1
Cangelosi, Vancouver*	.932	23	39	2	3	0
Carter, Phoenix	.981	23	51	0	1	0
Coachman, Tacoma	.917	12	18	4	2	0
Cochrane, Calgary	1.000	5	3	0	0	0
Cockrell, Calgary	.965	94	161	6	6	2
Colbert, Phoenix	.000	6	0	0	2	0
Cole, Colorado Springs*	.909	8	18	2	2	1
Coles, Phoenix	.971	26	33	1	1	0
Cooper, Tucson	.983	40	55	2	1	0
M. Davis, Edmonton	.982	111	207	9	4	2
Davis, Albuquerque	1.000	41	56	2	0	1
Dean, Tucson	.958	14	22	1	1	1
Fox, Tacoma*	.982	126	306	14	6	4
Goodwin, Albuquerque	.990	131	284	6	3	2
Grunhard, Edmonton*	.969	67	116	9	4	3
J. Hall, Vancouver	.974	18	35	2	1	0
Hawks, Las Vegas	.750	1	3	0	1	0
Heep, Vancouver*	1.000	11	19	0	0	0
Heffernan, Albuquerque	1.000	1	1	0	0	0
Higgins, Las Vegas	.946	23	33	2	2	0
Hill, Vancouver	.962	81	168	11	7	1
Hillemann, Las Vegas	.976	15	39	1	1	0
Hood, Calgary	.944	102	225	10	14	5
Howard, Las Vegas	.966	25	54	2	2	1
Howitt, Tacoma	.985	81	186	11	3	1
Jackson, Calgary	1.000	14	36	2	0	0
S. Jefferson, Colorado Springs	.968	20	27	3	1	0
Jelic, Las Vegas	.941	10	15	1	1	1
Jennings, Tacoma*	.940	82	145	11	10	0
Jeter, Vancouver	.934	35	81	4	6	0
L. Jones, 26 C.S.-57 Port.	.985	83	127	6	2	0
Kingery, Phoenix*	1.000	13	32	0	0	0
Kirby, Colorado Springs	.975	109	225	7	6	1
Komminsk, Tacoma	.992	67	124	6	1	0
Kutzler, Vancouver	1.000	1	1	0	0	0
Lampkin, Las Vegas	1.000	2	3	0	0	0
Lawton, Edmonton	1.000	12	28	1	0	0
Lee, Vancouver	.960	83	161	8	7	0
Lennon, Calgary	.951	67	113	3	6	1

Player, Team	Pct.	G	PO	A	E	DP
Leonard, Phoenix	.941	34	45	3	3	0
Lewis, Phoenix	.992	80	243	5	2	1
Lofton, Tucson*	.974	129	308	27	9	3
Lopez, Colorado Springs	1.000	5	9	0	0	0
Manto, Colorado Springs	1.000	2	3	0	0	0
Massarelli, Tucson	.917	9	10	1	1	1
McCray, Vancouver	.985	75	186	8	3	5
McGee, Phoenix	.909	4	10	0	1	0
McWilliam, Las Vegas	1.000	2	2	0	0	0
Mikulik, Tucson	1.000	1	1	0	0	0
Mondesi, Albuquerque	.000	2	0	0	1	0
Morgan, Portland*	1.000	3	2	0	0	0
Moses, Colorado Springs*	.993	61	140	8	1	3
Mota, Las Vegas	1.000	3	1	0	0	0
Munoz, Portland	.982	52	109	2	2	1
Naveda, Portland	.985	65	123	8	2	2
Neel, Tacoma	1.000	10	15	0	0	0
Newson, Vancouver*	1.000	31	53	1	0	0
Nixon, Colorado Springs	.909	9	10	0	1	0
Ortiz, Tucson	.941	23	43	5	3	1
Parker, Phoenix	.981	58	100	4	2	1
Peters, Edmonton	.985	72	120	8	2	1
A. Powell, Calgary	.983	51	106	8	2	0
Rhodes, Tucson*	.944	82	140	11	9	3
Ritchie, Phoenix*	.951	46	75	2	4	0
Rodriguez, Albuquerque*	.982	101	163	4	3	1
Rohde, Tucson	1.000	1	1	0	0	0
Roomes, Portland	1.000	46	66	6	0	2
Sammons, Tacoma	1.000	2	6	0	0	0
Sheaffer, Portland	.778	7	5	2	2	0
Simmons, Tacoma	.980	36	49	1	1	0
Simms, Phoenix	.977	48	82	3	2	1
Sorrento, Portland	1.000	7	8	2	0	1
Sosa, Vancouver	.970	30	95	2	3	0
Springer, Calgary	.950	14	19	0	1	0
Stevens, Edmonton*	.970	57	93	3	3	1
Tatis, Colorado Springs	1.000	3	4	0	0	0
Taylor, Las Vegas	.969	121	246	6	8	1
Vatcher, Las Vegas	.969	114	204	18	7	3
Waggoner, Vancouver	.982	48	109	1	2	0
Ward, Las Vegas	.964	72	129	3	5	2
T. Ward, Colorado Springs	.968	13	30	0	1	0
Wood, Phoenix*	.966	136	275	8	10	1
Young, Tucson	1.000	20	45	4	0	2
Zambrano, Colorado Springs	.957	29	42	2	2	0

CATCHERS

Player, Team	Pct.	G	PO	A	E	DP	PB
Afenir, Tacoma	.986	72	386	36	6	7	11
Alomar, Colorado Springs	.833	3	5	0	1	0	1
Bailey, Phoenix	.996	58	654	24	1	0	6
Bilardello, Las Vegas	.972	30	161	14	5	3	3
Brito, Tacoma	.984	22	113	13	2	2	5
Brooks, Albuquerque	1.000	7	15	0	0	0	1
Brown, Vancouver	.988	75	378	29	5	3	10
Brown, Colorado Springs	1.000	3	8	1	0	0	0
Buckley, Portland	1.000	3	7	1	0	0	0
Cochrane, Calgary	.949	23	115	14	7	1	3
Colbert, Phoenix	.991	25	100	16	1	0	4
D. Davis, Edmonton	.989	27	156	21	2	1	2
Decker, Phoenix	.994	26	156	16	1	0	3
Diaz, Colorado Springs	.983	35	160	17	3	4	1
Dorsett, Las Vegas	.990	31	188	16	2	0	1
Eusebio, Tucson	1.000	5	40	1	0	0	1
Fernandez, Phoenix	1.000	3	6	2	0	0	0
Gonzalez, Edmonton	.889	1	7	1	1	0	0
J. Hall, Vancouver	1.000	2	2	0	0	0	0
Heffernan, Albuquerque	.985	55	282	47	5	5	1
Hemond, Tacoma	.990	32	176	17	2	1	3
Hernandez, Albuquerque	.978	92	592	77	15	7	13
Higgins, Las Vegas	1.000	1	2	0	0	0	0
Howard, Calgary	.978	80	381	57	10	8	18
Johnson, Colorado Springs	.992	21	112	12	1	2	2
Lampkin, Las Vegas	.971	33	176	24	6	4	8
Liebert, Vancouver	1.000	18	66	2	0	0	3
Lyons, Edmonton	.972	26	153	22	5	5	4
Manto, Colorado Springs	.941	7	27	5	2	1	0
Manwaring, Phoenix	.975	22	100	15	3	2	3
Massarelli, Tucson	.970	27	143	17	5	1	4
McGriff, Tucson	.987	27	132	20	2	4	5
McGuire, Colorado Springs	.962	11	49	1	2	1	3
McNamara, Phoenix	.989	16	84	10	1	1	2
Nichols, Tucson	.985	34	237	30	4	8	7
Orton, Edmonton	.985	69	397	49	7	7	2
Rice, Albuquerque	1.000	1	6	1	0	0	0
Servais, Tucson	.985	57	350	33	6	5	6
Sheaffer, Portland	.984	53	286	20	5	2	7
Sinatro, Calgary	.960	40	199	17	9	4	9
Siwa, Portland	1.000	1	4	0	0	0	0
Taubensee, Colorado Springs	.975	89	412	47	12	5	11
Tejada, Tacoma	.980	20	128	17	3	1	0
Tingley, Edmonton	.961	17	65	9	3	0	2
Wakamatsu, Vancouver	.990	51	266	31	3	3	8
Walters, Las Vegas	.980	72	399	40	9	5	7
WEBSTER, Portland	.989	84	477	65	6	7	11

PITCHERS

Player, Team	Pct.	G	PO	A	E	DP
Abbott, Edmonton*	.976	27	13	28	1	4
Abbott, Portland	1.000	8	1	4	0	0
Aldrete, Phoenix*	.000	1	0	0	1	0
Allen, Tucson*	1.000	5	1	3	0	0
Allison, Tacoma*	.875	18	0	7	1	1
Anderson, Portland*	1.000	5	2	7	0	2
Ard, Phoenix	1.000	10	2	13	0	1
Baker, Tucson	.500	3	1	0	1	0
Balabon, Calgary*	.773	17	3	14	5	0
Bankhead, Calgary	1.000	5	0	1	0	0
Banks, Portland	.808	25	5	16	5	2
Barton, Calgary*	1.000	17	4	1	0	0
Beasley, Edmonton	1.000	23	4	20	0	0
Beck, Phoenix	.944	23	3	14	1	1
Bell, Colorado Springs*	1.000	4	2	2	0	0
Berrios, Edmonton*	1.000	17	3	2	0	0
Birkbeck, Colorado Springs	1.000	3	0	2	0	1
Bittiger, Colorado Springs	.889	27	12	20	4	0
Blair, Colorado Springs	.935	26	14	15	2	2
Bockus, Edmonton	.750	4	1	2	1	0
Bones, Las Vegas	.897	23	16	19	4	1
Boucher, Colorado Springs*	1.000	3	0	4	0	0
Bowen, Tucson	.957	18	8	14	1	2
Briscoe, Tacoma	.955	22	5	16	1	2
Brito, Vancouver	.909	19	8	12	2	1
Brundage, Calgary*	1.000	4	0	1	0	0
Bruske, Colorado Springs	1.000	7	2	1	0	0
Buckels, Edmonton	1.000	51	1	3	0	0
Burba, Calgary	.962	23	5	20	1	0
Burcham, Edmonton	.939	31	8	23	2	2
Burns, Tacoma	1.000	13	1	3	0	0
Campbell, Tacoma	1.000	35	5	14	0	1
Capel, Tucson	.867	30	5	8	2	0
Carter, Vancouver	1.000	41	3	11	0	1
Casian, Portland	1.000	34	1	7	0	1
Chamberlain, Colorado Springs	1.000	1	0	1	0	0
Childress, Tucson	1.000	7	1	1	0	0
Christopher, Albuquerque	1.000	63	6	10	0	0
Clark, Tucson	.872	26	10	24	5	7
Clements, Las Vegas*	1.000	11	0	3	0	0
Comstock, Calgary*	1.000	15	4	6	0	0
Cook, Albuquerque	.958	14	5	18	1	1
Cook, Calgary	1.000	10	3	7	0	2
Corbett, Edmonton*	.952	41	5	15	1	2
Costello, Las Vegas	.800	17	3	1	1	0
Cummings, Colorado Springs	.667	5	1	7	4	0
Curtis, Colorado Springs*	.778	20	3	4	2	0
Delkus, Portland	1.000	2	1	2	0	0
Dewey, Phoenix	1.000	10	1	4	0	0
Drahman, Vancouver	1.000	22	1	3	0	1
Drees, Vancouver*	.931	22	8	19	2	2
Dressendorfer, Tacoma	1.000	8	1	2	0	0
Drummond, Portland	.900	56	3	6	1	2
Dunne, Vancouver	1.000	17	0	9	0	0
Eave, Calgary	1.000	21	8	2	0	0
Edens, Portland	.972	25	14	21	1	4
Edwards, Vancouver*	1.000	14	4	11	0	1
Egloff, Colorado Springs	.900	15	3	6	1	2
Erb, Edmonton	1.000	31	0	4	0	0
Eskew, Tacoma	1.000	7	1	2	0	0
Fetters, Edmonton	.938	11	6	9	1	0
Freeland, Tucson	.929	22	2	11	1	0
Garces, Portland	1.000	10	1	5	0	1
Garcia, Tacoma	1.000	7	2	2	0	0
Garcia, Vancouver	.800	4	1	3	1	0
Gilmore, Las Vegas	1.000	26	10	7	0	0
Givens, Calgary*	1.000	3	0	2	0	0
Gozzo, Colorado Springs	.909	25	7	13	2	0
Grahe, Edmonton	.923	14	6	18	2	2
Gunderson, Phoenix*	.813	40	1	12	3	0
Guzman, Tacoma*	1.000	17	2	16	0	3
A. Hall, Colorado Springs*	.800	5	1	3	1	0
G. Hall, 19 Van.-3 C.S.*	.857	22	5	13	3	0
Hammaker, Las Vegas	1.000	3	0	6	0	1
Hanson, Calgary	1.000	1	0	1	0	0
Harris, Las Vegas	1.000	4	4	2	0	0
Harris, Tacoma	.929	16	4	9	1	1
Harris, Calgary	1.000	25	3	5	0	0
Hartgraves, Tucson*	1.000	16	1	8	0	3
Hartsock, Albuquerque	1.000	29	8	15	0	0
Hasler, Vancouver	.714	11	3	2	2	0
Heffernan, Albuquerque	1.000	2	1	1	0	1
Helton, Calgary*	.962	30	10	15	1	0
Hennis, Tucson	.786	11	3	8	3	1
Henry, Tucson*	.969	27	5	26	1	0
Heredia, Phoenix	.977	33	10	32	1	4
Hernandez, Tucson	1.000	16	2	5	0	1
Hernandez, Las Vegas	.955	56	6	15	1	2
Hernandez, Vancouver	.900	7	2	7	1	1
Hibbard, Vancouver*	1.000	1	0	4	0	0
Hickerson, Phoenix*	1.000	12	0	2	0	0
Holton, Albuquerque	.960	29	9	15	1	1
Horton, Colorado Springs*	1.000	22	0	6	0	2
Ilsley, Tucson*	.929	46	3	23	2	1
James, Albuquerque	.857	13	4	2	1	2
Jones, Calgary	.857	20	3	3	1	0
Jones, Albuquerque	1.000	29	6	11	0	2
D. Jones, Colorado Springs	1.000	17	4	7	0	0
Juden, Tucson	.889	10	2	6	1	0
Kennedy, Vancouver	.800	17	1	7	2	0
King, Colorado Springs	1.000	3	0	2	0	0
Kramer, Calgary	.929	16	5	8	1	1
Kramer, Colorado Springs	1.000	10	0	1	0	0
Kutzler, Vancouver	.973	29	14	22	1	0
Lambert, Las Vegas*	1.000	11	0	4	0	1
Leiper, Edmonton*	1.000	13	0	3	0	0
Lewis, Las Vegas	.850	48	8	9	3	1
Lewis, Edmonton	.926	17	9	16	2	1
Lilliquist, Las Vegas*	.929	33	5	8	1	0
Lovelace, Calgary*	.875	13	3	4	1	0
Lynch, Albuquerque*	1.000	33	5	9	0	1
Mahomes, Portland	.846	9	5	6	2	0
Mallicoat, Tucson*	.833	19	4	6	2	0
P. Martinez, Albuquerque	1.000	6	5	4	0	0
McAndrew, Albuquerque	.917	28	18	15	3	0
McCament, Las Vegas	1.000	30	8	7	0	0
McClellan, Phoenix	1.000	5	4	4	0	0
McCoy, Tacoma*	1.000	4	1	0	0	0
McMurtry, Phoenix	.842	27	12	20	6	2
Melendez, Las Vegas	1.000	9	0	5	0	1
Meyer, Calgary	.889	18	3	5	1	0
Mitchell, Calgary	1.000	2	0	2	0	0
Montalvo, Edmonton	1.000	25	0	7	0	1
Musselman, Tacoma*	1.000	25	6	21	0	3
Naveda, Portland	1.000	2	0	1	0	0
Neagle, Portland*	1.000	19	4	15	0	0
Neidlinger, Albuquerque	.967	23	18	11	1	3
Nelson, Calgary	1.000	28	2	4	0	1
Novoa, Phoenix*	.917	17	7	15	2	4
Olin, Colorado Springs	.923	22	2	10	1	0
Oliveras, Phoenix	1.000	3	3	2	0	0
Opperman, Albuquerque	.938	11	5	10	1	2
Otto, Colorado Springs*	1.000	17	4	17	0	1
Parker, Tucson	1.000	25	6	9	0	0
Pawlowski, Edmonton	1.000	10	0	1	0	0
Perschke, Vancouver	.906	27	10	19	3	1
Peterson, Las Vegas	1.000	8	2	3	0	0
Pico, Tacoma	1.000	45	5	14	0	0
D. Powell, Calgary*	.975	27	10	29	1	4
Prentice, Phoenix	1.000	1	0	1	0	0
Price, Las Vegas*	1.000	26	1	3	0	0
Rambo, Phoenix	1.000	3	2	0	0	0
Rasmussen, Las Vegas*	1.000	5	1	3	0	0
Reed, Phoenix	1.000	41	3	16	0	0
Remlinger, Phoenix*	.864	19	3	16	3	1
Rice, Calgary	.967	21	11	18	1	1
Richards, Calgary*	1.000	10	0	3	0	0
Rodriguez, Phoenix	1.000	3	0	1	0	0
Rojas, Calgary	1.000	16	1	2	0	0
Roscoe, Colorado Springs	1.000	3	2	0	0	1
Rosenberg, Las Vegas*	1.000	36	3	10	0	1
SAGER, Las Vegas	1.000	18	12	20	0	1
Salkeld, Calgary	1.000	4	0	4	0	2
Savage, Portland	1.000	38	8	4	0	2
Scheid, Vancouver*	.941	47	4	12	1	1
Schilling, Tucson	1.000	13	1	2	0	1
Schiraldi, Tucson	.909	15	5	5	1	2
Schock, Tacoma	1.000	16	4	9	0	3
Scott, Portland	.957	18	13	9	1	1
Scott, Las Vegas	.917	41	5	17	2	0
Seanez, Colorado Springs	.750	16	1	2	1	0
Sebra, Phoenix	1.000	30	3	5	0	1
Segura, Phoenix	1.000	32	0	8	0	1
Shaw, Colorado Springs	1.000	12	9	10	0	0
Shinall, Albuquerque	1.000	29	4	10	0	0
Show, Tacoma	.750	8	1	2	1	0
Slusarski, Tacoma	1.000	7	3	4	0	0
Smithberg, Las Vegas	.909	17	7	13	2	2
Sontag, Edmonton	1.000	3	1	1	0	0
Stephens, Vancouver	.840	53	5	16	4	0
Strebeck, Tacoma	.750	5	1	2	1	0
Tate, Phoenix	1.000	8	1	3	0	0
Thurmond, Phoenix*	1.000	26	0	8	0	0
Toliver, Edmonton	.938	18	3	12	1	0
Tsamis, Portland*	.944	29	8	43	3	0
Tunnell, Tucson	1.000	20	6	11	0	1
Turner, Tucson	1.000	13	0	2	0	0
E. Valdez, Colorado Springs*	.889	14	0	8	1	0
Valdez, Las Vegas	1.000	5	0	3	0	1
S. Valdez, Colorado Springs	.857	26	7	17	4	0
Valenzuela, Edmonton*	1.000	7	0	6	0	1
Vande Berg, Calgary*	.975	47	15	24	1	4
Veres, Albuquerque	1.000	57	6	11	0	1
Veres, Phoenix	.800	19	6	6	3	0
Vosberg, 12 Edm.-16 Cal.*	1.000	28	2	12	0	1
Walsh, Albuquerque	1.000	14	2	3	0	0
Walton, Tacoma	1.000	38	2	3	0	0

Player, Team	Pct.	G	PO	A	E	DP
C. Ward, Colorado Springs	.909	29	5	5	1	0
Wassenaar, Portland	1.000	40	3	18	0	2
Wayne, Portland*	1.000	51	0	7	0	0
Weber, Tacoma	.857	15	1	5	1	0
Wells, Albuquerque*	1.000	29	1	10	0	0
Wernig, Tacoma*	1.000	39	7	10	0	1
West, Portland*	1.000	4	0	1	0	0
Wetteland, Albuquerque	.923	42	5	7	1	2
Wickander, Colorado Springs*	1.000	11	0	3	0	0
Wilkins, Tucson	.864	65	5	14	3	0
Williams, Tucson	.818	7	5	4	2	0
Williams, Phoenix*	.875	30	1	20	3	2
Willis, Portland	1.000	3	2	2	0	0
Wood, Las Vegas	.909	47	10	10	2	2
York, Colorado Springs	.833	5	4	1	1	0
Young, Edmonton*	.938	34	5	10	1	0
Zappelli, Edmonton	.800	17	2	6	2	0

The following players did not have any fielding statistics at the positions indicated or appeared only as a designated hitter, pinch-hitter or pinch-runner: Bones, of; Coachman, p; Cochrane, 1b; Cockrell, c; Corsi, p; Cron, p; Engle, ph; Fleming, p; Fox, p; Garrison, p; Hamilton, dh; Heffernan, 2b; Henley, p; Hershiser, p; Hickey, p; Hill, 1b, p; Karros, 3b; Marquez, p; C. Martinez, 3b; Mielke, p; Noce, c; Peters, p; Pough, of; Pulido, p; Ritchie, p; Roomes, p; Sheaffer, p; K. Smith, of; Stephenson, dh, ph; Tatis, 3b; Tejada, p; Tolentino, p; Vatcher, p.

LEAGUE CHAMPIONS

Year	Team	Pct.
1903—	Los Angeles	.630
1904—	Tacoma	.589
	Tacoma§	.571
	Los Angeles§	.571
1905—	Tacoma	.583
	Los Angeles*	.604
1906—	Portland	.657
1907—	Los Angeles	.608
1908—	Los Angeles	.585
1909—	San Francisco	.623
1910—	Portland	.567
1911—	Portland	.589
1912—	Oakland	.591
1913—	Portland	.559
1914—	Portland	.574
1915—	San Francisco	.570
1916—	Los Angeles	.601
1917—	San Francisco	.561
1918—	Vernon	.569
	Los Angeles (2nd)x	.548
1919—	Vernon	.613
1920—	Vernon	.556
1921—	Los Angeles	.574
1922—	San Francisco	.638
1923—	San Francisco	.617
1924—	Seattle	.545
1925—	San Francisco	.643
1926—	Los Angeles	.599
1927—	Oakland	.615
1928—	San Francisco*	.630
	Sacramento§§	.626
	San Francisco§§	.626
1929—	Mission	.643
	Hollywood*	.592
1930—	Los Angeles	.576
	Hollywood*	.650
1931—	Hollywood	.626
	San Francisco*	.608
1932—	Portland	.587
1933—	Los Angeles	.610
1934—	Los Angeles z	.786
	Los Angeles z	.689
1935—	Los Angeles	.648
	San Francisco*	.608
1936—	Portland‡	.549
1937—	Sacramento	.573

Year	Team	Pct.
	San Diego (3rd)†	.545
1938—	Los Angeles	.590
	Sacramento (3rd)†	.537
1939—	Seattle	.589
	Sacramento (4th)†	.500
1940—	Seattle‡	.629
1941—	Seattle‡	.598
1942—	Sacramento	.590
	Seattle (3rd)†	.539
1943—	Los Angeles	.710
	S. Francisco (2nd)†	.574
1944—	Los Angeles	.586
	S. Francisco (3rd)†	.509
1945—	Portland	.622
	S. Francisco (4th)†	.525
1946—	San Francisco‡	.628
1947—	Los Angeles††	.567
1948—	Oakland‡	.606
1949—	Hollywood‡	.583
1950—	Oakland	.590
1951—	Seattle‡	.593
1952—	Hollywood	.606
1953—	Hollywood	.589
1954—	San Diego y	.604
1955—	Seattle	.552
1956—	Los Angeles	.637
1957—	San Francisco	.601
1958—	Phoenix	.578
1959—	Salt Lake City	.552
1960—	Spokane	.601
1961—	Tacoma	.630
1962—	San Diego	.604
1963—	Spokane	.620
	Oklahoma City a	.632
1964—	Arkansas	.609
	San Diego a	.576
1965—	Oklahoma City a	.628
	Portland	.547
1966—	Seattle a	.561
	Tulsa	.578
1967—	San Diego a	.574
	Spokane	.541
1968—	Tulsa a	.642
	Spokane	.586
1969—	Tacoma a	.589
	Eugene	.603

Year	Team	Pct.
1970—	Spokane a	.644
	Hawaii	.671
1971—	Salt Lake City	.534
	Tacoma	.545
1972—	Albuquerque	.622
	Eugene	.534
1973—	Tucson	.583
	Spokane a	.563
1974—	Spokane a	.549
	Albuquerque	.535
1975—	Salt Lake City	.556
	Hawaii a	.611
1976—	Salt Lake City	.625
	Hawaii a	.531
1977—	Phoenix a	.579
	Hawaii	.541
1978—	Tacoma b	.584
	Albuquerque b	.557
1979—	Albuquerque	.581
	Salt Lake City c	.541
1980—	Albuquerque	.578
	Hawaii	.539
1981—	Albuquerque*	.712
	Tacoma	.561
1982—	Albuquerque*	.594
	Spokane	.545
1983—	Albuquerque	.594
	Portland*	.528
1984—	Hawaii	.621
	Edmonton*	.486
1985—	Vancouver*	.522
	Phoenix	.563
1986—	Vancouver	.616
	Las Vegas*	.563
1987—	Calgary	.596
	Albuquerque*	.542
1988—	Vancouver	.599
	Las Vegas*	.529
1989—	Albuquerque	.563
	Vancouver*	.514
1990—	Albuquerque*	.641
	Edmonton	.553
1991—	Albuquerque	.580
	Tucson*	.564

*Won split-season playoff. †Won four-team playoff. ‡Won pennant and four-team playoff. §Tied for second-half title with Tacoma winning playoff. §§Tied for second-half title, with Sacramento winning playoff. ††Ended regular season in tie with San Francisco and won one-game playoff for pennant, then won four-club playoff. xWon playoff from first-place Vernon and awarded championship. yDefeated Hollywood in one-game playoff for pennant. zWon both halves, no playoff. aLeague was divided into Northern, Southern divisions in 1963, 1969-70-71, and Eastern, Western divisions in 1964 through 1968 and 1972 through 1977, won two-team playoff. bLeague divided into Eastern and Western divisions, Tacoma and Albuquerque declared co-champions following cancellation of four-team playoff due to continuing rain and wet grounds. cWon second-half title and defeated Hawaii in four-team playoff.

EASTERN LEAGUE

FINAL STANDINGS

Team	Har.	Hag.	Alb.	C.A.	Read.	Lon.	Wpt.	N.B.	W	L	T	Pct.	GB
Harrisburg (Expos)	....	12	8	15	11	15	11	15	87	53	0	.621	....
Hagerstown (Orioles)	8	....	13	8	12	13	12	15	81	59	0	.579	6
Albany (Yankees)	12	7	....	8	11	8	16	14	76	64	0	.543	11
Canton-Akron (Indians)	5	12	12	....	8	13	12	13	75	65	0	.536	12
Reading (Phillies)	9	8	9	12	....	10	10	14	72	68	0	.514	15
London (Tigers)	5	7	12	7	10	....	9	11	61	78	0	.439	25½
Williamsport (Mets)	9	8	4	8	10	10	....	11	60	79	0	.432	26½
New Britain (Red Sox)	5	5	6	5	7	6	9	....	47	93	0	.336	40

London club represented London, Ontario, Can.

Major league affiliations in parentheses.

Playoffs—Albany defeated Hagerstown, three games to none; Harrisburg defeated Canton-Akron, three games to one; Albany defeated Harrisburg, three games to none, to win league championship.

Regular-season attendance—Albany, 171,466; Canton-Akron, 218,397; Hagerstown, 193,753; Harrisburg, 233,423; London, 150,435; New Britain, 146,632; Reading, 250,610; Williamsport, 96,711. Totals—1,461,427. Playoffs (10 games)—12,598. All-Star Game at Huntsville—4,022.

Managers—Albany, Dan Radison; Canton-Akron, Ken Bolek; Hagerstown, Jerry Narron; Harrisburg, Mike Quade; London, Gene Roof; New Britain, Gary Allenson; Reading, Don McCormack; Williamsport, Clint Hurdle.

All-Star team—1B—J.T. Snow, Albany; 2B—Rodney Lofton, Hagerstown; 3B—Jim Thome, Canton-Akron; SS—Dave Silvestri, Albany; OF—Rob Katzaroff, Harrisburg; Bruce Dostal, Reading; Jeromy Burnitz, Williamsport; C—Bob Natal, Harrisburg; DH—Carlos Martinez, Canton-Akron; Util.—Matt Stairs, Harrisburg; RHP—Ed Martel, Albany; LHP—Arthur Rhodes, Hagerstown; Rel—Larry Stanford, Albany; Most Valuable Player—Matt Stairs, Harrisburg; Pitcher of the Year—Arthur Rhodes, Hagerstown; Manager of the Year—Mike Quade, Harrisburg.

BATTING

TEAM

Team	Avg.	G	AB	R	OR	H	TB	2B	3B	HR	RBI	SH	SF	HP	BB	Int. BB	SO	SB	CS	LOB
Hagerstown	.271	140	4738	704	554	1284	1747	225	41	52	624	29	52	42	618	25	913	165	45	1107
Harrisburg	.267	140	4759	683	483	1273	1841	196	45	94	620	63	39	54	493	32	853	167	79	1011
Albany	.267	140	4551	703	615	1215	1766	231	28	88	641	28	51	38	608	19	833	153	65	980
Reading	.260	140	4595	639	636	1196	1705	210	25	83	582	57	47	42	469	28	773	158	77	962
Canton-Akron	.253	140	4519	556	528	1145	1585	207	34	55	494	54	53	34	471	36	798	131	68	975
London	.251	139	4480	542	664	1123	1572	163	23	80	490	51	37	33	515	18	826	98	67	969
Williamsport	.238	139	4432	561	679	1053	1530	159	45	76	485	65	35	31	599	18	956	212	102	973
New Britain	.234	140	4481	439	667	1049	1395	181	21	41	382	38	36	26	530	12	851	101	68	1003

INDIVIDUAL

(Leading qualifiers for batting championship—378 or more plate appearances)

*Bats lefthanded.   †Switch-hitter.

Player, Team	Avg.	G	AB	R	H	TB	2B	3B	HR	RBI	SH	SF	HP	BB	Int. BB	SO	SB	CS
Stairs, Matt, Harrisburg	.333	129	505	87	168	257	30	10	13	78	2	3	3	66	8	47	23	11
Cianfrocco, Archi, Harrisburg	.316	124	456	71	144	212	21	10	9	77	2	2	9	38	2	112	11	3
Dostal, Bruce, Reading*	.313	96	364	68	114	150	11	5	5	34	1	4	5	58	5	55	38	16
Masse, Billy, Albany	.295	108	356	67	105	159	17	2	11	61	0	7	6	74	3	60	10	4
DeJardin, Bobby, Albany†	.295	129	482	74	142	169	21	0	2	53	8	1	2	62	1	55	18	13
Katzaroff, Rob, Harrisburg*	.290	137	558	94	162	196	21	2	3	50	9	1	5	54	1	61	33	18
Navarro, Tito, Williamsport	.288	128	482	69	139	162	9	4	2	42	12	4	1	73	2	63	42	19
Lofton, Rodney, Hagerstown	.284	118	437	78	124	143	6	5	1	33	9	2	3	48	1	74	56	10
Knoblauch, Jay, Albany	.284	97	335	52	95	148	16	2	11	50	2	4	3	42	1	69	16	8
Lehman, Mike, Hagerstown	.281	97	331	42	93	128	24	1	3	46	0	3	1	45	1	69	2	2

Departmental Leaders: G—Silvestri, 140; AB—Katzaroff, 558; R—Silvestri, 97; H—Stairs, 168; TB—Stairs, 257; 2B—Shamburg, 36; 3B—Burnitz, Cianfrocco, Stairs, 10; HR—Burnitz, 31; RBI—Burnitz, Phillips, 85; SH—Santangelo, 13; SF—Shamburg, Snow, 10; HP—Cianfrocco, 9; BB—Burnitz, 104; IBB—Carey, Stairs, 8; SO—Holland, 142; SB—Lofton, 56; CS—Brown, 20.

(All players—listed alphabetically)

Player, Team	Avg.	G	AB	R	H	TB	2B	3B	HR	RBI	SH	SF	HP	BB	Int. BB	SO	SB	CS
Agostinelli, Sal, Reading	.200	12	35	4	7	8	1	0	0	3	2	1	0	3	0	7	0	0
Alexander, Manny, Hagerstown	.333	3	9	3	3	4	1	0	0	2	0	1	1	1	0	3	0	0
Allison, Tom, Williamsport†	.225	31	89	13	20	26	4	1	0	9	2	1	1	11	0	19	2	1
Ausmus, Brad, Albany	.266	67	229	36	61	77	9	2	1	29	3	1	1	27	1	36	14	3
Austin, Pat, Reading	.289	91	329	57	95	130	21	1	4	39	2	1	0	41	1	47	21	8
Backs, Jason, Reading	.000	19	6	0	0	0	0	0	0	0	1	0	0	0	0	4	0	0
Balthazar, Doyle, London	.258	85	264	28	68	81	8	1	1	22	1	2	1	22	0	39	4	5
Barns, Jeff, Canton-Akron	.260	43	123	12	32	41	6	0	1	10	1	1	2	5	1	14	3	1
Barnwell, Richard, Albany	.263	5	19	4	5	5	0	0	0	0	0	0	0	1	0	6	2	0
Bautista, Ramon, Canton-Akron	.216	102	278	40	60	85	9	5	2	29	6	5	4	27	0	78	7	5
Beams, Mike, New Britain	.203	81	251	21	51	81	14	2	4	25	2	2	3	28	1	66	1	2
Bennett, Chris, Harrisburg	.000	28	4	1	0	0	0	0	0	0	1	0	0	1	0	0	0	0
Berthel, Dan, Hagerstown	.161	11	31	0	5	6	1	0	0	2	0	1	0	4	1	2	0	0
Beyeler, Arnie, London	.235	57	213	21	50	65	8	2	1	13	8	2	3	16	0	17	3	0
Blackwell, Juan, Albany	.195	21	41	6	8	10	2	0	0	1	0	1	1	2	0	15	0	0
Blosser, Greg, New Britain*	.217	134	452	47	98	149	21	3	6	46	0	4	1	63	0	114	9	4
Bogar, Tim, Williamsport	.251	63	243	33	61	83	12	2	2	25	2	4	2	20	0	44	13	8
Borland, Toby, Reading	.000	59	3	0	0	0	0	0	0	0	0	0	0	0	0	3	0	0
Brantley, Cliff, Reading	.222	11	9	1	2	2	0	0	0	0	1	0	0	0	0	3	0	0
Brennan, William, Harrisburg	.000	21	2	0	0	0	0	0	0	0	0	0	0	1	0	1	0	0
Brink, Brad, Reading	.143	5	7	0	1	1	0	0	0	1	0	0	0	0	0	0	0	0
Brogna, Rico, London*	.273	77	293	40	80	134	13	1	13	51	3	5	0	25	2	59	0	1
Bross, Terry, Williamsport	.000	20	1	0	0	0	0	0	0	0	0	0	0	0	0	1	0	0

— 390 —

Player, Team	Avg.	G	AB	R	H	TB	2B	3B	HR	RBI	SH	SF	HP	BB	Int. BB	SO	SB	CS
Brown, Dana, Reading	.244	88	271	39	66	81	5	2	2	25	3	3	4	28	0	51	24	20
Burnitz, Jeromy, Williamsport*	.225	135	457	80	103	232	16	10	31	85	0	8	4	104	4	127	31	13
Bushing, Chris, Harrisburg	.500	4	2	0	1	1	0	0	0	1	0	0	0	0	0	0	0	0
Byrd, Jim, New Britain	.240	79	292	28	70	81	9	1	0	15	5	2	1	28	1	53	14	10
Cabrera, Basilio, London	.127	29	71	10	9	14	1	1	3	1	0	3	0	3	0	17	3	0
Carey, Paul, Hagerstown*	.252	114	373	63	94	161	29	1	12	65	2	5	4	68	8	109	5	4
Carter, Andy, Reading*	.000	20	7	1	0	0	0	0	0	1	0	1	0	0	0	2	0	0
Cassels, Chris, Harrisburg	.222	84	297	35	66	120	15	0	13	48	1	3	2	19	1	61	1	3
Cianfrocco, Archie, Harrisburg	.316	124	456	71	144	212	21	10	9	77	2	2	9	38	2	112	11	3
Cinnella, Doug, Williamsport	.000	28	2	0	0	0	0	0	0	0	0	0	0	0	0	1	0	0
Contreras, Joaquin, Canton-Akron†	.225	70	240	27	54	76	13	3	1	19	1	0	1	16	1	33	1	0
Cook, Andy, Albany	.000	14	1	0	0	0	0	0	0	0	0	1	0	0	0	1	0	0
Cornelius, Reid, Harrisburg	.000	3	2	0	0	0	0	0	0	0	1	0	0	0	0	0	0	0
Cortes, Hernan, Williamsport*	.214	21	42	2	9	9	0	0	0	2	1	0	0	8	2	12	0	1
Costo, Tim, Canton-Akron	.271	52	192	28	52	71	10	3	1	24	0	6	0	15	0	44	2	1
Cruz, Ivan, London*	.248	121	443	46	110	158	21	0	9	47	1	2	4	36	5	73	3	3
Daulton, Darren, Reading*	.250	1	4	0	1	1	0	0	0	0	0	0	0	1	0	0	0	0
Davis, Glenn, Hagerstown	.250	7	24	4	6	10	1	0	1	3	0	1	0	1	0	2	0	0
Davis, Russ, Albany	.218	135	473	57	103	156	23	3	8	58	1	6	5	50	1	102	3	0
Davis, Steve, Williamsport*	.138	42	87	11	12	16	4	0	0	6	2	0	1	17	0	26	3	1
DeCillis, Dean, London	.267	59	225	25	60	73	8	1	1	32	0	7	0	18	0	27	2	3
Degifico, Vinnie, New Britain*	.231	75	199	12	46	62	4	0	4	19	1	1	0	37	2	51	0	2
DeJardin, Bobby, Albany†	.295	129	482	74	142	169	21	0	2	53	8	1	2	62	1	55	18	13
Dellicarri, Joe, Williamsport	.242	80	215	30	52	81	10	2	5	23	5	2	4	22	0	36	7	2
Dickerson, Bobby, Hagerstown	.238	90	302	34	72	95	12	4	1	36	4	5	6	9	0	44	2	0
Dixon, Colin, New Britain	.270	87	274	29	74	104	16	1	4	20	5	1	4	30	0	57	1	4
Dorante, Lou, New Britain	.265	58	181	21	48	63	12	0	1	22	3	3	4	24	1	34	2	0
Dostal, Bruce, Reading*	.313	96	364	68	114	150	11	5	5	34	1	4	5	58	5	55	38	16
Douma, Todd, Williamsport*	.250	10	8	1	2	2	0	0	0	0	0	0	0	0	0	3	0	0
Dozier, D.J., Williamsport	.278	74	259	49	72	119	11	6	8	30	0	1	1	39	2	88	25	6
Draper, Mike, Albany	.000	36	0	0	0	0	0	0	0	0	0	1	0	0	0	0	0	0
Dunnum, Rick, Reading	.000	55	5	0	0	0	0	0	0	0	0	1	0	0	0	4	0	0
Elli, Rocky, Reading*	.143	16	7	1	1	1	0	0	0	0	0	0	0	0	0	4	0	0
Epley, Daren, Canton-Akron*	.253	128	451	58	114	165	24	0	9	52	2	6	0	58	3	77	9	9
Escobar, Jose, Canton-Akron	.059	12	34	0	2	3	1	0	0	1	2	0	0	1	0	7	0	0
Fagnant, Ray, New Britain	.130	21	46	3	6	8	2	0	0	1	0	0	0	4	0	13	0	0
Faulk, Jim, Harrisburg	.251	78	267	32	67	98	10	3	5	47	1	1	1	37	6	54	22	12
Fernandez, Sid, Williamsport*	.000	1	3	0	0	0	0	0	0	0	0	0	0	0	0	0	1	0
Ferretti, Sam, Canton-Akron	.214	101	299	26	64	82	12	3	0	23	8	2	2	37	1	60	8	7
Flaherty, John, New Britain	.289	67	225	27	65	83	9	0	3	18	0	2	1	31	1	22	0	2
Fletcher, Paul, Reading	.143	21	7	0	1	1	0	0	0	0	0	1	0	1	0	1	0	0
Fox, Blane, New Britain*	.213	57	141	17	30	33	3	0	0	13	1	3	1	27	2	29	4	0
Frazier, Lou, London†	.239	122	439	69	105	131	9	4	3	40	3	1	1	77	6	87	42	17
Freed, Dan, Harrisburg	.100	26	10	4	1	1	0	0	0	1	3	0	0	4	0	1	0	0
Fulton, Greg, Harrisburg†	.293	55	157	18	46	55	7	1	0	18	1	2	2	12	1	29	4	4
Gaddy, Bob, Reading	.000	10	1	0	0	0	0	0	0	0	0	0	0	0	0	0	0	0
Galindo, Luis, London	.253	84	269	27	68	75	5	1	0	20	2	1	1	43	0	35	5	7
Gilbert, Roy, Hagerstown	.225	76	204	23	46	61	5	5	0	19	0	0	3	11	0	22	14	2
Gillette, Mike, London	.187	77	241	24	45	72	10	1	5	21	8	3	2	20	0	54	2	1
Gonzalez, Javier, Williamsport	.153	48	150	7	23	42	7	0	4	14	1	1	2	12	0	45	1	0
Gray, Elliott, Reading	.000	7	1	0	0	0	0	0	0	0	0	0	0	0	0	1	0	0
Grott, Matt, Harrisburg	.500	10	2	0	1	2	1	0	0	1	0	0	0	0	0	1	0	0
Gutierrez, Ricky, Harrisburg*	.236	84	292	47	69	83	6	4	0	30	3	2	2	57	0	52	11	0
Haney, Chris, Harrisburg*	.286	12	7	0	2	2	0	0	0	0	1	0	0	0	0	1	0	0
Hare, Shawn, London*	.272	31	125	20	34	58	12	0	4	28	0	0	1	12	1	23	2	2
Harrison, Phil, Harrisburg*	.333	23	3	1	1	1	0	0	0	0	0	0	0	0	0	0	0	0
Hendricks, Steve, New Britain	.211	100	336	20	71	85	10	2	0	33	3	4	2	33	1	48	8	9
Hernandez, Cesar, Harrisburg	.254	128	418	58	106	164	15	2	13	52	1	6	8	25	2	106	34	10
Hernandez, Rudy, Williamsport	.217	117	346	38	75	84	9	0	0	22	6	2	0	67	1	69	25	14
Hill, Chris, Williamsport*	.125	27	8	1	1	1	0	0	0	1	0	0	0	3	0	3	0	0
Hirsch, Chris, Harrisburg	.235	9	17	6	4	8	1	0	1	4	0	0	1	4	0	3	1	0
Hithe, Victor, Hagerstown	.277	69	260	46	72	93	11	5	0	26	0	0	1	40	0	48	20	2
Holcomb, Scott, Albany*	.000	27	1	0	0	0	0	0	0	0	0	0	0	0	0	0	0	0
Holdridge, David, Reading	.000	7	3	0	0	0	0	0	0	0	0	0	0	0	0	2	0	0
Holland, Tim, Hagerstown	.248	133	501	58	124	173	21	2	8	73	3	8	2	35	2	142	6	5
Housie, Wayne, New Britain†	.277	113	444	58	123	169	24	2	6	26	6	0	3	55	2	86	43	14
Howard, Tim, Williamsport*	.257	68	245	23	63	85	7	6	1	16	3	0	1	14	0	21	7	3
Howell, Pat, Williamsport†	.281	70	274	43	77	87	5	1	1	26	8	0	2	21	0	50	27	11
Hurst, Jody, London	.278	54	187	33	52	84	8	0	8	25	1	0	2	28	0	45	9	3
Hurst, Jonathan, London	.000	6	2	0	0	0	0	0	0	0	0	0	0	0	0	0	0	0
Ingram, Riccardo, London	.271	118	421	58	114	184	14	1	18	64	5	3	4	40	0	77	6	5
Jefferson, Reggie, Canton-Akron†	.280	6	25	2	7	8	1	0	0	4	0	0	0	1	0	5	0	0
Johnson, Brian, Albany	.000	2	1	0	0	0	0	0	0	0	0	0	0	0	0	0	0	0
Johnson, Chris, Harrisburg	.500	10	6	2	3	3	0	0	0	0	0	0	1	0	0	1	0	0
Johnstone, John, Williamsport	.167	27	12	0	2	2	0	0	0	0	1	0	0	1	0	4	0	0
Katzaroff, Rob, Harrisburg*	.290	137	558	94	162	196	21	2	3	50	9	1	5	54	3	61	33	18
Kilgo, Rusty, Harrisburg*	.000	14	1	0	0	0	0	0	0	0	0	0	0	0	0	0	0	0
Kimberlin, Keith, London†	.233	107	331	26	77	112	16	5	3	34	7	5	3	24	1	55	4	2
Kingwood, Tyrone, Hagerstown	.279	80	319	39	89	114	15	2	2	36	2	1	0	16	1	44	26	6
Kline, Doug, Williamsport	.000	50	1	0	0	0	0	0	0	0	2	0	0	0	0	0	0	0
Knoblauh, Jay, Albany	.284	97	335	52	95	148	16	2	11	50	2	4	3	42	1	69	16	8
Kosco, Bryn, Harrisburg*	.241	113	381	50	92	156	24	5	10	58	0	3	2	48	4	79	4	1
Lake, Ken, Harrisburg	.091	9	11	1	1	1	0	0	0	0	0	0	0	3	0	6	0	0
Laker, Tim, Harrisburg	.286	11	35	4	10	14	1	0	1	5	0	0	0	2	0	4	0	0
Lane, Nolan, Canton-Akron	.245	74	237	20	58	74	8	1	2	22	4	3	4	16	0	43	8	5
Lehman, Mike, Hagerstown	.281	97	331	42	93	128	24	1	3	46	0	3	1	45	1	69	2	2
Leonhardt, Dave, London	.200	7	15	5	3	3	0	0	0	0	2	0	0	4	0	4	0	0
Levis, Jesse, Canton-Akron*	.264	115	382	31	101	142	17	3	6	45	4	2	0	40	5	36	2	5
Lewis, Richie, Harrisburg	1.000	34	1	0	1	1	0	0	0	0	1	0	0	0	0	0	0	0
Lindsey, Darrell, Reading	.000	17	1	0	0	0	0	0	0	0	0	0	0	0	0	1	0	0
Lindsey, Doug, Reading	.259	94	313	26	81	97	13	0	1	34	4	2	2	21	0	49	1	0
Livesey, Jeff, Albany	.230	23	61	5	14	21	1	0	2	6	1	0	2	2	0	14	0	0
Lofton, Rodney, Hagerstown	.284	118	437	78	124	143	6	5	1	33	9	2	3	48	1	74	56	10
Longmire, Tony, Reading*	.288	85	323	43	93	144	22	1	9	56	1	4	2	32	6	45	10	7

Player, Team	Avg.	G	AB	R	H	TB	2B	3B	HR	RBI	SH	SF	HP	BB	Int. BB	SO	SB	CS
Magrann, Tom, New Britain	.105	28	76	5	8	12	1	0	1	3	2	1	0	17	0	14	0	0
Marchok, Chris, Harrisburg*	.000	41	1	0	0	0	0	0	0	0	0	0	0	0	0	0	0	0
Marigny, Ron, London	.271	25	85	14	23	28	3	1	0	6	2	0	1	15	0	17	2	1
Marsh, Tom, Reading	.263	67	236	27	62	105	12	5	7	35	3	3	1	11	0	47	8	4
Martel, Ed, Albany	.000	25	2	0	0	0	0	0	0	0	0	0	0	1	0	2	0	0
Martin, Chris, Harrisburg	.224	87	294	30	66	94	10	0	6	36	2	5	4	22	0	60	1	4
Martinez, Carlos, Canton-Akron	.329	80	295	48	97	156	22	2	11	73	0	7	2	22	3	47	11	4
Masse, Billy, Albany	.295	108	356	67	105	159	17	2	11	61	0	7	6	74	3	60	10	4
May, Lee, Williamsport†	.203	86	296	29	60	82	9	5	1	19	5	3	1	27	3	94	19	10
Mayo, Todd, Harrisburg*	.257	17	35	6	9	9	0	0	0	1	0	0	0	9	0	4	2	1
Maysey, Matt, Harrisburg	.000	15	10	0	0	0	0	0	0	0	1	0	0	1	0	4	0	0
McBride, Loy, Williamsport	.216	100	283	23	61	86	13	0	4	30	2	1	1	32	1	51	7	6
Meadows, Scott, Hagerstown	.300	33	120	18	36	48	7	1	1	11	0	1	1	34	0	22	1	4
Michel, Domingo, London	.269	49	145	18	39	51	4	1	2	14	0	2	0	43	2	42	1	1
Millette, Joe, Reading	.246	115	353	52	87	113	9	4	3	28	10	3	7	36	2	54	6	6
Milstien, Dave, New Britain	.278	86	309	36	86	106	6	1	4	31	2	5	1	46	1	38	3	5
Munoz, Omer, Harrisburg	.308	63	214	27	66	78	7	1	1	21	11	1	0	3	0	17	1	0
Natal, Bob, Harrisburg	.256	100	336	47	86	147	16	3	13	53	2	5	8	49	3	90	1	1
Navarro, Tito, Williamsport	.288	128	482	69	139	162	9	4	2	42	12	4	1	73	2	63	42	19
Newell, Tom, Albany	.000	9	1	0	0	0	0	0	0	0	0	0	0	0	0	1	0	0
Nivens, Toby, Williamsport	.071	28	14	0	1	1	0	0	0	1	3	0	0	0	0	6	0	0
Odor, Rouglas, Canton-Akron	.199	76	236	25	47	59	5	2	1	29	7	5	1	25	2	50	8	2
Paris, Juan, New Britain	.243	115	419	32	102	134	17	3	3	41	2	3	2	24	0	45	4	8
Pegues, Steve, London	.301	56	216	24	65	90	3	2	6	26	0	2	6	8	0	24	4	7
Phillips, Vince, Albany	.274	130	482	71	132	184	26	1	8	85	1	9	3	58	2	64	12	6
Pollack, Chris, Harrisburg*	.154	26	13	1	2	2	0	0	0	0	1	0	0	0	0	5	0	0
Powers, Scott, New Britain	.208	87	250	21	52	65	9	2	0	16	1	0	2	32	0	54	3	4
Proctor, Dave, Williamsport*	.500	9	4	2	2	4	0	1	0	2	1	0	0	0	0	2	0	0
Quintell, John, Albany*	.107	10	28	0	3	3	0	0	0	1	0	0	0	1	0	12	0	0
Raley, Tim, Hagerstown*	.244	80	234	39	57	81	9	3	3	31	1	1	2	30	2	56	2	0
Ramos, Ken, Canton-Akron*	.241	74	257	41	62	80	6	3	2	13	4	1	1	28	0	22	8	4
Randle, Randy, New Britain	.193	116	347	33	67	89	12	2	2	31	4	4	0	28	0	71	7	3
Reimink, Rob, London†	.258	89	279	37	72	89	9	1	2	18	4	1	1	51	1	67	2	4
Resetar, Gary, Canton-Akron*	.227	59	154	14	35	41	3	0	1	13	3	3	1	16	3	28	3	2
Riesgo, Nikco, Reading	.258	98	356	61	92	156	18	2	14	66	0	4	0	48	1	71	8	6
Ripken, Bill, Hagerstown	.600	1	5	1	3	3	0	0	0	0	0	0	0	0	0	0	0	0
Robbins, Doug, Hagerstown	.304	92	286	45	87	101	12	1	0	28	0	5	5	71	0	48	4	3
Robertson, Rod, Reading†	.245	117	416	52	102	148	19	0	9	51	6	4	2	33	0	74	20	6
Rodriguez, Ruben, 14 Lon.-23 N.B.	.270	37	100	11	27	41	5	0	3	9	1	0	1	8	0	19	1	1
Rogers, Bryan, Williamsport	.000	41	0	0	0	0	0	0	0	0	0	0	0	0	0	0	0	0
Rosado, Ed, Reading	.200	45	125	17	25	30	5	0	0	10	4	2	3	12	2	25	5	2
Roth, Greg, Hagerstown*	.345	38	119	21	41	62	4	1	5	24	2	2	1	12	1	26	1	0
Ryan, Sean, Reading†	.241	123	439	54	106	152	22	0	8	70	7	5	1	53	2	64	0	1
Sabino, Miguel, Canton-Akron*	.219	115	392	51	86	116	11	2	5	26	8	3	7	54	1	67	23	14
Santangelo, F.P., Harrisburg†	.245	132	462	78	113	154	12	7	5	42	13	4	7	74	0	45	21	7
Sarbaugh, Mike, Canton-Akron	.067	5	15	1	1	1	0	0	0	1	0	1	0	1	0	4	1	0
Scarsone, Steve, Reading	.306	15	49	6	15	24	0	0	3	3	0	0	0	4	0	15	2	0
Shamburg, Ken, Hagerstown	.275	116	426	59	117	187	36	2	10	82	0	10	3	69	5	61	3	2
Siddall, Joe, Harrisburg*	.230	76	235	28	54	65	6	1	1	23	2	3	1	23	2	53	8	3
Sieradzki, Al, Williamsport	.000	1	2	0	0	0	0	0	0	0	0	0	0	0	0	2	0	0
Silvestri, Dave, Albany	.262	140	512	97	134	238	31	8	19	83	2	2	2	83	3	126	20	13
Sims, Mark, Reading†	.000	14	1	0	0	0	0	0	0	0	0	0	0	0	0	1	0	0
Skeels, Andy, Albany*	.254	65	197	25	50	65	9	0	2	26	3	4	1	33	2	31	0	1
Snow, J.T., Albany†	.279	132	477	78	133	211	33	3	13	76	2	10	3	67	3	78	5	1
Sommer, David, Williamsport	.000	22	8	0	0	0	0	0	0	0	2	0	0	1	0	3	0	0
Spencer, Stanley, Harrisburg	.000	17	8	0	0	0	0	0	0	0	2	0	0	0	0	3	0	0
Stairs, Matt, Harrisburg	.333	129	505	87	168	257	30	10	13	78	0	3	3	66	8	47	23	11
Stanford, Don, Albany	.000	40	1	0	0	0	0	0	0	0	0	0	0	0	0	0	0	0
Tabaka, Jeff, Reading	.111	21	9	1	1	1	0	0	0	0	0	0	0	0	0	6	0	0
Talamantez, Greg, Williamsport	.000	32	2	0	0	0	0	0	0	0	1	0	0	0	0	2	0	0
Tatis, Bernie, Canton-Akron†	.333	8	30	5	10	13	3	0	0	3	0	0	2	1	0	3	0	1
Telgheder, Dave, Williamsport	.385	28	13	1	5	6	1	0	0	5	2	0	0	0	0	3	0	0
Thoden, John, Harrisburg	.200	5	5	1	1	1	0	0	0	0	2	0	0	0	0	5	0	0
Thomas, Andres, Canton-Akron	.290	45	169	15	49	65	14	1	0	20	1	1	0	11	3	17	2	1
Thome, Jim, Canton-Akron*	.337	84	294	47	99	138	20	2	5	45	0	3	4	44	4	58	8	2
Tinsley, Lee, Canton-Akron†	.295	38	139	26	41	61	7	2	3	8	2	0	4	18	2	37	18	5
Toale, John, Albany*	.000	2	2	0	0	0	0	0	0	0	1	0	0	0	0	0	0	0
Trevino, Tony, Reading	.253	43	83	10	21	29	6	1	0	12	2	1	2	6	0	23	1	0
Valentin, John, New Britain	.198	23	81	8	16	19	3	0	0	5	1	0	9	9	0	14	1	1
Vargas, Hector, Albany	.278	106	345	49	96	121	16	3	1	39	2	2	5	45	0	65	23	5
Vargas, Jose, Williamsport	.000	16	1	0	0	0	0	0	0	0	0	0	0	0	0	1	0	0
Viera, John, Albany*	.266	88	308	52	82	116	11	4	5	40	0	2	4	40	0	64	12	8
Voigt, Jack, Hagerstown	.244	29	90	15	22	25	3	0	0	6	1	0	2	15	1	19	6	0
Waller, Casey, Reading†	.261	118	402	64	105	168	25	1	12	52	2	2	7	54	6	47	2	0
Wallin, Les, New Britain	.202	28	89	13	18	30	8	2	0	9	0	0	0	11	0	29	0	0
Wardlow, Joey, Albany*	.133	5	15	1	2	3	1	0	0	1	0	0	0	0	0	4	0	0
Wearing, Melvin, Hagerstown	.299	35	107	18	32	47	6	0	3	24	0	1	4	17	0	28	1	0
Wedge, Eric, New Britain	.250	2	8	0	2	2	0	0	0	2	0	1	0	0	0	4	0	0
Whitfield, Ken, Canton-Akron	.240	69	200	24	48	70	9	2	3	24	0	0	3	21	5	52	5	1
Wiegandt, Scott, Reading*	.000	49	2	0	0	0	0	0	0	0	0	0	0	0	0	1	0	0
Williams, Cary, Reading	.278	116	421	55	117	162	21	3	6	62	3	5	6	27	3	69	12	1
Williams, Gerald, Albany	.286	45	175	28	50	80	15	0	5	32	1	3	0	18	2	26	18	3
Williams, Mike, Reading	.143	15	7	0	1	1	0	0	0	0	0	0	0	0	0	5	0	0
Williams, Paul, Williamsport	.259	133	463	62	120	175	29	1	8	72	0	5	4	69	2	75	0	4
Woodruff, Pat, London	.212	59	179	14	38	49	8	0	1	23	2	1	3	25	0	56	4	4
Yacopino, Ed, Hagerstown†	.343	69	268	51	92	122	16	4	2	47	2	4	1	35	2	42	4	5
Young, Pete, Harrisburg	.000	54	0	0	0	0	0	0	0	0	0	0	0	0	0	1	0	0
Zambrano, Roberto, Canton-Akron	.338	23	77	15	26	38	6	0	2	10	0	2	1	13	1	13	1	0
Zinter, Alan, Williamsport†	.220	124	422	44	93	145	13	6	9	54	2	2	3	59	1	106	3	3

The following pitchers, listed alphabetically by club, with games in parentheses, had no plate appearances, primarily through use of designated hitters:

ALBANY—Batchelor, Richard (1); Blueberg, Jim (8); Garcia, Victor (18); Gardella, Mike (53); Hartzog, Cullen (18); Manon, Ramon (3); Marris, Mark (8); Militello, Sam (7); Nielsen, Jerry (6); Perez, Pascual (2); Popplewell, Tom (52); Rub, Jerry (10); Smith, Willie (21); Springer, Russ (2); Stanford, Larry (52); Witt, Mike (1).

CANTON-AKRON—Bell, Eric (18); Birkbeck, Mike (21); Bruske, Jim (17); Chamberlain, Craig (2); Curtis, Mike (10); DiPoto, Gerard (28); Easley, Logan (6); Garcia, Apolinar (4); Hall, Grady (8); Horton, Ricky (25); Kiser, Garland (17); Kovach, Ty (11); Kramer, Tom (35); Meyer, Brian (14); Munoz, Oscar (15); Mutis, Jeff (25); Roscoe, Greg (13); Seanez, Rudy (25); Walker, Mike (45); Ward, Colby (4); Wickander, Kevin (20).

HAGERSTOWN—Bumgarner, Jeff (17); Burdick, Stacey (26); Codiroli, Chris (5); Constant, Andres (1); Culkar, Steve (3); Hickey, Kevin (15); Johnson, Dave (3); Jones, Stacy (12); Leinen, Pat (23); Linskey, Mike (16); McKeon, Joel (33); Milacki, Bob (3); Miller, Dave (14); Moore, Daryl (34); Oquist, Mike (27); Peraza, Oswaldo (19); Rhodes, Arthur (19); Schullstrom, Erik (2); Stephan, Todd (53); Williams, Jeff (39).

HARRISBURG—Holsman, Rich (4); Keliipuleole, Carl (6); Wainhouse, David (33).

LONDON—Cook, Ron (3); DeSilva, John (11); Doherty, John (53); Gohr, Greg (2); Groom, Buddy (11); Hansen, Mike (21); Hursey, Darren (35); Kerfeld, Charley (11); Knudsen, Kurt (34); Krumm, Todd (18); Lovelace, Vance (9); Marshall, Randy (27); Ramos, Jose (34); Rightnowar, Ron (15); Rivera, Lino (17); Stone, Eric (6); Vesling, Don (18); Willis, Marty (31); Wolf, Steve (17).

NEW BRITAIN—Allen, Tracy (4); Brown, Paul (12); Conroy, Brian (10); Davis, Freddie (46); Estrada, Pete (25); Finnvold, Gar (16); Fischer, Tom (22); Florence, Don (55); Hoy, Peter (47); Kane, Tom (41); Livernois, Derek (5); Manzanillo, Josias (7); O'Neill, Dan (2); Painter, Gary (15); Quantrill, Paul (5); Ryan, Ken (14); Sanders, Al (26); Taylor, Scott (4); Walter, Gene (3).

READING—Burgos, John (15); DiMichele, Frank (22); Limbach, Chris (18); Stevens, Matt (25); Wells, Bob (1).

WILLIAMSPORT—Trautwein, David (42); Vasquez, Aguedo (11).

GRAND SLAMS—Ausmus, Brogna, Carey, Epley, Faulk, Holland, Knoblauh, Martinez, Masse, Pegues, Phillips, Robertson, Silvestri, P. Williams.
AWARDED FIRST BASE ON CATCHER'S INTERFERENCE—None.

PITCHING

TEAM

Team	ERA	G	CG	ShO	Sv.	IP	H	R	ER	HR	HB	BB	Int. BB	SO	WP	Bk.
Harrisburg	2.97	140	13	16	44	1257.1	1161	483	415	68	37	452	16	916	59	9
Canton-Akron	3.15	140	17	14	38	1206.2	1066	528	423	43	35	499	27	854	73	10
Hagerstown	3.28	140	7	10	39	1231.1	1119	554	449	66	24	543	14	929	53	7
Albany	3.73	140	9	11	43	1205.1	1107	615	500	63	44	639	32	960	62	12
Williamsport	4.06	140	7	12	32	1197.1	1281	679	540	62	38	523	24	724	70	11
London	4.16	139	16	7	29	1194.1	1234	664	552	88	32	499	15	832	52	9
Reading	4.18	140	11	9	33	1203.0	1175	636	559	98	42	628	25	799	60	10
New Britain	4.19	140	9	10	23	1200.1	1195	667	559	81	48	520	35	789	58	13

INDIVIDUAL

(Leading qualifiers for earned-run average leadership—112 or more innings)

*Throws lefthanded.

Pitcher, Team	W	L	Pct.	ERA	G	GS	CG	GF	ShO	Sv.	IP	H	R	ER	HR	HB	BB	Int. BB	SO	WP
Mutis, Canton-Akron*	11	5	.688	1.80	25	24	7	0	4	0	169.2	138	42	34	0	6	51	2	89	3
Pollack, Harrisburg*	11	8	.579	2.75	26	25	3	1	2	0	157.0	147	59	48	3	0	68	0	83	8
Martel, Albany	13	6	.684	2.81	25	24	3	0	2	0	163.1	129	67	51	8	5	55	0	141	2
Burdick, Hagerstown	11	4	.733	2.99	26	21	0	1	0	0	135.2	99	67	45	7	1	100	0	102	5
Leinen, Hagerstown*	10	6	.625	3.03	23	21	2	0	0	0	148.2	143	63	50	7	3	33	0	63	1
Draper, Albany	10	6	.625	3.29	36	14	1	6	1	2	131.1	125	58	48	6	6	47	3	71	10
Fletcher, Reading	7	9	.438	3.51	21	19	3	1	1	0	120.2	111	56	47	12	1	56	3	90	6
Telgheder, Williamsport	13	11	.542	3.60	28	26	1	1	0	0	167.2	185	81	67	7	5	33	3	90	4
Willis, London	5	12	.294	3.64	31	23	3	4	0	0	155.2	154	75	63	7	2	69	2	98	3
Dipoto, Canton-Akron	6	11	.353	3.81	28	26	2	0	0	0	156.0	143	83	66	10	2	74	2	97	15

Departmental leaders: G—Borland, 59; W—Martel, Telgheder, 13; L—Sanders, 15; Pct.—Burdick, .733; GS—Johnstone, Marshall, 27; CG—Mutis, 7; GF—Borland, 50; ShO—Mutis, 4; Sv.—Borland, L. Stanford, 24; IP—Mutis, 169.2; H—Marshall, 186; R—Sanders, 101; ER—Sanders, 87; HR—Sanders, 16; HB—Kane, 11; BB—Burdick, 100; IBB—Hoy, 8; SO—Martel, 141; WP—Dipoto, 15.

(All pitchers—listed alphabetically)

Pitcher, Team	W	L	Pct.	ERA	G	GS	CG	GF	ShO	Sv.	IP	H	R	ER	HR	HB	BB	Int. BB	SO	WP
Allen, New Britain	0	1	.000	10.13	8	0	0	6	0	0	8.0	13	9	9	0	2	9	1	7	2
Backs, Reading	3	5	.375	7.36	19	13	0	0	0	0	69.2	101	66	57	10	9	40	0	36	1
Barns, Canton-Akron	0	0	.000	7.36	3	0	0	3	0	0	3.2	7	3	3	0	0	2	0	0	0
Batchelor, Albany	0	0	.000	45.00	1	0	0	1	0	0	1.0	5	5	5	0	0	1	0	0	0
Bell, Canton-Akron*	9	5	.643	2.89	18	16	1	0	0	0	93.1	82	47	30	1	2	37	1	84	6
Bennett, Harrisburg	5	6	.455	3.16	28	9	0	7	0	1	74.0	82	36	26	5	2	22	1	35	3
Birkbeck, Canton-Akron	2	3	.400	3.89	21	2	0	14	0	5	39.1	39	17	17	1	0	18	3	40	2
Blueberg, Albany	3	2	.600	3.18	8	8	0	0	0	0	45.1	43	22	16	4	5	21	0	37	2
Borland, Reading	8	3	.727	2.70	59	0	0	50	0	24	76.2	68	31	23	2	2	56	5	72	5
Brantley, Reading	4	3	.571	1.94	11	11	2	0	1	0	69.2	50	17	15	3	4	25	1	51	2
Brennan, Harrisburg	3	2	.600	3.12	21	0	0	6	0	1	34.2	35	21	12	1	4	30	1	33	9
Brink, Harrisburg	2	2	.500	3.71	5	5	0	0	0	0	34.0	32	14	14	3	1	6	0	27	1
Bross, Williamsport	2	0	1.000	2.49	20	0	0	16	0	5	25.1	13	12	7	1	0	11	0	27	1
Brown, New Britain*	1	1	.500	3.60	12	0	0	4	0	2	20.0	22	11	8	2	1	6	1	13	0
Bruske, Canton-Akron	5	2	.714	3.47	17	11	0	3	0	0	80.1	73	36	31	3	2	27	3	35	2
Bumgarner, Hagerstown	3	6	.333	4.54	17	11	0	0	0	0	73.1	84	44	37	5	4	35	0	45	5
Burdick, Hagerstown	11	4	.733	2.99	26	21	0	1	0	0	135.2	99	67	45	7	1	100	0	102	5
Burgos, Reading*	2	0	1.000	4.70	15	0	0	8	0	0	23.0	27	13	12	2	0	13	3	10	0
Bushing, Harrisburg	1	0	1.000	1.04	3	1	0	0	0	0	8.2	3	2	1	0	1	8	0	8	2
Carter, Reading*	11	5	.688	4.84	20	20	1	0	0	0	102.1	86	57	55	10	8	57	0	64	5
Chamberlain, Canton-Akron	0	0	.000	7.50	2	0	0	1	0	0	6.0	8	5	5	1	0	3	0	4	0
Cinnella, Williamsport	3	5	.375	3.71	28	6	0	11	0	2	77.2	92	41	32	2	1	38	4	45	5
Codiroli, Hagerstown	3	0	1.000	4.50	5	0	0	3	0	0	12.0	11	8	6	1	0	5	0	10	0
Conroy, New Britain	1	5	.167	3.02	10	10	1	0	1	0	65.2	51	27	22	6	4	26	2	34	3
Constant, Hagerstown	0	1	.000	18.00	1	1	0	0	0	0	2.0	7	4	4	0	0	1	0	1	0
Cook, Albany	6	3	.667	3.95	14	14	1	0	0	0	82.0	94	46	36	2	0	27	0	46	1
Cook, London*	0	1	.000	10.13	3	0	0	0	0	0	5.1	11	9	6	0	0	7	0	5	0
Cornelius, Harrisburg	2	1	.667	2.89	3	3	0	0	0	0	18.2	15	6	6	3	2	7	0	12	0
Culkar, Hagerstown	0	0	.000	0.00	3	0	0	3	0	0	5.0	1	0	0	0	0	1	0	4	0
Curtis, Canton-Akron*	2	0	1.000	1.83	10	0	0	4	0	2	19.2	20	6	4	2	2	10	0	20	1
Davis, New Britain	2	3	.400	5.45	45	0	0	26	0	0	77.2	102	51	47	4	1	29	7	42	4
DeSilva, London*	5	4	.556	2.81	11	11	2	0	1	0	73.2	51	24	23	4	0	24	0	80	1
Dickerson, Hagerstown	0	0	.000	0.00	1	0	0	1	0	0	1.0	0	0	0	0	0	3	0	0	0
DiMichele, Reading	0	2	.000	6.61	22	0	0	12	0	2	31.1	39	26	23	8	0	9	1	21	4

Pitcher, Team	W	L	Pct.	ERA	G	GS	CG	GF	ShO	Sv.	IP	H	R	ER	HR	HB	BB	Int. BB	SO	WP
Dipoto, Canton-Akron	6	11	.353	3.81	28	26	2	0	0	0	156.0	143	83	66	10	2	74	2	97	15
Doherty, London	3	3	.500	2.22	53	0	0	44	0	15	65.0	62	29	16	2	2	21	1	42	1
Douma, Williamsport*	2	4	.333	4.33	10	10	1	0	0	0	60.1	78	34	29	4	2	17	1	42	1
Draper, Albany	10	6	.625	3.29	36	14	1	6	1	2	131.1	125	58	48	6	6	47	3	71	10
Dunnum, Reading	6	5	.545	4.58	55	6	1	17	0	0	108.0	112	66	55	11	4	64	6	63	6
Easley, Canton-Akron	0	2	.000	3.60	6	0	0	3	0	1	15.0	11	7	6	2	0	1	0	14	1
Elli, Reading*	5	7	.417	3.15	16	14	1	0	0	0	74.1	65	33	26	6	1	33	0	48	0
Estrada, New Britain	2	12	.143	6.05	25	16	1	3	0	0	96.2	114	82	65	7	4	59	3	53	1
Fernandez, Williamsport*	0	0	.000	0.00	1	1	0	0	0	0	6.0	3	0	0	0	0	1	0	5	0
Finnvold, New Britain	5	8	.385	3.82	16	16	0	0	0	0	101.1	97	46	43	7	3	36	2	80	8
Fischer, New Britain*	8	11	.421	4.09	22	22	3	0	1	0	134.1	135	69	61	8	8	63	0	85	8
Fletcher, Reading	7	9	.438	3.51	21	19	3	1	1	0	120.2	111	56	47	12	1	56	3	90	6
Florence, New Britain*	3	8	.273	5.44	55	2	0	28	0	2	84.1	84	58	51	7	7	43	4	73	4
Fox, New Britain*	0	0	.000	10.80	1	0	0	1	0	0	1.2	3	2	2	1	1	2	0	1	0
Freed, Harrisburg	11	8	.579	4.32	26	26	0	0	0	0	162.1	176	84	78	12	5	41	0	83	4
Gaddy, Reading*	1	1	.500	4.71	10	2	0	3	0	0	21.0	20	12	11	2	2	15	0	16	1
Galindo, London	0	0	.000	7.36	3	0	0	3	0	0	3.2	5	6	3	2	1	2	0	4	2
Garcia, Canton-Akron	2	1	.667	1.96	4	4	0	0	0	0	18.1	22	13	4	0	1	7	0	10	4
Garcia, Albany*	5	5	.500	3.85	18	18	1	0	1	0	110.0	94	53	47	6	4	61	1	80	4
Gardella, Albany*	4	5	.444	3.82	53	0	0	27	0	11	77.2	70	37	33	1	1	55	6	76	3
Gohr, London	0	0	.000	0.00	2	2	0	0	0	0	11.0	9	0	0	0	0	2	0	10	0
Gray, Reading	0	2	.000	5.16	7	7	0	0	0	0	29.2	35	22	17	3	0	26	0	18	3
Groom, London*	7	1	.875	3.48	11	7	0	2	0	0	51.2	51	20	20	7	2	12	1	39	2
Grott, Harrisburg	2	1	.667	4.70	10	1	0	2	0	1	15.1	14	8	8	4	0	8	0	16	0
Hall, Canton-Akron	2	3	.400	3.26	8	7	2	0	0	0	47.0	39	23	17	2	0	11	0	24	7
Haney, Harrisburg*	5	3	.625	2.16	12	12	3	0	0	0	83.1	65	21	20	4	3	11	1	68	3
Hansen, London	4	5	.444	3.32	21	10	1	4	0	1	84.0	71	35	31	8	4	33	2	61	3
Harrison, Harrisburg*	7	1	.875	2.20	23	4	0	7	0	2	57.1	42	16	14	4	0	28	2	41	1
Hartzog, Albany	6	6	.500	5.80	18	18	0	0	0	0	90.0	100	63	58	4	0	55	0	64	4
Hickey, Hagerstown*	0	1	.000	1.83	15	0	0	11	0	3	19.2	15	6	4	1	0	6	0	20	0
Hill, Williamsport*	3	3	.500	4.69	27	12	1	3	0	1	88.1	115	59	46	8	1	40	2	42	5
Holcomb, Albany*	4	1	.800	1.41	26	0	0	12	0	1	32.0	20	5	5	1	0	22	4	28	2
Holdridge, Reading	0	2	.000	5.47	7	7	0	0	0	0	26.1	26	24	16	3	1	34	0	19	3
Holsman, Harrisburg*	0	0	.000	2.84	4	0	0	0	0	0	6.1	8	4	2	1	0	6	0	7	0
Horton, Canton-Akron*	1	2	.333	3.67	25	0	0	7	0	1	27.0	25	12	11	1	2	5	0	23	0
Hoy, New Britain	4	4	.500	1.46	47	0	0	40	0	15	68.0	47	20	11	2	0	22	8	39	1
Hursey, London*	2	2	.500	5.16	35	1	0	16	0	2	68.0	81	47	39	6	5	30	1	35	2
Hurst, Harrisburg	5	0	1.000	0.86	6	6	1	0	0	0	42.0	26	4	4	2	1	12	1	34	1
Johnson, Harrisburg	3	2	.600	3.34	10	10	1	0	1	0	56.2	59	25	21	2	1	28	0	42	2
Johnson, Hagerstown	3	0	1.000	1.00	3	3	0	0	0	0	18.0	13	3	2	0	0	3	0	9	0
Johnstone, Williamsport	7	9	.438	3.97	27	27	2	0	0	0	165.1	159	94	73	5	5	79	1	100	8
Jones, Hagerstown	0	1	.000	1.78	12	0	0	4	0	1	30.1	24	6	6	1	1	15	1	26	1
Kane, New Britain	4	8	.333	4.55	41	10	1	16	1	1	114.2	121	65	58	4	11	42	2	75	6
Keliipuleole, Harrisburg	0	1	.000	2.84	6	0	0	2	0	0	6.1	6	4	2	0	0	3	0	5	0
Kerfeld, London	1	1	.500	3.12	11	1	0	5	0	2	17.1	9	7	6	0	0	11	0	18	1
Kilgo, Harrisburg*	1	0	1.000	3.51	14	0	0	10	0	1	25.2	24	11	10	1	1	4	1	20	3
Kiser, Canton-Akron*	2	3	.400	2.03	17	4	0	6	0	0	44.1	35	13	10	1	1	11	2	34	3
Kline, Williamsport	2	5	.286	2.47	50	2	0	18	0	3	91.0	77	35	25	2	1	37	2	76	2
Knudsen, London	2	3	.400	3.48	34	0	0	18	0	6	51.2	42	29	20	1	1	30	2	56	4
Kovach, Canton-Akron	2	6	.250	6.02	11	11	0	0	0	0	58.1	72	44	39	2	4	28	2	30	8
Kramer, Canton-Akron	7	3	.700	2.38	35	5	0	13	0	6	79.1	61	23	21	5	1	34	3	61	3
Krumm, London	4	8	.333	7.10	18	12	1	2	0	0	77.1	103	70	61	10	3	42	2	61	10
Leinen, Hagerstown*	10	6	.625	3.03	23	21	2	0	0	0	148.2	143	63	50	7	3	33	0	63	1
Lewis, Harrisburg	6	5	.545	3.74	34	6	0	16	0	5	74.2	67	33	31	3	2	40	1	82	5
Limbach, Reading*	0	2	.000	5.68	18	0	0	11	0	3	19.0	20	13	12	2	0	6	1	17	0
Lindsey, Reading	3	1	.750	6.68	17	0	0	5	0	1	32.1	41	24	24	1	1	15	0	23	3
Linskey, Hagerstown*	6	5	.545	4.46	16	16	1	0	0	0	107.0	128	62	53	8	5	37	0	71	2
Livernois, New Britain	3	2	.600	3.25	5	5	0	0	0	0	27.2	28	14	10	1	0	10	0	31	3
Lovelace, London	1	0	1.000	5.52	9	0	0	1	0	0	14.2	18	14	9	2	0	9	0	12	4
Manon, Albany	0	2	.000	7.56	3	3	0	0	0	0	16.2	17	14	14	1	1	9	1	16	2
Manzanillo, New Britain	2	2	.500	2.90	7	7	0	0	0	0	49.2	37	25	16	0	1	28	1	35	2
Marchok, Harrisburg	4	2	.667	2.10	41	0	0	21	0	9	64.1	51	17	15	2	3	14	2	56	4
Marris, Albany	2	2	.500	4.35	8	4	0	2	0	1	31.0	35	15	15	4	2	9	0	17	0
Marsh, Reading	0	0	.000	0.00	1	0	0	1	0	0	2.0	0	0	0	0	0	1	0	0	0
Marshall, London*	8	10	.444	4.47	27	27	4	0	1	0	159.0	186	92	79	13	2	27	0	105	4
Martel, Albany	13	6	.684	2.81	25	24	3	0	2	0	163.1	129	67	51	8	5	55	0	141	2
Maysey, Harrisburg	6	5	.545	1.89	15	15	2	0	2	0	104.2	90	26	22	3	2	28	0	86	8
McBride, Williamsport	0	0	.000	0.00	1	0	0	1	0	0	1.0	1	0	0	0	0	1	0	0	0
McKeon, Hagerstown*	3	2	.600	4.19	33	0	0	17	0	0	62.1	72	36	29	1	3	27	2	34	4
Meyers, Canton-Akron	1	0	1.000	1.50	14	0	0	6	0	3	24.0	18	5	4	2	2	4	0	9	1
Milacki, Hagerstown	3	0	1.000	1.06	3	3	0	0	0	0	17.0	14	3	2	1	0	3	0	18	0
Militello, Albany	2	2	.500	2.35	7	7	0	0	0	0	46.0	40	14	12	3	3	19	0	55	0
Miller, Hagerstown	2	0	1.000	1.17	14	0	0	8	0	1	30.2	16	4	4	1	4	13	0	15	1
Moore, Hagerstown*	5	3	.625	3.38	34	0	0	13	0	3	32.0	21	16	12	3	0	19	2	47	0
Munoz, Canton-Akron*	3	8	.273	5.72	15	15	2	0	1	0	85.0	88	54	54	5	0	51	1	71	1
Mutis, Canton-Akron*	11	5	.688	1.80	25	24	7	0	4	0	169.2	138	42	34	0	6	51	2	89	3
Newell, Albany	1	0	1.000	4.73	8	0	0	3	0	1	13.1	14	15	7	2	2	12	0	13	1
Nielsen, Albany*	0	1	.000	5.63	6	0	0	2	0	0	8.0	9	6	5	1	0	8	1	5	0
Nivens, Williamsport	10	11	.476	4.19	28	25	2	1	1	0	144.0	156	85	67	8	8	63	4	72	12
O'Neill, Harrisburg*	0	2	.000	4.50	2	2	0	0	0	0	10.0	12	8	5	1	0	4	0	5	0
Oquist, Hagerstown	10	9	.526	4.06	27	26	1	1	0	0	166.1	168	82	75	15	0	62	4	136	7
Painter, New Britain	3	7	.300	4.84	15	15	1	0	0	0	87.1	89	54	47	10	0	35	0	51	4
Peraza, Hagerstown	6	7	.462	3.98	19	16	1	2	0	0	106.1	97	58	47	8	2	60	1	97	9
Perez, Albany	0	0	.000	1.69	2	2	0	0	0	0	5.1	5	1	1	0	0	1	0	6	0
Pollack, Harrisburg*	11	8	.579	2.75	26	25	3	1	2	0	157.0	147	59	48	3	0	68	0	83	8
Popplewell, Albany	4	10	.286	4.40	52	4	0	16	0	3	86.0	81	56	42	8	8	83	5	63	7
Proctor, Williamsport	0	2	.000	2.59	9	8	0	1	0	0	41.2	38	20	12	1	0	28	0	24	4
Quantrill, New Britain	2	1	.667	2.06	5	5	1	0	0	0	35.0	32	14	8	2	1	8	0	18	0
Ramos, London*	2	5	.286	3.80	34	4	0	9	0	0	64.0	67	37	27	4	5	25	1	43	4
Resetar, Canton-Akron	0	0	.000	18.00	1	0	0	1	0	0	1.0	0	3	2	0	0	4	0	0	0
Rhodes, Harrisburg*	7	4	.636	2.70	19	19	2	0	2	0	106.2	73	37	32	2	0	47	1	115	10
Rightnowar, London	2	1	.667	3.91	15	0	0	9	0	3	25.1	27	13	11	0	0	8	1	18	1
Rivera, London	2	2	.500	3.71	17	0	0	6	0	0	26.2	25	13	11	5	2	11	0	19	1
Rogers, Williamsport	6	8	.429	4.72	41	0	0	32	0	15	61.0	73	33	32	5	1	18	1	33	1
Rosado, Reading	0	0	.000	18.00	1	0	0	1	0	0	1.0	4	2	2	0	0	1	0	1	0

Pitcher, Team	W	L	Pct.	ERA	G	GS	CG	GF	ShO	Sv.	IP	H	R	ER	HR	HB	BB	Int. BB	SO	WP
Roscoe, Canton-Akron	6	2	.750	1.83	13	13	3	0	1	0	88.1	70	28	18	0	1	28	0	66	1
Rub, Albany*	1	0	1.000	2.45	10	0	0	3	0	0	11.0	7	7	3	0	0	17	2	17	2
Ryan, New Britain	1	2	.333	1.73	14	0	0	6	0	1	26.0	23	7	5	2	1	12	1	26	2
Sanders, New Britain	4	15	.211	4.95	26	26	1	0	0	0	158.1	160	101	87	16	2	77	3	80	8
Schullstrom, Hagerstown	1	0	1.000	2.77	2	2	0	0	0	0	13.0	11	5	4	0	1	3	0	9	1
Seanez, Canton-Akron	4	2	.667	2.58	25	0	0	18	0	7	38.1	17	12	11	2	1	30	1	73	1
Sieradzki, Williamsport	0	1	.000	9.00	1	1	0	0	0	0	7.0	8	7	7	1	0	5	0	2	0
Sims, Reading*	1	2	.333	2.52	14	0	0	4	0	0	25.0	23	7	7	1	1	5	0	20	0
Smith, Albany	7	7	.500	4.15	21	21	3	0	0	0	108.1	99	65	50	7	4	72	0	104	7
Sommer, Williamsport	4	7	.364	4.37	22	20	0	0	0	0	111.1	114	75	54	8	5	72	0	83	11
Spencer, Harrisburg	6	1	.857	4.40	17	17	1	0	0	0	92.0	90	52	45	6	4	30	0	66	2
Springer, Albany	1	0	1.000	1.80	2	2	0	0	0	0	15.0	9	4	3	0	0	6	1	16	0
D. Stanford, Albany	5	3	.625	4.50	40	0	0	18	0	0	68.0	68	42	34	3	3	31	7	42	2
L. Stanford, Albany	2	3	.400	1.89	52	0	0	41	0	24	62.0	41	18	13	2	0	36	3	61	12
Stephan, Hagerstown	5	5	.500	2.12	53	1	0	40	0	14	89.0	68	27	21	4	0	41	2	67	1
Stevens, Reading	5	1	.833	3.57	25	0	0	11	0	2	40.1	35	16	16	5	0	11	1	31	2
Stone, London	1	5	.167	5.74	6	6	0	0	0	0	26.2	26	18	17	0	0	25	0	10	1
Tabaka, Reading*	4	8	.333	5.07	21	20	1	0	1	0	108.1	117	65	61	8	4	78	2	68	11
Talamantez, Williamsport	3	2	.600	4.76	32	1	0	6	0	0	58.2	65	38	31	4	2	38	0	47	8
Taylor, New Britain*	2	0	1.000	0.62	4	4	0	0	0	0	29.0	20	2	2	0	0	9	0	38	1
Telgheder, Williamsport	13	11	.542	3.60	28	26	1	1	0	0	167.2	185	81	67	7	5	33	3	90	4
Thoden, Harrisburg	0	0	.000	2.59	5	5	0	0	0	0	31.1	30	9	9	2	0	3	0	19	0
Trautwein, Williamsport	3	9	.250	6.79	42	0	0	30	0	3	58.1	75	47	44	5	3	23	3	21	5
Vargas, Williamsport	2	1	.667	3.80	16	0	0	5	0	2	21.1	19	11	9	1	1	13	2	10	3
Vasquez, Williamsport	0	1	.000	3.97	11	0	0	7	0	1	11.1	10	7	5	0	2	7	1	5	0
Vesling, London*	7	8	.467	4.49	18	18	3	0	1	0	112.1	127	67	56	9	1	47	0	52	2
Wainhouse, Harrisburg	2	2	.500	2.60	33	0	0	27	0	11	52.0	49	17	15	1	4	17	2	46	3
Walker, Canton-Akron	9	4	.692	2.79	45	1	0	34	0	11	77.1	68	36	24	2	7	45	5	42	13
Walter, New Britain*	0	1	.000	3.60	3	0	0	1	0	0	5.0	5	2	2	1	1	0	0	3	1
Ward, Canton-Akron	0	1	.000	0.87	4	1	0	3	0	1	10.1	6	2	1	0	0	5	1	7	0
Wells, Reading	1	0	1.000	3.60	1	0	0	0	0	0	5.0	4	2	2	1	0	1	0	3	0
Wickander, Canton-Akron	1	2	.333	3.96	20	0	0	7	0	0	25.0	24	14	11	0	1	13	1	21	1
Wiegandt, Reading	2	3	.400	2.67	48	0	0	5	0	1	81.0	66	26	24	4	1	40	2	50	5
Williams, Hagerstown	3	5	.375	2.60	39	0	0	29	0	17	55.1	52	23	16	1	0	32	1	42	6
Williams, Reading	7	5	.583	3.69	16	15	2	0	0	0	102.1	93	44	42	1	2	36	0	51	2
Willis, London	5	12	.294	3.64	31	23	3	4	0	0	155.2	154	75	63	7	2	69	2	98	3
Witt, Albany	0	0	.000	9.00	1	1	0	0	0	0	2.0	2	2	2	0	0	2	0	2	1
Wolf, London	5	7	.417	4.80	17	14	2	0	2	0	101.1	109	59	54	8	2	63	3	67	6
Young, Harrisburg	7	5	.583	2.60	54	0	0	29	0	13	90.0	82	28	26	9	2	24	4	74	1

BALKS—Borland, Davis, Dipoto, Popplewell, Smith, Spencer, D. Stanford, 3 each; Birkbeck, Douma, Estrada, Hoy, Lewis, Marshall, Martel, Nivens, Peraza, Stephan, Wickander, Willis, 2 each; Backs, Bennett, Brantley, Bross, Carter, Cinnella, Doherty, Draper, Finnvold, Fischer, Fletcher, Florence, Gaddy, Gray, Haney, Horton, C. Johnson, Kane, Kline, Knudsen, Linskey, Manzanillo, McKeon, Munoz, Mutis, Oquist, Painter, Proctor, Ramos, Rivera, Talamantez, Telgheder, Thoden, Vargas, Wiegandt, Wolf, 1 each.

COMBINATION SHUTOUTS—Martel-Gardella 2, Blueberg-Stanford, Cook-Gardella-Stanford, Hartzog-Popplewell-Newell, Martel-Nielsen, Militello-Gardella, Albany; Bell-Kramer 2, Bell-Wickander-Walker, Bruske-Seanez, Kiser-Meyer, Kramer-Horton-Seanez, Munoz-Meyer-Easley-Ward, Roscoe-Horton-Birkbeck, Canton-Akron; Johnson-Miller-Moore, Linskey-Miller, Linskey-Williams, Oquist-Codiroli, Oquist-Moore, Oquist-Stephan, Peraza-McKeon, Rhodes-Stephan, Hagerstown; Bushing-Brennan-Kilgo, Freed-Lewis, Freed-Lewis-Young, Freed-Young, Hurst-Kilgo, Hurst-Marchok, Johnson-Wainhouse, Maysey-Wainhouse, Pollack-Marchok-Young, Spencer-Bennett-Marchok, Harrisburg; Gohr-Doherty, Groom-Willis-Doherty, London; Finnvold-Florence, Finnvold-Hoy, Fischer-Davis, Florence-Ryan-Hoy, Livernois-Kane, Taylor-Hoy, Taylor-Kane, New Britain; Brantley-Burgos-Dunnum, Brantley-Dunnum-Burgos, Carter-Burgos-Borland, Dunnum-Limbach, Fletcher-Wiegandt-Elli-DiMichele, Reading; Cinnella-Vargas, Hill-Kline-Vasquez, Johnstone-Cinnella, Nivens-Kline, Nivens-Rogers, Nivens-Talamantez, Proctor-Kline-Cinnella, Sommer-Trautwein, Telgheder-Hill-Rogers, Telgheder-Rogers, Telgheder-Vargas, Williamsport.

NO-HIT GAME—Conroy, New Britain, defeated Reading, 2-0, May 22.

FIELDING

TEAM

Team	Pct.	G	PO	A	E	DP	PB	Team	Pct.	G	PO	A	E	DP	PB
Harrisburg	.974	140	3772	1631	146	150	10	Canton-Akron	.968	140	3620	1635	172	137	16
Albany	.970	140	3616	1435	154	122	22	New Britain	.965	140	3601	1468	182	125	12
Reading	.969	140	3609	1471	163	162	16	Williamsport	.965	139	3592	1560	188	137	20
Hagerstown	.969	140	3694	1249	160	125	15	London	.964	139	3583	1505	191	116	22

Triple play—Reading.

INDIVIDUAL

*Throws lefthanded.

FIRST BASEMEN

Player, Team	Pct.	G	PO	A	E	DP
Allison, Williamsport	.946	4	32	3	2	2
Austin, Reading	1.000	3	32	0	0	4
Balthazar, London	1.000	2	11	1	0	0
Bogar, Williamsport	1.000	5	38	3	0	7
Brogna, London*	.984	40	331	44	6	28
Cianfrocco, Harrisburg	.990	115	1021	95	11	110
Cortes, Williamsport*	.991	16	101	9	1	8
Costo, Canton-Akron	.986	52	463	26	7	48
Cruz, London*	.987	98	845	49	12	87
Davis, Hagerstown	1.000	5	38	1	0	3
Degifico, New Britain	1.000	2	14	0	0	0
Dellicarri, Williamsport	.978	13	79	12	2	4
Dickerson, Hagerstown	.923	2	11	1	1	0
Dixon, New Britain	.985	23	187	8	3	16
Dorante, New Britain	.973	9	64	9	2	4
Epley, Canton-Akron*	.992	83	795	55	7	65
Fulton, Harrisburg	.989	11	86	6	1	2
Hendricks, New Britain	.987	87	738	44	10	77
Jefferson, Canton-Akron*	1.000	4	46	3	0	4

Player, Team	Pct.	G	PO	A	E	DP
Johnson, Albany	1.000	1	4	1	0	1
Kosco, Harrisburg	.972	19	161	11	5	15
Lehman, Hagerstown	.880	4	19	3	3	1
Martin, Harrisburg	1.000	1	1	0	0	0
Martinez, Canton-Akron	1.000	2	25	1	0	2
Michel, London	.963	3	24	2	1	1
Munoz, Harrisburg	.941	2	15	1	1	3
Quintell, Albany	1.000	1	2	0	0	0
Resetar, Canton-Akron	.970	4	43	4	0	2
Riesgo, Reading	.970	30	239	20	8	32
Robbins, Hagerstown	1.000	16	89	4	0	6
Roth, Hagerstown	1.000	13	61	4	0	3
Ryan, Reading	.989	103	850	63	10	105
Shamburg, Hagerstown	.987	107	810	79	12	91
Siddall, Harrisburg	1.000	5	33	3	0	4
Skeels, Albany	1.000	2	7	1	0	0
SNOW, Albany*	.993	131	1102	90	8	103
Trevino, Reading	1.000	6	35	1	0	2
Vargas, Albany	.971	10	59	9	2	5
Wallin, New Britain*	.977	26	194	15	5	14
Wearing, Hagerstown	.979	7	44	2	1	8
Williams, Williamsport	.982	117	991	82	20	100

SECOND BASEMEN

Player, Team	Pct.	G	PO	A	E	DP
Allison, Williamsport	.967	14	20	39	2	2
Austin, Reading	.968	46	104	139	8	39
Barns, Canton-Akron	1.000	14	16	32	0	5
BAUTISTA, Canton-Akron	.969	94	167	245	13	53
Beyeler, London	.960	47	105	137	10	36
Blackwell, Albany	.905	11	10	9	2	3
Bogar, Williamsport	.986	14	28	40	1	9
Davis, Albany	1.000	1	0	1	0	0
DeCillis, London	.942	20	47	50	6	6
DeJardin, Albany	.963	104	178	292	18	71
Dellicarri, Williamsport	1.000	6	11	13	0	3
Dickerson, Hagerstown	.958	31	55	82	6	12
Dorante, New Britain	1.000	1	1	1	0	0
Escobar, Canton-Akron	1.000	2	2	5	0	0
Ferretti, Canton-Akron	.958	21	37	55	4	9
Frazier, London	.921	15	29	29	5	4
Fulton, Harrisburg	1.000	2	1	1	0	0
Hernandez, Williamsport	.963	115	229	324	21	80
Kimberlin, London	.965	31	62	76	5	17
Leonhardt, London	.897	7	12	14	3	3
Lofton, Hagerstown	.967	111	211	285	17	80
Marigny, London	.938	11	16	29	3	7
Meadows, Hagerstown	1.000	3	3	2	0	0
Milstien, New Britain	.971	83	166	268	13	57
Munoz, Harrisburg	1.000	8	12	25	0	5
Odor, Canton-Akron	.973	15	29	42	2	9
Powers, New Britain	.962	36	64	88	6	17
Randle, New Britain	.980	22	46	51	2	10
Reimink, London	.964	19	32	49	3	13
Ripken, Hagerstown	1.000	1	2	1	0	0
Robertson, Reading	.969	86	192	239	14	70
Roth, Hagerstown	.833	4	5	5	2	1
Santangelo, Harrisburg	.971	70	144	186	10	36
Sarbaugh, Canton-Akron	.933	4	12	16	2	2
Scarsone, Reading	.970	15	43	54	3	21
Stairs, Harrisburg	.973	71	153	203	10	51
Tatis, Canton-Akron	.971	6	13	20	1	4
Vargas, Albany	.950	34	58	94	8	14
Wardlow, Albany	.929	5	1	12	1	1

Triple play—Robertson.

THIRD BASEMEN

Player, Team	Pct.	G	PO	A	E	DP
Allison, Williamsport	.923	6	1	11	1	2
Austin, Reading	.884	17	16	22	5	4
Barns, Canton-Akron	.829	13	5	24	6	1
Bogar, Williamsport	.943	44	27	88	7	5
DAVIS, Albany	.917	129	83	205	26	20
DeCillis, London	.667	1	2	0	1	0
DeJardin, Albany	.909	14	10	20	3	1
Dellicarri, Williamsport	.906	39	31	84	12	13
Dickerson, Hagerstown	.900	2	4	5	1	1
Dixon, New Britain	.893	52	22	86	13	8
Dorante, New Britain	.862	7	8	17	4	1
Ferretti, Canton-Akron	.947	33	16	74	5	6
Fulton, Harrisburg	.860	16	9	28	6	1
Galindo, London	.913	60	37	109	14	8
Holland, Harrisburg	.911	130	76	169	24	16
Howard, Williamsport	.914	61	38	101	13	7
Kosco, Harrisburg	.954	75	52	154	10	16
Marigny, London	.939	15	11	35	3	2
Milstien, New Britain	.833	2	4	1	1	0
Munoz, Harrisburg	1.000	4	3	2	0	0
Powers, New Britain	.911	45	29	73	10	9
Randle, New Britain	.904	46	22	72	10	2
Reimink, London	.914	69	52	119	16	11
Roth, Hagerstown	.917	8	4	7	1	0
Santangelo, Harrisburg	1.000	2	1	3	0	1
Shamburg, Hagerstown	.750	7	4	2	2	1
Stairs, Harrisburg	.925	50	37	111	12	16
Thomas, Canton-Akron	.892	23	11	55	8	5
Thome, Canton-Akron	.924	82	41	167	17	11
Trevino, Reading	.889	11	5	11	2	2
Vargas, Albany	1.000	4	0	2	0	0
WALLER, Reading	.917	114	83	205	26	26

Triple play—Austin.

SHORTSTOPS

Player, Team	Pct.	G	PO	A	E	DP
Alexander, Hagerstown	1.000	3	5	4	0	0
Allison, Williamsport	.909	4	3	7	1	0
Barns, Canton-Akron	.868	9	13	20	5	6
Beyeler, London	.883	12	18	35	7	6
Blackwell, Albany	1.000	2	3	2	0	1
Bogar, Williamsport	1.000	4	7	6	0	2
Byrd, New Britain	.957	78	167	235	18	49
Costo, Canton-Akron	1.000	1	1	3	0	0
DeCillis, London	.936	39	58	117	12	22
DeJardin, Albany	.974	16	11	26	1	1

Player, Team	Pct.	G	PO	A	E	DP
Dellicarri, Williamsport	1.000	10	12	32	0	4
Dickerson, Hagerstown	.944	53	82	152	14	29
Escobar, Canton-Akron	.917	9	9	24	3	2
Ferretti, Canton-Akron	.957	52	64	180	11	27
Fulton, Harrisburg	1.000	1	1	4	0	1
Galindo, London	.909	20	23	67	9	4
Gutierrez, Hagerstown	.941	84	158	196	22	54
Holland, Harrisburg	.714	3	1	4	2	0
Kimberlin, London	.947	77	118	221	19	53
Lofton, Hagerstown	1.000	2	0	2	0	0
Martin, Harrisburg	.960	81	124	240	15	56
Millette, Reading	.941	114	170	342	32	71
Munoz, Harrisburg	.970	48	59	138	6	27
NAVARRO, Williamsport	.950	125	233	353	31	83
Odor, Canton-Akron	.979	59	96	178	6	43
Powers, New Britain	.900	5	4	5	1	1
Randle, New Britain	.935	38	66	91	11	18
Robertson, Reading	.920	35	56	82	12	29
Santangelo, Harrisburg	.946	22	29	59	5	12
Silvestri, Albany	.948	132	218	362	32	84
Thomas, Canton-Akron	.961	23	34	65	4	21
Valentin, New Britain	.975	23	50	65	3	20

OUTFIELDERS

Player, Team	Pct.	G	PO	A	E	DP
Balthazar, London	1.000	1	4	0	0	0
Barns, Canton-Akron	.889	7	7	1	1	0
Barnwell, Albany	.933	5	13	1	1	1
Bautista, Canton-Akron	.000	2	0	0	1	0
Beams, New Britain	.960	63	115	5	5	0
Berthel, Hagerstown	1.000	10	13	0	0	0
Blackwell, Albany	1.000	2	0	1	0	0
Blosser, New Britain*	.946	108	178	15	11	3
Brogna, London*	1.000	19	37	2	0	0
Brown, Reading*	.968	46	88	2	3	1
Burnitz, Williamsport	.958	134	237	13	11	2
Cabrera, London	1.000	26	26	1	0	0
Carey, Harrisburg	.961	89	163	10	7	4
Cassels, Harrisburg	.949	60	87	6	5	2
Cianfrocco, Harrisburg	1.000	2	2	0	0	0
Contreras, Canton-Akron*	.953	46	79	3	4	0
Davis, Williamsport	1.000	24	34	2	0	1
Dostal, Reading*	.975	96	224	7	6	3
Dozier, Williamsport	.954	68	118	7	6	0
Epley, Canton-Akron*	.928	47	64	0	5	0
Faulk, Harrisburg*	.939	58	89	4	6	0
Ferretti, Canton-Akron	1.000	1	1	0	0	0
Fox, New Britain*	.925	31	57	5	5	0
Frazier, London	.964	95	181	7	7	0
Gilbert, Harrisburg	.975	70	150	5	4	1
Hare, London*	.952	28	55	5	3	2
Hernandez, Harrisburg	.980	124	222	21	5	3
Hithe, Hagerstown	.969	70	156	1	5	1
Housie, New Britain	.985	111	261	10	4	2
Howell, Williamsport	.985	69	186	5	3	1
Hurst, London*	.976	52	117	3	3	1
Ingram, London	.974	104	181	6	5	1
Katzaroff, Harrisburg	.974	135	319	13	9	2
Kingwood, Hagerstown	.966	74	196	5	7	0
Knoblauh, Albany	.934	64	109	5	8	0
Lake, Harrisburg	1.000	6	1	0	0	0
Lane, Canton-Akron	.978	73	125	6	3	3
Lehman, Hagerstown	1.000	1	1	0	0	0
Lofton, Hagerstown	1.000	7	18	0	0	0
Longmire, Reading	.972	82	134	3	4	0
Marsh, Reading	.986	53	142	3	2	1
Martinez, Canton-Akron	.857	8	12	0	2	0
MASSE, Williamsport	.990	104	184	7	2	1
May, Williamsport	.964	85	182	7	7	1
Mayo, Harrisburg*	1.000	12	13	2	0	0
McBride, Williamsport	.935	55	80	6	6	0
Meadows, Hagerstown	.965	31	55	0	2	0
Michel, London	1.000	19	30	1	0	0
Paris, New Britain	.970	108	213	10	7	1
Pegues, London	.986	36	69	4	1	0
Phillips, Albany*	.973	120	215	5	6	0
Raley, Hagerstown	1.000	21	23	0	0	0
Ramos, Canton-Akron*	.945	68	96	8	6	1
Randle, New Britain	.958	11	23	0	1	0
Riesgo, Reading	.967	41	56	2	2	0
Roth, Hagerstown	.971	15	30	3	1	0
Sabino, London*	.974	112	218	8	6	2
Santangelo, Harrisburg	.985	43	60	5	1	0
Stairs, Harrisburg	1.000	8	3	0	0	0
Tinsley, Canton-Akron	.966	38	56	1	2	0
Vargas, Albany	1.000	3	5	1	0	0
Viera, Williamsport*	.964	87	183	6	7	1
Voigt, Hagerstown	1.000	9	8	0	0	0
Whitfield, Canton-Akron	.940	27	44	3	3	0
C. Williams, Reading	.979	110	228	5	5	1
Williams, Albany	.974	45	109	4	3	0
Woodruff, London	.983	57	111	5	2	0
Yacopino, Hagerstown*	.966	67	139	3	5	0
Zambrano, Canton-Akron	.964	17	26	1	1	0

CATCHERS

Player, Team	Pct.	G	PO	A	E	DP	PB
Agostinelli, Reading	1.000	12	52	1	0	0	0
Ausmus, Albany	.992	63	470	56	4	4	9
Balthazar, London	.977	61	312	35	8	2	11
Daulton, Reading	1.000	1	6	2	0	0	0
Dorante, New Britain	.978	27	157	20	4	4	3
Fagnant, New Britain	.975	16	74	4	2	2	2
Flaherty, New Britain	.977	59	337	46	9	3	4
Gillette, London	.973	73	455	56	14	0	9
Gonzalez, Williamsport	.978	48	233	39	6	3	7
Hirsch, Harrisburg	.964	6	26	1	1	0	1
Johnson, Albany	1.000	2	6	1	0	0	0
Laker, Harrisburg	.959	10	67	4	3	0	0
Lehman, Hagerstown	.994	89	625	44	4	4	8
Levis, Canton-Akron	.984	110	644	77	12	8	10
DO. LINDSEY, Reading	.995	93	571	75	3	12	11
Livesey, Albany	.993	23	120	13	1	0	8
Magrann, New Britain	.980	26	175	23	4	1	2
Natal, Harrisburg	.992	70	453	45	4	3	5
Quintell, Albany	.966	6	28	0	1	0	1
Raley, Hagerstown	1.000	1	2	0	0	0	0
Resetar, Canton-Akron	.981	43	230	27	5	4	6
Robbins, Hagerstown	.992	57	343	27	3	3	7
Rodriguez, 13 Lon.-22 N.B.	.971	35	172	22	6	1	3
Rosado, Reading	.956	43	210	28	11	4	5
Siddall, Harrisburg	.984	61	401	36	7	5	4
Skeels, Albany	.987	57	359	35	5	1	3
Toale, Albany	1.000	1	2	0	0	0	1
Wedge, New Britain	1.000	1	6	1	0	0	0
Williams, Williamsport	.929	7	24	2	2	0	2
Zinter, Williamsport	.983	95	523	45	10	6	11

PITCHERS

Player, Team	Pct.	G	PO	A	E	DP
Allen, New Britain	1.000	8	0	3	0	0
Backs, Reading	.895	19	4	13	2	3
Batchelor, Albany	1.000	1	1	1	0	0
Bell, Canton-Akron*	.947	18	4	14	1	0
Bennett, Harrisburg	.889	28	4	12	2	1
Birkbeck, Canton-Akron	1.000	21	4	7	0	1
Blueberg, Albany	.929	8	7	6	1	0
Borland, Reading	.957	59	8	14	1	0
Brantley, Reading	1.000	11	5	15	0	1
Brennan, Harrisburg	1.000	21	2	8	0	1
Brink, Reading	1.000	5	1	6	0	0
Bross, Williamsport	1.000	20	2	4	0	0
Brown, New Britain*	1.000	12	3	6	0	0
Bruske, Canton-Akron	1.000	17	9	10	0	0
Bumgarner, Hagerstown	.900	17	2	7	1	0
Burdick, Hagerstown	.885	26	9	14	3	0
Burgos, Reading*	1.000	15	2	5	0	1
Bushing, Harrisburg	1.000	3	1	3	0	0
Carter, Reading*	1.000	20	3	11	0	0
Chamberlain, Canton-Akron	1.000	2	1	1	0	0
Cinnella, Williamsport	.958	28	10	13	1	2
Codiroli, Hagerstown	.750	5	2	1	1	0
Conroy, New Britain	1.000	10	6	10	0	0
Constant, Hagerstown	1.000	1	0	1	0	0
Cook, Hagerstown	1.000	14	4	13	0	0
Cornelius, Harrisburg	1.000	3	4	2	0	0
Culkar, Hagerstown	1.000	3	0	1	0	0
Curtis, Canton-Akron*	1.000	10	0	4	0	1
Davis, New Britain	1.000	45	3	14	0	0
DeSilva, London	.923	11	3	9	1	1
DiMichele, Reading*	1.000	22	0	5	0	0
Dipoto, Canton-Akron	.951	28	12	27	2	1
Doherty, London	.875	53	4	17	3	1
Douma, Williamsport*	1.000	10	1	10	0	0
Draper, Albany	.903	36	5	23	3	1
Dunnum, Reading	.947	55	6	12	1	2
Easley, Canton-Akron	1.000	6	3	1	0	0
Elli, Reading*	1.000	16	8	10	0	1
Estrada, New Britain	1.000	25	5	8	0	1
Finnvold, New Britain	.952	16	7	13	1	0
Fischer, New Britain*	.931	22	7	20	2	0
Fletcher, Reading	1.000	21	9	9	0	1
Florence, New Britain*	.917	55	3	19	2	1
Freed, Harrisburg	.974	26	11	26	1	4
Gaddy, Reading*	1.000	10	2	3	0	0
Garcia, Canton-Akron	.600	4	2	1	2	0
Garcia, Albany*	.944	18	6	28	2	0
Gardella, Albany*	1.000	53	2	20	0	0
Gohr, London	1.000	2	2	1	0	0
Gray, Reading	.800	7	0	4	1	1
Groom, London*	.923	11	5	7	1	0
Grott, Harrisburg*	1.000	10	1	1	0	0
Hall, Canton-Akron*	.882	8	2	13	2	0
Haney, Harrisburg*	1.000	12	8	21	0	2
Hansen, London	.950	21	5	14	1	1
Harrison, Harrisburg*	.905	23	5	14	2	0
Hartzog, Albany	1.000	18	4	11	0	0
Hickey, Hagerstown*	1.000	15	2	3	0	1
Hill, Williamsport*	.947	27	7	29	2	2
Holcomb, Albany*	1.000	26	0	1	0	1

Player, Team	Pct.	G	PO	A	E	DP
Holdridge, Reading	.500	7	0	1	1	0
Horton, Canton-Akron*	.889	25	3	5	1	0
Hoy, New Britain	.900	47	5	22	3	1
Hursey, London*	.947	35	7	11	1	0
Hurst, Harrisburg	.900	6	3	6	1	0
Johnson, Harrisburg	.909	10	4	6	1	2
Johnson, Hagerstown	1.000	3	2	1	0	0
Johnstone, Williamsport	.978	27	7	38	1	2
Jones, Hagerstown	1.000	12	0	5	0	0
Kane, New Britain	.968	41	10	20	1	3
Keliipuleole, Harrisburg	.000	6	0	0	2	0
Kerfeld, London	.500	11	1	0	1	0
Kilgo, Harrisburg*	1.000	14	2	7	0	1
Kiser, Canton-Akron*	1.000	17	1	9	0	0
Kline, Williamsport	.895	50	5	12	2	0
Knudsen, London	.889	34	2	6	1	0
Kovach, Canton-Akron	.857	11	2	10	2	1
Kramer, Canton-Akron	.905	35	4	15	2	4
Krumm, London	1.000	18	4	15	0	0
Leinen, Hagerstown*	.953	23	16	25	2	1
Lewis, Harrisburg	1.000	34	8	12	0	1
Limbach, Reading*	1.000	18	2	3	0	2
Da. Lindsey, Reading	1.000	17	3	2	0	0
Linskey, Hagerstown*	1.000	16	11	6	0	1
Livernois, New Britain	1.000	5	0	4	0	0
Lovelace, London*	1.000	9	4	3	0	0
Manon, Albany	.333	3	1	0	2	0
Manzanillo, New Britain	.857	7	3	3	1	0
Marchok, Harrisburg*	1.000	41	6	8	0	0
Marris, Albany	1.000	8	2	4	0	1
Marshall, London*	.971	27	9	25	1	1
Martel, Albany	.939	25	11	20	2	4
Maysey, Harrisburg	1.000	15	4	21	0	1
McKeon, Hagerstown*	1.000	33	0	8	0	0
Meyer, Canton-Akron	1.000	14	4	5	0	1
Milacki, Hagerstown	1.000	3	0	1	0	0
Militello, Albany	1.000	7	1	8	0	0
Miller, Hagerstown	1.000	14	3	4	0	1
Moore, Hagerstown*	.875	34	3	4	1	0
Munoz, Canton-Akron	1.000	15	7	4	0	0
Mutis, Canton-Akron*	.962	25	10	40	2	2
Newell, Albany	.667	8	0	2	1	1
Nielsen, Albany*	.750	6	1	2	1	0
Nivens, Williamsport	.863	28	11	33	7	7
O'Neill, New Britain*	1.000	2	0	2	0	0
Oquist, Hagerstown	1.000	27	14	17	0	2
Painter, New Britain	.938	15	6	9	1	1
Peraza, Hagerstown	.905	19	4	15	2	0
Perez, Albany	1.000	2	0	1	0	0
Pollack, Harrisburg*	.974	26	4	34	1	2
Popplewell, Albany	1.000	52	5	10	0	1
Proctor, Williamsport	.875	9	0	7	1	0
Quantrill, New Britain	.889	5	1	7	1	2
Ramos, London*	1.000	34	4	19	0	1
Resetar, Canton-Akron	1.000	1	1	0	0	0
Rhodes, Hagerstown*	.826	19	3	16	4	2
Rightnowar, London	1.000	15	3	4	0	0
Rivera, London	1.000	17	0	8	0	0
Rogers, Williamsport	1.000	41	4	15	0	3
Roscoe, Canton-Akron	.850	13	2	15	3	2
Rub, Albany*	1.000	10	0	1	0	0
Ryan, New Britain	.889	14	1	7	1	0
Sanders, New Britain	.964	26	11	16	1	0
Schullstrom, Hagerstown	1.000	2	1	0	0	0
Seanez, Canton-Akron	.600	25	1	2	2	0
Sieradzki, Williamsport	1.000	1	3	0	0	0
Sims, Reading*	1.000	14	2	7	0	0
Smith, Albany	.867	21	2	11	2	2
Sommer, Williamsport	.769	22	8	12	6	1
Spencer, Harrisburg	.958	17	8	15	1	1
Springer, Albany	1.000	2	1	2	0	0
D. Stanford, Albany	.917	40	7	4	1	0
L. Stanford, Albany	1.000	52	6	6	0	0
Stephan, Hagerstown	1.000	53	11	6	0	3
Stevens, Reading	.750	25	1	2	1	0
Stone, London	1.000	6	1	6	0	0
Tabaka, Reading	1.000	21	6	16	0	3
Talamantez, Williamsport	.950	32	10	9	1	2
Telgheder, Williamsport	.980	28	19	31	1	2
Thoden, Harrisburg	1.000	5	4	2	0	1
Trautwein, Williamsport	1.000	42	4	12	0	1
Vargas, Williamsport	.667	16	1	1	1	0
Vasquez, Williamsport	1.000	11	2	1	0	0
VESLING, London*	1.000	18	11	22	0	2
Wainhouse, Harrisburg	.933	33	4	10	1	0
Walker, Canton-Akron	1.000	45	6	14	0	0
Walter, New Britain*	1.000	3	0	1	0	0
Ward, Canton-Akron	1.000	4	2	2	0	1
Wickander, Canton-Akron*	.875	20	0	7	1	1
Wiegandt, Reading*	1.000	49	2	12	0	0
Williams, Hagerstown	1.000	39	7	6	0	0
M. Williams, Reading	1.000	15	8	14	0	1
Willis, London	.966	31	14	14	1	1
Witt, Albany	1.000	1	1	0	0	0
Wolf, London	1.000	17	9	10	0	0
Young, Harrisburg	.952	54	4	16	1	1

The following players did not have any fielding statistics at the positions indicated or appeared only as a designated hitter, pinch-hitter or pinch-runner: Barns, p; Beams, 3b; Blackwell, 3b; R. Cook, p; Dickerson, of, p; Fernandez, p; Fox, p; Fulton, c; Galindo, p; Hendricks, of; Hirsch, 1b; Holland, of; Holsman, p; Livesey, 3b, of; Marsh, p; McBride, p; Reimink, of; Rosado, p; Skeels, 3b, of; Tatis, of; Taylor, p; Thomas, 2b; Trevino, of; Wells, p.

LEAGUE CHAMPIONS

Year	Team	Pct.	Year	Team	Pct.	Year	Team	Pct.
1923—	Williamsport	.661	1950—	Wilkes-Barre‡	.652	1973—	Reading b	.551
1924—	Williamsport	.654	1951—	Wilkes-Barre‡	.612		Pittsfield	.551
1925—	York§	.583		Scranton (2nd)†	.562	1974—	Thetford Miners (2nd)c	.536
	Williamsport§	.583	1952—	Albany	.603		Pittsfield (2nd)	.496
1926—	Scranton	.627		Binghamton (2nd)‡	.562	1975—	Reading	.613
1927—	Harrisburg	.630	1953—	Reading	.682		Bristol*	.587
1928—	Harrisburg	.603		Binghamton (2nd)‡	.636	1976—	Three Rivers	.601
1929—	Binghamton	.597	1954—	Wilkes-Barre	.576		West Haven d	.576
1930—	Wilkes-Barre	.572		Albany (3rd)‡	.540	1977—	West Haven e	.623
1931—	Harrisburg	.597	1955—	Reading	.613		Three Rivers	.551
1932—	Wilkes-Barre	.561		Allentown (2nd)‡	.565	1978—	Reading	.642
1933—	Binghamton	.690	1956—	Schenectady†	.609		Bristol*	.580
1934—	Binghamton	.694	1957—	Binghamton	.607	1979—	West Haven f	.597
	Williamsport*	.603		Reading (3rd)‡	.529	1980—	Holyoke*	.561
1935—	Scranton	.657	1958—	Lancaster x	.568		Waterbury	.540
	Binghamton*	.580		Binghamton (6th)‡	.493	1981—	Glens Falls	.615
1936—	Scranton*	.609	1959—	Springfield†	.607		Bristol*	.577
	Elmira	.629		Springfield (3rd)y	.496	1982—	West Haven*	.614
1937—	Elmira†	.622	1960—	Williamsport y	.551		Lynn	.590
1938—	Binghamton	.622		Springfield (3rd)y	.496	1983—	Lynn	.554
	Elmira (3rd)‡	.522	1961—	Springfield	.612		New Britain‡	.518
1939—	Scranton†	.571	1962—	Williamsport	.593	1984—	Waterbury	.543
1940—	Scranton	.568		Elmira (2nd)‡	.514		Vermont‡	.536
	Binghamton (2nd)‡	.554	1963—	Charleston	.593	1985—	Albany	.540
1941—	Wilkes-Barre	.630	1964—	Elmira	.586		Vermont‡	.514
	Elmira (3rd)‡	.514	1965—	Pittsfield	.607	1986—	Reading	.566
1942—	Albany	.600	1966—	Elmira	.633		Vermont‡	.554
	Scranton (2nd)‡	.593	1967—	Binghamton z	.586	1987—	Pittsfield	.630
1943—	Scranton	.630		Elmira	.532		Harrisburg‡	.550
	Elmira (2nd)‡	.568	1968—	Pittsfield	.604	1988—	Glens Falls	.584
1944—	Hartford	.723		Reading (2nd)‡	.579		Albany‡	.522
	Binghamton (4th)‡	.474	1969—	York	.640	1989—	Albany‡	.657
1945—	Utica	.615	1970—	Waterbury a	.560		Harrisburg	.522
	Albany (3rd)‡	.564		Reading a	.553	1990—	Albany	.568
1946—	Scranton†	.691	1971—	Three Rivers	.569		London‡	.547
1947—	Utica†	.652		Elmira b	.561	1991—	Harrisburg	.621
1948—	Scranton†	.636	1972—	West Haven b	.600		Albany‡	.543
1949—	Albany	.664		Three Rivers	.559			
	Binghamton (4th)‡	.500						

*Won split-season playoff. †Won championship and four-team playoff. ‡Won four-team playoff. §Tied for pennant, York winning playoff. xLeague was divided into Northern, Southern divisions and played a split season; Lancaster over-all season leader. yPlayoff finals canceled after one game because of rain with Williamsport and Springfield declared playoff co-champions. zLeague was divided into Eastern, Western divisions; Binghamton won playoff. aTied for pennant, Waterbury winning playoff. bLeague was divided into American, National divisions; won playoff. cLeague was divided into American and National divisions; won four-team playoff. dLeague was divided into Northern, Southern divisions, won playoff. eLeague was divided into New England and Canadian-American divisions; won playoff. fWon both halves of split season (no playoffs). (NOTE—Known as New York-Pennsylvania League prior to 1938.)

FINAL STANDINGS

FIRST HALF

EASTERN DIVISION

Team	W	L	T	Pct.	GB
Greenville (Braves)	47	22	0	.681	......
Jacksonville (Mariners)	41	31	0	.569	7½
Carolina (Pirates)	37	35	0	.514	11½
Charlotte (Cubs)	35	37	0	.486	13½
Orlando (Twins)	33	36	0	.478	14

WESTERN DIVISION

Team	W	L	T	Pct.	GB
Birmingham (White Sox)	45	25	0	.643	......
Chattanooga (Reds)	35	32	0	.522	8½
Huntsville (Athletics)	28	44	0	.389	18
Knoxville (Blue Jays)	25	42	0	.373	18½
Memphis (Royals)	23	45	0	.338	21

SECOND HALF

EASTERN DIVISION

Team	W	L	T	Pct.	GB
Orlando (Twins)	44	31	0	.587	......
Greenville (Braves)	41	34	0	.547	3
Charlotte (Cubs)	39	33	0	.542	3½
Jacksonville (Mariners)	33	38	0	.465	9
Carolina (Pirates)	29	41	0	.414	12½

WESTERN DIVISION

Team	W	L	T	Pct.	GB
Knoxville (Blue Jays)	42	35	0	.545	......
Memphis (Royals)	38	38	0	.500	3½
Chattanooga (Reds)	38	39	0	.494	4
Huntsville (Athletics)	33	39	0	.458	6½
Birmingham (White Sox)	32	41	0	.438	8

COMPOSITE

Team	Grn.	Birm.	Orl.	Jax.	Char.	Chat.	Knox.	Car.	Mem.	Hunt.	W	L	T	Pct.	GB
Greenville (Braves)	....	10	11	10	11	10	10	9	9	8	88	56	0	.611	......
Birmingham (White Sox)	6	....	10	9	9	9	7	6	10	11	77	66	0	.538	10½
Orlando (Twins)	5	6	....	8	8	8	10	11	11	10	77	67	0	.535	11
Jacksonville (Mariners)	6	7	8	....	10	9	8	9	8	9	74	69	0	.517	13½
Charlotte (Cubs)	5	7	8	6	....	8	9	10	11	11	74	70	0	.514	14
Chattanooga (Reds)	6	7	8	7	8	....	11	6	10	10	73	71	0	.507	15
Knoxville (Blue Jays)	6	9	6	8	7	5	....	9	10	7	67	77	0	.465	21
Carolina (Pirates)	7	9	5	6	6	10	7	....	6	10	66	76	0	.465	21
Memphis (Royals)	7	6	5	8	6	6	6	10	....	7	61	83	0	.424	27
Huntsville (Athletics)	8	5	6	7	5	6	9	6	9	....	61	83	0	.424	27

Carolina's home games played in Zebulon, N.C.

Major league affiliations in parentheses.

Playoffs—Birmingham defeated Knoxville, three games to one; Orlando defeated Greenville, three games to none; Orlando defeated Birmingham, three games to one, to win league championship.

Regular-season attendance—Birmingham, 313,412; Carolina, 218,054; Charlotte, 313,791; Chattanooga, 186,285; Greenville, 222,038; Huntsville, 224,208; Jacksonville, 231,139; Knoxville, 123,361; Memphis, 185,409; Orlando, 110,131. Total, 2,127,828. Playoffs (11 games)—12,919. All-Star Game at Huntsville—4,023.

Managers—Birmingham, Tony Franklin; Carolina, Marc Bombard; Charlotte, Jay Loviglio; Chattanooga, Jim Tracy; Greenville, Chris Chambliss; Huntsville, Casey Parsons; Jacksonville, Jim Nettles; Knoxville, John Stearns; Memphis, Jeff Cox; Orlando, Scott Ullger.

All-Star team—1B—Elvin Paulino, Charlotte; 2B—Bret Boone, Jacksonville; 3B—Cheo Garcia, Orlando; SS—Alex Arias, Charlotte; OF—Reggie Sanders, Chattanooga; Fernando Ramsey, Charlotte; Kevin Koslofski, Memphis; Keith Mitchell, Greenville; C—Jim Campanis, Jacksonville; Util.—Vinny Castilla, Greenville; DH—Troy Neel, Huntsville; RHP—Pat Mahomes, Orlando; LHP—Wilson Alvarez, Birmingham; Most Valuable Player—Ryan Klesko, Greenville; Outstanding Pitcher—Mark Wohlers, Greenville; Manager of the Year—Chris Chambliss, Greenville.

BATTING

TEAM

Team	Avg.	G	AB	R	OR	H	TB	2B	3B	HR	RBI	SH	SF	HP	BB	Int. BB	SO	SB	CS	LOB
Chattanooga	.261	144	4599	575	595	1201	1724	211	48	72	510	55	37	29	420	23	894	104	64	955
Jacksonville	.251	143	4600	539	539	1153	1693	196	19	102	539	20	40	59	522	22	950	122	63	1005
Memphis	.249	144	4675	590	667	1165	1577	197	25	55	505	38	38	64	483	22	1023	129	81	982
Greenville	.248	144	4568	608	503	1131	1680	232	31	85	542	64	50	50	526	41	872	111	73	994
Charlotte	.245	144	4651	582	598	1140	1605	189	15	82	526	50	40	69	448	28	924	146	64	958
Orlando	.245	142	4522	529	494	1107	1502	172	29	55	468	34	37	67	482	22	709	121	59	1024
Carolina	.242	144	4510	486	526	1090	1456	175	37	49	441	43	44	47	427	22	869	96	63	946
Knoxville	.239	144	4483	529	525	1072	1536	183	34	71	471	64	35	34	487	25	1009	157	94	899
Birmingham	.238	143	4608	583	534	1097	1595	179	47	75	518	38	33	62	624	25	978	99	60	1092
Huntsville	.231	144	4623	576	671	1068	1464	188	20	56	487	50	45	52	598	34	976	137	74	1017

INDIVIDUAL

(Leading qualifiers for batting championship—389 or more plate appearances)

*Bats lefthanded.   †Switch-hitter.

Player, Team	Avg.	G	AB	R	H	TB	2B	3B	HR	RBI	SH	SF	HP	BB	Int. BB	SO	SB	CS
Bowie, Jim, Jacksonville*	.310	123	448	51	139	194	25	0	10	67	1	6	0	36	3	67	3	3
Laureano, Frank, Memphis	.298	99	359	58	107	137	17	2	3	34	2	5	7	61	1	51	12	4
Tedder, Scott, Birmingham*	.294	95	337	34	99	119	14	3	0	32	3	0	0	51	0	38	5	4
Klesko, Ryan, Greenville*	.291	126	419	64	122	192	22	3	14	67	3	4	6	75	14	60	14	17
Garcia, Cheo, Orlando	.282	137	496	57	140	199	24	4	9	75	1	7	10	45	3	48	13	4
Ross, Sean, Greenville*	.282	113	429	52	121	179	28	3	8	40	5	1	2	24	4	96	20	5
Colvard, Benny, Chattanooga	.281	124	463	62	130	220	23	8	17	68	1	1	2	17	0	111	11	4
Neel, Troy, Huntsville*	.277	110	364	64	101	191	21	0	23	68	0	7	5	82	18	75	1	3
Giannelli, Ray, Knoxville*	.276	112	362	53	100	141	14	3	7	37	5	2	2	64	6	66	8	5
Ramsey, Fernando, Charlotte	.276	139	547	78	151	199	18	6	6	49	7	2	3	36	0	89	37	17

Departmental leaders: G—Boone, Kent, Ramsey, 139; AB—Ramsey, 547; R—Coomer, 81; H—Ramsey, 151; TB—Colvard, 220; 2B—Kent, 34; 3B—Colvard, Pledger, R. Sanders, 8; HR—Paulino, 24; RBI—Paulino, 81; SH—Cedeno, 12; SF—Coomer, 8; HP—Crockett, 19; BB—Bolick, 84; IBB—Neel, 18; SO—Roberson, 129; SB—Gilbert, 43; CS—Gilbert, 19.

(All players—listed alphabetically)

Player, Team	Avg.	G	AB	R	H	TB	2B	3B	HR	RBI	SH	SF	HP	BB	Int. BB	SO	SB	CS
Abbott, Kurt, Huntsville	.253	53	182	18	46	54	6	1	0	11	1	1	1	17	0	39	6	3
Adams, Steve, Carolina	.000	8	1	1	0	0	0	0	0	0	0	0	0	0	0	0	0	0
Alborano, Pete, Memphis*	.257	51	183	11	47	56	7	1	0	16	1	0	1	18	1	27	2	1
Alicea, Ed, Greenville†	.333	13	42	6	14	20	3	0	1	5	0	0	0	6	1	5	1	0
Allen, Rick, Chattanooga	.251	123	382	52	96	125	15	1	4	26	4	1	0	35	4	61	5	1
Alva, John, Greenville	.207	68	256	27	53	73	12	1	2	24	3	2	0	15	1	49	0	2
Anderson, Mike, Chattanooga	.111	28	18	1	2	2	0	0	0	1	1	0	0	1	0	11	0	0
Antigua, Felix, Carolina	.091	3	11	1	1	1	0	0	0	0	0	0	0	0	0	2	0	0
Arguelles, Fernando, Jacksonville	.196	50	138	8	27	28	1	0	0	10	2	1	1	7	0	38	1	0
Arias, Alex, Charlotte	.275	134	488	69	134	172	26	0	4	47	3	3	3	47	2	42	23	9
Armas, Marcos, Huntsville	.226	81	305	40	69	111	16	1	8	53	2	4	0	18	1	89	2	1
Ayala, Bobby, Chattanooga	.154	40	13	3	2	2	0	0	0	0	0	0	0	0	0	7	0	0
Bafia, Bob, Huntsville	.255	14	51	4	13	17	4	0	0	8	0	1	0	6	0	9	0	1
Baldwin, Jeff, Charlotte*	.246	65	207	24	51	62	8	0	1	27	1	3	2	23	3	38	4	3
Baxter, Jim, Memphis	.219	67	187	25	41	61	11	0	3	22	1	2	5	27	0	62	1	2
Beeler, Pete, Chattanooga	.201	68	204	26	41	68	7	1	6	16	1	2	1	7	0	40	2	3
Bernhardt, Cesar, Birmingham	.272	26	103	15	28	39	2	0	3	16	0	0	2	12	0	8	3	4
Biasucci, Joe, Charlotte	.220	24	50	4	11	13	2	0	0	2	0	1	0	6	0	18	2	0
Blair, Paul, Charlotte†	.179	40	67	13	12	15	3	0	0	3	0	0	0	11	0	14	2	2
Bolick, Frank, Jacksonville†	.254	136	468	69	119	186	19	0	16	73	2	7	5	84	3	115	5	4
Booker, Eric, Huntsville	.257	30	113	12	29	35	6	0	0	17	0	1	0	15	1	20	0	0
Boone, Bret, Chattanooga	.255	139	475	64	121	198	18	1	19	75	1	3	5	72	2	123	9	9
Borrelli, Dean, Huntsville	.190	64	184	9	35	41	4	1	0	7	4	1	3	15	0	45	1	1
Bowie, Jim, Jacksonville*	.310	123	448	51	139	194	25	0	10	67	1	6	0	36	3	67	3	3
Branson, Jeff, Chattanooga*	.263	88	304	35	80	105	13	3	2	28	2	5	1	31	2	51	3	7
Bridges, Tony, Memphis	.224	113	371	34	83	103	11	0	3	30	6	2	1	34	3	106	18	5
Brito, Jorge, Huntsville	.202	65	203	26	41	55	11	0	1	23	2	1	4	28	0	50	0	1
Bryant, Scott, Chattanooga	.304	91	306	42	93	143	14	6	8	43	0	2	3	34	1	77	2	3
Buccheri, James, Huntsville	.212	100	340	48	72	87	15	0	0	22	5	4	7	71	0	60	35	7
Buckholz, Steve, Carolina	.091	21	11	2	1	1	0	0	0	0	0	0	0	0	0	2	0	0
Bullinger, Jim, Charlotte	.154	21	13	0	2	3	1	0	0	0	0	0	0	1	0	2	0	0
Burton, Chris, Greenville*	.208	58	144	18	30	40	3	2	1	9	1	1	0	14	1	33	8	4
Busby, Wayne, Birmingham	.162	67	198	18	32	42	3	2	1	14	4	0	3	28	0	75	2	5
Campanis, Jim, Jacksonville	.248	118	387	36	96	151	10	0	15	49	0	4	7	37	2	64	0	0
Campbell, Darrin, Birmingham	.221	94	289	39	64	98	7	3	7	32	1	3	7	27	0	94	0	1
Canan, Dick, Chattanooga	.214	34	84	10	18	25	2	1	1	10	1	1	0	9	0	24	3	1
Capellan, Carlos, Orlando	.241	117	365	41	88	100	10	1	0	29	4	4	2	24	2	29	12	5
Carcione, Tom, Huntsville	.122	17	49	4	6	8	0	1	0	4	0	0	1	8	0	17	0	1
Casarotti, Rich, Greenville†	.258	78	264	38	68	81	9	2	0	15	4	2	2	25	1	49	2	2
Castellano, Pedro, Charlotte	.421	7	19	2	8	8	0	0	0	2	0	1	1	0	0	6	0	0
Castilla, Vinny, Greenville	.270	66	259	34	70	114	17	3	7	44	2	4	2	9	1	35	0	1
Castleberry, Kevin, Birmingham*	.000	1	1	0	0	0	0	0	0	0	0	0	0	0	0	0	0	0
Cedeno, Domingo, Knoxville†	.223	100	336	39	75	97	7	6	1	26	12	1	1	29	1	81	11	6
Champion, Brian, Greenville	.226	113	332	45	75	115	17	1	7	35	0	2	3	49	3	77	1	0
Chasey, Mark, Birmingham*	.238	110	332	42	79	117	17	3	5	36	0	1	16	72	6	97	1	0
Chimelis, Joel, Huntsville	.214	68	238	26	51	68	10	2	1	16	7	3	0	18	0	30	4	3
Cole, Popeye, Chattanooga	.243	124	420	51	102	130	14	4	2	36	11	4	7	32	0	73	16	15
Cole, Victor, Carolina†	.000	20	1	0	0	0	0	0	0	0	0	0	0	0	0	1	0	0
Colvard, Benny, Chattanooga	.281	124	463	62	130	220	23	8	17	68	1	1	2	17	0	111	11	4
Conte, Mike, Huntsville	.228	104	359	36	82	107	10	0	5	30	5	3	1	25	1	58	8	4
Cooke, Stephen, Carolina	.000	9	8	0	0	0	0	0	0	0	0	0	0	0	0	6	0	0
Cooley, Fred, Huntsville	.125	13	40	3	5	6	1	0	0	6	0	1	0	3	0	10	0	0
Coomer, Ron, Birmingham	.255	137	505	81	129	205	27	5	13	76	6	8	1	59	1	78	0	3
Corbin, Archie, Memphis	.000	28	2	0	0	0	0	0	0	0	0	0	0	0	0	1	0	0
Correia, Rod, Huntsville	.221	87	290	25	64	79	10	1	1	22	8	1	6	31	0	50	2	4
Costo, Tim, Chattanooga	.280	85	293	31	82	122	19	3	5	29	0	2	4	20	0	65	11	5
Cox, Darren, Chattanooga	.184	13	38	2	7	8	1	0	0	3	1	1	0	2	0	9	0	0
Crockett, Rusty, Charlotte	.214	117	280	36	60	72	7	1	1	23	9	2	19	25	1	42	14	2
Crowley, Terry, Carolina†	.264	132	469	60	124	170	15	5	7	45	3	3	4	44	6	55	5	10
Cuevas, Johnny, Greenville	.190	68	205	22	39	59	11	0	3	21	1	1	1	13	1	47	1	0
Czarkowski, Mark, Jacksonville*	.500	20	2	0	1	1	0	0	0	0	0	0	0	0	0	0	0	0
Dattola, Kevin, Huntsville†	.235	77	285	38	67	84	13	2	0	18	2	3	5	35	5	58	15	14
Davis, Doug, Memphis	.169	31	89	9	15	18	3	0	0	4	0	0	3	11	0	20	0	5
Deak, Brian, Memphis	.201	73	204	31	41	80	9	0	10	41	1	5	3	53	4	51	0	1
de la Rosa, Juan, Knoxville	.215	122	382	37	82	107	11	1	4	33	3	2	3	17	0	94	17	11
DeLima, Rafael, Orlando*	.249	122	394	45	98	132	14	4	4	46	3	3	1	47	1	56	13	7
DeLoach, Bobby, Knoxville	.266	116	364	42	97	136	16	4	5	37	3	3	0	25	0	61	12	6
DiBartolomeo, Steve, Charlotte	1.000	45	1	0	1	1	0	0	0	0	0	0	0	0	0	0	0	0
Dodd, Bill, Chattanooga	.000	35	2	0	0	0	0	0	0	0	0	0	0	0	0	1	0	0
Edge, Greg, Carolina†	.220	102	350	43	77	94	10	2	1	22	8	1	3	36	0	22	13	10
Estep, Chris, Carolina	.243	97	300	34	73	106	17	2	4	34	1	5	4	33	0	111	4	6
Fajardo, Hector, Carolina	.167	10	6	0	1	1	0	0	0	2	1	0	1	0	0	2	0	0
Fansler, Stan, Carolina	.000	19	16	0	0	0	0	0	0	0	0	0	0	0	0	7	0	0
Figueroa, Fernando, Jacksonville*	.000	42	2	0	0	0	0	0	0	0	0	0	0	0	0	0	0	0
Foster, Lindsay, Birmingham†	.212	116	372	40	79	98	8	4	1	34	5	2	2	26	0	73	23	7
Garber, Jeff, Memphis	.250	61	200	24	50	56	4	1	0	19	7	0	4	26	0	44	7	2
Garcia, Cheo, Orlando	.282	137	496	57	140	199	24	4	9	75	1	7	10	45	3	48	13	4
Gardner, John, Charlotte	.174	30	23	2	4	6	2	0	0	0	1	0	0	0	0	12	0	0
Garner, Kevin, Birmingham*	.249	119	430	54	107	174	19	3	14	74	0	6	4	59	6	106	0	0
Garrison, Webster, Huntsville	.264	31	110	18	29	44	9	0	2	10	0	1	1	16	0	21	5	3
Gay, Jeff, Birmingham*	.193	26	83	5	16	20	4	0	0	6	1	1	1	5	1	19	1	0
Giannelli, Ray, Knoxville*	.276	112	362	53	100	141	14	3	7	37	5	2	2	64	6	66	8	5
Gilbert, Shawn, Orlando	.257	138	529	69	136	167	12	5	3	38	6	6	11	53	1	71	43	19
Gillum, K.C., Chattanooga*	.161	12	31	3	5	8	3	0	0	3	0	0	1	2	0	11	1	0
Gomez, Henry, Charlotte	.000	34	4	0	0	0	0	0	0	0	0	0	0	0	0	5	0	0
Gomez, Pat, Greenville*	.167	13	12	1	2	2	0	0	0	1	0	0	0	0	0	3	0	0
Gonzalez, David, Memphis	.129	23	70	9	9	10	1	0	0	6	0	1	0	8	0	17	1	2
Gonzalez, Ruben, Jacksonville	.237	94	308	27	73	99	14	0	4	41	1	5	6	37	0	53	0	1
Grace, Mike, Charlotte	.207	73	261	22	54	80	8	0	6	32	3	4	2	15	0	43	3	2

Player, Team	Avg.	G	AB	R	H	TB	2B	3B	HR	RBI	SH	SF	HP	BB	Int. BB	SO	SB	CS
Green, Tom, Carolina	.198	64	197	15	39	55	10	0	2	16	1	1	1	16	0	52	0	0
Griffin, Ty, Charlotte†	.164	42	116	16	19	23	4	0	0	12	0	6	3	27	2	37	4	3
Grifol, Pedro, Orlando	.150	6	20	0	3	3	0	0	0	2	0	0	0	0	0	6	0	0
Hamilton, Carl, Carolina*	.000	10	2	0	0	0	0	0	0	0	0	0	0	0	0	0	0	0
Hancock, Lee, Carolina*	.000	38	10	1	0	0	0	0	0	0	0	0	0	0	0	2	0	0
Hawblitzel, Ryan, Charlotte	.000	5	5	0	0	0	0	0	0	0	1	0	0	0	0	1	0	0
Hiatt, Phil, Memphis	.228	56	206	29	47	74	7	1	6	33	0	6	3	9	1	63	6	2
Hines, Tim, Carolina*	.204	34	98	8	20	25	2	0	1	7	1	1	2	6	0	21	0	0
Holley, Bobby, Jacksonville	.282	32	103	20	29	45	6	2	2	17	1	1	3	17	0	17	0	0
Hosey, Dwayne, Huntsville†	.245	28	102	16	25	34	6	0	1	7	1	1	1	9	1	15	5	4
Huyler, Mike, Carolina	.210	81	229	22	48	60	4	4	0	28	5	4	2	15	2	46	4	4
Imes, Rodney, Chattanooga	.500	8	2	1	1	1	0	0	0	0	1	0	0	0	0	0	0	0
Infante, Alexis, Knoxville	.227	9	22	3	5	6	1	0	0	1	0	0	0	0	0	3	0	2
Jackson, Bo, Birmingham	.308	4	13	2	4	4	0	0	0	0	0	0	0	4	0	2	1	2
Jaster, Scott, Birmingham	.265	104	362	40	96	139	14	4	7	44	1	6	5	36	1	73	1	4
Johnson, Judd, Greenville	.000	47	3	0	0	0	0	0	0	0	1	0	1	0	0	2	0	0
Jose, Manny, Chattanooga†	.302	63	169	22	51	77	8	6	2	17	4	1	0	22	1	37	13	10
Kelly, Pat, Greenville	.300	30	90	14	27	37	6	2	0	5	2	1	0	13	1	10	5	1
Kent, Jeff, Knoxville	.256	139	445	68	114	186	34	1	12	61	2	3	10	80	2	104	25	6
King, Bryan, Jacksonville	.080	13	25	2	2	2	0	0	0	0	1	0	1	4	0	6	1	0
Klesko, Ryan, Greenville*	.291	126	419	64	122	192	22	3	14	67	3	3	6	75	14	60	14	17
Knapp, Mike, Charlotte	.256	92	266	19	68	83	12	0	1	33	7	1	1	19	3	49	4	0
Knorr, Randy, Knoxville	.176	24	74	7	13	17	4	0	0	4	0	1	1	10	1	18	2	0
Kobza, Greg, Birmingham*	.000	1	4	0	0	0	0	0	0	0	0	0	0	1	0	2	0	0
Koslofski, Kevin, Memphis*	.324	81	287	41	93	135	15	3	7	39	4	4	4	33	3	56	10	13
Kowitz, Brian, Greenville*	.232	35	112	15	26	40	5	0	3	17	2	2	2	10	0	7	1	4
Kremblas, Frank, Chattanooga	.241	102	320	35	77	103	17	0	3	41	4	2	2	29	1	61	3	4
Kvasnicka, Jay, Orlando*	.271	99	292	48	79	107	12	2	4	27	3	0	1	54	2	40	23	11
Ladnier, Deric, Memphis†	.241	60	166	17	40	51	5	0	2	17	0	2	2	13	0	41	1	1
Laureano, Frank, Memphis	.298	99	359	58	107	137	17	2	3	34	2	5	7	61	1	51	12	4
Lee, Derek, Birmingham*	.325	45	154	36	50	79	10	2	5	16	0	1	6	46	5	23	9	7
Leslie, Reggie, Chattanooga	.000	1	1	0	0	0	0	0	0	0	0	0	0	0	0	1	0	0
Liebert, Allen, Birmingham*	.183	35	109	7	20	26	3	0	1	7	1	2	0	16	0	7	0	0
List, Paul, Carolina	.150	7	20	1	3	5	0	1	0	2	0	0	0	0	0	6	0	0
Logan, Todd, Orlando*	.184	18	38	5	7	9	2	0	0	3	0	0	0	8	0	9	0	0
Long, Kevin, Memphis*	.275	106	407	60	112	143	18	2	3	35	6	3	2	45	1	63	27	10
Lonigro, Greg, Chattanooga	.261	131	460	47	120	165	24	3	5	54	6	6	1	23	1	65	12	2
Lopez, Fred, Greenville	.264	23	53	5	14	20	3	0	1	6	0	0	0	6	0	10	0	0
Magrann, Tom, Carolina	.222	5	18	1	4	4	0	0	0	2	0	0	1	0	2	0	0	0
Maksudian, Mike, Knoxville*	.255	71	231	32	59	92	12	3	5	35	0	5	0	37	5	43	2	2
Maloney, Rich, Greenville	.261	43	111	12	29	37	6	1	0	13	3	4	0	10	1	8	0	0
Manahan, Tony, Jacksonville	.254	113	410	67	104	152	23	2	7	45	2	3	6	54	0	81	11	6
Martin, Al, Greenville*	.243	86	301	38	73	113	13	3	7	38	1	1	8	32	4	84	19	7
Marzan, Jose, Orlando	.262	84	229	29	60	83	13	2	2	22	2	2	5	28	2	29	2	1
Masteller, Dan, Orlando*	.246	124	370	44	91	130	14	5	5	35	3	2	3	43	6	43	6	4
Matos, Francisco, Huntsville	.194	55	191	18	37	42	1	2	0	19	5	0	2	17	1	28	12	2
Maynard, Tow, Jacksonville	.259	58	216	32	56	67	5	3	0	13	1	1	6	20	0	51	30	10
McAuliffe, Dave, Chattanooga	.000	33	2	0	0	0	0	0	0	0	0	0	0	0	0	2	0	0
McCarty, Dave, Orlando	.261	28	88	18	23	36	4	0	3	11	0	0	2	10	0	20	0	1
McCreary, Bob, Orlando†	.206	107	345	25	71	88	9	1	2	22	4	2	2	26	0	55	3	1
McDonald, Mike, Jacksonville*	.232	35	112	16	26	35	9	0	0	11	0	0	3	13	2	19	2	1
Merchant, Mark, Jacksonville†	.282	51	156	22	44	69	10	0	5	17	0	1	1	21	4	38	3	4
Merullo, Matt, Birmingham*	.214	8	28	5	6	12	0	0	2	5	0	0	0	2	0	4	0	0
Miller, Paul, Carolina	.250	16	8	0	2	3	1	0	0	1	0	0	0	0	0	4	0	0
Minor, Blas, Carolina	.000	4	3	0	0	0	0	0	0	0	0	0	0	0	0	2	0	0
Mitchell, Keith, Greenville	.327	60	214	46	70	121	15	3	10	47	3	5	1	29	0	29	12	8
Montalvo, Rob, Knoxville	.161	15	31	3	5	6	1	0	0	0	1	0	1	7	0	7	0	0
Monzon, Jose, Knoxville	.267	44	116	12	31	36	5	0	0	11	1	1	0	13	1	23	1	1
Morgan, Kenny, Orlando*	.239	58	184	24	44	64	7	2	3	17	0	1	2	27	0	35	2	2
Morris, Rick, Greenville	.240	115	338	50	81	114	16	1	5	43	4	7	9	75	1	55	2	3
Mount, Chuck, Charlotte	.000	17	0	0	0	0	0	0	0	0	0	0	0	0	0	0	0	0
Muh, Steve, Charlotte*	.000	21	0	0	0	0	0	0	0	0	0	0	0	1	0	0	0	0
Murphy, Pete, Carolina*	.000	35	6	1	0	0	0	0	0	1	0	1	0	2	0	2	0	0
Neel, Troy, Huntsville*	.277	110	364	64	101	191	21	0	23	68	0	7	5	82	18	75	1	3
Newfield, Marc, Jacksonville	.231	6	26	4	6	9	3	0	0	2	0	0	1	0	0	8	0	0
Nied, David, Greenville	.222	15	9	2	2	3	1	0	0	2	2	0	0	2	0	1	0	0
Nunez, Bernie, Knoxville	.197	82	234	16	46	71	11	1	4	24	4	3	1	11	2	71	4	4
Ocasio, Javier, Birmingham	.224	102	398	39	89	104	7	4	0	30	5	0	6	39	0	63	16	7
O'Halloran, Greg, Knoxville*	.254	110	350	37	89	132	13	3	8	53	2	6	0	27	3	46	11	6
Olmeda, Jose, Greenville†	.202	50	173	18	35	56	10	1	3	16	5	2	2	15	0	36	9	2
Olmstead, Reed, Orlando*	.196	38	107	12	21	33	6	0	2	11	1	0	1	15	0	28	0	0
Ortiz, Ray, Orlando*	.247	135	470	58	116	168	19	3	9	71	0	6	7	48	3	100	3	2
Osik, Keith, Carolina	.302	17	43	9	13	18	3	1	0	5	0	0	0	5	0	5	0	0
Paquette, Craig, Huntsville	.262	102	378	50	99	143	18	1	8	60	2	5	3	28	0	87	0	5
Parker, Tim, Charlotte	.133	24	15	2	2	2	0	0	0	0	0	0	0	1	0	3	0	0
Parks, Derek, Orlando	.215	92	256	30	55	87	14	0	6	31	2	3	12	31	1	65	0	0
Parnell, Mark, Memphis	.000	58	0	0	0	0	0	0	0	0	0	0	0	0	0	0	0	0
Paulino, Elvin, Charlotte*	.257	132	460	67	118	219	27	1	24	81	0	2	9	55	8	110	8	3
Pedre, Jorge, Memphis	.253	100	363	43	92	149	28	1	9	59	1	3	7	24	4	72	1	2
Pennington, Ken, Jacksonville	.244	91	320	32	78	114	14	2	6	29	1	1	2	27	1	57	3	3
Pennye, Darwin, Carolina	.257	122	455	53	117	166	20	7	5	43	5	2	7	23	0	85	19	8
Pennyfeather, William, Carolina	.275	42	149	13	41	46	5	0	0	9	1	1	1	7	0	17	3	2
Perez, Eduardo, Greenville	.250	1	4	0	1	1	0	0	0	0	0	0	0	1	0	0	0	0
Pezzoni, Ron, Jacksonville	.318	7	22	3	7	7	0	0	0	2	0	0	0	1	0	3	0	0
Pledger, Kinnis, Birmingham*	.218	117	363	53	79	138	16	8	9	51	4	1	4	60	3	104	15	10
Pose, Scott, Chattanooga	.274	117	402	61	110	131	8	5	1	31	7	3	2	69	3	50	17	13
Pugh, Tim, Chattanooga	.000	5	2	0	0	0	0	0	0	0	2	0	0	0	0	0	0	0
Ramsey, Fernando, Charlotte	.276	139	547	78	151	199	18	6	6	49	7	0	3	36	0	89	37	17
Ratliff, Daryl, Carolina	.215	24	93	10	20	23	3	0	0	9	1	0	0	6	0	16	8	3
Reese, Kyle, Memphis	.208	12	24	3	5	6	1	0	0	1	0	0	1	0	0	9	0	0
Risley, Bill, Chattanooga	.077	19	13	0	1	1	0	0	0	0	0	0	0	0	0	8	0	0
Rivera, Ben, Greenville	.154	26	13	1	2	2	0	0	0	0	2	1	0	0	1	5	0	0
Roberson, Kevin, Charlotte†	.256	136	507	77	130	215	24	2	19	67	0	5	9	39	1	129	17	3
Robinson, Darryl, Memphis	.285	99	351	42	100	128	16	3	2	35	4	1	4	17	2	34	0	5

Player, Team	Avg.	G	AB	R	H	TB	2B	3B	HR	RBI	SH	SF	HP	BB	Int. BB	SO	SB	CS
Robinson, Napoleon, Greenville	.043	29	23	2	1	1	0	0	0	0	2	0	1	1	0	13	0	0
Rodgers, Paul, Knoxville	.193	43	114	15	22	29	3	2	0	4	0	1	0	16	0	23	11	8
Rodriguez, Boi, Greenville*	.283	29	92	14	26	41	10	1	1	14	2	3	0	15	3	16	0	1
Roesler, Mike, Carolina	.000	20	1	0	0	0	0	0	0	0	0	0	0	0	0	0	0	0
Rogers, Jimmy, Knoxville	.000	29	0	1	0	0	0	0	0	0	0	0	0	0	0	0	1	0
Romero, Mandy, Carolina†	.217	98	323	29	70	91	12	0	3	31	2	2	1	45	4	53	1	2
Ross, Sean, Greenville*	.282	113	429	52	121	179	28	3	8	40	5	1	2	24	4	96	20	5
Roth, Greg, Birmingham*	.190	41	126	15	24	37	8	1	1	12	2	2	0	18	0	21	0	0
Rush, Eddie, Chattanooga	.165	32	91	11	15	15	0	0	0	3	1	0	1	9	0	11	0	0
Ryan, Colin, Memphis	.125	5	16	0	2	2	0	0	0	4	0	0	0	0	0	8	0	0
St. Peter, Bill, Charlotte	.192	44	146	14	28	39	2	0	3	9	1	0	0	14	0	39	4	3
Salles, John, Charlotte	.150	23	20	1	3	3	0	0	0	0	0	0	1	1	0	7	0	0
Sanders, Earl, Greenville	.333	48	3	1	1	2	1	0	0	0	0	0	0	0	0	1	0	0
Sanders, Reggie, Chattanooga	.315	86	302	50	95	150	15	8	8	49	1	4	1	41	5	67	15	2
Sanford, Mo, Greenville	.100	16	10	1	1	1	0	0	0	0	2	0	0	0	0	6	0	0
Santana, Ruben, Jacksonville	.200	5	15	2	3	6	0	0	1	3	0	0	0	1	0	3	0	0
Satre, Jason, Chattanooga	.250	8	4	0	1	1	0	0	0	0	0	0	0	0	0	2	0	0
Schock, Will, Chattanooga	.000	12	5	1	0	0	0	0	0	0	1	0	0	1	0	5	0	0
Schreiber, Bruce, Carolina	.243	108	325	25	79	95	11	1	1	22	3	2	1	21	0	64	4	4
Sellner, Scott, Chattanooga	.200	42	130	11	26	29	3	0	0	11	3	1	3	21	1	22	4	2
Shelton, Ben, Carolina	.231	55	169	19	39	56	8	3	1	19	0	1	4	29	0	57	2	1
Shockey, Scott, Huntsville*	.240	70	229	26	55	78	9	1	4	31	2	2	4	40	2	54	1	1
Sierra, Candy, Charlotte	.250	18	8	0	2	3	1	0	0	3	0	0	1	0	0	3	0	0
Simmons, Randy, Greenville*	.000	1	1	0	0	0	0	0	0	0	0	0	0	1	0	1	0	0
Simonds, Dan, Charlotte	.247	34	97	17	24	32	6	1	0	6	4	1	1	14	2	12	0	1
Siwa, Joe, Orlando	.191	61	157	11	30	35	2	0	1	14	3	1	5	11	0	25	0	0
Smith, Jack, Jacksonville	.212	38	104	17	22	35	2	1	3	11	1	2	0	7	0	22	1	2
Sodders, Mike, Charlotte	.000	9	1	0	0	0	0	0	0	0	0	0	0	0	0	1	0	0
Sparks, Greg, Carolina*	.273	69	220	19	60	85	10	0	5	35	0	4	1	39	5	55	0	2
Spradlin, Jerry, Chattanooga†	.400	48	5	2	2	4	0	1	0	2	0	0	0	0	0	2	0	0
Stargell, Tim, Jacksonville	.185	62	200	22	37	54	6	1	3	13	1	1	3	14	0	35	8	1
Sullivan, Carl, Birmingham	.234	45	128	11	30	47	6	1	3	12	3	0	5	6	0	32	2	0
Sutko, Glenn, Chattanooga	.286	23	63	12	18	30	3	0	3	11	2	0	0	9	2	20	0	0
Tatar, Kevin, Chattanooga	.200	12	5	0	1	1	0	0	0	1	0	0	0	2	0	1	0	0
Tatarian, Dean, Birmingham	.333	8	15	5	5	7	2	0	0	0	0	0	0	0	0	3	0	0
Taylor, Bill, Greenville*	.000	59	3	0	0	0	0	0	0	0	1	0	0	0	0	1	0	0
Taylor, Mike, Knoxville	.165	78	139	16	23	28	3	1	0	10	8	0	1	18	0	39	9	2
Taylor, Scott (Kan.), Green.	.000	8	2	0	0	0	0	0	0	0	0	0	0	1	0	1	0	0
Taylor, Scott (Ill.), Char.	.234	40	107	11	25	28	3	0	0	4	3	0	2	11	2	14	0	0
Tedder, Scott, Birmingham*	.294	95	337	34	99	119	14	3	0	32	3	0	0	51	0	38	5	4
Tejada, Wil, Huntsville	.200	6	20	2	4	4	0	0	0	3	1	0	0	1	0	4	1	0
Tellers, David, Carolina	.000	11	1	0	0	0	0	0	0	0	0	0	0	0	0	0	0	0
Thompson, Ryan, Knoxville	.241	114	403	48	97	141	14	3	8	40	5	3	4	26	2	88	17	10
Tinsley, Lee, Huntsville†	.224	92	303	47	68	93	7	6	2	24	1	4	3	52	1	97	36	14
Toale, John, Memphis*	.281	69	253	41	71	109	14	0	8	42	0	4	0	29	0	47	3	1
Torres, Jessie, Carolina	.067	14	30	3	2	2	0	0	0	1	0	1	0	10	3	12	0	0
Townley, Jason, Knoxville	.197	81	213	12	42	50	8	0	0	13	10	1	1	31	0	57	0	4
Tracy, Jim, Carolina	.200	16	5	1	1	1	0	0	0	0	0	2	0	0	0	2	0	0
Trafton, Todd, Chattanooga	.260	63	231	30	60	96	18	0	6	34	2	2	6	23	2	46	2	6
Tunison, Rich, Memphis†	.250	55	208	23	52	66	11	0	1	19	1	1	2	14	2	46	6	7
Turang, Brian, Jacksonville	.215	41	130	14	28	38	6	2	0	7	2	0	2	13	1	33	5	2
Turek, Joe, Chattanooga	.400	10	5	0	2	2	0	0	0	1	2	0	0	0	0	0	0	0
Upshaw, Lee, Greenville*	.133	19	15	0	2	3	1	0	0	3	0	0	0	0	0	4	0	0
Valdez, Frank, Orlando	.247	60	182	13	45	61	0	0	2	14	2	0	3	12	1	50	1	2
Vasquez, Luis, Chattanooga	.231	18	13	1	3	4	1	0	0	1	3	0	1	0	0	2	0	0
Vice, Darryl, Huntsville†	.244	97	287	46	70	83	11	1	0	28	2	1	5	63	3	60	3	2
Vitiello, Joe, Memphis	.219	36	128	15	28	34	4	1	0	18	0	1	1	23	0	36	0	0
Waggoner, Aubrey, Birmingham*	.230	69	248	39	57	85	11	4	3	21	2	0	1	54	2	56	20	6
Wakefield, Tim, Carolina	.133	26	15	2	2	3	1	0	0	0	1	0	0	4	0	6	0	0
Walk, Bob, Carolina	.000	1	2	0	0	0	0	0	0	0	0	0	0	0	0	0	0	0
Walker, Bernie, 8 Chat.-54 Mem.*	.232	62	185	38	43	61	4	4	2	18	2	1	2	36	0	46	13	4
Walker, Hugh, Memphis*	.231	117	407	40	94	134	16	6	4	43	1	2	12	29	3	107	13	9
Watkins, Daren, Memphis	.153	59	177	21	27	34	2	1	1	8	1	0	4	14	0	57	9	6
Watkins, Tim, Charlotte†	.250	52	8	1	2	2	0	0	0	1	2	0	1	0	0	1	0	0
Watson, Preston, Greenville	.500	49	2	0	1	1	0	0	0	0	0	0	0	0	0	1	0	0
Webb, Ben, Carolina	.000	37	2	0	0	0	0	0	0	0	1	0	0	0	0	2	0	0
Wehner, John, Carolina	.265	61	234	30	62	78	5	1	3	21	3	5	2	24	1	32	17	5
Welch, Doug, Charlotte	.241	131	444	45	107	163	17	0	13	65	2	3	8	25	2	107	7	6
Wendell, Turk, Greenville*	.150	25	20	1	3	3	0	0	0	0	0	0	0	0	0	8	0	0
Wetherby, Jeff, Jacksonville*	.288	76	264	39	76	116	15	2	7	36	0	3	3	35	4	44	6	4
White, Billy, Charlotte	.268	123	396	52	106	137	16	3	3	50	4	5	4	66	2	70	13	9
Williams, Ted, Jacksonville†	.219	70	269	47	59	87	10	3	4	16	2	1	4	21	0	73	34	13
Wilson, Brandon, Birmingham	.400	2	10	3	4	5	1	0	0	2	0	0	0	0	0	2	0	0
Wilson, Dan, Chattanooga	.257	81	292	32	75	104	19	2	2	38	1	4	0	21	0	39	2	2
Woodson, Kerry, Jacksonville	.000	13	0	0	0	0	0	0	0	0	0	0	0	0	0	0	0	0
Wright, George, Memphis†	.212	18	52	8	11	16	2	0	1	6	1	0	0	14	1	11	0	0
Yacopino, Ed, Carolina†	.224	42	147	19	33	37	2	1	0	14	0	2	0	21	0	26	3	1
Yan, Julian, Knoxville	.280	103	350	45	98	168	16	3	16	61	3	2	5	23	0	108	2	4
Young, Kevin, Carolina	.342	75	263	36	90	130	19	6	3	33	0	1	8	15	1	38	9	3
Young, Mark, Knoxville	.233	109	317	43	74	93	10	3	1	21	5	1	4	53	2	80	24	17
Zambrano, Eddie, Carolina	.253	83	269	28	68	100	17	3	3	39	2	7	4	22	0	56	4	2

The following pitchers, listed alphabetically by club, with games in parentheses, had no plate appearances, primarily through use of designated hitters:

BIRMINGHAM—Alvarez, Wilson (23); Bolton, Rodney (12); Brito, Mario (10); Chambers, Travis (10); Cortes, Conde (22); Davino, Mike (25); Garcia, Ramon (6); Hernandez, Roberto (4); Howard, Chris (38); Hudek, John (51); Kennedy, Bo (15); Keyser, Brian (3); Merigliano, Frank (36); Middaugh, Scott (12); Reynolds, Dave (19); Thomas, Larry (2); Ventura, Jose (25); Wickman, Robert (20).

CAROLINA—Ausanio, Joe (3); Duncan, Chip (6); Neely, Jeff (5); Tafoya, Dennis (40).

CHARLOTTE—Jaques, Eric (20); Jones, Shannon (4); Strauss, Julio (49); Stroud, Derek (4); Swartzbaugh, Dave (1).

CHATTANOOGA—Foster, Steve (17); Garcia, Victor (40); Hoffman, Trevor (14); McCarthy, Steve (12).

GREENVILLE—Bark, Brian (9); Borbon, Pedro (4); Strange, Don (4); Wohlers, Mark (28); Young, Mike (10).

HUNTSVILLE—Briscoe, John (2); Cormier, Russ (17); Erwin, Scott (19); Eskew, Dan (6); Garcia, Apolinar (13); Grott, Matt (42); Guzman, Johnny (7); Kuhn, Chad (44); Latter, Dave (58); Mielke, Gary (4); Mohler, Mike (8); Osteen, Gavin (28); Peek, Tim (56); Peters, Don (33); Phoenix, Steve (2); Revenig, Todd (12); Van Poppel, Todd (24); Weber, Weston (34); Zancanaro, David (30).

JACKSONVILLE—Balabon, Rick (10); Barton, Shawn (14); Blueberg, Jim (14); Eave, Gary (5); Evans, Dave (21); Fleming, Dave (21); Garcia, Marcos (6); Nelson, Jeff (21); Newlin, Jim (47); Pitz, Mike (36); Richards, Dave (10); Rojas, Ricky (15); Salkeld, Roger (23); Schooler, Mike (11); Wiggs, Johnny (6); Zarranz, Fernando (24); Zavaras, Clint (6).

KNOXVILLE—Blohm, Pete (3); Brown, Daren (3); Cromwell, Nate (16); Cross, Jesse (31); Hall, Darren (42); Horsman, Vince (42); Jones, Chris (12); Kizziah, Daren (11); Lloyd, Graeme (2); Ogliaruso, Mike (7); Sanchez, Alex (14); Thompson, Rich (10); Trlicek, Rick (41); Ward, Anthony (31); Weathers, Dave (24); Williams, Woody (18); Wishnevski, Rob (31).

MEMPHIS—Cruz, Andres (11); Duncan, Chip (22); Hopper, Brad (20); LeMasters, Jim (12); Moeller, Dennis (10); O'Neal, Randy (12); Perez, Dario (3); Peters, Doug (19); Pichardo, Hipolito (34); Pierce, Ed (31); Poehl, Mike (33); Roberts, Peter (25); Shifflett, Steve (59); Smith, Jim (16); Talbert, Lou (3); Taylor, Terry (6).

ORLANDO—Bangtson, Pat (26); Delkus, Pete (45); Garces, Rich (10); Johnson, Greg (53); Lind, Orlando (52); Mahomes, Pat (18); Muh, Steve (7); Newman, Alan (11); Richards, Rusty (19); Savage, Jack (6); Schwabe, Mike (6); Stowell, Steve (50); Trombley, Mike (27); Tsamis, George (1); Wassenaar, Rob (15); West, David (1); Wiese, Phil (21).

GRAND SLAMS—Armas, 2; Boone, Chasey, P. Cole, Coomer, Estep, Kent, Lonigro, Martin, Mitchell, O'Halloran, Paulino, Ross, Shockey, 1 each.

AWARDED FIRST BASE ON CATCHER'S INTERFERENCE—Crockett 2 (Cuevas, Monzon); Estep 2 (Gay, O'Halloran); Klesko 2 (Campbell, Siwa); Lee 2 (Arguelles, Campanis); McDonald 2 (Borrelli, Parks); Ross 2 (Campanis, Romero); Alva (Grifol); Bowie (Parks); Griffin (Arguelles); Hosey (Gay); Liebert (Maksudian).

PITCHING

TEAM

Team	ERA	G	CG	ShO	Sv.	IP	H	R	ER	HR	HB	BB	Int. BB	SO	WP	Bk.
Birmingham	2.93	143	20	16	32	1236.0	1049	534	402	61	56	493	16	885	59	14
Greenville	3.02	144	9	13	52	1238.2	1144	503	415	47	47	462	33	997	79	14
Orlando	3.04	144	22	14	31	1193.0	1068	494	403	60	32	442	21	955	43	3
Knoxville	3.07	144	17	18	32	1222.1	1043	525	417	52	57	548	28	972	83	16
Carolina	3.31	142	18	14	39	1211.1	1081	526	445	66	69	444	42	876	71	10
Jacksonville	3.38	143	19	15	35	1218.2	1145	539	457	90	61	400	10	965	69	14
Charlotte	3.75	144	25	16	24	1242.2	1150	598	518	92	45	523	45	847	50	11
Chattanooga	3.81	144	19	14	41	1203.2	1076	595	509	74	51	567	30	957	91	16
Huntsville	3.84	144	7	8	35	1251.1	1213	671	534	75	43	622	19	859	89	27
Memphis	4.21	144	10	6	32	1228.0	1255	667	574	75	72	516	20	891	69	12

INDIVIDUAL

(Leading qualifiers for earned-run average leadership—115 or more innings)

*Throws lefthanded.

Pitcher, Team	W	L	Pct.	ERA	G	GS	CG	GF	ShO	Sv.	IP	H	R	ER	HR	HB	BB	Int. BB	SO	WP
Mahomes, Orlando	8	5	.615	1.78	18	17	2	0	0	0	116.0	77	30	23	5	3	57	0	136	3
Alvarez, Birmingham*	10	6	.625	1.83	23	23	3	0	2	0	152.1	109	46	31	6	3	74	0	165	9
N. Robinson, Greenville	16	6	.727	2.27	29	28	0	0	0	0	174.2	172	61	44	6	10	48	2	107	4
Weathers, Knoxville	10	7	.588	2.45	24	22	5	0	2	0	139.1	121	51	38	3	8	49	1	114	7
Trombley, Orlando	12	7	.632	2.54	27	27	7	0	2	0	191.0	153	65	54	12	7	57	2	175	2
Wendell, Greenville	11	3	.786	2.56	25	20	1	3	1	0	147.2	130	47	42	4	6	51	5	122	11
Fleming, Jacksonville*	10	6	.625	2.64	21	20	6	0	1	0	140.0	129	50	41	7	2	25	2	109	6
Cross, Knoxville	10	9	.526	2.83	31	26	4	2	0	1	172.0	141	72	54	10	10	71	3	128	3
Wakefield, Carolina	15	8	.652	2.90	26	25	8	1	1	0	183.0	155	68	59	13	9	51	6	120	2
Salles, Charlotte	10	7	.588	3.00	22	22	4	0	1	0	150.0	141	59	50	10	2	37	2	74	2

Departmental leaders: G—Shifflett, B. Taylor, 59; W—N. Robinson, 16; L—Van Poppel, 13; Pct.—Wendell, .786; GS—Osteen, N. Robinson, Zancanaro, 28; CG—Bullinger, Wakefield, 8; GF—Parnell, 54; ShO—Anderson, Rogers, Ventura, 3; Sv.—Peek, 26; IP—Trombley, 191.0; H—Osteen, 176; R—Anderson, 94; ER—Corbin, 81; HR—H. Gomez, 19; HB—Ventura, 12; BB—Gardner, 97; IBB—Strauss, 8; SO—Trombley, 175; WP—Buckholz, 20.

(All pitchers—listed alphabetically)

Pitcher, Team	W	L	Pct.	ERA	G	GS	CG	GF	ShO	Sv.	IP	H	R	ER	HR	HB	BB	Int. BB	SO	WP
Adams, Carolina	2	2	.500	3.92	8	1	0	5	0	3	20.2	25	11	9	3	2	6	0	10	0
Alvarez, Birmingham*	10	6	.625	1.83	23	23	3	0	2	0	152.1	109	46	31	6	3	74	0	165	9
Anderson, Chattanooga	10	9	.526	4.40	28	26	3	1	3	0	155.1	142	94	76	8	8	93	2	115	17
Ausanio, Carolina	0	0	.000	0.00	3	0	0	3	0	2	3.0	0	0	0	0	0	0	0	2	0
Ayala, Chattanooga	3	1	.750	4.67	39	8	1	16	0	4	90.2	79	52	47	10	4	58	1	92	10
Balabon, Jacksonville	5	1	.833	3.09	10	10	0	0	0	0	64.0	60	31	22	5	1	26	0	42	4
Bangtson, Orlando	12	11	.522	3.44	26	25	3	0	2	0	162.0	161	79	62	6	5	42	1	110	5
Bark, Greenville*	2	1	.667	3.57	9	3	1	2	0	1	17.2	19	10	7	0	2	8	1	15	3
Barton, Jacksonville*	3	3	.500	3.12	14	4	1	3	1	0	34.2	36	16	12	0	1	8	0	24	0
Blair, Charlotte	0	0	.000	0.00	1	0	0	1	0	0	1.0	0	0	0	0	0	0	0	0	0
Blohm, Knoxville	1	0	1.000	1.69	3	0	0	0	0	0	10.2	7	2	2	1	0	4	1	6	0
Blueberg, Jacksonville	3	5	.375	2.72	14	13	2	0	0	0	89.1	75	36	27	8	6	23	0	67	3
Bolton, Birmingham	8	4	.667	1.62	12	12	3	0	2	0	89.0	73	26	16	3	8	21	1	57	3
Borbon, Greenville*	0	1	.000	2.79	4	4	0	0	0	0	29.0	23	12	9	1	3	10	0	22	2
Bowie, Jacksonville*	0	0	.000	0.00	1	0	0	1	0	0	2.0	3	0	0	0	0	2	0	0	0
Briscoe, Huntsville	2	0	1.000	0.00	2	0	0	2	0	1	4.1	1	2	0	0	0	2	0	6	0
Brito, Birmingham	2	4	.333	3.30	10	10	4	0	1	0	71.0	53	31	26	4	2	16	0	37	5
Brown, Knoxville	0	1	.000	10.80	3	0	0	2	0	0	3.1	6	4	4	1	0	1	0	2	0
Buckholz, Carolina	7	10	.412	4.66	21	21	3	0	0	0	133.1	135	74	69	11	9	53	1	85	20
Bullinger, Charlotte	9	9	.500	3.53	20	20	8	0	0	0	142.2	132	62	56	5	6	61	2	128	5
Canan, Charlotte	0	0	.000	9.00	1	0	0	1	0	0	1.0	0	1	1	0	0	4	0	0	0
Capellan, Orlando	0	0	.000	9.00	2	0	0	2	0	0	2.0	4	2	2	0	0	0	0	3	1
Chambers, Birmingham	0	0	.000	3.71	10	0	0	5	0	0	17.0	18	9	7	0	0	4	1	13	0
Champion, Greenville	0	0	.000	0.00	2	1	0	0	0	0	2.0	1	0	0	0	0	1	0	1	0
Cole, Carolina	2	2	.500	1.91	20	0	0	7	0	12	28.1	13	8	6	1	2	19	1	32	3
Cooke, Carolina*	3	3	.500	2.26	9	9	1	0	1	0	55.2	39	21	14	2	4	19	0	46	5
Corbin, Memphis	8	8	.500	4.66	28	25	1	0	0	0	156.1	139	90	81	7	8	90	1	166	13
Cormier, Huntsville	3	4	.429	5.64	19	9	1	2	0	0	67.0	75	52	42	8	3	31	1	29	6
Cortes, Birmingham	8	8	.500	3.31	22	22	0	0	0	0	133.1	126	63	49	9	5	61	1	71	7
Crockett, Charlotte	0	0	.000	0.00	2	0	0	2	0	0	3.0	1	0	0	0	1	1	0	1	0
Cromwell, Knoxville*	2	9	.182	4.95	16	16	0	0	0	0	80.0	73	53	44	5	5	53	0	61	8
Cross, Knoxville	10	9	.526	2.83	31	26	4	2	0	1	172.0	141	72	54	10	10	71	3	128	3

— 403 —

Pitcher, Team	W	L	Pct.	ERA	G	GS	CG	GF	ShO	Sv.	IP	H	R	ER	HR	HB	BB	Int. BB	SO	WP
Cruz, Memphis	1	7	.125	6.85	11	9	0	0	0	0	47.1	56	39	36	6	2	13	0	18	2
Czarkowski, Jacksonville*	4	9	.308	5.31	20	13	1	4	0	0	84.2	107	58	50	9	3	26	0	46	6
Davino, Birmingham	1	4	.200	3.45	25	0	0	18	0	4	47.0	41	23	18	0	1	16	1	27	3
Delkus, Orlando	5	5	.500	4.73	45	5	1	11	1	1	91.1	103	58	48	7	3	24	2	53	0
DiBartolomeo, Charlotte	4	3	.571	3.79	45	2	0	19	0	1	76.0	80	36	32	6	2	34	4	46	3
Dodd, Chattanooga	3	4	.429	4.32	35	2	0	14	0	7	75.0	68	41	36	3	1	40	6	64	12
Duncan, 6 Car.-22 Mem.	6	3	.667	4.89	28	9	2	11	1	1	88.1	99	50	48	12	4	32	0	67	6
Eave, Jacksonville	2	1	.667	1.69	5	5	1	0	0	0	26.2	15	6	5	3	2	10	0	18	0
Erwin, Huntsville	1	4	.200	3.63	19	0	0	10	0	2	22.1	15	10	9	0	0	17	2	30	6
Eskew, Huntsville	1	3	.250	3.92	6	6	0	0	0	0	39.0	37	20	17	1	1	17	0	29	4
Evans, Jacksonville	5	9	.357	5.21	21	20	1	0	0	0	115.2	118	74	67	15	9	49	0	76	12
Fajardo, Carolina	3	4	.429	4.13	10	10	1	0	0	0	61.0	55	32	28	4	0	24	0	53	3
Fansler, Carolina	6	6	.500	3.50	19	17	0	1	0	0	90.0	77	42	35	4	11	28	2	78	6
Figueroa, Jacksonville*	6	3	.667	2.53	41	2	0	21	0	5	64.0	57	22	18	3	3	24	2	55	4
Fleming, Jacksonville*	10	6	.625	2.64	21	20	6	0	1	0	140.0	129	50	41	7	2	25	2	109	6
Foster, Chattanooga	0	2	.000	1.15	17	0	0	16	0	10	15.2	10	4	2	0	3	4	0	18	2
Garces, Orlando	2	1	.667	3.31	10	0	0	5	0	0	16.1	12	6	6	0	2	14	2	17	0
Garcia, Huntsville	6	3	.667	3.18	13	13	0	0	0	0	79.1	76	36	28	3	4	22	0	40	3
Garcia, Jacksonville	3	2	.600	4.35	6	6	0	0	0	0	41.1	40	20	20	3	3	16	0	42	1
Garcia, Birmingham	4	0	1.000	0.93	6	6	2	0	1	0	38.2	27	5	4	0	3	11	0	38	1
Garcia, Chattanooga	5	3	.625	1.98	40	0	0	25	0	5	50.0	41	12	11	3	1	20	1	51	5
Gardner, Charlotte	7	8	.467	3.51	29	25	3	2	2	0	154.0	122	69	60	9	8	97	5	116	7
Gomez, Charlotte	5	8	.385	4.88	34	13	2	6	2	1	121.2	114	72	66	19	8	47	4	82	8
Gomez, Greenville*	5	2	.714	1.81	13	13	0	0	0	0	79.2	58	20	16	1	3	31	1	71	7
Grott, Huntsville	2	9	.182	5.15	42	0	0	23	0	3	57.2	65	40	33	6	0	37	7	65	6
Guzman, Huntsville*	2	1	.667	3.48	7	7	0	0	0	0	44.0	46	17	17	3	1	25	0	23	4
Hall, Knoxville	5	3	.625	2.60	42	0	0	24	0	2	69.1	56	23	20	5	2	27	2	78	9
Hamilton, Carolina*	3	4	.429	3.47	10	10	1	0	1	0	62.1	58	27	24	2	3	21	0	46	4
Hancock, Carolina*	4	7	.364	3.77	37	11	0	10	0	4	98.0	93	48	41	3	2	42	4	66	8
Hawblitzel, Huntsville	1	2	.333	3.21	5	5	1	0	1	0	33.2	31	14	12	2	3	12	3	25	0
Hernandez, Birmingham	2	1	.667	1.99	4	4	0	0	0	0	22.2	11	5	5	2	2	6	0	25	2
Hoffman, Chattanooga	1	0	1.000	1.93	14	0	0	13	0	8	14.0	10	4	3	0	0	7	1	23	1
Hopper, Memphis	1	1	.500	4.05	20	1	0	8	0	4	46.2	52	27	21	1	5	20	0	24	2
Horsman, Knoxville*	4	1	.800	2.34	42	2	0	17	0	3	80.2	79	23	21	2	0	19	5	80	3
Howard, Birmingham*	6	1	.857	2.04	38	0	0	24	0	9	53.0	43	14	12	2	3	16	1	52	2
Hudek, Birmingham	5	10	.333	3.84	51	0	0	42	0	13	65.2	58	39	28	4	6	28	7	49	5
Imes, Chattanooga	4	2	.667	5.13	8	8	0	0	0	0	47.1	48	29	27	5	3	17	0	25	0
Jaques, Charlotte*	3	1	.750	4.19	20	0	0	3	0	0	19.1	20	10	9	3	0	9	2	15	0
Johnson, Orlando	3	3	.500	2.40	53	0	0	49	0	25	56.1	40	18	15	3	0	28	5	61	5
Johnson, Greenville*	10	7	.588	3.56	47	9	0	19	0	6	98.2	108	42	39	4	2	15	0	66	7
Jones, Knoxville	2	2	.500	2.22	12	3	0	5	0	0	28.1	20	7	7	2	0	22	0	20	4
Jones, Charlotte	1	1	.500	6.52	4	2	0	2	0	0	9.2	5	9	7	0	1	11	0	12	2
Kennedy, Birmingham	10	3	.769	2.32	15	15	0	0	0	0	93.0	88	39	24	3	0	48	0	52	2
Keyser, Birmingham	0	1	.000	5.00	3	3	0	0	0	0	18.0	19	10	10	2	0	9	0	9	0
Kizziah, Knoxville	4	2	.667	0.89	11	2	1	4	0	1	30.1	26	11	3	0	0	11	2	19	1
Kremblas, Chattanooga	0	0	.000	0.00	3	0	0	2	0	0	3.1	1	0	0	0	0	2	0	1	0
Kuhn, Huntsville*	1	1	.500	5.96	43	0	0	12	0	0	51.1	50	38	34	4	3	40	0	49	10
Latter, Huntsville	6	4	.600	4.06	58	1	0	9	0	1	88.2	69	43	40	10	4	51	2	81	6
LeMasters, Memphis	2	2	.500	3.79	12	9	1	0	0	0	57.0	52	26	24	3	3	26	0	34	5
Leslie, Chattanooga	0	1	.000	18.69	1	1	0	0	0	0	4.1	8	9	9	0	0	3	0	4	4
Lind, Orlando	9	8	.529	2.67	52	7	2	22	1	3	108.0	96	40	32	5	3	39	4	110	5
Lloyd, Knoxville*	0	0	.000	0.00	2	0	0	1	0	0	1.2	1	0	0	0	0	1	0	2	1
Mahomes, Orlando	8	5	.615	1.78	18	17	2	0	0	0	116.0	77	30	23	5	3	57	0	136	3
McAuliffe, Chattanooga	4	6	.400	6.47	33	0	0	14	0	3	40.1	37	31	29	1	0	24	2	26	2
McCarthy, Chattanooga*	0	0	.000	6.75	12	0	0	2	0	0	9.1	17	9	7	1	0	9	0	9	3
Merigliano, Birmingham	3	2	.600	3.89	36	2	0	19	0	4	69.1	58	38	30	8	2	31	1	51	7
Middaugh, Birmingham	2	2	.500	3.41	12	1	0	2	0	1	34.1	27	20	13	0	1	14	1	27	2
Mielke, Huntsville	0	0	.000	1.93	4	0	0	0	0	0	4.2	4	2	1	0	0	3	0	4	0
Miller, Carolina	7	2	.778	2.42	15	15	0	0	0	0	89.1	69	29	24	4	3	35	4	69	5
Minor, Carolina	0	0	.000	2.84	3	2	0	1	0	0	12.2	9	4	4	0	7	0	18	1	
Moeller, Memphis*	4	5	.444	2.55	10	10	0	0	0	0	53.0	52	24	15	6	1	21	0	54	1
Mohler, Huntsville*	4	2	.667	3.57	8	8	0	0	0	0	53.0	55	22	21	5	2	20	0	27	3
Monzon, Knoxville	0	0	.000	5.40	1	0	0	0	0	0	1.2	2	1	1	0	0	1	0	4	0
Mount, Charlotte	4	5	.444	3.78	17	16	2	1	1	0	104.2	97	55	44	14	2	27	3	55	1
Muh, 7 Orl.-21 Char.*	1	1	.500	4.74	28	3	1	10	0	0	49.1	48	28	26	4	0	31	2	35	10
Murphy, Carolina	6	9	.400	3.41	32	7	1	9	0	0	97.2	96	44	37	3	6	35	5	49	4
Neely, Carolina	0	0	.000	6.75	5	0	0	4	0	0	4.0	5	4	3	2	0	4	0	5	0
Nelson, Jacksonville	4	0	1.000	1.27	21	0	0	20	0	12	28.1	23	5	4	0	0	9	0	34	2
Newlin, Jacksonville	6	5	.545	2.25	47	0	0	37	0	12	64.0	58	24	16	4	5	29	5	48	3
Newman, Orlando*	5	4	.556	2.69	11	11	2	0	0	0	67.0	53	28	20	0	1	30	1	53	8
Nied, Greenville	7	3	.700	2.41	15	15	1	0	0	0	89.2	79	26	24	0	6	20	3	101	1
Nunez, Orlando	0	0	.000	27.00	1	0	0	0	0	0	1.0	3	3	3	0	0	1	0	1	0
Ogliaruso, Knoxville	2	1	.667	3.69	7	6	2	0	0	0	39.0	31	18	16	0	3	18	0	24	5
O'Neal, Memphis	1	4	.200	4.33	12	12	0	0	0	0	54.0	48	31	26	8	11	22	0	29	2
Osteen, Huntsville*	13	9	.591	3.54	28	28	2	0	1	0	173.0	176	82	68	4	4	65	2	105	4
Parker, Charlotte	11	9	.550	3.73	24	24	4	0	2	0	144.2	131	70	60	6	4	73	2	74	9
Parnell, Memphis	4	5	.444	3.04	58	0	0	54	0	17	74.0	60	27	25	3	10	37	5	67	3
Peek, Huntsville	2	4	.333	3.26	56	0	0	49	0	26	66.1	65	31	24	5	1	15	3	52	2
Perez, Memphis	0	1	.000	8.53	3	2	0	1	0	0	12.2	15	12	12	5	0	5	0	12	2
Peters, Huntsville	4	11	.267	5.00	33	20	0	3	0	0	126.0	131	89	70	14	2	70	1	59	10
Peters, Memphis	5	8	.385	5.34	19	16	2	1	0	0	97.2	113	61	58	8	5	36	0	64	9
Phoenix, Huntsville	0	0	.000	6.00	2	0	0	1	0	0	3.0	7	3	2	1	0	1	0	3	0
Pichardo, Memphis	3	11	.214	4.27	34	11	0	5	0	0	99.0	116	56	47	4	4	38	5	75	6
Pierce, Memphis*	5	11	.313	3.84	31	20	2	4	0	0	136.0	136	73	58	6	2	61	1	90	3
Pitz, Jacksonville	1	5	.167	3.98	36	6	0	6	0	1	86.0	87	44	38	4	6	22	0	67	4
Poehl, Memphis	5	5	.500	4.13	33	10	1	8	1	0	93.2	100	55	43	1	6	39	1	53	7
Pugh, Chattanooga	3	1	.750	1.64	5	5	0	0	0	0	38.1	20	7	7	2	4	11	0	24	0
Revenig, Huntsville	1	2	.333	0.98	12	0	0	6	0	0	18.1	11	3	2	1	2	4	0	10	0
Reynolds, Birmingham	2	0	1.000	1.97	19	1	0	11	0	1	45.2	36	16	10	1	3	20	1	38	2
Richards, Jacksonville*	3	0	1.000	1.57	10	0	0	4	0	0	23.0	12	4	4	2	0	9	0	22	1
Richards, Orlando	6	7	.462	3.45	19	19	0	0	0	0	112.1	111	48	43	12	3	37	1	61	2
Risley, Chattanooga	5	7	.417	3.16	19	19	3	0	0	0	108.1	81	48	38	3	9	60	2	77	5
Rivera, Greenville	11	8	.579	3.57	26	26	3	0	2	0	158.2	155	76	63	13	3	75	4	116	8
Roberts, Memphis*	4	2	.667	2.67	25	0	0	6	0	2	33.2	31	14	10	1	5	14	0	29	2
Robinson, Memphis	0	0	.000	0.00	2	0	0	2	0	0	2.0	1	2	0	0	0	0	0	0	0

Pitcher, Team	W	L	Pct.	ERA	G	GS	CG	GF	ShO	Sv.	IP	H	R	ER	HR	HB	BB	Int. BB	SO	WP
Robinson, Greenville	16	6	.727	2.27	29	28	0	0	0	0	174.2	172	61	44	6	10	48	2	107	4
Roesler, Carolina	2	4	.333	4.91	20	0	0	14	0	6	25.2	20	15	14	4	1	15	5	31	1
Rogers, Knoxville	7	11	.389	3.31	28	27	4	0	3	0	168.1	140	70	62	7	6	90	0	122	11
Rojas, Jacksonville	1	3	.250	5.87	15	0	0	8	0	1	23.0	29	15	15	6	0	4	0	15	0
Salkeld, Jacksonville	8	8	.500	3.05	23	23	5	0	0	0	153.2	131	56	52	9	10	55	1	159	12
Salles, Charlotte	10	7	.588	3.00	22	22	4	0	1	0	150.0	141	59	50	10	2	37	2	74	2
Sanchez, Knoxville	4	2	.667	3.07	14	11	0	2	0	0	58.2	43	26	20	3	2	36	2	38	8
Sanders, Greenville	4	7	.364	3.65	48	0	0	16	0	0	79.0	82	37	32	3	0	51	4	85	9
Sanford, Chattanooga	7	4	.636	2.74	16	16	1	0	1	0	95.1	69	37	29	7	1	55	2	124	1
Satre, Chattanooga	1	7	.125	5.11	8	8	0	0	0	0	44.0	37	26	25	7	2	26	0	44	6
Savage, Orlando	2	1	.667	1.88	6	1	0	2	0	0	14.1	9	3	3	1	0	5	0	14	0
Schock, Chattanooga	6	3	.667	4.06	12	11	2	0	1	0	68.2	77	34	31	7	4	14	1	38	4
Schooler, Jacksonville	1	1	.500	5.56	11	2	0	3	0	0	11.1	13	9	7	2	0	3	0	12	0
Schwabe, Orlando	3	2	.600	1.77	6	6	3	0	2	0	35.2	24	12	7	0	1	7	0	34	1
Shifflett, Memphis	11	5	.688	2.15	59	1	0	35	0	9	113.0	105	34	27	4	5	22	6	78	1
Sierra, Charlotte	4	1	.800	3.78	18	6	0	3	0	0	47.2	45	24	20	4	3	22	0	24	1
Smith, Memphis	0	1	.000	7.04	16	0	0	5	0	0	23.0	24	19	18	0	2	18	0	20	3
Sodders, Charlotte*	0	2	.000	7.58	9	3	0	3	0	0	19.0	21	17	16	2	1	11	0	14	0
Spradlin, Chattanooga	7	3	.700	3.09	48	1	0	22	0	4	96.0	95	38	33	2	4	32	7	73	9
Stowell, Orlando*	2	1	.667	2.70	50	0	0	22	0	1	50.0	41	17	15	1	3	24	1	38	5
Strange, Greenville	1	0	1.000	13.50	4	0	0	1	0	1	4.2	9	7	7	1	0	2	0	8	1
Strauss, Charlotte	6	7	.462	2.69	49	0	0	30	0	9	73.2	63	30	22	3	1	27	8	57	3
Stroud, Charlotte*	0	0	.000	12.71	4	0	0	0	0	0	5.2	11	8	8	1	0	3	0	4	1
Swartzbaugh, Charlotte	0	1	.000	10.13	1	1	0	0	0	0	5.1	6	7	6	1	0	3	1	5	1
Tafoya, Carolina	1	3	.250	1.99	40	0	0	20	0	6	63.1	51	17	14	3	2	22	5	35	2
Talbert, Memphis	0	2	.000	7.62	3	3	0	0	0	0	13.0	21	13	11	0	0	10	1	3	1
Tatar, Chattanooga	3	8	.273	5.19	12	12	0	0	0	0	62.2	75	42	39	4	1	31	2	37	4
B. Taylor, Greenville	6	2	.750	1.51	59	0	0	44	0	22	77.1	49	16	13	1	3	15	2	65	3
Taylor, Knoxville	0	0	.000	0.00	2	0	0	1	0	0	2.0	2	0	0	0	0	0	0	1	0
S. Taylor, Greenville	3	4	.429	4.19	8	7	1	0	1	0	43.0	49	25	20	4	2	16	2	26	6
Taylor, Memphis	1	2	.333	5.55	6	6	1	0	0	0	35.2	51	22	22	1	0	16	0	17	2
Tellers, Carolina	0	2	.000	4.73	11	0	0	9	0	1	13.1	18	8	7	1	0	6	4	9	1
Thomas, Birmingham*	0	0	.000	3.00	2	0	0	2	0	0	6.0	6	3	2	0	0	4	1	2	0
Thompson, Knoxville	0	3	.000	3.55	10	0	0	8	0	3	12.2	13	7	5	0	1	2	2	11	0
Townley, Knoxville	0	0	.000	0.00	1	0	0	1	0	0	0.1	1	0	0	0	0	0	0	0	1
Tracy, Carolina	6	3	.667	2.45	16	12	2	3	0	1	88.1	80	30	24	3	4	21	1	72	2
Trlicek, Knoxville	2	5	.286	2.45	41	0	0	38	0	16	51.1	36	26	14	3	0	22	3	55	4
Trombley, Orlando	12	7	.632	2.54	27	27	7	0	2	0	191.0	153	65	54	12	7	57	2	175	2
Tsamis, Orlando*	0	0	.000	0.00	1	1	0	0	0	0	7.0	3	2	0	0	0	4	0	5	0
Turek, Chattanooga	4	5	.444	3.38	10	10	3	0	2	0	58.2	57	28	22	2	2	18	0	48	3
Upshaw, Greenville*	7	6	.538	3.36	19	19	2	0	0	0	115.1	117	55	43	4	2	43	1	87	5
Van Poppel, Huntsville	6	13	.316	3.47	24	24	1	0	1	0	132.1	118	69	51	2	6	90	0	115	12
Vasquez, Chattanooga	7	5	.583	3.12	17	17	6	0	2	0	121.1	104	50	42	9	4	43	0	64	3
Ventura, Birmingham*	8	10	.444	4.06	25	25	3	0	3	0	148.2	129	79	67	12	12	64	0	91	5
Vice, Huntsville	0	0	.000	9.00	2	0	0	2	0	0	2.0	4	2	2	0	0	2	0	2	1
Wakefield, Carolina	15	8	.652	2.90	26	25	8	1	1	0	183.0	155	68	59	13	9	51	6	120	2
Walk, Carolina	0	1	.000	1.80	1	1	0	0	0	0	5.0	5	1	1	0	0	2	0	3	0
Ward, Knoxville*	6	10	.375	3.73	31	18	1	2	0	0	128.0	122	64	53	7	10	53	2	110	7
Wassenaar, Orlando	2	2	.500	1.44	15	1	0	6	0	1	25.0	18	6	4	0	0	7	2	21	0
Watkins, Charlotte	8	6	.571	3.11	52	5	1	38	0	13	107.0	109	43	37	6	3	32	7	97	0
Watson, Birmingham	5	6	.455	4.24	49	0	0	18	0	1	80.2	74	48	38	4	4	44	7	53	6
Weathers, Knoxville	10	7	.588	2.45	24	22	5	0	2	0	139.1	121	51	38	3	8	49	1	114	7
Webb, Carolina	1	6	.143	3.15	37	1	0	21	0	3	68.2	61	35	24	2	10	30	4	38	3
Weber, Huntsville	2	3	.400	2.17	34	0	0	17	0	3	54.0	57	23	13	1	4	18	1	26	4
Wendell, Greenville	11	3	.786	2.56	25	20	1	3	1	0	147.2	130	47	42	4	6	51	5	122	11
West, Orlando*	0	0	.000	0.00	1	1	0	0	0	0	0.1	0	0	0	0	0	0	0	0	0
Wickman, Birmingham	6	10	.375	3.56	20	20	4	0	1	0	131.1	127	68	52	5	5	50	0	81	4
Wiese, Orlando*	6	9	.400	4.42	21	20	1	1	0	0	112.0	136	64	55	5	1	48	0	47	3
Wiggs, Jacksonville	1	0	1.000	4.05	6	0	0	3	0	0	13.1	14	6	6	1	0	2	0	14	1
Williams, Carolina	3	2	.600	3.59	18	1	0	8	0	3	42.2	42	18	17	1	1	14	0	37	0
Wishnevski, Knoxville	6	8	.429	2.94	31	10	0	11	0	3	101.0	78	46	33	2	9	53	5	58	11
Wohlers, Greenville	0	0	.000	0.57	28	0	0	27	0	21	31.1	9	4	2	0	0	13	0	44	3
Woodson, Jacksonville	4	6	.400	3.06	13	13	0	0	0	0	79.1	73	35	27	3	5	39	0	50	8
Young, Greenville*	0	0	.000	14.90	10	0	0	3	0	0	9.2	10	17	16	1	1	19	1	9	2
Zancanaro, Huntsville*	5	10	.333	3.38	29	28	0	1	0	0	165.0	151	87	62	7	6	92	0	104	8
Zarranz, Jacksonville	2	0	1.000	2.09	24	0	0	14	0	4	43.0	29	10	10	4	3	11	0	42	0
Zavaras, Jacksonville	2	2	.500	4.60	6	6	0	0	0	0	31.1	36	18	16	2	2	10	0	21	2

BALKS—Guzman, Risley, 5 each; Cormier, Cromwell, Don Peters, Rivera, Zancanaro, 4 each; Alvarez, Bullinger, Eskew, Shifflett, Ward, 3 each; Blueberg, Cole, Cortes, Cross, Czarkowski, Dodd, Fajardo, R. Garcia, Gardner, Latter, Osteen, Parker, Pitz, Poehl, Salkeld, Salles, Sanchez, Sanders, Tafoya, Tatar, Upshaw, Weathers, Wickman, Zarranz, 2 each; Anderson, Ayala, Bark, Barton, Buckholz, Duncan, Foster, V. Garcia, P. Gomez, Hamilton, Horsman, Howard, Imes, Jaques, Keyser, Kuhn, Merigliano, Miller, Moeller, Muh, Newlin, Parnell, Doug Peters, Pichardo, Pierce, Reynolds, D. Richards, N. Robinson, Rogers, Satre, Sierra, Smith, B. Taylor, Trombley, Van Poppel, Vasquez, Ventura, Wakefield, Watson, Weber, Wiese, Wishnevski, Woodson, Young, 1 each.

COMBINATION SHUTOUTS—Alvarez-Davino-Merigliano, Cortes-Howard, Cortes-Reynolds, Garcia-Merigliano, Kennedy-Hudek, Reynolds-Merigliano, Birmingham; Fansler-Webb 2, Buckholz-Cole, Buckholz-Hancock, Fansler-Hancock, Hamilton-Webb-Fansler, Miller-Cole, Murphy-Roesler-Ausanio, Tracy-Cole, Wakefield-Cole, Wakefield-Hancock-Roesler, Carolina; Salles-Strauss 2, Gomez-Watkins, Parker-Strauss, Salles-Watkins, Sierra-Gomez-DiBartolomeo, Watkins-Strauss, Charlotte; Dodd-Ayala, Pugh-McCarthy, Risley-Garcia-Foster, Risley-Spradlin-Ayala, Turek-Dodd, Chattanooga; Gomez-Taylor, Gomez-Wendell, Gomez-Wohlers, Nied-Bark-Taylor, Rivera-Sanders-Johnson, Robinson-Taylor, Upshaw-Robinson-Wohlers, Upshaw-Sanders-Watson, Wendell-Sanders-Wohlers, Greenville; Eskew-Grott, Osteen-Erwin, Osteen-Revenig-Peek, Peters-Erwin-Kuhn, Van Poppel-Latter-Kuhn-Peek, Zancanaro-Peek, Huntsville; Balabon-Newlin, Barton-Richards, Blueberg-Newlin, Czarkowski-Rojas-Nelson, Evans-Newlin-Nelson, Figueroa-Barton, Fleming-Richards, Fleming-Schooler-Nelson, Garcia-Merigliano, Pitz-Newlin, Salkeld-Richards-Newlin, Schooler-Evans-Figueroa-Newlin, Zavaras-Figueroa-Zarranz-Newlin, Jacksonville; Cross-Kizziah-Jones-Hall, Cross-Wishnevski, Horsman-Wishnevski, Rogers-Sanchez, Rogers-Trlicek, Rogers-Williams-Hall, Sanchez-Horsman, Sanchez-Horsman-Hall, Ward-Kizziah, Ward-Trlicek, Weathers-Hall-Horsman, Weathers-Horsman-Thompson, Wishnevski-Williams, Knoxville; Corbin-Shifflett, LeMasters-Corbin-Roberts, Pichardo-Parnell, Shifflett-Roberts-Parnell, Memphis; Bangtson-Wassenaar, Delkus-Johnson, Lind-Wassenaar, Mahomes-Johnson, Mahomes-Stowell-Johnson, Wiese-Lind, Orlando.

NO-HIT GAMES—Ventura-Howard-Hudek, Birmingham, defeated Charlotte, 4-1, April 18; Trombley, Orlando, defeated Knoxville, 3-0 (first game), August 8.

FIELDING

TEAM

Team	Pct.	G	PO	A	E	DP	PB
Greenville	.974	144	3716	1656	145	133	22
Chattanooga	.974	144	3611	1316	134	113	19
Charlotte	.973	144	3728	1453	144	140	14
Jacksonville	.972	143	3656	1492	147	131	19
Orlando	.971	144	3579	1427	151	111	7
Carolina	.970	142	3634	1498	158	125	22
Knoxville	.967	144	3667	1479	173	141	25
Birmingham	.964	143	3708	1497	192	125	26
Memphis	.964	144	3684	1506	192	112	26
Huntsville	.961	144	3754	1490	213	143	18

INDIVIDUAL

*Throws lefthanded.

FIRST BASEMEN

Player, Team	Pct.	G	PO	A	E	DP
Armas, Huntsville	.990	49	449	32	5	51
Baldwin, Charlotte*	.986	9	67	4	1	9
Beeler, Chattanooga	.978	5	44	1	1	2
Blair, Charlotte	1.000	6	34	2	0	0
BOWIE, Jacksonville*	.992	106	874	73	8	86
Campanis, Jacksonville	1.000	1	8	1	0	2
Canan, Charlotte	.977	7	41	2	1	9
Champion, Greenville	.986	38	316	24	5	22
Chasey, Birmingham*	.979	85	639	51	15	54
Conte, Huntsville	.970	9	55	9	2	5
Cooley, Huntsville	1.000	4	28	5	0	0
Coomer, Birmingham	1.000	3	19	2	0	1
Costo, Chattanooga	.992	69	481	25	4	46
Cuevas, Greenville	1.000	1	3	0	0	1
Davis, Memphis	.833	1	5	0	1	1
Garner, Birmingham	.989	66	606	38	7	58
Giannelli, Knoxville	1.000	8	17	1	0	1
Gonzalez, Jacksonville	1.000	35	281	17	0	24
Holley, Jacksonville	1.000	3	24	6	0	3
Klesko, Greenville*	.985	109	1043	57	17	97
Knorr, Knoxville	1.000	1	6	0	0	0
Kremblas, Chattanooga	.993	22	142	7	1	7
Maksudian, Knoxville	1.000	1	2	1	0	1
Maloney, Greenville	1.000	1	4	0	0	1
Martin, Greenville*	1.000	1	7	1	0	0
Marzan, Orlando	.988	69	471	31	6	39
Masteller, Orlando*	.987	66	516	25	7	49
Monzon, Knoxville	.941	2	16	0	1	0
Morris, Greenville	1.000	2	14	0	0	3
Neel, Huntsville	.987	42	335	34	5	33
Newfield, Jacksonville	1.000	2	11	0	0	2
Nunez, Knoxville	.984	18	120	4	2	25
O'Halloran, Knoxville	.993	36	257	22	2	27
Olmstead, Orlando*	.983	28	212	16	4	14
Paquette, Huntsville	1.000	1	6	0	0	0
Paulino, Charlotte	.989	130	1105	83	13	105
Pedre, Memphis	.989	13	86	4	1	7
Perez, Greenville	1.000	1	9	0	0	1
Robinson, Memphis	.985	16	119	11	2	5
Shelton, Carolina*	.982	53	460	27	9	38
Shockey, Huntsville*	.988	47	370	28	5	34
Sparks, Carolina*	.994	62	586	27	4	50
Stargell, Jacksonville	1.000	2	11	1	0	0
Toale, Memphis	.981	66	553	52	12	40
Torres, Carolina	1.000	2	13	0	0	1
Townley, Knoxville	.960	4	22	2	1	3
Trafton, Chattanooga	.990	54	446	27	5	43
Tunison, Memphis	.992	55	275	35	4	39
Vitiello, Memphis	1.000	1	14	1	0	0
Wehner, Carolina	.987	16	142	10	2	14
Yan, Knoxville	.984	96	812	64	14	71
Young, Carolina	.985	17	123	6	2	8

SECOND BASEMEN

Player, Team	Pct.	G	PO	A	E	DP
Allen, Chattanooga	1.000	3	2	6	0	1
Bernhardt, Birmingham	.961	26	48	76	5	18
Biasucci, Charlotte	.947	11	16	20	2	3
Blair, Charlotte	.982	20	24	30	1	4
Boone, Jacksonville	.974	127	288	339	17	91
Branson, Chattanooga	.991	26	54	62	1	17
Bridges, Memphis	.981	14	23	29	1	3
Buccheri, Birmingham	.921	8	14	21	3	3
Busby, Birmingham	.951	14	22	36	3	6
Capellan, Orlando	.957	115	253	286	24	61
Casarotti, Greenville	.980	75	155	229	8	49
Chimelis, Huntsville	.951	31	64	72	7	17
Correia, Huntsville	.949	31	63	67	7	11
Crockett, Charlotte	.981	35	58	95	3	25
Crowley, Carolina	.964	72	152	192	13	42
Edge, Carolina	.981	21	47	54	2	10
Garber, Memphis	.974	36	58	90	4	15
Garrison, Huntsville	.979	26	66	77	3	25
Gilbert, Orlando	.963	38	63	92	6	23
Gonzalez, Memphis	.800	1	1	3	1	1

Player, Team	Pct.	G	PO	A	E	DP
Holley, Jacksonville	1.000	3	5	2	0	0
Infante, Knoxville	1.000	1	0	1	0	0
Kelly, Greenville	.946	7	9	26	2	3
Kent, Knoxville	.957	139	249	395	29	96
Kremblas, Chattanooga	.918	27	37	52	8	7
Ladnier, Memphis	1.000	1	3	2	0	1
Laureano, Memphis	.957	99	172	255	19	44
Longiro, Chattanooga	.966	62	110	146	9	25
Maloney, Greenville	.987	20	23	51	1	12
Matos, Greenville	.857	3	4	8	2	4
Morris, Greenville	1.000	2	1	6	0	1
Ocasio, Birmingham	.966	96	204	252	16	56
Olmeda, Greenville	.978	49	93	174	6	28
Roth, Birmingham	.894	11	29	30	7	3
Rush, Chattanooga	1.000	1	0	3	0	0
Santana, Jacksonville	1.000	2	5	6	0	1
Schreiber, Carolina	.976	54	85	154	6	28
Sellner, Chattanooga	.941	38	88	88	11	25
Smith, Jacksonville	.944	3	8	9	1	2
Tatarian, Birmingham	1.000	1	1	1	0	0
Taylor, Knoxville	.944	6	5	12	1	1
Turang, Jacksonville	.953	13	28	33	3	3
Vice, Huntsville	.958	53	94	132	10	22
WHITE, Charlotte	.977	97	180	250	10	66
Wright, Memphis	1.000	1	0	1	0	0
Young, Knoxville	1.000	9	14	16	0	3

THIRD BASEMEN

Player, Team	Pct.	G	PO	A	E	DP
Allen, Chattanooga	.928	120	73	171	19	15
Bafia, Huntsville	.759	12	7	15	7	1
Beeler, Chattanooga	1.000	1	0	1	0	0
Bolick, Jacksonville	.953	135	87	255	17	21
Busby, Birmingham	.875	6	3	4	1	1
Campbell, Birmingham	1.000	2	0	3	0	0
Canan, Charlotte	.895	13	7	27	4	1
Castellano, Charlotte	1.000	7	2	11	0	0
Champion, Greenville	1.000	7	1	9	0	0
Chimelis, Huntsville	.928	27	24	53	6	6
Conte, Huntsville	.889	3	2	6	1	0
Coomer, Birmingham	.934	131	94	276	26	24
Correia, Huntsville	.920	10	6	17	2	2
Crockett, Charlotte	.857	6	5	4	1	2
Crowley, Carolina	.933	5	6	8	1	2
Edge, Carolina	1.000	2	0	1	0	0
Foster, Birmingham	1.000	1	0	1	0	0
Garber, Memphis	.914	22	14	39	5	2
GARCIA, Orlando	.954	135	93	281	18	19
Giannelli, Knoxville	.910	107	53	160	21	21
Gilbert, Orlando	.923	11	4	20	2	1
Gonzalez, Jacksonville	.500	1	0	1	1	0
Grace, Charlotte	.941	72	58	135	12	13
Hiatt, Memphis	.919	56	36	112	13	13
Holley, Jacksonville	.750	3	0	3	1	0
Infante, Knoxville	1.000	4	1	10	0	0
Kelly, Greenville	.960	11	3	21	1	3
King, Jacksonville	1.000	1	1	0	0	0
Kremblas, Chattanooga	1.000	3	2	5	0	1
Ladnier, Memphis	.950	7	10	9	1	0
Longiro, Chattanooga	.925	30	24	50	6	4
Maloney, Greenville	1.000	10	3	16	0	1
Marzan, Orlando	.750	5	2	1	1	0
Morris, Greenville	.942	102	53	190	15	11
Paquette, Huntsville	.917	67	45	132	16	11
Pedre, Memphis	.885	9	7	16	3	2
Pennington, Jacksonville	1.000	2	0	5	0	1
Robinson, Memphis	.942	59	44	102	9	7
Rodriguez, Greenville	.913	26	15	58	7	6
Roth, Birmingham	.929	10	3	10	1	1
St. Peter, Charlotte	.910	39	32	69	10	12
Schreiber, Carolina	.932	38	20	62	6	6
Smith, Jacksonville	.929	5	3	10	1	1
Tatarian, Birmingham	1.000	1	1	0	0	0
Taylor, Knoxville	.896	24	15	28	5	3
Vice, Huntsville	.823	27	13	52	14	5
Wehner, Carolina	.953	48	40	124	8	13
White, Charlotte	.966	14	10	18	1	3
Young, Carolina	.847	57	34	110	26	9
Young, Knoxville	.946	42	21	66	5	6

SHORTSTOPS

Player, Team	Pct.	G	PO	A	E	DP
Abbott, Huntsville	.951	53	89	164	13	42
Alva, Greenville	.954	68	99	214	15	52
ARIAS, Charlotte	.950	134	203	351	29	81
Bolick, Jacksonville	1.000	1	1	1	0	0
Boone, Jacksonville	.913	10	12	30	4	4
Branson, Chattanooga	.953	62	72	150	11	26
Bridges, Memphis	.946	100	178	260	25	50
Busby, Birmingham	.931	24	31	77	8	13
Canan, Charlotte	1.000	1	0	5	0	1
Castilla, Greenville	.965	66	86	221	11	39
Cedeno, Knoxville	.945	98	140	272	24	54
Chimelis, Huntsville	.760	7	7	12	6	4
Correia, Huntsville	.938	30	46	76	8	24
Costo, Chattanooga	.953	19	24	37	3	8
Crockett, Charlotte	1.000	3	3	3	0	1
Edge, Carolina	.970	73	96	193	9	40
Foster, Birmingham	.924	111	172	288	38	54
Garber, Memphis	1.000	3	5	16	0	3
Garrison, Huntsville	.806	6	10	15	6	2
Gilbert, Orlando	.959	51	62	127	8	32
Gonzalez, Memphis	.881	23	34	55	12	10
Holley, Jacksonville	.977	11	13	29	1	4
Huyler, Carolina	.950	76	89	196	15	33
Kelly, Greenville	1.000	4	7	16	0	2
King, Jacksonville	.967	9	15	14	1	8
Lonigro, Chattanooga	.947	42	60	119	10	23
Maloney, Greenville	.925	12	16	33	4	3
Manahan, Jacksonville	.938	99	142	278	28	66
Matos, Huntsville	.899	52	72	124	22	23
McCreary, Orlando	.940	107	132	274	26	50
Montalvo, Orlando	.962	14	21	29	2	12
Robinson, Memphis	.938	23	33	58	6	9
Roth, Birmingham	.929	8	9	17	2	4
Rush, Chattanooga	.981	31	29	74	2	13
Santana, Jacksonville	1.000	1	0	1	0	0
Schreiber, Carolina	1.000	1	0	3	0	1
Smith, Jacksonville	.891	28	28	54	10	11
Tatarian, Birmingham	.913	5	10	11	2	4
Taylor, Knoxville	.959	40	48	91	6	19
Vice, Huntsville	.824	4	6	8	3	2
White, Charlotte	.979	14	17	30	1	7
Wilson, Birmingham	1.000	2	4	7	0	1
Young, Knoxville	.852	8	7	16	4	3
McDonald, Jacksonville	1.000	29	61	5	0	2
Merchant, Jacksonville	1.000	41	61	3	0	1
Mitchell, Greenville	.963	60	99	4	4	1
Morgan, Orlando*	.967	45	80	7	3	2
Neel, Huntsville	.905	13	19	0	2	0
Newfield, Jacksonville	.833	4	5	0	1	0
Nunez, Knoxville	.962	64	96	6	4	2
Ortiz, Orlando*	.959	91	135	5	6	1
Pennington, Jacksonville	.975	77	114	4	3	0
Pennye, Carolina	.967	108	169	7	6	0
Pennyfeather, Carolina	.929	41	75	4	6	3
Pezzoni, Jacksonville	1.000	4	4	0	0	0
Pledger, Birmingham	.962	112	198	2	8	0
POSE, Chattanooga	.996	115	215	9	1	0
Ramsey, Charlotte	.971	138	358	14	11	3
Ratliff, Carolina	.977	22	43	0	1	0
Roberson, Charlotte	.985	132	259	7	4	0
Rodgers, Knoxville	.979	39	46	1	1	0
Ross, Greenville*	.970	104	156	4	5	0
Sanders, Chattanooga	.982	59	158	2	3	1
Shelton, Carolina*	1.000	1	3	0	0	0
Shockey, Huntsville*	1.000	2	4	0	0	0
Simmons, Greenville*	1.000	1	2	0	0	0
Smith, Jacksonville	1.000	1	1	0	0	0
Stargell, Jacksonville	1.000	47	68	3	0	0
Sullivan, Birmingham	.973	34	34	2	1	0
Tedder, Birmingham*	.994	94	152	4	1	2
Ry. Thompson, Knoxville	.983	111	222	5	4	0
Tinsley, Huntsville	.962	88	175	3	7	0
Trafton, Chattanooga	1.000	4	8	1	0	1
Turang, Jacksonville	1.000	26	45	2	0	0
Valdez, Orlando	.889	2	8	0	1	0
Vice, Huntsville	1.000	2	2	0	0	0
Vitiello, Memphis	.985	34	63	3	1	0
Waggoner, Birmingham	.981	68	153	1	3	1
B. Walker, 4 Chat.-40 Mem.	.955	44	79	6	4	0
H. Walker, Memphis	.958	115	178	3	8	0
Watkins, Memphis	.962	53	125	3	5	2
Welch, Charlotte	.973	77	105	5	3	0
Wetherby, Jacksonville*	.970	73	125	4	4	0
Williams, Jacksonville	.962	68	126	2	5	0
Wright, Memphis	1.000	10	29	0	0	0
Yacopino, Carolina*	.987	39	77	1	1	0
Young, Knoxville	.986	49	68	5	1	2
Zambrano, Carolina	.987	78	141	8	2	0

OUTFIELDERS

Player, Team	Pct.	G	PO	A	E	DP
Alborano, Memphis*	.950	26	37	1	2	0
Alicea, Greenville	1.000	12	16	0	0	0
Armas, Huntsville	.939	22	43	3	3	0
Baldwin, Charlotte*	1.000	30	51	1	0	0
Booker, Huntsville	.907	28	37	2	4	0
Bowie, Jacksonville*	1.000	2	1	0	0	0
Bryant, Chattanooga	.967	69	112	5	4	1
Buccheri, Huntsville	.991	91	211	5	2	1
Burton, Greenville	.965	40	52	3	2	0
Canan, Charlotte	1.000	1	1	0	0	0
Capellan, Orlando	1.000	2	1	1	0	0
Chasey, Birmingham*	1.000	1	1	0	0	0
Cole, Greenville	.975	111	147	12	4	3
Colvard, Chattanooga	.959	98	178	10	8	0
Conte, Huntsville	.991	88	200	13	2	6
Correia, Huntsville	1.000	21	27	2	0	0
Crockett, Charlotte	.972	62	98	5	3	1
Dattola, Huntsville	.967	77	144	2	5	0
Deak, Greenville	1.000	1	1	0	0	0
de la Rosa, Knoxville	.972	117	194	14	6	2
DeLima, Orlando*	.977	118	166	3	4	0
DeLoach, Knoxville	.962	105	147	5	6	3
Edge, Carolina	1.000	3	2	1	0	1
Estep, Carolina	.953	81	133	10	7	2
Figueroa, Jacksonville*	1.000	1	1	0	0	0
Garber, Memphis	1.000	5	9	1	0	0
Gilbert, Orlando	.970	60	118	11	4	1
Gillum, Chattanooga	.947	7	18	0	1	0
Green, Carolina	.992	56	109	8	1	0
Griffin, Charlotte	.962	30	48	2	2	1
Holley, Jacksonville	.962	22	49	2	2	0
Hosey, Birmingham	.974	99	218	7	6	2
Jaster, Chattanooga	.991	55	107	5	1	0
Jose, Chattanooga						
Kelly, Greenville	.923	10	10	2	1	1
Koslofski, Memphis	.974	81	176	12	5	1
Kowitz, Greenville*	1.000	35	56	2	0	0
Kremblas, Chattanooga	.938	40	71	4	5	0
Kvasnicka, Orlando*	.993	88	149	3	1	0
Lee, Birmingham	.986	43	65	5	1	2
List, Carolina	.727	7	7	1	3	0
Long, Memphis*	.970	82	148	11	5	6
Martin, Greenville*	.957	80	127	6	6	0
Masteller, Orlando*	.973	33	34	2	1	0
Maynard, Jacksonville	.985	55	129	3	2	1
McCarty, Orlando*	.977	28	38	4	1	0

CATCHERS

Player, Team	Pct.	G	PO	A	E	DP	PB
Antigua, Carolina	.950	3	18	1	1	0	0
Arguelles, Jacksonville	.986	46	248	29	4	3	6
Baxter, Memphis	.974	67	363	52	11	1	11
Beeler, Chattanooga	.989	42	255	24	3	3	7
Borrelli, Huntsville	.977	63	387	42	10	7	4
Brito, Huntsville	.986	65	371	42	6	5	8
Campanis, Jacksonville	.983	110	714	93	14	8	13
Campbell, Birmingham	.982	91	512	49	10	3	14
Carcione, Huntsville	.981	17	94	12	2	1	3
Cox, Chattanooga	.988	13	74	6	1	1	1
Cuevas, Greenville	.992	67	457	35	4	2	9
Davis, Memphis	.989	26	148	24	2	4	3
Deak, Greenville	.988	70	465	45	6	3	8
Edge, Carolina	1.000	1	3	2	0	0	1
Gay, Birmingham	.984	26	166	17	3	2	3
Grifol, Orlando	.976	5	39	2	1	0	0
Hines, Carolina	.982	29	143	22	3	1	2
Knapp, Charlotte	.987	91	496	48	7	3	7
Knorr, Knoxville	.986	20	130	16	2	3	2
Kobza, Birmingham	1.000	1	8	0	0	0	1
Kremblas, Chattanooga	1.000	4	9	1	0	0	3
Liebert, Birmingham	.982	35	188	26	4	1	6
Logan, Orlando	.981	17	101	4	2	1	0
Lopez, Orlando	1.000	19	102	4	0	0	5
Magrann, Carolina	1.000	5	43	2	0	0	0
Maksudian, Knoxville	.991	49	305	21	3	1	10
Marzan, Orlando	1.000	1	3	0	0	0	0
Merullo, Birmingham	.966	5	25	3	1	0	2
Monzon, Knoxville	.989	40	255	20	3	3	7
O'Halloran, Knoxville	.988	42	233	21	3	1	6
Osik, Carolina	.980	16	84	13	2	1	3
Parks, Orlando	.985	84	476	37	8	2	3
Pedre, Memphis	.989	51	322	41	4	5	8
Reese, Memphis	.963	11	48	4	2	1	1
ROMERO, Carolina	.994	86	552	63	4	6	14
Ryan, Memphis	.963	5	26	0	1	0	3
Simonds, Charlotte	.976	34	181	24	5	7	0
Siwa, Orlando	.985	59	367	38	6	1	3
Sutko, Chattanooga	.995	23	168	21	1	2	5
Taylor, Charlotte	.982	40	193	28	4	2	7
Tejada, Huntsville	1.000	6	36	8	0	0	3
Torres, Carolina	.975	11	73	6	2	2	0
Townley, Knoxville	.972	15	63	7	2	2	0
Wilson, Chattanooga	.993	72	486	49	4	3	3

PITCHERS

Player, Team	Pct.	G	PO	A	E	DP
Adams, Carolina	1.000	8	0	2	0	0
Alvarez, Birmingham*	.933	23	7	21	2	1
Anderson, Chattanooga	.962	28	9	16	1	0
Ausanio, Carolina	1.000	3	1	1	0	0
Ayala, Chattanooga	.941	39	2	14	1	1
Balabon, Jacksonville	.833	10	1	4	1	0
Bangtson, Orlando	.958	26	7	16	1	0
Bark, Greenville*	1.000	9	1	6	0	0
Barton, Jacksonville*	1.000	14	5	5	0	0
Blair, Charlotte	1.000	1	1	0	0	0
Blohm, Knoxville	1.000	3	1	1	0	0
Blueberg, Jacksonville	.818	14	6	12	4	0
Bolton, Birmingham	.947	12	7	11	1	2
Borbon, Greenville*	1.000	4	1	3	0	1
Brito, Birmingham	.880	10	6	16	3	2
Brown, Knoxville	1.000	3	0	1	0	0
Buckholz, Carolina	.944	21	5	12	1	1
Bullinger, Charlotte	1.000	20	9	25	0	1
Chambers, Birmingham	1.000	10	3	5	0	0
Cole, Carolina	1.000	20	3	7	0	3
Cooke, Carolina*	.833	9	1	9	2	1
Corbin, Memphis	.947	28	11	25	2	1
Cormier, Huntsville	1.000	17	7	11	0	3
Cortes, Birmingham	.944	22	14	20	2	1
Cromwell, Knoxville*	.917	16	2	9	1	2
Cross, Knoxville	.824	31	14	14	6	1
Cruz, Memphis	.929	11	1	12	1	1
Czarkowski, Jacksonville*	1.000	20	4	20	0	0
Davino, Birmingham	1.000	25	4	9	0	0
Delkus, Orlando	1.000	45	3	19	0	1
DiBartolomeo, Charlotte	.900	45	2	7	1	1
Dodd, Chattanooga	1.000	35	8	8	0	0
Duncan, 6 Car.-22 Mem.	.905	28	4	15	2	1
Eave, Jacksonville	1.000	5	3	0	0	0
Erwin, Huntsville	1.000	19	0	1	0	0
Eskew, Huntsville	1.000	6	2	6	0	0
Evans, Jacksonville	.871	21	9	18	4	1
Fajardo, Carolina	.833	10	3	2	1	1
Fansler, Carolina	1.000	19	3	14	0	1
Figueroa, Jacksonville*	1.000	41	6	13	0	0
Fleming, Jacksonville*	.977	21	7	35	1	2
Foster, Chattanooga	1.000	17	2	5	0	0
Garces, Orlando	1.000	10	1	2	0	0
Garcia, Huntsville	1.000	13	3	5	0	0
Garcia, Jacksonville	.875	6	2	5	1	0
Garcia, Birmingham	1.000	6	1	10	0	1
Garcia, Chattanooga	1.000	40	2	6	0	1
Gardner, Charlotte	.821	29	8	15	5	2
Gomez, Charlotte	1.000	34	7	8	0	0
Gomez, Greenville*	.905	13	2	17	2	1
Grott, Huntsville*	.846	42	1	10	2	0
Guzman, Huntsville*	1.000	7	3	3	0	0
Hall, Knoxville	1.000	42	5	10	0	1
Hamilton, Carolina*	.867	10	5	8	2	0
Hancock, Carolina*	.947	37	8	28	2	2
Hawblitzel, Charlotte	.889	5	3	5	1	1
Hernandez, Birmingham	1.000	4	3	1	0	0
Hopper, Memphis	1.000	20	7	7	0	1
Horsman, Knoxville*	.867	42	4	9	2	0
Howard, Birmingham*	.889	38	1	7	1	1
Hudek, Birmingham	.947	51	4	14	1	2
Imes, Chattanooga	1.000	8	5	10	0	1
Jaques, Charlotte*	1.000	20	1	3	0	0
Johnson, Orlando	.909	53	3	7	1	0
Johnson, Greenville*	1.000	47	9	11	0	1
Jones, Knoxville	.778	12	2	5	2	0
Jones, Charlotte	.500	4	0	1	1	0
Kennedy, Birmingham	.906	15	5	24	3	1
Keyser, Birmingham	1.000	3	0	5	0	1
Kizziah, Knoxville	.800	11	2	6	2	1
Kuhn, Huntsville*	1.000	43	3	3	0	0
Latter, Huntsville	1.000	58	9	17	0	1
LeMasters, Memphis	.909	12	3	7	1	0
Leslie, Chattanooga	.667	1	0	2	1	0
Lind, Orlando	1.000	52	4	20	0	1
Mahomes, Orlando	.950	18	11	8	1	0
McAuliffe, Chattanooga	.857	33	3	3	1	0
McCarthy, Chattanooga*	1.000	12	0	1	0	0
Merigliano, Birmingham	.833	36	6	9	3	0
Middaugh, Birmingham	1.000	12	1	4	0	0
Mielke, Huntsville	1.000	4	1	0	0	0
Miller, Carolina	.870	15	7	13	3	1
Minor, Carolina	.667	3	1	1	1	0
Moeller, Memphis*	.917	10	1	10	1	0
Mohler, Huntsville*	1.000	8	3	9	0	3
Mount, Charlotte	.824	17	5	9	3	1
Muh, 7 Orl.-21 Char.*	1.000	28	1	3	0	1
Murphy, Carolina	1.000	32	5	20	0	0
Nelson, Jacksonville	1.000	21	3	2	0	0
Newlin, Jacksonville	.870	47	5	15	3	2
Newman, Orlando*	.929	11	3	10	1	0
Nied, Greenville	.947	15	5	13	1	0
O'Neal, Memphis	1.000	12	0	7	0	0
Ogliaruso, Knoxville	.750	7	1	2	1	0
Osteen, Huntsville*	.978	28	15	29	1	2
Parker, Charlotte	.975	24	9	30	1	2
Parnell, Memphis	.813	58	2	11	3	1
Peek, Huntsville	1.000	56	4	14	0	0
Perez, Memphis	.857	33	11	19	5	0
Peters, Huntsville	1.000	19	4	9	2	0
Peters, Memphis	.867	19	4	9	2	0
Pichardo, Memphis	.808	34	9	12	5	0
Pierce, Memphis*	.963	21	1	25	1	0
Pitz, Jacksonville	.813	36	4	9	3	0
Poehl, Memphis	.952	33	7	13	1	1
Pugh, Chattanooga	1.000	5	1	8	0	1
Revenig, Huntsville	1.000	12	1	3	0	0
Reynolds, Birmingham	1.000	19	3	9	0	1
Richards, Jacksonville*	1.000	10	1	3	0	1
Richards, Jacksonville	1.000	19	6	20	0	2
Risley, Chattanooga	.955	19	6	15	1	1
Rivera, Greenville	.955	26	11	31	2	4
Roberts, Memphis*	1.000	25	3	6	0	0
Robinson, Greenville	.839	29	8	18	5	1
Roesler, Carolina	1.000	20	2	1	0	0
Rogers, Knoxville	1.000	28	11	23	0	0
Rojas, Jacksonville	1.000	15	1	1	0	0
Salkeld, Jacksonville	1.000	23	12	12	0	1
Salles, Charlotte	.962	22	17	34	2	3
Sanchez, Knoxville	1.000	14	6	19	0	1
Sanders, Greenville	.958	48	5	18	1	0
Sanford, Chattanooga	.929	16	5	8	1	0
Satre, Chattanooga	1.000	8	1	2	0	1
Savage, Orlando	1.000	6	1	0	0	0
Schock, Chattanooga	1.000	12	2	4	0	0
Schooler, Jacksonville	1.000	11	2	0	0	0
Schwabe, Orlando	.600	6	1	2	2	0
Shifflett, Memphis	.909	59	4	26	3	0
Sierra, Charlotte	1.000	18	1	9	0	0
Smith, Memphis	1.000	16	0	4	0	0
Sodders, Charlotte*	1.000	9	0	4	0	0
Spradlin, Chattanooga	.895	48	2	15	2	3
Stowell, Orlando*	.857	50	3	9	2	1
Strauss, Charlotte	.955	49	8	13	1	0
Tafoya, Carolina	1.000	40	3	13	0	1
Talbert, Memphis	1.000	3	0	1	0	0
Tatar, Chattanooga	.909	12	1	9	1	0
B. Taylor, Greenville	.929	59	1	12	1	1
S. Taylor, Greenville	1.000	8	1	7	0	1
Taylor, Memphis	.875	6	2	5	1	2
Tellers, Carolina	1.000	11	0	2	0	0
Thomas, Birmingham*	1.000	2	1	1	0	0
Ri. Thompson, Knoxville	1.000	10	0	2	0	0
Tracy, Carolina	1.000	16	6	11	0	0
Trlicek, Knoxville	1.000	41	4	5	0	0
Trombley, Orlando	.935	27	5	24	2	1
Tsamis, Orlando*	1.000	1	0	0	0	0
Turek, Chattanooga	.923	10	4	8	1	0
Upshaw, Greenville*	.920	19	4	19	2	0
Van Poppel, Huntsville	.848	24	8	20	5	1
Vasquez, Chattanooga	.966	17	5	23	1	1
Ventura, Birmingham	.879	25	8	21	4	0
Wakefield, Carolina	.912	26	9	22	3	3
Walk, Carolina	1.000	1	1	1	0	0
Ward, Knoxville*	.941	31	2	14	1	1
Wassenaar, Orlando	.857	15	2	4	1	2
Watkins, Charlotte	.957	52	7	15	1	0
Watson, Greenville	.870	49	4	16	3	0
Weathers, Knoxville	.943	24	13	20	2	3
Webb, Carolina	.944	37	3	14	1	3
Weber, Huntsville	.867	34	3	10	2	0
Wendell, Greenville	.939	25	13	18	2	2
Wickman, Birmingham	.917	20	19	14	3	0
Wiese, Orlando*	1.000	21	5	15	0	0
Wiggs, Jacksonville*	1.000	6	1	1	0	0
Williams, Knoxville	.846	18	2	9	2	0
Wishnevski, Knoxville	.941	31	13	19	2	2
Wohlers, Greenville	.714	28	1	4	2	0
Woodson, Jacksonville	.909	13	10	10	2	0
ZANCANARO, Huntsville*	1.000	29	6	35	0	0
Zarranz, Jacksonville	1.000	24	2	4	0	0
Zavaras, Jacksonville	.714	6	1	4	2	0

The following players did not have any fielding statistics at the positions indicated or appeared only as a designated hitter, pinch-hitter or pinch-runner: Arguelles, of; Biasucci, ss; Bowie, p; Briscoe, p; Campanis, 3b; Canan, p; Capellan, p; Castleberry, ph; Champion, p; Coomer, 2b; Costo, 2b; Crockett, p; Davis, of; Hoffman, p; Jackson, dh; Kremblas, ss, p; Laureano, ss; Lloyd, p; Montalvo, 3b; Monzon, p; Morris, of; Neely, p; Nunez, p; Osik, 3b; Phoenix, p; Reese, of; D. Robinson, p; Santana, of; Jac. Smith, c; Strange, p; Stroud, p; Swartzbaugh, p; M. Taylor, p; Townley, p; Valdez, 3b; Vasquez, of; Vice, p; West, p; Mi. Young, p.

LEAGUE CHAMPIONS

Year	Team	Pct.
1904—	Macon	.598
1905—	Macon	.625
1906—	Savannah	.637
1907—	Charleston	.620
1908—	Jacksonville	.694
1909—	Chattanooga*	.738
	Augusta	.702
1910—	Columbus	.588
1911—	Columbus*	.681
	Columbia	.710
1912—	Jacksonville*	.679
	Columbus	.632
1913—	Savannah	.754
	Savannah	.593
1914—	Savannah*	.667
	Albany	.650
1915—	Macon	.588
	Columbus*	.686
1916—	Augusta*	.617
	Columbia	.631
1917—	Charleston	.741
	Columbia*	.667
1918—	Did not operate.	
1919—	Columbia	.585
1920—	Columbia	.633
1921—	Columbia	.642
1922—	Charleston	.625
1923—	Charlotte*	.653
	Macon	.580
1924—	Augusta	.612
1925—	Spartanburg	.620
1926—	Greenville	.662
1927—	Greenville	.622
1928—	Asheville	.664
1929—	Asheville	.605
	Knoxville*	.634
1930—	Greenville*	.620
	Macon	.643
1931-35—	Did not operate.	
1936—	Jacksonville	.652
	Columbus*	.650
1937—	Columbus	.572
	Savannah (3rd)†	.565
1938—	Savannah	.574
	Macon (2nd)†	.570
1939—	Columbus	.601
	Augusta (2nd)†	.597
1940—	Savannah	.627
	Columbus (2nd)†	.583
1941—	Macon	.643
	Columbia (2nd)†	.636
1942—	Charleston	.620
	Macon (2nd)†	.585
1943-45—	Did not operate.	
1946—	Columbus	.568
	Augusta (4th)†	.547
1947—	Columbus	.575
	Savannah (2nd)†	.563
1948—	Charleston	.572
	Greenville (3rd)†	.549
1949—	Macon‡	.623
1950—	Macon‡	.588
1951—	Montgomery	.607
1952—	Columbia	.649
	Montgomery (3rd)†	.558
1953—	Jacksonville	.679
	Savannah (2nd)†	.571
1954—	Jacksonville	.593
	Savannah (2nd)†	.571
1955—	Columbia	.636
	Augusta (3rd)†	.543
1956—	Jacksonville‡	.621
1957—	Augusta	.636
	Charlotte (2nd)†	.562
1958—	Augusta	.550
	Macon (3rd)†	.500
1959—	Knoxville	.557
	Gastonia (4th)†	.504
1960—	Columbia	.597
	Savannah (3rd)†	.561
1961—	Asheville	.635
1962—	Savannah	.662
	Macon (3rd)†	.576
1963—	Augusta*	.661
	Lynchburg	.662
1964—	Lynchburg	.579
1965—	Columbus	.572
1966—	Mobile	.629
1967—	Birmingham	.604
1968—	Asheville	.614
1969—	Charlotte	.579
1970—	Columbus	.569
1971—	Did not operate as league—clubs were members of Dixie Association.	
1972—	Asheville	.583
	Montgomery§	.561
1973—	Montgomery§	.580
	Jacksonville	.559
1974—	Jacksonville§	.565
	Knoxville§	.533
1975—	Orlando	.587
	Montgomery§	.545
1976—	Montgomery x	.591
	Orlando	.540
1977—	Montgomery x	.628
	Jacksonville	.522
1978—	Knoxville x	.611
	Savannah	.500
1979—	Columbus	.587
	Nashville x	.576
1980—	Memphis	.576
	Charlotte x	.500
1981—	Nashville	.566
	Orlando x	.556
1982—	Jacksonville	.576
	Nashville x	.535
1983—	Birmingham x	.628
	Jacksonville	.531
1984—	Charlotte x	.510
	Knoxville	.483
1985—	Charlotte	.545
	Huntsville x	.542
1986—	Huntsville	.553
	Columbus x	.500
1987—	Charlotte	.586
	Birmingham x	.476
1988—	Greenville	.604
	Chattanooga x	.566
1989—	Birmingham x	.615
	Greenville	.504
1990—	Orlando	.590
	Memphis x	.507
1991—	Greenville	.611
	Orlando x	.535

*Won split season playoff. †Won four-club playoff. ‡Won championship and four-club playoff. §League was divided into Eastern and Western divisions; won playoff. xLeague was divided into Eastern and Western divisions and played split season; won playoff.

TEXAS LEAGUE

FINAL STANDINGS

FIRST HALF

EASTERN DIVISION

Team	W	L	T	Pct.	GB
Shreveport (Giants)	45	23	0	.662	.....
Jackson (Astros)	32	34	0	.485	12
Tulsa (Rangers)	24	43	0	.358	20 ½
Arkansas (Cardinals)	23	42	0	.354	20 ½

WESTERN DIVISION

Team	W	L	T	Pct.	GB
El Paso (Brewers)	45	23	0	.662	.....
Wichita (Padres)	39	29	0	.574	6
San Antonio (Dodgers)	31	37	0	.456	14
Midland (Angels)	30	38	0	.441	15

SECOND HALF

EASTERN DIVISION

Team	W	L	T	Pct.	GB
Shreveport (Giants)	41	27	0	.603	.....
Jackson (Astros)	38	32	1	.543	4
Tulsa (Rangers)	34	35	0	.493	7 ½
Arkansas (Cardinals)	26	45	0	.366	16 ½

WESTERN DIVISION

Team	W	L	T	Pct.	GB
Midland (Angels)	37	30	1	.552	.....
El Paso (Brewers)	36	32	0	.529	1 ½
Wichita (Padres)	32	35	1	.478	5
San Antonio (Dodgers)	30	38	1	.441	7 ½

COMPOSITE

Team	Shrv.	E.P.	Wich.	Jax.	Mid.	S.A.	Tul.	Ark.	W	L	T	Pct.	GB
Shreveport (Giants)	....	6	3	22	4	7	21	23	86	50	0	.632	.....
El Paso (Brewers)	4	....	22	4	21	17	5	8	81	55	0	.596	5
Wichita (Padres)	7	10	....	4	17	18	9	6	71	64	1	.526	14 ½
Jackson (Astros)	10	6	6	....	3	6	17	22	70	66	1	.515	16
Midland (Angels)	6	11	14	7	....	18	4	7	67	68	1	.496	18 ½
San Antonio (Dodgers)	3	15	14	4	14	....	4	7	61	75	1	.449	25
Tulsa (Rangers)	11	5	1	15	6	6	....	14	58	78	0	.426	28
Arkansas (Cardinals)	9	2	4	10	3	3	18	....	49	87	0	.360	37

Arkansas club represented Little Rock, Ark.

Major league affiliations in parentheses.

Playoffs—El Paso defeated Midland, two games to none; Shreveport defeated El Paso, four games to two, to win league championship.

Regular-season attendance—Arkansas, 265,268; El Paso, 273,438; Jackson, 114,660; Midland, 180,616; San Antonio, 185,336; Shreveport, 206,540; Tulsa, 260,864; Wichita, 200,217. Total—1,686,939. Playoffs (8 games)—14,350. Class AA All-Star Game at Huntsville—4,022. Texas League All-Star Game at El Paso—5,914.

Managers—Arkansas, Joe Pettini; El Paso, Dave Huppert; Jackson, Rick Sweet; Midland, Don Long; San Antonio, John Shoemaker; Shreveport, Bill Evers; Tulsa, Bobby Jones; Wichita, Steve Lubratich.

All-Star team—1B—John Jaha, El Paso; 2B—John Patterson, Shreveport; 3B—Juan Guerrero, Shreveport; SS—Royce Clayton, Shreveport; C—Dave Nilsson, El Paso; Ivan Rodriguez, Tulsa; OF—Shon Ashley, San Antonio; Ruben Escalera, El Paso; Steve Hosey, Shreveport; DH—Mark Howie, Midland; Util.—Jim Tatum, El Paso; P—Frank Seminara, Wichita; Don Vidmar, Midland; Paul McClellan, Shreveport; Chris Gardner, Jackson; Larry Carter, Shreveport; Most Valuable Player—John Jaha, El Paso; Pitcher of the Year—Paul McClellan, Shreveport; Manager of the Year—Don Long, Midland.

BATTING

TEAM

Team	Avg.	G	AB	R	OR	H	TB	2B	3B	HR	RBI	SH	SF	HP	BB	Int. BB	SO	SB	CS	LOB
El Paso	.303	136	4765	920	732	1443	2232	276	51	137	846	44	61	64	546	30	822	104	42	1057
Midland	.289	136	4633	813	797	1338	1965	235	46	100	744	38	34	41	552	30	821	164	68	973
Wichita	.272	136	4559	659	725	1240	1722	212	18	78	618	42	54	41	547	34	751	155	75	1024
Shreveport	.272	136	4478	725	540	1216	1800	242	42	86	640	70	30	57	562	52	881	208	96	991
San Antonio	.264	137	4486	643	677	1184	1695	220	33	75	574	51	42	44	531	29	802	182	91	993
Tulsa	.259	136	4424	568	676	1145	1665	210	53	68	520	45	41	32	474	23	839	61	58	943
Jackson	.254	137	4394	621	643	1114	1568	204	41	56	537	52	35	48	523	52	933	170	81	943
Arkansas	.244	136	4257	502	661	1040	1485	222	20	61	435	42	27	31	471	19	909	63	62	905

INDIVIDUAL

(Leading qualifiers for batting championship—367 or more plate appearances)

*Bats lefthanded.   †Switch-hitter.

Player. Team	Avg.	G	AB	R	H	TB	2B	3B	HR	RBI	SH	SF	HP	BB	Int. BB	SO	SB	CS
Howie, Mark, Midland	.364	130	516	101	188	278	32	2	18	123	0	5	5	56	5	49	7	6
Jaha, John, El Paso	.344	130	486	121	167	301	38	3	30	134	1	5	8	78	6	101	12	6
Guerrero, Juan, Shreveport	.334	128	479	78	160	261	40	2	19	94	0	4	5	46	2	86	14	10
Tatum, Jim, El Paso	.320	130	493	99	158	255	27	8	18	128	2	20	15	63	5	79	5	7
Escalera, Ruben, El Paso*	.316	114	443	101	140	198	26	7	6	67	10	2	11	61	5	73	9	3
Williams, Reggie, Midland†	.310	83	319	77	99	120	12	3	1	30	5	3	0	62	2	67	21	9
Ashley, Shon, San Antonio	.308	126	493	86	152	263	29	5	24	100	2	3	2	71	4	110	2	2
Prager, Howard, Jackson*	.305	109	357	57	109	172	26	2	11	65	4	3	2	52	6	75	9	6
Frye, Jeff, Tulsa	.302	131	503	92	152	218	32	11	4	41	5	3	1	71	1	60	15	8
Jackson, Kenny, El Paso	.302	114	427	77	129	223	25	9	17	66	3	2	3	31	2	81	9	3

Departmental leaders: G—Mikulik, 133; AB—Howie, 516; R—Jaha, 121; H—Howie, 188; TB—Jaha, 301; 2B—J. Guerrero, 40; 3B—Flora, 15; HR—Jaha, 30; RBI—Jaha, 134; SH—J. Cooper, 11; SF—Tatum, 20; HP—Tatum, 15; BB—Salmon, 89; IBB—Smiley, 9; SO—Salmon, 166; SB—Young, 70; CS—Young, 26.

(All players—listed alphabetically)

Player. Team	Avg.	G	AB	R	H	TB	2B	3B	HR	RBI	SH	SF	HP	BB	Int. BB	SO	SB	CS
Abreu, Frank, Arkansas	.238	89	256	24	61	78	12	1	1	20	2	3	3	47	1	66	5	3
Alfonzo, Ed, Midland	.277	26	83	13	23	38	1	1	4	13	2	0	1	2	0	7	0	0

Player, Team	Avg.	G	AB	R	H	TB	2B	3B	HR	RBI	SH	SF	HP	BB	Int. BB	SO	SB	CS
Allen, Harold, Jackson*	.100	26	10	0	1	2	1	0	0	1	0	0	0	0	0	5	0	0
Alvarez, Jorge, San Antonio	.298	66	225	33	67	94	14	2	3	23	2	1	3	18	2	32	9	7
Ansley, Willie, Jackson	.232	77	233	43	54	82	15	5	1	20	2	0	1	43	0	66	9	5
Ard, Johnny, Shreveport	.200	13	10	1	2	3	1	0	0	3	3	0	0	8	0	5	0	0
Ashley, Shon, El Paso	.308	126	493	86	152	263	29	5	24	100	2	3	2	71	4	110	2	2
Astacio, Pedro, San Antonio	.100	19	20	1	2	2	0	0	0	1	1	0	1	0	0	11	0	0
August, Sam, Jackson	.000	7	4	0	0	0	0	0	0	0	2	0	0	0	0	0	0	0
Baar, Bryan, San Antonio	.224	101	348	33	78	127	19	0	10	51	3	2	1	21	1	92	3	1
Baldwin, Jeff, Jackson*	.206	11	34	7	7	7	0	0	0	4	1	0	0	9	1	6	0	0
Barbara, Don, Midland*	.362	63	224	43	81	124	13	0	10	40	0	1	0	37	6	45	0	0
Barker, Tim, San Antonio	.292	119	401	70	117	151	20	4	2	46	8	5	6	80	2	61	32	13
Barns, Jeff, Midland	.219	10	32	5	7	7	0	0	0	3	0	0	1	0	5	0	0
Barron, Tony, San Antonio	.235	73	200	35	47	80	2	2	9	31	0	1	3	28	2	44	8	3
Basso, Mike, Wichita	.242	51	165	17	40	59	10	0	3	26	0	3	1	22	2	33	0	0
Bauer, Pete, Jackson	.000	46	4	0	0	0	0	0	0	0	0	0	0	0	0	0	0	0
Belcher, Kevin, Tulsa	.250	24	84	16	21	37	5	1	3	17	0	3	0	20	1	20	2	4
Berger, Mike, Tulsa	.185	9	27	2	5	6	1	0	0	2	0	0	0	3	0	7	1	0
Beuerlein, Ed, Jackson	.263	9	19	4	5	9	1	0	1	4	0	0	0	4	0	2	0	0
Biberdorf, Cameron, San Antonio	.000	14	1	0	0	0	0	0	0	0	0	0	0	0	0	0	0	0
Billmeyer, Mick, Midland*	.305	37	128	15	39	53	7	2	1	25	1	0	1	6	0	15	0	0
Bournigal, Rafael, San Antonio	.323	16	65	6	21	23	2	0	0	9	1	1	0	2	0	7	2	3
Brannon, Cliff, Arkansas	.281	119	399	46	112	152	26	1	4	44	4	3	0	30	1	94	11	6
Brocail, Doug, Wichita*	.200	36	20	3	4	4	0	0	0	3	3	0	0	0	0	4	0	0
Brown, Adam, San Antonio*	.270	15	37	3	10	14	1	0	1	4	0	0	2	1	0	11	0	0
Bryand, Renay, Wichita*	.000	37	5	0	0	0	0	0	0	0	0	0	0	0	0	1	0	0
Burgos, Paco, Tulsa†	.222	63	216	15	48	58	5	1	1	16	4	1	1	7	2	25	0	1
Burton, Mike, Tulsa	.241	106	361	43	87	130	18	2	7	49	2	2	2	56	3	88	0	2
Bustillos, Albert, San Antonio	.000	18	18	0	0	0	0	0	0	0	0	1	0	0	1	0	7	0	0
Byington, John, El Paso	.273	129	501	60	137	193	27	1	9	89	5	15	4	25	1	63	3	4
Carey, Frank, Shreveport*	.000	5	5	0	0	0	0	0	0	0	0	0	0	0	0	4	0	0
Carmona, Greg, Arkansas†	.182	13	33	1	6	6	0	0	0	1	0	1	0	5	1	9	0	2
Carter, Larry, Shreveport	.280	24	25	2	7	9	2	0	0	5	2	0	0	3	0	11	0	0
Cassidy, David, Arkansas*	.143	6	7	0	1	1	0	0	0	0	0	0	0	0	0	1	0	0
Castillo, Braulio, San Antonio	.300	87	297	49	89	138	19	3	8	48	1	3	6	32	2	73	22	11
Chavez, Rafael, Wichita	.600	38	5	0	3	4	1	0	0	2	0	0	0	0	0	1	0	0
Christian, Ric, Arkansas	.238	88	282	29	67	86	13	3	0	21	5	1	2	29	0	81	12	6
Cisarik, Brian, Wichita*	.284	115	384	68	109	154	24	3	5	52	2	4	2	66	5	65	27	8
Clark, Mark, Arkansas	.200	15	15	0	3	3	0	0	0	1	2	0	0	0	0	5	0	0
Clayton, Royce, Shreveport	.280	126	485	84	136	189	22	8	5	68	3	5	3	61	7	104	36	10
Coffman, Kevin, Jackson	.192	32	26	5	5	13	2	0	2	6	2	0	0	0	0	6	0	0
Colon, Cris, Tulsa†	.392	26	102	20	40	59	6	2	3	28	1	3	0	4	0	11	0	1
Conley, Greg, Wichita	.308	22	65	7	20	26	3	0	1	10	0	1	0	4	1	17	0	0
Cook, Dennis, San Antonio*	.667	7	9	1	6	12	1	1	1	4	1	0	0	0	0	1	0	0
Cooper, Craig, El Paso	.299	39	147	25	44	75	8	1	7	33	1	3	0	14	1	15	0	1
Cooper, Jamie, Shreveport	.230	105	374	57	86	105	9	2	2	25	11	1	1	34	4	109	25	7
Cromer, Tripp, Arkansas	.229	73	227	28	52	69	12	1	1	18	2	3	3	15	1	37	0	1
Cunningham, Everett, Wichita	.000	16	1	0	0	0	0	0	0	0	0	0	0	0	0	0	0	0
Davenport, Adell, Shreveport	.230	59	165	19	38	62	3	0	7	24	3	1	6	14	0	44	0	1
David, Greg, Wichita*	.255	90	306	42	78	107	11	0	6	46	0	3	1	41	3	42	5	5
Davis, Kevin, Midland	.346	51	153	30	53	69	12	2	0	25	5	1	0	10	0	26	8	3
Davis, Rick, Wichita	.000	50	3	1	0	0	0	0	0	0	1	0	0	1	0	1	0	0
Dean, Kevin, Jackson	.237	98	278	34	66	91	11	4	2	33	1	2	4	53	2	80	9	5
Dominguez, Frank, Midland	.222	5	18	2	4	5	1	0	0	1	0	1	0	0	0	2	0	0
Ealy, Tom, Shreveport	.201	85	199	29	40	62	5	4	3	21	1	0	2	32	2	45	1	0
Easley, Damion, Midland	.254	127	452	73	115	167	24	5	6	57	6	2	7	58	2	67	23	9
Ebel, Dino, San Antonio	.275	20	40	3	11	14	3	0	0	2	1	0	0	9	0	5	1	1
Ericks, John, Arkansas	.214	25	28	2	6	7	1	0	0	0	3	0	0	0	0	16	0	0
Escalera, Ruben, El Paso*	.316	114	443	101	140	198	26	7	6	67	10	2	11	61	5	73	9	3
Eusebio, Tony, Jackson	.261	66	222	27	58	78	8	3	2	31	4	2	4	25	5	54	3	4
Fanning, Steve, Arkansas	.241	59	158	19	38	48	7	0	1	14	2	0	4	29	1	45	3	5
Faulkner, Craig, El Paso	.307	77	267	39	82	130	18	0	10	46	1	1	2	19	0	57	1	1
Federico, Joe, Arkansas*	.209	48	110	12	23	35	7	1	1	13	0	0	1	13	3	38	0	1
Fernandez, Dan, Shreveport	.250	7	12	3	3	3	0	0	0	1	1	0	1	6	1	3	0	0
Fernandez, Joey, Arkansas*	.217	14	46	9	10	19	3	0	2	8	0	0	0	8	0	5	0	1
Fernandez, Jose, Arkansas*	.228	94	285	46	65	117	14	1	12	28	0	1	2	62	1	86	0	1
Finken, Steve, San Antonio	.288	116	386	53	111	154	20	4	5	48	4	7	1	54	3	65	8	4
Finn, John, El Paso	.300	63	230	48	69	91	12	2	2	24	5	2	2	16	0	27	8	4
Fiore, Mike, Arkansas	.263	123	453	60	119	182	31	4	8	50	3	4	7	44	2	55	7	11
Flora, Kevin, Midland	.285	124	484	97	138	218	14	15	12	67	3	3	3	37	0	92	40	8
Forrester, Tom, Jackson*	.231	26	39	4	9	12	3	0	0	5	0	2	0	6	0	9	0	0
Frye, Jeff, Tulsa	.302	131	503	92	152	218	32	11	4	41	5	3	1	71	1	60	15	8
Galindez, Luis, Wichita*	.000	17	16	1	0	0	0	0	0	0	2	1	0	0	0	5	0	0
Gardner, Chris, Jackson	.160	22	25	0	4	4	0	0	0	2	3	0	0	3	0	8	0	0
Garman, Pat, Tulsa	.224	28	98	9	22	34	6	0	2	16	0	1	1	10	1	21	0	1
Gilmore, Terry, Wichita	.500	9	2	0	1	1	0	0	0	0	0	0	0	0	0	1	0	0
Gonzales, Larry, Midland	.319	78	257	27	82	107	13	0	4	56	3	6	6	22	0	33	2	2
Gonzales, Todd, Arkansas	.000	3	2	0	0	0	0	0	0	0	0	0	0	0	0	0	0	0
Gonzalez, Freddy, San Antonio	.167	12	24	1	4	7	0	0	1	5	0	0	1	2	0	9	0	1
Green, Dave, Tulsa	.285	59	200	22	57	85	16	0	4	32	1	3	1	16	2	27	2	4
Greer, Rusty, Tulsa*	.297	20	64	12	19	35	3	2	3	12	0	0	1	17	0	6	2	0
Grovom, Carl, Jackson*	.000	10	3	0	0	0	0	0	0	0	0	0	0	0	0	1	0	0
Guerrero, Juan, Shreveport	.334	128	479	78	160	261	40	2	19	94	0	4	5	46	2	86	14	10
Guerrero, Mike, El Paso	.205	37	117	23	24	26	2	0	0	13	2	0	0	18	1	16	2	1
Hajek, David,	.191	37	94	10	18	24	6	0	0	9	0	1	0	7	2	12	2	0
Hannahs, Mitch, El Paso	.244	26	86	23	21	31	5	1	1	9	2	0	1	24	0	19	1	1
Harris, Donald, Tulsa	.227	130	450	47	102	168	17	8	11	53	7	2	7	26	1	118	9	8
Harris, Rusty, Jackson†	.240	51	150	21	36	45	9	0	0	18	3	3	2	22	4	26	0	0
Harris, Vince, Wichita†	.286	112	381	78	109	123	12	1	0	39	8	2	1	63	4	45	48	16
Hartgraves, Dean, Jackson	.154	19	13	2	2	2	0	0	0	0	2	0	0	1	0	4	0	0
Haslock, Chris, Wichita	.000	10	3	0	0	0	0	0	0	0	0	0	0	0	0	0	0	0
Hernandez, Jose, Tulsa	.239	91	301	36	72	100	17	4	1	20	5	4	1	26	0	75	4	3
Hershiser, Orel, San Antonio	.000	1	0	0	0	0	0	0	0	0	0	0	0	0	0	0	0	0
Hickerson, Bryan, Shreveport*	.500	23	4	0	2	2	0	0	0	0	1	0	0	1	0	1	0	0

Player, Team	Avg.	G	AB	R	H	TB	2B	3B	HR	RBI	SH	SF	HP	BB	Int. BB	SO	SB	CS
Hillemann, Charles, Wichita	.268	84	291	45	78	120	19	1	7	44	2	7	6	29	2	83	9	3
Hilton, Howard, Wichita	.000	26	1	0	0	0	0	0	0	0	0	0	0	0	0	0	0	0
Hosey, Steve, Shreveport	.293	126	409	79	120	202	21	5	17	74	5	4	6	56	5	88	26	11
Hostetler, Tom, Shreveport	.100	9	10	1	1	1	0	0	0	2	2	0	0	1	0	3	0	0
Howie, Mark, Midland	.364	130	516	101	188	278	32	2	18	123	0	5	5	56	5	49	7	6
Hubbard, Trent, Jackson†	.297	126	455	78	135	168	21	3	2	41	3	2	9	65	2	81	39	20
Hunter, Bert, Jackson†	.256	120	379	58	97	131	17	7	1	43	7	3	2	57	3	92	32	9
Iavarone, Greg, Tulsa	.148	12	27	2	4	4	0	0	0	1	0	0	1	3	0	8	0	0
Ingram, Garey, San Antonio	.000	1	1	0	0	0	0	0	0	1	0	1	0	0	0	1	0	0
Jacas, Dave, El Paso	.264	124	511	103	135	197	26	9	6	53	7	4	9	58	1	86	27	7
Jackson, Kenny, El Paso	.302	114	427	77	129	223	25	9	17	66	3	2	3	31	2	81	9	3
Jaha, John, El Paso	.344	130	486	121	167	301	38	3	30	134	1	5	8	78	6	101	12	6
James, Mike, San Antonio	.091	15	11	0	1	2	1	0	0	2	5	0	1	0	0	5	0	0
Jenkins, Bernie, Jackson	.260	109	335	42	87	124	14	4	5	36	2	3	4	26	1	83	21	8
Johnson, Erik, Shreveport	.219	58	146	27	32	45	7	0	2	20	4	0	1	16	4	20	6	2
Jones, Bobby, Midland†	.221	82	285	35	63	78	12	0	1	35	2	0	2	21	1	53	4	3
Jones, Todd, Jackson	.071	10	14	0	1	1	0	0	0	1	1	0	0	0	0	5	0	0
Juden, Jeff, Jackson	.105	16	19	1	2	3	1	0	0	2	2	0	0	1	0	8	0	0
Kaiser, Keith, Jackson†	.250	14	4	1	1	1	0	0	0	1	2	1	0	1	0	2	0	0
Kasper, Kevin, Shreveport	.250	33	72	13	18	23	2	0	1	9	1	0	0	6	0	12	2	0
Kellner, Frank, Jackson†	.270	83	311	47	84	105	7	4	2	25	2	2	0	29	2	37	6	5
Knox, Kerry, Wichita*	.000	28	13	0	0	0	0	0	0	0	1	0	0	2	0	6	0	0
Kreuter, Chad, Tulsa†	.234	42	128	23	30	43	5	1	2	10	0	0	1	29	4	23	1	0
Kuld, Peter, 29 Wich.-33 Tul.	.211	62	218	20	46	70	6	0	6	19	1	1	0	10	1	66	2	0
Larose, Steve, Jackson†	.000	26	2	0	0	0	0	0	0	0	0	0	0	0	0	1	0	0
Lawton, Marcus, Midland†	.287	114	439	76	125	181	25	8	5	53	4	2	6	29	3	62	29	10
Lepley, John, Arkansas*	.000	16	1	0	0	0	0	0	0	0	0	0	0	0	0	0	0	0
Lewis, Alan, San Antonio*	.109	16	46	3	5	9	1	0	1	5	0	0	0	6	0	8	0	0
Lewis, Dan, Shreveport*	.291	118	422	66	123	194	30	1	13	90	2	6	9	50	8	76	7	10
Liddell, Dave, El Paso	.205	13	39	5	8	12	1	0	1	6	1	0	1	6	0	9	0	0
Listach, Pat, El Paso	.253	49	186	40	47	56	5	2	0	13	2	0	5	25	0	56	14	2
Lopez, Luis, Wichita†	.268	125	452	43	121	143	17	1	1	41	4	4	8	18	3	70	6	8
Lynch, Dave, San Antonio	.000	11	1	0	0	0	0	0	0	0	0	0	0	0	0	0	0	0
Madsen, Lance, Jackson	.221	123	407	54	90	142	21	5	7	50	2	3	5	41	8	122	8	3
Magnusson, Brett, San Antonio	.265	110	358	69	95	155	23	2	11	66	2	4	4	67	1	69	5	5
Majer, Steffen, Arkansas	.042	34	24	1	1	1	0	0	0	1	0	0	0	0	0	10	0	0
Makarewicz, Scott, Jackson	.231	76	229	23	53	68	9	0	2	30	0	3	8	18	6	36	1	5
Mallicoat, Rob, Jackson*	.000	18	1	0	0	0	0	0	0	0	0	0	0	0	0	1	0	0
Marabell, Scott, San Antonio	.217	51	83	11	18	25	4	0	1	7	0	1	3	5	0	32	1	1
Marquez, Isidro, San Antonio	.000	35	2	0	0	0	0	0	0	0	0	0	0	1	0	0	0	0
Martinez, Luis, Arkansas†	.271	93	280	28	76	103	17	2	2	32	1	0	2	32	2	32	6	4
Martinez, Pedro, San Antonio	.000	12	13	0	0	0	0	0	0	0	0	0	0	0	0	6	0	0
Martinez, Pedro, Wichita*	.136	26	22	1	3	3	0	0	0	0	5	0	0	1	0	7	0	0
Massarelli, John, Jackson	.211	12	38	3	8	10	2	0	0	0	0	0	1	0	2	4	0	
McClellan, Paul, Shreveport	.071	14	28	3	2	2	0	0	0	4	0	0	0	0	0	6	0	0
McConnell, Walt, Midland*	.284	77	264	41	75	112	14	1	7	65	0	5	1	48	2	44	1	1
McCoy, Trey, Tulsa	.241	44	137	21	33	70	7	0	10	32	0	2	2	33	4	26	0	0
McLemore, Mark, Jackson†	.227	7	22	6	5	11	3	0	1	4	0	0	0	6	0	3	1	0
McNamara, James, Shreveport*	.275	39	109	13	30	48	8	2	2	20	1	1	0	21	3	11	2	1
McWilliam, Tim, Wichita	.296	94	307	40	91	134	20	1	7	56	0	3	5	34	2	45	1	3
Meier, Kevin, Shreveport	.320	33	25	3	8	9	1	0	0	5	1	0	0	4	0	9	0	0
Melvin, Scott, Arkansas	.288	34	52	3	15	18	0	0	1	7	0	1	0	3	1	18	0	0
Mikulik, Joe, Jackson	.293	133	492	76	144	214	17	4	15	94	0	5	4	41	8	62	20	8
Milchin, Mike, Arkansas*	.000	6	6	1	0	0	0	0	0	0	1	0	1	0	3	0	2	0
Miller, Orlando, Jackson	.186	23	70	5	13	22	6	0	1	5	2	0	2	5	1	13	0	0
Mondesi, Raul, San Antonio	.272	53	213	32	58	94	11	5	5	26	0	3	4	8	0	47	8	3
Morris, Rod, Tulsa*	.269	103	383	44	103	136	17	8	0	35	6	1	2	28	3	60	9	6
Morrow, Chris, San Antonio*	.360	24	89	13	32	44	6	0	2	8	0	0	0	4	0	14	1	2
Munoz, Jose, San Antonio†	.317	31	123	25	39	49	6	2	0	13	3	0	1	12	1	14	4	2
Myers, Jim, Shreveport	.000	62	3	0	0	0	0	0	0	0	0	0	0	0	0	0	0	0
Nilsson, Dave, El Paso*	.418	65	249	52	104	149	24	3	5	57	0	2	1	27	4	14	4	0
Osborne, Donovan, Arkansas†	.303	26	33	6	10	13	3	0	0	5	1	0	0	4	0	10	1	0
Ozuna, Gab, Arkansas	.000	17	1	0	0	0	0	0	0	0	0	0	0	0	0	0	0	0
Patterson, Dave, Shreveport	.350	61	177	35	62	83	15	0	2	29	2	2	4	44	2	16	3	5
Patterson, John, Shreveport†	.295	117	464	81	137	206	31	13	4	56	3	3	11	30	2	63	41	20
Pena, Jim, Shreveport*	.111	45	9	2	1	1	0	0	0	2	0	1	0	2	0	1	0	0
Perez, David, Tulsa	.000	25	1	0	0	0	0	0	0	0	0	0	0	0	0	1	0	0
Perez, Vlad, Shreveport	.000	27	1	0	0	0	0	0	0	0	0	0	0	0	0	0	0	0
Peters, Rex, San Antonio*	.204	39	108	19	22	27	2	0	1	7	0	1	2	16	3	13	0	2
Plemel, Lee, Arkansas	.333	53	3	0	1	1	0	0	0	0	0	0	0	0	0	0	0	0
Prager, Howard, Jackson*	.305	109	357	57	109	172	26	2	11	65	4	3	2	52	6	75	9	6
Prybylinski, Don, Arkansas	.185	48	119	13	22	30	8	0	0	13	1	1	0	8	1	28	0	0
Rambo, Dan, Shreveport	.136	26	22	1	3	3	0	0	0	3	0	0	0	4	0	4	0	0
Rapp, Pat, Shreveport	.000	10	8	0	0	0	0	0	0	0	3	0	0	0	0	5	0	0
Redington, Tom, Wichita	.284	116	394	54	112	150	23	0	5	57	0	6	3	67	2	66	2	3
Redman, Tim, Arkansas	.341	22	44	3	15	17	2	0	0	1	0	0	0	4	0	9	0	0
Reichle, Darrin, Wichita†	.167	14	6	0	1	1	0	0	0	0	3	0	0	0	0	2	0	0
Renteria, Ed, Jackson	.288	18	59	11	17	23	3	0	1	6	0	0	1	4	1	5	2	0
Resnikoff, Bob, Jackson*	.000	26	3	0	0	0	0	0	0	0	0	0	0	0	0	0	0	0
Reynolds, Shane, Jackson	.037	27	27	0	1	2	1	0	0	4	0	0	2	0	16	0	0	
Rice, Lance, San Antonio†	.200	78	215	23	43	60	8	0	3	28	2	3	1	31	2	30	2	1
Richards, Dave, San Antonio*	.500	29	4	0	2	2	0	0	0	1	0	0	0	0	1	0	0	
Rivers, Ken, Midland	.257	32	109	11	28	41	7	0	2	15	0	0	3	11	0	19	1	1
Rodriguez, Ivan, Tulsa	.274	50	175	16	48	68	7	2	3	28	1	5	1	6	0	27	1	2
Rogers, Kevin, Shreveport†	.087	22	23	0	2	2	0	0	0	2	1	0	0	3	0	8	0	0
Rohrmeier, Dan, Tulsa	.292	121	418	67	122	161	20	2	5	62	4	7	4	60	1	57	3	2
Ross, Mike, Arkansas	.247	68	255	31	63	102	18	0	7	28	0	3	14	0	39	2	4	
Sable, Luke, Tulsa	.289	95	339	32	98	124	12	7	0	33	5	2	2	25	0	53	9	11
Sager, A.J., Arkansas	.000	30	6	1	0	0	0	0	0	0	1	0	0	2	0	2	0	0
Salmon, Tim, Midland	.245	131	465	100	114	217	26	4	23	94	3	2	6	89	1	166	12	6
Sambo, Ramon, Midland†	.286	55	161	24	46	55	5	2	0	10	2	0	2	29	4	23	14	8
Samson, Fred, Tulsa	.208	69	207	31	43	63	12	1	2	15	3	1	4	25	0	63	2	3
Sconiers, Daryl, Midland*	.275	29	102	15	28	48	8	0	4	14	0	1	0	11	1	18	2	0
Sebra, Bob, Jackson	.000	1	1	0	0	0	0	0	0	0	0	0	0	0	0	0	0	0
Sellick, John, Arkansas	.245	116	387	57	95	171	18	2	18	63	0	4	4	43	2	109	3	4

Player, Team	Avg.	G	AB	R	H	TB	2B	3B	HR	RBI	SH	SF	HP	BB	Int. BB	SO	SB	CS
Seminara, Frank, Wichita	.077	27	26	1	2	2	0	0	0	1	3	0	0	0	0	8	0	0
Sherman, Darrell, Wichita*	.295	131	502	93	148	180	17	3	3	48	2	6	9	74	1	28	43	21
Shinall, Zak, San Antonio	.000	25	3	0	0	0	0	0	0	0	1	0	0	0	0	1	0	0
Shireman, Jeff, Arkansas†	.242	117	368	49	89	106	12	1	1	28	4	3	0	45	0	32	2	4
Simon, Rich, Jackson	.000	56	4	0	0	0	0	0	0	0	0	0	0	0	0	2	0	0
Smiley, Reuben, Shreveport*	.230	104	318	57	73	104	8	4	5	31	5	0	2	55	9	59	36	9
Smithberg, Roger, Wichita	.000	7	2	0	0	0	0	0	0	0	1	0	0	0	0	1	0	0
Snyder, Randy, El Paso†	.208	8	24	7	5	6	1	0	0	1	0	1	0	5	0	5	1	0
Springer, Dennis, San Antonio	.190	30	21	1	4	5	1	0	0	2	1	0	0	0	0	7	0	0
Stephenson, Phil, Wichita*	.471	12	34	4	16	21	5	0	0	8	0	2	0	6	1	2	0	0
Stewart, Tito, Wichita*	.000	7	1	0	0	0	0	0	0	0	0	0	0	0	0	0	0	0
Stone, Brian, Arkansas	.000	2	0	0	0	0	0	0	0	0	1	0	0	0	0	0	0	0
Tatum, Jim, El Paso	.320	130	493	99	158	255	27	8	18	128	2	20	15	63	5	79	5	7
Taveras, Ramon, San Antonio	.000	8	2	0	0	0	0	0	0	0	0	0	0	0	0	0	0	0
Taylor, Rob, Shreveport	.167	39	6	1	1	1	0	0	0	1	0	0	0	0	0	4	0	0
Taylor, Terry, Midland*	.196	32	102	15	20	28	6	1	0	8	1	2	0	18	3	22	0	2
Terrill, Jimmy, San Antonio*	.000	27	6	0	0	0	0	0	0	0	0	0	0	0	0	2	0	0
Traxler, Brian, San Antonio*	.256	103	379	50	97	142	24	0	7	61	0	5	3	53	8	44	1	2
Treadwell, Jody, San Antonio	.143	10	7	0	1	1	0	0	0	1	2	1	0	0	0	2	0	0
Trevino, Alex, Midland	.227	14	44	8	10	19	3	0	2	10	1	0	0	5	0	6	0	0
Trice, Wally, Jackson*	.000	20	2	0	0	0	0	0	0	0	0	0	0	0	0	2	0	0
Tucker, Scooter, Shreveport	.284	110	352	49	100	143	29	1	4	49	6	2	5	48	1	57	3	4
Valentin, Jose, Wichita†	.251	129	447	73	112	195	22	5	17	68	4	5	4	55	1	115	8	6
Velasquez, Guillermo, Wichita*	.295	130	501	72	148	243	26	3	21	100	0	7	1	48	6	75	4	2
Wallace, Tim, 35 Wich.- 18 E.P.†	.269	53	167	20	45	50	2	0	1	16	2	1	0	13	0	18	7	0
Weber, Pete, Shreveport*	.250	38	116	21	29	37	8	0	0	7	1	0	1	17	2	26	6	6
Weese, Dean, Arkansas	1.000	14	1	0	1	1	0	0	0	0	0	0	0	0	0	0	0	0
White, Charlie, Arkansas	.237	107	329	33	78	106	16	3	2	30	5	1	0	33	2	62	11	9
White, Mike, San Antonio*	.291	93	254	25	74	98	13	4	1	37	1	2	1	11	1	40	5	3
Wilkins, Mike, San Antonio	.167	23	18	0	3	5	2	0	0	3	2	0	0	0	0	11	0	0
Williams, Brian, Jackson	.000	3	4	0	0	0	0	0	0	0	1	0	0	0	0	0	0	0
Williams, Reggie, Midland†	.310	83	319	77	99	120	12	3	1	30	5	3	0	62	2	67	21	9
Windes, Rodney, Jackson*	.000	13	1	2	0	0	0	0	0	0	0	0	0	1	0	0	0	0
Wiseman, Dennis, Arkansas	.212	26	33	1	7	9	2	0	0	7	3	0	0	0	0	10	0	0
Wray, James, San Antonio	.000	43	1	0	0	0	0	0	0	0	0	0	0	0	0	0	0	0
Wrona, Rick, Tulsa	.159	27	82	4	13	24	0	1	3	7	0	0	0	5	0	18	0	2
Young, Eric, San Antonio	.280	127	461	82	129	163	17	4	3	35	8	1	2	67	0	36	70	26

The following pitchers, listed alphabetically by club, with games in parentheses, had no plate appearances, primarily through use of designated hitters:

ARKANSAS—Compres, Fidel (27); Corona, John (27); Kisten, Dale (36); Richardson, Dave (12); Salvior, Troy (13).

EL PASO—Alba, Gibson (3); Ambrose, Mark (19); Carter, Larry (1); Chapman, Mark (45); Czajkowski, Jim (43); Davino, Mike (12); Everson, Greg (7); Fortugno, Tim (20); Freeland, Dean (7); Gordon, Don (7); Green, Otis (10); Johnson, Chris (13); Kiefer, Mark (12); Lienhard, Steve (26); Mathews, Greg (2); McGraw, Tom (9); Miranda, Angel (38); Monson, Steve (17); Schwarz, Jeff (27); Smith, Mike (12); Sparks, Steve (4); Vann, Brandy (19); Wishnevski, Rob (7).

JACKSON—Freeland, Dean (1).

MIDLAND—Acosta, Clemente (37); Berrios, Hector (18); Bockus, Randy (12); Butcher, Mike (41); Carter, Glenn (8); Cobb, Marvin (42); Corbett, Sherman (13); Holzemer, Mark (2); James, Todd (27); King, Steve (5); Leftwich, Phillip (1); Martinez, Fili (15); Montalvo, Rafael (22); Pawlowski, John (15); Robertson, Doug (36); Shotkoski, Dave (23); Sontag, Alan (15); Valenzuela, Fernando (4); Vidmar, Don (22); Zappelli, Mark (32).

SAN ANTONIO—Allen, Steve (12); Brosnan, Jason (2); Calhoun, Ray (21); Coleman, Dale (32); Tapia, Jose (2).

SHREVEPORT—Peltzer, Kurt (5); Reed, Steve (15).

TULSA—Bohanon, Brian (2); Bronkey, Jeff (4); Brown, Rob (44); Campbell, Mike (23); Cunningham, Everett (22); Felix, Nick (11); Gies, Christopher (8); Gore, Bryan (27); Hayward, Ray (8); Hurst, Jon (5); Manuel, Barry (56); McCray, Eric (21); Menendez, Tony (3); Nen, Robb (9); Reed, Bobby (12); Romero, Brian (23); Rowley, Steve (10); Shaw, Cedric (26); Shiflett, Chris (4).

WICHITA—Hammaker, Atlee (5); Lewis, Jim (2); Wood, Brian (11).

GRAND SLAMS—D. Harris, 2; Alvarez, Ealy, Fanning, J. Fernandez, Flora, Garman, L. Gonzales, Gonzalez, Hosey, Howie, Jaha, D. Lewis, Madsen, McCoy, Prager, Salmon, Trevino, Valentin, 1 each.

AWARDED FIRST BASE ON CATCHER'S INTERFERENCE—Hosey 2 (Faulkner, Makarewicz); Barns (Baar); Burgos (Eusebio); Hunter (Faulkner); Rohrmeier (Tatum).

PITCHING

TEAM

Team	ERA	G	CG	ShO	Sv.	IP	H	R	ER	HR	HB	BB	Int. BB	SO	WP	Bk.
Shreveport	3.48	136	13	13	38	1177.0	1117	540	455	71	22	438	31	883	59	15
Jackson	4.00	137	7	8	32	1164.1	1039	643	518	61	61	679	22	947	120	12
San Antonio	4.27	137	14	12	20	1168.2	1234	677	554	94	38	500	43	858	42	19
Tulsa	4.41	136	15	6	35	1163.1	1161	670	570	98	54	547	25	821	66	26
Arkansas	4.42	136	13	5	22	1122.0	1191	661	551	63	41	486	78	805	68	14
Wichita	4.57	136	14	9	29	1187.0	1289	725	603	116	48	444	26	747	72	22
El Paso	4.70	136	8	4	32	1178.2	1283	732	616	54	41	604	36	950	91	14
Midland	4.90	136	11	3	29	1170.1	1406	797	637	104	53	508	8	747	83	14

INDIVIDUAL

(Leading qualifiers for earned-run average leadership—109 or more innings)

*Throws lefthanded.

Pitcher, Team	W	L	Pct.	ERA	G	GS	CG	GF	ShO	Sv.	IP	H	R	ER	HR	HB	BB	Int. BB	SO	WP
Larry G. Carter, Shreveport	9	8	.529	2.95	24	24	1	0	1	0	149.1	124	61	49	8	3	51	2	133	3
Gardner, Jackson	13	5	.722	3.15	22	22	1	0	1	0	131.1	116	57	46	6	8	75	1	72	10
Vidmar, Midland	13	5	.722	3.16	22	22	5	0	0	0	145.1	168	67	51	3	6	47	0	64	6
Brown, Tulsa	7	6	.538	3.29	43	4	1	17	0	4	117.2	130	59	43	3	6	39	5	86	6
Rogers, Shreveport*	4	6	.400	3.36	22	22	2	0	0	0	118.0	124	63	44	7	2	54	4	108	12
Seminara, Wichita	15	10	.600	3.38	27	27	6	0	1	0	176.0	173	86	66	10	9	68	0	107	12
Osborne, Arkansas*	8	12	.400	3.63	27	26	3	0	0	0	166.0	178	82	67	6	4	43	3	130	4
Rambo, Shreveport	12	6	.667	3.67	26	21	1	1	1	0	147.0	146	71	60	12	4	43	2	103	8

Pitcher, Team	W	L	Pct.	ERA	G	GS	CG	GF	ShO	Sv.	IP	H	R	ER	HR	HB	BB	Int. BB	SO	WP
Brocail, Wichita	10	7	.588	3.87	34	16	3	11	3	6	146.1	147	77	63	15	4	43	3	108	13
Shaw, Tulsa*	9	8	.529	4.06	26	23	1	1	0	0	142.0	142	76	64	9	3	66	0	111	14

Departmental leaders: G—Myers, 62; W—Seminara, 15; L—Wiseman, 15; Pct.—McClelland, .917; GS—T. James, Reynolds, Seminara, 27; CG—Seminara, 6; GF—Myers, 55; ShO—Ard, Brocail, Pedro J. Martinez, 3; Sv.—Manuel, 25; IP—Seminara, 176.0; H—T. James, 186; R—T. James, 104; ER—Pedro A. Martinez, 91; HR—Pedro A. Martinez, 21; HB—Cunningham, Romero, Seminara, 9; BB—Coffman, 101; IBB—Kisten, Plemel, 10; SO—Springer, 138; WP—Coffman, 30.

(All pitchers—listed alphabetically)

Pitcher, Team	W	L	Pct.	ERA	G	GS	CG	GF	ShO	Sv.	IP	H	R	ER	HR	HB	BB	Int. BB	SO	WP
Abreu, Arkansas	0	0	.000	27.00	1	0	0	1	0	0	1.0	3	3	3	1	0	1	0	0	0
Acosta, Midland*	0	6	.000	7.28	37	3	0	9	0	0	71.2	109	77	58	13	4	27	1	59	6
Alba, El Paso*	1	1	.500	11.57	3	0	0	1	0	0	2.1	5	3	3	1	0	4	0	2	0
Allen, Jackson*	4	7	.364	4.50	26	14	0	2	0	0	92.0	90	65	46	10	3	73	3	61	11
Allen, San Antonio	1	0	1.000	4.43	12	0	0	7	0	1	20.1	22	10	10	1	3	10	0	25	0
Ambrose, El Paso	10	6	.625	4.26	19	19	1	0	0	0	112.0	120	59	53	5	5	58	1	81	10
Ard, Shreveport	9	3	.750	2.74	13	13	4	0	3	0	88.2	77	31	27	4	2	36	0	58	4
Astacio, San Antonio	4	11	.267	4.78	19	19	2	0	1	0	113.0	142	67	60	9	3	39	3	62	4
August, Jackson	1	2	.333	5.24	7	7	0	0	0	0	34.1	27	22	20	2	2	19	0	25	1
Barns, Arkansas	0	0	.000	0.00	1	0	0	1	0	0	2.0	0	0	0	0	0	0	0	2	0
Bauer, Jackson	3	7	.300	3.81	46	0	0	15	0	1	78.0	50	36	33	6	3	33	3	80	8
Berrios, Midland*	2	1	.667	2.81	18	0	0	9	0	2	16.0	13	5	5	3	1	3	0	17	0
Biberdorf, San Antonio	0	3	.000	8.84	14	0	0	8	0	1	18.1	23	19	18	1	1	12	4	18	3
Bockus, Midland	3	0	1.000	7.27	12	0	0	7	0	0	17.1	28	15	14	3	1	6	1	10	1
Bohanon, Tulsa*	0	1	.000	2.31	2	2	0	0	0	0	11.2	9	8	3	0	0	11	0	6	0
Brannon, Arkansas	1	0	1.000	6.75	2	0	0	2	0	0	2.2	3	2	2	0	1	4	1	3	1
Brocail, Wichita	10	7	.588	3.87	34	16	3	11	3	6	146.1	147	77	63	15	4	43	3	108	13
Bronkey, Tulsa	0	0	.000	9.39	4	0	0	3	0	0	7.2	11	9	8	0	2	5	0	5	2
Brosnan, San Antonio*	0	1	.000	17.61	2	0	0	0	0	0	7.2	15	15	15	2	0	11	0	8	0
Brown, Tulsa	7	6	.538	3.29	43	4	1	17	0	4	117.2	130	59	43	3	6	39	5	86	6
Bryand, Wichita*	3	2	.600	3.09	37	1	0	14	0	1	55.1	53	23	19	3	2	14	5	34	3
Bustillos, San Antonio	5	5	.500	4.65	16	14	1	1	0	0	93.0	113	51	48	6	1	23	0	47	1
Butcher, Midland	9	6	.600	5.22	41	6	0	13	0	3	88.0	93	54	51	6	8	46	0	70	4
Calhoun, San Antonio	0	3	.000	6.37	21	0	0	11	0	1	29.2	34	26	21	2	1	18	3	11	1
Campbell, Tulsa	5	7	.417	5.23	23	15	3	2	0	1	108.1	104	68	63	14	1	51	5	90	3
Carter, Shreveport	9	8	.529	2.95	24	24	1	0	1	0	149.1	124	61	49	8	3	51	2	133	3
Carter, El Paso	0	0	.000	9.00	1	1	0	0	0	0	3.0	5	3	3	1	0	1	0	1	0
Carter, Midland	1	6	.143	8.26	8	8	0	0	0	0	40.1	69	46	37	5	0	26	1	13	3
Cassidy, Arkansas*	2	2	.500	7.62	6	6	0	0	0	0	28.1	44	26	24	3	2	15	1	15	0
Chapman, El Paso	4	3	.571	3.72	45	0	0	20	0	5	92.0	90	40	38	0	2	37	3	63	3
Chavez, Wichita	3	0	1.000	5.20	38	0	0	11	0	3	71.0	80	54	41	6	6	41	3	49	7
Clark, Arkansas	5	5	.500	4.00	15	15	4	0	1	0	92.1	99	50	41	2	2	30	4	76	0
Cobb, Midland	2	2	.500	4.04	42	0	0	19	0	3	78.0	73	49	35	9	3	45	1	72	8
Coffman, Jackson	8	7	.533	5.03	30	19	1	4	1	1	105.2	79	71	59	3	6	101	0	105	30
Coleman, San Antonio	1	2	.333	3.42	32	0	0	14	0	1	50.0	56	32	19	2	3	24	3	36	2
Compres, Arkansas	4	2	.667	3.94	27	0	0	26	0	9	32.0	37	17	14	2	0	12	3	18	2
Cook, San Antonio*	1	3	.250	2.49	7	7	1	0	0	0	50.2	43	20	14	2	1	10	1	45	0
Corbett, Midland*	0	1	.000	3.33	13	0	0	6	0	1	24.1	24	12	9	3	1	9	0	17	1
Corona, Arkansas*	0	2	.000	4.45	27	0	0	17	0	0	30.1	26	15	15	0	0	21	3	23	3
Cunningham, 21 Tul.- 16 Wich.	0	5	.000	7.43	37	1	0	15	0	0	66.2	77	65	55	7	9	41	3	48	9
Czajkowski, El Paso	5	2	.714	4.94	43	0	0	32	0	11	78.1	100	54	43	5	3	29	4	69	5
Davino, El Paso	1	1	.500	5.61	12	1	0	4	0	2	25.2	36	17	16	0	0	14	1	13	2
Davis, Wichita	5	6	.455	3.98	50	0	0	43	0	13	72.1	82	36	32	6	2	19	3	57	3
Ericks, Arkansas	5	14	.263	4.77	25	25	1	0	0	0	139.2	138	94	74	6	7	84	3	103	15
Escalera, El Paso*	0	0	.000	0.00	1	1	0	0	0	0	1.0	0	0	0	0	0	0	0	0	0
Everson, El Paso	0	0	.000	7.36	7	0	0	4	0	0	11.0	18	11	9	0	1	5	0	3	1
Faccio, Arkansas	7	8	.467	3.76	20	16	0	4	0	1	105.1	102	50	44	6	3	39	7	74	6
Felix, Tulsa*	0	0	.000	6.65	11	0	0	8	0	0	21.2	22	17	16	4	0	10	0	16	1
Fortugno, El Paso*	5	1	.833	1.99	20	3	0	13	0	1	54.1	40	15	12	1	0	25	1	73	3
Freeland, 1 Jack.- 7 E.P.	3	2	.600	4.76	8	6	0	1	0	1	39.2	46	23	21	2	3	17	1	25	7
Galindez, Wichita*	2	8	.200	6.41	17	17	0	0	0	0	85.2	116	73	61	14	2	43	0	43	3
Gardner, Jackson	13	5	.722	3.15	22	22	1	0	1	0	131.1	116	57	46	6	8	75	1	72	10
Gies, Tulsa	2	2	.500	4.82	8	7	0	1	0	0	37.1	51	29	20	4	2	13	0	25	1
Gilmore, Wichita	1	2	.333	6.04	9	2	0	1	0	0	25.1	28	19	17	6	1	7	0	18	2
Gonzales, Arkansas*	0	1	.000	3.86	3	1	0	0	0	0	9.1	6	4	4	1	0	10	0	5	0
Gordon, El Paso	0	0	.000	7.98	7	0	0	1	0	0	14.2	20	15	13	3	3	2	1	7	1
Gore, Tulsa*	7	8	.467	4.28	27	12	0	7	0	2	107.1	122	66	51	14	5	33	5	60	3
Green, El Paso*	3	3	.500	3.18	9	9	1	0	0	0	51.0	35	21	18	4	1	25	1	49	4
Grovom, Jackson*	1	1	.500	3.63	10	0	0	2	0	0	17.1	18	9	7	1	2	8	0	17	2
Hammaker, Wichita*	0	1	.000	3.52	5	0	0	1	0	0	7.2	10	3	3	0	0	4	0	9	0
Hartgraves, Jackson*	6	5	.545	2.68	19	9	3	5	0	0	74.0	60	25	22	3	2	25	3	44	4
Haslock, Wichita	0	0	.000	6.62	10	1	0	5	0	0	17.2	21	19	13	5	5	13	0	9	0
Hayward, Tulsa*	0	3	.000	4.45	8	3	1	2	0	0	28.1	33	16	14	1	0	13	0	21	4
Hershiser, San Antonio	0	1	.000	2.57	1	1	0	0	0	0	7.0	11	3	2	1	0	1	0	5	0
Hickerson, Shreveport*	3	4	.429	3.00	23	0	0	6	0	2	39.0	36	15	13	2	0	14	3	41	2
Hilton, Wichita	3	1	.750	4.78	26	0	0	12	0	3	37.2	37	26	20	2	2	17	3	31	3
Holzemer, Midland	0	0	.000	1.42	2	2	0	0	0	0	6.1	3	2	1	0	1	5	0	7	2
Hostetler, Shreveport	4	1	.800	3.55	9	9	0	0	0	0	45.2	39	19	18	0	1	20	0	33	0
Hubbard, Jackson	0	0	.000	0.00	1	0	0	0	0	0	1.0	0	1	0	0	0	0	0	0	0
Hunter, Jackson	0	0	.000	0.00	3	0	0	3	0	0	2.0	3	1	0	0	0	2	0	0	0
Hurst, Tulsa	2	1	.667	2.16	5	2	1	3	0	1	25.0	18	6	6	1	2	6	0	17	1
James, San Antonio	9	5	.643	4.53	15	15	2	0	1	0	89.1	88	54	45	10	4	51	1	74	4
James, Midland*	12	10	.545	4.81	27	27	4	0	1	0	161.0	186	104	86	10	5	73	0	94	17
Johnson, El Paso	4	4	.500	6.48	13	12	0	1	0	0	66.2	85	56	48	4	4	40	4	43	5
Jones, Jackson	4	3	.571	4.88	10	10	0	0	0	0	55.1	51	37	30	2	4	39	1	37	6
Juden, San Antonio	6	3	.667	3.10	16	16	0	0	0	0	95.2	84	43	33	4	3	44	0	75	0
Kaiser, Jackson	1	4	.200	11.54	14	9	0	0	0	0	39.0	40	62	50	3	8	71	1	41	21
Kiefer, El Paso	7	1	.875	3.33	12	12	0	0	0	0	75.2	62	33	28	4	1	43	2	72	6
King, Midland	0	3	.000	12.39	5	5	0	0	0	0	20.1	40	34	28	5	2	16	0	12	4
Kisten, Arkansas	1	5	.167	6.57	36	0	0	13	0	1	49.1	66	39	36	3	2	41	10	44	8
Knox, Wichita	4	4	.500	4.91	28	15	1	1	1	0	113.2	133	72	62	13	4	36	1	51	5
Kuld, Tulsa	0	0	.000	9.00	1	0	0	0	0	0	1.0	1	2	1	0	0	3	0	1	0

Pitcher, Team	W	L	Pct.	ERA	G	GS	CG	GF	ShO	Sv.	IP	H	R	ER	HR	HB	BB	Int. BB	SO	WP
LaRose, Jackson	1	3	.250	4.05	26	0	0	14	0	6	33.1	34	23	15	0	7	22	0	29	2
Leftwich, Midland	1	0	1.000	3.00	1	1	0	0	0	0	6.0	5	2	2	0	0	5	0	3	0
Lepley, Arkansas*	1	2	.333	4.41	16	0	0	9	0	0	16.1	17	8	8	2	0	14	4	7	3
Lewis, Wichita	0	0	.000	0.00	2	0	0	1	0	1	2.2	4	2	0	0	0	4	0	3	0
Lienhard, El Paso	9	9	.500	4.83	26	17	1	4	0	0	121.0	157	79	65	4	4	43	6	69	4
Lynch, San Antonio*	0	1	.000	6.75	11	0	0	7	0	1	13.1	17	11	10	2	0	6	0	10	1
Majer, Arkansas	4	6	.400	4.44	34	12	1	6	0	0	97.1	91	59	48	6	3	57	6	72	5
Mallicoat, Jackson*	4	1	.800	3.77	18	0	0	6	0	1	31.0	20	15	13	1	2	11	1	34	2
Manuel, Tulsa	2	7	.222	3.29	56	0	0	48	0	25	68.1	63	29	25	5	5	34	1	45	1
Marquez, San Antonio	4	1	.800	2.09	34	0	0	22	0	3	47.1	42	16	11	1	1	19	8	36	1
Martinez, Midland*	4	5	.444	6.44	15	15	0	0	0	0	81.0	104	72	58	16	3	50	0	42	3
Martinez, Wichita	11	10	.524	5.23	26	26	3	0	2	0	156.2	169	99	91	21	3	57	2	95	7
Martinez, San Antonio	7	5	.583	1.76	12	12	4	0	3	0	76.2	57	21	15	1	3	31	1	74	5
Mathews, El Paso*	0	0	.000	6.30	2	2	0	0	0	0	10.0	11	9	7	0	0	6	0	8	1
McClellan, Shreveport	11	1	.917	2.82	14	14	1	0	1	0	95.2	75	33	30	4	2	30	0	63	9
McCray, Tulsa*	4	3	.571	4.65	21	2	0	7	0	0	40.2	32	23	21	3	1	32	1	31	4
McGraw, El Paso*	1	1	.500	5.80	9	7	0	2	0	1	35.2	43	28	23	1	1	21	0	28	0
Meier, Shreveport	9	6	.600	5.04	33	18	2	3	0	0	135.2	157	86	76	15	1	38	2	79	10
Menendez, Tulsa	3	0	1.000	1.29	3	2	0	1	0	0	14.0	9	2	2	0	0	4	0	14	0
Milchin, Arkansas*	3	2	.600	3.06	6	6	1	0	1	0	35.1	27	13	12	1	0	8	2	38	1
Miranda, El Paso*	4	2	.667	2.54	38	0	0	24	0	11	74.1	55	27	21	2	1	41	1	86	8
Monson, El Paso	3	4	.429	5.91	17	10	1	4	0	0	64.0	84	49	42	1	0	28	3	38	2
Montalvo, Midland	5	1	.833	5.62	22	2	0	1	0	0	57.2	89	39	36	4	1	15	1	30	2
Myers, Shreveport	6	4	.600	2.48	62	0	0	55	0	24	76.1	71	22	21	2	2	30	5	51	4
Nen, Tulsa	0	2	.000	5.79	6	6	0	0	0	0	28.0	24	21	18	6	2	20	0	23	3
Osborne, Arkansas*	8	12	.400	3.63	26	26	3	0	0	0	166.0	178	82	67	6	4	43	3	130	4
Ozuna, Arkansas	0	2	.000	6.08	17	0	0	6	0	2	23.2	26	20	16	5	2	15	6	25	4
Pawlowski, Midland	1	3	.250	2.49	15	6	0	6	0	0	47.0	42	14	13	5	1	16	0	36	4
Peltzer, Shreveport*	0	1	.000	8.53	5	0	0	3	0	0	6.1	13	9	6	1	0	7	1	1	0
Pena, Shreveport*	7	4	.636	4.77	45	3	1	16	0	2	83.0	84	56	44	9	0	41	5	51	3
Perez, Tulsa	5	14	.263	4.22	25	24	4	0	2	0	147.0	130	76	69	11	4	69	3	97	5
Perez, Arkansas*	1	1	.500	3.35	27	0	0	11	0	1	43.0	40	16	16	0	0	19	1	22	0
Plemel, Arkansas	1	3	.250	3.30	53	1	1	17	0	3	84.2	87	41	31	4	4	25	10	57	11
Rambo, Shreveport	12	6	.667	3.67	26	21	1	1	1	0	147.0	146	71	60	12	4	43	2	103	8
Rapp, Shreveport	6	2	.750	2.69	10	10	1	0	1	0	60.1	52	23	18	1	3	22	0	46	1
Reed, Tulsa	4	4	.500	2.55	12	11	2	1	0	1	67.0	62	24	19	1	0	22	2	33	2
Reed, Shreveport	2	0	1.000	0.83	15	0	0	14	0	7	21.2	17	2	2	1	0	3	0	26	0
Reichle, Wichita	4	3	.571	5.02	14	14	0	0	0	0	57.1	63	37	32	3	1	27	1	32	6
Renteria, Jackson	0	0	.000	0.00	1	0	0	1	0	0	1.0	1	0	0	0	1	0	1	0	
Resnikoff, Jackson*	1	1	.500	3.00	26	0	0	7	0	1	42.0	40	18	14	3	2	13	1	34	3
Reynolds, Jackson*	8	9	.471	4.47	27	27	2	0	0	0	151.0	165	93	75	8	2	62	1	116	4
Richards, Jackson*	1	1	.500	2.66	29	0	0	11	0	1	44.0	30	13	13	3	2	22	1	55	1
Richardson, Arkansas*	1	2	.333	2.51	12	0	0	11	0	2	14.1	14	5	4	1	0	3	1	12	0
Robertson, Midland	2	2	.500	4.82	36	0	0	24	0	9	52.1	65	31	28	4	2	23	2	40	1
Rogers, Shreveport*	4	6	.400	3.36	22	22	0	0	2	0	118.0	124	63	44	7	2	54	4	108	12
Romero, Tulsa*	6	5	.545	4.98	23	14	2	5	0	1	94.0	92	61	52	11	9	52	1	79	4
Rowley, Tulsa	2	4	.333	6.02	10	8	0	0	1	0	43.1	48	32	29	5	6	27	0	24	7
Sable, Tulsa	0	0	.000	36.00	2	0	0	1	0	0	2.0	5	8	8	1	2	4	0	0	0
Sager, Wichita	4	3	.571	4.13	10	10	1	0	0	0	65.1	69	35	30	5	0	16	0	31	1
Salvior, Arkansas	0	2	.000	6.27	13	0	0	7	0	4	18.2	24	18	13	2	1	10	4	13	1
Schwarz, El Paso	11	8	.579	4.89	27	24	3	1	1	0	141.2	139	91	77	11	8	97	1	134	19
Sebra, Jackson	0	0	.000	0.00	1	0	0	1	0	0	2.1	1	0	0	0	0	0	0	3	0
Seminara, Wichita	15	10	.600	3.38	27	27	6	0	1	0	176.0	173	86	66	10	9	68	0	107	12
Shaw, Tulsa*	9	8	.529	4.06	26	23	1	1	0	0	142.0	142	76	64	9	3	66	0	111	14
Shiflett, Tulsa	0	0	.000	5.59	4	0	0	2	0	0	9.2	7	6	6	1	0	5	1	12	0
Shinall, San Antonio	2	4	.333	2.96	25	5	0	19	0	9	54.2	53	31	18	4	0	21	2	29	1
Shotkoski, Midland	5	11	.313	4.28	23	22	1	1	0	0	130.1	161	91	62	9	7	40	0	85	10
Simon, Jackson	4	2	.667	2.18	56	0	0	43	0	20	70.1	55	23	17	3	3	30	4	54	4
Smith, El Paso	3	3	.500	5.22	11	10	1	1	0	0	50.0	52	44	29	0	4	29	1	44	5
Smithberg, Wichita	2	3	.400	4.79	7	7	0	0	0	0	41.1	49	28	22	3	1	16	1	23	3
Sontag, Midland	2	3	.400	6.33	15	13	0	0	0	0	69.2	90	63	49	3	5	37	1	26	5
Sparks, El Paso	1	2	.333	9.53	4	4	0	0	0	0	17.0	30	22	18	1	0	9	0	10	2
Springer, San Antonio	10	10	.500	4.43	30	24	2	0	0	0	164.2	153	96	81	18	5	91	2	138	7
Stewart, Wichita*	0	0	.000	3.38	7	0	0	4	0	0	8.0	10	3	3	0	0	1	0	1	0
Stone, Arkansas	0	1	.000	7.11	2	2	0	0	0	0	6.1	9	6	5	0	1	6	0	6	0
Tapia, San Antonio	0	0	.000	9.00	2	0	0	2	0	1	2.0	4	2	2	1	0	0	0	2	0
Tatum, El Paso	0	0	.000	0.00	1	0	0	0	0	0	1.0	0	0	0	0	0	0	0	3	0
Taveras, San Antonio	0	1	.000	12.81	8	4	0	3	0	0	19.2	31	28	28	5	1	15	0	15	3
Taylor, San Antonio	3	3	.500	4.14	39	2	0	14	0	2	67.1	62	33	31	5	2	30	6	68	3
Terrill, San Antonio*	2	6	.250	3.25	27	7	1	6	1	0	72.0	69	34	26	2	2	33	3	36	5
Treadwell, San Antonio	3	3	.500	4.72	10	10	1	0	0	0	61.0	73	41	32	7	4	22	1	43	0
Trice, Jackson*	1	3	.250	4.18	20	0	0	12	0	1	23.2	26	12	11	2	0	5	0	27	0
Valenzuela, Midland*	3	1	.750	1.96	4	4	1	0	1	0	23.0	18	5	5	1	0	6	0	17	5
Vann, El Paso	2	3	.400	9.85	19	0	0	10	0	0	24.2	41	30	27	3	6	26	2	24	3
Vidmar, Midland	13	5	.722	3.16	22	22	5	0	0	0	145.1	168	67	51	3	6	47	0	64	6
Wallace, El Paso	0	0	.000	1.50	4	0	0	4	0	0	6.0	2	1	1	0	1	2	0	3	0
Weese, Arkansas	0	1	.000	9.61	14	0	0	4	0	0	19.2	27	23	21	4	2	14	3	15	1
Wilkins, San Antonio	6	6	.500	4.30	22	15	0	5	0	1	111.0	130	68	53	13	4	38	5	87	4
Williams, Jackson	2	1	.667	4.20	3	3	0	0	0	0	15.0	17	8	7	1	0	7	0	15	3
Windes, Jackson*	1	0	1.000	1.29	13	0	0	5	0	0	21.0	23	5	3	0	0	15	2	19	1
Wiseman, Arkansas*	6	15	.286	4.16	26	26	2	0	0	0	149.1	167	86	69	9	8	35	7	72	3
Wishnevski, El Paso	4	0	1.000	3.94	7	0	0	3	0	0	16.0	17	8	7	1	1	6	3	9	1
Wood, Wichita	4	2	.667	2.30	11	0	0	10	0	2	15.2	12	5	4	1	0	7	2	20	0
Wray, San Antonio	6	4	.600	3.48	43	0	0	18	0	1	67.1	58	32	26	4	1	25	6	56	0
Zappelli, Midland	2	2	.500	2.48	32	0	0	29	0	11	32.2	26	15	9	2	1	13	0	31	1

BALKS—Shaw, 9; Galindez, 6; Reichle, 5; Cook, Osborne, D. Perez, Romero, Terrill, 4 each; Davis, Ericks, Hayward, Rambo, Schwarz, Seminara, Shinall, 3 each; Alba, Astacio, Cassidy, Gore, Hilton, T. James, Jones, Juden, King, Knox, Mallicoat, Mathews, McClellan, Pena, Reynolds, Rogers, Shotkoski, Sontag, Taylor, Treadwell, 2 each; Ard, Bauer, Bryand, Bustillos, Campbell, G. Carter, Cobb, Corbett, Corona, Czajkowski, Everson, Fortugno, Freeland, Gardner, Gordon, Hershiser, Hickerson, Hostetler, Kisten, LaRose, Manuel, F. Martinez, Pedro J. Martinez, Milchin, Nen, Pawlowski, V. Perez, Richardson, Shiflett, Sparks, Tatum, Taveras, Vidmar, Windes, Wiseman, 1 each.

COMBINATION SHUTOUTS—Faccio-Ozuna, Faccio-Richardson, Osborne-Plemel, Arkansas; Ambrose-Miranda, Green-Chapman, Smith-Miranda, El Paso; August-Resnikoff-Grovom-Simon, August-Resnikoff-Simon, Coffman-Richards-Windes, Gardner-Hartgraves, Gardner-Simon, Hartgraves-Bauer-Trice-Simon, Jackson; Butcher-Corbett, Midland; Cook-Marquez, James-Shinall, Martinez-Calhoun, Martinez-Marquez,

Springer-Calhoun, Wilkins-Wray, San Antonio; Carter-Myers 3, Ard-Meier, Rambo-Myers, Taylor-Myers, Shreveport; Gore-Brown-Manuel, Reed-Shiflett, Romero-Hayward-Brown-Manuel, Shaw-Cunningham-Manuel, Tulsa; Brocail-Bryand-Davis, Martinez-Brocail, Wichita.

NO-HIT GAMES—Shaw-Cunningham-Manuel, Tulsa, defeated Arkansas, 2-0, April 18; Knox, Wichita, defeated Tulsa, 1-0 (second game), May 17.

FIELDING

TEAM

Team	Pct.	G	PO	A	E	DP	PB	Team	Pct.	G	PO	A	E	DP	PB
Shreveport	.971	136	3531	1328	143	128	14	Wichita	.967	136	3561	1537	172	118	18
Arkansas	.969	136	3366	1466	154	114	12	El Paso	.966	136	3536	1404	174	140	15
San Antonio	.969	137	3506	1498	160	141	24	Jackson	.964	137	3493	1479	188	126	20
Tulsa	.968	136	3490	1519	165	137	9	Midland	.961	136	3511	1549	203	126	18

INDIVIDUAL

*Throws lefthanded.

FIRST BASEMEN

Player, Team	Pct.	G	PO	A	E	DP
Baldwin, Jackson*	.992	11	110	11	1	7
Barbara, Midland*	.990	63	548	55	6	43
Brown, San Antonio	1.000	3	12	0	0	3
Burton, Tulsa	.989	105	920	66	11	99
Cisarik, Wichita*	1.000	25	198	13	0	16
Cooper, El Paso	.990	21	178	13	2	26
Davenport, Shreveport	.987	29	217	12	3	25
David, Wichita	1.000	1	5	0	0	0
Ealy, Shreveport	1.000	2	13	0	0	2
Escalera, El Paso*	.983	7	56	3	1	3
Faulkner, El Paso	1.000	1	6	0	0	1
Federico, Arkansas*	.981	29	193	12	4	16
Joey Fernandez, Arkansas	1.000	14	123	8	0	15
Finken, San Antonio	1.000	1	1	0	0	0
Gonzales, Midland	1.000	2	4	0	0	0
Gonzalez, San Antonio	1.000	3	3	1	0	0
Green, Tulsa	.968	10	86	6	3	7
Harris, Jackson	.955	3	21	0	1	5
Howie, Midland	.991	58	477	52	5	47
Hubbard, Jackson	1.000	1	1	0	0	1
Hunter, Jackson	.983	25	163	12	3	16
Jaha, El Paso	.992	109	880	81	8	92
Lewis, Shreveport*	.987	85	670	31	9	66
Magnusson, San Antonio	.978	7	41	3	1	2
Makarewicz, Jackson	1.000	3	6	1	0	1
McConnell, Midland	.952	11	72	8	4	6
McCoy, Tulsa	.981	21	194	9	4	15
McNamara, Shreveport	1.000	1	1	0	0	0
Melvin, Arkansas	1.000	1	1	0	0	0
D. Patterson, Shreveport	.991	30	194	19	2	22
Peters, San Antonio*	.997	34	277	26	1	26
Prager, Jackson*	.985	106	813	52	13	78
Renteria, Jackson	.955	3	18	3	1	4
Ross, Arkansas	.963	3	24	2	1	1
Samson, Tulsa	1.000	3	23	3	0	2
Sconiers, Midland*	1.000	12	94	7	0	11
Sellick, Arkansas	.984	101	814	73	14	61
Smiley, Shreveport*	1.000	2	7	0	0	1
Tatum, El Paso	1.000	1	10	1	0	1
TRAXLER, San Antonio*	.993	98	815	57	6	85
Velasquez, Wichita	.900	118	1092	69	12	93

SECOND BASEMEN

Player, Team	Pct.	G	PO	A	E	DP
Abreu, Arkansas	1.000	2	0	4	0	0
Alfonzo, Midland	1.000	6	16	14	0	3
Alvarez, San Antonio	.946	38	80	113	11	36
Bournigal, San Antonio	1.000	4	14	18	0	5
Burgos, Tulsa	.962	4	11	14	1	5
Byington, El Paso	1.000	3	6	4	0	3
Davis, Midland	.969	13	25	38	2	9
Ebel, San Antonio	1.000	4	9	1	0	0
Fanning, Arkansas	.965	54	112	133	9	35
Finn, El Paso	.974	61	126	177	8	45
Flora, Midland	.963	120	272	348	24	68
Frye, Tulsa	.957	127	262	322	26	80
Guerrero, Shreveport	.955	5	13	8	1	3
Guerrero, El Paso	.968	31	64	86	5	21
Hajek, Jackson	1.000	4	11	19	0	2
Hannahs, El Paso	.944	21	56	45	6	9
Harris, Jackson	.938	9	10	20	2	5
Harris, Wichita	1.000	5	8	10	0	2
Hillemann, Wichita	1.000	1	0	1	0	0
Howie, Midland	1.000	1	1	0	0	0
Hubbard, Jackson	.969	116	296	528	20	81
Johnson, Shreveport	.962	10	21	30	2	5
Kasper, Shreveport	.982	14	27	27	1	3
Listach, El Paso	.972	22	38	68	3	18
Lopez, Wichita	.960	121	273	332	25	80
McLemore, Jackson	1.000	7	27	24	0	10
Melvin, Arkansas	1.000	1	1	0	0	0

(continued, right column)

Player, Team	Pct.	G	PO	A	E	DP
D. Patterson, Shreveport	1.000	2	0	3	0	0
J. Patterson, Shreveport	.973	113	242	299	15	77
Renteria, Jackson	.970	6	20	12	1	3
Ross, Arkansas	.987	19	36	41	1	8
Sable, Tulsa	1.000	7	10	24	0	6
Samson, Tulsa	1.000	1	0	1	0	0
Shireman, Arkansas	.977	77	119	174	7	34
Wallace, 14 Wich. -3 E.P.	.925	17	35	39	6	15
YOUNG, San Antonio	.974	100	204	282	13	66

THIRD BASEMEN

Player, Team	Pct.	G	PO	A	E	DP
Abreu, Arkansas	.905	54	44	80	13	7
Alfonzo, Midland	.909	12	5	15	2	0
Alvarez, San Antonio	1.000	14	8	21	0	0
Barns, Midland	.931	9	10	17	2	4
Bournigal, San Antonio	1.000	7	6	6	0	2
Burgos, Tulsa	.925	33	25	61	7	4
Byington, El Paso	.925	112	75	222	24	30
Cooper, El Paso	.857	5	5	13	3	2
Davenport, Shreveport	.872	21	15	26	6	3
David, Wichita	.847	25	14	47	11	2
Davis, Midland	.900	27	10	53	7	10
Ebel, San Antonio	.800	5	3	1	1	0
Fanning, Arkansas	1.000	1	0	1	0	1
FINKEN, San Antonio	.930	102	78	199	21	24
Fiore, Arkansas	.909	39	19	71	9	4
Garman, Tulsa	.868	13	8	25	5	1
Guerrero, Shreveport	.871	80	39	109	22	5
Hajek, Jackson	.933	19	10	32	3	5
Harris, Jackson	.889	5	1	7	1	0
Howie, Midland	.943	45	40	93	8	8
Jaha, El Paso	.818	4	3	6	2	0
Johnson, Shreveport	.886	23	9	30	5	6
Jones, Midland	.000	1	0	0	1	0
Kasper, Shreveport	.929	9	3	10	1	2
Lewis, San Antonio	.897	15	11	24	4	2
Madsen, Jackson	.921	121	71	220	25	21
McConnell, Midland	.965	28	15	40	2	3
Melvin, Arkansas	.778	7	2	5	2	1
Munoz, San Antonio	.778	5	1	6	2	1
Nilsson, El Paso	1.000	6	5	13	0	0
D. Patterson, Shreveport	.927	30	13	38	4	5
Redington, Wichita	.928	114	77	257	26	21
Renteria, Jackson	.800	4	2	6	2	0
Rice, Midland	1.000	1	0	2	0	0
Ross, Arkansas	.906	51	37	89	13	5
Sable, Tulsa	.925	75	53	143	16	21
Samson, Tulsa	.927	25	10	41	4	5
Shireman, Arkansas	1.000	9	0	5	0	0
Tatum, El Paso	.857	14	9	15	4	1
Taylor, Midland	.897	32	16	62	9	7
Tucker, Shreveport	1.000	1	0	1	0	0
Wallace, Wichita	.941	4	3	13	1	1

SHORTSTOPS

Player, Team	Pct.	G	PO	A	E	DP
Abreu, Arkansas	.942	36	40	106	9	19
Alfonzo, Midland	.929	6	9	17	2	4
Alvarez, San Antonio	.933	6	6	8	1	4
Barker, San Antonio	.941	115	190	318	32	75
Barns, Midland	1.000	1	2	1	0	1
Bournigal, San Antonio	1.000	5	8	19	0	6
Burgos, Tulsa	.931	13	23	44	5	8
Byington, El Paso	.933	6	5	9	1	2
Carmona, Arkansas	.939	12	13	33	3	8
Clayton, Shreveport	.950	123	174	379	29	80
Colon, Tulsa	.917	26	50	82	12	23
Cromer, Arkansas	.969	71	117	198	10	41
Davis, Midland	.931	7	7	20	2	4
Easley, Midland	.924	127	186	388	47	69
Ebel, San Antonio	.967	10	10	19	1	2
Finken, San Antonio	1.000	2	1	1	0	1
Guerrero, El Paso	1.000	3	4	3	0	1

— 416 —

Player, Team	Pct.	G	PO	A	E	DP
Hajek, Jackson	.880	7	8	14	3	3
Harris, Jackson	.922	28	38	81	10	22
HERNANDEZ, Tulsa	.968	91	151	300	15	47
Johnson, Shreveport	.929	13	14	25	3	4
Kasper, Shreveport	.889	4	3	5	1	1
Kellner, Jackson	.942	82	116	226	21	41
Listach, El Paso	.854	29	48	63	19	17
Lopez, Wichita	.889	4	1	7	1	0
Miller, Jackson	.890	23	31	66	12	10
Munoz, San Antonio	.907	10	12	27	4	7
Renteria, Jackson	.957	6	7	15	1	4
Sable, Tulsa	.900	2	5	4	1	1
Samson, Tulsa	.909	5	10	20	3	6
Shireman, Arkansas	.949	32	39	90	7	17
Tatum, El Paso	.939	88	156	246	26	59
Valentin, Wichita	.939	129	176	442	40	73
Wallace, 8 Wich.- 15 E.P.	.963	23	41	62	4	11

OUTFIELDERS

Player, Team	Pct.	G	PO	A	E	DP
Alfonzo, Midland	1.000	1	1	0	0	0
Ansley, Jackson	.956	41	41	2	2	0
Ashley, El Paso	.960	85	141	4	6	2
Barron, San Antonio	.991	68	110	5	1	1
Belcher, Tulsa	.956	24	38	5	2	1
Brannon, Arkansas	.983	115	209	21	4	7
Castillo, San Antonio	.974	82	187	4	5	0
Christian, Arkansas	.981	86	147	6	3	0
Cisarik, Wichita*	.978	75	128	7	3	0
Cooper, Shreveport	.987	103	289	10	4	4
Cunningham, Tulsa	1.000	1	1	0	0	0
Davis, Midland	1.000	1	1	0	0	0
Dean, Jackson	1.000	86	121	12	0	1
Ealy, Shreveport	1.000	45	50	1	0	0
ESCALERA, El Paso*	.995	104	179	6	1	1
Federico, Arkansas*	1.000	1	1	0	0	0
Finken, San Antonio	.938	9	15	0	1	0
Finn, El Paso	1.000	2	3	0	0	0
Fiore, Arkansas	.985	81	124	8	2	0
Forrester, Jackson*	.900	7	7	2	1	0
Gonzalez, San Antonio	1.000	6	9	0	0	0
Green, Tulsa	1.000	18	21	1	0	0
Greer, Tulsa*	1.000	20	34	0	0	0
Guerrero, Shreveport	.976	59	79	4	2	0
Harris, Tulsa	.970	129	283	11	9	1
Harris, Wichita	.981	90	147	6	3	0
Hillemann, Wichita	.987	74	148	9	2	2
Hosey, Shreveport	.973	121	243	5	7	0
Hubbard, Jackson	.750	3	2	1	1	1
Hunter, Jackson	.979	95	178	7	4	1
Ingram, San Antonio	1.000	1	2	0	0	0
Jacas, El Paso	.957	122	257	7	12	2
Jackson, El Paso	.984	102	173	6	3	1
Jenkins, Jackson	.931	87	117	5	9	1
Jones, Midland	.938	68	106	14	8	4
Lawton, Midland	.970	108	219	6	7	1
Lewis, Shreveport*	1.000	1	3	0	0	0
Magnusson, San Antonio	.946	94	131	9	8	0
Marabell, San Antonio	.950	39	37	1	2	0
Martinez, Arkansas	.989	55	86	2	1	1
Massarelli, Jackson	1.000	2	2	0	0	0
McWilliam, Wichita	.981	54	101	3	2	0
Mikulik, Jackson	.972	120	200	6	6	1
Mondesi, San Antonio	.964	52	101	6	4	0
Morris, Tulsa*	.966	102	190	7	7	0
Morrow, San Antonio*	.909	22	39	1	4	0
Munoz, San Antonio	.939	19	25	6	2	0
Peters, San Antonio*	1.000	1	1	0	0	0
Rohrmeier, Tulsa	.984	103	168	12	3	0
Ross, Arkansas	1.000	1	1	0	0	0
Sable, Tulsa	1.000	2	1	0	0	0
Salmon, Midland	.966	130	265	16	10	2
Sambo, Midland	.979	26	43	3	1	1
Samson, Tulsa	.929	20	22	4	2	0
Sherman, Wichita*	.977	127	323	11	8	1
Smiley, Shreveport*	.977	94	165	2	4	1
Weber, Shreveport*	.973	31	70	3	2	0
White, Arkansas	.974	98	143	9	4	1
White, San Antonio	.962	76	97	3	4	1
Wilkins, San Antonio	1.000	1	1	0	0	0
Williams, Midland	.966	82	187	9	7	2
Wrona, Tulsa	1.000	4	3	0	0	0
Young, San Antonio	1.000	3	2	0	0	0

CATCHERS

Player, Team	Pct.	G	PO	A	E	DP	PB
Baar, San Antonio	.981	85	513	57	11	10	14
Basso, Wichita	.997	49	254	34	1	1	3
Berger, Tulsa	1.000	7	36	6	0	0	2
Beuerlein, Jackson	.944	6	31	3	2	0	0
Billmeyer, Midland	.990	37	185	16	2	4	8
Brown, San Antonio	.941	3	16	0	1	0	0
Conley, Wichita	.952	20	93	7	5	1	2
David, Wichita	.980	50	270	19	6	2	12

Player, Team	Pct.	G	PO	A	E	DP	PB
Dominguez, Midland	.970	5	30	2	1	0	0
Eusebio, Jackson	.985	62	424	48	7	7	13
Faulkner, El Paso	.989	73	467	58	6	8	12
Fernandez, Shreveport	1.000	6	20	2	0	0	1
Jose Fernandez, Arkansas	.979	89	538	58	13	8	7
Gonzales, Midland	.982	64	346	38	7	7	4
Iavarone, Tulsa	.965	11	50	5	2	0	1
Kreuter, Tulsa	.987	42	269	27	4	2	1
Kuld, 29 Wich. -22 Tul.	.989	51	321	27	4	0	2
Liddell, El Paso	.966	13	77	7	3	0	1
Makarewicz, Jackson	.974	70	481	44	14	2	6
Massarelli, Jackson	.977	7	35	8	1	1	1
McNamara, Shreveport	.991	35	204	19	2	2	2
Nilsson, El Paso	.979	50	343	33	8	0	1
Prybylinski, Arkansas	.981	45	222	38	5	6	2
Redman, Arkansas	.989	19	77	9	1	0	3
Rice, San Antonio	.993	61	363	61	3	8	10
Rivers, Midland	.948	27	145	20	9	2	4
Rodriguez, Tulsa	.988	37	210	33	3	6	2
Snyder, El Paso	1.000	8	45	2	0	1	0
Tatum, El Paso	.941	2	15	1	1	1	1
Trevino, Midland	.990	14	81	14	1	1	2
TUCKER, Shreveport	.995	106	673	70	4	9	11
Wrona, Tulsa	.984	22	107	14	2	0	2

PITCHERS

Player, Team	Pct.	G	PO	A	E	DP
Acosta, Midland*	.833	37	5	10	3	0
Alba, El Paso*	1.000	3	0	1	0	0
Allen, Jackson*	.957	26	3	19	1	2
Allen, San Antonio	1.000	12	3	1	0	0
Ambrose, El Paso	1.000	19	9	22	0	2
Ard, Shreveport	1.000	13	5	12	0	1
Astacio, San Antonio	.964	19	7	20	1	2
August, Jackson	1.000	7	2	3	0	0
Barns, Midland	1.000	1	1	0	0	0
Bauer, Jackson	.947	46	7	11	1	3
Berrios, Midland*	1.000	18	1	1	0	0
Bockus, Midland	1.000	12	2	4	0	0
Bohanon, Tulsa*	1.000	2	0	2	0	0
Brocail, Wichita	.920	34	5	18	2	0
Bronkey, Tulsa	1.000	4	1	1	0	0
Brown, Tulsa	.947	44	4	14	1	2
Bryand, Wichita*	.923	37	6	6	1	0
Bustillos, San Antonio	.964	16	8	19	1	2
Butcher, Midland	1.000	41	8	13	0	0
Calhoun, San Antonio	1.000	21	1	7	0	0
Campbell, Tulsa	.957	23	4	18	1	2
Carter, Shreveport	.920	24	5	18	2	0
Carter, Midland	.929	8	4	9	1	1
Cassidy, Jackson*	1.000	6	0	7	0	0
Chapman, El Paso	1.000	45	9	15	0	0
Chavez, Wichita	.917	38	1	10	1	0
Clark, Arkansas	.875	15	5	9	2	2
Cobb, Midland	.833	42	3	12	3	0
Coffman, San Antonio	.909	30	7	23	3	2
Coleman, San Antonio	1.000	32	2	17	0	2
Compres, San Antonio	1.000	27	2	2	0	0
Cook, San Antonio*	.917	7	3	8	1	0
Corbett, Midland*	1.000	13	1	4	0	0
Corona, Arkansas*	1.000	27	2	10	0	0
Cunningham, 21 Tul. - 16 Wich.	.941	37	5	11	1	0
Czajkowski, El Paso	1.000	43	4	9	0	1
Davis, Wichita	1.000	50	4	16	0	2
Ericks, Arkansas	.918	25	16	29	4	4
Everson, El Paso	.800	7	0	4	1	1
Faccio, Arkansas	.867	20	6	7	2	1
Felix, El Paso	1.000	11	1	2	0	0
Fortugno, El Paso*	.833	20	0	5	1	0
Freeland, 1 Jack. -7 E.P.	.800	8	1	11	3	1
Galindez, Wichita*	.850	17	3	31	6	0
Gardner, Jackson	.860	22	12	25	6	0
Gies, Tulsa	1.000	8	2	9	0	1
Gilmore, Wichita	1.000	9	2	3	0	1
Gonzales, Arkansas*	1.000	3	1	1	0	0
Gordon, Tulsa	.000	7	0	0	0	0
Gore, Tulsa*	1.000	27	2	20	0	1
Green, El Paso*	1.000	9	2	6	0	1
Grovom, Jackson*	1.000	10	0	3	0	1
Hammaker, Wichita*	1.000	5	1	0	0	0
Hartgraves, Jackson*	1.000	19	5	17	0	2
Haslock, Wichita	1.000	8	1	6	0	1
Hayward, Tulsa*	1.000	10	3	6	0	1
Hershiser, San Antonio	1.000	1	0	3	0	0
Hickerson, Shreveport*	.909	23	2	8	1	1
Hilton, Wichita	.750	26	3	3	2	0
Holzemer, Midland	1.000	2	0	1	0	0
Hostetler, Shreveport	1.000	9	3	2	0	1
Hurst, Tulsa	1.000	2	3	0	0	0
James, San Antonio	1.000	15	8	10	0	2
James, Midland*	.971	27	6	28	1	3
Johnson, El Paso	.875	13	3	4	1	0
Jones, Jackson	.875	10	1	6	1	0
Juden, Jackson	.905	16	5	14	2	0

Player, Team	Pct.	G	PO	A	E	DP
Kaiser, Jackson	.750	14	3	3	2	1
Kiefer, El Paso	1.000	12	4	10	0	0
King, Midland	.833	5	1	4	1	0
Kisten, Arkansas	1.000	36	5	15	0	0
Knox, Wichita*	1.000	28	5	21	0	1
LaRose, Jackson	.909	26	3	7	1	1
Leftwich, Midland	1.000	1	1	0	0	0
Lepley, Arkansas*	.750	16	1	2	1	0
Lewis, Wichita	1.000	2	1	0	0	0
Lienhard, El Paso	.958	26	5	18	1	0
Lynch, San Antonio*	1.000	11	1	0	0	0
Majer, Arkansas	.885	34	8	15	3	0
Mallicoat, Jackson*	1.000	18	2	4	0	0
Manuel, Tulsa	.909	56	6	4	1	0
Marquez, San Antonio	.923	34	2	10	1	1
Martinez, Midland*	.929	15	3	23	2	1
Martinez, Wichita	.960	26	3	21	1	0
Martinez, San Antonio	.706	12	2	10	5	0
Mathews, El Paso*	1.000	2	0	2	0	0
McClellan, Shreveport	.950	14	7	12	1	1
McCray, Tulsa*	.850	21	2	15	3	0
McGraw, El Paso*	1.000	9	3	6	0	1
Meier, Shreveport	.960	33	6	18	1	0
Menendez, Tulsa	1.000	3	0	4	0	0
Milchin, Arkansas*	1.000	6	1	3	0	0
Miranda, El Paso*	.846	38	4	7	2	1
Monson, El Paso	.867	17	5	8	2	0
Montalvo, Midland	.833	22	6	9	3	2
Myers, Shreveport	.955	62	6	15	1	1
Nen, Tulsa	.857	6	0	6	1	1
Osborne, Arkansas*	.979	26	14	32	1	1
Ozuna, Arkansas	1.000	17	1	3	0	0
Pawlowski, Midland	1.000	15	4	4	0	1
Peltzer, Shreveport*	1.000	5	0	3	0	0
Pena, Shreveport*	.955	45	4	17	1	2
Perez, Tulsa	.941	25	5	27	2	2
Perez, Shreveport	1.000	27	3	3	0	0
Plemel, Arkansas	.962	53	8	17	1	0
Rambo, Shreveport	.939	26	10	21	2	2
Rapp, Shreveport	.917	10	3	8	1	1
Reed, Tulsa	.947	12	5	13	1	1
Reed, Shreveport	1.000	15	3	4	0	1

Player, Team	Pct.	G	PO	A	E	DP
Reichle, Wichita	1.000	14	1	7	0	0
Resnikoff, Jackson*	.857	26	1	5	1	0
REYNOLDS, Jackson	1.000	27	12	25	0	1
Richards, Jackson*	1.000	29	1	2	0	0
Richardson, Arkansas*	.500	12	0	1	1	0
Robertson, Midland	1.000	36	5	5	0	0
Rogers, Shreveport*	.867	22	1	12	2	0
Romero, Tulsa*	.935	23	3	26	2	1
Rowley, Tulsa	.889	10	2	6	1	0
Sager, Wichita	1.000	10	2	7	0	0
Salvior, Arkansas	.857	13	2	4	1	1
Schwarz, El Paso	.875	27	13	15	4	1
Seminara, Wichita	.944	27	13	21	2	2
Shaw, Tulsa*	.905	26	5	33	4	1
Shiflett, Tulsa	1.000	4	0	1	0	0
Shinall, San Antonio	.944	25	4	13	1	1
Shotkoski, Midland	.914	23	12	20	3	3
Simon, Jackson	.909	56	4	6	1	0
Smith, El Paso	1.000	11	2	3	0	1
Smithberg, Wichita	1.000	7	2	8	0	0
Sontag, Midland	.760	15	9	10	6	2
Sparks, El Paso	.889	4	3	5	1	0
Springer, San Antonio	.967	30	8	21	1	0
Stewart, Wichita*	1.000	7	0	1	0	0
Taveras, San Antonio	1.000	8	1	5	0	0
Taylor, Shreveport	.818	39	2	7	2	0
Terrill, San Antonio*	.917	27	1	10	1	0
Treadwell, San Antonio	.917	10	2	9	1	0
Trice, Jackson*	.833	20	2	3	1	0
Valenzuela, Midland*	1.000	4	0	4	0	0
Vann, El Paso	.714	19	1	4	2	0
Vidmar, Midland	.895	22	16	18	4	3
Wallace, Wichita	1.000	4	0	1	0	0
Weese, Arkansas	1.000	14	2	1	0	0
Wilkins, San Antonio	.912	22	10	21	3	0
Williams, Jackson	1.000	3	1	0	0	0
Windes, Jackson*	1.000	13	3	3	0	0
Wiseman, Arkansas	.932	26	10	31	3	1
Wishnevski, El Paso	.857	7	2	4	1	1
Wood, Wichita	1.000	11	1	3	0	0
Wray, San Antonio*	1.000	43	4	9	0	0
Zappelli, Midland	1.000	32	5	4	0	0

The following players did not have any fielding statistics at the positions indicated or appeared only as a designated hitter, pinch-hitter or pinch-runner: Abreu, p; Biberdorf, p; Brannon, p; Brosnan, p; Burgos, of; Carey, 2b, 3b; Larry Carter (El Paso), p; Davino, p; Escalera, p; M. Guerrero, 3b; Hubbard, p; Hunter, p; Kuld, p; Renteria, p; Sable, p; Sebra, p; Sellick, of; Stephenson, dh, ph; Stone, p; Tapia, p; Tatum, p.

LEAGUE CHAMPIONS

Year	Team	Pct.
1888—	Dallas	.671
1889—	Houston	.551
1890—	Galveston	.705
1892—	Galveston	.741
	Houston	.613
1895—	Dallas	.754
	Fort Worth*	.750
1896—	Fort Worth	.757
	Houston*	.679
	Galveston	.548
1897—	San Antonio†	.657
	Galveston†	.717
1898—	League disbanded.	
1899—	Galveston	.632
	Galveston	.762
1900-01—	Did not operate.	
1902—	Corsicana	.866
	Corsicana	.682
1903—	Paris-Waco	.615
	Dallas*	.648
1904—	Corsicana*	.615
	Fort Worth	.800
1905—	Fort Worth	.545
1906—	Fort Worth	.677
	Cleburne x	.609
1907—	Austin	.629
1908—	San Antonio	.664
1909—	Houston	.601
1910—	Dallas†	.586
	Houston†	.586
1911—	Austin	.575
1912—	Houston	.626
1913—	Houston	.620
1914—	Houston†	.671
	Waco†	.671
1915—	Waco	.592
1916—	Waco	.587
1917—	Dallas	.600
1918—	Dallas	.584
1919—	Shreveport*	.677
	Fort Worth	.651
1920—	Fort Worth	.703
	Fort Worth	.750
1921—	Fort Worth	.691
	Fort Worth	.662

Year	Team	Pct.
1922—	Fort Worth	.694
	Fort Worth	.711
1923—	Fort Worth	.632
1924—	Fort Worth	.689
	Fort Worth	.763
1925—	Fort Worth	.711
	Fort Worth y	.653
1926—	Dallas	.574
1927—	Wichita Falls	.654
1928—	Houston*	.679
	Wichita Falls	.731
1929—	Dallas*	.588
	Wichita Falls	.620
1930—	Wichita Falls	.697
	Fort Worth*	.632
1931—	Houston a	.625
	Houston	.734
1932—	Beaumont*	.640
	Dallas	.727
1933—	Houston	.623
	San Antonio (4th)§	.523
1934—	Galveston‡	.579
1935—	Oklahoma City‡	.590
1936—	Dallas	.604
	Tulsa (3rd)§	.519
1937—	Oklahoma City	.635
	Fort Worth (3rd)§	.535
1938—	Beaumont	.635
1939—	Houston	.606
	Fort Worth (4th)§	.540
1940—	Houston‡	.652
1941—	Houston	.673
	Dallas (4th)§	.519
1942—	Beaumont	.605
	Shreveport (2nd)§	.576
1943-44-45—	Did not operate.	
1946—	Fort Worth	.656
	Dallas (2nd)§	.591
1947—	Houston‡	.623
1948—	Fort Worth‡	.601
1949—	Fort Worth	.649
	Tulsa (2nd)§	.584
1950—	Beaumont	.595
	San Antonio (4th)§	.513
1951—	Houston‡	.619

Year	Team	Pct.
1952—	Dallas	.571
	Shreveport (3rd)§	.522
1953—	Dallas‡	.571
1954—	Shreveport	.559
	Houston (2nd)§	.553
1955—	Dallas	.581
	Shreveport (3rd)§	.540
1956—	Houston‡	.623
1957—	Dallas	.662
	Houston (2nd)§	.630
1958—	Fort Worth	.582
	Cor. Christi (3rd)§	.507
1959—	Victoria	.589
	Austin (2nd)§	.548
1960—	Rio Grande Valley	.590
	Tulsa (3rd)	.528
1961—	Amarillo	.643
	San Antonio (3rd)§	.532
1962—	El Paso	.571
	Tulsa (2nd)§	.550
1963—	San Antonio	.564
	Tulsa (3rd)§	.529
1964—	San Antonio‡	.607
1965—	Tulsa	.574
	Albuquerque b	.550
1966—	Arkansas	.579
1967—	Albuquerque	.557
1968—	Arkansas	.586
	El Paso b	.562
1969—	Amarillo	.593
	Memphis b	.504
1970—	Albuquerque a	.615
	Memphis	.507
1971—	Did not operate as league—clubs were members of Dixie Association.	
1972—	Alexandria	.600
	El Paso b	.557
1973—	San Antonio	.590
	Memphis b	.558
1974—	Victoria b	.581
	El Paso	.555
1975—	Lafayette c	.558
	Midland c	.604
1976—	Amarillo b	.600
	Shreveport	.515

Year	Team	Pct.	Year	Team	Pct.	Year	Team	Pct.
1977—	El Paso	.600	1982—	El Paso	.559	1987—	Wichita d	.515
	Arkansas d	.485		Tulsa d	.515		Jackson	.515
1978—	El Paso d	.593	1983—	Jackson	.507	1988—	El Paso	.552
	Jackson	.567		Beaumont d	.500		Tulsa d	.522
1979—	Arkansas d	.571	1984—	Beaumont	.654	1989—	Arkansas d	.585
	Midland	.563		Jackson d	.610		Wichita	.537
1980—	Arkansas d	.596	1985—	El Paso	.632	1990—	San Antonio	.582
	San Antonio	.544		Jackson d	.537		Shreveport d	.489
1981—	San Antonio	.571	1986—	El Paso d	.630	1991—	Shreveport d	.632
	Jackson d	.507		Jackson	.533		El Paso	.596

*Won split-season playoff. †Won playoff for title. ‡Finished first and won four-club playoff. §Won four-club playoff. xTitle to Cleburne by default. yTied with Dallas in second half and won playoff for championship. zFort Worth disbanded. aTied with Beaumont at end of first half and won title in best-of-five series played as part of second-half schedule. bLeague divided into Eastern, Western divisions; won two-team playoff. cLeague divided into Eastern, Western divisions; declared co-champions when playoffs were not completed. dLeague divided into Eastern and Western divisions and played split-season; won playoffs. NOTE—Championship awarded to winner of four-team playoff, 1933-51; first-place team and playoff winner co-champions, 1952-64.

CALIFORNIA LEAGUE

FINAL STANDINGS

FIRST HALF

NORTHERN DIVISION

Team	W	L	T	Pct.	GB
San Jose (Giants)	45	23	0	.662	....
Stockton (Brewers)	42	26	0	.618	3
Modesto (Athletics)	35	33	0	.515	10
Reno (Independent)	31	37	0	.456	14
Salinas (Independent)	23	45	0	.338	22

SOUTHERN DIVISION

Team	W	L	T	Pct.	GB
Bakersfield (Dodgers)	45	23	0	.662	....
Palm Springs (Angels)	36	32	0	.529	9
High Desert (Padres)	31	37	0	.456	14
San Bernardino (Mariners)	28	40	0	.412	17
Visalia (Twins)	24	44	0	.353	21

SECOND HALF

NORTHERN DIVISION

Team	W	L	T	Pct.	GB
San Jose (Giants)	47	21	0	.691	....
Modesto (Athletics)	33	35	0	.485	14
Salinas (Independent)	32	36	0	.485	15
Stockton (Brewers)	29	39	0	.426	18
Reno (Independent)	28	40	0	.412	19

SOUTHERN DIVISION

Team	W	L	T	Pct.	GB
High Desert (Padres)	42	26	0	.618	....
Bakersfield (Dodgers)	40	28	0	.588	2
Visalia (Twins)	34	34	0	.500	8
Palm Springs (Angels)	29	39	0	.426	13
San Bernardino (Mariners)	26	42	0	.382	16

COMPOSITE

Team	S.J.	Bak.	H.D.	Sto.	Mod.	P.S.	Reno	Vis.	Sal.	S.B.	W	L	T	Pct.	GB
San Jose (Giants)	....	6	8	16	12	10	12	10	10	8	92	44	0	.676	....
Bakersfield (Dodgers)	6	....	11	7	11	8	6	15	9	12	85	51	0	.625	7
High Desert (Padres)	4	9	....	6	9	9	9	8	7	12	73	63	0	.537	19
Stockton (Brewers)	4	5	6	....	13	6	9	9	10	9	71	65	0	.522	21
Modesto (Athletics)	7	1	3	7	....	7	14	6	15	8	68	68	0	.500	24
Palm Springs (Angels)	2	10	10	6	5	....	7	10	6	9	65	71	0	.478	27
Reno (Independent)	6	6	3	9	5	5	....	8	9	8	59	77	0	.434	33
Visalia (Twins)	2	4	10	3	6	10	4	....	9	10	58	78	0	.426	34
Salinas (Independent)	9	3	5	8	3	6	12	3	....	6	55	81	0	.404	37
San Bernardino (Mariners)	4	7	7	3	4	10	4	9	6	....	54	82	0	.397	38

Major league affiliations in parentheses.

Playoffs—Stockton defeated San Jose, three games to one; High Desert defeated Bakersfield, three games to none; High Desert defeated Stockton, three games to two, to win league championship.

Regular-season attendance—Bakersfield, 147,655; High Desert, 204,438; Modesto, 77,287; Palm Springs, 64,871; Reno, 76,045; Salinas, 66,079; San Bernardino, 187,895; San Jose, 123,905; Stockton, 90,126; Visalia, 67,386. Total, 1,105,687. Playoffs (12 games)—32,431. All-Star Game at Palm Springs—1,237.

Managers—Bakersfield, Tom Beyers; High Desert, Bruce Bochy; Modesto, Ted Kubiak; Palm Springs, Nate Oliver; Reno, Mal Fichman; Salinas, Heide Koga; San Bernardino, Tommy Jones; San Jose, Ron Wotus; Stockton, Chris Bando; Visalia, Steve Liddle.

All-Star team—1B—Jay Gainer, High Desert; 2B—Frank Carey, San Jose; 3B—Jim Bishop, Salinas; SS—Ron Maurer, Bakersfield; OF—Matt Mieske, High Desert; Marc Newfield, San Bernardino; J.D. Noland, High Desert; C—Mike Piazza, Bakersfield; DH—Chris Delarwelle, Visalia; P—Rich Huisman, San Jose; Greg Hansell, Bakersfield; Gary Sharko, San Jose; Timber Mead, Reno; Most Valuable Player—Matt Mieske, High Desert; Pitcher of the Year—Rich Huisman, San Jose; Rookie of the Year—Matt Mieske, High Desert; Manager of the Year, Ron Wotus, San Jose.

BATTING

TEAM

Team	Avg.	G	AB	R	OR	H	TB	2B	3B	HR	RBI	SH	SF	HP	BB	Int. BB	SO	SB	CS	LOB
Bakersfield	.274	136	4616	738	528	1265	1876	234	34	103	636	58	53	62	543	33	899	148	100	1001
High Desert	.273	136	4616	873	772	1262	1921	220	50	113	766	34	50	75	690	34	941	240	93	1020
Modesto	.263	136	4603	723	689	1210	1714	221	29	75	638	45	41	45	698	21	996	155	94	1134
Reno	.262	136	4626	627	841	1210	1674	197	39	63	551	38	34	62	561	25	941	68	58	1115
San Jose	.260	136	4570	726	450	1190	1653	210	47	53	620	54	56	43	627	38	885	179	82	1075
San Bernardino	.261	136	4571	607	766	1193	1671	172	21	88	533	66	39	65	493	30	950	278	120	989
Visalia	.257	136	4602	654	739	1185	1690	178	27	91	547	35	40	57	583	24	924	209	81	1053
Salinas	.252	136	4541	587	784	1145	1575	190	30	60	516	73	41	58	521	32	950	131	82	1022
Palm Springs	.252	136	4473	586	647	1125	1569	180	36	64	504	66	26	48	579	34	971	122	99	1012
Stockton	.243	136	4480	639	544	1090	1585	176	41	79	535	51	50	71	663	33	926	149	92	1061

INDIVIDUAL

(Leading qualifiers for batting championship—367 or more plate appearances)

*Bats lefthanded.   †Switch-hitter.

Player, Team	Avg.	G	AB	R	H	TB	2B	3B	HR	RBI	SH	SF	HP	BB	Int. BB	SO	SB	CS
Mieske, Matt, High Desert	.341	133	492	108	168	261	36	6	15	119	0	4	13	94	6	82	39	12
Eppard, Jim, Salinas*	.339	89	313	55	106	146	27	2	3	43	0	1	4	62	14	24	12	4
de la Nuez, Rex, Visalia	.308	111	406	78	125	185	23	2	11	65	1	4	9	84	5	71	39	10
Meares, Pat, Visalia	.303	89	360	53	109	156	21	4	6	44	0	4	5	24	0	63	15	5
Santana, Ruben, San Bernardino	.302	108	394	55	119	152	16	4	3	43	9	5	6	26	4	74	34	12
Mifune, Hideyuki, Salinas	.300	132	493	85	148	185	17	1	6	49	16	5	5	53	0	69	30	11
Newfield, Marc, San Bernardino	.300	125	440	64	132	193	22	3	11	68	0	5	10	59	9	90	12	6
Ingram, Garey, Bakersfield	.297	118	445	75	132	183	16	4	9	61	5	6	14	52	4	70	30	13
Webb, Lonnie, Bakersfield	.291	87	340	71	99	141	18	3	6	36	6	3	5	46	2	76	22	16
Krumback, Mark, Reno†	.291	128	537	80	156	187	12	5	3	30	2	1	0	54	5	82	18	11

Departmental leaders: G—Bishop, Mieske, 133; AB—Krumback, 537; R—Noland, 114; H—Mieske, 168; TB—Mieske, 261; 2B—Mieske, 36; 3B—Noland, 12; HR—Gainer, 32; RBI—Gainer, 120; SH—Mifune, 16; SF—Gainer, 16; HP—Ingram, McFarlin, 14; BB—Mieske, 94; IBB—Eppard, 14; SO—Phillips, 144; SB—Noland, 81; CS—Noland, 23.

Player, Team	Avg.	G	AB	R	H	TB	2B	3B	HR	RBI	SH	SF	HP	BB	Int. BB	SO	SB	CS
Abbott, Kurt, Modesto	.255	58	216	36	55	76	8	2	3	25	2	4	1	29	0	55	6	3
Abercrombie, John, High Desert	.247	82	235	38	58	80	9	5	1	28	2	1	7	19	1	50	2	4
Alcantara, Francisco, Reno*	.000	64	1	0	0	0	0	0	0	0	0	0	0	0	0	0	0	0
Alfonzo, Edgar, Palm Springs	.277	81	292	43	81	112	11	4	4	38	10	2	1	38	3	32	5	7
Armas, Marco, Modesto	.279	36	140	21	39	70	7	0	8	33	1	5	2	10	0	41	0	0
Bass, Kevin, San Jose†	.105	5	19	1	2	4	2	0	0	1	0	1	2	1	3	2	0	0
Beard, Garrett, Bakersfield*	.276	48	152	22	42	74	14	0	6	30	5	1	2	27	0	30	0	1
Bellinger, Clay, San Jose	.258	105	368	65	95	152	29	2	8	62	7	6	11	53	3	88	13	4
Bethea, Steve, High Desert†	.277	80	206	43	57	72	8	2	1	33	3	2	1	37	0	44	9	5
Billmeyer, Mickey, Palm Springs*	.278	39	115	15	32	45	9	2	0	6	1	1	1	21	1	9	0	5
Bishop, Jim, Salinas	.278	133	478	68	133	207	19	2	17	106	2	6	4	81	3	132	3	2
Blackwell, Eric, Bakersfield*	.571	4	7	2	4	8	1	0	1	2	0	0	0	0	1	0	0	0
Blankenship, Shawn, Stockton†	.286	3	7	1	2	3	1	0	0	0	0	0	0	0	0	3	0	0
Bohringer, Helms, Bakersfield	.301	38	83	16	25	26	1	0	0	7	3	0	0	11	0	12	1	3
Bonner, Jeff, San Jose*	.217	83	226	39	49	65	5	4	1	21	4	2	2	46	2	28	13	5
Booker, Eric, Modesto	.288	74	271	59	78	110	20	3	2	44	1	2	4	63	3	52	6	1
Briggs, Kenny, Salinas†	.229	66	175	25	40	68	6	2	6	24	1	1	3	28	1	49	9	5
Brown, Matt, Visalia	.222	61	167	16	37	42	2	0	1	10	2	1	1	17	1	41	1	1
Bryant, Craig, San Bernardino	.309	25	81	12	25	38	7	0	2	10	1	0	2	6	0	18	3	2
Buckley, Troy, Visalia	.254	98	323	42	82	111	10	2	5	56	1	5	2	47	1	60	4	4
Busch, Mike, Bakersfield	.278	21	72	13	20	37	3	1	4	16	0	1	0	12	0	21	0	1
Cabrera, Juan, Stockton	.213	23	75	7	16	20	2	1	0	5	0	0	0	4	0	17	0	1
Calcagno, Dan, San Jose	.000	4	10	1	0	0	0	0	0	0	0	1	1	0	2	0	0	0
Cannon, Rob, Palm Springs	.153	24	59	5	9	12	3	0	0	7	0	2	0	13	0	16	0	2
Carcione, Tom, Reno	.259	64	220	24	57	71	6	1	2	13	3	0	1	28	1	62	1	1
Cardenas, Daniel, Bakersfield*	.238	80	265	32	63	96	15	3	4	32	4	3	3	9	1	85	8	4
Carey, Frank, San Jose*	.279	99	333	59	93	135	20	5	4	39	3	3	4	48	2	82	12	4
Carlson, Bill, Salinas	.292	53	185	29	54	78	9	3	3	23	2	3	1	18	2	30	4	5
Castaldo, Vince, Stockton*	.249	131	478	80	119	194	28	4	13	74	3	2	7	80	0	98	25	9
Chimelis, Joel, San Jose	.246	42	126	19	31	38	5	1	0	14	1	4	1	16	0	22	9	4
Clark, Tim, Stockton*	.274	125	424	51	116	170	19	4	9	56	1	5	8	57	4	60	9	7
Clayton, Craig, San Bernardino	.333	20	75	8	25	37	3	0	3	9	1	0	0	8	0	11	3	3
Clemens, Troy, Reno*	.224	69	152	22	34	45	5	0	2	19	0	1	1	30	1	21	0	1
Cohen, John, Visalia*	.244	52	180	22	44	54	10	0	0	6	1	0	1	19	1	40	11	4
Cole, Mark, 82 Reno - 17 Sto.	.254	99	354	36	90	114	16	4	0	29	2	2	3	36	2	51	10	8
Collier, Anthony, Bakersfield*	.281	129	498	75	140	191	24	3	7	59	1	5	2	42	3	83	14	13
Colon, David, Palm Springs	.258	96	326	41	84	190	8	1	2	44	6	5	4	41	2	43	6	12
Conley, Greg, High Desert	.182	33	99	9	18	21	3	0	0	7	0	0	4	12	0	29	2	3
Conte, Mike, Modesto	.375	11	40	5	15	21	4	1	0	7	0	0	1	3	0	7	3	0
Cooley, Fred, Modesto	.286	60	238	35	68	106	8	0	10	51	1	4	1	22	2	45	0	0
Cordova, Marty, Visalia	.212	71	189	31	40	69	6	1	7	19	2	0	2	17	0	46	2	4
Correia, Mike, Modesto	.263	5	19	8	5	5	0	0	0	3	1	0	0	2	0	1	1	0
Cortes, Rico, Reno*	.234	33	107	9	25	33	6	1	0	13	1	4	0	9	0	19	0	1
Couture, Jim, Stockton	.195	80	185	31	36	52	5	1	3	12	4	3	13	24	0	75	25	8
Crowe, Ron, San Jose	.290	106	369	50	107	141	19	3	3	58	1	9	3	46	6	47	6	6
Cruz, Fausto, Modesto	.207	18	58	9	12	13	1	0	0	0	0	0	1	8	0	13	1	2
Cruz, Todd, Salinas	.254	100	355	30	90	120	17	2	3	36	5	3	4	25	3	53	3	3
Dattola, Kevin, Modesto†	.293	63	256	43	75	107	19	2	3	39	3	1	5	42	5	53	29	14
Davenport, Adell, San Jose	.289	67	242	34	70	104	16	0	6	42	0	1	10	40	1	61	1	3
de la Nuez, Rex, Visalia	.308	111	406	78	125	185	23	2	11	65	1	4	9	84	5	71	39	10
Delarwelle, Chris, Visalia	.280	119	453	66	127	210	25	5	16	77	1	4	4	64	4	81	19	8
Diaz, Remigio, Stockton	.150	40	100	7	15	15	0	0	0	5	3	1	0	3	0	20	0	1
Dodge, Tom, Palm Springs†	.262	49	149	19	39	52	5	1	2	16	0	1	1	14	3	21	4	1
Dodson, Bo, Stockton*	.262	88	298	51	78	124	13	3	9	41	0	2	4	66	7	63	4	2
Dominguez, Frank, Palm Springs	.211	70	237	18	50	58	8	0	0	21	2	1	3	20	3	46	1	2
Dunn, Steve, Visalia*	.229	125	458	64	105	162	16	1	13	59	0	6	6	58	6	103	9	6
Ebel, Dino, Bakersfield	.312	31	93	15	29	42	10	0	1	13	3	0	1	10	0	13	0	1
Edmonds, Jim, Palm Springs*	.294	60	187	28	55	78	15	1	2	27	3	1	0	40	3	57	2	2
Eppard, Jim, Salinas*	.339	89	313	55	106	146	27	2	3	43	0	1	4	62	14	24	12	4
Faries, Paul, High Desert	.310	10	42	6	13	19	2	2	0	5	1	1	2	2	1	3	1	0
Farmer, Reggie, High Desert*	.274	76	175	40	48	77	12	1	5	31	0	1	3	27	0	48	3	3
Felix, Junior, Palm Springs†	.359	18	64	12	23	32	3	0	2	10	0	0	0	16	1	11	8	2
Fernandez, Dan, San Jose*	.244	37	90	14	22	29	5	1	0	11	0	2	0	29	1	26	0	2
Finn, John, Stockton	.256	65	223	45	57	71	12	1	0	25	6	3	9	44	1	28	19	9
Firova, Dan, Reno	.345	10	29	6	10	12	2	0	0	4	0	1	0	2	0	1	0	0
Fletcher, Rob, Modesto*	.237	58	198	30	47	70	10	5	1	15	2	0	2	22	0	24	11	3
Flores, Juan, Stockton	.152	12	33	2	5	6	1	0	0	4	1	0	0	0	0	11	1	1
Forbes, P.J., Palm Springs	.266	94	349	45	93	117	14	2	2	26	12	0	4	36	1	44	18	8
Gainer, Jay, High Desert*	.263	127	499	83	131	244	17	0	32	120	0	16	3	52	3	105	4	3
Galle, Mike, Bakersfield	.300	3	10	1	3	3	0	0	0	3	0	1	0	2	0	4	0	1
Gavin, Tom, Visalia	.213	43	150	16	32	52	3	1	5	14	1	2	0	15	0	27	3	3
Gieseke, Mark, High Desert†	.313	92	297	59	93	144	18	3	9	54	0	2	9	45	4	52	5	2
Gil, Danny, Palm Springs	.222	48	153	12	34	52	4	1	4	18	0	0	2	17	1	48	0	0
Gonzalez, Cliff, Reno*	.285	130	502	72	143	196	22	8	5	86	4	5	4	63	3	68	9	9
Gonzalez, Freddy, Bakersfield	.256	22	82	9	21	37	3	2	3	8	1	0	1	3	1	23	0	0
Gonzalez, Paul, High Desert*	.267	103	371	61	99	178	31	3	14	64	1	1	4	47	1	85	2	3
Gray, Dan, Bakersfield	.000	2	2	0	0	0	0	0	0	0	0	0	0	0	0	1	0	0
Green, Otis, Stockton*	.000	13	1	0	0	0	0	0	0	0	0	0	0	0	0	0	0	0
Gregory, Quinn, Reno	.150	14	40	4	6	13	1	0	2	5	0	1	1	4	0	17	0	0
Griffith, Tom, Salinas†	.108	21	65	8	7	9	2	0	0	2	2	1	2	9	0	24	1	4
Guerrero, Mike, Stockton†	.235	59	204	22	48	57	4	1	1	18	4	5	1	28	1	28	6	2
Hart, Chris, Modesto	.250	37	88	9	22	26	4	0	0	13	0	2	3	8	0	22	2	2
Haslock, Chris, High Desert	.000	21	1	0	0	0	0	0	0	0	0	0	0	0	0	0	0	0
Haugen, Troy, Stockton†	.203	65	128	25	26	30	0	2	0	13	6	0	2	40	0	31	9	8
Helfand, Eric, Modesto*	.256	67	242	35	62	100	15	1	7	38	2	2	2	37	2	56	0	1
Holbert, Ray, High Desert	.264	122	386	76	102	132	14	2	4	51	9	3	6	56	2	83	19	6
Hood, Randy, Stockton	.180	42	128	16	23	32	3	0	2	10	2	0	6	21	0	37	2	3
Hosey, Dwayne, Stockton*	.272	85	356	55	97	168	12	7	15	62	1	9	3	31	1	58	22	8
Hunter, Greg, San Bernardino*	.242	129	413	55	100	118	12	0	2	32	9	4	1	74	6	61	22	11
Ingram, Garey, Bakersfield	.297	118	445	75	132	183	16	4	9	61	5	6	14	52	4	70	30	13
Jackson, John, San Jose*	.295	14	44	8	13	17	0	2	0	3	0	0	1	8	0	5	1	2
James, Joey, San Jose*	.267	126	479	68	128	185	27	3	8	75	1	6	11	55	6	85	1	5
Johnson, Dodd, Reno	.276	94	330	42	91	131	16	3	6	52	0	5	9	44	0	67	2	1
Jones, Jimmy, Reno†	.204	45	103	19	21	35	5	0	3	12	1	0	2	22	0	22	3	1

Player, Team	Avg.	G	AB	R	H	TB	2B	3B	HR	RBI	SH	SF	HP	BB	Int. BB	SO	SB	CS
Kapano, Corey, Palm Springs	.286	120	419	63	120	173	23	3	8	52	1	1	4	72	5	86	13	7
Kappesser, Bob, 18 Vis.-79 Stock.	.216	97	259	36	56	68	6	3	0	17	11	2	2	44	1	57	10	9
Kasper, Kevin, San Jose	.267	22	45	11	12	15	3	0	0	7	1	1	2	11	0	10	3	3
Kawano, Ryo, Salinas	.202	89	243	25	49	69	10	2	2	17	7	2	7	20	2	55	1	3
Keathley, Don, Modesto	.000	4	2	0	0	0	0	0	0	0	0	0	0	0	0	2	0	0
Keitges, Jeff, San Bernardino*	.209	59	191	15	40	64	9	0	5	33	1	2	2	24	0	41	0	3
King, Bryan, San Bernardino	.171	50	105	13	18	24	4	1	0	12	5	1	1	26	0	20	10	4
Klavitter, Clay, San Bernardino*	.176	25	51	4	9	11	2	0	0	4	1	0	0	4	0	12	0	0
Kluge, Matt, San Bernardino	.236	28	72	4	17	20	0	0	1	13	1	1	1	2	0	24	0	0
Knabenshue, Chris, Palm Springs*	.200	11	30	5	6	10	1	0	1	5	1	0	0	8	1	11	0	0
Koeper, Chris, Salinas	.298	38	124	16	37	50	8	1	1	17	1	1	3	5	0	27	9	2
Kohno, Takayuki, Salinas	.143	16	42	5	6	9	0	0	1	1	3	0	0	3	0	6	1	0
Krumback, Mark, Reno†	.291	128	537	80	156	187	12	5	3	30	2	1	0	54	5	82	18	11
Laboy, Carlos, Palm Springs	.247	119	425	58	105	158	19	5	8	49	3	2	8	45	3	114	8	7
Lewis, Alan, Bakersfield*	.259	92	343	58	89	132	21	2	6	64	0	3	3	61	11	50	3	4
Lewis, Mica, Visalia	.283	115	420	69	119	180	18	5	11	57	8	5	3	60	1	103	38	5
Logan, Todd, Visalia*	.238	51	164	17	39	55	4	0	4	18	3	3	1	28	1	26	1	1
Lott, Billy, Bakersfield	.223	92	314	40	70	97	10	1	5	35	3	6	3	25	0	90	11	4
Lund, Ed, Bakersfield	.210	66	176	26	37	51	8	0	2	23	3	3	9	26	2	33	1	2
Lutticken, Bob, High Desert	.000	4	7	1	0	0	0	0	0	0	1	0	0	1	0	1	0	0
Magallanes, Bob, San Bernardino	.225	83	271	40	61	95	13	0	7	31	0	3	2	30	0	64	7	6
Manwaring, Kirt, San Jose	.000	1	3	1	0	0	0	0	0	0	0	0	0	1	0	1	0	0
Marrero, Oreste, Stockton*	.251	123	438	63	110	168	15	2	13	61	1	7	0	57	8	98	4	5
Marrero, Vilato, Stockton	.256	106	348	28	89	117	18	2	2	42	2	5	2	32	4	51	1	7
Marshall, Mike, Palm Springs	.250	3	8	1	2	3	1	0	0	2	0	1	0	2	0	3	0	0
Martin, Steve, High Desert	.268	98	343	82	92	138	13	6	7	58	5	5	9	59	4	77	42	11
Martinez, Manny, Modesto	.271	125	502	73	136	183	32	3	3	55	7	3	7	34	2	80	26	19
Martinez, Ray, Palm Springs	.270	106	371	58	100	129	13	5	2	41	7	0	6	66	3	64	10	7
Matos, Francisco, Modesto	.280	50	189	32	53	60	4	0	1	22	4	1	1	30	1	24	19	8
Maurer, Ron, Bakersfield	.290	129	442	59	128	180	21	5	7	53	13	3	3	63	3	68	8	8
Maynard, Tow, San Bernardino	.290	70	245	45	71	85	9	1	1	16	6	3	3	32	3	61	57	16
McCarty, Dave, Visalia	.380	15	50	16	19	31	3	0	3	8	0	0	3	13	0	7	3	1
McCray, Justin, Reno	.143	20	42	3	6	7	1	0	0	3	0	1	0	2	0	12	0	0
McFarlin, Jason, San Jose*	.233	103	407	65	95	121	10	5	2	33	10	2	14	47	2	72	46	20
Meares, Pat, Visalia	.303	89	360	53	109	156	21	4	6	44	0	4	5	24	0	63	15	5
Mercedes, Henry, Modesto	.258	116	388	55	100	135	17	3	4	61	3	3	2	68	1	110	5	8
Messer, Doug, Reno*	.000	25	2	0	0	0	0	0	0	0	0	0	0	0	0	0	0	0
Messerly, Michael, Modesto	.259	103	355	50	92	139	23	0	8	63	4	2	1	59	2	90	5	2
Mieske, Matt, High Desert	.341	133	492	108	168	261	36	6	15	119	0	4	13	94	6	82	39	12
Mifune, Hideyuki, Salinas	.300	132	493	85	148	185	17	1	6	49	16	5	5	53	0	69	30	11
Miller, Roger, San Jose	.274	108	369	59	101	140	10	1	9	59	9	3	6	52	5	38	4	0
Mitchell, Tommy, Reno	.265	119	411	65	109	174	20	6	11	61	3	4	13	71	2	108	0	2
Mondesi, Raul, Bakersfield	.283	28	106	23	30	50	7	2	3	13	0	1	3	5	1	21	9	4
Mota, Domingo, Bakersfield	.275	104	408	75	112	160	20	2	8	44	10	4	6	44	1	83	37	19
Munoz, Orlando, Palm Springs†	.270	36	122	16	33	37	4	0	0	10	7	0	3	15	0	23	3	3
Muramatsu, Arikato, Salinas	.208	121	318	46	66	79	7	3	0	17	9	2	2	17	0	72	10	5
Murray, Steve, San Bernardino†	.000	5	11	0	0	0	0	0	0	0	0	0	0	3	0	2	0	0
Nava, Lipso, San Bernardino	.271	86	258	19	70	91	5	0	2	33	3	2	6	20	0	43	5	4
Newfield, Marc, San Bernardino	.300	125	440	64	132	193	22	3	11	68	0	5	10	59	9	90	12	6
Noland, J.D., High Desert*	.277	128	495	114	137	196	23	12	4	67	5	4	2	78	5	96	81	23
Nunez, Alex, Visalia*	.212	106	364	44	77	84	3	2	0	16	7	0	2	20	0	87	19	9
Oberdank, Jeff, Palm Springs	.172	30	93	9	16	22	2	2	0	5	1	2	5	11	0	7	2	1
O'Leary, Troy, Stockton*	.263	126	418	63	110	153	20	4	5	46	1	3	5	73	5	96	4	9
Osinski, Glenn, Modesto	.268	111	373	67	100	163	20	2	13	69	4	7	3	59	0	77	4	10
Owens, Jay, Visalia	.245	65	233	33	57	94	17	1	6	33	0	2	8	35	1	70	14	6
Palma, Brian, Salinas*	.271	122	428	54	116	159	19	3	6	58	4	6	9	64	2	81	23	15
Parker, Brad, Modesto	.239	25	88	15	21	32	2	0	3	8	1	0	1	11	0	19	1	1
Partrick, Dave, Palm Springs	.202	97	302	32	61	81	5	3	3	24	7	1	1	14	0	118	15	12
Pattin, Jon, San Jose*	.269	36	78	10	21	21	0	0	0	11	0	0	0	13	0	16	0	0
Perez, Beban, Palm Springs*	.245	17	53	9	13	15	0	1	0	5	2	0	1	3	0	15	1	1
Peters, Rex, Bakersfield†	.297	81	276	48	82	105	12	4	1	50	0	5	0	57	2	42	4	3
Phillips, J.R., Palm Springs*	.248	130	471	64	117	203	22	2	20	70	1	2	3	57	4	144	15	14
Piazza, Mike, Bakersfield	.277	117	448	71	124	242	27	2	29	80	0	8	3	47	2	83	0	3
Pirkl, Greg, San Bernardino	.314	63	239	32	75	132	13	1	14	53	0	6	2	12	1	43	4	0
Postema, Andy, Reno	.211	111	413	51	87	108	13	4	0	40	4	1	8	42	1	82	6	4
Raabe, Brian, Visalia	.257	85	311	36	80	88	3	1	1	22	3	2	4	40	0	14	15	5
Raasch, Glen, San Bernardino	.000	2	4	0	0	0	0	0	0	0	1	0	0	0	0	3	0	0
Rabb, John, 34 Reno-3 Sal.	.273	37	132	27	36	60	6	0	6	17	1	0	3	22	0	32	3	2
Reid, Derek, San Jose	.269	121	454	72	122	169	23	6	4	65	6	10	1	37	2	91	27	9
Rivera, Rafael, Salinas	.200	75	150	18	30	43	5	1	2	17	2	1	2	13	0	51	1	0
Rodriguez, Edgal, Palm Springs	.214	10	28	3	6	8	2	0	0	2	0	0	1	1	0	6	1	0
Roebuck, Joe, Reno	.266	112	394	45	105	176	19	5	14	54	4	7	6	25	3	98	2	6
Rolen, Steve, San Jose	.255	102	321	56	82	126	13	8	5	49	4	1	8	45	1	86	16	6
Rumsey, Derrell, Visalia	.236	52	144	13	34	42	3	1	1	16	3	1	3	8	1	32	6	5
Salazar, Angel, Salinas	.254	22	67	12	17	19	2	0	0	7	3	1	1	7	1	5	1	0
Salazar, Carlos, Salinas	.262	30	103	10	27	45	4	1	4	22	0	0	1	4	1	28	1	0
Sanchez, Ozzie, High Desert*	.244	95	312	47	76	131	13	0	14	55	0	6	8	46	2	70	4	3
Santana, Ruben, San Bernardino	.302	108	394	55	119	152	16	4	3	43	9	5	6	26	4	74	34	12
Sheehy, Mike, Palm Springs	.000	7	15	1	0	0	0	0	0	0	0	0	0	4	0	4	0	0
Shelton, Harry, Salinas*	.218	92	326	41	71	91	8	3	2	33	1	2	4	31	1	53	12	12
Shepperd, Rich, Salinas	.136	28	81	8	11	19	3	1	1	4	3	0	2	5	0	21	2	0
Showalter, J.R., Palm Springs	.205	44	161	19	33	55	7	3	3	24	1	4	0	34	4	34	4	1
Simmons, Enoch, Modesto	.242	130	443	81	107	132	13	3	2	38	2	2	4	92	2	98	28	15
Sims, Gregory, Visalia	.133	4	15	3	2	2	0	0	0	0	0	0	0	0	0	6	1	0
Snyder, Randy, Stockton†	.256	82	223	33	57	90	11	2	6	33	4	3	9	37	1	77	7	2
Songini, Mike, Reno*	.235	20	51	6	12	13	1	0	0	4	0	0	2	5	0	8	1	1
Spires, Tony, San Jose	.213	77	230	30	49	54	5	0	0	18	6	0	3	25	0	44	7	2
Stahoviak, Scott, Visalia*	.278	43	158	29	44	58	9	1	1	25	2	0	3	22	2	28	4	3
Stephens, Brian, 54 Reno-56 S.B.*	.270	110	363	42	98	145	18	1	9	53	0	3	2	31	3	85	6	5
Stiner, Rick, Reno	.000	3	2	2	0	0	0	0	0	0	0	0	0	0	0	2	0	0
Sutherland, Alex, San Bernardino	.404	14	47	8	19	38	5	1	4	21	0	0	1	3	0	14	0	1
Swim, Greg, Salinas	.200	17	45	5	9	11	0	1	0	1	1	0	0	3	0	16	2	2
Tavarez, Jesus, San Bernardino	.283	124	466	80	132	164	11	3	5	41	13	1	4	39	1	78	69	20
Thomas, Delvin, San Bernardino	.229	124	389	64	89	148	16	2	13	43	7	3	12	50	2	101	24	11
Thomas, Royal, High Desert	.000	27	0	0	0	0	0	0	0	0	0	0	0	0	0	0	0	1

Player, Team	Avg.	G	AB	R	H	TB	2B	3B	HR	RBI	SH	SF	HP	BB	Int. BB	SO	SB	CS
Threadgill, George, Reno	.236	43	123	19	29	41	7	1	1	16	3	0	1	35	2	35	3	1
Turang, Brian, San Bernardino	.180	34	100	9	18	22	2	1	0	4	1	0	3	15	0	31	6	6
Turco, Frank, Reno	.173	38	104	7	18	23	3	1	0	4	3	1	2	7	0	28	3	0
Urbon, Joe, Reno*	.277	19	65	13	18	33	4	1	3	19	0	0	3	6	1	13	2	1
Uribe, Jose, San Jose†	.111	3	9	0	1	3	0	1	0	1	0	1	0	1	0	2	0	0
Uribe, Wilson, Reno†	.206	10	34	3	7	11	1	0	1	7	0	1	0	3	0	6	0	1
Verstandig, Mark, High Desert*	.240	68	171	26	41	48	4	0	1	17	2	1	0	55	3	35	3	3
Vranjes, Sam, San Bernardino*	.216	70	199	14	43	65	7	0	5	22	3	1	3	11	1	50	3	1
Waggoner, James, Modesto	.224	86	241	34	54	68	4	2	2	19	4	1	2	70	0	66	3	1
Walker, Dane, Modesto*	.273	22	66	11	18	22	2	1	0	5	1	1	0	14	0	9	2	3
Wallace, Tim, Reno†	.359	33	131	21	47	62	9	0	2	17	2	1	0	16	2	15	5	4
Watts, Burgess, Bakersfield	.278	16	54	7	15	21	3	0	1	7	1	0	0	1	0	10	0	0
Weaver, Trent, 27 Mod.-33 Stock.	.240	60	192	20	46	63	9	1	2	17	3	2	1	27	0	48	2	2
Webb, Lonnie, Bakersfield	.291	87	340	71	99	141	18	3	6	36	6	3	5	46	2	76	22	16
Weber, Pete, San Jose*	.284	71	271	56	77	108	16	3	3	40	1	5	4	38	4	63	18	6
Wilder, Willie, Reno	.261	31	69	14	18	26	2	0	2	7	0	0	2	7	0	19	1	2
Williams, Cliff, Reno	.267	15	30	5	8	9	1	0	0	0	0	0	0	0	0	10	0	0
Williams, Eddie, San Jose*	.260	25	77	8	20	26	2	2	0	11	0	0	0	13	2	13	0	1
Williams, Matt, Reno	.225	55	151	17	34	44	8	1	0	11	3	0	1	13	1	37	0	1
Williams, Reggie, Palm Springs†	.295	14	44	10	13	17	1	0	1	2	1	0	1	21	0	15	6	5
Witkowski, Matt, High Desert	.266	129	485	80	129	180	17	8	6	56	6	3	6	60	2	81	24	11
Wrona, Dave, Stockton†	.211	15	38	9	8	11	1	1	0	4	0	0	0	11	0	11	0	0
Yamanouchi, Kenichi, Salinas*	.242	90	223	16	54	69	12	0	1	14	4	1	3	30	0	58	2	3
Yasuda, Hideyuki, Salinas	.240	128	416	35	100	140	19	3	5	46	10	5	2	46	3	120	5	6
Young, Derrick, San Bernardino	.264	109	330	35	87	110	11	3	2	19	4	1	4	34	1	65	13	9
Young, Selwyn, Reno†	.333	4	6	0	2	2	0	0	0	2	0	1	0	1	0	2	0	0

The following pitchers, listed alphabetically by club, with games in parentheses, had no plate appearances, primarily through use of designated hitters:

BAKERSFIELD—Bustillos, Albert (11); Carroll, Donnie (15); Daspit, James (22); de la Hoya, Javier (27); Hansell, Greg (25); Helmick, Tony (5); Hershiser, Orel (2); Hoffman, Kevin (10); Kerr, C.J. (11); Martinez, Pedro (10); McFarlin, Terric (26); Mimbs, Mark (27); Mintz, Steve (28); O'Connor, Ben (16); Pascual, Jorge (5); Piotrowicz, Brian (33); Potthoff, Mike (4); Stryker, Ed (30); Tatis, Fausto (6); Tipton, Gordon (43); Treadwell, Jody (17).

HIGH DESERT—Bryand, Renay (10); DeVille, Dan (38); Estrada, Jay (21); Fredrickson, Scott (23); Galindez, Luis (11); Hammaker, Atlee (2); Lebron, Jose (5); Lifgren, Kelly (33); McKeon, Brian (29); Reed, Billy (21); Sanders, Scott (21); Silcox, Rusty (18); Smithberg, Roger (3); Soltero, Saul (34); Wilkinson, Brian (20); Worrell, Tim (11); Zinter, Ed (50).

MODESTO—Brock, Russ (4); Burns, Todd (2); Cormier, Russ (6); Erwin, Scott (11); Fermin, Ramon (3); Garland, Chaon (27); Hokuf, Ken (28); Honeycutt, Rick (3); Klink, Joe (3); Kracl, Darin (11); Lardizabal, Ruben (33); Love, Will (24); Mejia, Delfino (18); Miller, Rick (11); Miller, Russ (3); Mohler, Mike (21); Patrick, Bronswell (28); Phoenix, Steve (27); Rose, Scott (13); Show, Eric (1); Smith, Todd (33); Strebeck, Ricky (32); Sudbury, Craig (17).

PALM SPRINGS—Bannister, Floyd (7); Bennett, Erik (8); Berrios, Hector (10); Haffner, Les (22); Holzemer, Mark (6); King, Steve (32); Loubier, Steve (35); Martinez, Fili (5); Merriman, Brett (34); Montoya, Norm (17); Pakele, Louis (26); Peck, Steve (17); Powers, Randy (5); Saltz, Robert (20); Sontag, Alan (5); Swingle, Paul (43); Valenzuela, Fernando (1); Van Winkle, David (31); Vegely, Bruce (40); Vidmar, Don (6).

RENO—Beck, Dion (4); Buonantony, Rich (5); Crane, Rich (10); Easley, Logan (3); Everson, Greg (7); Gilles, Tom (10); Grove, Scott (2); Gunn, Clay (1); Johnson, Dom (26); Kracl, Darin (11); Lienhard, Steve (1); Lopez, Rob (7); Magill, Jim (1); McCray, Todd (38); McKeon, Kasey (2); Mead, Timber (24); Norris, Mike (6); Odekirk, Rick (25); Olker, Joe (6); Parisotto, Barry (31); Phillips, Lonnie (23); Pinon, Abdom (15); Roberts, Pete (10); Shaw, Shelby (17); Stewart, John (3); Stuart, Brad (5); Treanor, Dean (1); Vargas, Jose (9); Voit, David (8). Warren, Joe (15).

SALINAS—Arola, Bruce (41); Carrasco, Carlos (26); Dillard, Gordy (19); Fitzgerald, Dave (12); Ikesue, Kazutaka (28); Karasinski, Dave (24); Livingston, Dennis (14); Maye, Steve (13); McCreadie, Brant (11); Nishioka, Tsuyoshi (29); Ohta, Katsumasa (35); Ohtsubo, Yukio (41); Oka, Yukitoshi (13); Olson, Ken (3); Oshio, Kenichi (13); Stewart, John (33).

SAN BERNARDINO—Bankhead, Scott (3); Borski, Jeff (4); Cummings, John (29); Darwin, Jeff (16); Fitzer, Doug (30); Flynt, Bill (22); Garcia, Marcos (20); Givens, Brian (1); Gutierrez, Jim (17); Hampton, Mike (18); Holsman, Rich (4); Jones, Dennis (1); Kent, Troy (62); Knackert, Brent (2); Loe, Darin (9); McDonald, David (43); Mecir, Jim (14); Pena, Antonio (1); Pitcher, Scott (20); Rees, Sean (11); Rivas, Oscar (62); Rosenbalm, Marc (9); Wiley, Chuck (12); Woodson, Kerry (5); Youngblood, Todd (5); Zarranz, Fernando (11); Zavaras, Clint (11).

SAN JOSE—Aleys, Max (37); Benavides, Alvaro (30); Callahan, Steve (41); Dour, Brian (4); Hancock, Chris (9); Hanselman, Carl (25); Herring, Vince (39); Huisman, Richard (26); McGehee, Kevin (26); Ortiz, Angel (31); Pena, Pedro (16); Rapp, Pat (16); Sharko, Gary (54); Taylor, Rob (9); Whatley, Fred (9); Whitaker, Steve (6).

STOCKTON—Archer, Kurt (27); Berg, Rich (52); Cangemi, Jamie (54); Correa, Ramser (10); Dell, Tim (27); Drake, Sam (17); Fitzgerald, Dave (4); Grove, Scott (7); Holsman, Rich (30); Landry, Greg (5); McGraw, Thomas (11); Mikkelsen, Linc (27); Monson, Steve (15); Sandoval, Guillermo (5); Smith, John (5); Sparks, Steve (24); Tabaka, Jeff (4); Vancho, Robert (6); Vann, Brandy (23); Vargas, Jose (6).

VISALIA—Best, Jayson (27); Gregory, Brad (30); Gustafson, Ed (33); Henry, Jon (28); Hoppe, Dennis (9); Klonoski, Jason (18); Lewis, Mike (14); Lipson, Marc (49); Misuraca, Mike (21); Musselwhite, Darren (30); Nedin, Tim (12); Newman, Alan (15); Pulido, Carlos (57); Swope, Mark (13); White, Fred (39).

GRAND SLAMS—Mieske, 3; Delarwelle, Gainer, Martin, 2 each; Alfonso, Bryant, Busch, Collier, Cooley, Davenport, Dodson, Kluge, Lott, Messerly, Miller, Mitchell, Osinski, Piazza, Roebuck, Sanchez, Sutherland, W. Uribe, Witkowski, 1 each.

AWARDED FIRST BASE ON CATCHER'S INTERFERENCE—Witkowski 2 (Gil 2); Clemens (Yasuda); Dunn (Sutherland); Ingram (Brown); Martin (Kluge); Maurer (Kappesser); Mitchell (Couture); Rumsey (V. Marrero).

PITCHING

TEAM

Team	ERA	G	CG	ShO	Sv.	IP	H	R	ER	HR	HB	BB	Int. BB	SO	WP	Bk.
San Jose	2.67	136	16	18	41	1217.2	988	450	361	37	63	596	30	1080	90	11
Bakersfield	3.12	136	2	12	45	1216.1	1083	528	421	43	38	514	30	1137	65	12
Stockton	3.24	136	18	16	25	1209.1	1072	544	436	41	87	575	20	1065	92	18
Palm Springs	3.70	136	14	10	27	1194.0	1126	647	491	56	45	630	49	832	77	9
Modesto	4.29	136	6	6	36	1194.2	1195	689	569	104	47	596	39	841	90	10
Visalia	4.32	136	8	4	32	1195.0	1255	739	573	99	61	559	32	841	127	17
High Desert	4.53	136	10	7	30	1193.1	1245	772	601	102	57	631	26	942	95	13
San Bernardino	4.54	136	7	3	29	1200.2	1201	766	606	107	81	628	38	994	102	26
Salinas	4.87	136	21	5	25	1194.0	1352	784	646	99	68	570	11	801	108	21
Reno	5.13	136	15	7	31	1186.0	1358	841	676	101	79	659	29	850	102	15

INDIVIDUAL

(Leading qualifiers for earned-run average leadership— 109 or more innings)

*Throws lefthanded.

Pitcher, Team	W	L	Pct.	ERA	G	GS	CG	GF	ShO	Sv.	IP	H	R	ER	HR	HB	BB	Int. BB	SO	WP
Huisman, San Jose	16	4	.800	1.83	26	26	7	0	4	0	182.1	126	45	37	5	3	73	1	216	13
Mimbs, Bakersfield*	12	6	.667	2.22	27	25	0	1	0	0	170.0	134	44	42	2	3	59	2	164	4
McGehee, San Jose	13	6	.684	2.33	26	26	2	0	0	0	174.0	129	58	45	1	8	87	2	171	11
McFarlin, Bakersfield	14	6	.700	2.66	26	21	0	3	0	0	152.0	139	63	45	6	1	56	2	128	17
Dell, Stockton	10	9	.526	2.69	27	27	4	0	2	0	150.1	127	63	45	8	11	55	1	131	14
Mohler, Modesto*	9	4	.692	2.86	21	20	1	0	0	0	122.2	106	48	39	5	2	45	1	98	7
Hansell, Bakersfield	14	5	.737	2.87	25	25	0	0	0	0	150.2	142	56	48	5	5	42	1	132	3
Sparks, Stockton	9	10	.474	3.06	24	24	8	0	2	0	179.2	160	70	61	4	7	98	2	139	13
Patrick, Modesto	12	12	.500	3.24	28	26	3	1	1	0	169.2	158	77	61	9	1	60	4	95	7
Mead, Reno	13	7	.650	3.36	24	24	8	0	3	0	177.0	178	79	66	11	4	61	1	137	6

Departmental leaders: G—Alcantara, 64; W—Huismann, 16; L—Kent, Odekirk, Thomas, 13; Pct.—Green, .900; GS—Henry, 28; CG—Mead, Sparks, 8; GF—Kent, 50; ShO—Huismann, 4; Sv.—Sharko, 31; IP—Huismann, 182.1; H—B. McKeon, 197; R—Lardizabal, 115; ER—Lardizabal, 97; HR—Gustafson, 17; HB—Mikkelsen, Odekirk, 14; BB—Sparks, Van Winkle, 98; IBB—Kent, 15; SO—Huismann, 216; WP—Gustafson, 28.

(All pitchers—listed alphabetically)

Pitcher, Team	W	L	Pct.	ERA	G	GS	CG	GF	ShO	Sv.	IP	H	R	ER	HR	HB	BB	Int. BB	SO	WP
Alcantara, Reno*	6	3	.667	5.15	64	0	0	26	0	4	71.2	81	54	41	7	2	53	1	66	9
Aleys, San Jose*	5	1	.833	2.28	37	1	0	11	0	1	79.0	55	21	20	1	7	44	4	55	8
Archer, Stockton	2	4	.333	4.27	27	6	0	9	0	1	46.1	45	36	22	1	7	29	3	26	5
Arola, Salinas	2	6	.250	3.38	41	1	0	38	0	18	53.1	54	22	20	4	2	15	1	41	4
Bankhead, San Bernardino	0	1	.000	5.06	2	2	0	0	0	0	5.1	4	4	3	2	1	2	0	4	0
Bannister, Palm Springs*	0	3	.000	6.59	7	5	0	1	0	0	28.2	32	24	21	1	2	9	1	27	1
Beck, Reno*	0	1	.000	4.50	4	0	0	2	0	0	6.0	8	8	3	0	0	4	1	8	0
Benavides, San Jose	5	2	.714	1.30	30	0	0	11	0	0	34.2	23	7	5	0	8	16	3	21	1
Bennett, Palm Springs*	2	3	.400	2.51	8	8	1	0	0	0	43.0	41	15	12	2	3	27	0	31	0
Berg, Stockton	7	7	.500	2.33	52	0	0	21	0	2	96.2	81	34	25	1	10	41	4	82	4
Berrios, Palm Springs*	2	0	.000	4.94	10	0	0	3	0	0	23.2	23	16	13	1	1	11	1	29	2
Best, Visalia	1	5	.167	7.56	27	6	0	10	0	0	50.0	49	52	42	4	2	64	3	35	17
Bethea, High Desert	0	0	.000	6.75	1	0	0	0	0	0	1.1	1	1	1	0	0	2	0	1	0
Borski, San Bernardino	2	0	1.000	6.00	4	3	0	0	0	0	21.0	16	14	14	2	2	18	0	20	3
Brock, Modesto	1	2	.333	4.00	4	4	0	0	0	0	27.0	25	15	12	3	1	6	0	12	1
Brown, Visalia	0	0	.000	9.00	1	0	0	1	0	0	1.0	2	1	1	0	0	0	0	1	0
Bryand, High Desert*	3	1	.750	3.86	10	1	0	4	0	0	11.2	12	6	5	0	0	4	1	13	0
Buonantony, Reno	1	4	.200	7.33	5	5	0	0	0	0	23.1	26	25	19	4	3	25	0	15	3
Burns, Modesto	1	0	1.000	10.50	2	1	0	0	0	0	6.0	9	7	7	1	1	3	0	8	3
Bustillos, Bakersfield	2	3	.400	1.48	11	5	1	4	0	1	42.2	31	15	7	2	1	16	0	37	5
Callahan, San Jose*	5	5	.500	2.09	41	0	0	14	0	1	60.1	53	22	14	2	7	31	7	61	5
Cangemi, Stockton	4	7	.364	4.31	54	6	1	28	0	7	96.0	98	57	46	3	7	61	5	78	16
Carrasco, Salinas	9	10	.474	4.42	26	23	2	1	1	0	144.2	162	92	71	8	8	77	0	105	13
Carroll, Bakersfield*	0	1	.000	6.16	15	0	0	5	0	1	19.0	24	14	13	1	1	21	2	22	0
Clark, Stockton*	0	0	.000	0.00	1	0	0	0	0	0	1.0	1	0	0	0	0	0	0	1	0
Clemens, Reno	0	0	.000	16.62	3	0	0	2	0	0	4.1	5	8	8	0	0	10	0	3	1
Cormier, Modesto	4	2	.667	3.75	6	5	0	1	0	0	36.0	38	18	15	2	1	11	0	17	1
Correa, Stockton	2	1	.667	2.94	10	8	0	0	0	0	33.2	31	14	11	1	2	20	0	21	2
Crane, Reno*	1	1	.500	13.86	10	1	0	3	0	0	12.1	19	19	19	1	1	15	1	3	2
Crowe, San Jose	0	0	.000	0.00	3	0	0	3	0	0	2.1	0	0	0	0	0	2	0	3	0
Cummings, San Bernardino*	4	10	.286	4.06	29	20	0	2	0	1	124.0	129	79	56	7	3	61	1	120	15
Darwin, San Bernardino	3	9	.250	6.20	16	14	0	1	0	0	74.0	80	53	51	14	4	31	1	58	1
Daspit, Bakersfield	3	2	.600	3.20	22	9	0	6	0	2	64.2	58	29	23	1	1	36	2	47	6
Delahoya, Bakersfield	6	4	.600	3.67	27	11	1	7	0	2	98.0	92	47	40	6	1	44	1	102	3
Dell, Stockton	10	9	.526	2.69	27	27	4	0	2	0	150.1	127	63	45	8	11	55	1	131	14
Deville, High Desert	1	4	.200	5.63	38	1	0	14	0	0	70.1	76	61	44	8	2	49	2	49	4
Dillard, Salinas*	5	7	.417	4.80	19	19	3	0	0	0	114.1	124	76	61	7	8	53	2	83	12
Dour, San Jose	1	0	1.000	1.96	4	3	0	1	0	0	18.1	16	6	4	0	0	4	0	12	0
Drake, Stockton	2	3	.400	4.44	17	5	0	5	0	1	52.2	50	31	26	1	4	38	0	58	1
Easley, Reno	0	0	.000	2.70	3	0	0	2	0	1	3.1	2	3	1	0	0	2	0	2	0
Edmonds, Palm Springs*	0	0	.000	0.00	1	0	0	0	0	0	2.0	1	0	0	0	0	3	0	2	0
Eppard, Salinas*	1	0	1.000	0.00	1	0	0	0	0	0	1.0	1	0	0	0	0	1	0	0	1
Erwin, Modesto	1	0	1.000	2.70	11	0	0	9	0	2	13.1	7	4	4	1	0	6	0	22	4
Estrada, High Desert	2	1	.667	4.62	21	0	0	3	0	0	37.0	44	22	19	4	0	11	1	27	3
Everson, Reno	0	2	.000	4.38	7	0	0	6	0	1	12.1	14	11	6	2	2	7	0	5	0
Fermin, Modesto	1	0	1.000	4.38	3	2	0	0	0	0	12.1	16	7	6	1	1	3	0	5	0
Firova, Reno	0	0	.000	36.00	1	0	0	1	0	0	1.0	4	4	4	0	0	1	0	0	0
Fitzer, San Bernardino*	3	0	1.000	5.56	30	0	0	6	0	1	55.0	59	39	34	6	6	30	1	52	10
Fitzgerald, 4 Stock.- 12 Sal.*	4	6	.400	4.96	16	13	3	2	0	0	81.2	80	57	45	9	6	49	1	50	8
Flynt, San Bernardino*	1	0	1.000	4.50	22	0	0	7	0	0	38.0	46	27	19	1	4	25	0	40	5
Fredrickson, High Desert	4	1	.800	2.31	23	0	0	19	0	7	35.0	31	15	9	2	1	18	2	26	6
Galindez, High Desert*	4	3	.571	3.88	11	10	0	1	0	0	58.0	53	29	25	5	2	28	0	54	5
Garcia, San Bernardino	7	10	.412	3.46	20	20	4	0	2	0	130.0	97	57	50	7	7	62	1	123	5
Garland, Modesto	8	9	.471	4.32	27	24	1	1	0	0	156.1	159	88	75	15	9	61	0	117	7
Gilles, Reno	1	5	.167	6.36	10	8	1	2	0	0	46.2	67	40	33	9	3	16	2	28	4
Givens, San Bernardino*	1	0	1.000	1.80	1	1	0	0	0	0	5.0	4	2	1	0	0	1	0	4	0
Gonzalez, Reno	0	0	.000	13.50	2	0	0	2	0	0	2.0	5	3	3	1	0	0	0	1	0
Green, Stockton*	9	1	.900	1.92	12	11	2	0	2	0	75.0	41	18	16	1	5	33	0	106	4
Gregory, Visalia	6	2	.750	5.17	30	1	0	11	0	0	55.2	73	43	32	4	0	25	5	39	5
Grove, 7 Stock.-2 Reno	0	2	.000	6.75	9	1	0	6	0	0	13.1	16	12	10	1	0	11	1	6	2
Gustafson, Visalia	8	5	.615	4.97	33	18	0	10	0	4	130.1	134	93	72	17	6	86	2	120	28
Gutierrez, San Bernardino	4	4	.500	6.53	17	14	1	0	0	0	82.2	100	65	60	11	2	37	0	66	4
Haffner, Palm Springs	2	2	.500	5.53	22	0	0	4	0	0	42.1	48	33	26	1	3	31	2	29	5
Hammaker, High Desert*	0	0	.000	2.25	2	2	0	0	0	0	8.0	9	3	2	1	0	3	0	3	2
Hampton, San Bernardino*	1	7	.125	5.25	18	15	1	1	1	0	73.2	71	58	43	3	6	47	1	57	12
Hancock, San Jose*	4	3	.571	2.03	9	9	0	0	0	0	53.1	42	16	12	4	1	33	1	59	5
Hansell, Bakersfield	14	5	.737	2.87	25	25	0	0	0	0	150.2	142	56	48	5	5	42	1	132	3
Hanselman, San Jose	13	7	.650	3.80	25	24	5	0	1	0	156.1	152	71	66	11	4	66	0	88	5
Haslock, High Desert	1	1	.500	4.71	20	0	0	8	0	0	36.1	36	25	19	2	6	18	1	20	4
Helmick, Bakersfield	2	0	1.000	0.00	5	0	0	4	0	0	10.0	6	0	0	0	0	4	1	12	0

Pitcher, Team	W	L	Pct.	ERA	G	GS	CG	GF	ShO	Sv.	IP	H	R	ER	HR	HB	BB	Int. BB	SO	WP
Henry, Visalia	8	13	.381	4.48	28	28	4	0	0	0	172.2	174	103	86	13	12	60	2	110	11
Herring, San Jose*	11	3	.786	3.61	39	9	0	11	0	2	102.1	76	49	41	1	5	69	2	93	10
Hershiser, Bakersfield	2	0	1.000	0.82	2	2	0	0	0	0	11.0	5	2	1	0	0	1	0	6	0
Hoffman, Bakersfield*	1	0	1.000	6.98	10	1	0	4	0	0	19.1	20	15	15	1	0	12	1	20	1
Hokuf, Modesto	3	4	.429	4.17	28	0	0	15	0	7	45.1	38	24	21	2	4	25	2	43	3
Holsman, 4 S.B. - 30 Stock.*	4	9	.308	2.80	34	2	0	20	0	6	61.0	50	29	19	4	1	27	2	68	9
Holzemer, Palm Springs	0	4	.000	2.86	6	6	0	0	0	0	22.0	15	14	7	1	1	16	1	19	1
Honeycutt, Modesto*	0	0	.000	0.00	3	3	0	0	0	0	5.0	4	1	0	0	1	1	0	5	1
Hoppe, Visalia	2	0	1.000	6.48	9	0	0	4	0	0	16.2	15	13	12	1	0	10	0	10	1
Huisman, San Jose	16	4	.800	1.83	26	26	7	0	4	0	182.1	126	45	37	5	3	73	1	216	13
Hunter, San Bernardino	0	0	.000	0.00	1	0	0	1	0	0	1.0	0	0	0	0	0	3	0	1	0
Ikesue, Salinas	11	9	.550	5.71	28	22	2	1	0	0	134.0	171	102	85	12	4	63	1	76	5
Johnson, Reno	3	5	.375	3.25	25	9	1	5	0	2	72.0	65	31	26	3	4	38	0	63	7
Jones, San Bernardino*	0	0	.000	0.00	1	0	0	0	0	0	0.0	0	0	0	0	0	0	0	0	0
Kappesser, Stockton	0	0	.000	27.00	1	0	0	1	0	0	1.0	4	3	3	1	0	1	0	0	0
Karasinski, Salinas*	1	3	.250	4.28	24	2	0	7	0	0	48.1	62	33	23	5	0	12	0	22	4
Keathley, Modesto	0	0	.000	7.71	2	0	0	2	0	0	2.1	4	4	2	1	0	0	0	0	0
Kent, San Bernardino	7	13	.350	3.24	62	0	0	50	0	15	89.0	87	57	32	5	6	38	15	69	9
Kerr, Bakersfield	1	1	.500	5.40	11	0	0	6	0	2	10.0	6	8	6	0	0	8	1	10	0
King, San Bernardino	0	0	.000	0.00	2	0	0	2	0	0	2.0	1	0	0	0	0	1	0	1	0
King, Palm Springs	5	3	.625	2.39	32	9	1	19	1	9	98.0	71	33	26	1	6	67	5	110	10
Klink, Modesto*	0	0	.000	3.60	3	3	0	0	0	0	5.0	4	2	2	2	0	1	0	1	0
Klonoski, Visalia*	2	0	1.000	3.04	18	0	0	5	0	1	23.2	23	10	8	4	0	13	3	17	0
Knackert, San Bernardino	0	0	.000	2.08	2	2	0	0	0	0	4.1	3	1	1	0	1	3	0	7	0
Kracl, 5 Reno - 11 Mod.	3	8	.273	5.68	16	16	0	0	0	0	88.2	111	63	56	13	4	53	3	53	5
Landry, Stockton	0	0	.000	6.75	5	1	0	2	0	1	16.0	14	14	12	1	3	13	0	11	4
Lardizabal, Modesto	4	10	.286	6.45	33	18	0	9	0	0	135.1	159	115	97	10	7	91	4	65	10
Lebron, High Desert	0	3	.000	9.78	5	4	0	0	0	0	19.1	27	26	21	3	1	16	1	14	3
Lewis, Visalia*	3	1	.750	2.60	14	10	0	0	0	0	65.2	66	27	19	8	0	26	1	25	0
Lienhard, Reno	0	0	.000	3.00	1	0	0	0	0	0	3.0	4	2	1	0	0	0	0	1	0
Lifgren, High Desert	5	7	.417	4.36	33	10	0	2	0	0	99.0	101	63	48	8	1	55	3	87	4
Lipson, Visalia	5	4	.556	3.64	49	0	0	21	0	6	76.2	86	37	31	6	4	34	3	33	6
Livingston, Salinas*	0	2	.000	5.54	14	2	0	1	0	0	26.0	36	21	16	2	1	21	1	18	5
Loe, San Bernardino	0	1	.000	7.30	9	0	0	3	0	1	12.1	13	12	10	4	0	9	0	4	0
Lopez, Reno	0	1	.000	3.77	7	4	1	1	0	0	31.0	39	18	13	4	1	9	0	21	0
Loubier, Palm Springs	8	5	.615	3.40	35	11	1	7	1	1	111.1	105	55	42	3	7	56	8	60	10
Love, Modesto*	2	1	.667	5.18	24	0	0	8	0	1	41.2	44	28	24	5	0	28	2	39	7
Magill, Reno	0	0	.000	45.00	1	0	0	0	0	0	1.0	6	5	5	0	0	1	0	2	0
Marrero, Stockton	0	0	.000	45.00	1	0	0	0	0	0	1.0	4	6	5	1	0	1	0	0	1
Martinez, Palm Springs*	2	1	.667	2.10	5	5	1	0	1	0	30.0	17	9	7	1	1	16	0	23	1
Martinez, Bakersfield	8	0	1.000	2.05	10	10	0	0	0	0	61.1	41	17	14	3	5	19	0	83	1
Maye, Salinas	3	8	.273	5.61	13	12	5	0	0	0	85.0	98	64	53	8	5	52	0	48	6
McCray, Reno	1	5	.167	7.20	38	5	0	8	0	0	75.0	110	74	60	7	8	61	5	42	11
McCreadie, Salinas	0	2	.000	5.31	20	3	0	8	0	1	42.1	35	28	25	2	6	27	0	41	8
McDonald, San Bernardino*	2	3	.400	5.33	43	2	0	11	0	2	77.2	92	50	46	10	5	34	5	56	5
McFarlin, Bakersfield	14	6	.700	2.66	26	21	0	3	0	0	152.0	139	63	45	6	1	56	2	128	17
McGehee, San Jose	13	6	.684	2.33	26	26	2	0	0	0	174.0	129	58	45	1	8	87	2	171	11
McGraw, Stockton*	3	0	1.000	2.30	11	7	0	1	0	0	47.0	35	15	12	2	2	13	0	39	3
McKeon, High Desert	11	9	.550	5.15	28	26	0	2	0	0	159.0	197	107	91	12	10	67	2	123	4
McKeon, Reno	0	0	.000	36.00	1	0	0	0	0	0	1.0	5	4	4	0	0	2	0	0	0
Mead, Reno	13	7	.650	3.36	24	24	8	0	3	0	177.0	178	79	66	11	4	61	1	137	6
Mecir, San Bernardino	3	5	.375	4.22	14	12	0	2	0	1	70.1	72	40	33	3	3	37	0	48	8
Mejia, Modesto	2	2	.500	2.51	18	0	0	13	0	1	32.1	35	14	9	2	2	21	5	20	1
Mercedes, Modesto	0	1	.000	81.00	1	0	0	1	0	0	1.0	4	9	9	0	1	6	3	0	2
Merriman, Palm Springs	4	1	.800	1.96	34	0	0	17	0	2	41.1	36	20	9	0	2	30	5	23	4
Messer, Reno*	5	9	.357	6.10	25	15	1	5	0	3	90.0	113	72	61	7	2	52	1	39	4
Mikkelsen, Stockton	5	5	.500	3.42	27	16	0	5	0	0	121.0	116	51	46	3	14	42	0	103	5
Ri. Miller, Modesto*	1	2	.333	4.20	11	0	0	5	0	0	15.0	22	11	7	0	2	10	1	10	1
Ru. Miller, Modesto	0	0	.000	19.50	3	0	0	1	0	0	6.0	14	13	13	3	0	5	0	4	0
Mimbs, Bakersfield*	12	6	.667	2.22	27	25	0	1	0	0	170.0	134	49	42	2	3	59	2	164	4
Mintz, Bakersfield	6	6	.500	4.30	28	11	0	6	0	3	92.0	85	56	44	2	4	58	1	101	9
Misuraca, Visalia	7	9	.438	4.27	21	19	2	0	1	0	116.0	131	65	55	12	8	39	1	82	13
Mohler, Modesto*	9	4	.692	2.86	21	20	1	0	0	0	122.2	106	48	39	5	2	45	1	98	7
Monson, Stockton	7	2	.778	1.69	15	13	3	0	1	0	96.0	74	23	18	2	4	28	0	75	6
Montoya, Palm Springs*	4	7	.364	4.11	17	17	1	0	0	0	105.0	117	64	48	10	2	26	4	45	3
Murray, San Bernardino	0	0	.000	22.50	1	0	0	1	0	0	2.0	5	5	5	0	2	2	0	2	0
Musselwhite, Visalia	7	8	.467	4.03	30	17	1	2	0	0	138.1	163	71	62	8	6	34	2	67	8
Nedin, Visalia*	1	5	.167	3.98	12	12	1	0	1	0	63.1	58	38	28	8	4	31	0	48	4
Newman, Visalia	6	5	.545	3.51	15	15	0	0	0	0	92.1	86	49	36	2	6	49	2	79	11
Nishioka, Salinas	4	7	.364	4.07	29	18	1	3	0	2	130.1	147	74	59	14	6	50	1	106	7
Norris, Reno	0	3	.000	6.35	6	6	0	0	0	0	28.1	31	23	20	3	4	11	0	21	5
O'Connor, Bakersfield*	1	1	.500	3.70	16	0	0	4	0	0	24.1	28	12	10	1	0	12	2	26	0
Odekirk, Reno*	3	13	.188	4.26	25	25	2	0	1	0	150.0	161	82	71	12	14	65	1	114	6
Ohta, Salinas	6	10	.375	4.06	35	15	5	11	0	1	148.2	161	74	67	11	7	51	2	93	8
Ohtsubo, Salinas	3	5	.375	6.80	41	3	0	18	0	1	87.1	123	76	66	10	8	35	0	40	7
Oka, Salinas	1	2	.333	7.40	13	2	0	2	0	0	20.2	24	22	17	1	3	12	0	12	7
Olker, Reno*	2	2	.500	7.39	6	6	0	0	0	0	31.2	39	30	26	2	2	20	0	21	6
Olson, Salinas*	0	0	.000	9.00	3	1	0	2	0	0	3.0	3	3	3	0	2	6	0	0	3
Ortiz, San Jose*	3	2	.600	4.89	31	3	0	6	0	1	57.0	48	34	31	3	5	44	3	60	12
Oshio, Salinas	2	1	.667	6.47	13	2	0	6	0	0	32.0	42	24	23	2	2	29	1	23	5
Pakele, Palm Springs	7	11	.389	4.65	26	26	2	0	0	0	162.2	182	101	84	15	4	60	2	75	9
Parisotto, Reno	7	3	.700	3.91	31	0	0	19	0	7	50.2	39	25	22	3	2	38	9	43	5
Pascual, Bakersfield	0	0	.000	20.77	5	0	0	1	0	0	4.1	5	12	10	0	0	12	0	6	0
Patrick, Modesto	12	12	.500	3.24	28	26	3	1	1	0	169.2	158	77	61	9	1	60	4	95	7
Peck, Palm Springs	6	4	.600	2.09	17	8	0	3	0	2	69.0	57	28	16	2	1	16	0	67	3
Pena, San Bernardino	0	0	.000	0.00	3	0	0	0	0	0	4.2	4	0	0	0	2	4	0	3	0
Pena, San Jose	4	4	.500	3.26	16	14	1	1	1	0	88.1	71	41	32	3	2	38	0	88	8
Phillips, Palm Springs*	0	0	.000	4.50	2	0	0	2	0	0	2.0	3	1	1	0	0	3	0	0	0
Phillips, Reno	3	2	.600	2.25	23	1	0	19	0	11	28.0	20	12	7	1	3	16	2	31	4
Phoenix, Modesto	5	2	.714	3.74	27	3	0	10	1	2	84.1	87	44	35	13	5	33	4	65	3
Pinon, San Jose	2	3	.400	4.50	15	1	0	3	0	1	24.0	30	31	12	2	1	26	1	21	2
Piotrowicz, Bakersfield	2	6	.250	2.45	33	0	0	26	0	11	58.2	45	26	16	1	1	18	4	42	2
Pitcher, San Bernardino	2	4	.333	6.82	20	3	0	10	0	3	31.2	36	29	24	4	8	16	3	26	3
Potthoff, Bakersfield	0	1	.000	5.40	4	2	0	0	0	0	8.1	14	7	5	1	0	4	0	7	0
Powers, Palm Springs	3	7	.300	7.80	15	9	1	5	0	0	45.0	45	45	39	3	0	50	2	20	6

Pitcher, Team	W	L	Pct.	ERA	G	GS	CG	GF	ShO	Sv.	IP	H	R	ER	HR	HB	BB	Int. BB	SO	WP
Pulido, Visalia*	1	5	.167	2.01	57	0	0	32	0	17	80.2	77	34	18	2	0	23	2	102	3
Raabe, Visalia	0	0	.000	0.00	1	0	0	1	0	0	1.0	0	0	0	0	0	0	0	0	0
Rapp, San Jose	7	5	.583	2.50	16	15	1	0	0	0	90.0	88	41	25	1	10	37	0	73	1
Reed, High Desert*	0	0	.000	5.76	21	0	0	11	0	1	45.1	48	34	29	10	5	33	1	21	9
Rees, San Bernardino	3	3	.500	3.18	11	9	1	0	0	0	62.1	47	27	22	5	1	28	0	50	1
Rivas, San Bernardino*	7	5	.583	4.17	62	0	0	22	0	3	95.0	87	55	44	11	8	40	7	71	2
Roberts, Reno*	5	1	.833	2.30	10	8	0	1	0	0	58.2	50	17	15	3	3	20	1	46	5
Rose, Modesto	3	3	.500	4.39	13	13	0	0	0	0	67.2	66	45	33	7	2	38	1	31	7
Rosenbalm, San Bernardino	0	0	.000	4.35	9	0	0	5	0	0	10.1	14	9	5	2	1	4	0	4	2
Saitz, Palm Springs	2	0	1.000	4.28	20	1	0	9	0	0	33.2	32	19	16	3	2	17	1	27	1
Sanders, High Desert	9	6	.600	3.66	21	21	4	0	2	0	132.2	114	72	54	7	7	72	2	93	8
Sandoval, Stockton	1	0	1.000	9.00	5	1	0	2	0	0	10.0	12	10	10	1	1	4	0	13	0
Sharko, San Jose	2	0	1.000	1.32	54	0	0	48	0	31	68.1	61	14	10	1	3	18	6	39	0
Shaw, Reno	3	2	.600	5.23	17	11	1	2	0	0	75.2	85	49	44	11	3	36	0	46	4
Show, Modesto	0	1	.000	16.88	1	1	0	0	0	0	2.2	6	5	5	1	0	1	0	1	0
Silcox, High Desert	5	1	.833	5.24	18	16	0	1	0	0	80.2	92	58	47	12	3	45	1	67	7
Smith, Stockton	0	0	.000	9.00	5	0	0	1	0	0	9.0	13	11	9	0	0	8	0	1	0
Smith, Modesto	4	4	.500	2.97	33	0	0	23	0	4	60.2	41	25	20	6	1	42	6	88	9
Smithberg, High Desert	1	1	.500	1.50	3	3	0	0	0	0	18.0	12	6	3	0	1	6	0	11	0
Snyder, Stockton	0	0	.000	0.00	2	0	0	2	0	0	2.0	0	0	0	0	0	0	0	2	0
Soltero, High Desert	2	2	.500	2.64	34	0	0	13	0	4	58.0	46	23	17	2	6	22	2	53	3
Sontag, Palm Springs	2	0	1.000	1.74	5	5	1	0	1	0	31.0	22	11	6	0	3	9	0	15	1
Sparks, Stockton	9	10	.474	3.06	24	24	8	0	2	0	179.2	160	70	61	4	7	98	2	139	13
Spires, San Jose	0	0	.000	0.00	1	0	0	1	0	0	1.0	0	0	0	0	0	0	0	0	0
Stewart, 3 Reno-33 Sal.*	3	5	.375	3.10	36	0	0	16	0	2	52.1	46	25	18	4	2	23	3	53	6
Strebeck, Modesto	2	1	.667	1.83	32	0	0	29	0	17	44.1	28	10	9	2	2	37	2	35	5
Stryker, Bakersfield	3	1	.750	1.93	30	0	0	16	0	6	56.0	46	15	12	0	2	17	2	38	2
Stuart, Reno	0	0	.000	14.04	5	0	0	2	0	0	8.1	16	14	13	2	0	8	1	6	1
Sudbury, Modesto	3	2	.600	5.32	17	2	0	2	0	1	44.0	45	28	26	2	3	24	1	28	8
Swingle, Palm Springs	5	4	.556	4.42	43	0	0	28	0	10	57.0	51	37	28	2	1	41	8	63	11
Swope, Visalia*	0	7	.000	5.72	13	10	0	1	0	0	61.1	64	59	39	7	7	25	1	31	9
Tabaka, Stockton*	0	2	.000	5.19	4	4	0	0	0	0	17.1	19	11	10	1	0	16	0	19	2
Tatis, Bakersfield	0	0	.000	9.64	6	0	0	1	0	1	9.1	12	11	10	2	1	7	0	9	1
Taylor, San Jose	0	1	.000	5.06	9	0	0	8	0	4	10.2	14	6	6	0	0	4	0	13	2
Thomas, High Desert	8	13	.381	4.70	27	27	4	0	0	0	155.0	178	108	81	15	5	61	2	99	9
Tipton, Bakersfield	3	4	.429	3.13	43	0	0	37	0	14	63.1	58	28	22	1	8	34	7	61	4
Treadwell, Bakersfield	5	4	.556	3.74	17	14	0	0	0	0	91.1	92	46	38	8	4	34	2	84	7
Treanor, Reno	0	0	.000	27.00	1	0	0	1	0	0	1.0	1	3	3	0	1	3	0	0	2
Valenzuela, Palm Springs*	0	0	.000	0.00	1	0	0	0	0	0	4.0	4	1	0	0	0	3	0	2	1
Vancho, Stockton	0	1	.000	5.25	6	0	0	0	0	0	12.0	13	7	7	1	1	5	0	15	1
Van Winkle, Palm Springs	7	9	.438	4.03	31	19	2	5	0	0	138.1	136	79	62	6	3	98	4	78	5
Vargas, 6 Stock.-9 Reno	1	1	.500	6.03	15	3	0	5	0	0	37.1	48	30	25	4	5	12	1	21	7
Vegely, Palm Springs*	2	3	.400	3.36	40	0	0	19	0	3	59.0	57	33	22	2	2	36	5	59	3
Verstandig, High Desert	0	0	.000	0.00	1	0	0	1	0	0	1.0	0	0	0	0	0	0	0	0	0
Vidmar, Palm Springs	4	2	.667	1.40	6	6	3	0	2	0	45.0	31	9	7	1	1	6	0	25	1
Voit, Reno	0	1	.000	13.00	8	0	0	1	0	0	9.0	22	23	13	0	2	7	0	7	0
Warren, Reno	1	0	1.000	8.14	15	0	0	4	0	0	24.1	37	28	22	2	7	21	0	21	3
Whatley, San Jose	1	0	1.000	1.80	9	0	0	5	0	0	10.0	9	4	2	0	1	5	1	7	2
Whitaker, San Jose*	2	1	.667	3.38	6	6	0	0	0	0	29.1	25	15	11	2	1	25	0	21	3
White, Visalia	1	9	.100	5.80	39	0	0	30	0	10	49.2	54	44	32	3	6	40	5	42	11
Wiley, San Bernardino	1	0	.000	4.58	12	0	0	4	0	2	17.2	18	13	9	0	0	12	1	15	1
Wilkinson, High Desert	6	2	.750	5.60	20	5	0	6	0	0	45.0	48	33	28	5	1	35	1	39	6
Williams, Reno	0	0	.000	9.00	1	0	0	0	0	0	1.0	0	1	1	0	0	3	0	1	1
Woodson, San Bernardino	2	0	1.000	1.95	5	5	0	0	0	0	27.2	33	13	6	3	0	16	0	14	1
Worrell, High Desert	5	2	.714	4.24	11	11	2	0	0	0	63.2	65	32	30	2	2	33	0	70	3
Yamanouchi, Salinas*	0	0	.000	36.00	1	0	0	1	0	0	1.0	2	4	4	1	0	3	0	1	1
Youngblood, San Bernardino	1	0	1.000	7.15	4	1	0	0	0	0	11.1	15	10	9	2	4	8	0	12	2
Zarranz, San Bernardino	0	2	.000	3.57	11	0	0	0	0	0	22.2	21	12	9	1	2	14	2	18	1
Zavaras, San Bernardino	1	3	.250	3.79	11	11	0	0	0	0	40.1	35	25	17	2	3	37	0	38	7
Zinter, High Desert	6	6	.500	5.49	50	0	0	41	0	18	59.0	55	48	36	4	4	53	4	72	15

BALKS—Rees, 6; Ohtsubo, 5; Cummings, Dell, Gustafson, Mecir, Mikkelsen, Pakele, Vann, 4 each; Delahoya, Hampton, Huisman, Ikesue, Mead, Odekirk, Stuart, Van Winkle, Zarranz, 3 each; Arola, Deville, Galindez, Henry, Lardizabal, Lebron, McGehee, Mimbs, Nedin, Ohta, Oka, Sanders, White, 2 each; Best, Borski, Callahan, Cangemi, Carrasco, Cormier, Darwin, Daspit, Drake, Flynt, Garland, Gregory, Hanselman, Herring, Hoffman, Holzemer, Hoppe, Kent, Klink, Landry, Lewis, Lifgren, Livingston, Lopez, P. Martinez, Maye, McCray, McCreadie, McGraw, B. McKeon, Mejia, Messer, Mintz, Mohler, Montoya, Musselwhite, Nishioka, Norris, Oshio, P. Pena, Pinon, Potthoff, Pulido, Rivas, Rose, Sandoval, Sharko, Shaw, Silcox, J. Smith, Stewart, Strebeck, Sudbury, Swope, Thomas, Tipton, Treadwell, Whitaker, Woodson, Zinter, 1 each.

COMBINATION SHUTOUTS—Delahoya-Tipton, Hansell-Carroll-Daspit, Hansell-Daspit, Hansell-Helmick, Hansell-Stryker, Martinez-Bustillos, McFarlin-Daspit-O'Connor, McFarlin-Daspit-Tipton, McFarlin-Kerr, Mimbs-Piotrowicz, Mimbs-Tipton, Potthoff-McFarlin, Bakersfield; Galindez-Zinter, Lifgren-Soltero-Zinter, McKeon-Deville-Zinter, Thomas-Deville-Bryand-Zinter, Thomas-Zinter, High Desert; Brock-Love, Fermin-Strebeck, Honeycutt-Patrick-Hokuf, Mohler-Strebeck, Modesto; King-Haffner, Peck-King, Peck-Merriman, Van Winkle-Merriman-Swingle, Palm Springs; Johnson-McCray-Warren-Crane-Alcantara, Johnson-Messer, Kracl-Parisotto, Reno; Carrasco-Arola, Dillard-Ohta-Stewart-Arola, Dillard-Ohtsubo-Ohta, Oshio-Livingston-Ohtsubo-Arola, Salinas; Dour-Pena, Hancock-Aleys-Herring, Hancock-Callahan-Benavides, Huismann-Aleys, Huismann-Callahan, Huismann-Sharko, McGehee-Herring, McGehee-Ortiz, McGehee-Ortiz-Sharko, McGehee-Sharko, Rapp-Sharko, Whitaker-Aleys-Benavides-Herring, San Jose; Correa-Vann, Dell-Archer-Berg, Dell-Berg, Green-Cangemi, Green-Drake-Archer, McGraw-Holsman, McGraw-Landry, Mikkelsen-Vann, Monson-Vann, Stockton; Henry-Musselwhite-Pulido, Lewis-Pulido, Visalia.

NO-HIT GAMES—Vidmar, Palm Springs, defeated Bakersfield, 2-0 (first game), April 22; Martinez, Palm Springs, defeated Bakersfield, 4-0, May 25; Hampton, San Bernardino, defeated Visalia, 6-0, May 31.

FIELDING

TEAM

Team	Pct.	G	PO	A	E	DP	PB	Team	Pct.	G	PO	A	E	DP	PB
San Jose	.967	136	3653	1441	175	131	21	Stockton	.962	136	3628	1563	207	131	29
Bakersfield	.964	136	3649	1488	192	116	35	High Desert	.959	136	3580	1431	213	124	57
Modesto	.963	136	3584	1435	193	108	32	Palm Springs	.957	136	3582	1522	228	131	26
San Bernardino	.962	136	3602	1417	196	115	46	Salinas	.957	136	3582	1438	228	132	40
Visalia	.962	136	3585	1658	205	133	55	Reno	.955	136	3558	1505	240	136	34

Triple plays—Palm Springs, Stockton.

*Throws lefthanded.

FIRST BASEMEN

Player, Team	Pct.	G	PO	A	E	DP
Alfonzo, Palm Springs	1.000	1	10	0	0	1
Armas, Modesto	.985	14	120	11	2	11
Beard, Bakersfield	1.000	14	100	6	0	15
Bishop, Salinas	.974	9	75	1	2	13
Bohringer, Bakersfield	1.000	4	11	1	0	2
Buckley, Visalia	.982	6	51	5	1	4
Busch, Bakersfield	.962	18	161	17	7	13
Carcione, Reno	1.000	2	11	2	0	3
Carlson, Salinas	.988	40	292	24	4	25
Castaldo, Stockton	.985	8	57	10	1	2
Chimelis, San Jose	1.000	2	11	0	0	0
Clemens, Reno	.963	9	69	10	3	6
Cohen, Visalia*	1.000	1	1	0	0	1
Cooley, Modesto	.980	27	226	24	5	19
Cortes, Reno*	.982	24	202	22	4	26
Crowe, San Jose	.986	29	190	28	3	18
Davenport, San Jose	.982	7	55	1	1	1
Delarwelle, Visalia	.979	9	90	2	2	8
Dodson, Stockton*	.998	51	441	36	1	36
Dominguez, Palm Springs	1.000	5	43	4	0	3
DUNN, Visalia*	.9913	125	1122	131	11	111
Edmonds, Palm Springs*	1.000	2	9	0	0	2
Eppard, Salinas*	.994	72	582	33	4	53
Forbes, Palm Springs	1.000	1	3	0	0	0
Gainer, High Desert*	.976	101	813	77	22	80
Gieseke, High Desert*	.994	40	305	29	2	30
Gonzalez, Bakersfield	.972	17	159	13	5	19
Helfand, Modesto	1.000	1	7	0	0	1
Hunter, San Bernardino	.980	55	367	29	8	41
James, San Jose	.988	100	758	65	10	87
Dodd Johnson, Reno	.991	88	719	80	7	78
Kawano, Salinas	1.000	1	9	1	0	2
Keitges, San Bernardino	.981	52	389	30	8	32
Kohno, Salinas	1.000	1	4	1	0	0
Laboy, Palm Springs*	1.000	3	17	2	0	0
Lund, Bakersfield	.944	2	15	2	1	0
Magallanes, San Bernardino	1.000	2	8	2	0	0
O. Marrero, Stockton*	.983	65	491	39	9	50
V. Marrero, Stockton	1.000	17	112	11	0	17
Messerly, Modesto	.988	86	677	61	9	57
Mitchell, Reno	.977	11	80	5	2	5
Murray, San Bernardino	1.000	1	1	0	0	0
Nava, San Bernardino	1.000	1	2	1	0	0
Newfield, San Bernardino	.985	17	124	5	2	13
Palma, Salinas	.750	1	3	0	1	0
Pattin, San Jose	.975	8	35	4	1	1
Peters, Bakersfield*	.991	71	588	57	6	46
Phillips, Palm Springs*	.9906	130	1166	94	12	117
Piazza, Bakersfield	.981	17	143	13	3	9
Pirkl, San Bernardino	.991	16	108	6	1	10
Postema, Reno	1.000	2	12	0	0	2
Rivera, Salinas	1.000	4	22	1	0	3
Rolen, San Jose	.966	4	.25	3	1	6
Sanchez, High Desert*	.667	1	4	0	2	0
Santana, San Bernardino	.971	5	31	2	1	3
Simmons, Modesto	.984	20	114	8	2	8
Snyder, Stockton	.982	11	100	7	2	7
Thomas, San Bernardino	.966	17	104	9	4	3
Weaver, Stockton	1.000	1	4	0	0	0
M. Williams, Reno	1.000	10	49	5	0	3
Yamanouchi, Salinas*	.967	29	166	8	6	17

Triple play—Phillips.

SECOND BASEMEN

Player, Team	Pct.	G	PO	A	E	DP
Alfonzo, Palm Springs	.958	7	9	14	1	3
Bethea, High Desert	.973	12	18	18	1	7
Bohringer, Bakersfield	1.000	3	4	2	0	0
Briggs, Salinas	.923	18	26	34	5	8
Carey, San Jose	.950	86	179	203	20	45
Castaldo, Stockton	.966	23	30	55	3	15
Chimelis, San Jose	.985	17	33	31	1	14
Cole, 80 Reno-7 Stock.	.967	87	183	191	13	47
Correia, Modesto	1.000	2	5	2	0	1
Crowe, San Jose	.905	9	20	18	4	3
Cruz, Modesto	1.000	1	2	2	0	1
Diaz, Stockton	.833	6	1	4	1	0
Ebel, Bakersfield	.974	6	14	24	1	4
Faries, High Desert	.889	3	2	6	1	1
Finn, Stockton	.976	44	77	88	4	16
Fletcher, Modesto	.950	56	103	126	12	22
Forbes, Palm Springs	.968	91	213	276	16	56
Gregory, Reno	.900	3	5	4	1	0
Guerrero, Stockton	.951	14	24	34	3	8
Haugen, Stockton	.931	27	32	49	6	10
Hood, Stockton	.750	3	2	1	1	0
Hunter, San Bernardino	.978	23	39	51	2	7
Jones, Reno	.942	12	21	28	3	9

Player, Team	Pct.	G	PO	A	E	DP
Kappesser, Stockton	.919	10	17	17	3	6
Kasper, San Jose	.932	20	28	40	5	11
King, San Bernardino	1.000	6	4	7	0	3
Kohno, Salinas	.975	13	34	44	2	16
Krumback, Reno	.833	8	7	13	4	4
Mica Lewis, Visalia	.964	23	67	68	5	12
V. Marrero, Stockton	.962	34	58	69	5	17
R. Martinez, Palm Springs	.935	16	29	43	5	11
J. McCray, Reno	1.000	13	15	17	0	4
McKeon, Reno	1.000	1	0	1	0	0
Meares, Visalia	.959	58	130	174	13	52
Mifune, Salinas	.963	86	168	219	15	53
Mota, Bakersfield	.945	74	137	187	19	37
Munoz, Palm Springs	.955	21	28	56	4	13
Murray, San Bernardino	.857	1	2	4	1	0
Oberdank, Palm Springs	.964	13	29	25	2	7
Osinski, Modesto	.962	60	151	178	13	40
Postema, Reno	.903	13	31	34	7	10
Raabe, Visalia	.996	64	114	166	1	36
Rolen, San Jose	1.000	4	12	7	0	3
Salazar, Salinas	.933	8	16	26	3	6
Santana, San Bernardino	.952	54	114	144	13	30
Shelton, Salinas	.960	26	52	45	4	10
Spires, San Jose	.990	22	47	54	1	12
Swim, Salinas	1.000	3	3	2	0	0
Thomas, San Bernardino	.966	48	99	101	7	28
Turang, San Bernardino	.975	25	53	66	3	18
Turco, Reno	.933	25	42	55	7	7
Waggoner, Modesto	.975	27	48	69	3	10
Weaver, Stockton	.889	5	12	12	3	4
Webb, Bakersfield	.942	56	125	165	18	35
WITKOWSKI, High Desert	.969	129	302	344	21	74
Wrona, Stockton	1.000	2	4	5	0	1
Young, Reno	1.000	3	4	2	0	0

Triple plays—V. Marrero, Oberdank.

THIRD BASEMEN

Player, Team	Pct.	G	PO	A	E	DP
Alfonzo, Palm Springs	.909	17	16	34	5	3
Armas, Modesto	1.000	1	1	1	0	0
Beard, Bakersfield	1.000	2	2	3	0	0
Bethea, High Desert	.885	42	24	68	12	6
BISHOP, Salinas	.926	95	86	166	20	16
Bohringer, Bakersfield	.897	12	7	19	3	1
Briggs, Salinas	.848	14	11	28	7	3
Buckley, Visalia	.883	23	12	41	7	3
Cabrera, Stockton	.915	22	19	46	6	6
Carlson, Salinas	.842	5	6	10	3	0
Castaldo, Stockton	.910	79	57	146	20	9
Chimelis, San Jose	.938	24	19	57	5	9
Clayton, San Bernardino	.976	17	12	28	1	1
Colon, Palm Springs	1.000	1	1	0	0	0
Correia, Modesto	.857	3	2	4	1	0
Crowe, San Jose	.962	12	10	15	1	2
Cruz, Stockton	1.000	1	2	6	0	1
Davenport, San Jose	.889	46	31	65	12	9
Delarwelle, Visalia	.714	3	1	4	2	0
Dodge, Palm Springs	1.000	2	2	2	0	0
Ebel, Bakersfield	.915	21	16	38	5	3
Faries, High Desert	.500	2	2	1	3	0
Finn, Stockton	1.000	2	1	1	0	0
Galle, Bakersfield	.600	3	2	4	4	1
Gavin, Visalia	.900	32	20	70	10	3
Gonzalez, High Desert	.885	99	44	157	26	4
Gregory, Reno	1.000	2	2	4	0	1
Guerrero, Stockton	.857	5	1	5	1	0
Haugen, Stockton	1.000	1	0	1	0	0
Hunter, San Bernardino	.932	31	29	53	6	6
Dodd Johnson, Reno	.833	2	2	3	1	2
Jones, Reno	.941	18	18	30	3	2
Kapano, Palm Springs	.860	107	88	207	48	19
Kappesser, Stockton	1.000	1	0	1	0	0
King, San Bernardino	1.000	2	3	3	0	0
Koeper, Salinas	.625	3	3	2	3	0
Krumback, Reno	.500	1	1	1	1	0
Lewis, Bakersfield	.952	88	70	189	13	14
Mica Lewis, Visalia	.806	10	6	19	6	1
Lund, Bakersfield	1.000	2	2	2	0	2
Magallanes, San Bernardino	.918	79	42	137	16	10
V. Marrero, Stockton	.897	37	29	75	12	9
Martin, High Desert	.769	5	3	7	3	0
R. Martinez, Palm Springs	.857	6	1	5	1	1
J. McCray, Reno	1.000	6	2	5	0	1
Meares, Visalia	.831	22	14	50	13	5
Mercedes, Modesto	.875	14	10	11	3	0
Mifune, Salinas	.943	16	14	19	2	2
Mitchell, Reno	.884	92	82	185	35	19
Nava, San Bernardino	.896	16	13	30	5	3
Oberdank, Palm Springs	.944	14	8	26	2	3
Osinski, Modesto	.893	51	28	64	11	8
Parker, San Jose	.897	24	14	38	6	2

CALIFORNIA LEAGUE · CLASS A · CALIFORNIA LEAGUE

Player, Team	Pct.	G	PO	A	E	DP
Postema, Reno	.919	13	14	20	3	2
Raabe, Visalia	.974	10	6	32	1	1
Rivera, Salinas	.737	10	4	10	5	1
Rolen, San Jose	.963	59	36	93	5	7
Salazar, Modesto	.957	18	13	32	2	2
Shelton, Salinas	.667	1	2	2	2	0
Songini, Reno	.818	14	10	26	8	0
Spires, San Jose	.850	12	6	11	3	3
Stahoviak, Visalia	.909	42	31	89	12	14
Thomas, San Bernardino	.786	5	2	9	3	0
Waggoner, Modesto	.930	32	23	43	5	3
Watts, Bakersfield	.944	16	12	39	3	1
Weaver, 11 Mod. - 10 Stock.	.918	21	11	34	4	3

Triple play—Kapano.

SHORTSTOPS

Player, Team	Pct.	G	PO	A	E	DP
Abbott, Modesto	.959	45	78	130	9	21
Bellinger, San Jose	.934	97	157	297	32	56
Bethea, High Desert	.884	25	30	54	11	8
Blankenship, Stockton	.714	3	1	4	2	1
Bohringer, Bakersfield	.909	7	5	15	2	3
Briggs, Salinas	1.000	1	2	2	0	1
Bryant, San Bernardino	.918	23	38	63	9	15
Chimelis, San Jose	.889	4	5	11	2	1
Cole, Stockton	.918	10	22	34	5	11
Cruz, Modesto	.899	17	20	42	7	7
Cruz, Salinas	.937	96	135	239	25	48
Diaz, Stockton	.952	34	44	95	7	16
Ebel, Bakersfield	1.000	4	5	6	0	3
Faries, High Desert	.926	4	10	15	2	1
Finn, Stockton	.903	13	10	18	3	5
Forbes, Palm Springs	.857	1	2	4	1	1
Gregory, Reno	.800	1	0	4	1	1
Guerrero, Stockton	.954	44	58	107	8	24
Haugen, Stockton	.900	29	43	65	12	3
Holbert, High Desert	.934	121	196	331	37	69
Hunter, San Bernardino	.925	22	20	42	5	5
Jones, Reno	.907	9	11	28	4	3
Kapano, Palm Springs	1.000	1	4	7	0	2
King, San Bernardino	.928	39	43	98	11	13
Mica Lewis, Visalia	.889	41	69	99	21	21
Magallanes, San Bernardino	1.000	2	3	4	0	1
R. Martinez, Palm Springs	.914	88	137	247	36	53
Matos, Modesto	.950	49	87	141	12	26
MAURER, Bakersfield	.944	129	209	376	35	74
J. McCray, Reno	1.000	2	1	2	0	0
Mifune, Salinas	.947	34	58	86	8	26
Munoz, Palm Springs	.891	12	14	35	6	3
Nava, San Bernardino	.949	54	76	130	11	34
Nunez, Visalia	.938	105	156	310	31	59
Oberdank, Palm Springs	.929	5	5	8	1	1
Osinski, Modesto	1.000	7	1	1	0	1
Postema, Reno	.931	83	159	206	27	50
Salazar, Salinas	.500	1	1	2	3	1
Santana, San Bernardino	.944	19	29	56	5	8
Showalter, Palm Springs	.912	37	52	113	16	19
Spires, San Jose	.927	41	68	97	13	25
Swim, Salinas	.849	13	19	26	8	5
Turco, Reno	.905	9	8	11	2	1
Uribe, Reno	.921	10	12	23	3	7
Uribe, San Jose	1.000	3	5	6	0	2
Waggoner, Modesto	.962	30	48	79	5	19
Wallace, Reno	.934	33	64	106	12	26
Weaver, 1 Mod. - 14 Stock.	.938	15	17	44	4	9
Wrona, Stockton	.942	10	15	34	3	8
Yasuda, Salinas	.000	1	0	0	1	0

OUTFIELDERS

Player, Team	Pct.	G	PO	A	E	DP
Abercrombie, High Desert	.889	9	8	0	1	0
Alfonzo, Palm Springs	1.000	3	4	0	0	0
Armas, Modesto	1.000	11	23	1	0	0
Bass, San Jose	.889	5	7	1	1	0
Blackwell, Bakersfield	1.000	3	1	0	0	0
Bohringer, Bakersfield	1.000	3	3	0	0	0
Bonner, San Jose	.966	70	108	4	4	0
Booker, Modesto	.969	63	119	5	4	1
Briggs, Salinas	.963	18	26	0	1	0
Cannon, Palm Springs	.959	20	44	3	2	0
Cardenas, Bakersfield	.966	71	109	3	4	1
Carlson, Salinas	1.000	5	2	0	0	0
Castaldo, Stockton	.867	11	13	0	2	0
Clark, Stockton	.962	118	164	12	7	2
Clemens, Reno	.667	1	2	0	1	0
Cohen, Visalia*	.967	41	54	4	2	0
Collier, Bakersfield*	.965	120	156	9	6	0
COLON, Palm Springs	.988	93	163	6	2	2
Conte, Palm Springs	1.000	10	19	0	0	0
Cordova, Visalia	.923	51	58	2	5	0
Couture, Stockton	.949	64	89	5	5	1
Crowe, San Jose	.943	31	31	2	2	0
Dattola, Modesto	.945	57	96	7	6	0

Player, Team	Pct.	G	PO	A	E	DP
de la Nuez, Visalia	.965	106	184	10	7	3
Delarwelle, Visalia	.989	54	89	3	1	0
Edmonds, Palm Springs*	1.000	53	88	6	0	1
Eppard, Salinas*	1.000	18	20	1	0	0
Farmer, High Desert*	.985	53	63	2	1	1
Felix, Palm Springs	.968	17	30	0	1	0
Finn, Stockton	.977	21	38	4	1	2
Forbes, Palm Springs	1.000	3	2	1	0	0
Gavin, Salinas	1.000	11	10	2	0	1
Gieseke, High Desert*	1.000	6	3	0	0	0
Gonzalez, Reno	.954	117	205	21	11	3
Gonzalez, Bakersfield	1.000	1	2	0	0	0
Griffith, Salinas	.959	20	46	1	2	0
Guerrero, Stockton	1.000	1	1	0	0	0
Hart, Modesto	.958	27	44	2	2	0
Hood, Stockton	1.000	39	50	5	0	2
Hosey, Stockton	.938	73	112	8	8	1
Ingram, Bakersfield	.952	108	174	5	9	0
Jackson, San Jose*	.941	14	15	1	1	0
Kawano, Salinas	.910	77	121	11	13	1
King, San Bernardino	1.000	2	3	0	0	0
Klavitter, San Bernardino	.750	5	5	1	2	0
Knabenshue, Palm Springs	1.000	6	12	0	0	0
Koeper, Salinas	.909	32	56	4	6	0
Krumback, Reno	.974	123	277	18	8	8
Laboy, Palm Springs*	.939	109	160	8	11	1
Mica Lewis, Visalia	.958	48	88	3	4	0
Lott, Bakersfield	.956	87	126	5	6	1
Martin, High Desert	.980	87	196	5	4	0
Martinez, Modesto	.972	124	267	13	8	2
Maynard, San Bernardino	.957	60	111	0	5	0
McCarty, Visalia*	1.000	11	23	1	0	0
J. McCray, Reno	1.000	1	1	0	0	0
McFarlin, San Jose*	.972	102	202	9	6	1
Meares, Visalia	1.000	4	11	0	0	0
Messerly, Modesto	1.000	1	3	0	0	0
Mieske, High Desert	.948	132	258	14	15	3
Mifune, Salinas	1.000	2	2	0	0	0
Mondesi, Bakersfield	.940	27	42	5	3	2
Mota, Bakersfield	1.000	5	8	0	0	0
Muramatsu, Salinas	.962	114	245	8	10	2
Newfield, San Bernardino	.955	86	121	5	6	1
Noland, High Desert	.971	124	162	5	5	1
O'Leary, Stockton*	.982	120	163	4	3	3
Owens, Visalia	.992	64	123	6	1	1
Palma, Salinas	.947	95	184	13	11	1
Partrick, Palm Springs	.977	93	160	8	4	2
Perez, Palm Springs*	.966	16	25	3	1	2
Rabb, Reno	1.000	9	8	0	0	0
Reid, San Jose	.977	118	202	9	5	1
Rodriguez, Palm Springs	.929	6	12	1	1	0
Roebuck, Reno	.976	108	188	14	5	6
Rolen, San Jose	1.000	12	19	0	0	0
Rumsey, Visalia	.988	51	79	3	1	1
Sanchez, High Desert*	.939	36	45	1	3	0
Sheehy, Palm Springs	1.000	4	6	0	0	0
Shelton, Salinas	.951	67	133	4	7	1
Shepperd, Salinas	.946	25	51	2	3	0
Simmons, Modesto	.965	111	210	12	8	5
Sims, Visalia	1.000	4	9	1	0	0
Snyder, Stockton	1.000	2	4	0	0	0
Stephens, 30 Reno-34 S.B.	.954	64	72	11	4	2
Tavarez, San Bernardino	.964	111	231	9	9	1
Thomas, San Bernardino	.964	60	103	4	4	0
Threadgill, Reno	.833	5	5	0	1	0
Turang, San Bernardino	1.000	7	10	0	0	0
Turco, Reno	1.000	1	1	0	0	0
Urbon, Reno*	.893	17	23	2	3	0
Walker, Modesto	1.000	20	42	0	0	0
Weber, San Jose*	.973	65	100	9	3	2
Wilder, Reno	.938	25	30	0	2	0
Williams, San Jose*	.900	19	27	0	3	0
Williams, Palm Springs	.971	14	33	1	1	0
Young, San Bernardino	.969	87	150	4	5	0

CATCHERS

Player, Team	Pct.	G	PO	A	E	DP	PB
Abercrombie, High Desert	.976	63	374	39	10	2	27
Beard, Bakersfield	1.000	18	131	9	0	0	7
Billmeyer, Palm Springs	.978	37	201	17	5	0	6
Briggs, Salinas	1.000	3	7	2	0	0	0
Brown, Visalia	.977	59	309	31	8	1	23
Buckley, Visalia	.983	46	248	34	5	3	13
Calcagno, San Jose	1.000	4	25	5	0	2	2
Carcione, Reno	.971	61	343	62	12	8	10
Clemens, Reno	.948	40	179	23	11	0	11
Conley, High Desert	.985	29	176	15	3	2	8
Couture, Stockton	.933	3	12	2	1	0	0
Dodge, Palm Springs	.992	40	233	29	2	0	6
Dominguez, Palm Springs	.982	46	249	29	5	0	5
Eppard, Salinas*	1.000	1	1	0	0	0	0
Fernandez, San Jose	.983	29	215	21	4	2	6
Firova, Reno	.985	9	53	12	1	1	1
Flores, Stockton	.988	11	80	5	1	0	1

Player, Team	Pct.	G	PO	A	E	DP	PB
Gil, Palm Springs	.959	30	184	25	9	0	9
Gunn, Reno	1.000	1	1	0	0	0	0
Helfand, Modesto	.978	50	314	48	8	3	15
Hunter, San Bernardino	1.000	3	3	0	0	0	0
Kappesser, 15 Vis.-72 Stock...	.982	87	532	78	11	6	19
Keathley, Modesto	1.000	2	2	1	0	0	1
Klavitter, San Bernardino	1.000	9	23	5	0	0	1
Kluge, San Bernardino	.989	28	154	19	2	0	14
Logan, Reno	.967	37	200	34	8	2	12
Lund, Bakersfield	.986	57	435	43	7	2	14
Lutticken, High Desert	1.000	4	15	1	0	0	3
Manwaring, San Jose	1.000	1	16	0	0	0	0
V. Marrero, Stockton	.969	24	84	9	3	1	3
Mercedes, Modesto	.967	91	541	75	21	7	16
MILLER, San Jose	.991	104	819	98	8	12	11
Palma, Salinas	1.000	1	2	0	0	0	0
Pattin, San Jose	1.000	11	48	4	0	0	2
Piazza, Bakersfield	.981	75	580	56	12	6	14
Pirkl, San Bernardino	.971	46	304	27	10	3	14
Raasch, San Bernardino	.950	2	18	1	1	0	0
Rivera, Salinas	.958	31	120	17	6	2	11
Salazar, Modesto	.962	8	24	1	1	0	0
Snyder, Stockton	.977	66	485	58	13	7	13
Stiner, Reno	1.000	3	8	3	0	0	1
Sutherland, San Bernardino	.988	12	79	4	1	0	1
Verstandig, High Desert	.986	66	423	66	7	4	19
Vranjes, San Bernardino	.989	69	433	35	5	2	16
C. Williams, Reno	.933	14	38	4	3	0	1
M. Williams, Reno	.996	44	248	22	1	3	10
Yasuda, Salinas	.979	123	713	132	18	13	29

PITCHERS

Player, Team	Pct.	G	PO	A	E	DP
Alcantara, Reno*	.889	64	2	14	2	2
Aleys, San Jose*	1.000	37	10	20	0	1
Archer, Stockton	.818	27	2	7	2	1
Arola, Salinas	.917	41	1	10	1	0
Bankhead, San Bernardino	1.000	2	2	2	0	0
Bannister, Palm Springs*	1.000	7	1	6	0	0
Beck, Reno*	.500	4	0	1	1	0
Benavides, San Jose	1.000	30	5	5	0	0
Bennett, Palm Springs	1.000	8	2	10	0	0
Berg, Stockton	.931	52	3	24	2	0
Berrios, Palm Springs*	.625	10	2	3	3	0
Best, Visalia	.778	27	6	8	4	0
Borski, San Bernardino	1.000	4	1	5	0	0
Brock, Modesto	1.000	4	3	2	0	0
Brown, Visalia	1.000	1	0	1	0	0
Bryand, High Desert*	1.000	10	2	3	0	0
Buonantony, Reno	1.000	5	1	4	0	0
Burns, Modesto	1.000	2	1	0	0	0
Bustillos, Bakersfield	.952	11	8	12	1	0
Callahan, San Jose*	.933	41	5	9	1	0
Cangemi, Stockton	.958	54	12	11	1	0
Carrasco, Salinas	.938	26	7	23	2	1
Carroll, Bakersfield*	.667	15	1	1	1	0
Cormier, Modesto	1.000	6	0	3	0	0
Correa, Stockton	.857	10	2	4	1	0
Crane, Reno	.500	10	0	1	1	0
Cummings, San Bernardino*	.848	29	4	24	5	1
Darwin, San Bernardino	1.000	16	4	6	0	0
Daspit, Bakersfield	.917	22	6	5	1	1
Daughtry, Palm Springs	.833	6	1	4	1	0
de la Hoya, Bakersfield	1.000	27	6	14	0	0
Dell, Stockton	.885	27	14	32	6	3
DeVille, High Desert	.952	38	4	16	1	3
Dillard, Salinas*	.949	19	7	30	2	3
Dour, San Jose	1.000	4	1	4	0	1
Drake, Stockton	.778	17	0	7	2	1
Easley, Reno	1.000	3	0	1	0	0
Eppard, Salinas*	1.000	1	0	2	0	0
Erwin, Salinas	1.000	11	1	0	0	0
Estrada, High Desert	.923	21	5	7	1	1
Everson, Reno	.833	7	4	1	1	0
Fermin, Modesto	1.000	3	2	2	0	0
Fitzer, San Bernardino*	.800	30	1	3	1	0
Fitzgerald, 4 Stock.- 12 Sal.*	.960	16	7	17	1	2
Flynt, San Bernardino*	.889	22	0	8	1	0
Fredrickson, High Desert	1.000	23	3	4	0	0
Galindez, High Desert*	1.000	11	9	8	0	0
Garcia, San Bernardino	1.000	20	16	13	0	0
Garland, Modesto	.914	27	9	23	3	0
Gilles, Reno	.929	10	2	11	1	0
Givens, San Bernardino*	1.000	1	0	2	0	0
Green, Stockton*	1.000	12	5	12	0	1
Gregory, Visalia	.840	30	6	15	4	0
Grove, 7 Stock.-2 Reno	1.000	9	1	2	0	0
Gustafson, Visalia	.895	33	15	19	4	2
Gutierrez, San Bernardino	1.000	17	1	9	0	0
Haffner, Palm Springs	.917	22	5	6	1	0
Hammaker, High Desert*	1.000	2	0	1	0	0
Hampton, San Bernardino	.783	18	6	12	5	0
Hancock, San Jose*	1.000	9	1	9	0	0
Hansell, Bakersfield	.929	25	8	18	2	1

Player, Team	Pct.	G	PO	A	E	DP
Hanselman, San Jose	.947	25	12	24	2	2
Haslock, High Desert	.900	20	5	4	1	0
Helmick, Bakersfield	1.000	5	1	2	0	1
Henry, Visalia	.925	28	16	33	4	2
Herring, San Jose*	.958	39	6	17	1	2
Hershiser, Bakersfield	1.000	2	1	4	0	0
Hoffman, Bakersfield*	1.000	10	2	7	0	0
Hokuf, Modesto	.833	28	5	5	2	1
Holsman, 4 S.B.-30 Stock.*	.938	34	4	11	1	1
Honeycutt, Modesto*	1.000	3	0	1	0	0
Hoppe, Visalia	1.000	9	2	1	0	1
Huisman, San Jose	.909	26	14	16	3	2
Hunter, San Bernardino	1.000	1	1	0	0	0
Ikesue, Salinas	.960	28	8	16	1	2
Dom. Johnson, Reno	1.000	26	3	12	0	2
Karasinski, Salinas*	.867	24	3	10	2	2
Keathley, Modesto	1.000	2	0	1	0	0
Kent, San Bernardino	.839	62	5	21	5	4
King, San Bernardino	1.000	2	0	1	0	0
King, Palm Springs	.926	32	12	13	2	2
Klink, Modesto*	1.000	3	0	1	0	0
Klonoski, Visalia*	.909	18	2	8	1	1
Knackert, San Bernardino	1.000	2	0	1	0	0
Kracl, 5 Reno-11 Mod.	.750	16	4	14	6	0
Landry, Stockton	1.000	5	1	2	0	0
Lardizabal, Modesto	.941	33	11	21	2	2
Lebron, High Desert	1.000	5	1	2	0	0
Mich. Lewis, Visalia*	.950	14	5	14	1	3
Lienhard, Reno	1.000	1	0	3	0	0
Lifgren, High Desert	1.000	33	7	16	0	1
Lipson, Visalia	.974	49	14	24	1	2
Livingston, Salinas*	.833	14	0	5	1	1
Lopez, Reno	.889	7	2	6	1	0
Loubier, Palm Springs	.974	35	11	27	1	4
Love, Modesto	.833	24	1	9	2	1
F. Martinez, Palm Springs*	1.000	5	0	3	0	0
Martinez, Bakersfield	.900	10	3	6	1	0
Maye, Salinas	.957	13	6	16	1	1
T. McCray, Reno	.875	38	9	5	2	0
McCreadie, Salinas	.909	20	4	6	1	1
McDonald, San Bernardino*	.964	43	6	21	1	2
McFarlin, Bakersfield	.885	26	13	33	6	5
McGehee, San Jose	.923	26	10	14	2	0
McGraw, Stockton*	1.000	11	5	8	0	0
McKeon, High Desert	.946	28	17	18	2	3
Mead, Reno	.943	24	10	23	2	1
Mecir, San Bernardino	1.000	14	2	5	0	0
Mejia, Modesto	.933	18	6	8	1	1
Merriman, Palm Springs	.824	34	3	11	3	0
Messer, Reno*	.769	25	6	14	6	1
Mikkelsen, Stockton	.925	27	10	27	3	0
Ri. Miller, Modesto*	.800	11	2	2	1	0
Ru. Miller, Modesto.	1.000	3	1	0	0	0
Mimbs, Bakersfield*	.947	27	8	28	2	3
Mintz, Bakersfield	.875	28	6	8	2	0
Misuraca, Visalia	.971	21	16	17	1	1
Mohler, Modesto*	.975	21	8	31	1	2
Monson, Stockton	1.000	15	3	20	0	1
Montoya, Palm Springs*	.900	17	5	22	3	2
MUSSELWHITE, Visalia	1.000	30	12	29	0	0
Nedin, Visalia	.967	12	8	21	1	0
Newman, Visalia*	.929	15	7	19	2	2
Nishioka, Salinas	1.000	29	4	17	0	1
Norris, Reno	1.000	6	3	8	0	0
O'Connor, Bakersfield*	1.000	16	0	2	0	0
Odekirk, Reno*	.889	25	11	37	6	4
Ohta, Salinas	.963	35	7	19	1	0
Ohtsubo, Salinas	.926	41	3	22	2	4
Oka, Salinas	.800	13	2	6	2	1
Olker, Reno*	.750	6	1	5	2	0
Olson, Salinas*	1.000	3	0	1	0	0
Ortiz, San Jose*	1.000	31	3	10	0	0
Oshio, Salinas	.875	13	0	7	1	0
Pakele, Palm Springs	.921	26	13	22	3	2
Parisotto, Reno	1.000	31	5	7	0	1
Pascual, Bakersfield	1.000	5	1	0	0	0
Patrick, Modesto	.953	28	13	28	2	1
Peck, Palm Springs	1.000	17	6	5	0	0
Pena, San Bernardino	1.000	3	0	1	0	0
Pena, San Jose	.885	16	9	14	3	0
Phillips, Reno	1.000	23	2	8	0	3
Phoenix, Modesto	.846	27	2	9	2	0
Pinon, Reno	.889	15	4	4	1	2
Piotrowicz, Bakersfield	.929	33	5	8	1	0
Pitcher, San Bernardino	1.000	20	2	8	0	1
Potthoff, Bakersfield	.667	4	1	1	1	0
Powers, Palm Springs	.714	15	2	3	2	0
Pulido, Visalia*	.909	57	5	15	5	2
Rapp, San Jose	.913	16	8	13	2	4
Reed, High Desert*	.800	21	2	6	2	1
Rees, San Bernardino*	.941	11	3	13	1	0
Rivas, San Bernardino*	.862	62	6	19	4	0
Roberts, Reno*	.963	10	10	16	1	2
Rose, Modesto	.931	13	14	13	2	0
Rosenbalm, San Bernardino	1.000	9	0	1	0	1
Saitz, Palm Springs	.889	20	2	6	1	0

Player. Team	Pct.	G	PO	A	E	DP
Sanders, High Desert	.923	21	20	16	3	4
Sandoval, Stockton	.667	5	0	2	1	0
Sharko, San Jose	.857	54	4	8	2	0
Shaw, Reno	.941	17	8	8	1	0
Silcox, High Desert	.889	18	2	6	1	0
Smith, Stockton	1.000	5	0	1	0	1
Smith, Modesto	1.000	33	2	3	0	0
Smithberg, High Desert	.600	3	1	2	2	0
Soltero, High Desert	1.000	34	6	9	0	1
Sontag, Palm Springs	1.000	5	3	7	0	0
Sparks, Stockton	.960	24	19	53	3	10
Stewart, 3 Reno-33 Sal.*	1.000	36	0	2	0	0
Strebeck, Modesto	.875	32	5	2	1	0
Stryker, Bakersfield	1.000	30	3	7	0	0
Sudbury, Modesto	.895	17	7	10	2	0
Swingle, Palm Springs	1.000	43	2	3	0	0
Swope, Visalia	1.000	13	6	19	0	1
Tabaka, Stockton*	1.000	4	3	4	0	0
Thomas, High Desert	.911	27	12	39	5	2
Tipton, Bakersfield	.957	43	11	11	1	0
Treadwell, Bakersfield	.950	17	11	8	1	1
Vancho, Stockton	1.000	6	1	2	0	0
Vann, Stockton	.786	23	3	8	3	0
Van Winkle, Palm Springs	.848	31	11	17	5	0
Vargas, 6 Stock.-9 Reno	1.000	15	6	8	0	1
Vegely, Palm Springs*	.769	40	3	7	3	0
Vidmar, Palm Springs	1.000	6	6	8	0	0
Voit, Reno	1.000	8	1	4	0	0
Warren, Reno	1.000	15	1	4	0	0
Whatley, San Jose	.500	9	0	1	1	0
Whitaker, San Jose*	.900	6	1	8	1	0
White, Visalia	1.000	39	3	6	0	1
Wiley, San Bernardino	1.000	12	1	1	0	0
Wilkinson, High Desert	.846	20	3	8	2	0
C. Williams, Reno	1.000	1	0	1	0	0
Woodson, San Bernardino	1.000	5	1	7	0	0
Worrell, High Desert	.875	11	2	5	1	0
Zarranz, San Bernardino	1.000	11	0	2	0	0
Zavaras, San Bernardino	1.000	11	0	1	0	0
Zinter, High Desert	1.000	50	3	6	0	1

Triple play—Holsman.

The following players did not have any fielding statistics at the positions indicated or appeared only as a designated hitter, pinch-hitter or pinch-runner: Bethea, of, p; Bryant, 3b; Cabrera, 2b; Castaldo, ss; Clark, p; Clemens, p; Cooley, 3b; Crowe, p; Dodson, 3b; Edmonds, p; Eppard, 2b, 3b, ss; Firova, of, p; Fletcher, 3b; C. Gonzalez, p; Hunter, of; D. Jones, p; Kapano, of; Kappesser, p; Kerr, p; Kohno, 3b; Loe, p; Lund, of; Magill, p; O. Marrero, of; V. Marrero, p; Marshall, of; McCreadie, of; K. McKeon, p; Mercedes, p; Murray, p; Nishioka, of; C. Phillips, p; Postema, of; Raabe, p; Rivera, 2b, of; Show, p; Snyder, p; Spires, p; Stuart, p; Tatis, p; Taylor, p; Treanor, p; Valenzuela, p; Verstandig, p; Yamanouchi, p; Yasuda, of; Youngblood, p.

LEAGUE CHAMPIONS

Year	Team	Pct.	Year	Team	Pct.	Year	Team	Pct.
1914—	Fresno	.571		Reno	.643	1977—	Salinas	.564
1915—	Modesto	.857	1962—	San Jose§	.686		Lodi§	.579
1916-40—Did not operate.				Reno	.587	1978—	Visalia§	.698
1941—	Fresno	.643	1963—	Modesto	.589		Lodi	.607
	S. Barbara (2nd)*	.597		Stockton§	.687	1979—	San Jose§	.636
1942—	Santa Barbara†	.642	1964—	Fresno	.638		Reno	.525
1943-44-45—Did not operate.				Fresno	.600	1980—	Stockton§	.638
1946—	Stockton‡	.600	1965—	San Jose	.586		Visalia	.507
1947—	Stockton‡	.679		Stockton§	.614	1981—	Visalia	.621
1948—	Fresno	.607	1966—	Modesto	.577		Lodi§	.521
	S. Barbara (3rd)*	.529		Modesto	.671	1982—	Modesto§	.671
1949—	Bakersfield	.612	1967—	San Jose§	.676		Visalia	.586
	San Jose (4th)*	.543		Modesto	.586	1983—	Visalia	.621
1950—	Ventura	.607	1968—	San Jose	.629		Redwood§	.529
	Modesto (2nd)*	.586		Fresno§	.623	1984—	Modesto§	.597
1951—	Santa Barbara‡	.599	1969—	Stockton§	.600		Bakersfield	.486
1952—	Fresno†	.629		Visalia	.614	1985—	Fresno§	.575
1953—	San Jose‡	.664	1970—	Bakersfield	.667		Stockton	.566
1954—	Modesto‡	.623		Bakersfield	.671	1986—	Palm Springs	.613
1955—	Stockton	.733	1971—	Visalia§	.583		Stockton§	.585
	Fresno§	.718		Fresno	.500	1987—	Fresno§	.559
1956—	Fresno§	.650	1972—	Modesto§	.547		Reno	.535
1957—	Visalia x	.622		Bakersfield	.629	1988—	Stockton	.657
	Salinas (4th)*	.504	1973—	Lodi§	.657		Riverside§	.599
1958—	Fresno*	.639		Bakersfield	.571	1989—	Stockton	.627
	Bakersfield	.672	1974—	Fresno§	.607		Bakersfield§	.577
1959—	Bakersfield	.592		San Jose	.579	1990—	Visalia	.638
	Modesto§	.643	1975—	Reno	.614		Stockton§	.582
1960—	Reno	.614		Reno	.614	1991—	San Jose	.676
	Reno	.657	1976—	Salinas	.650		High Desert§	.537
1961—	Reno	.743		Reno§	.547			

*Won four-club playoff. †League disbanded June 28. ‡Won championship and four-club playoff. §Won split-season playoff. xWon both halves of split season.

CAROLINA LEAGUE

FINAL STANDINGS

FIRST HALF

NORTHERN DIVISION

Team	W	L	T	Pct.	GB
Prince William (Yankees)	38	32	0	.543	......
Lynchburg (Red Sox)	30	39	0	.435	7 ½
Salem (Pirates)	30	40	0	.429	8
Frederick (Orioles)	26	44	0	.371	12

SOUTHERN DIVISION

Team	W	L	T	Pct.	GB
Kinston (Indians)	45	23	0	.662	......
Winston-Salem (Cubs)	43	27	0	.614	3
Durham (Braves)	38	29	0	.567	6 ½
Peninsula (Mariners)	27	43	0	.386	19

SECOND HALF

NORTHERN DIVISION

Team	W	L	T	Pct.	GB
Lynchburg (Red Sox)	37	33	0	.529	......
Prince William (Yankees)	33	36	0	.478	3 ½
Salem (Pirates)	33	37	0	.471	4
Frederick (Orioles)	32	38	0	.457	5

SOUTHERN DIVISION

Team	W	L	T	Pct.	GB
Kinston (Indians)	44	26	0	.629	......
Durham (Braves)	41	29	0	.586	3
Winston-Salem (Cubs)	40	30	0	.571	4
Peninsula (Mariners)	19	50	0	.275	24 ½

COMPOSITE

Team	Kin.	W.S.	Dur.	P.W.	Lyn.	Sal.	Fre.	Pen.	W	L	T	Pct.	GB
Kinston (Indians)	....	14	9	15	11	11	13	16	89	49	0	.645	......
Winston-Salem (Cubs)	6	....	12	11	12	12	14	16	83	57	0	.593	7
Durham (Braves)	9	8	....	10	13	12	12	15	79	58	0	.577	9 ½
Prince William (Yankees)	5	9	10	....	9	13	10	15	71	68	0	.511	18 ½
Lynchburg (Red Sox)	9	8	6	11	....	12	10	11	67	72	0	.482	22 ½
Salem (Pirates)	9	8	8	7	8	....	13	10	63	77	0	.450	27
Frederick (Orioles)	7	6	8	10	10	7	....	10	58	82	0	.414	32
Peninsula (Mariners)	4	4	5	4	9	10	10	....	46	93	0	.331	43 ½

Peninsula club represented Hampton, Va.

Major league affiliations in parentheses.

Playoffs—Lynchburg defeated Prince William, two games to none; Kinston defeated Lynchburg, three games to none, to win league championship.

Regular-season attendance—Durham, 301,240; Frederick, 318,354; Kinston, 100,857; Lynchburg, 88,897; Peninsula, 41,131; Prince William, 208,166; Salem, 131,582; Winston-Salem, 111,333. Total, 1,301,560. Playoffs (5 games)—5,367. All-Star Game at Frederick—1,237.

Managers—Durham, Grady Little; Frederick, Wally Moon; Kinston, Brian Graham; Lynchburg, Buddy Bailey; Peninsula, Steve Smith; Prince William, Mike Hart; Salem, Stan Cliburn; Winston-Salem, Brad Mills.

All-Star team—1B—Willie Tatum, Lynchburg; 2B—Miguel Flores, Kinston; 3B—Pete Castellano, Winston-Salem; SS—Manny Alexander, Frederick; Util. IF—Ramon Caraballo, Durham; OF—Brian Giles, Kinston; Jeff McNeely, Lynchburg; Tracy Sanders, Kinston; Util. OF—John Jensen, Winston-Salem; C—Javy Lopez, Durham; DH—Chris Ebright, Winston-Salem; SP—Sam Militello, Prince William; RP—Mike Soper, Kinston; Most Valuable Player—Pete Castellano, Winston-Salem; Pitcher of the Year—Sam Militello, Prince William; Manager of the Year—Brian Graham, Kinston.

BATTING

TEAM

Team	Avg.	G	AB	R	OR	H	TB	2B	3B	HR	RBI	SH	SF	HP	BB	Int. BB	SO	SB	CS	LOB
Salem	.263	140	4624	634	696	1216	1755	185	39	92	560	30	30	47	466	13	974	170	67	981
Winston-Salem	.257	140	4501	666	561	1158	1726	218	34	94	596	47	43	55	591	25	1004	110	59	1052
Kinston	.257	138	4513	629	544	1158	1588	180	35	60	537	64	41	46	539	26	837	132	58	983
Frederick	.253	140	4692	603	603	1189	1650	195	31	68	523	42	34	50	483	20	844	193	76	1036
Lynchburg	.250	139	4497	560	575	1123	1545	195	25	59	494	42	28	42	527	17	967	114	80	979
Durham	.243	137	4346	587	473	1055	1566	164	31	95	505	33	40	34	457	17	901	194	122	827
Prince William	.239	139	4493	556	514	1074	1491	192	36	51	490	36	45	29	584	19	1005	136	84	1007
Peninsula	.237	139	4484	523	756	1064	1460	165	15	67	443	32	30	40	551	23	961	112	67	1050

INDIVIDUAL

(Leading qualifiers for batting championship—378 or more plate appearances)

*Bats lefthanded.   †Switch-hitter.

Player, Team	Avg.	G	AB	R	H	TB	2B	3B	HR	RBI	SH	SF	HP	BB	Int. BB	SO	SB	CS
McNeely, Jeff, Lynchburg	.322	106	382	58	123	161	16	5	4	38	4	1	4	74	4	74	38	21
List, Paul, Salem	.318	94	336	60	107	169	22	5	10	46	0	2	1	39	1	74	12	3
Giles, Brian, Kinston*	.310	125	394	71	122	148	14	0	4	47	3	3	2	68	2	70	19	7
Castellano, Pete, Winston-Salem	.303	129	459	59	139	200	25	3	10	87	2	5	3	72	4	97	11	10
Ratliff, Daryl, Salem	.293	88	352	60	103	125	8	4	2	23	2	1	0	27	0	43	35	9
Pezzoni, Ron, Peninsula	.289	106	405	57	117	146	8	3	5	43	2	4	4	44	2	54	21	3
Tatum, Willie, Lynchburg†	.287	126	421	54	121	178	25	4	8	54	2	6	12	61	4	89	15	8
Ebright, Chris, Winston-Salem*	.280	121	415	66	116	180	21	2	13	57	4	3	3	56	0	72	13	9
de los Santos, Alberto, Salem	.279	125	480	59	134	192	17	7	9	56	1	6	7	15	1	66	24	3
Easley, Mike, Kinston*	.277	109	386	64	107	137	20	5	0	43	5	2	1	57	1	65	6	4

— 431 —

Departmental Leaders: G—Jer. Williams, 137; AB—Jer. Williams, 550; R—Alexander, Jer. Williams, 81; H—Alexander, 143; TB—Jer. Williams, 213; 2B—Moore, 30; 3B—Jer. Williams, 11; HR—Sanders, 18; RBI—Castellano, 87; SH—Bethea, 12; SF—Oster, Walbeck, 10; HP—Tatum, 12; BB—Sanders, 83; IBB—Eiterman, Merchant, 6; SO—Jer. Williams, 147; SB—Caraballo, 53; CS—Caraballo, 23.

(All players—listed alphabetically)

Player, Team	Avg.	G	AB	R	H	TB	2B	3B	HR	RBI	SH	SF	HP	BB	Int. BB	SO	SB	CS
Alexander, Manny, Frederick	.261	134	548	81	143	175	17	3	3	42	3	1	2	44	0	68	47	14
Alstead, Jason, Frederick*	.260	77	177	33	46	50	2	1	0	12	4	2	6	30	1	39	15	5
Aude, Rich, Salem	.265	103	366	45	97	122	12	2	3	43	0	0	9	27	5	72	4	0
Ausmus, Brad, Prince William	.304	63	230	28	70	96	14	3	2	30	1	3	0	24	3	37	17	6
Bailey, Robert, Salem†	.235	75	213	30	50	63	7	0	2	19	4	1	0	23	0	69	15	5
Baker, George, Frederick†	.204	20	49	6	10	11	1	0	0	2	3	0	0	4	0	5	1	0
Bark, Brian, Durham*	.000	14	0	0	0	0	0	0	0	0	0	0	0	1	0	0	0	0
Beasley, Tony, Frederick	.248	124	387	50	96	130	11	10	1	34	6	3	6	27	0	75	29	8
Belyeu, Randy, Winston-Salem	.240	11	25	5	6	9	0	0	1	2	1	0	2	3	0	7	0	0
Berlin, Randy, Frederick	.233	84	227	22	53	63	4	0	2	29	1	2	0	19	0	37	4	3
Berni, Denny, Lynchburg*	.229	83	262	21	60	71	8	0	1	20	3	2	2	18	1	41	1	2
Berthel, Daniel, Frederick	.213	41	122	13	26	41	3	0	4	11	0	1	3	13	0	22	1	1
Bethea, Scott, Lynchburg*	.241	112	336	46	81	92	6	1	1	28	12	3	1	50	0	47	8	8
Biasucci, Joe, Winston-Salem	.275	67	211	35	58	77	10	3	1	34	4	3	4	30	0	58	2	3
Bosarge, Scott, Peninsula	.187	28	75	9	14	18	4	0	0	6	1	0	1	9	0	20	0	2
Bradford, Troy, Winston-Salem	.000	19	1	0	0	0	0	0	0	0	0	0	0	0	0	0	0	0
Bragg, Darren, Peninsula*	.224	69	237	42	53	76	14	0	3	29	1	1	2	66	0	72	21	9
Brakebill, Mark, Peninsula	.155	38	116	14	18	25	1	0	2	9	1	1	4	11	0	35	5	1
Brewington, Mike, Salem*	.164	28	61	6	10	11	1	0	0	7	0	1	0	11	0	18	3	0
Brust, Dave, Durham*	.221	94	253	36	56	96	5	1	11	33	1	2	3	23	0	70	7	6
Bryant, Craig, Peninsula*	.267	29	86	9	23	24	1	0	0	10	1	1	0	6	0	9	1	2
Buford, Damon, Frederick	.273	133	505	71	138	199	25	6	6	54	7	2	10	51	1	92	50	14
Bullett, Scott, Salem†	.333	39	156	22	52	75	7	5	2	15	0	0	8	1	0	29	15	7
Bullock, Renaldo, Peninsula	.340	14	47	4	16	19	0	0	1	2	1	0	0	2	0	13	5	4
Byrd, Jim, Lynchburg	.238	52	206	29	49	62	10	0	1	18	0	1	3	13	0	50	10	3
Cairo, Sergio, Frederick	.314	90	299	38	94	127	20	2	3	40	1	2	0	47	2	39	4	6
Canate, William, Kinston	.217	51	189	28	41	49	3	1	1	12	5	0	3	14	0	29	4	2
Caraballo, Ramon, Durham†	.250	120	444	73	111	158	13	8	6	52	3	2	3	38	1	91	53	23
Carpenter, Bubba, Prince William*	.280	69	236	33	66	100	10	3	6	34	1	3	2	40	3	50	4	1
Castellano, Pete, Winston-Salem	.303	129	459	59	139	200	25	3	10	87	2	5	5	72	4	97	11	10
Chick, Bruce, Lynchburg	.271	134	513	58	139	200	23	4	10	73	2	5	2	44	2	119	10	8
Clark, Jeff, Durham*	.116	18	43	4	5	5	0	0	0	1	0	0	0	5	0	5	4	1
Cole, Marvin, Winston-Salem	.272	86	276	41	75	104	17	3	2	29	5	2	6	17	2	12	5	3
Cudjo, Lavell, Peninsula	.246	60	171	22	42	55	8	1	1	17	1	1	3	19	0	59	2	6
Dando, Pat, Durham*	.143	25	70	2	10	11	1	0	0	5	0	0	1	3	1	16	2	1
Davis, Brad, Salem*	.278	9	18	2	5	7	2	0	0	3	0	0	0	1	0	4	0	1
DeJardin, Brad, Kinston*	.250	52	148	21	37	49	7	1	1	19	1	2	1	23	2	39	3	3
DeKneef, Mike, Lynchburg	.314	10	35	9	11	16	3	1	0	4	0	0	0	3	0	7	1	2
Delgado, Alex, Lynchburg	.212	61	179	21	38	46	8	0	0	17	1	1	2	16	0	19	2	1
de los Santos, Alberto, Lynchburg	.279	125	480	59	134	192	17	7	9	56	1	6	7	15	1	66	24	3
Delpozo, Roberto, Peninsula	.237	61	215	24	51	66	7	1	2	19	3	0	2	17	0	53	3	2
Devares, Cesar, Frederick	.251	74	235	25	59	85	13	2	3	29	2	1	4	14	0	28	2	2
Donahue, Tim, Kinston†	.283	34	99	14	28	36	8	0	0	10	2	1	4	10	1	12	5	0
Drew, Cameron, Kinston*	.000	3	2	0	0	0	0	0	0	0	0	0	0	1	0	1	0	0
Easley, Mike, Kinston*	.277	109	386	64	107	137	20	5	0	43	5	2	1	57	1	65	6	4
Ebright, Chris, Winston-Salem*	.280	121	415	66	116	180	21	2	13	57	4	3	3	56	0	72	13	9
Edge, Tim, Salem	.225	96	298	36	67	105	16	2	6	30	5	0	5	44	0	67	4	2
Eenhoorn, Robert, Prince William	.241	29	108	15	26	37	6	1	1	12	0	1	0	13	0	21	0	0
Eiterman, Tom, Kinston	.273	124	433	66	118	169	19	4	8	66	4	7	6	67	6	50	13	7
Erickson, Greg, Prince William	.204	47	152	14	31	40	5	2	0	9	2	0	1	22	0	32	2	3
Fermaint, Mike, Peninsula	.171	36	105	14	18	20	2	0	0	8	0	1	0	17	0	29	3	4
Figga, Michael, Prince William	.195	55	174	15	34	49	6	0	3	17	2	1	0	19	0	51	2	1
Flores, Miguel, Kinston	.268	124	425	61	114	154	19	3	5	40	7	6	9	34	1	45	29	7
Flowers, Doug, Frederick*	.275	63	193	22	53	76	14	0	3	22	2	1	1	13	3	50	0	2
Fox, Andy, Prince William*	.230	126	417	60	96	152	22	2	10	46	1	9	6	81	3	104	15	13
Franco, Matt, Winston-Salem*	.215	104	307	47	66	92	12	1	4	41	2	6	2	46	2	42	4	1
Gabbani, Michael, Winston-Salem	.239	41	109	12	26	35	6	0	1	8	3	0	1	2	0	37	0	1
Garland, Tim, Prince William	.150	27	80	4	12	15	1	1	0	7	0	1	0	7	0	22	3	0
Gilbert, Roy, Frederick†	.281	38	146	18	41	51	10	0	0	19	0	3	2	9	0	13	13	3
Giles, Brian, Kinston*	.310	125	394	71	122	148	14	0	4	47	3	3	3	68	2	70	19	7
Gillis, Tim, Durham	.246	120	395	48	97	144	26	3	5	59	2	9	3	58	3	86	6	7
Giovanola, Ed, Durham*	.254	101	299	50	76	103	9	0	6	27	0	3	2	57	1	39	18	11
Grace, Mike, Winston-Salem	.339	51	180	36	61	102	11	3	8	39	0	3	1	23	1	23	1	3
Graham, Greg, Lynchburg†	.196	82	275	31	54	65	6	1	1	24	4	1	1	36	1	65	6	7
Grayum, Richie, Winston-Salem*	.249	110	309	43	77	124	18	1	9	31	2	0	3	66	2	88	2	3
Griffin, Ty, Winston-Salem†	.242	88	314	71	76	112	21	3	3	25	0	3	1	72	2	80	26	4
Hale, Shane, Frederick	.000	18	0	1	0	0	0	0	0	0	0	0	0	0	0	0	0	0
Halland, Jon, Peninsula	.122	16	49	2	6	9	1	1	0	2	1	0	2	0	0	21	1	0
Hankins, Mike, Prince William†	.263	132	475	72	125	144	15	2	0	37	8	0	5	74	0	70	11	9
Hartung, Andy, Winston-Salem	.277	53	159	20	44	68	3	0	7	22	2	1	4	17	0	43	0	2
Hatteberg, Scott, Lynchburg*	.200	8	25	4	5	6	1	0	0	2	0	0	0	7	0	6	0	0
Hedge, Pat, Frederick	.191	90	235	20	45	64	5	1	4	24	5	1	1	28	1	76	5	5
Hernandez, Kiki, Prince William	.267	7	30	4	8	13	2	0	1	5	0	0	0	3	0	4	0	0
Holley, Bobby, Peninsula	.279	87	294	45	82	126	10	2	10	37	2	1	1	60	3	43	7	6
Horowitz, Ed, Frederick	.294	64	235	32	69	95	11	0	5	29	0	3	2	24	1	41	2	1
Huff, Brad, Winston-Salem	.000	7	8	0	0	0	0	0	0	0	1	0	0	0	0	4	0	0
Jarvis, John, Prince William*	.165	30	91	6	15	22	5	1	0	7	0	2	0	9	0	39	0	0
Jensen, John, Winston-Salem*	.256	128	446	68	114	186	26	2	14	78	0	1	8	73	5	119	9	5
Jimenez, Ramon, Prince William*	.254	102	350	38	89	112	13	2	2	41	1	3	2	45	3	98	2	4
Johnson, Mark, Salem*	.252	37	103	12	26	34	2	0	2	13	0	0	1	18	0	25	0	2
Kelly, Mike, Durham	.250	35	124	29	31	57	6	1	6	17	0	1	2	19	0	47	6	2
Kelly, Pat, Durham	.250	54	120	14	30	35	5	0	0	14	1	1	1	14	0	18	4	4
Kessinger, Keith, Frederick†	.179	26	56	5	10	13	3	0	0	4	1	0	0	8	0	12	2	0
Kluge, Matt, Peninsula	.155	18	58	3	9	11	2	0	0	3	0	0	0	3	0	24	0	0
Kostich, Bill, Peninsula*	.000	33	1	0	0	0	0	0	0	0	0	0	0	0	0	1	0	0
Kounas, Tony, Peninsula	.269	109	387	46	104	145	18	1	7	47	0	3	2	40	3	42	3	1
Kowitz, Brian, Durham*	.254	86	323	41	82	114	13	5	3	21	4	1	3	20	0	56	18	8
Lane, Nolan, Kinston	.305	31	95	14	29	51	6	2	4	13	1	1	0	9	0	14	2	3
Leach, Chris, Lynchburg*	.214	46	126	20	27	41	5	0	3	18	0	0	3	34	0	30	6	3
Leon, Johnny, Prince William	.228	51	162	18	37	57	6	1	4	14	1	0	0	10	0	39	0	0

Player. Team	Avg.	G	AB	R	H	TB	2B	3B	HR	RBI	SH	SF	HP	BB	Int. BB	SO	SB	CS
Letterio, Shane, Peninsula	.266	70	267	36	71	101	12	0	6	25	2	3	1	27	1	31	3	7
Lewis, T.R., Frederick	.208	49	159	18	33	44	7	2	0	7	2	1	1	19	2	25	1	1
List, Paul, Salem	.318	94	336	60	107	169	22	5	10	46	0	2	1	39	1	74	12	3
Livesey, Jeff, Prince William	.247	20	73	8	18	29	5	0	2	9	1	1	0	3	0	13	0	0
Lopez, Javy, Durham	.245	113	384	43	94	145	14	2	11	51	0	3	1	25	4	88	10	3
Losa, Bill, Kinston	.181	71	193	19	35	52	8	0	3	19	3	1	2	33	0	76	2	2
Luis, Joe, Lynchburg*	.264	43	106	9	28	31	3	0	0	6	2	0	1	14	0	16	0	1
Magallanes, Bob, Peninsula	.200	41	150	11	30	46	4	0	4	16	1	1	1	14	0	30	1	2
Manahan, Austin, Salem	.211	113	369	53	78	122	15	1	9	35	1	2	3	47	0	127	17	10
McCoy, Brent, Durham†	.247	92	288	37	71	90	8	1	3	27	5	2	1	38	1	45	6	7
McNeely, Jeff, Lynchburg	.322	106	382	58	123	161	16	5	4	38	4	1	4	74	4	74	38	21
Meade, Paul, Kinston†	.089	17	45	4	4	4	0	0	0	1	2	0	1	4	0	20	2	0
Merchant, Mark, Peninsula†	.252	78	270	31	68	96	8	1	6	34	0	0	0	51	6	70	11	4
Miller, Brent, Frederick*	.257	37	148	21	38	76	8	0	10	31	0	2	0	6	2	16	0	1
Moore, Boo, Lynchburg	.249	132	502	63	125	203	30	3	14	69	0	1	3	39	1	135	8	5
Morales, Jorge, Peninsula	.264	25	72	6	19	20	1	0	0	7	2	2	1	7	0	13	0	1
Mordecai, Mike, Durham†	.262	109	397	52	104	135	15	2	4	42	5	4	2	40	0	58	30	16
Mota, Carlos, Kinston	.235	69	196	18	46	56	5	1	1	23	8	1	0	14	1	49	9	2
Nieves, Melvin, Durham†	.264	64	201	31	53	91	11	0	9	25	0	1	5	40	2	53	3	8
Norris, Bill, Lynchburg*	.252	134	484	61	122	179	21	3	10	60	2	3	3	47	2	100	4	1
Obando, Sherman, Prince William	.264	42	140	25	37	71	11	1	7	31	0	2	2	19	2	28	0	1
O'Connor, Kevin, Durham*	.203	28	79	14	16	26	1	0	3	10	0	0	0	8	0	13	1	4
Osik, Keith, Salem	.270	87	300	31	81	113	12	1	6	35	3	2	3	38	0	48	2	3
Oster, Paul, Prince William†	.256	106	398	44	102	139	23	1	4	62	2	10	4	26	0	72	12	8
Pennyfeather, William, Salem	.266	81	319	35	85	132	17	3	8	46	1	2	1	8	0	52	11	8
Perez, Eddie, Durham	.271	92	277	38	75	114	10	1	9	41	2	3	3	17	2	33	0	3
Pezzoni, Ron, Peninsula	.289	106	405	57	117	146	8	3	5	43	2	4	4	44	2	54	21	3
Pineda, Jose, Prince William	.105	13	38	2	4	4	0	0	0	2	0	0	0	2	0	16	0	1
Pirkl, Greg, Peninsula	.264	64	239	20	63	97	16	0	6	41	0	3	7	9	0	42	0	0
Polewski, Steve, Salem†	.178	31	73	8	13	17	2	1	0	5	2	1	0	2	0	20	0	1
Porcelli, Joe, Winston-Salem†	.000	42	1	0	0	0	0	0	0	0	0	0	0	0	0	1	0	0
Postiff, James, Winston-Salem	.190	53	116	14	22	30	5	0	1	6	5	0	8	18	1	36	1	2
Pough, Clyde, Kinston	.167	11	30	2	5	6	1	0	0	2	0	0	1	1	0	9	1	0
Powell, L.V., Peninsula	.116	13	43	4	5	6	1	0	0	1	0	0	0	4	1	20	0	0
Raasch, Glen, Peninsula	.118	20	68	1	8	11	3	0	0	2	1	0	0	4	0	19	3	0
Ratliff, Daryl, Salem	.293	88	352	60	103	125	8	4	2	23	2	1	0	27	0	43	35	9
Reynolds, Doug, Frederick	.241	27	87	10	21	36	6	0	3	8	1	0	0	12	0	22	0	0
Riddle, David, Frederick	.000	52	1	1	0	0	0	0	0	0	0	0	0	0	0	0	0	0
Rigsby, Tim, Kinston	.202	85	263	24	53	78	12	2	3	25	3	0	3	13	0	77	1	3
Ripken, Bill, Frederick	.250	1	4	2	1	1	0	0	0	0	1	0	0	0	0	1	0	0
Robertson, Jason, Prince William*	.264	131	515	67	136	178	21	6	3	54	1	4	2	53	2	138	32	9
Rodarte, Paul, Peninsula	.222	65	216	19	48	54	4	1	0	13	1	2	0	32	0	56	5	1
Rodriguez, Roman, Salem	.224	133	451	62	101	123	10	0	4	59	9	5	4	63	0	92	9	7
Romay, Willie, Peninsula	.178	41	118	10	21	23	2	0	0	7	3	0	1	17	0	46	3	2
Saetre, Damon, Peninsula*	.282	90	277	37	78	99	16	1	1	19	2	2	1	44	5	34	7	3
St. Peter, Bill, Winston-Salem	.196	74	219	26	43	72	10	2	5	21	5	1	3	21	0	74	6	3
Sanchez, Daniel, Prince William	.138	33	80	6	11	17	2	2	0	8	1	0	1	4	0	23	1	0
Sanders, Tracy, Kinston*	.266	118	421	80	112	202	20	8	18	63	2	2	6	83	4	96	8	5
Sarbaugh, Mike, Kinston	.248	76	262	39	65	100	12	1	7	33	1	2	2	33	1	48	3	1
Scott, Rennie, Lynchburg	.000	50	2	0	0	0	0	0	0	0	0	0	0	0	0	1	0	0
Seda, Israel, Peninsula	.208	115	356	43	74	122	17	2	9	33	6	2	4	39	0	81	4	1
Shelton, Ben, Salem	.261	65	203	37	53	109	10	2	14	56	1	0	5	45	4	65	4	2
Simmons, Randy, Durham*	.221	106	290	30	64	103	16	4	5	34	6	3	1	23	0	84	14	7
Smith, Mark, Frederick	.250	38	148	20	37	56	5	1	4	29	0	3	2	9	0	24	1	3
Sprick, Scott, Frederick*	.179	34	84	4	15	21	6	0	0	8	0	1	0	6	0	16	0	3
Strickland, Ricky, Prince William†	.206	88	296	42	61	75	12	1	0	14	9	0	2	65	0	64	22	15
Sued, Nick, Kinston	.239	33	88	19	21	29	3	1	1	11	2	1	1	14	0	12	2	0
Swail, Steve, Durham	.100	32	50	2	5	5	0	0	0	3	0	0	0	6	0	15	0	1
Tallman, Steve, Frederick	.049	14	41	3	2	3	1	0	0	2	1	0	0	6	0	22	2	0
Tarasco, Tony, Durham*	.250	78	248	31	62	110	8	2	12	38	4	3	1	21	2	64	11	9
Tatum, Willie, Lynchburg†	.287	126	421	54	121	178	25	4	8	54	2	6	12	61	4	89	15	8
Tena, Paulino, Kinston	.252	127	433	43	109	132	9	4	2	52	10	7	0	27	1	65	12	11
Tepper, Marc, Kinston*	.271	109	384	40	104	126	12	2	2	56	4	5	3	33	5	53	9	1
Thomas, Kelvin, Peninsula*	.160	51	162	14	26	45	5	1	0	15	0	1	3	11	2	44	3	6
Torres, Jessie, Salem	.375	4	8	1	3	3	0	0	0	0	0	0	0	2	0	2	0	0
Torres, Paul, Winston-Salem	.115	27	87	9	10	17	1	0	2	7	0	1	2	11	0	30	4	0
Trusky, Ken, Salem*	.278	94	317	37	88	132	13	2	9	38	1	4	1	28	1	67	12	3
Tyler, Brad, Frederick*	.257	56	187	26	48	66	6	0	4	26	1	1	2	33	3	33	3	2
Viera, John, Prince William*	.200	48	165	25	33	57	4	4	4	17	0	1	1	27	2	41	13	6
Villalobos, Gary, Lynchburg	.203	62	172	14	35	41	4	1	0	9	3	0	0	6	0	46	2	1
Walbeck, Matt, Winston-Salem†	.269	91	260	25	70	90	11	0	3	41	3	10	2	20	3	23	3	2
Wardlow, Joe, Prince William*	.223	88	283	30	63	84	9	3	2	34	3	4	1	38	1	43	0	7
Wardwell, Shea, Lynchburg	.230	53	152	19	35	48	3	2	2	16	4	2	1	26	0	40	3	5
Washington, Kyle, Kinston	.333	3	12	1	4	6	0	1	0	0	0	0	0	2	0	5	1	0
Watkins, Darren, Durham	.213	22	61	12	13	24	3	1	2	9	0	0	0	3	0	20	1	1
Wawruck, Jim, Frederick*	.277	22	83	15	23	26	3	0	0	7	1	0	1	7	0	14	10	0
Wearing, Melvin, Frederick	.263	94	335	46	88	141	14	3	11	53	1	4	7	54	4	73	1	2
Williams, Dan, Kinston	.267	6	15	1	4	4	0	0	0	2	1	0	0	0	0	5	1	0
Williams, Jeff, Frederick	.000	12	1	0	0	0	0	0	0	0	0	0	0	0	0	1	0	0
Williams, Jerrone, Winston-Salem†	.258	137	550	81	142	213	19	11	10	64	7	4	2	33	3	147	23	8
Wilson, Bryan, Winston-Salem	.265	22	49	8	13	15	2	0	0	4	2	0	0	11	0	11	0	0
Wilson, Craig, Lynchburg	.223	98	310	43	69	104	23	0	4	37	3	2	4	39	2	77	0	3
Young, Kevin, Salem	.313	56	201	38	63	101	12	4	6	28	0	3	7	20	0	34	3	2
Zambrano, Jose, Lynchburg	.111	3	9	0	1	1	0	0	0	0	0	0	0	0	0	5	0	1

The following pitchers, listed alphabetically by club, with games in parentheses, had no plate appearances, primarily through use of designated hitters:

DURHAM—Borbon, Pedro (37); Burlingame, Dennis (26); Cronin, Jeff (37); DeLeon, Roberto (3); Hailey, Roger (5); Mattson, Rob (9); Mc-Michael, Greg (36); Minchey, Nate (15); Murray, Matt (2); Nied, David (13); Ritter, Darren (26); Ryder, Scott (8); Shiflett, Matt (16); Sottile, Shaun (6); Steinmetz, Earl (16); Strange, Don (38); Taylor, Scott (24); Vazquez, Marcos (4); Werland, Henry (8); Woodall, Brad (4); Young, Mike (13).

FREDERICK—Anderson, Matt (1); Blumberg, Rob (13); Carper, Mark (26); Constant, Andres (8); Culkar, Steve (6); Hays, Greg (30); Hebb, Mike (3); Hook, Mike (37); Kerr, Zack (8); Leinen, Pat (1); Miller, Dave (9); Moore, Daryl (22); O'Donoghue, John (22); Paveloff, Dave (5); Pennington, Brad (36); Plaster, Allen (4); Ricci, Chuck (30); Schullstrom, Erik (19); Williams, Steve (1); Yaughn, Kip (27).

KINSTON—Allen, Chad (26); Bryant, Shawn (29); Byrd, Paul (14); Charland, Colin (5); Johnson, Carl (32); Kiser, Garland (31); Kovach, Ty (4); Langdon, Tim (7); Leskanic, Curtis (19); Malley, Mike (9); Morgan, Scott (34); Munoz, Oscar (14); Neill, Scott (40); Person, Robert (11); Pettiford, Cecil (26); Phillips, Lonnie (6); Rivera, Roberto (10); Soper, Michael (62); Tatterson, Gary (1).

LYNCHBURG—Burgo, Dale (36); Dennison, Jim (30); Finnvold, Gar (6); Hoyer, Brad (52); Mosley, Tony (47); Plantenberg, Erik (20); Richardson, Ronnie (25); Riley, Ed (27); Rush, Andy (26); Smith, Tim (25); Uhrhan, Kevin (51).

PENINSULA—Converse, Jim (26); Czarkowski, Mark (6); Furcal, Manuel (29); Holman, Brad (47); King, Kevin (17); Lodding, Rich (28); Perkins, Paul (26); Pitcher, Scott (17); Schanz, Scott (27); Tegtmeier, Doug (50); Urso, Sal (46); Wiggs, Johnny (39).

PRINCE WILLIAM—Gilbert, Brent (31); Haller, Jim (46); Hitchcock, Sterling (19); Hodges, Darren (26); Hoffman, Jeff (34); Holcomb, Scott (10); Johnston, Dan (33); Militello, Sam (14); Ohlms, Mark (47); Ojala, Kirt (25); Prybylinski, Bruce (8); Ralph, Curtis (47); Rhodes, Ricky (15); Tucker, Steve (21).

SALEM—Arvesen, Scott (19); Bird, Dave (35); Buckholz, Steve (5); Carlson, Lynn (6); Cooke, Stephen (2); Fajardo, Hector (1); Futrell, Mark (10); Hope, John (6); McDowell, Tim (23); Parkinson, Eric (29); Robertson, Richard (12); Rychel, Kevin (11); Shouse, Brian (17); Tellers, David (40); Underwood, Bobby (15); Wagner, Paul (25); Watson, Dave (9); Way, Ron (25); White, Rick (13); Zimmerman, Mike (49).

WINSTON-SALEM—Caballero, Ed (32); Cheetham, Sean (6); Hawblitzel, Ryan (20); Hollins, Jessie (41); Jaques, Eric (30); Jones, Shannon (17); Melvin, Bill (41); Perez, Leopoldo (9); Sodders, Mike (11); Stroud, Derek (6); Swartzbaugh, Dave (15); Trachsel, Steve (12); Willis, Travis (53).

GRAND SLAMS—Jensen, Pirkl, 2 each; Brust, Chick, Devares, Eiterman, Franco, Grayum, Leon, Letterio, List, Magallanes, Moore, Jer. Williams, 1 each.

AWARDED FIRST BASE ON CATCHER'S INTERFERENCE—Eiterman (Kluge); Flores (Ausmus); Hankins (Horowitz); Pirkl (Devares).

PITCHING

TEAM

Team	ERA	G	CG	ShO	Sv.	IP	H	R	ER	HR	HB	BB	Int. BB	SO	WP	Bk.
Durham	2.91	137	13	18	38	1179.2	1076	473	381	49	48	435	28	946	75	11
Prince William	3.01	139	9	7	40	1209.2	1049	514	405	49	41	470	21	979	60	10
Kinston	3.10	138	7	14	51	1215.2	1056	544	419	64	42	601	18	1043	100	20
Lynchburg	3.38	139	13	11	31	1192.1	1170	575	448	68	42	385	12	864	77	5
Winston-Salem	3.53	140	16	16	40	1186.2	1087	561	466	71	43	564	17	900	99	13
Frederick	3.60	140	7	9	33	1212.2	1148	639	485	89	33	642	17	1050	84	16
Salem	4.30	140	17	6	27	1190.0	1182	696	568	107	55	520	23	891	91	13
Peninsula	4.66	139	13	4	22	1159.2	1269	756	601	89	39	581	34	820	67	18

INDIVIDUAL

(Leading qualifiers for earned-run average leadership—112 or more innings)

*Throws lefthanded.

Pitcher, Team	W	L	Pct.	ERA	G	GS	CG	GF	ShO	Sv.	IP	H	R	ER	HR	HB	BB	Int. BB	SO	WP
Smith, Lynchburg	12	9	.571	2.16	25	25	8	0	2	0	174.2	149	60	42	6	9	34	2	103	9
Hawblitzel, Winston-Salem	15	2	.882	2.42	20	20	5	0	2	0	134.0	110	40	36	7	7	47	0	103	8
Allen, Kinston	9	8	.529	2.48	26	25	2	0	1	0	152.2	146	58	42	7	3	51	2	82	7
Ojala, Prince William*	8	7	.533	2.53	25	23	1	0	0	0	156.2	120	52	44	5	4	61	1	112	3
Bradford, Winston-Salem	9	5	.643	2.59	19	19	4	0	2	0	118.0	103	44	34	10	2	48	2	72	10
Hitchcock, Prince William*	7	7	.500	2.64	19	19	2	0	0	0	119.1	111	49	35	2	3	26	0	101	5
Hodges, Prince William	6	8	.429	2.66	26	25	2	0	0	0	166.0	133	60	49	3	4	66	1	153	15
Leskanic, Kinston	15	8	.652	2.79	28	28	0	0	0	0	174.1	143	63	54	10	3	91	0	163	16
Hoffman, Prince William	12	5	.706	2.87	34	14	1	10	1	3	141.1	120	55	45	7	3	39	3	87	4
O'Donoghue, Frederick*	7	8	.467	2.90	22	21	2	1	1	0	133.2	131	55	43	6	2	50	2	128	8

Departmental leaders: G—Soper, 62; W—Leskanic, Hawblitzel, 15; L—Schanz, 17; Pct.—Hawblitzel, .882; GS—Ricci, 29; CG—Smith, 8; GF—Soper, 58; ShO—Bradford, Hawblitzel, Nied, Smith, Wagner, 2; Sv.—Soper, 41; IP—Smith, 174.2; H—Riley, 169; R—Perkins, 103; ER—Perkins, 84; HR—Parkinson, 18; HB—Zimmerman, 14; BB—Bryant, 106; IBB—Holman, Urso, 7; SO—Leskanic, 163; WP—Zimmerman, 20.

(All pitchers—listed alphabetically)

Pitcher, Team	W	L	Pct.	ERA	G	GS	CG	GF	ShO	Sv.	IP	H	R	ER	HR	HB	BB	Int. BB	SO	WP
Allen, Kinston	9	8	.529	2.48	26	25	2	0	1	0	152.2	146	58	42	7	3	51	2	82	7
Anderson, Frederick*	0	1	.000	6.75	1	1	0	0	0	0	5.1	7	5	4	0	0	6	0	6	1
Arvesen, Salem	5	10	.333	4.68	19	19	4	0	0	0	119.1	141	75	62	13	5	35	3	73	8
Bark, Durham*	4	3	.571	2.51	13	13	0	0	0	0	82.1	66	23	23	0	6	24	0	76	4
Beasley, Frederick	0	0	.000	4.50	3	0	0	2	0	0	2.0	2	1	1	0	0	4	0	1	1
Berlin, Frederick	0	0	.000	0.00	1	0	0	1	0	0	1.0	1	0	0	0	0	1	0	0	0
Bethea, Lynchburg	0	0	.000	9.00	1	0	0	0	0	0	3.0	5	3	3	0	0	2	0	0	1
Bird, Salem*	10	9	.526	4.17	35	15	1	8	0	1	131.2	151	75	61	10	3	44	2	111	5
Blumberg, Frederick*	7	2	.778	2.25	13	12	0	0	0	0	76.0	65	26	19	5	1	52	1	53	6
Borbon, Durham*	4	3	.571	2.27	37	6	1	21	0	5	91.0	85	40	23	2	2	35	2	79	4
Bradford, Winston-Salem	9	5	.643	2.59	19	19	4	0	2	0	118.0	103	44	34	10	2	48	2	72	10
Brust, Durham	0	0	.000	0.00	3	0	0	3	0	0	2.2	1	0	0	0	0	0	0	0	0
Bryant, Kinston*	11	9	.550	4.02	29	28	2	0	1	0	154.2	154	91	69	12	4	106	0	112	13
Buckholz, Salem	2	2	.500	2.67	5	5	0	0	0	0	33.2	23	14	10	1	2	11	0	28	4
Burgo, Lynchburg	5	3	.625	2.96	36	0	0	22	0	9	48.2	33	19	16	0	3	22	5	48	1
Burlingame, Durham	11	7	.611	3.01	26	26	3	0	0	0	161.1	143	60	54	5	8	80	0	95	10
Byrd, Kinston	4	3	.571	3.16	14	11	0	0	0	0	62.2	40	27	22	7	0	36	0	62	6
Caballero, Winston-Salem	6	7	.462	4.57	32	13	1	3	1	0	110.1	111	68	56	8	2	50	2	93	14
Carlson, Salem	1	1	.500	3.67	6	6	0	0	0	0	34.1	31	18	14	5	0	17	1	23	1
Carper, Frederick	3	8	.273	4.31	26	9	1	5	0	0	87.2	92	59	42	5	2	51	1	49	3
Charland, Kinston*	1	2	.333	1.80	5	5	0	0	0	0	20.0	10	7	4	0	3	8	0	19	1
Cheetham, Winston-Salem	5	6	.455	4.10	17	17	2	0	1	0	83.1	70	43	38	10	4	56	3	53	3
Constant, Frederick	3	5	.375	5.03	8	8	0	0	0	0	39.1	47	26	22	5	1	10	0	25	0
Converse, Peninsula	6	15	.286	4.97	26	26	1	0	0	0	137.2	143	90	76	12	2	97	2	137	6
Cooke, Salem	1	0	1.000	4.85	2	2	0	0	0	0	13.0	14	8	7	0	0	2	0	5	4
Cronin, Durham	9	5	.643	3.65	37	0	0	15	0	3	74.0	73	38	30	6	2	32	6	52	3
Cudjo, Peninsula	0	0	.000	19.29	3	0	0	2	0	0	2.1	5	5	5	0	0	2	0	1	1
Culkar, Frederick	0	0	.000	4.50	6	0	0	2	0	0	12.0	13	6	6	1	1	9	0	6	1
Czarkowski, Peninsula*	1	2	.333	3.46	6	6	0	0	0	0	26.0	32	15	10	2	1	6	0	12	2

— 434 —

Pitcher, Team	W	L	Pct.	ERA	G	GS	CG	GF	ShO	Sv.	IP	H	R	ER	HR	HB	BB	Int. BB	SO	WP
DeJardin, Kinston*	0	0	.000	27.00	1	0	0	1	0	0	1.0	2	3	3	0	0	2	0	0	1
DeLeon, Durham*	0	0	.000	5.06	3	0	0	2	0	0	5.1	10	4	3	1	2	1	1	4	0
Dennison, Lynchburg*	3	8	.273	3.38	30	19	0	6	0	0	133.1	134	61	50	11	5	32	1	68	5
Eiterman, Kinston	0	0	.000	0.00	3	0	0	3	0	0	2.2	2	1	0	0	0	2	0	0	0
Fajardo, Salem	0	1	.000	2.35	1	1	1	0	0	0	7.2	4	3	2	1	0	1	1	7	0
Finnvold, Lynchburg	2	3	.400	3.32	6	6	0	0	0	0	38.0	30	16	14	3	1	7	1	29	2
Furcal, Peninsula*	4	8	.333	5.98	29	14	1	4	1	0	90.1	121	68	60	8	2	23	2	62	3
Futrell, Salem	1	1	.500	3.98	10	0	0	5	0	1	20.1	22	14	9	2	0	12	0	17	1
Garland, Prince William	0	0	.000	0.00	1	0	0	1	0	0	1.1	3	6	0	0	0	2	0	0	0
Gilbert, Prince William	4	8	.333	4.60	31	9	0	8	0	0	78.1	95	48	40	5	5	35	3	36	6
Grace, Winston-Salem	0	0	.000	0.00	1	0	0	1	0	0	1.0	0	0	0	0	0	0	0	0	0
Graham, Lynchburg	0	0	.000	0.00	1	0	0	1	0	0	1.0	0	0	0	0	0	0	0	0	0
Hailey, Durham*	1	0	1.000	2.16	5	0	0	0	0	0	8.1	8	2	2	1	1	3	0	7	0
Hale, Frederick*	0	6	.000	3.42	16	9	0	3	0	1	71.0	61	45	27	5	6	34	0	72	5
Haller, Prince William	4	5	.444	1.95	46	2	0	21	0	6	74.0	68	35	16	2	2	41	4	61	6
Hawblitzel, Winston-Salem	15	2	.882	2.42	20	20	5	0	2	0	134.0	110	40	36	7	7	47	0	103	8
Hays, Frederick	2	3	.400	3.58	30	0	0	16	0	1	32.2	41	22	13	4	2	22	4	21	6
Hebb, Frederick	0	0	.000	2.25	3	0	0	2	0	0	8.0	7	2	2	0	0	8	0	5	0
Hitchcock, Prince William*	7	7	.500	2.64	19	19	2	0	0	0	119.1	111	49	35	2	3	26	0	101	5
Hodges, Prince William	6	8	.429	2.66	26	25	2	0	0	0	166.0	133	60	49	3	4	66	1	153	15
Hoffman, Prince William	12	5	.706	2.87	34	14	1	10	1	3	141.1	120	55	45	7	3	39	3	87	4
Holcomb, Prince William*	1	0	1.000	1.20	10	0	0	4	0	0	15.0	7	2	2	1	0	3	1	18	1
Hollins, Winston-Salem	4	8	.333	5.67	41	13	0	15	0	5	98.1	107	78	62	9	6	83	1	74	13
Holman, Peninsula	6	6	.500	3.22	47	0	0	35	0	10	78.1	70	34	28	4	2	33	7	71	5
Hook, Frederick*	0	3	.000	5.77	37	0	0	19	0	1	53.0	44	41	34	2	1	54	2	63	11
Hope, Salem	2	2	.500	6.18	6	5	0	1	0	0	27.2	38	20	19	5	0	4	0	18	0
Hoyer, Lynchburg*	1	5	.167	3.63	52	2	0	17	0	5	72.0	78	35	29	5	0	12	1	51	5
Jaques, Winston-Salem*	3	2	.600	3.00	30	0	0	16	0	4	45.0	37	15	15	1	1	22	1	33	3
Johnson, Kinston	6	1	.857	3.81	32	5	0	6	0	2	85.0	86	43	36	5	5	48	0	64	10
Johnston, Prince William	1	7	.125	3.50	33	8	1	11	1	3	82.1	69	36	32	3	6	42	2	46	3
Jones, Winston-Salem	8	6	.571	3.16	17	17	0	0	0	0	105.1	96	48	37	3	4	36	0	88	7
Kerr, Frederick	2	3	.400	5.04	8	3	0	2	0	1	25.0	30	21	14	3	1	15	1	14	0
King, Peninsula*	6	7	.462	4.37	17	17	2	0	1	0	92.2	99	55	45	8	0	38	0	59	5
Kiser, Kinston*	6	1	.857	1.49	31	0	0	12	0	5	48.1	35	11	8	2	1	14	2	52	3
Kostich, Peninsula*	1	5	.167	5.64	33	8	1	15	0	1	83.0	97	63	52	7	5	34	1	55	6
Kounas, Peninsula	0	0	.000	0.00	1	0	0	1	0	0	1.0	0	0	0	0	0	1	0	0	0
Kovach, Kinston	0	1	.000	7.30	4	4	0	0	0	0	12.1	15	13	10	1	1	17	0	11	1
Langdon, Kinston*	1	0	1.000	8.18	7	0	0	4	0	0	11.0	11	12	10	0	1	12	0	10	4
Leinen, Frederick*	0	0	.000	0.00	1	0	0	0	0	0	3.0	0	0	0	0	0	4	0	4	0
Leskanic, Kinston	15	8	.652	2.79	28	28	0	0	0	0	174.1	143	63	54	10	3	91	0	163	16
Lodding, Peninsula	0	1	.000	4.99	28	1	0	9	0	0	48.2	52	37	27	5	4	46	1	31	10
Malley, Kinston*	0	0	.000	10.19	9	1	0	4	0	0	17.2	25	25	20	0	3	25	0	17	5
Mattson, Durham	1	4	.200	4.34	9	8	2	1	0	1	45.2	48	23	22	2	0	9	1	32	3
McDowell, Salem	3	7	.300	5.56	23	14	3	4	1	0	103.2	127	74	64	9	5	41	0	71	8
McMichael, Durham	5	6	.455	3.62	36	6	0	13	0	2	79.2	83	34	32	3	3	29	6	82	6
Melvin, Winston-Salem	5	4	.556	3.33	41	3	0	15	0	4	100.0	89	50	37	5	1	49	4	94	12
Militello, Prince William	12	2	.857	1.22	16	16	1	0	0	0	103.1	65	19	14	1	4	27	1	113	1
Miller, Frederick	1	0	1.000	3.00	9	0	0	5	0	0	18.0	21	11	6	2	1	10	0	12	1
Minchey, Durham	6	6	.500	2.84	15	12	3	0	0	0	88.2	72	31	28	3	3	29	0	77	6
Moore, Frederick*	1	1	.500	1.32	22	1	0	11	0	5	47.2	28	8	7	1	0	15	2	44	0
Morgan, Kinston	7	2	.778	2.54	34	0	0	9	0	1	74.1	60	29	21	2	1	27	1	72	4
Mosley, Lynchburg*	4	4	.500	3.84	46	7	0	19	0	3	86.2	80	48	37	2	0	29	0	73	5
Munoz, Kinston	6	3	.667	1.44	14	0	0	6	0	0	93.2	60	23	15	2	5	36	0	111	6
Murray, Durham	1	0	1.000	1.29	2	2	0	0	0	0	7.0	5	1	1	0	0	0	0	7	0
Neill, Kinston	7	1	.875	2.73	40	0	0	16	0	1	69.1	67	32	21	4	6	16	2	56	8
Nied, Durham	8	3	.727	1.56	13	12	2	1	2	0	80.2	46	19	14	2	3	23	0	77	0
O'Donoghue, Frederick*	7	8	.467	2.90	22	21	2	1	1	0	133.2	131	55	43	6	2	50	2	128	8
Ohlms, Prince William	2	4	.333	2.65	47	0	0	42	0	26	51.0	44	22	15	2	0	28	1	55	2
Ojala, Prince William*	8	7	.533	2.53	25	23	1	0	0	0	156.2	120	52	44	5	4	61	1	112	3
Parkinson, Salem	9	10	.474	4.74	29	11	1	7	0	1	106.1	104	67	56	18	4	45	2	87	4
Paveloff, Frederick	0	0	.000	2.84	5	0	0	1	0	0	6.1	7	2	2	0	0	2	0	6	1
Pennington, Frederick*	1	4	.200	3.92	36	0	0	27	0	13	43.2	32	23	19	4	2	44	0	58	4
Perez, Winston-Salem	0	0	.000	7.24	9	0	0	5	0	0	13.2	13	12	11	0	5	17	0	9	2
Perkins, Peninsula	8	13	.381	5.23	26	24	2	0	0	0	144.2	149	103	84	14	3	68	2	86	3
Person, Kinston	3	5	.375	4.67	11	11	0	0	0	0	52.0	56	37	27	2	2	42	0	45	2
Pettiford, Kinston	8	2	.800	3.16	26	6	1	7	1	0	85.1	69	39	30	5	3	35	0	70	6
Phillips, Kinston	1	1	.500	3.00	6	0	0	4	0	1	9.0	4	3	3	1	0	1	0	11	1
Pitcher, Peninsula	3	8	.273	4.65	17	17	1	0	0	0	81.1	100	58	42	4	4	52	2	70	7
Plantenberg, Lynchburg*	11	5	.688	3.76	20	20	0	0	0	0	103.0	116	59	43	3	4	51	1	73	8
Plaster, Frederick	0	3	.000	11.00	4	2	0	1	0	0	9.0	13	14	11	2	0	8	0	10	0
Porcelli, Winston-Salem*	0	1	.000	4.53	41	0	0	20	0	1	59.2	65	38	30	1	3	34	0	29	10
Prybylinski, Prince William	4	2	.667	3.00	8	8	1	0	0	0	48.0	42	18	16	4	2	6	0	43	3
Ralph, Prince William	5	7	.417	3.31	47	0	0	24	0	6	65.1	51	28	24	5	4	22	4	61	1
Rhodes, Prince William	3	4	.429	5.45	15	14	0	0	0	0	67.2	69	44	41	5	1	40	0	52	8
Ricci, Frederick	12	14	.462	3.11	30	29	2	0	0	0	173.2	148	91	60	12	3	84	2	144	15
Richardson, Lynchburg	3	4	.429	4.46	25	6	1	8	0	0	70.2	81	49	35	4	3	38	0	44	5
Riddle, Frederick	2	4	.333	4.21	52	1	0	23	0	5	98.1	101	53	46	9	3	44	1	68	6
Riley, Lynchburg*	8	10	.444	3.53	27	27	2	0	0	0	163.0	169	80	64	10	6	56	0	122	7
Ritter, Durham	3	3	.500	3.40	26	0	0	13	0	2	53.0	44	23	20	5	3	26	4	44	5
Rivera, Kinston*	1	0	1.000	4.35	10	0	0	5	0	0	10.1	10	6	5	1	0	2	0	9	0
Robertson, Salem*	2	4	.333	4.93	12	11	0	0	0	0	45.2	34	32	25	2	3	42	0	32	4
Rush, Lynchburg	9	13	.409	4.11	26	26	2	0	0	0	149.0	145	75	68	13	5	47	0	144	14
Rychel, Salem	1	7	.125	6.02	11	11	0	0	0	0	49.1	48	44	33	7	3	27	0	34	10
Ryder, Durham	2	0	1.000	3.06	8	4	0	2	0	1	32.1	24	13	11	3	2	9	1	26	0
Schanz, Peninsula	2	17	.105	5.15	27	20	2	4	0	0	122.1	136	85	70	11	7	78	1	59	2
Schullstrom, Frederick	5	6	.455	3.05	19	17	1	0	1	0	85.2	70	32	29	5	1	45	1	73	4
Scott, Lynchburg	1	3	.250	3.36	49	1	0	21	0	2	75.0	84	45	28	2	5	28	2	51	10
Shiflett, Durham	1	3	.250	4.44	16	0	0	8	0	1	26.1	40	23	13	1	2	16	0	27	6
Shouse, Salem*	2	1	.667	2.94	17	0	0	9	0	3	33.2	35	12	11	2	0	15	2	25	1
Smith, Lynchburg	12	9	.571	2.16	25	25	8	0	2	0	174.2	149	60	42	6	9	34	2	103	9
Sodders, Winston-Salem*	8	1	.889	2.54	10	10	1	0	0	0	63.2	54	19	18	4	1	33	2	39	4
Soper, Kinston	3	2	.600	2.47	62	0	0	58	0	41	73.0	59	21	20	3	1	26	1	72	6
Sottile, Durham	1	0	1.000	6.75	6	0	0	1	0	0	8.0	19	11	6	0	1	3	0	4	1
Steinmetz, Durham	3	7	.300	4.00	16	15	0	1	0	0	72.0	74	38	32	7	3	24	1	58	0
Strange, Durham	0	0	.000	1.79	38	0	0	32	0	19	40.1	39	13	8	1	1	8	1	51	7

Pitcher, Team	W	L	Pct.	ERA	G	GS	CG	GF	ShO	Sv.	IP	H	R	ER	HR	HB	BB	Int. BB	SO	WP
Stroud, Winston-Salem*	0	3	.000	6.59	6	1	0	1	0	0	13.2	18	10	10	5	1	3	0	11	1
Swartzbaugh, Winston-Salem	10	4	.714	1.83	15	15	2	0	1	0	93.2	71	22	19	3	1	42	1	73	4
Tatterson, Kinston	0	0	.000	0.00	1	0	0	0	0	0	4.0	2	0	0	0	0	0	0	2	0
Taylor, Durham	10	3	.769	2.18	24	16	2	5	0	3	111.1	94	32	27	3	2	33	3	78	10
Tegtmeier, Peninsula	3	3	.500	5.35	50	1	0	16	0	1	77.1	95	64	46	5	1	30	5	56	4
Tellers, Salem*	6	4	.600	1.38	40	0	0	28	0	10	72.0	54	16	11	1	2	20	4	61	0
Tepper, Kinston*	0	0	.000	0.00	2	0	0	2	0	0	2.1	0	0	0	0	1	0	0	3	0
Thomas, Peninsula*	0	0	.000	0.00	2	0	0	2	0	0	2.1	2	0	0	0	1	0	0	0	0
Trachsel, Winston-Salem	4	4	.500	3.67	12	12	1	0	0	0	73.2	70	38	30	3	1	19	0	69	1
Tucker, Prince William*	2	2	.500	7.88	21	1	0	9	0	0	40.0	52	40	35	4	3	32	0	41	2
Uhrhan, Lynchburg	8	5	.615	2.91	51	0	0	32	0	12	74.1	66	25	24	5	2	27	0	58	5
Underwood, Salem*	0	3	.000	5.20	15	8	0	2	0	0	45.0	46	28	26	4	1	27	1	32	5
Urso, Peninsula*	0	3	.000	3.06	46	0	0	29	0	8	61.2	74	36	21	1	5	30	7	44	6
Vazquez, Durham	3	0	1.000	2.63	4	4	0	0	0	0	24.0	30	9	7	0	0	11	0	12	2
Wagner, Salem	11	6	.647	3.12	25	25	5	0	2	0	158.2	124	70	55	14	9	60	0	113	11
Watson, Salem*	0	1	.000	11.05	9	0	0	1	0	0	14.2	26	18	18	2	1	11	1	11	2
Way, Salem*	1	3	.250	4.26	25	1	0	10	0	1	57.0	68	34	27	8	3	25	1	44	1
Werland, Durham	5	2	.714	1.98	8	7	0	0	0	0	41.0	36	12	9	1	1	15	0	22	4
White, Salem	2	3	.400	4.66	13	5	1	4	0	1	46.1	41	27	24	2	0	9	3	36	2
Wiggs, Peninsula*	6	5	.545	3.19	39	5	3	9	1	2	110.0	94	43	39	8	3	42	4	77	4
J. Williams, Frederick	1	2	.333	2.70	12	0	0	11	0	6	16.2	17	6	5	1	0	6	0	20	0
S. Williams, Frederick*	0	1	.000	9.00	1	0	0	1	0	0	2.0	2	2	2	0	0	2	0	3	0
Willis, Winston-Salem	6	4	.600	4.05	53	0	0	48	0	26	73.1	73	36	33	2	3	25	1	60	7
Woodall, Durham*	0	0	.000	2.45	4	0	0	2	0	0	7.1	4	3	2	1	0	4	0	14	0
Yaughn, Frederick	11	8	.579	3.94	27	27	1	0	0	0	162.0	168	88	71	15	7	76	0	155	11
Young, Durham*	1	3	.250	3.62	13	3	0	4	0	1	37.1	32	21	15	2	3	21	2	22	3
Zimmerman, Salem	4	2	.667	4.37	49	1	0	44	0	9	70.0	51	47	34	1	14	72	2	63	20

BALKS—Byrd, 7; Bryant, 6; Hodges, 4; Bark, Hale, Hollins, Holman, Johnson, Kostich, Rychel, Schanz, Tellers, Trachsel, Wiggs, Yaughn, 3 each; Borbon, Caballero, Carper, Converse, Dennison, Hitchcock, Hook, Jones, King, Langdon, Mattson, McDowell, McMichael, Parkinson, Schul-lstrom, 2 each; Bethea, Carlson, Cooke, Cronin, Culkar, DeLeon, Hawblitzel, Johnston, Leskanic, Melvin, Militello, Mosley, O'Donoghue, Ojala, Person, Pitcher, Porcelli, Prybylinski, Ricci, Riddle, Tegtmeier, Uhrhan, Wagner, 1 each.

COMBINATION SHUTOUTS—Burlingame-Cronin-Strange, Burlingame-McMichael, Cronin-Strange, McMichael-Shifflett, Minchey-McMichael-Strange, Murray-Taylor, Nied-Cronin, Nied-Cronin-Taylor, Steinmetz-Borbon, Steinmetz-Minchey-Strange, Vasquez-McMichael-Strange, Werland-McMichael, Werland-Ritter, Werland-Ryder, Werland-Strange, Young-Cronin-Strange, Durham; Schullstrom-Pennington 2, Kerr-Moore, O'Donoghue-Carper, O'Donoghue-Riddle-Pennington, Ricci-Pennington, Ricci-Williams, Frederick; Byrd-Morgan-Soper 2, Allen-Neill, Bryant-Kiser-Soper, Bryant-Morgan-Kiser-Soper, Bryant-Morgan-Soper, Byrd-Johnson, Leskanic-Johnson, Leskanic-Morgan-Soper, Pettiford-Soper, Kinston; Plantenberg-Uhrhan 2, Rush-Hoyer-Burgo 2, Dennison-Uhrhan, Dennison-Uhrhan-Hoyer, Finnvold-Uhrhan, Plantenberg-Hoyer-Burgo, Rush-Mosley, Lynchburg; Schanz-Wiggs-Urso, Peninsula; Militello-Johnston-Hoffman-Ohlms, Militello-Ohlms, Ojala-Gilbert, Ojala-Ohlms, Ojala-Ralph-Haller, Prince William; Bird-Tellers, Buckholz-Tellers, Wagner-Tellers, Salem; Swartzbaugh-Jaques 2, Caballero-Melvin-Hollins, Hawblitzel-Willis, Jones-Melvin, Jones-Willis, Sodders-Hollins, Swartzbaugh-Melvin, Swartzbaugh-Melvin-Willis, Winston-Salem.

NO-HIT GAMES—Munoz, Kinston, defeated Prince William, 1-0, May 26; Schullstrom, Frederick, defeated Kinston, 2-0, July 3; Trachsel, Winston-Salem, defeated Peninsula, 4-2 (second game), July 12; Byrd-Morgan-Soper, Kinston, defeated Prince William, 1-0, August 23.

FIELDING

TEAM

Team	Pct.	G	PO	A	E	DP	PB	Team	Pct.	G	PO	A	E	DP	PB
Durham	.971	137	3539	1505	153	127	17	Kinston	.963	138	3647	1504	200	137	34
Winston-Salem	.969	140	3560	1492	164	121	19	Frederick	.961	140	3638	1412	207	138	21
Prince William	.964	139	3629	1606	198	133	22	Salem	.959	140	3570	1458	213	111	19
Lynchburg	.963	139	3577	1488	192	132	20	Peninsula	.956	139	3479	1379	226	108	25

Triple plays—Durham, Frederick, Peninsula.

INDIVIDUAL

FIRST BASEMEN

*Throws lefthanded.

Player, Team	Pct.	G	PO	A	E	DP
Aude, Salem	.980	64	554	34	12	37
Berlin, Frederick	.917	8	10	1	1	2
Berni, Lynchburg	.982	26	214	9	4	14
Bosarge, Peninsula	1.000	1	2	0	0	0
Brakebill, Peninsula	.956	10	78	8	4	3
Brust, Durham	.988	76	582	53	8	42
Cole, Winston-Salem	1.000	1	1	0	0	0
Dando, Durham*	1.000	7	42	4	0	6
Delgado, Lynchburg	1.000	2	11	2	0	2
Delpozo, Peninsula	1.000	1	5	0	0	0
Easley, Kinston	.988	78	678	36	9	65
Ebright, Winston-Salem*	.989	19	168	13	2	13
Eiterman, Kinston	1.000	7	35	2	0	4
Flowers, Frederick	.971	10	64	4	2	8
Franco, Winston-Salem	.989	84	706	44	8	53
Hartung, Winston-Salem	.988	35	236	19	3	29
Holley, Peninsula	.977	25	202	13	5	18
JIMENEZ, Prince William*	.987	99	933	81	13	85
Johnson, Salem*	.988	29	226	27	3	22
Kessinger, Frederick	1.000	2	3	0	0	1
Kounas, Peninsula	.982	39	292	33	6	26
Leon, Prince William	.991	26	218	14	2	20

Player, Team	Pct.	G	PO	A	E	DP
McCoy, Durham	.985	49	357	33	6	35
B. Miller, Frederick	.990	37	288	21	3	34
Moore, Frederick*	1.000	1	2	0	0	0
Oster, Prince William*	.976	20	159	5	4	16
Perez, Durham	.984	34	243	11	4	28
Pirkl, Peninsula	1.000	13	107	8	0	10
Polewski, Salem	1.000	1	1	0	0	0
Postiff, Winston-Salem	.992	17	117	5	1	18
Rodarte, Peninsula	1.000	5	35	5	0	2
Saetre, Peninsula*	.985	54	415	34	7	38
Sarbaugh, Kinston	1.000	6	39	5	0	7
Shelton, Salem*	.988	53	441	43	6	40
Sprick, Frederick	.964	8	26	1	1	2
Tatum, Lynchburg	.981	118	989	96	21	95
Tepper, Kinston*	.991	57	494	38	5	52
Wearing, Frederick	.983	94	702	65	13	67

Triple plays—McCoy, Saetre, Wearing.

SECOND BASEMEN

Player, Team	Pct.	G	PO	A	E	DP
Bailey, Salem	.944	17	26	41	4	7
Beasley, Frederick	.955	78	121	177	14	35
Berlin, Frederick	.937	15	25	34	4	9

Player, Team	Pct.	G	PO	A	E	DP
Bethea, Lynchburg	.967	87	164	219	13	54
Biasucci, Winston-Salem	.937	25	45	59	7	9
Bragg, Peninsula	.833	4	2	3	1	0
Caraballo, Durham	.952	115	217	341	28	73
Cole, Winston-Salem	.962	43	83	118	8	28
DeKneef, Lynchburg	1.000	2	4	4	0	1
Delgado, Lynchburg	.982	10	28	26	1	9
Donahue, Kinston	.966	7	14	14	1	5
Easley, Kinston	1.000	1	1	0	0	0
Fermaint, Peninsula	.961	34	73	101	7	16
FLORES, Kinston	.964	124	254	366	23	78
Giovanola, Durham	.965	25	46	65	4	14
Graham, Lynchburg	.850	6	8	9	3	3
Griffin, Winston-Salem	.953	73	175	188	18	48
Halland, Peninsula	.939	12	16	15	2	2
Hankins, Prince William	.965	66	115	186	11	40
P. Kelly, Durham	1.000	3	7	7	0	0
Kessinger, Frederick	.892	9	17	16	4	6
Letterio, Peninsula	1.000	4	5	15	0	4
Lewis, Frederick	1.000	1	1	4	0	2
Manahan, Salem	.952	111	187	310	25	42
Osik, Salem	.950	3	7	12	1	0
Polewski, Salem	.964	16	30	50	3	12
Rigsby, Kinston	1.000	1	1	3	0	0
Rodarte, Peninsula	.932	51	77	127	15	20
Sanchez, Prince William	.941	27	47	65	7	21
Sarbaugh, Kinston	.970	14	28	37	2	12
Scott, Lynchburg	1.000	1	1	0	0	0
Seda, Peninsula	.933	41	93	103	14	25
Sprick, Frederick	1.000	2	0	1	0	0
Tyler, Frederick	.943	53	93	139	14	26
Villalobos, Lynchburg	.963	51	63	119	7	22
Wardlow, Prince William	.971	56	110	154	8	37
Wilson, Winston-Salem	.967	5	12	17	1	3

Triple plays—Caraballo, Rodarte.

THIRD BASEMEN

Player, Team	Pct.	G	PO	A	E	DP
Aude, Salem	.762	10	4	12	5	2
Bailey, Salem	.886	34	20	50	9	2
Baker, Frederick	.875	2	2	5	1	2
Beasley, Frederick	.880	42	28	53	11	6
Berlin, Frederick	.923	57	35	73	9	6
Berthel, Frederick	.667	4	0	2	1	0
Biasucci, Winston-Salem	1.000	4	1	7	0	0
Brakebill, Peninsula	.782	26	17	26	12	2
Castellano, Winston-Salem	.956	67	46	128	8	15
Cole, Winston-Salem	.966	18	17	40	2	4
Delgado, Lynchburg	.947	12	11	25	2	4
Donahue, Kinston	.500	1	0	1	1	1
Easley, Kinston	.775	16	10	21	9	2
Eiterman, Kinston	1.000	1	0	1	0	0
Fox, Prince William	.920	126	85	247	29	19
Franco, Winston-Salem	.857	10	4	8	2	1
Gillis, Durham	.929	114	53	182	18	10
Giovanola, Durham	.913	29	17	46	6	7
Grace, Winston-Salem	.947	50	33	110	8	14
Graham, Lynchburg	1.000	2	1	0	0	0
Halland, Peninsula	.889	2	4	4	1	0
Hedge, Frederick	.667	4	1	1	1	1
Holley, Peninsula	.895	18	18	33	6	2
Johnson, Salem*	1.000	1	0	1	0	0
Kessinger, Frederick	.793	17	11	12	6	0
Leon, Prince William	.826	7	6	13	4	2
Letterio, Peninsula	.978	39	31	59	2	3
Lewis, Frederick	.861	33	23	39	10	6
Magallanes, Peninsula	.925	41	22	64	7	6
NORRIS, Lynchburg	.939	131	86	267	23	*24
Osik, Salem	.941	40	34	46	5	7
Polewski, Salem	.929	6	3	10	1	0
Postiff, Winston-Salem	1.000	2	1	2	0	0
Rigsby, Kinston	1.000	3	2	0	0	0
Sarbaugh, Kinston	.935	12	8	21	2	1
Seda, Peninsula	.868	19	14	32	7	0
Sprick, Frederick	.762	16	6	10	5	0
Sued, Kinston	1.000	1	0	1	0	0
Tena, Kinston	.915	116	77	223	28	26
Tyler, Frederick	1.000	2	0	1	0	0
Wardlow, Prince William	1.000	12	5	21	0	2
Young, Salem	.925	56	54	93	12	6

SHORTSTOPS

Player, Team	Pct.	G	PO	A	E	DP
ALEXANDER, Frederick	.951	134	226	393	32	93
Bailey, Salem	.840	13	16	26	8	5
Beasley, Frederick	.912	7	14	17	3	3
Bethea, Lynchburg	.829	9	8	21	6	2
Biasucci, Winston-Salem	.895	6	3	14	2	0
Bryant, Peninsula	.972	25	37	69	3	16
Byrd, Lynchburg	.915	45	62	131	18	31
Castellano, Winston-Salem	.939	65	86	190	18	31
DeKneef, Lynchburg	.969	8	13	18	1	6
Delgado, Lynchburg	.914	20	25	39	6	9

Player, Team	Pct.	G	PO	A	E	DP
Donahue, Kinston	.913	15	12	30	4	6
Eenhoorn, Prince William	.950	29	45	69	6	19
Erickson, Prince William	.947	47	82	151	13	32
Flores, Kinston	1.000	1	1	1	0	0
Franco, Winston-Salem	.667	1	1	1	1	1
Giovanola, Durham	.960	28	49	71	5	13
Graham, Lynchburg	.907	66	93	161	26	32
Hankins, Prince William	.935	69	87	213	21	46
Holley, Peninsula	.938	42	80	116	13	27
P. Kelly, Durham	.818	9	5	22	6	4
Kessinger, Frederick	1.000	4	1	4	0	1
Letterio, Peninsula	.950	26	39	57	5	15
Meade, Kinston	.900	17	25	47	8	12
Mordecai, Durham	.945	104	164	302	27	69
Polewski, Salem	.867	7	5	8	2	2
Rigsby, Kinston	.907	71	104	180	29	43
Rodarte, Peninsula	.960	9	7	17	1	2
Rodriguez, Salem	.943	133	210	371	35	63
St.Peter, Winston-Salem	.927	67	88	166	20	32
Sanchez, Prince William	.800	2	1	3	1	1
Sarbaugh, Kinston	.944	39	56	96	9	24
Seda, Peninsula	.872	46	77	107	27	15
Tena, Kinston	.939	13	13	33	3	7
Wilson, Winston-Salem	.909	12	8	32	4	5

Triple plays—Alexander, Holley, Mordecai.

OUTFIELDERS

Player, Team	Pct.	G	PO	A	E	DP
Alstead, Frederick	.972	61	91	12	3	5
Bailey, Salem	1.000	10	25	2	0	0
Berlin, Frederick	1.000	3	1	1	0	0
Berthel, Frederick	.946	36	50	3	3	0
Bethea, Lynchburg	.913	11	18	3	2	1
Bragg, Peninsula	.983	66	165	6	3	1
Brewington, Salem*	1.000	5	3	0	0	0
Buford, Frederick	.984	127	293	7	5	2
Bullett, Salem*	.957	39	87	3	4	1
Bullock, Peninsula	.750	11	11	1	4	0
Cairo, Frederick	.928	72	110	6	9	1
Canate, Kinston	.990	50	99	4	1	0
Carpenter, Prince William*	.963	62	98	7	4	2
Chick, Lynchburg	.959	129	243	12	11	3
Clark, Durham	.958	17	23	0	1	0
Cudjo, Peninsula	.949	52	86	8	5	0
DeJardin, Kinston*	.967	42	57	2	2	0
Delgado, Lynchburg	.857	5	6	0	1	0
de los Santos, Salem	.950	103	163	8	9	1
Delpozo, Peninsula	.957	41	64	3	3	0
Donahue, Kinston	1.000	1	1	0	0	0
Ebright, Winston-Salem*	.944	51	67	0	4	0
Eiterman, Kinston	.976	71	117	5	3	1
Garland, Prince William	.933	24	27	1	2	0
Gilbert, Frederick	1.000	38	77	5	0	0
Giles, Kinston*	.975	124	187	10	5	4
GRAYUM, Winston-Salem	.993	97	140	6	1	0
Hedge, Frederick	.992	79	117	4	1	0
Holley, Peninsula	1.000	1	2	0	0	0
Jensen, Winston-Salem	.971	128	188	12	6	4
Johnson, Salem*	1.000	2	1	0	0	0
M. Kelly, Durham	1.000	4	4	0	0	0
P. Kelly, Durham	.951	33	37	2	2	0
Kluge, Peninsula	1.000	1	1	0	0	0
Kostich, Peninsula*	1.000	1	1	0	0	0
Kounas, Peninsula	.889	10	15	1	2	0
Kowitz, Durham*	1.000	86	169	1	0	1
Lane, Kinston	.947	29	70	1	4	0
Leach, Lynchburg*	.984	38	59	1	1	0
List, Lynchburg	.893	34	48	2	6	1
McCoy, Durham	1.000	47	58	0	0	0
McNeely, Lynchburg	.968	103	237	5	8	1
Merchant, Peninsula	.989	66	87	2	1	0
Moore, Lynchburg	.965	96	158	9	6	2
Mota, Kinston	1.000	1	1	0	0	0
Nieves, Durham	.943	57	75	6	5	1
O'Connor, Durham	.971	27	31	2	1	0
Obando, Prince William	1.000	16	19	1	0	0
Oster, Prince William*	.944	72	111	7	7	1
Pennyfeather, Salem	.978	79	167	12	4	4
Pezzoni, Peninsula	.972	84	166	5	5	0
Pough, Kinston	1.000	8	4	0	0	0
Powell, Peninsula	.944	8	17	0	1	0
Ratliff, Salem	.951	83	181	15	10	3
Rigsby, Kinston	1.000	5	4	1	0	0
Robertson, Prince William*	.940	124	236	0	15	0
Romay, Peninsula	.982	40	111	1	2	0
Saetre, Peninsula*	.917	12	20	2	2	1
Sanders, Kinston	.947	113	153	8	9	1
Shelton, Salem*	.750	3	3	0	1	0
Simmons, Durham*	.977	102	166	2	4	0
Smith, Frederick	.980	29	49	1	1	1
Strickland, Prince William	.944	80	104	14	7	2
Tarasco, Durham	.977	66	119	6	3	2
Tepper, Kinston*	.750	5	3	0	1	0
Thomas, Peninsula*	.940	42	75	3	5	0

Player, Team	Pct.	G	PO	A	E	DP
Torres, Winston-Salem	.920	24	43	3	4	1
Trusky, Salem	.964	69	100	7	4	2
Tyler, Frederick	1.000	1	1	0	0	0
Viera, Prince William*	.976	45	79	2	2	0
Wardwell, Lynchburg	.960	49	94	3	4	0
Washington, Kinston	.714	3	5	0	2	0
Watkins, Durham	1.000	20	19	0	0	0
Wawruck, Frederick*	.941	13	16	0	1	0
Williams, Winston-Salem	.984	136	310	3	5	1

CATCHERS

Player, Team	Pct.	G	PO	A	E	DP	PB
Ausmus, Prince William	.990	54	419	54	5	2	6
Baker, Frederick	.949	18	88	5	5	2	4
Belyeu, Winston-Salem	1.000	11	56	10	0	1	1
Berlin, Frederick	1.000	1	2	0	0	1	0
Berni, Lynchburg	.988	13	78	5	1	0	3
Bosarge, Peninsula	.964	22	151	12	6	4	7
Davis, Salem	.938	9	28	2	2	1	0
Devares, Frederick	.990	68	443	70	5	6	9
Edge, Salem	.981	95	585	89	13	4	10
Figga, Prince William	.984	45	278	33	5	1	4
Flowers, Frederick	.985	25	126	7	2	2	4
Gabbani, Winston-Salem	.988	41	214	25	3	2	7
Hatteberg, Lynchburg	1.000	7	35	2	0	0	0
Hernandez, Prince William	1.000	7	57	8	0	1	2
Horowitz, Frederick	.982	30	203	10	4	1	2
Huff, Winston-Salem	1.000	5	7	0	0	0	0
Jarvis, Prince William	.979	6	43	4	1	0	0
Kluge, Peninsula	.958	17	104	10	5	3	2
Kounas, Peninsula	.984	33	162	18	3	2	10
Livesey, Prince William	.954	18	108	16	6	2	9
Lopez, Durham	.991	90	610	85	6	14	13
Losa, Kinston	.990	60	359	48	4	0	10
Luis, Lynchburg	.963	39	190	20	8	3	3
Morales, Peninsula	.942	17	87	11	6	1	1
Mota, Kinston	.991	64	399	46	4	2	12
Osik, Salem	.980	42	266	27	6	4	8
Perez, Durham	.987	44	254	44	4	6	3
Pineda, Prince William	1.000	13	80	11	0	0	1
Pirkl, Peninsula	.979	41	215	23	5	3	2
Postiff, Winston-Salem	1.000	32	151	14	0	0	4
Raasch, Peninsula	.986	19	126	15	2	2	3
Reynolds, Frederick	.958	15	85	7	4	4	0
Sued, Kinston	.981	30	235	21	5	1	9
Swail, Durham	.990	26	95	6	1	0	1
Tallman, Frederick	.992	14	109	12	1	3	2
Torres, Salem	.950	3	17	2	1	0	1
Walbeck, Winston-Salem	.978	85	473	64	12	5	7
Williams, Kinston	1.000	6	40	5	0	0	3
WILSON, Lynchburg	.994	93	585	71	4	10	14

Triple play—Perez.

PITCHERS

Player, Team	Pct.	G	PO	A	E	DP
Allen, Kinston	.974	26	8	30	1	5
Arvesen, Salem	.889	19	13	11	3	1
Bark, Durham*	.913	13	3	18	2	1
Beasley, Frederick	1.000	3	2	0	0	0
Bird, Salem*	.938	35	5	25	2	0
Blumberg, Frederick*	.938	13	7	8	1	0
Borbon, Durham*	.864	37	6	13	3	0
Bradford, Winston-Salem	.970	19	7	25	1	1
Brust, Durham	1.000	3	0	2	0	0
Bryant, Kinston*	.857	29	4	32	6	2
Buckholz, Durham	.778	5	1	6	2	0
Burgo, Lynchburg	1.000	36	3	10	0	0
BURLINGAME, Durham	1.000	26	18	28	0	5
Byrd, Salem	.867	14	3	10	2	0
Caballero, Winston-Salem	.902	32	19	18	4	2
Carlson, Salem	1.000	6	1	3	0	1
Carper, Frederick	.864	26	0	19	3	3
Charland, Kinston*	1.000	5	1	2	0	0
Cheetham, Winston-Salem	1.000	17	6	13	0	0
Constant, Frederick	1.000	8	5	5	0	0
Converse, Peninsula	.821	26	8	15	5	4
Cooke, Salem*	.000	2	0	0	1	0
Cronin, Durham	.905	37	8	11	2	1
Culkar, Frederick	1.000	6	2	1	0	0
Czarkowski, Peninsula	1.000	6	4	13	0	0
Dennison, Lynchburg*	.952	30	9	31	2	0
Finnvold, Lynchburg	1.000	6	2	4	0	0
Furcal, Peninsula*	.941	29	3	13	1	0
Futrell, Salem	1.000	10	2	1	0	0
Garland, Prince William	.000	1	0	0	1	0
Gilbert, Prince William	1.000	31	4	17	0	3
Hailey, Durham*	1.000	5	0	3	0	0
Hale, Frederick*	.909	16	0	20	2	0
Haller, Prince William*	.955	46	3	18	1	2
Hawblitzel, Winston-Salem	.943	20	7	26	2	1
Hays, Frederick	.900	30	5	4	1	0
Hitchcock, Prince William*	.852	19	5	18	4	0
Hodges, Prince William	.885	26	13	33	6	2

Player, Team	Pct.	G	PO	A	E	DP
Hoffman, Prince William	.946	34	12	41	3	3
Holcomb, Prince William*	1.000	10	0	1	0	0
Hollins, Winston-Salem	.857	41	9	9	3	1
Holman, Peninsula	.882	47	4	11	2	0
Hook, Frederick*	.917	37	0	11	1	0
Hope, Salem	.800	6	2	2	1	0
Hoyer, Lynchburg*	.929	52	5	8	1	1
Jaques, Winston-Salem*	.944	30	4	13	1	2
Johnson, Kinston	.800	32	3	9	3	0
Johnston, Prince William	.875	33	6	8	2	0
Jones, Winston-Salem	.789	17	7	8	4	1
Kerr, Frederick	.625	8	2	3	3	1
King, Peninsula*	.964	17	6	21	1	1
Kiser, Kinston*	1.000	31	2	9	0	0
Kostich, Peninsula*	1.000	33	5	12	0	0
Kovach, Kinston	1.000	4	0	2	0	0
Leinen, Frederick*	1.000	1	0	1	0	0
Leskanic, Kinston	.915	28	12	31	4	1
Lodding, Peninsula	1.000	28	4	7	0	1
Malley, Kinston*	1.000	9	4	3	0	0
Mattson, Durham	1.000	9	4	7	0	0
McDowell, Kinston	.920	23	11	12	2	1
McMichael, Durham	.913	36	5	16	2	1
Melvin, Winston-Salem	1.000	41	4	8	0	1
Militello, Prince William	.964	16	9	18	1	2
D. Miller, Frederick	.750	9	1	2	1	0
Minchey, Durham	.960	15	12	12	1	0
Moore, Frederick*	.909	22	2	8	1	0
Morgan, Kinston	.923	34	1	11	1	1
Mosley, Lynchburg*	1.000	46	9	15	0	0
Munoz, Kinston	.917	14	8	14	2	0
Murray, Durham	1.000	2	0	4	0	0
Neill, Kinston	.842	40	5	11	3	1
Nied, Durham	1.000	13	6	12	0	2
O'Donoghue, Frederick*	.960	22	6	18	1	3
Ohlms, Prince William	.857	47	3	15	3	1
Ojala, Prince William*	.972	25	8	27	1	2
Parkinson, Salem	.944	29	7	10	1	0
Pennington, Frederick*	.938	36	3	12	1	1
Perez, Winston-Salem	1.000	9	0	1	0	0
Perkins, Peninsula	.885	26	3	20	3	0
Person, Kinston	.778	11	2	5	2	0
Pettiford, Kinston	.905	26	3	16	2	1
Phillips, Kinston	.667	6	0	2	1	0
Pitcher, Kinston	1.000	17	10	10	0	0
Plantenberg, Lynchburg*	.969	20	7	24	1	1
Plaster, Frederick	.333	4	0	1	2	0
Porcelli, Winston-Salem*	1.000	41	3	7	0	1
Prybylinski, Prince William	1.000	8	2	8	0	1
Ralph, Prince William	1.000	47	4	7	0	0
Rhodes, Prince William	.818	15	6	3	2	0
Ricci, Frederick	.915	30	21	33	5	1
Richardson, Lynchburg	.885	25	13	10	3	1
Riddle, Frederick	.929	52	4	9	1	2
Riley, Lynchburg*	.969	27	7	24	1	0
Ritter, Durham.	1.000	26	5	11	0	1
Rivera, Kinston*	1.000	10	0	3	0	0
Robertson, Salem*	1.000	12	4	7	0	2
Rush, Lynchburg	.941	26	5	11	1	0
Rychel, Salem	.875	11	5	9	2	0
Ryder, Durham	1.000	8	1	7	0	0
Schanz, Peninsula	.909	27	10	20	3	2
Schullstrom, Frederick	.955	19	10	11	1	2
Scott, Lynchburg	.862	49	3	22	4	0
Shiflett, Durham	1.000	16	2	11	0	1
Shouse, Salem*	1.000	17	2	5	0	0
Smith, Lynchburg	.971	25	25	41	2	6
Sodders, Winston-Salem*	1.000	10	3	22	0	2
Soper, Kinston	1.000	62	4	7	0	0
Sottile, Durham	.500	6	0	1	1	0
Steinmetz, Durham	.933	16	4	10	1	0
Strange, Durham	1.000	38	1	5	0	0
Stroud, Winston-Salem*	1.000	6	1	3	0	0
Swartzbaugh, Winston-Salem	.875	15	3	19	0	0
Taylor, Durham	1.000	24	12	24	0	2
Tegtmeier, Peninsula	.947	50	4	14	1	0
Tellers, Salem	.905	40	3	16	2	0
Tepper, Kinston*	1.000	2	1	0	0	0
Trachsel, Winston-Salem	1.000	12	3	8	0	0
Tucker, Prince William*	.933	21	2	12	1	2
Uhrhan, Lynchburg	1.000	51	5	11	0	2
Underwood, Salem*	.875	15	2	5	1	1
Urso, Peninsula*	.955	46	2	19	1	1
Vazquez, Durham	.875	4	2	5	1	0
Wagner, Salem	.967	25	12	17	1	2
Watson, Salem*	1.000	9	2	5	0	0
Way, Salem*	.857	25	1	5	1	1
Werland, Durham*	1.000	8	5	4	0	1
White, Salem	.778	13	3	4	2	0
Wiggs, Peninsula*	.900	39	2	34	4	2
Williams, Frederick	1.000	12	0	2	0	0
Willis, Winston-Salem	.947	53	4	14	1	1
Yaughn, Frederick	.879	27	8	21	4	3
Young, Durham*	.909	13	3	7	1	0
Zimmerman, Salem	.933	49	2	12	1	1

The following players did not have any fielding statistics at the positions indicated or appeared only as a designated hitter, pinch-hitter or pinch-runner: Anderson, p; Beasley, 1b, of; Berlin, ss, p; Bethea, p; Brakebill, of; Brust, 3b; Buford, 3b; Cole, ss; Cudjo, p; DeJardin, p; DeLeon, p; Devares, of; Drew, ph; Eiterman, p; Fajardo, p; Giovanola, of; Grace, p; Graham, p; Griffin, of; Hebb, p; Horowitz, 3b; Jarvis, of; Kounas, p; Langdon, p; Mota, 3b; Paveloff, p; Ripken, dh; Seda, of; Sprick, ss; Tatterson, p; Thomas, p; Wardlow, of; S. Williams, p; Willis, of; B. Wilson, 3b; Woodall, p; Zambrano, dh.

LEAGUE CHAMPIONS

Year	Team	Pct.	Year	Team	Pct.	Year	Team	Pct.
1945—	Danville	.681		Kinston (2nd)†	.593	1976—	Winston-Salem	.618
1946—	Greensboro	.599	1963—	Kinston§	.538		Winston-Salem	.551
	Raleigh (2nd)†	.563		Greensboro§	.590	1977—	Lynchburg	.591
1947—	Burlington	.613		Wilson (2nd)†	.535		Peninsula‡	.556
	Raleigh (3rd)†	.574	1964—	Kinston§	.572	1978—	Peninsula	.696
1948—	Raleigh	.592		Winston-Salem§†	.590		Lynchburg‡	.614
	Martinsville (2nd)†	.570	1965—	Peninsula§	.597	1979—	Winston-Salem a	.607
1949—	Danville	.601		Durham§	.580	1980—	Peninsula‡	.714
	Burlington (4th)†	.500		Tidewater†	.528		Durham	.600
1950—	Winston-Salem*	.693	1966—	Kinston§	.547	1981—	Peninsula	.522
1951—	Durham	.600		Winston-Salem§	.586		Hagerstown‡	.507
	Wins-Salem (2nd)†	.583		Rocky Mount†	.533	1982—	Alexandria‡	.597
1952—	Raleigh	.581	1967—	Durham x (West.)	.536		Durham	.588
	Reidsville (4th)†	.536		Raleigh (East.)	.542	1983—	Lynchburg‡	.691
1953—	Raleigh	.593	1968—	Salem (West.)	.607		Winston-Salem	.529
	Danville (2nd)†	.572		Ral-Dur (East.)	.597	1984—	Lynchburg‡	.645
1954—	Fayetteville*	.628		HP-Thom. y (W.)	.493		Durham	.486
1955—	HP-Thomasville	.580	1969—	Rocky M (East.)	.569	1985—	Lynchburg	.679
	Danville (2nd)†	.533		Salem (West.)	.542		Winston-Salem‡	.417
1956—	HP-Thomasville	.591		Ral-Dur z (East.)	.560	1986—	Hagerstown	.655
	Fayetteville (4th)§	.523	1970—	Winston-Salem‡	.586		Winston-Salem‡	.594
1957—	Durham	.632		Burlington	.597	1987—	Salem‡	.576
	HP-Thomasville	.622	1971—	Peninsula‡	.647		Kinston	.536
1958—	Danville	.576		Kinston	.623	1988—	Kinston§	.629
	Burlington (4th)†	.511	1972—	Salem‡	.657		Lynchburg	.486
1959—	Raleigh	.600		Burlington	.632	1989—	Durham	.609
	Wilson (2nd)†	.550	1973—	Lynchburg	.588		Prince William‡	.522
1960—	Greensboro‡	.636		Winston-Salem‡	.557	1990—	Kinston	.652
	Burlington	.586	1974—	Salem	.671		Frederick‡	.544
1961—	Wilson	.594		Salem	.582	1991—	Kinston‡	.645
1962—	Durham	.636	1975—	Rocky Mount	.667		Lynchburg	.482
	Wilson	.600		Rocky Mount	.614			

*Won championship and four-club playoff. †Won four-club playoff. ‡Won split-season playoff. §League was divided into Eastern, Western divisions. xWon eight-club, two-division playoff. yWon eight-club, two-division playoff against Raleigh-Durham. zWon eight-club, two-division playoff against Burlington. aWon both halves of split season (no playoffs).

FLORIDA STATE LEAGUE

FINAL STANDINGS

FIRST HALF

EAST DIVISION

Team	W	L	T	Pct.	GB
Vero Beach (Dodgers)	42	23	0	.646	....
Miami (Independent)	35	29	0	.547	6½
Fort Lauderdale (Yankees)	32	30	0	.516	8½
West Palm Beach (Expos)	33	31	0	.516	8½
St. Lucie (Mets)	31	35	0	.470	11½

WEST DIVISION

Team	W	L	T	Pct.	GB
Clearwater (Phillies)	42	23	0	.646	....
Sarasota (White Sox)	38	29	0	.567	5
Charlotte (Rangers)	33	34	0	.493	10
Dunedin (Blue Jays)	29	36	0	.446	13
St. Petersburg (Cardinals)	24	40	0	.375	17½

CENTRAL DIVISION

Team	W	L	T	Pct.	GB
Lakeland (Tigers)	36	27	0	.571	....
Osceola (Astros)	31	33	0	.484	5½
Baseball City (Royals)	27	39	0	.409	10½
Winter Haven (Red Sox)	20	44	0	.313	16½

SECOND HALF

EAST DIVISION

Team	W	L	T	Pct.	GB
St. Lucie (Mets)	41	24	0	.631	....
West Palm Beach (Expos)	39	28	0	.582	3
Vero Beach (Dodgers)	37	29	1	.561	5½
Miami (Independent)	28	38	1	.424	13½
Fort Lauderdale (Yankees)	27	39	0	.409	16½

WEST DIVISION

Team	W	L	T	Pct.	GB
Clearwater (Phillies)	39	26	0	.600	....
Sarasota (White Sox)	37	27	0	.578	1½
Dunedin (Blue Jays)	30	36	0	.455	9½
Charlotte (Rangers)	29	36	0	.446	10
St. Petersburg (Cardinals)	23	44	0	.343	17

CENTRAL DIVISION

Team	W	L	T	Pct.	GB
Lakeland (Tigers)	36	29	0	.554	....
Baseball City (Royals)	35	30	0	.538	1
Osceola (Astros)	33	30	0	.524	2
Winter Haven (Red Sox)	23	41	0	.359	15½

COMPOSITE

Team	Clw	V.B.	Sar.	Lak.	WPB	StL	Osc.	Mia.	B.C.	Char.	Ft.L	Dun.	St.P	W.H.	W	L	T	Pct.	GB
Clearwater (Phillies)	....	3	8	7	3	5	5	3	3	12	5	9	13	5	81	49	0	.623	....
Vero Beach (Dodgers)	5	....	5	3	10	10	5	6	4	6	9	5	5	6	79	52	1	.603	2½
Sarasota (White Sox)	8	3	....	3	3	3	5	7	5	10	6	11	9	2	75	56	0	.573	6½
Lakeland (Tigers)	1	5	5	....	3	2	11	4	9	5	4	5	4	14	72	56	0	.563	8
West Palm Beach (Expos)	5	4	5	5	....	7	6	7	7	4	8	6	4	4	72	59	0	.550	9½
St. Lucie (Mets)	3	6	3	5	9	....	2	10	5	4	10	4	5	6	72	59	0	.550	9½
Osceola (Astros)	3	3	2	7	2	5	....	2	13	2	4	3	4	14	64	63	0	.504	15½
Miami (Independent)	4	7	1	3	9	6	5	....	2	4	9	3	6	4	63	67	1	.485	18
Baseball City (Royals)	5	4	2	7	1	3	6	6	....	3	5	2	5	13	62	69	0	.473	19½
Charlotte (Rangers)	4	2	6	2	3	3	5	4	5	....	3	11	9	5	62	70	0	.470	20
Fort Lauderdale (Yankees)	1	7	2	4	6	6	2	7	3	5	....	5	5	6	69	69	0	.461	21
Dunedin (Blue Jays)	7	3	5	3	2	4	4	5	5	1	....	12	3	59	72	0	.450	22½
St. Petersburg (Cardinals)	2	3	7	4	4	3	3	2	7	3	4	....	3	47	84	0	.359	34½
Winter Haven (Red Sox)	1	2	5	3	4	2	4	4	6	3	2	4	3	....	43	85	0	.336	37

Charlotte played home games in Port Charlotte, Fla.

Osceola played home games in Kissimmee, Fla.

Major league affiliations in parentheses.

Playoffs—West Palm Beach defeated Vero Beach, two games to one; St. Lucie defeated Sarasota, two games to one; West Palm Beach defeated Lakeland, two games to none; Clearwater defeated St. Lucie, two games to none; West Palm Beach defeated Clearwater, two games to none, to win league championship.

Regular-season attendance—Baseball City, 21,174; Charlotte, 97,399; Clearwater, 82,631; Dunedin, 67,040; Fort Lauderdale, 51,362; Lakeland, 51,464; Miami, 56,557; Osceola, 79,961; St. Petersburg, 155,946; Sarasota, 84,951; Vero Beach, 95,900; West Palm Beach, 105,787; Winter Haven, 20,323. Total, 1,018,836. Playoffs (12 games), 6,389. All-Star Game, 2,593.

Managers—Baseball City, Carlos Tosca; Charlotte, Bobby Molinaro; Clearwater, Lee Elia; Dunedin, Dennis Holmberg; Fort Lauderdale, Glenn Sherlock; Lakeland, John Lipon; Miami, Fredi Gonzalez; Osceola, Sal Butera; St. Lucie, John Tamargo; St. Petersburg, Dave Bialas; Sarasota, Rick Patterson; Vero Beach, Jerry Royster; West Palm Beach, Felipe Alou; Winter Haven, Mike Verdi.

All-Star team—1B—Scott Cepicky, Sarasota; 2B—Matt Howard, Vero Beach; 3B—Rey Noriega, Fort Lauderdale; SS—Troy Paulsen, Clearwater; Util. INF—Mike Lansing, Miami; LF—Robert Perez, Dunedin; CF—Nigel Wilson, Dunedin; RF—Rusty Greer, Charlotte; Util. OF—John Thomas, St. Petersburg; C—Brook Fordyce, St. Lucie; Miah Bradbury, Miami; DH—John Deutsch, Vero Beach; RHP—Tom Michno, Miami; Elliott Gray, Clearwater; LHP—Todd Douma, St. Lucie; Michael Mimbs, Vero Beach; Rel—Richard Batchelor, Fort Lauderdale; Julian Vasquez, St. Lucie; Most Valuable Player—Scott Cepicky, Sarasota; Manager of the Year—Lee Elia, Clearwater.

BATTING

TEAM

Team	Avg.	G	AB	R	OR	H	TB	2B	3B	HR	RBI	SH	SF	HP	BB	Int. BB	SO	SB	CS	LOB
Clearwater	.257	130	4141	596	443	1065	1450	172	39	45	528	56	51	51	501	27	692	110	58	927
Vero Beach	.256	132	4238	546	514	1083	1503	198	27	56	474	47	40	61	377	24	708	203	83	859
Lakeland	.251	128	4165	541	502	1046	1440	153	50	47	475	65	29	54	496	23	781	120	78	936
Sarasota	.251	131	4214	557	476	1058	1440	195	35	39	466	95	39	51	508	35	832	154	94	913
Charlotte	.244	132	4246	515	538	1037	1407	164	40	42	446	51	33	40	505	22	924	199	89	916
Fort Lauderdale	.244	128	4099	468	472	1000	1333	152	35	37	406	32	27	46	421	31	887	168	80	857
Osceola	.239	127	4061	484	455	970	1238	151	30	19	397	53	40	43	449	23	804	174	60	872

Team	Avg.	G	AB	R	OR	H	TB	2B	3B	HR	RBI	SH	SF	HP	BB	Int. BB	SO	SB	CS	LOB
Dunedin	.238	131	4195	438	492	998	1349	166	40	35	374	104	38	36	409	21	863	91	64	876
Miami	.238	131	4259	491	476	1013	1396	169	35	48	412	48	35	40	428	18	911	194	88	907
St. Lucie	.232	131	4245	463	404	983	1366	167	36	48	402	43	30	39	421	19	830	150	75	873
St. Petersburg	.230	131	4301	381	516	991	1284	151	32	26	328	26	24	37	399	18	746	48	41	928
Baseball City	.227	131	4135	446	461	938	1209	143	34	20	361	62	26	41	473	18	934	211	104	871
West Palm Beach	.218	131	4103	448	420	893	1264	143	33	54	381	23	40	48	411	21	861	136	69	817
Winter Haven	.217	128	3871	401	606	841	1089	139	20	23	347	60	37	40	482	18	918	127	76	816

INDIVIDUAL

(Leading qualifiers for batting championship—367 or more plate appearances)

*Bats lefthanded.   †Switch-hitter.

Player, Team	Avg.	G	AB	R	H	TB	2B	3B	HR	RBI	SH	SF	HP	BB	Int. BB	SO	SB	CS
Perez, Robert, Dunedin	.302	127	480	50	145	197	28	6	4	50	7	2	5	22	3	72	8	8
Wilson, Nigel, Dunedin*	.301	119	455	64	137	217	18	13	12	55	4	7	9	29	4	99	27	11
Deutsch, John, Vero Beach	.300	123	433	59	130	194	24	2	12	66	0	6	7	46	6	54	5	2
Thomas, John, St. Petersburg*	.298	116	433	52	129	172	14	10	3	46	0	3	5	36	0	71	9	8
Greer, Rusty, Charlotte*	.294	111	388	52	114	156	25	1	5	48	1	5	2	66	4	48	12	6
Cepicky, Scott, Sarasota*	.290	124	442	62	128	193	33	4	8	76	2	6	4	62	11	99	13	6
Paulsen, Troy, Clearwater	.288	122	441	62	127	157	21	3	1	47	8	6	5	31	1	45	2	5
Lansing, Mike, Miami	.286	104	384	54	110	162	20	7	6	55	1	6	4	40	1	75	29	7
Nuneviller, Tom, Clearwater	.283	124	446	77	126	173	31	5	2	54	8	5	9	48	2	52	16	9
Cornelius, Brian, Lakeland*	.279	121	438	57	122	174	16	9	6	59	6	5	3	45	4	67	4	6

Departmental leaders: G—Moore, 130; AB—Beanblossom, 508; R—Castleberry, 82; H—Perez, 145; TB—N. Wilson, 217; 2B—Cepicky, 33; 3B—N. Wilson, 13; HR—Noreiga, Oliva, 14; RBI—Cepicky, 76; SH—Montalvo, 21; SF—Taylor, 10; HP—Lukachyk, 15; BB—Noreiga, 78; IBB—Cepicky, 11; SO—Moore, 141; SB—Moore, 61; CS—M. Howard, 18.

(All players—listed alphabetically)

Player, Team	Avg.	G	AB	R	H	TB	2B	3B	HR	RBI	SH	SF	HP	BB	Int. BB	SO	SB	CS
Abare, Bill, Dunedin*	.180	117	350	24	63	103	19	3	5	31	3	1	1	45	3	127	0	2
Agostinelli, Sal, Clearwater	.250	32	80	9	20	22	2	0	0	8	3	1	0	16	0	10	1	2
Albright, Eric, Lakeland	.211	64	185	23	39	57	9	0	3	22	1	1	1	42	1	41	3	3
Alicea, Edwin, Miami†	.255	102	368	55	94	134	20	7	2	30	1	0	4	52	5	63	33	7
Allison, Tom, St. Lucie*	.162	22	74	7	12	13	1	0	0	7	3	2	0	9	0	24	8	1
Alvarez, Clemente, Sarasota	.206	71	194	14	40	57	10	2	1	22	7	1	4	20	0	41	3	2
Andrews, Jay, Baseball City†	.172	40	93	11	16	18	2	0	0	8	0	2	2	31	0	32	7	4
Anglero, Jose, Lakeland	.222	104	316	37	70	84	6	4	0	19	13	1	7	36	1	66	9	4
Angotti, Donald, Osceola	.000	5	7	1	0	0	0	0	0	0	0	1	0	1	0	3	0	0
Ansley, Willie, Osceola	.087	15	46	3	4	4	0	0	0	3	1	1	0	13	0	18	3	0
Ashley, Billy, Vero Beach	.252	61	206	18	52	88	11	2	7	42	0	1	0	7	0	69	9	2
Avent, Steve, Clearwater	.500	4	2	0	1	1	0	0	0	0	1	0	0	0	0	0	2	1
Ball, Jeff, Osceola	.246	117	391	53	96	132	15	3	5	51	3	4	10	49	4	74	20	8
Bargas, Rob, West Palm Beach†	.266	71	233	18	62	78	9	2	1	21	0	5	1	20	5	32	3	0
Barnwell, Rich, Fort Lauderdale	.292	86	298	50	87	123	15	3	5	37	6	0	9	43	2	76	31	7
Barry, Jeff, West Palm Beach†	.211	116	437	48	92	126	16	3	4	31	2	2	4	34	4	68	20	14
Beanblossom, Brad, St. Petersburg	.254	125	508	57	129	169	28	3	2	30	1	0	7	45	1	62	10	9
Bell, Jim, Osceola	.100	14	30	1	3	4	1	0	0	3	0	1	1	6	0	10	1	0
Berry, Perry, Osceola	.215	94	274	39	59	73	8	0	2	24	6	6	2	37	1	60	5	1
Beuerlein, Ed, Osceola	.224	62	192	23	43	75	8	0	8	23	1	1	4	28	1	59	1	0
Blackwell, Eric, Vero Beach*	.000	4	5	0	0	0	0	0	0	0	0	0	0	0	0	3	0	0
Blackwell, Juan, Fort Lauderdale	.171	27	82	8	14	16	2	0	0	7	0	1	3	8	0	24	0	4
Blanco, Henry, Vero Beach	.143	5	7	0	1	1	0	0	0	0	0	0	0	1	0	3	2	1
Bournigal, Rafael, Vero Beach	.242	20	66	6	16	18	2	0	0	3	1	0	1	3	0	3	2	1
Bradbury, Miah, Miami	.272	109	371	39	101	144	20	1	7	45	4	4	2	23	1	63	2	2
Bradish, Mike, 34 Mia.-36 Sar.	.258	70	190	19	49	66	12	1	1	18	2	1	1	30	0	50	2	6
Brady, Pat, Clearwater	.247	117	369	52	91	139	18	9	4	52	1	4	2	41	2	63	3	3
Brooks, Eric, Dunedin	.180	47	133	7	24	27	3	0	0	11	2	0	0	18	0	37	1	1
Brown, Adam, Vero Beach*	.284	58	183	26	52	82	10	1	6	35	0	3	3	25	4	29	1	1
Brown, Bryan, Winter Haven	.268	47	157	13	42	60	15	0	1	22	0	3	2	13	1	28	3	3
Brown, Randy, Winter Haven	.156	63	135	14	21	24	3	0	0	5	4	0	1	16	0	42	10	3
Burton, Chris, Miami*	.238	55	189	25	45	52	2	1	1	11	7	1	3	23	1	47	24	7
Butterfield, Chris, St. Lucie†	.225	121	426	41	96	143	24	7	3	40	6	2	2	53	4	87	8	8
Cabrera, Basilio, Lakeland	.286	74	266	29	76	108	15	4	3	34	4	1	7	16	1	41	17	6
Cameron, Stanton, St. Lucie	.185	83	232	25	43	56	7	0	2	26	3	1	4	46	0	82	2	1
Campas, Mike, St. Petersburg†	.245	35	94	10	23	26	0	0	1	8	0	1	0	20	1	15	2	1
Caraballo, Gary, Baseball City	.223	50	179	28	40	64	9	3	3	24	0	2	3	22	0	32	4	2
Carroll, Kevin, St. Lucie	.116	35	95	7	11	16	2	0	1	7	2	0	3	8	0	39	0	0
Carvajal, Jovino, Fort Lauderdale†	.231	117	416	49	96	123	6	9	1	29	3	1	0	28	5	84	33	17
Castleberry, Kevin, 20 Mia.-94 Sar.*	.263	114	410	82	108	148	18	5	4	43	8	7	4	63	3	63	31	10
Cepicky, Scott, Sarasota*	.290	124	442	62	128	193	33	4	8	76	2	6	4	62	11	99	13	6
Ciccarella, Joe, Winter Haven*	.232	32	99	12	23	26	3	0	0	11	2	4	1	18	0	29	1	1
Clinton, Jim, Charlotte	.193	86	244	19	47	64	12	1	1	17	4	0	3	16	0	63	16	8
Cole, Butch, Baseball City	.292	43	137	19	40	47	2	1	1	15	1	0	1	7	0	18	8	4
Coleman, Ken, Sarasota†	.280	44	118	15	33	44	6	1	1	15	0	2	1	20	0	21	5	3
Colon, Cris, Charlotte†	.313	66	249	33	78	106	9	5	3	27	5	0	3	9	2	44	4	5
Cornelius, Brian, Lakeland*	.279	121	438	57	122	174	16	9	6	59	6	5	3	45	4	67	4	6
Cramer, Bill, West Palm Beach	.211	61	147	13	31	42	8	0	1	12	0	1	1	34	1	34	1	0
Cromer, Tripp, St. Petersburg	.204	43	137	11	28	33	3	1	0	10	3	1	1	9	0	17	0	0
Cruz, Nandi, Dunedin	.224	64	219	15	49	57	6	1	0	18	8	0	3	10	0	42	3	7
Current, Matt, Clearwater*	.271	22	59	5	16	19	3	0	0	7	0	0	0	6	0	13	1	1
Curtis, Craig, Osceola*	.207	110	323	33	67	89	8	7	0	20	5	2	1	53	5	89	20	10
D'Alexander, Greg, Miami	.241	103	369	40	89	131	20	2	6	48	4	5	3	42	1	82	10	4
Dallas, Gershon, Osceola	.263	99	338	42	89	113	16	1	2	47	8	4	4	21	1	61	9	1
Dando, Pat, Miami*	.266	37	124	15	33	44	4	2	1	10	2	0	2	23	0	33	2	1
Davis, Brian, St. Lucie	.222	22	45	4	10	12	0	1	0	5	0	0	0	8	0	18	7	1
Davis, Tim, Winter Haven	.230	88	265	25	61	71	6	2	0	13	4	1	3	33	1	33	7	3
Davison, Scott, West Palm Beach	.168	82	250	19	42	59	6	4	1	24	5	1	3	31	0	66	11	5
Degifico, Vinnie, Winter Haven*	.265	11	34	4	9	9	0	0	0	1	0	0	0	6	0	9	0	0
DeKneef, Mike, Winter Haven	.242	104	372	36	90	117	20	2	1	35	8	1	1	28	0	39	13	9
Demerson, Tim, Fort Lauderdale	.280	42	125	18	35	38	3	0	0	12	1	0	2	13	0	24	12	6
Demus, Joe, Winter Haven	.110	43	73	4	8	9	1	0	0	1	2	0	1	11	0	23	1	0

Player, Team	Avg.	G	AB	R	H	TB	2B	3B	HR	RBI	SH	SF	HP	BB	Int. BB	SO	SB	CS
Deutsch, John, Vero Beach*	.300	123	433	59	130	194	24	2	12	66	0	6	7	46	6	54	5	2
Diaz, Alberto, St. Lucie	.217	108	391	43	85	101	8	4	0	26	7	2	2	39	0	57	21	12
Doffek, Scott, Vero Beach*	.261	94	268	28	70	101	16	3	3	32	2	2	3	13	1	24	5	3
Dorante, Lou, Winter Haven	.239	33	92	11	22	30	6	1	0	8	1	1	2	11	0	21	3	1
DuBose, Brian, Lakeland*	.200	15	35	7	7	12	2	0	1	6	0	0	1	10	0	12	0	1
Dukes, Willie, Winter Haven	.162	80	204	14	33	41	5	0	1	11	6	1	3	19	0	74	3	7
Durkin, Marty, West Palm Beach†	.110	30	73	3	8	11	1	1	0	3	0	2	1	3	1	21	3	2
Dziadkowiec, Andy, Miami*	.248	48	137	7	34	46	7	1	1	14	1	1	0	24	1	20	2	4
Ebel, Dino, Vero Beach	.205	43	112	12	23	28	5	0	0	8	4	2	2	7	1	17	1	1
Ellis, Paul, St. Petersburg*	.204	119	402	26	82	111	11	0	6	42	0	4	6	52	1	34	0	0
Escobar, John, Clearwater	.265	84	245	15	65	82	11	0	2	27	3	2	0	17	0	39	2	1
Evangelista, George, Charlotte	.227	14	22	1	5	5	0	0	0	0	0	0	0	2	1	9	1	0
Fanning, Steve, St. Petersburg	.222	53	189	19	42	57	7	1	2	14	3	0	1	29	1	27	1	3
Farmer, Randy, St. Lucie†	.250	1	4	0	1	1	0	0	0	0	0	0	0	0	0	0	0	1
Federico, Joe, St. Petersburg*	.250	11	28	6	7	12	2	0	1	3	0	0	1	5	0	8	0	0
Fermin, Carlos, Lakeland	.200	7	15	3	3	3	0	0	0	4	0	0	0	0	0	1	0	0
Fordyce, Brook, St. Lucie	.239	115	406	42	97	143	19	3	7	55	0	6	4	37	2	50	4	5
Foster, Julio, Sarasota	.333	8	9	0	3	3	0	0	0	0	0	0	0	3	0	3	0	0
Gaither, Horace, Sarasota*	.250	7	16	2	4	5	1	0	0	1	1	0	0	1	0	3	1	0
Gale, Bill, St. Petersburg	.222	24	18	7	4	4	0	0	0	1	0	0	0	2	0	8	2	0
Garces, Jesus, Clearwater	.100	7	10	0	1	1	0	0	0	2	1	0	0	1	0	2	0	0
Garcia, Anastacio, Dunedin†	.122	25	74	3	9	12	0	0	1	5	1	2	1	5	0	20	0	0
Garland, Tim, Fort Lauderdale	.240	44	129	11	31	37	4	1	0	12	0	2	1	7	0	37	7	3
Garner, Darrin, Charlotte	.229	68	188	37	43	49	6	0	0	19	6	1	0	40	0	30	11	6
Gay, Jeff, Sarasota*	.133	16	45	6	6	10	1	0	1	6	0	2	0	6	2	9	1	0
Gilcrist, John, Baseball City	.242	119	425	58	103	139	10	7	4	50	4	2	1	54	3	78	32	14
Gillette, Mike, Lakeland*	.275	17	51	8	14	17	3	0	0	6	1	1	0	5	0	13	0	1
Giordano, Marc, Miami*	.190	22	58	6	11	13	2	0	0	4	0	2	3	8	0	16	0	0
Gonzales, Rich, St. Petersburg	.204	34	98	5	20	26	6	0	0	2	0	1	1	7	0	26	0	0
Gonzalez, Pete, Vero Beach	.217	74	207	26	45	60	12	0	1	14	5	1	6	31	0	33	1	0
Goodale, Jeff, Lakeland	.233	31	90	8	21	23	2	0	0	4	0	0	3	18	2	24	1	1
Graham, Greg, Winter Haven†	.350	9	20	2	7	7	0	0	0	0	1	0	0	1	0	5	1	1
Grant, Larry, Winter Haven	.226	92	288	29	65	87	9	2	3	35	6	3	3	27	0	66	7	4
Green, Steve, Lakeland	.238	20	63	7	15	25	4	0	2	6	0	0	3	6	0	17	0	0
Greene, Willie, West Palm Beach*	.217	99	322	46	70	121	9	3	12	43	1	3	3	50	2	93	10	7
Greer, Rusty, Charlotte*	.294	111	388	52	114	156	25	1	5	48	1	5	2	66	4	48	12	6
Griffin, Marc, Vero Beach*	.240	115	400	69	96	121	15	5	0	33	5	1	4	55	3	60	42	12
Griffin, Tim, Vero Beach	.172	11	29	1	5	6	1	0	0	1	2	0	1	4	0	8	0	0
Guggiana, Todd, Charlotte*	.295	36	132	14	39	56	7	2	2	18	0	1	1	19	2	21	9	2
Hairston, John, Sarasota†	.204	51	93	10	19	30	4	2	1	13	1	0	1	12	1	44	3	1
Hajek, David, Osceola	.263	63	232	35	61	78	9	4	0	20	4	1	1	23	0	30	8	5
Hall, Andy, Miami	.175	39	120	9	21	23	2	0	0	6	2	0	0	14	0	33	0	1
Hamlin, Jonas, St. Petersburg	.210	121	442	36	93	136	23	4	4	45	0	4	0	24	1	107	1	9
Hanks, Chris, Winter Haven	.250	2	4	0	1	1	0	0	0	0	0	0	0	1	0	3	0	0
Harmes, Kris, Dunedin*	.250	16	44	4	11	14	3	0	0	3	3	0	0	9	1	7	2	0
Harris, James, St. Lucie	.243	101	321	35	78	106	10	0	6	28	1	3	3	36	0	33	0	2
Harris, Robert, Sarasota	.267	75	255	42	68	93	11	4	2	21	6	0	3	12	0	51	21	6
Hartwig, Rob, Clearwater†	.270	20	37	4	10	14	2	1	0	2	0	1	0	3	0	6	2	1
Hatteberg, Scott, Winter Haven*	.277	56	191	21	53	69	7	3	1	25	2	2	0	22	4	22	1	2
Hayden, Paris, Miami	.229	121	420	45	96	138	13	1	9	44	2	4	2	32	0	108	10	12
Helms, Tommy, Sarasota	.000	3	1	0	0	0	0	0	0	0	0	0	0	1	0	0	0	0
Henderson, Derek, St. Lucie	.241	83	282	31	68	86	10	4	0	15	2	0	3	20	0	51	2	7
Hennessey, Scott, Baseball City	.230	93	265	27	61	69	8	0	0	29	6	2	3	45	2	35	7	11
Herrera, Ezequiel, St. Petersburg	.243	121	465	31	113	134	11	5	0	28	4	2	3	16	1	72	1	5
Hiatt, Phil, Baseball City	.298	81	315	41	94	142	21	6	5	33	1	2	3	22	4	70	28	14
Hirsch, Chris, West Palm Beach	.176	15	34	2	6	7	1	0	0	2	1	1	1	6	0	7	1	0
Hodge, Lee, Charlotte	.000	1	0	0	0	0	0	0	0	0	0	0	0	0	0	0	0	0
Hodge, Tim, Dunedin*	.203	97	301	38	61	92	17	1	4	31	5	5	5	45	3	86	3	1
Hoffner, Jamie, St. Lucie*	.256	101	348	32	89	118	19	2	2	34	1	0	3	19	4	39	6	1
Holtzclaw, Shawn, Dunedin*	.245	90	277	26	68	92	16	1	2	30	5	2	1	41	3	52	2	2
Howard, Matt, Vero Beach	.261	129	441	79	115	151	21	3	3	39	14	6	10	56	2	48	50	18
Howard, Ron, Lakeland†	.243	109	350	53	85	123	14	6	4	37	7	1	5	34	0	77	14	7
Howard, Tim, St. Lucie*	.260	60	235	20	61	88	6	3	5	37	2	8	1	14	3	16	7	7
Howell, Dave, Fort Lauderdale*	.276	122	427	50	118	146	20	1	2	31	5	6	0	47	7	65	9	3
Howell, Pat, St. Lucie†	.220	62	246	36	54	66	8	2	0	10	6	0	3	14	0	47	37	9
Hulse, David, Charlotte*	.277	88	310	41	86	100	4	5	0	17	6	0	1	36	2	74	44	7
Hunter, Brian, Vero Beach	.240	118	392	51	94	118	15	3	1	30	5	5	1	45	2	75	32	9
Hyde, Mickey, Clearwater	.242	92	277	26	67	96	9	1	6	34	2	5	2	14	2	48	1	2
Jackson, Bo, Sarasota	.333	2	6	1	2	2	0	0	0	2	0	1	0	0	0	0	0	0
Jenkins, Garrett, Winter Haven	.239	83	218	35	52	64	6	3	0	25	4	1	0	41	1	63	21	11
Jennings, Lance, Baseball City	.235	10	34	1	8	9	1	0	0	5	0	0	2	3	0	9	0	0
Johnson, Brian, Fort Lauderdale	.239	113	394	35	94	116	19	0	1	44	2	3	6	34	2	67	4	6
Johnson, Luther, Osceola*	.146	44	96	5	14	17	3	0	0	5	0	0	0	12	0	33	2	2
Jones, Ron, Clearwater*	.158	12	38	8	6	13	4	0	1	6	0	0	0	13	2	8	0	0
Jordan, Kevin, Fort Lauderdale	.272	121	448	61	122	169	25	5	4	53	0	6	11	37	4	66	14	4
Kellner, Frank, Osceola†	.216	53	204	27	44	57	8	1	1	15	4	0	0	20	2	24	8	1
Kennedy, Jim, Charlotte	.103	23	68	5	7	10	3	0	0	4	1	2	2	5	0	11	0	0
Kidd, Dennis, Miami*	.243	115	408	49	99	147	18	6	6	38	6	2	6	24	3	95	23	9
King, David, Baseball City	.125	14	24	2	3	4	1	0	0	1	0	0	1	4	0	10	0	0
Kinyoun, Travis, Baseball City†	.098	24	41	3	4	6	0	1	0	1	0	1	1	5	0	15	1	0
Kite, Dan, Winter Haven	.000	32	1	0	0	0	0	0	0	0	0	0	0	1	0	1	0	0
Kizziah, Daren, Dunedin	.000	34	1	1	0	0	0	0	0	0	0	0	0	0	0	0	0	0
Kliafas, Stephen, Vero Beach	.260	31	73	11	19	20	1	0	0	6	1	0	0	5	0	10	1	3
Kobza, Greg, Sarasota*	.173	72	156	19	27	40	9	2	0	12	4	0	0	32	4	48	1	2
Krause, Ron, West Palm Beach*	.199	98	302	28	60	91	9	8	2	25	1	0	5	33	2	94	4	4
Lake, Ken, West Palm Beach	.200	76	250	27	50	82	7	2	7	35	1	2	1	23	0	68	7	7
Laker, Tim, West Palm Beach	.231	100	333	35	77	111	15	2	5	33	0	4	2	22	0	51	10	3
Langiotti, Fred, St. Petersburg	.197	31	61	6	12	15	3	0	0	2	0	0	0	6	0	13	0	1
Lansing, Mike, Miami	.286	104	384	54	110	162	20	7	6	55	1	6	4	40	1	75	29	7
Leach, Jalal, Fort Lauderdale*	.254	122	468	48	119	156	13	9	2	42	3	3	0	44	3	122	28	12
Ledinsky, Ray, Miami	.168	51	137	11	23	31	5	0	1	14	2	2	1	25	0	35	5	3
Lentz, Jim, Winter Haven	.217	14	46	4	10	13	3	0	0	2	0	0	0	4	0	20	0	0
Lewis, Anthony, St. Petersburg*	.230	124	435	40	100	149	17	7	6	43	0	2	2	50	7	101	5	5
Lieberthal, Mike, Clearwater	.288	16	52	7	15	17	2	0	0	7	1	1	3	0	0	12	0	0
Lockett, Ron, Clearwater*	.266	128	459	81	122	177	13	6	10	71	0	7	3	70	7	109	10	3

Player, Team	Avg.	G	AB	R	H	TB	2B	3B	HR	RBI	SH	SF	HP	BB	Int. BB	SO	SB	CS
Lohry, Adin, Fort Lauderdale*	.167	30	90	6	15	20	5	0	0	8	1	0	2	11	1	33	0	1
Lora, Jose, Winter Haven	.163	16	49	1	8	8	0	0	0	4	0	0	1	0		19	3	1
Lukachyk, Rob, Sarasota*	.271	125	399	63	108	166	27	2	9	49	8	3	15	63	4	100	22	8
MacArthur, Mark, 4 St.P.-44 Mia.	.204	48	157	14	32	42	4	0	2	7	0	2	0	10	1	45	9	4
Madril, Bill, Winter Haven	.176	10	17	2	3	4	1	0	0	3	0	1	1	3	0	3	1	1
Maldonado, Carlos, Lakeland	.167	26	54	7	9	10	1	0	0	2	5	0	0	3	0	7	1	0
Malzone, John, Winter Haven*	.249	103	265	40	66	84	11	2	1	28	3	4	4	60	4	56	2	5
Manning, Henry, Sarasota	.083	13	24	2	2	2	0	0	0	0	0	0		2	0	6	0	0
Marigny, Ron, Lakeland	.291	54	189	33	55	72	7	5	0	25	1	1	2	28	1	30	6	4
Marshall, Randy, Charlotte*	.223	77	242	24	54	66	10	1	0	35	2	4	1	38	3	57	1	2
Martinez, Angel, Dunedin	.184	12	38	3	7	8	1	0	0	3	2	0	1	7	0	7	0	0
Martinez, Hector, Dunedin	.083	6	12	1	1	3	0	1	0	0	2	0		2	0	3	0	0
Massarelli, John, Osceola	.309	51	194	27	60	72	9	0	1	22	2	2	4	16	2	34	18	8
Matilla, Pedro, Winter Haven	.130	29	77	2	10	11	1	0	0	4	1	0		10	0	18	0	1
Mayo, Todd, West Palm Beach*	.250	80	256	46	64	71	5	1	0	10	4	0	2	44	2	26	23	7
McCray, Justin, Sarasota	.095	21	21	3	2	2	0	0	0	1	0	0	1	3	0	8	0	0
McDonald, Chad, West Palm Beach	.253	112	384	44	97	140	16	3	7	48	1	4	7	37	2	67	10	0
McGough, Greg, Sarasota	.143	13	21	1	3	7	1	0	1	4	0	1	0	1	0	10	0	0
McKamie, Sean, Vero Beach	.263	67	194	25	51	62	8	0	1	12	5	1	5	8	0	33	11	3
McMullen, Kevin, Fort Lauderdale	.252	32	103	8	26	43	5	0	4	17	0	0	2	9	0	23	1	1
McMurray, Brock, Vero Beach	.210	107	343	46	72	128	14	3	12	51	1	4	2	45	1	87	17	5
McNamara, Denny, Lakeland	.237	64	207	39	49	78	11	3	4	34	2	3	1	41	1	35	11	3
Mendenhall, Kirk, Lakeland	.251	111	354	38	89	110	10	4	1	38	12	3	2	36	0	57	9	8
Mengel, Brad, Dunedin	.239	114	393	49	94	122	19	3	1	32	11	3	4	26	1	62	10	5
Miller, Orlando, Osceola	.298	74	272	27	81	96	11	2	0	36	2	3	8	13	0	30	1	3
Miller, Scott, Dunedin	.353	12	34	2	12	15	3	0	0	1	2	0	1	3	0	7	0	3
Millette, Joe, Clearwater	.255	18	55	6	14	16	2	0	0	6	3	2	1	7	0	6	1	2
Montalvo, Robert, Dunedin	.230	86	291	21	67	72	3	1	0	21	21	4	1	21	0	54	4	1
Monzon, Jose, Osceola	.215	46	144	14	31	46	6	0	3	17	6	2	0	17	0	31	2	0
Moore, Kerwin, Baseball City†	.210	130	485	67	102	123	14	2	1	23	5	1	3	77	0	141	61	15
Morillo, Cesar, Baseball City†	.173	62	226	11	39	47	8	0	0	13	7	2	2	13	0	68	6	5
Morrisette, James, 42 Mia.-65 St.L.	.244	107	390	49	95	125	18	0	4	44	1	4	4	33	3	81	14	5
Morrison, Jim, Winter Haven	.219	102	310	29	68	82	5	0	3	31	5	3	3	45	0	86	29	8
Morrow, Chris, Vero Beach*	.304	85	273	29	83	115	13	5	3	29	1	2	3	14	3	32	6	6
Morrow, Timmie, Charlotte	.251	119	463	65	116	171	24	8	5	59	8	5	1	33	0	123	33	13
Mota, Rafael, Osceola	.197	22	71	10	14	20	2	2	0	3	0	0	0	8	0	20	4	1
Myers, Rod, Baseball City*	.182	4	11	1	2	2	0	0	0	0	0	0	0	0	0	5	1	1
Neitzel, R.A., Clearwater*	.260	104	335	68	87	100	6	2	1	25	6	2	2	72	1	51	32	14
Newkirk, Craig, Charlotte	.233	109	343	33	80	101	18	0	1	21	4	3	3	61	2	71	4	6
Niethammer, Darren, Charlotte	.228	98	325	36	74	104	10	1	6	38	1	1	1	35	1	66	12	5
Noce, Doug, West Palm Beach	.231	9	13	2	3	3	0	0	0	0	0	0		1	0	4	0	0
Noriega, Ray, Fort Lauderdale†	.249	126	429	67	107	182	19	7	14	68	0	2		78	7	134	12	5
Nuneviller, Tom, Clearwater	.283	124	446	77	126	173	31	5	2	54	8	5	9	48	2	52	16	9
Nunez, Mauricio, St. Petersburg	.250	16	56	2	14	17	3	0	0	6	0	1	0	3	0	10	2	1
Nunez, Rogelio, Sarasota	.222	15	36	6	8	9	1	0	0	3	2	1	0	3	0	8	0	1
Ochs, Tony, St. Petersburg	.241	84	257	21	62	67	5	0	0	13	2	3	2	40	4	52	8	2
O'Donnell, Steve, Vero Beach	.256	114	383	52	98	134	21	0	5	49	1	7	8	31	3	80	13	6
O'Halloran, Greg, Dunedin*	.284	20	74	7	21	26	3	1	0	4	0	0		7	1	8	1	1
Oliva, Jose, Charlotte	.240	108	383	55	92	159	17	4	14	59	1	6	5	44	3	108	9	9
Olmstead, Reed, Osceola*	.238	49	168	10	40	59	12	2	1	23	0	2		17	1	31	0	1
Ortiz, Hector, Vero Beach	.228	42	123	3	28	30	2	0	0	8	0	3		5	0	8	0	0
Parese, Bill, Dunedin	.178	66	180	26	32	40	3	1	1	13	8	2	0	25	0	37	6	3
Parker, Stacy, Clearwater	.176	10	17	2	3	3	0	0	0	1	0	0		1	0	5	0	0
Paulsen, Troy, Clearwater	.288	122	441	62	127	157	21	3	1	47	8	6	5	31	1	45	2	5
Pemberton, Rudy, Lakeland	.229	111	375	40	86	114	15	2	3	36	6	2	9	25	2	52	25	17
Perez, Robert, Dunedin	.302	127	480	50	145	197	28	6	4	50	7	2	5	22	3	72	8	8
Pimentel, Wander, St. Petersburg	.142	80	261	14	37	44	7	0	0	7	3	1	0	8	0	56	1	1
Pineda, Jose, Fort Lauderdale	.143	4	7	0	1	1	0	0	0	0	0	0	0	0		3	1	0
Piskor, Kirk, Baseball City*	.182	4	11	1	2	2	0	0	0	0	0	0	0	1	0	1	0	0
Plemmons, Ron, Sarasota*	.239	128	444	49	106	137	17	4	2	64	9	5	1	66	4	67	9	16
Pollard, Damon, Baseball City†	1.000	13	1	0	1	1	0	0	0	0	0	0	0	0	0	0	0	0
Powell, Ken, Charlotte	.237	120	389	40	92	122	9	9	1	44	5	1	5	52	0	102	19	5
Prager, Howard, Osceola*	.279	14	43	6	12	18	2	2	0	7	2	1	1	10	1	10	2	0
Pride, Curtis, St. Lucie*	.260	116	392	57	102	164	21	7	9	37	3	0	2	43	4	94	24	5
Ramirez, J.D., West Palm Beach	.235	94	328	38	77	103	14	0	4	30	5	5	6	20	0	39	13	6
Rappoli, Paul, Winter Haven*	.000	4	5	2	0	0	0	0	0	0	0	0	0	0	0	0	0	0
Rendina, Mike, Lakeland	.214	115	359	36	77	100	7	2	4	41	2	3	4	54	5	62	2	2
Renteria, Ed, Osceola	.281	71	231	24	65	75	10	0	0	27	1	1	3	27	1	23	9	3
Reyes, Jimmy, Sarasota†	.000	1	1	0	0	0	0	0	0	0	0	0	0	0	0	0	0	0
Reyes, Victor, Charlotte	.250	6	8	0	2	2	0	0	0	0	0	0	0	0	0	3	0	1
Richison, David, Osceola	.000	4	5	0	0	0	0	0	0	0	1	0	0	1	0	5	0	0
Ricker, Troy, West Palm Beach	.222	105	293	35	65	85	8	0	4	21	2	4	5	28	0	81	15	9
Riesgo, Nikco, West Palm Beach	.278	5	18	4	5	9	1	0	1	1	0	0	0	1	0	5	0	1
Rijo, Rafael, Vero Beach	.233	83	262	27	61	81	14	0	2	20	6	2	1			65	23	17
Rivers, Mickey, Winter Haven†	.208	71	231	19	48	73	9	2	4	21	3	0	1	7	0	68	6	4
Roa, Hector, Miami	.199	87	286	32	57	73	3	5	1	18	3	1	3	15	1	50	17	9
Rodgers, Paul, Osceola	.216	41	139	21	30	31	1	0	0	4	0	0		13	0	27	12	1
Rodriguez, Andres, Fort Lauderdale	.207	86	256	26	53	59	6	0	0	16	6	1	2	23	0	47	12	8
Roman, Vincent, Osceola	.292	19	72	15	21	26	5	0	0	6	0	1	1	3	0	6	7	2
Rose, Pete, Sarasota*	.217	99	323	31	70	86	12	2	0	35	8	3	2	36	5	35	5	6
Russell, Fred, Baseball City†	.239	107	335	37	80	107	14	5	1	21	8	2	5	36	0	61	12	10
Ryan, Colin, Baseball City	.214	75	215	5	46	52	6	0	0	8	1	0	0	14	0	63	2	0
Saenz, Olmeda, Sarasota	.105	5	19	1	2	4	0	1	0	2	0	0	0	0	0	2	0	0
Sampson, Mike, Vero Beach	.000	30	1	0	0	0	0	0	0	0	0	0	0	0	0	0	0	0
Sanchez, Perry, West Palm Beach*	.119	32	84	3	10	11	1	0	0	5	0	1		8	1	12	0	0
Saunders, Doug, St. Lucie	.235	70	230	19	54	73	9	2	2	18	5	0	4	25	0	43	5	6
Savinon, Odalis, St. Petersburg	.272	28	92	11	25	31	4	1	0	7	3	1	2	12	0	18	1	4
Sawkiw, Warren, Lakeland†	.271	112	420	58	114	154	20	7	2	42	3	3		42	2	87	2	9
Schmidt, David, Winter Haven†	.175	63	177	25	31	42	4	2	1	16	3	4	3	37	2	66	0	2
Schreiner, John, Baseball City	.203	19	59	5	12	15	1	1	2	7	1	1		2		20	2	2
Scott, Kevin, Osceola	.214	104	341	31	73	81	8	0	0	27	7	5	2	33	2	84	12	4
Scott, Shawn, Dunedin†	.236	91	322	46	76	90	4	5	0	18	2	4	2	39	1	42	19	12
Sellers, Rick, Lakeland	.275	71	244	33	67	103	8	2	8	32	0	2	3	26	0	62	3	3
Shave, Jon, Charlotte	.228	56	189	17	43	52	4	1	1	20	2	4	5	18	1	31	7	7
Shields, Doug, Baseball City	.216	108	255	29	55	68	9	2	0	19	5	1	4	39	1	71	16	5

Player, Team	Avg.	G	AB	R	H	TB	2B	3B	HR	RBI	SH	SF	HP	BB	Int. BB	SO	SB	CS
Simons, Mitch, West Palm Beach	.180	15	50	3	9	13	2	1	0	4	0	0	0	5	0	8	1	0
Smith, Ed, Sarasota	.217	54	198	27	43	59	7	0	3	27	2	2	3	15	1	52	4	3
Smith, Ira, Vero Beach	.324	53	176	27	57	71	5	3	1	24	0	0	2	18	0	30	15	3
Solseth, Dave, Baseball City*	.235	121	400	42	94	120	13	5	1	43	5	3	2	45	6	63	9	8
Stewart, Andy, Baseball City	.231	77	268	27	62	88	15	1	3	35	4	2	4	7	1	56	6	3
Stewart, Brady, Baseball City	.237	42	131	14	31	41	7	0	1	9	3	0	2	11	0	40	2	2
Strickland, Dedrick, Fort Lauderdale†...	.222	9	27	4	6	6	0	0	0	3	1	0	0	5	0	6	1	0
Sullivan, Carl, Sarasota	.304	24	92	16	28	38	2	1	2	7	2	0	2	7	0	17	4	2
Surane, John, Miami	.230	68	187	27	43	43	2	0	0	13	6	0	4	37	0	37	10	9
Tackett, Tim, Winter Haven	.182	8	22	1	4	5	1	0	0	0	0	0	0	6	0	7	0	0
Tahan, Kevin, St. Petersburg	.130	13	46	4	6	6	0	0	0	1	0	0	0	4	0	10	0	0
Tannahill, Kevin, Charlotte	.135	15	37	2	5	5	0	0	0	1	1	0	1	1	0	12	1	0
Tatarian, Dean, Sarasota	.145	49	69	9	10	12	2	0	0	3	2	0	1	17	0	15	1	4
Taylor, Sam, Clearwater*	.259	115	367	51	95	153	20	7	8	73	2	10	6	55	6	52	3	3
Tedder, Scott, Sarasota*	.336	42	149	25	50	57	5	1	0	17	4	3	0	29	2	19	6	4
Teel, Garett, Vero Beach	.240	12	25	1	6	7	1	0	0	4	0	0	2	2	0	4	1	0
Tejada, Francisco, Clearwater..............	.500	1	4	0	2	3	1	0	0	2	0	0	0	0	0	1	0	0
Tejada, Leo, Sarasota	.252	109	333	40	84	104	9	4	1	19	17	1	4	20	0	44	9	8
Tewell, Terrance, Clearwater................	.210	81	248	32	52	82	9	0	7	39	7	2	3	17	0	63	0	0
Texidor, Jose, Charlotte	.282	13	39	8	11	14	1	1	0	3	1	0	1	2	0	6	1	1
Thomas, John, St. Petersburg*	.298	116	433	52	129	172	14	10	3	46	0	3	5	36	0	71	9	8
Thomas, Mark, St. Lucie	.218	84	275	34	60	103	14	1	9	28	1	4	3	31	0	99	13	7
Thomas, Orlando, St. Petersburg..........	.353	8	17	5	6	6	0	0	0	2	1	0	1	4	0	5	0	0
Tollison, David, Dunedin	.241	113	373	37	90	116	14	3	2	37	10	5	3	38	1	70	3	7
Torres, Gilberto, St. Petersburg	.252	39	111	5	28	31	3	0	0	6	2	0	3	9	0	20	1	0
Trevino, Tony, Clearwater	.280	26	93	13	26	35	3	0	2	17	0	1	5	10	0	15	0	1
Trujillo, Jose, St. Petersburg	.231	34	117	13	27	34	4	0	1	11	2	0	0	18	1	9	3	2
Twardoski, Mike, Winter Haven*	.143	4	14	2	2	3	1	0	0	2	0	1	0	0	0	3	0	0
Urbon, Joe, Clearwater*	.210	28	81	8	17	20	3	0	0	8	1	0	1	14	2	23	0	3
Urcioli, John, Miami	.233	73	236	19	55	69	8	0	2	24	4	3	2	12	0	49	2	2
Van Scoyoc, Aaron, Fort Lauderdale†	.228	79	250	12	57	66	9	0	0	14	3	1	0	16	0	41	3	3
Vargas, Julio, Clearwater	.222	4	9	0	2	2	0	0	0	0	0	0	1	0	0	3	0	0
Vargas, Victor, St. Petersburg	.107	12	28	0	3	3	0	0	0	1	2	0	2	3	0	8	1	0
Vazquez, Pedro, Baseball City†	.192	84	224	17	43	45	2	0	0	15	11	3	2	33	1	45	7	4
Ventress, Leroy, Clearwater†	.240	122	417	70	100	125	12	5	1	40	9	2	10	62	2	69	35	9
Walker, Larry, Fort Lauderdale	.127	48	150	15	19	32	1	0	4	17	0	1	3	18	0	35	0	0
Wallin, Les, Winter Haven*	.247	88	279	34	69	97	17	1	3	27	1	3	4	41	5	52	8	3
Wardwell, Shea, Winter Haven	.146	65	205	18	30	44	1	2	3	16	3	2	4	16	0	56	6	5
Wedge, Eric, Winter Haven	.238	8	21	2	5	8	0	0	1	1	0	0	3	0	7	1	0
Wiley, Skip, Baseball City*	.000	53	1	0	0	0	0	0	0	0	0	0	0	0	0	1	0	0
Williams, Brent, Vero Beach	.107	13	28	1	3	5	2	0	0	2	0	1	0	0	0	11	0	0
Wilson, Brad, Lakeland*	.100	10	10	0	1	1	0	0	0	0	0	0	2	1	2	0	0
Wilson, Nigel, Dunedin*	.301	119	455	64	137	217	18	13	12	55	4	7	9	29	4	99	27	11
Wilstead, Randy, West Palm Beach*	.000	1	0	0	0	0	0	0	0	0	0	0	0	0	0	0	0	0
Winford, Barry, Charlotte......................	.216	69	227	33	49	65	5	1	3	16	3	0	2	29	0	45	15	6
Wolak, Jerry, Sarasota	.291	110	326	36	95	123	17	1	3	22	13	0	3	14	0	62	22	8
Woodruff, Pat, Lakeland	.326	41	144	25	47	72	3	2	6	28	2	2	0	27	2	28	13	3
Woods, Tyrone, West Palm Beach	.220	96	295	34	65	101	15	3	5	31	0	3	3	28	0	85	4	4

The following pitchers, listed alphabetically by club, with games in parentheses, had no plate appearances, primarily through use of designated hitters:

BASEBALL CITY—Ahern, Brian (13); Berumen, Andres (7); Campbell, Jim (11); Centala, Scott (3); Chavez, Elbio (7); Conner, John (15); Diaz, Rafael (9); Dunn, Bubba (5); Gordon, Tony (19); Gross, John (17); Gutierrez, Rafael (1); Harris, Doug (19); Harvey, Greg (13); Hopper, Brad (19); Jacobs, Jake (19); Karchner, Matt (38); Long, Tony (47); McCormick, John (17); Russo, Tony (15); Shaw, Kevin (25); Toth, Robert (13).

CHARLOTTE—Alberro, Jose (5); Arner, Mike (24); Bickhardt, Eric (54); Bohanon, Brian (2); Buckley, Travis (28); Eischen, Joey (18); Felix, Nick (29); Goetz, Barry (46); Maldonado, Johnny (46); McCray, Eric (2); Oliver, Darren (2); Quero, Juan (34); Randle, Carl (29); Rowley, Steve (8); Saylor, Kyle (38); Steiner, Brian (30); Washington, Tyrone (12).

CLEARWATER—Adamson, Joel (5); Brink, Brad (2); Cox, Danny (3); Elliott, Donnie (18); Fletcher, Paul (14); Gaddy, Bob (34); Goedhart, Darrell (25); Gray, Elliott (20); Green, Tyler (2); Henderson, Ramon (1); Holdridge, David (15); Hurst, Charles (22); Langley, Lee (18); Limbach, Chris (39); Lindsey, Darrell (5); Malone, Chuck (10); Munoz, J.J. (2); Parris, Steve (43); Stevens, Matt (38); Sullivan, Mike (36); Wells, Bob (24); Wiegandt, Scott (11); Williams, Michael (14).

DUNEDIN—Brow, Scott (16); Brown, Daren (28); Brown, Tim (31); Dayley, Ken (3); Duey, Kyle (9); Ganote, Joe (4); Hotchkiss, Thomas (15); Kistaitis, Dale (1); Leiter, Al (4); Lloyd, Graeme (50); Martin, Gregg (13); Menhart, Paul (20); Moore, Marcus (27); Ogliaruso, Mike (22); Small, Aaron (24); Wanish, John (36).

FORT LAUDERDALE—Batchelor, Richard (50); Canestro, Art (21); Gogolewski, Doug (1); Greer, Ken (31); Hutton, Mark (24); Malone, Todd (6); Manon, Ramon (26); Marris, Mark (24); Munoz, Roberto (19); Nielsen, Gerald (42); Polak, Rich (40); Prybylinski, Bruce (13); Rumer, Tim (24); Springer, Russell (25); Wiley, Jim (4).

LAKELAND—Braley, Jeff (61); Cook, Ron (29); Drell, Tom (28); Ettles, Mark (8); Ferm, Ed (17); Garcia, Mike (25); Gonzales, Frank (25); Henry, Jimmy (6); Krumm, Todd (7); Leimeister, Eric (35); Lima, Jose (4); Lumley, Mike (43); Marcero, Doug (2); Radachowsky, Gregg (1); Ramos, Jose (12); Rivera, Lino (14); Schwarber, Tom (8); Torres, Leonardo (42); Warren, Brian (17); Wolf, Steve (9).

MIAMI—Asche, Scott (28); Bautista, Jose (14); Ericson, Mike (8); Fritz, John (14); Haslock, Chris (20); Hurst, Jonathan (15); Kerfut, George (34); Klancnik, Joe (21); Langley, Lee (23); Lemon, Don (10); Michno, Tom (29); Minchey, Nate (13); Reed, Billy (10); Rogers, Charlie (24); Whitworth, Ken (20); Williams, Ken (41).

OSCEOLA—Costello, Fred (5); Farmer, Gordon (17); Griffiths, Brian (18); Grovom, Carl (15); Hyson, Cole (25); Johnson, Lee (34); Jones, Todd (14); Kaiser, Keith (7); Luckham, Ken (27); Morman, Alvin (3); Phillips, Montie (44); Ponte, Edward (47); Resnikoff, Rob (8); Sebra, Bob (5); Small, Mark (26); Wall, Donnie (12); Williams, Brian (15); Windes, Rodney (45).

SARASOTA—Bolton, Rodney (15); Brutcher, Len (24); Chambers, Travis (2); Cortes, Argenis (5); Dabney, Fred (26); Galvan, Mike (14); Hoey, Andy (4); Johnson, Earnie (51); Keyser, Brian (28); Matznick, Danny (26); Mongiello, Michael (55); Reynolds, Dave (6); Ruffin, Johnny (26); Shepherd, Keith (18); Stevens, Scott (35); Wickman, Robert (7).

ST. LUCIE—Brady, Mike (8); Dorn, Chris (48); Douma, Todd (17); Fernandez, Sid (1); Freitas, Mike (5); Harriger, Denny (14); Hill, Chris (6); Kaplinghen, Greg (27); McCann, John (24); Proctor, Dave (6); Reich, Andy (54); Sample, Deron (13); Vasquez, Julian (56); Vazquez, Ed (1); Vitko, Joe (22); Walker, Peter (21); Wegmann, Tom (13).

ST. PETERSBURG—Baker, Ernie (38); Baker, Scott (19); Cassidy, David (21); Corona, John (15); Dixon, Steve (53); Faccio, Luis (8); Gorton, Chris (50); Green, Daryl (26); Hinkle, Mike (1); Lata, Tim (10); Nielsen, Kevin (1); Ozuna, Gabriel (31); Salvior, Troy (38); Shackle, Rick (21); Smith, Mark (20); Urbani, Tom (19); Weber, Ron (18).

VERO BEACH—Astacio, Pedro (9); Baumann, David (12); Bene, Bill (31); Biberdorf, Cam (33); Brady, Mike (37); Brosnan, Jason (11); Calhoun, Ray (27); Coleman, Dale (12); Freeman, Scott (25); Hoffman, Kevin (5); Jones, Kiki (9); Mimbs, Michael (24); Patrick, Tim (22); Snedeker, Sean (17); Sohn, Young Chul (1); Taveras, Ramon (22); Wengert, William (30).

WEST PALM BEACH—Barnes, Brian (2); Baxter, Bob (1); Bochtler, Doug (26); Bushing, Chris (46); Collins, Stacey (27); Cormier, Russ (5); Cornelius, Reid (17); Davis, Bret (22); Eddy, Jim (13); Eischen, Joey (8); Gideon, Brett (4); Kilgo, Rusty (33); Logan, Joe (24); Moya, Felix (19);

Polasek, John (52); Regira, Gary (12); Renko, Steve (4); Schmidt, Dave (9); Sieradzki, Al (1); Thoden, John (12); Tuss, Jeff (49); Wilkinson, Brian (8).

WINTER HAVEN—Allen, Tracy (27); Brown, Paul (35); Delgado, Rich (1); Dopson, John (6); Johnson, Jeff (7); Klvac, Dave (1); Maietta, Ron (3); Maloney, Ryan (16); Mitchelson, Mark (14); Niles, Thomas (25); Owen, Dave (1); Painter, Gary (9); Powers, Terry (25); Ryan, Ken (21); Santamaria, Silverio (45); Sele, Aaron (13); Vanegmond, Tim (13); Young, Brian (28).

GRAND SLAMS—Noriega, 2; Albright, Ashley, Brady, Cabrera, Colon, D'Alexander, Dallas, Davison, Gilcrist, Laker, Tewell, Wallin, Woodruff, 1 each.

AWARDED FIRST BASE ON CATCHER'S INTERFERENCE—Ashley 3 (B. Johnson 3); Kidd 3 (Gonzalez, Matilla, McMullen); Lockett 3 (Garcia, Monzon, Winford); Pride 3 (A. Brown, Kobza, McMullen); Hayden 2 (Gonzalez, B. Johnson); Anglero (H. Martinez); R. Harris (Agostinelli); Hunter (Ryan); Lake (Langiotti); Rendina (Alvarez); Schmidt (A. Stewart); Ventress (Garcia); Walker (Kinyoun); Wolak (Ortiz).

PITCHING

TEAM

Team	ERA	G	CG	ShO	Sv.	IP	H	R	ER	HR	HB	BB	Int. BB	SO	WP	Bk.
St. Lucie	2.58	131	13	17	39	1156.0	971	404	331	45	41	352	19	816	47	21
West Palm Beach	2.70	131	12	13	40	1124.2	941	420	338	35	42	416	18	771	40	23
Sarasota	2.89	131	20	15	39	1155.2	979	476	371	45	43	489	31	874	49	26
Baseball City	2.95	131	8	8	39	1135.1	963	461	372	27	57	490	36	742	91	23
Clearwater	2.95	130	6	18	40	1105.1	957	443	362	34	39	410	16	927	73	30
Miami	3.03	131	23	11	27	1135.1	1017	476	382	52	47	412	14	856	32	28
Osceola	3.03	127	11	14	32	1096.1	932	455	369	40	45	431	26	867	86	27
Dunedin	3.07	131	11	12	35	1149.2	1010	492	392	35	30	503	20	799	74	28
Fort Lauderdale	3.10	128	17	14	33	1100.2	910	472	379	39	51	434	29	842	64	20
Lakeland	3.36	128	6	10	34	1116.2	1007	502	417	38	49	414	12	806	53	23
Charlotte	3.38	132	9	9	34	1146.1	1038	538	430	46	62	505	51	875	70	16
Vero Beach	3.41	132	14	11	34	1133.2	1045	514	430	35	43	491	18	931	85	20
St. Petersburg	3.47	131	11	11	24	1142.1	1096	516	441	32	36	370	20	777	40	19
Winter Haven	4.18	128	18	8	19	1073.1	1050	606	499	36	42	563	8	808	107	42

INDIVIDUAL

(Leading qualifiers for earned-run average leadership—109 or more innings)

*Throws lefthanded.

Pitcher, Team	W	L	Pct.	ERA	G	GS	CG	GF	ShO	Sv.	IP	H	R	ER	HR	HB	BB	Int. BB	SO	WP
Wengert, Vero Beach	7	6	.538	2.06	30	13	2	8	2	3	127.0	100	36	29	3	6	42	2	114	8
Vitko, St. Lucie	11	8	.579	2.24	22	22	5	0	2	0	140.1	102	40	35	4	4	39	1	105	6
Keyser, Sarasota	6	7	.462	2.30	27	14	2	9	1	2	129.0	110	40	33	5	6	45	8	94	3
Urbani, St. Petersburg*	8	7	.533	2.35	19	19	2	0	1	0	118.2	109	39	31	2	2	25	0	64	3
Cornelius, West Palm Beach	8	3	.727	2.39	17	17	0	0	0	0	109.1	79	31	29	3	7	43	1	81	3
Michno, Miami	11	15	.423	2.42	29	29	13	0	3	0	216.0	175	77	58	12	5	66	1	190	1
Hutton, Fort Lauderdale	5	8	.385	2.45	24	24	3	0	0	0	147.0	98	54	40	5	11	65	5	117	4
Gray, Clearwater	10	4	.714	2.45	20	20	1	0	1	0	117.1	98	47	32	2	4	38	1	99	12
Harris, Baseball City	10	6	.625	2.47	19	18	3	0	1	0	116.2	92	38	32	3	3	27	4	84	4
T. Brown, Dunedin	8	3	.727	2.49	31	14	2	8	0	1	123.0	113	44	34	3	5	37	1	87	5

Departmental leaders: G—Braley, 61; W—Bochtler, Mimbs, 12; L—Michno, 15; Pct.—Bautista, J. Hurst, Warren, .800; GS—Michno, 29; CG—Michno, 13; GF—Braley, 50; ShO—Bautista, Buckley, Michno, 3; Sv.—Batchelor, Vasquez, 25; IP—Michno, 216.0; H—Michno, 175; R—Eischen, 86; ER—Young, 77; HR—Michno, 12; HB—Randle, 14; BB—Moore, 99; IBB—Bickhardt, 12; SO—Michno, 190; WP—Kite, 24.

(All pitchers—listed alphabetically)

Pitcher, Team	W	L	Pct.	ERA	G	GS	CG	GF	ShO	Sv.	IP	H	R	ER	HR	HB	BB	Int. BB	SO	WP
Adamson, Clearwater*	2	1	.667	3.03	5	5	0	0	0	0	29.2	28	12	10	1	1	7	0	20	2
Ahern, Baseball City	7	2	.778	2.00	13	13	2	0	0	0	81.0	71	20	18	1	3	27	1	34	2
Alberro, Charlotte	0	1	.000	9.53	5	0	0	0	0	0	5.2	8	9	6	0	1	7	2	3	3
Allen, Winter Haven	4	6	.400	3.88	27	11	0	8	0	1	95.0	96	49	41	6	1	43	0	56	12
Anglero, Lakeland	0	0	.000	9.00	2	0	0	2	0	0	2.0	3	2	2	0	0	2	0	0	1
Arner, Charlotte	8	8	.500	3.17	24	24	2	0	1	0	144.2	112	57	51	9	9	44	4	96	3
Asche, Miami*	8	7	.533	3.68	28	19	1	4	0	1	120.0	139	61	49	5	1	41	2	60	1
Astacio, Vero Beach	5	3	.625	1.67	9	9	3	0	1	0	59.1	44	19	11	0	1	8	0	45	2
E. Baker, St. Petersburg	0	4	.000	4.34	38	1	1	12	0	0	66.1	66	36	32	3	8	30	3	31	4
S. Baker, St. Petersburg	3	9	.250	4.42	19	16	1	2	0	0	93.2	98	47	46	2	3	42	0	50	5
Barnes, West Palm Beach*	0	0	.000	0.00	2	2	0	0	0	0	7.0	3	0	0	0	0	4	0	6	3
Batchelor, Fort Lauderdale	4	7	.364	2.76	50	0	0	41	0	25	62.0	55	28	19	1	1	22	5	58	4
Baumann, Vero Beach	0	0	.000	3.05	12	0	0	3	0	0	20.2	19	8	7	2	1	10	2	14	1
Bautista, Miami	8	2	.800	2.71	11	11	4	0	3	0	76.1	63	23	23	5	1	11	0	69	1
Baxter, West Palm Beach*	0	0	.000	20.25	1	0	0	0	0	0	1.1	4	3	3	0	0	0	0	1	0
Bene, Vero Beach	1	1	.500	4.15	31	1	0	12	0	0	52.0	39	37	24	0	2	65	1	57	21
Berumen, Baseball City	0	5	.000	4.14	7	7	0	0	0	0	37.0	34	18	17	0	4	18	0	24	5
Biberdorf, Vero Beach	4	2	.667	2.15	33	0	0	20	0	8	50.1	32	15	12	1	0	22	2	61	3
Bickhardt, Charlotte	5	5	.500	3.56	54	0	0	20	0	6	93.2	90	41	37	5	4	40	12	69	3
Bochtler, West Palm Beach	12	9	.571	2.92	26	24	7	1	2	0	160.1	148	63	52	6	6	55	2	109	7
Bohanon, Charlotte*	1	0	1.000	3.86	2	2	0	0	0	0	11.2	6	5	5	0	2	4	0	7	1
Bolton, Sarasota	7	6	.538	1.91	15	15	5	0	2	0	103.2	81	29	22	2	2	23	0	77	3
Brady, Vero Beach*	3	0	1.000	2.22	37	0	0	17	0	4	52.2	57	14	13	0	4	23	1	42	0
Brady, St. Lucie	0	0	.000	7.00	8	0	0	4	0	0	9.0	14	9	7	1	1	3	0	8	1
Braley, Lakeland	4	4	.500	2.63	61	0	0	50	0	24	72.0	65	28	21	0	7	25	3	50	2
Brink, Clearwater	2	0	1.000	0.69	2	2	0	0	0	0	13.0	6	1	1	1	0	3	0	10	0
Brosnan, Vero Beach*	1	2	.333	5.70	11	9	0	0	0	0	36.1	34	27	23	3	2	21	0	25	5
Brow, Dunedin	3	7	.300	4.78	15	12	0	1	0	0	69.2	73	50	37	5	2	28	1	31	2
D. Brown, Dunedin	6	5	.545	4.52	28	5	0	12	0	1	81.2	69	46	41	3	2	34	3	66	8
Brown, Winter Haven*	4	3	.571	3.17	35	0	0	26	0	8	65.1	52	27	23	2	1	25	2	56	7
T. Brown, Dunedin	8	3	.727	2.49	31	14	2	8	0	1	123.0	113	44	34	3	5	37	1	87	5
Brutcher, Sarasota	7	5	.583	4.54	24	19	0	2	0	0	103.0	106	64	52	8	7	62	1	68	4
Buckley, Charlotte	8	9	.471	3.23	28	21	3	3	3	1	128.0	115	58	46	7	6	67	4	131	4
Bushing, West Palm Beach	2	1	.667	1.94	46	0	0	26	0	9	65.0	41	15	14	1	1	40	3	68	4
Calhoun, Vero Beach	6	1	.857	2.56	27	0	0	25	0	12	31.2	22	10	9	1	1	13	2	26	2
Campbell, Baseball City*	2	2	.500	3.09	11	5	0	9	0	1	35.0	29	14	12	2	3	11	0	37	0
Canestro, Fort Lauderdale*	0	0	.000	3.98	21	2	0	9	0	1	40.2	42	21	18	2	3	16	0	27	3

Pitcher, Team	W	L	Pct.	ERA	G	GS	CG	GF	ShO	Sv.	IP	H	R	ER	HR	HB	BB	Int. BB	SO	WP
Cassidy, St. Petersburg*	3	9	.250	3.05	21	21	0	0	0	0	133.0	131	51	45	3	5	18	2	73	1
Centala, Baseball City	1	2	.333	5.73	3	3	0	0	0	0	11.0	13	9	7	1	2	8	1	5	1
Chambers, Sarasota	0	1	.000	2.08	2	0	0	2	0	0	4.1	2	1	1	0	0	2	0	3	0
Chavez, Baseball City	0	0	.000	4.40	7	0	0	3	0	0	14.1	6	7	7	0	0	13	0	7	3
Coleman, Vero Beach	2	0	1.000	0.42	12	0	0	9	0	5	21.1	17	1	1	0	0	5	0	23	1
Collins, West Palm Beach	5	6	.455	3.26	27	11	1	4	0	1	96.2	76	42	35	6	5	29	1	53	1
Conner, Baseball City	3	7	.300	6.22	15	9	0	2	0	0	50.2	68	43	35	1	5	29	0	23	5
Cook, Lakeland*	3	4	.429	3.30	29	1	0	13	0	1	43.2	47	23	16	2	2	13	1	27	1
Cormier, West Palm Beach	3	2	.600	3.80	5	5	0	0	0	0	23.2	33	16	10	2	2	6	0	8	0
Cornelius, West Palm Beach	8	3	.727	2.39	17	17	0	0	0	0	109.1	79	31	29	3	7	43	1	81	3
Corona, St. Petersburg*	2	1	.667	2.89	15	0	0	6	0	0	18.2	17	8	6	0	1	8	1	12	1
Cortes, Sarasota	2	0	1.000	2.09	5	5	1	0	1	0	38.2	31	12	9	2	1	10	0	19	0
Costello, Osceola	1	0	1.000	7.50	5	0	0	2	0	0	6.0	8	5	5	2	0	3	0	5	0
Cox, Clearwater	3	0	1.000	0.00	3	3	0	0	0	0	18.0	4	0	0	0	0	4	0	15	0
Dabney, Sarasota*	11	3	.786	2.99	26	8	1	5	1	1	96.1	88	45	32	6	4	44	1	72	2
Davis, West Palm Beach	1	3	.250	2.27	22	0	0	19	0	8	31.2	25	9	8	1	1	14	2	31	1
Davis, Winter Haven	0	0	.000	4.50	1	0	0	0	0	0	2.0	2	1	1	0	0	0	0	2	1
Dayley, Dunedin*	0	0	.000	0.00	3	2	0	1	0	0	6.0	1	0	0	0	0	2	0	2	0
Delgado, Winter Haven	0	0	.000	9.00	1	0	0	1	0	0	1.0	2	2	1	0	1	0	0	0	0
Diaz, Baseball City*	1	1	.500	2.93	9	1	0	2	0	0	15.1	12	7	5	0	0	11	0	5	2
Dixon, St. Petersburg*	5	4	.556	3.78	53	0	0	23	0	1	64.1	54	32	27	3	0	24	1	54	2
Dopson, Winter Haven	2	2	.500	3.38	6	6	0	0	0	0	26.2	26	14	10	0	1	8	0	26	2
Dorn, St. Lucie	6	7	.462	2.87	48	6	1	11	0	2	109.2	91	44	35	5	5	29	1	82	6
Douma, St. Lucie*	8	3	.727	2.27	17	13	3	2	2	0	99.0	83	30	25	2	4	16	0	84	3
Drell, Lakeland	6	10	.375	2.91	28	21	1	1	1	0	130.0	115	50	42	6	9	43	1	56	4
Duey, Dunedin	1	3	.250	2.87	9	0	0	4	0	0	15.2	19	10	5	0	0	12	2	8	2
Dukes, Winter Haven	0	0	.000	0.00	4	0	0	4	0	0	6.0	7	0	0	0	0	4	0	4	0
Dunn, Baseball City	0	3	.000	11.12	5	5	0	0	0	0	11.1	17	15	14	1	0	10	0	9	3
Eddy, West Palm Beach	0	2	.000	1.27	13	4	0	4	0	2	35.1	37	7	5	0	0	11	0	19	1
Eischen, 18 Char.-8 W.P.B.*	8	12	.400	3.87	26	26	2	0	1	0	146.2	134	86	63	8	6	79	1	106	11
Elliott, Clearwater	8	5	.615	2.78	18	18	1	0	1	0	107.0	78	34	33	1	1	51	0	103	10
Ericson, Miami	1	3	.250	2.70	8	8	0	0	0	0	36.2	29	12	11	1	0	8	0	21	2
Escobar, Clearwater	0	0	.000	9.00	1	0	0	1	0	0	1.0	3	1	1	0	0	0	0	1	0
Ettles, Lakeland	2	1	.667	4.76	8	1	0	0	0	0	17.0	19	11	9	2	1	6	0	14	1
Faccio, St. Petersburg	3	5	.375	3.04	8	8	1	0	0	0	53.1	44	21	18	1	1	15	0	40	3
Farmer, Osceola	7	5	.583	3.63	17	16	1	0	1	0	91.2	81	42	37	3	3	43	2	68	10
Felix, Charlotte*	3	8	.273	3.09	29	17	1	3	0	0	128.1	118	54	44	4	6	41	2	119	8
Ferm, Lakeland	4	8	.333	5.00	17	15	0	0	0	0	72.0	69	49	40	1	1	57	0	42	8
Fernandez, St. Lucie*	0	0	.000	0.00	1	1	0	0	0	0	3.0	1	0	0	0	0	1	0	4	0
Fletcher, Clearwater	0	1	.000	1.23	14	4	0	5	0	1	29.1	22	6	4	1	0	8	1	27	2
Freeman, Vero Beach	5	10	.333	4.30	25	25	4	0	1	0	150.2	154	85	72	6	8	55	3	102	13
Freitas, St. Lucie	0	1	.000	2.53	5	0	0	4	0	0	10.2	11	4	3	1	1	10	2	10	2
Fritz, Miami	0	2	.000	2.38	14	0	0	7	0	1	22.2	21	7	6	1	0	10	1	24	1
Gaddy, Clearwater*	4	1	.800	2.24	34	0	0	17	0	1	52.1	48	19	13	0	4	22	0	34	2
Galvan, Sarasota*	0	0	.000	4.32	14	0	0	7	0	0	16.2	19	9	8	0	1	8	0	13	1
Ganote, Dunedin	2	1	.667	3.08	4	4	1	0	1	0	26.1	26	10	9	1	1	9	0	13	0
Garcia, Lakeland	6	8	.429	3.13	25	24	0	0	0	0	144.0	130	63	50	5	6	41	2	109	3
Garner, Charlotte	0	0	.000	0.00	1	0	0	1	0	0	1.0	0	0	0	0	0	1	0	1	0
Gideon, West Palm Beach	0	0	.000	3.60	4	1	0	0	0	0	5.0	8	4	2	0	0	2	0	4	0
Goedhart, Clearwater	10	8	.556	4.21	25	23	1	0	1	0	117.2	136	65	55	5	5	44	2	86	4
Goetz, Charlotte	3	1	.750	2.41	46	0	0	33	0	12	56.0	56	24	15	1	0	24	2	42	6
Gogolewski, Fort Lauderdale	0	1	.000	3.00	1	1	0	0	0	0	3.0	3	1	1	0	0	0	0	5	0
Gonzales, Lakeland*	11	5	.688	3.39	25	25	1	0	1	0	146.0	130	62	55	4	3	55	0	99	3
Gordon, Baseball City*	1	0	1.000	1.90	19	0	0	4	0	0	23.2	20	11	5	1	0	24	1	27	0
Gorton, St. Petersburg	2	4	.333	3.07	53	0	0	20	0	1	73.1	71	32	25	1	3	24	5	58	3
Gray, Clearwater	10	4	.714	2.45	20	20	1	0	1	0	117.1	98	47	32	2	4	38	1	99	12
Green, St. Petersburg	5	10	.333	4.63	26	23	2	0	2	0	128.1	138	75	66	4	4	43	0	92	6
Green, Clearwater	2	0	1.000	1.38	2	2	0	0	0	0	13.0	3	2	2	0	0	8	0	20	2
Greer, Fort Lauderdale	4	3	.571	4.24	31	1	0	12	0	0	57.1	49	31	27	3	7	22	2	46	5
Griffiths, Osceola	4	3	.571	1.92	18	8	0	4	0	0	61.0	43	18	13	2	3	17	1	44	9
Gross, Baseball City	2	7	.222	4.50	17	16	0	1	0	0	80.0	73	47	40	6	5	52	2	55	7
Grovom, Osceola*	0	1	.000	1.51	15	3	0	1	0	0	35.2	24	9	6	3	2	11	0	35	5
Gutierrez, Baseball City	1	0	1.000	1.50	1	1	0	0	0	0	6.0	5	1	1	0	0	5	0	4	1
Harriger, St. Lucie	6	1	.857	2.27	14	11	2	1	2	0	71.1	67	20	18	2	1	12	0	37	1
Harris, Baseball City	10	6	.625	2.47	19	18	3	0	1	0	116.2	92	38	32	3	3	27	4	84	4
Harvey, Baseball City	3	5	.375	2.77	13	12	0	0	0	0	61.2	42	24	19	0	6	35	1	43	12
Haslock, Miami	1	2	.333	1.49	20	0	0	17	0	5	36.1	25	6	6	0	3	8	2	19	1
Henry, Lakeland*	0	0	.000	3.27	6	0	0	4	0	0	11.0	13	4	4	0	0	5	0	7	1
Hill, St. Lucie*	4	0	1.000	1.13	6	4	0	1	0	0	32.0	18	6	4	1	0	4	0	24	0
Hinkle, St. Petersburg	0	1	.000	3.60	1	1	0	0	0	0	5.0	7	3	2	0	2	0	0	2	0
Hoey, Sarasota	1	0	1.000	0.00	4	0	0	1	0	0	4.0	2	0	0	0	0	1	0	3	0
Hoffman, Vero Beach*	2	1	.667	10.80	5	0	0	2	0	0	6.2	9	12	8	0	0	6	0	9	1
Holdridge, Clearwater	0	0	.000	7.56	15	0	0	4	0	1	25.0	34	23	21	2	1	21	0	23	4
Hopper, Baseball City	0	2	.000	1.77	19	0	0	8	0	2	35.2	27	8	7	0	3	14	3	20	2
Hotchkiss, Dunedin	0	2	.000	2.14	15	0	0	9	0	0	33.2	25	16	8	0	1	21	0	13	3
Howell, Fort Lauderdale*	0	1	.000	4.50	2	0	0	1	0	0	2.0	1	1	1	0	0	1	0	1	0
Hurst, Clearwater	3	0	1.000	3.30	22	1	0	2	0	0	43.2	52	20	16	2	4	7	1	31	3
Hurst, Miami	8	2	.800	2.90	15	15	0	0	0	0	99.1	89	41	32	6	6	31	2	91	2
Hutton, Fort Lauderdale	5	8	.385	2.45	24	24	3	0	0	0	147.0	98	54	40	5	11	65	5	117	4
Hyson, Osceola	8	10	.444	4.18	25	23	3	1	0	0	131.1	134	68	61	6	5	63	1	91	16
Jacobs, Baseball City	3	2	.600	2.75	19	5	0	1	0	0	55.2	52	20	17	3	0	19	2	35	5
Johnson, Sarasota*	6	1	.857	1.75	51	0	0	22	0	7	51.1	41	17	10	0	3	17	6	42	3
Johnson, Winter Haven	0	1	.000	5.79	7	1	0	2	0	0	14.0	16	10	9	0	1	8	0	8	1
Johnson, Osceola	4	0	1.000	2.37	34	0	0	10	0	1	64.2	80	27	17	1	1	23	2	46	4
Jones, Vero Beach	3	1	.750	4.10	9	9	0	0	0	0	37.1	31	17	17	0	2	15	0	31	1
Jones, Osceola	4	4	.500	4.35	14	14	0	0	0	0	72.1	69	38	35	2	3	35	0	51	4
Kaiser, Osceola	0	5	.000	9.72	7	7	0	0	0	0	16.2	15	24	18	2	4	33	0	13	8
Karchner, Baseball City	6	3	.667	1.97	38	0	0	16	0	5	73.0	49	28	16	1	5	25	3	65	7
Kerfut, Miami	4	6	.400	2.30	34	5	1	12	0	3	97.2	70	32	25	3	9	28	2	72	2
Keyser, Sarasota	6	7	.462	2.30	27	14	2	9	1	2	129.0	110	40	33	5	6	45	8	94	3
Kilgo, West Palm Beach*	6	3	.667	1.58	33	1	0	10	0	5	74.0	56	14	13	1	2	24	1	47	1
Kistaitis, Dunedin*	0	0	.000	0.00	1	0	0	0	0	0	2.0	2	0	0	0	0	1	0	1	1
Kite, Winter Haven	3	2	.600	4.74	29	1	0	14	0	1	62.2	56	54	33	1	5	79	0	66	24
Kizziah, Dunedin	3	6	.333	2.39	34	0	0	17	0	3	60.1	52	28	16	0	2	38	3	47	4
Klancnik, Miami	3	0	1.000	3.74	21	0	0	9	0	0	33.2	36	18	14	3	2	21	1	28	6

Pitcher, Team	W	L	Pct.	ERA	G	GS	CG	GF	ShO	Sv.	IP	H	R	ER	HR	HB	BB	Int. BB	SO	WP
Klvac, Winter Haven*	0	1	.000	6.23	1	1	0	0	0	0	4.1	5	3	3	1	0	2	0	1	0
Krumm, Lakeland	3	3	.500	3.00	7	6	0	0	0	0	36.0	28	16	12	2	1	13	0	23	4
Langbehn, St. Lucie*	10	12	.455	2.52	27	27	1	0	0	0	175.1	149	53	49	7	4	44	3	106	7
Langley, 23 Mia. -18 Clear.*	5	4	.556	3.73	41	0	0	23	0	5	60.1	52	28	25	1	1	27	1	72	3
Lata, St. Petersburg	0	1	.000	2.93	10	0	0	2	0	0	15.1	15	5	5	0	0	11	0	10	1
Leimeister, Lakeland	2	2	.500	5.55	35	0	0	10	0	0	60.0	77	41	37	4	1	28	0	32	3
Leiter, Dunedin*	0	0	.000	1.86	4	3	0	0	0	0	9.2	5	2	2	0	1	7	0	5	1
Lemon, Miami	0	1	.000	5.19	10	1	0	1	0	1	17.1	23	15	10	1	2	4	0	13	1
Lima, Lakeland	0	1	.000	10.38	4	1	0	2	0	0	8.2	16	10	10	1	0	2	0	5	1
Limbach, Clearwater*	5	4	.556	2.05	39	0	0	18	0	6	48.1	27	13	11	0	0	14	0	54	3
Lindsey, Clearwater	1	2	.333	3.03	6	6	0	0	0	0	29.2	30	12	10	1	0	9	0	19	3
Lloyd, Dunedin*	2	5	.286	2.24	50	0	0	39	0	24	60.1	54	17	15	2	1	25	2	39	4
Logan, West Palm Beach	6	12	.333	3.18	23	22	3	0	0	0	141.1	117	65	50	4	5	52	1	90	3
Long, Baseball City*	7	3	.700	1.96	47	0	0	28	0	10	78.0	54	19	17	0	5	33	3	53	4
Luckham, Osceola	8	12	.400	3.89	27	27	3	0	0	0	162.0	158	80	70	4	7	61	1	91	10
Lumley, Lakeland	6	3	.667	2.84	43	3	0	20	0	6	69.2	55	30	22	0	5	27	3	72	6
Maietta, Winter Haven	0	1	.000	5.19	3	1	0	0	0	0	8.2	6	6	5	1	0	6	0	8	0
Maldonado, Lakeland	1	0	1.000	3.00	2	0	0	2	0	0	3.0	2	1	1	0	0	2	0	3	0
Maldonado, Charlotte	2	3	.400	1.98	46	0	0	31	0	14	50.0	47	14	11	2	2	16	4	40	1
Malone, Clearwater	3	5	.375	6.85	10	10	0	0	0	0	44.2	50	41	34	4	3	41	0	29	7
Malone, Fort Lauderdale*	1	1	.500	3.00	6	2	0	1	0	0	21.0	17	10	7	0	0	13	0	20	3
Maloney, Winter Haven*	0	5	.000	5.57	16	5	1	9	0	1	42.0	45	28	26	2	2	18	0	18	6
Malzone, Winter Haven	0	0	.000	6.75	4	0	0	5	0	0	9.1	14	8	7	2	0	4	0	1	1
Manon, Fort Lauderdale	10	8	.556	2.59	26	18	5	2	2	1	135.1	99	45	39	4	5	51	2	74	7
Marcero, Lakeland*	0	0	.000	40.50	2	0	0	0	0	0	1.1	5	7	6	0	1	2	0	0	0
Marris, Fort Lauderdale	4	6	.400	4.83	24	8	0	7	0	0	50.1	63	33	27	1	3	27	2	24	8
Martin, Dunedin	1	0	1.000	1.13	13	0	0	12	0	5	16.0	7	2	2	0	0	10	0	19	1
Matznick, Sarasota	5	12	.294	4.00	26	26	0	1	0	0	157.1	129	82	70	2	5	84	3	131	7
McCann, St. Lucie	2	3	.400	4.14	34	5	0	14	0	0	76.0	81	40	35	6	4	25	3	33	6
McCormick, Baseball City*	0	0	.000	3.12	17	0	0	7	0	0	26.0	19	13	9	0	0	15	3	19	4
McCray, Charlotte*	0	1	.000	5.79	2	2	0	0	0	0	9.1	11	8	6	0	1	6	1	7	1
Meinhart, Dunedin	10	6	.625	2.66	20	20	3	0	0	0	128.1	114	42	38	3	3	34	0	114	4
Michno, Miami	11	15	.423	2.42	29	29	13	0	3	0	216.0	175	77	58	12	5	66	1	190	1
Mimbs, Vero Beach*	12	4	.750	2.67	24	22	1	0	1	0	141.2	124	52	42	6	6	70	2	132	15
Minchey, Miami	5	3	.625	1.89	13	13	4	0	1	0	95.1	81	31	20	1	4	31	0	61	1
Mitchelson, Winter Haven*	4	7	.364	4.21	14	13	0	0	0	0	62.0	70	33	29	0	3	26	0	48	1
Mongiello, Sarasota	4	4	.500	2.25	55	0	0	44	0	23	68.0	51	26	17	1	1	34	5	62	5
Moore, Dunedin	6	13	.316	3.70	27	25	2	1	0	0	160.2	139	78	66	3	4	99	3	115	12
Morman, Osceola*	0	0	.000	1.50	3	0	0	1	0	0	6.0	5	3	1	0	0	2	0	3	1
Morrison, Winter Haven	0	0	.000	0.00	1	0	0	0	0	0	1.0	0	0	0	0	0	0	0	1	0
Moya, West Palm Beach	6	2	.750	1.94	19	15	0	2	0	0	88.0	73	33	19	2	1	33	0	57	2
Munoz, Clearwater*	0	0	.000	0.00	2	0	0	2	0	0	1.1	0	0	0	0	0	4	0	0	0
Munoz, Fort Lauderdale	5	8	.385	2.33	19	19	4	0	2	0	108.0	91	45	28	4	4	40	0	53	6
Newkirk, Charlotte	0	0	.000	27.00	1	0	0	1	0	0	0.2	2	2	2	0	0	2	1	1	0
Nielsen, Fort Lauderdale*	3	3	.500	2.78	42	0	0	14	0	4	64.2	50	29	20	2	3	31	4	66	7
Nielsen, St. Petersburg*	0	1	.000	5.06	1	1	0	0	0	0	5.1	7	5	3	0	0	2	0	4	1
Niethammer, Charlotte	0	1	.000	13.50	1	0	0	0	0	0	1.1	0	2	2	0	0	1	0	0	1
Niles, Winter Haven	3	14	.176	3.78	25	21	3	0	0	0	135.2	119	75	57	6	6	85	0	91	10
Ochs, St. Petersburg	0	0	.000	4.50	2	0	0	2	0	0	2.0	2	2	1	0	0	2	0	0	0
Ogliaruso, Dunedin	6	10	.375	3.36	22	22	1	0	0	0	128.2	114	64	48	5	2	74	2	86	12
Oliver, Charlotte*	0	1	.000	4.50	2	2	0	0	0	0	8.0	6	4	4	1	0	3	0	12	1
Owen, Winter Haven*	0	0	.000	4.50	1	1	0	0	0	0	4.0	3	2	2	0	0	2	0	5	0
Ozuna, St. Petersburg	2	3	.400	0.82	31	0	0	23	0	13	43.2	27	9	4	0	1	12	2	44	1
Painter, Winter Haven	2	5	.286	2.81	9	9	1	0	0	0	57.2	38	21	18	1	1	22	0	54	7
Parris, Clearwater	7	5	.583	3.39	43	6	0	8	0	1	93.0	101	43	35	1	9	25	4	59	3
Patrick, Vero Beach*	8	8	.500	5.52	22	12	1	5	0	0	93.0	122	66	57	2	2	32	1	59	6
Phillips, Osceola	2	5	.286	2.09	44	0	0	30	0	11	60.1	47	20	14	2	3	25	5	65	11
Polak, Fort Lauderdale	5	4	.556	3.67	40	0	0	19	0	2	54.0	50	24	22	0	2	23	4	50	3
Polasek, West Palm Beach*	6	4	.600	2.29	52	0	0	18	0	3	63.0	47	18	16	2	3	21	6	36	6
Pollard, Baseball City	1	1	.500	4.26	13	2	0	3	0	0	25.1	22	14	12	0	1	12	0	23	8
Ponte, Osceola	7	6	.538	1.78	47	0	0	32	0	10	76.0	43	21	15	4	5	21	9	82	2
Powers, Winter Haven	8	7	.533	4.60	25	15	3	5	0	0	105.2	108	66	54	1	3	54	1	76	7
Proctor, St. Lucie	2	0	1.000	1.52	6	6	0	0	0	0	29.2	16	6	5	0	2	22	0	19	2
Prybylinski, Fort Lauderdale	3	3	.500	2.30	13	1	0	4	0	0	31.1	22	8	8	0	1	4	2	35	0
Quero, Charlotte*	7	7	.500	2.88	34	10	0	9	0	1	84.1	88	35	27	0	2	31	4	57	2
Ramos, Lakeland*	2	0	1.000	1.31	12	0	0	4	0	0	20.2	12	3	3	0	1	8	0	13	2
Randle, Charlotte	3	8	.273	3.89	29	19	0	2	0	0	125.0	116	74	54	4	14	57	4	77	0
Reed, Miami*	0	2	.000	6.85	10	3	0	5	0	0	22.1	29	18	17	2	0	17	0	11	0
Regira, West Palm Beach	0	1	.000	4.61	12	1	0	4	0	0	13.2	13	10	7	0	0	19	0	14	1
Reich, St. Lucie	5	5	.500	2.67	54	0	0	26	0	4	104.1	86	35	31	4	6	40	6	76	4
Renko, West Palm Beach	0	1	.000	8.00	4	3	0	0	0	0	9.0	14	8	8	2	1	5	0	4	0
Resnikoff, Osceola*	0	0	.000	0.48	8	0	0	4	0	0	18.2	13	2	1	0	0	6	1	24	0
Reynolds, Sarasota	1	1	.500	1.23	6	0	0	4	0	2	14.2	14	3	2	0	2	6	2	14	0
Ricker, West Palm Beach	0	1	.000	4.50	1	0	0	1	0	0	2.0	2	2	1	0	0	0	0	3	0
Rivera, Lakeland	2	1	.667	3.38	14	0	0	12	0	3	16.0	18	7	6	0	2	9	0	17	2
Rogers, Miami*	6	7	.462	4.02	22	20	0	0	0	0	107.1	107	54	48	5	9	52	0	71	3
Rowley, Charlotte	7	1	.875	2.82	8	8	1	0	0	0	44.2	38	15	14	1	3	32	0	28	0
Ruffin, Sarasota	11	4	.733	3.23	26	26	6	0	2	0	158.2	126	68	57	9	5	62	0	117	10
Rumer, Fort Lauderdale*	10	7	.588	2.89	24	23	3	0	2	0	149.1	125	59	48	6	5	49	2	112	7
Russo, Baseball City	2	1	.667	1.64	15	0	0	11	0	4	22.0	9	5	4	0	3	9	2	20	1
Ryan, Winter Haven	1	3	.250	2.05	21	1	0	11	0	1	52.2	40	15	12	1	2	19	0	53	3
Salvior, St. Petersburg	2	3	.400	2.58	38	0	0	24	0	9	52.1	39	20	15	1	1	18	6	41	4
Sample, St. Lucie	1	2	.333	6.38	13	0	0	6	0	1	18.1	25	14	13	1	1	11	1	11	1
Sampson, Vero Beach	5	8	.385	4.99	30	10	1	10	1	2	88.1	78	54	49	5	4	59	1	56	3
Santamaria, Winter Haven	0	5	.000	4.33	45	1	0	18	0	3	62.1	65	38	30	1	1	57	2	59	12
Schmidt, West Palm Beach	1	1	.500	3.21	9	4	0	2	0	1	14.0	12	9	5	0	1	0	0	11	1
Schwarber, Lakeland	2	2	.500	6.26	8	5	0	1	0	0	23.0	22	16	16	4	1	17	0	18	1
Sebra, Osceola	1	0	1.000	2.77	5	2	0	3	0	1	13.0	11	4	4	2	3	5	0	13	0
Sele, Winter Haven	3	6	.333	4.96	13	11	4	1	0	1	69.0	65	42	38	2	6	32	2	51	5
Shackle, St. Petersburg	8	9	.471	2.65	21	21	2	0	2	0	129.0	125	44	38	4	1	36	0	94	2
Shaw, Baseball City	6	12	.333	2.88	25	24	3	1	1	0	137.1	144	59	44	6	5	39	3	55	15
Shepherd, Sarasota	1	1	.500	2.72	18	0	0	8	0	2	39.2	33	16	12	0	2	20	0	24	1
Sieradzki, West Palm Beach	0	0	.000	0.00	1	0	0	0	0	0	3.0	2	0	0	0	0	1	0	2	0
Small, Dunedin	8	7	.533	2.73	24	23	1	0	0	0	148.1	129	51	45	4	5	42	1	92	7
Small, Osceola	3	0	1.000	1.61	26	0	0	10	0	2	44.2	30	10	8	2	1	19	1	44	2

FLORIDA STATE LEAGUE

CLASS A

FLORIDA STATE LEAGUE

Pitcher, Team	W	L	Pct.	ERA	G	GS	CG	GF	ShO	Sv.	IP	H	R	ER	HR	HB	BB	Int. BB	SO	WP
Smith, St. Petersburg	2	4	.333	4.52	20	7	0	2	0	0	63.2	61	37	32	3	3	19	0	69	0
Snedeker, Vero Beach	7	3	.700	2.52	17	17	2	0	2	0	96.1	92	28	27	3	2	17	0	66	2
Sohn, Vero Beach	1	0	1.000	1.50	1	0	0	1	0	0	6.0	3	1	1	1	0	2	1	7	0
Spencer, Charlotte	4	4	.500	4.66	38	0	0	13	0	0	65.2	59	36	34	5	5	30	4	49	4
Springer, Fort Lauderdale	5	9	.357	3.49	25	25	2	0	0	0	152.1	118	68	59	9	6	62	1	139	6
Steiner, Charlotte*	2	2	.500	3.45	30	0	0	5	0	0	28.2	22	12	11	0	2	23	4	28	3
Stevens, Clearwater	0	3	.000	0.91	38	0	0	32	0	17	39.2	16	7	4	0	0	18	1	49	1
Stevens, Sarasota	8	10	.444	2.64	35	11	2	7	0	2	126.1	103	48	37	5	2	50	5	103	9
Sullivan, Clearwater	6	3	.667	2.61	36	7	0	20	0	11	76.0	58	29	22	3	2	36	2	64	4
Taveras, Vero Beach	7	2	.778	4.33	22	5	0	6	0	0	62.1	68	32	30	3	1	26	0	62	1
Taylor, Clearwater*	0	0	.000	9.00	1	0	0	1	0	0	1.0	2	1	1	0	0	1	0	1	0
Thoden, West Palm Beach	5	1	.833	2.22	12	11	0	0	0	0	56.2	45	15	14	1	1	4	0	32	0
Torres, Lakeland	4	2	.667	2.76	42	1	0	1	0	0	78.1	53	31	24	3	3	34	0	85	3
Toth, Baseball City	2	3	.400	2.83	13	10	0	0	0	0	63.2	53	24	20	1	2	23	2	42	0
Trujillo, St. Petersburg	0	0	.000	0.00	1	0	0	1	0	0	1.0	1	0	0	0	0	1	0	1	0
Tuss, West Palm Beach	6	4	.600	2.59	49	1	0	26	0	11	73.0	61	24	21	0	3	22	1	59	1
Urbani, St. Petersburg*	8	7	.533	2.35	19	19	2	0	1	0	118.2	109	39	31	2	2	25	0	64	3
Vanegmond, Winter Haven	4	5	.444	3.03	13	10	4	2	2	2	68.1	69	32	23	2	2	23	1	47	2
Vasquez, St. Lucie	3	2	.600	0.28	56	0	0	47	0	25	64.0	35	6	2	1	3	39	2	56	2
Vazquez, St. Lucie	0	0	.000	0.00	1	0	0	1	0	0	1.0	1	1	0	0	0	0	1	0	1
Vitko, St. Lucie	11	8	.579	2.24	22	22	5	0	2	0	140.1	102	40	35	6	4	39	1	105	6
Walker, St. Lucie	10	12	.455	3.21	26	25	1	0	0	0	151.1	145	77	54	9	4	52	2	95	7
Wall, Osceola	6	3	.667	2.09	12	12	4	0	2	0	77.1	55	22	18	3	2	11	1	62	1
Wanish, Dunedin	3	4	.429	3.02	36	1	1	17	0	1	80.1	70	29	27	4	1	29	2	61	8
Warren, Lakeland	8	2	.800	2.53	17	16	4	0	2	0	103.1	86	34	29	3	1	15	1	75	6
Washington, Charlotte	5	0	1.000	3.51	12	7	1	2	0	0	51.1	45	29	20	2	1	20	2	27	4
Weber, St. Petersburg*	2	9	.182	5.38	18	13	0	3	0	0	75.1	84	50	45	5	1	40	0	38	3
Wegmann, St. Lucie	4	3	.571	2.51	13	11	0	1	0	0	61.0	46	19	17	0	1	14	0	69	1
Wells, Clearwater	7	2	.778	3.11	24	9	1	3	0	0	75.1	63	27	26	5	4	19	4	66	6
Wengert, Vero Beach	7	6	.538	2.06	30	13	2	8	2	3	127.0	100	36	29	3	6	42	2	114	4
Whitworth, Miami	1	7	.125	3.75	20	7	0	4	0	1	69.2	59	38	29	4	4	35	0	37	4
Wickman, Sarasota	5	1	.833	2.05	7	7	1	0	1	0	44.0	43	16	10	2	1	11	0	32	1
Wiegandt, Clearwater*	0	1	.000	3.48	11	0	0	5	0	1	10.1	14	7	4	0	0	3	0	11	2
Wiley, Fort Lauderdale	0	0	.000	6.04	4	4	0	0	0	0	22.1	27	15	15	2	0	8	0	15	1
Wiley, Baseball City	4	2	.667	1.68	53	0	0	36	0	17	75.0	52	17	14	0	2	21	5	53	0
Wilkinson, West Palm Beach	1	1	.500	2.70	8	1	0	2	0	0	13.1	10	5	4	1	1	7	0	10	2
Williams, Osceola	6	4	.600	2.91	15	15	0	0	0	0	89.2	72	41	29	0	2	40	1	67	3
Williams, Miami*	3	5	.375	3.24	40	0	0	32	0	12	50.0	38	25	18	2	0	35	2	47	4
Williams, Clearwater	7	3	.700	1.74	14	14	2	0	1	0	93.1	65	23	18	5	3	14	0	76	2
Windes, Osceola*	3	5	.375	2.21	45	0	0	23	0	8	69.1	44	21	17	2	1	13	1	63	0
Wolf, Osceola	6	0	1.000	1.83	9	9	0	0	0	0	59.0	42	14	12	1	4	14	1	59	2
Young, Winter Haven	5	12	.294	5.87	28	20	2	4	1	1	118.0	146	80	77	7	6	50	0	77	6

BALKS—Mitchelson, 10; Moore, 9; Bushing, Freeman 7 each; T. Brown, Cornelius, Sele, S. Stevens, Wegmann, Whitworth, M. Williams, 6 each; Brow, Cormier, Dopson, Goedhart, Gorton, L. Johnson, Luckham, Niles, Rogers, B. Williams, Young, 5 each; Dabney, Hutton, Mongiello, Parris, Shaw, Wells, Wengert, Wolf, 4 each; Bickhardt, Cassidy, Collins, Ericson, Farmer, Ferm, Hotchkiss, K. Jones, Keyser, Langley, Michno, Mimbs, Ponte, Reich, Springer, Walker, Warren, W. Wiley, 3 each; Brutcher, Campbell, Canestro, Corona, Dixon, Dorn, Dunn, Felix, Garcia, Jacobs, J. Johnson, Kerfut, Kizziah, Lima, Limbach, Long, C. Malone, Minchey, R. Munoz, Newkirk, Polak, Polasek, Powers, Quero, Ruffin, Schwarber, Smith, Spencer, Vasquez, Washington, Wickman, Windes, 2 each; Adamson, Ahern, Allen, Asche, Bautista, Bolton, M.K. Brady, M.R. Brady, Braley, Brink, D. Brown, Buckley, Chavez, Conner, Cook, T. Davis, Drell, Eischen, Elliott, Ettles, Faccio, Fritz, Gaddy, Gogolewski, Gonzales, Gray, Griffiths, Harris, Harvey, Hoffman, Howell, C. Hurst, E. Johnson, Karchner, Langbehn, Lata, Leimeister, J. Maldonado, Maloney, Manon, Morris, McCann, McCormick, Menhart, Ogliaruso, Owen, Patrick, Phillips, Proctor, Prybylinski, Reed, Resnikoff, Reynolds, Rumer, Russo, Ryan, Salvior, Santamaria, Sebra, Shackle, Torres, Urbani, Vanegmond, Vitko, J. Wiley, K. Williams, 1 each.

COMBINATION SHUTOUTS—Harris-Long 2, Centala-Karcher-Hopper, Harris-Wiley-Long, Jacobs-Russo, Toth-Wiley, Baseball City; Arner-Goetz, Bohanon-Maldonado, Eischen-Spencer-Randle, Quero-Maldonado-Goetz, Rowley-Steiner-Felix, Charlotte; Brink-Sullivan, Cox-Gaddy, Cox-Limbach-Sullivan, Cox-Wells-Gaddy-Fletcher, Elliott-Langley, Elliott-Langley-Sullivan, Elliott-Stevens, Fletcher-Goedhart-Limbach-Sullivan, Goedhart-Wells-Wiegandt, Gray-Fletcher-Wiegandt-Stevens, Gray-Limbach, Gray-Stevens, Wells-Parris, Williams-Stevens, Clearwater; Brow-Dayley-Brown, Brow-Kizziah-Lloyd, Leiter-Brown-Kizziah-Graeme, Menhart-Brown, Menhart-Kizziah, Menhart-Lloyd, Moore-Kizziah-Lloyd, Ogliaruso-Brown, Ogliaruso-Lloyd, Small-Brow-Duey, Small-Lloyd, Dunedin; Rumer-Batchelor 2, Hutton-Batchelor, Hutton-Nielsen-Batchelor, Hutton-Polak-Batchelor, Marris-Greer-Polak, Munoz-Malone-Nielsen, Munoz-Marris-Batchelor, Fort Lauderdale; Drell-Lumley, Drell-Lumley-Rivera, Ferm-Henry, Garcia-Lumley, Garcia-Rivera, Krumm-Braley, Wolf-Braley, Lakeland; Asche-Kerfut-Fritz, Hurst-Williams, Kerfut-Haslock, Rogers-Whitworth, Miami; Farmer-Grovom-Ponte, Jones-Ponte, Jones-Resnikoff-Phillips, Jones-Small-Windes-Phillips, Kaiser-Johnson-Small-Ponte, Luckham-Phillips, Luckham-Ponte, Luckham-Windes, Phillips, Wall-Windes, Williams-Sebra, Osceola; Langbehn-Reich 2, Harringer-Reich, Hill-Vasquez, Langbehn-Dorn-Reich-Vazquez, Langbehn-McCann-Vasquez, Langbehn-Vasquez-Reich, Proctor-Douma, Walker-Dorn-Reich, Walker-Reich-Vazquez, Wegmann-Reich, St. Lucie; Cassidy-Gorton-Ozuna, Shackle-Baker, Shackle-Salvior, Shackle-Salvior-Ozuna, Urbani-Dixon-Ozuna, Urbani-Ozuna, St. Petersburg; Brutcher-Johnson, Brutcher-Johnson-Mongiello, Brutcher-Stevens-Johnson-Mongiello, Dabney-Shepherd, Matznick-Mongiello-Stevens, Ruffin-Mongiello, Sarasota; Freeman-Coleman-Calhoun, Patrick-Brady-Calhoun, Taveras-Calhoun, Vero Beach; Barnes-Bochtler, Collins-Kilgo-Moya-Schmidt, Cornelius-Bushing, Cornelius-Kilgo-Tuss, Logan-Schmidt, Moya-Kilgo-Tuss-Eddy, Moya-Polasek-Bushing-Tuss, Thoden-Kilgo, Thoden-Polasek, Wilkinson-Kilgo-Bushing, West Palm Beach; Allen-Santamaria, Mitchelson-Allen, Mitchelson-Ryan, Mitchelson-Ryan-Santamaria, Niles-Kite, Winter Haven.

NO-HIT GAMES—Cox-Gaddy, Clearwater, defeated Baseball City, 4-0, April 21; Ruffin, Sarasota, defeated Charlotte, 6-1 (second game), June 14; Dabney, Sarasota, defeated Baseball City, 6-0, August 3; Matznick, Sarasota, defeated Charlotte, 1-0 (nine no-hit innings in 15-inning game), August 26; Snedeker, Vero Beach, defeated St. Lucie, 3-0 (first game), August 28.

FIELDING

TEAM

Team	Pct.	G	PO	A	E	DP	PB	Team	Pct.	G	PO	A	E	DP	PB
St. Petersburg	.975	131	3427	1359	123	109	12	Lakeland	.967	128	3350	1410	161	115	18
Vero Beach	.973	132	3401	1344	130	124	24	West Palm Beach	.966	131	3374	1468	168	103	18
Clearwater	.971	130	3316	1314	137	122	12	Fort Lauderdale	.966	128	3302	1270	159	100	26
St. Lucie	.969	131	3468	1519	162	101	20	Miami	.966	131	3406	1325	167	120	17
Winter Haven	.968	128	3220	1304	149	108	43	Sarasota	.966	131	3467	1413	172	97	23
Dunedin	.968	131	3449	1530	166	113	26	Charlotte	.966	132	3439	1376	172	123	30
Baseball City	.968	131	3406	1329	159	105	23	Osceola	.964	127	3289	1397	174	109	20

Triple plays—None.

*Throws lefthanded.

FIRST BASEMEN

Player, Team	Pct.	G	PO	A	E	DP
Abare, Dunedin*	.984	112	986	89	18	84
Albright, Lakeland	.962	3	25	0	1	0
Anglero, Lakeland	1.000	2	5	0	0	0
Ball, Osceola	1.000	1	10	0	0	0
Bargas, West Palm Beach	.990	69	627	40	7	51
Barnwell, Fort Lauderdale	1.000	1	3	1	0	0
Beuerlein, Osceola	.951	8	52	6	3	3
Bradbury, Miami	1.000	8	49	2	0	8
Bradish, 33 Mia. - 12 Sar.	.989	45	338	28	4	31
Brady, Clearwater	1.000	3	22	0	0	2
Butterfield, St. Lucie	.962	3	24	1	1	1
Campas, St. Petersburg	.920	4	21	2	2	1
Castleberry, Miami	1.000	2	16	1	0	1
Cepicky, Sarasota	.988	95	769	80	10	58
Ciccarella, Winter Haven*	.996	31	234	10	1	22
Clinton, Charlotte	.984	19	111	16	2	14
Cornelius, Lakeland	.994	29	161	12	1	12
Cramer, West Palm Beach	.984	33	228	21	4	19
Curtis, Osceola*	.992	71	605	30	5	49
D'Alexander, Miami	1.000	1	1	1	0	1
Dando, Miami*	.982	36	267	13	5	26
DEUTSCH, Vero Beach*	.994	123	1045	77	7	99
Dorante, Winter Haven	.978	6	41	4	1	2
DuBose, Lakeland	1.000	3	14	2	0	1
Durkin, West Palm Beach	1.000	1	4	0	0	0
Federico, St. Petersburg*	1.000	6	39	8	0	5
Giordano, Miami*	1.000	17	128	12	0	9
Grant, Winter Haven	1.000	11	61	10	0	8
Greer, Charlotte*	.983	8	55	4	1	2
Guggiana, Charlotte	.983	31	258	31	5	28
Hall, Miami	.968	10	83	8	3	6
Hamlin, St. Petersburg	.986	119	1053	75	16	82
Harmes, Dunedin	1.000	4	40	1	0	4
Harris, St. Lucie	.992	96	869	80	8	62
Hennessey, Baseball City	1.000	1	1	0	0	0
Hoffner, St. Lucie	.990	42	356	25	4	30
Howard, Lakeland	1.000	1	0	1	0	0
Howell, Fort Lauderdale*	.989	116	1000	55	12	76
Hyde, Clearwater	1.000	2	3	0	0	0
Johnson, Fort Lauderdale	.989	9	84	10	1	6
Jordan, Fort Lauderdale	1.000	1	1	0	0	0
King, Baseball City	.945	10	43	9	3	4
Kobza, Sarasota	1.000	1	2	0	0	0
Lake, West Palm Beach	.983	22	163	15	3	11
Ledinsky, Miami	.971	34	279	22	9	23
Lewis, St. Petersburg*	1.000	2	9	0	0	1
Lockett, Clearwater*	.988	128	1053	95	14	105
Lukachyk, Sarasota	1.000	6	65	5	0	4
MacArthur, Miami	1.000	1	10	1	0	2
Marshall, Charlotte	.991	68	497	37	5	51
Matilla, Winter Haven	1.000	1	1	0	0	0
McDonald, West Palm Beach	.962	19	133	17	6	11
McMullen, Fort Lauderdale	.927	5	34	4	3	1
Mengel, Dunedin	.978	28	169	12	4	11
Montalvo, Dunedin	1.000	1	4	0	0	0
Morrisette, Miami	.889	1	7	1	1	0
Morrow, Vero Beach*	1.000	2	8	1	0	0
Newkirk, Charlotte	1.000	4	6	0	0	0
Niethammer, Charlotte	.981	21	136	20	3	14
Noce, West Palm Beach	1.000	1	4	0	0	0
O'Donnell, Vero Beach	.984	11	61	2	1	6
Ochs, St. Petersburg	.957	2	22	0	1	3
Olmstead, Osceola*	.985	45	365	31	6	30
Prager, Osceola*	.976	12	112	10	3	10
Rendina, Lakeland*	.989	112	961	61	11	81
Riesgo, West Palm Beach	.974	4	34	3	1	4
Sanchez, West Palm Beach	1.000	1	5	0	0	0
Schreiner, Baseball City	.991	15	106	10	1	10
Scott, Osceola	.958	3	22	1	1	3
Smith, Sarasota	1.000	25	239	19	0	18
Smith, Vero Beach	1.000	1	3	0	0	0
Solseth, Baseball City	.992	115	997	58	9	77
A. Stewart, Baseball City	1.000	1	10	1	0	0
Tahan, St. Petersburg	1.000	2	20	1	0	1
Tatarian, St. Petersburg	1.000	2	4	0	0	1
O. Thomas, St. Petersburg	1.000	1	6	0	0	0
Twardoski, Winter Haven*	1.000	2	17	2	0	4
Wallin, Winter Haven*	.983	85	685	58	13	55
Williams, Vero Beach	1.000	4	16	1	0	2
Wilstead, West Palm Beach*	1.000	1	3	0	0	0

SECOND BASEMEN

Player, Team	Pct.	G	PO	A	E	DP
Allison, St. Lucie	.970	5	15	17	1	6
Beanblossom, St. Petersburg	.973	115	160	242	11	47
Berry, Osceola	.941	91	170	260	27	52
Blackwell, Fort Lauderdale	1.000	2	2	4	0	0

Player, Team	Pct.	G	PO	A	E	DP
Castleberry, 14 Mia. - 74 Sar.	.964	88	176	228	15	35
Clinton, Charlotte	.963	12	26	26	2	6
Coleman, Sarasota	.947	28	47	78	7	16
Davis, Winter Haven	.949	41	58	108	9	11
Davison, West Palm Beach	1.000	4	3	5	0	0
DeKneef, Winter Haven	.987	36	67	90	2	21
Diaz, St. Lucie	.971	63	129	174	9	34
Doffek, Vero Beach	.913	19	17	25	4	5
Escobar, Clearwater	.969	34	79	79	5	23
Evangelista, Charlotte	.941	6	8	8	1	1
Fanning, St. Petersburg	.968	8	9	21	1	5
Fermin, Lakeland	.800	1	4	0	1	0
Foster, Sarasota	1.000	5	3	11	0	3
Garces, Clearwater	.786	5	2	9	3	2
Garner, Charlotte	.953	49	92	133	11	23
Graham, Winter Haven	1.000	1	1	3	0	0
Grant, Winter Haven	1.000	4	8	5	0	2
Hajek, Osceola	1.000	11	14	24	0	6
Hartwig, Clearwater	1.000	1	0	1	0	0
Helms, Sarasota	.500	3	0	1	1	0
Hodge, Charlotte	1.000	1	2	1	0	2
HOWARD, Vero Beach	.983	128	197	336	9	72
Howard, Lakeland	.972	94	177	243	12	50
Howard, St. Lucie	.934	15	29	42	5	5
Jordan, Fort Lauderdale	.968	114	181	306	16	56
Krause, West Palm Beach	.976	42	64	99	4	22
Lansing, Miami	.833	2	4	1	1	0
MacArthur, St. Petersburg	1.000	2	0	2	0	0
Marigny, Lakeland	.880	6	12	10	3	4
McCray, Sarasota	.813	9	6	7	3	1
McKamie, Vero Beach	1.000	2	2	1	0	1
Mendenhall, Lakeland	.956	8	18	25	2	5
Mengel, Dunedin	.966	53	132	151	10	34
Miller, Dunedin	.980	12	13	36	1	6
Montalvo, Dunedin	.972	18	28	41	2	13
Neitzel, Clearwater	.977	98	151	229	9	55
Newkirk, Charlotte	.965	59	105	142	9	37
Parese, Dunedin	.953	60	118	145	13	34
Paulsen, Clearwater	.971	9	13	20	1	4
Ramirez, West Palm Beach	.986	82	134	230	5	42
Renteria, Osceola	.957	35	49	83	6	14
Richison, Osceola	1.000	1	2	2	0	0
Roa, Miami	.984	56	96	145	4	34
Rose, Sarasota	1.000	2	4	9	0	0
Russell, Baseball City	.965	62	119	156	10	35
Saunders, St. Lucie	.986	54	113	163	4	34
Sawkiw, Lakeland	.907	40	66	70	14	17
Schmidt, Winter Haven	.966	60	93	164	9	23
Shave, Charlotte	.977	21	44	42	2	10
Simons, West Palm Beach	1.000	12	20	14	0	4
Surane, Miami	.987	52	106	115	3	19
Tatarian, Sarasota	.970	23	22	43	2	5
Tollison, Dunedin	1.000	1	1	0	0	0
Trevino, Clearwater	1.000	1	0	1	0	0
Trujillo, St. Petersburg	.980	9	21	27	1	5
Urcioli, Miami	.973	21	26	45	2	11
Van Scoyoc, Fort Lauderdale	.984	17	23	37	1	6
Vargas, St. Petersburg	1.000	4	4	3	0	2
Vazquez, Baseball City	.981	80	142	212	7	45
Wolak, Sarasota	.837	15	9	27	7	4

THIRD BASEMEN

Player, Team	Pct.	G	PO	A	E	DP
Allison, St. Lucie	.750	1	0	3	1	0
Anglero, Lakeland	.934	65	41	142	13	8
Ball, Osceola	.901	108	62	183	27	23
Blackwell, Fort Lauderdale	1.000	1	1	0	0	0
Blanco, Vero Beach	1.000	3	5	3	0	0
Bournigal, Vero Beach	1.000	5	1	6	0	0
Bradbury, Miami	1.000	2	1	2	0	0
Brady, Clearwater	.866	76	53	102	24	12
Butterfield, St. Lucie	.929	108	88	240	25	16
Campas, St. Petersburg	.950	17	12	26	2	2
Caraballo, Baseball City	.919	50	43	105	13	8
Clinton, Charlotte	.833	6	2	3	1	0
Coleman, Sarasota	.893	16	6	19	3	0
D'Alexander, Miami	.924	94	78	166	20	23
Davis, Winter Haven	.905	16	5	14	2	0
Doffek, Vero Beach	.900	29	10	35	5	1
Ebel, Vero Beach	1.000	7	0	6	0	1
Escobar, Clearwater	.941	41	28	52	5	4
Evangelista, Charlotte	.909	7	1	9	1	1
Fanning, St. Petersburg	.884	35	29	70	13	5
Fermin, Lakeland	1.000	2	0	1	0	0
Garner, Charlotte	.857	4	2	4	1	1
Grant, Winter Haven	.965	66	53	86	5	9
Greene, West Palm Beach	.891	90	71	182	31	19
Hajek, Osceola	.833	3	1	4	1	0
Harris, St. Lucie	1.000	1	0	1	0	0
Hiatt, Baseball City	.946	76	65	146	12	17
Howard, Lakeland	.846	12	4	18	4	1
Johnson, Fort Lauderdale	.500	2	0	1	1	0

FLORIDA STATE LEAGUE · CLASS A · FLORIDA STATE LEAGUE

Player, Team	Pct.	G	PO	A	E	DP
Lukachyk, Sarasota	.923	10	3	9	1	0
MacArthur, St. Petersburg	1.000	1	1	0	0	0
Maldonado, Lakeland	.970	14	4	28	1	1
Malzone, Winter Haven	.937	67	42	76	8	9
Marigny, Lakeland	.927	47	26	89	9	10
McCray, Sarasota	1.000	1	0	1	0	0
McDonald, West Palm Beach	.882	46	23	82	14	6
Mendenhall, Lakeland	1.000	1	0	1	0	0
Mengel, Dunedin	.987	30	22	56	1	1
Montalvo, Dunedin	.893	8	8	17	3	0
Morrisette, 9 Mia.-8 St.L.	.857	17	17	31	8	6
Newkirk, Charlotte	.920	38	23	57	7	7
Noriega, Fort Lauderdale	.918	123	87	204	26	21
O'DONNELL, Vero Beach	.953	105	77	189	13	23
Ochs, St. Petersburg	.892	55	31	118	18	5
Oliva, Charlotte	.940	91	79	154	15	15
Renteria, Osceola	.865	23	10	35	7	3
Richison, Osceola	1.000	2	0	2	0	0
Rose, Sarasota	.917	95	65	166	21	12
Russell, Baseball City	.882	5	6	9	2	1
Saenz, Sarasota	.842	5	5	11	3	0
Sanchez, West Palm Beach	.667	3	0	4	2	0
Saunders, St. Lucie	.872	16	11	30	6	2
Smith, Sarasota	.946	15	9	26	2	1
Tatarian, Sarasota	.909	9	4	6	1	0
Tollison, Dunedin	.932	99	64	169	17	8
Trevino, Clearwater	.925	25	19	43	5	4
Trujillo, St. Petersburg	.930	20	16	24	3	4
Urcioli, Miami	.916	33	21	55	7	2
Van Scoyoc, Fort Lauderdale	1.000	5	0	6	0	0
Vargas, St. Petersburg	1.000	7	6	11	0	0
Wolak, Sarasota	1.000	1	0	2	0	0

SHORTSTOPS

Player, Team	Pct.	G	PO	A	E	DP
Allison, St. Lucie	.938	9	13	32	3	8
Anglero, Lakeland	.933	22	35	62	7	15
Beanblossom, St. Petersburg	.927	14	22	29	4	9
Berry, Osceola	1.000	4	1	3	0	0
Blackwell, Fort Lauderdale	.857	5	4	14	3	2
Blanco, Vero Beach	1.000	1	1	1	0	0
Bournigal, Vero Beach	.987	17	28	50	1	10
R. Brown, Winter Haven	.933	52	90	148	17	28
Castleberry, Sarasota	.949	17	29	45	4	9
Clinton, Charlotte	.950	43	82	108	10	24
Coleman, Sarasota	.500	2	0	1	1	1
Colon, Charlotte	.932	65	118	157	20	39
Cromer, St. Petersburg	.986	43	79	134	3	32
Cruz, Dunedin	.953	64	103	204	15	34
Davis, Winter Haven	.923	11	12	24	3	4
Davison, West Palm Beach	.948	79	121	189	17	36
DeKneef, Winter Haven	.944	61	82	152	14	29
Diaz, St. Lucie	.933	41	62	106	12	15
Ebel, Vero Beach	.987	38	57	98	2	24
Escobar, Clearwater	1.000	10	5	12	0	3
Farmer, St. Lucie	1.000	1	0	4	0	0
Fermin, Lakeland	.909	4	2	8	1	1
Gaither, Sarasota	.857	4	6	6	2	2
Graham, Winter Haven	.923	8	7	17	2	6
Grant, Winter Haven	.902	15	10	27	4	3
Greene, West Palm Beach	.750	1	2	1	1	0
Hajek, Osceola	.929	4	4	9	1	3
Henderson, St. Lucie	.928	82	120	256	29	42
Howard, Vero Beach	1.000	6	0	2	0	0
Howard, Lakeland	1.000	1	1	2	0	0
Kellner, Osceola	.952	53	86	173	13	37
Kliafas, Vero Beach	.933	28	31	66	7	15
Krause, West Palm Beach	.961	52	81	143	9	18
Lansing, Miami	.941	99	144	272	26	54
Maldonado, Lakeland	.953	11	11	30	2	7
Marigny, Lakeland	.700	1	1	6	3	0
McCray, Sarasota	.857	4	0	6	1	0
McDonald, West Palm Beach	.882	4	5	10	2	1
McKamie, Vero Beach	.903	64	86	129	23	30
Mendenhall, Lakeland	.954	103	134	297	21	53
Mengel, Dunedin	.958	14	21	48	3	8
Miller, Osceola	.928	74	106	205	24	32
Millette, Clearwater	.963	18	27	51	3	7
Montalvo, Dunedin	.971	61	109	189	9	40
Morillo, Baseball City	.896	62	79	162	28	28
Neitzel, Clearwater	1.000	1	1	0	0	0
Noriega, Fort Lauderdale	1.000	1	1	0	0	0
Oliva, Charlotte	.000	1	0	0	1	0
PAULSEN, Clearwater	.965	108	160	311	17	79
Pimentel, St. Petersburg	.948	80	110	233	19	32
Ramirez, West Palm Beach	.879	4	12	17	4	6
Rijo, Vero Beach	1.000	1	0	1	0	0
Roa, Miami	.926	36	51	87	11	12
Rodriguez, Fort Lauderdale	.936	86	117	218	23	34
Russell, Baseball City	.914	35	45	93	13	15
Shave, Charlotte	.907	34	49	78	13	14
B. Stewart, Baseball City	.914	39	52	96	14	14
Tatarian, Sarasota	.778	10	8	6	4	2
Tejada, Sarasota	.932	109	159	277	32	48

Player, Team	Pct.	G	PO	A	E	DP
Urcioli, Miami	1.000	7	2	11	0	2
Van Scoyoc, Fort Lauderdale	.918	46	68	110	16	26

OUTFIELDERS

Player, Team	Pct.	G	PO	A	E	DP
Alicea, Miami	.982	79	156	6	3	2
Allison, St. Lucie	1.000	8	14	1	0	0
Andrews, Baseball City	1.000	5	7	0	0	0
Anglero, Lakeland	.914	20	30	2	3	1
Ashley, Vero Beach	1.000	27	39	1	0	0
Barnwell, Fort Lauderdale	.937	80	143	5	10	1
Barry, West Palm Beach	.968	110	200	14	7	0
B. Brown, Winter Haven	.967	46	80	8	3	3
Burton, Miami	.970	38	61	3	2	0
Butterfield, St. Lucie	.917	5	10	1	1	0
Cabrera, Lakeland	.993	72	144	4	1	3
Cameron, St. Lucie	.968	68	88	4	3	0
Campas, St. Petersburg	1.000	4	4	1	0	0
Carvajal, Fort Lauderdale	.983	117	223	13	4	4
Cepicky, Sarasota	1.000	3	3	0	0	0
Clinton, Charlotte	.905	7	19	0	2	0
Cole, Baseball City	.938	21	44	1	3	0
Cornelius, Lakeland	.944	97	161	9	10	0
Curtis, Osceola*	.967	36	57	2	2	0
Dallas, Osceola	.952	84	116	2	6	1
Davis, St. Lucie	.973	18	35	1	1	1
Davis, Winter Haven	1.000	4	1	0	0	0
Davison, West Palm Beach	1.000	1	1	0	0	0
DeKneef, Winter Haven	1.000	4	4	1	0	0
Demerson, Fort Lauderdale	.977	32	43	0	1	0
Dukes, Winter Haven	.941	56	78	2	5	1
Durkin, West Palm Beach	.964	23	26	1	1	1
Evangelista, Charlotte	1.000	1	1	0	0	0
Gale, St. Petersburg	1.000	8	23	0	0	0
Garland, Fort Lauderdale	.955	40	62	1	3	0
Garner, Charlotte	1.000	4	9	0	0	0
Gilcrist, Baseball City	.975	119	225	13	6	4
Gonzales, St. Petersburg	1.000	8	12	1	0	1
Goodale, Lakeland	.974	24	36	1	1	0
Grant, Winter Haven	1.000	5	4	0	0	0
Green, Lakeland	1.000	11	13	0	0	0
Greer, Charlotte*	.966	96	158	11	6	1
M. Griffin, Vero Beach	.981	108	201	10	4	3
Hairston, Sarasota	1.000	18	17	0	0	0
Hajek, Osceola	.983	42	52	5	1	0
Harris, Sarasota	.985	71	127	4	2	1
Hartwig, Clearwater	1.000	3	5	1	0	0
Hayden, Miami	.964	116	220	20	9	2
Hennessey, Baseball City	.963	46	73	5	3	3
Herrera, St. Petersburg	.991	120	314	21	3	7
Hodge, Dunedin	.948	65	91	1	5	0
Holtzclaw, Dunedin*	.902	58	104	6	12	1
Howard, St. Lucie	.975	33	38	1	1	0
Howell, St. Lucie	1.000	62	139	8	0	1
Hulse, Charlotte*	.978	71	129	6	3	1
Hunter, Osceola	.966	117	250	7	9	4
Hyde, Clearwater	.986	43	64	4	1	0
Jenkins, Winter Haven	.951	73	171	4	9	0
Luth. Johnson, Osceola*	.974	37	36	2	1	1
Jones, Clearwater	1.000	5	3	0	0	0
Kidd, Miami*	.995	101	200	8	1	2
Lake, West Palm Beach	.977	45	81	4	2	1
Leach, Fort Lauderdale*	.981	121	253	9	5	3
Ledinsky, Miami	.905	10	19	0	2	0
Lewis, St. Petersburg*	.988	121	240	13	3	4
Lora, Winter Haven	1.000	8	10	0	0	0
Lukachyk, Sarasota	.979	102	171	12	4	2
MacArthur, Miami	.987	42	74	3	1	0
Malzone, Winter Haven	1.000	4	6	1	0	0
Massarelli, Osceola	.961	27	48	1	2	1
Mayo, West Palm Beach*	.985	74	129	2	2	0
McMURRAY, Vero Beach	1.000	97	152	9	0	1
McNamara, Lakeland	.980	53	88	8	2	3
Mengel, Dunedin	1.000	2	1	0	0	0
Moore, Baseball City	.987	130	306	2	4	0
Morrisette, 17 Mia.-51 St.L.	.959	68	109	8	5	1
Morrison, Winter Haven	.967	98	166	10	6	2
Morrow, Vero Beach*	.976	66	121	2	3	1
Morrow, Charlotte	.989	116	267	9	3	4
Mota, Osceola	1.000	17	20	2	0	0
Myers, Baseball City*	1.000	2	4	0	0	0
Neitzel, Clearwater	1.000	1	1	0	0	0
Newkirk, Charlotte	.923	10	10	2	1	1
Niethammer, Charlotte	1.000	5	7	0	0	0
Nuneviller, Clearwater	.995	122	174	8	1	1
Nunez, St. Petersburg	1.000	2	6	0	0	0
Ochs, St. Petersburg	.833	11	9	1	2	1
Parker, Clearwater	1.000	4	1	0	0	0
Pemberton, Lakeland	.955	105	184	9	9	1
Perez, Dunedin	.971	97	160	10	5	1
Plemmons, Sarasota	.990	100	188	8	2	2
Powell, Charlotte	.973	96	137	9	4	2
Pride, St. Lucie	.981	109	199	5	4	1
Ramirez, West Palm Beach	1.000	1	2	0	0	0

Player, Team	Pct.	G	PO	A	E	DP
Rappoli, Winter Haven	1.000	3	3	0	0	0
Ricker, West Palm Beach	.991	97	205	11	2	1
Riesgo, West Palm Beach	1.000	2	3	0	0	0
Rijo, Vero Beach	.986	76	136	8	2	3
Rivers, Winter Haven	.965	60	77	6	3	1
Rodgers, Osceola	.959	41	66	5	3	0
Roman, Osceola	1.000	6	6	1	0	0
Sanchez, West Palm Beach	1.000	1	2	0	0	0
Savinon, St. Petersburg	1.000	15	46	0	0	0
Sawkiw, Lakeland	1.000	2	1	0	0	0
Scott, Dunedin	.966	73	161	7	6	2
Shields, Baseball City	.979	101	181	5	4	1
Smith, Vero Beach	.944	45	81	4	5	1
A. Stewart, Baseball City	1.000	1	1	0	0	0
Strickland, Fort Lauderdale	1.000	8	10	3	0	2
Sullivan, Sarasota	.962	24	46	4	2	3
Surane, Miami	1.000	7	10	1	0	0
Taylor, Clearwater*	.981	90	154	5	3	0
Tedder, Sarasota*	.983	36	58	1	1	0
Texidor, Charlotte	1.000	12	20	1	0	0
J. Thomas, St. Petersburg	.986	115	201	6	3	2
Thomas, St. Lucie	.979	61	86	6	2	1
Torres, St. Petersburg	1.000	6	2	0	0	0
Urbon, Clearwater*	.914	20	30	2	3	0
Vazquez, Baseball City	1.000	1	1	0	0	0
Ventress, Clearwater	.978	121	262	10	6	2
Wardwell, Winter Haven	1.000	64	115	2	0	0
Wilson, Dunedin*	.962	107	196	7	8	3
Wolak, Sarasota	.954	92	156	9	8	3
Woodruff, Lakeland	1.000	32	67	1	0	0
Woods, West Palm Beach	.957	74	85	5	4	0

CATCHERS

Player, Team	Pct.	G	PO	A	E	DP	PB
Agostinelli, Clearwater	.982	22	145	18	3	6	2
Albright, Lakeland	.982	59	393	39	8	4	7
Alvarez, Sarasota	.990	69	408	77	5	3	4
Angotti, Osceola	1.000	2	5	2	0	0	0
Avent, Clearwater	.857	4	6	0	1	0	0
Bell, Osceola	.983	9	56	2	1	0	1
Beuerlein, Osceola	.985	19	120	14	2	1	7
Bradbury, Miami	.990	90	594	71	7	8	9
Bradish, Sarasota	1.000	1	2	0	0	0	0
Brooks, Dunedin	.985	46	286	51	5	4	6
Brown, Vero Beach	.991	28	182	28	2	1	3
Carroll, St. Lucie	.973	35	202	15	6	2	5
Cramer, West Palm Beach	1.000	15	52	8	0	0	1
Current, Clearwater	.987	19	126	22	2	2	2
Demus, Winter Haven	.956	38	179	18	9	4	12
Dorante, Winter Haven	.988	24	140	20	2	4	2
Dukes, Winter Haven	1.000	5	11	0	0	2	5
Dziadkowiec, Miami	.973	25	169	14	5	2	2
ELLIS, St. Petersburg	.991	113	653	77	7	10	10
Fordyce, St. Lucie	.982	102	630	87	13	3	15
Garcia, Dunedin	.970	23	147	16	5	0	6
Gay, Sarasota	1.000	2	15	2	0	0	0
Gillette, Lakeland	.991	17	99	16	1	1	3
Gonzalez, Vero Beach	.977	67	468	42	12	5	12
Grant, Winter Haven	1.000	3	13	2	0	0	2
Hall, Miami	.973	25	126	16	4	2	6
Harmes, Dunedin	.989	12	82	12	1	0	4
Hartwig, Clearwater	1.000	1	1	0	0	0	1
Hatteberg, Winter Haven	.983	45	261	35	5	4	9
Henderson, Clearwater	1.000	1	1	0	0	0	0
Hirsch, West Palm Beach	.943	15	82	18	6	0	0
Jennings, Baseball City	1.000	10	63	7	0	0	1
Johnson, Fort Lauderdale	.985	97	654	54	11	8	16
Kennedy, Charlotte	.971	21	151	15	5	3	1
Kinyoun, Baseball City	.981	22	94	10	2	3	2
Kobza, Sarasota	.991	61	312	28	3	4	17
Laker, West Palm Beach	.979	97	560	87	14	4	14
Langiotti, St. Petersburg	.992	30	122	10	1	1	2
Lentz, Winter Haven	1.000	1	8	1	0	0	0
Lieberthal, Clearwater	.993	14	128	9	1	0	1
Madril, Winter Haven	.917	7	18	4	2	0	3
Manning, Sarasota	1.000	13	60	7	0	1	0
A. Martinez, Dunedin	.978	12	82	9	2	0	4
H. Martinez, Dunedin	1.000	6	26	3	0	0	3
Massarelli, Osceola	.987	18	130	21	2	1	4
Matilla, Winter Haven	.969	24	157	28	6	1	6
McGough, Sarasota	1.000	7	40	4	0	2	1
McMullen, Fort Lauderdale	.979	12	87	6	2	1	6
Monzon, Dunedin	.986	39	181	31	3	3	3
Niethammer, Charlotte	.984	44	274	34	5	3	10
Noce, West Palm Beach	1.000	5	12	1	0	0	0
Nunez, Sarasota	.967	15	79	8	3	0	1
O'Halloran, Dunedin	1.000	4	21	4	0	0	0
Ochs, St. Petersburg	1.000	5	8	0	0	0	0
Ortiz, Vero Beach	.974	33	238	28	7	0	7
Pineda, Fort Lauderdale	1.000	1	1	0	0	0	0
Piskor, Baseball City	1.000	4	19	1	0	0	1
Reyes, Charlotte	.958	6	21	2	1	0	1
Ryan, Baseball City	.978	75	387	52	10	5	15
Sanchez, West Palm Beach	.991	21	95	11	1	0	3

Player, Team	Pct.	G	PO	A	E	DP	PB
Scott, Osceola	.988	89	583	88	8	8	8
Sellers, Lakeland	.987	57	356	33	5	3	8
Solseth, Baseball City	1.000	3	8	0	0	0	0
A. Stewart, Baseball City	.996	42	221	40	1	1	4
Tackett, Winter Haven	1.000	7	56	1	0	0	2
Tannahill, Charlotte	.985	12	58	7	1	1	2
Teel, Vero Beach	.981	11	46	5	1	2	0
Tejada, Clearwater	1.000	1	7	2	0	0	0
Tewell, Clearwater	.979	80	511	55	12	7	6
O. Thomas, St. Petersburg	1.000	7	44	2	0	1	0
Vargas, Clearwater	1.000	3	8	1	0	0	0
Walker, Fort Lauderdale	.977	24	153	16	4	2	4
Wedge, Winter Haven	1.000	4	17	2	0	1	2
Williams, Vero Beach	1.000	5	23	1	0	0	2
Wilson, Lakeland	.917	6	11	0	1	0	0
Winford, Charlotte	.983	62	401	50	8	4	16

PITCHERS

Player, Team	Pct.	G	PO	A	E	DP
Adamson, Clearwater*	.909	5	1	9	1	1
Ahern, Baseball City	.950	13	3	16	1	0
Alberro, Charlotte	1.000	5	0	1	0	0
Allen, Winter Haven	1.000	27	9	15	0	0
Arner, Charlotte	.949	24	10	27	2	3
Asche, Miami*	.966	28	10	18	1	3
Astacio, Vero Beach	.909	9	7	13	2	2
E. Baker, St. Petersburg	.857	38	3	9	2	3
S. Baker, St. Petersburg*	1.000	19	3	11	0	3
Barnes, West Palm Beach*	1.000	2	1	2	0	0
Batchelor, Fort Lauderdale	.900	50	2	16	2	1
Baumann, Vero Beach	.750	12	1	2	1	0
Bautista, Miami	.905	11	5	14	2	1
Baxter, West Palm Beach*	1.000	1	0	1	0	0
Bene, Vero Beach	.600	31	1	5	4	1
Berumen, Baseball City	1.000	7	3	4	0	0
Biberdorf, Vero Beach	1.000	33	2	8	0	0
Bickhardt, Charlotte	.875	54	8	13	3	1
Bochtler, West Palm Beach	.918	26	17	28	4	2
Bohanon, Charlotte*	1.000	2	1	1	0	0
Bolton, Sarasota	.893	15	6	19	3	1
Brady, Vero Beach*	1.000	37	1	9	0	1
Brady, St. Lucie	1.000	8	2	1	0	0
Braley, Lakeland	1.000	61	5	14	0	0
Brink, Clearwater	1.000	2	0	2	0	1
Brosnan, Vero Beach*	.571	11	0	4	3	0
Brow, Dunedin	.969	16	8	23	1	3
D. Brown, Dunedin	1.000	28	11	11	0	1
P. Brown, Winter Haven*	.933	35	4	10	1	2
T. Brown, Dunedin	.900	31	11	16	3	1
Brutcher, Sarasota	.900	24	10	8	2	0
Buckley, Charlotte	.946	28	8	27	2	0
Bushing, West Palm Beach	.875	46	6	8	2	0
Calhoun, Vero Beach	1.000	27	4	9	0	0
Campbell, Baseball City*	1.000	11	3	4	0	0
Canestro, Fort Lauderdale*	1.000	21	3	14	0	2
CASSIDY, St. Petersburg*	1.000	21	13	51	0	1
Centala, Baseball City	.667	3	1	1	1	0
Chambers, Sarasota	1.000	2	1	0	0	0
Chavez, Baseball City	1.000	7	0	1	0	0
Coleman, Vero Beach	1.000	12	2	5	0	0
Collins, West Palm Beach	.957	27	13	32	2	2
Conner, Baseball City	1.000	15	2	4	0	0
Cook, Lakeland*	.813	29	3	10	3	0
Cormier, West Palm Beach	.800	5	1	3	1	0
Cornelius, West Palm Beach	.935	17	7	22	2	1
Corona, St. Petersburg*	1.000	15	2	3	0	0
Cortes, Sarasota	1.000	5	1	7	0	0
Costello, Osceola	1.000	5	1	0	0	0
Cox, Clearwater	1.000	3	1	0	0	0
Dabney, Sarasota*	.909	26	5	15	2	0
Davis, West Palm Beach	1.000	22	1	3	0	0
Davis, Winter Haven	1.000	1	0	1	0	0
Diaz, Baseball City*	.750	9	1	2	1	0
Dixon, St. Petersburg*	.944	53	1	16	1	0
Dopson, Winter Haven	1.000	6	0	3	0	0
Dorn, St. Lucie	.875	48	7	14	3	1
Douma, St. Lucie*	.969	17	5	26	1	1
Drell, Lakeland	.867	28	5	21	4	1
Duey, Dunedin	1.000	9	1	2	0	0
Dukes, Winter Haven	1.000	4	1	1	0	1
Dunn, Baseball City	.000	5	0	0	1	0
Eddy, West Palm Beach	1.000	13	1	11	0	4
Eischen, 18 Char.-8 W.P.B.*	.882	26	9	21	4	3
Elliott, Clearwater	1.000	18	6	8	0	0
Ericson, Miami	1.000	8	1	3	0	0
Ettles, Lakeland	1.000	8	1	3	0	0
Faccio, St. Petersburg	1.000	8	2	8	0	1
Farmer, Osceola	.944	17	3	14	1	0
Felix, Charlotte*	.900	29	5	31	4	0
Ferm, Miami	1.000	17	4	11	0	0
Fletcher, Clearwater	1.000	14	2	3	0	0
Freeman, Vero Beach	.900	25	12	15	3	1
Freitas, St. Lucie	1.000	5	0	3	0	0
Fritz, Miami	1.000	14	1	0	0	0
Gaddy, Clearwater*	.818	34	4	5	2	0

Player, Team	Pct.	G	PO	A	E	DP
Galvan, Sarasota*	1.000	14	1	1	0	0
Ganote, Dunedin	.857	4	2	4	1	0
Garcia, Lakeland	.941	25	5	11	1	0
Gideon, West Palm Beach	1.000	4	0	1	0	0
Goedhart, Clearwater	.900	25	6	12	2	0
Goetz, Charlotte	1.000	46	4	8	0	0
Gonzales, Lakeland*	.927	25	6	32	3	3
Gordon, Baseball City*	1.000	19	2	2	0	0
Gorton, St. Petersburg	1.000	53	7	11	0	0
Gray, Clearwater	.829	20	9	20	6	2
Green, St. Petersburg	.967	26	9	20	1	0
Green, Clearwater	1.000	2	1	4	0	1
Greer, Fort Lauderdale	1.000	31	1	10	0	1
Griffiths, Osceola	1.000	18	2	8	0	0
Gross, Baseball City	.929	17	3	10	1	2
Grovom, Osceola	.923	15	2	10	1	0
Gutierrez, Baseball City	1.000	1	0	1	0	0
Harriger, St. Lucie	.957	14	11	11	1	0
Harris, Baseball City	.944	19	4	13	1	0
Harvey, Baseball City	.923	13	5	7	1	0
Haslock, Miami	1.000	20	2	6	0	0
Henry, Lakeland*	1.000	6	1	1	0	0
Hill, St. Lucie*	1.000	6	3	8	0	0
Hinkle, St. Petersburg	.500	1	0	1	1	0
Hoey, Sarasota	1.000	4	0	1	0	0
Hoffman, Vero Beach*	.333	5	0	1	2	0
Holdridge, Clearwater	1.000	15	1	3	0	0
Hopper, Baseball City	.875	19	5	2	1	0
Hotchkiss, Dunedin	.857	15	4	8	2	0
Hurst, Clearwater	.929	22	3	10	1	2
Hurst, Miami	1.000	15	8	9	0	0
Hutton, Fort Lauderdale	.912	24	7	24	3	0
Hyson, Osceola	.920	25	8	15	2	1
Jacobs, Baseball City	1.000	19	4	4	0	0
Johnson, Sarasota*	.944	51	5	12	1	2
Johnson, Winter Haven	1.000	7	1	4	0	0
Lee Johnson, Osceola	.824	34	4	10	3	1
Jones, Vero Beach	1.000	9	3	9	0	1
Jones, Osceola	1.000	14	4	13	0	1
Kaiser, Osceola	1.000	7	1	1	0	1
Karchner, Baseball City	.900	38	5	13	2	0
Kerfut, Miami	.929	34	6	7	1	0
Keyser, Sarasota	.902	27	7	30	4	3
Kilgo, West Palm Beach*	1.000	33	6	24	0	2
Kistaitis, Dunedin*	1.000	1	1	0	0	0
Kite, Winter Haven	.905	29	5	14	2	1
Kizziah, Dunedin	.947	34	3	15	1	2
Klancnik, Miami	.625	21	1	4	3	0
Klvac, Winter Haven*	1.000	1	1	0	0	0
Krumm, Lakeland	1.000	7	5	5	0	0
Langbehn, St. Lucie*	.968	27	19	41	2	0
Langley, 23 Mia. - 18 Clear.*	.882	41	5	10	2	2
Lata, St. Petersburg	1.000	10	0	3	0	0
Leimeister, Lakeland	1.000	35	5	2	0	0
Leiter, Dunedin*	1.000	4	0	1	0	0
Lemon, Miami	1.000	10	3	1	0	0
Lima, Lakeland	1.000	4	1	1	0	0
Limbach, Clearwater*	1.000	39	2	6	0	0
Lindsey, Clearwater	1.000	6	2	5	0	0
Lloyd, Dunedin*	.962	50	4	21	1	1
Logan, West Palm Beach	.961	24	19	30	2	2
Long, Baseball City*	.963	47	6	20	1	0
Luckham, Osceola	.956	27	17	26	2	0
Lumley, Lakeland	.929	43	4	9	1	2
Maietta, Winter Haven	1.000	3	1	0	0	0
Maldonado, Lakeland	1.000	2	0	1	0	0
Maldonado, Charlotte	1.000	46	6	10	0	2
Malone, Clearwater	.800	10	1	7	2	0
Malone, Fort Lauderdale*	1.000	6	1	1	0	0
Maloney, Winter Haven*	1.000	16	2	5	0	2
Malzone, Winter Haven	1.000	6	0	1	0	1
Manon, Fort Lauderdale	.967	26	11	18	1	0
Marcero, Lakeland*	1.000	2	1	0	0	0
Marris, Fort Lauderdale*	.929	24	5	8	1	0
Martin, Dunedin	1.000	13	1	6	0	0
Matznick, Sarasota	.955	26	14	28	2	2
McCann, St. Lucie	.941	34	4	12	1	2
McCormick, Baseball City*	1.000	17	0	5	0	0
McCray, Charlotte*	1.000	2	0	3	0	0
Menhart, Dunedin	.938	20	12	18	2	1
Michno, Miami	.898	29	20	33	6	3
Mimbs, Vero Beach*	.969	24	6	25	1	2
Minchey, Miami	.933	13	5	9	1	0
Mitchelson, Winter Haven*	1.000	14	4	15	0	0
Mongiello, Sarasota	1.000	55	7	17	0	0
Moore, Dunedin	.923	27	11	25	3	0
Morman, Clearwater*	1.000	3	0	1	0	0
Moya, West Palm Beach	.833	19	11	9	4	1
Munoz, Fort Lauderdale	.919	19	7	27	3	1
Nielsen, Fort Lauderdale*	.867	42	4	9	2	1
Niethammer, Charlotte	1.000	1	0	1	0	0
Niles, Winter Haven	1.000	25	7	8	0	0
Ogliaruso, Dunedin	.875	22	10	18	4	1
Oliver, Charlotte*	1.000	2	1	0	0	0
Ozuna, St. Petersburg	1.000	31	6	5	0	1
Painter, Winter Haven	.895	9	7	10	2	2
Parris, Clearwater	.971	43	7	27	1	7
Patrick, Vero Beach*	.964	22	5	22	1	1
Phillips, Osceola	1.000	44	6	7	0	1
Polak, Fort Lauderdale	.923	40	1	11	1	1
Polasek, West Palm Beach*	1.000	52	7	22	0	1
Pollard, Baseball City	1.000	13	1	6	0	1
Ponte, Osceola	.846	47	1	10	2	0
Powers, Winter Haven	.952	25	7	13	1	2
Proctor, St. Lucie	1.000	6	2	4	0	0
Prybylinski, Fort Lauderdale	.818	13	3	6	2	0
Quero, Charlotte*	.926	34	5	20	2	0
Ramos, Lakeland*	1.000	12	2	5	0	0
Randle, Charlotte	.963	29	11	15	1	2
Reed, Miami*	1.000	10	2	3	0	0
Regira, West Palm Beach	1.000	12	2	4	0	0
Reich, St. Lucie	.882	54	14	16	4	1
Renko, West Palm Beach	1.000	4	1	2	0	0
Resnikoff, Osceola*	1.000	8	0	1	0	0
Reynolds, Sarasota	1.000	6	2	1	0	0
Ricker, West Palm Beach	.000	1	0	0	1	0
Rivera, Lakeland	1.000	14	1	4	0	0
Rogers, Miami*	.833	22	5	20	5	0
Rowley, Charlotte	1.000	8	3	8	0	1
Ruffin, Sarasota	.882	26	22	23	6	1
Rumer, Fort Lauderdale*	.951	24	7	32	2	0
Russo, Baseball City	1.000	15	2	2	0	0
Ryan, Winter Haven	1.000	21	2	11	0	1
Salvior, St. Petersburg	.917	38	4	7	1	0
Sample, St. Lucie	1.000	13	2	0	0	0
Sampson, Vero Beach	.929	30	2	11	1	2
Santamaria, Winter Haven	.950	45	7	12	1	2
Schmidt, West Palm Beach	1.000	9	1	0	0	0
Schwarber, Lakeland	1.000	8	1	6	0	0
Sebra, Osceola	1.000	5	1	0	0	0
Sele, Winter Haven	1.000	13	4	13	0	1
Shackle, St. Petersburg	.958	21	12	11	1	1
Shaw, Baseball City	.895	25	8	9	2	2
Shepherd, Sarasota	.917	18	5	6	1	1
Small, Dunedin	1.000	24	7	33	0	2
Small, Osceola	1.000	26	2	8	0	1
Smith, St. Petersburg	.909	20	4	6	1	0
Snedeker, Vero Beach	.923	17	8	16	2	3
Sohn, Vero Beach	1.000	1	0	2	0	0
Spencer, Charlotte	.889	38	5	3	1	0
Springer, Fort Lauderdale	1.000	25	14	17	0	2
Steiner, Charlotte*	.833	30	3	7	2	1
Stevens, Clearwater	1.000	38	4	4	0	0
Stevens, Sarasota	.806	35	7	18	6	0
Sullivan, Clearwater	.941	36	6	10	1	0
Taveras, Vero Beach	1.000	22	3	5	0	0
Thoden, West Palm Beach	1.000	12	5	15	0	1
Torres, Lakeland	1.000	42	2	7	0	0
Toth, Baseball City	.833	13	2	3	1	0
Tuss, West Palm Beach	1.000	49	2	11	0	1
Urbani, St. Petersburg*	.971	19	6	27	1	5
Vanegmond, Winter Haven	.933	13	5	9	1	0
Vasquez, St. Lucie	.929	56	8	5	1	0
Vazquez, St. Lucie	1.000	1	0	1	0	0
Vitko, St. Lucie	1.000	22	15	23	0	3
Walker, St. Lucie	.938	26	9	21	2	2
Wall, Osceola	.952	12	5	15	1	3
Wanish, Dunedin	1.000	36	7	14	0	1
Warren, Lakeland	.946	17	8	27	2	2
Washington, Charlotte	.818	12	3	6	2	1
Weber, St. Petersburg*	.929	18	1	12	1	0
Wegmann, St. Lucie	.900	13	4	5	1	0
Wells, Clearwater	.944	24	7	10	1	0
Wengert, Vero Beach	.933	30	12	16	2	2
Whitworth, Miami	.846	20	5	6	2	1
Wickman, Sarasota	.923	7	4	8	1	0
Wiley, Fort Lauderdale	1.000	4	1	0	0	0
Wiley, Baseball City	1.000	53	4	7	0	0
Wilkinson, West Palm Beach	.800	8	1	3	1	0
Williams, Osceola	.973	15	12	24	1	0
Williams, Miami*	.905	40	7	12	2	1
Williams, Clearwater	.966	14	9	19	1	1
Windes, Osceola*	1.000	45	4	19	0	0
Wolf, Lakeland	1.000	9	5	10	0	0
Young, Winter Haven	.964	28	11	16	1	0

The following players did not have any fielding statistics at the positions indicated or appeared only as a designated hitter, pinch-hitter or pinch-runner: Agostinelli, of; Albright, of; Anglero, p; Ansley, dh, ph; Bargas, 3b; Barnwell, 2b; E. Blackwell, ph, dh, pr; R. Brown, 3b, of; Butterfield, ss; Campas, 2b; Dayley, p; Degifico, dh, ph; Delgado, p; Demus, 1b; Doffek, of; Escobar, p; Fernandez, p; Garner, ss, p; Giordano, p; Gogolewski, p; T. Griffin, dh, ph; Hanks, dh, ph; D. Howell, of, p; Jackson, dh; Jenkins, 2b; Kite, of; Krause, of; Lohry, dh; Lukachyk, 2b; J. McCray, 1b; Morrison, p; J. Munoz, p; Newkirk, p; K. Nielsen, p; Niethammer, 3b; Noriega, of; Ochs, p; Owen, p; Radachowsky, c; Rendina, 2b; Renteria, 1b; J. Reyes, ph; David Schmidt (Winter Haven), 3b; Sieradzki, p; M. Sullivan, of; Surane, 3b; Taylor, p; Trujillo, p; Wiegandt, p.

LEAGUE CHAMPIONS

Year	Team	Pct.
1919—	Sanford*	.605
	Orlando*	.703
1920—	Tampa	.654
	Tampa	.722
1921—	Orlando	.635
1922—	St. Petersburg	.503
	St. Petersburg	.618
1923—	Orlando	.667
	Orlando	.678
1924—	Lakeland	.695
	Lakeland	.683
1925—	St. Petersburg	.667
	Tampa†	.696
1926—	Sanford	.647
	Sanford	.623
1927—	Orlando†	.600
	Miami	.661
1928-35—	Did not operate.	
1936—	Gainesville	.542
	St. Augustine (4th)†‡	.492
1937—	Gainesville§	.616
1938—	Leesburg	.626
	Gainesville (2nd)‡	.615
1939—	Sanford§	.787
1940—	Daytona Beach	.619
	Orlando (4th)‡	.507
1941—	St. Augustine	.659
	Leesburg (4th)‡	.488
1942-45—	Did not operate.	
1946—	Orlando§	.681
1947—	St. Augustine	.625
	Gainesville (2nd)‡	.584
1948—	Orlando	.643
	Daytona Beach (2nd)‡	.616
1949—	Gainesville	.635
	St. Augustine (3rd)‡	.556
1950—	Orlando	.629
	DeLand (3rd)‡	.590
1951—	DeLand§	.643
1952—	DeLand x	.704
	Palatka (3rd)‡	.569
1953—	Daytona Beach†	.657
	DeLand	.703
1954—	Jacksonville Beach	.629
	Lakeland†	.594
1955—	Orlando	.671
	Orlando	.643
1956—	Cocoa	.614
	Cocoa	.671
1957—	Palatka	.629
	Tampa†	.681
1958—	St. Petersburg	.732
	St. Petersburg	.681
1959—	Tampa	.591
	St. Petersburg†	.612
1960—	Lakeland	.731
	Palatka†	.614
1961—	Tampa†	.710
	Sarasota	.696
1962—	Sarasota	.689
	Fort Lauderdale†	.623
1963—	Sarasota	.645
	Sarasota	.667
1964—	Fort Lauderdale†	.629
	St. Petersburg	.594
1965—	Fort Lauderdale	.627
	Fort Lauderdale	.634
1966—	Leesburg†	.781
	St. Petersburg	.700
1967—	St. Petersburg y	.691
	Orlando	.638
1968—	Miami	.613
	Orlando z	.579
1969—	Miami a	.606
	Orlando	.606
1970—	Miami b	.662
	St. Petersburg	.600
1971—	Miami b	.667
	Daytona Beach	.586
1972—	Miami c	.562
	Daytona Beach	.606
1973—	St. Petersburg d	.575
	West Palm Beach	.580
1974—	West Palm Beach d	.598
	Fort Lauderdale	.626
1975—	St. Petersburg d	.652
	Miami	.581
1976—	Tampa	.559
	Lakeland d	.536
1977—	Lakeland d	.616
	West Palm Beach	.583
1978—	Lakeland	.565
	Miami§	.539
1979—	Fort Lauderdale	.643
	Winter Haven e	.577
1980—	Daytona Beach	.628
	Fort Lauderdale d	.606
1981—	Fort Myers	.554
	Daytona Beach f	.504
1982—	Fort Lauderdale f	.621
	Tampa	.546
1983—	Daytona Beach	.634
	Vero Beach f	.515
1984—	Tampa	.532
	Fort Lauderdale f	.521
1985—	Fort Myers g	.590
	Fort Lauderdale	.550
1986—	St. Petersburg g	.647
	West Palm Beach	.593
1987—	Fort Lauderdale g	.616
	Osceola	.576
1988—	Osceola	.606
	St. Lucie h	.532
1989—	Port Charlotte h	.540
	St. Petersburg	.540
1990—	West Palm Beach	.697
	Vero Beach h	.585
1991—	Clearwater	.623
	West Palm Beach h	.550

*Split-season playoff abandoned after each team won three games. †Won split-season playoff. ‡Won four-club playoff. §Won championship and four-club playoff. xWon both halves of split season. yLeague divided into Eastern and Western divisions with split season. St. Petersburg and Orlando won both halves of split season; St. Petersburg won playoff. zLeague divided into Eastern and Western divisions. Miami won regular-season pennant on basis of highest won-lost percentage. Orlando won four-club playoff involving first two teams in each division. aLeague divided into Southern and Central divisions. Miami won playoff between division leaders. (NOTE—Pennant awarded to playoff winner in 1936.) bLeague divided into Eastern and Western divisions. Miami won regular-season pennant on basis of highest won-loss percentage, and also won four-club playoff involving first two teams in each division. cLeague divided into Eastern and Western divisions. Won four-club playoff involving first two teams in each division. dLeague divided into Northern and Southern divisions. Won four-club playoff involving first two teams in each division. eLeague divided into Northern and Southern divisions. Same two clubs won both halves; won playoffs. fWon split-season playoff. gLeague divided into Western, Central and Southern divisions. Won four-club playoff. hLeague divided into Eastern, Western and Central divisions; played split-season. Won six-club playoff.

MIDWEST LEAGUE

FINAL STANDINGS

FIRST HALF

NORTHERN DIVISION

Team	W	L	T	Pct.	GB
Madison (Athletics)	39	29	0	.574	......
Rockford (Expos)	37	31	0	.544	2
Beloit (Brewers)	34	35	0	.493	5 ½
Appleton (Royals)	33	36	0	.478	6 ½
Kenosha (Twins)	32	37	0	.464	7 ½
South Bend (White Sox)	31	39	0	.443	9
Kane County (Orioles)	26	40	0	.394	12

SOUTHERN DIVISION

Team	W	L	T	Pct.	GB
Burlington (Braves)	41	26	0	.612	......
Quad City (Angels)	39	28	0	.582	2
Clinton (Giants)	38	31	0	.551	4
Cedar Rapids (Reds)	37	33	0	.529	5 ½
Waterloo (Padres)	34	34	0	.500	7 ½
Peoria (Cubs)	29	40	0	.420	13
Springfield (Cardinals)	28	39	0	.418	13

SECOND HALF

NORTHERN DIVISION

Team	W	L	T	Pct.	GB
Kane County (Orioles)	42	27	1	.609	......
Rockford (Expos)	39	30	0	.565	3
South Bend (White Sox)	38	31	0	.551	4
Madison (Athletics)	38	32	0	.543	4 ½
Beloit (Brewers)	36	32	0	.529	5 ½
Kenosha (Twins)	31	37	1	.456	10 ½
Appleton (Royals)	25	45	0	.357	17 ½

SOUTHERN DIVISION

Team	W	L	T	Pct.	GB
Clinton (Giants)	43	27	0	.614	......
Waterloo (Padres)	41	29	0	.586	2
Quad City (Angels)	35	35	0	.500	8
Peoria (Cubs)	33	36	0	.478	9 ½
Springfield (Cardinals)	30	40	0	.429	13
Cedar Rapids (Reds)	29	41	0	.414	14
Burlington (Braves)	26	44	0	.371	17

COMPOSITE

Team	Cln.	Mad.	Roc.	Wat.	Q.C.	Bel.	K.C.	S.B.	Bur.	C.R.	Ken.	Peo.	Spr.	App.	W	L	T	Pct.	GB
Clinton (Giants)	....	4	4	11	5	6	5	6	10	9	5	8	4	4	81	58	0	.583	......
Madison (Athletics)	4	....	6	4	4	7	8	5	3	6	8	5	7	10	77	61	0	.558	3 ½
Rockford (Expos)	4	8	....	4	4	7	9	7	4	2	7	6	6	8	76	61	0	.555	4
Waterloo (Padres)	3	4	4	....	7	4	3	7	9	8	4	11	7	4	75	63	0	.543	5 ½
Quad City (Angels)	9	2	4	7	....	5	5	4	7	5	8	6	9	3	74	63	0	.540	6
Beloit (Brewers)	2	7	7	4	3	....	7	6	6	5	5	3	5	10	70	67	0	.511	10
Kane County (Orioles)	3	6	4	4	3	7	....	6	5	4	6	7	5	8	68	67	1	.504	11
South Bend (White Sox)	2	5	9	7	1	4	7	8	....	3	4	7	3	5	69	70	0	.496	12
Burlington (Braves)	4	5	4	5	6	2	2	5	....	8	6	10	6	4	67	70	0	.489	13
Cedar Rapids (Reds)	5	2	6	6	9	3	4	4	6	....	5	7	7	2	66	74	0	.471	15 ½
Kenosha (Twins)	3	6	7	3	0	8	7	7	2	3	....	4	4	9	63	74	1	.460	17
Peoria (Cubs)	6	3	1	1	3	8	4	1	5	4	7	....	11	5	62	76	0	.449	18 ½
Springfield (Cardinals)	9	1	1	7	5	3	3	3	7	7	4	3	....	5	58	79	0	.423	22
Appleton (Royals)	4	4	6	4	5	4	5	5	4	6	5	3	3	....	58	81	0	.417	23

Kane County's home games played in Geneva, Ill.

Quad City's home games played in Davenport, Ia.

Major league affiliations in parentheses.

Playoffs—Madison defeated Kane County, two games to none; Clinton defeated Burlington, two games to none; Clinton defeated Madison, three games to none, to win league championship.

Regular-season attendance—Appleton, 72,601; Beloit, 77,487; Burlington, 81,811; Cedar Rapids, 132,820; Clinton, 83,943; Kane County, 240,290; Kenosha, 59,331; Madison, 92,663; Peoria, 212,159; Quad City, 242,322; Rockford, 66,524; South Bend, 221,071; Springfield, 175,017; Waterloo, 58,859. Total, 1,816,898. Playoffs (7 games), 12,633. All-Star Game, 2,993.

Managers—Appleton, Joe Breeden; Beloit, Bob Derksen; Burlington, Tim Tolman; Cedar Rapids, Frank Funk; Clinton, Jack Mull; Kane County, Bob Miscik; Kenosha, Joel Lepel; Madison, Gary Jones; Peoria, Bill Hayes; Quad City, Mitch Seone; Rockford, Pat Kelly (through June 2), Rich Dubee (June 3 through 4), Rob Leary (June 5 through end of season); South Bend, Tommy Thompson; Springfield, Mike Ramsey; Waterloo, Bryan Little. Managerial records of teams with more than one manager: Rockford, Kelly 27-21, Dubee 1-1, Leary 48-39.

All-Star team—1B—Roberto Arredondo, Waterloo; 2B—Fletcher Thompson, Burlington; 3B—Paul Russo, Kenosha; SS—Brandon Wilson, South Bend; OF—Darius Gash, Waterloo; Phil Dauphin, Peoria; Chris Hatcher, Burlington; C—Eric Christopherson, Clinton; DH—Jeff Kipila, Quad City; LHP—Lance Painter, Waterloo; RHP—Salomon Torres, Clinton; LH Rel—Wally Trice, Burlington; RH Rel—Rod Huffman, Clinton; Most Valuable Player—Salomon Torres, Clinton; Manager of the Year—Gary Jones, Madison.

BATTING

TEAM

Team	Avg.	G	AB	R	OR	H	TB	2B	3B	HR	RBI	SH	SF	HP	BB	Int. BB	SO	SB	CS	LOB
Madison	.258	138	4463	690	654	1152	1564	209	25	51	597	51	47	36	710	26	974	172	87	1091
Kane County	.256	136	4548	618	565	1163	1563	210	32	42	536	45	50	55	440	25	867	63	55	961
Waterloo	.254	138	4511	607	518	1148	1566	192	32	54	541	50	35	64	504	31	1026	123	62	993
Quad City	.249	137	4593	635	601	1143	1646	236	36	65	566	39	43	51	615	25	949	118	68	1094
Appleton	.249	139	4627	571	682	1150	1562	211	36	43	498	38	43	47	422	13	1004	159	73	989
Burlington	.248	137	4592	616	640	1138	1559	190	21	63	529	31	35	63	519	15	1033	121	65	1010
South Bend	.245	139	4546	567	576	1113	1472	190	38	31	478	77	38	51	499	24	1033	224	105	964
Beloit	.244	137	4422	616	577	1080	1504	192	17	59	504	62	38	50	608	31	1003	299	111	965
Peoria	.244	138	4581	577	678	1116	1609	225	20	76	499	51	34	67	516	28	955	91	50	1038
Kenosha	.243	138	4580	562	584	1114	1566	215	33	57	488	34	35	46	461	20	963	173	62	988
Clinton	.241	139	4456	596	465	1076	1483	177	40	50	513	63	42	63	570	26	1011	153	79	1016
Rockford	.241	137	4524	648	592	1090	1494	190	38	46	541	40	49	57	612	25	949	127	91	1037
Springfield	.238	137	4533	521	683	1078	1448	142	24	60	445	32	37	28	457	22	932	171	96	939
Cedar Rapids	.232	140	4546	584	593	1053	1463	179	21	63	510	29	48	45	576	20	951	159	64	993

INDIVIDUAL

(Leading qualifiers for batting championship—378 or more plate appearances)

*Bats lefthanded.   †Switch-hitter.

Player, Team	Avg.	G	AB	R	H	TB	2B	3B	HR	RBI	SH	SF	HP	BB	Int. BB	SO	SB	CS
Cummings, Midre, Kenosha†	.322	106	382	59	123	163	20	4	4	54	4	2	6	22	2	66	28	10
Wilson, Brandon, South Bend	.313	125	463	75	145	181	18	6	2	49	7	4	2	61	2	70	41	11
Gash, Darius, Waterloo†	.307	130	501	84	154	200	27	2	5	60	0	1	3	57	5	112	31	19
Coughlin, Kevin, South Bend*	.304	131	431	60	131	147	12	2	0	38	19	3	2	62	3	67	19	17
Murphy, Shaun, Rockford	.299	117	401	54	120	151	20	1	3	47	4	2	0	51	0	119	13	10
Dauphin, Phil, Peoria*	.296	120	426	74	126	196	27	5	11	49	4	7	4	72	9	66	15	7
Bish, Brent, Waterloo	.294	99	333	55	98	126	12	5	2	39	5	3	4	37	1	68	14	7
Henry, Scott, Madison*	.289	105	322	49	93	114	16	1	1	51	4	5	0	76	2	51	1	1
Singleton, Duane, Beloit*	.289	101	388	57	112	148	13	7	3	44	5	2	3	40	7	57	42	17
Sammons, Lee, Madison	.288	122	459	104	132	150	12	3	0	43	5	3	1	90	0	80	54	17

Departmental leaders: G—Burton, 134; AB—Burton, 531; R—Sammons, 104; H—Gash, 154; TB—Becker, 215; 2B—Becker, 38; 3B—Murray, 14; HR—Russo, 20; RBI—Russo, 100; SH—Coughlin, 19; SF—Russo, 10; HP—Weimerskirch, 19; BB—Hendley, Thompson, 104; IBB—Wilstead, 11; SO—Hatcher, 180; SB—Ozuna, 78; CS—Ozuna, 24.

(All players—listed alphabetically)

Player, Team	Avg.	G	AB	R	H	TB	2B	3B	HR	RBI	SH	SF	HP	BB	Int. BB	SO	SB	CS
Acta, Manny, Burlington	.257	78	276	27	71	93	14	1	2	35	0	3	3	16	0	40	0	1
Albert, Tim, Beloit*	.274	54	168	25	46	58	10	1	0	19	7	3	1	43	1	42	12	6
Anderson, Garret, Quad City*	.260	105	392	40	102	134	22	2	2	42	0	2	0	20	0	89	5	6
Anderson, Jonathan, Quad City	.190	26	63	8	12	16	2	1	0	6	2	0	2	7	0	12	0	0
Andrews, Jay, Appleton	.194	38	103	13	20	27	4	0	1	13	0	1	1	15	0	21	2	4
Andujar, Juan, Springfield†	.180	27	100	14	18	25	3	2	0	6	1	0	0	3	0	23	7	0
Arias, Amador, Cedar Rapids†	.186	21	59	5	11	13	0	1	0	4	0	0	1	4	0	14	7	3
Arland, Mark, Cedar Rapids	.160	36	100	18	16	24	5	0	1	9	1	0	1	16	0	46	5	2
Arredondo, Roberto, Waterloo*	.313	83	300	39	94	118	17	2	1	36	1	3	2	14	1	53	0	2
Audley, Jim, Kane County†	.260	70	289	50	75	94	3	5	2	27	2	2	4	32	2	53	4	4
Aversa, Joe, Springfield†	.234	78	184	19	43	48	2	0	1	14	5	0	0	43	0	37	5	6
Banton, Scott, Springfield	.167	82	186	27	31	45	2	3	2	13	2	0	1	43	3	41	6	7
Barbara, Don, Quad City*	.288	66	226	29	65	99	15	2	5	48	0	6	0	59	10	49	2	1
Beasley, Andy, Springfield*	.284	100	338	40	96	149	15	1	12	60	1	1	3	45	2	82	1	2
Beck, Wynn, Beloit*	.270	33	100	10	27	33	3	0	1	12	1	2	0	7	1	12	2	1
Becker, Rich, Kenosha†	.267	130	494	100	132	215	38	3	13	53	1	4	2	72	3	108	19	4
Beniquez, Juan, Appleton*	.400	5	10	0	4	4	0	0	0	0	0	0	0	4	0	2	1	0
Benjamin, Bobby, Beloit*	.260	107	338	60	88	148	19	1	13	58	1	5	3	93	3	95	20	8
Bennington, Jeff, Burlington	.185	36	92	7	17	25	5	0	1	6	1	2	2	7	0	20	0	1
Beuerlein, Ed, Burlington	.235	12	34	5	8	10	2	0	0	7	0	1	1	6	0	9	0	0
Bish, Brent, Waterloo	.294	99	333	55	98	126	12	5	2	39	5	3	4	37	1	68	14	7
Blakeman, Todd, Kenosha*	.205	113	381	27	78	101	14	3	1	40	2	2	4	30	3	92	2	3
Borgogno, Matt, Clinton*	.226	36	93	10	21	26	3	1	0	4	2	0	0	10	0	13	1	1
Brede, Brent, Kenosha*	.192	53	156	12	30	37	3	2	0	10	5	3	0	16	0	31	4	5
Brown, Alvin, Kenosha	.000	5	11	2	0	0	0	0	0	0	0	0	1	1	0	6	1	0
Bruno, Julio, Waterloo	.231	86	277	34	64	83	10	3	1	25	4	1	1	29	0	78	11	6
Bruno, Paul, Kenosha	.167	32	78	6	13	21	5	0	1	5	0	0	0	13	1	25	1	0
Burns, Michael, Burlington	.196	16	46	6	9	18	3	0	2	9	1	0	0	2	0	13	1	1
Burton, Darren, Appleton	.269	134	531	78	143	193	32	6	2	51	4	6	1	45	4	122	38	12
Byrne, Clayton, Kane County	.212	26	104	14	22	28	6	0	0	3	1	2	2	2	0	26	2	0
Cabrera, Juan, Beloit	.250	31	100	8	25	30	3	1	0	9	3	1	2	2	0	20	2	1
Calcagno, Dan, Clinton	.277	24	47	7	13	16	3	0	0	5	0	0	2	12	0	9	0	0
Callari, Ray, Rockford	.188	77	213	20	40	47	7	0	0	15	8	5	6	15	1	26	4	1
Calzado, Johnny, Springfield	.236	111	394	36	93	137	14	0	10	45	0	6	1	28	1	119	3	5
Cancel, Victor, Peoria	.219	105	342	45	75	100	17	1	2	28	3	4	7	37	2	92	22	10
Caraballo, Gary, Appleton	.251	79	275	39	69	93	16	1	2	44	0	7	7	34	0	33	13	1
Carlsen, Bob, Madison*	.311	92	299	57	93	121	23	1	1	54	3	5	0	67	1	38	5	2
Carter, Mike, Beloit	.279	123	452	62	126	164	24	4	2	40	2	3	4	26	5	42	46	13
Carter, Tim, Beloit	.229	113	385	51	88	150	13	2	15	64	3	4	10	47	3	125	10	5
Casper, Tim, Clinton†	.257	10	35	5	9	9	0	0	0	3	0	0	0	6	0	6	3	0
Cavazzoni, Ken, Cedar Rapids	.278	25	79	10	22	39	5	0	4	16	0	2	0	10	0	15	0	1
Cerda, Jose, Appleton	.224	44	143	17	32	45	7	0	2	18	2	1	3	18	2	37	0	2
Chavez, Raul, Burlington	.257	114	420	54	108	134	17	0	3	41	3	4	10	25	1	65	1	4
Christopherson, Eric, Clinton	.270	110	345	45	93	126	18	0	5	58	1	6	1	68	1	53	10	7
Christopherson, Gary, Burlington	.230	47	161	20	37	49	6	0	2	21	0	1	3	28	0	28	1	0
Ciesla, Ted, Rockford	.231	106	355	58	82	126	13	5	7	52	4	3	0	48	3	60	3	5
Clarke, Jeff, Appleton†	.227	81	242	25	55	66	7	2	0	14	3	3	1	19	2	37	5	8
Coffey, Stephen, Peoria	.167	11	30	2	5	5	0	0	0	0	0	0	0	1	0	10	0	1
Cohick, Emmitt, Quad City*	.274	112	350	52	96	169	22	9	11	53	2	3	5	56	3	97	8	4
Cole, Butch, Appleton	.237	53	190	20	45	61	7	0	3	24	0	1	2	8	1	27	10	5
Coleman, Ken, South Bend†	.346	8	26	5	9	10	1	0	0	4	1	0	0	4	0	4	0	0
Coleman, Paul, Springfield	.185	45	119	9	33	46	5	1	2	14	0	2	1	1	0	49	0	2
Cora, Joey, South Bend†	.200	1	5	1	1	1	0	0	0	0	0	0	0	0	0	0	0	0
Coss, Mike, Kane County	.182	3	11	1	2	2	0	0	0	0	0	0	1	0	0	1	0	0
Coughlin, Kevin, South Bend*	.304	131	431	60	131	147	12	2	0	38	19	3	2	62	3	67	19	17
Couture, Mike, Beloit	.333	1	3	0	1	1	0	0	0	0	0	0	0	0	0	0	0	0
Cox, Darron, Cedar Rapids	.267	21	60	12	16	20	4	0	0	4	1	0	4	9	0	11	7	1
Craig, Morris, Peoria*	.191	29	94	13	18	20	2	0	0	6	1	0	1	9	0	15	1	1
Cruz, Ruben, Burlington*	.278	114	418	49	116	163	15	4	8	59	1	3	3	26	1	64	4	1
Cummings, Midre, Kenosha†	.322	106	382	59	123	163	20	4	4	54	4	2	6	22	2	66	28	10
Cunningham, Earl, Peoria	.239	101	381	50	91	167	17	1	19	70	1	3	14	10	0	145	6	3
Dalesandro, Mark, Quad City	.273	125	487	63	133	181	17	3	8	69	0	4	6	34	1	58	1	7
Dauphin, Phil, Peoria*	.296	120	426	74	126	196	27	5	11	49	4	7	4	72	9	66	15	7
Davis, Allen, Kane County	.203	26	69	7	14	20	6	0	0	11	0	1	2	3	0	25	0	2
Davis, Courtney, Clinton	.196	56	143	22	28	40	4	1	2	12	3	0	3	23	0	49	11	3
Davis, Matt, Clinton†	.269	121	398	62	107	159	26	4	6	64	4	6	5	71	8	49	3	5
Davis, Nick, Burlington*	.187	55	171	26	32	52	6	1	4	19	0	1	0	32	0	65	1	0
Day, George, Appleton	.212	53	118	21	25	31	6	0	0	9	2	1	2	19	0	29	2	3
Dempsey, John, Springfield*	.180	36	100	3	18	24	1	1	1	7	1	0	2	5	0	22	0	2
Diaz, German, Peoria*	.252	105	317	36	80	102	12	2	2	23	7	1	4	41	4	80	7	2
Diaz, Steve, Beloit	.216	30	74	8	16	18	2	0	0	11	3	2	0	7	0	23	0	2
Diggs, Tony, Beloit†	.270	124	448	70	121	155	9	8	3	32	5	1	3	65	2	76	52	20
DiMarco, Steve, Kane County*	.252	37	107	10	27	32	5	0	0	13	1	1	0	9	0	21	1	2

Player, Team	Avg.	G	AB	R	H	TB	2B	3B	HR	RBI	SH	SF	HP	BB	Int. BB	SO	SB	CS
Dismuke, James, Cedar Rapids*	.254	133	492	56	125	186	35	1	8	72	2	9	4	50	3	80	4	2
Dodge, Thomas, Quad City†	.190	21	63	13	12	14	2	0	0	5	0	0	1	9	0	12	3	1
Donald, Tremayne, Springfield†	.250	77	292	36	73	83	8	1	0	22	3	3	1	34	1	45	38	15
Dotolo, Chris, Clinton	.125	3	8	2	1	2	1	0	0	1	0	1	0	0	0	2	0	0
Duffy, Darrin, Peoria	.200	8	25	1	5	5	0	0	0	3	0	1	2	3	0	4	1	3
Duncan, Andres, Clinton	.222	109	347	49	77	96	6	5	1	24	8	2	3	31	1	106	36	8
Duran, Ignacio, Springfield	.233	118	443	53	103	152	12	2	11	42	2	5	1	18	1	124	3	4
Durant, Mike, Kenosha	.203	66	217	27	44	60	10	0	2	20	2	1	3	25	0	35	20	5
Durkin, Marty, Rockford†	.000	4	8	2	0	0	0	0	0	0	1	0	1	0	0	4	0	0
Edwards, Mel, Waterloo*	.075	24	53	2	4	5	1	0	0	3	2	0	1	3	0	10	0	0
Edwards, Todd, Beloit*	.211	26	71	10	15	18	3	0	0	3	1	0	1	11	1	28	6	1
Elliott, Jim, Waterloo	.153	22	59	10	9	10	1	0	0	0	1	0	6	14	0	23	0	0
Enriquez, Graciano, Beloit†	.215	41	107	17	23	30	4	0	1	13	2	2	4	19	0	39	2	3
Erdman, Brad, Peoria	.254	83	280	33	71	104	19	1	4	26	8	1	3	32	1	59	5	0
Ettles, Mark, Waterloo	.500	14	2	0	1	1	0	0	0	0	0	0	0	0	0	0	0	0
Everly, David, Beloit	.250	2	4	1	1	2	1	0	0	1	0	0	0	2	0	3	1	1
Faneyte, Rikkert, Clinton	.255	107	384	73	98	144	14	7	6	52	3	4	9	61	1	106	18	11
Farlow, Kevin, Waterloo	.230	115	383	42	88	112	18	3	0	46	7	7	5	61	4	69	11	4
Farrell, Mike, Beloit*	.000	8	0	1	0	0	0	0	0	0	0	0	0	0	0	0	0	0
Fayne, Jeff, Springfield*	.245	78	241	23	59	74	12	0	1	24	2	1	2	31	4	56	5	2
Fernandez, Rolando, Peoria*	.281	108	302	35	85	100	9	0	2	40	2	1	2	50	6	34	2	5
Filotei, Bobby, Cedar Rapids	.216	102	328	44	71	83	5	2	1	20	4	6	2	48	1	89	13	7
Fitzpatrick, Rob, Rockford	.236	93	296	39	70	103	15	0	6	35	2	2	3	34	0	82	1	5
Flores, Juan, Beloit	.205	66	176	16	36	46	5	1	1	24	0	1	2	34	1	43	7	5
Flowers, Doug, Kane County*	.333	18	57	3	19	23	1	0	1	8	1	1	1	3	1	14	0	0
Forrester, Gary, Quad City	.150	10	20	1	3	3	0	0	0	2	2	0	0	2	0	7	0	0
Foster, Julio, South Bend	.188	28	85	7	16	18	0	0	1	5	1	0	0	5	0	22	4	4
Frias, Pedro, Clinton	.262	61	233	38	61	78	5	6	0	24	4	1	4	26	1	45	31	8
Friedland, Mike, Rockford	.087	12	46	3	4	4	0	0	0	2	0	0	0	5	1	18	1	2
Fuller, Jon, Cedar Rapids	.203	92	281	33	57	96	8	2	9	40	1	2	7	55	3	78	1	0
Gaither, Horace, South Bend*	.251	61	179	21	45	53	8	0	0	22	1	3	1	6	0	35	9	6
Gale, Bill, Springfield	.250	6	16	1	4	5	1	0	0	1	0	0	0	1	0	8	0	0
Garcia, Manuel, Kane County	.269	67	197	24	53	77	11	2	3	29	1	2	2	9	1	55	0	2
Gardner, Willie, Peoria	.143	9	21	2	3	4	1	0	0	0	1	0	0	0	0	11	0	0
Garrett, Clifton, Quad City*	.276	105	391	79	108	132	14	5	0	28	3	6	2	66	2	70	51	20
Gash, Darius, Waterloo†	.307	130	501	84	154	200	27	2	5	60	0	1	3	57	5	112	31	19
Gates, Brent, Madison†	.333	4	12	4	4	6	2	0	0	1	0	0	0	3	0	2	1	0
Gerald, Ed, Appleton	.244	101	348	49	85	141	15	10	7	46	3	4	2	49	1	107	18	2
Giegling, Matt, Cedar Rapids*	.206	48	107	3	22	27	2	0	1	10	0	0	0	14	2	26	1	2
Gil, Danny, Quad City	.103	14	39	2	4	6	2	0	0	2	0	1	0	5	0	12	0	0
Gill, Steve, Waterloo*	.258	116	383	54	99	151	18	8	6	48	7	3	9	39	2	86	20	4
Gillum, K.C., Cedar Rapids*	.246	126	452	62	111	170	22	8	7	43	1	2	7	51	2	105	19	6
Gilmore, Tony, Burlington	.272	82	276	25	75	90	12	0	1	27	5	1	3	25	2	45	2	2
Glenn, Leon, Beloit*	.174	51	161	23	28	52	2	2	6	27	3	2	0	13	0	62	18	3
Godin, Steve, Kane County	.269	93	346	48	93	129	12	3	6	38	3	6	3	23	1	66	10	3
Grahovac, Mike, Clinton	.206	26	68	7	14	19	2	0	1	4	3	0	1	4	0	19	1	1
Grebeck, Brian, Quad City	.245	121	408	80	100	126	20	3	0	34	15	4	10	103	0	76	19	10
Guanchez, Harry, Appleton	.279	109	376	40	105	127	16	0	2	50	0	4	10	24	0	52	0	2
Gumpf, John, Kenosha	.208	114	366	38	76	117	20	3	5	27	2	2	5	24	0	116	2	1
Hairston, John, South Bend†	.198	24	86	6	17	25	5	0	1	12	0	2	0	5	1	30	3	3
Hammargren, Roy, Cedar Rapids*	.210	53	167	20	35	65	6	0	8	20	2	0	2	19	1	47	1	0
Hargis, Dan, Rockford	.216	71	227	30	49	78	11	0	6	31	0	2	1	22	0	54	1	0
Harrel, Donny, Appleton	.231	82	242	22	56	75	14	1	1	19	3	1	5	26	0	62	2	0
Harris, Mike, Beloit*	.214	50	145	27	31	42	4	2	1	12	5	0	1	27	1	30	16	3
Hart, Shelby, Clinton	.222	52	162	15	36	44	8	0	0	12	2	2	11	8	0	40	4	1
Hartung, Andrew, Peoria	.218	28	101	9	22	32	3	2	1	11	0	0	2	8	0	16	0	1
Hatcher, Chris, Burlington	.233	129	497	69	116	188	23	5	13	65	0	4	9	46	4	180	10	5
Hattabaugh, Matt, South Bend	.000	4	7	0	0	0	0	0	0	1	0	1	0	1	0	1	0	0
Hauteman, Jeff, Beloit*	.000	19	1	1	0	0	0	0	0	0	0	0	0	0	0	1	0	0
Hawkins, Ty, South Bend*	.217	52	152	14	33	42	6	0	1	19	1	0	5	16	1	25	3	2
Hawks, Larry, Waterloo	.216	20	37	4	8	9	1	0	0	2	0	0	2	5	0	14	0	0
Henderson, David, Burlington	.199	75	211	27	42	64	7	3	3	20	0	4	10	30	1	71	9	4
Henderson, Lee, Waterloo	.213	61	169	6	36	40	4	0	0	7	0	0	1	14	0	53	0	0
Hendley, Brett, Madison*	.246	126	406	58	100	149	24	2	7	58	1	1	1	104	8	125	9	5
Henry, Scott, Madison*	.289	105	322	49	93	114	16	1	1	51	4	5	0	76	2	51	1	1
Hernandez, Carlos, Madison†	.221	121	375	59	83	109	14	3	2	46	12	5	0	59	1	98	23	13
Hicks, Aman, Kane County*	.238	49	164	25	39	48	6	0	1	7	2	0	2	16	1	28	8	5
Hocking, Denny, Kenosha†	.255	125	432	72	110	149	17	8	2	36	3	4	6	77	4	69	22	10
Holbert, Aaron, Springfield	.223	59	215	22	48	58	5	1	1	24	1	2	6	15	0	28	5	8
Hood, Randy, South Bend	.160	36	100	13	16	26	3	2	1	12	2	1	1	20	2	27	9	3
Houk, Tom, Kenosha	.209	101	253	16	53	73	10	2	2	25	3	0	2	39	0	57	3	6
Hrabar, Shaun, Kane County*	.161	68	180	12	29	37	6	1	0	14	5	4	1	13	1	32	2	4
Hyzdu, Adam, Clinton	.234	124	410	47	96	134	13	5	5	50	7	2	3	64	1	131	4	5
Javier, Vicente, Cedar Rapids	.217	58	152	22	33	38	2	0	1	14	4	1	1	8	0	26	4	5
Jennings, Lance, Appleton	.236	82	284	25	67	104	22	0	5	42	1	2	3	20	1	65	0	2
Johnson, Wayne, Rockford	.223	66	166	35	37	44	5	1	0	9	5	0	1	33	1	45	27	5
Jones, Motor-boat, Cedar Rapids	.227	98	352	58	80	104	7	1	5	42	0	3	0	62	2	43	26	6
Kasper, Kevin, Clinton	.269	21	78	10	21	25	4	0	0	6	1	0	1	9	0	8	0	0
Keighley, Steve, Rockford	.207	46	135	17	28	33	3	1	0	15	0	2	1	30	0	25	1	3
Kessinger, Keith, Cedar Rapids†	.204	59	206	15	42	50	5	0	1	15	5	1	3	23	1	46	0	1
Kinyoun, Travis, Appleton†	.311	25	74	12	23	32	3	0	2	15	1	2	0	10	2	15	0	0
Kipila, Jeff, Quad City	.274	112	401	64	110	199	35	0	18	77	0	9	4	58	1	99	4	2
Koelling, Brian, Cedar Rapids	.259	35	147	27	38	47	6	0	1	12	0	1	3	14	0	39	22	6
Kuehl, John, Waterloo†	.255	62	220	36	56	91	10	2	7	37	0	4	6	16	3	51	2	2
Lak, Carlos, Clinton†	.181	45	149	19	27	37	5	1	1	8	2	1	1	7	0	39	6	5
Lambert, Layne, Burlington*	.263	73	255	36	67	85	9	0	3	31	0	2	1	26	1	50	2	4
Lanfranco, Luis, Madison	.259	101	336	41	87	108	15	3	0	43	4	7	2	33	2	78	7	6
Lanfranco, Raphel, Burlington	.210	31	100	11	21	26	2	0	1	11	1	0	0	11	0	27	1	0
Little, Mike, Peoria	.274	122	413	59	113	175	28	2	10	61	3	4	1	58	1	90	3	0
Lopez, Pedro, Waterloo	.284	102	342	49	97	135	12	1	8	57	2	4	2	47	4	66	3	3
Lydy, Scott, Madison	.259	127	464	64	120	186	26	2	12	69	0	4	5	66	5	109	24	9
Malinoski, Chris, Rockford	.264	130	455	71	120	140	20	0	0	55	7	6	12	87	1	79	4	6
Manning, Henry, South Bend	.284	23	67	5	19	22	3	0	0	10	2	0	2	10	4	0	4	0
Martinez, Ray, Quad City	.238	6	21	3	5	6	1	0	0	1	0	0	0	4	0	5	0	0
McClain, Scott, Kane County	.222	25	81	9	18	18	0	0	0	4	1	0	0	17	0	25	1	1

Player, Team	Avg.	G	AB	R	H	TB	2B	3B	HR	RBI	SH	SF	HP	BB	Int. BB	SO	SB	CS
McConathy, Douglas, Kane County*	.246	35	122	16	30	37	7	0	0	17	1	2	3	16	1	18	0	0
McGonnigal, Brett, Clinton†	.211	35	109	18	23	31	3	1	1	7	4	2	0	14	1	35	2	2
McGough, Greg, South Bend	.204	58	157	13	32	39	5	1	0	18	2	2	4	21	4	50	2	1
Medina, Ricardo, Peoria	.302	14	43	5	13	19	3	0	1	5	0	0	1	6	0	2	1	0
Mejias, Teodulo, Clinton	.194	49	134	13	26	31	3	1	0	9	3	0	5	6	0	41	0	0
Mercado, Rafael, Madison	.242	123	446	52	108	144	15	3	5	53	6	4	3	23	3	92	3	4
Meury, Bill, Waterloo	.211	121	360	46	76	92	12	2	0	24	11	2	6	40	1	81	1	2
Millares, Jose, Kane County	.271	114	425	57	115	162	28	2	5	71	2	6	11	20	3	71	3	4
Miller, Barry, Clinton*	.244	117	397	43	97	135	19	2	5	51	5	5	3	53	5	66	1	1
Miller, Brent, Kane County*	.286	87	308	36	88	142	21	3	9	50	0	3	1	12	2	33	3	3
Miller, Damian, Kenosha	.232	80	267	28	62	84	11	1	3	34	2	3	2	24	1	53	3	2
Minnis, Billy, Quad City	.238	107	374	40	89	142	19	2	10	55	1	2	3	18	4	84	5	5
Miranda, Giovanni, Appleton	.236	122	416	57	98	113	11	2	0	27	11	2	4	33	0	67	28	12
Moberg, Mike, Rockford	.224	126	464	65	104	130	15	4	1	61	5	3	6	59	1	74	13	13
Molina, Islay, Madison	.282	95	316	35	89	116	16	1	3	45	1	4	6	15	1	38	6	4
Montgomery, Ray, Burlington	.252	120	433	60	109	148	24	3	3	57	11	2	8	37	1	65	16	14
Monzon, Dan, South Bend	.240	89	258	35	62	79	13	2	0	21	8	3	6	45	1	71	7	6
Moore, Tim, Peoria	.226	42	115	14	26	33	5	1	0	10	2	1	3	13	0	13	2	0
Morillo, Cesar, Appleton†	.250	63	236	35	59	77	9	3	1	17	1	1	1	38	0	54	9	8
Morse, Matt, Kenosha†	.226	87	266	26	60	73	9	2	0	13	6	0	0	19	1	41	1	1
Mota, Willie, Kenosha†	.279	94	344	23	96	120	18	0	2	32	1	2	3	8	1	44	3	1
Mundy, Rick, Peoria	.226	64	195	23	44	67	11	0	4	27	5	1	6	13	0	51	7	0
Muratti, Rafael, Quad City	.244	104	311	33	76	102	20	0	2	40	4	0	0	40	1	49	4	6
Murphy, Shaun, Rockford	.299	117	401	54	120	151	20	1	3	47	4	2	0	51	0	119	13	10
Murray, Glen, Rockford	.236	124	479	73	113	172	16	14	5	60	0	8	2	77	3	136	22	19
Musolino, Mike, Quad City*	.252	41	127	11	32	40	5	0	1	13	0	0	1	20	0	28	1	2
Myers, Eric, Madison†	.000	37	1	0	0	0	0	0	0	0	0	0	0	0	0	0	0	0
Nessmith, John, Clinton	.286	9	28	6	8	12	1	0	1	7	0	0	0	2	0	13	0	0
Nunez, Rogelio, South Bend†	.212	56	189	26	40	46	4	1	0	15	6	0	0	14	0	30	21	6
Oberdank, Jeff, Quad City	.219	58	169	31	37	51	5	0	3	11	5	0	5	22	1	32	7	2
Ortiz, Basilo, Kane County	.270	57	215	34	58	68	8	1	0	27	4	2	2	17	1	38	2	1
Ozuna, Mateo, Springfield	.252	115	437	69	110	138	11	4	3	35	3	3	3	46	1	39	78	24
Painter, Lance, Waterloo*	.000	28	1	0	0	0	0	0	0	0	0	0	0	0	0	0	0	0
Paredes, German, Kane County	.171	21	70	5	12	12	0	0	0	5	2	1	1	1	0	13	0	1
Perozo, Dan, Cedar Rapids	.216	31	111	10	24	28	0	2	0	5	2	0	0	5	0	20	12	3
Petagine, Roberto, Burlington*	.259	124	432	72	112	174	24	1	12	58	0	1	4	71	3	74	7	5
Pfeffer, Kurt, Kenosha	.200	13	35	2	7	7	0	0	0	0	0	0	0	2	0	12	0	0
Picketts, Bill, Madison†	.253	99	312	41	79	94	11	2	0	29	2	1	0	47	2	44	3	7
Piskor, Kirk, Appleton	.276	30	105	13	29	39	4	0	2	11	0	0	3	0	1	13	1	0
Poe, Charles, South Bend	.213	117	418	57	89	145	29	6	5	59	4	5	2	38	1	136	20	5
Polanco, Carlos, Quad City	.108	22	74	10	8	10	0	1	0	8	1	1	1	6	0	12	1	2
Postiff, James, Peoria	.235	14	51	3	12	16	1	0	1	3	1	0	1	5	0	14	1	0
Powell, Gordon, Beloit	.216	82	273	34	59	92	6	3	7	23	8	2	3	16	1	77	15	3
Pueschner, Craig, Waterloo*	.230	108	348	50	80	126	13	0	11	52	3	1	8	35	0	100	10	3
Pugh, Scott, Waterloo*	.255	38	145	16	37	42	5	0	0	14	1	2	1	10	2	21	1	1
Ramirez, Dan, Kane County	.264	120	402	59	106	129	19	2	0	40	11	3	12	34	1	66	9	6
Ramirez, Roberto, Clinton	.182	17	55	4	10	12	0	1	0	5	0	2	2	0	0	18	0	1
Ramos, Jorge, South Bend	.200	32	100	8	20	23	3	0	0	7	2	1	3	3	1	22	4	1
Reid, Greg, Madison*	.205	97	308	47	63	97	15	2	5	30	3	2	9	66	1	91	13	9
Reynolds, Doug, Kane County	.228	59	189	25	43	65	13	0	3	18	0	3	1	36	1	48	2	2
Riggs, Kevin, Cedar Rapids*	.268	118	406	72	109	140	21	2	2	42	3	5	3	91	2	51	23	8
Rivell, Bob, Waterloo	.278	20	54	6	15	20	5	0	0	7	1	0	1	7	0	8	1	2
Rivera, David, Kenosha†	.244	106	324	46	79	97	14	2	0	23	3	2	4	17	0	63	52	10
Rivers, Ken, Quad City	.198	28	96	8	19	29	5	1	1	14	0	3	3	3	0	28	0	0
Robertson, Mike, South Bend*	.329	54	210	30	69	92	16	2	1	26	3	3	3	18	3	24	7	6
Robledo, Nilson, South Bend	.289	40	142	15	41	65	7	1	5	20	1	1	0	9	0	42	3	2
Rodriguez, Ahmed, Springfield†	.231	57	169	18	39	53	6	1	2	24	3	2	2	6	0	51	1	5
Rodriguez, Beto, Springfield*	.283	79	244	34	69	93	6	6	6	18	2	0	2	54	2	52	0	1
Rodriguez, Edgal, Quad City	.258	46	120	19	31	52	8	2	3	14	0	1	0	16	0	25	0	1
Roso, Jimmy, Kane County	.307	58	189	23	58	73	13	1	0	30	2	3	2	24	1	42	1	3
Rosselli, Joe, Clinton	.000	23	0	1	0	0	0	0	0	0	0	0	0	0	0	0	0	0
Rumsey, Dan, Clinton*	.175	25	80	4	14	21	4	0	1	11	0	0	1	9	1	17	1	2
Rumsey, Derrell, Kenosha	.242	42	153	18	37	49	6	0	2	16	0	0	1	8	0	40	8	2
Rush, Eddie, Cedar Rapids	.254	80	323	43	82	99	17	0	0	43	2	3	1	37	1	36	4	3
Russo, Paul, Kenosha	.271	125	421	60	114	200	20	3	20	100	0	10	7	64	4	105	4	1
Saenz, Olmedo, South Bend	.245	56	192	23	47	65	10	1	2	22	1	2	5	21	0	48	5	3
Salazar, Julian, Madison	.209	95	273	31	57	69	12	0	0	14	7	1	6	41	1	73	10	4
Sammons, Lee, Madison	.288	122	459	104	132	150	12	3	0	43	5	3	1	90	0	80	54	17
Sass, James, Beloit	.212	23	66	5	14	17	3	0	0	4	0	0	1	9	0	12	3	2
Savinon, Odalis, Springfield	.249	59	205	23	51	59	5	0	1	9	1	1	0	15	0	44	7	7
Schmidt, Keith, Kane County*	.193	64	202	22	39	60	6	3	3	15	0	1	1	18	3	84	5	4
Seitzer, Brad, Kane County	.279	58	197	34	55	74	11	1	2	28	1	1	1	36	3	36	1	0
Sheppard, Don, South Bend	.208	83	178	24	37	49	5	2	1	11	1	1	1	21	0	57	7	2
Singleton, Duane, Beloit*	.289	101	388	57	112	148	13	7	3	44	5	2	3	40	7	57	42	17
Slater, Vernon, Appleton*	.125	15	32	3	4	5	1	0	0	0	0	0	0	2	0	16	0	1
Smith, Bryan, Burlington	.239	105	330	37	79	84	5	0	0	30	2	4	1	27	1	99	29	7
Smith, Dandy, Rockford	.227	105	374	38	85	127	12	3	8	44	0	3	4	29	2	81	3	3
Smith, Ed, Beloit	.261	61	218	31	57	86	13	2	4	37	1	3	1	21	2	41	5	2
Smith, Lance, Burlington	.250	3	12	0	3	4	1	0	0	0	0	0	0	0	0	3	0	0
Smith, Tom, Appleton†	.267	118	431	51	115	158	14	7	5	57	1	2	3	24	0	141	6	2
Solimine, Joe, South Bend	.158	17	38	4	6	9	3	0	0	1	3	0	0	1	0	13	0	6
Soto, Rafael, Peoria	.202	108	347	36	70	80	4	3	0	19	11	2	4	34	0	58	8	8
Spann, Tookie, Waterloo	.306	49	157	25	48	72	9	0	5	29	2	0	3	35	0	41	7	2
Stela, Jose, Quad City	.167	4	12	3	2	2	0	0	0	0	0	0	0	0	0	3	0	0
Stephens, Reggie, Waterloo	.164	34	67	10	11	12	1	0	0	3	2	0	0	7	0	18	11	3
Stewart, Brady, Appleton	.253	51	158	14	40	49	9	0	0	15	2	2	0	17	0	32	1	2
Strange, Keith, South Bend	.232	95	302	29	70	88	15	0	1	29	6	3	4	50	1	66	7	4
Strickland, Chad, Appleton	.173	28	81	5	14	21	4	0	1	5	1	1	0	2	0	12	2	1
Sudbury, Craig, Madison	.000	15	1	0	0	0	0	0	0	0	0	0	0	0	0	1	0	0
Tahan, Kevin, Springfield	.263	97	323	43	85	136	22	4	7	48	1	8	2	49	5	50	2	2
Tallman, Troy, Kane County	.125	6	16	2	2	3	1	0	0	1	0	0	0	4	0	6	0	0
Taylor, Scott, Peoria	.200	16	55	1	11	12	1	0	0	3	0	0	0	6	0	5	0	1
Taylor, Terry, Quad City*	.278	65	205	30	57	81	15	0	3	26	1	0	3	53	2	53	7	3
Tejero, Fausto, Quad City	.172	83	244	16	42	52	7	0	1	18	3	1	4	14	0	52	0	1
Thomas, Keith, 13 Mad.-74 App.†	.257	87	276	36	71	111	11	4	7	32	4	2	2	15	0	71	24	7

Player, Team	Avg.	G	AB	R	H	TB	2B	3B	HR	RBI	SH	SF	HP	BB	Int. BB	SO	SB	CS
Thomas, Orlando, Springfield	.095	9	21	3	2	2	0	0	0	2	0	0	0	2	0	8	0	0
Thompson, Fletcher, Burlington*	.271	116	428	85	116	152	15	3	5	33	5	2	5	104	0	115	37	16
Torres, Paul, Peoria	.213	99	352	60	75	145	24	2	13	50	3	0	9	48	2	91	6	2
Tyler, Brad, Kane County*	.271	60	199	35	54	79	10	3	3	29	1	2	1	44	1	25	5	3
Valrie, Kerry, South Bend	.215	87	331	47	71	104	11	2	6	29	3	0	3	23	1	78	32	6
Vargas, Victor, Springfield	.108	15	37	2	4	6	2	0	0	2	1	0	0	3	0	7	0	0
Vasquez, Chris, Cedar Rapids*	.267	50	195	33	52	94	13	1	9	37	0	4	3	14	1	41	5	4
Velez, Jose, Springfield*	.241	116	410	46	99	115	10	3	0	35	3	3	1	15	2	49	10	5
Velez, Noel, Cedar Rapids	.164	34	67	4	11	12	1	0	0	6	0	2	0	7	0	14	2	1
Vierra, Jose, Peoria	.265	132	513	52	136	191	37	0	6	55	1	7	2	48	3	78	3	3
Vogel, Mike, South Bend†	.278	14	36	1	10	13	3	0	0	4	0	0	0	5	1	8	1	0
Vondran, Steve, Cedar Rapids	.213	55	178	14	38	45	4	0	1	19	0	4	1	18	0	25	3	2
Walker, Dennis, South Bend	.221	122	394	48	87	130	10	9	5	38	5	1	7	42	2	109	18	15
Ward, Ricky, Clinton	.278	126	442	64	123	180	22	1	11	64	2	7	7	58	3	68	13	13
Weimerskirch, Mike, Rockford	.271	132	484	84	131	180	27	5	4	58	3	8	19	64	1	74	32	19
West, Jim, Waterloo	.214	5	14	0	3	3	0	0	0	0	0	0	1	0	2	0	0
Whalen, Shawn, Waterloo*	.229	99	306	39	70	118	16	4	8	52	1	4	1	33	8	72	0	2
Wheat, Chris, Beloit	.357	4	14	3	5	5	0	0	0	2	0	0	0	0	1	1	1
White, Darrin, Beloit*	.210	96	248	34	52	73	12	3	1	31	2	3	4	57	2	62	22	7
Wilson, Brandon, South Bend	.313	125	463	75	145	181	18	6	2	49	7	4	2	61	2	70	41	11
Wilson, Bryan, Peoria	.197	61	178	24	35	39	4	0	0	10	2	1	1	22	0	21	1	3
Wilson, Todd, Cedar Rapids*	.204	96	284	23	58	83	11	1	4	37	1	3	2	22	1	99	0	1
Wilstead, Randy, Rockford*	.254	121	421	59	107	159	26	4	6	57	1	5	1	58	11	72	2	2
Wrona, Dave, Beloit†	.249	62	209	31	52	65	10	0	1	24	3	1	1	28	0	39	7	3
Young, Ernie, Madison	.254	114	362	75	92	160	19	2	15	71	9	6	9	58	0	115	20	9
Young, Jason, Clinton	.235	93	311	32	73	106	13	4	4	32	3	1	5	26	3	78	8	2
Zaun, Gregg, Kane County†	.274	113	409	67	112	151	17	5	4	51	3	4	2	50	1	41	4	4

The following pitchers, listed alphabetically by club, with games in parentheses, had no plate appearances, primarily through use of designated hitters:

APPLETON—Ahern, Brian (10); Baez, Francisco (44); Berumen, Andres (13); Bryans, Jason (18); Chrisman, Jim (47); Dunn, Bubba (14); Fyock, Wade (17); Harris, Doug (7); Hierholzer, David (49); Lee, Anthony (6); Medrick, Chris (17); Milton, Herb (26); Myers, Rodney (9); Perez, Dario (34); Pineda, Gabriel (37); Pollard, Damon (16); Rea, Shayne (27).

BELOIT—Boze, Marshall (3); Brady, Mike (17); Brakeley, Bill (30); Bush, Chuck (6); Carter, Larry (30); Drake, Sam (14); Fitzgerald, Dave (9); Gamez, Francisco (25); Gibbs, Jim (2); Grove, Scott (13); Holmes, Darren (2); Hooper, Mike (13); Hvizda, Jim (3); Kellogg, Geoffrey (28); Mathews, Greg (7); Miller, Pat (33); Nunez, Edwin (5); Pruitt, Don (12); Smith, James (19); Smith, John (8); Souza, Brian (9); Stephens, Mark (4); Vazquez, Ed (7); Wegman, Bill (3); Zimbauer, Jason (11).

BURLINGTON—Allen, David (27); Anderson, Tom (6); Bjornson, Craig (6); Dovey, Troy (25); Gonzales, Ben (60); Gutierrez, Anthony (32); Hurta, Bob (56); Lane, Kevin (57); McDowell, Mike (17); Nieto, Roy (22); Normand, Guy (9); Scott, Tyrone (27); Trice, Wally (35); Wall, Donnie (16); Wheeler, Ken (25).

CEDAR RAPIDS—Berry, Kevin (37); Borcherding, Mark (26); Culberson, Calvain (18); Edwards, Ryan (37); Ferry, Mike (16); Griffen, Leonard (27); Hoffman, Trevor (27); Langford, Rich (14); Luebbers, Larry (28); Manon, Ramon (1); Margheim, Greg (35); McCarthy, Steve (32); Robinson, Scott (20); Satre, Jason (21); Steph, Rod (8).

CLINTON—Brummett, Greg (16); Carlson, Dan (27); Flanagan, Dan (44); Henrikson, Dan (29); Huffman, Rod (50); McLeod, Brian (15); Myers, Mike (11); Peltzer, Kurt (27); Reyes, Jose (30); Torres, Salomon (28); Yockey, Mark (36).

KANE COUNTY—Anderson, Matt (26); Blumberg, Rob (14); Borowski, Joe (26); Chatterton, Chris (10); Chouinard, Bobby (6); Dedrick, James (16); Eshelman, Vaughn (11); Farrar, Terry (12); Hebb, Mike (26); Martin, Tom (38); Paveloff, Dave (35); Pennington, Brad (23); Ryan, Kevin (1); Taylor, Tom (26); Tippitt, Bradley (18); Unrein, Todd (30); Wiley, Mike (23).

KENOSHA—Abel, Jackie (20); Best, Jayson (14); Bigham, Dave (49); Dixon, Dickie (25); Hoppe, Denny (38); Klonoski, Jason (33); Kohl, Jim (28); Mansur, Jeff (17); Persing, Tim (25); Peterson, Bart (24); Ritchie, Todd (21); Robinson, Bob (10); Russo, Pat (19); Swope, Mark (19); Taylor, Kerry (26); Taylor, Steve (18); Thelen, Jeff (26).

MADISON—Brimhall, Brad (28); Connolly, Craig (15); Dillon, Jim (28); Grimes, Mike (25); Gulledge, Hugh (39); Honeycutt, Rick (1); Johns, Doug (38); Kimball, Richard (2); McCarty, Scott (19); Mejia, Delfino (3); Mejia, Leandro (10); Phoenix, Steve (7); Revenig, Todd (26); Ross, Gary (10); Russell, Todd (20); Shaw, Curtis (28); Smith, Tim (1); Sturtze, Tanyon (27).

PEORIA—Alicano, Pedro (43); Belyeu, Randy (1); Bliss, Bill (20); Correa, Amilcar (39); Delgado, Tim (49); Doss, Jason (25); Gardner, Scott (3); Godfrey, Tyson (26); Kirk, Chuck (38); Krahenbuhl, Ken (23); Mann, Thomas (44); Perez, Pedro (7); Ross, Dave (39); Sutcliffe, Rick (1); Swartzbaugh, Dave (5); Taylor, Aaron (15); Weiss, Scott (14).

QUAD CITY—Adams, Dave (22); Craven, Britt (28); Edenfield, Ken (47); Fritz, John (25); Gamez, Bob (41); Haffner, Les (12); Hathaway, Hilly (20); Lachcnik, Joe (15); Lachemann, Bret (33); Leftwich, Phillip (26); Martin, Justin (27); Montoya, Norm (8); Neal, Dave (10); Parker, Rich (8); Scott, Darryl (47); Silverio, Victor (4).

ROCKFORD—Batista, Miguel (23); Baxter, Bob (45); Brewer, Billy (29); Collins, Stacey (7); Diaz, Ralph (38); Grewal, Ranbir (46); Howze, Ben (25); Jurado, Pat (21); Martinez, Martin (8); Mathile, Mike (17); Powell, Corey (26); Renko, Steve (16); Reyes, Rafael (3); Ryan, Bobby (49); Whitehead, Steve (22).

SOUTH BEND—Altaffer, Todd (21); Bere, Jason (27); Campos, Frank (37); Caridad, Rolando (53); Hoey, Andy (17); Hooper, Mike (11); Jean, Domingo (25); Jenkins, Jonathan (19); Locklear, Dean (13); Olsen, Steve (13); Perigny, Donald (56); Person, Robert (13); Ruffcorn, Scott (9); Shepherd, Keith (31); Tolar, Kevin (30); Woodfin, Chris (3); Young, Greg (13).

SPRINGFIELD—Anderson, Paul (27); Arias, Jose (8); Barreiro, Fernando (6); Botkin, Alan (39); Bowlan, Mark (28); Cimorelli, Frank (29); Eaton, Dann (39); Espinal, Willie (39); Fletcher, Dennis (56); Hammond, Allan (3); Keller, Clyde (45); Lata, Tim (5); Lucchetti, Larry (11); Nielsen, Kevin (26); Norris, David (12); Romanoli, Paul (16); Urbani, Tom (8).

WATERLOO—Altaffer, Todd (18); Banks, Lance (39); Bensching, Bruce (54); Devore, Ted (21); Florie, Bryce (23); Fredrickson, Scott (27); Hays, Rob (41); Ingram, Linty (16); Lebron, Jose (13); Mortensen, Tony (19); Sanders, Scott (4); Thibault, Ryan (42); Wilkinson, Brian (7); Worrell, Tim (14).

GRAND SLAMS—T. Carter, Ciesla, Little, 2 each; Becker, Blakeman, E. Christopherson, Cole, P. Coleman, Cruz, Cummings, Cunningham, C. Davis, Faneyte, Gash, Gumpf, Hartung, Hocking, Hyzdu, Lydy, Muratti, Murphy, Petagine, Pueschner, E. Smith, K. Thomas, Valrie, Ward, Weimerskirch, 1 each.

AWARDED FIRST BASE ON CATCHER'S INTERFERENCE—J. Velez 4 (Manning 2, Erdman, R. Lanfranco); Becker 3 (Cox, Fitzpatrick, Tejero); Morse 2 (J. Anderson, Fitzpatrick); Coffey (Dempsey); Gill (Mejias); Godin (Nunez); Harris (Reynolds); Malinoski (Hendley); Ba. Miller (S. Taylor); Weimerskirch (Hendley).

PITCHING

TEAM

Team	ERA	G	CG	ShO	Sv.	IP	H	R	ER	HR	HB	BB	Int. BB	SO	WP	Bk.
Clinton	2.74	139	25	17	43	1208.2	1013	465	368	41	30	449	20	1076	83	25
South Bend	3.17	139	7	17	38	1227.2	1005	576	433	43	53	638	18	1061	110	26
Waterloo	3.19	138	17	17	32	1197.0	1024	518	424	56	45	565	40	1045	73	15
Kenosha	3.29	138	14	8	32	1197.1	1142	584	438	50	63	514	15	783	86	23

Team	ERA	G	CG	ShO	Sv.	IP	H	R	ER	HR	HB	BB	Int. BB	SO	WP	Bk.
Beloit	3.44	137	13	6	38	1199.2	1123	577	459	55	50	478	23	987	75	26
Rockford	3.50	137	10	14	40	1208.1	1130	592	470	48	62	508	14	905	112	27
Kane County	3.52	136	9	10	33	1188.1	1107	565	465	53	38	538	21	1014	81	24
Cedar Rapids	3.53	140	19	14	27	1218.2	1122	593	478	65	62	493	24	903	79	19
Quad City	3.71	137	9	6	35	1209.0	1134	601	499	47	56	504	17	1131	92	25
Burlington	3.75	137	7	6	33	1202.1	1119	640	501	68	49	583	21	1060	105	33
Madison	3.83	138	4	11	40	1180.2	1101	654	502	46	60	596	26	945	109	14
Springfield	3.97	137	13	6	34	1198.2	1178	683	529	74	50	494	20	913	97	14
Peoria	4.00	138	11	4	29	1202.2	1225	678	534	52	61	530	19	947	78	41
Appleton	4.14	139	3	7	25	1194.2	1191	682	550	62	44	619	53	880	93	33

INDIVIDUAL

(Leading qualifiers for earned-run average leadership— 112 or more innings)

*Throws lefthanded.

Pitcher, Team	W	L	Pct.	ERA	G	GS	CG	GF	ShO	Sv.	IP	H	R	ER	HR	HB	BB	Int. BB	SO	WP
Torres, Clinton	16	5	.762	1.41	28	28	8	0	3	0	210.1	148	48	33	4	1	47	2	214	6
Painter, Waterloo*	14	8	.636	2.30	28	28	7	0	4	0	200.0	162	64	51	14	2	57	7	201	3
Ingram, Waterloo	8	4	.667	2.41	16	16	3	0	1	0	116.0	100	39	31	7	6	21	1	91	0
Mathile, Rockford	9	3	.750	2.47	17	17	5	0	2	0	116.2	100	45	32	3	4	19	0	66	4
Henrikson, Clinton*	12	8	.600	2.56	29	26	3	1	2	0	162.0	141	61	46	9	3	68	1	150	12
Satre, Cedar Rapids	8	6	.571	2.58	21	20	4	1	2	1	132.2	101	48	38	5	2	67	1	130	6
Brummett, Clinton	10	5	.667	2.72	16	16	5	0	2	0	112.1	91	39	34	2	3	32	2	74	5
Tolar, South Bend*	8	5	.615	2.83	30	19	0	6	0	1	114.2	87	54	36	3	8	85	0	87	6
Bere, South Bend	9	12	.429	2.87	27	27	2	0	1	0	163.0	116	66	52	8	5	100	0	158	11
Dovey, Burlington	7	6	.538	3.02	25	20	0	2	0	1	116.1	89	51	39	3	7	74	0	130	9

Departmental leaders: G—Gonzales, 60; W—Carlson, Torres, 16; L—P. Anderson, Cimorelli, Godfrey, T. Scott, 14; Pct.—Grewal, .846; GS—Cimorelli, 29; CG—Torres, 8; GF—Huffman, 49; ShO—Painter, 4; Sv.—Huffman, 36; IP—Torres, 210.1; H—Cimorelli, 202; R—T. Scott, 117; ER—T. Scott, 94; HR—Griffen, 15; HB—Borcherding, 13; BB—Bere, 100; IBB—Chrisman, 11; SO—Torres, 214; WP—Gutierrez, 22.

(All pitchers—listed alphabetically)

Pitcher, Team	W	L	Pct.	ERA	G	GS	CG	GF	ShO	Sv.	IP	H	R	ER	HR	HB	BB	Int. BB	SO	WP
Abel, Kenosha	1	2	.333	4.73	20	2	1	2	0	0	40.0	28	25	21	1	1	27	2	20	7
Adams, Quad City	8	8	.500	3.53	22	21	0	1	0	0	119.2	115	62	47	5	3	52	0	92	10
Ahern, Appleton	2	4	.333	4.93	10	9	1	0	1	0	49.1	53	29	27	4	4	24	1	22	6
Alicano, Peoria*	2	7	.222	3.52	43	9	0	16	0	6	99.2	88	52	39	2	3	35	0	79	9
Allen, Burlington	5	7	.417	5.22	27	18	1	2	1	0	108.2	134	73	63	11	2	37	1	73	5
Altaffer, 21 S.B.- 18 Wat.*	2	5	.286	3.65	39	1	0	18	0	2	56.2	57	29	23	5	2	30	1	54	6
Anderson, Kane County*	13	8	.619	3.03	26	26	5	0	2	0	169.1	135	65	57	9	5	62	0	160	6
Anderson, Springfield	9	14	.391	3.71	27	27	5	0	0	0	174.2	171	98	72	13	3	38	2	109	13
Anderson, Burlington	1	4	.200	6.40	6	6	1	0	0	0	32.1	38	27	23	2	4	14	0	28	2
Arias, Springfield	0	4	.000	8.36	7	5	0	0	0	0	28.0	35	28	26	2	0	17	0	14	9
Aversa, Springfield	0	0	.000	3.86	5	0	0	5	0	0	4.2	6	2	2	0	0	2	0	3	1
Baez, Appleton*	5	3	.625	3.31	44	0	0	19	0	2	70.2	74	36	26	1	0	35	10	59	8
Banks, Waterloo	4	2	.667	4.58	39	2	0	17	0	3	76.2	86	48	39	4	2	43	6	47	3
Barreiro, Springfield	0	0	.000	4.26	6	0	0	4	0	0	12.2	14	8	6	2	1	11	0	10	0
Batista, Rockford	11	5	.688	4.04	23	23	2	0	1	0	133.2	126	74	60	1	6	57	0	90	12
Baxter, Rockford*	6	5	.545	2.49	45	0	0	39	0	19	65.0	56	20	18	1	1	16	6	52	2
Bennington, Burlington	0	0	.000	0.00	1	0	0	1	0	0	1.0	1	0	0	0	0	0	0	1	0
Bensching, Waterloo	3	8	.273	2.44	54	0	0	33	0	12	66.1	53	26	18	1	4	33	8	85	6
Bere, South Bend	9	12	.429	2.87	27	27	2	0	1	0	163.0	116	66	52	8	5	100	0	158	11
Berry, Cedar Rapids	5	4	.556	3.36	37	0	0	25	0	3	64.1	50	28	24	3	1	26	1	60	11
Berumen, Appleton	2	6	.250	3.51	13	13	0	0	0	0	56.1	55	33	22	0	3	26	0	49	2
Best, Kenosha	0	0	.000	2.84	11	0	0	5	0	1	19.0	11	10	6	0	0	10	0	18	4
Bigham, Kenosha*	2	3	.400	1.98	49	0	0	23	0	2	59.0	47	19	13	3	1	29	1	36	2
Bjornson, Burlington*	1	2	.333	5.15	6	6	0	0	0	0	36.2	43	25	21	5	0	19	1	22	1
Bliss, Peoria	0	2	.000	3.72	20	0	0	19	0	6	19.1	20	10	8	1	0	5	1	23	0
Blumberg, Kane County*	3	4	.429	3.90	14	14	0	0	0	0	80.2	68	40	35	4	0	46	2	71	5
Borcherding, Cedar Rapids	9	8	.529	4.40	26	21	4	3	1	0	135.0	150	78	66	8	13	34	2	58	9
Borowski, Kane County	7	2	.778	2.56	49	0	0	28	0	13	81.0	60	26	23	2	3	43	2	76	4
Botkin, Springfield*	5	6	.455	3.27	39	3	0	12	0	0	63.1	53	31	23	2	0	29	4	52	2
Bowlan, Springfield	6	11	.353	4.49	28	20	2	2	1	0	134.1	136	75	67	8	3	62	3	97	10
Boze, Beloit	0	1	.000	5.68	3	1	0	2	0	0	6.1	8	4	4	0	0	7	0	4	0
Brady, Beloit	0	2	.000	4.11	17	4	0	6	0	1	50.1	50	30	23	5	1	33	0	48	4
Brakeley, Beloit*	10	6	.625	3.78	29	20	0	4	0	2	123.2	118	63	52	3	8	67	0	116	14
Brewer, Rockford*	3	3	.500	1.98	29	0	0	16	0	5	41.0	32	12	9	1	1	25	0	43	6
Brimhall, Madison	9	7	.563	5.70	28	17	0	4	0	0	102.2	101	77	65	4	5	71	0	89	17
Brummett, Clinton	10	5	.667	2.72	16	16	5	0	2	0	112.1	91	39	34	2	3	32	2	74	5
Bryans, Appleton	1	0	1.000	5.03	18	0	0	5	0	1	34.0	37	21	19	0	2	20	1	24	2
Bush, Beloit	0	0	.000	0.79	6	0	0	3	0	2	11.1	7	1	1	0	1	8	0	9	0
Campos, South Bend	7	9	.438	4.28	37	14	2	9	0	1	113.2	116	73	54	3	5	62	1	98	18
Caridad, South Bend	3	3	.500	2.19	53	0	0	39	0	17	70.0	48	20	17	3	1	40	3	76	15
Carlson, Clinton	16	7	.696	3.08	27	27	5	0	3	0	181.1	149	69	62	11	2	76	0	164	18
Carter, Beloit	14	3	.824	3.17	30	16	1	10	0	4	130.2	142	64	46	6	2	46	2	96	2
Chatterton, Kane County	2	0	1.000	5.23	10	0	0	4	0	0	10.1	13	9	6	0	1	5	0	8	2
Chouinard, Kane County	2	4	.333	4.64	6	6	1	0	0	0	33.0	45	24	17	3	2	5	0	17	3
Chrisman, Appleton	7	5	.583	2.55	47	0	0	19	0	4	88.1	61	30	25	2	2	47	11	90	3
Cimorelli, Springfield	8	14	.364	3.38	29	29	3	0	0	0	191.2	202	94	72	12	9	51	1	98	10
Cole, Appleton	0	0	.000	4.50	3	0	0	3	0	0	2.0	3	1	1	0	0	3	0	2	0
Collins, Rockford	1	0	1.000	3.04	7	2	0	0	0	0	23.2	25	11	8	3	1	5	0	10	0
Connolly, Madison	2	1	.667	4.34	15	3	0	0	0	0	37.1	39	19	18	1	4	11	1	49	3
Correa, Peoria	5	2	.714	2.96	39	1	0	11	0	2	79.0	59	35	26	4	1	50	2	75	9
Craven, Quad City	6	8	.429	4.17	28	14	1	4	0	0	105.2	116	63	49	2	1	38	1	78	5
Culberson, Cedar Rapids	6	8	.429	4.18	18	14	1	1	0	0	88.1	82	54	41	4	3	54	5	68	4
Davis, Clinton	0	0	.000	0.00	2	0	0	2	0	0	1.1	0	1	0	0	0	1	0	1	0
Day, Appleton	0	0	.000	0.00	3	0	0	3	0	0	4.0	2	0	0	0	0	4	0	6	0
Dedrick, Kane County	4	5	.444	2.95	16	15	0	0	0	0	88.1	84	38	29	2	5	38	1	71	5
Delgado, Peoria	7	2	.778	4.02	49	0	0	23	0	6	87.1	103	55	39	5	5	27	1	94	4
Devore, Waterloo	6	4	.600	3.08	21	21	1	0	1	0	122.2	113	53	42	5	3	73	4	111	14

CLASS A

MIDWEST LEAGUE

Pitcher, Team	W	L	Pct.	ERA	G	GS	CG	GF	ShO	Sv.	IP	H	R	ER	HR	HB	BB	Int. BB	SO	WP
Diaz, Rockford	4	6	.400	3.23	38	15	1	18	1	3	119.2	109	51	43	10	6	43	1	76	8
Dillon, Madison	3	2	.600	1.69	28	1	0	13	0	7	64.0	47	15	12	4	1	29	1	64	0
Dixon, Kenosha*	7	7	.500	3.59	25	25	2	0	0	0	153.0	161	79	61	6	5	68	0	86	7
Doss, Peoria	11	11	.500	3.34	25	24	1	0	0	0	142.2	136	65	53	3	8	68	1	154	3
Dovey, Burlington	7	6	.538	3.02	25	20	0	2	0	1	116.1	89	51	39	3	7	74	0	130	9
Drake, Beloit	2	2	.500	3.78	14	7	0	3	0	1	50.0	48	28	21	2	3	28	0	32	1
Dunn, Appleton	4	4	.500	3.39	14	12	0	2	0	0	79.2	68	44	30	3	1	49	2	53	7
Eaton, Springfield	2	1	.667	6.11	23	2	0	4	0	0	53.0	59	50	36	7	0	39	1	53	10
Edenfield, Quad City	8	5	.615	2.59	47	0	0	40	0	15	87.0	69	30	25	3	4	30	2	106	5
Edwards, Cedar Rapids	2	2	.500	2.22	37	1	0	15	0	2	56.2	52	23	14	0	4	23	3	63	5
Eshelman, Kane County*	5	3	.625	2.32	11	11	2	0	1	0	77.2	57	23	20	3	3	35	0	90	2
Espinal, Springfield	2	3	.400	5.24	39	0	0	19	0	0	56.2	57	44	33	5	8	55	1	38	5
Ettles, Waterloo	1	2	.333	2.25	14	0	0	14	0	8	16.0	6	5	4	2	0	6	2	24	2
Farrar, Kane County*	6	3	.667	3.70	12	11	0	1	0	0	65.2	73	33	27	4	6	28	1	35	6
Farrell, Beloit*	2	3	.400	1.98	6	5	0	1	0	0	36.1	33	13	8	2	2	8	0	38	1
Ferry, Cedar Rapids	2	2	.500	6.66	16	0	0	12	0	3	25.2	25	19	19	1	1	21	2	27	2
Fitzgerald, Beloit*	0	3	.000	12.46	9	0	0	3	0	0	13.0	23	18	18	2	1	8	2	9	6
Flanagan, Clinton	4	6	.400	2.09	44	0	0	19	0	3	69.0	49	20	16	0	8	35	9	57	3
Fletcher, Springfield	3	6	.333	3.95	56	0	0	25	0	2	73.0	76	34	32	3	5	21	3	99	5
Florie, Waterloo	7	6	.538	3.92	23	23	2	0	0	0	133.0	119	66	58	3	9	79	0	90	9
Fredrickson, Waterloo	3	5	.375	1.17	26	0	0	22	0	6	38.1	24	9	5	1	1	15	3	40	3
Fritz, Quad City	2	3	.400	3.67	25	5	0	9	0	0	61.1	52	27	25	3	4	24	1	72	2
Fyock, Appleton	2	6	.250	4.33	17	16	0	0	0	0	97.2	102	52	47	7	4	34	1	45	5
Gamez, Beloit	9	12	.429	3.63	25	24	1	0	0	0	146.1	140	76	59	2	11	57	2	92	7
Gamez, Quad City*	4	3	.571	3.64	41	0	5	11	0	1	76.2	75	38	31	6	3	38	4	83	10
Garcia, Kane County	0	0	.000	0.00	1	0	0	1	0	0	1.0	1	1	0	0	1	0	0	1	0
Gardner, Peoria	1	2	.333	5.25	3	3	1	0	0	0	12.0	16	9	7	0	2	7	0	6	1
Gibbs, Beloit	0	0	.000	4.50	2	0	0	1	0	0	2.0	3	1	1	0	0	0	0	3	0
Giegling, Cedar Rapids	0	0	.000	0.00	1	0	0	1	0	0	1.0	0	0	0	0	0	1	0	0	0
Godfrey, Peoria	7	14	.333	5.45	26	26	3	0	1	0	147.0	196	101	89	5	11	63	4	76	12
Gonzales, Burlington	7	7	.500	3.18	60	1	0	33	0	7	99.0	85	46	35	3	8	34	7	81	5
Grewal, Rockford	11	2	.846	2.98	46	0	0	17	0	5	96.2	85	40	32	3	7	44	1	97	13
Griffen, Cedar Rapids	5	10	.333	4.21	27	16	1	6	0	1	132.2	125	74	62	15	9	42	0	117	9
Grimes, Madison	6	3	.667	4.43	25	6	0	9	0	4	81.1	84	48	40	3	9	25	2	75	17
Grove, Beloit	2	2	.500	4.78	13	1	0	8	0	0	26.1	30	17	14	2	2	9	0	13	3
Gulledge, Madison	3	7	.300	4.70	39	0	0	25	0	6	76.2	67	52	40	1	6	54	6	67	10
Gutierrez, Burlington*	7	4	.636	2.69	32	13	0	2	0	0	107.0	78	46	32	5	5	62	2	126	22
Haffner, Quad City	1	1	.500	4.08	12	0	0	4	0	0	28.2	22	15	13	0	2	15	1	12	1
Hammond, Springfield	1	1	.500	11.70	3	2	0	0	0	0	10.0	13	13	13	2	4	7	0	4	2
Harris, Appleton	2	2	.500	2.20	7	7	1	0	1	0	45.0	41	14	11	1	1	10	1	39	2
Hathaway, Quad City*	9	6	.600	3.35	20	20	1	0	0	0	129.0	126	58	48	5	7	41	1	110	11
Hauteman, Beloit*	2	1	.667	3.61	19	1	0	7	0	1	42.1	37	18	17	5	1	16	0	38	5
Hawks, Waterloo	0	0	.000	0.00	1	0	0	1	0	0	1.0	1	0	0	0	0	1	0	1	0
Hays, Waterloo	2	3	.400	4.69	41	1	0	11	0	0	71.0	61	44	37	2	4	46	4	43	10
Hebb, Kane County	3	3	.500	5.15	26	6	0	5	0	0	73.1	87	50	42	4	1	42	4	52	7
Henrikson, Clinton*	12	8	.600	2.56	29	26	3	1	2	0	162.0	141	61	46	9	3	68	1	150	12
Henry, Madison	0	0	.000	1.69	5	0	0	4	0	0	5.1	8	2	1	0	0	2	0	3	1
Hierholzer, Appleton	5	7	.417	3.83	49	0	0	42	0	14	56.1	52	31	24	4	2	31	8	47	6
Hoey, South Bend	1	4	.200	4.05	17	2	0	2	0	0	40.0	41	22	18	0	2	22	0	20	3
Hoffman, Cedar Rapids	1	1	.500	1.87	27	0	0	25	0	12	33.2	22	8	7	0	1	13	0	52	2
Holmes, Beloit	0	0	.000	0.00	2	0	0	2	0	2	2.0	0	0	0	0	0	0	0	3	0
Honeycutt, Madison*	0	1	.000	18.00	1	1	0	0	0	0	1.0	4	2	2	0	0	0	0	2	0
Hooper, 13 Bel. - 11 S.B.	2	4	.333	2.44	24	1	0	9	0	1	44.1	40	19	12	2	1	20	0	36	2
Hoppe, Kenosha	2	5	.286	1.54	38	0	0	21	0	11	46.2	47	15	8	1	1	18	1	31	2
Houk, Kenosha	0	0	.000	0.00	1	0	0	1	0	0	1.0	2	0	0	0	0	1	0	0	0
Howze, Rockford	4	3	.571	4.22	25	10	0	10	0	0	81.0	90	56	38	1	3	60	0	39	8
Huffman, Clinton	1	6	.143	2.15	50	0	0	49	0	36	50.1	37	22	12	2	2	21	0	54	1
Hurta, Burlington*	6	2	.750	3.32	56	0	0	16	0	3	62.1	40	35	23	1	3	59	2	82	11
Hvizda, Beloit	0	1	.000	3.00	3	0	0	3	0	0	3.0	6	2	1	0	0	1	0	1	0
Ingram, Waterloo	8	4	.667	2.41	16	16	3	0	0	0	116.0	100	39	31	7	6	21	1	91	0
Jean, South Bend	12	8	.600	3.30	25	25	2	0	0	0	158.0	121	75	58	7	10	65	0	141	18
Jenkins, South Bend	6	7	.462	3.88	19	15	1	2	0	0	97.1	80	54	42	3	9	44	1	91	10
Johns, Madison*	12	6	.667	3.23	38	14	1	9	1	2	128.1	108	59	46	5	8	54	1	104	13
Jurado, Rockford	0	4	.000	3.95	21	1	0	6	0	2	41.0	45	23	18	2	2	17	2	27	1
Keller, Springfield	5	0	1.000	0.75	45	0	0	40	0	32	60.1	30	6	5	0	2	18	3	76	4
Kellogg, Beloit	8	6	.571	4.44	27	21	3	3	1	0	133.2	132	76	66	10	1	56	1	128	8
Kimball, Madison	0	0	.000	4.50	2	0	0	2	0	0	2.0	3	1	1	0	0	1	0	2	0
Kirk, Peoria	5	9	.357	3.60	38	17	2	17	0	4	137.2	147	73	55	13	3	42	2	108	4
Klancnik, Quad City	0	1	.000	9.27	15	0	0	10	0	0	22.1	24	25	23	3	5	20	0	17	7
Klonoski, Kenosha*	2	4	.333	2.45	33	0	0	21	0	8	36.2	34	11	10	0	2	19	4	38	2
Kohl, Kenosha	3	4	.429	3.32	28	0	0	11	0	2	40.2	44	27	15	1	1	10	1	26	6
Krahenbuhl, Peoria	7	8	.467	3.96	23	23	1	0	0	0	122.2	126	69	54	5	9	53	1	61	6
Lachemann, Quad City	9	4	.692	3.28	33	10	1	4	0	0	104.1	95	47	38	2	8	55	2	102	10
Lane, Burlington	6	3	.667	3.39	57	0	0	24	0	4	79.2	73	39	30	9	5	46	5	72	7
Lanfranco, Beloit	0	0	.000	0.00	1	0	0	1	0	0	0.1	0	0	0	0	0	0	0	0	0
Langford, Cedar Rapids	2	2	.500	2.42	14	0	0	9	0	1	26.0	24	9	7	2	3	11	0	19	5
Lata, Springfield	0	3	.000	11.21	5	5	0	0	0	0	17.2	31	28	22	2	0	12	0	8	5
Lebron, Waterloo	4	3	.571	4.60	13	12	0	0	0	0	62.2	59	36	32	5	1	33	0	38	2
Lee, Appleton	4	4	.500	3.38	6	6	0	0	0	0	34.2	28	17	13	1	1	18	0	30	2
Leftwich, Quad City	11	9	.550	3.28	26	26	5	0	1	0	173.0	158	70	63	6	3	59	0	163	8
Locklear, South Bend*	5	1	.833	2.97	44	0	0	21	0	0	60.2	40	27	20	3	3	31	2	47	2
Lucchetti, Springfield	1	4	.200	7.55	11	10	0	1	0	0	47.2	55	47	40	4	3	46	0	25	5
Luebbers, Cedar Rapids	8	10	.444	3.12	28	28	3	0	0	0	184.2	177	85	64	8	10	64	5	98	11
Mann, Peoria	5	4	.556	4.63	44	1	0	19	0	5	81.2	71	50	42	6	5	50	3	57	7
Manon, Cedar Rapids	0	0	.000	0.00	1	0	0	0	0	0	4.2	6	4	0	0	0	1	0	3	0
Mansur, Kenosha*	1	2	.333	5.46	11	0	0	9	0	1	28.0	34	17	17	2	0	10	1	25	1
Margheim, Cedar Rapids*	4	6	.400	4.13	35	13	1	9	0	2	104.2	103	61	48	7	6	46	0	44	3
Martin, Quad City	8	9	.471	3.89	27	18	1	1	1	0	134.1	128	69	58	4	12	57	1	118	7
Martin, Kane County*	4	10	.286	3.64	38	10	0	19	0	6	99.0	92	50	40	4	3	56	3	106	13
Martinez, Rockford	0	4	.000	5.50	8	8	0	0	0	0	36.0	33	27	22	3	8	25	0	27	7
Mathews, Beloit*	2	1	.667	2.06	7	7	1	0	1	0	39.1	28	11	9	0	0	10	0	45	2
Mathile, Rockford	9	3	.750	2.47	17	17	5	0	2	0	116.2	100	45	32	3	4	19	0	66	4
McCarthy, Cedar Rapids*	2	3	.400	4.17	32	1	0	14	0	2	45.1	37	26	21	2	3	27	3	43	5
McCarty, Madison*	4	5	.444	2.58	19	14	1	0	0	0	76.2	49	30	22	5	6	52	2	74	7
McDowell, Burlington	1	0	1.000	6.56	17	0	0	8	0	0	23.1	26	21	17	0	4	24	0	16	0

Pitcher, Team	W	L	Pct.	ERA	G	GS	CG	GF	ShO	Sv.	IP	H	R	ER	HR	HB	BB	Int. BB	SO	WP
McLeod, Clinton	2	4	.333	5.89	15	6	0	6	0	0	36.2	37	30	24	1	6	25	1	19	7
Medrick, Appleton*	0	0	.000	6.19	17	0	0	6	0	0	32.0	40	23	22	1	1	24	3	29	4
D. Mejia, Madison	1	0	1.000	0.00	3	0	0	2	0	1	4.2	3	1	0	0	0	6	2	4	0
L. Mejia, Madison	2	1	.667	4.04	10	9	1	0	0	0	35.2	39	21	16	3	1	15	1	17	1
Millares, Kane County	0	0	.000	0.00	1	0	0	1	0	0	0.2	0	0	0	0	0	2	0	0	0
Miller, Beloit	3	4	.429	1.63	33	1	0	24	0	9	99.1	70	23	18	2	2	24	9	64	2
Milton, Appleton	6	13	.316	6.69	26	24	0	0	0	0	122.1	142	110	91	9	6	80	0	62	15
Montoya, Quad City*	4	1	.800	5.13	8	8	0	0	0	0	40.1	55	27	23	2	0	12	0	22	4
Mortensen, Waterloo*	5	2	.714	3.10	19	6	0	3	0	2	52.1	38	23	18	3	2	30	0	53	1
Myers, Madison	5	8	.385	4.60	37	8	0	21	0	4	105.2	112	68	54	4	3	30	1	84	5
Myers, Clinton*	5	3	.625	2.62	11	11	1	0	0	0	65.1	61	23	19	3	0	18	0	59	4
Myers, Appleton*	1	1	.500	2.60	9	4	0	1	0	0	27.2	22	9	8	0	1	26	0	29	1
Neal, Quad City*	0	2	.000	8.87	10	5	0	4	0	0	22.1	31	26	22	4	2	16	0	12	2
Nielsen, Springfield*	10	9	.526	3.11	26	26	3	0	2	0	170.2	152	76	59	7	6	47	1	142	12
Nieto, Burlington	0	1	.000	3.09	22	0	0	8	0	0	43.2	38	22	15	0	0	23	0	31	5
Normand, Burlington*	0	5	.000	4.63	9	7	0	0	0	0	46.2	54	35	24	7	1	20	0	38	3
Norris, Springfield*	2	0	1.000	4.03	12	0	0	7	0	0	22.1	19	19	10	1	3	21	0	6	2
Nunez, Beloit	0	1	.000	4.00	5	1	0	3	0	1	9.0	9	5	4	1	1	0	0	9	1
Olsen, South Bend	5	2	.714	3.64	13	13	0	0	0	0	81.2	80	44	33	4	3	28	1	76	3
Painter, Waterloo*	14	8	.636	2.30	28	28	7	0	4	0	200.0	162	64	51	14	2	57	7	201	3
Parker, Quad City	0	1	.000	5.68	8	1	0	4	0	0	12.2	15	10	8	0	0	6	0	5	1
Paveloff, Kane County	6	1	.857	3.59	35	0	0	21	0	8	52.2	50	22	21	3	1	16	1	54	3
Peltzer, Clinton*	3	3	.500	4.07	27	0	0	14	0	2	42.0	38	21	19	3	0	17	3	33	8
Pennington, Kane County*	2	2	.500	5.87	23	0	0	19	0	4	23.0	16	17	15	1	0	25	0	43	6
Perez, Peoria	0	1	.000	5.59	7	1	0	3	0	0	9.2	10	11	6	2	0	9	0	4	0
Perez, Appleton	7	5	.583	3.24	34	9	0	6	0	0	100.0	86	45	36	7	4	41	0	73	10
Perigny, South Bend	6	4	.600	1.87	56	0	0	18	0	6	91.2	91	31	19	2	2	22	3	54	6
Persing, Kenosha	11	9	.550	3.43	25	25	2	0	2	0	157.1	125	79	60	10	11	71	0	84	9
Person, South Bend	4	3	.571	3.30	13	13	0	0	0	0	76.1	50	35	28	3	0	56	1	66	4
Peterson, Kenosha	4	3	.571	3.28	24	8	2	7	0	0	71.1	74	36	26	5	3	31	1	34	5
Phoenix, Madison	3	0	1.000	2.95	7	2	0	3	0	2	21.1	26	8	7	0	0	10	0	19	0
Pineda, Appleton	4	7	.364	4.91	37	8	0	23	0	3	88.0	98	58	48	6	2	41	5	72	5
Pollard, Appleton	3	3	.500	2.26	16	4	0	7	0	1	55.2	41	21	14	2	3	44	3	56	9
Powell, Rockford	12	8	.600	3.16	26	26	1	0	0	0	154.0	133	65	54	8	10	64	1	120	21
Pruitt, Beloit	7	4	.636	1.82	12	12	4	0	2	0	79.0	66	26	16	4	4	10	1	71	4
Rea, Appleton	7	11	.389	5.13	27	27	1	0	0	0	151.0	186	108	86	13	7	69	7	97	6
Renko, Rockford	4	5	.444	3.18	16	16	1	0	0	0	99.0	95	43	35	3	4	34	0	102	16
Revenig, Madison	1	0	1.000	0.94	26	0	0	22	0	13	28.2	13	6	3	1	0	10	2	27	1
Reyes, Clinton	1	2	.333	4.42	30	1	0	16	0	1	59.0	57	33	29	1	2	34	2	52	6
Reyes, Rockford	0	1	.000	5.56	3	3	0	0	0	0	11.1	14	8	7	1	3	2	0	10	0
Ritchie, Kenosha	7	6	.538	3.55	21	21	0	0	0	0	116.2	113	53	46	3	7	50	0	101	10
Robinson, Kenosha	1	1	.500	2.13	10	0	0	8	0	2	12.2	15	8	3	0	0	5	1	7	0
Robinson, Cedar Rapids	8	9	.471	3.77	20	19	2	0	1	0	126.2	122	57	53	5	2	48	3	75	4
Romanoli, Springfield*	1	1	.500	1.78	16	0	0	5	0	0	30.1	24	10	6	2	1	12	1	37	1
Ross, Madison	0	1	.000	14.09	10	0	0	5	0	0	15.1	25	28	24	1	2	16	1	15	3
Ross, Peoria*	4	1	.800	3.45	39	0	0	18	0	2	60.0	49	25	23	1	1	42	1	65	6
Rosselli, Clinton*	8	7	.533	3.10	22	22	2	0	0	0	153.2	144	70	53	5	1	49	0	127	11
Ruffcorn, South Bend	1	3	.250	3.92	9	9	0	0	0	0	43.2	35	26	19	1	2	25	0	45	1
Russell, Madison	5	0	1.000	5.36	20	1	0	6	0	0	45.1	60	39	27	2	2	30	0	24	4
Russo, Kenosha	3	0	1.000	3.51	19	0	0	8	0	3	25.2	28	14	10	0	3	12	0	21	0
Ryan, Kane County	0	0	.000	0.96	1	1	0	0	0	0	9.1	6	1	1	0	1	2	0	8	0
Ryan, Rockford*	5	7	.417	4.05	49	0	0	21	0	6	97.2	94	51	44	4	3	32	4	85	4
Salazar, Beloit	0	0	.000	0.00	1	0	0	1	0	0	1.2	0	0	0	0	0	1	0	0	0
Sammons, Madison	0	0	.000	0.00	2	0	0	2	0	0	2.1	2	1	0	0	0	0	0	1	0
Sanders, Waterloo	3	0	1.000	0.68	4	4	0	0	0	0	26.1	17	2	2	0	1	6	0	18	0
Satre, Cedar Rapids	8	6	.571	2.58	21	20	4	1	2	1	132.2	101	48	38	5	2	67	1	130	6
Scott, Clinton	4	3	.571	1.55	47	0	0	36	0	19	75.1	35	18	13	2	1	26	4	123	9
Scott, Burlington*	7	14	.333	5.94	27	27	0	0	0	0	142.1	179	117	94	12	5	89	1	98	18
Shaw, Madison*	7	5	.583	2.60	20	20	1	0	0	0	100.1	82	45	29	1	6	79	1	87	11
Shepherd, South Bend	1	2	.333	0.51	31	0	0	21	0	10	35.1	17	4	2	0	1	19	2	38	5
Silverio, Quad City	0	1	.000	7.16	4	0	0	0	0	0	16.1	18	16	13	0	1	15	0	16	0
Jim Smith, Beloit	2	2	.500	2.77	19	0	0	17	0	9	26.0	19	8	8	0	2	15	3	31	3
John Smith, Beloit	0	0	.000	2.82	8	1	0	3	0	3	22.1	18	7	7	1	0	8	0	14	0
Smith, Madison	0	1	.000	9.82	1	1	0	0	0	0	3.2	7	4	4	2	0	2	0	4	0
Souza, Beloit	0	3	.000	12.08	9	0	0	6	0	1	12.2	16	18	17	1	0	19	0	10	3
Steph, Cedar Rapids	4	3	.571	2.54	8	7	3	0	2	0	56.2	46	19	16	5	4	15	1	46	3
Stephens, Beloit*	0	0	.000	8.59	4	0	0	1	0	0	7.1	12	7	7	1	1	2	0	5	0
Sturtze, Madison	10	5	.667	3.09	27	27	0	0	0	0	163.0	136	77	56	5	5	58	5	88	10
Sudbury, Madison	4	8	.333	4.44	15	14	0	0	0	0	79.0	86	51	39	4	2	41	0	46	6
Sutcliffe, Peoria	0	0	.000	6.00	1	1	0	0	0	0	9.0	12	6	6	0	1	2	0	6	0
Swartzbaugh, Peoria	0	5	.000	1.83	5	5	1	0	0	0	34.1	21	16	7	0	2	15	1	31	2
Swope, Kenosha	6	3	.667	2.69	19	7	2	3	0	1	77.0	76	29	23	2	6	19	0	59	14
Taylor, Peoria	2	4	.333	5.17	15	14	1	1	0	0	78.1	99	60	45	4	5	27	1	42	8
K. Taylor, Kenosha	7	11	.389	3.82	26	26	2	0	1	0	132.0	121	74	56	4	10	84	1	84	11
S. Taylor, Kenosha	1	2	.333	3.00	18	0	0	3	0	0	30.0	31	13	10	2	0	15	1	27	0
Taylor, Kane County	4	11	.267	5.23	26	14	1	2	0	0	96.1	110	70	56	1	1	54	5	59	9
Thelen, Beloit	5	12	.294	3.17	26	23	3	2	0	0	150.2	151	75	53	10	8	35	1	86	6
Thibault, Waterloo*	4	6	.400	5.17	42	4	0	8	0	1	71.1	64	44	41	2	4	59	3	76	11
Tippitt, Kane County	4	6	.400	3.35	18	12	0	4	0	1	91.1	88	46	34	8	0	22	1	61	3
Tolar, South Bend*	8	5	.615	2.83	30	19	0	6	0	1	114.2	87	54	36	3	8	85	0	87	6
Torres, Clinton	16	5	.762	1.41	28	28	8	0	3	0	210.1	148	48	33	4	1	47	2	214	6
Trice, Burlington*	4	2	.667	0.99	35	0	0	33	0	18	45.2	23	7	5	1	1	9	0	53	5
Unrein, Kane County*	0	1	.000	3.40	30	1	0	19	0	1	50.1	51	24	19	2	2	15	1	44	1
Urbani, Springfield*	3	2	.600	2.08	8	8	0	0	0	0	47.2	45	20	11	2	2	6	0	42	1
Vazquez, Beloit	0	1	.000	2.16	7	0	0	6	0	1	16.2	13	8	4	1	1	7	1	7	0
Wall, Burlington	7	5	.583	2.03	16	16	3	0	1	0	106.2	73	30	24	4	4	21	1	102	5
Wegman, Beloit	0	2	.000	1.64	3	3	0	0	0	0	11.0	11	5	2	0	0	5	0	8	2
Weiss, Peoria	6	4	.600	3.83	13	13	1	0	0	0	82.1	72	41	35	1	5	35	1	66	7
Wheeler, Burlington	8	8	.500	3.34	25	23	2	1	1	0	151.0	145	66	56	5	0	52	1	107	7
Whitehead, Rockford	5	5	.500	4.89	22	16	0	0	0	0	92.0	93	66	50	4	3	65	0	61	10
Wiley, Kane County*	5	4	.556	2.43	23	9	0	3	0	0	85.1	71	26	23	3	4	41	0	59	5
Wilkinson, Waterloo	2	3	.400	1.43	7	7	1	0	1	0	37.2	27	12	6	0	2	16	1	22	4
Woodfin, South Bend	0	2	.000	5.79	3	0	0	2	0	1	4.2	5	4	3	0	0	5	3	5	3
Worrell, Waterloo	8	4	.667	3.34	14	14	3	0	2	0	86.1	70	36	32	5	3	33	0	83	1
Yockey, Clinton*	3	2	.600	2.89	36	2	0	7	0	1	65.1	60	29	21	0	1	27	0	72	2

Pitcher, Team	W	L	Pct.	ERA	G	GS	CG	GF	ShO	Sv.	IP	H	R	ER	HR	HB	BB	Int. BB	SO	WP
Young, South Bend	0	2	.000	5.47	13	1	0	4	0	0	26.1	33	19	16	0	1	10	1	14	3
Zimbauer, Beloit	5	4	.556	3.76	11	11	3	0	0	0	67.0	56	33	28	3	3	25	2	66	5

BALKS—Krahenbuhl, 11; Mann, 8; Caridad, Diaz, Farrar, Lane, Mathile, Pineda, 6 each; Alicano, Carlson, Jean, D. Perez, Sturtze, 5 each; M. Anderson, Bigham, Carter, Chrisman, Dovey, F. Gamez, Hays, Luebbers, Pollard, Rosselli, Steph, Torres, 4 each; Allen, Craven, Flanagan, Fritz, Fyock, Gutierrez, Hathaway, Jenkins, Kellogg, Lachemann, Margheim, Mathews, E. Myers, M. Myers, Olsen, Powell, Pruitt, Russo, Silverio, Swope, A. Taylor, Trice, Wheeler, 3 each; P. Anderson, T. Anderson, Arias, Barreiro, Batista, Bjornson, Borcherding, Correa, Dedrick, Delgado, Devore, Dixon, Dunn, Eaton, Eshelman, Fletcher, Fredrickson, Grewal, Griffen, Hoppe, Howze, Jurado, Kirk, Klonoski, Lee, Leftwich, Neal, Nieto, Normand, Perigny, Persing, Rea, J. Reyes, B. Robinson, D. Ross, Ruffcorn, T. Scott, Stephens, Swartzbaugh, K. Taylor, Unrein, Weiss, Wiley, Young, 2 each; Adams, Ahern, Banks, Bere, Berry, Berumen, Blumberg, Botkin, Boze, Brady, Brakeley, Brummett, Chouinard, Cimorelli, Collins, Connolly, Culberson, Doss, Edenfield, Espinal, Farrell, Florie, Godfrey, Gonzales, Grimes, Grove, Haffner, Hebb, Henrikson, Hierholzer, Hoffman, Honeycutt, Kohl, Langford, Lebron, Locklear, J. Martin, Martinez, McCarty, Medrick, Montoya, Mortensen, R. Myers, Painter, Peltzer, Renko, Revenig, Ritchie, D. Scott, Shepherd, John Smith, Sudbury, K. Taylor, Thibault, Tippitt, Urbani, Whitehead, Worrell, Yockey, Zimbauer, 1 each.

COMBINATION SHUTOUTS—Ahern-Chrisman, Berumen-Dunn, Milton-Bryans-Baez, Milton-Perez, Pollard-Chrisman, Appleton; Carter-Smith, Farrell-Bush-Smith, Beloit; Wheeler-Trice 2, Wall-Hurta-McDowell, Burlington; Griffen-Ferry, Luebbers-Hoffman, Luebbers-Langford-Griffen, Margheim-Hoffman, Robinson-Hoffman, Robinson-Margheim-Edwards, Satre-Ferry, Satre-Langford, Cedar Rapids; Myers-Flanagan-Huffman 2, Torres-Huffman 2, Carlson-Yockey-Huffman, Henrikson-Peltzer, Myers-Huffman, Clinton; Anderson-Martin, Blumberg-Borowski-Paveloff, Eshelman-Martin, Farrar-Chatterton, Farrar-Martin, Hebb-Paveloff-Wiley-Pennington, Martin-Borowski, Kane County; Persing-Hoppe, Persing-Robinson, Ritchie-Hoppe, Ritchie-Klonoski, K. Taylor-S. Taylor-Bigham-Hoppe, Kenosha; McCarty-Dillon, McCarty-Phoenix-Dillon, Phoenix-Brimhall-Gulledge, Shaw-Dillon, Shaw-Johns-Dillon, Shaw-Myers-Revenig, Sturtze-Gulledge, Sturtze-Revenig, Sudbury-Gulledge, Sudbury-Myers, Madison; Doss-Correa-Bliss, Krahenbuhl-Mann-Alicano, Weiss-Alicano, Peoria; Craven-Edenfield, Hathaway-Gamez-Edenfield-Scott, Lachemann-Scott, Silverio-Gamez-Lachemann-Scott, Quad City; Diaz-Whitehead-Brewer 2, Batista-Brewer, Collins-Ryan, Mathile-Howze, Powell-Baxter, Powell-Brewer, Powell-Diaz, Powell-Ryan, Whitehead-Baxter, Rockford; Bere-Perigny-Shepherd 2, Jenkins-Caridad 2, Bere-Campos-Tolar-Perigny, Bere-Hooper-Tolar, Bere-Tolar, Campos-Locklear, Campos-Perigny-Caridad, Jean-Altaffer-Perigny-Shepherd, Jean-Perigny-Locklear-Shepherd, Jenkins-Perigny, Jenkins-Shepherd, Person-Locklear-Hooper, Ruffcorn-Campos-Caridad, Tolar-Locklear-Caridad, South Bend; Bowlan-Keller, Nielsen-Fletcher-Keller, Nielsen-Keller, Springfield; Sanders-Fredrickson 2, Devore-Altaffer, Devore-Thibault, Florie-Bensching, Lebron-Thibault, Painter-Ettles, Sanders-Fredrickson-Bensching, Wilkinson-Hays-Bensching, Waterloo.

NO-HIT GAMES—Kellogg, Beloit, defeated Appleton, 6-0, June 18; Johns, Madison, defeated Burlington, 3-0, July 17.

FIELDING

TEAM

Team	Pct.	G	PO	A	E	DP	PB	Team	Pct.	G	PO	A	E	DP	PB
Waterloo	.970	138	3591	1506	159	127	20	Burlington	.958	137	3607	1327	217	100	42
Quad City	.969	137	3627	1455	163	114	23	Peoria	.958	138	3608	1364	220	110	21
Clinton	.966	139	3626	1440	178	136	21	South Bend	.957	139	3683	1491	231	123	37
Kane County	.961	136	3565	1400	199	107	16	Madison	.956	138	3542	1442	230	116	43
Cedar Rapids	.961	140	3656	1485	208	115	11	Appleton	.956	139	3584	1558	238	143	27
Beloit	.961	137	3599	1484	209	106	10	Kenosha	.955	138	3592	1590	242	131	18
Rockford	.961	137	3625	1640	216	132	20	Springfield	.955	137	3596	1509	239	111	38

Triple plays—Kane County, South Bend.

INDIVIDUAL

*Throws lefthanded.

FIRST BASEMEN

Player, Team	Pct.	G	PO	A	E	DP
Acta, Burlington	.976	6	39	1	1	4
Arredondo, Waterloo*	.987	60	508	33	7	45
Barbara, Quad City*	.997	64	560	38	2	44
Blakeman, Kenosha	.982	109	933	77	19	92
Bruno, Kenosha	.933	3	10	4	1	3
Burns, Burlington	1.000	4	27	0	0	2
Calzado, Springfield	.976	40	297	24	8	26
T. Carter, Beloit	.985	70	565	46	9	53
Cavazzoni, Cedar Rapids	1.000	1	1	1	0	0
Cohick, Quad City*	1.000	1	9	0	0	0
Coughlin, South Bend*	1.000	14	111	10	0	15
Dalesandro, Quad City	.992	21	126	6	1	8
M. Davis, Clinton	.983	18	106	10	2	17
Davis, Burlington	.992	15	115	8	1	8
Day, Appleton	.984	18	117	6	2	12
Dempsey, Springfield	1.000	2	6	0	0	0
Diaz, Beloit	1.000	1	5	1	0	0
Dismuke, Cedar Rapids	.981	121	1027	87	22	88
Duran, Springfield	1.000	1	4	0	0	0
Elliott, Waterloo	1.000	15	129	7	0	7
Erdman, Peoria	1.000	2	2	0	0	0
Farlow, Waterloo	.984	14	114	9	2	9
Fernandez, Peoria*	.976	11	77	4	2	3
Flowers, Kane County	.969	12	87	6	3	7
Giegling, Cedar Rapids	1.000	4	22	0	0	2
Glenn, Beloit	.987	34	267	28	4	22
Grahovac, Clinton	1.000	9	44	2	0	5
GUANCHEZ, Appleton	.9913	104	863	46	8	86
Hammargren, Cedar Rapids	1.000	1	6	0	0	2
Hargis, Rockford	1.000	7	44	3	0	5
Harrel, Appleton	.973	35	224	30	7	29
Harris, Beloit	.979	39	302	32	7	20
Hart, Clinton	.969	14	91	4	3	8
Hartung, Peoria	.990	26	190	11	2	18
Hawks, Waterloo	1.000	1	1	0	0	0
Henry, Madison	.995	25	172	9	1	19
Houk, Kenosha	1.000	12	55	8	0	3
Kellogg, Beloit	1.000	1	2	0	0	1
Kipila, Quad City	.986	61	493	18	7	44
Kuehl, Waterloo	.964	12	76	5	3	9
Lopez, Waterloo	1.000	6	55	5	0	7
McConathy, Kane County	1.000	35	239	21	0	16

Player, Team	Pct.	G	PO	A	E	DP
Medina, Peoria	1.000	9	74	7	0	7
Mercado, Madison	.977	122	945	100	25	82
Millares, Kane County	.957	2	19	3	1	0
Miller, Clinton*	.986	116	945	69	14	91
Miller, Kane County	.984	80	604	31	10	54
Miller, Kenosha	1.000	13	94	10	0	11
Monzon, South Bend	.889	1	7	1	1	0
Mota, Kenosha	.974	18	148	3	4	7
Mundy, Peoria	.978	17	119	13	3	10
Petagine, Burlington*	.978	119	940	60	22	75
Postiff, Peoria	.976	10	79	3	2	6
Pugh, Waterloo*	.995	38	353	10	2	33
Ramos, South Bend	1.000	1	1	0	0	0
Robertson, South Bend*	.993	51	403	40	3	32
B. Rodriguez, Springfield*	.981	67	577	35	12	39
Roso, Kane County	1.000	25	173	11	0	22
Smith, Rockford	.981	30	233	24	5	16
E. Smith, Beloit	.963	4	25	1	1	0
Solimine, South Bend	.976	6	39	2	1	3
Tahan, Springfield	.971	44	343	23	11	32
Tejero, Quad City	1.000	2	16	0	0	1
Torres, Peoria	.985	72	589	47	10	56
Vogel, South Bend	1.000	2	16	4	0	2
Vondran, Cedar Rapids	.987	8	71	3	1	6
Walker, South Bend	.989	73	598	42	7	54
Whalen, Waterloo*	1.000	1	8	1	0	1
Wilson, Cedar Rapids*	.979	10	85	7	2	8
Wilstead, Rockford*	.9911	115	1010	98	10	85

Triple plays—McConathy, Walker.

SECOND BASEMEN

Player, Team	Pct.	G	PO	A	E	DP
Acta, Burlington	.980	10	17	31	1	2
Arias, Cedar Rapids	.932	16	27	41	5	2
Aversa, Springfield	.947	22	29	60	5	10
Bish, Waterloo	.963	56	109	123	9	30
Borgogno, Clinton	.940	20	27	36	4	6
Calcagno, Clinton	1.000	1	1	0	0	0
Carlsen, Madison	.960	89	182	231	17	55
M. Carter, Beloit	1.000	2	7	5	0	1
Casper, Clinton	.941	8	8	24	2	3
Ciesla, Rockford	.931	37	63	99	12	22
Clarke, Appleton	.926	31	43	83	10	26

— 462 —

Player, Team	Pct.	G	PO	A	E	DP
Coleman, South Bend	.895	4	8	9	2	1
Cora, South Bend	1.000	1	2	4	0	1
Craig, Peoria	.918	14	25	31	5	3
M. Davis, Clinton	.973	39	50	94	4	18
Day, Appleton	.964	19	26	55	3	8
Diaz, Peoria	.956	80	145	203	16	32
Diggs, Beloit	.923	7	14	10	2	1
Dotolo, Clinton	1.000	1	2	3	0	1
FILOTEI, Cedar Rapids	.978	94	189	251	10	65
Foster, South Bend	.922	27	54	64	10	12
Frias, Clinton	.940	34	54	88	9	21
Gaither, South Bend	.952	38	69	109	9	25
Garcia, Kane County	.935	34	52	63	8	8
Grebeck, Quad City	.994	34	59	94	1	14
Hawks, Waterloo	1.000	2	3	2	0	1
Henderson, Burlington	.973	17	35	38	2	6
Houk, Kenosha	.968	42	85	129	7	28
Javier, Cedar Rapids	.975	15	33	45	2	7
Johnson, Rockford	.924	50	81	139	18	29
Kasper, Clinton	.962	13	21	30	2	6
Kessinger, Cedar Rapids	.975	8	19	20	1	6
Lak, Clinton	.957	44	87	113	9	29
Lanfranco, Madison	.800	2	0	4	1	1
Malinoski, Rockford	.943	49	86	144	14	26
Martinez, Quad City	1.000	1	1	2	0	0
Meury, Waterloo	.968	83	126	238	12	47
Millares, Kane County	.946	55	136	128	15	29
Minnis, Quad City	1.000	3	5	6	0	2
Miranda, Appleton	.955	101	210	276	23	65
Moberg, Rockford	.957	22	30	58	4	8
Monzon, South Bend	.955	74	154	211	17	38
Moore, Peoria	.935	22	42	44	6	17
Morse, Kenosha	.959	74	154	176	14	45
Oberdank, Quad City	.976	19	30	50	2	9
Picketts, Madison	.952	60	106	134	12	22
Polanco, Quad City	.926	22	41	34	6	9
Powell, Beloit	.951	54	113	159	14	30
Ramos, South Bend	.958	4	11	12	1	0
Riggs, Cedar Rapids	.941	7	15	17	2	3
Rivell, Waterloo	.930	18	32	34	5	11
Rivera, Kenosha	.951	41	71	102	9	16
A. Rodriguez, Springfield	.945	15	19	33	3	9
Rush, Cedar Rapids	.958	5	10	13	1	1
Salazar, Beloit	.949	22	45	49	5	12
Sass, Beloit	1.000	1	1	0	0	0
Soto, Peoria	1.000	1	2	0	0	0
Taylor, Quad City	.964	64	120	173	11	32
Thompson, Burlington	.961	113	226	271	20	62
Tyler, Kane County	.943	55	121	142	16	30
Vargas, Springfield	1.000	6	10	12	0	3
Velez, Cedar Rapids	1.000	1	1	2	0	0
Ward, Clinton	1.000	1	0	3	0	0
Wheat, Beloit	1.000	1	2	2	0	1
Wilson, Peoria	.949	43	89	97	10	23
Wrona, Beloit	.972	59	112	134	7	22

Triple play—Foster.

THIRD BASEMEN

Player, Team	Pct.	G	PO	A	E	DP
Acta, Burlington	.888	57	30	105	17	4
Bish, Waterloo	.903	40	18	84	11	8
Bruno, Waterloo	.932	85	48	172	16	13
Burns, Burlington	.857	1	1	5	1	0
Cabrera, Beloit	.934	26	19	38	4	3
Caraballo, Appleton	.947	79	63	187	14	20
Cavazzoni, Cedar Rapids	.500	2	1	0	1	0
Cerda, Appleton	.901	42	38	108	16	8
Chavez, Burlington	1.000	2	3	0	0	0
Christopherson, Burlington	.844	17	13	25	7	1
Ciesla, Rockford	.928	57	45	123	13	13
Clarke, Appleton	.838	13	4	27	6	2
Coleman, South Bend	.786	3	5	6	3	1
Coss, Kane County	.000	1	0	0	1	0
Dalesandro, Quad City	.913	103	72	180	24	18
M. Davis, Clinton	.919	15	6	28	3	1
Day, Appleton	.773	6	3	14	5	0
Diaz, Peoria	.773	10	4	13	5	0
Diaz, Beloit	1.000	1	0	3	0	0
Diggs, Beloit	.930	15	13	27	3	1
DiMarco, Kane County	.931	30	13	68	6	7
Duffy, Peoria	.909	3	3	7	1	0
Duran, Springfield	.860	106	78	211	47	24
Durant, Kenosha	1.000	1	1	1	0	0
Edwards, Waterloo	.962	24	12	38	2	5
Filotei, Cedar Rapids	.880	7	6	16	3	3
Flores, Beloit	.889	5	1	7	1	0
Forrester, Quad City	1.000	3	2	1	0	0
Frias, Clinton	1.000	2	1	5	0	0
Friedland, Rockford	.878	12	9	27	5	3
Gaither, South Bend	1.000	1	0	1	0	1
Gates, Madison	1.000	2	0	1	0	0
Grebeck, Quad City	.978	17	15	29	1	2
Hawks, Waterloo	1.000	1	0	0	0	0

Player, Team	Pct.	G	PO	A	E	DP
Henry, Madison	.971	60	27	107	4	8
Houk, Kenosha	.846	24	10	34	8	2
Javier, Cedar Rapids	.849	18	9	36	8	1
Kasper, Clinton	.769	5	3	7	3	2
Kessinger, Cedar Rapids	.924	40	36	74	9	6
Lambert, Burlington	.855	68	46	107	26	8
Lanfranco, Madison	.840	85	44	114	30	10
Malinoski, Rockford	.918	17	11	34	4	2
McClain, Kane County	.942	25	12	53	4	5
Medina, Peoria	.778	4	2	5	2	0
Meury, Waterloo	1.000	1	0	1	0	0
Millares, Kane County	.871	30	15	46	9	4
Miller, Kane County	.500	1	1	0	1	0
Minnis, Quad City	.833	15	10	15	5	1
Moberg, Rockford	.877	56	36	92	18	5
Monzon, South Bend	.889	7	7	9	2	1
Morse, Kenosha	.750	3	0	3	1	1
Oberdank, Quad City	.933	12	7	21	2	2
Picketts, Madison	.773	13	6	11	5	0
Postiff, Peoria	.800	1	1	3	1	0
Powell, Beloit	.833	25	17	48	13	4
Ramos, South Bend	.793	11	6	17	6	2
Riggs, Cedar Rapids	.813	41	29	49	18	5
Rivera, Kenosha	1.000	3	4	1	0	0
A. Rodriguez, Springfield	.871	31	15	39	8	1
Paul Russo, Kenosha	.917	124	62	237	27	19
Saenz, South Bend	.890	47	29	68	12	5
Salazar, Beloit	.898	23	15	29	5	7
Seitzer, Kane County	.908	58	51	116	17	12
E. Smith, Beloit	.943	51	39	111	9	9
Stephens, Waterloo	1.000	1	1	0	0	0
Strange, South Bend	.875	75	62	113	25	12
Tahan, Springfield	.500	3	0	1	1	0
Vargas, Springfield	.864	7	7	12	3	1
Vierra, Peoria	.893	127	102	199	36	14
Vondran, Cedar Rapids	.957	36	30	58	4	3
Walker, South Bend	.917	6	2	9	1	1
WARD, Clinton	.958	123	79	217	13	20
Wheat, Beloit	.818	3	3	6	2	1

SHORTSTOPS

Player, Team	Pct.	G	PO	A	E	DP
Andujar, Springfield	.929	27	27	78	8	9
Arias, Cedar Rapids	.727	4	0	8	3	0
Aversa, Springfield	.945	50	70	138	12	22
Bish, Waterloo	.875	3	2	5	1	1
Cabrera, Beloit	.769	5	6	4	3	2
Callari, Rockford	.944	74	114	207	19	46
M. Carter, Beloit	.897	98	122	252	43	39
Chavez, Burlington	.914	112	141	293	41	54
Clarke, Appleton	.881	22	30	44	10	9
Coffey, Peoria	.897	11	11	24	4	5
Coss, Kane County	.833	3	6	9	3	2
M. Davis, Clinton	.954	40	59	107	8	24
Diggs, Beloit	1.000	4	2	5	0	0
Dotolo, Clinton	1.000	2	2	2	0	1
Duffy, Peoria	1.000	2	0	1	0	0
Duncan, Clinton	.927	109	176	282	36	65
Everly, Beloit	.889	2	1	7	1	1
Farlow, Waterloo	.942	102	132	261	24	52
Filotei, Cedar Rapids	1.000	2	2	1	0	0
Forrester, Quad City	.778	5	4	10	4	3
Frias, Clinton	1.000	1	1	1	0	0
Gaither, South Bend	.842	12	13	19	6	3
Gates, Madison	1.000	4	6	9	0	4
Grebeck, Quad City	.973	69	87	200	8	39
Henderson, Burlington	.957	30	54	80	6	15
Hernandez, Madison	.914	121	161	327	46	60
Hocking, Kenosha	.923	104	193	308	42	65
Holbert, Springfield	.951	59	112	181	15	38
Houk, Kenosha	1.000	2	2	0	0	0
Javier, Cedar Rapids	.936	15	28	45	5	7
Johnson, Rockford	.800	1	1	3	1	1
Kasper, Clinton	.800	1	1	3	1	0
Kessinger, Cedar Rapids	.980	11	19	30	1	4
Koelling, Cedar Rapids	.945	35	64	92	9	22
Malinoski, Rockford	.945	79	114	210	19	38
Martinez, Quad City	1.000	5	7	12	0	1
Meury, Waterloo	.955	43	45	104	7	23
Millares, Kane County	.939	19	33	59	6	9
Minnis, Quad City	.913	66	81	180	25	27
Miranda, Appleton	.950	10	14	24	2	5
Monzon, South Bend	1.000	3	0	2	0	0
Moore, Peoria	.912	17	24	38	6	1
Morillo, Appleton	.916	62	93	191	26	47
Oberdank, Quad City	.938	5	4	11	1	3
Picketts, Madison	.887	24	30	56	11	15
Ramirez, Kane County	.935	120	155	303	32	44
Ramos, South Bend	.892	10	15	18	4	4
Rivera, Kenosha	.893	41	57	118	21	25
A. Rodriguez, Springfield	.804	10	14	23	9	4
Rush, Cedar Rapids	.944	75	131	222	21	55
Salazar, Beloit	.966	38	53	115	6	17
Soto, Peoria	.942	108	151	273	26	52

Player, Team	Pct.	G	PO	A	E	DP
Stewart, Appleton	.930	50	79	121	15	37
Vierra, Peoria	1.000	5	6	7	0	3
WILSON, South Bend	.950	123	203	353	29	75
Wilson, Peoria	.880	9	10	12	3	1
Wrona, Beloit	.857	4	1	5	1	1

Triple play—Millares.

OUTFIELDERS

Player, Team	Pct.	G	PO	A	E	DP
Albert, Beloit	.969	54	89	6	3	0
G. Anderson, Quad City*	.943	101	158	7	10	0
Andrews, Appleton	.750	11	8	1	3	0
Arland, Cedar Rapids	.983	26	58	0	1	0
Audley, Kane County	.988	70	158	6	2	3
Banton, Springfield	.944	71	113	4	7	3
Becker, Kenosha*	.963	124	270	19	11	2
Benjamin, Beloit	.979	88	132	8	3	1
Brede, Kenosha*	.988	49	79	3	1	1
Burton, Appleton	.971	132	288	16	9	4
Byrne, Kane County	.942	26	47	2	3	0
Calzado, Springfield	.977	38	83	3	2	0
Cancel, Peoria	.967	100	172	5	6	1
Cavazzoni, Cedar Rapids	.909	18	18	2	2	1
Cohick, Quad City*	.975	103	149	9	4	0
Cole, Appleton	.911	31	36	5	4	1
Coleman, Springfield	.906	44	71	6	8	1
Coughlin, South Bend*	.979	112	168	16	4	2
Couture, Beloit	.000	1	0	0	1	0
Cruz, Burlington	.926	85	106	7	9	1
Cummings, Kenosha	.930	95	166	6	13	0
Cunningham, Peoria	.960	97	164	6	7	0
Dauphin, Peoria*	.981	117	261	2	5	0
Davis, Kane County	.968	24	28	2	1	2
C. Davis, Clinton	.933	47	54	2	4	1
Day, Appleton	.500	4	1	0	1	0
Diaz, Peoria	.667	3	1	1	1	0
Diggs, Beloit	.963	104	223	8	9	2
Donald, Springfield	.962	76	173	4	7	1
Durkin, Rockford	1.000	3	3	0	0	0
Edwards, Beloit*	.976	25	37	3	1	0
Enriquez, Beloit	.932	37	63	5	5	0
FANEYTE, Clinton	.987	106	211	9	3	2
Fayne, Springfield	1.000	34	44	1	0	0
Fernandez, Peoria*	1.000	28	44	0	0	0
Gaither, South Bend	.000	4	0	0	1	0
Gale, Springfield	.833	4	4	1	1	0
Garcia, Kane County	1.000	13	16	1	0	0
W. Gardner, Peoria	.750	8	9	0	3	0
Garrett, Quad City*	.970	100	190	5	6	0
Gash, Waterloo	.980	128	237	13	5	5
Gerald, Appleton	.965	70	127	9	5	2
Giegling, Cedar Rapids	.900	4	9	0	1	0
Gill, Waterloo	.958	108	176	7	8	1
Gillum, Cedar Rapids	.952	124	207	9	11	1
Godin, Kane County	.971	74	124	12	4	1
Gumpf, Kenosha	.962	109	192	10	8	2
Hairston, South Bend	.833	2	5	0	1	0
Harris, Beloit	1.000	1	2	0	0	0
Hart, Clinton	.912	26	30	1	3	0
Hatcher, Burlington	.961	129	235	10	10	5
Hawkins, South Bend	.923	37	45	3	4	0
Henderson, Burlington	1.000	1	1	0	0	0
Hicks, Kane County*	.973	40	69	2	2	0
Hood, South Bend	.977	28	39	4	1	1
Houk, Kenosha	1.000	15	17	0	0	0
Hrabar, Kane County	.989	62	81	5	1	1
Hyzdu, Clinton	.955	120	185	8	9	1
Jones, Cedar Rapids	.976	97	195	5	5	0
Kipila, Quad City	.960	17	23	1	1	1
Little, Peoria	.960	65	92	3	4	0
Lydy, Madison	.967	122	222	14	8	3
McGonnigal, Clinton*	.977	27	36	6	1	1
Mercado, Madison	1.000	3	4	1	0	1
Millares, Kane County	1.000	2	3	0	0	0
Miller, Kenosha	.667	9	2	0	1	0
Moberg, Rockford	.962	43	71	4	3	2
Montgomery, Burlington	.985	118	249	12	4	2
Muratti, Quad City	.992	92	115	10	1	2
Murphy, Rockford	.951	108	172	23	10	6
Murray, Rockford	.970	115	222	5	7	2
Oberdank, Quad City	.957	16	21	1	1	1
Ortiz, Kane County	1.000	44	79	5	0	1
Paredes, Kane County	1.000	21	40	1	0	0
Perozo, Cedar Rapids	.983	31	56	1	1	0
Pfeffer, Kenosha	.833	6	5	0	1	0
Picketts, Madison	1.000	1	1	0	0	0
Poe, South Bend	.936	112	184	6	13	0
Pueschner, Waterloo	.979	95	126	15	3	2
Ramirez, Clinton	.944	15	17	0	1	0
Reid, Madison	.935	77	126	4	9	0
Riggs, Cedar Rapids	1.000	27	39	1	0	1
Rivera, Kenosha	1.000	2	2	0	0	0
Rodriguez, Quad City	.933	29	25	3	2	0
Rumsey, Clinton	.895	9	15	2	2	0
Rumsey, Kenosha	.947	38	71	1	4	0
Sammons, Madison	.974	117	224	5	6	2
Sass, Beloit	.957	20	20	2	1	0
Savinon, Springfield	.977	56	123	4	3	0
Schmidt, Kane County	.939	62	88	5	6	1
Sheppard, South Bend	.941	60	75	5	5	3
Singleton, Beloit	.968	100	155	25	6	1
Slater, Appleton*	1.000	9	12	1	0	1
B. Smith, Burlington	.971	103	194	7	6	1
Smith, Rockford	.938	24	28	2	2	0
Smith, Appleton	.946	114	199	13	12	1
Spann, Waterloo	.976	43	75	5	2	2
Stephens, Waterloo	.913	26	21	0	2	0
Tahan, Springfield	1.000	9	10	1	0	0
Thomas, Madison	.824	11	14	0	3	0
Thomas, Appleton	.968	59	114	8	4	1
Thomas, Madison	.951	70	128	8	7	1
Torres, Peoria	.966	26	53	3	2	1
Valrie, South Bend	.980	83	140	6	3	1
Vasquez, Cedar Rapids	.965	50	106	3	4	0
Velez, Springfield*	.977	115	196	12	5	4
Velez, Cedar Rapids	1.000	16	19	0	0	0
Walker, South Bend	.952	18	38	2	2	0
Weimerskirch, Rockford	.970	130	213	12	7	3
Whalen, Waterloo*	.962	47	49	2	2	0
White, Beloit	.933	10	14	0	1	0
Wilson, Cedar Rapids*	.940	47	60	3	4	1
Young, Madison	.968	101	204	9	7	3
Young, Clinton	.971	91	154	11	5	3

CATCHERS

Player, Team	Pct.	G	PO	A	E	DP	PB
J. Anderson, Quad City	.972	22	124	16	4	5	5
Beasley, Springfield	.975	100	648	87	19	3	23
Beck, Beloit	.969	11	57	6	2	1	1
Belyeu, Peoria	1.000	1	2	0	0	0	0
Bennington, Burlington	.975	26	148	8	4	1	3
Beuerlein, Burlington	.974	11	70	6	2	1	1
Brown, Kenosha	.947	4	16	2	1	0	0
Bruno, Kenosha	.982	22	92	15	2	1	4
Burns, Clinton	1.000	4	18	4	0	0	1
Calcagno, Clinton	.974	23	131	20	4	3	2
Christopherson, Clinton	.989	105	758	73	9	8	10
Cox, Cedar Rapids	.929	16	93	12	8	0	0
Dempsey, Springfield	.963	31	162	18	7	2	7
Diaz, Beloit	.978	26	167	8	4	3	1
Dodge, Quad City	.978	17	124	11	3	3	0
Durant, Quad City	.970	56	334	49	12	3	8
Elliott, Waterloo	1.000	1	12	0	0	0	0
Erdman, Peoria	.982	81	543	59	11	6	7
Fitzpatrick, Rockford	.980	70	403	49	9	8	10
Flores, Beloit	.994	44	275	43	2	6	3
Flowers, Kane County	1.000	3	21	2	0	0	0
Fuller, Cedar Rapids	.985	74	474	55	8	2	5
Giegling, Cedar Rapids	.979	31	160	23	4	2	0
Gil, Quad City	1.000	6	44	6	0	1	2
GILMORE, Burlington	.994	81	627	62	4	3	19
Grahovac, Clinton	1.000	10	52	11	0	0	2
Hammargren, Cedar Rapids	.962	33	209	19	9	2	6
Hargis, Rockford	.975	50	319	38	9	7	6
Harrel, Appleton	.931	8	25	2	2	0	1
Hattabaugh, South Bend	1.000	4	20	5	0	1	0
Hawks, Waterloo	1.000	9	24	3	0	0	2
Henderson, Waterloo	.989	60	393	38	5	4	10
Hendley, Madison	.983	58	363	36	7	3	24
Henry, Madison	.986	11	66	2	1	1	2
Jennings, Appleton	.987	77	481	57	7	6	6
Keighley, Rockford	.974	30	194	28	6	1	4
Kinyoun, Appleton	.975	22	137	18	4	2	6
Lanfranco, Burlington	.974	27	197	25	6	1	18
Lopez, Waterloo	.984	88	587	71	11	1	8
Manning, South Bend	.975	23	142	15	4	4	3
McGough, South Bend	.994	49	314	34	2	4	8
Mejias, Clinton	.985	28	121	7	2	2	6
Miller, Kenosha	.990	47	261	42	3	3	5
Molina, Madison	.987	83	530	63	8	8	17
Mota, Kenosha	.971	23	112	23	4	1	1
Mundy, Peoria	.966	45	308	34	12	2	8
Musolino, Quad City	.982	17	102	7	2	0	1
Nessmith, Clinton	1.000	5	26	1	0	1	1
Nunez, South Bend	.969	52	385	50	14	6	14
Piskor, Appleton	.971	23	116	18	4	1	8
Postiff, Peoria	1.000	3	23	2	0	1	1
Reynolds, Kane County	.981	25	194	15	4	3	4
Rivers, Quad City	.985	17	118	11	2	1	4
Robledo, South Bend	.976	16	108	15	3	0	6
Roso, Kane County	.974	12	105	8	3	0	1
L. Smith, Burlington	1.000	2	10	1	0	0	0
Solimine, South Bend	1.000	3	11	2	0	0	2
Stela, Quad City	1.000	4	29	3	0	1	0
Strange, South Bend	1.000	10	65	7	0	0	3
Strickland, Appleton	.978	28	150	24	4	5	6
Tahan, Springfield	1.000	14	73	6	0	0	0
Tallman, Kane County	.950	6	33	5	2	0	0

Player, Team	Pct.	G	PO	A	E	DP	PB
Sc. Taylor, Peoria	.970	16	120	9	4	2	5
Tejero, Quad City	.989	80	598	90	8	6	11
Thomas, Springfield	.977	8	38	5	1	0	1
Vogel, South Bend	.941	7	30	2	2	0	1
West, Waterloo	.976	5	39	1	1	1	0
White, Beloit	.983	85	519	65	10	4	5
Zaun, Kane County	.980	97	697	83	16	7	11

PITCHERS

Player, Team	Pct.	G	PO	A	E	DP
Abel, Kenosha	.875	20	1	6	1	1
Adams, Quad City	.882	22	7	23	4	2
Ahern, Appleton*	.889	10	5	11	2	3
Alicano, Peoria*	.933	43	4	24	2	1
Allen, Burlington	1.000	27	3	11	0	0
Altaffer, 21 S.B.- 18 Water.*	.800	39	4	8	3	1
Anderson, Kane County*	.964	26	8	19	1	2
Anderson, Springfield	.926	27	15	35	4	3
Anderson, Burlington	1.000	6	5	5	0	0
Arias, Springfield	1.000	7	1	1	0	0
Baez, Appleton*	.750	44	0	12	4	2
Banks, Waterloo	.952	39	6	14	1	2
Barreiro, Springfield	1.000	6	0	1	0	0
Batista, Rockford	.919	23	8	26	3	0
Baxter, Rockford*	.960	45	9	15	1	1
Bensching, Waterloo	1.000	54	6	7	0	1
Bere, South Bend	.894	27	13	29	5	0
Berry, Cedar Rapids	1.000	37	5	12	0	1
Berumen, Appleton	.818	13	2	7	2	0
Best, Kenosha	.500	11	1	0	1	0
Bigham, Kenosha*	.833	49	5	5	2	0
Bjornson, Burlington*	.857	6	0	6	1	0
Bliss, Peoria	1.000	20	0	1	0	0
Blumberg, Kane County*	1.000	14	3	10	0	0
Borchering, Cedar Rapids	.900	26	8	28	4	1
Borowski, Kane County	.875	49	3	18	3	1
Botkin, Springfield*	1.000	39	3	10	0	1
Bowlan, Springfield	.973	28	11	25	1	1
Boze, Beloit	1.000	3	0	1	0	0
Brady, Beloit	.909	17	4	6	1	3
Brakeley, Beloit*	.958	29	8	15	1	1
Brewer, Rockford*	.900	29	3	6	1	0
Brimhall, Madison	.913	28	6	15	2	0
Brummett, Clinton	.957	16	7	15	1	3
Bryans, Appleton	.818	18	2	7	2	0
Bush, Beloit	.667	6	1	1	1	0
Campos, South Bend	.939	37	13	18	2	2
Caridad, South Bend	.917	53	3	19	2	3
Carlson, Clinton	.905	27	7	12	2	0
L. Carter, Beloit	.886	30	9	22	4	4
Chatterton, Kane County	1.000	10	0	4	0	0
Chouinard, Kane County	.889	6	2	6	1	0
Chrisman, Appleton	.923	47	5	7	1	1
CIMORELLI, Springfield	1.000	29	16	28	0	1
Collins, Rockford	.846	7	2	9	2	1
Connolly, Madison	1.000	15	2	6	0	1
Correa, Peoria	1.000	39	7	12	0	1
Craven, Quad City	.933	28	3	11	1	0
Culberson, Cedar Rapids	.792	18	6	13	5	1
M. Davis, Clinton	1.000	2	0	1	0	0
Day, Appleton	.500	3	1	0	1	0
Dedrick, Kane County	.969	16	9	22	1	1
Delgado, Peoria	.750	9	2	10	4	0
Devore, Waterloo	.957	21	6	16	1	2
Diaz, Rockford	1.000	38	12	25	0	0
Dillon, Madison	1.000	28	5	10	0	0
Dixon, Kenosha*	.913	25	11	31	4	0
Doss, Peoria	.765	25	8	18	8	0
Dovey, Burlington	.773	25	7	10	5	1
Drake, Clinton	.727	14	2	6	3	1
Dunn, Appleton	.840	14	11	10	4	0
Eaton, Springfield	1.000	23	4	4	0	0
Edenfield, Quad City	.957	47	4	18	1	1
Edwards, Cedar Rapids	1.000	37	4	10	0	0
Eshelman, Kane County*	.909	11	4	16	2	0
Espinal, Springfield	.941	39	8	8	1	1
Ettles, Waterloo	1.000	14	0	4	0	0
Farrar, Kane County*	.938	12	3	12	1	0
Farrell, Beloit*	.889	6	0	8	1	2
Ferry, Cedar Rapids	1.000	16	1	2	0	0
Fitzgerald, Beloit*	1.000	9	2	4	0	0
Flanagan, Clinton	.895	44	2	15	2	1
Fletcher, Springfield	.900	56	2	7	1	1
Florie, Waterloo	.906	23	12	36	5	0
Fredrickson, Waterloo	1.000	27	4	5	0	0
Fritz, Quad City	.857	25	3	3	1	1
Fyock, Appleton	.885	17	10	13	3	0
Gamez, Beloit	.981	25	18	34	1	0
Gamez, Quad City*	.957	41	3	19	1	1
S. Gardner, Peoria	1.000	3	1	0	0	0
Godfrey, Peoria	.969	26	7	24	1	2
Gonzales, Burlington	.920	60	6	17	2	1
Grewal, Rockford	.955	46	10	11	1	1
Griffen, Cedar Rapids	1.000	27	14	18	0	0
Grimes, Madison	.958	25	10	13	1	0

Player, Team	Pct.	G	PO	A	E	DP
Grove, Beloit	1.000	13	2	5	0	0
Gulledge, Madison	.870	39	9	11	3	0
Gutierrez, Burlington*	.700	32	2	12	6	0
Haffner, Quad City	1.000	12	5	6	0	0
Harris, Appleton	.800	7	2	6	2	0
Hathaway, Quad City*	.833	20	4	21	5	4
Hauteman, Beloit*	1.000	19	3	12	0	3
Hays, Waterloo	.944	40	2	15	1	0
Hebb, Kane County	.923	26	3	9	1	2
Henrikson, Clinton*	.786	29	0	11	3	2
Henry, Madison	1.000	5	1	0	0	0
Hierholzer, Appleton	.905	49	4	15	2	2
Hoey, South Bend	1.000	17	5	3	0	0
Hoffman, Cedar Rapids	1.000	27	1	7	0	1
Hooper, 13 Bel.- 11 S.B.	1.000	24	1	6	0	1
Hoppe, Kenosha	1.000	38	1	11	0	0
Houk, Kenosha	1.000	1	0	1	0	0
Howze, Rockford	.870	25	8	12	3	2
Huffman, Clinton	.600	50	3	3	4	0
Hurta, Burlington*	.933	56	3	11	1	2
Hvizda, Beloit	1.000	3	1	0	0	0
Ingram, Waterloo	1.000	16	7	24	0	1
Jean, South Bend	.846	25	12	21	6	0
Jenkins, South Bend	1.000	19	5	13	0	3
Johns, Madison*	.952	38	9	31	2	2
Jurado, Rockford	1.000	21	6	11	0	0
Keller, Springfield	1.000	45	6	6	0	0
Kellogg, Beloit	.769	27	6	4	3	0
Kirk, Appleton	.892	38	11	22	4	2
Klancnik, Quad City	1.000	15	0	4	0	0
Klonoski, Kenosha*	.923	33	1	11	1	0
Kohl, Kenosha	.846	28	3	8	2	0
Krahenbuhl, Peoria	.949	23	8	29	2	3
Lachemann, Quad City	.769	33	3	7	3	0
Lane, Burlington	.813	57	2	11	3	1
Langford, Cedar Rapids	.800	14	1	7	2	0
Lata, Springfield	.857	5	2	4	1	0
Lebron, Waterloo	.882	13	4	11	2	2
Lee, Appleton	.667	6	0	2	1	0
Leftwich, Quad City	.956	26	12	31	2	3
Locklear, South Bend*	.947	44	4	14	1	1
Lucchetti, Springfield	.889	11	1	7	1	0
Luebbers, Cedar Rapids	.940	28	16	47	4	3
Mann, Peoria	.947	44	8	10	1	0
Mansur, Kenosha*	1.000	17	1	4	0	1
Margheim, Cedar Rapids*	.969	35	6	25	1	5
Martin, Quad City	1.000	27	8	21	0	4
Martin, Kane County*	.762	38	5	11	5	0
Martinez, Rockford	.875	8	8	6	2	1
Mathews, Beloit*	.909	7	3	7	1	0
Mathile, Rockford	1.000	17	8	13	0	0
McCarthy, Cedar Rapids*	.867	32	5	8	2	0
McCarty, Madison*	.800	19	6	10	4	0
McDowell, Burlington	.750	17	1	2	1	0
McLeod, Clinton	1.000	15	4	5	0	0
Medrick, Appleton*	.875	17	1	6	1	1
D. Mejia, Madison	1.000	3	0	1	0	0
L. Mejia, Madison	1.000	10	3	7	0	0
Miller, Beloit	.950	33	13	6	1	1
Milton, Appleton	.923	26	10	26	3	4
Montoya, Quad City*	.938	8	3	12	1	1
Mortensen, Waterloo*	.714	19	1	4	2	0
Myers, Madison	.967	37	9	20	1	2
Myers, Clinton*	.920	11	5	18	2	2
Myers, Appleton	1.000	9	2	8	0	0
Neal, Quad City*	1.000	10	0	8	0	0
Nielsen, Springfield*	.944	26	7	27	2	3
Nieto, Burlington	1.000	22	7	2	0	0
Normand, Burlington*	1.000	9	4	2	0	0
Norris, Springfield*	1.000	12	1	4	0	0
Nunez, Beloit	1.000	5	2	1	0	0
Olsen, South Bend	.941	13	6	10	1	0
Painter, Waterloo*	.972	28	19	50	2	2
Parker, Quad City	1.000	8	2	3	0	1
Paveloff, Kane County	1.000	35	1	11	0	0
Peltzer, Clinton*	1.000	27	5	9	0	0
Pennington, Kane County*	.500	23	0	2	2	0
Perez, Appleton	.950	34	5	14	1	0
Perigny, South Bend	.848	56	11	17	5	2
Persing, Kenosha	.955	25	17	25	2	0
Person, South Bend	.895	13	8	9	2	0
Peterson, Kenosha	.917	24	7	15	2	0
Phoenix, Madison	.833	7	2	3	1	0
Pineda, Appleton	.905	37	9	10	2	0
Pollard, Appleton	1.000	16	5	4	0	0
Powell, Rockford	.967	26	25	34	2	5
Pruitt, Rockford	1.000	12	10	15	0	1
Rea, Appleton	.962	27	9	16	1	1
Renko, Rockford	.962	16	10	15	1	1
Revenig, Madison	1.000	26	1	3	0	1
Reyes, Clinton	1.000	30	2	8	0	0
Reyes, Rockford	1.000	3	1	2	0	0
Ritchie, Kenosha	.927	21	9	29	3	2
Robinson, Kenosha	1.000	10	1	2	0	0
Robinson, Cedar Rapids	.951	20	12	27	2	0
Romanoli, Springfield*	.714	16	1	4	2	0

MIDWEST LEAGUE

CLASS A

MIDWEST LEAGUE

Player, Team	Pct.	G	PO	A	E	DP
Ross, Madison	.750	10	0	3	1	1
Ross, Peoria*	.929	39	4	9	1	1
Rosselli, Clinton*	.897	22	8	27	4	1
Ruffcorn, South Bend	.909	9	5	5	1	0
Russell, Madison	.929	20	5	8	1	1
Pasq. Russo, Kenosha	1.000	19	2	3	0	0
Ryan, Kane County	1.000	1	1	0	0	0
Ryan, Rockford*	.900	49	2	16	2	1
Salazar, Beloit	1.000	1	0	1	0	0
Sanders, Waterloo	1.000	4	1	6	0	0
Satre, Cedar Rapids	.923	21	9	15	2	2
Scott, Quad City	1.000	47	0	8	0	1
Scott, Burlington*	.861	27	9	22	5	1
Shaw, Madison*	.878	20	8	28	5	1
Shepherd, South Bend	.875	31	2	5	1	1
Silverio, Quad City	1.000	4	1	0	0	0
Ja. Smith, Beloit	.889	19	3	5	1	0
Jo. Smith, Beloit	1.000	8	0	4	0	0
Smith, Madison	1.000	1	3	0	0	0
Souza, Beloit	.500	9	0	1	1	0
Steph, Cedar Rapids	1.000	8	5	15	0	1
Stephens, Beloit*	.750	4	1	2	1	0
Sturtze, Madison	.878	27	20	23	6	2
Sudbury, Madison	.920	15	10	13	2	1
Sutcliffe, Peoria	1.000	1	1	0	0	0
Swartzbaugh, Peoria	.889	5	1	7	1	0
Swope, Kenosha	1.000	19	6	19	0	0
A. Taylor, Peoria	.955	15	5	16	1	1
K. Taylor, Kenosha	.829	26	13	16	6	3
St. Taylor, Kenosha	1.000	18	3	4	0	1
Taylor, Kane County	.850	26	7	10	3	0
Thelen, Kenosha	.886	26	12	19	4	1
Thibault, Waterloo*	1.000	42	3	8	0	0
Tippitt, Kane County	.929	18	10	16	2	2
Tolar, South Bend*	.867	30	6	20	4	1
Torres, Clinton	.918	28	21	24	4	1
Trice, Burlington*	.875	35	4	10	2	0
Unrein, Kane County*	1.000	30	2	10	0	1
Urbani, Springfield*	.889	8	0	8	1	0
Vazquez, Beloit	1.000	7	0	3	0	0
Wall, Burlington	1.000	16	4	18	0	1
Wegman, Beloit	1.000	3	1	3	0	0
Weiss, Peoria	1.000	13	2	16	0	2
Wheeler, Burlington	.968	25	8	22	1	0
Whitehead, Rockford	.903	22	11	17	3	2
Wiley, Kane County*	.938	23	4	11	1	0
Wilkinson, Waterloo	.786	7	4	7	3	1
Woodfin, South Bend*	.333	3	0	1	2	1
Worrell, Waterloo	1.000	14	5	11	0	0
Yockey, Clinton*	1.000	36	8	13	0	0
Young, South Bend	1.000	13	1	4	0	0
Zimbauer, Beloit	.933	11	5	9	1	0

The following players did not have any fielding statistics at the positions indicated or appeared only as a designated hitter, pinch-hitter or pinch-runner: Arredondo, of; Aversa, p; Beniquez, of; Bennington, p; Borgogno, ss; Cole, p; Durant, of; Flores, 2b; Garcia, p; Gibbs, p; Giegling, p; Guanchez, ss; Hammond, p; Hawks, p; Hendley, 1b; Holmes, p; Honeycutt, p; Kimball, p; Lak, of; L. Lanfranco, p; Manon, p; Millares, p; P. Perez, p; Powell, of; Sammons, p; Solimine, 3b; P. Torres, 3b; Vargas, ss; Vondran, c; J. Young, 2b.

LEAGUE CHAMPIONS

Year	Team	Pct.	Year	Team	Pct.	Year	Team	Pct.
1947—	Belleville	.667	1964—	Clinton	.629	1978—	Appleton a	.708
	Belleville	.672		Clinton	.667		Burlington	.500
1948—	West Frankfort*	.708		Fox Cities z	.667	1979—	Waterloo	.600
1949—	Centralia	.627	1965—	Burlington	.667		Quad Cities a	.579
	Paducah (4th)†	.454		Burlington	.677	1980—	Waterloo a	.610
1950—	Centralia‡	.675	1966—	Fox Cities z	.689		Quad Cities	.532
1951—	Paris§	.700		Cedar Rapids	.762	1981—	Wausau a	.636
	Danville (4th)†	.432	1967—	Wisconsin Rapids	.685		Quad Cities	.570
1952—	Danville x	.685		Appleton z	.587	1982—	Madison	.626
	Decatur (3rd)†	.584	1968—	Decatur	.656		Appleton b	.579
1953—	Decatur*	.576		Quad Cities z	.648	1983—	Appleton c	.635
1954—	Decatur	.587	1969—	Appleton	.648		Springfield	.576
	Danville (2nd)‡	.528		Appleton	.690	1984—	Appleton c	.640
1955—	Dubuque*	.587	1970—	Quincy z	.691		Springfield	.504
1956—	Paris y	.656		Quad Cities	.581	1985—	Kenosha b	.568
	Dubuque	.603	1971—	Appleton	.642		Peoria	.536
1957—	Decatur y	.683		Quad Cities a	.548	1986—	Springfield	.621
	Clinton	.623	1972—	Appleton	.598		Waterloo b	.557
1958—	Michigan City	.623		Danville a	.584	1987—	Springfield	.671
	Waterloo z	.613	1973—	Wisconsin Rapids a	.562		Kenosha b	.586
1959—	Waterloo	.613		Danville	.537	1988—	Cedar Rapids a	.621
	Waterloo	.613	1974—	Appleton	.593		Kenosha	.579
1960—	Waterloo	.629		Danville a	.517	1989—	South Bend a	.644
	Waterloo	.677	1975—	Waterloo a	.727		Springfield	.541
1961—	Waterloo	.613		Quad Cities	.624	1990—	Cedar Rapids a	.657
	Quincy z	.594	1976—	Waterloo a	.600		Quad City a	.579
1962—	Dubuque a	.667		Cedar Rapids	.595	1991—	Clinton a	.583
	Waterloo	.625	1977—	Waterloo	.580		Madison	.558
1963—	Clinton	.710		Burlington a	.511			

*Won championship and four-club playoff. †Won four-club playoff. ‡Playoff finals canceled because of bad weather. §Won both halves of split season. xWon first half of split season and tied Paris for second-half title. yWon first-half title and four-team playoff. zWon split season playoff. aLeague divided into Northern and Southern divisions and played split season. Playoff winner. bLeague divided into Northern, Central and Southern divisions. Playoff winner. cLeague divided into Northern, Central and Southern divisions; regular-season and playoff winner. (NOTE— Known as Illinois State League in 1947-48 and Mississippi-Ohio Valley League from 1949 through 1955.)

NEW YORK-PENN LEAGUE

FINAL STANDINGS

McNAMARA DIVISION-EASTERN

Team	W	L	T	Pct.	GB
Pittsfield (Mets)	51	26	0	.662	....
Oneonta (Yankees)	42	35	0	.545	9
Utica (White Sox)	39	37	0	.513	11½
Watertown (Indians)	27	50	0	.351	24

McNAMARA DIVISION-WESTERN

Team	W	L	T	Pct.	GB
Elmira (Red Sox)	47	30	0	.610	....
Auburn (Astros)	38	39	0	.494	9
Batavia (Phillies)	38	40	0	.487	9½
Geneva (Cubs)	35	43	0	.449	12½

STEDLER DIVISION

Team	W	L	T	Pct.	GB
Jamestown (Expos)	51	27	0	.654	....
Erie (Cardinals)	37	41	0	.474	14
Niagara Falls (Tigers)	36	42	0	.462	15
St. Catharines (Blue Jays)	35	42	0	.455	15½
Hamilton (Cardinals)	35	42	0	.455	15½
Welland (Pirates)	30	47	0	.390	20½

COMPOSITE

Team	Pit.	Jam.	Elm.	One.	Uti.	Aub.	Bat.	Erie	N.F.	S.C.	Ham.	Gen.	Wel.	Wat.	W	L	T	Pct.	GB
Pittsfield (Mets)	....	2	4	10	5	4	2	3	2	2	1	2	4	10	51	26	0	.662	....
Jamestown (Expos)	2	....	1	3	1	2	3	8	8	8	5	4	4	2	51	27	0	.654	½
Elmira (Red Sox)	0	3	....	3	3	5	8	3	1	3	2	9	3	4	47	30	0	.610	4
Oneonta (Yankees)	3	1	1	....	8	3	2	3	2	3	2	2	2	10	42	35	0	.545	9
Utica (White Sox)	7	3	1	4	....	3	2	1	3	2	1	2	3	7	39	37	0	.513	11½
Auburn (Astros)	0	2	8	1	1	....	4	2	4	0	3	6	3	4	38	39	0	.494	13
Batavia (Phillies)	2	1	4	2	2	8	....	1	2	2	2	9	1	2	38	40	0	.487	13½
Erie (Independent)	1	2	1	1	3	2	3	....	4	3	7	2	6	2	37	41	0	.474	14½
Niagara Falls (Tigers)	2	2	3	2	1	0	2	5	....	6	4	1	5	3	36	42	0	.462	15½
St. Catharines (Blue Jays)	2	1	1	1	1	4	2	7	2	....	5	1	5	3	35	42	0	.455	16
Hamilton (Cardinals)	3	4	2	2	3	1	2	1	5	5	....	0	6	1	35	42	0	.455	16
Geneva (Cubs)	2	0	3	2	2	6	5	2	3	3	4	....	1	2	35	43	0	.449	16½
Welland (Pirates)	0	4	1	2	0	1	3	3	5	4	4	3	....	0	30	47	0	.390	21
Watertown (Indians)	2	2	0	2	7	0	2	2	1	1	2	2	4	....	27	50	0	.351	24

Major league affiliations in parentheses.

Playoffs—Jamestown defeated Erie, one game to none; Pittsfield defeated Elmira, one game to none; Jamestown defeated Pittsfield, two games to none, to win league championship.

Regular-season attendance—Auburn, 58,233; Batavia, 43,247; Elmira, 79,546; Erie, 70,546; Geneva, 35,676; Hamilton, 69,872; Jamestown, 40,276; Niagara Falls, 62,157; Oneonta, 52,657; Pittsfield, 62,525; St. Catharines, 35,562; Utica, 70,150; Watertown, 58,394; Welland, 37,476. Totals—776,185. Playoffs (4 games)—5,312.

Managers—Auburn, Steve Dillard; Batavia, Ramon Aviles; Elmira, Dave Holt; Erie, Barry Moss; Geneva, Greg Mahlberg; Hamilton, Rick Colbert; Jamestown, Ed Creech; Niagara Falls, Gary Calhoun; Oneonta, Jack Gillis; Pittsfield, Jim Thrift; St. Catharines, Doug Ault; Utica, Mike Gellinger; Watertown, Gary Tuck (through July 8), Jim Gabella (July 9 through end of season); Welland, Lee Driggers. Managerial records of teams with more than one manager: Watertown, Tuck 5-16, Gabella 22-34.

All-Star team—1B—Derrick White, Jamestown; 2B—Rick Juday, Erie; 3B—Rob Grable, Niagara Falls; SS—Frank Rodriguez, Elmira; Util. IF—Tim Flannelly, Oneonta; OF—Robert Butler, St. Catharines; Lyle Mouton, Oneonta; Jim Austin, Jamestown; John Mabry, Hamilton; C—Mike Daniel, Jamestown; Jim Robinson, Geneva; DH—Eric Martinez, Auburn; LHP—Mark Loughlin, Auburn; Brian Looney, Jamestown; RHP—Chris Davis, Elmira; Heath Haynes, Jamestown; Player of the Year—Robert Butler, St. Catharines; Manager of the Year—Ed Creech, Jamestown.

BATTING

TEAM

Team	Avg.	G	AB	R	OR	H	TB	2B	3B	HR	RBI	SH	SF	HP	BB	Int. BB	SO	SB	CS	LOB
Jamestown	.266	78	2644	444	390	703	986	101	28	42	385	15	30	30	406	5	551	111	45	639
Pittsfield	.257	77	2600	437	342	668	879	108	23	19	343	26	23	26	409	6	503	93	36	613
Oneonta	.254	77	2541	426	428	646	957	113	30	46	367	18	35	50	364	10	583	66	42	573
Niagara Falls	.249	78	2557	377	376	636	854	109	14	27	309	21	24	41	367	5	541	77	47	637
Hamilton	.248	77	2573	345	367	639	891	130	13	32	301	10	19	37	301	7	535	92	48	578
Erie	.248	78	2700	400	414	669	1011	138	12	60	338	13	22	37	322	6	632	83	49	603
Auburn	.247	77	2557	365	382	632	865	94	26	29	303	22	28	36	284	11	572	144	64	545
Elmira	.246	77	2559	359	314	629	959	115	19	59	313	12	26	23	296	10	557	77	34	548
Batavia	.242	78	2575	366	369	622	860	96	23	32	304	35	16	42	250	5	464	122	47	498
Welland	.238	77	2587	328	382	616	876	97	20	41	276	10	15	29	258	4	592	88	46	527
Utica	.237	76	2461	358	341	583	784	93	33	14	298	22	23	41	316	7	564	108	43	554
St. Catharines	.234	77	2466	344	354	578	844	111	13	43	294	46	29	26	307	8	483	107	69	518
Geneva	.234	78	2612	336	355	612	844	103	12	35	276	26	27	37	295	4	511	61	36	575
Watertown	.228	77	2552	297	368	583	797	96	14	30	243	28	15	32	303	7	605	102	42	593

INDIVIDUAL

(Leading qualifiers for batting championship—211 or more plate appearances)

*Bats lefthanded. †Switch-hitter.

Player, Team	Avg.	G	AB	R	H	TB	2B	3B	HR	RBI	SH	SF	HP	BB	Int. BB	SO	SB	CS
Juday, Rick, Erie	.338	74	302	59	102	145	19	0	8	45	2	1	3	39	0	48	7	7
Butler, Robert, St. Catharines*	.338	76	311	71	105	152	16	5	7	45	6	3	2	20	5	21	33	15
White, Derrick, Jamestown	.328	72	271	46	89	125	10	4	6	50	0	2	7	40	0	46	8	3
Austin, James, Jamestown	.326	71	258	59	84	131	13	5	8	52	1	6	1	55	1	44	10	6
Campbell, Scott, Jamestown*	.324	69	241	53	78	85	7	0	0	33	4	3	1	56	0	38	6	5
Martinez, Eric, Auburn*	.320	73	278	40	89	138	20	1	9	58	0	6	5	19	5	32	4	1
Mouton, Lyle, Oneonta	.309	70	272	53	84	120	11	2	7	41	0	3	6	31	2	38	15	8

Player, Team	Avg.	G	AB	R	H	TB	2B	3B	HR	RBI	SH	SF	HP	BB	Int. BB	SO	SB	CS
O'Brien, John, Hamilton	.308	77	286	44	88	143	23	1	10	44	0	3	4	34	3	64	3	2
Cantu, Mike, Hamilton	.307	68	225	25	69	109	19	0	7	51	0	5	4	29	0	52	2	2
Grable, Rob, Niagara Falls	.303	73	251	48	76	119	18	2	7	48	1	2	2	47	0	55	2	4

Departmental leaders: G—O'Brien, Pratte, L. Rodriguez, 77; AB—Butler, 311; R—Curtis, 72; H—Butler, 105; TB—Butler, 152; 2B—O'Brien, 23; 3B—Mouton, 10; HR—Colon, Timmons, 10; RBI—Daniel, 62; SH—Lis, 9; SF—Schulte, Seefried, 7; HP—K. Thomas, 9; BB—Curtis, 60; IBB—Butler, Friedman, Martinez, 5; SO—Wilson, 72; SB—Mouton, 60; CS—Mouton, 18.

(All players—listed alphabetically)

Player, Team	Avg.	G	AB	R	H	TB	2B	3B	HR	RBI	SH	SF	HP	BB	Int. BB	SO	SB	CS
Adriana, Sharnol, St. Catharines	.206	51	170	27	35	58	8	0	5	20	1	4	5	26	0	33	9	4
Albrecht, Andrew, Oneonta*	.208	61	192	37	40	60	6	4	2	16	1	1	7	40	0	42	6	6
Allen, Matt, Jamestown	.168	40	125	16	21	34	0	2	3	16	0	3	0	20	2	36	4	1
Anderson, Steve, Oneonta*	.351	47	114	24	40	52	3	3	1	19	1	0	4	19	0	21	3	1
Andujar, Hector, Watertown	.273	3	11	1	3	3	0	0	0	0	0	0	0	1	0	4	0	0
Angotti, Don, Auburn	.192	20	52	3	10	17	1	0	2	7	0	0	1	3	0	11	1	1
Arias, Amador, Erie†	.230	52	200	24	46	70	14	2	2	17	1	2	0	18	1	42	13	5
Arredondo, Joe, Pittsfield	.256	42	117	23	30	37	7	0	0	19	1	1	1	21	0	13	1	0
Astacio, Rafael, Erie	.217	21	69	6	15	22	5	1	0	7	1	0	0	4	0	19	4	0
Austin, Corey, Utica	.273	44	150	24	41	47	4	1	0	15	2	1	3	6	0	33	7	5
Austin, James, Jamestown	.326	71	258	59	84	131	13	5	8	52	1	6	1	55	1	44	10	6
Babki, Blake, Jamestown*	.209	55	129	24	27	39	6	3	0	8	1	1	2	29	1	43	9	2
Bailey, Cory, Elmira	.000	28	1	0	0	0	0	0	0	0	0	0	0	0	0	1	0	0
Bates, Tommy, Watertown	.222	74	261	40	58	82	9	3	3	43	8	2	5	44	1	63	16	3
Beals, Gregory, Pittsfield	.212	39	132	22	28	35	4	0	1	14	2	0	1	24	0	16	2	2
Benbow, Louis, St. Catharines	.177	54	147	13	26	26	0	0	0	4	9	0	6	18	0	39	6	7
Billeci, Craig, Batavia	.267	68	247	37	66	115	14	1	11	45	0	1	8	16	1	46	2	5
Black, Keith, Hamilton	.243	51	136	15	33	43	5	1	1	10	1	1	1	15	1	28	8	3
Blanton, Garrett, Hamilton	.283	20	60	12	17	23	3	0	1	9	0	1	3	13	0	16	1	2
Bohrofen, Brent, Hamilton	.215	51	149	14	32	49	11	0	2	18	2	0	4	11	0	41	5	2
Bonifay, Ken, Welland*	.236	37	140	17	33	50	5	3	2	13	0	0	0	11	1	38	2	1
Brady, Stephen, Utica†	.235	65	226	37	53	71	6	3	2	31	3	4	1	31	0	31	21	6
Bright, Brian, Elmira	.237	61	194	22	46	67	9	0	4	21	1	1	0	17	0	47	3	1
Brito, Luis, Batavia†	.316	22	76	13	24	28	2	1	0	10	2	0	0	6	0	8	9	3
Brohm, Jeff, Watertown	.217	17	46	6	10	22	4	1	2	6	0	0	0	3	0	12	0	1
Brown, Jimmy, Niagara Falls†	.154	42	104	11	16	16	0	0	0	6	0	0	3	22	0	26	6	5
Buchanan, Shawn, Utica	.205	46	127	20	26	33	5	1	0	10	0	0	3	23	0	29	5	2
Burbank, Dennis, Oneonta	.111	27	9	2	1	1	0	0	0	0	0	0	0	2	0	6	0	0
Burguillos, Carlos, Niagara Falls	.275	54	167	22	46	57	11	0	0	18	0	3	1	22	0	18	1	3
Burnett, Roger, Oneonta	.276	62	232	36	64	86	6	2	4	28	0	2	8	17	0	39	3	4
Burton, Essex, Utica	.276	15	58	11	16	16	0	0	0	4	2	0	1	8	0	12	6	2
Butler, Robert, St. Catharines*	.338	76	311	71	105	152	16	5	7	45	6	3	2	20	5	21	33	15
Cabral, Irene, Erie*	.200	9	25	6	5	5	0	0	0	1	0	0	1	9	0	12	3	3
Cabrera, Miguel, Auburn	.226	35	124	10	28	34	2	2	0	9	1	0	1	5	0	30	6	4
Cacini, Ron, Auburn	.229	62	192	15	44	60	13	0	1	15	5	2	1	25	1	61	10	6
Campbell, Keiver, St. Catharines	.228	39	127	19	29	36	5	1	0	16	0	2	1	21	0	37	14	6
Campbell, Scott, Jamestown*	.324	69	241	53	78	85	7	0	0	33	4	3	1	56	0	38	6	5
Cantu, Mike, Hamilton	.307	68	225	25	69	109	19	0	7	51	0	5	4	29	0	52	2	2
Caple, Kyle, Erie	.129	9	31	5	4	12	2	0	2	6	0	0	0	0	0	8	0	0
Cardona, James, Welland*	.229	41	131	15	30	36	4	1	0	9	1	0	1	12	0	19	1	3
Charbonnet, Mark, Watertown*	.282	47	174	18	49	69	4	2	4	19	0	2	3	5	1	31	12	4
Cheek, Patrick, Batavia	.212	55	165	23	35	55	6	1	4	24	3	0	5	13	0	33	2	2
Cholowsky, Dan, Hamilton	.232	20	69	9	16	22	1	1	1	6	0	0	1	9	0	17	6	3
Coffey, Steve, Geneva	.167	14	42	4	7	8	1	0	0	2	1	0	0	5	0	19	1	1
Coleman, John, Oneonta	.143	20	7	1	1	4	0	0	1	3	0	0	0	0	0	3	0	0
Colon, Angel, Welland	.238	30	126	12	30	37	3	2	0	5	1	1	1	5	0	39	7	4
Colon, Felix, Welland	.249	63	205	32	51	95	8	0	12	41	0	1	3	32	1	57	0	2
Conger, Jeff, Welland*	.272	32	81	15	22	31	2	2	1	7	0	0	1	7	0	31	5	2
Coolbaugh, Mike, St. Catharines	.230	71	256	28	59	85	13	2	3	25	4	3	3	17	0	40	4	5
Craig, Dale, Geneva	.107	18	56	7	6	8	2	0	0	2	0	0	1	11	0	16	1	0
Craig, Morris, Geneva*	.136	7	22	2	3	3	0	0	0	3	1	0	0	2	0	4	0	1
Crowley, Jim, Elmira	.209	71	249	36	52	97	13	1	10	34	0	3	1	38	0	51	5	3
Cruz, Julio J., 16 Erie-25 Bat.	.189	41	143	19	27	41	8	0	2	21	2	1	2	20	1	33	1	1
Curtis, Randall, Pittsfield*	.289	75	298	72	86	106	12	1	2	33	3	2	2	60	1	63	26	9
Daniel, Mike, Jamestown	.253	66	221	37	56	94	9	4	7	62	0	6	0	51	1	53	2	0
Davenport, Jim, Hamilton	.178	35	90	14	16	26	5	1	1	6	0	0	5	9	0	39	2	4
Dennison, Scott, Jamestown	.100	17	40	10	4	5	1	0	0	6	0	0	1	16	0	6	1	1
DiFelice, Mike, Hamilton	.210	43	157	10	33	50	5	0	4	15	0	1	9	0	40	1	5	
DiMarco, Steve, Erie*	.223	62	229	28	51	74	9	1	4	24	0	3	2	38	1	47	2	2
Disarcina, Glenn, Utica*	.252	56	202	27	51	63	10	1	0	27	2	0	0	30	0	30	11	2
Doiron, Serge, Utica*	.192	29	73	3	14	16	2	0	0	6	1	1	1	10	0	20	1	0
DuBose, Brian, Niagara Falls*	.256	44	164	26	42	72	7	1	7	31	0	0	1	17	0	32	3	1
Dunn, Brian, Pittsfield	.231	4	13	1	3	3	0	0	0	0	0	0	0	0	0	2	0	0
Durham, Ray, Utica*	.254	39	142	29	36	52	2	7	0	17	2	1	2	25	0	44	12	1
Durkin, Chris, Auburn*	.256	69	246	31	63	94	10	3	5	35	0	2	2	30	1	64	20	7
Eason, Sam, Batavia	.314	15	51	8	16	22	3	0	1	4	0	0	0	8	0	2	1	1
Edwards, Jerome, Batavia	.273	67	242	37	66	83	9	1	2	25	3	2	4	29	0	42	23	10
Edwards, Otis, Watertown	.000	2	5	0	0	0	0	0	0	0	0	0	0	0	0	2	0	0
Eierman, John, Elmira*	.259	64	193	26	50	80	8	2	6	29	0	5	0	30	1	42	7	6
Ellsworth, Ben, Hamilton†	.202	43	119	10	24	31	5	1	0	8	1	1	0	11	0	20	2	1
Encarnacion, Angelo, Welland	.254	50	181	21	46	53	3	2	0	15	0	1	5	0	27	4	3	
Falco, Chris, Jamestown	.230	63	230	28	53	72	10	3	1	24	3	1	3	15	0	39	0	1
Farrell, Jonathan, Welland	.253	69	241	37	61	111	20	3	8	35	0	2	4	31	1	71	9	6
Feeley, Peter, Niagara Falls	.246	57	211	42	52	73	5	2	4	31	1	2	5	22	1	51	5	3
Flannelly, Timothy, Oneonta*	.272	65	268	46	73	116	19	3	6	46	1	5	3	19	3	41	1	3
Foster, Lamar, Batavia*	.236	49	127	17	30	48	7	1	3	13	1	1	1	18	1	30	3	1
Franklin, Micah, 26 Pit.-39 Erie†	.259	65	247	45	64	82	8	2	2	22	2	2	3	46	0	55	16	8
French, Ron, Hamilton	.188	51	138	23	26	36	7	0	1	8	0	1	1	21	0	41	14	4
Friedman, Jason, Elmira*	.273	70	253	36	69	110	13	2	8	36	1	2	3	35	5	43	3	2
Fryman, Troy, Utica*	.242	52	178	23	43	66	15	1	2	16	1	2	1	14	1	45	1	0
Garagozzo, Keith, Oneonta*	.500	15	2	0	1	1	0	0	0	0	0	0	0	1	0	0	0	0
Garces, Jesus, Batavia†	.251	55	179	30	45	51	4	1	0	19	5	1	3	28	0	11	9	3
Garcia, Guillermo, Pittsfield	.274	45	157	23	43	60	13	2	0	24	3	3	1	15	0	38	4	1

Player, Team	Avg.	G	AB	R	H	TB	2B	3B	HR	RBI	SH	SF	HP	BB	Int. BB	SO	SB	CS
Gardner, Willie, Geneva	.259	54	201	31	52	77	8	1	5	16	0	0	1	22	0	68	3	4
Garvey, Don, Welland	.229	50	157	26	36	47	8	0	1	19	0	0	2	16	0	19	3	4
Gibson, Tom, Niagara Falls	.153	30	85	10	13	16	3	0	0	5	0	0	0	11	0	30	4	1
Glanville, Doug, Geneva	.303	36	152	29	46	60	8	0	2	12	3	1	1	11	0	25	17	3
Gomez, Rudy, Geneva	.227	62	229	22	52	62	6	2	0	14	4	2	5	24	1	38	5	5
Grable, Rob, Niagara Falls	.303	73	251	48	76	119	18	2	7	48	1	2	2	47	0	55	2	4
Graham, Tim, Elmira*	.309	61	181	28	56	94	13	5	5	33	1	2	1	23	1	56	5	5
Grissom, Antonio, Batavia	.230	60	209	38	48	74	5	6	3	22	3	3	0	24	0	40	23	9
Grudzielanek, Mark, Jamestown	.262	72	275	44	72	93	9	3	2	32	3	3	3	18	0	43	14	5
Guerrero, Gustavo, Niagara Falls	.000	4	14	1	0	0	0	0	0	0	0	0	0	0	0	5	0	0
Haase, Dean, Utica*	.222	27	72	9	16	19	1	1	0	8	0	1	1	19	0	14	0	0
Haley, Ryan, Niagara Falls	.148	11	27	4	4	5	1	0	0	2	0	0	4	2	0	8	0	0
Harmes, Kris, St. Catharines*	.194	69	232	32	45	79	16	0	6	31	7	1	1	39	2	39	6	6
Hattabaugh, Matt, Utica	.205	26	73	5	15	16	1	0	0	10	0	0	4	17	0	12	0	1
Hawkins, Ty, Erie*	.212	17	66	9	14	21	4	0	1	5	0	0	2	5	0	17	0	1
Hayden, David, Batavia	.222	50	158	16	35	37	2	0	0	9	2	0	3	13	0	24	3	1
Heble, Kurt, St. Catharines	.172	55	128	19	22	46	6	0	6	18	0	1	2	20	0	44	0	2
Helms, Tommy, Utica	.221	35	113	13	25	34	6	0	1	8	2	1	3	11	0	30	3	1
Henderson, Pedro, Watertown	.257	47	140	19	36	48	4	1	2	14	1	0	2	20	0	44	6	2
Henry, Harold, Utica	.275	62	222	32	61	90	14	3	3	30	1	2	6	19	0	63	16	8
Herrera, Jose, St. Catharines*	.333	3	9	3	3	4	1	0	0	2	0	0	1	1	0	2	0	1
Higginbotham, Robin, Niagara Falls*	.265	49	166	15	44	64	5	0	5	21	0	2	5	10	1	34	7	0
Hines, Keith, St. Catharines	.237	73	249	36	59	85	13	2	3	31	4	3	1	21	0	52	16	8
Hinson, Dean, Welland	.150	7	20	4	3	4	1	0	0	4	0	0	0	5	0	9	0	0
Hobson, Todd, Auburn	.155	51	174	20	27	33	4	1	0	10	1	0	1	8	0	63	11	4
Hood, Randy, Erie	.288	16	66	14	19	33	3	1	3	15	2	1	0	10	0	17	9	4
House, Mitch, Welland	.173	57	191	23	33	50	3	1	4	19	1	1	5	26	0	55	1	1
Hubbard, Mark, Oneonta*	.237	73	278	45	66	84	13	1	1	26	2	4	5	51	3	71	4	1
Huston, Patrick, Geneva	.173	47	139	21	24	35	5	0	2	15	2	1	5	29	0	46	1	0
Inman, Bert, Oneonta	1.000	15	1	0	1	1	0	0	0	0	0	0	0	0	0	0	0	0
Jacobs, Frank, Pittsfield*	.233	74	287	51	67	116	12	5	9	50	0	2	0	46	3	56	5	2
James, Greg, Utica	.118	7	17	2	2	2	0	0	0	1	0	1	0	5	0	8	0	1
Jean, Archie, Jamestown	.211	19	38	6	8	9	1	0	0	1	0	0	1	8	0	11	0	2
Jenkins, Brett, Jamestown	.274	31	106	16	29	46	3	1	4	17	0	2	4	9	0	12	1	2
Johnson, A.J., Niagara Falls	.253	53	178	33	45	52	5	1	0	7	4	0	4	24	0	49	10	3
Juday, Rick, Erie	.338	74	302	59	102	145	19	0	8	45	2	1	3	39	0	48	7	7
Kantor, Brad, Watertown	.160	52	162	8	26	36	4	0	2	16	2	0	0	10	0	51	1	4
Koehler, Bart, Pittsfield	.224	16	49	7	11	13	2	0	0	4	0	0	1	4	0	23	0	0
Krevokuch, Jim, Welland	.226	58	195	22	44	58	8	0	2	17	0	4	7	27	0	30	8	6
Lammon, John, Elmira	.257	35	101	6	26	31	3	1	0	10	0	1	3	5	0	24	0	0
Larregui, Ed, Geneva	.248	71	270	34	67	86	12	2	1	28	2	2	5	15	0	29	13	3
Leatherman, Jeff, Welland†	.271	55	170	19	46	52	6	0	0	13	2	1	1	38	1	31	2	2
Leavell, Barry, Welland†	.122	15	49	3	6	7	1	0	0	4	0	1	0	1	0	12	0	2
Levangie, Dana, Elmira	.149	35	94	6	14	17	3	0	0	4	0	0	0	10	1	18	0	1
Linares, Mario, Auburn	.274	51	175	19	48	63	4	1	3	24	0	1	5	13	0	29	1	1
Lis, Joseph, St. Catharines	.291	66	206	36	60	89	12	1	5	27	4	4	4	41	0	19	4	3
Livesey, Steve, Oneonta	.143	39	119	14	17	28	2	0	3	15	1	0	2	6	0	43	1	2
Lora, Jose, Elmira	.119	25	59	12	7	9	0	1	0	3	1	0	0	5	0	24	4	2
Mabry, John, Hamilton*	.310	49	187	25	58	72	11	0	1	31	0	2	2	17	2	18	9	3
Madril, Bill, Elmira	.217	51	152	14	33	52	7	0	4	19	2	1	0	9	0	41	1	1
Mahony, Dan, Erie	.246	36	134	9	33	40	4	0	1	18	0	0	2	5	0	36	0	1
Manning, Henry, Erie	.159	12	44	3	7	8	1	0	0	8	0	2	0	2	0	7	0	0
Marin, Jose, Elmira	.213	22	61	7	13	14	1	0	0	6	1	0	1	5	0	12	7	2
Marrero, Ken, Erie	.191	30	110	10	21	32	5	0	2	11	1	1	0	7	0	30	0	0
Martindale, Ryan, Watertown	.230	67	243	34	56	75	7	0	4	25	1	1	6	21	3	50	7	4
Martinez, Eric, Auburn*	.320	73	278	40	89	138	20	1	9	58	0	6	5	19	5	32	4	1
Martorana, David, Utica	.210	66	243	35	51	69	8	2	2	35	3	3	2	13	0	38	7	2
Marx, Tim, Welland	.128	15	47	2	6	13	1	0	2	4	0	0	0	2	0	5	0	0
Matos, Domingo, Jamestown	.253	68	265	27	67	104	11	1	8	46	0	1	2	12	0	71	1	1
Maxwell, Pat, Watertown*	.182	16	55	5	10	10	0	0	0	5	1	1	0	3	0	9	1	1
McGlone, Brian, Auburn*	.241	58	187	27	45	48	3	0	0	16	4	3	0	19	1	44	8	3
McLin, Joe, Welland	.243	12	37	1	9	14	2	0	1	10	0	1	1	3	0	12	1	0
Mediavilla, Rick, Hamilton	.222	58	225	34	50	74	14	2	2	21	1	0	5	19	0	27	15	6
Medina, Facaner, Batavia†	.222	56	180	21	40	51	3	4	0	16	3	0	4	4	0	23	20	5
Medina, Ricardo, Geneva	.290	59	224	27	65	86	10	1	3	35	0	3	2	19	0	38	2	2
Meza, Larry, Hamilton*	.228	75	281	46	64	74	6	2	0	26	1	2	1	33	0	35	12	6
Millan, Bernie, Pittsfield†	.194	20	62	5	12	12	0	0	0	11	1	2	0	2	0	6	0	1
Miller, Kevin, Niagara Falls*	.288	45	146	23	42	59	12	1	1	23	0	1	4	22	0	40	1	1
Mitchell, Antonio, Welland†	.270	59	211	30	57	96	9	0	10	38	1	1	1	17	0	62	7	3
Mompres, Danilo, Pittsfield	.265	75	272	46	72	93	14	2	1	31	5	3	1	38	0	62	15	6
Montero, Sixto, Auburn	.217	41	143	18	31	41	4	0	2	19	3	1	0	14	0	23	1	1
Moore, Michael, Watertown	.193	31	83	7	16	20	4	0	0	6	3	1	1	7	0	23	0	0
Moore, Tim, Welland	.171	51	158	20	27	32	5	0	0	11	8	2	8	14	0	26	2	2
Moreno, Jose, Watertown	.235	14	34	6	8	10	2	0	0	2	1	0	1	4	0	3	0	0
Morgan, Kevin, Niagara Falls	.238	70	252	23	60	73	13	0	0	26	4	4	3	22	0	49	8	8
Morland, Michael, St. Catharines	.262	46	145	10	38	54	8	1	2	21	2	4	0	22	0	31	0	1
Morris, Aaron, Watertown*	.223	39	103	12	23	33	4	0	2	14	0	0	0	8	0	34	1	0
Motuzas, Jeff, Oneonta	.286	3	7	1	2	2	0	0	0	0	0	0	1	0	0	2	0	0
Mouton, James, Auburn	.264	76	288	71	76	117	15	10	2	40	3	3	7	55	1	32	60	18
Mouton, Lyle, Oneonta	.309	70	272	53	84	120	11	2	7	41	0	3	6	31	2	38	15	8
Murphy, Mike, Auburn	.167	25	66	5	11	11	0	0	0	3	0	1	0	11	1	11	0	0
Nace, Todd, Pittsfield*	.259	23	54	9	14	16	2	0	0	4	1	0	0	14	0	12	0	0
Nash, Rob, Batavia*	.245	31	98	13	24	30	3	0	1	14	1	0	0	12	0	16	2	1
Neff, Marty, Welland	.312	27	109	19	34	58	5	2	5	16	0	1	0	2	0	17	2	2
O'Brien, John, Hamilton	.308	77	286	44	88	143	23	1	10	44	0	3	4	34	3	64	3	2
Ochoa, Rafael, Utica	.257	64	191	30	49	66	3	4	2	25	1	2	2	36	1	64	13	5
O'Neill, Doug, Jamestown	.235	33	119	19	28	38	4	0	2	11	0	0	2	14	0	29	17	4
Otero, Ricardo, Pittsfield†	.292	6	24	4	7	7	0	0	0	2	0	0	0	2	0	1	4	0
Owen, Tommy, Jamestown	.208	27	48	5	10	10	0	0	0	2	0	1	1	11	0	21	1	0
Pena, Porfirio, Batavia	.194	23	72	8	14	26	4	1	2	9	0	2	2	3	0	24	0	0
Perez, Joe, Watertown*	.268	58	164	26	44	63	8	1	3	19	1	3	1	16	1	35	9	4
Perry, Herbert, Watertown	.212	14	52	3	11	13	2	0	0	5	0	0	0	8	0	7	0	0
Phillips, Steve, Oneonta*	.260	62	215	41	56	100	12	7	6	43	1	5	1	46	0	67	8	4
Pierce, Jeffrey, Utica	.241	50	158	22	38	56	10	4	0	24	0	1	1	25	2	26	4	2
Posada, Jorge, Oneonta†	.235	71	217	34	51	78	5	5	4	33	7	1	4	51	0	51	6	5

Player, Team	Avg.	G	AB	R	H	TB	2B	3B	HR	RBI	SH	SF	HP	BB	Int. BB	SO	SB	CS
Pratte, Evan, Niagara Falls†	.292	77	291	53	85	99	10	2	0	29	5	3	1	53	2	45	14	12
Quinlan, Craig, St. Catharines*	.130	23	54	4	7	17	1	0	3	4	0	0	0	8	0	26	1	1
Quintell, John, Oneonta*	.250	22	48	4	12	15	3	0	0	2	1	2	3	4	0	13	1	2
Radachowsky, Gregg, Niagara Falls	.000	2	3	1	0	0	0	0	0	0	0	0	0	3	0	1	0	0
Ragland, Trace, Welland*	.211	33	95	5	20	27	5	1	0	7	1	0	0	3	0	22	2	0
Ramirez, Omar, Watertown	.267	56	210	30	56	79	17	0	2	16	3	1	1	30	0	29	12	3
Rappoli, Paul, Elmira*	.263	69	209	37	55	81	15	1	3	19	2	2	6	34	0	37	11	3
Rea, Clarke, Niagara Falls*	.184	50	147	8	27	33	3	0	1	18	1	2	3	34	0	34	0	0
Richison, David, Auburn	.000	3	11	2	0	0	0	0	0	0	0	0	0	0	0	3	0	0
Robertson, Mike, Utica*	.167	13	54	6	9	13	2	1	0	8	0	0	0	5	0	11	1	1
Robinson, Dwight, Pittsfield*	.214	54	159	18	34	42	4	2	0	16	4	0	3	36	1	41	1	2
Robinson, Jim, Geneva	.284	64	215	31	61	84	11	0	4	27	3	4	3	40	0	26	2	4
Rodriguez, Frank, Elmira	.271	67	255	36	69	98	5	3	6	31	1	3	1	13	1	38	3	3
Rodriguez, Tony, Elmira	.257	77	272	48	70	87	10	2	1	23	2	4	3	32	0	45	29	4
Rojas, Roberto, Niagara Falls*	.214	7	14	2	3	4	1	0	0	0	0	0	0	0	0	6	1	0
Rollins, Pat, Utica	.204	24	49	11	10	15	2	0	1	6	1	1	7	11	0	11	0	1
Ruth, Pat, Batavia	.216	15	51	9	11	12	1	0	0	3	1	0	2	4	0	17	3	0
Saa, Humberto, Geneva	.225	50	160	18	36	42	6	0	0	18	1	2	1	17	0	23	4	4
Sadler, Sean, Niagara Falls	.192	43	151	13	29	36	7	0	0	17	0	2	1	17	0	29	0	0
Sandy, Tim, Pittsfield*	.282	72	259	56	73	90	13	2	0	24	3	3	5	59	0	39	10	4
Sarcia, Joe, Geneva*	.174	43	132	7	23	30	4	0	1	8	0	1	1	13	1	42	1	0
Schall, Gene, Batavia	.341	13	44	5	15	22	1	0	2	8	0	0	3	2	0	16	0	1
Schroeder, Todd, Welland*	.259	26	85	11	22	32	5	1	1	12	1	0	1	12	1	13	3	1
Schulte, Rich, Auburn*	.278	72	263	47	73	94	7	7	0	27	1	7	3	29	1	65	12	10
Sciortino, Mike, Pittsfield*	.250	54	196	23	49	63	10	2	0	26	0	2	1	13	0	38	1	1
Seefried, Tate, Oneonta*	.246	73	264	40	65	105	19	0	7	51	0	7	2	32	0	65	12	3
Seja, Aaron, Niagara Falls*	.125	12	24	2	3	3	0	0	0	0	1	0	0	3	0	6	2	0
Septimo, Felix, St. Catharines	.283	14	46	3	13	14	1	0	0	6	0	0	0	0	0	12	1	0
Sharts, Scott, Watertown	.159	61	207	14	33	55	7	0	5	20	1	2	1	24	1	68	2	2
Shirley, Mike, Watertown	.257	25	74	9	19	25	2	2	0	7	2	0	1	6	0	14	3	2
Shotton, Craig, Welland	.182	45	121	11	22	36	1	2	3	15	0	1	3	14	0	39	4	0
Siebert, Steve, Utica	.204	31	93	10	19	26	3	2	0	11	1	0	3	4	1	35	0	2
Simons, Mitch, Jamestown	.307	41	153	38	47	62	12	0	1	16	2	2	0	39	0	20	23	5
Smith, Robbie, Watertown	.188	51	128	14	24	28	4	0	0	7	1	0	2	28	0	53	8	3
Smolen, Bruce, Batavia	.214	69	234	26	50	59	5	2	0	22	3	3	3	24	0	39	4	2
Soto, Emison, Elmira	.225	33	80	13	18	27	7	1	0	4	0	1	1	8	0	21	0	2
Spencer, Shane, Oneonta	.245	18	53	10	13	17	2	1	0	3	3	0	1	10	0	9	2	2
Sprick, Scott, Erie*	.250	73	280	49	70	116	13	0	11	46	0	1	1	38	2	69	4	0
Stenta, Jeff, Erie	.202	40	119	15	24	28	1	0	1	9	1	1	0	22	0	25	8	4
Story, Jonathan, Utica	.176	12	34	6	6	10	0	2	0	3	0	0	0	8	0	9	1	0
Sullivan, Brian, Niagara Falls*	.302	48	162	40	49	73	8	5	2	27	4	3	4	36	1	23	13	6
Szczepanski, Joe, Geneva*	1.000	26	1	0	1	1	0	0	0	0	0	0	0	0	0	0	0	0
Tavarez, Hector, St. Catharines†	1.000	1	1	0	1	1	0	0	0	0	0	0	0	0	0	0	0	0
Taylor, Aaron, Geneva	.000	21	1	0	0	0	0	0	0	0	0	0	0	0	0	1	0	0
Taylor, Gary, Hamilton*	.240	45	100	21	24	27	3	0	0	14	0	1	1	32	1	18	2	2
Terilli, Joey, Geneva*	.259	66	243	45	63	101	13	5	5	32	0	4	1	45	2	51	4	4
Thomas, Kelvin, Erie*	.264	70	258	55	68	124	21	4	9	30	2	3	9	39	1	69	15	6
Thomas, Tim, Watertown	.000	3	6	0	0	0	0	0	0	0	0	0	0	0	0	3	0	0
Thompson, Brian, Auburn	.229	51	144	26	33	36	3	0	0	17	2	2	3	28	0	40	7	7
Thompson, Scott, Erie	.299	41	167	25	50	83	15	0	6	30	0	7	12	0	37	3	1	
Tijerina, Anthony, Pittsfield†	.243	44	144	16	35	42	5	1	0	17	1	2	4	15	0	13	2	1
Timmons, Osborne, Geneva	.221	73	294	35	65	113	10	1	12	47	0	4	2	18	0	39	4	3
Tokheim, David, Geneva*	.323	40	158	28	51	75	12	3	2	21	2	1	1	9	0	20	6	2
Tolliver, Jerome, Pittsfield	.272	73	268	41	73	103	6	3	6	52	0	2	5	33	0	59	7	4
Tooch, Chuck, Welland	.294	11	34	5	10	12	2	0	0	6	0	1	0	4	0	2	1	0
Turvey, Joe, Hamilton*	.174	38	132	12	23	26	1	1	0	14	0	1	1	11	0	36	1	1
Van Tiger, Tom, Watertown*	.240	59	183	19	44	56	7	1	1	13	0	1	2	35	0	36	14	4
Vargas, Julio, Batavia	.190	34	100	11	19	26	7	0	0	14	3	1	2	15	0	32	3	0
Velez, Noel, Erie	.258	47	163	29	42	60	5	2	3	18	0	1	4	16	0	43	6	2
Veras, Quilvio, Pittsfield†	.267	5	15	3	4	6	0	1	0	2	0	0	0	5	1	1	2	0
Vilet, Thomas, Batavia	.149	38	101	12	15	19	2	1	0	10	1	0	2	8	0	25	8	1
Vogel, Michael, Utica†	.271	23	59	6	16	20	1	0	1	9	1	1	1	14	2	19	0	2
Vosik, Bill, Watertown†	.260	66	192	24	50	59	5	2	0	23	3	1	4	27	0	32	10	5
Warner, Ron, Hamilton	.301	71	219	31	66	86	11	3	1	20	4	1	3	28	0	43	9	2
Weinke, Chris, St. Catharines*	.239	75	272	31	65	85	9	1	3	40	3	3	0	41	1	61	12	9
White, Derrick, Jamestown	.328	72	271	46	89	125	10	4	6	50	0	2	7	40	0	46	8	3
White, John, Jamestown	.242	41	124	16	30	39	5	2	0	9	1	0	2	13	0	38	14	7
Whitman, Jim, Erie	.232	63	224	21	52	77	11	1	4	37	3	6	3	26	1	54	5	7
Whitmore, Darrell, Watertown*	.368	6	19	2	7	11	2	1	0	3	0	0	0	3	0	2	0	0
Wilson, Thomas, Oneonta	.243	70	243	38	59	87	12	2	4	42	0	5	3	34	2	72	4	4
Winslow, Bryant, Auburn	.252	62	214	31	54	78	7	1	5	23	2	0	7	25	0	64	3	1
Womack, Anthony, Welland*	.277	45	166	30	46	52	3	0	1	8	2	0	0	17	0	39	26	6
Wynne, James, Jamestown	.000	18	1	0	0	0	0	0	0	0	0	0	0	0	0	1	0	0
Yorro, Jacinto, St. Catharines	.097	19	113	12	11	13	2	0	0	4	1	1	0	12	0	27	1	1

The following pitchers, listed alphabetically by club, with games in parentheses, had no plate appearances, primarily through use of designated hitters.

AUBURN—Anderson, Tom (9); Biehl, Rod (19); Evans, James (17); Gallaher, Kevin (16); Holliday, Brian (10); Lewis, Jim (7); Loughlin, Mark (15); Martinez, Luis (13); Miller, Tony (20); Rose, Heath (21); Sewell, Joe (9); Waring, Jim (21); White, Chris (26).

BATAVIA—Allen, Ron (8); Anderson, Chad (11); Blazier, Ron (24); Bojcun, Pat (20); Brown, Greg (16); Grace, Mike (6); Green, Tyler (3); Holman, Craig (15); Manicchia, Bryan (33); Nevill, Glenn (29); Sobocinski, Eric (13); Whisenant, Matt (11); Whisonant, John (23).

ELMIRA—Bennett, Joel (13); Brown, Ernie (1); Budrewicz, Tim (24); Caruso, Joe (21); Chafin, John (4); Davis, Chris (18); Delgado, Richard (13); Gonzalez, Melvin (20); Henkel, Robert (18); Konopki, Mark (17); Miller, Todd (11); Mitchelson, Mark (24); Pratts, Tato (4).

ERIE—Andrzejewski, Joe (16); Carter, David (21); Connolly, Matt (19); Jenkins, Jonathan (9); Konieczki, Dominic (24); Krippner, Curt (15); LeTourneau, Jeff (24); Lynch, Mike (16); MacNeil, Doug (12); Millerick, Edwin (5); Peskievitch, Tom (27); Pudlo, Scott (14); Roberts, Tim (10); Smith, Roosevelt (5).

GENEVA—Bliss, William (15); Burlingame, Ben (14); Davis, Steve (20); Kenny, Brian (15); Pacheco, Jose (8); Perez, Leo (13); Perez, Pedro (16); Schramm, Carl (15); Stevens, Dave (9); Tidwell, Mike (24); Trachsel, Stephen (2); Weiss, Scott (1); Young, Mike (23).

HAMILTON—Arias, Jose (2); Badorek, Mike (13); Beltran, Rigo (21); Boone, Antonio (20); Brumley, Duff (15); Castaldo, Joe (17); Creek, Doug (9); DeGrasse, Tom (17); Frascatore, John (30); Hisey, Jason (26); Longaker, Scott (18); Lucero, Kevin (31); Pasquale, Jeff (9); Simmons, Scott (15); Tanderys, Jeff (16); Watson, Al (19).

JAMESTOWN—Ashley, Duane (20); Braunecker, Derek (20); Ferguson, James (13); Figueroa, Matt (8); Haynes, Heath (29); Hostetler, Jeff (14); LaRosa, Mark (14); Looney, Brian (11); Paxton, Darrin (13); Pedraza, Rodney (7); Sproviero, Nick (22); Tarutis, Pete (21); Vanryn, Ben (6).

NIAGARA FALLS—Bergman, Sean (15); Blomdahl, Ben (16); Durussel, Scott (18); Henry, Jimmy (15); Kelley, Richard (15); LeMay, Bob (17); Martin, Doug (19); Miller, Henry (2); Reid, John (17); Reincke, Corey (11); Turri, Shawn (12); Undorf, Bob (15); Walsh, Dennis (18); Withem, Shannon (8).

ONEONTA—Croghan, Andrew (14); Floren, Whitney (4); Gully, Scott (26); Laviano, Frank (19); Long, Joe (1); Munda, Steven (16); Pettitte, Andy (6); Santiago, Sandi (8); Short, Benjamin (33); Sullivan, Grant (15); Thibert, John (3).

PITTSFIELD—Anaya, Mike (12); Carrasco, Hector (12); George, Chris (14); Lehnerz, Mike (3); Lindsay, Darian (25); Manfred, Jim (26); Reichenbach, Eric (15); Scheffler, Jim (22); Schorr, Brad (2); Shanahan, Chris (15); Smith, Ottis (15); Van Rynbach, Cap (17).

ST. CATHARINES—Barton, Paul (20); Burrell, Scott (2); Carrara, Giovanni (15); Ford, Alan (1); Gray, Dennis (15); Kotes, Christopher (16); Lindsay, Tim (16); Lopez, Freddy (1); Lugo, Angel (17); Manaure, Jose (2); Miller, Gary (14); Nolan, Darin (25); O'Connor, James (19); Spoljaric, Paul (4); Weber, Ben (16).

UTICA—Baldwin, Jim (7); Bertotti, Michael (14); Boehringer, Brian (4); Burrow, Jeff (9); Call, Mike (12); Ellis, Robert (15); Fritz, Gregory (17); Heathcott, Mike (6); Herrholz, John (9); Hoey, Andy (14); Kubicki, Marc (23); Levine, Alan (16); McGraw, Walter (3); Olsen, Stephen (2); Tagle, Henry (16); Thomas, Larry (11); Young, Greg (11).

WATERTOWN—Baker, Sam (22); Buzard, Brian (8); Davidson, Grady (11); Fleet, Joe (15); Fronio, Jason (3); Gajkowski, Steve (20); Jewell, Mike (21); Key, Wade (12); Knaplund, Greg (3); Logsdon, Kevin (13); Malley, Mike (6); Stemler, Andy (20); Sweeney, Mark (14); Tatterson, Gary (13); Walden, Alan (17).

WELLAND—Bradley, David (5); Bullard, Jason (6); Christiansen, Jason (8); Coombs, Glenn (13); Danner, Deon (9); de los Santos, Mariano (8); Douris, John (11); Evans, Sean (10); Harrah, Doug (11); Hope, John (3); Jones, Dan (9); Maguire, Michael (26); Martin, Jim (14); McCurry, Jeff (9); Pisciotta, Marc (14); Ramirez, Roberto (16); Roeder, Steve (24); Ruebel, Matt (6); Sparks, Shane (13); Teich, Michael (19).

GRAND SLAMS—Bates, Billeci, Cheek, F. Colon, Crowley, Flannelly, Heble, Linares, Livesey, Madril, Mitchell, Shotton, Sprick, S. Thompson, Tokheim, Tolliver, 1 each.

AWARDED FIRST BASE ON CATCHER'S INTERFERENCE—Hines 3 (DiFelice 2, Caple); Van Tiger 2 (Marrero, Vogel); Charbonnet (Marx); O'Neill (Marrero); F. Rodriguez (J. Robinson); Tokheim (Posada); Tolliver (Moreno); Velez (Encarnacion).

PITCHING

TEAM

Team	ERA	G	CG	ShO	Sv.	IP	H	R	ER	HR	HB	BB	Int. BB	SO	WP	Bk.
Elmira	3.11	77	5	5	24	682.1	577	314	236	30	45	259	3	579	58	5
Utica	3.37	76	6	5	17	651.2	579	341	244	23	31	301	0	545	50	12
Pittsfield	3.38	77	10	5	13	686.0	627	342	258	27	26	316	2	453	42	7
St. Catharines	3.54	77	6	5	17	668.1	641	354	263	35	29	267	9	561	49	15
Hamilton	3.62	77	1	2	16	668.2	620	367	269	44	33	274	1	599	48	23
Geneva	3.64	78	7	4	12	692.1	693	355	280	48	28	236	7	530	51	10
Welland	3.69	77	0	5	19	673.1	621	382	276	46	60	396	9	602	104	11
Batavia	3.69	78	1	9	21	682.1	612	369	280	66	35	301	16	596	74	18
Auburn	3.83	77	2	4	22	673.2	641	382	287	39	47	311	4	515	55	20
Niagara Falls	3.83	78	2	7	17	662.0	612	376	282	31	24	343	4	537	47	26
Watertown	3.85	77	5	3	13	670.1	613	368	287	16	36	399	17	551	66	13
Jamestown	3.93	78	5	4	20	691.0	660	390	302	32	28	348	13	608	66	21
Erie	4.26	78	7	1	16	694.2	644	414	329	53	37	405	5	579	70	10
Oneonta	4.35	77	5	3	21	674.1	676	428	326	19	28	322	5	438	66	14

INDIVIDUAL

(Leading qualifiers for earned-run average leadership—62 or more innings)

*Throws lefthanded.

Pitcher, Team	W	L	Pct.	ERA	G	GS	CG	GF	ShO	Sv.	IP	H	R	ER	HR	HB	BB	Int. BB	SO	WP
Looney, Jamestown*	7	1	.875	1.16	11	11	2	0	1	0	62.1	42	12	8	0	0	28	0	64	6
Call, Utica	6	1	.857	1.26	12	9	2	2	1	0	71.2	61	20	10	0	2	15	0	55	2
Thomas, Utica*	1	3	.250	1.47	11	10	0	0	0	0	73.1	55	22	12	2	0	25	0	61	3
Carrara, St. Catharines	5	2	.714	1.71	15	13	2	0	2	0	89.2	66	26	17	5	8	21	0	83	4
Holman, Batavia	6	2	.750	1.93	15	12	0	1	0	0	79.1	67	27	17	2	2	22	1	53	7
Loughlin, Auburn*	8	2	.800	2.01	15	15	1	0	1	0	94.0	73	32	21	4	7	32	0	78	7
Davis, Elmira	9	3	.750	2.19	18	16	0	1	0	1	98.2	91	35	24	4	0	23	1	65	1
Henry, Niagara Falls*	8	4	.667	2.22	15	15	2	0	2	0	97.1	73	34	24	1	4	54	0	79	6
Kotes, St. Catharines	6	5	.545	2.28	16	16	1	0	0	0	87.0	74	34	22	2	2	37	1	94	7
Henkel, Elmira	6	3	.667	2.34	18	11	0	2	0	2	77.0	58	34	20	3	4	33	0	87	14

Departmental leaders: G—Manicchia, Short, 33; W—Haynes, Shanahan, 10; L—Ellis, Maguire, 9; Pct.—Haynes, .909; GS—C. Davis, P. Perez, Kotes, 16; CG—Anaya, George, Konopki, Sweeney, 3; GF—Short, 33; ShO—Carrara, Henry, O. Smith, 2; Sv.—Bailey, 15; IP—O. Smith, 103.1; H—P. Perez, Weber, 105; R—Ellis, 66; ER—Croghan, 49; HR—Krippner, Nevill, 12; HB—Coombs, 13; BB—Andrzejewski, 65; IBB—Haynes, Manicchia, Nevill, 4; SO—Lynch, 102; WP—Coombs, 25.

(All pitchers—listed alphabetically)

Pitcher, Team	W	L	Pct.	ERA	G	GS	CG	GF	ShO	Sv.	IP	H	R	ER	HR	HB	BB	Int. BB	SO	WP
Allen, Batavia	3	3	.500	3.13	8	7	0	1	0	0	46.0	33	18	16	5	1	7	0	39	2
Anaya, Pittsfield	5	4	.556	2.79	12	12	3	0	1	0	80.2	73	35	25	2	2	28	0	40	5
Anderson, Batavia	3	3	.500	3.51	11	8	1	0	1	0	48.2	56	23	19	8	2	16	0	34	7
Anderson, Auburn	2	3	.400	3.64	9	9	0	0	0	0	54.1	51	23	22	3	1	18	1	44	1
Andrzejewski, Erie	1	5	.167	7.02	16	7	0	1	0	0	42.1	34	42	33	1	6	65	0	31	11
Angotti, Auburn	0	0	.000	4.50	1	0	0	1	0	0	2.0	2	2	1	0	0	4	0	0	0
Arias, Hamilton	0	2	.000	2.45	2	2	0	0	0	0	11.0	11	5	3	0	1	3	0	7	1
Ashley, Jamestown	1	2	.333	5.82	20	1	0	10	0	1	38.2	44	33	25	2	4	31	0	30	7
Badorek, Hamilton	2	5	.286	2.70	13	11	1	1	0	0	63.1	56	33	19	1	3	30	0	48	9
Bailey, Elmira	2	4	.333	1.85	28	0	0	25	0	15	39.0	19	10	8	2	3	12	0	54	2
Baker, Watertown	3	8	.273	2.74	22	7	0	14	0	5	72.1	54	35	22	2	1	38	1	48	8
Baldwin, Utica	1	4	.200	5.30	7	7	1	0	0	0	37.1	40	26	22	0	2	27	0	23	4
Barton, St. Catharines*	1	4	.200	5.93	20	0	0	8	0	0	27.1	30	20	18	2	0	18	2	18	0
Beltran, Hamilton*	5	2	.714	2.63	21	4	0	4	0	0	48.0	41	17	14	4	2	19	0	69	3
Bennett, Elmira	5	3	.625	2.44	13	12	1	0	1	0	81.0	60	29	22	3	6	30	0	75	7
Bergman, Niagara Falls	5	7	.417	4.46	15	15	0	0	0	0	84.2	87	57	42	1	2	42	0	77	5
Bertotti, Utica*	3	4	.429	5.79	14	5	0	3	0	0	37.1	38	33	24	2	2	36	0	33	9
Biehl, Auburn*	5	3	.625	3.48	19	8	0	0	0	0	77.2	51	36	30	4	4	55	0	75	8
Blazier, Batavia	7	5	.583	4.60	24	8	0	0	0	2	72.1	81	40	37	11	3	17	3	77	2
Bliss, Geneva	1	1	.500	5.40	15	0	0	14	0	2	20.0	24	12	12	0	1	4	1	24	5

Pitcher, Team	W	L	Pct.	ERA	G	GS	CG	GF	ShO	Sv.	IP	H	R	ER	HR	HB	BB	Int. BB	SO	WP
Blomdahl, Niagara Falls	6	6	.500	4.46	16	13	0	2	0	0	78.2	72	43	39	2	2	50	0	30	7
Boehringer, Utica	1	1	.500	2.37	4	4	0	0	0	0	19.0	14	8	5	0	2	8	0	19	0
Bohrofen, Hamilton	0	0	.000	0.00	1	0	0	1	0	0	1.0	0	0	0	0	0	0	0	0	0
Bojcun, Batavia	3	6	.333	5.81	20	8	0	6	0	3	69.2	83	60	45	10	5	33	2	53	4
Boone, Hamilton	1	0	1.000	4.50	20	1	0	3	0	0	22.0	16	13	11	2	2	14	0	12	2
Bradley, Welland	0	1	.000	6.28	5	3	0	0	0	0	14.1	17	11	10	1	0	13	0	8	1
Braunecker, Jamestown	4	4	.500	5.43	20	8	1	5	0	0	71.1	84	53	43	3	2	31	2	49	7
Brown, Elmira	0	0	.000	9.00	1	0	0	1	0	0	2.0	2	3	2	0	1	2	0	2	1
Brown, Batavia	1	4	.200	5.33	16	7	0	3	0	1	50.2	47	35	30	5	3	30	1	33	14
Brumley, Hamilton	2	6	.250	3.64	15	15	0	0	0	0	89.0	90	49	36	7	5	24	0	80	5
Budrewicz, Elmira	4	5	.444	4.18	24	6	0	7	0	1	60.1	63	41	28	0	8	30	1	51	6
Bullard, Welland	0	0	.000	0.00	6	0	0	6	0	4	7.0	4	0	0	0	0	4	0	7	0
Burbank, Oneonta	4	2	.667	4.14	23	0	0	8	0	1	50.0	62	29	23	1	2	11	1	32	1
Burlingame, Geneva	5	2	.714	2.84	14	5	0	4	0	1	50.2	49	22	16	2	1	12	0	38	1
Burrell, St. Catharines	0	2	.000	1.50	2	2	0	0	0	0	6.0	3	3	1	1	1	3	0	5	3
Burrow, Utica	1	1	.500	4.56	9	3	0	3	0	1	25.2	28	17	13	4	3	7	0	12	0
Buzard, Watertown*	1	0	1.000	0.59	8	0	0	7	0	3	15.1	9	4	1	0	1	9	0	14	0
Call, Utica	6	1	.857	1.26	12	9	2	2	1	0	71.2	61	20	10	0	2	15	0	55	2
Carrara, St. Catharines	5	2	.714	1.71	15	13	2	0	2	0	89.2	66	26	17	5	8	21	0	83	4
Carrasco, Pittsfield	0	1	.000	5.40	12	1	0	5	0	1	23.1	25	17	14	1	1	21	0	20	7
Carter, Erie	5	4	.556	5.17	21	0	0	9	0	1	47.0	41	28	27	1	4	25	1	29	7
Caruso, Elmira	2	1	.667	2.84	21	4	0	7	0	2	66.2	56	23	21	2	5	29	1	68	8
Castaldo, Hamilton	1	2	.333	7.13	17	1	0	5	0	0	24.0	31	26	19	3	4	15	0	11	5
Chafin, Elmira	0	0	.000	9.82	4	0	0	3	0	0	3.2	4	6	4	0	1	6	0	3	3
Cheek, Batavia	0	0	.000	0.00	1	0	0	1	0	0	1.0	0	0	0	0	0	1	0	1	0
Christiansen, Welland*	0	1	.000	2.53	8	1	0	1	0	0	21.1	15	9	6	1	1	12	1	17	5
Coleman, Oneonta	2	3	.400	2.91	18	5	0	4	0	1	52.2	44	22	17	1	1	30	0	36	4
Connolly, Erie	2	1	.667	4.32	19	0	0	9	0	1	41.2	39	23	20	1	2	26	1	43	5
Coombs, Welland	0	7	.000	7.71	13	12	0	0	0	0	44.1	37	54	38	5	13	62	0	43	25
Creek, Hamilton*	3	2	.600	5.12	9	5	0	1	0	1	38.2	39	22	22	2	3	18	0	45	3
Croghan, Oneonta	5	4	.556	5.63	14	14	0	0	0	0	78.1	92	59	49	6	2	28	0	54	5
Danner, Welland*	2	2	.500	2.96	9	9	0	0	0	0	48.2	44	22	16	4	6	17	0	24	5
Davidson, Watertown*	1	2	.333	6.86	11	0	0	3	0	0	21.0	22	16	16	0	5	20	0	29	5
Davis, Elmira	9	3	.750	2.19	18	16	0	1	0	1	98.2	91	35	24	4	0	23	1	65	1
Davis, Geneva	1	2	.333	8.20	20	1	0	6	0	0	26.1	45	28	24	4	0	17	0	16	5
DeGrasse, Hamilton	0	2	.000	2.93	17	2	0	3	0	0	27.2	33	19	9	1	4	11	0	17	0
Delgado, Elmira	0	1	.000	7.79	13	0	0	9	0	0	17.1	26	16	15	2	1	8	0	10	2
de los Santos, Welland	1	3	.250	5.51	8	6	0	0	0	0	32.2	41	24	20	6	3	21	0	22	7
Douris, Welland	4	1	.800	2.97	11	3	0	2	0	1	39.1	36	20	13	1	2	15	1	37	3
Durussel, Niagara Falls	3	0	1.000	4.64	18	1	0	10	0	3	33.0	38	25	17	1	3	17	2	23	5
Ellis, Utica	3	9	.250	4.62	15	15	1	0	1	0	87.2	86	66	45	4	6	61	0	66	13
Evans, Auburn	2	5	.286	3.65	17	4	0	9	0	2	44.1	39	25	18	2	5	23	1	28	9
Evans, Welland	1	1	.500	4.42	10	6	0	0	0	0	38.2	42	26	19	1	5	20	0	32	3
Ferguson, Jamestown	0	2	.000	6.37	13	5	0	2	0	0	29.2	39	30	21	0	2	25	0	18	9
Figueroa, Jamestown*	2	0	1.000	3.09	8	0	0	4	0	0	11.2	9	4	4	1	0	5	0	9	1
Fleet, Watertown	3	8	.273	4.38	15	15	0	0	0	0	86.1	79	54	42	3	2	54	3	63	14
Floren, Oneonta	0	0	.000	4.82	4	2	0	0	0	0	9.1	5	7	5	0	1	13	0	8	1
Ford, St. Catharines	0	0	.000	4.50	1	1	0	0	0	0	4.0	5	3	2	0	0	2	0	0	0
Frascatore, Hamilton	2	7	.222	9.20	30	1	0	7	0	1	30.1	44	38	31	3	2	22	1	18	1
Fritz, Utica*	4	1	.800	2.81	17	1	0	8	0	1	41.2	35	15	13	2	0	6	0	27	0
Fronio, Watertown	0	1	.000	19.64	3	0	0	2	0	0	3.2	6	8	8	1	0	4	0	1	0
Gajkowski, Watertown	3	3	.500	5.25	20	4	0	7	0	0	48.0	41	36	28	0	6	32	1	34	7
Gallaher, Auburn	2	5	.286	6.94	16	8	0	3	0	0	48.0	59	48	37	1	9	37	0	25	6
Garagozzo, Oneonta*	4	2	.667	4.40	15	15	0	0	0	0	75.2	66	50	37	1	2	62	0	55	9
Garvey, Welland	0	0	.000	10.80	1	0	0	1	0	0	1.2	1	2	2	1	0	0	0	0	0
George, Pittsfield*	6	3	.667	3.22	14	14	3	0	0	0	78.1	66	39	28	3	4	32	0	55	7
Gonzalez, Elmira	5	5	.500	3.72	20	10	1	3	1	1	67.2	54	36	28	5	2	21	0	38	5
Grace, Batavia	1	2	.333	1.39	6	6	0	0	0	0	32.1	20	9	5	3	1	14	1	36	1
Gray, St. Catharines*	4	4	.500	3.74	15	14	0	0	0	0	77.0	63	42	32	1	1	54	0	78	4
Green, Batavia	1	0	1.000	1.20	3	3	0	0	0	0	15.0	7	2	2	0	2	6	0	19	2
Gully, Oneonta	3	3	.500	4.53	26	0	0	17	0	4	43.2	46	28	22	2	3	14	2	38	5
Harrah, Welland	3	3	.500	3.06	11	7	0	0	0	0	47.0	51	22	16	4	4	10	0	48	1
Haynes, Jamestown	10	1	.909	2.08	29	0	0	23	0	11	56.1	31	15	13	3	4	18	4	93	4
Heathcott, Utica	3	1	.750	3.55	6	6	0	0	0	0	33.0	26	19	13	4	1	14	0	14	1
Heble, St. Catharines	4	4	.500	1.00	18	0	0	17	0	3	27.0	23	10	3	0	1	9	1	25	1
Henkel, Elmira	6	3	.667	2.34	18	11	0	2	0	2	77.0	58	34	20	3	4	33	0	87	14
Henry, Niagara Falls*	8	4	.667	2.22	15	15	2	0	2	0	97.1	73	34	24	1	4	54	0	79	6
Herrholz, Utica	0	0	.000	8.79	9	0	0	6	0	0	14.1	10	14	14	1	2	17	0	14	2
Hisey, Hamilton	4	4	.500	3.74	26	0	0	22	0	8	33.2	32	22	14	4	2	6	0	46	5
Hoey, Utica	2	0	1.000	2.66	14	0	0	8	0	3	20.1	26	7	6	1	1	6	0	17	2
Holliday, Auburn	2	3	.400	3.59	10	10	0	0	0	0	52.2	53	28	21	2	4	27	0	34	7
Holman, Batavia	6	2	.750	1.93	15	12	0	1	0	0	79.1	67	27	17	2	2	22	1	53	7
Hope, Welland	2	0	1.000	0.53	3	3	0	0	0	0	17.0	12	1	1	0	2	3	0	15	0
Hostetler, Jamestown*	3	4	.429	6.83	14	14	0	0	0	0	54.0	51	49	41	2	2	64	0	43	6
Inman, Oneonta	5	3	.625	4.08	15	15	0	0	0	0	90.1	75	56	41	1	4	41	0	42	12
Jenkins, Erie	3	3	.500	2.75	9	9	0	0	0	0	59.0	41	22	18	3	5	39	1	43	9
Jewell, Watertown	1	3	.250	3.94	21	0	0	13	0	1	45.2	44	23	20	2	2	24	2	42	2
Jones, Welland	2	2	.500	4.95	9	6	0	0	0	0	36.1	47	31	20	3	2	17	0	25	8
Kelley, Niagara Falls*	4	8	.333	3.32	15	13	0	1	0	0	81.1	75	38	30	7	1	33	1	78	4
Kenny, Geneva	5	7	.417	4.37	15	15	2	0	0	0	90.2	101	55	44	8	3	25	1	56	5
Key, Watertown	6	4	.600	2.67	12	7	1	3	0	0	60.2	48	19	18	3	1	19	2	45	3
Knaplund, Watertown*	0	0	.000	19.29	3	0	0	0	0	0	2.1	3	5	5	0	4	4	0	3	1
Konieczki, Erie*	2	5	.286	3.13	24	0	0	19	0	10	31.2	25	15	11	1	3	16	1	46	5
Konopki, Elmira	9	4	.692	2.64	17	14	3	2	0	1	95.1	76	36	28	4	9	23	0	66	4
Kotes, St. Catharines	6	5	.545	2.28	16	16	1	0	0	0	87.0	74	34	22	2	2	37	1	94	7
Krippner, Erie	3	6	.333	5.50	15	12	2	3	0	0	73.2	66	48	45	12	0	47	0	73	6
Kubicki, Utica	3	4	.429	2.91	23	0	0	17	0	3	43.1	24	18	14	0	5	28	0	56	4
LaRosa, Jamestown*	1	2	.333	3.71	14	12	0	1	0	0	63.0	68	41	26	1	0	16	0	57	8
Laviano, Oneonta	5	3	.625	4.65	19	3	2	4	1	0	62.0	56	36	32	4	2	31	0	31	10
Lehnerz, Pittsfield	0	0	.000	16.20	3	0	0	1	0	0	3.1	0	7	6	0	0	18	0	5	1
Lemay, Niagara Falls*	2	3	.400	2.88	17	1	0	11	0	1	34.1	27	17	11	0	0	21	0	32	1
LeTourneau, Erie	2	3	.400	4.79	24	5	0	10	0	1	62.0	71	46	33	9	4	23	1	44	4
Levine, Utica	6	4	.600	3.18	16	12	2	3	1	1	85.0	75	43	30	2	4	26	0	83	8
Lewis, Auburn	3	2	.600	3.76	7	7	0	0	0	0	38.1	30	20	16	3	3	14	0	26	2
Lindsay, Pittsfield*	7	2	.778	3.00	25	0	0	23	0	4	39.0	31	16	13	4	0	14	1	34	1

Pitcher, Team	W	L	Pct.	ERA	G	GS	CG	GF	ShO	Sv.	IP	H	R	ER	HR	HB	BB	Int. BB	SO	WP
Lindsay, St. Catharines	7	3	.700	3.01	16	11	1	2	0	0	89.2	73	44	30	5	1	27	0	65	10
Logsdon, Watertown*	2	5	.286	4.25	13	11	0	0	0	0	59.1	58	42	28	2	1	41	3	38	6
Long, Oneonta	0	1	.000	12.00	1	1	0	0	0	0	3.0	9	8	4	0	1	1	0	0	0
Longaker, Hamilton	0	2	.000	3.76	18	0	0	7	0	0	26.1	26	17	11	3	1	10	0	23	2
Looney, Jamestown*	7	1	.875	1.16	11	11	2	0	1	0	62.1	42	12	8	0	0	28	0	64	6
Lopez, St. Catharines*	0	0	.000	0.00	1	0	0	1	0	0	1.0	0	0	0	0	0	1	0	0	0
Lora, Elmira	0	0	.000	0.00	1	0	0	1	0	0	1.0	1	0	0	0	0	0	0	0	0
Loughlin, Auburn*	8	2	.800	2.01	15	15	1	0	1	0	94.0	73	32	21	4	7	32	0	78	7
Lucero, Hamilton*	1	0	1.000	3.79	31	0	0	15	0	4	35.2	28	19	15	0	2	18	0	46	3
Lugo, St. Catharines	2	3	.400	4.71	17	0	0	12	0	4	28.2	39	22	15	2	5	11	1	27	5
Lynch, Erie	6	3	.667	2.87	16	15	1	0	0	0	94.0	69	47	30	3	6	51	0	102	13
MacNeil, Erie	3	4	.429	5.47	12	8	2	3	0	0	51.0	59	35	31	7	2	21	0	46	4
Maguire, Welland*	5	9	.357	4.14	26	0	0	14	0	0	41.1	43	24	19	0	3	22	1	27	9
Malley, Watertown*	1	0	1.000	1.50	6	6	0	0	0	0	36.0	22	10	6	0	6	27	0	36	8
Manaure, St. Catharines	0	0	.000	0.00	2	0	0	1	0	1	3.0	4	0	0	0	0	1	0	4	0
Manfred, Pittsfield	6	4	.600	4.18	26	0	0	19	0	0	51.2	50	33	24	0	4	37	1	39	5
Manicchia, Batavia	2	3	.400	1.46	33	0	0	29	0	10	55.1	36	20	9	2	4	15	4	41	7
Martin, Niagara Falls	3	1	.750	4.73	19	2	0	8	0	2	45.2	47	33	24	3	4	16	1	26	3
Martin, Welland*	2	1	.667	3.66	14	0	0	4	0	0	32.0	32	18	13	1	3	23	0	26	5
Martinez, Auburn	2	2	.500	6.75	13	0	0	4	0	0	33.1	39	32	25	3	4	19	0	24	3
McCurry, Welland	2	1	.667	0.57	9	0	0	5	0	1	15.2	11	4	1	0	0	3	0	18	5
McGraw, Utica	0	2	.000	13.50	3	2	0	1	0	0	5.1	10	12	8	0	1	9	0	4	0
Miller, Auburn*	3	2	.600	4.61	20	1	0	14	0	7	27.1	29	18	14	1	1	20	0	36	2
Miller, St. Catharines	0	1	.000	7.20	14	1	0	1	0	0	25.0	36	21	20	4	0	21	0	18	6
Miller, Niagara Falls	0	0	.000	16.20	2	0	0	1	0	0	1.2	3	3	3	0	1	4	0	3	1
Miller, Elmira	2	0	1.000	4.50	11	4	0	4	0	0	32.0	34	20	16	3	1	12	0	17	1
Millerick, Erie	0	0	.000	8.59	5	0	0	0	0	0	7.1	8	7	7	1	0	10	0	4	0
Mitchelson, Elmira*	3	0	1.000	4.11	24	0	0	5	0	1	35.0	28	18	16	2	3	24	0	38	2
Moore, Watertown	0	0	.000	0.00	1	0	0	0	0	0	0.0	0	1	0	0	0	1	0	0	0
Munda, Oneonta	1	1	.500	3.90	16	0	0	4	0	0	32.1	37	19	14	0	3	15	0	14	4
Nevill, Batavia*	6	7	.462	4.33	29	1	0	12	0	4	72.2	67	41	35	12	5	39	4	59	11
Nolan, St. Catharines	0	6	.000	6.99	25	0	0	20	0	0	37.1	48	36	29	2	8	1	0	19	1
O'Connor, St. Catharines	0	3	.000	5.66	19	1	1	5	0	1	47.2	51	36	30	3	3	19	1	41	1
Olsen, Utica	1	0	1.000	0.64	2	2	0	0	0	0	14.0	3	3	1	0	0	4	0	20	1
Owen, Jamestown	1	0	1.000	3.00	5	0	0	3	0	0	9.0	7	3	3	2	0	6	0	5	1
Pacheco, Geneva	1	2	.333	3.04	8	8	1	0	0	0	47.1	53	21	16	2	1	7	0	24	1
Pasquale, Hamilton*	1	0	1.000	0.79	9	0	0	5	0	2	11.1	8	2	1	0	0	6	0	10	1
Paxton, Jamestown*	5	1	.833	2.01	13	6	0	1	0	0	58.1	37	13	13	2	3	27	1	62	2
Pedraza, Jamestown	3	1	.750	2.05	7	7	1	0	1	0	44.0	41	16	10	3	1	6	0	30	2
L. Perez, Geneva	0	0	.000	4.71	13	0	0	3	0	1	21.0	20	12	11	2	4	13	0	17	1
P. Perez, Geneva	4	4	.500	3.06	16	16	1	0	0	0	100.0	105	51	34	6	3	30	0	95	9
Peskievitch, Erie	5	3	.625	2.85	27	3	0	15	0	3	60.0	48	28	19	2	0	30	0	52	4
Pettitte, Oneonta*	2	2	.500	2.18	6	6	1	0	0	0	33.0	33	18	8	1	0	16	0	32	4
Pisciotta, Welland	1	1	.500	0.26	24	0	0	21	0	8	34.0	16	4	1	0	3	20	1	47	7
Pratts, Elmira	0	1	.000	6.35	4	0	0	2	0	0	5.2	5	7	4	1	2	6	0	5	2
Pudlo, Erie	5	3	.625	3.98	14	14	2	0	0	0	86.0	95	45	38	2	2	30	0	47	0
Ramirez, Welland*	2	6	.250	4.12	16	12	0	2	0	1	74.1	66	43	34	7	2	35	0	71	3
Reichenbach, Pittsfield	3	3	.500	4.26	15	15	1	0	1	0	80.1	78	43	38	2	3	33	0	35	2
Reid, Niagara Falls	0	0	.000	4.40	17	0	0	10	0	3	28.2	30	20	14	1	0	9	0	21	1
Reincke, Niagara Falls	0	3	.000	5.73	11	6	0	3	0	1	33.0	36	27	21	6	2	29	0	22	4
Roberts, Erie*	0	1	.000	4.30	10	4	0	1	0	0	29.1	42	24	14	5	0	13	0	14	0
Roeder, Welland	1	2	.333	2.14	24	1	0	8	0	2	46.1	29	24	11	0	7	38	0	55	2
Rose, Auburn*	7	4	.636	2.72	21	8	1	11	0	1	82.2	83	41	25	7	3	25	0	45	2
Ruebel, Welland*	1	1	.500	1.95	6	6	0	0	0	0	27.2	16	9	6	3	4	11	0	27	2
Santiago, Oneonta	2	1	.667	3.38	6	0	0	2	0	1	10.2	9	5	4	0	0	5	0	5	0
Scheffler, Pittsfield	5	2	.714	2.68	22	0	0	16	0	3	57.0	48	23	17	2	3	24	0	51	4
Schorr, Pittsfield	2	0	1.000	1.98	2	2	0	0	0	0	13.2	13	4	3	0	1	5	0	3	0
Schramm, Geneva	5	7	.417	3.41	15	15	2	0	1	0	97.2	80	47	37	7	7	33	1	63	9
Sewell, Auburn	0	1	.000	8.74	9	0	0	4	0	1	11.1	16	13	11	1	1	10	0	6	3
Shanahan, Pittsfield*	10	2	.833	2.92	15	15	1	0	0	0	101.2	96	39	33	5	2	31	0	57	3
Sharts, Watertown	0	1	.000	5.40	2	0	0	2	0	0	1.2	3	4	1	0	1	1	0	0	0
Short, Oneonta	2	4	.333	3.79	33	0	0	33	0	14	35.2	41	24	15	0	2	11	0	44	4
Simmons, Hamilton*	6	4	.600	2.59	15	14	0	0	0	0	90.1	82	34	26	4	1	25	0	78	1
Smith, Pittsfield*	7	2	.778	2.61	15	15	2	0	2	0	103.1	88	49	30	5	2	42	0	79	4
Smith, Erie	0	0	.000	2.79	5	1	0	1	0	0	9.2	6	4	3	0	3	19	0	5	2
Sobocinski, Batavia	0	0	.000	7.58	13	1	0	7	0	0	29.2	26	36	25	2	5	26	0	30	5
Sparks, Welland	0	2	.000	6.39	13	0	0	9	0	2	12.2	17	9	9	1	1	16	1	13	2
Spoljaric, St. Catharines*	0	2	.000	4.82	4	4	0	0	0	0	18.2	21	14	10	1	1	9	0	21	1
Sproviero, Jamestown	8	3	.727	3.72	22	0	0	7	0	2	55.2	61	31	23	4	1	26	3	36	1
Steler, Watertown*	0	3	.000	3.68	20	0	0	12	0	1	29.1	24	15	12	0	1	33	1	32	1
Stevens, Geneva	2	3	.400	2.85	9	9	1	0	0	0	47.1	49	20	15	3	2	14	0	44	2
Sullivan, Oneonta*	6	6	.500	4.29	15	15	2	0	0	0	94.1	92	56	45	2	5	38	2	45	5
Sweeney, Watertown	4	4	.500	3.44	14	10	3	2	1	1	70.2	68	30	27	2	4	35	2	66	4
Szczepanski, Geneva*	3	5	.375	2.82	26	2	0	20	0	4	51.0	46	22	16	6	1	17	2	46	1
Tagle, Utica*	3	1	.750	1.85	16	0	0	14	0	7	24.1	22	7	5	1	0	6	0	24	1
Tanderys, Hamilton	6	3	.667	3.16	16	13	0	2	0	0	77.0	61	36	27	8	1	36	0	43	6
Tarutis, Jamestown	2	2	.500	5.24	21	3	0	8	0	2	55.0	68	43	32	5	3	13	1	43	4
Tatterson, Watertown	0	1	.000	1.80	13	2	0	7	0	2	30.0	29	8	6	0	1	10	1	33	1
Taylor, Geneva	1	3	.250	3.63	21	1	0	14	0	3	34.2	32	15	14	1	2	9	1	30	2
Teich, Welland*	1	3	.250	4.61	19	2	0	4	0	1	41.0	44	25	21	3	2	27	1	40	4
Thibert, Oneonta	1	0	1.000	27.00	3	1	0	1	0	0	3.1	9	11	10	0	0	6	0	2	2
Thomas, Utica*	1	3	.250	1.47	11	10	0	0	0	0	73.1	55	22	12	2	0	25	0	61	3
Tidwell, Geneva*	4	3	.571	2.97	24	0	0	7	0	0	36.1	31	15	12	2	2	16	1	33	1
Trachsel, Geneva	1	0	1.000	1.26	2	2	0	0	0	0	14.1	10	2	2	0	0	6	0	7	0
Turri, Niagara Falls	0	1	.000	7.53	12	0	0	6	0	0	14.1	16	19	12	3	0	15	0	15	3
Undorf, Niagara Falls	2	1	.667	1.67	15	0	0	14	0	4	32.1	22	9	6	1	0	11	0	32	1
Van Rynbach, Pittsfield	0	3	.000	4.53	17	3	0	3	0	1	53.2	59	37	27	3	4	31	0	35	3
Vanryn, Jamestown*	3	3	.500	5.01	6	6	1	0	0	0	32.1	37	19	18	1	2	12	0	23	4
Walden, Watertown	2	7	.222	4.70	17	15	1	0	0	0	88.0	103	58	46	1	1	47	0	67	6
Walsh, Niagara Falls*	2	6	.250	3.73	18	9	0	8	0	3	70.0	60	39	29	5	3	31	0	82	4
Waring, Auburn	0	4	.000	3.84	21	7	0	12	0	3	61.0	70	39	26	5	2	10	1	56	2
Watson, Hamilton*	1	1	.500	2.52	8	8	0	0	0	0	39.1	22	15	11	2	0	17	0	46	1
Weber, St. Catharines	6	3	.667	3.24	16	14	1	2	0	0	97.1	105	43	35	3	4	24	2	60	7
Weiss, Geneva	0	0	.000	0.00	1	1	0	0	0	0	4.0	2	0	0	0	0	1	0	6	2
Whisenant, Batavia*	2	1	.667	2.45	11	10	0	1	0	0	47.2	31	19	13	2	0	42	0	55	4

Pitcher, Team	W	L	Pct.	ERA	G	GS	CG	GF	ShO	Sv.	IP	H	R	ER	HR	HB	Int. BB	SO	WP
Whisonant, Batavia*	3	4	.429	4.21	23	7	0	8	0	1	62.0	58	39	29	4	2	33	66	8
White, Auburn	2	3	.400	3.86	26	0	0	17	0	8	46.2	46	25	20	3	3	17	38	3
White, Jamestown	0	0	.000	31.50	1	0	0	1	0	0	2.0	6	7	7	1	0	3	0	1
Withem, Niagara Falls	1	2	.333	3.33	8	3	0	2	0	0	27.0	26	12	10	0	2	11	17	2
Wynne, Jamestown	3	1	.750	2.83	18	5	0	8	0	4	47.2	35	21	15	2	4	37	46	3
Yorro, St. Catharines*	0	0	.000	0.00	2	0	0	2	0	0	2.0	0	0	0	0	0	2	3	0
Young, Utica	1	1	.500	4.42	11	0	0	5	0	1	18.1	26	11	9	0	6	0	17	0
Young, Geneva	2	4	.333	4.76	23	3	0	3	0	1	51.0	46	33	27	5	1	32	31	7

BALKS—Beltran, 12; Bergman, LaRosa, 7 each; Blomdahl, 6; D. Martin, Short, Sullivan, C. White, 5 each; Gray, Kubicki, Peskievitch, Tarutis, M. Young, 4 each; T. Anderson, Bojcun, Haynes, Holliday, Knaplund, Nolan, Ramirez, Ruebel, Walsh, 3 each; Allen, Baker, Baldwin, Barton, Biehl, Boehringer, G. Brown, Brumley, Carrara, DeGrasse, Ferguson, Frascatore, Gajkowski, Grace, Loughlin, A. Miller, Nevill, Reichenbach, Reincke, Roeder, Schramm, Simmons, Sproviero, Steler, Szczepanski, Van Rynbach, Weber, Whisenant, 2 each; Andrzejewski, Ashley, Blazier, Boone, Braunecker, E. Brown, Burbank, Burlingame, Call, Castaldo, Coleman, Connolly, Davidson, Delgado, Durussel, Floren, Fritz, Gallaher, Gonzales, Henkel, Henry, Herrholz, Hisey, Holman, Jewell, Krippner, Laviano, Levine, Lewis, T. Lindsay, Lynch, Malley, Manicchia, J. Martin, Martinez, McCurry, G. Miller, Millerick, Mitchelson, Pedraza, Pisciotta, Pudlo, Reid, Scheffler, Shanahan, O. Smith, Sobocinski, Trachsel, Walden, Whisonant, 1 each.

COMBINATION SHUTOUTS—Biehl-Miller, Lewis-Evans-Miller, Loughlin-Rose, Auburn; Anderson-Sobocinski, Blazier-Allen, Brown-Bojcun, Green-Manicchia, Holman-Nevill, Whisenant-Anderson-Manicchia, Whisenant-Bojcun, Whisenant-Nevill, Batavia; Davis-Caruso-Bailey, Konopki-Henkel, Konopki-Miller, Elmira; Lynch-Connolly, Erie; Taylor-Burlingame, Trachsel-Bliss, Weiss-Szczepanski-Bliss, Geneva; Simmons-Frascatore-Boone, Watson-Beltran-Lucero-Frascatore, Hamilton; Hostetler-Ashley, Looney-Wynne, Jamestown; Bergman-Walsh 2, Blomdahl-Martin, Blomdahl-Reincke, Kelley-Durussel-Turri-Lemay, Niagara Falls; Garagozzo-Short, Inman-Short, Oneonta; Smith-Scheffler, Pittsfield; Carrara-Barton, Kotes-Heble, Kotes-Nolan, St. Catharines; Bertotti-Kubicki, Heathcott-Kubicki, Utica; Baker-Fronto, Key-Baker, Watertown; Coombs-Harrah-Douris-Sparks, Hope-Roeder-Ramirez, Ramirez-Douris-Sparks, Ruebel-Roeder-Pisciotta, Teich-Roeder, Welland.

NO-HIT GAMES—None.

FIELDING

TEAM

Team	Pct.	G	PO	A	E	DP	PB	Team	Pct.	G	PO	A	E	DP	PB
Jamestown	.962	78	2073	817	115	64	25	Niagara Falls	.956	78	1986	856	131	69	20
Pittsfield	.959	77	2058	869	125	70	10	Oneonta	.952	77	2023	886	146	69	35
Elmira	.958	77	2047	856	126	71	28	Auburn	.951	77	2021	784	144	57	19
Erie	.958	78	2084	819	127	51	21	Welland	.951	77	2020	866	149	58	30
Geneva	.957	78	2077	849	131	82	12	St. Catharines	.951	77	2005	858	149	62	20
Watertown	.957	77	2011	866	129	73	28	Hamilton	.950	77	2006	769	147	50	13
Batavia	.957	78	2047	810	129	64	28	Utica	.948	76	1955	807	152	59	23

Triple plays—Erie, Hamilton, Pittsfield, St. Catharines, Welland.

INDIVIDUAL

*Throws lefthanded.

FIRST BASEMEN

Player, Team	Pct.	G	PO	A	E	DP
Angotti, Auburn	1.000	2	11	1	0	0
Benbow, St. Catharines	1.000	1	1	0	0	0
Billeci, Batavia	.985	45	365	21	6	32
Bonifay, Welland	.997	34	285	22	1	22
Campbell, Jamestown	1.000	1	3	1	0	1
Cantu, Hamilton	.989	21	168	10	2	12
Colon, Elmira	.979	11	82	12	2	7
Coolbaugh, St. Catharines	.982	53	445	34	9	37
Cruz, Erie	1.000	3	27	1	0	0
Daniel, Jamestown	1.000	1	1	0	0	0
Disarcina, Utica	1.000	5	33	4	0	4
DuBose, Niagara Falls	.993	44	377	35	3	34
Foster, Batavia	.989	35	242	21	3	18
Friedman, Elmira*	.988	66	608	56	8	54
Fryman, Utica	.982	52	432	46	9	34
Grable, Niagara Falls	.957	5	42	3	2	3
Heble, St. Catharines	.965	23	200	21	8	15
House, Welland	.977	10	81	5	2	6
Huston, Geneva	1.000	6	50	4	0	3
Jacobs, Pittsfield*	.988	68	605	60	8	55
Leatherman, Welland	.989	14	85	4	1	9
Livesey, Oneonta	.968	8	57	4	2	10
Madril, Elmira	1.000	1	12	0	0	0
E. Martinez, Auburn*	.983	31	226	10	4	14
Matos, Jamestown	.970	35	272	24	9	25
McLin, Welland	1.000	8	58	5	0	6
Medina, Geneva	.996	35	243	27	1	24
K. Miller, Niagara Falls	1.000	4	25	1	0	2
Morris, Watertown*	.995	29	209	12	1	18
O'BRIEN, Hamilton	.993	59	514	21	4	32
Perez, Watertown*	.800	1	3	1	1	0
Quinlan, St. Catharines	1.000	3	20	0	0	1
Robertson, Utica*	.977	13	116	13	3	6
Rollins, Utica	1.000	12	77	15	0	6
Sadler, Niagara Falls	.974	30	241	20	7	20
Sarcia, Geneva*	.971	22	158	12	5	20
Schall, Batavia	1.000	4	28	5	0	3
Schroeder, Welland*	.973	20	171	10	5	8
Sciortino, Pittsfield*	.979	10	86	8	2	8
Seefried, Oneonta	.983	72	667	46	12	56
Sharts, Watertown	.991	59	511	29	5	46
Sprick, Erie	.984	70	629	42	11	42
Terilli, Geneva*	.974	25	210	13	6	27
Thomas, Watertown	1.000	2	13	0	0	1
Vargas, Batavia	1.000	4	17	2	0	4

Player, Team	Pct.	G	PO	A	E	DP
Velez, Erie	.955	6	40	2	2	2
D. White, Jamestown	.981	48	387	17	8	29
Winslow, Auburn	.979	48	398	26	9	31

Triple plays—Cantu, Coolbaugh, Jacobs, Sprick.

SECOND BASEMEN

Player, Team	Pct.	G	PO	A	E	DP
Adriana, St. Catharines	.958	4	11	12	1	0
Albrecht, Oneonta	.917	4	11	11	2	2
Anderson, Oneonta	.965	25	38	45	3	11
Andujar, Watertown	.889	1	5	3	1	2
Arias, Erie	.971	7	11	22	1	2
Astacio, Erie	.955	7	25	17	2	4
Black, Hamilton	.904	36	52	70	13	12
Brady, Utica	1.000	4	9	9	0	3
Brown, Niagara Falls	.800	5	3	5	2	1
Burton, Utica	.946	11	30	40	4	9
Cheek, Hamilton	.938	18	24	37	4	8
Cholowsky, Hamilton	.951	15	36	42	4	11
Colon, Welland	.933	8	10	18	2	3
Coolbaugh, St. Catharines	.980	14	13	36	1	3
M. Craig, Geneva	.844	6	13	14	5	3
Crowley, Elmira	.952	69	128	192	16	39
Dennison, Jamestown	.921	13	22	36	5	7
Durham, Utica	.928	38	54	101	12	16
Ellsworth, Hamilton	.942	39	50	79	8	12
Falco, Jamestown	.979	22	42	53	2	14
Franklin, 26 Pit. -3 Erie	.891	29	52	87	17	12
Garces, Pittsfield	.939	54	102	146	16	28
Garcia, Pittsfield	.979	45	120	117	5	32
Garvey, Welland	.917	39	63	103	15	21
Gomez, Geneva	1.000	1	5	3	0	2
Graham, Elmira	.000	1	0	0	1	0
Helms, Utica	.951	27	48	68	6	14
Jenkins, Jamestown	.959	15	32	39	3	8
Johnson, Niagara Falls	.909	3	3	7	1	3
Juday, Erie	.968	61	118	182	10	23
Kantor, Watertown	.899	16	31	40	8	3
Krevokuch, Welland	.946	33	57	82	8	17
Leatherman, Welland	1.000	1	3	0	0	0
LIS, St. Catharines	.972	62	135	183	9	38
Marin, Elmira	.935	9	16	13	2	4
Maxwell, Watertown	.954	15	34	49	4	16
McGlone, Auburn	.857	2	2	4	1	0
Meza, Hamilton	1.000	2	0	3	0	0
Millan, Pittsfield	.923	2	5	7	1	1

— 474 —

Player, Team	Pct.	G	PO	A	E	DP
Moore, Geneva	.929	29	69	76	11	16
Morgan, Niagara Falls	.750	1	2	1	1	0
Mouton, Auburn	.927	76	170	184	28	31
Posada, Oneonta	.943	64	131	197	20	42
Pratte, Niagara Falls	.953	73	157	210	18	36
Robinson, Pittsfield	1.000	2	3	3	0	2
L. Rodriguez, Elmira	.933	4	5	9	1	0
Saa, Geneva	.957	44	100	120	10	30
Siebert, Utica	1.000	1	1	1	0	0
Simons, Jamestown	.994	34	69	95	1	17
Smith, Watertown	.974	50	64	122	5	24
Smolen, Batavia	.972	14	23	46	2	3
Veras, Pittsfield	.958	4	12	11	1	6
Vosik, Watertown	.968	12	17	44	2	5
Womack, Welland	.947	5	6	12	1	0

Triple plays—Garcia, Garvey, Juday, Lis.

THIRD BASEMEN

Player, Team	Pct.	G	PO	A	E	DP
Andujar, Watertown	.667	1	0	2	1	0
Arredondo, Pittsfield	.915	32	29	57	8	10
Brown, Niagara Falls	.789	8	4	11	4	1
Cabrera, Auburn	1.000	1	0	1	0	0
Cacini, Auburn	.904	27	23	52	8	3
Campbell, Jamestown	.860	35	19	61	13	5
Cheek, Batavia	.902	37	19	55	8	2
Cholowsky, Hamilton	.789	6	10	5	4	0
Colon, Elmira	.913	18	4	17	2	1
Coolbaugh, St. Catharines	.778	3	2	5	2	1
DiMarco, Erie	.914	60	59	111	16	13
Disarcina, Utica	1.000	4	0	7	0	2
Ellsworth, Hamilton	.667	3	1	1	1	0
Falco, Jamestown	.935	35	27	59	6	8
Flannelly, Oneonta	.890	62	49	129	22	10
Garvey, Welland	.500	2	0	1	1	0
Grable, Niagara Falls	.912	45	33	71	10	7
Guerrero, Niagara Falls	1.000	3	0	5	0	0
House, Welland	.744	18	14	18	11	0
Huston, Geneva	.850	42	31	60	16	5
Jenkins, Jamestown	.909	15	12	28	4	2
Johnson, Niagara Falls	.926	22	16	34	4	4
Juday, Erie	.714	2	1	4	2	0
Kantor, Watertown	.890	37	21	52	9	7
Krevokuch, Welland	.919	30	15	42	5	1
Leatherman, Welland	.891	38	25	65	11	6
Livesey, Oneonta	.788	17	14	27	11	1
Marin, Elmira	.864	7	6	13	3	1
Martorana, Utica	.904	58	46	96	15	9
McGlone, Auburn	.920	9	4	19	2	3
Medina, Geneva	.898	26	19	69	10	13
Meza, Hamilton	.905	70	54	127	19	7
Millan, Pittsfield	1.000	1	1	0	0	0
Montero, Auburn	.890	41	35	103	17	9
Moore, Geneva	.872	13	12	22	5	2
Morgan, Niagara Falls	1.000	1	0	1	0	0
Pratte, Niagara Falls	.000	1	0	0	1	0
Richison, Auburn	.727	3	2	6	3	0
Robinson, Pittsfield	.861	50	31	99	21	10
L. RODRIGUEZ, Elmira	.929	63	43	102	11	10
Saa, Geneva	1.000	2	0	2	0	0
Siebert, Utica	.766	19	19	17	11	3
Smolen, Batavia	.874	48	33	71	15	8
Soto, Elmira	1.000	2	2	0	0	1
Vosik, Watertown	.902	51	24	96	13	5
Weinke, St. Catharines	.900	75	56	132	21	10
Whitman, Erie	.979	17	11	36	1	1

Triple play—Krevokuch.

SHORTSTOPS

Player, Team	Pct.	G	PO	A	E	DP
Adriana, St. Catharines	.853	36	54	97	26	19
Anderson, Oneonta	.924	22	27	58	7	8
Andujar, Watertown	1.000	1	0	1	0	0
Arias, Erie	.920	41	56	93	13	16
Bates, Watertown	.930	73	118	242	27	54
Benbow, St. Catharines	.916	45	64	132	18	18
Black, Hamilton	.917	14	17	27	4	1
Brady, Utica	.876	44	66	96	23	17
Brito, Batavia	.958	22	42	50	4	4
Brown, Niagara Falls	.667	3	1	1	1	4
BURNETT, Oneonta	.951	62	96	198	15	38
Cacini, Auburn	.913	35	46	69	11	11
Coffey, Geneva	.875	10	19	23	6	5
Colon, Welland	.886	23	35	66	13	17
Disarcina, Utica	.898	33	59	90	17	18
Falco, Jamestown	.952	8	13	27	2	2
Garcia, Pittsfield	1.000	2	0	3	0	2
Garvey, Welland	.882	9	7	23	4	3
Gomez, Geneva	.926	60	118	157	22	34
Grudzielanek, Jamestown	.933	72	112	206	23	40
Guerrero, Niagara Falls	1.000	1	0	3	0	0
Hayden, Batavia	.934	50	78	134	15	34
Johnson, Niagara Falls	.909	8	13	17	3	3
Juday, Erie	.556	1	1	4	4	1

Player, Team	Pct.	G	PO	A	E	DP
Lis, St. Catharines	1.000	1	3	6	0	2
McGlone, Auburn	.927	47	77	125	16	18
Millan, Pittsfield	1.000	2	3	0	0	0
Mompres, Pittsfield	.909	75	91	249	34	33
Moore, Geneva	1.000	7	11	16	0	6
Morgan, Niagara Falls	.944	67	114	204	19	37
Pratte, Niagara Falls	.929	2	7	6	1	2
F. Rodriguez, Elmira	.927	67	95	209	24	46
L. Rodriguez, Elmira	.932	15	17	38	4	4
Saa, Geneva	1.000	4	5	11	0	1
Smith, Watertown	1.000	2	2	6	0	0
Smolen, Batavia	.929	13	7	32	3	2
Stenta, Erie	.900	37	54	90	16	11
Tooch, Welland	.947	11	21	15	2	3
Veras, Pittsfield	1.000	1	4	5	0	1
Vosik, Watertown	1.000	4	5	6	0	1
Warner, Hamilton	.885	71	95	197	38	31
Womack, Welland	.918	40	72	97	15	20

Triple plays—Arias, Mompres, Warner.

OUTFIELDERS

Player, Team	Pct.	G	PO	A	E	DP
Albrecht, Oneonta	.982	50	104	3	2	2
Arredondo, Pittsfield	1.000	1	2	0	0	0
Astacio, Erie	.941	7	14	2	1	1
Austin, Utica	.964	38	50	4	2	1
Austin, Jamestown	.975	70	111	7	3	0
Babki, Jamestown	.955	47	61	2	3	0
Benbow, St. Catharines	1.000	10	9	1	0	0
Blanton, Hamilton	.962	18	22	3	1	1
Bohrofen, Hamilton	.967	44	58	0	2	0
Bright, Elmira	.962	56	70	6	3	0
Brohm, Watertown	1.000	16	12	1	0	0
Brown, Niagara Falls	.842	17	15	1	3	0
Buchanan, Utica	.971	42	66	2	2	2
Burguillos, Niagara Falls	.880	46	43	1	6	0
Burton, Utica	1.000	2	3	2	0	1
Butler, St. Catharines*	.981	76	147	8	3	1
Cabral, Erie*	1.000	9	24	1	0	0
Cabrera, Auburn	.899	33	61	1	7	0
Campbell, St. Catharines	.963	35	50	2	2	0
Campbell, Jamestown	.942	33	47	2	3	0
Cardona, Welland	.960	42	70	2	3	0
Charbonnet, Watertown*	.960	42	70	2	3	0
Coleman, Oneonta	.750	2	3	0	1	0
Conger, Welland*	.929	25	37	2	3	0
Coolbaugh, St. Catharines	1.000	1	1	0	0	0
Curtis, Pittsfield*	.969	75	213	4	7	2
Daniel, Jamestown	.944	9	17	0	1	0
Davenport, Hamilton	.929	29	48	4	4	1
Durkin, Auburn*	.969	63	121	6	4	2
Edwards, Batavia	.958	66	133	5	6	1
Edwards, Watertown*	.800	2	4	0	1	0
Eierman, Elmira	.964	61	101	6	4	3
Farrell, Welland	.957	51	85	3	4	0
Feeley, Niagara Falls	.959	54	90	3	4	0
Franklin, Erie	.936	20	41	3	3	2
French, Hamilton	.927	39	49	2	4	0
Gardner, Geneva	.960	46	71	1	3	0
Gibson, Niagara Falls	.895	25	29	5	4	1
Glanville, Geneva	1.000	36	77	4	0	1
Graham, Elmira	.953	54	100	2	5	0
Grissom, Batavia	.979	54	94	1	2	0
Hawkins, Erie	.813	14	13	0	3	0
Henderson, Watertown	.873	40	45	3	7	0
Henry, Utica	.990	56	98	1	1	0
Herrera, St. Catharines*	1.000	3	8	1	0	0
Higginbotham, Niagara Falls*	.902	40	68	6	8	1
Hines, St. Catharines	.926	72	106	7	9	1
Hobson, Auburn	.931	47	90	4	7	0
Hood, Erie	1.000	16	46	2	0	0
Hubbard, Oneonta*	.962	65	145	8	6	0
James, Utica	.857	6	6	0	1	0
Jean, Jamestown	1.000	17	21	0	0	0
Johnson, Niagara Falls	1.000	1	1	0	0	0
Larregui, Geneva	.960	61	111	8	5	2
Leavell, Welland	1.000	15	22	3	0	0
Lora, Elmira	.853	17	28	1	5	0
Mabry, Hamilton	.943	46	73	10	5	2
Mediavilla, Hamilton	.992	57	115	4	1	1
Medina, Batavia	.934	51	79	6	6	1
Medina, Geneva	1.000	1	3	0	0	0
K. Miller, Niagara Falls	.933	7	13	1	1	0
Mitchell, Welland	.974	52	68	6	2	0
Moore, Watertown	.923	2	3	1	0	0
Mouton, Oneonta	.957	56	106	5	5	1
Nace, Pittsfield*	1.000	19	21	1	0	0
Neff, Welland	.931	20	25	2	2	0
O'Neill, Jamestown	.963	33	74	5	3	1
Ochoa, Utica	.927	55	86	3	7	1
Otero, Pittsfield*	.923	4	11	1	1	0
Perez, Watertown*	.941	40	46	2	3	0
Phillips, Oneonta*	.967	53	83	4	3	0
Pierce, Utica	.939	34	46	0	3	2
Ragland, Welland	.917	26	41	3	4	2

Player, Team	Pct.	G	PO	A	E	DP
Ramirez, Watertown	.960	55	92	5	4	2
Rappoli, Elmira	.967	64	84	3	3	0
Rojas, Niagara Falls*	.750	5	3	0	1	0
Ruth, Batavia	.857	2	6	0	1	0
SANDY, Pittsfield	.993	72	131	2	1	2
Schroeder, Welland*	1.000	6	8	0	0	0
Schulte, Auburn	.971	70	162	4	5	0
Seja, Niagara Falls	.875	11	13	1	2	0
Septimo, St. Catharines	.857	13	17	1	3	1
Shirley, Watertown	.857	23	35	1	6	0
Shotton, Welland	.938	42	58	3	4	0
Siebert, Utica	1.000	3	6	0	0	0
Simons, Jamestown	1.000	8	8	0	0	0
Soto, Elmira	.850	17	17	0	3	0
Spencer, Oneonta	.917	6	11	0	1	0
Story, Utica	.923	7	12	0	1	0
Sullivan, Niagara Falls*	.967	47	85	2	3	0
Taylor, Hamilton	.971	27	24	9	1	0
Terilli, Geneva*	1.000	32	62	3	0	1
Thomas, Erie	.960	62	94	3	4	0
Thompson, Auburn	.959	31	46	1	2	0
Thomson, Erie	.976	39	80	1	2	0
Timmons, Geneva	.968	62	118	3	4	0
Tokheim, Batavia*	.954	38	79	4	4	2
Tolliver, Pittsfield	.961	69	119	4	5	2
Van Tiger, Watertown	.957	44	65	2	3	0
Velez, Erie	.939	30	43	3	3	0
Vilet, Batavia	.955	32	38	4	2	1
D. White, Jamestown	1.000	9	15	1	0	0
J. White, Jamestown	.931	37	54	0	4	0
Whitman, Erie	1.000	42	70	7	0	2
Wilson, Oneonta	.500	2	1	0	1	0
Yorro, St. Catharines*	.875	39	50	6	8	1

Triple plays—Butler, Curtis, Neff, Tolliver.

CATCHERS

Player, Team	Pct.	G	PO	A	E	DP	PB
Allen, Jamestown	.979	34	212	17	5	2	14
Angotti, Auburn	.988	16	77	6	1	0	2
Beals, Pittsfield	.979	39	258	25	6	2	6
Caple, Erie	.973	9	62	10	2	0	1
D. Craig, Geneva	1.000	1	1	0	0	0	0
Cruz, 11 Erie-23 Bat.	.982	34	252	19	6	3	9
Daniel, Jamestown	.981	39	278	29	6	5	6
DiFelice, Hamilton	.974	42	297	40	9	1	6
Doiron, Geneva	.978	26	120	16	3	1	7
Dunn, Pittsfield	1.000	4	16	0	0	0	0
Eason, Batavia	1.000	14	110	14	0	0	0
Encarnacion, Welland	.961	50	366	74	18	3	21
Farrell, Welland	.991	12	108	6	1	0	4
Haase, Utica	.980	27	184	17	4	1	7
Haley, Niagara Falls	.980	9	45	5	1	0	2
Harmes, St. Catharines	.981	45	324	43	7	4	14
Hattabaugh, Utica	1.000	26	184	22	0	1	2
Hinson, Welland	.962	5	19	6	1	0	0
Koehler, Pittsfield	.929	2	12	1	1	0	2
Lammon, Elmira	.953	9	36	5	2	0	0
Levangie, Elmira	.957	34	201	24	10	4	11
Linares, Auburn	.987	49	309	58	5	7	9
Madril, Elmira	.984	49	323	36	6	2	17
Mahony, Erie	.975	26	206	24	6	0	11
Maize, Welland	.986	15	128	11	2	0	5
Manning, Erie	1.000	7	49	9	0	2	1
Marrero, Erie	.968	27	180	34	7	3	5
Martindale, Watertown	.982	57	378	57	8	4	22
K. Miller, Niagara Falls	.995	27	169	17	1	0	8
Moore, Watertown	.967	15	84	3	3	0	5
Moreno, Watertown	.989	3	85	8	1	2	1
Morland, St. Catharines	.981	35	230	34	5	1	6
Motuzas, Oneonta	.952	3	19	1	1	1	0
Murphy, Auburn	.980	22	130	18	3	2	8
Owen, Jamestown	.986	19	127	13	2	2	5
Pena, Batavia	.980	15	128	16	3	2	4
Posada, Oneonta	.980	11	41	8	1	0	5
Quinlan, St. Catharines	1.000	5	7	0	0	0	0
Quintell, Oneonta	.980	22	86	14	2	0	5
Rea, Niagara Falls	.974	40	265	30	8	0	8
ROBINSON, Geneva	.994	62	404	77	3	7	5
Rollins, Utica	.985	12	59	7	1	1	8
Ruth, Batavia	.939	8	59	3	4	0	7
Sadler, Niagara Falls	.952	10	52	7	3	1	2
Soto, Elmira	.929	2	11	2	1	0	0
Tijerina, Pittsfield	1.000	36	176	25	0	1	2
Turvey, Hamilton	.976	38	298	23	8	1	7
Vargas, Batavia	.971	23	143	24	5	4	11
Vogel, Utica	.972	23	121	20	4	0	6
Wilson, Oneonta	.953	59	294	29	16	1	25

Triple play—Encarnacion.

PITCHERS

Player, Team	Pct.	G	PO	A	E	DP
Allen, Batavia	1.000	8	2	5	0	0
Anaya, Pittsfield	.950	12	8	11	1	1
Anderson, Batavia	.900	11	1	8	1	0

Player, Team	Pct.	G	PO	A	E	DP
Anderson, Auburn	1.000	9	7	10	0	1
Andrzejewski, Erie	.714	16	4	6	4	0
Arias, Hamilton	1.000	2	0	1	0	1
Ashley, Jamestown	.818	20	5	4	2	0
Badorek, Hamilton	.750	13	3	6	3	0
Bailey, Elmira	1.000	28	2	3	0	0
Baker, Watertown	.733	22	4	7	4	0
Baldwin, Hamilton	.700	7	0	7	3	0
Barton, St. Catharines*	.833	20	2	3	1	0
Beltran, Hamilton*	1.000	21	2	4	0	1
Bennett, Elmira	.933	13	4	10	1	3
Bergman, Niagara Falls	.960	15	9	15	1	1
Bertotti, Utica*	.917	14	1	10	1	0
Biehl, Auburn*	1.000	19	6	17	0	1
Blazier, Batavia	1.000	24	4	7	0	0
Bliss, Geneva	1.000	15	1	2	0	0
Blomdahl, Niagara Falls.	1.000	16	10	20	0	1
Boehringer, Utica	1.000	4	2	1	0	0
Bojcun, Batavia	.750	20	0	9	3	0
Boone, Hamilton	1.000	20	1	3	0	0
Bradley, Welland	1.000	5	0	4	0	0
Braunecker, Jamestown	1.000	20	4	8	0	0
Brown, Batavia	.778	16	3	4	2	1
Brumley, Hamilton	.750	15	3	6	3	0
Budrewicz, Elmira	1.000	24	5	11	0	2
Bullard, Welland	1.000	6	1	1	0	0
Burbank, Oneonta	1.000	23	4	10	0	0
Burlingame, Geneva	1.000	14	5	7	0	2
Burrow, Utica	.667	9	0	4	2	0
Buzard, Watertown*	1.000	8	1	1	0	0
Call, Utica	1.000	12	4	14	0	1
Carrara, St. Catharines	.880	15	6	16	3	2
Carrasco, Pittsfield	1.000	12	1	5	0	0
Carter, Erie	1.000	21	4	5	0	0
Caruso, Elmira	.889	21	6	10	2	2
Castaldo, Hamilton	.667	17	0	2	1	0
Chafin, Elmira	.667	4	2	0	1	0
Christiansen, Welland*	1.000	8	0	7	0	1
Coleman, Oneonta	.625	18	1	4	3	1
Connolly, Erie	.750	19	2	4	2	1
Coombs, Welland	.944	13	5	12	1	1
Creek, Hamilton*	.750	9	0	3	1	0
Croghan, Oneonta	1.000	14	5	9	0	0
Danner, Welland*	1.000	9	2	21	0	0
Davidson, Watertown*	1.000	11	0	1	0	0
Davis, Elmira	.862	18	8	17	4	2
Davis, Geneva	.600	20	0	6	4	0
DeGrasse, Hamilton	.917	17	0	11	1	0
de los Santos, Welland	1.000	8	1	9	0	0
Douris, Welland	.700	11	0	7	3	1
Durussel, Niagara Falls	.818	18	4	5	2	1
Ellis, Utica	.680	15	4	13	8	2
Evans, Auburn	1.000	17	2	9	0	0
Evans, Welland	1.000	10	1	3	0	0
Ferguson, Jamestown	1.000	13	2	3	0	0
Figueroa, Jamestown*	.800	8	0	4	1	0
Fleet, Watertown	.750	15	5	10	5	0
Floren, Oneonta	1.000	4	1	2	0	0
Ford, St. Catharines	1.000	1	1	0	0	0
Frascatore, Hamilton	.875	30	0	7	1	0
Fritz, Utica*	.909	17	0	10	1	0
Gajkowski, Watertown	1.000	20	1	5	0	0
Gallaher, Auburn	.818	16	2	7	2	1
Garagozzo, Oneonta*	.917	15	6	16	2	0
George, Pittsfield*	.947	14	3	15	1	0
Gonzalez, Elmira	1.000	20	6	13	0	2
Grace, Batavia	.786	6	3	8	3	0
Gray, St. Catharines*	.818	15	2	7	2	0
Green, Batavia	1.000	3	1	6	0	1
Gully, Oneonta	.938	26	4	11	1	0
Harrah, Jamestown	.889	11	3	5	1	0
Haynes, Jamestown	1.000	29	2	3	0	0
Heathcott, Erie	.938	6	5	10	1	1
Heble, St. Catharines	.750	18	0	3	1	0
Henkel, Elmira	.950	18	7	12	1	1
Henry, Niagara Falls*	.974	15	8	29	1	1
Herrholz, Utica	1.000	9	1	3	0	0
Hisey, Hamilton	1.000	26	2	2	0	0
Hoey, Utica	.889	14	2	6	1	0
Holliday, Auburn	.500	10	0	1	1	1
Holman, Batavia	.900	15	4	14	2	1
Hope, Welland	1.000	3	1	3	0	0
Hostetler, Jamestown*	1.000	14	2	4	0	0
Inman, Oneonta	.864	15	6	13	3	0
Jenkins, Erie	1.000	9	7	15	0	1
Jewell, Watertown	1.000	21	1	9	0	0
Jones, Hamilton	1.000	9	3	12	0	1
Kelley, Niagara Falls*	.962	15	4	21	1	3
Kenny, Geneva	.955	15	6	15	1	3
Key, Watertown	1.000	12	2	7	0	0
Konieczki, Erie*	.800	24	0	4	1	1
Konopki, Erie	1.000	17	12	22	0	0
Kotes, St. Catharines	.955	16	6	15	1	1
Krippner, Erie	1.000	15	1	7	0	1
Kubicki, Utica	.778	23	2	5	2	0
LaRosa, Jamestown*	.933	14	4	10	1	0

Player, Team	Pct.	G	PO	A	E	DP
Laviano, Oneonta	1.000	19	4	9	0	0
Lemay, Niagara Falls*	1.000	17	4	3	0	0
LeTourneau, Erie	.941	24	6	10	1	1
Levine, Utica	.886	16	15	16	4	0
Lewis, Auburn	1.000	7	3	3	0	0
Lindsay, Pittsfield*	1.000	25	0	10	0	0
Lindsay, St. Catharines	.931	16	11	16	2	3
Logsdon, Watertown*	1.000	13	4	12	0	1
Longaker, Hamilton	1.000	18	2	5	0	0
Looney, Jamestown	1.000	11	1	5	0	1
Loughlin, Auburn*	.786	15	0	11	3	0
Lucero, Hamilton*	.500	31	0	1	1	0
Lugo, St. Catharines	.769	17	3	7	3	0
Lynch, Erie	.941	16	4	12	1	0
MacNeil, Erie	.875	12	4	3	1	1
Maguire, Welland*	.900	26	4	5	1	0
Malley, Watertown*	1.000	6	4	5	0	0
Manaure, St. Catharines	.000	2	0	0	1	0
Manfred, Pittsfield	.923	26	6	6	1	0
Manicchia, Batavia	.938	33	5	10	1	2
Martin, Niagara Falls	.882	19	5	10	2	0
Martin, Welland*	1.000	14	2	4	0	0
L. Martinez, Auburn	.667	13	0	2	1	0
McCurry, Welland	.750	9	0	3	1	0
Miller, St. Catharines	1.000	14	1	6	0	1
H. Miller, Niagara Falls	1.000	2	0	1	0	1
Miller, Elmira	.917	11	4	7	1	0
Miller, Auburn*	1.000	20	2	2	0	0
Millerick, Erie	.667	5	0	2	1	0
Mitchelson, Elmira*	1.000	24	2	5	0	1
Munda, Oneonta	.727	16	2	6	3	1
Nevill, Batavia*	1.000	29	2	10	0	0
Nolan, St. Catharines	.889	25	3	5	1	0
O'Connor, St. Catharines	1.000	19	3	6	0	1
Owen, Jamestown	.667	5	0	2	1	0
Pacheco, Geneva	1.000	8	1	3	0	0
Pasquale, Hamilton*	.857	9	2	4	1	1
Paxton, Jamestown*	1.000	13	1	4	0	0
Pedraza, Jamestown	.875	7	1	6	1	1
L. Perez, Geneva	1.000	13	2	4	0	0
P. Perez, Geneva	.875	16	5	9	2	0
Peskievitch, Erie	.905	27	2	17	2	2
Pettitte, Oneonta*	1.000	6	1	2	0	0
Pisciotta, Welland	1.000	24	2	8	0	1
Pudlo, Erie	1.000	14	4	16	0	0
Ramirez, Welland*	.926	16	5	20	2	0
Reichenbach, Pittsfield	.857	15	11	7	3	0
Reid, Niagara Falls	1.000	17	0	3	0	1
Reincke, Niagara Falls	1.000	11	4	5	0	1
Roberts, Erie*	.800	10	2	2	1	0
Roeder, Welland	.889	24	1	7	1	1
Rose, Auburn*	.727	21	2	6	3	1
Ruebel, Welland*	1.000	6	1	11	0	0
Santiago, Oneonta	1.000	8	0	1	0	0
Scheffler, Pittsfield	1.000	22	5	7	0	0
Schorr, Pittsfield	1.000	2	0	4	0	0
Schramm, Geneva	.893	15	8	17	3	0
Sewell, Auburn	1.000	9	1	2	0	0
Shanahan, Pittsfield*	1.000	15	7	11	0	0
Sharts, Watertown	1.000	2	0	1	0	0
Short, Oneonta	1.000	33	3	2	0	1
Simmons, Hamilton*	.938	15	0	15	1	1
Smith, Pittsfield*	.974	15	15	22	1	0
Smith, Erie	1.000	5	0	1	0	0
Sobocinski, Batavia	1.000	13	1	0	0	0
Sparks, Welland	1.000	13	0	4	0	0
Spoljaric, St. Catharines*	.800	4	1	3	1	0
Sproviero, Jamestown	.900	22	3	15	2	3
Stemler, Watertown*	.500	20	0	1	1	0
Stevens, Geneva	1.000	9	2	8	0	0
Sullivan, Oneonta*	.938	15	3	12	1	0
Sweeney, Watertown	.941	14	7	9	1	0
Szczepanski, Geneva*	.909	26	0	10	1	1
Tagle, Utica*	.900	16	2	7	1	0
Tanderys, Hamilton	.947	16	7	11	1	1
Tarutis, Jamestown	.929	21	6	7	1	2
Tatterson, Watertown	1.000	13	2	3	0	0
Taylor, Geneva	.722	21	3	10	5	2
Teich, Welland*	.909	19	0	10	1	0
Thibert, Oneonta	1.000	3	0	2	0	0
Thomas, Utica*	.958	11	5	18	1	1
Tidwell, Geneva*	1.000	24	6	5	0	0
Trachsel, Geneva	1.000	2	4	2	0	1
Turri, Niagara Falls	1.000	12	1	3	0	1
Undorf, Niagara Falls	1.000	15	1	11	0	0
Van Rynbach, Pittsfield	.813	17	5	8	3	0
Vanryn, Jamestown*	1.000	6	0	8	0	0
Walden, Watertown	.818	17	4	5	2	1
Walsh, Niagara Falls*	.882	18	4	11	2	0
Waring, Auburn	.933	21	3	11	1	0
Watson, Hamilton*	.933	8	3	11	1	0
Weber, St. Catharines	.958	16	13	10	1	0
Weiss, Geneva	1.000	1	0	1	0	0
Whisenant, Batavia*	.813	11	2	11	3	0
Whisonant, Batavia*	1.000	23	4	8	0	1
White, Auburn	1.000	26	3	5	0	0
J. White, Jamestown	1.000	1	1	0	0	0
Withem, Niagara Falls	1.000	8	3	5	0	1
Wynne, Jamestown	1.000	18	5	12	0	0
Young, Utica	.750	11	1	2	1	0
Young, Geneva	1.000	23	4	9	0	0

Triple play—Jones.

The following players did not have any fielding statistics at the positions indicated or appeared only as a designated hitter, pinch-hitter or pinch-runner: Angotti, p; Bates, 2b; Black, 3b, of; Bohrofen, 3b, p; E. Brown, p; Burrell, p; Cheek, p; M. Craig, of; Delgado, p; Fronio, p; Garvey, p; Harmes, 1b; Knaplund, p; Lehnerz, p; Long, p; Lopez, p; Lora, p; McGraw, p; M. Moore, 1b, 2b, 3b, ss, p; T. Moore, of; Nash, of; Olsen, p; Perry, dh; Pratts, p; Radachowsky, dh, ph; D. Robinson, ss; Sciortino, of; Shirley, 3b; Tavarez, of; Tolliver, 3b; Whitmore, of; Yorro, p.

LEAGUE CHAMPIONS

Year	Team	Pct.	Year	Team	Pct.	Year	Team	Pct.
1939—	Olean*	.631	1959—	Wellsville†	.635	1978—	Oneonta	.729
1940—	Olean*	.625	1960—	Erie	.643		Geneva z	.718
1941—	Jamestown	.618		Wellsville (2nd)†	.535	1979—	Geneva	.725
	Bradford (2nd)†	.549	1961—	Geneva	.616		Oneonta z	.618
1942—	Jamestown*	.672		Olean (4th)†	.512	1980—	Oneonta y	.662
1943—	Lockport	.591	1962—	Jamestown	.580		Geneva	.649
	Wellsville (3rd)†	.532		Auburn (3rd)†	.521	1981—	Oneonta y	.658
1944—	Lockport	.608	1963—	Auburn	.585		Jamestown	.649
	Jamestown (2nd)†	.565		Batavia (3rd)†	.485	1982—	Oneonta	.566
1945—	Batavia	.677	1964—	Auburn§	.622		Niagara Falls y	.553
1946—	Jamestown‡	.672	1965—	Binghamton	.677	1983—	Utica y	.649
	Batavia‡	.672		Binghamton	.607		Newark	.649
1947—	Jamestown*	.690	1966—	Auburn x	.620	1984—	Newark	.622
1948—	Lockport*	.603		Binghamton	.646		Little Falls y	.587
1949—	Bradford	.635	1967—	Auburn	.667	1985—	Oneonta*	.705
1950—	Hornell	.653	1968—	Auburn	.645		Auburn	.603
	Olean (2nd)†	.568		Oneonta (2nd)*	.558	1986—	Oneonta	.766
1951—	Olean	.622	1969—	Oneonta	.662		St. Catharines z	.632
	Hornell (3rd)†	.568	1970—	Auburn	.623	1987—	Geneva y	.632
1952—	Hamilton	.659	1971—	Oneonta	.662		Watertown	.579
	Jamestown (2nd)†	.643	1972—	Niagara Falls	.686	1988—	Oneonta y	.632
1953—	Jamestown*	.704	1973—	Auburn	.667		Jamestown	.618
1954—	Corning*	.621	1974—	Oneonta	.768	1989—	Pittsfield	.697
1955—	Hamilton*	.656	1975—	Newark	.688		Jamestown y	.579
1956—	Wellsville*	.617		Newark	.714	1990—	Oneonta a	.667
1957—	Wellsville	.632	1976—	Elmira	.727		Geneva	.662
	Erie (2nd)†	.598		Elmira	.703	1991—	Pittsfield	.662
1958—	Wellsville	.556	1977—	Oneonta y	.671		Jamestown a	.654
	Geneva (2nd)†	.548		Batavia	.600			

*Won championship and four-club playoff. †Won four-club playoff. ‡Jamestown and Batavia declared co-champions; Batavia defeated Jamestown in final of four-club playoff. §Won championship and two-club playoff. xWon split-season playoff. yLeague divided into Eastern and Western Divisions; won playoff. zLeague divided into Wrigley and Yawkey Divisions; won playoff. aLeague divided into Eastern, Western and Stedler divisions; won playoff. (NOTE—Known as Pennsylvania-Ontario-New York League from 1939 through 1956.)

NORTHWEST LEAGUE

FINAL STANDINGS

NORTHERN DIVISION

Team	W	L	T	Pct.	GB
Yakima (Dodgers)	44	32	0	.579	.....
Everett (Giants)	37	39	0	.487	7
Bellingham (Mariners)	37	39	0	.487	7
Spokane (Padres)	24	52	0	.316	20

SOUTHERN DIVISION

Team	W	L	T	Pct.	GB
Boise (Angels)	50	26	0	.658	.....
Eugene (Royals)	42	34	0	.553	8
Southern Oregon (Athletics)	40	36	0	.526	10
Bend (Independent)	30	46	0	.395	20

COMPOSITE

Team	Boi.	Yak.	Eug.	S.O.	Ev.	Bel.	Bend	Spo.	W	L	T	Pct.	GB
Boise (Angels)	....	4	11	8	5	7	9	6	50	26	0	.658	.....
Yakima (Dodgers)	6	....	5	6	6	9	4	8	44	32	0	.579	6
Eugene (Royals)	1	5	....	4	6	8	9	9	42	34	0	.553	8
Southern Oregon (Athletics)	4	4	8	....	7	4	6	7	40	36	0	.526	10
Everett (Giants)	5	6	4	3	....	3	8	8	37	39	0	.487	13
Bellingham (Mariners)	3	3	2	6	9	....	5	9	37	39	0	.487	13
Bend (Independent)	3	6	3	6	2	5	....	5	30	46	0	.395	20
Spokane (Padres)	4	4	1	3	4	3	5	....	24	52	0	.316	26

Southern Oregon played home games in Medford and Cline Falls.

Major league affiliations in parentheses.

Playoffs—Boise defeated Yakima, two games to none, to win league championship.

Regular-season attendance—Bellingham, 60,484; Bend, 47,018; Boise, 132,611; Eugene, 130,039; Everett, 89,906; Southern Oregon, 70,164; Spokane, 130,111; Yakima, 81,835. Total—742,168. Playoffs (2 games)—5,878.

Managers—Bellingham, Dave Myers; Bend, Bill Stein; Boise, Tom Kotchman; Eugene, Tom Poquette; Everett, Rob Ellis (through August 11), Mike Bubalo (through end of season); Southern Oregon, Grady Fuson; Spokane, Gene Glynn; Yakima, Joe Vavra. Managerial records of teams with more than one manager: Everett, Ellis 26-27, Bubalo 11-12.

All-Star team—1B—Murph Proctor, Yakima; 2B—Eddy Diaz, Bellingham; 3B—Joe Randa, Eugene; SS—Brent Gates, Southern Oregon; OF—Mike Neill, Southern Oregon; Matt Brewer, Everett; Mark Johnson, Eugene; C—Frank Charles, Everett; DH—Leon Glenn, Bend; LHP—Mike Hampton, Bellingham; RHP—Julian Heredia, Boise; LH Rel—Ken Grundt, Everett; RH Rel—Troy Percival, Boise; Most Valuable Player—Joe Randa, Eugene; Manager of the Year—Tom Poquette, Eugene.

BATTING

TEAM

Team	Avg.	G	AB	R	OR	H	TB	2B	3B	HR	RBI	SH	SF	HP	BB	Int. BB	SO	SB	CS	LOB
Yakima	.271	76	2611	473	356	707	998	136	13	43	393	27	21	36	362	17	551	117	49	571
Southern Oregon	.264	76	2629	397	397	695	987	118	24	42	352	32	17	39	364	7	643	90	50	617
Everett	.261	76	2554	383	396	667	956	134	22	37	318	18	20	34	275	12	586	83	38	536
Boise	.254	76	2615	436	315	664	908	115	15	33	358	30	28	39	402	11	507	70	38	636
Eugene	.250	76	2641	394	370	661	976	127	16	52	340	16	21	40	365	22	576	117	41	628
Bend	.243	76	2505	386	478	609	855	115	22	29	306	11	16	31	324	4	602	104	67	524
Spokane	.243	76	2557	365	508	621	813	97	16	21	306	25	20	30	330	10	624	144	62	553
Bellingham	.227	76	2526	288	334	574	798	93	10	37	251	14	20	31	276	9	619	76	41	559

INDIVIDUAL

(Leading qualifiers for batting championship—205 or more plate appearances)

*Bats lefthanded.   † Switch-hitter.

Player, Team	Avg.	G	AB	R	H	TB	2B	3B	HR	RBI	SH	SF	HP	BB	Int. BB	SO	SB	CS
Neill, Mike, Southern Oregon*	.350	63	240	42	84	113	14	0	5	42	4	1	0	35	3	54	9	3
Brewer, Matt, Everett*	.347	68	239	48	83	136	21	1	10	48	0	2	3	35	3	38	4	0
Randa, Joe, Eugene	.338	72	275	53	93	150	20	2	11	59	0	4	6	46	4	29	6	1
Charles, Frank, Everett	.318	62	239	31	76	122	17	1	9	49	0	1	1	21	0	55	1	2
Turner, Ryan, Bend	.315	65	241	37	76	103	16	1	3	43	1	1	1	9	32	0	48	2	3
Johnson, Mark, Eugene*	.311	50	209	46	65	106	9	4	8	28	0	1	1	26	4	29	31	4
Proctor, Murph, Yakima†	.309	74	282	48	87	139	27	2	7	61	3	1	2	42	7	31	5	4
Jones, Dax, Everett	.306	53	180	42	55	87	5	6	5	29	1	3	1	27	0	26	15	8
Wolfe, Joel, Southern Oregon	.303	59	251	49	76	105	17	3	2	34	0	0	3	25	0	28	19	5
Spearman, Vernon, Yakima*	.290	71	248	63	72	80	8	0	0	17	7	1	4	50	0	37	56	9

Departmental leaders: G—Proctor, 74; AB—Hinton, 286; R—Spearman, 63; H—Randa, 93; TB—Randa, 150; 2B—Proctor, 27; 3B—Jones, Mashore, 6; HR—Glenn, 15; RBI—Proctor, 61; SH—Spearman, 7; SF—Clayton, 7; HP—Jackson, 12; BB—Sweeney, 51; IBB—Proctor, 7; SO—Glenn, 96; SB—Spearman, 56; CS—Pritchett, 13.

(All players—listed alphabetically)

Player, Team	Avg.	G	AB	R	H	TB	2B	3B	HR	RBI	SH	SF	HP	BB	Int. BB	SO	SB	CS
Adams, Tommy, Bellingham	.260	46	150	27	39	60	12	0	3	18	0	1	5	34	2	40	7	1
Andrews, Jay, Eugene†	.278	7	18	3	5	12	1	0	2	3	1	0	1	5	0	5	0	1
Anthony, Mark, Spokane	.278	64	212	24	59	74	4	4	1	26	4	0	1	32	0	61	24	6
Babbitt, Troy, Eugene*	.228	62	219	21	50	70	15	1	1	22	2	1	4	28	1	39	4	1
Bard, Mike, Bend†	.268	57	198	30	53	69	10	3	0	23	0	0	1	25	1	40	2	4
Barlow, Clem, Eugene	.157	42	115	14	18	21	1	1	0	2	3	0	2	18	0	52	5	7
Bellomo, Kevin, Everett	.243	38	107	13	26	29	3	0	0	8	0	3	3	13	2	29	0	0
Biancamano, John, Spokane*	.188	27	69	8	13	23	2	1	2	10	0	2	2	14	1	33	0	2
Blackwell, Jay, Yakima*	.133	5	15	1	2	2	0	0	0	0	0	1	0	2	0	7	1	0
Bobo, Elgin, Boise†	.285	49	172	40	49	70	10	1	3	29	1	0	5	31	0	26	4	1
Bond, Michael, Bellingham	.185	51	157	16	29	31	0	1	0	8	0	3	3	15	0	46	9	4

— 478 —

Player, Team	Avg.	G	AB	R	H	TB	2B	3B	HR	RBI	SH	SF	HP	BB	Int.BB	SO	SB	CS
Bonilla, Johnny, Bend*	.209	22	43	6	9	12	3	0	0	2	2	0	0	4	1	6	0	2
Bosarge, Scott, Bellingham	.259	9	27	4	7	10	1	1	0	2	0	0	0	1	0	4	0	0
Boudreau, Tommy, Bellingham	.160	49	144	11	23	28	5	0	0	11	2	0	2	23	0	29	1	2
Boykin, Tyrone, Boise	.210	52	162	26	34	58	8	2	4	22	1	2	0	33	0	54	4	1
Boyzuick, Mike, Yakima	.191	16	47	7	9	14	2	0	1	2	1	1	2	3	0	9	1	0
Bream, Scott, Spokane	.214	68	262	37	56	70	4	5	0	26	3	3	5	25	1	57	16	7
Brewer, Matt, Everett*	.347	68	239	48	83	136	21	1	10	48	0	2	3	35	3	38	4	0
Brookens, Andy, Eugene	.111	4	9	0	1	1	0	0	0	0	0	0	0	0	0	4	0	0
Brooks, Rayme, Eugene	.209	38	110	12	23	40	6	1	3	17	0	1	0	14	2	33	0	1
Cabrera, Juan, Southern Oregon†	.051	13	39	5	2	5	0	0	0	1	2	1	0	7	0	10	2	0
Calcagno, Dan, Everett	.167	4	6	0	1	1	0	0	0	0	1	0	0	0	0	1	1	0
Cannon, Rob, Boise	.277	15	47	9	13	23	5	1	1	5	0	0	0	13	1	17	2	1
Caple, Kyle, Bend	.194	22	62	4	12	14	2	0	0	2	0	0	2	8	0	18	0	1
Casper, Tim, Everett†	.170	25	53	7	9	10	1	0	0	4	1	1	0	8	0	8	0	1
Castro, Tony, Eugene†	.202	35	89	16	18	25	3	2	0	9	1	0	2	4	0	27	16	2
Charles, Frank, Everett	.318	62	239	31	76	122	17	1	9	49	0	1	1	21	0	55	1	2
Claus, Todd, Boise†	.213	59	178	27	38	44	6	0	0	8	5	1	7	25	1	43	6	5
Clayton, Craig, Bellingham	.264	43	159	16	42	61	10	0	3	22	2	7	1	15	3	30	0	1
Cookson, Brent, Southern Oregon	.000	6	9	0	0	0	0	0	0	0	0	0	0	0	0	7	0	0
Dana, Derek, Everett	.310	46	129	17	40	55	12	0	1	12	0	0	2	5	0	29	2	2
Demetral, Chris, Yakima	.283	65	226	43	64	81	11	0	2	41	5	1	1	34	2	32	4	3
Diaz, Eddy, Bellingham	.276	61	246	48	68	93	14	1	3	23	3	2	1	24	1	33	9	2
Edwards, Mel, Spokane*	.238	6	21	7	5	8	1	1	0	4	0	0	0	5	0	5	0	0
Endebrock, Kurt, Southern Oregon	.147	50	136	17	20	24	4	0	0	7	1	1	2	33	1	28	3	6
Erhard, Barney, Bellingham	.204	43	142	20	29	42	4	0	3	12	0	0	3	25	0	48	9	3
Farrish, Keoki, Yakima	.250	54	172	37	43	76	10	1	7	34	0	3	3	18	1	42	2	4
Feist, Ken, Eugene	.236	48	123	20	29	33	4	0	0	12	2	1	2	10	0	31	6	3
Fernandez, Julio, Bellingham*	.190	51	158	17	30	35	5	0	0	11	0	1	0	26	1	38	7	1
Florez, Tim, Everett	.249	59	193	33	48	64	8	4	0	25	2	1	1	12	1	33	7	1
Francisco, Vicente, Southern Oregon*	.289	15	38	8	11	12	1	0	0	3	1	0	0	7	0	11	0	0
Frias, Joe, Spokane	.144	50	153	15	22	27	5	0	0	8	1	1	2	14	1	34	4	1
Frias, Pedro, Spokane	.250	3	12	2	3	5	0	1	0	1	0	0	1	0	0	3	2	0
Frick, Tod, Southern Oregon	.125	7	16	0	2	2	0	0	0	1	0	0	0	1	0	1	0	0
Gates, Brent, Southern Oregon†	.288	58	219	41	63	83	11	0	3	26	5	2	2	30	2	33	8	2
Glenn, Leon, Bend*	.225	73	262	46	59	119	9	3	15	55	0	4	0	36	2	96	16	3
Gray, Daniel, Yakima	.252	45	135	29	34	56	8	1	4	28	1	2	3	30	0	25	1	3
Griffin, Tim, Yakima	.260	51	169	35	44	61	11	0	2	26	1	1	1	35	2	49	2	5
Gubanich, Creighton, Southern Oregon	.227	43	132	23	30	53	7	2	4	18	0	0	6	19	0	33	0	4
Haber, Dave, Eugene	.215	48	163	23	35	46	4	2	1	12	1	2	4	20	2	38	12	4
Hagy, Gary, Boise	.278	72	248	42	69	84	10	1	1	35	4	4	3	34	3	32	5	1
Hall, Tim, Spokane	.252	41	135	15	34	45	5	0	2	21	0	1	0	13	0	37	1	1
Halland, Jon, Bellingham	.231	60	216	18	50	70	6	1	4	24	1	2	2	4	0	65	5	2
Halter, Shane, Eugene	.233	64	236	41	55	69	9	1	1	18	2	1	3	49	1	60	12	6
Hart, Chris, Southern Oregon	.143	9	21	3	3	4	1	0	0	1	0	0	1	1	0	5	0	0
Hawks, Larry, 35 Bend-27 Spo.	.240	62	208	24	50	65	7	1	2	29	0	5	2	25	0	44	1	1
Henderson, Ken, Everett*	.159	38	88	10	14	19	2	0	1	11	0	0	3	8	0	32	1	0
Hinton, Steve, Eugene*	.283	71	286	37	81	111	15	0	5	39	0	0	2	25	2	36	4	1
Hollandsworth, Todd, Yakima*	.236	56	203	34	48	79	5	1	8	33	0	0	4	27	3	57	11	1
Hust, Gary, Southern Oregon	.276	64	246	42	68	113	5	5	10	49	3	0	8	24	0	94	8	5
Jackson, Ray, Everett	.257	66	241	43	62	81	11	4	0	20	2	4	12	30	0	54	22	6
Johnson, J.J., Yakima	.257	36	105	15	27	45	6	0	4	11	2	0	3	15	0	22	1	1
Johnson, Kevin, Spokane	.159	15	44	3	7	10	3	0	0	2	0	0	1	0	0	13	0	0
Johnson, Mark, Eugene*	.311	50	209	46	65	106	9	4	8	28	0	1	1	26	4	29	31	4
Jones, Dax, Everett	.306	53	180	42	55	87	5	6	5	29	1	3	1	27	0	26	15	8
Kaiser, Nick, Eugene	.238	47	172	19	41	47	6	0	0	17	0	2	6	19	1	31	9	6
Kennedy, Mike, Southern Oregon	.294	33	102	11	30	35	5	0	0	17	1	2	1	9	0	18	0	1
Klavitter, Clay, Bellingham	.206	33	107	10	22	31	6	0	1	13	0	0	1	11	1	29	0	1
Kliafas, Steve, Yakima	.279	49	165	28	46	57	7	2	0	18	2	2	4	10	0	30	7	3
LeBak, David, Spokane	.299	50	167	41	50	67	8	0	3	26	0	1	2	21	0	38	21	5
Lightner, Ed, Eugene	.305	37	105	15	32	36	4	0	0	11	0	1	1	12	0	14	6	2
Lisiecki, David, Bellingham	.000	21	1	0	0	0	0	0	0	0	0	0	0	0	0	1	0	0
Markiewicz, Brandon, Boise	.217	61	212	22	46	63	9	1	2	33	2	2	4	10	1	49	2	3
Mashore, Damon, Southern Oregon	.273	73	264	48	72	119	17	6	6	31	2	3	2	34	1	94	15	5
Mays, Terrance, Eugene	.252	28	107	13	27	34	5	1	0	8	2	0	1	15	1	19	6	5
McGee, Brian, Bend	.277	55	191	35	53	71	12	0	2	31	2	1	5	16	0	51	9	6
McGonnigal, Brett, Everett†	.156	15	45	4	7	7	0	0	0	2	2	0	0	6	1	11	2	1
Meyers, Don, Yakima	.312	50	141	20	44	63	11	1	2	18	0	1	3	14	1	34	1	4
Montgomery, Don, Everett	.240	61	196	16	47	74	15	0	4	36	0	3	1	31	1	53	0	1
Moody, Kyle, Spokane	.260	72	265	45	69	86	13	2	0	27	6	2	5	41	0	43	14	12
Morales, Jorge, Bellingham	.212	22	66	3	14	17	0	0	1	3	0	0	1	6	0	9	1	0
Mowry, Don, Spokane*	.232	39	142	16	33	46	7	0	2	22	1	2	2	23	2	37	3	2
Nash, Richey, Spokane	.316	5	19	5	6	8	0	1	0	1	0	0	0	2	0	5	1	1
Neill, Mike, Southern Oregon*	.350	63	240	42	84	113	14	0	5	42	4	1	0	35	0	54	9	3
Norman, Les, Eugene	.245	30	102	14	25	37	4	1	2	18	2	1	1	9	0	18	2	1
Norton, Rick, Southern Oregon*	.267	62	187	29	50	70	8	0	4	28	4	1	0	34	0	57	1	3
Ollison, Scott, Bend	.205	55	171	19	35	41	4	1	0	20	2	2	2	20	0	43	4	7
Palmeiro, Orlando, Boise*	.278	70	277	56	77	95	11	2	1	24	6	3	3	33	0	22	8	8
Parker, Stacy, Bend	.238	65	240	37	57	78	10	4	1	22	0	1	3	37	0	69	17	11
Perez, Eduardo, Boise	.288	46	160	35	46	62	13	0	1	22	1	1	4	19	0	39	12	3
Pinkney, Alton, Yakima*	.285	46	137	33	39	56	7	2	2	18	0	2	1	34	1	44	14	8
Polanco, Carlos, Boise	.172	36	58	6	10	13	3	0	0	4	1	0	1	13	0	9	1	0
Pritchett, Chris, Boise*	.267	70	255	41	68	111	10	3	9	50	0	3	2	47	3	41	1	0
Pritchett, Tony, Bend	.241	68	237	50	57	85	14	4	2	24	1	2	2	41	0	51	26	13
Proctor, Murph, Yakima†	.309	74	282	48	87	139	27	2	7	61	3	1	2	42	7	31	5	4
Pugh, Scotty, Spokane*	.317	36	139	20	44	61	8	0	3	20	1	1	1	14	2	11	1	2
Ramirez, Roberto, Everett	.229	53	153	20	35	52	10	2	1	10	0	0	0	19	0	51	7	6
Randa, Joe, Eugene	.338	72	275	53	93	150	20	2	11	59	0	4	6	46	4	29	6	1
Raven, Luis, Boise	.274	38	84	13	23	31	2	0	2	13	0	0	1	9	0	19	1	1
Richard, Ron, Yakima	.319	27	69	18	22	30	3	1	1	16	0	0	3	8	0	13	1	0
Ringgold, Keith, Bend	.125	8	24	3	3	3	0	0	0	0	1	0	0	5	0	10	1	0
Robertson, Shawn, Spokane	.284	60	208	44	59	85	14	0	4	38	0	2	4	48	0	49	25	7
Rodriguez, Albert, Everett	.248	34	101	14	25	27	2	0	0	3	1	0	0	13	2	10	1	1
Rountree, Jerrold, Spokane†	.200	54	160	22	32	36	4	0	0	16	6	0	0	23	1	47	16	5
Ruocchio, James, Boise	.208	37	120	10	25	36	5	0	2	13	1	2	0	4	0	37	0	1
Sanders, Paul, Eugene	.208	46	130	18	27	33	3	0	1	16	2	1	1	21	0	42	0	0

— 479 —

Player, Team	Avg.	G	AB	R	H	TB	2B	3B	HR	RBI	SH	SF	HP	BB	Int. BB	SO	SB	CS
Savage, Jim, Bend*	.223	57	197	30	44	62	7	1	3	18	1	1	0	26	0	30	8	5
Schoen, Jerry, Bend	.234	39	141	17	33	40	5	1	0	9	1	0	0	13	0	37	3	3
Sears, Jim, Boise	.233	41	90	19	21	23	2	0	0	14	1	1	0	24	0	15	4	1
Servello, Dan, Eugene	.243	53	173	29	42	72	10	1	6	21	0	3	5	32	3	64	5	0
Sheldon, Scott, Southern Oregon	.253	65	229	34	58	74	10	3	0	24	3	1	2	23	0	44	9	5
Slater, Vernon, Eugene*	.210	51	138	18	29	48	7	0	4	19	0	0	2	28	1	61	8	6
Smith, Bubba, Bellingham	.261	66	253	28	66	114	14	2	10	43	0	2	2	13	1	47	0	2
Speakman, Willie, Bellingham†	.167	38	102	5	17	23	3	0	1	6	0	0	0	13	0	34	1	2
Spearman, Vernon, Yakima*	.290	71	248	63	72	80	8	0	0	17	7	1	4	50	0	37	56	9
Stela, Jose, Boise	.295	33	112	13	33	41	3	1	1	15	4	1	1	10	0	13	1	4
Stephens, Reggie, Spokane†	.194	34	67	8	13	14	1	0	0	6	0	0	1	11	1	26	0	4
Strickland, Chad, Eugene	.161	34	118	13	19	29	7	0	1	11	2	2	2	13	0	16	1	1
Subero, Carlos, Eugene†	.174	6	23	2	4	5	1	0	0	2	1	0	0	0	0	7	0	0
Swank, Randy, Everett	.255	61	200	28	51	65	14	0	0	16	6	1	1	17	1	31	6	4
Sweeney, Mark, Boise*	.282	70	234	45	66	94	10	3	4	34	1	3	5	51	2	42	9	5
Sweeney, Roger, Yakima*	.241	11	29	3	7	8	1	0	0	2	0	0	0	1	0	9	1	0
Tallent, Ron, Boise	.209	25	43	6	9	12	3	0	0	8	0	0	1	14	0	17	0	1
Terrell, James, Bellingham	.286	65	248	26	71	92	6	3	3	22	3	0	2	15	0	42	2	3
Thielen, D.J., Everett	.228	65	237	35	54	86	8	3	6	31	0	2	3	17	1	86	7	2
Thomsen, Chris, Southern Oregon	.223	62	184	23	41	54	5	1	2	22	2	2	5	16	0	60	2	5
Thurston, Jerrey, Spokane	.214	60	201	26	43	55	9	0	1	20	2	2	2	20	1	61	2	2
Tramuta, Marc, Yakima	.242	32	66	4	16	17	1	0	0	9	0	1	0	8	0	21	0	1
Turco, Frank, Bend	.237	60	215	33	51	74	14	3	1	26	0	0	2	27	0	36	9	6
Turner, Chris, Boise	.227	52	163	26	37	48	5	0	2	29	2	5	2	32	0	32	10	2
Turner, Ryan, Bend	.315	65	241	37	76	103	16	1	3	43	1	1	9	32	0	48	2	3
Twitty, Sean, Everett	.209	27	91	11	19	31	3	0	3	12	0	1	1	13	0	20	18	2
Valencia, Max, Everett	.167	9	12	0	2	3	1	0	0	1	0	1	0	3	0	5	0	0
Van De Brake, Kevin, Yakima†	.225	30	89	10	20	28	5	0	1	13	1	2	0	5	0	13	1	0
Vaughn, Derek, Spokane	.271	49	192	21	52	64	5	2	1	17	1	0	2	15	0	47	15	7
Vitiello, Joe, Eugene	.328	19	64	16	21	41	2	0	6	21	0	2	1	11	1	18	1	1
Vorbeck, Eric, Yakima	.240	56	167	25	40	51	9	1	0	15	2	1	2	14	0	43	7	3
Walles, Todd, Bellingham	.211	45	133	14	28	36	2	0	2	18	0	1	4	20	0	48	1	3
Watts, Burgess, Yakima	.295	42	146	20	43	55	4	1	2	28	2	1	0	12	0	33	1	0
Wilder, Willie, Bellingham	.182	4	11	0	2	3	1	0	0	1	0	0	0	0	0	4	1	0
Williams, Cliff, Bend	.127	32	71	8	9	17	2	0	2	7	1	1	1	8	0	29	1	0
Williams, George, Southern Oregon†	.236	55	174	24	41	57	10	0	2	24	3	1	5	38	0	36	9	4
Wolfe, Joel, Southern Oregon	.303	59	251	49	76	105	17	3	2	34	0	0	3	25	0	28	19	5
Wood, Jason, Southern Oregon	.310	44	142	30	44	64	3	4	3	23	2	3	2	28	0	30	5	2

The following pitchers, listed alphabetically by club, with games in parentheses, had no plate appearances, primarily through use of designated hitters:

BELLINGHAM—Anderson, Doug (17); Bankhead, Scott (1); Borski, Jeffrey (8); Estes, Shawn (9); Foreman, Toby (17); Hampton, Mike (9); Mountain, Joe (8); O'Donnell, Erik (15); Polanco, Giovanni (21); Reyan, Julio (4); Rosenbalm, Marc (23); Russell, Lagrande (15); Weinbaum, Peter (11); Wiley, Chuck (5); Winzer, Kenny (2); Witte, Trey (27); Youngblood, Todd (15).

BEND—Boker, Mike (14); Cain, Tim (17); Castaneda, Rob (19); Cock, J.R. (22); Duke, Kyle (15); Finney, Mark (14); Fronio, Jason (5); Gibson, Monty (5); Goucher, Steve (14); Haddock, Darin (11); Knaplund, Greg (2); Minik, Tim (21); Murphy, Patrick (23); Person, Robert (2); Samuels, Geoff (15); Young, Greg (9).

BOISE—Butler, Mike (1); Dodd, Rob (6); Gledhill, Chance (21); Heredia, Julian (25); Keling, Korey (15); Mammola, Mark (23); Martinez, Eric (15); Percival, Troy (28); Powers, Randy (12); Purdy, Shawn (15); Ratekin, Mark (14); Robinson, Chris (27); Saitz, Robert (2); Van Dyke, Rod (20); Watson, Ron (18); Williard, Brian (1); Wylie, John (22).

EUGENE—Bailey, Mike (7); Bryans, Jason (7); Connolly, Chris (21); Downs, John (15); Farsaci, Dave (9); Fyhrie, Mike (21); Glaser, Kris (18); Johnson, Joel (17); Kobetitsch, Kevin (19); Landress, Roger (22); Lee, Thomas (14); Macias, Angel (15); Medrick, John (4); Miceli, Danny (25); Smith, Jeff (15); Yankow, Jeff (11).

EVERETT—Adams, Mike (3); Ayres, Lenny (16); Carrico, John (8); Grundt, Ken (29); Henrichs, Shawn (8); Hyde, Rich (26); Juelsgaard, Jarod (20); Luther, Tim (8); McLeod, Brian (11); Pote, Louis (5); Prentice, Tony (17); Stonecipher, Eric (10); Vanderweele, Doug (15); Vanlandingham, Bill (15); Wanke, Chuck (13); Wittcke, Darren (20).

SOUTHERN OREGON—Brock, Russell (8); Doyle, Tim (1); Evans, Michael (13); Ingram, Todd (17); Jensen, Jeff (5); Jiminez, Miguel (10); Kimball, Ricky (27); Misa, Joe (19); Morillo, Santiago (12); Nerat, Dan (24); Scharff, Tony (20); Smith, Tim (14); Stowell, Brad (3); Thees, Mike (21); Vizzini, Dan (14); Wojciechowski, Steve (16).

SPOKANE—Benhardt, Chris (27); Campbell, Jim (22); Ciocca, Eric (21); Corbitt, Cord (13); Davila, Jose (26); Eggleston, Scott (18); Grohs, Mike (12); Grygiel, Joe (22); Hanson, Craig (13); Long, Joey (13); Overholser, Drew (7); Ploeger, Tim (18); Samboy, Alvaro (15); Santiago, Jenny (2); Vazquez, Archie (1).

YAKIMA—Baumann, David (13); Bennett, Doug (14); Boggetto, Brad (20); Broyles, Jason (5); Carroll, Don (14); Castillo, Carlos (22); Crabtree, Chris (13); Hamilton, Kenny (15); Kerr, Jason (13); LeGendre, Bob (6); Maldonado, Albert (17); O'Connor, Ben (5); Osuna, Pedro (13); Sharp, Mike (26); Smith, Joseph (15); Thomas, Carlos (16).

GRAND SLAMS—Glenn, 3; Charles, 2; Adams, Hust, Montgomery, Neill, Slater, Wolfe, 1 each.

AWARDED FIRST BASE ON CATCHER'S INTERFERENCE—Boudreau (Charles); Hawks (Gubanich); Stephens (Dana); Swank (Kennedy); Vorbeck (Gubanich).

PITCHING

TEAM

Team	ERA	G	CG	ShO	Sv.	IP	H	R	ER	HR	HB	BB	Int. BB	SO	WP	Bk.
Boise	3.21	76	2	5	21	691.2	610	315	247	23	28	276	17	681	59	14
Bellingham	3.30	76	1	7	22	673.0	562	334	247	27	27	374	8	630	71	31
Yakima	3.81	76	0	4	20	677.1	615	356	287	35	32	330	13	684	46	16
Everett	3.86	76	1	3	19	660.1	617	396	283	43	52	360	17	570	95	24
Southern Oregon	3.89	76	3	4	18	680.2	640	397	294	32	34	322	15	592	65	19
Eugene	3.95	76	0	3	22	690.0	668	370	303	40	23	328	8	605	62	20
Bend	4.69	76	0	1	20	652.2	718	478	340	43	39	338	4	477	77	12
Spokane	5.50	76	3	0	13	667.1	768	508	408	51	45	370	10	469	89	25

INDIVIDUAL

(Leading qualifiers for earned-run average leadership—61 or more innings)

*Throws lefthanded.

Pitcher, Team	W	L	Pct.	ERA	G	GS	CG	GF	ShO	Sv.	IP	H	R	ER	HR	HB	BB	Int. BB	SO	WP
Heredia, Boise	8	1	.889	1.05	25	0	0	10	0	5	77.0	42	17	9	1	1	16	1	99	4
Vanderweele, Everett	6	4	.600	1.97	15	15	0	0	0	0	87.0	73	42	19	1	8	35	1	65	12
Hamilton, Yakima	7	4	.636	2.68	14	14	0	0	0	0	84.0	73	35	25	2	5	22	1	67	6
Youngblood, Bellingham	5	5	.500	2.75	15	15	0	0	0	0	95.0	82	41	29	3	6	40	1	84	6
Ayres, Everett	8	5	.615	2.85	16	16	1	0	0	0	98.0	85	46	31	7	10	46	1	74	7
Russell, Bellingham	6	7	.462	2.93	15	15	0	0	0	0	95.1	85	48	31	6	1	43	1	77	13
Purdy, Boise	8	4	.667	3.01	15	15	1	0	0	0	95.2	87	37	32	3	4	27	2	78	6
Keling, Boise	6	2	.750	3.04	15	14	0	1	0	1	83.0	71	31	28	3	3	30	0	96	5
Smith, Southern Oregon	5	2	.714	3.23	14	13	1	0	1	0	75.1	78	52	27	5	2	17	1	79	7
Ratekin, Boise	2	5	.286	3.34	14	13	1	1	0	0	70.0	59	31	26	1	3	22	0	49	3

Departmental leaders: G—Grundt, 29; W—Ayres, Baumann, Heredia, Purdy, Vanlandingham, 8; L—Long, 9; Pct.—Heredia, .889; GS—Ayres, 16; CG—Several pitchers tied with 1; GF—Hyde, Kimball, 24; ShO—Brock, O'Donnell, T. Smith, 1; Sv.—Percival, 12; IP—Ayres, 98.0; H—Boker, 93; R—Finney, 62; ER—Finney, 46; HR—Baumann, 11; HB—Grohs, 15; BB—Vanlandingham, 79; IBB—Grundt, Prentice, Robinson, 5; SO—Heredia, 99; WP—Vanlandingham, 25.

(All pitchers—listed alphabetically)

Pitcher, Team	W	L	Pct.	ERA	G	GS	CG	GF	ShO	Sv.	IP	H	R	ER	HR	HB	BB	Int. BB	SO	WP
Adams, Everett	0	1	.000	6.75	3	0	0	0	0	0	4.0	5	3	3	0	0	1	0	3	0
Anderson, Bellingham*	1	0	1.000	4.43	17	0	0	6	0	0	22.1	23	15	11	0	1	17	0	20	6
Ayres, Everett	8	5	.615	2.85	16	16	1	0	0	0	98.0	85	46	31	7	10	46	1	74	7
Bailey, Eugene	1	0	1.000	6.92	7	7	0	0	0	0	26.0	31	21	20	2	1	17	0	17	2
Bankhead, Bellingham	1	0	1.000	0.00	1	0	0	1	0	0	4.0	1	0	0	0	0	1	0	8	0
Baumann, Yakima	8	3	.727	5.23	13	12	0	0	0	0	72.1	89	43	42	11	3	21	0	68	1
Benhardt, Spokane*	3	3	.500	3.73	27	0	0	15	0	0	41.0	45	22	17	3	0	25	3	34	2
Bennett, Yakima	4	5	.444	3.30	14	12	0	0	0	0	57.1	31	26	21	1	7	45	0	65	3
Biancamano, Spokane	0	0	.000	6.75	1	0	0	1	0	0	1.1	3	1	1	1	0	0	0	1	0
Boggetto, Yakima	1	1	.500	3.65	20	1	0	12	0	1	37.0	25	19	15	2	5	20	4	26	6
Boker, Bend	7	6	.538	4.38	14	14	0	0	0	0	84.1	93	53	41	3	2	51	0	58	10
Borski, Bellingham	4	1	.800	0.90	8	7	0	0	0	0	50.0	36	9	5	0	2	11	2	32	1
Brock, Southern Oregon	4	0	1.000	3.12	8	8	1	0	1	0	43.1	37	19	15	2	1	12	1	48	4
Broyles, Yakima	0	0	.000	10.80	5	0	0	0	0	0	8.1	13	14	10	1	1	10	0	3	3
Bryans, Eugene	2	0	1.000	0.95	7	0	0	4	0	0	19.0	10	3	2	0	0	4	0	22	0
Butler, Boise*	0	0	.000	9.82	1	0	0	0	0	0	3.2	5	4	4	1	0	3	0	2	1
Cain, Bend	1	3	.250	5.71	17	6	0	4	0	0	58.1	65	49	37	2	4	25	0	59	8
Campbell, Spokane	2	2	.333	5.73	22	5	0	7	0	1	55.0	69	43	35	7	5	18	0	30	2
Carrico, Everett*	0	2	.000	4.74	8	4	0	1	0	0	24.2	34	21	13	2	0	15	0	14	1
Carroll, Yakima*	4	5	.444	3.80	14	14	0	0	0	0	68.2	80	44	29	5	1	30	0	50	3
Castaneda, Bend*	1	2	.333	3.86	19	0	0	7	0	2	32.2	40	15	14	1	0	11	1	16	2
Castillo, Yakima	5	3	.625	3.88	22	3	0	7	0	2	51.0	49	25	22	2	1	30	4	59	4
Ciocca, Spokane	0	3	.000	3.79	21	0	0	11	0	4	38.0	40	18	16	2	1	19	2	33	3
Clayton, Bellingham	0	0	.000	0.00	1	0	0	1	0	0	0.2	1	0	0	0	0	0	0	0	0
Cock, Bend	1	2	.333	2.84	22	0	0	12	0	2	31.2	26	14	10	1	1	18	0	25	1
Connolly, Eugene*	1	2	.333	3.71	21	0	0	5	0	2	51.0	40	30	21	1	2	41	0	45	10
Corbitt, Spokane*	1	2	.333	4.13	13	0	0	6	0	1	24.0	17	14	11	0	0	30	2	19	6
Crabtree, Yakima*	0	2	.000	6.23	13	0	0	1	0	0	26.0	32	19	18	3	1	10	0	35	4
Davila, Spokane	2	3	.400	8.06	26	1	0	12	0	0	44.2	54	43	40	5	5	26	3	28	8
Dodd, Boise*	0	1	.000	10.38	6	0	0	0	0	0	4.1	4	7	5	0	2	4	0	3	2
Downs, Eugene	3	4	.429	4.31	15	14	0	0	0	0	64.2	67	34	31	6	1	33	0	46	5
Doyle, Southern Oregon*	0	0	.000	0.00	1	1	0	0	0	0	3.0	0	0	0	0	0	1	0	2	0
Duke, Bend*	6	6	.500	3.44	15	14	0	0	0	0	81.0	79	50	31	2	1	51	0	70	11
Eggleston, Spokane	3	7	.300	4.48	18	12	1	4	0	1	66.1	72	45	33	4	6	32	0	38	7
Estes, Bellingham*	1	3	.250	6.88	9	9	0	0	0	0	34.0	27	33	26	2	1	55	0	35	6
Evans, Southern Oregon	1	3	.250	7.16	13	0	0	9	0	0	27.2	31	28	22	1	3	19	4	22	4
Farsaci, Eugene	0	1	.000	5.65	9	0	0	2	0	0	14.1	16	9	9	0	1	11	0	7	0
Finney, Bend	3	8	.273	7.53	14	14	0	0	0	0	55.0	76	62	46	3	6	47	1	31	15
Foreman, Bellingham*	0	1	.000	7.52	17	0	0	5	0	0	26.1	32	29	22	3	2	31	0	20	6
Fronio, Bend	0	0	.000	3.95	5	0	0	2	0	1	13.2	12	7	6	0	0	6	0	11	2
Fyhrie, Eugene	2	1	.667	2.52	21	0	0	13	0	5	39.1	42	17	11	0	1	19	1	45	1
Gibson, Bend	0	0	.000	5.02	5	0	0	3	0	0	14.1	17	12	8	1	0	9	0	11	4
Glaser, Eugene	5	2	.714	4.39	18	6	0	2	0	1	55.1	50	33	27	4	2	30	1	55	8
Gledhill, Boise	3	1	.750	3.53	21	4	0	4	0	0	43.1	37	21	17	3	1	18	0	34	2
Goucher, Bend	1	2	.333	6.46	14	3	0	6	0	0	39.0	51	35	28	4	3	9	0	18	5
Grohs, Spokane	2	4	.333	5.89	12	11	0	0	0	0	65.2	84	52	43	5	15	38	0	31	8
Grundt, Everett*	4	5	.444	2.33	29	0	0	15	0	0	54.0	55	27	14	3	3	16	5	58	3
Grygiel, Spokane*	2	6	.250	4.67	22	7	0	5	0	0	71.1	71	46	37	6	2	32	0	55	6
Haddock, Bend*	4	4	.500	5.57	11	11	0	0	0	0	51.2	72	42	32	7	2	10	0	37	5
Hamilton, Yakima	7	4	.636	2.68	14	14	0	0	0	0	84.0	73	35	25	2	5	22	1	67	6
Hampton, Bellingham*	5	2	.714	1.58	9	9	0	0	0	0	57.0	32	15	10	0	0	26	0	65	6
Hanson, Spokane	1	3	.250	6.49	13	10	1	2	0	0	61.0	76	56	44	2	0	24	0	39	11
Hawks, Spokane	0	1	.000	5.40	7	1	0	4	0	0	18.1	23	18	11	5	2	7	0	10	0
Henrichs, Everett	0	2	.000	8.01	8	7	0	1	0	0	30.1	31	33	27	5	2	23	1	22	6
Heredia, Boise	8	1	.889	1.05	25	0	0	10	0	5	77.0	42	17	9	1	1	16	1	99	4
Hyde, Everett	3	3	.500	4.42	26	0	0	24	0	7	36.2	37	20	18	3	4	8	0	25	1
Ingram, Southern Oregon	6	5	.545	3.43	17	12	1	1	0	1	81.1	72	39	31	4	6	39	0	64	5
Jensen, Southern Oregon	0	2	.000	5.79	5	0	0	0	0	0	4.2	3	3	3	0	0	7	0	3	0
Jiminez, Southern Oregon	0	2	.000	3.12	10	9	0	0	0	0	34.2	22	21	12	0	2	34	0	39	6
Johnson, Eugene	6	4	.600	3.48	17	12	0	0	0	0	75.0	69	39	29	7	2	21	0	85	10
Juelsgaard, Everett	3	5	.375	4.33	20	6	0	8	0	0	62.1	61	36	30	3	2	27	2	46	16
Keling, Boise	6	2	.750	3.04	15	14	0	1	0	1	83.0	71	31	28	3	3	30	0	96	5
Kerr, Yakima*	0	0	.000	1.57	13	0	0	7	0	0	23.0	13	4	4	0	1	17	1	34	2
Kimball, Southern Oregon	1	2	.333	2.97	27	0	0	24	0	11	33.1	26	18	11	1	2	14	0	44	3
Knaplund, Bend*	0	0	.000	27.00	2	0	0	1	0	0	3.1	7	15	10	2	1	11	0	2	2
Kobetitsch, Eugene*	1	2	.333	4.11	19	0	0	15	0	1	30.2	31	17	14	4	0	11	1	21	3
Landress, Eugene	7	3	.700	4.50	22	0	0	11	0	2	52.0	59	29	26	2	1	17	3	44	6
Lee, Eugene	1	3	.250	5.09	14	7	0	0	0	0	40.2	33	25	23	1	3	38	0	30	4
LeGendre, Yakima	0	1	.000	4.00	6	3	0	0	0	0	18.0	13	13	8	0	1	16	0	23	1
Lisiecki, Bellingham	0	1	.000	2.16	21	0	0	16	0	7	33.1	18	11	8	0	2	23	1	63	4

Pitcher, Team	W	L	Pct.	ERA	G	GS	CG	GF	ShO	Sv.	IP	H	R	ER	HR	HB	BB	Int. BB	SO	WP
Long, Spokane*	1	9	.100	6.99	13	11	0	0	0	0	56.2	78	57	44	2	2	39	0	40	8
Luther, Everett	1	3	.250	6.46	8	3	0	0	0	0	23.2	26	23	17	5	1	10	0	16	2
Macias, Eugene	6	1	.857	4.66	15	15	0	0	0	0	75.1	81	42	39	4	3	36	0	53	2
Maldonado, Yakima*	3	2	.600	2.38	17	0	0	7	0	3	45.1	32	14	12	3	1	12	0	58	0
Mammola, Boise*	3	1	.750	2.37	23	0	0	9	0	0	19.0	19	9	5	1	0	11	3	25	2
Martinez, Boise	5	2	.714	3.54	15	15	0	0	0	0	68.2	69	36	27	4	6	39	0	73	5
McLeod, Everett	0	2	.000	7.44	11	5	0	1	0	0	32.2	38	37	27	2	8	34	0	27	6
Medrick, Eugene*	1	0	1.000	3.18	4	0	0	3	0	1	5.2	7	2	2	0	0	2	0	5	0
Miceli, Eugene	0	1	.000	2.14	25	0	0	21	0	10	33.2	18	8	8	1	1	18	0	43	2
Minik, Bend	0	0	.000	2.31	21	0	0	19	0	10	23.1	18	8	6	1	2	13	0	18	2
Misa, Southern Oregon	5	4	.556	4.95	19	7	0	3	0	1	72.2	65	42	40	3	2	35	2	63	5
Morillo, Southern Oregon	1	2	.333	6.16	12	3	0	7	0	0	30.2	40	25	21	2	0	13	0	20	4
Mountain, Bellingham	1	1	.500	7.07	8	0	0	6	0	1	14.0	13	11	11	2	2	14	0	6	1
Murphy, Bend	3	3	.500	2.92	23	0	0	10	0	3	52.1	42	21	17	4	4	30	1	59	3
Nerat, Southern Oregon*	7	2	.778	4.54	24	0	0	11	0	2	37.2	36	27	19	2	0	25	1	31	3
O'Connor, Yakima*	1	1	.500	5.40	5	0	0	4	0	1	10.0	13	6	6	0	0	4	0	7	1
O'Donnell, Bellingham	5	4	.556	3.46	15	13	1	0	1	0	67.2	70	36	26	5	3	15	0	43	4
Osuna, Yakima	0	0	.000	3.20	13	0	0	11	0	5	25.1	18	10	9	1	4	8	0	39	1
Overholser, Spokane	1	1	.500	1.69	7	0	0	2	0	1	21.1	18	11	4	1	3	11	0	19	5
Percival, Boise	2	0	1.000	1.41	28	0	0	20	0	12	38.1	23	7	6	0	2	18	1	63	9
Person, Bend	1	1	.500	3.60	2	2	0	0	0	0	10.0	6	6	4	0	1	5	0	6	1
Ploeger, Spokane	4	7	.364	6.14	18	9	1	4	0	0	63.0	69	51	43	4	1	46	0	57	16
Polanco, Bellingham	2	4	.333	5.24	21	3	0	6	0	2	46.1	40	29	27	2	1	37	0	52	7
Pote, Everett	2	0	1.000	2.51	5	4	0	0	0	0	28.2	24	8	8	2	2	7	0	26	2
Powers, Boise	2	3	.400	6.05	12	10	0	0	0	0	38.2	41	31	26	1	1	34	2	35	11
Prentice, Everett	0	1	.000	2.38	17	0	0	7	0	3	22.2	13	10	6	0	4	17	5	18	0
Purdy, Boise	8	4	.667	3.01	15	15	1	0	0	0	95.2	87	37	32	3	4	27	2	78	6
Ratekin, Boise	2	5	.286	3.34	14	13	1	1	0	0	70.0	59	31	26	1	3	22	0	49	3
Reyan, Bellingham	0	1	.000	5.79	4	0	0	1	0	0	9.1	9	6	6	2	0	4	0	9	0
Robinson, Boise*	6	3	.667	2.13	27	0	0	11	0	3	38.0	33	13	9	1	0	10	5	41	1
Rosenbalm, Bellingham	2	3	.400	2.23	23	0	0	10	0	4	40.1	32	17	10	2	2	14	2	40	3
Russell, Bellingham	6	7	.462	2.93	15	15	0	0	0	0	95.1	85	48	31	6	1	43	1	77	13
Saitz, Boise	2	0	1.000	0.00	2	0	0	1	0	0	5.1	3	0	0	0	1	0	4	0
Samboy, Spokane	3	2	.600	5.96	15	10	0	3	0	0	54.1	66	43	36	9	5	26	0	44	6
Samuels, Bend	2	7	.222	4.21	15	11	0	1	0	0	62.0	79	58	29	4	7	20	1	35	2
Santiago, Spokane	0	0	.000	7.71	2	0	0	1	0	0	2.1	4	2	2	0	0	1	0	1	0
Scharff, Southern Oregon	3	4	.429	2.84	20	1	0	7	0	1	50.2	38	21	16	2	8	22	2	49	7
Sharp, Yakima	2	2	.500	2.16	26	0	0	20	0	5	41.2	35	17	10	0	1	14	3	52	2
Smith, Eugene	3	8	.273	3.94	15	15	0	0	0	0	77.2	88	46	34	5	3	21	0	74	5
Smith, Yakima*	7	3	.700	4.92	15	15	0	0	0	0	75.0	73	49	41	4	0	38	0	56	5
Smith, Southern Oregon	5	2	.714	3.23	14	13	1	0	1	0	75.1	78	52	27	5	2	17	1	79	7
Stonecipher, Everett	2	1	.667	2.37	10	1	0	6	0	1	19.0	12	7	5	1	0	9	1	26	1
Stowell, Southern Oregon	0	1	.000	3.00	3	0	0	1	0	0	6.0	7	4	2	0	0	5	0	0	2
Thees, Southern Oregon	3	2	.600	5.10	21	2	0	10	0	2	54.2	68	36	31	6	1	27	1	23	5
Thomas, Boise	2	0	1.000	3.93	16	2	0	5	0	0	34.1	26	18	15	0	0	33	0	42	4
Van Dyke, Boise	1	1	.500	4.35	20	2	0	2	0	0	41.1	42	23	20	1	2	18	1	18	5
Vanderweele, Everett	6	4	.600	1.97	15	15	0	0	0	0	87.0	73	42	19	1	8	35	1	65	12
Vanlandingham, Everett	8	4	.667	4.09	15	15	0	0	0	0	77.0	58	43	35	0	5	79	0	86	25
Vazquez, Spokane	0	0	.000	13.50	2	0	0	1	0	0	1.1	2	2	2	0	0	3	0	0	1
Vizzini, Southern Oregon*	2	2	.500	2.57	14	9	0	2	0	0	56.0	44	17	16	0	6	28	1	54	4
Wanke, Everett*	0	1	.000	5.16	13	0	0	5	0	0	22.2	18	19	13	7	2	17	0	25	5
Watson, Boise*	0	1	.000	6.23	18	3	0	7	0	0	26.0	35	28	18	1	3	15	0	27	3
Weinbaum, Bellingham	0	1	.000	0.00	1	0	0	0	0	0	0.1	1	1	0	0	2	0	0	0
Wiley, Bellingham	2	2	.500	3.30	5	5	0	0	0	0	30.0	29	18	11	0	2	9	0	28	2
Williams, Bend	0	1	.000	4.91	3	0	0	3	0	0	3.2	1	2	2	0	2	8	0	4	0
Williard, Boise	0	0	.000	4.91	1	0	0	0	0	0	3.2	2	2	2	0	0	3	1	4	0
Winzer, Bellingham	0	1	.000	13.50	2	0	0	1	0	0	2.0	4	3	3	0	0	3	0	3	1
Wittcke, Everett	0	0	.000	4.38	20	0	0	7	0	1	37.0	47	21	18	2	1	16	1	39	8
Witte, Bellingham	2	2	.500	2.20	27	0	0	22	0	8	45.0	27	12	11	0	0	31	1	44	5
Wojciechowski, So. Oregon*	2	5	.286	3.76	16	11	0	1	0	0	67.0	74	45	28	4	1	29	2	50	6
Wolfe, Southern Oregon	0	0	.000	0.00	1	0	0	1	0	0	2.0	0	0	0	0	0	0	0	1	0
Wylie, Boise	3	1	.750	3.28	22	0	0	8	0	0	35.2	38	18	13	2	0	7	1	30	0
Yankow, Eugene	3	2	.600	2.73	11	0	0	4	0	0	29.2	26	15	9	3	2	9	2	13	4
Young, Bend	0	0	.000	4.00	9	0	0	4	0	0	18.0	11	11	8	3	1	7	0	7	4
Youngblood, Bellingham	5	5	.500	2.75	15	15	0	0	0	0	95.0	82	41	29	3	6	40	1	84	6

BALKS—Estes, 10; Vanderweele, 7; Anderson, Grygiel, Jiminez, 6 each; Castillo, O'Donnell, Je. Smith, 5 each; Bailey, Juelsgaard, Keling, Long, 4 each; Downs, Hampton, Heredia, Ingram, Knaplund, Samuels, Joe Smith, Stonecipher, 3 each; Ciocca, Eggleston, Fyhrie, Glaser, Gledhill, Haddock, Hanson, Henrichs, Landress, Misa, Nerat, Overholser, Prentice, Ratekin, Robinson, Samboy, T. Smith, Thomas, Vanlandingham, Wiley, 2 each; Adams, Baumann, Borski, Brock, Broyles, Carroll, Connolly, Corbitt, Crabtree, Davila, Dodd, Duke, Finney, Foreman, Fronio, Grohs, Hyde, Jensen, Johnson, Kimball, LeGendre, Lisiecki, Luther, Maldonado, Minik, Ploeger, Polanco, Santiago, Wanke, Wojciechowski, Youngblood, 1 each.

COMBINATION SHUTOUTS—Hampton-Witte 2, Borski-Lisiecki, O'Donnell-Polanco-Lisiecki, Borski-Witte, Polanco-Rosenbalm-Anderson, Bellingham; Cain-Gibson-Minik, Bend; Keling-Van Dyke, Purdy-Heredia-Percival, Purdy-Robinson-Gledhill, Purdy-Saitz-Mammola-Percival, Van Dyke-Glednill-Ratekin, Boise; Downs-Connolly-Landress, Downs-Kobetitsch, Johnson-Bryans-Miceli, Eugene; Ayres-Grundt, Vanderweele-Hyde, Vanlandingham-Grundt, Everett; Ingram-Jensen-Kimball, Misa-Kimball, Southern Oregon; Bennett-Crabtree-Maldonado, Bennett-Crabtree-Osuna-Sharp, Hamilton-Sharp, Thomas-Maldonado, Yakima.

NO-HIT GAMES—None.

FIELDING

TEAM

Team	Pct.	G	PO	A	E	DP	PB	Team	Pct.	G	PO	A	E	DP	PB
Boise	.961	76	2075	837	117	76	24	Bellingham	.950	76	2019	834	150	65	31
Yakima	.956	76	2032	778	129	66	14	Spokane	.949	76	2002	901	156	72	27
Eugene	.951	76	2070	770	146	72	22	Everett	.948	76	1981	800	153	79	31
Southern Oregon	.951	76	2042	899	153	76	19	Bend	.944	76	1958	871	169	77	15

Triple plays—Bend 2.

INDIVIDUAL

*Throws lefthanded.

FIRST BASEMEN

Player, Team	Pct.	G	PO	A	E	DP
Babbitt, Eugene	.966	15	126	14	5	17
Bellomo, Everett*	1.000	4	9	0	0	0
Charles, Everett	.970	18	121	8	4	17
Dana, Everett	1.000	4	16	0	0	2
Endebrock, Southern Oregon	.979	11	88	4	2	7
Frias, Spokane	.947	7	32	4	2	2
Glenn, Bend	.989	72	650	49	8	65
Griffin, Yakima	1.000	3	16	0	0	2
Gubanich, Southern Oregon	1.000	1	1	0	0	0
Hawks, 2 Bend-2 Spo.	1.000	4	28	2	0	2
Hinton, Eugene*	.983	61	492	25	9	43
Hust, Southern Oregon	1.000	1	2	0	0	0
Johnson, Spokane	.667	1	4	0	2	0
McGee, Bend	1.000	3	18	0	0	2
Meyers, Yakima	1.000	7	23	4	0	2
Montgomery, Everett	.991	27	200	14	2	27
Mowry, Spokane*	.974	37	347	21	10	34
Norton, Southern Oregon	.979	6	45	2	1	4
Perez, Boise	1.000	5	36	4	0	4
PRITCHETT, Boise	.993	70	636	26	5	60
Proctor, Yakima*	.988	74	541	55	7	52
Pugh, Spokane*	.989	35	333	18	4	27
Ramirez, Everett	.982	41	303	17	6	23
Raven, Boise	.952	5	18	2	1	3
Sheldon, Southern Oregon	.983	7	55	3	1	5
Smith, Bellingham	.980	60	546	42	12	47
Tallent, Boise	1.000	5	25	3	0	4
Thomsen, Southern Oregon*	.991	62	502	33	5	44
Turco, Bend	1.000	1	7	1	0	2
Turner, Bend	1.000	1	11	0	0	1
Vitiello, Eugene	.944	3	17	0	1	2
Walles, Bellingham	.969	20	144	11	5	12
Williams, Bend	.947	4	16	2	1	3
Wolfe, Southern Oregon	.977	4	43	0	1	3

Triple plays—Glenn 2.

SECOND BASEMEN

Player, Team	Pct.	G	PO	A	E	DP
Babbitt, Eugene	1.000	6	6	8	0	3
Bard, Bend	.818	5	10	8	4	3
Brookens, Eugene	.875	4	2	5	1	1
Casper, Everett	.975	22	39	39	2	9
Claus, Boise	.916	48	59	105	15	17
Demetral, Yakima	.963	62	78	158	9	35
DIAZ, Bellingham	.973	56	100	155	7	33
Endebrock, Southern Oregon	.951	32	50	66	6	11
Erhard, Bellingham	.977	11	20	23	1	11
Florez, Everett	.963	57	108	176	11	37
Francisco, Southern Oregon	.940	11	20	27	3	5
Frias, Spokane	.938	19	44	46	6	7
Frias, Everett	1.000	1	2	5	0	1
Gates, Southern Oregon	.967	13	25	33	2	8
Haber, Eugene	.931	41	52	96	11	12
Halland, Bellingham	.943	13	21	29	3	2
Kaiser, Eugene	.933	41	69	84	11	21
Lightner, Bend	.949	10	24	13	2	5
Moody, Spokane	.951	59	122	171	15	43
Norton, Southern Oregon	1.000	2	3	0	0	0
Ollison, Bend	.937	48	86	152	16	35
Polanco, Boise	.955	36	45	60	5	14
Richard, Yakima	.933	7	7	7	1	4
Savage, Bend	.857	1	2	4	1	1
Sears, Boise	.946	27	35	52	5	13
Sheldon, Southern Oregon	.953	23	42	81	6	14
Stephens, Spokane	.875	3	5	2	1	0
Swank, Everett	.957	4	8	14	1	6
Turco, Bend	.989	18	31	62	1	11
Valencia, Everett	.800	1	1	3	1	0
Van De Brake, Yakima	.910	18	17	44	6	4
Wood, Southern Oregon	.979	12	26	21	1	7

THIRD BASEMEN

Player, Team	Pct.	G	PO	A	E	DP
Babbitt, Eugene	.775	16	10	21	9	1
Bard, Bend	.830	28	21	57	16	8
Biancamano, Spokane	.729	22	10	33	16	3
Bond, Bellingham	1.000	2	0	1	0	0
Boyzuick, Yakima	.897	16	11	15	3	0
Calcagno, Everett	1.000	1	0	1	0	0
Claus, Boise	.500	7	1	0	1	0
Clayton, Bellingham	.885	36	14	63	10	6
Edwards, Spokane	.778	6	7	7	4	0
Endebrock, Southern Oregon	1.000	1	2	1	0	0
Erhard, Bellingham	.875	4	4	10	2	2
Francisco, Southern Oregon	.857	2	0	6	1	1
Frias, Spokane	.882	23	14	31	6	6

Player, Team	Pct.	G	PO	A	E	DP
Frias, Everett	1.000	1	0	3	0	0
Gates, Southern Oregon	1.000	3	1	3	0	0
Glenn, Bend	1.000	1	0	2	0	0
Griffin, Yakima	.833	2	3	2	1	1
Gubanich, Southern Oregon	.500	3	1	2	3	0
Halland, Bellingham	.885	37	22	78	13	3
Hawks, 3 Bend-25 Spo.	.943	28	11	55	4	3
Kaiser, Eugene	1.000	1	0	3	0	0
Lebak, Spokane	.714	2	1	4	2	0
Lightner, Bend	.333	2	0	1	2	0
Markiewicz, Boise	.838	60	37	72	21	7
McGee, Bend	1.000	2	1	3	0	0
Meyers, Yakima	.925	26	17	32	4	2
Moody, Spokane	.846	4	5	6	2	0
Norton, Southern Oregon	.824	46	21	91	24	7
Ramirez, Everett	.917	5	3	8	1	0
RANDA, Eugene	.923	62	57	111	14	12
Robertson, Spokane	.800	3	2	6	2	1
Ruocchio, Boise	.913	23	8	34	4	2
Schoen, Bend	.852	36	22	70	16	6
Sheldon, Southern Oregon	.931	15	10	17	2	2
Speakman, Bellingham	.500	2	0	1	1	0
Swank, Everett	.917	9	6	16	2	2
Thielen, Everett	.814	65	46	98	33	8
Turco, Bend	.917	10	7	15	2	1
Valencia, Everett	.750	4	1	2	1	0
Van De Brake, Yakima	.692	2	4	5	4	0
Watts, Yakima	.906	42	28	68	10	6
Williams, Southern Oregon	.872	18	9	25	5	2

Triple play—Bard.

SHORTSTOPS

Player, Team	Pct.	G	PO	A	E	DP
Bond, Bellingham	.908	49	61	137	20	21
BREAM, Spokane	.964	68	100	247	13	46
Claus, Boise	.882	10	13	17	4	8
Diaz, Bellingham	.818	3	4	5	2	2
Erhard, Bellingham	.848	28	47	59	19	13
Francisco, Southern Oregon	.917	3	6	5	1	2
Frias, Everett	1.000	1	0	2	0	0
Gates, Southern Oregon	.937	41	51	141	13	21
Hagy, Boise	.931	72	105	221	24	46
Halter, Eugene	.928	64	118	154	21	40
Kaiser, Eugene	.886	9	10	21	4	3
Kliafas, Yakima	.939	49	75	124	13	22
Moody, Spokane	.929	12	18	34	4	4
Ollison, Bend	.828	5	9	15	5	3
Richard, Yakima	.854	14	9	26	6	6
Rodriguez, Everett	.926	33	47	79	10	21
Savage, Bend	.929	53	71	150	17	30
Sheldon, Southern Oregon	.884	11	15	23	5	4
Subero, Eugene	.938	6	9	21	2	3
Swank, Everett	.895	51	74	131	24	33
Tramuta, Yakima	.846	25	31	46	14	16
Turco, Bend	.883	23	45	76	16	16
Van De Brake, Yakima	.923	5	3	9	1	4
Wood, Southern Oregon	.912	34	38	96	13	18

Triple play—Savage.

OUTFIELDERS

Player, Team	Pct.	G	PO	A	E	DP
Adams, Bellingham	.948	41	67	6	4	2
Andrews, Everett	.833	6	10	0	2	0
Anthony, Spokane	.944	53	79	6	5	0
Bard, Bend	1.000	2	3	0	0	0
Barlow, Bellingham	.953	41	77	4	4	1
Bellomo, Everett*	.906	24	26	3	3	0
Blackwell, Bellingham	1.000	3	2	0	0	0
Bonilla, Bend*	.917	18	18	4	2	1
Boudreau, Bellingham	1.000	38	52	1	0	0
Boykin, Boise	.984	56	59	3	1	0
Brewer, Everett	.946	52	95	10	6	0
Cannon, Boise	1.000	15	28	1	0	1
Castro, Eugene	.943	29	31	2	2	0
Cookson, Southern Oregon	.857	5	6	0	1	0
Endebrock, Southern Oregon	1.000	8	10	0	0	0
Farrish, Yakima	.950	45	73	3	4	0
Feist, Everett	.975	30	39	0	1	0
Fernandez, Bellingham*	.929	47	72	7	6	1
Haber, Eugene	1.000	10	15	2	0	1
Hart, Southern Oregon	1.000	5	3	0	0	0
Hawks, 13 Bend-1 Spo.	.882	14	15	0	2	0
Henderson, Everett*	1.000	21	26	0	0	0
Hollandsworth, Yakima*	.939	51	106	1	7	0
Hust, Southern Oregon	.944	61	114	3	7	2
Jackson, Everett	.961	64	121	3	5	1
M. Johnson, Eugene	.974	50	110	4	3	1
Jones, Everett	.935	46	77	10	6	0
Kennedy, Southern Oregon	1.000	1	1	0	0	0

Player, Team	Pct.	G	PO	A	E	DP
Lebak, Spokane	.911	33	48	3	5	1
Lightner, Bend	.917	10	9	2	1	0
Mashore, Southern Oregon	.971	60	93	6	3	2
Mays, Eugene	.930	28	51	2	4	0
McGee, Bend	.875	5	7	0	1	0
McGonnigal, Everett*	1.000	9	11	0	0	0
Nash, Spokane	.800	4	7	1	2	0
Neill, Southern Oregon*	.945	50	81	5	5	1
Norman, Eugene	.959	30	65	5	3	1
PALMEIRO, Boise	.986	70	130	8	2	1
Parker, Bend	.943	65	98	2	6	0
Perez, Boise	.946	41	51	2	3	0
Pinkney, Yakima	.881	34	33	4	5	1
Pritchett, Bend	.917	63	103	7	10	2
Ramirez, Everett	1.000	4	3	0	0	0
Ringgold, Bend	1.000	5	6	0	0	0
Robertson, Spokane	.954	54	97	7	5	1
Rountree, Spokane*	.952	41	80	0	4	0
Schoen, Bend	1.000	1	1	0	0	0
Servello, Eugene	.967	43	85	4	3	0
Slater, Eugene*	.922	42	55	4	5	2
Spearman, Yakima*	.975	69	149	7	4	2
Stephens, Spokane	.833	10	5	0	1	0
Sweeney, Boise*	.954	67	81	2	4	1
Sweeney, Yakima*	.833	3	10	0	2	0
Tallent, Boise	1.000	12	4	0	0	0
Terrell, Bellingham	.944	58	80	5	5	0
Turco, Bend	.920	13	22	1	2	0
Turner, Boise	.750	6	3	0	1	0
Turner, Bend	.963	56	97	6	4	2
Twitty, Bellingham	.905	16	18	1	2	0
Vaughn, Spokane	.945	46	98	6	6	0
Vitiello, Eugene	1.000	15	32	4	0	0
Vorbeck, Yakima	.949	47	70	4	4	0
Wilder, Bellingham	.800	2	4	0	1	0
Williams, Bend	1.000	1	0	1	0	0
Wolfe, Southern Oregon	.944	46	47	4	3	0

Triple play — Pritchett.

CATCHERS

Player, Team	Pct.	G	PO	A	E	DP	PB
Bobo, Boise	.993	16	120	16	1	2	6
Bosarge, Bellingham	.987	9	68	6	1	0	1
Brooks, Eugene	.980	7	45	3	1	0	2
Calcagno, Everett	.929	3	12	1	1	1	0
Caple, Bend	.961	22	133	16	6	0	3
Charles, Everett	.975	39	277	37	8	4	13
Dana, Everett	.976	40	211	33	6	3	11
Frick, Southern Oregon	.946	6	34	1	2	1	1
Gray, Yakima	.983	45	372	39	7	5	8
Gubanich, Southern Oregon	.965	34	195	28	8	6	10
Hall, Spokane	.969	19	106	20	4	1	8
Hawks, Bend	1.000	4	25	6	0	1	2
Johnson, Yakima	.983	36	263	35	5	2	4
Johnson, Spokane	.982	10	51	5	1	0	3
Kennedy, Southern Oregon	.967	31	245	19	9	1	6
Klavitter, Bellingham	.979	23	177	7	4	1	15
McGee, Bend	.958	39	229	25	11	2	4
Meyers, Yakima	.981	12	48	4	1	1	2
Montgomery, Everett	.963	11	68	9	3	1	7
Morales, Bellingham	.983	17	105	10	2	1	6
Sanders, Eugene	.977	45	299	37	8	5	9
Speakman, Bellingham	.977	35	269	31	7	4	9
Stela, Boise	.981	26	187	22	4	1	5
Strickland, Eugene	.987	33	269	37	4	5	11
Thurston, Spokane	.974	56	330	48	10	2	16
TURNER, Boise	.997	44	357	39	1	1	13
Williams, Bend	.958	23	99	14	5	1	6
Williams, Southern Oregon	.993	18	117	19	1	2	2

Triple play — McGee.

PITCHERS

Player, Team	Pct.	G	PO	A	E	DP
Anderson, Bellingham*	.833	17	2	8	2	2
Ayres, Everett	.824	16	2	12	3	1
Bailey, Eugene	.600	7	0	3	2	0
Baumann, Yakima	1.000	13	2	7	0	2
Benhardt, Spokane*	.933	27	4	10	1	0
Bennett, Yakima	.875	14	4	3	1	0
Boggeto, Yakima	1.000	20	0	1	0	0
Boker, Bend	.889	14	5	19	3	1
Borski, Bellingham	.958	8	3	20	1	3
Brock, Southern Oregon	.846	8	2	9	2	0
Bryans, Eugene	1.000	7	1	6	0	0
Cain, Bend	.824	17	4	10	3	0
Campbell, Spokane	.889	22	6	10	2	1
Carrico, Everett*	1.000	8	1	3	0	0
Carroll, Yakima*	1.000	14	1	18	0	2
Castaneda, Bend*	1.000	19	1	2	0	0
Castillo, Boise	.846	22	5	6	2	0
Ciocca, Spokane	1.000	21	3	8	0	0
Cock, Bend	1.000	22	5	4	0	0

Player, Team	Pct.	G	PO	A	E	DP
Connolly, Eugene*	.714	21	1	9	4	2
Corbitt, Spokane*	.727	13	1	7	3	0
Crabtree, Yakima*	1.000	13	6	3	0	0
Davila, Spokane	1.000	26	4	3	0	0
Dodd, Boise*	.750	6	1	5	2	0
Downs, Eugene	.929	15	5	8	1	2
Doyle, Southern Oregon*	1.000	1	1	0	0	0
Duke, Bend*	.955	15	2	19	1	2
Eggleston, Spokane	.818	18	2	7	2	1
Estes, Bellingham*	1.000	9	1	9	0	0
Evans, Southern Oregon	.750	13	1	2	1	0
Farsaci, Eugene	.000	9	0	0	1	0
Finney, Bend	.727	14	2	6	3	0
Foreman, Bellingham*	.667	17	3	1	2	0
Fronio, Bend	1.000	5	0	1	0	0
Fyhrie, Eugene	1.000	21	6	8	0	1
Gibson, Bend	1.000	5	1	3	0	0
Glaser, Eugene	1.000	18	0	10	0	0
Gledhill, Boise	.800	21	3	5	2	0
Goucher, Bend	1.000	14	4	3	0	0
Grohs, Spokane	.864	12	7	12	3	2
Grundt, Everett	1.000	29	5	15	0	1
Grygiel, Spokane*	1.000	22	3	21	0	1
Haddock, Bend*	.900	11	4	5	1	1
Hamilton, Yakima	.960	15	13	11	1	2
Hampton, Bellingham*	.900	9	5	22	3	2
Hanson, Spokane	.938	13	4	11	1	0
Hawks, Bend	1.000	7	1	0	0	0
Henrichs, Everett	.750	8	2	1	1	0
Heredia, Boise	1.000	25	6	19	0	0
Hyde, Everett	.667	26	1	1	1	0
Ingram, Southern Oregon	.913	17	5	16	2	2
Jensen, Southern Oregon	1.000	5	1	1	0	0
Jiminez, Southern Oregon	.857	10	1	5	1	1
J. Johnson, Eugene	.833	17	1	9	2	0
Juelsgaard, Everett	.913	20	6	15	2	0
KELING, Boise	1.000	15	6	23	0	0
Kerr, Yakima*	1.000	13	3	2	0	0
Kimball, Southern Oregon	1.000	27	1	6	0	0
Knaplund, Bend*	1.000	2	1	1	0	0
Kobetitsch, Eugene*	.750	19	1	2	1	1
Landress, Eugene	.952	22	4	16	1	1
Lee, Eugene	.900	14	3	6	1	0
LEGENDRE, Yakima	.333	6	1	0	2	0
Lisiecki, Bellingham	.500	21	0	1	1	0
Long, Spokane	.833	13	2	13	3	2
Luther, Everett	1.000	8	2	0	0	0
Macias, Eugene	.818	15	4	14	4	2
Maldonado, Yakima*	1.000	17	1	6	0	0
Mammola, Boise*	1.000	23	2	6	0	1
Martinez, Boise	.727	15	2	6	3	0
McLeod, Everett	.333	11	0	1	2	0
Medrick, Eugene*	1.000	4	1	0	0	0
Miceli, Eugene	1.000	25	2	1	0	0
Minik, Bend	1.000	21	0	3	0	1
Misa, Southern Oregon	1.000	19	7	14	0	0
Morillo, Southern Oregon	.750	12	0	3	1	0
Mountain, Bellingham	1.000	8	1	4	0	0
Murphy, Bend	1.000	23	4	4	0	0
Nerat, Southern Oregon*	.778	24	0	7	2	1
O'Donnell, Bellingham	1.000	15	7	10	0	0
Osuna, Yakima	.800	13	1	3	1	0
Overholser, Spokane	1.000	7	0	2	0	0
Percival, Boise	1.000	28	3	4	0	1
Person, Bend	1.000	2	0	3	0	0
Ploeger, Spokane	.889	18	2	6	1	1
Polanco, Bellingham	.750	21	1	5	2	0
Pote, Everett	1.000	5	1	4	0	0
Powers, Boise	.857	12	1	5	1	1
Prentice, Everett	.625	17	1	4	3	0
Purdy, Boise	.929	15	0	26	2	4
Ratekin, Boise	.938	14	4	11	1	2
Reyan, Bellingham	1.000	4	0	3	0	0
Robinson, Boise*	.941	27	2	14	1	2
Rosenbalm, Bellingham	.800	23	2	6	2	1
Russell, Bellingham	.931	15	8	19	2	1
Samboy, Spokane	.786	15	1	10	3	0
Samuels, Bend	.929	15	5	21	2	3
Scharff, Southern Oregon	.913	20	3	18	2	4
Sharp, Yakima	1.000	26	1	6	0	1
Smith, Eugene	.706	15	4	8	5	1
Smith, Yakima*	.857	15	3	15	3	3
Smith, Southern Oregon	.923	14	8	16	2	1
Stonecutter, Everett	1.000	10	1	0	0	0
Stowell, Southern Oregon	1.000	3	0	3	0	0
Thees, Southern Oregon	1.000	21	2	11	0	0
Thomas, Yakima	.875	16	2	5	1	1
Van Dyke, Boise	1.000	20	2	10	0	0
Vanderweele, Everett	.895	15	3	14	2	3
Vanlandingham, Everett	.909	15	6	4	1	1
Vizzini, Southern Oregon*	1.000	14	1	10	0	0
Wanke, Everett*	1.000	13	0	2	0	0
Watson, Boise*	.778	18	4	3	2	0
Wiley, Bellingham	.700	5	4	3	3	0
Winzer, Bellingham	1.000	2	1	1	0	0
Wittcke, Everett	.667	20	0	2	1	0

Player, Team	Pct.	G	PO	A	E	DP
Witte, Bellingham	1.000	27	1	6	0	1
Wojciechowski, So. Oregon*	.769	16	7	13	6	2
Wylie, Boise	.923	22	1	11	1	0

Player, Team	Pct.	G	PO	A	E	DP
Yankow, Eugene	.833	11	2	3	1	1
Young, Bend	1.000	9	2	1	0	0
Youngblood, Bellingham	.970	15	8	24	1	0

Triple play—Boker.

The following players did not have any fielding statistics at the positions indicated or appeared only as a designated hitter, pinch-hitter or pinch-runner: M. Adams, p; Bankhead, p; Biancamano, p; Broyles, p; Butler, p; Cabrera, dh, ph; Clayton, p; Florez, 3b; Halland, ss; Klavitter, of; Lightner, ss; Markiewicz, ss; O'Connor, p; Proctor, of; Raven, of; Saitz, p; Santiago, p; C. Turner, 3b; Valencia, ss; Van De Brake, of; Vazquez, p; Walles, of; Weinbaum, p; C. Williams, p; G. Williams, of; Williard, p; Wolfe, p.

LEAGUE CHAMPIONS

Year	Team	Pct.
1901—	Portland	.675
1902—	Butte	.608
1903—	Butte	.578
1904—	Boise	.625
1905—	Vancouver	.586
	Everett*	.667
1906—	Tacoma	.600
1907—	Aberdeen	.625
1908—	Vancouver	.578
1909—	Seattle	.653
1910—	Spokane	.596
1911—	Vancouver	.628
1912—	Seattle	.600
1913—	Vancouver	.600
1914—	Vancouver	.632
1915—	Seattle	.564
1916—	Spokane	.622
1917—	Great Falls	.592
1918—	Seattle	.588
1919—	Seattle	.590
1920—	Victoria	.600
1921—	Yakima	.710
	Yakima†	.660
1922—	Calgary†	.600
1923-36—	Did not operate.	
1937—	Wenatchee	.603
	Tacoma*	.627
1938—	Yakima	.583
	Bellingham (2nd)†	.511
1939—	Wenatchee	.601
	Tacoma (2nd)†	.533
1940—	Spokane	.587
	Tacoma (4th)†	.500
1941—	Spokane	.669
1942—	Vancouver	.594
1943-45—	Did not operate.	
1946—	Wenatchee	.622
1947—	Vancouver	.566
1948—	Spokane	.614
1949—	Yakima	.660
	Vancouver (2nd)†	.615

Year	Team	Pct.
1950—	Yakima	.613
1951—	Spokane	.655
1952—	Victoria	.631
1953—	Salem	.635
	Spokane*	.590
1954—	Vancouver*	.636
	Lewiston	.629
1955—	Salem	.646
	Eugene*	.639
1956—	Yakima	.691
	Yakima	.619
1957—	Eugene	.576
	Wenatchee*	.647
1958—	Lewiston	.621
	Yakima*	.594
1959—	Salem	.623
	Yakima*	.563
1960—	Yakima	.638
	Yakima	.562
1961—	Lewiston*	.621
	Yakima	.600
1962—	Wenatchee*	.574
	Tri-City	.580
1963—	Lewiston	.594
	Yakima*	.613
1964—	Eugene	.636
	Yakima*	.611
1965—	Lewiston	.667
	Tri-City*	.681
1966—	Tri-City	.679
1967—	Medford	.607
1968—	Tri-City	.600
1969—	Rogue Valley	.633
1970—	Lewiston a	.538
	Coos Bay-No. Bend	.563
1971—	Tri-City a	.625
	Bend	.538
1972—	Lewiston a	.675
	Walla Walla	.513

Year	Team	Pct.
1973—	Walla Walla b	.638
	Portland	.563
1974—	Bellingham	.619
	Eugene c	.571
1975—	Portland	.545
	Eugene d	.684
1976—	Portland	.556
	Walla Walla d	.639
1977—	Bellingham e	.618
	Portland	.667
1978—	Grays Harbor f	.671
	Eugene	.514
1979—	Central Oregon d	.606
	Walla Walla	.571
1980—	Bellingham g	.643
	Eugene g	.529
1981—	Medford d	.600
	Bellingham	.557
1982—	Medford	.757
	Salem d	.486
1983—	Medford h	.735
	Bellingham	.588
1984—	Tri-Cities h	.622
	Medford	.608
1985—	Everett h	.541
	Eugene	.541
1986—	Bellingham h	.608
	Eugene	.608
1987—	Spokane c	.711
	Everett	.653
1988—	Southern Oregon	.605
	Spokane d	.553
1989—	Southern Oregon	.600
	Spokane d	.547
1990—	Boise	.697
	Spokane d	.645
1991—	Boise d	.658
	Yakima	.579

*Won split-season playoff. †Won four-club playoff. §League disbanded June 18. aLeague divided into Northern and Southern divisions, declared champion under league rules. bLeague divided into Eastern and Western divisions, declared champion under league rules. cLeague divided into Eastern and Western divisions; won two-team playoff. dLeague divided into Northern and Southern divisions; won two-team playoff. eLeague divided into Affiliate and Independent divisions; won two-team playoff. fDeclared league champion after winning one-game playoff. Balance of playoff canceled due to rain and wet grounds. gDeclared co-champion after winning one game. Balance of playoff canceled due to rain and wet grounds. hLeague divided into Washington and Oregon divisions; won two-team playoff. (NOTE—Known as Pacific Northwest League 1901-02, Pacific National League 1903-04, Northwestern League 1905-18, Pacific Coast International League 1919-22 and Western International League 1937-54.)

SOUTH ATLANTIC LEAGUE

FINAL STANDINGS

FIRST HALF

NORTHERN DIVISION

Team	W	L	T	Pct.	GB
Charleston (WVa.) (Reds)	46	26	0	.639	......
Greensboro (Yankees)	42	30	0	.583	4
Gastonia (Rangers)	32	40	0	.444	14
Fayetteville (Tigers)	30	38	1	.441	14
Spartanburg (Phillies)	30	40	1	.429	15
Sumter (Expos)	30	42	0	.417	16
Asheville (Astros)	24	45	0	.348	20 ½

SOUTHERN DIVISION

Team	W	L	T	Pct.	GB
Columbia (Mets)	47	27	0	.662	......
Macon (Braves)	42	28	0	.600	4 ½
Augusta (Pirates)	41	31	0	.569	6 ½
Columbus (Indians)	40	31	0	.563	7
Charleston (SC) (Padres)	34	38	0	.472	13 ½
Myrtle Beach (Blue Jays)	31	38	0	.449	15
Savannah (Cardinals)	26	44	0	.371	20 ½

SECOND HALF

NORTHERN DIVISION

Team	W	L	T	Pct.	GB
Charleston (WVa.) (Reds)	46	24	0	.657	......
Spartanburg (Phillies)	40	30	0	.571	6
Gastonia (Rangers)	37	33	0	.529	9
Sumter (Expos)	34	33	0	.507	10 ½
Greensboro (Yankees)	31	38	0	.449	17 ½
Asheville (Astros)	31	38	0	.449	14 ½
Fayetteville (Tigers)	28	41	0	.406	17 ½

SOUTHERN DIVISION

Team	W	L	T	Pct.	GB
Macon (Braves)	41	30	0	.577	......
Columbia (Mets)	39	30	0	.565	1
Savannah (Cardinals)	35	33	0	.515	4 ½
Charleston (SC) (Padres)	35	34	0	.507	5
Columbus (Indians)	33	38	0	.465	8
Myrtle Beach (Blue Jays)	29	41	0	.414	11 ½
Augusta (Pirates)	27	43	0	.386	12 ½

COMPOSITE

Team	CWV	C'ia	Mac.	Gbr.	C'us	Spar.	CSC	Gas.	Aug.	Sum.	Sav.	MB	Fay.	Ash.	W	L	T	Pct.	GB
Charleston (WVa.) (Reds)		5	0	21	0	5	4	20	0	2	0	5	12	8	92	50	0	.648	......
Columbia (Mets)	3		4	5	4	8	9	5	10	10	8	7	8	5	86	54	0	.614	5
Macon (Braves)	0	4		0	19	7	1	0	18	5	13	6	10	0	83	58	0	.589	8 ½
Greensboro (Yankees)	11	5	0		0	6	8	13	0	8	0	3	4	15	73	68	0	.518	18 ½
Columbus (Indians)	0	4	13	0		7	5	0	15	6	13	5	5	0	73	69	0	.514	19
Spartanburg (Phillies)	3	8	8	2	1		4	6	7	4	5	8	7	7	70	70	1	.500	21
Charleston (SC) (Padres)	4	7	3	4	6	6		5	1	7	8	11	1	4	69	72	0	.489	22 ½
Gastonia (Rangers)	12	3	0	15	0	6	3		0	5	0	3	3	19	69	73	0	.486	23
Augusta (Pirates)	0	2	10	0	13	5	7	0		6	15	7	3	0	68	74	0	.479	24
Sumter (Expos)	2	2	3	4	10	4	8	2	2		7	4	10	6	64	75	0	.460	26 ½
Savannah (Cardinals)	0	3	13	0	11	3	4	0	13	6		4	4	0	61	77	0	.442	29
Myrtle Beach (Blue Jays)	3	4	2	4	2	4	9	4	5	8	4		8	3	60	79	0	.432	30 ½
Fayetteville (Tigers)	4	4	2	0	3	5	3	5	3	6	4	12		6	58	79	1	.423	31 ½
Asheville (Astros)	8	3	0	13	0	4	13	0	2	0	4	4	4		55	83	0	.399	35

Playoffs—Columbia defeated Macon, two games to none; Columbia defeated Charleston (W.Va.), three games to none, to win league championship.

Regular-season attendance—Asheville, 117,625; Augusta, 100,141; Charleston (S.C.), 119,080; Charleston (W.Va.), 185,389; Columbia, 79,564; Columbus, 96,736; Fayetteville, 88,380; Gastonia, 44,060; Greensboro, 191,048; Macon, 107,059; Myrtle Beach, 62,885; Savannah, 99,399; Spartanburg, 54,489; Sumter, 45,639. Total—1,391,494. Playoffs (5 games)—11,386. All-Star Game—5,849.

Managers—Asheville, Frank Cacciatore; Augusta, Don Werner; Charleston (S.C.), Dave Trembley; Charleston (W.Va.), P.J. Carey (through May 5), Dave Miley (May 6 through end of season); Columbia, Tim Blackwell; Columbus, Mike Brown; Fayetteville, Gerry Groninger; Gastonia, Bump Wills; Greensboro, Trey Hillman; Macon, Roy Majtyka; Myrtle Beach, Garth Iorg; Savannah, Larry Milbourne; Spartanburg, Mel Roberts; Sumter, Lorenzo Bundy. Managerial records of teams with more than one manager: Charleston (W.Va.), Carey 17-7, Miley 75-43.

All-Star team—1B—Tom Raffo, Charleston (W.Va.); 2B—Joe Sondrini, Augusta; 3B—Butch Huskey, Columbia; SS—Chipper Jones, Macon; Util. IF—Howard Battle, Myrtle Beach; Jason Hardtke, Columbus; OF—Kyle Washington, Columbus; Steve Gibralter, Charleston (W.Va.); Rondell White, Sumter; Util. OF—Troy Hughes, Macon; DH—Kiki Hernandez, Greensboro; RHP—Jose Martinez, Columbia; LHP—Rafael Quirico, Greensboro; Most Valuable Player—Kiki Hernandez, Greensboro; Most Outstanding Pitcher—Jose Martinez, Columbia.

BATTING

TEAM

Team	Avg.	G	AB	R	OR	H	TB	2B	3B	HR	RBI	SH	SF	HP	BB	Int. BB	SO	SB	CS	LOB
Columbia	.265	142	4508	669	514	1196	1692	216	41	66	577	54	44	54	481	13	782	183	115	914
Columbus	.254	142	4666	727	710	1186	1791	219	52	94	621	34	55	74	658	27	968	217	68	1097
Charleston (W.Va.)	.250	142	4554	601	471	1139	1610	208	37	63	533	35	50	47	523	19	832	97	81	994
Greensboro	.247	141	4468	625	546	1105	1553	205	21	67	538	19	41	80	590	17	1145	180	125	973
Augusta	.247	142	4653	600	675	1149	1581	190	52	46	499	27	31	48	459	18	1087	214	109	964
Macon	.243	141	4505	722	577	1096	1606	201	45	73	613	33	53	33	534	11	923	264	102	877
Asheville	.241	138	4348	549	689	1047	1474	192	14	69	450	28	36	51	474	6	1068	107	73	915
Myrtle Beach	.239	142	4370	563	628	1044	1467	150	32	63	460	64	31	56	480	10	946	217	118	888
Gastonia	.239	142	4547	554	561	1085	1538	188	29	69	483	29	23	50	516	19	1020	123	85	965
Charleston (S.C.)	.238	141	4589	647	709	1090	1598	180	47	78	537	22	30	51	622	11	1133	232	110	1027
Spartanburg	.236	141	4406	563	525	1041	1415	192	22	46	471	47	31	56	455	4	992	170	66	928
Fayetteville	.235	138	4352	530	654	1024	1358	147	23	47	449	35	34	54	534	14	970	149	99	957
Sumter	.230	139	4478	599	629	1031	1531	179	42	79	500	18	37	47	513	9	1153	160	82	917
Savannah	.220	138	4402	589	650	969	1300	171	17	42	481	23	31	47	599	10	996	216	68	950

INDIVIDUAL

(Leading qualifiers for batting championship—389 or more plate appearances)

*Bats lefthanded. †Switch-hitter.

Player, Team	Avg.	G	AB	R	H	TB	2B	3B	HR	RBI	SH	SF	HP	BB	Int. BB	SO	SB	CS
Washington, Kyle, Columbus	.343	118	432	85	148	227	31	12	8	58	1	3	6	68	4	101	51	15
Hernandez, Kiki, Greensboro	.332	108	385	54	128	206	29	2	15	78	1	8	9	64	5	50	2	6

Player, Team	Avg.	G	AB	R	H	TB	2B	3B	HR	RBI	SH	SF	HP	BB	Int. BB	SO	SB	CS
Jones, Chipper, Macon†	.326	136	473	104	154	245	24	11	15	98	1	10	3	69	4	70	40	9
Sondrini, Joe, Augusta	.306	106	376	66	115	149	23	4	1	45	4	3	12	53	2	71	14	20
Pough, Clyde, Columbus	.304	115	414	77	126	200	35	3	11	73	2	9	8	62	2	62	11	5
Hughes, Troy, Macon	.300	112	404	69	121	184	32	2	9	80	1	5	3	36	1	75	23	15
Davis, Jay, Columbia*	.297	132	511	79	152	197	29	8	0	63	2	5	7	30	2	72	25	17
Lowery, David, Gastonia†	.294	133	507	55	149	199	15	4	9	49	1	1	6	57	0	66	32	22
Hardtke, Jason, Columbus†	.290	139	534	104	155	233	26	8	12	81	6	6	7	75	5	48	23	4
Huskey, Butch, Columbia	.287	134	492	88	141	256	27	5	26	99	1	7	4	54	5	89	22	10

Departmental leaders: G—Gibralter, 140; AB—Gibralter, 544; R—Hardtke, L. Jones, 104; H—Hardtke, 155; TB—Huskey, 256; 2B—Gibralter, 36; 3B—Washington, 12; HR—Huskey, 26; RBI—Huskey, 99; SH—Dotel, 17; SF—L. Jones, 10; HP—Everett, 23; BB—McDavid, 106; IBB—Posey, 7; SO—Turrentine, 163; SB—Bradshaw, 65; CS—Lowery, Vina, 22.

(All players—listed alphabetically)

Player, Team	Avg.	G	AB	R	H	TB	2B	3B	HR	RBI	SH	SF	HP	BB	Int. BB	SO	SB	CS
Adams, Dave, Charleston (S.C.)*	.236	96	276	26	65	74	5	2	0	42	1	2	4	48	0	40	7	2
Adams, Gary, Sumter*	.165	84	230	23	38	71	6	3	7	32	1	0	2	26	2	78	1	0
Alder, Jimmy, Fayetteville	.192	57	167	19	32	49	6	1	3	17	2	0	6	29	1	73	2	3
Allison, Tom, Columbia†	.322	43	121	26	39	56	10	2	1	10	3	0	4	17	0	24	9	2
Ambrosio, Ciro, Myrtle Beach	.167	5	6	0	1	1	0	0	0	0	0	0	0	0	0	3	0	0
Andrews, Shane, Sumter	.208	105	356	46	74	137	16	7	11	49	0	0	3	65	1	132	5	5
Andujar, Hector, Columbus	.189	14	37	5	7	7	0	0	0	3	0	0	1	3	0	8	0	0
Andujar, Jose, Savannah†	.213	100	320	40	68	96	9	5	3	29	5	1	1	28	0	80	27	4
Angotti, Don, Asheville	.111	5	9	0	1	1	0	0	0	0	0	0	0	0	0	0	0	0
Arace, Pascuale, Augusta*	.258	105	387	58	100	155	8	10	9	49	2	1	2	29	3	56	19	6
Arland, Mark, Charleston (W.Va.)	.278	7	18	2	5	7	2	0	0	4	0	0	2	1	6	1	0	
Avent, Steve, Spartanburg	.400	2	5	2	2	4	0	1	0	1	0	0	0	1	0	2	0	0
Ayala, Adan, Charleston (S.C.)	.181	71	204	21	37	60	4	2	5	23	1	3	3	23	0	54	1	8
Ballara, Juan, Savannah	.000	3	7	0	0	0	0	0	0	0	0	0	0	0	0	3	0	0
Battle, Allen, Savannah	.243	48	169	28	41	50	7	1	0	20	0	2	1	27	0	34	12	3
Battle, Howard, Myrtle Beach	.279	138	520	82	145	246	33	4	20	87	0	5	3	48	2	87	15	7
Bautista, Danny, Fayetteville	.192	69	234	21	45	62	6	4	1	30	4	3	1	21	1	65	7	7
Beck, Brian, Charleston (S.C.)*	.202	109	352	46	71	129	12	2	14	56	0	3	2	45	1	99	7	2
Bell, David, Columbus	.230	136	491	47	113	154	24	1	5	63	3	7	5	37	2	50	3	2
Bennett, Al, Spartanburg	.234	117	414	52	97	141	20	3	6	47	5	3	11	26	0	116	11	4
Bieser, Steve, Spartanburg†	.244	60	168	25	41	47	6	0	0	13	4	3	3	31	0	35	17	4
Bish, Brent, Charleston (S.C.)	.311	20	61	10	19	21	2	0	0	5	1	0	1	8	0	10	3	1
Blevins, Greg, Gastonia	.213	105	324	34	69	103	16	0	6	44	2	4	6	37	2	78	2	1
Bogues, Muggsy, Gastonia	.000	1	2	0	0	0	0	0	0	0	0	0	0	0	0	2	0	0
Bowers, Brent, Myrtle Beach*	.256	120	402	53	103	125	8	4	2	44	9	4	2	31	1	77	35	12
Bradshaw, Terry, Savannah*	.237	132	443	91	105	145	17	1	7	42	4	5	10	99	1	118	65	15
Bream, Scott, Charleston (S.C.)	.137	53	175	17	24	28	2	1	0	7	1	1	1	19	0	61	10	6
Brittain, Grant, Macon*	.221	94	272	63	60	94	8	7	4	36	2	4	2	69	0	58	15	8
Brown, A.B., Augusta	.241	65	216	18	52	63	9	1	0	21	3	0	0	30	1	48	9	9
Brown, Michael, Augusta*	.232	94	314	24	73	103	13	4	3	34	0	6	3	47	1	79	12	6
Bruce, Andy, Savannah	.184	20	76	6	14	21	4	0	1	6	0	0	0	4	1	27	0	0
Bryant, Pat, Columbus	.209	100	326	51	68	100	11	0	7	27	2	2	7	49	0	108	31	6
Bullett, Scott, Augusta†	.284	95	384	61	109	146	22	6	1	36	1	1	2	27	2	79	48	17
Bullock, Craig, Charleston (S.C.)	.234	121	418	55	98	153	25	3	8	50	1	1	10	57	1	122	2	8
Burns, Mike, Asheville	.246	72	244	26	60	95	12	1	7	40	0	2	2	21	1	60	2	1
Bustamante, Rafael, Char. (W.Va.)	.257	117	382	50	98	105	7	0	0	33	5	5	3	64	2	49	4	9
Cabrera, Jolbert, Sumter	.204	101	324	33	66	73	4	0	1	20	4	2	4	19	0	62	10	11
Campas, Mike, Savannah†	.206	54	180	32	37	49	9	0	1	12	2	1	3	34	0	44	2	1
Campusano, Genaro, Augusta	.240	82	296	38	71	125	15	0	13	47	0	3	3	28	0	133	4	1
Canate, William, Columbus	.240	62	204	32	49	78	13	2	4	20	7	3	4	25	0	32	14	5
Carlton, Drew, Myrtle Beach	.184	52	87	7	16	26	4	3	0	6	1	0	1	16	0	31	1	0
Castellano, Miguel, Gastonia	.233	114	360	34	84	102	9	0	3	33	4	1	2	31	0	46	2	2
Castillo, Alberto, Columbus	.277	90	267	35	74	109	20	3	3	47	5	5	5	43	0	44	6	5
Charbonnet, Mark, Columbus*	.246	37	118	20	29	43	5	3	1	17	0	1	2	5	0	23	3	1
Choate, Mark, Myrtle Beach	.183	71	164	25	30	41	5	0	2	12	3	1	7	16	0	34	7	5
Christopherson, Gary, Asheville*	.251	59	187	23	47	60	10	0	1	23	1	3	2	29	0	41	5	0
Cintron, Miguel, Augusta†	.241	61	195	26	47	58	8	0	1	9	1	1	1	22	1	45	6	0
Cooper, Tim, Greensboro	.242	85	252	40	61	80	15	2	0	26	0	1	2	43	1	63	11	6
Cotton, John, Columbus*	.227	122	405	88	92	160	11	9	13	42	3	3	3	93	1	135	57	14
Cox, Darron, Charleston (W.Va.)	.241	79	294	37	71	93	14	1	2	28	1	7	2	24	0	39	8	4
Creed, Clint, Sumter	.089	18	45	5	4	5	1	0	0	1	0	0	0	9	0	17	0	0
Crespo, Mike, Gastonia†	.180	44	133	16	24	40	10	0	2	15	1	2	0	11	0	34	0	0
Dando, Pat, Macon*	.061	11	33	2	2	3	1	0	0	2	0	0	0	0	0	9	0	0
Davis, Brad, Augusta*	.500	1	2	1	1	4	0	0	1	2	0	0	0	0	0	0	0	0
Davis, Jay, Columbia*	.297	132	511	79	152	197	29	8	0	63	2	5	7	30	2	72	25	17
Davis, Nick, Asheville*	.176	27	85	4	15	18	0	0	1	4	0	0	0	7	0	27	1	0
Delgado, Carlos, Myrtle Beach*	.286	132	441	72	126	202	18	2	18	70	1	3	8	75	2	97	9	10
Deller, Bob, Greensboro*	.252	84	254	44	64	76	10	1	0	19	0	2	5	58	3	51	15	14
Demerson, Tim, Greensboro	.000	2	2	0	0	0	0	0	0	0	0	0	0	0	0	0	0	0
Donahue, Tim, Columbus†	.000	2	2	0	0	0	0	0	0	0	0	0	0	0	0	0	0	0
Dotel, Mariano, Myrtle Beach†	.205	125	327	42	67	74	7	0	0	20	17	0	2	43	0	90	7	9
Doyle, Tom, Charleston (S.C.)*	.229	62	179	22	41	63	13	0	3	23	1	3	0	16	1	36	3	2
Drabinski, Marek, Macon	.167	45	102	13	17	22	5	0	0	4	0	1	0	12	0	24	0	0
Duncan, Enrique, Charleston (W.Va.)	.105	27	38	9	4	6	0	1	0	4	3	0	0	6	0	14	3	0
Dunn, Brian, Columbia	.238	46	143	18	34	42	5	0	1	13	0	2	0	15	1	28	5	3
Ealy, Tracey, Savannah†	.224	112	380	48	85	103	11	2	1	28	2	1	2	48	2	85	31	12
Eason, Tommy, Spartanburg	.279	27	86	10	24	36	9	0	1	10	0	0	2	6	0	7	1	0
Edwards, Mel, Charleston (S.C.)*	.219	14	32	6	7	12	2	0	1	3	0	0	1	5	0	11	0	0
Einhorn, Scott, Savannah	.216	67	194	29	42	67	9	2	4	24	0	3	3	18	0	47	3	2
Eldridge, Rod, Savannah	.237	126	451	53	107	163	29	4	6	64	0	3	3	38	1	83	3	1
Elliott, Jim, Charleston (S.C.)	.268	24	71	12	19	35	2	3	2	13	0	0	3	9	0	31	2	2
Erhardt, Herb, Charleston (W.Va.)*	.280	30	82	5	23	30	1	0	2	11	1	1	1	9	1	13	0	1
Eubanks, Craig, Charleston (S.C.)	.000	30	1	0	0	0	0	0	0	0	0	0	0	0	0	0	0	0
Everett, Carl, Greensboro†	.271	123	468	96	127	157	18	0	4	40	0	3	23	57	2	122	28	19
Farmer, Mike, Spartanburg	.238	132	483	65	115	177	16	5	12	77	2	7	4	32	0	130	33	6
Faw, Brian, Greensboro	.000	26	1	0	0	0	0	0	0	0	0	0	0	0	0	0	0	0
Fermin, Carlos, Fayetteville	.214	73	224	23	48	51	3	0	0	19	5	3	1	27	0	36	6	5
Flores, Jose, Asheville	.220	87	223	23	49	64	7	1	2	16	4	3	2	25	0	28	3	2
Fully, Ed, Columbia	.277	122	448	69	124	176	27	5	5	56	4	0	3	40	0	71	17	15

SOUTH ATLANTIC LEAGUE

Player, Team	Avg.	G	AB	R	H	TB	2B	3B	HR	RBI	SH	SF	HP	BB	Int. BB	SO	SB	CS
Gallardo, Luis, Greensboro	.247	114	392	54	97	160	20	2	13	77	2	6	4	54	3	99	9	4
Garcia, Omar, Columbia	.251	108	394	63	99	130	11	4	4	50	1	3	0	31	0	56	12	5
Gast, John, Charleston (W.Va.)	.233	19	60	7	14	25	2	0	3	14	2	1	1	9	1	8	0	0
Geisler, Phil, Spartanburg*	.163	36	129	19	21	27	3	0	1	8	1	0	0	14	0	36	0	0
Gibralter, Steve, Charleston (W.Va.)	.267	140	544	72	145	213	36	7	6	71	2	6	5	31	2	117	11	13
Gill, Chris, Charleston (W.Va.)	.232	106	370	57	86	108	18	2	0	28	4	5	6	46	1	45	15	14
Gilliam, Bo, Greensboro	.262	128	485	54	127	194	28	3	11	68	2	5	4	18	0	111	20	12
Givens, Jim, Fayetteville†	.248	60	226	27	56	61	5	0	0	15	0	0	0	17	0	31	13	11
Gomez, Fabio, Columbus	.227	12	44	4	10	12	0	1	0	6	0	0	0	4	0	8	0	1
Gonzales, John, Asheville	.185	15	27	4	5	6	1	0	0	2	2	0	0	0	0	8	2	1
Gonzales, Rich, Savannah	.242	64	240	34	58	82	10	1	4	37	0	3	2	26	0	40	5	2
Gonzalez, Wallace, Macon	.192	58	156	22	30	52	7	0	5	24	1	4	1	22	1	61	1	1
Goodale, Jeff, Fayetteville	.326	43	141	22	46	64	7	1	3	26	0	5	3	18	0	19	12	2
Gordon, Keith, Charleston (W.Va.)	.268	123	388	63	104	162	14	10	8	46	7	1	5	50	2	135	25	9
Green, Tom, Augusta	.349	41	129	30	45	72	13	4	2	24	0	2	3	20	0	24	3	5
Gress, Loren, Macon*	.209	43	129	15	27	45	7	1	3	15	0	3	1	15	0	37	2	2
Grissom, Antonio, Spartanburg	.172	33	93	12	16	16	0	0	0	3	0	1	1	19	1	22	13	4
Groppuso, Mike, Asheville	.183	63	197	31	36	62	12	1	4	25	0	0	3	34	1	60	3	1
Guerrero, Gustavo, Fayetteville	.056	10	18	3	1	1	0	0	0	0	0	0	0	4	0	6	0	1
Guzik, Robbie, Columbia	.116	38	43	2	5	6	1	0	0	1	0	0	1	7	0	19	1	2
Haley, Ryan, Fayetteville	.188	17	48	4	9	10	1	0	0	4	0	0	2	8	0	6	1	0
Hall, Billy, Charleston (S.C.)†	.301	72	279	41	84	106	6	5	2	28	0	2	0	34	1	54	25	9
Hammargren, Roy, Char. (W.Va.)*	.188	47	138	17	26	37	8	0	1	17	1	4	0	28	1	42	1	3
Hammond, Greg, Charleston (W.Va.)	.151	36	93	8	14	20	3	0	1	5	0	1	3	13	0	20	0	1
Hanel, Marcus, Augusta	.165	104	364	33	60	75	10	1	1	29	2	5	9	17	1	87	10	3
Hanlon, Larry, Gastonia	.244	71	225	25	55	68	11	1	0	13	3	0	7	36	0	45	16	6
Hardtke, Jason, Columbus†	.290	139	534	104	155	233	26	8	12	81	6	6	7	75	5	48	23	4
Harley, Al, Asheville*	.237	114	346	46	82	101	9	2	2	21	6	3	10	30	0	86	8	8
Hartwig, Robert, Spartanburg†	.244	37	131	13	32	40	4	0	1	17	1	1	2	24	0	19	6	2
Harvey, Raymond, Columbus*	.280	129	443	75	124	190	22	7	10	79	2	9	10	71	6	66	6	5
Hawkins, Darnel, Asheville	.417	5	12	0	5	5	0	0	0	2	0	1	1	3	0	2	0	1
Heath, Lee, Macon†	.236	126	399	55	94	118	9	3	3	44	9	3	5	29	0	82	62	21
Henderson, Pedro, Columbus	.143	4	7	1	1	1	0	0	0	1	0	0	0	0	0	4	0	0
Hernandez, Kiki, Greensboro	.332	108	385	54	128	206	29	2	15	78	1	8	9	64	5	50	2	6
Hernandez, Tom, Gastonia	.206	58	160	11	33	44	8	0	1	11	1	0	1	6	0	28	0	0
Hill, Lew, Greensboro†	.228	125	426	69	97	138	17	3	6	46	1	1	14	67	0	112	36	16
Hinson, Dean, Augusta	.179	13	39	3	7	7	0	0	0	2	1	0	0	1	0	17	0	0
Hirsch, Chris, Sumter	.119	15	42	7	5	10	2	0	1	5	0	1	0	6	0	14	2	0
Hodge, Lee, Gastonia	.185	55	178	12	33	45	3	0	3	20	3	3	1	10	0	40	2	2
Holifield, Rick, Myrtle Beach*	.219	114	324	37	71	99	15	5	1	25	1	1	7	34	1	94	16	15
Holland, Sid, Gastonia	.243	138	482	64	117	184	19	9	10	59	1	1	5	71	6	142	8	10
Horne, Tyrone, Sumter*	.266	118	428	69	114	170	20	3	10	49	1	4	2	42	1	133	23	12
Houston, Tyler, Macon	.231	107	351	41	81	127	16	3	8	47	1	3	1	39	0	75	10	2
Hughes, Troy, Macon	.300	112	404	69	121	184	32	2	9	80	1	5	3	36	1	75	23	15
Hurlbutt, Bob, Asheville	.209	76	206	17	43	58	9	0	2	17	2	2	4	11	0	59	0	3
Huskey, Butch, Columbia	.287	134	492	88	141	256	27	5	26	99	1	7	4	54	5	89	22	10
Hyers, Tim, Myrtle Beach*	.204	132	398	31	81	98	8	0	3	37	4	3	2	27	0	52	6	4
Hymel, Gary, Sumter	.198	34	116	7	23	36	5	1	2	15	0	0	1	5	0	46	1	1
Jackson, Jeff, Spartanburg	.225	121	440	73	99	134	18	1	5	33	3	1	6	52	0	123	29	14
Jackson, Miccal, Savannah	.214	65	173	22	37	46	6	0	1	18	0	0	3	36	0	40	8	8
Jaime, Juan, Myrtle Beach	.217	28	69	4	15	16	1	0	0	6	1	0	0	8	0	9	3	1
Jenkins, Anthony, Savannah	.233	51	150	25	35	54	5	1	4	15	2	0	1	32	0	60	9	3
Jesperson, Bob, Charleston (W.Va.)	.158	8	19	2	3	5	0	1	0	2	0	0	1	5	1	5	0	0
Jimenez, Vincent, Macon	.150	22	60	5	9	18	3	0	2	9	0	1	2	5	0	24	0	1
Johnson, Mark, Augusta*	.259	49	139	23	36	57	7	4	2	25	1	2	0	29	1	15	4	2
Jones, Chipper, Macon†	.326	136	473	104	154	245	24	11	15	98	1	10	3	69	4	70	40	9
Jones, Victor, Columbus	.174	25	69	10	12	16	0	2	0	10	2	0	3	16	1	17	6	3
Jordan, Tim, Savannah*	.195	74	210	19	41	51	4	0	2	22	0	4	2	22	2	43	4	3
Judson, Erik, Spartanburg	.209	82	234	36	49	66	12	1	1	24	3	2	2	28	0	76	10	1
Justice, David, Macon*	.200	3	10	2	2	8	0	0	2	5	0	1	0	2	1	1	0	0
Karcher, Rick, Macon*	.228	123	425	58	97	156	21	1	12	79	0	5	4	34	1	108	6	5
Keating, Dave, Fayetteville	.264	70	216	27	57	66	5	2	0	27	1	1	2	25	1	45	13	9
Kimbler, Doug, Fayetteville	.233	27	86	19	20	35	3	0	4	14	1	0	1	23	1	23	2	2
King, Jason, Columbia†	.267	108	277	47	74	84	10	0	0	21	15	2	2	73	1	37	12	13
Laake, Peter, Gastonia*	.218	94	266	48	58	78	11	0	3	24	3	3	6	52	1	74	2	2
Landinez, Carlos, Savannah	.148	46	128	19	19	20	1	0	0	7	0	0	2	19	0	40	7	2
Lanfranco, Raphael, Asheville	.138	18	29	2	4	4	0	0	0	2	0	0	0	9	0	8	0	1
Lantrip, Rick, Greensboro	.213	96	315	35	67	104	12	2	7	35	1	3	2	43	1	118	5	10
Ledesma, Aaron, Columbia	.339	33	115	19	39	50	8	0	1	14	3	3	4	8	0	16	3	2
Leonhardt, Dave, Fayetteville	.236	55	191	17	45	52	5	1	0	19	2	1	3	21	0	35	9	1
Lieberthal, Mike, Spartanburg	.305	72	243	34	74	91	17	0	0	31	0	3	5	23	0	25	1	3
List, Paul, Augusta	.273	12	33	7	9	15	3	0	1	10	0	2	0	7	1	10	1	0
Loeb, Marc, Myrtle Beach	.213	97	300	32	64	110	16	0	10	49	0	4	10	49	0	79	3	4
Long, Steve, Sumter	.000	63	1	0	0	0	0	0	0	0	0	0	0	0	0	1	0	0
Looney, Stephen, Fayetteville	.244	118	389	54	95	126	8	4	5	34	2	2	3	41	2	85	22	8
Lorms, John, Columbus*	.195	51	154	12	30	35	3	1	0	8	1	1	1	25	0	35	0	0
Lowery, David, Gastonia†	.294	133	507	55	149	199	15	4	9	49	1	1	6	57	0	66	32	22
Luce, Roger, Gastonia	.262	33	107	17	28	47	9	2	2	16	1	3	3	7	0	31	2	2
Mabry, John, Savannah*	.233	22	86	10	20	28	6	1	0	8	0	2	0	7	2	12	1	0
MacArthur, Mark, Savannah	.160	59	187	20	30	37	7	0	0	12	0	2	5	17	0	53	12	3
Maguire, Kevin, Augusta	.091	4	11	0	1	1	0	0	0	0	1	0	0	0	0	5	0	1
Maldonado, Carlos, Fayetteville	.253	50	190	24	48	68	14	0	2	19	3	3	1	15	0	27	3	7
Marabella, Tony, Sumter*	.239	107	348	42	83	112	12	1	5	42	3	4	3	41	2	48	5	4
Marshall, Randy, Gastonia*	.225	40	111	15	25	34	3	0	2	10	0	0	1	15	0	25	0	1
Martinez, Pablo, Charleston (S.C.)†	.267	121	442	63	118	156	17	6	3	36	6	2	2	42	1	64	39	19
Martinez, Ramon, Augusta	.255	106	345	51	88	99	7	2	0	13	6	0	2	10	0	82	35	7
Matachun, Paul, Gastonia*	.245	106	261	38	64	80	11	1	1	28	1	1	1	43	0	52	4	4
Mateo, Jose, Charleston (S.C.)†	.091	12	11	3	1	3	0	1	0	4	2	0	0	4	0	2	1	0
Matos, Malvin, Gastonia	.212	105	330	33	70	114	17	3	7	22	2	1	2	18	0	112	13	8
McCall, Rod, Columbus*	.217	103	323	34	70	101	14	1	5	35	0	1	3	61	3	128	2	2
McClinton, Tim, Columbia	.249	133	474	73	118	192	24	4	14	91	3	7	2	57	1	119	17	8
McDavid, Ray, Charleston (S.C.)*	.247	127	425	93	105	169	16	9	10	45	0	2	8	106	1	119	60	14
McKoy, Keith, Charleston (S.C.)*	.256	89	289	49	74	94	11	3	1	31	1	2	1	40	0	73	31	8
McMullen, Kevin, Greensboro	.260	23	73	10	19	22	3	0	0	5	0	1	1	11	0	22	2	1

Player, Team	Avg.	G	AB	R	H	TB	2B	3B	HR	RBI	SH	SF	HP	BB	Int. BB	SO	SB	CS
Meade, Paul, Columbus†	.202	29	89	11	18	36	4	1	4	8	0	0	1	9	0	24	0	1
Meyer, Rick, Spartanburg	.241	80	266	23	64	88	11	2	3	33	2	4	1	23	0	62	1	2
Millan, Bernie, Columbia†	.285	60	179	21	51	57	4	1	0	21	7	2	0	9	1	27	2	4
Miller, Scott, Myrtle Beach	.229	38	83	13	19	28	6	0	1	15	2	3	0	23	0	13	8	0
Mompres, Danilo, Columbia	.194	10	31	2	6	6	0	0	0	3	0	1	0	3	0	15	0	0
Montero, Alberto, Asheville	.216	48	153	13	33	47	8	0	2	10	0	1	0	14	0	45	2	2
Moore, Vincent, Macon†	.200	35	120	17	24	31	5	1	0	12	0	0	0	7	0	24	6	0
Morrison, Brian, Columbus	.222	6	18	1	4	5	1	0	0	2	0	0	1	3	1	3	0	0
Mulligan, Sean, Charleston (S.C.)	.260	60	215	24	56	83	9	3	4	30	1	1	6	17	0	56	4	1
Murray, Keith, Gastonia*	.243	104	338	38	82	123	8	6	7	44	3	1	2	28	3	90	18	10
Nash, John, Charleston (S.C.)	.202	44	119	12	24	32	5	0	1	8	2	1	1	12	0	30	1	1
Neff, Marty, Augusta	.160	27	106	8	17	35	6	0	4	17	0	0	0	2	0	34	3	1
Nevers, Tom, Asheville	.251	129	442	59	111	189	26	2	16	71	2	5	3	53	1	124	10	12
Noce, Doug, Sumter	.119	29	84	7	10	12	0	1	0	9	0	1	0	12	0	20	0	0
O'Connor, Kevin, Macon*	.250	90	312	58	78	96	11	2	1	31	2	6	3	48	1	36	32	10
Olmeda, Jose, Macon†	.275	81	305	66	84	125	16	8	3	30	2	1	1	38	0	38	34	6
O'Neal, Kelley, Fayetteville*	.251	114	395	66	99	118	10	3	1	26	3	1	10	48	1	75	22	11
Orr, Geoff, Macon	.204	81	235	37	48	64	6	2	2	22	3	0	1	28	0	49	11	4
Ortega, Hector, Sumter	.266	112	365	43	97	126	19	2	2	36	2	3	2	28	0	78	14	4
Ostermeyer, Bill, Charleston (S.C.)	.280	57	186	30	52	99	9	4	10	38	0	2	1	39	1	52	0	3
Ozoria, Claudio, Sumter	.211	91	289	43	61	103	6	9	6	28	0	4	6	26	0	95	18	6
Page, Sean, Savannah	.123	26	73	4	9	15	3	0	1	3	0	0	0	5	0	28	0	0
Pearce, Jeff, Charleston (S.C.)*	.277	117	415	63	115	169	25	4	7	65	0	5	4	40	3	100	24	16
Penn, Shannon, Gastonia†	.217	48	129	22	28	33	5	0	0	6	0	0	1	11	0	30	7	2
Perez, Eulogio, Spartanburg	.209	14	43	5	9	11	0	1	0	5	0	0	1	0	0	7	0	1
Perez, Jesus, Savannah	.098	25	51	4	5	6	1	0	0	2	3	1	0	8	0	13	0	0
Perez, Joe, Columbus*	.231	23	65	5	15	16	1	0	0	4	0	2	0	4	0	14	3	0
Perna, Bobby, Charleston (W.Va.)†	.248	136	460	71	114	175	24	5	9	57	2	5	0	83	3	71	7	10
Perona, Joe, Fayetteville	.265	46	147	25	39	68	7	2	6	25	2	2	4	23	1	19	5	2
Perozo, Ender, Columbia†	.186	95	296	32	55	74	6	2	3	18	4	0	8	37	0	77	6	4
Pimentel, Wander, Savannah	.278	27	90	10	25	32	5	1	0	8	2	0	0	7	0	15	1	0
Pinckes, Mike, Columbus	.154	8	13	3	2	3	1	0	0	4	0	1	0	6	0	5	0	1
Polewski, Steve, Augusta†	.281	49	167	25	47	62	4	4	1	15	1	1	1	19	0	34	12	5
Posey, Marty, Gastonia*	.247	128	421	63	104	165	22	3	11	60	0	2	5	63	7	99	4	4
Pough, Clyde, Columbus	.304	115	414	77	126	200	35	3	11	73	2	9	8	62	2	62	11	5
Quinones, Elliot, Charleston (W.Va.)	.231	120	428	57	99	163	22	6	10	64	0	4	5	30	0	67	7	3
Radachowsky, Gregg, Fayetteville	.143	5	14	2	2	3	1	0	0	1	0	0	0	5	0	7	1	1
Raffo, Tom, Charleston (W.Va.)	.277	133	473	63	131	196	22	2	13	68	1	5	8	39	3	81	2	4
Reams, Ron, Myrtle Beach	.249	126	446	54	111	144	23	2	2	31	7	3	1	14	1	81	30	9
Riggs, Kevin, Charleston (W.Va.)*	.500	1	2	0	1	1	0	0	0	0	0	0	0	1	0	0	0	0
Rivell, Bob, Charleston (S.C.)	.261	52	157	30	41	64	11	0	4	18	3	1	1	21	1	29	4	3
Roa, Hector, Macon	.306	34	121	17	37	53	10	0	2	16	4	2	1	9	0	22	2	1
Roberts, Lonell, Myrtle Beach	.222	110	388	39	86	103	7	2	2	27	10	2	2	27	1	84	35	14
Robinson, Raul, Macon	.214	42	103	17	22	26	4	0	0	10	1	1	0	20	1	16	3	4
Rodriguez, Abby, Sumter	.212	86	189	34	40	48	6	1	0	13	3	0	3	52	0	49	5	6
Rodriguez, Ernesto, Myrtle Beach†	.263	124	415	72	109	154	19	10	2	31	8	2	11	69	2	115	42	20
Rodriguez, Hector, Augusta	.215	112	353	40	76	102	13	2	3	30	2	0	2	39	1	102	3	8
Rogers, Danny, Fayetteville*	.230	112	391	39	90	144	17	2	11	67	0	3	3	41	2	132	1	2
Roman, Vince, Asheville	.279	91	298	51	83	109	15	1	3	16	4	0	7	27	0	48	23	5
Romano, Scott, Greensboro	.218	92	307	35	67	87	13	2	1	28	3	1	7	45	1	70	14	10
Ronan, Marc, Savannah*	.236	108	343	39	81	93	10	1	0	45	3	1	3	38	1	54	11	3
Ronca, Joe, Augusta	.234	105	381	35	89	113	13	4	1	49	0	2	1	21	0	81	14	9
Rudolph, Mason, Columbia	.228	64	219	18	50	69	11	1	2	20	1	0	1	11	1	61	4	3
Ruff, Dan, Fayetteville*	.256	60	203	18	52	76	10	1	4	35	0	4	2	21	2	41	3	2
Rumsey, Roger, Asheville	.291	60	175	33	51	75	7	1	5	21	1	1	2	24	0	21	10	7
Rusk, Troy, Spartanburg*	.284	19	67	9	19	30	5	0	2	11	0	1	0	7	0	16	0	1
Sadler, Sean, Fayetteville	.234	39	124	16	29	42	5	1	2	11	0	1	1	12	0	30	3	2
Salcedo, Edwin, Greensboro	.184	33	98	9	18	24	3	0	1	10	0	2	3	4	0	40	2	0
Saltzgaber, Brian, Fayetteville	.261	111	376	54	98	120	16	0	2	29	2	5	5	60	1	61	11	13
Samples, Todd, Sumter	.259	130	505	82	131	208	29	6	12	63	1	9	9	47	0	124	25	14
Sanchez, Daniel, Greensboro	.169	30	89	7	15	18	3	0	0	8	0	0	0	2	0	15	7	1
Santana, Raul, Sumter	.255	98	318	35	81	113	15	1	5	36	1	2	0	38	0	65	0	1
Santiago, Delvy, Columbus	.000	34	1	0	0	0	0	0	0	0	0	0	0	0	0	0	0	0
Santiago, Gus, Sumter	.108	19	65	6	7	8	1	0	0	1	0	0	2	8	0	32	0	1
Savage, Jim, Spartanburg*	.246	37	118	14	29	36	5	1	0	13	1	2	1	18	0	13	3	4
Schaefer, Cory, Augusta	.260	44	146	19	38	51	4	3	1	11	0	0	4	11	0	26	7	6
Schroeder, Todd, Augusta*	.297	26	91	12	27	32	5	0	0	10	0	1	1	10	3	20	0	0
Schulte, John, Augusta*	.215	35	107	15	23	34	4	2	1	9	1	0	1	22	1	23	10	3
Scott, Phil, Greensboro†	.133	20	45	3	6	7	1	0	0	3	0	0	1	7	0	6	0	2
Seja, Aaron, Fayetteville*	.179	37	106	6	19	19	0	0	0	5	0	0	0	18	0	37	1	2
Shave, Jon, Gastonia	.291	55	213	29	62	79	11	0	2	24	3	0	1	20	0	26	11	5
Silver, Roy, Savannah*	.167	23	60	5	10	14	1	0	1	12	0	0	0	5	0	3	1	1
Sirak, Ken, Spartanburg*	.255	80	251	25	64	89	14	1	3	31	2	2	1	15	2	41	0	2
Smith, Lance, Asheville	.280	104	346	34	97	129	20	0	4	41	3	7	1	30	1	44	1	0
Smith, Robbie, Columbus	.147	29	75	11	11	13	2	0	0	6	2	1	2	14	0	21	2	2
Sondrini, Joe, Augusta	.306	106	376	66	115	149	23	4	1	45	4	3	12	53	2	71	14	20
Spann, Tookie, Charleston (S.C.)	.172	33	93	12	16	23	2	1	1	6	0	0	0	24	0	25	2	3
Spivey, Jim, Savannah	.178	28	73	6	13	14	1	0	0	8	0	0	1	7	0	30	0	1
Steffens, Mark, Spartanburg*	.226	133	438	50	99	126	18	3	1	38	3	0	3	38	0	103	10	4
Stinnett, Kelly, Columbus	.263	102	384	49	101	160	15	1	14	74	1	5	10	26	2	70	4	1
Stocker, Kevin, Spartanburg†	.220	70	250	26	55	68	11	1	0	20	6	1	2	31	1	37	15	3
Swinton, Jermaine, Asheville	.219	110	338	42	74	118	13	2	9	41	1	0	3	44	0	149	6	4
Taylor, Mark, Savannah†	.240	44	96	14	23	34	6	1	1	14	1	2	2	18	0	24	0	0
Tejada, Francisco, Spartanburg	.206	36	97	12	20	26	3	0	1	9	0	1	0	12	1	25	0	0
Thomas, Corey, Spartanburg	.249	136	450	58	112	162	16	2	10	48	13	1	9	54	0	97	20	6
Thurston, Jerry, Charleston (S.C.)	.102	42	137	5	14	16	2	0	0	4	0	0	0	9	0	50	1	1
Tillman, Mark, Fayetteville*	.196	49	138	14	27	28	1	0	0	3	4	0	0	19	0	34	3	2
Torres, Jessie, Savannah	.250	23	72	7	18	23	3	1	0	12	1	1	0	10	0	16	0	0
Torres, Ramon, Columbus*	.056	5	18	2	1	1	0	0	0	1	0	0	1	0	0	2	0	1
Trujillo, Jose, Savannah	.288	65	222	31	64	80	10	0	2	35	0	1	4	56	0	20	14	4
Tsitouris, Marc, Sumter*	.247	96	308	37	76	107	14	1	5	34	1	3	3	20	3	51	1	0
Turner, Brian, Greensboro*	.268	123	425	58	114	158	18	1	8	63	2	4	2	59	1	93	10	11
Turrentine, Rich, Greensboro	.204	130	393	48	80	102	13	3	1	30	4	3	3	54	0	163	19	13
Van Scoyoc, Aaron, Greensboro†	.310	17	58	8	18	20	2	0	0	4	1	0	0	4	0	10	0	1

Player, Team	Avg.	G	AB	R	H	TB	2B	3B	HR	RBI	SH	SF	HP	BB	Int. BB	SO	SB	CS
Vasquez, Chris, Charleston (W.Va.) * ...	.252	51	163	15	41	50	6	0	1	15	1	1	1	9	0	40	3	1
Vazquez, Pedro, Charleston (S.C.)	.173	15	52	7	9	9	0	0	0	1	0	0	0	7	0	17	2	1
Veit, Steve, Asheville	.193	71	192	11	37	46	9	0	0	19	1	2	1	8	0	58	0	0
Vina, Fernando, Columbia*	.271	129	498	77	135	188	23	6	6	50	5	7	13	46	1	27	42	22
Virgilio, George, Macon†	.189	46	148	17	28	39	4	2	1	17	0	1	1	13	0	19	4	2
Vondran, Steve, Charleston (W.Va.)	.213	52	178	15	38	55	11	0	2	12	1	1	0	17	1	28	0	1
Waldron, Joe, Charleston (S.C.) *	.000	38	0	0	0	0	0	0	0	1	0	0	0	1	0	0	0	0
Wallace, David, Asheville	.254	123	402	62	102	125	12	1	3	36	3	0	5	62	0	100	23	6
Washington, Kyle, Columbus	.343	118	432	85	148	227	31	12	8	58	1	3	6	68	4	101	51	15
Weinberg, Michael, Fayetteville............	.217	45	157	14	34	49	7	1	2	11	1	1	6	15	0	47	6	4
Wentz, Lenny, Charleston (W.Va.)	.264	78	227	26	60	75	7	1	2	25	6	2	1	32	0	31	9	7
White, Jimmy, Asheville*	.256	128	437	66	112	162	22	2	8	43	0	2	5	43	2	133	12	16
White, Rondell, Sumter..........................	.262	123	465	80	122	196	23	6	13	68	1	4	7	57	3	109	50	17
Williams, Juan, Macon*	.233	106	347	44	81	100	12	2	1	32	6	2	3	39	1	100	13	11
Wilson, Brad, Fayetteville*	.193	55	171	16	33	46	10	0	1	16	0	0	0	23	1	36	3	2
Wilson, Dan, Charleston (W.Va.)	.315	52	197	25	62	84	11	1	3	29	0	1	2	25	0	21	1	1

The following pitchers, listed alphabetically by club, with games in parentheses, had no plate appearances, primarily through use of designated hitters:

ASHEVILLE—Barreiro, Efrain (18); Bjornson, Craig (5); Branconier, Paul (26); Brown, Duane (31); Daugherty, Jim (62); Fidler, Andy (33); Gobel, Donnie (15); Hernandez, Javier (30); Ketchen, Doug (27); Nieves, Fionel (3); Powers, Steve (36); Prats, Mario (33); Quijada, Ed (22); Reed, Dennis (40); Wilson, David (22).

AUGUSTA—Arvesen, Scott (8); Bullard, Jason (21); Carlson, Lynn (12); Cooke, Stephen (11); Danner, Deon (5); Douris, John (12); Fajardo, Hector (11); Futrell, Mark (41); Gobel, Donnie (30); Hooper, Troy (34); Hope, John (7); Hunter, Bobby (31); Jones, Dan (6); Latham, John (27); Lyle, Jeff (5); Miller, Kurt (21); Mooney, Joe (32); Redmond, Andre (7); Robertson, Richard (13); Ruebel, Mathew (8); Rychel, Kevin (8); Shouse, Brian (26); Sparks, Shane (6); White, Rick (34).

CHARLESTON (S.C.)—Beckett, Robbie (28); Bradley, Mike (2); Brown, Jeff (28); Cairncross, Cameron (24); Carlson, Lynn (5); Devore, Ted (12); Ettles, Mark (29); Garside, Russ (19); Hoeme, Steve (31); Ingram, Linty (12); Ivie, Ryan (37); Johnson, Bill (36); Newton, Steve (9); Overholser, Drew (21); Richmond, Ryan (8); Thompson, Charlie (34).

CHARLESTON (W.Va.)—Cecil, Tim (24); Doty, Sean (47); Duff, Scott (40); Ferry, Mike (22); Hook, Chris (45); King, Doug (30); Leslie, Reggie (44); McCarthy, Steve (1); Minutelli, Gino (2); Nieves, Ernie (27); Ray, John (28); Roper, John (27); Stewart, Carl (24); Tatar, Kevin (11).

COLUMBIA—Benson, Nate (25); Bristow, Rich (29); Butler, Chris (5); Carpentier, Rob (28); Castillo, Juan (28); Crawford, Joe (3); Engle, Tom (7); Fidler, Andy (4); Fiegel, Todd (2); Freitas, Mike (25); Harriger, Denny (2); Jones, Bobby (5); Martinez, Jose (26); Rees, Rob (20); Sample, Deron (12); Sieradzki, Al (9); Thomas, Mike (30); Thomas, Steve (37); Wegmann, Tom (7).

COLUMBUS—Alexander, Charles (17); Baker, Andy (25); Baker, Sam (4); Brown, Dickie (27); Buzard, Brian (6); Cofer, Brian (41); Embree, Alan (27); Gajkowski, Steve (3); McLochlin, Mike (15); Mlicki, Dave (22); Rivera, Roberto (30); Stone, Eric (9); Sweeney, Mark (3); Walden, Alan (12); Wertz, Bill (49); Winiarski, Chip (39).

FAYETTEVILLE—Bauer, Matt (4); Coppeta, Greg (28); Fazekas, Rob (24); Guilfoyle, Mike (40); Haeger, Greg (23); Kosenski, John (37); Lima, Jose (18); Lira, Felipe (15); Neidinger, Joe (37); Pfaff, Jason (14); Reincke, Corey (12); Rodriguez, Ed (32); Stidham, Phil (28); Stokes, Randy (38); Undorf, Bob (22); Warren, Brian (10); Withem, Shannon (11).

GASTONIA—Bouton, Tony (51); Buchheit, Scott (2); Burrows, Terry (27); Cardona, Jose (8); Curry, Dell (1); Dreyer, Steve (25); Erickson, Scott (14); Geeve, Dave (14); Giberti, David (9); Gies, Chris (19); Henson, Micky (8); Hurst, James (11); Kunz, Devin (20); Madrigal, Victor (10); McGough, Keith (16); Migliozzi, Tom (20); Ringkamp, Mark (17); Sadecki, Steve (16); Vlcek, Jim (29); Washington, Tyrone (11); Wells, Tim (13); Whiteside, Matt (48).

GREENSBORO—Dunbar, Matt (25); Frazier, Ron (25); Hines, Richard (26); Malone, Todd (29); Morphy, Pat (43); Perez, Cesar (30); Quirico, Rafael (26); Rivera, Mariano (29); Seiler, Keith (52); Siberz, Bo (42); Smith, Shad (38).

MACON—Chiles, Barry (40); Dare, Brian (25); Fowler, Dwayne (19); Francis, Don (10); Jewett, Earl (7); Leahy, Thomas (29); Lomon, Kevin (1); Mack, Ray (19); Mattson, Rob (23); Morrison, Keith (8); Potts, Mike (34); Ritter, Darren (14); Roa, Joe (30); Rohrwild, Shawn (26); Ryder, Scott (12); Saulter, Kevin (14); Smith, Pete (3); Sparma, Blase (13); Vazquez, Marcos (14); Werland, Henry (18); Williams, David (23).

MYRTLE BEACH—Aylmer, Robert (15); Bicknell, Greg (27); Burrell, Scott (5); Duey, Kyle (38); Flener, Huck (55); Ganote, Joe (20); Garcia, Rafael (39); Jordan, Ricardo (29); Karsay, Steve (20); Kistaitis, Dale (19); Lugo, Angel (12); Mandia, Sam (22); Singer, Thomas (27); Steed, Rick (28).

SAVANNAH—Bailey, Roy (73); Baker, Scott (8); Creek, Paul (5); Eversgerd, Bryan (72); Fusco, Tom (33); Gaston, Russ (9); Glover, Greg (8); Hammond, Allan (13); Jolley, Mike (23); Kelly, John (56); Kinney, Tom (17); Lata, Tim (1); Lopez, Jose (21); McGarity, Jeremy (27); Speek, Frank (48); Spiller, Derron (18); Tomso, Matt (5); Watson, Allen (3); Weber, Ron (7).

SPARTANBURG—Adamson, Joel (14); Allen, Ronnie (2); Bottalico, Ricky (2); Brink, Brad (3); Carlton, Scott (6); Desantis, Dom (3); Domecq, Ray (40); Elliott, Donnie (10); Gilmore, Joel (2); Goergen, Todd (24); Grace, Mike (6); Hassinger, Brad (21); Hill, Eric (27); Hurst, Charlie (12); Juhl, Mike (25); Manicchia, Bryan (12); Munoz, J.J. (20); Owens, Mike (16); Patterson, Jeff (35); Randall, Mark (43).

SUMTER—Alvarez, Tavo (25); Aucoin, Derek (41); Conley, Matt (10); Foster, Kevin (34); Gerstein, Ron (7); Kotch, Darrin (44); Martinez, Williams (39); Morrison, Keith (7); Norris, Joe (8); Ortega, Oscar (1); Pedraza, Rod (8); Perez, Carlos (16); Rueter, Kirk (8); Sieradzki, Al (15); Thomas, Mike (19); Vanryn, Ben (20); White, Gabe (24); Young, Pete (1).

GRAND SLAMS—Elliott, 2; G. Adams, Andrews, Arace, Bradshaw, R. Gonzales, Gonzalez, Goodale, Groppuso, Hodge, Huskey, Karcher, P. Martinez, McDavid, Neff, Nevers, O'Connor, Posey, Raffo, Ruff, Rumsey, Salcedo, Sirak, Steffens, Swinton, Virgilio, Wallace, R. White, 1 each.

AWARDED FIRST BASE ON CATCHER'S INTERFERENCE—Beck 3 (Jaime 2, Luce); Groppuso 3 (Salcedo 2, Gallardo); Ayala 2 (Houston, Sadler); Cooper 2 (Luce, Santana); Salcedo 2 (Rudolph, Santana); Deller (T. Hernandez); Hanel (Santana); Hughes (Taylor); J. Jackson (K. Hernandez); Pearce (Jaime); Thurston (K. Hernandez).

PITCHING

TEAM

Team	ERA	G	CG	ShO	Sv.	IP	H	R	ER	HR	HB	BB	Int. BB	SO	WP	Bk.
Charleston (W.Va.)	2.92	142	16	17	42	1222.1	1028	471	396	38	50	521	12	1079	81	7
Columbia	3.00	140	20	16	33	1198.2	1045	514	399	57	43	483	7	1079	87	26
Greensboro	3.01	141	19	15	26	1206.2	1051	546	404	54	50	502	17	1071	84	29
Spartanburg	3.29	141	17	12	34	1168.2	1033	525	427	71	33	415	3	1054	73	16
Macon	3.31	141	19	22	36	1201.1	1025	577	442	52	54	437	20	885	97	15
Gastonia	3.44	142	11	15	41	1215.0	1057	561	464	57	67	517	13	1070	56	25
Myrtle Beach	3.53	139	11	8	27	1169.0	1041	628	459	78	43	553	1	1099	101	28
Sumter	3.76	139	11	8	28	1189.2	1111	629	497	61	60	566	12	1073	93	28
Savannah	3.82	138	8	6	32	1183.2	1099	650	503	82	50	525	27	908	99	19
Augusta	3.85	142	10	18	29	1214.2	1074	675	519	45	83	716	17	982	126	36
Columbus	4.05	142	10	9	31	1222.1	1161	710	550	63	46	555	14	1053	75	17
Fayetteville..................................	4.11	138	5	3	29	1164.0	1162	654	532	69	42	496	4	867	80	25
Charleston (S.C.)...........................	4.32	141	10	8	39	1213.0	1154	709	582	86	57	646	20	960	91	39
Asheville.....................................	4.42	138	11	8	36	1143.1	1161	689	561	89	70	506	21	835	94	27

INDIVIDUAL

(Leading qualifiers for earned-run average leadership—115 or more innings)

*Throws lefthanded.

Pitcher, Team	W	L	Pct.	ERA	G	GS	CG	GF	ShO	Sv.	IP	H	R	ER	HR	HB	BB	Int. BB	SO	WP
Martinez, Columbia	20	4	.833	1.49	26	26	9	0	1	0	193.1	162	51	32	3	0	30	1	158	4
Roa, Macon	13	3	.813	2.17	30	18	4	2	2	1	141.0	106	46	34	6	5	33	4	96	3
Quirico, Greensboro*	12	8	.600	2.26	26	26	1	0	1	0	155.1	103	59	39	5	7	80	0	162	12
Roper, Charleston (W.Va.)	14	9	.609	2.27	27	27	5	0	3	0	186.2	135	59	47	5	4	67	0	189	8
Dreyer, Gastonia	7	10	.412	2.33	25	25	3	0	1	0	162.0	137	51	42	5	5	62	1	122	4
Frazier, Greensboro	12	6	.667	2.40	25	25	3	0	1	0	169.0	141	65	45	10	9	42	0	127	8
Brown, Charleston (S.C.)*	13	8	.619	2.45	28	25	4	2	2	1	165.0	134	55	45	10	7	45	2	152	4
Miller, Augusta	6	7	.462	2.50	21	21	2	0	2	0	115.1	89	49	32	6	4	57	0	103	13
Gies, Gastonia	10	3	.769	2.54	19	19	5	0	2	0	138.1	122	44	39	4	3	20	0	124	6
Jordan, Myrtle Beach*	9	8	.529	2.74	29	23	3	3	1	1	144.2	101	58	44	3	6	79	0	152	3

Departmental leaders: G—Bailey, 73; W—J. Martinez, 20; L—Beckett, 14; Pct.—J. Martinez, .833; GS—Several pitchers tied with 27; CG—J. Martinez, 9; GF—Long, 53; ShO—Faw, Roper, 3; Sv.—Kelly, 30; IP—J. Martinez, 193.1; H—Coppeta, 184; R—Beckett, C. Brown, 111; ER—Beckett, 100; HR—Singer, 15; HB—Bouton, Branconier, 13; BB—Beckett, 117; IBB—Speek, 7; SO—Roper, 189; WP—B. Johnson, 26.

(All pitchers—listed alphabetically)

Pitcher, Team	W	L	Pct.	ERA	G	GS	CG	GF	ShO	Sv.	IP	H	R	ER	HR	HB	BB	Int. BB	SO	WP
Adamson, Spartanburg*	4	4	.500	2.56	14	14	1	0	1	0	81.0	72	29	23	5	3	22	0	84	3
Alexander, Columbus*	0	0	.000	6.37	17	0	0	10	0	0	29.2	30	27	21	2	0	32	0	37	5
Allen, Spartanburg	2	0	1.000	3.21	2	2	2	0	0	0	14.0	14	5	5	1	0	4	0	7	0
Alvarez, Sumter	12	10	.545	3.24	25	25	3	0	1	0	152.2	151	68	55	6	11	58	0	158	4
Arvesen, Augusta	2	2	.500	2.82	8	8	0	0	0	0	44.2	46	25	14	1	3	20	0	33	3
Aucoin, Sumter	3	6	.333	4.28	41	4	0	8	0	1	90.1	86	55	43	5	10	44	3	70	6
Aylmer, Myrtle Beach*	1	1	.500	3.52	15	0	0	12	0	0	23.0	25	11	9	2	2	12	0	15	3
Bailey, Savannah	8	2	.800	2.49	73	0	0	24	0	0	86.2	65	28	24	6	3	33	1	78	3
A. Baker, Columbus	8	8	.500	4.05	25	24	2	1	1	0	144.1	116	75	65	7	6	84	1	118	17
S. Baker, Columbus	0	3	.000	4.09	4	2	0	2	0	0	11.0	15	10	5	0	1	6	0	12	1
Baker, Savannah*	2	3	.400	2.89	8	8	0	0	0	0	46.2	42	27	15	1	1	25	0	41	2
Barreiro, Asheville	0	3	.000	3.90	18	1	0	7	0	0	27.2	24	15	12	3	6	21	1	21	2
Bauer, Fayetteville*	1	0	1.000	1.80	4	0	0	1	0	0	10.0	7	2	2	0	0	3	0	9	0
Beckett, Charleston (S.C.)*	2	14	.125	8.23	28	26	1	0	0	0	109.1	115	111	100	5	3	117	0	96	20
Benson, Columbia	3	2	.600	2.28	25	1	0	13	0	1	59.1	49	19	15	4	0	38	1	38	6
Bicknell, Myrtle Beach	3	5	.375	4.43	27	4	0	10	0	1	61.0	68	45	30	8	0	20	0	60	8
Bieser, Spartanburg	0	0	.000	18.00	1	0	0	1	0	0	1.0	2	2	2	0	0	1	0	1	0
Bjornson, Asheville*	2	0	.000	6.19	5	1	0	0	0	0	16.0	17	12	11	2	2	6	0	11	3
Bottalico, Spartanburg	2	0	1.000	0.00	2	2	0	0	0	0	15.0	4	0	0	0	1	2	0	11	1
Bouton, Gastonia	9	6	.600	2.08	51	0	0	23	0	2	91.0	79	39	21	1	13	39	3	93	4
Branconier, Asheville	6	10	.375	3.57	26	25	3	0	0	0	141.1	142	77	56	12	13	36	1	96	8
Brink, Spartanburg	2	1	.667	1.65	3	3	1	0	0	0	16.1	13	3	3	1	0	5	0	16	1
Bristow, Columbia	2	0	1.000	3.21	29	2	0	12	0	1	47.2	41	26	17	2	7	38	1	36	7
Brown, Asheville	6	13	.316	4.43	31	20	2	5	0	1	146.1	163	86	72	11	11	44	3	78	7
Brown, Columbus	8	11	.421	5.44	27	26	1	1	1	0	152.1	167	111	92	11	10	61	2	109	6
Brown, Charleston (S.C.)*	13	8	.619	2.45	28	25	4	2	2	1	165.0	134	55	45	10	7	45	2	152	4
Buchheit, Gastonia	0	1	.000	8.10	2	0	0	1	0	0	3.1	7	4	3	1	0	3	0	4	0
Bullard, Augusta	2	2	.500	3.51	21	0	0	17	0	7	25.2	21	13	10	1	1	15	1	29	2
Burrell, Myrtle Beach	1	0	1.000	2.00	5	5	0	0	0	0	27.0	18	6	6	1	1	13	0	31	2
Burrows, Gastonia*	12	8	.600	4.45	27	26	0	0	0	0	147.2	107	79	73	10	5	78	0	151	6
Butler, Columbia	1	2	.333	10.50	5	3	0	0	0	0	12.0	10	15	14	2	1	19	0	7	11
Buzard, Columbus*	1	0	1.000	5.25	6	0	0	2	0	0	12.0	13	7	7	1	1	8	0	14	0
Cairncross, Charleston (S.C.)*	8	5	.615	3.56	24	24	2	0	1	0	131.1	111	72	52	10	7	74	0	102	6
Cardona, Gastonia	0	1	.000	1.65	4	0	0	5	0	1	16.1	14	3	3	1	0	18	0	18	0
Carlson, 12 Aug.-5 C (S.C.)	6	5	.545	2.88	17	17	0	0	0	0	90.2	64	34	29	8	7	48	0	86	4
Carlton, Spartanburg*	0	0	.000	10.80	6	0	0	3	0	0	10.0	10	16	12	2	0	11	0	10	2
Carpentier, Columbia	7	3	.700	4.06	28	8	0	12	0	3	93.0	102	49	42	8	1	24	1	58	4
Castillo, Columbia	12	9	.571	3.82	28	27	3	1	1	0	157.2	148	82	67	6	9	89	0	144	15
Cecil, Charleston (W.Va.)	8	4	.667	3.18	24	23	2	0	1	0	130.1	129	52	46	7	3	49	0	70	7
Chiles, Macon	3	7	.300	4.19	40	0	0	16	0	6	103.0	99	57	48	6	4	36	0	68	12
Cofer, Columbus	7	3	.700	2.62	41	0	0	35	0	12	58.1	50	19	17	1	1	25	1	42	4
Conley, Sumter	1	4	.200	9.00	10	6	0	0	0	0	33.0	33	42	33	1	0	44	0	32	5
Cooke, Augusta*	5	4	.556	2.82	11	11	1	0	0	0	60.2	50	28	19	0	5	35	1	52	3
Coppeta, Fayetteville*	11	10	.524	5.14	28	*27	0	1	0	0	150.2	184	95	86	12	1	48	0	96	4
Crawford, Columbia*	0	0	.000	0.00	3	0	0	2	0	0	3.0	0	0	0	0	1	0	0	6	0
Creed, Sumter	0	0	.000	0.00	1	0	0	0	0	0	1.0	0	0	0	0	0	1	0	0	0
Creek, Savannah*	2	1	.667	4.45	5	5	0	0	0	0	28.1	24	14	14	2	1	17	0	32	1
Curry, Gastonia	0	1	.000	3.00	1	0	0	0	0	0	3.0	3	1	1	0	0	1	0	4	0
Danner, Augusta*	1	2	.333	3.55	5	5	0	0	0	0	33.0	33	24	13	2	2	22	1	17	0
Dare, Macon*	3	1	.750	3.72	25	1	0	9	0	0	36.1	31	17	15	3	2	18	3	27	1
Daugherty, Asheville	3	1	.750	1.52	62	0	0	49	0	28	83.0	63	17	14	0	3	25	6	78	0
DeSantis, Spartanburg	0	2	.000	1.23	3	3	0	0	0	0	22.0	15	3	3	0	2	0	0	18	1
Devore, Charleston (S.C.)	2	3	.400	6.10	12	4	0	6	0	1	31.0	32	22	21	3	2	10	0	21	3
Domecq, Spartanburg	2	6	.250	3.00	40	1	0	35	0	13	57.0	38	23	19	3	3	42	1	45	3
Doty, Charleston (W.Va.)	4	2	.667	1.94	47	0	0	38	0	20	55.2	43	18	12	0	0	29	1	62	7
Douris, Augusta	0	3	.000	8.74	12	2	0	3	0	0	22.2	34	22	22	2	2	9	1	14	1
Dreyer, Gastonia	7	10	.412	2.33	25	25	3	0	1	0	162.0	137	51	42	5	5	62	1	122	4
Duey, Myrtle Beach	6	5	.545	3.27	38	1	0	18	0	5	82.2	77	42	30	4	2	31	0	84	7
Duff, Charleston (W.Va.)*	2	2	.500	2.72	40	0	0	30	0	15	49.2	29	16	15	1	2	32	1	53	7
Dunbar, Greensboro*	2	2	.500	2.22	24	2	1	14	0	1	44.2	36	14	11	1	3	15	0	40	2
Dunn, Columbia	0	0	.000	0.00	3	0	0	1	0	0	3.2	7	3	0	1	0	2	0	1	1
Elliott, Spartanburg	3	4	.429	4.24	10	10	0	0	0	0	51.0	42	37	24	1	3	36	0	81	6
Embree, Columbus*	10	8	.556	3.59	27	26	3	0	1	0	155.1	126	80	62	4	4	77	1	137	7
Engle, Columbia	3	2	.600	3.23	7	5	0	2	0	0	30.2	22	13	11	2	2	17	0	32	2
Erickson, Gastonia*	1	0	1.000	6.04	14	0	0	3	0	0	22.1	22	15	15	0	0	20	0	14	3
Ettles, Charleston (S.C.)	1	6	.143	4.78	30	0	0	18	0	4	49.0	55	29	26	6	2	28	1	34	1
Eubanks, Charleston (S.C.)	1	6	.143	4.78	30	0	0	18	0	4	49.0	55	29	26	6	2	28	1	34	1
Eversgerd, Savannah*	5	1	.167	3.47	72	0	0	22	0	1	93.1	71	43	36	7	3	34	4	97	11
Fajardo, Augusta	4	3	.571	2.69	11	11	0	0	0	0	60.1	44	26	18	1	2	24	0	79	3
Faw, Greensboro	11	7	.611	3.35	26	26	6	0	3	0	166.1	148	75	62	13	3	56	1	123	4

— 491 —

Pitcher, Team	W	L	Pct.	ERA	G	GS	CG	GF	ShO	Sv.	IP	H	R	ER	HR	HB	BB	Int. BB	SO	WP
Fazekas, Fayetteville	1	4	.200	1.98	24	0	0	22	0	6	27.1	28	12	6	1	1	20	1	32	1
Ferry, Charleston (W.Va.)	1	3	.250	4.47	22	1	0	11	0	2	44.1	41	23	22	2	1	21	2	51	4
Fidler, 4 C'bia-33 Ash.*	1	2	.333	4.48	37	0	0	16	0	2	60.1	53	38	30	4	0	65	0	56	11
Fiegel, Columbia*	0	1	.000	6.00	2	1	0	1	0	1	9.0	7	6	6	0	1	6	0	11	3
Flener, Myrtle Beach*	6	4	.600	1.82	55	0	0	44	0	13	79.0	58	28	16	2	0	41	0	107	7
Foster, Sumter	10	4	.714	2.74	34	11	1	9	1	1	102.0	62	36	31	3	9	68	1	111	5
Fowler, Macon	1	0	1.000	3.54	19	0	0	13	0	2	28.0	29	13	11	0	1	5	0	13	2
Francis, Macon	1	5	.167	5.35	10	5	0	1	0	0	35.1	43	34	21	3	1	6	0	38	3
Frazier, Greensboro	12	6	.667	2.40	25	25	3	0	1	0	169.0	141	65	45	10	9	42	0	127	8
Freitas, Columbia	5	8	.385	3.31	25	12	4	11	2	1	114.1	115	48	42	4	6	31	0	111	4
Fusco, Savannah*	4	1	.800	4.60	33	1	0	3	0	1	58.2	44	37	30	2	3	49	2	56	6
Futrell, Augusta	5	2	.714	2.92	41	0	0	18	0	4	77.0	65	31	25	2	6	23	0	55	6
Gajkowski, Columbus	0	0	.000	3.00	3	0	0	2	0	0	6.0	3	2	2	0	0	5	0	5	0
Ganote, Myrtle Beach	8	6	.571	3.42	20	20	3	0	1	0	118.1	104	61	45	9	1	46	0	127	10
Garcia, Myrtle Beach	4	12	.250	4.02	39	13	0	8	0	1	123.0	126	84	55	8	11	75	0	94	15
Garside, Charleston (S.C.)*	3	4	.429	3.17	19	7	0	3	0	0	59.2	59	32	21	4	3	25	2	21	1
Gaston, Savannah	2	3	.400	4.91	9	8	0	0	0	0	36.2	42	20	20	5	4	17	0	19	4
Geeve, Gastonia	6	4	.600	4.31	14	14	1	0	1	0	79.1	74	40	38	7	1	20	1	69	0
Gerstein, Sumter*	0	1	.000	0.00	7	0	0	5	0	1	9.1	5	1	0	0	0	5	0	6	0
Giberti, Gastonia*	1	2	.333	4.24	9	2	0	1	0	0	17.0	17	9	8	0	0	8	0	17	1
Gies, Gastonia	10	3	.769	2.54	19	19	5	0	2	0	138.1	122	44	39	4	3	20	0	124	6
Gilmore, Spartanburg	1	0	1.000	0.00	2	1	0	0	0	0	7.0	3	0	0	0	0	2	0	8	0
Glover, Savannah	1	3	.250	7.56	8	5	0	2	0	0	25.0	29	28	21	2	4	20	1	25	4
Gobel, 30 Aug.- 15 Ash.*	6	2	.750	4.83	45	0	0	13	0	1	59.2	60	37	32	4	6	41	1	58	3
Goergen, Spartanburg	7	8	.467	3.38	24	23	3	1	0	0	149.1	145	68	56	13	3	37	0	94	8
Grace, Spartanburg	3	1	.750	1.89	6	6	0	0	0	0	33.1	24	7	7	1	0	9	0	23	1
Guilfoyle, Fayetteville*	1	4	.200	2.66	40	0	0	34	0	8	47.1	41	22	14	3	5	26	1	44	2
Guzik, Columbia	0	4	.000	3.02	20	13	0	5	0	1	86.1	74	35	29	2	1	23	0	45	5
Haeger, Fayetteville*	4	10	.286	4.14	23	23	1	0	0	0	119.2	117	67	55	9	6	71	0	104	20
Hammond, Savannah	4	8	.333	5.21	13	13	0	0	0	0	65.2	63	42	38	0	6	50	1	52	14
Harriger, Columbia	2	0	1.000	0.00	2	2	1	0	1	0	11.0	5	0	0	0	0	2	0	13	0
Hassinger, Spartanburg	8	8	.500	3.20	21	21	4	0	2	0	123.2	121	54	44	5	4	31	0	87	6
Henson, Gastonia	3	4	.429	4.35	8	8	0	0	0	0	39.1	38	27	19	1	3	26	0	20	7
Hernandez, Asheville	3	8	.273	7.97	30	11	0	9	0	1	81.1	113	83	72	10	3	47	2	48	7
Hill, Spartanburg	7	10	.412	3.15	27	21	2	1	1	0	143.0	126	64	50	13	1	48	0	143	11
Hines, Greensboro*	8	9	.471	3.19	26	26	6	0	2	0	155.1	147	76	55	8	2	68	1	126	7
Hoeme, Charleston (S.C.)	7	1	.875	3.45	31	1	0	9	0	2	62.2	54	30	24	1	6	39	1	51	5
Hook, Charleston (W.Va.)	8	2	.800	2.41	45	0	0	19	0	2	71.0	52	26	19	0	11	40	1	79	8
Hooper, Augusta	3	5	.375	3.50	34	13	0	8	0	0	103.0	85	54	40	3	11	80	2	90	16
Hope, Augusta	4	2	.667	3.50	7	7	0	0	0	0	46.1	29	20	18	1	4	19	0	37	2
Hupe, Augusta	9	3	.750	4.08	31	8	0	8	0	1	81.2	71	47	37	4	5	50	3	54	7
Hurst, Spartanburg	2	2	.500	2.39	12	0	0	6	0	2	26.1	20	7	7	1	2	12	1	30	1
Hurst, Gastonia*	3	3	.500	2.26	11	8	0	1	0	0	51.2	41	18	13	0	2	14	1	44	0
Ingram, Charleston (S.C.)	5	6	.455	3.42	12	10	2	0	1	0	68.1	70	37	26	9	6	17	2	45	1
Ivie, Charleston (S.C.)*	5	5	.500	3.44	37	12	1	8	0	2	104.2	106	53	40	5	3	40	1	56	2
Jewett, Macon	1	0	1.000	3.60	7	0	0	5	0	0	10.0	8	5	4	0	2	6	1	9	5
Johnson, Augusta*	0	0	.000	0.00	1	0	0	0	0	0	2.0	2	1	0	0	0	2	0	2	0
Johnson, Charleston (S.C.)	3	4	.429	6.44	36	4	0	15	0	2	81.0	77	67	58	6	4	73	1	66	26
Jolley, Savannah	5	5	.500	4.87	23	11	0	1	0	0	81.1	101	63	44	5	6	32	2	48	12
Jones, Augusta	1	3	.250	4.15	6	6	1	0	0	0	39.0	44	24	18	1	2	11	1	25	4
Jones, Columbia	3	1	.750	1.85	5	5	0	0	0	0	24.1	20	5	5	2	2	3	0	35	0
Jordan, Myrtle Beach*	9	8	.529	2.74	29	23	3	3	1	1	144.2	101	58	44	3	6	79	0	152	3
Juhl, Spartanburg*	3	2	.600	2.92	25	0	0	13	0	1	49.1	43	23	16	5	1	7	0	45	0
Karsay, Myrtle Beach	4	9	.308	3.58	20	20	1	0	0	0	110.2	96	58	44	7	5	48	0	100	8
Kelly, Savannah	6	5	.545	1.38	56	0	0	50	0	30	58.2	43	14	9	5	0	16	6	62	2
Ketchen, Asheville	10	12	.455	4.27	27	27	2	0	1	0	151.2	166	99	72	9	11	62	1	95	21
King, Charleston (W.Va.)*	6	2	.750	3.45	30	14	0	6	0	1	107.0	102	56	41	5	3	43	2	78	5
Kinney, Savannah*	5	8	.385	3.99	17	17	2	0	0	0	106.0	120	61	47	5	3	29	1	55	11
Kistaitis, Myrtle Beach*	1	3	.250	4.45	19	2	0	10	0	0	32.1	33	23	16	2	3	21	0	27	8
Kosenski, Fayetteville	3	2	.600	2.69	37	1	0	9	0	2	73.2	59	32	22	3	4	45	1	42	4
Kotch, Sumter*	6	3	.667	3.11	44	1	0	16	0	3	75.1	65	33	26	3	4	47	3	85	10
Kunz, Gastonia*	1	3	.250	2.95	20	3	0	8	0	2	42.2	40	17	14	4	3	16	1	42	0
Lata, Savannah	1	0	1.000	3.00	1	1	0	0	0	0	6.0	3	2	2	0	0	1	0	7	1
Latham, Augusta*	1	2	.333	15.53	27	1	0	9	0	0	24.1	29	48	42	1	6	69	0	16	15
Leahy, Macon	8	5	.615	4.34	29	13	1	12	1	2	91.1	93	57	44	3	6	43	1	91	5
Leslie, Charleston (W.Va.)	5	0	1.000	1.83	44	2	0	15	0	2	93.1	66	21	19	1	4	39	2	91	6
Lima, Fayetteville	1	3	.250	4.97	18	7	0	4	0	0	58.0	53	38	32	4	1	25	0	60	2
Lira, Fayetteville	5	5	.500	4.66	15	13	0	2	0	1	73.1	79	43	38	8	1	19	0	56	2
Lomon, Macon	1	0	1.000	1.80	1	1	0	0	1	0	5.0	2	1	1	0	0	1	0	2	0
Long, Sumter	3	3	.500	3.18	63	0	0	53	0	17	76.1	72	34	27	2	5	31	1	79	15
Lopez, Savannah	2	6	.250	4.16	21	13	0	5	0	0	75.2	85	57	35	6	1	29	0	38	9
Luce, Gastonia	0	0	.000	21.60	2	0	0	1	0	0	1.2	4	4	4	1	2	0	0	2	0
Lugo, Myrtle Beach	1	2	.333	4.01	12	0	0	6	0	1	24.2	23	14	11	2	2	8	0	12	1
Lyle, Augusta	0	0	.000	5.02	5	0	0	1	0	0	14.1	13	11	8	1	1	9	1	8	1
MacArthur, Savannah	0	0	.000	18.00	1	0	0	1	0	0	1.0	2	3	2	0	0	3	0	0	0
Mack, Macon	0	2	.000	1.54	19	0	0	13	0	9	23.1	13	8	4	0	0	6	1	17	2
Madrigal, Gastonia	0	6	.000	5.36	10	10	0	0	0	0	47.0	47	32	28	5	3	32	0	40	4
Malone, Greensboro*	2	0	1.000	2.01	25	0	0	7	0	3	44.2	22	10	10	0	4	34	0	62	6
Mandia, Myrtle Beach	1	3	.250	3.86	22	0	0	17	0	5	32.2	25	21	14	5	0	16	1	37	0
Manicchia, Spartanburg	0	0	.000	4.94	12	0	0	4	0	1	31.0	28	17	17	4	2	12	0	34	1
Martinez, Columbia	20	4	.833	1.49	26	26	9	0	4	0	193.1	162	51	32	3	0	30	1	158	4
Martinez, Sumter	7	9	.438	3.16	39	8	0	11	0	0	108.1	109	53	38	5	4	39	4	84	4
Mattson, Macon	2	5	.714	2.82	23	7	3	4	1	0	76.2	61	29	24	1	4	17	1	51	5
McCarthy, Charleston (W.Va.)*.	1	0	1.000	0.00	1	1	1	0	1	0	9.0	6	0	0	0	0	0	0	13	1
McGarity, Savannah	7	12	.368	3.44	27	27	5	0	0	0	175.1	144	80	67	14	10	75	0	100	6
McGough, Gastonia	2	3	.400	7.98	16	0	0	5	0	0	29.1	39	28	26	0	4	19	1	14	1
McLochlin, Columbus	3	5	.375	4.52	15	15	1	0	0	0	89.2	96	52	45	5	1	35	0	54	7
Migliozzi, Gastonia	2	2	.500	3.69	20	0	0	9	0	1	31.2	23	15	13	3	3	24	2	37	4
Millan, Columbia	0	0	.000	54.00	1	0	0	0	0	0	1.0	3	6	6	2	2	2	0	0	0
Miller, Augusta	6	7	.462	2.50	21	21	2	0	2	0	115.1	89	49	32	6	4	57	0	103	13
Minutelli, Charleston (W.Va.)*.	1	0	1.000	0.00	2	2	0	0	0	0	8.0	2	0	0	0	0	8	0	7	0
Mlicki, Columbus	8	6	.571	4.20	22	19	2	1	0	0	115.2	101	70	54	3	6	70	1	136	10
Mooney, Augusta	3	6	.333	4.18	32	11	1	5	1	2	94.2	85	56	44	5	4	60	0	51	15
Morphy, Greensboro	4	8	.333	4.00	43	4	0	10	0	1	83.1	79	52	37	4	7	48	3	72	15
Morrison, 8 Mac.-7 Sum.	6	7	.462	3.66	15	15	2	0	0	0	78.2	77	43	32	5	2	17	0	51	2

Pitcher, Team	W	L	Pct.	ERA	G	GS	CG	GF	ShO	Sv.	IP	H	R	ER	HR	HB	BB	Int. BB	SO	WP
Munoz, Spartanburg*	8	6	.571	3.58	20	20	2	0	0	0	115.2	112	55	46	5	3	51	0	103	11
Nash, Charleston (S.C.)	0	0	.000	0.00	1	0	0	0	0	0	1.0	2	0	0	0	0	0	0	2	0
Neidinger, Fayetteville	5	11	.313	4.66	31	11	0	8	0	1	104.1	122	72	54	6	2	29	1	49	8
Newton, Charleston (S.C.)	2	0	1.000	5.11	9	0	0	4	0	3	12.1	13	7	7	1	0	4	0	10	1
Nieves, Charleston (W.Va.)	6	1	.857	2.98	27	10	0	7	0	0	87.2	96	38	29	1	7	32	2	53	3
Nieves, Asheville	0	2	.000	9.82	3	3	0	0	0	0	7.1	6	8	8	1	1	14	0	4	5
Norris, Sumter	1	3	.250	5.14	8	8	0	0	0	0	35.0	41	25	20	2	3	17	0	42	6
Ortega, Sumter*	0	0	.000	0.00	1	0	0	0	0	0	1.0	2	2	0	0	0	2	0	0	1
Overholser, Charleston (S.C.)	2	1	.667	5.45	21	1	0	14	0	6	38.0	42	26	23	3	5	29	2	21	2
Owens, Spartanburg*	3	1	.750	2.04	16	4	0	8	0	3	39.2	28	17	9	1	1	24	0	29	1
Patterson, Spartanburg	9	8	.529	4.42	35	10	2	22	1	9	114.0	103	60	56	7	4	41	0	114	2
Pedraza, Sumter	2	2	.500	4.41	8	8	1	0	0	0	49.0	61	29	24	3	1	10	0	22	5
Perez, Sumter*	2	2	.500	2.44	16	12	0	2	0	0	73.2	57	29	20	3	0	32	0	69	3
Perez, Greensboro	1	1	.500	2.65	30	0	0	24	0	1	37.1	26	17	11	4	3	20	0	48	7
Perozo, Columbia	0	0	.000	0.00	1	0	0	1	0	0	1.0	0	0	0	0	0	0	0	2	0
Pfaff, Fayetteville	3	6	.333	4.46	14	12	2	1	0	0	74.2	80	41	37	6	3	14	0	43	3
Potts, Macon*	8	5	.615	3.49	34	11	2	5	2	1	95.1	64	45	37	3	4	50	1	75	13
Powers, Asheville*	8	9	.471	4.36	36	15	1	4	1	0	126.0	122	74	61	12	4	59	1	100	7
Prats, Asheville*	4	1	.800	4.08	33	0	0	13	0	3	46.1	42	24	21	4	1	19	0	41	1
Quijada, Asheville	6	8	.429	3.77	22	13	3	5	1	2	88.1	75	44	37	8	3	28	1	59	3
Quirico, Greensboro*	12	8	.600	2.26	26	26	1	0	1	0	155.1	103	59	39	5	7	80	0	162	12
Randall, Spartanburg	4	7	.364	3.65	43	0	0	30	0	5	69.0	68	35	28	3	0	21	1	71	12
Ray, Charleston (W.Va.)	16	9	.640	3.36	28	27	3	0	0	0	171.1	161	72	64	9	9	57	1	120	3
Redmond, Augusta	0	1	.000	10.13	7	0	0	3	0	0	8.0	9	11	9	0	1	13	0	8	2
Reed, Asheville	4	2	.667	2.73	40	0	0	19	0	6	52.2	36	22	16	3	4	29	5	40	6
Rees, Columbia	6	8	.429	3.08	20	19	2	0	0	0	114.0	108	55	39	6	3	44	0	95	9
Reincke, Fayetteville	4	4	.429	5.40	12	12	0	0	0	0	58.1	56	43	35	6	4	36	0	43	7
Richmond, Charleston (S.C.)	0	0	.000	8.38	8	0	0	2	0	1	9.2	15	11	9	0	0	7	0	7	1
Ringkamp, Gastonia	0	3	.000	2.97	17	3	0	5	0	1	36.1	36	21	12	2	5	10	2	20	2
Ritter, Macon	0	2	.000	1.21	14	0	0	4	0	1	22.1	17	11	3	0	1	7	1	22	1
Rivera, Greensboro	4	9	.308	2.75	29	15	1	6	0	0	114.2	103	48	35	2	3	36	0	123	3
Rivera, Columbus*	7	1	.875	1.65	30	1	0	17	0	3	49.0	48	15	9	1	2	12	3	36	2
Roa, Macon	13	3	.813	2.17	30	18	4	2	2	1	141.0	106	46	34	6	5	33	4	96	3
Robertson, Augusta	4	7	.364	4.99	13	12	1	1	0	0	74.0	73	52	41	4	1	51	0	62	3
Rodriguez, Fayetteville*	7	8	.467	3.28	32	18	2	2	0	0	140.0	117	62	51	8	1	73	0	119	1
Rohrwild, Macon	0	3	.000	3.41	26	0	0	20	0	7	29.0	27	14	11	2	1	17	4	33	5
Roper, Charleston (W.Va.)	14	9	.609	2.27	27	27	5	0	3	0	186.2	135	59	47	5	4	67	0	189	8
Ruebel, Augusta*	3	4	.429	3.83	8	8	2	0	1	0	47.0	43	26	20	2	2	25	0	35	3
Rueter, Sumter*	3	1	.750	1.33	8	5	0	1	0	0	40.2	32	8	6	3	0	10	0	27	1
Rychel, Augusta	1	3	.250	5.57	8	6	1	1	1	0	32.1	30	24	20	1	7	24	0	26	11
Ryder, Macon	4	1	.800	1.62	12	2	0	7	0	2	33.1	25	7	6	1	2	14	1	23	4
Sadecki, Gastonia	4	4	.500	3.46	16	16	1	0	1	0	78.0	70	34	30	5	3	43	0	67	3
Sample, Columbia	4	2	.667	1.16	12	1	0	9	0	3	23.1	14	9	3	3	2	9	0	28	2
Santiago, Columbus	7	4	.636	3.56	34	11	1	7	1	3	118.2	109	64	47	7	4	30	0	111	6
Saulter, Macon	2	2	.500	3.12	14	0	0	9	0	3	17.1	17	6	6	1	0	7	0	18	0
Schaefer, Augusta	0	0	.000	0.00	1	0	0	1	0	0	2.0	1	0	0	0	0	3	0	1	0
Seiler, Greensboro*	7	5	.583	2.78	52	0	0	18	0	3	68.0	61	36	21	2	3	27	5	64	1
Shouse, Augusta*	2	3	.400	3.19	26	0	0	25	0	8	31.0	22	13	11	1	3	9	1	32	5
Siberz, Greensboro	6	5	.545	4.60	42	0	0	34	0	16	47.0	55	27	24	2	1	33	6	55	13
Sieradzki, 15 Sum. -9 C'bia	0	2	.000	5.93	24	0	0	12	0	1	27.1	38	23	18	2	2	23	0	19	5
Silver, Savannah	0	0	.000	0.00	3	0	0	3	0	0	3.0	6	5	0	2	0	0	0	3	0
Singer, Myrtle Beach*	3	8	.273	4.04	27	24	0	0	0	0	138.0	126	81	62	15	5	81	0	131	14
Smith, Macon	0	0	.000	8.38	3	3	0	0	0	0	9.2	15	11	9	1	0	12	0	14	2
Smith, Greensboro	4	8	.333	4.02	38	17	1	9	0	1	121.0	130	67	54	8	5	43	1	69	6
Sparks, Augusta	0	1	.000	5.87	6	0	0	2	0	0	7.2	8	6	5	0	1	8	1	6	2
Sparma, Macon	4	4	.500	5.59	13	13	1	0	0	0	66.0	74	51	41	4	6	33	0	34	13
Speek, Savannah	4	4	.500	2.42	48	2	0	15	0	4	78.0	57	31	21	6	1	37	7	78	0
Spiller, Savannah*	8	7	.533	4.32	18	18	1	0	0	0	106.1	102	62	51	9	4	32	2	77	12
Steed, Myrtle Beach	12	13	.480	4.03	28	27	4	0	0	0	172.0	161	96	77	10	5	62	0	122	15
Stewart, Charleston (W.Va.)	8	12	.400	4.56	24	24	2	0	0	0	136.1	117	73	69	6	4	88	0	135	18
Stidham, Fayetteville	0	1	.000	1.60	28	0	0	26	0	8	33.2	25	10	6	0	0	16	0	20	3
Stokes, Fayetteville	3	3	.500	4.22	38	2	0	14	0	0	74.2	66	37	35	1	3	28	0	55	7
Stone, Columbus	1	3	.250	2.94	9	9	0	0	0	0	49.0	42	20	16	3	0	19	0	37	1
Sweeney, Columbus	1	0	1.000	1.08	3	0	0	2	0	0	8.1	4	1	1	0	3	2	0	10	0
Tatar, Charleston (W.Va.)	6	3	.667	1.63	11	11	3	0	2	0	72.0	49	17	13	1	2	20	0	77	4
M. Thomas, 30 C'bia -19 Sum.*	8	3	.727	3.03	50	0	0	42	0	20	69.1	54	29	24	1	3	49	2	91	8
S. Thomas, Columbia	4	4	.500	4.01	37	9	0	17	0	5	110.0	92	55	49	6	2	51	1	116	9
Thompson, Charleston (S.C.)	3	6	.333	5.81	34	4	0	14	0	0	66.2	68	51	43	5	4	47	2	47	9
Tomso, Savannah	0	1	.000	2.45	5	0	0	2	0	0	7.1	3	2	2	1	0	3	0	3	0
Trujillo, Savannah	0	0	.000	0.00	1	0	0	1	0	0	1.0	0	0	0	0	0	0	0	0	0
Undorf, Fayetteville	4	1	.800	1.60	22	0	0	9	0	3	45.0	39	19	8	0	8	10	0	48	1
Vanryn, Sumter*	2	13	.133	6.50	20	20	0	0	0	0	109.1	122	96	79	13	6	61	0	77	10
Vazquez, Macon	7	4	.636	2.54	14	14	3	0	1	0	92.0	61	35	26	2	5	40	0	75	10
Vlcek, Columbus	1	2	.333	4.50	29	0	0	18	0	2	42.0	33	24	21	2	3	25	1	43	2
Walden, Columbus	1	4	.200	6.67	12	9	0	1	0	0	54.0	72	60	40	6	0	29	0	38	3
Waldron, Charleston (S.C.)*	10	6	.625	3.60	38	16	0	13	0	5	147.1	135	72	59	8	2	59	4	139	4
Warren, Fayetteville	3	1	.750	2.10	10	1	0	0	0	0	25.2	18	6	6	0	0	5	0	28	3
Washington, Gastonia	4	2	.667	2.72	11	7	1	2	1	2	53.0	49	16	16	3	2	13	0	40	4
Watson, Savannah*	1	1	.500	3.95	3	3	0	0	0	0	13.2	16	7	6	1	0	6	0	13	1
Weber, Savannah*	2	2	.500	5.83	7	6	1	0	0	0	29.1	37	24	19	3	0	15	0	25	0
Wegmann, Columbia	5	0	1.000	0.56	7	6	1	0	1	0	48.0	21	7	3	1	0	9	0	69	0
Wells, Gastonia	0	4	.000	4.66	13	0	0	7	0	2	19.1	16	13	10	1	2	15	0	14	2
Werland, Macon*	10	3	.769	3.12	18	16	2	0	2	0	112.1	83	43	39	9	2	34	1	78	3
Wertz, Columbus	6	8	.429	2.97	49	0	0	31	0	6	91.0	81	41	30	6	6	32	3	95	5
White, Sumter*	6	9	.400	3.26	24	24	5	0	0	0	149.0	127	73	54	7	5	53	0	140	8
White, Augusta	4	4	.500	3.00	34	0	0	18	0	6	63.0	68	26	21	2	1	18	3	52	4
Whiteside, Gastonia	3	1	.750	2.15	48	0	0	42	0	29	62.2	44	19	15	1	5	21	0	71	3
Williams, Macon	10	6	.625	3.15	23	20	2	1	1	0	131.1	116	64	46	5	6	56	1	76	8
Wilson, Asheville	1	9	.100	5.44	22	22	0	0	0	0	101.0	118	72	61	8	5	46	0	96	13
Winiarski, Columbus	5	5	.500	4.27	39	0	0	20	0	4	78.0	88	56	37	6	1	28	2	62	1
Withem, Fayetteville	2	6	.250	8.50	11	11	0	0	0	0	47.2	71	53	45	2	0	28	0	19	8

BALKS—Cairncross, Quirico, Waldron, 9 each; Branconier, J. Brown, 8 each; D. Brown, Burrows, Castillo, Garcia, D. Jones, Miller, Sparma, 6 each; Alexander, Alvarez, Jordan, Karsay, Ce. Perez, Sadecki, Spiller, 5 each; Carlson, Coppeta, Foster, Frazier, Hooper, B. Jones, Lima, Lira, Madrigal, Morphy, Morrison, Overholser, M. Thomas, S. Thomas, Vanryn, 4 each; Chiles, Conley, Faw, Gobel, Hassinger, Hill, Hines, B. Johnson, Ketchen, McGarity, McLochlin, Owens, Stidham, R. White, 3 each; Adamson, Bailey, Beckett, Daugherty, Eubanks, Fidler, Flener, Ganote, Henson, Hunter, J. Hurst, Kinney, Kistaitis, Kosenski, Long, Lyle, Mlicki, Norris, Pfaff, Powers, Rees, R. Rivera, Singer, Steed, Walden, Warren, Werland, 2 each; Allen, Arvesen, Aucoin, Aylmer, Barreiro, Benson, Brink, Bristow, C. Brown, Bullard, Cecil, Danner, Domecq, Duff, Dunn, Engle, Fajardo, Fowler, Freitas, Fusco, Gaston, Geeve, Gies, Goergen, Guilfoyle, Hammond, Hope, C. Hurst, Ingram, Ivie, Leslie, Lopez, Lugo, J. Martinez, W. Martinez, Mattson, Mc-Gough, Migliozzi, E. Nieves, Pedraza, Ca. Perez, Prats, Quijada, Reincke, Ringkamp, Robertson, Rodriguez, Roper, Siberz, Sieradzki, Stewart, Stokes, Stone, Tatar, Tomso, Vlcek, Watson, Weber, Wegmann, Wilson, Winiarski, 1 each.

COMBINATION SHUTOUTS—Brown-Daugherty, Brown-Prats, Ketchen-Daugherty, Powers-Daugherty, Wilson-Brown-Daugherty, Asheville; Carlson-Shouse 2, Arvesen-Futrell, Carlson-Gobel, Cooke-Gobel, Cooke-Mooney-Futrell, Cooke-White-Shouse, Fajardo-Mooney-Shouse, Hooper-Hunter-Futrell, Miller-Hunter-Futrell, Ruebel-Hunter, Rychel-Futrell-Bullard, Augusta; Beckett-Ivie, Carlson-Hoeme, Ivie-Ettles-Garside-Overholser, Waldron-Ettles, Charleston (S.C.); Cecil-Duff-Doty, King-Duff, Nieves-Hook-Doty, Nieves-Hook-Duff, Nieves-King-Doty, Ray-Duff, Ray-Leslie-Doty, Roper-Doty, Roper-Leslie, Tatar-Leslie-Doty, Charleston (W.Va.); Butler-Freitas, Castillo-S. Thomas, Castillo-S. Thomas-Freitas, Guzik-Sample, Harriger-Carpentier, Jones-Sample-Guzik-Benson, Jones-S. Thomas, Martinez-Carpentier, Martinez-M. Thomas, Rees-Benson, Columbia; A. Baker-Rivera, A. Baker-Santiago-Cofer, Embree-Rivera, McLochlin-Rivera, Stone-Cofer-Wertz, Columbus; Lira-Pfaff-Guilfoyle, Rodriguez-Stidham, Warren-Kosenski, Fayetteville; Burrows-Giberti-Vlcek, Dreyer-Cardona, Dreyer-Whiteside, Hurst-Bouton, Hurst-Ringkamp-Whiteside, Hurst-Whiteside, Sadecki-Whiteside, Sadecki-Ringkamp, Washington-Wells-Bouton-Whiteside, Gastonia; Dunbar-Perez, Faw-Seiler-Siberz, Morphy-Malone-Dunbar, Quirico-Dunbar-Perez, Quirico-Malone-Seiler-Siberz, Quirico-Morphy-Seiler-Perez, Quirico-Rivera-Malone-Perez, Rivera-Smith, Greensboro; Chiles-Leahy, Mattson-Potts-Chiles, Morrison-Mack-Rohrwild, Potts-Saulter-Leahy, Roa-Leahy, Ryder-Rohrwild, Vazquez-Ritter-Mack, Vazquez-Ritter-Rohrwild, Vazquez-Roa, Werland-Potts-Mack, Werland-Rohrwild, Williams-Leahy, Macon; Garcia-Lugo, Jordan-Duey-Mandia, Jordan-Garcia, Jordan-Mandia, Singer-Flemer-Mandia-Aylmer, Steed-Jordan, Myrtle Beach; Baker-Kelly, Creek-Eversgerd-Glover, Gaston-Fusco-Speek-Bailey, Gaston-Fusco-Bailey-Eversgerd-Kelly, Kinney-Kelly, Spiller-Kelly, Savannah; Brink-Owens, Elliott-Hurst-Domecq, Goergen-Randall, Hill-Juhl-Domecq, Hill-Randall, Munoz-Domecq, Munoz-Hurst, Spartanburg; Alvarez-Long, Foster-Martinez-Kotch-Long, Kotch-Long, Perez-Martinez-Long, Rueter-Aucoin, White-Aucoin-Kotch, Sumter.

NO-HIT GAMES—Mooney, Augusta, defeated Savannah, 1-0 (first game), May 31; Vazquez, Macon, defeated Sumter, 8-0 (first game), June 18; Quirico, Greensboro, defeated Charleston (S.C.), 2-0, July 21.

FIELDING

TEAM

Team	Pct.	G	PO	A	E	DP	PB	Team	Pct.	G	PO	A	E	DP	PB
Charleston (W.Va.)	.970	142	3667	1483	158	125	14	Macon	.958	141	3604	1523	223	112	41
Gastonia	.964	142	3645	1471	192	127	20	Augusta	.957	142	3644	1520	234	105	47
Columbia	.963	140	3596	1450	195	107	23	Sumter	.955	139	3569	1496	236	83	30
Spartanburg	.963	141	3506	1362	189	85	21	Asheville	.955	138	3430	1484	234	118	22
Charleston (S.C.)	.962	141	3639	1468	202	96	29	Columbus	.954	142	3667	1565	252	103	30
Savannah	.962	138	3551	1420	198	106	29	Greensboro	.951	141	3620	1435	258	105	32
Fayetteville	.958	138	3492	1437	214	102	27	Myrtle Beach	.944	139	3507	1343	289	89	46

Triple plays—Asheville, Columbus, Myrtle Beach.

INDIVIDUAL

*Throws lefthanded.

FIRST BASEMEN

Player, Team	Pct.	G	PO	A	E	DP
Adams, Charleston (S.C.)	.997	69	517	53	2	25
Allison, Columbia	1.000	5	41	2	0	4
Ayala, Charleston (S.C.)	.923	4	20	4	2	2
Bieser, Spartanburg	1.000	3	11	1	0	1
M. Brown, Augusta*	.975	65	559	34	15	41
Burns, Asheville	.990	48	389	22	4	37
Campusano, Augusta	.949	20	178	9	10	15
Carlton, Myrtle Beach	.983	27	109	8	2	6
Castellano, Gastonia	.992	59	443	29	4	38
Christopherson, Asheville	.984	29	235	17	4	17
Cooper, Greensboro	1.000	1	2	0	0	0
Dando, Macon*	.931	7	53	1	4	6
Davis, Asheville	1.000	18	153	10	0	14
Doyle, Charleston (S.C.)*	.990	38	268	15	3	24
Drabinski, Macon	1.000	2	5	0	0	0
Edwards, Charleston (S.C.)	1.000	3	22	2	0	2
Einhorn, Savannah	.964	16	75	6	3	8
Eldridge, Savannah	.983	119	1000	51	18	82
Elliott, Charleston (S.C.)	.977	23	160	8	4	15
Erhardt, Charleston (W.Va.)	1.000	10	63	6	0	10
Gallardo, Greensboro	.971	16	128	8	4	11
Garcia, Columbia	.988	105	858	72	11	69
Geisler, Spartanburg*	.990	36	293	18	3	17
Gonzalez, Columbia	.972	7	32	3	1	0
Gress, Macon	.983	29	211	17	4	18
Hammargren, Char. (W.Va.)	1.000	3	14	1	0	0
Hammond, Charleston (W.Va.)	1.000	4	34	4	0	7
Harvey, Columbus*	.977	61	471	44	12	39
Hernandez, Greensboro	.933	2	12	2	1	0
Hernandez, Gastonia	1.000	4	22	2	0	4
Hurlbutt, Asheville	1.000	4	9	1	0	0
Hyers, Myrtle Beach*	.986	126	915	84	14	73
Jimenez, Macon	1.000	10	51	3	0	3
Johnson, Augusta*	.975	40	319	33	9	25
Judson, Spartanburg	.972	12	62	8	2	5
Karcher, Macon*	.984	102	881	60	15	73
Laake, Gastonia*	.977	74	559	42	14	52
Loeb, Myrtle Beach	.978	14	78	11	2	7
MacArthur, Savannah	1.000	1	1	0	0	0
Marabella, Sumter	.962	13	61	14	3	3
Marshall, Gastonia	.990	27	171	18	2	18
McCall, Columbus*	.977	91	767	56	19	46
McMullen, Greensboro	.986	9	66	4	1	6
Millan, Columbia	.982	36	254	25	5	26
Noce, Sumter	1.000	4	26	3	0	1

Player, Team	Pct.	G	PO	A	E	DP
Orr, Macon	1.000	6	47	5	0	0
H. Ortega, Sumter	.975	46	338	51	10	24
Ostermeyer, Charleston (S.C.)	.972	29	186	22	6	12
Page, Savannah	.972	15	129	10	4	11
Perozo, Columbia	1.000	1	4	1	0	0
Pinckes, Columbus	.833	2	5	0	1	0
RAFFO, Charleston (W.Va.)*	.991	132	1079	72	11	92
Robinson, Macon	1.000	1	1	0	0	0
Rodriguez, Augusta	1.000	4	7	1	0	1
Rogers, Fayetteville*	.979	93	726	53	17	59
Ruff, Fayetteville	.988	41	381	23	5	25
Rusk, Spartanburg	.990	13	92	8	1	5
Sadler, Fayetteville	.952	4	18	2	1	1
Saltzgaber, Fayetteville	.974	5	36	1	1	4
Santiago, Sumter	.962	18	131	22	6	10
Schroeder, Augusta*	.981	19	147	11	3	13
Spivey, Savannah	1.000	1	3	0	0	0
Steffens, Spartanburg*	.993	84	661	47	5	52
Stinnett, Columbus	.947	2	17	1	1	0
Tsitouris, Sumter	.986	74	507	72	8	36
Turner, Greensboro*	.989	118	906	89	11	83
Veit, Asheville	.990	64	460	26	5	37
Vondran, Charleston (W.Va.)	1.000	3	13	1	0	2

Triple plays—Hyers, McCall, Veit.

SECOND BASEMEN

Player, Team	Pct.	G	PO	A	E	DP
Allison, Columbia	.955	9	8	13	1	4
Bieser, Spartanburg	.923	3	4	8	1	1
Bish, Charleston (S.C.)	.889	7	7	9	2	2
Brittain, Macon	.966	14	21	35	2	5
Campas, Savannah	.900	5	3	6	1	1
Choate, Myrtle Beach	.944	25	25	60	5	6
Cintron, Augusta	1.000	4	7	6	0	2
Cotton, Columbus	.933	113	186	305	35	55
Duncan, Charleston (W.Va.)	.943	15	25	25	3	5
Flores, Asheville	.959	46	78	111	8	22
Gill, Charleston (W.Va.)	.979	84	184	236	9	58
Givens, Fayetteville	1.000	1	1	0	0	0
Hall, Charleston (S.C.)	.941	59	114	140	16	26
Hardtke, Columbus	.944	20	33	52	5	9
Harley, Asheville	.948	105	190	270	25	56
Hodge, Gastonia	.985	54	80	121	3	24
Jackson, Savannah	.946	57	83	129	12	25
Judson, Spartanburg	1.000	1	3	5	0	2
Kimbler, Fayetteville	.857	5	9	9	3	3
King, Columbia	1.000	1	0	2	0	0

Player, Team	Pct.	G	PO	A	E	DP
Landinez, Savannah	.926	23	45	67	9	14
Lantrip, Greensboro	1.000	1	0	1	0	0
Leonhardt, Fayetteville	.945	13	30	39	4	9
Maldonado, Fayetteville	.911	13	25	26	5	7
Marabella, Sumter	.943	83	140	189	20	32
Martinez, Charleston (S.C.)	.964	54	97	119	8	27
Matachun, Gastonia	.982	67	96	123	4	24
Mateo, Charleston (S.C.)	.917	10	13	9	2	1
Millan, Columbia	.967	9	17	12	1	4
Miller, Myrtle Beach	.966	9	12	16	1	5
O'Neal, Fayetteville	.939	105	182	247	28	50
Olmeda, Macon	.969	80	139	231	12	37
H. Ortega, Sumter	1.000	3	3	4	0	0
Ozoria, Sumter	.894	33	47	63	13	7
Penn, Gastonia	.948	45	70	113	10	23
Perez, Savannah	.939	5	17	14	2	4
Perna, Charleston (W.Va.)	.917	2	3	8	1	0
Pinckes, Columbus	.833	2	4	1	1	0
Polewski, Augusta	.933	34	51	88	10	12
Rivell, Charleston (S.C.)	.914	26	39	46	8	9
H. Roa, Macon	.943	18	23	59	5	10
Rodriguez, Sumter	.935	39	59	71	9	11
Rodriguez, Myrtle Beach	.911	118	202	266	46	45
Rodriguez, Augusta	.857	2	3	3	1	1
Saltzgaber, Fayetteville	.938	9	12	18	2	5
Sanchez, Greensboro	.936	10	18	26	3	6
Schulte, Augusta	.945	13	25	27	3	2
Scott, Greensboro	.958	8	9	14	1	4
Shave, Gastonia	1.000	1	5	2	0	1
Sirak, Spartanburg	.960	7	11	13	1	3
Smith, Columbus	.957	21	36	53	4	10
Sondrini, Augusta	.965	95	153	282	16	48
Thomas, Spartanburg	.949	131	218	337	30	52
Trujillo, Savannah	.956	62	111	173	13	35
Turrentine, Greensboro	.927	119	222	284	40	51
Van Scoyoc, Greensboro	.984	12	24	36	1	9
VINA, Columbia	.965	126	194	385	21	61
Virgilio, Macon	.920	38	64	96	14	13
Wentz, Charleston (W.Va.)	.967	51	83	119	7	24

Triple plays—Flores, Rodriguez.

THIRD BASEMEN

Player, Team	Pct.	G	PO	A	E	DP
Adams, Charleston (S.C.)	1.000	10	0	10	0	0
Alder, Fayetteville	.873	55	43	101	21	3
Allison, Columbia	.938	8	4	11	1	0
Andrews, Sumter	.905	100	71	205	29	9
Andujar, Columbus	1.000	3	2	6	0	0
Battle, Myrtle Beach	.903	132	86	184	29	8
Bell, Columbus	.920	136	90	268	31	16
Bish, Charleston (S.C.)	.857	2	5	1	1	0
Brittain, Macon	.894	72	45	132	21	8
Bruce, Savannah	.907	18	22	27	5	1
Bullock, Charleston (S.C.)	.906	118	73	244	33	18
Bustamante, Char. (W.Va.)	1.000	1	0	1	0	0
Campas, Savannah	.893	49	45	106	18	7
Carlton, Myrtle Beach	.789	9	4	11	4	5
Castellano, Gastonia	.948	34	18	55	4	5
Choate, Myrtle Beach	.800	4	3	5	2	0
Christopherson, Asheville	.925	28	14	48	5	3
Cintron, Augusta	.929	57	48	136	14	14
Cooper, Greensboro	.893	48	34	83	14	6
Edwards, Charleston (S.C.)	.875	2	2	5	1	0
Erhardt, Charleston (W.Va.)	1.000	3	0	7	0	1
Flores, Asheville	.928	20	12	52	5	5
Gallardo, Greensboro	.824	7	6	8	3	4
Gast, Charleston (W.Va.)	.800	4	1	7	2	2
Givens, Fayetteville	.917	28	25	63	8	7
Gress, Macon	1.000	3	3	4	0	0
Groppuso, Asheville	.904	49	40	82	13	11
Hernandez, Gastonia	1.000	3	0	1	0	0
Huskey, Columbia	.912	128	102	218	31	21
Judson, Spartanburg	.888	43	17	62	10	2
Kimbler, Fayetteville	.912	12	6	25	3	1
Landinez, Savannah	.886	15	7	24	4	0
Leonhardt, Fayetteville	.899	39	31	85	13	7
Lowery, Gastonia	.904	106	59	177	25	14
MacArthur, Savannah	.918	59	43	102	13	6
Maldonado, Fayetteville	.870	5	4	16	3	2
Marabella, Sumter	.929	12	10	29	3	2
Matachun, Gastonia	.923	8	7	17	2	1
Meyer, Spartanburg	.889	80	53	131	23	5
Millan, Columbia	.857	9	6	6	2	1
Montero, Asheville	.867	46	41	89	20	9
Orr, Macon	.911	70	43	130	17	12
H. Ortega, Sumter	.909	29	25	55	8	5
Perez, Savannah	.333	2	1	0	2	0
PERNA, Charleston (W.Va.)	.935	115	75	186	18	19
Perona, Fayetteville	1.000	2	1	4	0	1
Pinckes, Columbus	1.000	1	1	3	0	0
Polewski, Augusta	.955	17	11	31	2	1
Rivell, Charleston (S.C.)	.946	14	11	24	2	3
H. Roa, Macon	.833	13	6	24	6	1
Rodriguez, Augusta	.903	75	54	123	19	2

Player, Team	Pct.	G	PO	A	E	DP
Romano, Greensboro	.843	90	45	154	37	11
Saltzgaber, Fayetteville	1.000	1	1	2	0	0
Sanchez, Greensboro	1.000	1	0	1	0	0
Savage, Spartanburg	.000	1	0	0	1	0
Sirak, Spartanburg	.891	20	17	24	5	4
Smith, Asheville	.667	1	1	1	1	0
Smith, Columbus	.909	6	1	9	1	0
Sondrini, Augusta	1.000	4	3	2	0	0
Trujillo, Savannah	1.000	1	0	2	0	0
Virgilio, Macon	.667	2	1	5	3	0
Vondran, Charleston (W.Va.)	.942	21	22	43	4	4
Wallace, Asheville	.667	2	0	2	1	0

Triple play—Bell.

SHORTSTOPS

Player, Team	Pct.	G	PO	A	E	DP
Allison, Columbia	.897	6	10	16	3	2
Ambrosio, Myrtle Beach	.857	5	1	5	1	1
Andujar, Columbus	.778	12	5	16	6	1
ANDUJAR, Savannah	.950	99	134	284	22	47
Bieser, Spartanburg	.909	3	3	7	1	1
Bish, Charleston (S.C.)	.977	9	15	27	1	6
Bream, Charleston (S.C.)	.958	52	91	115	9	21
Brittain, Macon	.941	12	18	14	2	4
Bustamante, Char. (W.Va.)	.926	116	165	310	38	65
Cabrera, Sumter	.934	101	141	256	28	39
Carlton, Myrtle Beach	1.000	1	0	1	0	0
Cooper, Greensboro	.927	20	34	55	7	8
Cotton, Columbus	.000	1	0	0	1	0
Dotel, Myrtle Beach	.884	122	188	270	60	50
Duncan, Charleston (W.Va.)	.900	3	5	4	1	0
Fermin, Fayetteville	.945	73	111	197	18	35
Flores, Asheville	.923	16	19	41	5	5
Gill, Charleston (W.Va.)	.952	19	10	49	3	9
Givens, Fayetteville	.938	31	47	88	9	17
Groppuso, Asheville	1.000	1	2	3	0	0
Guerrero, Fayetteville	.909	10	9	21	3	6
Hanlon, Gastonia	.933	71	92	214	22	40
Hardtke, Columbus	.927	111	162	293	36	41
Jackson, Savannah	1.000	2	0	3	0	0
Jones, Macon	.919	135	217	419	56	71
Kimbler, Fayetteville	.563	4	4	5	7	0
King, Columbia	.935	102	158	233	27	54
Landinez, Savannah	.923	3	6	6	1	2
Lantrip, Greensboro	.928	94	158	267	33	61
Ledesma, Columbia	.915	26	44	64	10	9
Maldonado, Fayetteville	.955	29	51	55	5	11
Martinez, Charleston (S.C.)	.928	67	123	186	24	23
Martinez, Columbus	.914	104	203	232	41	44
Matachun, Gastonia	.949	24	52	59	6	15
Mateo, Charleston (S.C.)	1.000	1	1	1	0	0
Meade, Columbus	.927	23	27	62	7	9
Millan, Columbia	.917	3	5	6	1	3
Miller, Myrtle Beach	1.000	2	1	1	0	1
Mompres, Columbia	.897	8	9	17	3	2
Nevers, Asheville	.916	127	205	349	51	69
O'Neal, Fayetteville	.750	3	3	0	1	0
H. Ortega, Sumter	.667	6	1	3	2	1
Perez, Spartanburg	.853	14	18	40	10	6
Perez, Savannah	.917	17	25	30	5	6
Pimentel, Savannah	.930	27	46	86	10	20
Rivell, Charleston (S.C.)	.897	10	11	15	3	3
H. Roa, Macon	1.000	3	1	0	0	0
Rodriguez, Sumter	.932	48	50	100	11	30
Rodriguez, Augusta	.899	37	55	87	16	20
Sanchez, Greensboro	.865	16	15	30	7	5
Savage, Spartanburg	.884	34	37	85	16	12
Scott, Greensboro	.969	10	13	18	1	2
Shave, Gastonia	.915	51	98	150	23	42
Sirak, Spartanburg	.915	21	33	42	7	10
Smith, Columbus	.947	3	6	12	1	3
Sondrini, Augusta	.895	9	16	18	4	6
Stocker, Spartanburg	.935	69	83	176	18	22
Thomas, Spartanburg	.818	3	4	5	2	2
Trujillo, Savannah	.923	4	6	6	1	0
Turrentine, Greensboro	.722	7	11	15	10	1
Van Scoyoc, Greensboro	.867	4	4	9	2	2
Vazquez, Charleston (S.C.)	.841	15	13	40	10	5
Wentz, Charleston (W.Va.)	.895	11	5	29	4	4

Triple play—Hardtke.

OUTFIELDERS

Player, Team	Pct.	G	PO	A	E	DP
Adams, Sumter*	.920	49	76	4	7	0
Adams, Charleston (S.C.)	1.000	8	11	0	0	0
Allison, Columbia	1.000	2	1	0	0	0
Arace, Savannah	.980	61	96	4	2	1
Arland, Charleston (W.Va.)	1.000	4	8	0	0	0
Battle, Savannah	.988	46	83	2	1	0
Bautista, Fayetteville	.973	67	137	6	4	2
Beck, Charleston (S.C.)*	.970	100	178	13	6	1

CLASS A

SOUTH ATLANTIC LEAGUE

SOUTH ATLANTIC LEAGUE

Player, Team	Pct.	G	PO	A	E	DP
Bennett, Spartanburg	.946	101	169	7	10	1
Bieser, Spartanburg	1.000	35	57	1	0	1
Bowers, Myrtle Beach	.966	114	199	1	7	0
Bradshaw, Savannah	.974	131	297	4	8	1
A. Brown, Augusta*	.966	61	80	6	3	0
Bryant, Columbus	.927	90	130	9	11	1
Bullett, Augusta*	.976	92	195	8	5	1
Burns, Asheville	.500	2	1	0	1	0
Canate, Columbus	.971	61	125	9	4	3
Castellano, Gastonia	.966	20	25	3	1	1
Charbonnet, Columbus*	.941	25	45	3	3	1
Cooper, Greensboro	.923	18	21	3	2	1
Davis, Columbia*	.932	128	222	10	17	1
Davis, Asheville	1.000	3	2	0	0	0
Deller, Greensboro*	.941	53	62	2	4	0
Demerson, Greensboro	1.000	1	1	0	0	0
Dotel, Myrtle Beach	1.000	4	6	0	0	0
Doyle, Charleston (S.C.)*	.875	2	6	1	1	0
Ealy, Savannah	.955	107	182	10	9	1
Einhorn, Savannah	1.000	3	4	0	0	0
Everett, Greensboro	.974	123	250	14	7	2
Farmer, Spartanburg*	.976	125	228	11	6	2
Fully, Columbia	.964	117	205	8	8	1
Gibralter, Charleston (W.Va.)	.961	136	234	15	10	3
Gilliam, Greensboro	.962	114	147	5	6	0
Gomez, Columbus	.952	10	19	1	1	1
Gonzales, Asheville	1.000	9	14	0	0	0
Gonzales, Savannah	.984	34	59	2	1	0
Goodale, Fayetteville	.984	41	57	4	1	0
Gordon, Charleston (W.Va.)	.965	118	208	11	8	3
Green, Augusta	.974	39	72	3	2	0
Grissom, Spartanburg	1.000	26	31	2	0	0
Guzik, Columbia	1.000	13	14	1	0	0
Hartwig, Spartanburg	1.000	5	4	0	0	0
Harvey, Columbus*	.985	61	63	3	1	1
Hawkins, Asheville	1.000	4	5	0	0	0
Heath, Macon	.966	123	276	5	10	1
Hill, Greensboro	.960	124	246	15	11	1
Hodge, Gastonia	1.000	1	3	0	0	0
Holifield, Myrtle Beach*	.970	99	152	8	5	0
Holland, Gastonia	.971	131	193	5	6	0
Horne, Sumter	.971	107	131	5	4	1
Hughes, Macon	.971	102	163	5	5	0
Jackson, Spartanburg	.976	117	235	8	6	2
Jenkins, Savannah	.962	32	47	4	2	0
Jesperson, Charleston (W.Va.)	1.000	8	14	0	0	0
Jones, Columbus	.958	23	45	1	2	1
Jordan, Savannah	.978	55	87	3	2	0
Justice, Macon*	1.000	2	1	0	0	0
Keating, Fayetteville*	.982	56	106	2	2	0
Laake, Gastonia*	.800	3	4	0	1	0
List, Augusta	1.000	8	13	0	0	0
Looney, Fayetteville	.984	116	180	10	3	0
Mabry, Savannah	.974	21	36	1	1	0
Matos, Columbus	.946	103	151	7	9	0
McClinton, Columbia	.934	113	144	11	11	0
McDavid, Charleston (S.C.)	.979	123	269	9	6	1
McKoy, Charleston (S.C.)	.955	54	83	2	4	0
Miller, Myrtle Beach	1.000	1	1	0	0	0
Moore, Macon*	.967	30	59	0	2	0
Murray, Gastonia	.963	102	171	11	7	3
Nash, Charleston (S.C.)	1.000	36	55	3	0	0
Neff, Augusta	.925	24	35	2	3	0
O'Connor, Macon	.978	88	126	5	3	1
H. Ortega, Sumter	.981	32	51	0	1	0
Ozoria, Sumter	.905	26	35	3	4	0
Page, Savannah	1.000	8	10	0	0	0
Pearce, Charleston (S.C.)*	.972	93	135	3	4	0
Perez, Columbus*	.895	18	31	3	4	0
Perna, Charleston (W.Va.)	1.000	19	29	2	0	0
Perozo, Columbia	.971	61	96	4	3	1
Posey, Gastonia	.987	91	145	5	2	2
Pough, Columbus	.926	62	79	8	7	3
Quinones, Charleston (W.Va.)	.972	112	168	8	5	2
Reams, Myrtle Beach	.944	113	161	9	10	1
Roberts, Myrtle Beach	.953	107	153	9	8	1
Robinson, Macon	.900	27	35	1	4	0
Roman, Asheville	.949	54	89	4	5	1
Ronca, Augusta	.923	95	132	11	12	1
Rudolph, Columbia	1.000	1	1	0	0	0
Ruff, Fayetteville	1.000	10	19	3	0	2
Rumsey, Asheville*	1.000	42	73	5	0	1
Saltzgaber, Fayetteville	1.000	12	27	1	0	0
Samples, Sumter	.962	128	248	29	11	3
Schaefer, Savannah	.947	42	85	4	5	0
Schroeder, Augusta*	1.000	4	5	0	0	0
Schulte, Augusta	.947	18	17	1	1	0
Seja, Fayetteville*	.973	36	70	3	2	2
Spann, Charleston (S.C.)	.984	30	56	6	1	2
Steffens, Spartanburg*	1.000	25	32	1	0	0
Swinton, Asheville	.927	99	112	15	10	0
Tillman, Fayetteville	.988	47	78	3	1	1
Torres, Columbus*	1.000	3	3	0	0	0
Turner, Greensboro*	1.000	4	4	1	0	1
Vasquez, Charleston (W.Va.)	.940	37	58	5	4	1

Player, Team	Pct.	G	PO	A	E	DP
Wallace, Asheville	.926	114	169	7	14	1
Washington, Columbus	.946	104	166	10	10	1
Weinberg, Fayetteville	.958	43	87	5	4	0
Wentz, Charleston (W.Va.)	1.000	4	4	1	0	0
White, Asheville	.978	109	214	12	5	2
RO. WHITE, Sumter	.987	96	215	6	3	1
J. Williams, Macon	.953	76	96	6	5	2

Triple play—Perez.

CATCHERS

Player, Team	Pct.	G	PO	A	E	DP	PB
Adams, Charleston (S.C.)	1.000	6	5	0	0	0	1
Angotti, Asheville	.947	3	18	0	1	0	0
Avent, Spartanburg	1.000	2	16	1	0	0	0
Ayala, Charleston (S.C.)	.990	57	364	41	4	2	17
Ballara, Savannah	1.000	3	14	2	0	0	0
Bieser, Spartanburg	.988	9	76	6	1	0	1
Blevins, Gastonia	.990	50	358	45	4	0	8
Burns, Asheville	.977	12	39	3	1	0	0
A. Castillo, Columbia	.982	89	734	86	15	5	14
Cox, Charleston (W.Va.)	.997	68	500	73	2	2	6
Creed, Sumter	.985	10	61	4	1	0	3
Crespo, Gastonia	.980	32	214	36	5	2	4
Davis, Augusta	1.000	1	6	1	0	0	0
Delgado, Myrtle Beach	.976	89	679	100	19	2	29
Drabinski, Macon	.983	31	146	25	3	2	9
Dunn, Columbia	.933	4	13	1	1	0	0
Eason, Spartanburg	.990	25	174	24	2	1	2
Gallardo, Greensboro	.988	44	326	17	4	3	13
Gonzalez, Macon	.955	29	159	10	8	0	11
Haley, Fayetteville	.963	8	45	7	2	1	1
Hammargren, Char. (W.Va.)	.992	15	108	12	1	2	4
Hammond, Char. (W.Va.)	.980	21	130	18	3	0	2
Hanel, Augusta	.985	104	732	120	13	10	34
HERNANDEZ, Greensboro	.989	77	582	69	7	2	11
Hernandez, Gastonia	.983	50	362	41	7	2	5
Hinson, Augusta	1.000	13	71	10	0	1	3
Hirsch, Sumter	.985	15	117	14	2	4	1
Houston, Macon	.985	99	591	75	10	3	21
Hurlbutt, Asheville	.982	63	332	51	7	4	4
Hymel, Sumter	.968	15	114	6	4	0	2
Jaime, Myrtle Beach	.959	25	153	10	7	0	4
Lanfranco, Asheville	.909	8	19	1	2	0	1
Lieberthal, Spartanburg	.984	72	565	68	10	3	10
Loeb, Myrtle Beach	.983	33	266	28	5	0	13
Lorms, Columbus	.980	51	395	44	9	8	9
Luce, Gastonia	.989	23	178	10	2	0	3
Maguire, Augusta	1.000	4	22	3	0	0	0
McMullen, Greensboro	1.000	2	6	0	0	0	0
Mulligan, Charleston (S.C.)	.977	52	327	48	9	0	5
Noce, Sumter	.988	21	152	12	2	1	4
Perona, Fayetteville	.984	34	221	18	4	1	6
Radachowsky, Fayetteville	1.000	4	44	3	0	0	1
Ronan, Savannah	.988	106	678	87	9	1	20
Rudolph, Columbia	.993	56	367	53	3	1	9
Rusk, Gastonia	1.000	3	14	2	0	0	0
Sadler, Fayetteville	.982	26	149	15	3	0	7
Salcedo, Greensboro	.972	29	191	20	6	1	8
Saltzgaber, Fayetteville	.983	39	260	38	5	1	7
Santana, Sumter	.976	93	655	87	18	5	20
Smith, Asheville	.968	77	430	77	17	4	17
Spivey, Savannah	.991	19	102	8	1	1	2
Stinnett, Columbus	.966	96	668	99	27	7	21
Taylor, Savannah	.971	30	119	15	4	0	7
Tejada, Spartanburg	.992	32	213	30	2	2	8
Thurston, Charleston (S.C.)	.982	42	292	30	6	7	6
Torres, Augusta	.980	23	165	29	4	1	10
Wilson, Fayetteville	.976	32	179	25	5	2	5
Wilson, Charleston (W.Va.)	.992	45	355	41	3	4	2

Triple play—Stinnett.

PITCHERS

Player, Team	Pct.	G	PO	A	E	DP
Adamson, Spartanburg*	.769	14	3	7	3	1
Alexander, Columbus*	.857	17	1	5	1	0
Allen, Spartanburg	1.000	2	1	3	0	1
Alvarez, Sumter	.932	25	13	28	3	2
Arvesen, Augusta	1.000	8	8	2	0	0
Aucoin, Sumter	.774	41	14	10	7	0
Aylmer, Myrtle Beach*	1.000	15	2	7	0	1
Bailey, Savannah	.923	73	2	10	1	0
A. Baker, Columbus	1.000	25	12	21	0	0
S. Baker, Columbus	1.000	4	0	2	0	0
Baker, Savannah*	.933	8	2	12	1	1
Barreiro, Asheville	.667	18	1	5	3	1
Bauer, Fayetteville*	1.000	4	1	3	0	0
Beckett, Charleston (S.C.)*	.852	28	3	20	4	0
Benson, Columbia	1.000	25	1	9	0	0
Bicknell, Myrtle Beach	.818	27	2	7	2	0
Bjornson, Asheville*	.800	5	1	3	1	0
Bottalico, Spartanburg	1.000	2	0	4	0	0
Bouton, Gastonia	.852	51	2	21	4	2

Player, Team	Pct.	G	PO	A	E	DP
Bradley, Charleston (S.C.)	1.000	2	0	1	0	0
Branconier, Asheville	.971	26	10	24	1	0
Brink, Spartanburg	1.000	3	0	2	0	0
Bristow, Columbia	1.000	29	3	10	0	0
Brown, Asheville	.947	31	11	25	2	2
Brown, Columbus	.967	27	14	15	1	0
Brown, Charleston (S.C.)*	.935	28	8	35	3	0
Buchheit, Gastonia*	.500	2	0	1	1	0
Bullard, Augusta	1.000	21	2	4	0	0
Burrell, Myrtle Beach	1.000	5	0	3	0	0
Burrows, Gastonia*	.920	27	8	15	2	1
Butler, Columbia	1.000	5	1	3	0	1
Buzard, Columbus*	1.000	6	1	1	0	0
Cairncross, Charleston (S.C.)* ..	.911	24	5	46	5	1
Cardona, Gastonia	1.000	8	1	5	0	0
Carlson, 12 Aug.-5 C.(S.C.)	.900	17	10	8	2	0
Carlton, Spartanburg*	1.000	6	2	0	0	0
Carpenter, Columbia	.962	28	8	17	1	1
J. Castillo, Columbia	.848	28	11	17	5	1
Cecil, Charleston (W.Va.)	.949	24	6	31	2	4
Chiles, Macon	.875	40	4	10	2	1
Cofer, Columbus	.949	41	10	27	2	2
Conley, Sumter	.857	10	4	2	1	0
Cooke, Augusta*	.923	11	3	9	1	0
Coppeta, Fayetteville*	.946	28	7	28	2	0
Creek, Savannah*	.714	5	0	5	2	0
Curry, Columbia	1.000	1	1	1	0	0
Danner, Augusta*	1.000	5	6	8	0	1
Dare, Macon*	1.000	25	1	4	0	0
Daugherty, Asheville	.914	62	7	25	3	1
DeSantis, Spartanburg	1.000	3	3	7	0	1
Devore, Charleston (S.C.)	1.000	12	2	3	0	0
Domecq, Spartanburg	.857	40	2	22	4	0
Doty, Charleston (W.Va.)	.941	47	5	11	1	0
Douris, Augusta	1.000	12	1	1	0	0
Dreyer, Gastonia	.939	25	13	33	3	3
Duey, Myrtle Beach	.875	38	8	13	3	0
Duff, Charleston (W.Va.)*	.933	40	5	9	1	0
Dunbar, Greensboro*	.800	25	1	3	1	1
Elliott, Spartanburg	.875	10	3	4	1	0
Embree, Columbus*	.977	27	8	34	1	3
Engle, Columbia	.800	7	2	2	1	0
Erickson, Gastonia*	.500	14	2	1	3	0
Ettles, Charleston (S.C.)	1.000	29	2	7	0	1
Eubanks, Charleston (S.C.)	.909	30	4	6	1	0
Eversgerd, Savannah*	.909	72	2	8	1	0
Fajardo, Augusta	.545	11	5	1	5	0
Faw, Greensboro	.925	26	18	19	3	1
Fazekas, Fayetteville	1.000	24	1	8	0	0
Ferry, Charleston (W.Va.)	1.000	22	1	4	0	0
Fidler, 4 C'bia-33 Ash.*	.786	37	5	6	3	0
Fiegel, Columbia*	1.000	2	0	1	0	0
Flener, Myrtle Beach*	.880	55	5	17	3	0
Foster, Sumter	.885	34	9	14	3	1
Fowler, Macon	.900	19	4	5	1	0
Francis, Macon	.750	10	2	1	1	0
Frazier, Greensboro	.849	25	14	31	8	3
Freitas, Columbia	.943	25	12	21	2	3
Fusco, Savannah*	.571	33	1	3	3	0
Futrell, Augusta	.955	41	5	16	1	2
Gajkowski, Columbus	1.000	3	0	1	0	0
Ganote, Myrtle Beach	.867	20	8	18	4	1
Garcia, Myrtle Beach	.946	39	13	22	2	2
Garside, Charleston (S.C.)*	.857	19	2	4	1	0
Gaston, Savannah	1.000	9	2	7	0	1
Geeve, Gastonia	1.000	14	0	9	0	1
Gerstein, Sumter*	1.000	7	2	2	0	0
Giberti, Gastonia*	1.000	9	0	6	0	1
Gies, Gastonia	.941	19	10	22	2	5
Glover, Savannah	.500	8	1	1	2	0
Gobel, 30 Aug.-15 Ash.*	1.000	45	5	6	0	1
Goergen, Spartanburg	.941	24	12	20	2	1
Grace, Spartanburg	1.000	6	1	8	0	1
Guilfoyle, Fayetteville*	.824	40	4	10	3	0
Guzik, Columbia	1.000	20	8	25	0	1
Haeger, Fayetteville*	1.000	23	8	16	0	0
Hammond, Savannah	1.000	13	1	7	0	1
Harriger, Columbia	1.000	2	0	2	0	1
Hassinger, Spartanburg	.968	21	8	22	1	0
Henson, Gastonia	.909	8	5	5	1	0
Hernandez, Asheville	.857	30	3	9	2	0
Hill, Spartanburg	.955	27	12	9	1	0
Hines, Greensboro*	.879	26	5	24	4	1
Hoeme, Charleston (S.C.)	.833	31	6	4	2	0
Hook, Charleston (W.Va.)	.867	45	1	12	2	1
Hooper, Augusta	.906	34	10	19	3	0
Hope, Augusta	.933	7	4	10	1	0
Hunter, Augusta	.929	31	1	12	1	2
Hurst, Spartanburg	1.000	12	1	3	0	0
Hurst, Gastonia*	.923	11	1	11	1	2
Ingram, Charleston (S.C.)	.962	12	5	20	1	5
Ivie, Charleston (S.C.)*	.971	37	8	25	1	5
Johnson, Charleston (S.C.)	.944	36	8	9	1	0
Jolley, Savannah	.889	23	1	7	1	1
Jones, Augusta	.909	6	3	7	1	0
Jones, Columbia	.875	5	0	7	1	0
Jordan, Myrtle Beach*	.784	29	9	20	8	1
Juhl, Spartanburg*	1.000	25	5	7	0	0
Karsay, Myrtle Beach	.806	20	8	21	7	0
Kelly, Savannah	1.000	56	2	7	0	1
Ketchen, Asheville	.921	27	4	31	3	2
King, Charleston (W.Va.)*	.906	30	6	23	3	1
Kinney, Savannah*	.967	17	4	25	1	1
Kistaitis, Myrtle Beach*	1.000	19	0	8	0	1
Kosenski, Fayetteville	.905	37	6	13	2	0
Kotch, Sumter*	.958	44	8	15	1	0
Kunz, Gastonia*	.929	20	2	11	1	1
Lata, Savannah	1.000	1	0	1	0	0
Latham, Augusta*	1.000	27	1	8	0	0
Leahy, Macon	.895	29	7	10	2	0
Leslie, Charleston (W.Va.)	.960	44	5	19	1	1
Lima, Fayetteville	.750	18	2	4	2	1
Lira, Fayetteville	1.000	15	4	18	0	0
Lomon, Macon	1.000	1	2	0	0	0
Long, Sumter	.963	63	11	15	1	0
Lopez, Savannah	.824	21	4	10	3	0
Lugo, Myrtle Beach	1.000	12	2	2	0	0
Lyle, Augusta	1.000	5	0	3	0	1
Mack, Macon	1.000	19	1	4	0	0
Madrigal, Gastonia	1.000	10	0	5	0	0
Malone, Greensboro*	1.000	25	0	5	0	1
Mandia, Gastonia	1.000	22	4	3	0	0
Manicchia, Spartanburg	1.000	12	1	4	0	1
Martinez, Columbia	.951	26	25	33	3	4
Martinez, Sumter	.895	39	6	11	2	0
Mattson, Macon	.923	23	7	5	1	0
McCarthy, Charleston (W.Va.)*	1.000	1	0	2	0	0
McGarity, Savannah	.971	27	7	26	1	0
McGough, Gastonia	.875	16	5	2	1	1
McLochlin, Columbus	1.000	15	7	15	0	0
Migliozzi, Gastonia	.667	20	0	2	1	0
Miller, Augusta	.958	21	6	17	1	0
Minutelli, Charleston (W.Va.)* ..	1.000	2	1	2	0	0
Mlicki, Columbus	.833	22	8	7	3	2
Mooney, Augusta	.848	32	5	23	5	3
Morphy, Greensboro	.826	43	1	18	4	1
Morrison, 8 Mac.-7 Sum.	.964	15	8	19	1	1
Munoz, Spartanburg*	.953	20	7	34	2	1
Neidinger, Fayetteville	.795	31	9	22	8	1
Nieves, Charleston (W.Va.)	.818	27	7	11	4	1
Nieves, Asheville	1.000	3	0	1	0	0
Norris, Sumter	1.000	8	1	3	0	0
O. Ortega, Sumter*	1.000	1	0	1	0	0
Overholser, Charleston (S.C.)	1.000	21	5	7	0	2
Owens, Spartanburg*	.933	16	4	10	1	0
Patterson, Spartanburg	.933	35	5	9	1	0
Pedraza, Sumter	1.000	8	6	9	0	2
Perez, Sumter*	.789	16	3	12	4	2
Perez, Greensboro	1.000	30	1	0	0	0
Pfaff, Fayetteville	1.000	14	6	21	0	0
Potts, Macon*	1.000	34	3	6	0	0
Powers, Asheville*	.905	36	3	16	2	1
Prats, Asheville	1.000	33	3	6	0	1
Quijada, Asheville	.917	22	6	16	2	0
Quirico, Greensboro*	.771	26	5	32	11	0
Randall, Spartanburg	1.000	43	2	9	0	1
Ray, Charleston (W.Va.)	1.000	28	12	18	0	2
Redmond, Augusta	1.000	7	0	1	0	1
Reed, Asheville	1.000	40	2	6	0	0
Rees, Columbia	.950	20	5	14	1	0
Reincke, Fayetteville	.923	12	7	5	1	1
Richmond, Charleston (S.C.)	1.000	8	0	1	0	0
Ringkamp, Gastonia	1.000	17	4	7	0	2
Ritter, Macon	1.000	14	1	1	0	0
Rivera, Greensboro	.958	29	4	19	1	2
Rivera, Columbus*	.917	30	2	9	1	0
J. ROA, Macon	1.000	30	14	29	0	4
Robertson, Augusta*	1.000	13	3	14	0	0
Rodriguez, Fayetteville*	1.000	32	5	16	0	0
Rohrwild, Macon	.818	26	5	4	2	0
Roper, Charleston (W.Va.)	.966	27	9	19	1	2
Ruebel, Augusta*	1.000	8	1	5	0	1
Rueter, Sumter*	1.000	8	8	11	0	0
Rychel, Augusta	1.000	8	1	4	0	1
Ryder, Macon	.833	12	2	3	1	0
Sadecki, Gastonia	.762	16	1	15	5	1
Sample, Columbia	1.000	12	0	5	0	0
Santiago, Columbus	1.000	34	6	8	0	0
Seiler, Greensboro*	.952	52	9	11	1	0
Shouse, Augusta*	1.000	26	2	7	0	1
Siberz, Greensboro	1.000	42	6	4	0	0
Sieradzki, 15 Sum.-9 C'bia	.333	24	0	1	2	0
Singer, Myrtle Beach*	.861	27	6	25	5	0
Smith, Macon	1.000	3	1	0	0	0
Smith, Greensboro	.941	38	13	19	2	1
Sparks, Augusta	1.000	8	0	2	0	0
Sparma, Macon	1.000	13	7	10	0	0
Speek, Savannah	.900	48	1	8	1	0
Spiller, Savannah*	1.000	18	1	5	0	1
Steed, Myrtle Beach	.783	28	10	37	13	3

SOUTH ATLANTIC LEAGUE

CLASS A

SOUTH ATLANTIC LEAGUE

Player, Team	Pct.	G	PO	A	E	DP
Stewart, Charleston (W.Va.)	.839	24	9	17	5	0
Stidham, Fayetteville	1.000	28	2	12	0	0
Stokes, Fayetteville	1.000	38	3	17	0	0
Stone, Columbus	.917	9	4	7	1	0
Sweeney, Columbus	1.000	3	1	0	0	0
Tatar, Charleston (W.Va.)	.933	11	3	11	1	0
M. Thomas, 30 C'bia-19 Sum.*	.833	49	2	8	2	0
S. Thomas, Columbia	.867	37	3	10	2	0
Thompson, Charleston (S.C.)	.909	34	3	7	1	1
Undorf, Fayetteville	1.000	22	3	12	0	1
Vanryn, Sumter*	.933	20	5	23	2	1
Vazquez, Macon	.958	14	7	16	1	1
Vlcek, Gastonia	.333	29	1	0	2	0
Walden, Columbus	.800	12	2	6	2	0
Waldron, Charleston (S.C.)*	.906	38	7	22	3	1
Warren, Fayetteville	.714	10	3	2	2	0
Washington, Gastonia	1.000	11	6	7	0	0
Watson, Savannah*	1.000	3	0	3	0	0
Weber, Savannah*	1.000	7	0	5	0	0
Wegmann, Columbia	.929	7	4	9	1	0
Wells, Gastonia	.750	13	2	1	1	0
Werland, Macon*	1.000	18	8	16	0	1
Wertz, Columbus	1.000	49	6	20	0	0
G. White, Sumter*	.939	24	8	23	2	1
White, Augusta	.909	34	1	9	1	0
Whiteside, Gastonia	.909	48	5	5	1	0
D. Williams, Macon	1.000	23	12	18	0	1
Wilson, Asheville	.864	22	7	12	3	2
Winiarski, Columbus	1.000	39	3	16	0	1
Withem, Fayetteville	.923	11	6	6	1	1

The following players did not have any fielding statistics at the positions indicated or appeared only as a designated hitter, pinch-hitter or pinch-runner: D. Adams, 2b; Angotti, 3b; Bieser, 3b, p; Bogues, 2b; A. Brown, ss; M. Brown, of; Crawford, p; Creed, p; Donahue, 2b; Dunn, p; Erhardt, of; Gill, 3b; Gilmore, p; Harley, of; Henderson, of; Jewett, p; M. Johnson, p; Karcher, of; Kimbler, of; Landinez, of; Lanfranco, 1b, of; Luce, p; MacArthur, p; Meyer, of; Millan, of, p; S. Miller, 3b; B. Morrison, dh, ph; Nash, p; Newton, of; Noce, 3b, of; O'Neal, 3b; Ozoria, ss; Perozo, p; Pough, 3b; Riggs, dh; Ronca, 3b; Saulter, p; Schaefer, p; Silver, p; C. Thomas, of; Tomso, p; Trujillo, c, p; Van Scoyoc, 3b; Veit, c; Wallace, 1b; Young, p.

LEAGUE CHAMPIONS

Year	Team	Pct.	Year	Team	Pct.	Year	Team	Pct.
1948—	Lincolnton*	.627		Spartanburg	.567	1980—	Greensboro	.590
1949—	Newton-Conover	.667	1968—	Spartanburg	.597		Charleston	.561
	Ruth'ford Co. (2nd)†	.627		Greenwood‡	.597	1981—	Greensboro‡	.695
1950—	Newton-Conover	.627	1969—	Greenwood‡	.587		Greenwood	.549
	Lenoir (2nd)†	.626		Shelby	.565	1982—	Greensboro‡	.681
1951—	Morganton	.645	1970—	Greenville	.576		Florence	.546
	Shelby (2nd)†	.604		Greenville	.619	1983—	Columbia	.620
1952—	Lincolnton	.649	1971—	Greenwood	.631		Gastonia‡	.587
	Shelby (2nd)†	.645		Greenwood	.759	1984—	Charleston	.549
1953-59—League inactive.			1972—	Spartanburg‡	.788		Asheville‡	.510
1960—	Lexington	.707		Greenville	.652	1985—	Florence‡	.599
	Salisbury (2nd)†	.650	1973—	Spartanburg‡	.646		Greensboro	.540
1961—	Salisbury	.627		Gastonia	.619	1986—	Columbia‡	.682
	Shelby (4th)†	.481	1974—	Gastonia	.606		Asheville	.643
1962—	Statesville	.563		Gastonia	.672	1987—	Asheville	.655
	Statesville	.700	1975—	Spartanburg	.543		Myrtle Beach‡	.597
1963—	Greenville†	.576		Spartanburg	.614	1988—	Charleston (S.C.)	.616
	Salisbury	.631	1976—	Asheville	.544		Spartanburg‡	.500
1964—	Rock Hill	.672		Greenwood‡	.600	1989—	Gastonia	.657
	Salisbury‡	.631	1977—	Greenwood	.557		Augusta‡	.535
1965—	Salisbury	.641		Gastonia‡	.590	1990—	Columbia	.580
	Rock Hill‡	.603	1978—	Greenwood	.614		Charleston (W.Va.)‡	.538
1966—	Spartanburg	.682		Greenwood	.565	1991—	Charleston (W.Va.)	.648
	Spartanburg	.767	1979—	Greenwood‡	.565		Columbia‡	.614
1967—	Spartanburg	.730		Spartanburg	.525			

*Won championship and four-club playoff. †Won four-club playoff. ‡Won split-season playoff. (NOTE—Known as Western Carolina League from 1948 through 1962 and known as Western Carolinas League through 1979.)

APPALACHIAN LEAGUE

FINAL STANDINGS

Team	Pul.	J.C.	Bur.	Eliz.	Kng.	Blu.	Mar.	Prn.	Hun.	Bri.	W	L	T	Pct.	GB
Pulaski (Braves)	....	6	2	8	6	1	2	2	10	8	45	23	0	.662	......
Johnson City (Cardinals)	6	....	2	5	7	1	1	9	1	8	40	26	0	.606	4
Burlington (Indians)	0	0	....	1	1	7	9	8	6	8	40	27	0	.597	4½
Elizabethton (Twins)	4	7	1	....	6	6	1	2	2	10	39	29	0	.574	6
Kingsport (Mets)	6	5	1	6	....	0	9	1	1	7	36	31	0	.537	8½
Bluefield (Orioles)	1	1	4	6	2	....	7	9	5	1	36	31	0	.537	8½
Martinsville (Phillies)	0	1	3	1	3	5	....	3	10	1	27	41	0	.397	18
Princeton (Reds)	0	1	4	0	1	3	9	....	5	1	24	40	0	.375	19
Huntington (Cubs)	2	1	6	0	1	7	2	6	....	0	25	42	0	.373	19½
Bristol (Tigers)	4	4	4	2	4	1	1	1	0	2	22	44	0	.333	22

Major league affiliations in parentheses.

Playoffs—Pulaski defeated Burlington, two games to none, to win league championship.

Regular-season attendance—Bluefield, 55,373; Bristol, 26,901; Burlington, 57,613; Elizabethton, 18,115; Huntington, 59,860; Johnson City, 31,442; Kingsport, 31,721; Martinsville, 72,703; Princeton, 25,203; Pulaski, 24,656. Total—403,587.

Managers—Bluefield, Gus Gil; Bristol, Juan Lopez; Burlington, Dave Keller; Elizabethton, Ray Smith; Huntington, Steve Roadcap; Johnson City, Chris Maloney; Kingsport, Andre David; Martinsville, Rollie Dearmas; Princeton, Sam Mejias; Pulaski, Randy Ingle.

All-Star team—1B—Lance Marks, Pulaski; 2B—Quilvio Veras, Kingsport; 3B—Andy Bruce, Johnson City; SS—Manny Jimenez, Pulaski; Util. IF—Ken Arnold, Huntington; OF—Ricky Otero, Kingsport; Manny Ramirez, Burlington; Clayton Byrne, Bluefield; Util. OF—Don Robinson, Pulaski; C—Pedro Grifol, Elizabethton; DH—Tom Mezzanotte, Bristol; RHP—Kevin Lomon, Pulaski; LHP—David Sartain, Elizabethton; RP—Chris Lemp, Bluefield; Most Valuable Player—Manny Ramirez, Burlington; Manager of the Year—Ray Smith, Elizabethton.

BATTING

TEAM

Team	Avg.	G	AB	R	OR	H	TB	2B	3B	HR	RBI	SH	SF	HP	BB	Int. BB	SO	SB	CS	LOB
Pulaski	.255	68	2281	352	266	582	820	107	19	31	288	27	12	30	244	8	573	134	44	483
Bluefield	.254	67	2198	329	272	559	797	99	14	37	266	12	18	47	240	5	518	78	66	469
Johnson City	.249	66	2147	352	273	534	796	128	16	34	268	7	29	23	297	10	498	64	41	462
Kingsport	.242	67	2137	307	265	518	735	88	21	29	252	15	18	38	215	12	478	101	41	465
Martinsville	.236	68	2236	299	323	527	713	86	11	26	246	15	16	32	261	5	585	64	26	502
Burlington	.234	67	2230	332	279	521	793	88	20	48	267	13	18	35	302	17	514	75	48	488
Elizabethton	.229	68	2201	316	270	505	778	102	15	47	260	6	23	31	245	8	545	107	30	442
Princeton	.221	64	2128	238	321	470	634	71	21	17	179	15	14	26	193	1	520	53	44	433
Huntington	.218	67	2224	248	366	485	638	65	17	18	194	26	17	49	233	10	567	85	30	490
Bristol	.208	66	2056	225	363	427	591	63	10	27	180	24	10	26	256	6	639	84	50	429

INDIVIDUAL

(Leading qualifiers for batting championship—184 or more plate appearances)

*Bats lefthanded. †Switch-hitter.

Player, Team	Avg.	G	AB	R	H	TB	2B	3B	HR	RBI	SH	SF	HP	BB	Int. BB	SO	SB	CS
Otero, Ricardo, Kingsport†	.343	66	236	47	81	124	16	3	7	52	1	6	2	35	5	32	12	4
Veras, Quilvio, Kingsport†	.336	64	226	54	76	98	11	4	1	16	5	0	7	36	0	28	38	11
Ramirez, Manuel, Burlington	.326	59	215	44	70	146	11	4	19	63	0	6	34	5	41	7	8
Byrne, Clayton, Bluefield	.321	54	221	39	71	97	9	4	3	25	2	1	2	18	0	38	8	17
Mezzanotte, Tom, Bristol†	.304	56	168	23	51	79	10	0	6	25	0	0	4	17	0	24	1	6
Deak, Darrel, Johnson City†	.302	66	215	43	65	119	23	2	9	33	0	4	6	42	1	44	1	6
Hawkins, Carla, Elizabethton†	.290	64	259	50	75	116	14	6	5	30	1	5	3	16	0	53	39	9
Maxwell, Pat, Burlington*	.289	45	166	41	48	67	8	4	1	12	3	1	0	26	2	15	7	4
Radziewicz, Doug, Johnson City*	.289	62	201	31	58	89	15	2	4	28	0	2	2	25	2	18	1	0
Larson, Danny, Martinsville*	.287	56	188	26	54	81	9	3	4	28	1	1	1	16	1	45	6	3

Departmental leaders: G—Brede, 68; AB—Hawkins, 259; R—Veras, 54; H—Otero, 81; TB—M. Ramirez, 146; 2B—Deak, 23; 3B—Jimenez, 7; HR—M. Ramirez, 19; RBI—M. Ramirez, 63; SH—Guerrero, 7; SF—Otero, 6; HP—Tillman, Wolff, 12; BB—Hazlett, 63; IBB—Daubach, Otero, M. Ramirez, 5; SO—An. Johnson, 69; SB—Hawkins, 39; CS—Byrne, 17.

(All players—listed alphabetically)

Player, Team	Avg.	G	AB	R	H	TB	2B	3B	HR	RBI	SH	SF	HP	BB	Int. BB	SO	SB	CS
Adams, Derek, Bluefield	.287	34	115	13	33	38	5	0	0	9	1	1	1	4	0	21	4	5
Alder, Jimmy, Bristol	.215	49	149	16	32	58	4	2	6	21	0	1	1	31	2	64	3	2
Alexander, Eric, Bluefield	.275	51	153	30	42	57	4	1	3	24	0	1	7	41	0	37	5	8
Archer, Carl, Pulaski	.189	50	159	23	30	48	9	0	3	21	3	1	3	20	0	35	3	1
Arendt, Jim, Princeton	.222	19	54	2	12	12	0	0	0	4	0	0	1	3	0	19	0	1
Arnold, Ken, Huntington	.275	61	229	28	63	105	16	4	6	43	3	2	1	20	0	33	4	2
Aubin, Kevin, Princeton	.134	31	97	7	13	17	4	0	0	9	1	1	4	10	0	37	0	1
Ayrault, Joe, Pulaski	.257	55	202	22	52	73	12	0	3	27	2	0	0	13	0	49	0	0
Battle, Allen, Johnson City	.387	17	62	26	24	32	6	1	0	7	1	0	1	14	0	6	7	1
Bell, Brent, Martinsville	.143	17	35	4	5	5	0	0	0	1	1	1	0	1	0	15	0	0
Belyeu, Randy, Huntington	.184	14	38	5	7	12	1	2	0	0	0	0	2	6	0	12	1	1
Bennett, Gary, Martinsville	.235	41	136	15	32	42	7	0	1	16	1	1	5	17	0	26	0	1
Bentley, Blake, Princeton	.197	42	122	13	24	32	6	1	0	6	0	0	2	20	0	39	5	3
Borzello, Mike, Johnson City	.333	3	3	0	1	2	1	0	0	0	0	0	0	0	0	1	0	0
Bowden, Merritt, Elizabethton	.234	49	171	24	40	61	7	1	4	20	0	1	1	18	0	39	5	3
Bradford, Vince, Bristol	.128	34	86	6	11	14	1	1	0	0	0	0	2	7	0	48	3	1
Brede, Brent, Elizabethton*	.241	68	253	24	61	83	13	0	3	36	2	4	1	30	2	48	13	4
Brito, Luis, Martinsville†	.268	31	123	17	33	38	5	0	0	9	1	2	2	5	0	21	5	2
Brock, Tarrick, Bristol*	.266	55	177	26	47	63	7	3	1	13	1	1	3	22	0	42	14	6
Brown, Alvin, Elizabethton	.203	57	172	26	35	49	7	2	1	11	0	0	5	26	0	65	6	2
Bruce, Andy, Johnson City	.283	50	198	34	56	104	21	0	9	42	0	5	2	13	2	50	1	2
Burritt, Mike, Burlington	.173	20	52	6	9	15	3	0	1	3	0	0	1	7	0	19	0	1
Byrne, Clayton, Bluefield	.321	54	221	39	71	97	9	4	3	25	2	1	2	18	0	38	8	17

— 499 —

Player, Team	Avg.	G	AB	R	H	TB	2B	3B	HR	RBI	SH	SF	HP	BB	Int. BB	SO	SB	CS
Cabral, Joaquin, Huntington*	.186	43	118	10	22	32	1	0	3	14	0	0	1	13	1	40	0	1
Caro, Jorge, Bristol†	.214	54	126	10	27	35	2	0	2	15	0	1	1	17	1	32	7	7
Casanova, Raul, Kingsport	.056	5	18	0	1	1	0	0	0	0	0	0	0	1	0	10	0	0
Cavazzoni, Kenneth, Princeton	.260	37	127	14	33	43	5	1	1	14	0	1	1	22	0	21	1	3
Chambers, Mark, Pulaski	.263	55	186	33	49	59	8	1	0	15	2	0	2	19	1	41	26	9
Chaney, Keith, Pulaski	.224	57	196	23	44	55	8	0	1	20	6	2	1	30	0	63	7	4
Chavez, Devin, Huntington	.227	42	128	9	29	34	3	1	0	9	0	0	2	18	0	29	2	2
Cherry, Lamar, Martinsville	.275	58	204	36	56	98	10	1	10	32	0	1	0	33	0	68	7	3
Chisum, David, Burlington*	.250	31	92	9	23	34	5	0	2	15	0	1	0	7	1	41	3	2
Coleman, Glenn, Bluefield	.200	48	150	25	30	43	7	0	2	12	0	1	6	18	0	55	8	3
Coleman, Ronnie, Burlington	.227	33	97	21	22	24	2	0	0	3	1	0	0	20	0	24	8	4
Colon, Hector, Johnson City†	.241	39	54	9	13	13	0	0	0	3	0	1	0	13	0	16	1	1
Concepcion, Yamil, Princeton	.175	32	103	12	18	23	2	0	1	9	0	2	2	8	0	36	0	0
Coss, Mike, Bluefield	.191	59	209	24	40	48	6	1	0	17	5	0	2	22	1	41	8	5
Crosnoe, Cory, Pulaski	.259	60	189	32	49	63	9	1	1	16	3	3	4	37	0	54	9	4
Daubach, Brian, Kingsport*	.243	65	218	30	53	85	9	1	7	42	1	2	6	33	5	64	1	3
Davis, Darwin, Kingsport	.194	53	186	17	36	51	8	2	1	17	0	4	1	14	0	47	8	1
Deak, Darrel, Johnson City†	.302	66	215	43	65	119	23	2	9	33	0	4	6	42	1	44	1	6
de los Santos, Reynaldo, Martinsville*	.236	54	178	24	42	54	1	4	1	20	1	2	1	21	0	42	10	1
Dempsey, John, Johnson City*	.234	49	145	13	34	42	8	0	0	18	1	1	1	13	0	36	0	1
Diaz, Carlos, Bristol	.130	38	92	12	12	12	0	0	0	6	0	1	1	15	0	26	2	2
Diaz, Cesar, Kingsport	.232	38	125	11	29	38	6	0	1	15	1	0	2	7	0	37	0	4
Dreisbach, Bill, Princeton	.167	22	60	7	10	14	2	1	0	1	1	1	1	3	0	11	1	0
Dudek, Steve, Johnson City*	.167	36	72	9	12	17	3	1	0	8	0	1	0	14	1	17	1	1
Duncan, Enrique, Princeton	.191	13	47	6	9	15	1	1	1	3	0	0	1	3	0	7	4	1
Duplesis, Dave, Burlington*	.233	30	103	18	24	47	1	2	6	24	0	2	5	14	2	30	3	3
Duran, Felipe, Burlington	.209	59	201	24	42	50	6	1	0	14	5	2	7	18	0	38	3	1
Edwards, Otis, Burlington	.162	27	74	8	12	18	4	1	0	7	0	1	0	14	0	23	3	3
Eicher, Michael, Johnson City	.273	8	22	5	6	7	1	0	0	1	0	0	0	4	0	4	1	0
Farmer, Randy, Kingsport	.230	57	209	24	48	64	10	0	2	25	1	2	2	10	0	27	13	2
Feoli, Mike, Johnson City†	.154	7	13	2	2	2	0	0	0	1	0	1	0	0	0	5	0	0
Fernandez, Jose, Huntington	.167	5	12	1	2	2	0	0	0	0	0	0	0	0	0	5	0	0
Fernandez, Michael, Elizabethton	.230	42	148	20	34	66	8	3	6	19	1	2	1	12	0	40	0	0
Garcia, Guillermo, Kingsport	.242	14	33	9	8	11	1	1	0	2	0	0	0	4	0	4	0	0
Garr, Ralph, Pulaski	.202	35	94	9	19	22	3	0	0	9	0	0	0	4	0	27	1	1
Garrow, David, Elizabethton	.161	9	31	3	5	9	1	0	1	2	0	0	0	2	0	12	0	0
Gast, John, Princeton	.277	36	137	17	38	56	6	0	4	12	1	0	1	8	0	17	1	1
Geisler, Phillip, Martinsville*	.325	32	114	22	37	45	5	0	1	18	0	0	1	23	1	25	1	0
Gilbert, Don, Bluefield*	.272	34	114	21	31	46	7	1	2	17	0	1	2	26	3	29	3	4
Gilligan, Lawrence, Johnson City	.253	48	87	15	22	35	4	3	1	9	1	2	1	7	0	14	2	1
Givens, Jim, Bristol†	.250	4	12	3	3	3	0	0	0	1	0	0	1	1	0	1	1	1
Graham, Gordie, Bluefield*	.144	38	104	10	15	30	6	0	3	10	0	0	1	6	0	41	0	2
Grejtak, Bryan, Bluefield	.257	46	148	26	38	68	7	1	7	20	0	2	3	28	1	44	4	2
Gresham, Kris, Bluefield	.239	34	117	16	28	37	5	2	0	16	1	3	4	5	0	19	6	4
Grifol, Pedro, Elizabethton	.262	55	202	24	53	86	12	0	7	36	0	4	2	16	0	33	0	1
Guerra, Pete, Burlington	.095	6	21	0	2	4	2	0	0	0	0	0	0	3	0	7	0	1
Guerrero, Gustavo, Bristol	.142	57	155	13	22	28	6	0	0	5	7	1	0	19	0	57	5	5
Hairston, Rodd, Burlington	.150	24	80	9	12	19	2	1	1	6	0	0	1	16	0	24	1	0
Hardy, Carlton, Martinsville	.133	36	105	13	14	20	6	0	0	9	0	1	2	11	0	35	2	0
Hawkins, Craig, Elizabethton†	.290	64	259	50	75	116	14	6	5	30	1	5	3	16	0	53	39	9
Hazlett, Steve, Elizabethton	.200	64	210	50	42	65	11	0	4	24	1	1	6	63	0	53	13	7
Hence, Sam, Burlington	.248	40	161	23	40	55	7	1	2	10	1	0	2	10	0	37	6	5
Hernandez, Crandall, Huntington	.077	15	13	2	1	1	0	0	0	1	0	0	0	4	0	8	0	1
Hernandez, Luis, Bristol	.215	41	130	20	28	41	6	0	3	16	3	0	1	14	2	34	9	1
Hernandez, Rafael, Kingsport	.213	47	150	11	32	38	6	0	0	10	1	0	4	12	0	40	0	2
Hopp, Dean, Martinsville	.196	20	56	9	11	15	1	0	1	5	0	1	1	5	0	16	0	0
Houston, Maceo, Huntington*	.187	44	139	10	26	33	2	1	1	13	1	0	0	10	1	47	1	1
Jackson, Miccal, Johnson City	.158	10	19	2	3	3	0	0	0	0	0	0	1	0	0	5	0	1
Jelinek, Joe, Martinsville†	.169	47	177	22	30	36	2	2	0	14	1	1	0	27	0	44	7	6
Jenkins, Demetrish, Princeton*	.257	59	230	31	59	76	6	4	1	18	7	1	1	8	0	30	2	7
Jimenez, Manny, Pulaski	.282	57	234	37	66	93	10	7	1	29	2	0	1	12	2	47	19	8
Johnson, Andre, Pulaski	.271	57	207	33	56	84	10	3	4	29	1	2	2	21	0	69	23	3
Johnson, Art, Bristol	.182	3	11	2	2	2	0	0	0	0	0	0	0	0	0	1	2	0
Johnson, Greg, Elizabethton	.229	46	170	19	39	44	2	0	1	14	1	2	3	8	0	29	10	0
Johnson, Wayne, Martinsville†	.245	31	94	16	23	30	7	0	0	9	0	0	1	14	0	26	4	3
Jones, Keith, Johnson City*	.281	66	228	43	64	90	13	2	3	31	0	5	2	29	0	35	21	5
Jordan, Tim, Johnson City*	.000	8	13	1	0	0	0	0	0	0	0	0	0	3	0	3	0	1
Keeline, Jason, Pulaski	.188	38	96	9	18	19	1	0	0	9	2	1	0	8	0	31	4	1
Kelliher, Paul, Pulaski	.214	4	14	1	3	3	0	0	0	0	0	0	0	0	0	4	0	0
Kimsey, Keith, Bristol	.159	53	164	10	26	38	3	0	3	17	1	1	1	14	0	60	2	3
Lara, Carlos, Pulaski	.237	33	97	14	23	36	5	1	2	17	1	0	6	10	0	11	5	2
Larson, Danny, Martinsville*	.287	56	188	26	54	81	9	3	4	28	0	1	1	16	1	45	6	3
Lawson, Cale, Burlington*	.191	35	110	14	21	40	4	0	5	15	0	0	0	12	1	27	0	3
Loyola, Juan, Princeton	.064	20	47	0	3	3	0	0	0	1	0	1	1	5	0	20	0	0
Luciano, Suliban, Kingsport	.203	53	172	23	35	56	7	1	4	14	4	1	1	6	0	42	3	0
Mallee, John, Martinsville	.237	39	135	15	32	40	8	0	0	14	1	0	2	19	0	25	5	0
Malpica, Omar, Princeton†	.205	30	83	11	17	20	3	0	0	7	1	2	1	26	0	23	0	2
Marks, Lance, Pulaski	.281	61	221	46	62	117	9	5	12	42	0	2	8	21	2	43	5	1
Mashore, Justin, Bristol	.203	58	177	29	36	48	3	0	3	11	2	0	0	28	1	65	17	6
Mauldin, Eric, Martinsville	.218	40	101	16	22	27	5	0	0	9	2	1	7	15	0	34	4	2
Maxwell, Pat, Burlington*	.289	45	166	41	48	67	8	4	1	12	3	1	0	26	2	15	7	4
McClain, Scott, Bluefield	.264	41	148	16	39	44	5	0	0	24	0	1	3	15	0	39	5	3
McConathy, Doug, Bluefield*	.402	27	92	17	37	57	10	2	2	18	0	2	3	13	0	14	2	4
McKinnon, Tom, Johnson City*	.167	7	6	0	1	1	0	0	0	0	0	0	0	0	0	4	0	0
Merritt, Joseph, Johnson City	.250	5	8	2	2	2	0	0	0	1	0	0	1	1	0	3	0	0
Meyer, Paul, Kingsport	.152	14	33	3	5	5	0	0	0	2	0	0	1	3	0	12	0	1
Mezzanotte, Tom, Bristol†	.304	56	168	23	51	79	10	0	6	25	0	0	4	17	0	24	1	6
Milne, Blaine, Johnson City	.263	10	19	2	5	6	1	0	0	3	0	0	1	1	0	2	0	1
Moore, Tim, Elizabethton†	.264	57	197	33	52	107	17	1	12	37	0	1	2	28	3	57	7	2
Moreno, Jorge, Bristol†	.197	49	122	10	24	26	2	0	0	6	1	1	3	11	0	43	0	4
Moreno, Juan, Kingsport	.291	23	86	11	25	38	1	3	2	16	0	1	0	4	0	22	3	1
Morgan, James, Burlington	.261	10	23	5	6	6	0	0	0	1	0	0	1	3	0	4	1	1
Morris, Rossi, Princeton	.113	26	53	7	6	6	0	0	0	0	1	0	0	4	0	25	5	0
Murphy, Mike, Martinsville	.218	44	156	15	34	36	2	0	0	7	2	0	1	11	0	40	9	2
Murray, Pat, Johnson City*	.120	30	50	8	6	10	1	0	1	3	0	0	0	8	0	22	1	0

Player, Team	Avg.	G	AB	R	H	TB	2B	3B	HR	RBI	SH	SF	HP	BB	Int. BB	SO	SB	CS
Norman, Kenny, Elizabethton†	.253	53	166	25	42	59	7	2	2	18	0	1	5	12	3	48	13	2
Ortiz, Basilio, Bluefield	.302	12	53	4	16	23	2	1	1	7	0	1	0	2	0	6	1	0
Otero, Ricardo, Kingsport†	.343	66	236	47	81	124	16	3	7	52	1	6	2	35	5	32	12	4
Patrizi, Mike, Kingsport	.194	32	103	14	20	25	2	0	1	6	0	0	3	7	0	18	2	2
Pena, Porfirio, Martinsville	.152	9	33	3	5	6	1	0	0	2	1	0	0	1	0	11	0	0
Perez, Richard, Huntington	.181	49	171	20	31	35	4	0	0	8	5	1	7	19	0	30	5	2
Perona, Joe, Bristol	.500	5	16	1	8	14	3	0	1	3	0	0	0	3	0	1	2	1
Prichard, Brian, Bristol	.109	28	64	6	7	12	0	1	1	3	2	0	1	11	0	34	0	0
Quillin, Ty, Kingsport*	.191	63	204	25	39	57	8	2	2	22	1	0	4	30	2	60	5	1
Radziewicz, Doug, Johnson City*	.289	62	201	31	58	89	15	2	4	28	0	2	2	25	2	18	1	0
Ramirez, Francisco, Elizabethton	.107	28	84	4	9	10	1	0	0	5	0	0	1	0	0	22	0	0
Ramirez, Manuel, Burlington	.326	59	215	44	70	146	11	4	19	63	0	3	6	34	5	41	7	8
Ramos, Martin, Princeton	.260	13	50	11	13	24	3	1	2	6	0	0	0	1	0	23	1	0
Reese, Calvin, Princeton	.238	62	231	30	55	78	8	3	3	27	0	2	0	23	0	44	10	8
Reeves, Mickey, Huntington	.100	28	60	5	6	6	0	0	0	2	0	0	1	2	0	17	2	0
Reinert, Greg, Pulaski†	.150	11	20	1	3	5	0	0	0	5	1	0	0	0	0	8	0	0
Reyes, Sergio, Huntington	.234	28	94	11	22	23	1	0	0	9	0	1	1	8	0	20	2	4
Rivas, Javier, Pulaski	.252	36	107	15	27	38	8	0	1	12	1	0	1	20	1	38	5	3
Robinson, Chuck, Huntington	.118	20	51	1	6	7	1	0	0	0	1	0	0	3	0	23	0	1
Robinson, Don, Pulaski*	.286	54	189	42	54	72	9	0	3	23	1	0	0	20	2	44	22	7
Robinson, Eli, Princeton	.214	43	140	10	30	33	3	0	0	8	0	1	3	12	0	55	2	3
Robles, Javier, Burlington	.125	12	32	5	4	7	0	0	1	3	0	1	0	9	1	10	2	0
Rojas, Roberto, Bristol*	.173	39	104	10	18	21	3	0	0	5	4	0	0	14	0	39	7	3
Root, Mitch, Huntington	.268	53	194	29	52	65	6	2	1	17	5	1	1	28	0	45	12	4
Rossler, Brett, Kingsport	.050	9	20	0	1	1	0	0	0	1	0	1	0	1	0	10	0	0
Ruff, Dan, Bristol*	.462	4	13	3	6	10	4	0	0	5	0	0	1	0	0	2	0	0
Ruiz, Stewart, Bluefield†	.257	47	175	29	45	49	4	0	0	11	2	1	5	4	0	28	11	6
Rumfield, Toby, Princeton	.274	59	226	22	62	90	13	3	3	30	1	4	5	9	0	44	1	7
Ruth, Pat, Martinsville	.268	36	127	16	34	49	7	1	2	15	1	1	3	14	0	46	4	1
Sallee, Andrew, Martinsville*	.235	56	187	24	44	65	9	0	4	27	2	2	2	18	2	33	0	0
Sanjurjo, Jose, Bristol	.078	32	64	7	5	6	1	0	0	7	0	1	7	1	0	21	2	0
Santiago, Jorge, Burlington	.094	15	32	1	3	4	1	0	0	2	0	0	0	2	0	10	0	0
Schmidt, Keith, Bluefield*	.233	52	172	26	40	65	11	1	4	17	0	0	4	16	0	50	2	4
Schorr, Brad, Kingsport	.000	11	2	0	0	0	0	0	0	0	0	0	0	0	1	0	0	0
Schultz, Bobby, Burlington*	.236	44	148	20	35	47	5	2	1	12	2	1	4	19	3	46	4	1
Seitzer, Brad, Bluefield	.289	12	45	5	13	24	2	0	3	5	0	0	0	5	0	10	1	1
Shabazz, Basil, Johnson City	.205	40	117	18	24	27	3	0	0	11	2	1	2	15	0	38	4	7
Shell, Scott, Elizabethton*	.040	8	25	2	1	1	0	0	0	1	0	1	0	1	0	9	0	0
Shirley, Mike, Burlington	.250	21	76	10	19	25	6	0	0	8	0	0	1	11	0	17	1	2
Smith, Calvin, Huntington	.225	54	182	28	41	44	3	0	0	9	4	0	1	37	1	47	16	3
Smith, Demond, Kingsport†	.250	35	116	28	29	43	3	4	1	12	0	1	6	12	0	24	16	7
Stovall, Darond, Johnson City†	.142	48	134	16	19	25	2	2	0	5	0	0	0	23	1	63	9	3
Strong, Kevin, Elizabethton	.154	17	39	5	6	9	0	0	1	3	0	0	0	6	0	14	0	0
Sued, Nick, Burlington	.255	43	157	18	40	52	6	0	2	23	0	2	1	13	0	10	3	5
Sutey, John, Bristol	.240	40	96	10	23	31	5	0	1	7	2	1	5	18	0	27	3	2
Taylor, Michael, Burlington	.225	18	40	5	9	12	0	0	1	3	0	0	0	10	0	10	0	1
Therrien, Dominic, Pulaski*	.500	6	16	4	8	9	1	0	0	7	1	0	0	5	0	2	0	0
Thomas, Mike, Bluefield	.224	41	147	20	33	53	8	0	4	26	1	3	3	12	0	35	7	0
Thomas, Rodney, Princeton	.100	33	90	12	9	15	1	1	1	6	0	0	0	6	0	36	9	1
Tillman, Darren, Huntington	.221	45	163	21	36	50	7	2	1	9	1	3	12	14	2	38	14	3
Ubina, Alex, Bristol	.296	12	27	1	8	9	1	0	0	2	0	0	0	1	0	4	0	0
Ugueto, Jesus, Johnson City	.187	55	166	16	31	42	8	0	1	22	1	4	0	14	0	45	0	3
Urbanek, Jason, Martinsville	.218	27	87	6	19	26	1	0	2	11	1	1	3	10	0	33	0	2
Valdez, Pedro, Huntington*	.289	49	152	17	44	57	11	1	0	16	0	5	2	17	3	30	5	1
Valette, Ramon, Elizabethton	.149	25	74	7	11	13	2	0	0	1	0	1	0	6	0	23	1	0
Veras, Quilvio, Kingsport†	.336	64	226	54	76	98	11	4	1	16	5	0	7	36	0	28	38	11
Virgilio, George, Pulaski†	.352	15	54	8	19	24	5	0	0	7	1	2	3	0	6	3	0
Vlasis, Chris, Johnson City*	.267	48	116	26	31	45	4	2	2	11	1	0	2	22	1	26	8	5
Walker, Steve, Huntington	.198	58	187	19	37	50	2	4	1	15	3	3	4	6	0	64	11	1
Walker, Tom, Huntington	.202	53	124	11	25	32	4	0	1	9	2	0	1	11	1	27	1	2
Waszgis, Robert, Bluefield	.229	12	35	8	8	18	1	0	3	8	0	0	1	5	0	11	3	0
Whitaker, Jeffrey, Burlington	.111	9	9	0	1	1	0	0	0	0	0	0	0	2	0	6	1	0
White, Andre, Burlington*	.200	42	140	13	28	34	4	1	0	14	0	2	2	13	1	17	15	3
Whitehurst, Todd, Burlington†	.281	23	64	12	18	35	3	1	4	12	0	0	1	9	1	23	0	0
Wilkerson, Wayne, Princeton*	.255	61	231	26	59	77	8	5	0	17	2	0	2	22	1	33	11	6
Williams, Edward, Johnson City†	.314	23	70	9	22	33	3	1	2	10	0	0	0	14	1	15	3	2
Wolff, James, Huntington	.207	50	169	21	35	50	3	0	4	20	1	1	12	17	1	52	5	2
Yelton, Rob, Bristol	.301	40	103	7	31	41	4	3	0	12	0	1	1	5	0	14	4	2
Young, Dmitri, Johnson City†	.256	37	129	23	33	49	10	0	2	22	0	2	2	21	1	28	2	1
Zollars, Mike, Burlington	.241	44	137	26	33	51	8	2	2	16	0	3	3	32	0	35	7	2

The following pitchers, listed alphabetically by club, with games in parentheses, had no plate appearances, primarily through use of designated hitters:

BLUEFIELD—Benge, Brett (23); Chouinard, Bobby (6); Eshelman, Vaughn (3); Farrar, Terry (3); Firsich, Steve (11); Gould, Frank (12); Krivda, Rick (15); Lemp, Chris (25); Mercedes, Juan (16); O'Connell, Shawn (19); Plaster, Allen (10); Ryan, Kevin (14); Sanders, Matt (17).

BRISTOL—Adams, Art (14); Bauer, Matt (15); Bussa, Todd (12); Cedeno, Blas (14); Durussel, Scott (6); Edmondson, Brian (12); Magrini, Paul (7); Miller, Trever (13); Nelson, Brian (8); Perpetuo, Nelson (8); Quiles, Henry (11); Raffo, Greg (19); Rodriguez, Alejandro (2); Schwarber, Tom (4); Sodowsky, Clint (14); Thompson, Justin (10).

BURLINGTON—Bluhm, Brandon (20); Colon, Jose (6); Coulter, Christopher (12); Crawford, Carlos (13); Doyle, Ian (25); Gibbs, Paul (16); Gonzalez, Jesus (5); Harris, Hernando (13); Hernandez, Fernando (14); Key, Wade (4); Knaplund, Greg (5); Koller, Rodney (2); Lopez, Albert (13); Maffett, Christopher (11); Resendez, Oscar (24).

ELIZABETHTON—Caridad, Ron (6); Carlson, Bob (27); Diaz, Sandy (13); Guardado, Eddie (14); Mieses, Melanio (22); Miller, Shawn (4); Pina, Rafael (16); Portillo, Luis (7); Roberts, Brett (6); Sartain, David (14); Schwartz, David (4); Sweeney, Dennis (16).

HUNTINGTON—Adams, Terry (14); Camarena, Miguel (16); Garcia, Mario (22); Gardner, Scott (7); Goodson, Kirk (17); Meyer, Jay (17); Morones, Eugenio (22); Pacheco, Yogi (5); Rodriguez, Cristobal (11); Sample, Frank (11); Sanchez, Adrian (14); Trinidad, Hector (12).

JOHNSON CITY—Arias, Jose (8); Avram, Brian (18); Barber, Brian (14); Chasin, Dave (16); Cochran, Jim (15); Gaston, Russell (8); Glover, Greg (4); Gonzalez, Cecilio (12); Hurst, Bill (2); Jeffcoat, Mike (2); Jones, Steve (24); Lucchetti, Lawrence (4); Rodriguez, Manuel (13); Romanoli, Paul (8); Santos, Gabriel (24); Slininger, Dennis (13); Tranbarger, Mark (4).

KINGSPORT—Corbell, Eric (16); Cotner, Andy (3); Crawford, Joe (19); Fiegel, Todd (11); Fitzgerald, Dave (7); Henderson, Jeff (10); Hokanson, Ed (17); Jacome, Jason (12); Perpetuo, Nelson (6); Ramirez, Hector (14); Seymour, Steve (8); Watson, Shaun (8).

MARTINSVILLE—Alexis, Juan (11); Anderson, Chad (5); Boldt, Sean (6); Bottalico, Rick (7); Brown, Dan (25); Coleman, Scott (16); DeSantis, Dominic (12); Edwards, Samuel (10); Gilmore, Joel (11); McIntyre, Joe (13); Mejias, Fernando (21); Mitchell, Robert (13); Page, Thane (16); Salamon, John (6).

PRINCETON—Balentine, Bryant (18); Brothers, John (3); Garcia, Fermin (14); Hrusovsky, John (26); Jarvis, Kevin (13); Miller, James (15); Morales, Armando (13); Murphy, Jeffrey (13); Reed, Chris (13); Rodriquez, Rory (13); Steph, Rod (7); Wiggins, James (14).

PULASKI—Behrens, Scott (3); Blair, Dirk (18); Butler, Jason (11); Carr, Brent (15); Dunlap, Travis (13); Ford, Stewart (18); Fowler, Dwayne (6); Francis, Scott (6); Hostetler, Michael (9); Kempfer, Jason (13); Lairsey, Eric (13); Lomon, Kevin (10); Nahas, Jim (4); Petit, Ricardo (5); Place, Mike (12); Ryder, Scott (2); Saulter, Kevin (8); Viarengo, Matt (6); Wilder, John (14).

GRAND SLAMS—Cherry, Moore, M. Ramirez, Reese, 2 each; Bruce, Duplessis, Geisler, Hazlett, Ju. Moreno, Otero, D. Robinson, M. Thomas, S. Walker, 1 each.

AWARDED FIRST BASE ON CATCHER'S INTERFERENCE—Adams 2 (Bennett, Taylor); Casanova (Prichard); Dempsey (Grifol); Grifol (Ce. Diaz); Vlasis (Ce. Diaz); T. Walker (Aubin); Waszgis (Brown).

PITCHING

TEAM

Team	ERA	G	CG	ShO	Sv.	IP	H	R	ER	HR	HB	BB	Int. BB	SO	WP	Bk.
Elizabethton	2.83	68	11	4	12	582.2	494	270	183	23	20	245	4	602	51	28
Bluefield	3.12	67	2	4	22	580.2	516	272	201	24	23	247	2	587	43	28
Kingsport	3.13	67	11	7	20	554.2	468	265	193	33	37	191	13	486	47	10
Pulaski	3.21	68	4	8	20	597.0	446	266	213	25	32	319	8	628	83	35
Burlington	3.30	67	2	6	19	600.0	515	279	220	29	42	242	3	605	76	13
Johnson City	3.55	66	7	6	18	570.0	465	273	225	36	36	212	4	564	46	18
Princeton	3.79	64	8	5	12	560.0	494	321	236	26	48	290	28	510	85	31
Martinsville	3.81	68	2	6	10	578.0	562	323	245	42	35	199	5	467	47	33
Huntington	3.86	67	9	3	13	596.2	620	366	256	32	39	244	1	468	50	20
Bristol	4.33	66	1	2	14	561.1	548	363	270	44	25	297	14	520	82	32

INDIVIDUAL

(Leading qualifiers for earned-run average leadership—54 or more innings)

*Throws lefthanded.

Pitcher, Team	W	L	Pct.	ERA	G	GS	CG	GF	ShO	Sv.	IP	H	R	ER	HR	HB	BB	Int. BB	SO	WP
Jones, Johnson City	3	4	.429	1.47	24	5	1	13	0	2	61.1	42	16	10	4	1	16	3	61	2
Gilmore, Martinsville	4	3	.571	1.53	11	9	0	2	0	0	59.0	45	16	10	3	1	14	1	51	2
Jacome, Kingsport	5	4	.556	1.63	12	7	3	5	1	2	55.1	35	18	10	1	0	13	2	48	6
Guardado, Elizabethton*	8	4	.667	1.86	14	13	3	1	1	0	92.0	67	30	19	5	2	31	0	106	6
Krivda, Bluefield*	7	1	.875	1.88	15	8	0	2	1	0	67.0	48	20	14	0	0	24	0	79	1
Fiegel, Kingsport*	5	4	.556	2.04	11	11	2	0	0	0	66.1	45	20	15	2	12	25	1	90	6
DeSantis, Martinsville	6	6	.500	2.19	12	12	0	0	0	0	78.0	64	34	19	3	6	14	0	55	2
Coulter, Burlington*	4	1	.800	2.30	12	7	0	2	0	1	62.2	49	16	16	2	3	18	0	49	7
Sartain, Elizabethton	9	4	.692	2.34	14	14	1	0	1	0	84.2	56	29	22	3	4	45	0	95	5
Jarvis, Princeton	5	6	.455	2.42	13	13	4	0	1	0	85.2	73	34	23	6	3	29	3	79	5

Departmental leaders: G—Carlson, 27; W—Sartain, 9; L—T. Adams, 9; Pct.—Blair, .889; GS—Sanchez, Sartain, 14; CG—Sanchez, 5; GF—Carlson, Hrusovsky, 25; ShO—Several pitchers tied with 1; Sv.—Santos, 14; IP—Sanchez, 104.2; H—Sanchez, 95; R—T. Adams, 56; ER—Barber, 44; HR—Cedeno, Edmondson, Harris, T. Miller, Perpetuo, 7; HB—Fiegel, 12; BB—Lairsey, 64; IBB—Rhodriquez, 6; SO—Guardado, 106; WP—Balentine, Morales, 14.

(All pitchers—listed alphabetically)

Pitcher, Team	W	L	Pct.	ERA	G	GS	CG	GF	ShO	Sv.	IP	H	R	ER	HR	HB	BB	Int. BB	SO	WP
Adams, Bristol	0	4	.000	4.35	19	5	0	9	0	3	49.2	48	36	24	2	0	33	2	57	11
Adams, Huntington	0	9	.000	5.77	14	13	0	0	0	0	57.2	67	56	37	1	6	62	0	52	4
Alexis, Martinsville	1	1	.500	6.91	11	0	0	4	0	0	27.1	37	24	21	4	1	8	0	16	2
Anderson, Martinsville	1	2	.333	2.91	5	5	0	0	0	0	34.0	28	12	11	4	3	2	0	30	1
Arias, Johnson City	4	3	.571	3.55	8	8	3	0	1	0	58.1	48	28	23	6	1	13	0	61	6
Avram, Johnson City	4	0	1.000	5.04	18	0	0	7	0	0	30.1	29	22	17	6	2	15	0	25	4
Balentine, Princeton*	0	3	.000	4.94	18	7	1	2	0	1	54.2	47	34	30	2	5	52	3	58	14
Barber, Johnson City	4	6	.400	5.40	14	13	0	0	0	0	73.1	62	48	44	5	5	38	0	84	4
Bauer, Bristol*	5	3	.625	3.19	15	2	0	10	0	4	36.2	33	15	13	1	5	8	1	39	1
Behrens, Pulaski	0	1	.000	10.45	3	3	0	0	0	0	10.1	14	12	12	2	0	6	0	3	1
Benge, Bluefield	4	1	.800	3.18	23	0	0	15	0	5	39.2	38	18	14	3	0	16	0	46	2
Blair, Pulaski	8	1	.889	3.35	18	1	0	10	0	4	45.2	47	21	17	2	0	15	0	41	5
Bluhm, Burlington*	5	1	.833	4.47	20	0	0	8	0	1	44.1	38	26	22	1	2	22	0	46	8
Boldt, Martinsville	0	0	.000	4.15	6	0	0	5	0	0	8.2	9	5	4	3	0	2	0	10	1
Bottalico, Martinsville	3	2	.600	4.09	7	6	2	0	0	0	33.0	32	20	15	2	1	13	0	38	2
Brothers, Princeton	3	0	1.000	0.95	3	3	0	0	0	0	19.0	13	4	2	1	2	4	0	16	2
Brown, Martinsville	3	0	1.000	1.72	25	0	0	23	0	10	36.2	23	7	7	0	1	10	2	38	2
Burritt, Burlington	0	0	.000	9.00	1	0	0	1	0	0	1.0	1	1	1	0	1	1	0	0	0
Bussa, Bristol	1	2	.333	2.73	12	1	0	7	0	1	29.2	28	16	9	0	1	17	1	26	2
Butler, Pulaski*	3	2	.600	4.70	11	8	0	0	0	0	38.1	30	24	20	3	0	32	0	58	10
Camarena, Huntington	2	1	.667	3.43	16	0	0	3	0	2	39.1	40	30	15	3	2	10	0	31	2
Caridad, Elizabethton	0	4	.000	4.87	6	6	0	0	0	0	20.1	24	19	11	0	0	13	0	17	4
Carlson, Elizabethton	3	3	.500	2.03	27	0	0	25	0	7	44.1	37	13	10	3	2	8	2	47	4
Caro, Bristol*	0	0	.000	0.00	2	0	0	2	0	0	2.1	2	0	0	0	0	0	0	0	0
Carr, Pulaski*	2	0	1.000	1.71	15	0	0	9	0	1	26.1	19	7	5	0	2	12	0	37	4
Cedeno, Bristol	1	4	.200	3.80	14	2	0	6	0	0	45.0	47	36	19	7	2	18	1	37	3
Chasin, Johnson City	2	3	.400	2.93	16	0	0	3	0	0	27.2	17	11	9	1	1	10	0	26	2
Chouinard, Bluefield	5	1	.833	3.48	6	6	0	0	0	0	33.2	44	19	13	1	2	11	0	31	1
Cochran, Johnson City	1	0	1.000	3.00	15	0	0	6	0	2	24.0	17	9	8	2	1	6	0	32	1
Coleman, Martinsville*	3	8	.273	5.05	16	12	0	3	0	0	73.0	92	51	41	5	4	23	1	44	5
Colon, Burlington	2	1	.667	3.50	6	5	0	0	0	0	18.0	12	8	7	2	2	12	0	17	1
Corbell, Kingsport	1	4	.200	6.37	16	4	1	8	0	0	41.0	42	37	29	2	5	25	1	27	5
Cotner, Kingsport*	0	0	.000	0.96	3	1	0	2	0	2	9.1	7	1	1	0	1	0	1	10	1
Coulter, Burlington*	4	1	.800	2.30	12	7	0	2	0	1	62.2	49	16	16	2	3	18	0	49	7
Crawford, Burlington	6	3	.667	2.46	13	13	2	0	1	0	80.1	62	28	22	3	9	14	0	80	6
Crawford, Kingsport*	0	0	.000	1.11	19	0	0	16	0	11	32.1	16	5	4	0	1	8	0	43	3
DeSantis, Martinsville*	6	6	.500	2.19	12	12	0	0	0	0	78.0	64	34	19	3	6	14	0	55	2
Diaz, Elizabethton	8	3	.727	3.38	13	10	2	1	0	0	74.2	61	35	28	5	0	30	0	92	7
Doyle, Burlington	2	4	.333	3.32	25	0	0	23	0	11	43.1	44	20	16	2	1	11	1	44	5
Dunlap, Pulaski	2	1	.667	2.54	13	0	0	10	0	4	28.1	20	13	8	1	2	15	0	42	6
Durussel, Bristol	0	0	.000	1.88	9	0	0	3	0	2	14.1	14	3	3	0	0	4	0	16	2

Pitcher, Team	W	L	Pct.	ERA	G	GS	CG	GF	ShO	Sv.	IP	H	R	ER	HR	HB	BB	Int. BB	SO	WP
Edmondson, Bristol	4	4	.500	4.57	12	12	1	0	0	0	69.0	72	38	35	7	3	23	1	42	5
Edwards, Burlington*	0	0	.000	0.00	1	0	0	1	0	0	1.0	2	0	0	0	0	1	0	0	0
Edwards, Martinsville	0	4	.000	4.98	10	1	0	5	0	0	21.2	22	17	12	2	0	10	1	11	0
Eshelman, Bluefield*	1	0	1.000	0.64	3	3	0	0	0	0	14.0	10	4	1	1	0	9	0	15	1
Farrar, Bluefield*	1	1	.500	4.15	3	3	0	0	0	0	13.0	11	9	6	1	2	6	0	17	1
Fiegel, Kingsport*	5	4	.556	2.04	11	11	2	0	0	0	66.1	45	20	15	2	12	25	1	90	6
Firsich, Bluefield	2	3	.400	5.16	11	4	0	2	0	0	29.2	28	21	17	1	3	20	0	25	0
Fitzgerald, Kingsport	1	0	1.000	2.76	7	1	0	3	0	0	16.1	13	8	5	1	1	7	2	9	2
Ford, Pulaski*	1	2	.333	4.42	18	0	0	8	0	0	36.2	30	22	18	0	9	29	4	36	10
Fowler, Pulaski	0	1	.000	2.03	6	0	0	4	0	1	13.1	9	6	3	1	0	2	0	9	0
Francis, Pulaski	5	0	1.000	0.90	6	6	1	0	1	0	40.0	17	5	4	0	2	11	0	33	0
Garcia, Princeton	2	2	.500	2.90	14	0	0	7	0	2	40.1	35	15	13	0	1	12	2	32	3
Garcia, Kingsport	0	0	.000	0.00	2	0	0	2	0	0	2.0	1	0	0	0	0	0	0	3	0
Garcia, Huntington	1	2	.333	2.19	22	0	0	20	0	6	37.0	34	18	9	3	3	8	0	33	4
Gardner, Huntington	2	3	.400	3.20	7	7	0	0	0	0	39.1	38	16	14	3	2	16	0	25	4
Gaston, Johnson City	1	4	.200	4.29	8	6	1	0	0	0	35.2	33	22	17	1	3	15	0	35	8
Gibbs, Burlington	3	0	1.000	1.22	16	1	0	8	0	0	37.0	25	9	5	0	2	13	0	54	1
Gilmore, Martinsville	4	3	.571	1.53	11	9	0	2	0	0	59.0	45	16	10	3	1	14	1	51	2
Glover, Johnson City	2	0	1.000	5.03	4	4	0	0	0	0	19.2	21	11	11	1	1	9	0	25	2
Gonzalez, Johnson City	6	3	.667	4.41	12	12	2	0	0	0	69.1	72	41	34	6	5	16	0	50	5
Gonzalez, Burlington	0	0	.000	14.14	5	0	0	1	0	0	7.0	11	12	11	2	0	9	0	8	2
Goodson, Huntington	0	4	.000	6.18	17	2	0	5	0	1	39.1	55	37	27	4	4	14	0	45	6
Gould, Bluefield*	3	6	.333	4.14	12	11	1	0	0	0	67.1	71	37	31	5	2	19	0	58	4
Guardado, Elizabethton*	8	4	.667	1.86	14	13	3	1	1	0	92.0	67	30	19	5	2	31	0	106	6
Harris, Burlington	4	3	.571	3.29	13	13	0	0	0	0	65.2	67	30	24	7	3	31	0	47	5
Henderson, Kingsport	3	2	.600	4.38	10	4	0	2	0	0	37.0	32	23	18	1	2	23	0	28	3
Hernandez, Burlington	4	4	.500	2.92	14	13	0	1	0	0	77.0	74	33	25	4	7	19	0	86	12
Hernandez, Kingsport	1	0	1.000	0.00	1	0	0	1	0	0	2.0	1	0	0	0	0	0	0	0	0
Hokanson, Kingsport	1	4	.200	5.17	17	0	0	10	0	4	38.1	37	28	22	3	2	20	3	29	3
Hostetler, Pulaski	3	2	.600	1.91	9	9	0	0	0	0	47.0	35	12	10	4	2	9	2	61	4
Hrusovsky, Princeton	4	4	.500	1.83	26	0	0	25	0	7	44.1	26	12	9	2	3	21	3	53	1
Hurst, Johnson City	0	0	.000	10.80	2	0	0	0	0	0	1.2	0	2	2	0	1	2	0	2	0
Jacome, Kingsport	5	4	.556	1.63	12	7	3	5	1	2	55.1	35	18	10	1	0	13	2	48	6
Jarvis, Princeton	5	6	.455	2.42	13	13	4	0	1	0	85.2	73	34	23	6	3	29	3	79	6
Jeffcoat, Johnson City	0	0	.000	6.75	2	0	0	0	0	0	1.1	2	1	1	0	0	1	0	2	1
Jones, Johnson City	3	4	.429	1.47	24	5	1	13	0	2	61.1	42	16	10	4	1	16	3	61	2
Kempfer, Pulaski	0	1	.000	3.34	13	1	0	8	0	3	29.2	24	14	11	0	2	20	0	20	8
Key, Burlington	2	1	.667	1.29	4	0	0	3	0	0	7.0	5	2	1	0	0	1	0	5	0
Knaplund, Burlington*	1	0	1.000	1.50	5	0	0	1	0	0	6.0	1	3	1	0	4	8	0	7	5
Koller, Burlington	0	0	.000	3.00	2	0	0	0	0	0	3.0	3	1	1	0	0	0	0	0	0
Krivda, Bluefield*	7	1	.875	1.88	15	8	0	2	0	1	67.0	48	20	14	0	0	24	0	79	1
Lairsey, Pulaski*	2	4	.333	5.44	13	13	1	0	0	0	44.2	25	35	27	1	4	64	0	48	12
Lemp, Bluefield	0	1	.000	2.06	25	0	0	23	0	12	39.1	22	14	9	0	2	24	0	43	6
Lomon, Pulaski	6	0	1.000	0.61	10	5	1	1	1	0	44.0	17	9	3	0	4	13	0	70	4
Lopez, Princeton	4	5	.444	3.44	13	13	0	0	0	0	73.1	61	33	28	4	3	23	0	81	4
Lucchetti, Johnson City	3	0	1.000	1.09	4	4	0	0	0	0	24.2	11	4	3	0	1	10	0	22	1
Maffett, Burlington	0	2	.000	11.05	11	1	0	2	0	0	22.0	27	31	27	2	3	27	2	17	9
Magrini, Bristol	1	3	.250	3.18	7	6	0	1	0	1	28.1	20	12	10	2	2	21	0	19	5
McIntyre, Martinsville*	2	3	.400	3.45	13	1	0	6	0	0	31.1	22	13	12	1	5	20	0	32	4
McKinnon, Johnson City	0	0	.000	3.52	5	2	0	1	0	0	7.2	2	3	3	0	3	9	3	2	2
Mejias, Martinsville	1	1	.500	3.53	21	0	0	12	0	0	51.0	53	31	20	3	3	17	0	40	2
Mercedes, Bluefield*	2	6	.250	3.98	16	8	0	5	0	1	52.0	45	28	23	2	1	28	0	60	2
Meyer, Huntington*	2	5	.286	3.04	17	7	0	4	0	1	68.0	75	37	23	2	2	25	0	41	2
Mezzanotte, Bristol	0	0	.000	32.40	1	0	0	1	0	0	1.2	8	6	6	2	0	0	0	0	0
Mieses, Elizabethton	1	1	.500	2.92	22	0	0	15	0	3	52.1	53	28	17	1	1	22	0	50	3
Miller, Princeton	1	6	.143	6.57	15	4	0	6	0	0	38.1	40	37	28	1	5	44	5	33	9
Miller, Elizabethton	1	1	.500	6.55	4	4	1	0	0	0	22.0	28	16	16	1	1	8	0	28	0
Miller, Bristol*	2	7	.222	5.67	13	13	0	0	0	0	54.0	60	44	34	7	2	29	0	46	9
Mitchell, Martinsville	0	6	.000	5.51	13	10	0	1	0	0	49.0	52	38	30	3	7	24	0	34	9
Morales, Princeton	3	2	.600	2.63	13	9	2	2	0	1	65.0	47	31	19	2	5	25	1	68	14
Morones, Huntington	2	3	.400	4.33	22	0	0	16	0	3	35.1	37	18	17	2	3	24	1	36	7
Murphy, Princeton	1	2	.333	8.04	13	0	0	3	0	0	31.1	43	31	28	2	4	11	1	13	3
Nahas, Pulaski	0	0	.000	12.46	4	2	0	1	0	0	8.2	13	13	12	3	0	9	0	4	2
Nelson, Bristol	0	2	.000	14.18	8	4	0	2	0	0	13.1	12	29	21	2	2	38	0	11	11
O'Connell, Bluefield	1	5	.167	3.73	19	0	0	11	0	1	41.0	47	25	17	2	4	16	1	37	7
Pacheco, Huntington	1	3	.250	3.12	5	5	1	0	0	0	34.2	30	14	12	1	1	8	0	21	0
Page, Martinsville	1	4	.200	5.67	16	6	0	5	0	0	46.0	52	37	29	5	0	22	0	49	10
Perpetuo, 8 Bris.-6 King.*	0	5	.000	6.86	14	0	0	9	0	1	21.0	29	18	16	7	2	6	1	17	1
Petit, Pulaski	2	0	.000	8.04	5	1	0	1	0	0	15.2	25	16	14	3	0	9	0	14	1
Pina, Elizabethton	4	5	.444	2.52	16	13	3	1	1	0	89.1	79	42	25	1	5	44	0	64	8
Place, Pulaski	1	2	.333	4.03	12	4	0	3	0	1	44.2	45	22	20	1	3	15	1	35	10
Plaster, Bluefield	4	1	.800	2.44	10	9	1	0	1	0	51.2	39	24	14	3	2	23	0	53	5
Portillo, Elizabethton	0	0	.000	2.31	7	0	0	7	0	0	11.2	9	3	3	1	0	3	0	9	2
Quiles, Bristol	1	1	.500	3.62	11	2	0	5	0	0	32.1	29	21	13	0	3	9	1	31	1
Raffo, Bristol	3	1	.750	4.59	19	1	0	10	0	2	49.0	47	25	25	3	1	27	3	63	12
Ramirez, Kingsport	8	2	.800	2.65	14	13	1	0	0	0	85.0	83	39	25	5	3	28	2	64	9
Reed, Princeton	3	6	.333	4.86	13	13	0	0	0	0	63.0	68	53	34	5	7	30	2	51	10
Resendez, Burlington	3	2	.600	2.68	24	1	0	15	0	6	50.1	33	26	15	0	2	31	6	62	11
Rhodriquez, Princeton	0	6	.000	4.91	13	8	0	3	0	0	51.1	43	36	28	4	7	37	6	39	12
Roberts, Elizabethton	3	0	1.000	2.25	6	6	1	0	0	0	28.0	21	8	7	0	0	10	0	27	2
Rodriguez, Bristol	0	0	.000	7.71	2	0	0	1	0	0	7.0	9	6	6	1	0	5	0	5	4
Rodriguez, Huntington	3	3	.500	4.31	11	7	1	2	1	0	48.0	51	37	23	0	4	15	0	39	4
Rodriguez, Johnson City	1	0	1.000	4.19	13	0	0	4	0	0	19.1	19	11	9	3	1	6	0	7	1
Romanoli, Johnson City*	2	0	1.000	0.77	8	0	0	1	0	0	11.2	7	1	1	0	1	4	0	19	1
Ryan, Bluefield	5	4	.556	2.59	14	11	0	3	0	1	76.1	71	26	22	3	1	24	0	71	6
Ryder, Pulaski	2	0	1.000	0.00	2	2	0	0	0	0	11.0	6	0	0	0	0	3	0	11	1
Salamon, Martinsville	2	1	.667	4.30	6	6	0	0	0	0	29.1	31	18	14	4	3	20	0	19	5
Sample, Huntington	1	1	.500	7.77	11	2	0	7	0	0	24.1	34	22	21	3	0	15	0	13	10
Sanchez, Huntington	5	5	.500	3.10	14	14	5	0	1	0	104.2	95	53	36	6	9	26	0	71	4
Sanders, Bluefield	1	1	.500	3.21	17	4	0	4	0	1	56.0	42	27	20	2	4	27	1	52	7
Santos, Johnson City	2	0	1.000	2.23	24	0	0	24	0	14	32.1	25	8	8	1	2	5	0	55	4
Sartain, Elizabethton*	9	4	.692	2.34	14	14	1	0	1	0	84.2	56	29	22	3	4	45	0	95	5
Saulter, Pulaski	0	2	.000	0.56	8	0	0	8	0	3	16.0	6	2	1	0	0	5	2	5	2
Schorr, Kingsport	5	6	.455	3.14	11	11	3	0	0	1	71.2	53	40	25	6	9	16	1	69	5
Schwarber, Bristol	2	0	1.000	0.00	4	0	0	2	0	1	10.0	7	2	0	0	0	2	1	15	1

Pitcher, Team	W	L	Pct.	ERA	G	GS	CG	GF	ShO	Sv.	IP	H	R	ER	HR	HB	BB	Int. BB	SO	WP
Schwartz, Elizabethton	0	1	.000	9.53	4	0	0	1	0	0	5.2	8	8	6	1	1	6	0	3	5
Seymour, Kingsport	3	1	.750	2.42	8	7	1	1	0	0	44.2	42	18	12	3	0	15	1	28	1
Slininger, Johnson City	4	3	.571	3.25	13	12	0	0	0	0	63.2	47	28	23	0	5	37	1	49	1
Sodowsky, Bristol	0	5	.000	3.76	14	8	0	3	0	0	55.0	49	34	23	3	2	34	0	44	8
Steph, Princeton	2	3	.400	3.11	7	7	0	0	1	0	46.1	37	19	16	1	4	11	0	52	4
Sweeney, Elizabethton*	2	3	.400	2.97	16	2	0	6	0	2	57.2	51	39	19	2	4	25	2	64	5
Thompson, Bristol*	2	5	.286	3.60	10	10	0	0	0	0	50.0	45	29	20	3	2	24	1	60	7
Tranbarger, Johnson City*	1	0	1.000	2.25	4	0	0	0	0	0	8.0	11	7	2	0	2	0	0	6	1
Trinidad, Huntington	6	3	.667	2.87	12	10	2	1	0	0	69.0	64	28	22	4	3	11	0	61	3
Viarengo, Pulaski	2	0	1.000	3.06	6	0	0	1	0	0	17.2	9	6	6	3	1	11	0	18	1
Watson, Kingsport	3	2	.600	3.88	8	8	0	0	0	0	46.1	50	21	20	3	1	9	0	30	2
White, Burlington*	0	0	.000	0.00	1	0	0	0	0	0	1.0	0	0	0	0	0	1	0	2	0
Wiggins, Princeton	0	0	.000	2.61	14	0	0	8	0	1	20.2	22	15	6	0	2	14	2	16	7
Wilder, Pulaski	8	2	.800	2.51	14	13	1	0	1	0	79.0	55	27	22	1	1	39	1	60	3

BALKS—Pina, 10; Lairsey, 8; DeSantis, Gilmore, 7 each; Barber, Lomon, Reed, Rhodriquez, Sartain, Thompson, 6 each; Benge, Gibbs, Meyer, Mitchell, Place, Salamon, Wilder, 5 each; T. Adams, Blair, Cedeno, Goodson, Jarvis, Krivda, Plaster, Raffo, Roberts, Ryan, Sanders, Sodowsky, 4 each; A. Adams, Balentine, C. Crawford, Farrar, Fiegel, Jones, Mejias, Morales, Quiles, C. Rodriguez, Steph, Sweeney, 3 each; Behrens, Chouinard, Edmondson, Gaston, C. Gonzalez, J. Gonzalez, Guardado, J. Miller, Nahas, Page, Watson, Wiggins, 2 each; Anderson, Arias, Bauer, Bluhm, Boldt, Bottalico, Bussa, Camarena, Caridad, Caro, Coleman, Corbell, Cotner, J. Crawford, Doyle, Francis, F. Garcia, M. Garcia, Gardner, Henderson, F. Hernandez, Hostetler, Jacome, Lemp, Mieses, S. Miller, T. Miller, Murphy, Nelson, O'Connell, Pacheco, Petit, A. Rodriguez, Romanoli, Santos, Slininger, Tranbarger, 1 each.

COMBINATION SHUTOUTS—Krivda-Benge, Krivda-O'Connell, Mercedes-Krivda, Bluefield; Magrini-Bauer, Miller-Adams, Bristol; Colon-Gonzalez-Doyle, Coulter-Doyle, Crawford-Doyle, Crawford-Resendez, Hernandez-Key-Doyle, Burlington; Guardado-Carlson, Elizabethton; Gardner-Garcia, Huntington; Barber-Santos, Gonzalez-Chasin-Cochran-Santos, Jones-Chasin, Lucchetti-Chasin, Slininger-Avram-Rodriguez-Cochran-Santos, Johnson City; Cotner-Fitzgerald, Fiegel-Henderson, Fiegel-Jacome, Jacome-Crawford, Schorr-Crawford, Watson-Corbell, Kingsport; DeSantis-Brown 2, Coleman-Brown, Gilmore-Coleman, Salamon-Brown, Martinsville; Brothers-Balentine-Wiggins-Hrusovsky, Jarvis-Balentine-Hrusovsky, Reed-Garcia, Princeton; Butler-Dunlap, Francis-Ford-Saulter, Hostetler-Butler-Lomon-Saulter, Ryder-Blair, Wilder-Viarengo-Ford, Pulaski.

NO-HIT GAMES—Francis, Pulaski, defeated Huntington, 9-0, July 13; Gibbs, Bristol, defeated Bluefield, 8-2, August 2; Guardado, Elizabethton, defeated Pulaski, 5-0, August 26.

FIELDING

TEAM

Team	Pct.	G	PO	A	E	DP	PB
Pulaski	.965	68	1791	780	93	62	23
Burlington	.961	67	1800	743	102	53	15
Kingsport	.959	67	1664	695	100	51	13
Johnson City	.958	66	1710	642	104	43	9
Bluefield	.956	67	1742	734	115	68	18
Bristol	.948	66	1684	713	131	44	19
Martinsville	.947	68	1734	675	136	50	16
Huntington	.944	67	1790	821	156	55	15
Elizabethton	.939	68	1748	638	155	39	7
Princeton	.937	64	1680	642	157	52	17

INDIVIDUAL

*Throws lefthanded.

FIRST BASEMEN

Player, Team	Pct.	G	PO	A	E	DP
Archer, Pulaski	.984	24	232	12	4	14
Aubin, Princeton	1.000	4	28	1	0	2
Bell, Martinsville	.978	9	42	3	1	3
Brede, Elizabethton*	1.000	6	36	2	0	1
Brown, Elizabethton	.963	50	368	19	15	25
Cabral, Huntington*	.960	32	275	15	12	27
Caro, Bristol*	.983	48	327	18	6	16
Cavazzoni, Princeton	.959	11	65	5	3	6
Chavez, Huntington	.984	10	56	6	1	2
Colon, Johnson City	.963	4	24	2	1	1
Daubach, Kingsport	.986	65	562	52	9	41
Dudek, Johnson City*	.923	4	24	0	2	2
Duplesis, Burlington*	.989	28	254	13	3	8
Garrow, Elizabethton	.882	2	14	1	2	2
Gast, Princeton	.986	16	131	10	2	14
Geisler, Martinsville*	.967	23	195	11	7	15
Gilbert, Bluefield	.981	24	196	15	4	17
Graham, Bluefield*	.970	24	185	12	6	16
Grejtak, Bluefield	1.000	1	9	1	0	0
Gresham, Bluefield	1.000	2	17	2	0	2
Grifol, Elizabethton	1.000	2	12	1	0	4
Hairston, Burlington	.978	24	201	17	5	19
Johnson, Elizabethton	.917	2	10	1	1	0
Keeline, Pulaski	.000	2	0	0	1	0
Kimsey, Bristol	1.000	1	2	0	0	0
Lawson, Burlington	.977	9	77	7	2	11
Marks, Pulaski	.984	46	419	20	7	39
McConathy, Bluefield	.995	22	188	14	1	27
Meyer, Kingsport	1.000	5	21	3	0	3
Mezzanotte, Bristol	.988	36	236	18	3	18
Moreno, Bristol	1.000	1	1	1	0	0
Murray, Johnson City*	.990	20	101	3	1	7
Prichard, Bristol	1.000	1	1	0	0	0
RADZIEWICZ, Johnson City*	.987	58	434	23	6	27
Ramirez, Elizabethton	.917	4	18	4	2	1
Robinson, Princeton	.963	39	322	12	13	26
Root, Huntington	1.000	3	34	1	0	1
Ruff, Bristol	1.000	1	8	1	0	4
Sallee, Martinsville	.971	45	320	18	10	26

Player, Team	Pct.	G	PO	A	E	DP
Shell, Elizabethton	1.000	8	61	4	0	1
T. Walker, Huntington	.987	44	276	18	4	22
White, Burlington*	1.000	1	6	0	0	1
Whitehurst, Burlington	.990	13	95	5	1	3
Wolff, Huntington	1.000	1	1	1	0	0
Yelton, Bristol	1.000	1	9	1	0	0

SECOND BASEMEN

Player, Team	Pct.	G	PO	A	E	DP
Chaney, Pulaski	.973	46	72	105	5	18
Chisum, Burlington	.961	27	46	52	4	10
Concepcion, Princeton	1.000	1	0	1	0	0
Deak, Johnson City	.973	52	108	144	7	30
Diaz, Bristol	.962	25	44	57	4	13
Duncan, Princeton	1.000	3	14	5	0	2
Duran, Burlington	.917	3	6	5	1	1
Feoli, Johnson City	1.000	1	1	0	0	0
Gilligan, Johnson City	.875	7	3	4	1	0
Givens, Bristol	1.000	2	4	7	0	0
Guerrero, Bristol	1.000	3	3	3	0	0
Hawkins, Elizabethton	.876	59	98	122	31	23
Hazlett, Elizabethton	.909	9	15	15	3	1
Hernandez, Bristol	.954	34	57	109	8	11
Hernandez, Kingsport	.972	10	12	23	1	5
Jackson, Johnson City	1.000	5	6	4	0	1
Jelinek, Martinsville	.941	45	69	124	12	27
Jenkins, Princeton	.932	54	108	138	18	25
Johnson, Elizabethton	1.000	4	2	7	0	1
Keeline, Pulaski	.984	16	16	47	1	3
Malpica, Princeton	.848	8	11	17	5	3
Maxwell, Burlington	.988	40	69	97	2	17
McClain, Bluefield	1.000	2	3	6	0	0
Moreno, Bristol	.875	12	13	29	6	3
Perez, Huntington	.914	32	69	91	15	14
Robles, Burlington	.941	4	5	11	1	2
Ruiz, Bluefield	.973	13	28	45	2	15
Santiago, Burlington	1.000	1	1	0	0	0
Smith, Huntington	.959	42	85	124	9	21
Urbanek, Martinsville	.893	26	46	46	11	5
Veras, Kingsport	.972	61	113	161	8	30
Virgilio, Pulaski	.923	13	16	32	4	8
Whitaker, Burlington	1.000	3	2	9	0	1

THIRD BASEMEN

Player, Team	Pct.	G	PO	A	E	DP
Adams, Bluefield	.867	6	3	10	2	1
ALDER, Bristol	.955	47	32	75	5	3
Bruce, Johnson City	.902	35	28	64	10	3
Burritt, Burlington	.909	18	11	29	4	2
Chaney, Pulaski	.917	11	10	23	3	1
Chavez, Huntington	.667	6	2	6	4	0
Cherry, Martinsville	.875	50	49	77	18	6
Colon, Johnson City	1.000	1	1	0	0	0
Concepcion, Princeton	.829	32	21	47	14	6
Coss, Bluefield	1.000	1	2	0	0	0
Crosnoe, Pulaski	.939	59	42	128	11	8
Davis, Kingsport	.850	40	21	64	i5	6
Duncan, Princeton	.852	7	7	16	4	3
Fernandez, Elizabethton	.742	9	6	17	8	2
Garrow, Elizabethton	.714	2	0	5	2	0
Gast, Princeton	.975	18	15	24	1	2
Gilbert, Bluefield	.895	6	5	12	2	2
Gilligan, Johnson City	1.000	4	0	3	0	0
Gresham, Bluefield	.944	5	9	8	1	1
Hardy, Martinsville	.921	22	9	26	3	5
Hazlett, Elizabethton	.786	9	5	17	6	2
Hernandez, Bristol	.727	6	2	6	3	1
Hernandez, Kingsport	.945	28	16	53	4	2
Johnson, Elizabethton	.903	40	29	73	11	8
Lara, Pulaski	.800	2	1	3	1	0
Malpica, Princeton	.919	11	7	27	3	0
McClain, Bluefield	.864	37	29	66	15	6
Mezzanotte, Bristol	1.000	4	1	2	0	0
Moreno, Bristol	.740	21	13	24	13	2
Perez, Huntington	.857	6	6	12	3	2
Ramirez, Elizabethton	.727	7	5	11	6	1
Robles, Burlington	.864	7	6	13	3	1
Root, Huntington	.869	44	31	82	17	5
Rossler, Kingsport	.667	3	2	2	2	0
Santiago, Burlington	.944	9	6	11	1	2
Seitzer, Bluefield	.935	12	7	22	2	1
Smith, Huntington	.824	13	6	22	6	5
Valette, Elizabethton	.500	2	0	2	2	0
T. Walker, Huntington	.833	4	1	9	2	1
Whitehurst, Burlington	.900	10	1	17	2	2
Young, Johnson City	.932	31	19	49	5	4
Zollars, Burlington	.843	37	14	61	14	8

SHORTSTOPS

Player, Team	Pct.	G	PO	A	E	DP
Adams, Bluefield	.874	25	26	71	14	16
Alder, Bristol	.600	2	1	2	2	0
ARNOLD, Huntington	.945	58	96	197	17	34
Brito, Martinsville	.921	31	51	89	12	15
Chaney, Pulaski	1.000	1	1	1	0	0
Chisum, Burlington	1.000	1	1	2	0	1
Coss, Bluefield	.939	6	18	13	2	4
Deak, Johnson City	1.000	3	1	1	0	0
Diaz, Bristol	.813	14	8	18	6	1
Duran, Burlington	.931	58	74	170	18	26
Farmer, Kingsport	.926	57	68	146	17	31
Garcia, Kingsport	.750	5	4	8	4	2
Garrow, Elizabethton	.857	3	1	5	1	0
Gilbert, Bluefield	1.000	3	3	5	0	1
Gilligan, Johnson City	.887	25	17	46	8	8
Givens, Bristol	1.000	2	0	5	0	0
Guerrero, Bristol	.897	57	70	140	24	23
Hazlett, Elizabethton	.912	47	68	108	17	17
Hernandez, Kingsport	.923	9	6	18	2	1
Jelinek, Martinsville	1.000	3	4	9	0	0
Jimenez, Pulaski	.938	54	73	155	15	38
Johnson, Bristol	.813	3	3	10	3	1
Keeline, Pulaski	.955	18	15	48	3	5
Mallee, Martinsville	.892	39	71	95	20	14
Malpica, Princeton	.880	7	10	12	3	2
Maxwell, Burlington	1.000	5	3	5	0	0
McClain, Bluefield	1.000	2	1	7	0	1
Moreno, Bristol	1.000	3	3	3	0	0
Perez, Huntington	.949	14	14	23	2	3
Reese, Princeton	.885	60	93	146	31	20
Robles, Burlington	1.000	1	0	1	0	0
Root, Huntington	1.000	2	1	4	0	0
Ruiz, Bluefield	.893	33	51	82	16	23
Santiago, Burlington	1.000	5	2	2	0	0
Ugueto, Johnson City	.925	55	59	125	15	20
Valette, Elizabethton	.909	21	19	41	6	7
Zollars, Burlington	.909	7	6	14	2	3

OUTFIELDERS

Player, Team	Pct.	G	PO	A	E	DP
Alexander, Bluefield	1.000	5	2	0	0	0
Archer, Pulaski	1.000	6	5	0	0	0
Arendt, Princeton	.862	19	22	3	4	1
Battle, Johnson City	1.000	16	29	0	0	0
Bentley, Princeton	.921	35	53	5	5	0

Player, Team	Pct.	G	PO	A	E	DP
Bowden, Elizabethton	.942	46	65	0	4	0
Bradford, Bristol	.917	22	31	2	3	0
BREDE, Elizabethton*	1.000	62	123	2	0	0
Brock, Bristol*	.891	35	49	0	6	0
Byrne, Bluefield	.979	54	90	5	2	2
Cavazzoni, Princeton	.938	27	28	2	2	0
Chambers, Pulaski	.981	51	52	1	1	0
Chisum, Burlington	.000	1	0	0	1	0
Coleman, Bluefield	.902	48	51	4	6	1
Coleman, Burlington	1.000	16	16	2	0	0
Colon, Johnson City	1.000	23	26	0	0	0
de los Santos, Martinsville	.946	44	82	5	5	1
Diaz, Bristol	1.000	1	1	0	0	0
Edwards, Burlington*	.958	21	22	1	1	1
Eicher, Johnson City	.778	5	6	1	2	0
Feoli, Johnson City	1.000	3	2	0	0	0
Fernandez, Huntington	1.000	4	7	0	0	0
Garr, Pulaski	.897	32	34	1	4	0
Hence, Burlington	.929	35	49	3	4	0
Houston, Huntington*	.861	21	29	2	5	1
Johnson, Pulaski	.896	54	63	6	8	1
Johnson, Martinsville	.950	29	56	1	3	1
K. Jones, Johnson City*	.954	63	78	5	4	1
Jordan, Johnson City	1.000	5	7	0	0	0
Kimsey, Bristol	.984	49	57	4	1	2
Larson, Martinsville*	.925	52	70	4	6	0
Loyola, Princeton	.920	16	19	4	2	0
Luciano, Kingsport	.953	38	38	3	2	0
Mashore, Bristol	.953	53	91	10	5	2
Mauldin, Martinsville	.947	31	50	4	3	0
Moore, Elizabethton*	.952	41	95	4	5	2
Moreno, Bristol	.905	12	17	2	2	0
Moreno, Kingsport	.917	23	41	3	4	0
Morgan, Burlington	.750	8	3	0	1	0
Morris, Princeton	.857	17	18	0	3	0
Murphy, Martinsville	.963	43	74	3	3	1
Norman, Elizabethton	.919	50	51	6	5	0
Ortiz, Bluefield	1.000	12	22	1	0	0
Otero, Kingsport*	.985	65	122	7	2	2
Quillin, Kingsport	.930	57	76	4	6	2
Ramirez, Burlington	.966	49	83	2	3	0
Ramos, Princeton	.833	12	11	4	3	0
Reeves, Huntington	.938	24	29	1	2	1
Reyes, Huntington	.827	27	41	2	9	0
Rivas, Pulaski	.958	24	21	2	1	0
Robinson, Pulaski	.966	52	80	4	3	0
Robinson, Princeton	.667	2	2	0	1	0
Rojas, Bristol*	.947	20	18	0	1	0
Ruth, Martinsville	1.000	20	44	2	0	2
Sanjurjo, Bristol	.957	20	20	2	1	0
Schmidt, Bluefield	.831	50	50	4	11	0
Schultz, Burlington	.974	39	35	2	1	0
Shabazz, Johnson City	.912	40	57	5	6	1
Shirley, Burlington	.968	20	29	1	1	0
Smith, Kingsport	.970	24	31	1	1	0
Stovall, Johnson City*	.934	46	69	2	5	0
Strong, Elizabethton	.882	12	15	0	2	0
Sutey, Bristol	.972	29	35	0	1	0
Therrien, Pulaski	1.000	6	3	1	0	0
Thomas, Bluefield	.886	40	31	8	5	1
Thomas, Princeton	.931	30	25	2	2	0
Tillman, Huntington	.920	45	67	2	6	0
Valdez, Huntington*	.921	47	66	4	6	0
Vlasis, Johnson City	.974	37	32	6	1	2
S. Walker, Huntington	.954	58	96	8	5	2
T. Walker, Huntington	1.000	6	4	0	0	0
White, Burlington*	.976	32	37	3	1	1
Wilkerson, Princeton*	.984	61	118	6	2	1

CATCHERS

Player, Team	Pct.	G	PO	A	E	DP	PB
Aubin, Princeton	.972	15	121	17	4	0	4
Ayrault, Pulaski	.988	47	425	64	6	7	12
Belyeu, Martinsville	.980	8	38	10	1	0	0
Bennett, Martinsville	.994	41	291	34	2	4	9
Borzello, Johnson City	1.000	3	5	0	0	0	1
Brown, Elizabethton	.951	7	48	10	3	1	1
Casanova, Kingsport	.975	5	35	4	1	1	1
Colon, Johnson City	1.000	1	6	0	0	0	0
Dempsey, Johnson City	.981	47	328	30	7	2	7
Diaz, Kingsport	.988	35	225	20	3	0	6
Dreisbach, Princeton	.992	17	111	15	1	3	4
GREJTAK, Bluefield	.995	38	320	44	2	4	12
Gresham, Bluefield	.991	24	190	24	2	0	5
Grifol, Elizabethton	.990	48	426	54	5	2	4
Guerra, Burlington	1.000	6	47	3	0	0	1
Hernandez, Huntington	1.000	1	18	1	0	0	2
Hopp, Martinsville	.972	16	96	10	3	0	2
Kelliher, Pulaski	1.000	4	28	5	0	1	0
Lara, Pulaski	.970	17	115	16	4	1	6
Lawson, Burlington	.988	12	70	9	1	3	1
Merritt, Johnson City	1.000	4	21	1	0	0	0
Mezzanotte, Bristol	.989	15	77	15	1	1	7
Milne, Johnson City	1.000	8	30	5	0	0	5
Patrizi, Kingsport	.983	32	215	20	4	0	5

Player, Team	Pct.	G	PO	A	E	DP	PB
Pena, Martinsville	.928	9	57	7	5	0	2
Perona, Bristol*	1.000	5	43	5	0	0	2
Prichard, Bristol	.974	23	166	19	5	0	6
Ramirez, Elizabethton	.972	18	124	15	4	2	2
Reinert, Pulaski*	1.000	8	43	2	0	0	5
Robinson, Huntington	.951	17	82	15	5	0	6
Rossler, Kingsport	1.000	3	11	2	0	0	1
Rumfield, Princeton	.970	38	283	35	10	1	9
Ruth, Martinsville	.971	5	30	3	1	1	3
Sued, Burlington	.988	43	364	47	5	6	8
Taylor, Burlington	.993	18	124	12	1	2	5
Ubina, Bristol	.943	11	39	11	3	0	1
Waszgis, Bluefield	.988	9	71	11	1	0	1
Williams, Johnson City	.969	21	163	26	6	0	2
Wolff, Huntington	.990	47	328	52	4	1	7
Yelton, Bristol	.985	33	178	18	3	3	3

PITCHERS

Player, Team	Pct.	G	PO	A	E	DP
Adams, Bristol	.933	19	3	11	1	0
Adams, Huntington	.864	14	5	14	3	1
Alexis, Martinsville	1.000	11	1	7	0	1
Anderson, Martinsville	1.000	5	3	3	0	0
Arias, Johnson City	.875	8	1	6	1	1
Avram, Johnson City	1.000	18	1	2	0	0
Balentine, Princeton*	.800	18	1	7	2	0
Barber, Johnson City	.857	14	3	9	2	1
Bauer, Bristol*	1.000	15	1	6	0	0
Behrens, Pulaski	1.000	3	1	2	0	0
Benge, Bluefield	1.000	23	1	2	0	0
Blair, Martinsville	.917	18	2	9	1	1
Bluhm, Burlington*	.778	20	3	4	2	1
Boldt, Martinsville	1.000	6	1	1	0	0
Bottalico, Martinsville	.857	7	1	5	1	0
Brothers, Princeton	1.000	3	4	3	0	0
Brown, Martinsville	.900	25	3	6	1	0
Burritt, Burlington	1.000	1	0	1	0	0
Bussa, Bristol	.625	12	1	4	3	1
Butler, Pulaski*	.833	11	0	5	1	1
Camarena, Huntington	.833	16	4	6	2	0
Caridad, Elizabethton	.750	6	2	4	2	0
Carlson, Elizabethton	1.000	27	3	10	0	1
Carr, Pulaski*	1.000	15	1	3	0	0
Cedeno, Bristol	.750	14	2	7	3	0
Chasin, Johnson City	1.000	6	2	5	0	0
Chouinard, Bluefield	1.000	6	0	2	0	0
Cochran, Johnson City	1.000	15	2	7	0	0
Coleman, Martinsville*	.947	16	2	16	1	1
Colon, Bristol	.833	6	3	2	1	0
Corbell, Kingsport	.875	16	6	8	2	3
Cotner, Kingsport*	1.000	3	0	1	0	0
Coulter, Burlington*	1.000	12	2	19	0	1
Crawford, Burlington	.828	13	4	20	5	1
Crawford, Kingsport*	.875	19	4	3	1	1
DeSantis, Martinsville	.972	12	10	25	1	0
Diaz, Elizabethton	.909	13	2	8	1	0
Doyle, Burlington	1.000	25	1	8	0	0
Dunlap, Pulaski	1.000	13	2	7	0	0
Durussel, Bristol	1.000	6	0	2	0	0
Edmondson, Bristol	1.000	12	5	16	0	2
Edwards, Martinsville	1.000	10	1	4	0	0
Eshelman, Bluefield*	1.000	3	1	1	0	0
Farrar, Bluefield*	1.000	3	1	1	0	0
Fiegel, Kingsport*	.857	11	4	8	2	1
Firsich, Bluefield	.857	11	0	6	1	1
Fitzgerald, Kingsport	.600	7	2	1	2	0
Ford, Pulaski*	.900	18	2	7	1	1
Fowler, Pulaski	1.000	6	3	0	0	0
Francis, Pulaski	.833	6	3	7	2	0
Garcia, Princeton	1.000	14	0	6	0	1
Garcia, Huntington	1.000	22	2	6	0	0
Gardner, Huntington	.882	7	4	11	2	0
Gaston, Johnson City	.818	8	2	7	2	0
Gibbs, Burlington	1.000	16	3	2	0	0
Gilmore, Martinsville	.923	11	0	12	1	0
Glover, Johnson City	.750	4	2	1	1	0
Gonzalez, Johnson City	.941	12	3	13	1	1
Gonzalez, Burlington	1.000	5	0	1	0	0
Goodson, Huntington	.667	17	1	3	2	0
Gould, Bluefield*	.941	12	0	16	1	0

Player, Team	Pct.	G	PO	A	E	DP
Guardado, Elizabethton*	.885	14	6	17	3	2
Harris, Burlington	.857	13	6	12	3	0
Henderson, Kingsport	.800	10	4	4	2	0
Hernandez, Burlington	.929	14	5	21	2	2
Hernandez, Burlington	1.000	1	0	1	0	0
Hokanson, Kingsport	1.000	17	2	4	0	0
Hostetler, Kingsport	.889	9	1	7	1	0
Hrusovsky, Princeton	.750	26	3	3	2	1
Hurst, Johnson City	1.000	2	0	1	0	0
Jacome, Kingsport*	.938	12	3	12	1	0
Jarvis, Princeton	.900	13	10	17	3	3
S. Jones, Johnson City	1.000	24	3	8	0	0
Kempfer, Pulaski	1.000	13	0	5	0	2
Key, Burlington	1.000	4	0	1	0	0
Koller, Burlington	1.000	2	1	2	0	0
Krivda, Bluefield*	.833	15	2	8	2	0
Lairsey, Pulaski*	.692	13	2	7	4	1
Lemp, Bluefield	.750	25	2	4	2	0
Lomon, Pulaski	1.000	10	1	6	0	2
Lopez, Burlington	.833	13	4	11	3	0
Lucchetti, Johnson City	.800	4	2	2	1	0
Maffett, Burlington	1.000	11	0	5	0	0
Magrini, Bristol	.625	7	1	4	3	1
McIntyre, Martinsville*	.600	13	0	3	2	0
McKinnon, Johnson City	1.000	5	0	2	0	0
Mejias, Martinsville	.846	21	3	8	2	0
Mercedes, Bluefield*	.929	16	0	13	1	0
Meyer, Huntington*	.944	17	3	14	1	0
Mezzanotte, Bristol	1.000	1	0	3	0	0
Mieses, Elizabethton	1.000	22	3	4	0	0
Miller, Princeton	.778	15	4	3	2	0
Miller, Elizabethton	1.000	4	1	4	0	0
Miller, Bristol*	1.000	13	4	9	0	1
Mitchell, Martinsville	.875	13	0	7	1	0
Morales, Princeton	.824	13	3	11	3	0
Morones, Huntington	.889	22	3	5	1	0
Murphy, Princeton	.875	13	2	5	1	0
Nahas, Pulaski	1.000	4	1	0	0	0
Nelson, Bristol	.800	8	2	2	1	0
O'Connell, Bluefield	.857	19	2	10	2	1
Pacheco, Huntington	1.000	5	1	3	0	0
Page, Martinsville	.800	16	0	4	1	0
Perpetuo, 8 Bris.-6 King.*	.750	14	0	3	1	0
Petit, Pulaski	1.000	5	2	1	0	0
Pina, Elizabethton	.917	16	8	14	2	1
Place, Bluefield	.917	12	2	9	1	0
Plaster, Bluefield	1.000	10	5	6	0	0
Portillo, Elizabethton	1.000	7	0	2	0	0
Quiles, Bristol	.800	11	2	2	1	0
Raffo, Bristol	.833	19	2	5	1	0
Ramirez, Kingsport	.958	14	5	18	1	1
Reed, Princeton	.800	13	1	11	3	1
Resendez, Burlington	.727	24	3	5	3	0
Rhodriquez, Princeton	.769	13	5	5	3	0
Roberts, Elizabethton	.800	6	1	3	1	0
Rodriguez, Bristol	1.000	2	0	1	0	0
Rodriguez, Huntington	.692	11	2	7	4	1
Rodriguez, Johnson City	.857	13	2	4	1	1
Romanoli, Johnson City*	1.000	8	1	2	0	0
Ryan, Bluefield	.920	14	5	18	2	1
Ryder, Pulaski	1.000	2	0	1	0	0
Salamon, Martinsville	1.000	6	3	3	0	0
Sample, Huntington	.667	11	1	3	2	0
Sanchez, Huntington	.909	14	4	26	3	2
Sanders, Bluefield	.950	17	8	11	1	4
Santos, Johnson City	.750	24	1	2	1	0
Sartain, Elizabethton*	.875	14	6	15	3	0
Saulter, Pulaski	1.000	8	4	0	0	1
Schorr, Kingsport	.900	11	5	13	2	1
Schwartz, Elizabethton	.500	4	1	0	1	0
Seymour, Kingsport	.941	8	5	11	1	0
Slininger, Johnson City	.941	13	4	12	1	1
Sodowsky, Bristol	1.000	14	1	16	0	1
Steph, Princeton	1.000	7	3	7	0	2
Sweeney, Elizabethton*	.923	16	1	11	1	0
Thompson, Bristol*	.833	10	2	8	2	0
Tranbarger, Johnson City*	.500	4	0	1	1	0
Trinidad, Huntington	.944	12	2	15	1	1
Viarengo, Pulaski	1.000	6	0	3	0	1
Watson, Kingsport	.955	8	5	16	1	1
Wiggins, Princeton	.846	14	1	10	2	1
WILDER, Pulaski	1.000	14	2	21	0	2

The following players did not have any fielding statistics at the positions indicated or appeared only as a designated hitter, pinch-hitter or pinch-runner: Caro, of, p; H. Colon, 2b; Dreisbach, of; Dudek, of; O. Edwards, p; G. Garcia, p; Jeffcoat, p; Knaplund, p; Mezzanotte, ss; Murray, of; Prichard, 2b; Reese, of; Ruiz, of; Schwarber, p; C. Smith, ss; Valdez, 1b; White, p.

Year	Team	Pct.	Year	Team	Pct.	Year	Team	Pct.
1921—	Greenville	.608		Bluefield z	.745	1974—	Bristol a	.754
	Johnson City*	.627	1951—	Kingsport‡	.659		Bluefield	.536
1922—	Bristol	.557	1952—	Johnson City	.595	1975—	Marion	.515
1923—	Knoxville	.635		Welch (3rd)†	.509		Johnson City a	.603
1924—	Knoxville*	.642	1953—	Welch*	.705	1976—	Johnson City a	.714
	Bristol	.607		Johnson City	.672		Bluefield	.600
1925—	Greenville	.667	1954—	Bluefield‡	.619	1977—	Kingsport	.623
1926-36—	Did not operate.		1955—	Salem**	.689	1978—	Elizabethton	.594
1937—	Elizabethton	.559	1956—	Did not operate.		1979—	Paintsville	.800
	Pennington Gap*	.580	1957—	Bluefield	.701	1980—	Paintsville	.657
1938—	Elizabethton	.664	1958—	Johnson City	.662	1981—	Paintsville	.657
	Greenville (3rd)†	.571	1959—	Morristown	.603	1982—	Bluefield a	.681
1939—	Elizabethton‡	.597	1960—	Wytheville	.614		Johnson City	.478
1940—	Johnson City§	.726	1961—	Middlesboro	.591	1983—	Paintsville	.653
	Elizabethton	.750	1962—	Bluefield	.671	1984—	Elizabethton b	.580
1941—	Johnson City	.614	1963—	Bluefield	.652		Pulaski	.536
	Elizabethton*	.661	1964—	Johnson City	.662	1985—	Bristol c	.638
1942—	Bristol	.667	1965—	Salem	.614	1986—	Johnson City	.667
	Bristol x	.660	1966—	Marion	.623		Pulaski b	.621
1943—	Bristol	.755	1967—	Bluefield	.627	1987—	Burlington b	.729
	Bristol y	.617	1968—	Marion	.583		Johnson City	.609
1944—	Kingsport‡	.575	1969—	Pulaski a	.576	1988—	Kingsport b	.644
1945—	Kingsport‡	.670		Johnson City	.544		Burlington	.529
1946—	New River‡	.675	1970—	Bluefield	.638	1989—	Elizabethton b	.691
1947—	Pulaski	.648	1971—	Bluefield a	.609		Pulaski	.618
	New River (3rd)†	.516		Kingsport	.559	1990—	Elizabethton	.761
1948—	Pulaski‡	.680	1972—	Bristol a	.588	1991—	Pulaski b	.662
1949—	Bluefield‡	.721		Covington	.586		Burlington	.597
1950—	Bluefield	.600	1973—	Kingsport	.757			

*Won split-season playoff. †Won four-team playoff. ‡Won championship and four-team playoff. §Johnson City, first-half winner, won playoff involving six clubs. xWon both halves and defeated second-place Elizabethton in playoff. yWon both halves, but Erwin won four-team playoff. zWon both halves, but Bristol won two-club playoff. **Salem and Johnson City declared playoff co-champions when weather forced cancellation of final series. aLeague was divided into Northern, Southern divisions; declared league champion, based on highest won-lost percentage. bLeague was divided into Northern, Southern divisions; won playoff for league championship. cBristol declared league champion based on regular-season record.

APPALACHIAN LEAGUE

SUMMER CLASS A

APPALACHIAN LEAGUE

ARIZONA LEAGUE

FINAL STANDINGS

Team	Ath.	Brew.	Mar.	Pad.	Car.	Ang.	Gia.	W	L	T	Pct.	GB
Athletics	....	5	7	6	6	7	8	39	21	0	.650	......
Brewers	5	....	3	5	9	5	7	34	26	0	.567	5
Mariners	3	7	....	4	6	5	8	33	27	0	.550	6
Padres	4	5	6	....	5	5	6	31	29	0	.517	8
Cardinals	4	1	4	5	....	6	9	29	30	0	.492	9½
Angels	3	5	5	5	3	....	8	29	30	0	.492	9½
Giants	2	3	2	4	1	2	....	14	46	0	.233	25

Games played in Mesa, Peoria, Scottsdale and Tempe.

Club names are major league affiliations.

Playoffs—No playoffs scheduled.

Regular-season attendance—No total official attendance figures reported.

Managers—Angels, Bill Lachemann; Athletics, Dickie Scott; Brewers, Wayne Krenchicki; Giants, Nelson Rood; Cardinals, Keith Champion; Mariners, Myron Pines; Padres, Ken Berry.

All-Star team—1B—David Mowry, Padres; 2B—Lino Connell, Angels; 3B—Jason Imperial, Brewers; SS—Manuel Cora, Padres; OF—Luinis Aracena, Athletics; Howard House, Brewers; Dennis McCaffery, Angels; C—James Bonnici, Mariners; DH—Steve Cerio, Cardinals; LHP—Brian Hancock, Brewers; RHP—George Glinatsis, Mariners; LH Rel—Charles O'Laughlin, Brewers; RH Rel—Troy Konemann, Cardinals; Most Valuable Player—Howard House, Brewers; Manager of the Year—Dickie Scott, Athletics.

BATTING

TEAM

Team	Avg.	G	AB	R	OR	H	TB	2B	3B	HR	RBI	SH	SF	HP	BB	Int. BB	SO	SB	CS	LOB
Brewers	.293	60	2095	442	376	614	832	69	40	23	365	16	36	35	327	4	408	72	40	505
Mariners	.286	60	2088	403	368	597	738	64	28	7	315	21	29	25	304	5	401	156	60	494
Padres	.283	59	2046	386	376	579	779	71	24	27	302	9	21	32	212	5	419	128	55	395
Athletics	.270	59	2012	411	334	544	688	65	17	15	315	16	28	31	333	7	364	84	22	488
Angels	.265	59	2023	353	353	536	706	62	39	10	284	21	20	28	314	5	449	62	26	500
Cardinals	.262	59	2044	351	394	535	744	84	22	27	283	5	21	37	287	9	426	56	38	474
Giants	.238	60	2011	296	445	479	619	79	17	9	239	5	23	35	301	7	496	93	50	468

INDIVIDUAL

(Leading qualifiers for batting championship—162 or more plate appearances)

*Bats lefthanded. •Switch-hitter.

Player, Team	Avg.	G	AB	R	H	TB	2B	3B	HR	RBI	SH	SF	HP	BB	Int. BB	SO	SB	CS
Stefanski, Michael, Brewers	.364	56	206	43	75	90	5	5	0	43	0	6	4	22	0	21	3	2
Cerio, Steve, Cardinals	.359	56	223	44	80	125	16	1	9	48	0	5	5	28	3	32	4	4
Keene, Andre, Giants*	.348	44	138	30	48	66	11	2	1	30	0	5	2	33	0	25	12	4
Cora, Manuel, Padres†	.347	49	199	38	69	87	8	5	0	32	1	4	2	17	0	27	12	10
Cabrera, Juan, Athletics†	.340	41	156	41	53	71	5	2	3	40	0	1	2	13	0	23	20	3
Aracena, Luinis, Athletics	.335	56	212	58	71	89	6	6	0	24	3	1	5	41	0	40	12	1
Bonnici, James, Mariners	.331	51	178	36	59	69	2	4	0	38	0	5	6	44	0	31	8	2
House, Howard, Brewers*	.330	55	209	54	69	111	8	8	6	45	1	1	1	38	1	45	9	6
Connell, Lino, Angels†	.324	56	216	43	70	104	8	10	2	40	6	1	1	30	0	64	6	5
Leary, Rob, Athletics*	.324	59	213	42	69	88	11	1	2	44	1	4	3	51	1	21	2	2

Departmental leaders: G—Leary, Simmons, 59; AB—K. House, 232; R—Aracena, 58; H—Cerio, 80; TB—Cerio, 125; 2B—Cerio, Wachter, 16; 3B—Connell, 10; HR—Cerio, 9; RBI—Cerio, 48; SH—Connell, 6; SF—F. Cruz, Valentin, 7; HP—Robinson, 8; BB—Leary, 51; IBB—Cerio, Jensen, Underwood, 3; SO—Bieri, 66; SB—Bullock, 35; CS—B. Rivera, 11.

(All players—listed alphabetically)

Player, Team	Avg.	G	AB	R	H	TB	2B	3B	HR	RBI	SH	SF	HP	BB	Int. BB	SO	SB	CS
Alcantara, Milciades, Mariners	.192	36	99	16	19	19	0	0	0	8	3	0	0	22	1	35	4	5
Alcaraz, Vlad, Angels	.223	51	157	24	35	49	5	3	1	24	0	3	3	39	2	28	2	0
Alimena, Charlie, Giants*	.251	50	179	19	45	65	10	2	2	33	0	4	2	21	2	44	5	5
Anderson, Jonathan, Angels	.211	17	57	4	12	12	0	0	0	7	0	1	1	6	1	13	0	0
Andrea, Leroy, Brewers	.300	4	10	2	3	3	0	0	0	1	0	0	0	1	0	4	2	1
Aracena, Luinis, Athletics	.335	56	212	58	71	89	6	6	0	24	3	1	5	41	0	40	12	1
Bailey, Reggie, Athletics	.212	13	33	7	7	13	3	0	1	3	0	0	1	5	0	9	0	1
Ballara, Juan, Cardinals	.216	53	185	25	40	66	7	5	3	26	0	0	2	20	1	61	1	3
Benschoter, Adam, Giants	.295	51	183	41	54	76	11	4	1	26	0	5	4	34	1	28	12	3
Bertucci, Joe, Angels	.170	30	100	15	17	24	3	2	0	10	0	2	0	11	0	27	3	1
Bieri, Chad, Brewers	.240	58	175	39	42	55	2	1	3	20	3	3	3	37	0	66	4	2
Blankenship, Kenny, Brewers†	.209	23	67	4	14	14	0	0	0	5	1	1	0	5	0	6	0	1
Blomeyer, Mike, Giants	.205	30	88	5	18	21	1	1	0	6	0	0	3	12	0	32	4	2
Bolivar, Rico, Giants	.129	26	85	3	11	15	2	1	0	7	0	2	2	0	0	33	0	1
Bonnici, James, Mariners	.331	51	178	36	59	69	2	4	0	38	0	5	6	44	0	31	8	2
Borzello, Mike, Cardinals	.222	9	18	3	4	6	2	0	0	2	0	1	1	2	0	2	0	0
Brannon, Paul, Mariners	.182	3	11	1	2	4	0	1	0	1	0	0	0	0	0	2	0	0
Buckler, Mark, Athletics	.213	43	122	18	26	26	0	0	0	13	0	3	4	16	0	25	5	1
Bullock, Renaldo, Mariners	.363	29	102	35	37	46	2	2	1	17	2	0	2	14	0	17	35	8
Bush, Homer, Padres	.323	32	127	16	41	48	3	2	0	16	0	0	1	4	1	33	11	7
Cabrera, Juan, Athletics†	.340	41	156	41	53	71	5	2	3	40	0	1	2	13	0	23	20	3
Callicott, Curt, Cardinals	.209	41	115	19	24	31	2	1	1	12	0	0	3	11	0	30	4	2
Carrion, German, Padres†	.275	33	120	17	33	35	2	0	0	13	1	1	6	9	1	14	6	3
Carty, Rico, Athletics	.362	16	47	4	17	21	2	1	0	9	0	0	0	5	0	2	0	1
Casey, Johnny, Brewers	.253	52	186	32	47	56	5	2	0	29	2	3	5	24	0	26	3	5
Casper, Tim, Giants	.286	11	42	6	12	15	3	0	0	2	1	0	0	3	0	7	6	1
Castro, Antonio, Angels	.191	19	68	7	13	14	1	0	0	10	0	3	0	7	0	23	1	2
Cerio, Steve, Cardinals	.359	56	223	44	80	125	16	1	9	48	0	5	5	28	3	32	4	4
Connell, Lino, Angels†	.324	56	216	43	70	104	8	10	2	40	6	1	1	30	0	64	6	5

Player, Team	Avg.	G	AB	R	H	TB	2B	3B	HR	RBI	SH	SF	HP	BB	Int. BB	SO	SB	CS
Cookson, Brent, Athletics	.000	1	1	0	0	0	0	0	0	0	0	0	0	0	0	1	0	0
Cora, Manuel, Padres†	.347	49	199	38	69	87	8	5	0	32	1	4	2	17	0	27	12	10
Creer, Jerry, Padres*	.310	10	29	9	9	11	2	0	0	0	0	0	0	7	0	10	8	0
Cruz, Fausto, Athletics	.278	52	180	38	50	60	2	1	2	36	3	7	3	32	0	23	3	0
Cruz, Javier, Mariners	.279	41	129	21	36	43	4	0	1	24	0	1	0	16	1	16	9	5
Cruz, Juan, Padres	.265	38	136	23	36	61	3	2	6	21	0	1	4	3	0	30	15	1
DeJesus, Anito, Padres	.355	23	93	18	33	45	2	2	2	11	0	0	1	4	0	5	0	1
de la Cruz, Marcelino, Padres	.212	19	66	13	14	17	1	1	0	11	0	0	1	5	0	15	1	0
DeLeon, Jose, Mariners	.268	24	71	12	19	22	1	1	0	9	1	0	0	5	0	11	0	1
Dilone, Juan, Athletics†	.222	48	153	26	34	36	2	0	0	21	1	4	0	37	2	45	5	3
Dobrolsky, William, Brewers	.292	5	24	3	7	11	4	0	0	5	0	0	0	3	0	3	0	0
Donati, John, Angels	.272	42	114	28	31	42	6	1	1	21	0	3	3	34	0	37	1	2
Dotolo, Chris, Giants	.179	13	39	5	7	8	1	0	0	6	0	0	1	7	0	12	3	0
Eicher, Mike, Cardinals	.295	48	183	33	54	77	5	6	2	31	1	2	1	24	0	26	0	2
Enriquez, Luis, Brewers†	.302	21	63	14	19	31	4	1	2	18	0	1	3	11	1	11	5	1
Foster, Ron, Giants	.226	35	124	15	28	39	8	0	1	13	0	0	0	16	0	33	4	1
Francisco, David, Athletics	.236	56	208	34	49	67	7	4	1	34	2	1	2	24	0	29	14	5
Francisco, Vicente, Athletics†	.202	33	119	18	24	32	3	1	1	9	2	1	1	13	1	26	2	0
Frazier, Julian, Giants	.176	32	85	9	15	15	0	0	0	3	0	0	0	17	0	36	5	2
Fults, Tony, Athletics*	.000	11	1	0	0	0	0	0	0	0	0	0	0	0	0	1	0	0
Furtado, Tim, Mariners	.381	37	113	27	43	50	5	1	0	16	0	1	0	21	0	9	3	3
Goins, Tim, Padres	.271	43	133	18	36	38	2	0	0	13	0	1	3	9	1	20	5	3
Greene, Charles, Padres	.284	49	183	27	52	84	15	1	5	38	2	6	3	16	0	26	6	1
Griffey, Craig, Mariners	.253	45	150	36	38	41	1	1	0	20	2	2	1	28	0	35	11	6
Guerrero, Pasquale, Brewers	.000	7	0	1	0	0	0	0	0	0	0	0	0	0	0	0	0	0
Hardwick, Joe, Angels	.220	43	127	30	28	32	0	2	0	12	6	1	5	28	0	36	15	4
Helms, Mike, Giants	.333	1	3	0	1	1	0	0	0	1	0	0	0	1	0	1	0	0
Henry, Antione, Cardinals	.263	42	160	40	42	47	5	0	0	15	0	1	3	33	0	33	12	7
House, Howard, Brewers*	.330	55	209	54	69	111	8	8	6	45	1	1	1	38	1	45	9	6
House, Ken, Brewers	.293	58	232	39	68	92	13	4	1	38	2	3	6	25	2	42	3	0
Imperial, Jason, Brewers	.341	33	129	38	44	62	8	5	0	33	0	4	4	23	0	25	0	2
Jensen, Marcus, Giants†	.284	48	155	28	44	64	8	3	2	30	0	4	5	34	3	22	4	2
Jones, Butter, Giants	.259	39	139	24	36	50	7	2	1	16	2	1	3	15	0	30	6	2
Keene, Andre, Giants*	.348	44	138	30	48	66	11	2	1	30	0	5	2	33	0	25	12	4
Konemann, Troy, Cardinals†	1.000	29	1	1	1	1	0	0	0	0	0	0	0	0	0	0	0	0
Lawson, David, Mariners*	.283	46	145	29	41	62	9	3	2	20	0	1	2	37	2	56	12	5
Leary, Rob, Athletics*	.324	59	213	42	69	88	11	1	2	44	1	4	3	51	1	21	2	1
Llanos, Victor, Cardinals	.250	42	168	24	42	56	14	0	0	23	0	2	2	13	1	46	0	1
Martin, Ronnie, Angels	.169	32	89	10	15	21	2	2	0	3	0	0	0	9	0	39	3	0
Martinez, Eduardo, Mariners	.247	31	93	10	23	26	3	0	0	8	0	1	2	11	0	24	3	3
Matos, Alberto, Padres	.245	31	98	21	24	32	3	1	1	11	1	0	1	6	0	29	3	5
McCaffery, Dennis, Angels	.323	54	220	46	71	84	5	4	0	37	1	2	4	25	0	18	6	4
Melendez, J.C., Mariners†	.276	44	134	24	37	48	9	1	0	24	2	1	1	14	0	20	4	1
Mendez, Ricardo, Athletics	.253	49	170	43	43	58	9	0	2	24	0	1	4	28	0	29	3	1
Mendoza, Francisco, Brewers†	.265	51	155	29	41	48	3	2	0	12	3	0	2	18	0	33	8	4
Millay, Keith, Athletics*	.000	18	1	0	0	0	0	0	0	0	0	0	0	0	0	0	0	0
Moncion, Manuel, Athletics	.232	35	112	11	26	35	7	1	0	16	1	2	1	7	0	30	3	0
Moncion, Pedro, Mariners	.230	34	87	17	20	21	1	0	0	10	2	2	0	18	0	17	2	1
Morgan, Charlie, Athletics	.000	6	1	0	0	0	0	0	0	0	0	0	0	0	0	0	0	0
Mota, Santo, Cardinals†	.238	26	101	16	24	29	3	1	0	10	1	0	1	11	0	17	12	4
Mowry, David, Padres*	.364	26	99	23	36	58	7	0	5	25	0	1	2	20	2	13	8	4
Musolino, Michael, Angels*	.154	4	13	1	2	5	0	0	1	2	0	0	0	3	0	1	0	0
Myers, Tom, Athletics*	.000	24	1	1	0	0	0	0	0	0	0	0	0	0	0	0	0	0
Oliver, Felix, Angels	.262	30	84	14	22	37	4	4	1	15	0	0	9	0	17	1	0
Pantoja, Thor, Giants	.248	36	117	14	29	35	3	0	1	10	0	0	3	12	0	32	4	5
Perez, Ralph, Padres*	.274	44	164	34	45	52	5	1	0	23	1	1	0	23	0	28	5	1
Perez, Susano, Padres	.217	20	69	10	15	25	1	3	1	10	1	1	0	8	0	23	2	1
Pineiro, Juan, Angels	.280	43	157	23	44	61	5	3	2	28	0	1	2	12	0	23	1	1
Powell, L.V., Mariners	.300	36	120	22	36	48	6	3	0	20	1	2	6	13	0	28	20	7
Preikszas, Dave, Brewers*	.339	16	62	12	21	31	2	1	2	12	0	1	1	6	0	12	4	1
Ramirez, Hiram, Giants	.163	26	49	5	8	9	1	0	0	4	0	1	1	6	0	17	0	2
Ramos, Martin, Mariners	.200	11	30	6	6	9	0	0	1	3	0	0	1	0	0	10	0	1
Relaford, Desmond, Mariners†	.270	46	163	36	44	57	7	3	0	18	1	5	1	22	1	24	17	2
Rivera, Alex, Padres	.194	12	31	11	6	8	0	1	0	6	0	0	0	6	0	8	1	1
Rivera, Bolivar, Mariners	.239	50	180	33	43	49	2	2	0	10	0	1	0	21	1	42	23	11
Roberts, John, Padres	.297	42	148	30	44	66	8	4	2	23	0	2	3	25	0	36	19	3
Robertson, Tommy, Mariners*	.331	34	142	28	47	66	3	5	2	30	1	3	0	10	0	11	8	4
Robinson, Alan, Cardinals	.246	50	138	30	34	40	2	2	0	15	1	0	8	26	0	26	14	2
Rodrigues, Cecil, Brewers	.234	29	111	19	26	29	3	0	0	7	0	1	1	25	0	19	11	5
Ross, Jackie, Brewers†	.297	40	158	47	47	59	3	3	1	24	0	1	3	38	1	21	14	5
Salazar, Elias, Giants	.119	22	67	9	8	10	2	0	0	5	0	0	0	5	0	26	0	2
Scott, Sean, Athletics*	.263	36	99	21	26	32	4	1	0	19	1	1	0	26	1	27	2	1
Serafini, Steve, Brewers	1.000	1	2	0	2	2	0	0	0	0	0	0	0	0	0	0	0	0
Sierra, Roberto, Angels	.255	45	161	30	41	50	4	1	1	20	3	0	1	33	0	20	3	4
Sievers, Jason, Giants	.247	29	73	10	18	22	4	0	0	14	1	0	3	16	0	14	1	2
Simmons, Mark, Angels	.294	50	228	48	67	79	6	3	0	17	3	0	2	43	0	61	17	3
Slattery, Don, Cardinals*	.244	53	172	28	42	56	7	2	1	20	0	2	0	42	1	27	2	2
Smith, Brandon, Athletics	.198	36	111	16	22	28	3	0	1	10	1	2	3	16	0	24	1	3
Sosa, Francisco, Mariners	.280	34	118	18	33	41	6	1	0	21	3	2	3	7	0	20	8	2
Stefanski, Michael, Brewers	.364	56	206	43	75	90	5	5	0	43	0	6	4	22	0	21	3	2
Stewart, Reggie, Padres	.313	41	112	26	35	39	4	0	0	14	1	0	4	12	0	27	11	7
Stillwell, Mark, Brewers*	.140	19	50	3	7	7	0	0	0	5	0	1	4	4	0	16	0	0
Strehlow, Robert, Cardinals	.200	29	60	7	12	16	1	0	1	5	0	0	4	8	0	20	1	4
Sumner, Chad, Cardinals	.281	38	146	23	41	58	5	3	2	26	0	3	0	18	0	25	2	1
Sutch, Rick, Athletics	.000	23	1	0	0	0	0	0	0	0	0	0	0	0	0	0	0	0
Thomas, Byron, Mariners	.246	40	134	24	33	38	3	1	0	17	3	3	1	16	0	31	12	3
Thomas, Juan, Giants	.000	1	3	0	0	0	0	0	0	0	0	0	0	0	0	1	0	0
Thompson, Paul, Padres*	.183	31	93	16	17	36	2	1	5	18	0	3	1	22	0	47	1	2
Trisler, John, Athletics	.000	8	1	0	0	0	0	0	0	0	0	0	0	0	0	1	0	0
Tucker, Rob, Brewers	.296	39	115	19	34	37	1	1	0	21	1	3	2	12	0	17	0	3
Ugueto, Hector, Cardinals	.207	54	179	30	37	45	6	1	0	13	1	0	4	29	0	49	4	2
Underwood, Curt, Cardinals*	.301	52	183	28	55	88	9	0	8	35	0	6	3	23	3	28	0	0
Valencia, Max, Giants	.209	26	86	16	18	19	1	0	0	5	0	2	2	8	0	19	1	4
Valentin, Jose, Brewers	.312	52	186	31	58	84	5	6	3	43	5	7	4	22	0	23	6	2
Valverde, Osvaldo, Mariners	.318	7	22	1	7	7	0	0	0	2	0	0	0	0	0	2	0	0

Player, Team	Avg.	G	AB	R	H	TB	2B	3B	HR	RBI	SH	SF	HP	BB	Int. BB	SO	SB	CS
Vazquez, Pedro, Padres	.288	20	73	15	21	24	3	0	0	9	1	0	0	5	0	14	6	2
Vega, Julio, Giants†	.257	37	113	14	29	33	4	0	0	16	0	0	2	15	0	20	2	1
Wachter, Derek, Brewers	.312	51	186	52	58	102	16	5	6	42	0	4	1	41	1	59	3	0
Walker, Dane, Athletics*	.373	29	118	37	44	53	3	0	2	22	1	0	2	24	1	11	12	1
Walton, Shelby, Cardinals	.250	4	12	0	3	3	0	0	0	2	1	0	0	1	0	4	0	4
Williams, Thurman, Giants	.111	24	63	10	7	7	0	0	0	2	1	0	3	10	0	22	1	1
Wyatt, Dwight, Padres	.178	22	73	21	13	13	0	0	0	8	0	0	0	11	0	14	8	3

The following pitchers, listed alphabetically by club, with games in parentheses, had no plate appearances, primarily through use of designated hitters:

ANGELS—Butler, Mike (11); Heusman, Theron (19); Knox, Jeff (6); Ledinsky, Mark (1); Merrill, Larry (6); Musset, Jose (10); Myers, Matt (21); Parker, Richard (15); Parra, Domingo (12); Rivera, Carlos (7); Sebach, Kyle (13); Severino, Blas (13); Sheehy, Mike (5); Williard, Brian (12); Young, Fred (8).

ATHLETICS—Acre, Mark (6); Fermin, Ramon (7); Lara, Nelson (14); Light, Jeff (2); Mejia, Delfino (4); Pierce, Rob (20); Rossiter, Mike (10); Sawyer, Zach (10); Shoemaker, Steve (8); Smock, Greg (15); Stowell, Brad (12).

BREWERS—Blair, Donnie (13); Browne, Byron (13); Christopher, Terry (2); Criminger, John (18); Farrell, Mike (6); Gorrell, Rob (7); Hancock, Mike (7); Jarvis, Rick (7); Ma, Young (11); Nicolau, Travis (13); O'Laughlin, Charles (13); Perez, Leo (2); Ramirez, Domingo (4); Rutter, Samuel (11); Vonderlieth, Scott (10); Wilkie, Jim (7); Wilstead, Judd (1); Zurn, Ricky (9).

CARDINALS—Balke, Peter (5); Busby, Ray (11); Davis, Clint (21); Davis, Ray (11); Dillman, Jeff (15); Guyton, Duffy (13); Jeffcoat, Mike (21); Lindauer, Dirk (19); Marchesi, Jim (12); McKinnon, Tom (1); Miller, Eric (15); Smith, Chad (14); Spencer, Charles (10); Tranbarger, Mark (23).

GIANTS—Brown, Kevin (7); Collins, Doug (13); Gambs, Chris (13); Gomez, Marcial (9); Guigni, Ramon (7); Henrichs, Shawn (5); Hernandez, Charlie (16); Israel, Kurtis (16); Locklear, Jeff (17); Martin, Jeff (12); Myers, Mike (1); Perez, Hector (10); Peysar, Charles (14); Pote, Louis (8); Stroth, Scott (14); Towns, Vince (12); Valdez, Carlos (13).

MARINERS—Dixon, Scottie (5); Ebert, Scott (12); Gargagliano, Dion (20); Glinatsis, George (12); Hartman, Kelly (15); Jenkins, Kevin (9); Lowe, Derek (12); Mantei, Matthew (17); Paulino, Angel (14); Pena, Antonio (2); Scales, Stan (5); Smith, Ryan (13); Soto, Luis (28); Sullivan, Daniel (25); Sylve, Bernard (9); Vandemark, John (1); Vargas, Carlos (16); Winzer, Kenny (1).

PADRES—Anthony, Greg (7); Barnes, Jon (12); Burns, Jerry (12); Compton, Robert (12); D'Amato, Brian (13); Diaz, Luis (18); Fjeld, Randy (16); Hollinger, Adrian (8); Loiselle, Richard (12); Narcisse, Tyrone (11); Santiago, Jenny (15); Spears, Chris (18); Vazquez, Archie (17).

GRAND SLAMS—Enriquez, Leary, 1 each.

AWARDED FIRST BASE ON CATCHER'S INTERFERENCE—Ballara (Tucker); Blomeyer (Ballara); Griffey (Jensen); Sievers (Bertucci); Walker (Anderson).

PITCHING

TEAM

Team	ERA	G	CG	ShO	Sv.	IP	H	R	ER	HR	HB	BB	Int. BB	SO	WP	Bk.
Athletics	4.27	59	1	3	16	516.0	475	334	245	22	31	302	4	422	41	28
Mariners	4.30	60	2	2	8	527.1	566	368	252	15	47	302	4	412	86	31
Angels	4.61	59	2	0	10	513.2	530	353	263	14	34	286	2	434	45	19
Brewers	4.80	60	4	0	12	524.2	523	376	280	11	32	319	9	461	54	31
Padres	4.89	59	1	3	16	513.2	551	376	279	23	29	293	17	406	45	25
Cardinals	5.42	59	0	0	17	524.2	611	394	316	13	28	247	1	460	44	23
Giants	6.14	60	0	0	5	522.0	628	445	356	20	22	329	5	368	57	31

INDIVIDUAL

(Leading qualifiers for earned-run average leadership—48 or more innings)

*Throws lefthanded.

Pitcher, Team	W	L	Pct.	ERA	G	GS	CG	GF	ShO	Sv.	IP	H	R	ER	HR	HB	BB	Int. BB	SO	WP
Glinatsis, Mariners	10	2	.833	2.19	12	12	0	0	0	0	74.0	63	35	18	1	8	32	0	80	17
Lowe, Mariners	5	3	.625	2.41	12	12	0	0	0	0	71.0	58	26	19	1	2	21	0	60	4
Hernandez, Giants	3	3	.500	2.42	16	4	0	10	0	0	48.1	44	16	13	1	3	25	0	26	3
Rutter, Brewers	5	2	.714	3.28	11	8	1	1	0	0	57.2	45	34	21	1	5	25	0	58	5
Millay, Athletics	6	1	.857	3.43	17	8	0	4	0	0	60.1	32	29	23	2	2	48	0	69	1
Busby, Cardinals	4	3	.571	3.51	11	11	0	0	0	0	59.0	67	35	23	1	2	29	0	71	3
Loiselle, Padres	2	3	.400	3.52	12	12	0	0	0	0	61.1	72	40	24	1	3	26	0	47	4
Zurn, Brewers	4	3	.571	3.53	9	9	0	0	0	0	51.0	34	26	20	0	4	27	1	49	7
Paulino, Mariners	3	3	.500	3.60	14	12	0	0	0	0	65.0	65	35	26	4	6	29	0	41	4
Smith, Cardinals	3	2	.600	3.72	14	10	0	0	0	0	67.2	67	39	28	0	11	0	54	4

Departmental leaders: G—Konemann, Soto, 28; W—Glinatsis, 10; L—Browne, Gomez, R. Smith, Williard, 6; Pct.—Millay, .857; GS—R. Smith, 13; CG—R. Smith, 2; GF—Konemann, 26; ShO—None.; Sv.—Konemann, 16; IP—R. Smith, 75; H—Marchesi, 89; R—Browne, 65; ER—Browne, 52; HR—Barnes, Burns, Paulino, Pierce, Sebach, Sutch, 4; HB—R. Smith, 11; BB—Browne, 67; IBB—Henrichs, Spears, 3; SO—Glinatsis, 80; WP—Glinatsis, 17.

(All pitchers—listed alphabetically)

Pitcher, Team	W	L	Pct.	ERA	G	GS	CG	GF	ShO	Sv.	IP	H	R	ER	HR	HB	BB	Int. BB	SO	WP
Acre, Athletics	2	0	1.000	2.70	6	0	0	2	0	0	10.0	10	3	3	0	0	6	0	6	0
Anthony, Padres	1	1	.500	1.65	7	7	0	0	0	0	27.1	17	8	5	1	4	17	0	22	1
Aracena, Athletics*	0	0	.000	0.00	1	0	0	0	0	0	1.0	1	0	0	0	0	1	0	0	0
Balke, Cardinals*	0	2	.000	17.05	5	0	0	0	0	0	6.1	10	12	12	1	0	14	1	5	0
Barnes, Padres	2	5	.286	5.19	11	11	1	0	0	0	52.0	52	37	30	4	4	25	1	42	7
Blair, Brewers	1	1	.500	8.03	7	7	0	0	0	0	24.2	35	27	22	1	1	10	0	12	2
Brown, Giants	0	3	.000	9.20	7	2	0	2	0	0	14.2	28	22	15	0	1	7	0	7	1
Browne, Brewers	1	6	.143	8.07	13	11	0	0	0	0	58.0	69	65	52	2	5	67	1	68	14
Buckler, Athletics	0	0	.000	0.00	3	0	0	3	0	0	4.1	1	1	0	0	0	2	0	3	0
Burns, Padres	4	3	.571	4.88	12	12	0	0	0	0	66.1	73	45	36	4	1	26	2	44	1
Busby, Cardinals	4	3	.571	3.51	11	11	0	0	0	0	59.0	67	35	23	1	2	29	0	71	3
Butler, Angels*	2	1	.667	4.11	11	7	0	4	0	0	50.1	50	29	23	2	1	26	0	57	5
Christopher, Brewers	0	0	.000	4.91	2	0	0	0	0	0	3.2	3	2	2	0	0	3	0	5	0
Collins, Giants	0	1	.000	11.63	13	2	0	5	0	0	21.2	27	34	28	2	1	28	0	13	13
Compton, Padres	1	1	.500	6.05	12	0	0	9	0	1	19.1	23	20	13	2	1	11	1	26	3
Criminger, Brewers	1	2	.333	5.82	18	0	0	18	0	3	21.2	26	18	14	1	0	8	1	31	2
D'Amato, Padres	1	2	.333	7.77	13	0	0	6	0	4	24.1	35	24	21	0	0	17	2	15	3
C. Davis, Cardinals	3	3	.500	5.74	21	0	0	9	0	0	26.2	35	23	17	0	3	12	0	25	1

— 510 —

Pitcher, Team	W	L	Pct.	ERA	G	GS	CG	GF	ShO	Sv.	IP	H	R	ER	HR	HB	BB	Int. BB	SO	WP
R. Davis, Cardinals	2	3	.400	6.75	11	10	0	0	0	0	54.2	71	47	41	2	1	24	0	31	3
DeLeon, Mariners	0	0	.000	13.50	1	0	0	0	0	0	0.2	2	1	1	0	0	0	0	0	0
Diaz, Padres	5	1	.833	3.04	18	0	0	12	0	5	47.1	39	23	16	3	4	16	2	33	3
Dillman, Cardinals	1	1	.500	6.18	15	1	0	3	0	0	27.2	44	25	19	2	1	6	0	28	1
Dilone, Athletics	0	0	.000	3.00	2	0	0	2	0	0	3.0	1	1	1	0	1	0	0	1	0
Dixon, Mariners	0	0	.000	2.57	5	0	0	1	0	0	7.0	7	2	2	0	1	4	0	4	5
Ebert, Mariners	0	1	.000	8.04	12	0	0	3	0	0	15.2	11	15	14	0	5	17	0	9	7
Farrell, Brewers*	2	1	.667	4.64	6	2	0	1	0	0	21.1	25	15	11	1	0	3	0	17	0
Fermin, Athletics	3	0	1.000	2.13	7	3	1	1	0	0	25.1	20	6	6	2	4	4	0	11	0
Fjeld, Padres	6	3	.667	5.33	16	5	0	3	0	0	50.2	56	42	30	2	4	30	2	37	5
D. Francisco, Athletics	0	0	.000	27.00	1	0	0	0	0	0	0.1	0	1	1	0	0	2	0	0	0
V. Francisco, Athletics	0	0	.000	0.00	1	0	0	1	0	0	0.2	0	0	0	0	0	2	0	0	0
Fults, Athletics*	1	2	.333	5.85	11	6	0	1	0	0	32.1	29	28	21	0	5	41	0	30	8
Gambs, Giants	1	5	.167	8.37	13	8	0	0	0	0	47.1	65	51	44	1	2	34	1	36	4
Gargagliano, Mariners*	1	0	1.000	8.22	20	1	0	3	0	0	23.0	28	27	21	1	4	23	0	28	4
Glinatsis, Mariners	10	2	.833	2.19	12	12	0	0	0	0	74.0	63	35	18	1	8	32	0	80	17
Gomez, Giants	1	6	.143	10.45	9	6	0	0	0	0	31.0	53	37	36	3	2	19	0	16	0
Gorrell, Brewers	1	3	.250	3.69	7	5	1	2	0	0	31.2	28	17	13	1	4	17	0	30	2
Guerrero, Brewers	0	1	.000	10.13	6	0	0	1	0	1	13.1	19	16	15	0	0	16	1	10	1
Guigni, Giants*	0	2	.000	12.71	7	1	0	2	0	0	11.1	19	19	16	3	1	9	0	6	4
Guyton, Cardinals	0	1	.000	8.89	13	0	0	4	0	0	26.1	40	29	26	2	1	12	0	12	0
Hancock, Brewers*	6	0	1.000	2.18	7	7	1	0	0	0	45.1	32	19	11	1	0	21	0	49	1
Hartman, Mariners	0	1	.000	7.31	15	0	0	2	0	0	16.0	23	15	13	1	0	19	0	15	1
Henrichs, Giants	0	0	.000	6.48	5	0	0	4	0	1	8.1	11	6	6	0	0	10	3	8	1
Hernandez, Giants	3	3	.500	2.42	16	4	0	10	0	0	48.1	44	16	13	1	3	25	0	26	3
Heusman, Angels*	4	1	.800	2.76	19	1	0	9	0	0	45.2	47	27	14	1	3	30	0	50	3
Hollinger, Padres	1	1	.500	12.75	8	0	0	3	0	0	12.0	21	20	17	1	0	16	2	14	1
Israel, Giants	1	2	.333	5.03	16	1	0	12	0	2	34.0	42	24	19	0	3	20	1	24	2
Jarvis, Brewers	0	2	.000	5.65	7	1	0	5	0	1	14.1	20	12	9	0	2	6	0	11	1
Jeffcoat, Cardinals	2	2	.500	6.08	21	0	0	5	0	1	26.2	24	21	18	0	4	8	0	32	2
Jenkins, Mariners	1	1	.500	9.90	9	1	0	4	0	0	10.0	18	14	11	1	0	11	0	7	6
Knox, Angels	0	4	.000	6.28	6	6	0	0	0	0	28.2	36	29	20	1	4	11	0	26	0
Konemann, Cardinals	1	2	.333	4.97	28	0	0	26	0	16	29.0	32	20	16	0	1	14	0	32	2
Lara, Athletics*	5	1	.833	3.79	14	10	0	2	0	0	54.2	52	31	23	1	3	26	0	31	2
Leary, Athletics*	0	0	.000	13.50	2	0	0	1	0	0	2.0	3	3	3	0	0	1	0	0	0
Ledinsky, Angels*	0	1	.000	10.80	1	0	0	1	0	0	1.2	3	2	2	1	0	0	0	0	0
Light, Athletics	0	0	.000	2.25	2	0	0	2	0	2	4.0	3	1	1	0	0	0	0	1	0
Lindauer, Cardinals	3	1	.750	4.33	19	1	0	2	0	0	35.1	33	18	17	2	1	24	0	36	1
Locklear, Giants*	2	3	.400	4.13	17	0	0	11	0	0	28.1	34	21	13	1	0	22	0	19	1
Loiselle, Padres	2	3	.400	3.52	12	12	0	0	0	0	61.1	72	40	24	1	3	26	0	47	4
Lowe, Mariners	5	3	.625	2.41	12	12	0	0	0	0	71.0	58	26	19	1	2	21	0	60	1
Ma, Brewers	2	0	1.000	2.22	11	0	0	4	0	1	24.1	26	13	6	0	3	9	2	11	1
Mantei, Mariners	1	4	.200	6.69	17	5	0	4	0	0	40.1	54	40	30	0	1	28	2	29	7
Marchesi, Cardinals	4	3	.571	4.22	12	12	0	0	0	0	64.0	89	45	30	2	3	18	0	49	3
Martin, Giants	4	2	.200	5.67	12	10	0	1	0	1	54.0	58	40	34	3	0	22	0	42	1
McKinnon, Cardinals	0	1	.000	19.13	3	3	0	0	0	0	8.0	9	20	17	0	4	16	0	5	13
Mejia, Athletics	2	1	.667	2.45	4	4	0	0	0	0	22.0	19	11	6	0	1	8	0	17	3
Merrill, Angels	0	2	.000	4.50	6	3	0	1	0	0	24.0	27	16	12	0	0	9	0	12	0
Millay, Athletics	6	1	.857	3.43	17	8	0	4	0	0	60.1	32	29	23	2	2	48	0	69	1
Miller, Cardinals	2	1	.667	1.96	15	1	0	6	0	0	23.0	23	7	5	0	1	7	0	11	0
Morgan, Athletics	0	0	.000	7.88	6	0	0	3	0	0	8.0	8	7	7	0	0	11	0	3	0
Mowry, Padres*	0	0	.000	9.00	1	0	0	1	0	0	1.0	2	1	1	0	0	2	0	1	0
Musset, Giants	1	1	.500	3.21	10	0	0	10	0	2	14.0	14	7	5	0	1	5	0	10	1
Myers, Angels	4	2	.667	4.45	21	4	0	6	0	1	58.2	55	35	29	3	5	19	0	46	5
Myers, Giants*	0	1	.000	12.00	1	0	0	0	0	0	3.0	5	5	4	0	0	2	0	2	0
Myers, Athletics*	2	4	.333	3.24	22	1	0	13	0	4	33.1	39	32	12	3	1	21	1	36	4
Narcisse, Padres	2	3	.400	7.47	11	10	0	0	0	0	37.1	43	41	31	1	4	37	0	23	5
Nicolau, Brewers	2	0	1.000	7.76	13	3	0	5	0	1	31.1	32	31	27	0	1	40	0	15	7
O'Laughlin, Brewers*	6	2	.750	3.80	13	4	1	4	0	0	66.1	61	35	28	2	3	26	1	44	6
Parker, Athletics	2	1	.667	2.70	15	0	0	15	0	5	16.2	13	6	5	0	0	8	0	8	2
Parra, Angels	0	1	.000	7.39	12	0	0	5	0	1	28.0	36	26	23	0	3	22	0	14	3
Paulino, Mariners	3	3	.500	3.60	14	12	0	0	0	0	65.0	65	35	26	4	6	29	0	41	4
Pena, Mariners	0	1	.000	0.00	2	0	0	0	0	0	2.0	4	4	0	0	0	2	0	0	1
Perez, Giants	0	3	.000	4.01	10	2	0	3	0	1	24.2	28	17	11	0	1	4	0	21	1
Perez, Brewers	0	0	.000	3.00	2	1	0	1	0	1	6.0	6	4	2	1	1	0	0	3	0
Peysar, Giants	0	1	.000	9.24	14	0	0	3	0	0	25.1	26	30	26	0	6	33	0	19	5
Pierce, Athletics	2	2	.500	5.60	20	2	0	5	0	2	53.0	59	48	33	4	5	30	2	34	9
Pote, Giants	2	3	.400	2.55	8	8	0	0	0	0	42.1	38	23	12	0	0	19	0	41	5
Ramirez, Brewers*	0	1	.000	8.84	4	1	0	0	0	0	9.2	16	11	9	0	1	7	0	7	0
Ramos, Mariners	0	0	.000	27.00	1	0	0	1	0	0	0.2	2	2	2	0	0	2	0	1	0
Rivera, Angels	4	3	.571	4.19	7	7	0	0	0	0	43.0	54	30	20	0	2	16	0	34	1
Ross, Brewers	0	0	.000	9.00	1	0	0	0	0	0	1.0	2	1	1	0	0	1	0	1	0
Rossiter, Athletics	3	4	.429	3.99	10	9	0	0	0	0	38.1	43	24	17	3	2	22	0	35	6
Rutter, Brewers	5	2	.714	3.28	11	8	1	1	0	0	57.2	45	34	21	1	5	25	0	58	5
Santiago, Padres	2	1	.667	8.91	15	0	0	6	0	1	33.1	39	36	33	1	1	29	1	33	8
Sawyer, Athletics	3	0	1.000	7.20	10	1	0	1	0	0	25.0	29	24	20	0	2	13	0	18	0
Scales, Mariners	0	0	.000	4.50	5	0	0	2	0	0	6.0	7	5	3	0	2	4	0	4	0
Sebach, Angels	3	5	.375	6.26	13	11	1	1	0	0	64.2	62	49	45	4	6	39	1	58	7
Severino, Angels	2	0	1.000	4.46	13	2	0	3	0	0	34.1	44	31	17	1	4	23	1	33	1
Sheehy, Angels	0	0	.000	3.86	5	0	0	3	0	1	7.0	6	4	3	0	0	3	0	3	0
Shoemaker, Athletics	2	1	.667	3.94	8	5	0	2	0	0	29.2	31	16	13	1	0	15	0	26	2
Smith, Cardinals	3	2	.600	3.72	14	10	0	0	0	0	67.2	67	39	28	0	3	11	0	54	4
Smith, Mariners	4	6	.400	4.56	13	13	2	0	0	0	75.0	87	59	38	3	11	42	0	51	10
Smock, Athletics*	1	1	.500	5.25	15	1	0	0	0	0	24.0	16	15	14	0	2	17	1	25	4
Soto, Mariners	3	2	.600	3.75	28	0	0	10	0	0	36.0	41	22	15	1	0	16	1	24	3
Spears, Padres*	3	3	.500	2.61	18	1	0	12	0	4	41.1	40	19	12	1	1	16	3	38	1
Spencer, Cardinals	1	5	.167	9.44	10	10	0	0	0	0	41.0	45	48	43	1	2	48	0	32	8
Stowell, Athletics	3	2	.600	3.55	12	7	0	3	0	0	45.2	36	24	18	2	1	18	0	43	1
Stroth, Giants	0	5	.000	4.81	14	5	0	1	0	0	43.0	43	28	23	1	1	27	0	29	4
Sullivan, Mariners	4	1	.800	4.36	25	1	0	18	0	6	43.1	56	39	21	0	3	28	1	30	10
Sutch, Athletics	3	2	.600	5.31	21	2	0	12	0	6	39.0	43	29	23	4	2	14	0	31	1
Sylve, Mariners	1	2	.333	4.00	9	3	0	0	0	0	18.0	17	14	8	1	3	11	0	14	2
Towns, Giants	1	1	.500	7.08	12	1	0	6	0	0	20.1	34	24	16	2	0	16	0	10	6
Tranbarger, Cardinals*	3	0	1.000	1.23	23	0	0	4	0	0	29.1	22	5	4	0	0	4	0	37	3
Trisler, Brewers	1	1	.500	1.26	8	0	0	6	0	1	14.1	10	5	2	0	1	11	2	10	1

Pitcher, Team	W	L	Pct.	ERA	G	GS	CG	GF	ShO	Sv.	IP	H	R	ER	HR	HB	BB	Int. BB	SO	WP
Valdez, Giants	2	3	.400	5.68	13	10	0	1	0	0	63.1	73	48	40	3	0	32	0	48	6
Valencia, Giants	0	0	.000	0.00	1	0	0	1	0	0	1.0	0	0	0	0	1	0	0	1	0
Vandemark, Mariners*	0	0	.000	40.50	1	0	0	0	0	0	1.1	2	6	6	0	0	5	0	1	2
Vargas, Mariners	0	0	.000	1.64	16	0	0	10	4	4	22.0	21	7	4	1	1	8	0	15	4
Vazquez, Padres	1	1	.500	2.48	17	1	0	6	0	1	40.0	39	20	11	2	2	25	1	31	3
Vonderlieth, Brewers*	1	0	1.000	4.15	9	0	0	5	0	1	17.1	19	13	8	0	1	10	0	17	2
Wilkie, Brewers	1	1	.500	5.23	7	0	0	2	0	0	10.1	15	11	6	0	0	9	0	10	0
Williard, Angels	5	6	.455	4.98	12	12	1	0	0	0	59.2	58	43	33	1	3	48	0	50	10
Wilstead, Brewers	0	0	.000	6.75	1	1	0	0	0	0	1.1	0	1	1	0	0	3	0	3	2
Winzer, Mariners	0	0	.000	0.00	1	0	0	0	0	0	0.1	0	0	0	0	0	0	0	0	0
Young, Angels	2	2	.500	2.89	8	6	0	1	0	0	37.1	25	19	12	0	2	27	0	35	5
Zurn, Brewers	4	3	.571	3.53	9	9	0	0	0	0	51.0	34	26	20	0	4	27	1	49	7

BALKS—Glinatsis, Mantei, 8 each; Burns, Lowe, Ma, 6 each; Dillman, 5; Barnes, Guerrero, Guigni, Martin, T. Myers, O'Laughlin, H. Perez, Shoemaker, Spencer, 4 each; Fults, Gambs, Gargagliano, Lara, Locklear, Loiselle, Merrill, Millay, Morgan, Narcisse, Williard, Young, Zurn, 3 each; Brown, Browne, Butler, Collins, D'Amato, C. Davis, Fjeld, Henrichs, Hollinger, Jeffcoat, Lindauer, Ramirez, Rivera, Sebach, Severino, C. Smith, Spears, Stroth, Sylve, Trisler, Vonderlieth, 2 each; Acre, Busby, Criminger, R. Davis, DeLeon, Dilone, Farrell, Fermin, Gomez, Gorrell, Hancock, Heusman, Israel, Konemann, Leary, Marchesi, Mejia, Miller, Nicolau, Parra, Paulino, Peysar, Pierce, Rutter, Santiago, Smock, Soto, Sullivan, Sutch, Towns, Tranbarger, Valdez, 1 each.

COMBINATION SHUTOUTS—Fermin-Smock-Sutch, Millay-Morgan-Fults, Shoemaker-Fermin-Smock-Myers, Athletics; Glinatsis-Scales, Paulino-Ebert-Mantei-Sullivan, Mariners; Burns-Santiago, Loiselle-Diaz, Narcisse-Fjeld-D'Amato, Padres.

NO-HIT GAME—Millay-Morgan-Fults, Athletics, defeated Angels, 9-0, August 29.

FIELDING

TEAM

Team	Pct.	G	PO	A	E	DP	PB	Team	Pct.	G	PO	A	E	DP	PB
Brewers	.949	60	1574	588	116	42	7	Padres	.944	59	1541	617	129	46	16
Angels	.948	59	1541	628	120	46	15	Giants	.940	60	1566	698	145	54	7
Cardinals	.947	59	1574	631	123	36	17	Mariners	.936	60	1582	715	157	63	14
Athletics	.946	59	1548	642	126	47	20								

INDIVIDUAL

FIRST BASEMEN

*Throws lefthanded.

Player, Team	Pct.	G	PO	A	E	DP
Alcaraz, Angels	.975	39	291	26	8	28
Alimena, Giants*	.983	50	432	41	8	39
Bailey, Athletics	1.000	3	15	4	0	1
Bieri, Brewers	.988	56	454	24	6	37
Bolivar, Giants*	.974	6	33	4	1	6
Bonnici, Mariners	.983	22	167	10	3	21
Cabrera, Athletics	1.000	2	3	0	0	0
Carty, Mariners	.976	11	70	11	2	6
Casey, Brewers	1.000	1	1	0	0	0
Cerio, Cardinals	1.000	12	91	8	0	6
Dobrolsky, Brewers	1.000	2	4	1	0	0
Donati, Angels	.986	30	206	9	3	13
Enriquez, Brewers	.800	1	4	0	1	1
D. Francisco, Athletics*	1.000	1	1	0	0	0
Furtado, Mariners	.963	12	98	5	4	12
Goins, Padres	.969	21	113	12	4	10
Greene, Padres	.993	17	132	6	1	14
Jensen, Giants	.955	3	20	1	1	3
Keene, Giants*	.981	6	48	4	1	4
Lawson, Mariners*	.996	25	220	4	1	16
Leary, Athletics*	.978	58	446	42	11	37
Llanos, Cardinals	.978	6	42	2	1	2
Mowry, Padres*	.980	25	232	14	5	15
Myers, Athletics*	1.000	2	2	0	0	0
Sievers, Giants	1.000	1	1	0	0	0
Slattery, Cardinals	1.000	5	42	4	0	1
Stefanski, Brewers	.958	3	22	1	1	1
Stillwell, Brewers*	.966	8	27	1	1	1
Thompson, Padres	.958	8	46	0	2	2
Tucker, Brewers	1.000	2	1	0	0	0
UNDERWOOD, Cardinals*	.992	44	359	17	3	20
Wachter, Brewers	1.000	2	5	0	0	0

SECOND BASEMEN

Player, Team	Pct.	G	PO	A	E	DP
Benschoter, Giants	.927	15	38	38	6	12
Blankenship, Brewers	1.000	1	1	1	0	0
Buckler, Athletics	1.000	1	1	0	0	0
Callicott, Cardinals	.977	9	21	21	1	4
Carrion, Padres	.963	20	37	41	3	8
Casey, Brewers	.931	6	14	13	2	1
Casper, Giants	.980	11	23	27	1	7
Connell, Angels	.938	51	97	129	15	29
Cora, Padres	1.000	1	4	2	0	2
Creer, Padres	.846	5	6	5	2	1
Cruz, Mariners	.961	23	58	64	5	18
de la Cruz, Padres	.982	10	26	30	1	9
Dilone, Athletics	.971	9	13	20	1	1
Dotolo, Giants	.769	5	9	11	6	1
D. Francisco, Athletics	.875	2	2	5	1	0

Player, Team	Pct.	G	PO	A	E	DP
V. Francisco, Athletics	.942	33	67	95	10	23
Helms, Giants	1.000	1	3	1	0	0
House, Brewers*	.000	1	0	0	1	0
Llanos, Cardinals	.750	1	4	2	2	0
Melendez, Mariners	1.000	1	2	0	0	0
Mendez, Athletics	.920	21	36	56	8	10
MENDOZA, Brewers	.939	47	76	92	11	18
Moncion, Mariners	.938	33	67	84	10	16
Relaford, Mariners	.905	15	18	39	6	10
Rivera, Giants	.833	2	3	7	2	0
Roberts, Padres	.925	25	52	59	9	9
Ross, Brewers	.855	14	21	26	8	3
Salazar, Giants	.939	12	26	20	3	3
Serafini, Brewers	1.000	1	0	2	0	0
Sierra, Angels	.833	5	8	12	4	1
Simmons, Angels	1.000	4	11	8	0	2
Ugueto, Cardinals	.914	53	89	123	20	18
Valencia, Giants	.931	20	38	57	7	13
Valentin, Brewers	.955	9	11	10	1	2

THIRD BASEMEN

Player, Team	Pct.	G	PO	A	E	DP
Alcantara, Mariners	.889	4	2	6	1	1
Benschoter, Giants	.881	30	25	64	12	2
Blankenship, Brewers	.875	8	2	12	2	1
Bonnici, Mariners	.862	10	9	16	4	0
Borzello, Cardinals	.778	4	0	7	2	0
Buckler, Athletics	.676	20	6	19	12	0
Bush, Padres	.895	31	25	60	10	3
Callicott, Cardinals	1.000	1	0	1	0	0
Carrion, Padres	.875	2	1	6	1	0
Cerio, Cardinals	.765	10	4	9	4	1
Cora, Padres	.972	8	10	25	1	1
Creer, Padres	.667	2	0	2	1	0
Cruz, Mariners	.800	1	8	16	6	2
de la Cruz, Padres	.941	6	6	10	1	0
DeLeon, Mariners	.818	23	11	34	10	3
Dilone, Athletics	.870	25	21	39	9	2
Donati, Angels	.917	5	5	6	1	0
Eicher, Cardinals	1.000	1	0	1	0	0
Foster, Giants	.875	32	26	65	13	10
Goins, Padres	.750	1	0	3	1	0
Greene, Padres	1.000	1	1	2	0	0
Imperial, Brewers	.942	33	27	71	6	6
Llanos, Cardinals	.786	6	3	8	3	0
Martinez, Mariners	.866	30	16	42	9	9
Mendez, Athletics	.922	18	14	33	4	2
Mendoza, Brewers	1.000	1	1	0	0	0
Roberts, Padres	.688	9	4	7	5	0
Scott, Athletics	1.000	3	2	5	0	0
SIMMONS, Angels	.905	55	41	93	14	8
Slattery, Cardinals	.800	11	4	20	6	0
Sumner, Cardinals	.868	36	30	69	15	4

Player, Team	Pct.	G	PO	A	E	DP
Valencia, Giants	.667	1	1	1	1	0
Valentin, Brewers	.808	23	11	31	10	1
P. Vazquez, Padres	.200	1	1	0	4	0

SHORTSTOPS

Player, Team	Pct.	G	PO	A	E	DP
Alcantara, Mariners	.922	32	46	108	13	16
Blankenship, Brewers	.957	13	13	31	2	4
Callicott, Cardinals	.922	27	32	62	8	5
Carrion, Padres	.882	4	7	8	2	1
Casey, Brewers	.898	45	65	128	22	24
Castro, Angels	.825	19	17	49	14	9
Cerio, Cardinals	.895	7	5	12	2	3
Connell, Angels	.864	5	3	16	3	3
Cora, Padres	.922	37	62	115	15	22
CRUZ, Athletics	.941	52	92	147	15	27
Cruz, Mariners	.973	8	12	24	1	7
de la Cruz, Padres	.727	3	4	4	3	1
Dotolo, Giants	.895	9	10	24	4	7
Llanos, Cardinals	.833	2	1	4	1	0
Mendez, Athletics	.894	14	19	23	5	6
Mendoza, Brewers	1.000	1	1	0	0	1
Mota, Cardinals	.908	26	34	84	12	9
Relaford, Mariners	.876	28	40	87	18	15
Rivera, Giants	.914	47	52	149	19	18
Salazar, Cardinals	.897	10	16	19	4	3
Sierra, Angels	.906	38	71	112	19	18
Sumner, Cardinals	.944	5	1	16	1	5
Valencia, Giants	.944	4	4	13	1	1
Valentin, Brewers	.742	5	8	15	8	0
P. Vazquez, Padres	.883	19	22	69	12	6

OUTFIELDERS

Player, Team	Pct.	G	PO	A	E	DP
Aracena, Athletics	.959	54	107	11	5	1
Bieri, Brewers	1.000	5	1	0	0	0
Blomeyer, Giants	.957	29	42	2	2	2
Bolivar, Giants*	.870	21	19	1	3	0
Buckler, Athletics	.808	17	18	3	5	2
Bullock, Mariners	.895	25	46	5	6	0
Cerio, Cardinals	1.000	5	7	1	0	0
Cruz, Padres	.976	36	76	7	2	0
Dilone, Athletics	.944	13	13	4	1	1
Eicher, Cardinals	.976	47	79	3	2	0
Enriquez, Brewers	.960	12	22	2	1	0
D. Francisco, Athletics	.985	55	126	6	2	0
Frazier, Giants	.911	32	46	5	5	2
Griffey, Mariners	.961	33	48	1	2	1
Hardwick, Angels	.943	42	78	4	5	1
Henry, Cardinals	.941	42	78	2	5	0
House, Brewers*	.976	45	81	1	2	0
House, Angels	.965	57	79	3	3	0
Jones, Giants	.956	34	79	8	4	1
Lawson, Mariners*	.750	15	11	1	4	0
Leary, Athletics*	1.000	2	1	0	0	0
Martin, Angels	.963	29	50	2	2	0
Matos, Padres	.965	29	52	3	2	1
McCAFFERY, Angels	1.000	53	103	12	0	1
Oliver, Angels	.852	13	23	0	4	0
Pantoja, Giants	.983	34	53	5	1	1
R. Perez, Padres	.936	40	69	4	5	2
S. Perez, Padres	.947	16	16	2	1	0
Powell, Mariners	.889	19	30	2	4	1
Preikszas, Brewers	1.000	12	17	2	0	0
Ramos, Mariners	.938	10	12	3	1	1
Rivera, Padres	.923	8	12	0	1	0
Robertson, Giants	.946	33	52	1	3	0
Robinson, Cardinals	1.000	49	86	5	0	0
Rodrigues, Brewers	.976	29	41	0	1	0
Ross, Brewers	.956	30	42	1	2	1
Scott, Athletics	.976	26	39	2	1	1
Slattery, Cardinals	.957	30	39	5	2	0
Sosa, Mariners	.982	30	50	5	1	0
Stefanski, Brewers	.750	10	3	0	1	0
Stewart, Padres	.913	34	41	1	4	0
Strehlow, Cardinals	.800	27	23	1	6	0
Thomas, Mariners	.857	35	48	0	8	0
Thompson, Padres	.818	7	8	1	2	0
Tucker, Brewers	.952	11	18	2	1	0
Valentin, Brewers	1.000	5	2	0	0	0
Valverde, Mariners	.667	4	2	0	1	0
Vega, Giants	.896	36	41	2	5	0
Wachter, Brewers	.964	44	76	5	3	0
Walker, Athletics	.975	23	37	2	1	0
Walton, Cardinals	.750	4	3	0	1	0
Williams, Giants	.943	23	49	1	3	1
Wyatt, Padres	.914	22	31	1	3	0

CATCHERS

Player, Team	Pct.	G	PO	A	E	DP	PB
Anderson, Angels	.963	12	61	17	3	3	3
Ballara, Cardinals	.973	49	355	47	11	2	13
Bertucci, Angels	.975	27	168	26	5	0	8
Bonnici, Mariners	.963	19	117	14	5	0	4
Borzello, Cardinals	1.000	4	13	0	0	0	1
Cerio, Cardinals	.966	16	103	9	4	0	3
DeJesus, Padres	.987	12	63	11	1	0	1
Dobrolsky, Brewers	1.000	2	12	1	0	0	0
Furtado, Mariners	.919	15	53	4	5	2	3
Goins, Padres	.982	22	150	14	3	2	4
Greene, Padres	.987	30	201	22	3	1	11
Jensen, Giants	.975	36	206	28	6	0	5
Melendez, Mariners	.976	43	242	43	7	1	7
Moncion, Athletics	.956	32	191	26	10	2	10
Musolino, Angels	.960	3	22	2	1	0	0
Pineiro, Angels	.957	25	179	20	9	0	4
Ramirez, Giants	.941	22	64	16	5	3	1
Sievers, Giants	.984	21	114	9	2	0	1
Smith, Athletics	.978	33	240	21	6	1	10
STEFANSKI, Brewers	.988	51	364	39	5	0	6
Tucker, Brewers	.965	19	102	7	4	0	1

PITCHERS

Player, Team	Pct.	G	PO	A	E	DP
Acre, Athletics	.000	6	0	0	1	0
Anthony, Padres	1.000	7	1	5	0	0
Balke, Cardinals*	1.000	5	1	6	0	0
Barnes, Padres	.900	11	2	7	1	0
Blair, Brewers	1.000	7	1	1	0	0
Brown, Giants	.625	7	4	1	3	1
Browne, Brewers	.909	13	2	8	1	0
Buckler, Athletics	1.000	3	0	1	0	0
Burns, Padres	.895	12	8	9	2	0
Busby, Cardinals	1.000	11	4	5	0	0
Butler, Angels*	1.000	11	4	10	0	0
Christopher, Brewers	1.000	2	0	1	0	0
Collins, Giants	.875	13	2	5	1	0
Compton, Padres	1.000	12	1	5	0	0
Criminger, Brewers	1.000	18	1	0	0	0
D'Amato, Padres	1.000	13	0	9	0	0
C. Davis, Cardinals	.667	21	0	2	1	0
R. Davis, Cardinals	.909	11	2	8	1	0
Diaz, Padres	1.000	18	3	4	0	1
Dillman, Cardinals	.800	15	2	2	1	0
Dixon, Mariners	1.000	5	0	1	0	0
Ebert, Mariners	1.000	12	3	2	0	0
Farrell, Brewers*	1.000	6	1	2	0	0
Fermin, Athletics	1.000	7	1	2	0	0
Fjeld, Padres	.688	16	2	9	5	0
Fults, Athletics*	.833	11	3	12	3	1
Gambs, Giants	1.000	13	7	7	0	1
Gargagliano, Mariners*	.786	20	1	10	3	0
Glinatsis, Mariners	.789	12	5	10	4	0
Gomez, Giants	1.000	9	6	2	0	0
Gorrell, Brewers	.286	7	0	2	5	0
Guerrero, Cardinals	1.000	6	0	1	0	1
Guigni, Giants*	.667	7	1	1	1	0
Guyton, Cardinals	.800	13	2	2	1	0
Hancock, Brewers*	1.000	7	2	6	0	1
Hartman, Mariners*	1.000	15	1	2	0	0
Hernandez, Giants	1.000	16	5	10	0	0
Heusman, Angels*	.929	19	2	11	1	0
Hollinger, Padres	.000	8	0	0	2	0
Israel, Giants	1.000	16	2	1	0	0
Jarvis, Brewers	1.000	7	1	3	0	0
Jeffcoat, Cardinals	.714	21	0	5	2	0
Jenkins, Mariners	1.000	9	0	1	0	0
Knox, Mariners	.833	6	1	4	1	0
Konemann, Cardinals	1.000	28	0	7	0	0
Lara, Cardinals*	.824	14	3	11	3	0
Light, Athletics	1.000	2	2	2	0	0
Lindauer, Cardinals	.909	19	2	8	1	0
Locklear, Giants*	.833	17	1	4	1	0
Loiselle, Padres	.615	12	3	5	5	0
Lowe, Mariners	.933	12	4	10	1	0
Ma, Brewers	.857	11	2	4	1	0
Mantei, Brewers	.889	17	1	7	1	0
Marchesi, Cardinals	.933	12	2	12	1	2
Martin, Giants	.941	12	6	10	1	1
McKinnon, Cardinals	1.000	3	2	0	0	0
Mejia, Athletics	.700	4	4	3	3	0
Merrill, Angels	1.000	6	0	7	0	0
Millay, Athletics	.917	17	3	8	1	1
Miller, Cardinals	1.000	15	1	5	0	0
Morgan, Athletics	.750	6	1	2	1	0
Musset, Angels	.909	10	0	1	0	0
Myers, Giants	.909	21	3	7	1	0
Myers, Athletics*	.923	22	2	10	1	0
Narcisse, Padres	.909	11	5	5	1	1
Nicolau, Brewers	.889	13	1	7	1	0
O'Laughlin, Brewers*	1.000	13	5	4	0	0
Parker, Angels	1.000	15	1	5	0	0
Parra, Angels	1.000	12	0	3	0	0
Paulino, Mariners	.692	14	2	7	4	2
Pena, Mariners	1.000	2	0	2	0	0
Perez, Giants	1.000	10	2	5	0	0

Player, Team	Pct.	G	PO	A	E	DP
Perez, Brewers	1.000	2	0	2	0	0
Peysar, Giants	.778	14	0	7	2	0
Pierce, Athletics	1.000	20	4	11	0	1
Pote, Giants	.750	8	1	5	2	0
Ramirez, Brewers*	.400	4	0	2	3	0
Rivera, Angels	1.000	7	2	10	0	0
Rossiter, Athletics	.833	10	2	3	1	0
Rutter, Brewers	.933	11	2	12	1	1
Santiago, Padres	.800	15	3	1	1	0
Sawyer, Athletics	.500	10	0	1	1	0
Scales, Mariners	.500	5	0	1	1	0
Sebach, Angels	1.000	13	5	6	0	1
Severino, Angels	.500	13	0	2	2	0
Sheehy, Angels	1.000	5	0	2	0	0
Shoemaker, Athletics	.857	8	2	4	1	0
Smith, Cardinals	.900	14	4	14	2	0
SMITH, Mariners	1.000	13	4	15	0	2
Smock, Athletics*	1.000	15	1	3	0	0
Soto, Mariners	1.000	28	1	5	0	0
Spears, Padres*	.909	18	3	7	1	1
Spencer, Cardinals	.875	10	2	5	1	0
Stowell, Athletics	.875	12	4	3	1	0
Stroth, Giants	.700	14	4	3	3	0
Sullivan, Mariners	.933	25	4	10	1	2
Sutch, Athletics	.778	21	4	3	2	1
Sylve, Mariners	.000	9	0	0	1	0
Towns, Giants	.667	12	0	4	2	1
Tranbarger, Cardinals*	1.000	23	2	7	0	1
Trisler, Brewers	1.000	8	1	3	0	0
Valdez, Giants	.824	13	4	10	3	2
Vandemark, Mariners*	.000	1	0	0	1	0
Vargas, Mariners	1.000	16	0	3	0	0
A. Vazquez, Padres	.833	17	0	5	1	0
Vonderlieth, Brewers*	.750	10	0	3	1	1
Wilkie, Brewers	.500	7	1	0	1	0
Williard, Angels	1.000	12	7	5	0	1
Winzer, Mariners	1.000	1	1	0	0	0
Young, Angels	.846	8	2	9	2	1
Zurn, Brewers	1.000	9	4	8	0	0

The following players did not have any fielding statistics at the positions indicated or appeared only as a designated hitter, pinch-hitter or pinch-runner: Andrea, 1b; Aracena, p; Blomeyer, 3b; Brannon, dh, ph; Cookson, of; DeLeon, p; Dilone, p; Dotolo, of; D. Francisco, p; V. Francisco, ss, p; Henrichs, p; Leary, p; Ledinsky, p; Llanos, of; Millay, 1b; Mowry, p; Mi. Myers, p; Ramos, p; Ross, p; Sievers, of; Sutch, of; J. Thomas, of; Tucker, 3b; Valencia, p; Wilstead, p.

LEAGUE CHAMPIONS

Year	Team	Pct.
1988—	Peoria Brewers	.690
1989—	Peoria Brewers	.732
1990—	Peoria Brewers	.679
1991—	Scottsdale A's	.650

GULF COAST LEAGUE

FINAL STANDINGS

CENTRAL DIVISION

Team	W	L	T	Pct.	GB
Expos	32	28	0	.533	....
White Sox	30	29	0	.508	1 ½
Pirates	30	29	0	.508	1 ½
Braves	30	29	1	.508	1 ½
Yankees	27	32	1	.458	5 ½

SOUTHERN DIVISION

Team	W	L	T	Pct.	GB
Orioles	35	24	0	.593	....
Blue Jays	31	28	1	.525	4
Rangers	30	29	0	.508	5
Twins	27	33	0	.450	8 ½
Mets	24	35	1	.407	11

NORTHERN DIVISION

Team	W	L	T	Pct.	GB
Red Sox	33	27	0	.550	....
Royals	31	29	0	.517	2
Dodgers	29	31	0	.483	4
Astros	27	33	0	.450	6

COMPOSITE

Team	Ori.	R.S.	Exp.	B.J.	Roy.	W.S.	Ran.	Pir.	Brv.	Dod.	Yan.	Twi.	Ast.	Met.	W	L	T	Pct.	GB
Orioles	....	0	0	7	0	0	7	0	3	0	0	9	0	9	35	24	0	.593	....
Red Sox	0	....	0	0	12	0	0	0	0	9	0	0	12	0	33	27	0	.550	2 ½
Expos	0	0	....	0	0	5	0	8	7	0	8	0	0	4	32	28	0	.533	3 ½
Blue Jays	6	0	0	....	0	0	6	3	0	0	0	8	0	8	31	28	1	.525	4
Royals	0	8	0	0	....	0	0	0	0	12	0	0	11	0	31	29	0	.517	4 ½
White Sox	0	0	9	0	0	....	0	3	5	6	0	7	0	0	30	29	0	.508	5
Rangers	7	0	0	8	0	1	....	0	0	0	0	6	0	8	30	29	0	.508	5
Pirates	0	0	6	1	0	9	0	....	7	0	7	0	0	0	30	29	0	.508	5
Braves	1	0	7	0	0	8	0	6	....	0	8	0	0	0	30	29	1	.508	5
Dodgers	0	11	0	0	8	0	0	0	0	....	0	0	10	0	29	31	0	.483	6 ½
Yankees	0	0	6	0	0	6	0	8	0	7	6	0	....	0	27	32	1	.458	8
Twins	5	0	0	6	0	0	8	0	0	0	2	....	0	6	27	33	0	.450	8 ½
Astros	0	8	0	0	9	0	0	0	0	10	0	0	....	0	27	33	0	.450	8 ½
Mets	5	0	0	6	0	0	5	0	0	0	0	8	0	....	24	35	1	.407	11

Games played in Bradenton and Sarasota, Fla.

Club names are major league affiliations.

Playoffs—Expos defeated Red Sox, one game to none; Expos defeated Orioles, two games to one, to win league championship.

Regular-season attendance—No official attendance figures reported.

Managers—Astros, Julio Linares; Blue Jays, Omar Malave; Braves, Jim Saul; Dodgers, Ivan DeJesus; Expos, Keith Snider; Mets, Junior Roman; Orioles, Ed Napoleon; Pirates, Woody Huyke; Rangers, Chino Cadahia; Red Sox, Felix Maldonado; Royals, Bob Herold; Twins, Dan Rohn; White Sox, Jaime Garcia; Yankees, Ken Dominquez.

All-Star team—1B—Joe Calder, Pirates; 2B—Ed Alfonzo, Mets; 3B—Elston Hansen, Yankees; SS—Keith Legree, Twins; OF—Abdiel Cumberbatch, Yankees; Angel Dotel, Dodgers; Duane Thomas, Orioles; C—Yabanne DeLeon, Royals; SP—Rich Forney, Orioles; RP—Bob Adkins, Blue Jays; Manager of the Year—Ed Napoleon, Orioles.

BATTING

TEAM

Team	Avg.	G	AB	R	OR	H	TB	2B	3B	HR	RBI	SH	SF	HP	BB	Int. BB	SO	SB	CS	LOB
Pirates	.267	59	1955	278	252	522	632	70	8	8	216	10	25	23	165	0	334	156	41	397
Royals	.259	60	1916	262	256	497	614	58	19	7	209	14	15	29	205	3	391	80	27	439
Dodgers	.257	60	1928	272	256	495	611	72	19	2	213	20	14	26	207	2	440	92	46	429
Yankees	.253	60	2043	286	281	516	633	75	9	8	234	19	24	24	243	0	432	109	26	484
Astros	.250	60	1886	227	303	472	586	51	21	7	188	21	14	23	147	4	379	106	62	356
Twins	.247	60	1872	260	258	462	643	68	37	13	193	8	25	19	191	2	388	100	49	361
Braves	.246	60	2002	271	313	492	649	77	25	10	222	13	16	28	176	1	429	72	35	419
Orioles	.245	60	1915	283	230	470	632	77	23	13	206	10	14	22	142	2	370	79	29	374
Rangers	.245	59	1945	233	218	476	663	90	26	15	199	3	13	19	189	1	418	73	16	484
Red Sox	.242	60	1935	299	245	468	630	60	21	20	244	13	19	39	269	3	477	117	47	408
Expos	.233	60	1948	276	280	453	630	79	22	18	223	10	17	33	201	2	448	93	40	405
White Sox	.226	59	1982	251	234	448	544	57	9	7	194	11	13	31	181	1	421	57	33	360
Blue Jays	.222	60	1897	213	230	421	592	79	28	12	173	20	7	14	149	3	429	93	34	372
Mets	.212	60	1815	222	277	385	496	61	19	4	156	16	22	15	199	1	429	93	34	372

INDIVIDUAL

(Leading qualifiers for batting championship—162 or more plate appearances)

*Bats lefthanded.   †Switch-hitter.

Player, Team	Avg.	G	AB	R	H	TB	2B	3B	HR	RBI	SH	SF	HP	BB	Int. BB	SO	SB	CS
Dotel, Angel, Dodgers*	.400	41	120	24	48	61	9	2	0	15	2	0	1	26	1	15	6	5
Ortiz, Luis, Red Sox*	.333	42	153	21	51	78	11	2	4	29	0	1	2	8	0	9	2	1
Wuerch, Jason, Yankees*	.333	38	150	24	50	58	8	0	0	18	2	4	3	9	0	23	2	4
Alfonzo, Ed, Mets	.331	54	175	29	58	74	8	4	0	27	4	6	2	34	0	12	6	4
Hansen, Elston, Yankees	.327	57	208	45	68	95	9	3	4	37	0	3	2	43	0	35	4	1
Long, Ryan, Royals	.311	48	177	17	55	61	3	2	0	20	0	1	2	10	0	20	6	4
Hawkins, Darnel, Astros	.309	45	139	25	43	57	4	2	2	23	0	0	0	16	0	14	11	6
Ochoa, Alex, Orioles	.307	53	179	26	55	72	8	3	1	30	3	1	1	14	0	19	9	2
Spencer, Shane, Yankees	.306	41	160	25	49	56	7	0	0	30	0	4	2	14	0	39	10	3
Stynes, Chris, Blue Jays	.306	57	219	29	67	96	15	1	4	39	1	4	3	39	0	39	10	3

Departmental leaders: G—Hardge, 60; AB—Hardge, 237; R—Hansen, Hardge, 45; H—Hansen, 68; TB—Nava, 97; 2B—Hardge, 18; 3B—Butler, Nava, Ogden, Wright, 7; HR—Thomas, 10; RBI—Calder, 45; SH—Goodwin, 5; SF—Calder, 8; HP—Collier, 14; BB—Ferreira, 49; IBB—Colon, Gerald, Hawkins, Polidor, 2; SO—Batista, 71; SB—Cumberbatch, 45; CS—Perez, 12.

(All players—listed alphabetically)

Player, Team	Avg.	G	AB	R	H	TB	2B	3B	HR	RBI	SH	SF	HP	BB	Int. BB	SO	SB	CS
Abreu, Bob, Astros†	.301	56	183	21	55	68	7	3	0	20	2	3	1	17	0	27	10	6
Acevedo, Jesus, Twins	.115	12	26	2	3	4	1	0	0	3	0	0	0	3	0	4	1	1
Aguado, Victor, Red Sox	.158	16	38	3	6	8	2	0	0	5	0	0	0	4	0	7	1	0
Albaladejo, Randy, Astros	.170	21	53	4	9	14	2	0	1	8	0	2	0	7	0	15	0	1
Albornoz, Rodolfo, Yankees	.195	31	82	7	16	18	2	0	0	6	3	1	0	10	0	15	0	1
Alfonzo, Ed, Mets	.331	54	175	29	58	74	8	4	0	27	4	6	2	34	0	12	6	4
Alicea, Ivan, Pirates*	.303	41	145	24	44	55	11	0	0	17	0	1	1	10	0	19	11	1
Arendt, James, Braves	.167	2	6	1	1	1	0	0	0	1	0	0	0	1	0	1	1	0
Asencio, Mattie, Orioles	.213	54	169	20	36	44	5	0	1	13	0	3	1	14	0	42	7	2
Austin, Corey, White Sox	.242	10	33	6	8	8	0	0	0	7	0	1	3	2	0	5	4	1
Awkard, Herman, Rangers	.227	38	128	16	29	43	5	0	3	18	0	1	2	2	0	35	7	0
Baez, Diogenes, Red Sox*	.268	41	153	30	41	56	6	3	1	16	1	0	2	13	0	27	8	2
Banks, Tony, Twins	.228	17	57	7	13	16	3	0	0	1	0	0	0	4	0	16	2	0
Batista, Juan, Expos	.201	51	189	19	38	53	7	1	2	19	1	1	1	11	0	71	9	7
Bell, Derek, Orioles†	.265	37	83	18	22	31	5	2	0	15	0	2	2	29	0	13	0	0
Beltre, Eddy, Mets	.210	40	119	12	25	37	8	2	0	14	0	2	1	14	0	22	0	0
Benitez, Yamil, Expos	.239	54	197	20	47	81	9	5	5	38	1	5	1	12	1	55	10	5
Bethke, Jamie, Rangers†	.141	20	64	5	9	11	2	0	0	4	0	0	1	4	0	13	1	1
Blanco, Pedro, Twins†	.333	9	21	3	7	9	0	1	0	1	0	1	0	3	0	3	2	1
Bogan, Victor, Twins	.160	28	81	5	13	13	0	0	0	6	0	0	1	2	0	20	2	3
Bonifay, Ken, Pirates*	.344	20	64	13	22	26	1	0	1	9	0	1	1	14	0	8	5	1
Borrero, Rikchy, Red Sox	.220	35	118	11	26	34	3	1	1	16	0	2	1	2	1	24	4	2
Bowrosen, Rich, White Sox	.233	53	172	25	40	60	10	2	2	13	0	0	3	18	0	61	1	1
Brookens, Andy, Royals	.225	30	71	12	16	22	4	1	0	4	0	1	1	9	0	26	6	1
Brown, Randy, Red Sox	.189	44	143	25	27	34	7	0	0	10	0	3	1	23	0	31	19	0
Bull, Bert, Mets	.167	43	138	12	23	25	2	0	0	8	1	0	2	11	0	29	5	4
Burgos, Carlos, Royals	.256	47	133	18	34	42	8	0	0	11	1	0	6	18	0	21	0	0
Burton, Essex, White Sox	.278	50	194	37	54	63	5	2	0	19	17	3	0	26	0	27	21	8
Burton, Steve, Rangers*	.295	50	176	18	52	72	12	4	0	24	0	3	0	12	0	24	1	1
Butler, Rich, Blue Jays*	.263	59	213	30	56	76	6	7	0	13	4	0	0	17	1	45	10	6
Calder, Joe, Pirates	.301	54	196	28	59	94	15	1	6	45	0	8	3	10	0	37	4	2
Calero, Enrique, Astros	.323	46	133	12	43	49	4	1	0	10	1	2	0	16	0	16	0	1
Cameron, Mike, White Sox	.221	44	136	20	30	33	3	0	0	11	1	0	4	17	0	29	13	2
Campos, Francisco, Astros	.147	21	34	4	5	8	1	1	0	3	0	0	2	6	0	7	1	1
Canda, Chad, Twins	.253	29	79	14	20	34	6	1	2	7	0	0	1	7	0	22	0	0
Carabba, Robbie, Expos	.247	30	93	17	23	28	5	0	0	8	0	0	1	18	0	22	8	4
Carbajal, Nilson, Expos	.000	6	4	1	0	0	0	0	0	1	0	0	0	2	0	2	0	0
Carlsen, Mike, Blue Jays	.198	26	91	7	18	30	6	0	2	15	0	2	1	4	1	18	1	4
Casanova, Raul, Mets	.243	32	111	19	27	35	4	2	0	9	1	1	2	12	0	22	3	0
Castillo, Rafael, Astros	.300	9	30	2	9	9	0	0	0	3	0	0	1	0	0	7	5	0
Cedeno, Edguardo, Astros	.191	33	110	11	21	25	4	0	0	10	2	0	2	2	0	36	7	2
Centeno, Henri, Astros†	.318	31	85	12	27	31	4	0	0	7	4	0	3	5	0	10	4	4
Cerda, Jose, Royals	.246	15	61	7	15	20	5	0	0	7	0	1	0	2	0	10	1	1
Ciccarella, Joe, Red Sox*	.304	8	23	5	7	12	2	0	1	6	1	1	2	6	0	3	0	0
Coakley, Derric, Twins	.189	21	53	11	10	16	0	0	2	4	1	0	2	7	0	11	5	2
Collier, Dan, Red Sox	.252	42	131	27	33	59	4	2	6	25	0	0	14	27	1	42	1	2
Colon, Angel, Pirates	.289	32	114	23	33	36	3	0	0	11	0	2	1	5	0	21	14	2
Colon, Dennis, Astros*	.238	54	193	20	46	61	5	2	2	28	1	1	1	10	2	28	4	7
Conger, Jeff, Pirates*	.324	15	37	5	12	12	0	0	0	4	0	0	0	4	0	8	8	2
Conner, Jamie, Orioles	.208	37	101	17	21	27	2	2	0	7	0	0	0	15	0	22	7	3
Correa, Miguel, Braves	.251	47	171	21	43	55	8	2	0	6	2	0	1	7	0	28	10	6
Cradle, Rickey, Blue Jays	.214	44	131	16	28	41	4	3	1	6	3	0	3	24	1	37	4	5
Crimmins, John, Red Sox	.321	18	53	7	17	22	2	0	1	6	0	0	1	7	0	15	1	1
Cumberbatch, Abdiel, Yankees†	.288	59	229	44	66	74	8	0	0	10	0	1	2	37	0	60	45	8
Cunningham, O'Brien, Pirates	.253	34	87	8	22	31	9	0	0	7	0	3	1	3	0	23	0	1
Curran, Shawn, Orioles	.172	36	99	16	17	22	5	0	0	8	1	1	2	17	0	34	0	1
Davidson, John, Dodgers	.000	16	1	0	0	0	0	0	0	0	0	0	0	0	0	0	0	0
DeLeon, Yabanne, Royals	.313	44	99	13	31	34	3	0	0	17	2	2	1	7	0	21	0	1
Dennison, Scott, Expos	.269	23	78	15	21	22	1	0	0	10	0	0	2	11	0	11	9	3
Devers, Ed, White Sox	.250	40	132	15	33	37	2	1	0	9	1	0	0	4	0	22	4	3
Diaz, Alejandro, Pirates	.140	24	57	8	8	10	2	0	0	4	0	0	4	8	0	21	0	0
Diaz, Jenny, Red Sox	.162	18	37	3	6	9	1	1	0	3	0	0	0	1	0	18	1	0
Dotel, Angel, Dodgers*	.400	41	120	24	48	61	9	2	0	15	2	0	1	26	1	15	6	5
Ducksworth, Ron, Pirates	.200	3	10	2	2	2	0	0	0	0	0	0	0	0	0	5	2	0
Dufault, Monty, Twins	.287	29	101	14	29	38	7	1	0	8	0	1	2	7	0	19	5	3
Durham, Ray, White Sox†	.304	6	23	3	7	8	1	0	0	4	0	0	0	3	0	5	5	1
Earl, Clyde, Pirates†	.233	26	73	11	17	18	1	0	0	8	2	1	0	6	0	14	9	0
Edmonson, Chris, Pirates	.254	42	138	19	35	43	5	0	1	14	0	1	2	21	0	24	1	2
Eenhoorn, Robert, Yankees	.350	13	40	6	14	23	4	1	1	7	0	0	0	3	0	8	1	0
Espinosa, Ramon, Pirates	.234	19	64	7	15	17	2	0	0	5	0	0	0	2	0	7	3	0
Evangelista, George, Rangers	.283	33	120	26	34	57	8	3	3	12	0	0	1	24	1	12	14	4
Evans, Glenn, Twins†	.236	50	165	25	39	47	2	3	0	13	3	1	1	32	1	31	12	7
Evans, Justin, Orioles	.187	35	91	8	17	21	4	0	0	7	0	3	2	10	0	22	0	2
Farmer, Ben, Expos	.198	34	96	16	19	32	4	3	1	8	0	1	0	20	0	30	1	3
Ferreira, Tony, Red Sox†	.255	48	157	36	40	42	2	0	0	14	1	1	0	49	0	30	17	3
Floyd, Cliff, Expos*	.262	56	214	35	56	89	9	3	6	30	1	1	5	19	1	37	13	3
Freitag, Mark, Expos	.179	26	78	6	14	17	3	0	0	4	0	0	7	0	0	12	3	1
Fryman, Troy, White Sox*	.231	7	26	2	6	9	3	0	0	3	0	1	0	4	0	7	1	0
Gainey, Ty, Pirates*	.500	3	8	2	4	4	0	0	0	1	0	0	0	1	0	2	3	0
Garcia, Adrian, Braves	.267	14	45	5	12	15	1	1	0	0	0	0	0	9	0	9	0	1
Garcia, Jose, Yankees	.222	21	45	6	10	16	4	1	0	12	2	1	0	0	0	13	0	0
Garcia, Luis, Twins	.250	15	4	1	1	1	0	0	0	0	0	0	0	1	0	2	0	0
Garr, Ralph Jr., Braves	.231	4	13	4	3	3	0	0	0	3	0	0	0	1	0	0	1	0
Garrow, David, Twins	.221	42	145	11	32	36	4	0	0	18	1	4	1	12	0	16	5	4
Gerald, Dwayne, Royals	.259	53	174	28	45	56	6	1	1	15	1	0	1	23	2	52	11	1
Gipner, Marcus, Yankees†	.153	39	131	6	20	21	1	0	0	12	3	2	1	12	0	23	1	0
Gonzalez, Alex, Blue Jays	.209	53	191	29	40	53	5	4	0	13	0	3	2	12	0	41	7	2
Gonzalez, German, Dodgers	.299	52	164	19	49	63	10	2	0	30	2	5	9	19	0	30	6	3
Gonzalez, Jimmy, Astros	.204	34	103	7	21	24	3	0	0	3	1	0	0	3	0	33	3	5
Gonzalez, Raul, Royals	.294	47	160	24	47	58	5	3	0	17	1	2	0	19	0	21	3	4
Good, Thomathon, Royals*	.198	36	81	11	16	16	0	0	0	5	1	0	0	9	0	17	5	0
Goodwin, Curtis, Orioles*	.258	48	151	32	39	44	5	0	0	9	5	0	1	38	0	25	26	5
Grapenthien, Danny, Astros	.000	2	7	1	0	0	0	0	0	0	0	0	0	1	0	3	0	0

Player, Team	Avg.	G	AB	R	H	TB	2B	3B	HR	RBI	SH	SF	HP	BB	Int. BB	SO	SB	CS
Griffin, Ryan, Blue Jays	.135	42	126	9	17	18	1	0	0	8	2	0	2	6	0	37	1	0
Grob, Robert, Braves*	.171	17	41	3	7	10	3	0	0	11	0	0	1	5	0	6	0	0
Hansen, Elston, Yankees	.327	57	208	45	68	95	9	3	4	37	0	3	2	43	0	35	4	1
Hardge, Mike, Expos	.253	60	237	45	60	93	18	3	3	30	0	4	2	23	0	41	20	7
Harris, Demarcus, White Sox	.176	30	74	9	13	13	0	0	0	0	3	0	3	8	0	24	2	2
Haughney, Trevor, Rangers*	.254	50	197	30	50	65	6	3	1	18	0	0	0	18	0	36	23	6
Hawkins, Darnel, Astros	.309	45	139	25	43	57	4	2	2	23	0	0	0	28	2	24	14	11
Heaps, Chris, Yankees	.264	42	148	16	39	45	6	0	0	11	1	1	1	11	0	29	18	4
Heidelberg, Khary, Expos*	.234	24	77	14	18	19	1	0	0	10	1	1	4	10	0	19	8	2
Henry, Santiago, Blue Jays	.207	55	213	22	44	60	10	3	0	14	1	2	0	11	0	40	7	4
Hiljus, Erik, Mets	.000	9	2	0	0	0	0	0	0	0	0	0	0	0	0	0	0	0
Hodge, Roy, Orioles	.267	36	90	10	24	31	4	0	1	13	0	1	1	19	0	17	1	0
Hollandsworth, Todd, Dodgers*	.313	6	16	1	5	5	0	0	0	0	0	0	0	0	0	6	0	0
Hurst, Jimmy, White Sox	.256	36	121	14	31	35	4	0	0	12	0	0	1	13	0	32	6	1
Hurtault, Roosevelt, Expos†	.175	20	57	6	10	12	2	0	0	4	0	0	4	1	0	15	5	1
Indriago, Juan, Royals†	.300	43	130	23	39	42	1	1	0	5	0	0	1	16	0	17	6	4
Isava, Jesus, Royals†	.113	31	62	6	7	10	0	0	1	7	1	0	2	13	0	24	1	1
Jackson, Lonnie, Dodgers*	.228	43	114	13	26	33	3	2	0	7	1	0	0	18	0	37	2	5
Jackson, Vince, Dodgers	.288	54	208	33	60	72	6	3	0	23	2	0	0	18	0	48	10	7
James, Bradley, Braves	.232	31	99	14	23	36	6	2	1	16	0	2	4	11	0	40	2	0
James, Nate, White Sox	.229	25	70	12	16	22	4	1	0	13	1	1	4	11	0	25	4	4
Jarad, Samir, Astros	.214	5	14	2	3	5	0	1	0	1	0	0	2	0	0	7	1	1
Johnson, J.J., Red Sox	.173	31	110	14	19	20	1	0	0	9	0	2	2	10	0	16	3	1
Johnston, Tom, Pirates	.208	8	24	3	5	6	1	0	0	6	0	0	0	3	0	4	2	1
Jones, Brian, Expos†	.250	33	92	7	23	26	3	0	0	5	4	2	1	3	0	24	3	5
Jones, Donny, Red Sox	.221	42	149	21	33	42	4	1	1	14	0	0	1	15	1	40	5	2
Keenan, Chris, Braves	.125	12	24	2	3	4	1	0	0	0	0	0	0	4	0	16	0	0
Kennedy, Darryl, Rangers*	.111	5	18	4	2	3	1	0	0	1	0	0	0	1	0	1	0	0
King, Karl, Twins	.189	49	148	16	28	31	3	0	0	11	0	1	3	19	0	20	3	2
Kiraly, John, Mets*	.233	40	129	13	30	36	6	0	0	10	1	3	1	11	0	36	0	4
Knowles, Eric, Yankees	.194	49	186	26	36	37	1	0	0	10	0	0	2	20	0	54	11	1
Koller, Jerry, Braves	.000	3	1	0	0	0	0	0	0	0	0	0	0	0	0	0	0	0
Latham, Chris, Dodgers*	.239	43	109	17	26	30	2	1	0	11	0	1	0	16	0	45	14	5
Ledee, Ricardo, Yankees*	.267	47	165	22	44	54	6	2	0	18	0	1	0	22	0	40	3	1
Lee, Angelo, Astros*	.170	18	53	4	9	11	0	1	0	1	1	0	0	4	0	20	4	1
Lee, Charles, Expos	.252	39	123	20	31	43	10	1	0	11	0	2	2	26	0	27	13	3
Legree, Keith, Twins*	.297	45	165	33	49	67	5	5	1	17	0	2	2	21	0	38	16	3
Leichmon, Sequnin, Braves	.353	15	34	7	12	14	2	0	0	5	0	1	1	3	0	6	0	1
Lentz, Jim, Red Sox	.222	9	27	5	6	9	1	1	0	2	0	0	0	7	0	11	0	0
Leonardo, Eddy, Braves	.239	54	184	13	44	52	4	2	0	25	0	3	1	12	0	23	5	4
Lewis, Brian, Yankees*	.257	50	179	15	46	55	4	1	1	18	5	2	2	13	0	29	1	3
Lindsay, Jon, Rangers*	.195	17	41	5	8	11	1	1	0	3	0	0	1	8	0	11	0	1
Livesey, Shanetone, Astros†	.245	46	151	20	37	43	2	2	0	14	1	0	2	20	0	23	13	9
Lloyd, Ron, Braves*	.280	28	93	12	26	28	2	0	0	7	1	0	0	4	0	15	4	3
Lohry, Adin, Yankees*	.240	8	25	4	6	8	2	0	0	8	0	0	0	6	0	5	4	1
Long, Ryan, Royals	.311	48	177	17	55	61	2	2	0	20	0	1	2	10	0	20	6	4
Lora, Jose, Red Sox	.000	3	9	2	0	0	0	0	0	0	0	0	0	0	0	4	1	0
Lorenzo, Odalis, Red Sox	.154	10	26	4	4	5	1	0	0	2	2	1	0	5	0	11	1	0
Machado, Robert, White Sox	.246	38	126	11	31	37	4	1	0	15	0	1	6	6	0	21	2	2
Maguire, Kevin, Pirates	.222	12	27	0	6	7	1	0	0	2	1	1	0	4	0	6	0	1
Mahay, Ron, Red Sox*	.273	54	187	30	51	70	6	5	1	29	2	2	4	33	0	40	2	0
Maize, Dave, Pirates†	.318	32	107	13	34	41	3	2	0	14	0	0	1	12	0	20	6	0
Malave, Jose, Red Sox	.322	37	146	24	47	61	4	2	2	28	0	3	1	10	0	23	6	1
Manrique, Marco, Orioles	.238	26	84	5	20	21	1	0	0	3	0	0	0	10	0	18	1	1
Maple, Marcus, Rangers	.182	14	33	4	6	6	0	0	0	3	0	0	0	3	0	12	1	0
Martinez, Hector, Braves	.257	38	136	15	35	50	7	1	2	12	1	0	1	6	0	14	4	1
Martinez, Javier, Pirates†	.306	41	98	16	30	32	2	0	0	8	1	0	3	7	0	13	16	6
Martinez, Ramon, Astros	.139	38	101	14	14	19	3	1	0	6	4	3	2	9	0	26	6	2
Martinez, Sandy, Dodgers†	.282	52	170	28	48	59	7	2	0	18	4	1	1	5	0	14	14	4
Mathis, Cory, Braves	.200	13	40	6	8	10	2	0	0	5	2	0	1	1	0	4	0	1
Mathis, Monte, White Sox	.139	14	36	2	5	5	0	0	0	2	0	0	1	0	0	7	1	1
Mays, Terrance, Royals	.312	31	77	16	24	32	4	2	0	16	1	1	1	13	0	14	11	1
McCollough, Mike, Rangers	.211	52	185	27	39	62	10	2	3	17	1	2	6	11	0	48	11	4
McCready, James, Mets	.000	16	2	0	0	0	0	0	0	0	0	0	0	0	0	2	0	0
McKeel, Walt, Red Sox	.133	35	113	10	15	23	0	1	2	12	0	4	1	17	0	20	0	0
McNabb, Buck, Astros*	.293	48	174	34	51	60	3	3	0	9	3	2	4	12	0	33	25	8
Mercedes, Feliciano, Orioles†	.227	53	185	34	42	56	4	5	0	15	1	0	2	29	0	45	12	5
Meyer, Paul, Mets	.161	15	56	5	9	14	3	1	0	4	1	0	1	3	0	11	1	0
Miley, Scott, Orioles	.250	21	76	5	19	23	4	0	0	4	0	0	2	6	0	18	0	0
Millege, Tony, White Sox	.186	30	86	13	16	25	4	1	1	10	0	1	0	8	0	24	1	1
Moore, Vince, Braves†	.400	30	110	28	44	66	4	6	2	22	0	1	0	13	0	19	7	2
Moreno, Juan, Mets	.200	31	100	14	20	27	3	2	0	6	1	1	1	8	0	40	11	0
Motuzas, Jeff, Yankees	.193	39	145	17	28	41	8	1	1	17	2	1	4	13	0	44	6	1
Myers, Roderick, Royals*	.278	44	133	14	37	48	2	3	1	18	0	1	5	6	1	27	12	2
Nalepka, Keith, Rangers	.283	48	166	23	47	69	13	0	3	31	1	4	2	19	0	28	2	0
Nava, Marlo, Twins	.301	56	209	30	63	97	14	7	2	27	1	3	1	7	0	20	7	3
Newhouse, Andre, Royals	.255	44	149	31	38	53	4	1	3	16	0	1	3	27	0	36	8	2
Obando, Sherman, Yankees	.294	4	17	3	5	7	2	0	0	1	0	0	1	0	0	2	0	0
Ochoa, Alex, Orioles	.307	53	179	26	55	72	8	3	1	30	3	1	1	16	0	14	11	6
Ogden, Jamie, Twins*	.320	37	122	22	39	68	9	7	2	25	0	4	0	11	0	30	8	4
Oliva, Jose, Rangers	.091	3	11	0	1	2	1	0	0	1	0	0	0	2	0	3	0	0
Ortega, Roberto, Royals*	.164	33	67	8	11	17	4	1	0	12	1	1	0	8	0	20	0	0
Ortiz, Luis, Red Sox	.333	42	153	21	51	78	11	2	4	29	0	1	2	8	0	9	2	1
Ortiz, Nick, Red Sox	.260	35	100	16	26	31	3	1	0	13	2	0	4	21	0	23	1	2
Osentowski, Jared, Mets	.250	51	168	14	42	46	2	1	0	19	2	2	0	16	0	36	5	3
Pages, Javier, Expos	.243	42	140	16	34	40	4	1	0	15	1	0	3	19	0	39	1	1
Payne, Jacob, Pirates†	.134	23	67	4	9	9	0	0	0	3	1	0	2	3	0	11	0	2
Peppers, Cedrick, Pirates*	.316	25	76	9	24	28	0	2	0	5	0	0	2	3	0	10	7	4
Perez, Luis, Twins	.271	59	188	27	51	60	3	3	0	16	1	3	3	25	1	38	17	12
Pierson, Larry, Expos	.194	20	67	3	13	13	0	0	0	6	0	0	1	7	0	20	1	0
Pineda, Jose, Yankees	.063	9	16	1	1	1	0	0	0	2	1	1	0	2	0	8	0	0
Pitts, Jon, Rangers	.063	7	16	1	1	2	1	0	0	2	0	0	1	1	0	3	0	1
Polidor, Wilfredo, White Sox†	.207	54	217	19	45	47	2	0	0	18	1	2	6	6	2	16	9	2
Polis, Pete, Blue Jays	.169	26	83	11	14	22	3	1	1	4	1	0	0	8	0	22	3	1

Player, Team	Avg.	G	AB	R	H	TB	2B	3B	HR	RBI	SH	SF	HP	BB	Int. BB	SO	SB	CS
Ponder, Marcus, Pirates	.275	43	142	20	39	47	6	1	0	14	1	2	0	13	0	22	32	5
Potskin, Joey, Braves	.000	1	3	0	0	0	0	0	0	1	0	0	0	0	0	0	0	0
Ramos, Eduardo, Astros	.277	54	202	22	56	78	8	4	2	29	1	1	3	5	0	44	1	2
Reese, T.J., Braves*	.250	18	32	8	8	11	1	1	0	3	0	0	1	5	0	9	0	0
Reyes, Angel, Yankees*	.143	10	14	1	2	2	0	0	0	1	0	0	0	1	0	3	0	0
Reyes, Jimmy, White Sox†	.183	33	93	14	17	19	2	0	0	9	0	3	0	12	0	27	5	2
Reyes, Tito, Pirates*	.226	35	93	14	21	24	1	1	0	12	1	1	2	5	0	13	3	1
Richardson, Eric, White Sox	.210	42	100	16	21	26	3	1	0	6	1	0	3	13	0	29	8	4
Richmond, Clarence, Dodgers†	.131	40	61	16	8	8	0	0	0	4	0	0	3	13	0	24	6	1
Riddle, Bradford, Braves	.269	13	26	2	7	7	0	0	0	1	1	0	1	2	0	9	2	1
Rivera, Melvin, Braves	.182	40	121	12	22	30	6	1	0	9	1	0	1	9	0	26	0	2
Robertson, Stan, Expos	.223	55	206	36	46	62	3	5	1	24	1	1	6	12	0	52	13	5
Robledo, Nilson, White Sox	.200	6	20	2	4	4	0	0	0	2	0	0	0	1	0	7	1	0
Rodriguez, Anthony, Dodgers	.157	29	51	3	8	10	2	0	0	2	0	0	1	9	0	20	0	1
Rodriguez, Felix, Dodgers	.266	45	139	15	37	53	8	1	2	21	0	0	1	6	0	32	1	0
Rodriguez, Frank, Red Sox	.500	3	14	3	7	9	0	1	0	3	0	0	0	1	0	1	0	0
Rodriguez, Jose, Braves	.181	23	72	6	13	13	0	0	0	4	0	0	0	6	0	21	0	0
Rodriguez, Nerio, White Sox	.225	26	89	4	20	21	1	0	0	8	0	0	1	6	0	12	0	0
Rodriguez, Noel, Astros	.164	22	55	4	9	10	1	0	0	6	0	0	1	2	0	11	2	0
Rossler, Brett, Mets	.176	15	51	9	9	13	2	1	0	6	1	3	0	2	0	12	1	1
Ruoff, Matt, Yankees*	.153	32	98	17	15	18	3	0	0	12	0	1	3	26	0	30	1	0
Salcedo, Edwin, Yankees	.200	3	5	1	1	4	0	0	1	4	0	1	1	0	0	1	0	0
Salvadore, Diego, Blue Jays*	.237	58	211	20	50	70	11	3	1	23	0	1	1	18	0	44	3	2
Santana, Francisco, Pirates†	.275	32	120	15	33	36	3	0	0	10	2	1	0	5	0	12	13	4
Santana, Jose, Astros†	.212	23	66	8	14	14	0	0	0	7	0	0	3	0	0	9	6	2
Santiago, Carlos, Blue Jays	.142	39	113	6	16	26	6	2	0	11	1	0	0	12	0	35	3	2
Santoya, Cristobal, Braves	.182	3	11	0	2	2	0	0	0	0	0	0	1	0	0	1	0	0
Saturnino, Sherton, Braves	.259	39	143	31	37	50	7	3	0	10	4	1	4	10	0	43	16	5
Shirley, Al, Mets	.176	51	187	21	33	47	3	1	3	13	0	0	2	14	0	62	17	4
Sly, Kian, Braves*	.236	39	127	16	30	46	7	3	1	13	0	1	4	9	1	34	3	3
Smith, J.J., Braves	.200	3	10	1	2	2	0	0	0	1	0	0	0	1	0	3	0	0
Soares, Todd, Dodgers	.238	55	193	26	46	54	6	1	0	29	4	2	1	11	0	33	0	0
Soto, Miguel, Braves	.273	45	154	12	42	54	8	2	0	20	0	1	1	8	1	21	1	1
Spencer, Shane, Yankees	.306	41	160	25	49	56	7	0	0	30	0	4	2	14	0	19	9	2
Steele, Steve, Mets	.110	28	82	7	9	9	0	0	0	2	0	0	0	8	0	19	0	1
Stephens, Bill, Dodgers*	.194	39	108	12	21	25	4	0	0	15	2	3	0	17	1	33	2	1
Strange, Keith, White Sox	.222	5	18	3	4	7	0	0	1	4	0	1	0	4	0	4	0	0
Strovink, Eric, Rangers	.266	44	158	11	42	63	10	4	1	18	0	1	4	18	0	36	1	5
Stynes, Chris, Blue Jays	.306	57	219	29	67	96	15	1	4	39	1	0	1	9	0	39	10	3
Subero, Carlos, Royals†	.262	53	183	19	48	62	6	4	0	24	5	2	5	8	0	36	5	2
Sweeney, Michael, Royals	.216	38	102	8	22	28	3	0	1	11	0	2	0	11	0	9	1	0
Sweeney, Roger, Dodgers*	.198	30	91	10	18	25	3	2	0	6	0	0	4	6	0	16	2	0
Tackett, Tim, Red Sox	.125	20	48	2	6	6	0	0	0	2	1	0	2	10	0	23	0	0
Tatro, Glenn, Orioles*	.301	34	83	14	25	33	2	3	0	5	0	0	12	0	0	20	2	2
Taylor, Jon, White Sox	.100	10	20	2	2	2	0	0	0	0	0	0	1	2	0	9	0	0
Tena, Dario, Pirates†	.224	15	49	6	11	11	0	0	0	4	0	1	1	6	0	9	4	2
Thacker, Pat, Blue Jays	.233	27	73	9	17	26	2	2	1	11	2	2	0	14	0	22	0	1
Thomas, Duane, Orioles	.224	45	147	26	33	77	2	1	10	32	0	0	5	24	0	62	8	3
Tolentino, Reynaldo, Rangers	.283	52	187	24	53	71	5	5	1	13	0	0	3	12	0	47	11	2
Torian, Vance, Braves	.208	55	202	25	42	47	5	0	0	18	2	1	1	21	0	36	7	1
Tosar, Miguel, Mets*	.210	40	119	18	25	32	5	1	0	9	3	0	0	21	0	21	7	2
Trevino, Gerald, Braves*	.281	58	199	32	56	78	10	3	2	25	0	1	2	33	0	36	8	3
Troncoso, Roberto, Rangers	.213	42	136	13	29	32	3	0	0	5	0	0	1	6	0	19	2	3
Valera, Roberto, Blue Jays	.196	30	97	10	19	24	3	1	0	7	2	1	2	8	0	27	4	2
Vilchez, Helimenes, Twins	.189	44	127	8	24	29	3	1	0	7	0	0	2	6	0	41	6	3
Vinas, Julio, White Sox	.225	50	187	21	42	60	9	0	3	29	0	2	2	19	0	40	2	3
Vivenzio, Augie, Braves*	.213	25	75	8	16	24	3	1	1	12	1	1	1	7	0	14	0	0
Vizcaino, Romulo, Twins†	.194	22	62	6	12	14	0	1	0	6	1	1	1	6	0	12	3	1
Vogel, Mike, White Sox†	.333	3	9	1	3	3	0	0	0	2	0	0	0	1	0	3	0	0
Walton, Carlo, Dodgers	.200	15	30	4	6	8	2	0	0	6	0	0	0	3	0	9	0	1
Warren, Mel, Dodgers	.252	43	135	14	34	40	2	2	0	10	1	2	3	11	0	46	7	5
Washington, Lamann, Orioles	.257	53	202	32	52	75	13	5	0	23	0	1	4	21	0	55	5	3
Wawruck, Jim, Orioles*	.378	14	45	6	17	20	1	1	0	6	0	0	6	4	0	4	2	2
White, Don, Mets	.240	54	196	32	47	61	10	2	0	12	1	2	3	24	0	37	30	7
Williams, Brent, Dodgers	.346	13	26	5	9	11	2	0	0	4	0	0	1	3	0	4	1	0
Williams, Rodney, Royals	.211	29	57	7	12	13	1	0	0	4	0	0	0	6	0	20	4	2
Williams, Terrell, Mets†	.180	33	100	8	18	25	2	1	1	12	0	2	0	9	0	34	4	2
Wilson, Desi, Rangers*	.160	8	25	1	4	6	2	0	0	7	0	1	0	3	0	2	0	0
Winget, Jeremy, Orioles*	.238	41	130	14	31	35	4	0	0	16	0	2	1	10	0	22	3	2
Winicki, Dennis, Braves	.267	45	146	26	39	47	6	1	0	10	1	0	3	17	0	20	18	8
Woodall, Kevin, Rangers	.215	39	130	13	28	34	2	2	0	8	0	0	4	0	0	19	4	0
Woods, Byron, Braves	.258	37	120	14	31	45	5	0	3	24	0	2	3	11	0	40	5	2
Wright, Lyndon, Twins†	.210	58	200	30	42	76	8	7	4	29	0	2	2	20	0	65	8	3
Wuerch, Jason, Yankees*	.333	38	150	24	50	58	8	0	0	18	2	4	3	9	0	23	2	2
Young, Tyson, Mets*	.125	27	80	9	10	15	3	1	0	5	0	0	0	12	0	34	3	2
Zahner, Kevin, Dodgers	.207	18	29	4	6	6	0	0	0	4	0	0	0	4	0	4	1	0
Zapata, Gustavo, Dodgers	.059	10	17	2	1	1	0	0	0	0	1	0	2	5	0	4	2	0
Zapata, Ramon, Pirates	.308	23	78	23	24	30	4	1	0	7	1	2	0	18	0	5	11	1

The following pitchers, listed alphabetically by club, with games in parentheses, had no plate appearances, primarily through use of designated hitters:

ASTROS—Bjornson, Craig (4); Blest, Ricky (16); Boatman, Steve (16); Bottoms, Derrick (16); Correa, Jorge (14); Dault, Donnie (3); Fesh, Sean (6); McLeod, Robert (9); Miller, Jeff (23); Morman, Alvin (11); Nix, David (9); Smith, Chuck (15); Spring, Josh (16); Vandemark, John (2); Young, Danny (13).

BLUE JAYS—Adkins, Rob (24); Beltran, Alonso (14); Burley, Travis (3); Doman, Roger (13); Jeffery, Scott (18); Leystra, Jeff (15); Mallory, Trevor (5); Meinershagen, Adam (11); Muir, Harry (17); Patterson, Rob (20); Pearlman, David (12); Perez, Jose (7).

BRAVES—Ayers, Rich (15); Burgess, Kurt (20); Carr, Brent (2); Garcia, Pedro (11); Giard, Ken (11); Havens, Willie (11); Jimenez, Luis (15); Maitland, Billy (12); Martineau, Yves (7); Nelson, Earl (11); Reyes, Carlos (20); Risdon, Craig (15); Roberson, Cody (11); Schmidt, Jason (11); Seelbach, Chris (4); Shafer, Bill (8); Wade, Terrell (10).

DODGERS—Cope, Gary (15); Fitzpatrick, Dave (16); Iglesias, Michael (8); Jones, Kiki (1); Lavigne, Martin (10); Minear, Clint (17); Osuna, Pedro (8); Salcedo, Jose (10); Smith, Kevin (10); Sohn, Young Chul (17); Sweeney, Robert (15); Valdez, Ismael (10); Watts, Brandon (12); Zerbe, Chad (16).

EXPOS—Alfonseca, Tony (11); Clelland, Rich (12); Conley, Matt (7); Cruz, Nelson (12); Easterling, Jamal (2); Fultz, Vince (9); Johnson,

Barry (7); Kerrigan, Mike (15); McDohald, Robert (9); Pacheco, Alex (15); Respondek, Mark (16); Reyes, Glen (1); Rueter, Kirk (5); Sanchez, Yonelvys (19); Stevens, Doug (20); Urbina, Ugueth (10).

METS—Belmonte, Pedro (14); Collier, Ervin (14); Finney, Tom (16); Hernandez, Hermes (6); Jones, Clifford (14); Kroon, Marc (12); Swanson, Dave (11); Teske, David (9); Williams, Scotty (11).

ORIOLES—Arias, Jose (18); Benitez, Armando (14); Chatterton, Chris (12); Conner, Scott (13); Cresencio, Arturo (7); DuBois, Brian (1); Forney, Rich (12); Fregoso, Daniel (12); Haynes, Jimmy (14); Jarvis, Matt (11); Kelley, Kent (13); Marquez, Ihosvany (10); Sachrison, Scott (1); Saneaux, Francisco (12).

PIRATES—Bonilla, Miguel (16); Carter, John (10); Christiansen, Jason (6); de los Santos, Mariano (9); Doorneweerd, David (10); Fairfax, Ken (11); Garcia-Luna, Francisco (12); Gernand, Daniel (6); Harrah, Doug (5); Knapp, Gene (15); Loaiza, Esteban (11); McCurry, Jeffrey (6); Perez, Gil (9); Pike, Dave (15); Pontbriant, Matt (14); Rosario, Francisco (14); Taylor, Michael (3); Thompson, Garrett (18); Valdes, Ramon (2).

RANGERS—Alberro, Jose (19); Andrews, Dave (4); Carew, Jeff (9); Chavarria, David (8); Curtis, Chris (7); Davis, Marty (5); Gandolph, Dave (7); Gerhart, Bert (10); Henderson, Daryl (17); Henson, Micky (2); Heredia, Wilson (17); Madrigal, Victor (10); O'Brien, Mark (9); Paramo, Paul (7); Patterson, Danny (11); Seaton, Billy (14); Ubiera, Miguel (13); Underhill, Patrick (4); Vallot, Joey (17); Vaughn, Heath (10).

RED SOX—Bailey, Phillip (1); Bennett, Joel (2); Bush, Craig (14); Caruso, Joe (2); Centeno, Luis (13); Henkel, Robert (1); Horn, Terry (7); Johnson, Jeff (4); Klvac, Dave (14); LeMaster, Matt (14); Maietta, Ron (13); Maloney, Ryan (3); Martinez, Cesar (13); Mejia, Jorge (13); Perez, Hilario (16); Pinango, Simon (4); Ring, Dave (5); Schoenvogel, Chad (15); Sosa, Jason (13); Vanegmond, Tim (3).

ROYALS—Acevedo, Milton (16); Bennett, Matthew (12); Bevil, Brian (13); Bovee, Michael (11); Brucato, Bob (1); Chavez, Elbio (11); Gutierrez, Rafael (16); Hodges, Kevin (9); Jacobs, John (12); Lee, Anthony (8); Pruitt, Jason (10); Sanchez, Jose (22); Schaefer, Chris (2); Shipley, Rich (1); Towns, Ryan (10); West, Eric (17); West, Paul (13).

TWINS—Belcher, Jay (14); Berson, Candy (15); Correa, Jose (27); Foster, David (2); Hawkins, Latroy (11); Hayes, Allen (3); Johnson, A.J. (19); Lidle, Cory (4); Miller, Shawn (10); Pfeffer, Kurt (3); Portillo, Luis (8); Radke, Brad (10); Stevens, Neil (12).

WHITE SOX—Andujar, Luis (10); Baldwin, James (6); Boehringer, Brian (5); Burrow, Jeff (5); Call, Michael (4); Chambers, Travis (6); Culberson, Don (19); de la Cruz, Carlos (10); Dunne, Mike (1); Harp, Keith (5); Hernandez, Roberto (1); Herrholz, John (7); Marshall, Ted (12); McGraw, Walt (7); Ruffcorn, Scott (4); Ruiz, Jorge (11); Schrenk, Steve (11); Soto, Juan (10); Starks, Fred (14); Tagle, Henry (2); Wood, Denny (6); Woodfin, Chris (13).

YANKEES—Carter, Tom (7); Cindrich, Jeff (13); Ferguson, Shane (14); Gogolewski, Doug (6); Kindell, Scott (21); Long, Joe (8); Parra, Luis (15); Paulino, Angel (19); Perez, Albert (20); Pettitte, Andy (6); Ramirez, Luis (17); Regalado, Victor (13); Santaella, Alexis (14); Santiago, Sandi (1); Smith, Sean (17); Sutherland, John (4); Thibert, John (8); Wiley, Jim (3).

GRAND SLAMS—Thomas, 2; Collier, Hardge, Hodge, Thacker, 1 each.

AWARDED FIRST BASE ON CATCHER'S INTERFERENCE—Beltre (Curran), G. Evans (Polis), Hardge (Grob), Hodge (Steele), Hurst (Pages), Legree (Manrique), Leonardo (Ne. Rodriguez), Ostentowski (Curran), Robertson (Payne), White (Curran).

PITCHING

TEAM

Team	ERA	G	CG	ShO	Sv.	IP	H	R	ER	HR	HB	BB	Int. BB	SO	WP	Bk.
White Sox	2.78	59	2	5	13	521.2	430	234	161	5	28	178	0	496	47	13
Rangers	2.89	59	5	5	21	507.2	408	218	163	15	31	191	0	448	40	29
Orioles	2.97	59	4	5	10	493.1	404	230	163	12	20	204	1	437	50	8
Blue Jays	3.02	60	4	5	15	503.2	455	230	169	10	13	194	0	377	40	19
Yankees	3.10	60	3	2	10	525.2	504	281	181	6	27	166	0	440	71	33
Red Sox	3.23	60	7	6	12	501.0	507	245	180	7	25	142	5	338	35	15
Dodgers	3.36	60	4	4	13	498.0	476	256	186	13	21	204	1	425	52	18
Pirates	3.40	59	3	4	10	500.2	481	252	189	11	28	166	1	397	49	26
Twins	3.46	60	3	2	11	496.2	463	258	191	8	17	192	1	395	34	18
Royals	3.49	60	5	6	14	495.0	473	256	192	6	39	204	3	421	53	19
Mets	3.50	60	13	4	16	488.2	469	277	190	12	20	188	8	382	56	20
Expos	3.61	60	4	3	16	510.2	508	280	205	9	28	205	0	401	62	17
Astros	3.95	60	3	3	12	496.2	476	303	218	10	32	278	3	444	78	33
Braves	4.29	60	0	7	17	516.1	523	313	246	20	21	239	2	388	72	28

INDIVIDUAL

(Leading qualifiers for earned-run average leadership—48 or more innings)

*Throws lefthanded.

Pitcher, Team	W	L	Pct.	ERA	G	GS	CG	GF	ShO	Sv.	IP	H	R	ER	HR	HB	BB	Int. BB	SO	WP
Marquez, Orioles	5	3	.625	1.12	10	8	1	1	1	0	64.1	31	11	8	1	2	33	0	70	4
Sohn, Dodgers*	7	0	1.000	1.27	17	3	0	6	0	2	49.2	39	10	7	0	1	8	0	54	1
Martinez, Red Sox*	3	2	.600	1.33	13	8	1	2	0	0	54.0	50	19	8	0	2	16	0	32	2
Haynes, Orioles	3	2	.600	1.60	14	8	1	4	0	2	62.0	44	27	11	0	0	21	0	67	7
Bevil, Royals	5	3	.625	1.93	13	12	2	1	0	0	65.1	56	20	14	0	2	19	0	70	3
McLeod, Astros	4	3	.571	1.93	9	9	2	0	0	0	51.1	39	19	11	1	3	13	0	39	6
Marshall, White Sox*	4	2	.667	1.99	12	12	1	0	0	0	63.1	58	25	14	1	3	17	0	44	5
Bovee, Royals	3	1	.750	2.04	11	11	0	0	0	0	61.2	52	19	14	1	1	12	0	76	4
Forney, Orioles	7	0	1.000	2.19	12	10	2	0	1	0	65.2	48	21	16	1	4	10	0	51	1
Muir, Blue Jays	3	5	.375	2.23	14	14	0	0	0	0	84.2	73	29	21	0	0	25	0	55	3

Departmental leaders: G—Jose Correa, 27; W—Berson, Forney, Sohn, 7; L—Belmonte, Chavarria, Finney, Gutierrez, 6; Pct.—Forney, Sohn, 1.000; GS—Muir, 14; CG—Belmonte, 4; GF—Adkins, 22; ShO—Several pitchers tied with 1; Sv.—Adkins, 10; IP—Muir, 84.2; H—Belmonte, Muir, Schoenvogel, 73; R—Clelland, 45; ER—Clelland, 39; HR—Belmonte, 5; HB—N. Stevens, 8; BB—Clelland, 48; IBB—Finney, 4; SO—Bovee, 76; WP—Clelland, 24.

(All pitchers—listed alphabetically)

Pitcher, Team	W	L	Pct.	ERA	G	GS	CG	GF	ShO	Sv.	IP	H	R	ER	HR	HB	BB	Int. BB	SO	WP
Acevedo, Royals*	2	1	.667	3.89	16	2	0	7	0	1	37.0	41	20	16	1	2	8	0	23	2
Adkins, Blue Jays	1	2	.333	1.82	24	0	0	22	0	10	34.2	19	9	7	0	3	29	0	52	5
Alberro, Rangers	2	0	1.000	1.48	19	0	0	16	0	6	30.1	17	6	5	1	5	9	0	40	1
Alfonseca, Expos	3	3	.500	3.88	11	10	0	0	0	0	51.0	46	33	22	2	3	25	0	38	2
Andrews, Rangers	0	0	.000	6.75	4	0	0	1	0	0	4.0	6	3	3	0	0	2	0	7	1
Andujar, White Sox	4	4	.500	2.45	10	10	1	0	1	0	62.1	60	27	17	0	4	10	0	52	2
Arias, Orioles	2	2	.500	3.79	18	0	0	13	0	1	19.0	18	10	8	0	1	6	0	13	2
Ayers, Braves	4	2	.667	5.06	15	0	0	2	0	0	26.2	27	15	15	0	0	15	0	13	4
Bailey, Red Sox	0	0	.000	0.00	1	0	0	1	0	1	2.0	2	1	0	0	1	0	0	1	0
Baldwin, White Sox	3	1	.750	2.12	6	6	0	0	0	0	34.0	16	8	8	1	1	16	0	48	3
Belcher, Twins	2	3	.400	5.54	14	4	0	6	0	1	37.1	46	30	23	1	1	14	0	15	2

Pitcher, Team	W	L	Pct.	ERA	G	GS	CG	GF	ShO	Sv.	IP	H	R	ER	HR	HB	BB	Int. BB	SO	WP
Belmonte, Mets	4	6	.400	4.42	14	12	4	1	1	0	73.1	73	42	36	5	3	23	0	56	5
Beltran, Blue Jays	2	0	1.000	1.91	14	3	0	7	0	3	33.0	26	9	7	0	1	7	0	30	1
Benitez, Orioles	3	2	.600	2.72	14	3	0	6	0	0	36.1	35	16	11	2	4	11	0	33	2
Bennett, Red Sox	0	0	.000	1.80	2	2	0	0	0	0	10.0	6	2	2	0	1	4	0	8	2
Bennett, Royals	2	5	.286	6.20	12	10	1	0	0	0	40.2	53	36	28	1	2	27	0	30	6
Berson, Twins*	7	3	.700	3.03	15	8	1	2	0	0	65.1	54	29	22	1	1	31	0	41	6
Bevil, Royals	5	3	.625	1.93	13	12	1	0	0	0	65.1	56	20	14	0	2	19	0	70	3
Bjornson, Astros*	2	0	1.000	0.00	4	3	0	1	0	0	25.0	12	0	0	0	1	6	0	24	0
Blest, Astros*	0	2	.000	7.67	16	1	0	7	0	0	27.0	32	26	23	2	1	22	0	17	6
Boatman, Astros	1	4	.200	6.14	16	4	0	11	0	1	36.2	45	38	25	0	2	24	1	20	9
Boehringer, White Sox	1	1	.500	6.57	5	1	0	2	0	0	12.1	14	9	9	1	0	5	0	10	3
Bonilla, Pirates	1	2	.333	4.41	16	2	0	11	0	4	34.2	31	21	17	2	3	12	0	26	2
Bottoms, Astros*	3	3	.500	2.93	16	2	0	9	0	6	30.2	29	16	10	0	2	16	2	29	4
Bovee, Royals	3	1	.750	2.04	11	11	0	0	0	0	61.2	52	19	14	1	1	12	0	76	4
Brucato, Royals	0	0	.000	0.00	1	0	0	0	0	0	1.0	1	0	0	0	0	1	0	2	0
Burgess, Braves*	1	0	1.000	1.52	20	0	0	17	0	8	29.2	20	8	5	1	1	7	0	25	2
Burley, Blue Jays	0	2	.000	5.54	3	2	0	0	0	0	13.0	12	8	8	1	2	9	0	10	1
Burrow, White Sox	1	0	1.000	2.00	5	0	0	2	0	0	9.0	6	2	2	0	1	2	0	4	1
Bush, Red Sox	5	4	.556	2.41	14	11	2	2	1	2	67.1	62	27	18	1	2	13	0	52	4
Call, White Sox	2	0	1.000	1.17	4	0	0	4	0	0	7.2	5	5	1	0	0	2	0	10	0
Canda, Twins	0	0	.000	0.00	1	0	0	1	0	0	1.0	1	1	0	0	0	1	0	1	0
Carew, Rangers	1	2	.333	3.00	9	1	0	2	0	0	18.0	16	11	6	0	2	7	0	11	3
Carr, Braves*	0	0	.000	2.57	2	2	0	0	0	0	7.0	6	2	2	0	3	3	0	10	1
Carter, Pirates	5	4	.556	3.29	10	9	0	0	0	0	41.0	42	20	15	0	4	13	0	28	5
Carter, Yankees*	0	0	.000	4.09	7	3	0	1	0	0	11.0	7	5	5	0	0	4	0	11	3
Caruso, Red Sox	2	0	1.000	4.50	2	0	0	0	0	0	6.0	6	3	3	0	0	4	0	4	0
Centeno, Red Sox	1	3	.250	4.50	13	1	0	9	0	1	30.0	35	20	15	1	3	8	0	15	4
Chambers, White Sox	0	0	.000	0.90	6	0	0	2	0	0	10.0	6	2	1	0	0	3	0	12	0
Chatterton, Orioles	5	1	.833	1.85	12	1	0	8	0	2	34.0	25	11	7	0	1	12	0	30	3
Chavarria, Rangers	0	6	.000	4.25	8	7	0	0	0	0	29.2	35	19	14	1	0	11	0	26	3
Chavez, Royals	3	1	.750	7.56	11	0	0	5	0	1	16.2	17	17	14	1	4	18	1	10	3
Christiansen, Pirates*	1	0	1.000	0.00	6	0	0	4	0	1	8.0	4	0	0	0	0	1	0	8	0
Cindrich, Yankees	4	5	.444	3.95	13	9	1	1	0	0	57.0	61	34	25	2	6	21	0	55	10
Clelland, Expos	5	4	.556	5.63	12	12	0	0	0	0	62.1	59	45	39	1	2	48	0	63	24
Collier, Mets	2	3	.400	2.38	14	6	2	4	0	0	56.2	57	20	15	0	2	13	2	26	4
Conley, Expos	2	2	.500	1.82	7	7	0	0	0	0	39.2	38	13	8	0	3	13	0	24	3
Conner, Orioles	1	4	.200	5.36	12	7	0	4	0	1	48.2	49	33	29	0	3	19	0	34	6
Cope, Dodgers*	1	4	.200	6.41	15	1	0	2	0	0	26.2	36	27	19	1	2	11	0	28	5
Correa, Astros	5	3	.625	3.48	14	11	0	0	0	0	67.1	59	36	26	2	2	42	0	56	10
Correa, Twins	2	2	.500	2.59	27	0	0	19	0	6	48.2	39	20	14	0	0	15	1	53	1
Cresencio, Orioles	1	1	.500	4.32	7	0	0	4	0	1	8.1	6	8	4	1	0	6	1	6	4
Cruz, Expos	2	4	.333	2.40	12	8	1	0	1	0	48.2	40	18	13	1	2	19	0	34	2
Culberson, White Sox	2	4	.333	2.45	19	2	0	16	0	4	33.0	20	13	9	0	1	14	0	33	1
Curtis, Rangers	4	0	1.000	2.06	7	7	0	0	0	0	35.0	27	9	8	1	2	9	0	23	0
Dault, Astros	0	0	.000	0.00	3	0	0	0	0	0	3.2	0	0	0	0	1	2	0	3	1
Davidson, Dodgers	2	3	.400	4.88	16	1	0	5	0	0	31.1	33	28	17	0	4	23	0	23	6
Davis, Rangers	3	0	1.000	1.30	5	5	0	0	0	0	27.2	17	4	4	0	1	4	0	22	0
de la Cruz, White Sox	0	2	.000	3.29	10	2	0	4	0	1	27.1	19	14	10	0	0	13	0	35	5
de los Santos, Pirates	3	2	.600	1.35	9	5	0	3	0	1	33.1	23	5	5	1	0	5	0	50	0
Doman, Blue Jays	2	2	.500	4.83	13	10	0	0	0	0	50.1	52	29	27	2	1	17	0	28	9
Doorneweerd, Pirates	3	1	.750	1.81	10	10	0	0	0	0	44.2	34	12	9	1	1	7	0	55	2
DuBois, Orioles*	0	0	.000	0.00	1	1	0	0	0	0	0.0	0	0	0	0	0	0	0	0	0
Dunne, White Sox	0	0	.000	0.00	1	0	0	1	0	0	3.0	0	0	0	0	0	1	0	5	0
Easterling, Expos	0	1	.000	19.29	2	0	0	0	0	0	2.1	6	8	5	0	0	3	0	2	0
Evans, Twins	0	0	.000	0.00	1	0	0	1	0	0	1.0	0	0	0	0	0	1	0	1	0
Fairfax, Pirates	3	5	.375	4.15	11	11	1	0	0	0	47.2	58	37	22	1	1	18	0	19	1
Ferguson, Yankees	2	1	.667	2.11	14	1	0	8	0	2	21.1	26	10	5	1	1	6	0	30	5
Fesh, Astros*	2	0	.000	2.19	6	0	0	2	0	0	12.1	5	4	3	0	0	11	0	7	4
Finney, Mets	2	6	.250	2.93	16	1	1	13	0	3	43.0	43	19	14	0	2	12	4	41	2
Fitzpatrick, Dodgers	1	2	.333	2.31	16	1	0	14	0	5	23.1	17	6	6	0	1	8	1	17	0
Forney, Orioles	7	0	1.000	2.19	12	10	2	0	1	0	65.2	48	21	16	1	4	10	0	51	1
Foster, Twins*	0	0	.000	6.00	2	0	0	0	0	0	3.0	4	3	2	0	0	3	0	4	2
Fregoso, Orioles	2	4	.333	4.22	12	10	0	0	0	0	53.1	43	29	25	4	3	33	0	53	13
Fultz, Expos	1	1	.500	5.95	9	1	0	1	0	1	19.2	27	16	13	0	2	4	0	12	1
Gandolph, Rangers*	0	3	.000	9.58	7	1	0	0	0	0	10.1	11	12	11	0	0	10	0	9	7
Garcia, Twins	1	2	.333	2.86	15	6	0	8	0	1	44.0	35	19	14	1	0	7	0	41	2
Garcia, Braves	3	2	.600	4.41	11	10	0	1	0	0	51.0	57	30	25	3	1	22	0	24	5
Garcia-Luna, Pirates	0	1	.000	3.16	12	0	0	4	0	0	25.2	24	15	9	0	1	11	0	16	5
Gerhart, Rangers	2	4	.333	1.94	10	8	0	0	0	0	41.2	31	14	9	0	3	13	0	22	0
Gernand, Pirates	0	1	.000	9.00	6	0	0	4	0	0	6.0	8	6	6	1	0	5	0	1	2
Giard, Braves	0	2	.000	3.79	11	10	0	0	0	0	38.0	42	21	16	3	0	13	0	24	2
Gogolewski, Yankees	2	1	.667	2.37	6	3	0	0	0	0	19.0	11	7	5	0	0	5	0	21	0
Gutierrez, Royals	4	6	.400	4.09	16	9	0	2	0	1	55.0	63	29	25	2	4	7	1	36	3
Harp, White Sox*	0	0	.000	1.80	5	0	0	3	0	0	5.0	5	2	1	0	2	1	0	4	0
Harrah, Pirates	1	2	.333	2.25	5	1	0	0	0	0	12.0	8	4	3	0	0	6	0	10	0
Havens, Braves	1	4	.200	8.67	11	7	0	1	0	0	27.0	35	31	26	0	1	21	0	15	5
Hawkins, Twins	4	3	.571	4.75	11	11	0	0	0	0	55.0	62	34	29	2	3	26	0	47	6
Hayes, Twins	0	2	.000	9.82	3	2	0	1	0	0	11.0	13	17	12	1	0	21	0	15	4
Haynes, Orioles	3	2	.600	1.60	14	8	1	4	0	2	62.0	44	27	11	0	2	21	0	67	7
Henderson, Rangers*	2	0	1.000	0.84	17	0	0	10	0	8	32.0	18	8	3	0	3	12	0	49	4
Henkel, Red Sox	1	0	1.000	1.80	1	1	0	0	0	0	5.0	4	1	1	0	0	1	0	7	0
Henry, Blue Jays	0	0	.000	0.00	1	0	0	1	0	0	1.0	0	0	0	0	0	0	0	0	0
Henson, Rangers	1	1	.500	18.00	2	0	0	1	0	0	5.0	14	11	10	0	1	2	0	5	0
Heredia, Rangers	2	4	.333	2.14	17	0	0	8	0	4	33.2	25	18	8	1	3	20	0	22	1
Hernandez, Mets	0	3	.000	1.72	6	0	0	3	0	0	15.2	21	11	3	0	0	5	0	11	5
Hernandez, White Sox	0	0	.000	0.00	1	1	0	0	0	0	6.0	2	0	0	0	0	7	0	0	0
Herrholz, White Sox	0	1	.000	3.07	7	0	0	4	0	0	14.2	13	6	5	0	3	1	0	15	0
Hiljus, Mets	2	3	.400	4.26	9	9	1	0	1	0	38.0	31	27	18	1	1	37	0	38	5
Hodges, Royals	1	2	.333	4.30	9	3	0	0	0	0	23.0	22	14	11	0	4	11	0	13	2
Horn, Red Sox	2	0	1.000	1.74	7	1	0	5	0	1	10.1	9	2	2	0	0	2	0	8	1
Iglesias, Dodgers	1	1	.500	4.70	8	6	0	1	0	0	23.0	26	13	12	1	0	17	0	17	2
Jacobs, Royals	2	0	1.000	2.77	12	1	0	1	0	0	26.0	24	12	8	0	2	3	0	16	1
Jarvis, Orioles*	3	1	.750	4.34	11	5	0	2	0	1	37.1	44	22	18	1	0	17	0	30	2
Jeffery, Blue Jays*	4	5	.444	4.02	18	2	0	7	0	1	53.2	52	31	24	1	0	12	0	31	1

Pitcher, Team	W	L	Pct.	ERA	G	GS	CG	GF	ShO	Sv.	IP	H	R	ER	HR	HB	BB	Int. BB	SO	WP
Jimenez, Braves	4	2	.667	6.15	15	1	0	6	0	0	33.2	45	28	23	4	4	16	1	30	7
Johnson, Expos	0	2	.000	3.86	7	1	0	3	0	0	11.2	10	9	5	0	4	6	1	11	3
Johnson, Red Sox	0	0	.000	0.00	4	1	0	3	0	1	6.0	2	0	0	0	2	0	0	5	0
Johnson, Twins	1	4	.200	2.81	19	0	0	9	0	1	48.0	41	23	15	1	0	19	0	47	4
Jones, Mets*	0	3	.000	3.09	14	4	0	7	0	2	35.0	31	19	12	0	8	1	34	6	
Jones, Dodgers	0	0	.000	0.00	1	1	0	0	0	0	5.0	4	0	0	0	1	0	10	0	
Kelley, Orioles	2	0	1.000	2.45	13	0	0	9	0	1	22.0	18	8	6	1	0	11	0	22	1
Kerrigan, Expos*	4	2	.667	2.80	15	1	0	4	0	0	35.1	38	20	11	1	0	0	29	2	
Kindell, Yankees*	0	4	.000	3.67	21	4	0	13	0	4	41.2	53	28	17	2	1	10	0	27	2
Klvac, Red Sox*	4	3	.571	2.35	14	10	3	2	1	0	69.0	63	23	18	1	4	20	0	47	4
Knapp, Pirates*	1	0	1.000	2.93	15	0	0	7	0	2	27.2	20	10	9	0	1	7	0	18	6
Koller, Braves	0	0	.000	3.38	2	2	0	0	0	0	8.0	9	6	3	0	0	3	0	10	1
Kroon, Mets	2	3	.400	4.53	12	10	1	2	0	0	47.2	39	33	24	1	4	22	0	39	10
Lavigne, Dodgers*	2	2	.500	2.38	10	10	1	0	1	0	53.0	44	23	14	1	2	26	0	49	4
Lee, Royals	1	1	.500	3.48	8	4	1	1	0	0	33.2	30	14	13	0	3	11	0	30	4
LeMaster, Red Sox	1	3	.250	5.70	14	1	0	5	0	0	36.1	45	30	23	1	3	13	1	12	4
Leystra, Blue Jays	4	2	.667	4.28	15	3	1	4	1	0	40.0	51	25	19	1	0	13	0	36	4
Lidle, Twins	1	1	.500	5.79	4	0	0	1	0	0	4.2	5	3	3	0	0	0	0	5	1
Loaiza, Pirates	1	0	.833	2.26	11	11	1	0	1	0	51.2	48	17	13	0	5	14	0	41	2
Long, Yankees	3	2	.600	2.61	8	6	0	1	0	0	38.0	39	23	11	0	3	7	0	27	4
Madrigal, Rangers	3	0	1.000	2.27	10	4	0	3	0	0	31.2	27	11	8	0	0	15	0	22	3
Maietta, Red Sox	2	4	.333	6.57	13	3	0	5	0	0	24.2	35	25	18	0	3	7	1	22	3
Maitland, Braves	1	1	.500	6.62	12	2	0	1	0	0	34.0	36	31	25	2	0	27	0	24	10
Mallory, Blue Jays	2	1	.667	2.01	5	5	1	0	1	0	22.1	24	6	5	1	2	4	0	16	2
Maloney, Red Sox	2	0	1.000	0.56	3	2	0	1	0	0	16.0	12	4	1	0	0	3	0	12	1
Marquez, Orioles	5	3	.625	1.12	10	8	1	1	1	0	64.1	31	11	8	1	2	33	0	70	4
Marshall, White Sox*	4	2	.667	1.99	12	12	1	0	0	0	63.1	58	25	14	1	3	17	0	44	5
Martineau, Braves	3	0	1.000	2.95	7	1	0	0	0	0	18.1	14	6	6	0	1	6	0	13	2
Martinez, Red Sox*	3	2	.600	1.33	13	8	1	2	0	0	54.0	50	19	8	0	2	16	0	32	2
McCready, Mets	6	4	.600	3.24	16	6	2	8	0	1	77.2	69	36	28	1	4	18	1	59	6
McCurry, Pirates	1	0	1.000	2.57	6	1	0	4	0	0	14.0	19	10	4	0	2	4	0	8	2
McDonald, Expos*	0	1	.000	4.82	9	1	0	4	0	0	18.2	21	15	10	0	2	13	0	10	3
McGraw, White Sox	2	3	.400	3.79	7	7	0	0	0	0	38.0	43	19	16	0	2	14	0	28	7
McLeod, Astros	4	3	.571	1.93	9	9	2	0	0	0	51.1	39	19	11	1	2	13	0	39	6
Meinershagen, Blue Jays	3	2	.600	3.51	11	8	0	3	0	0	41.0	39	28	16	1	2	19	0	21	9
Mejia, Red Sox	0	5	.000	7.12	13	6	0	4	0	1	36.2	52	35	29	0	1	11	0	18	1
Miller, Astros	5	2	.714	2.49	23	4	0	18	0	4	47.0	50	20	13	0	4	18	0	51	3
Miller, Twins	3	3	.500	2.59	10	9	2	1	1	0	55.2	54	22	16	1	1	6	0	33	2
Minear, Dodgers*	3	3	.500	2.90	17	1	0	8	0	1	31.0	25	12	10	0	2	12	0	20	2
Morman, Astros*	1	0	1.000	2.16	11	0	0	3	0	1	16.2	15	7	4	0	0	5	0	24	0
Muir, Blue Jays	3	5	.375	2.23	17	14	0	0	0	0	84.2	73	29	21	0	0	25	0	55	3
Nelson, Braves*	0	2	.000	4.18	11	7	0	0	0	0	32.1	29	21	15	0	1	12	0	28	0
Nix, Astros*	0	5	.000	6.34	9	6	0	0	0	0	32.2	44	27	23	1	4	14	0	24	4
O'Brien, Rangers*	1	2	.333	2.97	9	9	0	0	0	0	39.1	28	15	13	4	0	14	0	42	1
Osuna, Dodgers	0	0	.000	0.82	8	0	0	6	0	4	11.0	8	5	1	0	1	0	0	13	2
Pacheco, Expos	3	0	1.000	5.08	15	4	0	3	0	1	44.1	56	32	25	0	1	26	0	19	8
Paramo, Rangers*	1	2	.333	1.33	7	0	0	0	0	0	20.1	17	5	3	0	1	10	0	23	3
Parra, Yankees	0	0	.000	1.57	15	0	0	5	0	1	23.0	20	10	4	0	0	4	0	14	0
Patterson, Rangers	5	3	.625	3.24	11	9	0	0	0	0	50.0	43	21	18	0	3	12	0	46	4
Patterson, Blue Jays*	5	2	.714	2.76	20	0	0	9	0	0	42.1	44	22	13	1	1	15	0	34	3
Paulino, Yankees	4	1	.800	1.54	19	0	0	11	0	2	41.0	38	14	7	0	2	10	0	32	0
Pearlman, Blue Jays	3	3	.500	2.25	12	6	1	2	0	1	44.0	31	18	11	1	0	24	0	38	1
Perez, Yankees	1	1	.500	5.16	20	0	0	9	0	1	29.2	40	26	17	1	1	11	0	20	11
Perez, Pirates	0	2	.000	4.61	9	0	0	2	0	0	13.2	18	7	7	1	0	7	0	14	1
Perez, Red Sox	1	1	.500	3.28	16	0	0	6	0	2	24.2	27	10	9	0	1	12	1	15	1
Perez, Blue Jays	2	2	.500	2.38	7	7	1	0	1	0	41.2	32	16	11	1	1	19	0	25	1
Pettitte, Yankees*	4	1	.800	0.98	6	6	0	0	0	0	36.2	16	6	4	0	1	8	0	51	4
Pfeffer, Twins	1	0	1.000	2.70	3	0	0	0	0	0	3.1	4	1	1	0	0	1	0	4	0
Pike, Pirates	1	0	1.000	4.66	15	1	0	5	0	0	29.0	21	17	15	2	5	15	0	26	7
Pinango, Red Sox*	0	0	.000	4.50	4	0	0	1	0	0	4.0	7	5	2	0	0	2	0	1	0
Pontbriant, Pirates*	2	5	.286	3.57	14	8	1	4	0	2	53.0	62	27	21	1	1	14	0	41	7
Portillo, Twins	2	1	.000	2.21	8	0	0	6	0	1	20.1	17	7	5	0	1	5	0	19	1
Pruitt, Royals	2	3	.400	3.00	10	8	1	0	0	0	36.0	39	23	12	0	2	27	0	30	4
Radke, Twins	3	4	.429	3.08	10	9	0	1	0	1	49.2	41	21	17	0	2	14	0	46	0
Ramirez, Yankees	1	2	.333	6.55	17	1	0	9	0	0	22.0	27	20	16	0	1	8	0	21	2
Reese, Braves	0	0	.000	0.00	1	0	0	1	0	0	1.0	0	0	0	0	1	1	0	2	2
Regalado, Yankees	1	2	.333	3.12	13	0	0	4	0	0	26.0	28	10	9	0	2	8	0	20	0
Respondek, Expos*	3	1	.750	2.05	16	0	0	14	0	8	30.2	23	8	7	1	1	7	0	36	1
Reyes, Yankees*	0	0	.000	0.00	1	0	0	1	0	0	1.0	0	1	0	0	0	0	0	1	1
Reyes, Braves	3	2	.600	1.77	20	0	0	13	0	5	45.2	44	15	9	0	0	9	1	37	1
Ring, Red Sox	2	0	1.000	2.25	5	0	0	4	0	2	8.0	4	2	2	0	0	7	1	10	0
Risdon, Braves	2	1	.667	3.71	15	0	0	5	0	2	26.2	31	16	11	2	5	10	0	18	2
Roberson, Braves	3	5	.375	3.44	18	0	0	12	0	2	36.2	35	17	14	2	2	13	0	17	5
Rosario, Pirates	1	1	.500	4.10	16	0	0	7	0	0	26.1	30	20	12	1	1	9	0	9	1
Rossler, Mets	0	0	.000	18.00	1	0	0	1	0	0	1.0	2	2	2	1	0	1	0	0	0
Rueter, Expos*	1	1	.500	0.95	5	4	0	0	0	0	19.0	16	5	2	0	0	4	0	19	1
Ruffcorn, White Sox	0	0	.000	3.18	4	2	0	1	0	0	11.1	8	7	4	0	0	5	0	15	1
Ruiz, White Sox	3	1	.750	2.61	11	0	0	3	0	0	20.2	17	9	6	0	0	15	0	20	4
Sachrison, Orioles	0	0	.000	13.50	1	0	0	0	0	0	1.1	1	3	2	0	0	3	0	1	0
Salcedo, Dodgers	5	2	.714	4.33	10	9	2	0	0	0	52.0	63	30	25	2	2	8	0	38	6
Sanchez, Royals	2	3	.400	2.45	22	0	0	20	0	3	29.1	22	10	8	0	3	10	1	24	1
Sanchez, Expos	2	1	.667	4.82	19	1	0	10	0	2	37.1	41	23	20	0	3	22	0	34	10
Saneaux, Orioles	1	4	.200	3.95	12	6	0	4	0	1	41.0	42	31	18	1	3	22	0	27	5
Santaella, Yankees	0	2	.000	5.35	14	6	0	0	0	0	38.2	33	28	23	0	7	30	0	25	10
Santiago, Blue Jays	0	0	.000	0.00	1	0	0	0	0	0	2.0	0	0	0	0	0	1	0	1	0
Santiago, Yankees	0	0	.000	0.00	1	0	0	0	0	0	2.0	2	0	0	0	0	2	0	1	0
Schaefer, Royals	0	0	.000	3.00	2	2	0	0	0	0	3.0	4	2	1	0	1	0	0	1	0
Schmidt, Braves	3	4	.429	2.38	11	11	0	0	0	0	45.1	32	21	12	0	0	23	0	44	8
Schoenvogel, Red Sox	5	2	.714	3.25	15	11	1	1	0	0	72.0	73	29	26	3	3	13	1	49	5
Schrenk, White Sox	1	3	.250	2.92	11	7	0	2	0	0	37.0	30	20	12	0	5	6	0	39	1
Seaton, Rangers	1	0	1.000	3.05	14	3	0	5	0	0	41.1	24	15	14	2	4	9	0	27	1
Seelbach, Braves	0	1	.000	4.20	4	0	0	1	0	0	15.0	13	7	7	3	0	6	0	19	3
Shafer, Braves	0	1	.000	8.31	8	1	0	1	0	0	17.1	19	21	16	0	4	17	0	13	9
Shipley, Royals	0	0	.000	18.00	1	0	0	0	0	0	1.0	3	2	2	0	0	0	0	1	1

Pitcher, Team	W	L	Pct.	ERA	G	GS	CG	GF	ShO	Sv.	IP	H	R	ER	HR	HB	BB	Int. BB	SO	WP
Smith, Astros	4	3	.571	3.49	15	7	1	2	0	0	59.1	56	36	23	2	7	37	0	64	7
Smith, Dodgers*	1	4	.200	4.73	10	10	0	0	0	0	40.0	39	26	21	2	3	25	0	36	9
Smith, Yankees	2	4	.333	3.02	11	11	2	0	0	0	62.2	58	33	21	0	2	20	0	31	8
Sohn, Dodgers	7	0	1.000	1.27	17	3	0	6	0	2	49.2	39	10	7	0	1	8	0	54	1
Sosa, Red Sox	0	0	.000	4.50	3	0	0	2	0	0	4.0	7	6	2	0	1	2	0	1	1
Soto, White Sox	3	4	.429	3.35	10	10	0	0	0	0	53.2	44	30	20	1	5	23	0	36	6
Spring, Astros	1	4	.200	4.58	16	6	0	4	0	0	53.0	56	40	27	1	4	29	0	44	12
Starks, White Sox	3	2	.600	3.03	14	0	0	0	0	0	35.2	32	22	12	2	1	15	0	44	8
Stephens, Dodgers	0	0	.000	0.00	3	0	0	1	0	0	3.0	3	3	0	0	0	1	0	3	0
Stevens, Expos	3	2	.600	3.00	20	0	0	17	0	4	27.0	29	11	9	1	1	5	0	19	0
Stevens, Twins	2	5	.286	3.33	12	11	0	1	0	0	48.2	47	28	18	0	8	29	0	23	3
Sutherland, White Sox	0	2	.000	5.87	4	1	0	0	0	0	7.2	5	6	5	0	0	3	0	5	0
Swanson, Mets*	4	3	.571	2.64	11	10	2	0	0	0	64.2	58	28	19	2	1	24	0	52	10
Sweeney, Dodgers	3	3	.500	4.36	15	1	1	5	0	0	33.0	36	19	16	4	1	11	0	20	4
Tagle, White Sox*	0	0	.000	0.00	2	0	0	2	0	2	4.0	3	0	0	0	0	1	0	2	0
Taylor, Pirates*	0	0	.000	2.25	3	0	0	0	0	0	4.0	2	1	1	0	2	2	0	2	0
Teske, Mets*	0	1	.000	7.80	9	0	0	5	0	3	15.0	26	18	13	1	0	7	0	9	0
Thibert, Yankees	3	2	.600	0.91	8	6	0	0	0	0	39.2	29	13	4	0	0	11	0	40	9
Thompson, Pirates	2	1	.667	5.06	18	0	0	9	0	0	26.2	21	17	15	1	1	14	1	24	6
Towns, Royals	0	1	.000	7.59	10	1	0	3	0	0	10.2	5	9	9	0	1	23	0	13	10
Ubiera, Rangers	1	2	.333	3.90	13	3	0	6	0	0	27.2	31	18	12	0	2	18	0	19	3
Underhill, Rangers	1	0	1.000	1.00	4	1	0	3	0	1	9.0	4	2	1	0	0	4	0	11	4
Urbina, Expos	3	3	.500	2.29	10	10	3	0	1	0	63.0	58	24	16	2	4	10	0	51	2
Valdes, Pirates*	0	1	.000	32.40	2	0	0	0	0	0	1.2	8	6	6	0	1	2	0	1	0
Valdez, Dodgers	2	2	.500	2.32	10	10	0	0	0	0	50.1	44	15	13	0	0	13	0	44	0
Vallot, Rangers	0	0	.000	23.14	1	0	0	0	0	0	2.1	7	6	6	2	0	3	0	2	1
Vandemark, Astros*	0	0	.000	6.75	2	0	0	0	0	0	1.1	2	1	1	0	0	0	0	1	0
Vanegmond, Red Sox	2	0	1.000	0.60	3	2	0	1	0	1	15.0	6	1	1	0	1	1	0	20	2
Vaughn, Rangers	0	0	.000	3.38	10	0	0	5	0	2	18.2	10	10	7	3	1	7	0	20	3
Wade, Braves	2	0	1.000	6.26	10	2	0	0	0	0	23.0	29	17	16	0	0	15	0	22	3
Watts, Dodgers*	1	3	.250	4.64	12	5	0	4	0	1	33.0	28	20	17	1	2	25	0	30	5
E. West, Royals	1	1	.500	3.41	17	0	0	11	0	1	31.2	26	20	12	0	5	15	0	21	6
P. West, Royals	3	1	.750	1.93	13	3	0	4	0	2	23.1	15	9	5	0	3	12	0	25	3
Wiley, Yankees	0	2	.000	3.52	3	3	0	0	0	0	7.2	11	7	3	0	0	9	0	9	2
Williams, Mets	2	0	1.000	3.43	11	2	0	3	0	1	21.0	19	22	8	0	3	18	0	17	3
Wood, White Sox	0	1	.000	8.59	6	0	0	2	0	1	7.1	10	7	7	0	0	7	0	9	0
Woodfin, White Sox	1	0	1.000	2.39	13	1	0	10	0	4	26.1	19	7	7	0	0	7	0	24	0
Young, Astros	1	4	.200	7.99	13	7	0	0	0	0	32.2	32	33	29	1	2	39	0	41	12
Zerbe, Dodgers*	0	2	.000	2.20	16	1	0	4	0	0	32.2	31	19	8	1	0	15	0	23	6

BALKS—Gutierrez, Jeffery, A. Perez, Pettitte, 6 each; Boatman, Gandolph, Jimenez, Kroon, C. Smith, 5 each; Blest, Burgess, Culberson, C. Jones, McCready, Morman, Parra, Paulino, Rosario, K. Smith, Thibert, E. West, 4 each; Alberro, Berson, Bevil, Bonilla, Bush, T. Carter, Cindrich, Conley, Cruz, Davis, Garcia-Luna, Hawkins, Iglesias, Martineau, S. Miller, Nix, O'Brien, D. Patterson, Pinango, C. Reyes, Roberson, *Sanchez, Spring, Swanson, Urbina, 3 each; Bjornson, Burley, J. Carter, Chavarria, Collier, Jose Correa, Curtis, de los Santos, Fairfax, Forney, Harrah, Henderson, Heredia, Jacobs, Kerrigan, Lidle, Maitland, McGraw, Mejia, J. Miller, B. Patterson, Pearlman, Pontbriant, Radke, Risdon, Vanegmond, Wade, 2 each; Adkins, Andujar, Arias, Baldwin, Belmonte, Beltran, J. Bennett, Boehringer, Bottoms, Centeno, Cope, Jorge Correa, de la Cruz, Doman, Doorneweerd, Easterling, Evans, Fitzpatrick, Fregoso, P. Garcia, Gernand, Giard, Hayes, Haynes, Herrholz, Hiljus, Jarvis, F. Johnson, K. Jones, Klvac, Lee, Loaiza, Long, Madrigal, Mallory, Marquez, McCurry, McDonald, McLeod, Meinershagen, Minear, Muir, Osuna, G. Perez, H. Perez, J. Perez, Pike, Ramirez, Respondek, Ruffcorn, Saneaux, Schoenvogel, Seaton, Seelbach, Shafer, Stephens, Sutherland, Ubiera, Valdez, Vandemark, Vaughn, Watts, Woodfin, Young, 1 each.

COMBINATION SHUTOUTS—Bjornson-Miller, Bjornson-Smith-Miller-Morman, Correa-Morman, Astros; Beltran-Doman-Adkins, Meinershagen-Pearlman, Blue Jays; Giard-Maitland-Roberson, Havens-Burgess, Nelson-Martineau-Reyes-Burgess, Nelson-Martineau-Shafer-Reyes, Schmidt-Reyes, Schmidt-Risdon, Schmidt-Roberson, Braves; Fitzpatrick-Stephens-Davidson-Osuna, Smith-Sohn-Zerbe-Sweeney-Minear-Osuna, Sohn-Fitzpatrick, Dodgers; Reuter-Pacheco-Respondek, Expos; Belmonte-Finney, Mets; DuBois-Marquez-Kelley, Jarvis-Haynes, Marquez-Saneaux, Orioles; Carter-Gernand-Knapp-Christiansen, Carter-Knapp-Thompson, Doorneweerd-Perez, Pirates; Davis-Alberro, Gerhart-Alberro, Gerhart-Madrigal, Madrigal-Heredia-Vaughn, Patterson-Ubiera-Madrigal, Rangers; Bush-LeMaster-Sosa, Bush-Perez-Horn, Johnson-Schoenvogel-Martinez-Ring, Schoenvogel-Maietta, Red Sox; Bennett-Towns-Jacobs-Acevedo, Bevil-Jacobs, Bovee-Jacobs-Sanchez, Bovee-E. West-P. West, Gutierrez-E. West, P. West-Gutierrez-Acevedo-E. West, Royals; Miller-Garcia-Correa, Twins; Baldwin-Burrows-Culberson, Hernandez-Boehringer, Marshall-Woodfen, Soto-Herrholz, White Sox; Pettitte-Kindall, Smith-Ramirez-Paulino, Yankees.

NO-HIT GAMES—None.

FIELDING

TEAM

Team	Pct.	G	PO	A	E	DP	PB	Team	Pct.	G	PO	A	E	DP	PB
Rangers	.959	60	1523	643	92	40	17	Twins	.948	60	1490	566	112	32	17
Blue Jays	.957	60	1511	663	97	48	12	Orioles	.947	59	1480	644	118	38	19
Red Sox	.954	60	1503	703	107	46	18	Pirates	.945	59	1502	599	122	37	17
Dodgers	.952	60	1494	619	106	29	27	Yankees	.940	60	1577	697	146	40	14
Expos	.950	60	1532	706	117	45	12	Mets	.938	60	1466	623	139	44	14
Royals	.949	60	1485	664	116	47	19	Astros	.935	60	1490	613	145	38	25
White Sox	.949	59	1565	667	121	46	17	Braves	.933	60	1549	623	155	50	29

Triple plays—Dodgers, Expos, Royals.

INDIVIDUAL

*Throws lefthanded.
FIRST BASEMEN

Player, Team	Pct.	G	PO	A	E	DP
Bell, Orioles	1.000	10	60	4	0	2
Bonifay, Pirates	.986	8	67	4	1	4
Bowrosen, White Sox	1.000	1	10	0	0	1
Burgos, Royals	.981	34	245	9	5	17
BURTON, Rangers	.989	48	435	20	5	26
Calder, Pirates	.982	36	307	15	6	19
Calero, Astros	.986	46	346	19	5	21
Cerda, Royals	1.000	1	0	1	0	0
Ciccarella, Red Sox*	1.000	7	77	3	0	3
Colon, Astros	.983	15	105	11	2	6

Player, Team	Pct.	G	PO	A	E	DP
Crimmins, Red Sox	.975	12	114	3	3	7
Curran, Orioles	1.000	1	11	0	0	1
Diaz, Pirates	.974	22	137	10	4	7
Dotel, Dodgers*	1.000	4	20	1	0	3
Farmer, Expos	1.000	1	5	0	0	0
Floyd, Expos	.970	49	451	27	15	28
Fryman, White Sox	1.000	6	45	5	0	2
Garrow, Twins	.978	11	83	7	2	1
Gipner, Yankees	.950	3	18	1	1	0
Gonzalez, Dodgers	.980	23	178	18	4	8
Grapenthien, Astros	.955	2	20	1	1	5
Grob, Braves	1.000	1	2	0	0	0
Isava, Royals	.989	14	88	5	1	7

Player, Team	Pct.	G	PO	A	E	DP
James, Braves	.932	9	66	3	5	9
Jarad, Astros	.974	4	35	2	1	2
King, Twins	1.000	12	88	4	0	9
Kiraly, Mets*	.979	40	307	20	7	17
Lloyd, Braves	.900	7	41	4	5	5
Malave, Red Sox	.975	27	267	4	7	19
Manrique, Orioles	1.000	2	16	2	0	2
Matuzas, Yankees	.867	1	13	0	2	0
McKeel, Red Sox	1.000	4	23	0	0	1
Meyer, Mets	.941	11	102	9	7	10
Miley, Orioles	1.000	17	169	4	0	13
Nalepka, Rangers	1.000	14	114	5	0	8
Ogden, Twins*	.981	30	253	12	5	13
Ortega, Royals*	1.000	32	173	13	0	17
Pierson, Expos	.984	11	118	5	2	14
Polis, Blue Jays	1.000	2	6	0	0	1
Reyes, White Sox	.981	6	47	4	1	2
Rivera, Braves	.983	25	220	17	4	14
A. Rodriguez, Dodgers	1.000	1	4	1	0	0
Rodriguez, Astros	.600	1	3	0	2	0
Ruoff, Yankees	.979	27	218	12	5	16
Salcedo, Yankees	1.000	1	9	0	0	2
Salvadore, Blue Jays*	.981	58	551	30	11	42
Sly, Braves	.941	22	162	15	11	14
Smith, Braves	1.000	1	7	1	0	1
Soares, Dodgers	1.000	3	24	0	0	1
Soto, Rangers	1.000	1	3	0	0	0
Stephens, Dodgers	.978	35	245	17	6	14
Sweeney, Royals	.938	4	14	1	1	3
Tackett, Red Sox	.966	15	108	6	4	9
Taylor, White Sox	.970	9	57	8	2	2
Thacker, Blue Jays	1.000	1	2	0	0	0
Tosar, Mets	.980	5	45	3	1	7
Vilchez, Twins	.974	11	73	3	2	5
Vinas, White Sox	.968	43	366	28	13	32
Walton, Dodgers	1.000	1	3	1	0	0
Williams, Dodgers	1.000	1	7	0	0	1
Winget, Orioles*	.984	36	290	13	5	16
Wuerch, Yankees	.988	32	295	25	4	16
Young, Mets	.950	5	36	2	2	1

Triple plays—Burgos, Pierson.

SECOND BASEMEN

Player, Team	Pct.	G	PO	A	E	DP
Aguado, Red Sox	.950	7	6	13	1	2
Alfonzo, Mets	.987	39	79	71	2	12
Asencio, Orioles	.958	28	37	54	4	7
Beltre, Mets	1.000	3	3	1	0	0
Blanco, Twins	.967	6	10	19	1	3
Brookens, Royals	.986	20	31	39	1	9
Brown, Red Sox	.857	3	5	7	2	2
Burton, White Sox	.948	50	101	138	13	25
Carabba, Expos	1.000	3	1	0	0	0
Carlsen, Blue Jays	.864	12	19	32	8	12
Cedeno, Astros	.833	18	38	37	15	8
Centeno, Astros	.959	31	55	85	6	15
Cerda, Royals	.980	9	24	24	1	5
Colon, Pirates	.948	17	21	34	3	4
Colon, Astros	.944	18	27	40	4	2
J. Conner, Orioles	.918	31	41	71	10	11
Dennison, Expos	1.000	2	4	3	0	1
Diaz, Red Sox	.900	14	22	14	4	4
Dufault, Twins	1.000	2	4	8	0	1
Durham, White Sox	1.000	6	18	15	0	7
Earl, Pirates	.854	21	27	49	13	8
FERREIRA, Red Sox	.980	47	81	168	5	25
Garcia, Yankees	.930	17	21	32	4	6
Garcia, Twins	.667	1	1	1	1	0
Gerald, Royals	1.000	1	1	1	0	1
Hansen, Yankees	1.000	1	2	5	0	1
Hardge, Expos	.974	59	126	171	8	28
Heaps, Twins	.891	35	72	91	20	12
Henry, Blue Jays	.949	50	102	101	11	22
Indriago, Royals	.963	37	64	91	6	15
Knowles, Yankees	.972	16	27	42	2	7
Latham, Dodgers	.917	34	47	63	10	7
Martinez, Pirates	.872	13	15	19	5	3
Martinez, Dodgers	.978	32	55	81	3	12
Mathis, White Sox	.857	2	2	4	1	1
Mercedes, Orioles	.957	19	21	46	3	9
Nava, Twins	.959	51	96	117	9	20
Perez, Twins	1.000	1	2	0	0	1
Reyes, White Sox	.667	4	1	5	3	0
Subero, Royals	1.000	2	1	1	0	0
Tolentino, Rangers	.942	52	87	125	13	18
Torian, Braves	.945	34	76	97	10	19
Tosar, Mets	.975	23	36	41	2	8
Trevino, Braves	.944	28	53	64	7	13
Troncoso, Rangers	.871	8	9	18	4	2
Vilchez, Twins	1.000	1	2	2	0	0
White, Mets	1.000	1	0	1	0	0
G. Zapata, Dodgers	.941	6	17	15	2	2
R. Zapata, Pirates	.948	19	39	52	5	9

Triple play—G. Zapata.

THIRD BASEMEN

Player, Team	Pct.	G	PO	A	E	DP
Aguado, Red Sox	1.000	4	2	6	0	1
Albornoz, Yankees	.960	8	5	19	1	1
Alfonzo, Mets	.920	6	5	18	2	2
Asencio, Orioles	1.000	4	4	3	0	0
Awkard, Rangers	.909	4	2	8	1	0
Batista, Expos	.863	37	27	74	16	9
Bonifay, Pirates	1.000	3	2	1	0	0
Bowrosen, White Sox	.781	39	22	60	23	4
Brookens, Royals	.000	1	0	0	2	0
Brown, Red Sox	.870	9	6	14	3	0
Carlsen, Blue Jays	.800	1	0	4	1	1
Cedeno, Astros	.500	2	0	1	1	0
Cerda, Royals	1.000	5	2	15	0	1
Colon, Astros	.917	9	2	20	2	2
DeLeon, Royals	1.000	1	1	2	0	0
Dufault, Twins	.934	16	18	39	4	1
Edmondson, Pirates	.889	40	30	66	12	4
Evangelista, Rangers	.949	33	24	107	7	7
Evans, Twins	.846	7	4	7	2	0
Farmer, Expos	.882	28	12	48	8	4
Freitag, Expos	1.000	1	0	3	0	1
Garcia, Yankees	.000	1	0	0	1	0
Garrow, Twins	.742	14	12	11	8	1
Gerald, Royals	.833	16	11	24	7	2
Gonzalez, Dodgers	.882	8	8	7	2	0
Grob, Braves	.000	1	0	0	2	0
Hansen, Yankees	.883	54	37	106	19	8
Indriago, Royals	.667	3	0	2	1	0
Leonardo, Braves	.854	46	39	84	21	7
Long, Royals	.844	39	32	71	19	4
Lorenzo, Red Sox	.941	10	5	11	1	1
Manrique, Orioles	1.000	8	1	11	0	0
Martinez, Pirates	.818	27	12	33	10	1
Martinez, Dodgers	1.000	5	3	13	0	1
Mathis, White Sox	1.000	10	5	5	0	1
Oliva, Rangers	1.000	3	4	3	0	1
L. Ortiz, Red Sox	.933	32	30	67	7	2
N. Ortiz, Red Sox	.935	12	13	30	3	2
Osentowski, Mets	.809	50	53	112	39	11
Ramos, Astros	.833	53	26	94	24	4
Reyes, White Sox	.848	16	7	21	5	1
Rivera, Braves	.886	13	13	26	5	2
Rossler, Mets	.000	1	0	0	3	0
Smith, Braves	.833	2	2	3	1	0
Soares, Dodgers	.833	51	36	54	18	4
Soto, Rangers	.848	11	11	17	5	2
Stephens, Dodgers	1.000	2	2	1	0	0
Strange, White Sox	.909	5	3	7	1	0
STYNES, Blue Jays	.957	57	42	138	8	10
Trevino, Braves	.667	1	1	1	1	0
Troncoso, Rangers	1.000	3	0	6	0	0
Valera, Blue Jays	1.000	3	0	7	0	0
Vilchez, Twins	.839	30	23	50	14	1
Washington, Orioles	.824	50	39	92	28	7
T. Williams, Mets	.800	4	1	3	1	0
Woodall, Rangers	.750	7	0	9	3	0
Zapata, Dodgers	1.000	3	2	1	0	0

Triple play—Long.

SHORTSTOPS

Player, Team	Pct.	G	PO	A	E	DP
Abreu, Astros	.714	1	3	2	2	2
Aguado, Red Sox	.920	6	9	14	2	2
Albornoz, Yankees	.914	23	36	60	9	4
Alfonzo, Mets	.872	8	15	19	5	6
Asencio, Orioles	.898	24	32	56	10	7
Batista, Expos	.895	16	15	36	6	5
Beltre, Mets	.937	31	36	98	9	15
Blanco, Twins	1.000	2	0	3	0	0
Brown, Red Sox	.941	31	57	103	10	16
Carabba, Expos	.915	27	33	64	9	8
Cedeno, Astros	1.000	1	0	2	0	0
Colon, Pirates	.923	13	13	35	4	6
Colon, Astros	.500	2	0	1	1	0
Dennison, Expos	.944	21	23	61	5	3
Diaz, Red Sox	1.000	1	1	0	0	0
Ducksworth, Pirates	1.000	2	2	6	0	1
Dufault, Twins	.932	10	13	28	3	8
Earl, Pirates	.875	4	7	7	2	2
Eenhoorn, Yankees	.911	13	12	29	4	4
Ferreira, Red Sox	1.000	2	1	4	0	0
Garrow, Twins	.881	13	13	39	7	3
Gerald, Royals	.857	24	42	66	18	10
Gonzalez, Blue Jays	.915	51	66	160	21	23
Heaps, Yankees	.833	3	6	9	3	2
Johnston, Pirates	.875	8	9	12	3	1
Knowles, Yankees	.888	36	54	104	20	16
Latham, Dodgers	.913	8	10	11	2	3
Legree, Twins	.890	35	31	90	15	10
Leichmon, Braves	1.000	3	1	1	0	0
Leonardo, Braves	.811	10	17	13	7	2

Player, Team	Pct.	G	PO	A	E	DP
Livesey, Astros	.841	44	60	93	29	10
Martinez, Pirates	1.000	1	0	1	0	0
Martinez, Dodgers	.966	19	37	47	3	5
Mathis, White Sox	1.000	1	4	3	0	0
Mercedes, Orioles	.869	35	43	103	22	18
Nava, Twins	1.000	2	2	2	0	1
N. Ortiz, Red Sox	.902	21	40	61	11	8
Osentowski, Mets	1.000	1	1	1	0	1
Potskin, Braves	.500	1	0	1	1	0
PULIDOR, White Sox	.939	54	68	146	14	29
Reyes, White Sox	.878	9	12	24	5	4
Rodriguez, Red Sox	.950	3	9	10	1	5
Santana, Pirates	.921	32	45	95	12	12
Santana, Astros	.877	22	27	44	10	9
Santoya, Braves	.818	2	4	5	2	3
Subero, Royals	.911	40	65	129	19	24
Torian, Braves	.853	23	32	67	17	11
Trevino, Braves	.874	27	42	76	17	15
Troncoso, Rangers	.908	30	46	72	12	12
Valera, Blue Jays	.907	9	15	34	5	6
Washington, Orioles	1.000	5	2	8	0	0
T. Williams, Mets	.868	23	25	67	14	8
Winicki, Dodgers	.920	41	59	126	16	13
Woodall, Rangers	.906	34	48	87	14	11
Zapata, Dodgers	1.000	1	1	0	0	0
Zapata, Pirates	.840	6	7	14	4	3

Triple plays—Carabba, Subero, Winicki.

OUTFIELDERS

Player, Team	Pct.	G	PO	A	E	DP
Abreu, Astros	.963	52	67	11	3	1
Alicea, Pirates*	.977	28	40	2	1	0
Arendt, Braves	1.000	2	2	0	0	0
Austin, White Sox	1.000	10	5	0	0	0
Awkard, Rangers	.977	31	36	6	1	1
Baez, Red Sox	.963	39	74	3	3	0
Benitez, Expos	.967	52	85	2	3	1
Bogan, Pirates	.927	24	34	4	3	1
Bonifay, Pirates	1.000	3	4	0	0	0
Bull, Mets	.985	35	63	4	1	1
BUTLER, Blue Jays	.991	58	104	2	1	0
Cameron, White Sox	.951	43	55	3	3	1
Carlsen, Blue Jays	1.000	3	10	0	0	0
Castillo, Astros	.867	8	11	2	2	1
Coakley, Twins	.947	12	18	0	1	0
Collier, Red Sox	.923	11	12	0	1	0
Conger, Pirates*	.955	14	19	2	1	0
Correa, Braves	.968	41	88	4	3	1
Cradle, Blue Jays	.978	42	87	2	2	0
Cumberbatch, Yankees	.970	57	94	4	3	1
Cunningham, Pirates	.931	27	24	3	2	0
Devers, White Sox	.976	30	39	1	1	1
Dotel, Dodgers*	.955	24	40	2	2	0
Espinosa, Pirates	.960	18	22	2	1	0
Evans, Twins	.946	43	63	7	4	1
Evans, Orioles	.943	32	29	4	2	0
Garr, Braves	1.000	3	3	1	0	0
Gonzalez, Royals	.941	42	62	2	4	0
Good, Royals*	1.000	30	38	3	0	0
Goodwin, Orioles*	.988	39	77	5	1	1
Griffin, Blue Jays	.930	40	38	2	3	2
Hardge, Expos	1.000	1	2	0	0	0
Harris, White Sox	.955	22	20	1	1	1
Haughney, Rangers	.989	50	81	5	1	2
Hawkins, Astros	1.000	26	34	2	0	1
Heidelberg, Expos	.923	10	23	1	2	0
Hodge, Orioles	.962	32	20	5	1	1
Hollandsworth, Dodgers*	1.000	5	4	0	0	0
Hurst, White Sox	.976	27	37	4	1	2
Hurtault, Expos	.950	19	34	4	2	2
L. Jackson, Dodgers	.810	22	17	0	4	0
V. Jackson, Dodgers	.953	51	79	3	4	0
James, Braves	1.000	18	28	0	0	0
James, White Sox	.956	23	39	4	2	1
Jer. Johnson, Red Sox	.956	30	40	3	2	0
Jones, Expos	.976	32	38	2	1	0
Jones, Red Sox	.938	40	55	5	4	0
Keenan, Braves	.833	5	5	0	1	0
Ledee, Yankees*	.934	47	79	6	6	1
Lee, Astros	.889	14	8	0	1	0
Lee, Expos	.931	23	25	2	2	0
Leichman, Braves	.933	8	14	0	1	0
Lewis, Yankees	.927	42	48	3	4	0
Lloyd, Braves	1.000	16	23	1	0	1
Lora, Red Sox	1.000	3	4	0	0	0
Mahay, Red Sox*	.971	54	97	2	3	0
Malave, Red Sox	1.000	8	10	2	0	0
Maple, Rangers*	.950	14	19	0	1	0
Martinez, Astros	.957	38	66	1	3	0
Mathis, Braves	1.000	11	11	1	0	1
Mays, Royals	.952	28	38	2	2	1
McCollough, Rangers	.963	52	72	7	3	1
McNabb, Astros	.987	48	72	5	1	1
Miley, Orioles	1.000	1	1	0	0	0

Player, Team	Pct.	G	PO	A	E	DP
Millege, White Sox	1.000	12	12	0	0	0
Moore, Braves*	.967	26	57	2	2	0
Moreno, Mets	.981	30	46	6	1	3
Myers, Royals*	.979	43	45	2	1	0
Nava, Twins	1.000	2	4	1	0	0
Newhouse, Royals	.894	43	38	4	5	1
Ochoa, Orioles	.960	40	45	3	2	1
Ogden, Twins*	.800	3	4	0	1	0
Peppers, Pirates*	.969	22	29	2	1	1
Perez, Twins	.973	56	102	6	3	3
Ponder, Pirates	.952	40	76	4	4	1
Reese, Braves	1.000	1	2	0	0	0
Reyes, Yankees*	1.000	6	3	0	0	0
Reyes, Pirates*	.900	33	43	2	5	1
Richardson, White Sox	.932	39	67	2	5	1
Richmond, Dodgers	.935	33	28	1	2	0
Riddle, Braves	1.000	8	7	0	0	0
Rivera, Braves	1.000	2	3	0	0	0
Robertson, Expos	.938	51	80	11	6	2
Rodriguez, Astros	1.000	17	17	1	0	0
Santiago, Blue Jays	.957	38	58	8	3	1
Saturnino, Braves	.971	35	62	6	2	0
Shirley, Mets	.928	50	76	1	6	0
Sly, Braves	1.000	13	27	1	0	0
Spencer, Yankees	.959	37	64	6	3	2
Strovink, Rangers	.981	39	50	2	1	0
Rog. Sweeney, Dodgers*	.946	27	32	3	2	0
Tatro, Orioles*	.970	25	31	1	1	0
Tena, Pirates	1.000	14	28	2	0	0
Thomas, Orioles	.949	31	35	2	2	0
Vizcaino, Twins	.944	15	17	0	1	0
Walton, Dodgers	.800	8	4	0	1	0
Warren, Dodgers	.963	42	77	1	3	0
Wawruck, Orioles*	1.000	8	10	0	0	0
White, Mets	.979	53	93	1	2	0
Williams, Royals	.944	19	13	4	1	0
T. Williams, Mets	1.000	1	1	0	0	0
Wilson, Rangers*	1.000	3	2	0	0	0
Woods, Braves	.957	17	18	4	1	0
Wright, Twins	.931	58	119	3	9	1
Young, Mets	1.000	11	5	2	0	0

CATCHERS

Player, Team	Pct.	G	PO	A	E	DP	PB
Acevedo, Twins	1.000	6	18	0	0	0	2
Albaladejo, Astros	.949	21	134	16	8	1	11
Bell, Orioles	.982	29	147	21	3	0	8
Bethke, Rangers	.988	20	144	23	2	1	8
Borrero, Red Sox	.952	32	177	23	10	2	4
Burgos, Royals	.974	10	30	7	1	0	3
Campos, Astros	.966	21	98	15	4	1	9
Canda, Twins	.982	24	150	18	3	0	7
Carbajal, Expos	.923	6	12	0	1	1	1
Casanova, Mets	.979	32	211	24	5	0	4
Curran, Orioles	.968	31	188	24	7	0	6
DeLEON, Royals	1.000	43	195	26	0	0	8
Freitag, Expos	.958	22	140	18	7	1	4
A. Garcia, Braves	.991	14	94	17	1	1	5
Gipner, Yankees	.975	21	146	13	4	1	6
Gonzalez, Astros	.966	31	204	22	8	2	5
Grob, Braves	.958	11	63	6	3	0	7
Isava, Royals	.965	18	92	19	4	1	3
Jarad, Astros	1.000	1	3	0	0	0	0
Kennedy, Rangers	1.000	3	25	1	0	0	1
King, Twins	.985	37	243	20	4	0	8
Lindsay, Rangers	.984	16	112	10	2	0	4
Machado, White Sox	.977	38	287	54	8	1	10
Maguire, Pirates	1.000	12	68	6	0	0	3
Maize, Pirates	.970	32	206	19	7	3	5
Manrique, White Sox	.974	17	101	11	3	1	6
Martinez, Blue Jays	.981	37	226	34	5	3	6
Matuzas, Yankees	.983	37	246	35	5	1	6
McKeel, Red Sox	.978	28	127	52	4	2	14
Meyer, Mets	1.000	1	5	1	0	0	1
Pages, Expos	.969	40	240	39	9	0	7
Payne, Pirates	.968	22	139	11	5	1	9
Pineda, Yankees	.981	9	44	8	1	0	2
Pitts, Rangers	1.000	5	34	5	0	0	1
Polis, Blue Jays	.966	23	145	25	6	2	6
Reese, Braves	.950	6	17	2	1	0	4
Robledo, White Sox	1.000	1	4	0	0	0	0
A. Rodriguez, Dodgers	.972	28	122	19	4	0	8
F. Rodriguez, Dodgers	.973	32	161	18	5	0	10
Rodriguez, Braves	.952	23	122	18	7	1	8
Rodriguez, White Sox	.972	23	153	23	5	0	6
Rossler, Mets	.941	3	13	3	1	0	1
Soto, Rangers	.988	22	144	25	2	0	3
Sweeney, Royals	.977	20	110	15	3	0	5
Tackett, Red Sox	1.000	4	13	2	0	0	0
Thacker, Blue Jays	1.000	4	20	4	0	0	0
Vinas, White Sox	1.000	5	15	3	0	0	1
Vivenzio, Braves	.990	17	87	12	1	0	5
Vogel, White Sox	1.000	3	19	0	0	0	0

Player, Team	Pct.	G	PO	A	E	DP	PB
Walton, Dodgers	1.000	5	10	0	0	0	1
Williams, Dodgers	.986	11	66	6	1	0	5
Zahner, Dodgers	1.000	16	68	5	0	0	3

PITCHERS

Player, Team	Pct.	G	PO	A	E	DP
Acevedo, Royals*	.875	16	1	6	1	1
Adkins, Blue Jays	.750	24	0	3	1	0
Alberro, Rangers	1.000	19	0	3	0	1
Alfonseca, Expos	.929	11	4	9	1	0
Andujar, White Sox	.929	10	3	10	1	0
Arias, Orioles	1.000	18	0	10	0	0
Ayers, Braves	.750	15	2	4	2	0
Baldwin, White Sox	.857	6	1	5	1	1
Belcher, Twins	.833	14	1	4	1	0
Belmonte, Mets	.889	14	6	10	2	1
Beltran, Blue Jays	.833	14	1	4	1	1
Benitez, Orioles	.875	14	2	5	1	0
Bennett, Red Sox	1.000	2	1	2	0	0
Bennett, Royals	1.000	12	3	9	0	0
Berson, Twins*	1.000	15	1	12	0	0
Bevil, Royals	1.000	13	5	8	0	2
Bjornson, Astros*	1.000	4	1	5	0	0
Blest, Astros*	1.000	16	3	6	0	0
Boatman, Astros	.846	16	3	8	2	0
Boehringer, White Sox	.857	5	2	4	1	0
Bonilla, Pirates	1.000	16	2	11	0	0
Bottoms, Astros*	.900	16	4	5	1	0
Bovee, Royals	1.000	11	2	7	0	0
Burgess, Braves*	1.000	20	2	5	0	0
Burley, Blue Jays	1.000	3	0	2	0	0
Burrow, White Sox	1.000	5	1	1	0	1
Bush, Red Sox	1.000	14	0	3	0	0
Call, White Sox	1.000	4	1	2	0	0
Canda, Twins	1.000	1	0	1	0	0
Carr, Braves*	1.000	2	2	1	0	0
Carter, Pirates	.818	10	2	7	2	0
Carter, Yankees*	.500	7	0	1	1	0
Centeno, Red Sox	1.000	13	0	11	0	0
Chambers, White Sox	1.000	6	2	7	0	0
Chatterton, Orioles	1.000	12	2	5	0	0
Chavarria, Rangers	.800	8	3	1	1	0
Chavez, Royals	1.000	11	0	6	0	0
Christiansen, Pirates*	.000	6	0	0	1	0
Cindrich, Yankees	.625	13	0	5	3	0
Clelland, Expos	.960	12	5	19	1	0
Collier, Mets	1.000	14	3	9	0	1
Conley, Expos	1.000	7	4	9	0	0
S. Conner, Orioles	1.000	7	3	13	0	0
Cope, Dodgers*	.778	15	1	6	2	0
Correa, Astros	.800	14	5	7	3	1
Correa, Twins	.750	27	4	1	2	1
Cresencio, Orioles	.750	7	1	2	1	0
Cruz, Expos	.889	12	2	22	3	0
Culberson, White Sox	1.000	19	5	4	0	0
Curtis, Rangers	1.000	7	4	11	0	0
Dault, Astros	1.000	3	0	1	0	0
Davidson, Dodgers	.900	16	1	8	1	0
Davis, Rangers	1.000	5	1	6	0	0
de la Cruz, White Sox	1.000	10	2	7	0	0
de los Santos, Pirates	1.000	9	1	4	0	0
Doman, Blue Jays	.786	13	1	10	3	1
Doorneweerd, Pirates	1.000	10	0	7	0	0
Fairfax, Orioles	.846	11	1	10	2	1
Ferguson, Yankees	.714	14	1	4	2	0
Finney, Mets	.750	16	3	6	3	0
Fitzpatrick, Dodgers	1.000	16	1	7	0	0
Forney, Orioles	.917	12	10	12	2	0
Foster, Twins*	1.000	2	0	1	0	0
Fregoso, Orioles	.857	12	2	4	1	0
Fultz, Expos	.857	9	3	1	1	0
Gandolph, Rangers*	.500	7	1	0	1	0
Garcia, Twins	1.000	15	3	8	0	0
P. Garcia, Braves	.750	11	2	7	3	0
Garcia-Luna, Pirates	1.000	12	3	5	0	0
Gerhart, Rangers	.846	10	2	9	2	0
Giard, Braves	.900	11	2	7	1	1
Gogolewski, Yankees	.833	6	2	3	1	0
Gutierrez, Royals	.875	16	6	8	2	0
Harp, White Sox*	1.000	5	1	1	0	1
Harrah, Pirates	1.000	5	3	3	0	0
Havens, Braves	.667	11	2	0	1	0
Hawkins, Twins	.714	11	2	3	2	0
Hayes, Twins	.667	3	1	1	1	0
Haynes, Orioles	.929	14	7	6	1	0
Henderson, Rangers*	.500	17	0	2	2	0
Henkel, Red Sox	.667	1	0	2	1	1
Hernandez, Mets	.500	6	0	2	2	0
Hernandez, White Sox	1.000	1	0	2	0	0
Herrholz, White Sox	1.000	7	2	1	0	0
Hiljus, Mets	.667	9	3	9	6	0
Hodges, Dodgers	1.000	9	1	5	0	0
Horn, Red Sox	.750	7	1	2	1	0
Iglesias, Dodgers	1.000	8	3	0	0	0
Jacobs, Royals	.833	12	0	5	1	0
Jarvis, Orioles*	.846	11	0	11	2	0
Jeffery, Blue Jays*	1.000	18	3	7	0	0
Jimenez, Braves	.800	15	3	1	1	0
Johnson, Expos	.500	7	0	1	1	0
Johnson, Twins*	.643	19	3	6	5	0
Jeff Johnson, Red Sox	1.000	4	1	0	0	0
Jones, Mets*	.929	14	2	11	1	1
Jones, Dodgers	1.000	1	0	1	0	0
Kelley, Orioles	.857	13	0	6	1	0
KERRIGAN, Expos*	1.000	15	3	18	0	1
Kindell, Yankees*	1.000	21	2	6	0	0
Klvac, Red Sox*	.750	14	3	6	3	0
Knapp, Pirates*	.833	15	2	3	1	0
Koller, Braves	.500	2	1	0	1	0
Kroon, Mets	.706	12	4	8	5	0
Lavigne, Dodgers*	.895	10	2	15	2	1
Lee, Royals	1.000	8	2	6	0	0
LeMaster, Red Sox	.750	14	3	6	2	2
Leystra, Blue Jays	1.000	15	1	3	0	0
Loaiza, Pirates	1.000	11	4	6	0	0
Long, Yankees	.556	8	1	4	4	0
Madrigal, Rangers	.875	10	0	7	1	0
Maietta, Red Sox	.750	13	1	2	1	0
Maitland, Braves	.900	12	3	6	1	0
Mallory, Blue Jays	1.000	5	0	7	0	0
Maloney, Red Sox*	.333	3	1	0	2	0
Marquez, Orioles	.880	10	3	19	3	1
Marshall, White Sox*	.944	12	5	12	1	0
Martineau, Braves	1.000	7	0	2	0	0
Martinez, Red Sox*	.909	13	0	10	1	0
McCready, Mets	.939	16	11	20	2	2
McCurry, Pirates	.667	6	0	2	1	0
McDonald, Expos*	.800	9	1	3	1	0
McGraw, White Sox	.889	7	4	4	1	0
McLeod, Astros	.900	9	1	8	1	0
Meinershagen, Blue Jays	.917	11	5	6	1	1
Mejia, Red Sox	.875	13	2	5	1	0
Miller, Astros	.857	23	0	12	2	1
Miller, Twins	.800	10	3	9	3	0
Minear, Dodgers*	1.000	17	0	3	0	0
Morman, Astros*	1.000	11	3	4	0	0
Muir, Blue Jays	.833	17	4	11	3	0
Nelson, Braves*	.846	11	3	8	2	0
Nix, Astros*	1.000	9	1	4	0	1
O'Brien, Rangers*	.875	9	3	11	2	4
Osuna, Dodgers	1.000	8	2	3	0	0
Pacheco, Expos	.917	15	4	7	1	0
Paramo, Rangers*	.833	7	0	5	1	0
Parra, Yankees	1.000	15	3	3	0	0
Patterson, Rangers	.818	11	3	6	2	0
Patterson, Blue Jays*	1.000	20	1	11	0	0
Paulino, Mets	.923	19	3	9	1	0
Pearlman, Blue Jays	1.000	12	1	4	0	0
Perez, Yankees	1.000	20	2	3	0	0
Perez, Pirates	1.000	9	1	0	0	0
Perez, Red Sox	1.000	16	0	5	0	1
Perez, Blue Jays	.833	7	3	12	3	0
Pettitte, Yankees*	.875	6	1	13	2	1
Pfeffer, Twins	1.000	3	0	2	0	0
Pike, Pirates	1.000	15	0	6	0	0
Pinango, Red Sox*	.500	4	0	1	1	0
Pontbriant, Pirates*	.952	14	6	14	1	0
Portillo, Twins	1.000	8	1	1	0	0
Pruitt, Royals	1.000	10	3	8	0	0
Radke, Twins	1.000	10	3	12	0	0
Ramirez, Yankees	.800	17	0	4	1	0
Regalado, Yankees	1.000	13	3	1	0	0
Respondek, Expos*	.917	16	1	10	1	0
Reyes, Braves	1.000	20	4	5	0	0
Ring, Red Sox	.750	5	1	2	1	0
Risdon, Braves	.857	15	3	3	1	0
Roberson, Braves	1.000	18	5	5	0	0
Rosario, Pirates	1.000	16	2	4	0	1
Rueter, Expos*	1.000	5	2	7	0	2
Ruffcorn, White Sox	1.000	4	1	1	0	0
Ruiz, White Sox	1.000	11	0	3	0	0
Sachrison, Orioles	1.000	1	0	1	0	0
Salcedo, Dodgers	.750	10	2	13	5	0
Sanchez, Royals	.750	22	2	7	3	0
Sanchez, Expos	.900	19	2	7	1	0
Saneaux, Orioles	.778	10	0	7	2	1
Santaella, Yankees	.786	14	3	8	3	1
Schaefer, Royals	.500	2	0	1	1	0
Schmidt, Braves	.800	11	1	7	2	0
Schoenvogel, Red Sox	.944	11	3	14	1	0
Schrenk, White Sox	.917	11	3	8	1	0
Seaton, Rangers	1.000	14	0	6	0	0
Seelbach, Braves	1.000	4	1	2	0	0
Shafer, Braves	1.000	8	2	3	0	0
Shipley, Royals	1.000	3	0	1	0	0
Smith, Astros	.941	15	3	13	1	0
Smith, Dodgers*	1.000	10	2	7	0	0
Smith, Yankees	.810	11	5	12	4	0
Sohn, Dodgers	.947	17	5	13	1	2

Player, Team	Pct.	G	PO	A	E	DP		Player, Team	Pct.	G	PO	A	E	DP
Sosa, Red Sox	1.000	3	0	1	0	0		Underhill, Rangers	1.000	4	2	4	0	0
Soto, White Sox	.739	10	6	11	6	0		Urbina, Expos	.947	10	5	13	1	0
Spring, Astros	1.000	16	2	5	0	0		Valdes, Pirates*	1.000	2	0	1	0	0
Starks, White Sox	.846	14	4	7	2	0		Valdez, Dodgers	1.000	10	3	4	0	0
Stevens, Expos	.750	20	2	7	3	1		Vallot, Rangers	1.000	1	0	1	0	0
Stevens, Twins	1.000	12	5	7	0	0		Vanegmond, Red Sox	.750	3	1	2	1	0
Sutherland, Yankees	1.000	4	0	1	0	0		Vaughn, Rangers	.857	10	2	4	1	0
Swanson, Mets*	1.000	11	2	14	0	0		Wade, Braves*	.800	10	0	4	1	0
Rob. Sweeney, Dodgers	.917	15	2	9	1	0		Watts, Dodgers*	1.000	12	1	5	0	0
Tagle, White Sox*	1.000	2	2	1	0	1		E. West, Royals	.700	17	3	4	3	0
Teske, Mets*	1.000	9	1	5	0	1		P. West, Royals	.625	13	0	5	3	0
Thibert, Yankees	.800	8	2	10	3	0		S. Williams, Mets	.889	11	2	6	1	1
Thompson, Pirates	1.000	18	3	4	0	2		Wood, White Sox	1.000	6	0	2	0	0
Towns, Royals	1.000	10	2	0	0	0		Woodfin, White Sox	1.000	13	6	0	0	1
Ubiera, Rangers	.750	13	0	6	2	0		Young, Astros*	1.000	13	3	8	0	1
								Zerbe, Dodgers*	1.000	16	3	10	0	0

Triple plays—Urbina, Valdez.

The following players did not have any fielding statistics at the positions indicated or appeared only as a designated hitter, pinch-hitter or pinch-runner: Andrews, p; Bailey, p; Banks, of; Batista, of; Blanco, of; Brucato, p; S. Burton, of; Carew, p; Caruso, p; DuBois, p; Dunne, p; Easterling, p; G. Evans, p; Fesh, p; Gainey, dh; Gernand, p; Henry, p; Henson, p; Heredia, p; Indriago, of; Isava, of; C. Lee, 3b; Lentz, dh, ph; Lidle, p; Lohry, dh; Obando, dh; Ortega, of; Reese, p; A. Reyes, p; Rossler, of, p; C. Santiago, p; S. Santiago, p; Stephens, p; J. Taylor, c; M. Taylor, p; Vandemark, p; Vilchez, ss; Vinas, of; Wiley, p; Winicki, 3b.

LEAGUE CHAMPIONS

Year	Team	Pct.	Year	Team	Pct.	Year	Team	Pct.
1964—	Sarasota Braves	.610	1976—	Texas	.704	1986—	Reds	.548
1965—	Bradenton Astros	.632	1977—	Chicago AL	.731		Dodgers b	.541
1966—	New York AL	.667	1978—	Texas	.600	1987—	Dodgers b	.683
1967—	Kansas City	.614	1979—	Houston	.635		Royals	.635
1968—	Oakland	.650	1980—	Kansas City-Blue	.635	1988—	Yankees b	.714
1969—	Montreal	.585	1981—	Kansas City-Gold	.688		Royals	.619
1970—	Chicago AL	.600	1982—	New York AL	.667	1989—	Yankees c	.651
1971—	Kansas City	.755	1983—	Texas	.645		Dodgers	.635
1972—	Chicago NL a	.651		Los Angeles b	.617	1990—	Expos	.635
	Kansas City a	.651	1984—	White Sox	.651		Dodgers c	.603
1973—	Texas	.732		Rangers b	.571	1991—	Orioles	.593
1974—	Chicago NL	.702	1985—	Yankees d	.705		Expos e	.533
1975—	Texas	.774		Rangers	.532			

(Note—Known as Sarasota Rookie League in 1964 and Florida Rookie League in 1965.) aDeclared co-champions; no playoff. bLeague divided into Northern and Southern divisions; won one-game playoff for league championship. cLeague divided into Northern and Southern divisions; won best-of-three playoff for league championship. dYankees declared champion based on winning percentage when one-game playoff against Rangers was rained out. eLeague divided into Northern, Southern and Central divisions; won best-of-three playoff for league championship.

PIONEER LEAGUE

FINAL STANDINGS

NORTHERN DIVISION

Team	W	L	T	Pct.	GB
Great Falls (Dodgers)	46	24	0	.657	....
Helena (Brewers)	44	26	0	.629	2
Billings (Reds)	25	44	0	.362	20½
Medicine Hat (Blue Jays)	24	45	0	.348	21½

SOUTHERN DIVISION

Team	W	L	T	Pct.	GB
Salt Lake City (Independent)	49	21	0	.700	....
Idaho Falls (Braves)	39	30	0	.565	9½
Butte (Rangers)	29	41	0	.414	20
Pocatello (Independent)	21	46	0	.313	26½

COMPOSITE

Team	SLC.	G.F.	Hel.	IF.	But.	Bil.	MH.	Poc.	W	L	T	Pct.	GB
Salt Lake City (Independent)	....	5	4	6	12	6	5	11	49	21	0	.700	....
Great Falls (Dodgers)	2	....	4	6	6	11	9	5	46	24	0	.657	3
Helena (Brewers)	3	5	...	4	6	9	11	6	44	26	0	.629	5
Idaho Falls (Braves)	8	3	2	...	8	4	6	8	39	30	0	.565	9½
Butte (Rangers)	2	1	2	6	....	3	5	10	29	41	0	.414	20
Billings (Reds)	1	3	5	4	3	...	6	3	25	44	0	.362	23½
Medicine Hat (Blue Jays)	2	5	3	1	2	8	...	3	24	45	0	.348	24½
Pocatello (Independent)	3	2	1	5	4	3	3	...	21	46	0	.313	26½

Major league affiliations in parentheses.

Playoffs—Salt Lake City defeated Great Falls, two games to one, to win league championship.

Regular-season attendance—Billings, 80,242; Butte, 29,684; Great Falls, 79,176; Helena, 31,187; Idaho Falls, 71,292; Medicine Hat, 14,722; Pocatello, 25,468; Salt Lake City, 200,599. Total, 532,370. Playoffs (3 games), 7,545.

Managers—Billings, P.J. Carey; Butte, Dick Egan; Great Falls, Glenn Hoffman; Helena, Harry Dunlop; Idaho Falls, Steve Curry; Medicine Hat, J.J. Cannon; Pocatello, Rich Morales Jr.; Salt Lake City, Nick Belmonte.

All-Star team—1B—Andy Fairman, Helena; 2B—Dario Paulino, Idaho Falls; 3B—Jeff Cirillo, Helena; SS—Tony Graffagnino, Idaho Falls; OF—Rick Hirtensteiner, Salt Lake City; Kevin Grijak, Idaho Falls; Terrell Lowery, Butte; C—Ken Huckaby, Great Falls; DH—D.J. Boston, Medicine Hat; P—Jake Botts, Great Falls; Tyrone Hill, Helena; Brad Woodall, Idaho Falls; Manager of the Year—P.J. Carey, Billings.

BATTING

TEAM

Team	Avg.	G	AB	R	OR	H	TB	2B	3B	HR	RBI	SH	SF	HP	BB	Int. BB	SO	SB	CS	LOB
Idaho Falls	.304	69	2477	483	487	752	1094	127	19	59	430	21	22	33	281	10	468	89	44	525
Salt Lake	.302	70	2419	507	323	731	1015	124	29	34	436	19	30	41	368	8	436	91	38	586
Helena	.293	70	2433	464	331	713	1022	129	15	50	371	25	22	45	320	10	436	66	35	568
Pocatello	.279	67	2257	338	494	629	822	93	23	18	283	18	11	33	210	2	523	111	83	432
Great Falls	.272	70	2386	421	347	648	936	104	26	44	348	13	22	40	306	3	495	75	51	523
Butte	.269	70	2379	435	513	641	958	109	26	52	374	7	22	47	258	7	574	121	59	446
Medicine Hat	.261	69	2263	351	411	591	777	89	11	25	295	19	17	37	261	2	473	86	43	496
Billings	.236	69	2294	307	400	541	763	96	12	34	253	15	11	19	239	4	530	82	37	465

INDIVIDUAL

(Leading qualifiers for batting championship—189 or more plate appearances)

*Bats lefthanded.   †Switch-hitter.

Player, Team	Avg.	G	AB	R	H	TB	2B	3B	HR	RBI	SH	SF	HP	BB	Int. BB	SO	SB	CS
Fairman, Andy, Helena*	.373	70	268	57	100	148	22	1	8	62	0	4	0	48	3	27	3	1
Paulino, Dario, Idaho Falls	.371	64	244	39	89	106	12	1	1	38	3	0	4	18	0	39	3	5
Basse, Mike, Helena*	.367	55	218	55	80	112	15	4	3	26	1	2	5	29	1	43	16	9
Wong, Kevin, Pocatello	.365	56	203	35	74	94	13	2	1	41	1	2	2	19	0	27	7	8
Hirtensteiner, Rick, Salt Lake City*	.356	70	295	77	105	166	12	8	11	71	1	4	8	36	2	45	20	5
Cirillo, Jeff, Helena	.350	70	286	60	100	150	16	2	10	51	2	2	4	31	3	28	3	1
Garrigan, Pat, Pocatello	.348	50	178	33	62	83	10	4	1	33	2	3	3	20	1	30	5	8
Graffagnino, Tony, Idaho Falls	.347	66	274	53	95	131	16	4	4	56	2	2	3	27	0	37	19	4
Grijak, Kevin, Idaho Falls*	.337	52	202	33	68	109	9	1	10	58	2	4	1	16	1	15	4	1
Therrien, Dominic, Idaho Falls*	.327	53	223	48	73	106	15	0	6	37	3	1	1	21	0	38	10	6

Departmental leaders: G—Cirillo, Fairman, Hirtensteiner, 70; AB—Hirtensteiner, 295; R—Hirtensteiner, 77; H—Hirtensteiner, 105; TB—Hirtensteiner, 166; 2B—Castillo, 29; 3B—Hirtensteiner, 8; HR—Hirtensteiner, 11; RBI—Hirtensteiner, 71; SH—Whitford, 7; SF—Rolls, 8; HP—La. Williams, 12; BB—Fairman, Rolls, 48; IBB—Castillo, 4; SO—Zammarchi, 69; SB—Robinson, 31; CS—Lowery, 12.

(All players—listed alphabetically)

Player, Team	Avg.	G	AB	R	H	TB	2B	3B	HR	RBI	SH	SF	HP	BB	Int. BB	SO	SB	CS
Albert, Tim, Helena*	.350	5	20	6	7	9	2	0	0	5	0	0	0	4	0	2	1	0
Alvarez, Enenegildo, Medicine Hat	.163	34	86	7	14	16	2	0	0	3	4	0	2	6	0	26	3	2
Ambos, Willie, Salt Lake City	1.000	15	1	0	1	1	0	0	0	0	0	0	0	0	0	0	0	0
Anderson, Todd, Pocatello*	.244	43	119	17	29	32	1	1	0	10	1	1	6	9	0	31	8	4
Andrea, Leroy, 28 Poc. - 15 Hel.	.215	43	144	23	31	56	7	0	6	24	0	1	3	13	0	34	4	1
Andrews, Daniel, Great Falls*	.000	3	6	0	0	0	0	0	0	0	0	0	0	1	0	0	0	0
Aranzullo, Mike, Salt Lake City	.303	25	33	12	10	11	1	0	0	4	1	0	0	3	0	8	2	0
Atwater, Buck, Pocatello*	.307	48	153	30	47	65	9	3	1	16	0	0	0	14	0	40	9	10
Ayala, Reuben, Salt Lake City	.091	3	11	1	1	2	1	0	0	2	0	0	0	1	0	2	0	0
Baber, LaRue, Helena	.277	67	249	48	69	108	17	2	6	41	1	2	2	26	0	54	12	5
Banks, Dean, Pocatello	.324	48	148	26	48	61	7	0	2	16	4	0	4	14	0	14	9	7
Basse, Mike, Helena*	.367	55	218	55	80	112	15	4	3	26	1	2	5	29	1	43	16	9
Biggers, Brian, Salt Lake City	.257	49	148	29	38	40	2	0	0	23	3	1	4	22	0	27	2	1
Blanco, Henry, Great Falls	.255	62	216	35	55	79	7	1	5	28	2	3	1	27	0	39	3	6
Boston, D.J., Medicine Hat*	.280	59	207	34	58	73	12	0	1	25	1	1	2	33	0	33	4	7
Boyzuick, Mike, Great Falls	.203	26	64	9	13	21	1	2	1	3	1	0	4	7	0	10	0	1
Briggs, Stoney, Medicine Hat	.297	64	236	45	70	102	8	0	8	29	0	2	1	18	0	62	9	5
Brown, Mike, Great Falls	.149	27	67	4	10	12	2	0	0	6	0	0	1	5	0	18	0	1

Player, Team	Avg.	G	AB	R	H	TB	2B	3B	HR	RBI	SH	SF	HP	BB	Int. BB	SO	SB	CS
Bruno, Paul, Salt Lake City	.242	13	33	3	8	9	1	0	0	3	0	1	0	2	0	9	0	0
Burris, Pierre, Billings	.211	58	209	32	44	57	8	1	1	8	3	0	1	34	0	47	27	8
Carmona, William, Pocatello	.245	39	106	15	26	44	3	3	3	16	1	1	1	5	0	36	4	2
Castillo, Ben, Salt Lake City	.325	67	277	62	90	147	29	5	6	64	0	6	43	4	0	43	28	8
Castro, Juan, Great Falls	.276	60	217	36	60	71	4	2	1	27	3	2	0	33	1	31	7	6
Cirillo, Jeff, Helena	.350	70	286	60	100	150	16	2	10	51	2	2	4	31	3	28	3	1
Coates, Tom, Idaho Falls	.324	64	241	64	78	108	12	3	4	34	1	3	2	35	1	56	23	10
Cook, Doug, Idaho Falls	.000	19	1	0	0	0	0	0	0	0	0	0	0	0	0	0	0	0
Cooper, Jeff, Salt Lake City	.240	35	96	19	23	28	3	1	0	11	1	1	3	11	0	22	0	2
Crespo, Felipe, Medicine Hat	.310	49	184	40	57	88	11	4	4	31	2	2	3	25	0	31	6	4
Crespo, Mike, Butte†	.292	33	113	26	33	68	8	3	7	29	0	1	1	13	2	21	3	0
Cunha, Steve, Salt Lake City	.275	40	91	19	25	38	5	1	2	12	0	2	1	6	0	19	2	0
Daniels, Lee, Medicine Hat	.247	61	219	43	54	66	4	1	2	22	3	1	7	34	0	65	18	6
DeBerry, Joe, Billings*	.263	65	236	41	62	105	13	0	10	47	0	1	3	36	1	46	5	4
Dobrolsky, William, Helena	.161	9	31	2	5	7	2	0	0	2	0	0	0	3	0	5	0	0
Dreisbach, William, Billings	.167	6	18	3	3	3	0	0	0	0	0	0	0	3	0	5	0	0
Edwards, Mike, Butte	.312	66	218	56	68	111	11	1	10	42	0	3	2	38	1	45	9	4
Edwards, Todd, Salt Lake City*	.288	53	170	36	49	57	8	0	0	19	2	1	2	43	1	46	3	3
Estevez, Carlos, Salt Lake City*	.302	46	159	27	48	63	6	0	3	36	1	2	3	16	0	31	0	2
Everly, David, Helena	.163	19	43	7	7	8	1	0	0	1	1	0	3	8	0	18	0	1
Fairman, Andy, Helena*	.373	70	268	57	100	148	22	1	8	62	0	4	0	48	3	27	3	1
Fermaint, Mike, Pocatello	.333	28	90	22	30	33	3	0	0	8	2	0	1	14	0	17	4	1
Ferreira, Dan, Salt Lake City	.500	2	4	1	2	2	0	0	0	0	0	0	0	0	0	0	0	0
Ford, Andy, Billings	.155	22	71	9	11	17	3	0	1	6	1	1	1	6	1	25	0	1
Garrigan, Pat, Pocatello	.348	50	178	33	62	83	10	4	1	33	2	3	3	20	1	30	5	8
Gates, Todd, Butte†	.220	44	123	28	27	29	0	1	0	6	0	1	8	13	0	44	19	6
Ghostlaw, Derek, Helena	.206	17	34	4	7	7	0	0	0	1	0	0	0	2	0	11	0	0
Gil, Ben, Butte	.287	32	129	25	37	53	4	3	2	15	0	1	0	14	1	36	9	3
Gittmer, Joe, Helena	.207	40	145	20	30	40	2	1	2	17	2	3	3	8	0	26	1	0
Graffagnino, Tony, Idaho Falls	.347	66	274	53	95	131	16	4	4	56	2	2	3	27	0	37	19	4
Graham, Derrick, Billings	.233	60	215	22	50	63	10	0	1	24	0	1	3	18	0	57	11	2
Graves, Randall, Great Falls	.303	38	109	20	33	45	8	2	0	15	1	1	0	12	0	17	3	1
Gress, Loren, Idaho Falls*	.298	66	275	55	82	128	14	1	10	60	0	2	3	20	3	47	6	2
Grijak, Kevin, Idaho Falls*	.337	52	202	33	68	109	9	1	10	58	2	4	1	16	1	15	4	1
Hamm, Stacey, Pocatello†	.250	40	108	9	27	33	4	1	0	12	2	0	2	5	1	38	8	4
Harrison, Mike, Billings	.275	57	200	27	55	76	9	0	4	17	0	2	2	24	2	52	2	2
Hernandez, Ramon, Billings	.233	35	120	12	28	44	5	1	3	13	0	0	3	0	0	37	3	3
Herrera, Jose, Medicine Hat*	.245	40	143	21	35	45	5	1	1	11	1	0	3	6	1	38	6	7
Hirtensteiner, Rick, Salt Lake City*	.356	70	295	77	105	166	12	8	11	71	1	4	8	36	2	45	20	5
Hood, Randy, Helena	.250	9	32	9	8	8	0	0	0	4	0	0	0	11	0	6	2	0
Huckaby, Ken, Great Falls	.258	57	213	39	55	80	16	0	3	37	1	3	4	17	0	38	3	2
Jesperson, Bob, Billings	.273	40	132	18	36	47	7	2	0	15	0	2	2	25	0	30	7	2
Jimenez, Vincent, Idaho Falls	.267	25	101	23	27	54	7	1	6	22	1	1	3	12	1	22	2	0
Jones, Kevin, Salt Lake City	.111	6	18	2	2	2	0	0	0	0	0	0	0	2	0	5	0	1
Jones, Mike, Billings	.248	43	165	22	41	62	6	3	3	28	2	1	0	15	0	22	2	1
Joyce, James, Pocatello	.172	34	99	14	17	24	4	0	1	7	1	0	1	16	0	35	2	3
Kaelin, Kris, Pocatello*	.244	46	127	13	31	41	5	1	1	16	0	0	1	15	0	43	2	4
Kelliher, Paul, Idaho Falls	.115	10	26	3	3	3	0	0	0	1	0	0	0	9	0	7	1	0
Kirkpatrick, Jay, Great Falls*	.321	50	168	25	54	73	11	1	2	26	0	0	3	13	0	23	1	2
Koehler, James, Butte*	.261	56	180	34	47	80	13	1	6	38	0	1	3	26	0	32	8	5
Koelling, Brian, Billings	.353	22	85	17	30	45	7	1	2	13	0	1	0	14	0	23	6	2
Lacy, Kerry, Butte	.000	24	2	0	0	0	0	0	0	0	0	0	0	0	0	1	0	0
Landrum, Tito, Great Falls	.265	57	189	36	50	81	8	4	5	25	0	1	2	25	0	43	9	5
Langowski, Ted, Medicine Hat*	.285	37	123	17	35	47	9	0	1	26	0	2	0	24	0	16	1	1
Lawn, Mike, Helena	.297	59	202	36	60	78	7	1	3	34	4	1	10	29	0	44	9	5
Loftin, Bo, Billings	.178	47	163	19	29	50	6	0	5	23	0	0	3	11	0	62	1	1
Lombardi, John, Medicine Hat	.254	21	59	11	15	21	4	1	0	9	0	1	0	5	0	11	2	0
Lowery, Terrell, Butte	.299	54	214	38	64	97	10	7	3	33	0	2	1	29	0	44	23	12
Lutz, Brent, Medicine Hat	.270	41	115	23	31	48	4	2	3	23	1	0	7	21	0	34	6	1
Macrina, Eric, Salt Lake City	.289	26	76	15	22	27	3	1	0	9	1	3	2	13	0	29	0	1
Martin, Jim, Salt Lake City	.176	12	17	3	3	4	1	0	0	0	0	0	0	6	0	8	1	0
Martin, Matt, Billings†	.178	37	118	15	21	26	3	1	0	10	3	0	0	11	0	18	4	2
Martinez, Angel, Medicine Hat	.173	34	98	8	17	24	1	0	2	16	2	2	2	12	1	29	0	1
Martinez, John, Pocatello†	.192	34	99	12	19	22	3	0	0	12	0	1	0	7	0	13	1	4
Matheny, Mike, Helena	.285	64	253	35	72	92	14	0	2	34	5	1	6	19	0	52	2	4
McCune, Rob, Butte	.182	28	55	9	10	12	2	0	0	4	2	0	2	8	0	7	0	2
Mejia, Robert, Great Falls	.262	23	84	17	22	38	6	2	2	14	0	1	1	7	0	22	3	1
Mesa, Audy, Pocatello	.292	39	130	14	38	53	8	2	1	25	0	1	1	3	0	22	1	2
Miailovich, Rich, Salt Lake City	.222	13	45	9	10	12	2	0	0	2	0	0	1	7	0	9	0	1
Mill, Steve, Pocatello*	.000	16	0	1	0	0	0	0	0	0	0	0	0	0	0	0	1	0
Minter, Larry, Pocatello*	.323	40	130	19	42	49	5	1	0	9	0	0	4	0	0	35	3	6
Montgomery, Damon, Billings	.214	27	84	6	18	24	3	0	1	11	0	0	2	4	0	30	0	2
Morris, Marc, Pocatello	.088	19	34	1	3	4	1	0	0	1	0	0	2	6	0	19	1	0
O'Neill, Richard, Idaho Falls	.222	38	108	14	24	30	3	0	1	13	2	2	2	15	0	28	4	0
Ortega, Ed, Salt Lake City*	.382	37	123	19	47	55	6	1	0	15	3	2	0	10	0	13	7	2
Otanez, Willis, Great Falls	.288	58	222	38	64	95	9	2	6	39	1	4	2	19	0	34	3	3
Parra, Franklin, Butte†	.253	61	221	27	56	82	10	2	4	29	0	2	0	7	0	61	9	8
Paulino, Dario, Idaho Falls	.371	64	240	39	89	106	12	1	1	38	3	0	4	18	0	39	3	5
Philyaw, Dino, Pocatello	.059	7	17	2	1	1	0	0	0	1	0	0	1	0	0	6	0	2
Pinkney, Alton, Great Falls*	.214	6	14	1	3	3	0	0	0	2	0	0	0	6	0	6	1	1
Poyner, Pat, Butte	.143	20	42	3	6	8	2	0	0	9	1	0	1	6	0	17	0	1
Preikszas, Dave, Helena*	.184	30	98	19	18	32	2	0	4	17	0	2	2	15	0	24	3	1
Puchales, Javier, Great Falls*	.357	41	112	21	40	47	5	1	0	15	1	1	1	5	1	10	13	6
Radar, Keith, Salt Lake City	.203	21	69	8	14	24	2	1	2	14	0	1	1	11	0	18	0	0
Ramos, Jairo, Medicine Hat*	.267	35	116	15	31	38	7	0	0	10	1	2	0	8	0	11	8	2
Reed, Patrick, Great Falls	.296	45	152	31	45	65	5	3	3	19	0	3	5	22	0	48	6	4
Reinert, Greg, Idaho Falls†	.118	7	17	2	2	2	0	0	0	2	0	0	1	4	0	8	0	0
Ripplemeyer, Brad, Idaho Falls	.358	37	120	28	43	74	12	2	5	22	2	0	3	24	1	29	1	2
Roberts, Bryan, Butte	.274	52	190	32	52	82	7	4	5	29	2	2	8	10	0	52	3	3
Robinson, Terry, Pocatello*	.303	56	198	36	60	75	9	3	0	16	0	1	0	24	0	46	31	6
Rodriguez, Armando, Idaho Falls*	.294	36	109	17	32	53	8	2	3	16	1	1	0	10	0	23	0	2
Rolls, David, Salt Lake City	.326	66	224	58	73	108	21	1	4	46	1	5	8	48	0	37	4	3
Rosario, Gabriel, Medicine Hat	.250	49	164	23	41	46	3	1	0	21	2	2	0	16	0	33	7	4
Santoya, Cristobal, Idaho Falls	.273	3	11	2	3	4	1	0	0	1	0	0	0	0	0	1	0	0

Player, Team	Avg.	G	AB	R	H	TB	2B	3B	HR	RBI	SH	SF	HP	BB	Int. BB	SO	SB	CS
Scholzen, Jeffrey, Pocatello†	.236	38	110	10	26	33	3	2	0	9	1	1	2	12	0	34	8	5
Seals, Joe, Great Falls†	.264	29	72	13	19	34	4	1	3	13	0	1	0	24	0	20	1	0
Shaw, Kerry, Salt Lake City†	.301	23	73	19	22	27	2	0	1	14	1	0	0	15	0	5	0	0
Sisk, Kevin, Butte*	.295	51	193	35	57	68	5	0	2	37	0	3	1	23	1	20	5	6
Smith, Frank, Great Falls	.264	50	178	40	47	78	7	3	6	37	1	0	2	26	0	57	1	1
Smith, Willie, Salt Lake City	.222	21	36	5	8	8	0	0	0	2	0	1	0	4	0	11	0	0
Snead, Charles, Billings	.175	61	211	28	37	41	4	0	0	12	5	1	0	14	0	23	5	3
Stanton, Gary, Idaho Falls*	.000	4	4	1	0	0	0	0	0	0	0	0	1	0	0	3	0	0
Stefan, Todd, Salt Lake City	.303	64	231	48	70	88	6	6	0	51	3	3	0	36	0	28	8	6
Sullivan, Charlie, Butte*	.216	47	125	27	27	38	6	1	1	17	0	3	0	24	0	41	7	3
Swann, Pedro, Idaho Falls*	.276	55	174	35	48	65	6	1	3	28	1	2	2	33	1	45	8	5
Talanoa, Scott, Helena	.291	37	127	24	37	65	10	0	6	29	0	2	3	29	2	32	1	2
Tavarez, Hector, Medicine Hat†	.291	46	158	22	46	54	6	1	0	15	1	0	0	21	0	26	10	0
Taylor, Gene, Billings	.290	67	248	34	72	99	12	3	3	26	1	2	1	21	0	52	8	4
Taylor, Jon, Great Falls	.125	8	8	1	1	1	0	0	0	1	0	1	1	3	0	5	0	0
Texidor, Jose, Butte	.377	37	130	26	49	66	6	1	3	23	1	0	0	9	1	23	5	2
Therrien, Dominic, Idaho Falls*	.327	53	223	48	73	106	15	0	6	37	3	1	1	21	0	38	10	6
Tierney, Tom, Idaho Falls	.250	23	60	9	15	21	3	0	1	4	1	0	0	7	0	12	0	1
Todd, Theron, Salt Lake City	.317	52	189	35	60	96	13	4	5	38	1	3	1	33	1	21	14	3
Toth, David, Idaho Falls	.213	47	160	27	34	49	3	0	4	22	1	2	4	18	0	21	1	0
Tsoukalas, John, Medicine Hat*	.285	64	242	35	69	86	11	0	2	39	1	0	5	24	0	21	4	2
Tucker, Robert, Helena	.250	2	4	0	1	1	0	0	0	1	0	0	0	0	0	0	0	0
Vargas, Eric, Butte	.167	32	60	3	10	14	4	0	0	5	0	1	1	13	0	23	0	2
Walker, Johnny, Idaho Falls*	.315	18	73	22	23	36	4	3	1	11	0	1	2	9	2	12	7	4
Weldon, Paul, Pocatello*	.261	40	115	12	30	38	2	0	2	15	3	0	0	16	0	14	4	4
Wheat, Chris, Helena	.262	63	244	41	64	81	6	4	1	21	2	2	2	35	1	26	9	4
Whitford, Eric, Helena	.281	41	128	35	36	57	9	0	4	21	7	0	4	21	0	27	3	2
Wilburn, Trey, Billings†	.211	5	19	2	4	4	0	0	0	0	0	0	0	0	0	1	1	0
Wilke, Matt, Medicine Hat*	.159	34	113	7	18	23	2	0	1	15	0	2	4	8	0	37	2	1
Williams, Lanny, Butte	.269	62	186	38	50	84	12	2	6	37	0	2	12	15	1	61	11	2
Williams, Leroy, Great Falls	.297	23	74	10	22	36	5	0	3	14	0	0	2	10	1	11	0	1
Wiseman, Greg, Butte*	.242	60	198	28	48	66	9	0	3	21	1	3	4	10	0	46	10	0
Wong, Kevin, Pocatello	.365	56	203	35	74	94	13	2	1	41	1	2	2	19	0	27	7	8
York, Ronald, Idaho Falls	.224	22	58	8	13	15	2	0	0	5	1	1	3	0	0	25	0	2
Zammarchi, Erik, Great Falls	.249	61	221	45	55	77	6	2	4	27	2	1	7	47	0	69	21	10

The following pitchers, listed alphabetically by club, with games in parentheses, had no plate appearances, primarily through use of designated hitters:

BILLINGS—Carson, Mark (1); Coletti, John (12); Courtright, John (1); Dodd, Scott (18); Kendall, Phil (16); Langford, Rich (20); McClain, Charles (15); Quinones, Rene (11); Reeves, Drue (12); Tobin, Dan (13); Vivas, Domingo (22); Wyatt, Chuck (10); Zastoupil, Rich (25).

BUTTE—Ayala, Jason (20); Berthau, Terrell (21); Brownholtz, Joe (9); Buchheit, Scott (3); Curtis, Chris (6); Dalzochio, Paul (11); Davis, Marty (8); Giberti, Dave (17); Henson, Micky (5); Kennedy, Shawn (11); Madrigal, Victor (6); Magee, Bo (14); McGough, Keith (10); Paramo, Paul (14); Schuermann, Lance (30); Stuart, Brad (13); Underhill, Pat (9); Watson, Andy (1).

GREAT FALLS—Aronetz, Cam (24); Botts, Jake (13); Broyles, Jason (17); Castro, Nelson (14); Davis, Greg (13); Farnsworth, Ross (13); Gorecki, Rick (13); Jacinto, Larry (15); Maldonado, Albert (4); Parra, Jose (14); Sinacori, Chris (24); Strong, Stewart (19); Walkden, Mike (18); Williams, Todd (28).

HELENA—Benson, Matt (13); Boze, Marshall (16); Bush, Chuck (16); Criminger, John (2); Dennison, Brian (13); Farrell, Mike (5); Fetty, Pat (14); Fitzgerald, Dave (11); Hancock, Mike (5); Hauteman, Jeff (14); Hickox, Tom (14); Hill, Tyrone (11); Iwema, Todd (17); Lucas, Scott (5); Rugg, Rusty (8); Souza, Brian (14); Winawer, Larry (13).

IDAHO FALLS—Armstrong, Jim (14); Behrens, Scott (8); Dunlap, Travis (4); Kempfer, Jason (5); Koklys, Wayne (25); Koller, Jerry (9); Ledwik, Shannon (18); Majeski, Carl (25); Petit, Ricardo (10); Place, Michael (5); Rapp, Craig (20); Simoneaux, Wayne (2); Vasquez, Julio (9); Viarengo, Matt (11); Weber, Brent (16); Weeks, Ben (24); Woodall, Brad (28).

MEDICINE HAT—Baptist, Travis (14); Cardona, Isbel (9); Darley, Ned (12); Dolson, Andrew (13); Ermis, Chris (17); Ford, Alan (15); Lopez, Freddy (11); Manaure, Jose (19); Montoya, Albert (15); O'Halloran, Mike (13); Robinson, Ken (6); Sinclair, Steve (12); Taylor, Michael (14).

POCATELLO—Atwood, Derek (18); Callistro, Rob (9); Ekman, Rich (22); Gibson, Monty (14); Goucher, Steve (2); Grennan, Steve (23); Meyer, Jayson (14); Millerick, Ed (13); Schneck, Bruce (14); Stevens, Dale (24); Wechsberg, Von (13).

SALT LAKE CITY—Bergeron, Rob (8); Furmanik, Dan (14); Gilligan, John (25); Guidi, Jim (13); Guthrie, Joe (2); Harris, Gary (1); Knowles, Greg (3); Marcon, David (14); Matranga, Dave (13); McDonald, Kevin (15); Mirabella, Gene (7); Powers, Tad (5); Schultea, Chris (16); Stephens, Mark (18); Willard, Jon (16).

GRAND SLAMS—DeBerry, Koehler, 2 each; Fairman, Hirtensteiner, Mejia, Walker, 1 each.

AWARDED FIRST BASE ON CATCHER'S INTERFERENCE—Banks (Ripplemeyer); Harrison (Ripplemeyer); Preikszas (Rolls); Sisk (Lombardi); Le. Williams (A. Martinez).

PITCHING

TEAM

Team	ERA	G	CG	ShO	Sv.	IP	H	R	ER	HR	HB	BB	Int. BB	SO	WP	Bk.
Salt Lake	3.68	70	8	6	19	610.2	631	323	250	25	37	189	5	532	49	19
Great Falls	3.89	70	2	6	18	618.1	568	347	267	37	30	261	4	612	67	26
Helena	3.92	70	12	4	17	613.1	581	331	267	37	29	274	2	491	60	31
Billings	4.59	69	5	3	13	594.1	601	400	303	34	41	338	3	405	70	37
Medicine Hat	4.89	69	9	3	9	572.2	650	411	311	38	41	262	0	397	72	41
Idaho Falls	5.51	69	0	1	17	612.0	740	487	375	54	37	271	6	574	68	35
Butte	5.79	70	4	1	13	606.2	762	513	390	49	34	331	4	468	90	43
Pocatello	6.30	67	2	2	12	571.1	713	494	400	42	46	317	18	456	75	39

INDIVIDUAL

(Leading qualifiers for earned-run average leadership—56 or more innings)

*Throws lefthanded.

Pitcher, Team	W	L	Pct.	ERA	G	GS	CG	GF	ShO	Sv.	IP	H	R	ER	HR	HB	BB	Int. BB	SO	WP
Gilligan, Salt Lake City	6	1	.857	1.71	25	0	0	18	0	6	63.0	46	15	12	3	3	13	2	78	6
Stephens, Salt Lake City*	6	3	.667	2.43	18	8	4	3	0	0	77.2	51	30	21	1	5	20	1	89	9
Botts, Great Falls	5	3	.625	2.47	13	13	0	0	0	0	73.0	43	21	20	4	3	43	0	83	9
Souza, Helena	8	2	.800	3.04	14	14	2	0	1	0	83.0	80	35	28	4	1	34	0	70	3
McDonald, Salt Lake City	7	1	.875	3.05	15	15	0	0	3	0	82.2	84	36	28	2	2	32	0	85	12
Farnsworth, Great Falls*	8	3	.727	3.09	13	13	0	0	0	0	75.2	65	35	26	6	3	27	0	69	7
Taylor, Medicine Hat*	6	4	.600	3.11	14	10	2	1	0	0	75.1	70	37	26	3	7	34	0	58	4

Pitcher, Team	W	L	Pct.	ERA	G	GS	CG	GF	ShO	Sv.	IP	H	R	ER	HR	HB	BB	IBB	SO	WP
Hill, Helena*	4	2	.667	3.15	11	11	0	0	0	0	60.0	43	27	21	2	3	35	0	76	7
McClain, Billings	5	7	.417	3.38	15	12	2	3	0	0	80.0	63	47	30	6	5	51	0	62	10
Reeves, Billings	4	4	.500	3.47	12	11	2	0	0	0	62.1	61	42	24	5	5	31	0	33	6

Departmental leaders: G—Schuermann, 30; W—Farnsworth, Marcon, Souza, 8; L—Ermis, 8; Pct.—McDonald, .875; GS—McDonald, 15; CG—Montoya, 5; GF—Zastoupil, 24; ShO—McDonald, 3; Sv.—Woodall, 11; IP—Winawer, 91.2; H—Meyer, 104; R—Meyer, Miller, Patterson, 63; ER—Patterson, 58; HR—Meyer, 10; HB—Callistro, 10; BB—Dodd, 64; IBB—Grennan, 4; SO—Stephens, 89; WP—Ermis, 16.

(All pitchers—listed alphabetically)

Pitcher, Team	W	L	Pct.	ERA	G	GS	CG	GF	ShO	Sv.	IP	H	R	ER	HR	HB	BB	IBB	SO	WP
Ambos, Salt Lake City	7	4	.636	4.18	14	14	0	0	0	0	75.1	95	40	35	2	5	21	0	56	7
Armstrong, Idaho Falls*	3	5	.375	4.33	14	14	0	0	0	0	60.1	73	54	29	2	2	13	0	49	1
Aronetz, Great Falls*	4	1	.800	2.86	24	0	0	5	0	1	44.0	35	20	14	2	1	19	1	43	14
Atwood, Pocatello*	1	1	.500	6.31	18	1	0	5	0	1	25.2	32	20	18	0	2	13	2	19	8
Ayala, Butte	0	2	.000	4.35	20	2	0	8	0	0	31.0	38	23	15	2	2	25	1	21	5
Baptist, Medicine Hat*	4	4	.500	4.11	14	14	1	0	1	0	85.1	100	52	39	5	1	22	0	48	4
Behrens, Idaho Falls	1	0	1.000	10.29	8	0	0	1	0	0	14.0	20	18	16	2	2	14	0	11	1
Benson, Helena	1	0	1.000	4.20	3	2	1	1	0	1	15.0	15	7	7	2	2	5	0	6	1
Bergeron, Salt Lake City	1	1	.500	5.91	8	0	0	4	0	1	10.2	18	8	7	0	1	2	0	4	0
Berthau, Butte	3	7	.300	5.21	21	8	1	12	0	4	65.2	75	44	38	7	2	19	0	34	8
Botts, Great Falls	5	3	.625	2.47	13	13	0	0	0	0	73.0	43	21	20	4	3	43	0	83	9
Boze, Helena	3	3	.500	7.07	16	8	0	1	0	0	56.0	59	49	44	3	3	47	0	64	6
Brownholtz, Butte*	4	2	.667	3.72	9	8	1	1	1	1	46.0	43	26	19	4	1	15	0	42	1
Broyles, Great Falls	2	0	1.000	4.50	17	0	0	3	0	1	24.0	24	13	12	2	3	16	0	23	3
Buchheit, Butte*	0	0	.000	3.60	3	0	0	1	0	0	5.0	3	4	2	0	0	3	0	5	1
Bush, Helena	2	3	.400	5.00	16	0	0	8	0	3	27.0	27	17	15	2	3	11	0	19	4
Callistro, Pocatello	0	3	.000	5.92	9	7	0	1	0	0	48.2	62	43	32	6	10	20	1	50	7
Cardona, Medicine Hat	0	1	.000	9.42	9	0	0	5	0	1	14.1	18	17	15	2	2	15	0	14	5
Carson, Billings	0	1	.000	7.20	1	1	0	0	0	0	5.0	6	5	4	1	0	2	0	1	0
Castro, Great Falls	7	4	.636	5.26	14	14	1	0	1	0	75.1	81	51	44	7	5	13	0	63	2
Coletti, Billings*	0	3	.000	8.26	12	1	0	5	0	0	28.1	37	28	26	3	2	26	0	16	5
Cook, Idaho Falls	3	3	.500	6.06	18	5	0	2	0	0	52.0	66	39	35	3	4	14	0	54	3
Courtright, Billings*	1	0	1.000	0.00	1	1	0	0	0	0	6.0	2	0	0	0	1	0	0	4	0
Criminger, Helena	1	0	1.000	1.93	2	0	0	0	0	0	4.2	4	2	1	0	1	1	0	5	0
Curtis, Butte	0	2	.000	9.95	6	3	0	2	0	0	12.2	27	23	14	1	1	4	0	7	0
Dalzochio, Butte	1	0	1.000	8.62	11	0	0	3	0	0	15.2	26	17	15	1	3	6	0	8	5
Daniels, Medicine Hat	0	0	.000	0.00	1	0	0	1	0	0	1.1	1	0	0	0	0	0	0	2	0
Darley, Medicine Hat	2	6	.250	5.33	11	9	0	1	0	0	50.2	59	37	30	2	6	27	0	35	5
Davis, Great Falls	0	0	.000	8.50	13	0	0	6	0	0	18.0	24	23	17	1	2	15	0	19	6
Davis, Helena	1	5	.167	8.72	8	6	0	0	0	0	32.0	46	37	31	3	2	23	0	22	6
Dennison, Helena*	6	4	.600	4.32	13	12	1	0	0	0	73.0	83	45	35	4	2	25	0	47	3
Dodd, Billings*	1	7	.125	6.11	18	10	0	3	0	1	66.1	56	60	45	2	7	64	0	50	11
Dolson, Medicine Hat*	1	6	.143	5.50	13	9	0	3	0	0	55.2	73	42	34	3	5	24	0	30	8
Dunlap, Idaho Falls	0	1	.000	10.32	4	3	0	0	0	0	11.1	18	14	13	1	3	9	0	17	3
Ekman, Pocatello	1	4	.200	5.93	22	0	0	20	0	5	27.1	27	25	18	2	2	16	3	25	2
Ermis, Medicine Hat	1	8	.111	5.25	17	8	1	4	0	0	60.0	68	49	35	5	7	34	0	35	16
Farnsworth, Great Falls*	8	3	.727	3.09	13	13	0	0	0	0	75.2	65	35	26	6	3	27	0	69	7
Farrell, Helena	4	0	1.000	0.84	5	3	2	1	0	0	32.0	17	5	3	2	0	8	1	22	0
Fetty, Helena	1	0	1.000	1.96	14	0	0	13	0	2	18.1	10	5	4	1	0	6	0	23	1
Fitzgerald, Helena	1	1	.500	5.89	11	0	0	5	0	0	18.1	31	18	12	0	4	11	0	15	3
Ford, Medicine Hat	1	2	.333	5.31	15	2	0	10	0	2	39.0	42	29	23	4	1	17	0	19	4
Furmanik, Salt Lake City	4	0	1.000	4.29	14	1	0	9	0	3	21.0	26	12	10	0	0	8	1	21	2
Giberti, Butte*	5	1	.833	4.44	17	6	0	9	0	2	48.2	59	37	24	3	1	22	0	39	7
Gibson, Pocatello	2	0	.000	9.37	14	0	0	10	0	0	16.1	28	20	17	0	4	7	2	6	5
Gilligan, Salt Lake City	6	1	.857	1.71	25	0	0	18	0	6	63.0	46	15	12	3	3	13	2	78	6
Gorecki, Great Falls	0	3	.000	4.41	13	10	0	0	0	0	51.0	44	34	25	3	1	27	0	56	4
Goucher, Pocatello	0	1	.000	20.25	2	0	0	0	0	0	2.2	10	6	6	1	0	1	0	3	1
Grennan, Pocatello*	2	6	.250	4.14	23	6	0	8	0	0	54.1	43	32	25	3	2	32	4	64	5
Gress, Idaho Falls	0	0	.000	0.00	1	0	0	1	0	0	1.1	1	0	0	0	0	0	0	1	0
Guidi, Salt Lake City	2	2	.500	3.65	13	9	0	2	0	1	61.2	60	31	25	3	5	16	0	44	2
Guthrie, Salt Lake City	0	0	.000	12.00	2	0	0	1	0	0	3.0	4	6	4	2	0	3	0	2	0
Hancock, Helena*	2	2	.500	3.06	5	5	2	0	0	0	32.1	24	11	11	2	1	23	0	29	1
Harris, Salt Lake City	0	0	.000	27.00	1	0	0	0	0	0	0.1	1	1	1	0	0	2	0	0	0
Hauteman, Helena*	1	0	1.000	1.50	1	1	0	0	0	0	6.0	8	1	1	0	0	2	0	2	0
Henson, Butte	0	3	.000	10.80	5	5	0	0	0	0	18.1	34	32	22	1	2	18	0	13	5
Hickox, Butte	4	3	.571	3.16	24	0	0	23	0	10	37.0	33	16	13	3	3	14	1	14	0
Hill, Helena*	4	2	.667	3.15	11	11	0	0	0	0	60.0	43	27	21	2	3	35	0	76	7
Iwema, Helena	0	0	.000	3.97	17	0	0	6	0	1	34.0	37	21	15	5	0	17	0	36	4
Jacinto, Great Falls	0	0	.000	7.47	15	0	0	11	0	0	15.2	22	18	13	1	3	7	0	3	3
Kempfer, Idaho Falls	1	1	.500	9.56	5	5	0	0	0	0	16.0	24	18	17	3	2	8	0	7	1
Kendall, Billings	5	6	.455	4.19	16	11	1	2	0	2	81.2	98	54	38	4	6	22	0	53	5
Kennedy, Butte	4	3	.571	3.50	11	3	1	1	0	1	36.0	43	16	14	3	0	7	2	26	1
Knowles, Salt Lake City	1	0	.000	7.71	3	2	0	1	0	0	4.2	11	12	4	1	0	1	0	2	0
Koklys, Idaho Falls	3	1	.750	6.57	25	0	0	3	0	0	49.1	70	37	36	6	3	10	1	58	9
Koller, Idaho Falls	2	2	.500	6.25	9	9	0	0	0	0	36.0	49	29	25	1	1	14	0	29	7
Lacy, Butte	2	1	.667	5.59	24	2	0	6	0	1	48.1	47	34	30	6	4	36	0	45	15
Langford, Billings	3	4	.429	3.86	20	6	0	6	0	1	65.1	61	39	28	3	7	47	2	50	10
Ledwik, Billings	3	2	.600	4.23	18	0	0	5	0	2	38.1	40	19	18	3	3	16	0	26	5
Lopez, Medicine Hat*	1	0	1.000	8.34	11	0	0	2	0	0	22.2	33	28	21	4	1	19	0	14	8
Lucas, Helena*	0	1	.000	5.63	5	0	0	0	0	0	8.0	9	8	5	1	1	5	0	0	0
Madrigal, Butte	0	1	.000	8.77	6	5	0	0	0	0	25.2	35	29	25	4	5	13	0	17	4
Magee, Butte*	2	7	.222	4.80	14	14	0	0	0	0	69.1	76	45	37	3	3	57	2	51	6
Majeski, Idaho Falls	4	2	.667	4.50	25	0	0	13	0	3	34.0	33	29	17	6	1	23	2	49	6
Maldonado, Great Falls*	0	0	.000	1.23	4	0	0	3	0	1	7.1	4	1	1	0	0	0	0	9	0
Manaure, Medicine Hat	2	2	.500	4.46	19	0	0	13	0	4	40.1	38	30	20	1	4	20	0	40	4
Marcon, Salt Lake City*	8	2	.800	4.27	14	14	1	0	0	0	78.0	83	43	37	6	3	23	0	49	0
Matranga, Salt Lake City*	1	0	1.000	3.77	13	0	0	4	0	2	31.0	31	17	13	0	5	11	1	26	2
McClain, Billings	5	7	.417	3.38	15	12	2	3	0	0	80.0	63	47	30	6	5	51	0	62	10
McDonald, Salt Lake City	7	1	.875	3.05	15	15	3	0	3	0	82.2	84	36	28	2	2	32	0	85	12
McGough, Butte	0	1	.000	9.30	10	0	0	0	0	0	20.1	38	26	21	3	0	13	0	15	4
Meyer, Pocatello*	3	6	.333	5.27	14	13	1	0	0	0	82.0	104	63	48	10	7	41	0	57	7
Mill, Pocatello*	3	5	.375	7.95	15	12	0	0	0	0	60.0	84	63	53	2	2	29	0	43	11

Pitcher, Team	W	L	Pct.	ERA	G	GS	CG	GF	ShO	Sv.	IP	H	R	ER	HR	HB	BB	Int. BB	SO	WP
Millerick, Pocatello	0	3	.000	6.20	13	1	0	6	0	2	20.1	26	15	14	0	0	12	1	20	0
Mirabella, Salt Lake City	1	1	.500	6.67	7	7	0	0	0	0	28.1	38	24	21	0	2	15	0	23	2
Montoya, Medicine Hat*	5	7	.417	4.04	15	14	5	1	1	1	82.1	94	46	37	4	2	21	0	56	11
Morris, Pocatello	0	0	.000	9.00	3	0	0	2	0	0	3.0	4	3	3	0	0	3	0	3	0
O'Halloran, Medicine Hat	1	3	.250	6.98	13	0	0	9	0	1	19.1	25	21	15	3	2	13	0	14	1
Paramo, Butte*	0	0	.000	5.68	14	0	0	2	0	0	12.2	24	11	8	1	1	7	1	11	3
Parra, Great Falls	4	6	.400	6.16	14	14	1	0	1	0	64.1	86	58	44	5	2	18	0	55	0
Patterson, Pocatello	3	3	.500	7.18	16	9	0	1	0	0	72.2	94	63	58	9	2	36	2	63	4
Petit, Idaho Falls	0	0	.000	3.45	10	0	0	5	0	1	15.2	19	10	6	2	1	4	0	15	2
Place, Idaho Falls	2	1	.667	4.44	5	5	0	0	0	0	24.1	28	16	12	2	1	10	0	9	0
Powers, Salt Lake City	0	1	.000	4.50	5	0	0	4	0	1	8.0	6	5	4	1	3	4	0	9	1
Quinones, Billings*	1	4	.200	4.01	11	8	0	2	0	0	51.2	48	24	23	1	1	22	0	35	3
Rapp, Idaho Falls*	3	3	.500	3.81	20	9	0	3	0	0	59.0	62	29	25	6	2	14	1	57	5
Reese, Pocatello	2	3	.400	9.44	15	4	0	2	0	0	34.1	45	41	36	6	2	19	0	17	7
Reeves, Billings	4	4	.500	3.47	12	11	2	0	0	0	62.1	61	42	24	5	5	31	0	33	6
Robinson, Medicine Hat	1	1	.500	3.86	6	2	0	3	0	0	11.2	12	8	5	1	0	5	0	18	2
Rugg, Helena*	1	1	.500	7.94	8	1	0	0	0	0	17.0	19	20	15	2	2	8	0	7	2
Schneck, Pocatello*	0	0	.000	4.91	14	1	0	7	0	1	22.0	30	16	12	1	2	14	0	17	6
Schuermann, Butte*	4	4	.500	4.53	30	0	0	16	0	4	43.2	45	29	22	0	1	34	2	46	6
Schultea, Salt Lake City	2	2	.500	3.64	16	0	0	9	0	3	29.2	37	14	12	2	2	11	0	24	2
Simoneaux, Idaho Falls	0	0	.000	1.69	2	0	0	0	0	0	5.1	6	5	1	0	0	4	0	3	0
Sinacori, Great Falls	6	1	.857	1.57	24	0	0	19	0	7	34.1	22	9	6	0	1	16	1	35	4
Sinclair, Great Falls*	0	1	.000	6.75	12	0	0	8	0	0	14.2	17	15	11	1	3	11	0	14	0
Smith, Salt Lake City	0	0	.000	27.00	1	0	0	0	0	0	0.2	3	2	2	0	0	0	0	0	0
Souza, Helena	8	2	.800	3.04	14	14	2	0	1	0	83.0	80	35	28	4	1	34	0	70	3
Stanton, Idaho Falls*	0	0	.000	0.00	1	0	0	1	0	0	0.2	0	0	0	0	0	2	0	1	0
Stephens, Salt Lake City*	6	3	.667	2.43	18	8	4	3	0	0	77.2	51	30	21	1	5	20	1	89	9
Stevens, Pocatello	3	2	.600	7.71	24	0	0	6	0	0	30.1	46	32	26	1	2	28	1	24	6
Strong, Great Falls*	0	0	.000	3.95	19	0	0	4	0	0	27.1	23	19	12	2	5	13	0	34	8
Stuart, Butte	0	0	.000	6.91	13	0	0	4	0	0	27.1	39	31	21	2	3	12	0	21	4
Sullivan, Butte	0	0	.000	0.00	1	0	0	1	0	0	1.0	1	0	0	0	0	2	0	1	1
Taylor, Medicine Hat*	6	4	.600	3.11	14	10	2	2	1	0	75.1	70	37	26	8	3	34	0	58	4
Tobin, Billings	1	2	.333	7.86	13	3	0	5	0	0	34.1	40	35	30	5	1	31	0	23	8
Underhill, Butte	3	2	.600	6.65	9	8	1	0	0	0	46.0	61	42	34	5	1	15	0	40	8
Vasquez, Idaho Falls	3	2	.600	8.00	13	10	0	0	0	0	45.0	62	51	40	7	5	38	0	32	6
Viarengo, Idaho Falls	0	0	.000	7.90	11	0	0	7	0	0	13.2	23	20	12	1	1	12	0	17	3
Vivas, Billings	2	3	.400	3.95	22	1	0	9	0	0	54.2	69	32	24	3	0	8	0	32	1
Walkden, Great Falls*	5	1	.833	2.77	18	6	0	3	0	0	55.1	45	19	17	3	0	23	1	61	3
Watson, Butte	0	0	.000	0.00	1	0	0	1	0	0	1.1	0	1	0	0	0	0	0	4	0
Weber, Idaho Falls	4	4	.500	6.91	16	9	0	0	0	0	56.0	75	54	43	7	2	17	1	40	3
Wechsberg, Pocatello	3	7	.300	4.27	13	13	1	0	0	0	71.2	78	52	34	1	9	46	2	48	7
Weeks, Idaho Falls	3	2	.600	5.58	24	0	0	5	0	1	40.1	42	36	25	1	4	30	0	42	6
Willard, Salt Lake City*	4	2	.667	3.86	16	0	0	7	0	2	35.0	37	27	15	2	1	7	0	20	4
Williams, Great Falls	5	2	.714	2.72	28	0	0	14	0	8	53.0	50	26	16	1	1	24	1	59	4
Winawer, Helena	5	4	.556	3.63	13	14	3	4	0	2	91.2	82	44	37	4	3	22	0	56	5
Woodall, Idaho Falls*	4	1	.800	1.37	28	0	0	23	0	11	39.1	29	9	6	1	0	19	1	57	7
Wyatt, Billings	0	1	.000	6.00	10	3	0	5	0	0	21.0	17	16	14	0	4	25	0	10	8
Zastoupil, Billings	2	2	.500	4.06	25	1	0	24	0	9	37.2	43	18	17	1	3	8	1	36	3

BALKS—Atwood, 12; Dolson, 11; Dodd, 10; Montoya, 9; Weeks, 8; Ermis, Schuermann, 7 each; Armstrong, Dennison, Ford, Magee, Stuart, 6 each; Gorecki, Kendall, McClain, 5 each; Brownholtz, Castro, Grennan, Lacy, Meyer, Parra, Reeves, Robinson, Tobin, Winawer, 4 each; Aronetz, Benson, Bush, Cook, Curtis, Ekman, Farrell, Hauteman, Koklys, Madrigal, Matranga, Mill, Mirabella, Patterson, Schultea, Stephens, 3 each; Behrens, Botts, Boze, Coletti, G. Davis, M. Davis, Fitzgerald, Henson, Hickox, Koller, Langford, Ledwik, Majeski, Manaure, Marcon, McDonald, Reese, Schneck, Sinacori, Stevens, Vasquez, Vivas, Wechsberg, 2 each; Ayala, Baptist, Berthau, Buchheit, Carson, Courtright, Dalzochio, Farnsworth, Gibson, Guidi, Hancock, Hill, Kennedy, Knowles, Lucas, McGough, Millerick, O'Halloran, Petit, Powers, Rapp, Strong, Viarengo, Walkden, Weber, Williams, Woodall, Zastoupil, 1 each.

COMBINATION SHUTOUTS—McClain-Zastoupil, Quinones-Zastoupil, Wyatt-Vivas, Billings; Botts-Strong, Castro-Maldonado, Gorecki-Walkden, Gorecki-Walkden-Aronetz-Sinacori, Great Falls; Hill-Fetty, Helena; Cook-Majeski, Idaho Falls; Mill-Atwood-Schenck, Wechsberg-Grennan, Pocatello; Marcon-Gilligan, Marcon-Shultea-Gilligan, McDonald-Furmanik-Willard, Salt Lake City.

NO-HIT GAMES—None.

FIELDING

TEAM

Team	Pct.	G	PO	A	E	DP	PB	Team	Pct.	G	PO	A	E	DP	PB
Helena	.958	70	1840	750	114	62	10	Idaho Falls	.945	69	1836	747	150	65	18
Salt Lake	.957	70	1832	798	118	65	7	Butte	.943	70	1820	809	159	69	25
Great Falls	.953	70	1855	714	128	54	17	Pocatello	.941	67	1714	676	151	59	12
Billings	.946	69	1783	735	144	53	23	Medicine Hat	.939	69	1718	739	159	61	20

Triple play—Salt Lake City.

INDIVIDUAL

*Throws lefthanded.

FIRST BASEMEN

Player, Team	Pct.	G	PO	A	E	DP
Atwater, Pocatello	.903	6	23	5	3	5
Blanco, Great Falls	1.000	12	48	0	0	3
Boston, Medicine Hat*	.972	59	514	37	16	47
Boyzuick, Great Falls	.983	17	109	6	2	8
Bruno, Salt Lake City	.967	4	27	2	1	3
Cunha, Salt Lake City	.938	4	28	2	2	0
DeBerry, Billings*	.974	64	548	40	16	44
M. Edwards, Butte	1.000	1	7	1	0	0
T. Edwards, Salt Lake City*	.966	27	216	12	8	21
Estevez, Salt Lake City	.980	23	193	4	4	22
FAIRMAN, Helena*	.983	66	605	24	11	53
Ford, Billings	1.000	1	9	0	0	3

Player, Team	Pct.	G	PO	A	E	DP
Graham, Billings	1.000	3	27	1	0	2
Gress, Idaho Falls	.975	42	330	28	9	31
Jimenez, Idaho Falls	.975	25	212	24	6	23
Kaelin, Pocatello	.982	44	301	19	6	32
Kelliher, Idaho Falls	1.000	2	8	0	0	1
Kirkpatrick, Great Falls	.979	33	251	26	6	17
Koehler, Butte*	.978	50	375	33	9	41
Langowski, Medicine Hat*	.981	13	92	9	2	10
Loftin, Billings	.857	1	10	2	2	0
Macrina, Salt Lake City	.983	21	159	12	3	8
Martin, Billings	1.000	1	3	0	0	0
McCune, Butte	1.000	1	1	0	0	1
Poyner, Butte	.985	12	59	5	1	4
Radar, Salt Lake City	.846	1	9	2	2	1
Rodriguez, Idaho Falls*	1.000	5	29	1	0	3
Seals, Great Falls	.988	12	77	8	1	10

Player, Team	Pct.	G	PO	A	E	DP
Sisk, Butte	.945	10	62	7	4	6
Talanoa, Helena	.952	4	38	2	2	8
Tierney, Idaho Falls*	1.000	1	1	0	0	1
Weldon, Pocatello	.971	33	187	15	6	15
L. Williams, Great Falls	.985	17	130	4	2	11
Wiseman, Butte*	.974	14	106	7	3	11

Triple play—T. Edwards.

SECOND BASEMEN

Player, Team	Pct.	G	PO	A	E	DP
Atwater, Pocatello	.904	20	29	46	8	13
Banks, Pocatello	.925	15	25	37	5	7
Biggers, Salt Lake City	.969	38	55	100	5	15
J. Castro, Great Falls	.937	29	55	79	9	18
Coates, Idaho Falls	1.000	1	1	0	0	0
Cook, Idaho Falls	1.000	1	1	1	0	1
Cooper, Salt Lake City	.818	4	4	5	2	1
Crespo, Medicine Hat	.909	49	97	133	23	30
Fermaint, Pocatello	.949	27	58	72	7	13
Gates, Butte	.791	12	16	18	9	4
Graves, Great Falls	.910	26	35	87	12	16
Hood, Helena	1.000	3	7	9	0	0
Jones, Billings	.953	16	29	53	4	12
Martin, Billings	.891	10	15	26	5	5
McCune, Butte	.957	16	23	44	3	5
Mejia, Great Falls	.967	21	33	54	3	8
Mesa, Pocatello	.830	14	17	22	8	4
O'Neill, Idaho Falls	.938	16	17	43	4	7
Ortega, Salt Lake City	.974	32	62	89	4	19
Parra, Butte	.942	19	33	48	5	11
Paulino, Idaho Falls	.940	57	89	145	15	32
Rosario, Medicine Hat	.959	21	41	52	4	14
Santoya, Idaho Falls	.875	3	9	5	2	2
Shaw, Salt Lake City	1.000	2	6	2	0	0
Sisk, Butte	.981	26	47	58	2	17
Snead, Billings	.977	45	85	123	5	20
Sullivan, Butte	.971	15	25	42	2	8
WHEAT, Helena	.974	56	89	170	7	29
Whitford, Helena	.947	16	30	42	4	10

Triple play—Ortega.

THIRD BASEMEN

Player, Team	Pct.	G	PO	A	E	DP
Aranzullo, Salt Lake City	.647	9	5	6	6	0
Atwater, Pocatello	.786	10	13	9	6	3
Ayala, Salt Lake City	1.000	2	5	2	0	0
Banks, Pocatello	.955	13	8	13	1	2
BLANCO, Great Falls	.947	56	45	99	8	10
Boyzuick, Great Falls	.625	6	1	4	3	0
Cirillo, Helena	.916	62	60	104	15	8
Cooper, Salt Lake City	.899	32	18	53	8	6
Edwards, Butte	.927	60	52	100	12	6
Everly, Idaho Falls	1.000	7	2	8	0	1
Ferreira, Salt Lake City	.750	2	2	1	1	0
Ford, Billings	.868	16	10	23	5	1
Garrigan, Pocatello	.875	2	4	3	1	0
Graham, Billings	.742	10	7	16	8	0
Gress, Idaho Falls	.827	26	13	30	9	3
Harrison, Billings	.800	2	3	1	1	0
Hernandez, Billings	.619	7	6	7	8	0
Jones, Salt Lake City	.857	6	2	10	2	0
Jones, Billings	.946	27	33	54	5	4
Lutz, Medicine Hat	1.000	1	1	0	0	0
Martin, Billings	.962	12	5	20	1	2
Martinez, Pocatello	.800	4	2	2	1	0
McCune, Butte	.667	2	1	1	1	0
Mesa, Pocatello	.971	15	7	27	1	5
Miailovich, Salt Lake City	.939	13	10	21	2	4
O'Neill, Idaho Falls	.849	18	13	32	8	4
Ortega, Salt Lake City	.750	6	3	6	3	0
Otanez, Great Falls	.897	16	8	18	3	0
Parra, Butte	.889	6	7	9	2	1
Paulino, Idaho Falls	.750	10	5	10	5	1
Rosario, Medicine Hat	.778	3	1	6	2	0
Scholzen, Pocatello	.886	15	8	23	4	1
Shaw, Salt Lake City	.766	21	5	31	11	4
Sisk, Butte	.714	3	0	5	2	0
Sullivan, Butte	.750	9	6	9	5	0
Therrien, Idaho Falls	.845	26	15	56	13	5
Tsoukalas, Medicine Hat	.848	45	32	91	22	6
Wheat, Helena	.444	5	2	2	5	0
Wilke, Medicine Hat	.857	23	14	40	9	3
L. Williams, Great Falls	1.000	3	0	2	0	0
Wong, Pocatello	.922	19	17	30	4	5

SHORTSTOPS

Player, Team	Pct.	G	PO	A	E	DP
Aranzullo, Salt Lake City	1.000	1	1	0	0	0
Banks, Pocatello	.907	14	18	31	5	3
Biggers, Salt Lake City	.897	11	14	21	4	4

Player, Team	Pct.	G	PO	A	E	DP
J. Castro, Great Falls	.902	32	35	76	12	17
Everly, Helena	.913	12	9	12	2	2
GARRIGAN, Pocatello	.935	48	78	123	14	28
Gil, Butte	.914	32	61	88	14	23
Gittmer, Helena	.915	39	67	94	15	27
Graffagnino, Idaho Falls	.912	66	112	187	29	41
Hernandez, Billings	.874	22	52	52	15	9
Koelling, Billings	.951	21	35	43	4	8
Martin, Billings	.933	14	18	38	4	6
McCune, Butte	.882	4	10	5	2	2
Mesa, Pocatello	1.000	3	2	2	0	0
O'Neill, Idaho Falls	1.000	6	4	10	0	1
Otanez, Great Falls	.895	42	56	106	19	17
Parra, Butte	.897	29	52	79	15	17
Paulino, Idaho Falls	.833	1	3	2	1	2
Rosario, Medicine Hat	.939	23	34	43	5	7
Sisk, Butte	.959	10	16	31	2	7
Snead, Billings	.986	15	31	38	1	13
Stefan, Salt Lake City	.924	63	126	188	26	36
Tavarez, Medicine Hat	.892	45	68	146	26	32
Wheat, Helena	.818	3	4	5	2	1
Whitford, Helena	.886	23	27	66	12	10
Wilke, Medicine Hat	.857	6	8	22	5	3
Wong, Pocatello	.886	10	11	28	5	4

OUTFIELDERS

Player, Team	Pct.	G	PO	A	E	DP
Albert, Helena	1.000	5	10	0	0	0
Alvarez, Medicine Hat	.982	31	53	2	1	0
Anderson, Pocatello*	.960	42	90	7	4	2
Andrea, 9 Poc.-8 Hel.	.821	17	23	0	5	0
Andrews, Great Falls	1.000	2	2	1	0	1
Aranzullo, Salt Lake City	1.000	4	6	0	0	0
Baber, Helena	.943	67	112	3	7	0
Banks, Pocatello	.929	9	11	2	1	0
Basse, Helena	.942	49	79	2	5	1
Briggs, Medicine Hat	.906	64	113	2	12	0
Burris, Billings	.968	54	111	10	4	1
Carmona, Pocatello	.899	36	55	7	7	1
Castillo, Salt Lake City	.975	66	102	15	3	4
Cirillo, Helena	1.000	7	11	0	0	0
Coates, Idaho Falls	.962	55	96	5	4	1
Crespo, Butte	1.000	9	9	0	0	0
Cunha, Salt Lake City	1.000	16	6	0	0	0
Daniels, Medicine Hat	.961	58	117	5	5	1
Edwards, Salt Lake City*	1.000	13	15	0	0	0
Gates, Butte	.667	6	4	0	2	0
Graham, Billings	.911	40	68	4	7	0
Grijak, Idaho Falls	1.000	41	72	3	0	0
Hamm, Pocatello	.952	31	35	5	2	0
Herrera, Medicine Hat*	.948	38	50	5	3	1
Hirtensteiner, Salt Lake City*	.976	70	117	6	3	2
Hood, Helena	1.000	6	13	0	0	0
Jesperson, Billings	.978	38	89	2	2	1
Koehler, Butte*	1.000	3	4	0	0	0
Landrum, Great Falls	.926	54	82	5	7	0
Lawn, Helena	.982	59	102	8	2	1
Lowery, Butte	.943	54	92	7	6	0
Martin, Salt Lake City	1.000	5	3	0	0	0
Minter, Pocatello	.922	27	42	5	4	0
Montgomery, Billings	.952	17	19	1	1	0
Parra, Butte	.938	7	14	1	1	0
Philyaw, Pocatello	.909	5	9	1	1	0
Pinkney, Great Falls	1.000	9	9	1	0	0
Poyner, Butte	.000	3	0	1	1	0
Preikszas, Helena	.952	17	19	1	1	0
Puchales, Salt Lake City*	.933	16	14	0	1	0
Ramos, Medicine Hat*	.885	29	43	3	6	0
Reed, Great Falls	.967	42	59	0	2	0
Roberts, Butte	.933	47	72	11	6	0
Robinson, Pocatello*	.922	55	105	1	9	0
Rodriguez, Idaho Falls*	.889	15	7	1	1	0
Scholzen, Pocatello	.964	19	25	2	1	0
Smith, Great Falls	.905	43	54	3	6	0
Sullivan, Butte	1.000	7	4	0	0	0
Swann, Idaho Falls	.935	46	66	6	5	0
Taylor, Billings	.958	64	107	7	5	0
Texidor, Butte	.955	35	60	3	3	0
Therrien, Idaho Falls	.983	30	52	7	1	2
Tierney, Idaho Falls*	.963	18	25	1	1	0
TODD, Salt Lake City*	.986	52	67	4	1	1
Walker, Idaho Falls	.913	18	21	0	2	0
Weldon, Pocatello	1.000	3	3	0	0	0
Williams, Great Falls	.862	22	21	4	4	1
Wiseman, Butte*	.969	43	59	3	2	1
York, Idaho Falls	.857	8	11	1	2	0
Zammarchi, Great Falls	.973	59	103	4	3	0

CATCHERS

Player, Team	Pct.	G	PO	A	E	DP	PB
Brown, Great Falls	.980	24	137	8	3	0	2
Bruno, Salt Lake City	1.000	1	12	0	0	0	0
Crespo, Butte	.974	22	129	22	4	1	5

Player, Team	Pct.	G	PO	A	E	DP	PB
Dobrolsky, Helena	1.000	5	17	2	0	0	0
Dreisbach, Billings	.980	6	43	5	1	0	4
Ghostlaw, Helena	1.000	12	41	2	0	0	0
Harrison, Billings	.983	26	158	19	3	0	3
Huckaby, Great Falls	.977	55	456	48	12	1	12
Joyce, Pocatello	.976	34	219	26	6	5	3
Kelliher, Idaho Falls	1.000	3	20	0	0	0	0
Kirkpatrick, Great Falls	1.000	3	5	0	0	0	1
Loftin, Billings	.987	36	202	23	3	1	14
Lombardi, Medicine Hat	.991	19	105	6	1	0	0
Lutz, Medicine Hat	.985	33	167	26	3	1	12
Martinez, Medicine Hat	.982	24	141	19	3	1	8
Martinez, Pocatello	.975	30	178	21	5	2	5
MATHENY, Helena	.991	63	456	68	5	6	10
Montgomery, Billings	1.000	1	6	1	0	0	0
Morris, Pocatello	.941	15	77	3	5	0	4
Reinert, Helena	.956	7	39	4	2	1	7
Ripplemeyer, Idaho Falls	.968	24	196	14	7	1	7
Roberts, Butte	1.000	6	34	3	0	1	0
Rolls, Salt Lake City	.984	63	466	75	9	7	5
Seals, Great Falls	1.000	1	4	0	0	0	1
Smith, Salt Lake City	1.000	18	59	8	0	1	2
Taylor, Great Falls	.889	6	16	0	2	0	1
Toth, Idaho Falls	.981	44	334	35	7	0	4
Vargas, Butte	.989	32	158	25	2	2	8
Wilburn, Billings	.913	5	17	4	2	0	2
Williams, Butte	.967	31	161	16	6	0	12

PITCHERS

Player, Team	Pct.	G	PO	A	E	DP
Ambos, Salt Lake City	.846	14	5	17	4	2
Armstrong, Idaho Falls*	.792	14	2	17	5	1
Aronetz, Great Falls*	1.000	24	2	5	0	2
Atwood, Pocatello*	1.000	18	3	3	0	0
Ayala, Butte	.800	20	2	6	2	1
BAPTIST, Medicine Hat*	1.000	14	3	15	0	0
Behrens, Idaho Falls	.000	3	0	0	1	0
Benson, Helena	1.000	3	0	1	0	0
Bergeron, Salt Lake City	.667	8	0	2	1	0
Berthau, Butte	.920	21	4	19	2	1
Botts, Great Falls	.867	13	6	7	2	0
Boze, Helena	.900	16	2	7	1	0
Brownholtz, Butte*	.923	9	2	10	1	0
Broyles, Great Falls	.750	17	0	3	1	0
Buchheit, Butte*	1.000	3	0	1	0	0
Bush, Helena	.875	16	1	6	1	0
Callistro, Pocatello	.813	9	4	9	3	0
Cardona, Medicine Hat	1.000	9	3	2	0	0
N. Castro, Great Falls	.875	14	4	3	1	0
Coletti, Billings*	1.000	12	0	5	0	0
Cook, Idaho Falls	.933	18	4	10	1	1
Criminger, Helena	1.000	2	0	1	0	0
Curtis, Butte	.875	6	3	4	1	1
Dalzochio, Butte	.500	11	0	1	1	1
Darley, Medicine Hat	.818	12	2	7	2	0
Davis, Great Falls	1.000	13	1	0	0	0
Davis, Butte	1.000	8	4	4	0	1
Dennison, Helena*	.962	13	5	20	1	5
Dodd, Billings*	.824	18	7	21	6	2
Dolson, Medicine Hat*	.938	13	2	13	1	1
Dunlap, Idaho Falls	1.000	4	2	1	0	0
Ekman, Pocatello	1.000	22	2	6	0	0
Ermis, Medicine Hat	1.000	17	4	11	0	0
Farnsworth, Great Falls*	.813	13	1	12	3	0
Farrell, Helena*	.889	5	2	6	1	1
Fetty, Helena	1.000	14	0	1	0	1
Fitzgerald, Helena	1.000	11	1	1	0	1
Ford, Medicine Hat	1.000	15	1	0	0	0
Furmanik, Salt Lake City	1.000	14	0	1	0	1
Giberti, Butte*	.714	17	3	12	6	0
Gibson, Pocatello	.800	14	2	2	1	0
Gilligan, Salt Lake City	.941	25	3	13	1	2
Gorecki, Great Falls	1.000	13	5	4	0	0

Player, Team	Pct.	G	PO	A	E	DP
Grennan, Pocatello*	.923	23	2	10	1	1
Guidi, Salt Lake City	.923	13	2	10	1	1
Guthrie, Salt Lake City	1.000	2	0	1	0	0
Hancock, Helena*	1.000	5	0	9	0	1
Hauteman, Helena*	1.000	1	1	2	0	0
Henson, Butte	.250	5	1	0	3	0
Hickox, Helena	.813	24	1	12	3	2
Hill, Helena*	.813	11	1	12	3	1
Iwema, Helena	1.000	17	0	4	0	0
Jacinto, Great Falls	1.000	15	4	2	0	0
Kempfer, Idaho Falls	1.000	5	2	4	0	0
Kendall, Billings	.957	16	8	14	1	1
Kennedy, Butte	1.000	11	1	8	0	0
Koklys, Idaho Falls	1.000	25	1	6	0	0
Koller, Idaho Falls	.875	9	4	3	1	0
Lacy, Butte	.850	24	6	11	3	3
Langford, Billings	.643	20	4	5	5	0
Ledwik, Idaho Falls	.667	18	2	4	3	1
Lopez, Medicine Hat*	.333	11	0	1	2	1
Lucas, Helena*	.500	5	0	1	1	0
Madrigal, Butte	.833	6	0	5	1	0
Magee, Butte*	.950	14	4	15	1	0
Majeski, Idaho Falls	.857	25	1	5	1	0
Manaure, Medicine Hat*	.833	19	4	6	2	0
Marcon, Salt Lake City*	1.000	14	2	8	0	0
MATRANGA, Salt Lake City*	1.000	13	2	16	0	0
McClain, Billings	.714	15	1	14	6	2
McDonald, Salt Lake City	1.000	15	5	11	0	0
McGough, Butte	.700	10	2	5	3	1
Meyer, Pocatello	.920	14	8	15	2	0
Mill, Pocatello*	.615	15	1	7	5	0
Millerick, Pocatello	1.000	13	4	0	0	0
Mirabella, Salt Lake City	1.000	7	3	3	0	0
Montoya, Medicine Hat*	.950	15	1	18	1	3
O'Halloran, Medicine Hat	1.000	13	2	3	0	2
Paramo, Butte*	.750	14	1	2	1	0
Parra, Great Falls	.833	14	6	9	3	0
Patterson, Pocatello	.933	16	5	9	1	1
Petit, Idaho Falls	1.000	10	2	1	0	0
Place, Idaho Falls	.833	5	3	2	1	0
Quinones, Great Falls*	1.000	11	1	15	0	1
Rapp, Idaho Falls*	1.000	20	1	15	0	1
Reese, Pocatello	.714	15	2	3	2	0
Reeves, Billings	.786	12	5	17	6	1
Robinson, Medicine Hat	1.000	6	0	1	0	0
Rugg, Helena*	.889	8	1	7	1	1
Schneck, Pocatello	1.000	14	2	1	0	0
Schuermann, Butte*	.933	30	3	11	1	1
Schultea, Salt Lake City	1.000	16	1	9	0	0
Simoneaux, Idaho Falls	1.000	2	0	1	0	0
Sinacori, Great Falls	1.000	24	5	4	0	1
Sinclair, Medicine Hat*	1.000	12	1	2	0	0
Souza, Helena	.941	14	5	11	1	0
Stephens, Salt Lake City*	.955	18	4	17	1	1
Stevens, Salt Lake City	1.000	24	3	6	0	0
Strong, Great Falls*	1.000	19	1	2	0	0
Stuart, Butte	.857	13	2	4	1	0
Taylor, Medicine Hat*	.850	14	4	13	3	1
Tobin, Billings	.750	13	0	3	1	0
Underhill, Butte	.800	9	2	6	2	1
Vasquez, Idaho Falls	1.000	13	1	3	0	0
Viarengo, Idaho Falls	1.000	11	3	2	0	0
Vivas, Billings	.810	22	6	11	4	0
Walkden, Great Falls*	1.000	18	1	13	0	0
Weber, Idaho Falls	.800	16	1	7	2	2
Wechsberg, Pocatello	.862	13	7	18	4	2
Weeks, Idaho Falls	.900	24	4	5	1	0
Willard, Salt Lake City*	1.000	16	2	13	0	1
T. Williams, Great Falls	.882	28	4	11	2	1
Winawer, Helena	.919	13	9	25	3	3
Woodall, Idaho Falls*	.923	28	2	10	1	0
Wyatt, Billings	1.000	10	4	3	0	0
Zastoupil, Billings	.833	25	1	14	3	0

The following players did not have any fielding statistics at the positions indicated or appeared only as a designated hitter, pinch-hitter or pinch-runner: Carson, p; Courtright, p; Daniels, p; M. Edwards, of; Goucher, p; Graves, ss; Gress, p; Harris, p; Jimenez, c; Knowles, p; Maldonado, p; A. Martinez, 3b; Morris, p; Paulino, 1b; Powers, p; Seals, of; W. Smith, p; Stanton, p; Sullivan, p; Tucker, 2b; Watson, p; La. Williams, 3b.

LEAGUE CHAMPIONS

Year	Team	Pct.
1939—	Twin Falls*	.581
1940—	Salt Lake City	.608
	Ogden (4th)*	.492
1941—	Boise	.623
	Ogden (2nd)*	.598
1942—	Pocatello+	.690
	Boise	.683
1943-44-45—	Did not operate.	
1946—	Twin Falls‡	.585
	Salt Lake City+	.585
1947—	Salt Lake City	.618
	Twin Falls+	.600
1948—	Pocatello	.611
	Twin Falls (2nd)*	.595
1949—	Twin Falls	.624
	Pocatello (3rd)*	.595
1950—	Pocatello	.635
	Billings (3rd)*	.571
1951—	Salt Lake City	.618
	Great Falls (3rd)*	.559
1952—	Pocatello	.595
	Idaho Falls (2nd)*	.573
1953—	Ogden	.679
	Salt Lake City (4th)*	.527
1954—	Salt Lake City	.595
	Great Falls (4th)*	.530
1955—	Boise	.588
	Magic Valley (4th)*	.489
1956—	Boise	.561
1957—	Salt Lake City	.650
	Billings+	.582
1958—	Great Falls	.582
	Boise+	.615
1959—	Boise	.633
	Billings (2nd)*	.523
1960—	Boise	.686
	Idaho Falls	.650
1961—	Boise	.638
	Great Falls*	.571

Year	Team	Pct.
1962—	Boise§	.565
	Billings†	.706
1963—	Idaho Falls	.702
	Magic Valley†	.643
1964—	Treasure Valley	.615
1965—	Treasure Valley	.530
1966—	Ogden	.591
1967—	Ogden	.621
1968—	Ogden	.609
1969—	Ogden	.620
1970—	Idaho Falls	.629
1971—	Great Falls	.643
1972—	Billings	.694
1973—	Billings	.629
1974—	Idaho Falls	.569

Year	Team	Pct.
1975—	Great Falls	.577
1976—	Great Falls	.577
1977—	Lethbridge	.629
1978—	Billings x	.735
1979—	Helena	.623
	Lethbridge y	.559
1980—	Lethbridge y	.743
	Billings	.629
1981—	Calgary	.657
	Butte y	.557
1982—	Medicine Hat y	.629
	Idaho Falls	.600
1983—	Billings y	.614
	Calgary	.600
1984—	Billings	.691

Year	Team	Pct.
	Helena y	.647
1985—	Great Falls	.771
	Salt Lake City y	.657
1986—	Salt Lake City z	.643
	Great Falls	.571
1987—	Salt Lake City z	.700
	Helena	.657
1988—	Great Falls z	.754
	Butte	.629
1989—	Great Falls z	.791
	Butte	.621
1990—	Great Falls z	.706
	Salt Lake City	.618
1991—	Salt Lake City z	.700
	Great Falls	.657

*Won four-club playoff. †Won split-season playoff. ‡Ended first half in tie with Salt Lake City and won one-game playoff. §Ended first half in tie with Billings and Great Falls and won playoff. xBillings (first place) defeated Idaho Falls (second place) in First Place-Second Place playoff. yLeague divided into Northern and Southern divisions; won two-club playoff. zWon two-club playoff.

MINOR LEAGUE INDEX

OTHER BOOKS AVAILABLE
FROM THE SPORTING NEWS LIBRARY
Take your pick!

1992 Baseball Register
Available February 1992. #419..$11.95

The Complete Baseball Record Book — 1992
Available January 1992. #420..$14.95

1992 Official Baseball Rules
Available March 1992. #427 ....$3.95

Official 1991 American League Averages and Box Scores
Available January 1992. #428..$19.95

Official 1991 National League Averages and Box Scores
Available January 1992. #429..$19.95

American League 1992 Red Book
Available March 1992. #421 ....$10.95

National League 1992 Green Book
Available March 1992. #422 ....$10.95

The Complete Super Bowl Book — 1992
Available March 1992. #433 ....$11.95

1992 Pro Football Guide
Available July 1992. #434 ....$11.95

1992 Football Register
Available July 1992. #435 ....$11.95

1992-93 Official NBA Guide
Available September 1992. #436 ....$11.95

1992-93 Official NBA Register
Available September 1992. #437 ....$11.95

The Complete Hockey Book 1992-93
Available August 1992. #438..$15.95

Call 1-800-825-8508 to place an order with your Visa or MasterCard, or send check or money order to:

The Sporting News
Attn: Book Dept.
P.O. Box 11229
Des Moines, IA 50340

Please include $3.00 for the first book and $.50 for each additional book to cover the cost of shipping and handling. For Canadian orders, $6.75 for the first book and $.75 for each additional book. International rates available on request. Please apply sales tax: NY — 7.2%; IA — 4.0%; IL — 6.25%; MO — 5.725%. All U.S. and Canadian orders will be shipped UPS. No P.O. boxes, please.